LUTHERAN CYCLOPEDIA

A Concise
In-Home Reference
for the
Christian Family

LUTHERAN CYCLOPEDIA

A Concise In-Home Reference for the Christian Family

Edited by
Erwin L. Lueker

Concordia
Publishing House
St. Louis

Manufactured in the United States of America.

Library of Congress Cataloging in Publication Data
Main entry under title:
Lutheran cyclopedia
Includes bibliographical references.
1. Lutheran Church—Dictionaries. 2. Theology—Dictionaries. I. Lueker, Erwin Louis, 1914—ed.
BX8007.L8 1975 284'.1'03 75-2096
ISBN 0-570-03255-5

---

1 2 3 4 5 6 7 8 9 10 **KK** 93 92 91 90 89 88 87 86 85 84

From the Preface to the 1954 Edition

The LUTHERAN CYCLOPEDIA treats important aspects of the thought and life of the church. It includes the following areas: Bible interpretation, systematic theology, church history, life and worship in the church.

William F. Arndt, Richard R. Caemmerer, Otto A. Dorn, and Frederick E. Mayer served as editorial advisers.

The following served as consultants: William F. Arndt, Walter A. Baepler, Paul M. Bretscher, Walter E. Buszin, Richard R. Caemmerer, John H. C. Fritz, Theodore Graebner, Theodore Hoyer, John T. Mueller, Lando C. Otto, Jaroslav Pelikan, William G. Polack, Arthur C. Repp, Edward J. Saleska, George V. Schick, Otto H. Schmidt, Lewis W. Spitz, August R. Suelflow, John M. Weidenschilling, Emil C. Weis, Henry F. Wind.

The following supplied information and material, gave suggestions, or assisted the editor in other ways: John Bajus, Emil M. Biegener, Lorenz Blankenbuehler, T. O. Burntvedt, George Dolak, Elmer E. Foelber, William Graumann, Herman Harms, R. W. Heikkinen, Fred Hortig, Alfred Jensen, Hans C. Jersild, Julia Koenig, Herman H. Koppelmann, Karl Kretzmann, Robert Lange, P. G. Lindhardt, Anna Marie Lueker, Carl E. Lund-Quist, Enok Mortensen, Martin J. Neeb, Paul C. Nyholm, Arthur C. Piepkorn, F. Eppling Reinartz, A. A. Uppala, John Wargelin, Gilbert K. Wenger, Walter F. Wolbrecht, Leonard C. Wuerffel, Elmer C. Zimmermann.

Materials from *Concordia Cyclopedia* (CPH, 1927) were adapted and used. Theodore Graebner first suggested and outlined this work and served as a member of the editorial board until 1923. Ludwig Fuerbringer and Theodore Engelder served as editors from the beginning, and Paul E. Kretzmann replaced Theodore Graebner. The associate editors were Frederick Brand, William Dallmann, John H. C. Fritz, Theodore Graebner, Adolph Haentzschel, Edward Koehler, Karl Kretzmann, George W. Mueller, John T. Mueller, H. C. F. Otte, Theodore H. Schroedel, Franz C. Verwiebe. Some articles were written by William H. Behrens, John S. Bradac, Carl J. A. Hoffmann, J. A. Moldstad, H. K. Moussa, Frederick Wenger. Notes with varied suggestions by Ludwig Fuerbringer and other editors of *Concordia Cyclopedia* were made available to the editor.

In making a list of biographies it was considered best to follow the practice which places contemporary men into works like *Who's Who* rather than cyclopedias.

May the Lord of the church find use for the efforts which men who love Him have given to this work.

St. Paul's College, Concordia, Mo.
February 1, 1954 — ERWIN L. LUEKER

Preface to the Revised Edition

As soon as the previous edition of the LUTHERAN CYCLOPEDIA was published, I received numerous comments, corrections, suggestions, and criticisms. Thus many changes were entered into a master copy before it was decided to publish a revised edition. I hope that those who use this edition will also send us their suggestions for corrections.

The number of entries has been considerably increased, articles from the previous edition were carefully reworked, and the mechanics improved. Subjects on which information would be sought especially in a Lutheran cyclopedia are somewhat more complete than those on which information is available in many other reference works. Thus the length of an article is not necessarily a criterion of importance.

Special efforts were made to improve objectivity. I am grateful to those who pointed out unevenness and bias in some entries of the previous edition. Objectivity is not achieved merely by checking each entry for truthfulness. It involves also uniformity of treatment, skill of selection, sympathetic understanding, and a host of other factors. The experience of checking articles of many writers has impressed upon me the need for humble insight into problems of communication within the church.

This revision was begun while Otto A. Dorn was manager of Concordia Publishing House. His successor, Ralph L. Reinke, gave special attention to the cyclopedia and with wisdom, patience, and determination saw it to completion. Florence Flachsbart kept in touch with the work as it progressed and served as contact for the editor. We are indebted to many more at Concordia Publishing House who devoted hundreds of hours to this book.

Editors of Concordia Publishing House carefully checked all the entries, helped to devise the mechanics, and improved many of the items. These editors included Hilton Oswald, Erich Allwardt, John John, and William Olsen. Luther Poellot painstakingly checked the major portion of the entries and made many corrections and improvements. This task of checking and getting the material into final form was completed by Reinhold Stallmann.

The staff of Fuerbringer Library, Concordia Seminary, St. Louis, assisted me and my associates in many research problems. August R. Suelflow, Marvin A. Huggins, and others at Concordia Historical Institute helped with many entries pertaining to Lutheranism in America. The staffs of the Foundation for Reformation Research, of the Dept. of Research and Statistics (LCMS), and of other departments at the Lutheran Building and Concordia Publishing House were always ready to help. Colleagues and students, especially David W. Callies, John E. Groh, and L. Dean Hempelmann, helped obtain information and check entries.

There are many who contributed to the production of the cyclopedia whose names are not in the lists: Willard Allbeck, Elaine Allen, Thelda Bertram, Sarah Bischoff, Donna Busch, Dorothy Carmack, Nils A. Dahl, Elizabeth Danker, Anna Dorn, Norine Eggemeyer, William Fiess, Paul Friedrich, Edwin L. Frizen, Arnold H. Grumm, J. David Heino, Nyla Hesterberg, John W. Heussman, Rosemary Lipka, F. Dean Lueking, Geraldine Lutz, Martha MacLean, Jalo E. Nopola,

Albert W. Reese, Carl Schalk, Martin Schmidt, Armin Schroeder, Del Schulz, E. P. Schulze, Kristen E. Skydsgaard, Theodore G. Stelzer, Frank C. Streufert, Alice Suelflow, Nellie Turner, Leslie F. Weber, Robert C. Wiederaenders, Wilfried Willer, David Yagow, and others.

May she who shared so fully with me the concern and anxiety of producing this book sense in Christ that it is finished. My children lived practically all their lives in the context of this work.

ERWIN L. LUEKER

Abbreviations

*Person or thing thus starred in the body of the cyclopedia is separately listed

A. A.	Alcoholics Anonymous
AAPSS	American Academy of Political and Social Science
AB	Bachelor of Arts
ABC	American Broadcasting Company
ABCFM	American Board of Commissioners for Foreign Missions
abp.	archbishop
ABS	American Bible Society
AC	Augsburg Confession
acc.	according
ACCC	American Council of Christian Churches
ad.	addition
AD	Lat. *anno Domini,* after Christ
Adv.	Advent(ist); Adventism
AELC	American Evangelical Lutheran Church (formerly the Danish Evangelical Lutheran Church of America; not to be confused with the UELC and the Augustana Ev. Luth. Ch.)
Afr.	Africa(n)
ALC	American Lutheran Church (1930)
ALC, The	The American Lutheran Church (1960)
ALCW	American Lutheran Church Women
ALPB	American Lutheran Publicity Bureau
Alta.	Alberta
a. m.	Lat. *ante meridiem,* morning
a. M.	Ger. *am Main,* on the Main
Am.	America(n)
AM	amplitude modulation
A. M. A.	American Medical Association
A. M. E.	African Methodist Episcopal
AMORC	Ancient and Mystical Order Roseae Crucis; Rosicrucians
Anabap.	Anabaptist
ANF	*Ante-Nicene Fathers*
Angl.	Anglican
a. O.	Ger. *an der Oder,* on the Oder
Ap	Apology of the Augsburg Confession
A. P. U. C.	Association for the Promotion of the Unity of Christendom
Arab.	Arabia(n); Arabic
Aram.	Aramaic
archaeol.	archaeologist; archaeological; archaeology
archb.	archbishop
art.	article
assem.	assembly
assoc.	association; associate(d); associating
asst.	assistant
ASV	American Standard Version
ATS	American Tract Society
A. U. C.	Lat. *ab urbe condita,* from the founding of Rome (ca. 753 BC)
AV	Authorized Version
Ave.	Avenue
b.	born
BA	Bachelor of Arts
bap.	baptized
Bap.	Baptist
Bav.	Bavaria(n)
BC	before Christ
B. C.	British Columbia
bd.	board
BD	Bachelor of Divinity
Belg.	Belgium; Belgian
bet.	between
BFBS	British and Foreign Bible Society

Bible, Books of

	Gn	Jb	Jon	1 and 2	Co
	Ex	Ps	Mi		Gl
	Lv	Pr	Nah		Eph
	Nm	Ec	Hab		Ph
	Dt	SS	Zph		Cl
	Jos	Is	Hg	1 and 2	Th
	Ju	Jer	Zch	1 and 2	Ti
	Ru	Lm	Ml		Tts
1 and 2	Sm	Eze	Mt		Phmn
1 and 2	K	Dn	Mk		Heb
1 and 2	Ch	Hos	Lk		Ja
	Ez	Jl	Jn	1 and 2	Ptr
	Neh	Am	Acts	1–3	Jn
	Est	Ob	Ro		Jude
					Rv

Apocrypha

Tob	Tobit
Jdth	Judith
Ap Est	Apocryphal additions to Esther
Wis	The Wisdom of Solomon
Ecclus	Ecclesiasticus; The Wisdom of Jesus the Son of Sirach (or simply Sirach)
Bar	Baruch
L Jer	The Letter of Jeremiah
Ap Dn	Apocryphal additions to Daniel (The Prayer of Azariah and the Song of the Three Young Men)
Sus	Susanna
Bel	Bel and the Dragon
1 and 2 Mac	Maccabees
1 and 2 Esd	Esdras
Man	The Prayer of Manasseh

bldg.	building
Boh.	Bohemia(n)
bp.	bishop
Brit.	Britain; British
bros.	brothers
bus.	business
c.	century (pl. abbr. cents. or c.); copyright
ca.	circa; about

Abbreviations

Can.	Canada; Canadian
cand.	candidate
cat.	catechism
Cath.	Catholic
CBS	Columbia Broadcasting System
cen.	center; central
Cen. Am.	Central America
cents.	centuries
cf.	confer; compare; see
c. f.	condensed from
ch.	church; chapter (usually abbr. chap.)
chap.	chapter
CHIQ	*Concordia Historical Institute Quarterly*
chm. or chrm.	chairman
chs.	churches
CIC	*Codex Iuris Canonici*
CIM	China Inland Mission (succeeded 1964 by OMF)
CLC	Canadian Lutheran Council
CMA	Christian and Missionary Alliance
CMS	Church Missionary Society
Co.	County; Company
coed.	coeditor; coedited
coeduc.	coeducation(al)
col.	column(s)
coll.	college
com(m).	commission; committee; commonwealth
comm.	commonwealth
comp.	compile(d); compiler
Conc.	Concordia
conf.	conference; confession(al); confirm(ed)
cong.	congregation(al)
Cong.	Congregational(ist)
const.	constitution(al)
conv.	convention
CORE	Congress of Racial Equality
cotr.	cotranslator
cp.	compare
CPH	Concordia Publishing House
CR	*Corpus Reformatorum*
CSI	Church of South India
CSU	Christian Social Union
CTM	*Concordia Theological Monthly*
d.	died
D.	Domine (Lat. title given learned men in the Middle Ages); equivalent of Master
Dan.	Danish
days of the week	Sun. Mon. Tue. Wed. Thu. Fri. Sat.
DD	Doctor of Divinity
del.	delegate
dem.	democracy; democrat(ic)
Den.	Denmark
denom.	denomination(al)
dept.	department
D. g.	Lat. *Dei gratia,* by the grace of God
dir.	director(s); direct(ed); directing; directress
dist.	district
Dom. Can.	Dominion of Canada
Dr.	Drive
E or E.	east(ern)
ed.	edit(ed); edition; editor(ial); editing
educ.	educate(d); educating; education(al, -ally); educator
EELC	Estonian Evangelical Lutheran Church
e. g.	Lat. *exempli gratia,* for example
EKD	Evangelische Kirche in Deutschland
EKU	Evangelische Kirche der Union (1953)
ELC	Evangelical Lutheran Church (Norwegian)
ELCA	Evangelical Lutheran Church of Australia
ELCC	Evangelical Lutheran Church of Canada
ELS	Evangelical Lutheran Synod (Norwegian)
em.	Lat. *emeritus,* retired
emp.	emperor
ENE	east northeast
Eng.	England; English
enl.	enlarged
Ep	Epitome
Episc.	Episcopal(ian)
ESE	east southeast
ESEA	Elementary and Secondary Education Act
esp.	especially
est.	estimate(d); establish(ed, -es, -ing, -ment)
et al.	Lat. *et alii* (or *alia*), and others
etc.	Lat. *et cetera,* and so forth
Eur.	Europe(an)
ev.	evangelical(ly)
Ev. Rev.	*Evangelical Review*
ex.	executive
Ex. Com.	Executive Committee
FC	Formula of Concord
FCC (FCCCA)	Federal Council of the Churches of Christ in America
fed.	federal; federate(d); federation
ff.	and following
FHA	Federal Housing Administration
Fin.	Finland; Finnish
fl.	flourished
FM	frequency modulation
FMCNA	Foreign Missions Conference of North America
for.	foreign
Fr.	France; French
Frhr.	Freiherr
ft.	foot; feet
gen.	general(ly)
geog.	geographer; geographic(al, -ally); geography
Ger.	German(y)
Gk.	Greek
gov(t).	governor, government
grad.	graduate(d); graduating
Gt. Brit.	Great Britain
HE	*Historia Ecclesiastica*
Heb.	Hebrew
hist.	historian; historic(al, -ally); history; historico
hosp.	hospital
HQ	headquarters
hr.	hour
Hung.	Hungary; Hungarian
ib. or ibid.	in the same place
ICC	International Critical Commentary
i. e.	Lat. *id est,* that is, namely
IELC	India Evangelical Lutheran Church

Abbreviations

IFMA	Interdenominational Foreign Mission Association of North America, Inc.
IMC	International Missionary Council
in.	inch(es)
inc.	incorporated
indep.	independent(ly); independence
ins.	insurance; insured
inst.	institute(d); institution(al)
instn.	institution
instr.	instructor; instructed; instruction
interch.	interchurch
intercong.	intercongregational
interdenom.	interdenominational
internat.	international
intersyn.	intersynodical
introd.	introduce(d); introducing; introduction; introductory
is.	island(s); isle
It.	Italy; Italian
Jap.	Japan(ese)
Jeh. wit.	Jehovah's witnesses
Joh.	Johann(es)
Jr.	Junior
KJV	King James Version
km	kilometer
L. or Lat.	Latin
LB	Lutheran Brethren
LC	Large Catechism
LCA	Lutheran Church in America
LCC	Lutheran Church – Canada
LCIC	Lutheran Council in Canada
LCMS	Lutheran Church — Missouri Synod (adopted July 1947)
LCUSA	Lutheran Council in the U.S.A.
LCW	Lutheran Church Women
LDA	Lutheran Deaconess Association
LEA	Lutheran Education Association
LFC	Lutheran Free Church
Lith.	Lithuania(n)
LL	Late Latin
LLL	Lutheran Laymen's League
LMS	London Missionary Society
LPH	Lutheran Publication House
LQ	*Lutheran Quarterly*
lt.	lieutenant
Luth.	Lutheran
L. u. W.	*Lehre und Wehre*
LWC	Lutheran World Convention
LWF	Lutheran World Federation
LWML	Lutheran Women's Missionary League
LXX	Septuagint
m.	Lat. *meridies,* noon; married
MA	Master of Arts
Macm.	Macmillan
Man.	Manitoba
MAR	Master of Arts in Religion
math.	mathematician; mathematical; mathematics
MBS	Mutual Broadcasting System
MD	Doctor of Medicine
MDiv	Master of Divinity
ME	Middle English
M. E.	Methodist Episcopal
med.	medical
Medit.	Mediterranean
MELIM	Missouri Evangelical Lutheran India Mission
mem.	member; memorial
Meth.	Methodist
Mex.	Mexico; Mexican

mgr.	manager
mi.	mile(s)
miss.	mission(ary)
ML	Medieval Latin
mo.	month
Months	Jan. Feb. Mar. Apr. May June July Aug. Sept. Oct. Nov. Dec.
Mo. Syn.	Missouri Synod
MP	member of parliament
MPG	J. P. Migne, *Patrologiae cursus completus, series Graeca*
MPL	J. P. Migne, *Patrologiae cursus completus, series Latina*
MS (pl. MSS)	manuscript(s)
Mt.	Mount
n.	note
N or N.	north(ern)
NAACP	National Association for the Advancement of Colored People
NAE	National Association of Evangelicals
N. Am.	North America(n)
nat.	national
N. B.	New Brunswick
NBC	National Broadcasting Company
NCA	National Council on Alcoholism
NCC (NCCCUSA)	National Council of the Churches of Christ in the United States of America
n. d.	no date
NE	northeast(ern)
NEB	New English Bible
NELC	National Evangelical Lutheran Church (Finnish)
Neth.	Netherlands
Newf.	Newfoundland
NLC	National Lutheran Council
NLCA	Norwegian Lutheran Church of America
no.	number
nondenom.	nondenominational
Norw.	Norway; Norwegian
n. p.	name of publisher, printer, or place of publication not given
NPNF	*Nicene and Post-Nicene Fathers*
N. S.	Nova Scotia
NT	New Testament
NW	northwest(ern)
NYC	New York City
NYU	New York University
OE	Old English
OF	Old French
OMF	Overseas Missionary Fellowship (1964 successor to CIM)
Ont.	Ontario
op. cit.	Lat. *opere citato,* in the work cited
OT	Old Testament
p. (pl. pp.)	page(s)
par.	paragraph
patrol.	patrologist; patrologic(al); patrology
PEMS	Paris Evangelical Missionary Society
Pent.	Pentecost(al, -alism)
PhD	Doctor of Philosophy
philol.	philologist; philological; philology
philos.	philosopher; philosophic(al, -ally); philosophy

physiol.	physiologist; physiological; physiology
pl.	plural
p. m.	Lat. *post meridiem,* afternoon, evening
POAU	Protestants and Other Americans United for Separation of Church and State
pol.	politician; political(ly); politics
pop.	population; populated
Port.	Portugal; Portuguese
pref.	preface
pref. d.	preface date
prep.	preparatory
pres.	president
Presb.	Presbyterian
prim.	primitive
print.	printed; printing; printer
pro tem	Lat. *pro tempore,* temporary
prof.	professor
Prot.	Protestant
protect.	protectorate
psychol.	psychologist; psychological(ly); psychology
pub.	publish(er, -es, -ed, -ing); publication; public(ly)
q. v.	Lat. *quod vide,* which see
R.	River
RC	Roman Catholic
RCm	Roman Catholicism
RCs	Roman Catholics
Rd.	Road
reed.	reedited
reest.	reestablish(ed, -ing, -ment)
Ref.	Reformed
regt.	regiment
reinc.	reincorporate(d)
reintrod.	reintroduce(d)
rep.	republic(an)
reprint.	reprinted; reprinting
repub.	republish(ed, -ing)
resp.	respective(ly)
rev.	revise(d); revision; reviser
R. i. p.	Lat. *Requiescat in pace,* May he (or she) rest in peace
RMS	Rhenish Mission Society
RSV	Revised Standard Version
Russ.	Russia(n)
RV	Revised Version
S or S.	south(ern)
SA	Smalcald Articles
Salv. Army	Salvation Army
S. Am.	South America(n)
Sask.	Saskatchewan
sc.	Lat. *scilicet,* namely
SC	Small Catechism
Scand.	Scandinavia(n)
SCM	Student Christian Movement
Scot.	Scotland; Scottish; Scotch
SD	Solida Declaratio, Thorough Declaration
SE	southeast(ern)
secy.	secretary
sel.	selected; selection
SELC	Slovak Evangelical Lutheran Church; Synod of Evangelical Lutheran Churches
sem.	seminary
sess.	session
Skt.	Sanskrit
Slov.	Slovak(ia)
soc.	society; social(ly)
sociol.	sociologist; sociological; sociology
Sp.	Spain; Spanish
Span.	Spanish
SPCK	Society for Promoting Christian Knowledge
SPG	Society for the Propagation of the Gospel in Foreign Parts
sq.	square
Sr.	Senior
SS.	Saints
S. S.	Sunday school
SSR	Soviet Socialist Republic
SSW	south southwest
St.	Saint; Street
stand.	standard

States

Ala.	Ind.	Nebr.	S. C.
Alaska	Iowa	Nev.	S. Dak.
Ariz.	Kans.	N. H.	Tenn.
Ark.	Ky.	N. J.	Tex.
Calif.	La.	N. Mex.	Utah
Colo.	Maine	N. Y.	Vt.
Conn.	Md.	N. C.	Va.
Del.	Mass.	N. Dak.	Wash.
Fla.	Mich.	Ohio	W. Va.
Ga.	Minn.	Okla.	Wis.
Hawaii	Miss.	Oreg.	Wyo.
Idaho	Mo.	Pa.	D. C.
Ill.	Mont.	R. I.	

St. L. ed.	St. Louis (Concordia) edition of Luther's Works
STM	Master of Sacred Theology
stud.	studied; student
supt.	superintendent
SVM	Student Volunteer Movement
SW	southwest(ern)
Swed.	Sweden; Swedish
Switz.	Switzerland
syn.	synod(ical)
ThD	Doctor of Theology
The ALC	The American Lutheran Church (1960)
theol.	theologian; theological(ly); theology
Thor. Decl.	Thorough Declaration, Solida Declaratio (also abbr. SD)
TLH	*The Lutheran Hymnal*
TM	*Theological Monthly*
TQ	*Theological Quarterly*
TQS	*Theologische Quartalschrift*
tr.	translate(d); translating; translation; translator
Tractatus	Treatise on the Power and Primacy of the Pope
treas.	treasurer
Trig. or Trigl.	Triglot(ta)
Trin.	Trinity
TV	television
Twp.	Township
U.	University
UAC	Unaltered Augsburg Confession
UDELC	United Danish Evangelical Lutheran Church in America. Changed name 1945 to United Evangelical Lutheran Church.
UELC	United Evangelical Lutheran Church (see UDELC)
U. F. C. of Scot.	United Free Church of Scotland
ULC(A)	United Lutheran Church in America
UN	United Nations
undergrad.	undergraduate
UNIA	Universal Negro Improvement Association
univs.	universities
unpub.	unpublished

Abbreviations

US(A), or U. S. (A.)	United States of America
USSR	Union of Soviet Socialist Republics
v.	von; verse
VA	Veterans Administration
VBS	vacation Bible school
VELKD	Vereinigte Evangelisch-Lutherische Kirche Deutschlands
vice-pres.	vice-president
viz.	Lat. *videlicet,* namely
vol.	volume
vs.	versus
vv.	verses
W or W.	west(ern)
WA	*Weimar Ausgabe* of Luther's Works, main series
WA-Br	*Weimar Ausgabe* of Luther's Works, letters *(Briefe)*
WA-DB	*Weimar Ausgabe* of Luther's Works, Bible *(Deutsche Bibel)*
WA-T	*Weimar Ausgabe* of Luther's Works, table talk *(Tischreden)*
WCC	World Council of Churches
WCTU	Woman's Christian Temperance Union
WELS	Wisconsin Evangelical Lutheran Synod
WFB	World Fellowship of Buddhists
WW	World War
YMCA	Young Men's Christian Association
yr.	year
YWCA	Young Women's Christian Association
ZKG	*Zeitschrift für Kirchengeschichte*

Initials of Contributors

AAW	Arnold A. Wessler
ACM	Arnold C. Mueller
ACP	Arthur C. Piepkorn
ACR	Arthur C. Repp
ACS	August C. Stellhorn
AFK	Arnold F. Krentz
AHB	Arnold H. Bringewatt
AHH	Alvin H. Horst
AHJ	Allan Hart Jahsmann
AHN	Allen H. Nauss
AHS	Albert H. Schwermann
AJB	Andrew J. Buehner
AJCM	Albert J. C. Moeller
AK	Arne P. Kristo
AL	Arnolds Lusis
ALA	Arthur L. Amt
ALG	August L. Graebner
ALM	Arthur L. Miller
AlS	Alfred Schmieding
AM	Amadeo Molnár
AMA	Arthur M. Ahlschwede
AMR	Alfred M. Rehwinkel
AN	Arna Njaa
AOF	Alfred O. Fuerbringer
ARS	August R. Suelflow
AS	Anna K. Zink Springsteen
AvRS	Alfred von Rohr Sauer
AWG	Arthur W. Gross
BHJ	B. H. Jackayya
CaB	Carl Bergen
CAB	Charles A. Behnke
CAH	C. August Hardt
CAV	Carl A. Volz
CB	Conrad Bergendoff
CCS	Curtis C. Stephan
CEH	Curtis E. Huber
CK	Clarence E. Krumbholz
CML	Carl M. Lueker
CP	Clarence H. Peters
CSM	Carl S. Meyer
DF	Dorris A. Flesner
DGS	David G. Schmiel
DLD	Donald L. Deffner
DPM	Duane P. Mehl
DS	Delphin L. Schulz
DWL	David W. Lotz
ECW	Emil C. Weis
ECZ	Elmer C. Zimmermann
EDH	Emma D. Hoppe
EEF	Elmer E. Foelber
EER	Edward E. Ryden
EEY	Ernest E. Yunghans
EF	Earl Fuhrmann
EFE	Edward F. Eggert
EFK	Elmer F. Kraemer
EFP	Edward F. Peters
EFS	Eleanor Frances Sauer
EGS	Ernest G. Schwiebert
EH	Eva Huskey
EHK	Erich H. Kiehl
EJS	Edward J. Saleska
EK	Edgar M. Krentz
EL	Erwin L. Lueker
ELW	Edwin L. Wilson
EM	Elmer Maschoff
EMP	Ewald M. Plass
ER	Edmund C. Reim
ERB	Eugene R. Bertermann
ErR	Erhard H. Riedel
ES	Edmund Smits
EWG	Egon W. Gebauer
FEM	Frederick E. Mayer
FK	Fred Kramer
FLP	Fred L. Precht
FN	Frederick Nohl
FRW	Frederick R. Webber
FWD	Frederick W. Danker
FWM	Fred W. Meuser
GA	Gerhard Aho
GAA	Gustaf A. Aho
GH	Gunnar Hillerdal
GM	Gerhardt Mahler
GR	Gerhard Rost
GT	George Thomas
GVS	George V. Schick
GWH	George W. Hoyer
HAP	Herman A. Preus
HaWR	Harold W. Rast
HEH	Herbert E. Hohenstein
HFB	Hans F. Bruss
HFW	Henry F. Wind
HGC	Harry G. Coiner
HH	Henry Hamann
HHH	Herman H. Hohenstein
HHK	Herman H. Koppelmann
HJAB	Herbert J. A. Bouman
HLH	H. Lucille Hager
HLY	Harold L. Yochum
HM	Herman Mayer
HMK	Helen M. Knubel
HMZ	Herbert M. Zorn
HOK	Heino O. Kadai
HPH	Henry P. Hamann Jr.
HR	Henry W. Reimann
HRR	Henry R. Rowold
HS	Henry P. Studtmann
HT	Harry A. Timm
HTM	Herbert T. Mayer
HWD	Herb W. David
HWG	Herman W. Gockel
HWR	Herbert W. Rohe
IO	Iver Olson
JA	James Albers
JAH	James A. Hinz
JCC	James C. Cross
JD	John Daniel Jr.
JEG	John E. Groh
JEH	John E. Herrmann
JGM	James G. Manz
JHB	Julius H. Bodensieck
JHCF	John H. C. Fritz
JHS	James H. Shaud
JHT	John H. Tietjen
JJJ	James J. Johnson
JK	John W. Klotz
JMJ	John M. Jensen
JMW	John M. Weidenschilling
JP	Jaroslav Pelikan
JSB	John S. Bradac
JSD	John S. Damm
JTM	John T. Mueller
JTS	Jerome T. Schoel
JW	James M. Weis
JWC	John W. Constable
KHB	Kenneth H. Breimeier
KK	Karl Kurth
KW	Karl H. Wyneken
LB	Lambert Brose
LCW	Leonard C. Wuerffel
LDH	L. Dean Hempelmann
LEZ	Lester E. Zeitler
LFW	Lorenz F. Wahlers
LJM	Lambert J. Mehl
LJR	Louis J. Roehm
LJS	Louis J. Sieck
LP	Luther Poellot
LW	Lorenz Wunderlich
LWS	Lewis W. Spitz
LWSj	Lewis W. Spitz Jr.
MAH	Marvin A. Huggins
MAM	Myron A. Marty
MEM	Martin E. Marty
MHF	Martin H. Franzmann
MHS	Martin H. Scharlemann
MLK	Martin L. Kretzmann
MSF	Marianka S. Fousek
NEN	Norman E. Nagel
NG	Norman F. Gienapp
NH	Norman Habel
NST	Neelak S. Tjernagel
OAD	Otto A. Dorn
OCH	Oswald C. J. Hoffmann
OEF	Oscar E. Feucht
OES	Otto E. Sohn
OGM	O. G. Malmin
OHS	Otto H. Schmidt
OS	Omar Stuenkel
OTW	Oscar T. Walle
PFB	Paul F. Bente
PFS	Paul F. Siegel
PGL	Paul G. Lessmann
PHL	Philip H. Lochhaas
PHP	Paul H. Pallmeyer
PJS	Philip J. Schroeder
PLD	Paul L. Dannenfeldt
PR	Paul H. Riedel
PRP	Paul R. Picard
RAB	Ralph A. Bohlmann
RC	Robert L. Conrad
RDL	Richard D. LaBore
RDM	Robert Day McAmis
RDP	Robert D. Preus
RFG	Robert F. Gussick
RFM	Ray F. Martens
RGH	Robert G. Hoerber
RGL	Robert G. Lange

Initials of Contributors

RH	Rudolf Herrmann
RHL	Ralph H. Long
RJ	Richard Jungkuntz
RJS	Reuben J. Schmidt
RL	Richard H. Luecke
RLS	Roger L. Sommer
RPB	Richard P. Baepler
RPS	Robert P. Scharlemann
RR	Rudolf Rican
RRB	Robert R. Bergt
RRC	Richard R. Caemmerer
RRCj	Richard R. Caemmerer Jr.
RS	Richard Sommerfeld
RVS	Robert V. Schnabel
RWH	Reuben W. Hahn
SCY	Sigurd C. Ylvisaker
SFR	Sadie Fulk Roehrs
SP	Sirgirdur Palsson
TAG	Thomas A. Going
TC	Thomas Coates
TDM	Theodore D. Martens
TFN	Theodore F. Nickel
TG	Theodore Graebner
TGE	Theodore G. Eggers
TGT	Theodore G. Tappert
TH	Theodore Hoyer
TW	Theodore Wittrock
VAB	Victor A. Bartling
VEH	Victor E. Heinecke
WA	William F. Arndt
WAB	Walter A. Baepler
WAK	William A. Kramer
WAS	Walter A. Schultz
WB	Walter E. Bauer
WCG	Walter C. Gerken
WDU	Walter D. Uhlig
WEB	Walter E. Buszin
WED	Walter E. Dorre
WEG	William E. Goerss
WFG	Walter F. Geihsler
WFW	Walter F. Wolbrecht
WGM	William G. MacDonald
WGP	William G. Polack
WGR	Warren G. Rubel
WGT	Walter G. Tillmanns
WHM	Wallace H. McLaughlin
WHS	Walter H. Storm
WHW	Walter H. Wente
WJD	William J. Danker
WJH	William J. Hassold
WJK	William J. Kooimann
WK	Wi Jo Kang
WR	Walter R. Roehrs
WRB	W. R. Bulle
WS	William Schaller
WT	Wilfried Tappert
WW	Walter Wegner
WWO	Walter W. Oetting
WWW	Waldemar W. Wehmeier
WYJ	Won Yong Ji

LUTHERAN CYCLOPEDIA

A Concise In-Home Reference for the Christian Family

A

A and O. See *Alpha and Omega.*

à Becket, Thomas. See *Becket, Thomas à.*

A Mighty Fortress *(Ein feste Burg).* See *Amsdorf, Nikolaus von; Luther, Hymns of.*

Aachen, Synod of. See *Adoptionism.*

Aarhus, Rasmus Jensen of. See *Canada,* A 1; *Danish Lutherans in America,* 1.

Aaronic Blessing. See *Benedictions.*

Aasgaard, Johan Arnd (Apr. 5, 1876–Jan. 13, 1966). B. Alberta Lea, Minn. Educ. St. Olaf Coll., Northfield, Minn.; United (Norw. Luth.) Ch. sem. (see *Luther Theological Seminary,* 4). Pastor De Forest, Wis., 1901–11; taught at United Ch. sem. 1906–07. Pres. Conc. Coll., Moorhead, Minn., 1911–25. Pres. The Norw. Luth. Ch. of Am. (name changed 1946 to The Ev. Luth. Ch.) 1925–54. Helped lay groundwork for the merger that resulted in formation of The ALC 1960.

Abandonment, Malicious. See *Marriage,* II, III.

Abbadie, Jacques (1654–1727). Exponent of rationalistic-apologetic Calvinism; Dr. Theol. at age 17; pastor Paris 1671; organizer of Huguenot congregations in Berlin 1680; pastor of Fr. ch. in London, 1689; dean of Killaloe, Ireland, 1699.

Abbess. Originally the title of the superior of certain communities of nuns following the Benedictine rule but later extended to other superiors especially of the Second Franciscan Order.

Abbey. A monastic house governed by an abbot* or an abbess.* In the Middle Ages the living quarters of the monasteries were usually attached to the abbey ch.

Abbo(n) of Fleury (ca. 940–1004). Fr. scholar; during the decay of Anglo-Saxon culture he kept alive intellectual pursuits and, by emphasizing dialectics, directed theology toward scholasticism; his writings are source material on the papacy during the reign of Robert II. *MPL,* 139, 375–584.

Abbot (from Syrian *abba,* father). The superior in certain communities of monks of the Benedictine family or of certain orders of canons regulars. They receive solemn benediction from their diocesan bishop or (if abbot *nullius*) from any bishop. See also *Abbey; Roman Catholic Church,* C 4.

Abbot, Ezra (1819–84). Unitarian; prof. NT criticism at Harvard; probably his most important work is *The Authorship of the Fourth Gospel,* in which he defends the Johannine authorship and shows the relation of Justin Martyr* to this Gospel.

Abbot, George (1562–1633). Archb. of Canterbury; opposed Laud; supported Puritanism; one of those who prepared the KJV.

Abbot, Lyman (1835–1922). Cong. clergyman and writer; ed. *Outlook;* wrote exegetical and practical treatises which emphasized soc. reform and the "New Theology." Wrote *Dictionary of Bible Knowledge.*

Abd-Kelal. See *Middle East,* L.

Abdas. Bp. of Susa; in 414 destroyed a heathen temple and caused a persecution against Christians during the reign of Yazdegerd I.

Abdul Hamid II (1842–1918). Sultan (1876–1909); responsible for Armenian outrages.

Abdul Masih (servant of Christ). Name adopted by Sheikh Saleh after conversion by Henry Martyn in 1809. First native pastor of CMS in India. Ordained 1823.

Abeel, David (June 12, 1804–Sept. 4, 1846). B. New Brunswick, N. J.; went with Bridgman as pioneer (ABCFM) miss. to Batavia; instrumental in organizing Soc. for Promoting Female Educ. in the E. Returned to N. Y. 1845.

Abel, Félix Marie. See *Geography, Christian,* 8.

Abelard, Peter (1079–1142; Pierre de Palais). Studied under Roscellinus* (leading nominalist), William of Champeaux* (notable realist), Anselm of Laon,* and others; lectured at Corbeil and Paris; known because of romance with Heloise; used the method of logical analysis to arrive at religious realities, thus contributing to the flowering of scholasticism; in his *Sic et non* he showed the fathers to be contradictory, ambiguous, or both, thus arousing a critical attitude; in his Christology he emphasized the exemplary love manifested in Christ's death. Works include *Logica ingredientibus, Theologia Christiana, Sic et non, Historia calamitatum. Bruys, Pierre de;* see also *Conceptualism.*

J. G. Sikes, *Peter Abaelard* (Cambridge, 1932); *MPL,* 178.

Abelites. Small Afr. sect described by Augustine (*De haeresibus,* 87); married but practiced continence.

Abelly, Louis (1602–91). RC theologian; opponent of Jansenism* and Gallicanism.* Wrote *Medulla theologica* 1651.

Abeokuta. See *Crowther, Samuel.*

Abercius, Inscription of. Epitaph of Abercius Marcellus of Hieropolis (d. ca. 200), discovered by W. M. Ramsay 1883.

J. B. Lightfoot, *Apostolic Fathers,* II, i, 477–485.

Abgar, Letters of. Letters supposedly exchanged by Abgar V of Edessa* (4 BC–AD 50) and Jesus. Abgar, according to the legend, requested Jesus to heal him, and Thaddaeus or Addi* was sent by Thomas after the ascension (Eusebius, *HE,* I xiii; II, i, 6–7).

Abhiseka. 1. The Vedic rite of sprinkling rulers and officials. 2. The 10th Buddhic stage of perfection. 3. Hindu ceremonial bathing.

Abib. See *Nisan.*

Abjuration. 1. Renunciation of apostasy, heresy, or schism by oath. 2. An oath ordained by Charles II of Eng. abjuring doctrines of the RC ch.

Ablutions. The cleansing of the celebrant's mouth (since 5th c.) and of his fingers and the chalice (since 9th c.) after the Communion to insure that all of the consecrated species has been consumed. The practice persisted in the Luth. Ch. after the Reformation.

Abortion. Termination of pregnancy before independent viability of the fetus is attained. The practice has generally been condemned by Christians, e. g., Canon 306 of the Council of Elvira. In many parts of the world, medical codes and civil laws regard willful abortion as a criminal act. In most countries, however, therapeutic abortion (when the mother's health, life, or reason is endangered) is permitted. Many non-RC moralists and theologians approve this practice. RC moral theology condemns abortion as an end in itself but allows operations for other purposes which may also result in abortion. References to abortion may be found in works on ethics.*

Abraham, Testament of. See *Apocrypha,* A 4.

Abraham a Sancta Clara. Monastic name of Ger. preacher Hans Ulrich Megerle (1644–1709); educ.

by Jesuits and Benedictines; held high positions in order of barefooted Augustinians; a forceful preacher, appealing to popular fancy; among his writings *Auf, auf, ihr Christen* (against Turks), *Judas der Erzschelm* (an imaginary autobiography), *Grammatica religiosa* (compend of moral theology).

Abraham Ecchellensis (1600–64). Educ. Maronite Coll., Rome; taught Oriental languages at the Propaganda (Rome) and Coll. Royal (Paris). Published important works on Oriental languages and ecclesiastical literature.

Dictionnaire d'Histoire et de Géographie Ecclésiastiques, I (1912), 169–171.

Abraham Ibn Daud. See *Ibn Daud, Abraham.*

Abrahams, Israel (1858–1925). Prof. of Rabbinic literature, Cambridge; leader of "Liberal Judaism"; studied Christian origins in their relation to Rabbinic background.

Abrahamson, Laurentius G. (March 2, 1856–Nov. 3, 1946). B. Medáker, Swed.; brought to U. S. 1868; educ. Augustana Coll. and Sem.; ordained Aug. Syn. 1880; pastor Altona and Wataga, Ill., 1880–86; Chicago, 1886–1908; ed. *Augustana* (official Aug. Syn. Swed. organ), 1908–40; d. Rock Island, Ill.

Abreaction. See *Psychology,* J 7.

Abrenunciation. See *Renunciation.*

Absalon of Lund (1128–1201). Dan. soldier, statesman, archb. of Lund.

Absolute (Lat. "set free," "complete"). That which is self-sufficient. Philosophers used the term in various ways, Hegel, for example, applying it to the totality of the real. In cosmogony it is applied to the First Cause. Christians have applied the term to God.

Absolute Idealism. See *Hegel, Georg Wilhelm Friedrich; Idealism.*

Absolution. The formal act of an ordained clergyman in which, by virtue of his office and in the name and stead of Christ, he pronounces forgiveness of sins upon those who have confessed their sins, affirm their faith in Christ, and promise to amend their lives. The Biblical basis is Mt. 16:19; 18:18; Jn 20:19-23. In the primitive ch. (3d c. on) scandalous sinners who had been under public discipline received absolution at the time of their reconciliation to the ch. From the 5th c. on, notably in monastic communities, absolution was imparted privately. From the 10th c. on in the W. a public confession spoken by or in the name of the worshiping congregation was sometimes followed by absolution. While recognizing that private confession was a human (although highly praiseworthy and useful) institution, the Luth. Ch. retained individual absolution (normally after private confession) as "the living voice of the Gospel" and declared that it would be impious to abolish it. (AC XI; Ap. XI 2; SA-III VIII; SC V). Ap XIII 4 calls it "truly a sacrament" along with Baptism and the Sacrament of the Altar. FC SD XI 38 teaches that the individual can infer God's saving will toward him from private absolution. In a grave emergency, when an ordained clergyman cannot be had, a layman can act for the whole ch. in absolving a penitent (Tractatus 67). In some parts of the Luth. Ch. the confessor imparts individual absolution to the penitents by laying hands on each one after the group of penitents has spoken a general confession of sins together. While the general practice in the Luth. Ch. at present is still to administer absolution to all the penitents present at a public service, the old Luth. practice of private confession and individual absolution, which had disappeared almost wholly by the end of the 19th c., is slowly gaining ground again. The formula of absolution implied by the Luth. Symbols and in common use in the Luth. Ch. is *indicative* ("In the stead and by the command of my Lord Jesus Christ *I forgive* you all your sins . . ."). Until the 15th c. the *precative* form (*"May God forgive* you all your sins . . .") was almost universal; this form, still in exclusive use in E. Christianity, is used in the Luth. Ch. (as well as in the RC and Angl. communions) as a less formal kind of absolution. Absolution is usually, although not necessarily, a part of the preparation for receiving the Sacrament of the Altar.

The RC Church uses the term *absolutions of the dead* for a ceremony which follows a requiem mass. It consists of prayers for the departed, followed by the Lord's Prayer, during which the body is censed and aspersed with holy water. The ceremony originated in the Middle Ages. See also *Keys, Office of.* ACP

Absolutism. 1. A theol. term to designate the view held by exponents of an unconditional predestination,* that is, that God by an absolute decree destined certain men to eternal damnation. 2. In philosophy, a species of absolute idealism which emphasizes that complete reality belongs only to the absolute, while all short of the absolute is only appearance.

Abstinence. Refraining from indulgence in food, wine, and pleasure. Examples of abstinence in OT: blood (Lv 3:17), meats (Lv 11), parts sacred to the altar (Lv 3:9-17), meats consecrated to idols (Ex 34:15), special (Lv 9:10; Nm 6:5). The NT gives everyone liberty according to the dictates of conscience* and love regarding abstinence in adiaphora* (Ro 14: 1-3; 1 Co 8; Acts 15), condemns legalistic sects (1 Ti 4:3, 4), and enjoins abstinence from all that has the appearance of evil (1 Th 5:22). See also *Asceticism; Monasticism.*

Abstract of Principles. Statement of faith adopted by Southern Bap. Sem., Louisville, Ky. (1859), and Southeastern Bap. Theol. Sem. (1950). Its 20 articles treat fundamental doctrines and affirm the universal as well as the local ch.

Abstractive Cognition. See *Cognition.*

Abu-Bakr (573–634). Mohammed's father-in-law and successor.

Abu Hanifa (699–767). Persian Moslem; founder of Sunnite school of jurisprudence; liberal in interpretation of Koran.

Abu Qurra, Theodore (Abukara, 740–820). Christian writer of Asia Minor; wrote apologetics against Judaism and Islam.

Abuna. See *Ethiopic Church.*

Abyssinia. See *Africa* E 2; *Ethiopic Church.*

Abyssos. See *Hereafter,* C 6.

Acacian Schism. Schism (484–519) between Rome and the E. in the Monophysite Controversy.* See also *Acacius of Constantinople; Hormisdas.*

Acacians. See *Acacius of Caesarea.*

Acacius of Beroea (322–ca. 432). Gk. ch. father; friend of Basil of Caesarea* and Epiphanius;* opponent of John Chrysostom;* involved in Melitian Schism* and in Nestorian Controversy.

Acacius of Caesarea (d. ca. 366). Strict Arian and Homoean; deposed by Council of Sardica, 343; proposed Arian creed at Council of Seleucia (359) and drew up acts of Arian Syn. at Constantinople (360). Works exist only in fragments (Jerome, *De viris illustribus,* 98; Socrates *HE,* ii, 4). Followers called Acacians.

Acacius of Constantinople (d. 489). Patriarch of Constantinople; excommunicated 484* at Rome for supporting Peter Mongo. See also *Henoticon.*

Acarie, Mme. (1566–1618). Foundress of the Carmelites of the Reform in Fr.; beatified 1791.

Acathistus (Lat., from Gk. *akathistos* [sc. *hymnos*], "not sitting," i. e., standing; Akathist). Byzantine liturgical hymn or office, sung standing, in honor of Mary, another saint, or Christ. Esp. a certain hymn of 24 stanzas (each beginning with a different letter of the Gk. alphabet) based on the gospel accounts of

Christ's birth; written perhaps by Sergius* (d. 638) or Germanos* I.

Accentus (pron. a-CHEN-tus). The chanting of parts of a liturgical service by the officiant. The counterpart chant of the congregation is called *concentus.* It is a fixed principle of liturgical worship, embodied in the general rubrics of *The Lutheran Liturgy,* that the officiant shall chant (not speak) those portions of the service to which the choir or the congregation responds with chanting. The melodic variations in chanting are governed by traditional rules.

Acceptilation. A theol. term first applied in the Middle Ages to denote the acceptance by God of an atonement, not because it is in itself an equivalent but because God determines to accept it as such.

Accident. That which does not exist by itself essentially but subsists in another self-existent essence, e. g., original sin. (FC Ep I 23; SD 21, 54)

Accident Theory. See *Atonement, Theories of,* 1.

Accidia (accidie). See *Acedia.*

Accommodation. 1. Term early used by mystical interpreters of Scripture to indicate that certain passages of Scripture conveyed higher thoughts than implicit in the words. 2. Socinian writers used it to denote the equivocal character supposed to inhere in sacred writers. 3. In more recent times it was applied to OT quotations in the NT which seemed quoted out of context (e.g., Mt 13:35; 8:17; 2:17, 18, et al.). 4. It also designates a rationalistic theory according to which Christ (in the Bible) accommodated Himself to mental conditions and errors of the times. 5. In RC Ch. the Accommodation Controversy raged in 17th and 18th c. because Jesuits* had permitted Chinese and Indian converts to continue pagan practices, claiming these to be harmless accommodations. See also Nobili, Robert(o) de; *Popes,* 24. 6. In evolutionary hypotheses it is applied to the adjustments which an organism is held to achieve or perfect in the lifetime of an individual.

Acedia (accidia; accidie; Gk. Akedia). Sloth; ennui; indifference or repugnance to worship, considered one of the 7 deadly sins. Cf. Aristotle, *Ethics,* iv; LC I 99. See also *Sins, Venial and Mortal.*

Achad Haam (Asher Ginzberg, 1856–1927). B. in Ukraine; founder of cultural Zionism.

Achelis, Hans (1865–1937). B. Bremen; prof. Koenigsberg, Halle, Bonn, Leipzig; did extensive research on life and art in early ch. Chief work: *Die Katakomben von Neapel* (1936). His father, Ernst Christian (1838–1912), taught homiletics and practical theology at Marburg.

Achenbach, Wilhelm (Oct. 6, 1831–Feb. 24, 1899). B. Darmstadt, Hessen; grad. Conc. Sem., St. Louis; ordained and installed Grand Rapids, Mich., 1859; asst. prof. Fort Wayne 1863; pastor Venedy, Ill., 1871, and St. Louis (Carondelet), 1883.

Achrenius, Abraham. See *Finland, Lutheranism in,* 4.

Ackermann, Carl (Sept. 12, 1858–June 7, 1943). Educ. Capital U. and Theol. Sem.; held various pastorates in Ohio; pres., later prof., Lima (Ohio) Coll.; pres. Pacific Sem., Olympia, Wash.; prof. Capital U.

Acoemetae (Gk. "sleepless"). E. order of monks, founded by Abbot Alexander (ca. 350–ca. 430), which observed strict poverty, abstained from manual work, did miss. work, and by dividing into three choirs had 24-hour-a-day psalmody.

Acolyte. See *Clergy; Hierarchy.*

Acontius, James (d. ca. 1567). B. It.; became Prot.; fled to Basel; came to Zurich, where he associated with Ochino; came to London 1559; Mem. Dutch cong. in Austin-Friars. Wrote especially in area of Christian life (understood *fides* as *fiducia*). Sought to unify Protestants by insisting that only errors in doctrines essential for salvation were heresies.

Acosmism. See *Pantheism.*

Acquaviva, Claudio. See *Aquaviva, Claudio.*

Acrelius, Israel (1714–1800). B. and educ. Swed.; provost of the Swed. churches along the Del. and pastor at Fort Christina (Wilmington, Del.) 1749–55/56. Recalled to Swed.; pastor Fellingsbro, diocese of Västeras. Wrote *Description of the Former and Present Condition of the Swedish Churches in What Was Called New Sweden* (Stockholm, 1759). A friend of H. M. Muhlenberg, he defended him and his co-workers. See also *Parlin, Olaus; Reynolds, William Morton.*

Acrostics. See *Symbolism, Christian.*

Act of Amnesty at Nimes. See *France,* 6.

Act of Assembly. See *Presbyterian Churches,* 1.

Act of Separation and Deed of Demission. See *Free Church of Scotland.*

Act of Submission. See *Canon Law.*

Act of Supremacy. See *Church and State,* 9.

Act of Toleration. Act passed by Parliament under William and Mary (1689) relieving the legal disabilities of Prot. dissenters and protecting their worship; restricted the laws passed under Elizabeth, James I, Charles I, and Charles II. Papists and anti-Trinitarians were excepted from the act.

Act of Uniformity (1559). See *Roman Catholic Church,* D 9.

Act of Uniformity (1662). See *Presbyterian Churches,* 2.

Acta apocrypha. See *Apocrypha,* B 3.

Acta apostolicae sedis. Official publication of the papal see; formerly *Acta sanctae sedis,* privately published since 1865; made official by Pius X, 1904; renamed, 1909.

Acta facientes. See *Persecutions of Christians,* 4.

Acta historico-Ecclesiastica. Journal pub. at Weimar (1734–56) which gives information on contemporary Luth. beginnings in Am.

Acta martyrum. Accounts of the trials of early martyrs which were circulated and often read on their birthdays. Important early *Acta: Martyrium Polycarpi* (ca. 157), *Acta Justini et sociorum* (after 165), *Acta martyrum Scillitanorum* (ca. 185), *Passio Felicitatis et Perpetuae* (ca. 202). Beginning with the 4th c. the *Acta* were gathered in special books *(Martyrologia* or *Calendaria)* which came to be used in commemorative feasts in the RC Ch. The martyrology of Ado, compiled from a spurious source in 858, influenced the martyrology of Usuard (d. ca. 873), which was basic to the Roman martyrology issued by Gregory XIII in 1584.

Acta sanctorum. Multivolume edition of lives of the saints, in publication since 1643 by Belgian Jesuit scholars called Bollandists* after Jean de Bolland.*

Actiology. In philosophy, inquiry into causes.

Action. In the theol. axiom: "Nothing has the nature of a sacrament apart from the divinely instituted action." FC SD VII 83–87 describes the whole process involved in the celebration of the Sacrament of the Altar, including the setting apart of the elements, the consecration, the distribution, the reception, and the eating and drinking.

Action Sermon. The pre-Communion sermon in Scot. Presb. ch., the Lord's Supper being termed the *action.*

Active Obedience of Christ. See *Justification,* 5; *Priest, Christ as.*

Activism. In philosophy and religion, the view that action, especially spiritual activity, is the essence of reality; found in Aristotle's* conception of divinity, Leibnitz,* Fichte,* Maurice Blondel;* usually opposed to intellectual conceptions of truth; found expression in pragmatism, modernism, Soc. Gospel. The word has been extended to apply to any philosophy or theology which emphasizes activity.

Acton, John Emerich Edward Dalberg- (1834–1902). B. Naples; RC; studied under Doellinger and Ranke; friend of Gladstone; active in Brit. gov.; opposed Ultramontanism and papal infallibility; endeavored to establish Ref. Catholicism in Eng.; founded *Cambridge Modern History* and *English Historical Review.*

Acts of 1905. See *Presbyterian Bodies,* 1.

Acts of John (of Paul, Peter, Thomas, etc.) See *Apocrypha,* B 2–3.

Actual Grace. See *Gratia increata.*

Actual Sin. See *Sin.*

Actus dilectionis. In scholastic theology, an act of love elicited from God by works performed on the basis of natural reason (Ap IV 9).

Ad gentes. See *Vatican Councils,* 2.

Ad limina apostolorum (Lat. "to the thresholds of the apostles"). In RCm: 1. Pilgrimages to the traditional tombs of Peter and Paul in Rome. 2. Visits by bps. to Rome to venerate the tombs and report to the pope.

Adalar (d. 754). Co-worker, comartyr of Boniface.

Adalbert (ca. 1000–72). Archb. of Hamburg and Bremen; through the favor of Henry III became archb. and planned to unite N. Eur. under himself; this plan was frustrated by the papacy.

Adalbert of Prague; (Vojtech; ca. 939–997). While bp. of Prague, he played an important role in the Christian work in Slovakia and Hungary. Impeded in the free exercise of his episc. responsibilities by the rivalries between his family and the duke of Prague, he abdicated his see and became miss. bp. to the Baltic Prussians. Their hostility to Christian missions, which were tied up for them with the political encroachment of either Germans or Poles, led to his almost immediate martyrdom on his arrival in Prussia. See also *Danzig.*

Frantisek Dvornik, *The Slavs: Their Early History and Civilization* (Boston, 1956); H. G. Voigt, *Adalbert von Prag* (Berlin, 1898). MSF

Adaldag (d. 988). Chancellor of Otto I; archb. of Hamburg and Schleswig-Holstein.

Adalhard the Younger (9th c.) Pupil of Radbertus.

Adalram (9th c.). Archb. of Salzburg.

Adalward of Verden (d. 933). Anglo-Saxon miss.

Adam, William (Nov. 1, 1796–Feb. 19, 1881). B. Dunfermline, Fifeshire, Scot.; educ. St. Andrews; Bap. miss. to India 1817/18; assoc. with Ram* Mohan Roy; became Unitarian; severed connection with Bap. miss. soc. Mar. 1821; Unitarian minister Calcutta; made govt. survey of the state of educ. in Bengal 1835–38; to US 1838, Eng. 1841; d. Beaconsfield, Buckinghamshire, Eng. Ed. *Bengal Chronicle; Calcutta Chronicle; India Gazette; British India Advocate.* Other works include *The Law and Custom of Slavery in British India; East India Yearbook; Enquiry into the Theories of History.* LP

Adam Goddamus (d. 1358). Eng. Franciscan; pupil of Ockham. Wrote commentary and other works.

Adam of Bremen (d. after 1081). Wrote *Gesta Hammaburgensis ecclesiae pontificum,* important source for N. European ch. hist. (788–1072).

Adam of Fulda. See *Krafft, Adam.*

Adam of Marsh (d. ca. 1258). Eng. Franciscan theologian; friend of Robert Grosseteste;* defended national liberties.

Adam of St. Victor (d. bet. 1177 and 1192). Briton (Breton?) by birth; educ. Paris; entered monestery of Saint-Victor (see *Victorines*) Ca. 1130; sequence writer; mystic.

Adamites. A sect in N. Afr. (2d–3d c.) which claimed the primitive innocence of Adam, met naked in its meetings *(paradeises),* and condemned marriage. Similar sect in Bohemia (15th–18th c.).

Adamnan (ca. 624–704). Irish monk; wrote *Life of St. Columba, De locis sanctis;* upheld Roman date of Easter.

Adams, John Quincy (1767–1848). 6th Pres. of U. S.; wrote *Version of the Psalms* and hymns, some of which appeared in *Christian Psalmist* (1841).

Adams, Sarah (nee Flower; 1805–48). B. Harlow, Essex, Eng.; hymnist. Hymns include "Nearer, My God, to Thee."

Adams, Thomas (ca. 1590–ca. 1655). Pastor in Bedfordshire, Buckinghamshire, and London; Puritan preacher; influenced Bunyan.

Adapa. Mythical Babylonian hero.

Adat. See *Batak Protestant Christian Church.*

Addai. Traditional founder of ch. at Edessa. Eusebius (*HE,* I, xii, 3) identifies him with Thaddeus. See also *Abgar, Lethera of.*

Addis Ababa, Radio of. See *Africa* E 2.

Addison, Joseph (1672–1719). B. Milston, Wiltshire, Eng., son of Lancelot Addison.* Educ. Oxford; gave himself to the study of law and politics. Held important posts, e. g., Chief Sec. for Ireland. Married the Dowager Charlotte, Countess of Warwick, 1716. Known .for contributions to *The Spectator.* The leading literary light of his time; a devout Christian; used talents for hymn writing. 5 of his hymns appeared in *The Spectator,* 1712.

Addison, Lancelot (1632–1703). Father of Joseph Addison; dean of Lichfield; wrote devotional poems and hymns.

Addyman, John (Oct. 22, 1808–June 7, 1887). B. Yorkshire Co., Eng.; pioneer Meth. pastor in Can.; called into ministry of Meth. New Connexion 1833; established 177 churches.

Adelard of Bath (12th c.). Eng. philosopher, theologian, astronomer, natural scientist; wrote *Perdifficiles quaestiones naturales* (seeks to prove existence of God on basis of motion) and *De eodem et diverso* (doctrine of indifference; unity of Plato and Aristotle).

Adelberg, Reinhold (Nov. 9, 1835–Sept. 9, 1911). B. Arnstadt, Thuringia; came to Am. 1855; grad. Hartwick Sem. 1859; pastor Saugerties, N. Y., 1859–61; Albany, N. Y., 1861–69; Watertown, Wis., 1869–73; Milwaukee 1873–96; pres. N. Y. Ministerium 1867–69; asst. prof. Northwestern Coll., Watertown, 1869–73; special instr. in Eng. at Wauwatosa sem. 1896–1900; helped organize Gen. Council (1866) and Syn. Conf. (1872). Ed. Wis. Syn. *Gemeinde-Blatt.*

Adelmann von Adelmannsfelden, Bernhard (1459–1523). Humanist; friend of Reuchlin,* Erasmus,* Luther.*

Adelophagi (Gk. "eat in secret"). A sect (4th c.) holding that Christians should eat in secret as prophets supposedly did.

Aden. See *Middle East,* L 2.

"Adi Granth" (or simply "Granth"). Sacred book of Sikhs.*

Adiaphora (Gk. "indifferent things," *"Mitteldinge,"* "middle matters"). The Luth. Confessions speak of adiaphora as "church rites which are neither commanded nor forbidden in the Word of God." There is a definite province of activity which is not spefically covered by either God's command or God's prohibition. In the Old Dispensation, lives of believers were far more constricted than is the case today. Under the New Covenant God has lifted this yoke from us and has not framed all human activity with His commands and prohibitions but has consigned many acts to the discretion and judgment of the Christian (1 Co 6:12; 10:23; Ro 14:3, 6; Cl 2: 16, 17). While God has removed some matters from the domain of divine Law to the domain of adiaphora, it should, however, be noted that adiaphora *(in abstracto)* may cease to be adiaphora *(in concreto)* under ecrtain circumstances (e. g., when holding a life insurance policy springs from lack of trust in God; when smoking injures health; when drinking exceeds moderation; when immersion in Baptism is defended as the only correct mode; when cremation is an expression of atheism).

Pietists, in harmony with their doctrine of rebirth (*theologia regenitorum:* one reborn and having attained full spiritual manhood is free from sin), denied the existence of adiaphora, quoting such passages as 1 Co 10:31; Cl 3:17; Ro 14:23. They, however, confused the action itself with the life consecrated to God.

Adiaphora lie within the domain of Christian liberty, which may be defined as consisting of the freedom of believers from the curse (Gl 3:13) and coercion (Ro 6:14) of the Law, from Levitical ceremonies, and from human ordinances (Mt 23:8-10; Lk 22:26; Rv 5:10; 1 Ptr 2:8). This liberty is the direct result of justification (1 Ti 1:9; Ro 10:4; Jn 8: 31, 32, 36).

The doctrine of adiaphora is abused when it is made a springboard for loose living (Gl 5:13). Another abuse results from any attempt to make adiaphora a matter of conscience for others (Mt 23:4-8; 20:25, 26; 1 Co 3:5; 1 Ptr 5:3). Luth. principles differ widely from those of Catholicism and many representatives of Protestantism, who claim for the ch. the right to command or forbid things neither commanded nor forbidden by God. To be sure, ch. officials, bds., teachers, and pastors can effect desirable changes in the field of *Mitteldinge,* but it should be done by instruction and advice. Another abuse of this doctrine results when the question of offense to a weak brother is not taken into consideration (Ro 14:1, 2; 15:1; 1 Co 8:8, 11; 9:22). The guiding principle here as always must be love toward the weak (Ro 13:10; 1 Co 16:14; 9:19) without, however, bolstering weakness or covering malice and stubbornness (Gl 2:5). LW.

J. Schiller, *Probleme der christlichen Ethik* (Berlin, 1888); W. Trilhaas, "Adiaphoron," *Theologische Literaturzeitung,* LXXIV (1954), 457–462; Theo. Graebner, *The Borderland of Right and Wrong* (St. Louis, 1950).

Adiaphoristic Controversies. 1. Caused by the Augsburg Interim,* forced on the prostrate Lutherans in 1548 by the victorious emperor, which conceded the cup and clerical marriage but demanded the restoration of the mass, the 7 sacraments, the authority of the pope and bishops, etc., till matters might be finally adjusted. Melanchthon and others in the Leipzig Interim submitted and said these Romish ceremonies might be observed as matters indifferent in themselves. Prof. Flacius of Wittenberg, only 28, at the risk of losing his position, attacked the Interim, seconded by Wigand, Gallus, Brenz, and others. They held it wrong to observe even indifferent ceremonies when a false impression is thereby created. "Nothing is an adiaphoron when confession and offense are involved." The Passau Treaty of 1552 and the Augsburg Religious Peace of 1555 removed the cause; yet the controversy went on because the Adiaphorists continued to defend their position. FC X settled the controversy.

2. In 1681 another adiaphoristic controversy arose between orthodox and pietists regarding participation in amusements.

Joachim Westphal, *Luthers Meinung von den Mitteldingen* (1550); Joh. G. Walch, *Historische u. theologische Einleitung in die Religionsstreitigkeiten unserer Kirche v. d. Reformation bis auf jetzige Zeiten* (1730); standard histories; James W. Richard, *Philip Melanchthon, the Protestant Preceptor of Germany, 1497–1560* (New York, 1898), ch. 28.

Aditi. See *Brahmanism,* 2.

Adjuration. The act whereby one person imposes on another the obligation of speaking as under oath. (Jos 6:26; 1 Sm 14:24; 1 K 22:16; 2 Ch 18:15; Mt 26:63; Acts 19:13)

Adler, Alfred (1870–1937). Austrian psychologist ("individual psychology"). Opposed his teacher Freud's emphasis on sex and substituted man's "will to power." Emphasized the role inferiority feelings play in human action. Works include *Study of Organ Inferiority and Its Psychical Compensation; Social Interest.*

Adler, Felix (1851–1933). B. Alzey, Ger.; to US 1857; educ. Columbia U., NYC; founded N. Y. Soc. for Ethical* Culture; prof. Columbia U. 1902. Works include *The Moral Instruction of Children; The Reconstruction of the Spiritual Ideal; An Ethical Philosophy of Life Presented in Its Main Outlines.*

Adler, James George Christian (1756–1834). Prof. of Syriac and theology in Copenhagen; general superintendent of Schleswig and Holstein.

Adlung, Jacob (1699–1762). Erudite organist of the *Predigerkirche* in Erfurt. His *Musica mechanica organoedi, Anleitung zu der musikalischen Gelahrtheit,* and *Musikalisches Siebengestirn* establish him as an authority on 17th-c. musical culture and organ building.

Admadija. A Moslem sect founded when Mirza Admad offered himself as the Mahdi, or last Imam (1879).

Administration. See *Church Administration.*

Administration, Educational. See *Parish Education,* K.

Admiralty Islands. See *Bismarck Archipelago.*

Admonitio Christiana. See *Neostadiensum admonitio.*

Admonition. 1. The duty of admonishing is taught repeatedly in the NT (Mt 18:15-17; Ro 15:14; 1 Co 4:14; Eph 6:4; Cl 3:16; Tts 3:10; 1 Th 5:14). The early ch. frequently practiced admonition: privately in private offenses, publicly in public offenses. See *Keys, Office of.* 2. RC, a secret rebuke of a cleric by a prelate.

Adolescence. See *Young People's Organizations; Youth Work.*

Adonai Shomo Community. See *Communistic Societies,* 5.

Adopting Act. See *Presbyterian Confessions,* 5.

Adoptionism. The view that Christ according to His humanity is the Son of God by adoption only. Its first exponent was Theodotus* the Fuller, who came to Rome from Byzantium about 190, teaching that Jesus was a mere man, whose deity was only a miraculous power which as Christ or the Holy Spirit (identifying the two) came upon Him at His baptism. Paul of Samosata held similar views, declaring that Jesus was a mere man who, inspired by the *Logos* (Word), gradually acquired a divine dignity which eventually merited the designation "God" (260–272). In the days of Charlemagne, an Adoptionist Controversy was stirred up in Spain by Elipando,* bishop of Toledo, and Felix, bishop of Urgel, who contended that Christ as the 2d Person of the Trinity is the only-begotten Son of the Father, but as the Son of Mary He is the adopted Son of God. They were opposed by Beatus, a priest, and Heterius of Libana, a monk (785), who emphasized the divine Christ made man for us. Alcuin* wrote The Frankish Syn. at Regensburg (792), Frankfort (794), and Aachen (794) condemned the teachings of these Sp. theologians, as did Popes Hadrian I and Leo III. A similar controversy again arose in the 12th c., when Bishop Eberhard II of Bamberg defended Adoptionist views, accusing his opponents of Eutychianism. See also *Monarchianism,* A.

See references to hist. treatment under *Dogmatics;* A. Harnack, *Lehrbuch der Dogmengeschichte* (Freiburg, 1890); J. Bach, *Dogmengeschichte des Mittelalters* (Vienna, 1873–75).

Adoration. Primarily, worship directed to God in His majesty but also performed to idols and men. The OT forms of worship varied (e. g., Ex 3:5; Jos 5:15; Ps 2:12; Jb 31:26-28). In RCm the term is applied to the erroneous worship of Jesus in the Eucharist, for which a ritual drawn up by Thomas Aquinas is still used. See also *Worship,* 4, 5.

Adrian I. See *Pseudo-Isidorian Decretals,* 2.

Adrian IV. See *Popes,* 8.

Adult Education. Adult educ. is as old as civilization. Christ dealt chiefly with adults. The letters of the NT are lessons for adult Christians. However, the Christian church in the main limited its formal educ. to children and youth. The Scriptures impose no such limitation. The beginnings of adult educ., as it is thought of, go back to the Birmingham Sun. Soc. of 1789, Great Britain's labor colleges, Grundtvig's adult schools in Denmark; to lyceums, chautauquas, correspondence courses, university extension work; to Bible study groups, adult S. S., and miss. soc. The modern adult educ. movement is traceable to E. L. Thorndike's research into adult learning (ca. 1925), which reversed popular opinion that adults do not learn well, and to the organization of the Am. Assoc. of Adult Educ. (1926). The Prot. churches of Am., esp. through the United Christian Adult Movement (1936) initiated by the Internat. Council of Relig. Educ., spearheaded the development of relig. adult educ. Areas for study were set up, and "learning for life" courses developed. Textbooks were written for leadership training in the adult field. Steady progress has been made. Emphasis was placed on the young adult, family life training, the community, and the older adult. The churches discovered that people "learn as long as they live," that the church *is* a school, that Christian discipleship is lifelong growth in understanding, skills, and attitudes, and that it is the adult who sets the pattern of spiritual life for this generation and the next. Adults are the church's most influential teachers, its "living examples of Christian thought and practice."

Attention to adults does not lessen the needs of children and youth but simply recognizes the central role which adults play in our world. Adult educ. in the ch. is based on the doctrine of the priesthood of all believers and on the conviction that every Christian has a miss. in life to fulfill. Adults learn through all that happens in them, to them, and around them. Their whole environment is a part of their educ. In the churches, adult educ. is carried on through ch. services, cong. assemblies, committees, projects, activities, Bible classes, classes in Christian doctrine for adults, fellowship gatherings, organizations and groups within the parish; and in conventions, institutes, and the like outside the local church. Christian adult educ. should foster growth in 8 areas: Bible knowledge and skills, Christian doctrine and life, worship and the arts, Christian educ., Christian family life, the Christian in soc. and the church in the world (hist.), evangelism and miss., and Christian stewardship. Adult educ. in the ch. is strategic, because it (1) helps adults grow spiritually (Cl 1:9, 10), (2) helps them face life victoriously with Jesus (1 Jn 5:4), (3) strengthens Christian elementary educ. and makes it pay larger dividends because children follow adults (Mt 18:6), (4) builds stronger Christian homes (Lk 10:38-42), (5) provides more lay workers for the ch. (Lk 10:1), (6) lifts consecration and stewardship performance for the church's work at home and abroad (Mt 25:14-30), (7) helps to prevent spiritual indifference, nominal Christianity, and the loss of souls (Jn 15:2, 6), and (8) helps to stem the new secularism (Ps 10:4). What the home, the ch., and the nation are and what these will be in the future depends, under God, largely on the understanding, attitudes, skills, and spiritual responsiveness of the adult. OEF

Paul B. Maves, "The Christian Education of Adults," *Religious Education: A Comprehensive Survey,* ed. Marvin J. Taylor (New York, 1960); David J. Ernsberger, *A Philosophy of Adult Education* (Philadelphia, 1959); Earl F. Zeigler, *Christian Education of Adults* (Philadelphia, 1958); Hendrik Kraemer, *A Theology of the Laity* (Philadelphia, 1959); James D. Smart, *The Teaching Ministry of the Church* (Philadelphia, 1954); James R. Kidd, *How Adults Learn* (New York, 1959); Irene Smith Caldwell, *Responsible Adults in the Church School Program* (Anderson, Ind., 1963); Reuel L. Howe, *The Miracle of Dialogue* (Greenwich, 1963); Donald L. Deffner, *Toward Adult Christian Education,* LEA Yearbook (1962).

Adultery. See *Marriage.*

Advent. See *Church Year,* 1, 12; *Tempus clausum.*

Advent Christian Church. See *Adventist Bodies,* 3.

Advent of Christ. The church speaks of a threefold coming of Christ: (1) the lowly coming in the flesh (Zch 9:9; Mt 21:4; see *Incarnation*); (2) His spiritual coming in the hearts of the pious and His constant presence in the church (Jn 14:18, 23; see *Mystical Union);* (3) His return to judgment (Mt 24:30; see *Last Things*).

Adventist Bodies. 1. Adventism centers in the belief that there are 2 advents of Christ (both visible and personal), that the 2d coming of Christ is imminent, and that the central feature of this event is the establishment of His millennial reign. While Adv. has existed throughout the hist. of the ch., esp. in times of stress, the most significant Adv. movement of modern times originated with Wm. Miller (1782–1849). A former army officer, a farmer, a licensed Baptist preacher, and an ardent student of the "chronological portions" of the prophetic writings of the Bible, Miller believed that the dates for all important events in sacred hist. have been fixed in prophecy. Since the exact dates of the Flood, the sojourn of Israel in Egypt, the destruction of the Canaanites, the duration of the Exile had been foretold, the exact date of Christ's 2d coming must also have been prophesied. Miller believed that he found the date of Christ's 2d coming in Dn 8:13, 14, which speaks of 2,300 days until the cleansing of the sanctuary. He fixed the date of the beginning of this period in 457 BC, the year in which the command to rebuild Jerusalem was given, Dn 9:25, and following the practice of most time setters that according to Nm 14:34 a day in prophecy denotes a yr., he proclaimed that the cleansing of the sanctuary would occur within a yr. after March 21, 1843. The 70 weeks of Dn 9:24, totaling 490 yrs. and ending AD 33, would constitute the first part of the 2,300 "days," and the 1,335 days of Dn 12:12 would constitute the 2d part of this period and end in 1843. Miller held that the cleansing of the sanctuary was figurative language denoting the personal return of Christ to cleanse the world of all its pride and power, pomp and vanity and to establish the peaceful kingdom of the Messiah in place of the kingdoms of this world. In 1831 Miller opened a vigorous campaign to gain adherents for his views, and by 1843 his followers numbered 50,000. When March 21, 1844, passed without the Lord's visible return, there was keen disappointment, and Miller admitted his mistake. However, several prominent leaders believed that the coming of the Lord was to occur on the Festival of the Atonement, Oct. 22, 1844, and not on the Jewish New Year, as Miller had predicted. This encouraged the Adventists, and they made extensive preparations for the Lord's glorious appearance, only to be bitterly disappointed again.

2. The belief that Christ would appear at an early date to establish His millennial reign persisted, and in 1845 a group of Adventists met at Albany, N. Y., to define their position and to adopt principles embodying the views of Miller concerning the character of Christ's 2d advent, the resurrection, and the renewal of the earth. The salient points agreed on at Albany are: (a) The present world is to be destroyed by fire, and a new earth is to be created for the be-

lievers. (b) There are only 2 advents of Christ, both visible and personal. (c) The 2d advent is imminent. (d) The condition of sharing in the millennial reign of Christ is repentance and faith, a godly and watchful life. (e) There are 2 resurrections, that of the believers at Christ's 2d coming and that of the unbelievers after the millennium. (f) The departed saints do not enter Paradise in soul and spirit until the final blessedness of the everlasting kingdom will be revealed at Christ's 2d coming. However, differences arose within the group concerning the nature of Christ's coming, the immortality of the soul, the condition of the dead in the intermediate state, and the observance of the Sabbath. Controversies on these points led to the organization of various groups of Adventist bodies, the largest being the Seventh-day Adventist denomination, next in numerical strength the Advent Christian Church, and 3 numbering only a few congregations.

3. *Advent Christian Church.* After the disappointment of 1844, Jonathan Cummings and others predicted that the Lord would come in 1853 or 1854. This caused a division among Adv. When the prophecy remained unfulfilled, Cummings admitted his mistake and advised his adherents to reunite with the parent body. However, during the years of separation from the main body the followers of Cummings had developed ideas on the immortality of the soul which were at variance with the views of the majority. For this reason they organized a separate body in 1861 and have since then been known as the Advent Christian Church. They accept the Bible as the only divinely revealed truth; they repudiate the "inspired" writings of Mrs. Ellen White*; and they confess the doctrine of the Trin. Their distinctive tenet is the theory that man, who was created for immortality, forfeited his divine birthright through sin and that only believers in Christ will receive immortality. They believe that death is the state of unconsciousness and that all men will remain in this "soul sleep" until the 2d coming of Christ, when the righteous will receive everlasting life and the wicked will be annihilated. In common with other Adv. they believe that Christ will return visibly and rule personally in this world, which will be rejuvenated as the eternal home of the redeemed. They observe Sun. as the proper Sabbath and refuse to bear arms.

4. *Seventh-day Adventists.* The movement which resulted in the organization of the Seventh-day Adv. denomination originated with those Adv. leaders who believed that the date of the cleansing of the sanctuary had been fixed correctly by Miller but differed from him in interpreting the nature of this event. They held that the cleansing of the sanctuary did not refer to the rejuvenating of the world, as Miller had believed, but to Christ's "investigative judgment" in the sanctuary of heaven. According to this view Christ began in the fall of 1844 to judge the conduct of His chosen people according to the standard of the Decalog. In the meantime a congregation connected with the Adv. movement had come into contact with Seventh-day Bap., and this group insisted that the keeping of the OT Sabbath was God's everlasting commandment. Gradually an increasing number of Adv. held that Christ was cleansing the sanctuary according "to the fourth principle of the Decalog," that is, judging people as to their attitude over against the commandment to observe the Sabbath according to the Mosaic Law. In 1847 a female leader of the group, Ellen G. White,* nee Harmon (1827–1915), reported visions she had had in support of this doctrine. In one vision she saw two angels standing by the heavenly ark of the covenant in the "sanctuary" and Jesus raising the cover of the ark containing the Ten Commandments, the "fourth" being surrounded by a halo. In another vision she was informed that the third angel's message, Rv 14:9-12, referred to the papacy and that according to Dn 7:25 the great antichristian sin is the changing of the OT Sabbath into Sunday. Under Mrs. White's aggressive leadership, fortified by her vision of 1849 that her enemies were opposing not her but the Holy Spirit, the movement rapidly achieved its present basic form. A formal organization was effected in 1853. The founding of the group's 1st pub. house at Battle Creek, Mich., in 1855 marked the beginning of the movement's use of the printed word to disseminate its tenets. In 1863 the Gen. Conf. adopted a definitive constitution.

While Seventh-day Adv. have no formal creed, they believe that at the conclusion of His investigative judgment, begun in 1844 and based on man's attitude over against the Sabbath, Christ will return to this world, resurrect and translate all the just who have observed the Sabbath, consume the unjust who have kept the Sun., remove the just from this world, and leave the world desolate for 1,000 years. After the 1,000 years Christ and the saints will return to this world, the unjust will be raised, be granted a period of probation, and, if found unworthy, be annihilated with Satan. This earth will then become the rejuvenated home of the redeemed race of Adam. The Seventh-day Adv. believe it is their work to announce to all nations that the keeping of the Sabbath is man's only hope of preparing for the Lord's 2d coming. In the interest of this cen. doctrine they have developed their entire theology. (a) Although they claim to accept the Holy Scriptures as the only source of faith and practice, they actually base their cen. doctrine on the visions and revelations of Mrs. White, whom they consider to have been an inspired prophetess. (b) On the one hand they confess that the sinner is "justified by the Savior's grace, who cleanses from sin," but on the other hand they subscribe to Mrs. White's doctrine that the work of Christ consisted largely in showing that the Law of God could be kept by man. Obedience to such commandments as keeping the Sabbath, contributing the tithe, abstaining from pork, intoxicants, stimulants, and tobacco, and wearing modest clothes occupies a prominent place in their scheme of salvation. (c) In the doctrine of Christ's sacerdotal office they differ fundamentally from historic ev. doctrine. On the basis of Heb 8:1, 2 and similar passages they teach that the priestly office of Christ consists of 2 phases, the 1st extending from His ascension until 1844, the 2d inaugurated in the fall of 1844. The theory of the atonement is as follows: As the OT high priest pleaded for the congregation in the Holy Place of the temple throughout the yr., so Christ interceded for His people during the NT period; and as the high priest entered the Holy of Holies once a yr. and placed the sins of the congregation on the scapegoat, thus cleansing the sanctuary, so Christ entered the heavenly sanctuary in 1844 and is now placing the sins of His people on the devil. (d) Since the atonement is not completed until the sins have been removed from the sanctuary, the fate of the departed cannot be determined until Christ's 2d coming. In the interest of this theory they hold that all the dead, good and evil, are in a state of unconsciousness in the intermediate state. This is in line with their view that man is by nature mortal, that immortality will be given only to the believers, and that all wicked men will be entirely annihilated. When the world is rejuvenated, there will be no hell. Seventh-day Adv. reject infant baptism. They understand the ordinance of the Lord's Supper symbolically and observe it 4 times a yr. in conjunction with the rite of foot washing.

In recent yrs. an effort has been made by some denominational leaders to assimilate the Seventh-day Adv. into conservative Protestantism by minimizing the traditional differences in the Seventh-day Adv. doctrines of the Trin. and of the person and work of Christ. This effort has met with some resistance within the group and with skepticism on the part of some conservative Protestants, while other conservative Protestants have praised the development and have affirmed their willingness to recognize the Seventh-day Adv. as a basically Christian denomination. The group is marked by its energetic for. miss. activity (notably in Lat. Am. and in Afr.) with a total membership outside this country that exceeds the group's 335,765 members (1962) in U. S.; its use of mass media of communications (regular programs over nearly 1,000 radio and more than 150 television stations; nearly 50 pub. houses, printing in over 200 languages and putting out nearly 400 magazines); its stress on educ. (nearly 5,000 elementary and almost 300 secondary schools); its work in medicine and health (over 100 hospitals and sanatoria); its aggressive anti-RC polemics; and its emphasis on the absolute separation of relig. and gov.

5. The Church* of God (Seventh Day), Denver, Colo.

6. The Church* of God (Seventh Day), Salem, W. Va.

7. Church* of God of the Abrahamic Faith.

8. *Life and Advent Union.* Small denomination of Adv. which teaches that there will be no resurrection of the wicked.

See *Religious Bodies (U. S.), Bibliography.* FEM; ACP

Advocatus Dei, Advocatus Diaboli. See *Canonization.*

Advowson. The right of presentation to an ecclesiastical benefice, first mentioned in 441 (Council of Orange). In a presentative advowson a patron presents a candidate for the bp.'s endorsement; in a collative advowson the bp. himself is the patron.

Aegidius of Assisi (Giles; d. 1262). Companion of Francis of Assisi; his *Dicta* tr. into Eng.

Aegidius Romanus (Egidio Colonna; Giles of Rome; ca. 1245/47–1316). Augustinian theol.; studied under Thomas* Aquinas; became indep. thinker. His *De summi pontificis potestate* was the basis of Unam Sanctam (see *Bull*) of Boniface VIII (see *Popes,* 12). Other works include *Quodlibeta;* commentaries on Bible, Aristotle,* Peter* the Lombard. See also *Church and State,* 7.

Aelfric (ca. 955–1020). Eng. abbot; compiled grammar (hence called "The Grammarian"); tr. parts of OT; wrote homilies ("Lives of the Saints" most important); denied the Immaculate Conception.*

Aemilie Juliane (1637–1706), Countess of Schwarzburg-Rudolstadt. B. Heidecksburg, Schwarzburg-Rudolstadt, Ger.; orphaned at 5, adopted by her aunt, educ. in music and poetry; most productive of Ger. female hymnists, some 600 hymns being attributed to her; her hymns are full of a deep love for her Savior.

Aeneas of Gaza (d. 518). Alexandrian Christian Neoplatonist philosopher; wrote *Theophrastus* (defense of immortality of soul though denying Platonic preexistence).

Aenesidemus. See *Skepticism.*

Aeons. See *Gnosticism,* 5.

Aepinus, Johannes. See *Hoeck, Johann.*

Aerius. Presbyter and director of an asylum or hosp. at Sebaste in Pontus in 4th c.; opponent of strong hierarchical tendencies and of prayers for the dead; the "Aerians" named after him.

Aeschylus. See *Religious Drama.*

Aesthetics. The philosophical study of beauty as applied to art and nature. Plato and Aristotle regarded beauty as identical with order and proportion. Neoplatonism regarded beauty as belonging to all that exists as such. In the Middle Ages the transition to the modern theories of beauty took place. While the objective nature of beauty was held fast, the element of feeling evoked or pleasure experienced was added. The modern trend is to study aesthetics entirely from the subjective or psychological point of view. Thus Kant, in accordance with his system, did not regard beauty as adhering objectively in the object but only in the perception of the object. Present-day aesthetics centers on the "aesthetic experience," which may be defined as arising from "the disinterested and sympathetic attention to and contemplation of any object of awareness whatever, for its own sake alone" (Stolnitz). The chief theories of aesthetics may be classified as follows: "imitation" theories (Plato, Aristotle, Samuel Johnson); formalism (Clive Bell, Roger Fry); emotionalist theory (Tolstoi, Ducasse); the theory of aesthetic "fineness" (D. W. Gotshalk). Aesthetic evaluation and criticism is directed chiefly to painting, sculpture, architecture, literature, and music. – Aestheticism is a term applied to the theory which fails to distinguish between the beautiful and the good (true, to a certain extent, of the Greeks). While the Bible frequently uses connotations of beauty in describing the good (Eph. 5:27; Ps. 149:4; Is. 28:1; Rv. 21; and others), it carefully distinguishes between external beauty and moral uprightness (1 Ptr 3:3-5; Pr 11:22). See also *Architecture; Art; Music.*

Jerome Stolnitz, *Aesthetics and Philosophy of Art Criticism: A Critical Introduction* (Boston, 1960); Curt J. Ducasse, *Art, the Critics, and You* (New York, 1944); James L. Jarrett, *The Quest for Beauty* (Englewood Cliffs, 1957); Thomas Munro, *The Arts and Their Interrelations* (New York, 1949); Monroe C. Beardsley, *Aesthetics: Problems in the Philosophy of Criticism* (New York, 1958); Morris Weitz, *Problems in Aesthetics: An Introductory Book of Readings* (New York, 1959); Katherine E. Gilbert and Helmut Kuhn, *A History of Esthetics* (Bloomington, 1953). WHW

Aetius (d. ca. 370). Native of Antioch, bp. without a see; first to return to pure Arianism after 350; leader of Anomoeans;* wrote *On God Unengendered and on That Which Is Engendered.*

Afars and Issas, French Territory of the. See *Africa,* E 4.

Affirmation. See *American Lutheran Church,* V; *Brief Statement.*

Afghanistan. See *Middle East,* J.

Africa. A. General Description. 1. *Area:* ca. 11,700,000 sq. mi. *Pop.:* ca. 345,000,000. *Inhabitants: Berbers,* Caucasian in origin, aborigines of Sahara and Medit. states; *Arabs,* from W. Asia, in Egypt and N. Afr.; *Negroes,* chiefly in Sudan from Nile to Atlantic; *Bantu,* tribes S. of equator (Kaffirs; Zulus; Basutos; Bechuanas; Matabeles); *Pygmies, Bushmen, Hottentots* scattered through Bantu area.

Dynamic and drastic social, political, and cultural changes are in progress in Africa. Educ. is coming under govt. control; paganism is losing ground; the power of the witch doctor is disappearing.

2. *Religion.* About half the people are pagans, one third Muslims (see *Islam*), and one sixth Christians. RCs total about half of the Christian population, Prots. about two fifths, and Copts about one eighth. Alexandria* and Carthage* were early strongholds of Christianity (see *Clement, Titus Flavius; Origen; Tertullian*). But the ch., weakened by controversy, was almost annihilated by Muslim invasions in the 7th c.

3. The diversified forms of paganism usually embody 3 points: belief in a supreme being; belief in survival after death; belief in mana (impersonal force). Fetishism is a form of spirit worship connected with the use of fetishes. Animism and dynamism are prevalent. Fears and superstitions are connected with belief in demons and the conviction that objects are endowed with mysterious qualities by

means of magical rites. Ancestors are revered, consulted, and honored. Amulets are used extensively.

4. Christianity has made phenomenal penetrations of Afr. life and culture. The Afr. is deeply religious and able to grasp lofty spiritual truth.

5. Luth. work started 1585, when Duke Ludwig* of Württemberg sent an embassy to N. Afr. with miss. work as part of its assignment. Ernest* I of Saxe-Weimar sent Peter Heiling to evangelize Ethiopia, 1634. Georg Schmidt,* a Moravian, started miss. work in Capetown, 1737. He was opposed by the Ref. and returned to Holland. His work was resumed by Moravians, 1792. On Oct. 23, 1779, a Luth. ch. was organized in Capetown.

6. In 19th c. there were 5 avenues of approach to the heart of the continent. Miss. penetration from the south was started in 1799, when John T. Vanderkemp* of the LMS began work among Hottentots and Bushmen. He was joined by Robert Moffat* in 1817, and work extended to Bantus. Work from the north was started in Egypt and Ethiopia in 1825 by the CMS. In 1838 the workers were forced out of Ethiopia, and Johann Ludwig Krapf,* a Luth., went to Zanzibar and started a miss. on Mombasa. The Bap. Miss. Soc. began work in Sierra Leone 1795 but abandoned it 1797. The CMS took up the work, 1804. Henry M. Stanley's crossing of Afr. opened Cen. Afr. via the Congo R. In 1878 the Bap. Miss. Soc. and the Livingstone Inland Miss. entered the Congo.

B. SOUTH AFRICA. 1. *Angola. Area:* 481,351 sq. mi. *Pop.:* ca. 5,900,000. Discovered by Portuguese (1482) and controlled by them except 1641–48. RC Ch. is strong; its priests have status of state functionaries. Prot. miss.: Bap. Miss. Soc. (1878) has 250 places of worship (1960); ABCFM (1880), 1,400 miss. stations; Meth. (1884), 29,941 mem., established Taylor Institute; Plymouth Brethren (1889), 145 assem.; United Ch. of Can., 12,220 mem.; Can. Bap. Miss. (1954); S. Afr. Gen. Miss. (1918).

2. Former Fed. of Rhodesia and Nyasaland (included Northern and Southern Rhodesia and Nyasaland), est. 1953, ended 1963. Northern Rhodesia (indep. 1964) renamed itself *Rep. of Zambia* (*area:* ca. 290,584 sq. mi.; *pop.* [1972 est.]: ca. 4,500,000); mem. Comm. of Nations. *Southern Rhodesia* calls itself simply *Rhodesia* (*area:* ca. 150,332 sq. mi.; *pop.* [1972 est.]: 5,500,000). Nyasaland (indep. 1964) renamed itself *Rep. of Malawi* (*area:* figures vary from 36,100 to 45,747 sq. mi.; *pop.* [1972 est.]: 4,700,000); mem. Comm. of Nations.

Robert Moffat* began miss. work in S. Rhodesia (1859) for the LMS. In 1891, after G. Brit. had extended its control over the area (1890), the Ch. of Eng., the Meth. Miss. Soc., and the Dutch Ref. Ch. began work. The ABCFM entered the field 1893 and established Mt. Silinda Inst. and Pierce Mem. Hosp. Others followed: Seventh-day Adv., 1895; S. Afr. Gen. Miss., 1900; Am. Meth., 1899; Ev. Alliance Miss., 1942; S. Bap., 1950; in 1954 the Christian Conf. of S. Rhodesia was formed with 19 mem. bodies.

The Luth. Ch. of Swed. Miss. (W. Sköld) began work 1903; established large Mnene station, concentrating first on rural areas. The Luth. Ch. in S. Rhodesia has 16,103 mem. (1961), 164 lower primary, 16 upper primary, and one secondary schools, two for teacher training, one for nurses' training, and the Masingo Bible School.

Prot. Christianity in S. Rhodesia numbers 250,000 (1960).

Francis Coillard* began work in N. Rhodesia for the Paris* Ev. Miss. Soc. in 1885. It was followed by the LMS (David Livingstone*), which has the largest miss. in N. Rhodesia. Others: Seventh-day Adv., 1903; S. Afr. Gen. Miss., 1909; Universities' Miss. to Cen. Afr., 1910; Eng. Methodists. Salv. Army has 300 places of worship. Jeh. wit. (1948) are very active.

David Livingstone inspired 3 miss. in Nyasaland: Universities' Miss. to Cen. Afr. (1860) with ca. 40,000 communicants; Livingstonia Miss. of U. F. C. of Scot. (1875); miss. at Blantyre (1876), which operates the Henry Henderson Inst. The latter 2 form the Ch. of Cen. Afr., with ca. 130,000 mem. Others: S. Afr. Gen. Miss (1900); Seventh-day Adv.; Nat. Bap. Conv.

3. *Botswana* (formerly Brit. protectorate Bechuanaland), became fully indep. 1966. *Area:* figures vary from 219,815 to 231,804 sq. mi. *Pop.* (1972 est.): 700,000; mem. Comm. of Nations. R. Moffat* made frequent miss. journeys in Bechuanaland, and in 1864 John Mackenzie began work. Later the Hermannsburg Ev. Luth. Miss. entered the field. Its miss. baptized King Khama, native Christian ruler and reformer. Others: Dutch Ref. Soc., U. F. C. of Scot., Seventh-day Adv. See also *Paris Evangelical Missionary Society.*

4. *Mozambique* (Portuguese E. Afr.). *Area:* 302,328 sq. mi. *Pop.:* ca. 8,100,000. RC miss. entered, 1560. Brit. Meth. began work at Inhambane, 1883. Am. Meth. under Wm. Taylor* took over the work and operated Cen. Training School at Cambine. Swiss Miss. in S. Afr. came in 1870s; Ch. of Eng., 1893; S. Afr. Gen. Miss., 1936. Others: Meth. Ch. of S. Afr.; Pent. Assem. of Can.; Bap. Miss. of Mozambique; Free Bap. Miss.; SPG. Total Prots. about 60,000 (1960).

5. *Republic of South Africa.* Area: 472,359 sq. mi. *Pop.:* 22,000,000 (18,500,000 non whites; about 3,500,000 whites). Came into being in 1910 as indep. dominion in Brit. Commonwealth; became indep. rep., 1961. Apartheid policy (segregation and political and economic discrimination against non-European groups) supported by Dutch Ref. Ch. but opposed by other churches; same is true of Bantu Educ. Act (1953) and Group Areas Act.

The Moravians (George Schmidt,* 1709–85) entered the field, 1737; expelled by Dutch, 1743; reentered, 1792. John T. Vanderkemp* began work for LMS, 1799; followed by Robert Moffat,* John Philip,* David Livingstone,* Methodists (1816). Scot. Presb. (U. F. C. of Scot.) began 1818; founded famous Lovedale School. In 1826 Dutch Ref. Ch. ordained its first miss. to Afr. S. Afr. Gen. Miss. (Cape Gen. Miss.) began 1889. Luth. Rhenish Miss. Soc. and Berlin Miss. Soc. entered field in 1830s and gained firm foothold in Cape Colony. Hermannsburg Miss. (1850s) under Behrens* and Hohls made auspicious progress. Norw. Miss. Soc. sent Schreuder,* 1866; organized the Schreuder Miss., ultimately administered by the Ev. Luth. Ch. The Ch. of Swed. miss. began in 1870s. Other Luth. are the Hannoverian Free Ch. Miss. and the Bapedi Ch. In 1953 a council for churches having a Luth. basis was organized for all South Africa. The Ev. Luth. Ch. in Zulu, Xhosa, and Swaziland was formed July 7, 1960, by the Mankankanana Luth. Syn. (ELC), the Zula-Xhosa-Swazi Syn. (Berlin Miss. Soc. I), the Ev. Luth. Zulu Ch. (Ch. of Swed. Miss.), and the Norw. Luth. Zulu Syn. (Norw. Miss. Soc.); the name was soon changed to The Ev. Luth. Ch. in Southern Africa (South-Eastern Region). The Ev. Luth. Zulu Ch. of the Hermannsburg Miss. joined in a few yrs.

Others: ABCFM; Assem. of God; Ch. of Nazarene; Ev. Alliance Miss.; Mahon Miss.; Meth. Ch.; Salv. Army; Seventh-day Adv.; Mormons.

See also *Ministry, Education of,* XI A 3, 10–13; *Namaqualand.*

6. *Kingdom of Lesotho* (former Brit. protectorate Basutoland) became indep. 1966. *Area:* ca. 11,720 sq. mi. *Pop.* (1972 est.): 1,100,000; mem. Comm.

of Nations; surrounded by Rep. of S. Afr. Natives worship Modimo, regarded as supreme being. Tribes unified by Chief Moshesh, at whose invitation Paris* Ev. Miss. Soc. entered, 1833. Ch. of Eng. began work 1875. Others: A. M. E. Ch.; Nat. Bap. Conv.; Assem. of God.

7. *Kingdom of Swaziland* (former Brit. protectorate) became indep. 1968. *Area:* ca. 6,705 sq. mi. *Pop.* (1972 est.): 420,000; mem. Comm. of Nations. Meth. began Am. miss. work in 1880s. Others: S. Afr. Gen. Assemb. of God; A. M. E. Ch.; Internat. Child Evangelism Fellowship; Pilgrim Holiness Ch.

8. *South-West Afr.* (or *South West Afr.*), also called Namibia, a Ger. colony since 1884; became a South Afr. mandate 1920; UN Gen. Assem. resolved 1968 to revoke the mandate, but S. Afr. continued control. *Area:* ca. 318,260 sq. mi. *Pop.* (1971 est.): 650,000 (Ovambo, Herero,* Bergdamaras, Hottentots,* Bushmen, more than 96,000 whites.

LMS began among Hottentots, 1805. Others: Meth. Ch. of S. Afr.; Fin. Cong. Miss.

The Rhemish* Mission Soc. began 1829. H. K. Hahn* associated industrial and agricultural activity with his mission work. This soc. absorbed the work done by the London and Meth. societies. Oct. 4, 1867, the Rhenish Miss. Ch. constituted itself the Ev. Luth. Ch. in SW Afr. It has a training coll. for teachers and evangelists, the Paulinum, and 60 primary schools. Work on a second Paulinum and plans for a high school were initiated 1961. The Finish Miss. Soc. began 1870. It has the largest miss. and operates schools, seminaries, hospitals, and dispensaries in Ovamboland and the region of the Okovanggo (Okovango; Okavango) River. Martin Rautanen (d. 1926), its pioneer miss., tr. Bible into Ndango. The 123,000-member church is called the Ev. Luth. Ovambokavango Ch.

See also *Ministry, Education of,* XI A 14; *Namaqualand; Ovamboland.*

9. *Malagasy Republic* (Madagascar). *Area:* 230,035 sq. mi. *Pop.:* ca. 7,300,000. Island 250 mi. off E. coast of Afr.; French colony, 1896–1958; indep., 1958. Religion: animistic with traces of polytheism. Ancestor worship and witch doctor prevalent. Supreme being called "Fragrant One." Christianity and Islam are strong. Discovered by Europeans in 16th c. King Radama I invited missionaries; LMS began, 1818. In 1828 Queen Ranavalona I seized throne and persecuted Christians until 1861. In 1862 relig. freedom proclaimed. In 1868 Queen Ranavalona II was baptized. CMS and SPG entered 1864, Brit. Friends 1867. In 1896 a wave of persecution incited by Jesuits swept over the island.

In 1866 the Norw. Miss. Soc. sent John Engh and Nils Nilsen to work in Cen. Province. The Norw. Luth. Ch. of Am. began work 1892, the Luth. Free Ch. 1895. Lars Dahle* led in Bible translation work in 1870s and 1880s.

In 1871 a theol. sem. was founded. In 1950 the Luth. organized the Fiangona Loterana Malagasy (Malagasy Luth. Ch.). See also *Ministry, Education of,* XI A 7.

C. West Africa. 1. *Rep. of Senegal. Area:* ca. 75,750 sq. mi. *Pop.* (1972 est.): 4,100,000. Long a Fr. possession; part of Fr. Union 1946; autonomous rep. in the Fr. Community 1958; part of the short-lived Mali Fed. 1959–60; indep. rep. and mem. UN 1960. Animism and Islam are strong. RCs have done extensive miss. work.

The Paris* Ev. Mis. Soc. entered 1862. Its gains have been small. In the 20th c. the Worldwide Evangelization Crusade and Assem. of God Miss. entered the field.

2. *Mauritania. Area:* 419,229 sq. mi. *Pop.:* ca. 1,200,000 (Moors, Berbers, Negroes). Became indep. of France 1960. In 1534 a papal bull required the king of Portugal to support Cath. missionaries. Prots. had not yet entered the territory by 1960.

3. *Mali, Republic of* (formerly Sudanese Republic). *Area:* 464,874 sq. mi. *Pop.:* ca. 5,3000,000 (Bambaras, Malinkes, Sarakoles, Peulhs). Became indep. from Fr., 1960. Native religion animistic, but Islam made strong gains.

The Gospel Miss. Union began work 1919; tr. Bible into Bambara; emphasized medical work. Christian Miss. Alliance began at Sikasso, 1923; has Sudan Bible School at Ntoroso. Others: United World Miss.; Evangelistic Bap. Miss.

4. *Guinea. Area:* 94,926 sq. mi. *Pop.:* ca. 4,100,000 (most important tribes: Fullah, Mandingo, Susu). Islam is chief religion. In forest regions the Kissis, Tomas, and Guerzas are animistic and under power of fetish priests and sorcerers. At one time, Fr. penal colony. Became indep. (1958) and formed loose union, U. S. of Afr., with Ghana.

Jesuits began work at early date. Christian and Miss. Alliance began at Baro, 1918; headquarters at Kankan, where Mission Press serves all W. Afr.; established Bible school at Telekoro. Others: United World Miss.; Open Bible Stand. Miss.; Pongas Miss.; Jamaican Home and For. Miss. Soc.; SPG; Paris Ev. Miss. Soc.

5. *The Gambia. Area:* figures vary from 4,005 to 4,361 sq. mi. *Pop.* (1972 est.): 400,000 (Negroid Mandingos, Jolofs, Jolas). Former Brit. colony and protectorate; indep. Feb. 1965; mem. Comm. of Nations. Islam claims four fifths of population. Wesleyan Meth. began work 1821. In 1945 the govt. took over Meth., Angl., and RC primary schools and gave churches representation on the boards.

6. *Sierra Leone. Area:* 27,925 sq. mi. *Pop.:* ca. 2,800,000. Leading tribes are the Mendes (wholly Muslim), Uei, Bullom. Named and settled by Portuguese explorers in 15th and 16th c. Brit. colony (1808) and protectorate (1896) till granted independence in 1961. Islam is gaining rapidly.

Bap. Miss. Soc. began work 1795, Glasgow and Edinburgh societies 1797; both enterprises failed. CMS began at Rio Pongas 1807; transferred to Sierra Leone, 1816. One of its earliest miss. (1816–23) was the German William A. B. Johnson. An Am. Negro, Edward Jones, became principal of Fourah Bay Coll. Church organized on an indep. basis (1861) and Samuel Crowther* consecrated bp. Other miss.: Eng. Meth. (1811); Wesleyan Meth. Ch. of Am. (1889); United Brethren in Christ (took over work of the Am. Miss. Soc.); Bible Churchmen's Miss. Soc.; Assem. of God; United Pent. Miss. from Scot.; Miss. Ch. Assoc.

7. *Liberia. Area:* 43,000 sq. mi. *Pop.:* ca. 1,290,000 (Kru, Mandingos, Vai, Gola, Kissi). Animism is native religion; Islam strong in N and NW. Colonized in 1822 by the Nat. Colonization Soc., which sent 25,000 Negroes released from slavery in U. S. Declared its independence in 1847, patterned its constitution after that of the U. S.

First colonists were chiefly Meth. and Bap. Lot(t) Carey* and Colin Teague, Negro Bap., went to Liberia (1821) and formed the Bap. Gen. Conv. (successor: Lott Carey Bap. For. Miss. Conv. 1897). The Nat. Bap. Conv. is another Negro group at work in Liberia. Melville B. Cox* founded M. E. work, 1833. Meth. work is carried on by the A. M. E. and the Afr. Episc. Zion Ch. 1833 the Presb. (Presb. For. Miss. Soc) and Congr. (ABCFM) entered. The Am. Episc. Ch. began in 1820s. Bp. Samuel Ferguson* established educ. system. Cuttington Coll. and Divinity School opened in 1949. Morris Officer began work 1860 for ULC. Outstanding work was done by David and Emily Day. The Ev. Luth. Ch. in Liberia was organized 1948; see also *United Lutheran Church, The,* III. Other missions: Assem.

of God; several Pent. soc.; Bap. Mid-Miss.; Worldwide Evangelization Crusade; Liberian Inland Miss.

Africa's first miss. radio station, ELWA, opened at Monrovia, 1954.

See also *Ministry, Education of,* XI A 6.

8. *Republic of the Upper Volta. Area:* 105,869 sq. mi. *Pop.:* ca. 5,600,000 (mostly Mossis, animists who venerate ancestors and preserve tribal customs). Fr. colony, 1919; indep., 1960. RC Ch. strong. The Assem. of God began among Mossis, 1821; Christian and Miss. Alliance among Black Bobos, 1923. Others: Sudan Interior Miss.; Worldwide Evangelization Crusade; Upper Volta Miss.

9. *Ivory Coast. Area:* 124,502 sq. mi. *Pop.:* ca. 4,500,000 (animists except Dioula Muslims). Fr. protectorate since 1889; indep., 1960. An estimated 100,000 were converted by the Meth.-trained "prophet," Wm. Wada Harris* (1913–15). In 1924 Harris' churches were taken over by Eng. Wesleyans, but membership has dwindled. Others: Christian and Miss. Alliance (1930, established Central Bible School); Worldwide Evangelization Crusade, 1934; Conservative Bap. For. Miss. Soc., 1947.

10. *Niger. Area:* 489,806 sq. mi. *Pop.:* ca. 4,240,000 (chief tribes: Tuaregs; Tibbus; Hausa are Muslims). Fr. possession till indep., 1960. Edward F. Rice began work for Sudan Interior Miss., 1923. It was later joined by the Ev. Bap. Miss.

11. *Ghana. Area:* 92,100 sq. mi. *Pop.:* ca. 9,600,000 (about 50 tribes, mostly animists; Hausa are Muslims). Complete Bible in Ga, Twi, Fanti (1960).

Moravians began miss. work in 18th century. Basel miss. arrived 1828, 1832, but all except Riis succumbed to climate and fever. In 1843 Riis imported Moravian Christians from Jamaica and worked with success. After WW I the work passed to Free Ch. of Scot. The Ewe Presb. Ch. became indep. Thomas Thompson began work for the SPG, 1792. Thomas B. Freeman* began work for Meth. Miss. Soc., 1838. Others: Worldwide Evangelization Crusade, 1940; Bap. Mid-Miss., 1946; Assem. of God.

The Luth. Syn. Conf. began work in Ghana, 1958; first permanent miss. assigned 1961. Congregations established in Accra, the capital, and Tema, the newly developed seaport. A 2d miss. arrived 1962, established a congregation in the Kumasi area. The Ev. Luth. Ch. of Ghana was inc. 1961, accepted as a sister ch. of the LCMS 1971.

12. *Rep. of Dahomey. Area:* 43,483 sq. mi. *Pop.:* ca. 2,830,000 (chiefly Ewe and Bariba Negroes and Voltaic tribes). RC m has a strong hold; Islam is very influential. Eng. Meth. began work in middle of 19th c. Arthur E. Wilson and wife began work for Assem. of God, 1945. Sudan Interior Miss. began 1946.

13. *Togo. Area:* 21,853 sq. mi. *Pop.:* 2,000,000 (Ewe tribes predominate in S.; Hamitic tribes in N. are mostly Muslim). Indep., April 1960. The N. Ger. Miss. Soc. began among Ewe people 1847. During WW I this work was continued by native pastors and the U. F. C. of Scot. Others: Paris Ev. Miss. Soc.; Assem. of God.

14. *Nigeria. Area:* 356,669 sq. mi. *Pop.:* ca. 58,000,000 (250 tribes, among which Hausa, Fulani, Yoruba, and Ibo predominate). Islam gained strong foothold in the N. in 11th c. Brit. protectorate till Oct. 1960, then indep. The E region declared its indep. as Biafra 1967, succumbed 1970. In response to requests by repatriated Christian slaves, the Wesleyan Miss. Soc. and the CMS began work at Abeokuta, 1842. Names of Henry Townsend, Samuel Adjai Crowther,* and Mary Slessor* are prominent in hist. of Nigeria's missions. U. F. C. of Scot. began work 1846. The Qua Iboe Miss., started by Samuel A. Bill 1887, has been very successful in training national pastors.

The Sudan* Interior Miss. was founded as an indep. faith by Rowland V. Bingham in 1901. A. W. Banfield tr. Bible into Nupe dialect. A. P. Stirrett was pioneer medical miss.

The Dan. Sudan Miss. (Luth.) began work 1913. Others: Primitive Meth., 1893; Sudan United Miss., 1904; United Miss. Ch.; Dutch Ref. Ch. of S. Afr.; Salv. Army; Church Brethren; Christian Missions in Many Lands; Apostolic Ch.; Meth. Miss. Soc. (Eng.); Assem. of God; United Miss. Soc.

The Afr. Miss. Soc. of the Ev. Ch. of W. Af. supports over 100 national pastors. The Christian Council of Nigeria, representing 14 churches, was founded 1930.

In response to a plea from the Ibesikpo people, who had sent Jonathan Udoe Ekong to Am. to find a ch. to give them spiritual guidance, the Luth. Syn. Conf. in 1934 decided to send a 3-man delegation to explore the situation. Upon their favorable report Dr. Henry Nau, pres. of Immanuel Luth. Coll. of Greensboro, N. C., was sent to Afr. to begin the work. He was soon joined by others, and the work developed rapidly. A syn. was formed 1936 under the const. name "The Synod of the Evangelical Lutheran Church of Nigeria" and inc. under the name "The Evangelical Lutheran Church of Nigeria." WW II difficulty in getting new workers to the field resulted in the opening of a sem. and the training of a nat. ministry. 1949–53 saw the opening of a girls' school, a vocational training school, foundling home, high school, normal school, hosp., and the expansion of a bookstore and a printshop. 1963 const. name: "The Evangelical Lutheran Church of Nigeria." 1971 const. name: "The Synod of the Lutheran Church of Nigeria" The ch. was inc. as "Lutheran Church of Nigeria" 1972.

Statistics (1963) — baptized mem. 36,995, communicants 15,350, 12 districts, 209 congregations and preaching stations. Missionaries: 24 pastors, 11 teachers, 3 doctors, 5 nurses, 4 layworkers. Nat. workers: 17 pastors, 21 evangelists, 568 teachers, 15 medical workers. Institutions: 1 sem., 2 Bible institutes, 2 high schools, 87 elementary schools with 16,000 enrolled, 1 teacher-training coll., 2 hosp., school for missionaries' children.

See also *Ministry, Education of,* XI A 8–9.

15. *Portuguese Guinea. Area.:* 13,948 sq. mi. *Pop.:* ca. 600,000 (Mandingos, Fulas, Negroes, Bolams, Bulantas, Manjaks, Nalu, Biafare). RC predominates; Mandingos and Fulas are Muslims. The Worldwide Evangelization Crusade began work 1940.

16. *Madeira Islands. Area:* 308 sq. mi.; 400 mi. W. of Morocco. *Pop.:* ca. 268,700, mostly Eur. Uninhabited islands settled by Portuguese in 1419; RC dominant. Robert Reid Kalley, physician, began Prot. work in 1838 which resulted in an indigenous ch. functioning under the Presb. Joint. Com. on Ev. Cooperation in Portugal. M. E. Ch., began 1897.

17. *Cape Verde Islands. Area:* 1,538 sq. mi. *Pop.:* ca. 300,000 (mostly mulattoes). Discovered 1441 and annexed to Portugal 1456; predominantly RC. Ch. of the Nazarene began work in 1920s.

18. *Rep. of Equatorial Guinea* (former Sp. Guinea). Indep. 1968. *Area:* figures vary from 10,830 to 10,852 sq. mi. *Pop.* (1972 est.): 300,000. Discovered 1491. Am. Presb. began 1865 and worked under difficulties caused by the authorities. Its miss.: Mision Evangelica de Guinea Espanola. Others: Prim. Meth. Ch. (1870); Worldwide Evangelization Crusade (1933).

D. North Africa. 1. *Libya. Area:* 679,358 sq. mi. *Pop.:* ca. 2,000,000 (mostly Arabs, Berbers). Mentioned in Bible (Eze 30:5; Acts 2:10). Ruled by Phoenicians, Carthage, Rome, Vandals, Arabs (7th and 11th c.), Turks (1551), Italians (1912);

home of Barbary pirates; became federal kingdom Dec. 24, 1951, republic 1969. Islam is state religion. RC Ch. has It. and Maltese adherents. Christian miss. are restricted by the govt. The N. Afr. Miss. began work 1888 (William Reid). Others: Christian Miss. to the Jews; Seventh-day Adv.

2. *Tunisia. Area:* 48,332 sq. mi. *Pop.:* ca. 5,400,000 (mostly Muslim Arabs; 250,000 Europeans mostly RC). Ruled by Carthage, Rome, Arabs, Vandals, Fr. (1881); independent, 1956. Ramón Lull* (RC, 1235–1315) was pioneer miss. to Muslims of Tunis. The London Ch. Miss. to the Jews began work 1881. Others: N. Afr. Miss., 1882; Am. Meth., 1909.

3. *Algeria. Area:* 919,591 sq. mi. *Pop.:* ca. 15,200,000 (mostly Muslim Berbers and Arabs; 1,200,000 Europeans, mostly RC). Became Fr. colony in 1848, indep. rep. 1962/63. Edward H. Glenny (founder of N. Afr. Miss.) arrived in Algiers Nov. 5, 1881, with Henri Mayor and Salim Zeytoun. Others: Am. Meth. (1910); BFBS (whole Bible in Kabyle); Algiers Miss. Band; Ch. Miss. to Jews; Fr. Ev. Miss. to the Kabyles; Ev. Bap. Miss. The Luth. Dan. Israel Miss. began work among the Jews in Algiers.

4. *Morocco. Area:* 174,500 sq. mi. *Pop.:* ca. 16,500,000 (mostly Muslim Arabs, Moors, Berbers; 500,000 Europeans; 200,000 Jews; Negroes brought in from Sudan as slaves). In 1957 revisions in marital laws elevated the position of women. RCs number about 100,000. Arabs gained control of Morocco in AD 680. Fr. protectorate, 1912; indep. kingdom, 1956.

The Ch. Miss. to the Jews was the first soc. in Morocco (1875). The N. Afr. Miss. (1882), the S. Morocco Miss. (1889), and the Gospel Miss. Union are the largest societies in Morocco. Others: Mildmay Miss. to the Jews, 1889; Christian Miss. in Many Lands; Bible Churchmen's Miss. Soc.; Gospel Miss. Union, 1895; Light of Afr. Miss. A radio station, Voice of Tangier, broadcast from Tangier till private broadcasting was forbidden Dec. 31, 1959; thereafter it was located at Monte Carlo (Trans World Radio).

5. *Canary Islands. Area:* 2,808 sq. mi. *Pop.:* ca. 1,170,200 (mixture of Sp. and Guanches). Discovered in 15th c.; under Sp. control. RC predominant religion. Worldwide Evangelization Crusade began work 1946. Prot. preaching services prohibited.

6. *Rio de Oro.* Zone in Sp. Sahara (though sometimes the name is used for all of Sp. Sahara). *Area:* figures vary from 71,042 to 73,362 sq. mi. *Pop.* (perhaps ca. 2,000 settled inhabitants and perhaps ca. 19,000 to 25,000 nomadic tribesmen) consists mainly of Moors, Arabs, Berbers, Negroes. *Pop.* for all Sp. Sahara: perhaps ca. 55,000 to 60,000. Discovered by Sp., 1476, annexed, 1887. Islam is predominant religion. Neglected by Christian missions.

7. *Ifni.* Formerly part of Morocco; ceded to Sp. 1860; returned to Morocco 1969. *Area:* ca. 740/746 sq. mi. *Pop.* (1968): ca. 49,889 (chiefly Muslim). Neglected by Christian missions.

E. East Africa. 1. *Sudan* (formerly Anglo-Egyptian Sudan). *Area:* 967,500 sq. mi. *Pop.:* ca. 16,800,000 (two thirds Arabic-speaking Muslims in N. and Cen. sections, one third Negro tribesmen in south who speak 30 languages divided into 250 dialects). Ancient Cush and Nubia are contained in this territory. Arabs entered N. Sudan (Nubia) in 8th c., conquered it 1320, 1504. Khartoum was captured 1885 by Mahdists. Known as Anglo-Egyptian Sudan 1898–1955; indep., 1956. Constitution guarantees freedom of religion and conscience, but missionaries restricted. BFBS did pioneer work in Khartoum region in 1860s. Ch. Miss. Soc. opened station at Omdurman, 1899; in 1906 began work among southern tribes, where tens of thousands embraced Christianity as a result of emphasis on evangelism through educ. and indigenous churches. National pastors are trained at the Bishop Gwynne Coll. United Presb. Miss. established miss. at Khartoum in 1900 and at Doleib Hill in 1902, where the Ch. of Christ in the Upper Nile was established 1956. Sudan* United Miss. (organized by Lucy Guinness and Karl Kumm) began work 1907. Others: Sudan Interior Miss., 1936; Afr. Inland Miss., 1949.

2. *Ethiopia* (Abyssinia). *Area:* 471,778 sq. mi. *Pop.:* ca. 26,200,000 (mostly of Hamitic or Hamitic-Semitic stock mingled with Nilotic groups). Several millennia BC, Hamites of same stock as Egyptians invaded Ethiopia and pushed Negroes S. and W. In 1st millennium BC Semites from Yemen invaded the N. part, mingled with Hamites, and established the Aksumite kingdom, from which current rulers trace descent. About one third of the people are Ethiopian Christian (see *Ethiopic Church*); one third, Muslims; one third, animists; and a small group of Falasha Jews. The country is divided into "Ethiopic Church areas" and "open areas." Miss. work is permitted only in the latter. P. Heiling (see *Missions,* 4) began miss. work in 1634. In 1830 the CMS sent Samuel Gobat (1799–1879; after miss. efforts, bp. of Jerusalem) and others, who were expelled after 10 years. The London Soc. for Promoting Christianity Among the Jews and the Scot. Jewish Miss. began work among the Falasha Jews, 1860. Thomas A. Lambie of the United Presb. Ch. began work 1920, merged it with the Sudan Interior Miss. in 1927, which had 250 missionaries in Ethiopia 1960. Others: Bible Churchmen's Miss. Soc., 1932; E. Mennonite Bd. of Miss. and Charities; Bap. Gen. Conf.; Fin. Pent. Miss.; Christian Miss. in Many Lands; Red Sea Miss. Team; BFBS; SPG.

The Swed. Luth. *Fosterlandsstiftelse,* which had worked in Eritrea, began work at Addis Ababa (1904) and extended it to the Gallas (1923), to which the miss. had sent pupils from Eritrea in 1877 and where the Ethiopian Onesimus had done pioneer work. The Swed. soc. *Bibeltrogna Venner* began work 1911; the Ger. Hermannsburg Miss., 1927. Others: Dan. Ethiopian Miss.; Norw. Luth. Miss.; ALC. The LWF radio station at Addis Ababa was dedicated Feb. 26, 1963.

See also *Ministry, Education of,* XI A 4–5.

3. *Eritrea. Area:* 46,000 sq. mi. *Pop.:* ca. 1,000,000 (about half Muslim, [see E 2] half Abyssinian Orthodox). Under It. influence from 1885 to WW II. Federated with Ethiopia 1952, integrated with it 1962. 1866 the Swed. Luth. *Fosterlandsstiftelse* began work among Kunama tribe. Its Ev. Luth. Ch. of Eritrea has 4,752 mem. (1961). The Swed. Luth. *Bibeltrogna Venner* began 1911; closed during It. rule (715 mem., 1961). Others: Orthodox Presb. Ch.; Evangelistic Faith Miss.; Sudan Interior Miss.; Middle E. Gen. Miss.; Red Sea Miss. Team.

4. *Fr. Territory of the Afars and the Issas* (name changed 1967 from Fr. Somaliland. *Area:* figures vary from 8,494 to 9,000 sq. mi. *Pop.:* recent figures vary from 81,000 to 125,000. Territory in Fr. Community. RCs carry on work chiefly among Europeans. Prots. prevented from doing work by Fr. administration.

5. *Somalia* (formerly Brit. and It. Somalilands). *Area:* 265,000 sq. mi. *Pop.:* 2,930,000. Indep., 1960. Christianity probably introduced in 4th c., but in 9th c. Islam became dominant religion. The Swed. *Fosterlandsstiftelse* began work in 1875 but deported by Italians in late 1930s and missions given to RCs. Others: E. Mennonite Bd. of Miss. and Charities, 1952; Sudan Interior Miss., 1954.

6. *Kenya. Area:* 225,000 sq. mi. *Pop.:* ca. 11,900,000 (Bantu, Hamitic, and Sudan Negro stock; some Pygmies, Arabs, Europeans; Indians). Tribal religions and Islam prevail. Mau Mau movement

(political, religious, antiwhite) spread violence in 1950s. Brit. protect. 1890, indep. 1963. John L. Krapf began work for CMS at Mombasa, was joined by John Rebmann,* 1846. United Meth. Ch. began 1862. The miss. started by the E. Afr. Scot. Industrial Miss. (1891) was transferred to the Ch. of Scot., then to the Presb. Ch. of E. Afr. In Kenya Peter Cameron Scott* formed the Afr. Inland Miss. (1895), which has 100 missionaries in Kenya. Formed Afr. Inland Ch., 1941. Others: Pent. Assem. of E. Afr.; Salv. Army; Ch. of God; World Gospel Miss. (Nat. Holiness Assoc.); Bible Churchmen's Miss. Soc.; Elim Miss. Soc.; Norw. Pent. Assem.; Gospel Furthering Fellowship; Ind. Bd. for Presb. For. Miss.; Livingstone Pioneer Miss. Luth. work is carried on by the Swed. *Bibeltrogna Venner.*

7. *United Republic of Tanzania. Area:* 363,708 sq. mi. *Pop.:* ca. 14,000,000. Formed Apr. 26, 1964, by union of Tanganyika and Zanzibar. Most of the 315,000 inhabitants of the island of Zanzibar are Muslim. Tanganyika: pop. mostly Afr., 120 tribes, the largest the Sukuma; religions: animism and Islam; Portugal gained partial control (1498) but lost to Arabs and Turks; Ger. gained control (1884, 1890); after WW I mandated to Brit.; indep., 1961. The Universities' Miss. to Central Afr. (Angl.) began in Tanganyika in 1860, joined later by the CMS. The Angl. have 175,000 members and 800 Afr. workers (1960). In 1873 the CMS opened a field W. of Zanzibar. Others: Moravians (work started by LMS); Afr. Inland Miss. (40,000); Assem. of God; Seventh-day Adv.; Salv. Army; Mennonites; Christian Miss. in Many Lands; Gospel Furthering Fellowship; S. Bap.

During period of Ger. control slave traffic was abolished, and a number of Luth. soc. began work. The Bethel Miss. started work at Dar-es-Salaam, 1887, the Berlin Miss. in the Lake Nyasa region 1891; the Leipzig Miss. took over the work of the CMS in the Kilimanjaro area 1893. Later the Bethel Miss. began work in the Ruanda and Bukoba regions. During and after WW I Ger. miss. were expelled and the ch. were cared for in part by Scot. Presb., Afr. Meth., and Eng. Brethren. The League of Nations placed the country under Brit. rule, which gave the Luth. miss. to the Aug. Syn. (1921–22). After 1925 Ger. missionaries were permitted to return. In 1939 the Swed. opened missions in the southern highlands. They were later joined by the Fin. Miss. Soc. and Dan. Miss. The Norw. Miss. works in the north-cen. area. In 1961 the following Luth. ch. were in Tanganyika: Ev. Ch. of NW Tanganyika (55,385 members); Luth. Ch. of N. Tanganyika (158,615); Luth. Ch. of S. Tanganyika (90,728); Iraqu Luth. Ch. (2,097); Luth. Ch. of Central Tanganyika (18,190); Luth. Ch. of Uzaramo-Uluguru (5,374); Luth. Ch. of Usambara-Digo (32,150). The 1st joint conv. of Luth. was held in 1935. Thereafter the churches worked for unity and were ready for union in early 1960s. The Luth. Radio Center sends programs to various Afr. stations. Noted are the Luth. Theol. Coll. at Makumira and the Kilimanjaro Christian Medical Center.

See also *Ministry, Education of,* XI A 15.

8. See *Egypt.*

F. Central Africa. 1. *Uganda. Area:* 91,076 sq. mi. *Pop.:* ca. 10,450,000 (Bagandas, Pygmies, Bantus, Negroes, Hamites, Indians). Ganda native language. Africans are animists; Indians, Hindu; Islam is making gains. Brit. protect. 1894; rep. 1963. H. M. Stanley made the acquaintance of King Mtesa, who professed Christianity and asked for missionaries. Alexander Mackay* and 7 others were sent by the CMS (1876). Mackay was followed by H. P. Parker and Alfred R. Tucker. Anglicans have 100,000 baptized Christians and 2,500 places of worship (1960). Others: Afr. Inland Mission; Bible Churchmen's Miss. Soc.; Seventh-day Adv.

2. *Rep. of Zaïre.* Capital: Kinshasa (formerly Leopoldville). *Area:* figures vary from 905,328 to 905,568 sq. mi. *Pop.:* 23,300,000 (mostly Pygmies and Negroes). Languages: Kikonga, Lingala, Luba, Kingwana. In 1884 the Congo Free State was set up under Belg. king as absolute monarch; Belg. colony (called Belg. Congo) 1908; indep. 1960 as Democratic Rep. of the Congo; name changed 1971 to Rep. of Zaïre, after the 15th-c. Port. name for the Nzadi (Congo) R.; Congolese now called Zaïrois; all Congolese were required in the early 1970s to shed their Christian names. Long "slave pen" of W coast. Stanley descended the Congo to its mouth and wrote *Challenge to Christendom.* As a result the Livingstone Inland Miss. opened a station at Palabala in 1878, 6 years later transferred its work to the Am. Bap. Miss. Union (Am. Bap. For. Miss. Soc.). The Bap. Miss. Soc. began 1879 at Banzamanteke. In 1889 H. Grattan Guinness established the Congo Balolo Miss. Frederick S. Arnot (1858–1914) established miss. in SE Congo (Garenganze Ev. Miss.) for Plymouth Brethren, 1889. The Christian and Miss. Alliance established work 1884 (W. pocket). The S. Presb. started miss. at Luebo in 1891, have 70,000 communicants. Disciples of Christ entered 1899. Am. Meth. entered 1885 but did not become permanently established till 1914.

The Swed. *Missionsförbundet* originally assoc. its work with Livingstone Inland Miss., later extended its work on lower bank of the Congo.

Almost 50 soc. undertook work in the Congo, these operate 170 major medical institutions, 12,000 schools, large printing press. Entire Scriptures are available in 11 languages, the NT in 21 (1960). Prots. number over 2,000,000.

Pioneer RC miss.: Miss. du Saint Esprit; Belgian Miss.; New Miss. at Bangola (Jesuit); Miss. of the Peres D'Algerie. RCs number ca. 3,000,000 (1960).

3. *Central African Republic* (Ubangi-Shari). *Area:* 238,000 sq. mi. *Pop.:* ca. 1,500,000 (chiefly Manqia, Banda, Zandi, Banziri, Sari, M'Boom, Pambla, Boonga). Many Muslim nomads entered from Nigeria and the Cameroons. Colony of Fr. till 1958; rep., 1958; indep., 1960. Ch. of the Brethren sent 4 miss. 1918, has baptized membership of 20,660 (1960) and a Central Bible Institute. Bap. Mid-Miss. has been at work since 1920, Afr. Inland Miss. since 1924. Swed. Bap. Miss. Soc. has small miss.

4. *People's Rep. of the Congo* (Congo Rep.). *Area:* 132,046 sq. mi. *Pop.* (1972 est.): 1,000,000 (mainly Bateka and Banda). Explored by Fr. beginning in the 1870s. Brazzaville founded 1880 by explorer Pierre Paul François Camille Savorgnan de Brazza (1852–1905). Boundaries bet. Fr. and Belg. Congos est. 1885. The colony of Fr. Congo est. 1891. Known as Middle Congo from 1903. Linked with Chad, Gabon, and Ubangi-Shari to form Fr. Equatorial Afr. 1910, with Brazzaville capital. Overseas territory of Fr. 1946. Autonomous rep. in the Fr. Community 1958; fully indep. mem. of the community 1960. The Swed. *Missionsförbundet,* between Brazzaville and the sea, has 45,000 members. United World Miss. began work 1948.

5. *Gabon. Area:* 103,000 sq. mi. *Pop.:* ca. 500,000 (chiefly Bantu; small remnant of slave Pygmies). Muslims have entered. Under Fr. 1839–58; fully indep. of Fr. 1960. RCs began miss. 1844 (Libermann). Prot. miss.: ABCFM, 1842; Am. Presb., 1850; Paris Ev. Miss. Soc., 1892; Christian and Miss. Alliance, 1934. In 1913 Albert Schweitzer* came to Gabon and established his famous hosp. at Lambaréné.

6. *Chad. Area:* 495,000 sq. mi. *Pop.:* ca. 3,900,000 (mostly Negroes with some Semites,

Hausas and Fulani immigrants and Arabs). Language in N is Arabic, in S, Ngambai. Fr. colony until 1958; rep., 1958; indep., 1960. Islam is strong in N, animism in S. Bap. Mid-Miss. began at Fort Archambault, Christian Miss. in Many Lands at Fort Lamy, 1929, the Sudan United Miss., 1926. The Luth. Brethren Miss. is also at work. RCs became active in the 1930s.

7. *Cameroon* (Cameroun). *Area:* 200,000 sq. mi. *Pop.:* ca. 6,000,000 (Bantu and Sudan Negroes, Hausa, Fulani, Pygmies). Islam strong in N. Ger. protect. till 1916, when Fr. took five sixths, Eng. one sixth. In 1960 the Brit. section (except a small section that joined Nigeria) voted to join the E. section, which had become an indep. state. The Bap. Miss. Soc. began work 1841, reduced the language to writing, tr. Bible. Its outstanding missionary was Alfred Saker (1814–80). The Presb. Ch. in the U. S. A. extended its work to the Cameroons in the 1880s; organized the Presb. Ch. of Cameroun, 1957. The Ger. Bap., who began in 1890, turned their miss. over to the Am. Bap. Gen. Miss. Soc., 1935. The Sudan United Miss. (1911) has 10 stations (1960). The Ref. Ev. Ch. (Fr.) has 80,000 mem.; Seventh-day Adv., 3,000. RCs are very active in the area.

When Ger. assumed control (1887), the Bap. Miss. Soc. miss. were given to the Basel Ev. Miss. Soc. After WW I the miss. was given to the Paris Miss. and ultimately became a part of the Presb. Ch. The Luth. Brethren began work from Garoua to Lake Shad, 1920. In 1923 an indep. organization led by Adolphus Gunderson began work which was later taken over by the Ev. Luth. Ch. (U. S.). In 1925 the Norw. Miss. Soc. began miss. in the Ngaoundere area. These began to cooperate 1945. The Ev. Luth. Ch. of the Cameroons and the Cen. Afr. Rep. began its first year of constitutional life 1961. It has a sem. at Meiganga. EL (sections under Nigeria and Ghana by HM and KK)

See also *Church of the Lutheran Brethren of America; Ethiopianism; Kamerun; Ministry, Education of,* XI A 1–2.

Africa Inland Mission. See *Africa,* E 6.

African Methodist Episcopal Church. Began when Negroes under leadership of Richard Allen,* William White, and Absalom Jones withdrew from Saint George's Ch., Philadelphia, Nov. 1787 because of attempted racial segregation. In 1816 they withdrew from the M. E. Ch. and organized the ch. for the colored. The ch. has a sem. and coll. at Wilberforce, Ohio. See also *Methodist Churches,* 4 c.

African Methodist Episcopal Zion Church. See *Methodist Churches,* 4 c.

African Orthodox Church. Small body of Negro Episc. organized independently of the Prot. Episc. Ch. In doctrine it follows quite closely the High Ch. party in the Angl. Ch.

African Union First Colored Methodist Protestant Church, Inc. See *Methodist Churches,* 4 c.

Africanus, Sextus Julius. See *Julius Africanus, Sextus.*

Afrikaner. Chief in Union of S. Africa; welcomed Christian Albrecht into his country; enraged by imprudence of Christians, he destroyed mission at Warm Bath; later converted; miss. companion of R. Moffat.*

Agapastic Evolution. The view that attraction, sympathy, and purpose appear in the evolutionary process (Charles S. Peirce*).

Agape. 1. See *Love; Lund, Theology of.* 2. Love feast or common religious meal in early ch. (1 Co 11:17-34; Ignatius, letter to the Smyrnaeans, viii; Pliny's letter to Trajan).

Agapetae (Gk. "beloved"). In the early c., virgins who lived with men in a so-called state of spiritual love. Abuses led to condemnation at Elvira (ca. 306). Later a Gnostic sect was known by the same name (395).

Agatha. Sicilian noblewoman martyred by Quintianus, governor of Sicily, in 251.

Age See *Time.*

Age, Canonical. The age at which the RC Ch. (and, with variations, the Angl. Ch.) admits its subjects to various obligations and privileges. A child, upon attaining the "age of reason," about the 7th year, is held capable of mortal sin and of receiving the sacraments of penance and extreme unction, becomes subject to the law of the ch., and can contract an engagement of marriage. Shortly after, confirmation and Communion are administered. Girls may contract marriage at 12, boys at 14. The obligation of fasting begins at 21 and ends at 60. A deacon must be 22 years old, a priest 24, a bp. 30.

Age of Reason. 1. See *Age, Canonical.* 2. Name applied to 18th c. because of its rationalistic, antisupernaturalistic philosophies. See also *Natural Law,* 5.

Agil (us) (Ayeul; ca. 580–ca.650). B. Franche-Comté, Fr.; monk trained by Eustace* at Luxeuil; miss. with Eustace to Bav. ca. 617; 1st abbot at Rebais.

Agencies, Educational. See *Parish Education.*

Agenda (Lat. "things to be done"). In Eur. Lutheranism the handbook from which the clergyman conducts the services and ministrations of the ch. Eng.-speaking Lutheranism differentiates the agenda (orders for Baptism, confirmation, marriage, funerals, ordination, etc.) from the liturgy (orders for the pub. services). See also *Löhe, Johann Konrad Wilhelm; Service Books.*

Agenda Controversy. A controversy occasioned by the attempts of Frederick* William III of Prussia to introduce the "Prussian Liturgy." Some churches had as early as 1787 petitioned that the agenda be amended. In 1816 a liturgy for the Court and Garrison Ch. appeared without the author's name, but championed by the king. Opposition to this and other attempts to introduce a uniform agenda was led by Schleiermacher,* who upheld the right to vary from the agenda. See also *Prussian Union.*

Aggrey, James Emman Kwegyir (1875–1927). B. Gold Coast (now Ghana), Afr.; converted to Methodism; studied and later taught at Livingstone Coll., Salisbury, N. C. Studied educ. in Afr.; helped to establish Prince of Wales College at Achimota, now U. of Ghana. Labored for cooperation between whites and Negroes.

Aging and Infirm, Homes and Services for. Care of and services to the aging have been receiving increased study and attention in the past few decades. Simultaneously a standardization and professionalization of services has begun to take place. The result has been a substantial enrichment of programs of services and care, esp. through alternatives to institutional care which allow the older person to stay in his own home or immediate community.

In recent decades homes for the aging began to experience serious administrative and financial difficulties. While the Old Age Assistance and Old Age Survivors Ins. provisions of the Soc. Security Act of 1935 aided many residents and new applicants in making payments toward cost of their care, they also increased the possibilities for indep. living and for postponing applications for institutionalized care until the aging were in need of specialized and expensive nursing care in their later years. Few of the homes for the aging had been built and equipped or were sufficiently well supported to provide specialized and expensive care or to expand their facilities. Many proprietary nursing homes mushroomed into being; but without charitable contributions and tax exemption these tended to provide only substandard care for the medically ill and invalid. In recent yrs. federal and state legislatures have made provision for payment of extended medical care for the aging, and established standards for licensing, medical care, and soc. services which prevent exploitation of the aged and infirm. The increased life span and the corresponding increase in the aging population has multiplied not only the need for facilities and services for the aging, the ill, and the infirm but also for suitable and sufficient housing within the means of an aging population. Hence governmentally encouraged urban renewal housing programs are including many apartments specifically geared to the needs and the income of aging couples; and loans and grants are being made through FHA and through the Community Facilities Administration to voluntary and pub. groups to help supply the housing and nursing care needs of the elderly.

The 1963 report of the Com. on Aging of the A. M. A. states that most older people prefer to remain in their own homes as long as possible rather than in housing projects restricted to people of their own age, that four fifths of people over 65 are completely able to live independently in ordinary housing throughout the community, that more good housing for the entire population will meet the needs of these aging better than institutions, and that when special housing is needed it should emphasize community life.

The modern home for the aged has therefore been engaged in the process of converting its facilities to include nursing care for the aging and to enrich services to the aging by providing alternatives to institutional living either through direct extension of its own services or through referral to and use of other agencies and new services in the field. Alternative service programs that make early and complete institutionalization unnecessary include:

1. Counseling and casework services.
2. Home care programs, offering medical, visiting nurse, homemaker, dietary (meals on wheels), and other services.
3. Golden age clubs.
4. Friendly visiting services (volunteers).
5. Day care centers (opportunities for friendship, recreation, hobbies).
6. Foster home family care.
7. Home remodeling or renovation geared to the necessities of the aging and to their incomes.

The implications of this newer philosophy of care have begun to be widely recognized. Largely relieved of the fear of lack of care in illnesses or emergencies, the aging now seek to stay near their families or friends and in their own familiar environment, to remain as normally active and useful as possible, and if Christian, to enjoy the fellowship of their home congregation and own pastoral care. Communities and churches, on the other hand, are planning to retain the services, the experience, the capacities, and the wisdom of its aging population.

Sound professional consultation is essential for organizations planning new facilities and programing for the aging. A growing body of experience and knowledge, rapid urban and rural pop. changes, and new and changing criteria and developments in the building and service field require careful consideration. Voluntary and governmental agencies and organizations have been constituted to engage in studies, in programing and standard setting, and in the production of materials available for use by groups interested in services to the aging. Chief among these are the Nat. Council on the Aging, the Am. Assoc. of Homes for the Aging, the Am. Pub. Welfare Assoc., the Com. on Aging of the A. M. A., the Dept. of Health, Educ., and Welfare, the U. S. Pub. Health Service, and the President's Council on Aging. Most of these have their counterparts at regional, state, and local levels.

For a list of Lutheran homes and services see *Lutheran Health and Welfare Directory,* NLC, 50 Madison Avenue, New York, N. Y. 10010; *Statistical Yearbook* (CPH); *Lutheran Annual* (CPH). *Guidelines for the Establishment of Homes and Services for the Aging* and *The Responsibility of the Church for the Aging* (both prepared by and available from the Dept. of Soc. Welfare, The Luth. Ch. – Mo. Syn., 210 N. Broadway, St. Louis, Mo.); *A Guide for Lutheran Homes Serving the Aging,* Nat. Luth. Council, Division of Welfare, 50 Madison Avenue, New York, N. Y. 10010; *Homes and Services for the Aging,* Bd. of Soc. Miss., Luth. Ch. in Am., 231 Madison Avenue, New York, N. Y. 10016; *The Older American, 1963,* President's Council on Aging, Dept. of Health, Educ., and Welfare, Washington, D. C. 20025.

Pub. available from the Nat. Council on the Aging, Inc., 49 West 45th St., New York, N. Y. 10036: *Building for Older People — Construction, Location, Financing, Administration* (365 pp.); *Centers for Older People — Guide for Programs and Facilities* (120 pp.); *Flexible Retirement* (226 pp.); *Criteria for Retirement* (260 pp.); *Current Trends in Retirement; Planning Homes for the Aged* (119 pp.); *Older Employees* (72 pp.); *Library Service to the Aging; Maintaining Human Potential for Effective and Useful Living* (80 pp.); *Standards of Care for Older People in Institutions* (Sections I, II, and III, 112 pp. each).

Periodicals: *Aging,* U. S. Dept. of Health, Educ., and Welfare, Washington, D. C.; *Senior Citizens,* monthly ($5.00), Senior Citizens of Am., 1424 16th Street, N. W., Washington, D. C. 20006; *Nursing Homes,* monthly ($3.50), Am. Nursing Home Assoc., 1346 Connecticut Ave., N. W., Washington, D. C. 20006; *Professional Nursing Home,* monthly ($5.00), Miller Pub. Co., 2501 Wayzata, Minneapolis, Minn. 55405; *The Lutheran Welfare Quarterly* ($2.00), 50 Madison Ave., New York, N. Y. 10010; *Advance,* monthly ($2.00), magazine of practical churchwork, The Luth. Ch. – Mo. Syn., 210 N. Broadway, St. Louis, Mo. 63102. AHB

Agnes (3 or 4th c.). Martyr mentioned by numerous early fathers. Venerated as a model of purity. See also *Persecution of Christians,* 4; *Symbolism, Christian,* 4–5.

Agnew, Eliza (1807–83). First unmarried woman miss. to Ceylon; sent by ABCFM 1839; worked 43 years.

Agni. See *Brahmanism,* 2.

Agnoetae (Gk. "be ignorant of"). 1. Sect of 4th c. which denied the omniscience of God. 2. Sect of 6th c. maintaining there were things which Christ did not know.

Agnosticism (Gk. "not know"). Term first used by Huxley (1869) and applied to belief that certain knowledge in a particular field (e. g., religion) or in general has not been attained. In religion, agnosticism holds that certain knowledge of the existence and nature of God and of the supernatural world in general has not been reached. It differs from skepticism in that agnosticism usually grants the possibility of attaining knowledge. See also *Spencer, Herbert.*

Agnus Dei (pron. AHN-yus DAY-ee; L. "Lamb of God"). The Biblical basis is Jn 1:29; see also Is 53:7. 1. A prayer to Christ which occurs 3 times in the rite of the W. Ch. It is first sung in the Gloria in excelsis (with the additional address "Son of the Father" inserted after "O Lamb of God"). Since the 7th c. it has been sung after the consecration as a prayer to our Lord present in His body and blood in the Sacrament of the Altar; by the beginning of the 11th c. it was sung 3 times, with "grant us Thy peace" replacing the 3d "have mercy upon us." This change may reflect an accommodation to the giving of the kiss of peace at this point or to the calamities the ch. was suffering in the Middle Ages. At RC masses for the dead "grant them rest" replaces the 2d part of each line. In line with their denial of the sacramental union, the later Eng. reformers omitted the Agnus Dei from the Communion rite in the 1552 and subsequent ed. of the Book of Common Prayer. The opening words "O Christ" in our rite are not an integral part of the prayer but were added in 1525 to the version in John Bugenhagen's Brunswick Ch. Order partly to meet the exigencies of the musical setting. The Agnus Dei forms a regular part of the conclusion of litanies, including the one in our rite.

2. In Christian art, a representation of Christ the Victor in the form of a lamb (Rv 5:6-14), usually with nimbus and banner and standing or reposing on a book with seven seals.

3. In the RC Ch., a sacramental in the form of a molded wax medallion with the figure of a lamb which the pope blesses in the first yr. of his pontificate and at 7-yr. intervals thereafter. The custom goes back to the 9th c. ACP

Agobard of Lyons (779?–840). Sp.-born successor of archb. Leidrad of Lyons (816); severe critic of Emperor Louis the Pious, whom he forced to do public penance at Soissons (833). Agobard was deposed at the Council of Thionville (835) because he opposed the machinations of Empress Judith; was restored 2 years later. Wrote against adoptionism, speculative interpretations of the liturgy of Amalarius* of Metz, Fredegisius' doctrine of verbal inspiration of Scripture, idolatrous veneration of images, and the popular belief in witchcraft, magic, and trial by ordeal.

J. Allen Cabaniss, *Agobard of Lyons: Churchman and Critic* (Syracuse, 1953).

Agonizants. RC fraternity founded in Rome, It., ca. 1582/86 by Camillus de Lellis (1550–1614; b. Rome); given final approval 1591; popular name: Camillians; official name: Order of Clerics Regular, Servants of the Sick. Ministers to sick and dying.

Agrapha. A technical term for supposed sayings of Jesus which were handed down through oral tradition.

M. R. James, *The Apocryphal New Testament* (Oxford, 1924).

Agreed Statement on the Lord's Supper. Statement on Lord's Supper adopted (1955) by Ch. of S. India (CSI) and Federation of Ev. Luth. Churches (FELC).

Ev. Lutherische Kirchenzeitung, X (Apr. 1, 1956), 128; *Agreed Statements, The C. S. I.–Lutheran Theological Conversations, 1948–59* (Bangalore, 1960).

Agricola (Schneider), **Johann(es)** (1494–1566). B. Eisleben; educ. Wittenberg; kept minutes of Leipzig Debate (1519); sent by Luther to reform Frankfurt; taught at Eisleben (1525) and at U. of Wittenberg (1536); court preacher at Brandenburg (1540); one of authors of Augsburg Interim (1548). See also *Antinomian Controversy.*

G. Kawerau, *Joh. Agricola v. Eisleben* (Berlin, 1881).

Agricola, Kristian. See *Estonia,* 2.

Agricola, Martin (1486–1556). Cantor at cathedral school of Magdeburg; wrote works important for hist. of music during Reformation period.

Agricola, Michael (ca. 1510–57). Secy. of Martin Skytte, 1st Luth. bp. in Fin.; educ. Wittenberg 1536–39; rector of cathedral school in Aabo; coadjutor (1548), then bishop (1554) of Aabo. Regarded as creator of Fin. literary language; tr. NT and Psalms into Fin. Staunch follower of Luther, furthered planting of Lutheranism in Fin. The *Agricola-Luther Verein* is active in promoting Reformation studies. See also *Finland, Lutheranism in,* 2.

J. Gummerus, *Michael Agricola, der Reformator Finnlands* (1941).

Agricola, Rudolf (Huisman[n]; Huusman; Huysman[n]; Rodolphus; Rudolph; Roelof; Rudolf von Groningen; ca. 1443/44–1458). Humanist; b. Baflo, near Groningen, Neth.; educ. Erfurt, Cologne, Louvain, Pavia, Ferrara; scholar, painter, musican; active successively in Dillingen, Groningen, Brussels; lectured at Heidelberg; grasp of languages included Fr., Gk., Heb. Works include *De inventione dialectica; De formando studio.* See also *Humanism, Sixteenth-Century German; Reformed Churches,* 2.

Agricola, Stephan (Castenpauer, 1491–1547). Educ. Bologna, Venice, and Vienna; imprisoned (1522–24) for ev. preaching; pastor at St. Anna, Augsburg (1525); espoused Luth. reformation; preacher in Sulzbach (1543) and Eisleben (1545); participated at Marburg (1529), Smalcald (1537); signed Smalcald Articles.

Agricultural Society. See *Rural Church in America.*

Agrippa von Nettesheim, Henry Cornelius (1486–1535). Educ. Cologne and Paris; attended Council of Pisa (1511) as theologian of Emperor Maximilian; became interested in Reformation (ca. 1518) but felt Luther was too radical. His *Declamatio de incertitudine et vanitate scientiarum et artium* (influenced by Wessel* [Gansfort] and Nicolaus of Cusa*) espouses relativism and skepticism and attacks scholasticism and the veneration of saints and relics.

H. Morley, *The Life of Henry Cornelius Agrippa von Nettesheim* (1856); R. Stadelmann, *Vom Geist des ausgehenden Mittelalters* (Halle, 1929).

Ahimsa. See Jainism.

Ahlberg, Per August. (1823–87). B. Sweden; Luth. pastor and educator; head of Fgellsfeldt school, Uppsala; founded Miss. school at Ahlsborg, Smaaland; some of his students joined the Augustana Ch. in Am.

Ahlbrand, Albert H. (Apr. 27, 1872–Apr. 29, 1946). Buggy manufacturer; b. Seymour, Ind.; educ. Conc. Coll., Fort Wayne, Ind.; Fin. Secy., Cen. Dist., Mo. Syn.; member, Mo. Syn. Bd. of Dir., 1923. See also *Lutheran Laymen's League.*

Ahle, Johann Rudolf (1625–73). Like his contemporary, Andreas Hammerschmidt, Ahle wrote vocal and choral sacred dialogs which helped prepare the way for the ch. cantatas written by the Luth. composers of later generations. Ahle makes frequent use of the aria and of the ritornel, and his compositions distinguish themselves through their simplicity.

Ahlfeld, Johann Friedrich (1810–84). Luth. clergyman; 1847 succeeded rationalist Wislicenus at Halle; 1851–81 successor to Adolph von Harless at St. Nicolai, Leipzig; lectured in homiletics and pastoral theology to theol. candidates in Leipzig.

Ahlwardt Peter (1710–91). Prof. of logic at Greifswald treated Christian truths in terms of Wolffian philosophy.

Ahmadiya. See *Islam,* 5.

Aho, Gustav Axel (Oct. 9, 1897–Dec. 12, 1973). B. Sebeka, Minn.; educ. NELC sem. Ironwood, Mich.; pastor N. J., N. Y., Minn., Ohio, Ont., Mich.; chaplain East Ridge Retirement Village, Miami, Fla., 1968–72; pres. NELC 1931–53. Ed. *Auttaja.*

Ahriman. See *Zoroastrianism.*

Ahron ben Masche ben Ascher (10th c.). Palestinian Massorete.

Ahura Mazda. See *Zoroastrianism.*

Aichinger, Gregor (1564–1628). Ger. composer of the RC Church, whom August Ambros considers the superior to Jacob Handl (Gallus). Like his contemporary Hans Leo Hassler, he was a product of the Venetian School and served as organist of the Fugger family. In his last years he served as a priest in the ch. at Regensburg.

Aidan. (d. 651). Celtic bp. of Lindisfarne* (635); made extensive miss. journeys.

Ailly, Pierre d' (1350–1420). Fr. cardinal, theologian, reformer ("in head and members"); prominent at Council of Constance; placed Bible above canon law, council above pope.

Ailred. (1109–67). "Bernard of the North." Head of Cistercians in Eng. Wrote life of Edward the Confessor, *Speculum caritatis, De spirituali amicitia.*

W. Daniel, *The Life of Ailred of Rievaulx,* trans. F. M. Powicke (London, 1950); *MPL* 195, 209–796.

Aims, Educational. See *Christian Education,* G.

Ainslie, Peter (1867–1934). B. Dunnsville, Essex Co., Va.; educ. Transylvania Coll., Lexington, Ky.; preacher Newport News, Va., 1889–91; pastor Baltimore, Md. 1891–1934. Founded Council on Christian Union of the Disciples of Christ 1910 (name changed 1916 to Assoc. for the Promotion of Christian Unity, later to Council on Christian Unity); active in various movements (ecumenical, soc. betterment, racial equality, and pacifist). Cofounded *The Christan Union Quarterly* 1911. Other works include *God and Me; The Message of the Disciples for the Union of the Church; My Brother and I; The Scandal of Christianity; Working with God* (2 chaps. of which were later expanded and pub. separately under the title *Towards Christian Unity*); *Christ or Napoleon–Which?* See also *Disciples of Christ,* 3.

Ainsworth, Henry (1571–1623). Hebraist; champion of Eng. separatists; b. near Norwich; fled to Amsterdam 1593; teacher there of separatists till his death.

Ainu. Aboriginal people in N. Japan; perhaps of Caucasian origin; since WW II almost entirely assimilated into culture of Japan; perhaps ca. 100 "pure" Ainu left. Jesuit Hieronymus de Angelis visited them, 1616 and 1620. CMS began miss. work, 1876. Religion apparently originally monotheistic, now polytheistic (animism, goddess of fire, ancestor worship). Shin'ichiro Takakura, "Vanishing Ainu of North *Japan," Natural History, LXXV,* 8 (Oct. 1966), 16–25. See also *Missions, Bibliography.*

Aionios. See *Hereafter,* B 6.

Aitken, Robert (1734 [1735?]–1802). Printer; b. Dalkeith, Scot.; opened bookstore in Philadelphia, Pa., 1771; pub. 1st complete Eng. Bible known to be printed in Am. 1782 (an Eng. Bible and several Testaments are said to have been printed in Boston ca. 1750).

Aizanas. See *Ethiopic Church.*

Ajivikas. Adherents of religious system in India, similar to Jainism,* with humanistic tendencies; founded 6th c. BC.

Akathist (os). See *Acathistus.*

Akbar (1542–1605). Mogul emperor of Hindustan, N. India; Muslim by birth; known for tolerance and interreligion discussions. Founder of eclectic religion "Divine Faith."

Akiba ("Father of Rabbinic Judaism"; ca. 50–135). Systematized Halakah and evolved new principles of interpretation; increased range of Halakah. Influence also felt in philosophy, politics, and Haggada. On Halakah and Haggada see *Talmud.*

L. Finkelstein, *Akiba, Saint and Martyr* (New York, 1936).

Akron Rule. See *Galesburg Rule.*

Aksakov, Konstantin Sergeevich (1817–60). Russ. religious philosopher; Slavophile; protagonist of religious freedom.

al-Farabi. See *Arabic Philosophy.*

al-Ghazzali. See Arabic Philosophy.

al-Jahiz. See *Arabic Philosophy.*

al-Kindi. See *Arabic Philosophy.*

Alabama Lutheran Academy and College, Selma, Ala. See *Ministry, Education of,* VIII C 2 a; Young, Rosa.

Alacoque, Marguerite Marie (1647–90). Fr. nun; mystic; founder of devotion to Sacred* Heart of Jesus.

Alain de Lille (Alanus ab Insulis; ca. 1120–1202), Fr. philosopher, theologian, alchemist. Wrote *De planctu naturae; Anticlaudianus.*

Alais Peace of. See *France,* 10.

Alamanni. See *Alemanni; Germany,* A 1.

Alaric (ca. 370–410). Visigoth king (395–410); Arian. Conquest of Rome (410) was occasion of Augustine's *City of God.*

a Lasco, Johannes. See *Laski, Jan.*

Alaska (Eskimo *Alakshak,* "Mainland"; in popular belief "Great Land"). *Area:* 586,400 sq. mi.; *pop.:* ca. 250,000, of which ca. 40,000 are Eskimos and Indians. Sighted, 1732; effectively discovered by Russ. Vitus Jonassen Bering, 1741. Became center of fur trade under Russ. control; transferred to U. S., Oct. 18, 1867; became state, Jan. 3, 1959. Eskimos, Aleuts, and Indians (Tlingit, Tinneh) constituted original pop.; their villages still provide predominant place-names in interior and along Arctic and Bering Sea coasts. After 1867 most full-blooded Russians left. Many immigrants were from the Scand. countries. Anchorage is largest city, Juneau the capital.

During WW II the "Alcan" highway, an all-weather road, was built from Dawson Creek, B. C., through Yukon Terr. to Alaska. During and since WW II pop. in Alaska increased rapidly, mainly because of defense construction and coming of statehood.

Climate varies from extremely cold winters in some areas, where –50° F. readings are common, to summers when the same area has 24-hr. daylight and temperatures up to 90°. Fairbanks (only sizable city in interior) experiences extreme cold, but climate in forested areas of SW is comparable to that of Albany, N. Y.

Over 90 percent of Eskimo and Indian pop. professes Christianity. Denominations longest in Alaska include Presb., Episc., RC, and Luth. (Norw.). By 1950 many denominations and sects were represented. Russ. Orthodox churches still survive in S. coastal areas.

Mo. Syn. began work there in 1926, stepped it up in 1937. Congregations have since been established at Anchorage, Palmer, Fairbanks, Juneau, Chugiak, and Kenai. See *Missions, Bibliography.* OS

Alb. See *Vestments, Clerical.*

Alba. See *Bible Societies,* 6.

Alba, Duke of. See *Alva, Duke of.*

Alban. Legendary Brit. martyr. His death has been variously assigned to 249/251 (in a persecution under Decius), 283 or 286 (executed under martial law after protecting a priest, by whom he was converted, from persecutors), and 302/305 (in the persecution under Diocletian). Benedictine abbey founded ca. 793/794 at the site of his reputed martyrdom in Hertfordshire was named St. Albans in his honor. See also *England,* A 1; Persecution of *Christians,* 4.

Albania (Albanian *Shqipni*). Country in Balkan Peninsula on Adriatic Sea. *Area:* 10,629 sq. mi.; *pop.:* 1,660,000; mostly Muslim, though Gk. Orthodox Ch. is strong. See *Missions, Bibliography.*

Albanian Orthodox Archdiocese in America. See *Eastern Orthodox Churches,* 6.

Alber, Erasmus (ca. 1500–53). Ger. Luth. pastor; martyr of freedom of speech; highly regarded as hymnist; best-known hymn: "O Children of Your God, Rejoice."

Alber, Matthaeus (1495–1570). Reformer of Reutlingen. Educ. Tuebingen (1513–18); friend of Melanchthon; supported Luther in controversy with Zwingli on Lord's Supper; through his influence Reutlingen signed the AC; expelled during Interim; pastor of Stuttgart and collaborator of J. Brenz. See also *Lutheran Confessions,* B 1.

J. Hartmann, *Matthaeus Alber, der Reformator der Reichsstadt Reutlingen* (Tuebingen, 1863).

Albert (Albert II; the Younger; 1522–57). "The Warlike; German Alcibiades." Margrave of Brandenburg-Kulmbach; Prussian reformer; hymnist; at first supported Charles* V against the Schmalkaldic*

League; deserted the emp. and joined the league 1551. See also *Maurice of Saxony.*

Albert I (ca. 1165–1229). Also called Albert von Buxhoeveden (Bekeshövede) after his ancestral castle, and Alpert von Apelern (Apeldern; Appeldern) after a village near the castle; Albert of Riga. Canon at Bremen; bp. Livonia 1199; founded Riga 1201 and made it the bishop's seat; recognized as imperial prince 1207 and 1225. See also *Estonia,* 1.

Albert of Aachen (12th c.). Wrote hist. of 1st Crusade.

Albert of Brandenburg (1490–1545). Archb. of Magdeburg 1513; archb. and elector of Mainz 1514; cardinal 1518. Luther made his famous protest against sale of indulgences granted to Albert by the pope.

Albert of Prussia (1490–1568). First Hohenzollern duke of Prussia; converted to Lutheranism; founded U. of Koenigsberg 1544; supported Osiander of Nuernberg. In 1523, while Albert was Grand Master of Teutomic Knights (see *Military Religious Orders,* c), Luther advised him to marry and secularize his order; this he did.

Albert of Riga. See *Albert I.*

Albert of Saxony (d. 1390). Rector U. of Paris, 1353; 1st rector U. of Vienna 1365; bp. of Halberstadt 1366; nominalist; pupil of Buridan; wrote commentaries on Aristotle.

Albert the Blessed (de Vercelli; d. 1215). Patriarch of Jerusalem; drew up 1st rule for Carmelites, 1209.

Albert von Buxhoeveden. See *Albert I.*

Albert(i), Heinrich (1604–51). Studied under cousin Heinrich Schütz. Prolific composer of secular and sacred music. Hymnist; some hymns tr. into Eng. See also *Dach, Simon.*

Alberta. See *Canada.*

Alberdi, Heinrich. See *Albert, Heinrich.*

Alberti, Johann Friedrich (1642–1710). Luth.; devoted earlier yrs. to study of theology; later studied music; as organist and composer brought fame to Merseburg; rivaled in his day only by J. C. Bach.

Alberti, Julius Gustav (1723–72). Pastor, Hamburg; opposed J. M. Goeze.*

Alberti, Valentin (1635–97). Luth. theologian; lecturer at Leipzig; opposed Pietism.* See also *Frarecke, August Hermann.*

Albertini, John Baptist of (1769–1831). Leader of Moravians* (Unitas Fratrum); hymnist.

Albertus Magnus, (Albert the Great; 1193-1280). Founder of most flourishing period of scholasticism; b. Lauingen, Bavaria; educ. Padua, where he entered Dominican order; served as lector of convent scrols of his order in Ger.; studied theology, Paris; became gen. of his order for Ger., then bp. of Regensburg for 2 yrs.; many-sided author; called "Doctor Universalis"; wrote commentary on *Sententiae* of Peter* Lombard and *Summum theologiae;* prepared way for modern conflict between theology and false science.

Opera omnia, ed. A. Borgnet (Paris, 1890–99); ed. B. Geyer (Cologne, 1951–); G. v. Hertling, *Albertus Magnus, Beitraege zu seiner Würdigung* (Münster, 1914); H. C. Scheeben, *Der heilige Albert der Grosse* (Cologne, 1932) and *Albertus Magnus* (Bonn, 1932).

Albertz, Martin (1883–1956). B. Halle; prominent in *Bekennende Kirche* ("Confessing Church").

Albigenses. A branch of the Cathari* found chiefly in N. It. and S. Fr. They developed a New Manichaeism,* believing in a god of light and a prince of this world. The angels were "the lost sheep of the house of Israel," and Jesus' death was only apparent (see *Docetism*). Their anticlerical criticisms led to crusades against them (1181–82; 1208–29); some held out despite reverses and cruel treatment, did not disappear until middle of 14th c.

C. G. Coulton, *Inquisition and Liberty* (London, 1938); C. Schmidt, *Histoire de la secte des Cathares ou Albigeois* (Paris, 1849); H. J. Warner, *The Albigensian Heresy,* 2 vols. (New York, 1922–29).

Albinus, Johann Georg (1624–79). Ger. Luth. pastor and poet. Koch says his poetry was "distinguished by ease of style, force of expression, and liveliness of fancy" and that "his manner of thought was Scriptural and pervaded by a deep religious spirit." 3 of his hymns have been tr. into Eng.

Albo, Joseph (ca. 1380–ca. 1444). Span. Defended Judaism against Christianity *(Book of Principles).* Religion, he held, is based on 3 facts: existence of God; revelation; reward and punishment in the hereafter. Last of Jewish medieval philosophers.

Albornoz, Gil Alvarez Carillo de (Aegidius; ca. 1300–67). Sp. cardinal; archb. of Toledo; legate to Rome; secured restoration of authority in papal states; author of *Constitutiones Aegidianae.*

Albrecht. Ger. for Albert.*

Albrecht, Christian (d. 1815). Missionary of LMS to S. Afr. 1804–15. Among first missionaries (together with brother Abraham) to cross Orange R. and begin work of Christianizing Namaqualand.

Albrecht, Christian Johann (1847–1924). B. Württemberg; educ. St. Crischona; came to Minn., 1872; pastor Greenwood; New Ulm, 1882. Pres. of Minn. Syn. 1883–94; founder and 1st dir. of the coll. and practical sem. at New Ulm, 1884; taught some branches under dir. Hoyer as long as the school remained a theol. sem. (1893). Active in forming Joint Syn. of Wis. and Other States; pres. of China Miss. Soc., which sent E. L. Arndt as its first miss.

Albrecht, Hans (1902–61). Musicologist; lecturer (1947) and prof. (1955) U. of Kiel. Ed. complete works of J. S. Bach; *Musikforschung; Acta musicalogica;* pub. *Documenta musicalogica.*

Albrecht, Max John Frederick (Mar. 10, 1861–Oct. 21, 1943). B. Gross-Polzin, Pomerania; grad. St. Louis 1883; pastor Lebanon, Wis., 1883–88; Janesville, Wis., 1888–91; Fort Wayne, Ind., 1891–93; prof. 1893–1937, pres; 1893–1921 Conc. Coll., Milwaukee.

Albrecht, Walter William Frederick (Dec. 10, 1885–Nov. 16, 1961). B. Lebanon, Wis.; grad. Conc. Sem., St. Louis, 1906; pastor Redeemer, Didsbury, Alta., Can., 1906–07; St. John, Hubbell, Mich., 1907–13; Zion, Neshkoro, Wis., 1913–22; St. James, Shawano, Wis., 1922–27; prof. Conc. Sem., Springfield, Ill., 1927–61. Tr. F. Pieper's *Christliche Dogmatik (Christian Dogmatics),* 3 vols., compiled new index vol. (St. Louis, 1950–57).

Albrechtsberger, Johann Georg (1736–1809). Austrian contrapuntist and composer; taught Beethoven and Hummel; based 279 works on liturgical texts.

Albrechtsbrueder. See *Evangelical Church.*

Albright, Jacob. See *Evangelical Church.*

Albright, William Foxwell (1891–1971). Orientalist; b. Coquimb, Chile; educ. Upper Iowa U., Fayette, Iowa, and Johns Hopkins U., Baltimore, Md. Acting dir. Am. School of Oriental Research, Jerusalem, 1920–21; dir. 1921–29, 1933–36. Prof. Johns Hopkins U. 1929–58; research prof. Jewish Theol. Sem. Am. 1957–59. Led archaeol. expeditions. Pres. Palestine Oriental Soc. 1921–22, 1934–35; Am. Oriental Soc. 1935–36. Works include *From the Stone Age to Christianity; Archaeology and the Religion of Israel; The Archaeology of Palestine; History, Archaeology, and Christian Humanism; Yahweh and the Gods of Canaan.* See also *Geography, Christian,* 8.

Albright People. See *Evangelical Church.*

Alcoholics Anonymous. See *Alcoholism.*

Alcoholism. According to the National Council on Alcoholism, an alcoholic is a person whose drinking causes a continuing problem in his or her life. "For general purposes, alcoholics can be described as those people who drink in a very special way — that is, to excess, compulsively, without control, and self-destructively. The lack of control must be emphasized" (S. Vogel, "Psychiatric Treatment of Alcoholism," *Annals of the AAPSS,* Jan. 1958, p. 100). There are approximately 5½ million such drinkers in Am. today.

Alcoholism, the label given this uncontrolled drinking, has been classified as a sickness by the A. M. A. since 1936. It is generally believed to be symptomatic of unresolved emotional stress.

"The Twenty Questions Test," compiled by Johns Hopkins U. and available at all A. A. centers, is an excellent guide in determining whether or not one is an alcoholic. The NCA suggests a similar test of only 4 questions. Answering "yes" to any of the following should be considered a warning: Have you had blackouts (periods of temporary amnesia) after drinking? Do you need a drink in the morning? Has drinking interfered with your eating habits? Have you felt remorse after drinking?

Any philosophy basic to counseling the alcoholic should include the following points: 1. The alcoholic is a sick person. 2. The alcoholic can be helped, and he is worth helping.

"Alcoholics Anonymous is a fellowship of men and women who share their experience, strength and hope with each other that they may solve their common problem and help others to recover from alcoholism. The only requirement for membership is a desire to stop drinking. There are no dues or fees for A. A. membership; we are self-supporting through our own contributions. A. A. is not allied with any sect, denomination, politics, organization or institution; does not wish to engage in any controversy; neither endorses nor opposes any causes. Our primary purpose is to stay sober and help other alcoholics to achieve sobriety." *(44 Questions and Answers)*

See also *Temperance Movements and the Lutheran Church.*

Howard J. Clinebell, *Understanding and Counseling the Alcoholic* (Nashville, 1956); John C. Ford, *Man Takes a Drink* (New York, 1955); Albion R. King, *Basic Information on Alcohol* (Vernon, Iowa, 1953); Marty Mann, *Primer on Alcoholism* (New York, 1950); *Alcoholics Anonymous,* 2d ed. (New York, 1955); *44 Questions and Answers About the Program of Recovery from Alcoholism* (New York, 1952), p. 2. "Understanding Alcoholism," ed. S. D. Bacon, *Annals of the American Academy of Political and Social Science,* Jan. 1958. EFE

Alcuin (735–804). Educ. in cathedral school of York, Eng.; head of court school of Charlemagne; abbot Tours 796; revised Vulgate; sought to convert heathen by the Gospel, not force; opposed Adoptionism; greatest scholar of his age.

MPL, 100–101; E. S. Duckett, *Alcuin, Friend of Charlemagne* (New York, 1951); L. Wallach, *Alcuin and Charlemagne* (Ithaca, N. Y., 1959).

Aldhelm. (ca. 640–709). Eng. bp. and scholar; founded centers of learning; introduced Benedictine rule at Malmesbury; wrote extensively (101 riddles in Latin hexameter).

MPL, 89, 63–314; E. S. Duckelt, *Anglo-Saxon Saints and Scholars* (New York, 1947), pp. 3-97.

Aleandro, Girolamo (Hieronymus Aleander. 1480–1542). Nuncio of Leo X to Charles V. Urged Diet of Worms, 1521; sought to enforce its excommunication. Archb., Brindisi, 1524; cardinal, 1538.

Aleman, Louis d' (d'Allemand; ca. 1390–1450). Fr. cardinal; prominent at councils of Constance* and Basel*; opposed Eugenius* IV; deposed and banned 1439; reinstated 1449.

Alemanni. Ancient Germanic tribes bet. Danube and Main; attacked Romans, 213; conquered by Clovis,* 496. See also *Germany,* A 1.

Alembert, Jean Le Rond d' (1717–83). Fr. physicist and philosopher; forerunner of positivism.

Aleppo College. See *Middle East,* C.

Alès, Peace of. See *France,* 10.

Alesius, Alexander (Aless, or Alane. 1500–65). Scot. Educ. Edinburgh. Converted by Patrick Hamilton; imprisoned; fled to Ger.; became acquainted with Luther and signed AC; visited Eng. 1535; prof. Frankfurt on the Oder; active in Eng. under Edward VI; twice rector Leipzig U.

Althians. See *Shakers.*

Aleutian Islands. Part of Alas.; string of islands along coast and pointing towards Asia. Two of the islands invaded by Jap. during WW II, the only points of N. A. to come under enemy invasion. Thinly pop., mostly by people of Kamchatkan stock. Some miss. stations by Gk. Cath. Ch. See *Alaska; Missions, Bibliography.*

Alexander (ca. 273–328). Bp. of Alexandria. Opposed Arianism. Writings in *MPG,* 18, 523–608. See *Arianism.*

Alexander (ca. 350–ca. 430). Founder of Acoemetae.*

Alexander III. See *Popes,* 9.

Alexander IV. See *Augustinian Hermits.*

Alexander V. See *Schism,* 8.

Alexander VI. See *Popes,* 18.

Alexander VII. See *Jansenism.*

Alexander, Michael Solomon (1799–1845). B. Posen; rabbi Eng.; baptized 1825; prof. of Hebrew, King's Coll.; first Angl. bp. in Jerusalem, 1841.

Alexander, Natalis. See *Natalis Alexander.*

Alexander, Samuel (1859–1938). B. Australia; educ. Melbourne and Oxford; prof. Manchester 1893–1924. Philosopher; developed metaphysic of emergent evolution according to which materiality, secondary qualities, life, and mentality are emergent modifications of primal space-time. See also *Corupresence.*

Alexander, Thomas Theron (Oct. 8, 1850–Nov. 14, 1902). B. Horeb, Tenn.; sent by Presb. Bd. (N.) to Jap. 1877; opened new stations; taught theology in the Meiji Gakuin in Tokyo; d. Honolulu.

Alexander, William (1824–1911). Angl. primate of Ireland. Works include *Witness of the Psalms to Christ and Christianity;* contributions to *Speaker's Commentary.*

Alexander, William Patterson (1805–84). B. Paris, Ky.; grad. Princeton 1830; went to Hawaii as ABCFM miss. 1832; made preliminary surveys of Society Is. and Marquesas Is.; served at Waioli on Kauai Is.; cofounder of Ponahue School (Oahu Coll.); head of Lahainaluna Sem., Maui, 1843. Works include *Pastor's Manual;* S. S. books; *Evidences of Christianity; A System of Theology.*

Alexander Nevski (Alexander of Novgorod; ca. 1220–63). Russ. prince and saint. Defeated Swedes on the Neva, 1240. Opposed RCm.

Alexander of Hales (*Doctor irrefragabilis; Theologorum monarcha;* d. 1245). Educ. Hales; lectured at Paris; entered order of St. Francis (1236). Taught Bonaventura. His great work *Summa universae theologiae* teaches the *character indelebilis** and is a handbook of dialectic theology. He perfected the triple division of questions into *pro, contra,* and *resolutio,* which was adopted by scholasticism. His *Treasury of Merits* significant for indulgence* theory.

Alexander of Lycopolis (3d c.). Writer against Manichaeism. *MPG,* 18, 411–448.

Alexandria, School of. See *Commentaries, Biblical; Exegesis,* 3; *Schools, Early Christian,* 1.

Alexandrinus, Codex. See *Manuscripts of the Bible.*

Alexians. RC religious order of laymen originating from laymen who served during the Black Death (14th c.), named after Alexius (5th c.). They have several hospitals in the U. S.

Alexias. See *Comnena, Anna.*

Alfeld, Augustine (16th c.). Franciscan; opponent of Luther.

Alford, Henry (1810–71). B. London; educ. Cambridge; held numerous important positions, such as Fellow of Trinity, Hulsean lecturer, and Dean of Canterbury. While still young, he wrote several Lat. odes, a hist. of the Jews, and a series of homiletic outlines. His noblest undertaking was his ed. of the Gk. NT, the result of 20 years of labor. His poetical works are numerous and include "Ten Thousand Times Ten Thousand" and "Come, Ye Thankful People, Come." Ed. *Contemporary Review.* See also *Metaphysical Society, The.*

Alfred the Great (849–899). King of Eng.; gathered scholars and tr. portions of Bible and fathers (Boethius, Bede, Gregory the Great) into Saxon.

J. A. Giles, *The Whole Works of King Alfred the Great* (3 vols. London, 1858).

Alfvén, Hannes Olof Gösta. See *Evolution,* I.

Algeria. See *Africa,* D 3.

Algonquian. See *Primitive Religion.*

All Lutheran Youth Leaders' Council. See *Young People's Organizations,* II 5.

All Saints' Day. See *Church Year* 14, 16; Departed, *Commemoration of.*

All Souls' Day. *See Church Year* 14; *Departed, Commemoration of.*

Allah. See *Islam,* I.

Allatu. See *Babylonians, Religion of,* 5.

Alleghany Synod (Allegheny). See *General Synod of the Evangelical Lutheran Church in the United States of America, The; United Lutheran Church, Synods of,* 23.

Allegory. See *Exegesis,* 3–6; *Hermeneutics,* 3; *Preaching, Christian, History of,* 6, 8.

Allegri, Gregorio (ca. 1582–1652). It. composer of ch. music; priest at cathedral at Fermo, where his instrumental compositions attracted attention of Pope Urban, who appointed him to choir of Sistine Chapel. Best known for a *Miserere* for 2 choirs, of subtle and delicate sadness, traditionally sung in Rome during Holy Week.

Alleluia. See *Hallelujah.*

Allemand. See *Aleman.*

Allen, David Oliver (1799–1863). B. Barre, Mass.; educ. Amherst Coll. (1825) and Andover Sem. (1827); sent by ABCFM to India; active there in printing and Bible tr.

Allen, Horace Newton (Apr. 23, 1858–Dec. 11, 1932). Diplomatist; Presb. med. miss.; b. Delaware, Ohio; educ. Ohio Wesleyan U., Delaware, Ohio, and Miami Med. Coll., Oxford, Ohio; miss. in China; to Korea 1884; saved life of a prince and others in a revolution; med. officer to Korean Court; est. Prot. missions; held various govt. positions. Works include *A Chronological Index: Some of the Chief Events in the Foreign Intercourse of Korea from the Beginning of the Christian Era to the Twentieth Century; Korean Tales; Things Korean.* See also *Korea,* 5.

Allen, Oswald (1816–78). B. Kirkby-Lonsdale, Westmoreland, Eng.; invalid all his life, suffering from a diseased spine; manager of his father's bank; philanthropist. During severe winter of 1859–60 composed *Hymns of the Christian Life,* containing 148 hymns, including "Today Thy Mercy Calls Us."

Allen, Richard (1760–1831). B. Philadelphia, Pa.; slave near Dover, Del.; allowed to buy freedom 1777 by his master, who was converted as a result of services he allowed Allen to conduct in his (the master's) house; became Meth. 1777; moved to Philadelphia in the 1780s; licensed to preach 1784 by St. George's Meth. Ch., Philadelphia; organized Free African Soc. (a self-help and mutual-aid organization) Apr. 1787; withdrew with other Negroes from St. George's Ch. rather than submit to forced segregation Nov. 1787; ordained deacon by F. Asbury* 1799; helped found African* M. E. Ch. 1816 and was its bp. 1816–31.

Allen, Roland (1869–1947). Angl. miss. in N. China; active in World Dominion* movement.

Allen, William (1523–94). Sought to reintroduce RCm into Eng.; supported Philip II's invasion. Founded coll. at Douai (1568), Rome (1575–78), Valladolid (1589). Cardinal.

Allendorf, Johann Ludwig Conrad (1693–1773). Court preacher of Köthen; pastor Wernigerode and Halle; pietistic hymnist.

Allgemeine Evangelisch-Lutherische Konferenz. Organization of representatives of various Luth. groups of Ger.; met since 1868; 1st pres. was Harless, followed by Kliefoth. Its official organ, *Allgemeine Evangelisch-Lutherische Kirchenzeitung,* ed. for many yrs. by Luthardt. See also *Lutheran World Federation.*

Alliance, Holy. See *Holy Alliance.*

Alliance of the Reformed Churches Throughout the World Holding the Presbyterian System. Organized in London, 1875; membership ca. 46,000,000; includes practically all adherents of Presbyterianism. Ex. secy.'s office in Geneva, Swit. Also called World Presbyterian Alliance.

Alliances and Leagues, Holy. See *Holy Leagues and Alliances.*

Allies, Thomas William (1813–1903). Angl. theologian; participated in Oxford Movement; joined RC Ch.

Allix, Pierre (1641–1717). Ref. pastor in Paris; fled to London; wrote in defense of Reformation and Scriptural principle.

Allocution. Address delivered by pope to cardinals in secret consistory, often pub. later.

Alloeosis. Figure of speech by which Zwingli construed all passages of Scripture in which anything is ascribed to divine nature of Christ or to entire Christ which properly is property of human nature. Purpose of the *Alloeosis,* as used by Zwingli, was denial of the communication of attributes. He also used it in doctrine of absolution. Thus "Christ" in Lk 24:28 is referred only to His human nature since it is a mere figure of speech if the suffering and death of our Lord is ascribed to His divine nature.

Luther, *Vom Abendmahl Christi,* WA 25, 263–509; FC SD VIII 21, 38–45.

Allwardt, Henry August. (March 2, 1840–April 9, 1910). B. Wachendorf, Mecklenburg-Schwerin; to Am., 1853; educ. Conc. Coll., Fort Wayne; Conc. Sem., St. Louis, 1865; pastor, Marquette Co., Wis., 1865–73, Lebanon, Wis., 1874–1910. One of C. F. W. Walther's opponents in Predestinarian Controversy; joined Ohio Syn. with others. 1882; pres. of its NW Dist. till 1890 and of its successor, the Wis. Dist., till 1899; pres. Bd. of Luther Sem., Afton, later St. Paul, Minn., 1884–1910. D. D. Capital U., 1898.

F. W. Stellhorn, "D.[oktor] H. A. Allwardt," *Theologische Zeitblaetter,* XXIX (1910), 168–170.

Alms (Gk. *eleemosyne,* mercifulness, act of charity). Mt 6:1-4; Lk 11:41; 12:33; Acts 3:2, 3, 10; 10:2, 4, 31; 24:17. Word "alms" means gifts to poor and indigent, though in some sectors of early ch. so-called alms were divided into 4 equal parts: for the bp., priests, deacons and subdeacons, the poor. Almsgiving occupies important place in some primitive cultures (Aleuts, Eskimos, Egyptians, Sioux and Muskogee Indians) and has religious significance in Buddhism and Muhammadanism. OT stresses that all things belong to God and that the rule of conduct is: "Thou shalt love thy neighbor as thyself" (Lv 19:18, 34; cf. Ex 23:11; Lv 23:22; 25:25-28; Dt 15:9-11; Pr 14:20, 21; 21:13). After return from captivity increasing need caused increasing stress to be laid on almsgiving. The Apocrypha* made almsgiving a meritorious act, even an atonement for sin (Tob 12:

8, 9; Ecclus. 3:30). The NT opposes this apocryphal teaching (Mt 6:1-4) and emphasizes that man is saved by faith alone (Eph 2:8-10). In view of the fact that works are the fruits and evidences of faith (Mt 7:15-20; Ja 2), the NT speaks of rewards (Mt 6:4; 19:21; 25:34-40; Lk 14:14; Gl 6:9).

The ch. from its very beginning emphasized almsgiving (Acts 4:34, 35; 1 Co 16:1-3). The apocryphal idea of the efficaciousness of almsgiving crept into the ch. and is found in such early writers as Polycarp (*Epistola ad Philippenses,* 10; Hermas (*Similitudines,* 2); 2 Clement, 16; Cyprian (*De opere et eleemosynis);* Tertullian (*De poenitentia);* and Augustine (*De fide et operibus,* 26). These aberrations ultimately grew into the medieval system of almsgiving.

Luther restored almsgiving to its NT status as a pleasing work of the new life created through faith (WA 52, 433–434; 32, 407–413; LC I 247). This teaching is also in the Confessions (AC VI; Ap III; VI 42). See also *Charities, Christian.* EL

Almshouses. See *Child and Family Service Agencies,* 1.

Alogi. See *Monarchianism,* A 1.

Alpha and Omega. First and last letters of Gk. alphabet. Used to indicate that God in Christ is Beginning and End, Creator and Perfecter (Rv 1:17; 2:8; 22:13; cf. Is 44:6; 48:12).

Alpha Synod of the Evangelical Lutheran Church of Freedmen in America. Organized May 8, 1889, by 4 Negro pastors who had been ordained by N. C. Syn.: David Koonts, pres.; W. Philo Phifer, secy.; Sam Holt; Nathan Clapp. When Koonts died (1890), the syn. did not die with him. Phifer, in the name of the other 2 pastors, wrote to pres. Schwan of the Mo. Syn., 1891. The result was that the Syn. Conf. took up work among the Negroes in N. C., 1891.

Christopher F. Drewes, *Half a Century of Lutheranism Among Our Colored People* (St. Louis, 1927).

Alphonsus Liguori. See *Liguori, Alfonso Maria de.*

Alsace-Lorraine. See *France,* 15.

Alsted, Johann Heinrich (1588–1638). Ref. theologian; prof. Herborn (Nassau) and Weissenburg (Transylvania); at Synod of Dort, 1619. Polymath; chiliast. Pedagogical methods influenced Comenius.* Works include *Encyclopaedia septem tomis distincta; Distinctiones per universam theologiam;* and *Cursus philosophici encyclopaedia* (1630), which contains probably the earliest article on the use and abuse of tobacco.

Alt, Albrecht (1883–1956). Prof. of OT Greifswald, Basel, Halle, Leipzig; ex. of *Deutsches Ev. Institut für Altertumswissenschaft des Heiligen Landes zu Jerusalem* and *Deutscher Verein zur Erforschung Palästinas.*

Alt, Heinrich (1811–93). Educ. Berlin under Neander; teacher and preacher at the Charité Hospital, Berlin. Wrote *Der christliche Kultus.*

Altar. In Christian worship, the symbol of the divine presence in a church or chapel and the focus of devotion. The many forms it takes all derive ultimately from the table in the early places of worship to which members of the congregation brought their offerings and on which Holy Communion was celebrated. In best Luth. tradition it is covered to the floor on all sides and has on the mensa (table), in addition to the service book, only 2 candles and a crucifix (although these need not stand directly on the altar). When the altar stands against the back wall of the chancel, it may have behind it a reredos or a dossal curtain; the latter may extend around the sides of the altar (riddel curtains). Over the altar may be a canopy, called a ciborium, or a tester. Increasingly the liturgical denominations are returning to the ancient practice of placing the altar far enough away from the wall to permit the officiant to function behind it facing the people. Prior to the worship revival in contemporary Protestantism, altars were not generally used in these denominations; instead the service was conducted from the rostrum or pulpit, and a small table was brought out for use as necessary at Communion services. The principal altar is called high altar. ACP.

Altar Bread. Bread especially prepared for the Lord's Supper,* unleavened in W. and Armenian Ch., leavened in E. Ch. Also called wafer.

Altar Cards. 3 cards, containing parts of ritual of RC mass, placed on altar under crucifix at celebration of the mass and used by officiant in case of lapse of memory.

Altar Fellowship. The practice of communing at the same altar, which in the Luth. Ch. is a correlate of restricted (close) Communion, according to which only those who have been instructed, explored, and absolved are admitted to the Lord's Supper. Restricted Communion was also a protest against those who denied the Real Presence (see also *Grace, Means of,* IV 3). The practice was followed until establishment of the Prussian Union (1817). Luth. state churches continued to observe restricted Communion after 1817, though Ref. were more and more admitted to their Lord's Supper.

Among early Lutherans in Am. altar fellowship with Ref. was widely practiced. Reactions to the Prussian Union as well as the emigration of strict Lutherans, esp. in 19th c., led to more conservative practice. Restricted Communion was practiced by the Joint Syn. of Ohio, Ger. Syn. of Iowa, Syn. Conf., and Scand. synods. The Gen. Council expressed its position in the famous Galesburg* Rule. The Gen. Syn., believing "that the unity of the Church must be outwardly expressed," adhered "to the practice which marked the prevalent sentiment in America from the beginning, opening the privilege of the Lord's Supper to members, in good and regular standing, of other orthodox churches."

Generally speaking, men prominent in the struggle for confessionalism also advocated restricted Communion (C. P. Krauth, C. F. Walther, S. Fritschel), and the rising emphasis on Luth. confessionalism was marked by a stricter altar practice. In last decades of 19th c. and early in 20th, majority of Lutherans in Am. tended to follow organizational lines in practice of altar fellowship. See *Fellowship; Lutheran Confessions; Selective Fellowship; Unionism.*

W. Elert, *Abendmahl und Kirchengemeinschaft in der alten Kirche, hauptsächlich des Ostens* (Berlin, 1954); H. Sasse, *This Is My Body* (Minneapolis, 1959); *Church in Fellowship,* ed. V. Vajta (Minneapolis, 1963).

Altar Rail. Rail at entrance to or within chancel at which communicants can kneel to receive Sacrament of Altar. Traditional among Scand. Lutherans, it made its way among other Lutherans chiefly in the 20th c. In design it should be as transparent as possible so as not to present a visual barrier between worshipers and altar. ACP

Altdorfer, Albrecht (ca. 1480–1538). Painter, architect, engraver. Works include *Holy Family.*

Altenburg, Johann Michael (1584–1640). Ger. Luth. pastor. Composer of hymn tunes. "O Little Flock, Fear Not the Foe" is a favorite in Eng., U. S., and Germanic lands.

Altenburg Colloquy. Held Oct. 20, 1568–Mar. 9, 1569, at Altenburg, Ger., between Wittenberg theologians (Eber, Cruciger, and others) and Jena theologians (Wigand, Coelestin, Kirchner, and others). The Philippists (Wittenberg) defended the AC of 1540. Subjects discussed: justification, free will, and adiaphora. The colloquy led to no results. See also *Synergistic Controversy.*

Altenburg Conference (Colloquy; Interview). Discussion, or negotiation, primarily on indulgences, held early in Jan. 1519 bet. K. v. Miltitz* and M. Luther* in the house of G. Spalatin* at the Schlossberg, Altenburg, Ger., in presence of officials of the court of Frederick* III of Saxony. After the discussions Luther agreed to be silent on indulgences, provided his opponent did the same. It was also agreed that the bp. of Salzburg or bp. of Trier should arbitrate the matter.

Altenburg Debate. Debate, or disputation, held at Altenburg, Perry County, Missouri, in April 1841, on questions of church polity which had been agitating Saxon immigrants since deposition of Martin Stephan.* The two disputants were C. F. W. Walther* and Adolph Marbach,* an attorney. Walther drew the constructive conclusions, partially modifying the position which Carl Eduard Vehse* had taken. See also *Altenburg Theses.*

William J. Schmelder, "Walther at Altenburg," *CHIQ,* XXXIV (Oct. 1961), 65–81; P. E. Kretzmann, "The Altenburg Debate," *CTM,* XII (March 1941), 161–172.

Altenburg Theses. The theses which Walther defended in the Altenburg* Debate were:

I. The true Church, in the most real and most perfect sense, is the totality *(Gesamtheit)* of all true believers, who from the beginning to the end of the world from among all peoples and tongues have been called and sanctified by the Holy Spirit through the Word. And since God alone knows these true believers (2 Tim. 2:19), the Church is also called invisible. No one belongs to this true Church who is not spiritually united with Christ, for it is the spiritual body of Jesus Christ.

II. The name of the true Church belongs also to all those visible companies of men among whom God's Word is purely taught and the holy Sacraments are administered according to the institution of Christ. True, in this Church there are godless men, hypocrites, and heretics, but they are not true members of it, nor do they constitute the Church.

III. The name Church, and, in a certain sense, the name true Church, belongs also to those visible companies of men who have united under the confession of a falsified faith and therefore have incurred the guilt of a partial departure from the truth; provided they possess so much of God's Word and the holy Sacraments in purity that children of God may thereby be born. When such companies are called true churches, it is not the intention to state that they are faithful, but only that they are real churches as opposed to all worldly organizations *(Gemeinschaften).*

IV. The name Church is not improperly applied to heterodox companies, but according to the manner of speech of the Word of God itself. It is also not immaterial that this high name is allowed to such communions, for out of this follows:

1. That members also of such companies may be saved; for without the Church there is no salvation.

V. 2. The outward separation of a heterodox company from an orthodox Church is not necessarily a separation from the universal Christian Church nor a relapse into heathenism and does not yet deprive that company of the name Church.

VI. 3. Even heterodox companies have church power; even among them the goods of the Church may be validly administered, the ministry established, the Sacraments validly administered, and the keys of the kingdom of heaven exercised.

VII. 4. Even heterodox companies are not to be dissolved, but reformed.

VIII. The orthodox Church is chiefly to be judged by the common, orthodox, public confession to which its members acknowledge and confess themselves to be pledged. CSM

J. F. Koestering, *Auswanderung der sächsischen Lutheraner im Jahre 1838, ihre Niederlassung in Perry Co., Mo., und damit zusammenhängende interessante Nachrichten . . .* (St. Louis, 1867), pp. 51–52; Walter O. Forster, *Zion on the Mississippi* (St. Louis, 1953), pp. 523–525.

Altenburger Bibelwerk. M. Luther's* Bible tr., with his introductions and marginal comments, the summaries of V. Dietrich,* and the introductions and closing prayers of Franciscus Vierling. Preface to the reader dated Altenburg [Ger.] 1676; repub. at St. Louis, Mo., 1866. See also *Gönner, Johann Jakob.*

Altenburger Religionsgespraech. See *Altenburg Colloquy.*

Altenheim. See *Aging and Infirm, Homes and Services for.*

Althamer, Andreas (ca. 1500–ca. 1539). Luth. reformer. B. Brenz, Württemberg; d. Ansbach. Educ. Leipzig and Tübingen. Priest at Gmünd 1524; fled to Wittenberg 1525; went to Nürnberg 1526; pastor Eltersdorf 1527; deacon at St. Sebald, Nürnberg, 1528; called to Ansbach to aid Reformation in Brandenburg, 1528. His *Catechism in Question and Answer,* 1528, was first writing of that kind to be called a catechism. His selection of collects was widely used in S. Ger.

T. Kolde, *Andreas Althamer, der Humanist und Reformator in Brandenburg-Ansbach* (Erlangen, 1895).

Althaus, Adolf Paul Johannes (1861–1925). Father of P. A. W. H. Althaus;* b. Hannover, Ger.; educ. Erlangen and Göttingen, held several pastorates 1887–97, later prof. Göttingen; wrote *Die historische und dogmatische Grundlage der lutherischen Taufliturgie; Die Heilsbedeutung der Taufe im Neuen Testament.*

Althaus, Paul August Wilhelm Hermann (1888–1966). Son of A. P. J. Althaus*; b. Obershagen, Hannnover, Ger.; educ. Göttingen, Tübingen, and at the theol. sem. Erichsburg, Hannover; privatdocent Göttingen 1914; military chaplain 1915–18; taught Rostock 1920–25; prof. Erlangen from 1925. Influenced by A. v. Schlatter,* K. Heim,* K. M. A. Kähler,* W. Windelband,* et al. Had a broad philos. foundation, extensive knowledge of NT and M. Luther's thought; speaks of axiological eschatology, acc. to which eschatology is experienced already in this life; held that God reveals Himself in a gen. revelation outside salvation hist.; rejected natural theol.; held that proper relationship to God is est. only by Christian faith. Works include *Die letzten Dinge; Grundriss der Dogmatik; Grundriss der Ethik; Die christliche Wahrheit; Paulus und Luther über den Menschen; Die Theologie Martin Luthers; Die Ethik Martin Luthers; Der Brief an die Römer übersetzt und erklärt.*

Althusius, Johannes (1557–1638). Ger. jurist; defended democratic principle.

Alting. 1. *Johann Heinrich* (1583–1644). Son of Menso; prof. Heidelberg and Groningen; orthodox Calvinist. 2. *Jakob* (1618–79). Son of Henry; prof. of oriental languages and theology, Groningen; espoused literal exegesis. 3. *Menso* (1541–1612). Ref. pastor; b. Palatinate; fled to Neth.; opposed Lutheranism and advanced Ref. theology in E. Frisia.

Altlutheraner. See *Old Lutherans.*

Altnikol, Johann Christoph (1719–59). Pupil and son-in-law of J. S. Bach; compositions show unmistakable stamp of his mentor. Was at deathbed of Bach, who had become blind and dictated to Altnikol his last composition.

Altona Confession ("Altonaer Bekenntnis"; "Wort und Bekenntnis Altonaer Pastoren in der Not und Verwirrung des öffentlichen Lebens"). Issued Jan. 11, 1933, by pastors of Altona (now part of Hamburg), Ger., to give guidelines for Christian life on basis of Scripture in the confusing pol. situation; its 5 arts, deal with ch., boundaries for human behavior *(Grenzen des Menschen),* state, duties of the state,

God's commandments; harbinger of things to come in Confessing* Ch. and Kirchenkampf.*

Lutherische Monatshefte, VII (1968), 181–184.

Altruism. Term invented by Comte* to denote unselfish regard for welfare of others; opposed to egoism; considered by him to be the only moral principle of life.

Alumbrados. See *Illuminati.*

Alva, Duke of (Fernando Alvarez de Toledo; ca. 1508–ca. 1583). Sp. gen.; commander under Charles V and Philip II; defeated John Frederick of Saxony at Mühlberg (1547); suppressed Dutch revolt (1567); set up Council of Troubles (Blood Council) to punish enemies of Sp.

Alvelt, Augustine of (1480–ca. 1535). RC; b. Hannover; taught Leipzig; prior Halle; provincial for Saxony. Luther's opponent in controversy regarding papacy.

Alvinczi, Peter (1570–1634). Hungarian Ref. theologian; sought harmony between Lutherans and Ref. on doctrine of Lord's Supper.

Amalarius of Metz (ca. 780–ca. 850). Liturgical scholar; pupil of Alcuin; participated in Carolingian renaissance; chief work: *De ecclesiasticis officiis.*

Amalric of Bena (d. ca. 1207). Scholastic philosopher; prof. Paris; taught type of philosophy similar to Gnosticism. Teachings condemned by Synod of Paris (ca. 1209) and Lateran Council of 1215.

Amalricians. Followers of Amalric* of Bena.

Amama, Sixtinus (1593–1629). Succeeded Drusius as prof. of Heb. at Franeker, Neth.; textual critic; Bible tr.

Amana Society, or *Community of True Inspiration,* or *Inspirationists.* Ger. communistic religious soc. in Iowa. Traces its origin to 1714, when separatists in N. and W. Ger., stimulated by preaching of Fr. Camisard prophets, under leadership of Eberhard Gruber and Johann Rock, organized "congregations of the inspired." The movement flourished for a generation, then declined, but was revived, beginning 1817, in Hesse, Palatinate, and Alsace, through influence of Michael Krausert, Barbara Heinemann (illiterate Alsatian peasant girl), and Christian Metz.* When they refused to send their children to the state schools, swear allegiance, and bear arms, the govt. used repressive measures; as a result they began to emigrate to Am., 1842. They first settled near Buffalo and organized as Ebenezer Soc., 1843. In 1855 they removed to Iowa Co., Iowa, where they bought 26,000 acres of land, laid out 7 villages, of which the principal one is Amana, and incorporated (1859) as Amana Soc. The community was primarily religious, and communism, at first incidental, was made to serve this primary purpose. They held all property in common and carried on agriculture, manufacture, and trade. The entire govt. was vested in 13 trustees. In 1932 communism was abolished; civil affairs were taken over by a corporation called the Amana Soc.; ecclesiastical matters were put into hands of the Amana Ch. Soc. This change has not affected the religious tenets of the soc. Religiously the soc. was divided into 3 classes, graded according to their piety. Their main religious tenets, as contained in *Glaubensbekenntnis der wahren Inspirationsgemeinde* and *Katechetischer Unterricht von der Lehre des Heils,* included, besides fundamental doctrine of present-day inspiration, belief in Trinity, resurrection of the dead, the Judgment, justification through forgiveness of sins and holy life, perfectionism, and millenarianism. Sacraments are not regarded as means of grace. Baptism is rejected, and the Lord's Supper is celebrated about every 2 yrs., when the highest class also practices the rite of foot washing. It is held that there is a possibility of salvation after death and that the wicked are not punished eternally. Oaths are forbidden. The spiritual condition of each member is examined annually. See *Religious Bodies (U. S.), Bibliography.* FEM

Amandus (d. ca. 675). Merovingian apostle of Flanders; extensive miss. work in Flanders and Carinthia; bp. of Maastricht, 646.

Amandus, Johannes (d. ca. 1530). Originally RC; met Luther; pastor Königsberg 1523–25; supt. Goslar.

Amaterasu. Sun goddess of primitive Shinto, supposedly born from eye of Izanagi, the creator; from her descended Jimmu, 1st human ruler of Jap., 660 BC. See also *Shinto,* 1.

Ambivalence. In psychology, concepts which imply love and hate, attraction and repulsion. In religion, concepts (e. g., numinous, taboo) which imply wrath as well as kindness.

Ambo. See *Church Furniture,* 1

Amboise, Edict of. See *France,* 9.

Ambrogio Traversari (1386–1439). B. Portico, Romagna, It.; Camaldolese* theol. and general; humanist; attended Council of Florence.*

Ambrose (340–397). Noted leader and teacher of W Ch.; b. Trier; d. Milan. Educ. Rome for legal career; consular prefect for Upper It.; moved to Milan ca. 370. After death of Arian bp. Auxentius, appointee of Constantius, a dispute between orthodox and Arian parties caused a severe quarrel which threatened the peace of the city. Ambrose, as magistrate, was present to maintain order when the people, suddenly turning to him as a new candidate, transferred him from his official position to the episcopate. Since he was still a catechumen, he was baptized at once and 8 days later was consecrated bp. (374). Ambrose was distinguished for his defense of the catholic faith, opposing both paganism and heresy with equal zeal. When Theodosius I* attempted to force Christians to pay for rebuilding a synagog they had destroyed, and again when he massacred thousands of people in Thessalonica for opposing imperial authority, Ambrose rebuked him and took unprecedented step of excommunicating a Christian emperor. He also set a pattern for the Middle Ages by furthering the idea that it is the state's duty to support and further the work of the church and the church's duty to support and further the work of the state. Working together, both form the Corpus Christianum. Two of his major works are practical guides: *On Christian Faith* for the Christian prince; *On the Functions of the Ministry* for the clergy. All his writings demonstrate a pastoral approach. He was strong advocate of ascetic Christianity: celibacy, voluntary poverty, martyrdom. He was also active in development of liturgical music. See also *Ambrosian Music; Marcellina; Veni, Creator Spiritus.*

E. K. Rand, *Founders of the Middle Ages* (Cambridge, Mass., 1928); H. v. Campenhausen, *Ambrosius von Mailand als Kirchenpolitiker* (Leipzig, 1929); F. Dudden, *The Life and Times of St. Ambrose* (Oxford, 1935); J.-R. Palanque, *Saint Ambroise et l'Empire romain* (Paris, 1933); *MPL,* 14–17; *NPNF,* Ser. 2, X. WWO

Ambrose, Sisters of St. See *Annunciation, Orders of,* 3.

Ambrosian Music. Ambrosian chant is an older and in some ways more elaborate form of Lat. choral music than Gregorian chant. Ambrose introduced hymns and antiphons into the worship of the W and wrote some superb hymns still in use. Music of Ambrosian mass includes *ingressa* (counterpart of our Introit), *psalmellus* and versicle (corresponding to our Gradual), *cantus* (corresponding to Tract of our rite), alleluia, antiphon after the Gospel, Offertory, *confractorium* (where we have Agnus Dei), *transitorium* (equivalent of Communion chant). Characteristic of psalm tones is lack of an intonation and mediation. Ambrosian chant is largely limited in regular service use to Milan and a few areas of N It. ACP

Ambrosian Rite. One of few non-Roman Lat. rites to survive in RC Ch. Now used only in old archiepiscopal province of Milan. Exhibits marked differences from Roman rite. Named after Ambrose,* though no definite evidence connects it with him.

The Ambrosian Liturgy, tr. E. G. C. F. Atchley (London, 1909); W. C. Bishop, *The Mozarabic and Ambrosian Rites* (London, 1924), pp. 98–134.

Ambrosians. 1. Religious brotherhoods founded in region of Milan; given Augustinian rule by Gregory XI 1375; dissolved ca. 1646 by Innocent X. 2. 16th-c. Anabaptist sect which denied need of Bible or priests and claimed direct communication of the Spirit (Jn 1:9). See also *Annunciation, Orders of,* 3.

Ambrosiaster. Name first given by Erasmus to author of *Commentaria in XIII epistolas b. Pauli* (4th c.). Had been ascribed to Ambrose in Middle Ages.

MPL, 17, 45–535.

Ambrosius Catharinus. See *Catharinus, Ambrosius.*

Amen. Term derived from Heb.; root meaning "certainty"; signifies assent, confidence: "Verily," or, as Luther puts it: "Yes, yes; it shall be so." (SC III 21). See also *Response.*

Amen, Jacob. See *Ammann, Jacob; Mennonite Churches,* 3 a.

Amerbach, Bonifacius (ca. 1495–1562). Prof. of jurisprudence at Basel; humanist friend of Erasmus.

Amerbach, Veit (Veit Trolmann. 1503–57). Peasant's son; educ. Wittenberg; sympathized with Luther and Melanchthon but remained RC; taught at Wittenberg (1529–43), Ingolstadt (1543–57).

American and Foreign Bible Society. See *Bible Societies,* 5.

American Association of Adult Education. See *Adult Education.*

American Association of Group Workers. See *National Association of Social Workers.*

American Association of Medical Social Workers. See *National Association of Social Workers.*

American Association of Psychiatric Social Workers. See *National Association of Social Workers.*

American Association of Social Workers. See *National Association of Social Workers.*

American Association of Theological Schools. See *Ministry, Education of,* VI, B.

American Association of Visiting Teachers. See *National Association of Social Workers.*

American Asylum. See *Deaf,* 6.

American Baptist Association. See *Baptist Churches,* 14.

American Baptist Convention. See *Baptist Churches,* 8.

American Baptist Missionary Union. See *India,* 11.

American Baptist Publication Society. See *Baptist Churches,* 6.

American Bible Society. See *Bible Societies,* 5.

American Bible Union. See *Bible Societies,* 5.

American Board of Commissioners for Foreign Missions. Founded Sept. 5, 1810, by Gen. Assoc. of Cong. Churches of Mass., at Bradford, Mass. First missionaries: Adoniram Judson, Samuel Newell, Samuel Nott, and others, 1812, to India. In 1812 the Presb. churches resolved to work through the ABCFM; in 1814 the Associate Reform Ch. joined; in 1816 the Dutch Ref. Ch.; still later the Ger. Ref. Ch. In 1825 the Presb. United For. Miss. Soc., formed for work among the Indians, by resolution turned over its work to the ABCFM. A separation of the Old-school people took place in 1837. The New-school Presbyterians continued the relation until 1870, then withdrew to join the reunited Presb. Bd. In 1857 the Ref. Dutch withdrew to organize their own For. Miss. Bd. They were followed in quick succession by the Associate Ref. Presbyterians and the Ger. Ref. Ch. After 1870 the ABCFM represented practically only Cong. churches. See also *Hayslack Group; United Church Board for World Ministries.*

American Carpatho-Russian Orthodox Greek Catholic Church. See *Eastern Orthodox Churches,* 6.

American Catholic Church, The, Archdiocese of New York. See *Old Catholics,* 4.

American Catholic Church (Syro-Antiochian), The. Organized 1915; derives orders from the Syrian Patriarch of Antioch; uses RC liturgy in administering 7 sacraments; self-governed. HQ Miami, Fla.

American Christian Convention. See *United Church of Christ, The,* I B.

American Christian Missionary Society. See *Disciples of Christ,* 2 d.

American College for Girls. See *Armenia.*

American Council of Christian Churches. See *Union Movements,* 11.

American Ethical Union. See *Ethical Culture.*

American Evangelical Lutheran Church. See *Danish Lutherans in America,* 3-4.

American Holy Orthodox Catholic Apostolic Eastern Church. See *Eastern Orthodox Churches,* 6.

American Home Missionary Society. Name adopted 1826 by the United Domestic Missionary Society, undenominational, est. 1822. See also *Central Missionary Society of the Evangelical Lutheran Church in the United States.*

American Legion. See *Veterans Organizations.*

American Lutheran Church. Organized Aug. 11, 1930. Merger of Ohio, Iowa, and Buffalo synods. Pres.: Carl C. Hein 1930–37; Emmanuel F. Poppen 1937–50; Henry F. Schuh 1950–60. ALC merged with ELC and UELC (1960) to form The American* Lutheran Church.

I. Formation. Intersyn. friendship between Iowa and Ohio synods was stimulated in late 19th c. by identical positions on fellowship and secret societies, occasionally overlapping syn. boundaries, and mutual opposition to Mo. Syn. on doctrine of predestination. Doctrinal consultations at Richmond, Ind. (1883), Michigan City, Ind. (1893), Toledo, Ohio (1907, 1912), culminated in official fellowship, based on *Toledo Theses,** in 1918. This document pledged the synods to all "doctrines of faith" in Luth. confessions but recognized that absolute agreement in all areas of doctrine is not prerequisite for fellowship. Mechanics of merger were worked out 1924–30. Buffalo Syn. asked to be included in 1925. The only significant barrier to merger arose in 1926 over whether the new const. should ascribe inerrancy to every word of Scripture.

II. Doctrine. The const. affirmed:

1. *Scripture.* "The Church accepts the canonical books . . . as the inspired Word of God and the only infallible authority in all matters of faith and life . . . [and] believes that the canonical books . . . are, as a whole and in all their parts, the inspired and inerrant Word of God and accepts these books in the now generally recognized texts as substantially identical with the original texts and as the only inspired and inerrant authority, source, guide, and norm in all matters of faith and life."

2. *Confessions.* All Confessions of the Book of Concord are accepted "as the true exposition and presentation of the faith once for all delivered unto the saints."

3. *Fellowship.* Because unity in doctrine (in the sense of the Toledo Theses) and practice are the necessary prerequisites for ch. fellowship, the Galesburg Rule* is approved.

4. *Secret Societies.* "The Church is earnestly opposed to all organizations or societies, secret or open, which, without confessing faith in the Triune God and in Jesus Christ as the eternal Son of the eternal God, incarnate in order to be our only Savior from sin, are avowedly religious or practice forms of reli-

gion, teaching salvation by works. It declares such organizations and societies to be antichristian and rejects any fellowship with them."

III. Size and Structure. In 1930 the ALC had 2,064 congs., 1,554 clergymen, 506,819 bap. mem., 340,500 communicants. At time of 1960 merger it had 2,081 congs., 2,168 clergymen (1958 statistics), 1,059,195 bap. mem., 696,695 communicants. Because of many consolidations of congs., the total number increased only slightly in 30 years, but size of average cong. increased from 165 to ca. 330 communicants.

The ALC had strongly centralized syn. structure. Congs. owned their own property and remained their own highest authority but voluntarily obligated themselves to support the work of the whole ch., which was administered largely by cen. syn. bds. rather than by 13 geog. districts. One layman and 1 pastor from each precinct of 18 congs. served as delegates to biennial conventions. Severe financial crises during its 1st decade caused the ALC to develop very cautious financial policies and to center in its Bd. of Trustees an unusually great amount of authority in policy matters.

IV. Work. 1. *Education.* A few parochial schools (34 with ca. 3,000 students) existed in the ALC in 1960, but educ. emphasis in congs. was mainly on S. S. and instruction classes. In addition to its own sr. colleges (Capital, Wartburg, Texas Luth., and Luther [Regina, Sask.]) the ALC gave financial support to Pacific Luth. Coll. and to Calif. Luth. Coll. Its seminaries were Ev. Luth. (Columbus) and Wartburg (Dubuque). Its ministry to youth attending non-ch. colleges was carried out through the NLC's division of coll. and u. work.

2. *American Missions.* By 1955, though 415 congs. still had at least 1 Ger. service a yr., much of the orientation toward Ger. had been overcome. Bet. 1930 and 1960, 527 new congregations were founded, over one fourth of the 1960 membership. In 1957 the Mex. Luth. Conf. of the Tex. Dist. became an affiliate ch., La Iglesia Lutherana Mexicana, with headquarters and theol. sem., Augsburg, in Mexico City.

3. *World Missions.* Work in India was begun by the Ohio Syn. in 1913, when it was granted part of the Hermannsburg Society's work. By 1960 the field included 11 main stations, 4 high schools, a girls' industrial school, a hosp., and a leprosarium.

The much larger New Guinea field owes its origin to the Rhenish and the Neuendettelsau societies, whose work the Iowa Syn. helped support for many yrs. before part of the field was assigned to the ALC in 1932. Now the ALC and the Neuendettelsau fields are united in the Ev. Luth. Ch. of New Guinea. In 1958 there were 77 ordained missionaries, 88 lay workers, 82 national pastors, 1,232 national evangelists, 853 unregistered schools with 26,649 pupils and 887 national teachers, 11 secondary schools, 1 sem., 6 hospitals, and 4 nurses training schools.

In 1959 the ALC opened a new miss. field in Ethiopia with headquarters in Addis Ababa.

4. *Social Service.* Charitable institutions at Mars, Pa., Melville, Sask., Richmond, Ind., and Springfield, Minn., were owned by the ALC; those at Toledo, Ohio, and Muscatine and Waverly, Iowa, were partially supported; and those at Sterling, Nebr., Williston, Ohio, and Round Rock, Tex., were fully approved. The Bd. for Christian Soc. Action promoted soc. work and researched areas of vital soc. concern.

5. *Other.* Pub. house: Wartburg Press, Columbus. Official paper: *Lutheran Standard.* Ger. paper: *Kirchenblatt.* Organizations: Luther League, Women's Miss. Federation, Brotherhood.

V. Relationships with Other Churches. 1. *Lutheran.* No other Luth. syn. was as actively involved 1930–60 in promoting intra-Luth. unity on as many fronts. In 1930 the ALC entered into close fellowship of work and worship with 4 other "middle synods" in the Am. Luth. Conf.* The 1960 merger of The American Lutheran Church grew out of cooperation and fellowship in the Conf.

In 1934 the ALC resumed negotiations toward doctrinal unity which its constituent synods had carried on with the Mo. Syn. before 1930. In 1938 the ALC approved the Mo. Syn. *Brief Statement** plus its own appended *Declaration* as a basis for fellowship. However, neither these statements nor the unified *Doctrinal Affirmation* (1945) brought official doctrinal agreement or fellowship. Despite a 1946 resolution despairing "of attaining Lutheran unity by way of additional doctrinal formulations and reformulations" the ALC was soon back at work with the Mo. Syn. on a new statement, the *Common Confession.** By 1956 both synods had approved it, but fellowship failed to materialize because the ALC was ready to merge with the ELC and the UELC and because of a continuing difference of approach on prerequisites for ch. fellowship.

Negotiations with the ULCA produced the *Pittsburgh Agreement** (1940) on Scripture, fellowship, and secret societies. Both synods adopted the statement, but differences in interpretation of the document's function prevented establishment of pulpit and altar fellowship. In 1946 the ALC authorized "selective* fellowship" with Lutherans of other synods who agreed in doctrine and practice with the ALC const. Much local cooperation between ALC and ULCA congs. ensued. The ALC's 1950 rejection of a proposed merger of all NLC bodies reflected continuing uneasiness over the ULCA position on secret societies and fellowship with non-Lutherans.

On the wider Luth. scene the ALC prized highly the cooperative work of the NLC. The ALC was represented at the Luth. World Conv. of 1935 and has participated fully in work of the LWF.

2. *Non-Lutheran.* Strongly isolationist regarding non-Lutherans in 1930, the ALC gradually overcame some of its fear of ecumenical ventures. Its delegates committed it to WCC membership at Amsterdam in 1948, a decision which every subsequent ALC conv. reaffirmed. The ALC belonged to neither the FCCCA nor its more inclusive successor, the NCCCUSA. Yet some ALC boards utilized services of NCC agencies. An ALC committee was authorized to study and analyze implications of Council membership as prelude to possible future decision on membership. Membership in local councils of ministers and churches was left to cong. decision. Some took active role in these ventures, but no accurate statistics on degree of participation are available. FWM

See also *Lutheran Council in Canada,* 2.

Paul H. Buehring, *The Spirit of the American Lutheran Church* (Columbus, 1940); Fred W. Meuser, *The Formation of the American Lutheran Church* (Columbus, 1958); A. R. Wentz, *A Basic History of Lutheranism in America* (Philadelphia, 1955); Minutes of the biennial conventions 1930–60. Official archives of the ALC are at Wartburg Theol. Sem., Dubuque, Iowa.

American Lutheran Church, The. Organized Apr. 22, 1960. Began functioning Jan. 1, 1961. A merger of the ALC, the ELC, and the UELC. LFC became part of The ALC on Feb. 1, 1963. Headquarters: 522 S. 5th St., Minneapolis, Minn. Pres.: Fredrik Axel Schiotz 1960–70; Kent Sigvart Knutson 1970–73; David W. Preus 1973–.

I. Background. Though not the 1st merger of synods with diverse national backgrounds, the ALC was the 1st such large-scale combination in Am. It brought together groups which for generations had had strong orientation to Dan., Ger., and Norw. backgrounds in language and to a degree in patterns of piety. As evidence of Americanization of these originally for. language groups, the merger was a major event in Am. Luth. hist.

The ALC grew out of the close assoc. of these synods in the Am. Luth. Conf. Cooperative ventures (1930–50) paved the way for consideration of merger. Inasmuch as all the Conf. synods were also in the NLC there were two possible avenues to further unity. In 1949 the Aug. Syn. proposed an all-NLC merger, and the UELC a merger of the Conf. synods. In 1950 the ALC, the ELC, and the UELC approved the latter plan and rejected the more inclusive merger, partially at least because they wanted discussion of doctrinal and practical issues to precede any merger with synods outside the Conf. The Aug. Syn. (a Conf. synod) and the ULCA (non-Conf.), convinced that there were no unsolved important issues, continued to advocate the larger merger. Nevertheless, the Aug. Syn. participated in planning for the Conf. merger until 1952, withdrawing then because the merger was not inclusive enough and because it feared that ecumenical relationships would not receive adequate attention.

As evidence of unified approach to doctrine and ch. life the Conf. synods adopted *United* Testimony on Faith and Life* in 1952. A Joint Union Com. (1951–60) worked out merger details and a structure for the new ch. Its reports to the 1954, 1956, 1958, and 1960 conventions were approved by overwhelming majorities except in the LFC, where referendums in 1955 and 1957 failed by narrow margins. In 1961 an LFC referendum approved merger. On Feb. 1, 1963, the LFC became part of The ALC. A few LFC congregations protested the merger and continued independently as The Association* of Free Luth. Congs.

II. Doctrinal Basis and Spirit. 1. *Scripture.* The ch. accepts the Scriptures "as a whole and in all their parts as the divinely inspired, revealed and inerrant Word of God, and submits to this as the only infallible authority in all matters of faith and life." (Const.)

2. *Confessions.* "As brief and true statements of the doctrine of the Word of God, the Church accepts and confesses the following symbols, subscription to which shall be required of all its members, both congregations and individuals: 1) the ancient ecumenical creeds: the Apostolic, the Nicene, and the Athanasian; 2) the unaltered Augsburg Confession and Luther's Small Catechism. As further elaboration of and in accord with these Lutheran Symbols, the Church also receives the other documents in the Book of Concord. . . . The American Lutheran Church accepts without reservation the symbolical books of the evangelical Lutheran Church, not insofar as but because they are the presentation and explanation of the pure doctrine of the Word of God and a summary of the faith of the evangelical Lutheran Church." (Const.)

3. *Spirit.* The particular "spirit" is hard to define because the merged ch. is very young and contains diverse hist. emphases. The *United Testimony,* like the const., accepts the Bible as inspired and infallible revelation and the "inerrant and completely adequate source and norm of Christian doctrine and life" but also rejects "all rationalizing processes which would explain away either the divine or the human factor in the Bible." The *United Testimony* also: (1) decries separatistic spirit which ignores the existence of other Christian churches, (2) recognizes necessity of evangelism within the ch. as well as in the "world," (3) notes hist. variety of worship forms within its constituency, reminds members that liturgy is a reflection of doctrine, and commends current concern for liturgical uniformity while warning against equating form with faith, (4) encourages lay activity, including lay preaching, when it has approval of the proper authority, (5) notes diversity of conviction in regard to some forms of amusement, dress, food, and beverages.

III. Size and Structure. At the time of merger, The ALC had 4,941 congs., 4,884 clergymen, 2,306,780 bap. mem., 1,509,174 confirmed mem. It has congs. in Can. and in all states except Conn., Del., Miss., R. I., S. C., Vt. Heaviest concentration of membership is in Upper Midwest, especially Minn., Wis., N. Dak., Iowa. Property valuation in 1960: $514,699,668.

Although the const. ascribes "basic authority" as part of the ministry of Word and sacrament to the cong., it refrains from calling congs. sovereign, indep. units. Membership implies voluntary cong. participation in full work of the ch. Highest legislative authority is vested in the biennial gen. conv. of ca. 1,000 delegates, of whom ca. half are laymen. The Ch. Council, with clergy and lay representation from all districts, has special responsibility for spiritual welfare of the ch., the Bd. of Trustees for its bus. affairs. Together these 2 groups constitute the Joint Council, with power to act (legislate) in emergency situations between conventions.

The ch. has 19 geog. districts, each divided into conferences. As "the working unit of the Church in supervising clergy, congregations, and conferences in regard to both doctrine and practice," the district's major function is to promote work of The ALC and to foster harmony, cooperation, and fellowship in the ch.

IV. Work. About 60% of The ALC benevolence budget is devoted to miss., Am. and world miss. receiving nearly equal amounts. Some 75 new congs. have been established per yr. under the "package mission" plan, which lends money for a site, a 1st-unit bldg., and a parsonage down payment, plus adequate subsidy to carry the miss. to self-support. Special work is done in Mex. and Alaska (Eskimos). World miss. fields: India, New Guinea, Ethiopia, Colombia, S Afr., Madagascar, Cameroon, Japan, Taiwan, Hong Kong, Brazil, Nigeria. See also *Tokai Evangelical Lutheran Church.*

In higher educ. the ch. supports 11 colleges and universities: Augsburg, Augustana, Calif. Luth., Capital, Conc., Dana, Luther, Pacific Luth., St. Olaf, Tex. Luth., Wartburg; Waldorf (Jr.) Coll., Forest City, Iowa; Oak Grove Luth. High School, Fargo, N. Dakota. Sems.: The Ev. Luth. Theol. Sem., Columbus, Ohio; Luther Theol. Sem., St. Paul, Minn.; Wartburg Theol. Sem., Dubuque, Iowa; Pacific Lutheran Theol. Sem., Berkeley, Calif.

Other divisions of the ch.: Pensions, Charities (60 ch.-owned or ch.-related homes, mostly for children and aged), and Pub. (pub. house: Augsburg; official paper: *Lutheran Standard*).

Functioning directly under the Ch. Council are the Com. on Worship and Ch. Music, Com. on Relations to Luth. Churches, Commission on Evangelism, and Commission on Research and Soc. Action.

V. Affiliations and Relationships. 1. *With Other Lutherans.* As was to be expected, the merger conv. continued the affiliations which all the synods had with the NLC and LWF. The same conv. declared "willingness to enter into discussions looking toward pulpit and altar fellowship with any and all Lutheran Churches which confess their adherence to the Holy Scriptures as the Word of God in all matters of faith and life and subscribe to the Confessions of the Lutheran Church," and it encouraged congs. to cooperate in worship and work with congs. of other Luth. synods wherever there is agreement in confession and practice. In 1962 The ALC and the Mo. Syn. invited the LCA to discuss achievement of full fellowship, but the LCA Joint Commission declined until the three agree on exact nature of new cooperative agency to replace the NLC. The ALC and the Mo. Syn. est. fellowship with each other 1969.

2. *With Non-Lutherans.* Membership of the merged ch. in the WCC was a provision of the Articles of Union. To give opponents a fair hearing WCC membership was reevaluated in print and debate between 1960 and 1962. At the 1962 conv. WCC membership was reaffirmed by a vote of 647–307. Some vocal opposition continues. There has been no strong agitation for affiliation with the NCCCUSA even though some ALC divisions and commissions utilize its services.

Officially the ALC neither encourages nor restricts membership in local councils of churches and ministerial associations. *United Testimony* (1952) opens the door to such affiliation by recognizing that "so long as witness can be borne to the truth as we see it in Christ a measure of outward fellowship may be enjoyed even with such as differ with us in the apprehension of certain aspects of the truth." *United Testimony* also affirms the Galesburg Rule* as correct guiding principle, but since 1962 the Ch. Council has been restudying its meaning and applicability for the ch. in its present situation. FWM

See also *Lutheran Council in the United States of America, I.*

Handbook of the A.L.C. (1960); *Report of the Joint Union Committee* (1958, 1960); *Reports and Actions of the A. L. C.* (1962); R. C. Gremmels, *Unity Begins with You* (Columbus, 1958); *Documents of Lutheran Unity in America,* ed. R. C. Wolf.

VI. Districts. A. The ALC is divided into 19 districts on a territorial basis. These were organized in the interim between the constituting conv. of the ALC (Apr. 22–24, 1960) and Jan. 1, 1961. They represent mergers and/or realignments of old geog. districts and their conferences of the former ALC (1930–60), the ELC (1917–60), and the UELC (1896–1960). Pastors and congs. of the LFC (1897–1963) were added to the dist. rosters after its merger with the ALC, Feb. 1963.

B. Districts of the ALC serve "for the purpose of planning, promoting, and executing the program and work of the Church" (Dist. Const., Art. II, Sec. 4). Each dist. shall "(1) Exercise supervision over its clergy, congregations, and conferences in regard to doctrine and practice; (2) Admit, advise, discipline, and when necessary exclude congregations in accordance with the provisions of the Bylaws of The A. L. C., Part II; (3) Admit, advise, discipline, and when necessary exclude clergymen in accordance with the Bylaws of The A. L. C., Part III; (4) Authorize ordination to the Holy Ministry of candidates who have been approved by the Church Council and who have accepted calls within the district; (5) Establish and re-arrange the conferences of the district; (6) Elect its officers and committees; (7) Elect a lay representative of the district on the Church Council; (8) Elect its quota of delegates to the General Convention of The A. L. C., upon nomination by the several conferences at the district convention; (9) Establish its budget in harmony with the Bylaws of The A. L. C., Part VIII; (10) Prepare resolutions and recommendations to the congregations of the district; (11) Give consideration to resolutions and recommendations from conferences and congregations within the district; (12) Arrange for consideration of doctrinal and practical topics at district and conference meetings; (13) Consider matters which pertain to the life and program of The A. L. C., and transmit resolutions and recommendations to the General Convention; (14) Propose amendments to its constitution as provided in the Constitution and Bylaws of The A. L. C.; (15) Propose amendments to the Constitution of The A. L. C.; (16) Perform such other functions and duties as The A. L. C. may assign to its districts and as are necessary to fulfill the purpose of the district" (Art. V). Each district is divided into conferences whose objectives are to "(1) Study the Holy Scriptures and Christian doctrine, and promote such study within the congregations; (2) Quicken and deepen the spiritual life of clergy and laity; (3) Cultivate Christian fellowship; (4) Discuss methods of parish administration and the solution of parish problems; (5) Transact business matters relating to the congregational work of the conference; (6) Deliberate on the work and life of the Church and make these more effective within the congregations; (7) Support the total program of the Church and of the district in its application to the congregations of the conference." (Art. XI, Sec. 2)

C. Names and areas.

1. *Eastern:* states of Me., N. H., Vt., Mass., Conn., R. I., N. Y., Pa., N. J., Del., W. Va., Md., Va., N. C., S. C., Ga., Fla., D. C.; Can. from Lakehead to E Coast. Pres.: Gordon S. Huffman, 1961–.

2. *Ohio:* state of Ohio except Williams, Defiance, Fulton, Henry, Wood, Lucas, Ottawa counties; states of Ky., Tenn., Miss., and Ala.; counties of Ind. S of and including Madison, Blackford, and Jay, and counties E of and including Blackford, Madison, Hancock, Shelby, Decatur, Jennings, Scott, Clark, Floyd. Pres.: Kenneth Priebe, 1961–63; Paul Moeller, 1963–.

3. *Michigan:* state of Mich. except upper peninsula; and in Ohio the counties of Williams, Defiance, Fulton, Henry, Wood, Lucas, Ottawa. Pres.: Norman A. Menter, 1961–66, Robert L. Wietelmann, 1966–.

4. *Illinois:* state of Ill.; counties of Ind. W of and including Steuben, De Kalb, Allen, Adams, Wells, Grant, Tipton, Hamilton, Marion, Johnson, Bartholomew, Jackson, Washington, Harrison; counties of Mo. contiguous to Ill. Pres.: Elmer A. Nelson, 1961–.

5. *Northern Wisconsin:* counties in Wis. N of and including Trempealeau, Jackson, Wood, Portage, Waushara, Winnebago, Calumet, Manitowoc; upper peninsula of Mich. Theo. A. Ohlrogge, 1961–73, Vernon E. Anderson, 1973–.

6. *Southern Wisconsin:* counties in Wis. S of and including La Crosse, Monroe, Juneau, Adams, Marquette, Green Lake, Fond du Lac, Sheboygan. Pres.: M. C. Austinson, 1961–67, A. P. Nassen 1967–.

7. *Northern Minnesota:* counties in Minn. N of and including Wilkin, Otter Tail, Wadena, Cass, Crow Wing, Aitkin, Carlton. Pres.: A. E. Hanson, 1961–63; Tollef C. Hanson, 1963–67, Cecil M. Johnson, 1967–.

8. *Southeastern Minnesota:* counties in Minn. S and E of and including Pine, Kanabec, Mille Lacs, Sherburne, Wright, Carver, Scott, Le Sueur, Waseca, Freeborn. Pres.: E. C. Reinertson, 1961–63; Melford S. Knutson, 1963–72, J. Elmo Agrimson, 1972–.

9. *Southwestern Minnesota:* counties in Minn. S and W of and including Traverse, Grant, Douglas, Todd, Morrison, Benton, Stearns, Meeker, McLeod, Sibley, Nicollet, Blue Earth, Fairbault. Pres.: Edward A. Hansen, 1961–.

10. *Iowa:* state of Iowa. Pres.: H. W. Siefkes, 1961–66; Bruno Schlachtenhaufen 1966–.

11. *Eastern North Dakota:* counties in N. Dak. E of and including Rolette, Pierce, Wells, Stutsman, La Moure, Dickey. Pres.: L. E. Tallakson, 1961–73; Nelson F. Preus 1973–.

12. *Western North Dakota:* counties in N. Dak. W of and including Bottineau, McHenry, McLean, Kidder, Logan, McIntosh. Pres.: J. Elmo Agrimson, 1961–72; Roy W. Gilbertson, 1972–.

13. *South Dakota:* state of S. Dak. Pres.: E. O. Gilbertson, 1961–.

14. *Central:* states of Nebr., Colo., Kans., Okla., Mo. except counties contiguous to Ill.

15. *Southern:* states of Ark., La., Tex. Pres.: Erwin G. Fritschel, 1961–69; Archie L. Madsen, 1969–.

16. *Rocky Mountain:* states of Mont., Idaho, Wyo. Pres.: R. A. Daehlin, 1961–73, Norman G. Wick, 1973–.

17. *North Pacific:* states of Wash., Oreg., Alaska. Pres.: H. L. Foss, 1961–64, S. C. Siefkes, 1964–69; Clarence Solberg, 1969–.

18. *South Pacific:* states of Calif., Nev., Utah, N. Mex., Ariz., Hawaii. Pres.: Gaylerd Falde, 1961–.

19. *Canada:* Canada from Lakehead to Pacific Coast. Pres.: Karl Holfeld, 1961–66. See also *Canada,* A 26. WGT

American Lutheran Conference, The. 1. Recognition of unity and a sense of fellowship transcending nationalistic lines were expressed in forming this federation of 5 churches in 1930: ALC, Aug. Ev. Luth. Ch., ELC (Norw.), LFC, and UELC (Dan.). Its strength lay in upper Miss. valley, 2d- and 3d-generation descendants of Norw., Ger., Swed., and Dan. immigrants. In 1960 The American Lutheran Church* grew out of this federation.

2. Doctrinal basis of the Am. Luth. Conf. was a document known as the *Minneapolis Theses,** drawn up in 1925 by syn. representatives at a colloquium in Minneapolis and submitted for adoption to the bodies designated above. Incorporated are 8 points of doctrine quoted from the *Chicago Theses** of 1919, adopted by some of the bodies in 1920. On this basis these bodies voted to establish pulpit and altar fellowship with one another, individually adopted the proposed const. of the Am. Luth. Conf., and through their delegates organized as The Am. Luth. Conf. Oct. 29–31, 1930, at Minneapolis, Minn. (Documents are in Jan. 1941 issue of *Journal of Theology* of the Am. Luth. Conf.)

3. Spirit and purpose of the organizers is expressed in this quotation from the preamble of the const.: "In the providence of God the time appears to have come when Lutheran church bodies in America that are one in faith and that have declared pulpit and altar fellowship with one another should manifest their oneness by seeking to foster fraternal relations and by cooperating in the extension of the Kingdom of Christ. These church bodies believe that it is conducive to the attainment of these objectives to enter into an organization." Objectives stated in the const. are: "Mutual counsel concerning the faith, life, and work of the Church. Cooperation in matters of common interest and responsibility. . . ." Power was limited, each constituent body retaining autonomy; only such functions as were specifically assigned to the Conf. by its constituent bodies could be exercised by it. Conventions were held every 2 yrs., with representation based on communicant members and consisting of an equal number of pastors and laymen. Most of the work between conventions was done by commissions under direction of the Ex. Com.

4. Perhaps the most tangible project sponsored by the Conf. was Student Service. Careful coordination of efforts by constituent bodies led to growing unification of the work and consultation with the Bd. of Educ. of the ULCA. In 1944 the Conf. authorized unification of this enterprise and transfer of its direction to the NLC. See also *Students, Spiritual Care of,* B 4.

5. A Commission on Luth. Unity studied intersyn. relations and sought both to strengthen internal ties and to facilitate closer relationships with other Luth. bodies. An effort in this direction was the *Overture for Lutheran Unity,** pub. in Jan. 1944.

6. The Conf. sponsored biennial, all-Luth. seminars which brought together pastors of Luth. bodies generally in selected key cities.

7. Current soc. problems were studied and pertinent statements formulated by the Commission on Soc. Relations.

8. The Commission on Christian Higher Educ., Elementary or Parish Educ., and Youth Work enabled constituent bodies to share research and promotion and to coordinate activities.

9. The Commission on Common Liturgy made efforts to achieve uniformity of forms of public worship and a common hymnal.

10. Last official pub. of the Conf. was *Lutheran Outlook.*

11. Total bap. membership of the Am. Luth. Conf.: 2,465,839 (1954). Pres.: Otto Mees, 1930–34; Thaddeus F. Gullixson, 1934–38; Ernest E. Ryden, 1938–42; Harold L. Yochum, 1942–46; Laurence M. Stavig, 1946–50; Oscar A. Benson, 1950–52; Sigfrid E. Engstrom, 1952–54. The Conf. dissolved 1954. HLY

Journal of the American Lutheran Conference; Journal of Theology of the American Lutheran Conference; Lutheran Outlook; The Lutheran World Almanac and Encyclopedia 1934–1937, ed. R. H. Long et al. (New York, 1937); *The Lutheran Churches of the World* 1952, ed. A. R. Wentz (Geneva, 1952). See also bibliographies under articles on churches comprising the Am. Luth. Conf.

American Lutheran Education Association. See *Teachers,* 28.

American Lutheran Publicity Bureau (2112 Broadway, New York, N. Y.). Recognizing the need for presenting the Luth. Ch. in its true light to people outside the ch. itself, a group of laymen and pastors of the Mo. Syn. organized the ALPB on Jan. 21, 1914, in the S. S. auditorium of Immanuel Luth. Ch., 88th and Lexington Ave., New York, N. Y.

The bureau promoted publicity for Luth. churches when publicity was actually frowned on; when our fathers assoc. it with screaming sermon topics pub. by sectarian ministers in daily papers and with much that was vulgar and in bad taste in the religious field. At that time the bureau showed ch. people how to carry on publicity in an effective, dignified manner. Some of the earliest mediums of communication suggested were posters, road markers, special services, lectures, placement of books in pub. libraries, distribution of Gospel tracts, pub. important ch. events in the local papers.

The bureau's first Gospel tracts appeared in 1914; in 1915 a resolution was adopted to sponsor a Nat. Luth. Publicity Week; early in 1916 a clipsheet was issued and mailed to newspapers and press agencies; the 1st issue of the *American Lutheran* appeared in Jan. 1918.

J. F. E. Nickelsburg, engaged part time soon after the organizational meeting in 1914, became full-time worker in 1916. Some founders and earliest officers: H. P. Eckhardt,* pres.; F. C. Lang, treas.; Paul Lindemann, ex. secy. An office was opened Oct. 1, 1917, on E 62d St., New York. Two Luth. radio broadcasts were presented in July 1922 on the Westinghouse station, Newark, N. J.

In offering churches plans for house-to-house canvassing and for distributing tracts and other invitations, the bureau became important contributory factor in larger outreach of church's miss. work. The bureau was among first to recognize value of radio as means of proclaiming the Gospel. When many pastors were apprehensive of the effect of this new invention on ch. attendance, the bureau urged pastors to ask for radio time for services and sermons, for devotions and other means of "teaching all nations."

After more than 50 yrs. of service the ALPB continues a widespread program that may well be characterized by the slogan "A Changeless Christ for a Changing World." A number of practical programs for local churches are offered each yr. The pre-Lent and Lenten "Sharing Christ" plan has served thousands of Luth. congs. in efforts to carry on vigorous and effective evangelism. Nat. S. S. Week, introduced in 1940s, strengthens the outreach of the S. S. The Nov. Spiritual Life Crusade, introduced in 1956, offers materials and plans for educ. ch. members in stewardship. The Year-Round Ch. Attendance Plan (begun in 1960) offers a simple program designed to increase awareness of meaning of regular participation in worship. The Easter to Pentecost Ch. Attendance Crusade adopts a similar purpose but deals in depth with the significance of the post-Easter season. The Reformation Month program seeks to aid the understanding of what it means to be Luth. Distribution of tracts (begun in 1914) is still a primary service. *Lutheran Forum,* successor of the *American Lutheran,* provides an open forum for discussion of all phases of ch. life both practical and theoretical.

The ALPB receives considerable support from sale of materials used in connection with its various programs as well as from congs., societies, and individuals. TW

See also *Lamprecht, Theodore Henry; Lutheran Press.*

"American Lutheranism." Movement about the middle of the 19th c. which aimed at accommodating Lutheranism to its Am. environment. A reaction to the surge of Luth. confessionalism in Ger. and Am., it was an attempt to provide for greater fusion of Am. Lutheranism with the Puritanic and Methodistic ethos of Am. Resulted in part from revivalistic and reform movements of first half of 19th c.

Beginnings can be traced to 1844, when the Md. Syn.* resolved to prepare "Abstract of Doctrines and Practices of the Evangelical Lutheran Synod of Maryland." Benjamin Kurtz* was very influential in the preparation of the document; yet it was not accepted by the Md. Syn. Then a resolution of the Gen. Syn.* instructed a com. to formulate a "clear and concise view of the doctrines and practices of the American Lutheran Church." Samuel S. Schmucker* was chm. of the com.; the report was rejected by the Gen. Syn. In 1853 the Pa. Ministerium* was readmitted to the Gen. Syn., adding another confessional voice to this body. In 1855 the *Definite Synodical Platform** appeared.

Besides Kurtz and Schmucker, Samuel Sprecher* was a chief advocate of this movement. Largely through his influence 3 small Luth. synods adopted the *Definite Platform.* Kurtz was instrumental in organizing the Melanchthon Syn.* (1857), which dissolved in 1868. With few followers the move toward compromise, unionism, accommodation was defeated.

See also *Lutheran Church – Missouri Synod, The, V* 13; *United States, Lutheran (Confessional) Theology in.*

S. S. Schmucker, *Elements of Popular Theology* (Philadelphia, 1845); S. Sprecher, *A System of Ev. Luth. Theology* (Philadelphia, 1879); V. Ferm, *The Crisis in American Lutheran Theology* (New York, 1927); C. Mauelshagen, *American Lutheranism Surrenders to Forces of Conservatism* (Athens, Ga., 1936). CSM

American Moravian Youth Fellowship. See *Young People's Organizations, Christian,* III 15.

American Old Catholic Church. See *Old Catholics,* 4.

American Rescue Workers. This branch of the Salv. Army orig. Salvation* 1882, when Thomas E. Moore, who had come to Am. to superintend the work here, withdrew because of differences with Gen. Booth in regard to financial administration and began indep. work. Movement was incorporated in 1884, and in 1885 an amended charter was granted under the name "Salvation Army of America." Subsequent changes in the Salv. Army in the US resulted in return of a considerable number of officers to that organization, but about 25 posts refused to return and reorganized under the name "American Salvation Army." In 1913 the name was changed to "American Rescue Workers." In general doctrine and polity is very similar to the older body except that it is a ch. with the sacraments of Baptism and the Lord's Supper, rather than an evangelistic or philanthropic organization. However, the organization does gen. philanthropic work.

American Rite. See *Freemasonry,* 3.

American Society for Church Architecture. See *Art, Ecclesiastical and Religious,* 8; *Church Architecture,* 15.

American Sunday School Union. "The First Day or Sunday School Society," organized in Philadelphia, Jan. 11, 1791, by mem. of various denominations includ. Soc. of Friends, was 1st Am. gen. S. S. organization. Teachers were paid. N. Y. S. S. Union was organized 1816; Philadelphia Sun. and Adult School Union 1817. The latter in 1824 merged in Am. S. S. Union, which publishes S. S. literature, founds S. S., and distributes Bibles and tracts. See also *Sunday School.*

American Theological Society. See *Theological Society, American.*

American Theological Society – Midwest Division. See *Theological Society, American – Midwest Division.*

American Tract Society. See *Religious Tract Movement.*

American Unitarian Association. See *Unitarians.*

Americanism. Term used by Leo XIII (1899, *Testem benevolentiae*) in a pronouncement addressed to Cardinal Gibbons, condemning a tendency supposedly exalting natural virtues above passive obedience. The letter was indirectly aimed at the attempt to introduce into Eur. the Am. ideals regarding relationship of ch. and state.

Ames, Edward Scribner (1870–1958). B. Eau Claire, Wis.; educ. Drake U. (Des Moines, Iowa), Yale Divinity School (New Haven, Conn.), U. Chicago; prof. philos. and pedagogy Butler Coll., Indianapolis, Ind., 1897–1900; taught philos, till retirement U. Chicago 1900–35; pastor U. Ch. of Disciples of Christ, Chicago, 1900–40. Works include *Psychology of Religious Experience; Divinity of Christ; The Higher Individualism; The New Orthodoxy; Religion; Letters to God and the Devil.*

Ames, William (Wilhelm Amesius; 1576–1633). Calvinist moral theologian and controversialist. Educ. Cambridge; student of W. Perkins; strict Puritan; went to Holland; prominent in Remonstrant controversies; influential at Syn. of Dort; prof. Franeker. Works include *Medulla theologiae; Bellarminus enervatus; De conscientia, eius iure et casibus.*

Amesha Spentas. Class of beings in Zoroastrianism corresponding roughly to archangels.

Amesius, Wilhelm. See *Ames, William.*

Amiatinus, Codex. Lat. MS of the Vulgate written in Eng. ca. 700; used in preparation of Sistine ed.

Amice. See *Vestments, Clerical.*

Amiens, Cathedral of. See *Church Architecture,* 10.

Ämilie. See *Aemilie.*

Amish, The. See *Ammann, Jacob; Mennonite Bodies,* 3.

Amling, Wolfgang (1542–1606). Prot. theologian of Ger., known for opposition to the FC and for winning large portion of Anhalt to the Ref. Ch. Wrote *Confession of Anhalt.* See also *Reformed Confessions,* D 3 d.

Ammann, Jacob (ca. 1644–ca. 1730). Swiss Mennonite bp.; espoused strict practice of excommunication. Caused schism in Mennonite* Ch. in Swit. and Alsace (1693–97) by attempts to introduce

1632 Dordrecht* (Dort) Confession of Faith; followers called Amish.

Ammerbach, Elias Nikolaus (ca. 1530–97). Organist of St. Thomas Ch., Leipzig. Wrote *Orgel oder Instrument Tabulatur* and *Ein neu künstlich Tabulaturbuch.*

Ammon, Christoph Friedrich von (1766–1850). Court preacher and vice-pres. of consistory at Dresden; considered most skillful defender of popular rationalism.

Ammonius Saccas (d. ca. 242). Alexandrian; teacher of Plotinus; sought to synthesize Pythagoreanism and Platonism; reputed founder of Neoplatonism.*

Ammundsen, Valdemar (1875–1936). Dan. prof. and bp.; emphasized close connection bet. theology and Christian life; pres. World Alliance for International Friendship through the Churches.* Wrote on Lutheran Reformation, Kierkegaard, soc. Christianity, and (during WW I) war and the Christian.

Amnesty of Nimes. See *France,* 10.

Amora. Title of a teacher of the Mishnah, 250–500.

Amorality. Ethically neutral state or action.

Amphilochius (ca. 340–ca. 395). Bp. of Iconium; friend of Cappadocian Theologians.* Opponent of Euchites.*

MPG 39, 9–130.

Ampulla (Lat. diminutive from Gk. for "jar with 2 handles"). Vessel, usually vase or bottle shaped, anciently used for oil and perfumes. Since 4th c. the term denotes vessels in which consecrated oils are kept.

Amsdorf, Nikolaus von (Dec. 3, 1483–May 14, 1565). B. Torgau (?); d. Eisenach; mem. of noble Saxon family. Studied theol. at newly founded U. of Wittenberg 1502; earned master's degree 1504; lectured on theol. and philos. Befriended Luther; led by him to study Augustine.* Accompanied Luther* to Leipzig* 1519 and Worms* 1521. Called the Magdeburg 1524; reformed the city with Cruciger. Carried the Gospel to Goslar, Einbeck, Meissen, many other cities. Extensive correspondence with Luther (first mention of "A Mighty Fortress" 1527). John Frederick appointed him bp. of Naumburg-Zeitz (1542) because he was "gifted, scholarly, of noble birth, and without a wife." After Luther's death he was expelled from Naumburg (1547), joined other faithful Lutherans (Flacius, etc.) at Magdeburg in opposition to the Interim* and to Melanchthon's* compromising attitude. From 1552 on he lived in Eisenach, without defined office, yet as acknowledged "Secret Bishop of the Lutheran Church." Helped found U. of Jena. Involved in the Adiaphoristic,* Majoristic* Controversies (in the latter overshot the mark by asserting: "Good works are harmful to salvation"), was always concerned to remain faithful to the doctrine of Luther. Opposed Pfeffinger* and (with Melanchthon) Andreas Osiander.* See also *Synergistic Controversy.*

O. Lerche, *Amsdorf und Melanchthon* (Berlin, 1937); O. Nebe, *Reine Lehre: Zur Theologie des Niklas von Amsdorff* (Göttingen, 1935); W. Tillmanns, *The World and Men Around Luther* (Minneapolis, 1959), pp. 86–90 T. Pressel, *Nicolaus von Amsdorf,* in *Leben und Ausgewählte Schriften der Väter und Begründer der Lutherischen Kirche,* ed. J. Hartmann et al., VIII (Elberfeld, 1862), separate paging 1–164. WGT

Amsterdam Assembly. The meeting (Aug. 22–Sept. 4, 1948) which constituted the World Council of Churches.*

Amulets. Objects, or charms, believed to have magic powers to bring their wearer good fortune or protect him from harm. Their use has been almost universal among pagans at all times. The semipagan influence of the 4th c. brought them into the ch., where they were denounced as idols. But they survived under Christian coloring. Relics enclosed in costly cases, called phylacteries, were worn as potent protectors; holy water, blessed salt, and consecrated wafers were carried on the person. Contact with the E during the Crusades multiplied the talismans and charms.

Amusements. See *Recreation.*

Amyraldists. See *Amyraut, Moïse; Cameron, John.*

Amyraut, Moïse (Moses Amyraldus; 1596—1664). Pastor, later prof. Saumur, Fr.; notable Bible commentator and preacher; authored book on Christian ethics. In doctrine of predestination tried to harmonize universalism with particularism. Adopted doctrine of grace and free will of John Cameron.* Had many followers in colonial New England.

Anabaptist Creeds. See *Democratic Declarations of Faith,* 1.

Anabaptists (from Gk. for "rebaptize"). Term of reproach applied to radical reformers who did not recognize infant baptism; to them the term is false. It is hard, if not impossible, to determine their origin. 16th-c centers include Zurich, Switz.; Zwickau and Wittenberg, Saxony; Moravia; NW Ger. and the Low Countries; Münster, Westphalia; Rhineland and SW Ger. See also *Baptist Churches,* 2; *Denk, Johannes; Hetzer, Ludwig; Hofmann, Melchior; Hubmaier, Balthasar; Huter, Jakob; John of Leiden; Joris, David; Knipperdolling, Bernt; Luther, Controversies of,* d; *Manz, Felix; Menno Simons; Mennonite Churches,* 1; *Münster Kingdom; Münzer, Thomas; Sattler, Michael; Zwickau Prophets.*

Anacletus. After Linus, the 2d successor of Peter as bp. of Rome according to Cath. tradition.

Anagogic Interpretation. See *Exegesis,* 5.

Anahita. Ancient Persian goddess of fertility.

Analogia entis. Analogy of being; term used in philos. and theol. to show relationship between God and creature. Both have existence and essence. In God these are identical, but in creatures they are tension-in-synthesis (Augustine* of Hippo) or a view toward God which is essentially a view from God (Thomas* Aquinas). The *analogia entis* is rejected by some theologians (K. Barth*).

Analogy. The analogy of Scripture is that quality of Holy Writ according to which all its statements are in harmonious relation to one another, so that they mutually clarify and expound the doctrines concerned.

Analogy of Faith. Term drawn from Ro 12:6: ["Let us prophesy] according to the proportion [Gk. *analogia*] of faith." J. Gerhard,* Locus I, chap. xxv *(De interpretatione scripturae sacrae),* par. 531 (532): "All interpretation of Scripture should be analogus to [the] faith [*fidei analoga*]. This canon is set forth Ro 12:6; this [passage] means that the interpretation of Scripture should be undertaken and properly done [*conformari*] in such a way that it harmonizes [*consentiat*] with the whole [*perpetua*] thought set forth in Scripture concerning each article of the heavenly doctrine. . . . The articles of faith which the apostle here [cf. 2 Ti 3:15] means by ["faith"], which all must know in order to be saved, are taught in Scripture in clear and plain [*perspicuis*] words. . . . In interpreting Scripture, nothing whatever is to be propounded [*proferendum*] in conflict with this rule* of faith." This allows for aparent contradictions, e. g., with regard to predestination (see *Predestination,* I).

The view that restricts the analogl of faith to that which man finds harmonious and noncontradictory led to a broader use of Scripture and failure of free* Luth. confs. in Am. early in the 20th c.

See also *Exegesis,* 7; *Hermeneutics.*

Anamnesis (Gk. "memorial"). Used in accounts of institution of Lord's Supper (Lk 22:19; 1 Co 11: 24, 25); the part of many liturgies which commemorates the Passion, resurrection, and ascension; follows the Words of Institution.

Anan ben David (8th c. AD). Founder of Karaites.*

unsuccessfully tried to become exilarch. Wrote *Sepher ha-mitzvot* ("Book of Precepts").

Anaphora (Gk. "offering"). Central prayer in traditional Eucharistic liturgies. Begins with Salutation and Sursum corda and includes Sanctus, Consecration (Words of Institution), commemoration of Christ's Passion, resurrection, and ascension (Anamnesis), intercessions, and Lord's Prayer. Oldest surviving anaphoras are those of Hippolytus' *Apostolic Tradition* and of St. Serapion, bishop of Thmuis. Reduction of the anaphora in Luth. rites of 16th c. to at most the Sursum corda, Sanctus, Words of Institution, and Lord's Prayer is now widely felt to have been too radical, and a number of Luth. rites have restored a more inclusive anaphora for at least optional use.

Anarchism (Gk. "without rule"). Theory which regards govt. as source of soc. evils; would substitute spontaneous cooperation for political rule.

Anastasis (Gk. "resurrection"). Some early churches at Jerusalem and Constantinople were dedicated to the Anastasis of Christ.

Anat. See *Canaanites, Religion of.*

Anathema. Word used in NT and terminology of the church (like OT "accursed") as solemn curse, pronounced in God's name on heretics and ungodly (Gl 1:8, 9; 1 Co 16:22). Gen. designates eternal separation from God (Ro 9:3); also used as formula for sinful cursing, 1 Co 12:3; Acts 23:14. See also *Blessing and Cursing.*

Anatolia. Part of Turkey equivalent to peninsula of Asia Minor. See also *Middle East,* B.

Anatolius (d. ca. 282). Alexandrian; bp. of Laodicea; opponent of Paul of Samosata; wrote on date of Easter.

Eusebius, *HE,* VII, xxxii, 6—12; *MPG,* 10, 209 to 232.

Anaxagoras (ca. 500—ca. 428 BC). Author of *Peri phuseos;* brought philos. from Ionia to Athens; influenced Periclean age. Held that mind was an abstract being which arranged all. Explained and investigated many natural phenomena. See also *Philosophy.*

Anaximander (ca. 611—ca. 547). Gk. astronomer, geographer, philos. Held that first principle is eternal, indestructible, boundless matter. See also *Philosophy.*

Anaximenes of Miletus (6th c. BC). Gk. philos., held air is primary substance. See also *Philosophy.*

Ancestor Worship (Manism). Directed to deceased parents or forefathers. Cult is one of most ancient, is encountered in all parts of globe. Still survives where Christianity, Judaism, and Muhammadanism have not exerted their influence. Cult is based on universal belief in existence of an immaterial part of man which leaves the body at death. The deceased is also believed to have the same kindly interest in the affairs of the living as when alive and to interfere in the course of events for the welfare of the family or clan; or he may bring diseases, storms, or other misfortunes on them if his worship is neglected.

In ancient Rome, ancestor worship was a family religion. Masks or images, embodying the *manes,* i. e., the spirits of the deceased, who had become gods of the lower world, were set up in homes, altars erected, sacrifices made, and prayers offered to them in the same manner as to the *penates,* the protecting spirits of the household. The Hindus bring sacrifices to the *pitris (patres),* the divine spirits of deceased ancestors, and implore them for assistance.

In China, ancestor worship is universal. Tablets of wood bearing deceased's name and dates of birth and death are found in most homes; incense and spirit money are burned before them. From China, ancestor worship passed to Japan, where it also became firmly established.

Besides actual worship of spirits of the deceased, there has been among many races the custom of supplying the dead with things they enjoyed while alive. Among some savage races the dead man's wife, servants, and favorite animals were killed or buried alive with their former master.

Assoc. with ancestor worship is belief in possibility of communicating with spirits of the dead and obtaining their counsel and assistance in times of danger and misfortune through the agency of medicine men, wizards, or seers. There is also a widely prevalent belief that ancestors are reincarnated in newborn children.

See also *Religion, Comparative, Bibliography; Spencer, Herbert; Spiritism; Transmigration.*

Anchieta, Jose de (1533—97). "Apostle of Brazil." Port. Jesuit miss.

Anchor. Early symbol of sea voyage, then symbol of deliverance from sea disaster. In Heb 6:19 and early fathers it is symbol of Christian hope.

Anchorites. See *Hermits.*

Ancient Arabic Orders of Nobles of the Mystic Shrine. See *Freemasonry,* 9.

Ancient Free and Accepted Masons. See *Freemasonry.*

Ancient of Days. Title of Jahweh (Dan 7:9, 13, 22).

Anderson, Anton Marius (Mar. 8, 1847–1941). B. Hopballe, Jellinge, Jutland (Jylland), Den.; to US 1872; studied at Augsburg Sem. (see *Luther Theological Seminary,* 4); ordained by Norw.-Dan. Conf. 1874; pastor Nebr., Wis., and S. Dak.; resigned from Norw.-Dan. Conf. 1884; helped found Dan. Ev. Luth. Ch. Assoc. in Am. 1884 (gen. called Blair Ch.; see also *Danish Lutherans in America,* 5); founded Trin. Sem., Blair, Nebr., 1884 (prof. 1884–89, 1895–97). Ed. *Dask Luthersk Kirkeblad* 1877–84, *Danskeren* 1903–ca. 1920/21.

Andersen, Paul (1821—92). B. Norw.; to Am. 1843; educ. Beloit Coll., Wis.; ordained in Franckean Syn. 1848; 1st Scand. Luth. minister in Am. to hold regular Eng. services and establish a S. S.; organized 1st Norw. Luth. Ch. in Chicago; pres. N. Ill. Syn. 1857; prominent in organizing Scand. Aug. Syn. 1860; also in organizing Norw. Aug. Syn. 1870; pastor Milwaukee 1876—83.

Andersen, Rasmus (July 23, 1848–Aug. 18, 1930). Luth. cleric; b. Vedelshave, near Middelfart, on Fyn (Fyen; Fünen) Is., Den.; attended Ryslinge Mission School, near Ringe, on Fyn; sent to US 1871 as miss. among Danes by the Society* for the Propagation of the Gospel Among the Danes in N. Am.; educ. Augsburg Sem., Marshall, Wis. (moved to Minneapolis, Minn., 1872). Helped organize *Kirkelig Missionsforening* 1872 (see *Danish Lutherans in America,* 3). Pastor Waupaca, Wis., 1872–78; Perth Amboy, N. J., from June 1878 (also immigrant missionary Castle Garden (at the Battery) and later on Ellis Is., N. Y.; moved to Brooklyn, N. Y., Sept. 1878 and began serving also the Dan. Seamen's Miss.; also served a cong. at Lansingburgh, N. Y. Works include writings on Dan. ch. hist. See also *Immigrant and Emigrant Missions.*

Anderson, Charles Palmerston (1864–1930). Prot. Episc. bp. Chicago; active in ecumenical movement.

Anderson, Lars (Laurentius Andreae; 1480—1552). Swed. archdeacon won by Olaus Petri* for Reformation; ch. diplomat and politician, chancellor to Gustavus Vasa* (1523), arranging the 1st ref. polity of the Swed. ch.; with Petri condemned to death for resistance to presb. system (1540) but reprieved. Regarded as collaborator of Petri on 1526 Swed. NT.

Andhra, South. See *India,* 13.

Andhra Evangelical Lutheran Church. See *United Lutheran Church in America,* III.

Andover Controversy. Controversy in Cong. Ch. which spread in last 2 decades of 19th c. when the ABCFM refused to sanction missionaries who held the opinion of some Andover (Mass.) Theol. Sem.

profs. that heathen who died without hearing the Gospel would have 2d chance.

Andreä, Jakob (1528—90). Educ. Tübingen; at 18 preacher at Stuttgart; chancellor of Tübingen; active reformer in all S Ger.; confessed faith before King Anthony of Navarre at Paris and communicated it to Patriarch Jeremias* II of Constantinople; failed to unite Flacians and Philippists at Zerbst 1570; preached and pub. 6 sermons on disputed points; repeatedly revised the basis of the FC; the ch. owes the FC chiefly to Andreä and Chemnitz. See also *Lutheran Confessions*, C 2; *Montbiliard, Colloquy of*.

Johann V. Andreä, *Fama Andreana reflorescens* (Strasbourg, 1630).

Andreä, Johann Valentin (1586—1654). Grandson of Jakob A.; educ. Tübingen; insisted on pure morals as well as pure doctrine; called to Calw 1620; to Stuttgart as court preacher 1639; labored to educ. ministers and to introduce ch. discipline.

Andreae, Laurentius. See *Anderson, Lars*.

Andreen, Gustav Albert (March 13, 1864—Oct. 1, 1940). B. Porter, Ind.; educ. chiefly Aug. Coll., Rock Island, Ill., and Yale; instructor Aug. Coll. 1882—84; prof. of languages Bethany Coll., Lindsborg, Kans., 1884—94; prof. Yale 1894—1901; pres. Aug. Coll. 1901—35; ordained 1905. Wrote *Det Svenska Spraaket i Amerika; Studies in the German Idyl; History of the Educational Work of the Augustana Synod; The Early Missionary Work of the Augustana Synod in New York City; L. P. Esbjörn and the Pilgrim Fathers of 1849; History of Augustana College at Its 75th Anniversary*.

Andrew, Saint. See *Church Year*, 16.

Andrew of Crete (ca. 660—ca. 732). Native of Damascus; abp. Gortyna, Crete; involved with Monothelitism;* hymnist.

MPG, 97, 805—1444.

Andrewes, Lancelot (1555—1626). Angl. theol.; famous preacher; educ. Cambridge; dean of Westminster 1601; bp. Chichester 1605, Ely 1609, Winchester 1619; one of tr. of KJV; involved in controversy on Oath of Allegiance. Held that consecration changed elements in Lord's Supper without describing change; emphasized sacrificial concept; opposed to Calvinism. See also *High Church*.

Andrews, Lorrin (Apr. 29, 1795—Sept. 29, 1868). B. Windsor, Conn.; grad. Princeton Sem. 1825; sent by ABCFM as miss. to Hawaiian Is. 1828; stationed at Lahaina; established Lahainaluna Sem. 1831; severed connection with ABCFM 1842; served as judge and secy. of Privy Council. Wrote Hawaiian dictionary and grammar; tr. part of Bible into Hawaiian; did research into native folklore.

Anerio, Felice (1560—1614). Successor of Palestrina as composer of papal chapel; also maestro at Coll. in Rome; helped ed. *Editio Medicea* (1614) of Gregorian chant, which exerted great influence but fell into disrepute in 19th c. because of its untrustworthiness.

Angel of the Lord: The expression "the angel of the Lord" or "the angel of God" occurs more than 40 times in OT. "The angel of the Lord" appeared, for example, to Hagar in wilderness, Gn 16:7-14; later again, Gn 21:17; in company with two created angels visits Abraham in Mamre, Gn 18; appears to Abraham as he is about to sacrifice Isaac, Gn 22:11; to Jacob at Bethel, Gn 31:11-13; cf. 28:10-15; Jacob wrestles with Him at Peniel, Gn 32:24 (cf. Hos 12: 3-5); Jacob asks Him to bless the sons of Joseph, Gn 48:16; appears to Moses in burning bush, Ex 3; goes before camp of Israel, Ex 14:19; God warns Israel not to provoke Him, Ex 23:20-25; is again promised to Israel after they committed idolatry with golden calf, Ex 32:34; 33:1-12; leads them to Kadesh, Nm 20:16; appears to Balaam, Nm 22:22-35; appears to Joshua as Captain of the Lord's host, Jos 5:13 to 6:2; comes to Bochim, Ju 2:1-4; tells Israel to curse Meroz, Ju 5:23; appears to Gideon, Ju 6:11; to Manoah and his wife, Ju 13:2-5; name is used in proverbial expression, 1 Sm 29:9; 2 Sm 14:17, 20; 19:27; when David had numbered Israel, "the angel of the Lord" stretched hand over Jerusalem to destroy it, 2 Sm 24:16, 17; 1 Ch 21:15-30; appears to Elijah under juniper tree, 1 K 19:5-7; sends Elijah to Ahaziah, 2 K 1:1-3; smites 185,000 Assyrians, 2 K 19:35; 2 Ch 32:21; Is 37:36; David mentions Him, Ps 34:7; 35:5, 6; Isaiah calls Him angel of God's presence, Is 63:9; appears to Zechariah, who mentions His name, Zech. 1:8-21; 3; 12:8; and Malachi calls Him the Messenger, or Angel, of the covenant, Ml 3:1.

Commentators are divided in opinions regarding identity of "the angel of the Lord" in OT. Formula of earlier dogmaticians is still adhered to by some: Whenever the name of Jehovah or divine works and worship are ascribed to the Angel in Scripture, then this Angel must be understood as the Son of God. Accordingly, this angel is often referred to in dogmatic literature as the *Logos* or the *Angelus increatus*, and His appearances are regarded as appearances of the preincarnate Son of God.

Others hold that "the angel of the Lord" is not necessarily to be interpreted as reference to the preincarnate Christ but that manifestations of this "angel of the Lord" are none the less theophanies, or manifestations of God. Luther refrains from offering a specific identification of this angel.

Examination of passages cited above reveals that "the angel of the Lord" speaks at times as if He Himself were the Lord, at times as one who speaks in behalf of the Lord, in some instances appears in both roles interchangeably. OT Scriptures themselves offer no basis for definitive explication of precise nature of relationship between "the angel of the Lord" and the Lord Himself. Such NT occurrences of "the angel of the Lord" as Mt 1:24 and Lk 2:9 suggest that the NT writers did not relate this title to Jesus Christ. WW

Angela de Foligno (1248—1309). It. mystic; after worldly life, was converted ca. 1285; entered Third Order of St. Francis 1291; called *magistra theologorum*. Memoirs: *Liber sororis Lelle de Fulgineo*, or *Liber de vera fidelium experientia*.

Angela Merici. See *Ursulines*.

Angelic Hymn. The Gloria in excelsis ("Glory to God in the highest," Lk 2:14).

Angelico, Fra (Giovanni da Fiesole, originally Guido de Pietro; ca. 1400—55). It.; regarded one of greatest 15th-c. religious painters; b. Vicchio (Tuscany); joined Dominican order ca. 1418–20; priest ca. 1423—25; elected prior St. Domenico, Florence, 1449. His art depicts piety and contemplative spirit; paintings include frescoes at San Marco, Florence, and in Chapel of Pope Nicholas V, Rome.

Angelicus, Doctor. See *Aquinas, Thomas*.

Angelolatry. See *Angels, Veneration of*.

Angels, Evil. See *Devil*.

Angels, Good. 1. In both Heb. and Gk. the word for "angel" means "messenger." Both OT and NT use it to designate human messengers, e. g., Gn 32:3; Lk 7:24. The OT applies it also to prophet and priest (e. g., Is 42:19; 44:26; Ml 2:7) with obvious reference to their function as messengers sent by God. This may also be import of term "the angels of the seven churches" (Rv 1:20), where reference is evidently to the pastors of the 7 churches. In majority of passages, however, term angels designates those spiritual beings who were created in infinite numbers (cf. Dt 33:2; Dn 7:10; Heb 12:22) to serve God in various ways as His messengers. See also *Angel of the Lord*.

2. The OT creation accounts make no explicit reference to origin of angels. On basis of OT Gn 2: 1-3; Ex 20:11; NT Jn 1:3; Cl 1:16, Christian interpreters have concluded that creation of angels was

coterminous with creation of world. One poetic passage (Jb 38:4-7) refers to presence of angels ("the sons of God") when God "laid the foundation of the earth." Title "sons of God" (e. g., Jb 1:6; 2:1; 38:7; Ps 29:1 and 89:6 in Heb.) may also be seen as pointing to the angels' origin from God as well as their close relationship to Him.

3. Scriptures speak of angels as spiritual beings, at same time portray these noncorporeal beings as appearing in human form when, in their capacity as divine messengers, they manifest themselves to human beings. In each recorded instance they appear as men, not as women (e. g., Gn 19:1-22; 32:1; Mt 28:2-4; Acts 5:19). The 2 referred to by proper names similarly have masculine names: Gabriel and Michael (Dn 8:16; Lk 1:19, 26; Dn 10:13; Jude 9; Rv 12:7). Excluding references to cherubim and seraphim (see below), the Biblical statements lend no direct support to the popular view which ascribes wings to angels.

4. Angels, as superhuman beings, are described as possessing more than merely human attributes. In 3 passages speakers are quoted who refer to angels as "blameless" (1 Sm 29:9 RSV), as possessing ability "to discern good and evil" (2 Sm 14:17 RSV), and as having knowledge of "all things that are on the earth" (2 Sm 14:20 RSV). Ps 103:20 speaks of angels as "mighty men of strength" (Heb.). The moral perfection of angels is reflected in designation "holy ones," frequently applied in OT (e. g., RSV in Jb 5:1; Ps 89:5, 7; Dn 4:13; Zch 14:5). NT reinforces OT portrait of angels as creatures of holiness (Lk 9:26) and superhuman strength (2 Ptr 2:11). Attribute of immortality, implicit in OT writings, is explicitly ascribed in Lk 20:36.

5. Ranking of angels has been subject of much speculation. Pseudo-Dionysius (see *Dionysius the Areopagite,* 2) invented 27 ranks in an angelic hierarchy allegedly consisting of 3 major orders, each with 9 subdivisions. Later writers imitated or adapted this speculative ranking of angels, based to some extent on apocryphal and pseudepigraphal documents such as Tobit, Enoch, 2 Esdras, and the Testament of Levi. Biblical evidence, however, is limited to simple distinction between "angel" and "archangel" (occurring only twice: 2 Th 4:16; Jude 9), the latter meaning "chief angel." Dn 12:1 also designates archangel Michael as "the great prince" (cf. Rv 12:7); similarly in Jos 5:14 (RSV) reference is made to an angelic leader designated as "commander of the army of the Lord." It is assumed by some, though challenged by others, that such terms as principalities, powers, authorities, dominions, and thrones (cf. Ro 8:38; Eph 1:21; 3:10; Cl 1:16; 1 Ptr 3:22) are names of various angelic ranks.

6. The titles cherubim and seraphim, on the other hand, appear not to designate angelic ranks but rather special kinds of angelic beings. In OT the Lord is portrayed as enthroned above (or upon) the cherubim (e. g., RSV in 1 Sm 4:4; 2 K 19:15; Ps 80:1; 99:1), or as riding on a cherub or cherubim (e. g., 2 Sm 22:11; Ps 18:10; cf. Eze 1; 10). Cover (mercy seat) of the ark of the covenant, where the Lord promised to be present with His people, was embellished with figures of 2 cherubim with wings stretched out above the ark (cf. Ex 25:10-22). Embroidered representations of cherubim adorned the curtains of the tabernacle which housed the ark as well as the veil which enclosed the Most Holy Place. Figures of cherubim with outspread wings similarly stood in the Most Holy Place in Solomon's temple (1 K 6:23-28), and carved figures of cherubim embellished the temple walls and doors (1 K 6:29-35). Cherubim may thus be regarded as symbols of the presence of God, or as guardians of a sacred place, the latter definition being applicable to the guardian cherubim mentioned in Gn 3:24 and Eze 28:16. Archaeological evidence suggests that cherubim were represented pictorially as winged creatures having a human head and a lion's body. All Biblical occurrences of the term cherubim appear in OT, with the single exception of Heb 9:5.

7. Seraphim are mentioned by name only in Is 6:2-6, where they are described as 6-winged creatures who fly above the Lord's throne as they chant His praises. The winged "living creatures" (RSV) in the description of the heavenly throne room in Rv 4; 5 appear to be NT counterparts of the cherubim and seraphim of the OT.

8. Function of angels as God's messengers may be seen as fourfold: (1) conveying messages from God to men (e. g., Gn 31:11; Mt 2:13, 19, 20; Acts 27:23, 24); (2) foretelling special acts of God (e. g., Gn 16:11; Ju 13:3-5; Lk 1:11-20, 26-37; 2:9-12); (3) serving as agents of divine judgment (e. g., Gn 19:1, 11; 2 Sm 24:15-17; Mt 13:41, 42, 49, 50; Acts 12:23); (4) serving as agents of divine providence (e. g., 1 K 19:5-8; Ps 91:11, 12; Dn 6:22; Acts 5:19; 12:7). While the Scriptures do not specifically answer the question whether each believer, especially each believing child (see Mt 18:10), has one or more specially assigned guardian angels, they clearly assure God's people of the constant guardianship of His angelic messengers (Ps 91:11, 12; Heb 1:14). A further service rendered to God's people is recognized by the Luth. Confessions: "that the angels pray for us" (Ap XXI 8; cf. SA-II III 26). Biblical example of angelic intercession occurs in Zch 1:12. The invoking of angels is forbidden (Rv 22:8, 9; Mt 4:10; cf. SA-II III 26; see also *Angels, Veneration of*). Angels are also portrayed as praising God in holy worship (Ps 29:1, 2; 103:20, 21; Is 6:1-3; Lk 2:13, 14; Rv 7:11, 12).

9. While the Bible speaks of some angels who sinned (see *Devil*), the angels who faithfully served God are referred to in Scripture as "holy angels." Dogmaticians speak of these as angels who "persevered in holiness" and are now "confirmed in holiness." Such passages at Mt 18:10; 25:31; Mk 8:38 supply basis for the view that holy angels will persevere in their holiness for all time.

10. In NT, where Jesus Christ is portrayed as "the Head over all things," including the angels (cf. Eph 1:20-22; 1 Ptr 3:22), the ministry of the holy angels is given Christocentric emphasis. Angels announce Jesus' birth (Lk 1:26-35; 2:9-14), mediate providential guidance for infant Jesus (Mt 2:13, 19, 20), minister to Him as He performs redemptive work (Mt 4:11; Lk 22:43), are instantaneously available for His service (Mt 26:53); are heralds of His resurrection (Mt 28:2-7) and ascension (Acts 1:10, 11). Angels give attention to ministers of Christ's newly established church (Acts 5:19, 20; 8:26; 12:7-10; 27:23, 24) even as they continue to watch over and rejoice in progress of His church on earth (Lk 15:7, 10; 1 Ptr 1:12). Angels praise the ascended Christ before His throne (Rv 7:11, 12), will accompany Him and assist Him at final judgment (Mt 24:31; 25:31; 1 Th 4:16). It is in their relationship to Jesus Christ that all Christians become beneficiaries of Scriptural promises concerning attendant angels, who are "ministering spirits sent forth to serve for the sake of those who are to obtain salvation." (Heb. 1:14 RSV). WW

Angels, Veneration of. Cl 2:18 and Rv 22:8, 9 prohibit the adoration of angels; the primitive ch. down to pope Gregory the Great (590—604) condemned it. In RC and E. Orthodox popular piety the veneration accorded angels has sometimes exceeded tolerable limits. The Luth. Ch. keeps Sept. 29 in honor of St. Michael and All Angels and frequently refers to holy angels in its prayers; on the basis of Zch 1:12 the Luth. Symbols (Ap XXI 8; SA-II II 26) grant that angels pray for us, but hold that it would be idolatrous to invoke or adore them. ACP

Angelus. RC prayer repeated 3 times a day (morning, noon, and night), when the angelus-bell rings 3 strokes followed by a pause 3 times, and then 9 strokes. Consists of versicles, responses, 3 Hail Marys, and a prayer. In paschal time a hymn to Mary *(Regina Coeli)* is substituted.

Angelus increatus. See *Angel of the Lord.*

Angelus Silesius. See *Scheffler, Johannes.*

Angelus Temple. Cen. ch. of the Internat. Ch. of the Foursquare Gospel,* Los Angeles, Calif.

Anger. See *Sins, Venial and Mortal.*

Angilram (d. 791). Chaplain of Charlemagne.*

Anglican and Eastern Churches Association. Founded 1906 to pray for reunion of Angl. and E Orthodox Churches.

Anglican Catechisms. See *Anglican Confessions,* 9.

Anglican Chant. Music of psalms used in Angl. Ch.; derived from plainchant of 17th c. See also *Chant; Gregorian Music.*

Anglican Church. See *England.*

Anglican Confessions. 1. *The Ten Articles,* issued 1536 by Henry VIII ("Articles devised by the King's Highness' Majesty, to establish Christian quietness and unity among us, and to avoid contentious opinions; which Articles be also approved by the consent and determination of the whole clergy of the realm"), enjoin clergy to teach that the things in the Bible and the 3 Creeds are true, condemn all opinions condemned by the 1st 4 holy councils (I); teach that Baptism is necessary for attaining everlasting life, that infants and adults are to be baptized (II); penance consists of contrition, confession, amendment (III); in the Sacrament of the Altar the body and blood is corporally distributed under the "form and figure of bread and wine" (IV); justification is our acceptance into the grace of God attained by contrition and faith joined with charity (V); retain images (VI), honor of and prayers to saints (VII, VIII), traditional rites and ceremonies (IX), prayers for departed souls to relieve them of some of their pain (X).

2. *The Ten Articles* were followed by the *Institution of a Christian Man* (1537, *Bishops' Book*) which contained expositions of Apostles' Creed, Lord's Prayer, Ave Maria, Ten Commandments, 7 sacraments (Baptism, Penance, Lord's Supper given greater dignity than other 4), justification, use of images, royal supremacy, and other points of *The Ten Articles. The Erudition of a Christian Man* (1543; *The King's Book; A Necessary Doctrine and Erudition for any Christian Man; Pia et Catholica Christiani Hominis Institutio*) was a revision of the *Institution* (added material on free will, justification, predestination, transubstantiation, clerical celibacy).

3. *The Six Articles* (1539), which were to be definitive answers to 6 questions, held that "after the consecration there remaineth no substance of bread or wine, nor any other substance, but the substance of Christ," defended Communion under one kind, upheld celibacy, vows of chastity, private masses, and auricular confession.

4. In 1538 Eng. and Ger. scholars drafted *The Thirteen Articles* on basis of AC. Though never pub., they became basis for the Forty-two Articles.

5. Cranmer* continued to work for a Prot. creed, and in 1549 Parliament authorized Edward VI to appoint 32 persons (among the appointees: Cranmer,* Ridley,* Hooper,* Coverdale,* Peter Martyr,* and Justis Hales*) to draw up ecclesiastical laws. These drew up the *Forty-two Articles* (1553; Edwardine Articles), which were issued without formal authorization. Soon after their publication Edward VI died, and Cranmer and Ridley were burned under Mary.

6. After the death of Mary, Elizabeth gave Matthew Parker (1504—75) the task of recasting the *Forty-two Articles.* Using the AC and other Luth. and Ref. formulations, he revised the *Forty-two* into the *Thirty-nine Articles,* which received final revision by the Convocation of 1571. The same year an act was passed requiring subscription to them. The *Articles* give prominence to those tenets which separate Anglicans from Rome (supremacy of the pope; enforced celibacy; denial of the cup to the laity; councils; transubstantiation; sacraments; purgatory; adoration of relics and images; works of supererogation). They often lack clarity because of efforts at compromise between Luth. and Ref. theol. The theol. affinity of article on predestination has been much disputed; on Lord's Supper they are definitely Ref. Separation of American colonies from England made changes necessary in the *Articles.* The General Convention at Trenton (1801) adopted the *Thirty-nine Articles* but omitted the Athanasian Creed, "of the authority of general councils" (XXI), and made other changes necessitated by changed political conditions. See also *Presbyterian Confessions,* 4.

7. *Lambeth Articles.* After adoption of the *Thirty-nine Articles,* Calvinism gained strength in England. The *Lambeth Articles* (Nov. 20, 1595) are strong enunciation of Calvin's predestinarian system but never attained to symbolical authority. See also *Whitgift, John.*

8. *Irish Articles.* Drawn up chiefly by James Ussher and approved at the Convocation of Dublin (1615), these 104 articles revised the *Thirty-nine Articles* in a strongly Calvinistic direction (absolute predestination and perseverance, pope is Antichrist, Puritan view of Sabbath, no mention of episc. ordination) and became a basis for the Westminster Confession.

9. *Other Confessions.* The Anglican Catechisms must also be considered. Henry VII published a *Primer* based on 15th-c. *Prymer* (Lord's Prayer, Creed, Ten Commandments) with some additions. Cranmer's cat. was drawn from Luth. sources (1548). In the Prayer Books of Edward VI a cat. for children was included which underwent frequent alterations and is still used. See also *Book of Common Prayer; England; Presbyterian Confessions,* 3, 4; *Reformed Episcopal Church.* EL

P. Schaff, *Creeds of Christendom,* 3 vols. (New York, 1899); H. E. Jacobs, *The Lutheran Movement in England during the Reigns of Henry VIII and Edward VI* (Philadelphia, 1891); E. J. Bicknell, *A Theological Introduction to the Thirty-Nine Articles of the Church of England,* ed. H. J. Carpenter, 3d ed. (London, 1950); C. S. Meyer, *Elizabeth I and the Religious Settlement of 1559* (St. Louis, 1960); E. G. Rupp, *Studies in the Making of English Protestant Tradition* (Cambridge, 1947); *Creeds of the Churches,* ed. J. H. Leith (New York, 1963); J. H. Blunt, *The Reformation of the Church of England,* 2 vols. (London, 1870—72); P. Hughes, *The Reformation in England,* 3 vols. (New York, 1950—54).

Anglican Evangelical Group Movement. Organized 1906 by Anglicans who opposed unduly conservative theology and welcomed results of science and criticism. See also *Liberal Evangelicalism.*

Anglican Evangelicals. See *Evangelicals, Anglican.*

Anglican Scandinavian Conference. Held in Oslo, Norway, March 29—31, 1951, by representatives of Ch. of England and of Luth. churches in Denmark, Iceland, Norway. Purpose was to establish altar fellowship.

Church in Fellowship, ed. V. Vajta (Minneapolis, 1963), pp. 218—221.

Anglican Young People's Association. See *Young People's Organizations,* III 17.

Anglo-Catholics. Term applied to Tractarians,* to those emphasizing ritual, and to High Churchmen in gen. See also *Oxford Movement.*

Anglo-Israelism. Theory that Anglo-Saxon peoples are descendants of 10 lost tribes of Israel; first advanced by John Sadler, 1649; later developed by Richard Brothers (1757—1824); not in agreement with historical facts as known. See also *Ten Lost Tribes.*

Anglo-Saxons, Conversion of. See *England, Early Christianity in.*

Angola. See *Africa,* B 1.

Angra Mainyu. See *Zoroastrianism,* 3.

Angst (Anxiety). See *Existentialism,* 2 c.

Angiulla. See *Caribbean Islands,* E 5.

Anicetus (fl. 2d c. AD). B. Syria; pope ca. 154/157–166/168. Polycarp* came to Rome to discuss with him the date of Easter; no solution to the Easter* controversy was found, but Anicetus allowed Polycarp to continue the E tradition.

Animatism. See *Primitive Religion.*

Animism. See *Primitive Religion.*

Anker, Kristian (Oct. 29, 1848–Nov. 16, 1928). B. Odense, Den.; to US 1881; ordained 1881. Pastor Chicago, Ill.; Elk Horn Iowa; Blair and Lincoln, Nebr. Broke with Dan. Luth. Ch. 1894; helped organize The Dan. Ev. Luth. Ch. in N. Am. Pres. Dana Coll. and Trin. Sem. 1899–1905 (listed as Blair Coll. and Theol. Sem. 1899; referred to as Blair Coll. and Trin. Sem. 1900–01; designated as Trin. Sem. and Blair Coll. 1901–03; officially named Dana Coll. and Trin. Sem. 1903). See also *Danish Lutherans in America,* 3, 5; *Ministry, Education of,* VIII B 11; X P.

Anna Comnena (1083–ca. 1149). Daughter of Byzantine emp. Alexius I Comnenus; failed to secure empire for her husband, Nicephorus Briennius; her *Alexiad,* a hist. of her father's reign, is an important source for Byzantine hist. at time of 1st Crusade.

Annates. In RCm, 1st year's income from an ecclesiastical office which holder pays to papal curia. Practice began in 13th c. See also *Queen Anne's Bounty.*

Anne. See *Joachim.*

Annet, Peter (1693–ca. 1769). Eng. deist; schoolmaster; attacked credibility of the resurrection of Christ, miracles, and supernaturalism, and tried to discredit the work of Paul. Works include *The Resurrection of Jesus Considered.*

Annihilationism. Belief that the unrighteous pass out of existence after death. Some adherents hold that such annihilation is result of gradual disintegration occasioned by sin. Others hold that the wicked will suffer after death in expiation of their sins but that such suffering is followed by complete cessation of being. Origin of such teachings is to be found in the natural horror which men feel when confronted with idea of eternal punishment. For Scriptural doctrine opposing annihilationism see *Hereafter; Last Things.* See also *Conditional Immortality.*

D. M. Gilbert, "The Annihilation Theory Briefly Examined," *LQ,* IX (Oct. 1879), 613—648; J. H. C. Fritz, "Eine Gnadenzeit nach dem Tode, die Vernichtung aller Gottlosen und andere Irrlehren," *CTM,* VII (June 1936), 436—445.

Annoni, Jerome (1697—1770). Leader of Basel pietists.

Annulus Piscatoris. See *Ring of the Fisherman.*

Annunciades. See *Annunciation, Orders of.*

Annunciates of Lombardy. See *Annunciation, Orders of,* 3.

Annunciation, Feast of. Commemoration on March 25 of announcement of Gabriel to Mary that she was to become the mother of God (Lk 1:26-38). Also called Lady Day. See also *Church Year,* 13, 16.

Annunciation, Orders of. 1. *Annunciades.* Penitential order, founded 1502 by Jeanne de Valois (1464 to 1505), daughter of Louis XI of Fr., wife of Duke of Orleans (who became Louis XII). 2. *Annunciades, Celestial.* Religious order for women founded 1602 at Genoa by Maria Vittoria Fornari (1562—1617). 3. *Annunciates of Lombardy* (Ambrosians; Sisters of St. Ambrose; Sisters of St. Marcellina). Organized 1408 at Pavia by young women from Venice and Pavia. 4. *Annunciation, Archconfraternity of the.* Established 1460 in Rome to provide dowries for poor girls. Built chapel of Annunciation in Dominican Ch. of the Minerva. 5. *Annunziata.* Name by which Servites * are at times known because their chief monastery at Florence is dedicated to the Annunciation. 6. *Annunciation, Military Order of the.* Traces its origin to Order of the Collar, founded 1364 by Amadeus VI of Savoy. Its first dedication to the Virgin was by antipope Felix (Amadeus VIII) 1434. Transferred 1627 to monastery on the Mountain of Turin.

Annunziata. See *Annunciation, Orders of,* 5.

Anointing of the Sick. See *Unction.*

Anomoeans (Gk. *anomoios,* "dissimilar"). Arians who denied likeness of Son to Father; distinguished from Semi-Arians, who denied only the consubstantiality. Leaders were Aetius* and Eunomius.* See also *Arianism,* 1.

Anquetil-Duperron, Abraham Hyacinthe (1731 to 1805). Fr. Orientalist; tr. *Avesta.*

Ansegis (ca. 770—833). Abbot of Fontanelle; collected laws of Charlemagne* and Louis the Pious *(Capitularies).*

Anselm of Canterbury (1033—1109). Succeeded Lanfranc* as prior of monastic school at Bec,* Normandy, 1063, and as abp. of Canterbury. Studied Augustine extensively and lived himself into his spirit. In his *Cur Deus homo* he subjected the doctrine of the atonement to dialectical investigation and vindication. In the *Monologium* he developed an ontological argument for God. Had many difficulties with king of Eng. over rights and privileges. In character was humble, kind of heart, charitable. Was father of medieval scholasticism. See also *Barth, Karl.*

A. C. Welch, *Anselm and His Work* (London, 1901); M. Grabmann, *Geschichte der scholastischen Methode,* I (Berlin, 1956), 258—339; F. R. Hasse, *Anselm von Canterbury,* 2 vols. (Leipzig, 1843—52); R. W. Southern, *St. Anselm and His Biographer* (Cambridge, 1963); *Opera omnia,* ed. F. S. Schmitt (Edinburgh, 1946—); G. H. Williams, *Anselm: Communion and Atonement* (St. Louis, 1960).

Anselm of Laon (d. 1117). Theol.; b. Laon (near Paris), Fr.; taught at Laon. Works include *Glossa interlinearis.*

Anselm of Lucca (ca. 1036—1086). Partisan of Gregory VII; espoused ecclesiastical reforms.

Ansgar (Anskar; Anschar[ius]; Ansgarius; ca. 801–865). "Apostle of the North." B. near Corbie, N Fr.; Benedictine monk Corbie ca. 814; teacher and preacher Corvey, Westphalia, after 823; sent with an asst. by Louis* I to territory "beyond the Elbe" in the mid-820s in response to a request of Harold Klak (see also *Denmark*) and to Swed, ca. 829/830 in response to a request of the king of Swed.; bp. Hamburg 832, Bremen 847. See also *Sweden, Conversion of, to Christianity.*

Yngve Brilioth, *Ansgar, Sveriges Apostel* (Stockholm, 1955).

Ansgar Lutheran. See *Danish Lutherans in America,* 5.

Ansgarius Synod. See *Evangelical Covenant Church of America.*

Ante-Nicene Fathers. See *Patristics.*

Antediluvians. Name applied to people who lived before the Flood.

Antependium, See *Paraments.*

Antes, Henry. See *Congregation of God in the Spirit.*

Anthem. Sacred choral work whose text, though taken from Bible, is nonliturgical. While 17th-c. anthems were usually sung without accompaniment, modern anthems include instrumental accompaniment. Excellent anthems were written by Eng. master composers in 17th and 18th c. Use of anthems declined in some areas toward middle of 20th c. See also *Motet.*

Anthony (ca. 251—ca. 356). Saint. Father of Christian monasticism; b. Egypt. Reputedly hermit 80 yrs.; organized hermit colonies in which monks lived separately but met for religious services; left no written rule.

Anthony, Orders of St. Religious orders which claimed St. Anthony as their patron (Antonians, Hospital Brothers of St. Anthony, Armenian Antoians, Congregation of St. Anthony, Chaldean Antonians).

Anthony of Bourbon. See *Huguenots.*

Anthony of Padua (bap. name Ferdinand; 1195–1231). B. Lisbon, Port.; Augustinian ca. 1212; Franciscan 1220 at the friary of San Antonio in Coimbra (whence he took the name Anthony); miss. to Morocco; preached against heretics in N It. 1222–24, S Fr. 1223; preacher in It. 1227–31, specifically in Padua 1231. See also *Concordances, Bible; Preaching, Christian, History of,* 8.

Anthropocentrism. View that man is at center of all values and experiences.

Anthropolatry. Cult of human being conceived as God (Alexander the Great; Roman emperor; Shintoism).

Anthropology. That part of Christian dogmatics, or doctrinal theol., referring to man's creation, essential parts, fall, and subsequent sinfulness. Man was originally created in God's image, i. e., in concreate wisdom, holiness, and righteousness (Cl 3:10; Eph 4:24). Though positively good in both body and soul (Gn 1:31), man yet could fall (Gn 2:17), though question as to how this could be belongs to mystery of origin of sin. Man's fall was voluntary, for though Eve was deceived by the devil (1 Ti 2:14), she and Adam sinned against better knowledge (Gn 3:1-13). While the fall was foreseen by God, it was not willed by Him (Ps 5:4, 5). Scripture rejects all forms of determinism* and fatalism.* After the fall, man still retains a free will,* not only inasmuch as he is endowed with the faculty to will but also as he can exercise his free will in worldly affairs and in civil matters. But he has no free will in spiritual matters, i. e., he cannot by his own reason or strength believe in Jesus Christ and thus convert himself (Jn 1:13; 3:5, 6, 9; Cl 2:13). The Moral Law was originally written in the human heart (according to one interpretation of Ro 2:14, 15; 1:19-32), so that in state of innocence Adam knew God's will even without special revelation (Gn 2:18-24). After the fall, man still retains knowledge of God's Law and will, though it is obscured by sin (Ro 1:32). Conscience* is man's moral faculty which, on basis of natural law, judges between right and wrong. Since the fall has obscured the natural law and also weakened man's moral judgment, his opinions of moral and spiritual matters are often wrong; conscience therefore is no longer safe guide in doctrine and life but must be normed according to Scripture, the only source and rule of faith and life. See also *Dogmatics,* C. JTM

Anthropomorphism (Gk. *anthropos,* "man," and *morphe,* "form"). The Scriptural mode of speech by which the possession of human sense, limbs, and organs is attributed to God. God is spoken of as having face, eyes, ears, nose, heart, arm, hand, finger (Gn 3:8; Ex 6:6; 7:4; 13:3; Ps 10:17; 11:4; 18:8; 34:16; 63:8; 95:4; 139:16; Is 52:10; 62:8; Jer 27:5; Lk 11:20). Since God is not composed of material but is simply spirit, complete in His spiritual nature, the Bible, when it speaks of God as possessing human parts or affections (*anthropopathism,* Gk. "human feeling"), purposes to convey to the human mind some notion of ways of God in His universe (Is 55:8-11; Ro 11:33-36).

The term anthropomorphism is applied to heretical teachings which attribute actual body and human emotions to God. Thus Latter-Day Saints* hold that God is a material being, with human passions, who created man as men beget children. Those who thus ascribe human parts, attributes, and passions to God are called *anthropomorphites.*

Anthropopathism. See *Anthropomorphism.*

Anthroposophy. See *Steiner, Rudolf.*

Antichrist. 1. Term used in NT (1) of all false teachers (1 Jn 2:18; 4:3) and (2) of one outstanding adversary of Christ (1 Jn 2:18). Characteristics of Antichrist are taken from Dn 7; 8; 11:31-35; Rv 11; 13; 17; 18; writings of John; esp. 2 Th 2:3-12. His habitation is between the seas (Dn 11:45) and on seven hills (Rv 17:9-18); his power is growing already in time of apostles (1 Jn 2:18; 2 Th 2:7); he works with all power and signs and lying wonders (2 Th 2:9); a "falling away" precedes his coming (2 Th 2:3); he sits in temple of God (2 Th 2:4); he exalts self above God and shows self as God (2 Th 2:4); is a mystery of iniquity (2 Th 2:7, 8); is restrained in apostolic times (2 Th 2:7).

2. Word ἀντίχριστος occurs for first time in NT, there only in writings of John. Idea, however, is previously mentioned in NT, and roots go back into OT prophecy. Vain attempts have been made to seek origin of idea in heathen lands (e. g., battle of Ahura Mazda and Angra Mainyu). Antiochus IV was first historical figure to whom prophecies of Daniel (7:8, 19-25; 8:9-12; 11:21-45) were applied; later applied to Pompey, Herod, Caligula.

3. Bible passages generally applied to Antichrist were correlated early in Christian era. Polycarp (*Epistola ad Philippenses,* 7) quotes 1 Jn 4:3 in connection with those who do not confess Christ; *Didache* (16:4) speaks of Antichrist as world deceiver who is to come; Barnabas 4 speaks of "beast" as wicked one yet to come. Irenaeus (*Adversus haereses,* III—V) applies Jer 8:16; Dn 7:8-18; 2 Th 2; etc. to Antichrist. Hippolytus *(De Christo et antichristo)* quotes Gn 49:16, 17; Dt 33:22; Dn 11:31; 12:11-12; Rv 12; Mt 24:15-22; 2 Th 2; etc. as pertaining to Antichrist.

4. In early Christian times Antichrist was connected with expected return of Nero (Augustine, *De civitate Dei,* XX, 19; Commodian, *Instructiones,* 41; Lactantius, *De mortibus persecutorum,* II [Nero as forerunner of Antichrist]). In succeeding centuries the prediction of Antichrist and his characteristics remain relatively the same, but the external application changes. In 4th c. prediction of a "last Roman Emperor before Antichrist" became prominent. Antichrist apocalypses flourished in age of Islam and developed intensity during Crusades. The time came when people saw Antichrist in every political, nat., soc., or ecclesiastical opponent.

5. The Franciscans of the opposition assiduously held that the pope is the Antichrist. Bohemians Jan Milic* of Kromeriz and Matthias of Janow followed this view. Wycliffe and Purvey as well as Hus were firmly convinced that the pope is the Antichrist.

6. Luther regarded pope as Antichrist chiefly because papacy* substituted work-righteousness for grace in Christ (WA 40[I]:36, 37, 60, 61, 301; 20:673; 37:660, 661); also mentions that papacy substitutes man-made rules for divine Law (5:344; 40[I]:406, 407; forbids marriage and foods (54:113, 114); usurps power (5:195, 339—352; 52:666, 667); usurps position of Christ (42:635; 45:46; 52:220, 221; 50:4, 5); sits in temple (40[III]:421; 40[I]:71); exalts self above God (14:510; 50:4, 5); has other characteristics of Antichrist. Luther also spoke of the Turk (together with the pope) as Antichrist (42:634; WA, *Briefwechsel,* 1:270).

7. The AC does not speak of pope as Antichrist but indicates that subscribers are willing to continue

in RC system provided abuses are corrected (which included matters pertaining to temporal power, abuse of power, supremacy of councils, etc. — XXVIII: 28—78). The Ap shows that papacy has marks of Antichrist as depicted by Daniel (VII—VIII 24; XV 19; XXIII 25; XXIV 51) and by Paul (VII—VIII 4). Speaks of papacy as part of kingdom of Antichrist (XV 18). The SA hold that pope by his doctrine and practice has clearly shown self as Antichrist since he exceeds even Turks and Tartars in keeping people from their Savior. The FC quotes the SA on Antichrist.

8. Lutheran dogmaticians (Melanchthon, Chemnitz, Quenstedt, Baier, and others) regarded the teaching of the Antichrist as nonfundamental doctrine. C. F. W. Walther (*Lutheraner,* XXI [April 1, 1865], 113—115) and F. Pieper followed the opinion of the dogmaticians. EL

"Ist der Antichrist im Atheismus unserer Zeit zu suchen?" *Lehre und Wehre,* XV (Feb. 1869), 39 to 45; C. J. H. Fick, *Das Geheimniss der Bosheit im römischen Papstthum* (St. Louis, 1873); F. W. Stellhorn, "'Unsere Wege zur katholischen Kirche,'" *Lehre und Wehre,* XIX (April 1873), 97—108; W. Bousset, *The Antichrist Legend: a Chapter in Christian and Jewish Folklore,* tr. A. H. Keane (London, 1896); H. Preuss, *Die Vorstellungen vom Antichrist im späteren Mittelalter, bei Luther und in der konfessionellen Polemik* (Leipzig, 1906); A. Jeremias, *Der Antichrist in Geschichte und Gegenwart* (Leipzig, 1930); B. Rigaux, *L'Antéchrist et l'opposition au royaume messianique dans l'Ancien et le Nouveau Testament* (Paris, 1932); P. E. Kretzmann, "Papam esse verum Antichristum," *CTM,* IV (June 1933), 424—435; W. Hoenecke, "Vom Antichristen," *Theologische Quartalschrift,* XL (July 1943), 166—188, and "Der Antichrist," *Theologische Quartalschrift,* XLI (Jan. 1944), 91 to 109; P. Schuetz, *Der Anti-Christus* (Kassel, 1949); P. Althaus, *Die Letzten Dinge,* 5th ed. (Gütersloh, 1949), 282—297; H. Hamann, "A Brief Exegesis of 2 Thess. 2:1-12 with Guideline for the Application of the Prophecy Contained Therein," *CTM,* XXIV (June 1953), 418—433; E. Schlink, "Antichrist," *Religion in Geschichte und Gegenwart,* ed. K. Galling, 3d ed., I (Tübingen, 1957), 431—435.

Anticlericalism. 1. Opposition to activity or influence of clergy in secular affairs.

2. Any opposition to clergy.

See also *Freemasonry and the Church.*

Antigua. See *Caribbean Islands,* E 5.

Antilegomena (Gk. "spoken against, questioned"). Certain books of the NT concerning which there was no unanimity but some uncertainty in the early church regarding their canonicity. Distinguished from *homologoumena* (Gk. "universally accepted"). Because certain false teachers and other unauthorized persons tried to have their writings introduced into Christian congregations (cp. 2 Th 2:2), it was necessary for Christians to be alert, lest false gospels or letters be acknowledged, esp. by being ascribed to true apostles or disciples of apostles. It was due chiefly to this special vigilance that the following books were not accepted by the church everywhere before the latter part of the 4th c.: James, Jude, 2 and 3 John, 2 Peter, Hebrews, and the Apocalypse. The author of Hebrews is not definitely known; the identity of the James who is the author of the letter was not altogether certain, and the content of the letter was misunderstood; 2 and 3 John are addressed to private persons and were not made accessible to larger circles; 2 Peter was most likely written shortly before the death of the author and had no definite addressees; Jude is very short and has a very circumscribed message; and the Apocalypse was under suspicion on account of its nature. Over against these objections it is to be noted that all these books are mentioned at a very early date, some of them referred to as early as the beginning of the 2d c. as Apostolic writings, and all of them finally accepted by the church in the course of the 4th c. While doubts have been expressed regarding some of them even by orthodox Luth. teachers, in almost every case, the clear Apostolic doctrine, the depth of the admonitions and of the entire presentation, and the high prophetic insight into events of the future almost compel one to acknowledge them. Most of the objections voiced in recent centuries have been satisfactorily met by earnest searchers after the truth. See also *Canon, Bible,* 5, 6.

For gen. information see references under *Canon, Bible;* for position of Luth. dogmaticians see C. F. Walther, "Ist derjenige fuer einen Ketzer oder gefährlichen Irrlehrer zu erklären, welcher nicht alle in dem Convolut des Neuen Testamentes befindlichen Bücher für kanonisch hält und erklärt?" *L. u. W.,* II (July 1856), 204—216.

Antilles. See *Caribbean Islands.*

Antimission Baptists. See *Baptist Churches,* 11; *Missionary Baptists.*

Anti-Missouri Brotherhood. Organized in 1887 by group of ministers of the Norw. Syn. under the leadership of F. A. Schmidt.* Conducted a sem. at St. Olaf Coll., Northfield, Minn., 1886–90. In 1890 the Anti-Mo. Brotherhood became part of the United* Norw. Luth. Ch. in Am. See *Evangelical Lutheran Church,* 10.

Anti-National Religious Organization Movement. An antimiss. antibenevolent movement in the early 19th c. supported by Baptists (John Taylor, Daniel Parker, Alexander Campbell), Freethinkers, Universalists, Ref. Methodists, Unitarians, and others. The basic motive for the movement was the fear that religious authority would be concentrated as a result of the various undenominational benevolent associations and thus the separation of ch. and state be obliterated.

G. P. Albaugh, "Anti-missionary Movement in the United States," *An Encyclopedia of Religion,* ed. V. Ferm (New York, 1945), pp. 27—28.

Antinomian Controversy. Began 1527 when Melanchthon urged the Law to prevent abuse of free grace. Agricola of Eisleben held that the Law had no place at all in the ch.; the knowledge of sin and contrition to be wrought, not by the Law, but by the Gospel. Luther made peace bet. them. Prof. at Wittenberg in 1536 through Luther's influence, Agricola spread his antinomian views to Brandenburg, Frankfurt, and esp. in Freiberg, through Jacob Schenk. Luther stopped him from lecturing and printing. Agricola recanted and was reconciled (1538) but continued to spread his antinomian views. Luther repeatedly wrote against the Antinomians. Agricola attacked Luther and escaped trial by breaking his parole and fleeing to Berlin, where he again recanted (1541) but continued to defend his position.

Second Antinomian Controversy began 1556. Main issue: Third Use of the Law. Poach,* Anton Otto, and others denied that, with respect to good works, the Law was of any service whatever to Christians. Theses such as these were defended: "The Law does not teach good works. Evangelical preachers are to preach the Gospel only and no Law." Finally, following Melanchthon, the Philippists taught: "The Gospel alone is expressly and particularly, truly and properly, a preaching and a voice of repentance, or conversion," revealing the baseness of sin (Paul Crell*).

FC VI settled the matter by recognizing the triple use of the Law — (1) for outward decency, (2) for revealing sin, (3) for the rule of life to the regenerate, who need it on account of their Old Adam.

Antinomianism. View that Christians are free of all moral law. See also *Antinomian Controversy; Gnosticism,* 7 f.

Antinomy. A pair of contradictory propositions drawn from the same premise. It is often used to show that a given premise is false.

Antioch, School of. See *Commentaries, Biblical; Exegesis,* 4; *Schools, Early Christian,* 4.

Antioch, Synods of. Among the synods held at Antioch were the following: ca. 251, dealt with Novatianism of Fabius; 264—268, three synods dealt with Paul of Samosata;* ca. 330, deposed orthodox Eustathius of Antioch;* 341, "Dedication Council," attended by Constantius, Arians adopted 4 creeds to replace the Nicene. 344, deposed the Arian Stephen of Antioch for misconduct, adopted Semi-Arian creed; 354, 358, 361, 362 dominated by Arians; 363, 378 accepted Arian faith; 390, condemned Messalians.* Pelagianism,* Nestorianism,* and Monophysitism* were dealt with in synods of the 5th and 6th c.

Antiochene Rite. The collection of rules, liturgies, and traditions of the early ch. of Antioch from which the rites of the Monophysite Ch. are derived.

Antiochian Orthodox Archdiocese of Toledo, and Dependencies in N. A. See *Eastern Orthodox Churches,* 6.

Anti-organ. See *Disciples of Christ,* 2 e.

Antiphon. A response,* or versicle, sung in connection with Psalm, a lesson, or a collect, the pastor intoning the versicle by chanting the 1st part and the congregation answering by chanting its 2d part.

Antiphonary. A book of antiphons. See also *Service Books.*

Antipope. See *Papacy,* 4.

Anti-Saloon League. The Ohio Anti-Saloon League was organized at Oberlin 1893 in the interest of temperance and in opposition to all saloons in the state; a similar league was organized 1893 in the Dist. of Columbia. These and more than 40 similar organizations founded the Anti-Saloon League of Am. 1895, which pressed for adoption of the 18th Amendment to the US const. (adopted 1919; effective 1920; repealed 1933), became known as the Nat. Temperance League 1948, absorbed the Temperance Leagues of Am. and the Nat. Temperance Movement 1950.

Anti-Semitism (from Shem cf. Gn 10:1, 21-31 as ancestor of Jews). Prejudice, hostility, or opposition to Jews, Jewry, and Judaism.

Antisthenes. See *Cynicism.*

Antitactes. See *Gnosticism,* 7 j.

Antitrinitarianism. See *Unitarianism.*

Anton (Dalmatin). See *Dalmatin, Anton.*

Anton, Paul (1661—1730). Ger. Prot. theologian; one of the founders of the pietistic school at Halle; most important writing: *Collegium antitheticum.* See also *Francke, August Hermann.*

Antonelli, Giacomo (1806—76). Cardinal and prime minister; reestablished absolute power of papal administration.

Antonij (ca. 982—1073). Russian saint; established monastery at Kiev.

Antonine de Bourbon. See *Huguenots.*

Antoninus (1389—1459). Dominican; advisor of popes; most important work: *Summa theologica moralis.*

Antoninus Pius. See *Persecutions of Christians,* 3.

Antonius. See *Anthony; Norway, Lutheranism in,* 1.

Antwerp, Synod of (1563). See *Reformed Churches,* 2.

Antwerp Polyglot. See *Polyglot Bibles.*

Anxiety (Angst). See *Contrition; Existentialism,* 2 c.

Anxious Sent. See *Finney, Charles Grandison.*

Apaczai Csere, Janos (1625—59). Hung. theol. prof.; Presb.; Cartesian.

Apartheid. See *Africa,* B 5.

Aphraates (4th c.). "The Persian Sage"; probably b. of heathen parents; wrote 23 homilies on Christian doctrine and practice (337—345); important in the study of the Syriac text tradition because of his many quotations; seems to have taken the name Jacob; this later caused confusion in his identification.

J. Gwynn, "Aphrahat the Persian Sage," *NPNF,* Ser. 2, XIII, 152—162. Aphrahat, "Select Demonstrations," *NPNF,* Ser. 2, XIII, 343—412.

Aphrodite. See *Greek Religion,* 2.

Apocalypse of Paul, Peter, etc. See *Apocrypha,* B 5.

Apocalyptic Literature. Term applied to a type of literature produced in abundance by Jews after 200 BC and by Christians through AD 200. Samples of OT apocalyptic are in Zechariah, Daniel, the Psalms of Solomon, the Book of Jubilees, the Testament of Abraham, 2 Esdras, the Book of Enoch, and the Apocalypse of Baruch. NT apocalyptic occurs in the Apocalypse of John, the Shepherd of Hermas, and the Apocalypse of Peter.

Apocalyptic literature has theol. and literary characteristics. It presents the world caught in war between good and evil and offers hope of the victory of good in catastrophic action which destroys its enemies. It is marked by strong angelology and demonology and by fervent messianic hope which sometimes takes on an extreme political character. Only some of its images and visions are interpreted; some of its symbols are standard and have approximately the same meaning whenever they occur. All NT apocalyptic books except the Apocalypse of John are extra-canonical. (See *Canon*). Apocalyptic literature usually emerges from a downtrodden and oppressed people. Some of Luther's radical contemporaries produced apocalyptic writings.

The Apocrypha and Pseudepigrapha of the Old Testament in English, ed. R. H. Charles (Oxford, 1913); R. H. Charles, *A Critical History of the Doctrine of a Future Life in Israel, in Judaism, and in Christianity* (London, 1913); H. H. Rowley, *The Relevance of Apocalyptic* (New York, 1946). HTM

Apocatastasis. See *Restitution.*

Apocrisiarius (Gk. "answer"). Envoy of E Orthodox patriarchates.

Apocrypha (Gk. "hidden"). Term applied in later patristic literature to esoteric or otherwise obscure writings and to books whose authorship was unknown (extended to mean "spurious"); gradually came to be identified with 14 or 15 books excluded by Palestinian Jews from their canon as "outside books." In this sense the word Apocrypha as used by Jerome, e. g., is not negative or critical. Scholars of the Ref. period narrowed the meaning to the uncanonical books in the Vulgate (thence extended to books of the NT period). "Pseudepigrapha" is used by many to designate the vast number of other "outside books" written by Jews and early Christians.

A. 1. *Old Testament.* The Jews at an early date distinguished between canonical books for gen. use and others reserved ("hidden," hence "apocrypha") for the wise (cf. Josephus, *Against Apion,* I, 8; *Antiquities* XI, i—vi; 2 Esd 12:37, 38; 14:4-16, 42-47). The destruction of Jerusalem and the increasing prominence of Christian literature led Palestinian Jews to exclude the outside books from their canon at the Council of Jamnia, AD 90. The Hellenistic Jews, however, preserved these books in translations from which they passed into Christian usage and were gradually assimilated at various places in the OT canon. Alleged NT quotations from the Apocrypha have not been established (e. g., Mt 23:34, 35; Lk 11:49-51; 1 Co 2:9). But similarities are noticeable (2 Ptr 2:4; Ja 1:19; Heb 11:34 to 40). In Jude 6, 9, and 14-16 there seem to be references to two apocryphal books, the Assumption of Moses and the Book of Enoch. The earliest fathers, such as Clement, Barnabas, and Polycarp, quote the apocryphal books as equal in authority with the canonical books. Later fathers questioned the precise facts of their authorship.

2. Karlstadt *(Libellus de canonicis scripturis,* 1520) separated the Apocrypha from the canon, named a number of them *libri hagiographa* (following Jerome: Wisdom, Ecclesiasticus, Judith, Tobit, 1 and 2 Maccabees) and pronounced the rest unworthy of Christian use. Luther's edition (1534) placed all the Apocrypha after the OT with the remark: "Apocrypha: These books are not held equal to the Sacred Scriptures, and yet are useful and good for reading." A movement in Eng. (19th c.) led to their exclusion from Eng. Bibles. The RSV includes the OT Apocrypha in certain editions.

3. In familiar usage 14 books (in LXX and Vulgate) are included in the OT Apocrypha: 1 Esdras (compilation largely from Ezra); 2 Esdras (Esdras receives information about future events from an angel); Additions to Esther (dream of Mordecai, edict of Artaxerxes, etc.); Song of the Three Children (sung by Hananiah, Mishael, and Azariah after their deliverance), including the "Prayer of Azariah"; History of Susanna (a pious woman freed from an adultery charge by Daniel); Bel and the Dragon (Daniel shows the falseness of two idols); Prayer of Manasseh (cf. 2 Ch 33:18, 19); Baruch and the Epistles of Jeremiah (history and exhortations from Babylonian Captivity period); Tobit (Jew and Jewess aided by Raphael during Assyrian Captivity); Judith (a pious Jewess slays Holofernes and frees besieged "Bethulia"); 1 Maccabees (Jewish struggles for freedom under the Hasmonean brothers' leadership); 2 Maccabees; Ecclesiasticus, or Wisdom of Sirach (practical philosophy); Wisdom of Solomon (discussion of God-centered wisdom).

4. The Council of Trent (1546) reaffirmed the canonicity of all the above except 1 and 2 Esdras and the Prayer of Manasseh. Catholics call the Apocrypha "deuterocanonical" and reserve the word "apocrypha" for "outside books" not in the Vulgate (usually called "pseudepigrapha"). The most important of the latter are 3–4 Maccabees; Psalms of Solomon; Sibylline Books; Enoch; Assumption of Moses; Apocalypse of Baruch; Book of Jubilees*; Testament of the Twelve Patriarchs; Book of Adam and Eve; Martyrdom of Isaiah; Lives of the Prophets; Testament of Job; Testament of Abraham.

B. 1. *New Testament.* Here the terms "apocrypha" and "pseudepigrapha" are usually used interchangeably to designate all those writings produced within and without the church, many of which were regarded as possessing canonical authority at one time or another. Some were written in the name of a famed believer of the past in order to borrow his authority to secure the acceptance of the content of the document. Others were frankly written to disseminate false doctrines. The NT Apocrypha may be divided into 4 groups: Gospels, Epistles, Acts, and Apocalyptic.

2. The Gospels were usually written to cover *lacunae* in the life of Christ and advance private doctrines. They contain pure fiction, development of Gospel statements, words of Jesus tr. into action, traditions, parallels to OT miracles, literal fulfillment of prophecies. The most important are Gospel According to the Egyptians (ca. 130; ascetic); Gospel According to the Hebrews (ca. 130; many of the sayings, *logia,* of Jesus found at Oxyrhynchus seem derived from it); British Museum Gospel (ca. 135; condenses the 4 Gospels into 1); Gospel according to Peter (ca. 130; Docetic); Gospel of Thomas (the lost original was Gnostic; others by the same name are probably condensations); Traditions of Matthias (ca. 185; philosophical); Gospel of the Ebionites (ca. 200; Ebionite, opposed animal sacrifice, advocated vegetarianism); Gospel of James (ca. 200; perpetual virginity). Lesser Gospels are those of Pseudo-Matthew, of the Infancy, of Basilides, of Judas, of Truth, of Philip, of Nicodemus (Acts of Pilate), of Bartholomew, of Andrew, of Barnabas.

3. The apocryphal Acts were evidently used most extensively for the propagation of false views. The most important are: Acts of Paul (ca. 160; extends history of Acts); Acts of Paul and Tekla (ascribes to Tekla a prominent place alongside Paul in the ministry of the church; rejected by those who opposed a female ministry); Acts of John (ca. 180; Docetic); Acts of Peter (ca. 210; glorification of Peter, step in growing importance of Roman bishop); Acts of Thomas (ca. 220; ascetic); Acts of Andrew (ca. 250; ascetic).

4. Among the Epistles the most valuable is the so-called Epistle* of the Apostles. Others are certain Epistles of Mary, and of James, and supposed correspondence between Paul and Seneca. There is even mention (Eusebius) of a letter supposed to have been written by Christ to Abgar of Edessa.

5. The NT Apocalyptic literature includes such writings as the Shepherd of Hermas (105—135, which suggested a possibility of repentance for postbaptismal sins); the Apocalypse of Peter (ca. 130; canonical authority for a time in E churches); Sibylline Oracles (2d—3d c.; pagan, Jewish, Christian); Pistis Sophia (ca. 250; Gnostic); Apocalypse of Paul (cf. 2 Co 12:2-4). Others: Apocalypse of Bartholomew, of Mary, of Thomas. EL, HTM

The Apocrypha, tr. E. J. Goodspeed (Chicago, 1938); M. R. James, *The Apocryphal New Testament* (Oxford, 1924); C. C. Torrey, *The Apocryphal Literature* (New Haven, 1945); *The Apocrypha and Pseudepigrapha of the Old Testament in English,* ed. R. H. Charles (Oxford, 1913); R. Hofmann, "Apokryphen des Alten Testaments," *Realencyklopädie,* ed. A. Hauck, I (Leipzig, 1896), 622—670; B. M. Metzger, *An Introduction to the Apocrypha* (New York; 1957); T. Fritsch, "Apocrypha," *Interpreter's Dictionary of the Bible,* ed. G. A. Buttrick, I (Nashville, 1962), 161—166.

Apocrypha Controversy. See *Bible Societies,* 3, 4.

Apodeipnon. Name for compline in E Orthodox Ch.

Apollinarianism. Doctrine of Apollinaris* of Laodicsea and his followers.

Apollinarians. Followers of Apollinaris* of Laodicea.

Apollinaris, Claudius (2d c.). Bp. of Hierapolis; apologist; presented a defense of the Christian faith to Marcus Aurelius; also wrote *Against the Greeks (Gentiles), On Truth, Against the Jews,* and against the Montanists (Eusebius, *HE* IV, xxvii); only fragments extant.

J. Otto, *Corpus Apologetarum Christianorum,* IX (Jena, 1872), 479—495; *MPG,* 5, 1285—1302.

Apollinaris of Laodicea (the Younger; Apollinarius; ca. 310–ca. 390). Bp. Laodicea on the Syrian coast ca. 360. Opposed Arius; fell, however, into the error of teaching that Christ did not have a human soul, but the Logos in its stead; his teaching (Apollinarianism) was condemned as Docetism,* 381. When Julian forbade the Christians to teach the classics, Apollinaris reproduced the Scriptures in classic form. Followers called Apollinarians.

Apollinaris of Ravenna (d. ca. 75). According to legend, disciple of Peter and 1st bp. of Ravenna.

Apollinaris Sidonius, Gaius Sollius (ca. 430—ca. 487). B. Lyons, Fr.; bp. Clermont 469. Roman patrician and senator; converted to Christianity; author of books and poems valued as source material for 5th c.

Apollo. See *Greek Religion,* 2.

Apollonius of Tyana (ca. 3 BC—ca. AD 96). Gk. neo-Pythagorean soothsayer and magician. His biography, by Philostratus* the Athenian, is an idealizing romance with the apparent polemical aim of denying the exclusive claims of Christianity. Apollonius is pictured as a pagan Messiah who worked miracles, cast out demons, possessed knowledge of all languages, and raised the dead.

Apologetics (Christian). 1. *Definition.* Christian Apologetics is the scientific vindication of the truth and absoluteness of the Christian religion against unbelief. The expression "Christian Evidence" more properly denotes the scientific proof of the divine authority of Christianity. The term "Apology" denotes an argument in defense of a doctrine that has been attacked.

2. *Relation to Other Branches of Theology.** Apologetics is a branch of Systematic Theology. While Christian Dogmatics sets forth and expounds the Christian religion on the basis of Scripture, Apologetics vindicates its truth on grounds of reason, showing the unreasonableness of infidelity. Apologetics concerns itself with errorists outside the ch., Polemics with errorists within Christendom.

3. *History of Apologetics.* The hist. of Apologetics may be divided as follows: 1. the Apologetic Period, 70—250; 2. the Polemic Period, 250—730; 3. the Medieval Period, 730—1517; 4. the Modern Period, 1517 to date.

4. *Methodology of Apologetics.* The Apologetic method may be either hist. or philosophical, or it may combine both approaches. The 1st vindicates Christianity chiefly by defending Scripture, its fact and importance in human hist., and the value of its teachings in human soc. The 2d vindicates such fundamentals of Christianity as the doctrine of God, of man's ethical obligation, and the like, on the basis of pure reason. A simple, but very practical grouping is the following: Fundamental, Historical, and Philosophical Apologetics.

I. *Fundamental Apologetics.* A. *Being and Nature of God.* Christianity proclaims and defends the existence and rule of a divine, infinite, spiritual Being, absolutely 1 in essence, but 3 in Persons, endowed, with all divine attributes properly belonging to such a perfect, personal Spirit-Being against such antichristian theories as: 1. Atheism,* 2. Materialism,* 3. Pantheism,* 4. Deism,* 5. Rationalism,* 6. Idealism,* 7. Positivism,* 8. Agnosticism,* 9. Monism,* 10. Pluralism,* 11. Pessimism,* 12. Modernism,* teaching that deity is finite, 13. Natural Theology,* 14. Polytheism,* 15. Judaism,* and other forms of unbelief that deny that God is the 1st and ultimate and only divinely efficient Cause. God's existence is demonstrated not only by the specifically Biblical proofs, but also by corroborative arguments of sound reasoning, e. g., the theological, cosmological, teleological, moral, aesthetic, and ontological. See also *God, Arguments for the Existence of.*

B. *The Cosmological Problem.* 1. Christianity confesses and defends the creation* of all things by the Triune God within 6 days, to His glory and man's good. The doctrine of creation embraces 3 facts in agreement with reason and experience: a. Matter is not infinite, but finite; b. All things outside God were called into being out of nothing at the beginning of time by the omnipotent and all-wise Creator; c. Creatures are propagated according to fixed laws ("propagation after his kind"). 2. The doctrine of creation is denied by both atheistic and theistic evolution.* 3. Teleology* definitely supports the doctrine of creation. 4. Science and the Bible* are not in conflict with each other, though scientists and defenders of the Bible have been in conflict. Many conflicts have been caused by inaccurate perceptions or false conclusions based on the categories of science (*i. e.,* the sense world) on the one hand or by erroneous interpretations of the Bible on the other.

C. *The Anthropological Problem.* 1. Christianity declares that man is a personal, moral, free being, originally created in the divine image, which he lost through the Fall, by which he was deprived of his concreate wisdom, holiness, and righteousness, having become a sinner both as to original and actual sin. 2. With the brutes he has a certain relationship in physical things, but though fallen, he is still endowed with intelligence and free will.* He is not a development from brutes, but the lord or ruler of all things under God. 3. While he has lost his power of free will in spiritual things, he still retains it in earthly matters and the area of civil righteousness and so remains a free moral agent, though after the Fall he cannot do otherwise than sin. 4. Man is a religious being and seeks to worship higher beings or powers (Acts 17:26-28), though, unless converted, in a perverted form (Ro. 1:21-23). Such worship distinguishes man from the brutes as also does intelligence and will. 5. The doctrine of man, as proclaimed by Christianity, satisfies man's striving and furnishes him a goal for his efforts, while evolution also here proves itself an unsatisfactory and fruitless hypothesis.

D. *The Ethical Problem.* 1. Christianity teaches that at the creation of man God wrote into the human heart the Moral Law,* which, though obscured by sin, still is a criterion for conscience.* Through the Moral Law God rules man individually and collectively. Ethical norms are not mere conventions, but laws of God innate in man. 2. The universe is not ruled by chance, but by Law under Moral Government. 3. Christianity neither ignores sin nor attempts to explain its origin, but declares that God is not its author or abettor (though He permits it to occur), but rather forbids it, often prevents it. 4. Prompted by His goodness, God from eternity decreed to redeem sinful man through the vicarious active and passive obedience of His incarnate Son, whom He made man's Substitute and Redeemer. (See *Christ Jesus; Atonement.*) The denial of redemption contradicts the innate redemptive idea in man (as expressed, in corrupt form, in the traditions regarding "Champions" or "Saviors" of humanity).

E. *The Problem of Man's Immortality.* 1. Christianity teaches that man, redeemed by Christ and born again through the Holy Spirit, shall live with God throughout eternity in perfect happiness. 2. All who deny man's immortality do so contrary to all rational grounds and arguments (e. g., the metaphysical, teleological, ethical, hist.) and the widespread belief in immortality.

II. *Historical Apologetics.* A. *The Supernatural in History.* 1. Christianity holds that since God is the merciful Creator and hourly Benefactor of man, in whom man has his being (Acts 17:28; Cl 1:17), it is reasonable for Him to reveal Himself to man. 2. The necessity of the supernatural is grounded in man's need of God, its possibility in God's omnipotence, its reality in God's saving love, its purpose in God's desire to draw man to Himself. 3. The manifestation of the supernatural in hist. assumes the forms of revelation,* miracles,* and inspiration,* the latter esp. in Scripture.

B. *The Bible in History.* 1. The Bible is a special divine revelation, both possible and necessary. 2. It was given by divine inspiration,* and attests itself as God's Word by its authority,* efficacy, sufficiency, and perspicuity, an altogether unique Book. 3. It is further witnessed to as the divine truth by its internal and external proofs, its profound, convincing doctrines, its noble ethics,* its unity and consistency, its hist. character, its complete body of doctrines, its soberness of teaching, its wonderful Redeemer, its dependable writers, its spiritual appeal, its miraculous preservation, its prophecy and fulfillment, its remarkable attestation by archaeology.* 4. To these evidences must be appended its amazing miracles* (Christ, the Miracle of the ages; Paul's conversion), its uplifting influences, its superiority over man-made religions (Confucianism,* Taoism,* Brahmanism,* Buddhism,* Greek systems of philosophy, e. g., Stoicism,* Epicureanism,* Persian Dualism,* Muhammadanism,* and modern cults, all of which fail to supply man's spiritual needs).

C. *Christ in History.* 1. His wonderful incarnation*; 2. His amazing Person; His ethical purity, spiritual insight, divine love, patience, etc.; His marvelous claims, His unique redemption; His compassion upon lost sinners, His transformed Apostles; 3. As there is but 1 Holy Bible, so there is also only 1 divine Christ.

D. *The Church in History.* 1. Its supernatural origin; 2. its divine preservation in the midst of tribulation; 3. its glorious victories over its enemies; 4. its absolute religion, offering to men both the perfect truth and a perfect salvation*; 5. its manifold blessings to the world.

III. *Philosophical Apologetics.* A. *Definition and Scope of Philosophical Apologetics.* Philosophical Apologetics draws its material in the main from 1. the philosophy of religion; 2. the philosophy of hist.; 3. the psychology of religion; 4. the facts of Christianity itself. While Fundamental Apologetics deals with the problems belonging to natural theology, and Hist. Apologetics presents the evidences showing Christianity to be divine in its origin and existence, Philosophical Apologetics seeks its proofs from the very essence of religion itself.

B. *Philosophy of Religion.* The philosophy* of religion inquires into the general subject of religion from the philosophical point of view, that is, it employs critical analysis and evaluation for the defense of Christianity, treating such points as the nature, function, and value of religion; the nature of evil; the problem of the human spirit and its destiny; the relation of the human to the divine with special regard to the freedom and responsibility of the individual; the meaning of human existence; the nature of belief, and the like. See also *Religion Comparative.*

C. *Philosophy of History.** The philosophy of hist., in its stricter sense, denotes the explanation, from philosophical principles, of hist. phenomena in gen. or of the entire course of hist. development, treating as such also the origin, rise, and spread of Christianity and its influence in the world. Its value for Apologetics is therefore apparent, as it shows Christianity to be a mighty dynamic contributing toward the world's well-being.

D. *Psychology of Religion.* The psychology* of religion is concerned with man's religious consciousness, in particular, with beliefs as developments of human experience. While in itself it does not favor Christianity, it supplies valuable data used by the apologist for the defense of religious truth.

E. *The Facts of Christianity.* Christianity being factual and dynamic, it represents religious phenomena which may be evaluated for its own defense, e. g., the existence and nature of God, the immortality of the soul, the reality and objectivity of truth, the categorical nature of duty, the imperative of unselfish love, and the like. Christianity thus becomes its own best apology. JTM

See also *Christian Faith and the Intellectual.*

By the middle of the 20th c. Christian apologetics concerned itself more with the new physics (which often rejects materialistic naturalism and holds that morals and religion are compatible with physics) rather than with evolution. (B. H. Streeter). Furthermore, it concerned itself more with communication than with opposition. 4 areas were esp. discussed: world view *(Weltbild),* world outlook *(Weltanschauung)* (Karl Heim); anthropology (E. Brunner, R. Bultmann); correlation (P. Tillich); kerygmatic proclamation (H. Thielicke).

O. Zöckler, *Geschichte der Apologie des Christentums* (Gütersloh, 1907); H. C. Sheldon, *Unbelief in the Nineteenth Century* (New York, 1907); P. Carrington, *Christian Apologetics of the Second Century in Their Relation to Modern Thought* (London, 1921); W. Elert, *Der Kampf um das Christentum* (Munich, 1921); J. G. Machen, *The Origin of Paul's Religion* (New York, 1921); T. Graebner, *Evolution, An Investigation and a Criticism* (Milwaukee, 1929); G. A. Barton, *Archeology and the Bible* (Philadelphia, 1937); L. S. Keyser, *A System of Christian Evidence* (Burlington, Ia., 1939); A. Richardson, *Christian Apologetics* (New York, 1947); H. Thielicke, *Fragen des Christentums an die Moderne Welt* (Geneva, 1945); J. Finegan, *Light from the Ancient Past* (Princeton, 1946); Walter Künneth, "Zum Problem Christlicher Apologetik," *Schrift und Bekenntnis* (Hamburg and Berlin, 1950); P. Tillich, *Systematic Theology,* I (Chicago, 1951); H.-H. Schrey, "Apologetik III. Systematisch-theologisch," *Die Religion in Geschichte und Gegenwart,* ed. E. Kutsch, I (Tübingen, 1957), 486—490. EL

Apologists. 1. The classical period of Christian apology is the 2d c., a period of widespread persecution of Christians by Romans. The apologists defended Christianity against various charges: (a) that Christianity was irrational since the leaders continually repeat, "Only believe"; (b) that Christians were immoral when they gathered for worship and the agape; (c) that Christians sacrificed innocent children when they ate the body and drank the blood of the son of God *(pais theou);* (d) and that Christians were disloyal to the Roman authority, since they followed another king, Jesus. Christians were also forced to define their relationship to the Jew. Christians were easily confused with the Jews since they used the same Bible and their soc. attitudes were similar. Since the Jews were a rebellious people in the empire esp. after the middle of the 1st c., Christians tried to dissociate themselves from Jewish activities in the eyes of the Romans. But this was fraught with danger; it was only because Christians were confused with Jews (most of the earliest Christians were circumcised), that they were allowed under Roman law to propagate their views as freely as they did.

2. The 1st Christian who wrote specifically to the Romans in defense of the faith was Quadratus*.

3. Aristides presented his *Apology* to Antoninus Pius, emperor 138—161; some say to Hadrian ca. 125 (e. g. Euseb., *HE,* IV, iii, 3). After the revolt of the Jews (132) Christians pleaded to the Romans that they were not Jews. Aristides pointed out how Christianity is different not only from Judaism but also from other religions.

4. The apology that many consider to be the greatest was presented during the reign of Pius by Justin* Martyr, 150. The Roman rhetorician Fronto had presented an *Oration* against Christians accusing them of all the crimes listed above. Justin refutes these charges point for point. Justin was from Samaria and was martyred under Marcus Aurelius, 166. The son of heathen parents, he received a Hellenistic educ. and, he claims, sought for truth among the current systems of philosophy. He finally embraced Platonism, which seemed to bring him near the coveted goal — the vision of God and the eternal verities. At this juncture, however, while walking in silent meditation by the seashore, he encountered a venerable old Christian who, engaging him in conversation, shook his confidence in all human wisdom and directed him to the Prophets and Apostles as true teachers come from God. He also came to realize that Christians could not be lovers of pleasurable practices if they were willing to die for their religion. The ardent young Platonist became a Christian and, retaining his philosopher's mantle, devoted his life to the spread and vindication of

Christianity. An unordained lay preacher, he traveled from place to place, combating heathen, Jews, and heretics. Besides, he wielded a vigorous, if unpolished, pen. His principal works are his two *Apologies,* the *Dialog with Trypho the Jew,* not to mention doubtful or spurious works under his name. The central idea in Justin's theology, strongly biased by Platonic and Stoic speculation, is his Logos doctrine. The Logos, or universal Reason, familiar to the thought of the Stoa and the Academy, Justin boldly identifies with the historic Christ, in whom the divine Reason became incarnate. He interprets Christ in terms of heathen philosophy. Indeed, Christianity is to Justin the true philosophy and the highest reason. Moreover, the preincarnate Logos scattered seeds of truth, not only among the Jews, but among Greeks and barbarians as well. "The footsteps of the Logos are to be traced throughout the ages, faintly luminous among the Greeks, brighter among the Hebrews, shining with full effulgence only at the advent of our Savior." Thus Socrates, Heraclitus, and others, according to Justin, were Christians in fact, if not in name. On the practical side, Christianity is to Justin essentially a new law.

5. Many apologies were writtten during the reign of Marcus Aurelius (161—180) and immediately thereafter, the result of a number of added factors: (a) Some Christians seemingly participated in the revolutionary activities of Avidius Cassius (176) and were consequently accused of being unpatriotic; (b) In the 2d c. the Roman legions were on the defensive on all fronts and pestilence ravaged many areas of the Empire. The superstitious Romans seemingly blamed the Christians for these reversals; (c) A number of very able pagan intellectuals, including Celsus (*On the True Word,* 178) and the physician and metaphysical thinker Galen, addressed remarks against the Christians suggesting that if they desired to be recognized they should defend themselves in traditional philosophical patterns.

6. Athenagoras wrote *Plea Concerning Christians* (ca. 177), attempting to show that Christians were simply another school of philosophical inquiry and favorably disposed toward the Roman intellectual (not religious) traditions. He also wrote *On the Resurrection* in the Gk. tradition of demonstrating the natural immortality of the soul through rational arguments.

7. Melito, bishop of Sardis, wrote a *Petition* (only fragments exist in Eusebius, *HE,* IV, xxvi, 5—11) sometime after 176, suggesting that since the birth of Christ and the birth of Augustus took place at the same time these two forces, the religious and the political, ought to work together in building imperial destiny for the betterment of mankind. Melito also wrote works in other areas of theology but they are extant only in fragmentary form.

8. A disorganized work delineating the precise areas where Romans and Christians stand on common ground as well as those where they differ was *To Autolycus* by Theophilus,* bishop of Antioch, written sometime after 180. Theophilus may have been attempting to correct misconceptions created by the *Oration* of Tatian* the Syrian (ca. 177).

9. Apologies by Claudius Apollinaris,* Aristo* of Pella, and Miltiades* have not survived. The famous *Epistle to Diognetus** is possibly from this period.

10. These earlier apologies were written in Greek. Lat. apology began in the 3d c. Minucius* Felix wrote the apologetic dialogue *Octavius* ca. 200; it was patterned after similar philosophical dialogues by Cicero. Tertullian* (d. ca. 220) defended Christianity intellectually in *The Apology,* socially in many works dealing with various aspects of Christian living, and politically in letters to Roman officials.

11. The last of the classical Gr. apologists and perhaps the greatest was Origen,* who wrote 8 books *Against Celsus* (ca. 248). He refutes Celsus' attacks on the reliability of Scripture and the disciples as reporters of what happened, proceeds to defend the Incarnation and the Resurrection, and concludes by showing that the Christians are loyal in their own way to the Roman ideals. WWO

See also *Christian Church, History of,* I 2; *Lactantius Firmianus.*

J. Otto, *Corpus Apologetarum,* 9 vols. (Jena, 1847 to 1872); P. Carrington, *Christian Apologetics of the Second Century in Their Relation to Modern Thought* (London, 1921); *ANF,* I—IV; J. Quasten, *Patrology,* I (Westminster, Md., 1950); E. J. Goodspeed, *Index Apologeticus* (Leipzig, 1912); J. Geffcken, *Zwei griechische Apologeten* (Leipzig, 1907); "The Apology of Aristides on Behalf of the Christians," Syr. text ed. J. R. Harris, with appendix with Gk. text ed. J. A. Robinson, in Cambridge *Texts and Studies,* I, No. 1 (1891); Origen, *Contra Celsum,* tr. and ed. H. Chadwick (Cambridge, Eng., 1953); R. Grant, "Studies in the Apologists," *Harvard Theological Review, LI* (1958), 123—134; *MPG,* 2, 1159—86 (Diognetus); 6 (Justin, Tatian, Athenagoras, Theophilus); 11, 641—1632 (Origen, *Contra Celsum*); *MPL,* 3, 201—672 (Minucius Felix); see also bibliography under *Origen* and *Tertullian.*

Apology of the Augsburg Confession. See *Lutheran Confessions,* A 3.

Apology of the Book of Concord. See *Chemmitz, Martin; Kirchner, Timotheus; Selnecker, Nikolous.*

Apophthegmata Patrum (4th—5th c.). Sayings of Egyptian monks.

MPL, 73; 74, 10—516; *MPG,* 65, 71—440.

Aportanus, George (George of Deure; d. 1530). E Frisian reformer.

Apostasy (Backsliding; Gk., literally "from standing"). A total lapsing from principles or faith. The NT mentions as causes of apostasy: the putting away of faith and a good conscience (1 Ti 1:19, 20); listening to seducing spirits and doctrines of devils (1 Ti 4:1; 2 Ti 4:4); shallowness (Lk 8:13); lack of spiritual insight (Jn 6:63-65); love of the world (2 Ti 4:10; Mt 19:22). The OT gives, among others, the following reasons: absence of spiritual leaders (Ex 32:1); evil company (1 Ki 11:4); worldly success (Ps 78:57; Hos 6:4; Zph 1:6).

Apostles' Creed. See *Ecumenical Creeds,* A.

Apostolic Benediction. See *Benedictions.*

Apostolic Camera. See *Curia,* 2 f.

Apostolic Canon. See *Apostolic Constitutions.*

Apostolic Chancery. See *Curia,* 2 f.

Apostolic Christian Church (Nazarean). See *Evangelistic Association,* 2; *Holiness Churches,* 2.

Apostolic Christian Churches of America. See *Evanlistic Associations,* 2; *Holiness Churches,* 2.

Apostolic Church Directory. 35 articles pertaining to ch. morals and discipline written in the 4th c. but ascribed to the apostles.

Apostolic College. See *College Apostolic.*

Apostolic Constitutions (and *Canons*). Ancient collection of ecclesiastical precepts, ostensibly regulations for the organization and govt. of the church put out by the apostles. Some of the older sections may go back to the 4th c. and even beyond, but the present form goes back to about the 8th c. There are 8 books of the *Constitutions* and 85 *Canons,* the latter going back to a greater antiquity than the *Constitutions* and being possibly based upon traditions handed down from the early 2d c. The collection is interesting not only for its regulations, but esp. for its list of canonical books.

ANF, VII, 385—508; *MPG,* I, 510—1156; J. Quasten, *Patrology,* II (Westminster, Md., 1953.)

Apostolic Datary. See *Curia,* 2 f.

Apostolic Delegate. See *Legates.*

Apostolic Episcopal Church. See *Eastern Orthodox Churches,* 6.

Apostolic Faith Mission. See *Evangelistic Associations,* 3; *Holiness Bodies,* 2.

Apostolic Fathers. Significant Christian writers and writings of the period immediately following the NT. See also *Patristics,* 3.

1. *Clement of Rome.* A disciple of Peter and Paul; bp. of Rome, 92—101 (Eusebius); first of the "Apostolic Fathers." Many legends about him (consecrated by Peter; Clement of Ph 4:3; *Martyrium Clementis*). Of many writings ascribed to him, only the 1st Epistle to the Corinthians (in which he seeks to persuade a group of rebellious members of the congregation to be obedient to the presbyters who had been appointed by approved men) is considered authentic (ca. 96). He was well-read in the OT Scriptures, but his understanding of Pauline grace is not always clear and precise.

2. *Ignatius of Antioch.* 3d bp. of Antioch; martyred, acc. to tradition (Eusebius, *HE,* III, xxxvi), under Trajan, ca. 112. On his journey to Rome he wrote 7 letters (to the Ephesians, Magnesians, Trallians, Philadelphians, Smyrneans, Polycarp, and the Romans) which stress respect for bps. and oppose Docetism* and Judaizing tendencies. The letter to the Romans pleads with the Christians there not to prevent his martyrdom. The integrity of the epistles (of which there are various recensions) is established. They demonstrate Ignatius' determination to encourage the "monarchial episcopate" and influenced later developments within the ch.

3. *Polycarp* (ca. 69–ca. 156). Bp. Smyrna; disciple of John and friend of Ignatius; supported Asiatic view of celebration of Easter at Rome; burned at stake during persecution under Antoninus Pius; man of piety and zeal. Surviving work is a letter to the Philippians introducing the Epistles of Ignatius to them. Martyrdom described in a letter by the Smyrneans to the ch. of Philomelium.

4. *Papias* (ca. 150). Bp. of Hierapolis; disciple of John (?); friend of Polycarp; Eusebius accused him of chiliasm and other "strange sayings." Wrote *Exposition of the Lord's Oracles,* of which fragments remain. These treat the origin of Matthew and Mark. His statement concerning "presbyter John" occupies a prominent place in the isagogical discussion of the Fourth Gospel.

5. *Shepherd of Hermas.* Acc. to best scholarship written between 105 and 135 by a Roman Christian, Hermas, identified as the brother of Pius, bp. of Rome. Contains 5 visions, 12 mandates, 10 similitudes. Central thought is exhortation to repentance in view of impending Parousia. Assures 2d repentance for sins after Baptism. Though of slight literary merit, it was highly esteemed in early ch. and included at times in canon.

6. *Barnabas, Epistle of.* Originated in Egypt ca. 130; characterized by extreme allegorical interpretation of OT; enabled Christians to find Christ in every incident of OT. Written to Christians in danger of lapsing into Judaism. Ascription to Barnabas of NT considered false by modern scholars.

7. *Epistle to Diognetus.* Beautiful in style, this epistle is one of the earliest productions of the ch. which survives. Addressed to Diognetus,* perhaps the teacher of Marcus Aurelius. Last 2 chapters are by another hand (Hippolytus?). Compares relation of Christians and world with that of soul and body.

8. *The Didache (Teaching of the Twelve Apostles).* Written ca. 150 (some scholars hold that parts of it were written as early as 50); discovered by P. Bryennios* 1873; it was intended for use in instruction prior to Baptism. The first part (1—6) presents under the image of the two ways of life and death moral precepts which the catechumen was to know before Baptism. The 2d part (perhaps for after Baptism) gives instructions regarding Baptism, fasts, prayers, Eucharist, and "offices." The use of a somewhat different document in *Barnabas* and variant recensions indicate that the source for the *Didache* was some early Christian document for converts (perhaps based on a manual for Jewish proselytes). EL, HTM

J. B. Lightfoot, *The Apostolic Fathers,* ed. and completed J. R. Harmer (London, 1926); *The Apostolic Fathers,* ed. and tr. K. Lake, 2 vols. (London, 1925, 1930; T. F. Torrance, *The Doctrine of Grace in the Apostolic Fathers* (Edinburgh, 1948); Committee of the Oxford Society of Historical Theology, *The New Testament in the Apostolic Fathers* (Oxford, 1905); J. P. Quasten, *Patrology,* I (Westminster, Md., 1950); *The Apostolic Fathers, A New Translation and Commentary,* ed. R. M. Grant, 6 vols. in progress (Camden, 1964—).

Apostolic Lutheran Church of America (formerly Finnish Apostolic Lutheran Church). See *Finnish Lutherans in America,* 4.

Apostolic Lutherans. See *Finnish Lutherans in America,* 4.

Apostolic Overcoming Holy Church of God. See *Holiness Churches,* 2.

Apostolic See (Lat. "apostolic seat"). Term designating ch. center est. by apostle. RCm: see* or seat of papacy, namely Rome; also called Holy See, Roman See.

Apostolic Succession. Strictly speaking, the term describes the teaching of the E Orthodox, Monophysite, Nestorian, RC, Old Cath., Ch. of S India, and Swed. and certain other Luth. Christians that the ministry of their churches has come down from the apostles in an unbroken succession of bps. Of those named above, the Luths., the Ch. of S India, and some Anglicans regard the apostolic succession merely as a valuable symbol of continuity with the past, in a class with the creeds and the liturgy, and do not make it a test of the validity of a clergyman's ministry. E Orthodox, Monophysite, Nestorian, RC and some Angl. Christians gen. regard it as necessary to the existence of the church and to the valid ministration of most sacraments; RCs make a special point of the succession of the bps. of Rome from Peter. The hist. fact of the apostolic succession can be assumed with reasonable safety after the emergence of the monarchial episcopate as the normal form of govt. in the ch.; the demonstration of the hist. fact in the crucial period immediately after the apostles is beset with insurmountable difficulties.

Although the Luth. symbols affirm the desire to retain the apostolic succession and hist. episcopate (Ap XIV 1, 5) only a few canonically consecrated bps. accepted the Reformation and, except in Swed., political and other considerations prevented them from transmitting the apostolic succession to the Luth. community. Lacking bps. to ordain their candidates for the sacred ministry, the Luths. appealed to the patristically attested facts that originally bps. and priests constituted only one order; that the right to ordain was inherent in the priesthood (a principle on which a number of popes of the 15th c., among them Boniface IX, Martin V, and Innocent VIII, acted in authorizing Cistercian abbots who were only priests to ordain); that thence "an ordination administered by a pastor in his own church is valid by divine law" (Tractatus 65); and that when the canonical bps. refuse to impart ordination "the churches are compelled by divine law to ordain pastors and ministers, using their own pastors for this purpose *(adhibitis suis pastoribus)*" (ibid., 72). The succession of the ministry in the Luth. Ch. may therefore be presumed to be a valid presbyterial one.

Episc. polity does not imply apostolic succession;

the Luth. provincial churches in Ger. and the Meth. Ch. in the US are cases in point. In other cases, an episc. succession originated in a consecration by a clergyman in priest's orders, e. g., in the Luth. Ch. in Den., Nor., Iceland. The apostolic succession of the medieval Waldensians, and hence of the Moravian Unitas Fratrum, also rests on improbable legends. Many "wandering bishops" *(episcopi vagantes)* claim to stand in some Old Cath., E Orthodox, Nestorian, or Monophysite succession, but their competence validly to ordain and to consecrate is gen. denied by the bodies from whom they claim episc. descent.

The term "apostolic succession" is at times applied in a broad, nontechnical sense to a succession of doctrine or of believers from the apostles; but this is misleading.

A. Ehrhardt, *The Apostolic Succession in the First Two Centuries of the Church* (London, 1953); Hans Freiherr von Campenhausen, *Kirchliches Amt und geistliche Vollmacht in den ersten drei Jahrhunderten;* (Tübingen, 1953); E. Benz, *Bischofsamt und apostolische Sukzession im deutschen Protestantismus* (Stuttgart, 1953); T. W. Manson, *The Church's Ministry* (London, 1948); K. E. Kirk and others, *The Apostolic Ministry* (London, 1946); H. Brandreth, *Episcopi Vagantes and the Anglican Church,* 2d ed. (London, 1961). ACP

Apostolic Synod. See *Councils and Synods,* 1.

Apostolicam actuositatem. See *Vatican Councils,* 2.

Apotaxis. Renunciation of Satan at baptism (E Orthodox).

Apotelesmata. All official acts of Christ as Prophet, Priest, and King performed acc. to both, divine and human natures, e. g., dying for the sins of the world, destroying the works of the devil, being present with, and ruling and protecting, His ch. (FC SD VIII 46–47)

Apotheosis. Elevation of human beings to rank of gods. Instances found among Assyrians, Egyptians, and Persians in antiquity. Ancient Greeks deified mythical heroes, e. g., Hercules. Romans long accorded this token of respect alone to Romulus, founder of their city; later the emperor (e. g., Caesar, Augustus) and even women of the imperial court were given divine status by senate decree.

Appenzeller, Henry G. (Feb. 5, 1858—June 11, 1902). B. Souderton, Pa.; educ. Franklin and Marshall Coll. (Lancaster, Pa.) and Drew Theol. Sem. (Madison, N. J.); M. E. miss. to Korea 1885; pres. Pai Chai Coll., Seoul, and head of theol. dept.; pastor of 3 churches; ed. *Korean Christian Advocate;* helped tr. Bible into Korean; d. in sea accident.

W. E. Griffis, "Henry G. Appenzeller, of Korea," *The Missionary Review of the World,* Old Series, XXXV (April 1912), 271—282.

Approbation. Formal judgment of a Roman prelate declaring a priest fit to hear confession. Without it the absolution of a secular priest is held invalid.

Apse. That part of a ch., often semicircular and vaulted, in which the altar is situated on an elevated platform. See also *Church Architecture,* 3.

Aquaviva, Claudio (Claudius Acquaviva; 1543 to 1615). Jesuit 1567; 5th general of the order 1581; promoted *Spiritual Exercises* of Ignatius Loyola;* active in controversy on grace between Dominicans and Jesuits; under him the *Ratio atque institutio studiorum* (regulations for Jesuit officials and teachers) was put into final form (definitive ed. 1599) and imposed on the order; organized compilation of annual reports *(Litterae annuae;* 1583—). See also *Counter Reformation,* 8.

Aquila. See *Bible Versions,* A 2.

Aquila, Kaspar (Adler; 1488—1560). B. Augsburg; d. Saalfeld. Educ. Leipzig and Wittenberg. Pastor at Jengen, near Augsburg. Drawn to the Reformation by Luther's writings. In prison at Dillingen. Helped Luther tr. OT at Wittenberg. Pastor (1527) and Supt. (1528) at Saalfeld; dean Collegiate Inst., Schmalkalden, 1550. Engaged in controversy with Agricola, Osiander, and Major. See also *Sickingen, Franz von.*

Aquinas, Thomas. See *Thomas Aquinas.*

Arabia. See *Middle East,* L.

Arabic Bible Versions. See *Bible Versions,* F.

Arabic Philosophy. Arab. philosophy originated in Baghdad and is, in part, a synthesis of Hellenic and Oriental philosophies. Hellenic and Oriental writings were tr. into Arab. between 762 and 900 (the Gk. under Nestorian influence). The House of Wisdom, erected 832 under enlightened caliphs, had as its first famous scholar Hunain ibn-Ishaq (Johannitius, ca. 809—ca. 873). This revived learning came to Christians through Muslims in Sicily and Sp. Among outstanding Arab. philosophers were:

Averroes (1126—98); denied freedom of the will and immortality; commentary on Aristotle widely read by Christian scholars despite RC opposition; followed al-Farabi's theory of the soul.

Avicenna (ibn-Sina; 980—1037); famous chiefly as physician; metaphysical writings also widely read in Middle Ages.

al-Farabi (ca. 870–950); sought to support Muhammadan mysticism with Neoplatonism (soul is light emanating from divine intelligence); works include *De divisione philosophiae; De ortu scientiarum;* also wrote on the philosophy of Plato and Aristotle.

al-Ghazzali (1058–1111); "the Muslim Aquinas"; greatest theologian of Muhammadanism.

al-Jahiz (d. 896); attempted to show import in theology of natural phenomena.

al-Kindi (d. ca. 870); Neoplatonist; neo-Pythagorean; considered science and logic basic to theology.

Arab. philosophy influenced not only Jewish thinkers (Avicebron;* Maimonides*), but also Christian and contributed to the rise of scholasticism.*

Scripta Hierosolymitana, Vol. IX: Studies in Islamic History and Civilization, ed. U. Heyd (Jerusalem, 1961); D. B. Macdonald, *Development of Muslim Theology, Jurisprudence and Constitutional Theory* (London, 1903); De Lacy E. O'Leary, *Arabic Thought and Its Place in History* (London, 1939); *Beiträge zur Geschichte der Philosophie* [*und Theologie*] *des Mittelalters* (Münster, 1891—).

Arabs. See *Africa; Middle East.*

Arapaho. See *Indians, American,* 9.

Arator (d. ca. 550). Jurist at court of Ostrogoth king Athalaric; later deacon at Rome; Ligurian Christian poet. Wrote *De actibus Apostolorum.*

Arawaks. See *Caribbean Islands,* B.

Arbeitsgemeinschaft freier evangelisch-lutherischer Kirchen in Deutschland. See *Germany, Lutheran Free Churches in,* 14.

Arbousset, Jean Thomas (1810—1877). Fr. Prot.; educ. Montauban and Miss. House, Paris; miss. in Basutoland 1832; returned to Paris 1863; reorganized miss. in Tahiti; pastor Poitou, Fr. Wrote *Relation d'un voyage d'exploration au nord-est de la colonie du cap de Bonne-Espérance, entrepris dans les mois de mars, avril et mai 1836* and a description of Tahiti and adjacent islands.

Arcadia Association. See *Young People's Associations, Christian,* II 3.

Arcani Disciplina. See *Disciplina Arcani.*

Archaeological Periods. See *Time.*

Archaeology, Biblical. The task of Biblical archaeology is to find out how people in Bible times lived, built their homes, cooked their meals, buried their dead, and worshiped. For answers to these questions the archaeologist looks for a mound or a "tell" in the gen. area where a Biblical city once stood. Some important mounds (e. g., Ugarit and Mari in

Syria) were found by chance. Others beckoned because they were sites of such well-known ancient cities as Jerusalem and Jericho. Mounds like Gibeah and Mizpah were chosen for digging because they are conveniently located along the main highway. Soundings were made at other mounds because the surface sherds gave promise of important finds.

A basic unit of 6 natives probes into a mound. The pickman loosens the earth and exposes objects with a short-handled pick. The hoeman scrapes the loosened earth together with a hoe and sifts it for objects. Then he scoops the loosened earth into rubber baskets which 4 basket men carry to the excavation dump.

A trained field supervisor, responsible to the director, is in charge of each unit and cooperates with such other staff members as the photographer, architect, surveyor, and recorder.

The director and staff lay plans before the operation begins. Squares are laid out; measurements are taken; records are kept at strategic points on the mound. The first objective is to note where the surface level stops and a new layer of soil begins (recognized by the softness or hardness of soil, change in color, difference in texture). The potsherds and other objects found above such a level are sorted and kept separate from objects found lower. A change in the stratum may represent a shift in occupation. A hard surface may point to the fact that the floor level of a building has been reached; an effort is then made to find the walls of the building. Walls of mud, brick, or stone may be discovered first; then the floor must be correlated with the walls.

In the digging process any disturbances that occurred between floor levels must be noted. Later settlements often caused objects to shift from level to level. A cistern or a silo may cut directly through 3 or 4 lower levels. Such disturbances not only ruin valuable evidence but may lead the excavator to erroneous conclusions.

Potsherds, often broken into many pieces, are the most important objects to be sorted. On a large scale excavation as many as 100 baskets of potsherds are brought down from the mound daily. The handles, rims, and bases are separated from the body sherds and all are washed. The sorted pottery is laid out on straw mats and arranged for study at the end of the day. The director goes over the finds with the supervisor who guided their removal, notes where they were found, and has them packed and sent to headquarters. A pottery expert can tell within 50 to 100 yrs. to which archaeological age a piece of broken pottery belongs. When such information is correlated with the level or stratum at which it has been found, important conclusions for the hist. of the mound are drawn.

Each supervisor keeps records of the square in which he is working. He makes a top plan daily (diagram of the surface as it looks on each day of operation). Each of the 4 walls (sections) of the square reveals a set of lines representing the floors or occupation levels that have been dug through. The diagram of each section is drawn to scale to show the stratification. All artifacts found are recorded in 3 dimensions, so that a look at the floor plan or section drawing reveals exactly where the object was discovered.

No potsherd or artifact has been found that can be connected with the people of Israel prior to their entrance into the land of Canaan in the 13th c. B. C. The only reference to the Israelites in Egyptian literature is the stela of Merneptah from ca. 1220 BC.

Archaeology shows that the Genesis accounts concur remarkably with evidence noted in Palestine. Archaeological investigation has shown that the Middle Bronze Age (2200—1550 BC) was one of the most significant periods in the hist. of the ancient world, when the massive fortification systems of the Hyksos were built and when horses and chariots were introduced. In biblical terms this includes the time from the patriarchs to the sojourn in Egypt. Genesis 1—11 fits into this archaeological picture as a summary or review of everything in the ancient world prior to the Middle Bronze Age, including the great Early Bronze city states of 3000 BC, the proto-urban settlements of 4000 BC, and the period of the early Neolithic food gatherers and producers around 6000 BC.

There are close parallels between the findings of archaeology and the records of the Bible from the 13th c. BC on. Mounds reveal that Palestine was pillaged in the 13th c. BC. It may be reasonably concluded that this was done by the incoming Israelites. Remains of Adamah and Zarethan, which the Bible mentions in connection with the crossing of the Jordan, have been found 18 and 30 mi. N of Jericho (Jos 3:16). These cities were assoc. with the production of bronze vessels for Solomon's temple (1 K 7:45-46). Recent excavations at Zarethan and Succoth show that bronze ware was made there.

Help for understanding the time of the Judges has been unearthed by archaeology. Excavations at Shechem have uncovered the temple of Baal-berith (Ju 9:4) and shed light on the oak tree and the great stone (Jos 24:26). Operations at Taanach have called attention to a violent destruction there during the 12th c. This helps us understand Deborah's claim that in her fight with the kings of Canaan at Taanach they obtained no spoils of silver (Ju 5:19). It was the rise of the sea powers which put the Philistines into the advantageous position of maintaining a monopoly on iron, thus putting the Israelites at a disadvantage in defending themselves (1 S 13:19-20).

Both Megiddo and Hazor have shed light on the age of Solomon (cf. 1 K 9:15, 19). That Solomon converted Megiddo into a great chariot center is indicated by the complex of stables from his time found there. At Hazor a casemate wall and a city gate from the 10th c. show that Solomon strengthened the city as a defense for the Plain of Huleh.

Tirzah and Samaria (capitals of N Kingdom) have been excavated. Evidence of a destructive fire in the palace at Tirzah may point to Zimri, who took his own life rather than surrender to Omri (1 K 16:18). Omri probably chose to move his capital from Tirzah to Samaria, because the former had no outlet to the W and to commercial enterprises of the Medit. world (1 K 16:23-24). Excavations revealed that Omri and Ahab built a double wall around the strategic hill of Samaria; the wall explains why it took besiegers 3 yrs. to force Samaria to surrender (2 K 17:5-6).

Perhaps the best preserved of all important antiquities in Jerusalem is Hezekiah's tunnel (2 K 20:20). Ca. 1750 ft. long, built to provide water for Jerusalem in a siege, it leads from the Gihon spring to the pool of Siloam. The Siloam inscription was found on its walls. Recent digging in Jerusalem has confirmed the view that an earlier vertical shaft leading upward from the Gihon spring into the city was the passage which gave Joab access to the inner city to open the gates for David and his army (2 Sm 5:6-8).

Archaeological method has been improved and refined during the 20th c. The school established by W. F. Albright has shown that archaeology provides effective control over hypotheses of hist. and literary criticism and provides an excellent background for Bible study.

See also *Geography, Christian.*

W. F. Albright, *The Archaeology of Palestine* (Middlesex, 1949); K. Kenyon, *Archaeology in the Holy Land* (London, 1960); G. E. Wright, *Biblical Archaeology,* rev. and enl. ed. (Philadelphia, 1963); H. J. Franken and C. A. Franken-Battershill, *A*

Primer of Old Testament Archaeology (Leiden, 1963); L. H. Grollenberg, *Atlas of the Bible,* tr. and ed. J. Reid and H. Rowley (New York, 1956); R. E. M. Wheeler, *Archaeology from the Earth* (New York, 1954); A. G. Barrois, *Manuel d' archéologie biblique,* 2 vols. (Paris, 1939, 1953); *Ancient Near Eastern Texts Relating to the Old Testament,* ed. J. B. Pritchard (Princeton, 1950); *The Biblical Archaeologist,* pub. by the Am. Schools of Oriental Research, New Haven, Conn. AvRS

Archangel. See *Angels, Good,* 5.

Archbishop. Title given originally (4th c.) to patriarchs and bps. of important dioceses. Later designated a metropolitan* presiding over an ecclesiastical province. In the Luth. Ch. the chief bps. of Swed., Fin., Estonia, and Latvia bear the title. See also *Titular Bishop.*

Archdeacon. Originally (and still gen. in E churches) the title of the chief deacon in a diocese. In the W the title had by the 9th c. come to designate a priest in charge of an archdeaconry, an administrative subdivision of a diocese. To a degree this is still true of archdeacons (styled "Venerable") in the Angl. Ch., though their duties vary. In the RC Ch. it is usually only a title of honor that may be given to the ranking member(s) of a chapter.

Archdiocese. See *Archbishop.*

Archer, Frederic (1838—1901). B. Eng.; educ. London and Leipzig; organist London and (1881) New York; conductor Boston Oratorio Soc. and Pittsburgh Orchestra; deeply interested in liturgics and hymnology.

Arches, Court of (Arches Court). Angl. court of appeal for the Archdiocese or Province of Canterbury. Named after St. Mary of the Arches (Lat. *de Arcubus,* rare ablative plural of *arcus;* cf. Vulgate 2 Esd 4:13), London, where it formerly met; the ch. took its name from arches of the original 11th-c. ch. on the site.

Archimandrite. Head of monasteries; high ranking official in the E Ch.

Architecture, Ecclesiastical. See *Church Architecture.*

Archives. Records, resources, and hist. data have been preserved by the ch. through the ages, often with a view to their immediate usefulness and value to a parish, miss., ch. officials, or religious movement. Records and resources pertaining to the churches in Am. have been deposited in theol. sem. libraries, separate archives, and private collections. There are more than 500 such depositories in Am.

Accessibility of archives increases their value. Their completeness, the care with which they have been gathered, and the exhaustiveness of their research potential are important.

Though there are ca. 80 depositories of Luth. resources, basic records of Lutheranism in Am. may be found in ca. 6 chief collections.

The most complete depository of Luth. hist. resources is maintained by LCMS. Its Dept. of Archives and Hist., Conc. Hist. Inst., is at Conc. Sem., St. Louis; it includes archives of the former Nat. Ev. Luth. Ch. Its collections were begun in the 19th c.; a separate corporation was formed 1927. Its book, pamphlet, and periodical collection exceeds 37,000 volumes; its MS collections include several million items; its microfilm collection is in excess of 50,000 ft.; its museum collection includes more than 1,000 items. In conjunction with the library of Conc. Sem., St. Louis, a wide span of hist. resources are available.

The official archives of the former ALC are at Wartburg Sem., Dubuque, Iowa. Much original source material pertaining to the former Ohio Syn. is at Capital U., Columbus, Ohio. The archives of the former ELC are at Luther Theol. Sem., St. Paul, Minn. Both serve as depositories of the present ALC.

The archives of the LCA are at the Luth. School of Theol. at Chicago. Related collections are at Augustana Coll., Rock Island, Ill., with extensive resources pertaining to the Aug. Luth. Ch.; Grand View Coll., Des Moines, Iowa (esp. former AELC resources); Suomi Coll., Hancock, Mich. (materials pertaining to the former Fin. Ev. Luth. Ch.); and for the constituent parts of the former ULC, both at the Luth. Theol. Sem., Gettysburg, Pa., and the Luth. Theol. Sem., Philadelphia. Southern Luth. records are at the Luth. Theol. Southern Sem., Columbia, S. C.

Records and resources pertaining to the NLC, including resources on Luth. inter-ch. movements, are in the NLC library, New York. Additional archives are at Luther Coll., Decorah, Iowa; Augsburg Coll., Minneapolis, Minn.; Northwestern Luth. Theol. Sem., Minneapolis, Minn., and the Norw.-Am. Hist. Assoc., Northfield, Minn.

Regional, dist., or syn. collections are in the various ch. headquarters in the US and Can. The Luth. Hist. Conf., a cooperative agency for Luth. archivists, librarians, and historians, was organized 1962. Meeting biennially, the Conf. endeavors to coordinate and stimulate hist. efforts and provide channels of communication and cooperation for Luth. archivists, librarians, and historians.

The only journal of Luth. hist. in Am., *Concordia Historical Institute Quarterly,* has been pub. since 1928. ARS

A. R. Suelflow, *Directory of Religious Archival and Historical Depositories in America* (Church Records Committee, Society of American Archivists; mimeographed; Conc. Hist. Institute; St. Louis, 1963).

Archontics. See *Gnosticism,* 7 i.

Arensius, Bernhardus Antonius (variants include Ahrens; Arnzius; d. 1691). Luth. pastor NYC 1671-91; came from Holland; successor of Jacob Fabritus* at Trin. Luth. Ch., Broadway and Rector St.; directed the building of a 2d ch. after the 1st. erected 1671, was demolished 1673 by the Dutch; his gentle character contrasted favorably with the despotic tendencies of Fabritius.

Arenski, Anton (1861—1906). Russ. composer whose works, sacred and secular, are often catchy and pretty rather than virile and strong.

Ares. See *Greek Religion,* 2.

Aretius, Benedictus (Grecized from Marti; ca. 1522 to 74). Scientist and theologian; prof. of Gk. and Heb., later of theology, Bern; wrote in area of botany, classics, Heb., theology. Works include *Examen theologicum; Problemata theologica.*

Argentina. See *Lutheran Church – Missouri Synod, Districts of The,* B 2; *South America,* 1.

Argula von Grumbach (von Stauff). See *Grumbach, Argula von.*

Arianism. Heresy that engulfed many areas of the ch. esp. 320—380.

1. *Origin.* Arius (d. 336), a priest in a suburb of Alexandria, sought to combine the adoptionism of Paul of Samosata* with the Neoplatonic idea of divine transcendence and utter inaccessibility of God. God was described as an abstract monad, alone unbegotten, without equal, unchangeable, ineffable. Since God could not create the world directly because of His very nature, He created out of nothing, "before all times and eons," an intermediate being, exalted above other creatures, through whom He created the world. This intermediate being is the Logos, called "Son," who is not true God and not eternal. Some went so far as to teach that the Logos was dissimilar *(anomoios)* from the Father in essence. In time this being took human flesh, not inherently sinless, but capable of moral progress, choosing the good and continuing therein.

2. *Controversy.* Alexander, bp. of Alexandria,

called a council which deposed and excommunicated Arius, who continued to defend himself and found powerful supporters in Eusebius of Nicomedia* and Eusebius of Caesarea.* Emp. Constantine advised all involved to overlook trivia and agree on fundamentals. When this advice failed, perhaps on the advice of Hosius,* Constantine summoned the 1st ecumenical council to meet at Nicaea.* There the formula proposed by the Arians was laughed out of session. But the vast majority could not agree on a positive statement. One group, following Eusebius of Caesarea, did not agree with Arius, but did insist that the godhead was of 3 hypostasies. When the W bps. would not agree to this formula, fearing it would lead to Arianism, and insisted on the statement that God is One in essence *(homoousios),* a long standing suspicion between Gk. and Lat. teachers came to the surface. Those who insisted on the 3 hypostasies believed that a simple statement of *homoousios* would lead to modalism. Therefore they used the term *homoiousios* ("of like essence") to preserve the identity of each. These were later designated "Eusebians." They signed the Creed of Nicaea but only upon assurances from Constantine that it did not involve modalism.

3. *Issue.* After Nicaea there was constant quarreling between these 2 positions. The quarrel allowed the Arians to retain their positions. As long as Constantine lived, a balance was retained, but with his death and a redivision of the empire bet. his sons, one of whom supported the W and the other the E position, the teachers of the ch. fell into bitter provocation and acrimony. Athanasius even called the Gks. Semi-Arians. Constantius, who ultimately was dominant, had no interest in theology and was interested only in settlement. He deposed any bp. who stood for a strong position, especially the homoousians. Only with Constantius' death were the various parties to this dispute able to get together and settle the matter. This settlement, worked out by Hilary* of Poitiers and Ambrose of Milan in the W with Basil of Caesarea and Athanasius in the E, was formalized by the Council of Constantinople, 381. The godhead was designated *homoousios* made up of 3 distinct hypostasies, 1 substance in 3 persons. This council is also said to have drawn up what we call the Nicene Creed.

4. Prominent anti-Arians include the Cappadocian* Theologians.

See also *Jerusalem, Synoda of, Subordinationism.*

C. J. Hefele, *A History of the Councils of the Church,* tr. and ed. W. R. Clark, Vols. I, II (Edinburgh, 1894, 1896); H. M. Gwatkin, *Studies of Arianism,* 2d ed. (Cambridge, 1900) and "Arianism," *Cambridge Medieval History, Vol. I: The Christian Roman Empire,* ed. H. M. Gwatkin and J. P. Whitney (New York, 1924), pp. 118—142; J. N. D. Kelly, *Early Christian Creeds,* 2d ed. (New York, 1960); H. Lietzmann, *A History of the Early Church,* tr. B. L. Woolf, vols. III, IV (Cleveland, 1961). WWO

Arias Montano, Benito (1527—98). Sp. theologian; present at Council of Trent; chief ed. of Antwerp Polyglot. See also *Polyglot Bibles.*

Aristides (2d c.). Gk. Christian apoloigst. See also *Apologists,* 3.

Aristion (1st c.). Regarded by Papias as a primary authority (with "the Presbyter John") for the traditions of the Lord (Eusebius, *HE,* III, xxxix, 4).

Aristippus (ca. 435—ca. 356 BC). Gk. philosopher; originally of Cyrene; founder of Cyrenaic* school. See also *Socrates.*

Aristo of Pella (ca. 140). Apologist. Wrote *Disputation Between Jason and Papiscus Concerning Christ* (Origen, *Contra Celsum,* IV, lii; Eusebius, *HE,* IV, vi, 3). See also *Apologists,* 9.

Aristobulus (2d c. BC). Alexandrian, Jewish, Hellenistic, religious philosopher quoted by Clement, Origen, Eusebius. Claimed that the Torah, interpreted allegorically, contained the sum of Gk. philosophy.

Aristotle (384—322 BC). 1. Aristotle was born in the Gk. colony of Stagira on the Macedonian peninsula Chalcidice, the son of Nicomachus, court physician to Amyntas II, king of Macedon and father of Philip II of Macedon. In his 18th year Aristotle was sent to Athens, where he remained in close assoc. with the Academy for 20 years, until the death of Plato.* Leaving Athens, Aristotle resided with friends of the Academy first at Atarneus, in the Troad, and then at Mitylene, on the island of Lesbos, where he engaged in biological research. Invited by Philip to take charge of his son's educ., Aristotle became tutor to Alexander the Great, probably for the yrs. just preceding Alexander's appointment as regent for his father. In 335/4 Aristotle returned to Athens, where he labored 12 yrs. in the Lyceum, instituting and pursuing a program of investigation in almost every branch of human knowledge, and composing at least the more scientific portions of his now extant writings. An outburst of anti-Macedonian feeling at Athens in 323 precipitated Aristotle's flight — lest the Athenians should "sin twice against philosophy" — to Chalcis in Euboea, where he died in 322, within a little more than a yr. of the deaths of Alexander and Demosthenes.

2. The Aristotelian corpus, excluding doubtful and spurious works, includes (1) the logical treatises of the *Organon: Categories, De interpretatione, Prior analytics, Posterior analytics, Topics,* and *Sophistici elenchi;* (2) the treatises on natural science now distinguished as (a) physical science: *Physics, De coelo, De generatione et corruptione,* and *Meteorologica;* (b) psychology: *De anima* and a collection of shorter works known as *Parva naturalia;* (c) biology: *Historia animalium, De partibus animalium, De motu* and *De incessu animalium,* and *De generatione animalium; and* (d) *Problemata;* (3) first philosophy, or *Metaphysics;* (4) the treatises on practical science distinguished as (a) ethics: *Nicomachean Ethics* (named after his son Nicomachus) and *Eudemian Ethics* (named after Eudemus, one of his pupils); and (b) politics: *Politics, and Constitution of Athens;* (5) the treatises on productive science: *Rhetoric* and *Poetics,* both dealing with literary arts. The standard ed. of the Gk. text is that of Bekker (Berlin Academy, 1831—70). A complete Eng. tr. of the works included in the Berlin ed. was prepared under the editorship of W. D. Ross (Oxford, 1908—31).

3. The logic of Aristotle, by him called "analytic," is a discipline prior to all others, setting forth the requirements of scientific inquiry and proof. Science, in the strict sense, is demonstrated knowledge of the causes of things. Such demonstrated knowledge is obtained by syllogistic deduction from premises in themselves certain — thus science differs from dialectic, which employs probable premises, and from eristic, which aims not at truth, but at forensic victory. The Aristotelian logic of terms, propositions, and syllogisms depends not merely on formal relations exemplified in statement of proof, but on the possibility of discovering principles, i. e., universals and causes, which are true of nature. Aristotle is fond of tracing the transition in knowledge from the particulars of sense experience (the things more knowable to us) to the universals present in an inchoate way in sensation but grasped by intuitive reason or *nous* (the things more knowable in themselves). He claims to have accounted for human science without reducing knowledge to the motion of atoms, as had Democritus, or transforming things into ideas, as he thought Plato did.

4. The causes, which can be stated as connectives among terms because they are links among the phe-

nomena of nature, are of 4 sorts: material (the stuff of which a thing is made), formal (its essence or nature, *what* it is), efficient (the agency which brings it into being), and final (its end, or that for the sake of which it exists). Thus for Aristotle every sensible object is a union of 2 principles, matter and form — the matter in every case regarded as potentiality for the form which actualizes it. The fact of motion or change is then accounted for as a process by which potential being passes over, through form, into actual being. This analysis Aristotle regards as a triumph over Platonism, which, appealing only to form, left motion unintelligible as a passage from nonbeing to being, and over Democritean atomism, which, reducing scientific explanation to the discovery of material parts, simply assumed motion as a principle.

5. Aristotle proceeds, on the basis of the causes, to divide the sciences into the theoretic, the practical, and the productive. The theoretic sciences have as their end simply to know; as their subject matter "substances," things possessing an internal principle of motion or rest; as their form strict demonstration or necessity; as their agency the "intellectual" virtues of "intuitive reason" and "science" (combined in "philosophic wisdom"), the capacities of grasping first principles and demonstrating from them. The special theoretic sciences are differentiated according to differences found in their subject matters. Physics deals with "common sensible matter," with kinds of sensible natural objects — its subject matter is never purely formal, but always includes matter and motion. Mathematics treats of "intelligent matter," of numbers, points, lines, surfaces, volumes, which cannot exist apart from bodies, yet are abstracted in thought and treated separately in this science. Metaphysics investigates the first principles and causes which are assumed in the separate sciences, and therefore it treats of a substance which not only can be known apart, but which also exists apart from matter and motion, whose existence is established in the famous proof of the necessity of an unmoved mover as the cause of existence and motion. For if there were no separated substance, all sciences would be reduced to physics; and if forms and numbers existed separately, all philos. would be reduced to mathematics.

6. The practical and productive sciences have as their end action (i. e., doing and making, respectively) rather than knowledge; as their subject matter things done and things made, whose principle of motion is in an external agent and which have no natural definitions; their principles are established dialectically, hence their conclusions are only probable; and the virtues required to pursue these sciences are "practical wisdom" and "art." The practical sciences are differentiated as ethics, which treats of individual action, and politics, which treats of forms of community. In his ethics, Aristotle dialectically determines the good for man as the actualization or exercise of his distinctive faculty, reason, in the habitual subordination of appetite to rational principle — it is here that particular moral virtues are defined as means between extremes — and in the search for and contemplation of truth. In *Politics,* concerned with constitutions and forms of human associations which again have no natural definitions, a basis for proportional rules is found in the needs and interdependences of man for the ends of living and of living well — it is in this sense that man is by nature a "political animal." The productive sciences, finally, are differentiated according to their products, and the kinds of art according to the object, means, and manner of their imitation of nature. Thus in *Poetics* tragedy is distinguished by isolating its means of imitation, and the liberal arts are distinguished by their educative influence in preparing men for freedom.

7. The influence of Aristotle on subsequent philos. and science is incalculably extensive. This influence is rendered intricate by the fact that he has been read in widely different ways and adapted to modes of thought to which he explicitly opposed his own. During the Hellenistic period, when nearly all the philosophies reflected the impress of his thought, Aristotle was regarded as merely the most eminent of Plato's disciples, and "peritatetic" signified a specialist in science rather than a philos. In the early Middle Ages there was slight direct contact with his writings, and infiltrations of Gk. thought into Christian philos. was rather Neoplatonic than Aristotelian. In the 12th and 13th c., however, all the works of Aristotle were tr. into Lat. and were made the object of intense study and voluminous commentaries. The revolt of Renaissance philosophers against Aristotle was probably as much against this scholastic mode of discussion as against Aristotle's doctrine. A renaissance of Aristotelian studies in recent decades has been a result of the modern ed. of his works by the Berlin Academy and of the papal blessing of the work of Thomas Aquinas. Aristotle is alive today in neo-scholasticism, in behaviorist psychology, in the vitalism and dynamism of such thinkers as Bergson, and in much of the technical vocabulary, if not in the spirit, of modern science and philos. See also *Natural Law; Psychology,* C. RL

Arius. See *Arianism.*

Arles, Synod of (314). Called by Constantine; first syn. of W; in its 22 canons Donatism is condemned, the desire is expressed for a uniform date for Easter, and heretical baptism is rejected. The canons are esp. significant because of light they shed on ch.-state relations in this formative and critical period.

H. Lietzmann, *A History of the Early Church, Vol. III: From Constantine to Julian,* tr. B. L. Woolf, 2d ed. reprint (New York, 1961).

Armageddon. See *Messianic Hope.*

Armed Forces, Spiritual Care of. See *Armed Services Commission.*

Armed Forces Commission. See *Armed Services Commision,* 12.

Armed Services Commission. 1. Called into being by the Mo. Syn. convention, Cleveland, June, 1935. It organized Feb. 13, 1936. Chief duties are to give ecclesiastical endorsement to qualified pastors for commissions as chaplains in military service, to counsel chaplains, and to minister to the spiritual welfare of synod's members serving in armed forces, and patients in Veterans Administration (VA) Hospitals. The scope of the work increased when the numerical strength of the armed forces of the US was raised through the Selective Service Act in 1940; took on global aspects with WW II. Ex. offices were established 1940 in Chicago and a branch service office in Winnipeg, Canada, 1943. The ex. offices were moved to Washington, D. C., 1948, to be near the Chiefs of Chaplains. When the U. S. became involved in WW II, a comprehensive program was developed under the slogan "They shall not march alone." A unique feature is the roster and mailing list of Mo. Syn. military personnel from which names and addresses are forwarded to Mo. Syn. chaplains and contact and hosp. pastors.

2. The Commission also inaugurated a comprehensive literature program for the serviceman's private devotional life. The *Service Prayer Book* is sent to servicemen in an initial packet including names, addresses, and phone numbers of all Mo. Syn. contact pastors, a Luth. metal identification tag, Head of Christ wallet calendar, and several tracts. Since 1958 the Commission has provided each issue of *Portals of Prayer* for the serviceman's daily devotion. It sends him on request a mimeographed order of service including a meditation for each Sunday. Each month he receives *Loyalty — Christ and Country* (a printed order of service with

sermon), an appropriate tract, and names and latest addresses of Mo. Syn. military chaplains and Luth. Service Centers. During WW II, *At Ease,* a news letter written in a lighter vein, accompanied *Loyalty — Christ and Country.* Since 1951 *Double-Time,* a pocket-size picture magazine containing news of Luths. in service, their dependents, and US civilians stationed overseas, has been mailed to him quarterly. In all, the Commission distributes more than 60 different pieces of literature written specifically for men and women in the armed forces.

3. *The Lutheran Chaplain* has been pub. by the Commission since 1941: monthly during WW II, quarterly since 1954.

4. 359 Mo. Syn. and 2 SELC pastors have served as military chaplains since the beginning of WW II, many of them assigned to very responsible positions, including the post of Chief of Chaplains. In 1963 a Mo. Syn. pastor was appointed Chief of US Navy Chaplains, the first Luth. Chief of Chaplains. It was not uncommon during WW II and the Korean action for chaplains of our ch. to hold from 40 to 79 services a month.

5. At the close of WW II the Commission maintained 47 Luth. Service Centers and 44 Parish Centers, some alone, some with the NLC. In 1951 the Luth. Service Commission, a cooperative agency of the Mo. Syn. and the NLC, was established. This agency (comprising members of the Mo. Syn. and of churches affiliated with the NLC, and functioning under the supervision of the Armed Services Commission and of the NLC's Bureau of Service to Military Personnel) currently operates 43 Service Centers and Program Support Facilities in areas where large numbers of US military personnel are stationed. Service Centers, "homes away from home," staffed by service pastors or secretary-hostesses, provide opportunities for worship, Communion, Bible classes, fellowship with Christians, and soc. and recreational activities. WW II monthly attendances: from 3,000 to 50,000.

6. An important part of the Commission's program is the ministry to patients in VA Hospitals. Each of the 171 VA Hospitals and Facilities is served by a Mo. Syn. VA chaplain, or a full-time hosp. pastor salaried by the Commission, or a volunteer part-time hosp. pastor. Patients receive literature from the Commission each month.

7. Pursuant to a syn. resolution of the 1956 Saint Paul conv., the Commission assumed the added responsibility of ministering to military dependents overseas and to U. S. civilians living overseas at military bases. Their names and addresses are forwarded to the nearest Mo. Syn. chaplain or contact pastor; each month adults receive devotional literature from the Commission; children are provided with Sunday-School-Lessons-By-Mail and other appropriate materials on request.

8. "Christ Church Military Congregation" was established under the Commission's supervision in 1955. Newly baptized and/or confirmed military personnel not near a civilian ch. or whose residence status is so temporary that they cannot be transferred to such a ch. are enrolled in this Washington, D. C., congregation until transfer to a local congregation is feasible. Christ Luth. Ch. sends each mem. a certificate of membership, a Communion Record Card, and a variety of literature, including a personal message from the pastor each month.

9. Three directors serve the Commission: an ex. dir., a dir. of special services (since 1951), and a dir. of publications. At peak activity 50 full-time and 43 part-time persons were employed.

10. At the close of WW II the names of ca. 135,000 US members of the Mo. Syn., the SELC, and the ELS were on file in the Chicago office, and of 4,000 Canadian members in the Winnipeg office. Many more were on file during the war. 4,084 Mo. Syn. members were killed in action or died in service since the beginning of WW II.

11. The key figure is the home pastor, from whom the Commission receives the addresses of members. The Commission makes available to the home pastor, free of charge, 27 different printed items (change of address cards, Communion Record Cards, pre-induction pamphlets, etc.) PLD; LB.

12. First called Army and Navy Commission; name changed 1947 to Armed Services Commission; The name Armed Forces Commission adopted 1965.

Armenia. In W. Asia, bordering on Asia Minor, between the Black and the Caspian Sea and the Taurus and Caucasus Mountains, mainly high tableland. In 1918 the Rep. of Armenia was founded; recognized 1920 by the US, which, however, did not accept a mandate over it. In 1922 part of it, with Azerbaidzhan and Georgia, was incorporated with the Soviet States, but much of former Armenia is now part of Turkey. Area of the Armenian Soviet Socialist Republic: 11,306 sq. mi.; pop.: ca. 2,007,000 (1963).

Religion of Armenia originally much like that of Persia; sun and moon revered; male and female temple prostitutes. Christianity penetrated into this country early, probably from Antioch. Through the efforts of Gregory* the Illuminator, Christianity replaced paganism as the nat. ch. Ca. 420 the Bible was tr. into Armenian. The Armenians maintained their religion despite strenuous efforts of Zoroastrians and Turks to impose their beliefs by unspeakable persecutions, even in recent times. Armenians accept a strict Monophysite* doctrine. Head of the Armenian Ch. is the catholicos or supreme patriarch, elected by nat. council, residing at Echmiadzin; 2 lower patriarchs at Jerusalem and Constantinople. Colonies of Armenians are found in most larger cities in the world; usually remain faithful to their religion. Many emigrated to Am., esp. after the Turkish massacres near the beginning of this c., settling largely in the San Joaquin Valley, Calif. See *Armenians.*

Prot. miss. work was begun 1820 in Armenia by the ABCFM. The Presb. Ch. followed in 1870. Robert Coll., Istanbul, was begun 1863 by Cyrus Hamlin; the Am. Coll. for Girls was est. 1871 at Scutari. OHS

Armenian Bible Versions. See *Bible Versions,* G.

Armenian Evangelical Church in the Near East. See *Middle East,* C.

Armenians. Related to E Orthodox Ch. in doctrine, liturgy, and ch. govt. Holding Monophysite views, they separated from the other E churches at Chalcedon* 451. Turkish persecution 1894 brought many to Am., esp. New Eng., N. Y., and Calif. Some joined Prot. denominations; the majority attempt to perpetuate native language, customs, and religious views and organized The Armenian Apostolic Orthodox Ch. in Am. 1889. Armenian chs. in N. Am. include Armenian Apostolic Ch. of Am.; Diocese of the Armenian Ch. of N. Am. (including Diocese of Calif.); Armenian Apostolic Ch. of Am., Diocese of Can.; Armenian Ev. Ch. in Can.

Arminianism. Term embracing in gen. the teachings of Jacobus Arminius (Jacob Harmensen, or Hermansz, 1560—1609; minister Amsterdam; prof. theol. Leiden). The theol. views of Arminius and his followers were summed up in 5 points, briefly: 1. God from all eternity predestined to eternal life those of whom He foresaw that they would remain steadfast in faith to their end. 2. Christ died for all mankind, not only for the elect. 3. Man cooperates in his conversion by free will. 4. Man may resist divine grace. 5. Man may fall from divine grace. This last tenet was first held but doubtfully; but ultimately it was firmly accepted. The Syn. of Dort (1618—19) condemned the Arminian doctrines, and the civil powers, as was the gen. practice of the age, enforced the decrees of the council by pains and penalties. But the new view spread rapidly. In 1621 Episcopius (1583—1643), at the request of the leading Remonstrants* (Arminians), drew up a formula of faith in 25 chapters, which was widely circulated and subscribed by the most eminent men in Holland and Fr., such as Grotius,* Philip van Limborch (1633—1712; Dutch Remonstrant theol.), Jean Le Clerc (Johannes Clericus; 1657—1736; Swiss Prot. theol.), and Johann Jakob Wettstein* (1693–1754; NT scholar). In Fr. the effect of the controversy appeared in the modified Calvinism of Amyraut.* Abp. Laud introduced Arminianism into the Ch. of Eng., where it was adopted by Cudworth,* Jeremy Taylor,* Tillitson,* Chillingworth,* Pearson,* Whitby,* and others. Arminianism in the Ch. of Eng. at last became a negative term, implying the negation of Calvinism rather than any exact system of theol. Much of what passed for Arminianism was in fact Pelagianism, synergism in some form. A modified Arminianism arose again in Eng. in the Wesleyan Reformation of the 17th c.; its ablest expositions may be found in the works of John Wesley,* John Fletcher,* and Richard Watson; the other Eng. conformists and the Presb. in Scot. and elsewhere continued to be mainly Calvinists. See *Methodist Bodies,* 2; *Baptist Bodies,* 2; *Holiness Bodies; Reformed Churches,* 1; *Salvation Army,* 2. FEM

Armsdorf, Andreas (1670—99). Ger. organist and composer. B. Mühlberg; d. Erfurt. Studied law. Organist at Erfurt. Wrote chamber music and church music, including chorale variations.

Armstrong, Nicholas. See *Catholic Apostolic Church,* 1.

Armstrong, Richard (Apr. 13, 1805—Sept. 23, 1860). B. McEwensville, Pa.; Presb.; grad. Princeton Theol. Sem. 1830; sent to Hawaii by ABCFM 1831; stationed at Haiku and Wailuku, Maui, 1835—40; Honolulu 1840. Active in miss. and govt. affairs. Minister of Pub. Instruction; Pres. Bd. of Educ.; mem. House of Nobles and King's Privy Council; trustee Oahu Coll. and Queen's Hosp.; ex. officer Bible and Tract Soc.

Army and Navy Commission. See *Armed Services Commission,* 12.

Arnaud, Henri (1641—1721). Pastor and soldier. Led group of Waldenses to victory against Fr. and Savoyard armies.

Arnauld, Antoine (1612—94). B. Paris; d. Brussels. Illustrious mem. of famous Fr. family; noted for defense of Jansenism and for attacks on Jesuits.

Arnd(t), Johann (1555—1621). The most influential devotional author the Luth. Ch. has produced. Educ. U. of Helmstedt, Wittenberg, Strasbourg, and Basel; pastor Badeborn, Anhalt, in 1583. In 1590, when the territory became Ref., Arndt was deposed for insisting that he as a Luth. of the unaltered AC had the right to retain the exorcisms at Baptism. Pastor in Quedlinburg (influenced Johann Gerhard), Brunswick, and Eisleben; finally (1611) *Generalsuperintendent* in Celle. His *Four* (later *Five* and *Six*) *Books on True Christianity* and his *Little Garden of Paradise* have perennial and universal appeal; they have rarely been out of print in the original and have been tr. into many languages. Influenced by Luther, he stands solidly in the Luth. mystical tradition that goes back to the Middle Ages and demonstrates great skill in incorporating what is good from a variety of medieval (Tauler, the *Imitation of Christ,** Angela de Foligno,* John von Staupitz) and post-Reformation sources into his thought; speaking to a situation where "every one is very willing to be a servant of Christ, but no one will consent to be His follower" (*True Christianity,* I, Preface, 3), he combines theol. orthodoxy with a profound concern for the practical development of the Christian virtues. In the field of theol. he helped to fix the place of the doctrine of the mystical union of the believer with Christ in the Luth. dogmatic tradition. ACP

Johann Arnd, *Sechs Bücher vom wahren Christentum,* tr. A. W. Boehm, *True Christianity* (London, 1712), ed. C. F. Schaeffer (Philadelphia, 1868).

Arndt, Eduard Louis (Dec. 19, 1864–Apr. 17, 1929). B. Pomerania; grad. St. Louis 1885; pastor Saginaw, Mich., 1885—97; prof. Conc. Coll., St. Paul, Minn., 1897—1910; organized Ev. Luth. Miss. for China May 1, 1912; sent to China July 14, 1912; arrived Shanghai Feb. 25, 1913; est. missions and schools in Hankow territory. Mo. Syn. took over miss. 1917. Wrote *Our Task in China;* ed. *Missionsbriefe;* tr. hymns and sermons into Chinese. Buried Internat. Cemetery, Hankow. See also *China,* 8; *Riedel, Erhardt Albert Henry.*

Brief biography in "Important Events in Lutheran Church History for 1929," *CHIQ,* II (Jan. 1930), 98; E. H. A. Arndt, "The Beginnings of Our Work in China," *CHIQ,* V (Oct. 1932), 98—104; V (Jan. 1933), 137—144; VI (Apr. 1933), 19—24; VI (July (1933), 52—60.

Arndt, Ernst Moritz (1769—1860). Son of Ludwig N. Arndt. Educ. Greifswald and Jena. Prof. Greifswald and Bonn; rector Bonn. Opponent of Napoleon. Wrote hymns and patriotic songs; 14 hymns tr. into Eng.

Arndt, Johann Friedrich Wilhelm (1802—81). Pastor Berlin; famous preacher.

Arndt, William Frederick (Dec. 1, 1880–Feb. 25, 1957). B. Mayville, Wis.; d. Cambridge, Eng.; grad. St. Louis 1903; pastor Bluff City, Tenn., 1903–05; St. Joseph, Mo., 1905—10; Brooklyn, N. Y., 1910—12; prof. St. Paul's Coll., Concordia, Mo., 1912—21; Conc. Sem., St. Louis, 1921—57; on leave of absence to establish a pastoral training program for the Ev. Luth. Ch. of Eng. 1956—57. Secy. W Dist., Mo. Syn., 1912—21; mem. Mo. Syn. Bd. of For. Miss. 1921—56; mem. Com. for Luth. Union 1923—29, 1935—50. Ed. *Magazin für Ev.-luth. Homiletik und Pastoraltheologie* 1924—26; *Theological Monthly* 1926—30; coed. *Concordia Theological Monthly* 1930—38; managing ed. 1938—49; coauthor, *Popular Symbolics;* collaborator, *A Greek-English Lexicon of the New Testament,* a tr. and adaptation of W. Bauer's *Griechisch-Deutsches Wörterbuch.* Other works include *Does the Bible Contradict Itself? "Siehe, ich stehe vor der Tür!" Bible Difficulties; Christian Prayer; Fundamental Christian Beliefs; New Testament History; The Life of St. Paul; From the Nile to the Waters of Damascus; Bible Commentary: The Gospel According to St. Luke.* See also *Lexicons,* B. ARS

P. M. Bretscher, "William Frederick Arndt, 1880 to 1957," CTM, XVIII (June 1957), 401—408.

Arnobius (d. ca. 327). Teacher of rhetoric Sicca, Numidia; first a pagan and opponent of Christianity; after conversion wrote *Adversus nationes* as public avowal of sincerity (reveals great familiarity with classics, but deficient in Biblical and Christian knowledge). See also *Minucius Felix, Marcus.*

See bibliography under *Patristics.*

Arnold, Carl Franklin (1853—1927). B. Williamsfield, Ohio. Prof. ch. hist. Breslau. Wrote on persecutions of Christians (including Salzburgers) and a hist. of the ch. up to Charlemagne.

Arnold, Eberhard (1883—1935). Est. colony in Sannerz and Bruderhof at Fulda for ev. fellowship in life and work.

Arnold, Gottfried (1666—1714). Ger. ev. pietist; for a time follower of Spener, then of J. G. Gichtel (pupil of Böhme). Court preacher at Allstedt. Prolific author of devotional manuals and hymns, all tinged with mysticism. See also *Molinas, Miguel de.*

Arnold, Matthew (1822—88). Eng. poet, critic, and essayist; "the great English apostle of culture." B. Laleham, Middlesex, son of Dr. Thomas Arnold of Rugby; educ. Winchester, Rugby, and Oxford; private secy. to Lord Lansdowne 1847—51; inspector of schools 1851; prof. of poetry, Oxford 1857—67. As literary critic, Arnold propounded the need of maintaining the neglected qualities of dignity, harmony, and simplicity. Chief works: *On Translating Homer; Essays in Criticism* (first series, 1865); *Essays in Criticism* (second series, 1888); *Culture and and Anarchy; St. Paul and Protestantism; Literature and Dogma; God and the Bible; Last Essays on Church and Religion; a Friend of God.* Poems: *Resignation; Self-Dependence; The Scholar Gypsy; Requiescat; Sohrab and Rustum; Dover Beach; Thyrsis; The Last Word; Rugby Chapel.*

Arnold, Thomas (1795—1842). Broad Churchman; b. West Cowes; priest 1828; headmaster (famous for his stimulative influence) Rugby 1828; Prof. of Modern History, Oxford, 1841; d. Rugby. Wrote *History of Rome.*

Arnold of Brescia (ca. 1100—1155). B. probably at Brescia; said to have studied under Abelard; canon regular in It.; attacked worldliness of ch.; returned to Fr.; opposed by Bernard; condemned by Barbarossa; executed at Rome. See also *Waldenses.*

Arnold von Bruck. See *Bruck, Arnold von.*

Arnoldi, Bartholomäus, von Usingen (1462—1532). Teacher, fellow monk, and opponent of Luther. Influenced by William of Occam and the moralism of humanism, he criticized scholasticism and abuses in the ch. but remained in RC Ch. Participated in writing the *Confutation.*

Arnoldshain Theses *(Arnoldshainer Abendmahlsthesen).* Eight theses formulated and approved, November 1—2, 1957, after 1947—57 discussions of the meaning of the Lord's Supper by a commission of Luth., Ref., and *Union* theologians representing the Ev. Ch. of Ger.

The theses, prepared by theologians and not churches, were submitted for discussion to theologians, administrative groups, educators, and congregations of the Ev. churches of Ger. for discussion. The statements do not claim to offer a full exposition of the theol. of the Lord's Supper.

Thesis 4 reads: "The words which our Lord Jesus Christ speaks at the distribution of the bread and the cup tell us what He Himself gives in this meal to all who approach: He, the crucified and risen Lord, permits us, through His promissory Word, to receive Him, with bread and wine, in His body that was given into death for all and in His blood that was shed for all. Therewith, by virtue of the Holy Spirit, the Lord receives us into the victory of His lordship, so that by faith in His promise we might have forgiveness of sins, life, and salvation."

Text of theses in "Gemeinsam Formuliert und einmütig Angenommen," *Evangelisch-lutherische Kirchenzeitung,* XII (Sept. 15, 1958), 302, 303; Eng. tr. in P. M. Bretscher, "The Arnoldshain Theses on the Lord's Supper," *CTM,* XXX (Feb. 1959), 83 to 91; *Lutheran World,* VII (1960), 55—62; Hans Grasz, "Die Arnoldshainer Thesen und die lutherische Abendmahlslehre," *Neue Zeitschrift für systematische Theologie,* II (1960), 64—89; Albrecht Peters, "Zur Kritik an den Abendmahlsthesen von Arnoldshain," *Neue Zeitschrift für systematische Theologie,* II (1960), 182—219.

Arnzius. See *Arensius, Bernhard.*

Arrogance, Spiritual. See *Pride.*

Ars Moriendi (Lat. "art of dying [well]"). Type of devotional book that became popular in 15th c., largely under Franciscan and Dominican influence; designed to prepare Christians for a happy death. Best known is the *Ars moriendi* of Jean de Gerson. Related to this literature are the Dances of Death that about the same time became popular motifs in ch. decoration, MS illumination, and early printed books like *Chorea ab eximio macabro versibus alemanicis edita* (Paris. Guido Mercator pro Godeffredo de Marnef, 1490). A well-known 17th c. Eng. parallel is J. Taylor's *The Rule and Exercise of Holy Dying.*

Art, Ecclesiastical and Religious. 1. The specific area of artistic endeavor which relates to the decoration of ch. bldgs., performs as symbol and article of use in the acts of the liturgy, and relates individual and communal expression of a faith life. With the exception of a few brief but catastrophic periods of iconoclasm, the Christian faith has not only made room for, but welcomed the artist and craftsman into the service of the ch. Since the beginning of Christianity, the ch. has been the sponsor of art considered great not only in the context for which it was intended but as the highest expression of artistic feeling and craft. When the ch. did not sponsor good art, it did not express itself meaningfully to the world in any way.

2. Earliest Christian art came under many influences simultaneously. Palestine, Asia Minor, Alexandria, and Rome each brought some element of its own artistic heritage. In the W the dominant influence was Gk. classic art; in the E, Oriental art imposed its style on Christian subject matter. Technically, the art of the catacombs is more a type of writing than a style of art. Fresco painting included symbols of Christ such as the Chi Rho, the Alpha and Omega, and the fish. Rarely was the cross used, not only because it still held its context as an instrument of torture, but because the Christians at this time concerned themselves with a theol. of hope and deliverance rather than death. Themes for early paintings followed this line, depicting such stories as Jonah, the 3 men in the fiery furnace, Paul being let down the wall in a basket, and the Good Shepherd. When deemed proper, the early Christians were not adverse to utilizing pagan art for their own purposes. Thus the Roman god of the flocks, Hermes, provided a pattern for the Good Shepherd. Generally, however, the art of the early Christians can be described as abstract, geometric at times, symbolic and with no intention of depicting worldly reality. The human figure was deliberately distorted so that spiritual effect might take precedence.

3. Byzantine art, though a direct outgrowth of early Christian art, introduces a new style element, the Oriental, and becomes a style in itself. The chief capitol of this era, Constantinople, was on the border between E and W; its art was a mixture of these 2 elements. The imperial palace and court of the emp. became the influence for the decoration of the churches. Wealth and pomp were carried over to the ch. both in the materials used and in the subject matter depicted. Mosaic, with its gold and glitter, became the primary pictorial medium. In this medium, colored glass, very luminous and in the form of very small cubes called tesserae, are cemented into the white stucco of the wall. Gold tesserae, glass fused to gold leaf, were often set into the stucco at angles, thus catching light and reflecting it in various directions. The effect is an overall richess of color, light, and subject matter. Often the subject matter included the emperor and empress and members of the court. Symbolism was also used extensively, esp. in defining the sacraments. A formal plan for decorating churches was devised that determined what decorations should be used, where they should be placed, and by what technique. All Byzantine churches used this plan. Great works of Byzantine art are at the Hagia Sophia in Constantinople (Istanbul), in the 5th c. churches of Ravenna, It., done under the direction of Emp. Justinian who resided there when Ravenna was the capital of the W Empire, and in Sicily, particularly at Monreale. St. Mark's Cathedral, Venice, contains excellent examples of later Byzantine mosaic. This age also provided many fine examples of work in the minor arts, all of which rely heavily on the use of bril-

liant color and symbolism. Enamel ware, ivory carving, and precious metal were used in making plaques, icons, book covers, caskets, and liturgical items. A gen. description of this era would include the classical and Oriental influence, the rejection of the natural, and the use of wealth and light to transfer the observer's attention to the emotional and mystical elements of the liturgy.

4. Rome fell into utter ruin, and after the death of Charlemagne the ch. and its art went into hibernation. Awakening was due primarily to 3 influences: the monastic system, the Crusades, and the feeling of new life brought on by the passing of the year 1000 and its threat of the millennium. Monastaries maintained workshops for the express purpose of directing the skills of the artist towards the needs of the ch. Attempts were made, esp. in Fr., to encourage the style of the particular region rather than rely on a classical or Byzantine influence to dictate form. Thus each of various tribes which made up the Eur. complex provided a peculiar style to form a conglomerate whole. Esp. in painting we find considerable use of barbaric motifs. These worked their way into MS illuminations and provided strong influence for the resultant Gothic style. Since the ch. was now the patron of the arts, the state was removed as subject matter. God was the sole concern of the artist's work. There was very little attempt to create aesthetically pleasant work but rather to extend the work as a part of worship. Art now became an addition to the spoken word. Of all the art forms utilized at this time, sculpture can best be said to epitomize the age. Each ch. had its patron saint, sculpted and carried in procession on special occasions. The churches themselves were stark and massive and served also as fortresses. The sculptor's art kept them from being drab. The portal of the ch. provided the best arena for the sculptor, esp. at the tympanum. Here was depicted the Last Judgment, the Glorified Christ, or Christ surrounded by the 4 apocalyptic figures representing the Gospel writers. The sculptor was also called upon to execute crosses and crucifixes, many rivaling in wealth and beauty those done in the Byzantine age. The era can be summarized thus: ultra serious and devout, extremely inventive, with a concern for symbolizing truths that exist beyond the realm of human understanding and experience. Significant Romanesque art can be found in Fr. at Moissac, Chartres, Arles and Toulouse, in Ger. at Worms, Speyer and Hildesheim, in It. at Pisa and St. Ambrogio's in Milan, and in Eng. at Durham.

5. If the Byzantine age can be called majestic, and the Romanesque age devout, the Gothic age can be called intellectual, since art and architecture combined to convey intellectual concepts of God as He exists in nature. The Gothic artist looked to every aspect of life around him for subject matter. Reality itself was symbolic. The artist's task was to refine the forms of reality. Under the influence of Thomas Aquinas and his definition of beauty the artist sought to capture an ultimate in aesthetic perfection. There is today a tendency to regard this search as purely contemplative or religious. But the Gothic artists were concerned primarily with artistic problems. They brought to their work special influences that existed nowhere else. Their work contains N characteristics. It is not coincidental that the reach of the tall Fr. cathedrals towards the light occurs in a land of tall trees. It. did not strive for height in order to capture light. In the cold N, light was essential. It was an element in Aquinas's definition of beauty. The stained glass window was an attempt to capture and use this light. Paintings and MS illumination also attempted to utilize light with brilliant and vibrating color. Gothic art is essentially the art of the cathedral. Even many of the paintings utilized the cathedral as a setting. For the medieval artist the cathedral was the beginning and end of his life and livelihood. At the outset Gothic art expressed emotional mysticism; in the hands of fine artists it spoke to its time. Eventually it became aesthetic hack work, repetitious and devoid of spiritual significance. By the time of the Reformation and It. Renaissance, Gothic art was ready to succumb to the concepts of humanism. Works which remain as great statements of the Gothic ideal are in Fr. at Amiens, Reims, Chartres, Beauvais, and Paris. Cologne and Ulm hold fine examples of Ger. Gothic art. Salisbury and Canterbury are high peaks of the Gothic expression in Eng. In It. Gothic art never reached a pure expression. Orvieto and Siena contain some of the best examples; the Cathedral of Milan attempts to epitomize the best features of all Gothic art and becomes simply burlesque. (See *Church Architecture*)

6. The Gothic spirit was felt in It. primarily in painting. The Sienese school utilized the sense of humility and spirituality that was Gothic and yet incorporated a new feeling for emotion and human expression. The ultimate ideal of this school is found in the work of Giotto. His work in the Scrovegni Chapel in Padua is a display of utmost concern for spiritual feeling. The Renaissance begins with him. While it would be wrong to reject the work of the Renaissance artists out of hand, it would be equally wrong to categorize this era as Christian. Much art production at this time was religious or sacred in content, but its main purpose was to show the mastery of the artist over a particular art problem. As a result, churches tended to become museums.

7. The Prot. Reformation, while not anti-art, resulted in iconoclastic misunderstandings from which we are only now beginning to recover. Few artists painting under the influence of the Reformation created a specific Prot. style. Rembrandt* did. His work is often Christ-centered. But it is not the Christ of majesty; it is the Christ who heals the sick, who makes Himself known at the level of mankind. If distinctions are made between RC and Prot. art, they must begin historically at this point — the choice between the depiction of Christ's majesty and exalted state and the resultant majesty and glory of His followers, and His depiction as the suffering servant and the resultant servitude of His followers. This distinction is general, but ecumenical considerations seem to be reducing the division.

8. The ch. is again using the expression and craft of the artist. The artist in turn is finding in religious and ecclesiastical art an opportunity to devote his expression to a particular need. Such organizations as The Luth. Soc. for Worship, Music, and the Arts, and The Am. Soc. for Ch. Architecture encourage churches and artists to meet on common ground. The list of artists receiving extensive recognition while concentrating on religious and ecclesiastical art is growing steadily. RRCj

See also *Theology.*

G. G. Coulton, *Art and the Reformation,* 2d ed. (Cambridge, 1953); K. M. McClinton, *Christian Church Art Through the Ages* (New York, 1962); E. Male, *Religious Art from the Twelfth to the Eighteenth Century* (New York, 1963); E. Male, *The Gothic Image* (New York, 1958).

Artemis. See *Greek Religion,* 2.

Artemonites. See *Monarchianism,* A 3.

Articles of Agreement. See *Pittsburgh Agreement.*

Articles of Faith. See *Fundamental Doctrines.*

Articles of Faith (ca. 1611). See *Baptist Churches,* 2.

Articles of the Faith, The. See *Presbyterian Confessions,* 4.

Articles of Polity of the Church. See *Calvin, John,* 3.

Articles of Religion. See *Democratic Declarations of of Faith,* 6.

Articles of Visitation. In order to crush Crypto-Calvinism, which under Chancellor Nikolaus Crell* was again rearing its head in Electoral Saxony, a gen. visitation of churches and schools was ordered at Torgau 1592, to be conducted according to the Articles of Visitation, drawn up under the lead of Aegidius Hunnius* in 1593. Four articles treat the Lord's Supper, the Person of Christ, Holy Baptism, and the Election of Grace, each in from 4 to 6 terse, canonlike sentences in substantial agreement with the FC. To these are added just as terse statements of the errors of the Calvinists on these points. These Articles had to be confessed by all preachers and teachers and for a long time had a confessional character, esp. in Saxony.

For 1527 Arts. of Visitation see *Melanchthon, Philipp; Visitations, Church.*

Articles of War. See *Salvation Army,* 2.

Artman, Horace Greely B. (Sept. 23, 1857–Sept. 18, 1884). B. Zionsville, Pa.; d. Rajahmundry. Grad. Luth. Theol. Sem., Philadelphia; ordained Lancaster, Pa., May, 1880; miss. Rajahmundry, India, 1880; headmaster of miss. schools; started schools for native boys 1883 and 1884.

Artopaeus, Peter (1491—1563). Luth. theol. whose friendly attitude toward Osiander caused his deposition; wrote scholia on parts of OT and NT.

Arts, Seven Liberal. See *Quadrivium; Trivium.*

Aruba. See *Caribbean Islands,* E 7.

Arya Samaj. See *Hinduism,* 6.

Asbury, Francis (1745—1816). Sent by Wesley as miss. to Am.; first bp. of M. E. Ch. ordained in Am.; *Journals* reveal his zeal and wide miss. activity.

Ascension. Event in which the risen Christ removed His visible presence from the soc. of men and passed into the heavens. The doctrine of the Ascension is based on Acts 1:1-12; Mk 16:19; Lk 24:49-51 (which narrate the event); Jn 6:62; 20:17 (which look forward to it); Eph 4:8-10; 1 Ti 3:16; 1 Ptr 3:22; Heb 4:14 (which imply it). The Ascension is also implied in the references of Acts and the Epistles to Christ's being "seated at the right hand of God" (Acts 2:34; 5:31 RSV; 7:55, 56; Ro 8:34; Eph 1:20; Cl 3:1; Heb 1:3; 8:1; 10:12; 12:2). Throughout the apostolic age the Ascension is assumed as a fact among the other facts of Christ's life, as consistent with them, and as real.

The Ascension marks, for the Savior, the highest degree of exaltation, as it implies His session at the right hand of God, His entering into the full use, according to His human nature, of the divine attributes, of which He relinquished the full, continued, and unintermittent use and enjoyment during His State of Humiliation.

To the Christian the doctrine of the Ascension has manifold comforts. Faith and hope for the future of God's kingdom rest secure in the knowledge that Christ ascended and now is ever and everywhere present and governs and protects His church on earth. There is to be "a redemption of our body" (Ro 8:23); we shall "bear the image of the heavenly" (1 Co 15:49); "there is a spiritual body" (v. 44); our body shall be changed, "that it may be fashioned like unto His glorious body" (Ph 3:21); "our mortal bodies" are to be "quickened" (Ro 8:11). The future life is not to be one of pure spirit; it is to be "clothed upon" (2 Co 5:2). Best of all, we shall "see Him as He is" (1 Jn 3:2).

Ascension, Feast of. See *Church Year,* 5, 9, 16.

Ascension of Isaiah. See *Apocalypticism.*

Asceticism (Gk. "exercise," "practice," a term used by Gk. philosophers to denote moral discipline). Practiced by Essenes, Pythagoreans, Therapeutae, and other religious and philos. cults in pre-Christian times; found in varying degrees in almost all religions.

Outward asceticism was seldom practiced in OT (but cf. Nazarenes: Nm 6:2, 3, 13; Ju 13:5; 1 Sm 1:11; Lm 4:7; Am 2:11). In later Judaism it became a frequent practice (Tob 12:8; Mt 6:16; 9:14; Lk 18:22). The NT opposes workrighteous asceticism (Cl 2:16-23; 1 Ti 4:1-3). On the other hand, the Savior's command to each disciple to deny himself, take up his cross, and follow Him (Mk 8:34) brings out both aspects of an authentic Christian asceticism, the negative side of self-denial* and the positive side of the imitation of Christ (see Mt 9:15; 10:38, 39; 19:12, 21; 24:42; 25:13; Mk 10:28; Lk 9:57-62; Jn 12:25; Ro 8:13; 1 Co 9:26, 27; Gl 5:24; Col 3:5; 1 Jn 2:15, 16).

Some Gnostics and the Manichaeans practiced ascetic disciplines to free the soul from its entanglement in matter, which they regarded as evil. In varying degrees, these movements as well as others in the surrounding Gk. and Jewish world combined with the NT emphases to shape the ascetic practices of the early ch. and to influence the development of primitive and medieval monasticism.* Thus there were fixed times for fasting, fixed hours for prayer, regulations regarding food, abstinence from marriage, withdrawal from the world and similar practices (Clement of Alexandria, *Stromata,* VI, xii). Ascetic disciplines were widely used in the Middle Ages, often in reaction to the laxity and worldliness of both ch. and soc. Their proponents tended to emphasize, among others, the following notions: 1. the body's enjoyment of material things is evil; 2. the individual's duty is to gain his own blessedness; 3. satisfaction is accomplished through ascetic practices; 4. it is a God-pleasing work to imitate the suffering of Christ.

In *Freedom of the Christian Man* Luther opposed artificial asceticism by showing that works cannot justify and that the Christian can use all God's creatures but must obey the moral law. In addition, Luther frequently censures monks for work-righteousness (WA 40 I, 608, 609), for considering their mode of life higher than that of others (WA 31 I, 240; 20 I, 8; 33, 101; 46, 25; 40 II, 76), for leaving difficulties and duties of normal life for an invented mode of existence (WA 40 III, 208; 40 I, 342).

The Luth. Conf. oppose ascetic disciplines undertaken to merit grace and forgiveness and emphasize obedience to the moral law (e. g. AC XX 9, 10; XXVI 8). Positively, they teach that Christians will bear with patience, repentance, and faith the crosses that God sends them (Ap XV 45) and that they are to discipline themselves with bodily restraints, fasting, voluntary continence, almsgiving, and similar exercises as the Scriptures direct and for the kingdom of heaven's sake (AC XXVI 33—39; Ap IV 211, 277—284; XII 143; XV 46, 47; XXIII 36—40, 43, 44, 55, 65, 67—69; XXVII 9, 21, 22; SC VI 10; LC V 37). The revival of interest in an ev. and Biblical asceticism in non-RC Christianity is a significant phenomenon of the mid-20th c. EL, ACP

O. Zöckler, *Askese und Mönchtum,* 2 vols. (Frankfort, 1897); H. C. Lea, *History of Sacerdotal Celibacy in the Christian Church,* (New York, 1957); O. Hardman, *The Ideals of Asceticism* (New York, 1924); P. Pourrat, *Christian Spirituality,* various translators, 4 vols. (Westminster, Md., 1953—55); A. Brunner, *A New Creation,* tr. R. M. Bethell (New York, 1956); *Frei für Gott und die Menschen,* ed. L. Präger (Stuttgart, 1959); M. Thornton, *English Spirituality* (London, 1963); O. Wyon, *Living Springs* (Philadelphia, 1963).

Ash Wednesday. See *Church Year,* 4, 8, 16.

Asherah (Asherim). See *Canaanites, Religion of.*

Ashi, Rabbi (352—427). Jewish scholar; head of rabbinical school at Sura, Babylonia; chief ed. of Talmud.

Ashtaroth. See *Canaanites, Religion of.*

Asia. A. *Area:* ca. 17,094,666 sq. mi. *Pop.:* ca.

1,780,000,000. The largest continent and the one on which Christianity had its beginning; but large sections are still without knowledge of Christ. Some of the subdivisions and countries are treated separately as indicated by cross references.

B. *South Asia.* 1. See *India.*

2. Pakistan. *Area:* ca. 365,000 sq. mi. *Pop.:* ca. 127,942,000, about 85% Muslim. Till 1947 part of India; then dominion in British Commonwealth. Reorganized into E and W Pakistan 1955. Rep. within Brit. Commonwealth 1956. Revolt changed E Pakistan into indep. People's Rep. of Bangladesh (Bangla Desh; "Bengal[i] Nation") 1971; as a result, W Pakistan became simply Pakistan. Main languages: Bengali (official), Urdu, and Eng. in Bangladesh; Urdu (official), Eng., Hindi, and Punjabi in Pakistan.

C. W. Forman* of the Am. Presbyterian Miss. began work at Lahore, W Pakistan, 1848. This miss. emphasized educ. as miss. method, has institutions ranging from primary to coll., est. Gujranwala Theol. Sem. 1877. CMS began work at Karachi 1850. Others: Am. Meth., Brit. Meth., Salv. Army, Associate Ref. Presb. Ch., Woman's Union Miss. Soc., the Ev. Alliance Miss., Conservative Baptists, Pakistan Christian Fellowship, Internat. Miss., Inc. In W Pakistan the Bap. Miss. Soc. began work at Dinajpur 1795. Others: Australian Bap. Miss., S Bap., Assoc. of Bap. for World Evangelism, Ch. of God, Assem. of God, Seventh-day Adv., Worldwide Evangelization Crusade. 500,000 Christians, mostly converts of descendants from outcasts of Hinduism.

Maria Holst, Dan. Luth. doctor, worked among women 1903—17. In 1926 Jens Christensen joined Dan. Pathan Miss. In 1940s the Am. World Miss. Prayer League entered the field. The two formed Pakistani Luth. Ch. 1955. It works chiefly among Muslims. The Bangladesh Northern Ev. Luth. Ch. had 2,210 mems. 1973. See also *Norwegian Foreign Missions,* 3.

3. Ceylon. In 1972 named Sri Lanka ("great and beautiful island"). Island 31 mi. off S India. *Area:* 25,332 sq. mi. *Pop.:* ca. 13,273,000, Sinhalese (Buddhists), Tamil (Hindus), Moors and Malays (Muslim), Burghers. Veddas are aborigines. Under Port. (1505—1658), Dutch (1658—1796) and Brit. (1796 to 1948) control. Dominion, Feb. 4, 1948. Sinhalese is official language. Evangelized in early centuries. Cosmas Indicopleustes reported many Christians in 537. Port. introduced the RC Ch., which has 700,000 members. The Dutch Ref. Ch. was strong at one time, but is now small. The LMS began work 1804. James Chater (d. 1830) began work 1812 (Bap. Miss. Soc.); the Wesleyans 1814; Am. Ceylon Miss. (ABCFM) 1816; CMS 1817. In 1947 the churches of the S India United Miss. and Am. Ceylon Miss. formed the Jaffna Diocese of the Ch. of S. India. Others: Ceylon and India Gen. Miss. (1893); Salv. Army (1883); Seventh-day Adv.; Dutch Ref.; Christian Ref. Bd. of Miss.; Assem. of God; Conservative Bap.

Beginning in 1927 missionaries of the Mo. Syn. worked among Tamil-speaking members who had moved from its India missions to Ceylon. After Ceylon became indep., work was begun in Sinhalese. The work, supervised by the India Ev. Luth. Ch., centers in Colombo and Nuwara Eliya.

The total Prot. community is about 100,000.

4. Bhutan. *Area:* ca. 18,000 sq. mi. *Pop.:* ca. 1,100,000, chiefly Mongolian. The chief religion is Duk-pa Buddhism. Ruled by maharaja; for. policy controlled by India. Closed to missions.

5. Nepal. *Area:* ca. 54,000 sq. mi. *Pop.:* ca. 11,484,000, mixture of Mongolian and Indian. Ruled by Rana family 1846—1951; constitutional monarchy 1951. Opened to Christian missionaries 1950; United Miss. to Nepal (interdenominational) began educ. and medical work by contract with the govt. (Abode of Peace Hosp. at Katmandu). Later the Miss. to Lepers established a leprosarium at Bhangahan.

6. Tibet. *Area:* ca. 470,000 sq. mi. *Pop.:* est. 2,000,000 or 3,000,000, Mongolians. Ruled by lamas, Buddhist priests or monks, the supreme ruler being the Dalai Lama until 1951, when the Chinese communists entered. The Dalai Lama fled to India 1959.

RCs attempted to establish missions in 1845 but were expelled. In 1850s Moravians established a miss. on road leading from Punjab to Tibet. A Tibetan fugitive scholar and son, Joseb Gergan, tr. Bible with help of missionaries; printed 1948. Other border missions: Ev. Alliance; World Miss. Prayer League; Worldwide Evangelization Crusade; Cen. Asia Miss.; Miss. to Lepers; Mar Thoma Ch. of India.

7. Sikkim. *Area:* 2,745 sq. mi. *Pop.:* ca. 208,600. Buddhist country closed to missions.

C. *Southeast Asia.* 1. Burma. *Area:* ca. 261,700 sq. mi. *Pop.:* ca. 29,535,000 Burmese (Mongolian, 16,000,000), Chingpaw (3,700,000), Chin (300,000). Karen (2,400,000). Religion is Buddhism ("Land of Pagodas") mixed with animism. Ruled by Brit. for 120 yrs. Indep. since January, 1948. For several yrs. the govt. has restricted entrance of missionaries. About 100,000 Karen (mostly Bap.) are Christians. Only about 12,000 Buddhists have been converted. RCm entered in the 17th c.

Adoniram Judson (Am. Bap.) began work in 1814. By 1834 he had tr. Bible into Burmese. George Dana Boardman (Bap.) with the native Ko* Tha Byu opened station among Karen 1828. John E. Marks, a Jewish Christian, entered Burma for the Angl. SPG 1859. Anglicans operate St. John's Coll. and Holy Cross Coll. (sem.) at Rangoon. Others: Am. Meth. (1879); Eng. Meth. (Mandalay, 1887); Bible Churchmen's Miss. Soc. (1924); Salv. Army; Seventh-day Adv.; Pentecostal groups.

2. Malaya, Federation of. *Area:* ca. 50,600 sq. mi. *Pop.:* ca. 9,000,000, about 50% Malays, 38% Chinese, 11% Tamil. Religion: Islam (predominant), animism, Buddhism. Controlled successively by Port., Dutch, English, Domin. 1957. Joined Fed. of Malaysia 1963. Francis Xavier (RC) did miss. work middle of 15th c. There are about 86,000 RCs in Malaya.

The first Prot. miss. to Malaya was William Milne (LMS) who started (1815) at Malacca, and established the Anglo-Chinese Coll. Other Brit. Societies: SPG (1848); Presb. Ch. (1851); Soc. for the Promotion of Female Educ. in the E (1843); Christian Miss. in Many Lands; Salv. Army.

The Am. Meth. began work at Singapore 1885; branched out to Malaya and Indonesia. 62 primary and secondary schools enrolled 53,000 students (1960).

China was officially closed to for. miss. 1951; many workers moved to Malaya. The largest group belonged to the Overseas Miss. Fellowship. Many of these entered the New Villages established 1950 to 1953 to hinder communist infiltration. 14 missions worked in the New Villages 1960. The ULC on invitation by an E Asia Luth. Conf. in 1952 est. missions in some of the New Villages in the vicinity of Kuala Lumpur. The Tamil Luth. Ch. in India has had Tamil-speaking congregations in Penang, Kuala Lumpur, Singapore for over half a c. The Batak church has a diaspora parish in and near Singapore.

In 1948 the Malayan Christian Council was organized with headquarters at Singapore.

See also *Malaysia,* 3.

3. Singapore. Island off S end of Malay Peninsula. *Area:* 217 sq. mi. *Pop.:* ca. 2,187,000. Self-governing state in the Brit. Commonwealth, June,

1959. Joined Fed. of Malaysia 1963; withdrew 1965. The missions of Singapore are integrated with those of Malaya. See also *Malaysia,* 1, 3.

4. Thailand (Siam). *Area:* ca. 200,000 sq. mi. *Pop.:* ca. 39,089,000, Thai (originally Chinese), of which the Siamese are a subdivision; Shan Laos; Chinese. Buddhism is the state religion. People easygoing, yet advanced in civilization.

Thailand had an absolute monarchy until 1932, when a bloodless revolution introduced the Supreme Council of State which acts for the king.

Ann Hasseltine Judson (1789—1826) tr. Matthew, the Burman Cat., and a tract into Siamese with the help of Siamese prisoners at Rangoon (1815—20). Karl F. A. Gützlaff* (Neth. Miss. Soc.) landed in Bangkok, Aug. 23, 1828. He and his wife tr. Bible into Siamese and parts into Lao and Cambodian. The ABCFM sent David Abeel* in 1831. In 1833 John Taylor Jones, who tr. NT into Thai, was sent by the Am. Bap. Bd., and William Dean (organized first Prot. ch. in Far E at Bangkok, 1837) 2 yrs. later. In 1837 the Presb. Bd. of For. Miss. began work and developed the largest Prot. miss. In 1934 its churches organized the Ch. of Christ in Thailand. Their largest station is at Chiang Mai where they have Prince's Royal Coll., Dara Academy, McGilvary Theol. Sem., McCormick Hosp. and McKean Leprosy Colony. After China was closed, many of its missionaries went to Thailand. Some of the societies in Thailand are: Seventh-day Adv. (1918); Christian and Miss. Alliance (1929); Overseas Miss. Fellowship (CIM); Am. Bap.; S. Bap.; Pent. Miss.; New Tribes Miss.; Worldwide Evangelization Crusade; Oriental Boat Miss.; Internat. Child Evangelism Fellowship; Jeh. wit. The ABS (Thailand Bible House) has been active since 1837.

5. Cambodia. *Area:* est. 88,780 sq. mi. *Pop.:* ca. 7,410,000. Khmer civilization was established AD 435; Fr. protectorate 1863; assoc. state of the Fr. Union 1949; fully indep. 1955. Buddhism is the nat. religion; hill tribes are animists; Islam has ca. 100,000 adherents.

No Prot. miss. was admitted until 1922 (Christian and Miss. Alliance). Bible tr. into Cambodian (1956). BFBS active in Cambodia for some time.

6. Laos. *Area:* ca. 91,000 sq. mi. *Pop.:* 3,123,000, chiefly Laotians (originally from China) and aborigines. Buddhism is state religion but many are animists. Laos came under Fr. control (1893, 1904); free state in the Fr. Union 1946; indep. 1949.

Swiss mem. of Christian Miss. in Many Lands began work in S Laos, 1902. Workers of this miss. tr. Bible into Lao (1926, NT; 1932, whole Bible). Presb. from Thailand worked among the Kha tribes. The Christian and Miss. Alliance has worked with success in N Laos. Overseas Miss. Fellowship (CIM) entered Laos 1958.

7. Vietnam (formerly the Fr. Indochina states of Tonkin, Annam, and Cochin China). *Area:* ca. 65,700 sq. mi. *Pop.:* ca. 43,668,000, chiefly Annamese, a Mongolian people long influenced by Chinese, whose religion is Buddhism altered by Confucianism and Taoism. A new cult is that of Cao Dai; Caodaism combines elements from Buddhism, Confucianism, Taoism, RCm, and Islam. Fr. gained control ca. 1760. Indochina indep. at end of WW II. Vietnam divided at 17th parallel 1954. N Vietnam a communist "People's Republic"; S Vietnam a republic.

The RC Ch. gained a firm foothold during yrs. of Fr. control and has over 1,000,000 mem. The Christian and Miss. Alliance began work, 1911. It operates the John Olsen Mem. Studio, the Alliance Press, and Cen. Bible School. Portions of Bible tr. into several tribal languages. Other miss.: Seventh-day Adv.; Worldwide Evangelization Crusade; Wycliffe Bible Translators.

8. See *Indonesia.*

9. See *Philippine Islands.*

D. Far East. See *China; Japan; Korea; Mongolia; Taiwan.*

E. Middle East. See *Middle East.* EL

Asia Minor. The extreme W section of Asia, recently called Anatolia.*

Asoka. See *Buddhism,* 5.

Asperges (RC). The ceremony of sprinkling people with holy water before mass.

Assassins (Arab. *hashashin,* "hashish eaters"). Secret politico-religious Muslim sect of the Shi'ites*; founded 1090; flourished in Syria and Persia until suppressed in 13th c. Became terror by practicing "assassination." Head, "Old Man of the Mountain," had "assassins" drugged with hashish, intoxicating extract of hemp, before sending them on their murderous missions.

Assemblers. See *Camisards.*

Assemblies of God. Originated in the revival movement that began in the 20th c. Organized 1914 according to a combination of Cong. and Presb. principles, the movement emerged as the largest "Pentecostal" denomination in the US. Distinctive doctrines in addition to a core of ev. theol. are: (1) baptism in the Holy Spirit accompanied by the sign of speaking in other tongues; (2) divine healing of the body as a provision of the atonement; (3) the imminent premillennial coming of Christ. While not teaching the eradication of the old nature as do the "Holiness" bodies, high standards of practical holiness are practiced. Statistics (1964): 543,003 mem. in US; 1,004,796 enrolled in S. S. For. membership: 1,469,648.

I. Winehouse, *The Assemblies of God* (New York, 1959); C. Brumback, *Suddenly, from Heaven* (Springfield, Mo., 1961); K. Kendrick, *The Promise Fulfilled* (Springfield, Mo., 1961). WGM

Assembly. See *Reformed Churches,* 1.

Assig, Hans von (1650—94). Silesian nobleman, high official at Schwiebus in the Electorate of Brandenburg; hymnist.

Assignment Board. See *Teachers,* A 6.

Associate Presbytery. See *Associate Reformed Church.*

Associate Reformed Church. Has roots in the Ref. Presbytery (later called Ref. Presb. Ch.) organized Scot. 1743 under leadership of J. Macmillan* and Thomas Nairn(e) (ca. 1680–1764) by Ref. Presbyterians who traced their origin to 1733, when E. Erskine,* William Wilson (1690–1741), Alexander Moncrieff (1695–1761), and James Fisher (1697–1775) left the Est. Ch. and founded the Associate Presbytery (first called Assoc. Syn.; at times called Society People). Many emigrated to US. The 1st organization in the US was the Assoc. Presbytery of Pa., founded 1753. In 1774 the first Ref. Presbytery of Am. was organized. The Assoc. Presbytery of N. Y. was founded 1776. These 3 (except for a minority that continued till 1858 as the Assoc. Presb. Ch.) united 1782 as the Assoc. Ref. Presb. Ch., a syn. in polity. In 1802 it reorganized as 4 syns. (N. Y., Pa., Scioto, and the Carolinas) subordinate to a gen. syn. convened 1804. The syn. of the Scioto withdrew to form indep. Assoc. Ref. Syn. of the West 1820. In 1821 the syn. of the Carolinas was released to form Assoc. Ref. Syn. of the South 1822. After the disputed 1822 gen. syn. resolution to unite with the Presb. Ch. in the USA, the syn. of N. Y. continued indep. and reunited 1855 with syn. of the West as Gen. Syn. of the Assoc. Ref. Ch. This Gen. Syn. and the Assoc. Syn. (formed 1801; indep. of the Gen. Syn. of Scot. 1818) formed The United Presb. Ch. of N. Am. 1858. The Assoc. Ref. Syn. of the South continued indep. and became the Assoc. Ref. Presb. Ch. (Gen. Syn.). See also *Presbyterian Churches,* 1, 4. EL

Associate Reformed Presbyterian Church (General Synod). See *Associate Reformed Church.*

Associate Reformed Synod of the South. See *Associate Reformed Church.*

Associate Reformed Synod of the West. See *Associate Reformed Church.*

Associate Synod. See *Associate Reformed Church; Presbyterian Churches* 1.

Associated Lutheran Charities (Syn. Conf.). Known popularly as Assoc. Luth. Charities, this assoc. of charitable agencies was founded 1901 in Chicago by 3 pioneers in city or institutional miss. work: F. W. Herzberger* of St. Louis, August Schlechte (July 9, 1868—April 17, 1920) of Chicago, and F. C. T. Ruhland* of Buffalo. Men prominent in the movement in later yrs. included Carl Eissfeldt (Nov. 29, 1854—Mar. 14, 1935) of Milwaukee, a worker in the field of child welfare; Philipp Wambsganss Jr. (Feb. 16, 1857–Apr. 21, 1933) of Ft. Wayne, Ind., whose interests centered in hospitals and child welfare agencies; and Enno Duemling,* long-time institutional miss. in Milwaukee.

In the early days of the organization an annual conf. for mutual instruction and encouragement was the sole objective. Later other aims were added.

Assoc. Luth. Charities was instrumental in est. Bethesda Luth. Home for mentally retarded and epileptic children, Watertown, Wis., 1903. It also provided the impetus for founding the Deaconess Soc. 1919 and for est. undergrad. soc. work courses at Valparaiso U. Assoc. Luth. Charities took the leading role in sensitizing LCMS to its need for a Dept. of Soc. Welfare.

Several of the functions of Assoc. Luth. Charities became the responsibility of the synod's Dept. of Soc. Welfare. Such functions include consultative services to agencies and institutions. Previously the division of responsibility had been: 1. govt. responsibility for basic (chiefly financial) services relating to physical need; 2. ch. and voluntary community agency responsibility for professional services involving soc., emotional, and spiritual therapy. In recent yrs. govt. has begun to assume increasing responsibility for treatment services partly because of the inability of private agencies fully to assume that role and the desire on the part of govt. to focus on treatment and prevention rather than on palliative approaches. Apparently the role of govt. will continue to increase. Expenditures on the part of govt. and private sector of soc. welfare are in the ratio of 20 to 1 (1965).

In recent years new and experimental forms of soc. ministry have emerged. LCMS experiments involve "Ministers of Social Service," Luth. soc. workers with theol. training besides grad. soc. work educ., on staffs of inner city parishes. They engage in a generic ministry, sharing professional insights with other parish staff members. JCC

Association for the Promotion of the Unity of Christendom. See *Lee, Frederick George.*

Association for the Study of Community Organization. See *National Association of Social Workers.*

Association of Free Lutheran Congregations, The. Organized Oct. 1962 at Thief River Falls, Minn., by a group of congs. of the former Lutheran* Free Ch. which chose not to merge with The ALC, a few congs. from other ch. groups of Norw. background, and some congs. earlier affiliated with the Suomi Syn. The Assoc. started a sem. 1964 and a Bible School 1966 at 3110 E. Medicine Lake Blvd., Minneapolis, Minn. Miss. fields have included Sao Paulo, Brazil, and Nogales, Ariz. Summer Bible Camps are stressed. Official pub.: *The Ambassador.* IO

Association of Lutheran Brotherhoods. See *Laymen's Activity in the Lutheran Church.*

Association of Lutheran Secondary Schools. See *Teachers,* 19.

Association of Pentecostal Assemblies. Founded 1921 by Elizabeth A. Sexton, Hattie M. Barth, and Paul T. Barth. See also *International Pentecostal Assemblies.*

Association of Pentecostal Churches of America. See *Church of the Nazarene,* 2.

Assumption, Feast of. Feasts celebrating the Falling Asleep, that is, the death, of Mary have been celebrated in the E since the 4th or 5th c. Emperor Maurice (582—603) fixed the date for such celebrations on Aug. 15. The feast entered the W Ch. in the late 7th c. and became universal by the end of the 8th. Through the doctrine of Mary's bodily assumption seems first to have been upheld in the 8th or 9th c., it was officially declared a probable opinion in the RC Ch. only in the pontificate of Benedict XIV (pope from 1740) and it was only in 1950 that Pius XII in the bull *Munificentissimus Deus* defined it as a dogma that RCs must believe (but left open the question whether or not Mary died before being taken bodily into heaven). It has long been a RC holy day of obligation in many countries. The 1572 Luth. Ch. Order for Brandenburg still retained the feast by its traditional name; elsewhere in the 16th and 17th c. a number of Luth. Ch. Orders kept Aug. 15 as a festival, but commemorated the Visitation (otherwise kept on July 2) on it. ACP

Assumption of Mary. See *Munificentissimus Deus.*

Assumption of Moses. See *Apocrypha,* A 4.

Assurance. The firm persuasion of being in a state of grace. The Council of Trent anathematized the doctrine that a Christian may be sure of his salvation, but the Church of the Reformation upheld it. The Christian during his entire life will be cast about with many a doubt; he is to work out his salvation with fear and trembling. Yet he knows, being made divinely sure by the Holy Spirit, that "He which hath begun a good work in him will perform it" (Ph 1:6), the gift of the Spirit through the means of grace being an earnest of the inheritance laid up in heaven. By this assurance the Christian is upheld in tribulation and often rescued from utter despair. As Christians we have "full assurance of understanding" (Cl 2:2), that is, a perfect knowledge and entire persuasion of the truth of the doctrine of Christ. The "assurance of faith," Heb 10:22, is trust in the sacrifice and priestly office of Christ. The "assurance of hope," Heb 6:11, relates to the heavenly inheritance and implies a full persuasion that believers are the children of God and therefore heirs of His glory; from this passage it follows that such an assurance is what every Christian ought to aim at, and that it is attainable.

In a sense, assurance is the very essence of Christian faith. It expresses itself in such Scriptural terms as: "There is now no condemnation to them which are in Christ Jesus" (Ro 8:1); "Being justified by faith, we have peace with God" (Ro 5:1); "Ye have received . . . the Spirit of adoption, whereby we cry, Abba Father" (Ro 8:15). Compare the many passages expressing the confidence and joy of Christians, their union with God, and their assurance that sins are forgiven and the ground of fear of future punishment taken away.

The Luth. Conf. throughout agree with FC SD IV 12: "[Justifying] faith is a living bold [firm] trust in God's grace, so certain that a man would die a thousand times for it [rather than suffer this trust to be wrested from him]." See *Certainty, Religious.*

Assyria, Religion of. See *Babylonians, Religion of,* 7.

Assyrians, Church of the. See *Eastern Orthodox Churches,* 6.

Asterius the Sophist (d. after 341). Rhetorician and exegete; exponent of Arianism.

Astralism. Cult in which celestial bodies are objects of, or assoc. with, worship.

Astrology. Art which claims to forecast events by observation of stars, sun, moon, planets. Probably originated in Mesopotamia ca. 3,000 BC, spread to India, China (6th c. BC) and Greece (3rd c. BC). In Mesopotamia omens were drawn from celestial phenomena. This led to systematic observance of celestial bodies thus combining religion (astrology) and science (astronomy). In Mesopotamia, and later Egypt, astrology was connected with the ruling family and its predictions concerned the kingdom. When astrology came to the Greeks their world gods were changed to astral deities (catasterism); astrology was made personal, i. e., made prognostications for every person. Such prognostications were based on the zodiacal belt, probably a development of Greeks. In early Christianity astronomy and astrology were distinguished and the latter rejected by various councils. Astrology revived with Charlemagne and was given new impetus by Arab and Jewish scholars in the 12th c. In the 14th c. numerous universities had chairs in astrology (e. g., Paris, Florence). Astrology is still a popular pastime but is rejected by the intelligentsia as a serious science.

Astruc, Jean (1684—1766). Fr. physician and Biblical scholar; called father of documentary hypothesis because he was first to hold that use of Jahweh and Elohim in Pent. reveals different writers or sources. Works include *Conjectures sur les mémoires originaux dont il parait que Moyse s'est servi pour composer le Livre de la Genèse.* See also *Higher Criticism,* 12.

Astrup. 1. *Hans Jörgen S.* (Aug. 30, 1852–May 18, 1939). ELC miss. to Africa. B. Grue, Solör, Norw.; son of Nicolai Astrup; educ. Christiania U. (1870 to 76); Leipzig U. 1875—76, 1883—84, 1892—93; ordained 1878; pastor S Aurdal 1878—80; Jevnaker 1880; S Land 1881—84; miss. (originally of Schreuder Miss.) to Zulu at Entumeni, S Afr., 1884—1914; Entumeni and Eshowe 1914—39. Wrote numerous books, including Zulu school books and some on the Bible. 2. *Johannes* (Dec. 3, 1872—June 8, 1955). B. Christiania, Norw.; son of bp. Nils Astrup; to Natal 1883; USA 1890; educ. Luther Coll., Decorah, Iowa, 1890—93, Luther Sem., Robbinsdale (later at St. Paul), Minn., 1893—96. Miss. Untunjambili, Natal, S Afr. 1900—31; Supt. Schreuder Miss. 1918 to 1927; Supt. Am. Luth. Miss. in S Afr. 1927—47; wrote several pamphlets in Eng. and Zulu. Ed. paper in Zulu language. D. S Afr.

At Ease. See *Armed Services Commission,* 2.

Athanasian Creed. See *Ecumenical Creeds,* C.

Athanasius (ca. 293—373). Known in E tradition as "The Father of Orthodoxy." His life shows great heroism, fortitude, and faith. In 325 accompanied his bp., Alexander, to Council of Nicea as deacon; 3 yrs. later became bp. Alexandria. Known for defense of Nicene formula, which stressed that Jesus Christ is *homoousios* with the Father. Made little use of this term in early apologies of Christian faith, *Against the Gentiles* and *On the Incarnation;* but by 325 felt that it was the only one that would preserve the teaching of the ch. from the ravages of Arianism.* Though *homoousios* is not a Biblical term, he felt that it captured the witness of the Scriptures to the deity of Christ better than any of the specifically Biblical formulations that might have been substituted. His many works against the Arians include *The Decrees of the Council of Nicea; History of the Arians; Orations Against the Arians.*

Perhaps his most important contribution was made ca. the middle of the 4th c. when he brought together the Gk. theologians of the E, who emphasized that the Godhead is made up of 3 Persons, with the theologians of the W, who insisted that God is One. Athanasius' efforts, with those of such men as Basil and Hilary, led to settlement at Constantinople (381), where it was agreed that there is 1 true God, in whom there are 3 Persons, Father, Son, and Holy Spirit. WWO

MPG, 25—28; *NPNF,* Ser. 2, IV; J. N. D. Kelly, *Early Christian Creeds,* 2d ed. (New York, 1960).

Atheism. Denial of the existence of God. Term used in a variety of senses, depending on definition of God. Pagans applied it to early Christians because they rejected heathen idolatry. In theol. controversies of early ch. contending parties at times called each other atheists, and the RC Ch. justified the burning of heretics by applying this epithet to them. — Aside from this improper use the term has been variously used in scientific literature. In its widest sense it denotes the antithesis of theism and includes pantheism and deism. In a more restricted sense it denotes the denial of the Deity above and outside of the physical universe. In the most commonly accepted sense it is a positive dogmatic denial of anything that may be called God. The term is also used to express a merely negative attitude on the question of the existence of God, such as agnosticism* and the so-called "practical atheism," which is not based on scientific reasoning, but is merely a refusal to worship any deity.

The materialism of the 18th and 19th c. and biological evolution have given strong impetus to atheistic trends of thought. In Fr. the 18th c. produced many antitheistic writers, among them the Encyclopedists* Diderot,* Holbach,* and La Mettrie.* Voltaire* called Holbach's *Système de la Nature* the Bible of atheism. Ger. materialists of the 19th c.: Feuerbach,* Marx,* Vogt,* F. Büchner,* Haeckel,* were equally outspoken. Comte's Positivism,* Eng. Secularism (whose two main exponents are Holyoake* and Bradlaugh*), and continental Socialism are essentially atheistic. Of the great religions of the world, Buddhism,* Jainism,* and the Sankhya system of Brahmanic philosophy (see *Brahmanism*) deny the existence of a personal God.

It is not possible for a man to be an atheist, in the commonly accepted sense, in his innermost conviction. No amount of reasoning will erase from the human heart the God-given conviction that there is a Supreme Being; those who theoretically deny God's existence replace Him with something else. Likewise, no people has ever been found entirely devoid of religious belief. The difficulties which atheism involves are expressed by Bacon: "I had rather believe all the fabulous tales in the Talmud and the Koran than that the universal frame is without mind." The hopelessness of antitheism is apparent in the confession of Romanes, who speaks of "the appalling contrast between the hallowed glory of that creed which once was mine and the lonely existence as now I find it."

See also *Evolution.*

T. Graebner, *God and the Cosmos* (Grand Rapids, 1932); F. A. Lange, *The History of Materialism, and Criticism of Its Present Importance,* tr. E. C. Thomas (London, 1925); A. B. Drachman, *Atheism in Pagan Antiquity* (London, 1922); Fritz Mauthner, *Der Atheismus und seine Geschichte im Abendlande,* 4 vols. (Stuttgart, 1920—23; reprint Hildesheim, 1963).

Athena. See *Greek Religion,* 2.

Athenagoras (2d c.). Gk. Christian apologist and philos. of Athens; addressed apology to Marcus Aurelius Antoinus and his son Lucius Aurelius Commodus ca. 177. See also *Apologists,* 6.

Athirat (Athtart). See *Canaanites, Religion of.*

Atman. See *Brahmanism,* 3.

Atomism. Belief that there are discrete material elements (Democritus).

Atonement. Term employed by the KJV in tr. of Gk. *katallage,* Ro 5:11, often otherwise "reconciliation," Ro 5:10; 2 Co 5:19. At-one-ment properly reflects the core significance of the Gk. term, a mutual exchange, a drawing together of parties previously separated. Behind the concept lies the situation that the fall of mankind into sin, and the idolatry and rebellion of the individual sinner, set up a cleavage between God and man (Is 59:2) to which God's ultimate reaction is withdrawal, separation potentially permanent (Ro 1:18-32; Mt 8:12). Atonement is removal of this separation.

Emphases in the doctrine of the atonement vary as Biblical references are employed to answer the question: who reconciles whom? Does God reconcile men, or do men reconcile God, or does Jesus Christ reconcile God to men or men to God? Some teachers focus on the gravity of man's offense and of God's wrath against it (cf. Apology IV 80, "Christ is set forth to be the propitiator, through whom the Father is reconciled to us"). Such a position stresses the justice, in human dimensions, of God who cannot overlook sin but must punish it, and sees in the atonement the way by which God can be just and yet merciful. Other teachers stress that God the Father in love Himself moves in, despite His wrath for man's sin, on the need of man and gives His own Son to redeem man from sin, take the curse of sin on Himself, and work peace bet. God and man (2 Co 5:18-21; Cl 1:12-22; Jn 3:16). In this process the primary factor is that God for Christ's sake does not hold man's sin against Him (Ro 3:25; 2 Co 5:19), or forgives it. Here the OT concept tr. "atonement" is absorbed, namely to cover, *k'phar,* a sacrifice involving shedding of blood and giving up of life prefiguring the means by which God forgives man's sin (cf. especially Lv 16 and Heb 9). The process of the atonement in Christ is brought home to the individual through the "word of reconciliation" (2 Co 5:18-20; Cl 1:22-29), the Gospel of the cross of Christ by which the individual is moved to faith in God's atoning love in Christ. Luth. teaching of the atonement stresses that God's act is objective, taking the initiative (cf. the OT concept of the Covenant) in reaching out toward man, and that Christ's work is vicarious, in that He bears the burden of sin which is rightfully man's (Gl 3:10-13; cf. Is 53). See also *Justification; Redemption; Soteriology.*

F. Pieper, *Christliche Dogmatik,* vol. 2 (St. Louis, 1917), tr. T. Engelder, *Christian Dogmatics* (St. Louis, 1951); W. Elert, *Morphologie des Luthertums,* vol. 1 (Munich, 1952), tr. W. Hansen, *The Structure of Lutheranism* (St. Louis, 1962); J. M. Reu, *Homiletics,* 4th ed. (Columbus, 1934), pp. 351—354; W. J. Wolf, *No Cross, No Crown* (New York, 1957); V. Taylor, *The Atonement in New Testament Teaching,* 5th ed. (Chicago, 1950). RRC

Atonement, Day of. See *Judaism,* 4.

Atonement, Theories of. Among the theories of atonement, which objectors to the Scriptural doctrine of the vicarious atonement of Christ offer as substitutes, are 1. The *Accident Theory:* Christ's death was an accident, as unforeseen and unexpected as that of any other victim of man's hatred (Modernists); 2. The *Martyr Theory:* Christ gave up His life for a principle of truth which was opposed to the spirit of His day (Modernists); 3. The *Declaratory Theory:* Christ died to show men how greatly God loves them (Ritschl*): 4. The *Moral-Example Theory (Moral-Influence Theory; Moral-Power View of the Atonement):* Christ died to influence mankind toward moral improvement (Socinians, Horace Bushnell); 5. The *Governmental Theory:* God made Christ an example of suffering to exhibit to erring man that sin is displeasing to Him; or: God's govt. of the world made it necessary for Him to evince His wrath against sin in Christ (Hugo Grotius*; New* England Theology); 6. The *Guaranty Theory:* Reconciliation is based not on Christ's expiation of sin, but on His guaranty to win followers and thus conquer human sinfulness (Schleiermacher, Kirn, Hofmann); 7. The *Classic* or *Dramatic Theory:* the atonement as divine conflict and victory (Gustaf Aulén). All these and other man-made theories of atonement deny Christ's vicarious satisfaction and are based on the same leading thought: salvation by works, or salvation through personal sanctification, stimulated by Christ's death. See also *Christus Crucifixus; Lund, Theology of; Recapitulation; Sweden, Lutheran Church in,* 6. JTM

R. S. Franks, *A History of the Doctrine of the Work of Christ in Its Ecclesiastical Development,* 2 vols. (London, 1918) and *The Atonement* (London, 1934); G. Aulén, *Christus Victor,* tr. A. G. Hebert (London, 1931); Paul Althaus, *Die Theologie Martin Luthers* (Gütersloh, 1962), pp. 191 to 195, 2d ed. (Gütersloh, 1963) tr. R. C. Schultz, *The Theology of Martin Luther* (Philadelphia, 1966), pp. 218–223.

Atrium. See *Church Architecture,* 3.

Atterbury, Francis (1662—1732). Angl. prelate; controversialist; politician. B. Bedford; ordained 1687; bp. Rochester 1713; banished as Jacobite 1723; d. Paris.

Atticus (d. 425). Patriarch of Constantinople; for a time adherent of Pneumatomachianism; opponent of Chrysostom.

Attila. See *Geneviève.*

Attribute. 1. That which is indispensable to a substance. 2. Characteristic of God.* 3. That which is permanent or essential to a being. 4. The way in which feelings, images, or sensations differ.

Attrition. Term used by RC theologians: hatred of sin arising from love of the offended God is called perfect contrition; arising from other motives (fear of hell and of punishment, realization of the heinousness of sin), attrition. They teach that attrition alone does not justify, but that "by it the penitent, being assisted, prepares a way for himself unto justice" (Council of Trent, Sess. XIV, ch. 4), and that if, with attrition, he properly receives the sacrament of penance he is justified.

Attwood, Thomas (1765—1838). Eng. musician and composer; highly regarded by Mozart,* his teacher; organist St. Paul's Cathedral, London; among first in Eng. to recognize genius of Mendelssohn.

Auberlen, Karl August (1824—64). B. Fellbach; prof. theol. Basel; exponent of Swabian theol. of Bengel;* wrote *Der Prophet Daniel und die Offenbarung Johannis* and *Die göttliche Offenbarung.*

Aubigné, Jean Henri Merle d'. See *Merle d'Aubigné, Jean Henri.*

Auburn Affirmation. Document entitled "An Affirmation Designed to Safeguard the Unity and Liberty of the Presbyterian Church in the United States of America," signed by 1,274 Presb. ministers, pub. 1924, regarding toleration of divergence from traditional theol. views. The strict constructionist party within the ch. wanted the candidates for the ministry to affirm the 5 "essential and necessary" doctrines of 1910. The broadening influence within the ch. wanted to permit differing theories about the inspiration of the Bible, Incarnation, Atonement, Resurrection, and the continuing life and supernatural power of Christ. Pleading the safeguarding of liberty of thought, it opposed any attempt to elevate the 5 doctrinal statements to tests of ordination or of good standing in the ch. The signers of the affirmation declared that "these are not the only theories allowed by the Scriptures and our standards as explanations of these facts and doctrines of our religion" and asked for the preservation of the unity and the freedom of the ch.

L. A. Loetscher, *The Broadening Church: A Study of Theological Issues in the Presbyterian Church Since 1869* (Philadelphia, 1954). CSM

Auburn Declaration. Declaration adopted by New* School Presbyterians 1838 both as protest against the Plan of Union, an instrument to foster interdenominational miss. work, and as restatement of Calvinism against the charge of Arminianism.

Auburn Theological Seminary. Organized 1818 by those who thought Princeton too narrow; opened for students 1821 at Auburn, N. Y., under control of the Syn. of Geneva. An institution of The Presb. Ch. in the USA, it became assoc. with Union Theol. Sem., NYC, 1939.

Audians. Anthropomorphite followers of Audius, a Mesopotamian of the time of Arius, who founded this sect in protest against the worldly conduct of the clergy. It labored principally among the Goths.

Epiphanius, *Adversus haereses,* 70; Theodoret, *HE,* IV, ix.

Audientes. See *Catechetics,* 3.

Auer, John Gottlieb (1832—1874). B. Württemberg; educ. Miss. Training School, Basel; sent to W Afr. 1858; joined Episc. Ch. 1862; head of school at Cavalla, Liberia, 1867; ordained bp. of Cape Palmas 1873. Works include primer, dictionary, tr. of Psalms and other parts of Bible, hymnbook, prayer book in the Grebo language; primer and Bible hist. in the Kru language.

Aufklärung. See *Enlightenment.*

Augsburg, Friends of. See *Lutheran Free Church.*

Augsburg, Imperial Recess of. See *Schmalkaldic League.*

Augsburg, Religious Peace of (1555). Est. bet. Ferdinand I and the princes of the Ger. Empire at Augsburg Sept. 25, 1555. Since the Diet of Worms* the followers of Luther had been in a precarious position, in spite of the modifications at the Diet of Speyer* (1526). The formation of the Schmalkaldic* League and the desire of Charles* V to extirpate heresy led to the Schmalkaldic* War. With defeat of the emp. at Innsbruck and the Convention of Passau* (1552) settlement was made. Catholicism and Lutheranism (but not Calvinism) were recognized according to the principle of *cuius regio, eius religio:* the ruler of the territory chooses the religion which the subjects are bound to follow. Those who did not agree to the ruler's religion were permitted to emigrate. Both religions were allowed to continue in the Imperial cities, where already, established. By the *reservatum ecclesiasticum* (ecclesiastical reservation) a RC prelate who turned Lutheran was to give up his office. The pope protested but the emp. did not override the peace. It was, however, a concession to territorialism, not toleration. Some of the provisions of the "Peace" were among the factors which brought on the Thirty Years War.* It was superseded 1648 by the Peace of Westphalia.

Text in *Church and State Through the Centuries,* eds. S. Z. Ehler and J. B. Morrall (London, 1954), pp. 164–173; L. W. Spitz Jr., "Particularism and Peace: Augsurg - 1555," *Church History,* XXV (June 1956), 110–126. CSM

Augsburg Center. See *Mexico,* D 3.

Augsburg College. See *Ministry, Education of,* VIII B 1.

Augsurg Confession. See *Lutheran Confessions,* A.

Augsburg Diet (1518). Convened to obtain Ger. subsidy for the pope at war with Turks. M. Luther's enemies used the opportunity to prejudice princes and Maximilian* I against the Reformer, even forging theses on the papal ban and claiming they were by Luther. After the Diet, Cajetan* gave Luther a hearing (see *Luther, Martin,* 10). See also *Frederick III* (1463–1525).

Augsburg Diet (1530). See *Lutheran Confessions,* A 2.

Augsburg Interim. See *Interim; Lutheran Confessions,* C 1.

Augsburg Publishing House. See *Publication Houses, Lutheran.*

Augsburg Seminary. See *Ministry, Education of,* X G.

Augsburg Synod. A Luth. syn. of the Miss. Valley. The Ger. Augsburg Syn. of the Ev. Luth. Ch. was organized May 5, 1876. It consisted largely of people who did not feel at home among the liberal men of the Gen. Syn. It had congregations in Ohio, Ill., Pa., Mo., Ind., Iowa, Wis., Mich., Md., Ark., and Tenn. Its organ was *Der Sendbote von Augsburg.* In 1897 the Augsburg Syn. united with the Mich. Syn. after the latter's withdrawal from the Syn. Conf. But in 1900 the two synods separated again on account of doctrinal differences, and in 1902 the Augsburg Syn. was dissolved; many of its members entered the Ohio Syn. See also *Michigan Synod.*

August, Elector of Saxony (1526—1586). Succeeded his brother Maurice in 1553; staunch Lutheran, but, hoodwinked by the Crypto-Calvinists, he deposed the true Lutherans who opposed the Calvinizing Wittenberg Catechism and the Dresden Consensus. When, however, *Exegesis Perspicua* appeared in 1574, which actually attacked the Luth. doctrine of the Lord's Supper, he imprisoned the deceivers and spent 80,000 Taler to help bring into being the *Book of Concord* of 1580. See also *Lutheran Confessions,* C 2; *Peucer, Kaspar.*

Augustana. See *Lutheran Confessions,* A.

Augustana Book Concern. See *Publication Houses, Lutheran.*

Augustana College, Rock Island, Ill. See *Augustana Evangelical Lutheran Church,* 14; *Lutheran Church in America,* V; *Ministry, Education of,* VIII B 2.

Augustana College, Sioux Falls, S. Dak. See *Ministry, Education of,* VIII B 3.

Augustana Evangelical Lutheran Church. 1. After cong. beginnings 1848, The Scand. Ev.-Luth. Augustana Syn. in [or of] N. Am., or briefly, The Augustana Syn. *(den Skandinaviska Evangelisk-Lutherska Augustana Synoden i Nord Amerika, eller korteligen, Augustana Synoden)* was founded 1860 (see 2–8); adopted the name Augustana Ev. Luth. Ch. or, briefly, the Augustana Luth. Ch. 1948; merged with the AELC, The Finnish Ev. Luth. Ch. of Am., and the ULC June 28, 1962, Detroit, Mich., to form the LCA.

2. A small body of Swed. immigrants arrived 1845 in the Miss. Valley, settling in Jefferson Co., Iowa, calling their community New Sweden. Jan. 1848 they organized a cong. Because no ordained pastor was available, they called one of their own number, M. F. Hokanson [Haakanson*], to preach and administer the sacraments. He was a shoemaker who once had planned to be a miss. to the Laplanders. Though lacking theol. educ. and somewhat vacillating doctrinally, he was a fluent preacher. From the outset the cong. was beset by proselytizers who tried to shake the convictions of Hokanson and disrupt the flock. Only the timely arrival of stronger spiritual leaders from Swed. saved a remnant; thus New Swed. became the starting point of the future Aug. Luth. Ch.

3. The first ordained Swed. Luth. pastor to arrive in the Midwest was Lars P. Esbjörn. Strongly pietistic, like many of his fellow clergymen in Swed., he felt deeply distressed over the low state of morals and spiritual life in the Established Ch. Though thoroughly loyal to the Luth. theol. position, free ch. evangelistic movements based in Eng. influenced his thinking. Moved by reports of spiritual destitution among his countrymen who had migrated to Am., he determined to cast his lot with them. Together with 146 emigrants, many of whom were from his own parish of Östervaala, Esbjörn, accompanied by his wife and 6 small children, sailed from Gävle June 29, 1849, for the New World.

4. Before they reached their destination at Andover, Ill., 3 months later, many had succumbed to cholera and other diseases. Among the victims were 2 of Esbjörn's children. Esbjörn himself was stricken

with cholera in Chicago, but recovered. When he reached Andover, he found his party disintegrating. Some had moved to other places while others had deserted to sects. So hostile was the attitude of many Swed. immigrants toward the State Ch. of Swed. that Esbjörn was constrained to lay aside his clerical garb and use of liturgy. But his bitter experiences with the sects caused him to lose all enthusiasm for free church tendencies. In his first published appeal to Scandinavians he warned them against proselytizers and exhorted them to remain loyal to the AC and Luther's SC. It was not until March 18, 1850, that he effected the organization of a Luth. cong., and only 10 persons became charter members. Andover thus became the first congregation of the future Aug. Syn. to be organized and served by an ordained pastor.

5. Esbjörn's field of labor was soon extended to Moline, Rock Island, Galesburg, Princeton, Swedona, and other places. He also visited New Swed., where he gave encouragement to Hokanson. Beset by poverty and hardships, he made an extended trip in 1851 to Luth. centers in E states to gather funds for his work. He obtained $2,200, of which $1,500 was given by Jenny Lind, the "Swedish Nightingale," then touring Am. This money helped build small church structures at Andover and Moline, Ill., and New Swed., Iowa.

6. When the Ev. Luth. Syn. of N Ill.* was organized in Sept. 1851, Esbjörn became a mem., but only after taking exception to the doctrinal basis of the new body, which grudgingly acknowledged the AC as "mainly correct." On Esbjörn's request it was entered into the minutes of the Syn. that his congregations had written into their constitutions "that the Symbolical Books of the Lutheran Church contain a correct summary and exposition of the divine Word; wherefore we declare and adopt them as the foundation of our faith and doctrine, next to the Holy Scriptures." Esbjörn's correspondence from this period reveals his hope that with the arrival of more Scand. Luth. in the Midwest there would be a rising tide of confessional Lutheranism, and that the General Synod,* of which the Syn. of N Ill. became a part, would eventually be dominated by the conservative element.

7. When immigration began to reach flood tide, Esbjörn wrote urgent appeals to Peter Fjellstedt and Peter Wieselgren, pietist leaders in Swed., asking for help. In response, Tuve N. Hasselquist arrived in Galesburg, Ill., 1852. He was destined to be the leader of the future Aug. Syn. as pastor, ed., coll. pres., and syn. pres. Others who responded to the call were Erland Carlsson, who arrived in Chicago 1853; Jonas Swensson, who came to Sugar Grove, Pa., and Jamestown, N. Y., 1856, and O. C. T. Andren, who arrived at Moline 1856. Among theol. students from Swed. who also answered the call were Eric Norelius (future syn. historian), Andrew Andreen, P. A. Cederstam, and Peter Sjöblom, all subsequently ordained by the Syn. of N Ill.

8. With the arrival of more pastors from Swed. and Norw. the conservative Scand. elements soon dominated the Syn. of N Ill. Within the Syn. were a number of Norw. congregations organized as the Chicago Conf. The Swedes formed the Mississippi Conf. Friction developed between the Scand. and the "New Lutherans." In 1852 the Syn. of N Ill. had established an institution known as Ill. State U. at Springfield, and in 1858 Esbjörn had become a prof. at this institution. He soon found himself in conflict with the Neo-Luth. elements, and on March 31, 1860, resigned, advised the Scand. students to go home, and left for Chicago. At a meeting of the two Scand conferences in Chicago, April 23, 1860, Esbjörn's action was endorsed. An indep. syn. was planned. At Jefferson Prairie, Rock County, Wis., June 5—11, 1860, representatives of the Swed. and Norw. churches voted unanimously to found the Scand. Ev. Luth. Aug. Syn. in N. Am. The const. acknowledged the Holy Scriptures as "the revealed Word of God" and "the only infallible rule and standard of faith and practice," accepted the Apostolic, Nicene, and Athanasian Creeds, and declared adherence to "the unaltered Augsburg Confession as a short and correct summary of the principal Christian doctrines, understood as developed and explained in the other Symbolical Books of the Lutheran Church."

9. Hasselquist was elected pres. of the synod. Augustana Sem. was established at Chicago 1860, with Esbjörn as its head. In 1870 the Norw. withdrew peaceably from the syn., leaving the Swedes to work out their own destiny. See also *Norwegian-Danish Augustana Synod in America.*

10. The formation of the Aug. Syn. was regarded by many as presaging the breakup of the Gen. Syn. because of doctrinal laxity. This occurred 1867, when the Gen. Council was formed. Delegates of the Aug. Syn. attended meetings of the Council from the beginning. In 1870, the yr. of the Norw. withdrawal, the Aug. Syn. joined the Council. But when the Council merged with the Gen. Syn. and the United Syn. of the S 1918 to form the ULCA, the Aug. Syn. voted not to be part of the new body. In 1930 it participated with the ALC, the Norw. Luth. Ch. in Am. (later ELC), the LFC, and the United Dan. Luth. Ch. (later UELC) in forming the American Lutheran Conference* federation. When a movement was launched 20 yrs. later to form an organic union of the 5 Conf. bodies, the Aug. Syn. joined in the preliminary negotiations but later withdrew from the project, which issued 1960 in the formation of The American Lutheran Church.* The Aug. Syn., on the other hand, accepted an overture from the ULCA to join that church in inviting all other Luth. bodies to take part in conversations looking toward organic union. The Fin. Ev. Luth. Ch. and the AELC accepted the invitation. In June 1962 they met with the ULCA and the Aug. Syn. in a constituting conv. in Detroit to found the Lutheran Church in America.* In keeping with a tradition inherited from the Ch. of Swed., the Aug. Syn. throughout its hist. showed a deep interest in ecumenicity. In 1918 it was one of the founders of the National Lutheran Council.* In 1923 it helped organize the LWC, now the Lutheran World Federation.* In 1948 it was one of the founding churches of the World Council of Churches,* and in 1950 a charter member of the National Council of Churches of Christ in the United States of America.*

11. While Lutherans of other Eur. origins found themselves split into segments in Am., the Aug. Syn. never divided but remained the one Luth. gen. body of Swed. background in the US and Canada. Theol. controversies with the Evangelical Mission Covenant Church of America* over the doctrine of the Atonement marked the early hist. of the Aug. Syn.

12. During its 102-yr. hist. the Aug. Syn. extended its home miss. activities from the Atlantic to the Pacific and into Canada. Congregations were est. in 35 states and the Dist. of Columbia as well as 5 Can. provinces. The church's 13 major divisions, called conferences, were divided into districts. Originally under the jurisdiction of the conferences, home miss. became the responsibility of a syn. bd. 1938, beginning a strong centralization trend which continued till the Aug. Syn. became part of the LCA.

13. In for. miss. outreach the Aug. Syn. in its 2d yr. contributed funds to the Swed. Miss. Soc. in Stockholm and the Hermannsburg Miss. in Ger. When the Aug. Syn. became part of the Gen. Council 1870, it shared in the miss. work of that body in India and cooperated in Puerto Rico, where the

Luth. Ch. was planted by an Aug. Syn. pastor. An indep. China Miss. Soc., launched in Minn. 1902, was taken over by the syn. 1908. A large field was developed in China's Honan Province before the Jap. invasion and the following Communist revolution. In 1922 the Aug. Syn. took over the Leipzig Miss. in Tanganyika, Afr. When Ger. missionaries, expelled from Tanganyika in WW I, were permitted to return 1924, the Aug. Syn. opened a new field in Iramba. Under jurisdiction of the LWF the Aug. Syn. assumed principal responsibility for 3 large Ger. missions orphaned at the outbreak of WW II.

14. When it became part of the LCA, the Aug. Syn. was maintaining a theol. sem., 4 liberal arts colleges, and a junior college. Aug. Coll. and Theol. Sem. was founded in Chicago 1860, moved to Paxton, Ill., 1863, and to Rock Island, Ill., 1875. The sem. became a separate entity in 1948; in 1962 it was one of 4 theol. sems. of the merging LCA chs. to est. the Luth. School of Theol. at Chicago. Aug. Coll. is to take over the sem. buildings and remain in Rock Island. Gustavus Adolphus Coll. had its beginnings 1862 in Red Wing, Minn., was moved to E Union, Carver County, Minn., and in 1876 found a permanent home in St. Peter, Minn. Bethany Coll., noted for its "Messiah" festivals, was founded 1881 as an academy at Lindsborg, Kans. Upsala Coll., founded 1893, first had its home in Brooklyn churches, moved to Kenilworth, N. J., 1898, and finally located in E Orange, N. J. Luther Coll., Wahoo, Nebr., an academy and jr. coll. founded 1883, ceased to function with the formation of the LCA; its assets were absorbed by Midland Coll. The Aug. Syn. also cooperated with other Luth. bodies in maintaining a theol. sem. at Saskatoon, Sask., for training a Canadian ministry and supporting Pacific Luth. Coll., Tex. Luth. Coll., and Calif. Luth. Coll.

15. The Aug. Syn. and its conferences showed an early interest in charitable work. Immanuel Deaconess Institute, Omaha, Nebr., where deaconesses have been trained for many yrs., developed into a colony of mercy. When the Aug. Syn. merged with other churches in 1962, 11 hospitals, 17 homes for the aged, 10 children's homes, 9 hospices and inner miss. homes for young women, and 2 immigrant and seamen's homes were being supported. The number of summer camps was growing.

16. The first pub. of the Aug. Syn. appeared 1855 in Galesburg, Ill., when Hasselquist began printing a newspaper called *The Homeland: the Old and the New*. In 1856 he launched an exclusively religious paper called *The True Homeland,* the forerunner of *Augustana,* the church's Swed. pub. Its Eng. weekly, *The Lutheran Companion,* began 1892 as *The Alumnus,* merged 1950 with *Augustana* to form *The Augustana Lutheran.* But its new name was not popular and 1952 it reappeared as *The Lutheran Companion.* In 1963 it was absorbed by *The Lutheran.* Aug. Book Concern, Rock Island, Ill., founded as a private corporation, was taken over 1889 by the church. In 1963 it became an institution of the Bd. of Publication of the LCA.

17. Auxiliary organizations of the Aug. Syn. included the Aug. Luth. Ch. Women, formerly known as the Women's Miss. Soc., which for 70 yrs. gave strong support to the miss. program of the ch.; the Aug. Churchmen, a laymen's group; and the Aug. Luther League, the youth organization of the ch. All 3 groups were incorporated into the corresponding organizations of the LCA at the time of merger.

18. While the Aug. Syn. in polity and practice was theoretically congregational, it carried over from the State Ch. of Swed. a concept of the church as something more than the sum total of its local congregations. All candidates for the ministry were ordained at syn. meetings by the pres. of the church. While a call from a cong. was essential for ordination, the pastor through ordination became a mem. of the Aug. Ministerium and in that sense a minister of the ch. The syn. const. stated that the church "shall consist of all pastors and congregations regularly connected with it." The Aug. Syn. never adopted the episc. form of govt., which the Ch. of Swed. carried over from the pre-Reformation ch., but it constantly increased the authority of its pres. and its conf. executives, and the wearing of pectoral crosses became a prevailing practice among these officials.

19. Services in Swed., at first general in all pioneer churches, became increasingly rare following WW I and virtually ceased in all congregations by 1962. But much of the rich hymn heritage of the Ch. of Swed. is preserved in tr. in the Aug. hymnals of 1901 and 1925; some of it is retained in the *Service Book* ences of the Ch. of Swed.

20. Pres. of the Aug. Syn.: T. N. Hasselquist, 1860—70; Jonas Swensson, 1870—73; Eric Norelius, 1874—81; Erland Carlsson, 1881—88; S. P. A. Lindahl, 1888—91; P. J. Svärd, 1891—99; Eric Norelius, 1899—1911; L. A. Johnston, 1911—18; G. A. Brandelle, 1918—35; P. O. Bersell, 1935—51; Oscar A. Benson, 1951—59; Malvin H. Lundeen, 1959—62. Final statistics showed a baptized membership of 629,547. EER

See also *Lutheran Council in Canada,* 2.

E. Norelius, *De svenska luterska församlingarnas och svenskarnes historia i Amerika* (Rock Island, 1890); G. M. Stephenson, *The Religious Aspects of Swedish Immigration* (Minneapolis, 1932); *American Origin of the Augustana Synod,* eds. O. F. Ander and O. L. Nordstrom (Rock Island, 1942); *Century of Life and Growth: Augustana, 1848—1948,* hist. ed. O. N. Olson (Rock Island, 1948); A. R. Wentz, *Lutheran Church in American History,* 2d rev. ed. (Philadelphia, 1933) and *A Basic History of Lutheranism in America* (Philadelphia, 1955); O. N. Olson, *Augustana Lutheran Church in America, Vol. I: Pioneer Period, 1846—1860* (Rock Island, 1950); G. E. Arden, *Augustana Heritage* (Rock Island, 1963).

Augustana Synod. See *Augustana Evangelical Lutheran Church,* 8–20.

Augustana Theological Seminary. See *Augustana Evangelical Lutheran Church,* 9, 14; *Ministry, Education* of, X I.

Augusti, Johann C. W. (1772—1841). B. Eschenberga, near Gotha, Ger. Stud. theol. at Jena. Prof. philos. Jena 1800; prof. Oriental languages 1823; prof. theol. Breslau 1812, Bonn 1819; counselor of consistory Koblenz 1828; its pres. 1835. Wrote in field of archaeology, hist. of dogma, and introd. to OT.

Augustine of Ancona. See *Augustinus Triumphus.*

Augustine of Canterbury (d. ca. 604). Arrived Eng. 597 with ca. 40 other persons, including ca. 30 monks, a priest, and interpreters; after baptizing Ethelbert, king of Kent, converted and baptized many Anglo-Saxons; first abp. Canterbury. See also *Popes,* 4.

Augustine of Hippo (354—430). One of the greatest of the Lat. Ch. Fathers and one of the outstanding figures of all ages. B. Tagaste, d. Hippo, both in Afr. His father, Patricius, though a mem. of the council of his hometown, was not esp. distinguished for either learning or wealth and remained hostile to the Christian ch. till shortly before his death in 371, when he was baptized. His mother Monica was a consecrated woman, whose Christian virtues he praised in his writings. He was enrolled as a catechumen. Because of his fine progress in studies, a friend sent him to Madauros and Carthage for formal study. At Carthage he was drawn into sexual excesses, living with a mistress by whom he had a son, Adeodatus, 372. While studying rhetoric and philos. he came under the influence of Manichaeism,* holding its views for ca. 9 yrs. without becoming a formal convert. Later he wrote *Reply to Faustus the Manichaean,* showing the unscriptural nature of Manichaeism. He taught grammar at Tagaste and rhetoric first at Carthage and then Milan, where he met Ambrose.* But, rejecting Manichaeism, Augustine was influenced by Neoplatonism,* as his early writings, esp. *Of True Religion,* show. It is hard to determine from his writings when he was converted. His own account is in his *Confessions.*

In the spring of 387, after many sessions with Ambrose and study of the Bible, Augustine was baptized. Returning to Afr., he sold his possessions and founded a monastic-like clerical school. His Christianity remained strongly ascetic. In 395 he was consecrated as coadjutor to Bishop Valerius of Hippo and soon succeeded to the office. He was a pastor till death. His writings, esp. the letters, show that most of his time and thought was spent on pastoral concerns.

For more than 30 yrs. Augustine was also the leading theologian of Afr. Christianity. His influence at various synods was decisive. As the defender of the catholic faith he struggled against the Donatists and the Pelagians.* In his writings against the Donatists, esp. *On Baptism,* he develops his theol. on the nature of the ch. and the sacraments. But it is esp. in his writings against the Pelagians, e. g., *Of Grace and Free Will,* that Augustine makes his great contribution to catholic theol. He clearly asserts man's total inability to exercise his will favorably before God, and stresses on the other hand that God is absolutely sovereign, indeed irresistible, in His gracious activity. His formulations were the center of theol. discussion through the Middle Ages.

In 410 the Goths sacked Rome. The pagans blamed the Christians and their God for this disaster. Augustine put the capstone on his theol. activity by defending the Christians against this charge in *City of God.* He showed that the Father of Jesus Christ and the ch. of which He is the Head can never be identified with any one society, culture, or state. God directs all hist. toward a purpose that is beyond human structures, the City of God. WWO

See also *Philosophy; Preaching, Christian, History of,* 6; *Psychology,* C 2–3; *Time.*

MPL, 32—47; *NPNF,* Ser. 1, I—VIII; S. J. Grabowski, *The Church: An Introduction to the Theology of St. Augustine* (St. Louis, 1957); A. C. Pegis, *The Mind of St. Augustine* (Toronto, 1944); E. Gilson, *The Christian Philosophy of Saint Augustine,* tr. L. E. M. Lynch (New York, 1960); *A Companion to the Study of Saint Augustine,* ed. R. W. Battenhouse (New York, 1955).

Augustinian Hermits (Augustinian Friars; Hermits of St. Augustine. For Augustinian Canons see *Canons Regular*). Order formed 1256 by Pope Alexander IV by merging several small hermit bodies. Intended as counterpoise to growing power of older mendicant orders (Franciscans and Dominicans); linked more closely to papacy than they. The so-called Augustinian* Rule was the basis of its rather strict regulations. Soon the hermit character was exchanged for that of mendicancy, and the Augustinians became known as the 4th of the great mendicant orders (see *Mendicant Friars*). The order spread rapidly and in its prime had no less than 2,000 monasteries and 30,000 members. In the 14th c. a decline in discipline led to reforms; as a result part of the order became barefooted* monks. The Ger. "congregation" of the order was divided into 4 provinces. Luther entered the Erfurt monastery in the Saxon province 1505, tortured himself with rigorous privations of every kind, and went about with a sack as a mendicant. The provincial, Johann von Staupitz, referred him to Christ, encouraged him to study the Scriptures, caused him to be called to the U. of Wittenberg, and remained his friend, though he himself continued in the RC Ch. But so many other Augustinians, including Staupitz's successor, accepted Luther's doctrine, that the Ger. cong. of the order ceased to exist 1526; it was reestablished 1895 as a province. The Augustinians have been active chiefly as teachers and writers, but also as missionaries. They were the miss. pioneers in the Philippines. The motherhouse of the order in the US is at Villanova, Pa. See also *Luther Martin,* 3; *Recollects.*

Augustinian Rule. Basis of regulations of Augustinian* hermits; grew out of documents ascribed to Augustine* of Hippo. Chief teachings: love of God and neighbor; common life and the virtues necessary for it; abstinence; care of sick; authority; weekly reading for free followers of divine grace. See also *Dominicans.*

Augustinianism. Theology of Augustine* of Hippo.

Augustinus, Aurelius. Augustine* of Hippo.

Augustinus Triumphus (Augustine of Ancona; Agostino Trionfo; 1243–1328). Italian Augustinian hermit; versatile lecturer and preacher. Works include *Summa de potestate ecclesiastica* first comprehensive handbook of papacy; defended theory of power of ch. over state.

Augustus (Gaius Octavius; Gaius Julius Caesar Octavianus; 63 BC–14 AD). Grandnephew of Gaius Julius Caesar (100–44 BC; Roman statesman and gen.); stepfather of Tiberius*; b. Rome, It.; 1st Roman emp. 27 BC–14 AD; called Caesar Augustus Lk 2:1. "Augustus" became title also of other Roman emps. (e. g., Nero,* referred to Acts 25:21, 25).

Augustus II (1670–1733). "Augustus the Strong." King of Poland 1697–1704, 1709–33; b. Dresden, Ger.; elector of Saxony as Frederick Augustus I 1694–1733; joined RC Ch. to obtain Polish crown; wife and people remained Luth.; made alliance with Peter the Great of Russ. 1701; forced by Charles* XII of Swed. to give up crown 1704–09.

Auld Lichts. See *New Lichts.*

Aulén, Gustaf Emanuel Hildebrand. See *Christus Crucifixus; Lund, Theology of; Sweden, Lutheran Church in,* 6.

Aurelian (Lucius Domitius Aurelianus; ca. 212–275). "Restitutor orbis" (Lat. "Restorer of the world," i. e., of the Roman empire); b. Sirmium, Pannonia; Roman emp. 270–275; called "Lord and God." See also *Persecution of Christians,* 3.

Auricular Confession. See *Confession.*

Auriesville, New York. See *Pilgrimages,* 4.

Aurifaber, Andreas (1514—59). B. Breslau; d. Königsberg. Educ. Wittenberg. Rector Danzig and Elbing; prof. of physics and medicine Königsberg; son-in-law of A. Osiander* the elder and active mem. of his party. Opposed by M. Flacius* Illyricus.

Aurifaber, Johann (1517—68). B. and d. Breslau. Brother of Andreas. Educ. Wittenberg; friend of Melanchthon. Rector Breslau; prof. Rostock; chief author of Mecklenburg ch. order 1551—52; prof. Königsberg 1554; helped draw up Prussian ch. order; tried to mediate Osiandrian controversy; pastor and school inspector Breslau 1567.

Aurifaber, Johann (1519—75). Educ. Wittenberg 1537. Tutor to the count of Mansfeld 1540—44; Luther's famulus 1545; witnessed Luther's death 1546; court preacher Weimar 1550; went to Eisleben 1561; pastor Erfurt 1566. He was a coed. of the Jena ed. of Luther's works, ed. of 2 vols. of Luther's Lat. letters, and of the *Tischreden.* D. Erfurt.

Aurogallus (Goldhahn), Matthäus (ca. 1490–1543). B. Bohemia; prof. Heb. Wittenberg, 1521; publ. Heb. Grammar 1523—25, 1531; aided Luther in tr. OT esp. 1540 rev. Wrote Semitic hist. geog. *Reallexikon* 1526—39. Rector Wittenberg U. 1542.

Aurora Community. See *Communistic Societies, 5.*

Austin. Shortened form of Augustine, or Augustinian.

Austin Settlement. See *Madison Settlement.*

Australia, Evangelical Lutheran Church of. See *Australia, Lutheranism in,* A.

Australia, Lutheranism in. A. I. Lutheranism in Aus- began 1836, when Pastor Aug. A. I. Ludwig Christian Kavel* (1798–1860), of Klemzig, near Frankfurt on the Oder, Prussia, went to London to make arrangements for an entire cong. to emigrate to Am. or Australia. The reason for the contemplated emigration was the way the Prussian Union was forced on confessional-minded Lutherans. Emigration agents in London persuaded Kavel to take his flock to S Australia. The 1st group arrived at Port Adelaide in November 1838 and formed a short-lived settlement which they called Klemzig, a few mi. from what is now the center of Adelaide. In 1839 another colony of several hundred souls was planted at Hahndorf; and in 1841 Pastor G. D. Fritzsche* led another band of emigrants who founded Bethany and Lobethal. Other congregations were founded. With great zeal for the true worship of God and its perpetuation they est. a syn. soon after arrival. But the young ch. was soon disrupted by doctrinal controversies. Pastor Kavel's chiliastic teachings, his attitude toward the Luth. Confessions, and his views on ch. govt. led to a rupture in 1846. Henceforth the followers of Fritzsche and of Kavel pursued separate ways. In 1864, after both leaders had died, there was a brief *rapprochement;* but this "Confessional Union" did not lead to syn. reunion and was dissolved 1874 on the question of calling pastors from seminaries not genuinely Luth. (e. g., Basel). The followers of Kavel were now known as the Immanuel Syn. The antichiliastic party became the Ev. Luth. Syn. of S Australia; then, after the organization of other districts, the Ev. Luth. Syn. in Australia; finally, since 1941, the Ev. Luth. Ch. of Australia.

The body later known as the *Ev. Luth. Ch. of Australia* (ELCA) developed along sound, conservative Luth. lines and shows a steady, if slow, outward growth. Pastor Fritzsche had founded a coll. and sem. 1845 (Lobethal); but the doctrinal controversies then raging, as well as many other labors that claimed his time, caused the closing of the school 1855 after it had furnished 3 pastors. A number of missionaries were sent by the Dresden Miss. Soc. 1838—40 (Teichelmann, Schuermann, Meyer, Klose); later the ch. depended on Hermannsburg for ministers. In 1876 a private academy at Hahndorf was taken over by the syn. It turned out some good parish school teachers, but was closed 1885 because of lack of support.

2. With this decade began the "Missourian" influence in the hist. of the ELCA. Pastor Ernst Homann, having become acquainted with "Missouri" through *L. u. W.*, sought counsel from C. F. W. Walther. He became an enthusiastic "Missourian" and convinced others of the correctness of the position held by that ch. In 1881 Pastor Caspar E. Dorsch came as the first emissary of the St. Louis sem. and took charge of Bethlehem Ch., Adelaide. Others followed; but far greater was the number of young Australian Lutherans who received or completed their theol. training at various schools of the Mo. Syn.: Fort Wayne, St. Louis, Springfield. This movement was most pronounced at the turn of the c. when the 3d attempt to found a coll. and sem. (at Murtoa, Victoria, 1890) had not yet led to the inception of sem. classes nor of the higher preparatory classes. The abandonment of the Murtoa Coll. was staved off by the advice of A. L. Graebner, who visited Australia 1902 at the request of Ernst Homann (1838—1915). In 1903 C. F. Graebner, who had been called as principal of the coll., arrived and began his work. In 1905 the coll. was moved to Adelaide. For the next 25 yrs. all regularly called teachers (G. Koch, M. T. Winkler, Wm. Zschech, H. Hamann) were graduates of the St. Louis sem. The coll. is coeduc. since 1927. From 1912—65 Conc. Coll supplied ca. 200 theol. graduates and furnished most of the parish school teachers. In 1946 Queensland Conc. Coll., Toowoomba, a coeduc. secondary school, was founded. A new secondary school at Croydon, suburb of Melbourne, enrolled its first students 1964. Since 1958 Conc. Sem., on the same campus as Conc. Coll., Adelaide, is housed in its own buildings and is a separate institution.

3. The parish school system, maintained from the beginning of the ch., suffered greatly during WW I, when all schools in S Australia were closed by the govt. Rehabilitation was slow.

4. *Der Lutherische Kirchenbote* was pub. 1874–1917, 1925–40. *The Australian Lutheran* appeared 1913 as official organ of what was then known as Ev. Luth. Syn. in Australia (later Ev. Luth. Ch. of Australia), merged at end of 1966 with UELCA *The Lutheran Herald* in *The Lutheran,* which appeared 1967.

5. Home miss. work, which languished many yrs. because nearly all old settlers lived in the country, has been more energetically pursued in the last 30 yrs. Mission stations for work among aboriginals are maintained at Koonibba (since 1901) and Yalata (since 1954) on the so-called W Coast of S Australia. C. A. Wiebusch (St. Louis grad.) was the first miss. in charge at Koonibba. After supporting the work of the Mo. Syn. in China and India with means and some men, the ch. acquired a for. miss. field of its own 1936, the Rooke-Siassi islands NE of New Guinea. This enterprise suffered from the Japanese invasion in WW II, but the work of restoration proceeded rapidly. In 1951 the work was extended to the mainland of New Guinea.

B. 1. *The United Ev. Luth. Ch. in Australia* (UELCA) came into being in 1921 after a checkered hist. of secessions and reunions, of the affiliation and reaffiliation of various synods. The branch which followed Pastor Kavel experienced a secession movement 1860, the year of Kavel's death; the seceders linked up with the Ev. Luth. Syn. of Victoria (founded 1856 by Pastor Matthias Goethe). Goethe worked energetically among the many Germans who had come to Victoria for other than the religious reasons that had prompted the first immigration into S Australia. Full Luth. conviction was lacking; and through Goethe's successor in leadership, Pastor Herman Herlitz, the influence of the "United" *(unierte)* Basel Miss. Inst., as well as "United" influence in gen., became more pronounced. Hence the union of the Ev. Luth. Victoria Syn. with the Kavel branch, which took the name Ev. Luth. Immanuel Syn., was the signal for the dissolution 1874 of the "Confessional Union." The affiliation of the Immanuel Syn. and the Victoria Syn., known as the Ev. Luth. Gen. Syn., lasted till 1884. Its dissolution was caused by the same circumstance that had led the conservative Lutherans (later ELCA) to part from Immanuel 1874; the determination of the Victoria Syn. to continue calling "United" pastors from Basel. With the Victoria Syn. went a part of the Immanuel Syn. that called itself the Immanuel Synod *auf alter Grundlage* (a. a. G.). Continuing under the name of Ev. Luth. Gen. Syn., these were joined 1889 by the laxer of the two Luth. churches that had been organized 1885 in Queensland, where missionaries and lay helpers sent by "Father" Gossner had operated since 1838 and where a heavy Ger. immigration had later set in: the Ev. Luth. Syn. of Queensland. The more confessional-minded pastors (mostly Hermannsburg men), who had called their organization United Ger.-Scand. Ev. Luth. Syn. of Queensland, joined the Immanuel Syn. 1910 in the Ev. Luth. Ch. Union *(Kirchenbund),* which continued to secure ministers from Neuendettelsau and Hermannsburg. As a result of experiences during WW I the Gen. Syn. and the *Kirchenbund* joined to form the UELCA at Ebenezer, S Australia, Mar. 8, 1921. One small body that had separated from the ELCA 1902 was for a number of yrs. a dist. of the Ohio Syn. but joined the UELCA 1926. One reason for the merger was the situation in for. miss.: The Immanuel Syn., with the Iowa Syn., had long supported the work of the Neuendettelsau Miss. Soc. in what was then Ger. New Guinea. After WW I this territory was mandated to Australia, which was to dispose of the Ger. miss. Since the govt. would not give the miss. to a ch. outside Australia, the bodies mentioned formed a merger strong enough to handle the matter. In this they were supported by the Iowa Syn., which sent its pres., Fr. Richter, to advise the Australian Lutherans. When Ger. missionaries were permitted to return later, the field was divided bet. the Ger. miss. and the Iowa Syn. (later the ALC), the UELCA taking active part in the work under their Miss. Dir., F. O. Theile. The partnership with the ALC continued through and after WW II. The practical fellowship with the ALC which this work involved became a formally declared fellowship 1959. Connections with various Luth. churches in Ger. were maintained. ELCA and UELCA adopted Theses* of Agreement 1956, which became basis for merger forming the Luth. Ch. of Australia 1966.

2. A coll. was opened 1895 at Point Pass, S Autralia, remained small, and was devoted chiefly to training parish school teachers. As late as 1919 men went to Neuendettelsau, Ger., and Dubuque, Iowa, for theol. training. The formation of UELCA led to a small sem. at Tanunda, S Australia; but 1923 coll. and sem. were moved to N Adelaide (where Angas Coll. had been bought). After WW II a large property was acquired at Camden, suburb of Adelaide, where the coeduc. high school classes were quartered and taught; theol. classes are in the N Adelaide property. A coll. was opened at Brisbane, Queensland, 1945, and a boarding school with elementary and secondary classes at Walla Walla, New S Wales, 1948. In recent yrs. there has been a revival of the parish school, which had disappeared.

3. The ch. not only actively supports the New Guinea miss., but also maintains 2 miss. stations for aborigines: Hermannsburg, Cen. Australia, and Hope Valley, Queensland.

4. Official organ *The Lutheran Herald* merged at end of 1966 with ELCA *The Australian Lutheran* in *The Lutheran,* which appeared 1967.

5. Metropolitan congregations in Sydney and Melbourne left the UELCA 1923 and 1934 resp. and joined the *Reichskirche* 1929 and 1934. HH, HPH

A. Brauer, *Under the Southern Cross: History of Evangelical Lutheran Church of Australia* (Adelaide, 1956).

Australia, Missions in. 1. Mission work among the Australian aborigines has met with indifferent success. The original Australians are a dying race (estimated between 300,000 and 350,000 in 1788; 1961 census: 40,000 full-blooded natives). Their inveterate nomadic habits were formidable obstacles in the way of Christian evangelists. Miss. endeavors almost invariably took the form of the miss. station with ch., school, children's home, hospitals, and cottages for those who cared to stay. Men and women who cannot remain at the station are followed up by the missionaries at their places of work or cared for by the nearest resident pastor. So far it has not been found possible to create a real community and community life for the natives apart from the miss. station and supervised govt. camps. Yet the miss. stations have had good success in evangelizing the people as well as in lifting them to a higher soc. and economic level.

2. History. In 1823 the SPG expressed its willingness to assist in est. a miss. in New S Wales, but met with no success. In 1825 the London Miss. Soc. tried to win the aborigines in the vicinity of Sydney for Christ, but also with no success. In 1830 the CMS opened a station at Wellington Bay, ca. 200 mi. from Sydney. The mission was discontinued 1842. Missionaries sent by the Dresden Miss. Soc. came 1838 and 1840, but were compelled to relinquish their work and joined the ranks of the Luth. ministry. In 1840 the Gossner Miss. began to operate at Moreton Bay and at Keppel Bay (Queensland), but without lasting success. In 1851 the SPG opened stations in S Australia at Povindie on Spencer Gulf, with some success. The Moravians began a miss. 1859 in the Wimmera Dist. of Victoria. In the course of the following yrs. work was taken up by the Angl. Ch., the Presbyterians, the *Gesellschaft fuer innere und äussere Mission im Sinne der lutherischen Kirche,* various Luth. bodies, the Interdenom. Miss. Soc., the New S Wales Aborigines' Miss. Some stations had to be given up because of drought, illness, the trekking off or the dying out of natives. Of other non-Eur. peoples there are very few in Australia: Chinese, Hindus, Indians, Jap., Malays, S Sea Islanders, and others. Miss. work on a limited scale carried out among them by various religious bodies was not entirely without success. Of the excluded Kanakas not a few became Christians and returned to their native islands as witnesses for Christ. Comprehensive statistics not available. In 1962 the Koonibba miss. station (ELCA) numbered 579 souls and Yalata 250; reports on the 2 miss. stations of the UELCA show a total of 1,622. HH; HPH

Australia, United Evangelical Lutheran Church in. See *Australia, Lutheranism in,* B.

"Australian Lutheran, The." See *Australia, Lutheranism in,* A 4.

Austria. *Area:* ca. 32,376 sq. mi. *Pop.:* ca. 7,171,000. Rep. 1919—33; lost indep. in Eur. upheaval of 1930s and 1940s; reest. as rep. 1945. Austria covers the territory of the Roman provinces Raetia, Noricum, and Pannonia. Christianity was probably brought to Noricum by Christian legions. Florian* was martyred under Diocletian. Severin(us)* worked in Noricum in 5th c. Ch. given permanent structure in 8th c. The Benedictines, who were chiefly instrumental in evangelizing the country, founded elaborate monasteries and est. the ch.

Bet. 1483 and 1804 Austria, under the Hapsburgs, was most intimately concerned in all the fortunes of the Ger. Empire. Maximilian I really est. the empire and incidentally fixed its relation to the Pope, esp. by uniting Sp. and the Neth. under his dominion; as a result Philip II became one of the most powerful RC monarchs the world has ever seen.

Ev. pastors were active in Austria at time of Reformation (Speratus, Stiefel, Bünderlin, J. Strauss). Many students went to Wittenberg; by 1527 there were many demands for the pure Gospel. Countermeasures were taken. Kaspar Tauber, Leonhard Kaiser, and Hubmaier were martyred. Luther's writings were forbidden.

In 1568 Maximilian II est. a measure of toleration. The nobility and scholars supported the Reformation. Chytraeus* was called in to organize the evangelicals.

But the cause of Protestantism received a severe setback 1629 by the Edict of Restitution of Ferdinand II; the Ev. congregations had to fight for their very existence. So severe were the persecutions of the Protestants, that large areas of the country were almost depopulated by the zealotism of their rulers, as in the case of the Salzburgers.* From 1624 Prot. clergy were exiled. In 1628 ev. services were forbidden. Protestantism survived through private reading of the Bible and devotional books. Under Joseph II non-RCs were granted limited religious freedom by the Edict of Toleration 1781. The greatest victory for the hierarchy was the Concordat of 1855, which practically made the Pope the ruler of the country. But 6 yrs. later the Evangelicals won a pronounced victory, and the Patent guaranteeing them religious liberty and ecclesiastical indep. was followed 1870 by the recall of the Concordat.

The RC Ch. is both numerically and politically by far the strongest ch. in Austria. Of its pop. ca. 89% are RC. It has many societies, institutions, and foundations. In almost every parish there are brotherhoods and societies for prayer, associations for both sexes and all ages, societies of priests, congregations of Mary, Franciscan Tertiaries, and the Soc. of the Holy Family. Children and youth are cared for in protectories, kindergartens, orphan asylums, boarding schools, refuges, training schools for apprentices, and the like.

The Prot., or Ev., churches of Austria are a minority. The Luth., Swiss, and Anabaptist movements gained strong support at the time of Reformation but only a remnant remained. The movement away from Rome has gained some force in the Ger. sections of Steiermark. Among the institutions of the inner miss. of the Ev. Ch. the Deaconess Mother House of Gallneukirchen, over 85 yrs. old, is important. Lutherans and Ref. are under one administration in the Ev. Ch. of the Augsburg and Helvetic Confessions. The situation of the evangelicals had improved after WW I, but the 1933 Concordat brought new difficulties.

The govt. has recognized the following besides Luth. and Ref.: Gk. Orthodox 1781, Israelite 1781, Old Catholics 1877, Herrnhüter 1880, Islam 1912, Methodists 1951, Mormons 1955. Baptists and Mennonites are also active in Austria. Non-RC Christians participate in the Ecumenical Council, est. 1958.

Georg Loesche, *Geschichte des Protestantismus im vormaligen und neuen Österreich,* 3d ed. (Leipzig, 1930); H. Zimmermann, "Österreich," *Die Religion in Geschichte und Gegenwart,* ed. H. v. Campenhausen et al., IV (Tübingen, 1960), 1588—95.

Authenticity. See *Isagogics,* 1.

Authority. As in all spheres of human endeavor that impose or involve responsibilities, privileges, obligations, and duties, there is and must be authority, so there is authority also in the ch. This authority was bought and est. by the blood of Christ and is given to the ch. by Him, to be exercised by it as such or conferred by it on its individual members. Authority in the ch. is authority of the Word of Christ, which must always be the *norma normans* in confessing, teaching, and living. Authority must be in perfect accord with the Christian liberty which is ours through redemption in Christ Jesus. Since authority is given by the Bible to the spiritual priesthood of all believers (see *Keys, Office of*), of which, in fact, delegated authority is an emanation, those who have been given authority cannot lord it over the Christian cong. They are stewards rather than masters, servants rather than lords, and accountable to God. Though a cong. consist of only 2 or 3 members, it has all rights and spiritual powers. Those who exercise these powers for the cong. must administer such authority in the fear of God, for the welfare of the ch., in the interest of their fellowmen, and to the glory of God. HS

T. Coates, *Authority in the Church* (St. Louis, 1964); H. Studtmann, "Authority in the Church," *Abiding Word,* ed. T. Laetsch, I (St. Louis, 1946), 410—441; "Symposium on Church Authority," *American Lutheran,* XLIV (Dec. 1961), 318—322; XLV (Jan. 1962), 12—14+; (Feb. 1962), 43—49+; (Mar. 1962), 70—77+.

Authorized Version. See *Bible Versions,* L 10.

Autocephalous. Term used in early ch. to describe bps. superior; in modern E Orthodox Ch., nat. churches governed by own syn.

Auto-da-fé (Port. "act of faith"). Ceremony attending official final sentence of Inquisition, esp. in Spain.* Included procession to place of condemnation, sermon, reconciliation or sentence of condemnation, and handing over of recalcitrants to civil authority.

Automatism. Belief that animals and man are machines governed by mechanical laws. Advanced by Fr. physician and philos. Julien Offroy de La Mettrie* and later by S. Hodgson,* T. H. Huxley,* and W. K. Clifford.* Found in some forms of behaviorism. See also *Psychology,* J 4.

Auto redemption. Term used to describe belief (held by Unitarians, Modernists, and similar groups) that man saves himself.

Auxentius 1. D. ca. 374. Arian; bp. Milan; opposed Nicene Creed. 2. 4th—5th c. Pupil and biographer of Ulfilas.

Avatar. See *Hinduism,* 4.

Ave Maria (Lat. "Hail, Mary"). Also called the Angelic Salutation. Combined out of Lk 1:28, 42, it read originally "Hail, Mary, full of grace, the Lord is with thee; blessed art thou among women, and blessed is the fruit of thy womb, Jesus." As a memorial of Christ's incarnation, it has been in devotional use among Christians since the 11th c. In 1522 Luther wrote a commentary, often reprinted, on it (WA 10 II, 407–409; 17 II, 398–410; but see also 11, 59—61), and in a slightly modified form it is part of the gradual psalmodies for the Feast of the Annunciation (March 25) and of the Visitation (July 2) in our rite (*The Lutheran Hymnal* pp. 86, 87); there is also an echo of it in stanza 2 of Hymn 98, "Of the Father's Love Begotten." The objectionable addition — "Holy Mary, Mother of God, pray for us poor sinners now and in the hour of our death" — was not generally used until the 16th c. and became official even for RCs only in 1568. RCs make extensive use of the Ave Maria in their devotion, both as an indep. prayer, esp. after the Lord's Prayer, and as a frequently repeated part of the rosary.* ACP

Avenarius. See *Habermann.*

Aventrot, Joan. Neth. Prot.; burned Sp. 1632.

Averroes. See *Arabic Philosophy.*

Avesta. See *Zend-Avesta.*

Avicebrón (ibn-Gabirol: ca. 1020–ca. 1070). Sp. Jewish philos. Espoused pantheism which mingled Aristotelianism and Neoplatonism. Wrote *Fons vitae.*

Avicenna. See *Arabic Philosophy.*

Avidius Cassius. See *Apologists,* 5.

Avignon. City on Rhone, capital Vaucluse dept.; ca. 50 mi. N of Marseilles. Center of Albigenses* in 12th c. Papal property 1348. Seat of papal Babylonian* captivity.

Ávila, Juan de. See *John of Ávila.*

Awakening. See *Conversion,* II, 1; *Finland, Lutheranism in,* 4; *Great Awakening in England and America; Revivals,* 2.

Awakening of Confessional Lutheranism. See *Lutheran Confessions,* A 6.

Axiology (Gk. "science of value"). Theory of values which holds that results of psychology, religion, logic, philos., metaphysics, etc., are to be correlated. See also *Baden School; Windelband, Wilhelm.*

Axiom. Statement regarded as self-evident and accepted without proof. The modern tendency is to doubt axiomatic propositions. The existence of God is often treated as axiomatic in the Bible (Jn 14:1; Heb 11:6), though evidences are also treated.

Ayeul. See *Agil(us).*

Azariah, Vedanayakam Samuel (1874—1945). First Indian bp. of Angl. Ch.; educ. Madras Christian Coll.; active in miss. societies of India and formation of the Ch. of S India. Emphasized importance of Gospel preaching, need for well-trained ministry, and evangelism by every Christian; opposed caste system.

Azarias, Carolus. See *Flacius Illyricus, Matthias.*

Aztecs. See *Mexico;* A, B.

Azymite Controversy. The name *azymitai,* "users of unleavened bread," was given by the Gk. Ch. to the Lat. Ch. from the 11th c., because the latter used unleavened bread in the Lord's Supper, whereas the Gk. Orthodox Ch. insists on leavened bread. The W Ch. maintained it was immaterial which kind of bread was used. The Council of Florence decided 1439 that each ch. was to follow its own custom. See also *Schism,* 6.

B

Baader, Franz Xaver von (1765—1841). RC; deeply interested in Eckhart, St. Martin, and Böhme; left engineering profession to teach philos. theol. Munich. Considered God an everlasting process of activity, ethics the realization of divine life, and hist. the unfolding of God's redeeming love.

Baal. See *Canaanites, Religion of.*

Ball Shem-Tob (Baal Shem-Tov ["good (or kind) master of the Holy Name"]; real name Israel ben Eliezer; known also by acronym BEShT, formed from his initials; ca. 1700–60). Jewish teacher, healer; founded modern Hasidism* in Poland.

Babai the Great (d. 628). Teacher in Nisibis; Nestorian theol.

Babeuf, Francois Noel (Baboeuf; Gracchus; 1760–97). Fr. pol. agitator and journalist. See also *Communistic Societies,* 3.

Babists. See *Bahaism.*

Babst, Valentin (16th c.). Pub. Luther's *Geistliche Lieder.*

Babylas (d. ca. 250). Bp. Antioch; died in prison during Decian persecution. Chrysostom preached 2 sermons in his honor.

Babylonian Captivity. 1. Captivity of Jews in Babylon (2 K 24:14-16; 25:11; 2 Ch 36:22-23; Ez 1:1-4; Jer 25:11-12; 29:10; Dn 9:2; Zch 1:12; 7:5). 2. Metaphorically, period of popes at Arignon,* 1309–77 (Clement V, John XXII, Benedict XII, Clement VI, Innocent VI, Urban V, Gregory XI). After papal court was returned to Rome, antipopes Clement VII and Benedict XIII occupied Avignon. See also *Christian Church, History of,* II 3; *Popes,* 13, 14; *Schism,* 8. 3. Used metaphorically by Luther for subservience of ch. to Rome and abuses connected with the Mass. See also *Luther, Chief Writings of,* 4.

Babylonians, Religion of the. 1. Composite polytheistic form of religion in which the religious ideas current in the area of Babylon were ultimately merged with those prevailing in the city-states of the lower Tigris-Euphrates valley, when the latter were gradually absorbed into the Babylonian Empire under the 1st dynasty of Babylon (ca. 1800 BC). Marduk (Bel, i. e., Lord), chief deity of Babylon, the victorious city, emerged as head of the empire's pantheon. But homage was paid also to the gods of the conquered cities, chief among them Nabu (god of wisdom and writing) of Borsippa, Shamash (sun god) of Larsa and Sippar, Sin (moon god) of Ur, Ishtar (mother goddess) of Uruk, Ea (god of the watery deep) of Eridu, Enlil (storm god) of Nippur. As the names indicate, the arising religion included elements of Sumerian and Semitic origin. Worship of these gods included votive offerings, prayers which voiced the worshiper's praise of the respective god or presented petitions to him, the recitation of psalms of repentance, and, at the time of the spring equinox, the great ceremonial procession in connection with the New Year festival. On the latter occasion the king of Babylon took the hands of Marduk, a symbolic action to express that he was the god's adopted son.

2. The Babylonians further recognized the existence of a large number of demons, depicted in frightful form, which plagued mankind with disease and a host of other evils. To ward these off, the religious Babylonian wore amulets and resorted to incantations, the chanting of which was a specialty of a certain class of priests. There was, however, also a belief that there were beneficent genii, and each Babylonian was thought to have his particular patron god or goddess to whom he could appeal for help and protection and who would intercede in his behalf before the great gods. Witches and the evil eye were greatly feared.

3. The religious cult was in charge of a numerous priesthood grouped in many classes and ranks. Besides being in charge of the temple worship carried on in the sanctuaries of the various gods, the priests were the recognized authorities in the field of divination carried on by inspecting sheep's livers (hepatoscopy), reading the future in the stars (astrology), and interpreting dreams and omens of a wide variety (abnormalities of newborn children and animals; the shape assumed by a drop of sesame oil on water). The priests, however, were also the learned men of their time and devoted themselves to the preservation of religious and other literature, copying it for use in the temple libraries.

4. Imposing temples housed the images of the many gods, and kings considered it of special merit to erect such sanctuaries in the centers where each god was worshiped. A special feature in connection with some of these structures was the *ziggurat,* a square tower of as many as 7 stories of decreasing size, with a ramp running around the outside and serving as a staircase leading to the top. Famous is the temple-tower at Borsippa, forming part of the temple of Nabu. Today a large mound known as Birs Nimrud (Tower of Nimrod) marks the location.

5. Death to the Babylonian meant the separation of the soul from the body, the former entering the realm of the dead to continue a cheerless and shadowy existence in dark surroundings. Rulers of this nether world were the goddess Allatu, or Ereshkigal, and her husband Nergal, or Ninazu. In order that the soul might come to rest it was essential that the body be properly interred and not be disturbed in the grave.

6. Among the abundant remains of the religious literature of the Babylonians 2 are the most important: an epic glorifying Marduk and the so-called Gilgamesh epic. The former relates how the gods, the universe, and the human race came into being and how Marduk attained the position of leadership among the gods. The latter epic contains an account of the Flood which in many respects closely parallels the Biblical story.

7. The religious beliefs of the Assyrians were essentially the same as those of the Babylonians, with the exception that their chief god was Ashur. With the fall of Nineveh (612 BC) and the capture of Babylon by Cyrus (539 BC) the religion of the Babylonians and Assyrians fell into disuse. GVS

M. Jastrow, *The Religion of Babylonia and Assyria* (Boston, 1898) and *Die Religion Babyloniens und Assyriens,* 2 vols. in 3 (Giessen, 1905—12); R. W. Rogers, *The Religion of Babylonia and Assyria* (New York, 1908).

Bach, Johann Christian (1735—82). Regarded the most highly talented son of J. S. Bach; the first Bach to study in It. 1754; pupil of Padre Martini; organist Milan Cathedral 1760; joined RC Ch.; to London 1762; friend of Mozart, whom he influenced as composer.

Bach, Johann Christoph (1642—1703). Cousin of J. S. Bach's father; uncle of J. S. Bach's first wife. Noted for bold harmonies, inventive genius, and elaborate settings. Compositions include *Es erhub sich ein Streit; 44 Choräle zum Präambulieren; Ich lasse dich nicht.*

Bach, Johann Michael (1648—94). Father of first wife of J. S. Bach; writer of chorale preludes.

Bach, Johann Sebastian (Mar. 21, 1685—July 28, 1750). B. Eisenach; son of Johann Ambrosius Bach and his wife, Elisabeth, nee Lämmerhirt. His parents died before the end of his 10th year; he then lived with an older brother, Johann Christoph, a former pupil of Pachelbel. At 15 he became chorister at Lüneburg in the Michaelisschule, where he spent 3 yrs. and studied clavichord, violin, and composition and was probably a pupil of Georg Böhm, the organist of the Johanniskirche. In 1703 Bach became organist in Arnstadt, having spent some time in Weimar. In 1705 he was granted a month's leave of absence to become acquainted with Buxtehude and his work in Lübeck. Bach overstayed his leave by 3 months, incurring the displeasure of his superiors at Arnstadt. But his contacts with Buxtehude proved to be of great benefit. In 1807 he became organist at Mühlhausen and married Maria Barbara Bach, a distant cousin. Maria bore him 7 children, including 2 talented sons, Wilhelm Friedemann and Karl Philipp Emanuel. Intense strife had developed in Mühlhausen between orthodox Lutherans and Pietists. Bach was a profound believer in confessional Luth. orthodoxy, but had friends among the Pietists; a number of embarrassing situations developed which prompted him to leave the service of the ch. 1708 to become organist at Weimar at the court of Duke Wilhelm, a profoundly religious man, whose motto was "Alles mit Gott" and who was very devoted to his subjects. Bach wrote much organ music and many cantatas at Weimar. In 1717 he became Kapellmeister at Köthen at the court of Prince Leopold. Here Maria died in July, 1720, during Bach's absence from Köthen; Dec. 3, 1721, he married Anna Magdalena Wülcken, who had a beautiful soprano voice and a genuine appreciation of her husband's musical genius. In Köthen Bach composed his Brandenburg Concertos, much music for the clavichord, violin, and other instruments, and some ch. music. But the court at Köthen was Ref., not congenial to ch. music. Desiring again to compose more ch. and organ music and to send his older sons to a university, Bach left Köthen 1723 for Leipzig to become cantor of the Thomasschule and dir. of music at the Thomaskirche and Nikolaikirche. Here, despite many adversities and lack of appreciation and understanding on the part of his townspeople, he wrote much of his greatest music, including several cycles of ch. cantatas, his greatest organ music, the *Passions according to St. Matthew and St. John,* the *Christmas Oratorio,* several motets, the *B Minor Mass,* the *Musical Offering,* and *The Art of the Fugue.* In his own fields Bach has never been excelled or even equaled. Contrapuntal music found in him its greatest master; coupled with his skill and artistry one soon discovers a Luth. religiosity and theol. acumen which are astounding and which manifest themselves particularly in his music based on texts of the Bible, of Luth. chorales, and of Christian liturgies. Though at times the musicians' musician, Bach is today regarded as one of the great musicians of the people; he enjoys a popularity which surpasses that of any other great composer. He became blind in 1749. His greatness was not appreciated fully until more than a c. after his death. Bach is one of the most outstanding geniuses of Lutheranism, and his work, like that of Luther, is universal and timeless. See also *Oratorio; Passion, The; Schemelli, Georg Christian; Schubart, Johann Martin; Toccaha.* WEB

The Bach Reader, eds. H. T. David and A. Mendel (New York, 1945); W. Gurlitt, *Johann Sebastian Bach: the Master and His Work,* tr. O. C. Rupprecht (St. Louis, 1957); F. Hashagen, *Johann Sebastian Bach als Sänger und Musiker des Evangeliums und der lutherischen Reformation* (Emmishofen, Switz., 1925); G. Herz, *Johann Sebastian Bach im Zeitalter des Rationalismus und der Frühromantik* (Bern, 1935); H. Kretzschmar, *Bachkolleg* (Leipzig, 1922); C. H. Parry, *Johann Sebastian Bach,* rev. ed. (New York, 1934); A. Schweitzer, *Johann Sebastian Bach,* 10th ed. (Leipzig, 1934); P. Spitta, *Johann Sebastian Bach,* tr. C. Bell and J. A. Fuller-Maitland, 2 vols. in 1 (London, 1951); C. S. Terry, *Bach: A Biography,* 2d ed. (London, 1933) and *Bach: The Historical Approach* (New York, 1930); P. Wolfrum, *Johann Sebastian Bach,* 2 vols. (Leipzig, 1910); F. Blume, *Two Centuries of Bach* (New York, 1950) and "Johann Sebastian Bach," in *Die Musik in Geschichte und Gegenwart,* ed. F. Blume, I (Kassel, 1951), 962—1047; F. Hamel, *Johann Sebastian Bach: Geistige Welt* (Göttingen, 1951); F. Smend, *Bach in Köthen* (Berlin, [1951]); *The Little Bach Book,* ed. T. H. Nickel (Valparaiso, Ind., 1950); W. Schmieder, *Thematisch-systematisches Verzeichnis der Werke Johann Sebastian Bachs* (Leipzig, 1958).

Bach, Karl Philipp Emanuel (1714—88). Son of J. S. Bach; link bet. him and J. Haydn; assoc. with Klopstock; for a time in service of Frederick the Great. His *Versuch über die wahre Art das Klavier zu spielen* was the first well-organized treatise on playing keyboard instruments. His compositions often lack depth and show the influence of the Rationalistic Era; his *Fantasy and Fugue in C Minor* for organ represents him at his best. See also *Oratorio; Passion, The.*

K. P. E. Bach, *Essay on the True Art of Playing Keyboard Instruments,* ed. and tr. W. J. Mitchell (New York, 1948).

Bach, Wilhelm Friedemann (1710—84). Oldest son of J. S. Bach. Organist Dresden and Halle. Versatile composer.

Bach Gesellschaft. Organization founded Leipzig 1850 to make the works of J. S. Bach available. Dissolved 1900. Succeeded immediately by the Neue Bach Gesellschaft, which has popularized Bach's music and founded a Bach Museum in the Bachhaus, Eisenach.

Bachelor, Otis Robinson (1817—1901). B. Antrim, N. H.; d. New Hampton, N. H. Medical miss. to India for Free Bap. Miss. Soc. Stationed at Balasor 1840—51; Midnapur 1863—93. Principal of Midnapur Bible School.

Bachman, John (Feb. 4, 1790—Feb. 24, 1874). B. Rhinebeck, N. Y.; d. Charleston, S. C. Educ. Williams Coll. His theol. instructors were F. H. Quitman* and P. F. Mayer. Licensed to preach 1813; ordained 1814; pastor St. John's, Charleston, S. C., 1815; joined S. C. Syn.; its pres. Helped est. theol. sem. at Lexington, S. C., and Newberry Coll. Helped est. Gen. Syn. (pres. 1835, 1837) and Gen. Syn. South; helped in adoption of Book of Worship 1866; sympathized with Southerners during Civil War; contributed to Audubon's *Birds of America,* and collaborated with him on *Quadrupeds;* prof. of natural hist. in coll. of Charleston. Wrote *Unity of the Human Race* and *A Defense of Luther.*

Bachmann, Johannes Franz Julius. (1832–1888). B. Berlin; d. Rostock. Pupil of Tholuck and Hengstenberg; taught at Berlin 1856; prof. and U. preacher Rostock 1858; noted for knowledge of Luth. hymnology, biographer of Hengstenberg, and thorough work on the festival laws of the Pentateuch and on Judges 1—5.

Bachmann, Philipp Georg Otto (1864—1931). Luth.

theol. B. Geislingen; educ. Erlangen; prof. Systematic Theol. Erlangen 1902; collaborator on T. Zahn's NT commentary; chief contribution in area of religious education.

Backhaus, Johann Leonhard (Aug. 1, 1842—March 11, 1919). B. Amsterdam, Holland; educ. Teachers' Sem., Fort Wayne, Ind.; teacher Readfield, Wis., 1864; Bloomington, Ill., 1865—66; Venedy, Ill., 1867—82; St. Matthew's School, Chicago, 1883—84; prof. at Teachers' Sem., Addison, Ill., 1884—1915 (when he resigned); contributed articles to *Lutheraner* on educ. and schools.

Backsliding. See *Apostasy.*

Backus, Isaac (1724—1806). Congr.; opposed Saybrook* platform. Joined New Light separatists 1746. Withdrew over question of infant baptism. Bap. minister Middleborough, Mass., 1756 Championed religious freedom. Trustee Brown U. Active in Warren* Assoc. Wrote *A History of New England, with Particular Reference to the Denomination of Christians Called Baptists.* See also *Baptist Churches,* 22.

Bacmeister. 1 *Lucas* (1530–1608). B. Lüneburg; hymnist; educ. Wittenber; prof. and supt. Rostock; wrote *Von christl. Bann . . . aus Gottes Wort und D. M. Lutheri Schriften;* hist. of Rostock chs. 2. *Lucas* (1570–1638). B. Rostock. Son of preceding; prof. Rostock 1600; supt. Rostock 1604, Güstrow 1612; hymnist; works include *Disputationes contra decreta concilii Tridentini; Tractatus de lege; Disputationes de S. Trinitate.*

Bacon, Benjamin Wisner (1860—1932). Cong.; prof. of NT criticism Yale; wrote many works on introduction and exegesis.

Bacon, Francis (1561—1626). Eng. statesman and philos. Mem. Parliament; Lord Chancellor; peer. Convicted of taking bribes. Paved way for modern philos. by criticizing Scholastics for neglect of natural sciences and by advocating inductive (empirical) method. In *Novum organum* separated spheres of faith (theol.) and knowledge (philos.). Revelation sole source of faith. Experience source of knowledge. See also *Science, Secularism.*

Standard ed. of his works (14 vols.) by J. Spedding, R. L. Ellis, and D. D. Heath (London, 1857 to 1874); R. W. Church, *Francis Bacon* (New York, 1908); R. W. Gibson, Francis Bacon, *A Bibliography of His Works and of Baconiana to the Year 1750* (Oxford, 1950); G. W. Steeves, *Francis Bacon* (London, 1910).

Bacon, Roger (ca. 1220—ca. 1294). Called Doctor Mirabilis. Eng. philos. and scientist; Franciscan monk. Educ. Oxford and Paris. Settled at Paris. Opposed Scholasticism.* Insisted on supreme authority of Bible in theol., the right of the laity to the Bible, and the importance of its study in original languages; castigated corruption of priests and monks. Knowledge of physics, chemistry, and astronomy, gained by researches and experiments, put him far ahead of his times.

E. P. Cheyney, *The Dawn of a New Era, 1250 to 1453* (New York, 1936); T. Crowley, *Roger Bacon, The Problem of the Soul in His Philosophical Commentaries* (Dublin, 1950); S. C. Easton, *Roger Bacon and His Search for a Universal Science* (New York, 1952); H. O. Taylor, *The Mediaeval Mind: A History of the Development of Thought and Emotion in the Middle Ages,* 4th ed., 7th print., II (Cambridbe, Mass., 1959); E. Westacott, *Roger Bacon in Life and Legend* (New York, 1954).

Bad Boll. Place of Johann Blumhardt's* healing baths. After WW II the Mo. Syn. arranged theol. discussions with Ger. theologians at Bad Boll. See also *Germany,* C 6.

Bade, William Frederic (1871—1936). Prof. OT subjects Moravian Coll., Bethlehem, Pa., and Pacific School of Religion, Berkeley, Calif. Led archaeol. expeditions to Palestine. Works include *The Old Testament in the Light of Today.*

Baden, John H. (Dec. 20, 1823–July 10, 1897). B. Westeresch, Hannover. Studied theol. U. of Berlin. Asst. to Charles Stohlmann, New York; organized Luth. congregations at Mount Vernon and Hastings, N. Y., and St. Luke Ger. Ev. Luth. Ch., Brooklyn, which he served 24 yrs.; ed. *Herold,* organ of New York Ministerium, 1879; pres. of Ministerium 1881; helped est. Luth. Home for Immigrants in New York; dir. Luth. Theol. Sem., Philadelphia; on Bd. of Trustees, Wartburg Orphans' Home.

Baden, Lauridtz Ernst-Sön (1616—89). Dan. pastor and theol.; known for his devotional book *Himmelstige.*

Baden Disputation. See *Switzerland,* 2.

Baden School. Name of neo-Kantian trend in philos. which found main problems of philos. in axiology.* Chief representative was Wilhelm Windelband.*

Bader, Augustin (d. 1530). Anabap. leader in Augsburg; later broke with Anabaps. and held that his infant son was king of impending millennium, and that he himself was his son's reprensentative; tortured and executed on suspicion of plotting against the govt.

Bader, Johannes (1470/90–1545). Ref. theol.; pastor Landau; won for Reformation; excommunicated at Speyer 1524; opposed Anabaps.; his doctrine of Lord's Supper similar to that of M. Bucer*; influenced by K. v. Schwenkfeld.*

Bading, Johann (1824—May 24, 1913). B. Rixdorf, near Berlin; studied in Gossner* Missionary Society (1846) and under Louis Harms at Hermannsburg (1849) for miss. work in Afr.; deciding to go to Am., he left Louis Harms (1852) and completed studies at Barmen; sent to Am. by Langenberg Soc.; arrived Wis. 1853; ordained 1853 by John Muehlhauser* and Jacob Conrad; held pastorates at Calumet, Theresa, Watertown, Milwaukee, Wis.; pres. Wis. Syn. 1860—64, 1867—89; one of chief negotiators with representatives of Mo. Syn. in forming Synodical* Conference 1872; pres. Syn. Conf. 1882 to 1912; pres. Bd. of Trustees, Northwestern Coll., Watertown, Wis., 1865—1915; traveled in Ger. to raise funds for Northwestern 1863, 64; resigned pastorate in 1908 but remained asst. till 1913. Led Wis. Syn. to confessional Lutheranism. Instrumental in locating Northwestern Coll. at Watertown rather than Milwaukee.

Baeck, Leo (1873—1956). Rabbi; taught in Berlin; leader of Ref. Jewry. Works include *The Essence of Judaism* (rendition by I. Howe based on tr. from Ger. by V. Grubenwieser and L. Pearl).

Baepler, Andrew (July 28, 1850—Oct. 10, 1927). B. Baltimore; grad. St. Louis 1874; pastor Dallas, Tex., 1874, 75; near Cole Camp, Mo., 1875—79; at Mobile and Moss Point, Ala., 1879—82; Eng. miss. for W Dist., Mo. Syn., 1882, 83; prof. St. Paul's Coll., Concordia, Mo., 1884—87, 1899—1925; pres. Conc. Coll., Fort Wayne, 1888—94; pastor Little Rock, Ark., 1894—99; retired 1925.

Baepler, Walter August (Sept. 21, 1893—Oct. 9, 1958). B. Fort Wayne, Ind.; d. Springfield, Ill.; grad. Conc. Sem., St. Louis, 1914; pastor Haultain, Sask., 1915, 16; McEachern, Sask., 1916, 17; Moose Jaw, Sask., 1917–20; Winnipeg, Man., 1920–23; prof. Conc. Coll., Edmonton, Alta., 1923—36; Conc. Sem., Springfield, Ill., 1936–53; pres. there 1953 to 1958. Supt. of missions Man. and Sask. 1918 to 1921; vice-pres. Man. and Sask. Dist., Mo. Syn., 1922, 23; pres. Synodical* Conf. 1952–56. Works include *A Century of Grace: A History of the Missouri Synod, 1847—1947; A Century of Blessing, 1846 to 1946: Concordia Theological Seminary, Springfield, Illinois.*

Baetis, William (Wilhelm; Baetes; Batis; Betis; Petis; 1777–Aug. 17, 1867). Licensed by Pa. Ministerium

1809; served congs. in N. J. and Pa.; Pa. Ministerium Senior 1836.

Baetyl. Sacred rock (often meteor) used in heathen worship.

Baeumker, Clemens (1853—1924). Prof. philos. Breslau 1883, Bonn 1900, Strasbourg 1903, Munich 1912. Held that hist. is the evolution of the human spirit and that the past is immanent in the present and provides continuity. Wrote esp. on patristic and medieval philos.

Bager, John George (1725—94). Educ. Helmstedt. Pastor Palatinate; to Am. 1752; pastor New York, Baltimore, and Lebanon and York Cos., Pa.

Bagster's Polyglot. See *Polyglot Bibles.*

Bahaism. Mirza Ali Mohammed (1819—50) of Shiraz, Persia, assumed title Bab (Gate); proclaimed himself reformer of Islam 1844. Gained many followers (Babists) but was imprisoned and executed by Persian govt. 1850. In 1863 Bahaullah (Splendor of God), follower of the Bab, proceeded to formulate the sect's teachings while confined in Palestine by Turkish govt. After Bahaullah's death in 1892 his oldest son, Abdul Baha, Turkish prisoner till 1908, carried on; visited US 1912; d. Haifa 1921.

Bahaism is represented in Am. since the Chicago World's Fair of 1893. A magnificent temple, Mashrak-el-Azkar ("The Dawning Point of the Commemorations" of God), was erected at Wilmette, Ill.; designed by Louis J. Bourgeois; is 9-sided, with intricate ornamentation of exquisite beauty, was dedicated in 1942, and is open to the 9 great religions.

Bahaism has "no professional clergy, no ritualistic service"; proclaims itself a call to religious unity; and sets up as basic Bahai teachings: the oneness of mankind, independent investigation of truth, equality of men and women, universal peace, universal education, spiritual solution of the economic problem, a universal language, an international tribunal.

Bahaullah. See *Bahaism.*

Bahnmaier, Jonathan Friedrich (1774—1841). B. Oberstenfeld; pastor Ludwigsburg; prof. Tübingen 1815; hymnist. Works include *Meletemata de miraculis Christi;* sermons; works on asceticism; hymns include "Walte fürder, nah und fern."

Bahnsen, George Frederik. See *Danish Lutherans in America,* 1.

Bahrdt, Karl Friedrich (1741—92). Rationalistic Ger. Prot. theol.; dismissed from professorship at Leipzig and Erfurt for profligacy, at Giessen because of heretical tr. of NT. Wrote extensively. See also *Philanthropinism.*

Bahrein. See *Middle East,* L 5.

Bahya ibn-Paquda (11th c.). Rabbinical judge at Saragossa, Sp.; wrote *Guide to the Duties of the Heart,* one of the first systematic Jewish ethics.

Baier, Johann Wilhelm (1647—95). B. Nürnberg; d. Weimar. Prof. and rector Jena and Halle; gen. supt., court preacher, and city pastor at Weimar. Chief work, *Compendium theologiae positivae,* shows great influence in synergism Johann Musaeus,* his teacher and father-in-law, had on him; many editions; that of C. F. W. Walther (1879) included a rich collection of extracts from earlier Luth. theologians.

K. Heussi, *Geschichte der theologischen Fakultät zu Jena* (Weimar, 1954).

Baierlein, Eduard Raimund (Apr. 29, 1819—Oct. 12, 1901). B. Sierakowski, Posen, Poland; d. Ger.; arrived Frankenmuth, Mich., as miss. to Chippewa June 10, 1847; worked among Chippewa (Station Bethany, St. Louis, Mich.) 1847—53; left Bethany and became miss. to India in service of Leipzig Ev. Luth. Miss.; arrived Madras, India, Dec. 17, 1853; worked at Sadras, Cuddalore, and Tranquebar; discontinued because of poor health 1886. See also Miessler, Ernst Gustav Hermann.

E. R. Baierlein, *Im Urwalde: Bei den roten Indianern* (Dresden, 1889), *Nach und aus Indien* (Leipzig, 1873), and *Die Ev.-luth. Mission in Ostindien* (Leipzig, 1874); W. P. Schoenfuhs, "Eduard Raimund Baierlein: Lutheran Missionary to the Indians in America and Asia," *CHIQ,* XXVII (Oct. 1954), 133—141; (Jan. 1955), 145—162; XXVIII (Spring 1955), 1—26.

Baillie. 1. *Donald Macpherson* (1887—1954). Brother of John. B. Scot.; prof. St. Andrews U., Scot., 1935 to 1954. Opposed liberal theol. and attempts to reconstruct hist. Jesus; defended genuine incarnation; emphasized "I-Thou" encounter of faith. Wrote *Faith in God; God Was in Christ.* 2. *John* (1886 to 1960). Brother of Donald. B. Scot.; prof. theol. Auburn, N. Y., 1919, Toronto 1927, New York 1930; prof. divinity Edinburgh 1934; Moderator Ch. of Scot. 1943; rector New Coll., Edinburgh 1950; chaplain to Queen in Scot. 1954. Wrote extensively on revelation. Held all knowledge of God is based on God's self-disclosure (mediated immediacy); God is known to all men. Works include *Interpretation of Religion; And the Life Everlasting; Our Knowledge of God; The Belief in Progress; The Idea of Revelation in Recent Thought; The Sense of the Presence of God.*

Baius, Michael (1513—89). Flemish RC theol.; forerunner of Jansen*; had conflict with popes on questions of grace, free will, and sin; condemned by papal bulls (1567, 1579). In his system (Baianism) innocence is necessary component of human nature in original state; redemption restores original innocence; original sin is hereditary, habitual concupiscence.

Bake, Reinhard (1587—1657). Pastor Cathedral Ch., Magdeburg; remained staunch Luth. despite Jesuit attempts to convert him.

Baker, George. See *Father Divine.*

Baker, Henry Williams (1821—77). B. London; educ. Cambridge. Vicar of Monkland, Herefordshire. Best known as first ed. of *Hymns Ancient and Modern* (1861). Wrote 33 hymns, including "The King of Love My Shepherd Is."

Baker, John Christopher (1792—1859). Mem. Pa. Ministerium; held 3 pastorates, the last at St. Luke's, Philadelphia; able preacher and pastor.

Bakke, Nils J. (Sept. 8, 1853—May 8, 1921). Miss. to Am. Negroes. B. Norw.; d. Milwaukee; educ. Luther Coll., Decorah, Iowa, and Conc. Sem., St. Louis; grad. 1880; ordained Nov. 7, 1880; pastor "Sailors' Home," New Orleans, 1880; Concord, N. C., 1891; est. Immanuel Luth. Coll., Greensboro, N. C., 1903; prof. 1903—11; helped organize Immanuel Luth. Conf. 1900; field secy. for colored miss. of Ev. Luth. Syn. Conf. 1911. In Cincinnati 1911—13; St. Louis 1913—16; Oak Hill, Ala., 1916—20; Milwaukee 1920—21.

Bakker, Jan de. See *De Bakker, Jan.*

Baksay, Sándor (1832—1915). Bp. Ref. ch. Hungary. Wrote esp. on ethics.

Bakunin, Mikhail Aleksandrovich (1814—76). Russ.; worked with Marx and Engels. Developed Bakuninism, a theory of revolutionary anarchy, in *God and the State.*

Balder. In Norse mythology, son of Odin and Frigga; personification of sun's brightness; killed through treachery of Loki.

Balduin, Friedrich (1575—1627). Mem. philos. faculty, Wittenberg, 1601; preacher Freiberg 1602; supt. Oelsnitz 1603; prof. theol. Wittenberg 1604; supt. Wittenberg 1607. Works include a Lat. commentary on the Epistles of Paul and *Tractatus de casibus conscientiae.*

Baldung-Grien, Hans (ca. 1484—1545). Ger. artist and sculptor. Worked briefly with Dürer.* Works include high altar of Freiburg cathedral. Depicted Luther as very pious man in woodcut, 1521.

Bale, John (1495—1563). Bp. Ossory, Ireland. Wrote

mysteries and miracle plays. Used stage to promote Reformation.

Balfour, Arthur James (1848—1930). Brit. statesman and philos. Originator of Balfour Declaration (see *Middle East,* F). Wrote apologies for religious faith in which he held that all knowledge, including scientific, requires axioms which require religious faith. Works include *A Defence of Philosophic Doubt; The Foundations of Unbelief; Theism and Humanism; Theism and Thought.* See also *Metaphysical Society, The.*

Balfour, Edmund. See *Danish Lutherans in America,* 1.

Ball, Dyer (June 3, 1796—March 27, 1866). B. W. Boylston, Mass.; educ. Union Coll., New Haven, and Andover; sent by ABCFM as medical miss. to Singapore, then to Macao (1841) and Hongkong.

Balla, Emil (1885—1956). Prof. OT Münster, Leipzig, and Marburg. Works include *Das Ich der Psalmen; Der Erlösungsgedanke der israel-jüd. Religion; Die Droh- u. Scheltworte des Amos; Die Botschaft der Propheten.*

Ballagi, Mór (1815—91). Hung. Ref. theol. of Jewish descent; united 2 Prot. churches in Hungary; defended Prot. autonomy; promoted modern scientific theol.; ed. of journals; wrote commentaries and other works.

Ballantine, Henry (March 5, 1813—Nov. 9, 1865). B. near Albany, N. Y.; educ. U. of Ohio, and Princeton, Union (Va.), and Andover seminaries. Sent by ABCFM to India 1835; stationed at Ahmadnagar. Assisted in tr. Bible into Marathi. Tr. and wrote hymns in Marathi.

Balle, Nikolai Edinger. See *Denmark, Lutheranism in,* 7.

Baller, F. W. (1873—1922). Miss. of CIM. Wrote dictionary, primer, textbooks.

Ballou, Hosea (1771—1852). Clergyman. Often called "Father of American Universalism." Differed from J. Murray* in thoroughgoing anti-Calvinism. Most important work: *Examination of the Doctrine of Future Retribution.*

Balogh, Ferenc (1836—1913). Hung. Ref. Ch. hist.; espoused system of neoorthodoxy.

Balsamon, Theodore (ca. 1140—after 1195). Byzantine canonist; wrote *Scholia* on *Nomocanon* of Photius; collected E canon law. *MPG* 137, 138.

Baltic States. See *Estonia; Latvia; Lithuania.*

Baltimore, Councils of. See *Councils and Synods,* 6.

Baltimore, Lords. See *Calvert.*

Baltimore Catechism. See *Catechetics,* 14.

Baltimore Declaration. "Declaration on the Word of God and the Scriptures" adopted 1938 by the ULC at Baltimore, Md. Sets forth ULC position on the authority of Scripture, the meaning of "Word of God," and the inspiration of Scripture. See also *Lutheran Church in America,* II.

Documents of Lutheran Unity in America, ed. R. C. Wolf (Philadelphia, 1966), pp. 345, 357–359, 539.

Baltzer, Eduard Wilhelm (1814—87). Leader of *Lichtfreunde* in Ger.; espoused freedom of doctrine, political and social reform.

Bambara. See *Africa,* C 3.

Bambino. In art, name given to Jesus in swaddling clothes. It. diminutives for "child."

Ban. 1. Declaration of excommunication (see *Keys, Office of,* 3, 6, 7); 2. Fine imposed for sacrilege. 3. Interdict, the so-called greater excommunication, which imposed civil disabilities in addition to spiritual penalties. Luther placed the greater ban outside the jurisdiction of the church (SA-III IX).

Bancroft, Richard (1544–1610). Abp. Canterbury; held episcopacy is of divine origin; condemned Puritanism and Presbyterianism. Uncompromising at Hampton Court Conf.

Báñez, Domingo (1528—1604). Sp. Dominican noted for *banesianismus,* a theory of relation of grace and human freedom in good works.

Banfield, A. W. See *Africa,* C 14.

Bang, Jacob Peter (1865—1936). Dan. theol.; b. Rönne; d. Hellerup; prof. dogmatics and NT exegesis Copenhagen. Wrote in areas of hist. of doctrine and ethics. Ed. *Dansk kirketidende* (1903—16).

Bangladesh, People's Republic of. See *Asia,* B 2.

Bangor. Municipal borough, co. Down, N Ireland. Abbey (said to have sheltered 4,000 monks) est. there ca. 555 by Comgall, teacher of Columba.

Banks, A. A. See *Baptist Churches,* 31.

Banns. See *Marriage,* III.

Bantu. See *Africa,* A 1.

Baptism. See *Grace, Means of,* III.

Baptism, Heretical. See *Heretical Baptism.*

Baptism, Lay. Baptism performed by an unordained person. See also *Grace, Means of,* III; *Keys, Office of,* 5, 7.

Baptism, Liturgical. 1. The 2 constituent parts of baptism, water and the "word," or baptismal formula, are found in NT (Jn 3:5; Mt 28:19; Acts 2:38). Some scholars held that Baptism in at least some parts of the early ch. was "in the name of the Lord Jesus," (Acts 2:38; 10:48). In any case, the trinitarian formula soon became universal. The *Didache,* 7, describes the duties of the candidates for baptism and the method of administering it (trine immersion or infusion). Tertullian *(Adversus Praxean,* 26; *De Baptismo; De Corona Militis)* gives elaborate descriptions. In the 2d to 4th c. baptism was normally administered only at Easter and Pentecost. Epiphany and other feast days were added later. While the clergy were the ordinary ministers of the sacrament, baptism could be administered at any time and by any Christian in cases of grave emergency, though some fathers and councils discountenanced administration of baptism by women. The laying on of hands ("confirmation") or anointing ("chrismation") was an integral part of the baptismal rite in ch.

2. The medieval ritual of Baptism, as it had developed by the time of Gregory the Great, combined what had originally been separate stages in the preparation of adults for membership in the ch.; it remained practically unchanged thereafter. According to the *Mayence Manual (Agenda Moguntinensis)* of 1513 the Order of Baptizing Children *(Ordo ad baptizandum pueros)* comprised an introduction at the door of the ch. This included: asking for the candidate's name, sign of cross, prayers, tasting of salt *(gustus salis),* greeting of peace, further prayers, the Great Exorcism, the Holy Gospel, the Lord's Prayer, Ave Maria, the Apostles' Creed, the *ephphatha* ceremony, and the entrance into ch. The rite of Baptism proper took place at the baptistry, or font; Renunciation of the devil, the Creed, anointing the breast and back, an admonition to the sponsors, the 3-fold immersion (performed with child's head pointing to E, N, and S respectively), a prayer of thanksgiving, the putting on of the chrisom.* Other ch. orders prescribed kiss of brotherhood, the placing of a lighted taper into the hand of the child or a sponsor, and other ceremonies.

3. Luther's *Taufbüchlein verdeutscht* (1523) was essentially a tr. of the liturgy of Baptism then in use in Wittenberg. It included the lesser exorcism, the sign of the cross, prayers, the tasting of salt, the "Flood" prayer, the greater exorcism, further prayers, and the greeting of peace, the Holy Gospel from Mk 10, the Lord's Prayer, the *ephphatha* ceremony, procession into the church, renunciation of Satan, Creed, Baptism by 3-fold immersion, anointing (cross on head only), putting on of the chrisom, placing of the lighted taper in the hand of the child or sponsor. A simplification of this form published in 1526 became part of the Small Catechism in 1529 *(Die Begenntnisschriften der evangelisch-lutherischen Kirche,* 5th, rev. ed. [Göttingen, 1963], pp. 535–541); it underlies the normal Luth. baptis-

mal rite, though the greater exorcism and clothing with the chrisom were often omitted. See also *Baptism; Liturgics.* ACP.

Baptism for the Dead. Practiced by Mormons for salvation of others as ordinance inst. by God from eternity. But the Biblical way of salvation rules out vicarious Baptism, salvation being by personal faith and Baptism (Mk 16:15, 16; Acts 2:38; Mt 28:19, 20). Moreover, Heb 9:27 denies the possibility of salvation after death. Therefore 1 Co 15:29 cannot be quoted in favor of vicarious Baptism. The Greek preposition *hyper* here may mean *over* or *with reference to,* the Baptism of the early adult Christians thus being a confession of their hope of the resurrection of the body to eternal life. The Cath. Apostolic Ch. also practices baptism for the dead.

Baptism of Blood. Term used for martyrdom endured by unbaptized person for faith in Christ.

Baptism of Desire. In RCm, act of love for God by unbaptized person with desire to do all that is necessary for his salvation.

Baptism of the Holy Spirit. See *Pentecostalism.*

Baptismal Font. See *Church Furniture,* 1.

Baptismal Formula. See *Ecumenical Creeds,* A.

Baptismal Regeneration. See *Grace, Means of,* III.

Baptist Brethren. See *Brethren.*

Baptist Churches. 1. The basic principle of Baps. all over the world is "liberty of conscience." This principle manifests itself negatively in that Baps. reject subscription to human creeds, establishment of ecclesiastical organizations, and the teaching of any form of sacramentalism and sacerdotalism; and positively in that Baps. are enthusiastic, lay great emphasis on the competence and the responsibility of each individual soul in spiritual matters, accept only "believer's* Baptism," and vigorously maintain absolute separation of church* and state. Baps. do not consider creeds as tests of orthodoxy, but as evidences of unanimity. Since it is the inalienable right of the individual to formulate his own creed, there can be, strictly speaking, no heresy in Bap. bodies (*Democratic Declarations of Faith,* 3). Nevertheless, historically the Baps. are divided theologically into two large families, the Gen. and the Particular Baps., the former following Arminianism* and believing in universal salvation, the latter following Calvinism* and subscribing to the theory of a limited atonement.

2. The *General Baptists* are the spiritual descendants of the Anabaptists (see *Mennonite Churches,* 2), who misinterpreted the reformational principle of the universal priesthood* by making it applicable also to the political and soc. spheres. After the collapse of the Anabap. movement in 1535, the scattered remnants of these rebaptizers were gathered by Menno Simons and organized as the Mennonites. The theol. of the Mennonites was Pelagian; it stressed such errors as freedom of the will, a false enthusiasm or mysticism, asceticism,* and extreme literalism. The Mennonites placed great emphasis on the outward purity of the ch. and held that the restoration of apostolic Christianity must include Baptism* by immersion. Anabaptists came to Eng. as early as 1534, but were unable to gain a foothold because of the bitter persecutions resulting from the Act of Uniformity of 1559, which disenfranchised all religious non-conformists. John Smith* (Smyth), who had spent some time at Amsterdam and there with Thomas Helwys (ca. 1550—ca. 1616) had organized a Bap. cong., returned to Eng. 1611 and est. the 1st Eng. Bap. ch. Owing to Dutch Mennonite influence, these early Eng. Baps. were Arminian; they became known as Gen. Baps. However, the distinctive principle of all Baps., "liberty of conscience," was clearly enunciated in the Articles of Faith adopted ca. 1611: "The magistrate is not by virtue of his office to meddle with religious or matters of conscience, or compel men to this or that form of religion, for Christ only is King and Lawgiver of the Church and conscience." The *Particular,* or *Calvinistic,* Baps. trace their origin in part to the Separatist Movement in Eng. during the 16th c. Two groups of English Protestants, the Puritans* and the Separatists (see *United Church of Christ,* I A), opposed the Romanizing tendencies of the Est. Angl. Ch., the former holding that the reformation of the Angl. Ch. must be accomplished by remaining within the Est. Ch., the latter by complete separation. Both the Puritans and the Separatists, also known as Non-Conformists or Congregationalists, were agreed on the principles of Calvinism. They differed only in matters of ch. polity, the Puritans favoring Presbyterianism, the Separatists believing that the "Church should be a congregation of free men, founded after the pattern of the Apostolic Church, governing itself, not according to the laws of the State, but according to the Bible" (see *Polity, Ecclesiastical,* 7). In the course of time some of the Separatists adopted the view that only "believer's Baptism" by immersion was a valid Baptism; 1639 they organized the first Bap. Separatist cong. In theol. these early Calvinistic, or Particular, Baps. were in full accord with the Presbyterians* and the Congregationalists,* except on doctrines of the ch. and the sacraments. C. H. Spurgeon* is the outstanding Eng. Calvinistic Bap., and John Bunyan* the best-known Eng. Gen. Bap. Since 1891 the distinction bet. the Gen. and Particular Baps. no longer applies in Eng. since both groups have united on the basic principles of Bap. theol.: the supreme authority of Scripture, a regenerate membership, a democratic ch. govt., and believer's Baptism by immersion. On all other points great latitude of opinion is permitted. See also pars. 20-34; *Baptist Union of Great Britain and Ireland; Democratic Declarations of Faith,* 2.

3. The *American Baptist Churches* owe their origin very largely to the work of Roger Williams,* successively an Angl., Puritan, Separatist, Bap., Seeker. Coming to Mass. 1631, he was for a short season asst. pastor at Plymouth. In 1635 he was ordained pastor of the Salem ch. His Separatist views went far beyond those of the Salem Separatists and precipitated a bitter conflict with the ecclesiastical and secular authorities. Being an "arch-individualist," he maintained that the colonists had trespassed on rights of Indians in acquiring the respective land charters. This interest in civil and individual liberty helped crystallize his views of religious liberty. He was bitterly opposed to the theocratic govt. in the Puritan colonies, denied the magistrates jurisdiction over matters of conscience and religion, and contended for liberty of conscience, for separation of ch. and state, and for the right of the people to choose their own rulers. This led to Williams' banishment from the colony and his founding of a colony at Providence, R. I., in 1636. There "the Apostle of Liberty" put into practice the principles of civil and religious liberty which he later defended in *Bloody Tenent of Persecution for the Cause of Conscience.* In 1638 he and his followers adopted Baptism by immersion; the Providence ch. may therefore rightly be called the oldest Bap. ch. in Am. The distinctive tenet of this group was rigid individualism which manifested itself chiefly in stressing the inner religious experience of the individual. This tenet showed little, if any, interest in the visible ch. and considered all ecclesiastical organizations on a par with secular institutions. The Providence Baps. were in principle opposed to the adoption of any creedal statements and granted equal rights to members of Calvinistic and Arminian convictions. The Arminian group at Providence held that the "six principles" of Heb 6:1, 2 included the laying on of hands as a divine ordinance; in sub-

sequent controversy on this point the views of the Arminian Baps., later known as Gen. (or Old) Six-Principle Baps., gained gen. acceptance by 1652. While the Providence ch. is the oldest Bap. ch. in Am., the distinction of being the first Calvinist Bap. ch. in Am. is usually given to the Newport, R. I., ch. founded 1641 by John Clarke (1609–76). The Baps. in New Eng. states were Calvinists, while the majority of the early Baps. in the colonies favored Arminianism.* The Arminian, or General, Baps. failed to gain a foothold, because the majority of the early colonists were reared in the tradition of Calvinism. The Calvinistic, or Particular, Baps. laid greater emphasis on a trained ministry and were able to develop greater denominational consciousness than the Gen. Baps.

4. The Baps. developed their greatest strength in the Middle Colonies, owing largely to the influence of the Philadelphia Assoc. which adopted the Philadelphia Conf. 1742. This was a Calvinistic standard identical with the Conf. adopted 1677 by London Baps. The latter Conf. was in full agreement with the Westminster Conf. of 1644 and the Savoy Declaration of 1658 except in the statements concerning the Sacraments and the church (see *United Church of Christ,* I A 2; *Presbyterian Confessions,* 3). It is therefore correct to state that the theological antecedents of the vast majority of American Baps. are rooted in Calvinistic theol.; this accounts for the fact that formerly all and today many Particular Baps. subscribe to such doctrines as the total depravity of man, the necessity and sufficiency of Christ's atonement (limited to the elect), and unconditional election. Historians are agreed that the Bap. agitation for the separation of ch. and state played a prominent part in the adoption of the First Amendment of the Am. Const. The great period of expansion of the Bap. Ch. began ca. 1800. The vast majority of Baps. are known simply as Baps., sometimes also as "Regular Baptists," and have organized the American (Northern), Southern, and National (Negro) Conventions, comprising ca. 20,000,000 members. Other Bap. bodies use a descriptive adjective.

5. *Doctrine.* It is a distinct principle with Baps. that they acknowledge no human founder, recognize no human authority, and subscribe to no human creed. The competence of the individual soul under God is said to eliminate every extraneous thing between the soul and God. Included are ecclesiastical or civil order, ordinances, sacraments, preacher, and priest. Strictly speaking, there can be no heresy trial in the Bap. Ch., because there is no creedal subscription; there is no creedal subscription, because it is the inalienable right of every individual to form his own creed. This basic principle — in many points similar to that of the Cong. churches — is largely responsible for the fact that Baps., esp. those of the N Conv., grant equal rights to Modernists and Fundamentalists. The conservatives, who hold to the principles of the Philadelphia* and New* Hampshire Confessions, and the liberals, who have accepted the theories of Higher Criticism,* divine immanence, and the soc. gospel, are forced to recognize others' views according to the basic Bap. principle. The essentially distinctive feature of the Baps. is neither their practice of immersion nor their rejection of infant Baptism, but rather their insistence upon the right and competence of every individual, without the intervention of any outside agency, to acknowledge by faith the lordship of Christ and to profess such faith by immersion. Principles which distinguish Baps. from other Ref. denominations: 1. Independence of the local ch.; 2. separation of ch. and state; 3. rel. liberty an inalienable and inherent right of the soul; 4. the local ch. is a body of regenerated people, Baptism being the outward profession of their personal faith; 5. infant Baptism is fatal to the spirituality of the ch.; 6. immersion (a dramatic proclamation of the believer's spiritual death and resurrection); 7. the Scriptural ch. officers are pastors and deacons; 8. the Lord's Supper is observed in commemoration of Christ's death. The controversial points which originally separated Particular and General Baps. are no longer an issue among the "Regular" Baps., though they are still a live issue in some of the smaller Bap. churches.

6. *Polity.* In accord with its basic theol. principle, Bap. ch. polity is cong., the local cong. absolutely autonomous in fixing its doctrinal platform, discipline, and worship. All members have equal voting rights. Baps. are opposed in principle to every kind of ecclesiastical organization. This anticlericalism accounts in a large measure for the aggressive lay participation in ch. activities. Ordinarily Bap. churches unite as associations or state conventions; these bodies, however, have no legislative, judicial, or ex. powers. Formerly the miss. and educ. activities of the Baps. were carried on by various societies whose membership was not identical with the Bap. congregations, but was made up of those individuals who regularly contributed toward the respective soc. Toward the close of the 18th c. a number of such societies were founded for the purpose of spreading Bap. ideas and establishing Bap. churches in the territories which were opened after the Revolutionary War. In 1814 Baps. organized a soc. for for. missions; in 1824 the Am. Bap. Pub. Soc.; in 1832 the Home Miss. Soc. These societies were entirely indep. of ecclesiastical control and were responsible only to their membership. The various activities of the N Baps. have been reorganized somewhat along denominational lines in the hope that this move will eliminate duplication and work for greater efficiency.

7. *The Particular Baptists (7-19).* These bodies originally followed and to some extent still follow Calvinistic rather than Arminian theol. The N and S Conventions and the Negro Baps. constitute the vast majority of so-called Particular Baps. These 3 large bodies are agreed in doctrine and polity, but each group has retained its denominational identity for purposes of more efficient administration.

8. *American Baptist Chs. of the USA.* The hist. of this body until 1844 is described in the previous statement. In that yr. the state conventions of the N and the S split on the question of sending a slaveholding Bap. as a for. miss. It must be noted that the N Baps. were more willing to recognize the desirability of ecclesiastical organizations for effective and systematic ch. work. This willingness resulted in organizing the N Bap. Convention as a corporation in 1907 so that all churches, while retaining local autonomy and the independence of every other ch. and the Conv. itself, were united in carrying out the various Bap. activities. By uniting and coordinating the work of the many Bap. societies and bds., the N Baps. could expand their miss., educ., and philanthropic work considerably. In doctrine the N Baps. have become increasingly liberalistic. Their disregard for creeds and opposition to "regimentation of thought" has enabled theol. schools such as Colgate Rochester and the Divinity School of the U. of Chicago to introduce liberal theol. with Higher Criticism,* the theories of evolution and divine immanence, and the soc. gospel.* The N Baps. adopted the name Am. Bap. Conv. in Boston 1950. Present name adopted 1972. Inclusive membership (1973), 1,484,393. See also 26; *Missionary Baptists.*

9. *Southern Baptist Convention.* The center of activity of the early Baps. was in the New Eng. and the Atlantic seaboard area. When Bap. churches were planted in the S after the Revolutionary War by missionaries from the N it was natural that the S Baps. united with N Baps. in such activities as for. miss. The agency for this phase of Bap. work was

the Missionary Convention for Foreign Missions, organized 1814 with headquarters in Boston. This soc. opposed slavery, and refused to approve the appointing of a candidate for for. miss. work who was a slaveholder. Thereupon the state associations in the S withdrew from the N Conv., and 1845 organized the S Bap. Conv. at Augusta, Ga. In doctrine the S Baps. are much more conservative than the N, and gen. adhere to the Calvinistic New Hampshire Conf. Many of their churches practice close Communion. The seminaries, Southern Bap. at Louisville, Southwestern at Fort Worth, and Bap. Bible School at New Orleans, are fundamentalistic. The S Bap. Conv. has abstained from WCC and NCCCUSA. But the basic principle of all Baps., the right of the individual in all matters of conscience, permits the conservative S Baps. to interchange membership and ministry on terms of perfect equality with N Baps. The reason for the continued separation of the 2 bodies is not doctrinal, but administrative. Five denominational bds. have charge of home miss., for. miss., S. S. work, educ. institutions, and ministerial relief. Inclusive membership (1973), 12,065,333. See also *Missionary Baptists.*

10. *National Baptist Convention, U. S. A., Inc.* In the first 15 years after the Civil War Baptists claim to have gained ca. 1,000,000 adherents among the Negroes. The rapid expansion of the Bap. Ch. among the freed slaves was due in part to the Bap. principle of individual liberty, to the ease with which local churches could be formed, and to the low standard of indoctrination required. In 1880 the Negro Bap. churches organized the Nat. Bap. Conv. at St. Louis. The Nat. Bap. Conv. was incorporated in 1915. The *Nat. Bap. Conv. of the U. S. A., Inc.*, perpetuates the parent body. Inclusive membership (1958), 5,500,000. The *Nat. Bap. Conv. of Am.*, often called the "unincorporated" group, withdrew from the parent body in 1916.

11. *Primitive Baptists.* Following the Bap. principle that Christians must turn to the NT for doctrine and practice, including ceremonies and ch. rites, the Primitive Baps. hold that every form of ecclesiastical organization is sinful if not expressly prescribed in the NT. Since no miss. societies with a "money basis" are mentioned in the NT, a number of Bap. associations denounced the formation of all miss. societies and the pubs. of educ. bds. as contrary to the NT. In protest against what they viewed as anti-Scriptural ecclesiasticism, a number of associations, local groups of Bap. congregations, announced that they would no longer maintain fellowship with those associations which had "united themselves with the world" and, by their support of benevolent societies, had been "preaching a different Gospel." These associations are in principle opposed to every form of denominational organization, to state or nat. conventions. The only bond uniting the various associations is the exchange of the annual minutes. Any assoc. whose minutes are not approved is dropped from fellowship. Since there is no denominational organization, these Baps. have no official distinctive name, and have been known as "Antimission" (see also *Missionary Baptists*), "Hard Shell," "Old School," and most commonly as "Primitive" Baps. In polity they are extremely cong. Theol. training for pastors is not required; miss. work is not on an organized basis; instrumental music in the service, Sunday schools, and secret societies are not authorized. In theol. the "Primitive" Baps. are strictly Calvinistic. Inclusive membership of "Primitive" Baps. (1962) was 72,000.

12. *Nat. Primitive Bap. Conv., Inc.* (organized 1907). Formerly Colored Primitive Baptists, founded 1865. Later, and till the late 1960s, called Nat. Primitive Bap. Conv. in the U. S. A. Negro body with inclusive membership (1961) of 85,983.

13. *Two-Seed-in-the-Spirit Predestinarian Baptists.* This group teaches the Manichaean error that all mankind falls into two classes. One class is endowed with a good spiritual seed, implanted by God into Adam. This class is a spiritual generation existing in Christ before creation and are gathered into the Church which is Christ's resurrected body. This group is absolutely sure of salvation (which is by grace). In the spirit of the rest of mankind Satan planted an evil seed. This group numbered about 200 (1962).

14. *American Baptist Association.* A separate group of Baps. who withdrew from the various conventions because they considered the organization of such conventions as contrary to letter and spirit of NT; a Gen. Assoc. of Bap. Chs. was org. 1902; nat. fellowship (Bap. Gen Assoc.) formed 1905; present name adopted 1924. Believing their chs. alone are true, they claim to be "the divine custodians of the truth, and that they only have the right of carrying out the Great Commission, of executing the laws of the Kingdom, and of administering the ordinances of the Gospel." This assoc. is a cooperation of local congregations for the purpose of joint work, but its constituent members are so averse to ecclesiastical organizations and so zealous in preserving the rights of local congregations that the annual meetings are called "the meeting of the messengers [delegates] composing the American Baptist Association." In doctrine they are in harmony with the New* Hampshire Conf., but interpret Article XVIII concerning Christ's 2d coming according to modern premillennialism. They are represented chiefly in the South and Southwest. Inclusive membership (1973), 955,900. See also *Landmark Baptists.*

15. *General Association of Regular Baptist Churches.* Very similar to the Am. Bap. Assoc. in theol. and polity. Its churches are found chiefly in the N Cent. states. Left the N Bap. Conv. 1932. Inclusive membership (1973), 214,000.

16. *Seventh Day Baptists.* The first Seventh Day Bap. ch. was organized 1617 in London. Some members in both the Providence and Newport, R. I., Bap. churches shared the views of this London Bap. ch. and maintained fellowship with other Baps. until 1671, when Stephen Mumford organized the 1st Am. Seventh Day Bap. ch. The Sabbatarian Baps. have been unable to gain a large following. They have, however, been a large factor in determining the views of the Seventh-day Adventists* and the Ger. Seventh Day Baps. In ch. polity the Seventh Day Baps. agree fully with all Baps. thoroughly congregationalistic and uniting for joint work on a voluntary basis. In doctrine they follow the Calvinistic Baps. except in their view that the Sabbath was instituted at man's creation and sanctioned by Christ and the Apostles. However, their latitudinarianism permits fellowship with all immersionists. Inclusive membership (1963), 5,760.

17. *Seventh Day Baptists (German, 1728).* This group of Ger. Brethren, organized 1728 by J. C. Beissel,* est. as communistic* celibate society 1732, Ephrata, Pa., was characterized by extreme pietism, mysticism, and legalism. After a brief period of success as a monastic community with its flourishing industries, school, and printing press, the denomination dwindled to 150 members in 3 churches, 1962. In theol. and practice they agree with the Brethren.*

18. *Baptist General Conference.* Operated as a conf. since 1879; composed primarily of Swed. Bap. immigrants and their descendants. Formerly known as the Swed. Bap. Gen. Conf. of Am. Inclusive membership (1973), 111,364.

19. *Conservative Baptist Association of America.* Organized in N. J., 1947, this group regards the Bible as divinely inspired Word of God, infallible and of supreme authority. It stresses the autonomy

of the local cong. Inclusive membership (1963), 300,000.

20. *General Baptists* (20–34; see also 2). These are groups whose doctrinal position is closely related to that of the Anabaps. or who adopted Arminian theol. In contrast to the Particular Baps. they emphasize such doctrines as the universal Atonement and human responsibility. Many of the Gen. Baps. practice foot washing,* observe close Communion, and may be characterized as legalistic, pietistic, and given to enthusiastic expressionism. They are opposed to denominational and organized ch. work. The majority of the Gen. Baps. are united in associations or local federations for purposes of fellowship. Fellowship between the various associations is established and maintained by exchanging the annual minutes. The Arminian Baps. were unable to gain a large following because they were opposed to the organization of denominations, lacked denominational consciousness, and did not believe in a trained ministry. Many Arminian Baps. affiliated with the Calvinistic Baps.

21. *General Six-Principle Baptists.* The Arminian group in the Providence ch. (see 3 above) held that the laying on of hands was not only a ceremony, but a principle as essential as repentance, faith, Baptism, resurrection, judgment (citing Heb 6:1, 2). By 1652 the Six-Principle Baps. gained the majority of the Providence ch. and made the laying on of hands after Baptism the sign of the reception of the Holy Ghost, an indispensable condition for ch. membership. Though the Gen. (or Old) Six-Principle Baps. claim to be the original Bap. Ch. founded by Williams, they are rapidly disappearing. Three churches claim a membership of ca. 130 (1963).

22. *General Baptists.* While all those Bap. bodies which reject Calvinism of the Particular Baps. are called Gen. Baps. (see statement above), there is also a separate branch by this name. The origin of this group is probably due to the work of Robert Nordin and Thos. White, who were sent 1714 to the Arminian Baps. in Va. by the London Gen. Baps. But it was not until 1823 that Gen. Baps. appeared as a separate group. In recent yrs. this branch has attempted to unite with other Bap. bodies, and in 1915 formed a cooperative union with the N Conv. Inclusive membership (1973), 70,000.

23. *Regular Baptists.* While the term Regular Baps. is often used to denote the Particular Baps. in the 3 large conventions, there are also a number of smaller associations which claim to represent the original Eng. Bap. principles before a distinction was made between Particular and Gen. Baps. They are similar to Duck River Assoc. Baps. and are found in the S Atlantic states. In doctrine they are gen. Arminian, practice foot washing, observe close Communion, reject creeds and denominational organizations, and est. fellowship with like-minded associations. Inclusive membership (1962), 17,186. See also par. 4.

24. *Separate Baptists in Christ.* The origin of the Separate movement may be traced to the Whitefield revival, which caused the "New" and "Old Light" controversy among Congs., Presbs., and Baps., the "New Lights" overemphasizing the spiritual qualifications of the ministry. Under the leadership of the outstanding Bap. theol. Isaac Backus,* who occupied a mediating position between Calvinism and Arminianism,* many New Eng. Bap. churches withdrew from fellowship with the Regular Baps. This breach is now healed in New Eng. and practically so in Va. In 1754 New Eng. Separate Baps. under S. Stearns (1706–71) settled in N. C. and spread into adjoining states, forming several associations. These Separate Baps. are anti-Calvinistic, rejecting the limited Atonement and the double predestination; they lean toward Arminianism. In polity they follow strict Bap. principles and are opposed to all ecclesiastical organizations. Inclusive membership (1962), 7,496.

25. *Duck River (and Kindred) Associations of Baptists.* As a protest against the theory of a limited Atonement, a number of Bap. churches withdrew from the strictly Calvinistic Elk River (Tenn.) Assoc. and in 1825 organized the Duck River Assoc. This assoc. and smaller ones in the mountains of Tenn. occupy a mediating position between Calvinism and Arminianism, and are closely related to the Separate, United, and Regular Baps. These associations frown on every form of denominational organization and have no miss. or benevolent societies. Inclusive membership (1973), 8,909.

26. *Freewill Baptists.* The hist. of so-called Freewill Baps. is difficult to trace because they developed no real denominational consciousness and had no interest in organizing a denomination. The earliest group of Arminian Baps. known as Freewill Baps. was gathered 1727 by Paul Palmer in N. C. Subsequently the Philadelphia Assoc. exerted its Calvinistic influence, and during the 18th c. the Freewill Baps. almost disappeared. Toward the close of that c. John Randall, a Cong., who had embraced Arminian and Bap. views, was denied fellowship with the Regular Baps. in New Eng. and sought fellowship with the Freewill Baps. of the middle and S Atlantic states. This and other support from N Freewill Baps. enabled the Southern "Freewillers" to reorganize and gradually to expand their work considerably. In the course of time the Freewill Baps. of New Eng., also known as Free Baps., lost heavily to the Adventist* movement; the remnant united with N. Bap. Conv. 1911 (see also 8) and are no longer separate group. In doctrine Freewill Baps. accept "Five Points" of Arminianism,* stressing particularly free will, stating that "all men, at one time or another, are found in such capacity as that, through the grace of God, they may be eternally saved." Inclusive membership (1973), 203,000.

27. *United Free Will Baptist Church, The.* This is colored ch. corresponding in doctrine to the Freewill Baps. In polity this group grants greater authority to the assoc. or conf. than most Arminian Baps. Organized 1870, but apparently not clearly distinguished from white chs. Separate denomination organized 1901 as United Am. Free Will Bap. Ch. (Colored). "American" dropped in the 1950s. Inclusive membership (1962), 100,000.

28. *United Baptists.* The origin of this group is similar to that of Regular Baps. ignoring the distinction between Calvinistic and Arminian views. In recent yrs. many United Bap. churches, while retaining their hist. name and affiliation with their respective associations, are also enrolled with the N or S Bap. Conventions. Inclusive membership (1962), 63,641.

29. *Christian Unity Baptist Association.* A small group of Arminian Baps. in N. C.; separated from the Regular Baps. 1909. Inclusive membership (1963), 657.

30. *Independent Baptist Church of America.* Small group of Swed. Bap. churches following the Six-Principle Baps. They are conscientious objectors to war. Inclusive membership (1963), 25.

31. *National Baptist Evangelical Life and Soul Saving Assembly of the U. S. A.* Founded 1921 by A. A. Banks in Kansas City. Inclusive membership (1962), 57,647.

32. *Evangelical Baptist Church, Inc., General Conference of the.* Arminian, premillennial group, organized 1935; formerly known as Ch. of the Full Gospel, Inc. Inclusive membership (1960), 2,200; headquarters: Goldsboro, N. C.

33. *North American Baptist Association.* Organized in Little Rock, Ark., 1950. Theol. is ev.,

fundamental, missionary, and in the main premillennial. Inclusive membership (1960), 330,265.

34. *North American Baptist General Conference.* Emanating from Ger. Bap. immigrants, this group of churches is conservative, mission-minded, and partially bilingual. Inclusive membership (1963), 52,625.

35. Two Bap. groups were organized in the 1960s. Their classification is not given. The *Progressive National Baptist Convention, Inc.* was organized in Cincinnati, Ohio, 1961. Inclusive membership (1963), 500,000. *The Bethel Baptist Assembly, Inc.* was originally the Evangelistic Ministerial Alliance, founded in Evansville, Ind., 1934. Inc. as the "Bethel Baptist Assembly" in Ind., 1960. Inclusive membership (1962), 6,430.

36. Total Bap. membership in the US (1973): 28,764,903. FEM

See also *Religious Bodies (U. S.), Bibliography.*

Baptist General Conference. See *Baptist Churches,* 18.

Baptist Missionary Society. Organized Kettering, Northants, Eng., Oct. 2, 1792, as result of sermons preached by W. Carey.* Worked in India, Ceylon, China, Palestine, Afr., and W Indies.

Baptist Student Union. See *Students, Spiritual Care of,* A 3.

Baptist Training Union. See *Young People's Organizations,* III 1.

Baptist Union of Great Britain and Ireland. Formed 1891; united Gen. and Particular Baps. in Eng. and Ireland; leaders included J. Clifford.* See also *Baptist Churches,* 2; *Shakespeare, John Howard.*

Baptist World Alliance. See *Union Movements,* 10.

Baptist Young People's Union. See *Young People's Organizations,* III 3.

Baptist Youth Fellowship. See *Young People's Organizations,* III 2.

Baptistery. Building, ususally connected with ch., in which Baptism is performed. Earliest known (256) is that at Duro-Europos. The one at the Lateran is said to date from time of Constantine. See also *Church Architecture,* 5.

Bapuji Appaji (d. Jan. 16, 1894). Brahman of W India; converted to Christianity. Mem. Tr. Com. CMS; tr. books into Marathi.

Bar Cocheba. See *Christs, False.*

Bar-Hebraeus, Gregorius (Abulfaraj; 1226—86). Jacobite Syrian bp. and philos. of Jewish descent. Works include *Cream of Science; Granary of Mysteries; Scholia* on the Bible; *Chronicle.*

Bar Mitzvah (Heb. "son of the law"). Term applied to Jewish boy at 13; also the ceremony which recognizes the boy as a bar mitzvah.

Bar Sauma. See *Barsumas.*

Baradaeus (Baradai). See *Jacob Baradaeus.*

Baraita. Jewish book containing teachings of Tanna not included in the Mishnah.

Baraka. See *Primitive Religion.*

Barat, Madeleine Sophie (1779—1865). Fr. nun; founder of Soc. of the Sacred Heart.

Barbados. See *Caribbean Islands,* E 5.

Barbara. According to tradition, daughter of pagan in Nicomedia. Martyred by father after conversion to Christianity. Praised by John of Damascus (*MPG,* 96, 781—814); included in Menologion of Metaphrastes (*MPG,* 116, 301—316). Mentioned in Ap XXI 35.

Barbarossa. See *Frederick I* (Barbarossa).

Barbelo-Gnostics. See *Gnosticism,* 7 i.

Barbets. See *Camisards.*

Barclay, John (1734—98). Brit. founder of Berean Assembly at Edinburgh known for zealous study of Bible.

Barclay, Robert (1648–90). B. Gordonstoun (or Gordonstown), N Moray (or Morayshire), Scot.; educ. RC at Paris, Fr.; joined Soc. of Friends* 1667; repeatedly imprisoned. Works include *Truth Cleared of Calumnies; A Catechism and Confession of Faith; Theses theologicae; Theologiae vere Christianae apologia* (Eng. title *An Apology for the True Christian Divinity*). See also *Democratic Declarations of Faith,* 4; *Friends, Society of,* 1.

Bardenhewer, Otto (1851—1935). Patristic scholar; prof. OT exegesis Münster 1884—86); NT exegesis Munich 1886—1924. Chief work: *Geschichte der altkirchlichen Literatur.*

Bardesanes. See *Gnosticism,* 7 h.

Bardy, Gustave (1881–1955). Prof. patrology Besançon, Lille, and Dijon. Wrote on Paul of Samosata, Clement of Rome, and Irenaeus; surveys of Lat. and Gk. fathers.

Barebone, Praisegod (1596—1679). Opponent of Cromwell.

Barefooted Monks (and Nuns). Popular name for members of various orders who wear no footcovering whatsoever or only sandals. They are also known as "discalced" (e. g., discalced Carmelites), though this term is properly applied only to those who wear sandals. The custom was introd. in the W by Francis* of Assisi, probably with reference to Mt 10:10. It has been followed by the stricter branches of many orders, e. g., Capuchins, Poor Clares, Hermits of St. Augustine, Carmelites, Servites, and Passionists.

Baring-Gould, Sabine (1834—1924). Educ. Cambridge; held a number of positions as clergyman, last in Devonshire; wrote *Lives of the Saints* and numerous other works; best-known hymn: "Onward, Christian Soldiers."

Barmen Mission Society. See *Rhemish Mission Society.*

Barmen Theses. In harmony with the basic principle of the National Socialism* of Ger. an attempt was made by the so-called *Deutsche Christen* to make the people's state central in religion. They held that the Ger. Ev. Ch. should endorse the "social miracle" of the *Volkswerden* achieved through the nat. socialist revolution. They tried to express a new "Christ striving" in a "united people's community." The basic principle of the movement, *"die Volkskirche bekennt sich zu Blut und Rasse,"* was stated in the first of the *Twenty-Eight Theses* of the *Braune Synode* held in Saxony (prepared by Walter Grundmann-Dresden and others, 1933).

Various opposition fronts developed (e. g., *Notbund* of Niemöller). The most important were the opposition *Bekenntnissynoden.* On Jan. 3 and 4, 1934, 320 pastors gathered at Barmen-Gemarke. There Barth's* *Bekenntnis der freien Kirchensynode* was accepted as an answer to the *Twenty-Eight Theses.* In 5 parts (I. The Church in the Present Time; II. The Church under the Word of God; III. The Church in the World; IV. The Message of the Church; V. The Power of the Church) this confession fought against the aggrandizement of humanity in the ch. and stressed the need of submission to, and dependence on, God. Similar synods were held in various places in Ger.; Barth became a prominent leader among Ger. opponents of the *Deutsche Christen* until stopped by Hitler. EL

See also *Deutsche Evangelische Kirche; Germany,* C 4; *Kirchenkampf.*

K. D. Schmidt, *Die Bekenntnisse und grundsätzlichen Aeusserungen zur Kirchenfrage des Jahres 1933* (Vol. I). Vol. II: *Das Jahr 1934.* Vol. III: *Das Jahr 1935* (Göttingen, 1934—36); S. Herman, *It's Your Souls We Want* (New York, 1943); G. Niemöller, *Die erste Bekenntnissynode der Deutschen Evangelischen Kirche zu Barmen,* in *Arbeiten zur Geschichte des Kirchenkampfes,* ed. K. D. Schmidt, Vols. 5—6 (Göttingen, 1959).

Barnabas, Epistle of. See *Apostolic Fathers,* 6.

Barnabites *(Clerici regulares S. Pauli decollati).* RC religious order of clergy founded 1530 at Milan by

Antonio M. Zaccaria (d. 1539), Bartolommeo Ferrari, and Giacomo Antonio Morigia. See also *Counter Reformation,* 6.

Barnardo, Thomas John (1845—1905). B. Dublin; d. London. Founded Dr. Barnardo's Homes (for orphaned and destitute children); these homes cared for ca. 60,000 up to the time of Barnardo's death; the children were trained in the religion of their parents.

Barnby, Joseph (1838—96). Eng. composer of several hundred hymn tunes and of sacred choral music; ed. hymnbooks; organist and choirmaster; arranged for and conducted many performances of the works of J. S. Bach.

Barnes, Albert (1798—1870). Presb. theol.; exegetical writer. B. Rome, N. Y.; d. Philadelphia; pastor Philadelphia; leader of liberals at 1837 disruption of Presb. Ch. (reunited 1870). See also *Presbyterian* Churches, 4 a.

Barnes, Ernest William (1874—1953). Angl. churchman and mathematician; master of Temple; canon Westminster; bp. Birmingham. Held that religious beliefs must meet the test of rationality and that sciences pointed to spiritual interpretation of reality. Faith must be reformulated to conform to scientific findings. Rejected virgin birth and bodily resurrection of Christ. Wrote *Scientific Theory and Religion; The Rise of Christianity.*

Barnes, Robert (ca. 1495—1540). Educ. Louvain and Cambridge; prior of Augustinian monastery, Cambridge; leader of scholars and future reformers who met secretly at the White Horse Inn, Cambridge, ca. 1521—25. Convicted of heresy by Wolsey 1526, Barnes fled to Continent 1528; became close friend of Luther, Melanchthon, Bugenhagen, and others at Wittenberg. At Wittenberg he wrote a Lat. epitome of the main doctrines of the AC titled *Sententiae, A Supplication to the Most Gracious King Henry VIII* which included 10 doctrinal essays and a short *Lives of the Popes.* After the fall of Wolsey (1529) Barnes became royal chaplain and an important figure in the Anglo-Luth. diplomacy 1532 to 1540. Burned at Smithfield 1540 when that diplomacy collapsed, he made a fine confession of faith, printed at Wittenberg with a preface by Luther. He served the cause of the Eng. Reformation by helping to form *The Wittenberg* Articles of 1536* and *The Thirteen Articles of 1538.*

Definitive ed. of his works: *The Works of Tyndale, Frith and Barnes,* ed. John Foxe (London, 1572); *The Reformation Essays of Dr. Robert Barnes,* ed. N. S. Tjernagel (London, 1963); E. G. Rupp, *Studies in the Making of the English Protestant Tradition* (Cambridge, 1949). NST

Barnett, Samuel Augustus (1844—1913). Angl.; sought to reform soc. conditions along Christian lines. Founded Charity Organization Soc.; helped found Reform League.

Baronius, Caesar (1538—1607). RC theol.; studied theol. and law at Veroli and Naples; living in Cong. of the Oratory, Rome, he spent 30 yrs. gathering unpub. material in Vatican archives for *Annales ecclesiastici a Christo nato ad annum 1198,* RC reply to the *Magdeburg* Centuries.*

Baroque (Sp. *barrueco,* irregularly shaped pearl). Term used in architecture and art for fantastic, grotesque, florid, or incongruous styles which began with Michelangelo in the 16th c. and ended with rococo in the 18th c. (see *Church Architecture,* 13). In music it applies to the period from ca. 1600 to 1750.

Barrat, Thomas Ball (1862—1940). Meth.; prominent in Pent. movement.

Barrow(e), Henry (ca. 1550–93). Eng. Congregationalist; defended separatism and congregational independence; accused of circulating seditious tracts; hanged with J. Greenwood.*

Barrow, Isaac (1630—77). B. London. Angl. theol., mathematician. Ordained 1659; prof. math. Cambridge 1663 (resigned in favor of pupil Isaac Newton); vice-chancellor Cambridge 1675. Works include *A Treatise of the Pope's Supremacy.*

Barsom. Bundle of twigs or small metal-wire rods used by Parsees in sacrificial ceremonies.

Barsumas (ca. 435—ca. 489). Chief founder of Nestorianism in Persia; est. theol. school at Nisibis ca. 457. See also *Narsai.*

Barth, Christian Gottlob (1799—1862). Pastor Möttlingen 1824. Retired 1838 to devote life to missions. Helped found Basel Miss. Soc. Founded Württemberg Miss. Soc. Ed. *Calwer Missionsblatt.*

Barth, Gotthelf Christian (May 12, 1883—Feb. 17, 1965). Educ. Conc. Coll., Fort Wayne, Ind., and Conc. Sem., St. Louis (grad. 1905). Pastor Bertrand, Nebr., 1905—10, St. Louis, 1910—21; pres. Conc. Coll., Milwaukee, 1921—34; pastor Cincinnati, Ohio, 1934—45; pres. Conc. Sem., Springfield, Ill., 1945—52; pastor West Allis, Wis., 1952—56. Mem. Bd. of Dir. LCMS 1934—41; 3d vice-pres. LCMS 1941–44, 2d vice-pres. 1944–45. Pres. Synodical* Conf. 1950–52. Wrote *The Lord's Prayer; The Twenty-Third Psalm; The Life of Joseph;* devotional booklets.

Barth, Karl (1886–1968). B. Basel, Switz.; educ. Bern, Berlin, Tübingen, Marburg; asst. pastor Geneva 1909, Safenwil (Aargau canton) 1911; prof. Göttingen, Münster, Bonn, Basel. Influenced by K. G. A. v. Harnack,* neo-Kantians, socialism, S. A. Kierkegaard.*

Attacked attempts to fit the Christian message into man's preconceptions. Tried to keep Christianity from becoming an ideology, i. e., a product of culture. Opposed identifying human conclusions with Word of God and thereby destroying revelation. Held that theol. reflecting soc. and cultural situations lost its critical and prophetic role and that identification of a Weltanschauung (comprehensive conception of the world) with the Word of God rejected justification by grace.

Rejected natural theol. and the *analogia* entis* of Thomas Aquinas; held the analogy of faith and, with Anselm* of Canterbury, a *fides quaerens intellectum* (faith leads, reason follows). God is "wholly other." Interpretation of Scripture should not compromise with modern thought. Rejected metaphysical bases of theol. but used logical and linguistic aspects of philos. Regarded "religion" as a human product and distinguished it from revelation.

His theol. emphasizes a Christocentric approach to predestination. The work of Christ presupposes the work of the Father and has the work of the Spirit as a consequence. Beginning ca. 1925 he emphasized *deus dixit* (Lat. "God said") from a Calvinistic point of view.

Stressed importance of dogmatics in the ch.; its main function: to evaluate preaching. Dogmatics itself is tested by Scripture. Barth did not identify the Bible with the Word of God but stressed that it is a witness to the Word. His concept of relationship bet. Spirit and Word vitalizes Calvinism: when we hear the Word the Holy Spirit comes to us.

Works include *Der Römerbrief; Die kirchliche Dogmatik; Fides quaerens intellectum; Das Wort Gottes und die Theologie; Dogmatik im Grundriss; Nein! Antwort an Emil Brunner; Die christliche Lehre nach dem Heidelberger Katechismus; Evangelium und Gesetz; Christengemeinde und Bürgergemeinde.* EL

See also *Barmen Theses; Dialectical Theology; Existentialism; Kerygmatic Theology; Switzerland, Contemporary Theology in,* 3–8.

Barthel, Friedrich Wilhelm (Apr. 2, 1791—July 24, 1859). One of the few who, in that rationalistic age, retained the old faith, he still held an influential govt. position at Leipzig; his home became a center of true piety and Biblical Christianity, esp. for the serious-minded among the students of the U. Emigrated with Martin Stephan* 1838. First treas. Mo. Syn. His son, Martin C. Barthel (Feb. 12, 1838, to Feb. 26, 1899), was the first "gen. agent" of publishing interests of Mo. Syn. (1860) and first mgr. CPH 1869—91.

Bartholomaeus Anglicus (13th c.). Eng. Franciscan friar; prof. theol. Paris. Wrote *De proprietatibus rerum.*

Bartholomaeus de Martyribus (1514—90). Port. theol. Worked for reform at Trent. Wrote *Stimulus pastorum* and *Compendium spiritualis doctrinae.*

Bartholomew's Day Massacre. Early on Aug. 24, 1572, the tocsin rang in Paris, the signal for the massacre of Huguenot leaders. The massacre extended over the next 2 days and spread to the provinces. Estimates vary as to the number of victims. In Paris probably 3 or 4 thousand were killed; as many more were put to death in the provinces. The massacre was very likely determined by Catherine de Medicis, queen mother, for revenge on Gaspard de Coligny, who had supplanted her temporarily as dominant influence over Charles IX. The Duke of Guise had charge of the murder of Coligny and the Huguenot leaders, all of whom had been carefully designated beforehand. They were in Paris at that time for the wedding of Margaret, daughter of Catherine and the late Henry II, to Henry of Navarre on Aug. 18, 1572. This marriage was to reconcile the religious factions in Fr. which had been at war during much of the previous decade. The massacre, however, caused the 3d religious war. These wars were not ended until Henry of Navarre accepted RCm and issued the Edict of Nantes* 1598. The hist. controversy whether or not the massacre was a long-premeditated plan is one which cannot be resolved. In spite of some evidence that the plot goes back to 1565, no definite conclusions can be reached.

J. W. Thompson, *The Wars of Religion in France, 1559—1576* (Chicago, 1909); J. E. Neale, *The Age of Catherine de Medici,* reissue (New York, 1959); Jean H. Mariéjol. *Catherine de Médicis* (Paris, 1920); A. W. Whitehead, *Gaspard de Coligny, Admiral of France* (London, 1940). CSM

Bartolommeo, Fra (Baccio della Porta; 1475—1517). One of the principal painters of Florentine Renaissance. Came under influence of Savonarola in his youth and destroyed all except his religious paintings. Joined Dominican order 1500. Prior persuaded him to paint. Influenced by Leonardo da Vinci, Raphael, Bellini, Il Giorgione, Michelangelo.

Bartolus of Sassoferrato (1314—57). It. jurist; reformed dialectical method (already used by Odofredus); revived exegetical system of teaching law; wrote *Commentary on the Code of Justinian;* held ch. and state equal in authority; defended the principle *rex in regno suo est imperator regni sui.*

Barton, Clara. See *Red Cross.*

Barton, Elizabeth (ca. 1506—1534). Noted impostor at time of Henry VIII; used nervous disorder to stimulate inspired possession, esp. in interest of hindering progress of Reformation in Eng.; confessed to fraud; beheaded London. Called (Holy) Maid of Kent; Nun of Kent; Nun of Canterbury.

Barton, James Levi (1855—1936). B. Charlotte, Vt.; ordained Cong. ministry 1885; ABCFM miss. Harpoot, Turkey, 1885—92; prof. Miss. Theol. Sem. 1888—92; pres. Euphrates Coll., Harpoot, 1893; ABCFM for. secy. 1894 to death; mem. various committees and commissions for Middle East* missions and philanthropies; trustee of various Middle East colleges. Wrote numerous books on Middle East missions.

Baruch. See *Apocrypha,* A 3.

Bascom, John (1827—1911). Am. philos. writer; pres. U. of Wis.; prof. Williams Coll. Works include *Aesthetics; The New Theology; God and His Goodness.*

Basedow, Johann Bernhard (ca. 1724—90). Educ. reformer who advocated preparation of special textbooks and literature for children; emphasized pleasurable interest in teaching, object teaching, nature study, physical training. In his Philanthropinum at Dessau he was given opportunity to put his reform ideas into practice. Wrote *Methodenbuch; Elementarwerk.* See also *Philanthropinism.*

Basel Bible Society. See *Bible Societies,* 2, 4.

Basel, Confession of. See *Reformed Confessions,* A 5.

Basel, Council of (1431—49). Last of the councils of the conciliar movement (see *Councils and Synods,* 7), convoked by Martin* V, presided over by Card. G. Cesarini, whom Eugenius IV confirmed in this office when he continued the council. Objectives of the council as stated in the first session: 1. Extirpation of heresy; 2. Reunion of all Christians; 3. Make provision for instruction in Catholicism; 4. Settle disputes between Christian princes; 5. Reformation in head and members; 6. Reestablishment of discipline. Declared dissolved by Eugenius Dec. 18, 1431, the council nevertheless continued and reaffirmed the doctrine of the Council of Constance regarding the supremacy of the council over the pope. On Dec. 15, 1433, Eugenius IV again recognized the council by the bull *Dudum Sacrum.* But the anti-papal climate of the council brought on many restrictions of the papacy. In 1437 the council ratified the *Compactata,* granting the Bohemians the right to celebrate communion *sub utraque.* When the pope transferred the council to Ferrara (1437) to meet with the representatives of the E ch., a remnant remained at Basel, deposed the pope, and elected Amadeus VIII of Savoy as Pope Felix V. The Council of Ferrara met 1438-39, then was transferred to Florence, where it met 1439-42; then it was transferred to Rome, where it met 1442-45. In 1448 the rump council moved to Lausanne. After the death of Eugenius, Nicholas V was chosen pope and generally recognized. In 1449 Felix V abdicated and submitted to Nicholas V. See also *Florence, Council of.*

J. Hardouin, *Acta conciliorum,* VIII and IX (Paris, 1714—15); J. D. Mansi, *Sacrorum conciliorum nova et amplissima collectio,* XXIX—XXXI (Florence, 1788—98); J. Haller and others, *Consilium Basiliense: Studien und Dokumente,* 8 vols. (Basel, 1896—1936); P. Lazarus, *Das Basler Konzil* (Berlin, 1912); I. H. v. Wessenberg, *Die Grossen Kirchenversammlungen des 15. und 16. Jahrhunderts,* (Constance, 1840). CSM

Basel Missionary Society. Offshoot of *Deutsche Christentumsgesellschaft.** Founded as institute 1815 by C. F. Spittler,* N. von Brunn (1766—1849), and others, on impetus of K. F. A. Steinkopf.* C. G. Blumhardt* was its dir. till 1838. Est. as soc. 1822, when it first sent out missionaries on its own. F. J. Josenhans* (dir. 1850—79) systematized and industrialized the work of its missionaries and supervised erection of Basel *Missionshaus.* Female and medical missionaries were first sent out under O. Schott (dir. 1879–84). See also *Schmid(t), Friedrich.*

Basil, Liturgy of. See *Divine Liturgy.*

Basil I. See *Schism,* 5.

Basil Cathedral (Moscow). See *Church Architecture,* 6.

Basil of Ancyra (d. ca. 365). Bp. Ancyra; Semi-Arian.

Basil the Great (Basilius; ca. 330–ca. 379). Bp. Caesarea 370; one of the Cappadocian* theologians; known as opponent of Arianism* and other heresies.

Basileia; Basileus. See *King, Christ as; Kingdom of God.*

Basilians. 1. Name commonly given to most monks

of E Ch. in Middle Ages. Though Basil the Great* did not write a monastic rule (individual oriental monasteries had their own rules), his *Regulae fusius tractatae* (*MPG*, 31, 889—1306) influenced E monasticism. 2. Adherents of Basil of Ancyra* who opposed Arians at Syn. of Ancyra 358. 3. Soc. of priests founded 1800 in Fr. for training priests.

Basilica. See *Church Architecture,* 3.

Basilides. See *Gnosticism,* 7 e.

Basire, Isaac (1607—76). Anglo-Cath.; miss. in Near E; prof. Weissenburg.

Basis of Union. See *Canada,* B.

Bassler, Gottlieb (Dec. 10, 1813—Oct. 3, 1868). B. Langenthal, Switz.; to Am. at 4; printer 1826 to 1836; at 23 attended Pa. Coll. and the Luth. Theol. Sem., Gettysburg. Teacher, miss., pastor, dir. Licensed by W Pa. Syn. 1842; founded several Luth. congs.; secy. of meeting that founded Pittsburgh Syn., Jan. 1845; pres. Pittsburgh Syn. 1848 to 1850, 1856—58, 1865—67. Dir. Orphans' Farm School, Zelienople, Ohio, 1854—68. First pres. Gen. Council of the Ev. Luth. Ch. in N Am. 1867 to 1868.

Bastholm, Christian (1740—1819). Studied natural science, philos., and theol. Chief exponent of Enlightenment in Den.

Basutoland. See *Africa,* B 6.

Bataks. Bataks are a vital energetic people until recently untouched by Muslim influence, in the region of Lake Toba in N Sumatra (Indonesia). Lyman* and Munson,* Am. miss. who made the first attempt to reach the fierce Bataks, were killed 1834 as they approached the first village.

L. I. Nommensen,* sent by Rhenish* Mission Soc., entered the land alone 1864; he baptized 4 men with their wives and children (Aug. 27, 1865). In 1877 he est. a theol. training school (now at Siantar). Nommensen tr. NT into language of the Bataks (1878) and P. H. Johannsen the OT (1894).

The Batak Prot. Christian Ch. (Huria Kristen Batak Protestant) adapted the *adat* (ethical code of the Bataks), but its *Confession* rejects it as the basis of the ch. The AC and Luther's SC were included as conf. bases in the 1930 const. The Batak ch. drew up its own conf. *(Confession of Faith of the Huria Kristen Batak Protestant)* for admission into the LWF in 1951, probably because of resurgent nationalism. The conf. presents Luth. doctrine.

An ordained pastor is usually in charge of 8 to 14 Batak congregations, each of which has its own teacher-preacher assisted by lay presbyters. At the head of the ch. is the ephor.* The ch. has an extensive school system. Nommensen U. was est. 1954.

The Pungan Kristen (Batak Christian Ch.) was est. Djakarta (Jakarta; formerly Batavia), NW coast of Java, 1927; joined LWF 1972.

See also *Zending Batak.*

J. Ellwanger, "The Batak Protestant Christian Church," *CTM,* XXX (Jan. 1959), 1—17; J. Sarumpaet-Hutabarat, "Women under the Adat," *Lutheran World,* II (Summer 1955), 114—125; A. Bäfverfeldt, "Comparative Studies on Constitutions of Younger Churches," *Lutheran World,* I (Autumn 1954), 228 to 233; K. Bridston, "A Younger Church in Stormy Seas," *Lutheran World,* II (Spring 1955), 71—74; A. Lumbantobing, "Christian Education in the Batak Church," *Lutheran World,* II (Autumn 1955), 291 to 296; H. Meyer, "Study on the Transmission of our Faith as a Constitutive Element in the Growth of the Younger Churches," *Lutheran World,* I (Autumn 1954), 225—227; F. A. Schiotz, "A Visit Among the Bataks in Indonesia," *Lutheran World Review,* I (Jan. 1949), 1—14; F. A. Schiotz, "Lutheran World Missions," *The International Review of Missions,* XLIII (1954), 311—322; M. H. Bro, *Indonesia: Land of Challenges* (New York, 1954). *Theologische Existenz Heute,* new series, No. 137: L. Schreiner, *Das Bekenntnis der Batak-Kirche* (Munich, 1966). EL

Bates, William (1625—99). Presb. pastor London; lost benefice because of nonconformity 1662; failed to effect settlement bet. bps. and Dissenters. Wrote *Harmony of the Divine Attributes.*

Batiffol, Pierre (1861—1929). Fr. RC. Est. *Revue Biblique* with Lagrange. His book on the Eucharist (1905) was put on the Index (1911). Opponent of Modernism. Wrote hist. of RC Ch. and development of papal power.

Batizi, Andras (ca. 1510—ca. 1546). Hung. reformer; educ. Wittenberg (1542—43); leader at Syn. of Erdöd 1545; wrote one of the first ev. catechisms in Hung. Epic poet and hymnist.

Battle-Axe Experiment. See *Gates, Theophilus.*

Baudert, Samuel (1879—1956). Bp. Unitas Fratrum; held theol. and administrative positions at Niesky, Herrnhut, and Bad Boll. Wrote hist. of Herrnhut missions.

Baudissin, Wolf Wilhelm Graf (1847—1926). Prof. OT Strasbourg, Marburg, and Berlin.

Bauer, Bruno (1809—82). NT rationalistic critic; taught at Berlin until his *Kritik der evangelischen Geschichte des Johannes* and *Kritik der evangelischen Geschichte der Synoptiker* caused revocation of his license. Regarded Gospel story as figment of a single mind. See also *Lutheran Theology After 1580,* 10.

Bauer, Friedrich (1812—74). Helped Loehe* train men for Luth. ch. work in the US Midwest. Wrote Ger. grammar.

Bauer, Georg Lorenz (1755—1806). Prof. Altdorf 1789, Heidelberg 1805; orientalist and exegete. Exponent of hist. critical exegesis of Eichhorn.

Bauer, Johannes (1860—1933). Prof. practical theol. Marburg 1900, Königsberg 1907, and Heidelberg 1910. Wrote on practical topics (homiletics, agenda, religious instruction, catechism).

Bauer, Walter (1877—1960). Taught at Marburg 1903; prof. NT Breslau 1913, Göttingen 1916. Wrote in area of NT and early Christian Fathers. Works include *Griechisch-deutsches Wörterbuch zu den Schriften des Neuen Testaments und der übrigen urchristlichen Literatur.* Ed. *Theologische Literaturzeitung* 1930–39. See also *Lexicons,* B.

Bauernkrieg. See *Peasants' War.*

Baugher, Henry Lewis, Jr. (Aug. 6, 1840—Feb. 11, 1899). B. Gettysburg, d. Philadelphia; educ. Pa. Coll. and seminaries at Gettysburg, Pa., and Andover, Mass.; pastor Wheeling, W. Va., Norristown, Pa., Indianapolis, Ind., Omaha, Nebr.; prof. Gettysburg Coll. 1869—80, 1883—96; also taught at Howard U. 1883 and Gettysburg Sem. 1869—73, 1883; dir. Gettysburg Sem. 1889—99; pres. 1895 to 1896; pres. Gen. Syn. of the Ev. Luth. Ch. in the USA 1895—97; wrote commentary on Luke.

Baugher, Henry Lewis, Sr. (July 18, 1804—Apr. 14, 1868). B. Adams Co., Pa.; educ. Dickinson Coll. and Princeton and Gettysburg seminaries. Pastor Boonsboro, Md.; teacher at Gettysburg Coll. 1831; prof. Gk. Pa. Coll.; its 2d pres. 1850—68. In 1844 mem. of com. which formed "Abstract of the Doctrines and Practice of the Evangelical Lutheran Synod of Maryland," which omitted or rejected all distinctively Luth. doctrines.

Baum, Johann Wilhelm (1809—78). Prof. Strasbourg 1860—78. Notable hist. of the Swiss Reformation.

Bäumeler, Joseph Michael (Baumeler). See *Communistic Societies,* 5.

Baumgarten, Michael (1812—89). Ger. theol.; moved to religious life by Klaus Harms;* follower of Hengstenberg*; then influenced by Schleiermacher* and von Hofmann;* prof. Rostock; deposed for utterances and publications without having been given permission to defend himself and without having Scriptural evidence cited against him; this procedure was later severely criticized even by staunch Lutherans.

Baumgarten, Otto (1858—1934). Prof. practical theol. Jena 1890, Kiel 1894. Chm. Ev. Socialist Congress; mem. Ger. peace delegation 1919. Wrote books and ed. periodicals in area of practical theol. Coed. *Religion in Geschichte und Gegenwart* 1909 to 1913.

Baumgarten, Siegmund Jakob (1706—57). Prof. Halle; introduced philos. methods of Wolff* into theol.; this marked transition from Pietism to rationalism.

Baumgarten-Crusius, Ludwig Friedrich Otto (1788 to 1843). B. Merseburg; d. Jena. Studied theol. and philol. at Leipzig. U. preacher Leipzig 1810; prof. Jena 1812; lectured on all branches of theol. except ch. hist.; interested chiefly in hist. of dogma. Advocated rational supernaturalism; opposed crass rationalism, but also 95 theses of Klaus Harms.*

Baumstark, Carl Anton (1872—1948). RC; prof. Bonn 1921, Nijmegen 1923, Utrecht 1926, Münster 1930. Wrote chiefly in area of oriental Christian literature and liturgy.

Baur, Ferdinand Christian (1792—1860). Prof. Blaubeuren sem. 1817; prof. Tübingen 1826. Founder and chief representative of later Tübingen* school of theol.; applied Hegel's* principles of philos. to theol. The real essence of the Christian religion is to him the strictly ethical content of the teaching of Jesus, to the exclusion of the miraculous element; Peter represents the particularistic Jewish, Paul the universalistic heathen-Christian viewpoint of Christ's teaching; in the 2d c. these teachings were gradually brought into agreement; thus the Christian religion has a perfectly natural hist. development; of Paul's Epistles only those to the Romans, Corinthians, and Galatians are genuine; all the rest, because of their conciliatory tendency, are considered spurious. See also *Exegesis.*

Baur, Gustav Adolf Ludwig (1816—89). Prof. Giessen; pastor Hamburg; prof. Leipzig. Mem. commission for revising Luther's tr. of Bible.

Baur, Wilhelm (1826—97). Brother of Gustav. Ger. pastor and ch. administrator. Active in inner missions and hymnody.

Bauslin, David Henry (Jan. 21, 1854—Mar. 3, 1922). Am. theol. Educ. Wittenberg Coll., Springfield, Ohio; pastor Tippecanoe City, Bucyrus, Springfield, and Canton, Ohio; prof. hist. and practical theol. Hamma Divinity School, Springfield, Ohio, 1896 to 1922; dean of sem. 1911—22. Helped organize ULCA 1918. Ed. *Lutheran World* 1901—12; pres. Gen. Syn. 1905—07. Works include *Is the Ministry an Attractive Vocation?* and *The Lutheran Movement of the Sixteenth Century.*

Bautain, Louis Eugène Marie (1796—1867). Fr. philos. and theol.; prof. Strasbourg and Sorbonne; follower of Kant; rejected rational theistic arguments but was required to sign statements upholding the rationality of the existence of God, immortality, and revelation.

Bavarian Foreign Mission Society. See *Neuendettelsau Mission Society.*

Bavinck, Herman (1854—1921). Dutch Ref. theol.; prof. dogmatics Free U., Amsterdam. Most important work: *Gereformeerde Dogmatiek.*

Bavinck, Johan Herman (1895–1965). B. Rotterdam, Neth.; miss. Indonesia; prof. Amsterdam and Kampen, Neth. Works include *Inleiding in de Zendingswetenschap* (tr. D. H. Freeman, *An Introduction to the Science of Missions); The Church Between Temple and Mosque; The Impact of Christianity on the Non-Christian World.* See also *Indonesia,* 2.

Baxter, Richard (1615—91). Educ. Wroxeter; chaplain in one of Cromwell's regiments; chaplain to Charles II; refused bishopric of Hereford; afterwards took out license as Nonconformist minister; works include *Saints' Everlasting Rest.* Hymnist; wrote "Lord, It Belongs Not to My Care."

Bayle, Pierre (1647—1706). Fr. philos.; prof. Sedan and Rotterdam; skeptic; considered faith and reason exclusive realms; emphasized freedom of thought and toleration. Wrote *Pensées diverses sur la comète de 1680; Critique générale de l'Histoire du calvinisme du P. Maimburg; Dictionnaire historique et critique.*

Bayly, Lewis (ca. 1565—1631). Welsh Puritan; educ. Oxford; chaplain to James I 1616; bp. Bangor, Wales, 1616; imprisoned 1621. His *The Practice of Piety* influenced J. Bunyan.

Baynes, Paul (d. 1617). Taught at St. Andrews, Cambridge; deposed because of strict Puritanism.

Bazaars. See *Finances in the Church,* 5.

Beadle. 1. Mace-bearer attendant on ecclesiastical dignitaries. 2. Inferior parish officer with various minor duties connected with a ch. or vestry (chiefly in Eng.).

Beads, Use of. See *Rosary.*

Beatific Vision. See *Glory.*

Beatification. See *Canonization.*

Beaton, David (Bethune; ca. 1494—1546). Scot. cardinal, abp., chancellor. Responsible for arrest and execution of George Wishart. See also *Presbyterian Bodies,* 1.

Beatty, Alfred Chester. See *Manuscripts of the Bible,* 3 a.

Beatus of Liebana (ca. 730—798). Sp. priest, monk, geog.; opposed adoptionism.* His *Commentaria in Apocalypsin* (ca. 776) contains one of the oldest Christian world maps. Also wrote against Elipandus of Toledo and Felix of Urgel.

Beatus Rhenanus. See *Rhenanus, Beatus.*

Beaufort, Pierre de. See *Popes,* 14.

Beaulieu, Peace of. See *France,* 9.

Beausobre, Isaac de (1659—1738). Fr. Ref. pastor; fled from Paris to Rotterdam 1685; pastor Dessau 1686, Berlin 1694.

Bec. Norman Benedictine abbey founded 1034; made famous by Anselm* of Canterbury and Lanfranc.*

Bechmann, Fridemann (1628—1703). Prof. philos. 1656 and theol. 1668 Jena U. Works include *Institutiones theologicae; Haeresiographia; Theologia conscientiaria; Theologia polemica; Ad institutiones catecheticas Cunradi Dieterici annotationes uberiores.*

Bechuanaland. See *Africa,* B 3.

Beck, Albert H. (April 1, 1894—May 30, 1962). B. Baltimore, Ohio; d. River Forest, Ill. Grad. Teachers' Sem., River Forest, 1914. Instructor Concordia Teachers College, River Forest, 1914—23; prof. 1923—62. Composed *Fourteen Anthems for the Church Festivals; 76 Offertories on Hymns and Chorales; 36 Preludes on Hymns and Chorales.*

Beck, Johann Tobias (1804—78). B. Balingen; pastor at Waldthann near Crailsheim, and Mergentheim; prof. at Basel, 1836, and Tübingen, 1843. Opponent of the criticohistorical method as developed by Strauss and Baur; emphasized return to Bible and Biblical truth. Sought to build system of doctrine on Bible alone, avoiding historicotheol. terms and holding that even the Confessions were significant only because they performed a significant task in hist. Held that inspiration was the living, dynamic union and interpenetration of the human and divine spirit (3 levels of *theopneustia;** errors and contradictions in "irrelevant" matters in Scripture). The kingdom of God, he taught, was the supermundane economy of spirit and life (the heavenly reality), brought and revealed to man through Christ. The ethical or moral is the first and essential mark of the Christian. The above formal and material principles led to departures from Luth. orthodoxy in Beck's theol. system (emphasis on the psychol. in his doctrine of justification rather than on the objective act, seeing the saving hand of love rather than the majestic pronouncement of the Judge; faith, construed as the active ethical grasp of Christ — a dynamic gift producing personal righteousness — is the cause of justification). Influenced A. Schlatter.*

A. Schlatter, "Christus und Christentum. J. T. Becks theologische Arbeit," *Beiträge zur Förderung christlicher Theologie,* Vol. 8, No. 4 (Gütersloh, 1904); A. Sturhahn, "Zur systematischen Theologie Johannes Tobias Becks," *Beiträge zur Förderung christlicher Theologie,* Vol. 7, No. 6 (Gütersloh, 1903); G. Sentzke, *Die Theologie Johann Tobias Becks und ihr Einfluss in Finnland* (Helsinki, 1949).

Beck, Johan Vilhelm (1829—1901). Dan. pastor; leader of pietistic Ch. Soc. for Inner Missions in Den. Opposed Grundtvig. See also *Denmark, Lutheranism in,* 10.

Beck, William Frederick Henry (Wilhelm Friedrich Heinrich; Aug. 28, 1904–Oct. 24, 1966). B. Little Falls, Minn; educ. Conc. Sem., St. Louis, Mo.; pastor Clayton, Ill., 1930–43; in Mo. Syn. pub. relations work 1943–46; ed. CPH 1946–66. Works include *The New Testament in the Language of Today; We Bring Christ: Messages and Bible Studies for Preaching, Teaching, Reaching; The Christ of the Gospels; Bible Truth.*

Becker, Albert Ernst Anton (1834—99). Conductor of Berlin Cathedral Choir; composer of orchestral and choral music. His *Reformation Cantata* won for him a much-coveted prize in 1883.

Becker, Carl Heinrich (1876—1933). Ger. orientalist; prof. Hamburg 1908, Bonn 1913, Berlin 1930. Secy. of state in Prussia 1919, 1925; mem. Prussian cabinet 1921.

Becker, Cornelius (1561—1604). Pastor, prof. Leipzig. Put Psalter into hymn form attempting to offset the influence of Ambrosius Lobwasser.* Though used by Sethus Calvisius* and Heinrich Schütz,* Becker's texts lacked the popular appeal of texts prepared by Ludwig Helmbold.

Becket, Thomas à (ca. 1118—70). As chancellor of Eng. 1155—62, an ardent supporter of Henry II in his endeavor to obtain absolute mastery in state and ch.; as abp. Canterbury 1162 he sought to free the ch. from all civil jurisdiction; refused to sign the Constitutions of Clarendon and fled to Fr.; after an apparent reconciliation with the king he returned to Eng., but new difficulties ensued, and Becket was murdered by 4 retainers of Henry; within 3 yrs. after his death Becket was canonized by Alexander III (see *Popes,* 9); burial place was a shrine till Becket was stigmatized as traitor by Henry VIII.

Materials for the History of Thomas Becket, eds. J. C. Robertson and J. B. Sheppard, 7 vols. (London, 1875—85); M. D. Knowles, "Archbishop Thomas Becket. A Character Study," *Proceedings of the British Academy,* XXXV (1949), 177—205.

Beckman, Anders Frederik (1812—94). Prof. theol. Uppsala, Swed.; played important part in swaying faculty from neology to ev. theol. by his defense of the deity of Christ.

Becon, Thomas (ca. 1513—67). Eng. reformer; studied under Latimer;* assoc. with Cranmer.* Writings show influence of Luther till his exile 1553; later inclined to Zwingli.*

Beddome, Benjamin (1717—95). Bap.; from 1740 till his death minister at Bourton-on-the-Water, Gloucestershire; wrote "When Israel Through the Desert Passed" and many other hymns.

Bede ("the Venerable"; 673—735). B. Northumbria; educ. and taught at Jarrow; wrote scientific and theol. treatises, including commentaries (allegorical), books of hymns and epigrams, and *Historia ecclesiastica gentis Anglorum.* Though many of his pupils occupied prominent positions, he remained a simple monk. His influence spread through Eur., and he is often called "the Teacher of the Middle Ages." He dictated the last part of his Anglo-Saxon tr. of John on his deathbed. See also *John of Beverly.*

Works pub. in Paris 1521; J. A. Giles, *The Complete Works of the Venerable Bede* (London, 1843 to 1844); MPL, 90—95; E. S. Duckett, *Anglo-Saxon Saints and Scholars* (New York, 1947), pp. 217—336.

Bedlam (corruption of Bethlehem). Institution originally founded 1247 for housing visiting bps. and canons of St. Mary of Bethlehem; given by Henry VIII to city of London as hosp. for lunatics 1547; later became known for brutal treatment of insane people.

Beecher, Henry Ward (1813—87). B. Litchfield, Conn.; d. Brooklyn. Orator; author; lecturer. Son of Lyman Beecher; minister (Presb.) at Lawrenceburg and Indianapolis, Ind.; at Plymouth Ch. (Cong.), Brooklyn, N. Y., 1847; issued hymnal; made antislavery speeches; accepted evolution and Higher Criticism; was sued for adultery, but acquitted; withdrew, with his ch., from Cong. Assoc. 1882.

P. Hibben, *Henry Ward Beecher; an American Portrait* (New York, 1927); L. G. Crocker, *Henry Ward Beecher's Art of Preaching* (Chicago, 1934).

Beecher, Lyman (1775—1863). B. New Haven, Conn.; d. Brooklyn. Clergyman; author. Cong. pastor Litchfield, Conn., and Boston; Presb. pastor Cincinnati and pres. Lane Theol. Sem. there. Father of Harriet Beecher Stowe. See also *New Haven Theology; Revivals.*

Beehler, Jacob Matthias. See *Bühler, Jacob Matthias.*

Beethoven, Ludwig van (1770—1827). The master in whose hands the classical temper in music reached its highest development and who helped bring on the advent of Romanticism. B. Bonn; son of an irrational father who foolishly wanted to force Ludwig to become a child prodigy like the young Mozart, in order that he, the father, might live in financial security. Studied with Haydn, Albrechtsberger, and Salieri. In Vienna, music capital of his day, Beethoven soon won acclaim for ability as pianist; he was respected as a composer, but not understood. His deafness of later yrs. troubled him a great deal, though a blessing in disguise, since it caused him to concentrate on his inner self. Works include 9 symphonies, 5 piano concertos, 1 violin concerto, 32 piano sonatas, 9 sonatas for violin and piano, 17 string quartets, a large number of shorter works, the oratorio *Christus am Ölberge,* and *Missa Solemnis.* Beethoven may hardly be called a ch. composer; even *Missa Solemnis* was intended for the concert stage. See also *Passion, The.*

P. Bekker, *Beethoven,* tr. M. M. Bozman (New York, 1926); R. Bory, *Ludwig van Beethoven* (New York, 1964); J. N. Burk, *The Life and Works of Beethoven* (New York, 1946); G. Grove, *Beethoven, Schubert, Mendelssohn* (New York, 1951); R. Langer, *Missa solemnis: über das theologische Problem in Beethovens Musik* (Stuttgart, 1962); A. W. Thayer, *The Life of Beethoven,* rev. and ed. E. Forbes (Princeton, 1964).

Beffchen. See *Vestments, Clerical,* 3.

Beggars of the Sea. See *Gueux de mer.*

Beghards and Beguines. Semimonastic communities of W Eur. from 12th c. on. Beguines (sisterhood) are the original order; Beghards the male counterpart. Celibacy required as long as one remained a mem.; supported themselves by manual labor; devoted to devotional exercises and deaconess work. Persecuted for heresy and prosecuted for concubinage (13th c.), many joined the tertiaries of the mendicant orders. A few small communities of Beguines survive in the Neth. and Belgium.

Behavior. See *Educational Psychology; Psychology.*

Behaviorism. See *Educational Psychology,* D 4; *Psychology,* J 4.

Behm, Heinrich (1853—1930). Pastor Schlieffenberg

1883, Parchim 1887, Güstrow 1897; supt. Doberan 1900; bp. Mecklenburg-Schwerin 1922. Wrote *Die Innere Mission; Geschichte der Laienpredigt im Grundriss; Zur Frage der Weltanschauung.*

Behm, Johannes (1883–1948). Prot. theol.; b. Doberan, Mecklenburg-Schwerin, Ger.; prof. Königsberg 1920, Göttingen 1923, Berlin 1935. Coed. *Das Neue Testament Deutsch.* Other works include *Die Handauflegung im Urchristentum; Der Begriff Diatheke in Neuen Testament; Die Bekehrung des Paulus; Die mandäische Religion und das Christentum.*

Behm, Martin (1557—1622). B. Lauban, Silesia. After serving as private tutor in Vienna, studied at U. of Strasbourg; diaconus and eventually chief pastor Lauban. Renowned preacher; faithful pastor in times of famine, pestilence, war; prolific author; wrote ca. 480 hymns, which emphasize esp. the Passion of Christ.

Behnken, John William (Mar. 19, 1884–Feb. 23, 1968). B. Cypress, Harris Co., Tex.; educ. St. John's Coll., Winfield, Kans., and Conc. Sem., St. Louis, Mo.; ordained 1906; pastor Houston, Tex., 1908–35; pres. Tex. Dist. of Mo. Syn. 1926–29; pres. Mo. Syn. 1935–62. Active in Bad* Boll conferences and in est. LCUSA. Works include *Noonday Sermons; Mercies Manifold; This I Recall.*

Behrens, Henry William (Feb. 13, 1827—Apr. 22, 1900). B. Hermannsburg, Ger.; influenced in early youth by Louis Harms. Sent by Hermannsburg Soc. to Afr. Nov. 10, 1857; worked 6 yrs. among Zulu Kaffir in Natal, then among Bechuanas; founded Bethany Village; supervised work of Hermannsburg Soc. among Bechuanas. See also *Africa,* B 5.

Behrens, William Henry (Dec. 6, 1870—Mar. 29, 1943). B. St. Louis; grad. St. Louis 1893; pastor Salt Lake City, Utah, 1893—94; Tacoma, Wash. (doing miss. work in practically the entire state), 1894—98; Portland, Oreg., 1898—1909; Chester, Ill., 1909 to 1924; prof. Conc. Sem., Springfield, Ill., 1924—43; vice-pres. Oreg. and Wash. Dist. of Mo. Syn. 1899 to 1906; pres. 1906—09.

Beichtvesper. See *Confession.*

Being (in Aristotelian thought). Differing from Plato's extreme idealistic view that only ideas are the true and ultimate reality and "of the nature of Being" (R. B. Winn in Runes, *Dictionary of Philosophy*), Aristotle held that though Being, "as the essence of things" (R. B. W.) is in itself eternal, it could have no validity outside of things and minds. In other words, knowledge with any stability begins in sense-experience, in which individual existent things are revealed. Individuals are not to be deduced from ideas; on the contrary, abstract concepts devolve by induction from concrete instances.

Obviously Aristotle's method is to this extent empirical, and his parallel contribution to human thought of the distinction between percept and concept (object of sense-perception, object of abstract thought) and their interrelations has been most significant and helpful to later philosophers.

According to Aristotle the highest determinants of Being are actuality *(entelecheia)* and potentiality *(dynamis).* The first has been called perfection — the realization of the fulness of Being, and the second imperfection — incompleteness with, however, perfectibility.

Inevitably the question of Aristotle's position relative to the later classic scholastic terms for Being, *ens* and *esse,* is raised. *Ens* occurs in classic Lat. only once as a participle but quite often as a noun. "As a participle it is an essential predicate only in regard to God, in whom existence and essence are one, or whose essence implies existence" R. Allers in Runes, *Dictionary of Philosophy*). *Esse* "usually means existence which is defined as the *actus essendi,* or the reality of some essence. *Esse quid* or *essentia* designates the specific nature of some being or thing" (R. A.).

Aristotle could not agree with those who held that, since being is, nonbeing cannot exist or even be thought of as existing and therefore doubted the validity of all sense perception of the external world. He held that sense experience is a true source of conceptual knowledge. Since his basic concepts differ from those of the scholastics, his metaphysical statements, formulae, and predications also differ. It might be said that his categories and methodology bridged the gap between being and becoming and furnished sharp intellectual tools for succeeding ages. AJB

Beissel, Johann Conrad (1690–1768). B. Eberbach, Ger.; to Pa. 1720; est. (Ger.) Seventh Day Baps.; founded Ephrata Community near Reading, Pa.; wrote earliest vol. of Ger. poetry in Am.: *Göttliche Liebes und Lobestöne,* hymnist; mystic. See also *Baptist Churches,* 17; *Brethren,* 1; *Communistic Societies,* 5.

W. C. Klein, *Johann Conrad Beissel: Mystic and Martinet* (Philadelphia, 1942).

Bekennende Kirche. See *Confessing Church.*

Bekenntnis-Kirche in der Diaspora, Evangelisch-lutherische. See *Germany, Lutheran Free Churches in,* 13.

Bekenntnissynoden. See *Barmen Theses; Kirchenkampf.*

Bekker, Balthasar (1634—98). Dutch Ref. theol.; pastor Amsterdam 1679—92; opposed belief in witchcraft in *De betooverde Weereld.*

Bel and the Dragon. See *Apocrypha,* A 3.

Belgian Christian Missionary Church. See *Belgium.*

Belgian Congo. See *Africa,* F 2.

Belgian Gospel Mission. See *Belgium.*

Belgic Confession. See *Reformed Confessions,* C 1.

Belgium. Country N of Fr., formerly part of Neth.; since 1830 an indep. kingdom; the N part is Flemish, the S Walloon. *Area:* ca. 11,775 sq. mi. *Pop.:* 9,231,251 (1963).

The country was evangelized when N Fr. was gained for the Gospel and, in part, when the lowlands of Holland were Christianized. It became very strongly RC and has remained so. A few Prot. communions are survivals from the Reformation era; others are the result of immigration from adjacent countries, but mostly and mainly the result of evangelization. In 1963 one percent of the pop. was Prot.; 300 congregations and stations with 250 ministers and evangelists.

The Prot. Ev. Ch. (formerly: Union of Ev. Prot. Churches of Belgium) had 13,182 members 1963. The Belgian Christian Miss. Ch. had 8,529 members and the Belgian Gospel Miss. 4,710. Other denominations: Meth. 2,523; Ref. 1,614; Luth. (Ev. Luth. Free Ch.) 285; for. churches (among others, Scand. Luth.) 3,575. There is also a Prot. soc. for carrying on miss. work in the Congo (Ruanda). The Prot. Theol. Faculty in Brussels was officially recognized by the Belgian govt. 1963, when it was endowed with the *ius promovendi.* It is bilingual (Fr. and Dutch) and has 40 students (1964). The Ev. Luth. Free Ch. (2 pastors in 1964) is affiliated with the Syn. Conf.

The RC Ch. of Belgium was formally organized 1561, this date also indicating the cessation of foreign authority. After Belgium became an indep. country, an adjustment of boundaries was made. The priests are educ. at the episc. seminaries and at the U. of Louvain. The RC Ch. does not enjoy any particular legal prerogative. It receives a sum of money direct from the state as do also the Prot. Ev. Ch. and some indep. congregations. The archdiocese of Mechlin-Brussels (formerly: Mechlin diocese) coextensive with Belgium, was created 1559 by the pope. The most important bishoprics are:

Antwerp (recently created), Brugge, Gent, Liège, Namur, and Tournai. OHS, WJK

A. J. Bronkhorst, *Le Protestantisme en Belgique* (Amsterdam, 1958); *Annuaire des Eglises Evangéliques en Belgique* (Antwerp, 1963); J. Hazette, *Le Protestantisme en Belgique, sa situation actuelle,* ed. Ireniko (Chevetogne, 1960); Leon-E. Halkin, *La Reforme en Belgique sous Charles-Quint* (Brussels, 1957).

Believers. See *Brethren, Plymouth; Church; Faith.*

Believer's Baptism. The practice of considering as candidates for baptism only those who are already believers or are at least in a "covenant relation" through their birth of Christian parents. See also *Baptist Churches,* 1, 2; Reublin, Wilhelm.

Belize. See *Central America,* A.

Bell, George Kennedy Allen (1883–1958). Angl. theol.; dean Canterbury 1924; bp. Chichester 1929; chm. Ecumenical Council for Practical Christianity 1934–36; chm. Com. Ecumenical Council 1948–54, honorary chm. 1954. Wrote in area of hist. and on Christian unity.

Bell, Henry (fl. 1650). Employed in overseas affairs of state under James I and Charles I. Tr. Luther's *Tischreden* under the Eng. title *Dr. Martin Luther's Divine Discourses at His Table,* dedicated to Lord Mayor of London, authorized for printing 1646 by House of Commons, pub. 1652. (See also *Luther, Table Talk of.*)

G. Rupp, *The Righteousness of God* (New York, 1953), pp. 56–77.

Bell, Book, and Candle. Expression referring to symbolic actions formerly used in excommunication: shutting the pontifical book after pronouncing the curse, extinguishing a candle, and tolling the bell as for the dead. "Bell, book, and candle – candle, book, and bell, forward and backward to curse Faustus to hell" (C. Marlowe, *Doctor Faustus*). Agreement of the ceremony, the 1st instance of which is ca. 1190, with canon law has been questioned.

Bellamy, Edward (1850–98). Am. utopian author. Works include *Looking Backward,* which emphasized a materialistic equality and other socialistic factors which were later prominent in the social gospel.*

Bellamy, Joseph. See *New England Theology,* 4.

Bellarmine, Robert (Roberto Francesco Romolo Bellarmino; 1542–1621). B. Tuscany; d. Rome; nephew of Pope Marcellus II; Jesuit 1560; prof. Louvain 1570; prof. controversial theol. Collegium Romanum 1576; cardinal 1599; abp. Capua 1602–05; canonized 1930; doctor of the church 1931.

Bellarmine was an able scholar and controversialist. His chief work, *Disputationes de controversiis christianae fidei adversus huius temporis haereticos,* is a systematic apology for the RC position. It emphasizes the necessity of the magisterium (teaching office of the church) and tradition. Because its first vol. held that the papacy had only indirect power in temporal matters it was proposed for the Index of Prohibited Books* 1590. Other works: *Judicium de libro, quem Lutherani vocant concordiae; De translatione imperii romani a Graecis ad Francos, adversus Matthiam Flacium Illyricum.*

See also *Roman Catholic Confessions,* A 3.

Works in 12 vols. (Paris, 1870–74) and 8 vols. (Naples, 1872); autobiography (Rome, 1676). Primary sources are the biographies of J. Fuligatti (Rome, 1624), D. Bartoli (Rome, 1678) and N. Frizon (Nancy, 1708); J. Brodrick, *The Life and Work of Blessed Robert Francis Cardinal Bellarmine,* 2 vols. (London, 1928); E. A. Ryan, *The Historical Scholarship of Saint Bellarmine* (Louvain, 1936).

Belloc, Joseph Hilaire Pierre (Hilary; 1870–1953). Brit. RC writer; b. Paris, Fr.; educ. Oxford; Brit. citizen 1902. Works include *Characters of the Reformation; The Great Heresies.*

Bellows, Henry Whitney (1814–82). Unitarian; pastor in New York; pres. Nat. Unitarian Conf. 1865 to 1879. See also *Red Cross.*

Bells, Church. In early Christian ch. the faithful were summoned to worship by word of mouth; later trumpets were used, also large hammers, struck against wooden or iron instruments. Bells were introd. in 9th c., suspended at first in special bell towers, or campaniles, later in spires of churches themselves, their use meeting with great favor almost everywhere.

Ch. bells are commonly rung immediately preceding a service. Other uses have varied from time to time and place to place (e. g., ½ hr. before sunrise and ½ hr. before sunset; at noon; Sat. evening at 6 o'clock; at the death and/or burial of a ch. mem. [sometimes tolling his age]; at the beginning, middle, and end of the Lord's Prayer in a service; at confirmation; at the end of a service).

Beloit Seminary (Iowa). Began 1874 Springfield, near Decorah, Iowa, in a parsonage of The Norwegian*-Dan. Augustana Syn. in Am.; moved 1876 to Marshall, Wis., and operated in conjunction with Marshall Academy (est. there 1869 by the Scand. Ev. Luth. Syn. of [or in] N. Am.; see *Augustana Evangelical Lutheran Church,* 8); name Augustana Sem. adopted 1878; moved 1881 to Beloit, Iowa; merged 1890 with parts of Augsburg Sem., Minneapolis, Minn., and the sem. of the Anti-Missouri* Brotherhood at St. Olaf Coll., Northfield, Minn., to form the United (Norw.) Ch. Sem.

Beloit Seminary (Wis.). Popular name of an academy (or high school) opened 1843 for the instruction of young persons of either sex in science and literature.

Belot, Gustave (1859–1930). Fr. philos.; opposed science of morals because he held that metaphysics could not be used to est. morality; held that morality, like other culture, is a development or growth.

Beltane. Spring religious festival of Christian Celtic peoples.

Bema. See *Church Architecture,* 3.

Ben Naphtali, Mosche ben David (10th c.). Palestinian Masorete.

Bénard, Laurent (1573–1620). Benedictine monk. Founder of Maurists.*

Bender, Wilhelm (1845–1901). Prof. Boon; added the illusionistic critique to Ritschlian thought.

Benedetto da Mantova. See *Mantova, Benedetto da.*

Benedicite. See *Canticles.*

Benedict XII. See *Babylonian Captivity,* 2.

Benedict XIII. 1. *Pedro de Luna* (ca. 1328–1423). B. Aragon, Sp.: antipope at Avignon* 1394; deposed at Council of Pisa* 1409 and Constance* 1417. See also *Babylonian Captivity,* 2; *Gregory XII; Nicholas of Clémanges; Schism,* 8. 2. *Pietro Francesco Orsini* (1649–1730). B. Gravina, It.; scholarly, upright, peace-loving pope 1724–30.

Benedict XIV. See *Popes,* 24.

Benedict XV. See *Popes,* 31.

Benedict, Ruth Fulton (nee Ruth Fulton; 1887–1948). B. NYC; educ. Vassar Coll., Poughkeepsie, N. Y., and Columbia U., NYC; prof. anthropology Columbia U. Works include *Patterns of Culture.*

Benedict of Aniane (ca. 750–821). Visigothic monastic reformer supported by Charlemagne; wrote against Adoptionist Felix of Urgel; compiled monastic rules; gen. supervisor of Frankish monasteries.

MPL, 103, 355–1440.

Benedict of Nursia (ca. 480–ca. 543). Founder of Monte* Cassino (ca. 529); using earlier writings (of Basil, Cassian, and others), he worked out the Rule of 529, almost universally adopted in the Middle Ages by W monasteries. The rule shows excellence in organizing the worship, reading, and laboring activities of monks. See also *Benedictines.*

Benedictines (O. S. B.; *Ordo sancti Benedicti*). Monastic order founded on Rule of Benedict of Nursia,* father of W monasticism. This rule was based on earlier rules, and while strict in some respects, was, in gen., quite moderate. In addition to the 3 usual obligations of poverty, celibacy, and obedience it required manual labor of the monks and provided for daily reading and for convent libraries. Favored by Rome, the Benedictines absorbed the adherents of rival rules; by 811 only traces of rivals remained. Thereafter, for centuries, the Benedictine remained the normal monastic type. During the palmy days of the order (821–1200) its influence controlled the civilization of the entire Christian west. The Benedictines repaid with usury the favor extended them by the papacy. But the riches gathered by the monasteries brought into the order widespread corruption and immorality, which were only partly and temporarily checked by Cluniac, Cistercian, and other reforms. Inner decline and attacks from without reduced the 37,000 Benedictine houses of the 14th c. to only 50 in the early 19th c.

Benedict's sister, Scholastica, est. a convent, but it is doubtful whether that was the beginning of the Benedictine nuns. Certainly many women early adopted Benedict's rule, though they were not strictly enclosed. Benedictine nuns came to Ger. with Boniface.

The order was est. in US 1846. Statistics (1965): 27 abbeys, 4 priories, 1 miss. house, 1,966 priests, 371 clerics, 551 brothers, 218 students in major seminaries.

Benedictine Bibliography, ed. O. L. Kapsner. 2d ed., 2 vols. (Collegeville, Minn., 1962).

Benedictions. The *Aaronic* benediction, Nm. 6:24-26, was used in Temple and synagogue at the end of the liturgical part of the service. It was used in the early church (*Apostolic Constitutions*, II, 57) and was retained by Luther as the only one commanded by God. It conveys to the assembled cong., which has accepted the salvation of God in the means of grace, the blessing of the Triune God. The *Apostolic* benediction, 2 Co 13:14, is customarily used at the end of the minor services. The blessing in Gn 31:49 is called *Mizpah* benediction.

Benedictus. See *Canticles*.

Benefice. The right, granted to a cleric, of receiving the income from lands or other ch. property for performing spiritual duties. The value of benefices led to many abuses and much controversy in the Middle Ages. (See *Simony*.) Benefices are almost unknown in the US.

Beneficence. See *Alms; Charities, Christian.*

Benefit of Clergy. See *Clergy*.

Benevento, Synod of. See *Tempus Iausum*.

Benevolence. See *Alms; Charities, Christian; God; Social Work; Inner Mission; Deaconesses.*

Benevolent and Protective Order of Elks, The. See *Elks, The Benevolent and Protective Order of.*

Benevolent Societies. See *Aging and Infirm, Homes and Services for; Hospitals, Sanatoria, Homes for Convalescents and Chronically Ill; Child and Family Service Agencies.*

Benfey, Theodor (1809–81). Ger. Sanskrit scholar; prof. Göttingen 1848. Wrote Sanskrit grammar and Sanskrit-Eng. dictionary.

Bengel, Johann Albrecht (1687–1752). Foremost post-Reformation theol. in Württemberg; educ. Tübingen; prof. *Klosterschule* Denkendorf; pastor village cong. 1713; prelate Herbrechtingen 1741; prelate Alpirsbach and mem. of consistory, with residence at Stuttgart 1749. A man of eminent piety and vast and sound learning. In 1734 he pub. a Gk. NT with *apparatus criticus*, based on a careful study of the text in various MSS. Greatest work: *Gnomon Novi Testamenti*. Taught chiliasm; predicted millennium to begin 1836. See also *Textual Criticism*, 3.

J. C. F. Burk, *Dr. Johann Albrecht Bengels Leben und Wirken* (Stuttgart, 1831), tr. into Eng. 1837 R. F. Walker, *A Memoir of the Life and Writings of John Albert Bengel;* O. Wächter, *Johann Albrecht Bengel* (Stuttgart, 1865); E. Nestle, *Bengel als Gelehrter* (Tübingen, 1893); F. Nolte, *D. Johann Albrecht Bengel* (Gütersloh, 1913); R. F. Spieler, *The Theological Significance of Johann Albrecht Bengel* (Th. D. Dissertation, 1957; Conc. Sem. Library, St. Louis); G. Keller, *Johann Albrecht Bengel* (Basel, 1948).

Bennett, Cephas (Mar. 20, 1804–Nov. 16, 1885). B. Homer, N. Y. Sent by Am. Bap. Miss. Union to Burma as printer; printed Scriptures, tracts, and books in all the dialects of Burma.

Bennett, William Sterndale (1816–75). Eng. pianist and composer. Studied in Eng. and Ger. Schumann and F. Mendelssohn among his friends and admirers. Ability as performer, conductor, and composer were first recognized in Ger. Works include oratorio *Woman of Samaria*.

Benson, Louis Fitzgerald (1855–1930). Am. hymnologist; b. Philadelphia; educ. U. of Pa. Practiced law 7 yrs., then studied at Princeton Theol. Sem.; ordained to Presb. ministry 1886. After a 6-yr. pastorate he took up his lifework, that of hymnody and liturgics; ed. hymnbooks; works include *The English Hymn; The Hymnody of the Christian Church; Studies of Familiar Hymns* (2 vols.).

Bente, Gerhard Friedrich (Jan. 22, 1858–Dec. 15, 1930). B. Wimmer, Hannover; d. Redwood City, Calif.; buried Con. Cemetery, St. Louis. Grad. Saint Louis 1881; pastor Humberstone, Stonebridge, and Jordan, Ont., 1882–93; vice-pres. Can. Dist., Mo. Syn., 1885; pres. 1887–93; prof. Conc. Sem., Saint Louis, 1893–1926. Ed. *Lehre und Wehre;* coed. *Concordia Triglotta;* wrote *Was steht der Vereinigung der lutherischen Synoden Amerikas im Wege? Gesetz und Evangelium; Amerikanisches Luthertum: American Lutheranism* (2 vols.); *Historical Introductions to the Symbolical Books of the Evangelical Lutheran Church.*

J. Bente, *Biography of Dr. Friedrich Bente* (Saint Louis, 1936); L. Fuerbringer, "*D. F. Bente als Theolog*," *CTM*, II (June 1931), 416–423.

Bentham, Jeremy (1748–1832). Eng. philos., jurist, exponent of utilitarianism*; influenced thinking on govt., soc., and prison reform esp. through *An Introduction to the Principles of Morals and Legislation.* See also *Deontology*.

Bentley, Richard (1662–1742). Eng. clergyman, scholar, critic. B. near Wakefield. Founder of hist. philol. Master Trin. Coll., Cambridge, 1700; prof. theol. Cambridge 1716. Known for critical texts of classical authors. Delivered first Boyle lectures, *A Confutation of Atheism*, 1692.

Bentley, William Holman (1855–1906). Pioneer Afr. miss. of Baptist Missionary Society.* Reduced Congo language to writing; works include *Life on the Congo; Dictionary and Grammar of the Kongo Language as Spoken at San Salvador; Pioneering on the Congo;* tr. of NT.

H. M. Bentley, *W. Holman Bentley* (London, 1907).

Bentzen, Aage (1894–1953). Dan. theol.; prof. OT Copenhagen. Works include commentary on Isaiah and introd. to OT.

Benze, Charles Theodore (Sept. 19, 1865–July 3, 1936). Ordained 1897; pastor Beaver Falls, Pa., 1897–98; Erie, Pa., 1898–1908; pres. Pittsburgh Syn. (Gen. Council) 1908–10; pres. Thiel Coll. 1909–13; Am. prof. Kropp Sem., Ger., 1913–15; prof. Mount Airy, Pa., 1915–36; sent by Gen. Council as commissioner to India 1918; vice-pres. Bd. of For. Miss. (ULC) 1918; sent by NLC to Russia 1922 to est. relief work; contributor to *Lutheran, Lutheran Quarterly;* coauthor with T. E. Schmauk, *The Con-*

fessional Principle and the Confessions of the Lutheran Church.

Benzelius Family. See *Sweden, Lutheran Church in,* 2.

Berdyaev, Nikolai Aleksandrovich (1874–1948). B. Kiev. Educ. Kiev and Heidelberg. Russ. philos., at first Marxist, later leaning to Neo-Kantianism. Banished from Russ., he continued activity in Berlin and Paris, where he founded religiophilos. academy. Man is center of his teaching: human liberty and creativity. Wrote *Freedom and the Spirit; The Destiny of Man; Solitude and Society; Spirit and Reality.*

Berean Fundamental Church. Founded 1934 in Denver, Colo. Emphasizes conservative Prot. doctrines. Membership (1964): 1,450.

Berean Mission Incorporated. Interdenom. faith miss.; headquarters: St. Louis, Mo. Formed 1936; inc. 1937 as Berean Afr. Missionary Soc. Began work in Congo 1938. Also active in Ecuador, Barbados, Grenada, Philippine Is., Cuba, among Cuban refugees, and among the Navajo Indians in SW US. The soc. emphasizes Bible institutes and Bible study.

Bereans (See Acts 17:10, 11). 1. Religious group founded by J. Barclay* (hence also "Barclayites") at Edinburgh 1773. Barclay rejected natural theol. and held that Scripture is source of all truth. After Barclay's death most of his followers merged with Congregationalists. 2. The interdenom. Berean Band, which encouraged memorizing Scripture, was organized by Charles J. G. Hensman* of London 1905. 3. See *Berean Fundamental Church.* 4. See *Berean Mission Incorporated.*

Bérenger (de Tours; ca. 998-1088). B. Tours; canon of cathedral there and head of its school; the important facts of his life are connected with the second Eucharistic Controversy.* This controversy with Lanfranc ushered in the period of Scholasticism.*

Berg, Frederick (Mar. 20, 1856–Mar. 9, 1939). B. Logansport, Ind.; educ. Conc. Coll., Fort Wayne, and Conc. Sem., St. Louis; commissioned 1878 as first resident miss. and pastor of the Negro Luth. ch., Little Rock, Ark.; pastor Decatur, Ind., 1881 to 91; Beardstown, Ill., 1891–1911; prof. Immanuel Luth. Coll., Greensboro, N. C., 1911–36.

Berg Bible Society. See *Bible Societies,* 2.

Bergdamaras. See *Africa,* B 8.

Bergemann, Gustav Ernst (Aug. 9, 1862–May 13, 1954). B. Hustisford, Wis.; d. Fond du Lac, Wis.; educ. Northwestern Coll., Watertown, Wis., and the Milwaukee Sem. of Wis. Syn.; pastor Bay City, Mich., 1887–92; Tomah, Wis., 1892–99; Fond du Lac, Wis., 1899–1947; retired; mem. Indian Miss. Bd. 1903–17; pres. old Wis. Syn. 1908–17; pres. Joint Syn. of Wis. and Other States 1917–33.

Bergen Book (Bergic Book). See *Lutheran Confessions,* C 2.

Bergerac, Peace Treaty of. See *France,* 9.

Berggrav, Eivind (1884–1959). Bp. Oslo; educ. Oslo, Oxford, Cambridge, Marburg, and Lund; ed. *Kirke og Kultur* 1909; primate Norw. Ch. 1937; leader in ecumenical* movement; active in organizing resistance to Quisling govt. (puppet of Nazis); imprisoned 1942–45. Wrote *With God in the Darkness,* an account of Norw. Ch. conflict.

Bergh, Johan Arndt (Jan. 12, 1847–Feb. 5, 1927). B. Odemark, Norw.; to Am. 1860; grad. Aug. Coll. 1869, Augsburg Sem. 1871; pastor Fergus Falls, Minn., 1871–77; Waterloo Ridge, Iowa, 1877–82; Luther Valley, Wis., 1882–1912; Elliott, Ill., 1912 to 16; hosp. miss. St. Paul, Minn., 1916; supt. Chicago Dist., Norw. Luth. Conf., 1883–90; leader in organizing United Norw. Ch. 1890, Norw. Luth. Ch. 1917; chm. Madison Circuit, United Norw. Luth. Ch., 1897–1912. Wrote *Gammel og ny retning; Hans Egede; Livsbilleder fra kirken i Norden; Underfuld boenhoerelse; I sidste oieblik; I ledige stunder; Slaveristriden; Den norsk lutherske kirke i Amerika; Den norsk lutherske kirkes historie i Amerika; Se, det Guds lam.* Ed. *Ungeblad for kirken og hjemmet; Vort blad; Kirken og hjemmet.*

Bergh van Eysinga, Gustav Adolf van den (1874 to 1957). Dutch Ref. theol.; prof. NT exegesis and Israelite hist. Utrecht. Ed. *Nieuw theologisch tijdschrift; Tijdschrift voor wijsbegeerte.* See also *Dutch Radicals.*

Bergier, Nicolas Sylvestre (1718–90). Prof. theol. Besançon; encyclopedist; wrote against deism and materialism.

Bergius, Johann Peter (1587–1658). Educ. Heidelberg and Strasbourg; traveled in Eng., Fr., Holland; prof. Frankfurt an der Oder; court chaplain Berlin 1623. Together with Calixt worked for union of Luth. and Ref. Approached Luth. position on doctrine of predestination.

Bergmann, Christopher (1793–1832). B. Ebenezer, Ga.; studied under his father, J. E. Bergmann; pastor at Ebenezer; mem. Syn. of South Carolina and secy. 1825–32. Influenced by J. Bachmann to become Luth. minister; ordained 1824; succeeded his father at Ebenezer; held Salzburger chs. together and brought them into connection with the South Carolina Syn.

Bergmann, John Ernest (d. 1824). Last of the ministers sent to the Salzburgers in Georgia by S. Urlsperger* of Augsburg; labored in Georgia from 1785 to his death.

Bergson, Henri (1859–1941). Fr. Jew; philos.; b. Paris; prof. Coll. de Fr.; recipient of Nobel prize in literature 1927. In his philos. Bergson conceived of a vital impulse *(élan vital)* which is basic to all activity and the creative spirit of world-process. This god is itself not complete, but grows in goodness, knowledge, power, etc. He stressed the reality of time and the importance of change and evolution more than Hegel. Consciousness is continuous knowledge of the past and survives after death. Intuition was to him the highest source of truth, and in accordance with that view he took a special interest in mystics. Works include *Time and Free Will* (essay on immediate data of consciousness); *Matter and Memory; Creative Evolution; Spiritual Energy; The Two Sources of Morality and Religion.* See also *Time.*

Bergsträsser, Gotthelf (1886–1933). Luth. orientalist; b. Oberlosa, near Plauen, Ger.; educ. Leipzig; prof. Constantinople 1915, Königsberg 1919, Breslau 1922, Heidelberg 1923, Munich 1926. See also *Grammars,* A.

Berkeley, George (1685–1753). Irish philos.; lecturer at Dublin; dean at Derry 1724; lived in Am. 1728–31; bp. Cloyne, Ireland, 1734; spent last years in retirement at Oxford. The philos. of Berkeley champions idealism. Beginning with the observation that all knowledge comes through sense impressions, he sought to reduce matter to a complex of impressions and thus deny the existence of material substance. He believed, however, in the reality of spiritual being. Wrote *Essay Towards a New Theory of Vision* and *A Treatise Concerning the Principles of Human Knowledge.* See also *Protestant Episcopal Church,* 1 c.

J. D. Wild, *George Berkeley* (New York, 1962).

Berkemeier, Gottlieb Cleophas (1855–1924). Ger. secy. of Gen. Council; dir. Wartburg Orphans' Farm School, Mount Vernon, N. Y.; author, poet; ed. *Der deutsche Lutheraner.*

Berkemeier, Wilhelm Heinrich (William; Oct. 18, 1820–Mar. 7, 1899). B. Oerlinghausen, Lippe-Detmold, Ger.; Am. 1847; attended Gettysburg 1849–51; pastor Pittsburgh, Pa., Wheeling, W. Va., and Mount Vernon, N. Y.; active in immigrant miss.

work 1866–99. See also *Immigrant and Emigrant Missions.*

Berkenmeyer, Wilhelm Christoph (William Christopher; Willem; Berckenmeyer; Berkkenmeyer; Apr. 14[?], 1687–1751). B. Bodenteich, Lüneburg, Ger.; successor to Falckner in Hudson Valley chs. 1725. During his pastorate in New York, Trinity Ch., a substantial stone structure was built 1729. In 1731 he moved to Loonenburg (Looneburgh; later called Athens), in the N part of his extended parish. Representing the orthodox school of Lutheranism in Am., he became leader of the pastors in the Hudson Valley. In 1735 a *Kerck-Ordinantie,* drafted by him, bound the Dutch and Ger. chs. of New York and New Jersey together in a syn. that had only 1 meeting as far as the records show. Berkenmeyer sought to advance pure Luthtranism and prevent the ecclesiastical mingling of Luth. and Ref. Married Benigna Sibylla Kocherthal 1727. His journal, in Dutch, Ger., and Lat., contains much valuable hist. material.

H. J. Kreider, *Lutheranism in Colonial New York* (New York, 1942) and *History of the United Lutheran Synod of New York and New England,* Vol. 1 (Philadelphia, 1964).

Berlin Missionary Society I *(Gesellschaft zur Beförderung der evangelischen Missionen unter den Heiden).* The miss. movement in Berlin was inaugurated by "Father" J. Jänicke,* who founded a school for training missionaries 1800. Interest in this school led 10 men including J. Neander,* F. Tholuck,* O. v. Gerlach* to appeal for funds and organize a soc. 1824. Several yrs. later the soc. est. a training school; active esp. in Afr., E Indies, China.

Berlin Missionary Society II. See *Gossner Missionary Society.*

Bermondsey Settlement. See *Lidgett, John Scott.*

Bernadotte, Oscar Karl August (1859–1953). Swed. prince, naval officer, and statesman; promoted missions; founded Södertal Conf. for Deepening Spiritual Life; chm. Swed. section Ev. Alliance.

Bernanos, Georges (1888–1948). Fr. novelist; exponent of neo-Catholicism; opponent of totalitarianism.

Bernard (Silvestris; fl. ca. 1150). Poet, humanist, philos.; friend of Thierry of Chartres. Chief work: *De mundi universitate.*

Bernard of Chartres (d. bet. 1124 and 1130). Brother of Thierry* of Chartres; chancellor of School of Chartres 1119; sought to combine Plato's concept of ideas and Aristotle's forms.

Bernard of Clairvaux (1091–1153). Most influential man of his day; upright monk (Cistercian), spending himself in ascetic practices. His wise rule as first and lifelong abbot (1115–53) of the cloister he founded at Clairvaux, France, served to extend the order (now also called Bernardines) throughout Eur., and the influence of his eloquence and personality gave a new impetus to monasticism. He ended the papal schism in favor of Innocent II. In controversy with rationalistic Abelard (1140) he stood for the equally false principle of mysticism. He preached the 2d Crusade (1146), which, contrary to his prophecy, did not sweep back the Mohammedans, but swept Eugene III into office. He was an eloquent preacher, able writer of theol. treatises, composer of beautiful hymns, universal mediator, adviser of pope and king and common man. Despite his exaltation of monachism as the ideal of Christianity, his excessive glorification of Mary (whose "immaculate conception," however, he opposed), and his enthusiastic support of the papacy as the highest authority in the church, he was a sincerely pious, truly humble Christian, because he loved the Bible and because he believed in justification by faith, deploring on his deathbed, as throughout his life, the sinfulness of his life, and imploring the mercy of God for the sake of the righteousness gained by Christ – a psychological enigma indeed. Luther: "When Bernard is speaking of Christ, it is a pleasure indeed to listen to him; but when he leaves that subject and discourses on rules and works, it is no longer St. Bernard." See also *Preaching, Christian, History of,* 8.

J. A. W. Neander, *Der heilige Bernhard und sein Zeitalter* (Berlin, 1813), tr. M. Wrench, *The Life and Times of St. Bernard* (London, 1843); 2d Ger. ed. (Hamburg and Gotha, 1848); ed. S. M. Deutsch (Gotha, 1889); E. Vacandard, *Vie de Saint Bernard,* 2 vols. (Paris, 1895); H. Daniel-Rops, *Bernard of Clairvaux* (New York, 1964); E. H. Gilson, *The Mystical Theology of Saint Bernard,* tr. A. H. C. Downes (New York, 1955); *MPL,* 182–185.

Bernard of Cluny (Bernard of Morlaix; 12th c.). Benedictine monk in Abbey of Cluny when the monastery was at the height of its wealth and fame; composed *De contemptu mundi,* from which the hymns "Jerusalem the Golden," "Brief Life Is Here Our Portion," "For Thee, O Dear, Dear Country," and "The World Is Very Evil" are taken.

Bernard of Pavia (d. 1213). Teacher of canon law at Bologna. Compiled *Breviarium extravagantium.*

Bernardines. See *Bernard of Clairvaux; Cistercians.*

Bernardino of Siena (1380–1444). It. Franciscan monk; noted preacher; introduced strict Observatine Rule. See also *Symbolism, Christian,* 6.

Berneuchener Kreis. Group of ev. clergymen and laymen, founders and promoters of a High Ch. liturgical movement in Ger. The leader of the movement was Wilhelm Stählin. Its official periodical, *Berneuchener Buch,* was founded 1926.

Bernhard, Christoph (1627–92). Last and most important pupil of H. Schütz; Kapellmeister Dresden, where Schütz had been active. Studied also with Carissimi. Active for a time in Hamburg. Works reveal his skill as a composer and contrapuntist.

Bernhardi, Bartholomäus (1487–1551). Prof. physics and philos., and rector, Wittenberg; pastor Kemberg; friend of Luther; first Luth. married pastor.

Bernheim, Gotthardt Dellman (Nov. 8, 1827–Oct. 25, 1916). B. Prussia; to Am. 1831; grad. Luth. Sem., Lexington, S. C., 1849. Pastor Charleston, S. C., 1850–58; near Concord, N. C., 1858–60. Founded a female school Mount Pleasant, N. C.; it later became Mont Amoena Female Sem. Pastor Phillipsburg, N. J., 1883–93; Wilmington, N. C., 1893–95. Instructor Elizabeth Coll., Charlotte, N. C. Ed. *At Home and Abroad* 1881–88. Works include *The Success of God's Work; History of the German Settlements and of the Lutheran Church of North and South Carolina; Localities of the Reformation; The First Twenty Years of the History of St. Paul's Church, Wilmington.*

Berning, Wilhelm (1877–1955). RC bp. Osnabrück 1914; Apostolic Vicar N Ger. miss. 1914–30; titular abp.; spokesman for the Ger. Episcopacy with Nat. Socialism. Wrote on Eucharist and RCm in Ger.

Bernoulli, Carl Albrecht (1868–1937). Prof. ch. hist. Basel. Wrote on Overbeck, Nietzsche, and Bachofen.

Berquin, Louis de (1490–1529). Humanist and reformer in Fr.; tr. Erasmus' *Enchiridion* and Luther's *De votis monasticis.* Burned as heretic.

Bersier, Eugène (1831–89). Ref. pastor Paris; ch. hist. and reformer of liturgy.

Bertha of Kent (fl. ca. AD 600). Franconian princess; married Ethelbert of Kent; instrumental in reintroducing Christianity in Eng. 597. See also *Augustine of Canterbury.*

Berthelier, Philibert (d. after 1567). Opponent of Calvinism; condemned to death for liberalism; fled from Geneva.

Berthold of Hanover. See *Estonia.*

Berthold von Regensburg. See *Preaching, History of,* 8.
Bertholet, Alfred (1868–1951). Prof. OT Basel, Tübingen, Göttingen, and Berlin. Exponent of *Religionsgeschichtliche Schule.*
Bertling, Ernst August (1721–69). Ger. theol.; studied law; then theol.; prof. Helmstedt; rector of *Gymnasium* at Danzig. Works include devotional studies, summaries of Luther's doctrine, studies in moral and natural theol.
Bertram, Adolf Johannes (1859–1945). Cardinal 1916; abp. and metropolitan Breslau 1930. Leader of Ger. episcopate in the *Kirchenkampf.*
Beryllus. See *Monarchianism,* B 3.
Bes. Egyptian god of dancing and pleasure whose image the Gnostics adopted as an amulet.
Besa (ca. 400). Coptic writer.
Besant, Annie (1847–1933). Brit. theosophist; at first mem. Ch. of Eng.; later worked with Charles Bradlaugh* in free-thought movements; became pupil of Elena Blavatsky*; pres. Theosophical Soc. 1907; traveled widely in its interest, esp. in India; founded 2 schools for Hindus in Benares; est. Indian Home Rule League; vacillated in support of nationalist position; traveled in Eng. and Am. with Jiddu Krishnamurti, the "World Teacher." See also *Theosophy.*
Beskow, Frederik Nathanael (1865–1953). Swed. theol. Unordained, he preached in his own chapel at Djursholm. Opposed secularism with socially oriented gospel; pacifist; active in behalf of working man. Wrote hymns, including "Ack saliga dag." Founded workers settlement (Birkagarden) at Stockholm.
Besold, Hieronymus (ca. 1500–62). Pupil of Sebastian Heiden and Joachim Camerarius in Nürnberg; came to Wittenberg 1537; table companion of Luther and later of Melanchthon; returned to Nürnberg 1546; participated in reorganization of ch. of Zweibrücken 1557–58; participated in 2d ch. visitation in Nürnberg. Gathered table talks of Luther and participated in pub. of Luther's Genesis. Opposed Philippists.
Bessarion, Johannes (Basilius; ca. 1395–1472). Patriarch of Constantinople; abp. Nicaea; sought to reconcile E and W Chs.; friend of Eugenius IV, who made him cardinal; greatest scholar of his day, he extended speculative thought in theol. by his defense of Plato, *In calumniatorem Platonis.*
Besser, Wilhelm Friedrich (1816–84). Educ. Halle and Berlin; opposed Prussian Union; served as pastor of Luth. chs. in Pomerania and Silesia; mem. Breslau Syn. and its ruling bd.; wrote *Bibelstunden.*
Bestiaries. Books, popular in Middle Ages, which described animals (real and imaginary; often with illustrations) in verse or prose with added moral and religious lessons; developed from the *Hexameron* of Ambrose, *Etymology* of Isidore, and writings of Rabanus* Maurus. Much of the material comes from Aristotle, Pliny, and Solinus. Medieval Lat. bestiaries are traced to the earlier Gk. *Physiologus* ("Naturalist"). Animals described in these bestiaries are often used in ch. architecture.
Beta Sigma Psi. See *Students, Spiritual Care of,* A.
Betancourt (Betancur). See *Bethlehemites,* 3.
Bethany College, Lindsborg, Kans. See *Lutheran Church in America,* V; *Ministry, Education of,* VIII B 4.
Bethany Lutheran College and High School, Mankato, Minn. See *Ministry, Education of,* VIII C 2 b.
Bethany Lutheran Seminary, Mankato, Minn. See *Ministry, Education of,* X A.
Bethel Baptist Assembly, Inc. See *Baptist Churches,* 34.
Bethel Community. See *Communistic Societies,* 5.
Bethencourt. See *Bethlehemites,* 3.
Bethesda Lutheran Home. See *Associated Lutheran Charities.*
Bethlehemites. 1. Military order dedicated to Our Lady of Bethlehem; came from Palestine to Bohemia 1217; later devoted to care of sick and education. 2. Military religious order authorized 1257 by Henry III to open a house near Cambridge. 3. Followers of J. Hus sometimes called Bethlehemites after the name of the ch. in Prague where he preached. 4. Order of the Blessed Virgin Mary of Bethlehem founded 1459 by Pius II as Aegean defense against Turks. 5. Hospitaler order (Belemites) which grew out of Pedro de San José de Betancourt's (Betancur, Bethencourt; d. 1667) care of children, sick, and poor in Guatemala. Innocent XI placed it under Augustinian rule 1687.
Bethlen, Gabriel (1580–1629). King of Hungary 1620–29. Champion of Prot. cause against Hapsburgs in Thirty Years' War.
Bethune, George Washington (1805–62). Dutch Ref. clergyman. B. Greenwich, N. Y.; d. Florence, It. Educ. Dickinson Coll., Carlisle, Pa., and Princeton Sem.; miss. to Negroes, Savannah, Ga.; naval chaplain; pastor of Dutch Ref. chs. in various cities in N. Y. and Pa.; hymnist; tr. H. Malan's* "It Is Not Death to Die."
Betke, Joachim (1601–63). B. Berlin; d. Linum. Spiritualist. Assoc. rector Ruppin; pastor Linum; disciple of J. Arnd(t) and J. Böhme. Influenced Spener and F. Breckling.
Betrothal. See *Marriage.*
Bettex, Jean Frédéric (Friedrich; 1837–1915[1916?]). B. Morges, Vaud, Switz.; d. Stuttgart, Ger.; prof. science and apologetics. Of RC parentage; strongly Prot. in later life. Many of his books, often apologetic in nature, tr. into Eng. Works (and tr.) include *Das erste Blatt der Bibel (The First Page of the Bible); Die Bibel Gottes Wort (The Bible the Word of God); Naturstudium und Christentum ([Modern] Science and Christianity); Von der Grösse des dreieinigen Gottes (The Glory of the Triune God).*
Beurlin, Jakob (1520–61). Prof. theol. Tübingen; signed *Confessio Virtembergica* (see *Brenz, Johann; Lutheran Confessions,* A 5); tried to settle Osiandrian controversy.
Beuron, Abbey of. Benedictine abbey, SW Ger., on N bank of Danube ca. 8 mi NE of Tuttlingen. Originally est. as monastery for Augustinian Canons. Given to the brothers Maurus (1825–90) and Placidus (1828–1908) Wolter by Princess Katharina von Hohenzollern 1863; constituted an abbey 1868. Known for work in liturgical reform. Home of Palimpsest Institute.
Bewer, Julius August (1877–1953). Educ. Union Sem. (N. Y.), Columbia U., Basel, Halle, and Berlin; prof. OT exegesis Oberlin, Union, Columbia, and New Brunswick; worked on RSV; wrote extensively on OT canon, text, and exegesis.
Beyer, Christian (Baier; ca. 1482–1535). B. Kleinlangheim, Lower Franconia, W Bav., Ger.; lawyer; taught at Wittenberg beginning 1507; mayor Wittenberg 1513; Saxon chancellor 1528; read AC at 1530 Diet of Augsburg (see *Lutheran Confessions,* A 2).
Beyer, Hartmann (1516–77). Educ. Wittenberg; pupil of Luther and Melanchthon; corresponded with Bugenhagen, Jonas, Brenz, and other prominent Luths.; called to Frankfurt, where he zealously opposed the Augsburg Interim and checked the advance of Calvinism. Wrote 2 works against RCm (under pseudonyms Sigismund Cephalus and Andreas Epitimius) and a mathematical treatise *(De sphaera).* Sermons preserved in MS.
Beyer, Johann Paul (June 26, 1832–Jan. 19, 1905). Clergyman; b. Bavaria; attended Conc. Coll., Fort Wayne, and Conc. Sem., St. Louis; ordained Oct. 7, 1855; pastor Memphis, Tenn.; Altenburg, Mo.; Chicago, Ill.; Pittsburgh, Pa.; Brooklyn, N. Y.; secy. Synodical* Conf. 1872; pres. E Dist., Mo. Syn.,

1875–88; vice-pres. Mo. Syn. 1893 to 99; founder and ed. *Lutherisches Kinderblatt* (later *Lutherisches Kinder- und Jugenblatt*); wrote *Der Brief St. Pauli an die Epheser in Predigten.*

Beyschlag, Willibald (1823–1900). Prof. Halle 1860; led party that mediated bet. rigid orthodoxy and radical liberalism; opposed ultramontanism in Ger. See also *Evangelischer Bund.*

Beza, Theodore (Théodore de Bèze; 1519–1605). Fr. humanist; Ref. leader. B. Vézelay, Fr.; d. Geneva; renounced RCm at Geneva 1548; prof. Gk. Lausanne; prof. and pastor Geneva; defended burning of Servetus;* Calvin's second self and successor; strongly opposed Luth. doctrines of Eucharist and person of Christ; a power among Huguenots; real originator of *Textus Receptus;** gave Cambridge Codex D; works include *Vie de Calvin; Histoire ecclésiastique des églises réformées;* tr. of NT into Lat. with annotations. Completed C. Marot's* metrical Psalter. See also *Montbéliard, Colloquy of; Schmidt, Erasmus; Switzerland,* 2.

G. Friedlaender, *Beiträge zur Reformationsgeschichte* (Berlin, 1837); H. Heppe, *Theodor Beza,* in *Leben und ausgewaehlte Schriften der Vaeter und Begründer der reformirten Kirche,* VI (Elberfeld, 1861).

Bezae, Codex. See *Manuscripts of the Bible,* 3 a.

Bhagavad Gita. Section of *Mahabharata* (Sanskrit) which depicts the meeting of Arjuna with Krishna, who reveals himself as lord of creation. Confuses pantheism with monism, but still the greatest product of Hindu philos. See also *Hinduism,* 6.

Bhakti. See *Hinduism,* 5.

Bhikkus. See *Buddhism,* 4.

Biafra. See *Africa,* C 14.

Bibelstunden (Bible Hours). Devotional services, often informal, in which longer sections of Scripture are explained usually in the form of a homily. Such devotional services were common in the Luth. Ch. in Ger. (e. g., those by Louis Harms) and in Am.

Bible. See *Holy Scripture.*

Bible, Canon of. See *Canon, Bible.*

Bible, Inspiration of. See *Inspiration, Doctrine of.*

Bible, Poor Man's. See *Biblia Pauperum.*

Bible and Psychology. See *Psychology,* D.

Bible Belt. Term applied to S states because chs. there were opposed to liberalism and were fundamentalistic in their approach to Scripture.

Bible Christians. Also called Bryanites, organized 1815 in Eng. along Meth. lines by William O'Bryan (1778–1868); officially constituted 1831; merged with other Meths. in the United Meth. Ch. 1907. See also *Methodist Churches,* 1.

Bible Churchmen's Missionary Society. Organization formed 1922 in Eng. by conservative evangelicals when the CMS became predominantly liberal.

Bible Classes. See *Adult Education; Bible Study; Parish Education.*

Bible History. Often differentiated from Biblical history,* Bible hist. emphasizes use of Bible stories for instructional and religious values. In NT, knowledge of OT was communicated at home (2 Ti 3:15) or at pub. services (1 Ti 4:13). In the primitive ch., home reading, private instruction, and pub. services provided knowledge of Bible hist. (Eusebius, *HE,* VI, ii; Chrysostom on Eph 4:4; Cyril, *Catecheses,* IV, 35). Instruction in Bible hist. was almost forgotten during the Middle Ages (lack of common schools, cost of Bibles, dearth of Bibles in vernacular). Luther and Melanchthon stressed use of Bible hist. Otto Braunfels sought to introduce Bible hist. in his Lat. school *(Heldenbüchlein).* Luther's *Passionale* (1529; 11 OT, 38 NT pictures with explanatory notes) has been called the first Bible hist. for the home. With the establishment of Christian common schools, instruction in Bible hist. came into its own. Noted early texts were Justus Gesenius, *Biblische Historien* (1656) and J. Hübner,* *Zweimal 52 auserlesene biblische Historien* (1714). Since these were pub., use of Bible stories for instruction has been greatly expanded (core of S. S. training; special Bible histories for different ages; pictorial presentations of the Bible stories; films and slides; prominent in Sat. schools, summer schools, etc.).

J. M. Reu, *Quellen zur Geschichte des kirchlichen Unterrichts in der evangelischen Kirche Deutschlands zwischen 1530 und 1600, Part 2: Quellen zur Geschichte des biblischen Unterrichts* (Gütersloh, 1906) and *Catechetics,* 3d ed. (Chicago, 1931), pp. 289–308.

Bible in Education. See *Bible Study; Christian Education,* D.

Bible Institute Mission of Japan. See *Japan Evangelical Mission.*

Bible Institutes. See *Adult Education.*

Bible Manuscripts. See *Manuscripts of the Bible.*

Bible Presbyterian Church. See *Presbyterian Churches,* 4 e.

Bible Reading. See *Bible Study; Bible Societies; Bible Versions.*

Bible Revision. See *Bible Versions.*

Bible Societies. 1. The formal principle* of the Luth. Reformation brought about a renewed emphasis on Bible study, and the Prot. miss. activities of the 17th and 18th c. brought a philanthropic element into the distribution of Bibles which led to the organization of Bible societies in the 18th and 19th c.

2. *Germany.* Frhr. K. H. von Canstein* felt that the low spirituality of his times revealed a need for a Bible in every home. The funds he received as a result of his pleas enabled him to est. the *Canstein Bible Institute* 1710, the earliest organization created for the distribution of Bibles. The first *Nürnberg Bible Society,* founded 1804 with aid from the BFBS, was absorbed 1806 by the Basel Bible Society. In 1823 the *Central Bible Society* was est. in Nürnberg. The *Berlin Bible Society* was organized 1806 through the efforts of J. Jänicke for the purpose of providing Bibles for Bohemians in Berlin. Later it was expanded and called the *Prussian Bible Society* (1814). The *Württemberg Bible Society* was organized 1812 through the efforts of K. F. A. Steinkopf and others. Additional societies arose: *Saxon Bible Society* (1814), *Bible Society of Schleswig-Holstein* (1815), *Berg Bible Society* (1814), and others.

3. *England.* Various Christian organizations that included Bible distribution on their program arose out of the ev. movements of the 17th and 18th c. Among them: *Society for Promoting Christian Knowledge* (1698); *Society for the Propagation of the Gospel in Foreign Parts* (1701); *Society in Scotland for Propagating Christian Knowledge* (1709); *Society for Promoting Christian Knowledge among the Poor* (1750); *Naval and Military Bible Society* (1780; originally called *Bible Society*); *French Bible Society* (1792); *Trinitarian Bible Society; Society for Distributing the Holy Scriptures to the Jews.* The *Canadian Bible Society,* auxiliary to the BFBS, was formed 1904.

The suggestion to form the *British and Foreign Bible Society* was first made 1802; the soc. was founded Mar. 7, 1804, at a large interdenominational meeting at the London Tavern. Its object was "to promote the circulation of Holy Scriptures, without note or comment, both at home and in foreign lands." The first goal was to provide Wales with Bibles, but the soc. soon extended its activities to Eur., Asia, Afr., S Am., Can., and elsewhere. It helped est. Bible societies in Ger., Scand., and other countries (often as branches). The controversy regarding the Apocrypha caused much difficulty; when the soc. decided 1826 to discontinue printing the

Apocrypha, more than 50 branch organizations severed connections with it.

4. *Other Eur. Countries.* In *Scotland,* the *Edinburgh Bible Society* (1809) and the *Glasgow Bible Society* (1812) withdrew from the BFBS as a result of the Apocrypha controversy and united 1861 to form the *National Bible Society of Scotland.* In Ireland the *Hibernian Bible Society* was organized 1806. The most important societies of France: *Bible Society of France* (1864) and the *Bible Society of Paris* (1818). The *Netherlands Bible Society* was organized 1814. In Swed. an ev. soc. was organized 1809, which included Bible distribution in its work; later the king became the patron of the *Swedish Bible Society* (1814). The *Danish Bible Society* was organized 1814; the *Finnish Bible Society* 1812; the *Norwegian Bible Society* 1816. In Switz. the *Basel Bible Society* was founded 1804 by C. G. Blumhardt* and C. F. Spittler* with aid from BFBS; it absorbed the first Nürnberg Bible Society 1806; other Bible socs. in Switz. have included one at Saint Gall (1813). In S Eur. the *Malta Bible Society* (1817) played an important role. The *Russian Bible Society* (representing Protestants and Catholics) was organized by an imperial ukase 1813; when it was suppressed 1826, the *Evangelical Bible Society* was organized; the Russian Bible Society was reest. 1863.

5. In *America* the *Philadelphia Bible Society* was organized 1808 and the societies of Conn., Mass., N. Y., and N. J. in 1809, followed by many others.

The *American Bible Society* was organized in New York 1816 by 60 distinguished men. Invitations to the founding meeting had been sent out by the *Bible Society of New Jersey* at the suggestion of S. J. Mills.* The first pres. was E. Boudinot.* The object of the soc. was the circulation of the Holy Scriptures in the commonly received version (KJV) without note or comment. In 1822 the Bible House on Nassau Street was erected and in 1852 the Bible House on Astor Place. In 1835 Bap. missionaries tr. *baptismos* and *baptizo* with Burmese words meaning "to immerse." When the ABS refused to print the version, the *American and Foreign Bible Society* (Bap.) was organized 1836. When this soc. agreed to use the KJV in the distribution of the Bible in the Eng. language, seceders organized the *American Bible Union* 1850.

The *Christian Commercial Travelers' Association of Am., Internat.* (Christian Commerical Men's Assoc. of Am., Internat.; Christian Bus. Men's Assoc.; The Gideons Internat.; organized 1899) supplies hotel and hospital rooms and other public places with Bibles.

Bible Societies in Latin America (Sociedades Bíblicas en América Latina). Offices in Asunción, Bogotá, Buenos Aires, Caracas, Cochabamba, Cristóbal, Guatemala, Havana, Lima, Mexico, Montevideo, Quito, San Juan, Santiago.

The *German Evangelical Lutheran Central Bible Society for Missouri, Illinois, and Iowa, in St. Louis, Missouri* was organized Apr. 24, 1853, to promulgate Ger. Bibles and New Testaments.

6. Though Bible study was encouraged in some areas of the W Ch. before the Reformation (e. g., Spain), RC popes gen. opposed Bible reading in the vernacular because they held such action might lead to heretical views. Emphasis on Scripture by reformers led popes (Pius VII, Leo XII, Gregory XVI, Pius IX) to oppose Bible reading by laymen without theol. training. The principle that the Bible is not to be printed in the vernacular without explanation is still held. The first RC Bible institution was est. 1805 by G. M. Wittmann (1760–1833) at Ratisbon; dissolved 1817 by Pius VII. In It. the *Compagnia di San Paolo (Community of St. Paul),* founded 1563, encourages Bible reading. The *Pia Società San Girolamo (Pious Society of St. Jerome),* organized 1901 by Giacomo della Chiesa (later Benedict XV) prints and distributes the NT in Italian. The *Pia Società San Paolo (Pious Society of St. Paul),* founded at Alba, Cuneo, 1914, sponsors the *Società Cattolica Biblica Internazionale (Catholic International Bible Society),* which fosters reading and study of the Bible. After WW I, Bible movements became more gen. in the RC Ch., often connected with Catholic Action* and the liturgical revival. The *Katholisches Bibelwerk* (Germany 1933), *Catholic Biblical Association* (England 1940), and the *Catholic Biblical Association of America* (US 1936) are among leading RC Bible societies. Similar societies were organized in other countries of Eur. and Am. See also *Bible Study.*

7. Bible societies aid translators and publish and distribute Bibles and special books and phonograph records for the blind as widely as possible according to need. Bible societies and related agencies distribute ca. 25,000,000 Bibles or parts thereof annually.

8. *United Bible Societies.* Internat. fellowship of 23 Bible socs.; organized 1946. Its Council, to which each mem. soc. sends 1 representative, meets at least once in 3 yrs. Business of world organization conducted bet. Council sessions by Standing Com. The Secretariat: Gen. Secy.; Secy. for Promotion; two Study Secys.

E. Breest, "Bibelgesellschaften," in *Realencyklopädie für protestantische Theologie und Kirche,* 3d ed. J. J. Herzog and A. Hauck, II (Leipzig, 1897), 691 to 699; H. O. Dwight, *Centennial History of the American Bible Society* (New York, 1916); *The Bible in a Thousand Tongues,* comp. O. M. Norlie (Minneapolis, 1935); *The Book of a Thousand Tongues,* ed. E. M. North (New York, 1938); reports of Bible societies. EL, LP

Bible Study. Bible study is that activity by which a person comes to an understanding of the Bible text and its relation to Christ and personally reflects on the words he has read for a fuller application of God's will to his life. It comes to its climax when it is tr. into daily living. Bible study is not an end in itself, but a means used by the Holy Spirit to create and sustain faith in Christ. It equips the man of God to fulfill his mission in life. It is the means by which he develops into a mature Christian. True Bible study penetrates into whole divisions, periods, books, chapters as well as the individual verses and words of the Holy Scriptures.

Meditating on the words of Scripture was the immediate rule of life for every Jew (Jos. 1; 2 Ch 34; Neh 8; 1 Mac 2:67). Bible reading and study is the normal expression of intelligent Christian discipleship. This is clear from many passages of the NT and from the practice of the early ch. (Jn 5:39; Lk 24:27; Acts 17:11; 18:24-28; 2 Ti 3:14-17; Heb 5:12-14; 2 Ptr 1:19-21; 3:2).

The apostolic fathers and the early apologists are united in the belief "that the regular way to become a convinced Christian was to read the Holy Scriptures." Justin, Irenaeus, Tertullian, and Origen expected Bible study, not only of adults, but of children. The Bible was to them "the great public book of Christendom, to which all men must be introduced," so that they might feed their souls "from every Scripture of the Lord." Polycarp writes to the Philippian church: "I trust that ye are well exercised in the Holy Scriptures and that nothing is there hidden from you." This implies personal study. Chrysostom commended private Bible study classes. Like Augustine, he knew that the Bible is the church's best missionary.

Bible study declined, however, with the growing institutionalization of the ch. As time went on, the laity made less and less use of its right to a firsthand approach to Scripture. When in the 12th c. the Waldenses came forth with a Christianity growing out of private Bible study, it was too late. A ch. based on priesthood and mystery had not only crushed the development of Bible study, but had practically withdrawn the Book from the common people. This happened despite Jerome's warning: "Ignorance of the Scripture is ignorance of Christ."

With the Reformation a new day dawned for Scripture study. Luther appealed from the dicta of the church to the naked truth of Scripture alone. This renascence of Bible study was greatly aided by the invention of printing and Bibles in the vernacular. Adolf Harnack rightly says: ". . . the Reformation by placing the Bible into the hands of the layman has only returned to the simple confidence of the early church."

One of the basic assumptions of the Prot. faith is that those who embrace it will be able to read and interpret the Bible for themselves (the right of private judgment). But not always and not fully did the Prot. churches carry out the principles of the Reformation. Often there was too much study "about" the Bible and too little "in" the Bible. Bible histories, catechisms, and lesson materials have often supplanted personal Bible use. Strange as it may seem, the Bible has had to struggle to be received up to the present moment. Century after century it was relegated to 2d place by ecclesiasticism and clericalism of various forms and degrees.

Modern Bible study received a strong impetus from Pietism, particularly the popular Bible expositions of A. H. Francke,* which met the common need. Since 1685 Bible study has won a leading place within all Prot. denominations. Other factors contributing greatly to Bible study were the organization of Bible societies and the development of S. S. with classes for young people and adults devoted chiefly to Bible study. A revival of interest in the Bible at the beginning of the 20th c. suffered reverses at the hands of modern liberalism and higher criticism. Two world wars, the failure of materialism, and advances in gen. adult educ. stimulated various efforts to call people of the disordered world back to God through Bible study.

Some Bible study was carried on in the earlier days of the Mo. Syn. chiefly through *Bibelstunden* and young people's societies. The first regularly issued Bible study materials appeared 1912. Bible study classes were put on a firmer footing when they were received into the S. S. structure. A new advance in Bible study came with the Centennial Bible Study Program initiated 1947 by the Bd. of Parish Educ. and from the rise of Bible Institutes.

This advance has been intensified through leadership training for pastors, ch. bds., and over 25,000 laymen and women. It aimed at improving the quality of teaching, increasing the number of Bible classes (esp. small, face-to-face study groups), and reaching out to more people so that study group enrollments keep pace with numerical growth of churches. Two basic factors lie behind this new thrust: 1. the new expressions of materialism, secularism, hedonism, nihilism, moral decline, and mere religiosity call for an awakened laity sure of its convictions; 2. the realization that the church's power index is not its clergy but its people exercising their priesthood daily, wherever they are, in all situations in life, in all the world.

Two mid-20th c. phenomena have accelerated Bible study: the revival of Biblical studies in RCm and the appearance of a host of popular new Bible translations.

Bible study is essential for the vitality of the ch. and for the preservation of human freedom. Through Bible study, privately and in a class, the Scriptures become "the Book to live by."

There are 5 essentials of good method in Bible study: (1) good motivation; (2) intensive and repeated reading of the Bible text itself; (3) observing exactly what the text says; (4) finding Christ and doctrinal content; (5) assimilation through meditation. OEF

A. Harnack, *Bible Reading in the Early Church, New Testament Studies, V,* tr. J. R. Wilkinson (New York, 1912); F. Pieper, "Die Heilige Schrift," in *Christliche Dogmatik,* I (St. Louis, 1924), 233–444, tr. T. Engelder, "Holy Scripture," in *Christian Dogmatics,* I (St. Louis, 1950), 193–367; *The Encyclopedia of Sunday Schools and Religious Education,* ed. J. T. McFarland et al. (New York, 1915); O. Beguin, *Roman Catholicism and the Bible* (New York, 1963); monographs on Bible study by E. H. Robertson (Association Press, New York).

Bible Versions. A. *Septuagint.* 1. The earliest attempt to tr. the Scriptures is represented by the Gk. version of the OT commonly known as the Septuagint (LXX). It owes its name to the story (now discredited) that it is the work of 72 translators, 6 from each tribe of Israel, who at the request of King Ptolemy* Philadelphus II (285–246 BC) were sent to Egypt by the high priest Eleazar to prepare a version of the Jewish Law for the royal library at Alexandria. While there is doubtless a kernel of truth in this story and the bare fact of a tr. of the Law in the days of Ptolemy need not be questioned, the LXX as a whole exhibits such varying degrees of skill and accuracy that it can·be neither the product of a single body of translators acting in unison nor even the product of a single age. The tr. of the Pentateuch, for example, is pretty well done; that of Daniel is exceedingly poor (the early Christian ch. from ca. AD 200 on used the Gk. version of Theodotion in its stead); while the rendering of Ecclesiastes is so slavishly literal that it is little more than Grecized Hebrew. The most that can be said as to the origin of the LXX is that it was begun ca. 285 BC and completed before 132 BC (Cf. the Prolog of Ecclesiasticus.) The LXX differs strongly from the Hebrew in content and arrangement (Job, for instance, is ca. 400 lines shorter in the Gk.; the Gk. Jeremiah differs from the Heb. by addition, omission, and transposition) and presents also in its renderings innumerable divergences from our present Masoretic text. This is due in part, no doubt, to the arbitrary procedure of the translators, but also in some cases to the fact that the Heb. original differed from the text we possess today. This fact makes the LXX an invaluable aid, though to be used with caution, in the textual criticism of the OT.

2. The LXX was adopted by the Greek-speaking Jews, was used, as a rule, by the writers of the NT in citing the OT, and was regarded as authoritative, even inspired, by the early Christian Fathers. The constant appeal to it on the part of the leaders of the ch. to prove the Messiahship of Jesus aroused the antagonism of the Jews and gave rise, in the 2d c., to 3 rival translations: the strictly literal version of Aquila; the revision of the LXX by Theodotion; and the elegantly periphrastic version of Symmachus. These versions have been preserved only in isolated fragments.

B. *Targums.* The *Targums,* or Aramaic paraphrases, arose from the oral interpretation of the OT Scriptures which had become necessary since the days of the Exile, when Aramaic became the language of common intercourse in Palestine. These oral paraphrases were, in course of time, reduced to writing. The most important Targums are the Targum of Onkelos (1st or 2d c.) on the Pentateuch, which received its present form about the 3d c. after Christ, and the Targum of Jonathan ben Uzziel on the Prophets: Jonathan was a pupil of Hillel and lived in the 1st c. after Christ, but the

Targum associated with his name did not receive its final form until about the 5th c. The Targums are of value to the scholar in helping to determine the Heb. text employed in the early Synagog as well as in determining what interpretation the Jews gave to difficult passages.

C. *Syriac.* 1. For the OT, the oldest and most important version is the Peshitta. Whether this tr. is of Jewish or of Christian origin remains uncertain; at any rate, it was used early by the Syriac-speaking ch. and has remained the chief version of the Syriac OT. It is by various hands, though in fairly uniform style, and was made directly from the Heb. But there are traces of LXX influence.

2. Two later versions of the LXX OT, that by Philoxenus of Hierapolis (AD 508) and that by Paul of Tella (AD 616), were based on the LXX. Neither succeeded in displacing the Peshitta in common use.

3. Of the oldest Syriac tr. of the NT, dating from the 2d c., only the Gospels have been preserved. This old Syriac version is of the highest importance for the textual criticism of the Gospels, representing as it does a textual tradition indep. of the 2 great branches of the textual tradition represented by MSS B and D.

4. However, the version destined to become the standard version of the NT for the Syriac-speaking ch. was the Peshitta, a complete revision of the NT ascribed to Rabula,* bp. of Edessa. "It's style is beautifully smooth and clear, and it can claim to be one of the great literary achievements of the Eastern Church." (T. H. Robinson.)

5. Two later versions, or better, revisions, deserve notice because they contain those portions of the NT originally omitted from the Syriac Canon (2 Ptr, 2 and 3 Jn, Jude, Rv). That of Philoxenus of Hierapolis (AD 508) first included the 5 disputed books; it has hardly survived except for the 4 catholic Epistles, which are usually printed from this version. Similarly, the version by Thomas of Harkel, the NT counterpart to the OT version by Paul of Tella and of about the same date (AD 616), is used in Syriac Bibles only for Rv, though it is extant in its entirety.

D. *Egyptian.* There were 3 Egyptian, or Coptic (derived from Gk. *Aigyptios*) versions: Sahidic, dialect of Upper (southern) Egypt; Bohairic, of the W delta; and Fayumic of Cen. Egypt (of the NT only). Very little is known of the Fayumic at present. The Sahidic is the earlier of the 2 complete versions, having originated in the 2d or 3d c. after Christ. The Bohairic, now in ecclesiastical use among all Egyptian Christians, is considerably later, dated about AD 600. Both the Sahidic and the Bohairic are important for the textual criticism of the NT; the earlier Sahidic shows both "Neutral" and "Western" affinities, while the later Bohairic is more pronouncedly "Neutral." The OT portion of both these versions is based on the LXX, not on the original Heb.

E. *Ethiopic.* The *Ethiopic* version, still used by the Abyssinians, though Ethiopic has long ceased to be spoken, possibly dates from the 4th c. In the OT the tr. was made from the LXX, though it contains many variations from the Gk., the text in some MSS having been corrected from the Heb.

F. *Arabic.* Among the *Arabic* versions of the OT that of Saadia* ben Joseph, an Egyptian Jew (d. AD 942), was made directly from the Heb. text. It won great popularity among the Jews and was publicly read in the synagogs alongside of the Heb. text. However, only the Pentateuch, Isaiah, Canticles, Proverbs, and Job have been printed. The complete text of the OT in Arabic appeared in the Paris and London polyglots of the 17th c.; but it is of composite origin. The Pentateuch is the tr. of Saadia. Joshua, though also derived from the Heb., is by another hand. Judges, Samuel, Kings, Chronicles, and Job are based on the Peshitta; the Prophets, Psalms, and Proverbs are based on the LXX. As to the NT, Arabic versions have been made from the Gk., from the Peshitta, and from the Lat. The current Arabic NT is a translation, in the main, from the Bohairic dialect, with corrections and additions from the Gk. and Syriac.

G. *Armenian.* The *Armenian* version is ascribed by a 5th-c. Armenian writer, Moses of Chorene, to the patriarch Sahak (patriarch AD 390–428); his version was made from a Syriac text. Koriun, also of the 5th c., is authority for the statement that Mesrop (inventor of the Armenian alphabet) had by 411 translated the entire Bible from the Gk. He is said to have begun with Proverbs; this may indicate that the earlier books had been translated previously by unknown hands. Sahak and Mesrop later (after AD 431) revised the Armenian Bible on the basis of a Gk. Bible brought from Constantinople.

H. *Slavonic.* The *Old Slavonic* version, dating from the middle of the 9th c., is generally attributed to Cyril and Methodius, the apostles of the Slavs. The OT tr. is based on the LXX, that of the NT on the Gk. Except for fragments which survive in the official Slavonic Bible, the old version has been lost. See also *Bohemian Brethren,* 3; *Czechoslovakia,* 7.

I. *Gothic.* The *Gothic* version is the work of Ulfilas* (d. AD 381 or 388), bp. of the W Goths. Of the OT, which was based on the LXX, only the most meager fragments remain. Most of the NT, a literally faithful version, is preserved in various MSS, preeminent among which is the superb Codex Argenteus. The story that Ulfilas omitted from the tr. of the OT the Books of Kings for fear of exciting the warlike passions of the Goths is unworthy of credence, since such considerations would have barred Joshua and Judges as well. The probability is that Ulfilas did not live to finish the tr.

J. *Latin.* 1. *Latin* versions antedating the work of Jerome* are now commonly designated as the Old Lat. The term "Itala" formerly used and applied by Augustine to one of these versions is rightly avoided. The term Old Lat. designates a number of versions rather than *a* version, for if there was a single early version at all (and there is some evidence which points in that direction), it was probably not the work of one man, but rather the result of a process of accretion and revision, book being added to book and the resulting whole subjected to constant revision in various localities to meet local standards and needs. The Old Lat. versions probably originated in Afr., since Tertullian* of Carthage is the first to mention a Lat. version and his younger contemporary Cyprian* cites Scripture in a form that is identical with the oldest type of Old Lat. text found in existing MSS. The version, or versions, date from the 2d c. onward and are, therefore, valuable in textual criticism, since they enable the scholar to tap the stream of textual tradition at a point several centuries earlier than that of most extant Gk. MSS.

2. By the 4th c. there was such a welter of Lat. versions that Pope Damasus called on Jerome to produce an authoritative revision of the Old Lat. Bible. By 405 Jerome had completed the stupendous task. "The New Testament," he writes, "I have restored to the true Greek form; the Old I have rendered from the Hebrew." He began by tr. the OT from the LXX; the Gallican Psalter, which is the version included in the modern Vulgate, represents this rendering from the Gk. But Jerome became convinced as he proceeded that a satisfactory version could be made only from the Heb. directly, and the rest of the OT books in the Vulgate are a direct rendering of the original. Jerome's revisions of the Gospels appeared ca. 383, and it is possible that the rest of the NT was also revised at this time.

But there is some doubt as to the extent of Jerome's revision of the NT outside the Gospels. Jerome himself does not cite the Epistles, for instance, in the present Vulgate form – and Augustine, though he shows knowledge of the Vulgate Gospels and OT, seems not to have known the Epistles in their revised form. Jerome's new tr. encountered stubborn opposition, and it was not until the 6th or 7th c. that it won gen. acceptance in the ch. From the 13th c. on it is known as the *Vulgata*, a name which had formerly been applied to the LXX. In 1546 the Council of Trent decreed that it be used exclusively, and from then on it has been the official Bible of the RC ch. See also *Clement VIII; Popes, 22.*

K. Of the hundreds of modern versions only a few of the most important can be mentioned here. Since the Reformation the Bible has been tr. into all the languages and many of the dialects of Eur. Among the *French* versions that of J. Lefevre d' Etaples* (first printed completely in Antwerp, 1530), of Olivetan (Neuchatel, 1535), and esp. the Geneva Bible, a revision of Olivetan's work made by pastors of Geneva with the assistance of Beza* and others, deserve particular notice. The latter version, having undergone numerous revisions, still holds its place, though there are more recent translations. The principal *Dutch* version is the so-called States Bible (because authorized by the States General in 1594), pub. 1637 with sanction of the Council of Dort. It is still in use.

L. *English.* 1. Although portions of the Bible had been tr. into the vernacular in Anglo-Saxon times, and also after the Norman Conquest, the tr. known as Wycliffe's* was the first complete Eng. version. It was based on the Vulgate and appeared 1382–84. It is uncertain how much of the work is Wycliffe's. The greater part of the OT is probably the work of Nicholas* of Hereford. The NT is attributed to Wycliffe himself, but even this is not beyond doubt. A revision of Wycliffe's Bible, probably made by John Purvey, one of Wycliffe's followers, appeared not long after Wycliffe's death. This 2d version remained in common use until the beginning of the 16th c., when it was displaced by the work of W. Tyndale.*

2. The first Englishman to tr. the NT from the original Gk. was W. Tyndale. His tr. appeared on the Continent in 2 editions (3,000 copies each) before 1526. In 1530 Tyndale pub. his version of the Pentateuch and in the following yr. the Book of Jonah. In the OT, too, Tyndale worked from the original, using Luther and the Vulgate as aids.

3. In 1535 M. Coverdale* pub. at Zurich his tr. of the whole Bible "out of the Douche and Latin" (i. e., the Ger. of Luther and the Zurich Bible, and the Vulgate). This was the first complete printed Bible in Eng. and the first complete tr. by a single hand.

4. The so-called Matthew's Bible, essentially a compilation from Tyndale and Coverdale prepared by John Rogers,* appeared 1537, dedicated to "The most noble and gracyous Prynce Kyng Henry the Eyght and Queen Jane." Since it bore on its title page the inscription "Set forth with the Kinges most gracyous lycence," it may be considered the first Eng. authorized version.

5. Because of the deficiencies of both the Coverdale and the Matthew version, Coverdale, at the instance of Thomas Cromwell, undertook a fresh revision, which appeared 1539; because of the large proportions of the book (it measured 10 by 15 in.), it was known as the Great Bible. Its 2d ed., issued 1540, is called Cranmer's Bible because of his preface. (See also *Cranmer, Thomas*).

6. Richard Taverner's* version, a revision of Matthew's Bible, appeared 1539, but did not become popular.

7. During the persecution under Mary Tudor some Eng. reformers found refuge in Geneva. Here Whittingham, brother-in-law of Calvin, and his associates undertook a revision of Tyndale, collated with the Great Bible. Their work resulted in what is known as the Geneva Bible, completed 1560), most scholarly of the early Eng. versions. It won immediate popularity (Shakespeare used it extensively), no fewer than 120 editions appearing up to 1611. It did not, however, at once displace the Great Bible, but was used side by side with it until the appearance of the Bishops' Bible 1568 displaced the Great Bible.

8. The Bishops' Bible, revision of the Great Bible, owes its name to the fact that most of the revisers were bps. The revision was an attempt to counteract the popularity of the Geneva Bible, with its "pestilent glosses" or comments, often caustic. The Bishops' Bible, though never quite popular, passed through 20 editions, the last appearing 1606. This version is important historically, since the improved and revised ed. of 1572 is the basis of the revision that led to the KJV 1611.

9. The RC version pub. at Reims (NT 1582) and Douai (OT 1609–10) was based on the Vulgate and was very literal.

10. The King James Version of 1611 (also called Authorized Version) resulted from a suggestion by John Rainolds,* Puritan pres. of Corpus Christi Coll., at the Hampton Court Conference* called by James I to settle differences bet. Puritan and Angl. elements in the ch. James, interested in theol., ordered that a tr. be made of the whole Bible consonant to the original Hebrew and Greek, to be used in all chs. of Eng. To insure accuracy, the translators (54 were appointed, but only ca. 50 can be identified) were bound to observe no fewer than 15 specific rules. In particular, it was provided that the entire body of translators, divided into 6 companies, should approve the work of every member. The version is essentially a revision of the Bishops' Bible of 1572. See also *Textus receptus.*

11. The new version, appearing under royal authority and commended by the best scholarship of the age, though bitterly criticized in some quarters, soon won gen. favor. For 350 yrs. it has held its place as the Bible of the English-speaking world. The rare beauty and purity of its diction, its dignified and elegant simplicity, its reverential spirit and attitude have endeared it to millions of hearts and made it the most popular book in the Eng. tongue.

12. *The Revised Version.* The discovery and collation of numerous Biblical MSS in the first half of the 19th c., as well as the advances made in Gk. and Heb. scholarship, revealed some of the inaccuracies of the KJV and started the movement for revision about 1855. In 1870 a com. representing nearly all the churches in Eng. (no RCs were included) was entrusted with the work of preparing a revised version. The NT company began its work on June 22, 1870, and the OT company on June 30. In response to an invitation on the part of the Brit. revisers to participate in the task, an Am. revision committee was organized toward the close of the following year. The details of the plan of cooperation were, however, not fully arranged until 1875. The Eng. com. promised to give due consideration to all the Am. suggestions and renderings before the conclusion of its own labors and to permit the pub., in an appendix, of all important differences of rendering and reading which the Brit. reviewers should decline to accept. On the other hand, the Am. com. was to give its moral support to the Brit. editions "with a view to their freest circulation within the United States, and not to issue an edition of its own for a term of fourteen years." On May 17, 1881, the Eng. revised NT appeared in Eng. and a few days later in the US. In both countries the

demand was enormous, about 3 million copies being sold within a yr. of pub. The OT revision was completed 1884; the entire RV, bound in 1 vol., appeared 1885. The ASV, which embodied not only the readings which had appeared in the appendix to the Eng. RV, but also others which had been adopted by the Am. revisers later, appeared 1901. Neither the Brit. RV nor the ASV achieved the widespread acceptance that had been anticipated for them.

13. Of the many private versions that have appeared since 1901, the scholarly renderings of Ferrar Fenton (1903), R. F. Weymouth (NT 1902), James Moffatt (NT 1913; OT 1924), E. J. Goodspeed (NT 1923), E. J. Goodspeed and J. M. Powis Smith, with the assistance of other scholars (OT and NT 1935, Apocrypha 1938), deserve mention. *The New Testament in Modern English,* by J. B. Phillips (1958), and *The New Testament in the Language of Today,* by W. F. Beck (1963), endeavor to tr. into living English.

14. A widely accepted version completed in the 20th c. is the Revised Standard Version (RSV), of which the NT was pub. 1946, the OT 1952. This version is a revision of the 1901 ASV. The reception accorded the work has not been unmixed but is preponderantly favorable. The 1st RC ed. of the RSV NT was authorized 1964, appeared 1965; a complete RC RSV appeared 1966; the Oxford Annotated Bible, first pub. 1962, also received RC approval 1966.

15. In Oct. 1946 delegates of the Ch. of Eng., Ch. of Scot., and of Meth., Bap., and Cong. chs. recommended that a new tr. of the Bible be made. Later the Presb. Ch. of Eng., the Soc. of Friends, the Council of Churches for Wales, the United Council of Christian Churches and Religious Communions in Ireland, the BFBS, and the Nat. Bible Soc. of Scot. were represented on the committee. The NT of the *New English Bible* appeared 1961, the OT 1970.

16. The *Anchor Bible,* pub. of which began 1964 in New York, endeavors to give an exact tr. and extended exposition of the Bible. Translations of the Jewish Publication Soc. of Am. include *The Holy Scriptures According to the Masoretic Text,* OT only (Philadelphia, 1917, 1955, 1963) and *The Torah . . . The Five Books of Moses* (Philadelphia, 1962).

M. *German.* The Bible was tr. into Ger. as early as the 14th c. This tr. follows the Vulgate. After the invention of printing it appeared (1466–1521) in no fewer than 18 ed., 14 in the High and 4 – according to some, 5 – in the Low Ger. dialect. The origin of the pre-Lutheran Ger. Bible is still uncertain. That Luther was acquainted with it and made use of it has been est. Luther's version was made from the Heb. and Gk. and everywhere bears the stamp of originality. Its merits are well known. Schaff calls it "a wonderful monument of genius, learning, and piety." Its homely simplicity and rugged vigor, its idiomatic diction and rhythmic flow of language, its happily alliterative phrases (*Stecken und Stab, Dornen und Disteln, matt und müde,* etc.), and its freedom from all pedantic restraint have assured it a permanent place in the hearts of the Ger. people. Luther began his work on the NT in Nov. or early Dec. 1521 and completed it in the following March before he left the Wartburg. The tr. was pub. Sept. 1522. In the greater and more difficult task of tr. the OT, begun 1522, Luther had the assistance of Melanchthon, Bugenhagen, Cruciger, and others. The work was completed 1534, but Luther continued to improve his tr. with every new ed., esp. on the linguistic side. Luther's version not only formed the basis of several other versions (Dan., Swed., Icelandic, Dutch), but naturally gave rise to counter versions by the Catholics (H. Emser 1527;* J. Dietenberger 1534; J. Eck* 1537). The tr. of Dietenberger, rev. by Kaspar Ulenberg 1630 and by the clergy of Mainz 1662, became known as the "Catholic Bible." A revision of Luther's version known as the "Revidierte Bibel" appeared 1892 but has not met with gen. favor. Finally, several more recent scholarly translations deserve mention, notably those of E. F. Kautzsch* (OT) and K. H. v. Weizsäcker* (NT), which have also been pub. together in 1 vol., and those of W. M. L. DeWette,* J. F. Meier, F. E. Schlachter, and H. Menge.* A. Schlatter,* Wilhelm Michaelis, and others attempted to tr. the Bible into contemporary idiom.

N. As of 1964, 231 languages had entire Bibles; 290 more had the entire NT. Some parts of the Bible have been pub. in 1,216 languages and dialects, but over 1,000 mutually unintelligible languages and dialects have nothing of the Bible.

John Eliot's* Mohican tr. was the first Bible pub. in Am. (NT 1661; OT 1663). MHF

See also *Polychrome Bible; Theology.*

English Bible in America: A Bibliography of Editions of the Bible and the New Testament Published in America 1777–1957, ed. M. T. Hills (New York, 1961); *The Translated Bible 1534–1934,* ed. O. M. Norlie (Philadelphia, 1934); O. M. Norlie, *The Bible in a Thousand Tongues* (Minneapolis, 1935).

Bibles, Polyglot. See *Polyglot Bibles.*

Biblia pauperum (Lat. "Bible of the poor"). Books of late Middle Ages which attempted to illustrate with pictures the fulfillment of the OT in the NT (from Annunciation to crowning of Mary in heaven). NT picture is grouped with OT types and prophecies and explained with a biblical text. Title may refer to "spiritually poor" or to the fact that the *Biblia pauperum* was used by priests who preached to the poor. Among first books printed from blocks and type in Ger. and Neth. Copies in Lat. and Ger. extant. A similar work was called *Speculum humanae salvationis.* A work of Bonaventura* which arranged biblical events in alphabetical order was also called *Biblia pauperum.*

Bibliander, Theodor. See *Buchmann, Theodor.*

Biblical Canonics. That part of isagogics* which deals with the hist. side of the aim to determine what books constitute the Bible. See also *Canon, Bible.*

Biblical Commission. See *Commission, Biblical.*

Biblical Criticism. See *Higher Criticism; Simon, Richard; Textual Criticism.*

Biblical Hermeneutics. See *Hermeneutics.*

Biblical History. Biblical hist. follows the Bible in its chronology and treats the Jewish dispensation, life of Christ, life of the apostles, and the founding of the ch. to the end of the first century. The chief sources are the Bible, Apocryphal books, Philo, Josephus, some classical authors (Herodotus, Ctesias, Polybius, Diodorus, Siculus, Strabo, Plutarch, Livy, Tacitus), archaeological discoveries, patristic writings, papyri, and other MS discoveries. Biblical hist. treats all phases (political, economic, soc., religious) of the sacred narrative.

Biblical Isagogics. See *Isagogics.*

Biblical Philology. See *Philology, Biblical.*

Biblical Psychology. See *Psychology, D.*

Biblical Realism. See *Switzerland, Contemporary Theology in,* 7.

Biblical Textual Criticism. See *Textual Criticism.*

Biblical Theology. See *Theology, Biblical.*

Biblicism. Term used with negative connotation to describe the approach of some theologians to Scripture; used already 1883 by K. M. A. Kähler.* Attempts to identify theol. tendencies as biblicism proved futile. Often men like J. A. Bengel* and J. T. Beck* were classified as biblicists. H. Engelland (b. Föhrden, Schleswig, 1903; prof. theol. Hamburg Theol. Inst.) classifies A. H. Cremer,* Kähler, and A. Schlatter* as neo-biblicists. At times attempts were made to distinguish biblicism in the narrow and wide sense. It has been defined as a liberal use of the Bible that ignores context, figures of speech, and principles of interpretation. K. Barth regards biblicism as immediate approach to Scripture without use of dogma. R. Niebuhr regards biblicism as identical with bibliolatry. Calvin* is often classified as a biblicist whereas Luther's* emphasis on the Gospel protected him from a one-sided biblicism.

In a good sense Biblicism denotes thorough acquaintance with the Bible. In this sense a Bible scholar may be called a Biblicist.

Bibliolatry (Gk. "Bible worship"). Term applied, usually in reproach, to those who are regarded as giving too much reverence to the letter of the Scriptures.

Bibliology. That part of dogmatics* which deals with the essence and attributes of Holy Scripture in relation to mankind.

Bickell. 1. *Johann Wilhelm* (1799–1848). Authority on canon law. B. Marburg; d. Kassel. Studied law at Marburg and Göttingen. Prof. jurisprudence Marburg 1824–34; pres. supreme court Hesse-Cassel 1841; minister of state 1846. Upheld necessity of subscription of pastors to Confessions. 2. *Gustav* (1836[38?]–1906). Son of J. W. Bickell; theol. and linguist; taught Marburg and Giessen; joined RC Ch. 1865; prof. Münster, Innsbruck, and Vienna; works include translations and studies in area of Syriac and OT.

Bickersteth. 1. *Edward* (1786–1850). Angl. clergyman and hymnist. Ordained 1815; sent to Afr.; returned; secy. CMS 1816–30; rector Watton, Hertfordshire, 1830–50; helped found Evangelical Alliance*; compiled *Christian Psalmody* 1833, a collection of over 700 hymns. 2. *Edward* (1814–92). Nephew of E. Bickersteth (1786–1850); dean Lichfield; mem. of committee of NT revisers; works include commentary on Mark in *Pulpit Commentary.* 3. *Edward Henry* (1825–1906). Angl. clergyman; son of E. Bickersteth (1786–1850); educ. Cambridge; held a number of charges; bp. Exeter 1885 to 1900; hymnist; ed. hymnals. 4. *Edward* (1850 to 97). Angl. clergyman; son of E. H. Bickersteth; bp. S Tokyo. Educ. Cambridge; miss. to Japan; organized *Nippon Sei Kokwai* (Catholic Church of Japan); founded community missions of St. Andrew and St. Hilda.

Bickertonites. See *Latter Day Saints,* g 4.

Bidding Prayer. Ancient prayer, appointed esp. for Good Friday, with intercessions for various classes of men both in the ch. and without; so called because it bids people pray and mentions things to be prayed for.

Biddle, John (1615–62). Founder of Eng. Unitarianism; imprisoned several times for anti-Trinitarian views expressed in *Twelve Arguments* and *Confession of Faith Touching the Holy Trinity.* D. in prison in London.

Bidembach, Balthasar (1533–78). Provost Stuttgart. Attended Maulbronn* Colloguy 1564. With L. Osiander the Elder* wrote the Maulbronn Formula 1576, antecedent of the Formula of Concord. Successor of J. Brenz.* Wrote homiletic works on 1 Kings and Romans. Hymnist. See also *Lutheran Confessions,* C 2.

Biedermann, Alois Emanuel (1819–85). Swiss dogmatician; freethinker; Hegelian pantheist; held that spirituality and infinity were central in the idea of God; from 1850 to his death prof. Zurich.

Biedermann, Richard Daniel (Oct. 6, 1864–Mar. 8, 1921). Educ. Conc. Coll., Fort Wayne, and Conc. Sem., St. Louis (grad. 1885); pastor St. Paul, Minn.; Mobile, Ala.; Kendallville and Indianapolis, Ind.; pres. Conc. Sem., Springfield, Ill., 1914–21; secy. Mo. Syn. 1905–20.

Biel, Gabriel (ca. 1420–95). Ger. scholastic philos.; nominalist; taught at Tübingen; protagonist of semi-Pelagianism, mechanical theory of sacraments, "mighty dignity" of priests, and Immaculate Conception; position on ch. polity was that of the councils of Constance and Basel. Wrote commentary on *Sentences* of Peter Lombard. Writings were among first theol. works read by Luther.

F. X. Linsenmann, "Gabriel Biel und die Anfänge der Universität zu Tübingen," *Theologische Quartalschrift,* XLVII (1865), 195–226, and "Gabriel Biel, der letzte Scholastiker, und der Nominalismus," ib., 449–481, 601–676; *Friedrich Ueberwegs Grundriss der Geschichte der Philosophie,* ed. B. Geyer, 12th ed., II (Basel, 1951), 611–612, 786.

Bielefeld. See *Bodelschwingh, Friedrich von.*

Bienemann, Kaspar (Melissander; 1540–91). Gen. supt. Pfalz-Neuburg; tutor Weimar ducal court; pastor and gen. supt. Altenburg; hymnist.

Biewend, Adolf Friedrich Theodor (May 6, 1816–April 10, 1858). Pastor and educator. B. Rothehütte, Hannover. Educ. Clausthal 1828–35 and U. of Göttingen 1835–38. Tutor Grünenplan, Braunschweig, 1838–42. Applied to a miss. soc. in Stade, which was ready to send him to America. Encouraged by F. K. D. Wyneken to go to America. Ordained May 10, 1843, Hannover. Pastor Washington, D. C., 1843–47. Joined Pa. Synod. Resigned pastorate because cong. was not purely Luth., but a mixture of Luth., Ref., and RC elements. Taught Columbian Coll., Washington, D. C., 1847–49; prof. Ft. Wayne seminary as successor of C. L. A. Wolter 1849–50; prof. Conc. Sem., St. Louis, 1850–58. Promoted study and use of Eng. language and an Eng. academy in St. Louis. Advocated closer relations with other Luth. chs., esp. the Norw. and Tenn. Synods.

H. C. Wyneken, *Adolf Fr. Th. Biewend* (St. Louis, 1896).

"Big Bang" Theory. See *Cosmogony.*

Bigamy. Formal entering into second marriage while the first is undissolved. The normal form of marriage as instituted by God (Gn 1:27) and acknowledged and reaffirmed by Christ (Mt 19:4-6) is monogamy. Bigamy, accordingly, is a corruption of the original institution of marriage and is tolerated neither by the ch. nor, as a rule, by the state.

Bigg, Charles (1840–1908). Church historian; educ. Oxford. Wrote *The Christian Platonists of Alexandria; Neoplatonism; The Origins of Christianity.*

Bihlmeyer, Karl (1874–1942). B. Aulendorf; d. Tübingen. RC theol.; wrote in area of patristics and medieval mysticism.

Bill, Samuel A. See *Africa,* C 14.

Billerbeck, Paul (1853–1932). German pastor in Zielensig and Heinersdorf. Wrote (with H. L. Strack) *Kommentar zum Neuen Testament aus Talmud und Midrasch.*

Billicanus, Theobald (Gerlacher; Gernolt; ca. 1490–1554). Ger. theol.; favored Luther as early as 1518; later wavered between Luther, Zwingli, and Karlstadt; finally affirmed belief in RC doctrine. D. as prof. rhetoric Marburg.

Billick, Eberhard (ca. 1499–1557). RC theol. Chief RC opponent of Bucer. Participated in Regensburg* Conf. 1546 and Council of Trent.*

Billing, Einar Magnus (1871–1939). Son of Gottfrid Billing. Taught systematic theol. Uppsala 1900–20; bp. Västeraas 1920–39; outstanding Swed. theol.; one of the most original, creative thinkers of his time. Probably influenced Aulén and through him the so-called Lundensian school. His theol. research was chiefly directed toward the Bible and Luther. He originated the idea of the Swed. folk ch. (*folk-*

kyrkotanken), widely accepted among clergy and laity. Most important theol. works: *De etiska tankarna i urkristendomen* ("The Ethical Thoughts of the Primitive Church"); *Försoningen* ("The Atonement"); *Den svenska folkkyrkan* ("The Swedish Folk Church"). See also *Sweden, Lutheranism in,* 6.

G. Wingren, "Om Einar Billings teologi," in *Svensk teologisk kvartalskrift,* XX (1944), 271–301, and "Swedish Theology Since 1900," in *Scottish Journal of Theology,* IX (June 1956), 113–134; *Einar Billing in Memoriam,* by several authors (Stockholm, 1940). GH

Billing, Gottfrid (1841–1925). Swed. ch. leader and statesman; bp. Västeraas 1884, Lund 1898. Presided in the Swed. Ch. Assembly 1878–1920; played important role as promoter of Luth. confessions against liberal theology. Influential mem. of the Swed. parliament.

E. Rodhe, *Svenska kyrkan omkring sekelskiftet* (Stockholm, 1930). GH

Billot, Louis (1846–1931). Jesuit theol.; neo-Thomist; wrote on sacraments, Trin., ch., tradition, original sin, grace, *parousia.*

Bilney, Thomas (ca. 1495–1531). Eng. Prot. martyr. Mem. Trin. Hall, Cambridge; read Luther's writings in early 1520s. Converted by reading NT in Erasmus' ed. Said to have converted Hugh Latimer. Influenced Robert Barnes and Miles Coverdale. Preached against relics, pilgrimages, and cult of saints. Friend of M. Parker.* Arrested for heresy 1527; recanted. Arrested again 1531; burned at Norwich.

John Foxe, *Acts and Monuments,* ed. S. R. Cattley, IV (London, 1837), 619–656, 755–763.

Bilo Contagion. See *Demoniacal Possession.*

Bilocation. Term used to denote power to be in 2 places at the same time. In theol. bilocation receives consideration in the doctrine of Christology.

Biltz, Franz Julius (July 24, 1825–Nov. 19, 1908). B. Mittel-Frohna, Saxony; came to US as 13-yr.-old orphan with Saxons led by M. Stephan; one of the first students at Conc. Coll., Altenburg; ordained Mar. 12, 1848; served in Dissen (Friedheim), Cape Girardeau Co., Mo., Cumberland, Md., and Concordia, Mo. Missionary among Ger. immigrants; Pres. W Dist., Mo. Syn.; mem. Electoral Coll.; instrumental in founding St. Paul's Coll., Concordia, Mo.

Bimeler, Joseph Michael. (Bäumeler; Baumeler; Bimmeler). See *Communistic Societies,* 5.

Bination (from Lat. *bini*: twofold). Offering of mass twice on same day by same person.

Bindemann, Frederick Wilhelm. See *Canada,* A 6.

Binding and Loosing. See *Keys, Office of,* 3.

Bingham, Hiram (Oct. 30, 1789–1869). B. Bennington, Vt.; educ. at Middlebury Coll. and Andover Sem. Sent by ABCFM to Hawaii 1819; wrote a history of the mission in Hawaii down to 1845.

Bingham, Joseph (1668–1723). Eng. clergyman and archaeologist. B. Wakefield; d. Havant. Rector of Headbourne Worthy, near Winchester, and of Havant. Works include *Origines Ecclesiasticae; or The Antiquities of the Christian Church,* containing information on the hierarchy, organization, rites, discipline, and calendar of the early ch.

Binitarianism. Belief that there are only 2 persons in the Trinity,* Father and Son.

Binney, Joseph G. (1807–77). Bap. pastor; ABCFM (Cong.) miss. to Karens in Burma 1844–50, and Rangoon, Burma 1858–76.

Biogenetic Law. See *Haeckel, Ernst Heinrich.*

Biography, Bibliography of. I. *General. World Biography,* 5th ed. (Bethpage, N. Y., 1954); *Biographical Encyclopedia of America,* ed. J. C. Schwarz (New York, 1940); *Dictionary of American Biography,* ed. A. Johnson and D. Malone, new rev. pop. ed., 20 vols., with index and suppl. 1 (New York, 1943 to 1945), suppl. 2 ed. R. L. Schuyler and E. T. James, vol. 22 (New York, 1958); *Concise Dictionary of American Biography,* ed. F. Burkhardt et al. (New York, 1964); *Who's Who in America* (pub. since 1899 by the A. N. Marquis Co., Chicago); *Who Was Who in America* (A. N. Marquis Co., Chicago); R. W. Murphey, *How and Where to Look It Up: a Guide to Standard Sources of Information* (New York, 1958); excellent biographical materials have been prepared by R. R. Bowker Co., N. Y. (see *Directory of American Scholars,* 1963). Biographies and bibliographies are also given in encyclopedias.*

II. *Biblical.* Outstanding biographical material is given in Bible dictionaries* as well as in encyclopedias;* H. Morton, *Women of the Bible* (New York, 1941); L. Wangemann, *Biblische Biographien und Monographien* (Leipzig, 1899); H. Hunter, *Sacred Biography,* 6 vols. (Boston, 1794); R. Wenger, *Die Frauen des Neuen Testaments* (Stuttgart, 1927); J. Hastings, *Greater Men and Women of the Bible,* 6 vols. (New York, 1913–16).

III. *Early Christianity.* See references under *Patristics; Saints; Popes.* A. G. Rudelbach, *Biographien von Zeugen der christlichen Kirche* (Leipzig, 1850).

IV. *Christian (General).* W. Smith and H. Wace, *Dictionary of Christian Biography,* 4 vols. (London. 1877–87); M. Meurer, *Das Leben der Altväter der lutherischen Kirche* (Leipzig) 1861–64); M. Adam, *Vitae Germanorum theologorum* (Heidelberg 1620); A. G. Rudelbach, *Biographien von Zeugen der christlichen Kirche* (Leipzig, 1850) and *Christliche Biographie* (Leipzig, 1850); *Religious Leaders of America,* ed. J. C. Schwarz, Vol. I: *Who's Who In the Clergy, 1935–1936* (New York, 1936), Vol. II: *Religious Leaders of America, 1941–1942* (New York, 1941); R. F. Sample, *Beacon Lights of the Reformation* (Philadelphia, 1889); E. M. Harrison, *Heroes of Faith on Pioneer Trails* (Chicago, 1945); K. R. Hagenbach, *Leben und auserwählte Schriften der Väter und Begründer der Reformierten Kirche,* 10 vols. (Elberfeld, 1859–62); *Religion in American Life,* eds. J. W. Smith and A. L. Jamison (Princeton, 1961); *Dictionary of American History,* ed. in chief J. T. Adams, 6 vols. (New York, 1940); *The American Church History Series,* 13 vols. (New York, 1893–97); *The Yearbook of American Churches* (New York). Other good sources and bibliographies can be found in religious encyclopedias.*

V. *American Lutheran.* J. W. Richards, *Penn's Lutheran Forerunners and Friends* (Columbus, 1926); L. Fuerbringer, *Persons and Events* (Saint Louis, 1947); I. O. Nothstein, *Lutheran Makers of America* (Philadeplhia, 1930); A. R. Wentz, *History of the Gettysburg Theological Seminary* (Philadelphia, 1926); W. J. Finck, *Lutheran Landmarks and Pioneers in America* (Philadelphia, 1913); *Lutheran World Almanac* (pub. since 1921 by NLC); *Concordia Historical Institute Quarterly* (pub. since 1928 by Conc. Hist. Inst.); H. E. Jacobs and J. A. W. Haas, *The Lutheran Cyclopedia* (New York, 1899); J. C. Jensson, *American Lutheran Biographies* (Milwaukee, 1890); J. G. Morris, *Fifty Years in the Lutheran Ministry* (Baltimore, 1878); O. M. Norlie, *Prominent Personalities* (Northfield, Minn., 1942) and *School Calendar, 1824–1924* (Minneapolis, 1924); W. B. Sprague, *Annals of the American Lutheran Pulpit* (New York, 1869); *A Biographical Dictionary of Pastors of the American Lutheran Church* (Minneapolis, 1932); obituaries in church magazines and periodicals; American Lutheran church histories (by Graebner, Jacobs, Fritschel, Bente, Neve, Wentz, Wolf, and others). ARS

Bionomic Forces. In science and philosophy, extra-biological forces (all physical, chemical, and environmental factors) which affect living organisms in any way.

Biran, Maine de (1766–1824). Outstanding Fr. psychologist; defender of Fr. spiritualism; regarded religion as a matter of emotion rather than belief.

Biretta. Square cap with 3 or 4 projecting prominences and a tassel, worn by priests when approaching the altar for mass, and in choir, etc. A cardinal's biretta is red, a bishop's purple, that of other clerics black. See also *Vestments, Clerical.*

Birgitta. See *Bridget.*

Birinus (d. ca. 650). Apostle of W Saxons and first bp. Dorchester. Came to Eng. 634.

Birkedal, Wilhelm (1809–92). Educ. U. of Copenhagen; pastor Ryslinge, Den.; propagated theol. of Grundtvig*; est. a free cong. which, after 1868, functioned under the care of the bp. of the est. church.

Birken, Siegmund von (Betulius; 1626–81). B. Wildstein, Bohemia; because of religious persecution his family fled to Nürnberg, where he started his schooling. Studied law and theol. at U. of Jena. Because of his poetical gifts he was admitted as a mem. of the Pegnitz Shepherd and Flower Order; poet laureate. Tutor at Wolfenbüttel to the princes of Brunswick-Lüneburg; tutor at various courts. Wrote 52 hymns, including "Jesus, I Will Ponder Now" and "Let Us Ever Walk with Jesus."

Birkner, Henry Philip Ludwig (Feb. 26. 1857–Nov. 7, 1932). B. Brooklyn, N. Y.; grad. Conc. Sem., Saint Louis, 1878; attended N. Y. U. 1878–79; pastor Gordonville, Mo., 1879–86, St. Louis 1886–90, Boston 1890; vice-pres. Atlantic Dist., Mo. Syn., 1915 to 1918; pres. 1918–30.

Birmingham Sunday Society. See *Adult Education.*

Birth Control. See *Family Planning.*

Birth Control Federation of America, Inc. See *Family Planning,* 3.

Bischoff, Johann Gottfried (1871–1960). Leader of New Apostolic Church.

Bischoff, Rudolf Adam (May 16, 1847–Sept. 11, 1916). B. St. Louis; d. Bingen, Ind. Educ. Conc. Coll., Fort Wayne, Ind., and Conc. Sem., St. Louis; pastor Alexandria, Va.; prof. Conc. Coll., Fort Wayne, 1872–82, pres. 1882–86; pastor Bingen, Ind., 1886–89; prof. Conc. Coll., Fort Wayne, 1889 to 1904; ed. *Lutheran Pioneer* 1879–1912.

Bischop, Simon (Biscop). See *Episcopius, Simon.*

Bishop. (Gk. *episkopos,* "overseer"). 1. Used in NT for those who governed and directed the Christian communities. The NT does not distinguish between bps. and presbyters (Acts 14:23; 20:17, 28). In gen., "presbyter" indicated the office (Ro 12:8; 1 Th. 5:12) and "bishop" the function (Acts 20:28). The tendency toward investing one presbyter with overall responsibility may appear as early as the Pastoral Epistles (see 1 Ti 3:2, 5).

By the end of the 1st c. the bp. has become the head of the local ch. at least at Corinth (1 Clement, 44). In the *Didache* (XV) the bp. is preacher, teacher, and leader of worship. The bp. is the responsible leader of the cong. in the letters of Ignatius of Antioch (2d c.). In this monarchical episcopate, one bp. rules in each ch., maintains purity of doctrine, is the chief celebrant at the Eucharist, and presides at baptisms. Irenaeus* and Tertullian* are concerned with demonstrating the apostolic succession of episcopal offices. In Hippolytus* the "presbyter-bishop" has become the priest through whom the worshiping cong. at the Eucharist offers its sacrifice of praise, and to whom the responsibility of teaching and certain limited judicial functions belong. The bp. of the 3d c. is chosen by the community *(nos eligimus eum)* and is consecrated by the neighboring bps. assisted by the presbyters. The situation confronting Cyprian* of Carthage leads to an emphasis on the administrative and judicial functions of the bp. Each bp. is the representative of Christ and the contemporary embodiment of the apostles ("The bishop is in the church and the church in the bishop.").

2. Thus by the middle of the 3d c. the office of bp. had emerged as chief magisterial, liturgical, administrative, and judicial ministry of the ch. As Christianity moved out of the cities into the surrounding countryside jurisdiction of the bp. was extended beyond the original town limits to larger areas. When the Christian religion was recognized by Constantine, bps. were given the rank of an *illustris,* their right to distinctive garb was recognized, and their jurisdiction was conformed to the pattern of imperial administration. The distinctive features of the office of bp. were formalized by councils between Nicaea (325) and Chalcedon (451). From the 5th c. on the original parity of presbyters and bps. was more and more lost sight of. During the Middle Ages the bps. of the Christian West received functions of secular magistrates in many places.

3. In W canon law three things are necessary to est. a bp. in office: election, mission, and consecration. In RC theol., the office of bp. exists by divine right but jurisdiction is conceived of as conferred by the pope. At the present time RC bps. are usually selected by the pope; they receive their mission, or episc. powers, either directly from pope or through a metropolitan, and they are consecrated by a bp. assisted by two bps. The bp. swears allegiance to the pope and must periodically report to him *(visitatio liminum).*

4. In the Ch. of Eng. the cathedral dean and chapter elect a candidate nominated by the crown, and mission and consecration is by the metropolitan. In other parts of the Angl. communion the provisions of local canon law govern.

5. The chief duties of RC, Old Catholic, E Orthodox, and Angl. bps. are to administer those sacraments of which they alone are the ordinary ministers (ordination, confirmation) and serve as shepherd, priest, and teacher of the diocese.* The bps. of these communions claim apostolic* succession, although the validity of Angl. orders is not universally recognized.

6. The Hussite schismatics of Bohemia retained the title of bp., although without a demonstrable apostolic succession, and the episcopate was revived 1735 with the restoration of the Unitas Fratrum on the Saxon estates of Count von Zinzendorf. The title of bp. is gen. in Am. Methodism and related churches. Many smaller Prot. churches have adopted the title.

7. The Luth. symbols (AC XXVIII; Ap XXVIII; *Treatise on the Power and Primacy of the Pope,* 60–82; SA II iv 9; III x) recognized the rank of bps. and described their true function as preaching the Gospel, administering the sacraments, and exercising the keys. Though the symbols strongly express a desire to continue canonical govt., political factors prevented the perpetuation of the episcopate among the Luth. estates of the Holy Roman empire.

8. The office of bp. was kept in Swed. and Fin. (with apostolic succession); the title was restored in Den., Norw., Iceland, Transylvania, Slov. and Hung. In Ger. the supervision of the ch. was given to supts. In Luth. Ger. secular rulers often assumed the juridical functions of bps. and the style of *summus episcopus* of the ch. in their territories. The term *Landes bischof (episcopus territorialis)* was introduced in Nassau 1827. Several Luth. theologians (e. g. Stahl*, Löhe*) endeavored to reintroduce the office of bp. Efforts of the 18th and 19th c. Prussian kings to restore the episcopate in their domains climaxed in the shortlived joint Angl. and Prussian Union bishopric of Jerusalem.

9. When the office of *summus episcopus* was abolished after WW I, some Ger. territorial churches used the title "bishop" for their presiding officer. In 1933 the office was introduced throughout most of Ger. The prestige of bps. rose during the *Kirchenkampf** so that the office is regarded as self-evident in ch. orders and constitutions after 1945. The title has been rejected for the most part only in areas where Ref. influence is strong.

10. Ger. Ev. bps. are usually elected for life by synods or other ecclesiastical authorities. They usually have little or no legislative or administrative authority and their functions are largely spiritual (ordination, installation of pastors and prelates, visitation, consecration of churches, access to all pulpits of their territory, general oversight of the ch. and clergy, presiding over synods and other major administrative agencies).

11. In the 17th and 18th c. the RC Ch. began to consecrate indigenous bps. in India and China and the practice has now become gen. The first indigenous Angl. bp. was S. Crowther* of Afr. The episc. Luth. churches of Eur. often est. the episcopate in their missions, notably in India and Afr. The All Afr. Luth. Conf. (1955) expressed itself in favor of bps.

The episcopate was briefly est. among the Saxon Luth. immigrants to the US; Löhe designed his Franconian colony in Mich. to be episcopally governed, but his intention was never realized.

12. Today counselors, presidents of districts and synods in the Luth. churches of Am., and similar officers perform the function of bps. The extent of their administrative power may be greater or less than that exercised by their Eur. counterparts. EL, ACP

See also *Titular Bishop; Western Christianity 500–1500,* 8.

F. Haupt, *Der Episcopat der deutschen Reformation,* 2 vols. (Frankfurt/M, 1863–66); *Episcopacy, Ancient and Modern,* eds. C. Jenkins and K. D. MacKenzie (New York, 1930); *The Apostolic Ministry: Essays on the History and the Doctrine of Episcopacy,* ed. K. E. Kirk (London, 1946); A. Ehrhardt, *The Apostolic Succession in the First Two Centuries of the Church* (London, 1953); E. Benz, *Bischofsamt und apostolische Sukzession im deutschen Protestantismus* (Stuttgart, 1953); *The Historic Episcopate in the Fullness of the Church,* ed. K. M. Carey (London, 1954); *The Ministry in Historical Perspectives,* eds. H. R. Niebuhr and D. D. Williams (New York, 1956); K. Rahner and J. Ratzinger, *The Episcopate and the Primacy,* tr. K. Barker and others (New York, 1962); R. Caemmerer and E. Lueker, *Church and Ministry in Transition* (St. Louis, 1964).

Bishop Hill Colony. See *Communistic Societies,* 5.

Bishops' Bible. See *Bible Versions,* L 7.

Bishops' Book. See *Anglican Confessions,* 2.

Bismarck, Otto Eduard Leopold von (1815–98). See *Christian Socialism,* 1; *Kulturkampf.*

Bismarck Archipelago. E of Territory of New Guinea (of which it is politically a part); includes New Brit., New Ireland, Lavongai (New Hanover), and the Admiralty Islands, and ca. 200 other islands and islets. *Area:* ca. 22,920 sq. mi. *Pop.:* ca. 247,780, mostly Melanesians. Ger. protectorate 1884; after WW I under Australian control. George Brown of the Meth. Miss. Soc. of Australasia began work on New Brit. 1875. The Liebenzeller Miss. is at work on several islands of the Admiralty group. RC missions began 1889.

Bismillah (Arab. "In the name of Allah"). Formula at beginning of each sura (chapter) of Koran; commonly used by Muslim as pious expletive.

Bisschop, Simon. See *Episcopius, Simon.*

Bitter, Karl Hermann (1813–85). Prussian statesman and writer on music; biographer of J. S. Bach.

Bittle, David Frederick (Jan. 1811–Sept. 25, 1876). B. Frederick Co., Md.; educ. Pa. Coll. and Theol. Sem., Gettysburg, Pa.; United Synod pastor Va. and Md.; helped est. Roanoke Coll. and served as first pres. 1853–76.

Bitzius, Albert. See *Gotthelf, Jeremias.*

Bjarnason, Jon. See *Canada,* A 13; *United Lutheran Church, Synods of,* 6.

Bjarnason Academy. See *Canada,* A 13.

Björk, Eric Tobias (ca. 1668–1740). B. Westmanland. Swed.; ordained Uppsala; arrived Am. June 24, 1697, with Jonas Aureen and A. Rudman* to serve Swedes on Delaware. Under his pastoral leadership Swedes Lutheran Church, called Trinity Church (Old Swedes Church, Wilmington, Del.), was built; dedicated June 4, 1699. Recalled to Swed.; left Am. June 29, 1714. See also *Provost.*

Björling, Carl O. (1804–84). Swed. theol.; educ. Uppsala; bp. Västeraas; wrote a Christian dogmatics and other works which show his loyalty to the AC.

Björnson, Björnstjerne (1832–1910). Norw. novelist, poet, dramatist. Early writings sought to demonstrate ethical power of Christianity; influenced by Grundtvig*; opposed Ger. pietism; later turned from Christianity to positivism and naturalism; believed in triumph of good.

Black Art. See *Witchcraft,* 4.

Black Canons. Canons regular of Augustine of Hippo. So called because of black attire.

Black Cloister. See *Luther, Martin,* 3.

Black Fast. Fast during Lent and before ordination practices up to 10th c. Food was restricted and stipulated to be eaten in evening.

Black Friars. Name given Dominican Friars because of black attire. See also *Dominicans.*

Back Jews. See *Church of God and Saints of Christ; Falasha.*

Black Monks. Benedictine monks; so called because of black attire.

Black Muslim. See *Lost-Found Nation of Islam in the Wilderness of North America, The.*

Black Pope. Popular name for the Superior General of the Society* of Jesus.

Black Rubric. Name applied by High Churchmen to a statement introduced 1552 at the end of the Order of Holy Communion in the Anglican Book of Common Prayer; it reads in part: "[By kneeling] no adoration is intended, or ought to be done, either unto the Sacramental Bread or Wine there bodily received, or unto any Corporal presence of Christ's natural Flesh and Blood." When the practice of printing the rubrics in red was introduced in the 19th c., this statement, improperly called a rubric, was printed in black.

Black Stone. See *Kaaba.*

Blackstone, William Eugene (1841–1935). B. Adams, Jefferson Co., N N. Y.; Meth. businessman; interested in reest. Palestine as a Jewish state; helped est. Chicago Heb. Miss. Wrote *Jesus Is Coming.*

Blackwood, Andrew Watterson (1882–1966). B. Clay Center, Kans.; educ. Franklin Coll., New Athens, Ohio, Princeton (N. J.) Theol. Sem., and Xenia Theol. Sem. (see *Pittsburgh Theological Seminary*); ordained United Presb. 1908. Pastor Pittsburgh, Pa.; Columbia, S. C.; Columbus, Ohio. Prof. Presb. Theol. Sem., Louisville, Ky.; Princeton Theol. Sem.; Temple U., Philadelphia, Pa. Works include *Preaching from the Bible; Doctrinal Preaching for Today; The Growing Minister; Preaching from Prophetic Books; The Preparation of Sermons.*

Blahoslav, Jan (1523–71). Bohemian Brethren* bp.; hist., grammarian, musician, poet; reconciled Christianity and humanism; tr. NT into Czech.

Blair, James (ca. 1655–1743). B. Scot.; educ. Edinburg; Episc. Ch. of Scot. cleric; miss. to Va. 1685;

commissary for Va. (highest ch. office in the colony) 1689; cofounder Coll. of William and Mary, Williamsburg; its 1st pres. 1693–1743; pres. Va. Council, acting gov. Va. 1740–41; minister Jamestown Ch. 1694; rector Bruton Parish, Williamsburg. See also *Protestant Episcopal Church, The,* 1 a.

Blake, William (1757–1827). Eng. visionary, mystic, poet, artist, philos. Best-known works: *Songs of Innocence; Songs of Experience; The Everlasting Gospel; The Marriage of Heaven and Hell; The Four Zoas; Jerusalem; Prophetic Books; Milton.*

J. Bronowski, *William Blake and the Age of Revolution* (New York, 1965).

Blanchard, Charles Albert (1848–1925). B. Galesburg, Ill. Congregationalist. Educ. Wheaton Coll. and Chicago Theol. Sem.; agent and lecturer Nat.* Christian Assoc. 1870–72; principal Preparatory Dept. Wheaton Coll. 1872–74; prof. various subjects; pres. Wheaton Coll. 1882; pres. coll. section Ill. State Teachers Assoc. 1894; pres. Nat. Christian Assoc. 1903–04. Wrote *Modern Secret Societies; Light on the Last Days; Getting Things from God; Visions and Voices.*

Blandina (d. 177). Young female slave and Christian martyr; renowned for steadfastness and endurance while tormented to death during persecution at Lyons.

Blandrata, Giorgio (Biandrata; ca. 1515–88). It. physician; defended anti-Trinitarian views against Calvin and Beza; introduced Unitarianism in Poland and Transylvania. See also *Socinianism,* 1;*Socinus.*

Blankenbuehler, Lorenz F. (Feb. 7, 1886–Feb. 21, 1964). B. Webster City, Ia.; grad. Conc. Sem., St. Louis, 1911; prof. Conc. Coll., Portland, Oreg., 1911–21; Conc. Coll., St. Paul, Minn., 1921–41; head CPH ed. dept. 1941–52; prof. Conc. Sem., St. Louis, 1952–56; ed. *The Lutheran Witness* 1952 to 60; ed. em. 1960–64. Managing ed. *Lutheran Scholar* 1943–56; mem. Intersyn. Com. on Hymnology and Liturgics 1929–56; collaborator on *The Lutheran Hymnal.*

Blankenfeld, Johannes. See *Estonia,* 2.

Blarer, Ambrosius (Blaurer; 1492–1564). Educ. Tübingen; joined Luth. movement; later sided with Zwingli, whose extreme position on the Lord's Supper, however, he did not share; helped reform Württemberg; continued in mediating tendency; spent last yrs. in Switz. See also *Grynäus,* 1; *Schnepf, Erhard.*

Blarer, Thomas (1499–1570). Brother of Ambrosius. Studied under Luther and Melanchthon. Accompanied Luther to Worms 1521. Introduced reformation in Konstanz which ended with battle at Mühlberg.

Blasphemy. Speech, thought, writing, or action manifesting irreverence toward God or anything sacred (Ps 74:10, 18; Is 52:5; Rv 16:9, 11, 21). Expressions of contempt for destiny or deity are commonplace in primitive religion. False charges of blasphemy brought against Jesus (Mt 26:64-66; Jn 10:33), Stephen (Acts 6:11). Saul compelled Christians to blaspheme (Acts 26:11). Transgressions of God's people caused God's name to be blasphemed (Ro 2:24). Blasphemy is to be distinguished from atheism, sacrilege, and criticism of religion. But in moral theol., it is often regarded as a sin against the virtue of religion. In 16th and 17th c. Eng. it was dissent from the current religious dogma.

Blasphemy was severely punished under Jewish (Lv 24:16; 1 K 21:10), Greek (considered a crime against God and soc.), Justinian, medieval laws. In most countries it is still forbidden by law; since the Enlightenment, however, it is regarded as an offense against soc. rather than God. Christians regard it as a grave or mortal sin. EL

G. D. Nokes, *A History of the Crime of Blasphemy* (London, 1928).

Blass, Friedrich Wilhelm (1843–1907). Ger. classical scholar. Wrote *Grammatik des neutestamentlichen Griechisch* and *Philology of the Gospels.*

Blastares, Matthew (fl. 1335). Monk of Thessalonica; wrote handbook *Syntagma* of canon law.

MPG, 144, 960–1400.

Blaurer. See *Blarer.*

Blaurock, Georg (d. 1529). Monk; later leader of Swiss Anabaps.; burned in persecution at Innsbruck.

Blavatsky, Elena Petrovna (1831–91). Theosophist; b. Russia; d. London. Traveled extensively, esp. in Am. and India. Studied spiritism, occult and cabalistic literature, sacred writings of India. With Henry Steel Olcott founded the Theosophical Soc. in N. Y. 1875. Claimed miraculous powers, which were proved fraudulent. Wrote *Isis Unveiled; The Secret Doctrine; The Key to Theosophy.* See also *Theosophy.*

Bleby, Henry (Mar. 16, 1809–May 22, 1882). B. Winchcomb, Eng.; sent by Wesleyan Meth. Miss. Soc. to Jamaica; wrote on miss. work in W Indies.

Bleckmar Mission. See *Mission of the Evangelical Lutheran Free Churches.*

Bleek, Friedrich (1793–1859). Prof. Bonn; pupil of DeWette,* J. A. Neander,* and Schleiermacher.* Wrote critical studies of NT from conservative point of view.

Blemmydes, Nicephorus (1197–1272). E. Orthodox theol.; sought to reunite E and W church.

MPG, 142, 527–1622.

Blessedness. State of bliss of believers, veiled and imperfect in this life (Kingdom of Grace), perfect and eternal in heaven (Kingdom of Glory). Effected and sealed by the Gospel, appropriated and enjoyed by faith. Consists in spiritual joy, happiness, peace, hope, restoration of divine image in man, eternal glory (1 Co 2:9; Mt 5:3-12; Ro 4:6-8; Ps 16:11; 17:15; 23; 92:12-14; 128; Jb 36:11; Dt 28:1-14; Eph. 1:3; 2 Ptr 1:2-4; Rv 14:13; 1 Jn 3:2).

Blessig, Jean Laurent (1747–1816). Prof. U. of Strasbourg; mem. of bd. of dir. of "Church of the Augsburg Confession" in Alsace, the theol. and structure of which he strongly influenced.

Blessing and Cursing. Blessing (benediction) and cursing are both used effectively in Christ's kingdom, as will be evident on the Last Day (Mt 25:31, 41; 1 Co 16:22). God blessed by bestowing temporal and spiritual benefits on men (Nm 6:22-27; Gn 1:22; 2:3; 9:1-7; Ps 103). Men bless God by praising and thanking Him (Ps 103); they bless their fellow men by invoking God's favor on them (Gn 27:27-29; 48; 49; Dt 33; Ps 129:8).

Cursing is solely a prerogative of God (see *Anathema*). God's curse rests on sinners till they have forgiveness (Dt 27:15-26). All cursing by men, except their pronouncement of God's curse on sin and unbelief, is sinful and forbidden.

Blind. 1. Till 17th c., work among blind was regarded as charity. Since then educ. of blind has become highly developed science. Special laws protect and provide for blind; increasing numbers of vocations are open to them. Institutions for blind originated early in 19th c.; various organizations and associations are dedicated to their care.

2. Of ca. 20 million blind, most live in undeveloped countries. Hence Christian missions paid special attention to work among blind, as in China, where religion forbade acceptance of blind girls into the family. In US, Christian churches, Jewish organizations, YMCAs, service clubs (Lions, Rotary, etc.) work among the blind. Helen Keller* esp. directed attention to the blind.

3. In 1900 five systems of embossed type were in use among blind in US. In 1933 Grade 2 was adopted as standard Eng. Braille throughout the world. The ch. also began with systematic organized work among blind not many yrs. ago. The Soc. for Promotion of Ch. Work Among the Blind was orga-

nized in Prot. Episc. Ch. 1903. John Milton Soc., inc. 1928, serves most Prot. churches; RC branch inc. 1908.

4. In 1923 the Mo. Syn. directed the Miss. Bd. for the Deaf to investigate possibility of pub. religious magazine in Braille. In 1926 first issue of *Lutheran Messenger for the Blind* appeared. Special Bd. of Miss. for the Blind was elected 1947. Since then work among blind has expanded considerably. LCMS now has one of largest religious libraries for blind. Over 1,000 Braille vols. have been transcribed by volunteers. Large talking book dept. has been added, including tape recordings. LCMS now pub. 4 magazines for blind: *The Lutheran Messenger* in Braille; *The Lutheran Herald* in Moon; *Der Bote* in Ger., and *Teen Time*, which appears in Braille and Sight Saving. Ca. 500 volunteer transcribers emboss into Braille S. S. materials, library books, music notations, and special requests. Through its Board for the Blind the LCMS is able to supply religious Braille material to for. missionaries in almost any language.

The Luth. Braille Evangelism Assoc., Minneapolis, Minn., pub. the *Christian Magnifier* and other religious literature in Braille. WHS

H. Best, *Blindness and the Blind in the United States* (New York, 1934); G. Farrell, *The Story of Blindness* (Cambridge, Mass., 1956).

Bliss, Frederick Jones. See *Geography, Christian,* 6.

Blix, Elias (1836–1902). Norw. hymnist; prof. Christiania (Oslo) 1879; minister of culture 1884–88. Pub. *Nokre Salmar* and *Salmar og Songar*.

Blodget, Henry (1825–1903). Cong. for. miss. B. Bucksport, Me.; educ. Yale Coll. and New Haven and Andover Theol. Seminaries. Sent by ABCFM to China 1854; stationed at Shanghai, Tientsin, Peking. Mem. of com. which tr. NT into Mandarin; tr. 194 hymns and other theol. works.

Blomfield, Dorothy Frances (Mrs. G. Gurney; 1858–1932). Wrote "O Perfect Love, All Human Thought Transcending" for sister's wedding 1884.

Blondel, David (ca. 1590–1655). Huguenot ch. hist.; country pastor in Fr.; prof. Amsterdam. Wrote in defense of Ref. polity and against episcopacy. Most important work: *Pseudo-Isidorus et Turrianus Vapulans.* See also *Pseudo-Isidorian Decretola.*

Blondel, Maurice (1861–1949). Fr. philos.; devout RC. In *L'Action* he holds that the human will, which produces action, cannot be satisfied by finite good; hence a discrepancy bet. capabilities and will. From this point he developed an argument for existence of God based on volition. Assoc. with Modernist Movement.

Blondus, Flavius (1392–1463). Humanist; hist.; archaeologist; secy. to popes; important in development of modern historiography.

Blood Relationship. See *Impediments of Marriage, Scriptural and Natural.*

Bloody Sunday. See *Gapon, Jurij Apollonowitsch.*

Bloody Tenent of Persecution for the Cause of Conscience. See *Baptist Churches,* 3.

Blount, Charles (1654–93). Deist; b. Upper Holloway, Eng. Works include *Anima mundi; The Two First Books of Apollonius Tyaneus; Oracles of Reason; Great Is Diana of the Ephesians.* See also *Deism,* III 4.

Blow, John (ca. 1648[49?]–1708). Composer; b. North Collingham, Nottinghamshire, Eng.; teacher of H. Purcell*; organist Westminster Abbey 1669–80, 1695–1708. Works include services; anthems; secular compositions.

Bloxam, John Rouse (1807–91). Angl. assoc. of J. H. Newman. Originator of ceremonial revival in Angl. Ch. Leader in Tract Movement.

Blue Lodge. See *Freemasonry,* 3.

Blumhardt. 1. *Christian Gottlieb* (1779–1838). B. Stuttgart; d. Basel. Uncle of J. C. Blumhardt. Secy. *Deutsche Christentumsgesellschaft**; with C. F. Spittler founded Basel Bible Soc. 1804; dir. Basel Missionary Society.* Wrote *Versuch einer allgemeinen Missionsgeschichte der Kirche Christi,* 5 vols.; founded *Evang. Missionsmagazin* and *Heidenbote.* 2. *Johann Christoph* (1805–80). Educ. Tübingen; teacher at Basel Miss. Inst. 1830; pastor Möttlingen 1838. Gained fame as one who could cure by prayer; first reported cure was that of demoniac girl. In 1853 bought royal watering place Boll (Bad Boll), where all kinds of sufferers from all ranks of soc. and all countries flocked to be cured. In 1869 and 1872 he was joined by his sons. 3. *Christopher Friedrich* (1842–1919). Continued work of father Johann.

F. Zündel, *Johann Christoph Blumhardt, Ein Lebensbild,* rev. H. Schneider, 16th ed. (Giessen, 1954); E. Jäckh, *Blumhardt, Vater und Sohn und Ihre Botschaft* (Berlin, 1924–25).

B'nai B'rith. See *Students, Spiritual Care of,* A 3.

Board of Christian Education. See *Parish Education,* K 3.

Board of Parish Education. See *Christian Education,* E 13; *Parish Education,* M.

Boardman. 1. *Richard* (1738–Oct. 4, 1782). Meth. minister; b. and d. Ireland; to Am. as miss. with J. Pilmoor 1769; pastor N. Y. City; returned to Eng. 1774. 2. *George Dana, Sr.* (Feb. 8, 1801–Feb. 11, 1831). B. Livermore, Me.; educ. Andover Theol. Sem. Sent by Bap. Bd. of For. Miss. to India 1825; arrived Tavoy, Burma, Apr. 9, 1828; pioneer miss. to Karen. Made extensive jungle tours accompanied by native convert Ko* Tha Byu. See also *Judson, Sarah Hall.* 3. *George Dana, Jr.* (1828–1903). Am. Bap. pastor; b. Brit. Burma; son of G. D. Boardman, Sr.; educ. Brown U., Newton Theol. Institution; pres. Am. Bap. Miss. Union 1880–84; pres. Christian Arbitration and Peace Soc. of Am.; writings include *Titles of Wednesday Evening Lectures.*

Bobadilla, Nicolás Alfonso de (Nicholas; ca. 1509–90). B. Bobadilla, León, Sp.; educ. Valladolid and Alcalá de Henares, Sp., and Paris, Fr.; assoc. with I. (of) Loyola*; preacher and miss.; active in It., Ger., and Dalmatia.

Boccaccio, Giovanni (1313–75). Friend of Petrarch; humanist; student of Dante; because of his *Decameron* often considered first modern novelist.

Bocholt, Johannes (d. 1487). Founded Magdeburg House of the Brethren of the Common Life 1484; Luther visited it 1497.

Böckh, Christian Friedrich von (1795–1875). Pastor Nürnberg and Munich; eminent in liturgic researches; friend of J. K. W. Löhe; works include *Evangelisch-lutherische Agende.*

Böckman, Markus Olaus (Jan. 9, 1849–July 21, 1942). B. Langesund, Norw.; educ. Egersund High School, Aars and Voss Lat. School, U. of Christiania (Oslo); emigrated 1875; pastor near Kenyon, Minn., 1875–80; Gol and Moland 1880–88; prof. theol. Northfield 1886–90; Augsburg Sem. 1890–93; pres. United Norw. Ch. Sem. 1893–1917; pres. Luther Theol. Sem., St. Paul, Minn., 1917–30, prof. till 1937; retired. Knighted by Haakon VII of Denmark 1912.

Bocskay, István (1557–1606). Hung. nat. leader against Emperor Rudolf II; secured Treaty of Vienna, which gave religious freedom to Prots. of Hungary 1606.

Bodding, Paul Olaf (1865–1938). Miss. of Norw. Luth. Santal Miss. in India 1889–1933. Tr. Bible into Santali; wrote Santali grammar and dictionary and studies in Santali culture and folklore. See also *Norwegian Foreign Missions,* 3.

Bodelschwingh, Friedrich von (1831–1910). Ger. pastor; devoted many yrs. to inner miss. work at Bielefeld; est. number of institutions, including Bethel Home for Epileptics, schools for training deacons and deaconesses, and the first *Arbeiterkolonie,* at Wilhelmsdorf, to rehabilitate vagabonds. See also *Charities, Christian,* 5; *Christian Socialism,* 4.

Bodenschatz, Erhard (1576–1636). Luth. ed. and composer of ch. music; his *Florilegium Portense,* widely used in 17th and 18th c., included 265 motets by 93 composers.

Bodenstein, Andreas Rudolf. See *Karlstadt, Andreas Rudolf Bodenstein von.*

Body. The concept *body,* in sense of organized material of man, has frequently precipitated meditation and discussion regarding relationship of mind and body or interrelationship in trichotomy of soul, body, and spirit.

Materialists have it easy: body is matter; mind is simply matter in action – chemically, physiologically, or neurologically – or even electronically. Similarly, philosophical idealism oversimplifies by making the body merely the vehicle of consciousness.

Efforts to grapple with the problem include animistic views which consider the soul as inhabiting the body but with possibility of temporary or permanent separation. Descartes viewed body and soul as separate entities, having separate qualities, yet interacting with each other. This might be called beginning of interactionism, which with certain modifications is still popular.

In classic thesis-antithesis style a theory of parallelism arose, that relationship of mind and body is so close, even intimate, that both are considered manifestations of same substance (e. g. in Baruch Spinoza.)

Christian thought for a time seemed influenced by Greek dichotomies of mind and body, and mind was considered higher and body lower in man's nature. In more recent times the "whole man" concept is being stressed. When man fell into sin, the whole man fell; the whole man is restored by the redemptive activity of Jesus; the whole man partakes in the resurrection to eternal life; the whole man becomes more and more the temple of the Holy Spirit.

See also *Corporate Personality.* AJB

Boe, Lars Wilhelm (Dec. 27, 1875–Dec. 27, 1942). B. Calumet, Mich.; grad. St. Olaf Coll., Northfield, Minn., 1898; United Luth. Ch. Sem., Minneapolis, 1901; ordained 1901; pastor Lawler, Iowa, 1901–04, Forest City, Iowa, 1904–12, 1914–15; pres. Waldorf Coll. (prep. school), Forest City, 1904–15; mem. of House, Iowa legislature, 1909–11, of Senate 1913-15; gen. secy., bd. of trustees and bd. of regents United Norw. Luth. Ch. 1915–17; gen. secy. bd. of trustees and bd. of educ. Norw. Luth. Ch. 1917–18; pres. St. Olaf Coll. 1918–42; commissioner NLC and LWC; Knight (1926) and Commander (1940) of Order of St. Olav; vice-pres. Norw. Am. Hist. Assoc. 1939–42; pres. State Council of Minn. Colleges 1937–42.

Boecler, Otto Carl August (Nov. 3, 1875–Sept. 13, 1942). B. Memphis, Tenn.; grad. Conc. Sem., Saint Louis, 1898; pastor Ludington, Mich., 1898–1906; Grand Rapids, Mich., 1906–09; prof. Conc. Sem., Springfield, Ill., 1909–17; pastor Chicago 1917–25; prof. Conc. Sem., St. Louis, 1925–29; pastor Des Plaines, Ill., 1929–42. Author; managing ed. *Homiletic Magazine;* chm. Miss Bd. of Syn. Conf.; made miss. survey of Nigeria.

Boehm, Martin. See *United Brethren,* 1.

Boehne, John William (Oct. 28, 1856–Dec. 27, 1947). Manufacturer. B. Vanderburgh Co., Ind.; attended commercial coll.; Evansville councilman at large 1897–1901; mayor Evansville 1906–09; del. Dem. Nat. Conv., Denver, 1908; mem. 61st and 62d Congresses 1909–13; mem. Mo. Syn. Bd. of Dir.; helped organize Lutheran* Laymen's League.

Boethius, Anicius Manlius Torquatus Severinus (ca. 480–ca. 524). Christian statesman, writer, philosopher; influenced Theodoric toward benevolent rule; enemies at court brought about his downfall; sought to tr. Gk. classics into Lat. to assure their accessibility, a plan cut short by his early death; best-known work, *De consolatione philosophiae,* written while awaiting execution, develops theme that God is good and happiness consists in harmony with Him; wrote a short treatise on Trinity and a defense of Chalcedonian Christology. His 5 books *De musica* spell the end of antique musical science in the W world. With him, Cassiodorus, and Isidore of Seville began the medieval science of music. Idea that music constitutes a unit of mathematical science may be traced back to him. See also *Quadrivium.*

H. R. Patch, *The Tradition of Boethius: A Study of His Importance in Medieval Culture* (New York, 1935); first ed. of his works Venice 1492; *MPL,* 63, 64.

Bogatzky, Karl Heinrich von (1690–1774). B. Silesia. Studied law at Jena, then theol. at Halle under Francke. Poor health limited his activities to writing. Spent last 28 yrs. of life at Halle orphanage. Works include *Güldenes Schatz-Kästlein der Kinder Gottes* (Eng. title, *Golden Treasury*), *Meditations* (7 vols.), and the miss. hymn tr. into Eng. as "Awake, Thou Spirit Who Didst Fire."

Bogermann, Johannes (1576–1637). Exponent of strict Calvinism in Neth.; pastor Sneek 1599, Enkhuizen 1603, Leeuwarden 1604; chm. Syn. of Dort 1618–19; prof. Franeker 1636.

Bogomiles. Branch of Cathari,* numerous in 12th c. in Bulgaria and Constantinople; theol. a mixture of dualism and gnosticism; rejected Baptism and Lord's Supper; shunned chs. as seats of evil spirits; practiced much praying and strict asceticism. Survived severe persecutions. Found adherents in the W Ch.

Bogotá Theses. Four statements on the means of grace on which agreement was reached Oct. 1963 by pastors of Ev. Luth. Ch. – Colombia Syn., representatives of Caribbean Miss. Dist. of LCMS, LWF pastors of the Caribbean area, and 1 representative of the Mex. Luth. Church.

Noticiero de la Fe, XXIX, 3 (Dec. 1963), p. 20.

Bohairic Bible Version. See *Bible Versions,* D.

Bohatec, Josef (1876–1954). Ref. theol. in Hung. and Bohemia; exponent of neo-Calvinism. Did extensive research work on Calvin.

Bohemia. See *Czechoslovakia.*

Bohemia, Lutheran Theology in. 1. Movement inaugurated by Jan Hus* did not immediately issue in any definitive theol. formulation. In early yrs. the leader expressly directed the Bohemian* Brethren "to let the Law of God [the New Testament] suffice and believe it purely, forsaking all other writings." Thus, when Luther challenged authority of RC Ch., the Hussites were ready for a theol.

2. Luke* of Prague, bp. of the Brethren, was their doctrinal leader. His spiritualistic conception of Lord's Supper clashed with that of Luther, and until Luke's death the Brethren were torn between the two. In this connection Luther composed his treatise of 1523 "On the Adoration of the Sacrament." But when Luke died, the Luth. teaching prevailed among the Brethren, and after several consultations Luther expressed approval of their position.

3. The position was expressed in the confession of 1535. Despite differences in terminology and emphasis, it is strongly Luth., and from it we may date the half c. or so of official predominance of Luth. theol. in Boh. Protestantism. In doctrine of Lord's Supper the Brethren accepted the true presence of Christ but insisted on an interpretation of Christ's sitting on the right hand of the Father that differed from Luther's; they were also at variance with his view of Communion of the unworthy. But

Luther was willing to overlook these differences and in 1538 pub. the confession with his preface and endorsement. See also *Reformed Confessions,* E 3.

4. Meanwhile the Hussite* majority, the Utraquists, also experienced the impact of the Luth. Reformation. Most of them became Neo-Utraquists, i. e., Lutheran-minded. They expressed their new theol. position in the Boh. Confession of 1575, a combined confession of Neo-Utraquists and Boh. Brethren, seeking legal recognition from the king. He would give it only on the basis of a confession parallel to the AC. For this reason the Boh. Confession is not an accurate representation of the actual theol. situation among the Brethren at the time.

5. Alienated by both Philippism and Gnesio-Lutheranism and attracted by John Calvin's emphasis on discipline, the Brethren had begun to switch their theol. orientation from Wittenberg to Geneva. This can be seen in the thought and activity of their last bp., Comenius,* who quite consistently supported Ref. against Luth. theol.

Whatever chance there may have been for a rebirth of Luth. theol. in Boh. was crushed by the Battle of White Hill (1620) and the consequent victory of the Counter* Reformation. JP, MSF.

See also *Bohemian Brethren.*

G. Loesche, *Luther, Melanchthon und Calvin in Österreich-Ungarn* (Tübingen, 1909); E. Peschke, *Die Theologie der Böhmischen Brüder in ihrer Frühzeit,* I, 1–2 (Stuttgart, 1935–40).

Bohemia, Missions in. See *Czechoslovakia.*

Bohemian Brethren (Moravian Brethren). 1. The *Unitas Fratrum* (Union, or Unity of Brethren, usually referred to as Boh. Brethren), was founded 1457 in Boh. by men whose conscience could not find certainty of salvation in the Utraquist Ch., whose priests were giving the sacraments and thus "assurance of salvation" to anyone who requested them, regardless of any evidence of repentance. The Brethren had been influenced by the radical but pacifist Peter Chelcicky,* most original of Hussite* theologians. Following his ideas and those of Utraquist preacher John Rokycana, the Brethren left Prague to escape corruption of ch. and city life. They retired to a village under leadership of Gregory the Tailor and pastoral care of the strict local Utraquist priest. In 1467 they broke off from the Utraquist communion and est. their own ministry. Priests and bp. obtained their call through casting of lots and their "ratification" through laying on of hands by their local priest "authorized" by a Waldensian "senior." Group expanded by attracting other dissatisfied Utraquists and former Taborites (see *Hussites*). Priests were expected to live in apostolic poverty, to teach "in simplicity" according to "God's Law" (the NT), and to exercise strict pastoral discipline over their flock. Brethren were to avoid the "world" of secular offices, military service, and commerce. They lived in close fraternal community.

2. The 2d generation overthrew the old regime, feeling that the perfectionist expectations of the fathers overlooked God's grace and human realities. Secular offices, military service, and commerce were permitted and educ. encouraged. Above all, ch. discipline was modified, though still retained and emphasized. Lack of discipline in the early Luth. chs. prevented a *rapprochement* between Luke* of Prague, the Brethren's greatest theol., and Luther. But after Luke's death the Brethren became widely exposed to world Reformation currents, at first Lutheran (see also *Bohemia, Lutheran Theology in*), then Calvinist. A leader in the latter period was Jan Blahoslav.*

3. Brethren's excellent schools and tr. of the Bible, the Bible of Kralice, and rich hymnody were significant contribution to the wider Christian ch., including Luths. Their last bp., Comenius,* was pioneer of modern educ. The Counter* Reformation saw the suppression of the *Unitas* in Bohemia and its dissolution abroad. The Moravian* Church is a later attempt at a renewal of the *Unitas.* See also *Bohemia, Lutheran Theology in; Czechoslovakia; Moravian Church.*

P. Brock, *The Political and Social Doctrines of the Unity* (The Hague, 1957); M. S. Fousek, "The Perfectionism of the Early *Unitas Fratrum,*" *Church History,* XXX (Dec. 1961), 396–413. J. T. Mueller, *Geschichte der Brüderunität,* 3 vols. (Herrnhut, 1922–23); R. Rícan and A. Molnár, *Dejiny Jednoty bratrské* (Prague, 1957), tr. B. Popelár, *Die Böhmischen Brüder* (Berlin, 1961). MSF

Bohemian Confessions. See *Bohemia, Lutheran Theology in,* 3, 4; *Reformed Confessions,* E 2, 3.

Böhl, Eduard (1836–1903). B. Hamburg; prof. Ref. dogmatics Vienna.

Bohlin, Torsten Bernhard (1889–1950). Prof. systematic theol. Aabo 1925, Uppsala 1929; bp. Härnösand 1934. Wrote on Kierkegaard, Blaise Pascal, ethics, faith, and revelation.

Bohm, Edmund (Aug. 30, 1840–Dec. 24, 1895). B. Allstedt, Ger.; educ. Jena; to US 1868; active in N. Y. Ministerium; leader of educ. work of St. Matthew's Luth. Ch., NYC; joined Mo. Syn. and was ordained 1882; asst. pastor St. Matthew's Luth. Ch. 1882; dir. of the school that became Concordia* Coll., Bronxville, N. Y.

Böhm, Georg (1661–1733). Luth. composer of organ music; organist of the Johanniskirche, Lüneburg; influence on J. S. Bach is reflected in the latter's chorale partitas and *Orgelbüchlein.*

G. Frotscher, *Geschichte des Orgelspiels und der Orgelkomposition,* 2d ed. (Berlin, 1959); E. Valentin, "Georg Böhm," in *Die Musik in Geschichte und Gegenwart,* ed. F. Blume, II (Kassel, 1952), 11–15.

Böhme, Anton Wilhelm (1673–1722). Luth. theol.; educ. Halle; to Eng. 1701; court preacher of George of Den. and Anne and George I of Eng.; works include *The Duty of Reformation; The First Principles of Practical Christianity.*

Böhme, Jakob (1575–1624). Called *Philosophus teutonicus.* Ger. theosophist; mystic; shoemaker; b. near Görlitz; d. Görlitz. His theosophy attempts to explain origin of evil. God contains conflicting elements in His nature, harmoniously united; in the universe, which is an emanation of God, these conflicting elements separated, but can be harmoniously reunited through regeneration in Christ. Influenced Hegel, Schelling, and others. His influence spread to Eng., where a disciple, Jane Lead, founded the Philadelphians. Believed in Trinity, Incarnation, Atonement. Subscribed to Luth. Confessions shortly before death. Works include *Von den drei Prinzipien des göttlichen Wesens; Aurora oder die Morgenröte im Aufgang; Mysterium Magnum; Der Weg zu Christo.* See also *Theosophy.*

F. Hartmann, *The Personal Christianity: Doctrines of Jacob Boehme* (New York, 1957).

Böhmer, Arthur Heinrich (1869–1927). Prof. Bonn, Marburg, Leipzig; led studies in hist. of Reformation and life of Martin Luther; his *Der Junge Luther* tr. by J. W. Doberstein and T. G. Tappert as *Road to Reformation.*

Böhringer, Georg Friedrich (1812–79). B. Maulbronn; d. Basel. Ref. theol.; wrote *Die Kirche Christi und ihre Zeugen* (24 vols.).

Boileau-Despreaux, Nicolas (1636–1711). Fr. poet and art hist.; friend of A. Arnauld* and opponent of Jesuits.

Bois. 1. *Charles* (1826–91). Fr. Prot. theol.; prof. moral theol. and apologetics Montauban. See also *Reformed Confessions,* B. 2. *Henri* (1862–1924). Son of Charles. Prof. systematic theol. Montauban and Montpellier. Wrote on Christian certainty, life of Jesus, religious experience, and modern dogmatics. Ed. *Revue de Théologie.*

Boisgelin, Jean de Dieu Raymond de (1732–1804). Fr. RC bp. 1764, abp. 1770, cardinal 1803. Ultramontanist.

Boleyn, Anne. See *Parker, Matthew.*

Bolingbroke, Henry St. John (1678–1751). Eng. deist and statesman.

Bolivia. See *South America,* 3.

Bolland, Jean de (1596–1665). *B.* Julémont, near Liège; d. Antwerp. Jesuit; hagiographer, whose work was continued by Bollandists* after his death. Taught belles lettres at Ruremonde, Mechlin, Brussels, Antwerp; attached to Professed House of Antwerp as dir. of Lat. Cong. with assignment of preparing the *Acta* sanctorum* of H. Rosweyde* for pub. With co-workers Gottfried Henschen (ca. 1601—81) and Daniel Papebroch (1628–1714) extended Rosweyde's plan to include study of all materials and to print text with commentary. Work continued to present with interruption beginning 1794 (soc. reconstituted 1837; pub. resumed 1845).

Bollandists. Jesuit editors of *Acta Sanctorum;** named after Jean de Bolland.* The soc. publishes *Analecta Bollandiana* on hagiography.

Bolsec, Jérôme Hermès. See *Reformed Confessions,* A 9.

Bolshevism. See *Socialism and Communism,* 4.

Boltzius, Johann Martin (1703–65). Trained in Halle; selected with Israel Christian Gronau* to serve the persecuted Salzburgers and accompany them to Am.; pastor Ebenezer, Ga., from 1734 till his death; notable as preacher and pastor.

Bolzano, Bernhard (1781–1848). RC theol., philos., mathematician; prof. Prague 1805, deposed 1819. Held religion to be sum of all views which favor virtue or happiness. In ethics he combined virtue and happiness for the well-being of the whole. The function of logic is to present these *"Wahrheiten an sich."* Used a theory of uniform force *("sich gleichbleibende Kraftäusserung")* to demonstrate immortality and existence of God.

Bomberg, Daniel (ca. 1475–ca. 1549). Dutch printer of Hebrew books in Venice. Pub. first printed rabbinical Bible 1516–17, ed. Felix Pratensis.*

Bommelius, Henricus (Bomelius; Heinrich; Hendrick von Bommel; ca. 1500–70). Priest Utrecht 1522. Ev. preacher of lower Rhine. Pastor of Brethren of Common Life. Supported Wittenberg Concord; opposed views of later Lutherans. *Summa* (1st treatise on ethics of the Reformation) ascribed to him.

Bonaire. See *Caribbean Islands,* E 7.

Bonald, Louis Gabriel Ambroise de (1754–1840). Fr. viscount; philos.; defender of absolutism, papal infallibility, Jesuitism; held divine origin of language which, in his view, contains the essence of all truth.

Bonar, Horatius (1808–89). B. Edinburgh; ordained in the Est. Ch. of Scot. at Kelso 1837; joined Free Ch. of Scot. at its beginning 1843; pastor Chalmers Mem. Ch., Edinburgh, 1866. Hymnist; even before his ch. authorized hymn singing he pub. 7 tracts of hymns; wrote "I Heard the Voice of Jesus Say" and "I Lay My Sins on Jesus."

Bonaventura (1221–74). Called *Doctor seraphicus.* It. RC philos., cardinal, dogmatician, poet, mystic. Studied under Alexander of Hales; taught at Paris; gen. of Franciscans. Scholastic (realist); tried to prove that ch. doctrine agrees with reason; denied the doctrine of the immaculate conception of Mary. Works include *Speculum Mariae Virginis; Breviloquium.*

E. Bettoni, *Saint Bonaventure* (Notre Dame, Ind., 1964); J. G. Bougerol, *Introduction to the Works of Bonaventure* (Paterson, N. J., 1964).

Bond, Elias (d. July 24, 1896). B. Maine; educ. Bowdoin Coll. and Bangor Sem.; miss. to Hawaii; est. school for boys and girls at Kohala.

Bonhoeffer, Dietrich (1906–45). Ger. ev. theol.; studied under Harnack, Seeberg; also at Union Theol. Sem.; student pastor at technical high school and instr. at U. in Berlin; protested against *Deutsche Christen* (see *Barmen Theses*); accepted pastorate in London; Confessional Ch. (see *Kirchenkampf*) called him back to Ger. 1935 to lead the sem. at Finkenwalde (Pomerania); in US in summer of 1939 at invitation of R. Niebuhr; his activity in the opposition movement led to his imprisonment 1943; executed at Flossenbürg concentration camp. Tried to answer the question "Who is Christ?" in the ch. *(Communio Sanctorum),* in theologies of action and essence *(Act and Being),* in Biblical studies (*The Cost of Discipleship*), in the world (letters). His *Ethics* describes the Christian's conformation to Christ.

E. Bethge, *Dietrich Bonhoeffer: Gesammelte Schriften* (Munich, 1958–); J. D. Godsey, *The Theology of Dietrich Bonhoeffer* (Philadelphia, 1960); *The Place of Bonhoeffer,* ed M. E. Marty (New York, 1962).

Boniface (Winfrid; ca. 680–ca. 755). "Apostle of Germany." Eng. Benedictine miss. After a short stay in Friesland, commissioned 718 by pope as miss. to cen. Ger.; later made bp. Founded chs. in Hesse and Thuringia; est. sees and monasteries; expelled anti-RC Culdees. Est. 4 sees in Bavaria, but did not overcome anti-RC influence of Culdees. Called by Carloman and Pepin to regulate affairs of Frankish Ch.; had synods pass measures on introd. Roman laws, doctrines, and customs, extirpation of remnants of heathenism, and the "reformation" of the ch. Despite clergy opposition, the Ger. Nat. Council declared for submission to papal authority and expulsion of married clergy 742. Most bps. acknowledged papal supremacy 747; pope gave Boniface, "pillar of papal hierarchy," the see of Mainz. Founded Fulda monastery 744. In 754 resigned office in Mainz to continue work in Friesland, where met death at hands of heathen. See also *Germany* A 1; *Symbolism, Christian,* 4–5.

G. W. Greenaway, *Saint Boniface* (London, 1956); E. S. Duckett, *Anglo-Saxon Saints and Scholars* (New York, 1947), pp. 339–455; *Opera omnia,* ed. J. A. Giles, 2 vols. (London, 1844); *MPL,* 89, 597 to 892.

Boniface VIII. See *Popes,* 12.

Boniface, IX. See *Schism,* 8.

Bonnet, Charles (1720–93). Swiss naturalist and philos. Lawyer by profession; natural science his favorite pursuit; credited with discovery of parthenogenesis in aphids. Held doctrine of preexistent germs or particles created by Divine Being with inherent power for self-development in *Considérations sur les corps organises.* In *Palingénésie* taught immortality of all forms of existence. World is harmony directed by divine reason. Preformations of creation evolve to perfection. Organic life is a unity. Revelation is necessary. Christ taught resurrection and immortality.

Bonnivard, Francois de (ca. 1493–1570). Swiss reformer, politician; humanistic rather than Calvinistic. Imprisoned by Duke Charles of Savoy; hero of Byron's *Prisoner of Chillon.*

Bonnus, Hermann (1504–48). Low Ger. reformer, hymnist. Studied under Luther and Melanchthon. Friend of Bugenhagen and Hoeck. Ed. and revised several collections of Ger. and Lat. hymns.

Bonosians. Followers of bp. Bonosus (4th c.), who denied perpetual virginity of Mary.

Bonsen, Leopold Eberhard (1699–1788). Co-rector, rector, supt. of school at Montbéliard. Exponent of strict Luth. orthodoxy.

Bonwetsch, Gottlieb Nathanael (1848–1925). B.

Norka, Russ.; d. Göttingen. Prof. ch. hist. Dorpat, 1882, Göttingen 1891. Wrote in area of patristics and Russ. ch. Specialized in hist. of dogma in early ch. Prepared eds. and commentaries of Methodius of Olympus and Hippolytus. See also *Tschackert, Paul Moritz Robert.*

Book of Adam and Eve. See *Apocrypha,* A 4.

Book of Changes. See *Confucianism,* 2.

Book of Common Order. See *Presbyterian Churches,* 1.

Book of Common Prayer. 1. Official service book of the Ch. of Eng. and (with nat. variations) of the Angl. Communion. Contains all public rites and services of the Angl. Ch., including Morning Prayer, Evening Prayer, Communion, Baptism, Confirmation, Marriage, Burial, Psalter, ordination and consecration orders, 39 *Articles of Religion.*

2. The First Prayer Book of Edward VI, largely the work of Cranmer,* was confirmed by Parliament and made obligatory for all Eng. chs. through the Act of Uniformity 1549. Much of it was tr. from the Sarum* Rite (Salisbury). The first Prayer Book was also significantly influenced by the *Consultation,* a Ger. ch. order composed mostly by P. Melanchthon* and M. Bucer* and pub. by H. von Wied,* reforming abp. of Cologne.

3. After 1549 some extreme reformers became much more influential in Eng. As a result there was more agitation for a completely rev. Prayer Book. The Second Prayer Book of Edward VI appeared 1552. This rev., esp. influenced by the Swiss Reformation, was a radical departure from the 1549 ed.

4. In 1559, after the death of RC Queen Mary, Queen Elizabeth* restored the Prayer Book of 1552, with several significant conservative changes. This was the Third Prayer Book. In 1604 a Fourth Prayer Book appeared with only minor changes. The Fifth Prayer Book (1662), a rather thorough conservative rev., became the version still used in Eng.

The first American Prayer Book was issued 1789 by the first Gen. Conv. of the Prot. Episc. Ch., Philadelphia. In this version, suited to the Am. situation, one of the more significant changes from the Eng. version was the adoption of the Prayer of Consecration from the Scot. communion service. But the 1789 ed. differed in many respects from the Eng. version because of the influence of liberal elements in the Am. ch.

A thorough revision of the Am. version was made and adopted 1892. Changes in this version brought it into closer harmony with the Eng. ed. of 1662 and earlier versions. The Prayer Book now in use in US is the rev. of 1928. EFP

See also *Presbyterian Confessions,* 4.

M. H. Shepherd, Jr., *The Oxford American Prayer Book Commentary* (New York, 1950); W. K. L. Clarke and C. Harris, *Liturgy and Worship: A Companion to the Prayer Books of the Anglican Communion* (New York, 1932); *Ritual Notes* (London, 1956); E. Daniel, *The Prayer-Book: Its History, Language, and Contents* (London, 1889); F. Procter and W. H. Frere, *History of the Book of Common Prayer,* rev. and rewritten by W. H. Frere, new ed. (New York, 1915); J. W. Suter and G. J. Cleaveland, *The American Book of Common Prayer: Its Origin and Development* (New York, 1949); *The Annotated Book of Common Prayer,* ed. J. H. Blunt (London, 1895); E. L. Parsons and B. H. Jones, *The American Prayer Book: Its Origins and Principles* (New York, 1937); *The Tutorial Prayer Book,* eds. C. Neil and J. M. Willoughby (London, 1959); *The Two Liturgies, A. D. 1549, and A.D. 1552: with Other Documents Set Forth by Authority in the Reign of King Edward VI,* ed. J. Ketley (Cambridge, Eng., 1844); L. Pullan, *History of the Book of Common Prayer* (London, 1901).

Book of Concord *(Concordia).* Contains the Conf. Writings of the Luth. Ch., her Symbolical Books: the 3 Ecumenical Creeds (Apostles', Nicene, Athanasian); Unaltered AC 1530; its Apology; Luther's SC and LC; SA; Treatise on Authority and Primacy of the Pope; FC. J. Andreä's Ger. ed. appeared officially June 25, 1580, 50 yrs. after the presentation of the AC; the Lat. ed. appeared 1584.

For further information and important editions see *Lutheran Confessions* (esp. bibliography).

Book of Confutation. See *Konfutationsbuch.*

Book of History. See *Confucianism,* 2.

Book of Hours. Book containing offices or prayers appointed for canonical hours.*

Book of Mormon. See *Latter Day Saints.*

Book of Rites. See *Confucianism,* 2.

Book of Roots. See *Lexicons,* A.

Book of Rules and Order. See *Evangelical Church,* 3.

Book of Songs. See *Confucianism,* 2.

Book of the Dead. Collection of ca. 150 Egyptian spells intended to guide the soul in the next world and insure the safety and welfare of the deceased. See also *Negative Confession,* 1.

Books of Discipline. See *Discipline, Books of.*

Books of Homilies. Two books of homilies pub. in 16th-c. Eng. Written by T. Cranmer* and others to encourage ev. preaching.

Boone, William Jones (July 1, 1811–July 17, 1864). Born S. C.; d. Shanghai; educ. U. of S. C. and the Prot. Episc. Sem., Alexandria, Va. Medical miss. China 1837; bp. China 1844; mem. of committee which rev. Bible tr.

Boos, Martin (1762–1825). B. Huttenried, Bavaria. RC priest; experiences in asceticism resembled those of Luther; preached a doctrine of salvation by faith resembling that of Luther. Chaplain 1787. Driven out of Bavaria by ch. authorities; lived in Austria 1799–1816; forced to leave; returned to Bavaria; prof. Düsseldorf 1817; pastor Sayn 1819.

Booth, Ballington. See *Volunteers of America.*

Booth, William. See *Salvation Army,* 1.

Boquin, Peter (d. 1582). Prior Carmelite monastery, Bourges; embraced ev. faith; fled to Basel, Leipzig, and Wittenberg 1541. Taught at Strasbourg, Bourges, and Heidelberg. Inclined more and more to Reformed view. One of the writers of the Heidelberg Cat.

Bora, Katharina von. See *Luther, Family Life of.*

Boris (d. 1015). He and his brother Gleb, sons of Vladimir* I, were early Russ. saints.

Boris I (d. 907). First Christian ruler of Bulgaria ca. 853–889; converted to Christianity 865; accepted primacy of Rome; decided for Byzantine Ch. at Council of Constantinople 870; abdicated, retired to monastery 889; reckoned a saint by Orthodox Ch.

Bornemann, Friedrich Wilhelm Bernhard (1858 to 1946). Prof. Basel 1898; pastor Frankfort 1902; prof. Frankfort 1922. Works include *Die Thessalonicherbriefe; Historische und praktische Theologie.*

Borneo, North. See *Malaysia,* 5.

Borneo, West. See *Indonesia,* 5.

Bornholmers. 19th-c. Dan. Pietist sect on is. of Bornholm; founded by P. C. Trandberg.*

Borowski, Ernst Ludwig von (1740–1831). Ev. court preacher of Frederick William III 1815; bp. 1816; abp. 1829. Helped form Prussian Union. First biographer of Kant.

Börresen, Hans Peter (1825–1901). B. Den.; to Berlin 1852; civil engineer; persuaded by his wife Caroline (nee Hempel) to become a miss.; arrived India 1865; founded Santal miss. with L. O. Skrefsrud.* See also *Norwegian Foreign Missions,* 3.

Borrhaus, Martin (Cellarius; 1499–1564). Studied under Eck; friend of Melanchthon; won for Reformation by Luther's *On the Liberty of a Christian Man;* wrote against Anabaps. but finally joined Zwickau prophets; later gave up enthusiasm; to Basel; prof. rhetoric 1536, theol. 1544.

Borromeo, Carlo (1538–84). B. Arona; studied law

at Pavia; turned to theol. on accession of his uncle, Pius IV; cardinal and abp. Milan 1560; prominent at Council of Trent; founded seminaries for clergy; canonized 1610.

Borsippa. See *Babylonians, Religion of,* 1.

Borthwick, Jane Laurie (1813–97). B. Edinburgh, Scot. Hymn writer and tr. Many of her original hymns pub. in *Thoughts for Thoughtful Hours.* She and her sister, Sarah Findlater, pub. their first translations in *Hymns from the Land of Luther.* Some of her translations have been included in many hymnals pub. in Eng. and Am. Her translations include Hallelujah! Jesus Lives"; "Jesus, Lead Thou On"; "Be Still, My Soul."

Bortnyanski, Dmitri Stephanovich (ca. 1751–1825). "Father of Russ. ch. music," though his compositions are It. rather than Russ. in character. Catharine the Great sent him to It. (Venice, Rome, Naples) for training, that he might return to reform Russ. ch. music. After 11 yrs. in It. he returned and gave himself to the assigned task. Not a few of his compositions have been sung in Luth. and other Prot. chs.

Bosanquet, Bernard (1848–1923). Brit. absolute idealist; prof. St. Andrews 1903–08. Held that in finite existence there are only degrees of individuality and value which point to completion in the Absolute. Works include *The Principle of Individuality and Value; The Value and Destiny of the Individual; What Religion Is.*

Bosco, John. See *Salesians.*

Bosio, Antonio (ca. 1575–1629). It. archaeologist. "The Columbus of the Catacombs." Wrote *Roma sotterranea cristiana,* which laid basis for study of Christian antiquities.

Boso of Regensburg (d. 970). Miss. to Slavs; bp. Merseburg 968.

Bosse, Benjamin (Nov. 1, 1874–Apr. 4, 1922). B. Scott Twp., Ind.; manufacturer and banker; mayor Evansville; prominent in LLL; mem. Mo. Synod's Bd. of Control and Bd. of Dir.

Bossuet, Jacques Bénigne (1627–1704). Fr. RC prelate; canon, priest, and archdeacon Metz; bp. Meaux; tutor of dauphin of Fr. for some yrs. Noted controversialist against Fénelon* and separatists among Romanists. His 6 *Funeral Orations* rank high in the oratory of his ch. See also *Roman Catholic Confessions,* A 3.

Bost, Paul Ami Isaac David (1790–1874). Pastor Geneva; exponent of Enlightenment.* Miss. under auspices of London Continental Soc. for ca. 35 yrs. Hymnist. Works include revision and tr. into Fr. of C. G. Blumhardt's *Versuch einer allgemeinen Missionsgeschichte der Kirche Christi.*

Boston, Declaration of Synod of. See *Democratic Declarations of Faith,* 2.

Boston, National Council of. See *Democratic Declarations of Faith,* 2.

Botswana. See *Africa,* B 3.

Botticelli, Sandro (ca. 1444–1510). It. painter; pupil of Fra Filippo Lippi; assisted in decorating Sistine Chapel; after 1497 follower of G. Savonarola.*

Bottome, Margaret. See *King's Daughters.*

Bouck, William C. (Jan. 7, 1786–Apr. 19, 1859). B. Fulton, Schoharie Co., N. Y.; elected 4 times to Assembly of N. Y.; state senator; finished difficult section of Erie Canal; built 5 other canals; gov. N. Y. 1842; Asst. Treas. US; participated in councils of N. Y. Ministerium.

Boudinot, Elias (1740–1821). Am. lawyer, philanthropist, statesman, author. 'First pres. ABS. Works include *The Age of Revelation* (reply to T. Paine*); *The Second Advent; A Star in the West* (sets forth the view that the Am. Indians are the 10 lost tribes of Israel).

Bouglé, Célestin Charles Alfred (1870–1940). Fr. scholar; held religion responsible for caste system in India; held that morality cannot be satisfactory as long as it depends on religion.

Boulogne, Edict of. See *France,* 9.

Bourdaloue, Louis (1632–1704). Often called founder of Fr. eloquence, Voltaire ranking him above Bossuet; entered Jesuit order at 16; occupied chairs of rhetoric, philos., and moral theol.; known for piety and honesty.

Bourges, Pragmatic Sanction of. See *Pragmatic Sanction.*

Bourignon, Antoinette (1616–80). Quietist who gathered followers in Neth., Fr., and Scot.; convent life and efforts at orphans' work failures due to distrust of human nature; attacked religious organizations of every type; denied divine foreknowledge, atonement, need of Scriptures. See also Poiret, Pierre.

Bousset, Johann Franz Wilhelm (1865–1920). B. Lübeck; d. Giessen; prof. NT exegesis Göttingen 1896, Giessen 1916. Prot. theol. of *Religionsgeschichtliche* Schule.* Works include *Hauptprobleme der Gnosis; Religion des Judentums im neutestamentlichen Zeitalter;* various studies on the Antichrist.

Boutroux, Étienne Émile Marie (1845–1921). Fr. philos.; prof. Sorbonne. Denied omnipotence of causality. Science deals with only part of reality. There is in reality "a certain degree of contingency"; science deals with selected data but reason must consider the wholeness of things in their quality, value, and significance for life and include spiritual interpretation. Works include *On the Contingency of the Laws of Nature; Natural Law; Science and Religion in Contemporary Philosophy.*

Bovon, Jules (1852–1904). Ref. theol.; educ. Lausanne and Berlin; prof. NT on theol. faculty Lausanne. Described God in twofold aspect: incomprehensible in work of creation and preservation, comprehensible in relation to spiritual life.

Bowen, George (Apr. 30,1916–Feb. 5, 1888). B. Middleburn, Vt.; educ. Union Theol. Sem. Sent by ABCFM to India 1847; stationed at Bombay; supported himself; secy. Bombay Tract Soc. and ed. Bombay *Guardian.* Excerpts of writings pub. in 3 vols.

Bowne, Borden Parker (1847-1910). Am. Meth. philos. Educ. New York, Halle, Göttingen, Paris; prof. philos. Boston. Formulated philos. of personalism.* The real is that which acts or can be acted on, namely person. God is the supreme Person, active and creative. Works include *Metaphysics; The Principles of Ethics; Theism; Personalism; The Essence of Religion.*

Bowring, John (1792–1872). B. Exeter. Eng. statesman, linguist, hymnist; Unitarian. Said to have acquired mastery of 200 languages and dialects and speaking knowledge of 100. Served in various govt. positions at home and abroad. Writings pub. in 36 vols. Hymns include "In the Cross of Christ I Glory" and "Watchman, Tell Us of the Night."

Boxer Uprising. See *China,* 7.

Boy Scouts. First organized 1908 in Eng. by Robert Stephenson Smyth (1857–1941), 1st Baron Baden-Powell of Gilwell. Introduced into US 1910. According to charter granted by Congress 1916, the purpose of the organization is to "promote, through organization and cooperation with other agencies, the ability of boys to do things for themselves and others, to train them in Scoutcraft, and to teach them patriotism, courage, self-reliance, and kindred virtues, using the methods which are now in common use by Boy Scouts," by emphasizing the Scout Oath or Promise and Law for character development, citizenship training, and physical fitness. Stress is also laid on the effort made by the organization to further love for outdoor life; for this purpose so-called hikes are made, and some time is spent in summer camps. Such outdoor life is also intended to contribute to health and practical educ.

The Scout Law, to which obedience must be promised, says that the scout must be trustworthy, loyal, helpful, friendly, courteous, obedient, cheerful, thrifty, brave, clean, and reverent. Scouts are required to "do a good turn daily." The scout idea is to instill in the boy love and duty to God, home, and country.

In its initial stages, scouting could be charged with possessing a religious character but refraining from the use of the Christian Gospel for the building up of a God-pleasing character; that is to say, with trying to serve God without a true regeneration of the heart and without being guided by the principles of Holy Scripture. The position on religion was later clarified and modified. The organization does maintain that "no boy can grow into the best kind of citizenship without recognizing his obligation to God. . . . The recognition of God as the ruling and leading power in the universe and the grateful acknowledgment of His favors and blessings are necessary to the best type of citizenship, and wholesome precepts in the education of the growing boy." However, while recognizing the religious element in the training of the boy, scouting refrains from giving religious training or even announcing a program of such training but assigns to the church whatever spiritual guidance and religious instruction the boy is to receive. The official stand of the scout movement towards religious and moral training is defined as follows: Whatever scouting has to say about religion refers to "civil righteousness" – termed "character building and citizenship training," "good citizenship through service." The oath: "The Boy Scout 'Pledge' is a promise, not an oath in the Scriptural sense of the term. The upraised hand, with three fingers extended, has reference to the threefold pledge, not to the Trinity." (*Scouting in the Lutheran Church,* pub. 1943 by Boy Scouts of America.)

"We recognize that there is no Boy Scout authority which supersedes the authority of the local Pastor and the Congregation in any phase of the program affecting the spiritual welfare of Lutheran men and boys in Scouting." (Elbert Fretwell, chief Scout executive)

Various committees of the Mo. Syn. at different times made reports on their dealings with scout authorities and this led to a resolution approving the committee's report in 1944: "Your Committee believes that the matter of scouting should be left to the individual congregation to decide and that under the circumstances Synod may consider her interests sufficiently protected." *(Proceedings of the Thirty-ninth Regular Convention of the Ev. Lutheran Synod of Missouri, Ohio, and Other States* [St. Louis, 1944] p. 257) TG

Boyce, William (1710–79). Eng. master of ch. music; compositions for organ and choir enjoy wide use esp. in Angl. circles.

Boyle, Robert (1627–91). B. Ireland; educ. Eng.; devoted to science (Boyle's Law) and theol.; founded Boyle Lectures, 8 lectures delivered annually in London against unbelievers. See also *Society for Advancing the Christian Faith in the British West India Islands.*

Bradford, John (ca. 1510–55). Prot. martyr. B. Manchester, Eng.; prebendary St. Paul's; chaplain to Edward VI; popular preacher; burned at Smithfield; wrote many short works.

Bradford, William (1590–1657). Leader of Pilgrim Fathers. See also *United Church of Christ,* I A 1.

Bradlaugh, Charles (1833–91). Brit. atheist; soc. and pol. reformer. Ed. and pub. *National Reformer* in defense of freethinking; prosecuted 1876 with Annie Besant* for repub. Malthusian *Fruits of Philosophy* but won case; elected mem. of Parliament but not seated till 1886 (first because he refused to take oath and later forbidden); promoted soc. and pol. reform in India; developed secularism* into atheism.

Bradley, Dan Beach (July 18, 1804–June 23, 1893). B. Marcellus, N. Y.; d. Bangkok; pioneer med. miss. to Thailand (formerly Siam); sent by ABCFM 1834; ordained 1838; returned to US 1847; sent out again 1849 by Am. Miss. Assoc.; tr. portions of Bible and wrote extensively in Eng. and Siamese.

Bradley, Francis Herbert (1846–1924). Brit. philos.; in *Ethical Studies* held that man must first find himself as a whole and then bring himself in line with the universe; in *Appearance and Reality* held that ultimate fact is experience which is unity with the perceived; but since absolute spirit is beyond finite minds, judgments err.

Bradwardine, Thomas (ca. 1290–1349). Called *Doctor Profundus;* lecturer at Oxford; fearless confessor to Edward III; abp. Canterbury 1349; his *De causa Dei contra Pelagium* prepared Wycliffe for his work.

Brady Nicholas. See *Psalter, English.*

Braeuninger, Moritz (Dec. 2, 1836–1860). B. Crimmitschau, Saxony. Trained by Löhe; sent to Am.; studied at Wartburg Sem., St. Sebald (later Dubuque), Iowa; miss. to Indians; spent 2 months with J. J. Schmidt in camp of Crow Indians near Fort Sarpy, Mont., 1858; again left St. Sebald July 5, 1859, with other missionaries to work among Indians; erected station on Powder River (E Oregon) 1860. According to report, shot by one of a group of Indians with whom he was last seen July 22, 1860.

Brahma. See *Brahmanism,* 2; *Hinduism,* 4.

Brahma Samaj. See *Hinduism,* 6; *Ram Mohan Roy.*

Brahman. See *Brahmanism; Hinduism,* 4.

Brahmanas. Prose ritualistic writings (legends, hist. records, hymns, and rituals) which arose ca. 800 BC from oral traditions regarding particular East Indian Vedas*; explained and interpreted the relations of sacred text and ceremonial; added symbolical meanings. See also *Brahmanism; Hinduism.*

Brahmanism. 1. The religion of the Brahmans, the priestly caste in India, esp. one stage in its development. Though the terms Brahmanism and Hinduism* are sometimes used interchangeably to denote the entire development of orthodox religious thought in India, beginning with the period that follows the composition of the Rig-Veda (see *Veda*) down to modern times, the term Brahmanism is today often applied to the period following ancient Vedic Hinduism, when the Brahmanas* with their ceremonialism were much in evidence.

2. *The Vedic Period.* The earliest religion of the Aryan invaders of India, as we find it portrayed in the Rig-Veda, was of a polytheistic nature, particularly in the popular mind. But the Rig-Veda, most ancient sacred book of the Hindus, also shows remains of an earlier monotheism similar to that found in many ethnologically ancient peoples. This is strikingly brought out in the Rig-Veda creation hymn X. lxxxii. 1-3 and X. cxxi. 1-5 with its similarities to Gn 1 and 2. According to one authority, in the Rig-Veda the god Varuna (Gk. *ouranos*), the sky that covers all, is already on the wane and boisterous Indra, the sky that rains (thundergod), is in the ascendancy. Dyu or Dyaus Pitar, "Father Heaven," the sky that shines, has often been related to Greek *Zeus Pater,* Latin *Iuppiter* (Diespiter), Teutonic *Tiu,* and German *Zio.* Prithivi Matar, his wife, is "Mother Earth." Agni (Lat. *ignis*) is the fire god. Soma, originally an intoxicating drink used for libations, is the god to whom all the hymns of one book of the Rig-Veda are addressed. Aditi is the limitless sky and her sons the Adityas are the suns of the different months of the year. In time many new gods were added and there was considerable overlapping of functions. Vishnu, originally the sun crossing the sky in 3 steps (rising, zenith, setting) grew in importance in a later period. In all

the Vedas (the Rig-Veda, Sama-Veda, the two Yajur-Vedas, and the Arthava-Veda) mystical and symbolical terms abound. A creator-god may appear as Purusha, Visvakarman, Hiranyagarbha, Brahma, or Prajapati. The Vedic gods, with the exception of Rudra, storm-god (later Siva, the destroyer), were beneficent. Sacrifices of food, esp. of melted butter and soma, were made to them. Their help was implored against the multitudes of demons and evil spirits, which were believed to cause disease and misfortune of all kinds. The Vedic eschatology included belief in heaven and hell, to which, at death, the good and the evildoers pass respectively.

3. *Brahmanism Proper.* In earliest times there were neither temples nor holy places nor priests. But toward the end of the Vedic period and with the advent of the Brahmanas* a priesthood developed. The Brahman (or Brahmin) priests interpreted the sacred writings, gained priestly power, and (it is generally believed) introduced and supported the caste system as the Aryans moved southward. Formerly the Aryan invaders had occupied only the northwestern part of India, the Punjab, or "five-river" country. The mixture of Aryans and darker-skinned aborigines brought with it the beginning of the caste system, a prominent feature in Hinduism. The traditional four castes: Brahman, or priestly caste, which became socially supreme; Kshatriya, or warrior caste; Vaisya, or agricultural caste; Sudra, or servile caste. The prominence now given to the idea of an impersonal deity marks the end of the Vedic period of Indian religious development and the beginning of Brahmanism. During the period that followed, the main features of the Vedic religion were retained, essentially the same gods were worshiped, and the Veda was regarded as a divine revelation; but the Brahmans gained ever greater importance, until they were regarded as "gods on earth." The priestly speculation which marks this period was a reaction against the numerous sacrifices, and to some extent against the ritual, which had become a burden. The essential feature of this speculation, which was philos. rather than religious, was the belief in an eternal, unchangeable principle, or world soul. This principle, called Brahman or Atman (i. e., "Self"), lies at the basis of the universe, and all beings are manifestations of it. Man emanated from it and eventually returns to it. During this period the doctrine of the transmigration* of souls was also developed and found expression in the Upanishads,* the 3d group of sacred Indian texts. According to this doctrine a man is reincarnated immediately at death, and the deeds in his previous existence determine the character of his rebirth. He is reincarnated in a higher state if his previous deeds are good, but in a lower state, even in animal form, as that of a pig, ass, etc., if his previous deeds are evil. As rebirth means continued suffering, the great aim is to be released from rebirth. But it is desire that leads to rebirth, therefore all desire must be abolished. To abolish all desires that fetter the soul to the world and to become one with Brahman-Atman is the great object of human endeavor. This final union with the infinite is called *moksha,* salvation.

4. Six major systems of Brahmanic philos. were developed, which are based on the Upanishads and are considered orthodox. Each taught its own way of salvation, i. e., how to be released from rebirth. They are Sankhya, Yoga, Nyaya, Vaisheshika, Mimamsa, and Vedanta. The Sankhya is atheistic and dualistic. It teaches that on the one hand there is the soul (or an infinite plurality of individual souls), on the other, matter. Release from rebirth comes to him who recognizes the absolute distinction between these two. The Vedanta, the most important system, appears in various schools of interpretation. It teaches the identity of the ego with the infinite, unchangeable Brahman. He alone exists; the multiplicity of phenomena is an illusion. He who attains this knowledge has *moksha* (release from rebirth and merging with the universal soul). Vaisheshika (atomic philosophy), Mimamsa (return to Vedic rites), and Nyaya (logic) are minor systems. Followers of Charvaka denied the authority of the Vedas,* considered soul merely intelligence in the body, and considered pleasure the highest good. For later religious development in India see *Hinduism.*

R. C. Dutt, *The Civilization of India* (London, 1900); J. N. Farquhar, *A Primer of Hinduism* (New York, 1914); A. A. Macdonell, *A History of Sanskrit Literature* (New York, 1929); D. S. Sarma, *What Is Hinduism?* (Madras, 1945); J. T. Wheeler, *Ancient and Hindu India* (Calcutta, 1961). AJB

Brahmo Samaj. See *Hinduism,* 6; *Rasn Mohan Roy.*

Brahms, Johannes (1833–97). With Bach and Beethoven, one of the 3 great B's of the music world. Lived at close of Romantic Era; did not fall under spell of such Romanticists as von Weber, Chopin, Berlioz, Wagner, Liszt; composed in style of classical masters; studied music of Bach assiduously; enriched classical idiom with new type of lyricism, originality, and rhythm; produced such gigantic works as his 4 symphonies, 2 piano concertos, his violin concerto, 3 string quartets, and other outstanding literature. Was a freethinker. Though his *Ein deutsches Requiem* is a great masterpiece of concert music, it was not meant to be a Luth. work. When selecting Bible texts for this work, Brahms avoided every passage which mentioned Christ by name (Ger. text); translations have not always reflected the composer's determination to refrain from using the word "Christ."

A. Einstein, *Greatness in Music,* tr. César Saerchinger (New York, 1941) and *Music in the Romantic Era* (New York, 1947); K. Geiringer, *Brahms: His Life and Work,* tr. H. B. Weiner and Bernard Miall (New York, 1936); W. Niemann, *Brahms,* tr. C. Phillips (New York, 1929); H. Gal, *Johannes Brahms,* tr. J. Stein (New York, 1963).

Braille. See *Blind.*

Brainerd. 1. *David* (Apr. 20, 1718–Oct. 9, 1747). B. Haddam, Conn.; friend of and missionary to Indians. Commissioned by Soc. in Scot. for Propagating Christian Knowledge (see *Bible Societies,* 3) to work among Indians near Stockbridge, Mass., but chief work was among Indians of Delawer River basin. Memoirs, pub. under titles *Mirabilia Dei inter Indicos and Divine Grace Displayed,* influenced later missionaries including Henry Martyn and Wm. Carey. 2. *John* (1720–81). Brother of David; miss. among Indians.

Brakel, Dirk Gerryts (Theodori à; 1608–69). Dutch Ref. theol.; mystical pietistic writings influenced Ger. Pietism.

Bramante (Lazzari; Donato d'Agnolo or d'Angelo; 1444–1514). It. architect; planned and executed buildings connecting Belvedere and Vatican; plans for reconstruction of St. Peter's carried out only in part.

Bramhall, John (1594–1663). Angl. prelate Ulster; bp. Derry 1634; abp. Armagh 1661 (vacant since Ussher's death). Opposed Hobbes on freedom of will.

Brand, Frederick (Sept. 9, 1863–Jan. 1, 1949). Son of Peter Brand. Grad. Conc. Sem., St. Louis, 1886; pastor Braddock, Pa., 1886–93; Pittsburgh, Pa., 1893 to 1903; Springfield, Ill., 1903–20; pres. Cen. Ill. Dist., Mo. Syn., 1907–17; vice-pres. Mo. Syn. 1917 to 1929; Dir. For. Miss. 1920; visited China and India 1921–22, China 1926; wrote *Foreign Missions in China.*

Brand, Peter (Nov. 3, 1839–Jan. 11, 1918). B. Ansbach; educ. Cologne and Neuendettelsau; to Am. 1857; miss. St. Clair, Mich. (Iowa Syn.); pastor Eden Valley, Farnham, and Buffalo, N. Y. (Buffalo Syn.); opposed Grabau on doctrine of ch.; one of the commissioners at the Buffalo "Colloquium" 1866; pastor Washington, D. C. (Mo. Syn.) 1869; Pittsburgh, Pa. (Ohio Syn.) 1876. In protest against stand of Ohio Syn. on doctrines of election and conversion, he and his congregation left Ohio Syn. and helped form Conc. Syn.; later joined Mo. Syn. Pres. Conc. Syn.; pres. E Dist., Mo. Syn., 1888; vice-pres. Mo. Syn. 1899; mem. of its Bd. for For. Miss.

W. Bröcker, "Pastor P. Brand," *Lutheraner,* LXXIV (Feb. 26, 1918), 75–77.

Brandelle, Gustaf Albert (Mar. 19, 1861–Jan. 16, 1936). Educ. Augustana Coll. and Theol. Sem., Rock Island, Ill.; grad. and ordained 1884; pastor Denver, Colo., 1884–1918, Rock Island, Ill., 1918 to 1923; pres. Ev. Luth. Aug. Syn. 1918–35; pres. em.; pres. NLC 8 yrs.; mem. Bd. of Miss., Aug. Syn.; ed. *Augustana Journal* 1897–1906; delegate LWC Eisenach 1923, Copenhagen 1925.

Brandrud, Andreas (1868–1958). Prof. ch. hist. Oslo. Works include *Kirkens historie.*

Brandt, Christian Philip Heinrich (1790–1857). Luth. pastor Bavaria; defended orthodox faith against rationalism, esp. that of Gustav Friedrich Dinter; active in home miss.; wrote *Schullehrer-Bibel;* ed. *Homiletisch-Liturgisches Korrespondenzblatt.*

Brandt, Nils Olsen (Jan. 29, 1824–1921). B. Norw.; grad. U. of Norway, Christiania; ordained 1851; to Am. 1851; pastor Wis., Minn., and Decorah, Iowa, 1851–82 (resigned); taught language and religion at Luther Coll., Decorah, Iowa, beginning 1865; helped organize Norw. Syn. 1853; its vice-pres. 1857–71; coed. *Kirketidende* beginning 1869.

Brandt, Olaf Elias (Feb. 19, 1862–Feb. 20, 1940). Son of N. O. Brandt; b. near Oconomowoc, Wis.; grad. Luther Coll., Decorah, Iowa, 1879; Northwestern Coll., Watertown, Wis., 1880; Conc. Sem., St. Louis, 1883; U. of Leipzig 1897. Pastor Cleveland, Ohio, 1883–92, Chicago 1892–96, Minneapolis 1905–11; prof. Luther Sem., St. Paul, Minn., 1897 to 1936; assoc. ed. *Kirketidende* 1897–1902; Commander Order of St. Olav 1924; mem. Norw. Syn. and Norwegian Lutheran Church of America.

Brant, Sebastian (ca. 1458–1521). Prof. jurisprudence Basel; city clerk for Strasbourg; humanist and reformer of morals; most famous work: *Das Narrenschiff* 1494, satire on vices and foibles of age, culturally and poetically most significant, source of Alexander Barclay's *The Shyp of Folys (The Ship of Fools).*

Brastberger, Immanuel Gottlob (1716—64). *Spezialsuperintendent* Nürtingen; 85th ed. sermons on Gospels, *Evangelische Zeugnisse der Wahrheit,* Reutlingen 1883.

Bratt, Torbjörn Olafssön. See *Norway, Lutheranism in,* 2.

Brauer, August G. (May 20, 1857–Sept. 26, 1932). B. Pittsburgh, Pa.; d. St. Louis, Mo.; son of E. A. Brauer; manufacturer; attended the Luth. high school which later became Walther Coll., St. Louis; mem. Bd. of Control, Conc. Sem., St. Louis, 1893 to 1932; secy. LLL 1917–32.

Brauer, Ernst August (Apr. 19, 1819–Sept. 29, 1896). B. Northeim, Hannover; studied theol. Göttingen and Berlin. Moved by appeal of Wyneken, and on advice of L. A. Petri* and Löhe,* went to Am. with Sievers* and his group of miss. emigrants 1847. C. A. T. Selle, of Chicago, prevailed on him to take charge of the newly organized cong. in Addison, Ill. Here he did pioneer work 10 yrs.; pastor Pittsburgh, Pa., 1857; active in controversy with Grabau; prof. exegesis, logic, and isagogics Conc. Sem., St. Louis, 1863–72; pastor Trinity Ch., St. Louis, 1872–78; Crete, Ill., 1878; contributor to *Der Lutheraner* and *Lehre und Wehre;* for a time ed. the latter; wrote tracts.

Albert Brauer, *Lebensbild des weiland ehrwürdigen Pastor Ernst August Brauer* (St. Louis, 1898).

Brauer, Karl (Jan. 10, 1831–May 12, 1907). B. Lissberg, Hesse; d. N Tonawanda, N. Y. Educ. Frankfort on the Main and Friedberg. To Am. 1850. Teacher Philadelphia, St. Louis, Cleveland, Baltimore. Prof. music Teachers' Sem., Addison, Ill., 1866–97; first full-time Mo. Syn. prof. music. Issued *Mehrstimmiges Choralbuch* 1888.

Braun, Anton Theodor (d. March 1814). B. Treves; RC miss. among Indians in Can.; convert to Lutheranism, preaching in Frontenac and Dundas, Ont.; formally received into Luth. Ch. by J. C. Kunze, Christ Ch., New York; ministered to chs. of Schoharie parish 1790–93; pastor Albany 1794 to 1797, Schoharie 1798–1800, Troytown, Guilderland, and New Brunswick, N. Y., 1800–14; secy. N. Y. Ministerium 1793–97; one of few conservative men who opposed rationalistic views of F. H. Quitman.

Braun, Johannes (1628–1708). Ref. prof. theol. Nijmegen 1665, Groningen 1680. Pupil of J. Cocceius*; exponent of federal theology.*

Braun, Joseph (1857–1947). Jesuit; prof. Christian art, archaeology, and liturgics Valkenburg (Neth.), Frankfort on the Main, Pullach. Wrote *Liturgisches Handlexikon.*

Braune, Karl (1810–79). Pastor near Torgau; gen. supt. Altenburg; active in miss. work; wrote *Unsere Zeit und die innere Mission.*

Braunfels, Otto (Otho Brunfels; 1488–1534). B. Mainz, Ger.; Carthusian monk and humanist turned reformer; ev. preacher and teacher; supported Anabaps.; friend of Luther,* Karlstadt,* and Zwingli.*

Bräuninger. See *Braeuninger.*

Bray, Thomas (1656–1730). Educ. Oxford; sent by bp. Compton of London to help order ch. affairs in Md.; arrived 1700; tried to est. library in each parish; founder of SPCK and SPG; works include *Bibliotheca catechetica; Bibliotheca parochialis; Papal Usurpation and Persecution* (often called *Martyrology*).

E. L. Pennington, *The Reverend Thomas Bray* (Philadelphia, 1934); H. P. Thompson, *Thomas Bray* (London, 1954).

Brazil. See *Help for Brazil Mission; Lutheran Church – Missouri Synod, Districts of The,* B 1; *South America,* 4.

Breckling, Friedrich (1629–1711). Dan. Luth. theol. Educ. Rostock, Königsberg, Helmstedt, Wittenberg, Leipzig, Jena, Giessen. Influenced in turn by J. Arnd(t)* for mysticism, J. Böhme* for theosophy, J. Betke* for spiritualism, and C. Hoburg* for syncretism. Became father's asst. Wrote violent attack on Flensburg clergy. Deposed; taken into custody; escaped to Amsterdam. Pastor Zwolle; dismissed under cloud of scandal. Friend of P. J. Spener* and G. Arnold.*

Bredal, Erik. See *Lapland.*

Bredt, Johann Viktor (1879–1940). Prof. state, ch., and internat. law Marburg. Wrote on ch. law and relationship bet. ch. and state.

Breeches Bible. Geneva Bible 1560; so called because of tr. "made themselves breeches" Gn 3:7.

Breithaupt, Joachim Justus (1658–1732). Prof. theol. Halle 1691; gen. supt. Magdeburg 1705; co-worker of A. H. Francke; pietist.

Breitinger, Johann Jakob (1575–1645). Ref. leader Zurich; took part in Synod of Dort; noted for organizational ability.

Breklum Missionary Society. Organized 1876 by Christian Jensen.* Missionaries sent to India 1881, Afr. 1912, China after WW I. Work in Afr. interrupted by WW I, resumed after WW II. Work in

China ended by Communist revolution. See also *Sevenringhaus, John Dietrich.*

Brendan (d. ca. 577). Said to have est. monasteries in Ireland and Brittany.

Brent, Charles Henry (1862–1929). Prot. Episc. bp. Philippine Is. 1901–18, W New York 1918–26, in charge of churches in Eur. 1926–28; opposed opium traffic; leader in ecumenical movement; pres. first World Conf. on Faith and Order 1927. See also *Ecumenical Movement, The,* 7.

Brentano, Franz (1838–1917). Ger. philos.; Dominican priest; liberal; seceded from ch. 1873 in protest against dogma of papal infallibility. Opposed "content" psychology of Wundt with "act" psychology, which holds that all mental life is activity and that experience is a way of acting; the task of psychology is to find meaning of act.

Brenz, Johann (June 24, 1499–Sept. 11, 1570). B. Weil der Stadt, near Stuttgart; d. Stuttgart. Educ. Heidelberg. Lectured on philol., philos., and Mathew when he met Luther* (Heidelberg Disputation*) 1518. Preached Luth. doctrine; forced to flee 1522. Settled at Hall, Swabia. Tried to help peasants after their defeat in Peasants' War* 1525. Celebrated Luth. Lord's Supper at Christmas 1525; wrote large and small catechisms 1528. Consistently supported Luther in Communion Controversy. Coauthor *Syngramma Suevicum* against Oecolampadius 1525. Attended Marburg Colloquy* Oct. 1529. Supported Augsburg Confession* 1530 against S Ger. mediating theologians (Bucer, etc.) and Zwingli. Introd. Luth. ch. orders in Brandenburg-Ansbach, Nürnberg, Dinkelsbühl, and Heilbronn 1532. Recalled to Swabia after restoration of Duke Ulrich 1534; chief reformer of Württemberg. Reformed the U. of Tübingen 1537. Attended meeting at Schmalkalden Feb. 1537 (see *Lutheran Confessions,* B 2) and various colloquies: Hagenau* 1540, Worms* 1540–41, Regensburg* 1546. Work in Hall interrupted by Schmalkaldic War* 1546–47 and Interim* 1548. Forced to flee by Charles V* Dec. 16, 1546; returned Jan. 4, 1547. Narrowly escaped arrest June 24, 1548; hidden first at Hohenwittlingen Castle, later at Mömpelgard. Met Calvin.* Returned secretly to Stuttgart after his wife's death, but had to remain in hiding 18 months. Pardoned, he prepared the *Confessio Virtembergica,* which he took to the Council of Trent, Mar. 1552; was not allowed to read it to the Council. Opposed Calvinist encroachment in Württemberg. Reformed the Palatinate 1553. Provost of Cathedral of Stuttgart 1554. Despite his staunch Lutheranism he retained a lively interest in Waldensians* and Huguenots.* Went to Paris and met Cardinal de Guise to obtain peace for Prots. in Fr., but in vain. In last yrs. (1568–69) helped Duke William of Jülich and Duke Julius of Brunswick-Wolfenbüttel introd. Luth. ch. orders. Buried under cathedral pulpit; Jesuits destroyed grave.

Brenz was Luther's most reliable friend in S Ger. Declined many calls in order to help safeguard confessional Lutheranism in Württemberg. Est. excellent educ. facilities for pastors (prep. schools still in existence). Orders of service simple. His was a deep piety, with pastoral concern for all Christians, but without compromise. WGT

W. Köhler, *Bibliographia Brentiana* (Berlin, 1904); J. Hartmann and K. Jäger, *Johann Brenz,* 2 vols. (Hamburg, 1840–42); H. Hermelink, "Johannes Brenz als lutherischer und als schwäbischer Theologe," in *Evangelisch-Lutherische Kirchenzeitung,* III (Aug. 31, 1949), 242–246; W. G. Tillmanns, *The World and Men Around Luther* (Minneapolis, 1959), pp. 146–147; *Confessio Virtembergica,* ed. E. Bizer (Stuttgart, 1952); *Predigten des Johannes Brenz,* ed. E. Bizer (Stuttgart, 1955); F. K. Wild, "Johannes Brenz's Leben," in *Das Leben der Altväter der lutherischen Kirche,* ed. M. Meurer, IV (Leipzig, 1864), 161–297; *Magister Johannes Brenz* (St. Louis, 1894).

Bres, Guy de (1522–67). Reformer of S Neth.; fled to Eng. 1548, to Switz. 1556; executed at Valenciennes 1567. See also *Reformed Confessions,* C 1.

Breslau Synod. The Evangelical Lutheran (Old Lutheran) Church in Prussia. See also *Germany, Lutheran Free Churches in,* 1–3.

Brethren (Dunkers; Ger. Bap. Brethren). 1. The Ger. Brethren movement had its origin in the Pietistic revival inaugurated by P. J. Spener* during the 2d half of the 17th c. While most Pietists hoped to reform the ch. by retaining their membership in the various state churches, Alexander Mack (1679 to 1735), a Calvinist, and E. C. Hochmann (1670 to 1721), a Halle Pietist, believed that a mere protest against the cold formalism of the churches and the laxity of morals was insufficient. They withdrew from the state ch. 1708 and organized a separate cong. at Schwarzenau, Westphalia. In line with his Calvinistic and legalistic background, Mack believed that a Christian must enter a covenant relation with Christ est. by triple immersion; hence the names Täufer, Tunker, Dunker, Dompelaars, Ger. Bap. Brethren. While the Brethren are opposed to written creeds, they have worked out a system of doctrine, practice, and ch. govt. in line with their enthusiastic, pietistic, mystic, and ascetic views. Like the Friends* and Mennonites,* with whom they have often been erroneously identified, they place greater emphasis on rites and regulations which they find prescribed in the NT than on doctrine, believing that they have reestablished the simplicity of life which marked the apostolic ch. The following rites and practices have been observed by various groups: Baptism by triple forward immersion followed immediately by confirmation while kneeling in the water; the Eucharist, celebrated only in the evening and preceded by foot washing and the love feast; "veiling" of women in the public service; anointing of sick with oil; excommunication according to Mt 18; total abstinence; nonparticipation in war; opposition to use of oath and civil litigation; simplicity in attire; some forbid cutting the beard. – The movement spread rapidly to various parts of Ger., Holland, and Switz. Because of pol. persecution some Brethren emigrated to Pa. 1719; by 1729 practically all had come to Am. Because they retained many Eur. customs and dialects, they were considered illiterate by their Eng. neighbors, though the many publications issuing from the presses of C. Sauer (see *Publicity, Church*) at Germantown prove the opposite. A serious defection occurred 1728 when J. C. Beissel* founded the monastic community at Ephrata, Pa., whose members until recently were classified as Brethren, but are now listed with Baps. (see *Baptist Churches,* 17). In the 19th c. the Brethren were disturbed by several controversies on matters of ch. govt. and practice, which led to the formation of several groups.

2. *Church of the Brethren* (Conservative Dunkers). The largest group. Its ch. polity is quasi-presbyterian. Formerly the clergy was largely untrained and was expected to be self-supporting; in recent yrs. an agressive program in educ. and miss. was launched. Inclusive membership (1972) 182,614.

3. *Old German Baptist Brethren.* Organized 1881 in protest against the introduction of specially organized missions, Sunday schools, training of ministers, which they consider as opposed to essential Christianity.

4. The original Brethren body in the US split 1881–83. The *Brethren Ch.* resulted. A 1939 split of the Brethren Ch. resutled in the Ashland group (see 6) and the *Nat. Fellowship of Brethren Chs.*

(also known as the "Grace" group), which favors modern methods in ch. work and autonomy of local congs. Inclusive membership (1972) 33,239.

5. *Church of God* (New Dunkers). Small group founded 1848; accepted no denominational name other than "Church of God." Disbanded Aug. 1962.

6. *Brethren Church* (Ashland, Ohio). Withdrew from Ch. of Brethren 1882. Inclusive membership (1972) 17,114.

See also *Religious Bodies (US), Bibliography.* FEM

Brethren, Bohemian. See *Bohemian Brethren.*

Brethren, Plymouth. Also popularly called Darbyites; members insist on such names as "Believers," "Christians," "Brethren," and "Saints." Originated in Eng. and Ireland during the 2d and 3d decades of the 19th c. Dissatisfied with the schismatic conditions of Christendom and particularly the mingling of ch. and state in the Ch. of Eng., John Nelson Darby (1800–82) and others held that subscription to creeds, adoption of denominational names, and setting up ecclesiastical organizations were inherently sinful. Darby believed that instead of joining organized denominations Christians must follow the pattern of the NT ch., gather in local "brotherhoods" to give expression to their "spiritual communion" by the breaking of bread and prayer, await the direction of the Holy Spirit, and listen to anyone who feels called to preach. Rejecting every form of regular ministry, creeds, rituals, and ecclesiastical organization, they organized "meetings," the largest at Plymouth. Darby was joined by men of outstanding ability, chiefly G. F. Müller,* father of Eng. orphanages, and S. P. Tregelles* (1813–75), exegete. The theol. position of the Brethren is fundamentalistic-literalistic with strong Calvinistic tendencies. Its distinctive doctrine is the belief that the visible Christian ch. must be one. They ascribe to the visible ch. all the marks which the NT predicates of the holy Christian ch. and say that membership in a denomination is a denial of the "one body." In line with this false conception of the ch. the Brethren hold two major errors: 1. Since only true believers can belong to a "meeting," the Holy Spirit directly governs the assembly when it accepts a member; 2. a person once incorporated into the "visible body of Christ" can never be lost. The Brethren have no regular ministry, frequently not even ch. bldgs. The services are primarily for the purposes of praise and the "breaking of bread" as an act of obedience, testimony, fellowship, and hope. Darby and his co-workers were the forerunners of modern premillennialism. The Brethren came to Am. about the middle of the 19th c. and are now represented by ca. 665 chs. Instead of presenting a united Christian ch., they have added to the schisms. The differences are largely concerning matters of discipline. Some "meetings" are known as "Open Brethren"; others are "Exclusive Brethren" because they exclude from fellowship those with whom they disagree in doctrine or in practice and sometimes even all the members of a "meeting" which has not repudiated an allegedly heterdox "meeting." See also *Religious Bodies (US), Bibliography.* FEM

A. C. Piepkorn, "Plymouth Brethren (Christian Brethren)," *CTM,* XLI (1970), 165–171.

Brethren, River. Three small denominations, Brethren in Christ; Old Order River Brethren, or Yorker; and United Zion Church (formerly United Zion's Children), collectively known as River Brethren, trace their beginning to Swiss Mennonites* who settled in Lancaster Co., Pa., 1752. During the revival of 1770 conducted by P. W. Otterbein and M. Boehm (see *United Brethren,* 1) among Baps., Luths., and Mennonites, differences of opinion arose concerning the mode of Baptism. The groups advocating triple immersion were opposed to formal ch. organizations and designated their congs. merely as "brotherhoods," each known by its respective locality. The largest was near the Susquehanna; hence the name River Brethren. Brethren have not adopted a creed but follow in gen. the principles and practices of Mennonites and Dunkers. They adhere to a legalistic and literalistic interpretation of such portions of the NT as seem important to them, e. g., triple immersion; anointing the sick; veiling women in the public service; foot washing, love feast, and Eucharist observed in evening; unsalaried ministry; nonresistance; nonconformity to the world in dress and soc. customs. Discussions have arisen in their midst about such trivial points as whether the same person should both wash and dry the feet in the ceremony of foot washing. Brethren in Christ Ch. is the largest and most progressive group. Old Order, or Yorker, River Brethren numbered 291 in 1936 and apparently disbanded sometime thereafter. United Zion Ch. numbered 880 in 1972.

Brethren, United. See *United Brethren.*

Brethren Church (Ashland, Ohio). See *Brethren,* 6.

Brethren Church (Progressive). See *Brethren,* 4.

Brethren in Christ. See *Brethren, River.*

Brethren of the Common Life. An assoc. of pious priest and laymen founded by Gerhard Groot(e)* of Deventer (Neth.) and Florentius* Radewijns (1350 to 1400). The Sisters of the Common Life, together with two cloisters for regular canons (see *Clergy*), were founded soon afterwards. The theol. of the Brethren of the Common Life was that of practical mysticism;* their object, the furtherance of piety; their occupation, the study of Scripture, copying and circulating useful books, manual labor, preaching, and popular educ. Their organization was monastic, but without lifelong vows. Their spreading of the Scriptures and piety (commended by Luther) exerted a wholesome influence; but, emphasizing Christ in us to the virtual exclusion of Christ for us, they were unable to effect a real Reformation. See also *Luther, Martin,* 2; *Thomas a Kempis.*

A. Hyma, *Brethren of the Common Life* (Grand Rapids, 1950).

Bretkunas, Jonas. See *Lithuania,* 2.

Bretscher, Paul Martin (Nov. 11, 1893–Aug. 10, 1974). B. Wausau, Wis.; educ. Conc. Sem., Saint Louis, Am. Conservatory of Music, Chicago, U. of Chicago; ordained LCMS 1918; asst. prof. Conc. Teachers Coll., River Forest, Ill., 1915–18; pastor Gospel Luth. Ch., Milwaukee, 1918–23; prof. Conc. Teachers Coll., River Forest, 1923–41; prof. Conc. Sem., St. Louis, 1914 until retirement 1969; acting pres. Conc. Sem., 1952–53. Mem. and chm. synodical Commission on Fraternal Organizations. Chm. synodical Bd. for Parish Education. Mem. ed. bd. of *Cresset, Lutheran Education, Concordia Theological Monthly, This Day.* Involved in Mo. Syn.-Eur. conferences held in Ger., Fr., Swed., Eng. in the late 40s and early 50s. Works include *The Lutheran Elementary School: An Interpretation; The History and Cultural Significance of the Taschenbuch Urania; The Church in Its Relation to Freemasonry and Related Orders; Luke 17:20-21 in Recent Investigations; Review of "Bad Boll" Conferences; Toward a Lutheran Philosophy of Education.*

Bretschneider, Karl Gottlieb (1776–1848). Gen. supt. Gotha; held to rational supernaturalism; wrote in field of dogmatics; pub. works of Melanchthon; founded *Corpus reformatorum;* prepared lexicon on NT.

Breve (Brief). Called *"Litterae Apostolicae"* in *Acta Apostolicae Sedis.* Less formal papal release than bull* or encyclical* but often dealing with important matters (honorary privileges, beatification).

Usually written in Lat., signed by secy. of briefs, and sealed (or stamped) with the papal signet ring (see *Ring of the Fisherman*).

Breviary. RC liturgical book containing all that is necessary to enable a cleric to recite daily Divine Office assigned to the canonical* hours. Divided into 4 books for the 4 seasons. The primitive office consisted of Psalms and Scripture lessons. Under Ambrose hymns and antiphons were added; responsories, canticles, collects, and other elaborations began with Benedict of Nursia.* In the Middle Ages lives of saints tended to replace Psalms and the Scriptures. Recited by priests and clerics. Many religious orders have their own breviaries. See also *Popes,* 21; *Service Books.*

Brevis Confessio. See *Mennonite Churches,* 2.

Brewster, William (ca. 1560–1644). Regarded by many as the outstanding leader of the Pilgrims; organized Separatist Ch. of Scrooby, Eng.; to Holland 1608; to Am. on *Mayflower;* ruling elder till Ralph Smith arrived. See also *Robinson, John.*

Briçonnet, Guillaume (ca. 1470–1534). Educ. Navarre; bp. Lodève 1504; abbot St. Germain-des-Prés, Paris, 1507; bp. Meaux 1516. Attended Council of Pisa. In effort to improve morals of his clergy introd. ev. preachers (J. Lefèvre, Roussel, Farel) and Fr. tr. of Gospels and Epistles. Charged by the Cordeliers (see *Cordeliers,* 1) before Parliament of Paris with being in sympathy with Luther (1525–26). Two of his preachers (Pouvan and Saunier) burned at stake. Wrote *Synodalis oratio;* correspondence with Margaret of Navarre.

Bridaine, Jacques (1701–67). Fr. preacher; educ. Jesuit Coll. and Miss. Sem. of St. Charles de la Croix, Avignon. Works include *Cantiques Spirituels* and 5 vols. of sermons.

Bridge, William (ca. 1600–70). Puritan pastor Norwich, Eng., 1636; nonconformist; fled to Holland; pastor Rotterdam; ret. to Eng. 1642; prominent in movement of Cromwell; Presb. pastor Great Yarmouth 1643–62.

Bridges, Matthew (1800–94). Author; hymnist. Educ. in Ch. of Eng.; joined RC Ch. 1848; hymns include "Crown Him with Many Crowns."

Bridget (Brigit, Birgitta, Brigitta; ca. 1303–73). Swed. RC nun and mystic; patron saint of Swed.; mother of Catherine* of Sweden. Her *Revelationes,* accounts of visions she claimed to have had, contain evangelical tendencies. See also *Brigittines.*

Bridget of Kildare. See *Brigid.*

Bridgewater Treatises. Eight treatises on various aspects of "the power, wisdom, and goodness of God, as manifested in the Creation"; written by T. Chalmers,* J. Kidd, W. Whewell, C. Bell, P. M. Roget, W. Buckland, W. Kirby, W. Prout; pub. 1833–40 under bequest of the 8th Earl of Bridgewater.

Bridgman, Elijah Coleman (Apr. 22, 1801–Nov. 2, 1861). B. Belchertown, Mass.; d. Shanghai, China; educ. Amherst Coll. and Andover Theol. Sem. Sent by ABCFM to China 1829; arrived 1830; worked with D. Abeel*; ed. *Chinese Repository;* pub. *Chinese Chrestomathy;* active in Bible translation and revision.

Brief. See *Breve.*

Brief Statement (1932). Based on the formulation by F. Pieper, "Ich glaube, darum rede ich" (1897). In its report, which advocated that the *Chicago Theses** be not accepted in the form submitted, the Committee on Intersyn. Matters at the 1929 conv. of the Mo. Syn. recommended the creation of a committee instructed "to formulate theses, which, beginning with the *status controversiae,* are to present the doctrines of Scripture and the Lutheran Confessions in the shortest and simplest manner." The committee appointed by Pres. F. Pfotenhauer (F. Pieper,* F. S. Wenger,* E. A. Mayer, L. A. Heerboth, Th. Engelder*) issued the *Brief Statement of the Doctrinal Position of the Missouri Synod* in 1931. This document treated Holy Scripture, God, Creation, Man and Sin, Redemption, Faith in Christ, Conversion, Justification, Good Works, Means of Grace, Church, Public Ministry, Church and State, Election of Grace, Sunday, Millennium, Antichrist, Open Questions, Symbols of the Lutheran Church. This Brief Statement was adopted by the 1932 Mo. Syn. convention. Efforts toward unity with the ALC continued. The 1938 Mo. Syn. conv. accepted the *Brief Statement,* the *Declaration* (prepared by the ALC commissioners), and the entire report of the floor committee of the conv. as a basis for future fellowship with the ALC, and the ALC adopted the *Brief Statement* and the *Declaration.* The 1941 Mo. Syn. conv. felt that the ALC had not done everything possible to carry out the 1938 resolutions (esp. in view of the Sandusky Resolutions,* Pittsburgh Agreement,* and failure to persuade the Am. Luth. Conf.); the Mo. Syn. had, also, been informed that its own sister synods were not yet favorable to active fellowship, and it therefore (at the request of synods of the Syn. Conf. 1940) instructed the committee to formulate one document in which "we do not mean to dispense with any doctrinal statement made in our *Brief Statement.*" In 1944 this document (the *Doctrinal Affirmation*) was in preparation. It was presented to the ALC 1946 and declared unsatisfactory. A similar position was taken by the Mo. Syn. 1947. The Mo. Syn. also reaffirmed the *Brief Statement* 1947 but declared that the 1938 resolutions be no longer considered a basis for establishing fellowship. At the same time it instructed its committee to continue discussion with the ALC, using the *Brief Statement* and other existing documents (and documents to be formulated) and thus try to arrive at one document. See also *Common Confession; Intuitu fidei; Sunday.* EL

Proceedings of the Mo. Syn. 1929, p. 113; 1932, pp. 154, 155; 1938, pp. 221–233 (contains ALC *Declaration*); 1941, pp. 277–304 (refers to ALC Sandusky Resolutions); 1944, pp. 228–252 (contains ALC Mendota Resolutions); 1947, pp. 476 to 515 (contains Mo. Syn. *Brief Statement*); *CTM,* II (May 1931), 321–336 (*Brief Statement* in German), 401–416 (English): *Reports* of the ALC conventions, 1938, pp. 255, 256; 1940, pp. 312-315; *Lutheran Standard,* XCVIII (Dec. 7, 1940), 4, 5; *Lutheran Companion,* XLIX (Nov. 28, 1940) 507, 508; *Proceedings* of the Syn. Conf., 1940, pp. 81–88. An analysis of the situation as it obtained after the 1941 Fort Wayne conv. of the Mo. Syn. is given by M. Reu in *Kirchliche Zeitschrift,* LXV (Oct. 1941), 577–607; *Doctrinal Declarations* (St. Louis, 1957), pp. 43–57; *CTM,* XVI (Jan. 1945), 1–5; (April 1945), 265; (Nov. 1945), 787–788; C. S. Meyer, "The Historical Background of 'A Brief Statement,'" *CTM,* XXXII (July 1961), 403–428; (Aug. 1961), 466–482; (Sept. 1961), 526–542; C. S. Meyer, "The Role of *A Brief Statement* Since 1932," *CTM,* XXXIII (April 1962), 199–209; F. H. Pralle, "A Brief Statement, 1932–1959," *Lutheran Education,* XCVII (June 1962), 442–453.

Brieger, Johann Friedrich Theodor (1842–1915). Ev. theol.; prof. Halle, Marburg, Leipzig; scholar of Reformation hist.

Briesmann, Johann(es) (1488–1549). Monk at Wittenberg and Frankfort on the Oder; won for Luther by the disputation at Leipzig and by Luther's writings of 1520; spread the Gospel in Königsberg and Riga. "First disseminator of the pure doctrine in Prussia."

Briggs, Charles Augustus (1841–1913). Am. Biblical scholar. Presb. minister; prof. Heb. and Biblical theol. Union Theol. Sem.; suspended from ministry 1893 by Gen. Assem. for liberal views on place of reason in religion; joined Prot. Episc. Ch. ca. 1900.

Joint ed. *International Critical Commentary.* See also *Brown, Francis; Lexicons,* A.

Brightman, Edgar Sheffield (1884–1953). Philos.; prof. Boston 1919. Advocated personalism. God is creative, supreme, personal, but also limited, or finite; involved in cosmic evolution; time enters His very being. Since existence exhibits conflict, God is involved in struggle and victory, thus including redemption by the cross. Works include *Religious Values; The Problem of God; Moral Laws; A Philosophy of Religion; Person and Reality.*

Brigid of Kildare (Bridget, Brigit, Brighid, Bride; ca. 453–523). Patron saint of Ireland; child of a bondmaid and a prince of Ulster; freed from parental control by King of Ulster, she founded Kildare and 3 other monasteries; remains placed beside those of Patrick and Columba.

Brigittines. *Ordo Sanctissimi Salvatoris.* Order founded ca. 1346 in Swed. by Bridget* as an instrument to spread the kingdom of God on earth. The monasteries were double, one part for monks, the other for nuns. The order contributed to the civilization of the North, but was nearly obliterated by the Reformation.

Brilioth, Yngve Torgny (1891–1959). B. Västra Ed, Kalmar Co., Smaaland province, Swed.; prof. ch. hist. Turku (Aabo), Fin., 1925; prof. Lund, Swed., 1929; bp. Växjö, Kronoberg Co., S Swed., 1947; abp. Uppsala 1950; active in ecumenical movement. Works include *Nyanglikansk renässans* (tr. *The Anglican Revival: Studies in the Oxford Movement); Nattvarden i evangeliskt gudstjänstliv* (tr. [rev. and shortened] A. G. Hebert, *Eucharistic Faith and Practice, Evangelical & Catholic); Predikans historia* (tr. K. E. Mattson, *A Brief History of Preaching*).

Brinck, Sven Dideriksen (1665–1728). Educ. Christiania, Uppsala, Copenhagen; army chaplain; pastor first Dan.-Norw. Luth. ch. in London 1692; returned to Den. 1702.

Brinckerinck, Jan (1359–1419). Popular preacher of Brethren and Sisters of the Common Life; ordained priest 1393; introd. discipline for house for women founded at Deventer by Groote.*

Bring, Ragnar. See *Lund, Theology of.*

British and Foreign Bible Society. See *Bible Societies,* 3.

British Columbia. See *Canada,* A 11, 18, 20, 24, 27, 28.

British Council of Churches. Formed 1942 by Prot. chs. in Eng., Scot., Wales, and Ireland for discussion and joint action.

British Guiana. See *South America,* 12.

British Honduras. See *Central America,* A, D 2, K.

British Isles. See *Great Britain; Ireland.*

British Israelism. Name for Anglo-Israelism* in Eng.

British Jews Society. See *International Society for the Evangelization of the Jews.*

British Museum Gospel. See *Apocrypha,* B 2.

British Society for the Propagation of the Gospel Among the Jews. See *International Society for the Evangelization of the Jews.*

British Syrian Mission. See *Middle East,* C.

British West Indies. See *Caribbean Islands,* E 5.

Brito-Pictish Church. See *Celtic Church,* 12.

Brixius Northanus (thon Noirde; ton Orde; Thonwerde; d. 1557). Lived in Schoppingen, East Friesland; pastor Soest and Lübeck; signed SA (WA 38, 388–389).

Broad Church. Angl. liberals. See also *High Church; Protestant Episcopal Church,* 7.

Broadcasting. See *Radio and Television Evangelism, Network; Radio Stations.*

Broadus, John Albert (1827–95). Bap.; b. Va.; prof. U. of Va.; pastor Charlottesville, Va.; prof. S Bap. Theol. Sem., Greenville, S. C., 1859; its pres. Louisville, Ky., 1888; gave Lyman Beecher Lectures at Yale. Works include *Preparation and Delivery of Sermons.*

Brobst, Samuel Kistler (Nov. 16, 1822–Dec. 23, 1876). B. Albany Twp., Berks Co., Pa., of an old Ger. family, which had come to Pa. at end of 17th c. Educ. Allentown Academy, Marshall Coll. (Lancaster) and Washington Coll. (in W Pa.). Agent for Am. S. S. Union. Licensed June 4, 1847, in Philadelphia, by Ministerium of Pa. Ed. *Der Jugend Freund; Lutherische Zeitschrift; Theologische Monats-Hefte.* Started *Der Lutherische Kalender;* also issued an Eng. calendar. Helped est. theol. sem. at Mount Airy (Philadelphia) and Muhlenberg Coll., Allentown. Pastor Allentown 1867–76.

Brochmand, Jesper Rasmussen (1585–1652). Prof. Copenhagen; bp. Sjælland. Works include *Universae theologiae systema* and apologetic, polemic, and devotional works.

Brockelmann, Carl (1868–1956). Prof. Breslau, Königsberg, Halle, Berlin. Wrote Syriac lexicon and grammar; comparative grammar of Semitic languages; hist. of Arab. literature; hist. of Islamic peoples.

Brockhaus, Carl (1882–99). Cofounder *Ev. Gesellschaft für Innere Mission;* exponent of Darbyites in Germany.

Brockmann, Johann Heinrich (Feb. 8, 1833–Jan. 20, 1904). B. Bergen, near Celle, Ger.; as young man attended services at Hermannsburg; entered Hermannsburg* miss. school; examined, ordained, came to Am. 1862; joined Wis. Syn.; pastor Algoma, Mosel (near Sheboygan), Fort Atkinson, and Watertown, (all in Wis.); mem. Wis. Syn. Indian Miss. Board.

Broders, Christan James (Nov. 22, 1867–Nov. 27, 1932). B. New Orleans, La.; educ. Conc. Coll., Fort Wayne, Ind., and Conc. Sem., St. Louis, Mo. Pastor of various congs. Military chaplain 1898 in Sp.-Am. War. Miss. to Brazil 1900–01 (see also *Lutheran Church – Missouri Synod, District of The,* B 1).

Brodhead, Augustus (1831–87). B. Milford, Pa.; d. Bridgeton, N. J.; educ. Union Coll. and Princeton Theol. Sem. Sent by Presb. Ch. in USA as miss. to India 1858. Wrote extensively; ed. miss. magazine; tr. hymns.

Brohm, Theodore (Apr. 10, 1846–Apr. 27, 1926). B. New York City. Son of Theodore Julius Brohm. Educ. Conc. Coll., St. Louis, later Fort Wayne; grad. Conc. Sem., St. Louis, 1866; postgrad. work New York U.; pastor East Boston; prof. Northwestern Coll., Watertown, Wis., 1871; prof. Teachers' Sem., Addison, Ill., 1879–1913, dir. 1906–13; retired; instr. Calif. Conc. Coll., Oakland, till 1925.

Brohm, Theodore Julius (Sept. 12, 1808–Sept. 24, 1881). B. Oberwinkel, near Waldenburg, Saxony; studied theol. in Leipzig 1827–32; after grad. he became attached to Martin Stephan;* refused to accept a position in state ch.; emigrated with Stephan to Am.; his private secy.; cofounder Conc. Coll., Altenburg, Mo.; instr. till 1843; pastor Trin. Luth. Ch., New York, 1843–58; Holy Cross Ch., St. Louis, 1858–78; resigned; assisted in teaching at Teachers' Sem., Addison, Ill., 1879–81.

Brömel, Albert Robert (1815–85). B. Teichel, Schwarzburg; d. Ratzeburg, Prussia. Supt. duchy of Lauenburg 1854; mem. Luth. consistory at Kiel 1876. Works include *Der Grund der Kirche; Homiletische Charakterbilder.*

Bromley, Thomas (1629–91). Eng. mystic and chiliast; fololwer of J. Böhme*; with Jane Lead(e),* J. Pordage,* and F. Lee* organized The Philadelphian* Society for the Advancement of Piety and Divine Philosophy.

Brommer, Carl Frederick (Mar. 30, 1870–Oct. 18, 1949). B. Württemberg; d. San Diego, Calif.; educ. Conc. Coll., Fort Wayne, and Conc. Sem., St. Louis (grad. 1891); pastor Gotha and Tampa, Fla., 1891 to 1896; Houston, Tex., 1896–1902; Cheyenne, Wyo., 1902–04; Beatrice, Nebr., 1904–11; Hampton, Nebr., 1911–24; pres. Nebr. Dist., Mo. Syn., 1915 to 1922, S. Nebr. Dist. 1922–24; pres. Conc. Teachers Coll., Seward, Nebr., 1924–41, instr. 1941 till retirement 1944.

Bronxville Concordia Collegiate Institute. See *Ministry, Education of,* VIII, C, 2, j.

Bronze Age. See *Time.*

Brook Farm. See *Communistic Societies,* 5.

Brooke, Graham Wilmot (1866–Mar. 5, 1892). B. Aldershot, Eng.; d. Lokoja, Afr.; studied medicine St. Thomas' hosp.; went to Afr. as indep. miss. but failed to reach Sudan; ret. to Eng.; sent as lay miss. with J. A. Robinson by CMS to Sudan 1890; worked at Lokoja; quickly mastered the Hausa language and preached over wide areas.

Brooke, Stopford Augustus (1832–1916). Irish preacher; Ch. of Eng. clergyman; seceded 1880; became indep. clergyman with Unitarian inclinations; works include histories of Eng. literature and studies of authors and plays.

Brooks, Charles Timothy (1813–83). Educ. Harvard and Cambridge; Unitarian minister in several cities, at last in Newport, R. I. The Am. version of the hymn "God Bless Our Native Land" seems to be based on his free tr. of a Ger. patriotic song.

Brooks, Phillips (1835–93). B. Boston. Educ. Harvard. A failure at teaching, he studied at the Episc. Theol. Sem., Alexandria, Va.; rector Ch. of the Advent, Philadelphia; rector Trin. Ch., Boston; bp. Mass. Wrote "O Little Town of Bethlehem."

Brorson, Hans Adolf (1694–1764). One of Denmark's greatest hymnists; ordained 1722; bp. Ribe 1741; popular preacher; pietist.

Brotherhood and Sisterhood. Terms denoting groups of men or women participating in a common center, primarily family, then also in race, humanity, fellowship, purpose; used in religious literature esp. with reference to unity of man in origin and structure and to designate disciples of a charismatic personality. Brotherhoods and sisterhoods develop in religious groups for cultivation of piety and achievement of goals through community life. In Christianity the terms describe those who participate in the fellowship* of Christ; in RCm esp., they denote religious orders united by common vows, life, and goals; similar orders have multiplied in Anglo-Catholic, Prot., and Luth. churches. The terms also apply to some secular and religious associations. See *also Sisterhoods.*

Brotherhood of St. Andrew. Organization of laymen in Prot. Episc. Ch. in US, the Ch. of Eng., and their branches. Purpose of the soc. is "the spread of Christ's kingdom among men, especially young men." Organized in St. James' Ch., Chicago, Saint Andrew's Day, Nov. 30, 1883. Two rules were adopted: 1. "To pray daily for the spread of Christ's kingdom among men"; 2. "to make an earnest effort each week to bring at least one young man within the hearing of the Gospel of Jesus Christ as set forth in the services of the church and in young men's Bible classes." 35 such groups organized 1886 as the Brotherhood of St. Andrew.

Brothers Hospitallers of St. John of God. RC order; developed out of work for the sick in Granada by John* of God. Pius V approved the order 1572. The Hospital of St. John Calybita, Rome, was given to the order 1584 by Gregory XIII and became the motherhouse.

Brothers Marists. See *Marists.*

Brothers of Charity. See *Congregation of the Brothers of Charity.*

Brothers of Christ. See *Christadelphians.*

Brothers of the Common Life. See *Brethren of the Common Life.*

Brothers of the Sword. See *Estonia,* 1.

Brouwer, Annéus Marinus (1875–1948). Rector Neth. Miss. School, Rotterdam, 1910; prof. ch. hist. and miss., later of NT, Utrecht.

Brown, Abel J. (1817–94). B. near Lincolnton, N. C.; grad. Emory and Henry Coll., Emory, Va.; taught at Jefferson Male Academy, Blountville, Tenn., and Greeneville (Tenn.) Coll.; deacon 1836; ordained pastor 1837; pastor N and S Carolina, and for 36 yrs. Sullivan Co., Tenn.; leader Tenn. Syn.; one of founders of Holston Syn.; pres. of diet of Salisbury, N. C., which led to the organization of The United* Synod of the Evangelical Lutheran Church in the South.

Brown, Charles Lafayette (Dec. 3, 1873–Dec. 5, 1921). B. Iredell Co., N. C.; educ. Roanoke Coll., Salem, Va., and Mount Airy Sem., Philadelphia, Pa.; ordained 1898; miss. to Japan 1898–1916; founded and organized Kyushu Gakuin, boys' school at Kumamoto, Japan, with 2 depts.: middle school and theological; taught at the school till his return to Am. 1916; acting gen. secy. Bd. of For. Miss. of United* Synod of the Evangelical Lutheran Church in the South 1916–18; taught at Southern Theol. Sem., Columbia, S. C., 1918; one of 3 gen. secretaries of United* Lutheran Church 1918–21; visited Luth. miss. fields in India and Afr. 1921; d. Sanoghie, Liberia.

In Memoriam: Charles Lafayette Brown, prepared by E. K. Bell, L. B. Wolf, and G. Drach (Baltimore, 1922).

Brown, Ford Madox (1821–93). Eng. painter; studied at Brugge, Gent, Antwerp, Paris; assoc. with Pre-Raphaelite Brotherhood, but not mem. of it; worked chiefly in secular field. Paintings include "Christ Washing St. Peter's Feet."

Brown, Francis (1849–1916). B. Hanover, N. H. Educ. Dartmouth Coll., Union Theol. Sem., U. of Berlin, Ger. Prof. Union Theol. Seminary. Dir. Am. School for Oriental Study and Research in Palestine (Jerusalem) 1907–08. Ed. with cooperation of C. A. Briggs* and S. R. Driver,* *A Hebrew and English Lexicon of the Old Testament;* joint ed. and tr. *Teaching of the Twelve Apostles;* other works include; *Assyriology: Its Use and Abuse in Old Testament Study.*

See also *Lexicons,* A.

Brown, James Allen (Feb. 19, 1821–June 19, 1882). B. Lancaster Co., Pa., of Quaker lineage; educ. Pa. Coll., Gettysburg; baptized in Presb. Ch.; studied theol. privately; licensed 1845 by Md. Syn.; pastor Baltimore, Md., and York and Reading, Pa.; prof. theol. Newberry Coll., S. C.; pres. 1860; left because of his Union sentiments; chaplain 87th Pa. Regiment and of US Army Hosp., York, Pa.; S. S. Schmucker's successor at Gettysburg 1864; pres. Gen. Syn. 1866; coed., with M. Valentine, *The Quarterly Review of the Evangelical Lutheran Church,* 1871–75, ed. 1876 to 1879; disabled by paralysis 1879.

Brown, John (1722–87). Scot. clergyman and commentator. B. Carpow; poor and largely self-taught; herdboy; peddler; soldier; schoolteacher; proficient in several modern and ancient languages; preacher at Haddington during entire ministry; prof. theol. Works include *Self-interpreting Bible.*

Brown, John Newton (1803–68). Am. Bap. preacher; prof. theol.; ed. secy. Am. Bap. Publication Soc. 1849 to death; most important work: *Encyclopedia of Religious Knowledge.* See also *Democratic Declarations of Faith,* 3.

Brown, Nathan (June 22, 1807–Jan. 1, 1886). Am. Bap. Conv. miss. to India. B. New Ipswich, N. H. To Burma 1832; est. miss. at Assam 1835, then in other areas; returned to Am. 1855; to Yokohama 1873; worked there 6 yrs. Works include NT in Assamese and Jap.; parts of OT in Assamese and Shan; catechism in Assamese and Shan; hymns in Assamese and Burman; *Grammar of the Assamese*

Language; arithmetic in Burman and Assamese; comparative vocabulary of ca. 50 Indian languages and dialects. Ed. *Orunódoi,* monthly magazine.

Brown, Samuel Robbins (June 16, 1810–June 20, 1880). B. E Windsor, Conn.; educ. Yale Coll. and Columbia Theol. Sem., S. C.; sent to China by ABCFM 1838; returned to Am. 1847; to Jap. under Ref. (Dutch) Ch. of Am. 1859. Persuaded many Chinese and Jap. (including princes) to study in Am. Assisted in Jap. Bible tr.

Brown, William Adams (1865–1943). Educ. Yale, Union Theol. Sem., and in Ger., Scot., and Eng.; instructor 1892, then prof. Union Theol. Sem.; ordained Presb. 1893; author; liberal theol.; exponent of ecumenicity.

Browne, Robert. See *United Church of Christ, The,* I A 1.

Browne, Thomas (1605–82). Eng. physician, author. B. London; d. Norwich. Aided in condemnation of 2 women as witches 1664. Works include *Religio Medici* (blending religious feeling and skepticism); *Urne-Buriall.* See also *Deism,* III 2.

Browning, Elizabeth Barrett (1806–61). Wife of Robert Browning. Remembered most for her *Sonnets from the Portuguese.* For many yrs. many people thought her greater than her husband. Some of her hymns are in use in the US.

Browning, Robert (1812–89). B. Camberwell, suburb of London; considered the most intellectual and erudite of Victorian poets. Son of a London banker, received main training under private tutors; read voluminously. Interested in music, painting, sculpture, poetry; never unsympathetic with people, but essentially analytical in his attitudes. Sought to express spiritual values in dogmas and contemporary philos.; emphasized the soul and future life. Chief works: *Paracelsus; Sordello; Pippa Passes; A Blot in the 'Scutcheon; A Soul's Tragedy; My Last Duchess; The Pied Piper of Hamelin; How They Brought the Good News from Ghent to Aix; The Lost Leader; The Bishop Orders His Tomb at Saint Praxed's Church; The Confessional; The Glove; Fra Lippo Lippi; Saul; Rabbi Ben Ezra; Caliban upon Setebos,* or, *Natural Theology in the Island; Prospice; The Ring and the Book.*

Brownists. See *United Church of Christ, The,* I A 1.

Brownson, Orestes Augustus (1803–76). Am. clergyman, author. B. Stockbridge, Vt.; d. Detroit. Presb. at 19. Preacher (Universalist, Unitarian, Soc. for Christian Union and Progress). RC 1844; apologist.

Bruck, Arnold von (ca. 1490–ca. 1554). Composer; b. Bruck, Austria; dean Laibach (Ljubljana, or Lyublyana; ancient Emona; Slovenia, NW Yugoslavia); royal Kapellmeister. Works include sacred and secular songs, motets,* miserere.*

Brück, Gregorius (Gregor; Georg? Real name Heinse, Henisch, or Heincz; latinized Pontanus; ca. 1484–1557). Jurist; b. Brück, near Wittenberg, Ger.; educ. Wittenberg and Frankfurt an der Oder; councillor of Frederick* III ("the Wise"); later chancellor. See also *Lutheran Confessions,* A 2.

Bruckner, Anton (1824–96). RC Austrian composer and organist. Wrote only symphonies (9) and religious choral works (e. g., masses). Admirer of Richard Wagner*; relations between Bruckner and Brahms* were notoriously hostile. Regarded by many as last of great composers of RC ch. music.

W. Wolff, *Anton Bruckner, Rustic Genius* (New York, 1942); D. Newlin, *Bruckner, Mahler, Schoenberg* (New York, 1947); E. Doernberg, *The Life and Symphonies of Anton Bruckner* (New York, 1961); H. F. Redlich, *Bruckner and Mahler,* rev. ed. (London, 1963).

Brückner, Benno Bruno (1824–1905). Educ. Leipzig; pastor Hohburg, near Wurzen; pastor and prof. Leipzig; canon Meissen; consistorail councillor Prussia; provost, prof., and gen. supt. Berlin; canon Brandenburg; chief interest in ch. govt.

Brüdergemeine. Ger. name for renewed Unitas Fratrum. See also *Moravian Church.*

Bruderhof Communities. See *Communistic Societies,* 5.

Brüderunität. Name used for both old and renewed *Unitas Fratrum.* See also *Bohemian Brethren; Czechoslovakia; Moravian Church.*

Bruhns, Nicolaus (1665–97). Organist, violinist, composer. Pupil of D. Buxtehude.* Works include religious cantatas and ch. music for organ.

Bruis. See *Bruys.*

Brumder, George (May 24, 1839–May 9, 1910). Luth. layman; b. Alsace, near Strasbourg; d. Milwaukee; father taught school; to Am. 1857; pub. first hymnal of Wis. Syn. and Ger. journals and newspapers including *Familienfreund; Haus- und Bauernfreund; Hausfreund; Germania; Germania-Herold; Milwaukee-Herold; Die Rundschau.*

Brun, Johan Lyder (1870–1950). Prof. NT Oslo. Founded *Norsk teologisk tidsskrift.* Works include *Jesu Evangelium; Apostelkonzil und Aposteldekret; Die Auferstehung Christi in der urchristlichen Überlieferung.*

Brun, Johan Norda(h)l. See *Norway, Lutheranism in,* 10.

Brunelleschi, Filippo (Brunellesco; ca. 1377–1446). It. artist and architect. Designed and constructed dome of Cathedral in Florence. Pioneer of Renaissance art.

Brunfels. See *Braunfels.*

Brunn, Arthur Johann Conrad (July 10, 1880–Aug. 27, 1949). B. Chicago, Ill.; grandson of F. A. Brunn*; grad. Conc. Coll., Fort Wayne, Ind., 1900; Conc. Sem., St. Louis, 1903; pastor Brooklyn 1903–49; mem. Mo. Syn. Army and Navy Com. during WW I; pres. Mo. Syn. Atlantic Dist. 1930–41; vice-pres. Mo. Syn. 1941–49; mem. Bd. of Dir. ALPB; assoc. ed. *The American Lutheran;* ex. secy. Wartburg Luth. Home for the Aged, Brooklyn; mem. Bd. of Dir. Bethlehem Luth. Children's Home, Staten Is.; mem. Bd. of Trustees Conc. Collegiate Inst., Bronxville, N. Y.

Brunn, Friedrich August (1819–1895). B. Castle Schaumburg, Duchy of Nassau; educ. Leipzig, Bonn, and the theol. sem. Herborn; entered ministry 1842; severed connection with state ch. of Nassau 1846; with a number of families organized indep. cong. Steeden; 1846–60 yrs. of development; break with Breslau Syn. 1865; with Immanuel Syn. 1870; with Luth. state ch. 1875. First meeting of Ev. Luth. Free Ch. of Saxony, which Brunn joined, was held 1877. Brunn's first contact with Missourians probably 1846, when he received a letter from G. Loeber. Walther's visit to Ger. 1860 gave impetus to opening the preparatory institution at Steeden 1861, which furnished the Mo. Syn. ca. 235 men. Works include *Gottes Wort und Luthers Lehr'; Vom Gefühlschristentum; Die Lehre von den Gnadenmitteln; Die Lehre von der Kirche; Thesen über die Lehre von der Rechtfertigung; Mitteilungen aus meinem Leben.* See also *Germany, Lutheran Free Churches in,* 4–5.

R. D. Drews, *The Relation of Friedrich Brunn to the German Free Churches and the Missouri Synod, 1846–1876* (STM Thesis, Conc. Sem., St. Louis, 1962); "Leichenreden für den ehrw. Pfarrer Friedrich August Brunn" and "Zum Ehrengedächtnis des sel. Pfarrer Brunn," in *Die Evangelisch-Lutherische Freikirche,* XX (May 1895), 85–92.

Brunn, Nikolaus von. See *Basel Missionary Society.*

Brunner, Heinrich Emil (1889–1966). B. Winterthur, Switz.; educ. Zurich, Berlin, and N. Y.; taught in 1916–24; prof. Zurich, Switz., 1924–53; lectured in Eng. 1913; pastor Obstalden, Canton Glarus, Switz., US and Jap.; helped est. dialectical* theol.; opposed theol. of experience; emphasized use of Word of God in approach to modern man; with M. Buber* and F. Ebner* he emphasized confrontation with God in an I-Thou relationship; involved in ecumenical* movement. Works include *Erlebnis, Erkenntnis und Glaube; Wahrheit als Begegnung* (tr. A. W. Loos, *The Divine-Human Encounter*); *Der Mensch im Widerspruch* (tr. O. Wyon, *Man in Revolt*); *Das Gebot und die Ordnungen* (tr. O. Wyon, *The Divine Imperative*); *Dogmatik* (tr. O. Wyon, *Dogmatics*); *Das Ewige als Zukunft und Gegenwart* (tr. H. Knight, *Eternal Hope*). See also *Dogmatics,* B 5; *Switzerland, Contemporary Theology in,* 6–8.

Brunner, Leonhard (ca. 1500–58). Luth. pastor Worms and Landau. Opposed Anabaps.

Brunner, Peter. See *Dogmatics,* B 13.

Brunnholtz, Peter (d. 1757). Dan. Luth. pastor. B. Schleswig; educ. Halle; assisted H. M. Mühlenberg,* serving at Philadelphia and Germantown 1745–51; at Philadelphia alone 1751–57; cofounder Pa. Ministerium; zealous worker but suffered from poor health. See also *Koch, Peter; Liturgics.*

Bruno I (the Great; 925–965). Youngest son of Ger. Emp. Henry I (the Fowler). Under reign of his brother Otto I (the Great) chancellor 940, abp. Cologne 953; regent of empire 961 with William, abp. Mainz, on Otto's 2d expedition into Italy. Promoted close alliance bet. episcopate and crown.

Bruno, Filippo Giordano (ca. 1548–1600). It. philos.; put to death by Inquisition for cosmological theories based on Copernicus; opposed Aristotelianism; held theory of animate monads; taught relativity of space, time, and motion; influenced J. Böhme, Spinoza, Leibnitz, Descartes, Schelling, Hegel.

Bruno of Cologne (ca. 1030–1101). B. Cologne; educ. Cologne, Reims, Tours; head of cathedral school at Reims and overseer of diocesan schools 1057; chancellor diocese 1075; deposed and forced to flee by archbishop Manasses; returned after Manasses' deposition 1080 but soon withdrew to mountains near Grenoble and founded Carthusian* order.

Bruno of Querfurt (Bonifacius; ca. 970–1009). Saxon nobleman; ordained ca. 997 Rome; sent by Sylvester II as miss. to Slavs esp. in Poland and Prussia; suffered martyrdom Lithuania.

Bruno of Würzburg. See *Catechetics,* 5.

Brunstäd, Friedrich (1883–1944). Prof. philos. Erlangen; systematic theol. Rostock. Wrote in area of philos. and theol.; works include *Reformation und Idealismus; Theologie der lutherischen Bekenntnisschriften.*

Brush Run Baptist Church. See *Disciples of Christ,* 2 b.

Bruys, Pierre de (Bruis; Petrus Brusius; d. ca. 1126 [or 1132/33?]). Fr.. reformer; pupil of P. Aberlard,* but was condemned by him for subverting the ch.; advocated abolition of ch. bldgs., prayers for the dead, infant baptism, veneration of the cross; ascetic; burned by people enraged at his burning of crosses. Followers called Petrobrusians. Se also *Waldenses.*

Bryan, William Jennings (1860–1925). Am. lawyer, statesman, orator; Presb.; in wide demand as Chautauqua lecturer; strong advocate of Fundamentalism in religion. Died a few days after the end of the Scopes trial in Tennessee, at which he defended the truth of revealed religion against attacks of evolutionism, winning the case for the state.

Bryant, William Cullen (1794–1878). Am. poet; educ. Williams Coll.; practiced law 1815–25, then followed literary pursuits; hymns include "Look from Thy Sphere of Endless Day."

Bryennios, Philotheos (ca. 1833–1914 [1918?]). B. Constantinople; d. Chalcis; educ. Chalcis, Berlin, Munich, and Leipzig; E Orthodox prof. ch. hist. Chalcis; metropolitan of Serrae in Macedonia and of Nicomedia. Discovered *Didache* and MSS of other early Christian writings.

Bryzelius, Paul. See *Canada,* A 2.

Buber, Martin (1878–1965). Jewish religious thinker; national universalist. B. Vienna; spent most of first 14 yrs. in Poland with grandfather, Salomon Buber, outstanding Haskalah* student; educ. secondary school in Lwów and univs. of Vienna and Berlin. Prof. U. of Frankfurt 1923–33, Hebrew U. of Jerusalem 1938–51. Early in life participated in Zionist movement and regarded founding of political state as phase of Jewish Renaissance; influenced by H. Cohen*, G. Landauer*, G. Simmel*, W. Dilthey*, Nietzsche*, Kierkegaard*, Dostoevski*, Oriental philosophers.

In his early phase he was interested in mysticism* (e. g., writings of Meister Eckhardt* and J. Boehme*), which absorbs finite Self in Infinite because it concentrates on life energies and creative vitality.

Withdrew from writing and lecturing 1904 to devote 5 yrs. to study of Hasidism.* Thereafter strongly influenced by Kierkegaard, whose existentialism he modified in direction of Hasidism. Rejected mysticism as delusion; replaced earlier emphasis on unity by stress on diversity.

His mature philos. is in *I and Thou* (1923), which emphasizes relationship as central meaning of existence. There are 2 primary attitudes: "I–It" attitude (subject–object) objectifies experience and is never spoken with whole being; "I–Thou" attitude (subject–subject) is best seen in dialogue between 2 persons but also takes place with nature. God, the eternal Thou, is supreme partner of dialogue and underlying power in all other "I-Thou*" encounters. Man relates to God with basic drives (hunger, sex, will) and institutions (politics, economics) that comprise material of his existence.

Buber often spoke of his own involvement with character of Jesus of Nazareth, whom he called "my great brother"; endeavored to understand the impulses of His Jewish being; strove to recover Him for Judaism; regarded Him as the incomparably purest figure in the hist. of Jewish messianism – but not as the Messiah.

Works include *I and Thou; Between Man and Man; Two Types of Faith; Origin and Meaning of Hasidism; Hasidism and Modern Man; Israel and Palestine; Israel and the World; Paths in Utopia; The Prophetic Faith; Moses.* EL

M. Friedman, *Martin Buber: the Life of Dialogue* (New York, 1960); M. L. Diamond, *Martin Buber: Jewish Existentialist* (New York, 1960); M. Buber, *Werke,* 3 vols. (Munich, 1962–63); H. v. Balthasar, *Martin Buber and Christianity,* tr. A. Dru (New York, 1961).

Bucanus, Wilhelm (d. 1603). Prof. theol. Lausanne; exponent of Calvinism. See also *Dogmatics,* B 5; *Grace, Means of,* IV 3.

Bucer, Martin (Butzer; Kuhhorn; 1491–1551). Ger. Prot. reformer. B. Sélestat; d. Cambridge. Dominican; studied theol., Gk., and Heb. at Heidelberg. Erasmus inclined him towards Protestantism; views influenced by Luther at Heidelberg disputation 1518. Introd. Reformation at Strasbourg 1523. To avoid theol. divisions, he advocated compromises and used dubious expressions. In disputes bet. Luther and Zwingli he adopted a middle course, trying to reconcile both; but his views of the Lord's Supper, approaching those of Zwingli, exposed him to Luther's criticism. At Augsburg 1530 he gen. agreed with Luth. views but declined to subscribe to the AC; later helped draw up Tetrapolitan Confession (Strasbourg, Konstanz, Memmingen, Lindau). At Diet of Regensburg* he tried to unite Prots. and RCs. Refusing to sign the *Interim,* he accepted an invitation of Abp. Cranmer to teach theol. at Cambridge and to help in furthering the Reformation in Eng. See also *Lutheran Confessions,* B 1; *Reformed Confessions,* D 1; *Regensburg Book; Regensburg Conference; Sickingen, Franz von.*

J. W. Baum, *Capito und Butzer, Strassburgs Reformatoren,* in *Leben und ausgewählte Schriften der Väter und Begründer der reformirten Kirche,* III (Elberfeld, 1860).

Buchanan, George (1506–82). Scot. humanist; joined Ref. movement; fled to Fr.; taught Montaigne; Calvinist protagonist on return to Scot.; moderator Gen. Assem.

Buchheimer, Louis Balthaser (Mar. 23, 1872–Aug. 1, 1953). B. Detroit; d. St. Louis. Grad. Conc. Sem., St. Louis, 1893; prof. Conc. Coll., Conover, N. C., 1893–96; pastor Memphis, Tenn., 1896–1902; Saint Louis 1902–37; dean theol. Immanuel Coll., Greensboro, N. C., 1937–39; assoc. pastor Detroit 1939–46; retired and returned to St. Louis. Vice-pres. Eng. Dist. of Mo. Syn. 1918–21. Works include *Faith and Duty; From Advent to Advent; Things New and Old; Sermons on Romanism; The Christian Warfare; The First Gospel and Other Sermons; Wholesome Words; Comfortable Words; Gracious Words; Emblems in the Gospels;* ed. *Great Leaders and Great Events.* ARS

Buchholtz, Andreas Heinrich. See *Bucholtz, Andreas Heinrich.*

Buchman, Frank Nathan Daniel. See *Buchmanism.*

Buchmanism (Oxford Group Movement; First Century Christian Fellowship; Moral Re-Armament). Founded by Frank N. D. Buchman (1878–1961), grad. Mount Airy Luth. Theol. Sem. (ULC), Philadelphia. After a few years in the Luth. ministry Buchman was led at Keswick, Eng., to a "new career of service," emphasizing absolute honesty, purity, unselfishness, and love. According to Buchmanism, the barrier of sin is removed by "sharing" (complete confession of all sins and witnessing this confession before others), "surrender," "restitution," and receiving and following immediate "guidance" from God. Thus Buchmanism tries to "revitalize" Christianity and supply men with "moral rearmament."

G. C. Gast, *Oxford Group Movement* (Columbus, n. d.); W. G. Schwehn, *What Is Buchmanism?* (St. Louis, 1940); C. I. Benson, *The Eight Points of the Oxford Group* (New York, 1936); A. W. Eister, *Drawing Room Conversion* (Durham, N. C., 1950); P. Howard, *Frank Buchman's Secret* (New York, 1962).

Buchmann, Theodor (Bibliander; ca. 1500–64). Swiss theol. and Oriental scholar; Zwingli's successor as prof. Prot. theol. Zurich 1531–60; opposed Calvin's doctrine of predestination.

Buchner, Charles (1842–1907). B. Irwinhill, Jamaica; d. Herrnhut; Moravian bp.; dir. Teachers Sem., Niesky; mem. Miss. Bd., Berthelsdorf.

Büchner, Friedrich Karl Christian Ludwig (1824–99). Ger physician and philos.; lecturer U. of Tübingen. In *Kraft und Stoff* he tried to reduce everything to a single material source.

Büchner, Gottfried (1701–80). B. Rüdersdorf, Saxe-Altenburg; educ. Jena; rector Querfurt, Saxony; wrote *Biblische Real- und Verbal-Hand-Concordanz.*

Bucholtz, Andreas Heinrich (Buchholtz; 1607–71). Luth. theol.; educ. Wittenberg and Rostock; rector Lemgo 1637; instructor 1639, prof. poetry 1641 and theol. 1645 Rinteln; preacher 1647 and supt. 1664 Braunschweig. Works include hymns and the romances *Herkules* and *Herkuliskus.*

Buchrucker, Karl von (1827–99). Leading Bavarian Luth. clergyman; supt. Munich; consistorial councillor 1885; founded *Neue Kirchliche Zeitschrift;* ed. cat. which became official in Gen. Syn. of Bavaria.

Büchsel, Friedrich (1883–1945). Prof. NT Rostock. Works on theol. of NT include *Theologie des Neuen Testaments.*

Büchsel, Karl Albert Ludwig (1803–89). Ger. Luth. positive theol. Educ. Prenzlau and Berlin. Pastor Schönfeld 1828–41; pastor and supt. Brüssow 1841 to 1846; pastor Berlin 1846–53; gen. supt. Neumark and Niederlausitz 1853–84; influential in Prussian Union, with Luth. leanings. Works include *Erinnerungen aus dem Leben eines Landgeistlichen,* 5 vols.

Buchwald, Georg Apollo (1859–1947). Pastor Zwickau and Leipzig; supt. Rochlitz. Active in Luther research; ed. materials for Weimar and Erlangen eds. Luther's works.

Buck, Dudley (1839–1909). B. Hartford, Conn. Studied in Leipzig, Dresden, and Paris; organist Hartford, Chicago, Boston, Brooklyn, and New York. Works include organ compositions, cantatas, and ch. music for both liturgical and choir use.

Buck, Henry W. (Feb. 28, 1906–Apr. 20, 1960). Grad. U. of Kans. Law School 1928; sr. partner law firm Morrison, Hecker, Buck, and Cozad. Mem. Ex. Bd. Lutheran Laymen's League 1937–39, 1941–43, 1947 to 1948; pres. Internat. Walther League 1939–47; mem. Bd. of Dir. Wheat Ridge Foundation 1939–60; mem. Bd. of Dir. The Lutheran Church – Missouri Synod 1951–60; secy. The Lutheran Church – Missouri Synod Foundation 1959–60; mem. Implementation Committee of the Synodical Survey Commission 1959–60; guest lecturer U. of Kans. Law School and U. of Mo. at Kansas City.

Buckley, James Monroe (1836–1920). Am. Meth. Episc. author and clergyman; ed. *Christian Advocate* 1880–1912.

Budde, Karl Ferdinand Reinhard (1850–1935). Ger. Prot. theol.; prof. OT Strasbourg and Marburg; Orientalist. Works include *Religion of Israel.*

Buddeus, Johann Franz (1667–1729). Ger. Luth. theol. and scholar. Prof. Wittenberg, Jena, Coburg, and Halle; mediated bet. orthodox Lutheranism and Pietism; several times rector Jena U. Works include *Institutiones theologiae dogmaticae; Isagoge historico-theologica ad theologiam universam.*

Buddha, Fellowship Following. See *Fellowship Following Buddha.*

Buddha, Gautama. See *Buddhism; Gautama Buddha.*

Buddhism. 1. Religious system founded by Gautama* Buddha, 6th c. BC, in N India; revolt against Brahmanism.* Denies authority of the Vedas, rejects Brahmanic caste system, ritual, and philos. speculations, and offers a new way to salvation. The 2 canonical languages of Buddhism: Pali, of S or Hinayana (Theravada) Buddhism, and Skt., of N or Mahayana Buddhism.

2. The texts on which our knowledge of early Buddhism is based are sacred books found in Ceylon, written in Pali and called *Tipitaka* (Skt. *Tripitaka*), that is Three Baskets (Pitaka), namely the Baskets of Vinaya, Sutta, and Abhidhamma (monastic rules and disciplines, teachings of the Buddha, and Buddhist higher philos., resp.). Other books come from Nepal, written in Skt., and from China and Tibet, written in the languages of those countries. In a way, Gautama's doctrine is not religion but practical atheism. Of the 5 requisites of religion, i. e., "the belief in a divine power, the acknowledgment of sin, the habit of prayer, the desire to offer sacrifice, and the hope of a future life" (F. M. Müller*), not one is found in Gautama's system. Though he did not deny existence of traditional gods, yet he held that prayer and sacrifice to them were of no avail, as they, like men, were subject to death and rebirth and in rebirth might sink to the level of inferior beings, while men in rebirth might rise to the level of gods. In anatta (absence of soul) he likewise denied the existence of the soul (see *Transmigration of Souls*). But, in common with Brahmanism, he held the pessimistic view that life was not worth living; that in his "five aggregates" of being (corporeality, feeling, perception, mental formations,

and consciousness), man was subject to a continuous round of rebirths; that a man's karma, i. e., his acts in one existence, determined his lot in future existences; that salvation consisted not in escape from sin and hell (neither of which are recognized by Indian philosophies), but in obtaining freedom from rebirths; and that ignorance (avidya) is the cause of all evil. But as he rejected the Vedas and taught a new way of destroying ignorance and obtaining freedom from rebirth, his doctrine, like Jainism,* was considered a heresy by the Brahmans. He was also against the caste system.

3. Buddha's entire doctrine is based on the so-called "four noble truths," which speak 1. of the universality of suffering, 2. of the causes of suffering, 3. of the cessation of suffering, and 4. of the path that leads to the cessation of suffering. Birth, decay, disease, death, separation from what we love, contact with what we hate, and failure to attain what we desire – all is suffering. This suffering is caused by "thirst," i. e., craving for life and its pleasures, and this attachment causes rebirth and continued misery. Freedom from rebirth and consequently from suffering can be obtained if this craving is completely destroyed. The path that leads to this end is the "noble eightfold path," namely, "right belief, right aspirations, right speech, right conduct, right means of subsistence, right effort, right mindfulness, right meditation." This path is called the "middle path," as it is removed from the extremes of a sensuous life and of asceticism. He who follows this path to its end becomes an arhat, or saint. He has destroyed his ignorance, become perfect by knowledge, and broken the fetters that bind him to the wheel of life. The supreme and final goal of this spiritual discipline is nirvana (Pali nibbana), literally "a blowing out," namely of the desires and passions that lead to rebirth. As the old karma is exhausted and no new karma is added, the round of rebirths ceases and ends in an unconscious state. Whether this is equivalent to the annihilation of personality was not stated by Gautama, but many Buddhist texts interpret it in this sense. Nirvana may in a certain sense be obtained in this life by the arhat, but it is entered upon completely only at death.

4. The followers of Gautama soon were organized into a mendicant order open to all men over 20, physically and legally fit, without caste distinction. The monks (Pali *bhikkus;* Skt. *bhikshus,* i. e., "beggars") obligated themselves to keep 10 commandments forbidding 1. taking of life, 2. theft, 3. sexual impurity, 4. lying, 5. use of intoxicating liquors, 6. eating at forbidden times, i. e., bet. noon and the following morning, 7. taking part in dancing, singing, music, theater, 8. using ornaments and perfume, 9. sleeping on beds raised from the floor, 10. receiving gold or silver. Every monk had to take the vow of absolute celibacy and poverty. Great stress was laid on the virtues of benevolence (even to animals), patience, and humility. Twice a month he had to confess his faults before the assembled brethren. He had to dress only in rags, beg food with an alms dish in his hand, live much of the time in forests, and spend many hours in contemplation. Thus an elaborate system of rules governed his entire life. Subordinated to the monks were the nuns, whom Gautama, according to tradition, admitted to the order only with great reluctance. Beside this monastic order also a lay membership was organized. But the rules for the lay members were far less strict. They were obligated to observe only the first 5 of the 10 commandments mentioned above and to practice benevolence and charity at all times. As Buddhism is atheistic in principle, it makes no provision for a cult or priesthood. Wherever these are found in modern forms of Buddhism, they are a later development.

5. Shortly after Gautama's death the first great council, attended by 500 arhats, met at Rajagaha (Rajagriha, modern Rajgir) to decide and take measures to preserve the authoritative teachings of the Buddha; here the canonical *Tipitaka (Tripitaka)* was formulated. A hundred yrs. after the death of the Buddha, after certain schismatic monks had been defeated, the 2d great council met at Vesali, under King Kalasoka's patronage. Zealous Buddhist Emperor Asoka convened the 3d great council at Pataliputra (modern Patna). Heretics were expunged and missionary plans were laid. Asoka sought the extension of Buddhism throughout his empire and the entire world. Other great councils were held ca. 25 BC, AD 1871, and 1954–56. A council called by King Kaniska (Kanishka) in the first c. AD is not recognized by the Theravada (see 6) but apparently left its mark on Buddhism in Tibet and China.

6. The later hist. of Indian Buddhism is marked by the great conflict bet. the schools called Hinayana ("Little Vehicle") and Mahayana ("Great Vehicle"). This led to a permanent division into 2 sects. The Hinayana (Theravada) is the conservative system. It is based on the Pali canon, holds to the original teachings of Buddhism, regards Gautama as a mere man, and teaches that salvation can be obtained by only few mortals. It maintained itself in the S part of the Buddhist sphere (Ceylon, Burma, Siam). Mahayana Buddhism, on the other hand, called so because it claimed to be the better vessel to take man across the stream of existence to nirvana, follows the Skt. scriptures. It transformed Gautama into a god or an incarnation of the Absolute. It is the N form of Buddhism (Tibet, China, Korea, Japan). The peculiar hierarchical form into which it developed in Tibet is called Lamaism.* The last phase of decadent Indian Buddhism is that called Tantrayana, which developed from the Mahayana Buddhism of Tibet and introduced esoteric worship and magic and even sensual practices which weakened Buddhism and made revival almost impossible after the Muslim invaders destroyed the Mahayana temples and monasteries. Buddhism apparently lost out in India to Hinduism (which converted Buddhist temples into Hindu temples) and to Islam (which opposed Buddhism with violence); internal decay also contributed to the temporary disappearance of Buddhism from India. But it continued in Ceylon, Burma, Thailand, China, Indo-China (Vietnam), the East Indies (Malaya, Sumatra, Java, Bali, and Borneo), Korea, and Japan, and reached into the W world. After WW II it made some converts in India among the scheduled castes or untouchables; also some intellectuals showed interest.

7. The 6th conf. of the World Fellowship of Buddhists (WFB) in Phnom Penh, Cambodia, Nov. 1961, increased world interest in Buddhism. The WFB, est. 1950, has attempted to secure unity among the branches of Buddhism in teachings and in cultural, educational, and missionary activities. A 1958 conference in Thailand dropped the distinction between Theravada and Mahayana Buddhism, but differences bet. them were strongly in evidence at the 1961 conference. Political problems of the nations represented (e. g., disarmament and differing regimes) disturbed the delegates, but joint work continued on the *Encyclopaedia of Buddhism* as planned in 1955.

8. In China Buddhism became intertwined with Taoism* and Confucianism,* in Japan with Shinto.*

See also *Chinese Philosophy,* 5; *Nichiren; Sacred Literature; Soka Gakkai; Theosophy.*

K. W. Morgan, *The Path of the Buddha: Buddhism Interpreted by Buddhists* (New York, 1956).

AJB

Buehler. See *Bühler.*

Buenger, Johann Friedrich. See *Bünger, Johann Friedrich.*

Buenger, Theodore Henry Carl (Apr. 29, 1860–Sept. 9, 1943). B. Chicago; grad. Conc. Sem., St. Louis, 1882; miss. NW Wis. 1882–84; pastor Tinley Park and Orland Park, Ill., 1884–91; St. Paul, Minn. 1891–93; taught at Conc. Coll., St. Paul, Minn., 1893–1943; temporary dir. there 1893, dir. 1896, pres. 1905–27.

Buffalo Colloquy. Discussion bet. C. F. W. Walther,* W. Sihler,* H. C. Schwan,* J. C. D. Römer of St. Louis, Mo., J. Keil of Pittsburgh, Pa., and J. C. Theiss of Altenburg, Mo., of the Mo. Syn., and H. K. G. v. Rohr,* C. F. (W.) Hochstetter,* P. Brand,* C. Krull of Neubergholz, N. Y., E. Schorr of Buffalo, N. Y. (alternate for F. Groth of Cedarburg, Wis.), and H. A. Christiansen of Detroit, Mich., of the Buffalo* Syn.; held Buffalo, N. Y., Nov. 20–Dec. 5, 1866. Items discussed: ch., ministry, excommunication, adiaphora, ordination. See also *Lutheran Church – Missouri Synod, The,* V 15.

Das Buffaloer Colloquium, abgehalten vom 20. November bis 5. December 1866, das ist, die schlieszlichen Erklärungen der die Synode von Buffalo und die von Missouri, Ohio u. a. Staaten vertretenden Colloquenten über die bisher zwischen beiden Synoden streitigen und besprochenen Lehren, rev., signed, and pub. by the collocutors (St. Louis, 1866), known also as *Protokoll über die Verhandlungen des Colloquiums gehalten in Buffalo . . .* from heading on first page; R. A. Suelflow, "Buffalo-Missouri Colloquy," in "The Relations of the Missouri Synod with the Buffalo Synod up to 1866," *CHIQ,* XXVII (1954–55), 127–132.

Buffalo Declaration. See *Washington Declaration.*

Buffalo Synod. 1. Till 1886 its official name was "The Synod of the Lutheran Church Emigrated from Prussia." Its original mems. had left Ger. 1839 under J. A. A. Grabau* of Erfurt in protest against the Prussian Union.* Small groups settled in New York City and Albany, the majority in the Buffalo area, and another group near Milwaukee. Only a few immigrants came later, because royal pressure in behalf of the Prussian Union faded after 1840. The syn. was organized June 25, 1845, at Milwaukee by 4 pastors and 18 lay dels.

2. At first there were high hopes of combining Grabau's adherents with the Saxon immigrants of 1839 and the Luths. affiliated with Loehe's* enterprises; in opposition to the other Luth. syns. of that day these groups were all unequivocally committed to the Luth. Confs. But such hopes were frustrated by disagreements that developed, esp. on the doctrine of the ministry.

3. Grabau held that ordination is a divine inst. performed by previously ordained men, through which God confers the authority of the ministry on men whom the proper officials of the ch. have found qualified for office. For the sake of good order pastors could demand cong. obedience in all matters not contrary to the Word of God. Grabau was convinced that his view was biblical and confessional and that it could help check the growing spirit of sectarian congregationalism. When his 1840 *Hirtenbrief* came to the Saxons, who had a much more congregational view of the ministry and ordination, controversy ensued. Bitter strife continued for many yrs., esp. because the Missouri Synod* felt bound to give pastoral care to individuals and groups that were unwilling to submit to Grabau's views. All efforts at reconciliation were in vain because the starting point of the groups and the basis of their appeal to each other were so different. Grabau regarded Mo.'s doctrine as sectarian; Mo. regarded Grabau's as hierarchical and romanizing. 1859 the Buffalo Syn., in what amounted to a decree of excommunication, renounced all fraternal relations with Mo.

4. Resistance among Buffalo Syn. clergy to Grabau's views and methods led 1866 to a heresy trial of Grabau by his own syn., which rejected his distinctive views and asked him to renounce them. Schism followed on his refusal and suspension. 3 pastors remained loyal to Grabau. 12 joined the Mo. Syn. 6 formed an indep. anti-Grabau group that claimed to be the real Buffalo Syn.; it disbanded 1877, most pastors and congs. joining the Wis. Syn. See also *Buffalo Colloquy.*

5. After 1866, and even more after Grabau's death 1879, the Buffalo Syn. gradually modified its views on the ministry, pastoral authority over congs., the strict practice of private conf., and frequent use of the ban and excommunication. It always retained its deep loyalty to the Luth. Confs.

6. Grabau's *Hirtenbriefe* and the *Kirchliches Informatorium* were voices of the syn. before the schism. After 1866 the official ch. paper was *Wachende Kirche.* The syn.'s Martin Luther Coll. and Sem., est. 1840, furnished a steady small supply of pastors and teachers. When Buffalo became part of the American Lutheran Church* 1930 it had 44 pastors, 51 congs., 10,341 bap. mems. in N. Y., Can., Pa., Mich., Wis., Ill., and Minn.

See also *Iowa and Other States, Evangelical Lutheran, Synod of,* 1. 5, 9.

P. H. Buehring, *The Spirit of the American Lutheran Church* (Columbus, 1940); J. F. Köstering, *Auswanderung der sächsischen Lutheraner im Jahre 1838,* 2d printing (St. Louis, 1867), pp. 84–112; R. A. Suelflow, "The Relations of the Missouri Synod with the Buffalo Synod up to 1866," *CHIQ,* XXVII (Apr., July, Oct., 1954), 1–19; 57–73; 97–132; *Protokoll über die Verhandlungen des Colloquiums gehalten in Buffalo, N. Y., vom 20. November bis 5. December 1866,* alternate title *Das Buffaloer Colloquium . . .*, rev., signed, and pub. by the collocutors of both sides (St. Louis, 1866); complete hist. of the Buffalo Syn. pub. intermittently in *Wachende Kirche,* LIV (June 15, 1920) – LXIII (Dec. 1929). FWM

Buffon, George Louis Leclerc de. See *Evolution,* I.

Bugenhagen, Johann (Pomeranus; Dr. Pommer; June 24, 1485–Apr. 20, 1558). B. Wolin, Pomerania; educ. U. of Greifswald; at 18 appointed rector of Latin school Treptow on the Rega; ordained priest 1509; appointed lecturer on Bible and church fathers 1517. Became follower of Luther 1520 after reading *Babylonian Captivity* (see *Luther, Chief Writings of*). Married 1522. Pastor Wittenberg 1523–58; Luther's confessor. Lectured on Psalms at Wittenberg. Helped pub. Low Ger. ed. NT 1524. Officiated at Luther's wedding (see *Luther, Family Life of*). First Wittenberger to oppose Zwingli* 1525. Great organizer of Luth. Ch. In 1526 reformed Hamburg, Brunswick 1528, Lübeck and Lower Saxony 1530. His ch. order was introd. also in Minden, Osnabrück, Göttingen, Soest, Bremen, and many other places. Called to Pomerania 1534; succeeded in introd. Reformation against much opposition. Christian III* called him to Denmark* 1537; reformed the ch. and U. of Copenhagen; crowned the king and queen; called back 1542 to reform Schleswig-Holstein; busy also in Brunswick and Hildesheim. After declining 3 bishoprics and all other calls he was made gen. supt. of Saxony 1539. Preached funeral sermon for Luther. After Imperials captured Wittenberg, Charles V treated him with surprising mildness. Bugenhagen, in turn, did not oppose the Augsburg Interim.* He helped draft Leipzig Interim. But 1550 he returned to strict Lutheranism with *Commentary on Jonah,* in which he protested against RC error. Shortly before his retirement 1557 he warned all pastors against compromises. One of greatest scholars of Reformation era. Praised by Luther for 1524 commentary on whole Psalter (WA, 15, 8). Helped Luther rev. Bible 1539; stood at his side in Antinomian Controversy* 1539–40. In controversies after Luther's death he suffered much *Anfechtung* (spiritual anxiety) besides grievous physical pain toward the end of life. Greatest contribution to Reformation was his indefatigable zeal and his ability to organize Luth. churches and schools; he is called the father of the *Volksschule*. Works include *Pomerania; Von dem Christenloven und rechten guden Werken;* letter to Christians in England. See also *Christian Education,* D 5; *Lutheran Confessions,* B 1; *Pack, Otto von.*

Bugenhagiana. Quellen zur Lebensgeschichte des D. Joh. Bugenhagen, Vol. I: Bibliotheca Bugenhagiana. Bibliographie der Druckschriften des D. Joh. Bugenhagen, ed. G. Geisenhof (Leipzig, 1908); H. Hering, *Doktor Pomeranus, Johannes Bugenhagen* (Halle, 1888); W. M. Ruccius, *John Bugenhagen Pomeranus* (Philadelphia, 1924); W. Tillmanns, *The World and Men Around Luther (Minneapolis,* 1959), pp. 90–93. WGT

Bugge, Fredrik Wilhelm Klumpp (1838–96). Norw. theol.; prof. theol. Christiania 1870–93; bp. Christiania 1893–96; one of revisers of Norw. Bible; wrote esp. in field of NT isagogics.

Buhl, Frants Peder William Meyer (1850–1932). Prof. OT Copenhagen 1882, Leipzig 1890; of Semitic languages Copenhagen 1898. Wrote on canon and text of OT and on geog. and sociology of Palestine. Collaborated on eds. of H. F. W. Gesenius,* *Hebräisches und aramäisches Handwörterbuch über das Alte Testament.* See also *Lexicons,* A.

Bühler, Jacob Matthias (Beehler; Aug. 8, 1837–Aug. 28, 1901). Pioneer Mo. Syn. pastor on US Pacific coast. B. Baltimore, Md.; grad. Conc. Sem., Saint Louis, 1860; pastor San Francisco 1860. Because of his firm stand for confessional Lutheranism a split ensued, and St. Paulus was organized 1867, mother ch. on Pacific coast. Organized day school 1872, of which J. H. Hargens was in charge for over 40 yrs. Pres. Calif. and Oreg. Dist. of the Mo. Syn. 1887–99, Calif. and Nev. Dist. 1899–1901. Excellent preacher, wise counselor, ardent lover of the Lord, friend of children, splendid organizer.

J. H. Theiss and J. W. Theiss, *Lebenslauf und Charakterbild des seligen Präses J. M. Bühler* (Oakland, Calif., 1902); R. T. Du Brau, *The Romance of Lutheranism in California* ([St. Louis, 1959]).

Building, Church. See *Church Architecture.*

Building Program, Parish. Religious and evangelistic act undertaken by a cong. in which a ch. home for its people and a house for God is planned and built. The bldg. program includes everything a cong. does and decides that finally leads to adequate facilities for its purposes.

Since each cong. is unique, there can be no plan that would suffice for all programs. Desire for uniformity has resulted in much mediocrity in contemporary ch. architecture. A ch. should not be built until the cong. knows how, whom, and why it worships; what its entire program of parish educ. entails; how it can best advance Christian witness; what new methods of worship and educ. can be adopted. The pastor usually guides and directs the study of these problems.

Publications to guide pastor and people include *Architecture and the Church,* issued by the Commission on Ch. Architecture of the LCMS (St. Louis, 1965); *Manual for the Building Enterprise,* ed. E. S. Frey, LCA Comm. on Ch. Architecture (New York, 1965); C. H. Atkinson, *How to Get Your Church Built* (New York, 1964); A. Biéler, *Architecture in Worship* (London, 1965); D. J. Bruggink and C. H. Droppers, *Christ and Architecture: Building Presbyterian/Reformed Churches* (Grand Rapids, 1965); A. W. Christ-Janer and M. M. Foley, *Modern Church Architecture* (New York, 1962); V. H. Fiddes, *The Architectural Requirements of Protestant Worship* (Toronto, 1961); E. S. Frey, *This Before Architecture* (Foundation Books, Jenkintown, Pa., 1963); P. Hammond, *Liturgy and Architecture* (New York, 1961); J. R. Scotford, *When You Build Your Church,* 2d ed. (Great Neck, N. Y., 1958); *Church Buildings and Furnishings,* ed. J. G. Sherman (Greenwich, Conn., 1958); J. F. White, *Protestant Worship and Church Architecture* (New York, 1964); periodicals *Anno Domini, Liturgical Arts,* and *Your Church.*

A ch. should be built from the inside out. Many congs. in hurry to have a bldg. are still pondering the problems of fitting their liturgical needs into a meaningless shell. Much time and prayerful consideration must be given to the meaning of worship before the architect can even be chosen, much less commissioned. A cong. cannot be reminded too often that what it builds is not the end, but a place of corporate and individual worship and a means of witnessing to the Truth, which is the Source of all Being. RRCj

See also *Church Architecture.*

Bulgakov, Sergei Nikolaevich (1871–1944). Russ. theol. Warm, but critical, adherent of ecumenical movement. Emphasized doctrine of man as image of God. Christ is God-Man in which all mankind participates. There is that in God's nature which is the image of God in man, the primordial manhood in God (divine God-manhood); the creaturely God-manhood is the divine in man. This is Sophiology (describes relation of man and God); Sophia is the Godhead, a living, loving substance, ground, and principle. Creaturely Sophia is image of God in in world. Emphasized sobornost.* Works include *The Orthodox Church; The Wisdom of God; Du Verbe incarné; Le Paraclet; Die Tragödie der Philosophie.*

Bulgaria. Balkan country W of Black Sea. Under control of USSR since WW II. *Area:* 42,796 sq. mi. *Pop.* (1960 est.): 7,867,000; Gk. Orthodox 84.4%, Muhammadan 13.5%, Jewish .8%, RC .8%, Armenian and Prot. .5%. Won for Christianity under Boris* chiefly by Cyril* and Methodius of Gk. Ch. ca. AD 864. Placed ecclesiastically under Rome by Boris (contributing cause of Great Schism*); returned to allegiance of Constantinople 1869. Bulgarian Ch. restored 1870–72 with exarch in Constantinople. Methodists began miss. work 1857; ABCFM later. In recent times National Ch. disest.; hospitals and schools prohibited.

Bulgarian Eastern Orthodox Church. See *Eastern Orthodox Churches,* 6.

Bull *(Litterae apostolicae sub plumbo).* The most solemn and formal written mandate of the pope; used for releases of universal significance, canonization, universal papal laws, changes in ch. provinces, creation of orders, and matters of similar importance. Lat. *bulla,* "bubble," was the lead or wax stamped to seal and authenticate mandates since 6th c. Since 1878 only consistorial bulls (signed by pope and cardinals) are thus sealed; less important ones are stamped and signed by the Cardinal Chancellor, a lesser official, and 2 notaries. Bulls begin with name of pope (without numeral), followed by *"episcopus servus servorum Dei,"* greeting, addresses, message. Bulls are designated by their first words. Important bulls are *Clericis Laicos* (Boniface VIII, 1296), threatening Fr. and Eng. kings with excommunication because of their high taxes; *Unam Sanctam* (Boniface VIII, 1302), containing the most sweeping claims ever advanced by the papacy (see also *Two Swords*); *In Coena Domini* (Urban V, 1362), excommunicating heretics, etc., by name (published with additions every Maundy Thursday till 1773); *Exsurge, Domine* (Leo X, June 15, 1520), the bull which Luther burned; *Decet Romanum Pontificem* (Jan. 3, 1521), excommunicating Luther; *Dominus ac Redemptor Noster* (Clement XIV, 1773), abolishing the Jesuits, and *Sollicitudo Omnium* (Pius VII, 1814), reestablishing them; *Ineffabilis* (Pius IX, 1854), proclaiming the dogma of the Immaculate Conception; *Pastor Aeternus* (Pius IX, 1870), defining papal primacy and infallibility; *Munificentissimus Deus* (Pius XII, 1950), promulgating the Assumption of Mary. EL

See also *Golden Bull; Reformation, Lutheran,* 9.

Bull, George (1634–1710). Angl. theol.; bp. Saint David's, Wales; exponent of old Anglo-Catholicism. Works include *Defensio Fidei Nicenae.*

Bull, John (ca. 1562–1628). Eng. RC organist and composer of the Madrigalian Era; wrote much ch. music. Though not equal to Gibbons and Byrd, he enjoys a fame that puts him above the rank and file of Eng. composers.

Bullarium. Collection of bulls.*

Bullen. See *Pullus, Robert.*

Bullinger, Johann Heinrich (1504–75). Swiss reformer. B. Bremgarten (Aargau); d. Zurich. Left RC Ch. 1522. Succeeded Zwingli as chief pastor of Zurich and leader of Reformation in Ger. Switz. 1531. Helped draw up *First Helvetic Confession;* concluded with Calvin the *Consensus Tigurinus;* other works include *Second Helvetic Confession; History of the Reformation.* See also *Religious Drama,* 3; *Switzerland,* 2.

Zwingli and Bullinger, sel. tr. with introd. and notes by G. W. Bromiley (Philadelphia, 1953).

Bultmann, Rudolf. See *Demythologization; Existentialism,* 1.

Bünger, Johann Friedrich (Jan. 2, 1810–Jan. 23, 1882). B. Etzdorf, near Rosswein, Saxony; scion of family of clerics reaching back to the Reformation. At Leipzig he came under influence of an elderly, retired candidate of theology named Kühn; private tutor Pirna and Dresden; to US with Martin Stephan;* gave practical assistance to colonists in Perry Co., Mo.; one of the founders of the coll. at Altenburg. Teacher Trinity school, St. Louis 1841; asst. pastor Trinity 1844; pastor Immanuel 1847. Walther called him the Am. Luth. Valerius Herberger.* His practical nature was exemplified in his pastoral work. Pres. W Dist., Mo. Syn., 1863–75. Friend of miss.; "Father" of Syn. Conf. Negro Miss. Founder of Luth. Hosp. and Orphan's Home, St. Louis.

C. F. W. Walther, *Kurzer Lebenslauf des weiland ehrwürdigen Pastor Joh. Friedr. Bünger* (St. Louis, 1882).

Bünger, Theodore Henry Carl. See *Buenger, Theodore Henry Carl.*

Bunsen, Christian Karl Josias von (1791–1860). Ger. scholar and diplomat; friend of Frederick William III and IV of Prussia; assisted in preparation of Prussian* Union agenda; ed. hymnbook; wrote on theol. and philos. themes.

Bunyan, John (1628–88). Eng. preacher and author; joined Bedford nonconformist ch. 1653; soon began to preach; came into conflict with G. Fox and Quakers; at the Restoration he was ordered to stop preaching; refused; was thrown into jail, where he remained ca. 11½ yrs. and wrote some of his works, which include *Grace Abounding to the Chief of Sinners; The Life and Death of Mr. Badman; The Holy War; The Heavenly Footman; Pilgrim's Progress.*

J. Brown, *John Bunyan,* Tercentenary ed., rev. F. M. Harrison (London, 1928); W. Y. Tindall, *John Bunyan, Mechanick Preacher* (New York, 1964); O. E. Winslow, *John Bunyan* (New York, 1961).

Buonarotti. See *Michelangelo.*

Burce, Willard Lewis. See *New Guinea,* 7.

Burchard (ca. 965–1025). Bp. Worms 1000; compiled *Decretum,* important collection of canon law.

Burchard, Samuel Dickinson (1812–91). Presb. clergyman in N. Y. city; his remarks associating the opponents of J. G. Blaine with "rum, Romanism, and rebellion" probably caused Blaine to lose New York's votes and the presidential election 1884.

Burck, Joachim à (Burgch; Burgk; Möller; Moller; Müller; 1546–1610). Ger. Luth. organist and composer. Sought to write music on basis of Scripture texts. See also *Passion, The.*

Burckhardt. See *Spalatin, Georg.*

Burckhardt, Jakob Christoph (1818–97). Swiss hist. and writer on It. Renaissance; prof. Basel; instr. Zurich. Works include *Die Zeit Konstantins des Grossen; Geschichte der Renaissance in Italien.*

Bure, Idelette de. See *Calvin, John,* 4.

Burg, Johann Friedrich (1689–1766). B. Breslau, Ger.; educ. Leipzig; pastor Breslau 1735; mem. of high consistory Breslau 1742. Ed. hymnals; coed. Hirschberger* Bibel.

Burger, Carl Heinrich August von (1805–84). Mem. high consistory Munich; with G. C. A. v. Harless* made ch. of Bavaria a model Luth. ch. in doctrine, worship, and use of sacraments; wrote studies of Gospels and Revelation; prevented Loehe's break with state ch.; supported Gustav Adolf Verein.* His hymbook, liturgy, and Bible studies used in America.

Bürger, Ernst Moritz (Feb. 17, 1806–Mar. 22, 1890). B. Saxony; educ. Dresden and Leipzig; pastor Rochsburg and Lunzenau; joined Saxon emigrants under M. Stephan* (1777–1846); pastor Seelitz, Perry Co., Mo.; in the confusion resulting from doubts regarding the doctrine of ch. and ministry he resigned as pastor at Seelitz; after the 1841 Altenburg* Debate he left Mo.; en route to Ger. he stopped at Buffalo and was persuaded to remain as pastor of former followers of L. F. E. Krause; charter mem. Mo. Syn.; pastor Buffalo and W. Seneca, N. Y., Washington, D. C., and Winona, Minn.

Memoirs of Ernst Moritz Buerger, tr. by E. J. Buerger (Lincoln, Mass., 1953).

Burger, Johann Georg (July 4, 1816–Mar. 26, 1847). B. Nördlingen, Bav. Entered teacher training under J. K. W. Löhe* as his 2d student 1841. To US 1842 with J. A. Ernst.* Attended the Ohio Syn. sem. at Columbus, Ohio. Licensed by the Ohio Syn. 1844. Served a cong. in Hancock Co., Ohio. Withdrew from Ohio Syn. 1845 (see *Document of Separation*); ordained at that time. Pastor Willshire, Van Wert Co., and in Mercer Co., Ohio, 1846. Attended the July 1846 meeting in Fort Wayne, Ind., that concerned itself with drafting the Mo. Syn. const. (see *Lutheran Church – Missouri Synod, The,* I 1, III 1. See also *Ohio and Other States, The Evangelical Lutheran Joint Synod of,* 5.

Burgh, William George de (1866–1943). Brit. philos.; Prof. Reading 1907–34. Exponent of ethical theism. The antinomies of morality can only be resolved on the religious level which implies communion with God. The frustration of moral striving is resolved by the supervention of divine grace. Wrote *The Legacy of the Ancient World; Towards a Religious Philosophy; From Morality to Religion.*

Buri, Fritz. See *Demythologization.*

Burial. 1. Burial practices are usually assoc. with conceptions of life, nature of soul, death, and hereafter. But customs are often preserved when beliefs and practices change. Fear, love, and awe are attitudes of the living toward the dead and determine burial practices.

2. In OT the body was often buried in cave, shaft, ground, etc. (e. g., Gn. 23:19; 25:9; 35:19). Even criminals and enemies were not denied burial (Jos 8:29; 10:26, 27; 2 Sm 21:12-14). Cremation* was obnoxious (Am 2:1) and usually reserved for executed criminals (Jos 7:25; Lv 20:14; 21:9). The

corpse was usually placed on a bier (2 Sm 3:31; Lk 7:12-14). In NT bodies were washed (Acts 9: 37), anointed (Mk 16:1), wrapped in linen (Mt 27: 59), hands, feet, and head wrapped in cloth (Jn 11: 44). Graves were regarded as unclean.

3. Christians early showed care for the dead. The church became responsible for the burial of its mems. Candles, incense, and psalms expressed joyful hope of resurrection. Corpses often were dressed in white or in official garments. Prayers for the dead* and eucharists in their honor occurred at an early date. According to Augustine, proper burial expressed faith in the resurrection. It is more a comfort to the living than a service to the dead (*De civitate Dei,* I, xi, xiii).

4. By the late Middle Ages customs which are still in the Roman rite had become fixed. The Office of the Dead came to consist of the Placebo* (Vespers), the Dirige, or Dirge* (Matins), and the Requiem* Mass. The early note of joy had also changed to sadness (liturgical color: black).

In the E Orthodox Ch. the corpse is carried from the house to the ch. with the singing of Psalms followed by relatives and friends bidding Godspeed. After the funeral *troparia* (hymns) the body is buried, the priest throwing earth on the coffin and praying for the eternal memory of the dead.

Luther opposed the Office of the Dead, masses for the dead, vigils, formal mourning, and related customs. He emphasized comfort, forgiveness of sins, rest, sleep, life, and resurrection (WA 35, 478–479). He held that it is the duty of the ch. to provide Christian burial for its mems. (WA 44, 203). The marks of Luth. burial: proclamation of hope that the departed will be raised to eternal life; manifestation of love; reminder of death and preparation for it. Ringing the bell, accompanying the body from house to ch., interment with prayer and songs were preserved. The Luth. and Angl. committal services are very similar. A divine service with sermon often took the place of the Office of the Dead.

In Am. Protestantism the sermon (often eulogy) is a prominent feature of burial. EL

Buridan, Jean (ca. 1300–ca. 1359). Fr. scholastic philos.; pupil of William of Occam; teacher of Albert of Saxony; held that will and intellect are essentially identical; reputed (perhaps erroneously) to have posed hypothetical dilemma ("Buridan's Ass") in which an ass, set midway bet. 2 equal heaps of hay, is unable to decide bet. them and dies of starvation. Wrote *Compendium logicae.*

Burk, Philipp David (1714–70). Son-in-law of J. A. Bengel,* by whom he was influenced; espoused analytic, biblical, pietistic preaching; pub. new ed. of Bengel's *Gnomon.* Other works include: *Gnomon in Duodecim Prophetas Minores; Die Rechtfertigung und deren Versicherung im Herzen nach dem Worte Gottes betrachtet.*

Burkitt, Francis Crawford (1864–1935). Prof. divinity Cambridge. Did original work on Syriac versions of NT. Works include *The Old Latin and the Itala; Early Eastern Christianity; The Gospel History and Its Transmission.*

Bürkner, Richard (1856–1913). Ger. pastor; wrote in area of ch. architecture and liturgics.

Burma. See *Asia,* C 1.

Burman, Frans (1628–79). Prof. dogmatics and ch. hist. Utrecht; espoused federal theol. of Cocceius.*

Burnet, Gilbert (1643–1715). Eng. bp. and hist. B. Edinburgh; d. London; prof. divinity Glasgow; preacher London 1675; bp. Salisbury 1689. Works include *History of the Reformation; History of My Own Time.*

Burning Bush. See *Evangelistic Associations,* 10.

Burns, William Chalmers (Apr. 1, 1815–Apr. 4, 1868). B. Dun, Scotland; d. Newchwang; educ. Aberdeen and Glasgow. First miss. of Eng. Presb. Miss. Soc. to China 1847; stationed at Hong Kong, Canton. Amoy, Shanghai, Swatow, Foochow, Peking, Newchwang; made exploratory trip into Manchuria. Tr. Bunyan's *Pilgrim's Progress* into Amoy and Pekingese; tr. hymns and psalms into various dialects. Influenced J. H. Taylor.*

Burruss, K. H. See *Churches of God, Holiness.*

Bursche, Julius (1862–1942). Gen. supt. 1905 and bp. 1937 Ev. Augsburg Ch. in Poland; prisoner 1939.

Burton, Ernest DeWitt (1856–1925). Am. Bap. theol. and educ.; pres. U. of Chicago 1923–25; ed. *Biblical World; American Journal of Theology;* works include *Syntax of the Moods and Tenses in New Testament Greek.*

Burton, Robert (1577–1640). Eng. divine. Prolific essayist. Influenced many writers. Treats religious melancholy. Works include *The Anatomy of Melancholy.*

A. Brownlee, *William Shakespeare and Robert Burton* (Berkshire, Eng., 1960).

Burruss, K. H. See *Churches of God, Holiness.*

Busch, Ian (1399–ca. 1480). B. Zwolle; prof. Windesheim. Leader and prominent writer of Brethren of the Common Life.

Buschbauer, Hans. See *Hoffmann, Francis Arnold.*

Busche, Hermann von dem (1468–1534). Ger. humanist, scholar; prof. Marburg; active in Luth. reformation of Westphalia. Works include *Vallum humanitatis.*

Busembaum, Hermann (1600–68). Ger. Jesuit theol.; teacher Cologne; rector Hildesheim and Münster; Jesuit moral theol. embodied in *Medulla theologiae moralis.*

Bushido. Unwritten Jap. code of honor requiring extreme loyalty to superiors, simplicity of life combined with dignity, and complete indifference toward suffering and death. Approved suicide as escape from disgrace.

Bushmen. See *Africa,* A 1, 6; B 8.

Bushnell, Albert (1818–79). ABCFM miss. to Afr. 1844; stationed at Gaboon; returned to US 5 times because of ill health; d. Sierra Leone.

Bushnell, Horace (1802–76). Am. Cong. clergyman; pastor Hartford, Conn., 1833–59; resigned because of ill health. In *Christian Nurture* he criticized revivals with their emphasis on definite knowledge of the moment of conversion and held that a child should be trained as a Christian from the very beginning. Other works include *God in Christ; Christ in Theology; Nature and the Supernatural; Forgiveness and Law; The Vicarious Sacrifice.*

Life and Letters of Horace Bushnell, ed. M. A. Cheney (New York, 1903); B. M. Cross, *Horace Bushnell* (Chicago, 1958); W. A. Johnson, *Nature and the Supernatural in the Theology of Horace Bushnell* (Lund, 1963); A. J. W. Myers, *Horace Bushnell and Religious Education* (Boston, 1937); T. T. Munger, *Horace Bushnell, Preacher and Theologian* (Boston, 1899).

Buskirk, Jacob van (Feb. 11, 1739–Aug. 5, 1800). Of Dutch descent; b. Hackensack, N. J.; studied theol. under J. A. Weygand,* at Princeton Coll., and under H. M. Mühlenberg*; probably first Am.-born Luth. pastor in US; helped improve relations between Dutch in N. J. and Germans in Pa.; mem. Bd. of Trustees, Franklin Coll., Lancaster, Pa.

Buskirk, Lawrence van (1775–Apr. 21, 1797). Studied Heb. and Ger. under J. C. Kunze* at Columbia Coll., N. Y.; his 6 published sermons probably the first Eng. Luth. sermons printed in America.

Buszin, Walter Edwin (Dec. 4, 1899–July 2, 1973). B. Milwaukee, Wis. Educ. Conc. Sem., St. Louis, Mo. Studied at Am. Conservatory of Music, Chicago, Ill.; Northwestern U. School of Music, Evanston, Ill.; Columbia U. and Union Theol. Sem., NYC; Chicago U. Divinity School. Taught at Conc. Sem., Springfield, Ill., 1925–27. Prof. Bethany Lutheran

Coll., Mankato, Minn., 1929–35; Conc. Coll., Fort Wayne, Ind., 1937–46 (high school dept. 1937–39). Ordained by Mo. Syn. 1946. Prof. Conc. Teachers Coll., River Forest, Ill., 1946–47; Conc. Sem., St. Louis, 1947–66. After retirement, music librarian Boys Town, Omaha, Nebr. *Cantors at the Crossroads,* ed. J. Riedel (St. Louis, 1967) was pub. in his honor. Ed. *Response in Worship – Music – the Arts.* Prepared and compiled *God's Own Sacrifice Complete: An Order of Meditation and Worship based on the Seven Words of Jesus Christ on the Cross and intended chiefly for use in a Tre Ore Service conducted in Christian Churches on Good Friday;* ed. *The Introits for the Church Year* and coed. *The Graduals for the Church Year,* both in *The Concordia Liturgical Series for Church Choirs.* Other works include *Luther on Music; The Doctrine of the Universal Priesthood and its Influence upon the Liturgies and Music of the Lutheran Church.*

Butler. 1. *John George* (1754–Dec. 12, 1816). B. Philadelphia; served in Revolutionary War; studied theol. under J. H. C. Helmuth*; licensed to preach ca. 1880; pastor at Carlisle and Slippensburg, Pa.; itinerant miss. in Pa., Va., Tenn.; pastor Cumberland, Md. 2. *John George* (Jan. 28, 1826–Aug. 2, 1909). Grandson of 1.; b. Cumberland, Md.; educ. Alleghany Coll., Cumberland, Md., and Pa. Coll. and Theol. Sem., Gettysburg, Pa.; pastor St. Paul's Eng. Luth. Ch. 1849–73 and Luther Place Memorial Ch. 1873–1909, both Washington, D. C.; chaplain 5th Regt., Pa. Volunteers, in Civil War; appointed hosp. chaplain by A. Lincoln; chaplain US House of Representatives and Senate.

Butler, Joseph (1692–1752). Eng. theol.; b. Wantage; d. Bath; son of Presb. parents; became Angl. in his youth; bp. Bristol 1738, one of the poorest sees in Eng.; of Durham 1750, richest see. Works include *Analogy of Religion, Natural and Revealed, to the Constitution and Course of Nature.* See also *High Church.*

Butler, William (1818–99). Meth. miss. B. Dublin, Ireland; d. Newton Centre, Mass.; educ. Hardwick Street Mission Sem. and Training School, Dublin, and Didsbury Coll., near Manchester, Eng.; to US 1850; sent to India 1856 by M. E. Ch. to found miss.; worked at Bareilly; returned to US; miss. to Mex. 1873. Works include *The Land of the Veda.*

Buttlar, Eva Margaretha von (ca. 1665/70–ca. 1717/21). Leader of extreme apocalyptic and libertine group. B. Eschwege, Hesse; d. Altona; claimed to be mother of all, the divine *sophia* (wisdom).

Buttstett, Johann Heinrich (1666–1727). Ger. organist and composer; pupil of J. Pachelbel;* organist in various Erfurt chs., including one RC; master of counterpoint.

Butzer, Martin. See *Bucer, Martin.*

Buxtehude, Dietrich (1637–1707). Organist and *Werkmeister* (gen. overseer) of Marienkirche, Lübeck, 1668, succeeding Franz Tunder,* his father-in-law. Under Buxtehude's direction the *Abendmusiken* (evening concerts; originated ca. 1646) were presented Sundays at the end of the Trinity season and in Advent and gained great renown, attracting also young J. S. Bach,* who thus became a pupil of Buxtehude. Many of Buxtehude's cantatas and much of his organ music were written for these concerts. His greatness comes to light esp. in his organ works. His works are imbued with the spirit of Lutheranism as well as with the spirit of the North and of the Baroque* Era. He may be regarded as the most typical representative of the great North Ger. School of Luth. organists. See also *Toccata.*

M. Bukofzer, *Music in the Baroque Era* (New York, 1947); W. E. Buszin, "Dietrich Buxtehude," *Musical Quarterly,* XXIII (Oct. 1937), 465–490; P. H. Lang, *Music in Western Civilization* (New York, 1941).

Buxtorf. 1. *Johann* (The Elder; 1564–1629). B. Kamen, Westphalia; Heb. scholar and authority on rabbinical literature; prof. Heb. at Basel 1591–1629. Works include *Lexicon Hebraicum et Chaldaicum; Biblia sacra Hebraica et Chaldaica cum Masora . . . ac . . . Commentariis.* 2. *Johann* (The Younger; 1599–1664). Son of 1.; prof. Lausanne; succeeded father at Basel. Finished and pub. father's *Concordantiae Bibliorum Hebraicae et Chaldaicae* and *Lexicon Chaldaicum, Talmudicum, et Rabbinicum.* Other works include *Tractatus de Punctorum Vocalium, et Accentuum, in Libris Veteris Testamenti Hebraicis, Origine, Antiquitate, & Authoritate.* Through their insistence on the absolute dependability of the Masoretic text, the Buxtorfs laid the foundation for the doctrine of inspiration in *Helvetic Consensus Formula* (see *Reformed Confessions,* A 10).

Buzacott, Aaron (Mar. 4, 1800–Sept. 20, 1864). Born S Molton, Eng.; educ. Hoxton Academy; LMS miss. to S Seas 1827; stationed at Tahiti, then Rarotonga; with J. Williams* and Charles Pitman tr. Bible into language of Rarotonga.

Byington, Theodore L. (Mar. 15,1831–June 18, 1888). B. Johnsonsburg, N. J.; educ. Princeton Coll. and Union Theol. Sem.; ABCFM miss. to Turkey 1858; stationed at Eskizaghra; returned to US because of ill health 1867; to Constantinople 1874. Wrote *Evidences of Christianity;* ed. *Zornitsa.*

Byrd, William (ca. 1540–1623). Eng. organist and typical composer of Madrigalian* Era. RC; persecuted for his religious convictions; great polyphonist; music characterized by wide variety of expression, by grace, massiveness, and shifting tone colors. He and Orlando Gibbons* were musical giants of Eng.

E. H. Fellowes, *William Byrd* (New York, 1923); E. Walker, *A History of Music in England* (London, 1924).

Byzantine Art. See *Art, Ecclesiastical and Religious,* 3.

Byzantine Church. See *Eastern Orthodox Churches.*

Byzantine Liturgy. See *Liturgies.*

Byzantine Text. See *Lucian of Antioch.*

C

Caaba. See *Kaaba.*

Cabala (Cabbala[h], Kabala, Kabbala[h], Qabbala[h]; Heb. "received or traditional lore"). System of Jewish theosophy which interpreted the OT by esoteric methods to reveal hidden doctrines. The interpretation was to some extent literal, allegorical, anagogical, and homiletical, but noted for permutation of letters and combination of numbers. In the course of its development it was influenced by various philosophies and religions including Gnosticism,* Neo-Platonism,* and Pythagoreanism.*

Cabalism probably originated in Palestine; it experienced significant development in Babylonia (550 to 1000), moving to Eur. in the 9th and 10th centuries. *Zohar* ("brightness"; commentary on the Pentateuch), compiled by Moses de Leon (ca. 1250 to ca. 1305) of Granada, Sp., attributed in large part by him to Simeon* ben Yohai (bar Yochai; 2d c.), and pub. ca. 1300, was long regarded holiest of cabalistic writings.

Cabalism blossomed in the 16th c. and exerted marked influence also in the 17th and 18th c. in Palestine and Poland. Important Cabalists: Isaac ben Solomon Ashkenazi Luria (1534–72), Hayyim Vital (1543–1620). R. Lully,* Pico* della Mirandola and J. Reuchlin* were Christian scholars interested in Cabalism.

Cabalists tried to explain the nature of deity (*En-Sof:* "Infinite") and its manifestations. They connected the finite universe with the infinite God through a system of emanations and tried to account for evil and achieve perfection of life.

Cabasilas, Nicolas (Nickalaos Cavasilas; 14th c.). E mystic*; probably layman; not to be confused with the anti-RC churchman of Thessalonica (also 14th c.). Works include *De vita in Christo,* in which ascent of soul corresponds to sacraments.

MPG, 150, 355–772.

Cabet, Étienne (1788–1856). Fr. socialist; views on taxation, compulsory labor, and old-age pension treated in his *Voyage en Icarie* (connects socialism with religion); bought land for an Icarian settlement in Texas, but later moved the settlement to Nauvoo, Ill.

Cabrera, Juan Baptista (1837–1916). Bp. *Iglesia Española Reformada;* leader of ev. movement in Spain.

Cabrol, Fernand (1855–1937). Benedictine* monk; b. Marseilles; prior Solesmes; abbot Farnborough, England. Wrote in area of liturgics; ed. with H. Leclercq* *Dictionnaire d' archéologie chrétienne et de liturgie.*

Cadman, Samuel Parkes (1864–1936). Cong. clergyman; liberal theol.; pastor Millbrook, Yonkers, New York, and Brooklyn, N. Y.; pres. FCCCA; radio preacher. Works include *Charles Darwin and Other English Thinkers; Christianity and the State; Imagination and Religion; Pursuit of Happiness.*

Caecilia. See *Cecilia.*

Caecilian(us) (d. ca. 345). Bp. Carthage ca. 311 or 307; involved in Donatism. See also *Donatist Schism, The.*

Caedmon (d. ca. 680). Eng. Christian poet; according to Bede* he was the first to compose Bible stories in Old Eng. verse.

Caelestius. See *Celestius.*

Caeremoniale Episcoporum. RC liturgical book containing ceremonies to be observed by bps. and other ecclesiastics in metropolitan, cathedral, and collegiate churches. A rev. ed. promulgated by Clement VIII (1536–1605; pope 1592–1605) by bull *Cum novissime* 1600. See also *Pontificale Romanum.*

Caeremoniale Romanum (The Roman Ceremonial). Book of ceremonies of the Roman Curia compiled in the 15th c.; contains directions for the ceremonies of nominating and crowning the pope, canonizing saints, creating cardinals, and other papal functions.

Caerularius, Michael. Patriarch of Constantinople 1043–ca. 1058; brought to completion the schism between the Roman and the Gk. Ch. 1054; excommunicated by Leo X 1054; exiled ca. 1058 by Emp. Isaac I Comnenus to Imroz, where he died. See also *Schism,* 6.

Caesar Augustus. See *Augustus.*

Caesarean School. See *Schools, Early Christian.*

Caesarius of Arles (ca. 470–ca. 542). RC; entered monastery at Lérins; bp. Arles 502; presided at Council of Orange, which defended Augustine's* doctrines against Pelagianism and semi-Pelagianism; introduced many ecclesiastical reforms; founded several monasteries.

MPL, 39; 67, 998–1166; *Sancti Caesarii episcopi Arelatensis Opera omnia nunc primum in unum collecta,* 2 vols., ed. *G. Morin* (1937–42);*Caesarii Arelatensis opera, I: Sancti Caesarii Arelatensis sermones,* ed. G. Morin, 2d ed., in *Corpus Christianorum, Series Latina,* vols. 103–104 (Turnhout, 1953).

Caesarius of Heisterbach (ca. 1180–ca. 1240). Preacher at Cologne. Wrote *Dialogus miraculorum; Libri VIII miraculorum; Vita sancti Engelberti.*

Caesaropapism. See *Church and State,* 4, 5.

Cahenslyism (from Peter Paul Cahensly [1838–1923; b. Limburg, Ger.], who proposed it 1890). Plan to assign RC bps. and priests to US dioceses and parishes to match the majority of the people in nat. origin and language; abandoned under pub. pressure. See also *Ireland, John.*

Cainites. See *Gnosticism,* 7 i.

Cainnech. See *Celtic Church,* 6.

Caird, Edward (1835–1908). Scot. philos.; prof. Glasgow 1866; master Balliol Coll., Oxford, 1893; gave theistic interpretation to Hegelianism (see *Hegel, Georg Wilhelm Friedrich*); taught unity of man because he shares a common rationality and evolutionary development; classified religions as objective (Gk.), subjective (Jewish), and universal (Christian). Works include *Hegel; The Critical Philosophy of Immanuel Kant; The Evolution of Religion; Lay Sermons and Addresses.*

Caird, John (1820–98). Brother of Edward; Scot. theol. and philos.; principal and vice-chancellor Glasgow; held thought to be the reality; works include *Introduction to the Philosophy of Religion.*

Cajetan (It. Gaetano; real name Tommaso de Vio; Jacopo Vio; ca. 1468–1534). B. Gaeta (hence Gaetano, or Cajetan); joined Dominican* order 1484; held disputation with Pico* della Mirandola in Ferrara 1494; taught philos. and theol. at Padua; gen. of Dominican order 1508–18; cardinal 1517; bp. Gaeta 1519. Urged reform at Lateran* Council V of 1512 to 1517; papal legate in Ger. 1518–19; urged crusade against Turks at Diet of Augsburg; reasoned with Luther* after Diet 1518; supported election of Charles V* and Hadrian VI; opposed divorce of

Henry VIII.* Wrote commentary on *Summa theologiae* of Thomas Aquinas.* See also *Augsburg Diet* [1518]; *Luther Martin,* 10.

J. F. Groner, *Kardinal Cajetan* (Louvain, 1951).

Cajetan of Thiene (1480–1547). RC priest; secy. of Julius II; tried to reform the clergy; cofounder of Theatines*; active in Counter* Reformation.

Calamy, Edmund (1600–66). Eng. clergyman; noted preacher; leader of Puritan* pastors; deposed 1662.

Calas, Jean (1698–1762). Fr. Prot.; accused of murdering son because latter intended to become RC; died on wheel, goods confiscated; later decision reversed, property restored.

Calendar, Ecclesiastical. See *Church Year.*

Calendar, Gregorian and Julian. See *Gregorian Calendar; Julian Calendar.*

Calendar, Lutheran Church. See *Church Year,* 16.

Calendaria. See *Acta Martyrum.*

Calhoun, Simeon Howard (Aug. 15, 1804–Dec. 14, 1875). B. Boston, Mass.; d. Buffalo, N. Y. Missionary ABCFM 1843; head of miss. sem. on Mount Lebanon, Syria, 1844–75; assisted W. Goodell in tr. Bible into Turkish.

California, Synod of. See *United Lutheran Church, Synods of,* 21.

California Concordia College, Oakland, Calif. See *Ministry, Education of,* VIII C 2 c.

California Lutheran College, Thousand Oaks, Calif. See *Lutheran Church in America,* V; *Ministry, Education of,* VIII B 5; *United Lutheran Church, Synods of,* 21.

Caliph (Arab. "successor"). Successor of Muhammad as head of the Islamic empire and religion. Orthodox Caliphate: Abu-Bakr* 632–634, Omar 634–644, Othman 644–656, Ali 656–661; Omayyad Caliphate 661–750; Abbasid Caliphate 750–1256; Omayyad Caliphate of Córdoba 756–1031; Fatimid Caliphate of Egypt 909–1171.

Calixt, Friedrich Ulrich (1622–1701). Prof. theol. Helmstedt; involved in crypto-Catholicism.

Calixtines. See *Hussites.*

Calixtus I. See *Monarchianism,* B 2.

Calixtus II. See *Concordat,* 2.

Calixtus, Georg (Callisen; 1586–1656). Educ. Helmstedt; traveled in Ger., Neth., Eng., Fr. 1609–13; prof. theol. Helmstedt 1614; it became center of his irenic school. Patristic scholar; influenced by Melanchthon* (esp. his humanism); acquainted with Ref. scholars; tried to reestablish the *consensus* quinquesaecularis* by differentiating bet. fundamental and non-fundamental doctrines; separated dogmatics and ethics; followed analytic method in dogmatics; held that only doctrinal matter of Scripture is inspired, but writers kept from error also in other matters. At Colloquy of Thorn sided with Reformed. His doctrine characterized as syncretistic by Calov. See also *Syncretism.*

E. L. T. Henke, *Georg Calixtus und seine Zeit,* 2 vols. (Halle, 1853–60); H. Leube, *Kalvinismus und Luthertum im Zeitalter der Orthodoxie,* I (Leipzig, 1928); H. Schüssler, *Georg Calixt: Theologie und Kirchenpolitik: Eine Studie zur Ökumenizität des Luthertums* (Wiesbaden, 1961); J. Wallmann, *Der Theologiebegriff bei Johann Gerhard und Georg Calixt* (Tübingen, 1961).

Call. See *Ministerial Office,* 5; *Conversion,* II 1; *Teachers,* 3, 8, 10; *Vocation.*

Callenberg, Johann Heinrich (1694–1760). Prof. Halle; known for the extensive miss. work among Jews and Muslim which he inaugurated. See also *Institutum Judaicum.*

Callistus. See *Calixtus.*

Calov(ius), Abraham (1612–86). B. East Prussia. Educ. Königsberg and Rostock; prof. and pastor Königsberg; supt. of schools and churches 1641; pastor Danzig; pastor Wittenberg and gen. supt. of the district; head prof. and dean of faculty Wittenberg.

A man of great administrative ability and indefatigable industry, active in almost every phase of the church's work: administration, preaching, teaching, and writing. An effective teacher, lecturing to as many as 500 students at times. Wrote scores of books on every area of theol., 28 works on the Syncretistic* Controversy alone. Greatest work is his immense *Biblia illustrata* (1672–76), a commentary on the Bible which treats both individual verses and longer passages. Next in importance is his *Systema locorum theologicorum* (1655–77), in 12 vols., one of the most original and scholarly, if also tedious, dogmatic works of the day. *Isagoges ad ss. theologiam* (1652) was a very important contribution in the development of dogmatic prolegomena. All his works evince prodigious learning and great breadth of knowledge. Was particularly well versed in mathematics, philos., law, Heb., and patrology.

A controversial figure, a stubborn man, highly respected by his partisan colleagues, but despised by his theol. adversaries. Chief proponent of confessional Luth. orthodoxy against the syncretists of his day. His polemics were more tenacious than bitter; Kunze remarks that his continuous involvement in controversy has left a misleading impression of him. See also *Syncretism.*

J. W. Kunze, "Calovius," *Realencyklopädie für protestantische Theologie und Kirche,* ed. A. Hauck, 3d ed., III (Leipzig, 1897), 648–654; A. Tholuck, *Der Geist der lutherischen Theologen Wittenbergs im Verlaufe des 17. Jahrhunderts* (Hamburg and Gotha, 1852); G. Walch, *Historische und Theologische Einleitung in die Religions-Streitigkeiten der Evangelisch-Lutherischen Kirchen von der Reformation an bis auf jetzige Zeiten,* 5 vols. (Jena, 1730 to 1739). RDP

Calvert. 1. *George* (ca. 1580–1632). 1st Baron Baltimore; Brit. secy. of state 1619; announced conversion to RC faith 1625; granted territory of Md., but died before charter issued. 2. *Cecilius* (1605 to 1675). Son of George; received charter for Md., which became haven for RCs. 3. *Leonard* (1606 to 1647). Son of George; gov. Md. province 1634 to 1647. 4. *Charles* (1637–1715). Son of Cecilius; gov. Md. 1661–75; proprietor 1675–1715. See also *United States of America, Religious History,* 5.

Calvin, John (July 10, 1509–May 27, 1564). 1. B. Picardy; son of a fiscal official employed by the local bishop. As a young man he began studies for the priesthood at Paris, but soon transferred to law, studying Orléans and Bourges. He early came in contact both with humanism and with the ev. movement initiated by Luther. The exact details of his conversion to Protestantism are absent from his writings, but it is apparent that it occurred no later than 1533. As a result of espousing the Prot. cause, he fled Fr., arriving Basel 1535, where he planned to devote himself to scholarship.

2. Aroused by the persecution of the Prots. in Fr., he issued 1536 a treatise in their behalf, addressed to Francis I. This was the famous *Institutio religionis christianae* (tr. as *Institutes of the Christian Religion*), the classic exposition of Calvin's theology. A 2d ed. appeared 1539, and the first Fr. ed. 1540. The *Institutes,* which show a close dependence on Luther, present Calvin's theol. in lucid, systematic, and exhaustive form and established him at the age of 27 as a theol. of the first rank.

3. While passing through Geneva in 1536, Calvin was prevailed upon by the local Prot. leader Farel* to remain. His first major accomplishment there was *Articles concernant l'organisation de l'eglise et du culte a Genève,* 1537. With Farel he prepared a confession of faith (which they expected all to accept) and a catechism. This created wide resent-

ment, and Calvin was forced to leave Geneva when the city council turned against him. He planned to return to Basel, but at the insistence of Bucer he went instead to Strasbourg.

4. Calvin was impressed by Bucer's emphasis on the community character of the ch. in Strasbourg. Under Bucer's influence, too, his doctrinal views concerning predestination and ch. order came to maturity during his Strasbourg sojourn. There, too, in 1541, he married a widow, Idelette de Bure, whom he called "the excellent companion of his life." She died 1549, leaving Calvin to rear two stepchildren. Calvin's natural austerity was accentuated by domestic troubles.

5. Meanwhile, in 1541, Calvin was called back to Geneva, where Farel's Prot. party had succeeded in regaining control of the city. As a condition of his return, Calvin insisted on complete authority as leader of the Genevan "theocracy." Under him Geneva became the "city of God."

6. At Calvin's direction, 4 ch. orders were est.: ministers, elders, teachers, deacons. The former 2 constituted the ecclesiastical consistory, with full power of ch. discipline. Calvin was unyielding in his efforts to extirpate heresy; in a notable case, the city council in 1553, at Calvin's insistence, executed M. Servetus* on charges of heresy.

7. Calvin's authority in Geneva was now unquestioned and his influence spread throughout Europe. Though subject to a chronic illness, he engaged in prodigious work. He lectured and preached several times a week; wrote exegetical and homiletical commentaries, besides innumerable theol. tracts and opinions; carried on a voluminous correspondence; and supervised successive eds. of *Institutes*. In 1559 he founded the Academy of Geneva, which attracted thousands of students from all parts of Europe. Always frugal and plain in his manner of life, he usually slept no more than 4 hrs. a night. He died in the arms of his friend Beza.*

8. Calvin was a systematic theol., and the *Institutes* bear the impress of his logical and comprehensive theol. method. This work originally contained 4 main chapters: Commandments, Creed, Prayer, and Sacraments. He continued to revise and expand the *Institutes,* so that the final definitive ed. of 1559 contains 80 chapters divided into 4 books: Of the Father; Of the Son; Of the Holy Spirit; Of the Church.

9. His theol. orientation is consistently Biblical, and Luther's influence on his doctrinal formulations is undeniable. There existed, nevertheless, a distinct difference bet. the two reformers, characterized by Calvin's predominantly formal and legalistic approach to Christianity in contrast to Luther's warm and ev. spirit. "Luther stresses the glory of God's love; Calvin stresses God's love of glory."

10. The idea of the sovereignty, honor, and glory of God is paramount in Calvin's system. He emphasizes God's love of "docility" and speaks of Him as "spiritual legislator." In the doctrine of justification, Calvin is close to Luther, though his approach is more intellectual and judicial. He accepts the Bible as the sole and infallible source of divine truth. Man, since the fall of Adam, is totally depraved and is redeemed only by the blood of Christ, whom he must accept through faith engendered by the Holy Spirit. He conceives of the church as the total number of the elect and insists on the 4 orders of ch. govt. (see 6 above; *Polity, Ecclesiastical,* 7). He believes the 2 sacraments to be efficacious means of grace. He understands the real presence of Christ in a spiritual sense. The state is God's instrument, subject to His sovereignty, and its laws must conform to His; thus Calvin regards every mem. of the state as also under the discipline of the church.

11. In his doctrine of predestination, the "horrible decree," Calvin is swayed by logic: Since only some are elect, he deduces that the others must be reprobate. The Scripture passages on universal grace he applies only to the elect. Concerning this doctrine he asserts that "God will be glorified in His own way." See also *Double Predestination.*

12. The influence of Calvin spread throughout Switz., and in 1549 the Consensus Tigurinus (see *Reformed Confessions,* A 8) provided a doctrinal basis for the unification of Zwinglians and Calvinists in that country. From Geneva Calvinism branched out into all parts of Eur. and gave rise to the Fr. Huguenots,* the Dutch Reformed (see also *Netherlands; Reformed Churches,* 2, 4), the Scotch Presbyterians (see also *Presbyterian Churches,* 1), and the Eng. Puritans.* TC

T. Beza, "Life of John Calvin," J. Calvin, *Tracts and Treatises on the Reformation of the Church,* tr. H. Beveridge, I (Edinburgh, 1844), reprint with addition of hist. notes and introd. by T. F. Torrance (Grand Rapids, Mich., 1958), lvii–cxxxviii; J. Calvin, *Institutes of the Christian Religion,* tr. F. L. Battles, ed. J. T. McNeill, *The Library of Christian Classics,* XX–XXI (Philadelphia, 1960); W. Walker, *John Calvin* (New York, 1906); J. Mackinnon, *Calvin and the Reformation* (New York, 1962); G. Harkness, *John Calvin; the Man and His Ethics* (New York, 1931).

Calvinism. The term, derived from the name of J. Calvin,* is employed variously to denote the individual teachings of Calvin; the doctrinal system confessed by the "Reformed" or "Calvinistic" churches; the entire body of conceptions, theol., ethical, philos., soc., and pol., which owe their origin to Calvin. Sometimes also the term comprehends his views regarding both theological doctrine and ecclesiastical polity. At other times it is limited to the former, esp. to his view on the doctrine of grace. These views are sometimes called the Five Points of Calvinism: 1. particular election (supralapsarianism); 2. particular redemption; 3. moral inability in the fallen state; 4. irresistible grace; 5. final perseverance. These Five Points were opposed by the rival system of Arminianism,* which was presented by the Remonstrants at the Synod* of Dort. In 1618 to 19 the Syn. of Dort condemned the Arminian doctrines and enforced adherence to Calvinism. In addition to a doctrine of grace, Calvin held the spiritual presence of Christ in the Lord's Supper but not the doctrine of the real presence of Christ's body in the sacrament. He stressed the sovereignty of God. His views of ch. govt. were essentially such as are now called Presbyterian. Holding that the ch. should be spiritually indep. of the state, he yet was willing that the discipline of the ch. should be carried out by the civil magistrates.

The *Institutes of the Christian Religion,* first pub. 1536, were the earlier systematic presentation of Calvin's thought. Various Prot. chs. adopted Calvin's theol. views, together with his ecclesiastical polity. Thus J. Knox* carried both Calvin's theol. and polity to Scot., where the first Presb. Gen. Assem. was held 1560. The early reformers of the Eng. Ch. mostly held Calvin's doctrine of grace, which prevailed to the end of Queen Elizabeth's reign. When the rival system of Arminius was brought to trial 1618 at the Syn. of Dort, Holland, the Eng. clerical representatives cast Calvinistic votes. In spite of this, Arminianism took deep root in the Eng. Ch. and elsewhere. Abp. Laud* was its warm friend and advocate, as was the High Ch. party gen.; Low Churchmen continued Calvinistic. The ecclesiastical polity of Calvin was embraced by the Puritan* party, but never enjoyed the favor of the majority of the Eng. people. Of the 2 great Eng. revivalists of the 18th c., Whitefield* was Calvinistic (Calvinistic Methodists), and J. Wesley* was Arminian (Wesleyan Methodists). Most Eng. Baps. are Calvinistic. The theol. tenets and ecclesiastical polity of Calvin have nearly always been dominant in Scot., though the sterner features of both have been softened.

Calvinistic chs. include Calvinistic Bap., Calvinistic Meth., Cong., Ev. Ch., Ger. Ref., Presb.

See also *Grace, Means of,* I 7; *Scotland, Reformation in,* 1.

J. Calvin, *Institutes of the Christian Religion,* tr. F. L. Battles, ed. J. T. McNeill (Philadelphia, 1960); E. F. K. Mueller, *Die Bekenntnisschriften der Reformierten Kirche* (Leipzig, 1903); J. Calvin, *Tracts and Treatises,* tr. H. Beveridge, ed. T. F. Torrance (Grand Rapids, 1958); J. T. McNeill, *The History and Character of Calvinism* (New York, 1954).

Calvinism and the Means of Grace. See *Grace, Means of,* I 7.

Calvinistic Methodism. G. Whitefield* separated from J. Wesley,* with whom he had been assoc. in the great revival of Eng., on the question of predestination and free will. Wesley was Arminian; Whitefield was Calvinist. The Countess of Huntingdon, interested in the religious revival of Methodism, took Whitefield under her special patronage and became responsible for organizing the Calvinistic Methodists, also known as Lady Huntingdon's Connection. Calvinistic Methodism is found chiefly in Wales, where it is known as Welsh Methodism.

Calvinizing Churches. See *Calvinism.*

Calvisius, Sethus (Kallwitz; 1556–1615). First cantor of St. Thomas, Leipzig, to enjoy wide fame; versatile scholar, excelling in music, mathematics, chronology, astrology, linguistics, and musicology. Fostered simple music, notably through his *Harmonia cantionum ecclesiasticarum* (1597), in 4-part harmony and containing some of Luther's hymns; active in disposing the youth of the ch. to good music.

F. Blume *Die evangelische Kirchenmusik* (Potsdam, 1931); E. Koch, *Geschichte des Kirchenlieds und Kirchengesangs* (Stuttgart, 1866–76); S. Kümmerle, *Encyklopädie der evangelischen Kirchenmusik,* 4 vols. (Gütersloh, 1888–95); C. von Winterfeld, *Der evangelische Kirchengesang* (Leipzig, 1843–47).

Calvör, Caspar (1650–1725). Learned theol. of the school of Calixt*; interested in liturgics; works include *Rituale ecclesiasticum,* homiletical part of which is of continuing interest.

Camaldolese (Camaldolites; Camaldulians; Camaldulensians). Strict monastic order, originally eremitic, later partly cenobitic, founded by Romuald (ca. 952 to 1027) ca. 1012 at Camaldoli, near Arezzo, Italy. See also *Counter Reformation,* 6; *Hermits.*

Cambodia (Khmer Rep.). SE Asia, in S part of Indochina; *area:* 69,898 sq. mi.; *pop.* (1972 est.): 7,600,000. Fr. protectorate 1863; Theravada Buddhist (see *Buddhism,* 5–6) kingdom 1946; autonomous 1949; fully indep. 1953; rep. 1970. RC contacts began in the 16th c., Prot. missions 1922 (Christian and Miss. Alliance); other Christan work includes BFBS colporteur and Seventh-day Adv. The Bible in Cambodian was pub. 1956.

Cambrai, League of. See *Popes,* 19.

Cambrai, Peace of (Ladies' Peace). Peace concluded at Cambrai 1529 by Louise of Savoy, mother of Francis I, and Margaret of Austria, aunt of Charles V, in behalf of the 2 monarchs. The treaty gave Spain unquestioned supremacy in Italy and left French territory undiminished. See also *Charles V; Speyer, Diets of,* 2.

Cambridge Arminians. See *Latitudinarians.*

Cambridge Platform. See *Democratic Declarations of Faith,* 2; *United Church of Christ, The,* I A 2.

Cambridge Platonists. Latitudinarian* school founded by Benjamin Whichcote, Ralph Cudworth,* John Smith, and Henry More in the 17th c.; tried to reconcile reason and religion; believed that good and evil exist apart from God; views led to mysticism and transcendentalism; held data of revelation could be judged by reason because God dwells in the mind.

Cambridge School. English philosophers influenced by G. E. Moore, prof. Cambridge; defended "common-sense" and opposed idealism.

Camera. See *Curia, Roman.*

Camerarius, Joachim (1500–74). Educ. Leipzig and Erfurt; prof. Nürnberg, Tübingen, and Leipzig; Gk. classicist; friend of Melanchthon* and Luther; assisted Melanchthon in preparing material for the *Apology;* favored the Leipzig Interim, Dec. 1548; present at the Religious Peace of Augsburg and the Diet of Regensburg; wrote biographies of Melanchthon and H. E. Hessus.* See also *Religious Drama,* 3.

Cameron, James (Jan. 6, 1800–Oct. 3, 1875). B. Scot.; sent by LMS to Madagascar; erected cotton factory and printing press; assisted in erecting chs.; active in exploration, surveying, and cartography.

Cameron, John (d. 1446). Secy. of James I 1424; keeper of Privy Seal 1425; chancellor Scot. ca. 1426; bp. Glasgow 1428. Supported king in attack on ecclesiastical courts; prominent at Council of Perth; excommunicated by Eugenius IV for refusing to come to Rome to answer charges; active at Council of Basel.

Cameron, John (ca. 1579–1625). Prot. theol.; educ. Glasgow; taught at Bergerac and Sedan, Fr.; tutored at Paris, Geneva, Heidelberg; pastor Bordeaux 1608; prof. Saumur 1618; returned to Eng. 1620; principal Glasgow 1622; supported James (VI) I; returned to Saumur 1623; prof. Montauban 1624. Advocated passive obedience to government. Held that God's action on will is moral, not physical. Followers called Cameronites, and sometimes Amyraldists, because Aryraut* adopted Cameron's doctrine of grace and free will.

Cameron, Richard. See *Cameronians.*

Cameronians. Also called Society People. Group of Scot. Presbyterians founded by R. Cameron (d. 1680). Held that the Solemn League and Covenant was perpetually binding; opposed efforts of Charles II to enforce the episc. form of government. J. Macmillan* was their 1st minister. See also *Presbyterian Churches* 1.

Cameronites. See *Cameron, John* (ca. 1579–1625).

Cameroon. See *Africa,* F 7.

Camillians. See *Agonizants.*

Camillus de Lellis. See *Agonizants.*

Camisards. Name of uncertain origin. Also called Barbets, Assemblers, Vagabonds, Children of God, Fanatics. French Prot. sect in Cévennes; some of its members experienced trances and convulsions; ecstatic phenomena included prophecies. After the revocation of the Edict of Nantes 1685 Louis XIV tried to suppress them; in a counter move the Abbe du Chayla was assassinated; war followed (1702–05) in which J. Cavalier* became a famous Camisard leader. Clement XI issued a bull against the sect 1703. In 1705 the Camisards were decisively defeated and suppressed.

Cämmerer. See *Kemmerer.*

Camp Fire Girls. Founded 1910 by a group of educators under the leadership of Luther Halsey Gulick and his wife to perpetuate ideals of the home, initiate and develop habits making for character and health, and train girls to be useful homemakers and citizens. The program is designed to serve 4 age brackets: Blue Birds (7–8), Camp Fire Girls (9–11), Junior Hi Camp Fire Girls (12–13), and Horizon Club Girls (14 through high school). Membership in individual groups in the first 3 age brackets ranges from 6 to 20, and in the 4th from 10 to 30. Each group is led by a woman volunteer. Some Camp Fire groups are organized and sponsored by chs. with the pastor as spiritual leader. Publications include *The Book of the Camp Fire Girls* and a periodical, *Camp Fire Girl.*

Camp Meetings. Religious meetings held outdoors and usually lasting several days. Probably first held by Presb. and Meth. pastors in Ky. 1799; later almost exclusively by Methodists and Baptists. At first participants lived in temporary shelters; later, permanent camps were built.

Campanella, Tommaso (Giovanni Domenico; 1568 to 1639). Italian philos.; joined Dominicans* ca. 1582; his first book, *Philosophia sensibus demonstrata,* because of disavowal of Aristotelianism, aroused suspicion of ecclesiastical authorities; he was accused of conspiracy against the Sp. govt., arrested 1599, condemned to life imprisonment 1602; freed by Spanish 1626, definitively by Urban VIII 1629. Held that individual consciousness is fact of existence. Doubting results of senses and reasoning, he held that the fact of one's own existence is the basis of inferences. Equally certain was the awareness of an external world to which sensual experiences referred. Works include also *Prodromus philosophiae instaurandae, seu de natura rerum* and *De sensu rerum et magia.*

Campanile (from LL *campana,* "bell"). Bell tower, usually freestanding, as originated in Italy. Most famous example: leaning tower of Pisa. Others are at Florence, Cremona, and Bologna.

Campanius, Johan (Johannes; John; Aug. 15, 1601 to Sept. 17, 1683). B. Stockholm; educ. U. of Uppsala; ordained 1633; to Am. with Johan B. Printz (1592 to 1663), gov. of New Sweden, arriving Feb. 15, 1643. Lutheran pastor to Swedes on Delaware. Printz est. the seat of govt. on Tinicum, a Delaware river island below Philadelphia, and caused to be built for the Swedes who settled there a Luth. ch., which Campanius dedicated Sept. 4, 1646, and served. Campanius' work among Indians antedated that of J. Eliot* a few years. Returned to Swed. 1648; navy chaplain for a yr.; then served in the Uppsala diocese. Translated Luther's Small Catechism into so-called American-Virginia (Indian) language; completed it after return to Sweden; it was pub. Stockholm 1696 with 2 Indian-Swedish vocabularies also prepared by him.

Campanus, Johannes (ca. 1500–ca. 1575). B. in bishopric of Liège. Anti-Trinitarian and Anabaptist. Held that Holy Spirit is not divine; Son not coeternal with Father. Imprisoned more than last 20 yrs. of his life.

Campbell, Alexander (1788–1866). Son of T. Campbell*; b. Ballymena, Co. Antrim, Ireland; studied U. of Glasgow; to US 1809; began preaching 1810; joined his father in Christian Assoc. of Washington, Pa.; helped organize Disciples* of Christ. Works include *The Christian System.*

Campbell, David Elliott (June 7, 1825–June 13, 1857). B. Pa.; grad. Western Theol. Sem., Allegheny, Pa., 1849; went to India under Presb. Bd. of For. Miss. 1850. With wife and 2 children put to death at Cawnpore by order of Nana Sahib, rebel chief.

Campbell, John McLeod (1800–72). Scot. divine; taught that Christ was representative of humanity in repentance rather than substitute under penalty of its sin. Excluded from Presb. Gen. Assem. 1831. Followers sometimes called Campbellites, but not to be confused with Disciples* of Christ.

Campbell, Reginald John (1867–1956). Eng. Cong., later Ang., preacher. His *New Theology* (1907), which tried to harmonize Christian beliefs with modern critical views, gained wide attention. Other works: *A Faith for Today; Problems of Life; Christianity and the Social Order. See also New Theology.*

Campbell, Robert (1814–68). Educ. Glasgow and Edinburgh; advocate; joined Episc. Ch. of Scot., later RC Ch.; poet; among his hymn translations: "Christians, Come, in Sweetest Measures."

Campbell, Thomas (1763–1854). Father of A. Campbell*; b. Glasgow, Scot. (or in Ireland?); educ. U. Glasgow; minister Secession Ch. (see *Erskine, Ebenezer*); to US 1807; formed Christian Assoc. of Washington, Pa. (see *Disciples of Christ,* 2 a); helped found Disciples of Christ. Works include *Declaration and Address of the Christian Association of Washington.*

Campbellites. See *Campbell, John McLeod; Disciples of Christ,* 2 b.

Campeggio, Lorenzo (ca. 1474–1539). Ordained priest 1510 after death of his wife; bp. Feltre 1512; nuncio at imperial court 1513–17; cardinal 1517; papal legate to Eng. 1518; sent to Ger. to enforce Edict of Worms*; abp. Bologna; leader at Regensburg 1524; at Augsburg with Charles V* 1530, where he tried to bribe Melanchthon.*

Campello, Enrica de (1831–ca. 1902). RC priest 1855; canon St. Peter's, Rome, 1868. Most important exponent of Old Catholicism in It.; founded Ref. It. Cath. Ch. 1882; returned to RC Ch. 1902.

Campus Crusade for Christ International. Founded 1951. Object: to "present the Gospel of the Lord Jesus Christ to the students of the colleges and universities of the United States and also foreign countries." See also *Students, Spiritual Care of,* A 5.

Campus Ministry, National Lutheran. See *Lutheran Council in the United States of America,* III.

Camrose Lutheran College. See *Canada,* A 20; *Ministry, Education of,* VIII C 2 d.

Canaanites, Religion of. The inhabitants of Palestine W of the Jordan at the time of the Israelite conquest were called Canaanites. For several hundred yrs. after that time many Israelites were tempted to accommodate, modify, or neglect the covenant religion of Israel in favor of the religion of the Canaanites. A series of discoveries at Ras Shamra (ancient Ugarit) in N Syria, beginning 1929, included a number of clay tablets describing the myths and rites of the ancient gods of Canaan. According to these myths the patriarch of the 70 gods (or "holy ones") of the Canaanite pantheon was the majestic god El, "the father of years." El also was one of the names given to the God of Israel in the OT. The female consort of El and the mother god of the pantheon was Athirat, who is designated Asherah in the OT (2 K 23:4 RSV). The Asherim (plural of Asherah) were common wooden female cult pillars of the Canaanites used during the Israelite occupation of Canaan. (Ex 34:13 RSV)

Probably the most popular of the Canaanite gods was Baal, the god whom many of the Israelites worshiped as late as the time of Jeremiah. Baal had a variety of significant titles or names. He was sometimes dubbed "Zebul (Prince), Lord of heaven and earth" (cf. "Beelzebul" Mt 12:24 RSV). He was sometimes called "Son of Dagon," grain god of the Philistines (1 Sm 5:2). Baal's title "Rider of the Clouds" is also applied to Yahweh, God of Israel (Ps 68:4 RSV). A fourth title, "Baal the Victor," underscores the role of Baal as the conqueror of Prince Yam (Heb. and Canaanite word for sea) or Judge River (cf. Hab 3:8); of the chaos monster Leviathan, who is described as the twisting serpent both in the Ras Shamra tablets and in Is 27:1; and of Mot (Heb. and Canaanite word for death). In one of the texts from Ras Shamra, Baal is recognized as king of the gods because of his decisive victory over Yam, sea or chaos god, who appeared as foe of the gods. It is of interest to note that the first time Yahweh, God of Israel, is acclaimed King in Israel is after His decisive victory over Egypt, terrifying foe of Israel (Ex 15:1-18). After Baal had won his kingship, he built a house or temple-palace in the great mountain of the gods in the far North. Comparable imagery is employed to describe Jerusalem as "Mount Zion, in the far north, the city of the great King" (Ps 48:2 RSV). It was from this great temple in the clouds of the far North that Baal was thought to appear as the mighty storm god, brandishing his thunder club in one hand and his spear of lightning in the other. Baal was therefore considered a god of life, nature, and fertility who needed to be placated to ensure adequate rainfall. Included among cultic objects of Baal worship mentioned in the OT are altars for animal sacrifice (Ju 6:25) and stone pillars (Ex 34:13). Sacred prostitution was also associated with the fertility rites of Baal and his female consorts (Hos 4:14). Of these consorts, Anat, the goddess of love and war, is the most prominent in the myths of Ras Shamra. However, the female goddess most frequently represented among the finds of archaeologists in Palestine is Astarte (Ashtoreth). The Ashtaroth (plural of Ashtoreth) are mentioned many times in the OT (Ju 2:13). According to another Ras Shamra text Baal died and entered the netherworld of Mot, god of death. Thereupon El gashed himself in a ritual lamentation similar to that of the Baal prophets on Mt. Carmel (1 K 18:28), and Anat fought with Mot, ripped him open, and scattered him across the fields. Baal then returned to life, and El cried aloud, "I know that the victor Baal lives." A similar portrait of the conquest of death is employed in the OT (Is 25:8). The dying and rising of Baal was thought to correspond with the annual death and rebirth of nature; in other Baal texts, however, the battle with Mot is fought every 7 yrs. This cycle of death and rebirth of a deity is a common feature of ancient mythologies. In stark contrast to this phenomenon stands the biblical portrait of Yahweh, God of Israel, as the "living" God who is in no sense restricted by the boundaries of nature. Yahweh is portrayed as the creator of fertility, nature, the sea, and the entire earth. Moreover, the activity of Yahweh was not concerned primarily with the cycles of nature or the rebirth of creation, but with the course of the hist. of His covenant people Israel. It is probable that the major religious function of the Canaanites was a New Year festival revolving around the rebirth of the god of nature. There is considerable evidence to indicate that the Canaanites had an organized priesthood and that they offered animal sacrifices and vows similar to those mentioned in the OT. In addition, numerous Canaanite shrines, temples, and fertility cult objects have been discovered by archaeologists in recent yrs. Baal was frequently portrayed as a bull or calf, an image employed by the Israelites at various times (Ex 32:4). Oher Canaanite deities include Shachar, the dawn or morning star (cf. Is 14:12), and Resheph, god of pestilence (cf. Hab 3:5). It was this mythical religion of the Canaanites that held such attraction for the Israelites and that came into direct conflict with the religion of Yahweh as the Israelites entered the promised land and committed their covenant allegiance to Yahweh, the unseen, unbound Creator-God. (Jos 24)

G. R. Driver, *Canaanite Myths and Legends* (Edinburgh, 1956); J. Gray, *The Legacy of Canaan* (Leiden, 1957); C. F. Pfeiffer, *Ras Shamra and the Bible* (Grand Rapids, 1962); N. C. Habel, *Yahweh Versus Baal* (New York, 1964). NH

Canada. A. *Lutheranism in.*

1. The first clergyman to conduct a Luth. service on Can. soil was Rasmus Jensen of Aarhus (d. 1620; first Luth. pastor in Am.), chaplain of an expedition sent out by Christian IV of Den., which entered Hudson Bay and reached the Churchill River in Sept. 1619. In 1749 a wave of immigrants, among them many Ger. Luths., landed at Halifax, N. S.; the first documentary evidence of the existence of a cong. there bears the date Oct. 12, 1752. Here was erected 1755 St. George Luth. Ch., the first Luth. ch. on Can. soil. But not till 1783 did these Luths. obtain their own pastor, B. M. Hausihl* (1727–99); meanwhile they were served by a pious layman and later occasonally by an Angl. rector.

2. Lunenburg, N. S., was founded June 7, 1753, with the arrival of an expedition including many Ger. Lutherans. According to Andreas Jung, historian of the period, Paul Bryzelius (1713–73), a Swede, ordained by the Ch. of Eng., began to serve these Luths. 1767. About 1770 they tried to obtain pastoral services through H. M. Mühlenberg* of Philadelphia, but without success. Frederick Schultz became pastor of the group 1772 and dedicated Zion Luth. Ch. there 1772. In 1775 the cong. had 185 families. It has the longest continuous hist. of any Luth. cong. in Canada.

3. The Nova Scotia Conf. of the Pittsburgh Syn. was organized 1876 and the Ev. Luth. Syn. of Nova Scotia 1903 (mem. Gen. Council 1903; ULC 1918; Atlantic Dist., E Can. Syn., LCA, 1962). Represented in New Brunswick, Newf., and Nova Scotia.

4. Forty Ger. Luth. families joined other Loyalists in leaving the Mohawk Valley and emigrating to the neighborhood of Kingston, Ont.; there 2 congs. were organized 1783, one at Bath, the other at Ernestown. Barren soil caused the community to resettle near the present town of Morrisburg; there Zion Luth. Ch. was completed at Riverside 1789, the first Luth. ch. in Ont., dedicated by Samuel Schwerdtfeger,* newly called pastor of Albany, N.Y., and former mem. of the Pa. Ministerium, who had moved to Williamsburg, Dundas Co., Ont. Later many of these St. Lawrence Luths. were lost to Angl., Meth., and pseudo-Luth. congs. New life was brought into this rapidly disintegrating community when Herman Hayunga (d. 1872) resigned his chair at Hartwick Sem. and accepted a call to the Saint Lawrence Luths. 1826; during a ministry of 46 yrs. he gathered a sizable cong. at St. John's, Riverside, and est. St. Peter's, N Williamsburg. These congs. and those in York Co. had joined the Can. Syn. but later severed their connections to join the syns. of New York and New Eng., from which the Eng.-speaking congs. again withdrew to form the Ev. Luth. Syn. of Cen. Can. 1908, mem. of the Gen. Council 1909 and of the ULC 1918; merged 1925 into the Ev. Luth. Syn. of Can. (see *United Lutheran Church, Synods of,* 1).

5. Another group of ca. 60 Ger. Luth. families moved from the Genesee Valley, New York, and settled in Markham Twp., ca. 20 mi. N. of Toronto 1793. According to the record in the Nat. Archives and Library, Ottawa, No. 3987, congs. were organized at Unionville and Buttonville 1794; their first pastor was G. S. Liebich. After a vacancy of nearly 16 yrs., an aged Christian, Adam Keffer, traveled several hundred mi., mostly on foot, to Kleckner-ville, Pa., to plead with the Pittsburgh Syn. for a pastor. His first visit brought no results other than a visit 1849 by G. Bassler,* pres. of the syn. But when Keffer appeared again 1850 with more insistent pleas, C. F. Diehl was sent in Sept. to the congs. in the Markham and Vaughan area.

6. Luths. from Hesse, Alsace, and Württemberg began to settle in Waterloo Co., Ont., in the early part of the 19th c. and were served for ca. 30 yrs. by the aggressive miss. Frederick Wilhelm Bindemann (1790–1865), Ref. in name and liberal in doctrine. Bindemann organized many congs., but many conservative Luths. refused his ministrations; after a visit by J. H. Bernheim in Kitchener 1836, missionaries were sent from the Pittsburgh Syn. and the Pa. Ministerium.

7. The Canada Conf. of the Pittsburgh Syn. was

organized 1853; it in turn became the Ev. Luth. Can. Syn. (Gen. Syn.) 1861. It was one of the synods forming the Gen. Council 1867; joined ULC 1918.

8. St. Peter Ch., Kitchener (E Can. Syn.), founded 1863, is the largest Luth. cong. in Can.

9. On Waterloo Luth. Sem. and Waterloo Coll. see *United Lutheran Church, Synods of,* 1.

10. The E Dist. of the Mo. Syn. began work in Ont. through J. A. Ernst,* who made miss. journeys into the Rhineland and Fisherville area from his home in Eden, N. Y., and organized congregations 1854 at Rhineland in Feb. and at Fisherville in May. The Rhineland cong. thus became the mother ch. of the Mo. Syn. in Can.; it obtained official membership in this syn. 1854. Forced by illness to resign his charge in N. Y. 1860, he went to Euclid, Ohio, then (1863) to Lecon and Elmira, Waterloo Co., Ont. (then called Canada West), where he served ca. 18 yrs. and, with pastors Johann E. Roeder (d. Feb. 21, 1902) and C. Henry Sprengeler (June 25, 1819–Oct. 10, 1903), organizing many congs. in the Waterloo area. When the Can. Dist. of the Mo. Syn. was formed 1879, he became its first president. The name of this Dist. was changed 1923 to Ontario Dist.

11. Under the direction of the Minn. Dist. the Mo. Syn. began work in W Can. 1879, when E. Rolf* of St. Paul, Minn., came to serve Luths. at Berlin (Ossowo), Manitoba. Candidate H. Bügel was called to Winnipeg 1891 and was the first resident missionary. Candidate Emil Eberhardt began the work of pioneering in Alta. at Stony Plain 1894, after F. Eggers of Great Falls, Mont., had explored the territory. The congs. of the 2 W provinces were organized into the Alberta and Brit. Columbia Dist. 1921; the Man. and Sask. Dist. was formed 1922. Since 1921 the Mo. Syn. maintains Conc. Coll. at Edmonton, a residential high school and jr. college. Luth. radio (esp. Luth. Hour) and TV programs have been widely used.

12. The activity of the Wisconsin* Synod in Can. was for a number of yrs. confined to the work of Ewald Herrmann. He left the state ch. of Hannover, Ger., 1894 and came to Saskatchewan (Assiniboia) as a mem. of the General* Council, serving congs. at Josephsburg, Neudorf, and Wellesley. He was colloquized by F. Pfotenhauer* 1903 and became a mem. of the Mo. Syn. In 1905 he accepted a call to Lake Mills, Wis., and joined the Wis. Synod. Then he accepted a call extended by a small group of families in Regina, Sask. While in Regina he joined the Nebr. Dist. of the Wis. Syn. Supported by that syn. he remained pastor of Grace Luth. Ch., Regina, till 1924, when he resigned because of advancing age. His cong. had requested relations with the Mo. Syn. Another cong. of the Wis. Syn., Our Savior, Sault Ste. Marie, Ont., was organized 1956. – In Edmonton, Alta., a group of people left St. Paul Ch. (Mo. Syn.) under protest and on Jan. 18, 1963, founded St. Matthew Luth. Ch. as an indep. cong. under the leadership of student Dieter Mueller. The cong. was accepted into membership by the Wis. Syn. in its 1963 conv. at Milwaukee. A ch. bldg. was completed Dec. 1963.

13. Icelanders arrived at Gimli, Man., in Oct. 1875; the first Icelandic service in Can. was conducted in their midst in Aug. 1876 by Paul Thorlaksson (1849–82), grad. of Conc. Sem., St. Louis; Oct. 1877 he accepted the call to 3 congs. comprising ca. 120 families. His conservative theol. did not find favor with 5 other congs. of 130 families; these 5 called Jon Bjarnason (1845–1914) in 1877. This latter group adopted the name The Icelandic Syn. of Am.; the former were known as The Icelandic Cong. in New Iceland. In 1885 Icelandic congs. on both sides of the internat. boundary formally organized the Icelandic Ev. Luth. Syn. in (N) Am. In 1913 the Jon Bjarnason Academy was est. in Winnipeg and operated continuously up to 1940, when a change in the educ. policy of the province brought its closing. Most of the Icelandic pastors received their theol. training in ULC seminaries. This syn. joined the Can. Syn., LCA, 1962.

14. With the advent of the transcontinental railroad 1885, many Luths. arrived in W Can., esp. from Bucovina, Rumania, Galicia, the W provinces of Russia, and Ger. In 1888 forty Ger. Luths. of Winnipeg addressed a request for help to the Can. Syn. In response, Pres. F. Veit visited them and organized Trin. Ger. Ev. Luth. Cong. in Winnipeg Dec. 16, 1888. Heinrich C. Schmieder, asst. pastor at St. Paul Ch., Philadelphia, Pa., grad. of Kropp Sem., Ger., accepted the call as first pastor 1889. The long distance from the Can. Syn. in Ont. made the founding of a separate syn. in W Can. imperative; 4 pastors met July 22, 1897, in Winnipeg to org. a Ger. Ev. Luth. Syn. of Manitoba* and the NW Territories (entered ULC 1918); in 1947 it was changed to Ev. Luth. Syn. of W Can. The Gen. Council, to which the Man. Syn. belonged, was not able to supply enough missionaries for the rapidly growing field, and so an agreement was made bet. the Gen. Council and Paulsen's Sem., Kropp, Ger., whereby the latter institution furnished many pastors for work in the Man. Syn. – In 1912 Spruce Grove, Alta., became the birthplace of the Luth. Coll. and Sem. That yr. several young men received some preliminary training in the home of Juergen Goos. In 1913 the institution was moved to S Edmonton, Alta., by the Ger. Ev. Luth. Syn. of Man. and other Provinces (see *Manitoba and the Northwest Territories, Synod* of); moved to Saskatoon, Sask., 1914; merged 1965 with Luther Theol. Sem. (see 20) to form Lutheran Theol. Sem. (see *Ministry, Education of,* X L). The Ev. Luth. Syn. of W. Can. became the W Can. Syn., LCA, 1962.

15. The work of the Nat. Ev. Luth. Ch. (Fin.), affiliated with the Syn. Conf., dates back to 1895. In that year Juho Heimonen began to preach at Fort William, Ont. As first miss. and first resident pastor he organized First Luth. Ch. in Fort William 1896 and the following yr. another cong. in Port Arthur, extending his activities also into Sask. Merged with LCMS Jan. 1, 1964.

16. The Finnish Suomi Synod, with headquarters in Hancock, Mich., has been interested in the spiritual welfare of the Finns in Can. ever since its founding 1890; but its work has always been handicapped by a shortage of ministers. Hence it sought assistance from the ULC. A plan of cooperation was approved by both chs. (1921–30). Beginning 1930 the syn. authorized the ULC to send and support men to work among Finns in Can. In 1931 all Fin. work of this syn. was integrated with the Can. syns. of the ULC. See also *Finnish Lutherans in America,* 2.

17. First Eng. Luth. Ch., Winnipeg, the only Can. cong. of the Eng. Ev. Luth. Syn. of the NW (ULC), joined the Cen. Can. Syn., LCA, 1962.

18. The 2 congs. of the Pacific Syn. (ULC) in Brit. Columbia merged with the W Can. Syn., LCA, 1962. The Slovak Zion Syn. (LCA) has 2 congs. with 329 souls.

19. The Joint Syn. of Ohio began its work in Can. when part of a former cong. of the Man. Syn. in Winnipeg appealed to H. Ernst, then pres. of the Minn. Dist. of the Ohio Syn., to supply them with a pastor. G. Gehrke, later pres. and mission supt., accepted this call to Winnipeg 1905. In the fall of 1906 there were 14 pastors who ministered to many mission parishes throughout the prairie provinces; these parishes formed the Can. Conf., which in 1908 was organized into the Can. Dist. of the Ohio Syn., later a dist. of the ALC. In 1913 an academy was

erected at Melville, Sask., and relocated 1926 in Regina. Luther Coll. includes grade 9 to first yr. university and is affiliated with the U. of Saskatchewan. – In 1840 the Buffalo Syn. entered Ont. and organized St. John Ch., Gas Line. Later this body joined the ALC, and its parishes in Ont. are now mems. of the E Dist. of the ALC.

20. The Norw. Luth. Ch. began work in Can. at Parry Sound, Ont., 1876, when the Jarlsberg cong. was organized; in 1889 miss. work was begun in Vancouver and New Westminster, Brit. Columbia. With the exception of some work done by the Norw. Syn. in Man., aggressive work was started 1895. Work had been carried on indep. by the Norwegian Synod (see *Evangelical Lutheran Church,* 7–10), the United* Norwegian Lutheran Church (see also *Evangelical Lutheran Church,* 10–11), and the Hauge Norwegian Ev. Luth. Church (see *Evangelical Lutheran Church,* 4–6). In 1917 the parishes of these 3 bodies were organized into the Can. Dist. of the Norw. Luth. Ch. in Am.; in 1922 the Dist. was incorporated by an Act of Parliament under the name "The Norwegian Lutheran Church of Canada." This body has 3 institutions of higher learning in Can.: Outlook Coll. in Sask., organized 1916, closed 1936 because of drought conditions and the depression, reopened 1939 under the name The Sask. Luth. Bible Inst., known today as Luth. Collegiate Bible Institute (151 students enrolled 1962–63), operating as a high school and a 2-yr. Bible school; Luther Theol. Sem., Saskatoon, Sask., conducted cooperatively with Luth. Coll. and Sem. of the Man. Synod (LCA) since 1939, merged 1965: Lutheran Theol. Sem., Camrose Luth. Coll., Alta., with high school and commercial courses, opened 1911. In 1959 Camrose Luth. Coll. began first yr. university work. – This ch. with its institutions merged with the Ev. Luth. Ch. of Canada, ALC, 1960.

21. In 1885 the Minn. Conf. of the Aug. Syn. resolved to begin home miss. work in Can. At Stockholm, Sask., the first cong. was organized 1889. In 1913 the Can. Conf. of the Ev. Luth. Aug. Syn. was formed. A school for training ministers was opened 1912 at Percival, Sask., but was closed several yrs. later because of financial difficulties. Joined W. Can. Syn., LCA, 1962.

22. The work of the UELC (Dan.) was begun 1904 at Dickson, Alta., by J. G. Gundeson and later organized under the W. Can. Dist. of the United Dan. Luth. Ch. In the 1960's some congs. merged with the W Can. Syn., LCA, others with the Ev. Luth. Ch. of Can., ALC; some remained indep.

23. The Dan. Ev. Luth. Ch. has several congs. and is supported by the Dan. Ch. in For. Lands.

24. The Luth. Free Ch. has been active in Can. since 1895, when Christian Sangstad, with a group of ca. 80 Norwegians from Crookston, Minn., went to Bella Coola, Brit. Columbia, where he founded a cong. In 1903 work was begun in Alberta and in 1904 in Sask. This group merged with The Ev. Luth. Ch. of Can., ALC, 1963.

25. In 1928 John Horarik of the Slovak Ev. Luth. Ch. began to minister to Slovak people in Montreal, Toronto, Hamilton, and Oshawa.

26. The Ev. Luth. Ch. of Canada. The Can. Dist. of the ALC was constituted July 7, 1960; a charter was granted by Parliament at Ottawa, incorporating and est. the Can. Dist. as The Ev. Luth. Ch. of Can.; it began to function as an autonomous body Jan. 1967. The Ev. Luth. Ch. of Can. covers the territory from the Lakehead, Port Arthur, to the Pacific Coast. Congs. in E Can. are mems. of the E Dist. (US) of the ALC.

27. The LCA – Can. Section was organized in Toronto in Apr. 1963, a result of the merger in 1962, which in the US involved the Am. Ev. Luth. Ch., the Aug. Ev. Luth. Ch., the Suomi (Fin.) Luth. Ch., and the ULC. The LCA – Can. Section is divided into 3 syns.: the E Can. Syn. (Ont., Quebec, and the Maritimes); the Cen. Can. Syn. (Man. and Sask.); and the W Can. Syn. (Brit. Columbia, Alta., and the Yukon). Mem. of Lutheran* Council in Can.

28. Lutheran Church – Canada. A federation of syn. districts of the LCMS in Can., namely the Alta. and Brit. Columbia Dist., the Man. and Sask. Dist., the Ont. Dist., and the Can. Conf. of the Eng. Dist. Membership open to all groups affiliated with the Syn. Conf. Article III of the const. mentions as objects of the federation: 1. To promote the extension of the Kingdom of God and the work of the Lutheran Church – Canada; 2. To speak unitedly and with authority (a) in matters of public relations, (b) in conferring with the federal and/or provincial governments, and (c) in dealing with other church bodies; 3. To work toward doctrinal unity with other church bodies; 4. To study the matter of the formation of an indep. Lutheran Church – Canada to be affiliated with the LCMS. Article V adds that membership in Lutheran Church – Canada shall in no wise alter the relationship of a Dist. or cong. to its parent body, nor shall it interfere with the prevailing constitutional, administrational, or any other regulations of said parent body. The const. requires for representation at the annual conv. one delegate for each 4,000 communicants or fraction thereof, with equal representation bet. pastors and lay members. The LCC was organized in Winnipeg Sept. 11–12, 1958. Here the const., previously approved by the 3 Can. Dists., was adopted. The first officers, elected for 3 yrs., were A. H. Schwermann, pres.; Arne Kristo, Eng. Dist., vice-pres.; Maynard F. Pollex, Ont., secy.; Clarence Kuhnke, Man., treas.; David Appelt, Sask., mem.-at-large. A Dominion Charter was granted by Parliament, Ottawa, June 1959. At the time of the organization 1958 all the parishes of the LCC numbered 75,827 souls, 47,237 communicants, 184 pastors, and 321 congregations. The question "Shall the federation become an independent synod?" was placed before all congs. in Can. in spring 1964. Out of 274 congs., 214 voted in favor. 93.5% exercised their right to cast a ballot. Of the total vote, 78% were in favor of independence, with the understanding that an indigenous syn. would remain in close assoc. with the LCMS. District-wise the favorable vote was: Alberta and Brit. Columbia 90.4%; Manitoba and Sask. 80.1%; Ont. 50%; Eng. Conf. 75%. The voting regulations agreed on by the Dists. called for a 66⅔% majority in each District. Since the Ont. Dist. split with a 50-50 vote, the proposed action to become an autonomous syn. was defeated; the LCC will continue as a federation within the LCMS. Mem. of Lutheran* Council in Can.

29. Canadian Luth. World Relief is an agency for immigration and material aid sponsored by the ALC, LCA, and the LCMS. Aid has been given to needy in Algeria, Austria, Jordan, Yugoslavia, the Crown Colony of Hong Kong, and elsewhere.

30. The Canadian Luth. Council, organized in 1952, was superseded by the Lutheran* Council in Can. 1967.

31. Lutheran institutions of mercy in Can. include Good Samaritan Hosp. (inter-Luth.), Edmonton, Alta.; Bethany Chronic Hosp. (ALC), Calgary, Alta.; Bethany Old Folks Home (ALC), Calgary, Alta.; Bethany Home and Hosp. (ALC), Camrose, Alta.; Luth. Home for the Aged (LCA), Wetaskiwin, Alta.; Luth. Sunset Home (ALC), Saskatoon, Sask.; St. Paul Luth. Home (ALC), Melville, Sask.; Bethany Pioneer Village (LCMS), Middle Lake, Saskatchewan. AHS

Directory, Lutheran Churches in Canada (1960 to 1964); H. Engen, *A History of the Evangelical Lutheran Church of Canada* (1955); V. J. Eylands, *Lutherans in Canada* (Winnipeg, 1945); E. G. Goos, *Pioneering for Christ in Western Canada;* Heinz-Lehmann, *Das Deutschtum in West Canada* (Berlin, 1939); J. E. Herzer, *Homesteading for God* (Edmonton, 1946); F. Malinsky, *Grace and Blessing: A History of the Ontario District of The Lutheran Church — Missouri Synod* ([1954]); K. K. Olafson, *The Icelandic Lutheran Synod: Survey and Interpretation;* A. M. Rehwinkel, "Laying the Foundation of a New Church in Western Canada," *CHIQ,* XXXVIII (April 1965), 3–15; D. L. Roth, *Acadie and the Acadians* (Philadelphia, 1890); E. R. W. Schultz, "Tragedy and Triumph in Canadian Lutheranism," *CHIQ,* XXXVIII (July 1965), 55–72; A. H. Schwermann, "The Life and Times of Emil E. Eberhardt, Pioneer Missionary of Alberta and British Columbia," *CHIQ,* XXXIV (Jan. 1962), 97–128; P. E. Wiegner, *The Origin and Development of the Manitoba-Saskatchewan District of The Lutheran Church – Missouri Synod* (n. p., 1957); *Jubiläums-Buchlein: Festschrift zur Feier des 50-Jährigen Jubiläums der evang.-luther. Synode van Canada* (n. p., 1911); C. R. Cronmiller, *A History of the Lutheran Church in Canada, I* (n. p., 1961).

B. *Protestantism in.*

Protestantism, represented chiefly by the Angl., Presb., Meth., and Cong. churches, is predominant in the West and Midwest.

As far back as the close of the 19th c. repeated attempts were made to unite the various Prot. denominations into one strong Canadian church. In sparsely settled areas many considered denominations unnecessary and wasteful. In 1904 a Joint Committee on Ch. Union was appointed by the Cong., Meth., and Presb. chs. to work toward amalgamation of these denominations. Doctrinal controversies and theol. issues were avoided as irrelevant and secondary in the face of the practical problems pressing on the church. After much deliberation a Basis of Union was drawn up and adopted by the 3 bodies; thus the United Ch. of Can. came into being June 10, 1925.

The Basis of Union guaranteed that there should be no disturbance of the local ch. in its freedom of action and form of govt.; yet there were upheavals in almost every community. Methodists were not prepared to accept Presb. ministers; Presbs. were not ready to sing out of Cong. hymnals.

Eventually all Meth. and Cong. chs., with isolated exceptions, joined the United Ch. of Can. and ceased to exist as denominations in Canada. Many Presb. chs. were divided and declined to join the merger. Comparatively few Presb. chs., except in the West, escaped disruption. HM

See also *Canadian Council of Churches; Union Movements,* 7.

C. *Roman Catholic Church in.*

Since the territory now included in the Dom. of Can. was largely settled by pioneers of the RC persuasion, the entire E section of the country is predominantly RC. Jacques Cartier took possession of the Labrador region in the name of Fr. 1534 and ascended the St. Lawrence as far as Montreal 1535 to 1536. When the first permanent settlement was made at Quebec 1608 under the leadership of Samuel de Champlain, the settlement with its outposts was strongly RC from the beginning; the RC religious hist. of the Dom. may properly be said to begin 1625, when the Jesuits (see *Society of Jesus*) arrived, immediately beginning their educ. and miss. endeavors. For a while, after the country had come under Eng. control 1763, the number of Prots. increased rapidly in the E part of the Dom.; during the 18th c. immigration from Ireland was steady; the Fr. Cath. population was increased after the Franco-Prussian War by a number of Alsatians. There is no state ch. in the Dom. of Can., but the RCs of Quebec are guaranteed the privileges which they enjoyed before the Eng. became masters of the country; RC schools have always received recognition before the law, but private schools conducted by Prot. bodies have often been conducted under a handicap which wrought much harm. 1871–1941 ca. 40% of the pop. of Can. was RC. The 1961 percentage was 45.7% (8,347,826), the highest percentage being in Quebec. Can. has an apostolic delegate, who resides at Ottawa. AHS

Canada, Evangelical Lutheran Church of. See *Canada,* A 26.

Canada Conference. See *Canada,* A 7.

Canada Congregational Foreign Missionary Society. Organized 1881; collaborated with ABCFM; worked in W Cen. Afr.

Canada Synod. See *Canada,* A 7–9; *United Lutheran Church, Synods of,* 1.

Canadian Bible Society. See *Bible Societies,* 3.

Canadian Council of Churches. Organized 1944. Mem. chs. 1973: The Angl. Ch. of Can.; The Armenian Ch. of Am. – Diocese of Can.; Bap. Fed. of Can.; Christian Ch. (Disciples of Christ); Gk. Orthodox Archdiocese of N. and S. Am. – 9th Dist. (Can. and Alaska); LCA – Can. Section; Presb. Ch. in Can.; Ref. Ch. in Am. – Classis of Ont.; Religious Soc. of Friends – Can. Yearly Meeting; Salv. Army – Can. and Bermuda; United Ch. of Can. Affiliated institution: Ecumenical Institute of Can.

Canadian Lutheran Council. See *Canada,* A 30; *Lutheran Council in Canada,* 2.

Canadian Lutheran World Relief. See *Canada,* A 29.

Canadian Order of Foresters. See *Foresters.*

Canal Zone. See *Central America,* C.

Canary Islands. See *Africa,* D 5.

Cancelli. In the ancient Christian basilica, barriers bet. the nave and the chancel. The railing sometimes (as in San Clemente, Rome) enclosed the seats of the lower clergy as well as the ambos (reading desks). In the E Orthodox Ch. the cancelli developed into the iconostasis. The rood screen of the medieval chs. shows another form of the development. In the West the epistle ambo was moved back (eastward) into the rood screen; preaching was done from there. *Kanzel,* a Ger. word now used for the pulpit alone, is derived from the word cancelli.

Candelabra. See *Church Furniture,* 2.

Candida Casa. See *Celtic Church,* 3.

Candidate (Lat. *candidatus,* "one clothed in white as an aspirant to office"). One who presents himself, or is presented, for membership, office, position, right, or honor.

In Germany students who had passed their *pro ministerio* examination received the title *candidatus reverendi ministerii* (candidate for the sacred ministry). In Scandinavia a prospective minister becomes a "candidate of theol." after passing a series of tests (usually in biblical thought and languages, religion, philos., and theol.). In the Dutch Ref. Ch. a "candidate" is a licentiate who seeks ordination as a minister. The word is used in various ways in Am. churches. It designates a student preparing for the ministry as also an applicant for a pulpit engagement.

Candidatus reverendi ministerii (crm) is used in Luth. chs. in Am. for a student who has been officially declared a qualified candidate for the ministry and for a pastor who is temporarily in an inactive status.

Candidus, Pantaleon (1540–1608). B. Austria; fled to Ger.; city pastor and gen. supt. Zweibrücken 1571; with Heinrich Schwebel, son of Johann Schwebel,* led Zweibrücken back to a decided Ref. position. Works include *Dialogus de unione personali duarum in Christo naturarum.*

Candlemas. See *Church Year,* 13.

Candler, David (d. 1744). Early Luth. pastor in Md. and Pa.; activities extended from the Susquehanna to the Potomac.

Candles. 1. Used in worship by chs. of E and W, esp. on altar; may have developed from lights carried in procession and placed beside altar. 2. Votive candles are lit before shrines and statues in RC Church.

Cane Ridge Camp Meeting. See *United States, Religious History of the,* 13.

Canisius, Peter (1521–97). Prominent Jesuit of Ger.; educ. Cologne, where he founded the first Jesuit colony, the order spreading rapidly through Ger.; noted for his catechisms.

Canitz, Friedrich Rudolph Ludwig von (1654–99). German statesman and poet. Pietist; educ. Leiden and Leipzig; traveled in Eng., Holland, It., and France. Close friend of P. J. Spener. * Wrote hymns, one of which, "Come, My Soul, Awake, 'Tis Morning," tr. by C. Winkworth.*

Cannegieter, Tjeerd (1846–1929). Prof. dogmatics Utrecht 1878–1916; wrote in area of systematics and liturgics; taught that religion is revelation and experience of God in the heart.

Canon. 1. In E Orthodox matins, a liturgical sequence* or chain of troparia* ordered in 9 series. The initial troparion of each series is called the *Catavasia.* During the singing the worshipers descend from their stalls. 2. Ecclesiastical title of secular clergy belonging to a cathedral or collegiate church. 3. In music, a kind of perpetual fugue,* in which different parts, beginning one after another, repeat the same melody. See also *Tallis, Thomas.* 4. See *Rule of Faith.*

Canon, Bible. 1. Canon is a Gk. word meaning "rule" or "list." Since the time of Athanasius (d. 373) "canonical" has come to mean "authoritative, inspired, divine." The word is used to denote the collection of inspired books of the Bible.

2. Originally it was the prophet's word which was "inspired." As the prophetic oracles were incorporated in written records, many of them achieved canonical status after the voice of prophecy became silent in the 4th c. BC. Discovery of the "Book of the Law" 621 BC had stimulated the canonical consciousness, though the Pentateuch as we know it today did not achieve canonical status until ca. 400 BC. In addition to the Law and the Prophets, a 3d division known as Hagiographa * (Gk.) or Kethubim (Heb. "Writings"), consisting of Job, Psalms, Proverbs, Song of Songs, Ruth, Lamentations, Ecclesiastes, Esther, Daniel, Ezra, Nehemiah, and 1 and 2 Chronicles, was included in the canon of the OT. From Jewish utterances (Synod of Jamnia *) we can conclude that the OT canon was complete ca. AD 100 with canonization of the Writings. Divergences are found among the mems. of the Dead Sea community (see *Dead Sea Scrolls*) at Khirbat Qumran who recognized or used books rejected by the rabbis. The Jews in Alexandria were more liberal than their Palestinian brothers and included in their canon Wisdom of Solomon, Ecclesiasticus, additions to Esther, Judith, additions to Daniel, 1 and 2 Maccabees, 1 and 2 Esdras, Baruch, and the Prayer of Manasses. These writings are known as the OT Apocrypha.* Jesus and His disciples appear to have adhered to the more limited Palestinian canon. Paul and his converts relied heavily on the LXX, whose inspiration was viewed by many early Christians as equal to that of the Heb. originals. Almost all OT Scriptures, with the probable exception of Song of Songs, Ruth, Lamentations, Ecclesiastes, Esther, and Ezra, are either quoted or alluded to in the New Testament. References to apocryphal writings are also made (Ja 1:19 [Ecclus 5:11]; Mt 27:43 [Wis 2:13, 18-20]; Eph 6:11, 13-17 [Wis 5:17-21]). Occasionally also Pseudepigrapha are cited. Jude 14–16 quotes Enoch 1:9. Jerome says the quotation in Mt 27:9 was taken from a writing attributed to Jeremiah, but there is strong possibility that in this passage we are dealing with scribal interpretation. There has been no unanimous agreement in the Christian ch. on the extent of the OT canon. Jerome preferred to exclude the Apocrypha and transmit in the Vulgate * the Jewish canon of the 39 books contained in most Eng. translations. Because of well-est. use of the Apocrypha, these writings gradually became part of the Vulgate and were used also by the framers of the Book of Concord, who make no pronouncements on the extent of the OT canon. Luther's dictum on the Apocrypha expressed in his tr. of the Bible 1534, "These are books which are not held equal to the sacred Scriptures and yet are useful and good for reading," influenced subsequent generations; we find the Apocrypha excluded from the sacred canon in the translations gen. used in Luth., Angl., and Ref. churches (though the KJV originally included them).

3. The canon of 27 books in the NT was fixed gradually. It took some time before all NT books were universally known and recognized as inspired. The ch. proceeded cautiously, concerned to est. the apostolic credentials of each writing.

4. Most scholars agree that all NT books had been written by the middle of the 2d c.; some think that the yr. 100 is the terminal date. Apostolic writings were gradually gathered into collections (cf. 2 Ptr 3:16), encouraged by the prestige these writings enjoyed in the worshiping community (see Cl 4:16; 1 Th 5:27; 2 Th 2:15), and by the use of the codex or book in place of scrolls. By the end of the 2d c. the 4 gospels, Acts, the Pauline letters (exclusive of Hebrews), 1 John, and 1 Peter seem to have enjoyed universal recognition. Most of these are attested by the Muratorian* Canon, dating from the latter half of the 2d c. In the earliest yrs. of the formation of the NT canon the question of authorship was not a major concern. Conflicts with heretics, however, prompted the ch. to emphasize apostolicity as a criterion for canonical status. Little difficulty was encountered with books that had est. themselves throughout the ch. from time immemorial (such as the 4 gospels), but Hebrews, James, 2 Peter, 1 and 2 John, Jude, and Revelation were special objects of debate because of their limited use in certain areas of the church. Their canonical status, however, was recognized by the Synod of Laodicea,* and the persecutions begun by Diocletian* in 303 may have been a strong contributing factor. See also *Carthage, Synods and Councils of.*

5. The classification of Origen* into *homologoumena* (universally recognized), *antilegomena** (not universally recognized), and spurious (mostly uncanonical gospels; the newly discovered Coptic Gospel of Thomas qualifies for this category) is paralleled substantially by Eusebius.* But Eusebius includes under the category *antilegomena* (1) disputed books (James, 2 Peter, 2 and 3 John, Jude) and (2) spurious (Acts of Paul, Shepherd of Hermas, Apocalypse of Peter, Barnabas, Didache). Eusebius expresses no personal doubts about Hebrews, which he classifies as a *homologoumenon;* but he is not sure whether Revelation belongs among the "spurious" books. Eusebius' doubts about Revelation reflect the more conservative attitude of the Syrian chs. which have gen. adhered to a shorter canon of 22 books (lacking 2 Peter, 2 and 3 John, Jude, and Revelation).

6. Throughout the Middle Ages there was no doubt as to the divine character of any book of the NT. Luther again pointed to the distinction bet. *homologoumena* and *antilegomena** (followed by M. Chemnitz* and M. Flacius*). The later dogmati-

cians let this distinction recede into the background. Instead of *antilegomena* they use the term deuterocanonical. Rationalists use the word canon in the sense of list. Lutherans in Am. followed Luther and held that the distinction bet. *homologoumena* and *antilegomena* must not be suppressed. But caution must be exercised not to exaggerate the distinction.

See also *Higher Criticism; Isagogics; Theology.* WA FWD

F. Buhl, *Kanon und Text des Alten Testamentes* (Leipzig, 1891), tr. J. Macpherson, *Canon and Text of the Old Testament* (Edinburgh, 1892); H. E. Ryle, *The Canon of the Old Testament,* 2d ed. (London, 1895); W. R. Smith, *The Old Testament in the Jewish Church,* 3d ed. (New York, 1912); C. R. Gregory, *Canon and Text of the New Testament* (New York, 1907); B. F. Westcott, *A General Survey of the History of the Canon of the New Testament,* 7th ed. (London, 1896); T. Zahn, *Introduction to the New Testament,* tr. under direction and supervision of M. W. Jacobus and C. S. Thayer, 3d ed., 3 vols. (New York, 1909); W. H. Green, *General Introduction to the Old Testament: the Canon* (New York, 1916); A. H. McNeile, *An Introduction to the Study of the New Testament,* 2d ed., rev. C. S. C. Williams (New York, 1953); E. J. Goodspeed, *The Formation of the New Testament* (Chicago, [1926]) and *The Meaning of Ephesians* (Chicago, 1933); A. Souter, *The Text and Canon of the New Testament,* 2d ed., rev. C. S. C. Williams (London, 1954); K. Aland, *The Problem of the New Testament Canon* (London, 1962).

Canon, Little. See *Offertory.*

Canon Law. 1. Rules or laws relating to faith, morals, and discipline, imposed by ecclesiastical authority.

2. The body of laws grew out of decisions of councils which originally had varying degrees of authority. The 20 canons of Nicaea were authoritative in E and W. Others were added, e. g., those of Sardica (343) in the W. Collections existed in the 5th c. The Council of Chalcedon (451) cites those of the Council of Antioch (341 or 330). Early collectors were John Scholasticus (E), Dionysius* Exiguus (W), and the author of the Hispana Collection. Later, canonical letters of bps. (e. g., Dionysius* of Alexandria, Gregory* Thaumaturgus, Basil the Great) and decretals of popes attained canonical authority. In the 4th and 5th c. collections were ascribed to fictitious authors (e. g., apostolic canons to Hippolytus).

3. The *Decretum* (collection of Gratian, ca. 1140) marks the dividing line bet. *ius antiquum* (ancient canon law) and *ius novum* (contemporary canon law). Gratian's canon was supplemented by later collections: one, composed by Raymond of Peñafort, promulgated by Gregory IX bet. 1230 and 1234; the *Sext,* added by Boniface VIII; the *Clementines,* by Clement V, promulgated 1317 by John XXII; the *Extravagantes* of John XXII; the *Extravagantes Communes* (decrees of popes bet. 1261 and 1471). The canons of Trent are called *ius novissimum.*

4. The standard text of canon law is the *Codex Iuris Canonici,* begun 1904 by Pius X, promulgated 1917 by Benedict XV. Official RC canon law is interpreted by a commission of cardinals created 1917. See also *Corpus Juris Canonici.*

5. While the RC canon law was binding in England* in the Middle Ages, it was supplemented by provincial decrees of Canterbury. In 1433 the Syn. Constitutions of S. Langton* (1222) and H. Chichele (1416) were issued in the *Provinciale* by W. Lyndwood. Henry VIII by the Act of Submission made all canons dependent on the king's assent, 1532. *The Book of Canons,* a collection of 151 canons, was passed under the influence of Abp. R. Bancroft by the Convocation of Canterbury 1604 and of York 1606. In 1939 a Canon Law Commission was created to produce an "operative" body of canon law.

6. Calvin* regarded law as a gift of God and the external structure as a necessary element of the church's existence, for which rules and laws are necessary. He held that the state had the duty to uphold the commandments; it was to be concerned with the *exteriora* of the ch., while the *interiora* were the concern of preachers, elders, and deacons.

7. Luther differentiated bet. the spiritual kingdom of Christ and the kingdom of the world; he justified law for the ch. in the world on the basis of *ius naturale divinum* and *ius spirituale divinum.* The function of ch. law was to support Christians in the fulfillment of the commandments. Luther held that the creation of ch. law should be in the hands of mems. of the ch.; Christian secular govt. should have a concern for religion and remove abuses.

8. The Lutheran* Confessions contain no canon law but provide basic and theol. principles for ch. law (AC V, VII, XIV, XV, XXVIII).

9. The actual formulation of Luth. ch. law devolved upon secular rulers. The ch. orders of the 16th and 17th c. are largely governmental regulations. In the 19th and 20th c. the legislative functions came more into the hands of the Prot. and Luth. churches. Lay participation in legislative ch. assemblies also increased.

10. In Am., constitutions and other official statements of Luth. and Prot. bodies perform the function of canon law.

F. Lauchert, *Die Kanones der wichtigsten altkirchlichen Concilien nebst den apostolischen Kanones* (Freiburg, 1896); J. F. von Schulte, *Die Geschichte der Quellen und Literatur des canonischen Rechts von Gratian bis auf die Gegenwart,* 3 vols. (Stuttgart, 1875–80; reprint Graz, 1956); E. Eichmann, *Lehrbuch des Kirchenrechts auf Grund des Codex Iuris Canonici,* ed. K. Mörsdorf, 9th ed., 3 vols. (Paderborn, 1958–59); J. A. Abbo and J. D. Hannan, *The Sacred Canons,* 2 vols. (St. Louis, 1952); J. Johnson, *A Collection of the Laws and Canons of the Church of England,* 2d ed., 2 vols. (Oxford, 1850); J. Heckel, *Lex charitatis, Eine juristische Untersuchung über das Recht in der Theologie Martin Luthers* (Munich, 1953). EL

Canon of Hippo Regius. See *Carthage, Synods and Councils of.*

Canon of the Mass. That part of the mass* which begins with the prayer *Te igitur* after the *Sanctus* and ends just before the *Pater noster* (according to others, with consumption of the sacred species). It is called "canon" (Gk. *kanon,* "rule") because it follows a fixed rule.

Canoness. Word *canonica* (Lat. from Gk. "one living under rule"; *virgo Deo sacrata* [virgin dedicated to God]; *sanctimonialis* [consecrated one]) traced back to 4th c. in E and 8th c. in W. Used in W (e. g., Council of Chalon-sur-Saône* 813) for mem. of community of women who professed common life but did not bind themselves to full rule of Augustine (vowed chastity, obedience, but not poverty; vow not perpetual). Beginning with 11th c. canonesses regular are female counterpart of canons regular.*

Canonical Age. See *Age, Canonical.*

Canonical Hours. See *Hours, Canonical.*

Canonicity. See *Canon, Bible.*

Canonics. See *Biblical Canonics.*

Canonization. In RCm, definitive sentence by which the pope declares a faithful departed (previously beatified) to have entered eternal glory and establishes a cult for the saint. Beatification allows only limited public veneration, whereas canonization establishes such veneration throughout the church.

In the early ch., martyrs were publicly venerated; later, also confessors. Local bps. controlled the cults of saints in their diocese; such control later devolved upon the pope. Canonization follows a long legal procedure (CIC, 1999–2141) in which the *promotor fidei (advocatus diaboli,* "devil's advocate") produces arguments against canonization, while the *postulator (advocatus Dei,* "God's advocate") urges the claims of the candidate. In the Russ. Ch. canonization was performed by the Holy Synod.

A. D. Severance, "Beatification and Canonization with Special Reference to Historic Proof and the Proof of Miracles," *American Society of Church History Papers,* ed. W. W. Rockwell, 2d series, vol. 3 (New York, 1912), 41–62; G. Oesterle, "Heiligsprechung," *Lexikon für Theologie und Kirche,* V (Freiburg, 1960), 142–143; E. W. Kemp, *Canonization and Authority in the Western Church* (New York, 1948).

Canons of the Church of England. See *Canon Law,* 5.

Canons Regular *(canonici regulares).* Canons living under rule which originated with reform movements of Gregory VII (11th c.). Largely adopted rule of Augustine.

Canossa. See *Church and State,* 6.

Canstein, Karl Hildebrand Frhr. von (1667–1719). Founded Canstein Bible Institute in Halle. See *Bible Societies,* 2.

Canstein Bible Institute. See *Bible Societies,* 2.

Cantata. While, in the early hist. of the Luth. Ch., the mass, passion, and motet continued to play the important part they had played in ch. music of pre-Reformation days, the cantata began to flourish as Luth. music during the Baroque* Era. The cantata is a composite form which may include an instrumental prelude or overture, recitatives, arias, duets, and choruses. Cantatas are usually accompanied by an organ or orchestra. They may be lyrical or dramatic, secular (*cantata da camera*) or sacred (*cantata da chiesa*). The Luth. cantata, which differs from the RC cantatas of It. and Fr. and from the Angl. and Ref. types of Eng. and Am., became an integral part of Luth. worship in the 17th and 18th c. It was sung bet. the Epistle and Gospel of the day and was related directly to the same, presenting and interpreting the texts of the lections. Former liturgical texts were neglected to such an extent that often only the Kyrie and Gloria remained.

Cantatas based on chorales were known as chorale cantatas. Cantatas of this type were written largely by such masters as F. Tunder,* J. P. Krieger,* J. Kuhnau,* and esp. by J. S. Bach.* D. Buxtehude* preferred to base his cantatas on free poetic texts and relate them to the It. baroque style; but he by no means ignored the chorale.

Bach wrote no fewer than 5 cycles of cantatas (ca. 295) for the ch. yr.; of these, ca. 195 have been preserved. Among the Luth. antecedents of the cantata we find *Gespräche zwischen Gott und einer gläubigen Seele,* by A. Hammerschmidt,* and numerous works by H. Schütz,* notably his *Symphoniae sacrae* of 1629. After Bach, the cantata was practically absorbed by the oratorio*; cantatas of some sort were written by the masters of the Classical and Romantic Eras and by Eng. and Am. composers. WEB

G. Adler, *Handbuch der Musikgeschichte* (Frankfurt, 1924); W. Apel, *Harvard Dictionary of Music,* 9th print. (Cambridge, Mass., 1955); F. Blume, *Die evangelische Kirchenmusik,* in *Handbuch der Musikwissenschaft* (Potsdam, 1931); *Grove's Dictionary of Music and Musicians,* ed. E. Blom, 5th ed., 9 vols. (London, 1954), supplementary vol. 10 (London, 1961); H. Kretzschmar, *Führer durch den Concertsaal,* 7 editions, 2 parts in 4 vols. (Leipzig, 1887 to 1939); S. Kümmerle, *Encyklopädie der evangelischen Kirchenmusik,* 4 vols. (Gütersloh, 1888–95); H. J. Moser, *Geschichte der deutschen Musik,* 5 editions, 3 vols. (Stuttgart, 1920–30).

Cantate. See *Church Year,* 14.

Cantate Domino (Lat. "O sing ye unto the Lord"). 1. Psalm 98, from its first words in Latin. 2. Papal bull. See also *Council of Florence,* 3.

Canterbury. Metropolitan see of Eng.; headquarters of Augustine's miss. work among Anglo-Saxons 597; primacy in Eng. est. by Vitalian (pope 657–672), confirmed by Alexander III (pope 1159–81).

Canterbury, Nun of. See *Barton, Elizabeth.*

Canterbury Club. See *Students, Spiritual Care of,* A 3.

Canticles. Non-metrical spiritual songs, Psalms, or hymns, taken directly from Scriptures and used in the ch. from the earliest times, usually chanted at prescribed place in the services. In some cases the Bible text has been paraphrased to some extent; in others it has remained unchanged. Canticles in use in the ch. include the *Gloria Patri* ("Glory be to the Father"), based on the baptismal formula Mt 28:19, a paraphrase in use since the 1st c. and known as the Lesser Doxology; the *Gloria in excelsis,* or song of the angels, Lk 2:14, enlarged into a hymn of adoration celebrating God's glory as manifested in the gift of His Son, the Greater Doxology; the *Tersanctus,* or *Sanctus,* "Holy, Holy, Holy," at the service of celebration of the Holy Supper, a combination of the hymn of the seraphim before the throne of God, Is 6:2, 3, and of the song of the multitudes as they went forth to meet Christ at the time of His triumphal entry into Jerusalem, Mt 21:9, the section chanted by the people being taken from the great Hallel of the Jewish festival season, Ps 118:25, 26; the *Nunc dimittis* of the aged Simeon, Lk 2:29 to 32, his joyful thanksgiving for the salvation manifested and bestowed in Christ Jesus, sung at the close of the Communion service as well as at Vespers; the *Te* Deum laudamus,* a hymn of praise, whose authorship is ascribed to either Athanasius or Ambrose, including praise, confession of faith, and petition, sung in the morning service, or Matins; the *Benedicite,* beginning, "O all ye works of the Lord, bless ye the Lord," from the Song of the Three Holy Children, in the Apocrypha; the *Magnificat,* beginning, "My soul doth magnify the Lord," Mary's song of praise, Lk 1:46-55, used in Vespers* since the earliest times; the *Benedictus,* beginning, "Blessed be the Lord God of Israel," the song of praise of Zacharias after the birth and circumcision of John the Baptist, Lk 1:68-79, used in festival services, esp. at Christmastide.

Cantionale. Collection of ecclesiastical chants used either in the chief service of the day or as choruses appointed for Sundays and holidays, arranged in the order of the ch. year. Some of the best examples are the collections by J. Spangenberg,* L. Lossius,* Johannes Keuchenthal, Matthäus Ludecus, and B. Helder.* See also *Service Books.*

Cantor. The precentor, or chief singer, of a section of the choir in an Angl. ch.; more loosely applied to an organist and choirmaster in Ger. chs., also in synagogs.

Cantus; Cantus Choralis; Cantus Firmus; Cantus Planus. See *Ambrosian Music; Gregorian Music.*

Canute IV (Knut; Knud; Cnut; ca. 1040–86). "The Saint." King of Den. 1080–86; supported ch.; tried to invade Eng.; patron saint of Den.

Canzone (canzona). 1. Serious lyrical poem of It. of the 13th to 17th c. 2. Lyrical song of the 18th and 19th c., or instrumental music of a simple character. 3. Forerunner of the fugue*; at times, notably among the Germans, the term was synonymous with fugue. Cf. J. S. Bach's *Organ Canzona in D Minor.*

Caodaism. Syncretistic Indo-Chinese religion; resulted from alleged revelation of the god Cao-dai; officially established 1926.

Cape of Good Hope. Called Cape Colony before 1910. See also *Africa,* B 5.

Cape Verde Islands. See *Africa,* C 17.

Capernaitic Eating. Term derived from literal interpretation of Jesus' discourse at Capernaum on the bread of life (Jn 6:26-58). See also *Grace, Means of,* IV 4.

Capital and Labor. The industrial revolution and the development of the modern capitalistic system led to problems bet. owners and financiers of industrial enterprises (capital) and those carrying out the actual production (labor). The problems are complicated on the level of capital by the fact that those financing the operations are frequently concerned only by way of investment and return of interest or dividends, while the management of the operations is entrusted to employees; and on the level of labor by the modern organization of labor into unions, headed by professional leaders, who bargain with the management for the most advantageous wage and working conditions and enforce their demands by strikes. – The Christian is concerned with these problems on two levels. On the 1st level he is mindful of the behavior of the Christian who is himself an owner or stockholder in industry, a unit in the management, or a worker. That behavior will be conditioned by Christian love. The Holy Spirit at work in the Christian because of the redemption of Jesus Christ will actuate in him the readiness to be concerned for the other person at the expense of personal sacrifice, if need be, and to look at his relationship as a field of calling in which he can glorify God through his acts of love. In these situations the Christian confronts reactions of his own flesh and patterns of selfishness in the world around him, in which disregard for the interests of the other party is rationalized. Since folkways of behavior and attitudes of class consciousness are deeply rooted, it behooves the Christian to be doubly alert and sober in maintaining the watchfulness of love, and in carrying out the principles of love (Eph 6:5-9; Cl 3:22 to 25; 4:1).

On the 2d level the Christian is concerned for the welfare also of those who do not profess the Christian religion, and for his fellow Christians under the influence of those who are not Christians. That means that he will be interested in the leadership of corporations, the techniques of management and labor relations, and the operations of labor unions. He will be anxious to have Christians be influential in their direction. He will be interested in the part which the govt. will play in the conciliation of labor disputes, the regulation of securities, the supervision of labor unions. He will be anxious that the right ethical guidance will be imparted in the schools and universities of the land. – Christians recognize that capital property is not in itself a sin, but are aware of the Savior's warnings that it can become a snare for the soul (Mk 10:23-31; cf. 1 Ti 6:17). On the other hand, while understanding that the drudgery of labor is one of the curses of sin, they are aware of the dignity of work and put the capacity of the spiritual man to work in a zestful carrying out of the opportunities of labor (Eph 4:28). RRC

J. Daniel, *The Church and Labor-Management Problems of Our Day* (Bethlehem, Pa., 1947) and *Labor, Industry, and the Church* (St. Louis, 1957); *Christianity and Property,* ed. J. F. Fletcher (Philadelphia, 1947).

Capital Sins. Sins which cause other sin; sometimes listed as pride, covetousness, lust, anger, gluttony, envy, sloth. In SA-III 1 original sin is described as capital sin. See also *Sin; Sin, Original; Sins, Venial and Mortal.*

Capital University. See *Ministry, Education of,* VI C; VIII A 1; X E; *Universities in the United States, Lutheran,* 2.

Capitalism. Term used to denote numerous economic systems in which the instruments of production and capital goods are owned by private individuals or corporations, investments determined by private decision, and production and prices largely set in a free market. Capitalism is at times regarded as the opposite of socialism* or communism. Some theologians and chs. have discussed capitalism from the viewpoint of social ethics* and human rights. See also *Capital and Labor.*

Capito, Wolfgang Fabricius (Köpfel; 1478–1541). Received degree in medicine at U. of Freiburg; turned to law, then to theol.; cathedral preacher at Basel 1515; preacher at Mainz 1519; espoused Reformation doctrines; to Strasbourg 1523, where he was chief preacher of the Ch. of St. Thomas. Instrumental in drawing up Tetrapolitan Conf. 1530. Helped with Wittenberg* Concord 1536, achieving agreement with Luth. party. See also *Reformed Confessions,* A 6; D 1; *Regensburg Book.*

J. W. Baum, *Capito und Butzer, Strassburgs Reformatoren, in Leben und ausgewählte Schriften der Väter und Begründer der reformirten Kirche,* III (Elberfeld, 1860).

Cappa. Cape, esp. as part of ecclesiastical or academic garb.

Cappa Magna. In RCm, cloak with hood and long train, lined with fur, worn by cardinals, bps., and other dignitaries.

Cappadocian Theologians. Three great teachers of the ch. who worked in Cappadocia in the 4th c.: Basil* the Great, his friend Gregory* of Nazianzus, and Basil's brother Gregory* of Nyssa. Champions of the faith of Nicaea,* they carried on the work of Athanasius* and brought it to a climax. The virtual defeat of Arianism* at the Second Ecumenical Council in Constantinople 381 was largely due to their efforts. As ecclesiastical statesmen and organizers, impassioned orators, and skilled theologians they shaped a large part of the theol. and practice of the E Church.

1. *Basil the Great* (ca. 330–ca. 379). One of 10 children in a prominent family in Cappadocian Caesarea. Three became bps.: Basil, Gregory of Nyssa, Peter of Sebaste. Their sister, Macrina the Younger, devoted herself to ascetic life. Basil was early exposed to zealous Christianity by his grandmother, Macrina the Elder, and mother, Emmelia. His studies of rhetoric took him to schools at Caesarea, Constantinople, and after 351 to Athens, where his friendship with Gregory of Nazianzus flourished. Returning to Caesarea 356, he became a teacher of philos. and other subjects. A yr. later he embraced ascetic life and was baptized. He observed monasteries during a visit to Egypt and propagated monastic movements in Asia Minor. The cloister est. by him in Pontus became a pattern for E monasteries. In 358 he collaborated with Gregory of Nazianzus on *Philocalia,* an anthology of Origen's works, and the 2 *Regulae,* detailed and abbreviated principles for monastic life. Persuaded by Eusebius of Caesarea to become a priest ca. 364, he succeeded Eusebius as bp. of Caesarea 370. Supported the orthodox position in the Trinitarian controversies and actively opposed Arianism.* His refutation of the latter and Macedonianism (see *Pneumatomachi*) may be found in *Adversus Eunomium* (363–365) and *Liber de Spiritu sancto* (ca. 375), both of which affirm the consubstantiality of the Son and the Holy Spirit with the Father. Though threatened with confiscation and exile by the Arian Emp. Valens, he remained resolute. His contributions to liturgics and hymnology are valuable. The Byzantine Liturgy is traditionally ascribed to him. His Christian devotion led him to help establish hospitals, homes for the poor, and hospices for travelers and strangers. He himself lived in the humblest manner. The tasks of ecclesiastical administration and organization did not keep him from becoming a great theol., as his works attest. Besides the works

mentioned, he wrote a treatise on the Christian attitude toward pagan literature and learning, and many sermons and letters.

2. *Gregory of Nazianzus* (ca. 330–ca. 390). Oldest of 3 children in a wealthy Cappadocian family near Nazianzus, where his father was bishop. His mother, Nonna, consecrated him to Christian service before his birth. He studied rhetoric at Cappadocian Caesarea, continued his educ. at Christian schools of Caesarea in Palestine and Alexandria in Egypt, and completed it at Athens. Refusing a position as teacher of rhetoric in Athens, he went home ca. 357 after baptism in preparation for the journey. Gregory's attempts to shun public life in favor of monastic solitude were not honored. His efforts were enlisted ca. 362 to check the spread of a semi-Arian formula in his father's diocese. Popular sentiment and the insistence of his father forced him into the priesthood. He fled in protest to the monastery of his friend Basil, later returning to take up his duties at Nazianzus. His *Oratio* 2 *(Apologetica)* is a defense of this flight and return. After the death of his father 374, he retired to Seleucia in Isauria only to be summoned 379 by the orthodox party in Constantinople to allay a rampant Arianism* in that city. His eloquent protests against Arianism (cf. the 5 *Orationes* [27–31] in defense of the Nicene doctrine of the Trinity) led to his consecration as bp. of Constantinople 381. Objections to his appointment from the Egyptian and Macedonian hierarchy caused him to resign the position within a few days and return to his native diocese. His friend Eulalias was consecrated bp. of Nazianzus 384; Gregory devoted the rest of his life to study and monastic practices at the family estate in Arianzus. He is best remembered as the great orator and rhetorician of the Cappadocian theologians. Works include 45 orations, 244 letters, and ca. 400 poems.

3. *Gregory of Nyssa* (ca. 331–ca. 396). Younger brother of Basil the Great, who was chiefly responsible for his education. After serving as lector in the ch., he embarked on a worldly career as a teacher of rhetoric. His marriage to Theosebia did not deter him from entering the Basilian monastery in Pontus under the influence of Basil and Gregory of Nazianzus. Named bp. of the small Cappadocian town of Nyssa by his brother 371; the position soon revealed his administrative inadequacies. A syn. of Arian bps. meeting at Nyssa 376 convinced Emp. Valens to depose Gregory on the charge of misappropriation of funds. After Valens' death 378, Gregory was welcomed back to his former diocese. On a visit to Pontus ca. 379 he was elected abp. of Sebaste against his will. With Gregory of Nazianzus he played a prominent role in the Second Ecumenical Council at Constantinople 381, which repudiated Arianism. Frequent visits to the capital followed, the last in 394. Lacking administrative and oratorical qualities, he nonetheless distinguished himself as the most gifted thinker and theol. of the 3 Cappadocians. Works include *Oratio catechetica magna* and *De anima et resurrectione dialogus qui inscribitur Macrinia* (dogmatic); *De hominis opificio* and *Explicatio apologetica . . . in hexaemeron* (exegetical).

1. General: F. W. Farrar, *Lives of the Fathers,* 2 vols. (London, 1889); J. Quasten, *Patrology,* III (Westminster, Md., 1960); H. v. Campenhausen, *The Fathers of the Greek Church,* tr. S. Godman (New York, 1959); H. Weiss, *Die Grossen Kappadocier: Basilius, Gregor von Nazianz und Gregor von Nyssa als Exegeten* (Braunsberg, 1872); K. Weiss, *Die Erziehungslehre der drei Kappadozier,* in *Strassburger theologische Studien,* ed. A. Ehrhard and E. Müller, V, 3-4 (Freiburg, 1903).

2. Special: M. M. Fox, *The Life and Times of St. Basil the Great as Revealed in His Works,* in *The Catholic University of America Patristic Studies,* LVII (Washington, 1939); G. L. Prestige, *St. Basil the Great and Apollinaris of Laodicea,* ed. H. Chadwick (London, 1956); R. T. Smith, *St. Basil the Great* (New York, 1908); C. Ullmann, *Gregorius von Nazianz, der Theologe,* 2d ed. (Gotha, 1867); T. A. Goggin, *The Times of Saint Gregory of Nyssa as Reflected in the Letters and the Contra Eunomium,* in *The Catholic University of America Patristic Studies, LXXIX* (Washington, 1947); W. W. Jaeger, *Two Rediscovered Works of Ancient Christian Literature: Gregory of Nyssa and Macarius* (Leiden, 1954); W. Völker, *Gregor von Nyssa als Mystiker* (Wiesbaden, 1955). *MPG,* 29–32 (Basil the Great); 35–37 and 38, 9–846 (Gregory of Nazianzus); 44–46 (Gregory of Nyssa). HAWR

Cappel, Louis (1585–1658). Prof. Heb. Saumur; OT textual critic; pointed out late origin of vowel signs and textual corruptions. Works include *Critica Sacra.* See also *Reformed Confessions,* A 10.

Capuchins *(Ordo Fratrum Minorum S. Francisci Capuccinorum).* Offshoot of Franciscan* order, founded in It. ca. 1528. Its mems. wear a pointed cowl *(capuche),* sandals, and beard. Its severe Rule had the purpose of restoring the rigor and simplicity of the Franciscan Rule. The severity of the Rule has been mitigated in practice. Active in Counter Reformation.

Caraccioli, Galeazzo (Marquis de Vico; 1517–86). Nephew of pope Paul IV; left Naples because of his sympathy for Reformation; deacon, mem. of council and consistory at Geneva.

Caraffa, Giovanni Pietro. See *Paul IV.*

Carbon Theory. See *Haeckel, Ernst Heinrich Philipp August.*

Carbonari (It. "charcoal burners"). Secret political and pseudo-religious organization in It. and Fr.; arose ca. 1800; existed till ca. 1840. Opposed absolutism in politics; espoused natural religion.

Cardale, John Bate (1802–77). B. London; d. Albury. "Apostle" of Catholic* Apostolic Church.

Cardinal Doctrine. Basic, chief, essential, fundamental teaching, e. g., justification* by grace through faith in Christ, the 3 principles of the Reformation (grace alone, faith alone, Scripture alone), fundamental articles of faith treated in creeds and other accepted confessions.

Cardinal Virtues. Plato (*Republic,* iv, 427) regarded prudence, fortitude, temperance, and justice as the cardinal virtues. Ambrose, according to tradition, and other Christian writers adopted these. The "theological" virtues (faith, hope, charity) were added, but in contrast to the four "natural" virtues. Some combine them all as seven cardinal virtues.

R. Schwarz, *Fides, spes und caritas beim jungen Luther* (Berlin, 1962).

Cardinals. RC dignitaries ranking immediately after the pope; his chief counselors. Three ranks: cardinal bps., cardinal priests, and cardinal deacons. In a series of increases 1959–69 their number was raised from 70 to 134. They form the Sacred Coll., over whose meetings (consistories) the pope presides. Cardinals are created by the pope; all nations are supposed to be considered, but more cardinals are from It. than from any other country. Though the pope is not bound to ask or accept their advice, he consults them in all important matters, both in consistory and otherwise. The cardinals take an active part in the govt. of the RC Ch. through the offices they hold in the Curia* and various commissions. They frequently serve as legates. Since the 11th c. they elect the popes (see *Conclave*). Though in theory anyone, even a layman, is eligible to the papal chair, no one who was not previously a cardinal has been elected since Urban VI (1378). Cardinals wear red birettas and robes, are styled Your Eminences, and claim the right of addressing emperors and kings as "brothers." See also *Western Christianity 500–1500,* 7.

Care of Souls. See *Pastor as Counselor.*

Carey, Lot(t) (ca. 1780–1828). B. Va. as slave; d. Liberia. First Am. Negro miss. to Africa. Converted 1807; bought freedom 1813; founded miss. soc. in Richmond, Va.; with Colin Teague, another Negro preacher, to Liberia 1821; est. school at Monrovia; acting gov. of Liberia. See also *Africa,* C 7.

Carey, William (1761–1834). Pathfinder in Eng. for modern missions. Shoemaker by trade; early interested in missions; studied theol.; pastor of Bap. chs.; gave impetus to founding Bap. Miss. Soc. Oct. 2, 1792. To India 1793. Finding Eng. doors closed, he went to Serampore, Dan. India, and with J. Marshman* and W. Ward* founded a press. Translated Bible into Bengali; instrumental in tr. and pub. Bible in whole or in part in numerous other languages and dialects. See also *Serampore Trio.*

F. D. Walker, *William Carey: Missionary Pioneer and Statesman* (Chicago, 1951); J. C. Marshman, *The Life and Times of Carey, Marshman, and Ward,* 2 vols. (London, 1859).

Caribbean Islands. A. *Historic Formation.* When Columbus discovered the new world, he touched shore on this chain of islands, the W Indian Archipelago, ca. 3,000 islands and islets extending over 1,600 mi. from the tip of Fla. to the NE coast of S Am., encircling what is now called the Caribbean Sea. The islands first came under Sp. rule, later fell prey to various seafaring adventurers from Eng., Fr., and Holland; these countries affected the present geog. divisions. The islands form the Greater and Lesser Antilles. The Greater Antilles include 4 islands, home of 4 indep. nations (Cuba, Jamaica, Dominican Rep., and Haiti; the latter 2 occupy the island of Hispaniola*) and Puerto Rico.

B. *General Description. Area:* 93,770 sq. mi. The original Indians, of S Am. origin, were branches of the Arawaks and Caribs, the latter giving their name to the islands and the sea. But in the period of conquest and the later colonial era the Indians either died because of the clash of civilizations or were transplanted to the mainland of Cen. or S America. Negro slaves were brought from Afr. to work the mines and plantations. This created a heavy mixture of Negro and Creole blood, esp. in the Sp.-speaking colonies; other islands, chiefly under Fr. and Eng. control, became almost wholly Negro. On some islands are found large numbers of E Indians who immigrated from colonies of the Far East. The language spoken on each island reflects its historic political connections.

C. *Social and Political Aspects.* Independence came relatively late to the nations in this area. Haiti, occupying one-third of Hispaniola, was under French rule. The Haitians won indep. 1804, but the Dominican Republic did not enjoy full pol. freedom till 1844. Cuba and Puerto Rico were under Sp. rule till 1899. Cuba then formed its own govt., but Puerto Rico remained under stateside control, enjoying a voluntary commonwealth status within the US. The Lesser Antilles enjoy various degrees of internal self-govt. either within the Brit. Commonwealth, or as overseas depts. of the Fr. Community, or as autonomous states within the kingdom of the Neth., or as territories within the US. However, esp. since WW II, pol. experiments of various kinds are being tried in testing local responsibility for govt. and soc. improvement. They range from purely socialistic revolution in Cuba to a cooperative venture bet. govt. and private capital in Puerto Rico, and from the status of islands such as Jamaica, Trinidad, and Tobago to the paternalistic pattern often followed in Fr. possessions.

D. *Religion.* Development of the dominant religion in each area was influenced by the respective formative colonial period. Islands under Sp. and Fr. control have gen. retained outward religious allegiance to RCm, but with less religious fervor apparent than in other areas of Lat. America. Islands developed under Brit. rule are predominantly Prot., as also to a lesser degree the Neth. Antilles. The Virgin Islands, formerly under Dan. rule, have an est. Luth. tradition. Where the Negro pop. is strong, active resurgence of Afr. animism is apparent in voodoo rites.

E. *Individual countries.* 1. *Cuba. Area:* 44,218 sq. mi. *Pop.:* 8,823,000 (1973 est.). Language: Spanish. Religion: mostly RC. Of 28 Prot. denominations reporting, the largest are Bap., Pent., Prot. Episc., Meth., Seventh-day Adv., and a number of faith missions. Lutheran work began 1910, when a Luth. pastor emigrated from the US to the Isle of Pines for health reasons and began miss. work among N Am. and Ger. settlers. An Eng. miss. field developed as a result under the auspices of the Mo. Synod. In 1946 the outreach was extended to Havana, with services also in Spanish. North Am. personnel remained till 1961. Since then the work is under the leadership of resident workers.

2. *Dominican Republic. Area:* 18,703 sq. mi. *Pop.:* 4,554,000 (1973 est.). Language: Spanish. Religion: ca. 95% RC (state religion). Prot. community includes Pent., Seventh-day Adv., Dominican Ev. Ch., Assemblies of God, Free Meth. Ch. of N Am., Christian Missions to Many Lands, and the Prot. Episc. Church. See also *Hispaniola.*

3. *Haiti. Area:* 10,714 sq. mi. *Pop.:* 5,099,520 (1973 est.). Language: Fr. and Creole, a local patois. Religion: mostly RC (state religion). Prot. community includes Bap., Church of God (Cleveland, Tenn.), The Church of God of Prophecy, Seventh-day Adv., W Indies Miss., Unevangelized Fields Missions, Pent., and Methodists. See also *Hispaniola.*

4. *Puerto Rico. Area:* 3,435 sq. mi. *Pop.:* 2,712,033 (1970). Free commonwealth assoc. with US. Language: Sp. and Eng. jointly. RCm predominates. Prot. community includes Assemblies of God, Meth. Ch. of the US, Am Baps., United Christian Miss. Soc., Disciples of Christ, United Ev. Ch. of Puerto Rico, Cong. Chs., Ch. of God (Cleveland, Tenn.), and Caribbean Syn. of the LCA. The first Prot. service in Puerto Rico was conducted by a Luth. seminarian from Ill. near the end of 1898. This field was later adopted by the Gen. Council of the Luth. Ch. in the US and eventually incorporated in the ULC. With sister chs. in the Virgin Islands (see E 8), this miss. in 1952 became the Caribbean Syn., now of the LCA.

5. *British West Indies.* Islands in West Indies which comprise or comprised Brit. colonies or dependencies. Following are or were included: Brit. Virgin Islands, Turks and Caicos Islands, Cayman Islands, Bahamas, Brit. West Indies Fed. (the latter, formed 1958, dissolved 1962, included Antigua, St. Christopher [Kitts]-Nevis-Anguilla, Montserrat, Dominica, St. Lucia, Grenada, St. Vincent, Barbados, Jamaica, and Trinidad and Tobago). The West Indies Associated States (not a pol. entity), self-governing territories in free assoc. with the United Kingdom, were est. 1967 and consisted of Antigua, Dominica, Grenada, St. Christopher (Kitts)-Nevis-Anguilla, St. Lucia, St. Vincent (autonomy for the latter delayed because of local pol. uncertainties). Language: English. Protestantism predominates. Chs. include RC, Angl., Moravian, Ch. of God (Cleveland, Tenn.), Ch. of God of Prophecy, Disciples of Christ, Internat. Ch. of the Foursquare Gospel, Meth., Pent. Assemblies of Can., United Christian Missionary Soc., United Ch. of Can., Wesleyan Meth.

6. *French West Indies.* Comprise Guadeloupe, Martinique, and surrounding islands. *Area:* 1,118 sq. mi. Language: French. RCm predominates. Prot. work listed only for Seventh-day Adv. and the W Indies Mission. Restrictions on the entry of non-RC missions have been relaxed in recent years.

7. *Netherlands Antilles.* Three Windward Islands (Curaçao, Aruba, and Bonaire) and 3 Leeward Islands (St. Martin, St. Eustatius, and Saba). *Area:* ca. 385/394 sq. mi. *Pop.:* ca. 230,000 (1972 est.). Language: dialect of mixed origins, called Papiamento. RCm predominates. Prots. include Prot. Union Ch., Dutch Ref., Meth., Angl., Seventh-day Adv., and Salv. Army. Lutheran services are conducted on Aruba and Curaçao, where the Norw. Seamen's Miss. maintains centers with resident pastors.

8. *Virgin Islands of the United States.* About 50 Leeward* Islands east of Puerto Rico; 3 largest: St. Thomas, St. John, and St. Croix (Santa Cruz). *Area:* 133 sq. mi. *Pop.:* ca. 63,200. Language: English. Prot. Chs. include Prot. Episc. Ch., Meth. Miss., Moravian Ch., and Caribbean Syn. of the LCA. Under Dan. rule till 1917, the islands were purchased by the US. The Luth. Ch., formerly under Dan. supervision, was then transferred to a Luth. Ch. in the US; now part of the Caribbean Syn. of the LCA. See also E 4; *United Lutheran Church, Synods of,* 2.

See *Missions, Bibliography.* RFG

Caribbean Synod. See *Caribbean Islands,* E 4, 8; *United Lutheran Church, Synods of,* 2.

Caribs. See *Caribbean Islands,* B.

Carlile, Wilson (1847–1942). Founded Ch. Army in Westminster, Eng., 1882; it works in slums, prisons, and workhouses.

Carlowitz, Christoph (1507–78). Saxon chancellor; follower of Erasmus.*

Carlsen, Niels Christian (June 1, 1884–Feb. 6, 1950). Luth. clergyman. B. Den.; to US 1894; grad. Trin. Sem., Blair, Nebr., 1910; ordained 1910; 1910–30 pastor in Duluth, Minn., in Superior, Milltown, and Bone Lake, Wis., and in Royal, Iowa; vice-pres. UELC 1921–25; pres. 1925–50 (full-time 1930–50). Active in NLC, Am. Luth. Conf., and LWC. Fostered negotiations that led to organization of Am. Luth. Ch. 1960.

Carlsson, Erland (Aug. 24, 1822–Oct. 19, 1893). B. Suletorp, Smaaland, Swed.; grad. U. of Lund 1848; pastor Vexio and Lessebo, Swed., 1849–53; in Chicago 1853–75; at Andover, Ill., 1875–87; pres. Aug. Syn. 1881–88; bus. mgr. Aug. Coll. and Sem., Rock Island, Ill., and one of its directors from its founding; for many yrs. ed. *Missionaeren.*

Carlstadt. See *Karlstadt; Draconites.*

Carlyle, Alexander ("Jupiter"; 1722–1805). Scot. theol. Educ. Edinburgh, Glasgow, and Leiden. Pastor Inveresk 1748–1805. Leader, with William Robertson and John Home, of the predominant moderates in the Scot. ch. in 2d half of 18th c.

Carlyle, Thomas (1795–1881). B. Ecclefechan, Dumfriesshire, Scot.; educ. Annan Academy and Edinburgh U. Taught math. Looked forward to the career of a minister; then abandoned both the idea of the ministry and Christian faith. Studied German and worked his way through an extensive reading course in hist., poetry, romance, and other fields. Works may be divided into 3 main groups: I. Literary Criticism. A. German works include *The Life of Friedrich Schiller; Wilhelm Meister's Apprenticeship and Travels; German Romance.* B. English. *Essay on Burns; Boswell's Life of Johnson; Sir Walter Scott.* II. Philosophical and Social Writings. *Sartor Resartus: The Life and Opinions of Herr Teufelsdröckh* ("Sartor Resartus" is Latin and means "The Tailor Retailored"; depicts Carlyle's spiritual struggle and is most representative of his genius; contains chapters on "The Everlasting No," "Center of Indifference," and "The Everlasting Yea"); *Chartism; On Heroes, Hero-Worship, and the Heroic in History* (includes an essay on Luther; sets forth Carlyle's view that human affairs are shaped by great leaders); *Past and Present* (like *Chartism,* attacks the principle of *laissez faire;* advocates governmental directive for both capital and labor, profit sharing, and educational legislation). III. Historical Writings. *The French Revolution: A History; Oliver Cromwell's Letters and Speeches; The Life of John Sterling; History of Frederick II of Prussia.* ECW

Carlyle, Thomas (1803–55). See *Catholic Apostolic Church,* 1.

Carmelites (Order of Our Lady of Mount Carmel). Founded as a hermit colony on Mount Carmel ca. 1154. Primitive rule laid down by Albert of Jerusalem 1209 prescribed absolute poverty, solitude, and total abstinence from meat. After the Crusades many mems. of the order went to Eur. and reorganized as a mendicant order. An Order of Carmelite Sisters was founded in the Low Countries 1452. The mystics Teresa* and John* of the Cross were Carmelites. The order stresses devotion to Mary and the child Jesus; early defended Immaculate Conception. Habit: dark brown; brown scapular; white mantle (hence "White Friars"). See also *Mendicant Friars.*

R. McCaffrey, *The White Friars* (Dublin, 1926).

Carneades (ca. 215–ca. 129 BC). Gk. skeptic philos.; opposed stoics; founded New (3d) Academy; advanced doctrine of logical probabilism.

Carnival (probably from Lat. *carnem levare,* "put away meat"; some derive it from *carne vale,* "O flesh, farewell!"). Period before Lent (either 3 days before Lent or Feb. 3 to Ash Wed.); eating meat in this period is prohibited in RC Ch.

Caro, Joseph ben Ephraim (1488–1575). B. Sp. or Port. Jewish jurist; works include *Shulhan Aruk (Table Prepared),* authoritative work on Jewish laws and ceremonies.

Carol. Popular spiritual song for festive occasions, esp. a spiritual folk song for the Christmas season; best ones came into vogue in Ger., Eng., and Fr. in the Middle Ages and after the Reformation.

Caroli, Peter (ca. 1480–after 1545). Fr. follower of J. Lefèvre d'Étaples;* fled to Geneva 1535; Calvinist pastor Neuenburg and Lausanne 1536; opposed Calvin; deposed 1537; returned to Fr. and RC Ch.

Caroline Books *(Libri Carolini).* Treatise compiled ca. 790–792; ascribed to Charlemagne.* Attacked Iconoclastic* Council (754) and Nicaea* II (787).

MPL, 98, 942–1550.

Caroline Islands. Large archipelago in W Pacific Ocean; includes 550 to 680 islands (depending on what is called an island). *Area:* ca. 550 sq. mi. Inhabitants Polynesian. Formerly belonged to Ger.; under Jap. control 1914–44; part of Trust Territory of the Pacific Islands; assigned to US 1947. Missions by ABCFM; Liebenzeller Miss. (before WW I). The RC Ch. is also active. See also *Micronesia.*

Carpatho-Russian Orthodox Greek Catholic Church, American. See *Eastern Orthodox Churches,* 6.

Carpenter, William (1762–1833). Luth. pastor; b. near Madison, Va.; soldier in Revolutionary War; pastor Madison Co., Va., and Boone Co., Ky. See also *Streit, Christian.*

Carpocrates. See *Gnosticism,* 7 f.

Carpov, Jakob (1699–1786). Lecturer at Jena and Weimar on Wolffian philosophy; sought to demonstrate dogmatics by math. method; wrote *Theologia revelata dogmatica methodo scientifica adornata.*

Carpzov. Family of Ger. lawyers and theologians including 1. *Benedikt* (1595–1666). Prof. and judge Leipzig; in *Jurisprudentia ecclesiastica seu consistorialis* he est. scientifically the "episcopal system" of ch. polity. 2. *Johann Benedikt the Elder* (1607 to 1657). Brother of preceding; prof. Leipzig; wrote

Isagoge in libros ecclesiarum luth. symbolicos. 3. *Johann Benedikt the Younger* (1639–99). Son of preceding; prof. Leipzig; opponent of Pietism, esp. of Spener* and A. H. Francke.* 4. *Samuel Benedikt* (1647–1707). Brother of preceding; Spener's successor as court preacher at Dresden. 5. *Johann Gottlob* (1679–1767). Son of preceding; supt. Lübeck; very learned; wrote *Introductio in libros canonicos bibliorum Veteris Testamenti* and treatises against Pietists and Moravians. 6. *Johann Benedikt* (1720 to 1803). Grandson of Johann Benedikt the Younger; prof. Leipzig and Helmstedt; opponent of rationalism.

Carranza, Bartolome de (1503–76). B. Miranda; d. Rome. Sp. Dominican theol. influenced by Juan de Valdes;* participated in Council of Trent; imprisoned 17 yrs. for Luth. tendencies in his doctrines.

Carroll, John (1735–1815). Jesuit. B. Upper Marlboro, Md.; educ. Fr.; returned to US 1774; miss. in Md.; named prefect apostolic by Pius VI; named bp. of Baltimore 1789, consecrated 1790; abp. 1808; founded Georgetown Academy. See also *Roman Catholic Church,* E 3.

P. K. Guilday, *The Life and Times of John Carroll* (Westminster, Md., 1954).

Carter, Marmaduke Nathaniel (Mar. 7, 1881–Oct. 14, 1961). B. Hanover Co., Va.; entered Mo. Syn. ministry by colloquy 1917; pastor Chicago, Ill., 1928–57; frequent guest preacher. Works include *Lutheran Customs.*

Cartesianism. The philos. of R. Descartes.*

Cartesius, Renatus. See *Descartes, René.*

Carthage, Canon of. See *Carthage, Synods and Councils of.*

Carthage, Synods and Councils of. Center of N Afr. Christianity for several centuries, Carthage was the scene of many important meetings already in the days of Cyprian.* Beginning ca. 350, a number of councils and synods were held there in connection with the Donatist* schism. A gen. Afr. council held 393 at Hippo Regius, near Carthage, is notable for its complete list of NT books, confirmed 397 at Carthage. An important synod was held 418 at Carthage because of the hesitation of Zosimus of Rome to condemn Caelestius* and Pelagius.* It adopted theses against Pelagianism on original sin, the absolute necessity of divine grace for salvation, and the reality of sin in Christian life. See also *Pelagian Controversy,* 5.

Carthage College. Beginnings date to a school opened by Luths. 1847 at Hillsboro, Ill.; moved to Springfield, Ill., as Ill. State U. 1852; closed as a result of Civil War; reest. as Carthage Coll. 1869/70 at Carthage, Ill., by the Ev. Luth. Syn. of Cen. Illinois,* the Ev. Luth. Syn. of N. Illinois,* and the Ev. Luth. Syn. of Iowa (see *United Lutheran Church, Synods of,* 9); 2d campus est. at Kenosha, Wis., 1961/62; Carthage, Ill., campus closed 1964. See also *General Synod of the Evangelical Lutheran Church in the United States of America, The,* 8; *Lutheran Church in America,* V; *Ministry, Education of,* VIII B. 6.

Carthusians. Monastic order, noted for uncommon severity in its practices. Disheartened with degeneracy in the ch., Bruno* of Cologne formed a colony of hermits 1084 and founded La Grand Chartreuse (whence the name Carthusians), until 1903 chief house of the order, in a lofty valley near Saint-Pierre-de-Chartreuse, ca 12½ mi. N of Grenoble, Fr. Though he did not intend to found an order and wrote no rule, the order grew from his example and was officially recognized 1170. It boasts that it is the only monastic order which never required reforms. Its rule prescribes practical isolation not only from the world but also from brother monks. Each has his own cell. Manual labor, study, prayer, and contemplation follow in prescribed order. The smallest details of life are regulated. Not even the sick receive meat. Never very large, the order has ca. 20 monasteries.

Cartwright, Peter (1785–1872). Am. Meth. preacher; b. Amherst Co., Va.; little formal educ.; licensed exhorter 1802; deacon 1806; presiding elder 1812; moved from Ky. to Ill. 1824; known for vigorous sermons and "muscular" Christianity.

Cartwright, Thomas (1535–1603). Eng. Puritan*; b. Hertfordshire; d. Warwick; prof. Cambridge; attacked prelacy, presently to be defended by R. Hooker*; championed Presb. polity; with Walter Travers drew up *Holy Discipline* for Presb. congs.

Carus, Paul (1852–1919). Ed., author, and philos. B. Ilsenburg, Ger.; educ. Strasbourg and Tübingen; to US ca. 1884; ed. *The Open Court* and *The Monist;* in religious (esp. Oriental) and philos. writings held that religion must be purified by scientific criticism.

Cary, Lott. See *Carey, Lot(t).*

Cary, Phoebe (1824–71). Sister of Alice Cary, with whom she moved from Ohio to N. Y. City; their mutual affection attracted much interest; poetical gift of both about equal; both wrote hymns; most popular hymn of Phoebe: "One Sweetly Solemn Thought."

Caryophylles, John (Caryophilus). See *Eastern Orthodox Standards of Doctrine,* A 3.

Casa Publicadora Concordia. See *Lutheran Church – Missouri Synod, Districts of,* B 1.

Casalis, Eugène (1812–91). Fr. Prot. miss. in Basutoland; dir. Paris* Evangelical Missionary Society.

Casas, Bartolomé de las. See *Las Casas, Bartolomé de.*

Casaubon, Isaac (1559–1614). B. Geneva of Fr. parents. Classicist; ranks immediately after J. J. Scaliger*; Ref. theol.; prof. Gk. Geneva 1582, Montpellier 1596; sublibrarian of royal library, Paris, 1604; prebendary Canterbury and Westminster 1610.

Case, Shirley Jackson (1872–1947). Bap. clergyman, educator, liberal theol.; b. Hatfield Point, N. B., Can.; d. Lakeland, Fla.; educ. Acadia U., Wolfville, N. S., Can.; Yale U.; Marburg U.; taught math St. Martins (N. B.) Sem. and Horton Collegiate Academy, Wolfville, N. S., Can.; Gk. at New Hampton (N. H.) Lit. Instn.; hist. and philos. of religion at Bates Coll., Lewiston, Maine; ch. hist. and NT interpretation at Chicago U.; religion at School of Religion, Lakeland, Fla. Dean Chicago Divinity School 1933–38, (Fla.) School of Religion 1939–47. Ed. *A Bibliographical Guide to the History of Christianity.* Other works include *Makers of Christianity from Jesus to Charlemagne; The Evolution of Early Christianity; Jesus: A New Biography; The Social Origins of Christianity.*

L. B. Jennings, *The Bibliography and Biography of Shirley Jackson Case* (Chicago, 1949).

Casel, Odo (1886–1948). RC theol.; entered Benedictine abbey Maria Laach. Wrote in area of liturgics; emphasized mysterious element in worship.

Caselius, Johannes (1533–1613). Ger. humanist; pupil of Melanchthon and Camerarius; prof. rhetoric Rostock 1563 and Helmstedt 1589.

Casework, Social. See *Social Work,* C.

Caspari, Carl Paul (1814–92). Luth. theol. B. Dessau, of Jewish parents; educ. Leipzig 1834–38; converted 1838; lector 1847, prof. 1857 Christiania. Followed exegetical methods of Hengstenberg.* Grundtvig's* views led him to investigate the development of early creedal statements and to write *Ungedruckte, unbeachtete und wenig beachtete Quellen zur Geschichte des Taufsymbols und der Glaubensregel* (3 vols.) and *Alte und neue Quellen zur Geschichte des Taufsymbols und der Glaubensregel.* Other works include an Arabic grammar, several commentaries, studies in OT and patristic hist.; tr. *Book of Concord* into Norw.; active in OT tr.

Caspari, Karl Heinrich (1815–61). Luth. pastor Munich. Wrote in area of practical theol. (catechetics, homiletics); also *Der Schulmeister und sein Sohn.*

Caspari, Walter (1847–1923). Ger. Luth. theol.; educ. Munich, Erlangen, and Leipzig; pastor Memmingen and Ansbach. Tried to combine adherence to Luth. confessions with scientific theology. Works include *Die evangelische Konfirmation, vornämlich in der lutherischen Kirche; Die geschichtliche Grundlage des gegenwärtigen Evangelischen Gemeindelebens, aus den Quellen im Abriss dargestellt.*

Caspari, Wilhelm (1876–1947). Prof. OT Breslau 1915, Kiel 1922. Works include *Die israelitischen Propheten.*

Cassander, Georg (ca. 1513–1566). Taught theol. Brugge and Gent; advisor of Ferdinand I and Maximilian II; RC exponent of meditating theol.; lived in retirement at Cologne.

Cassel, Colloquy of. Religious conf. held July 1–9, 1661, at Cassel, Hesse; arranged by landgrave William VI of Hesse bet. Ref. and Luth. theologians, the former from the U. of Marburg, the latter from the U. of Rinteln. Sebastian Curtius and Johannes Hein were the spokesmen for the Ref., Johannes Henichius and Peter Musaeus* for the Luths. Topics discussed: Baptism, the Lord's Supper, the person of Christ, predestination. Some measure of agreement was reached; polemics, it was agreed, should be minimized. However, the good intentions of the collocutors were not tr. into gen. action among the clergy in the Ger. states. In the final analysis the dialog belongs to those which were without far-reaching effect. See also *Syncretism.* CSM

Cassianus, Johannes (John Cassian; Massiliensis; Eremita; ca. 360–ca. 345). Monk and theol.; lived among monks of Egypt for a time; ordained deacon by Chrysostom; founded monastery and convent at Marseilles. Opposed Augustine's view of predestination on the one hand and Pelagianism on the other. Works include *De institutis coenobiorum* (introduced E monastic ideals in W); *Collationes patrum; De incarnatione Domini. MPL,* 49 and 50. See also *Semi-Pelagianism.*

Cassiodorus, Flavius Magnus Aurelius (Senator; ca. 485–ca. 583). Statesman, author, and educator. Held various high offices in Ostrogothic Italy. Retired to the Monasterium Vivariense or Castellense which he founded ca. 540 on the Gulf of Squillace. Works include a treatise on the soul, an exposition of the Psalter, an encyclopedia of religious and profane knowledge, commentaries on NT books, a grammar, and a ch. history. Furthered theol. educ.; set up a curriculum which is largely the basis for the quadrivium and trivium of medieval schools, antecedent of modern liberal arts education. Works include *Deartibus,* which contains a chap. on music.

The Letters of Cassiodorus, ed. T. Hodgkin (London, 1886); A. Momigliano, "Cassiodorus and Italian Culture of His Time," *Proceedings of the British Academy,* XLI (London, 1955), 207–245; *MPL,* 69, 421–1334; 70.

Cassirer, Ernst (1874–1945). Ger. philos.; taught at Berlin, Hamburg, Oxford, Göteborg, Yale, and Columbia. Developed neo-Kantian philos. of Marburg School into philos. of culture. Held that physical sciences have developed a symbolism which must be placed alongside of other symbols (art, religion); man is *animal symbolicum* rather than *animal rationale.* Works include *Philosophie der symbolischen Formen; Das Erkenntnisproblem in der Philosophie und Wissenschaft der neueren Zeit; Substanzbegriff und Funktionsbegriff; Sprache und Mythos; An Essay on Man.*

Cassock. See *Vestments, Clerical.*

Caste. Hereditary class in the soc. of India.* See also *Brahmanism,* 3; *Hinduism,* 3.

Castell, Edmund. See *Lexicons,* A.

Castellio, Sebastianus (Sébastien Chatillon or Chateillon; 1515–63). B. Saint-Martin-du-Fresne; d. Basel. French Ref. theol.; won for Protestantism by Calvin*; rector Geneva school; religious differences separated him from Calvin; to Basel, where he became prof. Gk.; opposed burning of Servetus*; works include *De haereticis* and tr. of Bible into Lat. and Fr.

Castenpauer (Kastenbauer). See *Agricola, Stephan.*

Casti Connubii. See *Encyclicals; Family Planning,* 6.

Castigationes Paternae. Chastisements of God, which flow not from wrath but from love (Ps 94:12; Heb. 12:6; Rv 3:19).

Castro, Balthasar Isaak Orobio de (ca. 1620–87). Neth. Jewish philos.-physician; converted; reverted to Judaism and became bitter opponent of Christianity.

Casualism. Doctrine that all things exist, or are ruled, by chance.

Casuistry. Branch of theol. knowledge related to pastoral theol., though usually regarded as a branch of ethics, dealing with the solution of doubtful cases of conscience or questions of right and wrong according to Scripture.

The Talmud* shows the minute differentiations to which casuistry may attain. The RC system of penance and absolution led to the writing of books on casuistry which listed sins and weighed circumstances with dialectical skill. One of the earliest of such works is Raymond of Peñafort's *Summa de casibus poenitentiae.* Others followed: *Astesana, Angelica, Pisana* (or *Pisanella,* also called *Bartholina* or *Magistruccia*), *Pacifica, Rosella, Sylvestrina.* Jesuits introduced the term "moral theology" for casuistry (e. g., Liguori,* *Theologia moralis*). Luther's *Von der Freiheit eines Christenmenschen* struck at the very roots of RC casuistry by emphasizing that the individual must stand or fall by himself. Melanchthon's *Consilia* is an example of Luth. casuistry. Other Luths. who wrote on casuistry: Balduin,* J. F. König,* J. K. Dannhauer.* Early Ref. work: W. Perkins,* *The Whole Treatise of Cases of Conscience, Distinguished into Three Books.* Modern Luth. treatments of casuistry are to be sought in books on pastoral* theology, ethics,* and works treating phases of Christian life.

Casula. See *Vestments, Clerical,* 1.

Caswall, Edward (1814–78). Eng. hymnist. Educ. Oxford; curate near Salisbury; joined RC ch. 1847; from 1850 lived in Oratory, Edgbaston; among his translations of Lat. hymns: "O Jesus, King Most Wonderful."

Catacombs. Caverns, grottoes, and subterranean passages, partly natural, partly enlarged by excavating the tufa and sandstone beneath and near certain cities, chiefly in the countries bordering on the Medit. Sea, many of them having their origin in quarries. The most noted catacombs are those of Rome. They consist of galleries extending beneath the city and the neighboring country for hundreds of miles in a number of stories of passageways. Along the corridors are horizontal excavations in the walls, which are often widened out into cells or small rooms. Here an estimated 6 million dead were deposited, usually in sarcophagi. After 410, when the invasion of Alaric took place, the catacombs were no longer used as burial places, and a few centuries later even the crypts of the martyrs were abandoned, their bones having meanwhile, in most cases, been removed to the altar crypts of various chs. which bore their names. During the siege of Rome by the Lombards the catacombs were in part destroyed and soon after became entirely inaccessible and were practically forgotten. The first excavations in recent times were made in the 16th c. The catacombs are of particular significance today because of the information they provide about early Christian worship, art, and veneration of martyrs. See also *Bosio, Antonio.*

E. Bock and R. Goebel, *The Catacombs,* 2d ed.

(London, 1962); M. Gough, *The Early Christians* (New York, 1961); W. Lowrie, *Monuments of the Early Church* (New York, 1923).

Catalog of Testimonies *(Catalogus Testimoniorum; Vorzeichnüs der Zeugnissen).* Scripture passages and quotations from ch. fathers on the person of Christ, esp. the *genus maiestaticum,* added as an appendix, but not as material subscribed, to the Book* of Concord. Written by Jakob Andreä* and M. Chemnitz* and added at suggestion made by Chemnitz Jan. 1580 to forestall charges that the FC in the article on the person of Christ introduced "strange, self-invented *phrases* and dangerous *modi loquendi.*"

Cataphrygians. See *Montanism.*

Catasterism. See *Astrology.*

Catavasia. See *Canon,* 1.

Catechetical Schools. See *Schools, Early Christian.*

Catechetics. 1. Branch of religious educ. dealing with the theory and method of teaching Christian doctrine, particularly to children and to such adults as are candidates for ch. membership. The term is derived from the Gk. word κατηχέω, meaning "to instruct by word of mouth"; it first referred esp. to oral instruction, usually of an informal type. By the 13th c. catechetics had acquired the connotation of instruction in the form of questions and answers. In Luther's time the word *catechismus* came to be applied to a book; A. Althamer's* 1528 catechism was the first book with the word in its title. Luther used the term because he felt such a book would meet the needs of oral instruction. In the course of time, catechetics has become assoc. with systematic questioning on the basis of a catechism.

2. Since Christ commanded His followers to build the ch. by teaching and baptizing, it was self-evident from the outset that instruction in doctrine be a most important consideration of the church. In the apostolic ch. there were 2 patterns of educ., one for the Jewish converts and one for Gentiles. The former was quite simple; it had 2 phases: (1) to recognize Jesus as the promised Messiah and (2) to understand the place of the Law in the NT church. Traces of a pattern for Gentile converts can be seen in Paul's references to instruction in Christian faith (Ro 16:17; 1 Co 15:3-4) and morals (Ro 6:17; Eph 4:20-32).

3. Up to the time of the persecutions (ca. AD 200) the type of instruction seems to have been of a more informal nature, though the earlier writings show that the ch. fathers tried to systematize doctrines. Under persecution the ch. became more cautious in receiving new members. The time of probation and preparation was extended. One result was the "catechumenate," beginnings of which are reflected in the writings of Origen.* Inquiry into the character and life of a catechumen and a course of instruction preceded entry into the catechumenate, both classes of which attended the *missa catechumenorum*: (1) *audientes* (Lat. "hearers") or beginners, who had not yet obtained the mark of complete purification, and (2) *competentes* (Lat. "those qualified"), who had given sufficient evidence of sincerity. The latter were given instruction for baptism, received by that sacrament into full membership, and admitted to the *missa fidelium** and the Lord's Supper. After the persecutions the catechumenate declined for many reasons, chief of which was this, that the large number of persons following the popular trend to become Christians made thorough instruction impossible.

4. From the 7th to the 12th c. religious educ. waned. Mass baptisms and group decisions made it practically impossible to carry on a systematic form of catechetics. A few protested. Men like Pirmin,* Alcuin,* Charlemagne,* and Rabanus* Maurus drew up instructions for training ch. mems., but their influence was limited.

5. Catechetical works in the stricter sense date back to the Weissenburg catechism (ca. the end of the 8th c.), which contained the Lord's Prayer, a section on capital sins, the Creed, and liturgical matter. The catechism of Notker* Labeo was used till the 12th c. The first catechism in the form of questions and answers was written by Bruno, bp. of Würzburg (d. 1045).

6. Among pre-Reformation sects the Waldenses* and the followers of J. Hus* prepared catechisms in the form of questions and answers. These catechisms consisted chiefly of 3 parts explaining the Ten Commandments, the Creed, and the Lord's Prayer; the RC catechism in the Middle Ages as a rule had 2 divisions: the Lord's Prayer and the Creed.

7. With the Reformation many catechisms came on the scene. J. Bugenhagen,* P. Melanchthon,* and J. Brenz* are a few of many who pub. various types of catechisms, some for the people, others for the clergy. Luther's *Der kleine Katechismus,* which first appeared 1529, is the oldest catechism of the ch. still in use. It was the culmination of several series of sermons beginning 1516. It soon outstripped others in influence and importance and was tr. into practically all Eur. languages. Its deeply evangelical note, which was not satisfied with simple historic faith but emphasized functional living Christianity, is doubtless the reason for its popularity. Luther's *Der grosse Katechismus* also appeared 1529. See *Catechisms, Luther's.*

8. Pursuant to action of the Council of Trent 4 theologians were appointed to draw up a catechism to serve chiefly as a manual for catechists and preachers. Result of their effort was the *Catechismus Romanus* (see *Roman Catholic Confessions,* A 3).

9. After the Reformation throughout Luth. countries the catechism of Luther or those of other reformers came to play an important part in family worship and in the curriculum of ch. and school. But despite earnest efforts, catechetical instruction began in many sections to degenerate into rote learning of the chief parts of the catechism. When Pietism* entered the Ger. ch., notably through P. J. Spener,* special measures were taken to avoid this intellectualism. But the rationalism* which followed this period blighted the ch. in Europe. The theory of rationalists was that instruction in religion should not concern itself so much with imparting truths, but should follow the Socratic method of drawing the needed truths out of the child. They failed to see that a Christian teacher deals not only with reason and experience but also with revelation, the truths of which must be imparted. They also overlooked the fact that they were not dealing with mature minds but with children. By mid-19th c. Luther's catechism was welcomed back into most schools of Germany. In the Scand. chs. Luther's catechisms never lost their hold and are still in use in upper grades of pub. elementary and secondary schools.

10. The RC Ch. also felt the impact of rationalism. Its catechisms were criticized as too dry, too impractical, too scholastic, and not Christian enough. Dissatisfaction culminated in attempts to produce more satisfactory texts, most of which bore the mark of rationalism. In reaction to this, a spirit of romanticism came into the RC Ch., showing respect to antiquity and esp. to the Middle Ages.

11. When Luths. came to Am. they at first used catechisms of their native land. Among these catechisms was the so-called *Kreuz-Katechismus* of Dresden. But Am. translations and explanations of Luther's *Small Catechism* began to appear in the 17th c. J. Campanius* tr. it into an Am. Indian language. German and Eng. eds. probably came from Benjamin Franklin's press 1749. Since then

many hundreds of eds. have been pub. in Am. in nearly all languages spoken in the country. Among those of important influence were reprints and revisions of the Dresden catechism and Ger. and Eng. eds. of J. K. Dietrich's* catechism which included material from the Dresden catechism. Other explanations of Luther's catechism used in Am. include those by J. K. W. Löhe,* J. Stump,* J. M. Reu,* H. J. Schuh* (d. 1934), C. F. W. Gausewitz,* Jacob A. Dell, Henry P. Grimsby, Otto Frederick Nolde, and Jacob Tanner; among Norwegians, E. Pontoppidan's* catechism and Harald Ulrik Sverdrup's catechism, abridged ed., tr. by Emil Gunerius Lund (1852–1938) have been preferred; the H. C. Schwan* ed. was popular in the Mo. Syn. till a new synodical catechism appeared 1943.

12. The catechism enjoyed a prominent position also in the Ref. branches of the Prot. church. In Scotland, Calvin's 1545 catechism held a dominant place, but was supplanted 1648 by act of Parliament by the *Westminster Shorter Catechism,* used by Presbyterians, Baptists, and Congregationalists in Gt. Britain. In Holland and in the Palatinate, where Dutch Ref. and Ger. Ref. were prominent, the *Heidelberg Catechism* was used (see *Reformed Confessions,* D 2).

13. When mems. of various denominations came to Am., they brought their catechisms with them. In the course of time these catechisms were supplemented by the writings of J. Cotton,* B. Harris,* and I. Watts. Much of Cotton's catechism was incorporated in *The New-England Primer.* Other early catechisms were by J. Davenport,* J. Eliot,* T. Shepard,* R. Mather,* J. Norton,* and S. Stone.*

14. For many yrs. the outstanding catechism of the RC Ch. in Am. was the 1885 *Baltimore Catechism,* later revised by a committee of bps. and printed in graded eds. Since 1959 *A Catholic Catechism,* Eng. version of the *Katholischer Katechismus,* official for all dioceses of Ger., has found widespread use in the US.

15. While catechetics has disappeared in many sections of the Christian ch., it still holds an important place among Luths. and RCs. Among the latter there is a definite trend away from formalism and toward leading the catechumen to personal, living, active faith. Catechetical renewal has been linked with the liturgical renewal in that church. Impetus was given to this movement by the Congress for Mission Catechetics, Eichstätt, Ger., July 21—28, 1960. Among the leaders in this trend are Johannes Hofinger, Josef Andreas Jungmann, Gerard S. Sloyan, and Josef Goldbrunner.

16. Some of the more important trends in the Luth. Ch. are evident in the Ger. writings of Kurt Frör, Karl Witt, Karl Hauschildt, and Alfred Niebergall. In the US, the LCA's parish educ. curriculum (ed. W. Kent Gilbert) and the LCMS's catechism series (ed. Walter M. Wangerin) give evidence of a departure from formal questioning and a return to the concept of catechetics which combines discussion and the expository method in such a way that doctrine becomes personal and functional. ACR

See also *Theology.*

I. Historical Studies. J. M. Reu, *Catechetics, or Theory and Practice of Religious Instruction,* 3d ed. (Chicago, 1931), *Quellen zur Geschichte des kirchlichen Unterrichts in der evangelischen Kirche Deutschlands zwischen 1530 und 1600,* a multivolume work (Gütersloh, 1904–35), and *Dr. Martin Luther's Small Catechism: A History of Its Origin, Its Distribution, and Its Use* (Chicago, 1929); L. J. Sherrill, *The Rise of Christian Education* (New York, 1944).

II. Recent Roman Catholic Studies. J. Goldbrunner, *Teaching the Cath. Catechism,* tr. B. Adkins, 3 vols. (New York, 1959–60); J. A. Jungmann, *Handing on the Faith* (New York, 1959); *Shaping the Christian Message,* ed. G. Sloyan (New York, 1958); *Teaching All Nations,* ed. J. Hofinger, rev. and partly tr. by C. Howell, 3d print. (New York, 1962).

III. Recent Lutheran Studies. K. Frör, *Erziehung und Kerygma* (Munich, 1952); O. Hammelsbeck, *Der kirchliche Unterricht* (Munich, 1947); K. Witt, *Konfirmandenunterricht,* 3d ed. (Göttingen, 1964); A. C. Repp, *Confirmation in the Lutheran Church* (St. Louis, 1964).

Catechism of Geneva. See *Reformed Confessions,* A 7.

Catechisms. See *Catechetics; Catechisms, Luther's.*

Catechisms, Luther's. Two books of religious instruction written by Luther for old and young. In 1516 he preached a series of sermons on the Ten Commandments; 1517 he preached and wrote on the Lord's Prayer, 1518 on the Ten Commandments, and in the next 10 yrs. issued many studies on the Catechism and related subjects. Visiting Saxon chs. 1528, Luther found the people sunk in superstition and the pastors in ignorance and immorality. He preached a series of sermons on the 5 chief parts of Christian doctrine (May, Sept., Nov., Dec. 1528; Mar. 1529). These sermons provided background for the *Deutsch Katechismus* (later called *Der grosse Katechismus*), which he began to write in the fall of 1528. He began on the *Enchiridion: Der kleine Katechismus* in Dec. 1528; it appeared on large charts Jan. 1529 and in booklet form ca. the middle of May 1529. The *Deutsch Katechismus* appeared in book form Apr. 1529. The *Enchiridion* in the form we have it dates from 1531 to 1542. The parts on the Office of the Keys and Confession were added later. The "Christian Questions" were added after Luther's death; though often ascribed to him, there is no evidence of his authorship of them.

The Christian faith is not only to be learned, but also to be lived; how it is to be lived in various walks and stations of life is plainly shown in the "Table of Duties," probably suggested by J. Gerson's* *Tractatus de modo vivendi omnium fidelium,* reprinted 1513 at Wittenberg. Probably Luther did not write "What the Hearers Owe to Their Pastors" and "What Subjects Owe to the Magistrates."

The transcendent merits of both catechisms gave them instant entrance into home, school, and ch.; they were soon confessed "as the Bible of the laity, wherein everything is comprised which is treated at greater length in Holy Scripture, and is necessary for a Christian man to know for his salvation" (FC Ep Summary 5). The *Small Catechism* has been called the greatest book of instruction ever written and the explanation of the Second Article the greatest sentence from a pen not inspired. It is a confession of faith and can be prayed. It was soon tr. into other languages and for over 400 yrs. has been in constant use to train the young. Some claim that it has wider circulation than any other book except the Bible.

The *Large Catechism* was written to aid pastors and fathers in teaching. It is practical, popular, and, at the same time, theologically developed. In the Decalog we come to the knowledge of our sins, in the Creed to justification by faith in Christ, and in the Lord's Prayer is manifested the new life in the Spirit.

K. Bornhäuser, *Der Ursinn des Kleinen Katechismus D. Martin Luthers* (Gütersloh, 1933); J. Meyer, *Historischer Kommentar zu Luthers Kleinem Katechismus* (Gütersloh, 1929); see also references under *Catechetics.*

Catechismus Romanus. See *Roman Catholic Confessions,* A 3.

Catechumen. See *Catechetics,* 3; *Christian Education,* E 10; *Missa catechumenorum.*

Catechumenate. See *Catechetics,* 3.

Categorical Imperative. Universal and unconditional moral command or obligation; distinguished from hypothetical imperative, which is conditional and depends, e. g., on expediency, practical necessity, or desire. See also *Ethics,* 6; *Kant, Immanuel,* 7.

Catena (chain). Commentary composed of extracts from different authors elucidating a text, esp. the Bible. This type of commentary dates from the 5th c. to the close of the Middle Ages. Many extracts of otherwise unknown works have thus been preserved. See also *Florilegium; Patristics,* 2, 7; *Procopius of Gaza.*

Cathari. Manichaean sect practically identical with the Albigenses*; found in W Eur., N It., Fr., Ger., and Flanders. Not sound in the doctrine of the Trin.; believed in a baptism of the Spirit in a very peculiar sense connected with ordination; claimed to have a perfect degree of purity in doctrine and life; flourished chiefly in the 11th and 12th centuries. Innocent III proclaimed a crusade against them, but they flourished under persecution. See also *Bogomiles; Manichaeism,* 3; *Saints, Veneration of,* 7.

Catharinus, Ambrosius (Lancelot Politi; ca. 1484–1553). B. Siena, It.; studied philos. and law; taught law Siena; entered papal service Rome 1513; influenced by writings of G. Savonarola*; Dominican 1517; opposed M. Luther* from 1520; prominent at Council of Trent* 1545–47; bp. Minori, It., 1546; abp. Conza (Consa; Compsa), It., 1552. Defended immaculate* conception and other views opposed to Dominican tradition; supported absolute papal authority.

Catharsis. See *Psychology,* J 7; *Psychotherapy,* 2, 6.

Cathedral. Church containing official seat (Gk. *kathedra*) or throne of bp.; hence mother ch. *(ecclesia matrix)* of diocese. Formerly also called dome (Lat. *domus episcopi,* "house of bp."); hence Ger. *Dom* and It. *duomo.* Originally a cathedral was served by a bp.; gradually services were delegated to a separate body of clergy (see *Chapter*); other chs. in diocese called parish churches. In the Luth. Ch. the word cathedral is used in a wider sense and includes various significant churches. See also *Church Archi-*

Catherine de Médicis (1519–89). Fr. queen; 3 of her 4 sons were rulers of Fr.; through them her influence was felt. Her unscrupulousness is shown by the way she played one side against the other in the religious wars and her responsibility for the Bartholomew's* Day Massacre. See also *France,* 9; *Medici.*

tecture; Western Christianity 500–1500, 8.

Catherine of Alexandria (d. ca. 307). According to legend, a virgin of noble blood; protested against persecution of Christians by Maxentius (thus in early MSS; probably Maximinus); condemned to torture on a spiked wheel (hence the name Catherine wheel); beheaded. According to legend her body was discovered on Mount Sinai ca. 800. Removed from RC calendar 1969. See also *Church Year,* 17.

MPG, 116. 275–302.

Catherine of Genoa (1447–1510). B. Genoa, It.; RC mystic.

Catherine of Siena (1347–80). B. Siena, It.; RC mystic noted for visions and revelations. See also *Jörgensen,* 2.

Catherine of Sweden (ca. 1331–81). Daughter of Bridget*; head of Brigittines* (1374–81).

Catholic (Gk. "universal"). 1. Universal as distinct from local. First applied to Christian ch. as a whole in a letter of Ignatius (ca. 110): "Where Christ is, there is the catholic Church" (*Ad Smyrnaeos,* viii, 2). 2. Orthodox as distinguished from heretical or schismatic. 3. Universal as applied to the ch. before the schism* bet. E and W. 4. Used in distinctive names of various ch. bodies: RC Ch., Anglo-Catholic Ch., Old Cath. Ch., Cath. Apostolic Ch. 5. In Luth. theol. (as in early Christendom) the word is often used of the one holy cath. (Christian) and apostolic ch. that transcends temporal, geog., and all other barriers.

Catholic Action. Cooperation of the RC laity and bps. in furthering the cause of the church. See also *Pallottine Fathers; Popes,* 32; *Youth Organizations,* V 2.

Catholic Apostolic Church. 1. Also known as Irvingites. Originated under the preaching of the Scot.-Presb. pulpit orator E. Irving.* The soc., pol., and religious upheavals of 1790–1820 in Eur., esp. the Fr. Revolution and the Napoleonic wars, led many to look for the immediate return of Christ. But they felt that the ch. was not ready for the Lord's 2d coming, because it did not have the NT charismatic gifts. Irving believed that the return of Christ was dependent on the presence of a living and active apostolate. He held that the premillennial coming of Christ was impossible as long as the ch. continued in the crime of neglecting to reestablish the 5-fold office of apostles, prophets, evangelists, pastors, and teachers according to Eph 4:11. He interpreted Acts 1:11 to mean that there must be 12 apostles at Christ's return as there were 12 at His ascension. In 1830 a number of individuals claimed to have received apostolic charismatic gifts, e. g., speaking in tongues, the gift of prophecy, and divine healing; this raised the hope that soon also 12 apostles would be appointed by the Holy Spirit. On July 14, 1835, twelve men who claimed to have been appointed as apostles were commissioned to inaugurate the real apostolic mission to the Gentiles, of which Paul, as one born out of due time, 1 Cor 15:8, had only barely made the beginning. The first apostles were J. B. Cardale,* Henry Drummond* (1786–1860), Spencer Perceval (son of prime minister Spencer Perceval), Henry Dalton (d. 1871), Thomas Carlyle (1803–55), Francis V. Woodhouse, Nicholas Armstrong, William Dow, Henry King (d. 1865), Duncan Mackenzie (d. 1855), Frank Sitwell, John Tudor. In London 7 congs. were organized according to the pattern of the 7 Asiatic congs.; a manifesto was issued by the hierarchy to the heads of the Eur. states to prepare for the Lord's imminent coming and the establishment of the millennium by accepting the decrees of this newly formed hierarchy and submitting to the "holy sealing" by the apostles as a condition of salvation. Romanizing trends were introduced in the cultus (elaborate vestments), in doctrine (the Lord's Supper a sacrifice, transubstantiation), and in ch. govt. (a hierarchy with presumptuous claims). The movement spread to the Continent, particularly Germany. But when one after another of the "twelve apostles" died before the Lord's return, a sharp division of opinion arose as to the number of apostles, some contending that there were only 12 in the NT ch., so there can be no more or fewer than 12 in the end period. This party believed that as the first apostolate was unable to prepare the world for the millennium, so also the apostolate of the 19th c. was unable to cope with the wickedness of the world. This party, now known as the Cath. Apostolic Ch., has no "living apostles," the last having died 1901 and no ordinations to the priesthood or the episcopate being possible today. The local chs. are governed by "angels" and "priests," and the mems. await patiently and inactively the Lord's further directions.

2. In Ger., F. W. Schwartz (d. 1895) and his successors, Fritz Krebs (1832–1905) and Hermann Niehaus (1848–1932), headed a group which contended that as apostles were added to the original 12, e. g., Paul, Barnabas, and Silas, so the Holy Spirit may at any time inspire new selections "through the spirit of prophecy." Later Schwartz, Krebs, Niehaus, and others in Saxony, and John Erb (d. 1942) of Chicago were selected as apostles. This group was later called

New Apostolic Ch. and has the New Apostolic Ch. of N Am. as a branch. Their theol. centers in the belief that an apostolate is essential to the church. The apostles are viewed as spiritual canals that supplement the Bible with their teaching, complete the work of the atonement, govern the ch., give efficacy to the sacraments, impose the tithe as due Christ the High Priest and Chief Apostle, and through the laying on of hands, the "holy sealing," prepare men for Christ's 2d coming.

See also *Scotland, Reformation in,* 5.

P. E. Shaw, *The Catholic Apostolic Church* (Morningside Heights, N. Y., 1946). FEM.

Catholic Biblical Association. See *Bible Societies,* 6.

Catholic Biblical Association of America. See *Bible Societies,* 6.

Catholic Church. See *Roman Catholic Church.*

Catholic Church, Liberal. See *Liberal Catholic Church.*

Catholic Clubs. See *Students, Spiritual Care of,* A 3.

Catholic Directory, Official. Pub. annually by P. J. Kenedy and Son, N. Y.; contains information on the hierarchy and various activities and institutions of the RC Ch.

Catholic Education in the United States. See *Roman Catholic Education in the United States.*

Catholic International Bible Society. See *Bible Societies,* 6.

Catholic Lay Societies, Religion Orders, etc. See *Roman Catholic Lay Societies; Orders in the United States.*

Catholic Reformation. See *Counter Reformation.*

Catholic University of America. See *Popes,* 29.

Catholicon. Term for nave, or center of ch., in E Orthodox Ch.

Catholicos. Title of Nestorian and Armenian patriarchs. Formerly applied to head of a group of monasteries in one city. Used in some E chs. originally as honorary title given certain exarchs ranking below patriarchs but above metropolitans.

Causa secunda (Lat. "second cause"). Cause caused by something else. Used of second causes by which God (often referred to as First Cause) preserves and directs His creation (Ps. 127:1). Luth. dogmaticians have pointed out that in the divine act of concurrence both God works and the means work. Furthermore, the divine concurrence is not previous *(actio praevia),* but the operation of God and that of the means is numerically one *(una numero actio).*

Causality. 1. In gen., cause is that which in any way exerts a positive influence in the production of a thing; it is the ground, occasion, or agency for an event, that without which effects (consequents) cannot be.

2. Newton formulated the 2d law of motion with a mechanical notion of force: force is proportional to the rate of change of momentum with respect to time, where momentum depends on mass and velocity jointly. Causation is an interaction which conforms to the laws of motion, and to the same natural effects we must, as far as possible, assign the same causes. J. S. Mill insisted, however, that there may be a plurality of causes producing an effect.

3. Modern science gen. has tended to conceive cause as a productive force, with cause and effect as regularly connected processes or changes, but since Hume the notion of "productive force" often has been replaced by causation conceived simply as an invariant relation, or universal conjunction, of events in space and time.

4. Contemporary analysis operationally interprets causality as correlation of phenomena, or invariant relation, or functional dependency. Thus it is viewed variously as a relation, in a time series, bet. events, processes, or beings such that (a) when one occurs, the other necessarily follows (sufficient condition) and when the latter occurs, the former must have preceded (necessary condition), and when one occurs under certain conditions, it is the contributory cause; (b) when one occurs, the other invariably follows (invariable antecedence, invariant relation); (c) one has the efficacy to bring about or change the other; (d) one part is functionally dependent on the whole or on another part, and when motion is described in quantitative terms the dependence of motion on conditions is expressed by functional relations which constitute the mathematical form of the laws of mechanics.

5. According to Ernst Mach, causality signifies functional relation between variables which characterize physical phenomena; e. g., causality as regularity of sequence is expressed in terms of functional relation between variables which describe the state of a system.

6. According to the statistical view of natural law, the same causes are followed by distributed effects (frequency distributions). Some modern physicists regard cause-effect as a useful tautology (analytic judgment) and hold that laws of quantum mechanics do not necessarily involve reference to, or even differentiation of, a law of connection of cause and effect, and that such laws can be restricted to first- and second-order differential equations.

See also *Cause.*

D. Bohm, *Causality and Chance in Modern Physics* (New York, 1961); R. B. Braithwaite, *Scientific Explanation* (London, 1953); M. Bunge, *Causality* (Cambridge, Mass., 1959); *Readings in the Philosophy of Science,* eds. H. Feigl and M. Brodbeck (New York, 1953); V. F. Lenzen, *Causality in Natural Science* (Springfield, Ill., 1953); *Readings in Philosophy of Science,* ed. P. P. Wiener (New York, 1953). RVS

Causative Authority. Term used in describing the power of the Bible of attesting itself as the divine truth, independently of any external proof (1 Co 2:4, 5; 1 Th 2:13, 14; 1 Co 1:5, 6; Jn 7:17).

Cause. 1. "Cause" and "effect" are correlative terms denoting any two distinguishable but related (antecedent, consequent) phases of experienced reality in a time series, such that whenever the temporally prior ("cause") ceases to be, the temporally posterior ("effect") appears.

2. Pre-Socratic used *arche* to denote a thing existent prior to and along with others, and without which others would not be. Plato used *arche* to denote a reason why a thing has its essential qualities so that we call it by a certain name.

3. Aristotle used *aitia* to denote reasons or principles of explanations: (1) efficient cause: the productive agent or force bringing forth an effect; (2) final cause: the purpose or end of a thing, that for the sake of which it possesses certain qualities or was produced by some intelligence; (3) formal cause: the essence accounting for the thing's nature, the qualitative characteristics making it what it is, distinguishing it from other things and making it like similar things; (4) material cause: that from which something arises, is fashioned, or produced. Medieval scholastics employed and modified these principles.

4. With the Renaissance growth of natural science, "substance" replaced material cause, and formal cause was set aside; "cause" was interpreted mainly as efficient cause.

5. Hume, who assumed that every idea is copied from some preceding impression or sentiment, traced belief in the "necessary connection" of cause-effect to the recurrence of certain experiences of uniform sequence (constant conjunction) which create in the perceiver a habitual expectation, a custom of anticipation whereby the mind habitually passes from perception of antecedent to expectation of consequent.

6. To rescue science from Humean psychologism,

Kant posited the principle of causality as an a priori, necessary category (form) of the understanding which is not dependent on, but is constitutive of, experience. It is through this form of understanding that empirical knowledge of nature becomes possible. (See *Kant, Immanuel*).

7. J. S. Mill identified regularity of sequence as the essence of causality, "cause" being defined as the antecedent, or concurrence of antecedents, on which an event is invariably and unconditionally consequent.

8. J. H. Poincaré and P. Frank adopt a conventionalist view of causality as a definition (or regulative canon of procedure) of a state of a system.

See also *Causality*.

Plato, *Phaedo* and *Timaeus;* Aristotle, *Metaphysics;* D. Hume, *Treatise of Human Nature,* III, and *An Enquiry Concerning Human Understanding;* I. Kant, *Critique of Pure Reason;* J. S. Mill, *System of Logic;* P. Frank, *Philosophy of Science: The Link Between Science and Philosophy* (Englewood Cliffs, N. J., 1957); J. H. Poincaré, *Science and Hypothesis,* tr. W. J. G. (New York, 1952) and *Science and Method,* tr. F. Maitland (New York, 1952). RVS

Cavalier, Jean (Chevalier; ca. 1681–1740). Leader of Camisards*; fought in Fr., It., Neth., and Sp.; lt. gov. of the island of Jersey; gov. of the Isle of Wight.

Cavasilas, Nickalaos. See *Cabasilas, Nicolas.*

Cave, William (1637–1713). Angl. patristic scholar. B. Pickwell; d. Windsor. Rector London; canon Windsor; vicar Isleworth. Works include: *Apostolici; Ecclesiastici; Scriptorum ecclesiasticorum historia literaria.*

Cawood, John (1775–1852). Educ. Oxford; held various positions as clergyman, the last as incumbent at Bewdley, Worcestershire; among his hymns: "Hark! What Mean Those Holy Voices"; "Almighty God, Thy Word Is Cast."

Caxton, William (ca. 1422–91). 1st Eng. printer; also translator. His 1st known piece of printing in England is an indulgence issued 1476.

Cayenne. See *South America,* 14.

Cayman Islands. See *Caribbean Islands,* E 5.

Cazalla, Augustino (1510–59). B. and d. Valladolid. Sp. martyr. Accompanied Charles V to Ger. at beginning of Schmalkaldic war 1546; lost faith in RCm; arraigned by Inquisition; executed as a Luth. heretic in 1st auto-da-fé.

Cecilia (2d–3d c.). Christian martýr of Rome; patron saint of music, esp. ch. music; according to legend, invented the organ.

Celano, Thomas of. See *Thomas of Celano.*

Celebes. See *Indonesia,* 1, 6.

Celestial Element. True body and blood of Jesus Christ present in, with, and under the bread and wine in the Lord's Supper.

Celestine I. See *Ephesus, Third Ecumenical Council of; Palladius* (5th c.).

Celestines. 1. Branch of Benedictines, originally called Hermits of St. Damian or Hermits of Murrone (Morone), after Pietro di Murrone (became Celestine V 1294), who founded community of hermits on Mount Murrone 1235–38 and Mount Majella 1240–43; Urban IV gave them Benedictine rule. The order spread through It., Fr., Neth., Bohemia, and Ger., but fell victim to the Reformation and the Fr. Revolution.

2. It. reform cong. of spiritual Franciscans who received permission 1294 from Celestine V to live according to the order of St. Francis independently of the mother group. The privilege was revoked 1302 by Boniface VIII. Remnants of the order went to Narbonne, Fr.

Celestius (Caelestius; Coelestius; 5th c.). Advocate at Rome whom Pelagius* persuaded to give up secular pursuits. In opposition to the low morality of their day, Celestius and Pelagius emphasized individual responsibility and free will. Celestius taught innocence of newborn infants. His teachings were condemned by Councils of Carthage (412) and Ephesus (431).

Celibacy. Obligation not to marry or to use marriage rights. The idea that celibacy was more perfect and holy than marriage may have roots in Jewish (Essenes,* Therapeutae*) and pagan conceptions. The notion is present in the apocryphal Acts of Paul and Tekla. Many Christians soon looked for this "perfection" in their pastors and gave preference to unmarried pastors. The first Council of Nicaea* refused to prohibit the marriage of clergy. The Syn. of Gangra* raised its voice against those who refused to accept the ministrations of married clerics. In the W the Syn. of Elvira* required bps., priests, and all who served the altar to live in continence even if married. Siricius forbade the marriage of priests 386. Later popes and councils of the W confirmed this edict. For 600 yrs. the priesthood struggled openly and in secret against celibacy. Rome considered wives to be concubines, and children bastards. The Syn. of Pavia* 1018 passed severe judgment against them. Gregory VII took decisive action against the marriage of priests. (See *Popes,* 7). He upheld the principle that a married priest who said mass and a layman who took Communion from him be excommunicated. When married priests opposed Gregory's enactments, he incited the nobility and people against them. Severe penalties were imposed on those who did not conform.

The Reformation called attention to the vicious results of celibacy (AC XXIII; Ap XXIII). Emp. Ferdinand and the rulers of Fr., Bavaria, and Poland asked the Council of Trent* to consider the repeal of celibacy. It decreed: "If anyone says that clerics constituted in sacred orders . . . can contract marriage, and that, contracted, it is valid . . . let him be anathema" (Sess. XXIV, canon 9); "If anyone says . . . that it is not better and more blessed to remain in virginity or celibacy than to be united in matrimony, let him be anathema" (ib, canon 10). It made special rules regarding "illegitimate sons of clerics" (Sess. XXV, Decree Concerning Reform, ch. 15). RC arguments for celibacy were based on Mt 19:11, 12; 1 Co 7:25, 26, 38, 40.

See also *Asceticism.*

H. C. Lea, *History of Sacerdotal Celibacy in the Christian Church* (New York, 1957); O. Hardman, *The Ideals of Asceticism* (New York, 1924); E. C. Butler, "Monasticism," in *Cambridge Medieval History,* ed. H. M. Gwatkin and J. P. Whitney, I (New York, 1924), 521–542.

Cella. Chapel erected in early Christian times in cemeteries, chiefly for commemorating the dead.

Cellarius, Johannes (Keller; Kellner; 1496–1542). Prof. Heb. Wittenberg and Leipzig; pastor Frankfurt, where he introduced proper administration of the Lord's Supper, with part of the service in Ger.; 1st Luth. supt. Dresden; staunch supporter of the Luth. Reformation.

Cellarius, Martin. See *Borrhaus, Martin.*

Cellerier, Jacob Elisée (1785–1862). Prof. oriental languages Geneva; mem. Geneva consistory; advocated modified liberal Calvinism.

Celsus (2d c.). Platonist philos.; opponent of Christianity. Wrote *Alethes logos* (True Word), known through Origen's reply *Kata Kelsou (Contra Celsum).*

Celsus, Aulus Cornelius. See *Paracelsus.*

Celtic Church. 1. Many facts regarding the Celtic Ch. have been brought to light in the 20th c. It was once regarded as a half-mythical organization, whose true hist. was obscured by traditions and contradictions. Careful hist. research has revealed a religious organization of great influence and of almost unmatched miss. achievement. It played an important role in the evangelization not only of the Brit. Isles, but of Gaul, Switz., and even It. and the Germanic lands.

2. Martin (ca. 315–ca. 399); bp. Tours; a founder of the Celtic Ch.; had little sympathy with Lat. Christianity; est. monastery at Ligugé and a Celtic miss. training school near Tours; the latter was called *Logo-Tigiac* ("bright white house"). A great opponent of Arians, Martin was flogged by order of the magistrates of Milan for speaking out against Arianism. See also *Wales.*

3. Ninian (ca. 360–ca. 432); one of Martin's most famous pupils; b. Pictland (now Scot.); educ. Tours; sent by Martin to Pictland; est. miss. training school (Celtic *muinntir,* "community"), called *Candida Casa* (Lat. "bright white house"), at Whithorn, SW Scot., ca. 397; trained hundreds of missionaries who went throughout the Brit. Isles.

4. Piran (ca. 352–ca. 430; some say a c. later). Irish Pict; est. a ch. and training center at Perranzabuloe, Cornwall; trained men who were then sent on preaching tours throughout W Eng. and Cornwall. Ruins of his ch. were discovered 1835.

5. Patrick.* Celtic, not RC, miss. to Ireland; built on foundations laid by Ninian's missionaries.

6. Finbar (ca. 490–578); Irish Pict; est. training school at Maghbile, Ulster; sent missionaries to Britain; founded colony and churches at Dornoch; friend of Comgall. Cainnech (ca. 515–600); Irish Pict; labored as miss. among W Picts and in Pictland of Alba; est. training center at Achadh-Bo, Ireland. Ferghil; trained by Cainnech; miss. to Salzburg. Kentigern (Mungo, "the beloved one"; ca. 518–603); eloquent preacher; pioneer in miss. expansion; est. miss. training school at Glasgow. Petrock (fl. ca. 550); Celtic miss. to Cornwall and probably Devon.

7. Columbia (ca. 521–597). B. Donegal; d. Iona*; Celtic miss.; "Apostle of Caledonia"; est. training school on Iona 563; sent missionaries to Britain and the Continent; founded Gaidhealic Ch., which succeded Pictish Ch.; built on foundations laid by Ninian, Piran, Patrick, and others. See also *Symbolism, Christian,* 4–5.

8. Comgall the Great (ca. 516–ca. 601). Famous preacher; founded influential school at Bangor of the Ards, Ulster. Among those trained were Columbanus* and Gall.*

9. Other famous Celtic leaders were Moluag,* Aidan,* Maelrubha,* Kilian,* Servanus,* Drostan,* and Dewi.* Kilian became a noted miss. to Würzburg and Heilbronn. Dewi, now called David, was the great miss. to Wales.

10. The Celtic Ch. fl. 4th–9th c. It long antedated the Lat. Ch. in N Eur. and was a powerful rival of Rome. Its date of Easter was different; it rejected the Roman type of tonsure, knew nothing of bps. as the Lat. Ch. understood them, rejected the jurisdiction of the pope, and knew nothing of the worship of Mary, intercession of saints, purgatory, transubstantiation, Communion in one kind, and other typical Roman traditions.

11. Perhaps the most notable characteristic of the Celtic Ch. was its fiery miss. zeal. It maintained a far-flung chain of *muinntirs,* which were miss. training schools. Here men were trained who made their way throughout the Brit. Isles and to the Continent, reaching places as far away as Austria, S Ger., Switz., and Italy. They were missioners, not pastors. They made little attempt to found permanent congs., but were content to be "awakeners," going two by two on lengthy preaching tours. Each great training center maintained a dozen or more communities where a "family" of preachers lived and from which they went out on their preaching missions.

12. The Celtic Ch. has a multitude of "saints," but in the old Celtic languages this word means merely "cleric" or "missionary," nothing more. The Celts did not canonize their noted men; nor did they dedicate their chs. to apostles, martyrs, or noted leaders. The Celtic Ch. was composed of several divisions, the more important of which were the Brito-Pictish Ch., the Iro-Pictish Ch., and the Ch. of the Gaidheals. The Picts and the Gaidheals regarded each other as erring groups.

13. The older accounts of the Celtic Ch. present a maze of contradictions and anachronisms; this led many to declare that its true hist. was lost beyond recovery. But considerable progress has been made by a group of careful historians. A. Macbain, W. D. Simpson, A. R. MacEwen, and A. B. Scott deserve special mention. These and others have made available an abundance of material on the Celtic Ch. and have done much to purge it of the thick veneer of legend, idle speculation, and confusion that until recently obscured its true hist. The *Transactions* of the Gaelic Society of Inverness also furnish much material.

14. The Celtic Ch. is important for its great miss. achievements and its ev. character. Its hist. fills in what was once a strange gap of 450 yrs. bet. the end of the apostolic and patristic era and the time of the rise in influence of the RC Ch. Many famous MSS of the NT were due to the industry of Celtic scribes, to whom we owe the preservation of such treasures as the Muratorian Fragment, the Codex Boernerianus, and the Codex Sangallensis. FRW

See also *Cerne, Book of; Culdees; Druids.*

A. B. Scott, *The Pictish Nation: Its People and Its Church* (Edinburgh, 1918) and *St. Ninian, Apostle of the Britons and Picts* (Edinburgh, 1916); W. D. Simpson, *Saint Ninian and the Origins of the Christian Church in Scotland* (Edinburgh, 1940), *The Historical Saint Columba,* 2d ed. (Aberdeen, 1927), and *The Celtic Church in Scotland* (Aberdeen, 1935); N. Chadwick, *Celtic Britain* (New York, 1963); M. Anderson, *St. Ninian: Light of the Celtic North* (London, 1964).

Cemetery (Gk. *koimeterion,* "sleeping place"). Burial ground. The Gk. word originally was used exclusively of Christian burial places. RC, Luth., and other chs. have endeavored to have their own cemeteries, usually restrictively or primarily for their own members.

Cennick, John (1718–55). Eng. hymnist; appointed by J. Wesley to teach in a school for colliers' children, Kingswood; joined Moravian Ch. 1745; deacon London 1749.

Cenobites (from Gk. *koinos bios,* "common life"). Monks living together under a common rule (distinguished from hermits*).

Censor. See *Index of Prohibited Books.*

Central African Republic. See *Africa,* F 3.

Central Agency for Foreign Missions. Est. 1883 by bps. of the Ch. of Eng. to receive special funds for for. missions.

Central America. A. *Historic Formation.* Before gaining indep. from Spain, Cen. Am. was divided into pol. areas which today comprise the 5 reps., viz., the captaincy gen. of Guatemala and the dependent divisions of Chiapas, San Salvador, Nicaragua, Honduras, and Costa Rica. During the colonial period, sections of the Caribbean coast in Honduras and Nicaragua were settled by Eng. buccaneers. In 1786 Sp. recognized Brit. sovereignty over Belize (Brit. Honduras). After gaining indep. from Sp. in 1821, Chiapas became part of Mexico. The 5 other provinces eventually split into the present nations of Guatemala, El Salvador, Honduras, Nicaragua, and Costa Rica. Panama, which occupies the remainder of the isthmus, was part of Colombia till 1903, when it declared its independence. Though not technically part of Cen. Am., Panama is usually considered together with the other 5 reps. because of its geog. and economic similarities.

B. *Inhabitants. Indians,* chiefly of Mayan background, concentrated mostly in Guatemala; *Mestizos,* people of mixed Indian and Sp. blood; *Negroes,* settled along Caribbean coast; *Europeans* and *North Americans,* immigrants residing chiefly in larger cities; *Orientals,* forming small colonies in urban areas.

C. *Social and Political Aspects.* After gaining indep. 1821, the 5 reps. passed through periods of violent revolution and enforced calm under strong dictators. Since WW II there has been an awakened sense of soc. responsibility, with solutions for regional problems sought by more democratic means. Reactionary pressures, both from the conservative right and the extremist left, are still apparent. Panama has had special blessings, as well as problems, because of proximity to the US-operated Canal Zone, a 10-mile-wide concession through which the canal was completed 1914.

D. *Religion.* 1. The pre-Columbian religions are still in evidence where larger concentrations of Indians hold to their primitive cultures. The Spaniards brought the pre-Reformation RCm of their land. Many of the priests were consecrated men who desired to learn the languages of the Indians and bring them the Gospel. But govt. policies often hindered such work. With the decline of Sp. power the number of priests became very limited. As a result, where the Indian cultures remained strong a type of syncretism developed in which ancient preconquest rites were combined with RC ritual.

2. Eng. Prot. work was begun 1825 by Wesleyans among Negro settlers in Honduras, Costa Rica, and Panama. Anglicans began 1844 in Brit. Honduras. The Moravian miss. among the Indians on the Mosquito (Mosquitia) Coast of Nicaragua dates from 1848. American Presbyterians opened a Sp.-language field in Guatemala 1882 at the invitation of the president. Using CIM as model, C. I. Scofield* founded the Central* Am. Miss. 1890. In the 20th c. many others entered the area, esp. since WW I.

3. Lutheranism came with Ger. settlers at end of 19th c. The first attempt to form a Luth. cong. in Guatemala was made 1908. The Ger. pastor also visited Luth. settlers in other neighboring countries. During both World Wars this work was disrupted. In 1947 LCMS, on invitation by the people, sent the first N Am. miss. to Guatemala to work among scattered Germans in Guatemala City, to serve Eng.-speaking Negroes in Puerto Barriòs (since the Anglicans had withdrawn during WW II), and to initiate Sp. work in the rural area surrounding Zacapa. After 1950 the staff was augmented and the work extended into the other republics. In 1941 a Luth. miss. was formally opened in the Canal Zone to serve N Americans stationed there. By 1957 under the auspices of the Armed Services Commission of LCMS this parish also included work in Spanish in the Rep. of Panama. The only other Luth. effort in Cen. Am. is centered in Costa Rica, where a pastor has worked in cooperation with LWF since 1958 to serve Ger.-speaking Luths. in Costa Rica, Nicaragua, Honduras, and El Salvador.

E. *Guatemala. Area:* 42,042 sq. mi. *Pop.:* 5,685,000 (1973 est.). Most RC. Largest Prot. group is the Ev. Ch. in Guatemala, which grew chiefly out of efforts of the Cen. Am. Miss. and has its Bible School and headquarters there. Others in descending order of membership: Ch. of God (Cleveland, Tenn.); United Presb. Ch.; Assemblies of God; Seventh-day Adv.; Ch. of the Nazarene; S Bap. Conv.; Soc. of Friends; Ch. of God of Prophecy. LCMS works in several areas. Guatemala City is also headquarters for the Caribbean Miss. Dist. of LCMS, with a resident counselor and bus. mgr. Also stationed there is the dir. for theol. studies, who supervises the preparation of nat. pastors through an in-service training program. The Luth. Hour office for Cen. Am. is in Antigua.

F. *El Salvador. Area:* 8,259 sq. mi. *Pop.:* 3,914,000 (1973 est.). Most RC. Largest Prot. groups are Pentecostals and Assemblies of God. Others follow in size: Cen. Am. Miss.; Ch. of God (Cleveland, Tenn.); Am. Bap. Home Miss. Societies; Seventh-day Adv.; Nat. Bap. Conv.; Soc. of Friends. The Luth. missions under LCMS are in the capital, San Salvador, and in the E section bordering on Honduras.

G. *Honduras. Area:* 44,482 sq. mi. *Pop.:* 2,870,000 (1973 est.). Most RC. Among Prots., Meth. miss. is largest, followed by Seventh-day Adv. and Ch. of God (Cleveland, Tenn.). Others are the Moravians, United Ch. of Christ, Assemblies of God, Christian Missions in Many Lands, and 12 other groups. LCMS stationed the first resident miss. 1963 to serve scattered village groups.

H. *Nicaragua. Area:* 57,145 sq. mi. (est.). *Pop.:* 2,183, 600 (1973 est.). RCm predominates. Among Prots., the Moravian miss. is largest followed by Am. Bap. Home Miss. Societies, Nat. Bap. Conv., Assemblies of God, Seventh-day Adv., Ch. of the Nazarene, Cen. Am. Miss., and LWF Ger. cong.

I. *Costa Rica. Area:* 23,421 sq. mi. (est.). *Pop.:* 1,902,000 (1973 est.). Rcm predominates. Among Prots., the Prot. Episc. Ch., whose bp. for Cen. Am. resides in San Jose, the capital, has the largest following. Next are Seventh-day Adv., Lat. Am. Miss. (whose sem. and editorial center is also in San Jose), SPG, S Bap. Conv., Meth. Miss., and LWF Ger. cong. Since 1963 LCMS has a miss. working in Spanish.

J. *Panama. Area:* 29,129 sq. mi., including Canal Zone. *Pop.:* 1,560,000 (1973 est.). RCm predominates. Among Prots., highest membership is reported by Internat. Ch. of the Four-Square Gospel, Prot. Episc. Ch. (bp. in the Canal Zone), Seventh-day Adv., Meth. Miss., Ch. of God (Cleveland, Tenn.), S Bap. Conv., and Union Chs. of the Canal Zone. LCMS's only parish serves both Canal Zone and rep.; the first miss. to work in Spanish took up residence in the Rep. of Panama 1963.

K. *Belize* (formerly called Brit. Honduras). *Area:* ca. 8,867 sq. mi. *Pop.:* 132,000 (1974 est.). RCm predominates. Among Prots., the Angl. Ch. of the Province of the W Indies, with a resident bp., is the largest; then follow the Seventh-day Adv., Meth. Ch., Ch. of the Nazarine, and others. RFG

See *Missions, Bibliography.*

Central American Mission. Founded 1890 by C. I. Scofield*; began work 1891 in Costa Rica. See also *Central America,* D 2.

Central and Southern Illinois Synod. See *Illinois. Evangelical Lutheran Synod of Central and Southern.*

Central Bible Society. See *Bible Societies,* 2.

Central Canada, Evangelical Lutheran Synod of. See *Canada,* A 4; *United Lutheran Church, Synods of,* 1.

Central Canada Synod (LCA–Can. Section). See *Canada,* A 27.

Central China Wesleyan Lay Mission. Committee which worked under the direction of the Wesleyan* Methodist Missionary Society.

Central Conference Mennonite Church. See *Mennonite Churches,* 3.

Central Evangelical Holiness Association. See *Church of the Nazarene,* 2.

Central Illinois Synod. See *Illinois, Evangelical Lutheran Synod of Central.*

Central Lutheran Theological Seminary. See *Ministry, Education of,* X B; *United Lutheran Church, Synods of,* 3; *Western Theological Seminary,* 1.

Central Missionary Society of the Evangelical Lutheran Church in the United States. By 1833 the Ev. Luth. Syn. and Ministerium of N. C., the Ev.

Luth. Syn. of West Pa., the Ev. Luth. Syn. of Md., and the Ev. Luth. Syn. of Va. had each est. a miss. soc. In Oct. 1835 the Cen. Miss. Soc. of the Ev. Luth. Ch. in the US was est. at Mechanicsburg, Cumberland Co., Pa. Purpose: "to send the gospel of the Son of God, to the destitute portions of the Lutheran Church in the United States, by means of missionaries, and by assisting for a season, such congregations of said church as are not yet able to support the gospel, and ultimately to co-operate in sending it to the heathen world." Socs. in mem. syns. of The General* Syn. of the Ev. Luth. Ch. in the USA became branches of this cen. soc., which by 1836 est. connection with the American* Home Miss. Soc. See also *Heyer, Johann Christian Friedrich.*

Central Pennslyvania Synod. See *United Lutheran Church, Synods of,* 23.

Central Schools. See *Christian Education,* E 7; *Parish Education,* I.

Central States Synod. See *United Lutheran Church, Synods of,* 3.

Central Virginia Synod. See *Virginia Synod, Central.*

Central Yearly Meeting of Friends. See *Friends, Society of,* 9.

Centuries, Magdeburg. See *Magdeburg Centuries.*

Cephalus, Sigismund. See *Beyer, Hartmann.*

Cerdo (ca. 140). Syrian Gnostic; according to Hippolytus and Irenaeus, the teacher of Marcion*; held that only the soul will be raised.

Cerecloth. Cloth treated with wax and placed on altar to prevent soiling of linen cloths above.

Ceremonial Law. See *Grace, Means of,* II 2.

Ceremonial Worship. See *Worship,* 8.

Ceremonies in the Lutheran Church. See *Adiaphora; Adiaphoristic Controversies; Agenda; Liturgics;* articles on individual liturgical acts (e. g., *Baptism; Lord's Supper*).

Ceremony. See *Worship,* 8.

Cerinthus. See *Gnosticism,* 7 b.

Cerne, Book of. Collection of nonliturgical, chiefly Celtic,* prayers dating from 8th–9th c.

Certainty, Religious. A true believer can be certain of his salvation. The faith that justifies is itself a certainty of salvation; its essence is "a being sure of God's grace in Christ Jesus" *(fiducia cordis),* Heb 11:1; Jn 3:36; Ro 4:20, 21; Eph 2:5; 4:30; 2 Ti 1:12. In *Introduction to Romans* Luther defines faith as "a living, moving confidence in God's grace" (WA-DB 7, 10). It is an indication of a weak faith when a Christian has doubts and feels uncertain that he is in a state of grace and will be saved. See Luther, WA 12, 386–399; 10 Ia, 331; Ap IV 322–355. See also *Apologetics,* II B.

A. Kurz, *Die Heilsgewissheit bei Luther* (Gütersloh, 1933); J. T. Mueller, "Die Heilsgewissheit nach der Konkordienformel," *CTM,* V (March 1934), 172 to 178.

Certosa. It. name for Carthusian* religious house, esp. as developed at Pavia and Florence.

Cerularius. See *Caerularius.*

Cesarini, Julian (1398–1444). Cardinal; papal legate in Ger. 1431, Hungary 1442. Influential at Ferrara-Florence Council.

Ceylon. See *Asia,* B 3.

Ceylon and India General Mission. Founded in Scot. 1893; fields include Pakistan.

Chad. See *Africa,* F 6.

Chafer, Lewis Sperry (1871–1952). Am. Presb. clergyman and educ.; conservative and dispensational in theol.; founder (1924) and pres. Dallas (Texas) Theol. Sem.; ed. *Bibliotheca Sacra.* Works include *Satan; Systematic Theology* (8 vols.).

Chair of Peter. In NT "chair" used as symbol of authoritative teaching and exercise of authority (Mt 23:2 NEB). In early ch. apostolic chair or see *(sedes apostolica)* was bishopric allegedly founded by apostle (e. g., at Rome, Alexandria, Antioch, Jerusalem). Roman see early traced back to Peter; hence called "Peter's chair" *(cathedra Petri;* also *sedes sancta, papalis, Romana).* Chair on which Peter supposedly sat preserved at Rome (origin usually ascribed to much later period). In the 4th c. Feb. 22 came to be celebrated as the date on which Peter ascended the chair. Jerome* placed celebration of Peter's chair at Antioch on Feb. 22, at Rome on Jan. 18; latter made official by Paul IV (pope 1555–59).

Chairetismoi. See *Pan-Ecclesiastical Ceremonies.*

Chakko, Sarah (1905–54). Syrian orthodox Christian; b. India; dir. Isabella Thoburn Coll., Lucknow, India, 1945; emissary of Student Christian Movement, and chm. in India, Burma, Ceylon; chm. of Committee for Life and Work of Women in the Ch., Ecumenical Council, Amsterdam, 1948; elected to praesidium of Ecumenical Council 1951.

Chalcedon, Council of. The 4th Ecumenical Council was held 451 at Chalcedon, Bithynia, on the Bosporus, opposite Constantinople. This Council climaxed the 4th stage in the discussions about the person of Jesus Christ (see *Christology*) which caused great difficulty ca. AD 200–600. This controversy was triggered by Eutyches.* In effect he seemed to deny that true manhood remained in Jesus Christ after the personal union had taken place. He held that Christ was *of* two natures (in origin?), but that He did not exist *in* two natures after the incarnation. The hist. of the ch. in this period is marked by corrupt ecclesiastical politics and by fearful rivalry among the E sees of Alexandria, Antioch, and Constantinople, and bet. E and W. Roman bp. Leo the Great (see *Popes,* 2) brought considerable pressure to bear on E churchmen and finally secured adoption of his "tome" as the official doctrine about the 2 natures in Christ. The final creed of Chalcedon reads:

"We, then, following the holy Fathers, all with one consent, teach men to confess one and the same Son, our Lord Jesus Christ, the same perfect in Godhead and also perfect in manhood; truly God and truly man, of a reasonable [rational] soul and body; consubstantial [coessential] with the Father according to the Godhead, and consubstantial with us according to the Manhood; in all things like unto us, without sin; begotten before all ages of the Father according to the Godhead, and in these latter days, for us and for our salvation, born of the Virgin Mary, the Mother of God, according to the Manhood; one and the same Christ, Son, Lord, Only-begotten, to be acknowledged in two natures, *inconfusedly, unchangeably, indivisibly, inseparably;* the distinction of natures being by no means taken away by the union, but rather the property of each nature being preserved, and concurring in one Person and one Subsistence, not parted or divided into two persons, but one and the same Son, and only-begotten, God the Word, the Lord Jesus Christ; as the prophets from the beginning [have declared] concerning him, and the Lord Jesus Christ himself has taught us, and the Creed of the holy Fathers has handed down to us."

The authoritative role played by Leo enhanced his standing in the entire ch. Unfortunately many E nat. chs. could not agree to this formula; so the Christians of Armenia, Syria, and Egypt remained Monophysite* [only one nature] and thereby isolated themselves from orthodox Christianity.

See also *Armenians; Simony; Theotokos.*

J. W. C. Wand, *The Four Councils* (London, 1951); P. Schaff, *The Creeds of Christendom,* 6th ed. (New York, 1931), II, 62–65; M. H. Scharlemann, "The Case for Four Adverbs," *CTM,* XXVIII (Dec. 1957), 881–892. HTM

Chalice. Cup used to contain wine at celebration of Lord's Supper. Has been made of glass or precious metal; since the 4th c. some were decorated with precious stones. See also *Church Furniture,* 3.

Chalice Veil. Square of colored brocade or similar material, often richly embroidered, used to cover the chalice (and paten) before the offertory and after the communion. First introduced into the W Ch. ca. the 16th c., the chalice veil was adopted in different parts of the ch. at different times. At an earlier date, a 2d corporal* was often (and is still occasionally) used to veil the chalice after the communion, with the chalice left unveiled before the offertory.

Chalmers, James (Aug. 4, 1841–Apr. 8, 1901). B. Scot.; son of stonemason; blessed with rugged physique, courage, and abundant energy; called "Great Heart of New Guinea" by R. L. Stevenson. Sent to Rarotonga, Cook Is., by LMS 1866; went to New Guinea 1877; made explorations and est. chain of miss. stations along coast; landed with Oliver Tomkins and others on Goaribari Is., where they were clubbed to death and eaten by natives. Wrote *Work and Adventure in New Guinea; Pioneering in New Guinea; Pioneer Life and Work in New Guinea, 1877—1894.*

James Chalmers: His Autobiography and Letters, ed. R. Lovett, 5th ed. (London, 1903); K. Moxon, *Tamate, Peacemaker of New Guinea* (Washington, 1960); W. Robson, *James Chalmers of New Guinea* (London, [1933]).

Chalmers, Thomas (1780–1847). Scot. theol.; noted preacher; mathematician; philanthropist. B. Anstruther, Scot.; educ. St. Andrews U.; minister at Kilmany 1803, Glasgow 1815; prof. of moral philos. at St. Andrews U. 1823; of theol. at Edinburgh 1828; left Est. Ch. with many followers and est. Free* Church of Scotland 1843; principal and prof. of theol. at New College, Edinburgh, 1843. Promoted Sunday and day schools for educ. poor; active in welfare work. Calvinistic in theol. Works include the first of the Bridgewater* Treatises; *Institutes of Theology. See also Scotland, Reformation in,* 2.

W. Hanna, *Memoirs of the Life and Writings of Thomas Chalmers,* new ed., 2 vols. (Edinburgh, 1878); H. Watt, *Thomas Chalmers and the Disruption [of the Church of Scotland]* (Edinburgh, 1943); F. R. Webber, "Thomas Chalmers, the Walther of Scotland," *CTM,* XVIII (June 1947), 411–429.

Chalon-sur-Saône. City E cen. Fr. Several important provincial councils held there in Middle Ages, one of most prominent being that ordered 813 by Charlemagne.* Its 66 canons included directives on educ. of clergy and on use of confession and Lord's Supper, and opposed abuses, esp. those deriving from greed.

Chamberlain, George W. (Aug. 13, 1839–July 31, 1902). Miss. in Brazil under Presb. Bd. North.

Chamier, Daniel (1565–1621). Huguenot* theol.; defender of Calvinism in Fr.; strove for union of all Prots. in Fr.; made academy of Montauban a center for Ref. theol.

Chaminade, Guillaume Joseph. See *Marianists.*

Champagnat, Marcellin Joseph Benoît (1789–1840). Founder of Marists.*

Chance. 1. Event that occurs indeterminedly without discernible human or divine intention or direction and not in assoc. with observable pattern, natural necessity, or causal relation. Chance events are occurrences not caused by conscious or unconscious teleology. 2. Assumed impersonal determiner of chance events.

Chancel. Originally the sanctuary or space immediately around the altar. Later the entire area set apart by an arch or screen, or the entire area in the ch. E of nave and transepts. See also *Choir* (architectural).

Chancery. *Episcopal chancery* is office of diocese in which, under direction of bp. or his representative, all documents of diocese are drafted and processed. Office in charge of chancellor. *Roman chancery* (papal chancery, Apostolic chancery, *Cancellaria Apostolica*) was that branch of Roman curia* which drafted and expedited papal bulls (see *Bull*) and briefs (see *Breve*). Cardinal called chancellor was at its head.

Chandieu, Antoine de la Roche (1534–91). Ref. pastor; of noble extraction; won by Calvin for Protestantism; pastor Paris 1557–62; fled to Switz. after Bartholomew's* Day Massacre; chaplain to Henry of Navarre 1585; pastor Geneva 1588. See also *Reformed Confessions,* B.

Chandler, John (1806–76). B. Witley, Surrey, Eng.; d. Putney. Educ. Corpus Christi Coll., Oxford; ordained deacon and priest; succeeded his father as vicar of Witley 1837; later Rural Dean; wrote numerous sermons and tracts; one of the earliest and most successful of modern translators, esp. of Lat. hymns.

Ch'ang. In philos. of Lao-tzu (see *Taoism*) the eternal laws or principles.

Chang Tao-ling. See *Taoism,* 4.

Change, Philosophy of. See *Bergson, Henri; Heraclitus.*

Changes, Book of. See *Confucianism,* 2.

Channing, William Ellery (1780–1842). Am. Unitarian clergyman. Pastor Boston 1803; rejected Biblical doctrines of inspiration, Trinity, atonement, total depravity, devil, but accepted Christ's sinlessness, miracles, resurrection. His creed is in a sermon he preached at Baltimore at the installation of Jared Sparks* 1819. See also *Unitarianism.*

Chant (Lat. *cantus,* "song"). The liturgy (Order of the Holy Communion) and the minor offices are often chanted, i. e., recited in a sung-spoken manner. The Luth., Angl., RC, Gk. Orthodox, and Russ. Orthodox are the main chs. which offer wide possibility for chanting the liturgy. Liturgical chant derives from W and E traditions. The former begins with Ambrosian* (Milanese, 4th c.), Gregorian,* Mozarabic,* Gallican,* and Sarum* chants. These can be placed under the common heading of plainsong. Early E traditions are called Byzantine, or Gk. Orthodox; Russ. developments came later. Both E and W forms can be traced through Jewish traditions to Egyptian and Indian ethos. All these branches and practices are monophonic, gen. unaccompanied, and, in the true sense of chant, free-rhythmic music. These features are found in music within and without the ch., though largely developed within the ch. After the Reformation Eng. developed her own manner of chanting. Chanting Psalms and Canticles at Morning and Evening Prayer developed into Angl. chant, which is to be sung in 4-part harmony; it may be sung in unison only with accompaniment. The reciting-note features are common to plainsong and Angl. chant, but the manner of making a cadence differs widely in melody and rhythmic pattern. Luther's *Formula missae* (1523) and *Deudsche Messe* (1526) helped set the tone and attitude toward use of plainsong in the Luth. services of worship. In early and developing periods of Lutheranism plainsong was widely used in chanting the propers* and the ordinary* of the Order of the Holy Communion. It has remained in the decorum and habit of the ch. To chant the liturgy is a manner of prayer; it is a mark of the ch. in action to express God's sacramental work and respond sacrificially in praise and thanksgiving. See also *Liturgics; Luther, Liturgies of.*

Handbuch der deutschen evangelischen Kirchenmusik, ed. K. Ameln, C. Mahrenholz, W. Thomas, and C. Gerhardt, I in 2 parts: *Der Altargesang* (Göttingen, 1941–42); W. Apel, *Gregorian Chant* (Bloomington, Ind., 1958); *Schatz des liturgischen Chor- und Gemeindesgesangs,* ed. L. Schoeberlein,

2 vols. (vol. 2 in 2 parts) (Göttingen, 1865–72). RRB

Chantal, Jeanne Françoise Fremiot de (1572–1641). Fr. religious; founded Order of the Visitation of Mary (Visitation* Nuns).

Chantepie de la Saussaye. 1. *Daniel* (1818–74). Ref. pastor Leeuwarden, Leiden, and Rotterdam; prof. Groningen 1872; espoused ethical orthodox theol. 2. *Pierre Daniel* (1848–1920). Son of Daniel; prof. hist. of religion Amsterdam 1878, Leiden 1899; investigated phenomenology of religion. Works include *Lehrbuch der Religionsgeschichte.*

Chanukah (Chanukkah). See *Judaism,* 4.

Chapel. The word chapel originally (7th c.) probably denoted the temporary sanctuary which housed the cape (LL *cappa*) of Martin of Tours when it was carried along on military campaigns; later, any sanctuary containing relics; then building which differed in some ways from chs. (e. g., places of worship for schools, colleges, hospitals), special parts of chs. having their own altar (Chapel Royal and Chapel of Ease in Eng.), and private chs.; in Am. at times synonymous with ch.

Chaplain. Clergyman, usually with special, limited functions, as one employed in a private chapel to read the lessons and to preach; in Am. esp. men opening or conducting religious services in an assembly of a pub. or semipub. nature, as in legislature assemblies, pub. institutions, and the armed forces. See also *Armed Services Commission.*

Chaplet. One third of a rosary,* namely 55 beads, for 50 Ave* Marias and 5 Paternosters.*

Chapman, John (1865–1933). Educ. Oxford; deacon Ch. of Eng. 1889; joined RC Ch. 1890. Entered Benedictine Order (see *Benedictines*) 1892; NT and patristic scholar; defended priority of Matthew.

Chapman, John Wilbur. See *Revivals,* 2.

Chappuis, Jean (fl. 1500). Fr. canonist; compiled *Extravagantes Johannis XXII* and *Extravagantes communes.*

Chappuis, Paul Gabriel (1892–1930). Ref. pastor Paris 1916, L'Auberson 1917, Etoy 1922, Geneva 1929. Wrote on the problem of religious knowledge and on influence of Stoicism on early Christian thought.

Chapter. From custom of reading a chapter at meetings of monks, the place of meeting and assembly received name chapter. Later monks of a region (provincial) and of whole order (general) were called chapters. Then name extended to include mems. of corporate body responsible for ecclesiastical institution, more specifically a cathedral (cathedral chapter) or large ch. (collegiate chapter). In late Middle Ages, cathedral chapters received increasing role in function of bp., right of electing him, and ultimately became indep. of episcopal control. Council of Trent partially restored authority of bp. over chapter. In Angl. Ch. chapters are practically indep. of bps.

In Luth. chs. which preserved episcopacy (e. g., in Scand.) chapter is head of diocese and includes bp. (chm.), dean, and additional mems., of whom at least some are elected by clergy and laity.

Ex. head of chapter usually called dean or provost.

Chapter, Little. Short Scripture lesson read at canonical hours* except Matins.*

Chapters and Verses of the Bible. Before the time of Christ the Jews divided the OT into parashoth and haftaroth for reading in the synagog on the Sabbath. The NT books were also divided at an early date into *titles* and *chapters.* S. Langton* is gen. considered as having introduced the present chapter divisions into the Vulgate ca. 1205. Verse divisions were first indicated 1551 by R. Estienne* I, a printer, in his 4th ed. of the NT. Verse divisions were introd. a few yrs. later in the whole Bible.

Character indelebilis. Term used in RC theol. to denote a certain spiritual mark said to be impressed on recipients of certain sacraments. "If anyone says that in three sacraments, namely, baptism, confirmation, and order, there is not imprinted on the soul a character, that is, a certain spiritual and indelible mark, by reason of which they cannot be repeated, let him be anathema" (Council of Trent, Sess. VII, can. 9 on the sacraments in gen.). The "character" of Baptism is said to distinguish the baptized (including Prots.) as soldiers of Christ and subject them to the pope and canon law, and the "character" of order is said to set apart clergy from laity. Sometimes called sacramental seal. See also *Sacraments Roman Catholic.*

Characterology (Gk. *charassein,* "cut into, engrave," and *logos,* "word, reason"). Study of character, esp. its development and difference. Character is evident in a person's behavior. Some regard character as a result of organic structure, including the form of the body. Others place greater stress on influence of environment. Rationalistic approaches regard character as a result of convictions or sense of values. Environment, convictions, and values are often religious.

Chardin, Pierre Teilhard de. See *Teilhard de Chardin, Pierre.*

Charismata. See *Gifts of the Spirit.*

Charities, Christian. 1. *The Term.* The word charity (pl. charities) is derived from Lat. *caritas,* used by Jerome* in the Vulgate for Gk. *agape.* But in KJV charity, the Anglicized form of *caritas,* is occasionally used when *agape* indicates love of man for his fellowmen (1 Co 13). It denotes primarily not such outward evidences of love as almsgiving, but love itself, an inner principle or attitude, a motive which determines man's relation to his fellowman and bestows a peculiar value on all his activities. Thus 1 Co 13 describes it as the greatest and most enduring Christian virtue.

2. *Later Usage.* As the ch. lapsed into legalism and as monastic ideals of morality developed, *caritas,* or charity, gradually assumed a meaning just the opposite of *agape.* In the Middle Ages it meant simply "giving of goods to feed the poor," which "profits nothing" without the motive of Christian love (1 Co 13). In present usage the word charity means A. Christian love*; B. an attitude of sympathy toward those who are suffering from misfortune; C. liberality in caring for the poor and handicapped; D. tolerance in judging others. It has even acquired an obnoxious connotation of paternalistic benevolence with doubtful motivation and purpose. It is primarily because of these implications that modern revisers of the NT have substituted the word love for charity in tr. *agape.*

3. *Institutional Usage.* A "charity" is an eleemosynary institution or agency, founded and operated to assist the poor, sick, handicapped, orphaned, etc., without charge. In the 19th c. the concept of "charities" was broadened, and particular emphasis was laid on the natural "right" of the individual to benefit by the bounty of his fellowmen. It was out of this enlarged concept (which includes justice) that the Charity Organization movement was born 1869 in London; the first Charity Organization society in the US was founded 1877 in Buffalo. Much modern soc. work has developed from this source. The word charity in an institutional sense has now practically disappeared from the vocabulary of secular soc. work and has been largely replaced by "service," a word more nearly expressive of motivation and methods used in our age to assist those in distress. (See *Social Work*). The word charity is still used, with diminishing emphasis, by such ch.-sponsored organizations for soc. service as Cath. Charities and Associated* Lutheran Charities.

4. *Historical Development.* In the OT the "charity" to be practiced by God's children was prescribed

in many laws and ordinances. With the coming of Christ these rules were abrogated. The virtue of love for the neighbor was enjoined in the NT, but the expression of this attitude in deeds of love became a matter of Christian liberty. In the apostolic age, besides the bread and wine, used for celebrating the Lord's Supper, Christians brought to the altar products of every kind to be distributed among the poor. Ca. 550 oblations were restricted for use of the clergy, and gifts for the poor were deposited in a special place. With the disintegration of morals attendant on the collapse of the Roman Empire and the economic crises into which soc. was plunged, the masses became pauperized; monasteries and such charitable institutions as hospitals became central points in dispensing charity. Rules and regulations were gradually est. Ca. one fourth of the income of of the ch. was set aside for charity in early centuries. The amount and character of charity dispensed by the ch. in following centuries varied, but the ch. remained as the only friend and benefactor of the poor and handicapped. Gradually the practice of charity came to be regarded as a meritorious service rewarded by God with special favors. The close of the Middle Ages saw Christian charity degenerate into crassest work-righteousness. With the Reformation a new day dawned for Christian charity. Luther championed the liberty of a Christian under God to express Christian love in conformity with Gl 6:9-10. Christians were again enjoined to practice charity as an expression of love to God and their fellowmen and as evidence of gratitude for unmerited grace bestowed through Jesus Christ.

5. The 19th c. esp. saw a great expansion of the work of organized Christian charity, originated and conducted largely through efforts of Luths. Deaconess* work was begun 1833 in Kaiserswerth, Ger., largely through efforts of T. Fliedner; Kaiserswerth produced many agencies and institutions of charity, aiding sick, forsaken, fallen, orphaned, and aged in almost every country of Eur. Also in 1833 there was est. in Hamburg "Das Rauhe Haus," a great center of charitable work founded by Johann Hinrich Wichern,* father of the German Inner Mission movement. The orphanage at Halle, founded by A. H. Francke* and the colony for epileptics at Bielefeld, founded by F. von Bodelschwingh,* deserve special mention. In Eng. A. A. Cooper* (1801–85), T. J. Barnardo, and G. Müller* promoted great charitable enterprises. Den., Norw., Swed., and other Prot. countries shared in this greatest development of organized Christian charity since the days of the early ch.

6. The early hist. of the Luth. Ch. in the US includes reports on the charitable work of the only Luth. ch. in N. Y. in 1674. This report, with similar items in following yrs., reveals the fact that Luth. congs. in the early days of the US did not shirk their charitable obligations. In those days cong. action for relief of the poor seems to have been the universal custom, since the simple economy of life in a new country did not call for large, specialized agencies of charity. But with great pop. increase in the 18th and 19th c., such agencies were gradually est. W. A. Passavant* and J. F. Bünger* deserve special mention in this connection.

7. In 1945 almost 500 agencies and institutions of mercy operated under Luth. auspices in the US. The existence of such a large Luth. network of professional welfare services, together with a wide variety of governmental and voluntary community welfare services fostered the ill-founded belief that the individual Luth. cong. need not be directly concerned with ministry to the troubled neighbor. But since 1950 congs. have increasingly recognized charity or soc. welfare as an integral element of witness and ministry. Most Luth. congs. have soc. welfare or soc. ministry committees which serve as catalysts bet. mems. of the cong. and those in need. Luth. welfare bds. have stimulated concern through theol. essays, educ. materials, and workshops. This partnership of cong. and agency in soc. welfare has furthered the ministry of compassion.

8. Since 1950 there has been a decided change in the relative roles and responsibilities of govt. on the one hand, and ch.-related and voluntary community and inst. chaplains on the other; surveys of existing and projected agencies have been made; interpretive materials have been pub.

9. In 1965 Assoc. Luth. Charities comprised 114 mem. agencies, classified in 4 groupings: 1. City and Inst. Missions; 2. Family and Child Care; 3. Care of the Aged; 4. Health and Hospitals. An Ex. Bd. of 9 elected mems. conducts the affairs of the organization. Officers include a pres., 1st and 2d vice-presidents, secy., treasurer, and bus. mgr.

10. The assoc. sponsors a biennial nat. conv. in odd-numbered yrs.; regional meetings are held in even-numbered yrs. in various major Luth. pop. centers in the US. Since 1953 both the nat. and regional meetings have been held under joint auspices of Assoc. Luth. Charities and The Luth. Welfare Conf. in Am. (NLC), insofar as gen. sessions and workshops are concerned. The bus. sessions of each group are held separately because most Luth. health and welfare agencies are inter-Luth. in their auspices. The joint nat. convs. are called Luth. Health and Welfare Forums. The assoc. publishes *Proceedings,* containing membership roster, reports, and papers delivered at biennial convs.; *Proceedings* of the regional meetings; and *The Good News,* a religious monthly distributed in hospitals and other institutions by pastors and missionaries.

See also *Aging and Infirm, Homes and Services for; Associated Lutheran Charities; Child and Family Service Agencies; Hospitals, Sanatoria, Homes for Convalescents and Chronically Ill; Inner Mission; Social Work.* HFW, JCC

Charity (Christian love). Greatest theol. virtue (1 Co 13). See also *Charities, Christian,* 1, 2.

Charity, Brothers of. See *Congregation of the Brothers of Charity.*

Charity, Sisters of. See *Sisters of Charity.*

Charity Organization Society. See *Charities, Christian,* 3.

Charity Organizations. See *Charities, Christian; Aging and Infirm, Homes and Services for; Child and Family Service Agencies; Hospitals, Sanatoria, Homes for Convalescents and Chronically Ill.*

Charlemagne (Charles the Great; Charles I; Ger. *Karl der Grosse;* Lat. *Carolus Magnus;* ca. 742–814). Founder of the Holy Roman Empire. Son of Pepin* the Short (founder of Carolingian dynasty). D. Aachen. Anointed (together with his father and his brother Carloman) king of the Franks 754; coruler with Carloman after Pepin died 768; sole ruler after Carloman died 771; crowned emp. of the Romans by Leo III Dec. 25, 800. After his father and brother died he carried out the projects of his father and grandfather, bringing the Lombards into subjection in support of the papacy and assuming the Lombard crown. He then turned N to the task of conquering and Christianizing the Saxons, accomplishing this task after ca. 33 yrs. of successive campaigns. On extending the boundaries of his realm, he provided for speedy Christianization of acquired territory by covering the country with Christian institutions and forcing people to submit to Baptism and to full agreement with the cultus of the RC Ch. He considered such conversion of the whole pop. essential to the attainment of his pol. ends. To improve the moral and intellectual standards of the clergy, he required bps. and abbots to found schools in their cathedrals and monasteries. He summoned the most eminent educators of his own land and those of It., Sp., and Brit. (including Alcuin* of York) to direct an educ. program. Through monasteries and chs. he sought to spread civilization throughout his realm; promoted ch. music, previously neglected in Ger.; encouraged revival of Christian art; opposed iconoclasm and image worship.

J. Lord, *Beacon Lights of History,* III (New York, 1921), 55–91; C. W. Previté-Orton, *The Shorter Cambridge Medieval History,* rev. P. Grierson, I (London, 1953), pp. 303–333; H. Lamb, *Charlemagne* (New York, 1954); L. Wallach, *Alcuin and Charlemagne* (Ithaca, N. Y., 1959); R. Winston, *Charlemagne* (Indianapolis, 1954).

Charles I (king of Gt. Brit, and Ireland). See *Presbyterian Confessions,* 1.

Charles I. Holy Roman emperor. See also *Charlemagne.*

Charles II (king of Gt. Brit. and Ireland). See *England,* C 1.

Charles II (823–877). Called "Charles the Bald"; Fr. *Charles le Chauve.* Holy Roman emperor 875–877. King of Fr. (Charles I) 840–877. See also *Inquisition,* 2.

Charles V (1500–58). Holy Roman emperor; elected 1519, crowned 1530. King (Charles I) of Sp. 1516 to 1566. Greatest ruler of the house of Hapsburg. His treatment of the Reformers was conditioned by his political and military needs in the struggle with the Fr. and Turks. He condemned Luther in the Edict of Worms* 1521; was tolerant toward the Lutherans at Speyer* 1526 because the League of Cognac and the menace of the Turks created an unfavorable situation for him; took a firm stand against the Lutherans at Speyer* 1529 because he felt strengthened by the Peace of Cambrai.* At the time of the Augsburg Diet 1530 he needed support of Ger. princes against the Turks and therefore could not afford to crush Lutheranism. The Religious Peace of Nürnberg* 1532 gave the Lutherans religious liberty for a year. The alliance bet. the Turks and the Fr. doubtless motivated the emp. to make further concessions to the Lutherans at Speyer 1541 and 1544. He crushed the Schmalkaldic* League 1547 but was constrained through the efforts of Maurice* of Saxony to sign the Passau Treaty 1552. Permitted the passage of the Religious Peace of Augsburg* 1555. Resigned 1556; spent his remaining days at the monastery of San Jerónimo de Yuste, Estremadura, Spain.

E. Armstrong, *The Emperor Charles V,* 2 vols. (London, 1902); K. Brandi, *The Emperor Charles V,* tr. C. V. Wedgwood (New York, 1939); R. Tyler, *Emperor Charles the Fifth* (Fair Lawn, N. J., 1956); G. von Schwarzenfeld, *Charles V: Father of Europe,* tr. R. M. Bethell (Chicago, 1957).

Charles VII (of France). See *France,* 3.

Charles IX (of France). See *France,* 9.

Charles IX (1550–1611). Son of Gustavus* I; regent of Swed. 1599–1604, king 1604–11. See also *Lapland; Sweden, Lutheran Church in,* 1.

Charles X Gustavus (1622–60). King of Swed. 1654 to 1660. See also *Sweden, Lutheran Church in,* 2.

Charles XI (1655–97). King of Swed. 1660–97. See also *Sweden, Lutheran Church in,* 2.

Charles XII (1682–1718). Called "The Alexander of the North" and "Madman of the North." King of Swed. 1697–1718. See also *Sweden, Lutheran Church in,* 2, 3.

Charles, Elizabeth (nee Rundle; 1828–96). Eng. author of popular works on various periods of ch. hist.; works include *The Chronicles of the Schönberg-Cotta Family;* original hymns; translations of hymns from Lat. and Ger.

Charles, Robert Henry (1855–1931). B. Ireland; educ. Belfast and Dublin; prof. Biblical Gk. Dublin; lecturer Oxford; canon Westminster 1913, archdeacon 1919; scholar of Jewish eschatological, apocryphal, and apocalyptic writings; ed. *Apocrypha and Pseudepigrapha of the Old Testament in English;* other works include *Religious Development Between the Old and the New Testaments; A Critical History of the Doctrine of a Future Life, in Israel, in Judaism, and in Christianity.*

Charles, Thomas (1755–1814). Angl. pastor, then Meth. traveling preacher; founded Calvinistic Meth. Ch. in Wales.

Charles the Bald. See *Charles II.*

Charles the Great. See *Charlemagne.*

Charms. See *Amulets.*

Charnock, Stephen (1628–80). Puritan*; b. and d. London; proctor Oxford; chaplain to Henry Cromwell in Dublin; returned to Eng. ca. 1660 as preacher without reg. charge; joint pastor with Thomas Watson of a Presb. cong., London. Wrote *Existence and Attributes of God.*

Charterhouse (Fr. *maison chartreuse*). Carthusian* religious house. Most famous one est. 1371 in London by Walter de Manny, endowed 1611 by Thomas Sutton.

Chartres Cathedral of. See *Church Architecture,* 10.

Chartres, School of. School of the 7 liberal arts and classical learning founded by Fulbert.* Other important leaders of the school included Bernard* of Chartres, his younger brother Thierry* of Chartres, Bernard* (Silvestris), William* of Conches, Gilbert* de la Porrée, and John* of Salisbury.

Charvakas. See *Brahmanism,* 4.

Chasidism. See *Hasidism.*

Chastity (Lat. *castitas,* from *castus,* "pure, chaste, continent, holy"). Adherence to religious or moral standards in matters pertaining to sex; often abstention from sexual intercourse.

Theologically, chastity is regulated sexual activity based on Gn 1:27; 2:18-25 which precludes arbitrary refusal of sex acts (1 Co 7:2; 1 Ti 4:3; Heb 13:4) or autonomous use (Mt 5:28; Ro 1:24-32; 6:15-20; 1 Th 4:3-8). In marriage chastity integrates sex with the whole personal and spiritual relationship bet. marriage partners (1 Co 7:39; Eph 5:25-33) and outside marriage requires abstention from use of powers of propagation and all forms of fornication (Ro 1:24-32; 1 Co 6:15-20). Transgressions of the laws of chastity occur in thought or desire (Mt 5:28), word (Eph 5:3, 12), and deed (1 Co 6:15).

In opposition to dualistic conceptions, Christian ethics regards natural sexual desires as good and their use in marriage a virtue (1 Co 7; Heb 13:4). In non-Christian cults sexual relations are often considered taboo and forbidden at certain times or to certain people.

In Christian ethics abstinence* may be practiced for certain purposes (Mt 19:12; 1 Co 7).

Chasuble (Fr. from LL *casubla,* "hooded garment"). Ecclesiastical vestment in form of wide sleeveless cloak that slips over the head but remains open at sides; its color varies with season or occasion; worn by celebrant at eucharistic service in RC and E Orthodox and in some Angl., Episc., and Luth. chs. See also *Vestments Clerical.*

Chateaubriand, François René de (1768–1848). Fr. writer and statesman. Works include *Génie du christianisme; Les Martyrs; Essai sur les révolutions.*

Chatillon, Sébastien (Chateillon). See *Castellio, Sebastianus.*

Chaucer, Geoffrey (ca. 1340–1400). Eng. poet. Works include *Canterbury Tales;* prose tr. of Boethius's* *De consolatione philosophiae.*

Chauncy, Charles (1705–87). Am. liberal clergyman; educ. Harvard; pastor First Ch., Boston, 1727–87; opposed Whitefield* revival movement and attempt to impose Angl. liturgy and episcopacy on America.

Chautauqua. The methods and ideas of the Chautauqua movement are traceable to the Chatauqua Lake Sunday School Assembly and its first season at Chautauqua Lake, N. Y., Aug. 4–18, 1874. The program was soon enlarged to include all branches of popular educ., presented in a variety of courses, lectures, religious addresses, entertainments, and concerts. See also *Vincent John Heyl.*

Chelcicky, Peter (Peter of Chelcice; ca. 1390 to ca. 1460). B. and d. Chelcice, S Bohemia. Extremely creative Hussite* lay theologian; social radical; writings wielded formative influence on the first-generation Bohemian* Brethren. Taught absolute separation of believers and the world; demanded strict adherence to Sermon on the Mount, central law of Christian life, which springs from baptismal regeneration and radical lifelong repentance. True believers, always a minority, are to flee communion with nominal Christians, esp. priests who administer Office of the Keys carelessly. Since a Christian may not use the sword, Chelcicky rejected Hussite warfare. Works include *Postilla* and *Sit' viry* (net of faith; *Netz des Glaubens*).

P. Brock, *The Political and Social Doctrines of the Unity of Czech Brethren in the Fifteenth and Early Sixteenth Centuries* (The Hague, 1957); J. Goll, *Quellen und Untersuchungen zur Geschichte der Böhmischen Brüder,* II (Prague, 1882); M. Spinka, "Peter Chelcicky," *Church History, XII* (Dec. 1943), 271-291. MSF

Chemnitz, Martin (Chemnitius; Chemnicius; Kemnitz; Kemnitius; Kemnicius; 1522–86). B. Treuenbrietzen, Brandenburg; weaver's apprentice 1538; educ. Magdeburg 1539–42, U. Frankfurt an der Oder 1543–44, U. Wittenberg 1545–47, U. Königsberg (Kaliningrad) 1547–48; taught school Calbe 1542–43, Wriezen an der Oder 1544–45, Kneiphof school (Königsberg) 1548–49. At Wittenberg and Königsberg assoc. with a relative, Georg Sabinus (1508–60), son-in-law of Melanchthon. Melanchthon impressed on him the importance of the proper distinction bet. Law and Gospel. With Sabinus to Salfeld during pestilence 1549; studied Lombard* and Luther*; to Königsberg 1550; castle librarian under Albert* of Prussia 1550 to 1552; interest shifted increasingly from astrology, which he began to study at Magdeburg, to theology; opposed A. Osiander in justification controversy; in intricacies of this controversy he resigned post at end of 1552; to Wittenberg Apr. 1553; guest at Melanchthon's table; mem. U. Wittenberg faculty Jan. 1554; lectured on Melanchthon's *Loci* till Oct. 20; ordained by Bugenhagen Nov. 25; to Brunswick as coadjutor of J. Mörlin* Dec. 1554; conducted public disputations twice a yr.; continued lecturing on Melanchthon's *Loci;* 1557 with Mörlin to Wittenberg in connection with adiaphoristic and synergistic controversies, and to Worms, where RCs and Luths. met; wrote widely accepted *De Coena Domini* 1560.

Struggles with Jesuits began 1562 when Chemnitz attacked Cologne Jesuits in *Theologiae Jesuitarum praecipua capita;* Diego de Paiva d'Andrada (1528 to ca. 1576) answered with *Orthodoxarum explicationum de controversiis religionibus capitibus libri decem.* Chemnitz replied with *Examen Concilii Tridentini* (1565–73). Concentrating on dogmatic decrees, Chemitz spared himself the effort of discussing decrees of reform. He canonized for his readers the extreme conservative interpretation of Trent's decrees by taking d'Andrada's work as his commentary on the council's decrees. The theol. of *Examen* is that of a disciple of Luther and Melanchthon; its methodology is that of Biblical theol. somewhat suspicious of scholastic philos.; however, there is wide use of patristic evidence.

Chemnitz returned with Mörlin 1567 to Prussia to prepare a collection of symbolic books for the Luth. Ch. in Albert's domain; supt. Brunswick 1567; aided in claiming predominantly RC Brunswick-Wolfenbüttel for Lutheranism beginning 1568; issued theol. opinion regarding Majoristic* controversy 1568. With Chytraeus* reworked Jakob Andreä's *Swabian Concordia* 1574–75 to produce *Swabian-Saxon Concordia;* participated in Torgau Conf. 1576, and in Bergen Abbey Conf. 1577, in which FC was produced; with N. Selnecker* and T. Kirchner* prepared *Apologia oder Verantwortung des christlichen Concordienbuchs,* pub. 1582. Helped Julius* of Brunswick-Wolfenbüttel organize U. Helmstedt 1575–76. Rift in friendship occurred 1578 when Julius had his 14-yr.-old son made bp. of Halberstadt and 2 other sons tonsured according to RC ritual. Chemnitz urged cautious adoption of Gregorian calendar 1582. His *Loci theologici quibus Ph. Melanchthonis communes loci perspicue explicantur pub.* 1591 by P. Leyser*; other works include *De duabus naturis in Christo* (1570). A popular adage runs: "If Martin [Chemnitz] had not come along, Martin [Luther] would hardly have survived" (Lat. *Si Martinus non fuisset, Martinus vix stetisset*). ACP

See also *Lutheran Confessions,* C 2; *Neostadiensium admonitio.*

The Doctrine of Man in Classical Lutheran Theology, ed. H. A. Preus and E. Smits (Minneapolis, 1962); A. G[räbner], "An Autobiography of Martin Kemnitz, Translated from the German and Latin," *TQ,* III (Oct. 1899), 472-487; R. Mumm, *Die Polemik des Martin Chemnitz gegen das Konzil von Trent* (Leipzig, 1905); A. C. Piepkorn, "Martin Chemnitz' Views on Trent: The Genesis and the Genius of the Examen Concilii Tridentini," *CTM,* XXXVII (Jan. 1966), 5–37; T. Pressel, *Martin Chemnitz,* in *Leben und Ausgewählte Schriften der Väter und Begründer der lutherischen Kirche,* ed. J. Hartmann and others, VIII (Elberfeld, 1862), separate paging 1–75; P. J. Rehtmeyer, *Antiquitates ecclesiasticae inclytae urbis Brunsvigae,* III (Brunswick, 1710), 273–536 and supplement 118–464; *Vita Martini Chemnicii* in *Examen concilii Tridentini per Martinum Chemnicium scriptum,* ed. E. Preuss (Berlin, 1861), pp. 925–958.

Chemnitz Conference. Conf. formed 1878 in Chemnitz, Saxony, by Luths. who upheld their confessions of faith and opposed the Prussian* Union, sects, and separatists.

Ch'eng. In Chinese thought beginning with Confucius: honesty; sincerity; reverence; absolute true-self; fulfillment of self; being true to nature of being.

Cheng Ching-yi (1881–1940). B. Peking; d. Shanghai. Cong. pastor; participated in World Miss. Conferences; active in union efforts; pres. Chinese Miss. Soc.; emphasized Christian life.

Ch'eng Hao (Master Ming-tao; 1032–86). Chinese philos.; with his brother Ch'eng Yi (Master of Yi-ch'uan; 1033–1107) developed a system of neo-Confucianism.

Chenoboskion, Gnostic Texts of. See *Gnosticism,* 8.

Cherokees. See *Indians, American,* 7.

Cherubim. See *Angels, Good,* 3, 6.

Cherubini, Maria Luigi Carlo Zenobio Salvatore (1760–1842). It. composer of opera and sacred music; childhood genius evident in 3 masses, an oratorio, 3 cantatas, and several smaller works, all composed before he was 16. In his 2d period of composition he wrote numerous operas. Later, on appointment to the Fr. Chapel Royal 1816, he returned to sacred music. Greatest works include *Mass in F; Mass in A; Requiem in C Minor; Requiem in D Minor.*

Chesterton, Gilbert Keith (1874–1936). Eng. author; joined RC Ch. 1922; wrote many works in its defense; mystical in approach to religious thought. Works include *Heretics; The Catholic Church and Conversion; The Everlasting Man; Orthodoxy.*

Chevalier, Jean. See *Cavalier, Jean.*

Cheyennes. See *Indians, American,* 11.

Cheyne, Thomas Kelly (1841–1915). B. London; d. Oxford. Eng. clergyman and biblical critic; educ. Oxford and Göttingen; disciple of G. H. A. Ewald; mem. OT rev. bd. 1884; prof. interpretation of Scripture, Oxford, 1885–1908; wrote on OT; joint ed., with J. S. Black, *Encyclopaedia Biblica.*

Ch'i (Chinese; originally "vapor, gas"; later used in physical, metaphysical, psychological, physiological senses). 1. Concrete thing or definite object as contrasted with Tao (unitary first principle with no spatial restriction or concrete form). 2. Material force as opposed to principle. Used with regard to intangible, invisible, ineffable thing or force. Before neo-Confucianiasm, "vital force" denoting psychophysiological power associated with breath and blood. 3. Variety of meanings: vital force in operation of active (yang) and passive (yin) principles; morale; five forces (metal, wood, water, fire, soil); reality of ultimate vacuity; principle of differentiation and individuation; undifferentiated matter transcending shape and features.

Chi-Rho. See *Constantine I.*

Chiao. In Chinese philos. and religion: teaching; system of doctrine.

Chiapas. See *Central America,* A.

Chicago Lutheran Divinity School. See *Northwestern Lutheran Theological Seminary.*

Chicago Lutheran Theological Seminary. See *Indiana Synod,* 2; *Ministry, Education of,* X I.

Chicago School of Theology. An approach to theol. developed at Chicago U. under leadership of men like S. Mathews* and S. J. Case.* It made soc. experience central and basic to all theol. systems.

Chicago Synod of the Evangelical Lutheran Church. Name adopted 1895 by Indiana* Syn. (II). Divided 1920 among following ULC syns.: Ill., Ind., Mich., Ohio (see *United Lutheran Church, Synods of,* 7, 8, 12, 19).

Chicago Theological Seminary (United Ch. of Christ). Est. 1857 by delegates from Cong. chs. in Ill., Ind., Iowa, Mich., Mo., and Wis.; inc. 1855; began work 1858; affiliated with U. of Chicago 1915. Institutes assoc. with the sem.: Ger., est. 1882; Dan.-Norw., founded 1884; Swed., begun 1885, all reorganized as institutes 1893.

Chicago Theses. Theses formulated at Chicago, March 11–13, 1919, by representatives of the Aug. Syn., the Iowa Syn., the Joint Syn. of Ohio, the LFC, the NLCA, the UDELC, and the ULC; all these groups were mems. of the NLC. The theses were later reexamined and incorporated as section IV of the Minneapolis* Theses.

CTM, I (Sept. 1930), 688–691, and XV (Mar. 1944), 194–197; *Journal of Theology of the American Lutheran Conference,* VI (Jan. 1941), 14–17; *TM,* VII (Apr. 1927), 114–117; R. C. Wolf, *Documents of Lutheran Unity in America* (Philadelphia, 1966), pp. 293, 298–301.

Chicago Theses (Intersynodical Theses; Theses for Union). Intersynodical confs. 1903–06 at Watertown and Milwaukee, Wis., Detroit, Mich., and Fort Wayne, Ind., failed to solve the differences on predestination and conversion. The Iowa Syn. suggested gen. and open confs. for discussion of points at issue 1913. Pastors of the disputing syns. signed the St. Paul Theses at St. Paul, Minn., 1916, and demanded that the matter be taken up officially. A colloquy began 1917, with representatives of the syns. concerned participating. As a result, the *Chicago Thesen über die Bekehrung, Prädestination und andere Lehren* were unanimously adopted April 15, 1925, at Chicago by representatives of the Buffalo, Iowa, Mo., Ohio, and Wis. Syns. Agreement on the article of predestination was brought about by G. Fritschel,* who accepted G. Stoeckhardt's* view. Representatives of Ohio, Iowa, and Buffalo Syns. and the NLCA adopted the Minneapolis* Theses Nov. 18, 1925, at Minneapolis, Minn. An intersynodical committee revised the Chicago Theses at St. Paul, Minn., Aug. 2, 1928. This revision was presented to the Mo. Syn. conv. at River Forest, Ill., 1929. The Mo. Syn. mems. of the intersynodical committee held that fraternal relations were "at present excluded by the connections into which . . . these synods have entered," but urged, at the same time, that action be taken on the Theses. An examining committee had recommended that the Theses be rejected. The floor committee on intersyn. matters recommended in its report that the Theses be not accepted "in their present form" and that the syn. instruct a committee "to formulate theses which, beginning with the *status controversiae,* are to present the doctrine of the Scriptures and the Lutheran Confessions in the shortest, most simple manner." The report was adopted. See also *Brief Statement; Free Lutheran Conferences,* 2–5; *Instuitu Fidei.*

Chicago Thesen über die Bekehrung, Prädestination und andere Lehren: Angenommen von Vertretern der Synoden von Buffalo, Iowa, Missouri, und Wisconsin, 2d ed. (n. p., 1926); *Chicagoer Thesen über die Bekehrung, Prädestination und andere Lehren* (St. Louis, n. d.); *TQS,* XXVI (Oct. 1929), 250–273; "Schlussbericht des Intersynodalen Komitees," *TQS,* XXV (Oct. 1928), 266–288; *Proceedings* of Mo. Syn. convs., esp. 1929 (St. Louis, 1929), pp. 110–113. EL

Chickasaws. See *Indians, American,* 7.

Chien ai. See *Chinese Philosophy,* 4.

Chiesa Libera Christiana in Italia. See *Gavazzi, Alessandro.*

Child and Family Service Agencies. 1. Child welfare activities in the US began with provisions for homeless or neglected children. In the colonial period such children were either placed in mixed almshouses (public institutions in which the mentally ill, epileptic, alcoholic, aged, and others were also housed) or in families as apprentices or indentured servants. In the early 1800s the number of homeless children increased as a result of wars and epidemics of cholera and yellow fever. The inherent evils of almshouse care led to the establishment of children's institutions or orphanages, primarily under religious and nonsectarian auspices. Pub. provision was greatly expanded after the Civil War with the creation of homes for soldiers' and sailors' orphans and of state schools for dependent children. From the beginning, most state institutions placed children into family homes as soon as possible. In 1853 the Children's Aid Soc. of N. Y. City became the first special agency for child placement in the US. In subsequent decades many such agencies were est. under private auspices. Beginning with the 1909 White House Conf. on the Care of Dependent Children, there was concern for keeping the child at home, even if the home was poverty-stricken. Beginning 1911 with Ill., most states soon est. a system of pub. aid for children in their own homes. These programs were superseded by the act entitled Aid to Dependent Children, inaugurated 1935 by the federal Social Security Act. This program and other provisions of the Soc. Security Act have greatly helped prevent child dependency.

2. Pub. agencies are concerned largely with financial assistance to dependent children and families. Private agencies, religious and nonsectarian, concentrate primarily on placement and counseling services. Most child welfare agencies originally operated by or affiliated with denominations have become nonsectarian either in effect or in fact. Exceptions include the RC, Jewish, Luth., and Episc. agencies.

3. Child welfare was first undertaken by Luths. in Am. 1737, when refugees from Salzburg, resettling in Ga., set up an asylum for the needy. That yr.

a plague of fever left many orphans who were cared for at Ebenezer, the first Prot. orphanage in Am. Later developments in Luth. welfare are noted in the following hist. and analysis of child and family services offered by agencies related to the LCMS.

4. The first structured concern for dependent children in the Mo. Syn. was a fruit of faith of the Luth. Charities Assoc., an agency composed of congs. in the St. Louis, Mo., area. The assoc. was est. and incorporated 1863 under leadership of C. F. W. Walther* to plan, structure, and coordinate the health and welfare ministry of the ch. Under guidance of the assoc. the first orphanage in the syn. was est. 1868 at Des Peres, Mo. By 1900 eight orphanages had been est. in various sections of the country, primarily in the Midwest and Great Plains states. For almost 30 yrs. institutional care was the predominant form of service offered by Luth. agencies to dependent children.

5. A significant development occurred 1896 in the founding of the Children's Friend Soc. of Wis., the first syn. agency concerned with placement of children in foster families (either private homes in which children would be cared for till reunion with parents could be effected, or homes in which children would become permanent members of families through legal adoption). Ten more agencies for foster care were created in a decade. Then building new orphanages ceased. While institutional care was to remain the primary service rendered to dependent children for many yrs., foster care programs of all agencies steadily increased in significance. The turning point was reached in the early 1940s, when for the first time the number of children in foster care exceeded those in congregate care. Increased awareness of the prime importance of the Christian family as the major influence on the soc., emotional, and spiritual development of children led to this change in emphasis.

6. Out of the awareness that no single service program could meet the needs of every dependent child, multifunction agencies began to arise in the late 1930s. Some were created through merger of previously separate orphanages and foster care agencies, others through broadening the range of agency services. All child welfare agencies affiliated with the syn. and est. since 1943 have offered a wide range of service programs.

7. The first child care programs of Luth. agencies tended to focus almost exclusively on children rather than on the family units of which they were part. This emphasis was understandable and realistic because most children served were orphans either in reality or in effect. Rehabilitiation of the family unit was impossible in most cases. This has changed dramatically. In 1951 less than 1 percent of the children in the care of Luth. agencies were either full or half orphans. Since the Great Depression of the 1930s the primary reasons for acceptance of new children into agency care have included severe marital discord, parent-child relationship problems, and similar social-emotional factors. Parental death and desertion have been insignificant factors since WW II. Thus today's dependent children do have families; Luth. agencies minister to the whole family. Family casework (counseling services designed to strengthen family life and help family mems. with their problems of adjustment) is now an integral service of almost all Luth. welfare agencies.

8. The typical Luth. agency offers these services: temporary foster care for children, adoptive placements, unwed mother services, and family counseling. In addition, some children's services offer institutional care for severely emotionally disturbed children. A few Luth. agencies also maintain group-care facilities for emergency shelter of dependent children, pending placement in suitable foster homes. Institutions or orphanages for long-term care of stable, healthy dependent children no longer exist in the Luth. Ch.

9. The ministry of Luth. agencies to dependent children operates on these principles: (1) the primary service focus is to rehabilitate the family unit, restoring the home to maximum spiritual, social, and emotional effectiveness; (2) prevention of the need for placement of the child away from the family unit wherever possible; (3) provision of a placement situation appropriate to the child's special needs, if placement proves to be necessary; (4) permanent adoptive placement of a child in a Luth. family when his own home cannot be restored. All Luth. agencies are family focused (primarily on the child's own family, and on substitute family experiences when these resources become necessary).

With rare exceptions, all Luth. welfare agencies are directly related to the welfare ministry of the congs. under whose auspices the services are rendered. The purpose of the agencies is to render services that the congs. are unable to provide because of state law requirements, extent of financial needs, professional skills required, or demands of confidentiality. Luth. welfare agencies supplement, but never supplant, the welfare ministry of the cong.

10. For a complete and current listing of Luth. child and family service agencies consult latest ed. of *Lutheran Health and Welfare Directory* (Nat. Luth. Soc. Welfare Conf., New York, N. Y.); latest ed. of *Lutheran Annual* (CPH, St. Louis, Mo.). For information concerning trends and developments in these welfare fields consult latest ed. of *The Social Work Yearbook* (Russell Sage Foundation, New York, N. Y.), issued in odd-numbered years. JCC

See also *Charities, Christian,* 5; *Inner Mission.*

Child Welfare Associations. See *Charities, Christian; Child and Family Service Agencies.*

Children, Dependent, Care and Training of. See *Charities, Christian; Child and Family Service Agencies.*

Children of God. See *Camisards.*

Children of Light; Children of Truth. See *Friends, Society of.*

Children's Crusade. See *Crusades.*

Children's Friend Society. See *Child and Family Service Agencies,* 5.

Children's Special Service Mission. Organized 1868 in Eng. to supplement the work of the ch., S. S., and home among children; distributed literature in Eng., Fr., Dutch, Dan., Swed., Tamil; pub. *Our Own Magazine; Our Boys' Magazine.*

Chile. See *South America,* 5.

Chiliasm. See *Millennialism.*

Chillingworth, William (1602–44). Anglican. B. Oxford; d. Chichester. RC 1630; Angl. again 1634; Arminian; chancellor Salisbury 1638; chaplain in royal army; captured; d. in captivity. Wrote *The Religion of Protestants a Safe Way to Salvation,* vindicating the sole authority of the Bible and the individual's right to study it. See also *Christian Church, History of,* III 10.

China (LL *Sinae*). 1. E Asia; probably ancient Seres; medieval Cathay; rep. 1911; *area,* including outlying territories: 3,760,339 sq. mi.; *pop.:* 850,000,000 (1973 est.). Latitude ca. the same as that of N Am. countries (Hudson Bay to Nicaragua); climate similar to that of N Am. Greater part of the country is mountainous, but there are large tracts of fertile soil, chiefly on the plains and in the valleys of the great rivers. Most important rivers are the 3,200-mi. Yangtze; the 2,700-mi. Hwang Ho or Yellow; the 1,780-mi. Amur; the 1,200-mi. Si or West. The 1,000-mi. Grand Canal, from Hangchow to Peking, connects the Yangtze and the Hwang Ho.

2. The Chinese belong to the Mongoloid race. Civilization early reached a high stage of develop-

ment in China, but then remained at a standstill for centuries, with the country closed to for. influences. Educ. was held in highest esteem but was not common. Rigorous examinations in the classical literature of the country were required for pol. preferment. But after the 1911 revolution, educ. was opened to the masses, including women, and W science was introd.

3. Early Chinese hist., highly elaborated and embellished by Chinese historians, is obscure. Many dynasties are recorded of which no tangible trace appears. But China was a civilized nation when all Eur. nations were steeped in barbarism. Its culture antedates that of Greece and Rome. The oldest dynasty bordering on hist. domain appears to be the Shang dynasty (ca. 1766–ca. 1122), followed by the Chou dynasty (ca. 1122–ca. 255), founded by Wu Wang. During the latter dynasty Confucius* and other prominent men, whose writings are still extant, flourished.

4. The 3 hist. religions of China are Taoism,* Buddhism,* and Confucianism.* Other non-Christian religions that entered China include Zoroastrianism,* Manichaeism,* Islam,* and Judaism.* All over China there is a multitude of temples; ritualistic acts are constantly performed by gen. ignorant priests and monks. The average Chinese lives in constant dread of evil spirits, whose malicious intentions he must thwart, whose anger he must appease. Ancestor worship is an outstanding feature of Chinese cultus.

5. In the early hist. of Christianity, Christian thought appears to have penetrated into China. Nestorianism,* which, according to an 8th c. tablet discovered ca. 1625 near Sian, entered China in the 6th or 7th c., survived there till ca. the 14th c., when it succumbed to persecution.

6. Marco Polo, famed 13th c. traveler, mentions Christian chs. in China. John* of Montecorvino entered China 1294. In the 16th c. M. Ricci* and others came. Dominicans came from Mexico to Macao (Heungshan) 1587; Coqui (Cocchi) reached the mainland 1630. Dominicans and Franciscans lodged protests in Rome against Jesuitic accommodation to paganism. In 1645 Innocent X issued a decree against the practices of the Jesuits as described by Morales, a Dominican. In 1656 Alexander VII sanctioned the practices as described by the Jesuits. In 1692 Emp. K'ang-hsi legalized dissemination of the Christian religion throughout the empire. In 1704 Clement XI confirmed a decree issued by the Inquisition forbidding the use of *Shang-ti* and *T'ien* and approving *T'ien Chu;* it forbade tablets bearing the characters *Ching T'ien* in churches; it prohibited Christians from taking part in sacrifices to Confucius or to ancestors; it proscribed ancestral tablets with characters calling them the throne or seat of the spirit of the deceased, but permitted tablets with merely the name of the dead. (See also *Chinese Term Question.*) Yung Chêng (emp. 1723–35), son and successor of K'ang-hsi, inaugurated persecutions that continued many yrs. Many anti-Christian laws were promulgated. Later, under Fr. colonial policy, RCm was reborn in China.

7. Prot. missions did not enter China till the beginning of the 19th c. R. Morrison* came to China Sept. 7, 1807, followed 1813 by W. Milne.* E. C. Bridgman* arrived at Canton 1830. K. F. A. Gützlaff* reached China 1831. After the Opium War bet. Eng. and China 1842, China was forced to open 5 port cities: Shanghai, Ningpo (now Ninghsien), Fuchow (Fowling), Amoy, and Canton; a new era for commercial and miss. endeavor resulted. Later wars opened new ports but also increased Chinese opposition to for. commercial and religious contact; this led to frequent persecutions and culminated in the Boxer outbreak 1900. The Boxers were a Chinese secret society that stirred up antiforeign action in N China. In the uprising ca. 200 mems. of miss. families and thousands of Chinese Christians lost their lives.

8. In the 19th c. missions were opened in China by organizations in Eur., Am., and Australia and by the CIM. The Mo. Syn. entered the field 1917 when it took over the work begun by E. L. Arndt* 1913. A sem. est. 1922 at Hankow moved 1938 to Wanhsien, returned to Hankow 1947, closed 1949. See also *Riedel, Erhardt Albert Henry.*

9. Though China appeared to offer excellent opportunities for miss. endeavor after WW II, the govt. of the Chinese People's Republic (est. Oct. 1, 1949) forced withdrawal of miss. personnel. By the close of 1952 only ca. 30 Prot. missionaries were known to be in China. The last LCMS worker left China June 1952. The regime on the mainland of China controls, if not censors, all religious work and worship of Prots., RCs, and other Christians. Buddhism, Taoism, and Mohammedanism have been proscribed. Many missionaries once assigned to China have opened new areas occupied heavily by Chinese, esp. Malaya, Indonesia, and Formosa (Taiwan*).

OHS; ErR

See also *Hsin I Hui.*

A. C. Moule, *Christians in China Before the Year 1550* (London, 1930) and *Nestorians in China* (London, 1940); P. Y. Saeki, *The Nestorian Documents and Relics in China* (Tokyo, 1937); K. S. Latourette, *A History of Christian Missions in China* (London, 1929); J. Schmidlin, *Das gegenwärtige Heidenapostolat im fernen Osten,* Part 1 (Münster, 1929); P. M. d'Elia, *The Catholic Missions in China* (Shanghai, 1934); C. Cary-Elwes, *China and the Cross: Studies in Missionary History* (London, 1957); P. A. Varg, *Missionaries, Chinese, and Diplomats: The American Protestant Missionary Movement in China, 1890 to 1952* (Princeton, 1958); F. P. Jones, *The Church in Communist China: A Protestant Appraisal* (New York, 1962); W. G. Polack, "Christian Missions in China Before Morrison," *CTM,* III (April and June 1932), 274–281, 410–416.

China, Evangelical Lutheran Mission for. See *Arndt, E. L.*

China, Religions of. See *Buddhism; China, 4–9; Chinese Philosophy; Confucianism; Taoism.*

China Evangelical Lutheran Church, The. See *Taiwan.*

China Inland Mission. June 25, 1865, J. H. Taylor* resolved to form a soc. for evangelizing the interior of China. An organizational structure was set up in Eng. 1865–66. Interdenom. and internat. in scope, it soon had branches in Ger., Scand., Switz., and Eng. speaking countries. Emphasized miss. preaching, teaching, and works of mercy. Some of its missions formed regional feds. Forced to withdraw from China 1951; headquarters moved from Shanghai first to Hong Kong, then Singapore. Name changed in the mid-1960s to Overseas* Missionary Fellowship.

L. T. Lyall, *A Passion for the Impossible: The China Inland Mission 1865–1965* (Chicago, 1965).

Chinese Blind, Mission to the. Organized 1887 in Scot. to support work of Wm. Murray* among blind* in China.*

Chinese Evangelization Society. See *Taylor, James Hudson.*

Chinese Philosophy. 1. Chinese philos. aims at the highest kind of life and ideally embraces both otherworldliness and this-worldliness, sublime and common, absolute and essential, transcendent and immanent.

2. Taoism* opposed nature to man and glorified Tao (way), which emphasized spontaneity and "inaction" (non-artificiality) in the sense of following nature by simplicity, tranquillity, and enlightenment. It is the way of sageliness within and kingliness

without, aiming at attainment of the sublime and performance of common tasks. Great teachers of Taoism were Lao-tzu* and Chuang-tzu.*

3. Confucianism* advocated human-heartedness *(jen),* righteousness *(yi),* superior man *(chun-tzu,* "moral man, noble man"), the cultivation of life *(hsiu shen;* it results in harmony in family, state, world). This resulted in moralistic and humanistic teaching (*chung,* "being true to your nature") which climaxed in *chung yung* (golden mean; find central clue of your being and live harmoniously with the universe). Outstanding teachers were Confucius,* Mencius,* and Hsün Tzu.*

4. Mohism (Moism), founded by Mo Ti (Mo-tzu; Micius; 5th–4th c.), taught universal love, pacifism, and utilitarianism. Yang Chu (ca. 440–360) emphasized "keeping essence of our being intact"; often compared with Epicurus.* Sophists (dialecticians; logicians), early called *ming chia,* literally "name school," concentrated on relationship bet. substance and quality. The Yin-Yang school (400–200) emphasized contrasting but complementary principles. *Yang* (active; positive; male) pertains to all things in origination; *yin* (passive; negative; female) pertains to all things at time of their responding.

5. In the Middle period there was a fusion of Chinese philos. and development of Buddhism.* Liu An (Huai-nan Tzu; d. 122 BC; Taoist) and Tung Chung-shu (ca. 177–104; Confucian) fused Yin-Yang with Confucianism and combined Taoist metaphysics with Confucian ethics. This led to superstition, which was combated by Wang Ch'ung (27–97). Though not free of all superstition, he promoted a critical spirit.

6. Neo-Confucianism developed in 3 phases that emphasized reason (960–1368), mind (1368–1644), and moral law (1644–1911). Vital force and reason are basic in all phases. Greatest neo-Confucian was Chu Hsi (1130–1200). EL

Yu-Lan Fêng (Fung Yu-Lan), *A History of Chinese Philosophy,* tr. D. Bodde, rev. reprint, 2 vols. (Princeton, 1952–53) and *The Spirit of Chinese Philosophy,* tr. and ed. E. R. Hughes (London, 1947); *A Source Book in Chinese Philosophy,* comp. and tr. Wing-Tsit Chan (Princeton, 1963); A. Forke, *Geschichte der alten chinesischen Philosophie,* in *Abhandlungen aus dem Gebiet der Auslandskunde,* XXV (Hamburg, 1927), *Geschichte der mittelalterlichen chinesischen Philosophie,* in *Abhandlungen aus dem Gebiet der Auslandskunde,* XLI (Hamburg, 1934), and *Geschichte der neueren chinesischen Philosophie,* in *Abhandlungen aus dem Gebiet der Auslandskunde,* XLVI (Hamburg, 1938).

Chinese Term Question. Controversy regarding the proper name for God in China that came to a head with M. Ricci*; he used the names *Shang-ti* (or *Shang-di;* it means high ruler) and *T'ien* (heaven; divinity), terms for God found in ancient Chinese classics. His successor, Niccolò Longobardi (Longobardo; ca. 1566–1655), rejected the term *Shang-ti,* holding that it was the name of an idol. Dominicans and Franciscans opposed the use of *Shang-ti;* Clement XI ruled 1704 that it should not be used. Since then RCs have used *T'ien Chu* (Lord of heaven). R. Morrison* and Joshua Marshman* used *Shen* (heavenly spirits; spiritual power) in their Bible translation. About 1840 other Prot. missionaries used *Shang-ti* for the true God and *Shen* for idols and for the true God when discriminating adjective is added (e. g., 1 Jn 5:20). Missionaries of the Mo. Syn. at first did likewise. Soon the controversy about the propriety of using an idol name *(Shang-ti)* for God involved them also; a conf. paper (1924) advocated the use of *Shen* alone. The Mo. Syn. Miss. Bd. in 1928 allowed use of *Shen* but allowed no missionary to refuse to use miss. literature having the term *Shang-ti.* The faculty at Conc. Sem., Saint Louis, the Bd. of For. Miss., the syn. committee, and the missionaries ultimately agreed that *Shang-ti* could be divested of its heathen connotation and filled with Biblical content. EL

See also *China,* 6.

1935 *Proceedings* of the Mo. Syn. (St. Louis, 1935), pp. 168–176.

Ching. In Chinese philos.: 1. Classic Confucian or Taoist standards. See also *Confucianism,* 2. 2. Essence; purity; spirit. 3. Tranquillity.

Chiniquy, Charles Paschal Telesphore (1809–99). B. Kamouraska, Quebec; RC priest 1833–58; "Apostle of Temperance of Canada"; est. RC colony in Kankakee Co., Ill., 1851; left RC Ch. and joined Can. Presbyterians 1858; lectured extensively, also in Eng. and Australia; wrote tracts on temperance and books bitterly hostile to RC Ch.

Chippewa. See *Indians, American,* 5, 9, 10.

Chlodowech; Chlodwig. See *Clovis I.*

Choctaw. See *Indians, American,* 7.

Choice. Act of free* will in deciding betw. 2 or more alternatives.

Choir (architectural). The part of a ch. separated from the nave* on the one hand and the sanctuary on the other. The word choir is often used in a wider sense to include the sanctuary and the area on the lower level immediately W of the communion rail. Singers are often placed in this part of a ch.; hence the term choir. See also *Chancel; Church Architecture,* 3. RRB

Choir (musical). Group of singers taking part in ch. services. In the OT a sacred choir was organized by David (1 Ch 6:31-47) and continued by Solomon (2 Ch 5:12, 13). In both Jewish and early Christian services a solo voice over against a singing group chanted the Psalms. The cong. responded with a refrain. This arrangement of solo voice, choir, and cong. influenced the place and function of the choir in the beginning and early development of the plainsong period in the Christian ch. The all-male choir (boys and men) developed after Constantine's conversion and was securely est. in the *Schola cantorum* of Gregory I (see *Gregorian Music; Popes,* 4). The choir schools at Metz and St. Gall are of equal importance in the 8th c. The choir was of such importance in medieval times that the study of music is in essence the study of ch. music. The new music, the polyphony of the 12th c., brought about a new concept and organization of the choir. Previously the choir, composed of male clerics or at least boys strictly trained under ecclesiastical direction in a home attached to the cathedral, performed in the sanctuary. The music was monody chant, and the cong. sang little or nothing. Gregory XI introd. the *Collegio dei Capellani Cantori,* trained and directed by laymen; it sang either from a choir loft or the W gallery. The cong. did not participate in the singing of the liturgy in medieval times. Female voices were tolerated in some parishes even before the Reformation. Both traditions, male and mixed choirs, are found in Angl., RC, and Luth. chs. The Ch. of Eng. has tried to preserve a male choir, mems. of which are considered lower clergy who function in the chancel. The Luth. Ch. preserves a lay concept of the choir. The choir is gen. placed best in the W gallery (with organ console and organ chests) for acoustical rather than liturgical reasons. Proper choir vestment is cassock and white surplice for all. Female singers preferably wear black skullcaps. The Luth. Ch. preserves these chief functions of the choir: to sing the propers* that are beyond the ability of the cong.; to assist the cong. in singing liturgy and hymns; to sing music appropriate to the Ch. year, i. e., motets, cantatas, and anthems. RRB

M. Pierik, *The Song of the Church* (New York, 1947) and *Dramatic and Symbolic Elements in Gregorian Chant* (Tournai, Belgium, 1963); D. Johner,

Choralschule, rev. M. Pfaff, 8th ed. (Regensburg, 1956); W. Apel, *Gregorian Chant* (Bloomington, Ind., 1958); E. A. Wienandt, *Choral Music of the Church* (New York, 1965).

Choisy, Jacques Eugène (1866–1949). Prof. ch. hist. Geneva; studied role of women in the ch.; did research on Calvin; pioneer in ecumenical movement.

Chomjakow, Alexej Stepanowitsch (1804–60). Russ. theol.; ardent defender of the E Orthodox Ch., which he regarded as the only true ch.

Chorale (Ger. *Choral;* It. *corale;* ML *choralis;* from Gk. *choros,* Lat. *chorus,* "group of dancers and singers"; "chorale" came into use in the 2d half of the 16th c. and is usually preferred to "choral" in Eng.). Hymn or psalm sung by cong. and/or choir to a traditional or composed melody. In ecclesiastical usage it denotes the choral plainsong *(cantus planus)* of the RC office and the hymn style that became classic in the Luth. Ch. of Germany.

The chorale developed from the *cantus choralis* (choral chant) introd. at the time of Gregory I (see *Gregorian Music; Popes,* 4). This *cantus choralis* was structurally monotonic, in part merely graduated, stereotyped, and recitative music. Its musical pattern was determined not with reference to the rhythm of words or to grace and expression of melody, but simply by textual notation.

From Rome choral singing of this type spread to Eng. and to the empire of Charlemagne,* who founded schools for singing N of the Alps. The most renowned of these schools, at Metz, was under the management of Rabanus* Maurus.

The chorale was the peculiar interest of the Luth. Ch.; the Ref. regarded the Psalter as the proper hymnbook and disapproved of original hymns. The Luth. chorale continued the simplicity of the Gregorian chorale. Luther used 4 sources for his chorales: official Lat. hymnody, pre-Reformation popular hymns, secular folk songs, and original hymns.

W. Apel, *Gregorian Chant* (Bloomington, Ind., 1958) and *Harvard Dictionary of Music,* 9th print. (Cambridge, Mass., 1955); *Dictionary of Music and Musicians,* ed. G. Grove, 5th ed., E. Blom (New York, 1954), II, 269–275; A. T. Davison and W. Apel, *Historical Anthology of Music,* rev. ed., 2 vols. (Cambridge, Mass., 1949–50); W. E. Buszin, *The Doctrine of the Universal Priesthood and Its Influence upon the Liturgies and Music of the Lutheran Church* (St. Louis, n. d.); E. Liemohn, *The Chorale Through Four Hundred Years of Musical Development as a Congregational Hymn* (Philadelphia, 1953). JTS

Chorale Cantata. See *Cantata.*

Chorale Prelude. Organ prelude based on a chorale.* The theol. faculty at Wittenberg officially approved use of the organ in Luth. worship services 1597. Soon thereafter hymn preludes began to play an important part in Luth. worship services. Though the Thirty* Years' War brought a halt to most organ building in Ger., the chorale prelude was born in those yrs. S. Scheidt* is regarded as "the father of the chorale prelude," but the chorale fantasies of M. Praetorius* and the chorale variations of the composers of N Ger. helped bring the chorale prelude into existence. By and large, the Luth. masters, esp. of N and Cen. Ger., were at their best in organ composition when writing chorale preludes. This was largely due to the fact that the chorale was to them a vital part of their worship life. The chorale preludes of men like J. G. Walther,* D. Buxtehude,* J. Pachelbel,* and the Bachs* are among the finest gems of all organ literature.

Chorepiscopus. Bp. appointed by diocesan bp. to assist in rural areas.

Chosen. See *Korea.*

Chrischona (Christi[a]na; 9th–10th c.). Legendary saint; d. on return from pilgrimage to Rome; buried on Dinkelsberg near Basel; chapel erected in her honor; pilgrimages to St. Chrischona popular in Middle Ages. C. F. Spittler* founded *Pilgermission St. Chrischona* (headquarters at St. Chrischona) primarily to train laymen for miss. work: colporteurs, city missionaries, evangelists, deacons, housefathers, teachers, preachers (esp. in Am.) and missionaries (e. g., to Falasha*). One of its missioners est. the Syrian orphanage *(Syrisches Weisenhaus)* in Jerusalem. Connected with CIM since 1895. See also *United Lutheran Church, Synods of,* 28; *Vetter, Jakob.*

Chrism. 1. See *Oils, Holy.* 2. Sacrament of E Orthodox Ch. corresponding to confirmation.* 3. See *Unction.*

Chrismation (anointing). Term for confirmation in E Orthodox Ch. Immediately after baptism the priest anoints the baptized person with myron* as an indissoluble continuation of baptism. See also *Unction.*

Chrismon. Monogram made of the first 2 Gk. letters of *Christos* (XP).

Chrismon (ME "cloth"). White robe, cloth, or mantle put on a person at baptism as a symbol of innocence.

Christ, Brothers of. See *Christadelphians.*

Christ, Lives of. See *Jesus, Lives of.*

Christ Church Military Congregation. See *Armed Services Commission,* 8.

Christ Figure. See *Literature and Theology.*

Christ Jesus. The Son of God who became man, incarnate by the Holy Ghost of the Virgin Mary, and suffered and died for the sins of the world. He rose again from the dead, ascended into heaven, sits at the right hand of God, and will return to judge the world. All who believe in Him and accept Him as their Savior are the children of God and receive eternal life.

Christ is referred to by many different names in the Bible. These names are not mere titles, but accurate descriptions of His person. "Jesus" (derived via Gk. from Heb.) means Savior (Mt 1:21; cf. Acts 4:12). "Christ" (derived from Gk.; "Messiah," equivalent in meaning, is derived from Heb.) means Anointed. He was anointed with the Holy Spirit at His baptism (Jn 1:32, 33; Is. 11:2). "Messiah" is the name the Jews used after the Babylonian Captivity in referring to the Savior who was to come. (Jn 1:41; 4:25)

I. *Person of Christ.* Christ Jesus is true God, begotten of the Father from eternity, and also true man, conceived by the Holy Ghost and born of the Virgin Mary.

A. *Deity.* So completely is the doctrine of Jesus' deity the foundation of the Christian faith, that Jesus recognizes only that faith which acknowledges Him as the Son of God (Mt 16:16). Christ is at times identified with the Angel* of the Lord, Jehovah, Lord in the OT (cf. 1 Co 10:4 with Ex 13:21; 14:19; Jn 12:41 with Is 6:1-5; Heb 12:18-26 with Ps 68:7, 8, 17, 18). The NT naturally provides clearer evidence of the deity of Christ. The Gospel of John was written "that ye might believe that Jesus is the Christ, the Son of God" (Jn 20:31). Because of the unity of His essence with the Father, Jesus could say: "I and My Father are one." (Jn 10: 30; cf. Jn 14:9)

Christ is begotten or born of the Father from eternity (Jn 1:14, 18; Ro 1:3; 8:32; 1 Jn 1:7; 1 Ptr 1:3; 1 Th 1:1; Heb 1:5; Mi 5:2; Ps 2:7). The words "this day" (Ps 2:7) refer to the eternal day of the Father. In His eternal life the Father generated the Son, who is also eternal.

Those who deny the deity of Christ (Cerinthus, Arius, some modern theologians) reject the foundation of the Christian faith.

B. *Humanity.* Jesus was conceived by the Holy Ghost and born of the Virgin Mary (Is 7:14; Mt 1:

23-25; Lk 1:35; Heb 2:14; Mt 1:16). He was miraculously (Lk 1:37) made of a woman (Gl 4:4) as had been prophesied (Gn 3:15). The conception of Jesus was a sinless conception (Lk 1:35). The question of how a sinless nature could originate out of the sinful blood of Mary caused RCs to evolve the doctrine of the immaculate conception of Mary (see *Roman Catholic Confessions,* C), and others to hold that God preserved a sinless flesh from the time of Adam (both ideas are contrary to Scripture, Jn 3:6; Ro 5:18). M. Chemnitz* held that the Son of God assumed our human nature, which in conception was cleansed from sin. ("De Peccato Originali," in *Enchiridion;* cf. WA 44, 311–314)

By His birth Jesus became a man in the full sense of the word. He took part of the flesh and blood of children (Heb 2:14; Ro 9:5; Jn 1:14), had a real body and soul and a human will, ate, drank, grew weary, and died a real death (cf. WA 52, 815–816). Only in one respect did Jesus differ from His brethren: He was without sin (original as well as actual, Heb 7:26; Ro 5:18, 19; 2 Co 5:21) and hence free from the germ of death (Ro 6:23; Jn 10:18). The humanity of Christ is essential for our salvation, for the Redeemer of the world had to assume the guilt and penalty of the Law which was binding on all men; this was possible only if He became like us in all things, in a perfect human nature. (Gl 4:4)

Though otherwise a human nature is also a person, it is peculiar to the human nature of Christ that it does not constitute a separate being and never existed by itself. The human nature did not receive the divine, but the divine assumed the human.

C. Jesus Christ is true God and true man in one person (Jn 1:14; 1 Ti 2:5), in which person the human nature and the divine nature are united in the most intimate communion (1 Ti 3:16; Ro 1:3, 4). This uniting of God and man in one being is called the personal union *(unio personalis)* and is expressed in the axiom: Neither is the flesh without the Word, nor the Word without the flesh.

But despite the intimacy of the union of the 2 natures in Christ, each nature remains intact, just as soul and body remain what they are, though united in 1 person (Cl 2:9). There is no commingling of the natures. By the union of God and man in Christ there did not originate a 3d nature, the divine-human nature. Because the 2 natures are so closely conjoined in Christ, the dogmaticians speak of *propositiones personales* (personal propositions, statements that express or describe the personal union). Thus one can say on the basis of Scripture: this man is God; and: this God is man. (Lk 1:31, 32; 2:11; Gl 4:4; Acts 20:28; Ro 5:10; 1 Ti 3:16)

See also *Perichoresis.*

D. *Communication of Attributes.* Though in the person of Jesus Christ each nature retains its essenial attributes unchanged and undiminished in kind and number, yet each nature also communicates its attributes to the other in the personal union, so that the divine nature participates in properties of the human nature and vice versa. The FC and most Lutheran dogmaticians distinguish 3 kinds *(genera)* of Scripture statements teaching the communication of attributes *(communicatio idiomatum): genus idiomaticum, genus maiestaticum,* and *genus apotelesmaticum.* See also *Idiomata.*

1. Scripture passages classified as statements or the *genus idiomaticum,* the genus of appropriation, are those whereby attributes of either nature are ascribed to the entire person of Christ. (Jn 8:58 and Lk 3:23; Jn 21:17 and Lk 2:52; Cl 1:16 and Jn 18:12)

2. Propositions of the *genus maiestaticum,* the genus of glory, deal with the divine attributes showing forth the glory of the only begotten of the Father. Though the human nature of the person of Christ remains truly human, yet all divine properties and perfections and the honor and glory pertaining to this divine nature are communicated to His human nature; the divine perfections, which the divine nature has as essential attributes, the human nature has as communicated attributes. In Christ dwells all the fullness of the Godhead bodily (Cl 2:9; Heb 1:3). By virtue of the personal union the Son of Man, while on earth and in conversation with Nicodemus, was also in heaven (Jn 3:13); and now, though ascended into heaven, He, the Son of Man, is also with His church on earth to the end of the world (Mt 28:20). By communication of attributes Jesus was an omnipotent man; in Him there dwelt eternal life, infinite wisdom, immutable holiness and righteousness, boundless power, love indivisible and everlasting as God Himself. Although Christ, according to His human nature, was exposed to temptation, this human nature, by communicated holiness, was not only sinless, but absolutely impeccable.

3. The term *genus apotelesmaticum* is derived from the Gk. word for the performance of a task. Scripture texts under this head assert a union by which, in official acts, each nature performs what is peculiar to itself with the participation of the other. Not only did the entire person, Christ, die for our sins (1 Co 15:3), but we were reconciled to God by the death of His Son (Ro 5:10). The obedience of the child Jesus was a fulfillment of the 4th Commandment rendered by the Son of God. He suffered and died; this passion and death was endured by His human nature in communion with His divine nature. The 3d genus, particularly, might appear as an unnecessary burdening of Christian dogmatics. It is, like the Luth. treatment of Christology in gen., occasioned by the Ref. opposition. Ref. theol. separates Christ's actions as man from His actions as the Son of God.

II. *The States of Humiliation and Exaltation.* 1. For the work of redemption Christ, the God-Man, humbled Himself (Ph 2:8). To humble oneself is to forgo prerogatives which one might rightfully claim. Christ humbled Himself according to the human nature, the divine nature as such not being capable of humiliation or exaltation or any other change of state or condition. Yet it was not the man Christ, independent of the Logos, who humbled Himself (for thus the man Christ never existed) but the indivisible person Jesus Christ. This humiliation did not consist in the assumption of the human nature by the divine nature, for then His exaltation must have consisted in an abandonment of the human nature by the divine nature and a dissolution of the personal union (the error of the Gnostics*); in this case the Son of Man would not now sit at the right hand of the Father Almighty. The humiliation of the God-Man rather was that self-denial by which He forbore using and enjoying fully and constantly the divine majesty communicated to His human nature. When He might have deported Himself as the Lord of Lords, He took upon Himself the humble form of a servant. Being rich, He took upon Himself poverty. He who fed the thousands by the lakeside suffered hunger in the desert and thirst on the cross. It was the Lord of Glory who was crucified, the Prince of Life who was killed. Lastly, the body of the Holy One of God was laid in another man's grave. Through all the yrs. of His humiliation, from the night of His nativity to the night which shrouded Golgotha in darkness at midday, rays and flashes of the glory of the Only-Begotten of the Father bore witness to the majesty of the Son of Man. He knew what was in Nathaniel's heart, read the past hist. of the Samaritan woman, and saw the thoughts of the disciples as well as of His enemies. He was in heaven while He taught Nicodemus by night.

The purpose of this humiliation of the God-Man

was the redemption of the world. The Holy One of God humiliated Himself and became obedient unto death to make atonement for our rebellious disobedience. God in His righteousness demanded that man should fulfill the Law in perfect love toward God and his neighbor. Hence man's Substitute was "made under the Law" (Gl 4:4). But as the continued use of His divine majesty would have placed Jesus beyond the power of His human enemies, it was necessary for Him to forgo full and constant use of His divine power and majesty, in order that the work of redemption might be performed and the Scriptures fulfilled. (Mt 26:53, 54)

2. The resumption and continuation of such full and constant use of His divine attributes according to His human nature was and is the exaltation of Christ, the God-Man (Eph 4:8; Heb 2:7). Before coming forth from the tomb He, according to His human nature, descended to hell and manifested His glory to the spirits condemned because of their unbelief (1 Ptr 3:18-20. See *Descent into Hell*). Christ's resurrection was the public proclamation of His victory over sin and death. By His ascension He visibly entered according to His human nature into His heavenly kingdom. Sitting at the right hand of God the Father Almighty, He exercises dominion also according to His human nature over all creatures, esp. over His church. The form of a servant has been forever put away; when His exaltation will culminate, He will come again, indeed, as the Son of Man, but in His glory and will sit on the throne of His glory with power and great glory. (Mt 25:31; Lk 21:27)

III. *The Office of Christ.* Strictly speaking, "Christ" is not a proper name but designates a person as set apart by anointing for a special office, purpose, and task; our Lord is "the Anointed" who functioned and functions in an absolutely unique sense as Prophet, Priest, and King. While Luther, Melanchthon, and other early Luth. theologians do not use this distinction technically, it appears even in Eusebius. It was introduced into Luth. theol. by J. Gerhard.* "Anointed" means that Jesus received the office to which He was divinely appointed (Heb 5:4-10), qualified (He received the Spirit "without measure," Jn 3:34, C. K. Williams' tr.), commissioned (Jn 20:21; cf. Is 49:6), and accredited (Acts 2:22), and for this office He received the gift of the Holy Ghost. (Acts 10:38)

1. *Prophet.* Jesus is the great Revealer of divine Truth, both in His own person and by His Word; the Logos of God to man, revealing to lost mankind the holiness and, above all, the mercy and love of God. See also *Prophet, Christ as.*

2. *Priest.* By His spotless, perfect obedience unto death He propitiated, in the place of all mankind, the offended majesty of God. "Himself the Victim and Himself the Priest," He has by His vicarious life and suffering fulfilled all righteousness and atoned for all sin. See also *Atonement; Faith; Justification; Priest, Christ as.*

3. *King.* Possessed of "all power in heaven and on earth," Jesus, also according to His human nature, is now "Lord of all," so that all external events in the world of man and of nature and all spiritual influences are equally under His control. As King He carries into full effect the great purpose of His revelations as Prophet and of His atoning sacrifice as High Priest. Particularly, He governs and protects the ch. and rules the world in the interest of the ch. Also in the last judgment and to eternity He rules supreme over all; there is no appeal from His verdict. The saints and angels in heaven are His Kingdom of Glory. See also *King, Christ as.*

See also *Ascension; Descent into Hell; Filioque Controversy; Last Things Logos; Symbolism, Christian,* 1, 6; *Trinity.*

J. Bodensieck, "The Person and the Work of Christ," *What Lutherans Are Thinking,* ed. E. C. Fendt (Columbus, 1947), pp. 192–218; O. Cullmann, *Christology of the New Testament,* tr. S. Guthrie and C. Hall (Philadelphia, 1959); W. Elert, *Morphologie des Luthertums,* tr. W. A. Hansen, *The Structure of Lutheranism,* I (St. Louis, 1962), pp. 222–253; O. C. J. Hoffmann, "Office, or Work, of Christ," *The Abiding Word,* ed. T. Laetsch, II (St. Louis, 1947), 112–144, 769; T. S. Kepler, *Contemporary Thinking About Jesus* (New York, 1944); L. J. Roehm, "The Person of Christ," *The Abiding Word,* ed. T. Laetsch, I (St. Louis, 1946), 18–38, 583; J. Schaller, *Biblical Christology* (Milwaukee, 1919); bibliography and notes on FC SD VIII, in *Die Bekenntnisschriften der evangelisch-lutherischen Kirche,* 5th ed. (Göttingen, 1964), 1017–49; see also references under *Dogmatics; Jesus, Lives of.*

"Christ-Myth." See *Drews, Arthur Christian Heinrich; Jesus, Lives of.*

Christadelphians. Anti-Trinitarian sect that originated ca. 1848 under leadership of J. Thomas.* Originally in the Disciples* of Christ movement, Thomas withdrew, partly because he disagreed with A. and T. Campbell* on the doctrine of the Trinity. He claimed that the existing denominations were apostate and that the chs. must return to primitive Christianity in doctrine and practice as defined in the Bible. Though he claimed to accept the inspiration of the Bible, he denied the cardinal doctrines of the Bible, esp. 1. the doctrine of the Trinity, teaching a dynamic Monarchianism*; 2. the immortality of man, teaching that men are dead in the intermediate state, that the unrighteous will be annihilated, while immortality will be given only to the righteous; 3. the Scriptural doctrine of the final coming of Christ, teaching that Israel will be restored in Palestine during a millennium, which will be preceded by the resurrection of the "responsibles" and followed by the judgment, the just receiving immortality and the unjust being destroyed; 4. the doctrines of the devil and hell. At the time of the Civil War the followers of Thomas, compelled to adopt a name to secure exemption from military service, selected the name Christadelphians, "Brothers of Christ."

R. Roberts, *Dr. Thomas: His Life and Work* (London, 1884).

Christaller, Johann Gottlieb (Nov. 19, 1827–Dec. 10, 1895). B. Württemberg; sent to Afr. by Basel* Miss. Soc.; on Gold Coast 1853–58, 1862–68; in Württemberg 1868–95. Founded scientific study of W Afr. languages. Tr. Bible into Twi (Tshi); also studied many other W Afr. languages. Works include *Grammar of the Asante and Fante Language Called Tshi; Sprachproben aus dem Sudan; Die Töne der Negersprachen; Dictionary of the Asante and Fante Language.*

Christening. Synonym for baptism. See also *Baptism, Liturgical; Grace, Means of,* III.

Christenlehre. See *Parish Education,* F 5.

Christentumsgesellschaft, Die Deutsche. Founded Aug. 30, 1780, by J. A. Urlsperger*; headquarters Basel. First called *Deutsche Gesellschaft thätiger Beförderer reiner Lehre und wahrer Gottseligkeit,* later *Deutsche Gesellschaft zur Beförderung christlicher Wahrheit und Gottseligkeit.* Originally organized to oppose attacks on the Bible, it soon devoted its energies to missions and charities. K. F. A. Steinkopf* and C. F. Spittler* were prominent in its work.

E. Beyreuther, "Neue Forschungen zur Geschichte der Deutschen Christentums-gesellschaft," *Theologische Literaturzeitung,* LXXXI (May–June 1956), 355–358.

Christian I (1560–91). Elector of Saxony; father of John* George I; influenced by Nikolaus Crell,* he rejected strict Lutheranism in favor of Melanchthonianism and Crypto-Calvinism (see *Crypto-Calvinistic Controversy*).

Christian II (1481–1559). "The Cruel." King of Den. and Norw. (1513–23) and Swed. (1520–23); married Isabella, sister of Charles* V; responsible for "Stockholm* Blood Bath" Nov. 8–10, 1520, in which over 80 Swed. nobles were slain. Driven out of Sw. 1521, out of Den. to the Neth. 1523. Interested in humanistic reforms in the ch. Defeated by Gustavus* I in Swed.

Christian III (1503–59). King of Den. and Norw. (1534–59). See also *Denmark, Lutheranism in,* 2; *Norway, Lutheranism in,* 2.

Christian (of Prussia; d. 1245). Cistercian*; miss. ca. 1209; bp. of Prussians 1215.

Christian Alliance. See *Evangelistic Associations,* 5.

Christian and Missionary Alliance, The. See *Evangelistic Associations,* 5.

Christian Art. See *Art, Ecclesiastical and Religious.*

Christian Association of Washington, Pa. See *Disciples of Christ,* 2 a.

Christian Beacon. See *Union Movements,* 11.

Christian Brothers (Brothers of the Christian Schools). Noted and influential RC educ. brotherhood, founded 1680 at Reims by Jean* Baptiste de la Salle. Its mems. take the 3 simple vows,* are pledged to teach without compensation, and wear a special habit. Priests with theol. training may not become mems. Organization and discipline recall that of the Jesuits, but there is no official connection with that order.

Christian Catholic Church (Dowieites). Followers of J. A. Dowie,* who organized the Christian Catholic Apostolic Church in Zion 1896, supposedly on the plan of the apostolic ch. He bought ca. 10 sq. mi. of land on Lake Michigan 42 mi. N of Chicago and 1901 founded there a partly religious, partly industrial community called Zion City, of whose financial and ecclesiastical affairs he had complete control. He est. schools, a coll., and many industries. He had extraordinary success both as bus. mgr. and religious leader, assuming the title "Elijah the Restorer" 1901 and "First Apostle" 1904. He demanded of his followers repentance of sins and faith in Christ, but the most prominent tenet was that of faith healing, he himself claiming to possess remarkable powers. He held that all diseases are produced by the devil, and as Christ came to destroy the works of the devil, so this power is still bestowed today. Other tenets were baptism by immersion; millenarianism; abstinence from pork, tobacco, and intoxicating liquors. Dowie est. branches in other states and sent missionaries to other countries. In 1906 the movement claimed 17 branches, 35 ministers, and 5,865 mems. After failure of miss. campaigns in N. Y. City and visits by Dowie to Eng., unrest developed; Dowie was accused of immorality and mismanagement and deposed 1906. He was succeeded in office by W. G. Voliva.* Zion City ceased to be an exclusive community. Principles were modified, and chs. and indep. businesses welcomed. The Zion Conservatory of Music and Art attracts many students unaffiliated with the ch. The Zion Passion Play, first presented 1935, attracts many visitors. Periodical: *Leaves of Healing.*

Christian Catholic Church of Switzerland, The. Name used by Old* Catholics in Switz.; 1st syn. held at Olten 1875. See also *Herzog, Eduard; Küry, Adolf.*

Christian Church. See *Disciples of Christ; United Church of Christ,* I B.

Christian Church, History of. Jesus Christ is the central figure in all hist. The time preceding His birth was one of preparation for His coming; the time following it is one of planting and growth in His Kingdom of Grace. Ch. hist. is the record of this planting and growth, sometimes in the face of great obstacles. The hist. of the NT ch. may be divided into 3 periods: ancient (1–590), medieval (590–1517), and modern (1517–).

I. *Ancient.* 1. *Apostolic Era* (1–ca. 100). The disciples of Jesus, Founder and Head of the ch., were to be witnesses to Him in Jerusalem, in all Judea, in Samaria, and to the uttermost part of the earth (Acts 1:8). During the 1st c. there were 3 great centers in Asia: Jerusalem (30–44), Antioch in Syria (44–68), Ephesus (68–100). The mother ch. at Jerusalem was dispersed, Acts 8:1-4. Antioch became the center of Gentile Christianity (disciples first called Christians there, Acts 11:26) and the home base for missions, Acts 13:1-3. The ch. at Ephesus, founded by Paul, continued to flourish under John, who is said to have gone there from Jerusalem during the Jewish War of 66–70. Before the siege of Jerusalem in 70, mems. of the ch. there fled to Pella in Decapolis (Eusebius, *HE,* III, v, 3). Before the end of the Apostolic Era the ch. was firmly planted in the W, e. g. in Rome, where Peter is said to have been crucified in 64 and Paul beheaded in 66.

2. *Post-Apostolic Era* (ca. 100–ca. 170). In this period were produced the writings of the Apostolic* Fathers. The anonymous *Epistle to Diognetus** may have been written in this period. To this period belong also the apologists* Quadratus,* Aristides,* Melito,* Claudius Apollinaris,* Miltiades,* Athenagoras,* Theophilus* of Antioch, Tatian,* Aristo* of Pella, and Justin* Martyr; they defended the Christian faith against assaults of paganism and Judaism from without and against those of Gnosticism* from within.

Perverters of Christianity: Ebionites,* Elkesaites,* leaders of Gnosticism,* Encratites.* These were opposed by Irenaeus,* Tertullian,* and Hippolytus* (anti-Gnostic Fathers). Marcion* charged conflict bet. OT and NT. Montanism* opposed by Alogi (see *Monarchianism,* A 1). Against the Montanists the ch. declared revelation closed.

3. *Ante-Nicene Era* (ca. 170–325). Uninterrupted succession of bps. emphasized to secure valid transmission of apostolic tradition and unity of episcopacy and of the ch. The ch. recognized a canon (see *Canon, Bible*) of the OT (following that of the Jewish Syn. of Jamnia*) and of the NT and a rule of faith (see *Ecumenical Creeds,* A 3, 4). A beginning of scientific theol. was made in the Alexandrian catechetical school (Pantaenus,* Clement* of Alexandria, and Origen.* See also *Exegesis,* 3; *Schools, Early Christian,* 1). Great leaders in the W were Tertullian,* Cyprian,* Irenaeus,* and Hippolytus.* To this period belongs also the apologist Marcus Minucius* Felix.

Heresies threatened the ch.: Monarchianism* (opposed by Tertullian*) and Arianism* (opposed by Alexander,* Athanasius,* Gregory* of Nazianzus, Basil* the Great, Gregory* of Nyssa, and Hilary* of Poitiers and condemned by the Council of Nicea.* See also *Cappadocian Theologians*).

4. *Post-Nicene Era* (325–590). This era marks new conquests for Christianity and additional formation of doctrine. In 391 Theodosius* I forbade all heathen sacrifices; in 529 Justinian* I closed the school of philos. in Athens. A number of barbaric kingdoms, planted on the soil of the decrepit Roman Empire, turned to Christianity. Heresies were combated. Arianism continued to trouble the ch. but was finally defeated 381 at the 2d Ecumenical Council (Constantinople*; see also *Ecumenical Creeds,* B 1 b). This council also condemned the Macedonians, or Pneumatomachians,* who denied that the Holy Spirit was of an essence equal to that of the Father and of the Son, and Apollinarianism (Apollinaris* of Laodicea). Nestorianism,* converting the 2 natures of Christ into 2 persons, was condemned 431 at Ephesus (see *Ephesus, Third Ecumenical Council of*). Monophysitism* was condemned at

Chalcedon 451 and Constantinople 553 (see *Chalcedon, Council of; Constantinople, Councils of,* 2; *Monophysite Controversy*). Monothelitism* was condemned 680 at Constantinople (see *Constantinople, Councils of,* 3). Donatism (see *Donatist Schism*) was opposed by Augustine* of Hippo. Pelagianism was opposed by Augustine* of Hippo and condemned 431 at Ephesus (see *Ephesus, Third Ecumenical Council of; Pelagian Controversy*).

5. Eminent in this period: Ambrose,* Chrysostom,* Augustine* of Hippo, and Jerome.* Near the end of this era there was a great change in ch. organization. The clergy became a special order, economically indep. and exempt from the jurisdiction of secular courts. Canon laws and traditions began to be codified. The power and prestige of the bp. of Rome grew. Monasticism* continued to develop (Anthony,* Simeon* Stylites, Benedict* of Nursia). But spiritual life deteriorated.

II. *Medieval* (590–1517). This period may be divided according to the fortunes of the papacy*: its rise (Gregory I–VII), its supreme power (Gregory VII–Boniface VIII), and its decline (Boniface VIII to Leo X). See also *Popes,* 4–20. The first division of the Medieval Period may also be dated as ending ca. 1050, in view of the 1054 schism bet. E and W.

1. 590–ca. 1050. The ch. suffered tremendous losses. Islam overran Asia, N Afr., and Sp., but was turned back 732 at Tours by Charles Martel. But for the W it was a time of great miss. expansion. Patrick,* Columba,* Columbanus,* Augustine* of Canterbury, Willibrord,* Boniface,* and Ansgar* were miss. to the Brit. Isles and the Continent. Cyril* and Methodius went to the Slavs in Moravia. Vladimir* I Christianized Russia. The iconoclastic* controversy created much disturbance in the E and was a contributory factor leading to the schism* bet. E and W 1054. The spurious *Donation* of Constantine* pretended to justify the pope's temporal power, first est. 756 by Pepin III (the Short). The *Pseudo-Isidorian* Decretals* further strengthened papal power.

The second Council of Nicaea* (787), defining the doctrine of the veneration of images, terminated a period of doctrinal development in the E Orthodox Ch. In the W, *filioque* ("and the Son") appeared in the Nicene Creed at the Council of Toledo* 589. Gregory I developed the doctrine of purgatory and applied to it the idea of the sacrifice of the mass, taught invocation and intercession of saints and angels, and fostered veneration of relics and images. (See also *Popes,* 4). Doctrinal controversies concerned adoptionism,* Gottschalk's doctrine of predestination (see *Presdestinarian Controversy*), and Berenger's* opposition to the doctrine of transubstantiation. Odo* of Cluny gave new impetus to monasticism and reform. Lat. hymnists of this period: Gregory I, V. Fortunatus,* Bede,* Notker* Balbulus, and P. Damiani.*

2. Ca. 1050–1294. This age includes the great investiture* struggle; the crusades* (1096–1270); rise of the military* religious orders; founding of the mendicant* orders; Scholasticism*; rise of the universities (see *Higher Education,* 4).

3. 1294–1517. Boniface VIII (1294–1303) in the bull *Unam* Sanctam* reached the peak of papal claim to world supremacy and failed. Clement V (1304–14), creature of Philip IV (the Fair), transferred the curia to Avignon,* beginning the Babylonian Captivity (1309–77; see also *Babylonian Captivity,* 2), which resulted in the papal schism* (1378 to 1417), ended by the Council of Constance* (1414 to 1418). Conciliarism (Reform Councils: Pisa* 1409, Constance 1414–18, Basel* 1431–49) failed to est. reforms. Reformers appeared: Marsilius* of Padua; William of Ockham*; J. de Gerson*; Nicholas* of Cusa; mystics J. Eckhart* and J. Tauler.* Greater than these were J. Wycliffe,* J. Hus,* and G. Savonarola.* See also *Popes,* 12–20; *Councils and Synods,* 7.

III. *Modern* (1517–). 1. The Luth. Reformation.* Leo X (see *Popes,* 20) appointed Albert* of Brandenburg chief manager in one district of Ger. for the sale of indulgences.* Albert appointed J. Tetzel* indulgence seller. Oct. 31, 1517, Luther* nailed 95 Theses* to a door of the Castle Ch., Wittenberg. Luther was called to account before cardinal Cajetan at the 1518 Diet of Augsburg. The Leipzig* Debate, 1519. Bull *Exsurge, Domine* burned 1520. Bull of excommunication, *Decet,* issued 1521. Luther at the Diet of Worms,* 1521. NT tr. into Ger. 1522. Peasants'* War, 1525. Diets of Speyer,* 1526 and 1529. Marburg Colloquy, 1529. Catechisms, 1529. Diet of Augsburg and AC, 1530. Complete Bible tr. into Ger., 1534. Controversies in Ger. Luth. chs., 1548–77. Book* of Concord pub. 1580. See also *Catechetics,* 7; *Catechisms, Luther's; Luther, Martin,* 6-20; *Lutheran Confessions.*

2. H. Zwingli* protested against Bernhardin Samson's promotion of the sale of indulgences* 1519; broke with Rome 1522; abolished mass 1525; died in battle of Kappel 1531. Zwinglianism absorbed by Calvinism.*

3. J. Calvin's* 1st stay at Geneva 1536–38; *Institutes of the Christian Religion* 1536; 2d stay at Geneva 1541–64. Cardinal principles of his Reformation: sovereignty of God, absolute supremacy of the Bible as norm for life and doctrine; justification by faith in Jesus Christ; universal priesthood of all believers.

4. The Luth. Reformation outside Germany. Frederick I, king of Den. 1523–33, favored Lutheranism. H. Tausen,* the "Danish Luther." Diet of Odense, 1527. The "forty-three articles of Copenhagen," 1530. Christian III made Lutheranism the religion of Den. and Norway. Diet of Copenhagen legalized the Reformation 1536. (See also *Denmark, Lutheranism in,* 1-4). The Reformation was introduced in Iceland by G. Einarsson* 1540. Lutheranism was planted in Swed. by O. Petri* and L. Petri.* Gustavus* I, elected king of Swed. 1523, favored the Reformation; the 1529 council at Örebro marked its legal introduction. The Reformation was introduced in Fin. by M. O. Agricola.*

5. The Reformation spread rapidly in Poland but was curtailed by Sigismund III. In Bohemia and Moravia the Reformation was checked by the Jesuits.* The Counter* Reformation curbed the spread of the Reformation in Croatia, Slavonia, and It. See also *Bohemian Brethren; Czechoslovakia; Yugoslavia; Moravian Church.*

6. The Swiss Reformation spread to nearly all countries of Eur. The first Ref. syn. was held in Paris 1559 *(Confessio Gallicana).* Prots. in Fr. were called Huguenots.* Calvinism became dominant also in the Netherlands. Scotland turned to Calvinism largely under leadership of J. Knox.* The Scot. parliament officially proclaimed the Ref. faith the religion of Scot. 1560. See also *Reformed Confessions,* B.

7. W. Tyndale's* NT, smuggled into Eng. 1526, prepared the way for Protestantism there. The marital troubles of Henry VIII (king 1509–47) caused the break with Rome; he issued the Ten Articles 1536. The Six Articles of 1539 constituted a reaction against Protestantism. During the reign of Edward VI (1547–53) Protestantism of the Ref. type was firmly planted and the Forty-two Articles adopted. The reaction under Mary (1553–58) was not able to uproot it. Under Elizabeth (1558–1603) the Thirty-nine Articles were adopted; Puritans* and Independents* multiplied. See also *Anglican Confessions; England,* B 1-6.

8. Various radical groups sprang up in Eur. in the

days of the Reformation (Anabaptists; Unitarians*). See also *Baptist Churches,* 2; *Mennonite Churches.*

9. The Counter* Reformation. Organizations opposing the Reformation: Theatines,* Jesuits.* The Inquisition* was continued. The Council of Trent* formulated RC dogma and anathematized Prot. doctrine. Religious wars worked hardships on RCs but esp. on Prots. Wars in Fr. 1562–98, Neth. 1572 to 1609, Ger. 1546–55 and 1618–48. Prot. disunity often aided the Counter Reformation, as in Poland, Hungary, and, to some extent, the Netherlands. Arminianism* opposed strict Calvinism* and was condemned at the Syn. of Dort* 1619.

10. Prot. doctrines were formulated in a more systematic way in the 17th c. (J. Gerhard,* Luth.; G. Voet,* Ref.). Latitudinarians* and advocates of syncretism* reacted against orthodoxy (W. Chillingworth*; G. Calixtus*). The same c. produced such groups as the Quakers* and theosophists (see *Theosophy,* 1).

11. The age of orthodoxy was followed by Pietism* (P. J. Spener*; A. H. Francke*; H. A. Brorson*; E. Pontoppidan*). Swed. curtailed Pietism by royal decree 1726. N. L. von Zinzendorf* made Herrnhut the center of the Moravian* Ch. In Eng. J. and C. Wesley* and G. Whitefield* founded Methodism (see *Methodist Churches*).

12. Pietism's indifference to doctrine merged into the age of rationalism.* The 18th c. made reason the test of all things; Eng. Deism* regarded it as the chief source of knowledge. Unitarianism* spread. Jansenism* and Quietism,* 17th and 18th c. movements in the RC Ch., were opposed by Jesuits.* In the 2d half of the 18th c. the Jesuits were suppressed in RC countries, only to come back strong in the 19th c. and to add greatly to the victory of Ultramontanism.*

13. E Orthodox chs. were largely left untouched by the stirring events of the W. Thoroughly conservative in doctrine and cultus, they were influenced chiefly by political events (rise of the Balkan States; changes in Russia).

14. The 19th and 20th cents. saw several religious streams flowing side by side or merging. Romanticism* was a reaction against rationalism.* F. D. E. Schleiermacher* became the father of Protestant Modernism.* Luth. confessionalism, led by C. Harms,* opposed the Prussian* Union.

15. The Ch. of Eng. produced the Oxford* movement. The 19th c. was marked by social reforms. World missions, begun in the 18th c., were expanded in the 19th c.; many miss. societies were organized. R. Raikes* promoted and popularized the Sunday school.

16. Pius IX defined the dogma of the Immaculate Conception 1854. Vatican Council I defined the dogma of papal infallibility 1870. Pius XII defined the dogma of the Assumption of Mary 1950. John XXIII convoked Vatican Council II 1962.

17. WW I and II and global unrest dispelled the optimism of the early 20th c. Resurgence of paganism challenged the ch. in wide areas. But distress of the times encouraged Christians to collaborate for relief of the needy. Despite strong anti-Christian forces (communism, materialistic humanism, evolutionism) the ch. moved forward. See also *Ecumenical Movement.* LWS

See also *Theology.*

G. P. Fisher, *History of the Christian Church* (New York, 1887); R. H. Nichols, *The Growth of the Christian Church,* rev. 1-vol. ed. (Phidadelphia, 1941); L. P. Qualben, *A History of the Christian Church,* rev. and enl. ed. (New York, 1958); W. Walker, *A History of the Christian Church,* rev. C. C. Richardson (New York, 1959).

Christian Church of North America, General Council. Formed by merger of the Italian Christian Churches of North America (founded Chicago 1907 by Louis Francescon) and the General Council of the Italian Pentecostal Assemblies of God (founded Chicago 1904 by Rocco and John Santamaria). First gen. council held Niagara Falls, N. Y., 1927. Originally called Unorganized Italian Christian Churches of North America. "Unorganized" dropped 1939; "Italian" dropped 1942. Inc. 1948. Membership ca. 8,500 (1973).

Christian Churches (Disciples of Christ), International Convention. See *Disciples of Christ.*

Christian Commercial Travelers' Association of America, International (Christian Commercial Men's Association of America, International; Christian Business Men's Association). See *Bible Societies,* 5.

Christian Congregation. See *Evangelistic Associations,* 4.

Christian Deaf Fellowship. See *Deaf,* 8.

Christian Education. A. *Christian Educ. Defined.* Christian educ. is as old as Christianity. It comprises the efforts of Christians to transmit their beliefs and religious practices to the next generation. The term Christian educ. is used in various meanings. It may cover the entire teaching program of the ch., including preaching and the instruction and training given in a Christian home. Thus used, the term Christian educ. embraces all activity for the conversion and strengthening of souls. In its strict sense, Christian educ. begins after a person becomes a child of God; it seeks to nourish, strengthen, protect, and perfect him by means of the Word of God. The term Christian educ. is most commonly used to describe the work of individuals or organizations that devote themselves to teaching the tenets of Christianity. Christian educ. is the work of man insofar as he teaches and applies the Word of God; it is the work of God insofar as the Holy Spirit alone makes the Word of God effective in the heart of man.

Religious educ. may or may not be Christian educ. The term may be used to describe the educ. efforts of any Christian or non-Christian religious group.

B. *Early Christian Educ.* Early Christians were faced with the problem of teaching the tenets of their religion in a world in which they were a small and persecuted minority. At first Christian instruction was given individually, with parents, deacons, and other mems. of the ch. teaching. But catechumen schools were soon opened. These were in session at stated periods during the week, in some cases every day. Instruction extended over a period of several yrs. Instruction in secular subjects was received from parents, private tutors, and in secular schools. Schools entirely in charge of Christian teachers came later, perhaps at the end of the 2d c. An effort was made to train teachers in catechetical schools. See also *Catechetics,* 2, 3.

C. *Educ. in the Middle Ages.* After ca. AD 500, formal educ. deteriorated and almost disappeared. Some monasteries taught reading and writing, some preserved and copied MSS. Judged by modern standards, these educ. activities were extremely meager.

Ca. AD 800 Charlemagne* sponsored a movement for improved and more gen. educ. He brought to his court scholars, including Alcuin,* to promote and supervise schools. As a result, monastic schools increased in quantity and quality. Some offered educ. also for youths not preparing for monastic life. But there was no gen. pub. demand for educ., and the ch. failed to emphasize its importance.

Beginning with 12th c., schools became more numerous. Chantry schools were taught by priests. Sometimes only a select group of children were admitted, sometimes all who would come. In some cases instruction was free, in others a fee was required.

Guild schools were also organized, est. by merchants or craft guilds, chiefly for children of guild mems., though others also attended. In many communities these schools gradually became borough or town schools, supported by civic authorities. In many cases they were taught by priests. Subjects were largely reading and writing in the vernacular and Lat., arithmetic, and some geog. and hist. Much teaching was drill work. There were no textbooks; the teacher gen. dictated what the pupils were to learn. In gen., educ. was inadequate and reached comparatively few people.

Medieval schools emphasized the 7 liberal arts, including the trivium* and quadrivium.*

D. *Luther and Educ.* 1. Modern Christian educ. stems from the Reformation. The people of Luther's day were unschooled and ignorant, the papacy interested in educ. only insofar as it served to produce faithful and obedient subjects of the ch. Luther's proclamation of the Biblical doctrines of justification by faith and of the universal priesthood of believers liberated the individual from the domination of the ch. Thus educ. became an urgent necessity. Luther therefore advocated universal educ., that each individual might be prepared for faithful discharge of his duties toward God and man.

2. Luther's most important educ. treatises are *An die Ratherren aller Städte deutsches Lands, dass sie christliche Schulen aufrichten und erhalten sollen* (1524) and *Eine Predigt, dass man Kinder zur Schule halten solle* (1530). In these and other writings Luther insisted on adequate educ. for all children. He encouraged educ. on all levels. He emphasized *Christian* educ.: "Where Holy Scripture does not rule, I certainly advise no one to send his child" (WA 6, 462). He accepted the union of ch. and state of his day as a matter of expedience, urging the state to carry on and enforce a program of gen. educ. At the same time he continually reminded parents and the ch. of their duties in child training.

3. Luther's educ. principles may be summarized briefly: Parents are primarily responsible for the educ. of their children; universal educ. is a right and necessity; it is the duty of the state to est. schools and require regular attendance; the foundation of all school instruction is the Christian religion, but in addition children need to learn Lat., Gk., hist., math, singing, physical training, and the practical duties of life; boys should learn a trade, girls housework; children should be taught according to laws of learning, e. g., the knowledge of a thing should precede its name; the teacher must be properly trained; parents and children owe the teacher due respect, and he should be duly remunerated; the teacher, in turn, should by precept and example show himself worthy of respect; pastors need pedagogical training and teaching experience before entering a pastorate, because they are responsible for the school of their cong.; every school should have a library.

4. Luther helped provide textbooks for study in religion. Chief of these was the *Small Catechism* (see *Catechisms, Luther's*), which already in its 1st ed. recognized the value of visual aids; it included a number of illustrations. Luther's tr. of the Bible into the vernacular made its use possible in school. He urged use of the Bible as the chief and most frequently used reading book in both primary and high schools. The very young were to be "kept in the gospels." Luther's hymns were also used in school.

5. On request of the Duke of Mansfeld, Luther took active part in est. 2 schools in Eisleben, one for primary, the other for secondary instruction. In their courses of study and in methods these schools became models for others. Great organizers of Luth. schools were P. Melanchthon* and J. Bugenhagen.* Melanchthon worked esp. in the interest of secondary educ. in Cen. and S Ger., Bugenhagen in N Ger. and Den.

6. Wherever the Reformation spread, educ. was part of it; Luther exerted great influence on parochial, private, and pub. schools of all Prot. countries. He also gave impetus to educ. in the RC Ch., inasmuch as the Reformation forced the RC Ch. to engage in gen. educ. as a measure of self-defense.

E. *Luth. Educ. Since the Reformation.* 1. Since the Reformation, Luth. schools have followed Lutheranism the world over. Before WW II they were found in Austria, Hungary, Swed., Norw., Den., Russia, Fin., Iceland, Australia, Can., the US, and S Am., and in Luth. for. miss. fields in India, China, Afr., and elsewhere.

2. Where the Luth. Ch. is the state ch. (e. g., Norw. and Swed.), Luth. doctrine may be taught in pub. schools. In other countries (e. g., the US and Can.), indep. schools are maintained by Luth. congs.

3. The 1st known Luth. school in Am. was est. by Swedes who settled on the Delaware 1638. Salzburgers est. a school at Ebenezer, Ga., 1734 and built up a system of Luth. schools; J. A. Treutlen,* 1st gov. of Ga., was a product of one of these schools. H. M. Mühlenberg* was instrumental in organizing many chs. and schools. Luth. schools of Scand., Ger., and Dutch origin fl. in N. Y., Pa., N. J., Md., the Carolinas, Va., and Ga. in the US colonial and early nat. period.

4. The oldest school in the Mo. Syn. is St. Matthew's, NYC, est. 1752 or 1753. Other early schools of the Mo. Syn: Immanuel, Cole Camp, Mo., 1834; Zion, Addison (Bensenville), Ill., 1837; St. Paul's, Fort Wayne, Ind., 1837; St. John's, Marysville, Ohio, 1838; schools est. by Saxons in St. Louis and Perry Co., Mo., 1839, and by Bavarians in the Saginaw Valley, Mich., 1845. See also *Parish Education,* D.

5. Early Luth. schools were often taught in parsonages by pastors and were in session only 3 or 4 days a week because of other demands on the pastor's time. As congs. became more stable, school bldgs. were erected, and full-time teachers were called in most cases.

5. Some Luth. groups discontinued their schools. Today there are wide differences in the various Luth. chs. in the emphasis placed on Christian educ. and on the agencies and means whereby Christian educ. is to be achieved. Apart from S. S. and VBS, some Luth. bodies maintain practically no schools, except ministerial training schools and for. miss. schools. Others emphasize a complete system of Luth. educ. including elementary schools, high schools, and colleges.

7. Luth. elementary schools are usually maintained by individual congs., though some are interparish schools (central schools). Luth. high schools are gen. maintained as cen. schools by associations of congs. because they require a larger constituency. Seminaries, teachers' colleges, and preparatory schools are maintained by synods. Valparaiso U., Valparaiso, Ind., is maintained by an assoc. of individuals.

8. Teachers for LCMS schools are trained at Conc. Teachers Coll., River Forest, Ill., Conc. Teachers Coll., Seward, Nebr., and Conc. Coll., St. Paul, Minn. Junior colleges (see *Ministry, Education of,* IX) provide pre-ministerial and pre-teacher educ. Students in the theol. seminaries at St. Louis, Mo., and Springfield, Ill., receive some pedagogical training, because pastoral work involves teaching. For training teachers the Wis. Syn. maintains Dr. Martin Luther Coll., New Ulm, Minn. The ALC trains its teachers at Wartburg Coll., Waverly, Iowa.

9. All Luth. ch. bodies in the US maintain S. S., VBS, released-time classes, Sat. schools, or other types of classes. The S. S. is the most popular of these. It was introd. early in the Luth. bodies that discontinued their parochial schools, but eventually in all Luth. synods. The S. S. usually provides a pro-

gram of Christian educ. for all ages, from preschool to adult. Teacher training depts. are conducted in connection with most Luth. S. S. See also *Parish Education,* B, H 2–3, K 6.

10. The Luth. pastor is held to provide a special course of instruction prior to confirmation, which normally occurs at the age of ca. 13 or 14, but which may occur also at any time during adulthood. Those enrolled in a class that is being prepared for confirmation are called catechumens. Confirmation* admits the individual to communicant membership in the ch., but it is not to mark the end of Christian instruction.

11. The various Luth. ch. schools are frequently called agencies of Christian educ. In most cases these agencies are made to serve the twofold purpose of instruction for mems. of the cong. and winning the unchurched in the community. See also *Parish Education,* H.

12. Administration and supervision of Christian educ. rests chiefly in the local cong., which commonly elects a bd. of educ. to carry on its work under regulations contained in the constitution of the cong. or set up in greater detail apart from the constitution. As a rule, the regulations make the bd. responsible for the organization, management, and supervision of all educ. agencies and activities in the cong.; for increasing enrollments both of mems. and nonmembers; for executing resolutions of the cong. in educ. matters; for reporting regularly to the cong.; and for proposing changes and improvements in the cong. program of Christian educ.

13. The cong. bds. and committees of educ. are aided by official syn. and dist. bds. whose duty is the gen. supervision and promotion of parish educ. Most of the syn. bds. of parish educ. have staffs of full-time workers who counsel congs. in the promotion and improvement of their agencies and who prepare study materials for the various types of schools. They engage in research in Christian educ. and make their findings available, seeking to est. sound principles and policies of Christian educ. In the LCMS the Bd. of Parish Educ. is responsible for the larger program of parish educ., dealing only indirectly with the individual congs., though it publishes and promotes most of the educ. and promotional publications that serve the local cong. Dist. Bds. of Parish Educ. serve in specified geog. areas of the syn. and are in close touch with the work of the individual congs. Most districts have supts. who visit and counsel congs.

F. *Statistics.* 1. In 1972 Luth. chs. in the US and Can. conducted 17,818 S. S. with 2,296,145 pupils, 296,854 officers and teachers.

2. In 1973 LCMS enrolled 694,333 in S. S., 151,590 in 1,239 elementary schools, 345,392 in VBS, 148,021 in weekday religion classes. Except for elementary schools, enrollments in other Luth. bodies were gen. proportionate.

3. In 1973 LCMS enrolled 13,219 in 33 community high schools.

G. *Philos. of Luth. Educ.* 1. Philosophies of educ. have their source in the view which men hold of God; of the origin, nature, and destiny of man; of truth; of the ch.; of the state; and of other related factors. Thus a philos. of educ. forms a pattern whereby those who are engaged in educ. seek to pass on to future generations a particular set of beliefs and a program of life consistent with these beliefs. Any philos. of Christian educ. is so largely determined by theol. that theol. outranks scientific investigation and the postulates of reason as a determinant of the philos.

2. The Luth. philos. of educ. is rooted in divine revelation. It gives place to findings of science and postulates of reason not at variance with divine revelation; e. g., educ. principles and practices that grow out of the origin and destiny of man are derived from revelation, which is divine and irrevocable truth to the Luth. educator. Principles and practices that grow out of the nature of man are derived in part from revelation (e. g., the fact that man is a sinful being), in part from reason or experience (e. g., certain facts which deal with the physical and psychological makeup of man).

3. The Luth. philos. of educ. recognizes the need of consistency in educ. and the desirability of educ. in nonconflicting environments, particularly in the case of the young. That is the reason for its insistence on Luth. schools for Luths. who engage in formal educ. (Luth. elementary schools, Luth. high schools, and Luth. coll. and universities), schools that foster the same educ. ideals as the Christian home. The Luth. philos. holds that home and ch. have rights and responsibilities in educ. prior to those of the state.

4. On the basis of revelation, Luth. educators hold that there is one Triune God, who created man and the universe; that man, rational and distinct from the animals, has a body and soul and has the commission to subdue the earth (Gn 1:28), that is, to make it useful for his own good and the good of his fellow men; that Adam and Eve, the first human beings, were created perfectly holy and righteous; that Adam and Eve sinned and that through their disobedience all mankind has become sinful; that the gracious God sacrificed His own Son Jesus Christ for the sins of mankind; that the believer in Christ's redemptive work has pardon for his sins and is saved and will finally go to heaven; that the believer, being a new creature in Christ and the dwelling-place of God's Holy Spirit, loves God and serves Him by prayer and worship, by hearing and reading God's Word, and by living and working in accordance with it; and that in Scripture God est. absolute standards of right and wrong. The Luth. educator's philos. revolves about God's grace, Christ's redemptive work, the faith of the believer, and eternal salvation.

5. At the same time Luth. education recognizes that the Christian lives in the world and faces such practical problems as making a living, discharging the duties of family life, getting along socially with his fellow men, keeping himself healthy, using his powers for the good of soc., and living a satisfying cultural life. The Luth. philos. of educ. therefore provides not only for teaching the way to salvation, but also for teaching the common requirements of life which are inherent in man's physical, soc., economic, cultural, and charitable duties and privileges. This calls for attitudes and skills which cover the entire range of man's intellectual, physical, emotional, and volitional life, and Luth. educ. seeks to train for these necessary attitudes and skills.

6. Due to its grounding in revelation, Luth. educ. is conservative and not easily swayed by new theories of thought. For example: Though it has recognized the contributions of "progressive education" in the field of methods and techniques, it has never accepted its underlying and motivating theory of the natural goodness of man and the perfectibility of man by human means. Because this theory is anti-Scriptural and anti-Christian, Luth. educ. rejects it.

7. Luth. educ. places a high value on the individual in accordance with the Biblical doctrine of the universal priesthood.

8. While the philos. of Luth. educ. calls for Luth. schools for all Luths. who engage in the pursuits of formal educ. (elementary schools, high schools, colleges, and univs.), the practice has not been everywhere consistent with the ideal. Insufficient concentration of Luth. pop. in a given area, unsatisfactory economic circumstances of the Luth. constituency, or other factors have made the ideal impossible of attainment in many communities. It stands never-

theless as an ideal and as a goal, at least in the Luth. bodies that maintain a system of complete ch. schools on all levels.

9. S. S., VBS, released-time classes, Bible classes, and other ch. schools and classes are part of the larger educ. program of the ch. and are maintained and promoted to achieve those aims and objectives of Luth. educ. which can be achieved by these means, as well as to reach those mems. of the ch. who cannot be reached by any other means. As to these agencies, the Luth. Ch. holds that people of all ages are in need of Christian educ. that they might "grow in grace and in the knowledge of our Lord and Savior Jesus Christ" (2 Ptr 3:18). For that reason classes are maintained for all age levels, from nursery age to adulthood.

H. *Aims and Objectives of Christian Educ.* 1. The ultimate aim of Christian educ. is the perfect restoration of the image of God which was lost in the fall of man. This aim is achieved partially when man comes to faith in Christ and will be fully achieved when the believer enters heaven through a blissful death. All intermediate aims of Christian educ. center about the ultimate aim. The purpose of Christian educ. for life on earth is to restore the Christian to his former blessed state as completely as possible; it is to train men and women who know God as well as He can be known by sinful man, men and women who are sure of their faith in Jesus Christ and of their salvation, and who find their greatest joy in serving God and their fellow men. In short, the aim is an ever-increasing degree of sanctification, which C. F. W. Walther* described as follows: "1. An ever-increasing *enlightenment of the mind;* 2. an ever-increasing *purification and renewal of the heart;* 3. an ever-increasing *zeal in a life of good works*" (*Das walte Gott!* pp. 146–147).

2. The purpose of Christian educ. and training is to guide, direct, preserve, and strengthen the learner, all in keeping with the Word and will of God; to help him develop a Christian view of life; to prepare him for service in home, ch., country, and occupation; and to strengthen all other Christian virtues in him. Christian educ. seeks to develop the individual so that he may become an effective priest for his own person and his own household, as well as an effective witness to the unbelievers about him.

3. Statements of the objectives of Christian educ., organized systematically and set forth in varying degrees of detail, are found scattered through the publications of the ch. Most of these statements agree in the fundamentals, though they vary greatly in form and in organization. Briefly, they emphasize knowledge of Scriptural truths and the application of these truths to daily living; preparation for worthy membership in the Christian home and family; active and intelligent ch. membership; active participation in the evangelization of the unchurched community; and the application of Christian principles to the soc., economic, and pol. problems of the community and nation.

I. *Teaching Materials.* 1. The Bible is basic in any program of Christian educ., and its content and teaching are emphasized in the teaching materials, though the Bible itself may not always be used by the class. In Luth. parochial schools, Luther's *Small Catechism* (see *Catechisms, Luther's*) is commonly used for systematic instruction in doctrine. This catechism and its exposition contain a summary of the chief Bible doctrines. A shorter or longer Bible History containing selections from the Bible, usually in Bible language, may be used to teach the most important Biblical historical data in chronological order. Additional Bible reading or Bible study is carried on. In confirmation instruction, Luther's *Small Catechism* is the basic textbook. Luth. schools use other modern materials in their religion classes, including workbooks, films, pictures, and similar materials. If a trend can be noted, it is in the direction of more direct study of the Bible itself.

2. Due to varying conditions (length of school term, length of instruction period, different types of students) in the separate agencies, most larger ch. bodies provide materials that meet as nearly as possible the distinctive needs of the various agencies, such as the parochial school, S. S., VBS, released-time classes, or Bible classes. This condition poses difficult problems of coordination of materials, because many pupils are enrolled in 2 or more agencies.

3. The preparation of materials for parochial schools presents the greatest problem, because the parochial school is more than a school to which a course in religion has been added; it is a school in which the Word of God runs like a golden thread through everything that is taught and learned. This is esp. true in such subjects as hist., geog., civics, literature, sociology, art, and science.

4. The LCMS publishes materials for the religion classes of its parochial schools, a gen. curriculum guide, curricula for all school subjects, a ch. hist. textbook, a reading series, an art series, a textbook in physical educ., a music reader and music collections, record forms, and other materials, besides a number of professional books for the teacher.

J. *Legislation Pertaining to Christian Educ.* 1. Even in a country that maintains the separation of ch. and state, such as the US, there are a number of areas in the field of Christian educ. where the interests of ch. and state meet, and where legislation is necessary to clarify issues, insure justice, and assure orderly procedure. This legislation deals chiefly with educ. standards and supervision, and with provisions for needed soc. services.

2. There have been times when unfavorable legislation threatened the existence of parochial schools in a number of states. During and after WW I, private and parochial schools on the elementary level were opposed by some as un-American, partly because of for. languages taught in some of them. A number of schools were closed unlawfully by violence. After this war, the opponents sought to close them by legal means. A number of states passed laws to prohibit the use of any but the Eng. language in the elementary school grades. All such laws were declared unconstitutional when the US Supreme Court 1923 ruled against the for.-language laws of Nebr. and other states. Oregon passed a law 1922 outlawing all private and parochial schools on the elementary level. In 1925 also this law was declared unconstitutional by the US Supreme Court. The unconstitutionality of the various laws was found chiefly in their restriction of the rights of parents to choose the school and the educ. for their children. Unfavorable legislation which appeared in Can., notably in the province of Alta., during the same period, was later likewise repealed.

3. Legislation pertaining to standards of bldgs., equipment, and the school subjects outside of religion in many cases has been a means of improving the educ. program of parochial schools.

4. The question of fed. aid for parochial schools had long been debated when, in 1965, the US Congress passed the Elementary and Secondary Education Act (ESEA), which provided some funds to benefit children in these schools. The framers of the Act intended that children in ch.-related and private schools should benefit the same as pub. school children in similar circumstances. The benefits may take many forms: remedial reading, dual enrollment whereby children enrolled in ch.-related schools may attend some classes in pub. schools, welfare services, and others aimed at equalizing educ. opportunity. Because of emphasis on equalizing educ. opportunity,

the larger appropriations under ESEA are for educ. deprived children. Loan of library books and other materials is also provided for. All services are provided under pub. auspices; books or materials used by parochial school children are on loan from the pub. agency. Administrators and teachers in ch.-related and private schools often participate in planning projects for all schools in a district. Since 1944 the Mo. Syn. has held that the ch. may accept aid for its soc. service program. In 1965 it resolved "that federal aid for children attending nonpublic schools, as authorized by the Congress and defined by the courts, be deemed acceptable so long as it does not interfere with the distinctive purposes for which such schools are maintained" (*Proceedings of the 46th Regular Convention,* pp. 153–154). Aid to parochial schools is opposed by many in the US on the ground that it violates the principles of separation of ch. and state and that it jeopardizes the welfare of pub. schools. ESEA represents compromise legislation in that it makes the aid available only to children and not to schools directly (child benefit theory).

5. State laws and local ordinances permit release of pub. school pupils to the ch. of their choice for religious instruction. Pub. school authorities in many communities are glad to offer school time for such released-time instruction. The management of released-time classes is the responsibility of the ch. which sponsors them. But the school usually requires 1. that parents request in writing the release of their children for a specified time; 2. that the ch. conducting the classes furnish the school with enrollment attendance reports; 3. that teachers instructing released-time classes be qualified to teach. These requirements deal with standards and with maintenance of good order and are not designed to control the educ. program of the participating ch. In 1962 and 1963 the US Supreme Court declared unconstitutional arrangements providing for and/or requiring Scripture reading, Lord's Prayer, and/or another prayer in pub. schools.

K. *Judging Results of Christian Educ.* 1. Judging results of Christian educ. in terms of doctrinal knowledge and other subject matter presents no great problem, but Christianity deals ultimately with attitudes and beliefs, with such elements as spiritual advancement, faith, and Christian life. These are difficult, if not impossible, to judge scientifically by existing instruments of measurement.

2. To some extent, results of Christian educ. may be judged by observation. Strengths and weaknesses of a ch. body mirror to a large extent its educ. system. Behavior of pupils in school, the attitude of an individual toward sin, his attitude when he has committed a wrong, his willingness to confess his Savior by word and deed, his trust in God in the time of trouble and need, his prayer life, his love toward God and His Word, his desire to lead a godly life – these are to a certain degree measurable elements for the observant educator. In the case of adults the observer may also judge on the basis of faithfulness in hearing God's Word and partaking of Communion, active participation in ch. work, contributions in money and service, the quality of home life, zeal in witness-bearing, and similar evidences that Christian instruction has been effective.

3. In all these judgments it must be remembered that the final aim for a Christian is eternal life, that also weak faith saves, and that the Old Adam at times creates embarrassing situations for even the best of Christians. Viewed in this light, Christian educ. is seen in terms of souls won for Christ, each of which is worth more than all the riches of the world.

4. In gen., Christian educators take for granted that results correspond largely to the quantity and quality of the Christian educ. received. Earnest Christian homes, Christian chs. that cling firmly to the Word of God, and schools in which the Word of God runs like a golden thread through all that is taught, ordinarily combine, by the grace of God, to develop strong Christians, willing witnesses for God, loyal members of the home, faithful ch. mems., and good citizens. WAK

See also *Parish Education; Protestant Education in the United States; Schools, Church-Related.*

W. H. Beck, *Lutheran Elementary Schools in the United States,* 2d ed. (St. Louis, 1965); P. Bretscher, "Toward a Lutheran Philosophy of Education," *CTM,* XIV (1943), 8–33, 81–95; A. W. C. Guebert, "Luther's Contribution to Modern Elementary Education," *Lutheran School Journal,* LXXIV (Nov. 1938), 100–106; A. H. Jahsmann, *What's Lutheran in Education?* (St. Louis, 1960); E. W. A. Koehler, *A Christian Pedagogy* (St. Louis, 1930); *The Lutheran One-Teacher School,* ed. W. A. Kramer (St. Louis, 1949); *Religion in Lutheran Schools,* ed. W. A. Kramer (St. Louis, 1949); *Lutheran Elementary Schools in Action,* ed. V. C. Krause (St. Louis, 1963); E. A. W. Krauss, "The Missouri Synod and Its Parochial School System," in *Ebenezer,* ed. W. H. T. Dau (St. Louis, 1922), pp. 208–228; O. P. Kretzmann, "Christian Education in the Second Century," *Lutheran School Journal,* LXXXII (June 1947), 438–444; P. E. Kretzmann, *A Brief History of Education* (St. Louis, [1920]) and "The Aims of Christian Education," *CTM,* VII (Nov. 1937), 842–848; J. C. W. Lindemann, "Luther als Reformator des deutschen Schulwesens," *Evangelisch-Lutherisches Schulblatt,* I (1866), 129–140, 161–171, 193–205, 225–233, 257–260, 289–293, 321–330, 353–361; II, 6–10, 33–37, 65–73; (1867), 129–133, 161–165, 193 to 196, 257–261, 289–295, 321–334, 353–362; A. G. Melvin, *Education* (New York, 1946), pp. 108–140; A. C. Mueller, "The Call to Teach Secular Subjects," *Lutheran Education,* LXXXVIII (Oct. 1952), 59–65; F. Nohl, *A Curriculum Guide for Lutheran Elementary Schools,* 3 vols. (St. Louis, 1964); F. V. N. Painter, *Luther on Education* (St. Louis, 1928); *100 Years of Christian Education,* ed. A. C. Repp (River Forest, Ill., 1947); D. C. Schilke, "The Christian Philosophy of Education," *Lutheran School Journal,* LXXII (June 1937), 439–444; A. C. Stellhorn, *The Meaning of a Lutheran Education,* 2d ed. (St. Louis, 1928), and *Schools of The Lutheran Church — Missouri Synod* (St. Louis, 1963); H. C. Theiss, "Distinctive Lutheran Ideals in the Field of Education," *American Lutheran,* XXIII (Dec. 1940), 7–8; see also bibliography under *Catechetics.*

Christian Endeavor. The 1st young people's Christian Endeavor soc. was organized Feb. 2, 1881, by F. E. Clark* in the Williston Cong. Ch., Portland, Maine. As socs. multiplied the movement became interdenom. The United Soc. (nat. union of the US and Can.) was organized 1885. Soon socs. sprang up in India, China, Eng., Australia, and elsewhere. The Internat. Soc. of Christian Endeavor covers N and S Am. The World's Christian Endeavor Union, organized 1895, is the overall organization. At the 1906 Geneva world convention a platform was adopted requiring active mems. to pledge faith in Christ, open acknowledgment of Christ, service for Christ, loyalty to Christ's ch. The organization stresses spirituality, catholicity, loyalty, fellowship, missions, philanthropies. Headquarters: Columbus, Ohio. Periodical: *The Christian Endeavor World.*

Christian Ethics. See *Ethics,* 2.

Christian Faith and the Intellectual. 1. In the church's proclamation of the Lord Jesus Christ, Christian faith has ever heard a decisive word of divine judgment on a world alienated from its Creator (Jn 12: 31) and a decisive word of divine reconciliation with that world (2 Co 5:18-21). That world has been judged and redeemed from beyond by the eternal Word, who became flesh in the fullness of time and dwelt among us (Jn 1:14; Gl 4:4-5; Eph 1:9-10). Christian faith has embraced Him who was folly to the Greek and a stone of stumbling to the Jew; its Spirit-impelled testimony to Him is the saving power of God for both Jew and Greek (Ro 1:16-17; 1 Co 1:22-25). Christian faith has seen God's Light dispel spiritual darkness and has proclaimed that through Him alone God's redemptive purposes have become clear and the meaning of life laid bare (Jn 1:1-18; Eph 3:7-12). It has attested that in Christ a dying world has been created anew, so that the finite and fallen might bear the Infinite and Holy (Ro 8:9; 1 Co 3:16; 2 Co 5:17). In a Christian, godless reason has been transformed, set free from its spurious claims to autonomy (1 Co 2:14-16; 2 Co 10:5), and placed in the service of God. Out of this tension between judgment and reconciliation, darkness and light, reason and faith, Christian faith has addressed itself to the human situation, esp. to the intellectual.

2. The witness of the early ch. to Greco-Roman intelligentsia took 2 primary forms: 1st, the ch. was compelled to est. the sanctity of Christian morals in answer to those cultured despisers who accused it of such abominations as cannibalism, incest, infanticide, sorcery, and, in gen., "hatred of the human race" (Tacitus, *Annales,* XV, 44); 2d, Christian witness asserted the divine truth of its doctrine. It opposed dualistic and pantheistic polytheism; in this it joined forces with leading pagan literati of the times (at least in rejecting crude mythologies). But more: as evinced in writings of the Apologists, the new faith claimed fullness of truth. Justin* Martyr, e. g., conceded that the greatest of the pagans may have participated in the truth; but he held that Christians alone possess it in entirety. They alone have perfect truth because they alone have the Logos incarnate. In extended defense and exposition of doctrine the fundamental problem of the church's best thinkers from apostolic times to Augustine* of Hippo was elaboration of strict monotheism within a Trinitarian framework. Attempts to solve this problem gave rise to Trinitarian* and Christological* controversies. Among instruments used by the Fathers to effect a solution were categories derived from Hellenistic philosophy. Faith and reason operated closely together; but the Scriptures were always the point of departure. The Fathers regarded "reason," or Hellenistic philosophy, as propaedeutic to Christianity and an instrument in doctrinal exposition. Pagan philos. contained certain anticipations of Christian truth (which the Fathers largely attributed to borrowings from the OT); but it was beset by serious aberrations of human speculation. Christianity was accordingly heralded as the one true wisdom.

3. The hist. of Christian witness to the intellectual from Augustine of Hippo to the late Middle Ages and Renaissance is the hist. of increasing rapprochement of theol. and philos., since the great thinkers of the time were primarily theologians or theologian-philosophers. Christian faith became, in the words of Anselm* of Canterbury, *fides quaerens intellectum,* "faith in search of understanding." Insofar as faith reflected on the content of revelation with the help of reason it developed Scholastic theology (see *Scholasticism*); in reflecting on presuppositions of revelation it developed natural theology,* i. e., proofs for God's existence. Faith, however, was not construed as incomplete without proof, but as the key factor in the search for a comprehensive vision of life; philos. was the handmaid in this quest, which culminated in the synthesis of Gk. philos. (particularly Aristotelianism; see *Aristotle*) and Christian revelation by Thomas* Aquinas in the 13th c. This synthesis was occasioned by the discovery and tr. of Aristotle's complete works; it afforded the Christian "answer" to those intellectuals (e. g., the Latin Averroists; see *Arabic Philosophy*) who saw in Aristotle an inclusive rational system independent of Christian revelation. Reacting to the latter, Aquinas solved the relation of faith and reason by incorporating them in a uniform system of "natural" and "supernatural" truth. Architecturally this synthesis was given expression in the Gothic cathedral; in literature by Dante's *Divine Comedy;* in politics by the desideratum of harmony bet. papacy and empire. But the synthesis was precarious and was called into question in the late Middle Ages by William of Ockham* and representatives of the so-called *via moderna* who favored terminological analysis rather than metaphysical synthesis, and criticism rather than speculation. They drove a wedge bet. theol. and philos. and broke apart the 13th c. synthesis by a theory of "double truth" in which faith and ecclesiastical authority were posited as superior to reason. Luther and the Reformers gen. shared in the Ockhamist reaction against the *via antiqua,* but Luther's critique of reason was theol. rather than epistemological, i. e., the "theol. of the cross" is foolishness to the sin-darkened intellect of natural man. This theological critique of reason has since been shared by such Christian thinkers as Pascal,* Kierkegaard,* and K. Barth.

4. The Middle Ages ended with philos. and theol. each claiming autonomy; this, with the growth of empirical science, set the stage for the modern period. Christian witness to the intellectual since the Renaissance has been normed by two "attacks" from philos. and science, both of which had been freed from original ties to the church. Christian response has been marked by diversity and subtlety and by concern to speak responsibly to the modern situation (the latter emphasized by theological liberalism). This response has primarily been an informed apologetic recognizing changing philosophical and scientific attitudes and inferences (rather than specific conclusions, though these too have been involved). Pascal and Kierkegaard opposed, respectively, the rationalism of Descartes* and Hegel* and the attempt to subsume Christian revelation within a "system." Joseph Butler* and W. Paley* answered 18th c. deism* and upheld the "Book of God" over against the self-sufficiency claimed for the "Book of Nature." Schleiermacher* addressed the early 19th c. cultured despisers of religion in terms of the very premises of the philos. and natural science of his day; he sought affirmation of Christianity as the highest value of life. Following his cue, 19th c. theol. concerned itself mainly with reconciling Christ and culture. In the 20th c., with its frightful legacy of 2 world wars and the threat of imminent atomic holocaust, Christian theologians have been challenged to answer the atheistic existentialism of such thinkers as Nietzsche,* Sartre, and Camus. Paul Tillich* responded to Nietzsche's charge that "God is dead" by presenting God as the "Ground of Being," i. e., the presupposition for all life and for "authentic existence." In an age dominated by science and technology, Christian thinkers have also addressed the scientifically educated in terms of the contemporary picture of the physical universe. K. Heim's *Der evangelische Glaube und das Denken der Gegenwart* (5 vols.) is the most notable of such ventures. Rudolf Bultmann's program of "demythologization" may be seen as an attempt to preserve the Christian message for modern man by paring "prescientific" trappings off the NT. Christian apologists have also had to consider the positivists' contention that only that is true which can be demonstrated by scientific method. Related to this is the problem of the nature and validity of religious language and the verifiability of theological claims.

From apostolic times to the present, Christian theologians and defenders of the faith have recognized themselves to be "under obligation both to Greeks and to barbarians, both to the wise and to the foolish" (Ro 1:14 RSV).

See also *Apologetics, Christian.*

C. N. Cochrane, *Christianity and Classical Culture,* rev. ed. (New York, 1944); B. A. Gerrish, *Grace and Reason: A Study in the Theology of Luther* (New York, 1962); H. R. Niebuhr, *Christ and Culture* (New York, 1951); J. Pelikan, *The Christian Intellectual* (New York, 1966); A. Richardson, *Christian Apologetics* (New York, 1947); P. Tillich, *Theology of Culture* (New York, 1959). DWL

Christian Faith Society. See *Society for Advancing the Christian Faith in the British West India Islands.*

Christian Geography. See *Geography, Christian.*

Christian Holiness Association. See *National Holiness Association.*

Christian Humanism. See *Humanism.*

Christian Literature Society for China. See *Society for the Diffusion of Christian and General Knowledge Among the Chinese.*

Christian Literature Society for India. Organized 1858 in Eng. as the Christian Vernacular Educ. Soc. for India to train native teachers, instruct native children, and pub. school books and Christian literature.

Christian Methodist Episcopal Church. See *Methodist Churches,* 4 c.

Christian Missions. See *Missions;* see also names of various countries.

Christian Nation Church U. S. A. See *Holiness Bodies,* 2.

Christian Quakers. See *Keith, George.*

Christian Reformed Church. See *Netherlands,* 2; *Reformed Churches,* 4 c.

Christian Science. See *Church of Christ, Scientist.*

Christian Social Union. Founded June 14, 1889, in Eng. by C. Gore* and H. S. Holland*; B. F. Westcott* was 1st pres. Objectives: to claim for Christian law the ultimate authority to rule soc. practice; to study applications of Christian truths and moral principles to contemporary soc. and economic problems; to present Christ as Master and King, enemy of wrong, power of righteousness and love. Spread socialist teaching and was influential at Pan-Angl. Congress and Lambeth Conf. 1908.

G. C. Binyon, *The Christian Socialist Movement in England* (London, 1931), pp. 158–179.

Christian Socialism. 1. Revolts of the masses in mid-19th c. Eur. and theories assoc. with these revolutions occasioned a religious response called Christian socialism. It appeared in different forms in various parts of W Eur. and N Am.; it usually involved an effort to include many ideals of soc. reform in a framework of liberal Christian theol. and popular action. The movements have been described as attempts to socialize Christianity and Christianize socialism by making Christianity the religion of which socialism is the practice. Christian socialism gen. represented an attack on *laissez-faire* economics and the clerical *status quo.* In the case of Bismarck's (1815–98) Christian socialism (or state socialism) the term was taken over for opposite purposes, namely to denote an attempt on the part of the govt. to provide for some of the needs of workers.

2. Christian socialism in Eng. was prefigured in the soc. program of R. Owen.* As a formal movement it was founded 1848 by J. M. F. Ludlow,* C. Kingsley,* T. Hughes,* and particularly by J. F. D. Maurice.* This group provoked hostility on the part of the est. forces of the Ch. of Eng. and suffered from failure to rally secular socialist forces. A workingmen's coll. was est. in London 1854. But by 1858 the movement had spent most of its force. Several times since, the Brit. Isles have seen Christian socialism in action, e. g., the Guild of St. Matthew, beginning 1877, and the Ch. Socialist League, founded 1906. In gen. these movements grew out of the High Ch. party and were motivated by a proclamation of divine sovereignty over all realms of life, against a background of evolutionary optimism.

3. On the Continent Christian socialism included more varied emphases than in Eng., from Bismarck's inversion of its use to the Russ. (A. S. Khomyakov*; F. M. Dostoevski*) apocalyptic form, to Ottokár Prohászka's* (1858–1927) program in Hungary in the 1920s, or E. Dollfuss'* partisan use of the term in Austria in the 1930s. The latter reflected RC emphasis sanctioned by some liberalizing soc. emphases of Leo XIII and Pius XI (who, however, called Christian socialism as a philos. a contradiction in terms).

4. Most consistent interest in Christian socialism has been shown in Germany. J. H. Wichern* and F. von Bodelschwingh* considered themselves Christian socialists, though their efforts for redress of soc. evils appeared in a conservative pol. framework. The Ritschlian school of theol. (see *Ritschl, Albrecht*), in the yrs. just before WW I, produced a number of Christian socialist tendencies, but the movement came under criticism by Karl Barth, who had earlier found it congenial but later considered it pervaded by humanism. Shortly after WW I, under P. Tillich* and others, the movement was revived, with increased interest in Marxist sources, under the name Religious Socialism; but it failed to win wide support of clergy or masses and disintegrated in the face of Hitler's National Socialism.

5. Some emphases of Christian socialism were assumed by the Life and Work branch of the Ecumenical* Movement through efforts of N. Söderblom* of Swed. and others. In the US the Social* Gospel of W. Rauschenbusch* and others provided a parallel to Eur. interests in seeing the Lordship of Christ asserted in various causes of soc. reform and revolution.

See also *Stoecker, Adolf.*

G. C. Binyon, *The Christian Socialist Movement in England* (London, 1931); C. E. Raven, *Christian Socialism, 1848—1854* (London, 1920); P. Tillich, *The Protestant Era,* tr. J. L. Adams (Chicago, 1948). MEM

Christian Symbolism. See *Symbolism, Christian.*

Christian Union. Founded 1864, when local unions or feds. of Christian (see also *United Church of Christ, The,* I B) and Disciples* of Christ chs. banded together under James F. Given, J. V. B. Flack, and others to achieve freedom from pol. and ecclesiastical interference in worship. The group has no binding creed and endeavors to grant every individual the right to his own interpretation of the Bible without controversy on disputed theol. questions, but stresses 7 principles: oneness of the ch., headship of Christ, Bible only rule of faith and practice, fruits of faith condition of fellowship, Christian union without controversy, autonomy of local cong., avoidance of pol. preaching. Ordains men and women. Speaks of baptism and Lord's Supper as ordinances. Local groups differ somewhat in name. Gen. organization includes a Gen. Council. See also *Churches of Christ in Christian Union.*

In 1886 R. G. Spurling* Sr. and others organized an indep. body called Christian Union.

Life History of J. V. B. Flack, ed. J. Clevenger (Excelsior Springs, Mo., 1912); H. Rathbun and A. C. Thomas, *Christian Union and Bible Theology* (Excelsior Springs, Mo., 1911).

Christian Union. See *Young People's Organizations, Christian,* III 8.

Christian Union (Tenn.). See *Church of God,* 2.

Christian Unity. See *Altar Fellowship; Ecumenical Movement, The; Fellowship; Union Movements.*

Christian Unity Baptist Association. See *Baptist Churches,* 29.

Christian Vernacular Education Society for India. See *Christian Literature Society for India.*

Christian, William. See *Church of the Living God,* 1.

Christian Workers for Fellowship. See *Church of the Living God,* 1.

Christian Worship. See *Worship,* 2.

Christianity. See *Christian Church, History of; Church.*

Christians of the Universal Brotherhood. See *Russian Sects.*

Christiansen, Gottlieb Bender (Oct. 27, 1851–Sept. 27, 1929). B. Vejlby, near Assens, Fyn, Den.; to US 1877; educ. Augsburg Theol. Sem., Minneapolis, Minn.; ordained 1881 by Norw.-Dan. Conf.; pastor in Iowa, Minn., Nebr.; prof. Trin. Sem., Blair, Nebr., 1890–96; pres. United Dan. Ev. Luth. Ch. in Am. 1896–1921.

Christina (1626–89). Queen of Swed. 1632–54. Daughter of Gustavus* II. B. Stockholm; d. Rome. Trained, after death of her father, by Axel Oxenstierna to become ruler; crowned 1644; abdicated 1654; joined the RC Ch. 1655. See also *Vatican City.*

Christina, Fort. Settlement of Swed. Luths. made 1638 on the present site of Wilmington, Del. When R. Torkillus* arrived, services were held at the fort until a chapel was built 1641 or 1642.

Christlieb, Theodor (1833–89). B. Birkenfeld, Württemberg; d. Bonn. Helped found Ger. Evangelistic Union 1883, Johanneum* 1886. With P. R. Grundemann* and G. A. Warneck* founded *Allgemeine Missions-Zeitschrift* 1874.

Christmas. Earliest certain mention of celebration on Dec. 25 is in the Philocalian Calendar of 354, which gives the Roman practice in 336. Commemoration of the Nativity on Jan. 6 originated in the E and was combined (e. g., in Jerusalem) with commemoration of Jesus' baptism. By the 5th c. most E chs. accepted the Roman date, though Jerusalem celebrated the Nativity Jan. 6 till 549 or later.

Most customs connected with Christmas are borrowed from pagan sources. The Roman Saturnalia, marking return of the sun with the practice of giving and receiving presents, as well as Yuletide customs of people of N Eur., left their mark on the outward observance of Christmas. Possibly the use of evergreens, holly, ivy, mistletoe, and rosemary was suggested by non-Christian customs, though they soon received Christian significance. Burning the Yule log was an important part of Christmas festivities in Eng. The domestic Christmas tree first appeared in Ger. in the 16th c. From Ger. the custom came to Eng. and Am. Festivities connected with Santa* Claus derived from Christian and pagan sources. The use of lights and bells accords well with the spirit of the festival. See also *Church Year,* 1, 16 b; *Schwan, Heinrich Christian.*

H. K. Usener, *Das Weihnachtsfest* (Bonn, 1911); F. X. Weiser, *The Christmas Book* (New York, 1952); L. Fendt, "Der heutige Stand der Forschung über das Geburtsfest Jesu am 25. XII. und über Epiphanias," *Theologische Literaturzeitung,* LXXVIII (Jan. 1953), columns 1–10; *Celebrating Christmas Around the World,* ed. H. H. Wernecke (Philadelphia, 1962); *Christmas: An American Annual of Christmas Literature and Art,* ed. R. E. Haugan (Minneapolis, 1931–); W. G. Polack, "The First Christmas Tree in an American Church Service," *CHIQ,* XVII, No. 1 (Apr. 1944), 4–6.

Christmas Conference. Meeting at Baltimore Dec. 24, 1784, at which ca. 60 lay preachers formed the M. E. Ch.

Christoffel, Ernst J. (d. 1955). Est. homes for blind, crippled, and orphaned in Turkey (Malatya 1908 to 1919) and Iran (Tabriz 1925; Isfahan 1928). Worked esp. with blind; created oriental alphabet for blind and educ. them as evangelists, teachers, etc.

Christological Controversies. Controversies pertaining to the Scriptural doctrine of the person and work of Christ. See also *Adoptionism; Christ Jesus; Doctrine, Christian, History of,* 2; *Apollinaris of Laodicea; Arianism; Eutychianism; Lutheran Theology After 1580,* 2; *Monarchianism; Monophysite Controversy; Monothelitism; Nestorianism; Pneumatomachi; Three Chapters, Controversy of.*

Christology. That part of dogmatics, or doctrinal theol., which treats of the person of Jesus Christ as the God-man, with the human nature and the divine nature included in one person. See also *Christ Jesus.*

Christomonism. Term used to describe the view (e. g., of Karl Barth) that revelation comes to us only in the incarnation.

Christoph (1515–68). Duke of Württemberg 1550–68. Worked for unity of Ref. and Luth. theologians. Laid foundation for ev. ch. govt. Used income from chs. and monasteries for support of chs. and schools.

Christopher. Patron saint of travelers, ferrymen, etc. Acc. to tradition, a 3d c. martyr. A legend refers the name Christopher (Gk. *Christophoros,* "Christbearing") to his carrying Christ, in the form of a child, across a river.

Christotokos. See *Nestorianism,* 1.

Christs, False. Those who make the false claim of being the promised Christ. Jesus prophesied that deceivers of that kind would appear (Mt 24:5, 23-28; Mk 13:22). Men of this nature before the destruction of Jerusalem were possibly Simon the sorcerer (Acts 8:9), Theudas, mentioned in Josephus as causing trouble in the days of gov. Fadus (*Antiquities,* XX, 5, 1), the Egyptian mentioned Acts 21:38, and Dositheus and Menander, whose names are reported by somewhat later writers. In the 2d c. appeared Bar Cocheba, a leader of the Jews in the disastrous insurrection of 132–135. See also *Simon Magus.*

Christ's Sanctified Holy Church. Began in Colored M. E. Ch. in La. with preaching by white evangelists; organized ca. 1903/04 as Colored Ch. South. See also *Holiness Churches,* 2.

Christus Crucifixus; Christus Victor. Terms popularized by Gustaf Aulén, who referred *Christus Crucifixus* to the eschatological drama of redemption including the work of Christ finished on the cross, namely the act of divine love through which God establishes reconciliation bet. Himself and the world. *Christus Victor* is used for the finished work that appears to faith as a victory over those demonic powers that have enslaved humanity and is the victorious breakthrough of the divine will and the establishment of "the new covenant." See also *Lund, Theology of.*

Christus Victor. See *Christus Crucifixus.*

Christus Victor. Fellowship of Cong. pastors in US organized 1942 to promote neoorthodox and Trinitarian theol.

Chrodegang. B. early in 8th c.; d. 766. Frankish Christian leader. Bp. Metz ca. 742; abp. 754. Reestablished relationship bet. his country and Rome. Known for efforts in behalf of ch. discipline and morals. Strictly enforced the rule of Benedict* of Nursia. Helped spread Roman customs through Ger. Works include *Regula.*

Chronology, Biblical and Ecclesiastical. Science of fixing dates and chronological sequence of events in sacred and ecclesiastical hist. See also *Time.*

Chrysanthos, Notaras (d. 1731). Metropolitan of Caesarea 1702; patriarch of Jerusalem 1707 as successor of his uncle Dositheus*; author of confession signed by Gk. bps. at the 1727 council at Constantinople.

Chrysippus. See *Stoicism.*

Chrysologus, Peter. See *Peter Chrysologus.*

Chrysoloras, Manuel (1355–1415). Humanist. B.

Constantinople; sent to It. and Eng. to seek help against Turks; settled in It. ca. 1396; taught at Florence and other It. cities; works include a Gk. grammar.

MPG, 156, 9–60.

Chrysostom, John (ca. 345–407). Patriarch of Constantinople. Name Chrysostom (from Gk. *chrysostomos,* "goldenmouthed") not applied to him till after his death. Mem. of a rich patrician family; studied rhetoric and philos.; intended to follow law, but turned to the Bible instead, leading the life of a strict ascetic in the first yrs. after his baptism; priest in Antioch 12 yrs.; patriarch of Constantinople 398. Immediately inaugurated needed reforms and laid the foundation for systematic charitable work. But his position became increasingly insecure because of enemies he made by his rigorous rules and fearless attacks on luxury. Under auspices of Eudoxia, Theophilus* of Alexandria assembled the Syn. ad Quercum* 403 that deposed and banished Chrysostom. After his recall another syn., at Constantinople, again condemned him; banished by force to Asia Minor; died at Comana, Asia Minor, before reaching destination. Fame rests chiefly on his sermons, in which he reached great heights of oratory. Writings may be divided chiefly into homilies, treatises, and letters and include *On the Priesthood; On Penance; On Celibacy.*

C. Baur, *John Chrysostom and His Time,* tr. M. Gonzaga, 2 vols. (Westminster, Md., 1959–60); J. A. W. Neander, *Der heilige Johannes Chrysostomas und die Kirche,* 2 vols., 3d ed., new and improved print. (Berlin, 1858), Vol. I: *The Life of St. Chrysostom,* tr. J. C. Stapleton (London, 1838); W. R. W. Stephens, *Saint John Chrysostom: His Life and Times,* 3d ed. (London, 1883). ACR

Chrysostom, Liturgy of St. John. See *Divine Liturgy.*

Chu Hsi. See *Chinese Philosophy,* 6.

Chuang-tzu (4th-3d c. BC). Chinese philos.; teacher of Taoism*; stressed love of nature, logic, and the attention of the sages to the sublime and the common. See also *Chinese Philosophy,* 2.

Chubb, Thomas. See *Deism,* III 5.

Chuma. See *Susi.*

Chun-tzu. See *Chinese Philosophy,* 3.

Chung. See *Chinese Philosophy,* 3.

Church. 1. The word "church" is commonly applied to the whole number of true believers, the communion of saints, the invisible ch. of Christ; any particular denomination of Christian people; particular congs. of any Christian denomination; the religious establishment of any particular nation or govt. (e. g., Ch. of Eng.); the sum total of the various Christian denominations in a country; and the house of Christian worship.

2. *Biblical meaning.* The word "church" is derived from the Gk. *kyriakos,* "of, or belonging to, the Lord." In the OT 2 words were used for the idea of assembly: *edah* and *qahal* (Lv 4:13, 14; cf. Heb 12:23). In the NT the term is *ekklesia,* derived from *ekkalein,* "call out"; hence the term describing the town meeting of the Gk. city is transferred to the gathering of those who have been summoned by the call of God and His Spirit to belong to His people in Christ (Eph 1:22, 23; 4:1-6). The 80-plus instances of the term in the NT designate the body of all believers in all the world, or the believers gathered in a particular place (e. g., Gl 1:2; "ch. in the house" Cl 4:15; Ro 16:5). In no case is the term used of gatherings in which also unbelievers are essentially numbered, unless Rv 2–3 is so interpreted. The picture of the ch. used by Paul (cf. 1 Co 12; Eph 4:1-16; Ro 12:4-18; 14:1; 15:1) and probably implied by Jesus (Mt 25:31-46), that the mems. of the ch. are the body of Christ on earth, stresses that they stand in a functional relation toward each other, namely that they "edify" (1 Co 14:26; Eph 4:12) or build up one another in faith for life. This mutual relation is termed *koinonia* ("sharing") and involves mutual care expressed in forgiveness and admonition (cf. Mt 18; Eph 5:19, 20), the Lord's Supper (1 Co 10:16, 17), and care for physical need (2 Co 8:4). The breaking of this mutual activity receives vivid rebuke (Ro 16:17, 18; 3 Jn 9-11). Other analogies for the ch. stress that it is the place where God is worshiped (Eph 2:19-22), the means by which God is glorified to the world (1 Ptr 2; Ph 2:14-16).

3. *Visible and invisible.* In reaction to RC stress on the political quality of the ch. in its submission to the pope, the concepts of "visible" and "invisible" ch. were developed, though the terms are not in the Bible and the Luth. confessions. The term "invisible" is a useful adjective for the ch., if it denies a political essence to the ch. (Ap VII and VIII, 23–28), reminds of the worldwide community in which true Christians should live together, and denotes God's own recognition of each believer (2 Ti 2:19); it is harmful if it makes of "church" an abstract idea without counterpart in fact (Ap VII and VIII, 20) or allows the assumption that a perfect unity already exists that does not need the careful ministry of every mem. of the ch. (cf. Eph 4:1-16). The term "visible" is useful if it sets up a sphere of activity in which Christians genuinely labor for each other and in witness to their world; it is harmful if activism is allowed to replace Word and Sacrament as the means of propulsion of the ch. See also *Luther, Chief Writings of,* 7.

4. *Marks.* In contrast to the position that the episcopate or apostolic succession are the *esse* of the ch., the Luth. symbols have developed the concept of the Gospel and the Sacraments as the marks of the ch. (AC V, VIII, XIII). Special ministers of the Word are significant for the ch. as they use Gospel and Sacraments and train Christians for their mutual ministry (Eph 4:7-13).

See also *Church Militant; Church Triumphant.*

C. Bergendoff, *The Doctrine of the Church in American Lutheranism* (Philadelphia, 1956); R. R. Caemmerer, *The Church in the World* (St. Louis, 1949); R. R. Caemmerer and E. L. Lueker, *Church and Ministry in Transition* (St. Louis, 1964); F. E. Mayer, "The Proper Distinction Between Law and Gospel and the Terminology Visible and Invisible Church," *CTM,* XXV (Mar. 1954), 177–198; P. S. Minear, *Images of the Church in the New Testament* (Philadelphia, 1960); F. Pieper, *Christliche Dogmatik,* III (St. Louis, 1920), 458–534, Eng. tr. *Christian Dogmatics,* III, ed. W. W. F. Albrecht (St. Louis, 1953), 397–435; H. A. Preus, *The Communion of Saints* (Minneapolis, 1948).

Church, Institutional. See *Institutional Church.*

Church Administration. 1. There is growing need in the ch. for good administrative procedure. S. W. Blizzard, "The Minister's Dilemma," *Christian Century,* LXXIII (April 25, 1956), 508–510, showed that though Prot. ministers put administration at the end of the list of preferred pastoral tasks, it was first on the list in terms of time consumed. Since administration is a necessity, it should be viewed in its proper perspective and carried out with maximum efficiency and minimum time.

2. The word "administration" occurs in some form only twice in the NT RSV, representing 2 Gk. words. In 1 Co 12:28 "administrators" are among God-appointed ch. functionaries; here the Gk. word means "those who steer, pilot, direct"; in this sense administrators give proper direction to an enterprise. 2 Co 8:20 speaks of administering the gift given by the chs. for the poor in Jerusalem; here the Gk. word means "serving" (cf. Mt 20:28); in this sense administrators are servants; their greatest service is speaking and sharing God's Word.

3. If an administrator is to function effectively as leader and servant, (1) he must help people see and set goals indicated in the Bible; the ch. is the people of God, who are to carry out God's will through worship, nurture, service, and witness in the world. (2) An administrator should help people analyze the situation in the ch. in order to see where they are and where God's goals indicate they should be; such analysis should consider resources of the group for meeting the goals. (3) People should be involved in determining functions that need to be performed and planning means or structures by which these functions can be performed. (4) People should be organized for the tasks to be done; they need to be asked, trained, and put to work in the functions that have been determined as necessary. (5) Provision should be made for supervision, to help assure progress and offer resources to increase efficiency. (6) Evaluation should ask: "How are we doing in the light of our goals?" Everything going on in the ch. should be critically viewed as measured by effectiveness in helping people reach God-given goals.

H. Coiner, "The Pastor as Administrator of the Christian Fellowship," *CTM,* XXXV (May 1964), 271–283; R. R. Caemmerer, *Feeding and Leading* (St. Louis, 1962); O. Tead, *Democratic Administration* (New York, 1945) and *The Art of Administration* (New York, 1951). RC

Church Advertising. See *Public Relations; Publicity, Church.*

Church and Ministry, Walther's Theses on. Theses from C. F. W. Walther's* *Die Stimme unserer Kirche in der Frage von Kirche und Amt;* an elaboration of his 1841 Altenburg* Theses. The 1850 Mo. Syn. conv. authorized preparation of a formal reply to the Buffalo* Syn. and its leader, J. A. A. Grabau,* in regard to the controversy that had arisen bet. the 2 syns. on ch. and ministry. Walther submitted theses and an outline for a book to the 1851 Mo. Syn. conv.; they were discussed and approved. Shortly thereafter Walther and F. C. D. Wyneken* went to Ger. to confer with authorities there on the dispute, to do further research for the book at the Erlangen library, and to arrange for its pub.; it appeared in Erlangen 1852. It contains copious testimonies from the ch. fathers and orthodox Luth. theologians and is regarded as a classic statement on ch. and ministry.

The 9 theses on the ch. distinguish bet. the ch. in the proper *(eigentlich)* sense of the term, i. e. the communion of saints or the totality of believers in Christ, and the ch. in a figurative *(uneigentlich)* sense, i. e., visible groups, or congs. (particular chs.). The ch. in the proper sense may be described as invisible, though its presence may be identified by concrete marks, namely the Word of God purely preached and the Sacraments administered according to Christ's institution. Walther was contesting the view of Grabau that tended to identify the community of true believers, known only to God, with a particular empirical or institutional form of the ch.

The 10 theses on the office of the pub. ministry were directed in part against what were considered hierarchical tendencies in Grabau's position. They begin by affirming vigorously that the pub. ministry (1) is different from the ministry of the royal priesthood common to all believers, (2) is a divine, not a human institution, and (3) is obligatory, not optional, for the ch. Walther avoided the view (e. g., of J. W. F. Höfling*) that the pub. ministry is merely a derivation of the gen. priesthood, a soc. expediency, a dispensable feature of ch. order left to human discretion. But he held that, though God created the office and calls ministers, the pub. ministry is not a special class in the ch.; it is not an autonomous, self-perpetuating institution, indep. of and superior to the gen. priesthood of believers. Rather, the pub. ministry is transmitted *(übertragen;* hence: *Übertragungslehre,* doctrine of transference or transmission) by God through the cong., the possessor of ch. powers. The ministry exercises in pub., on behalf of the corporate body, the same powers that any spiritual priest may exercise privately. The theses guard the rights and responsibilities of the laity and preserve the divine institution, distinctiveness, and inalterability of the pub. office of the ministry.

C. F. W. Walther, *Die Stimme unserer Kirche in der Frage von Kirche und Amt,* [5th ed.] (Zwickau, Saxony, 1911) and "The Church and the Ministerial Office," tr. A. G.[räbner], *TQ,* I (July 1897), 271 to 276; W. Dallmann, W. H. T. Dau, and T. Engelder (editor), *Walther and the Church* (St. Louis, 1938), pp. 47–86. KW

Church and State. 1. Relations bet. ch. and state, individual Christians and govts., organized chs. and civil forms have varied through the centuries.

2. When Christianity first appeared in the Medit. world of the Roman Empire it was confused with Judaism. But soon the distinctions were noted, and Christianity was classified as an unlawful religion *(religio illicita).* Though the early Christians were respectful in submission to the pagan state, their refusal to acknowledge the divinity of the emp. could be construed as disloyalty. Trajan's instructions to Pliny est. a pattern of dealing with Christians, discountenancing Christianity, but not allowing measures against it to become exaggerated. Yet at times violent persecutions broke out. See also *Persecutions of Christians.*

3. The Edict of Milan* (313) by Contantine* I gave official toleration to the Christians, but not preference over other religious bodies. Theodosius* I outlawed pagan worship and declared the Christian religion the religion of the empire (380). Domination of ch. over state, of state over ch., or coexistence of the two seemed to be possible lines of development.

4. In the E Byzantine Empire caesaropapism was adopted; the absolute monarchy obtained supreme control over the ch. and exercised its dominion even in matters normally reserved for ecclesiastical authorities; the ch. in effect became a dept. of the state.

5. In the W, Valentinian III and Theodosius II recognized the pope as head of the W Ch. 445. The decentralized govts. after the "fall" of the Roman Empire (see *Papacy,* 3) permitted the RC Ch. to gain preeminence. In 494 Gelasius I formulated his view on the relationship bet. ch. and state: two powers governed Christendom, the secular and the spiritual, each with its own sphere of action in which the other was not to interfere, the spiritual comparatively the higher of the two. But by 800, with the revival of imperial dignity by Charlemagne,* the W Ch. was threatened at least with a mild form of caesaropapism. About this time the RC Ch. began to augment its territorial holdings, a factor in the relationship bet. the RC Ch. and various states from the 9th to the 20th c.

6. Disintegration of the Carolingian Empire and invasions of the N tribes and Saracens brought on moral and pol. decay, from which the emergence of feudalism rescued Eur. The Cluniac* reform movement and the Hildebrandian papacy (see *Popes,* 7) set aside dominance over the papacy by the Roman aristocracy or the revived *imperium;* Henry IV stood before Gregory VII at Canossa 1077 as a penitent for pol. faults. Acknowledgment of papal suzerainty by R. Guiscard* (1059) and John of Eng. (1213) illustrate the extent of the power of the ch. in the feudal Middle Ages. Resistance of secular rulers may be illustrated by the Constitutions of Clarendon* (1164), enacted by Henry II of Eng., and the

efforts of Frederick* I (Barbarossa) to control the papacy. See also *England,* 3.

7. The 13th c. saw the zenith of papal pol. power in the struggle bet. the *imperium* and the *sacerdotium.* Innocent III defined the *plenitudo potestatis* of the papacy. See *Popes,* 10.) The formulations of Aegidius* Romanus and Augustinus* Triumphus bolstered the "two* swords" theory of papal supremacy. In *Unam sanctam* (1302) Boniface VIII (see *Popes,* 12) claimed that all power, spiritual and temporal, was given to the ch., which controlled temporal power also when exercised by princes. Dante* in *De monarchia* looked for control of all temporal power by a universal monarchy alongside the papacy with its supreme spiritual power. Marsilius* of Padua, together with John* of Jandun, wrote *Defensor pacis* 1324, the classic treatise on supremacy of state over ch.

8. Growth of nationalism and the rise of strong monarchies in W Eur. in the later Middle Ages gave rise to measures against papal claims, including the Pragmatic* Sanction of Bourges 1438.

9. During the Reformation the right of princes to determine the religion of their territories was firmly acknowledged in the Peace of Augsburg* 1555 and reaffirmed in the Peace of Westphalia* 1648. In Eng. Henry VIII's control of the ch. was confirmed 1534 in the Act of Supremacy (reenacted 1559 in revised form under Elizabeth I). Also in RC countries the monarchs obtained a large measure of control over the ch.

10. Luther permitted the princes to take over affairs of the ch. as *Notbischöfe.* This led to Luth. state chs. in Ger. The Scand. Luth. countries, likewise, continued state control of the ch. AC XXVIII set forth distinction bet. the two powers. (See *Luther and Civil Government.*)

11. J. Calvin* upheld a theocratic polity, subjecting state to ch. In the words of the 2d Helvetic Conf. 1566, it is the duty of the magistrate to "advance the preaching of the truth and the [pure and] sincere faith." (See also *Reformed Confessions,* 6.) He has authority, "and it is his duty to take order," according to the Westminster Conf. 1647, "that unity and peace be preserved in the Church, that the truth of God be kept pure and entire," and that ecclesiastical discipline be carried out; the ch. was to be determinative in all the matters. (See also *Presbyterian Confessions,* 3, 4.)

12. Against extreme Calvinism, T. Erastus* in *Explicatio gravissimae quaestionis* maintained ascendancy of state over ch. in ecclesiastical matters. Erastianism* was defended 1594 by R. Hooker* in *Ecclesiastical Polity.* In Ger. it was modified by collegialism.* T. Hobbes* in *Leviathan* set forth a system of pol. absolutism that in its theories of ch.-state relations virtually embraced Erastianism. Under impact of growing secularism and development of toleration extreme Erastianism was modified, as were extreme theocratic views.

13. Views of Anabaptist, Independents, Separatists, and like-minded sectaries also contributed to acceptance of theories that favored separation of temporal and spiritual powers.

14. Such separation was effected in the First Amendment to the Constitution of the US: "Congress shall make no law respecting an establishment of religion, or prohibiting the free exercise thereof." The presence of many nationalities and varied forms of religious belief prevented formation of close ties bet. any one ch. and the state. Writings of J. Wise,* labors of I. Backus,* and efforts of T. Jefferson* and others brought about the establishment and recognition of the voluntary principle. The Virginia Statute of Religious Liberty 1785–86 was the first enactment in the states to grant freedom of conscience. The abolition of support to the Cong. Ch. in Mass. 1833 marked the end of state support for chs. in the US. In the 19th and 20th c. there have been various attempts to subvert the First Amendment. But Supreme Court decisions have maintained separation bet. ch. and state. POAU is among militant groups organized to further separation of ch. and state. Other groups in the US staunchly supporting separation of ch. and state include Baps., Seventh-day Adv., and Jeh. wit. See also *Public Aid to Church-Related Elementary and Secondary Schools.*

15. In Eur. the struggle for separation of ch. and state was esp. violent in Fr., where the Revolution first set aside RCm and replaced it with the cult of reason. The 1801 Concordat* restored RCm, but throughout the 19th c. anticlericalism opposed ultramontanism.* Separation of ch. and state was accomplished in Fr. 1905. In It. and Sp. RCm is the state religion (1966). Port. allows freedom of worship, though RCm is predominant. In Lat. Am. ch. and state are gen. separate. See also *Kulturkampf.*

16. Resurgence of world religions (e. g., Buddhism,* Shinto,* Islam*) has been coupled with nationalism. Esp. the aggressiveness of Islam has worked for union of that religion with the states in which it is predominant.

17. Atheistic Marxist-Leninist socialism has been antagonistic to Christianity esp. in Russia and China. Totalitarianism, esp. Nazism, advanced the omnicompetent state and a nat. religion. In the US in the 20th c. a religion of "Americanism" began to develop. CSM

See also *United States, Religious History of the,* 10.

AC XVI and related literature; G. Hillerdal, *Gehorsam gegen Gott und Menschen: Luthers Lehre von der Obrigkeit und die moderne Staatsethik* (1954); F. E. Cranz, *An Essay on the Development of Luther's Thought on Justice, Law, and Society,* extra number of the *Harvard Theological Review* (Cambridge, Mass., 1959); W. Künneth, *Politik zwischen Dämon und Gott: Eine christliche Ethik des Politischen* (Berlin, 1954); A. P. Stokes, *Church and State in the United States,* rev. ed. by the author and L. Pfeffer, 3 vols. in 1 (New York, 1964); *Church and State Under God,* ed. A. G. Huegli (St. Louis, 1964).

Church Architecture. 1. That specific area of architecture which relates to the construction of houses of worship, concerns the housing of specific liturgies, and acts, as does religious art, as individual and communal expression of faith life. This article deals specifically with architecture executed for the Christian faith, though Hebraic, pagan, and secular influences on Christian architecture could not be ignored in a more elaborate dissertation.

2. From apostolic times to the end of the 15th c. the hist. of architecture was the hist. of ch. bldg. The decline of the ch. at the time of the It. Renaissance (15th–16th c.) also saw a gen. decline in architecture that is only now beginning to abate.

3. The decision of Constantine* I to make Christianity the state religion had momentous effect on Christian art and architecture. Congregations assembled openly rather than in homes of mems. Increase in membership was met with new and impressive architectural settings. Constantine brought much power and wealth to bear. Large, imperially sponsored chs. were soon built in Rome, Constantinople, and throughout the empire. Their basic form was basilican, a combination house, temple, and assembly hall. But this new form was more than a derivation. It had qualities of original creation. Many authorities consider the basilica the most important single architectural form. It was gen. oriented on a longitudinal axis running from W to E. Before entering the ch. proper, the atrium, a colonnaded court, had to be traversed. The far side of the

atrium formed the narthex.* Then came the nave* with its large center aisle and 4 side aisles, 2 on either side. At the E end of the nave was the great (triumphal) arch that framed the altar and the vaulted apse beyond. The altar stood in a separate compartment that was at right angles to the nave and aisles and was called the bema. See also *Orientation of Churches; Trausept.*

4. An important aspect of early Christian architecture was the marked contrast bet. exterior and interior. The exterior was left unadorned, merely a shell whose shape reflected the space enclosed. This ascetic treatment of the exterior gave way very often to utmost richness on the interior.

5. One other type of structure entered the tradition of Christian architecture in the time of Constantine I, namely the round, or polygonal, bldg. crowned with a dome. This type of bldg., developed by the Romans (e. g., the Pantheon), was by the 4th c. given Christian meaning in baptisteries and funerary chapels.

6. Though there is no clear-cut division bet. early Christian and Byzantine art, we find the latter evidencing a more E or oriental influence and style. This shift to the E was completed during the reign of Justinian* I, an art patron equal to Constantine* I. Churches built during his reign exist with much of their original splendor today. The most beautiful examples of chs. built in this First Golden Age survive in Ravenna, It., not in Constantinople, where much was destroyed by iconoclasts. In many respects the most interesting ch. in Ravenna is S. Vitale, completed 547. Of octagonal plan with a domed central core, only the merest remnants of the longitudinal axis of the early Christian basilica remain. From the time of Justinian* I, domed central-plan chs. were to dominate the world of Orthodox Christianity, while the basilica plan dominated the architecture of the medieval W. The most important ch. from this period existing in Constantinople is Hagia Sophia (St. Sophia; Holy Wisdom), one of the outstanding creative triumphs of all time; in Byzantine architecture it is unmatched in monumental ambitions and engineering genius. See also *Schism,* 6. Other important structures include St. Mark's, Venice, a fine example from the Second Golden Age, lavishly decorated and beautifully situated, and the cathedral of St. Basil, Moscow, with its fairyland domes.

7. The Middle Ages marked the shift of the center of Eur. civilization from the Medit. to the N boundaries of the Roman world. Many factors account for this shift, e. g., the split bet. the RC and Orthodox faiths and the impact of invasions by Germanic tribes. These factors also contributed to artistic and architectural changes in Eur. The Carolingian age under Charlemagne* produced fine chs., particularly the Palace Chapel at Aachen and Abbey Ch. of Saint-Riquier, Fr. But 1000 marks an important point in the development of ch. architecture. Possibly expectation of the millennium led to few chs. built 600–1000. Certainly the Crusades* and simultaneous growth of religious enthusiasm created desire for new chs. New wealth and the new middle class of craftsmen and merchants helped recapture the power and imaginative bldg. of ancient Rome; hence the name Romanesque. Chs. not only became more numerous but also were gen. larger, more richly decorated, and looked more "Roman" since their naves used vaults and, unlike any previous ch. styles, used architectural ornamentation and sculpture on exteriors. Romanesque chs. of importance are scattered throughout what was at that time the RC world: from N Sp. to Ger., from Cen. It. to N Eng. The finest, most inventive, and greatest variety are in Fr. Of these a few bear special mention: St. Sernin, Toulouse, illustrates a high degree of regularity in its plan; Notre-Dame-la-Grande, Poitiers, is particularly noteworthy for its elaborately bordered arcades; St. Etienne (Abbaye-aux-Hommes), Caen, is important because of systematic use of the ribbed groin vault above the nave. The cathedral at Durham, Eng., chiefly in Norman Romanesque, is noted for the proportionate disposition of its masses. The design of the imperial cathedral at Speyer helps convey a feeling of sheer enormity. The cathedral at Pisa is unique for the delicacy and color of its exterior. All these chs. displayed extraordinary inventiveness by architect-engineer and artist. Use of buttresses, ribbed groined vaults, and sculpture, plus striving for height and light, mark this 200-yr. period as one of the most inventive times, architecturally speaking, since ancient Greece.

8. It would be wrong to describe Gothic as a synthesis of Romanesque traits. Such an idea would not explain the new spirit of Gothic, the emphasis on strict geometric planning, and the search for delicacy and luminosity. There was a kind of quest for sacred mathematic. Harmony (the perfect relationship among parts in terms of mathematical proportions and ratios) was the source of beauty, symbolizing the laws according to which, in Gothic thought, divine reason constructed the universe. The search for height and light reached its crest, and light streaming through stained glass became symbolic of mystic revelation of the Spirit of God.

9. The engineering "experiments" of the Romanesque era were continued and refined. Architectural details were more rationally planned and executed. Rather than using a "horseshoe" or rounded arch with its restrictions, Gothic architects used the pointed arch, which could be more loftily extended. Vaulting became more flexible; areas of any shape could be covered. Buttressing was now more fully understood, and the resultant delicacy achieved on exteriors created a more successful aesthetic solution than that found in Romanesque structures. Use of sculpture as architectural detail, begun by Romanesque architects, was carried to a precise and refined role on Gothic chs. Particularly facades used niches and piers onto and into which sculpture was placed, making the entire structure a kind of carving.

10. The most significant Gothic cathedrals are in Ile-de-France. Cathedrals at Paris, Chartres, Reims, Rouen, and Amiens compete as national monuments. Such concentrated expenditure of effort and money has seldom been seen. It was an expression of the combined religious and patriotic fervor of the Gothic age that reached its peak by the middle of the 13th c. Then work slowed, projects became less ambitious, and architectural concerns deteriorated to concentration on decoration rather than structure. See also *Notre Dame Cathedral of Paris, France.*

11. Outside Fr. the Gothic style received wide acceptance. Eng. proved very receptive to it; excellent examples are found at Salisbury, at Gloucester, and in Henry VII's Chapel, Westminster Abbey, London. From ca. 1250 Gothic had strong impact in Ger. The cathedral at Cologne was begun 1248 but not completed till modern times. The ch. of St. Sebald, Nürnberg, is an excellent example of Ger. Gothic. But It. had great difficulty with Gothic. The closer one gets to Rome, the less good Gothic is found. Probably the most truly Gothic ch. in It. is the Milan cathedral. Though ambitious, the building lacks cohesion and has come to be one of the world's architectural jokes.

12. The It. Renaissance cannot be said to have contributed any great concepts to the development of church architecture. Humanism overtook the ch., and its architecture shows it. St. Peter's, Rome, is spectacular; that is why it was built. No uniform spiritual motivations are evidenced. The importance

of bldg. seemed to be to display theories that had been expounded 1,500 yrs. earlier.

13. It is not right to reject out of hand all chs. built from the Renaissance to the present. St. Paul's, London, was rebuilt in Eng. Renaissance style according to designs of C. Wren* after the Great Fire of 1666. Even the rococo style produced some amazing chs. The Ch. of Our Lady, Zwiefalten, S. Ger., is an amazing blend of painting, sculpture, and architecture; but one must ask if it is a ch. or simply the reply of the Counter* Reformation.

14. It is a rare event when a ch. is built that shows true architectural inventiveness as well as understanding of the building's function. New technical advances and materials have resulted in new approaches and solutions. Often results have shown lack of sincerity either in the client or architect, or both. Successful examples show proper and vital approach to the liturgical function of the place and not simply architectural ingeniousness. Eur. has provided the most successful chs., designed by such architects as Auguste Perret and Le Corbusier of Fr., and Dominikus Böhm, Rudolf Schwarz, and Otto Bartning of Ger. These showed great architectural ability, responsibility to the time in which they worked, and knowledge of liturgies involved.

15. Outstanding US ch. architects of the past and present include Ralph Adams Cram, Eero Saarinen, Pietro Belluschi, Edward A. Sovik, Charles Stade, Gyo Obata, and Edward Dart; these, and a few others, have shown rare ability to design a ch. from the inside out. Such men as Adalbert R. Kretzmann and Edward S. Frey have done much to keep theol. concerns foremost in ch. bldg. The Am. Soc. for Ch. Architecture and the Ch. Architectural Guild of Am. provide resources for those interested in knowing more about ch. architecture. No one form will answer the problem of ch. design. Various forms arise at the intersection of God's action toward man and man's response to God in community with his fellowmen. Only God, in His rightful place in the lives of people, can make a bldg. a ch. RRCj

See also *Art, Ecclesiastical and Religious; Building Program, Parish; Theology; Transept.*

A. Christ-Janer and M. M. Foley, *Modern Church Architecture* (New York, 1962); K. M. McClinton, *The Changing Church* (New York, 1957); J. Pichard, *Modern Church Architecture,* tr. E. Callmann (New York, 1960); J. I. Sewall, *A History of Western Art* (New York, 1953).

Church Army. See *Carlile, Wilson.*

Church Assembly. See *England,* C 9.

Church Buildings. See *Church Architecture.*

Church Calendar, Lutheran. See *Church Year,* 16.

Church Center. See *Denmark, Lutheranism in,* 8–9.

Church Commissioners. See *England,* C 9.

Church Conflict. See *Berggrav, Eivind; Kirchenkampf.*

Church Congress. Unofficial meeting of lay and clerical delegates of the Ch. of Eng.; first such congress was held 1861.

Church Discipline. See *Discipline, Church.*

Church Expectant. See *Church Suffering.*

Church Extension Fund. See *Finances in the Church,* 7.

Church Fathers. See *Fathers of the Church.*

Church Festivals. See *Church Year.*

Church Furniture. 1. In the furniture of the chancel* the altar* stands first, not because a special intrinsic value attaches to it, but because it is the place of prayer and the table for the distribution of the Lord's Supper (1 Co 10:21; in the E Orthodox and Angl. liturgies the altar is called the "Lord's Table," a term occasionally found in gen. Prot. circles). Its antecedents were altars for sacrifice and tables for incense. The mensa* is used for service books and the Communion vessels, a special shelf usually holding the cross (see *Cross,* 4) and candelabra (see 2). The reredos is the screen, or partition wall, behind the altar and is often elaborate with ornament and religious symbolism, usually triptych in form (3 compartments side by side). Altar paintings or statues are usually placed high so as not to interfere with the cross. The pulpit (elevated preaching stand) is, as a rule, on the Gospel* side of the chancel (formerly in the center in many Prot. chs.). Some Prot. chs. used merely a desk on a raised platform; more formal chs. built pulpits that rise from a single shaft or stem and are richly decorated. Panels of the railing may be carved in rich effects or constructed in the form of niches, with statues of the evangelists or major prophets (see *Prophecy*). The baptismal font should have a definite, permanent place, either in a special baptismal chapel or at the entrance of the sanctuary, but not so as to interfere with movement of communicants. Some fonts are sculptured of marble with a cover of like material or of ebony wood. Simplest fonts consist of a pedestal and basin holder; others are elaborate with sculpture. The lectern (reading desk from which Scripture lessons are read) takes the place of the ancient ambo (elevated pulpit in early Christian chs.; often there were two, one for reading the Gospel, one for the Epistle). Among forms of lecterns is that of an eagle with wings partly extended, symbol of John the Evangelist. See also *Epistle Side of Altar.*

2. A special shelf above the mensa (see 1) is designed to hold the cross (see *Cross,* 4) or crucifix* and candelabra (branched candlesticks, usually ornamented). Though the Luth. Ch. defended the crucifix against iconoclastic tendencies, many of its mems. have advocated return to the plain cross.

3. The pieces of a regular Communion set are chalice,* or cups for distributing the wine, flagon,* paten,* and ciborium.*

See also *Piscina; Symbolism, Christian.*

E. Geldart, *A Manual of Church Decoration and Symbolism* (London, 1899); J. C. Cox, *English Church Fittings, Furniture, and Accessories* (London, [1923]); E. J. Weber, *Catholic Ecclesiology* (Pittsburgh, 1927); F. R. Webber, *The Small Church,* rev. ed. (Cleveland, 1939); J. B. O'Connell, *Church Building and Furnishing* (Notre Dame, Ind., 1955); P. F. Anson, *Fashions in Church Furnishings 1840 to 1940* (London, [1960]); J. F. White, *Protestant Worship and Church Architecture* (New York, 1964); P. H. D. Lang, *What an Altar Guild Should Know* (St. Louis, 1964).

Church Government. See *Polity, Ecclesiastical.*

Church History. See *Christian Church, History of.*

Church Invisible. See *Church,* 3.

Church Law of 1686 (Sweden). See *Sweden, Lutheran Church in,* 2.

Church Militant. Ecclesiastical term denoting mems. of the ch. on earth as distinguished from the church* triumphant.

Church Mission Society (Dan.). See *Danish Lutherans in America,* 3.

Church Missionary Society (Angl.). Founded at London Apr. 12, 1799, as Soc. for Missions in Afr. and the E; preparations for a med. miss. dept. began 1882; women's dept. fully organized 1895. Fields include Afr., Ceylon, India, Pakistan, Iran, Palestine, and the Far E.

Church Modes. See *Modes, Ecclesiastical.*

Church Music. See *Music, Church.*

Church of Central Africa. See *Africa,* B 2.

Church of Christ (Latter Day Saints). See *Latter Day Saints,* g 3.

Church of Christ (Holiness) U. S. A. Organized 1896 at Jackson, Miss., by C. P. Jones, a Bap. preacher. Episc. govt. Emphasizes original sin, atonement, gift of the Holy Ghost, baptism by immersion,

Lord's Supper, foot washing, and divine healing.

Church of Christ (Temple Lot). See *Latter Day Saints,* g 3.

Church of Christ, Scientist. Founded by Mary Morse (nee Baker) Eddy,* who claimed to have experienced a miraculous healing at Lynn, Mass., after reading Mt 9:1-8. Of this experience she says: "It was in Massachusetts, in the year 1866, that I discovered the Science of Divine Metaphysical Healing, which I afterwards named Christian Science. The discovery came to pass in this way. During twenty years prior to my discovery I had been trying to trace all physical effects to a mental cause; and in the latter part of 1866 I gained the Scientific certainty that all causation was Mind, and every effect a mental phenomenon" (*Retrospection and Introspection* [Boston, 1891], p. 32). "I knew the Principle of all harmonious Mind-action to be God, and that cures were produced in primitive Christian healing by holy, uplifting faith; but I must know the Science of this healing, and I won my way to absolute conclusions through divine revelation, reason, and demonstration." (*Science and Health,* p. 109)

She spent 1866–75 in retirement and preliminary work. *Science and Health with Key to the Scriptures* was pub. 1875; all authorized eds. have uniform paging. Scholars have explored the connection bet. the tenets of this book and the metaphysical method of healing of P. P. Quimby,* oriental religions and philosophies, Neoplatonism,* mysticism,* and Gnosticism.*

The Church of Christ, Scientist, was founded in Boston 1879. Christian Scientists from other areas were at first added to this cong. In 1892 the ch. was reorganized and est. as The Mother Church, The First Church of Christ, Scientist; all other Christian Science chs. (ca. 3,200) are branches of it. Its *Church Manual* forbids numbering its mems. and reporting such figures for pub.

The Church of Christ, Scientist, has no clergy; *readers* conduct services; *teachers* instruct classes in Christian Science; *practitioners* engage in healing.

The fundamental principles of Christian Science are: "1. God is All-in-all. 2. God is good. Good is Mind. 3. God, Spirit, being all, nothing is matter. 4. Life, God, omnipotent good, deny death, evil, sin, disease. – Disease, sin, evil, death, deny good, omnipotent God, Life" (*Science and Health,* p. 113). God is "the divine Principle," individual but not personal, reflected by everything real and eternal; as mind He fills all space. Life, truth, and love constitute the trinity. The atonement of Christ exemplifies "man's unity with God, whereby man reflects divine Truth, Life, and Love." (*Science and Health,* p. 18)

Christian Science holds that all reality is in God and His creation, which is good. The only reality of sin, sickness, and death is the fact that unrealities seem real to erring human belief. Its adherents are taught to overcome evil by regarding it as unreality.

Publications: *The Christian Science Journal,* founded 1883; *Christian Science Quarterly,* 1890; *Christian Science Sentinel,* 1898; *The Herald of Christian Science,* 1903, pub. in various languages; *The Christian Science Monitor,* 1908. EL.

See also *New Thought.*

Church of Daniel's Band. See *Evangelistic Associations,* 6; *Holiness Bodies,* 2.

Church of England. See *England.*

Church of England Book Society. Organized 1880 to circulate Christian literature in English and other languages.

Church of England Zenana Missionary Society. Organized 1880 to support CMS work among Indian women.

Church of God. 1. Ca. 200 religious groups in the US use this name in some form, including Pent., Adv., Dunker, Holiness, Winebrennerian, and Mennonite groups. Many are not listed because they object to pub. statistics and other information.

2. Many Pent. reject the use of any name except Ch. of God. Many of these trace their origin to the Latter* Rain Movement started 1886 by R. G. Spurling* and R. G. Spurling, Jr. The father organized a fellowship first called Christian Union in Monroe Co., Tenn. (See *Church of God [Cleveland, Tenn.]*). In 1892 R. G. Spurling, Jr., led a revival near Turtletown, Tenn.; another meeting was held by this group at the home of W. F. Bryant, a Meth. preacher, at Camp Creek, on Burger Mountain, Cherokee County, N. C. The Christian Union was reorganized as the Holiness Ch. 1902. A. J. Tomlinson* joined the group 1903; overseer 1909; impeached 1923; organized Tomlinson Ch. of God (name changed 1953 to Church* of God of Prophecy). When A. J. Tomlinson died 1943, his son Milton A. Tomlinson continued this group; another son, Homer A. Tomlinson, organized followers as The Church* of God.

3. These chs. are agreed in insistence on reestablishing the so-called apostolic ch. order, holding that the Holy Spirit must govern the ch. as He did in apostolic times. They are inclined toward theocratic ch. govt.

4. These chs. stress such fundamental doctrines as inspiration of the Bible, deity of Christ, His atonement, resurrection of the body. They also teach entire sanctification as an instantaneous experience (different from and subsequent to conversion), charismatic gifts in preternatural form (e. g., speaking in tongues), faith healing, imminent return of Christ, and His premillennial reign. In gen. they reject denominational creeds, though some (e. g., at Cleveland, Tenn.) pub. declarations of faith. They gen. adhere to literalistic interpretation of the Bible.

See also the *Church of God* entries that follow.

E. T. Clark, *The Small Sects in America,* rev. ed. (Nashville, 1949); C. W. Conn, *Like a Mighty Army Moves the Church of God, 1886–1955* (Cleveland, Tenn., 1955); see also works listed under *Religious Bodies (US), Bibliography.*

Church of God (Adventist). See *Church of God (Seventh Day), The.*

Church of God (Anderson, Ind.). Founded ca. 1880 by D. S. Warner.* Opposes ecclesiasticism; looks for the ideal NT ch. in a concrete embodiment of Christ's spiritual body. The Prot. Reformation is said to have restored the NT purity of doctrine; the Ch. of God is said to be restoring the NT form of ch. govt. This group holds that the visible ch. must be Spirit-filled and Spirit-directed and that the Holy Spirit will restore such gifts of the early ch. as prophecy, baptism with the Holy Ghost, and divine healing. Pub. house at Anderson, Ind. 1973 inclusive membership: 152,787.

Church of God (Apostolic), The. See *Evangelistic Associations,* 17.

Church of God (Cleveland, Tenn.). Organized Aug. 19, 1886, as Christian Union by R. G. Spurling,* Monroe Co., Tenn.; reorganized 1902 as Holiness Ch.; renamed Ch. of God 1907. Govt. is centralized; state assemblies and annual gen. assemblies; chs. elect their officers. Operates Lee College (Cleveland, Tenn.), 3 Bible schools, 1 preparatory school. Fundamental and Pentecostal in doctrine; emphasizes entire sanctification; regards baptism, Lord's Supper, and foot washing as ordinances; practices divine healing; rejects use of alcohol, tobacco; opposes membership in secret societies. 1973 inclusive membership: 287,099. See also *Church of God,* 2; *Spurling, Richard G.; Tomlinson, Ambrose Jessup.*

Church of God (Greenville, S. C), The. Founded 1925 by J. R. Martin, J. R. Lamb, and Elma S.

Davis. Emphasized that the whole Bible is the Word of God.

Church of God (New Dunkers [Dunkards]). See *Brethren, 5.*

Church of God, The. Organized by Homer A. Tomlinson,* son of A. J. Tomlinson, after the latter's death 1943, as a continuation of the Church* of God movement. Episc. in govt.; officers appointed. Stresses sanctification, baptism of the Holy Ghost, speaking with tongues, miraculous healing. 1973 inclusive membership: 75,890.

Church of God (Seventh Day), The. Two groups withdrew from Seventh-day Adventists (see *Adventist Bodies,* 4) because of disagreement over the name of a new press. They were joined by another group that objected to Mrs. E. G. White's* status as prophetess. These formed the Ch. of God (Adv.) and est. headquarters at Stanberry, Mo. Later this body split into 2 groups centering in Denver, Colo., and Salem, W. Va.

See also *Adventist Bodies,* 4; *Church of God (Seventh Day), Denver, Colo., The; Church of God (Seventh Day), Salem, W. Va., The.*

Church of God (Seventh Day), The (Denver, Colo.). Claims to continue The Church* of God (Seventh Day). Keeps Sat. as Sabbath; believes in imminent, personal, and visible return of Jesus, and that the righteous will inherit the earth forever. Pub. house at Stanberry, Mo.

Church of God (Seventh Day), The (Salem, W. Va.). Governed by an "apostolic council" of 12 "apostles." Ministry supported by tithes. Leaders chosen by drawing names from a hat, because democratic election is considered unbiblical. Seventh day observed as Sabbath. A. N. Duggan, a leader of this group, went to Jerusalem, which he called The World Headquarters of the Church of God. See also *Church of God (Seventh Day), The.*

Church of God, Inc., The (Original). Organized 1886. Claims to be the first ch. organized according to the apostolic pattern. "(Original)" included in name 1917. Headquarters Chattanooga, Tenn. 1973 inclusive membership: 20,000.

Church of God and Saints of Christ. Sometimes called Black Jews; organized 1896 by W. S. Crowdy at Lawrence, Kans.; nat. headquarters at Philadelphia 1900, internat. headquarters at Belleville (near Portsmouth, Va.) 1917. Crowdy and his successors are accepted as prophets divinely called and in true communication with God. This ch. holds the Negro race to be descended from the lost 10 tribes of Israel; claims to follow the Bible rigidly; observes OT customs, esp. the Jewish calendar, Sabbath, OT festival days, tithing, marriage within their own group; also observes baptism by immersion, Lord's Supper, and foot washing.

Church of God as Organized by Christ. See *Evangelistic Associations,* 7; *Holiness Bodies,* 2.

Church of God by Faith. Founded 1919 in Fla. by John Bright. Holds that Christ is only mediator bet. man and God; places hope of salvation in the Word of God as interpreted by Jesus Christ. Teaches regeneration; sanctification; baptism of the Holy Ghost and with fire; speaking in tongues; one Lord, faith, and baptism; isolation of willful sinners from the ch. Gen. Assembly meets 3 times a yr. Officers: bp., overseer, ex. secy.

Church of God General Conference, Oregon, Ill. See *Church of God of the Abrahamic Faith.*

Church of God in Christ (Mennonite). See *Mennonite Churches,* 3 a.

Church of God in Christ, The. Founded 1895 in Ark. by Mason Charles Haerison; inc. 1897. Teaches doctrine of the Trinity, repentance, regeneration, justification. Stresses holiness as prerequisite for salvation, speaking in tongues, divine healing. Regards baptism by immersion, Lord's Supper, and foot washing as ordinances. Its ch. structure (bps., apostles, prophets, evangelists, pastors, elders, overseers, teachers, deacons and deaconesses, missionaries) is regarded as deriving from Scripture. Conducts annual nat. convs.

Church of God in Christ, The, International. Organized 1969 Kansas City, Mo., by bps. of The Church* of God in Christ (organized 1895) as a result of disagreement over polity and governmental authority; Wesleyan in theol.; stresses gift of tongues as evidence of full baptism of the Holy Ghost. 1973 inclusive membership 501,000. See also *Pentecostalism.*

Church of God of All Nations. Small group that withdrew 1957 from Church* of God of Prophecy under leadership of Grady R. Kent in Cleveland, Tenn.

Church of God of Prophecy, The. Traces its origin to 1903, when A. J. Tomlinson* of Culbertson, N. C., was ordained pastor of holiness people who met at Camp Creek, Cherokee Co., N. C., by R. G. Spurling, Jr., and W. F. Bryant. Tomlinson moved to Cleveland, Tenn., 1904; became leader in Christian Union movement (see *Church of God,* 2). Impeached, he organized the Tomlinson Church of God (name changed 1953 to The Church of God of Prophecy). His son, Milton A. Tomlinson, succeeded him as overseer. Doctrines emphasize regeneration, sanctification, baptism with Holy Ghost, divine healing, premillennial return of Christ. Headquarters Cleveland, Tenn.

Church of God of the Abrahamic Faith. Adv. body organized 1888 in Philadelphia as Churches of God in Christ Jesus; permanent Conference organized 1921; corporate name: Church of God General Conference, Oregon, Ill. 1973 inclusive membership: 7,200.

A. G. Huffer, *Systematic Theology* (Oregon, Ill., 1960).

Church of Illumination, The. Organized 1908 by Reuben Swinburne Clymer (b. 1878). Tries to harmonize philos. with religious truth. Teaches spiritual, esoteric, philos. interpretation of the Bible. "Seekers" initiated into mysteries of divine law are the "priesthood of Melchizedek." Holds that man must unearth his soul (called Christos and regarded as a spark of the divine) from deep debris and bring it into consciousness in a process called regeneration. Headquarters Quakertown, Pa.

R. S. Clymer, *The Teachings of the Masters: The Wisdom of the Ages,* enl. and rev. ed. (Quakertown, Pa., 1952) and *Manual: Order of Service and Ritual: Church of Illumination* (Quakertown, Pa., 1952).

Church of Jesus Christ (Bickertonites). See *Latter Day Saints,* g 4.

Church of Jesus Christ (Cutlerites). See *Latter Day Saints,* g 5.

Church of Jesus Christ (Strangites). See *Latter Day Saints,* g 6.

Church of Jesus Christ of Latter-day Saints. See *Latter Day Saints.*

Church of Jesus Christ of Latter Day Saints, Reorganized. See *Latter Day Saints,* g 2.

Church of North India. Inaugurated Nov. 29, 1970, at Nagpur. United the Ch. of India, Pakistan, and Ceylon (Angl.); United Ch. of Northern India (a Presb.-Cong. union); Meth. Ch. (Brit. and Australian conferences); Conference of Bap. Chs. in North India; Disciples Ch.; Ch. of the Brethren. See also *England,* C 12.

Church of Our Lord Jesus Christ of the Apostolic Faith, Inc. Organized in Ohio; moved to New York, N. Y., 1919. Claims to be the true ch. according to apostolic basis.

Church of Revelation, The. Organized 1930 by Janet Stine Wolford at Long Beach, Calif.; practices various forms of healing. 1973 inclusive membership; 750.

Church of Scotland. See *Presbyterian Churches,* 1.

Church of South India. Formed Sept. 27, 1947, by the Angl. chs. of S India, Burma, and Ceylon, most of the S India United Ch. (Congregationalists, Presbyterians, Evangelicals), and Meth. chs.; membership ca. 1,000,000. See also *India,* 14.

Church of Sweden Mission, The. See *Swedish Missionary Societies,* 3.

Church of the Air, Columbia. See *Radio and Television Evangelism, Network,* 3.

Church of the Brethren (Conservative Dunkers). See *Brethren,* 2.

Church of the Brethren Youth Fellowship. See *Young People's Organizations,* III 16.

Church of the Desert. See *France,* 10.

Church of the Disciples. See *Clarke, James Freeman.*

Church of the East (Assyrians). Aramaic-speaking Am. branch of the E Orthodox Ch.; patriarch resides at Seleucia-Ctesiphon, Chaldea, Mesopotamia. See also *Eastern Orthodox Churches,* 6.

Church of the Foursquare Gospel, The International. See *Foursquare Gospel, The.*

Church of the Full Gospel, Inc. See *Baptist Churches,* 32.

Church of the Gospel. Organized 1911 Pittsfield, Mass. Stressed holiness of heart, discipleship, baptism by immersion.

Church of the Living God. 1. The Church of the Living God (Motto: Christian Workers for Fellowship) was organized 1889 at Wrightsville, Ark., by William Christian (b. Miss. 1856; d. Memphis, Tenn., 1928), who claimed a divine call to create the office of chief. He held that Freemasonry has the true mode of religion, called his group an "organism . . . known as operative Masonry" with baptism, Holy Supper, and foot washing as its "first three corporal degrees." Other features include tithing and believer's baptism by immersion; chs. are called temples.

2. In 1919 a group seceded from the Church of the Living God, largely because of differences regarding management, and adopted the name House of God, Which Is the Church of the Living God, the Pillar and Ground of the Truth, Inc.

See also *Holiness Churches,* 2.

Church of the Lutheran Brethren of America. Organized 1900 at Milwaukee, Wis., by Norwegians influenced by revival that swept through the Norw. settlements in the 1890s; 5 congs. were original nucleus; 1st spiritual leader was K. O. Lundeberg.* Emphasizes conscious experience of conversion, godly life, nonliturgical forms of worship, lay activity, miss. work. Accepts only those into membership who profess personal experience of salvation. Has done extensive miss. work in China, Afr., Jap., and Formosa. Operates Broen Memorial Home, Fergus Falls, Minn., and Sarepta Home, Sauk Centre, Minn. Seminaries: 1. Luth. Brethren Schools (Hillcrest Luth. Academy) est. 1903 at Wahpeton, N. Dak., as Luth. Bible School; to Grand Forks, N. Dak., 1915; to Fergus Falls, Minn., in the 1930s. 2. École Biblique Centrale, Kaélé, Cameroon, Afr. 3. École Biblique Centrale, Gouna Gaya, Chad, Afr. 1972 inclusive membership: 9,960. See also *Africa,* F 7; *Ministry, Education of,* VIII C 2 1; XI A 1, 16.

Church of the Lutheran Confession. This group of Luths., mostly from the Wis Syn., the ELS, the Orthodox Luth. Conf., and the LCMS, adopted a const. at Watertown, S. Dak., Aug. 9–12, 1960 (additions Aug. 6–11, 1964); formally organized and elected the 1st permanent officers (1st pres.: Paul Albrecht) Jan. 1961, at Sleepy Eye, Minn. The const. lists the following purposes: A. To aid its mems. so that all things may be done decently and in order; B. To afford its membership additional opportunities and facilities for the exercise of Christian stewardship in the service of the Lord Jesus Christ, in accordance with the commands and promises of His Word; C. To facilitate the exercise of true Christian fellowship and to help maintain the same through mutual strengthening and fraternal vigilance, in keeping with the will of God; D. To protect this fellowship against encroachment of error and unionism through united testimony and doctrinal discipline.

This ch. accepts the canonical Scriptures as verbally inspired; 3 ecumenical creeds; Book of Concord of 1580; Brief* Statement of 1932. It defines its position in the statements *Concerning Church Fellowship; Theses on the Relation of Synod and Local Congregation to the Holy Christian Church;* and *Theses on the Ministry of the Keys and the Public Ministry.* It owns and controls Immanuel Luth. Coll., Eau Claire, Wis., and pub. the *Journal of Theology.* It has a miss. in Tokyo, Japan. 1973 inclusive membership: 9,490. Its greatest concentration of chs. is in Wis. and S. Dak.

Church of the Nazarene. 1. One of the larger groups emerging from the holiness movement (see *Holiness Churches,* 1). Organized Pilot Point, Tex., 1908. Its theol. and doctrinal foundations are in holiness and sanctification as taught by J. Wesley.*

2. In Brooklyn, N. Y., the Utica Ave. Pent. Tabernacle was founded 1894, the Bedford Ave. Pent. Ch. and the Emmanuel Pent. Tabernacle 1895; these 3 formed the Assoc. of Pent. Chs. of Am. 1895; were joined 1896 by chs. of the Cen. Ev. Holiness Assoc., a New Eng. group.

3. In 1895 a First Ch. of the Nazarene was organized in Los Angeles, Calif.; it formed an organization called Ch. of the Nazarene with related chs. as far E as Chicago; this group united 1907 with the Assoc. of Pent. Chs. of Am. at Chicago to form the Pent. Ch. of the Nazarene. *Basis of Union* was the merger document.

4. In 1894 a Ch. of Christ was organized in Tenn. and spread through Ark. and W Tex. Holiness chs. were organized 1898 in Tex., the first Indep. Ch. of Christ 1900. These groups merged 1904 to form the Holiness Ch. of Christ, which joined the Pent. Ch. of the Nazarene at Pilot Point, Tex., Oct. 1908. This is usually considered the beginning of the Ch. of the Nazarene.

5. Holiness people of Tenn. formed the Pent. Alliance (later called Pent. Miss.) 1898; joined the Pent. Ch. of the Nazarene 1915; Pentecostals of Scot. also joined the group 1915.

6. Name changed 1919 to Ch. of the Nazarene. "Pentecostal" was dropped to avoid confusion with "tongue talking" groups.

7. The *Manual* is largely influenced by the Meth. *Discipline.* Since mems. came from Episc., Cong., Presb., and Meth. backgrounds, the *Basis of Union* sought a middle course by giving organized chs. the right of indep. action subject to Gen. Assembly approval and at the same time entrusted the care of the chs. to supts.

8. Teaches divine inspiration of the canonical Scriptures; Trinity; deity of Christ; atonement; justification; regeneration; 2d coming of Christ; resurrection; judgment; eternal bliss; and damnation. Holds that original depravity is corruption by reason of which everyone is "very far gone" so that no one can convert himself without the grace of God by Christ assisting him. Distinctive tenets are divine healing (but not to exclusion of medical agencies), entire sanctification (as 2d work of grace subsequent to regeneration), Holy Spirit's witness to such sanctification. Baptism (adults and children; pouring, sprinkling, or immersing) and the Lord's Supper (only unfermented grape juice used) are

divine ordinances. Opposes use of tobacco and alcohol. Applicants for membership are required to show evidence of salvation by following rules of behavior in *Manual.*

9. 1973 inclusive membership: 394,197.

Manual of the History, Doctrine, Government, and Ritual of the Church of the Nazarene, 1923, 4th ed. (Kansas City, 1924); *Journal of the Sixth General Assembly of the Church of the Nazarene,* eds. E. J. Fleming and C. A. Kinder (Kansas City, [1923]); J. B. Chapman, *A History of the Church of the Nazarene* (Kansas City, 1926); E. T. Clark, *The Small Sects in America,* rev. ed. (Nashville, 1949); see also *Religious Bodies (US), Bibliography.* EL

Church of the New Jerusalem. See *Swedenborgians.*

Church of the Seven Ecumenical Councils. See *Eastern Orthodox Churches,* 1.

Church of the United Brethren in Christ, The. See *United Brethren.*

Church Orders *(Kirchenordnungen).* Regulations, under the gen. ecclesiastical const. of a state, by which canonical ch. forms that had previously prevailed in a land or city were modified in agreement with directions drawn up by men representing the Reformation, while the newly developing ch. system became progressively est. Those of the 16th c. are the most important. They usually open with a statement of the doctrinal position of the country or state or city, followed by regulations concerning the liturgy, the appointment of ch. officers, and the whole administration of the various congs. included in the resp. jurisdiction. Since later compilations often used earlier, acknowledged forms, the orders are grouped in families, by countries or districts.

L. D. Reed, *The Lutheran Liturgy,* rev. ed. (Philadelphia, [1960]); C. Daib, "Church Order and the Confession," *CTM,* XVII (Feb. 1946), 128–138.

Church Peace Mission. Formed 1950 in Detroit by Quakers, Mennonites, and Brethren to coordinate peace efforts.

Church Peace Union. See *Council on Religion and International Affairs.*

Church Polity. See *Polity, Ecclesiastical.*

Church School. See *Parish Education.*

Church Social League. See *Christian Socialism,* 2.

Church Society for Inner Mission. See *Denmark, Lutheranism in,* 10.

Church Struggle. See *Kirchenkampf.*

Church Student Movements. See *Students, Spiritual Care of.*

Church Suffering (Church Expectant). RC term denoting the souls in purgatory.*

Church Tones *(Kirchentöne).* See *Modes, Ecclesiastical.*

Church Triumphant. 1. Ecclesiastical term denoting the mems. of the ch. who enjoy bliss of union with Christ in the hereafter. (See also *Hereafter,* A, C 1, 2). In the terminology of the E Orthodox Ch. the ch. triumphant is equivalent to the ch. invisible (see *Church,* 3).

2. See *Communistic Societies,* 5.

Church Usages. See *Adiaphora; Agenda; Liturgics.*

Church Visible. See *Church,* 3.

Church World Service. Dept. of the National* Council of the Churches of Christ in the USA that engages in relief work in war-stricken and other needy areas. Founded 1946.

Church Year. 1. The ch. yr. may be divided into 6 seasons, opening with Adv. The early part of this season is devoted to discussion of eschatological subjects in the lessons and liturgy; in the latter part, esp. on and after the 4th Sun. in Adv., the Christmas theme is prominent. The Christmas Festival, Dec. 25 in the W, is the 1st primary festival, with 2 or 3 days at times devoted to its observance (see also *Christmas*). It is followed by the feasts of St. Stephen (Dec. 26), St. John the Evangelist and Apostle (Dec. 27), and the Holy Innocents of Bethlehem (Dec. 28). Thus the feast of the birth of the King of martyrs is followed by the "heavenly birthdays" of the first martyr in will and in deed, the apostolic martyr in will but not in deed, and the infant martyrs in deed but not in will.

Note: "Feast" and "festival" are synonymous in this context; both reflect the Lat. *dies festus;* "feasts and festivals" indicates only that both words are used in reference to certain special days other than fast days.

2. The octave of Christmas is the Festival of the Circumcision and the Name of Jesus; it concurs with the New Year's Day of the civil yr. In the W the festival of Epiphany, Jan. 6, recalls the episode of the Magi*; the feast has an octave. The number of Suns. in the post-Epiphany season varies with the date of Easter.

3. The season of pre-Lent (Septuagesima, Sexagesima, and Quinquagesima, the 3 Suns. before Ash Wed., take their names from Lat. words indicating that they fall resp. within 70, 60, and 50 days before Easter) partakes of some of the characteristics of Lent. See also par. 18.

4. The season of Lent, beginning on Ash Wed., is a period of penitential reflection. It climaxes in Passiontide (the last 2 weeks of Lent: Passion Week, the 2d week before Easter; and Holy Week, also called Great Week, formerly called Passion Week, in which Palm* Sun. and the "3 great days," Maundy Thu., Good Fri., and Holy Sat. [also called the Great Sabbath] receive most attention. See 8.).

5. The Easter* season begins on Easter Sun., the 2d great festival of the ch., with 2 or 3 days at times devoted to the contemplation of the resurrection of the Lord; it extends to Ascension Day (see 9). Ascensiontide is followed by Pent. (see 10), the 3d great festival of the ch., at times observed with 2 or 3 festival days. See also *Judaism,* 4.

6. In the 2d part of the ch. yr., the post-Trin. season, there are no festivals of the 1st rank. The number of Suns. after Trin. (or after Pent.) varies with the date of Easter. See also par. 18.

7. The ch. yr. developed slowly. At first the Good Friday–Easter event was thought of as being commemorated every week. The 1st festival commemorated annually was Easter. An early controversy about the date of Easter was settled 325 by the Council of Nicaea,* which decreed that Easter be celebrated on the 1st Sun. after the 1st full moon on or after the spring equinox, or one week later if the full moon falls on Sun. See also *Easter Controversy.*

8. From early days Easter was preceded by a period of preparation called Lent. The custom of fasting* during this time was gen. at an early date, but the length of the fast varied. Finally the fast was extended to 40 days, after the analogy of the period of the Lord's temptation, Mt 4:2. Ash Wed. (so called from the custom of daubing the foreheads of worshipers on that day with ashes of the previous yr.'s palms, in token of penitence and human mortality) has been the 1st day of Lent since the Gelasian* Sacramentary. The season of preparation for Easter closed with the Great Week, also called Holy Week. Wed. of Holy Week was formerly call Spy Wed. by some because of the preparations of Judas for betraying Christ. Thu. of Holy Week commemorated the institution of the Lord's Supper; it was called Holy Thu. by some; its Ger. name is *Gründonnerstag** (Green Thursday); since the Gospel of the day was Jn 13:1-15, the day was also known as the Day of Foot Washing; its present Eng. name, Maundy Thu., is derived either from the words of Jn 13:34 (Lat. *Mandatum novum do vobis*) or from the custom of carrying gifts to the poor in maunds

(hand baskets) on that day. Good Fri. (Ger. *Karfreitag,* a name expressing sorrow) was a day of deep mourning, with a complete fast till 3 or 6 o'clock in the afternoon.

9. Forty days after Easter (Acts 1:3) came the Festival of the Ascension, which seems to have originated in the 4th c.

10. Pent. (from Gk. *pentekostos,* "fiftieth"), the 50th day after Easter, can be traced to the 3d c. It is also called Whitsunday (very likely from white garments worn on that day), esp. in Eng. Tertullian* calls the whole time from Easter to Pent. by the latter name and gives each day of the entire period the importance and dignity of a Sun.

11. In the early ch. less stress was laid on the birthday of the Lord than on the fact that the Son of God became man (Jn 1:14). Accordingly we find a festival celebrating this fact as early as Clement* of Alexandria (beginning of the 3d c.). The 6th of Jan. was the accepted date for the Festival of Epiphany, or the Manifestation of the Lord, at the end of the 3d c.; it commemorated not only the birth of Christ, but also His baptism and, in some cases, His first miracle, thus expressing very well the gen. idea of the revelation and manifestation of the divinity of Christ in His humanity.

12. Just as Easter had its special season of preparation, so a similar period was set aside before Christmas. The length of the Adv. season varied according to the ancient Comites (see *Comes*), Milan observing 5 Suns., Rome only 4. Finally the custom of having 4 Suns. was gen. accepted.

13. After the 5th c. the number of festivals in the ch. increased rapidly. With increasing veneration of Mary her festivals gained ground. The Festival of the Annunciation (also called Lady Day), celebrating the conception of our Lord, was fixed for Mar. 25, and that of the Presentation of Our Lord and the Purification of Mary for Feb. 2; the latter festival is known in Eng. as Candlemas, from the custom of blessing candles, carrying them in procession, and holding them lighted during the reading of the Gospel and from the Sanctus through the Communion. Mary's meeting with Elizabeth is commemorated on the Feast of the Visitation, July 2.

14. Naturally the feasts of Apostles and Evangelists were soon celebrated, esp. those of Peter and Paul. With the rising tide during the Middle Ages came the many saints' and martyrs' days. All Saints' Day, Nov. 1, commemorated all the saints together and All Souls' Day, Nov. 2 (Nov. 3 when Nov. 2 is a Sun.), commemorated the faithful departed. Many of the Suns. of the ch. yr. are known by special names, usually after the first words of their resp. introits, the names of the Suns. in Lent being: Invocavit (Ps 91:15 in some old Lat. versions; Vulgate: *clamabit*); Reminiscere (Ps 25:6); Oculi (Ps 25:15); Laetare (Is 66:10); and Judica* (Ps 43:1). The name Palm Sun. is derived from the traditional use of palms in ceremonies of the day. The first 4 Suns. after Easter are Quasimodogeniti (1 Ptr 2:2), or Low* Sun., or Dominica* in albis; Misericordia(s) Domini (Ps 33:5); Jubilate (Ps 66:1); Cantate (Ps 98:1). Rogate precedes the Rogation* Days, from which it takes its name. Exaudi (Ps 27:7).

15. The Luth. reformers of the 16th c. gen. retained the ancient festivals in honor of Christ and the Triune God as a matter of course, preferring also to regard Marian commemorations as Christ festivals. Relatively few commemorations of extra-Biblical saints survived. Economic considerations played a prominent role in reducing the number of saints' days. The Festival of the Reformation, Oct. 31, commemorating the posting of the 95 Theses,* goes back to the 17th c.

16. The ch. calendar in gen. use in the Luth. Ch. may be said to include the following Suns., festivals, and days: A. *Movable.* Four Sundays in Advent; Septuagesima; Sexagesima; Quinquagesima; the Suns. after the Epiphany, ending with the Transfiguration (also kept Aug. 6); Ash Wed.; Invocavit; Reminiscere; Oculi; Laetare; Judica; Palm Sun.; Mon., Tue., and Wed. of Holy Week; Maundy Thu.; Good Fri.; Holy Sat.; Easter and the 2 days following; Quasimodogeniti; Misericordia(s) Domini; Jubilate; Cantate; Rogate; Ascension; Exaudi; Pent. (or Whitsunday); Trin.; and the Suns. after Trin. B. *Fixed.* St. Andrew, Nov. 30; St. Thomas, Dec. 21; Christmas, Dec. 25; St. Stephen, Dec. 26; St. John the Evangelist and Apostle, Dec. 27; Holy Innocents, Dec. 28; Circumcision and the Name of Jesus, Jan. 1; Epiphany, Jan. 6; Conversion of St. Paul, Jan. 25; Presentation and Purification, Feb. 2; St. Matthias, Feb. 24; Annunciation, Mar. 25; St. Mark, Apr. 25; SS. Philip and James the Less, May 1; Birth of St. John the Baptist, June 24; SS. Peter and Paul, June 29; Visitation, July 2; St. Mary Magdalene, July 22; St. James the Elder, July 25; St. Bartholomew, Aug. 24; St. Matthew, Sept. 21; Michaelmas, Sept. 29; St. Luke, Oct. 18; SS. Simon and Jude, Oct. 28; Reformation, Oct. 31; All Saints, Nov. 1.

17. Other commemorations observed by Luths. have included: St. Nicholas, Dec. 6; Christmas Eve, Dec. 24; the Baptism of Our Lord, Sun. after New Year; St. Gregory I (the Great), Mar. 12; the Presentation of the AC, June 25; St. Lawrence, Aug. 10; the Beheading of St. John the Baptist, Aug. 29; the Birth of Mary, Sept. 8; Holy Cross Day, Sept. 14; St. Martin, Nov. 11; St. Catherine* of Alexandria, Nov. 25. The Festival of Harvest (Harvest Home) is often kept on the Sun. after Michaelmas, a Day of Humiliation and Prayer on the Wed. before the last Sun. after Trin., Thanksgiving* Day on the 4th Thu. in Nov. in the US and on the 2d Mon. in Oct. in Can., and the commemoration of the Faithful Departed on All Souls' Day, Nov. 2 (Nov. 3 when Nov. 2 is a Sun.).

18. In the 1970s a movement arose to extend the Epiphany season to the Sun. before Ash Wed. and to have the 2d part of the ch. yr. more gen. recognized as an "after Pent." rather than "after Trin." season. ACP

See also *Departed, Commemoration of; Post-Pentecost Season; Quadragesima; Porate Masses; Thanksgiving Day; Tre ore.*

A. A. McArthur, *The Evolution of the Christian Year* (Greenwich, Conn., 1953); L. Eisenhofer and J. Lechner, *The Liturgy of the Roman Rite,* tr. from the 6th Ger. ed. by A. J. and E. F. Peeler, ed. H. E. Winstone (New York, 1961); G. Rietschel and P. Graff, *Lehrbuch der Liturgik* (Göttingen, 1951); G. Kunze, "Die gottesdienstliche Zeit," *Leiturgia,* I (Kassel, 1954), 437–534; E. T. Horn III, *The Christian Year* (Philadelphia, 1957); L. D. Reed, *The Lutheran Liturgy,* rev. ed. (Philadelphia [1960]).

Churches of Christ. This assoc. of congs. traces its hist. to the Great* Revival under B. W. Stone* and others opposed to every form of denominationalism and "ecclesiasticism." The congs. banded together as the Chs. of Christ must be viewed less as a denomination than as an assoc. of congs. The movement received impetus through the work of T. and A. Campbell,* who held that creeds, confessions, and unscriptural words and phrases contributed to moral decline in Christendom. (See *Disciples of Christ,* 2 a, b). Originally the names of Churches of Christ and Disciples of Christ were used interchangeably by congs. which held that nothing could be tolerated in NT chs. unless it is expressly sanctioned in the Bible. Claiming to follow the example of the primitive ch., they rejected the use of denominational names, creeds, ecclesiastical terminology, and ch. govt. Each local cong. is considered autonomous; ecclesiastical govt. or supervision is viewed as contrary to the NT. When miss. societies were organized on a "money basis" with membership on the basis of fixed annual contributions, when some of the chs. introd. instrumental music and others adopted "unscriptural means of raising money," the Conservatives gradually separated from the Progressives; there is a clear line of demarcation bet. the Disciples of Christ ("Progressives," modernistic) and the Chs. of Christ ("Conservatives," fundamentalistic). The latter group is strong esp. in Tex., Tenn., and Ark. The All-Can. Committee of the Chs. of Christ (Disciples) was organized 1922.

Churches of Christ (Disciples), All-Canada Committee of the. See *Churches of Christ.*

Churches of Christ in Christian Union. Organized 1909 in Ohio by a group that separated from the parent Council of Christian* Union Chs. Holds the 4 basic Holiness principles of regeneration, entire sanctification, divine healing, and the premillennial coming of Christ. Ref. Meth. Ch. (see *Methodist Churches,* 4b) merged with the group 1952. 1973 inclusive membership: 8,771. See also *Holiness Churches,* 3.

Churches of God, Holiness. Organized 1914 in Atlanta, Ga., by a group of 8 under leadership of K. H. Burruss in the interest of Holiness doctrines. See also *Holiness Churches,* 2.

Churches of God in Christ Jesus. See *Church of God of the Abrahamic Faith.*

Churches of God in North America (General Eldership). Organized 1830 in Harrisburg, Pa., by 7 men under leadership of J. Winebrenner* (hence also called Winebrennerians) as Gen. Eldership of the Ch. of God; name changed 1845 to Gen. Eldership of the Ch. of God in N Am., and in 1896 to Gen. Eldership of the Chs. of God in N Am. Local eldership, held to be divinely instituted, consists of a teaching and a ruling elder. Doctrine, set forth in *Twenty-Seven Points of 1849* and *Doctrinal Statement of 1925,* is Arminian. Distinctive views: that sectarianism is anti-Scriptural; that each local ch. should be called Ch. of God; that all such things as ch. offices and customs should be given names drawn from the Bible; that baptism by immersion, the Lord's Supper, and foot washing are obligatory. No written creed is recognized. The Bible is accepted as the only rule of faith and practice. 1973 inclusive membership: 35,833.

Churching of Women. Public thanksgiving in ch. by women after childbirth. The custom is based on Lv 12:6 and is mentioned in a letter by Augustine* of Canterbury to Gregory I. The rite varies in Angl., RC, and Luth. chs.

Churchwarden. Laymen appointed in the Angl. Ch. to assist in managing the temporal affairs of the ch.

Churfürstenbibel. See *Weimarische Bibelwerk, Das.*

Chytraeus, David (Kochhafe; 1531–1600). B. Ingelfingen, Württemberg; studied law, philol., philos., and theol. at Tübingen (influenced by J. Camerarius,* E. Schnepf,* J. Heerbrand*), theol. at Wittenberg (under P. Melanchthon,* M. Luther,* P. Eber*); taught languages at Heidelberg 1546; returned to Tübingen 1547; lectured on rhetoric, astronomy, and Melanchthon's *Loci communes* at Wittenberg 1548; traveled abroad ca. 1550; prof. of religion 1551, theol. 1553 at Rostock. Present at Diets of Augsburg 1555 and 1566, Consultation of Worms* 1557; with other theologians at the 1561 Convention of Naumburg* he warned against "the acceptance of the later editions" of the AC; wrote reactions of Rostock U. to Weimar* Confutation 1567; helped prepare *Kirchenordnung* for Lower and Upper Austria 1569, Styria 1574; mem. of consistory of Rostock 1570; rewrote articles on free will (II) and Lord's Supper (VII) for *Swabian-Saxon Concordia* 1574; one of 17 who prepared *Torgau Book* 1576; produced *Bergen Book* with J. Andreä,* M. Chemnitz,* N. Selnecker,* A. Musculus,* and C. Körner.* Works include *Chronicon Saxoniae; Historia Augustanae Confessionis;* Commentaries. See also *Lutheran Confessions,* C 2. JWM

O. Krabbe, *David Chytraeus* (Rostock, 1870); J. W. Montgomery, *Chytraeus on Sacrifice* (St. Louis, 1962); T. Pressel, *David Chyträus,* in *Leben und ausgewählte Schriften der Väter und Begründer der lutherischen Kirche,* ed. J. Hartmann and others, VIII (Elberfeld, 1862), separate paging 1–48.

Ciborium (Gk. *kiborion:* seed vessel of some Indian and Egyptian plants). 1. Receptacle for the host* of the Lord's Supper. See also *Church Furniture,* 3. 2. Canopy over altar of some chs.

Cicero, Marcus Tullius (106–43 BC). Roman statesman, orator, and eclectic philos. Quaestor in Sicily 75; praetor 66; consul 63; banished 58; recalled 57; proconsul in Cilicia 51–50. Sided with Pompey; later reconciled with Caesar; slain under 2d triumvirate. Fostered study of Gk; noted for his orations, eclectic treatment of philos. and religious subjects. Works include *De natura deorum; De finibus bonorum et malorum; De divinatione; De officiis; De amicitia.*

Cincture. See *Vestments, Clerical,* 1.

Circuit Counselor and Education. See *Parish Education,* L 3.

Circumambulation. Walking round a person or an object to exert influence or bestow honor. Examples are found among people of Indo-Eur. origin. Keeping the object on the right side is believed to produce a beneficial effect; keeping it on the left is thought to have an evil effect.

Circumcellions. See *Donatist Schism.*

Circumcision. See *Judaism,* 1.

Circumcision and the Name of Jesus, Festival of the. See *Church Year,* 2, 16B.

Circumincession; circuminsession. Indwelling of the persons of the Trin. in each other; cf. Jn 10:30, 38; 14:11; 17:21.

Cisneros, Francisco, Jiménez de. See *Jiménez de Cisneros, Francisco.*

Cistercians. Monastic order founded on the Benedictine rule 1098 at Cîteaux, E Fr., by Robert de Molesme (ca. 1029–1111) to counteract the laxity that had overtaken the Cluniac* monks. Also called White Monks because of the color of their habit. Observed extreme simplicity of life, even poverty. Bernard* of Clairvaux entered the order 1112; under his influence and prestige it enjoyed remarkable development; mems. sometimes called Bernardines. The order spread quickly through W Eur. and to Eng. and Wales. It played an important part in Eng. sheep farming and in agricultural development, including horse and cattle breeding, in N and E Eur. But wealth and internal strife combined to result in decline. The most important reform movement launched in the 17th c. to remove these weaknesses was that of the Trappists.*

Cithara Sanctorum. See *Czechoslovakia,* 7.

City Missions. Effort by the ch. to reach with the Gospel the unchurched in poorer sections, slums, and pub. institutions (e. g., hospitals, prisons) of large cities; usually in charge of city missionaries, deaconesses, and soc. workers under ch. supervision.

Civil Constitution of the Clergy. See *France,* 5.

Civil Government. Civil govt. is a divine inst. comprising the whole number of those through whom by divine ordinance the legislative, judicial, and ex. powers necessary for governing a commonwealth are administered in accord with the form of govt. obtaining in that commonwealth (Gn 9:6; Ex 3:1-22; Nm 27:15-23; Jos 1:1-9; 1 Sm 9:16; 1 K 19:15; 2 K 8:13; Dn 2:21, 37; 4:17; Jn 19:10-11; Ro 13:1-6). The duties of civil govt. are to promote the welfare of its people by protecting individuals and groups in their civil rights and to defend the state against dangers from within and without (1 Ti 2:2; Gn 9:6; Mt 26:52; Ro 13:4). Hence the power of the ch. and the civil power must not be mingled or confused (Jn 18: 36; Mt 22:21; Acts 18:12-17. Cf. AC XXVIII). In the administration of its duties, govt. makes use of all ways and means necessary and suitable for the proper discharge of its obligations. In carrying out its functions, govt. follows natural* law, the dictates of reason, experience, and common sense. The relation of mems. of a commonwealth to their govt. is that of subjects to authority. As subjects, they are, for conscience' sake to render their govt. honor, obedience, and service as far as this can be done without violating God's law. See also *Church and State.* PFS

Civil War. See *Slavery and Lutheranism in America; United States, Religious History of the* 14–16.

Clairvoyance. See *Psychical Research.*

Clandestine Engagement. See *Marriage,* II, III.

Clare of Assisi (1194–1253). It. nun; founded, with Francis* of Assisi, the Poor Clares 1212, an order committed to poverty, penance, and contemplation. See also *Franciscans.*

Clarenbach, Adolf (ca. 1500–29). Ref. martyr with Anabap. tendencies. Humanist. Studied at Münster and Cologne; conrector at Wesel 1524; banned; taught Lat. and NT at Osnabrück 1525; banished and went to Lennep 1527. Wrote dogmatic treatise with polemic against Rome. Rejected law; held that faith, hope, and love alone are truth. Arrested at Cologne Apr. 3, 1528; in prison with P. Fliesteden* and burned with him Sept. 28, 1529. Some scholars regard him as Waldensian, others as Luth.

Clarendon, Constitutions of. Sixteen articles, or constitutions, drawn up 1164 at Clarendon, Eng., by advisers of Henry* II. They gave the king much authority in matters of patronage, crimes of clergymen, ecclesiastical trials, ecclesiastical property, election of higher clergy, and other matters. Alexander III (see *Popes,* 9) condemned 10 of the articles, tolerated the others. See also *Becket, Thomas à.*

Clark, Ephraim Weston (Apr. 25, 1799–July 16, 1878). B. Haverhill, N. H. Grad. Dartmouth Coll., Hanover, N. H., 1824, Andover (Mass.) Theol. Sem. 1827; ABCFM miss. to Sandwich Islands (Hawaii); arrived Honolulu in Mar. 1828; helped start miss. in Micronesia 1852; worked on Bible rev.; tr. Bible dictionary.

Clark, Francis Edward (1851–1927). Cong. pastor; founded Christian* Endeavor. Born Francis Edward Symmes at Aylmer, Quebec; orphaned; adopted by uncle; educ. Dartmouth Coll., Hanover, N. H., and Andover (Mass.) Theol. Sem. Pastor Williston Ch., Portland, Maine, 1876; S Boston 1883. Full-time pres. United Soc. of Christian Endeavor 1887; pres. World's Christian Endeavor Union 1895.

Clarke, Adam (ca. 1762–1832). B. Ireland; d. London; studied in Eng.; Meth. 1778; sent out as preacher 1782; traveled throughout Gt. Brit.; denied "the eternal sonship" of Christ; thrice pres. Brit. Conf.; scholar of comprehensive attainments; assisted in preparing an Arab. Bible; wrote an 8-vol. commentary on the Bible.

Clarke, James Freeman (1810–88). Am. Unitarian cleric; grad. Harvard; helped est. the Ch. of the Disciples, a Unitarian ch. in Boston founded in the interest of freedom of individual belief and to apply the Christian religion to soc. problems; secy. Unitarian Assoc.; prof. natural theol. and Christian theol. at Harvard. Works include *Ten Great Religions; Orthodoxy: Its Truths and Errors;* ed. *The Western Messenger.*

Clarke, John. See *Baptist Churches,* 3.

Clarke, Samuel (1675–1729). Eng. divine and metaphysician; chaplain to bp. of Norwich and Queen Anne; disciple of I. Newton*; opposed Cartesianism, deism,* materialism,* freethinkers,* doctrine of Trinity.* Works include *A Discourse concerning the Being and Attributes of God, the Obligations of Natural Religion, and the Truth and Certainty of the Christian Revelation; The Scripture-Doctrine of the Trinity.*

Clarke, William Newton (1841–1912). Am. Bap. clergyman; prof. theol. Colgate U., Hamilton, N. Y., 1890–1908, Christian ethics 1908–12; helped popularize Modernism in Am. theol. sems.; disciple of A. Ritschl*; exponent of the theol. of experience. Works include *An Outline of Christian Theology; The Christian Doctrine of God.*

Class Meeting. Distinctive feature of Methodist* chs.; introd. by J. Wesley in London 1742. A cong. is divided into classes, over each of which the pastor appoints a leader to see each person in his class to inquire concerning his soul's welfare, to advise, reprove, comfort, or exhort, and to receive contributions.

Class Struggle. See *Marx, Karl Heinrich.*

Classic Theory of Atonement. See *Atonement, Theories of.*

Classis. In Ref. chs. (e. g., Dutch and Ger. Ref. chs. in Eur. and Am.) a ruling body corresponding to the presbytery.* See also *Reformed Churches,* 1.

Clauberg, Johann Christoph (1622–65). Prof. Leiden, Herborn, Duisburg; exponent of Cartesian philos.

Claude, Jean (1619–87). B. SW Fr.; d. The Hague; leader of Fr. Ref. Ch.; pastor Nimes, Montauban, and Paris. Works include *Traité de la composition d'un sermon.*

Claudianus Mamertus (ca. 425–ca. 474). Younger brother of Mamertus.* Christian monk and philos.; held soul is immaterial. His *De statu animae* shows influence of Augustine* of Hippo and Neoplatonism.*

MPL, 53, 697–786.

Claudius I (Tiberius Claudius Drusus Nero Germanicus; 10 BC–54 AD). Roman emp. 41–54; expelled Jews from Rome ca. 50–52 and thus helped put Aquila and Priscilla in touch with Paul. (Acts 18:1-2)

Claudius (d. ca. 830). Bp. Turin; noted for Bible commentaries and iconoclasm.

MPL, 104, 609–928.

Claudius, Matthias (1740–1815). Pseudonym: Asmus. Luth. lay poet; defended faith in age of rationalism; ed. *Wandsbecker Bothe.*

Clausen, Claus Laurits (Lauritz; Nov. 3, 1820–Feb. 20, 1892). B. Den.; teacher; lay preacher; went to Norw. 1841; to Am. 1843 to work among Norwegians; ordained by Buffalo Syn. Oct. 18, 1843; pastor in Wis., Iowa, Minn., Va., and Pa.; elected to Iowa state legislature 1856; Commissioner of Immigration 1856–59; army chaplain 1861–62. With A. C. Preus* and H. A. Stub,* the elder, organized Norw. Ev. Luth. Ch. in Am. 1851; helped organize Syn. for the Ev. Luth. Ch. in Am., commonly called Norw. Syn., 1853; its vice-pres.; helped organize The Conf. for the Norw.-Dan. Ev. Luth. Ch. in Am. 1870; its pres.; ed. and author. See also *Danish Lutherans in America,* 3; *Evangelical Lutheran Church,* 7, 8; *Norwegian Evangelical Lutheran Synod of America.*

O. M. Norlie, *Prominent Personalities,* mimeographed (Northfield, Minn., 1942); H. F. Swansen, *The Founder of St. Ansgar: the Life Story of Claus Laurits Clausen* (Blair, Nebr., 1949).

Clausen, Henrik Nikolai (Nicolai; 1793–1877). Dan. theol. Educ. U. Copenhagen; traveled in Eur. 1818 to 1820; influenced by Schleiermacher*; impressed by Rome; lector 1821, prof. NT 1822–74 and dogmatics 1831–74 U. Copenhagen; promoted modified rationalism*; engaged in controversy with N. F. S. Grundtvig.* Works include *Catholicismens og Protestantismens Kirkeforfatning, Laere og Ritus; Christelig Troeslaere.*

Clausnitzer, Tobias (ca. 1619–84). Swed. Luth. cleric, author, and hymnist; chaplain 1644 in Thirty* Years'

War; pastor Weiden, W Ger., 1649–84; mem. of consistory and district inspector there; hymns include "Liebster Jesu, wir sind hier" and "Wir glauben all' an einen Gott."

Claver, Peter. See *Peter Claver.*

Clay, Albert Tobias (Dec. 4, 1866–Sept. 14, 1925). Archaeologist; orientalist. B. Hanover, Pa.; educ. Franklin and Marshall Coll., Lancaster, Pa., and at Mount Airy Sem. and U. Pa., Philadelphia; Assyrian fellow 1892–93, instr. Heb., U. Pa. 1892–95; ordained 1892; pastor Philadelphia and South Bethlehem, Pa., and Chicago, Ill.; instr. OT theol., Chicago Luth. Sem., 1895–99; instr. Heb., Mount Airy Sem., 1905–10; lecturer in Heb., Assyrian, and Semitic archaeology 1899–1903, asst. curator Babylonian and Semitic antiquities 1899–1910, asst. prof. Semitic philol. and archaeol. 1903–09, and prof. 1909–10, U. Pa.; prof. Assyriology Yale 1910–25; curator Yale Babylonian Collection 1912–25; Reinicker lecturer Episc. Theol. Sem., Alexandria, Va., 1908; annual prof. Am. School of Oriental Research, Jerusalem, 1919–20. Ed. cuneiform texts. Works include *Business Documents of Murashu Sons of Nippur dated in the Reign of Artaxerxes I; An Old Babylonian Version of the Gilgamesh Epic on the Basis of Recently Discovered Texts; Amurru, the Home of the Northern Semites; The Empire of the Amorites; A Hebrew Deluge Story in Cuneiform; The Origin of Biblical Traditions.*

Cleanthes (3d c. BC). Gk. Stoic philos.; succeeded Zeno* of Citium. See also *Stoicism.*

Clemen, Ferdinand (d. 1847). Luth. pastor Lemgo, W Saxony; exponent of the Christian awakening* or reaction against the Enlightenment.*

Clemen, Otto Konstantin (1871–1946). Historian. Instr. Zwickau gymnasium; honorary prof. ch. hist. Leipzig 1928; authority on Reformation; contributed to WA; pub. selections of Luther's works with Albert Leitzmann.

Theologische Literaturzeitung, LXXVIII (Aug.–Sept. 1953), 541–560.

Clement I (Clemens Romanus; Clement of Rome). See *Apostolic Fathers,* 1.

Clement III (antipope). See *Henry IV* (Ger.).

Clement V (Bertrand de Got; 1264–1314). B. near Bordeaux, Fr.; pope 1305–14. See also *Babylonian Captivity,* 2; *Christian Church, History of,* II 3; *Decrees and Decretals; Military Religious Orders,* b. *Vienne, Council of.*

Clement VI. See *Babylonian Captivity,* 2; *Jubilees.*

Clement VII. 1. Robert of Geneva (ca. 1342–94); antipope 1378–94 (see *Babylonian Captivity,* 2; *Schism,* 8).

2. Giulio de' Medici (1478–1534). Nephew of Lorenzo the Magnificent and cousin of Leo X (see *Popes,* 20); b. Florence, It.; cardinal 1513; pope 1523–34; taken prisoner 1527 when Rome was sacked by imperial troops; released; returned to Rome 1528; made peace with Charles V; refused to sanction divorce of Henry* VIII from Catherine of Aragon. See also *Holy Leagues and Alliances,* 5; *Medici.*

Clement VIII (antipope). See *Schism,* 8.

Clement VIII (Ippolito Aldobrandini; 1536–1605). B. Fano, It.; pope 1592–1605; issued the Clementine ed. of the Vulgate 1592, standard RC Lat. Bible. See also *Bible Versions,* J 2; *Curia,* 2 d.

Clement XI. See *Unigenitus.*

Clement XIV. See *Popes,* 25.

Clement of Alexandria (Titus Flavius Clemens; ca. 150–ca. 215). Gk. ch. father. Regarded as founder of Alexandria school of theol. Hymnist. B. probably Athens. Date and manner of conversion not known. After conversion he studied in It., Greece, Syria, Palestine, and elsewhere. In Alexandria he succeeded his master Pantaenus* as head of the school ca. 190–ca. 202, when he fled to Palestine under persecution; his pupil Origen* succeeded him as head of the school. Clement agreed with Gnosticism* in emphasis on knowledge but disagreed as to content of true knowledge. For him true knowledge presupposed the apostolic faith of the ch., based on divine revelation; regarded the OT and Gk. philos. as parallel streams leading Jews and Gks. to Christ; sometimes accused of universalism.* Works include *Exhortation to the Heathen; Instructor;* and *Stromata;* all written to show Christianity as the true philos. centered in Christ, the Logos, Mediator of knowledge and immortality to man. Hymns ascribed to him include "Shepherd of Tender Youth," one of the oldest Christian hymns. See also *School Early Christian,* 1; *Tradition.*

R. B. Tollinton, *Clement of Alexandria,* 2 vols. (London, 1914); C. Mondésert, *Clément d'Alexandrie* (Paris, 1944); J. Quasten, *Patrology,* II (Westminister, Md., 1953), 5–36; *MPG,* 8–9. EK

Clementines. 1. Writings ascribed to Clement* I include 2 Letters to the Corinthians; Apostolic* Constitutions; 2 Letters to Virgins; Apocalypse of Clement (Apocalypse of Peter); letters in the Pseudo*-Isidorian Decretals; an Arab. Apocalypse; and 3 specifically called Clementines by convention: Homilies; Recognitions; Epitomes. Only the 1st letter to the Corinthians is considered authentic. See also *Apocrypha* B, 5; *Apostolic Fathers,* 1.

2. See *Canon Law,* 3.

Clerc, Laurent. See *Gallaudet, Thomas Hopkins.*

Clerestory (clearstory). In the basilica and later forms of ch. architecture, the roof of the nave proper was often raised higher than that of the outer aisles; this gave rise to the clerestory: the outside wall, with windows, that supports the center roof; the corresponding interior space is also called clerestory.

Clergy. Those separated to the work of the Christian ministry. The apostolic ch. knew of no ranks in the clergy (see Acts 20:17, 28: "elders" identified with "overseers," i. e. "bishops"). From the time of Cyprian,* father of the hierarchical system, the distinction of clergy (from laity) as an order in the ch. and of ranks in the clergy became universal. In the RC Ch. the clergy became not only a separate order but were regarded as a priesthood with the office of mediatorship bet. God and men. To the distinction of presbyters (elders*) and bps., as differentiated in rank, was added the distinction of various classes of sacerdotal clergy: higher (subdeacon, deacon,* priest, bishop,* metropolitan,* patriarch,* pope*); lower (doorkeepers, lectors, exorcists [see *Exorcism*], acolytes*). Beginning in the later Middle Ages the regular clergy were mems. of monastic orders (under a *regula,* "rule"), the secular* clergy those who live in the world. "Benefit of clergy" was the privilege granted clergymen because of their office, e. g., exception from trial in civil courts (see Ap XXVIII 1, 2); the term refers also to the ministration or sanction of the ch. In Am. the clergy are gen. not considered a separate caste under civil law. See also *Hierarchy; Ministerial Office.*

Clericalism. 1. Principle that gives clergy control over pub. affairs in such areas as educ., marriage laws, and charities. 2. Championing the ch. in conflicts with the state. 3. Assumption by the clergy for its exclusive right of certain functions that belong to the universal priesthood.

Clericis Laicos. See *Bull.*

Clericus, Johannes. See *Arminianism.*

Clerks Regular. In RCm men who combine duties of secular clergy with vows of monks (e. g., Jesuits*).

Clermont, Council of (1095). Presided over by Urban* II; Clermont (ancient Augustonemetum; S cen Fr., ca. 88 mi. E of Limoges; episc. see 4th c.; scene of several councils) was the scene of the launching of the 1st Crusade (see *Crusades,* 1).

Clermont-Ganneau, Charles. See *Geography, Christian,* 5.

Clifford, John (1836–1923). Leader of Baps. in Eng.; concerned with soc. justice; a founder of the Nat. Council of the Ev. Free Chs.; its pres. 1898–99; first pres. Bap. World Alliance (see *Union Movements,* 10) 1905–11; pres. World Brotherhood Federation 1919–23. See also *Baptist Union of Great Britain and Ireland.*

J. Marchant, *Dr. John Clifford* (London, 1924).

Clifford, William Kingdon (1845–79). Brit. mathematician and philos.; educ. Cambridge; prof. applied mathematics U. Coll., London, 1871–79. Held mind is ultimate reality; consciousness built of particles of "mind-stuff." Ethics influenced by evolutionary theory. Conscience and moral law development of "self." Works include *Body and Mind.* See also *Metaphysical Society, The.*

Cloister (ML *claustrum,* "room in a monastery"). 1. Monastery* or convent.* 2. Covered passage on side of a court with one side walled and the other open, usually connecting bldgs. around an open court.

Cloppenburg, Johannes (Cloppenburch; 1592–1652). Neth. Ref. theol.; prof. Harderwijk and Franeker; opposed Mennonites, Arminians, and Socinians; forerunner of federal* theol.

Close Communion. Policy whereby communion fellowship is limited to mems. of a syn. or denomination. See also *Altar Fellowship; Fellowship; Galesburg Rule.*

Closed Season. See *Tempus clausum.*

Clöter, Ernst Ottmar (Ottomar; Apr. 25, 1825–Mar. 17, 1897). B. Bayreuth, Bav.; d. Valley Creek, Minn.; educ. Erlangen, Leipzig; one of Löhe's* missioners; arr. Am. 1849; pastor Saginaw, Mich., 1849 to 1857; miss. to Chippewa (Ojibwa) at Gabitaweegama, ca. 14 mi. N of Brainerd, Minn., W of the Mississippi R., bet. the river and Mission Lake. After the Aug. 1862 Indian uprising laid the miss. station waste, new headquarters were est. at Crow Wing, Minn.; miss. work discontinued here 1868. Pastor Stillwater (Zionsberg; Afton; Lakeland; Valley Creek), Minn., 1868–97; pres. Minn. and Dak. Dist. of the Mo. Syn. 1882–85.

Clovis I (Chlodowech; Chlodwig; ca. 466–511). King of Salian Franks; founded Frankish monarchy; his wife Clotilda persuaded him to be baptized 496; built Ch. of Holy Apostles (later called St. Geneviève), Paris; convoked first Council of Orleans* 511. See also *France,* 1.

Cluniac Reform. The Cluniacs were not properly a distinct order, but were Benedictines* remodeled by the reform movement issuing from Cluny* in the 10th c. This reform purposed to restore the original strictness of the rule of Benedict* of Nursia, esp. as expounded by Benedict* of Aniane. Till then each monastery was an indep. unit; but the houses affiliated with Cluny were absolutely subject to its abbot. Gregory VII used the Cluniac movement in forcing celibacy* on the clergy. By the 12th c. the Cluniac movement was spent and in need of reform. The Cluniac order was dissolved 1790. See also *Cistercians; Majolus.*

Cluny. Commune E cen. Fr. Benedictine* monastery founded there 910 by William I (the Pious; 886 to 918), duke of Aquitaine. From the middle of the 10th to the middle of the 12th c. it was the religious center of W Eur. Bernard* of Cluny was among its outstanding figures. See also *Cluniac Reform; Odilo; Odo.*

Clutz, Jacob Abraham (Jan. 5, 1848–Sept. 7, 1925). B. Adams Co., Pa.; grad. Pa. Coll., Gettysburg, 1869; Luth. Theol. Sem. Gettysburg, 1872; pastor Newville, Pa., and Baltimore, Md., 1872–83; Gettysburg 1904–09; secy. Bd. of Home Miss., Gen. Syn., 1883–89; pres. Midland Coll., Atchison, Kans., 1889 to 1904; prof. Western Theol. Sem., Atchison, 1894 to 1904; Luth. Theol. Sem., Gettysburg, 1909–25; mem. various committees and bds. of Gen. Syn. and ULC; active in formation of ULC. Coed. *Lutheran Missionary Journal* and *Lutheran Quarterly.*

Coadamites. Human beings believed by some opponents of the Scriptural account of creation to have been contemporaries of Adam and Eve, though of different origin; the theory is related to the suppositions of evolutionism. See also *Preadamites.*

Coadjutor. Asst. to a cleric, esp. to an infirm diocesan bp.

Coan, George Whitefield (Dec. 30, 1817–Dec. 21, 1879). Presb. miss. B. Bergen, N. Y.; d. Wooster, Ohio; educ. Williams Coll., Williamstown, Mass., and Union Theol. Sem., NYC; sent to Persia by ABCFM 1849; worked in villages of Persia and Kurdistan.

Coan, Titus (Feb. 1, 1801–Dec. 1, 1882). B. Killingworth, Conn; d. Hilo, Hawaii; educ. Auburn (N. Y.) Theol. Sem.; sent to Patagonia 1833 by ABCFM; returned 1834; arrived Honolulu June 6, 1835; worked at Hilo and Puna, Hawaii; the religious awakening that began 1837 is attributed to his preaching. Works include *Adventures in Patagonia; Life in Hawaii.*

Coat of Arms, Luther's. See *Luther, Coat of Arms or Seal of.*

Cobham, Lord. See *Oldcastle, John.*

Cocceius, Johannes (Coccejus; Koch; 1603–69). Dutch Ref. theol.; b. Bremen; d. Leiden; taught sacred philol. Bremen 1630, Franeker 1636; prof. theol. Franeker 1643, Leiden 1650. Allegorizing and mysterizing exegete; brought covenant theol. (see *Federal Theology*) to its apex. His view that Christian Ch. hist. is foreshadowed in the OT is called Cocceianism. Works include *Summa doctrinae de foedere et testamento Dei; Lexicon et commentarius sermonis hebraici et chaldaici.*

Cochlaeus, Johannes (Dobeneck; Dobenek; Dobneck; Wendelstinus; 1479–1552). RC anti-Luth. controversialist; educ. Nürnberg, Cologne, and in It.; friend of K. v. Miltitz* and G. Aleandro.* See also *Regensburg Conference.*

Cochran, Joseph Gallup (Feb. 5, 1817–Nov. 2, 1871). B. New York state; d. Persia; educ. Amherst (Mass.) Coll. and Union Theol. Sem., NYC; Presb. miss. of ABCFM to Nestorians in Persia; taught at Seir sem. 1851–57; principal 1857–65. Author and tr. in Syriac. Works include schoolbooks; books on Bible geog. and hist., pastoral theol., and homiletics.

Cochrane, Thomas (1866–1953). Studied medicine at Glasgow; sent by LMS as medical miss. to Mongolia; founded Peking Union Medical Coll. 1904; its first head 1906–15; after return to Eng. he founded the periodical *World Dominion* 1923, the Survey Application Trust 1924, and the Movement for World Evangelism 1930. Collaborated with Roland Allen* on *Missionary Survey;* other works include *The Task of the Christian Church.*

Cock, Hendrik de. See *De Cock, Hendrik.*

Codex. (Lat. "trunk of tree; tablet of wood; book"). Bound or unbound MS sheets as distinguished from scrolls. See also *Manuscripts of the Bible,* 2 c, 3 a.

Codex Iuris Canonici. See *Canon Law,* 4.

Codrington, Robert Henry (1830–1922). Brit. miss. in Melanesia and Australasia; ethnologist; linguist.

Coelestius. See *Celestius.*

Coena Domini, In. See *In Coena Domini.*

Coerper, Heinrich (1863–1936). Founded Liebenzeller* mission.

Coffey, Peter (1876–1943). RC neo-Thomist; prof. Maynooth, Ireland, 1902–43. Held that there can be only 1 true philos., namely that which harmonizes natural and revealed truth; regarded Aquinas as starting point for all philos. Works include *The*

Science of Logic; Ontology; Epistemology. See also *Neo-Thomism.*

Coffin, Charles (1676–1749). Fr. RC hymnist; rector Paris U. 1718. Hymns include "On Jordan's Bank the Baptist's Cry"; "The Advent of Our God."

Coffin, Henry Sloane (1877–1954). Am. cleric. Educ. Yale, Edinburgh, Marburg, and Union Theol. Sem., NYC; held pastorates in NYC; pres. Union Theol. Sem. 1926–45; moderator Presb. Ch. in the U. S. A. (see *Presbyterian Churches,* 4a) 1943–44; liberal. Works include *The Creed of Jesus; God Confronts Man in History.*

This Ministry: The Contribution of Henry Sloane Coffin, ed. Reinhold Niebuhr (New York, 1945); M. P. Noyes, *Henry Sloane Coffin: The Man and His Ministry* (New York, 1964).

Cogito, ergo sum. See *Descartes, René.*

Cognac, Holy League of. See *Holy Leagues and Alliances,* 5.

Cognition. Intellectual process whereby knowledge is derived from nonpropositional apprehension (e. g., perception, memory) or ideas (propositions or judgments). Scholasticism* held that all knowing is affection of senses by objects through mediums that supply material foundations for forms within the mind. Abstractive cognition is cognition through other things (e. g., God through creation, Ro 1:20). Quidditative cognition is knowledge of the essence of an object.

Cohen, Hermann (1842–1918). Ger. philos.; prof. Marburg. His neo-Kantianism was thoroughly rationalistic; held that philos. has 3 parts: logic (mathematics), ethics (socialism), and aesthetics (pure feeling). Works include *System der Philosophie; Religion der Vernunft aus den Quellen des Judentums; Ethik des reinen Willens; Der Begriff der Religion im System der Philosophie.*

Coherence Theory. See *Truth.*

Coillard, François (1834–1904). Miss. of the Paris* Ev. Miss. Soc. Worked 20 yrs. in Basutoland before heading up an indigenous miss. organized 1877 by Basuto for work among the Barotse in the Rhodesias. See also *Africa,* B 2, 6.

Coke, Thomas (1747–1814). Welsh cleric. B. Brecon (Brecknock), Wales; Angl. pastor 1770–76 Somersetshire; joined Wesley movement 1777; itinerant minister in and about London; 1st pres. Irish conf. 1782; drafted Meth. miss. program; to Am. with J. Wesley's instructions for organization of Am. Meth. ch. and as supt. 1784; ordained F. Asbury* as supt. of Am. chs. 1784; made 9 trips to Am. 1784–1803; tried to unite Angl. and Meth. chs. in Eng. and Episc. and Meth. chs. in Am.; headed 1st Meth. miss. committee; its pres. 1804–14; successful in for. miss. efforts. See also *Methodist Churches,* 4.

Colani, Timothée (1824–88). Pastor Strasbourg; prof. Fr. literature and philos. at the Strasbourg Prot. sem. 1861 and of homiletics on theol. faculty of the U. 1864. Noted preacher; liberal theol.

Colegio Concordia, Crespo, Entre Rios, Argentina. See *Lutheran Church – Missouri Synod, Districts of The,* B 2.

Colegio Concordia, Obera, Misiones, Argentina. See *Lutheran Church – Missouri Synod, Districts of The,* B 2.

Colenso, John William (1814–83). Angl.; b. Cornwall; educ. Cambridge; 1st bp. Natal 1853; condoned polygamy among converts; denied eternal punishment and traditional authorship and hist. accuracy of Pentateuch and Jos. Deposed 1863 by metropolitan Robert Gray* of Cape Town, but upheld by Judicial Committees of Privy Council. Works include *The Pentateuch and the Book of Joshua Critically Examined;* commentary on the Epistle to the Romans.

Coleridge, Samuel Taylor (1772–1834). Eng. poet, critic, philos., and dramatist. Fond of weird and unusual romantic themes. Deeply impressed by Luther's writings. Borrowed without leave a copy of H. Bell's* version of Luther's Table Talk from Charles Lamb and made notes in its margins; this copy, in the Brit. Museum, is regarded by some as the most precious of all vols. of Luther in English. Viewed Luther as "the only fit commentator for St. Paul . . . not by any means such a gentleman as the apostle, but almost as great a genius." Works include *Aids to Reflection,* a defense of Trinitarian Christianity.

G. Rupp, *The Righteousness of God* (New York, 1953), pp. 49–50.

Colet, John (ca. 1467–1519). Eng. theol.; educ. Oxford; intimate friend of Erasmus*; dean St. Paul's 1504; founded St. Paul's School; humanist.

Colgate Rochester Divinity School. See *Baptist Churches,* 8; *Ministry, Education of,* XII.

Coligny, Gaspard (II) de (ca. 1519–72). Fr. admiral; saved Paris by holding Saint-Quentin 17 days against forces of Philip II of Sp.; captured; converted to Protestantism while imprisoned; released 1559; leader of Huguenots with Louis I de Bourbon, Prince de Condé. Attempted to est. Huguenot colonies in Rio de Janeiro, in Fla., and at what is now Port Royal, S. C.; first victim in Bartholomew's* Day Massacre.

Colin, Jean Claude Marie. See *Marists.*

Cölius, Michael (1492–1559). Friend of M. Luther.* B. Döbeln, Ger.; educ. Leipzig; taught at Döbeln and Rochlitz; ordained priest 1518; opposed, then accepted teachings of Luther; ev. preacher Pensau 1523; persecuted; fled 1525; court preacher of Count Albrecht of Mansfeld 1525; with Luther in the latter's last illness. Wrote, with J. Jonas,* *Vom christlichen Abschied des ehrwürdigen Herrn D. Martini Luthers.*

Collect. Terse, comprehensive prayer. Name derived from Lat. *collectus,* "gathered, bound together," indicates that needs of the ch. are collected and assembled in this prayer of assembled worshipers. The great classic collects gen. contain only 1 petition and are usually addressed to God the Father. The 5 parts of a collect: Invocation (address to God); relative clause (ground on which prayer is offered); petition; purpose (benefit hoped for as result); Trinitarian ending (mediation and ascription). Not all 5 parts need always be present.

Collections in Churches. See *Finances in the Church.*

Collective and Individual. See *Corporate Personality.*

College, Apostolic. 1. RC term for the apostles under the supposed primacy of Peter. 2. RC institutions immediately subject to Rome and under its direction and protection, e. g., the College of Propaganda and certain national colleges, including the Eng.

College and University Work, Commission on. See *Students, Spiritual Care of,* c 2.

College of Cardinals. See *Cardinals.*

College of Life. See *Communistic Societies,* 5.

College of the Bible. See *Ministry, Education of,* XII.

Colleges. See *Higher Education; Ministry, Education of,* VI–VIII.

Collegialism (Collegial System). Ch.-state relations based on natural rights (see *Natural Law,* 5) and voluntarism,* rather than presuppositions of divine institutions. Collegialism holds that the state is a corporate unity formed by a pact of union *(pactum unionis)* in which free men have agreed to be subjects by a pact of subjection *(pactum subjectionis);* the state is an object in itself, existing for the common welfare of its subjects. The ch. is a voluntary, indep. assoc. existing for the spiritual welfare of its mems.; its right of self-govt. *(iura sacrorum collegialia)* can be voluntarily relinquished and right of govt. transferred by tacit or express agreement *(pacto vel tacito vel expresso)* to the ruler of the state; this right of govt., then, is not an inherent right of the ruler of the state, who has inherent right only of supervision of the ch. *(iura sacrorum maiestatica).* Basic concepts of collegialism are traced to S. von Pufendorf,* C. Thomasius,* and, to a lesser degree, H. Grotius.* Its logical conclusions and applications were formulated by C. M. Pfaff.* Other names associated with collegialism are Justus Henning Böhmer (1674–1749) and his son Georg Ludwig Böhmer (1715–97), J. L. v. Mosheim,* G. W. V. Wiese,* and F. D. E. Schleiermacher.* CSM

Collenbusch, Samuel (1724–1803). Ger. lay theol.; b. Schwelm; d. Barmen; leader of a mystic, biblicistic, pietistic movement; his theol. emphasized ethics.

Collin, Nicholas (ca. 1746–1831). Swed. Luth. pastor; arrived in Am. May 12, 1770; pastor Raccoon (Swedesboro) and Penn's Neck (Pennsneck), N. J., and Wicaco (Gloria Dei), Philadelphia, Pa. Prominent in the annals of the Swedes on the Delaware.

The Journal and Bibliography of Nicholas Collin, tr. A. Johnson, introd. by F. H. Stewart (Philadelphia, 1936).

Collingswood Synod of the Bible Presbyterian Church. Organized 1956 by a group representing ca. one-fifth of the membership of the Bible Presb. Ch. (see *Presbyterian Churches,* **4 e**).

Collingwood, Robin George (1889–1943). Brit. archaeol., hist., and philos.; representative of historicism; prof. Oxford. Held that a hist. event has an "inside" and an "outside"; the purpose of hist. is exploration of the human spirit; the presuppositions of religion are hist. conditioned, yet are to be approached with unquestioning acceptance. Works include *Religion and Philosophy; Speculum Mentis; Essay on Philosophical Method; Essay on Metaphysics; the New Levianthan; The Idea of Nature; The Idea of History.*

Collins, Anthony (1676–1729). Deist, freethinker*; b. Heston, near Hounslow, Middlesex, Eng.; educ. Cambridge; friend of J. Locke*; denied OT prophecy, canonicity of NT, immortality of the soul. Works include *Essay on the Use of Reason; A Discourse of Free-Thinking; A Philosophical Inquiry Concerning Human Liberty; Discourse of the Grounds and Reasons of the Christian Religion; The Scheme of Literal Prophecy Considered.* See also *Deism,* III 5.

Colloquy. In the original polity of the Fr. Ref. Ch. a body corresponding to the presbytery*; replaced 1852 by consistory.* Also the name given to a formal theol. discussion.

Collyer, Robert (1823–1912). Cleric and author; b. Keighly, Eng.; to US 1850; blacksmith and M. E. lay preacher; Unitarian 1859; pastor Chicago 1859 to 1879, NYC 1879–1903. Works include *Clear Grit; Some Memories; Thoughts for Daily Living.*

Collyer, William Bengo (1782–1854). B. Blackheath, Eng.; educ. Homerton Coll.; began ministry 1800 at Cong. ch., Peckham, London (the ch. was later enl., then rebuilt and called Hanover Chapel); ordained 1801; also served Salters' Hall Chapel since ca. 1813; preached ev. sermons in contrast to contemporary formalism and Arian doctrine. Compiled a hymnbook containing 57 of his hymns and a wedding book containing 89 of his hymns; hymns include "Morning Breaks upon the Tomb" and "Return, O Wanderer, Return"; other works include lectures on Scripture facts, prophecy, miracles, parables, doctrines, and duties.

Cologne, Cathedral of. See *Church Architecture,* 11.

Cologne Reformation in. See *Hermann von Wied.*

Colombia. See *South America,* 6.

Colonial America, Church in. See *United States of America, Lutheran Theology in,* 1–3; *United States of America, Lutheranism in,* 1–2; *United States of America, Religious History,* 1–11.

Colonial and Continental Church Society. Organized 1823 by chs. of Eng., Scot., and Ireland for work among Eng. residents in colonies and on the Continent; headquarters London.

Colonial Missionary Society. Organized 1836 in Eng. for miss. work in Brit. colonies; headquarters London.

Colonna, Egidio. See *Aegidius Romanus.*

Colored Church, South. See *Christ's Sanctified Holy Church.*

Colored Cumberland Presbyterian Church. See *Presbyterian Churches,* 4 b.

Colored Methodist Church in Louisiana. See *Christ's Sanctified Holy Church.*

Colored Methodist Episcopal Church. See *Methodist Churches,* 4 c.

Colored Primitive Baptists. See *Baptist Churches,* 12.

Colors, Liturgical. Little is known of the origin of their use. Order for their RC use was est. by Innocent III and Pius V (see *Popes,* 10, 21). The basic colors have been retained in Angl. and Luth. chs.

White symbolizes innocence and holiness, majesty and glory, festivity and joy; red, color of fire and blood, symbolizes the Holy Ghost, martyrdom, fervor, and love; green symbolizes hope, peace, and life; violet is the color of penitence and mourning; black symbolizes humiliation, sadness, deep mourning, and death. RC usage also includes rose on Gaudete (3d Sun. in Adv.) and Laetare (4th Sun. in Lent), and allows gold instead of white, red, and green, and silver instead of white.

Basic directives for use of liturgical colors: violet from and with Vespers on the Eve of Advent up to, but not including, Vespers on Christmas Eve; white from and with Vespers on Christmas Eve through the Epiphany Octave, including Vespers on Jan. 13; green from and with Matins on Jan. 14 up to, but not including, Vespers on the Sat. before Septuagesima; violet from and with Vespers on the Sat. before Septuagesima up to, but not including, Vespers on the Sat. before Easter; white from and with Vespers on the Sat. before Easter up to, but not including, Vespers on the Sat. before Pent.; red from and with Vespers on the Sat. before Pent. up to, but not including, Vespers on the Sat. before Trin. Sun.; white from and with Vespers on the Sat. before Trin. Sun. through the Trin. Octave, including Vespers on the 1st Sun. after Trin.; green from and with Matins on Monday after the 1st Sun. after Trin. up to, but not including, Vespers on the Eve on Adv. If special days are observed, the color for the day should be used.

White is proper for Circumcision and the Name of Jesus, John the Apostle and Evangelist, Transfiguration, Conversion of Paul, Presentation, Annunciation, Ascension, Nativity of John the Baptist, Visitation, Mary Magdalene, Michael and All Angels, All Saints' Day, Dedication of a ch. and its anniversary, days of gen. or special thanksgiving; may be used on Maundy Thu. if Communion is celebrated. Red is proper for Reformation and its Octave and on commemorating the death of martyrs: Thomas, Stephen, Holy Innocents, Matthias, Mark, Philip and James, Peter and Paul, James the Elder, Bartholomew, Luke, Simon and Jude, Andrew. Violet is proper for the Day of Humiliation and Prayer. Black is proper for Good Friday.

Some use green from Septuagesima through Shrove Tue. (see *Shrovetide*); in that case it is proper to use white from Matins on Jan. 14 up to, but not including, Vespers on the Sat. before Septuagesima. Violet may be used from Matins on the Mon. after Rogation Sun. up to, but not including, Vespers on the Wed. before Ascension Day, and on Holy Innocents' Day when it falls during the week.

If a day is observed by a service on the preceding evening (e. g., a Thanksgiving Eve service) it is proper to use the color of the day that is being observed. If there is a conflict (e. g., when St. Andrew's Day falls on the 1st Sun. in Adv.), consult a liturgical calendar; where none is available, let good judgment apply. New Year's Eve, New Year's Day as such, Mother's Day, Mission Festival, weddings, funerals, confirmation services, Communion, and similar occasions are not part of the liturgical yr. and as such have no colors assigned to them; the colors that are normally in season may be used. LP

Colportage. Sale (usually at low rates) or free distribution of Bibles and other religious publications by colporteurs (peddlers of miss. materials).

Columba. See *Celtic Church, 7.*

Columban (Columbanus; ca. 543–615). Irish monk; preached in Burgundy and in what is now Switz.; spent last yrs. in N It.; est. Monasteries at Anegray and Luxeuil, Fr., and Bobbio, It.

Columbia Church of the Air. See *Radio and Television Evangelism, Network,* 3.

Columbia Theological Seminary. See *Ministry, Education of,* XII.

Columbus Conference. Meeting at Columbus, Ohio, Jan. 20, 1941, attended by representatives of the NLC, of 8 of its constituent bodies, and of the Mo. Syn. It coordinated support of orphaned missions and spiritual care of draftees by the Mo. Syn. and the NLC.

L. Meyer, "Meeting on War Relief," *Lutheran Witness* (Feb. 4, 1941), 43; G. V. Schick, "The Columbus Conference and Its Repercussions," *Lutheran Witness* (May 13, 1941), 168–169.

Comba, Emilio (1839–1904). Founded cong. of Waldenses* in Venice 1867; prof. ch. hist. Waldensian faculty, Florence, 1872; founded and ed. *La Rivista cristiana.* Tried to trace true ch. through various forms and movements from apostolic days.

Comenius, John Amos (Jan Amos Komenský; 1592 to 1670). Chief representative of the 17th c. Czech Reformation cultural development; last sr. bp. of the Czech branch of the *Unitas fratrum* (see *Bohemian Brethren*); forced into exile by the victory of the Counter* Reformation in Czech lands (see *Czechoslovakia*). Comenius' universalism, based on the eschatological hope of Christ's second coming, led him to view the theol., scientific, and pol. development of the time from the perspective of the oneness of the created world. It was from this new vantage point that he saw the task of educ. He rightly saw his ambitious plan for the reform of human soc. relations, *De rerum humanarum emendatione consultatio catholica,* 7 vols., as his most distinctive achievement; but it was never pub. To his contemporaries he was famous as an educ.; his theory of language educ. was esp. renowned. His pedagogical works are collected in his 1657 *Opera didactica omnia.* The books he wrote for the spiritual comfort of his fellow believers show him as a talented writer and poet. The christocentric piety of the writings is in some ways a foretaste of pietism. One of them, the allegorical *Labyrinth of the World,* is an outstanding jewel of Czech prose. He exerted great effort on the ecumenical reconciliation and unification of Prot. chs. and countries. He was convinced that the different Reformation movements were to be followed by an integral reformation of the whole ch. He was led to his endeavors also by the circumstances of his life, which put him in contact with the most varied forms of Eur. Protestantism. After leaving his country 1628, he lived in Leszno, Poland. From there he went to Eng., where he spent the winter of 1641–42. This was followed by his stay in Elbing, W Prussia, where he labored on the Swed. educ. system till 1648, when he went to Poland. In 1650–54 he was active in Sárospatak, Hung. Postwar chaos, which took away his hope of returning to his homeland, and the great fire in Laszno in 1656 drove him to Amsterdam, where he died. His suggestions for a future organization of all mankind culminated in an ecumenical council of chs. *(consistorium oecumenicum),* an internat. academy of scholars and teachers, and an internat. peace court; he reinterpreted theol. motifs from the *Unitas fratrum* and applied them universally. *Bequest of the Unitas fratrum,* written 1650, reflects his conviction that his ch. was about to die, only to sprout again like a seed and lead to greater unity of mankind.

J. V. Novák and J. Hendrich, *Jan Amos Komenský* (Prague, 1932); K. Schaller, *Die Pädagogik des Johann Amos Comenius und die Anfänge des pädagogischen Realismus im 17. Jahrhundert* (Heidelberg, 1962); M. Spinka, *John Amos Comenius* (Chicago, 1943); A. Molnár, "Esquisse de la théologie de Comenius," *Revue d'Histoire et de Philosophie Religieuses,* XXVIII and XXIX, 2 (1948–49), 107–131. AM (tr. MSF)

Comes (pl. *comites*). Lectionary fixing readings for Suns., festivals, and ferial services of the ch. yr. See also *Pericope.*

Comgall. See *Celtic Church,* 8.

Coming of the Bridegroom. In E Ch., name for the Vigils of Passion Week.

Comma Johanneum. See *Johannine Comma.*

Commandments of the Church. Certain moral and ecclesiastical precepts imposed by the RC Ch. on its mems. (e. g., Communion in Easter season; annual confession; hearing mass on Sun. and certain feast days; days of fasting and abstinence). Also in a broad sense certain other laws or precepts issued by the RC Ch.

Commendation of the Dying (Lat. *commendatio animae,* "commendation of the soul"). Name often given to the prayer spoken at the bedside of a dying person. Luth. agendas contain prayers that usually ask God to forgive the sins of the departing one and receive him into heaven.

Commentaries, Biblical. Two major schools of interpretation, Antiochene and Alexandrian, thrived in the early centuries. The Antiochenes, including notably 2 pupils of Diodorus,* Theodore* of Mopsuestia and John Chrysostom,* may be said to be the precursors of modern historicocritical method with their accent on the literal and hist. sense. But the Alexandrians, including Pantaenus,* Clement* of Alexandria, Dionysius* of Alexandria, Cyril* of Alexandria, and Origen* set the pattern for more than a millennium with their fanciful allegorical exegesis inherited from interpreters of Homer (Plato,* Philo* Judaeus, and the Stoics*; see also *Exegesis,* 3, 4; *Schools, Early Christian,* 1, 4). The Victorines,* esp. Hugh* of St. Victor, briefly recovered the Antiochene spirit. Much patristic exegesis, both astounding and depressing, is preserved in medieval catenae (see *Catena*), notably by Theophylact* and Euthymius* Zigabenus. Definite originality appears first in the work of M. Luther,* whose 1535 commentary on Gl is a classic. Luther's comments are often homiletically conditioned; J. Calvin* offers more objective comment on the original sense of a passage in his masterful expositions of almost every book of the Bible. The peculiar theol. accents for which Calvin is known are, of course, evident.

Among more significant commentaries prior to the 19th c.: M. Poole's* *Synopsis Criticorum,* 5th ed., 6 vols. (1709–12), a learned but uncritical collection of opinions; J. J. Wetstein,* *Novum Testamentum graecum,* 2 vols. (1751–52) enjoys great prestige for its unparalleled collection of rabbinic and classical quotations; M. Henry,* *An Exposition of the Old and New Testament,* 5 vols. (1708–10), a popular work completed (Ro to Rv) by his nonconformist colleagues.

In contrast to the prolix "intellectual crockery" (as Spurgeon termed it) of the 17th c. Eng. commentators, J. A. Bengel's* 1742 *Gnomon Novi Testamenti* is a model of perspicuity and brevity.

W. M. L. De* Wette's commentaries pub. early in the 19th c. reflect the considered refinement of the Antiochene school and its purge of allegorical and subjective approaches. The writings of E. W. Hengstenberg* mark a reaction to the exegetical method of De Wette and is characterized as retrogressive by F. W. Farrar.* F. Delitzsch,* working jointly with J. Keil,* earned great respect for his series on the OT. The mediating influence of F. D. E. Schleiermacher* is apparent in F. A. G. Tholuck's* works. Among Eng. works of this period, those of C. J. Ellicott,* J. B. Lightfoot,* and B. F. Westcott* deserve mention.

The vast number of publications in the 20th c. fall into 3 groups:

1. One-vol. commentaries. The usefulness of 1-vol. commentaries is limited, but *Peake's Commentary on the Bible,* ed. Matthew Black and Harold H. Rowley (1962), offers a broad survey of the critical spectrum; *The New Bible Commentary,* ed. Francis Davidson, 2d ed. (1954), accents Ref. viewpoints.

2. Commentary series. *The International Critical Commentary on the Holy Scriptures of the Old and New Testaments* (1895–) is authoritative, though some vols. have been superseded by fresh investigations. *The Interpreter's Bible* (1952–57) contains much superfluous material, but is excellent for such books as Dt, Ps, and Is. Fresh translations mark *The Anchor Bible* (1964–), which is uneven in its exposition of the text but includes new philol. data, esp. on Ps. and Jb. *The New International Commentary* (NT 1951–, OT 1965–) presents fundamentalist viewpoints. The Prot. theol. faculty of the U. of Strasbourg is ed. *Commentaire de l'ancien testament* (1963–) and *Commentaire du nouveau testament* (1949–). For the NT only, *The Expositor's Greek Testament,* 5 vols. (1897–1910), supersedes H. Alford,* *The Greek Testament,* 4 vols. (1849–60), and is a useful reference set if used with such later works as *The Tyndale New Testament Commentaries* (1956–) and the *Cambridge Greek Testament Commentary* (1957–). Bible students not trained in Heb. and Gk. find the following useful: *Westminster Commentaries* (1899–); *The Moffatt New Testament Commentary,* 17 vols. (1926–50); the *Torch Bible Commentaries* (1948–); *Harper's New Testament Commentaries* (1958–); *The Layman's Bible Commentary* (1959–); *Cambridge Bible Commentary: New English Bible* (1963–). Of the Ger. series, *Biblischer Kommentar: Altes Testament,* ed. Martin Noth et al. (1955–), is one of the most ambitious ever undertaken and will rank in painstaking scholarship with the *Göttinger Handkommentar zum Alten Testament* (1892–), which includes H. Gunkel* on Gn and the Ps. *Kommentar zum Alten Testament,* ed. Ernst Sellin et al. (1913–39), took a fresh start with Wilhelm Rudolph's commentary on Ru, SS, and Lm (1962). The *Kritisch-exegetischer Kommentar über das Neue Testament,* begun 1829 by H. A. W. Meyer,* is the outstanding work in any language; recent eds. include such notable contributions as those of Rudolf Bultmann on Jn and Ernst Lohmeyer on Ph, Cl, and Phmn. *Theologischer Handkommentar zum Neuen Testament* (new series 1957–), *Herders Theologischer Kommentar zum Neuen Testament* (1953–), and *Handbuch zum Neuen Testament* (1960–), a counterpart to *Handbuch zum Alten Testament,* ed. O. Eissfeldt (1934–), are worthy rivals. Bible students not trained in Heb. and Gk. find a wealth of pondered thought in *Das Alte Testament Deutsch* (1949–; tr. of some vols. are in *The Old Testament Library* [1961]; includes such fresh treatments as that of John Gray on 1 and 2 K) and *Das Neue Testament Deutsch* (1932–; in continuous revision). Among notable Fr. series is *Études Bibliques,* begun 1903 by Marie-Joseph Lagrange; includes Ceslaus Spicq on Heb.

3. Commentaries not in series. Many excellent commentaries do not appear in series. Notable are George Adam Smith, *Jeremiah,* 4th ed., rev. and enl. (1929), and *The Book of the Twelve Prophets* (1929; rev. ed. 1960); *A Critical and Exegetical Commentary on the Book of Amos,* ed. Richard S. Cripps, 2d ed. (1955); Vincent Taylor, *The Gospel According to St. Mark,* 2d ed. (1966), superseding Henry Barclay Swete, *The Gospel According to St. Mark,* 3d ed. (1909); John Martin Creed, *The Gospel According to St. Luke* (1930); William F. Arndt, *The Gospel According to St. Luke* (1956); B. F. Westcott,* *The Gospel According to St. John,* appeared in the *Speaker's Commentary* 1880, separately 1883, and ed. with a tr. by A. Westcott, 2 vols. (1908); *The Beginnings of Christianity, Part I: The Acts of the Apostles,* eds. Frederick John Foakes-Jackson and Kirsopp Lake, 5 vols. (1920–33); Joseph Armitage Robinson, *St. Paul's Epistle to the Ephesians,* 2d ed. (1909); *The Epistle of St. James,* ed. Joseph Bickersteth Mayor, rev. 3d ed. (1913); *The First Epistle of St. Peter,* ed. Edward Gordon Selwyn, 2d ed. (1947); *The Epistle of St. Jude and the Second Epistle of St. Peter,* ed. Joseph Bickersteth Mayor (1907).

Much gen. inaccessible information is collected in Frederick Danker, *Multipurpose Tools for Bible Study,* 2d, rev. ed. (St. Louis, 1966); includes a select list of commentaries on each book of the Bible (pp. 239–272) and a bibliography (p. 240, n. 1). On older commentaries see Friedrich Bleek, *An Introduction to the Old Testament,* eds. Johannes Bleek and Adolf Kamphausen, tr. from the 2d ed. by G. H. Venables, ed. E. Venables, 2 vols. (London, 1875 to 1882); James Moffatt, *An Introduction to the Literature of the New Testament,* 3d ed. (New York [1918]). For more recent literature see Robert H. Pfeiffer, *The Books of the Old Testament* (New York [1957]) and *Peake's Commentary on the Bible,* eds. Matthew Black and Harold H. Rowley (London, 1962). FWD

Commination Service (from Lat. for "to threaten"). Name sometimes used for the Angl. service on Ash Wed. in which God's anger and judgments against sinners are proclaimed. See also *Discipline, Church.*

Commissary Court. See *Consistory,* 2.

Commission, Biblical. Est. 1902 by Leo XIII because of liberal tendencies in biblical studies of RC scholars; composed of cardinals and consultants; chief functions are to foster Bible study and defend the truth of Scripture; in 1907 Pius X gave the same authority to its decisions as is ascribed to doctrinal decisions of Roman congs.

Commissions, Ecclesiastical. Bodies appointed for special functions or duties in the ch. The Ecclesiastical Commissioners (since 1948 Ch. Commissioners for Eng.) of the Angl. Ch. manage its estates and revenues. Two parliamentary commissions on Eng. Ch. courts were est. 1830 and 1881. The Royal Commission on Ecclesiastical Discipline, est. 1904, investigated alleged breaches in the conduct of the Angl. Divine Service. In RC Ch., commissions consist of ecclesiastics appointed by pope (papal) or bp. (diocesan). Papal commissions either consist chiefly of cardinals (e. g., Biblical Commission*) or are presided over by a cardinal. In Luth. and other Prot. chs., commissions are usually permanent or of longer duration and greater importance than committees.

Committee on Friendly Relations Among Foreign Students. See *International Student Service.*

Commixture. The placing of a small portion of the host into the chalice during the celebration of the mass. The practice originated in the medieval W ch.

and is perpetuated esp. by RCs and some Anglo-Caths. Not to be confused with intinction.*

Committal Services. See *Burial,* 4.

Commodianus (ca. 3d c.). Christian Lat. poet; chiliast and patripassianist; works include *Instructiones adversus gentium deos; Carmen apologeticum.*

MPL, 5, 201–262.

Commodus, Aelius Aurelius. See *Marcus Aurelius.*

Commodus, Lucius Ceionius. See *Marcus Aurelius.*

Common Confession. 1. After the Mo. Syn. adopted the 1938 resolutions regarding fellowship with the ALC, attempts were made to unite the contents of the *Brief* Statement* and the *Declaration.* The resulting document, *Doctrinal Affirmation,* was adopted by neither of the bodies. The 1947 Mo. Syn. (LCMS beginning 1947) conv. instructed its Committee on Doctrinal Unity "to make every effort to arrive ultimately at one document which is Scriptural, clear, concise, and unequivocal." (*Proceedings,* p. 510)

2. After meeting with the union committees of the syns. of the Synodical* Conf., the Committee on Doctrinal Unity met with the Fellowship Commission of the ALC May 17, 1948. Subsequently both groups selected subcommittees to draw up doctrinal theses. After lengthy study and criticism of preliminary drafts, a plenary meeting of the committees of the 2 chs. was held Dec. 5–6, 1949, at the end of which the theses were unanimously approved. This *Common Confession,* Part I, was accepted 1950 by the LCMS and the ALC.

3. The 12 topics of the *Common Confession,* Part I, treat the doctrines of God, man, redemption, election, means of grace, justification, conversion, sanctification, the ch., the ministry, the Luth. confessions, the last things.

4. The *Common Confession,* Part II, was unanimously adopted by the official committees of the ALC and the LCMS Feb. 9, 1953, at a joint meeting in Chicago, Ill.

5. The purpose of Part II was to supplement and clarify Part I. Under the gen. heading "The Church in the World" it treats i. The Church's Mission; ii. The Church's Resources; iii. The Ch. and Its Ministrations; iv. The Ch. and the Home; v. The Ch. and Vocation; vi. The Ch. and Educ.; vii. The Ch. and Govt.; viii. The Ch. and Ch. Fellowship; ix. The Ch. and Anti-Christian Organizations; x. The Ch. and the World to Come.

6. The *Common Confession,* Part II, was approved and the confession in its entirety was adopted by the ALC 1954. The 1956 LCMS conv. resolved that "the *Common Confession* (Parts I and II) be not regarded or employed as a functioning basic document toward the establishment of altar and pulpit fellowship with other church bodies" and "that the *Common Confession,* one document composed of Parts I and II, be recognized as a statement in harmony with the Sacred Scriptures and the Lutheran Confessions." (*Proceedings,* p. 505)

Proceedings, LCMS, 1950, pp. 566–587; 1953, pp. 10, 11, 14–15, 485–490, 494–544; 1956, pp. 491 to 517; *Official Reports . . . Convention of the American Lutheran Church,* 1950, pp. 281, 286; 1954, pp. 331–344, 351; *Doctrinal Declarations* (St. Louis, 1957), pp. 71–91; *Church in Fellowship,* ed. V. Vajta (Minneapolis, 1963), pp. 63–65; *Moving Frontiers,* ed. C. S. Meyer (St. Louis, 1964), pp. 418 to 420; R. C. Wolf, *Documents of Lutheran Unity in America* (Philadelphia, 1966), pp. 323, 381, 408 to 444, 449, 608–609. EL

Common Grace *(gratia communis).* According to Ref. doctrine (Calvinistic), the elect are converted and preserved in the state of faith and salvation by special or irresistible grace; to all others the sovereign God grants only common grace, which is resistible. See also *Calvinism; Grace.*

Common Law Marriage. See *Marriage, Biblical and Christian,* III.

Common Life, Brethren of the. See *Brethren of the Common Life.*

Common Prayer, Book of. See *Book of Common Prayer.*

Common Service. See *Liturgics.*

Commonsense Realism. Philos. school, founded by T. Reid*; tried to est. a realistic philos. in opposition to G. Berkeley* and D. Hume*; based on an alleged universal common consciousness ("common sense").

Communication of Attributes *(communicatio idiomatum).* See *Christ Jesus,* I D; *Idiomata.*

Communio sanctorum (Lat. "communion of holy people [things]"). Phrase added to the Apostles' Creed probably ca. the 4th c., perhaps in Gaul. Its original meaning is debated. Traditional intepretation holds that *sanctorum* is masculine and that the phrase means "communion of holy people." The words can be variously understood: communion with departed saints and martyrs; communion with all believers (living and departed); fellowship of holy people (descriptive of the church*); communion of holy people in holy things. Since the end of the 19th c. the view that regards *sanctorum* as a neuter referring to the sacraments and other holy things of the ch. has become prominent. Evidence from the ancient and medieval ch. can be used in support of various meanings.

Luther tr. the phrase "die Gemeine der Heiligen" (communion of saints), taking *sanctorum* as masculine and referring the phrase to the fellowship that exists in Christendom. "Communion in holy things" and "communion of saints" are not necessarily divergent. "Communio" is dynamic rather than static, a participation with other Christians in holy things that make them one.

See also *Fellowship; Koinonia; Niceta(s).*

T. v. Zahn, *The Apostles' Creed,* tr. C. S. Burn and A. E. Burn, based on 2d ed. (London, 1899); W. Elert, *Abendmahl und Kirchengemeinschaft in der alten Kirche hauptsächlich des Ostens* (Berlin, 1954), tr. N. Nagel, *Eucharist and Church Fellowship in the First Four Centuries* (St. Louis, 1966); F. J. Badcock, *The History of the Creeds,* 2d ed (London, 1938), pp. 243-272; J. N. D. Kelly, *Early Christian Creeds,* 2d ed. (London, 1960), pp. 388–397. EL

Communion, Holy. See *Grace, Means of,* IV.

Communion of Brethren. Alternate name for Bohemian* Brethren.

Communion of Natures *(communio naturarum).* See *Christ Jesus,* I C; *Idiomata.*

Communion of Saints. See *Communio sanctorum.*

Communion Service. See *Lord's Supper.*

Communion Set. See *Church Furniture,* 3.

Communion Tokens. Tokens of metal stamped with texts, initials, etc., given in some chs. to mems. entitled to partake of Communion. Some chs. use cards instead of tokens.

Communism. See *Socialism,* 4.

Communist Manifesto. See *Marx, Karl Heinrich.*

Communistic Societies. 1. Religious groups that sought to organize their life and property according to collective ideals were in existence in Palestine (Essenes*), Egypt (Therapeutae*), and other lands at the time of Christ. The collectivism practiced in the early ch. at Jerusalem was not an absolute, total, or compulsory community of goods. The individuality of each mem. was guarded (Acts 5:4). Love was the only law by which each was bound.

2. Beginning in the 3d c., Manichaeans (see *Manichaeism*) practiced a type of communism assoc. with asceticism.* Benedictines* observed communistic practices. Before the Reformation, groups that opposed the papacy often organized on a collective basis (Cathari,* Albigenses,* Waldenses,* Beghards*

and Beguines, Lollards,* Taborites, Moravian Brethren; see also *Bohemian Brethren*). In the days of the Reformation, Anabaptists often formed communistic societies (e. g., at Münster).

3. Few religious communistic groups have existed in modern Eur. F. N. Babeuf* advocated communistic theories (Babouvism) during the Fr. Revolution; R. Owen* was active in Eng. in the 1st part of the 19th c. Am. has seen many such experiments, some primarily religious, others only soc. and economic. Most of the largest successful ones were of Ger. origin. A few existed over a c.; many dissolved sooner for various reasons (failure to solve the problem of family life, the injunction of celibacy, secession of the young, lack of personal liberty, killing individual initiative and endeavor, etc.)

4. The first communistic organization in Am. was formed by Labadists (followers of J. Labadie*) who settled 1679 on the Hudson in New York and ca. 1683 at Bohemia Manor, near the present site of Elkton, Md., but soon sacrificed their religious convictions to the profit motive. Johann Kelpius (1673 to 1708) led the followers of Johann Jakob Zimmermann (1644–93) from Rotterdam to Germantown (Philadelphia). They called themselves the colony of the Contented of the God-loving Soul; others called them the Soc. of the Woman in the Wilderness because they aspired to become the beloved of the woman in Rv 12.

5. The more important Am. socs.: Amana* Soc.; House* of David; Oneida* Community; Rappists*; Shakers.* The Ephrata Community, near Reading, Pa. founded ca. 1732 by J. C. Beissel,* dissolved 1814; the remaining mems. inc. as (Ger.) Seventh Day Baptists (see *Baptist Churches,* 17; *Brethren,* 1). Icaria was founded 1848 by Fr. settlers under E. Cabet* in Tex., later moved to Nauvoo, Ill., then to Iowa, where a division in 1879 gave rise to New Icaria; Icaria soon dissolved, New Icaria in 1895. In Württemberg, Ger., those who separated from the State Ch. under leadership of the mystic Barbara Grubermann founded the Separatists; after her death the group, under Joseph Michael Bimeler (Bäumeler; Baumeler; 1778–1853) emigrated to Am. and founded Zoar, Ohio, 1817; dissolved 1898. The Bethel, Mo., and Aurora, Oreg., communities were founded 1844 and 1855 resp. by Wilhelm Keil of Nordhausen, Prussia; dissolved 1880 and 1881 resp. Many communistic socs. resulted from, or were influenced by, plans promoted by François Marie Charles Fourier (1772–1837; Fr. socialist); best known: Brook Farm (1841–47; at West Roxbury, Mass.; known for its prominent mems. and visitors, including R. W. Emerson,* N. Hawthorne,* and H. Greeley*) and the North American Phalanx (1843–56; near Red Bank, N. J.). The Adonai Shomo (Heb. "the Lord is there") community (Adv.) was formed 1861 by Frederick I. Howland, settled first at Athol, then at Petersham, Mass., chartered 1876, dissolved 1896. Swedes emigrated to Am. 1846 under Eric Janson (see also *Sweden, Lutheranism in,* 5) and founded the Bishop Hill Colony, Ill.; Janson, who claimed to be Christ reincarnate, was assassinated 1850; the colony was dissolved 1862. Perhaps the oldest communistic socs. are the Bruderhof communities founded by J. Huter*; Huterites migrated from S Russia to S Dak. and settled at Wold Creek and Bon Homme 1874 and Elm Spring 1877. Koreshanity was founded 1886 at Chicago by Cyrus (Heb. Koresh, whence the name) R. Teed; moved 1903 to Estero, Fla.; principal divisions: Ch. Triumphant, Coll. of Life, and Society Arch-Triumphant.

Community Chests. See *Social Work,* D 3.

Community Churches. As a rule a community ch. is an indep., undenominational, or interdenominational cong. representing the union of several small or weak denominational chs.; it ordinarily has no creedal platform; its program of ch. work is chiefly this-worldly and varies to meet the soc. and cultural interests of the resp. constituency. See also *Independent Churches,* 2.

Community of St. Paul. See *Bible Societies,* 6.

Community Social Work. See *Social Work,* C 1.

Commutation of Penance. In the RC Ch., a change made in a prescribed penance,* often with relaxation. See also *Indulgences.*

Comnena, Anna. See *Anna Comnena.*

Compactata (of Prague). See *Basel, Council of; Hussites.*

Compagnia di San Paola. See *Bible Societies,* 6.

Comparative Religion. See *Religion, Comparative.*

Comparative Symbolics. See *Symbolics.*

Competentes. See *Catechetics,* 3.

Competence of the Individual Soul. See *Baptist Churches,* 5.

Compline (complin; from Lat. for "complete"). Last of the canonical hours.*

Complutensian Polyglot. See *Lexicons, B; Polyglot Bibles.*

Compostela, Order of. Sp. RC military order; founded ca. 1161; assisted in expelling Muslim; dissolved 1835.

Compresence. Togetherness of several items, e. g., coexistence of elements in the unity of consciousness; developed in S. Alexander's* *Space, Time, and Deity.*

Comstock Laws. See *Family Planning,* 5.

Comte, Auguste (1798–1857). Fr. philos. and math.; founded positivism*; in *Cours de philosophie positive* he sought to est. 3 stages of mental evolution: theol., metaphysical, scientific; sought to remove the supernatural from religion and make it a force for secular and soc. reforms. Other works include *Catechisme positiviste; Systime de politique positive.* See also *Altruism.*

Conatus. Drive or urge that aims at self-preservation in a thing.

Concentus. See *Accentus.*

Conception, Immaculate. See *Mariolatry; Mary Festivals; Roman Catholic Confessions,* C.

Conceptualism. Theory in philos. first expounded by P. Abelard* as a mediating position bet. nominalism* and realism,* postulating that concepts in the mind are predicates that may be affirmed of reality or subjects of discourse.

"Concerning Church Fellowship." See *Church of the Lutheran Confession.*

Conciliar Movement; Conciliarism. Conciliarism is the view that the ch. should be governed by councils and that councils are superior to the pope. See also *Councils and Synods,* 7.

Conclave. Place where the cardinals* assemble to elect a pope*; also, the assembly itself. The conclave begins 15 to 18 days after a pope's death or resignation. A large part of the Vatican is walled off and divided into rooms or cells. All entrances except one are closed, not to be opened till an election is made. Each cardinal may take with him a secy. and a servant (conclavist), sworn to secrecy.

Concomitance. RC doctrine that both body and blood of Christ exist in each element of the Lord's Supper, so that both are received by communicating in one kind (bread or wine) only.

Concordances, Bible. Books containing words of the Bible in alphabetic order, with their context usually given, and references by chapter and verse. The 1st concordances were of the Vulgate; tradition ascribes the 1st, *Concordantiae morales,* to Anthony* of Padua; Hugh* of St. Cher prepared an authentic concordance, reputedly with the aid of 500 monks; other concordances to the Vulgate include F. P. Dutripon, *Condordantiae bibliorum sacrorum* (Paris, 1838; rev. G. Tonini 1861; 7th ed. 1880). The 1st Heb. concordance, *Meir Natib* ("Light of the Way"), was completed by Isaac (or Mordecai) Nathan ca. the middle of the 15th c. (pub. Venice, 1524); other Heb. concordances include S. Mandelkern, *Veteris Testamenti concordantiae Hebraicae atque Chaldaicae,* 2 vols. (Leipzig, 1896–1900), 3d ed. corrected and supplemented by Moshe Henry Goshen-Gottstein, 1 vol. (Jerusalem and Tel-Aviv, 1955); G. Lisowsky and L. Rost, *Konkordanz zum hebräischen Alten Testament* (Stuttgart, 1958). The 1st Gk. concordance to the NT was that of the Luth. Sixt Birck (Xystus Betuleius; 1500–54) (Basel, 1546); the 2d was that of Robert I Estienne* and Henry II, *Concordantiae Graeco-Latinae Testamenti Novi* (Paris, 1594; 2d ed. 1624); Erasmus Schmidt* (Schmied), *Tamieion* ("Treasury") (Wittenberg, 1638), was the basis of subsequent similar works; other concordances to the Gk. NT include W. F. Moulton and A. S. Geden, *A Concordance to the Greek Testament* (Edinburgh, 1897; 4th ed. 1963 includes corrections by John F. Recks); O. Schmoller, *Handkonkordanz zum griechischen Neuen Testament* (Stuttgart, 1868; A. Schmoller ed. 12th ed. 1960); J. B. Smith, *Greek-English Concordance to the New Testament* (Scottdale, Pa., 1955). Konrad Kircher pub. a concordance to the LXX (Frankfurt, 1607) with the Heb. words in alphabetic order; Abraham van der Trommen pub. a concordance to the LXX (Utrecht, 1718) with the Gk. words in alphabetic order and with additional helps; E. Hatch* and H. A. Redpath* issued *A Concordance to the Septuagint and the Other Greek Versions of the Old Testament (Including the Apocryphal Books),* 3 vols. (Oxford, 1892–1906). The 1st large Ger. concordance was by Conrad Bawr (Lat. Agricola) (Nürnberg, 1609); other Ger. concordances include that of G. Büchner* (Jena, 1750; many later eds.). The 1st concordance to the NT in English was pub. London ca. 1535 by Thomas Gybson; the 1st Eng. concordance to the whole Bible was that of John Marbeck* (London, 1550); Alexander Cruden's concordance to the whole Eng. Bible, completed 1737 (pub. London, 1738), was remarkably accurate and has been improved in its many eds. chiefly by addition of new features (e. g., Gk. and Heb.); other Eng. concordances include J. B. R. Walker, *The Comprehensive Concordance to the Holy Scriptures* (Boston, 1894; reissued repeatedly); J. Strong, *The Exhaustive Concordance of the Bible* (copyrighted 1890, but 1st ed. New York, 1894; 25th print. 1963); R. Young, *Analytical Concordance to the Bible* (Edinburgh, 1879; many later eds.); Nelson's *Complete Concordance of the Revised Standard Version Bible* (New York, 1957); *Concordance to the New English Bible: New Testament,* comp. E. G. Elder (London, 1964; Grand Rapids, Mich., 1965).

Readers who lack knowledge of Gk. and Heb. but desire to know the meaning of the original underlying a given Eng. word will find a list of concordances designed for that purpose with guidance in their use in F. Danker, *Multipurpose Tools for Bible Study,* 2d ed. (St. Louis, 1966). For a detailed list of older concordances see "Concordance," J. M'Clintock and J. Strong, *Cyclopaedia of Biblical, Theological, and Ecclesiastical Literature,* II (New York, 1894), 454–456. EL, FWD

Concordat. 1. Agreement bet. civil and ecclesiastical authorities, particularly bet. the pope and civil govts., to regulate ecclesiastical matters. Concordats are pub. as civil law on ratification by the state and as canon law on ratification by the ch. The 3 theories regarding the nature of concordats: (1) the legal theory, that the state as superior grants the ch. certain privileges revocable at will; (2) the compact theory, that state and ch. as equals make an agreement abrogated only by mutual consent; (3) the privilege theory, that the ch. grants concessions and indults to the state, which acknowledges duties toward the ch.

2. The 1122 Concordat of Worms, usually cited as the 1st concordat, consisted of 2 declarations. Calixtus II (Guido of Vienne; Guido of Burgundy; d. 1124; pope 1119–24) addressed emp. Henry V without mentioning his successors, but the effect of the concordat was felt for centuries. Henry's declaration was made to the pope and the Holy Roman Ch. The declarations regulated the conferring of regalia and the consecration of bps. and abbots. See also *Investiture Struggle.*

3. In the 1448 Concordat of Vienna bet. Nicholas V (Tommaso Parentucelli; Tommaso da Sarzana; ca. 1397–1455; pope 1447–55) and emp. Frederick III free canonical election of abps., bps., and some abbots was permitted; some papal reservations were allowed for lesser benefices, and the payment of annates was regulated.

4. The 1516 Concordat of Bologna bet. Leo X (see *Popes,* 20) and Francis I of Fr. influenced affairs of the RC Ch. in Fr. for centuries. It revoked the Pragmatic* Sanction of Bourges (see *France,* 3; *Gallicanism*). The king, in gen., received the right to nominate candidates for all important ecclesiastical positions.

5. The 1801 concordat bet. Pius VII (see *Popes,* 27) and Napoleon* I, First Consul since 1799, recognized the restoration of the RC Ch. in Fr. after the revolution. It acknowledged that "the Catholic, Apostolic, and Roman religion is the religion of the vast majority of French citizens." Diocesan reorganization was conceded; all bps. were required to resign. Ch. property remained in the hands of the state, but ample provision was made for maintenance of bps. and priests. The 1802 "Organic Articles" by Napoleon unilaterally modified the concordat, which, however, remained in force till 1905. See also *Consalvi, Ercole; France,* 5, 6; *Roman Catholic Church,* D 8.

6. Concordats with Guatemala, San Salvador, Honduras, Nicaragua, Costa Rica, Haiti, Ecuador, Venezuela, and Colombia in the 2d half of the 19th c. recognized RCm as the state religion.

7. The 1929 Lateran Treaty bet. Pius XI (see *Popes,* 32) and It. restored the pope's temporal power by creating the state of Vatican* City and recognizing the pope as a sovereign prince, thus settling the "Roman Question" (see *Popes,* 28). The 1929 concordat, attached to the Lateran Treaty, dealt with relations bet. the Vatican and the kingdom of It.; it guaranteed the clergy free exercise of religion, but prohibited them from engaging in political activity in opposition to the state.

8. The 1933 concordat bet. Pius XI and the Nazi govt. of Ger. allowed the RC Ch. authority in religion, but excluded it from politics. Freedom of communication within the ch., its educ. interests, and the assocs. of Catholic* Action were guaranteed. But encroachments of the Ger. govt. led to the 1937 encyclical *Mit brennender Sorge.*

9. Pius XI also completed concordats with Latvia 1922, Bavaria 1924, Poland 1925, Romania 1927, Lithuania 1927, Prussia 1929, Baden 1932, and Austria 1933. The 1940 concordat bet. Pius XII and Port. recognized RC ethics and morals as basic to state activity; at the same time it recognized separation of ch. and state in principle. The 1953 concordat bet. Pius XII and Sp. names RCm as the state religion but grants some freedom of worship and religion to non-Caths.; ecclesiastical courts were allowed competence in some causes. CSM

Concordia. See *Book of Concord.*

Concordia Academy and Junior College. See *Ministry, Education of,* VIII C 2.

Concordia College, Bronxville, N. Y. (formerly Conc. Collegiate Institute). See *Lutheran Church – Mis-*

souri Synod, The, V 7; *Ministry, Education of,* VIII C 2 j.

Concordia College, Conover, N. C. Est. in the late 1870s as a high school by mems. of the Tenn. Syn. Chartered 1881 as Conc. Coll. First pres. P. C. Henkel (see *Henkels, The,* 3) 1881–86. Taken over 1893 by The Eng. Ev. Luth. Syn. of Missouri* and Other States. Closed 1935.

Concordia College, Edmonton, Alta., Can. See *Ministry, Education of,* VIII C 2.

Concordia College, Fort Wayne, Ind. See *Ministry, Education of,* VIII C 2.

Concordia College, Milwaukee, Wis. See *Lutheran Church – Missouri Synod, The,* V 7; *Ministry, Education of,* VIII C 2.

Concordia College, Moorhead, Minn. See *Ministry, Education of,* VIII B.

Concordia College, Portland, Oreg. See *Ministry, Education of,* VIII C 2.

Concordia College, St. Louis, Mo. See *Ministry, Education of,* X C.

Concordia College, Saint Paul, Minn. See *Ministry, Education of,* VIII C 2.

Concordia College (Colegio Concordia), Obera, Misiones, Argentina. See *Lutheran Church – Missouri Synod, Districts of The,* B 2.

Concordia College, California, Oakland, Calif. See *Ministry, Education of,* VIII C 2.

Concordia College of Texas, Lutheran, Austin, Tex. See *Ministry, Education of,* VIII C 2.

Concordia Collegiate Institute. See *Concordia College,* Bronxville, N. Y.

Concordia Historical Institute. See *Archives.*

Concordia Institute (Instituto Concordia), Sao Paulo, Brazil. See *Lutheran Church – Missouri Synod, Districts of The,* B 1.

Concordia Lutheran College, Ann Arbor, Mich. See *Lutheran Church – Missouri Synod, The,* VII 12; *Ministry, Education of,* VIII C 1 a.

Concordia Lutheran College of Texas. See *Ministry, Education of,* VIII C 2 m.

Concordia Middle School, Chia Yi, Taiwan. See *Taiwan.*

Concordia Publishing House. See *Publication Houses, Lutheran.*

Concordia Seminary, Adelaide, Australia. See *Ministry, Education of,* XI B.

Concordia Seminary, Formosa (Taiwan), Rep. of China. See *Ministry, Education of,* XI B.

Concordia Seminary, Kowloon, Hong Kong. See *Ministry, Education of,* XI B.

Concordia Seminary, Nagercoil, Madras State, S India. See *Ministry, Education of,* XI B.

Concordia Seminary, Saint Louis, Mo. See *Lutheran Church – Missouri Synod, The,* I 4; V 2; VI 7; *Ministry Education of,* VI C; X C.

Concordia Seminary, Springfield, Ill. See *Ministry, Education of,* X D.

Concordia Seminary (Seminario Concordia), Porto Alegre, Brazil. See *Lutheran Church — Missouri Synod, Districts of The,* B 1.

Concordia Seminary (Seminario Concordia), Villa Ballester (José León Suárez since 1970), Buenos Aires, Argentina. See *Lutheran Church – Missouri Synod, Districts of The,* B 2.

Concordia Senior College, Fort Wayne, Ind. See *Lutheran Church – Missouri Synod, The,* VII 12; *Ministry, Education of,* VIII B 8, C 2 f.

Concordia Synod of Pennsylvania and Other States, Evangelical Lutheran. Organized at Pittsburgh, Pa., June 7, 1882, by 14 pastors, 6 lay delegates, and 1 teacher; these had withdrawn from the Ev. Luth. Joint Syn. of Ohio* and Other States after it left the Ev. Luth. Synodical* Conference of North America 1881 in the controversy on election and conversion. P. Brand* of Pittsburgh was made pres. and *The Lutheran Witness* and *Der Lutheraner* the organs. The syn. became a mem. of the Syn. Conf. Oct. 1882; in 1886 it resolved to disband and unite with the Mo. Syn. (see *Lutheran Church – Missouri Synod, The*).

Concordia Synod of the West. Organized 1862 by Frederick William Wier, Leberecht Friedrich Ehregott Krause, D. J. Warns, and C. F. Jungk. Applied for membership in the Ev. Luth. Joint Syn. of Ohio* and Other States. Application rejected 1865 because the Ohio Syn. saw no need for such a branch syn. The Conc. Syn. of the W. dissolved soon thereafter; its mems. were absorbed by other Luth. syns.

Concordia Synod of Virginia, Evangelical Lutheran. Organized 1868 at Coyner's Ch., Augusta Co., Va. Pastors present: George Schmucker (elected pres.), James E. Seneker, and Henry Wetzel; 6 laymen from 5 congs. present; *The Lutheran and Missionary* was recommended as reading matter to the mems. of the congs. Joined The Ev. Luth. Synodical* Conference of North America 1876. Became the Conc. Dist. of the Ev. Luth. Joint Syn. of Ohio* and Other States 1877; brought with it 17 congs. and 9 miss. stations; merged with the E Dist. of the Ohio Syn. 1920.

Concordia Teachers College, River Forest, Ill. See *Lutheran Church – Missouri Synod, The,* V 6; *Ministry, Education of,* VIII B 9.

Concordia Teachers College, Seward, Nebr. See *Ministry, Education of,* VIII B.

Concordia Theological Seminary. See *Concordia Seminary.*

Concupiscence. The word *concupiscentia* is used in the Lat. text of AC II in the definition of original sin.* Ger. text: "voll boser Lust und Neigung." Following Augustine* of Hippo, Bonaventura,* Hugh* of St. Victor, and others, Ap II says that concupiscence seeks and loves carnal things (not only sinful lusts of the body but also carnal wisdom and righteousness), ignores and despises God, lacks fear and trust in Him, hates His judgment and flees it, is angry at Him, despairs of His mercy, and trusts in temporal things (Ro 7:7, 23; 1 Co 2:14); it rejects the claim that concupiscence is a penalty and not a sin.

W. Elert, *Morphologie des Luthertums,* I (Munich, 1931; 1952 print.), 25–31, tr. W. A. Hansen, *The Structure of Lutheranism, I* (St. Louis, 1962), 28–35.

Concurrence. Falling of festivals on consecutive days, thus causing 2d vespers of one to coincide with 1st vespers of the other. Ordinarily the more important festival, or the festival beginning, takes precedence.

Concursus Dei (Lat., "concurrence of God"). Term used in dogmatics to describe God's cooperation in all that occurs; described as moral (in actions of rational beings) and physical (in all creation).

With respect to good acts a distinction must be made bet. civil good works *(iustitia civilis)* done by unregenerate in God's kingdom of power and rewarded with temporal blessings, and works God does in His kingdom of grace in the regenerate by the gracious operation of the Holy Ghost *(iustitia spiritualis).* See also *King, Christ as,* 4, 5.

God concurs in evil works only insofar as they are acts *(quoad materiale),* not insofar as they are evil *(quoad formale);* thus evil acts are not done without God nor is God made the cause of evil.

Condé, Louis I de Bourbon, Prince de (1530–69). Leader of Huguenots.* See also *France,* 9.

Conder, Claude Reignier. See *Geography, Christian,* 4.

Conder, Josiah (1789–1855). B. London; ed. and author; pub. numerous prose and poetical works; contributed 3 hymns to W. B. Collyer's* collection 1812; ed. the *Congregational Hymn-Book;* poems and hymns pub. 1856 under the title *Hymns of Praise.*

Condignity. See *Merit.*

Condillac, Étienne Bonnot de (1715–80). Fr. philos.; abbé of Mureaux; influenced by D. Diderot,* J. J.

Rousseau,* and J. Locke.* Rejected innate faculties and ideas and held that all human knowledge is transformed sensations. Though he held in his psychology that personality is aggregate of sensations, he nevertheless affirmed reality of soul and rejected atheism.

Conditio sine qua non. Condition without which a cause does not produce an effect.

Conditional Immortality. Belief which holds that immortality is conditioned on behavior of soul during earthly life. See also *Annihilationism.*

Conditional Morality. Morality based on a hypothetical imperative; the necessity of moral actions depends on the desired goals of the agent.

Condorcet, Marie Jean Antoine Nicholas de Caritat, Marquis de (1743–94). Fr. math., philos., encyclopedist.*

Confederate States of America, The General Synod of the Evangelical Lutheran Church in the. See *General Synod of the Evangelical Lutheran Church in the United States of America, The,* 4: *United Lutheran Church, Synods of,* 5; *United Synod of the Evangelical Lutheran Church in the South, The,* 1.

Conference for the Norwegian-Danish Evangelical Lutheran Church in America, The. See *Clausen, Claus Laurits; Evangelical Lutheran Church,* 10; *Norwegian-Danish Augustana Synod in America; United Norwegian Lutheran Church in America, The.*

Conference of Boards of Public Charities. See *National Conference on Social Welfare.*

Conferences. (Lat. *confero,* "bring together." Used by some classical authors of pub. conferences and discussions. Early used in connection with religious discussions. Cf. Gl 2:6). Beginning in the 11th c., meetings (often called *calendae* because held on the 1st of the month) of priests were held to discuss religious topics, perhaps because the diocese as such had become too large for frequent meetings of all mems. Such meetings of priests declined in the 13th c. and have never been fully revived in the RC Ch., though officially endorsed.

In the Prot. Ch. no fixed meaning attaches to the word "conference" (see *Methodist Churches,* 3, 4a; in Congregationalism it designates the voluntary organization of chs. in a dist.). The term has been variously used in Am. Lutheranism. In the earliest days it was applied to the meetings of syns. as well as to less formal gatherings. Pastoral conferences have often been held in Prot. chs. of Eur. and Am.

Confessing Church *(Bekennende Kirche; Bekenntniskirche).* Organized 1933 as the *Pfarrernotbund* (Pastors' Emergency League) under leadership of Martin Niemöller to oppose Ger. Christians controlled by Nazis. After WW II the movement continued. It adheres to the ancient creeds and Barmen* Theses. The "Confessing Church" professes adherence to the AC and other Reformation symbols. It is governed by a Bruderrat (Council of Brethren), consisting of representatives from various territories. See also *Barmen Theses; Kirchenkampf.*

D. Schmidt, *Pastor Niemöller,* tr. L. Wilson (New York, 1959): C. S. Davidson, *God's Man: The Story of Pastor Niemoeller* (New York, 1959); W. Niemöller, *Kampf und Zeugnis der Bekennenden Kirche* (Bielefeld, 1948). EL

Confessio Augustana (Augsburg Confession). See *Lutheran Confessions,* A.

Confessio Gallicana. See *Christian Church, History of,* III 6; *Reformed Confessions,* B.

Confessio Hafnica (Hafniensis). See *Denmark, Lutheranism in,* 2.

Confessio Pentapolitana. See *Lutheran Confessions,* A 5.

Confessio Rhaetica. See *Rhaetian Confession.*

Confessio Saxonica. See *Lutheran Confessions,* A 5.

Confessio Tetrapolitana (Tetrapolitan Confession). See *Reformed Confessions,* D 1.

Confessio Virtembergica. See *Brenz, Johann; Lutheran Confessions,* A.

Confession. 1. Profession or open acknowledgment of one's faith in anyone or anything, esp. in Christ and His Gospel (Mt 10:32; Lk 12:8; 1 Jn 2:23; 4:15). The meaning that became prevalent in the early ch., i. e. the act of a confessor* or martyr,* is found already in the NT (1 Ti 6:13).

2. That which is confessed: creed, confession, symbol (see *Creeds and Confessions*).

3. Acknowledgment, admission, or disclosure of one's own sins. In the OT confession of sin is both formal (Lv 5:5; Nm 5:6-8) and personal, private, or spontaneous (Ps 32; 51). In the NT, confession of sins is prominent in the ministry of John the Baptist (Mt 3:6) as well as in the early ch. (Acts 19:18; Ja 5:16; 1 Jn 1:9). The *Didache* (4, 14; 14, 1) stresses the importance of confession in the ch., that worship may be pure. The mode of confession or the person to receive it is not indicated in the NT or sub-apostolic writings. Tertullian and Cyprian already assoc. acts of reparation with the act of confessing mortal sins, notably murder, idolatry or apostasy, and gross sexual offenses. Subsequently in the W, Celtic influence on the Continent was decisive in bringing about the substitution of private confession of sins before a priest for pub. discipline of gross offenders.

4. In modern RCm, confession may refer to any self-examination and contrition; usually it refers to the formal act *(confessio)* which, with absolution, is cen. in the sacrament of repentance (penance*). The power of the priest to forgive sins in the sacrament of penance is deduced from Jn 20:22-23; Mt 16:19; 18:15-18. The material of penance is contrition,* confession, and satisfaction.* Confession is necessary when a believer has fallen from baptismal grace (thereby losing sanctifying grace) by committing mortal sin (see also *Sins, Venial and Mortal*). Forgiveness of mortal sins may be secured without confession and priestly absolution by an act of perfect contrition (which includes the desire for formal confession). Venial sins need not be confessed. The form of penance is absolution,* a judicial act. The sacrament is properly administered by a priest who has both the authority of his priestly order and the authority of jurisdiction in the given case. Since 1215 at least an annual confession has been required of each communicant. See also *General Confession.*

5. The Luth. symbols rejected the necessity and possibility of enumerating all sins in confession (AC XI, Ap XI, SA III iii), but insisted on the retention of private confession, though they granted that it was a human institution. The absolution that followed confession they regarded as the "living voice of the Gospel." (Ap XI; SC V)

6. Early in the Luth. Reformation, individual confession before Communion became predominantly an exploration to determine if the individual had adequate knowledge for worthy reception of Holy Communion. In the era of Pietism, individual confession fell into disuse and was replaced by general* confession.

7. Ref. and Angl. chs. rejected private confession and absolution as a sacrament in the 16th c.

8. In Am., the Definite Platform (1855) held that no one should be admitted into the General Syn. who believes in private confession and absolution. But C. F. W. Walther, like many supporters of the Confessional Revival in Eur., felt that both should be retained. In the 20th c. periodic attempts have been made to restore individual confession in the Luth. Ch. in the spirit of the symbols. But the most common form of confession remains the gen. pub.

confession and absolution in the course of the Eucharistic service or immediately before it.

9. In E Orthodoxy, individual confession plays a more restricted role than it does in the W.

EL, ACP

Sources of Christian Theology, ed. P. F. Palmer, II: *Sacraments and Forgiveness* (Westminster, Md., 1959); K. Aland, "Die Privatbeichte im Luthertum von ihren Anfängen bis zu ihrer Auflösung," *Kirchengeschichtliche Entwürfe* (Gütersloh, 1960), pp. 452 to 519; L. Klein, *Evangelisch-lutherische Beichte: Lehre und Praxis* (Paderborn, 1961); P. H. D. Lang, "Private Confession in the Lutheran Church," *Una Sancta,* XXII, 1 (Resurrection, 1965), 18–40; F. L. Precht, *Changing Theologies of Private and Public Confession and Absolution* (unpub. ThD dissertation, Conc. Sem., St. Louis, 1965).

Confession of Faith. See *Creeds and Confessions.*

Confession of Faith (Zwingli's 1530). See *Reformed Confessions,* A 3.

Confesion of 1967. See *Presbyterian Confessions,* 4.

Confession of Seven Baptist Churches in London. See *Democratic Declarations of Faith,* 3.

Confession of 1680. See *Democratic Declarations of Faith,* 2.

Confession of 1688. See *Democratic Declarations of Faith,* 3.

Confession of Somerset. See *Democratic Declarations of Faith,* 3.

Confessional Church, Evangelical Lutheran. See *Germany, Lutheran Free Churches in,* 13.

Confessional Lutheran Church of Finland. See *Finland, Lutheranism in,* 5.

Confessional Lutheranism, Awakening of. See *Luther Renaissance; Lutheran Confessions,* A 6, D; *United States, Lutheran Theology in,* 6–11.

Confessional Subscription. See *Lutheran Confessions,* D 3.

Confessions. See *Creeds and Confessions; Theology.*

Confessor. 1. One who avows faith. 2. Martyr in the early ch. 3. One who is known for a holy life, esp. under persecution. 4. One (e. g., priest or pastor) who hears confession* and pronounces absolution.* See also *Keys, Office of,* 8 b; *Saints, Veneration of,* 3.

Configuration. See *Psychology,* J 5.

Confirmation. 1. In the early ch., confirmation was part of the rite of Baptism. After the candidates were baptized Easter Eve, they were "confirmed" with chrism,* prayers, the sign of the cross, and the laying on of hands; Easter morning they were allowed to make their 1st communion (see *Catechetics,* 1–3). A remnant of this early practice survived in Luther's *Taufbüchlein;* it is found in the current post baptismal prayer in which God is implored to strengthen, i. e., confirm, the child "with His grace unto life everlasting."

2. With the growth of the ch., and esp. with the increased number of infant baptisms, bps. began to delegate authority to priests, permitting them to baptize anytime. In the E, priests were permitted also to confirm, provided they used chrism blessed by the bp. But in the W, Rome forbade confirmation except by a bp. Where the RC liturgy came into use, Baptism and confirmation became distinct and separate rites. Because of this separation the idea gradually emerged in medieval times that confirmation was a complement to Baptism. At first the rite was greatly to be desired because it gave a Christian the added gift of the Holy Spirit; later it was deemed necessary for salvation. Already in the 1st half of the 12th c. Hugh* of St. Victor referred to confirmation as the 2d sacrament. Confirmation was made part of the RC sacramental system by the Council of Florence* 1439; it was said to bestow grace and a "certain spiritual and indelible sign" necessary for salvation, equal in power to all other sacraments. In March 1547 the Council of Trent* fixed the RC doctrine and anathematized the Prot. substitution for confirmation.

3. The question whether confirmation should precede 1st Communion has been a knotty one in the RC Ch. At different times and places, esp. in Lat. Am. chs., 1st Communion has preceded confirmation on the premise that the Eucharist is supernatural food, whereas confirmation is supernatural growth. In gen., the hierarchy has favored the precedence of confirmation, esp. since instruction has become part of preparation for the rite.

4. The Gk. Cath. chs. regard confirmation as a sacrament and administer it at the same time as Baptism or as soon as possible after it, even in the case of infants. In the Angl. (Prot. Episc.) Ch. confirmation is a formal rite administered by the bp.; the High Ch. regards it as a sacramental rite conveying the gift of the Holy Ghost, the low Ch. as essentially a personal renewal of the promises made by others for the subject in Baptism. The High Ch. urges the age of 5–6, the Low Ch. prefers the age of 14–16 for confirmation.

5. Contrary to popular opinion, the Luth. Ch. lacks a universally accepted definition of confirmation and a consistent approach to it. It unanimously rejected the RC view (see 2) but was not in agreement as to whether the rite should be reest., ref., or abolished.

6. Luther did little to encourage an ev. type of confirmation, though he approved the 1540 Brandenburg Ch. Order and subscribed to the 1545 Wittenberg Reformation. His emphasis on instruction, esp. in preparation for the Lord's Supper, proved to be a major contribution to a new type of confirmation assoc. not only with Baptism but also with the Lord's Supper. Only in the few cases where confirmation was introd. as a substitute for the RC sacrament was the assoc. with the Lord's Supper not made.

7. The development of confirmation in the Luth. Ch. followed no uniform pattern. Most Luths. in the 16th c. wanted nothing to do with confirmation and regarded the very word as a "Romanizing" offense. But even in those parts of Ger. and Scand. where the rite as such was rejected, need for instruction connected with Baptism and the Lord's Supper led to a Luth. rite. Efforts were made in a few chs. to reest. confirmation (Hesse) or ref. it (Pomerania). Local circumstances varied; at some places confirmation could be quickly est., elsewhere it was delayed; it was not pub. observed in Hamburg till 1832. See also *Denmark, Lutheranism in,* 6.

8. In the development of confirmation in the Luth. Ch. there were at least 6 gen. types: catechetical, traditional, hierarchical, sacramental, pietistic, and rationalistic. The first 4 appeared in the 16th c., the last 2 in the 17th and 18th c. In practice it is difficult to find any of these in pure form (except occasionally in an initial stage), because more than 1 influence was often at work. In the latter part of the 19th c. and esp. in the 20th c. it is not unusual to see the impact that all 6 types have made, esp. in the New World and in the younger chs.

9. Where confirmation is assoc. with Baptism and the Lord's Supper, as is usually the case, 3 essential elements of confirmation are: (1) a course of instruction preceding the rite; (2) profession of faith, usually made through an examination and summarized in formal questions in the rite; (3) intercessory prayers by the cong., normally with imposition of hands.

10. In Am., Luth. children are confirmed when they are 12–14; such confirmation usually takes place on Palm Sun. or Pent. Adults are often privately catechized in a less formal manner, and pub. confirmed. When children's 1st Communion is separated from confirmation, the latter usually occurs later,

with confirmation regarded as a partial fulfillment of the obligation imposed at the time of Baptism to rear children in the Christian faith. Preparation for 1st Communion is then also preceded by instruction; such instruction, though less extensive, shows that the children (usually bet. 8 and 10) can examine themselves (1 Co 11:28) and are able to exercise the right to partake of the Lord's Supper.

11. Baptism, not confirmation, normally marks the beginning of one's membership in the ch. If a person has come to faith by the Gospel prior to Baptism, the sacrament becomes for him a confirmation. Hence a person is not baptized and confirmed in the same ceremony. In such cases confirmation is superfluous and detracts from Baptism.

12. The practice of confirmation has received considerable attention in the Luth. Ch. since WW II. The LWF made confirmation a matter of particular study in order to divest it of for. elements and reconstruct it for present-day circumstances. Similar studies are being carried on by other groups. ACR

See also *Catechetics; Christian Education,* E 10.

RC: M. Bohen, *The Mystery of Confirmation* (New York, 1963); B. Neunheuser, *Baptism and Confirmation,* tr. J. J. Hughes (New York, 1964). *Angl.:* G. W. H. Lampe, *The Seal of the Spirit* (New York, 1951); *Confirmation: History, Doctrine, and Practice,* ed. K. B. Cully (Greenwich, Connecticut, 1962). *Luth.:* Commission on Education, Lutheran World Federation, *Confirmation: A Study Document,* tr. W. G. Tillmanns (Minneapolis [1963]); A. C. Repp, *Confirmation in the Lutheran Church* (St. Louis, 1964); *Zur Geschichte und Ordnung der Konfirmation in den lutherischen Kirchen,* ed. K. Frör (Munich, 1962).

Confirmation Instruction. See *Confirmation; Parish Education,* F 4.

Confiteor (Lat. "I confess"). Confession of sins used in the RC Ch. in sacrament of penance,* at beginning of mass,* and on other occasions. The form of the RC *Confiteor* adopted 1314 by the Council of Ravenna was authorized 1570 in the missal of Pius V (see *Popes,* 21). In it confession is made to God and the saints. Though not in the Book of Common Prayer, it has been widely adopted in the Angl. Ch. In the Luth. Ch., the part of the service commonly called the Confession of Sins, extending inclusively from the Exhortation to the Declaration of Grace, is often called *Confiteor.*

Confractorium. See *Ambrosian Music.*

Confraternity. In the wider sense, RC assoc. having as its object some particular religious work (e. g., personal sanctification; care of poor, sick, orphans; performance of last rites). Hincmar* prescribed rules for them. Fl. 13th c.

RC canon* law restricted use of name "confraternity" to unions that have increase of pub. worship as at least part of their purpose and calls such other assocs. as described above "sodalities" or "pious unions."

Confucianism. 1. The system of thought growing out of the teachings of Confucius,* who profoundly influenced China's ethics, religion, educ., and pol. systems for more than 2,000 yrs.

2. Writings of Confucianism include 5 sacred books called *Ching: Book of History, Book of Songs, Book of Changes, Spring and Autumn Annals, Book of Rites;* a 6th, *Book of Music,* is said to have been lost in the Han dynasty. Of these 6, Confucius probably wrote only the *Spring and Autumn Annals;* the *Book of Rites* and parts of the *Book of Changes* may have been written as late as the 3d c. BC. Neo-Confucianists of the Sung dynasty (960–1279) added 4 books called *Shu: Analects* of Confucius, *Golden Mean, Great Study,* and *Works of Mencius.**

3. Confucius enunciated many ethical precepts and sayings of China's past without organizing them into a coherent system. As Aristotle* later, so Confucius stressed the golden mean bet. extremes. Inevitably Confucianism blended with China's ancient universalism and its antitheses of *yin* and *yang,* world souls or forces representing the female (negative) principle and the male (positive) principle in the universe, and associated also, e. g., with cold and heat, darkness and light. Yang divides itself into innumerable *shen* (good spirits) abiding, e. g., in sun, moon, stars, rivers, mountains. The *shen* of one's ancestors are regarded as included among the gods. Yin is divisible into innumerable *kwei,* evil spirits or demons that harass men and must be driven away. Heading up all the spirits is *T'ien,* heaven, also called *Ti,* emp., or *Shang-ti,* supreme emp. In its animist, ancestor worship, polytheism, and polydemonism Confucianism has affinities with some schools of Hinduism.

4. From 200 BC to AD 900 Taoism* and Buddhism* greatly influenced Confucianism; the neo-Confucianism resulting during the Sung dynasty had epistemological and metaphysical foundations for its ethics. The religious leadership of the people rested with the emp., called Son of Heaven, until the fall of the empire 1912.

The welfare of the nation was regarded as depending on the proper observance by the emp. of the religious rites, esp. the worship of heaven and earth at the winter and summer solstices resp., at the great altars S and N of Peking. On these occasions the emp., also sacrificed at the tablets of his ancestors and to the sun, moon, stars, winds, rain, clouds, and thunder. Other gods in the pantheon of the state religion were the corn spirits, various mountains and streams in China, the principal seas, famous men and women of antiquity (e. g., Confucius and his disciples), the emp. who taught the people agriculture, the first breeder of silkworms, and the planet Jupiter. Still other gods were worshiped by the mandarins and authorities in the provinces, e. g., physicians of ancient times, a star that is regarded as patron of classical studies, the gods and goddesses of walls and moats, cannons, water, rain, architecture, kilns, and storehouses. Three annual sacrifices were brought for the repose and refreshment of the souls of the departed in gen. There are numerous temples throughout the empire; though there is no priesthood, religious observances are thoroughly ritualistic and attended by great pomp. Sacrifices include swine, cattle, goats, and silks.

5. In his concern for the welfare of the state Confucius preserved what he thought was best in traditional teachings. He made his ethics revolve around *jen* (human-heartedness, or love; one of his 3 universal virtues, wisdom, love, and courage, and one of his 5 constant virtues, love, righteousness, propriety, wisdom, and sincerity). His 5 cardinal relations included those of prince and minister (or ruler and subject), husband and wife, father and son, older brother and younger brother, and friend and friend. His Golden Rule took a negative form: "Do not to others what you do not want done to yourself." He produced no philos. or theol. system. His teachings were entirely ethical; he did not speak of God, immortality, or sin and its remedy; punishment for wrongdoing is confined to this world; salvation comes by effort. His teachings met little success in his lifetime, but Confucian writings were hidden and escaped the Burning of the Books under Shih Huang Ti ca. 212 BC and thereafter gained in influence. State worship of Confucius began 195 BC under Liu Pang, founder of the Han dynasty, and ended 1912; imperial worship ceremonies were resumed at the Temple of Heaven by the president at the winter solstice 1914.

Confucianism spread to other countries, including Annam and Korea*; it entered Japan* at ca. the same time as Buddhism (6th c. after Christ) and was considerably altered by Jap. influences; e. g., in China the emp.'s rule as Son of Heaven was contingent on the pleasure and support of the people; in Jap. the emp. ruled as Son of Heaven theoretically by right of descent from Amaterasu,* practically by conquest and power; this lends significance to the denial of Hirohito, Jap. emp., in a Jan. 1, 1946, rescript, that he is divine.

See also *Chinese Philosophy; Religion, Comparative, Bibliography; Sacred Literature.* AJB

Confucius (K'ung Fu-tzu; Kung Fu-tse; K'ung Ch'iu; ca. 551–ca. 479 BC). Chinese philos. B. Lu (now Shantung). Prime minister of Lu. Resigned ca. 495 in protest against ruler's evil ways. See also *Chinese Philosophy; Confucianism.*

Confutatio Pontificia. See *Lutheran Confessions,* A 3.

Confutation, Book of. See *Konfutationsbuch.*

Congo. See *Africa,* F 2, 4.

Congregation. See *Authority; Church; Keys, Office of; Lutheran Congregation; Polity, Ecclesiastical.*

Congregation of God in the Spirit, The. Group organized by Henry Antes (1701–55) in Pa. 1742 in effort to unite ev. Christians, esp. Luths., Ref., and Moravians.

Congregation of the Brothers of Charity *(Frères de la charité).* RC religious order founded ca. 1807 at Ghent, Belgium, by Pierre-Joseph Triest (1760–1836; canon of St. Bavon of Ghent) to sanctify its mems. by the exercise of works of charity that embrace every phase of physical and moral suffering. The rule and constitutions were approved and confirmed by Leo XIII 1899.

Congregation of the Daughters of Mary Immaculate. See *Marianists.*

Congregation of the Index. See *Index of Prohibited Books.*

Congregation of the Little Sisters of the Poor. See *Sisterhoods.*

Congregation of the Mission. See *Lazarists.*

Congregational Christian Churches, General Council of. See *United Church of Christ,* I.

Congregational Christian Churches, National Association of. Organized 1955 in Detroit, Mich., by Cong. Christian Chs. that did not merge with United* Church of Christ; no doctrinal requirements. 1965 inclusive membership: 110,000.

Congregational Christian Student Fellowship. See *Students, Spiritual Care of,* A 3.

Congregational Holiness Church. Separated from the Pent. Holiness Ch. 1921 in protest against episc. form of govt. and to retain holiness doctrines (see *Holiness Churches,* 3). 1962 inclusive membership: 5,212.

Congregational Independence. See *Polity, Ecclesiastical,* 3, 4.

Congregational Methodist Church. See *Methodist Churches,* 4 b.

Congregational Methodist Church of the U. S. A. See *Methodist Churches,* 4b.

Congregational Union (Scot.). See *Scotland, Reformation in,* 4.

Congregationalism. See *United Church of Christ,* I A 1.

Congregations, Roman. See *Curia.*

Congress, Church. See *Church Congress.*

Congress of Racial Equality (CORE). An organization that seeks to gain rights for Negroes chiefly through passive resistance. Organized 1942 Chicago by James Leonard Farmer, former program dir. of NAACP; he was influenced by *War Without Violence,* written by Krishnalal Shridharani, pupil of Gandhi. The passive resistance movement was aided by Martin L. King,* Jr. (see also *Southern Christian Leadership Conference*). In 1961 CORE conducted the first Freedom Rides into Ala. and Miss. Farmer resigned from CORE effective 1966 to head the Center for Community-Action Education, Inc.

W. H. Burns, *The Voices of Negro Protest in America* (New York, 1963).

Congruity. See *Merit.*

Connecticut Asylum. See *Gallaudet, Thomas Hopkins.*

Connectionism. See *Educational Psychology,* D 3.

Connolly, Richard Hugh (1873–1948). Patristic scholar; educ. Cambridge; priest 1899; head of Benet House, Cambridge, 1904–16; ed. patristic writings.

Connor, Ralph. See *Gordon, Charles William.*

Conrad III (1093–1152). King of Ger. 1138–52; founded Hohenstaufen dynasty of Holy Roman emps., but was not crowned emp.; a leader of 2d Crusade (see *Crusades,* 3).

Conrad, Frederick William (Jan. 3, 1816–Apr. 10, 1898). B. Pine Grove, Pa.; educ. Gettysburg Sem. 1837–40; pastor Waynesboro, Pa., 1841–44; St. John's, Hagerstown, Md., 1844–50; prof. Wittenberg Coll., Springfield, Ohio, 1850–55; pastor First Luth. Ch., Dayton, Ohio, 1855–62; Trinity Luth. Ch., Lancaster, Pa., 1862–64; Chambersburg, Pa., 1864. Part owner and ed. *Lutheran Observer,* Baltimore, Md., 1863; chief ed. 1866–98; ed. Luther's Catechism; joint author *Lutheran Manual and Guide.* See also *General Synod,* 7.

Conrad of Gelnhausen. See *Konrad von Gelnhausen.*

Conrad of Marburg. See *Konrad von Marburg.*

Conradi, Ludwig Richard (1856–1939). Leader of Adventists in Ger. and Russ. Works include *Das Geheimnis enthüllt; Der Seher von Patmos; Weissagung und Weltgeschichte.*

Consalvi, Ercole (1757–1824). It. cardinal; opponent of Fr. Revolution; chief negotiator of 1801 Concordat. See also *Concordat,* 5.

Consanguinity. See *Impediments of Marriage, Scriptural and Natural.*

Conscience. In gen. usage the term applies to the moral feeling, the urge to do the right thing and avoid the wrong. Figuratively the word is used loosely to denote man's intuition of right and wrong; or the sensitiveness of individuals or groups to moral right or wrong. In gen. literature the term has a usage far from standard or uniform.

The NT uses a standard word for conscience, *syneidesis;* despite variations in NT authorship, a unified pattern of meaning emerges. Twice (1 Ptr 2:19; Ro 13:5) the term seems to imply in gen. man's moral conscience toward God, the realization that God is concerned for the goodness of man's actions. But in most cases the word is given a more specialized meaning. Peter, the writer to the Hebrews, and particularly Paul often refer to "the good conscience." By this they imply the awareness, satisfying in feeling, of the rectitude of one's conduct and intimate that conscience involves or presupposes recognition of a standard. Conversely the writer to the Hebrews and Paul speak of a bad conscience, i. e., one aware of a moral lapse and offense against an acknowledged standard. This process of recognizing a standard and comparing action with it is explicit and central in Paul's use of the term in the epistles to the Corinthians (1 Co 10:25-29; 2 Co 1: 12; 5:11). There Paul describes the results of this process of judgment as imperfect and unhappy where the standard of judgment is faulty. He speaks of a "weak" conscience (1 Co 8:10, 12) as one that is not feeble or sluggish in its activity, but hampered by a faulty norm. Interesting is the word "seared" (1 Ti 4:2), which some have imagined to mean "calloused" or "insensitive"; more consistently it implies "branded" in the sense of permanently harmed. Paul speaks of conscience serving as a witness (Ro 2:15; 9:1), i. e., to the recognition of moral responsibility.

In Luth. literature much has been made of the "terrors of conscience" (contrition*), induced by the indictment of the law of God, as the indispensable prerequisite and preparation for the Gospel. The Biblical concept appears to be more limited to the intellectual and emotional reflex accompanying particularly such actions as are consciously contrary to standard. The NT emphasizes man as living with a sense of responsibility toward God, who sets the standard. In the cure of souls, the Christian is interested in removing the tensions of an evil conscience with the guarantee of a good conscience, i. e., forgiveness in Christ Jesus, and in equipping the individual with that vitality for living which fosters the good conscience, i. e., the life of the Spirit through Jesus Christ. RRC

See also *Baptist Churches,* 1, 2.

E. W. A. Koehler, "Conscience," *CTM,* XIII (May 1942), 337–364; C. A. Pierce, *Conscience in the New Testament* (London, [1955]); C. Scaer, *A Treatise on Conscience* (Boston, 1927); J. Stelzenberger, *Syneidesis im Neuen Testament* (Paderborn, 1961) and *Syneidesis, Conscientia, Gewissen* (Paderborn, 1963); A. Gräbner, "Die Lehre vom Gewissen," 1894 *Proceedings* of the Nebraska District, LCMS, pp. 9 to 77.

Consecration of the Elements. See *Worship, Parks of,* 12.

Consensus Formula, Helvetic. See *Reformed Confessions,* A 10.

Consensus Gentium; Consensus Omnium (unanimity of the races; unanimity of all). Terms often used in apologetics,* esp. in connection with the doctrine of God and immortality. Thus the gen. belief in a supreme being is held to support the argument for the existence of God.

Consensus of Bremen *(Consensus ministerii Bremensis ecclesiae).* Calvinistic doctrinal statement prepared by C. Pezel* and others; signed 1595; made confession of Bremen by its council 1644.

Consensus of Dresden *(Consensus Dresdensis).* Prepared 1571 by crypto-Calvinists as an apology of their position before Elector August.* (See also *Crypto-Calvinistic Controversy*).

Consensus of Geneva *(Consensus Genevensis).* See *Reformed Confessions,* A 9.

Consensus of Sandomierz *(Consensus Sendomirensis).* See *Poland, Lutheranism in,* 3.

Consensus of Zurich. See *Reformed Confessions,* A 8.

Consensus Omnium. See *Consensus Gentium.*

Consensus Patrum. Unanimity of ch. fathers on a matter of faith or morals.

Consensus Quinquesaecularis. Term describes hist. theory of G. Calixtus,* who held that till 500 the ch. was marked by unity and doctrinal purity. He argued that the only proper basis for ch. union in his day was the unanimous belief of the first 5 cents. Term was popular among some Latitudinarians* and is used occasionally to describe one possible basis of future reunion of the ch. See also *Vincent of Lérins.*

G. Calixtus, *De veritate unicae religionis Christianae et autoritate antiquitatis ecclesiasticae dissertationes* (Helmstedt, 1658); O. Ritschl, *Dogmengeschichte des Protestantismus,* IV (Göttingen, 1927), 400–423; H. Sasse, " 'The Future Reunited Church' and 'The Ancient Undivided Church,' " *The Springfielder,* XXVII, 2 (Summer 1963), 8–21. HTM

Consensus Repetitus Fidei Vere Lutheranae. Confession prepared 1655 by A. Calov* and others against the syncretism* of G. Calixtus.*

Consensus Tigurinus (Zurich Consensus). See *Calvin, John,* 12; *Reformed Confessions,* A 8.

Conservative Amish Mennonites. See *Mennonite Churches,* 3.

Conservative Baptist Association of America. See *Baptist Churches,* 19.

Conservative Congregational Christian Conference. Organized 1948 in Chicago by Cong. Chr. Chs. and ministers who wished to maintain traditional Cong. doctrines and polity. 1972 inclusive membership: 19,416.

Conservative Dunkers. See *Brethren,* 2.

Conservative Judaism. See *Judaism,* 3.

Conservative Mennonite Conference. See *Mennonite Churches,* 3 a.

Consilia Evangelica. See *Evangelical Counsels.*

Consistent Empiricism. See *Logical Positivism.*

Consistory. 1. In RCm, assembly of cardinals* convoked by and meeting in the presence of the pope. 2. In Ch. of Eng., the bp.'s court for administration of ch. law in his diocese (but "Commissary Court" in the diocese of Canterbury). 3. The lowest court in many Presb. chs., consisting of the minister and elders of a local ch. (Kirk-session in Scot.). 4. In some Luth. and Ref. chs., an administrative bd. consisting entirely, or chiefly, of clergy; often attached to the bp. of a diocese. See also *Reformed Churches,* 1.

Consolamentum. Cathari* rite of laying on of hands by which spiritual baptism was administered and apostolic succession conferred; usually performed shortly before death, making the candidate one of the "perfect."

Consolation. 1. Alleviation of sorrow. 2. Evening meal of monks.

Consolidated American Baptist Missionary Convention. Formed 1840 in N. Y.; included almost all colored Bap. chs. of northern US; worked esp. in Haiti.

Constance, Council of (1414–18). The 2d of three 15th-c. councils intended to bring about a reformation of the ch. (see *Councils and Synods,* 7); held under John* XXIII and Sigismund.* The most influential members of the session were P. d'Ailly* and J. de Gerson.* The papal schism* that began 1378 was settled: John XXIII and Benedict* XIII were deposed; Gregory* XII abdicated; Martin* V was elected. J. Hus* and Jerome* of Prague were burned. Reforms were urged by lower clergy, monks, doctors, and professors, led by d'Ailly and Gerson and supported by the emp. But the would-be reformers disagreed among themselves and their agitation practically came to naught, largely because the abuses they attacked concerned such matters as papal procedure, administration and income of vacant benefices, simony, indulgences, and dispensations, from which the pope, cardinals, and other Roman ch. officials received much of their income.

H. Finke, *Forschungen und Quellen zur Geschichte des Konstanzer Konzils* (Paderborn, 1889); *Acta concilii Constanciensis,* eds. H. Finke, J. Hollnsteiner, and H. Heimpel, 4 vols. (Münster in Westfalen, 1896–1928).

Constance, Peace of. See *Frederick I,* Holy Roman emp.

Constantine I (ca. 280–337). "The Great." Roman emp. 306–337; son of Constantius I (Flavius Valerius; Chlorus, "the Pale"; ca. 250–306; Roman emp. 305–306) and Helena. Sent to the court of Diocletian* 292; Constantius succeeded Diocletian 305 as W emp. and proclaimed Constantine his successor (caesar). The army acclaimed Constantine as Augustus on the death of Constantius at York, Brit., 306; but he was not est. as sole emp. of the W till 312, when he defeated rival Maxentius at the Mulvian Bridge near Rome. On this occasion, according to tradition, he saw the sign of the cross in the sky with words often given in Gk. as *en touto nika* ("conquer by this") and in Lat. as *in hoc signo vinces* ("by this sign thou shalt conquer"). On his standard, called labarum,* Constantine replaced the pagan emblems with the Chi-Rho (initial letters of *Christ* in Gk.). In 313 he and E emp. Licinius issued the so-called Edict of Milan* granting equal toleration to all religions. Licinius later renewed persecutions of Christians, but was decisively defeated 324 by Constantine, who became sole Roman emp. 325. Constantine convened the Council of Nicaea* (see also *Arianism; Councils and Synods,* 4). Beginning in 326 he moved the seat of govt. from Rome to Byzantium, which he rebuilt and 330 renamed Constantinople. Baptized by Eusebius* of Nicomedia shortly before death. In the E Ch. he is venerated as a saint and regarded as equal with the apostles, or as the 13th apostle.

The most diverse opinions have been held on Constantine's personal relations to Christianity and the motives that governed his imperial policy. The extreme view of the E Ch. referred to above was held by Eusebius* of Caesarea in *Life of Constantine.* The other extreme (first put forward by Ammianus Marcellinus [ca. 330–ca. 400], a pagan writer) sees in Constantine nothing but a shrewd, calculating politician, who allied himself with the new religion in order to realize his imperial ambitions. Though Constantine's conduct in gen. was determined by policy rather than by principle, his preference for Christianity was not only prudential but also personal. His life is stained with crimes, but the softening and humanizing effects of Christianity are evident in his legislation. His concern for the unity of the ch., threatened with division by Arianism,* was probably subordinate to higher concern for the unity of the empire. He was drawn to Christians by his interest in purity of life, his genuine humanity, and shrewd statesmanship. He ascribed his victory over Maxentius to the vision of the cross mentioned above, exempted the clergy from military and municipal duties, abolished some practices offensive to pub. morality, est. asylums for foundlings, mitigated slave laws, and placed restrictions on concubinage and divorce. Patron of science and art.

Constantine's importance for the hist. of the ch. lies in 3 areas. He was the 1st emp. to grant Christianity legal standing and imperial support. He set a pattern of imperial interest in ecclesiastical concerns that easily became policy of imperial control for his successors. He moved the seat of govt. to the E, forcing the Roman bp. to become the pol. and administrative as well as spiritual leader in the W.

See also *Church and State,* 3; *Courts, Spiritual.*

M. A. Huttmann, *The Establishment of Christianity and the Proscription of Paganism* (New York, 1914); N. H. Baynes, *Constantine the Great and the Christian Church* (London [1931]); C. N. Cochrane, *Christianity and Classical Culture* (Oxford, England, 1940); L. B. Holsapple, *Constantine the Great* (New York, 1942); A. Alföldi, *The Conversion of Constantine and Pagan Rome,* tr. H. Mattingly (Oxford, England, 1948); A. H. M. Jones, *Constantine and the Conversion of Europe* (London [1948]); H. Dörries, *Das Selbstzeugnis Kaiser Konstantins* (Göttingen, 1954); H. Dörries, *Constantine and Religious Liberty,* tr. R. H. Bainton (New Haven, Conn., 1960); *MPL,* 8, 9–672. HTM

Constantine IV (Pogonatus, i. e. the Bearded; 648 to 685). E Roman emp. 668–685; convoked 6th ecumenical council (see *Constantinople, Councils of,* 3).

Constantine VI. See *Theodore of Studion.*

Constantine (Cyril). See *Cyril and Methodius,* 1.

Constantine, Donation of. See *Pseudo-Isidorian Decretals,* 2.

Constantinople, Councils of. Following councils often considered ecumenical met at Constantinople:

1. The 2d ecumenical council, 381, called by Theodosius* I. Meletius* of Antioch, Gregory* of Nazianzus, and Nectarius* of Constantinople successively presided. Gregory was made bp. of Constantinople; when he resigned, he was replaced by Nectarius. Ca. 150 orthodox bps. attended the council. They produced a doctrinal statement, now lost, on the consubstantiality of the 3 persons of the Trin. and accepted a creed that was more developed than that of Nicaea (Nicaeno-Constantinopolitanum; creed, or faith, of the 150 fathers; see also *Ecumenical Creeds,* B 1 b). 4 canons were adopted; 3 additional ones accepted in the E are probably spurious. The 1st canon condemns Arianism,* Apollinarianism (see *Apollinaris of Laodicea*), and Macedonianism*; the 2d imposed observance of diocesan and patriarchal limits on bps.; the 3d declared that because Constantinople was the new capital its bp. should have preeminence after the bp. of Rome; the 4th invalidated the consecration of Maximus as bp. of Constantinople. See also *Schism,* 4.

2. The 5th ecumenical council was called 553 by Justinian* I to condemn the so-called Three Chapters. The proceedings were dominated by the emp. See also *Three Chapters, Controversy of; Origenistic Controversy.*

3. The 6th ecumenical council, 680–681, was called by Constantine* IV. It adopted dyothelitism* and condemned and anathematized Honorius I (pope 625–638) on grounds of Monothelitism.*

4. The council of 869–870, often regarded as the 8th ecumenical council, though rejected by the Gk. Ch., dealt with the Photian Schism. See *Photius; Schism,* 5.

See also *Acacius of Caesarea; Arianism; Councils and Synods,* 4; *Eastern Orthodox Confessions,* A 3; *Quinisext Synod.*

See bibliography for *Councils and Synods;* J. N. D. Kelly, *Early Christian Creeds,* 2d ed. (New York, 1960); E. Honigmann, *Trois mémoires posthumes d'histoire et de géographie de l'Orient chretien,* ed. P. Devos (Brussels, 1961); A. M. Ritter, *Das Konzil von Konstantinopel und sein Symbol: Studien zur Geschichte und Theologie des II. Ökumenischen Konzils* (Göttingen, 1965). EL

Constantinopolitan Creed. See *Ecumenical Creeds,* B.

Constitutio Dogmatica Prima de Ecclesia Christi. See *Vatican Councils,* 1 b.

Constitution, Westminster. See *Westminster Standards.*

Constitution civile du clergé (Civil Constitution of the Clergy). See *France,* 5.

Constitution Northwestern Holiness Association. See *Methodist Churches,* 4 b.

Constitution on the Catholic Faith. See *Vatican Councils,* 1 a.

Constitution on the Sacred Liturgy. See *Vatican Councils,* 2.

Constitutions. Term derived from Roman law, where it designated enactments of the emp. in decree, letter, or ordinance having force of statute. Hence, in canon law, ordinances of the ch. Gen. used of ecclesiastical constitutions issued by gen. councils and by the Roman see. Episc. constitutions are issued by bps. individually or assembled in syn.

Constitutions, Apostolic. See *Apostolic Constitutions.*

Constitutions, Church. See *Church Orders; Polity, Ecclesiastical,* 6.

Consubstantiation. View, falsely charged to Lutheranism, that bread and body form 1 substance (a "3d substance") in Communion (similarly wine and blood) or that body and blood are present, like bread and wine, in a natural manner. See also *Grace, Means of,* IV 3.

Consul, Stipan (Stephan Konsul; b. 1521). B. Pinguente, Istria; priest; expelled from Carniola for ev. sympathies 1549; guest in home of P. Truber* 1552–53; teacher in Upper Palatinate 1553; Truber brought Consul into contact with J. Ungnad* von Weissenwolf, with whom Consul est. an institute at Urach for tr. and printing; works include tr. of AC 1562 and NT 1562 to 1563 into Serbo-Croatian with A. Dalmatin* and P. Truber.

Consultation. See *Book of Common Prayer,* 2.

Consultation of Worms. See *Worms, Consultation of.*

Consultation on Church Union. See *Ecumenical Movement, The.* 14.

Contarini, Gasparo (1483–1542). Educ. Padua; Venetian ambassador at court of Charles* V; present at Diet of Worms*; cardinal 1535; mem. of commission to prepare for Council of Trent*; sought to reconcile RCs and Luths. at Regensburg 1541 (see *Regensburg Conference*); works include *Confutatio articulorum seu quaestionum Lutheri; Consilium de emendanda ecclesia; Epistola de justificatione.*

Contemplation. See *Mysticism.*

Continence (Lat. *continentia*). Gk. equivalent is usually tr. "temperance" and denotes the virtue of one able to govern self, i. e., master and control his desires and passions (Acts 24:25; 1 Co 9:25; Tts 1:8; 2 Ptr 1:6). Such temperance is enjoined and spoken of as a gift of the Spirit (Gl 5:23). The Eng. word "continence" refers to control of animal appetites as spoken of 1 Co 7:5, 9; 1 Ptr 2:11. The sex urge is not in itself evil, but a gift of God for holy matrimony (Pr 18:22; 1 Ti 3:12; 5:14; Heb 13:4); esp. the incontinent are enjoined to marry (1 Co 7). The Bible opposes all legalistic human ordinances (Cl 2: 16-23; 1 Ti 4:1-3), upholds Christian liberty (1 Co 6:12; 10:23), and considers the practice of continence a voluntary act in harmony with circumstances (1 Co 7:1-5, 26), individual gifts (1 Co 7:6-9), and Christian vocation (1 Co 9:1-6). See also *Asceticism; Celibacy.*

Continental Society. See *Oncken, Johann Gerhard.*

Contingency. See *Boutroux, Étienne Émile Marie.*

Contract, Social. See *Government; Natural Law,* 5.

Contributions, Church. See *Finances in the Church.*

Contrition. Movement of heart prior to conversion, namely, "that the heart perceive sin, [and] dread God's wrath" (FC SD II 70). Before the time of Luther, teachings pertaining to contrition and repentance were admittedly confused (Ap XII 4–7). In rabbinic Judaism, repentance (Heb. *teshubah,* "return") was often man's self-redemption from the thralldom of sin. The RC Ch. teaches that "perfect contrition justifies the sinner even without the Sacrament of Penance" (E. J. Hanna, "Attrition," *The Catholic Cyclopedia,* II [New York, 1907], 66; see also *Canons and Decrees of the Council of Trent,* sess. XIV, Sacrament of Penance, ch. 4). By "perfect contrition" RCs mean detestation of sin that arises from love of God. That which arises from any other motive (e. g., fear of losing salvation) is considered attrition.* In rationalism contrition is the first step toward self-improvement, which it regards the essence of salvation. In many Prot. circles the view prevails either that contrition procures forgiveness of sins or, in milder form, that contrition has an influence on God, moving Him to forgive.

Two truths are taught in Scripture regarding contrition: 1. The nonexistence of conversion where contrition has not preceded (FC SD II 70). Contrition is the indispensable preparation for conversion. Fear of God's wrath and damnation always precedes faith (Jl 2:12; Mk 1:15; Lk 15:18; 18:13; 24:47; Acts 2:37; 16:29; FC SD II 54, 70). One who does not experience such anguish of conscience (*terrores conscientiae,* result of awareness of God's law), despises God's grace (Lk 5:31-39; Ap XII 51; XIII 21; AC XII). Luther emphasized that true contrition is not active *(activa contritio),* i. e., fabricated remorse, but passive *(passiva contritio),* i. e., true sorrow of the heart, suffering, and pain of death (SA III iii 2). But from this it is not to be concluded that contrition is a cause of forgiveness (Ro 3:28). 2. Contrition in no way brings about, implements, or occasions justification through faith (WA 6, 545; 52, 271; 48, 335; FC SD III 30–31). Good works do not justify (Eph 2:8); the contrition of the unconverted person is not even a good work, since it is joined with hatred toward God (God justifies the ungodly, Ro 4:5). As soon as one longs for divine grace, faith exists in the heart (Is 42:3; Mk 9:24; cf. FC SD II 14). Faith is engendered by the Holy Spirit through the Word (see *Conversion,* II 2–3). EL

T. Engelder, "Zur Lehre von der Reue," *CTM,* V (1934), 218–227, 369–382, 445–455, 497–509, 584 to 596, 657–668; W. Elert, "Angst," *Morphologie des Luthertums,* I (Munich, 1931; improved print., 1952), 39–44, tr. W. Hansen, "Fear," *The Structure of Lutheranism,* I (St. Louis, 1962), 43–49.

Controversy of the Three Chapters. See *Three Chapters, Controversy of.*

Convalescents, Homes for. See *Hospitals.*

Convent. Bldg(s). in which a body of religious dwell, or the community itself; tends to be restricted to female communities.

Conventicle. In the early ch., a house of prayer or religious meeting. Later a cabal of monks to secure election of a favorite as superior. In England applied to J. Wycliffe's followers and, contemptuously, to meetings of Dissenters.*

Conventicle Act. See *Presbyterian Churches,* 2.

Conventuals. Branch of Franciscans* that favored accumulation of property and followed a less strict rule.

Conversion. The doctrine of conversion is of paramount importance in the total body of Scriptural teaching and Christian belief, since it shows how the salvation won for us by Christ is brought into the possession of the individual sinner for his soul's eternal salvation.

I. *Necessity of Conversion.* It is God's good and gracious will that every human being should be saved (Jn 3:16; 1 Ti 2:4; Tts 2:11); Jesus fulfilled the Law in our stead and provided a sufficient ransom from sin, death, and the devil (Jn 1:29). But it is not in the power of anyone to take for himself the fruits of Christ's redemption. Faith in Christ, deliverance from the power of darkness, and translation into the kingdom of the Son cannot be achieved by any human being for himself (Eph 2:1). The 1st disobedience brought dire consequences to the entire human race. Man lost his perfect knowledge of God (1 Co 2:7-9; 13:9-10). After the Fall man is still a rational being, with understanding and a will, able to acquire intellectual knowledge of the truths of the Gospel; but he cannot of himself acquire the spiritual grasp that accepts, believes, and trusts in what has been heard and learned (1 Co 1:23; 2:14). Man's will is free in worldly affairs (Ap XVII 4, 7, 9), but there is nothing in the mind and heart of natural, unconverted man that could incline his will toward God (Gn 8:21; Jn 6:44; Ro 8:5). This corruption of the mind and will is not merely a relative loss of righteousness, but natural man no longer has a remnant of the divine image or of his original powers (Mk 16: 16; Jn 1:5; 8:34, 37; 15:5; Ro 3:12; 8:7; 1 Co 2:14; 2 Co 3:5; Eph 2:1-2, 12; Ph 2:13; 2 Ti 2:26; FC SD II 7, 12–14, 20–21). See also *Free Will; Image of God.*

II. *Nature of Conversion.* 1. The word "conversion" (Gk. *epistrophe*) is taken from Scripture (Ps 51: 13; Is 60:5; Acts 3:19; Ja 5:19-20); tr. "turn" (Acts 9: 35; 11:21; 14:15; 26:18; 2 Co 3:16), "return" (1 Ptr 2:25). Luther commonly tr. it with *Bekehrung.* Various synonyms are used in Scripture (e. g., regeneration, new birth, second birth, awakening, illumination, call, repentance), all denoting the act of divine grace by which the sinner is delivered from the power of darkness and tr. into the kingdom of Christ. (Cl 1:13)

2. The word "conversion" is used in Scripture in a wider and a narrower sense. In the wider sense it designates the entire process whereby man is transferred from his carnal state into a spiritual state of faith* and grace* and then enters, and under the continued influence of the Holy Spirit continues in, a state of faith and spiritual life.

3. Conversion in the narrower sense is essentially

the bestowal of faith *(donatio fidei)* in God's promise of salvation for Christ's sake. It takes place in the heart and consists in this, that a heart, broken and contrite because of sin, comes to faith in Christ and trusts in Christ for grace and forgiveness (Acts 11:21). It takes place when the Holy Spirit engenders faith in the hearts of penitents through the Word of God (Law and Gospel) and the Sacraments. (Is 55: 10-11; Jn 1:45-50; 6:63; Acts 8:34-38; 16:13-34; Ro 1:16; 10:17)

4. Though conversion is a divine miracle that cannot be understood through psychological observation and introspection, Scripture speaks of distinct "inner motions" of the heart, namely contrition* and faith; when these are present, conversion has taken place; these inner motions are described by dogmaticians by the words *motus interni, quibus conversio absolvitur* (Is 42:3; Mk 9:24). Contrition does not form a beginning of, or half of, conversion, nor does it produce a better spiritual condition in the sinner, since of itself it can only lead to despair (2 Co 7:10); but it is the indispensable preparation for conversion. The converted person may be sure of his conversion. (2 Co 13:5; 1 Jn 3:14)

5. Conversion is sometimes spoken of as being gradual; but in that case the term is used in a wide sense to include certain outward acts that commonly precede conversion and only prepare for conversion. Conversion proper is the matter of an instant, the moment when the Holy Spirit through means of grace* engenders faith in a contrite heart.

6. Since God's mighty power (2 Co 4:6; Eph 1:19) works through means in conversion, it can be resisted. (Mt 23:37; Acts 7:51)

7. Concerning the fact that some passages of Scripture speak of God's converting man, others of man's converting himself (Jer 24:7; 31:18; Acts 3:19), J. W. Baier* says: "The word 'conversion' is taken in a double sense in the Scriptures, inasmuch as at one time God is said to convert man and, at another, that man is said to convert himself, though as to the thing [itself] the action is one and the same." (*Compendium,* III, 191)

8. Men may fall from grace after conversion (David, Peter, Hymenaeus, Alexander). Unless the sin against the Holy Ghost be committed, they may again be converted ("reiterated conversion"; David, Peter; Eze 18:23-32). See also *Sin, The Unpardonable.*

III. *Effects of Conversion.* Through conversion and faith the believer is made a child of God (Gl 3: 26); enters the kingdom of God; is, for Christ's sake, declared just and absolved from all guilt and punishment (Ro 3:28; 8:33); has peace, boldness, confidence, comfort (Ro 5:3-5), and hope of eternal life (Ro 5:21; 8:30). The Holy Spirit, who creates justifying faith in the heart of the sinner, also, from the moment that this faith has been wrought, sets in motion the divine work of sanctification* (Ro 6: 16; 8:14; 13:10) until in the ch. triumphant the divine image of perfect righteousness will be completely restored (Heb 12:23). WHW

See also *Justification; Synergism; Synergistic Controversy.*

F. W. Stellhorn, "Conversion," *The Lutheran Cyclopedia,* ed. H. E. Jacobs and J. A. W. Haas (New York, 1899), pp. 136—141; "Conversion," *The Concordia Cyclopedia,* eds. L. Fuerbringer, T. Engelder, and P. E. Kretzmann (St. Louis, 1927), pp. 181—182; C. Kleiner, "Conversion," *The Encyclopedia of the Lutheran Church,* ed. J. Bodensieck (Minneapolis, 1965), I, 618–619. In *Proceedings* of LCMS District Conventions: C. F. W. Walther, "Thesen über die Bekehrung des Menschen zu Gott," Northern 1873, pp. 19–58; J. Frosch, "Thesen über den rechten Gebrauch der Gnadenmittel im Werke der Bekehrung," Canada 1882, pp. 12–37; H. Hanser, "Thesen über die Lehre von der Bekehrung," Eastern 1882, pp. 24–50; R. H. Biedermann, "Thesen über die Lehre von der Bekehrung," Nebraska 1882, pp. 7 to 48; F. Pieper, "Thesen über die Lehre von dem gänzlichen Unvermögen des natürlichen Menschen in geistlichen Dingen in ihrer Wichtigkeit für das christliche Leben," Southern 1882, pp. 6–61; C. F. W. Walther and R. H. Biedermann, "Thesen über die Rechtfertigung des sündigen Menschen vor Gott nach dem Evangelium," Nebraska 1883, pp. 10–72; A. Gräbner, "Von der Wiedergeburt oder Bekehrung," Southern 1894, pp. 10–79; H. A. C. Paul, "Die schriftgemässe Lehre von der Bekehrung," Oregon and Washington 1901, pp. 12–54; C. M. Zorn, "Vom freien Willen und von der Bekehrung," Central 1906, pp. 11–53; W. H. Bewie, "Der zweite Artikel der Konkordienformel: Vom freien Willen oder menschlichen Kräften," Texas 1919, pp. 56–130. F. W. Stellhorn, *Worum handelt es sich eigentlich in dem gegenwärtigen Lehrstreit über die Gnadenwahl?* tr. G. H. Schodde, *What Is the Real Question in the Present Controversy on Predestination?* (Columbus, Ohio, 1881); C. F. W. Walther, *Beleuchtung des Stellhorn'schen Tractats über den Gnadenwahlslehrstreit* (St. Louis, 1881); F. W. Stellhorn, *Prüfung der "Beleuchtung" Hrn. Dr. Walther's* (Columbus, Ohio, 1881); *The Error of Modern Missouri: Its Inception, Development, and Refutation,* tr. from the Ger., ed. G. H. Schodde (Columbus, Ohio, 1897); C. M. Zorn, *Bekehrung und Gnadenwahl* (St. Louis, 1902); F. Pieper, "Eine deutschländische Disputation über die Lehre von der Bekehrung," *L. u. W.,* XLVIII (1902), 289–298, 327–333, *Die Grunddifferenz in der Lehre von der Bekehrung und Gnadenwahl* (St. Louis, 1903), *Zur Einigung der amerikanisch-lutherischen Kirche in der Lehre von der Bekehrung und Gnadenwahl* (St. Louis, 1913), tr. *Conversion and Election: A Plea for a United Lutheranism in America* (St. Louis, 1913), and *Christian Dogmatics,* II (St. Louis, 1951), 452–503; J. T. Mueller, *Christian Dogmatics* (St. Louis, 1934), pp. 336–366; G. J. Fritschel, *Zur Einigung der amerikanisch-lutherischen Kirche in der Lehre von der Bekehrung und Gnadenwahl* (Chicago, 1914); L. S. Keyser, *Election and Conversion* (Burlington, Iowa, 1914); O. Hallesby, *Infant Baptism and Adult Conversion* (Minneapolis, 1924); T. Engelder, "Let Us Get Together on the Doctrines of Conversion and Election," *CTM,* VI (July 1935), 539–543; H. E. Brunner, *Wahrheit als Begegnung,* tr. A. W. Loos, *The Divine-Human Encounter* (Philadelphia, 1943); W. H. Wente, "Conversion," *The Abiding Word,* I, ed. T. Laetsch (St. Louis, 1946), 168–187; C. G. Carlfelt, "The Work of the Holy Spirit," *What Lutherans Are Thinking,* ed. E. C. Fendt (Columbus, Ohio, 1947), pp. 219–246; E. S. Jones, *Conversion* (Nashville, 1959); J. Baillie, *Baptism and Conversion* (New York, 1963); W. Barclay, *Turning to God: A Study of Conversion in the Book of Acts and Today* (Philadelphia, 1964).

Conversion of St. Paul. See *Church Year,* 16 B.

Convocation. See *England,* C 9.

Conybeare, Frederick Cornwallis (1856–1924). Fellow of University Coll., Oxford; Armenian scholar; specialized in early ch. hist. and textual criticism of the LXX and NT. Works include *Myth, Magic, and Morals: A Study of Christian Origins; The Historical Christ.*

Conybeare, William John (1815–57). Eng. clergyman and author; educ. Westminster and Trin. Coll., Cambridge; Whitehall preacher 1841; 1st principal Liverpool Collegiate Institution [Liverpool Coll.] 1842; vicar Axminster, Devonshire; resigned because of illness 1854. Wrote *The Life and Epistles of St. Paul* with J. S. Howson*; other works include *Essays Ecclesiastical and Social.*

Cook, Stanley Arthur (1873–1949). Eng. orientalist; taught Heb. and comparative religion at Cambridge.

Coed. *Cambridge Ancient History* and *Encyclopaedia Britannica;* wrote on Code of Hammurabi and on Palestinian religions; other works include *An Introduction to the Bible.*

Cook, Thomas (Nov. 22, 1808–July 19, 1892). B. Melbourne, Derbyshire, Eng.; Bap. miss. Rutlandshire; founded Thomas Cook & Son tourist agency, which gave rise to the term "Cook's tour."

Cook Islands. S Pacific islands inhabited by Polynesians; dependency of New Zealand. *Area:* 84 sq. mi. *Pop.:* ca. 18,000. Discovered by James Cook 1773 to 1777; annexed to New Zealand 1901. J. Williams* was pioneer miss. in Rarotonga. Missions throughout the islands by the LMS. Many converts have been zealous as evangelists, even as far as the Loyalty Islands. The RC Ch. also has missions. See also *Polynesia.*

See *Missions, Bibliography.*

Cooke, Henry. See *Presbyterian Churches,* 3.

Coolhaes, Caspar Janszoon (Kaspar Koolhaas; Koolhaes; ca. 1534–1615). Neth. theol.; mem. nat. syn. of Dordrecht* 1574; differed from strict Ref. position on the doctrine of predestination; emphasized piety and tolerance; believed in salvation of unbaptized children.

Cooper, Anthony Ashley. See *Shaftesbury, Anthony Ashley Cooper, 3d Earl of.*

Cooperation in Conversion. See *Contrition; Conversion; Synergism.*

Cooperative Grace. See *Grace.*

Coornhert, Dirck Volkertszoon (1522–90). Neth. pol. and author; Calvin opposed his tolerance and theol. conviction. Works include *Zedekunst, dat is Wellevenskunste,* a book on ethics with stoic and mystic characteristics.

Cope. See *Vestments, Clerical.*

Copenhagen, Diet of. See *Christian Church, History of,* III 4; *Denmark, Lutheranism in,* 2; *Norway, Lutheranism in,* 2.

Copernicus, Nicolaus (Koppernigk; 1473–1543). B. Thorn [Torun], Prussian Poland. Father of modern astronomy. Educ. Cracow and Bologna; studied medicine, philos., and math; lectured on math and astronomy at Rome. Returned to Prussia 1505; at Heilsberg (Lidzbark Warminski) and Frauenburg formulated the theories later pub. in *Commentariolus* and *De revolutionibus orbium caelestium* [*coelestium*]; in his preface to the latter, A. Osiander* the Elder states that the conclusions are to be regarded as hypothetical; it was put on the Index* of Prohibited Books 1616 and was not removed for many yrs. Copernicus regarded the sun rather than the earth as the center of solar system; prepared the way for J. Kepler,* Galileo,* I. Newton,* and F. G. Bruno.*

Coptic Church (derived from Gk. Aigyptos, "Egypt"). 1. Mark, Barnabas, and Peter are associated in various traditions with the founding of the ch. in Egypt. Tradition also names Anianus (Annianus; d. ca. 84; bp. Alexandria ca. 61–ca. 84) as the first bp. of Alexandria. The break with Rome came at the Council of Chalcedon 451. The Copts denied the 2 natures of Christ, "the property of each nature being preserved, and concurring in one Person and one Substance" (see *Chalcedon, Council of*), and maintained Monophysitism.* Dioscurus* I was deposed at Chalcedon. He retained many followers, but the others of his people elected Proterius patriarch. The latter was murdered because of his harshness and replaced 457 by Timothy, also called Ailuros (Gk. "the Cat"; d. 477). In 567 two lines of patriarchs were est.: the orthodox Cath., whose following consisted of a for. minority, and the Egyptian Monophysites, or the Coptic Ch. The seat of the patriarch was moved to Cairo by Christodulos, patriarch 1047–77.

2. The Coptic Ch. as such never reunited with Rome. It was reduced by internal troubles, persecution, and the Persian invasion (ca. 618-627). It saw relief from Byzantine persecution in the Arab conquests ca. 640. In the Muslim massacre of 832 many Copts were slain. For several cents. thereafter, Egypt was ruled alternately by Arabs, Turks, and Syrians. Saladin, a Kurd of Armenia, became sultan of Egypt 1174; he moderated opposition to Christians, but during the Crusades the Copts were persecuted by Muslim.* The Turks regained power over Egypt 1517 and remained until overcome by Napoleon I. After the Eng. defeated the Fr. in Egypt 1801, Mehemet (or Mohammed) Ali (1769–1849; viceroy of Egypt 1805–48) became ruler; under his reign the Copts attained peace. In 1741 the Coptic bp. of Jerusalem joined the RC Ch., giving rise to the Uniate Coptic Ch. See also *Egypt; Ethiopic Church; Uniates.* ECZ

Coptic Evangelical Church in the Nile Valley. See *Egypt.*

Corbinian (ca. 670–ca. 725). Frankish miss. in Bavaria and S Tyrol; a predecessor of Boniface*; allegedly consecrated bp. by Gregory II (d. 731; pope 715–731); settled at Freising, Bavaria.

Cordatus, Conrad (ca. 1476–1546). Educ. Vienna and Ferrara; to Ofen 1510; deposed and repeatedly imprisoned for ev. preaching in Hung. Spent some time in Wittenberg; teacher Liegnitz 1527; preacher Zwickau 1529; pastor Niemegk 1532, Eisleben 1537; supt. Stendal 1540. Gathered Luther's table talks; opposed Melanchthonians in Synergistic* Controversy.

Cordeliers (Fr. *cordelle,* "small cord or rope"). 1. Franciscan monks est. 1217 in Fr. by Philip II (Philip Augustus; 1165–1223; king 1180–1223); Louis IX (St. Louis; 1214–70; king 1226–70) gave them custody of the Holy Land. 2. Friars Minor (Observants) who followed the rule of Paulet of Foligno (d. 1390). The name is still used in Fr.-speaking regions of Switz. 3. Fr. name for Cordigeri, founded 1585 by Sixtus V (Felice Peretti; 1521–90; pope 1585–90); so-called from girdle worn as sign of penance (see Lk 12:35). 4. Order of noble ladies (Cordelières) est. ca. 1498 by Queen Anne de Bretagne (1477–1514). 5. Pol. club founded 1790; active in 1st Fr. Revolution; met in old Franciscan convent in Paris.

Cordes, Johann Heinrich Karl (1813–92). B. near Lüneburg; educ. Dresden Luth. Miss. Sem. and at Erlangen; miss. to India 1840; involved in securing the former Dan.-Halle Miss. remnants and property for the Leipzig Miss.; connected with work of miss. bd. at Leipzig 1872; retired 1887. See also *Schwarz, Johann Michael Nikolous.*

Cornelius (fl. 3d c. AD). Bp. Rome (pope) 251–253; exiled under Roman persecution. See also *Novatian.*

Cornelius, Peter Joseph von (1783–1867). Ger. painter; studied in Rome; assoc. with J. F. Overbeck* and F. W. v. Schalow*-Godenhaus; works include portrayals of *Creation, Redemption, Sanctification,* and the *Last Judgment* in the Ludwigskirche, Munich; sketched plans for frescoes, depicting sin and grace, for a projected royal mausoleum in Berlin. See also *Nazarenes,* 3.

Cornelius a Lapide (Cornelis Cornelissen van den Steen; 1567–1637). Flemish exegete; became Jesuit 1592; prof. Louvain 1596, Rome 1616. Wrote commentaries on all Biblical books except Jb and Ps; works noted for erudition, spirituality, clarity, allegory, and mysticism.

Cornerstone. Stone lying at the foundation of a principal angle or placed in the most prominent corner of a bldg.; usually hollowed to receive documents, coins, and other items of historic interest.

Cornerus, Christophorus (Corner; Christoph Körner; Korner; 1518–94). Called *Oculus Universitatis.* B. Franconia; prof. Frankfort on the Oder; gen.

supt. Brandenburg; worked on FC at Torgau 1576, Bergen 1577. Works include commentaries on Ps, Acts, Ro, Gl, on selected hymns of OT and NT, on the ecumenical creeds, and on the orations of Cicero; study on the syllogism of Aristotle. See also *Lutheran Confessions,* C 2.

Corporal (from Lat. *corpus,* "body," i. e., of the Eucharist). Linen cloth, ca. as wide as the depth of the mensa* from its front edge to the retable* and originally ca. twice as long; the sacred vessels of the Eucharist were set on part of it, the other part being brought forward to cover them and the offerings of the faithful. Later 2 cloths were used; the vessels were set on one; from the other developed the pall.* The symbolism of the corporal is drawn from Mk 15:46. Beginnings of the corporal can be traced to the 4th c. The chalice veil, and the Communion veil of sheer linen or silk used to cover all the sacred vessels, are of comparatively recent origin. See also *Paraments.*

Corporate Personality. Term describing the instinctive unification of the soc. group and the individual in ancient cultures ("law of participation"), differing from the modern W antithesis bet. the collective and the individual.

H. W. Robinson* tried to demonstrate corporate personality in the OT. Just as the individual implicated the entire group in his reprobation or blessing among primitives, so also, argued Robinson, such an oscillation of unification bet. the individual and the group (family, tribe, nation) is to be found in the OT. Achan implicated his entire family when he plundered Jericho; his family suffered with him for his crime (Jos 7). Descendants of Saul were executed to expiate the Gibeonite blood Saul had shed. (2 Sm 21)

Robinson held that hist. individual Israelites who figuratively represented the nation demonstrated corporate personality by their representative functions. Abraham, Isaac, Jacob, the king, the prophet, the priest, or even a layman (Neh. 1:6) are such representatives. Some scholars suggest that the concept of corporate personality provides the key to understanding the "I" of the Psalms as an individual-collective fluidity differing from the modern antithesis bet. the collective and the individual. Ps 44 may provide an example of such fluidity. Others contend that the Servant Songs of Is (42:1-9; 49: 1-9a; 50:4-11; 52:13–53:12) are best understood as examples of fluid corporate personality. For many yrs. debate has raged as to the nature of the Servant in these Songs; corporate personality enables the Servant to be both individual and nat. in character.

Only if the group is considered primary may the phenomenon of corporate personality occur. Israel's fluid interdependence of the individual and the group arose not from a blood relationship in the group, but primarily because the covenant with Yahweh was the *people's* covenant. In view of the unifying covenant, Amos (3:1) addressed his contemporaries as those whom Yahweh brought out of the land of Egypt. The covenant group, with maximum fluidity bet. the individual and the collective, was bound by no time barriers; corporate personality erased the strictures of time. On the other hand, the individual was not lost within the covenant-people. The Decalog* was directed to individuals.

Bible scholars have tried to use the concept within the NT. T. W. Manson* understands some of the "Son of Man" sayings of Jesus in this light. According to some, the Adam-Christ parallel of Ro 5 and Paul's understanding of the ch. as the body of Christ are more readily apprehended in the light of corporate personality. Others hold that the "body" of 2 Co 5 is to be understood in this way.

O. Eissfeldt, "The Ebed-Jahwe in Isaiah xl.-lv. in the Light of the Israelite Conceptions of the Community and the Individual, the Ideal and the Real," *The Expository Times,* XLIV (1932–33), 261–268; A. R. Johnson, *The One and the Many in the Israelite Conception of God,* 2d ed. (Cardiff, 1961), pp. 1–22; E. Jacob, *Theology of the Old Testament,* tr. A. W. Heathcote and P. J. Allcock (London, 1958), pp. 153–156; T. W. Manson, *The Servant-Messiah* (Cambridge, 1953); J. A. T. Robinson, *The Body: A Study in Pauline Theology* (London, 1952), pp. 55–67; H. W. Robinson, *Corporate Personality in Ancient Israel,* ed. J. Reumann (Philadelphia, 1964); L. Lévy-Bruhl, *How Natives Think,* tr. L. A. Clare (New York, 1926). JEG

Corporate Worship. See *Worship,* 7.

Corporation Act of 1661. Act of the Eng. parliament under Charles II (1630–85; king 1660–85) excluding Dissenters* from municipal corporations. Fell into desuetude after 1718, when the Occasional Conformity and Schism acts were repealed (Occasional Conformity Act: passed 1711 to prevent Dissenters* from receiving Communion in the Angl. Ch. in order to qualify for govt. posts; Schism Act: passed 1714 to prevent Dissenters from keeping schools or engaging in tuition). Repealed 1828. See also *Test Act.*

Corpus Catholicorum. 1. Organization of RC states of the Holy Roman Empire that furthered RC interests; formed ca. 1524; countered by the Corpus* Evangelicorum; ended 1806 at the dissolution of the empire. 2. Published series comprising works of prominent RC writers of the Reformation period (e. g., J. Eck,* H. Emser,* and J. Cochlaeus*). The soc. for pub. was organized 1917 at Münster by J. Greving and transferred later that yr. to Bonn. The soc. also pub. *Reformationsgeschichtliche Studien und Texte.*

Corpus Christi. RC festival in honor of the local presence of Christ in the host*; celebrated on Thu. after Trin. Sun. Ca. 1230 the Augustinian nun Juliana of Liège (1193–1258) in a vision saw the ch. as a full moon with one dark spot, the lack of such a festival. Urban IV (pope 1261–64) est. the festival 1264. The procession, dating from ca. 1275, was originally not connected with the feast. Since the 14th c. the host is carried in the procession in a monstrance.* Miracle plays and mystery plays (see *Religious Drama,* 2) came to be assoc. with the occasion. M. Luther* considered it the most harmful of medieval festivals (WA 17 II, 438); the Council of Trent* gloried in it as a "triumph over falsehood and heresy" (13th Sess., The Holy Eucharist, ch. V). It was one of the first festivals rejected by Luther and was also removed from the Angl. calendar at the time of the Reformation.

Corpus Doctrinae Christianae. Systematized body (Lat. *corpus*), or collection of writings, on Christian doctrine. The term is not always used in exactly the same sense; but it gen. stands for doctrinal standards accepted by special denominations or by the whole ch. The ecumenical* creeds (see also *Creeds and Confessions*) are a *corpus doctrinae* for the whole ch. The Book of Concord is a *corpus doctrinae* for the Luth. Ch., since it contains the specific confessions universally recognized as Luth. A popular, though not orthodox, *corpus doctrinae* was the Corpus Philippicum (1560), which contained the 3 ecumenical creeds, the altered AC, the Ap, P. Melanchthon's* *Loci,* and his other chief doctrinal writings. See also *Lutheran Confessions,* C 1.

Corpus Evangelicorum (Corpus Sociorum Augustanae Confessionis). Organization formed gradually by delegates from ev. states in the Holy Roman Empire to imperial diets; its purpose was to defend and promote ev. interests. From the outset evangelicals made common cause in religious matters at the diets and occasionally made pacts (e. g., at Regensburg 1524, Torgau 1526). The Corpus Evangelicorum was formally organized July 22, 1653; its presidency became permanently attached to Saxony; it ended 1806 at the dissolution of the empire. See also *Corpus Catholicorum.*

Corpus Iuris Canonici. Main collection of RC canon* law antedating the Codex Iuris Canonici; included the *Decretum* of Gratian, decretals of Gregory IX, the *Sext,* the *Clementines,* the *Extravagantes* of John XXII, and the *Extravagantes Communes.*

Corpus Misnicum. See *Lutheran Confessions,* C 1.

Corpus Philippicum. See *Corpus Doctrinae Christianae.*

Corpus Wittenbergense. See *Lutheran Confessions,* C 1.

Corpus Sociorum Augustanae Confessionis. See *Corpus Evangelicorum.*

Corregio, Antonio Allegri da (1489 [some say 1494] –1534). It. Renaissance painter; master of delicacy, lights, and shadows; *Ecce Homo,* dome frescoes at Parma, and *Holy Night* are characteristic.

Correspondence School. See *Ministry, Education of,* X C.

Correspondence Theory. See *Truth.*

Corvinus, Antonius (Rabe; 1501–53). B. Warburg; d. Hanover. Expelled from cloister because of his Lutheranism 1523; preacher in Goslar 1528, Witzenhausen 1529; advanced Reformation in Northeim, Hildesheim, and Calenberg-Göttingen; opposed Augsburg Interim*; imprisoned 1549–52; works include sermons on the Gospels and Epistles.

Corvinus, Jakok. See *Raabe, Wilhelm.*

Cosmic Intelligence. See *Rosicrucians.*

Cosmic Religion. See *Einstein, Albert.*

Cosmogony (Gk. *kosmos,* "world"; *gonos,* "a begetting"). Part of the science of astronomy; deals with the origin of the universe; esp. the study of various theories (and the theories themselves) regarding the beginning of the world. The Scripture account is also called cosmogony.

The idea of creation* out of nothing was practically unknown in early heathen cosmogonies. Most early cosmogonies consider *matter* eternal and attribute the *form* to the activity of a deity. Others, including those who identify deity and matter, regard both matter and form eternal. The Scriptures attribute both matter and form to the Creator.

Prominent at the middle of the 20th c. were the "big bang" theory (originated 1922 by G. A. Friedmann; universe consists of galaxies flying away from each other as result of titanic explosion of dense, hot blob of matter billions of yrs. ago) and the "steady-state" theory (originated 1948 by Fred Hoyle, Thomas Gold, and Herman Bondi; universe is infinite, uniform, and changeless, without beginning and end, with density constant; Hoyle changed view 1965 to hold that known universe is oscillating finite region in an infinite universe).

Cosmological Argument. See *God, Arguments for the Existence of.*

Cosmology. That part of dogmatics* and philosophy* which deals with the origin, structure, and preservation of the universe, with special reference to man.

Cosmos (Gk. "order"). Name given to universe by Gks. because they first regarded it as ordered by fate, later (Plato*; Aristotle*) by intelligence. Religion regards the universe as ordered by deity. Science usually assumes an "order of universe" with or without religious implications.

Costa Rica. See *Central America,* A, D 2, I.

Cotta. See *Vestments, Clerical,* 2.

Cotta, Ursula (d. 1511). Wife of Kunz of Eisenach. See also *Luther, Martin,* 2.

Cotton, John (ca. 1584–1652). "The Patriarch of New England." Puritan*; b. Derby, Eng.; educ. Cambridge; dean Emmanuel Coll., Cambridge, 1606–12; ordained deacon and priest in Ch. of Eng. 1610; vicar St. Botolph's Ch., Boston, Lincolnshire, Eng., 1612–33; summoned to appear before Court of High Commission for changing liturgy of Ch. of Eng. to simpler Puritan form 1632; to Am. with T. Hooker* and S. Stone* 1633; teacher Puritan Ch., Boston, 1633–52; leader of Congregationalism in New Eng.; participated in banishment of A. Hutchinson* and R. Williams*; favored strong govt. by the few; held that magistrates should have authority over spiritual and secular affairs of citizens. Works include *The Keyes of the Kingdom of Heaven; The Way of the Churches of Christ in New England; Milk for Babes.*

L. Ziff, *The Career of John Cotton: Puritanism and the American Experience* (Princeton, N. J., 1962).

Council for Western Asia and Northern Africa. See *Egypt.*

Council of Reformed Churches in the United States. See *Union Movements,* 5.

Council of Trent. See *Trent, Council of.*

Council on Religion and International Affairs. Organized 1914 as Ch. Peace Union at instigation of Andrew Carnegie; name changed 1961; includes non-Christian religious pracifists; headquarters New York City.

Councils and Synods. 1. Ecclesiastical assemblies convened for discussion and settlement of questions affecting the faith and discipline of the ch. Ecumenical conventions are called councils; assemblies representing smaller areas are called either councils or syns. Councils have been distinguished as follows: ecumenical (representing the entire Christian world; the RC Ch. applies this term to councils representing all areas of the RC Ch.), East or West (representing only one of these areas), patriarchal (representing a patriarchate), national (representing a nation; often called syn.), plenary (representing a nation or several provinces; presided over by papal legate), primatial (representing the territory of a primate), neighboring provinces (representing neighboring provinces, but not all the provinces subject to the primate), provincial (representing a province; under a metropolitan), diocesan (representing a diocese; under a bp.; usually called syn.), mixed (composed of civil and ecclesiastical dignitaries gathered to settle secular as well as ecclesiastical matters), councils at Constantinople (consisted of bps. from any part of the world who happened to be in the city at the time of the council), Synod of Bishops (Apostolic Synod; announced by Paul VI [see *Popes,* 35] in the *motu proprio* "Apostolica Sollicitudo" Sept. 15, 1965; consists of representative bps. chosen to advise and assist the pope, by whom it is convoked, to whom it is directly and immediately subject, and who assigns its agenda and gives its members deliberative and advisory power). In Protestantism the word "synod" has various technical meanings.

2. Attempts to trace later councils directly to the 1st council of Christians (Acts 15) have proved futile. Early syns. apparently developed out of enlarged cong. meetings (in earliest times delegates were sent from one cong. to another; 1 Clement, 63; Ignatius, "To the Philadelphians," 10, "To the Smyrnaeans," 11, "To Polycarp," 7) or were called, to meet a difficult and widespread problem. According to an account quoted by Eusebius (*HE,* V, xvi, 10), the "faithful" in Asia met often in many places throughout Asia to consider Montanism.* His own account (*HE,* V, xxiii, 2) speaks of "synods and assemblies of bishops" held near the end of the 2d c. in connection with the Easter* controversy, but they may not have been gatherings of bps. exclusively.

3. *Provincial Synods.* As the teaching of apostolic* succession became prominent, bps. acted as successors of the apostles rather than as representatives of the chs. In the 3d c. bps., presbyters, deacons, and laymen attended syns.; responsibility for decisions gravitated to the bps. Provincial syns. became fixed institutions in the 3d c., when annual meetings came to be held. The 325 Council of Nicaea* (canon 5) called for 2 meetings a yr. The metropolitan called and presided over the provincial syn.

4. *Ecumenical Councils.* Ecumenical councils did not develop out of provincial syns. but were created by Constantine* I. In connection with the Donatist* controversy he called a meeting of bps. at Rome 313 and a larger meeting of bps. at Arles* 314. In the case of these assemblies, as well as that of Nicaea, Constantine determined place and time, summoned the bps., paid expenses, and gave the decisions binding force (Eusebius, *HE,* X, v, 20). Thus real power in early ecumenical councils did not stem from bps. as apostolic successors, but from a secular ruler. Following are often regarded as ecumenical councils (Prots. usually do not consider those after Chalcedon ecumenical): Nicaea* I (325), Constantinople* I (381), Ephesus* (431), Chalcedon* (451), Constantinople* II (553), Constantinople* III (680–681), and Nicaea* II (787). The RC Ch. adds Constantinople* IV (869–870), Lateran* I (1123), II (1139), III (1179), IV (1215), Lyons* I (1245), II (1274), Vienne* (1311–12), Constance* (1414–18), Basel*-Ferrara-Florence* (1431–43), Lateran V (1512–17), Trent* (1545–63), Vatican I (1869–70), II (1962–65). (See also *Vatican Councils*)

5. National Councils. Often called syns. In the early Middle Ages the ch. of the Germanic nations functioned on a nat. basis. Provincial syns. met rarely. The nat. ruler held a prominent position in ch. affairs. Kings usually called or sanctioned the syns. and reserved the right to alter or set aside decisions. After the middle of the 7th c., kings or their delegates attended syns. and influential men of the state were mems. This development was esp. seen in the Frankish kingdom. In Sp., under Arian influence, provincial syns. were most frequent. In the nat. ch. framework, bishoprics changed from city-centered to territorial units with diocesan meetings.

6. *Roman Catholic Synods.* At an early date bps. at Rome, holding that they had primacy in the ch., tried to extend jurisdiction of their provincial syns. to the entire ch. Julius I invited E bps. to a syn. at Rome 341; Gallic bps. attended the syn. called by Damasus 369. Roman pontiffs held that decisions of their syns. were binding because the popes were Peter's successors. Prestige of papal syns. was lessened by recognition given to syns. held by the Carolingian emps. N of the Alps.

With the ascendancy of papal power under Leo IX, papal syns. increased in prestige and were considered ecumenical by the hierarchy (see 4). But they were essentially different from the early ecumenical councils which were controlled by secular power. The popes tried to bring the councils completely under their domination and held that papal authority confirmed the decisions of councils.

Reform councils and the Reformation caused the papacy to view councils with distrust. Only pressing need of a counterreformation led to the Council of Trent.* The papacy reest. the essence of councils along lines developed before the reform councils, with higher clergy as mems. and with control securely in papal hands. At Vatican I (Dec. 8, 1869–Oct. 20, 1870) the papacy obtained absolute primacy in the decree of infallibility. Vatican II (Oct. 11, 1962–Dec. 8, 1965) was called by John XXIII (see *Popes,* 34) for renewal of the ch., to return to the liturgical, biblical, and Christian sources of faith. (See also *Roman Catholic Confessions; Vatican Councils*)

In Am. the RC Ch. has held provincial councils (1829, 1833, 1837, 1840, 1843, 1846, and 1849) and plenary (1852, 1866, and 1884) councils at Baltimore, Md. The abp. of Baltimore presided at all these councils. The plenary councils were attended by prelates from the entire US; their decisions, sanctioned by the pope, were binding for Am. RCm. See also *Roman Catholic Church,* E 8.

7. *Reform Councils.* John* of Paris promoted the conciliar* movement. Marsilius* of Padua held that councils should be summoned by the emp., represent all Christendom, be of highest authority in ecclesiastical matters, and be composed of clergy and laity. W. of Ockham* also held that the gen. council and not the pope was the highest authority in ecclesiastical matters. A solution to the papal schism of 1378 was sought in the views of John, Marsilius, and W. of Ockham. Konrad* von Gelnhausen, Henry* of Langenstein, P. d'Ailly,* and J. de Gerson* led the movement for reform councils. The Council of Pisa* failed to end the schism. The Council of Constance* ended the schism and tried to est. universal councils as the highest authority in the ch. and to have such councils meet regularly. Though endorsed at Basel, this Constance plan failed because of the opposition of the papacy. (See also *Basel, Council of*)

8. *Luther on Councils.* M. Luther* subordinated councils to the Word of God, which is self-sufficient (WA 50, 614–615, 631). The truth of the Gospel cannot be est. by councils (WA-T 3, 149). The Holy Spirit is not bound by conciliar decisions (WA 15, 584; 39 I, 186). Since articles of faith, doctrine, and works existed before councils, the latter cannot est. or decree doctrine, but, as all men, must show that what they say is in harmony with God's Word (WA 21, 471; WA-T 4, 457–458); if their pronouncements show such harmony, they are accepted for the Word's sake (WA 8, 57–58; 10 Ib, 337; 17 II, 29; 39 I, 187; 50, 551–552, 604, 618). As individual mem, so also councils erred. (WA 2, 405–406; WA-Br 1, 470–471; WA-Br 3, 374)

Luther pointed out that the Holy Spirit dwells in the hearts of believers, and if council mems. are selected from the people of God, there is a true council ruled by the Spirit (WA 50, 643–644). Luther favored a free (WA 54, 206–207) Christian (WA 54, 212–213) council (WA 47, 127; 50, 288 to 289; 52, 760; 54, 208). Such a true council is a gathering of pious people for the preservation among them of the pure Word (WA 51, 529). The duty of judging doctrine is a matter for all Christians (WA 45, 380), and hence councils of such Christians also judge doctrine and works and arrange externals (WA-T 3, 694–695). Thus Luther opposed the "pope-in-council" ("head and mems.") idea of Romanists (WA 52, 760; 54, 206–209). Luther regarded Nicaea I, Constantinople I, Ephesus, and Chalcedon as ecumenical councils (WA 54, 221; WA-T 4, 269). He held that councils up to Gregory I (see *Popes,* 4) were still somewhat pure; from Gregory I to Charlemagne* the pope was a spiritual lord and introduced superstitions; thereafter the pope usurped the 2 swords. (WA-T 4, 255)

9. In Luth. and Ref. chs., the theol. basis for councils and syns. is found Acts 15. In syns., congs. converse with each other and express unity in doctrine, order, and life. The authority of councils and syns. derives from the activity of the Spirit.

10. In the early yrs. of the Reformation Luther

emphasized the priesthood of believers and a ch. structure evolved from the cong. After the Peasants' Revolt and the activity of the enthusiasts, Luther counseled that the clergy take the lead and proceed with deliberate caution in giving direction to matters of ch. order. (WA-Br 4, 158)

11. The Homberg Synod (Hesse, 1526) proposed the est. of syns. of pastors and cong. delegates to examine candidates for the ministry, supervise visitations, and answer questions put by congs.

12. P. Melanchthon,* with his emphasis on the visible ch., regarded syns., or *conventus docentium,* as instruments for preserving unity in pure doctrine. Not only clergymen but also pious and learned laymen and secular rulers and their representatives should attend syns. Synods should consider not only Scripture but also the fathers.

13. During his life, Luther and the faculty at Wittenberg decided important issues. Synods therefore were primarily meetings of pastors to discuss teaching and discipline. The actual govt. of the ch. was in the hands of secular rulers and structured through consistories.

14. During the controversies following Luther's death, syns. were structured in various ways (e. g., they often consisted of rulers and their representatives and theologians) to solve theol. problems. Melanchthon opposed solving such questions by majority vote.

15. During the period of Luth. orthodoxy the Scriptural concept of syn. was discussed without definitive formal result.

16. In the 19th c. Luth. syns. began to develop in Ger. and Switzerland. F. D. E. Schleiermacher* proposed a syn. structure evolved from congs. The 1835 Church Order for the Rhineland and Westphalia took on directive importance. Syns. became of increasing importance after WW I. Participation of pastors and laymen in syns. during the *Kirchenkampf* increased the prestige of syns.

17. Fr. Prots., influenced by J. Calvin,* early developed a syn. structure consisting of a local consistory, semiannual provincial syn., and gen. syn. Regional syns. (colloques) were added 1572. This structure influenced Ref. Ch. polity in Scot., Neth., Ger., Eng., and Am.

18. By the middle of the 20th c. most Ger. territories and the EKD, VELKD, and EKU had regional and nat. syns. Such syns. consist of pastors, laymen, and representatives of theol. faculties and of organizations for ch. work. In practically all syns. laymen form the majority (also in the Finnish Ch. Assembly). They are usually legislative, supervisory, and/or advisory.

19. In Am. Lutheranism syn. convs. were important from the 18th c. on. While some (e. g., the Pa. Ministerium and the N. Y. Ministerium) consisted of pastors, laymen gen. had a prominent role. Functions of such convs. varied. C. F. W. Walther* regarded syns. as advisory to congs. C. P. Krauth* held that congs. act in syn. through their representatives. Though syn. convs. still perform some administrative functions, they are gen. regarded as legislative, supervisory, and advisory. EL

See also *Church; Keys, Office of; Neocaesarea, Council of; Pisa, Council of; Priesthood, Universal;* Qunisext Synod.

W. Bright, *Notes on the Canons of the First Four General Councils* (Oxford, 1882); *The Twentieth Century Encyclopedia of Catholicism,* ed. H. Daniel-Rops, LXXXII: F. Dvornik, *The Ecumenical Councils* (New York, 1961); C. J. von Hefele, *Conciliengeschichte,* 7 vols., vols. 8–9 by J. Hergenröther (Freiburg, 1855–90), tr. and ed. W. R. Clark et al., *A History of the Councils of the Church* [2d ed. of vol. 1 entitled *A History of the Christian Councils*] (Edinburgh, 1883–96); E. F. Jacob, *Essays in the Conciliar Epoch,* 3d ed. (Notre Dame, Ind., 1963); H. Jedin, *Ecumenical Councils of the Catholic Church,* tr. E. Graf (New York, 1960); E. H. Landon, *A Manual of Councils of the Holy Catholic Church,* 2 vols. (Edinburgh, 1909); H. Liermann, "Amt und Kirchenverfassung," *Gedenkschrift für D. Werner Elert,* ed. F. H. Hübner, W. Maurer, and E. Kinder (Berlin, 1955), pp. 359–372; M. Luther, "Von den Konziliis und Kirchen" (WA 50, 509 to 563; Eng. tr. "On the Councils and the Churches," *Works of Martin Luther,* V [Philadelphia, 1931], 131–300), *"Convocatio concilii liberi Christiani,* Ausschreibung eines heiligen freien christlichen Concilii" (WA 38, 284–289), "Von den Concilien" (Walch ed., St. Louis, 1887, XXII [*Tischreden*], 1349–70), and *"Disputatio de potestate concilii,* Vom vermögen unnd gewalt eins gemeynen Concilij" (WA 39 I, 184–197); Ap XII 167; Tractatus; P. Melanchthon, *Corpus Reformatorum,* ed. C. G. Bretschneider, III (Halle, 1836), 468–472; C. Raab, *The Twenty Ecumenical Councils of the Catholic Church* (Westminster, Md., 1959); *Theologische Existenz heute,* new series, ed. K. G. Steck and G. Eichholz, No. 37: H. Storck, *Das allgemeine Priestertum bei Luther* (Munich, 1953); R. Stupperich, "Kirche und Synode bei Melanchthon," *Gedenkschrift für D. Werner Elert,* ed. F. Hübner, W. Maurer, and E. Kinder (Berlin, 1955), pp. 199 to 210; *Councils & Synods, with Other Documents Relating to the English Church,* ed. F. M. Powicke and C. R. Cheney, II, in 2 parts (Oxford, 1964).

Counselor in Parish Education. See *Parish Education,* L 4.

Counsels, Evangelical. See *Evangelical Counsels.*

Counsels of Perfection. See *Evangelical Counsels.*

Counter Reformation. 1. Also called Cath. Reformation. A movement in the RC Ch. toward reform and renewal, having its rise in the late 15th c. but receiving its greatest impetus and acceleration from the Prot. Reformation.

2. In the Low Countries the *devotio* moderna* was carried forward esp. by the Brethren* of the Common Life. The *Imitation* of Christ* and the revival of Augustinianism* are products of this movement. Nicholas* of Cusa and D. Erasmus* were educ. by the Brethren; both protested against evils in the RC Ch. and furthered reform.

3. In Sp., F. Jiménez* de Cisneros promoted drastic reform measures in Castile, esp. among the Conventuals*; opened U. of Alcalá de Henares 1508; instrumental in comp. and pub. the *Complutensian Polyglot.* Cardinal Francisco de *Quiñones** ca.(1475–1540) compiled the *Breviarum Sancti Crucis,* which gave new emphasis to Scripture reading and influenced T. Cranmer* and the Book* of Common Prayer.

4. In It. the Oratory of Divine Love, founded ca. 1517, banded together ca. 60 clerics and laymen of an austere life, given to regular formal worship, charitable works, fasting, and pilgrimages, who were determined to renew the RC Ch. The group included Gian Matteo Giberti,* Cajetan* of Thiene (Gaetano da Tiene), Jacopo Sadoleto,* Giovanni Pietro Caraffa (later Paul* IV), and Luigi Lippomano (bp. Verona 1548). After the sack of Rome 1527, they went to Venice, where they were joined by G. Contarini,* R. Pole,* Giovanni Morone,* and others.

5. A commission was created by Paul* III which, under leadership of Contarini, prepared a scheme of reform, *Consilium delectorum cardinalium et aliorum prelatorum, de emendanda ecclesia,* 1537 to 1538. The commission included Contarini, Caraffa, Gregorio Cortese, Giberti, Sadoleto, Federigo Fregoso, Pole, G. Aleandro,* and Tommaso Badia;

aged Bartolomeo Guidiccioni was also appointed and required to supply material for discussion, but permitted to stay home. The report of the commission stated that the ch. was almost in ruins; it condemned various evils, including abuses in the RC curia, absenteeism of bps., and corruption in religious orders.

6. The Camaldolese* were expanded and fl. in the 1st part of the 16th c. The Theatines* concerned themselves with reform of secular clergy. The Capuchins,* Barnabites,* Clerks* Regular of St. Paul, and Clerks Regular of Somascha* belong to the movement that revitalized Romanism. Orders for women (e. g., Ursulines*) were also prominent in the movement.

7. The Cong. of the Oratory, a cong. of secular priests authorized 1575, founded by F. de' Neri,* gave attention to forms of pub. worship and to scholarship; among its mems. were G. P. de Palestrina* and C. Baronius.*

8. The Society* of Jesus, founded by I. of Loyola* and approved 1540, included among its early mems. F. Xavier*, A. Salmerón,* C. Jajus,* D. Laynez,* and P. Favre*; dedicated to missions and educ., it was one of the most powerful forces in the renewal of Romanism. Xavier is noted for his missions in the Orient. Loyola est. the Collegium Romanum 1551, the Collegium Germanicum 1552; the latter supplied men for reconverting Prot. Germany. P. Canisius* comp. catechisms, founded schools, achieved much RC success in N Ger. Poland also was regained with the help of the Jesuits. C. Aquaviva* was one of the foremost generals of the order; R. Bellarmine* and F. Suarez* were among its outstanding theologians.

9. The Jesuits, observing strict obedience, became valuable allies of the reformed popes that followed the earlier Renaissance papacy. Paul* III, Julius* III, Paul* IV, Pius* IV, and Pius V (see *Popes,* 21) rehabilitated the papacy and made it a moral as well as a political force.

10. All of these popes used the Roman Inquisition,* founded 1542 by Paul III. An adaptation of an older institution used in Sp., it was operative esp. in It. in suppressing Protestantism.

11. The 1st Index* of Prohibited Books was issued 1559 under Paul IV, another step in efforts to counter Protestantism.

12. The Council of Trent* was one of the most important factors in this movement. Summoned by Paul III, it met in 3 assemblies, 1545–47, 1551–52, 1562–63. In the 1st, Giammaria del Monte (later Julius III), Marcello Cervini (later Marcellus II, 1555), and R. Pole were papal legates; D. Laynez was perhaps most influential. Doctrine and reform were treated concurrently. The acceptance of the traditional Canon (including the Apocrypha), the authorization of the Vulgate, and the definition of Scripture and tradition as the sources of religious truth were determined. Rejection of imputed righteousness in the doctrine of justification gave direction to RC doctrine. In the 2d assembly, canons on the Eucharist, Penance, and Extreme Unction were est. The last assembly, guided till Mar. 1563 by Cardinal Girolamo Seripando, repeated the reemphasis of the 6th session on residence in their dioceses as a divine obligation for bps.; the sacrifice of the mass, orders, and the est. of seminaries were among the matters in which decisions were reached by this assembly. Anathemas on Prot. doctrines and affirmations of RC teachings, with the success of reform decrees, mark the importance of the Council of Trent in the Counter Reformation.

See also *Czechoslovakia,* 6; *Hungary; Roman Catholic Confessions,* A; *Sweden, Conversion of, to Christianity.*

B. J. Kidd, *The Counter-Reformation, 1550 to 1600* (London, 1933); H. Jedin, *Geschichte des Konzils von Trient,* vols. I-II (Freiburg, 1949–57), tr. E. Graf, *A History of the Council of Trent,* vols. I–II (St. Louis, 1957–61) and *Der Abschluss des Trienter Konzils, 1562–63* (Münster, 1963); *Canons and Decrees of the Council of Trent,* ed. and tr. H. J. Schroeder (St. Louis, 1941); H. Boehmer, *The Jesuits,* tr. from 4th rev. ed. P. Z. Strodach (Philadelphia, 1928); P. Janelle, *The Catholic Reformation* (Milwaukee, 1949); P. Dudon, *St. Ignatius of Loyola,* tr. W. J. Young (Milwaukee, 1949); L. Pastor, *The History of the Popes,* various translators and editors, vols. VI–XXXV (St. Louis, 1923–49). CSM

Country Church. See *Rural Church in America.*

Court, Antoine (1696–1760). Father of Court* de Gebelin; "Restorer of Protestantism in Fr."; b. Villeneuve-de-Berg, Vivarais, Fr.; founded and dir. sem. Lausanne 1729–60. See also *France,* 10–11.

Court de Gebelin, Antoine (1725–84). Son of A. Court*; b. Nîmes, Fr.; educ. Lausanne and Geneva, Switz.; cleric, scholar. Works include *Le Monde primitif.*

Courts, Spiritual (Church Courts; Ecclesiastical Courts). Since the RC Ch. claims the right of legislating for its "subjects," it consistently claims also the judicial powers necessary to enforce its laws and to exact penalties from transgressors. These powers are exercised through spiritual courts. Recognition of the Christian Ch. by Constantine I led to the development of such courts and enabled them gradually to enlarge their jurisdiction. Eventually not only all matters with even a remote bearing on the ch. or religion were taken from the civil courts, but clerics of every degree were exempted from civil jurisdiction in the W Ch., and all cases to which a cleric was a party were tried in spiritual courts. Three courts of judgment are recognized: that of the bp. or his vicar-gen., that of the metropolitan (abp.), and that of the pope. Appeal may be made from lower to higher courts. But some cases are in the 1st instance reserved to the pope. Ecclesiastical courts have been limited in their powers, even in RC countries, and with their jurisdiction their importance has dwindled. (See also *Church and State; Clergy; Curia,* 2 d, e)

Courveille, Jean Claude. See *Marists.*

Cousin, Victor (1792–1867). Fr. philos.; opposed sensationalism*; leader of eclectic school that combined elements of T. Reid's* philos. with Germanic thought and Cartesianism.* Works include *Fragments philosophiques.*

Covenant. 1. The most frequent OT Heb. word for covenant is *b'rith;* it may be derived from an Akkadian word meaning "fetter." Its rarity in the earliest sections of the OT leads one to conclude that Israel's covenant with Yahweh was probably designated in terms other than *b'rith.* "The Ten Words," oldest designation for the Decalogue, has covenant connotations (Ex 34:28); in the ancient Near East covenants were called and regarded as "words" of the suzerain. In the light of this fact it is possible that the phrase "Word of God" was originally bound up with the covenant. The LXX and NT Gk. word for *b'rith* is *diatheke* (usual meaning: last will and testament).

2. In antiquity covenants were gen. est. as a basis for human relationships that were not kinship ties: suzerainty covenant, in which a superior binds an inferior to obligations set down by the superior; parity covenant, in which both parties are bound by oath; patron covenant, in which the superior party binds himself to some obligation for the benefit of an inferior; promissory covenant, which does not est. a new relationship bet. 2 parties, but guarantees future performance of stipulated obligations. With all these covenants, 2 conditions were necessary: there

had to be witnesses, and an oath was taken to insure keeping of the covenant.

3. The covenant concept is rooted in Israel's election by Yahweh. One might say that the covenant is the working extension and implementation of election, the formal and continual application of what is implicit in election, namely the concrete responsibilities assumed by the Elector and the obligation of the electee undertaken in response.

4. Various covenants are referred to in the OT: the covenant with Noah, in which God promises the patriarch and his family deliverance from the flood (Gn 6:18-21); God's covenant with the earth, in which He binds Himself never again to destroy the world by a flood (Gn 9:13-17); God's covenant with Abraham, Isaac, and Jacob, in which He swears to make the descendants of these men a mighty nation and to give them Palestine for their possession (Gn 15:18-21); the Mosaic covenant, which formed the basis of Israel's laws and cultic life (Ex 24:7-8); God's covenant with David, in which the Lord promises the king an eternal dynasty (2 Sm 7); the new covenant outlined Jer 31:31-34.

5. The heart of the covenant concept may be expressed in the words: "I am your God, and you are My people" (Ex 6:7; Jer 7:23; Eze 37:26-27). In the covenant the God who of His own free will and grace brought Israel into existence, created her out of the nothingness of Egyptian slavery through the deliverance of the Exodus, and thus made her a people, this same Redeemer-God through the covenant now bound Himself to be Israel's Father, Husband, Shepherd, and Lord. In the covenant relationship Israel was bound to be this Redeemer-God's obedient son, faithful wife, submissive flock, and loyal servant. The nation's weal or woe depended on its faithful adherence to the covenant obligations. Thus the revelation of Yahweh in the covenant relationship was one that confronted Israel with obligations and responsibilities. From the beginning, Israel knew herself to be accountable. There was no theophany without obligation, no meeting God without meeting the urgency of a demand.

6. Together with her unshakable conviction that she was the chosen of Yahweh, the covenant gave Israel her consciousness of being the elect community of God. The election and covenant made and maintained Israel as a nation and gave it solidarity. God's covenant was with the *people* of Israel; individuals enjoyed the blessings of the covenant relationship only as long as they remained within the covenant community.

7. In the NT the word "covenant" appears in connection with the Lord's institution of the Holy Eucharist. Is it possible to connect the Lord's Supper with OT covenant traditions? The very brief account yields little, but conjecture points to numerous possibilities. The purpose of a covenant was to bind 2 parties together in a firm relationship; this becomes the whole of the NT covenant bet. Christ and the ch. The Lord's Supper was regarded as a formal act that est. a lasting relationship bet. the community and Christ, in analogy to the Mosaic covenant, but combining with it a number of motifs from OT sources, including the sacrificial animal, the Suffering Servant (Is 53:11-12; Mt 26:28), and the new covenant of Jer 31:31-34.

8. Since the individual relationship to Christ is basic to the content, form, and obligation of the covenant, all the detailed prescriptions of Jewish law are unnecessary and (for Paul) inimical to Christianity (Gl 4:21-31; 2 Co 3:6). The Letter to the Hebrews uses the covenant tradition much more frequently but in almost exactly the same way as Paul. Every possible argument is drawn to show that the new covenant fulfills and abrogates the old.

9. The surprising infrequency of references to covenant in the NT is understandable. The covenant for Judaism meant the Mosaic law, and for the Roman Empire a covenant meant a secret soc. This 2-sided conflict made it nearly impossible for early Christianity to use the term meaningfully.

P. Heinisch, *Theology of the Old Testament,* tr. W. Heidt (Collegeville, Minn., 1950); G. E. Mendenhall, "Covenant," *The Interpreter's Dictionary of the Bible,* I (New York, 1962), 714–723; G. E. Wright, in "The Faith of Israel," *The Interpreter's Bible,* I (New York, 1952), 354–357. HEH

Covenant Church of America. See *Evangelical Covenant Church of America.*

Covenant Code. See *Law Codes,* 2.

Covenant Theology. See *Federal Theology.*

Covenanters. Groups of evangelicals in Scot. bound themselves by covenant ca. 1556–ca. 1562 to maintain the Reformation. The 1581 covenant, known as the King's Confession, was signed by people of all classes because of fear of revival of Romanism. Charles I's attempt to introduce the 1637 Scottish Prayer Book led to the 1638 National Covenant, which revived and expanded that of 1581. The 1643 Solemn League* and Covenant was an agreement bet. Scots and the Eng. Parliament against Charles I. Its objectives: maintenance of Presbyterianism in Scot.; reformation of the Ch. of Eng.; uniformity of chs. of Brit. Isles; eradication of popery and prelacy; maintenance of liberties, rights of Parliament, and rightful power of king. See also *Presbyterian Churches,* 4 f; *Presbyterian Confessions,* 1.

See also *Cameronians; Federal Theology; Presbyterian Confessions,* 1, 3.

J. K. Hewison, *The Covenanters: A History of the Church in Scotland from the Reformation to the Revolution,* 2 vols., rev. and corrected ed. (Glasgow, 1913); P. Y. De Jong, *The Covenant Idea in New England Theology, 1620–1847* (Grand Rapids, Mich., 1945).

Coverdale, Miles (ca. 1488–ca. 1568). Educ. Cambridge; his tr. of the Bible pub. 1535 and his 2d version of the NT in 1538; pastor of a Luth. cong. at Bergzabern, Ger., 1545; *Goostly Psalmes and Spirituall Songes,* usually ascribed to him, contains a number of Luther's hymns. See also *Bible Versions,* L 3.

Covetousness. The word appears often in the Bible. The corresponding Heb. term is used in an expression tr. "given to covetousness" in Jer 6:13; 8:10 and used of those who rob and defraud others by extortion and oppression. The Gk. term *pleonexia* (covetousness, grasping selfishness) is used to describe the character and conduct of a greedy person. Hence covetousness is often the desire to gain at the expense of another.

Covetousness is often forbidden and condemned in the OT (Ex 20:17; Jos 7:21; Pr 21:26); to deprive a man of property was to deprive him of his God-given inheritance in the promised land.

Covetousness was recognized as a prominent vice by the Gks. in their ethical writings; it was counted one of the 3 most disgraceful vices.

Christ warned against covetousness Lk 12:15. He indicates that covetousness causes a man to center his life around possessions that become his god. Paul calls a covetous man an idolater and says that such a man has no inheritance in the kingdom of Christ and of God (Eph 5:15); he has no such inheritance because he is not a Christian. Paul also warns against assoc. with one called a brother if he is immoral or covetous (1 Co 5:11).

Some feel that the frequent assoc. of immorality with covetousness implies that covetousness overlaps with, or leads to, immorality. Some NT passages refer only to coveting material possessions; others include immorality, esp. in regard to another's spouse. The 9th and 10th Commandments reflect this dual meaning; the 9th forbids coveting a neighbor's possessions, the 10th esp. forbids coveting a neighbor's wife or any of his living possessions. There are many examples of covetousness leading to immorality, e. g., David and Bathsheba (2 Sm 11) and Herod and Herodias (Mt 14:3-4).

Luther describes the insidious ways of covetousness: "Such is nature, that we all begrudge another's having as much as we have. Everyone acquires all he can and lets others look out for themselves. Yet we all pretend to be upright. We know how to put up a fine front to conceal our rascality. We think up artful dodges and sly tricks (better and better ones are being devised daily) under the guise of justice. We brazenly dare to boast of it, and insist that it should not be called rascality but shrewdness and business acumen." (LC I 297–298)

See also *Sins, Venial and Mortal.*

W. F. Arndt and F. W. Gingrich, *A Greek-English Lexicon of the New Testament* (Chicago, 1957), p. 673; S. D. F. Salmond on Eph 5:3, in *The Expositor's Greek Testament,* ed. W. R. Nicoll (London, New York, Toronto, 1897–1910), III, 351–352; E. R. Achtemeier, "Covetousness" and "Desire," *The Interpreter's Dictionary of the Bible,* various eds., I (New York, 1962), 724, 829–830; *A Theological Word Book of the Bible,* ed. A. Richardson (London, 1950), p. 64. RC

Cowl. Hood worn by mems. of religious orders and developed into great cloak with hood. Benedict* of Nursia ordered his monks to wear heavy cowl in winter and light one in summer. Benedict* of Aniane forbade his monks to wear a hood that extended below the knees. Servites* and Canons* Regular of St. Augustine wear hoods separated from cloaks.

Cowper, William (1731–1800). B. Hertfordshire, Eng.; pre-Romanticist poet; deeply religious; given to attacks of melancholy. Lived at Olney 1767–86; collaborated with J. Newton* on the *Olney Hymns,* contributing 67 of them, including "There Is a Fountain Filled with Blood"; "God Moves in a Mysterious Way"; "God of My Life, to Thee I Call." Other works include *The Task.*

Cox, Frances Elizabeth (1812–97). B. Oxford; tr. 56 hymns from the Ger., including "Jesus Lives! No Longer Now"; also wrote original hymns.

Cox, Melville Beveridge (1799–1833). B. Hallowell, Maine; 1st for. miss. of the Meth. Ch. (Am.); arrived Liberia 1833; d. ca. 4 months later.

Coxe, Arthur Cleveland (1818–96). B. Mendham, N. J.; prelate, author, poet; educ. U. of N. Y.; Episc. rector St. John's, Hartford, Conn., 1842, Grace, Baltimore, Md., 1854, Calvary, NYC, 1863; bp. W diocese of N. Y. 1865; provisional bp. Haiti 1872 to 1874. Ed. and rev. the first 9 vols. of the Am. print. of the *Ante-Nicene Fathers;* hymns include "Savior, Sprinkle Many Nations."

Coyner, Martin Henry (Jan. 15, 1890–Feb. 13, 1962). B. Waynesboro, Va.; d. St. Louis, Mo. Grad. Conc. Coll., Conover, N. C., 1910; Conc. Sem., St. Louis, Mo., 1913. Taught at Conc. Coll., Conover, 1913 to 1928; prof. Conc. Sem., Springfield, Ill., 1928–60. Works include essays and devotional materials.

Cracow, Georg (1525–75). Prof. Roman law, Wittenberg; chancellor under August of Saxony 1565; imprisoned on charges of Crypto-Calvinism 1574.

Cradle Roll. See *Parish Education,* B 2, 3.

Crämer, Friedrich August (May 26, 1812–May 3, 1891). B. Kleinlangheim, Bavaria; studied theol. Erlangen 1830–32; mem. of a Patriotic Students' Soc. (Burschenschaft); imprisoned for participation in the 1833 Frankfort Insurrection; released 1839, but remained under police surveillance; studied Gk., Ger., Fr., and Eng.; tutor to the only son of Count Carl von Einsiedeln 1841–43; tutor of the children of Lord and Lady Lovelace (the latter a daughter of Lord Byron), Devonshire, Eng., 1843; tutor of Ger. language and literature Oxford 1843. Took issue with Tractarianism* there and followed F. K. D. Wyneken's* appeal for Luth. ch. workers in Am.; this took him first to J. K. W. Löhe* in Neuendettelsau 1844; traveled through N Ger. in the interest of miss. in Am.; ordained by T. F. D. Kliefoth* in the cathedral of Schwerin Apr. 4, 1845. Founded miss. colony at Frankenmuth, Mich., 1845; mem. Michigan* Syn., but left it 1846 in protest against liberalism; helped found Missouri* Syn. 1847; continued till 1850 as pastor and Indian miss.; succeeded A. Wolter* as prof. at the Practical Sem., Fort Wayne, Ind., 1850 and later became pres. of the sem.; when it was combined 1861 with the Theoretical Sem. at St. Louis, C. F. W. Walther* and he for a while were the faculty. For the sake of the many Norw. students he studied Norw. In 1875 he went with the Practical Sem. to Springfield, Ill., as sole prof.; he was chief instructor after the arrival of H. C. Wyneken* 1876 and became dir. 1878. His activities included as many as 23 lectures a week; in summer vacations he often prepared emergency workers to be sent out in fall. While in Fort Wayne he also served the country cong. at Cedar Creek; while in St. Louis he founded and served the cong. at Minerstown; while in Springfield he served as vacancy pastor and as assistant pastor of the local cong., and at Chatham, 10 mi. SSW of Springfield.

See also *Detzer, John Adam; Ministry, Education of,* XI.

L. Fuerbringer, "Friedrich August Crämer," *L. u. W.,* LXVIII (1922), 1–8, 33–40; F. Lochner, "Ehrengedächtniss des seligen Herrn Friedrich August Crämer," *Der Lutheraner,* XLVII (1891), 147 to 149, 155–157, 173–174, 181–182, 190–191, 197 to 198, 203–205; XLVIII (1892), 3–5, 12–13, 27–28, 39–40, 48–49, 55–56, 70–72, 79–80, 85–86.

Cramer, Johann Andreas (1723–88). Luth. theol. and hymnist. Preacher Cröllwitz, near Lützen, 1748; court preacher Quedlinburg 1750, Copenhagen 1754; prof. theol. Copenhagen 1765, Kiel 1774.

Cramer, Malinda E. See *Divine Science.*

Cramer, Samuel (1842–1913). B. Middleburg, Neth.; Mennonite preacher; teacher at Mennonite Sem. and prof. U. of Amsterdam 1890.

Cranach (Kranach; Kronach). Family of Ger. painters that apparently took its name from Kronach in Upper Franconia. 1. *Lucas the Elder* (1472–1553). B. Kronach; d. Weimar; influenced by humanists while at Vienna (ca. 1503); court painter under Frederick* III (the Wise) ca. 1505 and under John* the Constant and John* Frederick. Friend of Luther; active in arrangements and formalities of his marriage; sponsor of his oldest son. Mem. of the council and mayor of Wittenberg. Influenced by A. Dürer* and painters of Bavaria and Austria. Painter of princes of Saxony and N Ger. and of the Reformation. Works include portraits, altar pieces, woodcut designs, copperplate engravings, and sketches for dies. Early espoused cause of Reformation; his art shows ev. understanding of Scripture and ch. Painted portraits of Luther and practically all important Luth. reformers. Noted also for secular paintings (e. g., Venus and Cupid; Judgment of Paris; Jealousy). 2. *Hans* (d. 1537). D. Bologna; son of 1; worked with father; after his death Luther addressed words of comfort to his father. 3. *Lucas the Younger* (1515–86). B. and d. Wittenberg; son of 1; worked with father and continued his style.

Cranmer, Thomas (1489–1556). B. Aslacton, Nottinghamshire, Eng. Educ. Cambridge. In 1529 came to the attention of Henry VIII by suggesting that the question of annulment of the royal marriage be referred to the canonists and universities. Sent on an embassy to Charles* V 1531. At Nürnberg he became acquainted with A. Osiander* the Elder, whose niece Margaret he married 1532. Abp. Canterbury

1533. Annulled marriage of Henry VIII and Catherine of Aragon; this was a preliminary step to the 1534 Act of Supremacy, which dissolved the obedience of Eng. to the pope. Cranmer supported Erastianism.* Opposed the Six Articles of 1539 (see *Anglican Confessions,* 3). Changed his views on the Lord's Supper from belief in the Real Presence to belief in the spiritual eating and drinking, similar to beliefs held by H. Zwingli,* J. Calvin,* and M. Bucer.* (See also *Calvinism; Grace, Means of,* IV 3). Promoted reading of the Scriptures; the 1540 Bible (see *Bible Versions,* L 5) is known as "Cranmer's Bible" because of his preface. "Cranmer's Catechism," entitled *A Short Instruction into Christian Religion,* is a tr. of J. Jonas's* Lat. Brandenburg-Nürnberg catechism, which was a tr. of Ger. sermons (mostly by A. Osiander the Elder) for children. He helped draw up the Forty-two Articles (see *Anglican Confessions,* 5). His greatest contribution was the first Book* of Common Prayer. His 4 sermons in the 1547 *Homilies* were on salvation, faith, good works, and Bible reading. When Mary* I came to the throne 1553 he was condemned for treason but pardoned by the queen, only to be condemned for heresy 1555; deposed as abp. Feb. 14, 1556; signed a series of recantations, but finally retracted them all; burned at the stake Mar. 21.

Writings and Disputations of Thomas Cranmer, ed. J. E. Cox (Cambridge, 1844); *Miscellaneous Writings and Letters of Thomas Cranmer,* ed. J. E. Cox (Cambridge, 1846); *Cranmer's Selected Writings,* ed. C. S. Meyer (London, 1961); G. W. Bromiley, *Thomas Cranmer, Archbishop and Martyr* (London, 1956) and *Thomas Cranmer, Theologian* (New York, 1956); A. F. Pollard, *Thomas Cranmer and the English Reformation, 1489–1556,* new ed. (New York, 1926); J. G. Ridley, *Thomas Cranmer* (London, 1962). CSM

Cranmer's Bible; Cranmer's Catechism. See *Cranmer, Thomas.*

Crashaw, Richard (ca. 1613–49). B. London; son of a Puritan poet and clergyman; metaphysical poet; often shows great genius in treating religious subjects despite excessive use of figures of speech called conceits. Refused to accept the Solemn League and Covenant (see *Presbyterian Confessions,* 1); fled to Fr.; embraced RCm. Works include *Steps to the Temple.*

Crasselius, Bartholomäus (1667–1724). Ger. clergyman and hymnist; b. Wernsdorf, Saxony; pastor Nidda and Düsseldorf; hymns include "Dir, dir, Jehovah, will ich singen."

Crato von Crafftheim (Johann Krafft; 1519–85). B. Breslau; educ. Wittenberg; intimate of Luther 6 yrs.; gathered material later pub. in Luther's *Table Talk* (see *Aurifaber, Johann* [1519–75]); studied medicine at Leipzig and Padua; became famous as a physician at Breslau; physician of emp. Ferdinand I, Maximilian II, and Rudolf II; influential in the cause of Protestantism in Austria; first of Melanchthonian persuasion, he later inclined to Ref. views.

Cratylus of Athens (5th–4th c. BC). Disciple of Heraclitus*; teacher of Plato*; chief speaker in Plato's *Cratylus.*

Created Grace. See *Gratia increata.*

Creation. The first book of the Bible begins with the affirmation that God created the heaven and the earth (Gn 1:1) and the last hymns adoration to the Creator God. (Rv 4:11)

In the OT there are numerous short references to creation, usually as axiomatic bases from which something is deduced (e. g., 1 Sm 2:8; 2 Kgs 19:15; 1 Ch 16:26; Jb 12:7-10; Neh 9:6; Ps 24:1-2; 74:16; 95:3-6; 121:2; 124:8; 136:1-9; 146:5-6; Pr 3:19; 22:2; 30:4-5; Is 37:16, 20; 44:9, 24; 45:9-10, 17-18; 48:12-13; Jer 10:10-13; 51:15-16; Hos 8:14; Zch 12:1), and some longer sections on creation (e. g., Gn 1–2 [often divided, as in the RSV, into 2 sections: 1–2:4a and 2:4b-25]; Jb 38–41; Ps 104; Pr 8; Is 40:18-26; Is 51:9-16). The Bible speaks of creation by fiat (Ps 148:5), creation by Word (Ps 33:6), creation in the past (Gn 1:1; Jb 38–41), creation in the sense of providence, or preservation, in the present (Neh 9:6; Jb 10:8-12; 38–41; Ps 95; 104), and creation of events (Is 48:3-7). God's entire creation and preservation is connected with trust, adoration, judgment, and mercy. (SC II; LC II)

The NT also emphasizes creation and preservation. Jesus and His contemporaries presuppose both (Mt 5:45; 6:26, 30; 19:4); the prayer of early Christians Acts 4:24-30 begins with a declaration of faith in God as Creator; in the sermons of Acts 14:15-17 and 17:24-28 Paul emphasizes God's continual creative work. Creation is referred to for various purposes (e. g., comfort, Acts 4:24; show the nature of faith, Heb 11:3). Creation's close relation to salvation and redemption stated in the OT (e. g., Is 45:17-18) is emphasized, and creation is explicitly connected with Christ in the NT; in "the Word" who became flesh and "by Him" (or "through Him") and "for Him" all things are created (Jn 1:1-3; Cl 1:15 to 17). Creation out of nothing *(ex nihilo)* is based on such passages as Gn 1:1; Ro 4:17; Heb 11:3. In Pr 8 wisdom is personified in terms related to Jn 1:1-18 and is connected with creation (Pr 8:24-30). Wisdom is identified or associated with Jesus (1 Co 1:24, 30; Cl 2:3). As the Word, so the Spirit (wind, breath) was active in creation (Jb 26:13; Ps 33:6). In the work of Jesus Christ and of the Holy Spirit creation reaches its climax. (Mt 3:16; Lk 1:15-17, 35; 4:18; Jn 3; Ro 8:18-27; 1 Co 12; 2 Co 5:17-21; Rv 21)

In the early ch., esp. against gnosticism, creation of the world by the one, good, all-ruling, omnipotent Father was emphasized. There is one Creator, the Father of the world, the Father of Jesus Christ; with His Word and Wisdom, His Son and Spirit, He created all things visible and invisible out of nothing. The nature and role of the Trin. in creation became a matter of discussion in the 3d c. (see *Adoptionism; Arianism; Monarchianism*). Differences on other matters connected with creation did not develop into serious controversies in the early church. Some fathers held a creation out of nothing; others assumed a preexistent or precreated material. Some (e. g., Clement* of Alexandria, *Fragments,* XII 1) held that God's creative activity ceased after the 6th day; others (e. g., Origen,* *De Principiis,* III vi 7) held that the created universe is in process of transmutation and transformation. The 6 days of creation were conceived as 1,000 yrs. (Barnabas 15:4) or long periods (E Orthodox Ch.), or as an instant (Athanasius, *Contra Arianos,* II 60); Augustine relates time to form, order, and change (*Confessions,* XII xii 15; XII xiii 16; XII xv 22; XII xxix 40). Rational reconstruction of the how of creation differed in the early ch.

The Reformers spoke of 6 days of creation, though their interpretations differed. Luther emphasizes that the personal, holy, almighty God, Creator, Redeemer, and Vivifier, is his Lord. This God is still creatively active and is the Source of all action. Man and world are creatures of the Creator, dependent on and responsible to Him. Luther stresses the role of Christ, the Word, in creation. He lauds the present creative work of God. The beginning and the present is often held in tension by Luther, as when he speaks of man's birth as unconnected with the beginning of creation, yet holds that in God's sight he was born already at the beginning of the world. He relates natural birth to spiritual rebirth. Man and Satan are God's creatures even after the fall, but God is not responsible for sin (FC SD I 54–62 follows some of the early fathers in solving this problem by distinguishing substance and accident). Because the world and total man are God's creation, Luther rejected the division of life into spiritual and earthly duties. Finally, according to Luther, God, veiled in His creatures *(larvae dei)*, actively confronts man. In the Luth. Confessions the doctrine of creation is treated at length in Luther's explanation of the 1st Article of the Apostles' Creed. (SC II 2; LC II 10-24)

Theistic creation has frequently been challenged in modern times. Idealists tend to despise the material world and favor Platonic idealism. Materialists regard only the empirical and material as real and often ally with atheistic evolutionists.

Christians have at times joined humanists or idealists in opposition to materialism. When they have placed the Bible in opposition to science, they have at times wrongly interpreted some statements of the Bible; yet there must be proper Christian apologetics and even polemics.

Some have applied the personalist emphases of existentialism in such a way that creation becomes only an affirmation of one's creation in the present. In the middle of the 20th c. a tendency to emphasize the soteriological significance of God's revelations regarding creation became prominent.

W. F. Albright, *The Biblical Period from Abraham to Ezra* (New York, [1963]); D. Bonhoeffer, *Creation and Fall* (London, 1959); L. F. Gruber, *Creation ex nihilo* (Boston, 1918) and *The Six Creative Days* (Burlington, Iowa, 1941); A. Heidel, *The Babylonian Genesis* (Chicago, [1942]); E. Jacob, *Theology of the Old Testament* (London, 1958); J. W. Klotz, *Genes, Genesis, and Evolution* (St. Louis, 1955) and *The Challenge of the Space Age* (St. Louis, 1961); P. L. Maier, *Test-tube Theology: A Postscript on the Conflict Between Science and Religion . . . or IS There a Conflict?* (St. Louis, 1963); M. Metzger, *Die Paradieserzählung, die Geschichte ihrer Auslegung von J. Clericus bis W. M. L. De Wette* (Bonn, 1959); H. W. Reimann, "Luther on Creation," *CTM*, XXIV (Jan. 1953), 26–40 and *Let's Study Theology: An Invitation to the Excitement of Christian Thought in the 20th Century* (St. Louis, 1964), pp. 23–31; H. Renckens, *Israel's Concept of the Beginning: The Theology of Genesis 1–3* (New York, 1964); A. Richardson, *The Bible in the Age of Science* (Philadelphia, 1961); W. R. Roehrs, "The Creation Account of Genesis: Guidelines for an Interpretation," *CTM*, XXXVI (May 1965), 301–321; H. Thielecke, *How the World Began* (Philadelphia, 1961); B. Vawter, *A Path Through Genesis* (New York, [1956]); G. Viehweg, "The Doctrine of Creation," *The Abiding Word*, I (St. Louis, 1946), 1–17; W. Wegner, "Creation and Salvation," *CTM*, XXXVII (Sept. 1966), 520–542; C. Westermann, *The Genesis Accounts of Creation*, tr. N. E. Wagner (Philadelphia, 1964); *Darwin, Evolution, and Creation*, ed. P. A. Zimmerman (St. Louis, 1959).

Creationism. The theory that every human soul is created by a special divine act. This view is rejected by traducianism.*

Credence. See *Divine Liturgy*.

Credner, Karl August (1797–1857). B. Waltershausen, cen. Ger. Prof. ch. hist. and NT exegesis Giessen 1832; rationalist; works include the unfinished *Einleitung in das Neue Testament*.

Credo. See *Creeds and Confessions*.

Credo quia absurdum (Lat. "I believe because it is absurd"). Expresses the view that to believe the absurd shows greater faith than manifested by belief in the logical or rational.

Credo ut intelligam (Lat. "I believe in order that I may understand"). Expresses the view that belief precedes understanding or philos.; held, e.g., by Augustine* of Hippo and Anselm* of Canterbury.

Creed of Pius IV. See *Roman Catholic Confessions*, A 2.

Creeds and Confessions. A creed (*credo*, σύμβολον, *regula fidei*) is a confession of faith for pub. use or a form of words setting forth with authority certain articles of belief. Creeds do not precede faith, but follow it. Christian creeds express the convictions of the believer toward Christ and His Word. Confession is, then, the outward manifestation of a deed and gift of God. A conf. is subjective inasmuch as faith springs from the heart and objective inasmuch as such faith can be characterized only by its foundation and content.

Creeds were used as summaries of doctrine, bonds of union, safeguards against error, and means of instruction. Creeds have, to a remarkable degree, inc. the basic principles of their confessors, and an understanding of creeds is indispensable in the study of ch. cultures. In the RC Ch. creeds are regarded as absolute and infallible in authority. In Prot. chs. creeds *(norma* normata)* are relative to the Bible *(norma* normans)*. As instruments, creeds have been nobly used (in proclaiming, teaching, defending, preserving the truth) but also abused (in compulsion, persecution, suppression, misdirection).

Creeds arose from the gen. ch. (e.g., Apostles' Creed), from councils (e.g., Nicene Creed), from syns. (e.g., Westminster Conf.), from committees (e. g., FC), from an individual (e. g., Luther's Catechism), or from an individual acting for a group (e.g., AC). They developed from precedents beginning with NT creedal statements: Jesus is Christ, God, Lord, Savior (Mt 16:16; Mk 8:29; Lk 9:20; Acts 4:12; 8:37; Ro 1:3; 10:9; 1 Co 12:3; Heb 4:14; 1 Jn 4:15; 5:5; amplified in 1 Co 15:3-4; 2 Ti 2:8; Ph 2:5-11; 1 Ptr 3:18-22); the fish was early used as a symbol for this confession because the letters of the Gk. word for fish *(ichthys)* are the first letters of *Iesous Christos Theou (H)yios Soter* (Jesus Christ, God's Son, Savior). In the history of creeds may be traced the unfolding of Scriptural thought (not a development of Scriptural doctrine, but, as Luther said in speaking of the Apostles' Creed, honey gathered from many flowers) as well as the development of false religious premises. In their stress creeds bear the impress of their age and purpose. Though they may not give the Bible's answer to unforeseen crises at all times, their hist. is a demonstration of the fact that they contain basic principles from which new formulations continually proceed. Thus ecumenical creeds (one or more) are usually considered basic by Christian chs. and later creeds extend or explain them.

After the ecumenical* creeds (the term indicates coextension with the visible ch. but the 3 creeds have not been equally received in all Christendom) had been written, few creeds were written until the Reformation era. The creeds of that era incorporated the principles which were developed in the succeeding age. The creeds of the 16th c. bore the impress of the profound theol. controversies. When the controversies subsided, a climax in creed making had been reached, and a reaction is indicated in the brief, popular, and practical creeds of succeeding ages.

Many platforms and statements have been formulated in modern times, though none has attained paramount importance. One trend is indicated by statements which seek to reunite Christendom on the simplest formulations. Diametrically opposed to such statements are attempts to develop creeds in greater detail in whole or part. In the late 19th and early 20th c. there was a trend away from creedal subscription in some chs. This trend was reversed by the middle of the 20th c., and a new interest in creeds and confessions became evident.

Creeds have been classified as ecumenical, E Cath., RC, Prot., national or regional, democratic declarations, and statements of principles.

See also *Anglican Confessions; Democratic Decla-*

rations of Faith; Eastern Orthodox Standards of Doctrine; Ecumenical Creeds; Lutheran Confessions; Presbyterian Confessions; Reformed Confessions; Roman Catholic Confessions; Theology. American sects and cults listed by individual name. EL

P. Schaff, *The Creeds of Christendom,* 6th ed. (New York, 1931); W. Elert, *Morphologie des Luthertums,* I (Munich, 1931; 1952 print.), 176–185, tr. W. A. Hansen, *The Structure of Lutheranism,* I (St. Louis, 1962), 200–210; H. Heppe, *Die Bekenntnisschriften der altprotestantischen Kirche Deutschlands* (Cassel, 1855); F. W. Bodemann, *Vergleichende Darstellung der Unterscheidungslehren der vier christlichen Hauptkonfessionen* (Göttingen, 1869); W. A. Curtis, *A History of Creeds and Confessions of Faith in Christendom and Beyond* (New York, 1912); *Creeds of the Churches,* ed. J. H. Leith (Chicago, 1963); *Die Bekenntnisschriften der evangelisch-lutherischen Kirche,* 4th rev. ed. (Göttingen, 1959); E. L. Lueker, "Functions of Symbols and of Doctrinal Statements," *CTM,* XXXII (May 1961), 274–285; T. G. Tappert, "The Symbols of the Church," *What Lutherans Are Thinking,* ed. E. C. Fendt (Columbus, Ohio, 1947), pp. 343–367; *The Church and the Confessions,* ed. V. Vajta and H. Weissgerber (Philadelphia, 1963).

Crell, Nikolaus (Krell; ca. 1550–1601). B. Leipzig; brought into govt. 1580 by August* of Saxony; councilor of Christian* I 1586; chancellor of Saxony 1589; sought to reintroduce Crypto*-Calvinism into Saxony by removing the oath of obligation to the FC and exorcism at baptism; autocratic; opposed the Hapsburgs and supported the Fr.; condemned by court of appeals at Prague after Christian's death; beheaded.

Crell, Paul (Crellius; Krell; 1531–79). Taught at Wittenberg. With P. Eber* he rejected the ubiquity* of Christ but taught the real presence (see *Grace, Means of,* IV 3).

Crell, Samuel (1660–1747). Unitarian preacher in Ger., Eng., and Neth.; proponent of Socinianism.*

Cremation. The practice of burning corpses. Early practiced by Hindus, by Gks. in the Homeric age, and by Etruscans in It. Christianity, continuing Jewish custom, fostered burial. Charlemagne* forbade cremation 784. An attempt was made to introd. the custom in Eng. 1874. Though the RC Ch. and others, including Luths., viewed cremation negatively, esp. when assoc. with denial of the resurrection of the body, active opposition has waned in recent yrs. See also *Burial.*

Cremer, August Hermann (1834–1903). Luth. theol.; b. Unna, Westphalia; educ. Halle and Tübingen; pastor Ostönnen 1859; prof. systematic theol. Greifswald 1870. Works include *Die paulinische Rechtfertigungslehre; Biblisch-theologisches Wörterbuch der neutestamentlichen Gräeität.* See also *Lexicons,* B.

Crescas, Chasdai ben Abraham (ca. 1340–ca. 1410). Jewish philos. in Sp.; opposed cosmogony of Aristotle; held probability of infinite space; opposed rationalism of Maimonides*; made love an attribute of God.

Creutziger; Creutzinger; Creuziger. See *Cruciger.*

Crischona. See *Chrischona.*

Crisis, Theology of. See *Switzerland, Contemporary Theology in,* 5.

Critical Idealism. I. Kant's* designation for his theory of knowledge. See also *Idealism.*

Critical Monism. The philos. which in ontology* holds that reality is one, yet embraces multiplicity; in epistemology* holds unity of subject and object.

Critical Realism. Term used in epistemology* to define a position distinguished from naive realism.* Critical realists agree that there is a difference bet. an object and the perception of an object. But there is wide disagreement as to the nature of the media, vehicles, or essences that convey knowledge and by means of which, or through which, we perceive and think.

Criticism, Higher. See *Higher Criticism.*

Criticism, Textual. See *Manuscripts of the Bible; Textual Criticism.*

Critop(o)ulos, Metrophanes. See *Metrophanes Kritop(o)ulos.*

Croce, Benedetto (1866–1952). It. philos. Held that spirit, an immanent process, is the only reality; rejected both naturalism* and theism.*

Crocius. 1. *Johannes* (1590–1659). B. Laasphe, Westphalia; educ. Herborn and Marburg; prof. theol. Marburg 1617; rector U. of Cassel 1633, Marburg 1653; exponent of mediating Calvinism; present at Leipzig Colloquy (see *Reformed Confessions,* D 3). Works include commentaries; sermons; polemics against RCs and Luths. 2. *Ludwig* (1586–1655). B. Laasphe, Westphalia; brother of Johannes; educ. Marburg and Basel; pastor and supt. Bremen; prof., later rector, *Gymnasium Illustre,* Bremen; attended Syn. of Dort* 1618–19; proponent of Ger. Ref. theol. (see *Reformed Churches,* 3). Works include *Syntagma sacrae theologiae.*

Croft, William (Crofts; ca. 1677–1727). Eng. composer; pupil of J. Blow*; organist Westminster Abbey and Chapel Royal; helped found Academy of Vocal Music 1725; pub. choral works as *Musica Sacra,* 2 vols., 1724, claimed to be the first engraved in full score on plates.

Crol, Bastiaen. See *Reformed Churches,* 4 b.

Cromlech. 1. Columns of unhewn stone supporting a tabular block and forming a chamber that covered a burial place or perhaps was a place of worship. 2. At times cromlech designates a stone circle as distinguished from dolmen.*

Cromwell, Oliver (1599–1658). Eng. soldier and statesman. B. Huntingdon; descended from Richard Williams, who took the maiden name of his mother, T. Cromwell's* elder sister; mem. of parliament for Huntingdon 1628, for Cambridge 1640; championed cause of Puritans and Independents; prominent in parliament struggle with Charles I; an effective leader of the New Model army; signed Charles I's death warrant; suppressed Irish and Scot. revolts; appointed Lord Protector 1653; buried in Westminster Abbey; disinterred and hung after Charles II became king. See also *England,* B 7.

Cromwell, Thomas (ca. 1485–1540). Adviser of T. Wolsey*; after the latter's fall 1529, in the service of Henry* VIII; vicar gen. 1535; chief adviser and agent of the king in ch. affairs; Earl of Essex 1540; supported Eng. Protestantism; planned and executed the pol. maneuvers that gave the Ch. of Eng. indep. from Rome; these maneuvers included support of the king's marriage to Anne Boleyn, negotiations with the Luth. Schmalkaldic princes, dissolution of monasteries, and pub. of the Eng. Bible. When the internat. pol. situation 1540 made Henry VIII seek the goodwill of Charles V, the king repudiated his Prot. policy of the 1530s; his marriage to Anne of Cleves was annulled; Cromwell was condemned to death by a parliamentary act of attainder and beheaded.

R. B. Merriman, *Life and Letters of Thomas Cromwell,* 2 vols. (Oxford, 1902); A. G. Dickens, *Thomas Cromwell and the English Reformation* (New York, 1959); N. S. Tjernagel, *Henry VIII and the Lutherans* (St. Louis, 1965). NST

Cronenwett, Emanuel (Feb. 22, 1841–Mar. 9, 1931). Luth. clergyman and hymnist; educ. Capital U., Columbus, Ohio; ordained Woodville, Ohio; pastor Carrollton, Waynesburg, Wooster, and Delaware, Ohio, and Butler, Pa.; hymns and poems pub. 1926; translations include "Lord God, We All to Thee Give Praise," "Lord Jesus Christ, Thou Hast Prepared," and "Lord, as Thou Wilt, Deal Thou with Me"; original hymns include "We Have a Sure, Prophetic Word" and "Invited, Lord, by Boundless Grace."

Crosby, Fanny. See *Van Alstyne, Frances Jane.*

Crosier (crozier; pastoral staff; *baculus pastoralis;* OF *crocier,* from *crosse,* shepherd's staff). Staff curved at top, straight in middle, pointed at end. Shepherd's staff early became symbol of authority to rule flock. Also given to abbots at their consecration. Though its presentation to abbesses at consecration has been discontinued, it is still used by them in some cases as symbols of their office.

Cross. 1. In NT times the cross was used to torture and kill. It is used figuratively in the NT for suffering (Mt 10:38; Mk 8:34; 10:21; Lk 9:23; 14:27) and as a symbol of Christ's atoning death (e. g., 1 Co 1:17; Gl 6:12, 14; Eph 2:16; Ph 3:18; Heb 12:2).

2. Over 50 forms of the cross have been distinguished and used in symbolism, including *crux decussata* (St. Andrew's cross, or saltire, shaped like the letter X); *crux commissa,* or tau cross (St. Anthony's cross, shaped like the letter T; the *crux ansata,* or ankh, is a tau cross with a loop at the top); *crux immissa* (Lat. cross, shaped like the symbol +).

3. In RC chs. on Good Fri. a ceremony called adoration, or veneration, of the cross, or creeping to the cross, is observed, in which the worshipers remove their shoes, kneel, and kiss a crucifix,* clergy preceding laity.

4. The practice of making the sign of the cross may be traced at least to the time of Tertullian,* who wrote of it as a custom of Christians everywhere, observed as a reminder of the crucified Savior on all ordinary occasions of life. In the 2d c. superstitious use was made of the sign of the cross. The Luth. Ch. condemned superstitious abuse of the symbolic act, but retained its proper use. Luther (SC VII 1, 4) recommends the use of the sign of the cross in connection with the morning and evening prayer. The cross is also found in Christian art as the most significant and eloquent symbol of Christianity. In some chs. it lies flat on the altar or is suspended from the ceiling of the apse.* In the Luth. Ch. a crucifix may stand on a shelf above the mensa (see *Church Furniture,* 1 and 2). A cross may also be used as ornament on other furniture and on ch. bldgs. See also *Images; Invention of the Cross, The; Symbolism, Christian,* 1.

Crotch, William (1775–1847). Eng. composer; played the organ in pub. in London at age of 4; prof. music Oxford 1797; 1st principal Royal Academy of Music 1822; works include the oratorios *Palestine* and *The Captivity of Judah.*

Crotus Rubianus (Rubeanus; Johannes Jäger; Venator[ius]; ca. 1480–ca. 1545). Ger. humanist; b. Dornheim, Thuringia; ed. Erfurt; head of Fulda monastery school 1510; friend of Ulrich von Hutten* and J. Reuchlin*; one of the authors of *Epistolae obscurorum virorum* (see *Letters of Obscure Men*); for a time attracted to Luther; later opposed *Reformation.*

Crowdy, William Saunders. See *Church of God and Saints of Christ.*

Crowley, Robert. See *Psalter, English.*

Crowther, Samuel Adjai (ca. 1810–91). 1st native Angl. bp. in Afr.; b. Yorubaland, W Afr.; enslaved; rescued by Brit.; studied at Bathurst (Sierra Leone) and London; 1st student enrolled at Fourah Bay Coll. (founded 1827 by CMS), Sierra Leone; taught at schools in Sierra Leone, including Fourah Bay Coll.; attended CMS coll., London; ordained 1843 in Eng.; miss. in Yorubaland and esp. at Abeokuta; made bp. of the Niger 1864 in Canterbury Cathedral. Works include a grammar of the Yoruba language; vocabularies of the Ibo and Yoruba languages; Bible tr. See also *Africa,* C 6.

Crucifix. Representation of Christ on cross,* painted or sculptured in W Ch., only in painted form in E Ch. Probably not used gen. and pub. by Christians in 1st five cents., though figures of a lamb or bust of Christ on cross occur in the 5th c. Crucifixes in strict sense used from the last part of the 6th c. on. Came into gen. use as central piece of altar in 16th c. Frequently used also by Luths. See also *Symbolism, Christian,* 1.

Cruciger (Creutziger; Creutzinger; Creuziger; Crutziger). 1. *Caspar* (Kaspar; 1504–48). The Elder; b. Leipzig; d. Wittenberg. Enrolled U. of Leipzig 1513; attended Leipzig* Debate; became follower of Luther; to Wittenberg 1521; studied theol., math, and botany at U. of Wittenberg; married Elisabethe von Meseritz (see 3); rector St. John's School, Magdeburg, 1525; helped make Magdeburg a Luth. stronghold; recalled to Wittenberg as prof. and pastor of the Castle Ch. 1528; secretary to Luther; aided Luther in tr. Bible; took part in theol. debates; willing to compromise with Zwinglians and RCs; helped draft Leipzig Interim* but died before it was pub. Works include *In epistolam Pauli ad Timotheum priorem Commentarius; Enarratio Psalmi 116–118; Der XX. Psalm für christliche Herrschaft zu beten; In Evangelium Johannis Apostoli Enarratio; Enarratio Psalmi: Dixit Dominus [110] et aliquot sequentium; Comment. in Matthaeum; In Epistolam Pauli ad Romanos Commentarius; De iudiciis piarum Synodorum sententia; Enarrationis Symboli Nicaeni articuli duo, de Synodis et tribus personis Divinitatis.* See also *Lutheran Confessions,* B 1.

E. W. Löhn, *Dr. Caspar Creutziger oder Cruciger, der Schüler, Freund u. Amtsgenosse Luther's u. Melanchthon's* (Leipzig, 1859); T. Pressel, *Caspar Cruciger nach gleichzeitigen Quellen* (Elberfeld, 1862); H. Petrich, *Caspar Cruciger* (Hamburg, 1904); W. G. Tillmanns, *The World and Men Around Luther* (Minneapolis, 1959), pp. 94–98. WGT

2. *Caspar* (Kaspar; 1525–97). The Younger; b. Wittenberg; son of Caspar the Elder (see 1) and Elisabethe (see 3); supported P. Melanchthon*; imprisoned; banished from Saxony as Philippist 1576; turned Reformed; pastor, and pres. of consistory, in Kassel.

3. *Elisabethe* (nee von Meseritz; ca. 1504–35). Married C. Cruciger the Elder (see 1) 1524; wrote the hymn "Herr Christ, der einig' Gott's Sohn."

Cruden, Alexander (1701–70). B. Aberdeen, Scot.; educ. Marischal Coll., Aberdeen; Presb.; life marked by eccentricities; London bookseller to Queen Caroline 1735; compiled Bible concordance 1736–37; spent last yrs. in efforts to reform nat. morals.

Cruet. Vessel to hold wine or water for altar service.

Crüger, Johann(es) (Krüger; 1598–ca. 1662). B. Prussia; d. Berlin. Studied music at Regensburg under Paul Homberger; organist St. Nicholas Ch., Berlin, 1622; chorale* compositions include "Auf, auf, mein Herz, mit Freuden"; set many of P. Gerhardt's* hymns to music; contributed ca. 37 melodies to *Geistliche Lieder und Psalmen;* hymn collections include *Newes vollkömmliches Gesangbuch Augsburgischer Confession; Praxis pietatis melica; Geistliche Kirchenmelodien.*

Crull, August (Jan. 27, 1845–Apr. 17, 1923). B. Rostock, Ger.; educ. Rostock, Fort Wayne, and St. Louis; asst. pastor Trin. Luth. Ch., Milwaukee, 1865; dir. Luth. high school, Milwaukee; pastor Grand Rapids, Mich., 1871; prof. Ger. and Fr., Conc. Coll., Fort Wayne, 1873; lived in Milwaukee after retirement 1915; poet; hymn tr. include "The Lord Hath Helped Me Hitherto," "The Lord, My God, Be Praised," and "Come, Thou Precious Ransom, Come"; ed. collections of poetry entitled *Gott segne Dich!* and *Gott tröste Dich!;* ed. *Das walte Gott!,* a book of devotions drawn from C. F. W. Walther's* sermons; other works include *Lehrbuch der deutschen Sprache* and *Kurze Gestenlehre.*

Crusades. 1. Military expeditions initiated by the ch. against Muslim and others. They are variously numbered. Their purpose was to recover the Holy Land for Christianity. Ca. 1074 Gregory VII (see *Popes,* 7) gathered an army for war against the infidels, but his plans were not carried out, first because of the hostility of R. Guiscard,* later because of the struggle about investiture.* At the end of the c. the time seemed more propitious; Urban* II preached a crusade against Islam* 1095, stirring the Council of Clermont* to a frenzy of enthusiasm further fanned by the fanaticism of Peter* the Hermit. Peasants, lower clergy, runaway monks, women, and children joined the movement and gave the advance guard of the crusading army the character of a mob; it came to a miserable end in Hungary and across the Bosporus.

2. The armies that set out 1096 on the 1st Crusade lacked unity in motives, but were successful in this, that Nicaea* was taken 1097; the sultan of Iconium (now Konya, or Konia), another city in Asia Minor, was defeated soon thereafter; Antioch in Syria was captured June 1098; Jerusalem fell July 15, 1099. But increasing prosperity of the armies of occupation and of the It. merchants who settled in Syrian ports led to debility and internal strife, with disastrous consequences. The frontier fortress of Edessa (now Urfa, SE Turkey) was captured by Zangi, atabeg of Mosul, Dec. 25, 1144, and the spirit of battle and conquest on the part of the Christians was decidedly quenched.

3. The 2d Crusade was organized 1147; its leaders were Louis* VII of France and Conrad* III of Ger.; it failed; by 1149 its armies returned to Eur.

4. When Saladin (1138–93) came to power in Egypt, he made it his object to drive the Christians out of Palestine. He took Jerusalem 1187 and restricted Christian power to Antioch in Syria, Tripoli, Tyre, and the Hospitalers'* fortress at Margat by 1189. News of the fall of Jerusalem led immediately to the organization of the 3d Crusade, with Frederick* I of Ger., Richard* I of Eng., and Philip* II of Fr. as its leaders. But Frederick drowned 1190 in the Calycadnus (now Göksu) river near Selefke (Seleucia); after Acre was taken in 1191 by Richard and Philip, they quarreled; Philip left for Fr. immediately; Richard left for Eng. 1192. The Crusade failed in its object, but ended in a 3-yr. peace with Saladin, saved Antioch, Tripoli, and a coastal strip for the Christians, and secured permission for small groups of Christians to visit Jerusalem.

5. The following Crusades came to be marked by profoundly different aims and methods. The 4th Crusade (1202–04) was first promoted by Innocent III (see *Popes,* 10) along the old lines. But Philip* of Swabia and the Venetians under leadership of their doge, Enrico Dandolo (ca. 1108–1205), turned the Crusade to their own purposes; Zadar (It. Zara), an Adriatic port that had been taken by the Hungarians, was conquered 1202; Constantinople was taken and sacked 1204, the empire being divided bet. Venice and the Crusaders.

6. In 1212 an outburst of fanatical enthusiasm led to the Children's Crusade, an ill-conceived and disastrously executed venture led by Stephen, a 12-yr.-old Fr. shepherd, and Nicolas, an 8-yr.-old Ger. Hardship, death, and moral and literal shipwreck took their toll; many Fr. children fell into the hands of slavers.

7. Sporadic attempts were made in the next yrs. to rouse the original spirit of the Crusades, but defeat and ignominy resulted. The 5th Crusade (1218–21) was the last begun under Innocent III. Frederick* II of Ger. led the 6th Crusade 1228–29. His diplomacy achieved unexpected success. Bethlehem, Nazareth, and most of Jerusalem, as well as the pilgrim route from Acre to Jerusalem, were given to the Christians for a treaty period of 10 yrs. On expiration of the treaty, Thibaut IV (1201–53), count of Champagne and king of Navarre, led an expedition to Acre 1239 in an attempt to retain Jerusalem. He was joined 1240–41 by forces of Richard of Cornwall (1209 to 1272), king of the Romans. But the Christians were defeated and lost Jerusalem 1244.

8. The last efforts of Christian monarchs to gain control of the Holy Land were the 7th and 8th Crusades, undertaken by Louis* IX of Fr. On the 7th Crusade (1248–54) he reached Egypt 1249 via Cyprus; was defeated, captured, and released on ransom; went thence to Acre 1250; tried to strengthen Christian holdings in the Holy Land; returned to Fr. 1254 on the death of his mother. On the 8th Crusade (1270) Louis IX went with his brother, Charles of Anjou, to Tunis; Louis died there of the plague; Charles ended the Crusade by successful negotiation. But with the fall of Caesarea and Arsuf 1265, Antioch and Joppa 1268, Tripoli 1289, and Acre 1291, Christians lost all ground they had gained in the Crusades.

9. Two results of the Crusades were increase of papal power because of the leading role played by popes in inaugurating these expeditions, and growth of the spirit of religious intolerance. This latter spirit found expression in the Inquisition.* Other crusades were against Poland, the Utraquists,* Taborites, Cathari* (e. g., Albigenses,* Bogomiles*). Stedingers,* and others (see also *Hussites; Bohemian Brethren*). The force of the crusader spirit in connection with inquisitorial measures abated only gradually.

T. A. Archer and C. L. Kingsford, *The Crusades: The Story of the Latin Kingdom of Jerusalem* (New York, 1894); *The Cambridge Medieval History,* planned by J. B. Bury, ed. J. R. Tanner, C. W. Previté-Orton, and Z. N. Brooke, V (New York, 1926; reprinted with corrections 1929), 265–333; D. C. Munro, *The Kingdom of the Crusaders* (New York, 1935); S. Runciman, *A History of the Crusades,* 3 vols. (Cambridge, Eng., 1951–54); *A History of the Crusades,* ed.-in-chief K. M. Setton, 2 vols., I ed. M. W. Baldwin, II ed. R. L. Wolff and H. W. Hazard (Philadelphia 1955, 1962); R. Pernoud, *The Crusaders,* tr. E. Grant (Philadelphia, 1964). HTM

Crusius, Christian August (1715–75). Ger. theol. and philos.; b. Leuna; d. Leipzig; prof. Leipzig; theol. position similar to that of J. A. Bengel*; opposed C. Wolff* and G. W. Leibnitz*; tried to prove that positive revelation harmonizes with reason; highly regarded by I. Kant.* Works include *Entwurf der nothwendigen Vernunftwahrheiten; Hypomnemata ad theologiam propheticam,* 3 vols.; *Weg zur Gewissheit und Zuverlässigkeit der menschlichen Erkenntnis.*

Crusius, Martin (Kraus; 1526–1607). B. Grebern; d. Tübingen; prof. Lat. and Gk. at Tübingen 1559; promoted study of modern Gk. in Germany; with Jakob Andreä* and L. Osiander* the Elder he sought through imperial ambassador David Ungnad von Weissenwolf (d. 1600), Joachim von Sintzendorff, and S. Gerlach* to lead Jeremiah II, patriarch of Constantinople, to accept the Luth. faith. Works include *Annales Suevici; Turcograecia; Germanograecia.* See also *Eastern Orthodox Churches,* 5; *Eastern Orthodox Standards of Doctrine,* A 2, 5.

Crutziger. See *Cruciger.*

Crux ansata. See *Cross,* 2.

Crypt. Vault under the apse* and high altar* of a ch., containing the remains of the martyr after whom the ch. was named; burial vault, or basement, of some chs.

Crypto-Calvinistic Controversy. Divides into two stages: 1552–74 and 1586–92. In his vacillating position on the Lord's Supper, P. Melanchthon* was the father of Crypto-Calvinists (name derived from Gk. *krypto,* "hide"). His followers tried to suppress Luther's views and replace them with Calvin's views while professing loyalty to Lutheranism. G. Major,* P. Eber,* P. Crell,* and K. Peucer* were leading Crypto-Calvinists. J. Westphal* saw the menace and sounded warning 1552 in *Farrago confusanearum et inter se dissidentium opinionum de coena Domini, ex sacramentariorum libris congesta* ("Medley of Confused and Mutually Dissenting Opinions on the Lord's Supper, Gathered from the Books of the Sacramentarians"). He was aided by Johann(es) Timan(n) of Bremen, E. Schnepf,* N. Gallus,* M. Flacius,* J. Brenz,* Jakob Andreä,* M. Chemnitz,* P. von Eitzen,* and others. August,* Elector of Saxony, was influenced by his advisers to fill all positions with Philippists.* In 1567 he recognized the *Corpus doctrinae Christianae,* or *Philippicum* (so called after Philipp Melanchthon; also called *Misnicum,* after the Lat. name for the territory of Meissen); it included the 3 ecumenical creeds and such writings of Melanchthon as the altered AC, the altered Ap, and the altered *Loci communes theologici.* Those who refused to subscribe were deposed, jailed, or banished. In 1573 Duke John William, patron and protector of faithful Luths., died; August became guardian of his sons and immediately deposed and banished J. Wigand,* T. Hesshus,* and others, in all ca. 100 true Luth. preachers and teachers. In 1574 the Philippists pub. the anonymous *Exegesis perspicua et ferme integra controversiae de sacra coena* with its Sacramentarian errors. When the Elector saw that he, too, was to be drawn into the Calvinistic camp, he drove the Philippists from power and jailed and banished their leaders. True Lutheranism was restored 1574 by the Torgau Confession *(Confessio paucis articulis complectens summam doctrinae de vera praesentia corporis et sanguinis Christi in coena dominica).* Unmasking of the Philippists led also to adoption of the Maulbronn Formula, parts of which were embodied in the FC (see *Lutheran Confessions,* C 2), which deals with Sacramentarianism in VII and VIII.

Christian* I made N. Crell* chancellor 1589. Crell put Calvinists into places of power. Luth. books were suppressed; a new catechism was Calvinistic; exorcism was abolished. Many Luth. leaders, including N. Selnecker* and P. Leyser,* were deposed, jailed, and banished. On the death of Christian I (1591) the administrator, Duke Frederick William, suppressed Calvinism and reest. true Lutheranism by the Saxon Visitation* Articles.

Crypto-Kenotic Controversy (1619–27). B. Mentzer* the Elder, of Giessen, writing against the Reformed, said that omnipresence was not "simple *presence" (adessentia simplex),* but always *"operative* presence" *(omnipraesentia operativa)* and that omnipresence was not to be predicated of the human nature of Christ in the state of humiliation. M. Hafenreffer,* of Tübingen, appealed to by Mentzer, disapproved of his position. Soon Tübingen and Giessen were engaged in pub. controversy. The question was on the use made by Christ in the state of humiliation, according to His human nature, of the divine majesty communicated to His human nature in the personal union (see *Idiomata*). The theologians of Giessen (Mentzer and J. Feuerborn*) denied the presence of Christ with creatures according to His human nature, or at least refused to call it omnipresence; they were inclined also to exclude Christ according to His human nature from the work of preserving and governing the universe (see also *Decisio Saxonica*). They were called kenoticists from a Gk. word meaning "to empty," because they took the word in Ph 2:7 to mean that Christ emptied Himself according to His human nature of a measure of divine majesty. Their position is untenable (Jn 5:17), though they admitted some use of divine majesty and did not hold, as modern kenoticists do, that Christ according to His divine nature emptied Himself of His divine attributes, or *absolutely* renounced use of divine majesty. The Tübingen theologians (L. Osiander* the Younger, M. Nicolai,* T. Thumm*) ascribed to the human nature of Christ, in the state of humiliation, the sitting at the right hand of the Father, Christ having thus made full use, in this respect, of the divine majesty, though in a hidden way. This view was called crypto-kenoticism, from Gk. *krypto,* "hide." The position is untenable in the light of Scripture passages that ascribe the sitting at the right hand of God to Christ, also according to His human nature, in the state of exaltation. Those who held it admitted that Christ, in His sacerdotal office, in His suffering and dying, renounced the full use of the divine majesty communicated to His human nature. Modern theories of kenoticism are traced to W. F. Gess,* C. Gore,* and G. Thomasius.*

W. Sanday, *Christologies Ancient and Modern* (New York, 1910), pp. 71–78; O. Bensow, *Die Lehre von der Kenose* (Leipzig, 1903); F. Loofs, "Kenosis," *Realencyklopädie für protestantische Theologie und Kirche,* eds. J. J. Herzog and A. Hauck, 3d ed., X (Leipzig, 1901), 246–263; F. Pieper, *Christliche Dogmatik,* II (St. Louis, 1917), 337–358, tr. T. Engelder, *Christian Dogmatics,* II (St. Louis, 1951), 296–301; J. T. Mueller, *Christian Dogmatics* (St. Louis, 1934), pp. 290–291.

Cuba. See *Caribbean Islands,* C, E 1.

Cudworth, Ralph (1617–88). Cambridge Platonist; b. Aller, Somerset, Eng.; prof. Cambridge; rector Ashwell; prebendary Gloucester. In *The True Intellectual System of the Universe* he held that the Christian religion is the only source of knowledge; set forth 3 principles: 1. reality of divine intelligence and the spiritual world it created; 2. eternal reality of moral ideas; 3. reality of moral freedom and responsibility.

Cuffs. Rounded cloth cuffs that can be tightened, worn as part of clerical vestments* by priests and deacons of the Eastern* Orthodox Chs. over wide sleeves of the dalmatic* or sticharion*; symbolize trust in the mighty right arm of God.

Cuius regio, eius religio. See *Augsburg, Religious Peace of.*

Culbertson, Michael Simpson (1819–62). B. Chambersburg, Pa.; educ. West Point and Princeton Theol. Sem.; miss. to China* for Presb. Bd. 1844; at Ningpo 1845–51, Shanghai 1851–62; worked on Chinese Bible tr. Wrote *Darkness in the Flowery Land.*

Culdees (probably derived from old Irish *céle dé,* "companion of God," rather than Lat. *cultores dei,* "worshipers of God"). An ancient monastic order (origin obscure) with settlements in Ireland and Scot. Probably originated in Ireland. Their societies were often formed by 13 mems.: the Abbot, Prior, or Head, and 12 others, on the analogy of Christ and His disciples. St. Moling (founded an abbey at Achad Cainigb called Tech Moling; d. ca. 697) and St. Carthage the Younger (Carthach; Mochuda; est. monasteries at Rahan [or Rathin] and Lismore; d. ca. 637) are called Culdees in early records.

Early Culdees had the marks of anchorites, but gradually became similar to secular canons; probably helped preserve Scot. Christianity bet. the 7th and 12th cents.; later corrupted; superseded by canons* regular; perhaps the last remnants of the Celtic* Ch.; disappear in the 1st part of the 14th c.

W. Reeves, *The Culdees of the British Islands, as They Appear in History* (Dublin, 1864); T. J. Parry, "Culdees," *Encyclopaedia of Religion and Ethics,* ed. J. Hastings, IV (Edinburgh, 1911), 357–358.

Cullmann, Oscar. See *Dogmatics,* B 13.

Cult. 1. A form of religious worship or devotion, as

distinguished from the teaching or creed of a religious organization; a system of religious rites and observances, such as the cult of Mary or the saints, in the RC Ch. 2. The term is often used as synonym of "sect" (always in a derogatory sense); applied by various Prot. chs. to smaller religious groups, esp. those that emphasize a peculiar tenet.

Cultus. See *Worship,* 8.

Cumberland Methodist Church. See *Methodist Churches,* 4 b.

Cumberland Presbyterian Church. See *Presbyterian Churches,* 4 b.

Cumberland Youth Fellowship. See *Young People's Organizations, Christian,* III 7.

Cummings, Jonathan. See *Adventist Bodies,* 3.

Cummins, George David (1822–76). B. near Smyrna, Kent Co., Del.; Prot. Episc. cleric 1845–74; asst. bp. Ky. 1866; opposed emphasis on ritual; organized Reformed* Episc. Ch. 1873. See also *Protestant Episcopal Church, The,* 4 c.

Cupola. Rounded vault, or dome, on circular or other base and forming roof or ceiling. Became characteristic of the Byzantine style of church* architecture.

Curacao. See *Caribbean Islands,* E 7.

Curaeus. See *Cureus.*

Curate (Lat. *curatus,* "one who has the care of souls"). In *Book of Common Prayer* curate (like Fr. *curé*) is a clergyman who has care of souls; used of rector, vicar, or perpetual curate, or their assistants, and of clergyman temporarily in charge of parish; perpetual curates (incumbents of parishes in which tithes are impropriate and no vicarage has been endowed) are now gen. called vicars.

Curäus. See *Cureus.*

Curcelläus, Stephanus (Curcellaeus; 1586–1659). Prof. at Sem. of Remonstrants, Amsterdam; Arminian (see *Arminianism*).

Cure of Souls. See *Pastor as Counselor.*

Cureton, William (1808–64). Eng. Syriac scholar; educ. Oxford; on staff of Brit. Museum 1837–49; discovered Syriac text of 3 letters of Ignatius,* the Curetonian text of the Gospels, and the Festal Letters of Athanasius.*

Cureus, Joachim (Scheer; 1532–73). B. Silesia; educ. Wittenberg, Padua, and Bologna; close friend of P. Melanchthon* and K. Peucer*; physician in Glogau; strongly inclined to Ref. position on Lord's Supper; his *Exegesis perspicua et ferme integra de Sacra Coena,* pub. 1574, caused August,* Elector of Saxony, to take action against Crypto-Calvinists; other works include a hist. of Silesia.

Curfew. The practice of calling people, esp. children and young people, off the streets and away from other pub. places at a certain hour of the night in the interest of decency and pub. welfare.

Curia. 1. Secular. In ancient Rome, a division of the people. In medieval Lat., synonymous for "court," designating either a solemn assem. called by a king, or any court of law.

2. a. *Curia Romana.* In the canonical sense, depts. and officials used by the pope to administer RC govt. In a broader sense the term includes all dignitaries and officials forming the immediate entourage of the pope.

b. Before Constantine, the bp.* of Rome was assisted in his administrative duties by the presbytery at Rome and neighboring bps. From Constantine until the Middle Ages, Roman syns. handled important or difficult affairs. In the Middle Ages the papacy made increasing use of cardinals. Tribunals, congs., and offices were gradually formed. Sixtus V, by the constitution *Immensa,* Jan. 22, 1588, est. 15 congs. His system remained substantially the same until Pius X reorganized the curia by the constitution *Sapienti consilio,* June 29, 1908.

c. In the strict sense the curia consists of congs., tribunals, and offices.

d. *Congregations.* Norms specified by the pope determine the discipline and bus. of congs. No important bus. is to be transacted without knowledge of the pope. All mems. are bound to secrecy regarding official matters. Only cardinals are mems. of congs., but they are staffed by major and minor officials and provided with consultors. Their competence is primarily administrative and executive; judicial power is reserved to tribunals, and legislative to the pope. Congs. do not share in papal infallibility. There are 12 congs.:

Sacred Congregation for the Doctrine of the Faith. In the 13th c. Innocent III (see *Popes,* 10) commissioned legates as the Holy Office of the Inquisition; this function was given to the Dominican Order by Gregory IX (see *Popes,* 11) 1231, and to the Friars Minor by Innocent* IV 1243–54. Paul* III est. permanent cong. 1542. Pope is prefect. Called Cong. of the Holy Office by Pius X (see *Popes,* 30); present name 1965 by Paul VI (see *Popes,* 35); competency includes matters of faith and morals; negatively, it condemns error; positively, it promotes orthodox doctrine; advises regarding doctrinal content of books (see also *Index of Prohibited Books*).

Sacred Congregation for Bishops (formerly Sacred Consistorial Cong.). Est. 1588 by Sixtus V (see *Popes,* 22); powers extended 1908 by Pius X and 1952 by Pius XII (see *Popes,* 33). Pope is prefect. Competency includes preparation of agenda for consistories; control of all that pertains to the founding, preservation, and condition of dioceses not subject to the Sacred Congregations for the Propagation of the Faith and for the Oriental Church; deciding competency of other congs. except that of the Doctrinal Cong.

Sacred Congregation for the Discipline of the Sacraments. Est. 1908 by Pius X. Competency includes regulation of discipline of sacraments; matrimonial cases; est. of validity and obligations of orders; legitimation of birth.

Sacred Congregation for the Clergy (formerly Sacred Cong. of the Council). Est. 1564 by Pius* IV as Sacred Cong. of the Cardinals Interpreters of the Council of Trent.* Competency includes discipline of clergy and faithful; review of acts of councils and episc. conferences.

Sacred Congregation of Religious and Secular Institutes. Est. 1586 by Sixtus V (see *Popes,* 22); confirmed 1588. Competency includes matters pertaining to institutes of religious, third orders, and secular institutes.

Sacred Congregation for the Evangelization of Nations or for the Propagation of the Faith. Originated as commission of cardinals by Gregory* XIII; modified by Clement* VIII to promote reconciliation with E Christians. Permanently est. 1622 by Gregory* XV. Competency includes authority, with exceptions, over religious missionaries and over mission territories in which a hierarchy is not fully constituted.

Sacred Congregation for Divine Worship. Functions and title determined 1969 by Paul VI; has gen. competence over ritual and pastoral aspects of worship in RC and other Lat. Rites. Its duties formerly performed by Cong. of Rites (est. 1588 by Sixtus V; powers extended 1930 by Pius XI [see *Popes,* 32]).

Sacred Congregation for Catholic Education (formerly Sacred Cong. of Seminaries and Universities). Est. 1915 by Benedict XV (see *Popes,* 31); functions extended 1931–32 by Pius XI, and by Pius XII (see *Popes,* 32 and 33) 1941 and 1949. Competency includes authority, with exceptions, over sems. and univs.

Sacred Congregation for the Oriental Churches. Est. 1862 by Pius IX (see *Popes,* 28) – though congs. with similar functions had existed before – and united to Sacred Cong. for the Propagation of the Faith; made autonomous 1917 by Benedict XV (see *Popes,* 31); functions extended 1938 by Pius XI; John XXIII (see *Popes,* 34) appointed 6 patriarchs to it, 5 of the E Rite; Paul VI named consultors from all E Rite groups 1963. Pope is prefect. Competency includes control of dioceses, bps. and other clergy, religious, and faithful of the E Rite.

Sacred Congregation for the Causes of the Saints. Est. 1969 by Paul VI; handles all matters connected with beatification and canonization and with preservation of relics (affairs formerly under Cong. of Rites).

Former Congs. include: *Sacred Cong. of Ceremonies;* est. 1588 by Sixtus V; its functions were transferred in the 1960s to the Prefecture of the Apostolic Palace. *Sacred Cong. for Extraordinary Ecclesiastical Affairs;* est. 1793 by Pius VI (see Popes, 26) as Cong. for Extraordinary Affairs from the Kingdom of the Gauls; powers extended 1814 by Pius VIII (see *Popes,* 27); its duties were taken over in the 1960s by the Sacred Council for the Pub. Affairs of the Ch. *Sacred Cong. of the Basilica of St. Peter;* permanently est. by Clement VIII; reduced in rank in the 1960s.

e. *Tribunals:*

Sacred Apostolic Penitentiary. Originated in the 12th c.; reorganized 1569 by Pius V. Has jurisdiction over matters affecting the private spiritual good of individuals.

Sacred Roman Rota. Originated in Apostolic Chancery; reorganized 1908 by Pius X; revised 1934 by Pius XI. Court for appeals to Holy See.

Supreme Tribunal of the Apostolic Signatura. Existed since the 15th c.; reorganized 1908 by Pius X. Competency includes certain cases involving personnel of Rota; annulment of decisions by Rota; jurisdiction of lower courts.

f. *Offices:*

*Apostolic Chancery.** Originated in the 4th c. office of notaries of the Roman Ch. Forwarded decretal letters of canonization, papal bulls, documents concerning creation of dioceses, and similar important matters. Abolished 1973; its functions transferred to Secretariat of State.

Apostolic Datary. Dates from the 15th c. Handles matters pertaining to nonconsistorial benefices.

Apostolic Camera. Originated in the 11th c.; functions defined 1934 by Pius XI. Administers temporal goods and rights of Holy See.

Secretariat of State. Originated in the 15th c. Processes affairs bet. Holy See and civil govts., and other special matters.

Secretariat of Briefs to Princes. Originated in the 15th c. Drafts papal encyclicals, letters to heads of state, and other major documents.

Secretariat of Latin Letters. Originated in the 15th c. Drafts less formal papal letters.

See also *Pontifical Commissions.*

3. *Diocesan Curia.* Court through which bp. governs diocese.

Curitiba Conference (1951). 1st Lat. Am. Luth. Conf.; held at Curitiba, Brazil, on invitation by the Synodical Federation of Brazil, encouraged by the NLC; present: delegates of "immigrant" chs. and missions, and representatives for the home chs. in N. Am., Eur., and LWF.

Curriculum. See *Parish Education,* D 5.

Cursing. See *Blessing and Cursing.*

Cursives. See *Manuscripts of the Bible,* 3 b.

Curtius, Sebastian. See *Cassel, Colloquy of.*

Cusa, Nicholas of. See *Nicholas of Cusa.*

Cutlerites. See *Latter Day Saints,* g 5.

Cuttington College and Divinity School. See *Africa,* C 7.

Cuyler, Theodore Ledyard (1822–1909). Presb.; b. Aurora, N. Y.; educ. Princeton Coll. and Princeton Theol. Sem.; pastor Brooklyn 1860–90; works include *From the Nile to Norway; Recollections of a Long Life.*

Cybele. Goddess of prehistoric Phrygian empire (more extensive than Roman province); symbol of the fruitful earth; cult was attended with wild ceremonies, some of which were included in the mystery* religions.

Cynewulf (Cynwulf; Kynewulf; fl. 750). Anglo-Saxon poet; nothing known of his life. Works include *The Ascension* (middle section of *The Christ*); *Juliana; Elene; The Fates of the Apostles.*

Cynicism. Philosophy of the Cynics, probably so called from Cynosarges, the place in Athens where Antisthenes (ca. 444–370 BC), founder of the school, taught, though the name was soon assoc. with the unconventional, "doglike" (Gk. *kynikos*), shameless, and aggressive habits of the adherents of the sect. Diogenes (ca. 412–323 BC), called "the Dog," was the best-known representative of the Cynics. They hold that virtue is the supreme good and requires limiting desires and appetites to essentials of life; the wise man is sufficient unto himself. Pride in asceticism and a contempt for all the amenities and, sometimes, even for the decencies of life were marked characteristics of some Cynics. See also *Cyrenaics; Socrates.*

Cyprian (ca. 200 [some say 210]–258). B. probably at Carthage; taught rhetoric; became Christian ca. 246; bp. Carthage by popular acclaim ca. 248; fled during Decian persecution; returned 251 under Gallus, successor of Decius; condemned and beheaded under Valerian (see *Persecutions of Christians,* 4). According to his view, bps. are successors of the apostles and, like them, specially endowed with the Holy Spirit. The properly elected and ordained bp. was supreme in his own ch. Cyprian endeavored to check presbyteral or other infringements on episc. authority. Presbyters participated in sacerdotal functions as delegated by the bp. The episcopate is a unity, each bp. representing the whole office. From the unity of the episcopate springs the unity of the ch., outside of which there is no salvation. Cyprian's conception of the ch. makes every schismatic also a heretic. He recognized the primacy of Peter in representing the unity of the ch., but not in authority and jurisdiction, and regarded other bps., including the bp. of Rome, as his colleagues. See also *Stephen I* (of Rome).

E. W. Benson, *Cyprian: His Life, His Times, His Work* (London, 1897); J. A. Faulkner, *Cyprian: The Churchman* (Cincinnati, 1906); H. Koch, *Cyprian und der römische Primat: Eine kirchen- und dogmengeschichtliche Studie,* in *Texte und Untersuchungen zur Geschichte der altchristlichen Literatur,* ed. A. Harnack and C. Schmidt, XXXV, part 1 (Leipzig, 1910); B. Poschmann, *Ecclesia Principalis: Ein kritischer Beitrag zur Frage des Primats bei Cyprian* (Breslau, 1933); J. H. Fichter, *Saint Cecil Cyprian: Early Defender of the Faith* (St. Louis, 1942); *MPL,* 3–4.

Cyprian (of Antioch in Pisidia; 3d-4th c.). Legendary character; according to one account beheaded with Justina in Diocletian* persecution. See also *Persecutions of Christians,* 4.

Cyprian (5th c. AD). Christian poet; probably Gallic; composed metrical Lat. tr. of OT.

Cyprian (d. ca. 549). Bp. Toulon 516; pupil of Caesarius* of Arles; present as bp. at numerous syns.; opposed semi*-Pelagianism; in letter to bp. Maximus of Geneva he shows knowledge of *Te* Deum,* justifies the statement "the God-man suffered," and defends himself against charge of theopaschitism.*

MPL, 67, 1001–24.

Cyprian, Ernst Salomon (1673–1745). B. Ostheim,

Franconia. Dir. and prof. theol. Casimir Coll., Coburg; mem. of the consistory at Gotha; staunchly opposed and frustrated the plan of uniting the Luth. and Ref. chs. advocated by Frederick William I (1688–1740; king 1713–40) of Prussia. Works include *Historie der Augsburger Confession.*

Cyprus. See *Middle East,* E.

Cyran. See *Du Vergier de Hauranne.*

Cyrenaics. Followers of Aristippus,* who took an opposite view to that of the Cynics,* holding that man can rise above human appetites only in hedonism,* tasting all possible sensual pleasures.

Cyril and Methodius. Apostles of the Slavs; b. Thessalonica in the 820s.

1. The Byzantine Ch. and Empire in the 9th c. chose evangelization as the way to win the friendship and alliance of the Slavs (hitherto pagan), esp. of the Russians and Bulgarians threatening Constantinople and its territories. Cyril (Constantine; d. 869) and Methodius (d. 885), brothers of high rank and educ., were chosen for the task, the former as scholar and linguist, the latter as administrator. Cyril is reputed to have devised a Slavic alphabet, based principally on Gk. letters; he initiated tr. of liturgical as well as important theol. and legal texts into Macedonian Slavic (Old Church Slavonic). This became the basis of Slavic literature.

2. In the 860s, after bringing the Gospel to the Khazars, NE of the Black Sea, Cyril and Methodius went to the Bulgarians and to Great Moravia (see *Czechoslovakia,* 1, 2), whose prince Rastislav had asked Byzantine emp. Michael III (839–867; emp. 842–867) for Christian missionaries, in order to counteract Frankish influence by giving the people the Gospel and its ministry in their own language.

3. Cyril and Methodius' missionary work was favored by Rome, which approved the liturgy in the vernacular; after Cyril's death, Adrian II (792–872; pope 867–872) appointed Methodius abp. of Sirmium, with jurisdiction over Moravia, Pannonia, and Serbia. He was violently opposed by Frankish bps. and banned and imprisoned 870–873. Appeals by John VIII (ca. 820–882; pope 872–882) secured his release and reinstatement. But subsequent intrigues (esp. after the death of Methodius) involving Franks, Magyars, and Moravians issued in the fall of Great Moravia by ca. 906–907 and the end of Byzantine missions there.

4. Disciples of Methodius, driven out of Great Moravia, took refuge in Bulgaria, which became the seat of a flourishing Byzantine Ch. and culture that influenced Serbs, Russians, and Romanians; all these, with the Bulgarians, became Eastern Orthodox after the schism* bet. E and W, retaining the vernacular liturgy. The E Orthodox Slavs also retained an adapted form of Cyril's alphabet.

F. Dvornik, *The Slavs: Their Early History and Civilization* (Boston, 1956) and "The Medieval Cultural Heritage of the Mid-European Area," *Review of Politics,* XVIII (Oct. 1956), 487–507. MSF

Cyril Lucaris. See *Lucaris, Cyril.*

Cyril of Alexandria (ca. 376–444). Succeeded his uncle Theophilus* as abp. of Alexandria 412; under him that see reached its height of power; opposed Nestorius,* whose deposition he brought about; also opposed Arians, Novatians, Jews, and Neoplatonists; final formulation of the doctrine of the Trinity was his work. Works include *De adoratione in spiritu et veritate; Glaphyra; Thesaurus de sancta et consubstantiali Trinitate;* commentaries. See also *Ephesus, Third Ecumenical Council of; Mariology; Mark, Liturgy of Saint; Nestorianism.*

Cyril of Jerusalem (ca. 315–ca. 386). Bp. Jerusalem ca. 350; deposed and exiled several times. Works include *Catecheses,* lectures on Christian faith and practice. See also *Ecumenical Creeds,* B 1 b. *MPG,* 33, 9–1272; *Cyril of Jerusalem and Nemesius of Emesa,* ed. and tr. W. Telfer (Philadelphia, 1956).

Czechoslovakia. Cen. Eur. country composed of 19 regions formerly (before Jan. 1, 1949) Boh., Moravia, Slovakia, and part of Silesia; inhabited largely by a Slavic pop. speaking 2 closely related languages, Czech (in the W) and Slovac (in the E).

1. Great Moravia, which included Boh. and other cen. Eur. territories, was introd. to Christianity in the 9th c. by the Byzantine missionaries Cyril* and Methodius and their disciples; but it soon took on W orientation as a result of pol. and economic ties.

2. With the fall of Great Moravia by ca. 906-907, the name Moravia was limited to the W part of the former empire, which continued as a province attached to Boh. and was later included in Czechoslovakia. Boh. built a rich culture on its Byzantine Moravian heritage; it became a center of Christian influence on its pagan neighbors and was probably responsible in part for the conversion of Hung. and Poland. Wenceslas I (Václav; ca. 907–ca. 929; duke of Boh. ca. 921–ca. 929; Slavic saint) and Adalbert* of Prague gave Boh. an honored place in the medieval Christian commonwealth.

3. Slovakia was conquered by the Magyars ca. 906–907, with resultant adverse effects on the subsequent cultural and economic development of the Slovaks. Strong cultural ties with the Czechs proved valuable sustaining factors in the cents. of Hung. rule.

4. In the 14th c. Boh. experienced a cultural and spiritual renaissance, reaching its "Golden Age" under Charles IV (1316–78; King of Ger. and Boh. and Holy Roman emp. 1347–78) in a flowering of literature and art; the founding of Charles U. 1348 est. Prague as cultural center of cen. Eur. The *Devotio* moderna* also helped prepare the way for the Hussite* reform of the 15th c.

5. Religious vitality, drained by yrs. of strife and warfare, was regained by the *Unitas Fratrum* (see *Bohemian Brethren*). The Utraquist (see *Hussites*) majority ch. found new life with the coming of Luth. influence to Boh. The Luth. impact was strong also in Silesia and Slovakia, and for a time on the Boh. Brethren.

6. The Counter* Reformation had a devastating effect on Czechoslovak Christianity. Protestantism was almost wiped out in Boh.-Moravia, annexed 1620 by the Austrian Hapsburgs; it fared somewhat better in Hungarian Slovakia, where persecution was shorter and not uniformly imposed. Among the Czech religious exiles was J. A. Comenius.* The refugees joined Prot. chs. abroad.

7. The work of **Jirí Tranovský*** (Tranoscius; ca. 1592–1637), gave Luths. in Slovakia spiritual resources that helped them through religious oppression and the suppression of Czech culture after 1620. The Czech tr. of the Bible (Bible of Kralice; see also *Bohemian Brethren,* 3) and Tranovský's hymnal (*Cithara Sanctorum,* or *Tranoscius,* which preserved the Luth. liturgical heritage and the rich Czech Reformation hymnody in Slovakia) have provided the main spiritual nurture of Slovak Luths. See also *Synod of Evangelical Lutheran Churches,* 13.

8. The Enlightenment* brought toleration to Luths. and Ref. in the Austro-Hung. Empire. The creation of the Czechoslovak Republic 1918 brought full religious liberty. This was followed by large-scale defections from the RC Ch. on the part of Czech clergy and laity. A large group of them formed the modernist (see *Modernism*) nat. Czechoslovak Ch. 1920. Somewhat rationalistic at first, it experienced a partial conservative renaissance after 1927. The Czech Luths. and Ref., largely descendants of Boh. Brethren, merged into one body, the

Ev. Ch. of Czech Brethren. This ch. took for its conf. basis the old Boh. confessions (see *Bohemia, Lutheran Theology in*). But the stronger Slovak Luth. Ch. (founded 1921) maintained its indep. Many Czechs became churchless. Most Czechs remained RC, devout in rural areas, but largely nominal in cities.

9. Antichristian measures of Communists, in power since 1948, have effected further loss to the RC Ch. There has been little open persecution, but the govt. exercises considerable pressures to make it difficult to be a Christian, esp. for the young. The hostile regime has forced Christians to dig deeper into the meaning of Christian faith. Best-known Ev. spokesman is Josef L. Hromádka (b. 1889).

See also *Moravian Church; Slovakia, Lutheran Theology in.*

The Cambridge Medieval History, planned by J. B. Bury, ed. J. R. Tanner, C. W. Previté-Orton, and Z. N. Brooke (New York, 1936), VI, 422–472, and VIII, 1–157, 556–619; R. W. Seton-Watson, *A History of the Czechs and Slovaks* (London, 1943); F. Dvornik, *The Slavs: Their Early History and Civilization* (Boston, 1956) and *The Slavs in European History and Civilization* (New Brunswick, N. J., 1962); R. Rican, *Das Reich Gottes in den Böhmischen Ländern,* tr. B. Popelar (Stuttgart, 1957). MSF

Czeglédy, Sándor (1883–1944). Ref. OT theol. in Hung. Tr. NT (1924, 2d ed. 1930) and, with S. Raffay, the whole Bible (1938) into Hung. The Ref. and Luth. Bible Commission used his tr. as a basis for a new Hung. tr.

Czerski, Johann(es) (1813–93). B. W Prussia; founded *Christlich-apostolisch-katholische Gemeinde.*

D

"D." In Biblical criticism the letter "D" is the symbol for one of the alleged sources of the Pentateuch. See also *Higher Criticism,* 6–13.

Dach, Simon (1605–59). Ger. poet. B. Memel; educ. Königsberg, Wittenberg, and Magdeburg; private tutor Königsberg, asst. in Cathedral school 1633, conrector 1636, prof. poetry at the U. 1639, repeatedly dean philos. faculty, rector at the U. 1656–57; invalid; prominent mem. of group of poets at Königsberg; H. Alberti* and J. Stobäus* contributed music for some of his poems; hymns include "Ich bin bei Gott in Gnaden" and "O wie selig seid ihr doch, ihr Frommen."

Dächsel, Karl August (1818–1901). B. Naumburg; educ. Leipzig and Halle; Luth. pastor Hirschfeld, Neusalz, and Steinkirche. Works include a somewhat chiliastic 7-vol. commentary on the Bible, including the Apocrypha.

Dachstein, Wolfgang (ca. 1487–ca. 1561). Studied at Erfurt; Dominican monk at Strasbourg; left order and joined Reformation movement ca. 1524; organist at Strasbourg cathedral 1541; remained there and served RC Ch. after Interim* became effective in Strasbourg 1549; composer; hymnist; coed. *Kirchenampt.*

Da Costa. 1. *Isaac* (1798–1860). B. Amsterdam; of Port. Jewish descent; studied law at Leiden; poet; converted to Christianity 1822; supported orthodoxy and opposed liberalism and Groningen* School. 2. *Uriel* (1585–1640). Freethinking Port. Jewish philos.; fled to Amsterdam; condemned by Port. Jews 1618; regarded by some as forerunner of B. Spinoza.*

Daetrius, Brandanus (1607–99). B. Hamburg. Supt. of city of Brunswick; pres. Brunswick regional consistory; supported G. Calixtus.*

Dagobert I. See *France,* 1; *Netherlands,* 1.

Dahl, Theodor(e) Halvorson (Apr. 2, 1845–Jan. 18, 1923). B. Baastad, Norw.; educ. Christiania, Norw.; to Am. 1865; studied theol. Paxton, Ill., at the Augustana school moved to Rock Island, Ill., 1875; pastor Litchfield, Minn., Green Bay, Wis., Stoughton, Wis.; pres. Norw. Dan. Conf. 1881–86; pres. United Norw. Luth. Ch. in Am. 1902–17. Works include *Saloonforretningern* and *Fred og Strid.*

Dahle, Lars Nilsen (1843–1925). B. Stavanger, Norw.; miss. of Norw. Miss. Soc. to Madagascar 1870 (see *Africa,* B 9); supt. Madagascar; gen. secy. Norw. Miss. Soc. 1889–1920; helped tr. Malagasy Bible and create native theol. literature. Works include *Madagaskar og dets beboere; Specimens of Malagasy Folk-Lore; Livet efter döden* (Ger. tr. O. Gleiss, *Das Leben nach dem Tode;* Eng. tr. J. Beveridge, *Life After Death*); *Et tilbakeblik paa mitliv.*

Dahomey, Republic of. See *Africa,* C 12.

Daillé, Jean (Dallaeus; 1594–1670). Fr. Ref. pastor; hist.; controversialist; mediating theol.

d' Ailly, Pierre. See *Ailly, Pierre d'.*

Dake, Vivian A. See *Evangelistic Associations,* 13.

Dakota. See *Indians, American,* 5, 9.

Dalai Lama. See *Asia,* B 6.

Dale, James Gary. See *Mexican Indian Mission.*

Dale, Robert William (1829–95). Eng. Cong. minister; noted for pol. and educ. activity. Works include *The Atonement,* in which he maintains penal doctrine against liberals but emphasizes the ethical rather than the forensic.

d' Aleman. See *Aleman.*

d' Alembert. See *Alembert.*

d' Allemand. See *Aleman.*

Dallmann, Charles Frederick William (Dec. 22, 1862 to Feb. 2, 1952). B. Neu Damerow, Pomerania; to Am. 1868; grad. Conc. Sem., St. Louis, Mo., 1886; pastor Marshfield (Mo.), Baltimore, New York City, Milwaukee; pres. Eng. Ev. Luth. Syn. of Mo. and Other States 1899–1901, vice-pres. 1901–05; vice-pres. Mo. Syn. 1926–32; ed. *The Luth. Witness* 1891 to 1895. Works include *John Hus; John Wiclif; William Tyndale; Martin Luther; Kate Luther; The Christian; The Ten Commandments; The Lord's Prayer; The Battle of the Bible with the "Bibles"; The Titles of the Christian in the New Testament; My Life; John; Peter; Paul.*

Dalman, Gustaf Hermann (Marx; 1855–1941). B. Silesia; prof. Leipzig 1895; dir. Ger. Ev. Inst. for Archaeology of the Holy Land in Jerusalem 1902; prof. Greifswald 1917; engaged in research into 1st c. Judaism; held that Christ ordinarily spoke Aramaic. Works include *Arbeit und Sitte in Palästina.*

Dalmata. See *Dalmatin, Anton.*

Dalmatic (dalmatica). Ecclesiastical outer vestment worn originally by deacons, now also such dignitaries as bps. See also *Tunicle; Vestments, Clerical.*

Dalmatin, Anton (Dalmata; 16th c.). Croatian ev. theol.; with S. Consul* and P. Truber* tr. NT and AC into Serbo-Croatian.

Dalmatin, Georg (Juri[j]; Jurj; ca. 1547–89). Slovene ev. clergyman in Carniola; tr. Bible into Slovene; hymnist.

Dalton, Henry. See *Catholic Apostolic Church,* 1.

Damascus Fragments. Heb. documents found 1896 in genizah (archives of synagog) at Cairo, Egypt, by S. Schechter.* The fragments describe religious faith and life of Zadokites.*

Tr. in *The Apocrypha and Pseudepigrapha of the Old Testament,* ed. R. H. Charles, II (New York, 1913), 785–834.

Damasus I. See *Fides Damasi.*

Damiani, Pietro (Peter Damian; 1007–72). B. Ravenna, It.; studied at Ravenna, Faenza, Parma; entered Benedictine monastery at Fonte Avellana, near Gubbio, It., 1035; prior ca. 1043; cardinal bp. Ostia 1057. Est. penitential exercises for hermits; opposed simony and other vices of clergy. Works include *Liber Gomorrhianus; Liber gratissimus; Disceptatio synodalis.*

Damien de Veuster, Joseph (1840–89). Belgian RC; Miss. in Hawaii 1864; cared for lepers on Molokai Is. 1873; d. of leprosy.

Damnation. See *Hereafter,* B.

Dan, Adam (Feb. 8, 1848–May 6, 1931). B. Odense, Den.; sent 1869 by Chrischona Miss. Soc. to the Gallas, E Afr., to Jews of Khartoum, Egypt, and Palestine 1870–71; to Am. 1871; pastor Racine (Wis.) 1871–80, Salinas and San Francisco (Cal.) 1880–84, Minneapolis 1884–93, Chicago 1893–96, Cedar Falls (Iowa) 1896–1900, Boston 1900–02, Chicago 1902 to 1926, Clinton (Iowa) 1926–31; helped found *Kirkelig Missionsforening* (see *Danish Lutherans in America,* 3); its 1st pres. 1872; knighted by Christian X of Den.; founded and ed. *Kirkelig Samler;* ed. *Dansk Börneblad.* Works include novels, hymns, and books of poetry and travel.

Dana College. See *Ministry, Education of,* VIII B 11.

Dance. 1. In the widest sense, a springing or leaping in evidence of great emotion (e. g., joy or elation, Jn 11:34; 21:21, 23; Jb 21:11; Eccl 3:4; Mt 11:17), stern determination (e. g., in certain war dances), or religious fervor and ecstasy (e. g., 2 Sm 6:14).

2. The dance plays a prominent part in primitive cultures, where it is often assoc. with religion or romantic love. The ancient Gks. developed the artistic qualities of the dance, and festive choruses tried to express the beauty of harmony, often in correlation with poetry and music.

3. The U. of Wittenberg permitted dances for the sake of discipline, so that students might learn propriety and modesty in conversation and behavior. Dances were also to teach students how to show proper attention to females. Luther reportedly said: "When young ladies and their boyfriends engage in round dances and it is done with decent music and conduct, it is an urbane exercise that pleases me very much" (WA-T 2, 100, No. 1434). He would not condemn the dance, except when it is excessive, indecent, or immoderate, and held that dancing itself could not be properly blamed if sin is connected with it at times (WA 17 II, 64). Older people should attend dances to watch over the young. (WA 32, 209; see also WA 24, 418–419; 34 II, 214; 43, 315; 47, 361)

4. That the dance may become a vehicle of sin, as Luther pointed out (WA 1, 498; 24, 418–419), is evident from the development of the dance in decadent periods of hist.

5. Christian chs. in the 19th and 20th cents. often opposed certain types of dancing. C. F. W. Walther* and other Luths. in Am. opposed dancing that included close embrace, suggestive gestures and acts, and accompanying music that tended to inflame passions. The dance of the daughter of Herodias was often cited as sensuous (Mk 6:22). Such warnings of Scripture as 2 Sm 11:2-4; Pr 5:20-21; Jer 17:9; Mt 5:28; 15:19; 1 Co 10:12; 2 Ti 2:22; Ja 1:14-15 were applied.

6. After 1918 renewed emphasis was placed on purification of the dance and on its recreational and artistic values. But as some other arts, so also some dances of more recent yrs. express a confused outlook on life. Though the dance continues to be watched with suspicion by many religious groups and mems of chs., some ch. groups have used forms of dancing.

C. Andresen, "Altchristliche Kritik am Tanz," *Zeitschrift für Kirchengeschichte,* LXXII (1961), 217–262; F. Bowers, *The Dance in India* (New York, 1953); *Religion and the Dance: A Report of the Consultation on the Dance* (sponsored by the Dept. of Worship and the Arts, Nat. Council of the Chs. of Christ in the USA, New York 1960; mimeographed 1961); M. Berndt, *Adaptation of the Religious Dance and Similar Physical Movements in the Indigenous Church* (STM thesis, Conc. Sem., St. Louis, 1961 [1962]); C. F. W. Walther, *Tanz und Theaterbesuch* (St. Louis, 1885); J. T. Crane, *An Essay on Dancing* (New York, 1853); C. F. Hafermann, "The Evils of Dancing," *Lutheran Standard,* XCVIII, 39 (Sept. 28, 1940), 3; T. Graebner, *The Borderland of Right and Wrong,* 9th rev. ed. (St. Louis, 1956); T. G. Tappert, "Luther in His Academic Role," *The Mature Luther,* Martin Luther Lectures, III (Decorah, Iowa, 1959), 6–8. EL

Daneau, Lambert (Danaeus; Dannaeus; 1530–95). Fr. Prot. Studied law at Orléans; to Geneva 1560; met J. Calvin*; joined Ref. Ch.; pastor Gien, Fr., 1561; prof. Geneva 1574, Leiden 1581; thereafter at Gent (Belgium) and Orthez, Lescar, and Castres (Fr.). Strict Calvinist. Wrote in area of philos., law, and theol.

Danicic, Duro (Djuro; Georg; 1825–82). Serbian philol.; continued language reforms begun by V. S. Karadžić. Works include lexicography, OT tr.

Daniel, Hermann Adalbert (1812–71). Prof. and inspector Halle. Works include *Thesaurus hymnologicus; Codex liturgicus;* geog. textbooks.

Danish Bible Society. See *Bible Societies,* 4.

Danish Church Mission. Est. 1903; worked in Arabia; combined colportage and evangelistic work with med. and educ. work; merged 1946 with the Danish* Miss. Soc.

Danish Evangelical Lutheran Church Association in America *(Det Danske Evangeliske Lutherske Kirkesamfund i Amerika).* See *Danish Lutherans in America,* 5.

Danish Evangelical Lutheran Church in [of] America. See *Danish Lutherans in America,* 3.

Danish Evangelical Lutheran Church in North America, The. See *Danish Lutherans in America,* 3.

Danish Evangelical Lutheran Free Church. See *Denmark, Evangelical Lutheran Free Church of.*

Danish-Halle Mission. See *Missions,* 5–6.

Danish Lutherans in America. 1. The 1st Luth. minister in Am. was the Dan. pastor Rasmus Jensen of Aarhus. He came 1619 with the Jens Munk expedition to Nova Dania on Hudson Bay, at the mouth of the Churchill River, and died there Feb. 20, 1620. A number of Danes settled in New Amsterdam (later NYC) with the Dutch in the 17th c. Lauritz Anderson Rhodesius was ordained 1656 for work in the Dan. W Indies. Dan. Luth. pastors served there till 1918. Many Danes, including Luth. pastors, joined the Moravian Ch. Some Dan. Luth. laymen became Moravian pastors. Two Dan. pastors became Moravian bps.: John Christian Jacobsen (went to Nazareth, Pa., 1816; ordained bp. 1854; d. 1870) and George Frederik Bahnsen (1805–69; pastor Bethany, N. C., 1834; ordained bp. 1860). Moravian missionaries reached the W Indies 1732 and Greenland 1733. A number of Luths. who became Moravians went to Labrador. Otto Christian Krogstrup (b. 1714; ordained 1741), a Dan. Luth. pastor who joined the Moravians, went to Philadelphia, Pa., 1753. Others who went to Am. in the 18th and 19th cents. included Michael Knoll,* Peter Brunnholtz,* J. C. Leps,* H. Hayunga, A. R. Rude, and Edmund Balfour. All served Eng. or Ger. congs. except where a native tongue had to be used.

2. The chief wave of Dan. immigration began ca. 1850. During the next 80 yrs. ca. 331,000 Dan. immigrants came to the US. Many joined Mormon, Adv., Bap., and Meth. chs.; others joined Norw., Swed., and Ger. Luth. chs.; many remained unchurched.

3. C. L. Clausen* helped lay the foundation for Dan. Luth. work in Am. As a result of his influence a commission (known as *Udvalget*) to assure the preaching of the Gospel among Danes in N Am. was organized in Den. 1869; Norw. Luth. pastors had organized several congs. among Dan. settlers. In 1871 the commission, which was leaning toward Grundtvigianism (see *Denmark, Lutheranism in,* 8), sent pastor A. C. L. Grove-Rasmussen, lay preacher A. S. Nielsen, and student Rasmus Andersen* to survey the field among the Danes. They met Clausen, pres. of The Conf. for the Norw.-Dan. Ev. Luth. Ch. in Am. (see *Norwegian-Danish Augustana Synod in America, The)* founded 1870. Nielsen was called to serve the Danes at Cedar Falls, Iowa, and was ordained by Calusen 1871. Nielsen, Andersen, A. Dan,* and N. Thomsen* rejected cooperation and fellowship with The Conf. for the Norw. Dan. Ev. Luth. Ch. in Am. and organized the *Kirkelig Missionsforening* (Ch. Miss. Soc.) 1872. The name was changed unofficially 1874 and officially 1878 to The Dan. Ev. Luth. Ch. in Am. *(Den Danske Evangeliske Lutherske Kirke i Amerika).* Doctrinal differences in-

volving Grundtvigianism led to the exclusion of more than 20 conservative pastors and their congs. 1894. These pastors and congs. formed The Dan. Ev. Luth. Ch. in N. Am. 1894 (also known as North Ch.). The Dan. Ev. Luth. Ch. in Am. helped form the NLC 1918; changed name to The Dan. Ev. Luth. Ch. of Am. 1945, to Am. Ev. Luth. Ch. 1953. HQ Des Moines, Iowa, where it had Grand View Coll. and Sem. Official papers: *Kirkelig Samler* and *Lutheran Tidings.* In 1962 the AELC merged with 3 other chs. to form the Lutheran* Ch. in Am.

4. Pres. of *Kirkelig Missionsforening,* The Dan. Ev. Luth. Ch. in [of] Am., and the AELC: A. Dan 1872–74, J. A. Heiberg* 1874–79, A. S. Nielsen* 1879 to 1883, T. Helveg* 1883–85, A. S. Nielsen 1885–87, J. Pedersen 1887–88, A. L. J. Söholm 1888–91, A. S. Nielsen 1891–93, O. L. Kirkeberg* 1893, A. S. Nielsen 1893–94, K. C. Bodholdt 1894–95, P. Kjölhede 1895–1903, K. C. Bodholdt 1903–11, N. P. Gravengaard 1911–18, K. C. Bodholdt 1918–22, S. D. Rodholm 1922–26, H. Jörgensen 1926–36, A. Jensen 1936–60, A. N. Farstrup 1960–62. Final bap. membership 23,808 in 76 congs.

5. In 1884 the Dan. pastors and congs. of the Norw.-Dan. Conf. withdrew and formed The Dan. Ev. Luth. Ch. Assoc. in Am. *(Det Danske Evangeliske Lutherske Kirkesamfund i Amerika).* Headquarters: Blair, Nebr., where the ch. est. Trin. Sem. 1884 and added a coll. 1899 (first called Blair Coll., but called Dana Coll. since 1903). In 1896 the Dan. Ev. Luth. Ch. in N. Am. merged with the Ch. Assoc. of 1884 to form the United Dan. Ev. Luth. Ch. in Am. (name changed in 1945 to United Ev. Luth. Ch.). Its periodicals included *Dansk luthersk Kirkeblad* (1877–1920) and *Danskeren* (1892-1920), which merged to form *Luthersk Ugeblad. De Unges Blad i Amerika* (1896–1918) became bilingual and changed name to *Our Lutheran Youth;* it became all-Eng. 1921 and was absorbed into *The Ansgar Lutheran* 1927. See also *Publication Houses, Lutheran.*

6. Pres. of United Dan. Ev. Luth. Ch. in America and the UELC: G. B. Christiansen* 1896–1921, M. N. Andreasen 1921–25, N. C. Carlsen 1925–50, Hans C. Jersild 1950–56, William Larsen 1956–60. Final statistics: ca. 73,000 bap. mems. in ca. 182 congs. The UELC merged with 2 other chs. to form The American* Luth. Ch. as of Jan. 1, 1961. JMJ

Danske i Amerika, 2 vols. (Minneapolis, 1908, 1916); P. S. Vig, *Dansk Luthersk Mission i Amerika i Tiden för 1884* (Blair, Nebr., 1917); E. Mortensen, *Stories from Our Church* (Des Moines, Iowa: The Committee on Publications of the Dan. Ev. Luth. Ch. of America. Blair, Nebr.: LPH, 1952); P. C. Nyholm, *The Americanization of the Danish Lutheran Churches* (Copenhagen, 1963); J. M. Jensen, *The United Evangelical Lutheran Church: An Interpretation* (Minneapolis, 1964).

Danish Missionary Society. Founded 1821 Taarbaek, Den.; supported work of the Basel* Miss. Soc. in Afr.; engaged in work in India beginning 1863, Manchuria 1896. Merged 1946 with the Danish* Ch. Miss. in Arabia. Began work in Tanzania 1948. Taiwan ca. 1948, Jap. 1957.

Danish Sudan Mission. See *Africa,* C 14.

Dankbrand. See *Thangbrand.*

Dannaeus, Lambert. See *Daneau, Lambert.*

Dannenfeldt, Paul Louis (Mar. 7, 1887–Aug. 14, 1971). B. Bennet(t), Nebr.; educ. Conc. Sem., St. Louis, Mo.; miss. in Wyo., based at Wheatland, 1910–15; miss. for Nebr. Dist. (included Wyo.) of the Mo. Syn. 1915–16. Pastor Jonesville, Ind., 1916–21; Cincinnati, Ohio, 1921–27; Fort Wayne, Ind., 1927–56. Chm. Mo. Syn. Army and Navy Commission (name changed 1947 to Armed Services Commission) from 1940. Ed. *The Central District Messenger* 1927–33.

Dannhauer, Johann Konrad (1603–66). B. Köndringen, Ger.; educ. Strasbourg, Marburg, Altdorf, and Jena; prof. Strasbourg. Opposed RC and Ref. theol.; rejected theol. of G. Calixtus* as syncretism.* Theologian of the Luth. orthodox tradition; influenced P. J. Spener.* Works include *Hodosophia christiana sive theologia positiva; Liber conscientiae apertus sive theologia conscientiaria; Katechismusmilch.* See also *Dogmatics,* B 6; *Inspiration, Doctrine of,* B 3 c; *Lutheran Theology After 1580,* 3, 4.

Danovius, Ernst Jakob (Danow; 1741–82). Educ. Danzig, Helmstedt, and Göttingen; prof. Jena; specialties were NT exegesis, symbolics, moral theol., and esp. dogmatics.

Dante Alighieri (Durante; 1265–1321). It. poet. B. Florence; first sided, with his family, with the Guelphs, then assoc. with the Ghibellines, then broke with both; received good educ. typical of patrician youths in Florence; met Beatrice (possibly Bice Portinari; 1266–90) ca. 1274; memory of her became a semireligious, mystical longing that found mature expression in the *(Divina) Commedia* (three parts: *Inferno, Purgatorio, Paradiso).* Because of his involvement in pol. dissensions as adherent of the "White" party and opposition to Boniface VIII (see *Popes,* 12), Dante was accused of corrupt practices and hostility to the pope; banished 1302; spent rest of life wandering from one It. city to another (including Verona, Bologna, Padua, and Ravenna). His *De Monarchia* advocated secular monarchy to match spiritual monarchy of pope. Other works include *Vita Nuova; Convivio; Rime* (or *Canzoniere,* a collection of canzoni, ballate, and sonnets).

Le Opere di Dante, ed. M. Barbi et al., 2 vols. (Florence, 1921–22); *Le Opere di Dante Alighieri,* ed. E. Moore, rev. and reed. P. Toynbee, 4th ed. (Oxford, 1924); *The World of Dante,* eds. S. B. Chandler and J. A. Molarino (Toronto, 1966).

Danzig. First mentioned 997 as the Polish town of Gdansk (Gyddanyzc); Gospel preached there 997 by Adalbert* of Prague; Reformation gained entrance 1525 and, though retarded by Sigismund I of Poland, continued to advance and was firmly est. by 1540; captured by Russia 1734; annexed to Prussia 1793; free state from 1919 to WW II; inc. in Ger. 1939; made part of Poland 1945.

Darby, John Nelson. See *Brethren, Plymouth.*

Darbyites. See *Brethren, Plymouth.*

Dark Age(s). Term originating ca. the 18th c. and designating either Eur. hist. ca. 5th–ca. 11th c. or all Middle* Age(s).

Darkness. See *Light and Darkness.*

Darling, David (1790–1867). Sent by LMS as miss. to S Seas 1816; stationed at Eimeo and Tahiti; began miss. on Marquesas 1834; helped tr. Bible into Marquesan.

Darwin, Charles Robert (1809–82). Eng. naturalist; Christian in youth, later freethinker.* Works include *On the Origin of Species by Means of Natural Selection, or the Preservation of Favored Races in the Struggle for Life,* which substitutes mechanical (natural) for supernatural explanation of origin of varied forms of life. Held that in the struggle for existence the fittest survive and new species emerge as a result of natural selection. In *The Descent of Man* Darwin specifically included in his theory the human race as descended from an anthropoid animal. His theory of the origin and perpetuation of new species is called Darwinism.

Darwin, George Howard. See *Evolution,* I.

Dass, Petter (1647–ca. 1708). Norw. cleric and poet; b. on the is. of Nord Herö, on the N coast of Norw.; son of a Scot. father and Norse mother; educ. Copenhagen; ordained ca. 1673; pastor Alstahaug 1689.

See also *Norway, Lutheranism in,* 7.

Datary. See *Curia, Roman,* 2 f.

Dathenus, Petrus (ca. 1531–ca. 1590). B. Cassel, Flanders; Calvinist theol.; pres. 1578 Syn. of Dordrecht.*

Dau, William Herman Theodore (Feb. 8, 1864–Apr. 21, 1944). B. Lauenburg, Pomerania; to Am. 1881; grad. Conc. Sem., St. Louis, 1886; pastor Memphis, Tenn., 1886–92; pres. Conc. Coll., Conover, N. C., 1892–99; pastor Hammond, Ind., 1899–1905; prof. Conc. Sem., St. Louis, 1905–26; pres. Valparaiso (Ind.) U. 1926–29; ed. *The Lutheran Witness;* ed. Eng. part of *Magazin für Ev.-Luth. Homiletik und Pastoraltheologie;* managing ed. *Theological Quarterly* and *Theological Monthly;* consulting ed. *Alma Mater;* ed. *Four Hundred Years; Ebenezer.* Works include *At the Tribunal of Caesar; The Great Renunciation; He Loved Me, and Gave Himself for Me; The Leipzig Debate in 1519; Luther Examined and Reexamined;* joint author with A. L. Graebner* and L. Wessel* of *The Proof Texts of the Catechism with a Practical Commentary;* coed. and co-tr. with G. F. Bente* of *Concordia Triglotta.*

d'Aubigné, Jean Henri Merle. See *Merle d'Aubigné, Jean Henri.*

Daub, Karl (1765–1836). Ger. Prot. theol.; tried to est. philos. reconstruction of orthodoxy; influenced by I. Kant,* F. W. J. von Schelling,* G. W. F. Hegel,* and P. K. Marheineke.* See also *Theology, Speculative.*

Daud, Abraham Ibn (1110–80). Jewish hist. and philos. of Toledo, Sp.; works include *Emunah Ramah* ("Exalted Faith").

Daughters of Charity of St. Vincent de Paul. See *Vincent de Paul.*

Daughters of Mary. See *Marianists.*

Davenport, Charles Benedict. See *Eugenics.*

Davenport, John (1597–1670). Brit. clergyman; pastor in Eng. 1615–25. Puritan sympathizer; helped procure charter for Mass. Colony 1629; to Boston 1637; founded New Haven Colony 1638 and became its pastor; made laws for colony with Theophilus Eaton; pastor First Church, Boston, 1668.

Davenport Theses. Early in the hist. of the Iowa Syn. controversies arose bet. it and the Mo. Syn. (see *Lutheran Church – Missouri Synod*) on the function of the Luth. Confs., the nature of "open* questions," and doctrines (e. g., church and ministry). In 1873 the N Iowa Conf. requested the Iowa Syn. in session at Davenport, Iowa, to state its position toward the Mo. Syn., esp. for the sake of those pastors who had recently joined and were not acquainted with the course of the controversy. As a result the Iowa Syn. adopted 21 theses that sought to show the status of the controversies at the time by indicating on what points the syns. had approached agreement and on what points there was still divergence. Following doctrines are treated in the theses: Church and Ministry 1–5; Confessions 6–7; Antichrist 8–10; Chiliasm 11–15; Open Questions 16–21. See also *Iowa and Other States, Evangelical Lutheran Synod of; Madison Theses; Toledo Theses.*

J. Deindörfer, *Geschichte der Evangel.-luth. Synode von Iowa und anderen Staaten* (Chicago, 1897); G. J. Fritschel, *Quellen und Dokumente zur Geschichte und Lehrstellung der ev.-luth. Synode von Iowa u. a. Staaten* (Chicago, n. d.); J. L. Neve, *A Brief History of the Lutheran Church in America,* 2d rev. and enl. ed. (Burlington, Iowa, 1916); R. C. Wolf, *Documents of Lutheran Unity in America* (Philadelphia, 1966).

David (Dewi). See *Celtic Church,* 9.

David, Christian (1691–1751). Revivalist; co-worker of N. L. von Zinzendorf.*

David of Augsburg (ca. 1200–ca. 1272). Ger. mystic; outstanding preacher; co-worker of Berthold von Regensburg (see *Preaching, History of,* 8); works include Lat. and Ger. treatises.

David of Dinant (d. after 1215). Aristotelian pantheistic philos.; taught at Paris; held that all being (material, spiritual, intellectual) has one essence, namely God.

Davidis, Franz (Franciscus; ca. 1510–79). Supt. of Luth. Ch. in Hung. ca. 1556; Ref. 1564; bp. of Unitarians (see *Unitarianism*) 1568; imprisoned 1579.

Davidists. See *Joris, David.*

Davidson, Andrew Bruce (1831–1902). Scot. divine; prof. oriental languages at New Coll., Edinburgh; mem. OT Rev. Committee 1870–84; exegetical works include a commentary on one third of Jb, regarded by some as 1st scientific commentary on the OT in the Eng. language; other works include *An Introductory Hebrew Grammar.*

Davidson, Samuel (ca. 1807–98). Irish Presb., later Cong.; prof. Biblical literature at Lancashire Indep. Coll., Manchester, 1842–57; later mem. of the OT Rev. Committee; rationalistic in theol.; works include *An Introduction to the Old Testament; An Introduction to the New Testament; The Canon of the Bible.*

Davies, Richard (ca. 1501–81). Welsh Biblical scholar; bp. of Saint David's; helped tr. NT into Welsh; rev. Dt and 2 Sm for Bishops' Bible.

Davies, Samuel (ca. 1723–61). Am. educ. and noted preacher; ordained Presb. 1747; raised funds in Eng. for The Coll. of N. J. (Princeton); pres. Princeton 1759–61.

Day, David Alexander (Feb. 17, 1851–Dec. 17, 1897). Luth. miss. and doctor in Liberia, where he served ca. 24 yrs. See also *Africa,* C 7.

Day, Emily. See *Africa,* C 7.

Day, Samuel Stearns (1808–71). B. Ontario, Can.; sent by Am. Bap. Miss. Union to the Telugu people, India, 1835; est. miss. at Nellore.

Day of Atonement. See *Judaism,* 4.

Day of Foot Washing. See *Church Year,* 8.

Day of Prayer for Missions. See *Woman in Christian Society,* III D 1.

Dayananda Sarasvati. See *Sarasvati, Dayananda.*

Dayman, Edward Arthur (1807–90). Hymnist; b. Cornwall; educ. Oxford; held positions in the Angl. Ch.; hymns include "Almighty Father, Heaven and Earth."

Deaconess Association, Lutheran. See *Deaconesses,* 10, 11, 14.

Deaconess Homes. See *Deaconesses,* 5, 14.

Deaconesses. 1. Female servants in the ch., formerly unmarried or widowed (some contemporary diaconates permit married women to serve as deaconesses); a special ministry in the ch.; "Phoebe, a deaconess." (Ro 16:1 RSV)

2. Custom and usage of the ancient world forbade intimate assoc. of the sexes in pub. assemblies. Functions of deaconesses in the early ch. were to instruct female catechumens, assist at the baptism of women, care for sick or impoverished women, minister to women martyrs and confessors in prison, and act as ushers for women in chs.

3. The 4th c. was the Golden Age of the female diaconate. Forty deaconesses served in the cong. of J. Chrysostom* in Constantinople. Among the deaconesses of that time was Olympias.*

4. When the diaconate came to be regarded as a meritorious work, its deterioration began. Escape sought from a corrupt world resulted in monastic life. By the 12th c. deaconesses had nearly disappeared.

5. The modern career woman in ch. work looks back to 1833 for the beginnings of her work. T. Fliedner,* planning ways to meet the needs of people in distress, opened a door for women who wanted to use their talents for the ch. He est. the first motherhouse 1836 at Kaiserswerth, Ger., where he trained ca. 425 deaconesses. J. K. W. Löhe* est. a motherhouse at Neuendettelsau 1854. Among others in Eur. were those at Bielefeld, Basel, Paris,

and St. Petersburg. The diaconate was introd. also in Eng. and Scand.

6. Among chs. that have deaconesses are the Ch. of Eng., the Ch. of Scot., the Episc., Presb., Ref., Meth., Mennonite, and Bap. chs. Many deaconesses are active throughout the world.

7. W. A. Passavant* introd. the diaconate in Am. He est. a Luth. hosp. in Pittsburgh, Pa., 1849, and on his request Fliedner brought 4 deaconesses from Ger. to be nurses in this "Pittsburgh Infirmary," later called Passavant Hosp. One of the 4 deaconesses was Maria Elizabeth Hess, later wife of Philipp Wambsganss, Sr. (Dec. 19, 1823–Oct. 1, 1901).

8. Motherhouses were est. at Philadelphia 1884 and Baltimore 1895. In Omaha, E. A. Fogelström organized the Ev. Immanuel Assoc. for Works of Mercy 1889; a hospital opened 1890; home for deaconesses built 1891; Immanuel Deaconess Assoc. formed 1892. The Milwaukee motherhouse, later connected with the ALC, was est. ca. 1893. Other deaconess homes include those est. in Chicago, Minneapolis, Brooklyn, Brush (Colo.), and Axtell Nebr.). See also *Wenner, George Unangst.*

9. F. W. Herzberger* helped est. the deaconess movement in the Syn. Conf. He was ably supported by P. Wambsganss, Jr., pres. of the *Ev.-Luth. Wohltätigkeitskonferenz.*

10. The Luth. Deaconess Assoc. of the Ev. Luth. Syn. Conf. of N. Am. (LDA) was organized in Aug. 1919 at Fort Wayne, Ind. Deaconess training was given in connection with the Luth. Hosp., Fort Wayne. First grad.: Ina Kempff 1922. First deaconess sent to a for. field: Louise Rathke, to India 1926.

11. LDA Pres.: P. Wambsganss, Jr., 1919–33; Walter Klausing 1933–55; Edgar H. Albers 1955–. Supts. (called Ex. Dir. beginning in 1957): Bruno Poch 1923–32; Herman B. Kohlmeier 1932–41; Arnold F. Krentz 1941–61; Walter C. Gerken 1961–67; Arne P. Kristo 1968–71; Lucille Wassman 1971–. Dir. of Training: Arne P. Kristo 1961–17. Dir. of Deaconess Educ.: Lucille Wassman 1971–. Over 300 deaconesses have been trained since 1920.

12. Deaconess schools: Fort Wayne, Ind., 1920 to 1943; Beaver Dam Hosp., Beaver Dam, Wis., 1922 to 1935; Luth. Hosp., Hot Springs, S. D., 1924–27; Bethesda Luth. Home, Watertown, Wis., 1925–35. In 1935 the Fort Wayne school separated its program from the Luth. Hospital and the 3 schools were combined into one at Fort Wayne. The courses at that time emphasized intensive 1-yr. religious educ. for those who had specialized in nursing, educ., or social work.

13. In 1941 training was lengthened to 2 yrs.; courses in sociology and psychol. at Ind. U. Extension, Fort Wayne, and 6 mo. practical work were required.

14. In 1943 the LDA sold its Fort Wayne home, on hosp. grounds, to the Luth. Hosp Assoc. Deaconess educ. was transferred to Valparaiso (Ind.) U. In 1946 training was extended to a 4-yr. coll. course leading to a BA degree with a major in theol. Since 1961 deaconess students have been required to spend 1 yr. internship bet. the jr. and sr. yrs. Since 1959 LCMS jr. colleges have been opened to students interested in deaconess training; the first 2 yrs. training are available there, as at Valparaiso U.; the last 2 yrs. are available only at Valparaiso U.

15. Deaconesses wear modern uniforms, are paid full salaries, and participate in the LCMS pension plan.

16. Though many deaconesses in various chs. serve in nursing, soc. welfare, institutional work, and for. missions, a growing number are being trained to serve as assistants to parish pastors; most deaconesses in the Syn. Conf. are parish deaconesses.

E. Beyreuther, *Geschichte der Diakonie und inneren Mission in der Neuzeit,* 2d ed. (Berlin, 1962); K. Bliss, *The Service and Status of Women in the Churches* (London, 1952); C. Dentzer, *Deaconess Work* (Milwaukee, n. d.); F. U. Gift, *The Ministry of Love* (Philadelphia, 1928); C. Herzel, *On Call* (New York, 1961); H. B. Kohlmeier, *History of the Lutheran Deaconess Association* (mimeographed; Fort Wayne, Ind., 1944); P. E. Kretzmann, *A Handbook of Outlines for the Training of Lutheran Deaconesses* (St. Louis, n. d.); J. Mergner, *The Deaconness and Her Work,* tr. Mrs. A. Spaeth (Philadelphia, 1911); F. Meyer, *Von den Diakonissen und ihrem Beruf* (Munich, 1892); J. F. Ohl, *The Inner Mission* (Philadelphia, 1911); W. A. Passavant, Jr., "The Beginnings and Some Principles of the Deaconess Motherhouse," *The First General Conference of Lutherans in America,* ed. H. E. Jacobs (Philadelphia, 1899), pp. 216–227; N. N. Rönning and W. H. Lien, *The Lutheran Deaconess Home and Hospital, Fiftieth Anniversary* (Minneapolis, 1939); F. S. Weiser, *Love's Response* (Philadelphia, 1962); A. R. Wentz, *Fliedner the Faithful* (Philadelphia, 1936).

AFK, AK, WCG

Deacons. Officers of the ch., particularly of the local cong., who, according to apostolic example and precept (1 Ti 3:8-13), have charge of certain administrative work, notably that of assisting the servants of the Word in governing the ch., taking care of its charitable endeavors, and otherwise occupying a leading position of service in the cong. See also *Diaconus; Elders,* 3.

Dead, Commemoration of. See *Departed, Commemoration of.*

Dead, Prayers for. Prayers for the dead can be traced back to early Christian times (*Apostolic* Constitutions,* VIII, 41–42; Cyril* of Jerusalem, *Catechesis XXIII, Mystagogica V,* 9–10; Tertullian,* *De corona militis,* 3, and *De oratione,* 29). Augustine held that prayers for the dead could help only those who had led pious lives (*De verbis apostoli, sermo* CLXXII XXXII, 2). Prayers for the dead were assoc. with the celebration of the Lord's Supper (*Apostolic Constitutions,* VI, 30). RC doctrine "regarding prayers for the dead is bound up inseparably with the doctrine of purgatory and the more general doctrine of the communion of saints" (*The Catholic Encyclopedia,* 1908 ed., p. 653; cf. *Canons and Decrees of the Council of Trent,* Session XXV, "Decree Concerning Purgatory"). The RC *locus classicus* is 2 Mac 12: 40-45 (cf. 1 Co 15:29).

Luther's position is best summarized: "Nothing has been commanded or enjoined upon us concerning the dead. Therefore all this may be safely omitted, even if it were no error and idolatry" (SA-II II 12). He inclines to a cautious toleration of the practice, points out that we have no command to pray for the dead, inasmuch as those who are in heaven do not need prayers, and those who are in hell cannot be helped thereby, and suggests that Christians make their prayers conditional (WA 10-III, 194–195, 409 to 410; 11, 130; 12, 596; 26, 508; 44, 203). The Ap states: "We know that the ancients speak of prayer for the dead, which we do not prohibit" (XXIV, 94). Luther and the confessions vigorously oppose purgatory and attempts to gain forgiveness of sins for the dead, esp. through such works as masses and almsgiving (see *Opus operatum*). M. Chemnitz* regarded ancient prayers for the dead as exhortations and consolations for the living (*Examen Concilii Tridentini, III, Locus III: De purgatorio,* Section II, vii, 12). Most Luth. theologians regarded prayers for the dead as useless or unpermitted; others emphasized the mystical union of believers and regarded prayers for the dead (though not for their salvation) permissible.

See also *Departed, Commemoration of.*

L. Dahle, *Das Leben nach dem Tode,* tr. O. Gliess

(Leipzig, 1895); [C. H.] Stirm, "Darf man für die Verstorbenen beten?" *Jahrbücher für Deutsche Theologie,* VI (1861), 278–308. EL

Dead, Realm of. See *Hereafter,* C 3 (2).

Dead, Vespers of. See *Burial,* 2.

Dead Sea Scrolls. In spring 1947 an Arab found ancient parchment MSS in a cave near the NW shore of the Dead Sea. One of the scrolls, a Heb. copy of Is, measures 24 ft. by 10 in. It was probably written ca. 100 BC; it is perhaps the oldest copy of any book of the Bible. Most of the other scrolls were sacred writings of an ascetic Jewish community of ca. 200 people (gen. regarded as Essenes*) who lived there at Khirbet Qumran ca. 100 BC to AD 68.

At least 10 more caves, containing MSS, pottery fragments, and coins, have been found in that area. The discoveries are significant for OT textual studies and NT faith and life.

The scrolls have shown that the Bible was transmitted with a high degree of accuracy. The Qumran Is seems to be ca. 1,000 yrs. older than the next oldest known copy of this book. But there are very few differences bet. the two. This lends added assurance that our common OT Heb. text is indeed essentially the same as that which Christ used.

The scrolls have shown a similarity bet. the faith and life of the Qumran community and that of the early NT ch. It was pointed out that the "Teacher of Righteousness" resembled Christ. The Fr. scholar A. Dupont-Sommer claimed that this Teacher was portrayed as a divine being who had become man, who was put to death by his enemies, and whose resurrection from the dead was anticipated. Some Am. writers created a stir by publicizing the unwarranted conclusion that the doctrines of the incarnation, the vicarious suffering, and the resurrection of Jesus were not new and unique, but were borrowed from the teachings of the Qumran community.

Organization in the Qumran community has been compared to that in the early Christian Ch. An inner Qumran group including 12 laymen calls to mind the 12 disciples. Both communities pooled their property for the benefit of all mems. Writings of both groups refer to anger with a brother without a cause, personal admonition in case of a grievance, and refraining from pub. charges unless they could be proved by witnesses. Both groups observed ritual washings and a sacred meal involving bread and wine; but the Qumran rites seem more closely connected with the OT cultus than with the NT sacraments.

Some early views on the scrolls and their origin were subjective. The contention that the scrolls made a new evaluation of the Christian religion necessary is now considered both premature and greatly exaggerated. The literature of the Qumran community will no doubt have a prominent place among the apocryphal writings that were produced bet. the OT and NT. Its theol. seems to be more closely related to Moses and the prophets than to the Gospel of Jesus Christ. The value of the scrolls both for OT textual studies and for NT faith and life will undoubtedly increase as the unpub. contents of the caves are made available. AvRS

F. F. Bruce, *Second Thoughts on the Dead Sea Scrolls* (Grand Rapids, Mich., 1956); M. Burrows, *The Dead Sea Scrolls* (New York, 1955); F. M. Cross, Jr., *The Ancient Library of Qumran and Modern Biblical Studies* (Garden City, N. Y., 1958); H. E. Del Medico, *The Riddle of the Scrolls,* tr. H. Garner (New York, 1959); *The Dead Sea Scriptures,* tr. T. H. Gaster, rev. and enl. ed. (Garden City, N. Y., 1964); Y. Yadin, *The Message of the Scrolls* (New York, 1957).

Deadly Sins. See *Sins, Venial and Mortal.*

Deaf. 1. In OT, deaf were protected by law (Lv 19: 14). In NT, Jesus healed deaf (Mk 7:32-37). Word "ephphatha" ("be opened"), often used in work among deaf, was spoken by Jesus (Mk 7:34). Deafness is also ascribed to those who hear but do not understand (Is 42:18; 43:8; Mt 13:14). Healing deaf a sign of messianic kingdom. (Mt 11:5; Lk 7:22)

2. The condition of the deaf in the Greco-Roman world was deplorable. They were often regarded as defective and their rights were curtailed. Augustine* of Hippo held on the basis of Ro 10:17 that deafness hinders faith (*Contra Julianum,* III iv 10). For cents. the ch. made no organized effort to reach the deaf.

3. J. R. Pereire* originated a method of signing the alphabet with one hand. C. M. de l'Épée* perfected this method. T. H. Gallaudet* and L. Clerc brought this sign language to the US.

4. In the 19th c. institutions for the deaf were est. in many parts of the world. Govts. and such educators as H. Mann* became interested in educ. of deaf. The RC Ch. est. the St. Joseph Inst. for the Deaf, St. Louis, Mo., 1837.

5. In the 19th c. ministers of the Gospel led in bringing educ. to the deaf. Many clergymen served as administrators and teachers in residential schools. As educ. of deaf became more specialized, the clergy withdrew from school staffs and concentrated on Gospel ministry.

6. Thomas Gallaudet (1822–1902), son of T. H. Gallaudet, while serving on the faculty of the Institution for the Instruction of the Deaf and Dumb, NYC, organized a Bible class and began conducting religious services for deaf; it soon became St. Ann's Ch. for Deaf-Mutes, inc. 1854. Edward Miner Gallaudet (1837–1917), another son of T. H. Gallaudet, was a noted teacher of deaf-mutes in the Am. Asylum, Hartford, Conn., and head of a school for deaf-mutes, Washington, D. C.; part of the latter school became Gallaudet Coll. 1894. Henry Winter Syle, a deaf man, was ordained to the Episc. priesthood 1883.

7. The Southern Bap. Conv. does extensive work among deaf in the South. The Meth. Ch., Ch. of Christ, Assemblies of God, and other Prot. chs. are active in deaf work.

8. The Christian Deaf Fellowship is an interdenom. organization that began work in Akron, Ohio, in the early 1940s and is spreading to other parts of the US and Can. The United Ch. of Can. has missions in Ont. and a large ch. in Toronto.

9. The Desoms (Deaf Sons of Masons) were organized in the 1940s.

10. In 1873 an assoc. of Mo. Syn. congs. founded an institute for deaf-mutes in connection with an orphanage in Royal Oak, Mich.; its 1st dir. and teacher was G. P. Speckhard.* New property for the Royal Oak inst. was acquired 1874 at Norris, Mich., near Detroit. At the instigation of Edward J. Pahl (d. Nov. 4, 1945), a grad. of the Detroit school, adult work among deaf was begun. Among Mo. Syn. pioneers in work among deaf were Hermann Daniel Uhlig (Nov. 8, 1847–Aug. 15, 1913; dir. of the Detroit inst. 1879–1900) and E. A. Duemling.* A. Reinke* conducted the 1st Mo. Syn. service for deaf Mar. 4, 1894; within a few months he conducted services for deaf in Fort Wayne and Elkhart, Ind.; he requested the Mo. Syn. at its 1896 conv. to undertake miss. work among deaf and a syn. commission for deaf was est.; he also urged students at the St. Louis sem. to study sign language under tutelage of a Mrs. Jacobi. Two students, Hermann Adam Bentrup (Nov. 24, 1872–Oct. 29, 1948) and Traugott Martin Wangerin (Oct. 21, 1873–Sept. 9, 1951), were sent out in the 1st yr. By 1897 three missionaries were conducting services in 14 cities; total average attendance: 300.

11. In 1965 the LCMS had nearly 60 workers among deaf. Deaf were served in over 200 cities and numbered over 5,000 communicant mems. Pas-

tors also minister to deaf in state hospitals and other govt. institutions. Training programs are conducted at Conc. Sem., St. Louis, Mo.; Conc. Sem., Springfield, Ill.; Conc. Sr. Coll., Fort Wayne, Ind.; and several prep. schools. The work is supervised by the Bd. for Miss.

12. For. work among deaf by the LCMS was begun 1964 in the Far East under the direction of William Reinking as resident counselor in Hong Kong. Contacts for work among deaf have been made in Australia, Brazil, Nigeria, New Guinea, and elsewhere.

13. The Luth. Friends of the Deaf est. the Luth. School for the Deaf, Mill Neck, N. Y., 1951; it publishes educ. materials (e. g., the John of Beverley Series of religious workbooks).

14. The Ephphatha mission of The ALC centers its work in the midwestern states among Scand. people. This miss. began 1898 when the United Norw. Luth. Ch. in Am. first considered expanding its home miss. work to include deaf and blind. Gilbert H. Bakken became its 1st part-time and H. O. Bjorlie the 1st full-time pastor to deaf.

15. Beginnings of work among deaf by the LCA date back to the early part of the 20th c. in E Pa. and centered in Philadelphia, where students from the sem. conducted classes and services for children in the Pa. School for the Deaf, Mount Airy, Pa. HWR

K. W. Hodgson, *The Deaf and Their Problems* (New York, 1954); H. Best, *Deafness and the Deaf in the United States* (New York, 1943).

Dean, William. See *Asia,* C 4.

Death. Temporal death is cessation of natural life; universal (Heb 9:27); results from sin (Gn 2:17; Ro 5:12-14); for believers prelude to eternal bliss (2 Co 5:1; Ph 1:23; 2 Ti 4:6-8; Ja 1:12); described as separation of spirit from body (Ec 12:7; 2 Co 5:1-5; 2 Ptr 1:14), departure (2 Ti 4:6); introduced into the world by Satan (Heb 2:14; Jn 8:44); occurs once (Heb 9:27); certain (Jb 14:1-2).

Fear of death and of what lies beyond is a source of anxiety and alarm to a guilty conscience. But Jesus has taken away the sting of death, 1 Co 15:55-57, and has given to His own the assurance that death leads to a state of endless bliss, Ps 16:11. That man was not destined for a life ending in death is clear from the penalty for sin, Gn 2:17. It was possible for man not to sin *(posse non peccare)* and hence not to die. According to theol. statements based on the analogy of the angels confirmed in holiness, he might have attained the inability to sin *(non posse peccare),* hence the absolute state of deathlessness. The dominion of death over man is ascribed to sin, Ro 5:12.

Spiritual death is the alienation of sinful man from the holy God. *Temporal* death is so called because it takes place in time and for the duration of time. *Eternal* death, or the "second death" (Rv 20:14), is the fate of those who meet temporal death unjust, impenitent, unbelieving; they are forever separated from God and will rise only to hear their doom and experience it in body and soul (Mt 10:28; 25:41-46). But death has no eternal claim on those who meet temporal death in spiritual life; they will rise to eternal life (Mt 25:31-40, 46; Jn 5:29).

See also *Hereafter.*

Death and Funeral Practices. See *Burial.*

De Bakker, Jan (Jan van Woerden; Pistorius; 1499 to 1525). B. Woerden, Neth.; educ. Utrecht and Louvain; entered priesthood at Utrecht; pastor Woerden 1523; arrested for departing from traditional doctrine; imprisoned; released; went to Wittenberg to contact Luther; returned; summoned to Utrecht, he fled to Holland, married, and as layman taught the Gospel; imprisoned at the Hague; burned at stake.

Debrecen. City in E Hungary*; prominent in Prot. ch. hist.; noted for confessions of faith formulated there 1560–62 and 1567. See also *Reformed Confessions,* E 6.

de Bres, Guy. See *Bres, Guy de.*

Debrunner, Johann Albert (1884–1958). B. Basel; educ. Göttingen and Basel; taught at Zurich 1917–18, Greifswald 1918–20, Bern 1920–25, Jena 1925–35, Bern 1935–54. Mem. of the Ev. Ref. Ch. Revised F. W. Blass,* *Grammatik des neutestamentlichen Griechisch;* ed. *Indogermanisches Jahrbuch* 1927–39 and *Indogermanische Forschungen* 1948–58.

Decalog. The fundamental moral law in the form of 10 sentences (LXX: *deka logoi* Ex 34:28). When God created man, He wrote the Law into his heart. According to Ro 2:14-15, Gentiles who have not the decalog carry out its precepts by nature and thereby show that the works of the Law are written in their hearts. (Cf. Gn 1:27; Eph 4:24)

In order to lead Israel to worship only Him, God gave His holy will in Ten Commandments from Sinai (Ex 19:1–20:17; Dt 5) and later wrote them on 2 tables (Ex 24:12; 31:18) which were to be placed into the "ark of the testimony" (Ex 25:21-22). also called "ark of the covenant" (Nm 10:33) and "ark of God" (1 Sm 3:3). Moses broke the 1st set of tables when he came down from the mountain (Ex 32:19). New tables were prepared (Ex 34) and put into the ark (Dt 10:1-5; 1 K 8:9; Heb 9:4). The tables may have been lost when Nebuchadnezzar destroyed the temple. (2 K 25)

That the 10 Commandments do not concern Gentiles and Christians, but only Jews, as Luther said (WA 16, 424), is true of the form in which they were given (Ex 20:1-17; Dt 5:6-21). Luther, following NT precedent (cf. Mt 19:18-19; Mk 10:19; Eph 6:2-3; Cl 2:16-17), omitted ceremonial elements (the word "Sabbath" and ceremonial commands of the 3d Commandment), the mention of iconolatry (1st Commandment), and the threat attached to the 2d Commandment, and made other changes (e. g., in the 10th Commandment, Ex 20:17; Dt 5:21; and in placing the part that he used as the Close of the Commandments, Ex 20:5b-6; Dt 5:9b-10).

The 10 Commandments tell us what we are to do and not to do and how we are to be and not to be. Man cannot be saved by the Law (Gl 2:16); but the Law serves as a curb, a mirror, and a rule. It serves as a curb "to maintain external discipline against unruly and disobedient men" (FC Ep VI 1; cf. 1 Ti 1:9-10; Ps 32:9). It serves as a mirror by showing man what he is (Is 64:6; Ro 3:20; 7:7; Gl 3:24). It serves as a rule in showing what God expects of man.

No mere man has perfectly fulfilled the Law as God demands (Gl 3:10; 1 Jn 1:8); all are sinners (Eph 2:3; Ro 3:22-23), subject to temporal and eternal punishment (Lv 26:14-43; Dt 27:14-26; 28:15-68; Ro 6:23). But Christ fulfilled the Jewish ceremonial and pol. laws as well as the moral law (Mt 22:21; Luke 2:22-39; 1 Ptr 2:21-22). He also bore the punishment for our sins (1 Co 15:3; Gl 3:13; 1 Ptr 2:24). The Christian, then, is no longer under the Law. (Ro 6:14; Gl 5:18)

The Bible neither numbers the Commandments nor determines their respective position (cf. Ex 20:17 and Dt 5:21; Mt 19:18-19 and Mk 10:19). The Jews make Ex 20:2 the 1st Commandment, Ex 20:3-6 the 2d, and Ex 20:17 the 10th. The E Orthodox and the Ref. Chs. make Ex 20:2-3 the 1st, Ex 20:4-6 the 2d, and Ex 20:17 the 10th. The Luths. and RCs draw the 2d from Ex 20:7, the 3d from Ex 20:8-11, and make Ex 20:17a the 9th and Ex 20:17b the 10th. Jews divide the 10 Commandments into 2 groups of 5 each. Luths. and RCs assign 3 Commandments to the 1st table and 7 to the 2d. E Orthodox and Ref. Chs. assign 4 to the 1st and 6 to the 2d. RH, LP

R. Herrmann, "The Decalog and the Close of the

Commandments," *The Abiding Word,* I (St. Louis, 1946), 124–145; F. W. C. Jesse, *Catechetical Preparations, Part I: The Decalog* (St. Louis, 1919); E. G. W. Keyl, *Katechismusauslegung aus Dr. Luthers Schriften und den symbolischen Büchern,* I (Nördlingen, 1853); M. Reu, "The Significance of the Law and the Example of Jesus for the Formation of the New Life," *Christian Ethics* (Columbus, Ohio, 1935), pp. 114–122.

Decet Romanum pontificem (bull). See *Bull; Reformation, Lutheran,* 9.

Decisio Saxonica. Decision rendered 1624 by theologians including Höe* von Höenegg in a dispute bet. the theologians of Tübingen and Giessen. The former held that in Christ's State of Humiliation the God-Man retained both the possession and the use of all His divine attributes, though He applied them only in secret; the latter held that the Lord had the possession and the functions of His divine attributes, but did not use them according to His human nature. The decision declared that in working miracles the God-Man temporarily stepped out of His *kenosis.**

Decius, Gaius Messius Quintus Trojanus (Caius; 201–251). B. Budalia, near Sermium, Pannonia; Roman emp. 249–251. See also *Persecution of Christians,* 3–4; *Philip the Arabian.*

Decius, Nikolaus (Deeg; ca. 1485–after 1546). Pastor, poet, and musician. Seems to have been a native of Hof, Upper Franconia; educ. Leipzig; monk; spiritual leader of Benedictine nunnery (Steterburg); became Luth. ca. 1522; rector at Hanover 1522; then teacher in Brunswick 1522; wrote perhaps the first hymns of Lutheranism for the Reformation of Brunswick; entered U. of Wittenberg 1523; 2d pastor at Stettin ca. 1524, later 1st pastor of *Nikolaikirche* there; asst. pastor Liebstadt, E Prussia, 1530; at Mühlhausen 1534; sympathetic to Calvinists; cantor and teacher of Lat. school, Bartenstein; asst. cantor and preacher at court in Königsberg 1540; returned to Mühlhausen 1543; regarded as restless and unstable. Author and composer of "Allein Gott in der Höh sei Ehr" and "O Lamm Gottes, unschuldig." Other works include *Summula* (on passages from Mt).

Declaratio Solida (Solid Declaration). See *Lutheran Confessions,* C 2.

Declaration (American Lutheran Church). See *American Lutheran Church,* V 1; *Brief Statement.*

Declaration and Address. See *Disciples of Christ,* 2 a.

Declaration of Faith (Bap. Conv., N. H.). See *Democratic Declarations of Faith,* 3.

Declaration of Faith (Foursquare Gospel). See *Foursquare Gospel, The.*

Declaration of Faith (Society of Friends). See *Friends, Society of,* 2.

Declaration of Faith and Order (Cong.). See *Democratic Declarations of Faith,* 3.

Declaration of Faith of English People Remaining at Amsterdam in Holland, A. See *Democratic Declarations of Faith,* 3.

Declaration of Faith of the Reformed Church in France (1872). See *Reformed Confessions,* B.

Declaration of Independence. See *Natural Law,* 5.

Declaration of Synod of Boston. See *Democratic Declarations of Faith,* 2.

Declaration of the Faith, Church Order, and Discipline of the Congregational or Independent Dissenters. See *Democratic Declarations of Faith,* 2.

Declaration of the Representatives of the American Lutheran Church (1938). See *American Lutheran Church, V; Intuitu fidei.*

Declaration of the Rights of Man and of the Citizen. See *France,* 11.

Declaration on Christian Education. See *Vatican Councils,* 2.

Declaration on Religious Freedom. See *Vatican Councils,* 2.

Declaration on the Relationship of the Chruch to Non-Christian Religions. See *Vatican, Councils,* 2.

Declaratory Acts. Two acts, 1879 and 1892, of the Presb. Ch. of Scot. allowing ministers some freedom in some items in Ref. confessions. See also *Free Church of Scotland; Presbyterian Churches,* 1; *Presbyterian Confessions,* 4.

Declaratory Statement. Adopted 1903 by Gen. Assem. of the Presb. Ch. in the USA; purpose was to bring God's decree of election into harmony with universal grace. See also *Presbyterian Churches,* 4 a.

Declaratory Theory. See *Atonement, Theories of.*

De Cock, Hendrik (1801–42). Dutch Ref. pastor; leader in organization of Christian Ref. Ch.; minister at Eppenhuisen and Noordlaren 1824; Ulrum 1829; influenced by Willem Bilderdijk (1756–1831), poet, scholar, and critic, to oppose rationalism and formalism of Ref. Ch. in the Neth.; suspended, he announced his separation from the est. Ref. Ch. 1834; with Hendrik Pieter Scholte (1805–68) and others organized the Christian Ref. Ch. *(Christelijke Gereformeerde Kerk)* 1836. See also *Netherlands,* 2.

Decoration, Church. See *Art, Ecclesiastical and Religious.*

Decrees and Decretals. Decretals are collections of decrees or laws, esp. of papal laws and rules. The term is derived from the Lat. *decretalis,* "containing a decree"; cf. the Lat. *decretum,* "decree." The singular, "decretal," denotes any authoritative decree or a letter embodying such a decree. Decretals include the *Decretum* of Gratian* and decretals of Gregory IX (see *Popes,* 11), Boniface VIII (see *Popes,* 12), and Clement* V. Such decretals are part of canon* law *(Corpus* Iuris Canonici).* See also *Decretals, False; Pseudo-Isidorian Decretals.*

Decrees of God. The essential internal acts of God: decree of creation, redemption, and predestination. God decreed to create the world. Foreseeing that man would fall into sin, He decreed to send Christ as the universal Savior from all sins, from death, and from the power of the devil. He also decreed to save and to preserve unto eternal life certain persons through Christ. The decrees of God cannot be frustrated. See also *Creation; Predestination; Redemption.*

Decrees of the Council of Trent. See *Roman Catholic Confessions,* A.

Decrees of Vatican II. See *Vatican Councils,* 2.

Decretals, False. Compilations of alleged laws and resolutions within the RC Ch. to support false claims. See also *Pseudo-Isidorian Decretals.*

Decretum Gelasianum. Early Lat. document; author unknown; erroneously ascribed to Gelasius I (pope 492–496); contains 5 sections: Christ and the Holy Ghost, canonical Scripture, the Roman Ch., orthodox councils and fathers, and approved patristic and apocryphal writings.

Decretum of Gratian. See *Canon Law,* 3; *Decrees and Decretals; Gratian* (canonist).

Decretum of Gratian. See *Canon Law,* 3.

Decretum pro Armenis. See *Florence, Council of,* 3.

Dedekennus, Georg (Dedekendus; Dedeken; 1564 to 1628). Luth. theol.; b. Lübeck; d. Hamburg; pastor Neustadt; preacher in Hamburg; works include *Thesaurus consiliorum et decisionum; De peccatorum causis.*

Dedication. Religious ceremony whereby anything is dedicated or consecrated to the service of God. In OT the tabernacle (Ex 40; Nm 7), Solomon's temple (1 K 8; rededication 2 Ch 29), Zerubbabel's temple (Ez 6:16-17) were dedicated. This custom was followed by Maccabaeus (1 Mac 4:52–59) and Herod (Josephus, *Antiquities,* XV, xi, 6). Cities, walls, gates, houses were also consecrated (Dt 20:5; Ps 30, title; Neh 12:27).

Eusebius describes the dedication of the cathedral

at Tyre ca. 315 (*HE,* X, iv). By the 13th c., dedication consisted of 6 parts: blessing outside, blessing in middle of ch., preparation for altar consecration, altar consecration, procession of relics, blessing of altar vessels and furnishings.

In the RC Ch. solemn consecration (permanent chs.) is only by bp., blessing (temporary chs. and those of metal or wood) by priest. The ceremony consists of prayers, sprinkling with holy water, followed by mass.

Luther rejected concepts of magic and superstition in dedicatory act (WA 50, 644–645). Preaching and prayer sanctify and dedicate chs. (WA 49, 588–615). Scripture readings, hymns, and prayers occupy a prominent place in Luth. ceremonies of groundbreaking, cornerstone laying, dedication, and consecration.

The Minister's Handbook of Dedications, ed. W. H. Leach (New York, 1961); *English Orders for Consecrating Churches in the Seventeenth Century, Together with Forms for the Consecration of Churchyards, the First Stone of a Church, the Reconciliation of a Church, and the Consecration of Altar Plate,* ed. J. W. Legg (London, 1911); R. W. L. Muncey, *A History of the Consecration of Churches and Churchyards* (Cambridge, Eng., 1930).

Deed of Demission. See *Free Church of Scotland.*

Defectives, Care of. See *Charities, Christian; Hospitals, Sanatoria, Homes for Convalescents and Chronically Ill.*

Defender of the Faith *(Fidei Defensor).* Title used by rulers of Eng.; first conferred 1521 by Leo X on Henry VIII for his treatise against Luther defending the doctrine of 7 sacraments.

Defense of Greek Orthodoxy. See *Eastern Orthodox Standards of Doctrine,* A 2.

Defenseless Mennonites, Conference of. See *Mennonite Churches,* 3 b.

"Defensor pacis." See *Marsilius of Padua.*

Definite Synodical Platform *(Definite Platform, Doctrinal and Disciplinarian, for Evangelical Lutheran District Synods; Constructed in Accordance with the Principles of the General Synod).* Document born of "American Lutheranism"; pub. anonymously Sept. 1855; S. S. Schmucker* was instrumental in drawing it up. It included an "American Recension of the Augsburg Confession." Its chief object was to obviate the influence of confessional Lutheranism. The *Definite Platform* charges the AC with error in approval of the ceremonies of the mass, private confession and absolution, denial of the divine obligation of the Christian Sabbath, baptismal regeneration, the real presence of the body and blood of the Savior in the Eucharist. The descent into hell is omitted from the Creed. The Athanasian Creed is not included. The other Luth. symbols are rejected because of their length and alleged errors.

Though drafted by leaders of the General* Synod, the *Definite Platform* was adopted by only 3 district syns.: the Wittenberg Syn. of the Ev. Luth. Ch. of Ohio, the Olive Branch Syn. of the Ev. Luth. Ch. of the State of Ind., and the Eng. Luth. Syn. of Ohio (later known as the E Ohio Syn.). The other constituent syns. either refused to adopt the document or rejected it altogether. The Gen. Syn. as such, therefore, cannot be held responsible for the *Definite Platform.* The authors and supporters of the document had mistaken a half-developed tendency for a final result.

Definite Platform, Doctrinal and Disciplinarian, for Evangelical Lutheran District Synods; Constructed in Accordance with the Principles of the General Synod, 2d ed. (Philadelphia, 1856); E. L. Lueker, "Walther and the Free Lutheran Conferences of 1856–1859," *CTM,* XV (1944), 529–563; V. Ferm, *The Crisis in American Lutheran Theology* (New York, 1927); C. Mauelshagen, *American Lutheranism Surrenders to Forces of Conservatism* (Athens, Ga., 1936).

Defoe, Daniel (ca. 1660–1731). Eng. pioneering novelist, pamphleteer, journalist. Works include *The Shortest Way with the Dissenters,* which shows the absurdity of religious intolerance; *Robinson Crusoe.*

Degrees, Prohibited. See *Prohibited Degrees.*

Degrees of Glory. See *Hereafter,* A 6.

Degrees of Punishment. See *Hereafter,* B 4.

Dei filius. See *Vatican Councils,* 1 a.

Dei gratia. Lat. "by the grace of God"; abbreviated D. g. Found 1 Co 15:10. First used at the Third Ecumenical Council of Ephesus*; later secular rulers used the expression in connection with their titles to indicate that they held their office by divine grace and will.

Dei verbum. See *Vatican Councils,* 2.

Deicide. Literally a slayer of a god; term sometimes used to designate esp. those who took part in the crucifixion of Christ.

Deification. See *Apotheosis.*

Deindörfer, Johannes A. (1828–1907). B. Rosstal, near Nürnberg; educ. Nürnberg and Neuendettelsau; to Frankenhilf (now Richville), Mich., as an emissary of J. K. W. Löhe* 1851; joined Missouri* Syn. 1852; with G. M. Grossmann* to Iowa 1853 because of differences with the Mo. Syn.; helped found Iowa* Syn. 1854; pastor Iowa, Wis., and Ohio 1853–93; pres. Iowa Syn. 1893–1904; prominent in the opposition of his syn. to the Mo. Syn. Works include *Geschichte der Evangel.-Luth. Synode von Iowa und anderen Staaten; Denkschriften* commemorating the 10th, 25th, and 50th anniversaries of the founding of the Iowa Syn.

Deinzer, Johannes (Sept. 2, 1842–Jan. 25, 1897). B. Ger.; taught at the institute of the Neuendettelsau* miss. soc.; asst. of J. K. W. Löhe; to Am. 1879, at the 25th anniversary of the Iowa* Syn., representing its friends in Ger.; sent out ca. 100 missionaries, many to the Iowa Syn.; ed. *Wilhelm Löhe's Leben* and J. K. W. Löhe, *Agende,* 3d ed., 1884.

Deism. System of belief which holds either that the universe is a self-sustained mechanism from which God withdrew immediately after creation or that God is still active in the universe, but only through the laws of nature.

I. Antecedents. The sources on which deism drew were many. 1. Some arguments of deists were taken from early opponents of Christianity (Celsus,* Porphyry,* Philostratus*), from statements made in the course of early controversies (Gnostic [see *Gnosticism*], Trinitarian and Christological,* Pelagian,* Arminian [see *Arminianism*]), and from pre-Christian philosophers (Socrates,* Plato,* Democritus,* Leucippus,* Epicurus,* M. T. Cicero,* Plutarch*). 2. Discoveries and explorations of the 15th and 16th cents. brought information to Eur. regarding various religions; this stimulated comparative religion. 3. Scientific discoveries undermined many views held in the medieval ch. I. Newton's* scientific works led deists to conclude that observation of laws est. by God is a sufficient basis for religious conviction. 4. Many arguments of deists were taken from contemporary controversies, with RCs quoted against Prots. and vice versa. 5. Deists criticized abuses in the ch., "lifeless dogmatism," ritualism, and the lack of true spiritual life. 6. Deists criticized the narrow scholasticism of RCs, but developed scholastic statements concerning God into a conception of a master mechanic who created the world and then let it operate on its own. 7. Deists drew heavily on results of textual* criticism and higher* criticism. 8. Dissatisfaction with fanaticism and atrocities ascribed to religious communions prepared the way for many deistic arguments. See also *Rationalism.*

II. Method. Much writing of the deists is negative. Inspiration, text of Scripture, miracles, prophecies, deity of Christ, Bible characters, ordinances, institutions, rites and doctrines of the ch., character of the clergy, and other religious matters were subjected to their attacks. The smaller part of their writings was devoted to developing a religion of nature.

III. History. 1. Deism is gen. considered as beginning with E. Herbert* (ca. 1583–1648) and ending with Thomas Jefferson (1743–1826; Am. statesman; works include *The Life and Morals of Jesus of Nazareth,* often called "The Jefferson Bible"). Herbert granted the possibility of revealed religion, but held that perception occurs through the correspondence of objects with ideas innate in the mind; held 5 principles to be common to all religions: (1) rationally derived belief in the existence of deity; (2) obligation to worship deity; (3) close connection bet. worship and practical morality; (4) obligation to repent of sin and abandon it; (5) divine recompense in this world and the next. T. Hobbes* (1588–1679) held that religion arises out of fear and superstition and is to be controlled by the state. Deists disliked Hobbes's intolerance but were influenced by his rationalism.

2. T. Browne* (1605–82) regarded faith and reason as hostile forces, and tried to keep them apart; opposed dependence on authority and adherence to antiquity. J. R. Tillotson* (1630–94) opposed intolerance; regarded ethics and reason as chief elements in religion.

3. J. Locke* (1632–1704), though not a deist, was extensively quoted by deists and gave new directions to deistic thought. His empiricism replaced Herbert's doctrine of innate ideas. His statement that it was difficult to prove the soul immaterial was seized on by deists, as well as his remark that time weakened evidence for traditional revelation.

4. C. Blount* (1654–93) marks the transition bet. Herbert's doctrine of innate ideas and Locke's empiricism; opposed revelation by trying to parallel Bible narratives with heathen legends; held that what is necessary for salvation must be known to all since there is no special revelation. J. Toland* (1670 to 1722) est. deism on the empiricism of Locke. A. A. Cooper (1671–1713), 3d Earl of Shaftesbury,* emphasized natural ethics and introd. wit and mockery as weapons.

5. M. Tindal* (ca. 1656–1733) reduced Christianity to naturalism*; regarded it unreasonable to hold that truth is withheld from most of mankind. Other Eng. deists: Thomas Woolston (ca. 1670–ca. 1733); A. Collins* (1676–1729); H. St. J. Bolingbroke* (1678–1751); Thomas Chubb (1679–ca. 1747; works include *The Supremacy of the Father Asserted; A Discourse Concerning Reason; The True Gospel of Jesus Christ Asserted*); Thomas Morgan (1680–1743; works include *The Moral Philosopher*); P. Annet* (1693–ca. 1769).

6. H. Dodwell, Jr. (see *Dodwell,* 2), paved the way for transition from deism to skepticism; denied reason a place in religion. This trend was accelerated by D. Hume's* denial of causality* as a force (see also *Cause,* 5).

IV. Factors in the decline of deism: Christian apologies (G. Berkeley,* J. Butler,* W. Law,* J. Leland,* G. Lyttelton,* W. Paley,* G. West*); differences among deists; exhaustion of the subject of deism; Meth. revival (see *Methodist Churches,* 1).

V. Eng. deism influenced men in Fr. (J. J. Rousseau,* Voltaire*), Ger. (J. K. Dippel,* I. Kant,* G. E. Lessing,* M. Mendelssohn,* H. S. Reimarus,* C. Wolff*), and Am. (B. Franklin, T. Jefferson [see also par. III 1 above], T. Paine*). It influenced philos., Modernism,* and Freemasonry* in the 19th and 20th cents. and is studied by antichristian movements. EL

See also *Freethinker.*

J. Orr, *English Deism: Its Roots and Its Fruits* (Grand Rapids, Mich., 1934); S. G. Hefelbower, *The Relation of John Locke to English Deism* (Chicago, 1918); H. M. Morais, *Deism in Eighteenth Century America* (New York, 1960); L. Stephen, *History of English Thought in the Eighteenth Century,* 3d ed., 2 vols. (New York, 1902; repr. 1927); G. A. Koch, *Republican Religion: The American Revolution and the Cult of Reason* (New York, 1933; repr. Gloucester, Mass., 1964).

Deissmann, Gustav Adolf (1866–1937). Prof. NT Heidelberg and Berlin; showed that NT Gk. was that of the papyri; pointed out the value of papyri for study of NT Gk. Works include *Bibelstudien; Licht vom Osten.* See also *Lutheran Theology After 1580,* 13.

de la Place, Josué. See *Place, Josué de la.*

Delaware. See *United States, Religious History of the,* 6.

Delehaye, Hippolyte (1859–1941). Belgian Jesuit; pres. Bollandists* 1912.

Delitzsch. 1. *Franz* (1813–90). B. and d. Leipzig; prominent theol. of the Erlangen school (see *Lutheran Theology After 1580,* 11); prof. Rostock, Erlangen, and Leipzig; special field was exegesis; acquainted with founders of the Mo. Syn.; enthusiastic Lutheran; later, influenced by modern scientific theol., opposed literalistic use of FC. Works include commentaries on OT books in a series to which J. F. K. Keil also contributed; tr. NT into Heb.

2. *Friedrich Conrad Gerhard* (1850–1922). Assyriologist; b. Erlangen; d. Langenschwalbach; son of Franz; prof. Berlin 1899; lectures *Babel und Bibel,* in which he maintained that OT ideas originated in Babylonia, caused noted controversy; opponents showed that Biblical OT religion had unique divine origin. Works include *Assyrische Grammatik; Assyrisches Handwörterbuch.*

Delk, Edwin Heyl (Aug. 15, 1859–Feb. 8, 1940). Luth. clergyman; b. Norfolk, Va.; ordained 1882; pastor Schoharie, N. Y., 1882–85, Hagerstown, Md., 1885 to 1902, Philadelphia, Pa., 1902–29; pres. Philadelphia Fed. of Chs. 1910–14; trustee Luth. Theol. Sem. and Luth. Deaconess Motherhouse. Works include *Three Vital Problems; The Need of a Restatement of Theology;* ed. *The Life and Works of Rev. Charles S. Albert, D. D.*

Della Robbia. See *Robbia.*

Deluge. See *Flood.*

Demantius, Johannes Christoph (1567–1643). B. Reichenberg (Liberec), Boh.; Luth. composer of sacred and secular music; works include *Passion According to St. John.* See also *Passion, The.*

Demeter. See *Greek Religion,* 2.

Demetrius (d. ca. AD 231). Bp. Alexandria 189; first a friend, then opponent, of Origen* (Eusebius, *HE,* VI, iii, viii, xix, xxvi).

Demetrius of Thessalonica (Demetrius Mysos; Demetrius of Thrace; Demetrius Rascianus; 16th c.). Highly literate Serbian deacon; in service of patriarch of Constantinople; for several months P. Melanchthon's* houseguest in Wittenberg 1559; entrusted by Melanchthon with delivery of Gk. version of AC and a personal letter to Patriarch Joasaph but on the way became engrossed in Prot. work in Wal(l)achia (now part of Romania) and apparently did not reach Constantinople. See also *Eastern Orthodox Churches,* 5.

Demiurge. See *Gnosticism,* 5.

Demme, Karl Rudolph (Apr. 10, 1795–Sept. 1, 1863). B. Ger.; educ. Altenburg, Göttingen, and Halle; to Am. 1818; licensed 1819 by Pa. Ministerium to serve at Hummelstown, Pa.; assoc. pastor St. Michael and Zion Ch., Philadelphia, Pa.; ed. Ger. tr. of the works of F. Josephus*; active in liturgical and hymnological work. See also *Schaeffer, Charles Frederick.*

Demmel, Joseph (1846–1913). Old Cath. pastor Bonn; bp. Old Cath. Ch. 1906. See also *Old Catholics.*

Democratic Declarations of Faith. Under this head are included the creeds evolved by Prot. denominations after the period of conf. writing based on involved theol. thought had come to an end; they are considered exhibitions of unity rather than binding symbols. In gen., these creeds are less theol., more popular, and more permissive of private judgment. Many are of the nature of a covenant and emphasize voluntary agreement for the achievement of a common purpose.

1. Creeds of this type may be traced to such Anabaptist statements as the *Schleitheim Confession,* entitled *Brüderlich Vereinigung etzlicher Kinder Gottes sieben Artikel betreffend* (adopted 1527 by Swiss Anabaptists); *Rechenschafft unserer Religion, Leer und Glaubens* (drafted 1540 by Peter Riedemann*); the *Waterland Confession* entitled *Korte Belydenisse des Geloofs* (1577); and the *Dordrecht* Confession.* (See also *Mennonite Churches,* 2)

2. Congregationalists weaken gen. creeds and emphasize particular creeds. Each cong. has the right to formulate its own creed. Prominent among their gen. declarations: *Savoy Declaration* (1658; first 2 parts: preface, and revision of the *Westminster Confession* [see *Presbyterian Confessions,* 3, 4]; the pref. emphasizes "a forbearance and mutual indulgence unto Saints of all persuasions, that keep unto, and hold fast the necessary foundations of faith and holiness, in all other matters *extra fundamental,* whether of Faith or Order"; the 3d part is a Platform of Discipline); *Declaration of the Faith, Church Order, and Discipline of the Congregational or Independent Dissenters* (also called *Declaration of Faith and Order;* summary of leading Cong. doctrines of faith and order; adopted 1833 by the Congregational Union of Eng. and Wales). In Am. the following are noteworthy: *Cambridge Platform* (1648; approved in substance the doctrinal parts of the *Westminster Confession* but not its articles on discipline); *Declaration of Synod of Boston* (also called *Confession of 1680;* modified *Savoy Declaration;* approved *Cambridge Platform* in substance); statements of the Synod of Saybrook (1708; approved the *Confession of 1680;* adopted Heads* of Agreement; drew up the Saybrook Platform of discipline) and of the National Council of Boston (1865; adopted the "Burial Hill Declaration," which expressed adherence to faith and order substantially as embodied in the *Cambridge Platform* and in the *Confession of 1680,* and a brief statement of polity). (See also *United Church of Christ, The,* I A 1, 2)

3. Two large bodies emerged in early 17th c. Bap. hist. in Eng.: Arminian (also called Gen. because they believed in gen. or universal atonement) and Calvinist (also called Particular, because they believed in particular redemption). (See also *Baptist Churches,* 2). Baptists do not consider creeds as tests of orthodoxy, but as portrayals of unanimity. Creeds of Particular Baptists include: *London Confession* ("The Confession of Faith of those Churches Which are Commonly [though falsely] called Anabaptists"; adopted by 7 Bap. chs. 1644); *Somerset Confession* ("A Confession of the Faith of Several Churches of Christ in the County of Somerset, and of Some Churches in the Counties Neer Adjacent"; 1656); *Second London Confession* ("Confession of Faith Put Forth by the Elders and Brethren of Many Congregations of Christians [Baptized Upon Profession of Their Faith] in London and the Country"; 1677; reprinted 1688; reaffirmed 1689; sometimes called *Confession of 1688;* based on *Westminster Confession* [see *Presbyterian Confessions,* 3]); *Philadelphia Confession (Second London Confession* with the addition of Art. XXIII and XXXI; pub. authorized 1742 by the Philadelphia Bap. Assoc., organized 1707; printed 1743). Some early important declarations of Arminian (Gen.) Baps.: *Short Confession of Faith in XX Articles by John Smyth,* ca. 1609; *A Declaration of Faith of English People Remaining at Amsterdam in Holland* (1611; election conditioned by foreknown faith; reprobation by foreknown unbelief; perseverance denied); *The Faith and Practise of Thirty Congregations, Gathered According to the Primitive Pattern,* adopted 1651 by congs. of Lincolnshire, Leicestershire, and adjoining counties; *Midland Association Confession* ("Sixteen Articles of Faith and Order Unanimously Assented to by the Messengers Met at Warwick, the 3rd Day of the 3rd Month, 1655"); *The Standard Confession* (also called *London Confession;* "A Brief Confession or Declaration of Faith," adopted 1660 at London); *An Orthodox Creed* ("An Orthodox Creed, or A Protestant Confession of Faith, Being an Essay to Unite and Confirm All True Protestants in the Fundamental Articles of the Christian Religion, Against the Errors and Heresies of Rome"; endorsed 1678; approaches Calvinism). More recent statements by Baps.: *Declaration of Faith* (drawn up by J. N. Brown* and others ca. 1833; pub. by N. H. Bap. Conv.; widely accepted in Am.); *Abstract* of Principles;* and *Statement of Committee on Baptist Faith and Message* (adopted by S Bap. Conv. 1925).

4. Quakers acknowledge no platform or creed of binding authority. Some follow R. Barclay's* *Catechism and Confession of Faith* and *Apology.* See also *Friends, Society of.*

5. Moravians have no confession of faith as such but endorsed the AC. An expression of their theol. is found in A. G. Spangenberg,* *Idea fidei fratrum.* See also *Moravian Church.*

6. Meth. creeds allow for development. In addition to the Bible, Methodists recognize 3 classes of confessional guides or standards: a. *Twenty-five Articles of Religion* (adopted 1784 at Baltimore; prepared by J. Wesley from *Thirty-nine Articles* [see *Anglican Confessions,* 6]); b. Wesley's *Sermons and Notes on the New Testament;* c. *Book of Discipline* and several catechisms (1852, 1868). See also *Methodist Churches.*

7. Practically all groups that reject creeds have statements of principles (e. g., *Articles of War* of the Salvation* Army and T. Campbell's* *Declaration and Address* [see *Disciples of Christ,* 2 a, 3]).

W. Walker, *The Creeds and Platforms of Congregationalism* (New York, 1893); P. Schaff, *The Creeds of Christendom,* 6th ed., 3 vols. (New York, 1931); T. B. Neely, *Doctrinal Standards of Methodism, Including the Methodist Episcopal Churches* (New York, 1918); J. C. Wenger, *The Doctrines of the Mennonites* (Scottdale, Pa., 1950); W. L. Lumpkin, *Baptist Confessions of Faith* (Chicago, 1959); *Creeds of the Churches,* ed. J. H. Leith (Chicago, 1963). EL

Democritus (ca. 460–ca. 371 BC). B. Abdera, Thrace; known as "Abderite" and "Laughing Philosopher." Adopted the atomistic philos. of Leucippus* and developed it into the first important materialist philos. of nature; held that the soul is material and perishes with, and in the same sense as, the body. See also *Philosophy.*

DeMolay, Order of. See *Freemasonry,* 8.

Demon. The word originally meant "a deity." In later Gk. usage it became a term for a spirit, either good or evil. In the NT, demons are evil spirits or devils. See also *Devil.*

Demoniac Possession. Possession is the condition in which a person is controlled by an evil, foreign being, which maltreats and tortures the body in various ways, sometimes causing the features to become distorted into ferocious mocking and often causing the victim to express disrespect for religion in a bold, cynical way. The demoniac at Gadara (Lk 8:26-39) showed the following characteristics of possession:

He recognized Jesus as his opponent and knew His divine nature; he had supernatural strength; the demons in him desired to escape into swine.

Some object that such an account as Lk 8:26-39 cannot be accepted at face value but that Jesus only humored a notion of the time in seeming to recognize the existence of demons, that demons do not really exist, and that He only seemed to cast them out.

Some commentators attribute these struggles bet. Christ and demons to limitations of knowledge on the part of Jesus. But it is apparent that Christ recognized Satan's power and that the evil spirits recognized Jesus as the Son of God, the Messiah.*

Instances of demoniac possession are occasionally reported in contemporary times. TG

See also *Demonology; Devil.*

T. Graebner, "Demoniacal Possession," *CTM,* IV (Aug. 1933), 589–603.

Demonology. Study of demons or of beliefs in demons or evil spirits. Ancient Egyptians, Assyrians, Babylonians, Gks., and others believed in demons. In the NT, demons are evil or unclean spirits opposed to God; they constituted the hierarchy of Satan and took possession of people (Mt 8:16; 12:22-29; Mk 1:32; 5:1-20; Lk 8:26-39). See also *Demoniac Possession; Devil.*

Demythologization (Ger. *Entmythologisierung*). Term used by Rudolf Bultmann (b. 1884; Ger. theol.; prof. Marburg) for a way of interpreting Scripture in the categories of modern man. It tries to remove ancient "myths" (e. g., the "mythical *Weltbild*") and state the message of Scripture in relevant contemporary language. He defined "myth" as a representation according to which the transcendent and divine appears as immanent and human, the invisible as visible.

The issue was discussed 1941 by Bultmann in a study entitled *Offenbarung und Heilsgeschehen.* He believes that hidden in the myth* is a *kerygma,** which can be set free by demythologization and proclaimed in existential terms (see *Existentialism*). The hist. core of Christianity is in the crucifixion of Jesus, which is also in a mythological setting.

Fritz Buri (b. 1907; Swiss theol.; prof. Basel) endorses Bultmann's existentialism and demythologization, but faults him for halting with the *kerygma.* Consistency, he holds, requires also a "dekerygmatization" of the Christian message.

Kerygma and Myth: A Theological Debate, ed. H. W. Bartsch, tr. R. H. Fuller, 2 vols. (London, 1953–62); W. Arndt, *"Entmythologisierung," CTM,* XXII, No. 3 (Mar. 1951), 186–191; R. R. Caemmerer, "More on *Entmythologisierung," CTM,* XXII, No. 10 (Oct. 1951), 769–770; P. M. B[retscher], "Bultmann and Goldammer," *CTM,* XXV, No. 9 (Sept. 1954), 692–694; O. Cullmann, "Rudolf Bultmann's Concept of Myth and the New Testament," *CTM,* XXVII, No. 1 (Jan. 1956), 13–24; P. Althaus, Jr., *Fact and Faith in the Kerygma of Today,* tr. D. Cairns (Philadelphia, 1959); J. Macquarrie, *The Scope of Demythologizing: Bultmann and His Critics* (London, 1960); L. M. Petersen, *A Historical Critical Analysis of Rudolf Bultmann's Form Criticism as Related to His Demythologization* (Th. D. Thesis, Conc. Sem., St. Louis, 1960); L. Malevez, *Le message chrétien et le mythe* (Brussels, 1954), tr. O. Wyon, *The Christian Message and Myth* (London, 1958); R. Marlé, *Bultmann et l'interprétation de Nouveau Testament* (Paris, 1956). EL

Denck, Hans. See *Denk, Johannes.*

Denham, John (1615–69). Eng. poet. Successfully extended the couplet to descriptive poetry. Works include *The Sophy; Cooper's Hill;* tr. of the Psalms.

Denicke, David (1603–80). Hymnist; b. Zittau, Saxony; lectured at Jena and Königsberg; tutored the two oldest sons of Duke Georg of Brunswick-Lüneburg; mem. Hanover consistory. Hymns include "Kommt, lasst euch den Herren lehren"; "Wenn ich die heil'gen zehn Gebot"; "Wir Menschen sind zu dem, o Gott." With J. Gesenius* ed. Hanoverian hymnals 1646–59.

Denifle, Heinrich Seuse (Josef Anton; 1844–1905). Austrian RC theol. Sought to reconcile mysticism* and scholasticism*; studied medieval univs.; founded with Franz Ehrle the *Archiv für Literatur- und Kirchengeschichtedes Mittelalters* 1885.

Denis (Denys; 3d–4th c.). Apostle to the Gauls; 1st bp. of Paris; patron saint of Fr.; beheaded at Paris; identified in popular belief with Dionysius* the Areopagite (Acts 17:34).

Denison, George Anthony (1805–96). Tractarian* and Anglo*-Catholic; vicar Broadwindsor and East Brent; archdeacon Taunton.

Denk, Johannes (Hans Denck; ca. 1495–1527). B. Heybach (Habach), Bavaria; befriended by J. Oecolampadius*; expelled from Nürnberg on charge of heresy 1525; joined Anabaps.; expelled from Augsburg and Strasbourg 1526, Worms 1527; with L. Hetzer* tr. OT prophets. See also *Socinianism,* 1.

Denmark. Christianity apparently first came to Den. in the 6th and 7th cents. through contacts incidental partly to commerce, partly to raids on Ireland. Willibrord* entered Den. ca. 700, but his work seems to have had little lasting success. Ebo* and Halitgar (bp. Cambrai ca. 817; d. ca. 830) entered Den. ca. 822. Ebo returned to Den. several times in the following yrs. for further miss. work with some success. Harald Klak, prince of Jutand, expelled from his country 826, took refuge with Emp. Louis I and was baptized, with his household and retinue. When he returned to Den., he was accompanied by Ansgar,* who est. missions in Schleswig and Ribe. The 1st Christian ch. in Den. was built at Haddeby (Hedeby), near Schleswig, ca. 847. Ansgar's death was followed by a period of transition that ended with the decisive adoption of Christianity, usually dated ca. 950 at the baptism of King Harold Bluetooth (d. ca. 986).

King Sweyn II (Sweyn Estrithson) organized the Dan. Ch. into 9 bishoprics ca. 1060. A metropolitan see for Scand. was est. at Lund ca. 1104. The king was the most powerful figure in the ch. till the 12th c., when the prelates of the ch., under leadership of the abp. of Lund, gained freedom and power for the higher clergy. Power struggles resulted bet. kings and prelates in the 13th and 14th cents.

The ch. of the later Middle Ages was characterized by moral decay, formalized piety, pessimism, and futile attempts at reform.

See also *Thirty Years' War.*

Denmark, Evangelical Lutheran Free Church of. Organized Nov. 4, 1855, in Copenhagen, Den., by N. P. Grunnet* for confessional reasons; organized at a time when practically all religious restrictions had been removed in Den. and when rationalism,* Grundtvigianism (see *Denmark, Lutheranism in,* 8), and S. A. Kierkegaard's* attacks on "official Christianity" were making an impact on the ch. Many critics remained in the ch.; some joined sectarian movements; others became enemies of the ch.; a few joined the Luth. free ch. movement.

In 1882 the Ev. Luth. Free Ch. of Den. est. ch. fellowship with the Luth. Free Ch. of Saxony and thus came into contact with the Mo. Syn.

In 1888 N. P. Grunnet's son Waldemar, who had studied in Am., became his father's asst. When he came to be regarded as his father's successor, some withdrew 1895 and formed the United Ev. Luth. Free Congs. of Den. (*De forenede evangelisk-lutherske frimenigheder i Danmark*). In 1900 J. M. Michael, who had studied at Conc. Sem., St. Louis, and had been sent as miss. to Hamburg, Ger., was called to serve at Helsingör (Elsinore). In 1967 the Ev. Luth. Free Ch. in Den. numbered 7 congs., 212 mems. This body is supported by the LCMS.

W. J. Michael, *Den evangelisk-lutherske Frikirke i Danmark ved 100-ars jubiläet: 1855–1955* (pub. by W. J. Michael, n. d.).

Denmark, Lutheranism in. 1. At the beginning of the 16th c. the ch. in Denmark was in great need of reform. Many of its leaders were worldly and corrupt, not interested in the spiritual life of the people. The humanist Poul Helgesen (Paulus Helie; Heliae; Eliae; ca. 1485–ca. 1535) unsuccessfully tried reform from within and opposed the Reformation. The ch. was more indep. of Rome than that of many other countries. Aage Jepsen (Sparre) was endorsed as abp. of Lund by royal councillors 1526 and given authority to appoint bps. without consulting Rome. The intention was, however, to remain RC. See also *Christian II; Reformation, Lutheran,* 10.

2. H. Tausen* began to preach Luth. doctrine 1525 at Viborg. Despite a pledge to be true to Rome, Frederick I protected Tausen. Others, including Claus Mortensen, began to preach and initiate reforms at various places, including Malmö. Tausen went to Copenhagen 1529. Dan. Luth. hymnals were pub. 1528, 1529, and 1533. Luths. under leadership of Tausen presented a statement of their faith at the 1530 Diet of Copenhagen in the 43 articles of the *Confessio Hafnica* (or *Hafniensis;* name taken from Hafnia, 11th c. Lat. name of Copenhagen). Tausen pub. a Gospel and Epistle postil 1535. After the 1534–36 civil war Christian III (1503–59; king of Den. and Norw. 1534–59) was in financial distress. The RC chs. were wealthy. The king saw that the Reformation was gaining ground. At the 1536 Diet of Copenhagen much RC wealth was confiscated and the country made Luth.

3. In 1537 J. Bugenhagen* crowned the king and queen and ordained 7 new supts., later called bps. This broke apostolic succession in Denmark. Calvinistic tendencies were not tolerated. P. Palladius* (1503–60) was a prominent bp. The Bible was tr. into Dan. 1550 by C. Pedersen* and others; called the Christian III Bible.

4. N. Hemming(sen),* a follower of P. Melanchthon,* exerted humanistic influence and sought compromise with Calvinism.*

5. After 1600 humanistic theol. was sharply attacked by Luth. orthodoxy, which dominated the ch. in the 17th c. Pastors were better trained and were required to pledge adherence to the AC, instead of committing themselves vaguely, as formerly, to ev. teaching. The family altar was emphasized. But there was a tendency to separate faith and life. Intolerance was prevalent, ignorance and superstition strong. Witches were burned at the stake. In the midst of this was a deep mystic religiosity that found expression in devotional literature and in emphasis on penitence and prayer. T. H. Kingo* was the great hymnist of the time.

6. Pietism* came to Den. from Ger. ca. 1703 and found expression through its pastors and hymnists (e. g., H. A. Brorson*) and in groups that met for prayer and Bible reading. The first Luth. for. miss. was launched 1705 by the Dan. king in cooperation with Halle pietists; B. Ziegenbalg* and H. Plütschau* were sent to India. Some orthodox pastors were worldly; throughout the 18th c. there was a struggle bet. dead orthodoxy and pietism. The Dan. common school was begun with erection of ca. 240 schools. Children were given a thorough instruction in religion. Confirmation was introd. 1736.

7. The subjective elements of the pietistic period melted into the optimistic views of the Enlightenment.* Faith in God was replaced by faith in man, and the voice of conscience by reason. Men were not directly opposed to Christianity, but under the influence of R. Descartes,* J. J. Rousseau,* and naturalism* in gen., the dogmas of the ch. were disregarded; emphasis was on faith in providence, a demand for a good life, gratitude to God for His gifts, and the hope of eternal life after death. To be a good citizen was enough to gain God's favor. The educ. classes drifted away from Christianity, ch. attendance declined, religious indifference was gen. Some (e. g., Nikolai Edinger Balle, 1744–1816; prof. theol. Copenhagen 1772; bp. Sjaelland 1782) stood firm on the Bible. Some Bible reading groups also continued.

8. Rationalism* held sway at the beginning of the 19th c. But N. F. S. Grundtvig* sought in the spoken Word and in the sacraments the clear and unchanging expression of true and pure Christianity as it had come down from Christ Himself through the cents. In reaction against small Bible reading groups he held that the Bible was a "dead word" over against the "living word" of the Apostles' Creed. He influenced the Dan. Ch. esp. by his view of life, hymns, emphasis on cong. life and singing, and the effect of his message esp. in rural areas. His great love for Den. and his vision of its hist. destiny gave his movement a national spirit. Christian, national, pol., and cultural subjects were discussed in great folk mass meetings. As a result, Grundtvigianism became the most liberal of the 3 main groups in the Dan. Ch. (the other 2: *Centrum,* or Church Center, and *Indre Mission,* or Inner Mission; see 9 and 10 below).

9. J. P. Mynster* led the educ. classes to a confessional form of Christianity. His view on the ch. gave direction to the Church Center group. H. L. Martensen,* Mynster's successor as bp. of Sjaelland, combined Luth. orthodoxy with Hegelianism and built a vast dogmatic and ethical system on a Christian idealistic philos.

10. When pious groups of the mid-19th c. found they could not in good conscience cooperate with Grundtvigians because their view of Scripture and their attitude toward the world were so different, a group of laymen organized Inner Mission, based on Luth. confessions, to stimulate spiritual life. The soc. grew slowly. J. V. Beck* attended the 1861 annual meeting and preached on Peter's Draught of Fishes (emphasizing fishing for men by both laity and clergy, Lk 5:1-11). The soc. was reorganized under the name *Kirkelig Forening for Indre Mission* (Church Society for Inner Mission). Beck became its leader. Both pastors and laymen were to preach. Miss. halls were built in nearly all parishes (ca. 400 halls by 1900); informal meetings were held. Beck remained leader of the movement till his death. He was orthodox, but had been stimulated by S. A. Kierkegaard's* attack on the official ch. and by his demands for deeper spiritual life. Beck was eloquent; great revivals swept the country as a result of his preaching and that of other men of the movement. They demanded Christian life separated from the world. Out of the Ch. Soc. for Inner Miss. grew such activities as dissemination of Christian literature, works of charity, and, indirectly, for. missions. The movement is faithful to Luth. doctrine. In its high esteem of the sacraments and frequent use of the Lord's Supper it has been influenced by Grundtvig. It is the 3d and strongest main group in the Dan. Ch.

11. The gen. secularization of culture in Eur. also engulfed Den. The theol. of Mynster and Martensen was not strong enough to counter the influence of positivism* and socialism* after the middle of the 19th c. A gap developed bet. Christianity and modern culture. Secularization became an open fact. People divided over the issues but remained nominal mems. of the ch.

12. Barthianism influenced the theol. of the 20th c. Most important names in theol. discussions: N. F. S. Grundtvig* and K. Barth (see *Switzerland, Contemporary Theology in*). Most of the clergy are influenced by one or both of these. A High Ch. movement has gained some ground. Theol. is confessional and ch. centered. Luther study has been revived. The ch. was in strong opposition to Nazism during the Ger. occupation 1940–45; its most famous champions: Kaj Munk (1898–1944), pastor and poet, and his fellow pastor and martyr, Tage Schack (d. 1945).

13. Kierkegaard's influence was felt only a short time in mid-19th c., but reappeared in the 20th c., largely through Barth, and has left its mark on existential theol. and philos.

14. The Dan. Ch. is governed by parliament and is supported by income from investments and by taxation. There are 10 dioceses and ca. 2,000 pastors. 96 percent of the pop. is Luth. The king appoints pastors nominated by the minister for ecclesiastical affairs from a list of 3 selected by the congs. Dan. Luth. pastors subscribe to the 3 ecumenical* creeds, the AC, and Luther's SC (see *Catechisms, Luther's; Lutheran Confessions*). JMJ

See also *Danish Lutherans in America; Denmark, Evangelical Lutheran Free Church of.*

L. N. Helveg, *Den Danske Kirkes Historie til Reformationen,* 2 parts (Copenhagen, 1857–70); L. P. Fabricius, *Danmarks Kirkehistorie,* 3 parts in 2 vols. (Copenhagen, 1934–35); *Den Danske Kirkes Historie,* eds. H. Koch and B. S. Kornerup, 8 vols. projected (Copenhagen, 1950–); E. H. Dunkley, *The Reformation in Denmark* (London, 1948); F. Münter, *Kirchengeschichte von Dänemark und Norwegen,* 3 vols. (Leipzig, 1823–33).

Denny, James (1856–1917). Prof. theol. Glasgow Free Ch. Coll. 1897; moved from a liberal to an ev. position; works include *The Death of Christ; Jesus and the Gospel.* See also *Presbyterian Churches,* 1.

de Nobili, Robert(o). See *Nobili, Robert(o) de.*

Denominationalism in the United States. See *United States, Religious History,* 11–13.

Dens, Peter (1690–1775). Belgian RC theol.; works include *Theologia moralis et dogmatica.*

Denys. See *Denis; Dionysius.*

Deo gratias (Lat. "thanks to God"). Liturgical formula used in W Ch.

Deontology. Ethics of duty rather than right or goodness. The term was the title of book by J. Bentham.*

Departed, Commemoration of. In the early ch., feasts of apostles and evangelists were soon celebrated, esp. those of Peter and Paul, though those of John and James were also favorites. Later, martyrs and all other saints were commemorated Nov. 1 (All Saints' Day) and the departed in purgatory Nov. 2 (All Souls' Day; Nov. 3, if Nov. 2 fell on Sun.). In the E Orthodox Ch., this festival is observed the Sat. before Pent. or the last Sun. of the ch. yr. In the Moravian Ch., Easter morning is dedicated to the memory of those who died during the yr. In the Ev. Ch. of Prussia, the last Sun. of the ch. yr. was set aside for commemorating the dead, and this day or Dec. 31 has been adopted by many Luths. See also *Church Year,* 14, 17. *Dead, Prayers for; Totenfest.*

Dependent Children. See *Child and Family Service Agencies.*

Deposition from Ministerial Office. In RCm, clergy can be deposed by their superiors. In the Luth. Ch., the act of deposition is declarative, as an exercise of the office of the keys.* In Am. Lutheranism, syns. usually pronounce sentences of deposition against pastors and teachers. In the LCMS, "1. Members who act contrary to the confession laid down in Article II and to the conditions of membership laid down in Article VI or persist in an offensive conduct, shall, after previous futile admonition, be expelled from Synod. 2. Expulsion shall be executed only after following such procedure as shall be set forth in the Bylaws of the Synod. 3. If the member expelled is a pastor or teacher in a congregation of Synod, such congregation, unless it has already done so, is held to depose him from office and to deal with him in accordance with the Word of God, notwithstanding an appeal. If it persistently refuses to do so, the respective District is to deal with it. If all negotiations and admonitions fail of their purpose, such congregation forfeits its membership in Synod. 4. Because of their expulsion those so expelled forfeit their membership and all share in the property of Synod. The latter holds good also with respect to those who for any reason themselves sever their connection with Synod." (*Constitution,* Art. XIII, in *Handbook of The Lutheran Church – Missouri Synod,* 1973 ed., p. 24).

Depositories, Lutheran Historical. See *Archives.*

Depravity. See *Sin.*

de' Rossi, Giovanni Battista. See *Rossi, Giovanni Battista de'.*

Derschau, Bernhard (Derschow; 1591–1630). Prof. theol. and pres. consistory, Königsberg; hymnist; hymns include "Herr Jesu, dir sei Preis und Dank."

Dervish (Persian, "beggar"; synonymous with Arab. "fakir"). Mem. of an Islamic order whose practices include dances and self-castigation. There are many orders; some live in monasteries, others go about ordinary occupations and carry on the practices of their order only on special occasions. The dancing (whirling) and the howling dervishes are most widely known. See also *Islam.*

Descant. Melody or counterpoint added to a melody and usually lying above it.

Descartes, René (Renatus Cartesius; 1596–1650). B. La Haye, Touraine; d. Stockholm. Fr. RC philos.; educ. Jesuit coll., La Flèche. In Holland 1629–49, Swed. 1649–50. System (Cartesianism*) differs in many respects from Thomism (see *Scholasticism*). He is called father of modern philos. because he broke the sway of Scholasticism with his initial doubt, mathematical deduction generalized, and opposition to Aristotelianism. Held that all knowledge is open to initial doubt, except reality of self. Was convinced of his own existence by force of the sequitur: If there is a thought, there must be one who thinks it. This he expressed in the maxim: *"Cogito, ergo sum,"* i. e., "I think, therefore I exist." Generalizing mathematical deductions, he envisaged a mechanistic world from which he exempted the human soul and God, who is the infinite substance; space and motion were basic realities. Cartesian dualism* maintains the absolute duality of *res cogitans* (mind) and *res extensa* (matter). Works include *Discours de la méthode; Meditationes de prima philosophia; Principia philosophiae; Les Passions de l'ame.*

Descent into Hell. The doctrine of the descent of Christ into hell is based primarily on 1 Ptr 3:18-20, a difficult passage. Various interpretations hold that Christ went to the realm of the dead, or to the prison of wicked men and angels. Some Calvinists say His descent included the sufferings on the cross, others that it took place after death; the prominent Luth. view is that it took place after vivification. It is regarded as having taken place according to the soul; according to body and soul. It is held that Christ preached to souls who had had no chance in life, or to the damned and the evil angels. Some say His preaching was Gospel, others say it was Law, judgment, and a proclamation of victory. Augustine of Hippo,* Thomas* Aquinas, T. Beza,* et al. held that 1 Ptr speaks of a sermon of Christ before His incarnation.

The descent into hell did not take place immediately after death, because the soul of Jesus went to paradise (Lk 23:43). It is gen. regarded as taking place before Christ left the tomb. In 1 Ptr 3:19 "prison" (Gk. *phylake;* on this word see also Rv 18:2; 20:7; cf. 2 Ptr 2:4; Jude 6; it is used many times in the NT for an earthly prison) designates the abode of lost souls and evil angels to whom Christ proclaimed His victory (Cl 2:15).

See also *Presbyterian Confessions,* 3; *Protestant Episcopal Church,* 5.

G. Stoeckhardt, *Kommentar über den Ersten Brief Petri* (St. Louis, 1912), pp. 134–181; F. W. Farrar, *Mercy and Judgment* (New York, 1881), pp. 75–81; J. Pearson, *An Exposition of the Creed,* new ed. (London, 1880), pp. 346–386; FC Ep and SD IX; J. T. Mueller, "Notes on Christ's Descent into Hell," *CTM,* XVIII (Aug. 1947), 610–617; M. H. Scharlemann, "He Descended into Hell," *CTM,* XXVII (Feb. 1956), 81–94.

Desertion, Malicious (malicious abandonment). See *Marriage,* II; III.

Desiderius. Last king of Lombards (ca. 757–774); attacked papacy; overthrown by Charlemagne.*

Design, Argument from. See *Teleology.*

Desires. See *Lust.*

de Soto, Hernando. See *Roman Catholic Church,* E 1.

Dessau, League of. Organized in July 1525 by Joachim* I Nestor of Brandenburg, Albert of Mainz (see *Albert of Brandenburg*), George* the Bearded of Saxony, and Erich I and Henry II (the Younger) of Brunswick-Wolfenbüttel to oppose the spread of Protestantism. Prots. countered with the League of Torgau.*

Dessler, Wolfgang Christoph (1660–1722). Hymnist; educ. Altdorf; proofreader; amanuensis; conrector of School of the Holy Ghost, Nürnberg. Hymns include "Wie wohl ist mir, o Freund der Seelen"; "Ich lass dich nicht, du musst mein Jesus bleiben."

Determinism. Theory that all is absolutely determined by causes that lie outside of itself; opposed to indeterminism,* which declares man's will to be free. Forms of determinism include theological (as in Calvinism*), mechanical (as in materialism*), fatalistic (see *Fatalism*), economic (see *Marx, Karl Heinrich*), and others.

Detzer, John Adam (1817–Nov. 24, 1903). Ger. baker; to Am. with F. A. Crämer,* F. Lochner,* P. J. Trautmann,* 1845; advisory pastor 1847 in Missouri* Syn., which he helped found; worked in NW Ohio; founded ca. 18 congs.

Deus absconditus; Deus revelatus (Lat. "God hidden; God revealed"). God* rules in every event but is different ("wholly other") from every perceptible reality and is in that sense hidden *(absconditus);* He is revealed (*revelatus*) as fatherly love in Jesus Christ and as He enters into the realities of our life. God in His bare majesty is unapproachable and is perceptible only in creative acts as signs and symbols (Is 55:8; Ro 1:19-20; 11:33-36).

M. Luther* agrees with W. of Ockham* that God's essence is incomprehensible to reason and makes *absconditus* and *revelatus* significant in his doctrine of sin and grace. God, who is active in all events, does not relieve His creatures of responsibility. Sin separates man from God.

In Christ, God is revealed as a God of love. The Gospel invites to faith in Christ. In Christ, His power and glory are hidden under the lowliness and shame of the cross, His love under wrath; He is revealed only to faith and remains hidden to reason and unbelief. EL

See also *God; Revelation.*

J. Dillenberger, *God Hidden and Revealed* (Philadelphia, 1953); H. Bandt, "Luthers Lehre vom verborgenen Gott: Eine Untersuchung zu dem offenbarungsgeschichtlichen Ansatz seiner Theologie," *Theologische Arbeiten,* ed. H. Urner, VIII (Berlin, 1958).

Deus ex machina (Lat. "god from a machine"). In ancient drama, the introd. of a representation of a god or goddess (usually suspended by a machine) to provide a supernatural solution for dramatic difficulty; hence, a person or thing suddenly introd. in a story or play to provide an artificial solution to an otherwise insoluble problem.

Deus incarnatus. See *God.*

Deus incognitus. See *God.*

Deus loquens (Lat. "God speaking"). Term used by M. Luther* and others to emphasize the living, active contemporaneity of the Word of God, thus continuing the manifestation of God in creation, mercy, judgment, and salvation as the Word of God. It is often used in contrast with, but not exclusive of, the perfect tense, *Deus dixit* ("God spoke").

Deus revelatus. See *Deus absconditus; God; Revelation.*

Deuterocanonical. See *Apocrypha.* A 4; *Protocanonical.*

Deuteronomic Code. See *Law Codes.*

Deuteronomist Writer. See *Higher Criticism,* 6–13.

Deutsche Christen. See *Barmen Theses; Kirchenkampf.*

Deutsche Christentumsgesellschaft. See *Christentumsgesellschaft, Die Deutsche.*

Deutsche Evangelische Kirche (Ger. Ev. Ch.). Organized 1933 in Ger.; predecessor of Evangelische Kirche in Deutschland (see *Germany,* C 5; *Union Movements,* 8–9). See also *Barmen Theses; Marahrens, August.*

Deutsche Messe. See *Chant.*

Deutsche Theologie. See *German Theology.*

Deutschmann, Johann(es) (ca. 1625–1706). B. Jüterbog; son-in-law of A. Calov*; prof. Wittenberg; opposed syncretism* of F. U. Calixt* and pietism* of P. J. Spener* and espoused strict Luth. orthodoxy.

Dévay, Mátyás Biró (Dévai; ca. 1500–45). Hung. reformer; originally RC; Luth. 1529; educ. Wittenberg; called "Hungarian Luther"; later went to Switz. and worked for Calvinism.*

Deveuster, Damian (De Veuster). See *Damien de Veuster, Joseph.*

Devil. Term meaning literally "accuser," 1 Ptr 5:8; in Scripture usually a descriptive name of Satan; also used in the plural for the fallen angels (demons [see *Demon*], evil spirits, unclean spirits), the chief of whom is called Satan by way of eminence (Mt 12:24-26). Satan himself, for whose subjugation Christ came, is the originator of all wickedness (Eph 2:2), an opponent of the kingdom of God. He is the tempter of the faithful (1 Ptr 5:8-9); he led Eve into sin and so became the originator and king of death (Heb 2:14). Originally created good, the evil spirits fell through their own fault (2 Ptr 2:4). That the devil is a personal being is clear from the Gospels and Epistles. Jesus calls him "evil one" and "enemy" (Mt 13:19, 28; 1 Ti 5:14). Other terms: "Adversary" (1 Ptr 5:8), "Satan" (Lk 22:31), "Beelzebub" or "Beelzebul" (Mt 10:25; 12:24; Mk 3:22; Lk 11:15, 18, 19), "prince" of devils and demons (Mt 12:24), "ruler of this world" (Jn 12:31; cf. Eph 6:12). Everlasting punishment was prepared for the devil and his angels (Mt 25:41). See also *Demonology; Demoniac Possession.*

Devil's Advocate. See *Canonization.*

Devotio moderna. Spiritual revival that began in Holland in the 14th c.; led esp. by G. Groote*; spread to Ger., Fr., It., and elsewhere. See also *Counter Reformation,* 2; *Czechoslovakia,* 4; *Hussites.*

Devotional Literature. See *Literature, Lutheran,* 3.

De Wette, Wilhelm Martin Leberecht (1780–1849).

Ger. theol.; influenced by H. E. G. Paulus,* J. F. Fries,* and F. D. E. Schleiermacher*; prof. Basel; championed Fragment Theory of Pentateuch; ed. Luther's works; other works include OT introd. and commentaries. See also *Higher Criticism,* 13.

Dewey, John (1859–1952). Am. philos. and educ.; prof. Minnesota 1888, Michigan 1889, Chicago 1894, Columbia 1904–30; adherent of pragmatism* of C. S. Peirce* and W. James,* but modified it in the direction of naturalism* and positivism.* His conception of man was drawn from biology, psychology, and sociology; organs of the body are instruments for dealing with environment; mind and its ideas provide tools for dealing with human situations (instrumentalism). The hypothesis that works is the true one. Truth is an abstract noun applied to the collection of cases that are confirmed by their consequences; hence experimentation enters into the determination of every warranted proposition; propositions in themselves are "if-then" predictions that have reality in their operations (operationalism). Works include *Studies in Logical Theory; Essays in Experimental Logic; Democracy and Education; Reconstruction in Philosophy; Experience and Nature; The Quest for Certainty; A Common Faith; Logic; The Theory of Inquiry.* See also *Psychology,* J.

Dewi (David; b. probably ca. 520; died perhaps ca. 589, some say ca. 601). Patron saint of Wales; gen. reckoned among its early missionaries.

Dexter, Henry Martyn (1821–90). Educ. Yale and Andover theol. sem.; Cong. pastor Manchester (N. H.) and Boston; authority on hist. of Congregationalism; tr. hymn "Shepherd of Tender Youth" from Gk.

Deyling, Salomon (1677–1755). Luth. prof. Leipzig. Works include *Institutiones Prudentiae Pastoralis.*

Diaconate. See *Deaconesses; Deacons.*

Diaconics. Dept. of theol. that deals with the work of home missions as administered by pastors and deacons. See also *Theology.*

Diaconus (Ger. *Diakonus;* related to "deacon"). Term used variously in reference to a pastor, 2d pastor, supply pastor, asst. minister, preacher, and deacon. Related Ger. terms: *Pfarrverweser; Prediger.*

Diadochus (5th c.). Bp. Photice, Epirus. Works include homily on ascension; 100 *Capita Gnostica* on the way of spiritual perfection.

MPG, 65, 1139–1212.

Diakonus. See *Diaconus.*

Dialectic (from Gk. *dialektos,* "discourse"). Theory and practice of logical analytic thought and discussion. Aristotle* held that Zeno* of Velia (Elea), It., discovered the dialectic method. But Heraclitus used a dialectic method before Zeno. He held that law and harmony in the universe exists because opposites are halves of one and the same thing. Dialectic as the art of debating is usually assoc. with Socrates.* Plato* used the dialectic method to analyze ideas. Aristotle held that the purpose of dialectics is to examine the foundations of science. He distinguished bet. dialectical reasoning (which proceeds syllogistically) and demonstrative reasoning (which begins with primary premises). As a result of the Stoics' division of dialectics into logic and rhetoric, dialectic was, till the end of the Middle Ages, regarded as synonymous with logic or as part of it. G. W. F. Hegel* held that all reality is divided into opposite poles, and that truth must be sought through thesis, antithesis, and synthesis. K. Marx* applied dialectic to soc. theories, holding that every class calls into being an opposite class (rulers – subjects; capital – labor), and that progress results from the struggle. (See also *Dialectical Materialism*). I. Kant* used the dialectical method to show that criteria applied to phenomena cannot be applied to the *Ding an sich.* K. Barth (see *Switzerland, Contemporary Theology in*) operates with the dialectical method inasmuch as he shows opposite poles in the "yon-side" and the "this-side" (God – man; eternal – temporal); the synthesis in Barth's thinking does not rise per se from opposite poles but comes from the "yon-side." See also *Dialectical Realism; Dialectical Theology; Historicism,* 3. EL

Dialectical Materialism. School of philos. founded by K. H. Marx* and F. Engels*; holds that matter (nature) is real in its own right, apart from supernatural source. The term "dialectical" refers to dynamic interconnectedness of things and to the radical character of the universality of change. Its basic hypotheses: law of interpenetration, unity, and strife of opposites; law of transformation bet. quantity and quality; law of negation of negation, i. e., each stage of development resolves the contradictions in a preceding synthesis. See also *Evolution,* III.

Dialectical Realism. Name given by W. Temple* to the procedure whereby one begins with the natural process, traces it to the highest level (spirit), and turns back and interprets the unity of the whole process in terms of spirit.

Dialectical Theology. Term used to describe the theol. method of K. Barth* (see *Switzerland, Contemporary Theology in*), who stressed that God is transcendent, the "Wholly Other," so that He cannot be characterized in some simple formula. Statements about God must perhaps be paradoxical, with each affirmation balanced by a negation to do justice to God's infinite transcendence. See also *Brunner, Heinrich Emil; Neoorthodoxy; Niebuhr, Reinhold.*

Diamper, Synod of. Held 1599 at Diamper (or Udiamperur), India; Port. pressure brought Syrian Christians temporarily into RC Ch. as Malabar Uniate Ch. See also *India,* 6; *Malabar Christians; Uniate Churches.*

Diaspora. 1. Jews living outside the borders of the Holy Land. 2. Scattered Christians. 3. Luths. living in non-Luth. regions. See also *Gustav-Adolf Society; Lutherischer Gotteskasten.*

Diatessaron (Gk. "through four"). Harmony of the 4 Gospels written to make a continuous narrative; esp. applied to that of Tatian.* See also *Harmony of the Gospels,* 1.

Diaz, Juan (d. 1546). B. Cuenca, Sp., native town of A. and J. de Valdes*; studied theol. 13 yrs. at Paris; converted to Lutheranism by J. Enzinas (see *Enzinas, Francisco de*); to Geneva 1545; cordially received by J. Calvin*; friend of M. Bucer* at Strasbourg; accompanied Bucer to the 1546 Regensburg* Conference; settled in Neuburg, Bavaria, where he pub. *Christianae Religionis Summa.* His brother Alfonso, an officer at the papal court, tried to persuade him to return to RCm; failing, Alfonso had Juan killed. Charles* V and Paul* III did not press charges against Alfonso, since he had killed a heretic. Alfonso later committed suicide.

E. Boehmer, *Spanish Reformers of Two Centuries from 1520,* I (Strasbourg, 1874), 185–216; M. Bataillon, *Érasme et l'Espagne* (Paris, 1937), pp. 551 ff., 1st Span. ed., *Erasmo y España,* tr. A. Alatorre, II (Mexico, 1950), 98—100; G. Gutbrod, *Römische Bruderliebe: Eine Geschichte aus der Reformationszeit* (Leipzig, [1890]). WGT

Dibble, Sheldon (Jan. 26, 1809–June 22, 1845). ABCFM miss. to Hawaiian Is. B. Skaneateles, N. Y.; educ. Hamilton Coll. and Auburn Theol. Sem.; ordained and sent to Hawaii 1830; stationed at sem. at Lahainaluna 1836. Tr. part of OT. Other works include a hist. of Hawaii and of phases of its missions; textbooks on grammar, natural hist., and sacred hist. in Hawaiian language.

Dibelius, Martin Franz (1883–1947). Ger. theol.; b. Dresden; prof. Heidelberg 1915; specialist in early Christian hist.; belongs to the *Formgeschichtliche*

Schule (see *Isagogics,* 3), but holds that the Passion narrative was essentially a continuous account from earliest times. Works include commentaries; *Die Formgeschichte des Evangeliums; Urchristentum und Kultur; Die Botschaft von Jesus Christus; Evangelium und Welt; Botschaft und Geschichte; Paulus* (Eng. tr. F. Clarke, *Paul*); *Jesus* (Eng. tr. C. B. Hedrick and F. C. Grant, *Jesus*).

Dibelius, Friedrich Karl Otto (1880–1967). B. Berlin; cousin of Martin Franz; educ. Berlin; pastor Crossen on the Oder, Scot., Danzig, Lauenburg (Lebork; in Pomerania), Berlin; gen. supt. of the Kurmark; dismissed from all offices by Nazis 1933; a leader of the *Bekennende Kirche* (see *Kirchenkampf*); ev. bp. Berlin 1945; pres. EKD council 1949; pres. WCC 1954. Works include *Das Jahrhundert der Kirche; Vom Erbe der Väter; Grenzen des Staates; Vom ewigen Recht.*

Dictatus papae. Document dictated or drafted by a pope; esp. 3 letters and 27 theses on the supremacy of the pope and RC Ch., ascribed to Gregory VII (see *Popes,* 7), but contested as to authenticity and hist. and pol. significance.

Dictionaries. See *Encyclopedias and Dictionaries; Lexicons.*

Didache. See *Apostolic Fathers,* 8.

Didascalia Apostolorum. Ancient Christian writing; mixture of moral and ecclesiastical instruction; probably written in Syria in the 3d c.

Diderot, Denis (1713–84). "Pantophile"; Fr. philos.; educ. by Jesuits; became deist, then materialist, finally pantheistic naturalist; forerunner of positivism*; as ed.-in-chief of the *Encyclopédie* he greatly influenced the Enlightenment.* Works include polemics against Christianity. See also *Deism; Encyclopedists; Freethinker; Materialism; Naturalism; Pantheism.*

Didymus of Alexandria (ca. 313–ca. 398). Blind from age 4; leader of catechetical school in Alexandria. Works include *De Trinitate; De Spiritu Sancto; Contra Manichaeos;* commentaries.

MPG, 39, 131–1818.

Didymus, Gabriel. See *Zwilling, Gabriel.*

Dieckhoff, August Wilhelm (1823–94). Ger. Luth. theol.; b. Göttingen; d. Rostock; prof. Göttingen and Rostock; wrote against J. C. K. v. Hofmann* and A. Ritschl*; in the controversy on election and conversion he sided with the opponents of the Mo. Syn. Wrote esp. on the hist. of Luth. doctrine.

Diedrich, Julius (1819–99). Seceded from the Prussian* Union to join the Breslau* Syn. because of differences on polity; he and 6 other pastors withdrew from the Breslau Syn. and formed the Immanuel Syn. 1864.

Dieffenbach, Georg Christian (1822–1901). Ger. Luth. theol. and poet. B. Schlitz, Hesse; educ. Giessen and Friedberg; taught at Darmstadt; vicar Kirchberg and Vielbrunn; asst. pastor Schlitz 1855, chief pastor 1873. Helped found *Evangelische Konferenz – hauptsächlich für die Lutheraner in der Landeskirche* 1876. Issued *Für unsere Kleinen,* an illustrated monthly, 1884–98. Contributed to liturgical literature.

Diehl, C. F. See *Canada,* A 5.

Diehl, Wilhelm (1871–1944). Pastor Darmstadt and Hirschhorn 1895; prof. Friedberg sem. 1913; pres. Hesse state ch. 1920, prelate 1923; deposed for pol. reasons 1933; historian of Hesse-Darmstadt. Works include *Hassia sacra.*

Diekamp, Franz (1864–1943). RC Thomistic theol.; patrol.; prof. Münster. Works include 3-vol. dogmatics.

Diem, Hermann. See *Dogmatics,* B 13.

Dies dominica (Lat. "Lord's day"). Ecclesiastical term for Sunday.

Dies irae (Lat. "day of wrath"). Medieval sequence,* or hymn, ascribed to Thomas* of Celano; opening words drawn from Zph 1:15 (Vulgate); expresses hope of redemption through Christ. See also *Millennium,* 4.

Diest. 1. *Heinrich van* (1595–1673). B. Altona, Ger.; educ. Herborn and Heidelberg; Ref. pastor Emmerich 1624; prof. Heb. and theol. Harderwijk 1627, Deventer 1629; follower of J. Cocceius.* 2. *Samuel van* (1631–94). Son of Heinrich; Ref. theol.; educ. Deventer, Leiden, and Utrecht; prof. Duisburg, Harderwijk 1664, and Deventer 1681; follower of Cocceius; opposed Cartesianism.*

Diesterweg, Friedrich Adolf Wilhelm (1790–1866). Ger. educ.; introd. J. H. Pestalozzi's* educ. ideas and methods into Ger. Works include *Wegweiser zur Bildung für deutsche Lehrer.*

Diet. The diet (deliberative assembly) of the Holy Roman empire originated in the Frankish annual spring meeting of all degrees of men, to deliberate on military matters and other great affairs of state, with the king presiding. By the time of Charlemagne* there had also developed a smaller body composed of lay and clerical leaders. The imperial diet *(Reichstag)* of the Middle Ages arose from this smaller body and was composed of lay and clerical princes *(Fürsten)* of Ger. (sometimes from It.). Seven electors (the abps. of Mainz, Trier, and Cologne; the king of Bohemia; the count palatine of the Rhine, the duke of Saxony, and the margrave of Brandenburg) became a separate element of the diet (finalized by the Golden* Bull of 1356). In the last half of the 13th c. representatives of imperial and episc. towns were added to the diet. It dealt with such matters as taxes, legislation, and military expeditions. Its acts as compiled and enunciated at its close were called "recess" *(Reichsabschied).*

After the Peace of Westphalia* (1648), which acknowledged Ger. as a confederacy of sovereign princes, the diet was a congress of envoys. The N Ger. confederation (1867–70) had a *Bundesrat* (congress of envoys) and a *Reichstag* (elected representatives), an arrangement continued in the constitution of Ger. after 1870.

Diet of Augsburg. See *Lutheran Confessions,* A 2.

Diet of Speyer. See *Speyer, Diets of.*

Diet of Worms. See *Worms, Diet of.*

Dietenberger, Johannes (ca. 1475–1537). B. Frankfort on the Main; mem. of Dominicans*; present at Augsburg 1530; among those chosen to refute the AC; prof. Mainz 1532; tr. Bible into Ger.

Dieterich, Albrecht (1866–1908). B. Hersfeld, Ger.; prof. classical philol. Giessen 1895, Heidelberg 1903; adherent of *Religionsgeschichtliche* Schule.*

Dietrich, Christian (1844–1919). B. Gschwend, Ger.; dir. *Evangelisches Töchterinstitut,* Stuttgart. Works include *Die Privaterbauungsgemeinschaften der evangelischen Kirchen Deutschlands;* ed. *Philadelphia Organ für Gemeinschaftspflege.*

Dietrich, Fritz (1905–ca. 1945). B. Pforzheim, Ger.; Luth. musicologist. Works include articles on organ works of J. S. Bach*; *Geschichte des deutschen Orgelchorals im 17. Jahrhundert.*

Dietrich, Johann Konrad (Conrad Dieterich; 1575 to 1639). B. Gemünden on the Wohra, Ger.; chaplain Marburg 1600; deposed and exiled by the Ref. govt. for staunch Lutheranism 1605; prof. and dir. Giessen; supt. and dir. Ulm. Works include *Institutiones catecheticae,* an exposition of M. Luther's* catechism, tr. into Ger. by F. W. A. Notz*; a shorter ed., long used in Ger. and Eng. tr. by the Ev. Luth. Synodical* Conf. of N Am.

Dietrich, Sixt(us) (ca. 1492–1548). B. Augsburg, Ger.; Luth. composer; a number of his chorale-based works were pub. by G. Rhau.*

H. Zenck, *Sixtus Dietrich* (Leipzig, 1928).

Dietrich, Veit (1506–49). B. and d. Nürnberg; educ. Wittenberg; M. Luther's* secy. 1527; with Luther at Marburg 1529 and at Coburg 1530 (see *Lutheran Confessions,* A 2); private instructor; mem. Wittenberg philos. faculty; pastor Nürnberg 1535; attended 1546 Regensburg* Conference; involved in pol. of Schmalkaldic* War; removed from office 1547; opposed Interim* in Nürnberg. Works include *Summaria über die ganze Bibel; Agendbüchlein;* joint author with Luther of *Hauspostille.* See also *Luther, Table Talk of; Medler, Nikolaus.*

Dietrich von Bern. See *Theodoric.*

Dietrich von Niem (Nieheim; Nyem). See *Niem.*

Dietrichson, Johannes Wilhelm Christian (Apr. 4 [or Aug. 23], 1815–Nov. 14, 1883). Luth. cleric; b. Fredrikstad, Norw.; educ. Christiania (Oslo); ordained Feb. 26, 1844; to Am. later in 1844; organized congs. in Wis.; to Norw. 1845 and persuaded some pastors to come with him to Am.; returned to Norw. 1850, held 2 pastorates, and served as postmaster at Porsgrund 1876–82. Works include *Reise blandt de norske emigranter i "De Forenede nordamerikanske fristater" (Travels among the Norwegian Emigrants in "The United North American Free States").*

Diets, Lutheran, in America (Dec. 27–28, 1877; Nov. 5–7, 1878; Dec. 27–29, 1898). Free assemblies in Philadelphia, Pa., of clergy and laity of various syns.; purpose was educational. At the first two, ca. 100 pastors and as many laymen attended; none officially represented a particular Luth. body; papers read and discussed were later pub. in 2 vols. The 3d was called "The First General Conference of Lutherans in America." Similar conferences were held 1902 and 1904. See also *United Lutheran Church in America, The,* I.

First Free Lutheran Diet in America, ed. H. E. Jacobs (Philadelphia, 1878); *Second Free Lutheran Diet in America,* eds. W. M. Baum and J. A. Kunkelman (Philadelphia, 1879); *The First General Conference of Lutherans in America,* preface by H. E. Jacobs (Philadelphia, 1899).

Diffusionism. Theory in anthropology which holds in contrast to the theory of evolution* that cultural similarities prove hist. contact.

Digambara. See *Jainism.*

Diggers. Equalitarian group of Levellers* led by Gerrard Winstanley (1609–52). Fl. 1649–50. Cultivated common lands in protest against private property.

Dignitatis Humanae. See *Vatican Councils,* 2.

Dilfeld, Konrad Georg (Conrad Dielefeld; d. 1684). B. Nordhausen, Ger.; defender of the Luth. confessions, esp. against pietism. Works include *Theosophia Horbo-Speneriana* (see also *Horb, Johann [es] Heinrich)* against P. J. Spener's* view that only the converted could effectively teach and administer the sacraments.

Dilherr, Johann Michael (1604–69). B. Themar (near Meiningen), Ger.; prof. Jena 1631; dir. gymnasium at Nürnberg 1642; pastor St. Sebald ch., Nürnberg, 1646; wrote commentary on Jb for *Das Weimarische* Bibelwerk;* hymnist.

Diller, Michael (ca. 1500–70). Little known about early youth; matriculated Wittenberg 1523; prior Augustinian monastery at Speyer ca. 1530. Began preaching justification by faith, but did not engage in polemics. The city council, recognizing the need of regular services for people who had broken with Rome, appointed him pastor 1538 and protected him against pressures from his superiors. When Charles* V came to Speyer (1541, 1544, 1548), Diller left. Introd. Communion under both kinds 1543. During the Interim* was in Switz. Chaplain of Count Palatine Ottheinrich 1553. The count became elector, and Diller went with him to Heidelberg 1556; helped write Heidelberg and Baden ch. orders and took part in ch. visitations 1556; attended Consultation of Worms* 1557; elector Frederick III (see *Frederick III,* 3), who succeeded Ottheinrich 1559, retained Diller as adviser. In the controversies of the times he followed a mediating course; rebuffed by T. Hesshus,* he sided more and more with the Reformed, e. g., at the 1564 colloquy at Maulbronn; appeared little in pub. during last 6 yrs. of his life; d. Heidelberg. WGT

Dilliger, Johann (Dillinger; 1593–1647). B. Eisfeld, Ger.; to Magdeburg 1611; entered Wittenberg U. 1618; to Coburg 1625; pastor Gellershausen 1633; deacon St. Moritz, Coburg, 1634; composer.

Dillmann, Christian Friedrich August (1823–94). B. Illingen, Ger.; ev. Biblical scholar and orientalist; prof. Tübingen, Kiel, Giessen, and Berlin; known for work on the Ethiopic Bible and commentaries on OT books.

Dilthey, Wilhelm Christian Ludwig (1833–1911). Ger. hist. and philos.; prof. Basel, Kiel, Breslau, Berlin; student of biography; constructed new methodology and interpretation of soc. and culture.

Held that in natural sciences we are spectators describing phenomena without entering into their inner essence; in human sciences we know the subject matter from the inside and can describe the reality of its process and content. The individuality of human sciences is overcome by the common structure of the human spirit expressed in "objective mind," that is, all things belonging to civilization and culture (e. g., instruments, towns, laws, literature, art, language).

Religion is a manifestation of metaphysical consciousness which seeks solutions for enigmas of life. Metaphysical systems can be divided into 3 worldviews: naturalism,* objective idealism,* idealism of freedom (subjective idealism).

Works include *Einleitung in die Geisteswissenschaften; Das Wesen der Philosophie; Der Aufbau der geschichtlichen Welt in den Geisteswissenschaften; Das Leben Schleiermachers.*

See also *Historicism,* 4; *Philosophy.*

H. A. Hodges, *The Philosophy of Wilhelm Dilthey* (London, 1952); W. Kluback, *Wilhelm Dilthey's Philosophy of History* (New York, 1956); W. Dilthey, *Gesammelte Schriften,* 12 vols. (Berlin, 1914 to 1936; reissued Göttingen and Stuttgart, 1957 to 1960). EL

Dimitrij of Rostov (Danilo Touptala; Daniil Savic Tuptalo; 1651–1709). E. Orthodox hagiographer; opposed raskolniks*; metropolitan of Serbia 1701, Rostov 1702.

Ding an sich (thing-in-itself). Term used by I. Kant* to denote the real objects that underlie phenomena and exist outside of consciousness, in distinction from phenomena (appearance) by which they become perceptible to the senses.

Dinsmore, Charles Allen (1860–1941). Am. Cong. minister; lecturer at Yale U. Divinity School 1920; Dante scholar. Works include *The Teachings of Dante; Aids to the Study of Dante; Life of Dante; Atonement in Literature and Life.*

Dinter, Christian Gustav Friedrich (1760–1831). Ger. cleric and educ.; pastor at Kitzscher, near Borna, 1787; dir. normal school, Dresden, 1797; pastor Görnitz 1807; mem. of consistory and of educ. council, Königsberg, Prussia, 1816; prof. theol. there 1817. Works include *Schullehrerbibel; Die vorzüglichsten Regeln der Katechetik.*

Diocesan Curia. See *Curia,* 3.

Diocese (Gk. *dioikesis,* "housekeeping; administration"). Territory administered by a bishop* normally assisted by lesser clergy; usually divided into parishes.

The word "diocese" was originally used in the Roman empire for an administrative subdivision. In the reorganization of Diocletian* and Constantine* I the empire was divided into 12 (later 14) "dioceses" of which provinces were subdivisions.

The ecclesiastical use of "diocese" was derived from the civil, beginning in the 3d—4th c. Originally ecclesiastical dioceses tended to correspond to civil units also beyond the territory of the empire. But once established, the area of dioceses tended to remain fixed despite civil change. The word became prominent for the territory of a bp. in the 9th c. and was used interchangeably with *paroecia* or *parochia* (Lat. for Gk. *paroikia*, "parish") until the 13th c. Thereafter "diocese" is the territory of a bp. and "parish" is a subdivision thereof.

See also *Cathedral; Curia,* 2 d, f; 3; *Eparchy.*

Diocletian (Gaius Aurelius Valerius Diocletianus; Jovius; ca. 245–313 [some say 316]. Father-in-law of Galerius*; Roman emp. 284–305; coemperor with Maximian* from 286; inst. longest and most severe of the early persecutions* of Christians. Abdicated.

Diodati, Giovanni (1576–1649). Calvinist theol. of noble It. extraction; pastor Geneva; prof. Heb. and theol. Geneva; attended Syn. of Dordrecht* 1618 to 1619; tr. Bible into It. and Fr.

Diodorus of Tarsus (Diodore; d. ca. 392). Bp. Tarsus 378; a leader of the Antioch school (see *Schools, Early Christian,* 4); fought Arianism*; opposed Apollinaris* of Laodicea; condemned as Nestorian 499 (see *Nestorianism).*

Diogenes. See *Cynicism.*

Diogenes of Babylonia (or of Seleucia). See *Stoicism.*

Diognetus (2d or 3d c.). Addressee of *Epistle to Diognetus;* identity not est. See also *Apologists,* 9; *Apostolic Fathers,* 7; *Christian Church, History of,* I 2.

Dionysius. See also *Denis.*

Dionysius (3d c.) Pope 259–268 (some say 260–267); reorganized Roman ch. after Valerian persecution; sent help to ch. of Caesarea when it was invaded by barbarians; accepted defense of Dionysius* of Alexandria against charges of tritheism.*

MPL, 5, 99-136.

Dionysius Exiguus (fl. 1st half of 6th c.). Scythian monk; computed probable dates of great events in world hist., esp. that of the birth of Christ; introd. the division of world hist. into periods BC and AD, which is still used, though several yrs. in error (i. e., Christ was born several yrs. "BC"); made a collection of canon law. See also *Pseudo-Isidorian Decretals,* 1 a; *Time.*

Dionysius of Alexandria (Denis; ca. 190–ca. 264). "The Great." B. of heathen parents; pupil of Origen*; head of catechetical school at Alexandria (see *Schools, Early Christian,* 1) ca. 232; bp. Alexandria ca. 247; fled ca. 250 in Decian persecution (see *Persecutions of Christians,* 4); returned ca. 251; banished in Valerian persecution 257 (see *Persecutions of Christians,* 4); returned 260. Involved in controversies. Readmitted lapsed into the ch. Opposed Sabellianism and Paul* of Samosata. Accused of tritheism* but defense accepted by Dionysius* of Rome. Athanasius defended his orthodoxy. Works include *On Nature* (against materialism* of Epicureanism*) and *On the Promises* (against Chiliasm; see *Millennium,* 3). See also *Monarchianism,* B 6.

MPG, 10, 1233–1344 and 1575–1602.

Dionysius of Corinth (fl. ca. 170). Bp. Corinth. Works include letters dealing with dogmatic, ethical, exegetical, polemical, and disciplinary topics written to chs. in Lacedaemon, Rome, Athens, Nicomedia, Pontus, and Crete.

Eusebius, *HE,* II, xxv, 8; IV, xxiii, 10-12.

Dionysius the Areopagite. 1. Converted by Paul at Athens (Acts 17:34); tradition regards him as the 1st bp. Athens (Eusebius, *HE,* III, iv, 11; IV, xxiii, 3). 2. Unknown author (ca. AD 500), long identified wrongly with Paul's convert. Works include *The Celestial Hierarchy; The Divine Names.* Called "Pseudo-Areopagite" and "Pseudo-Dionysius."

Dionysius the Carthusian (1402–71). Also called Denys van Leeuwen, or de Leeuwis, after his family name, and Denys van Rijkel (Rickel, Ryckel) after his birthplace in Belgian Limburg. Mystic and theol.; works include commentaries on books of the Bible; editions of the fathers; books on moral theol.; homilies.

Dionysus. See *Greek Religion,* 3 b.

Dioscorus (Dioscurus; d. 454). Patriarch of Alexandria 444–451, as successor of Cyril* of Alexandria; supported Eutyches*; deposed, but not condemned as heretic, by council of Chalcedon* 451; exiled. See also *Coptic Church,* 1; *Ephesus, "Robber Synod" of.*

Dioscorus (Dioscurus; d. 530). Antipope; b. Alexandria; deacon; emissary to Theodoric* the Great; prominent in delegation to Constantinople that ended the Acacian* schism; antipope to Boniface II (b. Rome; pope 530–532) Sept. 22–Oct. 14, 530.

Diphysites. See *Dyophysites.*

Diplomatics. Branch of archaeol. that deals with such ancient writings as literary and public documents, letters, charters, and decrees, esp. with regard to their decipherment, authenticity, signatures, and dates.

Dippel, Johann Konrad (1673–1734). Ger. physician, alchemist, and Pietist theol.; lived for a time in the Neth., Altona (Den.), and Swed. Works include *Ein Hirt und Eine Heerde;* most of his writings were pub. 1747 under the title *Eröffneter Weg zum Frieden.*

Diptychs. Lists of names of those included in special pub. prayers in RC and E Orthodox chs. The term is derived from the 2-leaved folders on which the names were written. Reading of the names in the canon* of the mass led to the term "canonization.*"

Dircksz, Willem (d. 1525). Lived in Utrecht, Neth.; martyred for Luth. views, antipapalism, sacramentarianism.

Direction. See *Radio and Television Evangelism, Network,* 5.

Director of Christian Education. See *Parish Education,* L 4.

Directory for the Public Worship of God. Compiled 1645 by Westminster* Assem.; designed on Presb. principles to replace the Book* of Common Prayer. See also *Henderson, Alexander.*

Directory of Church Government. See *Presbyterian Bodies,* 2.

Directory of Worship. See *Norway, Lutheranism in,* 3.

Dirge. Technical name for the Office of the Dead derived from the antiphon *"Dirige Domine Deus meus in conspectu tuo viam meam"* (Ps 5:8) in the 1st nocturn of the office. More commonly the word means a lyrical or musical composition expressing grief.

Discernment of Spirits. Gift possessed in apostolic times whereby the sources of prophecy (divine, human, or demonic) were discerned (1 Co 12:10; 1 Jn 4:1). It was a gift needed at a time when many false prophets were in the world (2 Jn 7). Later (by Ignatius [see *Apostolic Fathers,* 2] and in the *Didache* [see *Apostolic Fathers,* 8]), rules for judging prophets were given.

Disciple. 1. One who receives instruction from another, accepts doctrines of another, and implements and spreads them. In Scripture the word is used for a follower of a prophet (Is 8:16), of Jesus (Mt 5:1; 8:21), of John the Bap. (Mt 9:14), of the Pharisees (Mt 22:16). 2. One of the 12 apostles (Mt 10:1; 11:1; 20:17). 3. Adherent of a school (e. g., in theol., philos., pol., and art). 4. Mem. of the Disciples* of Christ.

Disciples of Christ (Christian Churches [Disciples of Christ], International Convention; name changed 1968 to Christian Church [Disciples of Christ]). Am. religious body organized to restore primitive Christianity and to unite all Christians on the basis of the Bible alone.

1. *Antecedents.* Though the Disciples originated in Am., similar movements arose at ca. the same time in Scot., Ireland, Eng., and Wales. a. J. Locke* emphasized that Christians should unite on the basis of such teachings as the Holy Spirit has in Scripture declared, in express words, to be necessary for salvation. b. The Glassites (Glasites), founded by John Glass (Glas; 1695–1773), opposed connection of ch. with state and sought to conduct affairs of the ch. after the primitive Christian pattern; also known as Sandemanians (Robert Sandeman, 1718–71, son-in-law of Glass, modified teachings of the group). A similar movement was led by Robert Haldane (1764–1842; Cong. evangelist and author) and his brother, James Alexander Haldane (1768–1851; 1st Cong. cleric in Scot.). The chs. in these movements were often called Churches* of Christ. See also *Scotland, Reformation in,* 4.

2. *History.* a. T. Campbell* formed the Christian Association of Washington, Pa., 1809, and wrote *Declaration and Address,* regarded as the *Magna Charta* of the Disciples.

b. A. Campbell* joined his father Thomas 1810 and soon led the movement, headquarters at Brush Run, Pa.; the Brush Run ch. joined the Redstone Bap. Assoc. of Pa. 1813 and led a reform movement in the Bap. Ch.; as a result of disagreements, the Baps. excluded the followers of the Campbells, who repudiate the name Campbellites.

c. Chs. with the simple name "Christian" originated 1801 in the Cane Ridge Camp Meeting, Ky. They adopted principles similar to those of the followers of the Campbells (emphasis on primitive Christianity, autonomy of the local cong., and the spiritual indep. and competence of the laity). By 1832 the Christian Churches under B. W. Stone* had merged with the main current of the Disciples.

d. The followers of the Campbells joined the Mahoning Bap. Assoc. 1823. W. Scott* (1796–1861) began his work in the Assoc. 1827; his formula for salvation: 1. faith (persuasion based on rational evidence); 2. repentance; 3. baptism by immersion; 4. remission of sins; 5. gift of the Holy Spirit and eternal life. He regarded the first three as within human power, the last two as works of God. The reform movement led to the separation bet. the followers of the Campbells and the Baps. that began before 1830 and was completed ca. 1833; because it was a gradual process involving various groups, the beginning of the Disciples as such cannot be dated precisely. During the following yrs. the Disciples continued to grow, without organization and without headquarters, and developed a sense of unity. Need for consolidation came to be felt, but first efforts at it met resistance in antipathy against human organizations. The 1st nat. conv. met Cincinnati 1849 and created the Am. Christian Miss. Soc.; but most miss. work continued to be done by individuals and local groups.

e. 1860–75 may be called "the era of controversy" in the hist. of the Disciples. The group passed through the Civil War without division, but questions, e. g., of open communion, instrumental music, creeds, clergy, and miss. socs. caused dissension. Later a group of conservatives withdrew because of their opposition to miss. socs. and instrumental music.

f. Succeeding yrs. were marked by expansion, organization of miss. socs. (merged 1920 into the United Christian Missionary Soc.), and federation.

3. *Doctrine.* Since their fundamental purpose is to restore in faith, spirit, and practice the Christianity of Christ and the apostles, the Disciples endeavor to avoid all ecclesiastical terminology, creeds, and ch. names not found in the NT. Their position and message are set forth in T. Campbell, *Declaration and Address,* which advocates Christian unity, regards creeds as useful for instruction but not as tests of fitness for membership, holds the NT to be a perfect const. for worship, discipline, and govt. of the NT ch., and holds full knowledge of revealed truth unnecessary for membership; A. Campbell, *The Christian System;* P. Ainslie,* *The Message of the Disciples for the Union of the Church;* and Isaac Errett (1820–88), *Our Position.* The Disciples define the Trin. as the revelation of God in a 3-fold personality. They deny total depravity and the election of grace as contrary to reason. Christ is viewed as King with universal authority and leadership; the distinction bet. Law and Gospel consists in rejecting the binding character of the OT and making the NT the perfect const. for the worship, discipline, and govt. of the NT ch.; baptism by immersion is viewed as an act of obedience for the remission of sins; the Lord's Supper is celebrated every Sun. as a memorial feast. In recent yrs. liberalism has gained the upper hand among the Disciples.

4. The polity of the Disciples is cong. The local ch. is usually called "Christian Ch." The chs. unite in dist. and state convs., but these are advisory. The Internat. Conv., composed of individual mems. of the chs., meets annually and is advisory.

5. Bacon Coll., est. 1836 at Georgetown, Ky., moved 1839 to Harrodsburg, Ky., subsequently became Transylvania Coll., Lexington, Ky.; Bethany Coll., Bethany, W. Va., was est. 1840; Butler U., Indianapolis, Ind., grew out of Fairview Academy, est. 1843.

6. The Disciples have played a prominent role in interdenom. movements. Inclusive membership (1972): 1,386,374.

See also *Christian Union; Churches of Christ; Foreign Christian Missionary Society; United Church of Christ,* I B.

W. E. Garrison and A. T. DeGroot, *The Disciples of Christ* (St. Louis, 1948); J. DeF. Murch, *Christians Only* (Cincinnati, 1962); O. R. Whitley, *Trumpet Call of Reformation* (St. Louis, 1959); see also entries under *Religious Bodies (US), Bibliography.* EL

Disciplina arcani (Lat. "discipline of the secret"). Term used since the 17th c. for the withholding of certain parts of Christian teaching and worship from pagans and from catechumens till the last stages of their preparation. Some scholars find an approach to this practice in some NT books (e. g., Rv). Justin* seems not to know the practice but there may be evidences of it in the ch. order ascribed to Hippolytus* of Rome. The most extensive use occurs in the era of mass conversions after the end of the persecutions AD 313 (see *Persecutions of Christians,* 4). At this time it included the rites, ceremonies, and statements of the significance of Baptism and Holy Communion, and such liturgical forms as the Creed and the Lord's Prayer. The arcane discipline disappeared almost wholly in the 5th c. ACP

Discipline (Meth.). See *Methodist Churches,* 2.

Discipline, Books of. 1. The *1st Book of Discipline* was drafted 1560 at Edinburg on govt. request by J. Knox* et al. Dealt with doctrine; sacraments; abolition of idolatry; ministers and their lawful election; provision for ministers; rents and patrimony of the ch.; ch. discipline; election of ch. officers; gen. ch. policy. Signed by some nobles but not ratified by the Privy Council. See also *Presbyterian Churches,* 1. 2. The *2d Book of Discipline* was drawn up in the 1570s by A. Melville* et al. Dealt with relation bet. ch. and state; province, duties, relations, and election of ch. officers; operation of Ch. of Scot. Gen. Assem., syns., and presbyteries. Sanctioned and endorsed by Gen. Assem. but never received full civil recognition. 3. For other disciplines see *Methodist Chruches,* 2; *Presbyterian Confessions,* 3.

Discipline, Church. In its ecclesiastical sense the word "discipline" denotes actions partly of a penal and partly of a reformatory nature directed against one who has offended against ch. law or morality. Discipline existed in the ch. in early and medieval times. At the beginning of Lent those convicted of notorious sins were put to pub. penance for their spiritual benefit and as warning to others. When the papacy was at its height, excommunication was a weapon so formidable that even powerful kings quailed at the thought that it might be directed against them. In the Ch. of Eng. excommunication has given place to the commination service on Ash Wed. In Presb. chs., discipline is exercised by the session, an appeal being allowed to the presbytery or syn. and thence to the Gen. Assem. In the constitutions of the Ref. chs. of Am. (e. g., Ger. and Dutch) the principles and rules of discipline laid down are very similar to those of the Presb. Ch. In the Luth. Ch., discipline is administered by the local cong. on the basis of the Word of God (Mt 18). In the M. E. Ch., discipline is by admonition, followed by trial and expulsion if convicted; appeal is allowed to a judicial conf. and thence to the gen. conf. See also *Keys, Office of; Penitential Discipline; Polity, Ecclesiastical; Western Christianity 500–1500,* 8.

Disinterested Benevolence. See *New England Theology,* 3.

Dispensation. Relaxation of a law in a special case by the legislator or another authorized by the legislator to dispense. By the 5th c. AD dispensations were granted by bps. of Rome and, to a more limited extent, by other bps., councils, and priests. By the late Middle Ages the right of dispensation belonged to the pope. This view was upheld by the Council of Trent.* Dispensations in specific instances from universal laws are regarded as necessary in a just administration.

In RCm, the pope, as vicar of Christ, has communicated to him the right to dispense from all ecclesiastical laws and self-imposed obligations (vows, oaths). The ch. cannot dispense from *ius naturale* or *ius divinum.* The pope delegates some of his dispensing rights to bps. and other officials. A sufficient cause is required for a dispensation from a superior's law to be both valid and licit. Dispensation is void if a false statement has been made in securing it. A bp. can dispense from his own laws and those of his predecessors. Vicars-gen. have the ordinary dispensing power of bps. The parish priest by his own ordinary right can dispense in particular cases from the observance of fasting, abstinence, holy days, and certain diocesan statutes.

Henry VIII abolished the pope's dispensing power in Eng. and conferred it in restricted form on the Abp. of Canterbury 1534. In 1838 the right was restricted still more.

F. Suárez, *Tractatus de legibus ac de Deo legislatore* (Coimbra, Port., 1612); J. Brys, *De dispensatione in iure canonico praesertim apud decretistas et decretalistas usque ad medium saeculum decimum quartum* (Brugge, Belgium, 1925); M. A. Stiegler, *Dispensation, Dispensationswesen und Dispensationsrecht im Kirchenrecht* (Mainz, 1901); W. J. S. Simpson, *Dispensations* (London, 1935); E. M. Riley, *The General Norms of Dispensation* (Washington, 1939). EL

Dispensationalism. *The Scofield Reference Bible,* which advocates dispensationalism, defines a dispensation as "a period of time during which man is tested in respect of obedience to some *specific* revelation of the will of God." Elements of millennialism are found in Jewish opinions in OT times and in some early Christian writers. Among the forerunners of modern millennialism: the Shakers* and J. N. Darby (see *Brethren, Plymouth*). Modern dispensationalists divide the hist. of man into 7 dispensations, the last constituting the millennial reign of Christ on earth. They hold that in previous dispensations God and Christ could not carry out the divine plan for mankind because of man's perversity and that God will therefore test man's obedience in a final dispensation. Premillennialists say that because of man's disobedience in gen. and the Jews' obstinacy in particular, Christ was unable to fulfill many Messianic prophecies, e. g., that of the reest. of the throne of David, conversion of the Jews, and building of His kingdom. Therefore He founded only the ch. as the kingdom of God during His first coming and awaits the est. of His own kingdom at His 2d advent, at the beginning of the final dispensation. In this final period of God's special revelation the Jewish race will accept Christ as its king, est. a glorious kingdom in Palestine, and rule with Christ 1,000 yrs. All nations will recognize Christ's sovereign rule. In support of these vagaries many premillennialists appeal to the theory that God's will is revealed in 7 dispensations, and that as God created the world in 6 days and rested on the 7th, so the hist. of man must comprise 6 periods of labor and 1 of rest. Prominent dispensationalists, e. g., C. I. Scofield* and W. E. Blackstone,* see in the number 7 the sacred rock on which their whole Scripture interpretation seems to be built. Levitical worship, they say, revolved about the week. There was a "week of weeks" (Lv 23:15-16), a "week of months" (Lv 23:27-28), a "week of yrs." (Lv 25:4), and a "week of weeks of yrs." (Lv 25:8-12). All millennialists assume that 2 Ptr 3:8 ("one day is . . . as a thousand years") applies in prophecy. Dispensationalists therefore claim that each day of the creation week prophetically typifies a corresponding 1,000 yrs. in world hist. But they are not agreed in fixing the chronology of the "world-week." Some divide the hist. of man into 7 periods of 1,000 sun yrs. each. The yr. 6,000 since the creation is said to be imminent, and the beginning of the world-Sabbath may be expected momentarily. Some say that each dispensation begins with catastrophe and ends with new revelation, even as in Gn 1 evening is mentioned before morning. Most hold that every dispensation begins with revelation and ends with catastrophe (the latter as punishment for man's disobedience), some dispensations being relatively short, others long.

The most popular theory identifies these dispensations: 1. The state of innocence, ending with the fall. 2. Man is governed by conscience, proves unfaithful again, and is punished by the Flood. 3. The period of civil govt., Gn 9:6, ending with the destruction of Sodom and Gomorrah. 4. God revealed the messianic promise to the patriarchs; the destruction of Pharaoh shows the inadequacy of this dispensation. 5. In the Mosaic period God revealed Himself as the covenant-God; the crucifixion was the catastrophic end of this period. 6. We are in the period of grace (also called the period of mystery because of Rom 16:25; Eph 3:3-6; Cl 1:24-27), in which Christ reveals Himself through the Gospel; this period will end with the great tribulation and the 2d coming of Christ, the judgment of the nations as to their attitude toward Christ's brethren (the Jews), and the destruction of Antichrist. 7. The dispensation of manifestation, the millennium, corresponding to the Sabbath of creation week; it is to last 1,000 yrs.; but even in this period not all will obey; the world-Sabbath will end with judgment at the white throne and the destruction of Satan and the earth, Rv 20: 11-15; the believers will now enter heaven and the unbelievers eternal destruction. FEM

See also *Millennium.*

O. T. Allis, *Prophecy and the Church* (Philadelphia, 1945); C. N. Kraus, *Dispensationalism in America* (Richmond, Va., 1958); C. B. Bass, *Backgrounds to Dispensationalism* (Grand Rapids, Mich., 1960); W. E. Cox, *An Examination of Dispensa-*

tionalism (Philadelphia, 1963); C. C. Ryrie, *Dispensationalism Today* (Chicago, 1965).

Displaced Persons. People deported or forced to leave their native land by war or persecution. After WW II, chs. gave much attention to material and spiritual needs of displaced persons.

Disruption, The. See *Presbyterian Churches,* 1; *Scotland, Reformation in,* 2.

Disselhoff, Julius August Gottfried (1827–96). B. Soest, Westphalia; educ. U. of Halle; ev. theol.; T. Fliedner's* helper at Kaiserswerth institute for deaconesses; after Fliedner's death, dir. his institutions.

Dissenter (from Lat. *dissentire,* "to disagree"). In its broadest sense, one who disagrees in matters of opinion or belief; hence one who departs from an est. or state ch.

Gen. refers to a mem. of a religious body in Eng. which has separated from the Est. Ch.; usually restricted to the Prots. (e. g., Presbs., Congs., Baps., Quakers) referred to in the Act* of Toleration of 1689 (which did not include RCs and Unitarians). See also *Puritans.*

Because the term acquired a contemptuous connotation it was replaced by "nonconformist.*" Later groups not assoc. with state or est. chs. were called "free chs."

See also *Conventicle; Nonconformist.*

Distler, Hugo August (1908–42). B. Nürnberg; composed choir and organ music; organist in Lübeck (St. Jacobi) 1931, Stuttgart 1933, Berlin 1940. Works include *Mörike-Chorliederbuch.* See also *Passion, The.*

L. Palmer, *Hugo Distler and His Church Music* (St. Louis, 1967).

Districts. See *American Lutheran Church, The,* VI; *Lutheran Church – Missouri Synod, Districts of The; Wisconsin, Evangelical Lutheran Joint Synod of,* V.

District Boards of Education. See *Parish Education,* L 2.

District Superintendents. See *Parish Education,* L 4.

Diterich, Johann Samuel (1721–97). B. Berlin; pastor Berlin; advocated a rationalism that left room for revelation; hymnist.

Ditheletism. See *Dyotheletism.*

Divination. An occult art practiced extensively in ancient and modern times; claims ability to discover the will of the gods, to forecast the future from certain indications and auguries, and to decide from phenomena of an alleged supernatural kind the correct course of action to be followed in a given instance. The power of divination was often ascribed to persons in an abnormal state of mind, either ecstasy or demoniac* possession; but it was usually assoc. with the office of priests, who used such objects as waves of the sea, twigs of trees, intestines of animals, and flames of fire, and such phenomena as motions of stars and planets, movements of fish, and casting of lots.

Divine Comedy ([Divina] *Commedia*). See *Dante Alighieri.*

Divine Healing. See *Healing.*

Divine Image. See *Image of God.*

Divine Liturgy. Regarded as the chief and crowning service by the E Orthodox Ch. Divided: 1. Credence, in which the eucharistic elements are prepared on the prothesis* (side table); 2. Liturgy of the Catechumens, in which the cong. by Psalms and other Bible passages, sermon, and hymns prepares for the sacramental act; 3. Liturgy of the Faithful, from which catechumens and unbaptized persons are excluded and in which the faithful receive the Lord's Supper.

Liturgical services: 1. That of James (oldest and longest) is rarely celebrated, perhaps only at Jerusalem; 2. That of Basil, shorter than that of James, used 10 times a yr., esp. in Lent; 3. That of J. Chrysostom,* still shorter, the most usual; 4. That of the Presanctified, shortest, used on Wed. and Fri. in Lent (in RCm only on Good Fri.), with elements consecrated on preceding Sun.

Divine Love, Oratory of. See *Counter Reformation,* 4.

Divine Nature of Jesus. See *Christ Jesus.*

Divine Office. See *Hours, Canonical.*

Divine Plan of the Ages. See *Jehovah's Witnesses,* 2.

Divine Right. Theory of kingship according to which the right to rule inheres by divine inst. in the person of the king and his heirs to the throne; advocated in Eng. esp. by the Stuarts. See also *Roman Catholic Church,* D 2.

Divine Science. New* Thought group. Its principles and practice were worked out by 3 sisters from Denver, Colo.: Althea Brooks Small, Fannie Brooks James, and Nona Lovell Brooks, with Malinda E. Cramer of San Francisco, Calif. Divine Science Coll., Denver, was inc. 1898, and the 1st Divine Science Ch., Denver, founded 1899. In 1957 many Divine Science chs. and colleges organized the Divine Science Federation International.

Divine Service. See *Liturgics; Worship.*

Divines. See *Ministerial Office,* 1.

Divorce. See *Marriage,* III.

Dix, Gregory (George Eglinton Alston Dix; 1901–52). Angl. liturgical scholar; Benedictine monk; works include *The Shape of the Liturgy,* which popularized liturgical study.

Dix, William Chatterton (1837–98). B. Bristol, Eng.; educ. Grammar School, Bristol, for a mercantile life; hymnist. Hymns include "Come unto Me, Ye Weary"; "As with Gladness Men of Old."

Doane, Edward Topping (May 30, 1820–May 15, 1890). B. Tompkinsville, Staten Is., N. Y.; educ. U. Theol. Sem.; ABCFM miss. in Micronesia 1855–90.

Doane, George Washington (1799–1859). B. Trenton, N. J.; educ. Union Coll., Schenectady, N. Y.; Prot. Episc. cleric; prof. Trin. Coll., Hartford, Conn.; rector Trin. Ch., Boston; bp. of N. J.; founded Burlington (N. J.) Coll.; hymnist; hymns include "Thou Art the Way, to Thee Alone"; issued *Songs by the Way* 1824.

Dober, Johann Leonhard (1706–66). B. Münchsroth, Swabia; Moravian miss., with D. Nitschmann* II, to Dan. W Indies (Virgin Islands of the United States beginning 1917); arrived St. Thomas 1732; then to St. Croix; left for Eur. 1734, arrived 1735; superintending elder of cong. at Herrnhut 1735; miss. to Jews, Amsterdam, 1738; bp. 1747; hymnist. See also *Caribbean Islands,* E 8.

Dobschütz, Ernst Adolf Alfred Oskar Adalbert von (1870–1934). B. Halle; educ. Leipzig, Halle, and Berlin; prof. NT Jena 1899, Strasbourg 1904, Breslau 1910, Halle 1913. Works include *Die Thessalonicher-Briefe; The Eschatology of the Gospels; The Influence of the Bible on Civilization; Der Apostel Paulus; Das apostolische Zeitalter; Das Kerygma Petri kritisch untersucht;* reworked E. Nestle, *Einführung in das griechische Neue Testament.*

Docetism (probably from Gk. *dokein,* "appear, seem"). Ancient and modern view that Christ had no real but only an apparent body and that He therefore did not really suffer but only apparently; related to Gnosticism.* Among those assoc. with Docetism: Apollinaris* of Laodicea. The name "Docetae" (Gk. *doketai*) occurs in Serapion of Antioch (Eusebius, *HE,* VI, xii, 6), Clement* of Alexandria (*Stromata,* III, xiii; VII, xvii), Hippolytus,* and Theodoret.*

Docta ignorantia (Lat. "learned ignorance"). Term traced to Augustine* of Hippo; used by Nicholas* of Cusa for man's limited insight into the incomprehensibility of the infinite; applied to men's knowledge of God gleaned from phenomenal world.

Dr. Martin Luther College. See *Luther College,* 3; *Ministry, Education of,* VIII B 12.

Doctor of the Church. Title given to eminent fathers of the ch. Gk. doctors: Athanasius,* Basil the Great, Gregory of Nazianzus, J. Chrysostom*; Lat. doctors include Ambrose,* Jerome,* Augustine* of Hippo, Gregory I (see *Popes,* 4). See also *Cappadocian Fathers.*

Doctrinal Affirmation. See *American Lutheran Church,* V 1; *Brief Statement.*

Doctrinal Theology. 1. Systematic presentation of doctrine including such disciplines as Biblical theol. and confessional theol. 2. Often another term for dogmatics.*

Doctrine, Christian, History of. 1. Jesus commanded His disciples to teach all nations to observe all that He commanded them (Mt 28:20). What the disciples taught was Christian doctrine. When men teach what Jesus commands, they teach the truth; when they teach anything contrary to His commands, they teach error or heresy. The teachers of the ch. soon found it necessary to defend the truth of their faith against error in their midst and against attacks from Jews and pagans. This made it necessary for them to formulate their doctrine so that it would be clear to others. This led to the fixation of dogma. Those who taught error also formulated their doctrine; as the cents. passed, error increased in scope and variety. The hist. of doctrine is the record of the development of doctrinal forms and the fixation of dogma in the ch.

2. The earliest pronouncements of doctrine subsequent to the books of the NT are in the writings of the Apostolic* Fathers. These are followed by the writings of the so-called Gk. Apologists* (Epistle to Diognetus,* Quadratus,* Aristides,* Melito,* Claudius Apollinaris,* Miltiades,* Athenagoras,* Theophilus* of Antioch, Tatian,* and Justin* Martyr; see also *Patristics,* 3–4; *Christian Church, History of,* 2). These defended the faith in an era of persecution. But in praising Christianity as the highest form of philos. wisdom and truth, they weakened its power as the only means of salvation. During this period the ch. also had to defend itself against error in its midst (Gnosticism*; Encratism*; Montanism*; Monarchianism*). Controversy with errorists led to the declaration that revelation and prophecy had ceased and to fixation of the NT canon (see *Canon, Bible,* 3–5). During this time the schools of Alexandria and Antioch were founded, marking the beginning of scientific theol. (see *Exegesis,* 3–4). Tertullian* became the father of Lat. theol. He, Irenaeus,* and Hippolytus* were among the principal anti-Gnostic writers. The development of scientific theol. coincides with serious attacks on fundamental Christian doctrine, but also with the correct formulation of the challenged doctrines and their successful defense. The doctrine of the Trin. was attacked by Monarchianism* and Arianism* (see also *Christological Controversies*). The resulting controversy led to the first Council of Nicaea* 325 and to the Nicene Creed (see *Ecumenical Creeds,* B), which also took note of the error of the Macedonians or Pneumatomachi,* who denied the deity of the Holy Ghost. Apollinarianism (see *Apollinaris of Laodicea*) was condemned by the 381 council at Constantinople.* Nestorianism* denied the unity of Christ's person. Cyril* of Alexandria brought about the condemnation of Nestorius* at the council at Ephesus* 431. Eutychianism* taught that Christ, after the incarnation, had only 1 nature. The ensuing controversy was settled by the council at Chalcedon* 451. The resulting agreement is found in the Athanasian Creed (see *Ecumenical Creeds,* C). The Chalcedonian settlement was unsuccessfully challenged by Monophysitism (see *Monophysite Controversy*) and Monothelitism.* Summary: Nicaea 325, Christ is divine; Constantinople 381, Christ is human; Ephesus 431, Christ 1 in person; Chalcedon 451, Christ 2 in nature. A fierce anthropological controversy was stirred up by Pelagius* (see *Pelagian Controversy*), who taught freedom of the will in spiritual matters and salvation by works. Augustine* of Hippo was one of his chief opponents. Persecutions* of Christians by Decius and Diocletian* and the problem of the lapsed gave rise to Novatianism and Donatism (see *Novatian, Schism of; Donatist Schism, The*).

3. The early Middle Ages found the E and W Ch. in controversy regarding the use of images (iconoclastic* controversy) and the addition to the Nicene Creed of the words "and the Son" (see *Filioque Controversy*). The 2d Council of Nicaea* 787 marked the virtual end of development of doctrinal forms in the E Ch. In the W Ch. the adoptionist controversies (see *Adoptionism*), predestinarian* controversy, and eucharistic* controversies are to be noted.

4. In the later Middle Ages, philos. became the handmaid of theol. The great scholastics aimed to harmonize various doctrines of the ch. by the dialectic* method (see also *Scholasticism*). The sacramental and sacerdotal system that had developed in the course of cents. was fortified and papal supremacy explained. The number of sacraments grew from 2 to 7 (see *Sacraments, Roman Catholic*). Augustinianism* gave way to semi-Pelagianism (see *Pelagian Controversy,* 7–10). The immaculate conception of Mary was still being debated, but the trend was in favor of the dogma (defined 1854). The papal victory over the conciliar movement (see *Councils and Synods,* 7) prepared the way for the definition of papal infallibility 1870. Debates centering around the terms "realism,"* "nominalism,"* and "conceptualism"* influenced the development of doctrine in the medieval ch. The Council of Trent* (1545–63) crystallized RC dogma.

5. Earlier reformers (P. Waldo,* J. Wycliffe,* J. Hus*) had not been able to change the direction of RCm. The greatest challenge to RC doctrinal aberrations came with Prot. Reformation. Prot. doctrinal formulation is linked with M. Luther,* H. Zwingli,* and J. Calvin.* The name Luther suggests his 2 catechisms,* the AC, and the SA (see *Lutheran Confessions,* A, B 2). Zwingli's views are set forth in his 67 theses of 1523 and in a modified way in the Tetrapolitan Confession (see *Reformed Confessions,* D 1). Calvinism gave rise to many symbolic expressions (e. g., the Zurich Consensus, the Gallican Confession, the Heidelberg Catechism, the Thirty-nine Articles, the Lambeth Articles; see *Reformed Confessions,* A 8, B, C 1; *Anglican Confessions,* 6, 7). Arminianism* was a synergistic protest against Calvinism (Remonstrants* vs. Counter-Remonstrants). Post-Reformation controversies in the Luth. Ch. (Interimistic or Adiaphoristic,* Majoristic,* Antinomian,* Osiandrian* or Stancarian, Synergistic,* Flacian [see *Flacius Illyricus, M.*], Crypto*-Calvinistic) led to the FC and the Book* of Concord (see *Lutheran Confessions,* C 2), the last dogmatic formulation of the Luth. Ch. as such. For the Calvinistic Ref. Ch. the final dates are 1619 (Syn. of Dordrecht) and 1643 (Westminster Assembly). The last 2 cents. have been as marked by deviations from accepted standards as by adherence to them (Deism,* Ecumenical* Movement, Evangelicalism,* Fundamentalism,* Liberalism,* Modernism,* Rationalism*). Unfaithfulness to the Word of God has led to innumerable doctrinal aberrations and the rise of many religious sects and cults, each with its own doctrinal idiosyncrasies. But by the grace of God there is still a host of believers faithful to His Word.

See also *Christian Church, History of; Christian Faith and the Intellectual; Dogmatics; Theology.* LWS

E. H. Klotsche and J. T. Mueller, *The History of*

Christian Doctrine (Burlington, Iowa, 1945); J. L. Neve, *A History of Christian Thought,* 2 vols. (Philadelphia, 1943–46); R. Seeberg, *Lehrbuch der Dogmengeschichte,* 4 vols. in 5 books, 2d and 3d ed. (Leipzig, 1913–23), tr. C. R. Hay, *Text-Book of the History of Doctrines* (Grand Rapids, Mich., 1952); A. v. Harnack, *History of Dogma,* 7 vols., tr. from the 3d Ger. ed. by N. Buchanan (Boston, 1899–1903).

Doctrine of the Faith, Sacred Congregations for The. See *Curia,* 2 d; *Inquisition,* 7.

Document of Separation. Statement signed at Cleveland, Ohio, Sept. 18, 1845, by 9 men including W. Sihler,* J. A. Ernst,* J. G. Burger,* and C. A. T. Selle,* giving reasons for withdrawal from the Ohio* Syn. The reasons: 1. Lax confessionalism and unionistic practices of the syn.; 2. Repeal by the syn. of the resolution that guaranteed the fundamental Ger. character of the sem. at Columbus, Ohio. See also *Lutheran Church – Missouri Synod, The,* I 1-2.

Documentary Hypothesis. See *Higher Criticism,* 6–13.

Dodd, Charles Harold. See *Isagogics,* 3.

Dodd, Edward Mills (June 22, 1824–Aug. 20, 1865). Educ. Princeton Coll. and Union Theol. Sem., NYC; ABCFM miss. to Jews at Salonika 1849; to Armenians* 1855.

Doddridge, Philip (1702–51). B. London; educ. at a nonconformist sem. at Kibworth, Leicestershire; minister Kibworth 1723; minister and head of a sem. at Northampton 1729; author and poet; works include *The Family Expositor;* hymns include "Hark the Glad Sound! the Savior Comes."

Döderlein, Christian Albrecht (1714–89). B. Seyringen, Ger.; pastor Halle 1753; prof. Rostock 1758, Bützow 1760; adherent of Halle pietism.*

Döderlein, Johann Christoph (ca. 1745–92). B. Windsheim, Ger.; educ. Altdorf; prof. theol. Altdorf 1772, Jena 1782; stood at point of transition bet. orthodoxy and rationalism. Works include *Institutio theologi christiani.*

Dods, Marcus (1834–1909). Scot. Biblical scholar; b. Belford, Northumberland, Eng.; educ. Edinburgh; minister Glasgow; prof. NT exegesis at New Coll., Edinburgh; ed. J. P. Lange's *The Life of the Lord Jesus Christ* and works of Augustine* of Hippo; other works include commentaries on Gn and 1 Co in *The Expositor's Bible;* articles in the *Encyclopaedia Britannica* and in J. Hastings, *A Dictionary of the Bible.*

Dodwell. 1. *Henry, Sr.* (1641–1711). Irish theol. and hist.; educ. Dublin; prof. hist. Oxford 1688–91; removed because he refused to swear allegiance to William and Mary; joined nonjurors*; returned to Angl. Ch. 1710. Wrote in area of hist., dogmatics, patristics, and philol.

2. *Henry, Jr.* (ca. 1700–84). Deist. Works include *Christianity Not Founded on Argument.* See also *Deism,* III 6.

Doedes, Jakobus Isaak (1817–97). B. Langerak, Neth.; educ. Utrecht; pastor Hall 1843, Rotterdam 1847; prof. NT Utrecht 1859; exponent of hist. apologetics (see *Apologetics, Christian,* II).

Doehring, Bruno (1879–1961). B. Mohrungen, E Prussia; pastor Fischau, W Prussia; court and cathedral pastor Berlin 1914; prof. Berlin 1947; wrote on contemporary ch. situation in Ger.; works include *Die deutsche Volkskirche; Gott, das Leben und der Tod.*

Dogma. See *Doctrine, Christian, History of; Dogmatics.*

Dogmatic Constitution on Divine Revelation. See *Vatican Councils,* 2.

Dogmatic Constitution on the Church. See *Vatican Councils,* 2.

Dogmatics. Systematic and critical arrangement of the faith and message of the ch. derived from the Word of God in the OT and NT. The Bible was revealed to man in the course of cents. through different penmen; statements of divine truth are found in various parts of the Bible. Christian dogmatics tries to bring all teachings concerning each divine truth together and to arrange these truths in a systematic way. Thus the truths of the Bible must first be studied and understood (see *Exegesis; Hermeneutics*); then they may be stated and arranged.

A. *Nature and Function.* 1. Dogmatics (from Gk. *dogma,* "that which one holds to be true"; *dokei moi,* "methinks") deals not only with that which seems best and right, but also that which is determined and to be held or believed. The term is used in the LXX for decrees and laws (Est 3:9; Dn 2:13; 6:9-10). In the NT it is used for Mosaic law (Cl 2:14; Eph 2:15) and for decisions of the Jerusalem council (Acts 16:4). In the ch. fathers it is used for est. truths of Christianity (e. g., Ignatius, *Epistle to the Magnesians,* xiii, 1; Clement of Alexandria, *Stromata,* VII, xvi) and for heretical doctrines (e. g., Origen,* *Homilia XVI in Jeremiam,* 9 [*MPG,* 13, 449]). For some time after the Reformation the terms *sacra doctrina* and *theologia* (cf. the *Loci* theologici* of P. Melanchthon* and others) included not only religious truths taken from the Word of God but also ethical principles (e. g., among scholastics). After the science of morals or ethics* had been separated from that of dogmas (chiefly as a result of G. Calixtus,* *Epitome theologiae moralis,* 1634), the name "dogmatic theology" *(theologia dogmatica)* was given (e.g., by L. F. Reinhart,* J. Hildebrand,* F. Buddeus,* and C. M. Pfaff*) to that part of theology* which presents Bible doctrines in systematic arrangement.

2. Particularly after the age of rationalism* there was widespread discussion regarding the scope and purpose of dogmatics. RCs continued to emphasize the position expressed by the Council of Trent* that Scripture and tradition determine doctrine. Prots. for some time after the Reformation gen. held that the Bible is normative, but views championed since that time include: (a) dogmatics is the systematizing of Bible doctrine; (b) it is the systematizing and evaluation of doctrines held by the ch. throughout hist.; (c) it is the systematizing of the creed of a particular ch. in which the material principle is basic and cent.; (d) it is the systematizing of the doctrines held by a ch. in a particular period of hist.; (e) it is the systematizing of religious truths as perceived by the individual dogmatician.

3. For Luth. dogmaticians the principle laid down 1521 by P. Melanchthon* in his *Loci communes* was formative: *Evangelium est promissio,* not *philosophia coelestis* or *lex Christi.* Melanchthon also emphasized the center of Luth. dogmatics: God's grace in Christ appropriated through faith *(gratia universalis* [see *Grace*], *sola* gratia, sola* fide)* as revealed in the Word *(sola* Scriptura).*

B. *History.* 1. From earliest times the ch. tried to systematize its teachings, though few treatments were complete systematizations. Religious and Platonic elements were prominent in the treatises of Clement* of Alexandria and Origen.* Athanasius,* Gregory of Nyssa (see *Cappadocian Theologians,* 3), and Cyril* of Jerusalem made the Trin. and esp. Christ cen. in their treatments. John* of Damascus was 1st to attempt a complete system of dogmatics (I. Trinity; II. Anthropology; III. Christology; IV. Ascension of Christ, Faith, Prayer, Sacraments, Resurrection). Gregory* of Nazianzus, Cyprian,* Hilary* of Poitiers, and Augustine* of Hippo also made important contributions to dogmatics.

2. In the 9th c. J. S. Erigena* gave Scholasticism* a Neoplatonic (see *Neoplatonism*) character. Later

the influence of Aristotle became prominent. The scholastic movement caused dogmatics to become a logical system of deductions and dialectical elaborations. See *Abelard, P.; Albertus Magnus; Alexander of Hales; Anselm of Canterbury; Biel, Gabriel; Bonaventura; Duns Scotus; Ockham, William of; Peter the Lombard; Roscellinus.*

3. RC dogmatics is concerned with *veritates revelatae* (revealed truths) blended with the *veritas* (truth) of philos. Hence Aristotelian logic and philos. are united with the content of revelation in Thomas* Aquinas. Systematicians like R. Bellarmine* and Cajetan* (ca. 1468–1534) wrote in the Reformation era. Some prominent modern RC systematicians: Karl Adam, Hans Urs von Balthasar, Marie Joseph Congar (originally George Ives, or Yves), Jean Daniélou, Hans Küng, F. Diekamp,* Joseph Pohle, Erich Przywara, Peter Lengsfeld, Karl Rahner, Edward (Henry) Cornelis Florentius Alfons Schillebeeckx, Michael Schmaus, Dominikus Thalhammer, Gustave Thils, Gustave Weigel.

4. M. Luther* attacked the ontological orientation of dogmatic thought. But J. Calvin* and P. Melanchthon* operated with the unity of truth that used Aristotelian thought.

5. The *Loci* of Melanchthon and *Institutes* of Calvin laid the foundation for Luth. and Ref. orthodoxy. Some Ref. systematicians of the classical period: H. Bullinger,* W. Musculus,* B. Aretius,* Peter* Martyr, H. Zanchi,* T. Beza,* L. Daneau,* M. Virel,* W. Bucanus,* Z. Ursinus,* C. Olevian(us),* P. Boquin,* J. J. Grynaeus,* J. Piscator,* C. Pezel,* A. Polanus,* von Polansdorf, G. Sohn(ius),* B. Keckermann,* J. H. Alsted,* M. Martini,* L. Crocius (see *Crocius,* 2), J. H. Alting and son Jakob (see *Alting,* 1, 2), L. Trelcatius,* Sr. and Jr., G. Voet,* W. Perkins,* W. Ames,* J. Cocceius,* H. Wits,* and J. H. Heidegger.* Some more recent or contemporary: C. Hodge,* H. F. Kohlbrügge,* Karl Barth* (see *Switzerland, Contemporary Theology in*). Gerrit Cornelis Berkouwer, H. E. Brunner,* Arnold Albert van Ruler, Reinhold Niebuhr.*

6. Luth. dogmaticians in the age of orthodoxy (see *Lutheran Theology After 1580,* 3, 4, 5) tried to separate anti- and extra-Biblical teachings from Biblical truth. They are noted for their Scriptural learning, accuracy of statement, and devout application of theol. Outstanding Luth. dogmaticians of the 16th and 17th cents., M. Luther,* P. Melanchthon,* M. Chemnitz,* A. Hunnius,* L. Hutter,* J. Gerhard,* J. F. König,* A. Calov,* J. A. Quenstedt,* D. Hollaz,* J. W. Baier,* J. R. Brochmand.*

7. The age of orthodoxy was followed by emphasis on piety, emotional warmth, and correct living (see *Pietism*) rather than correct doctrinal formulation (P. J. Spener,* A. H. Francke,* J. A. Freylinghausen*). The overemphasis on man led to rationalism,* which first sought to explain doctrine rationally, then treated the doctrines themselves rationally (e. g., J. S. Semler,* J. C. Döderlein*), and finally used Scripture only to corroborate logical deductions (J. F. Röhr,* J. A. L. Wegscheider*). Since this method could not lead to comprehension of God, F. D. E. Schleiermacher* turned the investigation to a consideration of the experience of man. G. W. F. Hegel* turned the investigation toward revelation by seeking a God who seeks to reveal Himself. This position influenced the dogmaticians known as "mediating theologians" (see *Mediating Theology*). The 19th c. produced more positive men, though their emphases varied, J. T. Beck,* A. Hahn,* K. I. Nitzsch,* K. A. v. Hase,* P. K. Marheineke,* A. D. C. Twesten,* Julius Müller,* I. A. Dorner,* H. L. Martensen,* and K. F. A. Kahnis.* More positive still: E. W. C. Sartorius,* G. Thomasius,* F. A. Philippi,* C. E. Luthardt,* H. F. F. Schmid,* F. H. R. Frank,* A. F. C. Vilmar,* and A. v. Oettingen.*

8. In Scand., theol. followed the pattern of Ger. in the 17th and 18th cents. In the 19th c. distinctive characteristics developed.

9. In the 19th c. in Fin., A. F. Granfelt* approached the mediating theol. of H. L. Martensen* and I. A. Dorner,* tried to reconcile Christianity and culture, faith and reason. In the 19th and 20th cents.: G. Johansson* opposed liberal theol., materialism, and positivism with the theol. of J. T. Beck*; noted for loyalty to Scripture. His successor was G. G. A. Rosenqvist,* philos. and student of cultural ethics; espoused critical hist. approach to Scripture. A. J. Pietilä,* successor of Rosenqvist, is regarded by some as the greatest dogmatician in Fin. in the 1st half of the 20th c. (see also *Finland, Lutheranism in*).

10. The liberal movement in Norw. led to the est. of a free faculty at Oslo 1908. O. Hallesby,* leader of the free faculty for many yrs., advocated a theol. that combined orthodoxy and pietism.* At the U., dogmatics was taught by J. Ording,* C. Ihlen,* and H. N. H. Ording.* See also *Norway, Lutheranism in.*

11. In Den., Grundtvigianism, pietism,* and liberalism influenced theol. in the 19th c. In the middle of the 19th c. S. A. Kierkegaard* attacked the humanism and socialism of the ch. Toward the end of the 19th c. Olfert Ricard advocated a theol. of the ideal personality. After WW I the reaction against Christian idealism and humanism was very pronounced. Theol. was influenced by Kierkegaard and K. Barth (see *Switzerland, Contemporary Theology in*). Noted 20th c. theologians: Regin Prenter (b. 1907 Frederikssund, Den.; pastor Hvilsager and Aarhus; prof. dogmatics Aarhus 1945), Kristen Ejner Skydsgaard (b. 1902 Fünen, Den.; prof. dogmatics Copenhagen 1942), and N. H. Söe. See also *Denmark, Lutheranism in.*

12. Outstanding theologians in Swed. in the 19th–20th cents.: N. Söderblom* and E. M. Billing.* See also *Lund, Theology of; Sweden, Lutheranism in.*

13. In the 20th c. K. Barth strongly influenced Luth. and Ref. theol., and the existentialism* of R. Bultmann (see also *Demythologization*) is debated. The theol. of D. Bonhoeffer* influenced Eur. and Am. theol. Prominent Ger. Luth. dogmaticians (or systematicians) of the middle 20th c.: P. Althaus,* Sr. and Jr., Peter Brunner (b. 1900 Arheilgen, Ger.; prof. systematic theol. Heidelberg 1947), Oscar Cullmann (b. 1902 Strasbourg; prof. NT Strasbourg 1930, ch. hist. Strasbourg 1936, ch. hist. and NT Basel 1938, ch. hist. Paris 1949, NT Paris 1951), Hermann Diem (b. 1900 Stuttgart; prof. systematic theol. Tübingen 1957), Gerhard Ebeling (b. 1912 Berlin; prof. ch. hist. Tübingen 1946; prof. systematic theol. Tübingen 1954, Zurich 1956, Tübingen 1965), W. Elert,* Gerhard Gloege (b. 1901 Crossen on the Oder; prof. systematic theol. Jena 1946, Bonn 1961), Ernst Kinder (b. 1910 Barmen; prof. systematic theol. Neuendettelsau; prof. dogmatics and hist. of dogma Münster 1953), Walter Künneth (b. 1901 Etzelwang; prof. systematic theol. Erlangen 1953), Wolfhart Pannenberg (b. 1928 Stettin; prof. systematic theol. Wuppertal 1958, Mainz 1961), Edmund Schlink (b. 1903 Darmstadt; prof. systematic theol. Heidelberg 1946), Helmut Thielicke (b. 1908 Barmen; prof. systematic theol. Tübingen 1945, Hamburg 1954), Wolfgang Trillhaas (b. 1903 Nürnberg; prof. Göttingen 1946, prof. systematic theol. Göttingen 1954).

C. *Arrangement.* The material of dogmatics has been variously arranged. A popular arrangement: 1. Bibliology (doctrine of the Bible); 2. Theology (in the narrow sense: doctrine of the natural knowledge of God, the Trin., God's essence and attributes); 3. Cosmology (doctrine of creation, preservation, divine providence); 4. Angelology (doctrine of angels); 5. Anthropology (doctrine of man in his relation to God, of the image of God, state of innocence, fall, sin, free will); 6. Christology (doctrine of Christ's person, state, office); 7. Soteriology (doctrine of salvation); 8. Pneumatology (doctrine of the Holy Spirit and His work); 9. Sacramentology (doctrine of the means of grace); 10. Ecclesiology (doctrine of the ch.); 11. Eschatology (doctrine of the last things).

See also *Christian Faith and the Intellectual; Doctrinal Theology; Doctrine, Christian, History of.*

Historical treatments: E. H. Klotsche and J. T. Mueller, *The History of Christian Doctrine* (Burlington, Iowa, 1945); J. L. Neve, *A History of Christian Thought,* 2 vols. (Philadelphia, 1943–46); W. Rohnert, *Die Dogmatik der evangelisch-lutherischen Kirche* (Braunschweig, 1902); F. Loofs, *Leitfaden zum Studium der Dogmengeschichte,* 4th ed. (Halle, 1906); R. H. Grützmacher, *Textbuch zur systematischen Theologie und ihrer Geschichte im 16., 17., 19., und 20. Jahrh.,* 2d ed. (Leipzig, 1923) and *Textbuch zur deutschen systematischen Theologie und ihrer Geschichte vom 16. bis 20. Jahrhundert,* ed. G. G. Muras, 4th ed., 2 vols. (vol. 1 Gütersloh, 1955; vol. 2 Bern and Tübingen, 1961); H. W. Bartsch, *Handbuch der evangelisch-theologischen Arbeit 1938 bis 1948* (Stuttgart, 1949); H. L. J. Heppe, *Die Dogmatik der evangelisch-reformierten Kirche,* ed. E. Bizer (Neukirchen, 1958); F. Diekamp, *Katholische Dogmatik nach den Grundsätzen des heiligen Thomas,* ed. K. Jüssen, 12th and 13th ed. vol. 1, 11th and 12th ed. vols. 2–3 (Münster, 1954–59); R. F. Weidner, *Theological Encyclop(a)edia and Methodology,* 2d ed., 2 vols. (Chicago, 1898–1910).

Works by Luths. in Am.: S. S. Schmucker, *Elements of Popular Theology,* 5th ed. (Philadelphia, 1845); C. Löber, *Evangelisch-Lutherische Dogmatik,* with foreword by C. F. W. Walther (St. Louis, 1893); J. W. Baier, *Compendium theologiae positivae,* ed. C. F. W. Walther (St. Louis, 1879); S. Sprecher, *The Groundwork of a System of Evangelical Lutheran Theology* (Philadelphia, 1879); C. P. Krauth, *The Conservative Reformation and Its Theology,* first issued 1871 (Philadelphia, 1913); H. E. Jacobs, *Elements of Religion* (Philadelphia, 1894) and *A Summary of the Christian Faith* (Philadelphia, 1905); H. Schmid, *The Doctrinal Theology of the Evangelical Lutheran Church,* tr. C. A. Hay and H. E. Jacobs, 3d ed. (Minneapolis, 1961); W. Linsenmann, *Die Dogmatik der Evangelisch-Lutherischen Kirche,* 2 vols. (Saginaw, Mich., 1901–02); M. Valentine, *Christian Theology,* 2 vols. (Philadelphia, 1906); A. L. Graebner, *Outlines of Doctrinal Theology* (St. Louis, 1910); A. Hoenecke, *Ev.-Luth. Dogmatik,* 4 vols. plus index vol. (Milwaukee, 1909–17); A. G. Voigt, *Biblical Dogmatics* (Columbia, S.C., 1917); *The Distinctive Doctrines and Usages of the General Bodies of the Evangelical Lutheran Church in the United States,* 4th ed. (Philadelphia, 1914); J. Schaller, *Biblical Christology* (Milwaukee, 1919); C. E. Lindberg, *Christian Dogmatics and Notes on the History of Dogma,* tr. C. E. Hoffsten (Rock Island, Ill., 1922); F. Pieper, *Christliche Dogmatik,* 3 vols. plus index (St. Louis, 1917–28), tr. T. E. W. Engelder, W. W. F. Albrecht, F. E. Mayer, L. F. R. Blankenbuehler, *Christian Dogmatics,* 3 vols. plus new index vol. by W. W. F. Albrecht (St. Louis, 1950–57); W. E. Schramm, *What Lutherans Believe* (Columbus, Ohio, n. d.); G. H. Gerberding, *Lutheran Fundamentals* (Rock Island, Ill., 1925); E. Hove, *Christian Doctrine* (Minneapolis, 1930); P. L. Mellenbruch, *Doctrines of Christianity* (New York, 1931); J. Stump, *The Christian Faith* (New York, 1932); C. H. Little, *Disputed Doctrines* (Burlington, Iowa, 1933); J. T. Mueller, *Christian Dogmatics* (St. Louis, 1934); E. C. Fendt, *Christian Dogmatics* (Columbus, Ohio, 1938); H. Sasse, *Here We Stand,* tr. T. G. Tappert (New York, 1938); E. W. A. Koehler, *A Summary of Christian Doctrine,* 2d ed. (n.p., 1952); J. M. Reu, *Lutheran Dogmatics,* mimeographed (Dubuque, Iowa, 1941–42); T. E. W. Engelder, *Scripture Cannot Be Broken* (St. Louis, 1944); *The Abiding Word,* 3 vols., vols. 1–2 ed. T. F. K. Laetsch (St. Louis, 1946–60); W. J. Kukkonen, *Faith of Our Fathers* (New York, 1957); E. H. Wahlstrom, *God Who Redeems* (Philadelphia, 1962). EL

Dogmatism. 1. An incorrect use of the logical-dialectical method, often not beginning with the matter under consideration, but applying concepts and categories elsewhere derived. 2. Any persistent promulgation or defense of an idea that is false or for which there is little or no evidence.

Dole, Daniel (Sept. 9, 1808–Aug. 26, 1878). B. Bloomfield (now Skowhegan), Maine; educ. Bowdoin Coll. (Brunswick, Maine) and Bangor (Maine) Theol. Sem.; ABCFM miss. to Hawaii 1840; pres. Oahu Coll.

Doleantie. See *Netherlands,* 2.

Doles, Johann Friedrich, Sr. (1715–97). Pupil of J. S. Bach* while student of theol. at U. of Leipzig; cantor at the Thomasschule, Leipzig, 1756–89; great admirer of Bach.

F. Blume, "Doles, Johann Friedrich (sen.)," *Die Musik in Geschichte und Gegenwart,* III (Kassel and Basel, 1954), col. 627–639; H. J. Moser, *Geschichte der deutschen Musik,* vol. 2, part 1 (Stuttgart, 1922); P. Spitta, *Johann Sebastian Bach,* tr. C. Bell and J. A. Fuller-Maitland, 3 vols. (London, 1951); H. Banning, *Johann Friedrich Doles* (Leipzig, 1939).

Dölger, Franz Joseph (1879–1940). B. Sulzbach, Ger.; RC priest 1902; prof. Münster, Breslau 1926, Bonn 1929. Wrote on baptism, exorcism, confirmation, and eucharist in the early ch.

Dollfuss, Engelbert (1892–1934). Austrian chancellor 1932; opposed Nazis; proclaimed dictatorship 1933; shot by Nazi rebels. See *Christian Socialism,* 3.

Döllinger, Johann(es) Joseph Ignaz von (1799–1890). B. Bamberg, Ger.; ch. historian. At first supported ultramontanism.* Factors contributing to break with Rome included nationalism, his fear of scholasticism,* definition of the Immaculate* Conception 1854, pub. of the 1864 Syllabus* of Errors, definition of papal infallibility* 1870. Excommunicated 1871. Became a leader of Old* Catholics. Ed. *Beiträge zur politischen, kirchlichen und Cultur-Geschichte der 6 letzten Jahrhunderte.* Works include *Kirche und Kirchen, Papstthum und Kirchenstaat; Geschichte der Moralstreitigkeiten in der römisch-katholischen Kirche seit dem sechzehnten Jahrhundert; Beiträge zur Sektengeschichte des Mittelalters.*

J. Friedrich, *Ignaz von Döllinger: Sein Leben auf Grund seines schriftlichen Nachlasses,* 3 vols. (Munich, 1899–1901).

Dolmen. See *Cromlech,* 1.

Domenico, Giovanni. See *Campanella, Tommaso.*

Domestic and Foreign Missionary Society. See *Protestant Episcopal Church,* 4.

Dominic. See *Dominicans.*

Dominic Gundisalvi (Dominicus Gundissalinus; fl. ca. AD 1175). Archdeacon of Segovia, Sp.; tr. Aristotle, al-Ghazzali, Avicebron, and Avicenna; 1st to combine Aristotelian-Arab. philos. and Christian scholasticism.

Dominica. See *Caribbean Islands,* E. 5.

Dominica in albis. One of the Lat. names of the 1st Sun. after Easter. In full: Dominica in albis deponendis (or depositis). Reference is to laying aside white robes used in connection with Baptism at Easter. See also *Church Year,* 14; *Low Sunday.*

Dominical Letter. See *Sunday Letter.*

Dominicale. White linen veil worn by women to Communion. Term applied both to the veil worn gen. in ch. and the napkin with which women were to receive Communion, the bread being laid on it instead of on the bare hand.

Dominican Evangelical Church. See *Caribbean Islands,* E 2.

Dominican Republic. See *Caribbean Islands,* A, E 2; *Hispaniola.*

Dominicans (*Ordo Praedicatorum,* "Order of Preachers"; also called *Fratres Praedicatores,* "Friars Preachers," Black* Friars [in England], and Jacobins*). The Spaniard Dominic (Dominicus; Domenico; Domingo; Dominikus; ca. 1171–1221; RC priest; canon at Osma), while engaged in efforts to convert the Albigenses* of S Fr., founded the order 1215. It adopted the Augustinian* rule and was committed to poverty (see also *Mendicant Friars*) and dedicated to teaching, preaching, and scholarship; but the rule of poverty was soon disregarded and was abrogated for the whole order by 1477. The order grew rapidly, esp. in cities. It engaged in missions, but its chief purposes were strengthening faith and combating heresy. The Inquisition* was largely, but not exclusively, staffed by Dominicans. They preached crusades. Notable Dominicans include Albertus* Magnus, Fra Angelico,* Fra Bartolommeo,* T. de Torquemada (see *Inquisition,* 6), Pius V (see *Popes,* 21), G. Savonarola,* J. Tetzel,* and Thomas* Aquinas. Attached to the Dominicans are a Second* Order and Tertiaries.*

Dominicum. Term used in the early ch. to designate bldgs. in which Christian services were held (in this sense also *dominica*); also applied to the wealth or treasury of the ch. and to the celebration of the Lord's Supper.

Dominis, Marco Antonio de (1560 [or 1566]–1624). It. ecclesiastic; Jesuit; bp. Senj (Zengg), Croatia; abp. Split (Spalato); joined Angl. Ch. 1617; returned to RC Ch. 1622; sought unity through episc. conception of the ch.

Dominus ac Redemptor Noster. See *Bull.*

Domitian (Titus Flavius Domitianus Augustus; 51–96). Roman emp. 81–96; caused severe persecution of Christians (see *Persecution of Christians,* 3).

Dommer, Arrey (ca. 1828–ca. 1905). B. Danzig; musicologist and music critic. Works include *Handbuch der Musikgeschichte.*

Dompelaars. See *Brethren,* 1.

Donatello (Donato de Nicolò di Betto Bardi; ca. 1386–1466). It. sculptor after the style of F. Brunelleschi. Works include the Evangelist John on the facade of the Dome of Florence and St. George at Or San Michele, Florence.

Donatio Fidei. See *Conversion,* II 3.

Donation of Constantine (*Constitutum* or *Donatio Constantini*). Forged document, probably of the 8th–9th c.; presents Constantine* I as giving the pope and his clergy great temporal and spiritual powers. See also *Popes,* 1; *Pseudo-Isidorian Decretals,* 1 a, 2; *Valla, Lorenzo.*

Donation of Pepin. See *Pepin the Short.*

Donatist Schism, The. Grew out of conflict of views as to discipline of lapsed, esp. traditores (who had surrendered the Scriptures to persecutors). When on the death of Mensurius,* bp. of Carthage (d. ca. 311 or 307), who had frowned on voluntary martyrdom, the moderate party hastily elected his archdeacon Caecilian(us)* bp., the rigoristic-fanatical party (led by Donatus of Casae Nigrae) excommunicated him on the plea that consecrating bp. Felix of Aptunga (Aptonga; Aptungi; Aptungis) was a traditor. They set up Majorinus, a lector, as rival bp. An ecclesiastical commission and the syn. of Arles* decided against the Donatists. Ca. 315 Majorinus died and was succeeded by Donatus the Great (of Carthage; d. ca. 355; perhaps not the same as Donatus of Casae Nigrae). In 316 Constantine* I took a stand against the Donatists and initiated persecution. But they held that to be persecuted was a mark of the ch. and under leadership of Donatus spread throughout N Afr. They also held that sacraments administered by one deserving excommunication were invalid, that the Cath. Ch., failing to excommunicate such, had ceased to be the true ch., that its Baptism was invalid, and that they themselves alone were the true ch. (see AC VIII 3 and Ap VII–VIII 49). In 321 Constantine* I gave the Donatists freedom of faith and worship. But Flavius Julius Constans (ca. 323–ca. 350), his successor in Afr. 337, resumed persecution. The Donatists, now allied with the Circumcellions (vagabond mendicant monks that terrorized the countryside; named after the Lat. *cellas circumientes rusticorum,* "wandering about among peasant cottages"), increased in violence. Constantius II (317–361; succeeded Constans in the E 351) continued the persecution. Donatus the Great died in exile. Under Julian* the Apostate the Donatists regained freedom of religion and flourished accordingly. But later they suffered from dissension reflecting reaction against extremism and from renewed persecution. The writings of Augustine* of Hippo against the Donatists, advocating spiritual measures against them, appeared 393–412. At a conference in Carthage 411 bet. 286 Cath. and 279 Donatist bps. the imperial commissioner decided against the Donatists; severe restrictions were imposed on them, including a prohibition even to assemble, under pain of death. Augustine now tried to justify the use of force for bringing heretics into the fellowship of the ch.; he appealed, wrongly, to Lk 14:23. Vandals persecuted both Caths. and Donatists ca. 429. The schism ended in the 7th c. with the destruction of the ch. in Afr. by Saracens. See also *Optatus.*

G. G. Willis, *Saint Augustine and the Donatist Controversy* (London, 1950); W. H. C. Frend, *The Donatist Church: A Movement in Protest in Roman North Africa* (Oxford, 1952); S. L. Greenslade, *Schism in the Early Church* (London, 1953).

Donatus of Casae Nigrae. See *Donatist Schism, The.*

Donatus the Great (of Carthage). See *Donatist Schism, The.*

Donne, John (1573–1631). B. London; brought up RC; joined Angl. Ch.; dean St. Paul's, London; poet. Works include *Devotions upon Emergent Occasions.*

Donum concreatum. See *Donum superadditum.*

Donum gratiae. See *Gratia increata.*

Donum superadditum; donum supernaturale. These terms denote the RC scholastic doctrine of "superadded, supernatural" grace given to Adam in addition to his natural powers and lost by him through the Fall. According to this doctrine, man lived in moral communion with God by virtue of an original righteousness that exalted him above merely human nature. According to RC doctrine, Mary, the mother of Jesus, was preserved from the stain of original sin (Immaculate* Conception) and for others all that was lost by the Fall is restored by Baptism: "If anyone . . . says that [in Baptism] the whole of that which belongs to the essence of sin is not taken away . . . let him be anathema" (*Canons and Decrees of the Council of Trent,* Session V, "Decree Concerning Original Sin," 5).

Luth. doctrine knows no such "superadded, supernatural" gift, but regards the original wisdom, righteousness, and holiness of man in his first estate as concreate (*donum concreatum*). Accordingly, man's nature (including that of Mary) after the Fall is corrupt, and the image of God, which was lost by man in the Fall and renewal of which is begun in believers on earth, will be fully restored only in heaven (Ap II, IV 351–352; FC SD I).

Dooley, Thomas Anthony III (Jan. 17, 1927–Jan. 18, 1961). B. St. Louis, Mo.; educ. Notre Dame (South Bend, Ind.) premedical school and St. Louis (Mo.) U.; participated as US navy doctor in evacuation of N Vietnamese; received Legion of Merit medal 1955; resigned from navy 1956. Began medical miss. work in Laos in fall 1956; it later expanded into the Medical Internat. Cooperation Organization (MEDICO). Works include *Deliver Us from Evil; The Edge of Tomorrow; The Night They Burned the Mountain.*

A. W. Dooley, *Promises to Keep: The Life of Doctor Thomas A. Dooley* (New York, 1962).

Doopsgesinde (Doopsgesint; Doopsgezind[en]; Doopsghesinde). See *Mennonite Churches,* 1; *Netherlands,* 4.

Doorkeeper. See *Clergy; Hierarchy.*

Dordrecht, Synods of. 1. June 16–28, 1574; provincial syn. of Ref. chs. of N Holland, S Holland, and Zeeland. Passed 91 acts pertaining to ch. structure and doctrine. Resolutions include that 14 classes be formed, that consistories consist of ministers and elders only (deacons under exceptional conditions), that consistories elect pastors (with possible participation of male members of ch.), that ministers and teachers subscribe only the Belgic Conf. (see *Reformed Confessions,* C 1), and that only the Heidelberg Catechism be used; the ch. order of Emden was approved in substance.

2. June 2–18, 1578; 1st nat. syn. in the Neth.; P. Dathenus* presided; a ch. order was est.; it was resolved that profs. of theol. subscribe the Belgic Conf. (see *Reformed Confessions,* C 1); use of the Geneva Catechism and of the Heidelberg Catechism (see *Reformed Confessions,* A 7, D 2) was sanctioned.

3. Nov. 13, 1618–May 29, 1619; convened by the States Gen.; condemned Arminianism*; endorsed Belgic Conf. and Heidelberg Catechism. See also *Reformed Churches,* 2; *Reformed Confessions,* C 1-2, D 2.

Dordrecht Confession. Adopted by Mennonites* at Dordrecht, Apr. 21, 1632. Its 18 articles, which represent the mature development of Anabaptist thought, are a comprehensive statement of belief and express the distinctive ch. order and practice of Mennonites.

Dorn, Louis William (Oct. 15, 1865–Apr. 4, 1918). B. Boeuf Creek, Franklin Co., Mo.; grad. Conc. Sem., St. Louis, Mo., 1885; asst. pastor to his father in Pleasant Ridge, Ill.; pastor at Rockford, later at Belleville, Ill.; prof. of mathematics and natural sciences 1900, later of Ger. and hist., Conc. Coll., Fort Wayne, Ind.; ed. *Lutherisches Kinder- und Jugendblatt* 1905; contributor *Magazin für ev.-luth. Homiletik* [*und Pastoraltheologie*] and *Der Lutheraner.*

Dorner. 1. *Isaak August* (1809–84). B. Neuhausen, Ger.; educ. Tübingen; prof. Tübingen, Kiel, Königsberg, Bonn, Göttingen, and Berlin; mediating theol.; influenced by F. D. E. Schleiermacher.* Works include *Entwicklungsgeschichte der Lehre von der Person Christi.* See also *Mediating Theology.*

2. *August Johann(es)* (1846–1920). B. Schiltach, Ger.; son of Isaak August; educ. Göttingen, Tübingen, and Berlin; lectured at Göttingen; prof. and co-dir. Wittenberg 1874; prof. systematic theol. Königsberg 1889; writings reveal his speculative-critical theol.

Dort. See *Dordrecht.*

Dositheus. Samaritan heretic(s) dated 3d c. BC to 1st c. AD. Sources are confused on beliefs, practices, and pertinent hist.; it has been assumed that there were 2 heretics and sects bearing the name, the earlier denying, the later affirming the resurrection of the dead. Followers, called Dositheans, used name Elohim (God) instead of Jahweh (Lord) and a 30-day calendar; practiced asceticism and Levitical purity.

Dositheus (Dositheos; 1641–1707). B. near Corinth; uncle of N. Chrysanthos*; metropolitan of Caesarea 1666; patriarch of Jerusalem 1669. See also *Eastern Orthodox Standards of Doctrine,* A 2.

Dostoevski, Fedor Mikhailovich (1821–81). B. Moscow; Russ. novelist; suffered for advocacy of soc. reform; contributed to reaction in literature and theol. against humanism and materialism.

Doty, Elihu (1812–65). Educ. Rutgers Coll. and the theol. sem. of the Ref. Prot. Dutch Ch. (see *Reformed Churches,* 4) at New Brunswick, N. J. Mem. of 1st ABCFM and Ref. Prot. Dutch Ch. miss. to Java 1836; transferred to Borneo 1840, to China Amoy Miss. 1844.

Douai Version. See *Bible Versions,* L 9.

Double Effect Principle. Principle that seeks to determine when an action from which both evil and good result may be performed.

Double Monastery. Monastery* for both men and women.

Double Predestination (Absolute Predestination). Predestination according to which, in the belief of some, God determined by eternal decree who is to be damned as well as who is to be saved. See also *Calvin, John,* 11; *Predestinarian Controversy; Presbyterian Confessions,* 3; *Preterition; Reformed Confessions,* A 9.

Double Procession of the Holy Spirit. Procession of the Holy* Spirit from the Father and the Son. See also *Filioque Controversy.*

Double Reference Theory of the Atonement. View of M. Amyraut* of a gen. or universal reference in the atonement* of Christ to all men that is theoretical or hypothetical, and of a limited reference to the elect, the saved, that is practical and real.

Double Standard of Morals. Term denoting the view that grants greater license in sexual matters to men than to women.

Double Truth. Theory which holds that a proposition may at the same time be true in one area (e. g., theol.) and false in another (e. g., philos.).

Douglas, Charles Winfred (1867–1944). B. Oswego. N. Y.; Prot. Episc. cleric. organist, composer; studied ch. music in Eng., Fr., Ger. Works include *Church Music in History and Practice.* See also *Gregorian Music,* 3.

Doukhobor. See *Russian Sects.*

Doumergue, Emile (1844–1937). B. Nîmes, Fr.; Ref. cleric; prof. ch. hist. Montauban 1880. Wrote extensively on J. Calvin.*

Dow, William. See *Catholic Apostolic Church,* 1.

Dowie, John Alexander (1847–1907). B. Edinburgh, Scot.; to S Australia 1860; returned 1867; finished educ. at U. of Edinburgh; ordained Cong. pastor 1870; preacher at Alma and Sydney, Australia, 1870; during plague began ministry of divine healing*; left Cong. Ch. 1878; organized a Divine Healing Assoc. at Melbourne, Australia; to San Francisco, Calif., 1888; to Evanston, Ill., 1890; to Chicago 1893; founded Christian* Cath. Ch. 1896; proclaimed himself Elijah the Restorer 1901; deposed 1906.

Dowieites. See *Christian Catholic Church.*

Downton, Henry (1818–85). B. Shropshire, Eng.; educ. Cambridge; held various positions as clergyman; rector Hopton 1873; poet; hymns include "For Thy Mercy and Thy Grace."

Doxa (Gk. "opinion"). Term used for the simple certainty of belief and modifications of such belief.

Doxology (Gk. *doxologia,* "praise, laudation"; from *doxa,* "glory," and *logos,* "word, speech, speaking"). Stately and exultant hymn of praise addressed to the Triune God or to a single person of the Godhead, as in Paul's letters, e. g., Ro 16:27; Eph 3:21; in particular, the Greater Doxology *(Gloria in Excelsis),* the Lesser Doxology *(Gloria Patri),* and the long-meter doxology ("Praise God, from Whom All Blessings Flow").

Drabík, Nikolaus (Drabicius; 1588–1671). B. Strassnitz, Moravia; leader of exiled Bohemian* Brethren in Hung.

Drach, John George Peter (Sept. 3, 1873–Oct. 2, 1957). B. Greenport, Long Island, N. Y. Educ. Wagner Coll.; Luth. Theol. Sem., Mount Airy, Philadelphia, Pa. Asst. pastor Reading, Pa.; pastor West Philadelphia. Secy. Bd. of For. Miss. of the General* Council of the Ev. Luth. Ch. in N. Am. 1905 and of the ULC Bd. of For. Missions. Ed. *The Foreign Missionary.* Coauthor (with C. F. Kuder*), *The Telugu Mission.* Other works include *Forces in Foreign Missions; Seeing Things in the Far East; Kingdom Pathfinders.*

Draconites, Johann(es) (Drach; Draco; Trach; Carlstadt; 1494–1566). B. Karlstadt on the Main; educ. Erfurt; canon in Erfurt; joined Luther; pastor Miltenberg and Waltershausen; prof. theol. Marburg, Lübeck, and Rostock; attended the 1541 Regensburg* Conference; signed the Schmalkaldic Articles (see *Lutheran Confessions,* B 2). Ed. a partially printed polyglot* Bible in Heb., Chaldee, Gk., Lat., and Ger.

Dracontius, Blossius Aemilius (5th c. AD). According to early tradition, of Sp. origin; possibly b. Carthage; lawyer Carthage; Christian poet. Works include *De laudibus Dei;* epics; an elegy; 2 epithalamiums.

Dragonnades (Dragonades; Dragoonades; from Fr. *dragon,* "dragon"). Some trace the name to an emblem on a standard, others to ornamentation on a weapon, others to the dragon-like spitfire action of the weapon. Dragonnades were persecutions of Prots. in Fr. at the hands of dragoons, mounted infantrymen, under Louis XIV (1638–75; king 1643–1715). See also *France,* 10; *Huguenots.*

Drama, Religious. See *Religious Drama.*

Dramatic Theory of Atonement. See *Atonement, Theories of.*

Dräseke, Johann Heinrich Bernhard (1774–1849). B. Brunswick, Ger.; d. Potsdam; educ. Helmstedt; pastor Mölln 1798, Ratzeburg 1804, Bremen 1814; eminent pulpit orator; advocated humanistic Christianity; was impressed with Freemasonry; worked for conciliation of Pietism* and Rationalism.*

Dravidian. In Indian usage, the name of a "southern" group of Brahmans (see *Brahmanism*). The term is also more gen. applied to a group of Indian languages that includes Tamil* and Malayalam.*

Dream. See *Psychical Research; Revelation.*

Dreier, Christian (1610–88). B. Stettin, Ger.; Luth. theol.; educ. Jena, Wittenberg, and Rostock; prof. Königsberg (called Kaliningrad since 1946); participated in 1645 Colloquy of Thorn* (see *Reformed Confessions,* D 3 c); follower of G. Calixtus.*

Dresden Cross Catechism *(Kreuz-Katechismus).* See *Catechetics,* 11.

Dresden Evangelical Lutheran Mission. See *Leipzig Evangelical Lutheran Mission.*

Drese, Adam (Dresen; ca. 1620–1701). Probably b. Thuringia; Luth. hymnist and composer; studied music at Warsaw; dir. of the court chapel, Weimar; later held similar positions at Jena and Arnstadt; pietistic; hymns include "Seelenbräutigam, Jesu, Gotteslamm."

Dressler, Gallus (1533–after 1580). B. Nebra, Ger.; Luth. composer; succeeded M. Agricola* in Magdeburg; adopted views of P. Melanchthon*; deacon St. Nikolai ch., Zerbst. Works include *Ausserlesene teutsche Lieder mit vier und fünff Stimmen.*

S. Kümmerle, *Encyklopädie der evangelischen Kirchenmusik,* I (Gütersloh, 1888), 337; C. v. Winterfeld, *Der evangelische Kirchengesang,* I (Leipzig, 1843), 190, 341, 416.

Dreves, Guido Maria (1854 [some say 1845]–1909). B. Hamburg; Jesuit; collected Lat. ch. songs. Ed. *Analecta Hymnica Medii Aevi,* 55 vols.

Drewes, Christopher Frederick John (Jan. 12, 1870–Mar. 3, 1931). B. Wolcottsville, N. Y.; grad. Conc. Sem., St. Louis, Mo., 1892; pastor Memphis, Tenn., 1892–94, Hannibal, Mo., 1894–1905, St. Louis, Mo., 1905–17; mem. Syn. Conf. Bd. of Colored Missions 1908–17; its dir. 1917–31; ed. *Missions-Taube* 1911 to 1931 and Concordia Sunday School literature. Other works include *Dr. Martin Luther's Small Catechism Explained by Way of Questions and Answers; Half a Century of Lutheranism Among Our Colored People; Mission-Stories; Introduction to the Books of the Bible.*

Drews, Christian Heinrich Arthur (1865–1935). Ger. philos.; disciple of K. R. E. v. Hartmann*; held a monism* conceived as process, with God immanent; taught "Christ-myth" method, which assumes that Gospels are books for edification which tell nothing about a hist. Jesus; held that astralism provides the background of the NT. Works include *Die Christusmythe; Der Sternhimmel in der Dichtung und Religion der alten Völker und des Christentums; Die Entstehung des Christentums aus dem Gnostizismus.*

Driesch, Hans Adolf Eduard (1867–1941). Ger. biologist and philos.; experiments led him to support a dynamic vitalism which held that life cannot be explained as physical or chemical phenomena, but that every organism has its own entelechy (something that contains or realizes an end or final cause). Works include *Leib und Seele.*

Driessche, Jan van den. See *Drusius, Johannes.*

Driver, Samuel Rolles (1846–1914). B. Southampton, Eng.; d. Oxford; Angl.; Biblical critic; successor of E. B. Pusey* as prof. Heb. and canon, Christ Ch., Oxford, 1883; mem. OT revision committee 1876 to 1884. Joint ed. with F. Brown* and C. A. Briggs,* *A Hebrew and English Lexicon of the Old Testament,* based on the lexicon of W. Gesenius, tr. E. Robinson; jt. ed. with A. B. Davidson and H. B. Swete, *A Dictionary of the Bible,* ed. J. Hastings and J. A. Selbie; other works include *Introduction to the Literature of the Old Testament.* See also *Lexicons,* A.

Drozdov, Vasili Mikhailovich. See *Eastern Orthodox Standards of Doctrine,* A 4.

Druids. Priests of Celts of ancient Gaul, Brit., and Ireland; their learning, transmitted orally, was a mixture of religion, natural science, and medicine; among their objects of veneration were the oak and mistletoe. Though prominent politically and socially, Druids succumbed to the advance of Roman civilization in Gaul and S. Brit. and to the influence of Christianity in N. Brit. and Ireland. See also *Celtic Church.*

Drummond, Henry (1786–1860). See *Catholic Apostolic Church,* 1.

Drummond, Henry (1851–97). Scot. ev. writer; lecturer on science and prof. theol. at the Glasgow coll. of the Free Ch. of Scot. Works include *Natural Law in the Spiritual World.*

Drummond, William Hamilton (1863–1945). Eng. Unitarian. Ed. *The Inquirer.*

Druses. See *Druzes.*

Drusius, Johannes (Jan van den Driessche; 1550 to 1616). B. Audenarde, Belgium; Ref. exegete and orientalist; prof. oriental languages at Oxford 1572, Leiden 1577; prof. Heb. at Franeker 1585.

Druthmar. 1. *Christian of Stavelot* (Grammaticus; 9th c.). Probably b. Burgundy; priest at Stavelot; gave exegetical lectures at Stavelot and Malmédy, Belgium; wrote *Expositio in Matthaeum. MPL* 106, 1259—1520. 2. *Druthmar of Lorsch* (d. 1046). Monk of Lorsch, Ger.; abbot of Corvey, Westphalia;

noted for learning, zeal, strict observance of discipline; canonized.

Druzes (Druses). Religio-ethnic group; originated in the 11th c.; named after Muhammad ibn-Ismail al-Darazi, who held that al-Hakim (985–1021; 6th Fatimid caliph of Egypt 996–1021) was the last incarnation of the deity; believed to be of mixed Aramaic and Arabic descent; settled esp. in Lebanon, Anti-Liban, and the Hauran; some believed to be in China; religious system is monotheistic and contains elements drawn from various sources (e. g., Judaism, Christianity, and Islam); slaughtered ca. 2,500 Maronites* 1860.

Dryden, John (1631–1700). Eng. poet, dramatist, satirist, critic; a chief formulator of modern Eng. prose. Joined RC Ch. 1685. Works include *Religio Laici* (defense of Anglicanism) and *The Hind and the Panther* (defense of RCm).

Dualism. In metaphysics, assumption of 2 mutually hostile superior beings, one representing everything good and beneficial to man, the other the source of all sin and evil, as in Zoroastrianism* (see also *Parsees*) and in Gnosticism.* In philos., the view that in the world there are 2 principles, or substances, which are wholly indep. and totally different from each other: the spiritual and the corporeal, mind and matter. Theistic, or Biblical, dualism asserts essential difference bet. Creator and creation. Dualism is opposed to monism,* pluralism,* and some forms of pantheism.* See also *Descartes, René.*

Dubcansky, Johann (fl. ca. 1500). Czech reformer.

Du Bois, William Edward Burghardt. See *National Association for the Advancement of Colored People.*

Dubois, Clément Francois Théodore (1837–1924). Fr. composer; organist and prof. Paris. Works include *Les Sept paroles du Christ.*

Dubourg, Anne (ca. 1520–59). B. Riom, Fr.; prof. civil law U. of Orleans ca. 1547; *conseiller clerc* Parliament of Paris 1557; Prot. ca. 1559; pleaded in Parliament for persecuted Prots.; imprisoned; hanged and burned Dec. 23 at Paris. His fortitude decisively impressed F. Hotman.*

Dubs, Rudolph. See *Evangelical Church,* 1.

Dubuque Theses *(Thesen über den Lehrstreit von der Gnadenwahl).* Seven theses prepared by S. Fritschel* and adopted by the Iowa* Syn. at Dubuque, Ia., 1882. They deal with predestination and conversion. They reject the position that particular election is not the extension of the gen. decree of grace and salvation to the individual people in whom it attains realization, but an essentially *(thatsächlich)* different decree which is the cause of the salvation of the elect. Furthermore, they reject the position that predestination is election "according to the mere pleasure of divine will" *(nach dem blossen Wohlgefallen des göttlichen Willens)* without consideration of human behavior, and favor the view that election took place in view of faith. See also *Chicago Theses; Lutheran Church — Missouri Synod,* V; *Thirteen Theses.*

J. Deindörfer, *Geschichte der Evangel.-Luth. Synode von Iowa und anderen Staaten* (Chicago, 1897); *Quellen und Dokumente zur Geschichte und Lehrstellung der ev.-luth. Synode von Iowa u. a. Staaten,* comp. G. J. Fritschel (Chicago, n.d.); S. F[ritschel], "Aus den Verhandlungen der Versammlung unserer Synode zu Dubuque, Iowa, über den Lehrstreit von der Gnadenwahl," *Kirchen-Blatt der evangelisch-lutherischen Synode von Iowa,* XXV (1882), 114–115, 123–124, 132–133.

Duchesne, Louis Marie Olivier (1843–1922). Fr. RC ch. hist.; prof. Institut Catholique, Paris, 1877; dir. Fr. school of archaeol., Rome 1895; specialized in Christian archaeol. and early ch. hist.

Ducis, Benedictus (Duch; Hertoghs; Herzog; ca. 1485 to 1544). B. near Constance, Ger.; Luth. composer; pastor Stubersheim 1533; Schalkstetten 1535; works pub. esp. in such collections as G. Rhau,* *Neue deutsche geistliche Gesänge.*

Duck River Baptists. See *Baptist Churches,* 25.

Duden. 1. *Gottfried* (b. 1785). Ger. author and traveler. Wrote geog., sociol., and pol. descriptions of Am. His *Bericht über eine Reise nach den westlichen Staaten Nordamerikas und einen mehrjährigen Aufenthalt am Missouri* persuaded many Ger. Luths. to settle in Mo. 2. *Konrad Alexander* (1829 to 1911). Ger. philol.; works include *Rechtschreibung der deutschen Sprache und der Fremdwörter.*

Dudum Sacrum. See *Basel, Council of.*

Duemling, Enno A. (Dümling; Jan. 6, 1875–Oct. 22, 1946). B. Fort Wayne, Ind.; son of Hermann; grad. Conc. Sem., St. Louis, Mo., 1896; pastor Detroit, Mich., 1896–1902; organized miss. for deaf in Detroit 1896; inst. miss. of Syn. Conf. in Milwaukee, Wis., 1902–46; pres. Assoc. Luth. Charities. Works include *The Lutheran Ministrant.*

Duemling, Hermann (Dümling; Oct. 5, 1845–Mar. 11, 1913). B. Schönebeck, Ger.; educ. Halle and Heidelberg; instructor Luth. high school, Milwaukee, Wis.; prof. Ev. Luth. Teachers Sem., Addison, Ill., 1870 to 1874; prof. Conc. Coll., Fort Wayne, Ind., 1874 to 1899; ed. *Die Abendschule* 1871–99; ed. *Germania* 1899–1913. Works include *Bau, Leben und Pflege des menschlichen Körpers; Illustrirtes Thierleben,* 2 vols.; *Bilder aus der Natur; Bismarck und seine Zeit;* arithmetic books.

Illustrated obituary by "W." in *Die Abendschule,* LIX, 18 (Apr. 3, 1913), 548–551.

Duff, Alexander (1806–78). First miss. of the Est. Ch. of Scot. to India 1830. With the help of Ram* Mohan Roy founded a school in Calcutta 1830 which later became a center of W educ. in India. At the 1843 division of the Ch. of Scot. he went with the Free Ch. Helped found U. of Calcutta. Returned to Scot. 1864 because of ill health; continued to work for for. miss. until his death. Helped found *Calcutta Review* and ed. it 1845–49.

O. G. Myklebust, *The Study of Missions in Theological Education,* I (Oslo, 1955).

Duffield. 1. *George, Jr.* (1818–88). B. Carlisle, Pa.; educ. Yale Coll., New Haven, Conn., and Union Theol. Sem., NYC; Presb. pastor; hymnist. Hymns include "Stand Up, Stand Up for Jesus." 2. *Samuel Augustus Willoughby* (1843–87). B. Brooklyn, N.Y.; son of George, Jr.; educ. Yale Coll., New Haven, Conn.; Presb. pastor; hymnist. Works include *Warp and Woof: A Book of Verse; English Hymns: Their Authors and History; The Latin Hymn-Writers and Their Hymns.*

Duhm, Bernhard (1847–1928). B. Bingum, Ostfriesland; Prot. theol.; prof. Göttingen and Basel; exponent of Religionsgeschichtliche* Schule; friend of J. Wellhausen*; proposed Trito-Isaiah theory of authorship of Is 56–66. Works include *Die Theologie der Propheten; Israels Propheten;* commentaries on Jb, Ps, Is, Jer, and Hab.

Dühring, Karl Eugen (1833–1921). Ger. philos.; exponent of positivism.*

Dukhobor. See *Russian Sects.*

Dulia. See *Latria.*

Dulles, John Welsh (1823–87). ABCFM miss. to Madras, India; est. work at Arcot; returned to Am. 1852. Ed. *American Presbyterian* 1855; other works include *Life in India; The Ride Through Palestine; The Soldier's Friend.*

Dümling. See *Duemling.*

Dunant, Jean Henri (1828–1910). Swiss philanthropist; founded Red* Cross.

Dunkers (Dunkards). See *Brethren.*

Dunowas. See *Middle East,* L.

Duns Scotus, John (ca. 1265–ca. 1308). *"Doctor subtilis; Doctor maximus; Doctor Marianus."* B. Duns,

Scot. Franciscan teacher at Oxford, Paris, and Cologne; opposed intellectualistic and deterministic system of Thomas* Aquinas. Followers called Scotists. See also *Scholasticism*, 3; *Via antiqua.*

E. Bettoni, *Duns Scotus: The Basic Principles of His Philosophy,* ed. and tr. B. Bonansea (Washington, 1961); R. Seeberg, *Die Theologie des Johannes Duns Scotus* (Leipzig, 1900); É. H. Gilson, *Jean Duns Scot: Introduction à ses positions fondamentales* (Paris, 1952); *R. P. F. D. S. . . . opera omnia,* 12 vols. (Lyons, Fr., 1639); *Opera omnia* (Rome, 1950–); *Duns Scotus: Philosophical Writings,* ed. and tr. A. Wolter (Edinburgh, 1962); J. F. Bonnefoy, *Le Ven. Jean Duns Scot* (Rome, 1960); R. R. Effler, *John Duns Scotus and the Principle Omne quod movetur ab alio movetur* (Louvain, Belgium, 1962); J. F. Boler, *Charles Peirce and Scholastic Realism* (Seattle, Wash., 1963).

Dunstable, John (Dunstaple; ca. 1370 [some suggest as late as ca. 1400]–1453). Eng. composer, mathematician, and astronomer; important in 15th c. Eng. music; contributed significantly to the development of counterpoint. Works include motets, masses, antiphons, and songs.

Dunstan (ca. 909 [some suggest as late as ca. 925] to 988). B. near Glastonbury, Eng.; abbot Glastonbury; bp. Worcester and London; abp. Canterbury; introd. monastic reforms based on rule of Benedict* of Nursia; promoted educ. of clergy.

Du Pin, Louis Ellies (Dupin; 1657–1719). Fr. RC cleric and hist.; favored Gallicanism*; exiled on charges on Jansenism*; returned after retraction. Works include *Nouvelle bibliothèque des auteurs ecclésiastiques; Traité de la puissance ecclésiastique et temporelle.*

Duplessis-Mornay. See *Mornay.*

Duraeus. See *Durie.*

Durandus de Sancto Porciano, Gulielmus (Lat. form of French Guillaume Durand de Saint-Pourçain; ca. 1270/75–ca. 1332/34). "Doctor modernus; Doctor resolutissimus." B. Saint-Pourçain-sur-Sioule, Fr.; scholastic Dominican theol.; bp Limoux 1317, Le Puy 1318, Meaux 1326; developed nominalism* in opposition to the realism* of Thomas* Aquinas; anticipated the terminism (see *Terminism,* 2) of W. of Ockham*; distinguished bet. realms of reason and faith; opposed pope in the question of beatific vision.

Durani Empire. See *Middle East,* J.

Duräus. See *Durie.*

Dürer, Albrecht (1471–1528). Ger. painter and engraver. B. Nürnberg; studied under M. Wohlgemuth*; court painter under Maximilian I and Charles* V. Several of his paintings include Reformation figures. Works include woodcuts illustrating the Book of Revelation and the passion; an engraving portraying St. Jerome in his study; paintings entitled *Adoration of the Christ Child* and *Adoration of the Magi.*

W. Waetzoldt, *Dürer and His Times,* tr. R. H. Boothroyd, enl. ed. (London, [1955]); E. Panofsky, *The Life and Art of Albrecht Dürer* (Princeton, 1955); M. Brion, *Dürer: His Life and Work,* tr. J. Cleugh (New York, 1960); W. Scar, *Albrecht Dürer and the Lutheran Reformation* (BD thesis, Conc. Sem., St. Louis, Mo., 1945); H. T. Musper, *Albrecht Dürer* (New York, 1966).

Durham Cathedral. See *Church Architecture,* 7.

Durie, John (Duraeus; Duräus; Dury; 1596–1680). Scot. cleric; planned to reunite all non-RCs, esp. Luths. and Calvinists; helped draft the Westminster Confession (see *Presbyterian Confessions,* 3) and Westminster* Catechisms.

Durkheim, Emile (1858–1917). Fr. philos. Held a sociol. positivism*: Society is cen. to this philos.; truth and falsehood are objective when they express collective thought; soc. is not simply the sum of its individuals, but a kind of entity; religion is soc. activity, and its primitive form is best seen in totemism.* Works include *Les formes élementaires de la vie religieuse* (Eng. tr. *The Elementary Forms of the Religious Life); Les règles de la méthode sociologique* (Eng. tr. *The Rules of Sociological Method).*

Dury. See *Durie.*

Dutch East Indies. See *Indonesia, Republic of.*

Dutch Guiana. See *South America,* 13.

Dutch Missionary Societies. See *Netherlands,* 7; *Netherlands Lutheran Society for Home and Foreign Missions; Netherlands Missionary Society; Netherlands Missionary Union; Netherlands Reformed Missionary Association.*

Dutch Radicals. Term applied to 19th and 20th c. theologians in Holland including A. Pierson,* A. D. Loman,* and G. A. van den Bergh van Eysinga. Views of the school included the hypothesis that Jesus and Paul never lived and that no writings of the NT antedated the 2d c.

Dutch Reformed Church. See *Netherlands; Reformed Churches,* 2, 4.

Duties, Table of. See *Haustafel.*

Du Vergier de Hauranne, Jean (Duvergie[r]; Du Verger; 1581–1643). "St. Cyran." Fr. theol.; b. Bayonne; abbot Benedictine monastery of St. Cyran in the province of Berry, Fr., 1620; dir. Port* Royal 1636; friend of C. Jansen; cofounder of Jansenism.*

Dwight, Harrison Gray Otis (1803–62). B. Conway, Mass.; ABCFM miss.; traveled with E. Smith* from Malta through Asia Minor, Armenia, Persia, and back to Malta 1830–31; joined W. Goodell* in miss. at Constantinople 1832.

Dwight, John Sullivan (1813–93). B. Boston; educ. Harvard Coll. and Divinity School, Cambridge, Mass.; grad. 1836; Unitarian pastor; joined Brook Farm 1841. Est., owned, and ed. *Dwight's Journal of Music* (founded 1851, discontinued 1881).

Dwight, Timothy (1752–1817). B. Northampton, Mass.; grandson of J. Edwards* the elder; Cong. cleric and educ.; educ. Yale U., New Haven, Conn.; chaplain US army; pastor Greenfield Hill (near Fairfield), Conn.; one of "Hartford Wits," a group of literary and professional men centered in Hartford, Conn.; pres. Yale 1795–1817; poet. Works include *The Triumph of Infidelity: A Poem; Theology Explained and Defended;* hymns include "I Love Thy Kingdom, Lord." See also *New Haven Theology; Revivals.*

Dwight, Timothy (1828–1916). B. Norwich, Conn.; grandson of Timothy; Cong. cleric and educ.; pres. Yale U., New Haven, Conn., 1886; resigned 1898. Works include *Thoughts of and for the Inner Life.*

Dwinell, Israel Edson (1820–90). Prof. Pacific* School of Religion, Berkeley, Calif.; assoc. ed. *Bibliotheca Sacra.*

Dyaus Pitar. See *Brahmanism,* 2.

Dyer, Samuel (Jan. 20, 1804–1843). B. Greenwich, Eng.; LMS miss. to Malacca and Penang (1827–43). Invented movable metallic type for printing Chinese Scriptures. Helped tr. Bible into Chinese.

Dykes, John Bacchus (1823–76). B. Hull, Eng.; cleric and composer; hymn tunes include Alford, Beatitudo, Nicaea, St. Agnes, St. Cross, St. Mary Magdalene, and Vox dilecti; other works include many services and anthems.

Dylander, Johan (ca. 1709–41). B. Swed.; to Am. 1737; served Swed. chs. along the Del. 1737–41; preached in English, German, and Swedish; helped organize Ger. congs. at Germantown and Lancaster, Pa.; often preached in Episc. chs.; one of the most influential Swed. Luth. pastors in Am.

Dynamic Monarchianism. See *Monarchianism,* A.

Dynamic Psychology. See *Phychology, Dynamic.*

Dynamic Religion. See *Switzerland, Contemporary Theology in,* 3.

Dynamism (from Gk. *dynamis,* "power"). Philos. system which holds that all phenomena are manifestations of force; distinguished from mechanism.* Examples: 1. The view of Anaximenes* of Miletus (of the Ionian school of philos.) that things grow by condensation and rarefaction, or heat and cold; 2. G. W. v. Leibnitz'* explanation of substance; 3. I. Kant's* explanation of matter as forces of attraction and repulsion; 4. Arnold van Gennep's (1873–1957) description of an attitude of the savage mind toward the sacred and hidden; 5. The view of W. Ostwald,* exponent of energetics; 6. The *élan vital* (vital force) of H. Bergson* and the philos. of organism of A. N. Whitehead.*

Dyophysites (Diphysites; from Gk. *dyo,* "two," and *physis,* "nature"). Those who held that in Christ 2 natures, divine and human, coexist as expressed by the Council of Chalcedon.* Opposed the Monophysites (see *Monophysite Controversy*).

Dyothelitism (dithelitism; from Gk. *dyo,* "two," and *thelema,* "will"). The doctrine that in Christ there are 2 wills, divine and human; Christ had a human soul (Mt 26:38) and a human, but sinless, will (Mt 26:39). The doctrine was upheld by orthodox theology against monothelitism.* See also *Constantinople, Councils of,* 3.

Dyu. See *Brahmanism,* 2.

Dzu-Nowas. See *Middle East,* L.

E

"E." In Biblical criticism the letter "E" is the symbol for one of the alleged sources of the Pentateuch. See also *Higher Criticism,* 6–13.

Ea. See *Babylonians, Religion of,* 1.

Eadmer. See *Edmer.*

Eadmund. See *Edmund.*

Eagles, Fraternal Order of. Organized 1898 in Seattle, Wash., for mutual benefit, protection, improvement, and soc. enjoyment; requires belief in a Supreme Being; stresses betterment of lives. Ritual, initiation, and memorial services are set in a religious framework that promises eternal salvation in the Grand Aerie beyond to all mems. of the order. Local branches are called "aeries" and the headquarters "grand aerie." The order offers beneficial (sick and death benefits) and nonbeneficial memberships, both only on basis of initiation into the order. 1967 membership ca. 850,000. PHL

Earlier Awakening. See *Finland, Lutheranism in,* 4.

East, Liturgical. The direction of the altar from the nave of a ch. See also *Orientation of Churches.*

East and West Schism. See *Schism,* 4, 6.

East Indies. See *Indonesia, Republic of.*

East London Institute for Home and Foreign Missions. Founded 1873 in London, Eng., by H. G. Guinness* to train for. missionaries; worked esp. in Afr.; united with Livingstone Inland Mission to form The Regions* Beyond Missionary Union 1899.

East Ohio Synod of the Evangelical Lutheran Church. See *United Lutheran Church, Synods of,* 19.

East Pakistan. See *Asia,* B 2.

East Pennsylvania Synod. See *United Lutheran Church, Synods of,* 22, 23.

Easter. The day of Christ's resurrection from the dead. "Easter duty" obligates RCs to receive Holy Communion at Easter time (1st Sun. in Lent to Trin. Sun. in the US; Ash Wed. to Low* Sun. in Eng.; Ash Wed. to the octave of SS. Peter and Paul [July 6] in Ireland; 1st Sun. in Lent to the octave of the Ascension in Scot., or in some places to Low Sun.). See also *Church Year; Easter Controversy; Pasch; Sunday Letter.*

Easter Controversy. Arose from lack of uniform time of celebrating the Christian Passover. The E Ch. commemorated the death of Christ on the 14th (hence "Quartodecimans," from Lat. for "14th") of Nisan, and as a result on any day of the week; the W commemorated the death of Christ on a Fri. and the resurrection on the Sun. following. The former practice emphasized Christ's death, the latter His resurrection. The difference was discussed by Polycarp* and Anicetus.* Under Victor* I it almost led to a schism. The Council of Nicaea* declared itself against the Quartodecimans, who were henceforth treated as heretics. In the W the controversy was ended by the Syn. of Whitly.* See also *Church Year,* 7; *Polycrates; Sunday Letter.*

Easter Dates. Gregory* XIII ordered the Julian calendar revised 1582 in this way, that Thu., Oct. 4, be followed by Fri., Oct. 15, giving the month 21 days that yr.; the Eng. parliament adopted this New Style when it ordered that in 1752 Wed., Sept. 2, be followed by Thu., Sept. 14, giving the month 19 days that yr. The resultant calendar in common use among us is New Style Gregorian (see *Gregorian Calendar*), with Easter dates ("M" is March, "A" is April):

1875 M 28	1917 A 8	1959 M 29
1876 A 16	1918 M 31	1960 A 17
1877 A 1	1919 A 20	1961 A 2
1878 A 21	1920 A 4	1962 A 22
1879 A 13	1921 M 27	1963 A 14
1880 M 28	1922 A 16	1964 M 29
1881 A 17	1923 A 1	1965 A 18
1882 A 9	1924 A 20	1966 A 10
1883 M 25	1925 A 12	1967 M 26
1884 A 13	1926 A 4	1968 A 14
1885 A 5	1927 A 17	1969 A 6
1886 A 25	1928 A 8	1970 M 29
1887 A 10	1929 M 31	1971 A 11
1888 A 1	1930 A 20	1972 A 2
1889 A 21	1931 A 5	1973 A 22
1890 A 6	1932 M 27	1974 A 14
1891 M 29	1933 A 16	1975 M 30
1892 A 17	1934 A 1	1976 A 18
1893 A 2	1935 A 21	1977 A 10
1894 M 25	1936 A 12	1978 M 26
1895 A 14	1937 M 28	1979 A 15
1896 A 5	1938 A 17	1980 A 6
1897 A 18	1939 A 9	1981 A 19
1898 A 10	1940 M 24	1982 A 11
1899 A 2	1941 A 13	1983 A 3
1900 A 15	1942 A 5	1984 A 22
1901 A 7	1943 A 25	1985 A 7
1902 M 30	1944 A 9	1986 M 30
1903 A 12	1945 A 1	1987 A 19
1904 A 3	1946 A 21	1988 A 3
1905 A 23	1947 A 6	1989 M 26
1906 A 15	1948 M 28	1990 A 15
1907 M 31	1949 A 17	1991 M 31
1908 A 19	1950 A 9	1992 A 19
1909 A 11	1951 M 25	1993 A 11
1910 M 27	1952 A 13	1994 A 3
1911 A 16	1953 A 5	1995 A 16
1912 A 7	1954 A 18	1996 A 7
1913 M 23	1955 A 10	1997 M 30
1914 A 12	1956 A 1	1998 A 12
1915 A 4	1957 A 21	1999 A 4
1916 A 23	1958 A 6	2000 A 23

See also *Sunday Letter.*

Easter Duty. See *Easter.*

Eastern Canada Synod. See *Canada,* 3, 27.

Eastern Orthodox Catholic Church in America. See *Eastern Orthodox Churches,* 6.

Eastern Orthodox Churches. 1. Developed in E (Byzantine; Oriental) part of Roman Empire as distinguished from the W (Roman; Occidental) part; often referred to collectively as the Oriental Ch., Gk. Ch., Greco-Slav Ch., E Orthodox Ch., Orthodox Cath. Ch., Orthodox Cath. Ch. of the E. Ch. of the 7 Ecumenical Councils, Holy Orthodox Cath. Apostolic E Ch.; to be distinguished from Assyrian (or Nestorian; see *Nestorianism*) and Monophysite* chs. of the E.

2. *History.* Almost from the beginning a difference of opinion bet. the E and W parts of the ch. appeared which may, in part, be accounted for by differences in language and temperament. Though the E produced most of the prominent early fathers, e. g., Ignatius, Polycarp, Papias (see *Apostolic Fathers,* 2, 3, 4), Basil the Great, Gregory of Nazianzus, Gregory of Nyssa (see *Cappadocian Theologians*), Clement* of Alexandria, Origen,* Eusebius* of Caesarea, Athanasius,* John Chrysostom,* Cyril*

of Alexandria, and Cyril* of Jerusalem, and though it had the strong sees of Antioch, Jerusalem, Alexandria, and Constantinople (earlier name: Byzantium) to represent it at ecumenical councils, in the first 7 of which it largely assumed theol. leadership (see *Councils and Synods,* 4), yet its productive period did not survive the attack of Islam*; the W Ch., with only one great see, Rome, became the more influential in Christendom. Evidences of difference in spirit appeared in the Easter* Controversy and at the Council of Nicaea,* which failed to settle the Arian controversy and led to further conflict; it became more pronounced in the Iconoclastic* Controversy; it became more bitter in the Filioque* Controversy and the veiled accusation of heterodoxy attending its discussions; it culminated in the mutual recriminations and condemnations and attending declarations of excommunication in 1054 (see *Schism,* 4, 6). Meanwhile John* of Damascus, last great theol. of the E Orthodox Ch., had summed up results of labors of some of the fathers in a fairly complete system of theology. Between the 1054 schism and the fall of Constantinople 1453 there were such teachers as Theophylact* and Euthymius* Zigabenus. During this period, in the 9th and 10th c., the E Orthodox Ch. made a great conquest in the conversion of Slavs, in whose territory it has maintained itself to the present. The Russian (Bolshevik) Revolution of 1917 all but liquidated the E Orthodox Ch. in Russia. But since 1941 there has been a recovery of the ch., and the Soviet state again tolerates it. See also *Russia.*

3. *Doctrinal Position.* During the period of the first 7 ecumenical councils (see *Councils and Synods,* 4) the E Ch. was orthodox in doctrine, except for rejecting the procession of the Holy Ghost from the Father *and the Son* (see *Ecumenical Creeds,* B 1 c; *Filioque Controversy*). For almost 9 cents. after the 787 Council of Nicaea the E Ch. accepted no further symbols and made no collection representing its doctrinal position. Its chief characteristic has been a tenacious adherence to old forms. Innovations were viewed as heresies. No changes in liturgy, doctrinal formulations, and ch. polity were countenanced. This accounts for the fact that the E Ch. has not followed the RC Ch. in such innovations as priestly despotism of the penitential system, introduction of sacerdotal celibacy, and absolute supremacy and infallibility of the pope (see *Roman Catholic Confessions*). The mysteries (sacraments) are the heritage of Christ or the apostles; in them a visible sign is combined with some invisible factor; both soul and body are benefited. Christian piety is systematized. Icons are used. Intercession, invocation, and veneration of saints is taught. See also *Eastern Orthodox Standards of Doctrine.*

4. *Liturgy.* The purpose of all services, mysteries (sacraments), and sacramentals, and of the veneration of relics and icons is to unite the believer mystically with God. The belief that the sacraments impart the divine life is reflected esp. in pub. worship. Union with God is est. through visible and tangible means. The Divine Liturgy is regarded as the crowning service, because all others draw their central sanctification from it, because it was celebrated by Christ, and because it joins the believer, by communion of the body and blood of Christ, to the source of all graces. See also *Divine Liturgy.*

5. *Polity.* E Orthodox chs. are a group of self-governing chs. without centralized organization. The ancient patriarchates: Constantinople, Alexandria, Antioch, and Jerusalem; Constantinople is regarded by many as having primacy of honor. Patriarchates formed later: Bulgaria 917, Serbia (Yugoslavia) 1346, Moscow 1589, and Romania 1925. The chs. of Cyprus, Sinai, Greece, Poland, Albania, and Czechoslovakia are indep. (autocephalous*). Others (Finland, Estonia, Latvia, Hungary, China, Japan, Macedonia, 3 Russ. chs. outside Russ., Ukrainians, and Ruthenians abroad) have some self-govt. and are called autonomous, though canonically bound to a patriarchate. Bps. constitute the highest authority (singly in diocese; jointly in larger territories).

Relation to the Reformation. In the last half of the 16th c. leaders of the Luth. Ref. est. contact with the patriarch of Constantinople. A Gk. tr. of the AC sent to Joasaph 1559 apparently did not reach him. In 1569–84 D. Chytraeus* issued information on the E Orthodox Church. In 1573–81 M. Crusius,* Jakob Andreä,* L. Osiander,* and others corresponded with Jeremias* II. C. Lucaris* favored Ref. doctrine; he gathered no great permanent following. In the 2d half of the 17th c. a reaction against Protestantism set in. In the 19th and 20th cents. overtures of the Angl. Ch. to est. fraternal relations with E Orthodox Chs. have helped to break down the wall that formerly separated E Chs. from the Prot. Chs. of Europe. Some E Orthodox Chs. took part in the Faith and Order Movement and in the WCC (see also *Ecumenical Movement,* 8, 10, 11; *Union Movements,* 15). See also *Demetrius of Thessalonica.*

6. *American Eastern Orthodox Bodies.* In Am., the E Ch. is represented by the Albanian Orthodox Archdiocese in Am., ca. 62,000 (1972); Albanian Orthodox Diocese of Am., 5,000 (1972); The Am. Carpatho-Russ. Orthodox Gk. Cath. Ch., ca. 106,900 (1972); Antiochian Orthodox Archdiocese of Toledo, Ohio, and Dependencies in N. A., ca. 30,000 (1972); The Antiochian Orthodox Christian Archdiocese of N. Y. and All N. Am., 125,000 including Can. (1972); Bulgarian E Orthodox Ch. (Diocese of N. & S. Am. and Australia), 86,000 (1962); Ch. of the E (Assyrians), 3,200 (1952); E. Orthodox Cath. Ch. in Am., 275 (1972); Gk. Orthodox Archdiocese of N. & S. Am., 1,950,000 (1972); Holy Orthodox Ch. in Am. (E Cath. and Apostolic), 260 (1967); Holy Ukrainian Autocephalic Orthodox Ch. in Exile, 4,800 (1967); The Romanian Orthodox Episcopate of Am., 50,000 (1972); The Russ. Orthodox Ch. Outside Russ., 55,000 (1951); The Orthodox Ch. in Am., 1,000,000 (1972); Serbian E. Orthodox Ch. for the USA and Can., 50,000 (1963); Syrian Orthodox Ch. of Antioch (Archdiocese of the USA and Can.), 30,000 (1972); Ukrainian Orthodox Ch. of Am. (Ecumenical Patriarchate); Ukrainian Orthodox Ch. in the USA.

S. N. Bulgakov, *The Orthodox Church* [ed. D. A. Lowrie, tr. E. S. Gram] ([London] 1935); R. M. French, *The Eastern Orthodox Church* (London, 1951); *Die Orthodoxe Kirche in griechischer Sicht,* ed. P. I. Bratsiotis (Mpratsiotes), 2 vols. (Stuttgart, 1959–60); C. N. Callinicos, *The Greek Orthodox Catechism* (New York, 1953; 2d print. 1960); N. Zernov, *Eastern Christendom* (New York, 1961); D. Attwater, *The Christian Churches of the East,* rev. ed., 2 vols. (Milwaukee, 1961–62); J. Meyendorff, *The Orthodox Church,* tr. J. Chapin (New York, 1962); E. Benz, *The Eastern Orthodox Church,* tr. R. and C. Winston (Chicago, 1963); A. Schmemann, *The Historical Road of Eastern Orthodoxy,* tr. L. W. Kesich (New York, 1963); T. Ware, *The Orthodox Church* (Baltimore, 1964); D. J. Constantelos, *The Greek Orthodox Church: Faith, History, and Practice* (New York, 1967).

Eastern Orthodox Standards of Doctrine. The whole E Orthodox Ch. accepts the doctrinal decisions of the 7 oldest ecumenical councils (see *Councils and Synods,* 4). Some add the Quinisext* (ca. 691–692) and the one held 879–880 at Constantinople under Photius.* After these councils the doctrinal system in the E Orthodox Ch. remained fixed till manifestos were evoked against Romanism and Protestantism in the 17th c.

A. *Confessions Formally Endorsed.* 1. The *Orthodox Confession of the Faith of the Catholic and Apostolic Eastern Church,* written ca. 1640 by P. Mogila* as a catechism for the Russ. Ch., revised, sanctioned 1643 by a Gk. and Russ. syn., sanctioned again 1672 at Jerusalem, was a defensive measure against RCm (Jesuits*) and Protestantism (Calvinism,* promoted by C. Lucaris*; see par. C below). It treats doctrine under 3 heads: Faith (Nicene Creed), Hope (Lord's Prayer, Beatitudes) and Love (virtues, vices, and the Decalog).

2. *Decrees of the Synod of Jerusalem, or Confession of Dositheus** (1672). The 1672 syn. at Jerusalem is the most important in the modern hist. of the E Ch. and may be compared to the Council of Trent.* It issued a new *Defense,* or *Apology,* of E Orthodoxy directed chiefly against the Calvinism of C. Lucaris* and his followers. It endorsed the answers given by Jeremias* II to M. Crusius,* sanctioned the confession of P. Mogila,* and condemned that of C. Lucaris.* It consists of *Six Chapters* and *Confession of Dositheus.* The latter contains 18 decrees: (1) single procession of the Spirit; (2) Scripture not of private, but ecclesiastical interpretation; (3) double election is conditioned on man's use of his free will; (4) creation; (5) providence; (6) sin, with Christ and Mary exempt; (7) incarnation, death, resurrection, ascension, and judgment of Christ; (8) work of Christ – He is the only Mediator, but Mary, saints, and angels bring petitions to Him; (9) faith, which works by love, alone saves; (10) Cath. and Apostolic Ch. contains all believers, and bps. are necessary; (11) mems. of the ch. are those who hold the faith of Christ, apostles, and holy syns.; (12) the Cath. Ch. cannot err or be deceived; (13) man justified by faith and works; (14) in the fall man did not lose his intellectual and moral nature or free will; (15) 7 sacraments; (16) necessity and effect of Baptism; (17) Eucharist both a sacrament and a sacrifice; (18) souls of dead are either at rest or in torment (those dying in penitence but without satisfaction go to Hades, whence they may be delivered by prayers of priests, alms, unbloody sacrifice of the mass).

3. *Synods of Constantinople* (1672, 1691). The 1st adopted a statement in harmony with the *Confession of Dositheus;* the 2d condemned logothete John Caryophylles, who accepted views of C. Lucaris.*

4. *Russian Catechisms.* Platon's* Catechism shows a tendency to go directly to the Bible; Philaret's* Catechism of 1823 is one of the best summaries of E Orthodoxy.

5. *Answers of Patriarch Jeremias II of Constantinople to Lutherans.* When Jakob Andreä* and M. Crusius* sent the AC to Jeremias* II they received in his *Answers* (1576) a rejection of nearly all distinctive Luth. doctrines.

B. *Private Confessions.* 1. Of *Gennadius* II* (1453). Prepared for the Sultan after the fall of Constantinople; philos. in approach.

2. Of *Metrophanes* Kritop(o)ulos* (1625). Metrophanes was sent by C. Lucaris* to study theol. in Eng. and on the Continent; became close friend of G. Calixtus,* at whose request he prepared the confession, which opposed Romanism but was conciliatory to Protestantism.

C. *Confession of C. Lucaris** (1631); tried to graft Ref. teachings on Orthodox creeds. First 8 chaps. are Orthodox, last 10 Ref. in spirit. EL

See also *Eastern Orthodox Churches,* 3.

P. Schaff, *The Creeds of Christendom,* rev. eds., 3 vols. (New York, vol. 1 preface date 1931); W. Walther, *Lehrbuch der Symbolik* (Leipzig, 1924); C. N. Callinicos, *The Greek Orthodox Catechism* (New York, 1953; 2d print. 1960); *Die Orthodoxe Kirche in griechischer Sicht,* ed. P. I. Bratsiotis (Mpratsiotes), 2 vols. (Stuttgart, 1959–60); N. Zernov, *Eastern Christendom* (New York, 1961).

Eastern Star. See *Freemasonry,* 5.

Eastvold, Carl Johan (Mar. 19, 1863–July 23, 1929). B. Höiland, near Stavanger, Norw.; to Am. 1880; educ. Red Wing (Minn.) Sem. and Chicago Luth. Sem.; pastor Minn., Iowa, and S. Dak.; pres. Hauge* Syn. 1904–10, 1917; pres. Jewell (Iowa) Luth. Coll. ca. 1911–ca. 1912; mem. of bds. for for. missions; pres. Stavangerlag (fed. of immigrants and their descendants of the Stavanger diocese of Norw.).

Ebbinghaus, Hermann. See *Psychology,* G 4.

Ebbo. See *Ebo.*

Ebed Jesu (Abdhiso bar Berikha; ca. 1250–1318). Metropolitan of Nisibis, Armenia; one of the last prominent Nestorians (see *Nestorianism*) who wrote in Syriac. Works include *The Pearl* (a dogmatic work); poetry; catalog of Syriac authors; collection of ecclesiastical canons.

Ebel, Johann(es) Wilhelm (1784–1861). B. Passenheim, E Prussia; theosophist (see *Theosophy*); Luth. pastor Königsberg 1810; deposed 1841; found refuge with pietists in Ludwigsburg. Influenced by J. H. Schönherr*; taught pneumatologic harmony of knowledge and faith. Emphasized dualism ("light nature – darkness nature"), primary *(haupt)* and secondary *(neben)* natures. Aimed at restoration of the "divine image" and renewal of the cosmos.

Ebeling, Gerhard. See *Dogmatics,* B 13.

Ebeling, Johann Georg (1637–76). B. Lüneburg, Ger.; musical dir. and teacher at St. Nicholas Ch., Berlin; composed melodies for many of P. Gerhardt's* hymns; prof. music and Gk. at Gymnasium Carolinum, Stettin 1668. Issued *Pauli Gerhardi geistliche Andachten,* a collection of 120 sacred songs.

Ebenezer, Ga. See *Child and Family Service Agencies,* 3.

Ebenezer Society. See *Amana Society.*

Eber, Paul (1511–69). B. Kitzingen, Bavaria; educ. Nürnberg and Wittenberg; prof. Lat. 1541, Heb. 1557 Wittenberg; castle preacher, later city preacher and gen. supt. of electorate 1558; assoc. with Melanchthon; poet. Hymns include "Helft mir Gott's Güte preisen"; "Herr Gott, dich loben alle wir"; "Wenn wir in höchsten Nöten sein"; "Herr Jesu Christ, wahr'r Mensch und Gott."

C. H. Sixt, *Dr. Paul Eber, der Schüler, Freund und Amtsgenosse der Reformatoren* (Heidelberg, 1843); T. Pressel, "Paul Eber," in *Leben und ausgewählte Schriften der Väter und Begründer der lutherischen Kirche,* ed. J. Hartmann et al., VIII (Elberfeld, 1862), separate pagination 1–108; G. Buchwald, *D. Paul Eber, der Freund, Mitarbeiter und Nachfolger der Reformatoren* (Leipzig, 1897).

Eberhard II (Bp. of Bamberg). See *Adoptionism.*

Eberhard, Johann August(us) (1739–1809). B. Halberstadt, Ger.; rationalist; pastor Halberstadt 1763, Berlin 1768; prof. philos. Halle 1778. Works include *Neue Apologie des Sokrates.*

Eberhard(t) of Béthune (d. ca. 1212). B. Béthune, Fr.; teacher and literary historian of Flanders. Works include *Graecismus de figuris et octo partibus orationis,* a long Lat. poem on rhetoric, prosody, grammar, and syntax; also ascribed to him: *Liber antihaeresis,* against Cathari* and Waldenses.*

Eberhardt, Christoph Ludwig (Jan. 3, 1831–Apr. 27, 1893). B. Lauffen, Württemberg; educ. Basel Miss. Inst. (see Basel Missionary Society); to Ann Arbor, Mich., 1860 in response to F. Schmid(t)'s* plea for help; Mich. Syn. miss.; pastor St. Paul's, Saginaw, 1861; stood for sound Lutheranism; "Father of Mich. Sem."; helped found 2d Mich. Syn. and was its pres. 1881–90. See also *Michigan Synod.*

Eberhardt, Emil. See *Canada,* 11.

Eberlin, Johann (von Günzburg) (ca. 1468–1533). B. Kleinkötz, near Günzburg, Bavaria; Franciscan preacher Tübingen, Ulm, and Freiburg; gained for Reformation through Luther's writings; strove for peace and order during Peasants'* War. Works include *Wie sich ein Diener Gottes Worts in all seinem Thun halten soll.*

Eberlin, Johann Ernst (1702–62). B. Jettingen, Bavaria; composer; organist Salzburg. Works include oratorios, toccatas and fugues, masses, motets, sonatas, and preludes.

Ebert, Jacob (1549–ca. 1614). B. Sprottau, Silesia, Ger.; prof. Heb., ethics, and theol. Frankfort on the Oder; hymnist. Hymns include "Du Friedefürst, Herr Jesu Christ."

Ebionites (Heb. "poor"). Term perhaps first applied to Christians in gen., then esp. to Jewish Christians at Jerusalem (cf. Gl 2:10). Origen uses it for Jewish Christians. It was applied also to an extreme Judaistic sect of the 2d c. that gen. professed loyalty to the Torah* reinterpreted to harmonize with tenets of varying groups and that apparently practiced severe asceticism. Jesus was regarded as the Messiah but not divine, nor born of a virgin; Paul was rejected; they used a Heb. Gospel apparently based on Matthew.

Ebner, Christina (1277–1356). Of Nürnberg; not related to Margareta; prioress Dominican nunnery Engeltal, near Nürnberg; mystic, prominent in the Friends* of God movement.

Ebner, Ferdinand (1882–1931). B. Wiener Neustadt, Austria; teacher, Gablitz, Austria; exponent of an "I*–Thou" philosophy; according to his view man is a personality because he can address and be addressed by a "Thou"; for the "I" to shut itself off from the "Thou" is the essence of sin and leads to "I-loneliness." Works include *Das Wort und die geistigen Realitäten.*

Ebner, Margareta (1291–1351). Of Donauwörth; not related to Christina; Dominican mystic; lived in nunnery Medingen, near Dillingen; prominent in the Friends* of God movement.

Ebo (Ebbo; ca. 775–851). Abp. Reims 816; librarian of Louis* I (the Pious); his miss. work in Den. prepared way for Ansgar.*

Ebrard, Johann(es) Heinrich August (1818–88). B. Erlangen; educ. Erlangen and Berlin; prof. Zurich and Erlangen; held mediating position bet. orthodoxy and F. D. E. Schleiermacher*; his doctrine on the Lord's Supper and predestination tried to reconcile Luths. and Ref.; justification explained in light of regeneration.

Eccard, Johann(es) (1553–1611). B. Mühlhausen in Thüringen, Ger.; Luth. composer; pupil of O. di Lasso*; musician in household of Johann (Hans) Jakob Fugger (1516–79; patron of art; counselor of Duke Albert IV of Bavaria) at Augsburg 1578; court musician Königsberg 1579–1608, Berlin 1608–11. Works include songs, cantatas, motets, and settings for hymns.

Handbuch der Musikwissenschaft, ed. E. Bücken, vol. X: F. Blume, *Die evangelische Kirchenmusik* (New York, 1931); H. J. Moser, *Geschichte der deutschen Musik,* 3 vols. in 4 (Stuttgart, 1920—24); C. G. A. V. v. Winterfeld, *Der evangelische Kirchengesang und sein Verhältnis zur Kunst des Tonsatzes,* 3 vols. (Leipzig, 1843–47).

Eccard, Johannes (Meister Eckhart). See *Eckhart, Johannes.*

Ecce Homo (Lat. "behold the man"). Title of various representations of the suffering Jesus before Pilate as described Jn 19:5.

Ecclesia; Ekklesia. See *Church,* 2.

Ecclesia docens; ecclesia discens (Lat. "teaching church," "learning church"). RC terms for clergy *(ecclesia docens)* and laity *(ecclesia discens).*

Ecclesia plantanda (Lat. "The church must be planted"). Favorite motto of H. M. Mühlenberg.* indicating his determination to est. the Luth. Ch. in Am.

Ecclesiastical Commissions. See *Commissions, Ecclesiastical.*

Ecclesiastical Courts. See *Courts, Ecclesiastical.*

Ecclesiastical Modes. See *Modes, Ecclesiastical.*

Ecclesiastical Ordinances. Code of ch. discipline proposed by Calvin and rev. and adopted by Geneva 1541.

Ecclesiastical Polity. See *Polity, Ecclesiastical.*

Ecclesiastical Reservation. See *Augsburg, Religious Peace of.*

Ecclesiasticus. See *Apocrypha,* A 3.

Ecclesiology. 1. That part of dogmatics or doctrinal theol. which treats of the concept of the ch. chiefly according to its internal religious aspect, "the holy Christian Ch., the communion of saints." 2. Science of bldg. and decorating chs. 3. Science of ecclesiastical institutions in society. 4. Science of soc. phenomena resulting directly from religious motives.

Echo Park Evangelistic Association. See *Evangelistic Associations,* 20.

Echter, Julius, von Mespelbrunn (1545–1617). B. Mespelbrunn, Ger.; RC prince-bp. Würzburg; founded U. there; carried out Counter* Reformation with Jesuits.*

Eck, Johann (Johann Maier, or Mayer; 1486–1543). B. Eck (now Egg) on the Günz, Swabia, Ger.; d. Ingolstadt; RC controversialist; educ. Heidelberg, Tübingen, Cologne, and Freiburg im Breisgau; at Freiburg came under influence of U. Zasius*; prof. Ingolstadt 1510–43. On friendly terms with M. Luther* 1517; soon turned against him; pub. *Obelisks* against Luther's theses 1518; Luther answered with *Asterisks.* The Leipzig* Debate was a turning point in the Reformation. Eck was unsuccessful in his plan to burn Luther's books (J. Reuchlin* opposed him at Ingolstadt). Wrote *De primatu Petri adversus Ludderum* ca. 1519 and went to Rome to get papal action against Luther; Leo X (see *Popes,* 20) issued the bull* *Exsurge, Domine* (see *Reformation,* 9; *Index of Prohibited Books,* 1), which threatened Luther and others (e. g., W. Pir[c]kheimer* and L. Spengler*) with excommunication. In 1530 Eck wrote 404 articles against Luther and his co-workers and was one of the main authors of the RC *Confutatio* (see *Lutheran Confessions,* A 3). Attended various colloquies (Hagenau* 1540, Worms* 1540, Regensburg* 1541). Issued a Ger. tr. of the Bible; other works include many treatises against Luther. See also *Switzerland,* 2.

T. Wiedemann, *Dr. Johann Eck* (Regensburg, 1865).

Eckard, James Read (Nov. 22, 1805–Mar. 12, 1887). B. Philadelphia, Pa.; educ. Princeton Theol. Sem.; ABCFM miss. to Ceylon 1833–43.

Ecke, Gustav (1855–1920). B. Erfurt, Ger.; ev. theol.; prof. Königsberg 1900, Bonn 1903; followed the theol. of C. M. A. Kähler.* Works include *Die evangelischen Landeskirchen Deutschlands im neunzehnten Jahrhundert; Die theologische Schule Albrecht Ritschls und die evangelische Kirche der Gegenwart; Unverrückbare Grenzsteine.*

Eckhardt, Ernst (Mar. 26, 1868–Jan. 24, 1938). B. Frankenberg, Saxony, Ger.; to US 1884; educ. Conc. Sem., St. Louis, Mo. Pastor near Byron, Nebr., 1891–1904; Blair, Nebr., 1904–11; Battle Creek, Nebr., 1911–21. Mo. Syn. statistician 1921–38. Literary ed. *Amerikanischer Kalender für deutsche Lutheraner; Lutheran Annual.* Other works include *Homiletisches Reallexikon nebst Index Rerum.*

Eckhardt, Henry Philip (Jan 31, 1866–May 11, 1949). B. Reisterstown, Baltimore Co., Md.; educ. Conc. Sem., St. Louis, Mo. Pastor Cleveland, Ohio, 1889; joined The Eng. Ev. Luth. Syn. of Missouri* and other States 1898; pastor Jersey City, N. J., 1909; Mo. Syn. pastor Pittsburgh, Pa., 1911. Pres. The Eng. Ev. Luth. Syn. of Mo. and Other States 1905–11; Mo. Syn. Eng. Dist. 1911–12; Mo. Syn. vice-pres. 1917–26; pres. ALPB. Works include *Confirmation Booklet; The English District.*

Eckhart, Johannes (Meister Eckhardt; Eckart; Eckardt; Eccard; Eckehart; ca. 1260–ca. 1327). B. Thuringia; Ger. Dominican theol., mystic, preacher; founded Ger. mysticism and philos. language. Magister theol. Paris 1302; Dominican provincial, Saxony, 1303; vicar-gen. Bohemia, with power to reform convents 1307; taught at Paris, Strasbourg, Cologne (H. Suso* and J. Tauler* his pupils); charged at Cologne with teaching pantheism, but disclaimed it. Tried to explain the mysteries of the Trin. and the relation bet. Creator and man. Influenced by Aristotle,* Augustine* of Hippo, Neoplatonism,* Avicenna (see *Arabic Philosophy*), Thomas* Aquinas, et al. Works include *Opus tripartitum;* commentaries; sermons.

Meister Eckhart, ed. F. Pfeiffer, tr. C. de B. Evans (London, 1924); *Meister Eckhart,* tr. R. B. Blakney (New York, 1941); H. Bornkamm, *Eckhart und Luther* (Stuttgart, 1936); J. Ancelet-Hustache, *Master Eckhart and the Rhineland Mystics,* tr. H. Graef (New York, 1957); *Meister Eckhart: Die deutschen und lateinischen Werke,* pub. under auspices of Deutsche Forschungsgemeinschaft (Stuttgart, 1936–).

Eclecticism. Selecting that which seems best from various systems of religion, philos., psychol., etc. In the 1st half of the 20th c. eclectics in Am. stressed mystical and oriental religions.

Economic Determinism (Economic Interpretation of History). Philos. which holds that the economy of a society determines the course of its soc., pol., and intellectual development. See also *Marx, Karl Heinrich.*

Economic Interpretation of History. See *Economic Determinism.*

Ecstasy (religious enthusiasm*). Abnormal mental condition or state of exaltation or rapture that preoccupies mind and feelings. In the practice of some heathen religions narcotics, intoxicants, and other means are used to experience the ecstatic state. Some Christian sects use fasting, contemplation, music, psychol., emotional appeals. See also *Mysticism.*

Ecthesis (Ekthesis; Gk. "a setting forth"). Edict issued 638 by E Roman emp. Heraclius (ca. 575–641; emp. 610–641); accepted by syns. of Constantinople 638 and 639; forbade mentioning either 1 "energy" or 2 "energies" in the person of Christ; advocated monothelitism.* See also *Sergius* (d. 638).

Ectoplasm. Term used in spiritualism (spiritism*) to designate the supposed emanation from a medium.

Ecuador. See *South America,* 7.

Ecumenical Councils. See *Councils and Synods,* 4.

Ecumenical Creeds. Creeds called ecumenical: Apostles', Nicene, and Athanasian. Ecumenical means worldwide, gen., or universal. Though not all these creeds are used by all chs., they are used by chs. throughout the world.

The Apostles' Creed is characteristically Western. The Nicene Creed in its original form (without *filioque* [see *Filioque Controversy*]) is the chief confession in the E Ch. The Athanasian Creed has been in the Russ. liturgy since the 17th c. and was used for a time in the Gk. liturgy beginning 1780.

The Luth. (see *Book of Concord*), Angl. (see *Anglican Confessions,* 1), and RC Chs. (see *Roman Catholic Confessions*) have included the 3 creeds in their Confessions. But the Prot. Episc. Ch. in the US refused to include the Athanasian Creed in its liturgy 1785, 1786, 1789 (see also *Protestant Episcopal Church,* 5). The Ref. bodies, though gen. endorsing the Christological doctrines of the Nicene and Athanasian Creeds, adhered chiefly to the Apostles' Creed and inc. it in their catechisms, e. g., the Heidelberg Catechism (see *Reformed Confessions,* D 2).

A. *Apostles' Creed.* 1. This creed was not formulated by councils of theologians but grew spontaneously out of the needs of the living ch.

2. The tradition that the Creed was composed on Pent. or shortly thereafter by the 12 apostles, each contributing an article, is stated, e. g., by T. Rufinus* ca. 403 in *Commentarius in symbolum apostolorum* and in the *Explanatio symboli ad initiandos,* usually ascribed to Ambrose.* This view was embodied in the *Catechismus Romanus* (see *Roman Catholic Confessions,* A 3). Some Luths. defended the tradition. The theory was attacked by L. Valla* and D. Erasmus* and ultimately proved false on basis of intrinsic improbability, silence of the Scriptures, silence of ante-Nicene fathers, and various forms extant in the early ch.

3. The Creed grew from NT beginnings (e. g., Mt 10:32-33; Jn 1:49; 6:69; 11:27; 20:28; Acts 8:37; 14:15; 2 Co 13:14; 1 Ptr 1:2). The confession of Peter (Mt 16:16) and the baptismal formula (Mt 28:19) influenced the development of the Creed esp. More developed creedal statements are found in such ch. fathers as Ignatius of Antioch (see *Apostolic Fathers,* 2) and Justin* Martyr. For a long time the Creed was usually memorized but not written (*disciplina* arcani*). It was explained to the catechumens in the last stages of their preparation. The ante-Nicene fathers called the early forms of the Creed the "rule* of faith," "rule of truth," "apostolic tradition," and "symbol." Such "rules of faith" are mentioned by Irenaeus,* Tertullian,* Novatian,* Cyprian* of Carthage, and Origen.*

4. That the Creed developed indep. in different regions is shown by the differences existing among early creeds. The Old Roman creed read: "I believe in God the Father Almighty; and in Christ Jesus, His only (begotten) Son, our Lord; and in the Holy Spirit, the holy church, the forgiveness of sins, (and) the resurrection of the flesh." A longer form finally became standard in the West. T. Rufinus* gives a Lat. version; Marcellus* of Ancyra gives it in Gk. Later additions were made ("descended to hell" in a 4th c. creed; "catholic" from Eastern usage; "communion of saints" [see *Communio sanctorum*] in a commentary on the creed by Niceta[s]* of Remesiana) until the present form triumphed in the W (6th–8th c.) as a result of RC efforts.

5. Though secondary in the E Ch., the Apostles' Creed is a strong bond of union bet. all ages and sections of Christianity. It was highly regarded e. g. by Augustine* of Hippo, M. Luther,* and J. Calvin.* Attacking this creed is tantamount to attacking Scripture.

B. *Nicene Creed (Symbolum Nicaeno-Constantinopolitanum).* 1. Represents the E development of the baptismal formula and shows directly the results of the Arian Controversy (see *Arianism*). Three forms may be distinguished:

a. The Nicene Creed of 325 grew out of the immediate necessity of safeguarding the apostolic teaching concerning the deity of Christ against the Arian heresy. It closed with the words "and in the Holy Ghost" but added an anathema against Arians.

b. The Constantinopolitan Creed is so called because, when presented to the Council of Chalcedon* 451, is was ascribed to the 381 Council of Constantinople.* It differs slightly from the Nicene Creed of 325 and has a long 3d article asserting the true deity of the Holy Spirit.

c. The 3d form differs from the others by including the word *filioque.* The E Orthodox Ch. held to the *monarchia* ("sole rule") of the Father and the single procession of the Spirit; it differentiated the latter from the temporal mission of the Spirit from the Father and the Son. The addition of *filioque* emphasized the procession from the Father and the Son. In the 11th c. the RC Ch. added the word to the Creed; this led to the great schism* bet. E and W (see also *Filioque Controversy*).

2. The Nicene Creed, more than the Apostles' Creed, echoes sharp distinctions (e. g., "begotten, not made") drawn by the orthodox against heresies.

C. *Athanasian Creed (Symbolum Quicunque).* 1. The 3d and last of the creeds called ecumenical. Its origin is obscure. Since the 9th c. it has been ascribed to Athanasius*; this view has been contested since the 17th c. and is today rejected (early councils do not mention this creed; it was written in Lat., whereas Athanasius wrote in Gk.; it presupposes later heresies: Nestorianism,* Eutychianism*). It seems to have originated in Gaul or N Afr. as a summary of the doctrinal decisions of the 1st 4 ecumenical councils. It also seeks to state the doctrine of the Trinity* in Augustinian terms.

2. By the 9th c. this creed was in the liturgy in Ger. and was used at prime (see *Hours, Canonical*). Luther regarded it as possibly the grandest production of the ch. since the time of the apostles. EL

See also *Te Deum.*

F. J. Badcock, *The History of the Creeds,* 2d ed. (London, 1938); H. A. Blair, *A Creed Before the Creeds* (New York, 1955); A. E. Burn, *An Introduction to the Creeds and to the Te Deum* (London, 1899); J. H. Crehan, *Early Christian Baptism and the Creed* (London, 1950); O. Cullmann, *The Earliest Christian Confessions,* tr. J. K. S. Reid (London, 1949); F. W. Danker, *Creeds in the Bible* (St. Louis, 1966); P. Feine, *Die Gestalt des apostolischen Glaubensbekenntnisses in der Zeit des Neuen Testaments* (Leipzig, 1925); A. Hahn, *Bibliothek der Symbole und Glaubensregeln der alten Kirche,* ed. G. L. Hahn, 3d ed. (Breslau, 1897); F. Kattenbusch, *Das apostolische Symbol,* 2 vols. (Leipzig, 1894—1900); J. N. D. Kelly, *Early Christian Creeds,* 2d ed. (New York, 1960) and *The Athanasian Creed* (New York, 1964); H. Lietzmann, *Symbole der alten Kirche* (Bonn, 1914); P. Schaff, *Creeds of Christendom,* 3 vols., first issued 1877, vol. 1 6th ed., vol. 3 4th ed. (New York, 1919); T. Zahn, *Das apostolische Symbolum* (Leipzig, 1893).

Ecumenical Movement, The. 1. The Ecumenical Movement, a major 20th c. ecclesiastical development, is a many-sided effort to overcome existing divisions in the ch. and to manifest the unity of the ch. as the Body of Christ. It finds its text in Jesus' prayer: "that they may all be one; even as Thou, Father, art in Me, and I in Thee." (Jn 17:21)

2. Though the term "Ecumenical Movement" is applied to a 20th c. development, the phenomenon that it describes has always been present in the ch. Even before Christians were separated into major denominational families the ch. put forth considerable effort to maintain unity in the face of heresy and schism; unity was a primary purpose of the early ecumenical councils (see *Councils and Synods,* 4). After the ch. split into E and W (see *Schism,* 6) there were several unsuccessful attempts at reunion, culminating at the Council of Ferrara-Florence, 1438–39 (see *Basel, Council of*).

3. At the time of the Reformation and afterward numerous efforts to overcome resulting fragmentation of the ch. were gen. unsuccessful in healing the breach bet. RCs, Luths., Ref., and Anglicans. In 19th-c. Protestantism there were several major unitive efforts: the Prussian* Union of 1817 and other instances of Luth.-Ref. union; Angl. efforts to est. intercommunion with other chs.; voluntary movements that united Christians of all denominations increasingly interested in the miss., educ., and moral concerns of the ch.; the Evangelical* Alliance, an assoc. of individuals committed to basic ev. theol. and opposition to RCm; the formation of world fellowships.

4. In the 20th c., concern for ch. unity developed into a full-fledged, comprehensive movement that affected all chs., including those that remained outside ecumenical organizations (e. g., the RC Ch., LCMS, S Baps.). The Ecumenical Movement is composed of many movements, including efforts to unite Christians for miss. work, Christian service, and theol. discussions. It tries to bring Christians of separate denominations together in councils, agencies, and federations and achieve organic union both bet. chs. of the same denomination and bet. those of different denominations. The movement reaches also beyond ecumenical organizations into theol. dialog and other exchanges bet. local groups of Christians.

5. Impetus for the modern Ecumenical Movement can be traced to the 1910 World Missionary Conference, Edinburgh. The Ecumenical Movement arose from the miss. movement; the church's concern for miss. has nurtured the concern for unity. The Edinburgh conf. was a consultative assem. that brought together delegates of miss. socs. at work in non-Christian lands. It was the result of a demonstrated need for cooperation in carrying out the church's miss.; from it flowed 3 main streams of ecumenical activity: cooperation in missions, discussions of faith and order, and a common concern to apply the Christian faith to practical problems.

6. From a continuation committee est. by the 1910 conf. the Internat.* Missionary Council emerged 1921 under leadership of John Raleigh Mott (1865–1955), chm. of the 1910 conf. and a dominant figure in the Ecumenical Movement in its 1st decades. Composed of official representatives of miss. associations, the Internat. Miss. Council served as an agency for coordination and cooperation on miss. fields, for study of common miss. problems, and for counsel to missionaries and miss. chs. It sponsored several miss. conferences and was integrated with the WCC 1961 as its Commission on World Mission and Evangelism.

7. Episc. miss.-bp. Charles Henry Brent (1862–1929) came away from the 1910 Edinburgh conf. convinced that it was time for chs. to take up issues of faith and order in an attempt to resolve differences. Under his leadership the Prot. Episc. Ch. in the US extended an invitation to all chs. of the world to join in sponsoring a World Conference on Faith and Order. WW I and post-war problems delayed the conf., held 1927 at Lausanne. It brought together official representatives of all major denominations except RC, to discuss uniting and dividing issues for the 1st time.

8. The success of the Lausanne Conf. initiated the Faith and Order Movement, which tries to bring official ch. representatives together for systematic theol. discussion. Other world confs. on Faith and Order: Edinburgh 1937, Lund 1952, Montreal 1963. The Faith and Order Movement was absorbed by the WCC 1948. Faith and Order confs. demonstrated both how much unity in faith exists and how great the difficulty is in resolving differences in faith and order.

9. The 1910 Edinburgh conf. showed that cooperation bet. Christians is possible despite division. Some held that chs. should cooperate in areas other than miss. In 1914 threat of major war led to formation of the World Alliance for Promoting International Friendship Through the Churches. At the close of WW I this organization led the way in bringing ch. representatives together for consideration of other internat. and soc. problems. A conference on Life and Work was held 1920 Geneva. Under leadership of Luth. Abp. N. Söderblom* of

Uppsala, a Universal Christian Conference on Life and Work was held in Stockholm 1925 to encourage Christian cooperation in treating soc. ills. Under the assumption that Christians could and should cooperate in works of love and service despite differences in faith, the Universal Christian Council for Life and Work was organized a few yrs. later (name adopted 1930) to strengthen the fellowship of chs. in the application of Christian ethics to modern soc. problems. A 2d Conf. on Life and Work was held at Oxford 1937 to deal with ch-state problems.

10. It soon became evident that the Faith and Order and the Life and Work movements needed to be more closely related. Leadership in both was often the same; theol. differences often were at the root of differences in how to deal with soc. and internat. problems. Therefore the 1937 Faith and Order and Life and Work confs. recommended formation of a World* Council of Churches incorporating the activity of both movements. Delayed by WW II, the WCC came into being 1948 at Amsterdam with a membership of 147 Prot., Episc., Luth., and E Orthodox chs.

11. The WCC works through an Assem. consisting of official representatives of mem. chs. The Assem. meets ca. every 6 yrs. Assemblies since Amsterdam: Evanston, Ill., 1954; New Delhi 1961; Uppsala, Sweden, 1968. Between assemblies WCC affairs are handled by a Central Committee of ca. 100. The WCC has 3 commissions: The Commission on Faith and Order, which holds confs. for theol. discussion; The Commission of the Churches on International Affairs, which continues in a new form the work of the Life and Work movement; The Commission on World Mission and Evangelism, which incorporates the concerns and activity of the former Internat. Miss. Council.

12. The Ecumenical Movement is broader and more diverse than the WCC. It includes less official – but influential – internat. and interdenominational organizations, e. g., the Young* Men's Christian Association and the Young* Women's Christian Association, the Student* Christian Movement, and the World* Council of Christian Education and Sunday School Association. As counterpart of efforts to unite Christians in world organizations, local and nat. councils of chs. have been formed. The NCC was organized 1950, incorporating the Federal* Council of the Churches of Christ in America and other agencies of cooperation (see *Union Movements,* 13).

13. A major phase of the Ecumenical Movement is the effort to bring about organic union of separated chs. Too many mergers have taken place since 1910 to mention in detail. Merger efforts in gen. have been successful in bringing together separate chs. within a denominational family. The est. and the United Free Ch. of Scot. merged 1929; the major Meth. chs. of the US united 1939; several mergers produced The American* Lutheran Church 1960 and the Lutheran* Church in America 1962.

14. Some important mergers have crossed denominational lines. In 1925 the United Ch. of Can. resulted from mergers of 40 bodies after 19 acts of union (see *Canada,* B). In 1947 the Church* of South India was formed out of Angl., Meth., Presb., Cong., and Ev. components, a notable union because of its disposition of the episcopacy question. In Ger. in 1948 Luth., Ref., and union chs. est. a fed., the *Evangelische Kirche in Deutschland* (EKD; Ev. Ch. in Ger.), which does not, however, include intercommunion (see *Union Movements,* 8–9). In the US a Consultation on Church Union has brought representatives of major Prot. chs. together to consider organic union.

15. For decades the RC Ch. remained aloof from the Ecumenical Movement. It declined an invitation to take part in the Lausanne Conf. on Faith and Order; in 1928 Pius XI (see *Popes,* 32) stated in effect in the encyclical *Mortalium Animos* that the one way to unity was through return to the RC Ch.; RCs were forbidden to attend the Amsterdam Assem. of the WCC 1948.

16. Vatican* Council II produced a major change in attitude toward the Ecumenical Movement among RCs. John XXIII (see *Popes,* 34) stated that Christian unity was one of the major aims of the Council and invited other chs. to send official observers, calling non-RC Christians "separated brothers." Official RC observers attended the 1961 WCC Assem. at New Delhi. The Secretariat for Promoting Christian Unity, est. 1960, became an instrument for directing ecumenical discussion. As a result of the action of pope and council, RCs everywhere entered the Ecumenical Movement. Though the RC Ch. has not become part of any major ecumenical organizations, it has developed an approach to dialog with the WCC and the Lutheran* World Federation and engages in considerable dialog on a local level.

17. Involvement of the RC Ch. in the Ecumenical Movement has important implications for the future of the movement. RC participation raises new problems and new possibilities as chs. continue efforts for unity.

A History of the Ecumenical Movement, 1517–1948, ed. R. Rouse and S. C. Neill (Philadelphia, 1954); N. Goodall, *The Ecumenical Movement* (London, 1961); S. McC. Cavert, *On the Road to Christian Unity* (New York, 1961); W. R. Hogg, *Ecumenical Foundations: A History of the International Missionary Council And Its Nineteenth-Century Background* (New York, 1952) and *One World, One Mission* (New York, 1960); J. T. McNeill, *Unitive Protestantism,* rev. ed. (Richmond, Va., 1964). JHT

Ecumenicity. Conception or structure of the ch. in its universal character. Often used of interdenom. and interconfessional fellowship. See also *Ecumenical Movement, The.*

Ecumenics. Study of the nature and miss. of the ch. as a worldwide fellowship. See also *Ecumenical Movement, The.*

Eddas. Two 13th-c. collections of Icelandic mythology and legend. See also *Iceland; Sveinsson, Brynjulf.*

Eddington, Arthur Stanley (1882–1944). Eng. astronomer; prof. Cambridge 1913; dir. university observatory 1914. Known for research on motion and evolution of stars; elucidated theory of relativity; held world of physical science is a symbolic world, construction of the mind; ultimate reality is spiritual; dangerous to build a theol. on constantly changing concepts of science; positive evidence for religion is mystical. Works include *The Nature of the Physical World; Science and the Unseen World; New Pathways in Science; The Philosophy of Physical Science.*

Eddy, Mary Morse (nee Baker; 1821–1910). B. Bow, N. H.; founded Church* of Christ, Scientist; married George Washington Glover (d. 1844) 1843, Daniel Patterson 1853 (divorced 1873), Asa Gilbert Eddy (d. 1882) 1877.

Edel, Eugen (1872–1951). Leader of Pent. movement in Ger.; active in evangelistic union endeavor.

Edelmann, Johann Christian (1698–1767). B. Weissenfels, Ger.; studied theol.; developed negative attitude toward official chs.; went to Moravians at Herrnhut 1735, mystic separatists at Berleburg 1736; later became individual separatist. Taught that religion should be based on nature and reason. Works include *Die Göttlichkeit der Vernunft.*

Edersheim, Alfred (1825–89). B. Vienna; Jew converted to Christianity; studied theol. at Edinburgh and Berlin; Presb. minister 1846; Angl. curate 1875;

lecturer Oxford. Works include *The Life and Times of Jesus the Messiah.*

Edessa. City in NW Mesopotamia (now Urfa in SE Turkey in Asia); adopted Christianity before the end of the 2d c.; became a center of oriental Christian culture and theological activity. Its theol. school, est. ca. 363 and made famous by Ephraem,* furnished ministers for Mesopotamia and Persia; championed orthodoxy, though for a while after the death of Ephraem it was influenced by Arianism*; later succumbed to Nestorianism* and Monophysitism*; closed 489 by Bp. Cyrus II at the direction of Zeno (426–491; E. Roman emp. 474–491). Though Ephraem adopted many things from Origen and used allegories freely, other representatives of the school emphasized the critical and philol. aspects of exegesis. See also *Exegesis,* 4; *Schools, Early Christian,* 6.

Edict of Amboise. See *France,* 9.

Edict of Boulogne. See *France,* 9.

Edict of Fontainebleau. See *France,* 8.

Edict of Milan. See *Constantine I; Milan, Edict of.*

Edict of Nantes. See *France, 10; Nantes, Edict of.*

Edict of Poitiers. See *France,* 9.

Edict of Restitution. See *Restitution, Edict of.*

Edict of Saint-Germain. See *France,* 9.

Edict of Toleration. (1) 313. See *Constantine I; Milan, Edict of.* (2) 1781. See *Hungary; Joseph II and Josephinism; Roman Catholic Church,* D 14.

Edict of Worms. See *Worms, Edict of.*

Edification. See *Worship,* 5.

Edinburgh Bible Society. See *Bible Societies,* 4.

Edinburgh Conference. (1) 1910. Convened as World Missionary Conf.; attended by ca. 1,200 delegates of various chs. and miss. bds.; forerunner of ecumenical movement. See also *Ecumenical Movement, The,* 5. (2) 1937. Second World Conf. on Faith and Order; subjects discussed: Grace, Word of God, Communion of Saints, Ministry and Sacraments, Church's Unity in Life and Worship. See also *Ecumenical Movement, The,* 8.

Edinburgh Medical Missionary Society. Organized 1841 to encourage medical men to work with missionaries throughout the world.

Edmer (Eadmer; ca. 1060–ca. 1124). Eng. Benedictine monk, hist., and theol. Works include biographies of Anselm* of Canterbury, Dunstan, and other saints; chronicle of contemporary events (ca. 1066–ca. 1122).

Edmeston, James (1791–1867). B. Wapping, London; surveyor, architect, hymnist; joined Angl. Ch.; warden St. Barnabas Ch., Homerton, Middlesex; interested in the London Orphan Asylum; fondness for children inspired many children's hymns. Hymns include "Savior, Breathe an Evening Blessing."

Edmund (Eadmund; ca. 841–870). "The Martyr." King of E Anglia 855–870; according to legend killed in Dan. invasion for refusal to renounce Christianity.

Education, Adult. See *Adult Education; Parish Education,* H.

Education, Aims and Objectives. See *Christian Education,* G, H.

Education, Bible in. See *Adult Education; Bible Study; Christian Education,* G; *Parish Education,* H.

Education, Christian. See *Christian Education.*

Education, Evaluation of. See *Christian Education,* K; *Parish Education,* L, M.

Education, History of. See *Catechetics; Christian Education,* B–E; *Confirmation; Schools, Early Christian.*

Education, Legislation Pertaining to. See *Christian Education,* J.

Education, Philosophy of Lutheran. See *Christian Education,* G.

Education, Statistics of Lutheran. See *Christian Education,* F; *Parish Education,* D 7–9, E 10, F 4–5, G 3; *Teachers,* A 1.

Educational Agencies. See *Parish Education,* B–H.

Educational Conferences. See *Parish Education,* M 5–7; *Teachers,* A 10.

Educational Journals. See *Teachers,* A 9; *Theological Journals.*

Educational Psychology. A. 1. Educ. may be defined as man's systematic efforts to control and direct change in behavior through learning.

2. Educ. psychology* is a science in the broad sense of the word. It deals with processes involved in educ., is largely experimental in nature, and has accumulated or developed a vast store of factual knowledge, a system of fundamental principles, and a variety of techniques. Its aim is to understand, predict, and control human behavior.

3. Historically the roots of educ. psychol. lie in associationism, which explains the process of learning as the combination and recombination of elemental components of "mind-stuff." This philos., which antedates Aristotle* (e.g., Plato*), was formed, reformed, and transformed by a succession of thinkers even into the present century. J. F. Herbart,* 1st to emphasize dynamics of learning and apply mathematics to associationism in an attempt to explain learning, is often called father of educ. psychol. His theory of apperception and 5 formal steps in teaching still have considerable influence. But experimentalists (e. g., J. Dewey*) of the late 19th and early 20th c. prepared the way for a scientific approach to the study of psychology involving research and investigation of the nature and processes of learning.

4. Prominent among methods of educ. psychol. are experimentation, controlled observation, rating, testing, measuring, interviewing, clinical and case study, questionnaires, and normative developmental studies. Data obtained are, when possible, submitted to rigid statistical refinement and interpretation. Much valuable information is gleaned from laboratory studies, but many investigators prefer to study behavior in actual life situations (e.g., school and classroom).

B. *The Nature of the Human Organism.* 1. The raw material with which educ. psychologists work is the human organism. God created man a body and soul in one functional unity.

2. What we know of the soul is a matter of Scripture and faith. Since the soul is beyond reach of scientific research techniques, it is ignored by most educ. psychologists. But concern for the soul is fundamental in Christian educ.; understanding and educ. the whole man, body and soul, remains the goal.

3. Under God, man is the product of 2 determining forces, heredity and environment. Information on heredity is furnished chiefly by geneticists: psychologists also frequently investigate its effects. Psychologists concentrate most of their experimentation on the effect of environment on behavior and development, since environmental factors may be controlled and manipulated more readily. The question of the effect of environment on native abilities has provoked animated debate among scientists. For all practical purposes one may operate on the principle that heredity est. the individual's potentials, and environment determines to what degree his development will approach those potentials in any or all particulars.

4. In the fact that no 2 persons have both identical heredity and identical environment lies the basis for individual differences. Understanding and adjusting to individual differences are prime imperatives for effective educ.

5. Christian educators see the hand of God working through natural laws on finite matter. Therefore they cannot hold that one is what he is solely because of heredity and environment. God's love,

wisdom, and power to perform wonders will not be denied.

C. *Human Development.* 1. Human development involves physical, mental, emotional, soc., and spiritual growth and integration. It continues in one form or another from conception to death.

2. Postnatal growth is relatively slow in man. It is continuous, not sporadic or capricious; it proceeds at different rates from time to time. The several types of growth may occur in phases and at rates apparently independent one of another. Growth normally results in changes of behavior, at times sudden.

3. Physical growth proceeds through predictable stages, but there is no rigid timetable for such development. Individual differences are extensive and significant. Physical growth often influences children's abilities, interests, and adjustments. Such physical characteristics as body build, appearance, strength and energy levels, awkwardness, handicaps, and anomalies may seriously affect personality development. It is important that a child learns to accept himself and to be objective toward his assets and limitations. Christian educ. teaches a child to honor his body and to care for it and use it as the temple of God.

4. Mental development is very rapid in infancy and the preschool yrs. It continues more slowly into the 20s. Some yrs. later a gradual recession sets in. But not until one is well past the physiological prime of life does mental ability decrease appreciably. Then factual, technical, or cultural acumen may more than offset loss in speed of learning. This augurs well for adult educ. in advanced yrs.

5. Emotions involve the function of the entire system. The emotional development of a child depends on his physiological nature and his past experience. From an infant's original emotional state, best described as gen. excitement, develop varieties of emotional expression related to conditions of delight or distress. These are further specialized by training into definite patterns of likes and dislikes, feelings, attitudes, interests, appreciations, and soc. attitudes and motives. Emotional balance is intimately assoc. with feelings of acceptance, security, and personal worth. Successful guidance toward emotional maturity requires full cooperation of parents with school. Together they try to train a child to control his emotional life and to channel his emotional energies toward achievement of socially worthy and God-pleasing goals.

6. A newborn child is unsocial and egocentric. His 1st step toward socialization is realization of himself as apart from the gen. confused pattern of persons and things about him. At first wholly dependent on others, he becomes an increasingly indep. soc. being as he learns to recognize, communicate, cooperate, follow, and lead. His personality is turned outward, and he develops interest in and concern for others. Such soc. development is gradual and often subtle.

7. The exact nature of spiritual growth defies scientific analysis. Spiritual life is a gift of God, a work of the Holy Ghost. It is nourished by Word and Sacrament. Human agencies (parents, pastors, teachers, etc.) are frail implements in the hand of the Spirit as He works in a child faith, justification, and sanctification of life. Without such spiritual growth total development is never achieved. If a child is to mature into a happy and adjusted individual, every aspect of his personality and life must be integrated about spiritual growth, faith, and spiritual values. Christian psychologists acknowledge significance of spiritual development and in this area turn to Scripture for answers to questions. [These facts are often quoted by mems. of the LCMS in favor of its system of schools. Ed.]

D. *The Nature of Learning.* 1. When behavior is modified by structural or physiological development, maturation has taken place. When change in behavior is correlated with experience or with stimuli outside the organism, learning has occurred.

2. Learning may be cognitive, psychomotor, or affective in nature. It may be typed according to the various levels at which it occurs, often on more than one level at the same time. The most prominent explanations of learning are trial and error behavior, conditioning, insight, identification, and imitation.

3. Various experimental psychologies have offered explanations of the learning process. The 1st influential theory was the connectionism of E. L. Thorndike* and his followers. Repudiating the assoc. of ideas theory, they postulated a bond bet. stimulus and response. Three prime laws of learning were formulated: readiness, exercise, and effect. Later such explanatory terms as belongingness, impressiveness, polarity, identifiability, availability, and mental systems were added. Connectionism had immediate appeal to educators as a set of working principles that could readily be taken over into classroom methodology. Readiness, repetition, effect, drill, etc., came to be bywords in the Am. school.

4. Behaviorism rose as a revolt against structuralism and mentalistic functionalism. Under J. B. Watson,* its founder, behaviorism was thoroughly materialistic and mechanistic. The reflex and its conditioning constituted the complete and final answer to behavior. Even thought was defined in terms of bodily movement. Complex behavior was simply a chain or pattern of many conditioned responses. Laws of conditioning were laws of learning. Reinforcement insured permanence, and extinction accounted for forgetting. Many experimenters carried behaviorism forward far beyond Watson, with great influence. See also *Psychology*, J 4.

5. W. Köhler* and K. Koffka* popularized Gestalt psychology (see*Psychology*, J 5). The Gestalt and field theories emphasize the dynamic role of the whole organism reacting not to isolated stimuli but to whole situations or configurations. For the configurationists, perception, insight, goal consciousness, and goal striving are the cues to the nature of learning. The field theory has also been applied to the study of personality. See also *Psychology*, J 5.

6. Among other psychol. systems that have influenced Am. education: functionalism,* dynamic psychology,* purposivism,* personalism,* and psychoanalysis.* The influence of the latter has been most profound for its emphasis on the dynamics of the self and what it consciously or unconsciously brings to the learning situation.

7. Each of the psychologies mentioned has provided helpful facts and theory on the nature of the learning process, but no one theory is totally correct and sufficient to the exclusion of others.

E. *Conditions Favorable to Learning.* 1. Educ. psychologists have suggested certain principles or guidelines for maintaining conditions favorable to effective learning.

2. The physical nature of the school and the classroom should meet state requirements. A child learns more effectively and enjoys school much more in hygienic and pleasant surroundings conducive to and convenient for learning.

3. It appears that, barring excessive fatigue, any hour can be as effective for studies as another.

4. Readiness for school or for any phase of learning is most essential. It may depend on physical maturation, emotional and soc. development, gen. ability, previous experience, information, prerequisite skills, interests, and other factors.

5. The healthy organism profits most in learning. The school should be alert to the health needs of

pupils, esp. where health, visual, or auditory handicaps are involved.

6. Adjustment and emotional security affect learning. The school should study the personality needs of each pupil, cooperating with the home in striving for patterns of best adjustment.

7. Have a learning situation before trying to teach. Active interest and attention are essential to almost all learning activities in school.

8. Effective learning depends on clear initial impressions. Be definite, clear, concise, patient, and sympathetically understanding and helpful.

9. Appeal to as many avenues of sense impression as possible. Use visual and auditory aids as well as active and concrete experience.

10. Be guided by psychol. considerations rather than simply by logical order in presenting new material.

11. When possible, the learning material should be arranged and presented in a form or system. Unit organization is most helpful. This applies also to teaching religion.

12. Except for lengthy passages of difficult material, the whole method of memorizing seems better for brighter and experienced pupils. In certain cases the part method may be more effective.

13. Occasionally it may be better to begin with the unknown and proceed to the known, though the opposite is a good gen. rule. Spontaneous interest is often aroused by the unknown. When ability to recognize or cope with the unknown depends on previously learned skills or facts, it may be mandatory to proceed from the known to the unknown.

14. At times it may be advantageous to proceed from the complex to the simple, though the opposite is gen. indicated.

15. Encourage such pupil activity as laboratory exercises, field trips, class discussions, and group planning and execution of projects. Children learn best by doing.

16. Active rehearsal of material to be mastered will facilitate learning and enhance retention. Free and spontaneous class discussion provides opportunity for active rehearsal and review.

17. Mastery of techniques is characteristic of certain studies. Meaningful drill based on individual need may precede and accompany the study of subjects that require application of definite skills. Practice must be motivated, controlled, and reinforced.

18. Distribution of practice into several short periods is more effective than the same amount of practice confined to one long period. Avoid fatigue.

19. Individual differences among pupils demand adjustments to individual needs, interests, and capacities. Independent study and homogeneous grouping should be used when applicable. Suitable tests should be used for diagnostic and remedial purposes.

20. Cooperative learning can be very beneficial. Pupils should have opportunity to plan and to learn together in both homogeneous and heterogeneous groupings. Such groupings should always be flexible.

21. Encourage self-discipline in the interest of the group. Rules should be few, clear, and consistently enforced. Enforced discipline should not be lacking where self-discipline is not forthcoming. Imposed discipline should be ev. motivated; careful applications of both Law and Gospel are necessary.

22. Motivation can hardly be overestimated. Motives initiate, sustain, and direct activity toward goals. Intrinsic motivation, derived from pleasure in the task itself, is a powerful, self-sustaining drive to learning. Extrinsic motivation, derived from interest in the goal, reward, or other consequence outside the activity itself, may also be used; in fact, it may be necessary until intrinsic motivation can take over.

23. Effectiveness of reward and punishment varies with the situation, the child, and the way the matter is handled. Whenever positive incentives (praise or reward) are used, they should never be allowed to replace the real goal for children. Neither should children be trained to expect punishment or reward and to live accordingly.

24. Knowledge of one's progress can be an incentive to learning. If grades are used, they should be given and interpreted objectively. Children should be trained in objective self-evaluation.

25. Since motivation involves goal striving, pupils should be helped to see purpose in learning activity. Such purposes relate to the objectives of educ. It is most helpful to express educ. objectives in terms of anticipated behavioral outcomes.

26. Some useful things may be learned incidentally or accidentally, but the teacher should not rely on this. Incidental or accidental learning may be the source of spontaneous interest but may also lead to error, misfortune, bad habit, and later unpleasantness.

27. The school should not foster individual rivalry bet. pupils to stimulate learning. Group competition (characterized by fair play and brotherly consideration) and competition with one's own previous achievement are stimulating and valuable.

28. Recent experimentation has proved the value of electronic devices, television, teaching machines, programmed instruction, and team teaching in educ. Schools should make increasing use of them, but they must be recognized simply as valuable aids to teaching. Such devices and techniques will never replace a good, effective classroom teacher.

29. To insure transfer of training in schoolwork or transfer of learning to life, the school should teach for transfer. Also the religious training of children should be life-related and must be taught for transfer.

30. Teach children how to study. Allow for a good measure of initiative, creativity, and freedom in work. Encourage productivity.

31. Though children should be taught to be realistic and to expect normal frustrations and difficulties in life, they should be trained to the habit of success. Children should be taught to view their successes and legitimate mistakes and failures objectively.

32. Attitudes and values should be deliberately cultivated. Though they may be acquired by the pupil in various ways, the school should not leave it to chance. A Christian school, working with a Christian home, will strive purposefully to impart God-pleasing attitudes and values.

33. A Christian child's predominant motive in school and in life gen. should be love for God and love for his fellowman.

34. The school has become the great coordinator of various educ. influences that confront the modern child. But no agency can relieve parents of their God-given responsibilities for training their child.

F. *Educational Psychology and the Work of the Church.* The ch. has much to gain from encouraging and sponsoring scientific study of teaching, learning, and measurement, esp. in the area of religious growth. No man can directly observe, much less measure, the spiritual life of another, but helpful inferences may be drawn from a careful study of what it produces. Faith and new life are the work of the Spirit, but there is also a human element in religious training. In order more thoroughly to eliminate human error and interference in Christian educ. and to improve its own educ. programs and techniques, the ch. welcomes scientific study of human development and learning.

See also *Psychology.*

H. W. Bernard, *Psychology of Learning and Teaching,* 2d ed. (New York, 1965); M. L. Bigge,

Learning Theories for Teachers (New York, 1964); L. J. Cronbach, *Educational Psychology,* 2d ed. (New York, 1963); K. C. Garrison, A. J. Kingston, and A. S. McDonald, *Educational Psychology,* 2d ed. (New York, 1964); H. J. Klausmeier, *Learning and Human Abilities: Educational Psychology* (New York, 1961); M. R. Loree, *Psychology of Education* (New York, 1965); J. M. Sawrey and C. W. Telford, *Educational Psychology,* 2d ed. (Boston, 1964); L. M. Smith and B. B. Hudging, *Educational Psychology* (New York, 1964); H. Sorenson, *Psychology in Education,* 4th ed. (New York, 1964); J. M. Stephens, *The Psychology of Classroom Learning* (New York, 1965). EEY

Edward VI. See *England,* B 4.

Edwardian Theory of the Atonement. See *New England Theory of Atonement.*

Edwardine Articles. See *Anglican Confessions,* 5.

Edwards, Jonathan (the Elder; 1703–58). B. E. Windsor, Conn.; pastor Northampton, Mass.; led revivals of 1734 and 1740; miss. to Indians and Cong. pastor, Stockbridge, Mass., 1751; wrote his most important works there; pres. Coll. of N. J. (now Princeton U.) 1757. Writings defended Calvinism* against Arminianism,* opposed Half-Way* Covenant, defended New Eng. revivals, and initiated the New* Eng. Theol. See also *Great Awakening in England and America.*

The Works of President Edwards, 1st Am. ed., 8 vols. (Worcester, Mass., 1808–9); A. Miller, *Jonathan Edwards,* in *American Biography,* ed. J. Sparks, I (New York, 1902); D. J. Elwood, *The Philosophical Theology of Jonathan Edwards* (New York, 1960); L. Howard, *"The Mind" of Jonathan Edwards: A Reconstructed Text* (Berkeley and Los Angeles, 1963).

Edwards, Jonathan (the Younger; 1745–1801). B. Northampton, Mass.; son of Jonathan (the Elder); pastor; pres. Union Coll., Schenectady, N. Y., 1799–1801; held governmental theory of atonement (see *Atonement, Theories of,* 5). See also *New England Theology,* 4.

Edzard(us) (Edzardi). 1. *Ezra* (Esra; Esdras; 1629–1708). Ger. orientalist; active in miss. to Jews. 2. *Sebastian* (d. 1736). Son of Ezra; with his brother Georg continued the miss. work of their father.

Eekhof, Albert (1884–1933). B. Steenwijk, Neth.; Ref. pastor Diemen 1910; prof. ch. hist. Leiden 1924. Works include *De Hervormde Kerk in Noord-Amerika (1624–1664).*

Eerdmanns, Bernardus Dirks (1868–1948). Semitic scholar; prof. Leiden 1898. Wrote numerous books on OT.

Efficient Cause. See *Cause,* 3.

Egbert (ca. 639–ca. 729). B. Northumbria; monk and bp. Lindisfarne; to Ireland; helped organize evangelization of Ger. See also *Suidbert.*

Egede. 1. *Hans Povelsön* (Povelsen; Poulsen; Paulsen; Pavelsen; 1686–1758). "Apostle of Greenland; Apostle of the Eskimos." B. Trondenes, near Harstad, on E Hinnöy of the Vesteraalen group of islands, N Norw.; d. Stubbeköbing, on Falster Is., Den.; educ. Copenhagen; Luth. pastor Vaagen, on one of the Lofoten Is.; to Greenland 1721, intending to evangelize descendants of early Norse settlers; found only Eskimos; miss. Greenland till 1736; tr. SC; assisted by Albert Topp 1723, and soon thereafter by others, including his own sons Paul and Niels and a native worker; to Copenhagen 1736, to head a Greenland miss. training sem.; supt. (or bp.) Greenland 1740; to Stubbeköbing 1747; buried Copenhagen.

2. *Paul* (1708–89). Son of Hans; succeeded his father in the Greenland miss. and as dir. of the sem.; completed the Innuit (Eskimo) version of the NT.

L. T. A. Bobé, *Hans Egede: Colonizer and Missionary of Greenland* (Copenhagen, 1952); E. N. Rolfsrud, *White Angakok: Hans Egede and the Greenlanders* (Rock Island, Ill., 1952).

Eginhard. See *Einhard.*

Egippius. See *Eugipius.*

Egli, Emil (1848–1908). Swiss Ref. theol.; pastor; prof. ch. hist. and archaeol. Zurich; cofounder of *Zwingliana* 1897 (periodical devoted to study of H. Zwingli* and Swiss Reformation). Ed. *Aktensammlung zur Geschichte der Zürcher Reformation in den Jahren 1519–1533.*

Egli, Henry (Egly; 1824–90). B. Baden, Ger.; to US 1837; Amish Mennonite pastor 1854; bp. 1858; organized Defenseless Mennonite Ch. ca. 1865 (later called Conf. of the Ev. Mennonite Ch.). See also *Mennonite Churches,* 3 a.

Egli, Raphael (Eglinus Iconius; 1559–1622). Swiss Ref. theol.; prof. NT Zurich 1592; prof. theol. Marburg 1606.

Ego. 1. *Empirical:* self conceived as series of conscious acts and contents. 2. *Pure:* non-empirical; e. g., the soul theory that regards the pure ego as a permanent spiritual substance, and the transcendental theory that considers the self an inscrutable subject. 3. In S. Freud,* the *ego* is a narrower region than the *id,* which is the unconscious region in which basic instincts jostle together with no sense of order or value. The *ego* aims at self-preservation and maintains contact with the external world. The *superego* is the deposit of parental influences of childhood. 4. Ethical egoism holds that each individual should seek his own welfare. 5. Psychological egoism holds that the determining motive of voluntary action is concern for one's own welfare. See also *Psychology,* J 7. EL

Egranus, Johannes Wildenauer (Sylvius; d. 1535). Follower of M. Luther*; broke with him on the doctrine of justification, Lord's Supper, free will; regarded D. Erasmus* highly; held fast to the unity of the ch.

Egypt. *Area* (1965): 386,198 sq. mi. *Pop.* (1965 est.): ca. 29,600,000; Islam* is the state religion (ca. 91% of the people are Muslim); most of the rest are mems. of the Coptic* Ch.; there are 161,347 RCs (1965), some Orthodox, and other Christians. Ruled by Gt. Brit. 1882–1922, then indep.; army forced King Faruk I to abdicate 1952; Egypt became a rep. 1953. Feb. 1, 1958, the United Arab Rep. was formed by Egypt and Syria, with Yemen as a federated mem. Syria withdrew Sept. 30, 1961; Yemen Dec. 26, 1961.

Christianity probably came to Egypt in the 1st c. Angl. (CMS) work began 1825 in hope of cooperation with the Coptic* Ch. but was given up 1862–82. Key miss. in developing CMS work in the early 20th c.: W. H. Temple Gairdner.* The United Presb. Miss. (also called Am. Miss.), which built on work begun 1854 by the Assoc. Ref. Syn. of the W (see *Associate Reformed Church*), won many converts among Copts. From it grew the Coptic Ev. Ch. in the Nile Valley, which became autonomous 1958.

Eur. Luths. began pastoral, hosp., and miss. work chiefly in Alexandria and Cairo in the late 1850s.

The Egypt Gen. Miss. (originally Egypt Mission Band), organized on the initiative of Annie Van Sommer, began work 1898. Home for girls, hosp. and dispensary, and the Nile Mission Press, also called Arabic Christian Publishers, are outgrowths of Van Sommer's work. After Egypt seized the Suez 1956 the name Egypt Gen. Miss. was changed to Middle* East Gen. Miss.; its Brit. workers were transferred to Lebanon, then to Eritrea; the Nile Miss. Press moved to Beirut; the US Council of the miss. continued work with non-Brit. missionaries under the name Egypt Gen. Miss.; use of this name continued also after the miss. merged with Unevangelized* Fields Miss. at the end of 1964. Other miss. include Bap. and Assemblies of God.

The Egypt Inter-Mission Council, formed 1921 by 14 for. miss. societies, ceased activity 1956 except some welfare work. The Near* East Council of Chs., founded 1927 as Near East Christian Council (name changed 1964), also known as Council for Western Asia and Northern Africa, is active in Egypt. EL

See also *Missions, Bibliography.*

Egypt General Mission. See *Middle East General Mission.*

Egypt Inter-Mission Council. See *Egypt.*

Egyptian Mysteries, See *Mystery Religions.*

Ehrenberg, Friedrich (1776–1852). B. Elberfeld, Ger.; Ref. pastor; confidant of Frederick William III, but opposed him in Agenda* Controversy.

Ehrenfels, Maria Christian Julius Leopold Karl v. (1859–1932). B. Rodaun, Austria; prof. philos. and psychol. Prague; helped introd. the term *Gestalt* into psychol. (see also *Educational Psychology,* D 5; *Psychology,* J 5). Held that desire is fundamental in valuation and sought to trace the way in which desires and motives produce values. Works include *Über Gestaltqualitäten; System der Werttheorie.*

Ehrhard, Albert (1862–1940). B. Herbitzheim, Alsace; RC hagiographer and patristic scholar; taught ch. hist. at Strasbourg 1889, Würzburg 1892, Vienna 1893, Freiburg 1902, Strasbourg 1903, Bonn 1920. Works include *Liberaler Katholizismus?*

Ehrle, Franz (1845–1934). B. Isny, Württemberg; RC hist.; prefect of Vatican library; with H. S. Denifle* started *Archiv für Litteratur- und Kirchengeschichte des Mittelalters;* pioneer in scientific study of the hist. of Scholasticism.*

Eich, Friederich. See *New Guinea,* 5.

Eichelberger, Lewis (Aug. 25, 1801–Sept. 16, 1859). B. Frederick Co., Md.; educ. at the Gen. Syn. theol. sem. at Gettysburg, Pa.; pastor Winchester, Va.; principal of women's sem. there; prof. S. C. Syn. theol. sem., Lexington, S. C.

Eichhorn. 1. *Albert* (1856–1926). B. Garlstorf, near Lüneburg, Ger.; prof. ch. hist. Halle 1888, Kiel 1901. Helped found *Religionsgeschichtliche* Schule.* 2. *Johann Gottfried* (1752–1827). B. Dörrenzimmern, Württemberg, Ger.; Prot. theol.; hist.; educ. Göttingen; prof. oriental languages Jena 1775, philos. Göttingen 1788. See also *Higher Criticism,* 12. 3. *Karl.* See *Germany, Lutheran Free Churches in,* 9.

Eichmann, Eduard (1870–1946). B. Hagenbach, Ger.; RC hist. and canonist; specialized on the relationship of ch. and state in the Middle Ages. Works include *Lehrbuch des katholischen Kirchenrechts auf Grund des Codex iuris canonici.*

Eidetic Science. Term used by E. Husserl* to denote a knowledge of universal essences.

Eielsen, Elling (1804–83). B. Voss, Norw.; Luth. lay preacher in Norw. and elsewhere in Scand. 1832–39; to Am. 1839; ordained 1843 by F. A. Hoffmann*; helped organize the Eielsen* Syn.; its pres. 1846–83. Works include a catechism.

Eielsen Synod (The Ev. Luth. Ch. in [or of] Am.; also called Elling Syn.; Ellingian Syn.; Ellingianerne). Organized 1846 at Jefferson Prairie, Wis., by E. Eielsen* and others. The constitution, written by Eielsen and adopted April 13–14, made proof of conversion a condition of membership. In 1875–76 changes in emphasis led to revision of the constitution and change of name to Hauge's Norw. Ev. Luth. Syn. in Am. In 1876 a separation occurred, Eielsen and his followers reorganizing under the old constitution and name. The syn. disbanded 1965. See also *Evangelical Lutheran Church, The,* 5–6, 12; *Hauge Synod.*

Eifrig, Charles William Gustav (Sept. 23, 1871–Nov. 1, 1949). B. Waldheim, Ger.; to Am. 1878; educ. Fort Wayne, Ind., and St. Louis, Mo.; pastor McKees Rocks, Pa., 1895–99, Cumberland, Md., 1899–1903, Ottawa, Ont., Can., 1903–9; president of Can. Dist. of the Mo. Syn. 1906–09; prof. natural science at the Addison (Ill.) Teachers Sem. and Conc. Teachers Coll., River Forest, Ill. (see *Teachers,* A 5), 1909–42. Works include *Our Great Outdoors,* 2 vols.

Eigenkirche. In Germany, a ch. in which the local ruler or owner, spiritual or secular, appointed the clergy. See also *Investiture, Struggle About.*

Ein' feste Burg ("A Mighty Fortress"). "Battle Hymn of the Reformation"; written by M. Luther. See also *Amsdorf, Nikolaus von; Luther, Martin,* 15.

Einarsson, Gissur (Gizur; ca. 1508–48). First Luth. bp. of Iceland 1540–48; attended cathedral school, Skalholt; Ögmundur Palsson, RC bp. Skalholt, sent him to Ger. for further study; attracted to Lutheranism, but did not tell Palsson, who approved the election of Einarsson as his successor; went to Den. and received consent of Dan. king for Luth. ordination; on Einarsson's return, Palsson was arrested and taken to Den., dying perhaps en route; Einarsson was ordained in Copenhagen 1542; energetic, an efficient administrator, and poet. SP

Einhard (ca. 770–840). Confidant and biographer of Charlemagne*; architect; abbot.

Einsiedeln, Abbey of. See *Meinrad; Pilgrimages,* 4; *Switzerland,* 2.

Einstein, Albert (1879–1955). B. Ulm, Ger.; naturalized Swiss at 15; prof. Zurich 1909–11, Deutsche U., Prague, 1911–12, Berlin 1914; adopted Ger. citizenship; to US 1933; mem. Inst. for Advanced Study, Princeton, N. J., 1933–45; naturalized Am. Contributions to science include special (1905) and gen. (1916) theory of relativity; formula for laws of gravitation and electromagnetism; formula for Brownian movement; law of photoelectric effect. Held the external world can only be grasped by speculative means since sense-perception gives only indirect information of it. Distinguished 3 stages in religious development: anthropomorphic, moral, and stage of "cosmic religion"; the last is the belief that the world is rationally ordered and that God is impersonal. Judaism, he held, is no transcendent religion; its God is "negation of superstition." Works include *The World As I See It.* See also *Time.*

Eire. See *Ireland.*

Eiriksson, Magnus (1806–81). B. Iceland; educ. Copenhagen; private tutor in Copenhagen; Unitarian; engaged in bitter polemics against H. L. Martensen.*

Eisegesis. Opposite of exegesis.* Reading thoughts into a text (as of the Bible) rather than drawing thoughts from it.

Eisenacher Bund. Founded 1902 as Eisenacher Konferenz by G. Lepsius,* S. Keller,* and T. Jellinghaus.* A. Schlatter,* M. Kähler,* and others joined the movement. Original purpose was to foster fellowship. Became Eisenacher Bund 1905; opposed sectarianism* and modernism.*

Eisengrein. 1. *Martin* (1535–78). Originally ev.; RC ca. 1558; leader of Counter* Reformation in Bavaria. 2. *Wilhelm* (1534–84). RC ch. hist.; nephew of Martin; wrote against Magdeburg Centuries of M. Flacius* Illyricus.

Eisenmenger, Johann Andreas (1654–1704). B. Mannheim, Ger.; prof. oriental languages Heidelberg. Ed. unpointed OT 1694 with J. Leusden; other works include *Entdecktes Judenthum* (tr. J. P. Steckelin, *The Traditions of the Jews*).

Eissfeldt, Carl. See *Associated Lutheran Charities.*

Eitzen, Paul von (1522–98). Educ. Wittenberg and Rostock; friend of M. Luther* and P. Melanchthon*; Gen. Supt. Schleswig. In 1574 introd. Gottorper ordination oath, which pledged loyalty to AC, Ap, Luther's Catechism, and SA; rejected FC for personal reasons.

Ekklesia. See *Church,* 2.

Eklund. 1. *Johan Alfred* (1863–1945). Swed. Luth. pastor, teacher, bp., and hymnist. 2. *Pehr Gustav*

(1846–1911). Prof. Lund. Works include *Den apostoliska tron i M. Luthers katekesutläggning.*

Ekman. 1. *Erik Jakob* (1842–1915). Swed. state ch. pastor 1864–79 under influence of J. T. Beck*; became supporter of P. P. Waldenström*; left state ch. after being reprimanded for refusing to confirm non-spiritually-minded children; active 1879–1904 in Svenska Missionsförbundet (see *Swedish Missionary Societies*); held Ref. view of Lord's Supper; later rejected infant baptism and doctrine of eternal punishment, resigned from leadership of Svenska Missionsförbundet, and became dir. of a life insurance assoc. 2. *Johan August* (1845–1913). Swed. Luth. theol.; prof. OT Uppsala; bp. Västeraas 1898, abp. 1900.

Ekong, Jonathan Udo. See *Africa,* C 14.

Ekthesis. See *Ecthesis.*

El. See *Canaanites, Religion of.*

El Salvador. See *Central America,* A, F.

Élan vital. See *Bergson, Henri.*

Elberfeld Mission Society. See *Rhenish Mission Society.*

Elbogen, Ismar (1874–1943). B. Schildberg, Poland; Ger. Jewish theol.; to Am. 1938. Works include *Der jüdische Gottesdienst in seiner geschichtlichen Entwicklung; Geschichte der Juden seit dem Untergang des jüdischen Staates* (tr. A. I. Shinedling, *History of the Jews After the Fall of the Jewish State*); *A Century of Jewish Life,* tr. M. Hadas.

Elbrecht, Paul George (Sept. 30, 1921–Jan. 16, 1972). B. Cleveland, Ohio; educ. Conc. Sem., Springfield, Ill.; pastor Lubbock, Tex., 1954–58; taught at Conc. Sem., Springfield, Ill., 1958–66. Pres. Ala. Luth. Academy and Coll., Selma, Ala., 1966–70; Conc. Luth. Coll. of Tex., Austin, Tex., 1970–72. Works include *The Christian Encounters Politics and Government.*

Elders. 1. Term derived from OT and NT (Ex 3:16; Lk 7:3). The Gk. word *presbyteros* ("elder") in the NT is a synonym for "bishop (overseer)" (Acts 20:17, 28), "ruler" (1 Ti 5:17), "pastor (or shepherd)" (1 Ptr 5:1-4). Large congs. had a number of presbyters or elders (Ja 5:14; Jerusalem Acts 15:4, 6, 23; 21:18; Ephesus Acts 20:17, 28). At least some elders preached and taught (1 Ti 5:17). In course of time differences in rank were introd. into ch. offices, with elders in the lower ranks.

2. In the modern ch., eldership is characteristic of Presb. chs., which derive their name from this institution. Two classes of elders, teaching and ruling, are distinguished. The former are the pastors; the latter are laymen set apart as assistants to pastors in overseeing and ruling the congs. Pastor and ruling elders form the "session," lowest of the ruling powers of the ch.; the Gen. Assem., composed of representatives of elders and pastors, is the highest legislative body of the ch. See also *Polity, Ecclesiastical,* 7; *Reformed Churches,* 1.

3. In the Luth. Ch. the terms "elders" and "deacons*" are often used synonymously with reference to laymen chosen by a cong. for a specified term to assist the pastor in his official duties. They and the pastor form the Board of Elders; with reference to the cong. they have only advisory or executive, not legislative, power. The office of trustee is often united with that of elder, trusteeship being prescribed by law when congs. are inc. Duties of trustees concern property management and maintenance.

Eleatic School. Gk. school of philos. at Velia (or Elea), S It.; founded, according to tradition, by Xenophanes*; Parmenides* and Zeno* were among its leaders. It held that the world is in a state of rest, not motion; being is real and eternal.

Election. See *Chicago Theses; Predestinarian Controversy; Predestination.*

Electors. See *Diet.*

Eleemosynary Agencies. See *Charities, Christian.*

Elementary Education. See *Christian Education; Parish Education.*

Elements, Heavenly and Terrestrial. See *Grace, Means of,* IV 4.

Elephantine Papyri. Found toward the end of the 19th and early in the 20th c. at Elephantine, an is. in the Nile, Upper Egypt; date from the 5th c. BC; furnish information on a syncretistic Jewish colony.

Elert, Werner (1885–1954). Ger. historical and systematic theol. B. Heldrungen; d. Erlangen. Educ. Breslau, Erlangen, Leipzig, 1906–12; pastor and army chaplain 1912–19; dir. Old Luth. free ch. sem. Breslau 1919–23; prof. Erlangen 1923.

Made Erlangen world-famous center of neo-Lutheranism. Though critical of classical Luth. dogmaticians including P. Melanchthon,* Elert regarded M. Luther,* the Confessions, and classical dogmaticians as being essentially in harmony. His theol. is oriented in the ev. thought of Luther and in the dialectic of Law and Gospel. Though Luth. and confessional (often called *Lutheranissimus*), he was in constant dialog with his age and emphasized the task of theol. and the ch. in the contemporary world. He based his findings on thorough Biblical and hist. research.

Works include *Der Kampf um das Christentum; Der christliche Glaube; Das christliche Ethos* (tr. C. J. Schindler, *The Christian Ethos*); *Morphologie des Luthertums,* 2 vols. (Vol. I tr. W. A. Hansen, *The Structure of Lutheranism*); *Abendmahl und Kirchengemeinschaft in der alten Kirche, hauptsächlich des Ostens* (tr. N. E. Nagel, *Eucharist and Church Fellowship in the First Four Centuries*); *Zwischen Gnade und Ungnade: Abwandlungen des Themas Gesetz und Evangelium; Der Ausgang der altkirchlichen Christologie,* ed. W. Maurer and E. Bergsträsser.

Beiträge zur historischen und systematischen Theologie: Gedenkschrift für D. Werner Elert, ed. F. Hübner, W. Maurer, E. Kinder (Berlin, 1955). EL

Elevation. Ceremony of elevating the consecrated elements in the celebration of Holy Communion; may occur several times in a service; the term usually refers to elevation after consecration of each element. The practice was inst. in the 13th–14th c. M. Luther* permitted the practice to continue for the sake of the weak *(um der Schwachen willen),* because it could have a good meaning (WA 54, 163). In 1542 he did not oppose abolishing elevation in Wittenberg (he did not want to oppose J. Bugenhagen*), though personally he would rather have had it retained (WA 54, 122). In 1544 he favored retention of it as witness against sectarians who denied the Real* Presence (WA 54, 162–167). Many 16th c. orders retained the practice. Today most Luth. chs. do not follow it. Luths. who retain it regard it as a visible witness to the church's faith that the consecrated bread and wine are the body and blood of Christ (see also *Grace, Means of,* IV 3). EFP

Elgar, Edward (1857–1934). Eng. RC composer; organist St. George's Ch., Worcester. Works include *Pomp and Circumstance,* a march; oratorios: *The Apostles; The Kingdom.*

Elias. 1. *of Cortona* (ca. 1180–1253). B. near Assisi, It.; d. Cortona, It.; studied law; early companion of Francis* of Assisi; 1st Franciscan provincial of Syria 1219; vicar of the order 1221; gen. of the order 1232; deposed and banished 1239. 2. *Levita.* See *Levita, Elijah.*

Eligius. See *Eloi.*

Elijah Muhammad. See *Lost-Found Nation of Islam in the Wilderness of North America, The.*

Eliot, Charles William (1834–1926). B. Boston, Mass.; educ. Harvard U., Cambridge, Mass.; asst. prof. Harvard 1858–63, prof. (Cambridge) Mass.

Inst. of Technology 1865–69; pres. Harvard 1869–1909; made divinity school nonsectarian. Works include *The Religion of the Future;* ed. *Harvard Classics.*

Eliot, John (1604–90). "Apostle to the Indians" of N Am.; b. Eng.; Puritan; to Am. 1631; teacher in the ch. at Roxbury, Mass. 1632; first preached to Indians in their own tongue 1646; his Mahican Bible (NT 1661, OT 1663) was the 1st Bible pub. in Am.; founded 13 chs. (no. of converts est. 1674: ca. 4,000); educ. many native workers, including 24 preachers; received financial help from a miss. corporation in Eng.; many results of his work destroyed by King Philip's War (1675–76; named after Indian chief Philip, son of Massasoit).

Missionary Explorers Among the American Indians, ed. M. G. Humphreys (New York, 1913), pp. 1–28; W. G. Polack, *John Eliot: The Apostle to the Indians* in *Men and Missions,* ed. L. Fuerbringer, I (St. Louis, 1924); J. T. Adams, "John Eliot," *Dictionary of American Biography,* ed. A. Johnson and D. Malone, VI (New York, 1943), 79–80.

Eliot, Thomas Stearns (1888–1965). Am.-born Brit. poet, dramatist, ed., pub., essayist, pol. lecturer. B. St. Louis, Mo.; d. London; buried E Coker, Somerset, home of his ancestors; grandson of W. G. Eliot*; educ. Smith Academy (a dept. of Washington U., St. Louis), Milton (Mass.) Academy, Harvard, the Sorbonne, Ger., and Oxford; London resident 1914; Brit. subject 1927.

Eliot became major influence in modern poetry through pub. of *The Waste Land* 1922. Voiced concern over depressing situation of modern man: his aimlessness, maladjustments, frustrations, and lack of faith.

Eliot's belief that the only way out of the "waste land" is Christianity moved him to join the Ch. of Eng. 1927. *Ash-Wednesday* (1930) portrays his religious beliefs. In it he describes the progress from disillusionment to faith, from hopelessness to hope, but not a hope for pol. and soc. progress.

An excellent craftsman, Eliot adapted the poetic technique begun by the Fr. symbolists Charles Pierre Baudelaire (1821–67), Stéphane Mallarmé (1842–98), and Jules Laforgue (1860–87); shows influence of Dante,* J. Donne,* and Ezra Loomis Pound (b. 1885); influential in reviving verse plays.

In his *Weltanschauung* the pessimism and agnosticism of the post-WW I generation gives way to Christian faith.

Works include *The Waste Land; Ash-Wednesday; After Strange Gods; Murder in the Cathedral; The Idea of a Christian Society; Four Quartets; The Cocktail Party; Selected Essays; The Elder Statesman; Collected Poems, 1909–1962.* EEF

F. O. Matthiessen, *The Achievement of T. S. Eliot: An Essay on the Nature of Poetry,* 3d ed. (New York, 1959); G. Smith, *T. S. Eliot's Poetry and Plays: A Study in Sources and Meaning,* 1st Phoenix ed. (Chicago, 1960); H. Howarth, *Notes on Some Figures Behind T. S. Eliot* (Boston, 1964).

Eliot, William Greenleaf (1811–87). Grandfather of T. S. Eliot*; b. New Bedford, Mass.; educ. Columbian Coll., Washington, D. C., and Harvard Divinity School, Cambridge, Mass.; ordained 1834; to Saint Louis, Mo., and est. First Congregational Society 1835, dedicated The Church of The Messiah 1851; founded Eliot Sem. (now Washington U.) 1853, Mary Institute 1859; advocated emancipation of slaves, woman suffrage, and temperance reform. Works include *Discourses on the Doctrines of Christianity; The Story of Archer Alexander: From Slavery to Freedom.*

Elipando (Elipandus; ca. 717–808). Abp. Toledo, Sp.; held that Christ is son of God by adoption, not by nature. See also *Adoptionism.*

Elisabeth of Brunswick-Lüneburg (1510–58). Wife of Duke Eric of Brunswick-Lüneburg (Calenberg); after his death 1540 she helped A. Corvinus* introd. the Reformation into her land.

Elisabeth of Schönau (ca. 1129–64). Rhenish Benedictine visionary. Works include *Visiones; Liber viarum Dei.*

Elisabeth of the Trinity (Elisabeth of Dijon; Marie-Joséphine Catez; 1880–1906). Carmelite mystic at Dijon convent. Works include *Écrits spirituels,* tr. Benedictines of Stanbrook, *The Praise of Glory.*

Elizabeth (1207–31). Wife of Landgrave Louis IV of Thuringia; devoted herself to religion and charitable works; emphasized mystical love of Christ and His presence in the poor; canonized.

Elizabeth I (1533–1603). Queen of Eng. 1558–1603. Daughter of Henry VIII and Anne Boleyn. Steered middle course in religion; completed establishment of Angl. Ch., that is, it was made the state ch.; in 1563 she authorized the Lat. text of the Thirty-nine Articles adopted 1562; excommunicated 1570; took severe measures against dissenters. See also *England,* B 6; *Popes,* 21.

Elizabethan Settlement. The Eng. Ch. as organized under Elizabeth* I. See also *England,* B 6.

Elk River Association. See *Baptist Churches,* 25.

Elkesaites. See *Gnosticism,* 7 d.

Elks, Benevolent and Protective Order of. Organized 1866, the Elks lodge originally catered to those in pursuit of soc. enjoyment; benevolent and protective features added later to est. the "fraternal" character of the order.

Activities of Elks include an obligation to charity, justice, and brotherly love; religious principles stressed in the ritual have salvation by works as their dominant note.

A blessed hereafter is assured to all mems. in good standing, burial and memorial rituals stressing an eternity of bliss in reward for faithfulness in charity, justice, and brotherly love.

In some places "Elks Clubs" have been organized which offer soc. membership without obligating on any ritual. Such membership is unauthorized by the Order and uses the "Elks" name without sanction.

1967 membership ca. 1,361,455. PHL

Eller, Elias. See *Ellerians.*

Ellerians (Ronsdorf Sect; Zionites). Founded 1726 in Elberfeld, Ger.; removed 1737 to Ronsdorf by Elias Eller (1690–1750), who declared that his 2d wife was divinely designated as "mother of Zion" and that she would give birth to the Savior a 2d time. After Eller's death the sect declined.

Ellermann, Louise Elisabeth (Aug. 3, 1884–Jan. 11, 1957). B. Evansville, Ind.; trained for nursing Evansville; to India as 1st Mo. Syn. med. miss. 1913; discontinued work in India 1926 and returned to US; resigned from miss. service 1927.

Ellerton, John (1826–93). B. London; educ. King William's Coll., Isle of Man, and Trin. Coll., Cambridge; held various appointments; hymnist. Works include *Notes and Illustrations of Church Hymns;* hymns include "Savior, Again to Thy Dear Name We Raise."

Ellicott, Charles John (1819–1905). B. Whitwell, near Stamford, Eng.; educ. Cambridge; ordained deacon 1846, priest 1847. Prof. King's Coll., London, 1858; also Cambridge 1860. Dean Exeter 1861; bp. Gloucester and Bristol 1863. Chairman of group that worked on NT RV. Other works include *Historical Lectures on the Life of Our Lord Jesus Christ.*

Elliott, Charlotte (1789–1871). Angl. hymnist; b. Clapham, London; invalid 1821; hymns include "Just as I Am, Without One Plea."

Elliott, Julia Anne (d. 1841). Wife of Henry Venn Elliott, brother of Charlotte Elliott*; hymnist, hymns include "Hail, Thou Bright and Sacred Morn" (known in altered versions as "Great Creator, Who This Day" and "Father, Who the Light This Day").

Ellis, William (Aug. 29, 1794–June 9, 1872). B. London; LMS miss. to South Seas 1816; est. printing press at Tahiti; to Sandwich Islands 1822; to Eng. 1825; visited Malagasy Rep. (see *Africa,* B 9) in attempt to reintroduce Christianity 1853, 1854, 1856; reest. miss. 1862; to Eng. 1865. Works include *Polynesian Researches; The Martyr Church: A Narrative of the Introduction, Progress, and Triumph of Christianity in Madagascar.*

Eloheimo, John William (Dec. 9, 1847–Dec. 8, 1913). B. Sahalaks, Fin.; educ. *Turku, Porvoo, and Helsinki;* ordained 1874; to US ca. 1887/88. Pastor Astoria, Oreg., 1888; Calumet, Mich., 1889. Helped found Suomi Syn. See also *Finnish Lutherans in America,* 1–3.

Elohist Writer. See *Higher Criticism,* 7–13.

Eloi (Eligius; ca. 588–ca. 660). Patron saint of goldsmiths and metalworkers; skilled metalworker; served under Merovingian kings Clotaire II and Dagobert I; later bp. Noyon, Fr., and active as miss. among Franks and Frisians.

El Salvador. See *Central America,* A, F.

Elven, Cornelius (1797–1873). Bap. pastor Bury Saint Edmunds, Suffolk, Eng.; wrote the hymn "With Broken Heart and Contrite Sigh."

Elvira, Synod of. Convened ca. 306 at Elvira (Illiberis, or Eliberis, probably near modern Granada, Sp.); dealt with disciplinary matters; strongly condemned heathen immorality; forbade sacred pictures on walls of ch. bldgs.; approved E custom that forbids unmarried priests to marry after ordination; enjoined continence on clerics already married. See also *Usury,* 3.

ELWA (radio station). See *Africa,* C 7.

Elwert, Eduard (1805–65). B. Cannstatt, Ger.; prof. ch. hist. and hist. of dogma Zurich; as exegete, endeavored to overcome atomistic-supernatural approach to Scripture by hist.-individual approach to doctrine of inspiration; indebted to J. G. v. Herder* and F. D. E. Schleiermacher.*

Elzevir Text. See *Textual Criticism,* 2.

Emanation. System of oriental origin holding that all being is derived through a process of descending radiations from the godhead; opposed to creation out of nothing. See also *Gnosticism,* 5; *Neoplatonism.*

Ember, Pál (1660–1710). Hung. Ref. pastor and ch. hist.; educ. at Debrecen, Hung., and at Leiden and Franeker, Neth.; moderate adherent of J. Cocceius.*

Ember Days. See *Quatember.*

Embury, Philip (ca. 1728–ca. 1773). Of Ger. descent; b. probably Ballingrane, Ireland; converted by J. Wesley* 1752; to Am. 1760; built 1st Am. Meth. ch. in N. Y.; cousin of B. Heck.*

Emergence. Term used to denote hypothesis of emergent evolution. In C. L. Morgan* it refers to appearance of novelties in evolution. In W. Temple* it is the emergence of the distinct levels of matter, life, intelligence, spirit.

Emeritus (from Lat. *emereri,* "to serve one's time"). One retired from professional life or free of its duties, usually because of age or disability, but holding the rank of his last office.

Emerson, John S. (1800–67). B. Chester, N. H.; educ. Dartmouth Coll., Hanover, N. H., and at Andover (Mass.) Theol. Sem.; ABCFM miss. to Sandwich Islands 1831: stationed at Wailua, on Oahu; prof. Lahainaluna Sem. 1842–46; returned to Wailua 1846; pub. (with W. P. Alexander,* Artemus Bishop [1795–1872], and S. M. Kamakan) an Eng.-Hawaiian dictionary.

Emerson, Ralph Waldo (1803–82). B. Boston, Mass.; ancestry formed an unbroken line of clergymen reaching back to early New Eng. hist.; educ. Harvard Coll. and Divinity School, Cambridge, Mass.; pastor, Second Ch., Unitarian, Boston, 1829; resigned 1832 because of unwillingness to administer the Lord's Supper; traveled abroad 1832–33; personally acquainted with S. T. Coleridge,* W. Wordsworth,* and T. Carlyle* (b. 1795); settled in Concord, Mass., 1833; essayist, lecturer, poet. His 1st vol., *Nature* (1836), in which he announced his transcendentalist viewpoint, met with only mild reception. But 2 significant addresses, *The American Scholar* (1837) and *The Divinity School Address* (1838), secured him a wide following. Common themes move through his essays, addresses, and poetry: man can know truth intuitively through Reason, which links him to the progressively unfolding revelation of the Oversoul* in nature; man, Am. man particularly, should exercise the private capacities of mind and esp. his moral qualities, an emphasis Emerson felt was lacking in prominent thinkers of his time. Emerson's ability to convince his audiences and readers of the individual's great personal worth has led to his being considered a moral teacher, effective essayist, inspiring speaker, and experimental poet. Works include *Nature; The American Scholar; The Divinity School Address; Essays* (2 series); *Poems; Representative Men; English Traits; The Conduct of Life.* See also *Idealism; Transcendentalism.* WGR

R. L. Rusk, *The Life of Ralph Waldo Emerson* (New York, 1949); *The Transcendentalists: An Anthology,* ed. P. Miller (Cambridge, Mass., 1950); S. E. Whicher, *Freedom and Fate: An Inner Life of Ralph Waldo Emerson* (Philadelphia, 1953).

Emigrant Missions. See *Immigrant and Emigrant Missions.*

Emilie. See *Aemilie.*

Emmeram (Haimrham[m]; 7th or 8th c.). Itinerant preacher in Bav.

Emmerich, Anna Katharine (Emmerick; 1774–1824). B. near Coesfeld, Westphalia; Augustinian nun, ecstatic, and mystic at Dülmen, Westphalia; stigmata of the passion appeared in her body; Clemens Brentano's accounts of her stigmatization* and meditations are subjects of prolonged debate.

Emmons, Nathanael. See *New England Theology,* 4.

Emory, John (1789–1835). B. Spaniard's Neck, Queen Annes Co., Md.; studied law; ordained M. E. deacon ca. 1812, elder ca. 1814; held various pastorates; agent of the Meth. Book Concern 1928; changed *The Methodist Magazine* into *The Methodist Magazine and Quarterly Review* and ed. it 1830–32; ed. works of J. Wesley*; other works include *Defence of "Our Fathers," and of the Original Organization of the Methodist Episcopal Church Against the Rev. Alexander M'Caine and Others.*

Emotion. See *Educational Psychology,* C 5.

Empaytaz, Henri Louis (Empeytaz; 1790–1853). Prominent figure in Geneva awakening that began in Société de Amis, a pietistic Bible circle organized 1810 by Empaytaz and fellow theol. students but soon disbanded under pressure of local rationalistic clergy. Expelled from theol. study for holding unauthorized religious meetings, Empaytaz came under spell of mystic Baroness B. J. v. Krüdener* and became her companion on mission journeys to Paris, Alsace, and Switz. Later pastor Geneva. Works include *Considerations sur la divinité de Jesus-Christi* against "Arianism" of Geneva clergy.

Empedocles (ca. 490–ca. 430 BC). B. Agrigento Sicily; Gk. pluralist philos., statesman, and religious thinker; sought to reconcile logically immutable, single being (see *Parmenides*) with sensible world of change and motion (see *Heraclitus*) in a cosmological doctrine of 4 elements (earth, air, fire, and water) moved by love (attraction) and strife (repulsion). See also *Psychology,* B 2; *Transmigration of Souls.*

Empirical Theology. Theol. system that eliminates all norms outside experience. Deity and ethics exist only in experience, final criterion of religious value. Schools of empirical theologians: 1. those who evaluate experience in all fields; 2. those who evaluate experience in the moral field; 3. those who restrict themselves to religious experience. F. D. E. Schleiermacher is the father of the last-named school, which includes intuition and mysticism in its category of experience.

Empiricism. Philos. theory according to which experience is the only source of knowledge; denies the possibility of supernatural source of knowledge; leads to criticism of Christian ethics and religion. See also *Logical Positivism; Sensationalism.*

Emser, Hieronymus (ca. 1477–1527). B. Ulm, Ger.; educ. Tübingen and Basel; RC opponent of M. Luther* and H. Zwingli*; plagiarized Luther's NT tr.; helped organize a ref. RC Ch. in Ger.

Emser Punktation. Name applied to series of 23 articles drawn up 1786 at Ems, Ger., by the abps. of Mainz, Trier, Cologne, and Salzburg in protest against establishment of a papal nunciature at Munich; ecclesiastical princes regarded such a nunciature as an infringement on their rights. Ultimate aim of the Punktation to est. an indep. nat. ch. in Ger. was not attained because of clerical and pol. opposition.

Enckhausen, Heinrich Friedrich (1799–1885). B. Celle, Ger.; dir. of the Singakademie and court organist, Hanover; composed orchestral and piano music, ch. music, and an opera.

Encolpion (enkolpion; from Gk. for "on" and "bosom"). Medallion with sacred picture worn on the breast by bps. of E. Orthodox Ch. See also *Panagia,* 2.

Encontre, Daniel (1762–1818). Orthodox Calvinist; pastor 1790; prof. Montpellier 1808, Montauban 1814.

Encounter. Term used for contact or meeting bet. man and God or man and man. In M. Buber* it describes the relation of subject to subject ("I–Thou"). Hans Urs von Balthasar (b. 1905; Swiss RC theol.) finds the norm of all knowledge in the meeting of persons. The importance of encounter with God has been stressed by such men as J. Baillie,* D. M. Baillie,* Herbert Henry Farmer (b. 1892; Eng. theol.), R. Niebuhr* (b. 1892; Am. theol.). K. Barth (see *Switzerland, Contemporary Theology in*), and Emil Brunner (b. 1889; Swiss theol.).

Encratism. "Encratites" (from Gk. *enkrates,* "self-disciplined") denotes those Gnostics, Ebionites,* and Docetists that rejected wine, flesh, and often marriage. See also *Gnosticism; Docetism; Tatian.*

Encyclicals. Circular or gen. letters addressed to many people or a whole order. The name formerly included letters sent by bps. to their people, but now applies almost exclusively to formal pastoral letters addressed by the pope to the RC Ch. To be distinguished from briefs (see *Breve*), bulls,* rescripts,* constitutions,* and decrees.* Pub. in *Acta Apostolicae Sedis.* Named from the first words of the official, pub. text. Some important encyclicals: *Quanta Cura* (1864; against the 80 errors rejected in the 1864 Syllabus* of Errors; see *Roman Catholic Confessions,* D); *Aeterni Patris* (1879; commended study of philos., esp. Thomism*); *Rerum Novarum* (1891; against socialism*); *Pascendi* (1907; against modernism*); *Casti Connubii* (1930; on marriage*); *Quadragesimo Anno* (1931; 40th anniversary of *Rerum Novarum;* on reconstruction of the social order); *Divini Redemptoris* (1937; against atheistic communism; see *Socialism,* 4).

Encyclopedia, Theological. The preliminary exposition or branch of learning which sets forth in basic concept the gen. order and contents of theol. science. An early Luth. work on the order of a theol. encyclopedia was A. Calov's 1673 *Encyclopaedias disciplinarum realium ideae.* Best-known works were those of the Ref. theol. K. R. Hagenbach* and of the Luth. J. C. K. v. Hofmann.* See also *Methodology, Theological.*

R. F. Weidner, *Theological Encyclop(a)edia and Methodology,* 2d ed., 2 vols. (Chicago, 1898–1910); R. Pieper, *Wegweiser durch die Theologischen Disciplinen und deren Litteratur* (Milwaukee, 1900); G. R. Crooks and J. F. Hurst, *Theological Encyclopaedia and Methodology,* in *Library of Biblical and Theological Literature,* ed. G. R. Crooks and J. F. Hurst, III (New York, 1884); A. Kuyper, *Encyclopedia of Sacred Theology: Its Principles,* tr. J. H. de Vries (New York, 1898).

Encyclopedias and Dictionaries. 1. The 1st encyclopedias were works of 1 author and were designed to summarize the knowledge and thinking of the time. Aristotle* wrote many encyclopedic treatises. The *Historia Naturalis* of Pliny the Elder, dating from AD 77–79, the oldest encyclopedia in existence, is regarded by many as the 1st encyclopedia because of its method of compilation. Isidore* of Seville, Vincent* of Beauvais, and R. Bacon* tried to cover every branch of knowledge. In 1630 the 1st modern encyclopedia (one of the 1st to bear the title *Encyclopaedia*) was pub. by J. H. Alsted.* The 1st notable alphabetic Eng. cyclopedia was issued 1704 by John Harris. Ephraim Chambers' *Cyclopaedia* 1st appeared 1728 in 2 vols. The *Encyclopedia Americana,* 1st pub. 1829, was the 1st successful venture of its kind originating in Am.

2. By derivation, encyclopedia means instruction in the circle of arts and sciences regarded by the Gks. as essential to a liberal educ. Classical Gks. understood *enkyklios* ("in a circle") *paideia* ("learning") as referring to a complete system of instruction. Apparently *Enkyklopaideia* was not used in book titles till the 16th c., when it usually designated philos. or pedagogical works rather than comprehensive compilations.

3. In the 14th–16th c. the encyclopedia developed in 2 ways: 1. a combination of different modes of organizing knowledge; 2. the separation of the function of the encyclopedia from biographical, hist., lexicographical, philos., philol., and pedagogical works.

4. Modern encyclopedias purport to be repositories of information on one or more branches of knowledge. They are usually organized alphabetically for rapid and easy use.

5. Earliest important Christian dictionary was the *Onomasticon* of Eusebius* of Caesarea, a geog. dictionary of the Bible. Jerome* (d. 420) wrote *De nominibus Hebraicis* and *De viris illustribus.* Many dictionaries and cyclopedias have been compiled in recent cents.

6. Gen. religious encyclopedias: *Realencyklopädie für protestantische Theologie und Kirche,* ed. J. J. Herzog and A. Hauck, 3d ed., 21 vols. plus index vol. and 2 supplementary vols. (Leipzig, 1896–1913); *The New Schaff-Herzog Encyclopedia of Religious Knowledge* [based on *Realencyklopädie für protestantische Theologie und Kirche,* ed. J. J. Herzog and A. Hauck], ed. and tr. P. Schaff et al., 12 vols. plus index vol. (Grand Rapids, Mich., reprint 1949–53); *Twentieth Century Encyclopedia of Religious Knowledge* [extension of *The New Schaff-Herzog Encyclopedia of Religious Knowledge,* ed. and tr. P. Schaff et al.], ed. L. A. Loetscher (Grand Rapids, Mich., 1955); *Encyclopaedia of Religion and Ethics,* ed. J. Hastings, 12 vols. plus index vol. (New York, 1908–26; 4th impression 1956–60); J. G. Frazer, *The Golden Bough,* 3d ed., 11 vols. plus index vol. and supplementary vol. (London, 1907–15, 1937); *A Dictionary of Religion and Ethics,* ed. S. Mathews and G. B. Smith (New York, 1921); *An Encyclopedia of Religion,* ed. V. Ferm (New York, 1945); A. Bertholet and H. v. Campenhausen, *Wör-*

terbuch der Religionen (Stuttgart, 1952); *Nordisk teologisk uppslagsbok för kyrka och skola* (Lund and Copenhagen, 1952–57); F. König, *Religionswissenschaftliches Wörterbuch* (Freiburg, 1956); *Weltkirchenlexikon,* ed. F. H. Littell and H. H. Walz (Stuttgart, 1960); *Die Religion in Geschichte und Gegenwart,* ed. K. Galling, 3d ed., 5 vols. plus index vol. (Tübingen, 1957–65).

7. Christianity – for. works: *Encyclopédie théologique,* ed. J. P. Migne, 3 series, 168 vols. in 170 (Paris, 1845–66); *Kirke-leksikon for Norden,* ed. F. Nielsen, 4 vols. (Copenhagen, 1900–29); *Dictionnaire d'histoire et de géographie ecclésiastiques,* ed. A. Baudrillart, vols. 1–17 (Paris, 1912–71, in progress); *Dictionnaire pratique des connaissances religieuses,* ed. J. Bricout, 6 vols. plus supplement (Paris, 1925–29); *Dictionnaire de spiritualité ascétique et mystique, doctrine et histoire,* ed. M. Viller, et al., 7 vols. (Paris, 1932–71, in progress); *Enciclopedia ecclesiastica,* ed. A. Bernareggi, vols. 1–6 (Milan, 1942–55, in progress); *Theologisch Woordenboek,* ed. H. Brink, 3 vols. (Roermond, Neth., 1952 to 1958); *The Oxford Dictionary of the Christian Church,* ed. F. L. Cross (London, 1957); *Evangelisches Kirchenlexikon,* ed. H. Brunotte and O. Weber, 3 vols. plus index vol. (Göttingen, 1956–61).

8. Christian antiquities: *A Dictionary of Christian Antiquities,* ed. W. Smith and S. Cheetham, 2 vols. (Hartford, Conn., 1880); *A Dictionary of Christian Biography, Literature, Sects and Doctrines,* ed. W. Smith and H. Wace, 4 vols. (London, 1877–87); *A Dictionary of Christian Biography and Literature to the End of the Sixth Century A. D., with an Account of the Principal Sects and Heresies,* ed. H. Wace and W. C. Piercy (London, 1911); *Dictionnaire d'archéologie chrétienne et de liturgie,* ed. F. Cabrol, H. Leclerq, and H. Marrou, 15 vols. in 30 parts (Paris, 1903–53); *Reallexikon für Antike und Christentum,* ed. T. Klauser, F. J. Dölger, H. Lietzmann, et al., vols. 1–7 (Stuttgart, 1950–69, in progress).

9. Bible: *A Dictionary of the Bible,* ed. J. Hastings, 4 vols. plus extra vol. with indexes (Edinburgh, 1898–1904); *Encyclopaedia biblica,* ed. T. K. Cheyne and J. S. Black, 4 vols. (New York, 1899–1903); *A Dictionary of Christ and the Gospels,* ed. J. Hastings, 2 vols. (New York, 1906–08); *The International Standard Bible Encyclopaedia,* ed. J. Orr, 5 vols., rev. M. G. Kyle (Chicago, 1930); *Dictionary of the Apostolic Church,* ed. J. Hastings, 2 vols. (New York, 1916); J. D. Davis, *A Dictionary of the Bible,* 4th ed. (Philadelphia, 1924); *A New Standard Bible Dictionary,* ed. M. W. Jacobus et al., 3d ed. (New York, 1936); J. D. Davis, *The Westminster Dictionary of the Bible,* rev. H. S. Gehman (Philadelphia, 1944); M. S. Miller and J. L. Miller, *Encyclopedia of Bible Life,* rev. ed. (New York, 1955); *Dictionnaire de la Bible,* ed. F. G. Vigouroux, L. Pirot, et al., 5 vols. plus 8 supplementary vols. (Paris, 1895–1912; 1928–72, in progress); *Encyclopaedia Biblica [Entsiqlopediyah Miqra'it],* 6 vols. (Jerusalem, 1954–71, in progress); *A Theological Word Book of the Bible,* ed. A. Richardson (New York, 1950); *Bibel-Lexikon,* ed. H. Haag, 8 parts (Einsiedeln, Switz., 1951–56); *Encyclopedia of Biblical Interpretation,* ed. M. M. Kasher, 8 vols. (New York, 1953–70, in progress); *Biblisch-theologisches Handwörterbuch zur Lutherbibel und zu neueren Übersetzungen,* ed. E. Osterloh and H. Engelland (Göttingen, 1954); J. E. Steinmueller, *Catholic Biblical Encyclopedia* (New York, 1950); M. F. Unger, *Unger's Bible Dictionary* (Chicago, 1957); J.-J. v. Allmen, *Vocabulaire Biblique,* 2d ed., Eng. *A Companion to the Bible,* tr. P. J. Allcock et al. (New York, 1958); W. Corswant, *Dictionnaire d'archéologie biblique,* ed. É. Urech (Neuchatel, 1956), tr. A. Heathcote, *A Dictionary of Life in Bible Times* (New York, 1960); *The Interpreter's Dictionary of the Bible,* ed. G. A. Buttrick, 4 vols. (Nashville, 1962); *The Cambridge History of the Bible,* ed. P. R. Ackroyd, C. F. Evans, G. W. H. Lampe, and Greenslade, 3 vols. (Cambridge, Eng., 1963–70); A. van den Born, *Bijbels Woordenboek,* 2d rev. ed. (Roermond, Neth., 1954–57), adapted and tr. L. F. Hartman, *Encyclopedic Dictionary of the Bible* (New York, 1963).

10. Denominational. A. Protestant: *The Mennonite Encyclopedia,* ed. H. S. Bender and C. H. Smith, 4 vols. (Scottdale, Pa., 1955–59); *Encyclopedia of Southern Baptists,* ed. C. J. Allen et al., 2 vols. (Nashville, Tenn., 1958); *Encyclopaedia of the Presbyterian Church,* ed. A. Nevin (Philadelphia, [1884]).

B. Luth. in Am.: *The Lutheran Cyclopedia,* ed. H. E. Jacobs and J. A. W. Haas (New York, 1899); *The Concordia Cyclopedia,* ed. L. Fuerbringer, T. Engelder, P. E. Kretzmann (St. Louis, 1927); *Lutheran Cyclopedia,* ed. E. L. Lueker (St. Louis, 1954); *The Encyclopedia of the Lutheran Church,* ed. J. Bodensieck, 3 vols. (Minneapolis, 1965).

C. Roman Catholic: *Wetzer und Welte's Kirchenlexikon,* ed. J. Hergenröther and F. Kaulen, 2d ed., 12 vols. plus index vol. (Freiburg, 1882–1903); *The Catholic Encyclopedia,* ed. C. G. Herbermann, 15 vols. plus index vol. and 2 supplementary vols. (Supplement II in 2 parts) (New York, 1907–51); *Lexikon für Theologie und Kirche,* ed. J. Höfer and K. Rahner, 2d ed., 10 vols. plus index vol. and *Das zweite Vatikanische Konzil,* (Freiburg, 1957–68, in progress); *New Catholic Encyclopedia,* ed. W. J. McDonald (New York, 1967); *Dictionnaire apologétique de la foi catholique,* ed. A. d'Alès, 4 vols. plus index vol. (Paris, 1911–31); *A Catholic Dictionary,* ed. D. Attwater, 2d ed., rev. (New York, 1949); *Enciclopedia cattolica,* 12 vols. (Vatican City, 1948 to 54); *Dictionnaire de Théologie Catholique,* ed. A. Vacant, E. Mangenot, and É. Amann, 15 vols. plus 3-vol. index (Paris, 1909–49; 1953–72); *The New Catholic Dictionary,* ed. C. B. Pallen and J. J. Wynne (New York, 1929), reissued without rev. as *Catholic Encyclopedic Dictionary* (New York, 1941).

11. Jewish: *The Universal Jewish Encyclopedia,* ed. I. Landman, 10 vols. plus index vol. (New York, 1939–44); J. R. Rosenbloom, *A Biographical Dictionary of Early American Jews* (Lexington, Ky., 1960); *The Standard Jewish Encyclopedia,* ed. C. Roth (New York, 1959); *The New Jewish Encyclopedia,* ed. D. Bridger (New York, 1962).

12. Philosophy: R. Eisler, *Handwörterbuch der Philosophie,* ed. R. Müller-Freienfels, 2d ed. (Berlin, 1922); *Dictionary of Philosophy and Psychology,* ed. J. M. Baldwin, 2d ed., 2 vols. (New York, 1925); *A Lexicon of St. Thomas Aquinas Based on the* Summa Theologica *and Selected Passages of His Other Works,* ed. R. J. Deferrari and M. Barry, 5 fascicles (Washington, D. C., 1948–49); *Enciclopedia filosophica,* 4 vols. (Venice, 1957); *The Concise Encyclopedia of Western Philosophy and Philosophers,* ed. J. O. Urmson (New York, 1960); *The Encyclopedia of Philosophy,* ed. P. Edwards, 8 vols. (New York, 1967). HLH

See also *Encyclopedists; Lexicons.*

Encyclopedists. Editors and collaborators of the *Encyclopédie ou Dictionnaire raisonné des sciences, des arts et des métiers* (1751–80), an alphabetically arranged Fr. reference work in 35 vols. covering the whole field of knowledge. Editor D. Diderot* and his co-workers, including J. L. R. d'Alembert,* P. H. D. d'Holbach,* J. J. Rousseau,* and Voltaire,* advocated religious toleration and democracy, and many of them natural theol.

J. Morley, *Diderot and the Encyclopaedists,* new ed., 2 vols. (London, 1886); *The Encyclopédie of*

Diderot and d'Alembert: Selected Articles, ed. J. Lough (Cambridge, Eng., 1954).

Endemann, Samuel (1727–89). Ref. pastor and churchman; prof. theol. Marburg 1782; opposed neology and the Enlightenment.* Wrote compends of dogmatic and moral theol.

Endogamy. Marriage within a group, esp. as required by custom or law, in distinction from exogamy.*

Endress, Christian Frederick Lewis (Mar. 12, 1775–Sept. 30, 1827). B. Philadelphia; mem. Pa. Ministerium; pastor Frankford, Pa., Cohenzy, N. J., Easton, Pa., Lancaster, Pa.; helped form General* Syn.

Energism. Ethical theory that right action lies in efficient exercise of normal human capacities, the aim being self-realization rather than happiness or pleasure.

Engagement. See *Marriage, Biblical and Christian.*

Engagement Ring. See *Ring, Engagement and Wedding.*

Engelbert of Admont (ca. 1250–1331). Learned Austrian Benedictine* abbot. B. Volkersdorf, Styria, Austria; entered Benedictine abbey, Admont, Austria, ca. 1267; studied at cathedral school of St. Vitus at Prague and U. of Padua; probably abbot of St. Peter, Salzburg; abbot of Admont 1297; poet; eclectic philos.; writings include works on theol. and natural science.

Engelbrecht, Ernst Henry (Dec. 23, 1870–Feb. 28, 1944). B. Farmers Retreat, Ind.; educ. Ev. Luth. Teachers Sem., Addison, Ill., Columbia U., NYC, and the U. of Chicago; teacher Kendallville, Ind., 1891–1901, in NYC at Immanuel Ch. 1901–11 and at St. Matthew's Ch. 1911–15; prof. Conc. Teachers Coll., River Forest, Ill., 1915–44; pres. and field secy. Walther League.

Engelbrecht, Hans (1599–1642). Pious mystic of Brunswick; lay preacher in Lower Saxony and Holstein; much persecuted despite efforts to work peaceably with clergy.

Engelder, Theodore Edward William (Jan. 21, 1865 to June 23, 1949). B. Olean, N. Y.; educ. Conc. Coll., Fort Wayne, Ind., and Conc. Sem., St. Louis, Mo.; pastor Sugar Grove and Logan, Ohio, 1886–90, and Mount Clemens, Mich., 1890–1914; pres. Mich. Dist., Mo. Syn., 1912–14; prof. Conc. Sem., Springfield, Ill., 1914–26, Conc. Sem., St. Louis, Mo., 1926–46. Staunch defender of verbal inspiration; molded thinking of Mo. Syn. clergy along dogmatical lines. Contributed to *L. u. W., TM,* and *CTM;* other works include *Scripture Cannot Be Broken; Reason or Revelation?*

"Theodore Engelder, 1865–1949," *CTM,* XX (Aug. 1949), frontispiece and pp. 561–563.

Engelhardt, Gustav Moritz Konstantin von (1828–81). Studied under F. A. Philippi*; prof. ch. hist. Dorpat; tried to adhere to Luth. Confessions; pupils included A. Harnack,* R. Seeberg,* and G. N. Bonwetsch.* Works include a life of V. E. Löscher*; *De Jesu Christi tentatione.*

Engelhardt, Johann Georg Veit (1791–1855). Prof. ch. hist, Erlangen; engaged in research in mysticism, patristics, and ecclesiastical and dogmatic hist.; influenced Erlangen confessionalism. See also *Lutheran Theology After 1580,* 11.

Engels, Friedrich (1820–95). Founder with K. H. Marx* of Marxian socialism.* From pietistic Ger. family; lost faith at age 21; in Eng. 1842–44; there became acquainted with industry and the proletariat; explained socialism in the light of a universal dialectical* materialism. Ed. and pub. vols. II and III of K. H. Marx, *Das Kapital.* Works include *Herrn Eugen Dührings Umwälzung der Wissenschaft* (also called *Anti-Dühring); Ludwig Feuerbach und der Ausgang der klassischen deutschen Philosophie; Der Ursprung der Familie, des Privateigenthums und des Staats;* introductions to many works of Marx.

Engelsbrüder. See *Gichtelians.*

Engert, Thaddäus Hyazinth (1875–1945). B. Ochsenfurt, Ger.; ordained RC priest 1899; hist.-critical approach to OT studies led to conflicts with RC Ch.; became Prot. 1910.

England. A. *Early History.* 1. There may have been Christians in Brit. already in the 2d c. During the persecution of Diocletian,* most severe 303–305, also the Christians in Brit. suffered, Alban* reportedly among them. But persecution in Gaul and Brit. seems to have been less severe than elsewhere, perhaps because Constantius I (d. York, Eng., 306), father of Constantine* I, had some sympathy for Christians. Britons attended the Syn. of Arles 314.

2. When Gothic conquests in Gaul and It. led to release of Brit. from Roman control, Christianity was pushed N and W in Brit. It swung back in the work of Columba (see *Celtic Church,* 7), who sent missionaries from Iona into Scot. and N Brit. He came from Ireland, where Patrick* had worked earlier. Augustine* of Canterbury, sent by Gregory I (see *Popes,* 4), arrived in Eng. 597. Aidan* went from Iona to Northumbria and est. his see at Lindisfarne.* Strife bet. Celtic and RC factions led to the 664 Syn. of Whitby,* which decided in favor of Rome.

3. Papal control increased in Eng. under Theodore* of Tarsus and his successors, then declined in the wake of Danish invasions. After the Norman Conquest (1066), ties with the Continent, including Rome, were strengthened and episc. power increased, though William I (called William the Conqueror; 1027–87; king 1066–87) resisted the pretensions of Gregory VII (see *Popes,* 7). Lanfranc* was abp. Canterbury 1070–89; Anselm* succeeded him 1093. John (often called John Lackland; ca. 1167–1216; king 1199–1216) defied Innocent III (see *Popes,* 10) over the election of S. Langton* as abp. Canterbury, and Eng. was put under the interdict 1208. John surrendered his crown to the papal legate and received it back as a vassal of the pope.

4. The prestige of the popes suffered from their exile in Avignon,* their supposed subservience to the King of Fr., and strife bet. papal contenders. In the 14th c. parliament asserted Eng. indep. by curtailment of papal jurisdiction, appointments, and exactions.

B. *Reformation Period.* 1. These curtailing laws were appealed to as the spirit of nationalism grew and blossomed under the Tudors. When Clement* VII would not grant an annulment of Henry VIII's (1491–1547; king 1509–47) marriage to Catherine of Aragon, Henry succeeded in attaining qualified recognition as head of the Ch. of Eng. 1531. He could count on considerable national feeling and resentment against the exactions and interference of Rome. T. Wolsey* had been papal legate. See also *Regalism.*

2. The Lollards* had been forced underground but were receptive to the ev. doctrine that came down the Rhine and through the Low Countries to Eng. Men who became leaders in the Eng. Reformation gathered at the White Horse Inn, Cambridge, to study banned works of M. Luther.* Luths. of various strength may be found among the Eng. reformers. The most Luth. of them, R. Barnes,* was a friend of Luther and the Wittenberg reformers and represented Henry VIII in negotiations with the Schmalkaldic* League. Henry later had him burned at the stake, and Luther mourned "St. Robert." Much of W. Tyndale's* theol. was akin to Luther's. T. Bilney* came to the Gospel much as did Luther. M. Coverdale* was a Luth. pastor in Bergzabern, Ger. T. Cranmer,* a priest, married a niece of A.

Osiander* the Elder, but his theol. had only a Luth. phase (ca. 1532–48). Luth. influence is apparent in most of the Henrician formularies and can be seen also in the Thirty-nine Articles and the Book of Common Prayer.

3. Henry VIII did not want doctrinal renovation. For his writing against Luther, Leo X (see *Popes,* 20) gave him the title Defender* of the Faith. But he was for a time interested in assoc. with the Schmalkaldic* League against Charles* V, nephew of Catherine of Aragon. Anglo-Luth. doctrinal confs. were held 1536 and 1538; through them Lutheranism influenced Eng. religious formulas under Henry VIII and his successors. Henry VIII's later reaction is reflected in the Six Articles of 1539 and the King's Book of 1543 (see *Anglican Confessions,* 2–4). See also *Lutheran Confessions,* A 5.

4. Henry VIII had found a submissive servant in T. Cranmer,* whom he made abp. of Canterbury. Cranmer's most abiding work, the Book* of Common Prayer, was pub. 1549 under Edward VI (1537–53; king 1547–53), rev. in a Swiss direction 1552. The Forty-two Articles were drafted 1552, pub. 1553; on them were based the Thirty-nine Articles adopted 1562, rev. 1571 (see *Anglican Confessions,* 5, 6). They remain in effect but have long since lost confessional force except for the Ev. party. During Edward VI's reign the regency council under his uncle, Edward Seymour (ca. 1506–52), Duke of Somerset, moved the Eng. ch. to Protestantism, and this more radically under John Dudley (ca. 1502–53), Duke of Northumberland, who displaced Seymour.

5. With Mary Tudor (1516–58; queen 1553–58; see also *Mary I*) there came to the throne a good RC and a poor queen. Some Prots. went into exile. T. Cranmer,* N. Ridley,* and H. Latimer* were burned at the stake. Mary's readiness to persecute on religious grounds, her restoration of papal obedience, and her unfortunate for. policy, motivated by religion, alienated her people with their growing relish for indep. and being Eng. They finally wanted no more of what Mary stood for and enthusiastically acclaimed Elizabeth* I.

6. Elizabeth I sought with great skill to arrange the ch. so that all her people would be in it. She was under strong pressure from the Marian exiles, who out-Calvined Calvin, to do away with what remained of "popery" from Cranmer's day. There was much opposition to altars, kneeling, and vestments, and considerable support for Presbyterianism. Elizabeth insisted on bps. R. Hooker* justified episcopacy as Scriptural and reasonable and gave later Angl. theol. a philos. slant with dominant interest in the Incarnation, in sharp contrast to the Reformers' concern with the cross. The Elizabethan Settlement of 1559 had the typical Angl. characteristics of comprehensiveness, acknowledgment of the role of reason, and insistence on bps.

7. The divine necessity of bps. was asserted by the High* Church party, which developed in opposition to Puritan* deprivations. The Stuart kings were sympathetic to RCs. Charles I (1600–49; king 1625–49) and W. Laud* were beheaded under O. Cromwell.* Parliament est. Presbyterianism 1646 (see *Presbyterian Churches,* 2).

C. *Restoration and Later History.* 1. Anglicanism was vigorously restored with Charles II (1630–85; king 1660–85; see also *Scotland, Reformation in,* 3) but James II (1633–1701; king of Eng., Scot., and Ireland 1685–88) was turned out of the country for his unparliamentary notions and Romanism.

2. With the accession of William III (1650–1702) and Mary II (1662–94) in 1689 the Prot. succession was est. The Act* of Toleration (1689) granted freedom of worship to nonconformists* except RCs and Unitarians, though no nonconformists might hold pub. office. The SPCK was founded 1698, the SPG 1701 (see also *Bible Societies,* 3). See also *Nonjurors.*

3. When the Hanoverians came to the throne, beginning with George I (1660–1727; king 1714–27), the king was officially Luth. in Hanover, Angl. in Eng., and Presb. in Scot. The 18th c. was the heyday of rationalism*; theol. and ch. life reached an all-time low (see also *Deism,* III).

4. C. and J. Wesley* and G. Whitefield* brought new life into this wilderness of the Latitudinarians.* Their fervent Gospel preaching and call for personal religion evoked widespread response. Their influence among industrial masses helped spare Eng. a Fr. Revolution. The Wesleys wished to keep the movement in the Ch. of Eng., but establishment of separate places of worship and J. Wesley's ordination of presbyters and a supt. (bp.) for Methodists in Am. and Brit. led to formation of a separate denomination (see also *Methodist Churches,* 1).

5. Many within the Ch. of Eng. were affected by the Wesleyan movement. R. Raikes* popularized the S. S. in the 1780s. Ev. clergy founded the Church* Missionary Soc. 1799. The interdenominational BFBS was founded 1804 (see also *Bible Societies,* 3). W. Wilberforce* worked successfully for abolition of the slave trade.

6. The yr. 1828 saw the removal of restrictions from nonconformists, 1829 from RCs (diocesan hierarchy restored 1850), 1858 from Jews.

7. The vitality of the Ev. movement waned, and the privileged Ch. of Eng., weakened by internal divisions, latitudinarianism, ineffectual clergy, and parliamentary action, greatly needed reform. Ch. renewal by recovery of RC elements was the goal of the Oxford Movement begun by an 1833 sermon of J. Keble* protesting suppression of certain bishoprics. Publicists of the Oxford Movement produced 90 tracts, or pamphlets, urging doctrine and discipline according to the example of the ancient ch. In the last and most controversial J. H. Newman* interpreted the Thirty-nine Articles in a RC sense. Weary of the doctrinal chaos in the Ch. of Eng. he sought refuge with Rome 1845. Leadership passed to E. B. Pusey,* followed by C. Gore*; the latter formed a bridge with men of the High* Church who imported much liberal theol. to the great distress of those reared on the Bible. The second wave of the Oxford Movement was much engaged in ritualistic innovation. Lawcourts were invoked to suppress this, as they had been against George Cornelius Gorham's (1787–1857) denial of baptismal regeneration. When the courts proved ineffective, the chaos was almost complete.

8. With the decline of liberalism and the harvesting of the good fruits of both Ev. and Oxford movements, a good measure of common sense has resisted party strife and narrow labels. But wide divergences persist with the debilitating effect of compromise and the absence of any operative confession. While the Thirty-nine Articles are highly regarded only by the Low* Ch. (or Ev.) party (see *High Church*), episc. polity remains a common bond together with the Book* of Common Prayer, which gen. though variously provides the common form of worship.

9. The proposed revision of the Book of Common Prayer in 1927–28 failed due to Prot. opposition in Parliament, which is still the supreme authority in the affairs of the Ch. of Eng. The crown gives dean and chapter authority to elect a bp., nominates a candidate, and endorses the elected candidate. Each province has its own abp. and a Convocation made up of an Upper House (bps). and a Lower House (representative clergy). Each bp. is supreme in his

diocese. The curate of a parish is removed only by resignation, promotion to another benefice, or because of some disgraceful offense. Convocations deal with doctrine, liturgy, and canon law. In 1919 the Ch. Assem. was added, made up of a House of Bps. (combined Upper Houses of both Convocations), a House of Clergy (combined Lower Houses of both Convocations), and a House of Laity elected by diocesan confs. Its business is legal and administrative. It prepares measures for Parliament's approval and deals with financial matters, though much influence is also exercised by the variously appointed Church Commissioners, who are trustees of properties and funds.

10. Eng. Christianity has a noble miss. hist. Boniface* was apostle to N Eur., J. Eliot* to Am., W. Carey* and H. Martyn* to India, S. Marsden* to New Zealand, R. Moffat* and D. Livingstone* to Afr., and J. Chalmers* to the South Sea Islands.

11. The worldwide Angl. communion emerged from such miss. work and the formation of the Brit. Empire. Since 1867 the bps. have met ca. every decade at Lambeth* Palace, London residence of the abp. of Canterbury. These confs. have only deliberative and advisory function, but their findings enjoy considerable influence. In 1888 the Lambeth Quadrilateral (rev. ed. of the 4 Arts. agreed on at the Gen. Conv. of the [Angl.] Prot. Episc. Ch. held at Chicago 1886) stated the Angl. program for unifying Christendom: Bible, Apostles' and Nicene Creed, 2 Sacraments, and hist. episcopate. On this basis intercommunion has been est. with Old* Catholic and Eastern* Orthodox chs. Reciprocal arrangements have been made with Luth. chs. of Scand. in the Swed. episc. succession, though these arrangements have been strained by Scand. ordination of women.

12. Anglicans have played a leading role in the Ecumenical* Movement, commending to other chs. as the unifying way their comprehensive view of the ch., their doctrinal elasticity, and their episcopate. The last has been a roadblock to reunion with Methodists and Presbyterians in Brit. The Church* of South India, est. 1947 under a compromise formula, gained gen. approval 1948, but comparable union projects for N India/Pakistan and Ceylon were received with fewer reservations 1958. For N India/Pakistan a 4th rev. ed. of the 1951 Plan of Ch. Union was approved 1965 by the Negotiating Committee and submitted to the negotiating chs. with request for response by 1969. For Ceylon a 4th rev. ed. of Scheme of Church Union was pub. 1963 and presented for voting. For further developments see *Church of North India.* A program of larger mutual helpfulness among Angl. chs. was agreed on at Toronto 1963.

13. Ch. attendance is small on an average Sun. There is much soul-searching on the part of some with respect to ch. life. The current "new theol." of the Broad Ch. holds little promise.

14. After Mary, Calvinism was dominant. Then the High Ch. harked back to the RC heritage. Its doctrinal theol. since that time has operated largely with RC and Ref. alternatives, with little understanding of the Luth. position.

15. Use of the Strangers' Ch. *(Ecclesia peregrinorum)* was given to Eur. Prots. in London under Edward VI and again from Elizabeth I on. The Lutherans' right to their own ch. was granted by the 1669 Latin Charter of Charles II, who was interested in helping trade. Trin. Luth. Ch., London, was dedicated 1673, the yr. of the Test* Act. After the Act* of Toleration (1689) the Luths. split into nat. groups. Most Eur. Luth. chs. now have outposts in Brit. serving Luths. in their own for. tongue. The Hanoverian kings had Luth. chaplains, but this practice declined and finally ended.

16. Eng.-speaking Lutheranism goes back to the beginning of the Ev. Luth. Ch. of Eng. 1896. Six Ger. bakers did not feel at home in the liberalism and nationalism of the Ger. Luth. Ch. of their day and called a pastor from the Missouri* Synod. This ch. became Eng.-speaking, and after WW II it began energetically to face its responsibilities among a largely unchurched people.

17. After WW II help was needed by Luth. refugees from Poland, Latvia, Estonia, and Ger. The Luth. Council of Gt. Brit. was founded 1948 under leadership of E. G. Pearce of the Ev. Luth. Ch. of Eng. to sustain and draw these Luths. together. Funds were provided equally by the LCMS and the NLC. Later the whole burden was assumed by the LWF and the Luth. Council became its nat. committee. Efforts continue to draw the various Luths. closer together. Pastors meet twice a yr. under auspices of the Luth. Free Conf. The Ev. Luth. Ch. of Eng. trains pastors at its Westfield House, Cambridge; the Council has attached a theologian to Mansfield Coll., Oxford, for similar purposes.

18. Exact statistics not available. Recent figures: 70 Luth. pastors in Gt. Brit.: 15 Ger., 15 Ev. Luth. Ch. of Eng., 9 Latvian, 6 Swed., 5 Norw., 5 United Luth. Syn., 4 Polish, 4 Dan., 3 Estonian, 2 Fin., and 2 Hung. The United Luth. Syn. is a product of the Council and cares for the Eng.-speaking children of refugees and for unchurched Brit. people. NEN

J. R. H. Moorman, *A History of the Church in England* (London, 1953); *An Ecclesiastical History of England,* ed. J. C. Dickinson, 5 vols. (London, 1961–); C. S. Meyer, *Elizabeth I and the Religious Settlement of 1559* (St. Louis, 1960); E. G. Pearce, *The Lutheran Church in Britain* (London, 1953).

England, Free Church of. Traces its beginning to a quarrel in 1843 bet. Henry Phillpotts* (1778–1869), bp. Exeter and High Churchman who espoused Tractarianism,* and James Shore, one of his clergy and who opposed the movement. The ch. received definite shape in 1863 in assoc. with the Calvinistic Methodists known as the Countess of Huntingdon's Connexion. It adopted the Thirty-nine Articles. Later in the c. it became assoc. with the Reformed* Episcopal Church, formed in the US by G. D. Cummins, through which it obtained episc. orders.

English District Synod of Ohio. See *General Synod of the Evangelical Lutheran Church in the United States of America, The,* 3.

English (Evangelical) Lutheran Conference of Missouri, The. See *Missouri and Other States, The English Evangelical Lutheran Synod of.*

English (Evangelical) Lutheran Conference of Missouri and Other States, The General. See *Missouri and Other States, The English Evangelical Lutheran Synod of.*

English Evangelical Lutheran Synod of Missouri and Other States, The. See *Missouri and Other States, The English Evangelical Lutheran Synod of.*

English Evangelical Lutheran Synod of the Northwest. See *General Council of the Evangelical Lutheran Church in (North) America,* 3; *United Lutheran Church, Synods of,* 17.

English Lutheran Publication Society of St. Louis, Mo. Organized 1888 to tr. into Eng. standard Luth. books, tracts, and works of persons of ability in the Syn. Conf.

English Northwest Synod. See *United Lutheran Church, Synods of,* 17.

English Ohio Synod. See *Ohio and Other States, The Evangelical Lutheran Joint Synod of,* 4.

Engnell, Karl Ivan Alexander (1906–64). B. Linköping, Swed.; prof. Lund and Uppsala. Coed. *Svensk bibliskt uppslagsverk.* Other works include *Studies in Divine Kingship in the Ancient Near East;*

Gamla Testamentet: en traditionshistorisk inledning; Profetia och tradition; The Call of Isaiah.

Enlightenment (Ger. *Aufklärung*). 1. Philos. movement that began toward the end of the Renaissance,* flowered esp. in the 2d half of the 18th c., and began to decay in the 19th c.; its elements were individualistic, rationalistic, and subjective; its goal was independence, also from authority of Biblical revelation; affected every phase of life; marked the beginning of modern secular culture; spread from Eur. to N and S Am.

2. Humanism began and developed in It. in the 15th-16th c. Its influence was temporarily restricted by religious interest aroused by the Reformation but revived and found expression in R. Descartes,* B. Spinoza,* P. Bayle,* and Deism.* In the Fr. Enlightenment upper classes became frivolous and regarded RCm and Protestantism as equally ridiculous. Its leading exponents were the Encyclopedists.* It attacked religious, pol., and soc. traditions and reached its climax in the Fr. Revolution (see *France,* 2).

3. Ger. Enlightenment was influenced by the Eng. and the Fr. It drew strength from Freemasonry* and the philos. of C. v. Wolff.* Prominent factors in the Ger. movement were the influence of the skeptical Frederick II, C. F. Nicolai's* *Allgemeine Deutsche Bibliothek,* and the writings of M. Mendelssohn,* H. S. Reimarus,* and G. E. Lessing.* Theol. became grossly rationalistic. But vulgar features were sloughed off by J. W. v. Goethe* and I. Kant,* who criticized shallowness and led Ger. literature and philos. to their greatest heights. Ger. Enlightenment was followed by an influential philos. idealism.*

See also *Secularism.*

J. G. Hibben, *The Philosophy of the Enlightenment* (London, 1910); E. Cassirer, *The Philosophy of the Enlightenment,* tr. F. C. A. Koelln and J. P. Pettegrove (Princeton, N. J., 1951); *Das Zeitalter der Aufklärung,* ed. W. Philipp, in *Klassiker des Protestantismus,* VII, ed. C. M. Schröder (Bremen, 1963); H. G. Nicolson, *The Age of Reason: The Eighteenth Century,* in *The Mainstream of the Modern World Series,* ed. J. Gunther (New York, 1961).

Enlil. See *Babylonians, Religion of the,* 1.

Ennodius, Magnus Felix (ca. 473–521). B. probably Arles; taught rhetoric Milan; bp. Pavia ca. 514; held that the pope is *de jure* superior to human judgment; tried to reconcile E and W chs., pagan culture and Christian faith; hymnist. Works include a biography of Epiphanius, bp. Pavia.

MPL 63, 13–364.

Enoch. See *Apocrypha,* A 4.

Ens. See *Being.*

En-Sof (En-Soph). See *Cabala.*

En-soi (in itself). Term used by the Fr. existentialist Jean-Paul Sartre (b. 1905) for material things; the *en-soi* is characterized by being.

Entelechy (Gk. *entelecheia*). In Aristotle: 1. form, essence, or function that makes matter a real thing; 2. mode of being of a thing whose essence is completely realized. See also *Being.*

Entered Apprentice. See *Freemasonry,* 3.

Entfelder, Christian (16th c.). Pupil of J. Denk*; Anabap. preacher Eibenschitz (Bohemia) 1527, Strasbourg 1529, Königsberg 1544; mystic; pantheist.

Enthusiasm (from Gk.; fanaticism from Lat.; Ger. *Schwärmerei*). Belief that people receive special revelations of the Holy Spirit. Enthusiasts expect God to draw, enlighten, justify, and save them without means of grace.* Cf. FC Ep II 13; SD II 4, 46, 80. See also *Ecstasy; Mennonite Churches,* 2.

Envelope System. See *Finances in the Church,* 4.

Environment. See *Educational Psychology,* B, 3–5.

Envy. Sinful jealousy.* See also *Sins, Venial and Mortal.*

Enzinas, Francisco de (Grecized: Dryander; Ger.: Eichmann; Fr.: Duchesne; known in Holland as Van Eyck; ca. 1520–ca. 1552). B. Burgos, Sp.; educ. Louvain (Belgium) and Wittenberg; tr. NT into Sp., pub. Antwerp 1543; gave copy to Charles* V; imprisoned in Brussels; escaped to Wittenberg ca. 1545; to Eng. via Strasbourg and Basel; prof. Cambridge; returned to Strasbourg 1549. Works include *Historia vera de morte sancti viri Ioannis Diazij.* His brother Jaime wrote a Sp. ev. catechism pub. Antwerp 1545 and was burned in Rome as heretic 1547.

Eoban (Eoba; Eobo; Eaba; d. 754). Co-worker and amanuensis of Boniface*; sent to Eng. by Boniface; accompanied him on last visit to Frisia; martyred with him at Dokkum; sometimes called diocesan bp. of Utrecht or Maastricht 753.

Eobanus Hessus. See *Hessus, Helius Eobanus.*

Éon of Stella (Éon de l'Étoile; Eudo de la Stella; Eons; Euno; Evus; d. ca. 1148). B. probably Loudéac, Brittany; enthusiast; traveling preacher; followers plundered chs. and monasteries; was condemned by the Syn. of Reims 1148; imprisoned.

Eparchy. Term equivalent to diocese* in Eastern* Orthodox Churches.

Épée, Charles Michel de l' (1712–89). Fr. abbé; obtained manual alphabet from J. R. Pereire*; perfected one-hand sign alphabet for deaf and dumb; founded institution for deaf and dumb at Paris.

Ephesus, "Robber Synod" of (Called *Latrocinium,* Lat. "highway robbery," by metonymy "a band of robbers"; 449). By brutality and violence and support of imperial troops Dioscorus* (d. 454) obtained temprary restoration of Eutyches* and condemnation of Flavian,* Eusebius* of Dorylaeum, Theodoret* of Cyrrhus (in Syria), et al; decisions reversed by Council of Chalcedon.*

Ephesus, Seven Sleepers of. See *Seven Sleepers of Ephesus.*

Ephesus, Third Ecumenical Council of (431). Convoked by E Roman Emp. Theodosius II (401–450; emp. 408–450; grandson of Theodosius* I), who favored Nestorius.* Opening of the council was postponed from day to day for 15 days because John of Antioch and other bps. from Syria and elsewhere in the E (adherents of Nestorius) and the representatives of Rome had not arrived. On June 22 Cyril* of Alexandria, chief opponent of Nestorius, refusing to wait longer, opened the council; the same day it condemned, deposed, and excommunicated Nestorius. The doctrine that Mary is *Theotokos** (mother of God), and that God the Word was born, suffered, and died in the flesh, was adopted. The legates of Celestine I of Rome (pope 422–432), arriving later, joined in the condemnation of Nestorius July 10–11, trying to use the occasion in the interest of the primacy of Rome. The council also condemned Pelagianism* (in the doctrine of Celestius*) and the Messalians (Euchites*). See also *Councils and Synods,* 4.

Ephor (Gk. "magistrate," esp. in Sparta). Term used for several ecclesiastical officials with supervisory functions. In Luth. chs. it is used for officials whose functions correspond to those of bp. or supt., e. g., in Saxony. See also *Batak Protestant Christian Church.*

Ephphatha. See *Deaf,* 1, 14.

Ephraem (Ephraim; Ephrem; Ephraem Syrus, i. e. the Syrian; ca. 306–ca. 373). B. Nisibis; possibly accompanied Jacob* of Nisibis to Nicaea 325 AD; after cession of Nisibis to Persia 363, went to Edessa.* Exegetic, dogmatic, controversial, and ascetic writings, mostly in verse, reveal efforts to be a Scriptural theol. Wrote hymns for feast days and funerals, against heretics, and on the Last Judgment. Enjoined devotion to saints, esp. Mary, whose sinlessness he taught. Called "Harp (or Lyre, or Zither) of the Holy Ghost; Prophet of the Syrians." See also *Manuscripts of the Bible,* 3 a; *Schools, Early Christian,* 4–6.

J. Alsleben, *Das Leben des heiligen Ephraem, des Syrers* (Berlin, 1853); *Des heiligen Ephräm des Syrers ausgewählte Schriften,* vol. 1 ed. O. Bardenhewer, tr. S. Euringer and A. Rücker, vol. 2 ed. and tr. A. Rücker, *Bibliothek der Kirchenväter,* series vols. 37 and 61, ed. O. Bardenhewer, K. Yeyman, and J. Zellinger (Kempten and Munich, 1919, 28); A. Vööbus, *Literary, Critical, and Historical Studies in Ephrem the Syrian* (Stockholm, 1958).

Ephraemi, Codex. See *Manuscripts of the Bible,* 3 a.

Ephrata Community. See *Baptist Churches,* 17; *Communistic Societies,* 5.

Epiclesis. Petition in E anaphora* asking God the Father to send the Spirit on the bread and wine of the Lord's Supper to change them into the body and blood of Christ.

Epictetus (ca. 50–ca. 130). B. probably Hierapolis, Phrygia; Gk. Stoic (see *Stoicism*) philos.; concentrated on ethics, stressing the fatherhood of God and brotherhood of men; mentions Christians only once, contemptuously.

A. F. Bonhöffer, *Epictet und die Stoa* (Stuttgart, 1890), *Die Ethik des Stoikers Epictet* (Stuttgart, 1894), and *Epictet und das Neue Testament,* in *Religionsgeschichtliche Versuche und Vorarbeiten,* X, ed. R. Wünsch and L. Deubner, (Giessen, 1911); D. S. Sharp, *Epictetus and the New Testament* (London, 1914); *Epictetus: The Discourses as Reported by Arrian, the Manual, and Fragments,* ed. and tr. W. A. Oldfather, 2 vols., in *The Loeb Classical Library,* ed. E. Capps, W. H. D. Rouse, and T. E. Page (New York, 1925–28). EK

Epicureanism. The philos. system of Epicurus.* The community that he est. at Athens was called The Garden from the garden in which he taught. Though he is said to have written voluminously, only 3 letters and numerous aphorisms survive. From these remains and from the works of such followers as Lucretius* and Philodemus it is evident that the school's chief tenets were organized under a few main heads: canonic (Epicurean logic), physics, and ethics. Of these divisions the first two interested Epicurus only to the extent that they provided a basis for the 3d. Prominent among his principles: The only avenue to knowledge is sense-perception, which all men have in common. Through sense-perception we learn that there are only 2 things in the universe whose existence is certain and enduring: atoms and void. From these primordial, eternal atoms of matter and their chance combination everything else arises: this world with its human inhabitants and an infinite number of other worlds, with anthropomorphic gods inhabiting the empty regions bet. the worlds and beyond. The gods are blissfully and immortally free of all concern for this world or any other. Man, on the other hand, is characterized by mortality. When he dies, the atoms of his body patently begin slow dissolution; the atoms of his soul, being much finer, are dispersed at once. Consequently, after death there is no life or consciousness; for when we are, death is not, and when death is, we are not. Therefore man's proper concern is with this life only, in which pleasure is the greatest good of man's nature and as such the aim of human existence. Pleasure must not be understood in the crass sense but as a peaceful, indep. state of body and mind, free from pain and trouble, resulting in imperturbability. In fact, "imperturbability" rather than "pleasure" is the catchword that marks Epicurus' ambition to free men from the fears that rob them of happiness: fear of death and fear of gods or of mysterious powers in nature. To maintain the imperturbability for which he believed his physics furnished a basis, Epicurus counseled shunning pub. life and withdrawing from the world.

Epicurea, ed. H. K. Usener (Leipzig, 1887); *Epicurus: The Extant Remains,* ed. and tr. C. Bailey Oxford, 126); *The Philosophy of Epicurus: Letters, Doctrines, and Parallel Passages from Lucretius,* ed. and tr. G. K. Strodach (Evanston, Ill., 1963). RJ

Epicurus (ca. 341–ca. 270 BC). B. Samos; Gk. philos.; founded Epicureanism*; probably studied under Pamphilus (Platonist) and Nausaphanes (Democritean); character changed from aggressive to gentle and considerate; founded school at Mytilene, on the is. of Lesbos, and at Lampsacus, Mysia; ca. 306 founded school at Athens.

N. W. DeWitt, *Epicurus and His Philosophy* (Minneapolis, 1954); A. M. J. Festugière, *Epicurus and His Gods,* tr. C. W. Chilton (Oxford, 1955); *Epicurus: Letters, Principal Doctrines, and Vatican Sayings,* ed. and tr. R. M. Geer (Indianapolis, 1964).

Epigonation (from Gk. for "on" and "knee"). Rhombic vestment worn on right hip by bps. and some other ecclesiastical dignitaries of the E Orthodox Ch.

Epigonus. See *Monarchianism,* B 5.

Epiphanes. See *Gnosticism,* 7 f.

Epiphanius (ca. 315–403). B. near Eleutheropolis, Palestine; Gk. ch. father; bp. Salamis (Constantia), Cyprus, 367; highly esteemed for monastic asceticism, learning, piety, self-denying care for the poor, and zeal for orthodoxy (but zeal not always according to knowledge; see *Origen*); his polemical treatises have hist. value.

MPG, 41; 42; 43, 9–664.

Epiphany (Gk. "manifestation"). Term applied to the birth, Baptism, appearance of the star, and similar events in Christ's life. It is also applied to Jan. 6, celebrated in commemoration of the visit of the Magi. See also *Church Year,* 2, 11, 16.

Episcopacy (from Gk. *episkopos,* "overseer, bishop"). Govt. of ch. by bps.

See also *Bishop; Hierarchy; Polity, Ecclesiastical,* 6.

Episcopal Church, The. See *Protestant Episcopal Church.*

Episcopal Inquisition. See *Inquisition,* 3.

Episcopal Synod (Diocese of Jordan). See *Middle East,* C.

Episcopal Throne. In E Orthodox Ch., place from which bp. supervises the people when he is not in the sanctuary.

Episcopalians. See *Protestant Episcopal Church.*

Episcopius, Simon (Bischop; Biscop; Bisschop; 1583–1643). B. Amsterdam; educ. Leiden; influenced by Arminius; prof. Leiden 1612; with other Remonstrants deposed and excommunicated 1619 by Syn. of Dordrecht* and expelled from the country; prof. Arminian Coll., Amsterdam, 1634. Works include a confession of faith and liturgical forms for Remonstrant Brotherhood. See also *Arminianism.*

Epistemology (Gk. "study of knowledge"). Branch of philos. that investigates the possibility, limits, origin, kinds, structure, and other problems of knowledge and tries to determine the nature of truth. See also *Philosophy,* 3, 6.

Epistle of the Apostles *(Epistola Apostolorum).* 2d c. apocryphal writing containing supposed conversations of the risen Christ with the apostles; directed against gnosticism* and docetism*; Coptic tr. found 1895 in Cairo by Carl Schmidt (1868–1938).

Epistle Side of Altar. Liturgical south*; right as one faces the altar. See also *Church Furniture,* 1.

Epistolae obscurorum virorum. See *Letters of Obscure Men.*

Epitimia. E Orthodox term denoting fasting, praying,

giving alms, reading sacred books, etc. imposed on great sinners.

Epitimius, Andreas. See *Beyer, Hartmann.*

Epitome. See *Lutheran Confessions,* C 2.

Epitrachelion (from Gk. for "on" and "neck"). Long narrow stole worn by priests and bps. in the E Orthodox Ch. See also *Vestments, Clerical.*

Epoche. In E. Husserl,* suspension of judgment, or reduction of object to pure phenomenon.

Epworth League. Organization for young people in Meth. chs. of Am., named after J. Wesley's* birthplace, Epworth, Eng. Organized 1889 at Cleveland, Ohio, by merging 5 organizations into 1. See also *Young People's Organizations, Christian,* III 12.

Equatorial Guinea. See *Africa,* C 18.

Equiprobabilism. Theory in ethics which holds that, when 2 divergent judgments are equally defensible, either may be followed; developed by A. M. de' Liguori.*

Era. See *Time.*

Erasmus, Desiderius (ca. 1469–1536). "Prince of the humanists." B. probably Rotterdam; educ. Deventer and 's Hertogenbosch; spent several yrs. in the Augustinian monastery at Steyn (or Emmaus; near Gouda); ordained priest 1492; entered the service of the bp. of Cambrai; studied philos. and theol. in Paris 1495–96; acquired a distaste for scholasticism*; returned to Holland because of illness; in Paris with interruptions 1496–99; on the 1st of 3 visits to Eng. (1499–1500) he met J. Colet,* who influenced him in the direction of Christian humanism; in Fr. and Holland 1500–05, Eng. 1505–06, It. 1506–09, Eng. 1509–14, Basel 1514–16, Neth. 1516–21, Basel 1521–29, Freiburg 1529–35, Basel 1535–36.

Relationship of Erasmus to the Reformation was ambivalent. He approved of Luther's* assault on abuses; opposed innovations in doctrine and ch. life; avoided siding openly with Luther in hope of maintaining a more influential role as a neutral. Many of Erasmus' friends joined the Reformation; hist. moved beyond him, leaving this moderate idealist an isolated and tragic figure during his last years.

Works include *Adagia* (ancient Lat. sayings elucidated); *Moriae Encomium* ("Praise of Folly"); *De Libero Arbitrio; Colloquies; Enchiridion;* editions of the NT and of ch. fathers.

See also *Synergistic Controversy.*

P. S. Allen, *The Age of Erasmus* (Oxford, 1914); J. Huizinga, *Erasmus and the Age of Reformation,* tr. F. Hopman, with a selection from the letters of Erasmus, tr. B. Flowers (London, 1952); P. Smith, *Erasmus: A Study of His Life, Ideals, and Place in History* (New York, 1923); A. Renaudet, *Études érasmiennes, 1521–1529* (Paris, 1939); R. E. Reynolds, *Thomas More and Erasmus* (London, 1965); M. M. Phillips, *Erasmus and the Northern Renaissance* (New York, 1965); L. Bouyer, *Erasmus and the Humanist Experiment,* tr. F. X. Murphy (London, 1959). LWSj

Erastianism. View according to which the state is supreme in ecclesiastical affairs. Term derived from name of T. Erastus,* who held that Christian rulers are responsible for external govt. of the ch. and hence could judge men's conduct, settle disputes, and work with pastors in reproving those living immoral lives, but could not debar from the Sacrament. Erastianism has aspects beyond the principles of Erastus, who did not make the ch. subservient to the state but tried to curtail the former's legal and pol. functions. See also *Church and State,* 12.

Erastus, Thomas (original name Lieber, Liebler, or Lüber; ca. 1524–83). Ger.-Swiss Zwinglian physician and theol.; prof. Heidelberg and Basel; as Zwinglian opposed both Calvinists and Luths.; present at theol. confs. bet. Luths. and Ref. at Heidelberg 1560, Maulbronn* 1564; helped introd. Heidelberg Catechism (see *Reformed Confessions,* D 2); *Explicatio gravissimae quaestionis* (written 1568; pub. 1589) places external affairs of ch., but not its spiritual functions (ministry of Word and Sacraments), under Christian ruler. See also *Church and State,* 12; *Erastianism.*

Erb, John. See *Catholic Apostolic Church,* 2.

Erb, Matthias (1494–1571). B. Ettlingen, Ger.; humanist; joined Reformation 1520; chaplain of the troops of Bern in war against RC cantons; pastor Baden; friend of M. Bucer*; supt. and reformer of Alsace; deposed 1560 for opposing Luth. ch. order of Duke Christopher.

Erdmann, Christian Friedrich David (1821–1905). B. Güstebiese, Ger.; educ. Berlin; ev. theol.; prof. Königsberg 1856; gen. supt. of ch. in Silesia 1864.

Erdös, Joseph (1856–1946). Hung. Ref. theol.; prof. NT Debrecen 1888–1928; espoused orthodox confessional theol., but advocated freedom in NT research.

Erdösi. See *Sylvester, Johannes.*

Eremites. See *Hermits.*

Ereshkigal. See *Babylonians, Religion of the,* 5.

Erfurtsche Buch. See *Neostadiensium admonitio.*

Eric IX. See *Sweden, Conversion of, to Christianity.*

Erich I (1470–1540). Duke of Brunswick-Lüneburg; fought against Turks 1493; regarded Reformation as disobedience of estates to empire, rather than reform endeavor or matter of conscience; admired M. Luther* for his stand at Worms (see *Worms, Diet of, 1521*).

Eridu. See *Babylonians, Religion of the,* 1.

Erigena, Johannes Scotus (Ierugena; Eriugena; ca. 815–ca.877). B. and educ. probably in Ireland; probably principal of court school of Emp. Charles* II 847; his doctrine is an early attempt at occidental speculative dogmatics; he is a connecting link bet. Gk. and occidental philos.; influenced Scholasticism* and mysticism.* Tr. some of the writings of Gk. ch. fathers into Lat. Works include *De divisione naturae.*

Erikssön, Jörgen (1535–1604). "Norway's Luther"; 3d Luth. bp. Stavanger 1571–1604; b. Haderslev, Den.; educ. Copenhagen and Wittenberg; firmly est. Lutheranism in his territory. See also *Norway, Lutheranism in,* 2.

Eritrea. See *Africa,* E 3.

Erk, Ludwig Christian (1807–83). B. Wetzlar, Ger.; music teacher in Mörs and at the Royal Seminary, Berlin; dir. liturgical cathedral choir, Berlin; organized the Erk male choral soc. and the Erk mixed chorus esp. to foster folk songs; ed. *Vierstimmige Choralsätze der vornehmsten Meister des 16. und 17. Jahrhunderts* and many other collections.

Erlangen School. See *Lutheran Theology After 1580,* 11.

Ermelo Missionary Society. Organized at Ermelo, Holland, 1856. Mission fields included Indonesia, South Sea Islands, and Egypt.

Ernest (Ernst; 1497–1546). "The Confessor." B. Uelzen, Prussia; Duke of Brunswick-Lüneburg; nephew of Frederick* the Wise; introduced Lutheranism into duchy 1527; signed AC 1530.

Ernest I (Ernst; 1601–75). "Der Fromme" ("the Pious"); "Bet-Ernst" ("Praying Ernest"). B. Altenburg, Ger.; Duke of Saxe-Weimar 1620–40, Saxe-Gotha 1640–75; Luth.; felt responsible for both temporal and eternal welfare of subjects; est. schools and compulsory educ. to achieve piety and practical training. Works pub. under him include a Ger. hymnal; *Das Weimarische* Bibelwerk; Cantionale sacrum.* See also *Africa,* A 5.

Ernest of Hessen-Rheinfels (Ernst; 1623–93). B. Kassel, Ger.; educ. as strict Calvinist; after a colloquy bet. RCs and Luths. in 1652 he joined RC Ch.; advocated ch. union, international court for adjustment of differences bet. RC nations, tolerance.

Ernesti, Johann August (1707–81). B. Tennstedt, Ger.; educ. Schulpforte, Wittenberg, and Leipzig; prof. Leipzig; mediating theol.; tried to hold to inspiration of the Bible and to Luth. Symbolical Books, but made concessions to rationalism. See also *Grammaticohistorical Method; Lutheran Theology After 1580,* 8; *Nösselt, Johann August.*

Ernestinische Bibel. See *Weimarische Bibelwerk, Das.*

Ernst, August Friedrich (June 25, 1841–Aug. 8, 1924). B. Eddesse, Hannover; educ. Celle and Göttingen; instructor Clausthal Gymnasium; to Am. to serve Luth. Ch.; ordained Pottstown, Pa., 1864; pastor Brooklyn and Albany, N. Y.; prof. Northwestern U. (later Northwestern Coll.), Watertown, Wis., 1869, pres. 1871; served this school over 50 yrs. and made it an Am. school with Luth. ideals of the best Ger. traditions; 1st pres. Joint Synod of Wisconsin and Other States 1892–1901 (see *Wisconsin Evangelical Lutheran Synod*). Works include *Aus der Geschichte der lutherischen Kirche in Nord-Amerika,,* bound with T. Schlüter, *Luthers Leben* (Milwaukee, 1917), pp. 189–250; textbooks for parish schools.

Ernst, Christoph Friedrich Wilhelm (1765–1855). B. Jesberg, Ger.; court preacher Kassel 1795; gen. supt. 1845; influenced by I. Kant* and F. W. J. v. Schelling*; espoused a form of supernaturalism*; emphasized mystery of God; held Christianity is beyond the realm of reason.

Ernst, Johann Adam (Nov. 27, 1815–Jan. 20, 1895). "Father of Missouri Lutheranism in Canada." B. Öttingen, Ger.; cobbler by trade; entered teacher training under J. K. W. Löhe* 1841 as his 1st student; to Am. with J. G. Burger* 1842; mem. Ohio Syn. (see *Ohio and Other States, Evangelical Lutheran Joint Synod of*) 1842–45; suggested organizing new syn. to C. F. W. Walther* 1845; signed "document* of separation" from Ohio Syn. Sept. 18, 1845, at its Cleveland, Ohio, conv.; signed W. Sihler's* original draft of the Missouri* Syn. const. in St. Louis, Mo., May 20, 1846, and was among the founding fathers of the Mo. Syn. at the meeting at Fort Wayne, Ind., July 1846 and Chicago, Ill., Apr. 1847. Pastor Neudettelsau, Union Co., Ohio, 1848; in and near Marion, Marion Co., Ohio, 1848; Town Eden, Erie Co., N. Y., 1849; Euclid, near Cleveland, Ohio, 1860; Lecon and Elmira, Waterloo Co., Ont., Can., 1863; Euclid, Ohio, 1881. See also *Canada,* A 10; *Lutheran Church – Missouri Synod, Districts of The,* A 9.

Ernst. See also *Ernest.*

Erntedankfest. See *Thanksgiving Day.*

Eros. See *Love; Lund, Theology of.*

Errett, Isaac. See *Disciples of Christ,* 3.

Error. See *Fundamental Doctrines; Heresy.*

Erskine, Ebenezer (1680–1754). B. Berwickshire, Scot.; educ. Edinburgh; ordained by Kirkcaldy presbytery 1703; minister Portmoak 1703–31; refused to take Oath of Abjuration (see Abjuration, 2); minister Sterling and moderator Sterling and Perth 1731; opposed 1732 Patronage Act of Assem. (see *Presbyterian Churches,* 1), which ignored rights of laity in elections to vacant chs.; suspended from ministry by Gen. Assem. 1733; with William Wilson of Perth, Alexander Moncrieff of Abernethy, and James Fisher of Kinclaven formed an Associate Presbytery 1733; formally deposed from the est. ch. and formed Secession Ch. 1740. See also *Associate Reformed Church; Scotland, Reformation in,* 1.

Erskine, Thomas (1788–1870). Scot. theol.; interpreter of the mystical side of Calvinism. Works include *Essay on Faith; The Unconditional Freeness of the Gospel.*

Erudition of a Christian Man, The. See *Anglican Confessions,* 2.

Esbjörn, Lars Paul (1808–70). B. Delsbo, Swed.; educ. Uppsala; pastor in Swed.; to Am. 1849; pastor in Ill. 1849–58; Scand. prof. theol. at Ill. State U., Springfield, 1858–60; pres. and prof. Augustana Sem., Chicago, 1860–63; pastor in Swed. 1863–70. See also *Publication Houses, Lutheran.*

G. Andreen, *L. P. Esbjörn and the Pilgrim Fathers of 1849* (Rock Island, Ill., 1925).

Esch, Johann (Esschen; van Esch; van Essen; Nesse; d. 1523). Augustinian monk of Antwerp; follower of M. Luther*; burned at the stake in Brussels with H. Voes*; commemorated by Luther in the poem "Ein neues Lied wir heben an."

Eschatology. Part of dogmatics* that treats of the last* things. See also *Dispensationalism; Millennium.*

Escobar y Mendoza, Antonio (1589–1669). Sp. Jesuit; b. Valladolid; noted for asceticism and energy as preacher. Works include *Liber theologiae moralis; Historia de la Virgen Madre de Dios Maria;* commentaries.

Esdras. See *Apocrypha,* A 3.

Eskil (ca. 1100–ca. 1181). Bp. Roskilde, Den., 1134; abp. Lund, Swed., ca. 1138–77; assoc. with Fr. reformers, esp. Bernard of Clairvaux; championed ideas of Gregory VII (see *Popes,* 7); conflicts with kings led to yrs. of exile in Fr.

Eskimos (In[n]uit). Ca. 45,000 native inhabitants of N coast of N Am. and neighboring islands, esp. Greenland.* Usually live close to seashore; language is polysynthetic (word elements combine into single words equivalent to a sentence); soc. structure communistic anarchistic (raw material and some manufactured items common property; govt. structure usually absent; soc. action controlled by pub. opinion); cheerful, lighthearted people. According to native religion, all things, animate and inanimate, have a spirit. Men and animals have souls that continue after this life. A sky god and sea goddess are most important deities. There is also a cult of game animals.

H. Egede* began Christian missions among Eskimos of Greenland 1721. His son Paul completed tr. of the NT into Innuit. The Moravian Ch. began work in Greenland 1733 (this miss. given to Dan. Luths. 1899), Labrador 1764. Oblates of Mary Immaculate have worked among Eskimos near Hudson Bay since ca. 1860. The CMS worked till 1920 on the continent. The E Orthodox Ch. pioneered among Eskimos in Alaska. The Am. branch of the Moravian Ch. began in Alaska 1885, the Am. branch of the Swed. Miss. Soc. 1897. Jesuits have worked among Eskimos since 1786.

The Luth. Eskimo Miss. of The ALC has stations at Nome, Alaska, on Bering Sea, and Arctic Ocean coastline. Episcopalians, Presbyterians, and Quakers also carry on miss. work among Eskimos.

Espen, Zeger Bernhard von (1646–1728). Belgian canonist; b. Louvain; prof. canon law Louvain 1675; defended Gallican theories (see *Gallicanism*); defended Jansenism*; fled to Belgium. Works include *Jus ecclesiasticum universum.*

Ess, Leander van (Johann Heinrich van Ess; 1772–1847). Ger. RC theol.; Benedictine monk; tr. Bible into Ger.; criticized decree of Council of Trent* on Bible publication.

Esse. See *Being.*

Essence. See *Being.*

Essenes. Etymology of the term disputed. Jewish ascetic monastic group mentioned by Philo* Judaeus, F. Josephus,* and Pliny* the Elder. Seem to have originated ca. 2d c. BC and existed into 2d c. AD. Most important settlement on the W shore of the Dead Sea. Emphasized simplicity, piety, sacramental meals, fixed times for prayer. Taught dualism of light and darkness and had own solar festive calendar. Regarded themselves as people of new covenant. Classes: priests, Levites, mems., novitiates. The view that John the Baptist and Jesus were connected with Essenes is gen. rejected. See also *Dead Sea Scrolls.*

Established Church. See *State Church.*

Esther, Additions to. See *Apocrypha,* A 3.

Esther, Feast of. See *Judaism,* 4.

Esthetic Argument. See *God, Arguments for the Existence of.*

Estienne, Robert, I (Étienne; Stephanus; 1503–59). B. Paris; printer to Francis I of Fr. (1494–1547; king 1515–47) 1539; to Geneva; joined Ref. Ch.; pub. Lat. and Gk. classics, patristic writings, Lat.-Fr. dictionary, various eds. of the Bible, concordance. See also *Chapters and Verses of the Bible; Textual Criticism,* 2.

Estius, Gulielmus (Willem; Wilhelm; Hessels van Est; 1542–1613). B. Gorcum, Holland; studied at Utrecht and Louvain; prof. primarius Douai 1582, chancellor 1595. Works include *In omnes beati Pauli et septem catholicas apostolorum epistolas commentarii.*

Esto mihi. Another name for Quinquagesima* Sun.; first Lat. words of the traditional Introit* for the day (Ps 31:2b, 3, 1).

Estonia. 1. *Christianity before the Reformation.* Estonia, a Baltic country at the outfall of the Finnish Gulf, N continental Eur., experienced its 1st contacts with Christianity in the 11th c. Russ. Prince Yaroslav's (ca. 988–1054) "Christianizing" activities ca. 1030 failed, as did efforts of the Fr. Cistercian miss. Fulco, consecrated Bp. of the Estonians by Abp. Eskil* of Lund ca. 1164. The 1st successful miss. effort among Livonians and Estonians came from Germany. Meinhard (or Meinhart; d. 1196), an Augustinian monk from Holstein, landed ca. 1180 at the mouth of the Düna river; his efforts resulted 1184 in a ch. at Ikskile; he was made Bp. of Livonia 1186 by Abp. Hartwig II of Bremen. He was succeeded by Berthold of Hanover (d. 1198), who advocated a crusade against the Baltic people and died in it as a warrior. The next Bp. of Livonia, Albert* I, sailed up the Düna 1200 with military protection and dedicated the territory to Mary (Marienland). The Knights of the Sword *(Fratres militiae Christi)* were organized ca. 1201, confirmed by Innocent III 1204, absorbed by Teutonic Knights in 1237. Albert I won a major battle 1217 over Estonian forces led by Lembitu. In the summer of 1219 King Waldemar II of Den. est. a foothold in N Estonia. In connection with his campaign, Dietrich, Bp. of Estonia, was killed. The succession was contested between Wescelin (or Guecelin), Waldemar's candidate, and Hermann, Albert's candidate and brother, with the former recognized by Rome. By 1220 Järvamaa and Virumaa (the suffix "-maa" means "region") were in Dan. hands; by 1227 the whole country was under Christian rule, with Christian baptism enforced. During the Middle Ages 4 powers emerged: the Livonian branch of the Teutonic Knights (Knights of the Sword), the prince-bps., the nobles, and the cities. Most natives belonged to a politically powerless and economically exploited 5th estate.

2. *The Reformation and subsequent history.* Reformation ideas reached Livonia and Estonia from cen. and N Ger. in the 1520s. Reformation in Estonia was influenced by the ideas of A. Knöpken,* Sylvester Tegetmeyer,* and M. Hofmann* (or Hoffmann). Luth. teachings gained adherents early. Estonia lacked an outstanding reformer, but Johann Lange (d. 1531), Zacharias Hasse (d. 1531), and Hermann Marsow (came to Tartu [Dorpat] ca. 1523) were leading evangelicals. Lange and Hasse preached in Tallinn [Reval] since ca. 1523. In 1524 *Christliche Ordnung im kirchlichen Regiment* est. the organization of the ev. ch. in that city (see also *Lutheran Confessions,* A 5). Though Bp. Johannes Blankenfeld's spirited opposition arrested early spread of ev. ideas in Tartu, the outside help of Tegetmeyer and Hof[f]mann turned the tide. Little is gen. known of the spread of the ev. movement in smaller towns. Real evangelization of the countryside occurred in the 17th and 18th cents.

The ev. climate promoted pub. of catechetical helps (the catechism of Simon Wanradt and Johann Koell 1535; Franz Witte's catechism 1554). The NT appeared in 2 dialects 1686 and 1715; Anton Thor Helle's whole Bible *(Piibli Raamat)* appeared 1739.

In 1558 Russ. attacked and annexed Tartumaa, Viljandimaa, Järvamaa, and Virumaa. Swed. acquired Tallinn and Harjumaa-Virumaa. The Northern War (1563–70) resulted in a Prot.-RC curtain that halved the country. Swed. took possession of the mainland 1629, adding the islands 1645. Under Swed. rule Bp. Kristian Agricola provided directives for a clearly defined ch. organization ca. 1585; a Prot. university was est. at Tartu 1632; Estonian religious literature prospered; Swed. ch. statutes became effective in Estonia 1692. After the Great Northern War (ca. 1700–21) Estonia was occupied by Russians. Moravian Brethren (see *Moravian Church*) appeared; though outlawed 1743 they reached a height of influence in the 1st half of the 19th c. In the middle of the 19th c. the Russ. govt. initiated a policy of Russification that led to persecution of Luths.

3. *The Estonian Evangelical Lutheran Church.* Est. of the indep. Rep. of Estonia 1918 resulted in an indep. Estonian Ev. Luth. Ch. The 1919 Gen. Assem. of the EELC approved a constitution which maintains that the EELC is a free people's ch. Its teachings are based on Scripture and the Confessions of the Ev. Luth. Ch. The ch. is governed by a primate (Jakob Kukk 1919; Hugo Bernhard Rahamägi 1934; Johan Köpp [b. 1874] 1939). In 1937 the EELC had ca. 900,000 mems. and 250 pastors. Official pub.: *Eesti Kirik.* The EELC is a mem. of LWF and WCC.

WW II and for. occupations (Russ. 1940–41; Ger. 1941–44; Russ. 1944–) have impeded the work and development of the EELC. Köpp fled to Swed. 1944. Mems. of the EELC in Exile are scattered in many different countries and not formally organized or incorporated; 1957 membership: ca. 66,000. Bp. J. O. Lauri of Stockholm (b. 1891; educ. Dorpat; ordained 1917; bp. 1943; to Ger. 1944; then to Swed.) succeeded Köpp as head of the EELC in Exile.

Since Oct. 1967 Abp. Alfred Tooming (ordained 1934; rector St. Paul's parish, Viljandi, and dean of the Estonian Ch.'s Viljandi district 1949) headed the 350,000-mem. EELC in the Soviet Union. HOK

See also *Virginius, Adrian.*

E. Uustalu, *The History of Estonian People* (London, 1952); J. Köpp, *From Established Church to Free People's Church* (Stockholm, 1949); *Baltische Kirchengeschichte,* ed. R. Wittram (Göttingen, 1956); L. Arbusow, *Die Einführung der Reformation in Liv-, Est-, und Kurland,* in *Quellen und Forschungen zur Reformationsgeschichte,* III (Leipzig, 1921); O. Sild, *Eesti kirikulugu vanimast ajast olevikuni* (Tartu, 1938); A. Torma, *The Church in Estonia,* reprint bound with H. Perlitz, *The Fate of Religion and Church Under Soviet Rule in Estonia 1940–41* (New York, 1944); *Papers of the Estonian Theological Society in Exile, No. 15: Estonia Christiana* (Wetteren, Belgium, 1965); J. Aunver, *Religious Life and the Church in Estonia* (Stockholm, 1961).

Estonian Evangelical Lutheran Church. See *Estonia,* 3; *Estonian Lutherans in the US.*

Estonian Lutherans in the US. 1. *Missionary period* (until 1949). Work among Estonian immigrants in the US began as part of the for. language inner miss. endeavor of the LCMS. Best-known Estonian miss. in the early 20th c. was Hans Rebane; he worked mainly in Boston, New York, Philadelphia, and Baltimore. Conrad Klemmer (d. 1956) worked as the only Estonian miss. in the US 1913–56, serving congs. in New York, Boston, and Bogota and Paterson, N. J. Despite faithful labors of the missionaries the spiritual needs of Estonians could not be met adequately.

2. *Period of organization* (1949–53). After WW II many Estonians made their home in the US, Swed., Can., Eng., Australia, and elsewhere. Fourteen congs. were est. in the US and 7 in Can. Most Estonian congs. belong to the Estonian Ev. Luth. Ch. in Exile (see *Estonia,* 3).

3. *EELC in Exile in the US.* Since 1953 Estonian Luth. congs. in the US are divided into First Bishopric, led by Dean Aleksander Hinno (b. 1904), and Chicago Bishopric, led by Dean Rudolf Kiviranna (b. 1912). 1955 statistics: 8,007 mems. served by 18 pastors. HOK

Eternal. Existing forever, without beginning or end in time. See *God; Hereafter.*

Eternal Life. Spiritual life; the union of a Christian with God through faith in Christ Jesus, esp. the perfect enjoyment thereof in heaven. That eternal life is a present possession of every Christian is clearly taught in Scripture (Jn 3:16; 6:47; 1 Jn 5:11). Eternal life begins for us when the Father reveals the Son to us and enables us to call Him Lord by the Holy Ghost (1 Co 12:3). See also *Hereafter.*

Eternal Object. Term in A. N. Whitehead's* philos. corresponding to "idea" in Plato* or "form" in Aristotle.*

Eternal Punishment. See *Hereafter,* B.

Eternally Begotten. Term used to describe the eternal generation of the Son by the Father. See *Christ Jesus,* I A.

Ethelbert (Aethelber[h]t; Aedilberct; ca. 552–616). King of Kent ca. 560; married Bertha (a Christian), daughter of Frankish king Charibert (Haribert); baptized by Augustine* of Canterbury 597; 1st Christian Eng. king.

Ethelbert (Aethelberht; Aegelbriht; Albert; d. ca. 794). King of East Angles and Christian martyr; said to have wooed Elfthryth, daughter of Offa of Mercia, and to have been slain at the instigation of Offa or Offa's queen, Cynethryth; buried at Hereford.

Ethelbert (Aethelber[h]t; d. 866). King of Kent 855, Wessex 860.

Ethical Argument. See *Immortality, Arguments for.*

Ethical Culture. Movement begun 1876 when F. Adler* founded the N. Y. Soc. for Ethical Culture, based on 3 assumptions: sex, purity, and the principle of devoting the surplus of one's income beyond that required for one's own needs to the elevation of the working classes and continued intellectual development. He called the soc. the new religion of humanity, whose heaven is on earth, whose god is the good, and whose ch. is the universe. The soc. approached religion from the practical moral standpoint and encouraged its adherents to live a good life by following the dictates of duty. The movement declared its indep. of all creeds, called for deed rather than creed, and required of its mems. only recognition of the ethical aim as the highest goal of life.

Ethical culture socs. were organized in Chicago 1882, Philadelphia 1885, St. Louis 1886, Brooklyn 1906. Other socs. and fellowship groups were est. elsewhere in Am. The Am. Ethical Union was formed in the late 1880s; 1966 membership: ca. 5,500; its organ: *Ethical Culture Today.*

Socs. were est. in Ger., Fr., It., Eng., Austria, Japan, Switz., India, New Zealand, and other countries. The Internat. Union of Socs. for Ethical Culture was est. 1896 but survived among Eur. nations only in Eng. The Internat. Humanist and Ethical Union was formed 1952 in Amsterdam.

Stress is laid on moral instruction of the young. Ethical culture schools open to all were est. in NYC. Ethical culture socs. have been active also in soc. reform.

Services include music, inspirational readings, meditations (instead of prayer), and addresses.

After Adler's death John Lovejoy Elliott (1868–1942) was sr. leader of the N. Y. soc. After Elliott's death it was headed by 5 leaders.

See *Religious Bodies (US), Bibliography.*

Ethical Formalism. Term applied to the method of rational reflection of I. Kant* whereby he tried to determine ethical standards.

Ethical Problem. See *Apologetics,* I D.

Ethics. 1. Term for a. discipline concerned with such concepts as good, bad, duty, obligation; b. set of moral principles or values; c. philos. study of behavior and principles of conduct. J. M. Reu* defined ethics as "the science of the moral as it is to be realized first of all in the life of the individual and then also within the community of other personal beings."

2. Ethics has been variously classified, e. g., naturalistic ethics bases moral principles on empirically verifiable factors; theistic ethics claims approval of deity for moral principles; Christian ethics emphasizes voluntary acceptance of the divine will as norm by free human personalities and application of that will in individual and soc. life. These designations are not mutually exclusive. See also *Theology.*

3. Early Gk. thinkers often compared physical and moral health. Socrates* stressed close relationship bet. proper behavior and proper thought. Plato* built ethics on a metaphysical basis but conceived of it largely as citizenship in a free state in which individuals are guided by wisdom, courage, temperance, and justice. Aristotle* gives a list of virtues that form a golden mean bet. vices (see also *Eudaemonism*). Epicureans advocated a life of simple, refined pleasures. Early Stoics (see *Stoicism*) favored a life of virtue and inner equilibrium affected by neither pleasure nor pain. Later Stoics (e. g., Epictetus* and Marcus* Aurelius) considered each man a part of the whole world and condemned class distinctions as irrational. Skeptics (see *Skepticism*) questioned all knowledge and actions. Neo-Platonists regarded mystic union with the ultimate One, the Absolute, as the highest good. See also *Neo-Platonism; Plotinus.*

4. J. J. Rosseau* held that man should obey his impulses in a strictly natural environment. L. A. Feuerbach* also developed a principle of egoism, holding that ethics consists in obeying the natural impulse. E. H. Haeckel * added altruism (duty to society) to egoism. Utilitarianism* (T. Hobbes,* J. Bentham*) holds that whatever is useful is good and that the highest good for the individual or the greatest happiness of the greatest number must be selected by reason. See also *Mill, John Stuart.*

5. The ethics of evolutionism* is in a continual state of flux. That which is considered ethical today is the result of acts with favorable results in past evolutionary stages, and both past and present are parts of development toward an ideal (H. Spencer*). Elements of naturalism,* utilitarianism,* and evolutionism are present in empiricism.* See also *Aesthetics.*

6. I. Kant* sought a universal principle for behavior and found it in superindividual reason and the categorical* imperative. Later theologians (e. g., F. D. E. Schleiermacher*) took cognizance of his philos. ethics in their presentations. Am. representatives of idealistic ethics include B. P. Bowne,* W. E. Hocking,* and J. Royce.*

7. RC morality is a matter of works; the higher form of morality culminates in vows of poverty, chastity, and obedience; the lower form allows unrestricted use of all things natural. Ref. theol. makes salvation depend on an absolute divine decree and considers God's will as revealed in Scripture to be the unconditional law for moral development. Modernism was nomistic in its emphasis on the Sermon on the Mount.

8. Luth. theol. emphasizes that man does not become good by doing good, but must be good before he can do good (see also *Justification*). Love created in the heart by the Holy Spirit motivates Christian life. Christian ethics is not submission to God's will but harmony with it.

9. RC ethics in the 1960s stressed personal freedom, sought a middle way bet. unrestrained capitalism and totalitarian socialism, and continued to emphasize natural law. Angl. ethics stressed the doctrine of incarnation, emphasized that the incarnate Christ incorporates us in a new society, and sought synthesis bet. faith and reason. Luth. ethics usually distinguishes bet. society under law and the Christian believer under grace. Prots. in gen. emphasize freedom and justice. Reinhold Niebuhr and others stress relevance of sin and grace to politics.

10. Situation(al)* ethics emphasizes importance of love in determining proper action in given situations.

See also *Decalog; Grace, Means of,* II 2; *Moral Philosophy; Moral Theology; Social Ethics.* EL

L. S. Keyser, *A System of General Ethics,* 3d ed., rev. (Burlington, Iowa, 1926); N. Hartmann, *Ethics,* tr. S. Coit, 3 vols. (London and New York, 1932); O. A. W. Piper, *Die Grundlagen der evangelischen Ethik,* 2 vols. (Gütersloh, 1928–30); A. Nygren, *Filosofisk och kristen etik* (Lund, 1923); H. E. Brunner, *Das Gebot und die Ordnungen* (Tübingen, 1932), tr. O. Wyon, *The Divine Imperative* (London, 1937); J. M. Reu and P. H. Buehring, *Christian Ethics* (Columbus, Ohio, 1935); H. Thielicke, *Theologische Ethik* (Tübingen, 1951–), abridged and tr., *Theological Ethics,* ed. W. H. Lazareth (Philadelphia, 1966–); N. H. Söe, *Kristelig etik,* 4th ed. (Copenhagen, 1957), tr. *Christliche Ethik,* ed. W. Thiemann, 2d ed. (Munich, 1957); D. Bonhoeffer, *Ethics,* ed. E. Bethge, tr. N. H. Smith (New York, 1955); W. Elert, *The Christian Ethos,* tr. C. J. Schindler (Philadelphia, 1957); G. Hillerdal, *Teologisk och filosofisk etik* (Stockholm, 1958); R. Niebuhr, *Essays in Applied Christianity,* sel. and ed. D. B. Robertson (New York, 1959); A. Gyllenkrok, *Systematisk teologi och vetenskaplig metod, med särskild hänsyn till etiken,* with Eng. summary, *Systematic Theology and Scientific Method with Particular Reference to Ethics* (Uppsala, 1959); M. Warnock, *Ethics since 1900* (London, 1960); H. R. Niebuhr, *The Responsible Self* (New York, 1963); R. M. Hare, *The Language of Morals* (New York, 1964).

Ethics, Social. See *Social Ethics.*

Ethiopia. See *Africa,* E 2; *Ethiopic Church.*

Ethiopian Church. See *Coptic Church; Ethiopic Church; Nonchalcedonian Churches,* 6.

Ethiopianism. Movement among natives of cen. and S Afr. aimed at dethronement of white supremacy. Began ca. 1892, when the Afr. membership of the Wesleyan Meth. Ch. (British) in Pretoria, Transvaal, withdrew and, under leadership of M. M. Mokone, founded an indep. Ethiopian ch.; its slogan: "Africa for the Africans." In 1896 this ch. applied for membership in the African* Methodist Episcopal Church. James Mata Dwane was sent to Am. to unite with the A. M. E. Ch. on behalf of this ch. He represented only part of the Ethiopian Movement, in which ca. 15 different organizations sprang up. He returned as authorized supt. of the work in S Afr. The S Afr. or Cape Colony Conf. was organized 1897. Am. Bp. Henry McNeal Turner (1834–1915) organized the Transvaal Conf. 1898; later he organized the Sierra Leone, Liberia, and S Afr. confs. By 1904 Bp. Levi J. Coppin organized several Annual Conferences. Meanwhile Dwane approached the Angl. Ch., which formed the "Ethiopian Order" 1900, ordained Dwane deacon, and made him Provincial of the order. Much religious, racial, and social unrest among the natives resulted from the Ethiopian Movement.

Ethiopic Bible Version. See *Bible Versions,* E.

Ethiopic Church (Abyssinian Church). Tradition associates the origin of Christianity in Ethiopia (Abyssynia) with the return of the treasurer of Queen Candace (Acts 8:26-39) to his homeland. But Christianity did not take permanent root in Ethiopia until the 4th c., when Hezana ('Ezana; Aizanas; [Ta]zana), king of Aksum, is said to have become Christian, probably under influence of Frumentius.* By ca. 500 the ch. in Aksum was apparently Monophysite (see *Monophysite Controversy*), perhaps partly as a result of an influx of those exiled from the Roman Empire for religious reasons, partly as a result of dependence for apostolic succession on the Coptic* Ch. of Alexandria. The Aksumite empire disappeared from hist. after the 6th c.; Muhammadanism spread; the ch. declined. We know little about the Abyssinian Ch. from ca. 650–1268, when, after several changes of govt., the old dynasty was restored; under an able, energetic, and ambitious patriarch (abuna) the ch. then took a new lease on life. From the 13th to the 17th c. and in the 19th c. the RC Ch. tried to gain control of the Ethiopic Ch. In 1951 the Coptic* Ch. freed the Abyssinian Ch. from the requirement that the abp. be a Copt; a native Abyssinian, Basil, was made abp. In 1959 a separate patriarchate, under the "Pope of Alexandria, Patriarch of the See of St. Mark," was est. for Ethiopia. Head of the Ethiopic Ch. is called catholicos-patriarch. There are many monastic communities for men; cloisters for women are rare. The typical ground plan of Abyssinian chs. is round or octagonal. Saints, esp. Mary, are venerated. The order of service perpetuates with variations the Egyptian form of the E rite. There is a colony of the Abyssinian Ch. in Jerusalem. Ties to the imperial throne of Ethiopia are traditionally very close. The Abyssinian Ch. belongs to the WCC. Recent yrs. have seen a measure of assimilation to E Orthodoxy. See also *Africa,* E 2; *Jacob Baradaeus; Mark, Liturgy of Saint.* ACP.

Ethos. Character; moral nature; guiding beliefs; ideals; standards.

Étienne, St. See *Church Architecture,* 7.

Étienne, Robert I. See *Estienne, Robert I.*

Etiology (from Gk. *aitia,* "cause"). Science, investigation, or theory of causes.

Etten, Edwin van. See *Radio and Television Evangelism, Network,* 1.

Eucharist. See *Covenant,* 7; *Grace, Means of,* IV; *Lord's Supper.*

Eucharistic Congresses. Gatherings of RC clergy and laity for celebrating the Eucharist and deepening understanding of it and devotion to it. Marie Marthe Emilia Tamisier (1834–1910) promoted pilgrimages to Avignon and other sanctuaries in Fr. where Eucharistic miracles allegedly had occurred. An internat. Eucharistic meeting was held at Lille 1881. Other Eucharistic congresses, internat., nat., regional, and local, followed.

Eucharistic Controversies. The theory that during Holy Communion bread and wine are changed into the body and blood of Christ (later called transubstantiation*) and that the mass is a sacrifice, which had been gaining ground, was championed by P. Radbertus,* who argued from the authority of the fathers and alleged miracles. Ratramnus,* asked for his opinion by Charles* II of Fr., condemned the treatise of Radbertus and stressed figurative and mysterious aspects of the Sacrament. Rabanus* Maurus and J. S. Erigena* held similar views; Hincmar* of Reims and others sided with Radbertus; the Scriptural doctrine of the real presence (see *Grace, Means of,* IV 3) was lost sight of. The theory of Radbertus prevailed.

Berenger* elaborated the theory of Ratramnus; denied that unworthy communicants receive the body and blood of Christ; was opposed by Lanfranc*; condemned unheard by a syn. in Rome 1050; condemned, while in prison, by a syn. in Vercelli 1050, which also had the book of Ratramnus on the Eucharist burned; condemned again in a council at Paris 1050 or 1051; satisfied the papal legate Hildebrand (see *Popes,* 7) with an evasive declaration 1054; was compelled in Rome to burn his writings and accept a Capernaitic* formula 1059; repudiated this confession and answered Lanfranc with his chief work, *De Sacra Coena adversus Lanfrancum liber posterior;* was compelled 1079 at Rome, by Gregory VII (see *Popes,* 7), to abjure his view and sign a formula in which the words *substantialiter converti* (a statement of transubstantiation) appear for the first time in official context; on return to Fr. he again repudiated his submission to Rome, but was brought to heel again at a council at Bordeaux 1080; died a solitary penitent. Transubstantiation came to be gen. accepted, stated in the 4th Lateran* Council 1215, the 2d Council of Lyons* 1274, and the Council of Florence* 1439, and confirmed by the Council of Trent* 1551 (Sess. XIII, chap. IV; divergent views anathematized in related canons).

M. Luther* rejected transubstantiation and defended the real presence.

See also *Calvinism; Crypto-Calvinistic Controversy; Grace, Means of,* I 7, IV 3; *Impanation; Lutheran Confessions.*

Eucharistic Sacrifice. See *Mass.*

Euchites (Gk. "praying ones"). Also called Messalians, after a corresponding Syriac word. Adherents of enthusiastic-spiritualistic movement that originated in Syria ca. 350 and spread to Asia Minor. Their ascetic dualism was probably influenced by Manichaeism.* Held that the devil, still present in the baptized, is to be overcome by prayer, through which grace and mystic union with God are achieved. Depreciated sacraments. Some trace the movement to Eustathius* of Sebaste, others to a Symeon of Mesopotamia. See also *Ephesus, Third Ecumenical Council of.*

Eucken, Rudolf Christoph (1846–1926). Ger. philos.; prof. Jena 1874–1920; received Nobel prize 1908; exchange prof. Harvard 1912–13. Held a philos. of ethical activism: truth must satisfy the needs of the whole of life (this approach called noological method); in spiritual existence man relates himself to the universal Spirit. See also *Luther Society.*

Euclid(es) of Megara (ca. 450–374 BC). B. Megara, Greece; founded Megarian school of philos.; defended the unity of goodness. See also *Socrates.*

Eudaemonism. Ethical theory that makes well-being (*eudaemonia, apatheia,* or *euthymia,* the happy condition of the *daimon* [soul or spirit]) the highest aim in life. Regarded by Aristotle* as highest good. Hedonism* and utilitarianism* are related but not synonymous concepts.

Eudes, Jean (1601–80). Fr. RC; priest 1625; founded Congregation of Jesus and Mary (known as Eudists) and Congregation of Our Lady of Charity of the Refuge. See also *Sisterhoods.*

Eudoxius (ca. 300–370). Anomoean Arian leader; bp. Constantinople 360. See also *Anomoeans; Arianism,* 1.

Eugenics. Science dealing with factors affecting improvement of hereditary qualities; esp. emphasizes selective human mating. Plato* advocated that the state mate best with best and worst with worst, the children of the former to be reared by the state, those of the latter to be rejected. Aristotle* also advocated selective mating.

Francis Galton (1822–1911), Eng. scientist, coined the word "eugenics," founded the science, and provided endowments for the study of eugenics. Eugenics education societies were organized in various countries. An internat. conf. was held in London 1912.

Charles Benedict Davenport (1866–1944), Am. zoologist, was founder and dir. of the Eugenics Record Office, Cold Spring Harbor, N. Y. The Eugenics Research Assoc. was organized 1913. The Am. Eugenics Soc., organized 1926 to promote research on human differences and provide information on heredity and qualitative aspects of pop., draws membership from geneticists, physicians, psychiatrists, educators, nurses, and laymen interested in heredity and pop.

Eugenics suggests reduction of the number of defectives by segregation, sterilization (usually vasectomy for males, salpingectomy for females), and birth control (see *Family Planning*).

Eugenicus, Mark (ca. 1392–1445). B. Constantinople; metropolitan of Ephesus ca. 1436; procurator of the patriarchate of Alexandria; scholastic; attended Council of Florence*; chief Gk. opponent of union bet. E and W chs.

Eugenius IV (Gabriele Condolmieri; Gabriel Condulmer; ca. 1383–1447). B. Venice; pope 1431–47; engaged in struggle with Council of Basel*; lived at Florence ca. 1431–43; transferred the council to Ferrara 1437, to Florence (see *Florence, Council of*) 1439, to Rome 1443; deposed 1439 by that part of the council which refused to leave Basel; continued to exert recognized authority.

Eugipius (Egippius; Eugepius; Eugipp[ius]; Eugyp[p]ius; ca. 455–ca. 538). B. Carthage; abbot Lucullanum, near Naples; pupil and biographer of Severinus* of Noricum; compiled *Thesaurus ex S. Augustini operibus. MPL* 62, 549–1200.

Euhemerism. View of Euhemerus* that gods are deified mortals and that religious myths are distorted accounts of hist. events.

Euhemerus (Euemerus; Evemerus; 4th c. BC). B. Sicily; Gk. mythographer. Works include *Sacred History.* See also *Euhemerism.*

Euler, Leonhard (1707–83). B. Basel; physicist, mathematician; opposed deism* and naturalism*; espoused revelation; supported neology.* Writings include works on astronomy.

Euloghitaria (from Gk. *eulogetos,* "blessed"). In E Orthodox Ch., parts of Matins which begin "Blessed art Thou, O Lord; teach me Thy statutes." (Ps 119: 12)

Eulogius 1. *of Alexandria* (d. 607); patriarch Alexandria 580–607; opposed Novatians and Monophysites. *MPG,* 86:2, 2907–64 (some ascribe 2913–38 to Sophronius of Jerusalem). 2. *of Córdoba* (ca. 810–859). B. *Córdoba;* opposed Islam* in Sp. *MPL,* 115, 703–966. 3. *Georgiewski* (1868–1946). E Orthodox; bp. Chelm (Cholm; Kholm), Poland, 1905; abp. Volhynia 1914; mem. All Russian Council and Holy Synod 1917; to Serbia, Berlin, and Paris 1920–22; leader of Russ. Orthodox Ch. in W Eur.

Eunomius (ca. 335–ca. 394). B. Cappadocia; Anomoean leader; bp. Cyzicus in Mysia. See also *Anomoeans; Arianism,* 1.

Euripides. See *Religious Drama.*

Eusebius of Caesarea (called Pamphili; ca. 260–ca. 339). "The father of ch. hist." Pupil and friend of Pamphilus* of Caesarea; bp. Caesarea ca. 313; high in favor with Constantine* I; provisionally excommunicated under charge of Arianism* at a council at Antioch ca. 324; convinced the 325 Council of Nicaea of his orthodoxy by submitting a creed, probably that which his ch. at Caesarea had been using. Works include *Chronicon,* a universal chronological hist.; *De martyribus Palaestinae,* an account of martyrdoms in Palestine 303–310; *Evangelica demonstratio* and *Evangelica praeparatio,* apologetic works; *Historia Ecclesiastica,* which preserves many quotations from early churchmen and presents a reasonably reliable account of the growth of the early ch., esp. in the E; *Vita Constantini,* which develops the philos. of hist. that the Christian emp. represented the final triumph of God acting in hist. See also *Geography, Christian,* 3; *Socrates* (surnamed Scholasticus).

D. S. Wallace-Hadrill, *Eusebius of Caesarea* (London, 1960); *Eusebius, Bishop of Caesarea: The Ecclesiastical History and the Martyrs of Palestine,* tr. and annotated by H. J. Lawlor and J. E. L. Oulton, 2 vols. (London, 1927–28). HTM

Eusebius of Dorylaeum (d. ca. 452 AD). Gk. theol.; bp. Dorylaeum (near modern Eskisehir), Asia Minor, 448; protested teaching of Nestorius* 428, of Eutyches* 448; imprisoned 449; escaped to Rome; reinstated and played prominent role at Council of Chalcedon* 451.

Eusebius of Emesa (ca. 295–ca. 359). B. Edessa*; probably a disciple of Eusebius* of Caesarea; outstanding exegete; sympathized with Semi-Arians; bp. Emesa (now Homs), W Syria, ca. 340; there forced to defend himself against charges of Sabellianism (see also *Monarchianism,* B 6).

Eusebius of Nicomedia (d. ca. 341 AD). Gk. Arian theol.; bp. Nicomedia ca. 318; signed the confession of Nicaea* only under pressure from Constantine and after long opposition; patriarch Constantinople ca. 339. See also *Arianism,* 2.

Eusebius of Samosata (d. ca. 379 AD). Bp. Samosata ca. 361; opposed Arianism*; killed by tile from a roof.

Eusebius of Vercelli (ca. 283–371). B. Sardinia; bp. Vercelli ca. 340; opposed Arianism*; banished to E after Syn. of Milan 355; recalled by Julian*; lived with his clergy under rule. *MPL,* 12, 9–972.

Eustace (ca. 560–ca. 629). B. Burgundy; monk at Luxeuil under Columban*; abbot at Luxeuil ca. 612; miss. with Agil(us)* to Bav. ca. 617. See also *Germany,* A 1.

Eustathius of Antioch (d. ca. 337 AD). Bp. Beroea (now Alep, or Aleppo), Syria; patriarch Antioch, Syria; opposed school of Origen*; opposed Arians at Nicaea* 325; deposed at Arian syn. of Antioch* ca. 330 and exiled to Thrace; followers (called Eustathians) in Antioch refused to recognize bps. of Arian consecration, thus occasioning the Eustathian, later Meletian,* schism.

Eustathius of Sebaste (ca. 300–ca. 377). Pupil of Arius*; abp. Sebaste, in Pontus, ca. 356; vacillated in attitude on Nicene creed; interested in monasticism*; followers called Eustathians.

Eustathius of Thessalonica (d. ca. 1193 AD). Byzantine scholar and leader; abp. Thessalonica ca. 1175; works include commentaries on Homer and Pindar and an account of the Norman conquest of Thessalonica.

Euthalius (4th or 7th c.). Alleged ed. of Acts, Epistles of Paul, and Catholic Epistles and author of introd. material (prologue, description of content, and life of Paul).

Euthanasia. Intentional cutting short of human life in cases of misery regarded as incurable. Though called "mercy killing," Christian chs. usually object to it for various reasons: it breaks the 5th Commandment; man's life is given by God (Jb 10:8-12; Ps 139:13-16), who alone has right to take it again (Jb 1:21; Acts 17:26; 1 Jn 3:15); when man takes human life he must have Scriptural reasons (e. g., Mt. 26:52; Ro 13:4). In recent yrs. some doctors have repeatedly raised questions regarding the extent to which medical science should be applied to extend human life artificially indefinitely.

J. H. C. Fritz, "Euthanasia," *CTM,* XVIII, 2 (Feb. 1947), 94–100; J. F. Fletcher, *Morals and Medicine* (Princeton, N. J., 1954).

Eutherius. Abp. Tyana, Cappadocia; Nestorian opponent of Cyril* of Alexandria; deposed at Ephesus* 431.

Euthymius Zigabenus (Zigadenus; Zygadenus; 12th c.). Gk. Orthodox monk and theol. Works include *Panoplia dogmatica;* commentaries on Ps, the Gospels, and the Epistles of Paul. *MPG,* 128–131.

Eutyches (ca. 378–ca. 454). Archimandrite of E Ch. in Constantinople; opposed Nestorius*; condemned and deposed 448 at a council at Constantinople; reinstated 449 as priest and abbot at the "Robber Synod" of Ephesus*; exiled ca. 452. See also *Eutychianism.*

Eutychianism. 5th-c. heresy taking its name from Eutyches,* who asserted that there were 2 natures in Christ before, but only 1 after, the incarnation. In opposition to Nestorianism,* Eutyches taught that the human nature in Christ was absorbed, swallowed up, by the divine nature; thus his doctrine was an expression of Monophysitism.* See also *Christological Controversies; Chalcedon, Council of.*

Evagrius Ponticus (ca. 346–ca. 399). B. Pontus; deacon and noted preacher at Constantinople; retired as monk to Nitrian desert; friend and disciple of Macarius*; through his writings influenced Palladius,* J. Cassianus,* Maximus* the Confessor, and others. *MPG,* 40, 1213–86.

Evagrius Scholasticus (ca. 536–ca. 600). B. Coele-Syria; ch. historian of 431–594. *MPG,* 86:2, 2405–2886.

Evangeliary. See *Evangelistary.*

Evangelical (from Gk. for "Gospel"). Term meaning loyal to the Gospel of Jesus Christ. The Luth. Reformation was evangelical. Later the term described those who emphasized the doctrine of atonement for sin. Evangelicals are known for miss. work, personal piety, and opposition to ritualism and modernism. In the 20th c. a liberal ev. movement tried to combine the zeal of evangelicals with liberalism. In Eng. the term is applied to the Low* Ch.

Evangelical Alliance. Assoc. formed London 1846. Attendance of ca. 800 at the organizational meeting included J. A. James,* E. Bickersteth (see *Bickersteth,* 1), F. W. Krummacher (see *Krummacher,* 3), F. A. G. Tholuck,* A. Monod (see *Monod,* 3), J. H. Merle* d'Aubigné, L. Beecher,* and S. S. Schmucker.* Purpose of the Alliance was to unite ev. Christians, champion liberty of conscience and tolerance, and oppose RCm and Tractarianism.* Doctrinal articles adopted: 1. the divine inspiration, authority, and sufficiency of the Scriptures; 2. the right and duty of private judgment; 3. the unity of the Godhead and the Trinity of the divine persons; 4. the total depravity of human nature as a result of the Fall; 5. the incarnation of the Son of God, His work of redemption for sinful mankind, mediatory intercession, and kingship; 6. justification only by faith; 7. the work of the Holy Spirit in converting and sanctifying the sinner; 8. the immortality of the soul, the resurrection of the body, the final judgment by the Savior, receiving the righteous into eternal life and condemning the ungodly to eternal perdition; 9. the divine institution of the office of the ministry and of the sacraments (Baptism and the Lord's Supper). The Alliance did not try to unite the chs. organically but simply to bring about a closer fellowship of individual Christians. Every mem. was asked to pray for the common cause on the morning of the 1st day of every week and during the 1st week of every yr. *Evangelical Christendom,* founded London 1847, was one of its early publications. US branch est. 1867. The internat. movement now called World's Ev. Alliance. See also *Evangelischer Bund; Macleod, Norman; Schaff, Philip.*

Evangelical Alliance Mission, The. Began 1890 with a Bible and miss. training course conducted by F. Franson* in Brooklyn, N. Y. First called The Scand. Alliance Miss. of N. America; name changed 1949 to The Ev. Alliance Miss. (acronym TEAM). The first field was China; other fields: Japan, India, S Afr., Mongolia, Venezuela-Colombia, Port., Neth. Antilles, Rhodesia, W Pakistan, Tibetan Frontier, Taiwan, W Irian, Austria, Fr., Sp., Korea, Ceylon, Arabian Gulf, Peru, SE Eur., Trinidad, Lebanon. Mem. IFMA.

Evangelical and Reformed Church. See *United Church of Christ, The,* II.

Evangelical Association. See *Evangelical Church,* 1.

Evangelical Awakening. See *Great Awakening in England and America.*

Evangelical Baptist Church, Inc., General Conference of the. See *Baptist Churches,* 32.

Evangelical Bible Society. See *Bible Societies,* 4.

Evangelical Church (Albrights; The So-called Albright People; Albrechtsbrüder). 1. Organized 1803 by Jacob Albright (Albrecht; 1759–1808; b. near Pottstown, Pa.; confirmed Luth.; joined Meth. Ch. 1792). Under his instruction 20 converts from among the Ger.-speaking people in SE Pa. formed 3 groups, called classes, in 1800 to pray with and for each other. Albright did not intend to found a new ch., but language barriers kept his group from uniting with Meths. In 1803 an ecclesiastical organization was effected at a gen. assem. Albright was consecrated and ordained as minister of the Gospel by laying on of hands in solemn prayer by his 2 associates, John Walter and Abraham Lieser. The 1st annual conf. was held Kleinfeltersville, Lebanon Co., Pa., Nov. 1807. Albright was elected bp.; articles of faith were adopted. The 1st gen. conf. was held Buffalo Valley, Union, Co., Pa., Oct. 1816; the name Evangelical Association was adopted. With increased use of Eng., work spread throughout the N part of the US from New Eng. to the Pacific and into Tex. and Can. A Gen. Miss. Soc., organized 1839, worked in the US, Can., Ger., Switz., Poland, Latvia, Afr., China, Japan, Fr., Estonia. A Woman's Miss. Soc. was organized 1883. A division in 1891 resulted 1894 in the organization, by the minority group, of the United Ev. Ch. under Bp. Rudolph Dubs, Naperville, Ill. The 2 bodies reunited (see also *Evangelical Congregational Church*) 1922 as the Ev. Ch., which merged 1946 with the Ch. of the United* Brethren in Christ to form the Ev.* United Brethren Ch.; 1964 inclusive membership: 735,723. A pub. house was founded 1815; *Der Christliche Botschafter,* early official organ, was founded 1836. 1968 publications included *Builders; Church and Home; The World Evangel.* In 1968 the Ev. United Brethren Ch. became a part of The United Meth. Ch.

2. In doctrine the ch. is Arminian (see *Arminianism*); its articles of faith correspond closely to those of the Methodist* Chs.

3. Albright began a book of rules and order which was finished by George Miller (1774–1816) and adopted 1809. A connectional polity was est. Bps. were elected by the Gen. Conf.

R. W. Albright, *A History of the Evangelical Church* (Harrisburg, Pa., 1942); see also *Religious Bodies (US), Bibliography.*

Evangelical Church in Germany (Evangelische Kirche in Deutschland). See *Union Movements,* 8–9.

Evangelical Church of Czech Brethren. See *Czechoslovakia,* 8.

Evangelical Church Society of the West. See *German Evangelical Church Society of the West, The.*

Evangelical Congregational Church. Formed 1922 by mems. of the United Ev. Ch. (see *Evangelical Church,* 1) who did not join in the 1922 reunion; first continued separate existence under their old name; adopted name Ev. Cong. Ch. 1928; Arminian; evangelistic; Methodistic in ch. govt.; ch. property owned by local congs.; 1967 inclusive membership 29,744.

Evangelical Continental Society. Organized London 1845 to support and found evangelical societies for evangelistic work in Eur.

Evangelical Counsels (Counsels of Perfection). Term applied, esp. by RCs, to voluntary poverty, perfect chastity, and obedience to a religious superior. NT support for chastity (virginity) is sought in Mt 19: 11-12; Lk 14:26; 18:29; 1 Co 7:7, 25-40; for poverty in Mk 10:17-22; for obedience in Mk 9:34; 10:43. The counsels are usually regarded as works of supererogation* which aid the soul to avoid the carnality described 1 Jn 2:16 and achieve perfection (Mt 5:48). The counsels form the basis of nearly all monastic orders.

Evangelical Covenant Church of America, The. Swed. immigrants, who came from free Luth. chs. or miss. socs. formed as a result of revivals in Swed., organized indep. congs. in Am. Some of these, esp. in Ill., formed the Swed. Ev. Luth. Mission Syn. 1873; others formed the Swed. Ev. Luth. Ansgarius Syn. 1874, which joined The General* Syn. of the Ev. Luth. Ch. in the USA 1875. The 2 united 1885 to form the Swed. Ev. Mission Covenant Ch. of Am. The present name was adopted 1957. The ch. stresses the necessity of spiritual life, essential unity of Christians, consecrated living, miss. work. It finds inspiration and guidance in hist. creeds but adopts no fixed creeds. Mems. confess Jesus Christ as Lord and Savior and receive the OT and NT as the record of God's revelation of Himself through various acts of love and judgment, as His special revelation, and as the only perfect rule of faith, doctrine, and practice.

C. W. Biorklund, H. J. Ekstam, K. A. Olsson, and D. C. Frisk, *According to Thy Word* (Chicago, 1954).

Evangelical Foreign Missions Association. Organized and inc. 1945 as voluntary assoc. of denominational and nondenominational miss. agencies; affiliated with Nat. Assoc. of Evangelicals (see *Union Movements,* 12). Membership in the 1960s: ca. 70 agencies.

The assoc. holds that the Bible is infallible, inspired, authoritative Word of God; doctrine of trinity, deity, virgin birth, sinless life, miracles, vicarious death, bodily resurrection, ascension of Jesus Christ; regeneration by Holy Spirit; resurrection of saved and lost; unity of believers in Christ.

Publishes *Missionary News Service;* functions as service agency for its mems.; cooperates with Interdenominational* For. Miss. Assoc. of N Am., with which it publishes the *Evangelical Missions Quarterly.*

Headquarters Washington, D C.

Evangelical Free Church Association. See *Evangelical Free Church of America.*

Evangelical Free Church of America. Formed 1950 by merger of the Swed. Ev. Free Ch. and the Ev. Free Ch. Assoc.

A fellowship was organized 1884 at Boone, Iowa, by indep. congs. and some congs. of the Swed. Ev. Luth. Mission Syn. and of the Swed. Ev. Luth. Ansgarius Syn.; did not join in the organization of the Swed. Ev. Mission Covenant Ch. of Am. 1885 (see *Evangelical Covenant Church of America*); inc. 1908 as Swed. Ev. Free Ch.

The Ev. Free Ch. Assoc. began with a cong. organized 1884 in Boston. A western miss. assoc. was formed 1891, an eastern miss. assoc. 1898. The 2 merged 1912 to form the Norw. and Dan. Ev. Free Ch. Assoc. (later called Ev. Free Ch. Assoc.).

The Ev. Free Ch. of Am. tries to be fundamental without being fanatic; no decision bet. Arminianism and Calvinism; Zwinglian on Lord's Supper; mode of baptism and age for baptism open; receives mems. not by baptism but by personal confession of faith. 1967 inclusive membership: 50,312.

A. T. Olson, *Believers Only: An Outline of the History and Principles of the Free Evangelical Movement in Europe and America Affiliated with the International Federation of Free Evangelical Churches* (Minneapolis, 1964) and *This We Believe* (Minneapolis, 1961).

Evangelical Law. In E Orthodox theol., the law preached by Christ and the apostles; completes and is superior to OT law. Mosaic law is negative; ev. law prescribes positive virtues of which Christ is the incarnation. It is esp. in the Sermon on the Mount.

Evangelical Lutheran Church, The. 1. Name adopted 1946 by The Norw. Luth. Ch. of Am. (see pars. 13–14).

2. Membership of the ELC was midwestern, with more than 70% of it in Wis., Ill., Minn., Iowa, N. Dak., S. Dak., the rest in other states, Can., and Mex.

3. Large-scale Norw. migration to Am. began 1825 when the sloop "Restaurationen" landed in N. Y. with 53 immigrants. The stream increased till ca. 1890, then tapered off to the present trickle. The Ev. Luth. Ch. drew its strength largely from these people and their descendants.

4. Among characteristics of Norw. Luths. in Am.: loyalty to the Word of God; deep-seated piety colored by the Haugean movement (see *Norway, Lutheranism in,* 10); confessionalism.

5. Two gen. tendencies developed among Norwegians in Am., one "low ch.," the other liturgical, each with added features.

6. The "low ch." tendency developed under E. Eielsen,* a product of the Haugean movement in Norw., but not as sympathetic with the nat. ch. as H. N. Hauge* had been. Among Eielsen and his followers little emphasis was placed on the hist. liturgy of Norw. Lutheranism, much on the priesthood of believers and on development of spiritual gifts; training leaders was not given as much prominence as in other groups of Norw. Luths.

7. The liturgical tendency developed under leadership of ordained pastors trained in the Ch. of Norw. Among those connected with this tendency: N. O. Brandt,* C. L. Clausen,* J. A. Ottesen,* A. C. Preus,* H. A. Preus,* and H. A. Stub.*

8. In 1851 The Norw. Ev. Luth. Ch. in Am. was organized at the Luther Valley Ch., Rock Prairie Settlement, Wis., by A. C. Preus, H. A. Stub, C. L. Clausen, and 30 representatives of 18 congs. This organization was dissolved 1852. In 1853, under leadership of A. C. Preus, The Norw. Ev. Luth. Ch. in Am. was organized at Koskonong, Wis. its name was changed 1867/68 to The Syn. for the Norw. Ev. Luth. Ch. in Am.; it is also known as Norw Syn. Represented at the 1866 Reading, Pa., convention (see *General Council of the Lutheran Church in [North] America,* 2) but not represented 1867 at the 1st conv. of the Gen. Council.

9. Characteristics of this Norw. Syn.: strict Luth. orthodoxy; sovereignty of the local cong.; requirement of a cong. call for anyone to preach in a cong.; use of the clerical vestments and liturgy of the Ch. of Norw. Helped form the Ev. Luth. Synodical* Conf. 1872.

10. The Norw. Syn. was larger and stronger than the Eielsen group. But in Jan. 1880 F. A. Schmidt* publicly attacked statements of C. F. W. Walther* on predestination; as a result of subsequent controversy the Norw. Syn. left the Synodical* Conf. 1883; ca. one-third of the Norw. Syn. withdrew 1887 and est. the Anti-Missouri* Brotherhood. In 1890 the Brotherhood, The Conf. for the Norw.-Dan. Ev. Luth. Ch. in Am., and the Norw.-Dan. Augustana Syn. united to form The United* Norw. Luth. Ch. in Am.

11. The Lutheran* Free Ch. was organized 1897 as a result of controversy in the United Norw. Luth. Ch. in Am. over control of Augsburg Sem., Minneapolis, Minn., and over the nature of ministerial training.

12. At the beginning of the 20th c. Norw. Luths. in Am. were divided into the Norw. Syn., organized 1853; Hauge's Norw. Ev. Luth. Syn. (see *Eielsen Synod; Hauge Synod*); the United Norw. Luth. Ch. in Am., organized 1890; the Luth. Free Ch., organized 1897; the Eielsen* Syn.; and the Church* of the Luth. Brethren of Am.

13. In 1905 Hauge's Norw. Ev. Luth. Syn. invited Norw. ch. bodies to hold discussions with possible union in view. The invitation was favorably received by the Norw. Syn. and the United Norw. Luth. Ch. in Am., but it was not till 1917 that the 3 chs. merged, forming The Norw. Luth. Ch. of Am. A small minority of the Norw. Syn. declined to enter the merger and in 1918 formed The Norw. Syn. of the Am. Ev. Luth. Ch. (see *Evangelical Lutheran Synod*). See also *Madison Settlement.*

14. The Norw. Luth. Ch. of Am. experienced steady growth and healthy development. In 1946 its name was changed to The Ev. Luth. Ch.

15. It helped form the NLC 1918, the LWC 1923, the Am. Luth. Conf. 1930, and the LWF 1947. It became the 3d-largest gen. Luth. body in Am. (after the ULC and the LCMS). Total 1959 membership: over 1 million; ca. 2,000 pastors. Pres.: H. G. Stub* 1917–25; J. A. Aasgaard* 1925–54; F. A. Schiotz 1954–60.

16. The ELC became part of The American* Luth. Ch. at the end of 1960. OGM

See also *Eielsen Synod; Lutheran Council in Canada,* 2; *Norwegian Evangelical Lutheran Synod of America; Tokai Evangelical Lutheran Church; United Norwegian Lutheran Church.*

C. Anderson, *The Doctrinal Position of the Norwegian Synod: A Brief Survey of the Position in Doctrine and Practice Held by the Old Norwegian Synod Prior to the Merger of 1917* (n.p., n.d.).

Evangelical Lutheran Church in Southern Africa. See *Africa,* B 5.

Evangelical Lutheran Church in Southwest Africa. See *Africa,* B 8.

Evangelical Lutheran Church in (of) [North] America. See *Eielsen Synod; Hauge Synod.*

Evangelical Lutheran Church in the Confederate States of America, The General Synod of the. See *United Synod of the Evangelical Lutheran Church in the South,* 1.

Evangelical Lutheran Church of Canada, The. See *Canada,* A 26.

Evangelical Lutheran Church of England. See *England,* C 16–18.

Evangelical Lutheran Church of New Guinea. See *New Guinea,* 5.

Evangelical Lutheran Church of the Augsburg Confession. See *France,* 15.

Evangelical Lutheran Church–Synod of France and Belgium. See *France,* 15.

Evangelical Lutheran Concordia Synod of Pennsylvania and Other States. See *Concordia Synod of Pennsylvania and Other States, Evangelical Lutheran.*

Evangelical Lutheran Confessing Church. See *Germany, Lutheran Free Churches in,* 13.

Evangelical Lutheran Free Church. See *Belgium; Germany, Lutheran Free Churches in.*

Evangelical-Lutheran Free Church in Saxony, Synod of the. See *Germany, Lutheran Free Churches in,* 4–7.

Evangelical Lutheran Free Church of Baden. See *Germany, Lutheran Free Churches in,* 9.

Evangelical Lutheran General Synod in North America, The. See *United Synod of the Evangelical Lutheran Church in the South,* 1.

Evangelical Lutheran General Synod South, The. See *United Synod of the Evangelical Lutheran Church in the South,* 1.

Evangelical Lutheran Institute for the Deaf. See *Deaf,* 10.

Evangelical Lutheran Joint Synod of Wisconsin. See *Wisconsin, Evangelical Lutheran Joint Synod of.*

Evangelical Lutheran Mission for China. Miss. organization est. 1912 by E. L. Arndt.*

Evangelical Lutheran (Old Lutheran) Church. See *Germany, Lutheran Free Churches in,* 1.

Evangelical Lutheran Ovambokavango Church. See *Africa,* B 8.

Evangelical Lutheran Seminary of Canada. See *Ministry, Education of,* XI B.

Evangelical Lutheran Synod. 1. This syn. regards itself as the spiritual successor of the Norw. Syn. that was organized 1853 (see *Evangelical Lutheran Church, The,* 8–13).

2. The minority which disagreed with the Madison* Settlement of 1912 and the Austin Settlement 1916–17 organized The Norw. Syn. of the Am. Ev. Luth. Ch. 1918, joined the Syn. Conf. 1920, adopted the name Ev. Luth. Syn. 1958, and withdrew from the Syn. Conf. 1963 because of doctrinal differences.

The group originally numbered ca. 13 voting pastors and a number of congs. In 1966 it numbered 43 parish pastors, 15,798 bap. mems. During the first 10 yrs. the young men of the syn. received their training for the ministry and for teaching in the ch. at institutions of the Mo. and Wis. Syns. Since 1927 the Norw. Syn. owns and conducts Bethany Luth. Coll. and (since 1946) Theol. Sem., Mankato, Minn. Christian day schools are operated in the syn. Official pub.: *Lutheran Sentinel.*

3. The syn. has, esp. in the 1st yrs. of its existence, tried to reach as many individuals and smaller groups as possible who found themselves alone after the 1917 merger. Gradually the synod's work fell into the normal groove of est. home and for. miss. work. The syn. cooperated with the Ev. Luth. Synodical* Conf. in colored missions in Am. and Nigeria. SCY

Pres.: Bjug Harstad (pres. pro. tem., 1917; 1918–21); George Albert Gullixson (1921–26); Christian Anderson (1926–30); Helge Matthias Tjernagel (1930–34); Norman A. Madson (1934–35); Christian A. Molstad (1935–37); Henry Ingebritson (1937–42); Norman A. Madson (1942–46); Adolph M. Harstad (1946–50); C. Monrad Gullerud (1950–54); Milton H. Otto (1954–56); Milton Tweit (1956–62); Theodore A. Aaberg (1962–63); Joseph N. Peterson (1963–66); Juul B. Madson (1966–).

Evangelical Lutheran Synod of Missouri, Ohio, and Other States, The. See *Lutheran Church – Missouri Synod, The.*

Evangelical Lutheran Synod of The Southwest. See *Southwest, Synod of the.*

Evangelical Lutheran Theological Seminary. See *Ministry, Education of,* VI C; X E.

Evangelical Lutheran Zulu Church. See *Africa,* B 5.

Evangelical Mennonite Brethren Conference. See *Mennonite Churches,* 3.

Evangelical Methodist Church. See *Methodist Churches,* 4 b.

Evangelical Mission Covenant Church of America. See *Evangelical Covenant Church of America.*

Evangelical Protestant Conference of Congregational Churches. Formed 1911 by merger of Ger. Ev. Prot. Ministers' Assoc. and Ger. Ev. Ministers' Conf. Known for extreme liberalism, rationalism, and Unitarianism. United with Cong. chs. 1925.

Evangelical Protestantism. See *United States, Religious History of,* 17.

Evangelical Society of Geneva. See *Société évangélique de Genève.*

Evangelical Synod of North America. See *United Church of Christ, The,* II B.

Evangelical Synod of Syria and Lebanon. See *Middle East,* C.

Evangelical Synod of the West. See *German Evangelical Church Society of the West, The.*

Evangelical Union. James Morison (1816–1893), minister of a United Secession cong., was suspended from it 1841 for teaching that Christ made atonement not only for the elect but for all mankind. Later his father (Robert Morison; d. 1855), Alexander Cumming Rutherford, and John Guthrie were also suspended. These 4 pastors and 9 laymen, representing 3 chs. and 2 preaching stations, formed the Evangelical Union at Kilmarnock, Scot., 1843. Other suspended pastors and students later joined the movement. Those who shared Morisonian views were called Morisonians; their position was called Morisonianism.

Evangelical Union of South America. Formed 1911 by amalgamation of several S. Am. missions.; mem. IFMA.

Evangelical United Brethren Church, The. Formed 1946 at Johnstown, Pa., by merger of the Evangelical* Church and the Church of the United* Brethren in Christ. Arminian in doctrine. Methodistic in govt. Merged 1968 with The Methodist* Church to form The United Meth. Ch. (see *Methodist Churches,* 1).

Evangelicalism. In a wide sense, loyalty to the Gospel of Jesus Christ. In various hist. contexts the term has taken on more specific meanings. Moravianism (see *Moravian Church*), Pietism,* and federal* theol. preceded the founding of Eng. Evangelicalism by C. and J. Wesley* and G. Whitefield.* Adherents of Evangelicalism are called Evangelicals.* See also *Evangelical.*

Evangelicals. 1. Those who emphasize the Gospel of salvation by faith in Jesus Christ and, as a result, are committed to presenting that Gospel to all individually or in groups.

2. Followers of M. Luther,* who emphasized the doctrine of justification* by faith.* Many Luth. chs. include the word Evangelical in their name. At times the term was used of Luths. to distinguish them from Ref.

3. Prots. as distinguished from RCs. The Prussian* Union created an "Evangelical" Church. Prot. chs. of Ger. organized a fed. 1948 called Evangelische Kirche in Deutschland (see *Union Movements,* 8–9).

4. Adherents of the Evangelical Revival in Eng. which is traced to activities of J. and C. Wesley* and G. Whitefield.* The movement was never separatist but tried to work within the Ch. of England.* Eng. Evangelicals organized the Church* Miss. Soc. (see also *Bible Churchmen's Missionary Society*), the Colonial* and Continental Ch. Soc., the Religious Tract Soc. (see *Religious Tract Movement*), and the Brit. and For. Bible Soc. (see *Bible Societies,* 3). Opposed Tractarianism.*

5. In the US the term has been used for those advocating closer cooperation among denominations adhering to fundamental doctrines. The American* Bd. of Commissioners for For. Miss., Am. Bible Soc. (see *Bible Societies,* 5), and an Am. branch of the Evangelical* Alliance were organized by Evangelicals. S. S. Schmucker* and P. Schaff* were leaders in the movement.

6. After organization of the Federal* Council of the Chs. of Christ in Am., Evangelicals tended

toward fundamentalism* under leadership of such men as J. G. Machen* and B. B. Warfield.* Because fundamentalism often emphasized anti-intellectualism and literalism and took a negative attitude toward sciences, many conservatives preferred to be called Evangelicals. Nat. organizations: Am. Council of Christian Chs. (see *Union Movements,* 11); Nat. Assoc. of Evangelicals (see *Union Movements,* 12).

A. C. Zabriskie, *Anglican Evangelicalism* (Philadelphia, 1943); G. R. Balleine, *A History of the Evangelical Party in the Church of England,* new ed. (London, 1951); L. E. Elliott-Binns, *The Early Evangelicals* (London, 1953); R. H. Nash, *The New Evangelicalism* (Grand Rapids, Mich., 1963); *Contemporary Evangelical Thought, IV: Christian Faith and Modern Theology,* ed. C. F. H. Henry (New York, 1964); C. F. H. Henry, *Evangelicals at the Brink of Crisis* (Waco, Tex., 1967); B. L. Shelley, *Evangelicalism in America* (Grand Rapids, Mich., 1967).

Evangelicals for United Action. See *Union Movements,* 12.

Evangelisch-christliche Einheit (Union protestante chrétienne). Fr. and Ger. Christians organized Oct. 14, 1920, by Jules Rambaud for overcoming nat. hatred and distrust bet. Germans and Fr.

Evangelisch-Johannische Kirche. Founded 1926 by Joseph Weissenberg (1855–1941) as the Evangelisch-Johannische Kirche nach der Offenbarung St. Johannis. Dissolved and proscribed 1935; revived 1946 under Frieda Müller (b. 1911), successor of Weissenberg. Gnostic-dualistic. Headquarters in Berlin.

Evangelische Kirche in Deutschland. See *Germany,* C 5; *Union Movements,* 8–9.

Evangelischer Bund. Organized 1886 in Erfurt by W. Beyschlag,* G. A. Warneck,* and others to promote interconfessional discussion and clarify the relationship of ch. and state. In 1886 it est. a press that printed a membership journal, tracts, etc. till 1941. It tried to give the Los* von Rom movement in Austria an ev. basis and pub. the periodical *Die Wartburg* 1902–41 for this purpose.

The Bund urged ev. chs. not to rely on the state but develop independence and tried to help the state find its proper stance esp. toward RCm.

Regarding the Reformation as a permanent standard for Ger. hist., the Bund concerned itself also with free thought, sectarianism, and soc. religious movements. In the Kirchenkampf* it refused to be drawn into the Deutsche Christen (see *Barmen Theses*) movement and remained indep. In the difficult time of reconstruction and indifference after 1945 it est. a new base of operations in Konfessionskundliches Institut, Bensheim, 1947. In confessional encounter it emphasizes ev. self-evaluation over against RCm. Related in purpose to the Evangelical* Alliance.

Evangelism. Etymologically, evangelism means preaching the Gospel; literally: Gospelism. It is that activity of Christians which tries to bring unregenerate mankind under the influence of the Gospel and to win and keep souls for Christ.

Historically, the ch. began as an evangelistic movement (Acts 8:4). It was the evangelistic fervor of the early ch. that enabled it to achieve remarkable success with God's blessing.

As the ch. became more formal in its organization and more institutional in its operation, it lost its pristine zeal for evangelistic activity. The lowest ebb of evangelistic fervor was reached in the Middle Ages, but a revival was born with the dawn of the Prot. Reformation.

In modern times, esp. in the 19th c. and particularly in Eng. and Am., the evangelistic program of the ch. was given great impetus by such men as G. Whitefield,* C. and J. Wesley,* W. Booth (see *Salvation Army,* 1), D. L. Moody,* and I. D. Sankey.* Large meetings were held in tents or auditoriums or out in open spaces, to which the gen. pub. was invited and at which unconverted were called to repentance and faith by highly emotional addresses. See also *Great Awakening in England and America; Revivals.*

It would be hist. inaccurate to say that these evangelistic meetings were without good results. God used them to accomplish His purpose (Is 55:11). Unfortunately the emotional extravagance and insincere professionalism that characterized many meetings brought them into disrepute and subjected the entire movement to suspicion of spiritual fraud.

The evangelistic spirit has revived in Am. Protestantism esp. since WW II. Intensive evangelism programs were launched by many chs. 1945–49. Many laymen enrolled in courses designed to make them more proficient in witness for Christ. Thousands were trained in visitation evangelism (house-to-house visits made to unchurched). Millions were won for the ch. in the early post-war yrs. By means of radio, printing press, motion picture, television, and other modern media, and personal witness the LCMS has contributed to evangelization. HWG

See also *Evangelical.*

D. C. Bryan, *A Workable Plan of Evangelism* (New York, 1945); *Your Church at Work,* comp. and ed. L. Meyer (St. Louis, n. d.); S. W. Powell, *Where Are the People?* (New York, 1942); T. B. Kilpatrick, *New Testament Evangelism* (New York, 1911); D. M. Dawson, *More Power in Soul-Winning* (Grand Rapids, Mich., 1947); R. A. Torrey, *Personal Work* (Chicago, 1901); H. W. Wood, *Winning Men One by One* (Philadelphia, 1908); A. W. Blackwood, *Evangelism in the Home Church* (New York, 1942); J. M. Bader, *Evangelism in a Changing America* (St. Louis, 1957); E. A. Nida, *Message and Mission: The Communication of the Christian Faith* (New York, 1960); *Why We Must Speak: A Discussion on Evangelism at the Third Assembly of the World Council of Churches, New Delhi, 1961* ([Geneva], 1961); E. A. Kettner, *Adventures in Evangelism* (St. Louis, 1964); A. S. Wood, *Evangelism: Its Theology and Practice* (Grand Rapids, Mich., 1966).

Evangelist. 1. Author of a NT Gospel. 2. Mem. of primitive ch. who brought the Gospel to new territories. 3. Person responsible for conversion of a group or nation. 4. Traveling missionary. 5. Denominational minister or layman who is an itinerant preacher or performs other ch. service. 6. Revival preacher.

Evangelistary. 1. Book containing the Gospel lessons. 2. Book containing the complete Gospels.

Evangelistic Associations. Chs. characterized esp. by evangelistic work. Many have holiness leanings or are Meth. The following may be included:

1. *Apostolic Christian Churches of America.* Ger.-Swiss group of chs. founded ca. 1847 by Benedict Wyeneth; pacifists; 1967 inclusive membership: 8,740.

2. *Apostolic Christian Church* (Nazarean). Teaches entire sanctification; denies reconversion.

3. *Apostolic Faith Mission.* Originated 1900 at Topeka, Kans., in the revival work of several evangelists including Miss Minnie Hanson and Mrs. M. White. Stands for "restoration of the faith once delivered to the saints, the old-time religion, camp meetings, revivals, missions, street and prison work, and Christian unity everywhere." Missions in Japan, China, Korea, S. Am., and other countries. Disbanded 1957.

4. *The Christian Congregation.* Organized 1887 in Ind.; revised incorporation ca. 1898 at Kokomo, Ind.; congregational in doctrine and polity; centers teaching and work in the "new commandment" of

Jn 13:34-35; 1967 inclusive membership: 44,914.

5. *The Christian and Missionary Alliance.* Originated under leadership of A. B. Simpson* (1844–1919), Presb. pastor, who resigned his charge in NYC, withdrew from the presbytery of NY, and entered indep. evangelistic work among unchurched. In 1887 two societies were organized: Christian Alliance (inc. 1890), for home work, esp. among neglected classes in towns and cities of the US; International Missionary Alliance (inc. 1889). In 1897 the 2 socs. merged in The Christian and Miss. Alliance. It has no strict creed but emphasizes Christ as Savior, Sanctifier, Healer, and Coming Lord. It has no close ecclesiastical organization, though it has an overall gen. conf., called Gen. Council, and dists. with branches. Missions in many countries. 1967 inclusive membership: 68,829.

6. *Church of Daniel's Band.* Organized 1893 at Marine City, Mich.; 1951 inclusive membership: 200.

7. *Church of God as Organized by Christ.* Organized 1886 under leadership of P. J. Kaufman, Mennonite; opposes "hireling ministry," revivals, creeds, tobacco, lodges, fine clothing, theaters; observes baptism, communion, and foot washing but has no binding form for their observance. 1938 inclusive membership: 2,192.

8. *Hephzibah Faith Missionary Association.* Under this name a number of indep. chs. were organized 1892 in Iowa; reorganized 1935; subsequently dissolved; new organization formed 1948. Purposes: preaching the doctrine of holiness, developing miss. work at home and abroad, and promoting philanthropic work. Ministers usually supported by freewill offerings.

9. *Lumber River Annual Conference of the Holiness Methodist Church.* Organized 1900 at Union Chapel Ch., Robeson Co., N. C. Originally called Lumber Mission Conference of the Holiness Methodist Ch.; 1959 inclusive membership: 360.

10. *The Metropolitan Church Association.* Began in Chicago as Metropolitan Holiness Church in an 1894 revival movement; current name adopted 1899. Has no specific creed, no definite form of ch. organization; does not pay salaries. Wesleyan in theol. Official pub.: *The Burning Bush.* 1958 inclusive membership: 443.

11. *Missionary Church Association.* Organized 1898 at Berne, Ind., to promote full teaching of the Word of God and engage in aggressive miss. work. Claims to stand for the evangelical truths of Christianity and to be interdenominational. 1967 inclusive membership: 9,475.

12. *Peniel Missions.* Organized 1886 by T. P. Ferguson in Los Angeles, Calif.

13. *Missionary Bands of the World.* Grew out of a miss. soc. of young people formed 1885 in the Free Meth. Ch. under leadership of Vivian A. Dake; indep. 1898 as Pentecost Bands of the World. Meth. in character. Present name adopted 1925. Merged 1933 with the Church of God (Holiness), Fort Scott, Kans., and 1958 with the Wesleyan* Meth. Ch. of Am.

14. *Pillar of Fire.* Organized 1901, inc. 1902 as Pentecostal Union under leadership of Mrs. Alma White, wife of a Meth. minister; 1st headquarters were at Denver, Colo. Believing it impossible to carry out the miss. work of the ch. in connection with est. denominations and claiming to have received a vision of worldwide evangelism, Mrs. White est. missions in a number of cities and a training school in Denver. Headquarters were moved 1908 to Zarephath, near Bound Brook, N. J. The name Pillar of Fire was adopted 1917. Doctrinal beliefs include divine healing, premillennialism, restoration of Jews, eternal punishment, everlasting life. 1948 inclusive membership: 5,100.

15. *Free Christian Zion Church of Christ.* Organized 1905 under leadership of E. D. Brown, Negro, at Redemption, Ark.; in doctrine gen. agrees with Meths. 1961 inclusive membership: 19,826.

16. *The Gospel Mission Corps.* Inc. 1962 in N. J.; organized along military lines; believer's baptism and holy communion are observed.

17. *The Church of God (Apostolic).* Organized 1897 by Thomas J. Cox at Danville, Ky., as Christian Faith Band Ch.; inc. 1901; present name adopted 1915, inc. 1919. Foot washing and immersion are practiced. 1954 inclusive membership: 600.

18. *Fire Baptized Holiness Church.* Organized 1898 in Atlanta, Ga., as part of the interracial Fire Baptized Holiness Assoc. of Am.; the Negro membership separated 1908 and became the Fire Baptized Holiness Ch. of God 1922; 1958 inclusive membership: 988.

19. *The Fire Baptized Holiness Church (Wesleyan).* Organized ca. 1890 as The Southeast Kansas Fire Baptized Holiness Assoc. Present name adopted 1945; episc. in ch. organization; 1957 inclusive membership: 1,007.

20. *Echo Park Evangelistic Association.* Founded 1921 by A. S. McPherson* at Los Angeles, Calif.

See also *Foursquare Gospel, The; Pentecostalism.* See *Religious Bodies (US), Bibliography.*

Evangelistic Ministerial Alliance. See *Baptist Churches,* 35.

Evangelistics. That branch of theol. knowledge which treats the hist. and science of the propagation of Christianity.

Evangelization. Mission work. See also articles under *Mission* and related terms.

Evans, Christmas (1766–1838). B. on Christmas Day at Ysgaerwen, Cardiganshire, W Wales; Presb. in his youth, he became Bap. 1788; ordained ca. 1789; famous for eloquence.

Evans, James (1801–46). B. Eng.; "Apostle of the North"; came to Can. as a young man; teacher for a time; miss. to Indians in Ont.; supt. of a Meth. miss. in the West; invented syllabic system of the Cree language.

Evanson, Edward (1731–1805). B. Warrington, Lancashire, Eng.; Angl. clergyman; espoused Unitarianism*; influenced by H. S. Reimarus* and H. E. G. Paulus.* Works include *The Dissonance of the Four Generally Received Evangelists.*

Evensong. Name for Vespers* in medieval Eng.; now often used as a name for the Angl. service of Evening Prayer.

Everlasting Life. See *Hereafter, A.*

Evidence, Christian. See *Apologetics, Christian,* 1.

Evil. That which is harmful or morally bad. Often used as synonym for sin.*

Evodius. The 1st bp. of Antioch, according to Eusebius* of Caesarea.

Evolution. Naturalistic theory according to which the universe in gen., the solar system specifically, and the earth in particular, with all animate and inanimate objects existing thereon, have been evolved or developed, over millions or billions of yrs., in accord with existing natural laws, from some form of primitive mass that contained all materials needed to form the chemical elements now found in the universe. The atheistic branch of evolution states that everything now existing came into being only through existing natural laws. Theistic evolution accepts existence of a supernatural being who called into being the primitive mass and drew up fundamental laws of nature and who may, from time to time, step in to give evolution a helping hand. In gen., evolutionists are not concerned with origins but with development from a simple to a more complex state. Evolutionary theories have been applied to such areas of knowledge as anthropology, ethnology, sociology, history, comparative religion, and metaphysics.

I. *Inorganic Evolution.* Most theories proposed to explain development of the inorganic universe form 2 classes: monistic and dualistic.

Monistic or uniformitarian theories assume that the solar system developed as a closed system, isolated from other similar groups in the universe. I. Kant,* influenced by speculations of Thomas Wright (1711–86) of Durham, Eng., advanced a nebular hypothesis for the origin of the universe. Pierre Simon de Laplace (1749–1827; Fr. astronomer and mathematician) set forth a nebular hypothesis that became popular. Revisions of it include, e. g., those of Hannes Olof Gösta Alfvén (b. 1908; Swed. prof. of plasma physics), Karl Friedrich von Weizsäcker (b. 1912; Ger. physicist and philos.), Fred Lawrence Whipple (b. 1906; Am. astronomer), and Gerard Peter Kuiper (b. 1905 in the Neth.; Am. astronomer).

Dualistic or catastrophic theories assume interaction of the sun with other stars or celestial bodies. An early theory in this class was proposed by George Louis Leclerc de Buffon (1707–88; Fr. naturalist). Thomas Chrowder Chamberlin (1843–1928; Am. geologist) and Forest Ray Moulton (1872–1952; Am. astronomer) formulated the planetesimal or spiral-nebula hypothesis that involved a close approach of our sun and another star. Theories of James Hopwood Jeans (1877–1946; Eng. astronomer, mathematician, physicist), Harold A. Jeffreys (b. 1891; Eng. astronomer, geophysicist), George Howard Darwin (1845–1912; son of C. R. Darwin*; Eng. astronomer, mathematician), Henry Norris Russell (1877–1957; Am. astronomer), and Raymond Arthur Lyttleton (b. 1911; Eng. astronomer) are also included in this class. In recent yrs. the Big Bang theory (according to which the universe began billions of yrs. ago with the explosion of a hot, dense blob of matter), originated by Alexantrovich Friedmann (1888–1925; Russ. mathematician), modified by Martin Ryle (b. 1918; Eng. radio astronomer) and others, has been challenged by the Steady State theory (according to which the universe is infinite, uniform, changeless, without beginning and end), formulated 1948 by Fred Hoyle (b. 1915; Brit. astronomer, mathematician), Thomas Gold (b. 1920; Am. astronomer [formerly Brit.; b. Austrian]), and Hermann Bondi (b. 1919; Brit. mathematician), and modified 1965 by Hoyle to incorporate evidence for an oscillating universe with varying density.

II. *Organic Evolution.* Development of life from inorganic materials and continued evolvement of life to present-day forms. The concept of organic evolution can be traced back to Gks. and Romans. Jean Baptiste Pierre Antoine de Monet, chevalier de Lamarck,* was the forerunner of C. R. Darwin* in modern evolutionary theory. Lamarck's theory (1809) included inheritance of acquired characteristics and the Use and Disuse theory. Darwin advanced the theory of natural selection 1859 in *On the Origin of the Species by Means of Natural Selection, or the Preservation of Favoured Races in the Struggle for Life.* Hugo de Vries (1848–1935; Dutch botanist) formulated a theory of mutation that supplied the mechanism for Darwin's theory.

Evolutionists cite as evidence in support of the theory:

1. Similarity in embryological development. This is considered evidence of common descent. Divergence bet. invertebrates and vertebrates has also led to theories of parallel evolution.

2. Animal groups can be arranged in an order of increasing complexity. This is regarded as proof that they have evolved from the simple to the complex.

3. Similarity in physiology and biochemistry. This is taken to indicate that organisms are related by common descent.

4. Comparative anatomy. Here the argument is based on resemblances bet. organisms and certain parts of their bodies.

5. Plants and animals geog. isolated differ from those of other regions. This is held to indicate that they have evolved along different lines.

6. Rocks and fossils can be arranged in a time table. This is taken to indicate that organisms have evolved from simple to complex.

7. Results of studies of uranium disintegration. These are held to indicate that the earth is ca. 2 billion yrs. old. This is said to allow enough time for development of forms of life known today.

8. Color patterns of animals. It is believed by evolutionists that present organisms evolved in course of time from relatively simple patterns and neutral colors. Today there are those with (a) protective resemblance, (b) warning coloration, (c) mimicry coloration, and (d) colors that serve sexual selection.

9. The science of genetics. Mutations can create varieties; hence it is postulated that they can create species. Chromosome aberration (chromosomes added or subtracted, number doubled or halved, fragments added or subtracted) experiments have been classified by some as new species. But here no new contribution has been made, only a rearrangement of material already present. Also: addition or subtraction of whole chromosomes is usually harmful and deletions are usually fatal.

III. *Evolution in Other Fields.* Basic ideas of evolution have been applied to many fields. In metaphysics the theory of emergent evolutionism (C. Lloyd Morgan [1852–1936; Eng. biologist and philos.] and Samuel Alexander [1859–1938; Brit. realist metaphysician]) holds that in the sequence of events new levels appear which go beyond regrouping of previous events. Thus the whole is more than the sum of its separate parts. In comparative religion evolutionary scholars try to show that higher forms of religion evolved from lower forms (animism, etc.). In anthropology evolutionists held that the psychic unity of mankind leads to indep. progress and that all elements of culture must pass through the same stages of development. The dialectical* materialism of K. H. Marx* and F. Engels,* maintaining that everything is made of opposing factors whose internal movement leads to progress, has influenced ethics, sociology, and evolutionary views of history. The ethics of evolutionists is in a continual state of flux; that which is considered ethical today is the result of acts with favorable results in past evolutionary stages. JK, EF

See also *Time.*

Evolutionism. Adherence to one or more theories of evolution* or the application of such theories to specific areas (e. g., ethics). See also *Ethics,* 5.

Ewald, Georg Heinrich August (1803–75). B. Göttingen; orientalist; prof. Göttingen 1827–37, Tübingen 1838–48, Göttingen 1848–67; helped found Protestantenverein (Protestant* Union) 1863. In opposition to the romantic conceptions of J. G. v. Herder* and J. G. Eichhorn* he interpreted the OT prophets idealistically; approach to the NT opposed that of F. C. Baur* and D. F. Strauss.* Works include *Geschichte des Volkes Israel.* See also *Higher Criticism,* 14.

Ewald, Johann Ludwig (1748–1822). Ger. Ref. pastor and prof. Espoused supernaturalism.*

Ex cathedra (Lat. "from the chair"). In the exercise of or by virtue of one's office, e. g., when the pope is said to speak infallibly ex cathedra. See also *Infallibility, Papal.*

Ex opere operantis (Lat. "by deed of doer"). Term used to present the view that the condition of the person performing an act affects its efficacy; thus the moral condition of the administrant or recipient has a role and value in causing or receiving sacramental grace. Not to be confused with *ex opere operantis* *ecclesiae,* which refers to the efficacy of liturgical prayer due to the action of the ch.

Ex opere operato. See *Grace, Means of,* I 8; *Opus operatum.*

Exaposteilaria (from Gk. for "send forth"). Part of E Orthodox matins; subject: sending forth of the apostles.

Exapsalmos. Six psalms at beginning of E Orthodox matins.

Exarch. In the E Ch.: head of a chief see or province in the early ch.; bp. lower than a patriarch but higher than a metropolitan; patriarch's deputy; head of an indep. ch.

Exaudi. See *Church Year,* 14.

Exclusive Particles. Words that exclude from conversion and justification all cooperation of unconverted man. " 'Exclusive terms,' that is, . . . words of the holy apostle Paul which separate the merit of Christ completely from our own works and give all glory to Christ alone. Thus the holy apostle Paul uses such expressions as 'by grace,' 'without merit,' 'without the law,' 'without works,' 'not by works,' etc. All these expressions say in effect that we become righteous and are saved 'alone by faith' in Christ." (FC Ep III 7).

Excommunication. Act whereby one is excluded from the communion of the ch.

See also *Keys, Office of,* 9.

Execrabilis. 1. Constitution (some call it a bull) issued 1317 by John XXII (see *Popes,* 13); restricted pluralism (one clergyman holding two or more benefices at one time) by limiting each clergyman to two benefices (one with, one without care of souls), cardinals and kings' sons excepted; expanded and consolidated practice of reservation.*

2. At an assembly of Christian princes at Mantua 1459 Gregory of Heimburg opposed the crusade proposed by the pope against the Turks. When the pope saw how things were going, he issued the bull Execrabilis Jan. 1460. Gregory appealed from the pope to a gen. council. The bull, which excommunicated such appellants, was applied against Gregory. See also *Popes,* 15.

Exegesis. 1. The Gk. word *exegesis* is used of the art of Biblical interpretation or exposition. Hermeneutics* studies principles and formulates rules for interpretation; exegesis uses the principles and rules to determine the meaning of the text. The Bible is a clear book (see *Perspicuity of Scripture*). But it was written long ago in languages and in a cultural situation strange to most of us, who live in a different kind of society, with concepts and values other than those of old Palestine. Even people who stood much closer to the sacred authors in terms of language, culture, and time needed explanations. Philip interpreted Is 53 for the eunuch of Ethiopia (Acts 8:26-35). Jesus explained the OT to His disciples (Lk 24:27).

2. Several tendencies in exegesis soon developed in the early ch. By the end of the 1st c. divergent modes of interpretation were current.

3. The School of Alexandria (Clement* of Alexandria is regarded as the founder of the theol. school; Pantaenus* was the 1st teacher of the catechetical school), esp. Origen,* sponsored allegorical interpretation. It held that the passages of Scripture that relate hist. events or speak of earthly things have deep meaning other than literal. Accordingly we must distinguish bet. the literal, the allegorical or mystical, and the moral sense. The literal sense, it was held, is at times unworthy of the Scriptures, e. g., in the story of Noah's drunkenness (Gn 9:20-27); hence we must assume that a deeper meaning was intended. The existence of a literal sense was not denied, but it was held that this sense often must be disregarded or discarded. See also *Millennium,* 3.

4. Allegorical interpretation was opposed by the School of Antioch, whose representatives included J. Chrysostom,* Diodorus* of Tarsus, John* of Antioch, Lucian,* Paul* of Samosata, Theodore* of Mopsuestia, and Theodoret* of Cyrrhus. They held that the literal sense is usually the intended sense and must be adhered to unless it is plain that an allegory is intended, e. g., in parables. Influenced School of Edessa.*

5. In the Middle Ages, up to the Reformation, the allegorical method was gen. followed and even extended. Passages were declared to have a 4-fold meaning: literal, allegorical or mystical, moral, and anagogic. The anagogic (from Gk. for "lead upwards") meaning involved the hope of heaven; e. g., the Sabbath law (Ex 20:8) signifies (a) the 7th day must be kept as a day of rest; (b) Christ rested in the grave; (c) the Christian must rest from sin; (d) true rest awaits us in heaven. Much ingenuity and nonsense entered into this kind of exegesis.

6. The revival of learning and study of Heb. and Gk. introd. a change. M. Luther* freed himself of the spell of allegorical interpretation and became an interpreter honored throughout Christendom. Calvin also rejected the medieval system and became an exegete of extraordinary ability. Through the reformers the principle that the native, natural sense, is the sense intended by God was vindicated and became the directive for Prot. theologians. Thus the foundation was laid for later achievements in exegesis.

7. Unfortunately, some exegetical insights of the Reformation were soon lost. Luth. orthodoxy (see *Lutheran Theology After 1580*) developed a dogmatic kind of exegesis, whose method consisted of applying categories of doctrine to the art of interpretation. In that period the analogy* of faith was identified with the doctrinal content of summaries extracted from clusters of passages put together without full regard to their context. Pietism* revolted against this kind of exegesis and returned interpretation to the practice of such obvious principles as letting the sacred documents speak for themselves. J. A. Bengel* was an early exponent of Heilsgeschichte,* careful grammatical analysis, textual* criticism, quest for the hist. Jesus, millennialism,* and an interest in concepts and terms of the kind that led to G. Kittel's* *Theologisches Wörterbuch zum Neuen Testament.* Other and later pietists resorted to devotional interpretation that looked for spiritual incentive in every passage and influenced other devotional writing.

8. Ref. 17th-c. exegesis suffered for a time from the excessive typology of men like J. Cocceius.* Among more moderate practitioners of this art were P. Fairbairn* and M. S. Terry.* There is revival of interest in typology modified in form, depending largely on recapitulation in the Biblical account of God's revelatory activity.

9. Recent decades have been marked by emphasis on the historicocritical* method that followed the Enlightenment* and its concern for determining the actual nature of the events recorded in the Scriptures. Proponents of this method (e. g., K. H. Graf,* J. Wellhausen,* and H. E. Fosdick*) at first attempted to apply principles, derived in a gen. way from biological evolution, to interpretation of Scripture. In the 20th c. the view became prominent that the worshiping and teaching community of Israel and the early ch. produced the Biblical documents, as we know them, on the basis of oral tradition and earlier liturgical, catechetical, and homiletical materials.

10. Interest in comparative religion as part of preparation for Biblical interpretation has been abandoned in favor of emphasis on Biblical theol. in its uniqueness. In recent yrs. the RC Ch. has concentrated on Biblical interpretation, with the way prepared by Pius XII's (see *Popes,* 33) 1943 encycli-

cal *Divino afflante Spiritu.* Counterpart to this encyclical is the World Council's *Guiding Principles for the Interpretation of the Bible* accepted by the ecumenical Study Conference 1949. WA, MHS

See also *Theology*.

R. H. Grant, *A Short History of the Interpretation of the Bible,* rev. ed. (New York, 1963); J. Wood, *The Interpretation of the Bible* (London, 1958); R. M. Grant, J. T. McNeill, and S. Terrien, "History of the Interpretation of the Bible," *The Interpreter's Bible,* I, ed. G. A. Buttrick et al. (New York, 1952), pp. 106–141.

Exegesis perspicua. See *Cureus, Joachim.*

Exegetical Theology. See *Theology.*

Exemplarism. Doctrine that divine ideas are the ontological bases of finite realities.

Exhorters. Lay persons licensed to exhort but usually not to preach. They may hold meetings for prayer and exhortation wherever opportunity is afforded.

Existential Analysis. See *Psychotherapy,* 13.

Existentialism. 1. Existentialism is a technical philos. position popularized in the thought of S. A. Kierkegaard.* It developed with the aid of insights derived from the skeptical epistemology* of Brit. empiricism* and influenced by the phenomenology* of E. Husserl.* Principal doctrines of existentialism concern the epistemological, axiological, and psychological aspects of human being or reality. Modern exponents include Gabriel Marcel (1889–1973; Fr. RC teacher and writer), Jean-Paul Sartre (b. 1905; Fr. teacher, novelist, and dramatist), Martin Heidegger (b. 1889 Messkirch, Baden; prof. Marburg 1923–28, Freiburg 1928–45), and K. Jaspers.* Some contemporary theologians (e. g., Rudolf Karl Bultmann [b. 1884 Wiefelstede, Ger.; prof. Marburg 1921–51; see also *Demythologization*] and K. Barth* [see also *Switzerland, Contemporary Theology in*]) have been influenced by one or more phases of it.

2. Though existentialists develop views in divergent ways and complex jargon, there are some common basic features in their views which may be regarded as necessary conditions of a developed existential philosophy. The following deals primarily with these features.

a. Existence and essence. Contrary to the deterministic Aristotelian view which holds that objects of thought have an essence, or defining constituents (*genus* and *differentia*), which can be known through rational processes of reflection or inquiry, existentialists gen. insist that in the case of man no such essence is prior in time to the actual existence of human consciousness. Though the blueprint or concept of an artifact may precede its manufacture, thus determining its essence prior to its actual existence, man's being is not so determined. Here existentialist views diverge, depending on the theistic or atheistic orientation of the writer. For Kierkegaard, man's essence is known by God. But since we cannot know by processes of reason that which God knows, we can discover only the essence we have made for ourselves after coming to exist. Atheistic existentialists agree with this conclusion, not on the grounds of skepticism regarding our knowledge of God, but on the ground that God does not exist. In this case man has no essence at all except that which he himself creates by means of his conscious choices after he has come to exist. Since each new choice alters his "essence," it is always incomplete until he is dead. This incompleteness of human reality and its irrevocable termination is gen. assoc. with existentialist emphasis on the contingency and frailty of human life.

b. Freedom. The denial of any human essence ontologically prior to concrete human beings is the source of the emphasis on human freedom. If no such essence objectively exists or is known, man is free to make of himself what he chooses to be. Present choices merely limit the range of future possibilities but do not determine which of the remaining possibilities he will choose. No other person, no environment or passion can thus be claimed to be the causal determinant of one's being what he is. Hence man *is* his freedom and is responsible for his nature and all his choices.

c. Anxiety *(Angst).* Such freedom is the ground of the existentialists' preoccupation with anxiety or anguish. Facing an undetermined future, man becomes anxious because he is responsible but cannot know the consequences of his decisions. Man is thus a subject "condemned to be free" (Sartre). In such circumstances some men make a leap (Ger. "Sprung") at a certain stage in life (Kierkegaard), committing themselves to Jesus Christ, whom they cannot intellectually grasp (and who is therefore called "absurd") as their only hope. For most existentialists man tries to flee from freedom and responsibility in various ways, e. g., by sensual pursuits or belief in some form of psychological determinism. This is "bad faith" (Sartre) or "inauthenticity" (Heidegger); man then refuses to accept himself and his responsibility for what he has made of himself.

d. Subjective source of value. To be an authentic person requires that one realize and courageously accept the fact that human freedom necessarily gives rise to anxiety, which affects all one's knowledge and volition. Authentic man is therefore an unhappy consciousness (Sartre). Even for the Christian, sickness is a natural state (Kierkegaard). Once man accepts this fact, his conscious decisions are intensified and his choices made with passionate inwardness (Kierkegaard) that attends the freely-chosen acts of the total personality. Such decision-processes, accompanied by the values of courage and fortitude, exhibit man as the source of value.

e. Human solidarity. If man acts as an authentic person, he also chooses to do what accords with his image of man as he ought to be; for men are together in the world and are intuitively aware of this fact of human existence, as the experience of shame shows. Since human existence implies communion (Marcel) or being with others, each man is responsible for all. This fact also explains why each man is regarded as a threat to the existence of others. The choices he makes invariably affect others. Choices desirable for the individual are therefore regarded as those that strengthen human solidarity (Marcel) or those that are appropriate in the situation (Sartre). In the latter view, others are injured in some way by one's choices, and so "hell is other people." Kierkegaard's existentialism is not incompatible with this latter view. But Marcel more eloquently expresses the humanistic concern of existentialism by emphasis on the benefits of human coexistence, cooperation, and concern for others. CEH

Kierkegaard's Concluding Unscientific Postscript, tr. D. F. Swenson and W. Lowrie (Princeton, 1941); M. Heidegger, *Being and Time,* tr. J. Macquarrie and E. Robinson (New York, 1962); J.-P. Sartre, *Being and Nothingness,* tr. E. Barnes (New York, 1956) and *Existentialism,* tr. B. Frechtmann (New York, 1947); E. Mounier, *Existentialist Philosophies,* tr. E. Blow (London, 1948); H. J. Blackham, *Six Existentialist Thinkers* (New York, 1952); R. G. Olson, *An Introduction to Existentialism* (New York, 1962); *Christianity and the Existentialists,* ed. C. Michaelson (New York, 1956).

Exogamy. Marriage outside a group, esp. as required by custom or law, in distinction from endogamy.*

Exorcism (from Gk. for "out" and "adjure"). Expelling or banning of evil spirits. Exorcism in the broad sense by rite and ritual is widely practiced in many religious cults. In the narrow sense it is a Christian ceremony.

Jesus expelled demons with a simple command

(Mk 1:23-26; 9:14-29; Lk 11:14-26). The apostles continued the practice with the power and in the name of Jesus (Mt 10:1; Acts 19:11-16).

Special formulas of exorcism were developed in the early ch. The practice was early assoc. with baptism and preceded it. The RC Ch. and the E Orthodox Ch. preserved the rite of exorcism. The Luth. Ch., following M. Luther's* "Taufbüchlein," gen. kept exorcism until the 18th c. S. S. Schmucker* and others rejected exorcism. C. F. W. Walther* advised congs. that practiced exorcism not to abolish it in haste and those that did not have it not to reintroduce it.

See also *Baptism, Liturgical,* 2, 3.

Exorcist. See *Clergy; Hierarchy.*

Experimentalism. See *Pragmatism.*

Explicit Faith. See *Fides explicita.*

Exposition, Biblical. See *Exegesis.*

Exposition of the Christian Faith. See *Reformed Confessions,* A 4.

Exsultet. 1. *Exsultet iam angelica turba* (Lat. "Now let the angelic host rejoice"; first words of the *praeconium paschale* ["paschal praise"] or *laus [consecratio, benedictio] cerei* ["praise (consecration, blessing) of the candle"]). RC hymn originating ca. 7th c. or earlier; sung by deacon on Holy Sat. (see *Church Year,* 4) at blessing of candle into which are inserted 5 grains of incense representing the wounds of Jesus. 2. *Exsultet orbis gaudiis* (Lat. "Let the earth with joy resound"). RC hymn in divine office for vespers and lauds on feasts of apostles and evangelists outside the Easter season.

Exsurge, Domine. See *Bull; Christian Church, History of,* III 1; *Luther, Martin,* 13; *Reformation, Lutheran,* 9.

External Works of God. See *Father, God the.*

Externalism. See *Formalism.*

Extravagantes. See *Canon Law,* 3; *Chappuis, Jean.*

Extreme Unction. See *Unction.*

Exultate Deo. See *Bull; Florence, Council of,* 3.

Eyck, van. *Hubert* (or Huybrecht; ca. 1366–1426) and *Jan* (ca. 1370–ca. 1441), brothers; reputedly born Maeseyck, Belgium, whence their name; founded Flemish school of painting. Hubert's only known work (and one on which he collaborated with Jan) is an altarpiece at Ghent. Jan's other works include a "Madonna and Child."

Eylert, Ru(h)lemann Friedrich (1770–1852). B. Hamm, Westphalia; ev. theol.; court preacher at Potsdam (1806) of Frederick* William III; encouraged the king to initiate inauguration of the Prussian Union.

Ezekiel, Apocryphal. Additions to Eze 37; taught universal resurrection; quoted in some ch. fathers; probably originated bet. 50 BC and 50 AD.

Ezra, Abraham Ibn (1093–1167). B. Sp.; Jewish philos.; influenced by Neoplatonism* and Avicebrón.*

F

Faber, Basilius (ca. 1520–ca. 1575). B. Sorau, Lower Lusatia; studied at Wittenberg under P. Melanchthon*; rector Nordhausen, Tennstädt, Magdeburg, and Quedlinburg; dismissed from the last post for refusing to sign the Corpus Philippicum (see *Corpus doctrinae Christianae*); dir. Rathsgymnasium at Erfurt. Tr. M. Luther's* commentary on Gn 1–25 into Ger.; collaborator on first 4 vols. of the "Magdeburg Centuries" (see *Flacius Illyricus, Matthias*).

Faber, Ernst (Apr. 25, 1839–Sept. 26, 1899). B. Coburg, Ger.; d. Tsingtao, China; left for China 1864 in service of Rhenish* Miss. Soc.; discharged 1880; joined Allgemeiner Evangelisch-Protestantischer Missionsverein (see *German East Asia Mission*) 1885. Works include *Der Lehrbegriff des Konfuzius; China in historischer Beleuchtung.*

Faber, Frederick William (1814–63). B. Calverley, Yorkshire, Eng.; hymnist and theol.; educ. Oxford; rector Elton, Huntingdonshire; RC 1845; est. a religious community at Birmingham called Wilfridians, or Brothers of the Will of God, which merged with the Oratorians*; est. a branch in London 1849. Hymns include "Sweet Savior, Bless Us Ere We Go"; "The Pilgrims of the Night."

Faber, Jacobus. See *Lefèvre d'Étaples, Jacques.*

Faber, Johannes (Fabri; Heigerlin; 1478–1541). B. Leutkirch, Ger.; son of a smith (hence his name); called "Malleus Haereticorum" (Lat. "Hammer of Heretics") after one of his works; vicar-gen. Constance 1518; humanist friend of D. Erasmus*; participated in disputations at Zurich 1523 and Baden (in Aargau, Switz.) 1526 against H. Zwingli*; bp. Vienna ca. 1530. Wrote against M. Luther,* J. Oecolampadius,* B. Hubmaier,* K. Schwenkfeld.*

Faber, Petrus. See *Favre, Pierre.*

Faber, Wendalinus (1st half 16th c.). Teacher at Eisleben; by 1537 court preacher of Count Gebhard von Mansfeld at Seeburg; signed SA and Tractatus; opposed J. Agricola* in Antinomian* Controversy.

Faber, Zachäus (1583–1632). B. Röcknitz, near Wurzen, Ger.; deacon Dippoldiswalde 1604, pastor Somnitz 1609, supt. Chemnitz 1611; wrote the hymn "Herr, ich bin ein Gast auf Erden."

Fabordone. See *Fauxbourdon.*

Fabri, Friedrich Gotthardt Karl Ernst (1824–91). B. Schweinfurt, Ger.; ev. theol.; inspector of the Rhenish* Miss. Soc. 1857–84; espoused Biblicism rather than confessionalism; opposed Darwinism and materialism; advocated separation of ch. and state.

Fabri, Jacobus. See *Lefèvre d'Étaples, Jacques.*

Fabri, Johannes. See *Faber, Johannes.*

Fabricius, Jacob (1593–1654). B. Köslin, Pommerania; chaplain to Gustavus* II of Swed.; hymnist. His part in writing the hymn "Fear Not, O Little Flock, the Foe" ("O Little Flock, Fear Not the Foe") was apparently this, that he versified the prose form of Gustavus III; J. M. Altenburg* is gen. regarded as having made the Ger. version that C. Winkworth* tr. into Eng.

Fabricius, Johann(es) (1644–1729). B. Altdorf, near Nürnberg; prof. Altdorf 1677, Helmstedt 1697; sought to minimize confessional differences. Works include *Consideratio variarum controversiarum.*

Fabricius Johann Albert (1668–1736). B. Leipzig; classical scholar, bibliographer, and philologist; educ. Leipzig; private librarian at Hamburg 1693; prof. ethics and rhetoric at gymnasium 1699. Works include *Codex pseudepigraphus; Centifolium Lutheranum.*

Fabricius, Johann Philipp (1711–91). B. Kleeberg, near Frankfurt am Main; Luth. miss. among Tamil-speaking people of S India; revised the Ziegenbalg-Schultze Tamil Bible 1758 and issued his own tr. of the NT; pub. Luth. hymnal and other books. See also *India,* 10.

Fabritius, Jacob (Fabricius; d. 1693). Sent 1669 by Luth. consistory of Amsterdam to New Amsterdam (New York); dismissed because of despotic and irascible nature at Albany and later NYC; pastor of a Swed. ch., Wilmington, Del., 1671; pastor Wicaco (Philadelphia), 1677—93. See also *Arensius, Bernhard.*

Faburden. See *Fauxbourdon.*

Facundus (d. ca. 571). Bp of Hermiane, Afr. Defended the Three Chapters (see *Three Chapters, Controversy of*).

MPL, 67, 521—878.

Fagius, Paul (Phagius; ca. 1504–49). Fagius is Lat. for "beech," which is also the basic meaning of his Ger. family name Büchlein, or Büchelin; Phagius reflects the Gk. for "oak." B. Rheinzabern, The Palatinate; pastor at Isny, Württemberg, 1538; est. a Heb. press there; collaborator of E. Levita*; pastor Konstanz ca. 1543; pastor and prof. OT Strasbourg 1544; to Eng. 1549 as a result of Interim*; prof. OT Cambridge; friend of M. Bucer.*

Fahling, John Adam (June 19, 1892–Nov. 28, 1945). B. Conklin, Mich.; educ. Conc. Sem., St. Louis, Mo. Pastor McAlester and Wellston, Okla., 1914–20; Sawyer, Mich., 1920–24; Hamtramck, Mich., 1924–39; Milan, Mich., 1945. Ex. secy. Detroit (Mich.) Luth. Center 1939–45. Works include *The Life of Christ; A Harmony of the Gospels; Behold the Savior in Sacred Art* (Lenten sermons); *German Gospel Sermons with English Outlines.* See also *Jesus, Lives of.*

Fairbairn, Andrew Martin (1838–1912). Scot. Cong. minister; principal Airedale Coll. at Bradford and Mansfield Coll. at Oxford; lectured in Am. univs. Works include *Catholicism, Roman and Anglican; The Place of Christ in Modern Theology.*

Fairbairn, Patrick (1805–74). Scot. Presb. theol.; joined Free Ch. 1843; prof. Free Ch. coll., Aberdeen; principal Free Ch. coll., Glasgow; mem. OT rev. company. Works include *The Typology of Scripture;* ed. *The Imperial Bible Dictionary.*

Faith. 1. Objectively, body of truth found in creeds (*fides quae creditur;* Lat. "the faith that is believed"). 2. The human response to divine activity (*fides qua creditur;* Lat. "the faith by which one believes"). Faith as response is supernatural. 3. Faithfulness as a virtue.

See also *Faith, Justifying; Grace; Grace, Means of; Justification;* articles beginning with the word *Fides.*

E. L. Wilson, "Faith," *The Abiding Word,* I, ed. T. F. K. Laetsch (St. Louis, 1946), 188–220; A. v. Schlatter, *Der Glaube im Neuen Testament,* 2d ed. (Stuttgart, 1896); A. Koeberle, *The Quest for Holiness,* tr. J. C. Mattes (New York, 1936); J. Pelikan, "The Relation of Faith and Knowledge in the Lutheran Confessions," *CTM,* XXI (May 1950), 321–331; W. F. Beck, "The Basis of Our Faith," *CTM,*

XXIII (June 1952), 418–427, "The Growth of Our Faith," *CTM,* XXIII (July 1952), 498–508, and "Our Life of Faith," *CTM,* XXIII (Aug. 1952), 583–590; F. Gogarten, *The Reality of Faith,* tr. C. Michalson et al. (Philadelphia, [1959]); R. Bring, *Das Verhältnis von Glauben und Werken in der lutherischen Theologie* (Munich, 1955); H. E. Brunner, *Faith, Hope, and Love* (Philadelphia, 1956); C. A. Skovgaard-Petersen, *Faith and Certainty,* tr. A. W. Kjellstrand (Rock Island, Ill., 1957); J. H. Bavinck, *Faith and Its Difficulties,* tr. W. B. Eerdmans, Sr. (Grand Rapids, Mich., 1959); H. Bars, *Faith, Hope and Charity,* tr. P. J. Hepburne Scott, in *The Twentieth Century Encyclopedia of Catholicism,* XXVII (New York, 1961); R. K. Bultmann and A. Weiser, *Faith,* tr. D. M. Barton, ed. P. R. Ackroyd, in *Bible Key Words,* X (London, 1961); G. Ebeling, *The Nature of Faith,* tr. R. G. Smith (Philadelphia, 1961) and *Word and Faith,* tr. J. W. Leitch (Philadelphia, 1963); R. Schwarz, *Fides, Spes und Caritas beim jungen Luther* (Berlin, 1962); K. Bendall and F. P. Ferré, *Exploring the Logic of Faith: A Dialogue on the Relation of Modern Philosophy to Christian Faith* (New York, 1962); N. F. S. Ferré, *The Finality of Faith; and, Christianity among the World Religions* (New York, 1963); M. E. Marty, *Belief and Unbelief as Modern Problems* (San Francisco, 1963; mimeographed); C. Michalson, *The Rationality of Faith* (New York, 1963); D. M. Baillie, *Faith in God and Its Christian Consummation,* foreword by J. McIntyre, new ed. (London, 1964); see also references under *Creeds and Confessions; Dogmatics; Ecumenical Creeds.*

Faith, Explicit and Implicit. See *Fides explicita; Fides implicita.*

Faith, Justifying *(fides justificans; fides salvifica).* The act by which one enters into that right relation to God which the all-atoning work of Christ has est. for the whole world.

Man needs new life through faith because of sin, which separates from God (Is 59:2). The remedy for sin comes entirely from God (Eph 2:5, 8). His gracious plan of salvation is revealed in Scripture and is received by faith (Ro 4:13, 16).

The Bible uses many images to portray faith (e. g., coming to Christ, Mt 11:28; seeing Christ, Jn 14:9; obedient hearing of Christ, Jn 10:27; keeping Christ's Word, Jn 8:51; laying hold on eternal life, 1 Ti 6:12).

Faith as a soteriological factor *(fides salvifica)* may be defined or described as consisting of knowledge, assent, and confidence. Each of these concepts is a definition of faith if it is understood to imply also the other two.

Faith as *knowledge* is the grasp with the mind, or the mental possession of that which is communicated (Lk 1:77; Jn 14:7; 17:3; Ro 10:14, 17; 1 Ti 2:4; 2 Ptr 1:3). This salutary knowledge is not mere intellectual acquaintance (Ja 2:19) or technical knowledge (1 Co 2:14), but a product of divine grace which permeates the whole heart (1 Co 2:12; 2 Co 4:6; 2 Ti 1:12).

Faith as *assent* is an act of the will which accepts the exalted phenomena presented to the mind. Hence, the preaching of faith is hortatory, pleading, persuasive in its message (Acts 26:28; 28:23). Since man is by nature dead in trespasses and sins (Eph 2:1; Cl 2:13), his coming to spiritual life is the work of God (Jn 6:29; Eph 2:1-10).

Faith as confidence means that faith is that certainty, that assurance, which is as great and as firm as though we actually had the promised things in our possession, as though we could see, feel, and handle them, as though we had not only the prospect but the substance of these things (Jn 17:8; Ro 4:18-21; 8:24; 2 Ti 1:12; Tts 3:7; Heb 11:1; 1 Ptr 1:3, 13; Ap IV, 48, 50).

Faith is also thought of as a *state.* In this respect faith is viewed as the continued possession of the gifts and blessings of God, in and through Christ, through an enduring, abiding confidence in His complete and all-sufficient redemption (Lk 22:32; 2 Co 13:5; Gl 2:20; Cl 2:7; 1 Ti 4:7; 2 Ti 4:7). Christian faith can increase in intensity (2 Co 10:15) and extension (1 Co 1:5).

Justification by grace through faith est. a new relationship bet. God and man and produces new attitudes, desires, objectives, and ideals (Gl 2:20; Ph 4:8; Tts 2:12-13). True faith is a living, energizing, motivating power that propels and urges to action (Mt 17:20; 1 Jn 5:4-5). ELW

See also *Ethics; Faith; Good Works; Grace, Means of; Material Principle; Opus operatum; Sola fide.*

Faith, Rule of. See *Rule of Faith.*

Faith, Sacred Congregation for the Doctrine of the. See *Curia,* 2 d.

Faith and Message, Statement of Committee on Baptist. See *Democratic Declarations of Faith,* 3.

Faith and Order Movement. See *Ecumenical Movement, The,* 8, 10, 11; *World Council of Churches.*

Faith Healing. See *Healing.*

Faithful, Mass of the. See *Missa. fidelium.*

Faithful Departed, Commemoration of. See *Church Year,* 17.

Fakir (from Arab. *faqir,* "poor"). Muslim word also used in Hinduism* instead of *bhikshu* and older terms (see also *Buddhism,* 4). Some fakirs practice asceticism and self-torture. Hindu fakir orders include yogis (see *Yoga*). See also *Dervish.*

Falasha (Ethiopic for "immigrant"). "Jews of Abyssinia." Group of people in Ethiopia (Abyssinia) whose religion bears marks of Jewish influence. Theories of their hist. include that they descended from Menelek, alleged son of Solomon by the Queen of Sheba; that their ancestors came from Judaea with the Queen of Sheba; that they descended from the ten* lost tribes of Israel; that they came to Abyssinia in the 1st c. AD. Their religious life centers in synagogue worship (reading of Torah; prayers); strict Sabbath observance; chief Jewish festivals observed (but not Purim or dedication of temple); have OT and other sacred books in Geez (Semitic language formerly used in Ethiopia); priests and deacons appointed by community; avoid contact with Christians; monastic system. Est. number ranges from ca. 50,000 to ca. 200,000. Sometimes called Black Jews. See also *Judaism.*

Falckner, Daniel, Jr. (1666–ca. 1741). B. Saxony; grandson of pastor Christian Falckner; son of pastor Daniel Falckner, Sr.; brother of Justus Falckner*; studied theol. at Erfurt; follower of A. H. Francke*; to Am. 1694; assoc. with Ger. pietists in Pa.; to Ger. 1698; returned to Germantown (Philadelphia), Pa., with his brother Justus and others 1700; agent of the Frankfort Land Co.; organized and served 1700–08 a cong. in Falckner's Swamp (New Hanover), Pa.; lost all through intrigues of his bus. partners; in later yrs. served congs. in N. J. and N. Y.

Falckner, Justus (Nov. 22, 1672–1723). Luth. clergyman; hymnist; b. Saxony; brother of D. Falckner,* Jr.; educ. Halle; to Germantown (Philadelphia), Pa., 1700 with his brother, and attorney with him of the Frankfort Land Co.; ordained in Gloria Dei Ch., Wicaco(a), Philadelphia, Nov. 24, 1703; pastor N. Y. and N. J. 1703–23. Works include *Grondlycke Onderricht;* hymns include "Auf! ihr Christen, Christi Glieder."

J. F. Sachse, *Justus Falckner* (Philadelphia, 1903); D. W. Clark, *The World of Justus Falckner* (Philadelphia, 1946); H. J. Kreider, "Justus Falckner," *CHIQ,* XXVII (July 1954), 86–94; "Justus Falckner's Ordination Certificate," tr. J. G. Glenn, *CHIQ,* XXVII (Oct. 1954), 141–143.

Falconer, See *Keith-Falconer.*

Falk, Johann(es) Daniel (1768–1826). Author; philanthropist; hymnist; b. Danzig; studied theol. and philos. at Halle 1787; organized Gesellschaft der Freunde in der Not 1813 to provide family care for orphaned and neglected children; later est. school for such children. Wrote the hymn "O du fröhliche."

Falk, Paul Ludwig Adalbert. See *May Laws.*

Falk Laws. See *May Laws.*

Falkland Islands. See *South America,* introd. par.

Fall of Man. The act of the first parents of our race by which they sinned, through which, by imputation, all men were constituted sinners, and which had the result that thereby their nature and the nature of all descended from them became corrupt and subject to sin, having lost the divine image of perfect holiness and true knowledge of God (Gn 3; Ro 5:12-19). Man had been placed in a state of probation, possessing the ability not to sin (Lat. *posse non peccare*). The test of this probation was obedience to the divine law. While in this state, man was tempted by the devil*; the temptation accomplished its intent when man, exercising free will, ate of the forbidden fruit. Separation from God resulted, since man now had become alienated from the life of the Spirit, seeking in self and in the world that whereby he might live. Thus man had been brought to know good and evil, though in a different sense from that which he had desired. Only through the second Adam, Christ, were the ravages of the fall and its consequences (God's wrath and displeasure, temporal death, and eternal damnation) abundantly made good and the means of pardon and grace provided for all men. See also *Sin; Sin, Original.*

Fallot, Tommy (1844–1904). B. Fouday, Steinthal, Fr.; studied theol. in Strasbourg; pastor of the free ch. Chapelle du Nord, Paris, 1875; active in evangelism, moral reform, and ecumenical endeavor.

False Decretals. See *Decretals, False.*

Falso bordone. See *Fauxbourdon.*

Fami(g)lia pontifica. See *Papal Household.*

Familists (Family of Love). Founded by Hendrik Niclaes*; he taught that the world had seen 2 dispensations (of Law and of faith) and regarded himself as the prophet of the 3d (love); Familists lived in the 3d dispensation and were antinomian; main field of activity was in Britain.

Family Altar. See *Prayer,* 1.

Family Life Education. Christian family life education is a term denoting a program of service to child, youth, and adult which helps to better equip them for living in the Christian family. It aims to enrich the spiritual life of the home, to give parents a better understanding of their children and the skills for their Christian nurture, to make personal and family worship increasingly effective, to supply counsel in problems of family relationships, and to help lift the entire spirit and purpose of the home.

The aim of Christian family life educ. is that every family by the grace of God become a spiritually growing, responsible, Christian family unit. It is an intensification of the ministry of pastor to people, and families to each other, to help families fulfill their God-given mission. It embraces: helping parents in the Christian nurture of their children; helping families est. and maintain meaningful family devotions; guiding and inspiring families to be Christian households, living by Christian standards; helping child, youth, and adult develop a Christian view of sex; preparing youth and adults for marriage as a godly vocation. It also includes winning, assimilating, conserving families for Christ; serving the founding, expanding, shrinking, and aging family throughout life; helping incomplete families, single adults, and couples. It is both preventive and remedial, nursing sick marriages back to health and referring problem cases to the best resources in the community. It involves restudy from the Biblical view of such areas as mate selection, engagement and marriage, divorce and remarriage, family structure and authority, sexual ethics, and birth control. More than a program of services, it is a concern, emphasis, and family-conscious dimension of the modern ministry.

God made the home the center of worship and religious training. It not only conveys physical life but is God's primary institution to insert the life in Christ into each generation (Gn 18:19; Dt. 6:6-7; Eph 6:1-4). The home is the cradle of personality, the most potent teaching agency, the chief unit in evangelism, the best barrier against evil, the keeper of culture, the bulwark of the ch., and the cornerstone of the nation. Correlation bet. consistent Christianity and successful marriage is very high. New strains and stresses have been placed on the family by world-shattering changes in society. Modern life has greatly increased the incidence of separation, divorce, broken homes, and child delinquency. Home and ch. need each other more than ever before. Research by psychologists, sociologists, and welfare workers has cast new light on family relations. It is logical that the ch. should take the lead, because it alone has the regenerating power of the Gospel of Christ, the love and concern of the Good Shepherd, and the teaching facilities and agencies to carry out a balanced program of family life guidance. OEF

See also *Parish Education,* H 3.

Helping Families Through the Church, ed. O. E. Feucht (St. Louis, 1957); O. E. Feucht, *Ministry to Families* (St. Louis, 1963); *Sex and the Church,* ed. O. E. Feucht et al. (St. Louis, 1961); *Engagement and Marriage,* ed. O. E. Feucht et al. (St. Louis, 1959); R. W. Fairchild and J. C. Wynn, *Families in the Church* (New York, 1961); W. H. Lazareth, *Luther on the Christian Home* (Philadelphia, 1960); W. E. Hulme, *The Pastoral Care of Families* (Nashville, 1962); E. R. Duvall and R. L. Hill, *Being Married* (New York, 1960).

Family Planning. 1. Term widely used for processes whereby size of family is controlled; often preferred to "birth control" because it includes techniques of achieving as well as avoiding conception. "Planned parenthood" is registered in the US patent office as a service mark. The term "birth control," first used 1914 by Margaret Sanger (b. 1883; nurse) in the *Woman Rebel,* a monthly magazine, in a wide sense designates any method of limiting family size, in a narrow sense prevention of conception by chemical or mechanical means.

2. In 1798, in *An Essay on the Principle of Population as It Affects the Future Improvement of Society,* T. R. Malthus* advocated pop. control by late marriage and continence. Francis Place (1771–1854; Brit. tailor; soc. reformer; helped pass Reform bill 1832; drafted People's Charter) advocated use of contraceptives. R. D. Owen* gave information on method in *Moral Physiology.* The Am. physician Charles Knowlton (1800–50) was jailed 1832 for explaining birth control in *Fruits of Philosophy.* In 1877 A. Besant* and C. Bradlaugh* were acquitted of immorality on republishing this tract in England. Publicity attending the trial led to formation of a Malthusian* league in England. Similar leagues were est. in the Neth., Belgium, Fr., and Ger. in the 1880s.

3. Aletta Jacobs (1849–1929; 1st Dutch woman physician to practice in Holland; suffragist) est. the world's 1st birth-control clinic 1878 at Amsterdam. M. Sanger est. 1st US birth-control clinic 1916 in Brooklyn, organized 1st Am. Birth Control conf. 1921, and founded the Am. Birth Control league. The Margaret Sanger Research Bureau (1st permanent birth-control clinic in the US; founded 1923) provided contraceptive services and did research in

infertility and marriage counseling. The league and Research Bureau merged 1939 to form the Birth Control Federation of America, Inc. (changed 1942 to Planned Parenthood Federation of America, Inc., New York). The Internat. Planned Parenthood federation was organized at Stockholm, Swed., 1953.

4. The A. M. A. and allied specialty groups endorsed birth control 1937.

5. Legal opposition to birth control changed to endorsement and sponsorship. In the US the so-called Comstock laws of 1873 prohibited sending contraceptive information and devices through the mail (virtually nullified in the 1930s by Fed. court decisions). N. C. was the 1st state in which pub. health facilities made birth control services available (1937); other states soon followed. By 1957 only Conn. and Mass. enforced laws forbidding physicians to offer contraceptive information; later they also permitted contraceptives for prophylactic purposes, Conn. being the last to abandon prohibition of contraceptives (1965). In the early 1960s ca. 17 states restricted dissemination of information regarding prevention of conception, but all exempted medical practice. The US Pub. Health Service assists in child-spacing and family planning programs proposed by any state. In the 1950s govts. of other nations (e. g., India, Japan, Egypt, China) began sponsoring birth control.

6. Religious groups formerly opposed birth control. While continuing to oppose abortion,* many endorse or allow contraceptives. The Cen. Conf. of Am. Rabbis (Reform), the Rabbinical Assem. of Am. (Conservative), Unitarians, and Universalists were among early proponents of birth control in the US. Through its Committee on Marriage and the Home the FCC in 1938 pub. *Moral Aspects of Birth Control* favoring birth control. By 1960 most Prots. and Luths. in Am. favored or allowed contraceptives. The encyclical* *Casti Connubii* (Pius XI, 1930; see *Popes,* 32) declared that birth control methods that deliberately frustrate the act of matrimony in its natural power to generate life offend the law of God and nature. The encyclical permits abstinence under certain circumstances as a means of child spacing and family limitation. More liberal positions are advocated by some RCs.

J. T. Landis and M. G. Landis, "Family Planning," *The Marriage Handbook* (New York, 1948), pp. 367–400, and *Building a Successful Marriage,* 4th ed. (Englewood Cliffs, N. J., 1963); R. M. Fagley, *The Population Explosion and Christian Responsibility* (New York, 1960); *Religion and Birth Control,* ed. J. C. Monsma (New York, 1963); A. M. Rehwinkel, *Planned Parenthood and Birth Control in the Light of Christian Ethics* (St. Louis, 1959); A. W. Sulloway, *Birth Control and Catholic Doctrine* (Boston, 1959); J. T. Noonan, Jr., *Contraception: A History of Its Treatment by the Catholic Theologians and Canonists* (Cambridge, Mass., 1965). EL

Family Services. See *Child and Family Service Agencies.*

Family Worship Hour. See *Worship Hour, Family.*

Fanaticism. Irrational zeal (displaying many characteristics of monomania) which prevents deliberation or consideration on the basis of either Scripture or reason (cf. Lk 9:53; Jn 19:15; Acts 7:57; 9:1). See also *Enthusiasm.*

Fanatics. See *Camisards; Enthusiasm.*

Fandrey, Gustav Adolf (Dec. 20, 1866–July 14, 1930). B. Samter, Posen, Ger.; educ. Neuendettelsau Miss. School 1881–84; to Am. 1884; prof. Wartburg Sem., Mendota, Ill., 1884–85; pastor Fort Madison, Iowa 1885–89, Chicago 1889–1930; pres. Ev. Luth. Syn. of Iowa* and Other States 1927–30.

Fanon. 1. Vestment like a short cape worn by the pope at solemn pontifical mass. 2. Napkin used in handling holy vessels and bread for the Eucharist.

Far East Broadcasting Company. Inc. 1945 Calif.; operates a number of radio transmitters (the 1st est. 1948 Manila, Philippines) broadcasting the Gospel in many languages.

Far Eastern Bible Institute and Seminary. See *Far Eastern Gospel Crusade.*

Far Eastern Gospel Crusade. Formed 1947 in Denver, Colo., by merger of 2 organizations formed in the mid-1940s by GIs in the Far East (GI Gospel Crusade; Far Eastern Bible Institute and Seminary). Fields of work include Cambodia, Japan, Okinawa, Philippines. Mem. IFMA. Headquarters: Detroit, Mich.

Farabi, al-. See *Arabic Philosophy.*

Farel, Guillaume (1489–1565). B. Dauphiné, Fr.; Prot. reformer; follower of J. Lefèvre* d'Étaples; held M. Luther's* views on grace and justification; fled Fr. 1523; active in Meaux, Basel, Montbéliard, Strasbourg, Berne, Aigle, Neuchâtel, and Geneva; persuaded J. Calvin* to settle in Geneva; banished with Calvin 1538; pastor Neuchâtel. See also *Neuchâtel, Independent Evangelical Church of; Switzerland,* 2.

Farkas, Joseph (1833–1908). Hungarian Ref. theol.; prominent ch. historian, esp. on Hungary.

Farmer, James Leonard. See *Congress of Racial Equality.*

Farner, Oskar (1884–1958). Prof. ch. hist. Zurich 1939; authority on H. Zwingli.* Works include *Huldrych Zwingli.*

Farnese, Alesandro. See *Paul III.*

Farnovius, Stanislaus (Farnowski; Farnesius; d. ca. 1615). Influenced by It. anti-trinitarian critics; accepted personality but rejected invocation of Holy Spirit; defended preexistence and metaphysical deity of Christ.

Farquhar, John Nicol (1861–1929). Sent by LMS to India; entered service of YMCA 1909 for work among non-Christian coll. students in India; prof. comparative religion Victoria U. of Manchester, Eng., 1923; wrote extensively on India and Hinduism.

Farrad Muhammad. See *Lost-Found Nation of Islam in the Wilderness of North America, The.*

Farrant, Richard (fl. 1564–ca. 1580). Eng. composer. Works include "Hide Not Thou Thy Face"; "Call to Remembrance."

Farrar, Frederic William (1831–1903). B. Bombay, India; canon Westminster 1876; archdeacon Westminster 1883; dean Canterbury 1895; known for writings on Bible times; questioned eternal punishment. Works include *The Bible: Its Meaning and Supremacy; The Early Days of Christianity; The Life and Work of St. Paul; The Life of Christ; Lives of the Fathers; History of Interpretation;* commentaries on OT and NT books.

Fascism. See *Socialism,* 3.

Fasting. Fasting is mentioned often in the OT. It was undertaken voluntarily or by pub. prescription. Pharisees considered fasting meritorious (Lk 18:12); their "twice in the week": Mondays and Thursdays. Jesus speaks of fasting as a common practice which, in itself, He does not condemn (Mt 6:16-18); but His disciples did not fast (Mt 9:14), and He did not command it. The apostles fasted at times (Acts 13:2; 14:23). In conformity with Jewish custom many in the early ch. fasted twice a week: Wednesdays and Fridays. Under influence of monastic ideas the practice gradually lost its voluntary character and was imposed on all Christians as obligatory and God-pleasing.

To fast meant, at first, to abstain from all food till evening. The E Orthodox Ch. keeps its fasts with considerable strictness; the RC Ch., as early as the Middle Ages, permitted fasting to become a very tolerable experience. RC rules regarding abstinence and fasting have been changed several times in the 20th c. (e. g., 1957, 1966).

Luth. Confessions teach that right fasting is a fruit of repentance commanded by God in the same way as right praying and right alms-giving; that fasting is useful for keeping the flesh in check; and that it is a fine external training in preparation for receiving Holy Communion. (Ap XII 139, 143; XV 47; SC VI 10)

See also *Church Year,* 8; *Quatember.*

Fatalism. Belief that events are inevitably determined; hence often spoken of as a blind doctrine. It is decidedly anti-christian, denying possibility of personal relation bet. believer and God; leads to pessimism.* It is a prominent feature of Islam.*

Father, God the. The term Father as used in Scripture ordinarily refers to the God of the covenant in His relation to believers and in this sense refers to the divine essence without distinction of Persons (see *Fatherhood of God*). But in many passages the Persons are differentiated. The Father, personally so named (e. g., Jn 3:35; 5:20; 15:9; 17; 20:17; 1 Ptr 1:3), is specifically described as unbegotten (Jn 5:26) but generating eternally the Son (Ps 2:7; Acts 13:33; Heb 1:5) and sending forth the Holy* Spirit (Gl 4:6). The act of generating, or begetting, the Son, of which the human mind can form no adequate notion, is a true act, but internal (terminating within the Godhead, the Son also being God, of one same and indivisible essence with the Father, Jn 10:30). The eternal procession of the Spirit from the Father and the Son (see *Filioque Controversy*) is also an internal act. Generation and procession indicate the relation bet. Father and Son and bet. Father, Son, and Spirit. These acts involve no time factor, as if the Father existed before the Son was generated, or as if the Father and Son existed before the Spirit proceeded ("the Spirit . . . proceedeth from the Father," Jn 15:26). The difference bet. generation and procession transcends our comprehension. The external, or outward, works of God, which relate to the universe, include these: the Father sent the Son to redeem man (Jn 3:16-17) and gives, or sends, the Spirit (Jn 14:26); creation, ascribed to the Father: redemption, ascribed to the Son; sanctification, ascribed to the Spirit.

See also *Filioque Controversy; God; Procession of the Holy Spirit; Trinity.*

Father Divine (original name believed to be George Baker; ca. 1880–1965). Negro cult leader; b. probably Hutchinson Island, near Savannah, Ga.; itinerant worker; asst. to evangelist Samuel Morris in Baltimore; ca. 1907 Morris took the name Father Jehovia and the title God in the Fathership Degree and gave Baker the name Messenger and the title God in the Sonship Degree; traveling preacher in the South 1912–15; to NYC 1915; operated an employment agency; purchased home 1919 in a white community at Sayville, Long Island, under name of Major Morgan J. Devine and made it a communal dwelling, his first "heaven"; operated an employment agency; changed name to Father Divine 1930; arrested with followers for disturbing peace 1931; released on bail and moved to Harlem 1932; opened first Harlem "heaven" 1933; sued by an apostate and moved to Philadelphia 1941; est. "kingdom" including many properties; movement called Peace* Mission; defined deity: "God is not only personified and materialized. He is repersonified and rematerialized. He rematerialized and He rematerialates. He rematerialates and He is rematerializatable. He repersonificates and He repersonifitizes."

Fatherhood of God. The term Father is applied to the triune divine essence in Scripture in a 2-fold sense. God is Father (Ps 68:5) in the sense of Creator (Is 64:8). But the word Father more commonly involves concepts of love, mercy, and grace and is equivalent to "God of the covenant." As such he is Father of those who have entered covenant relations with Him. The correlate idea is not humanity as such, but mankind redeemed, esp. believers, who have received the blessings of the covenant. In this sense Israel was taught to regard God as Father (Ex 4:22; Dt 32;6; Ps 89:26-27; Is 63:16; Jer 31:9; Jn 5:45; 8:41; 2 Co 6:18). Believers are children of God by adoption (Jn 1:12-13; Ro 8:14-16). In this sense Jesus speaks of God as the Father of believers (Mt 6:4, 8, 9, 15, 18). The idea of a divine fatherhood as implying a relation to all mankind, and apart from the covenant of grace, is foreign to Scripture (Jn 8:44; Ro 9:8). See also *Father, God the; Filioque Controversy; God; Procession of the Holy Spirit; Trinity.*

Fathers of the Church. Recognized teachers of the ch. from the close of the apostolic age to a terminal date variously set from the 7th to the 9th c.

Fathers of the Faith of Jesus. See *Paccanarists.*

Fatiha(h). See *Koran.*

Fátima. Parish in cen. Port.; site of famous Marian shrine est. because Mary (said to have called herself (Our Lady of the Rosary) allegedly appeared 6 times May 13–Oct. 13, 1917, to 3 shepherd children (Lucia dos Santos [b. 1907], and her cousins Francisco [1908–19] and Jacinta [1910–20]) in the natural depression Cova da Iria.

Fauré, Gabriel Urbain (1845–1924). Fr. composer; dir. Paris Conservatory of Music 1905. Works include *Requiem.*

Faustus of Mileve (d. ca. 400). Manichaean. Visited Carthage 383. Augustine* of Hippo turned from Manichaeism* when he found him a fraud.

Faustus of Riez (ca. 408–ca. 490). See *Pelagian Controversy,* 10.

Fauxbourdon (Fr. for "false bass"; Middle Eng.: *faburden;* It.: *falso bordone;* Sp.: *fabordone).* Term for 3-voice setting in which the lowest voice mostly falls a 3d higher than the root of the chord, or true bass; the middle voice is consistently a 4th lower than the top voice. Date of origin unknown; some hold as early as the 10th c.; in MSS of ca. 1300. Often used in connection with plainsong (see *Gregorian Music*); used by such masters as J. S. Bach,* L. v. Beethoven,* J. Brahms,* and W. A. Mozart.*

Favre, Pierre (Lefèvre; Petrus Faber; 1506–46). Fr. Jesuit theol.; b. Villaret, Savoy, near Geneva. To Paris 1525; assoc. with F. Xavier* and I. of Loyola*; priest 1534; helped found Jesuits.*

Fawcett, John (1740–1817). Eng. clergyman and hymnist; b. Lidget Green, Yorkshire; became Meth. under G. Whitefield's* influence ca. 1756; became Bap. ca. 1759; ordained 1765 at Wainsgate, Yorkshire; pastor Hebden Bridge, Yorkshire. Works include a devotional commentary on the Bible; hymns "How Precious Is the Book Divine" and "Blest Be the Tie That Binds."

Fawkes, Guy. See *Gunpowder Plot.*

Faye, Eugène de (1860–1929). B. Lyons, Fr.; Ref. theol. and patristic scholar; prof. Paris 1912. Works include *Clément d'Alexandrie; Étude sur les origines des églises de l'âge apostolique; Gnostiques et gnosticisme; Origène, sa vie, son oeuvre, sa pensée.*

Fayumic Bible Version. See *Bible Versions,* D.

Feast of Asses *(festum asinorum).* 1. Another name for Feast* of Fools. 2. Festival of the Flight to Egypt, within the Epiphany* octave.* Perhaps innocent in origin; but by 13th c. burlesque elements were prominent. Braying by participants at mass, bringing ass into ch., use of the so-called Prose of the Ass were made part of mass and canonical office. 3. The ass at times also figured in Palm* Sun. processions and commemorating the story of Balaam's ass.

Feast of Esther. See *Judaism,* 4.

Feast of Fools. 1. Feast* of Asses. 2. Mock religious festival begun ca. 12th c. by subdeacons of cathedrals and held ca. the Feast of the Circumcision

(Jan. 1). 3. Name also given collectively to the series of mock festivals in the Christmas season (by deacons on Feast of St. Stephen [Dec. 26], priests on St. John's Day [Dec. 27], choir boys on Holy Innocents [Dec. 28], and subdeacons on or about Circumcision [Jan 1]). Perhaps a Christian adaptation of the Roman Saturnalia, the celebrations were characterized by masquerades, extravagances, excesses. Council of Basel* imposed severe penalties for the observances 1435.

Feast of Harvest (Jewish). See *Judaism,* 4.

Feast of Lights. See *Judaism,* 4.

Feast of Tabernacles. See *Judaism,* 4.

Feast of Trumpets. See *Judaism,* 4.

Feast of Weeks. See *Judaism,* 4.

Feasts. See *Church Year.*

Febronianism. Movement in the RC Ch. in Ger. to undergird nationalization of the ch. Real power of the ch. was to reside in bps. Johann Nikolaus von Hontheim (1701–90), leader of the movement, wrote *De statu ecclesiae et legitima potestate Romani pontificis* under pseudonym Justinus Febronius. See also *Roman Catholic Church,* D 2; *Ultramontanism.*

Fechner, Gustav Theodor (1801–87). Ger. philos., physicist, and psychol.; formulated Fechner's law: "In order that the intensity of a sensation may increase in arithmetic progression, the stimulus must increase in geometric progression"; considered God the soul of the universe and natural laws the modes of the unfolding of His perfection. See also *Psychology,* G 3.

Fecht, Johannes (1636–1716). B. Sulzburg, near Freiburg, Baden, Ger.; Luth. theol. and opponent of Pietism*; gen. supt. Baden-Durlach 1688; prof. and supt. Rostock 1690. Works include *Philocalia sacra; De vera rerum sacrarum notitia; De origine et superstitione missarum, in honorem sanctorum celebratarum.*

Federal Council of Evangelical Free Churches. See *Free Church Federal Council.*

Federal Council of the Churches of Christ in America. Organized in Philadelphia Dec. 1908; 30 denominations represented; combined membership ca. 25 million. Purpose, according to the constitution: 1. to express the fellowship and catholic unity of the Christian church; 2. to bring the Christian bodies of America into united service for Christ and the world; 3. to encourage devotional fellowship and mutual counsel concerning the spiritual life and religious activities of the churches; 4. to secure a larger combined influence for the churches of Christ in all matters affecting the moral and social condition of the people, so as to promote the application of the law of Christ in every relation to human life; 5. to assist in the organization of local branches of the Federal Council, to promote its aim in their communities. The constitution stated that the Council was to have "no authority over the constituent bodies adhering to it. It has no authority to draw up a common creed or form of government or of worship, or in any way to limit the full autonomy of the Christian bodies adhering to it." Various depts. dealt with missions, research, educ., race relations, radio, soc. service, armed services, prisoners of war, etc. It was absorbed 1950 into the National Council of Churches of Christ in the United States of America (see *Union Movements,* 13).

E. B. Sanford, *Origin and History of the Federal Council of the Churches of Christ in America* (Hartford, Conn., 1916); J. A. Hutchison, *We Are Not Divided: A Critical and Historical Study of the Federal Council of the Churches of Christ in America* (New York, 1941).

Federal Council of Evangelical Free Churches. See *Free Church Federal Council.*

Federal Emergency Relief Administration. See *Social Work,* D 1.

Federal Social Security Act. See *Social Work,* D 1.

Federal Theology (Föderaltheologie; from Lat. *foedus* and *theologia*). Covenant theol.; roots traced by some to concepts in Epistle of Barnabas (see *Apostolic Fathers,* 6), Irenaeus,* Clement* of Alexandria, and Augustine* of Hippo; reached its apex in the theol. of J. Cocceius.*

H. Zwingli* speaks of a covenant of God with Adam, renewed with Noah and Abraham. He emphasizes esp. the covenant with Abraham in which God promises grace and requires righteousness of life. This covenant is one and the same as the NT covenant. The sacraments are signs of the covenant. Zwingli's thought is developed by J. H. Bullinger.* Both emphasized the covenant role of sacraments. P. Melanchthon* in *Examen ordinandorum* made baptism a *mutuum foedus* and *mutua obligatio* bet. God and the person baptized. J. Calvin* also makes the covenant a part of his system. Other Ref. theologians followed the lead of Zwingli, Bullinger, and Calvin. The covenant idea is found in early Ref. confessions and is prominent in the Heidelberg Catechism (see *Reformed Confessions,* D 2) and the Westminster Confession (see *Presbyterian Confessions,* 3–4). M. Martini* and J. Cloppenburg,* teachers of Cocceius, distinguished a "natural covenant" (old covenant of the Law) and a "covenant of grace" (new covenant of the Gospel).

The classic treatment of fed. theol. is J. Cocceius' *Summa doctrina de foedere et testamento Dei.* A *foedus* is a covenant in which both parties *(conjurati)* bind themselves; it has visible signs *(signa notabilia)* and command and promise. When God establishes a covenant it involves Law and promise. The covenant is initially not mutual, as human covenants are, but is est. by God. It becomes mutual when man agrees to it. The covenant of works (natural covenant) was made before the Fall; its Law was written in Adam's heart. The command not to eat of the tree of the knowledge of good and evil is the beginning of all of God's commandments; the promise of life bound man to believe and love God. The tree of life is a sacrament of justification by works. There are 5 nullifications *(Abschaffungen)* of the covenant of works. The first 2: sin and the covenant of grace. The covenant of grace commands contrition and faith. In eternity the Father made a compact with the Son in which the Son binds Himself to obedience unto death and the Father promises Him a kingdom and a spiritual seed. Salvation is offered the elect by the command to believe in Christ and by the promise of life. After the fall man is by nature dead in sin; rebirth is wrought by Christ. This new covenant of grace is immutable and eternal. The final goal of the covenant is the glory of God. The 3d nullification of the covenant of works is by the proclamation of the New Testament. The covenant of grace is divided into 2 economies: *in expectatione Christi* (OT) and *in fide Christi revelati* (NT). OT sacraments: circumcision and the Passover lamb. NT sacraments: Baptism and the Lord's Supper. The 4th nullification of the covenant of works is the death of the body. The 5th is the resurrection of the body.

Anabaptists used the term covenants for brotherhoods whose mems. dedicated themselves in faith to the Lord's service.

Covenant theol. of Luth., Ref., and Anabap. origin was later modified.

See also *Braun, Johannes; Burman, Frans; New England Theology.*

G. Schrenk, *Gottesreich und Bund im älteren Protestantismus* (Gütersloh, 1923); P. Y. De Jong, *The Covenant Idea in New England Theology, 1620–1847* (Grand Rapids, Mich., 1945). EL

Federated Churches. Congs. composed of 2 or more denominational units conducting local work together but maintaining separate denominational affiliation.

A fed. ch. was formed 1887 in Mass. Federated chs. usually have 1 minister and joint S. S., services, policy, and governing bd.

Federated Lutheran Seminary, Taichung, Taiwan. See *Ministry, Education of,* XI B 23; *Taiwan.*

Federation for Authentic Lutheranism. Formed Nov. 1971 Libertyville, Ill., by a small group of pastors and congs., most of whom had been LCMS mems.

Federation of Latvian Lutheran Congregations. See *Latvia.*

Federation of Evangelical Lutheran Churches in India. See *India,* 16.

Federation of Rhodesia and Nyasaland. See *Africa,* B 2.

Feet Washing. See *Foot Washing.*

Feigenbutz, Konrad. See *Figenbocz, Chunradus.*

Felgenhauer, Paul (1593–ca. 1677). B. Pu(t)schwitz, Boh.; educ. Wittenberg; influenced by K. Schwenkfeld (see *Schwenkfelders*), V. Weigel,* and J. Böhme.* Exponent of a type of mysticism, tolerance, and pacifism.

Felician Sisters. See *Sisterhoods.*

Felicissimus, Schism of. Arose from the hostility of certain presbyters under leadership of Novatus* against Cyprian, bp. Carthage. During Cyprian's absence in the Decian persecution, and without his knowledge and consent, Novatus ordained Felicissimus deacon 250. Felicissimus and others challenged Cyprian's strictness by indulgence toward the lapsed and refused to comply with an order for ch. visitation and offering for poor issued by absent Cyprian. The schismatics were condemned by a council at Carthage 251.

Felicity (Lat. *felicitas,* "happiness; good fortune"). 1. Roman martyr (2d c.); according to legend, martyred with 7 sons. 2. Afr. martyr (d. ca. 202); companion of Perpetua,* who also suffered martyrdom.

Felix of Cantalice. See *Sisterhoods.*

Félix of Urgel. See *Adoptionism.*

Fell, John (1625–86). Bp. Oxford. Ed. "Oxford text" of Cyprian.

Fellowship. A. *Nature of Christian Fellowship.* Christian fellowship is common sharing in the Gospel (Ph 1:5), in faith (Phmn 6), and in other spiritual and mutual gifts. God creates it by calling us into fellowship or partnership with His Son so that we share in all Christ's works, blessings, glory, and goods (1 Co 1:9; 10:16; 1 Jn 1:3, 6, 7). It is a union of believers in Christ through fellowship of the Spirit (2 Co 13:13 [14]; 1 Jn 1:7). This communion of believers is unity or "oneness" in Christ (Jn 17:11, 21-22) which transcends race, soc. position (Gl 3:28; Ja 2:1), and death (1 Th 4:13-18). Non-relatives are called father, mother, brother, and sister (Mt 12:49-50; 1 Ti 5:1-2).

Christian fellowship involves participation in the experiences of Christ (Jn 14:9; Ro 6:1-8; 14:8; Ph 1:21; 3:10) and of fellow Christians. Out of basic communion in the Gospel of Christ comes the communication of spiritual and material gifts (Acts 2:42-45; Ro 15:25; 2 Co 8:4; 9:13; Heb 13:16).

As faith always produces fruit, so fellowship of the Spirit in Christ manifests itself in action. Christian fellowship is activity in the Gospel (Gl 2:9). Its mark is love (1 Co 13; 1 Ptr 1:22; 1 Jn). It causes Christians to treat each other as close relatives (1 Ti 5:1-2). It is a fellowship of feelings (2 Co 11:29), burdens (Gl 6:2; Heb 13:3), and a communication of help (Acts 20:35; Ja 1:27). It is activated by desire to bring others into its fellowship (1 Jn 1:3) and avoid or heal schism within itself (1 Co 1; 3:1-11; Eph 4:3). A climax is in the Lord's Supper (1 Co 10:16).

The ideal of fellowship was portrayed by Christ when He spoke of the ch. as one flock under one Shepherd (Jn 10:16) and of individual Christians and chs. as branches growing on one Vine (Jn 15:1-6). In His great prayer on the eve of His death the Savior prayed for unity among His followers (Jn 17:20-23).

The apostles tried to maintain Christian fellowship (1 Co 12:12-27; Eph 4:1-16; cf. also Acts 2:42; Ro 12:5; 1 Co 1:10; 10:17; 2 Co 13:11; Gl 3:28; Ph 1:27; 1 Ptr 3:8; 1 Jn 1:7), condemned schisms under various leaders (1 Co 1:10-17; 3:3-9), and tried to solve difficulties through deliberation and discussion (Acts 15:1-35).

B. *Fellowship of Churches.* In the early ch., unity was exemplified by fellowship in worship. Pastors in one part of the ch. were recognized in other parts and, if present at a service, were invited to take part (cf. custom of Judaism in NT times: Mt 9:35; Lk 4:16-27; Acts 13:5, 15; 14:1-3; 16:13; 18:24-28). Rise of heretics and impostors led to rules and safeguards, e. g., Apostolic* Constitutions and Canons. Cf. Mt 7:15-23; Gl 1:8-9; 1 Ti 1:5-7; 4:1-7; 6:3-5; 2 Ti 4:3-4; Tts 1:10-16; 2 Ptr 2. The schismatic spirit continued to be condemned (cf. 1 Clement) and unity praised. Ignatius makes unity flow from loyalty to the bp., e.g., *Ad Ephesios,* IV; *Ad Trallianos,* III; cf. Cyprian, *De unitate ecclesiae.*

With the growth of the hierarchical system, fellowship was more and more determined by the hierarchy. Disagreement was revolt and for hundreds of yrs. a capital crime.

The schism bet. E and W (see *Schism,* 4, 6) destroyed fellowship that could not be restored at Lyons 1274 (see *Lyons, Councils of,* 2) and Florence 1439 (see *Florence, Council of*). The traditional RC position made fellowship depend on unity of faith, govt., worship, and acknowledgment of the supreme authority of Rome. The 2d Vatican* Council recognized chs. and ecclesiastical communities outside the RC Ch. and fostered an ecumenical spirit.

M. Luther* at first tried to maintain fellowship with the RC Ch., but his excommunication made it impossible (see *Reformation, Lutheran,* 7–9). Fellowship bet. Luther and the Ref. was not hastily cut off. The ideal of a unified ch. is strongly emphasized in the preface to the AC. Luther's own efforts for peace are shown in his letter to Cardinal Albrecht of Mainz (WA 30 II, 397–412; cf. WA 30 II, 268–356).

The statement of AC VII, "to the true unity of the Church it is enough to agree concerning the doctrine of the Gospel and the administration of the Sacraments," is variously stated in Luther's writings (e. g., unity springs from agreement in Word and doctrine, WA 34 II, 387; it springs from the inner spirit, WA 10 II, 219; 22, 57–59; from the sacraments, WA 10 II, 219–220. Love avails nothing where unity in faith and spirit are lacking, WA 40 II, 136–137).

Beginning 1530 the AC was considered by those who subscribed to it a unifying document, criterion of fellowship, and safeguard against Ref. and RC teaching. Fellowship was usually not denied whole Luth. state chs. that held this confession but did not formally subscribe to the whole Book of Concord. Later efforts at restoring fellowship with the Ref. were unsuccessful (Wittenberg* Concord 1536; Thirteen Articles 1538 [see *Anglican Confessions,* 4]; Regensburg* Conference 1541; Interims* 1548; Thorn Conference 1645 [see *Reformed Confessions,* D 3 c]; Prussian* Union 1817; modern movements). Decisions of the Council of Trent* completed the breach bet. Luths. and RCs (see *Counter Reformation; Roman Catholic Confessions,* A).

Early Luths. in Am. had few or no bonds of union, no important rules regarding fellowship with other Christians. They were a prey of many religious propagandists. H. M. Mühlenberg* strove to est. consciousness of Luth. unity and loyalty to the Luth. Confessions. But in this period limited fellowship with other bodies (esp. Episcopalians) was practiced. Then followed a period in which confessional distinctions were more and more disregarded and wider fellowship with other chs. sought (often following cultural or language lines). Beginning ca. 1820, S. S. Schmucker* labored to reunite Luths. and reintroduce the AC and subscription to its "fundamental" doctrines.

Reactions to the Prussian* Union, immigration of Luths. from Eur., and other things led to gradual formulation of fellowship rules in the 19th c. Growth of confessional consciousness by mid-c. is indicated by widespread opposition to the Definite Platform (see *Definite Synodical Platform*). When the General* Council of the Luth. Ch. in N. Am. was formed 1867, the Mo. Syn., the Joint Syn. of Ohio, and the Ger. Syn. of Iowa had misgivings. The Joint Syn. of Ohio asked the Gen. Council for a statement on chiliasm, altar fellowship, pulpit fellowship, and secret societies; this led to the Pittsburgh Declaration 1868, Akron Rule 1872, Galesburg* Rule 1875, and the action taken at Pittsburgh 1889 (see also *Four Points*). C. F. W. Walther* and others at the Free* Luth. Conferences tried to est. gen. Luth. fellowship based on loyalty to the AC, holding that the other Luth. confessions were not sufficiently known in Am. to serve as basis.

Doctrinal controversies among Luths. in the 2d half of the 19th c. underlined doctrinal differences, alienated Luths. from each other, strengthened syn. walls, and occasioned restatements of the boundaries of fellowship. The Mo. Syn. instructed its delegates to the Syn. Conf. not to deliberate with persons who had accused the Mo. Syn. of Calvinism (1881 *Synodal-Bericht,* p. 45). *L. u. W.,* LI (Feb.-Mar. 1905), 49–53, 97–115, citing Jer 23:31-32; Mt 7:15; Lk 21:17; Ro 16:17; 2 Co 6; 1 Ti 6:3, 5; Tts 3:10; 2 Jn 10-11; and other passages, upheld refusal of Mo. Syn. delegates to pray with those of the Iowa and Ohio syns. at the Free Conference at Detroit, Mich., Apr. 6–8, 1904.

While the gen. trend in Am. Lutheranism at the end of the 19th c. was to make confessional loyalty the basis of fellowship, there was no complete unanimity. Some, emphasizing the unity of the ch., advocated gen. Christian fellowship. This view was strenuously opposed, esp. by those who emphasized the confessional nature of altar fellowship.

The 1st half of the 20th c. was marked by many efforts toward Luth. unity and fellowship. Many statements were issued to show doctrinal positions as well as doctrinal agreement or disagreement. Principles and methods varied. Some tried to adhere to the principles of M. Luther and C. F. W. Walther. Others demanded agreement on all formulated doctrines and such as are to be formulated, holding that all joint work and worship is indicative of indifference toward, or agreement with, error. Selective* fellowship has been advocated by some; others oppose it for the sake of order and hold that the individual pastor or ch. has foregone the right of selective fellowship. Distinctions are also made bet. various types of fellowship (e. g., work, private and pub. prayer, pulpit, altar). Following the precedent set by C. F. W. Walther, the Mo. Syn. Coll. of Presidents called for free Luth. conferences 1949.

See also *Church; Ecumenical Movement, The; Free Lutheran Conferences; Fundamental Doctrines; Lutheran Confessions; Union and Unity Movements, Lutheran, in the United States; Union Movements; Unionism.* EL

Patristic writings; standard ch. histories; Luther's works; V. Ferm, *The Crisis in American Lutheran Theology* (New York, 1927); F. Pieper, "Einige Sätze über den Unionismus," in 1924 *Synodal-Bericht,* Oregon and Washington District, Mo. Syn., pp. 4–39; C. P. Krauth, *Theses on the Galesburg Declaration on Pulpit and Altar Fellowship,* prepared by an 1876 order of the General Council, dated Philadelphia 1877, and reprint. in *The Lutheran Church Review,* XXVI (July and Oct. 1907), 515–527, 740–748; XXVII (Jan. and Apr. 1908), 129–137, 321–330; F. Bente, *Was steht der Vereinigung der lutherischen Synoden Amerikas im Wege?* (St. Louis, 1917); *The Distinctive Doctrines and Usages of the General Bodies of the Evangelical Lutheran Church in the United States,* 4th ed. (Philadelphia, 1914); T. C. Graebner, *The Problem of Lutheran Union and Other Essays* (St. Louis, 1935); T. F. Gullixson, *The Fellowship Question* (Minneapolis, Minn., n.d.); T. C. Graebner and P. E. Kretzmann, *Toward Lutheran Union* (St. Louis, 1943); M. Reu, *In the Interest of Lutheran Unity* (Columbus, Ohio, 1940); H. E. Jacobs, "Some Considerations Involved in the Discussion of the Fellowship Question," *The Lutheran Church Review,* VIII (Oct. 1889), 243–279; M. V.[alentine], "Altar-Fellowship" and H. E. J.[acobs], "Pulpit Fellowship," *The Lutheran Cyclopedia,* ed. H. E. Jacobs and J. A. W. Haas (New York, 1899), pp. 9, 399–400; W. Brenner, *Dangerous Alliances or Some Peace Snags* (Toledo, Ohio, n d.); J. H. C. Fritz, *Union or Unity?* (St. Louis, n.d.); C. A. Hardt, "Christian Fellowship," *CTM,* XVI (July 1945), 433–466; W. A. Arndt, "Selective Fellowship," *CTM,* XVII (June 1946), 455–457, and "Missouri's Insistence on Acceptance of the Word of God and the Confessions of the Lutheran Church as a Condition of Church Fellowship," *CTM,* XVIII (Mar. 1947), 171–177; R. T. DuBrau, "New Testament Fellowship: A Study in Semantics," *CTM,* XXII (May 1951), 334–342; M. Schulz, "The Question of Altar Fellowship According to the Halle Resolutions," tr. and condensed by F. E. M.[ayer], *CTM,* XVIII (July 1947), 534–537; E. L. Lueker, "Walther and the Free Lutheran Conferences of 1856–1859," *CTM,* XV (Aug. 1944), 529–563; W. G. Polack, "Lutheran Unity: The Present Status," *The Lutheran Witness,* LXVIII, (June 14, 1949), 194–196; *What Lutherans Are Thinking,* ed. E. C. Fendt (Columbus, Ohio, 1947); E. Rinderknecht, "Lutheran Unity and Union from the Point of View of the United Lutheran Church," *The Lutheran Church Quarterly,* XIX (Jan. 1946), 13–34; A. H. Grumm, "Church Fellowship," *The Abiding Word,* II (St. Louis, 1947), 517–537; W. Elert, *Abendmahl und Kirchengemeinschaft in der alten Kirche hauptsächlich des Ostens* (Berlin, 1954), tr. N. E. Nagel, *Eucharist and Church Fellowship in the First Four Centuries* (St. Louis, 1966); *Four Statements on Fellowship,* presented by the constituent synods of the Synodical Conference for study and discussion (St. Louis, 1960); *Church in Fellowship,* ed. V. Vajta (Minneapolis, Minn., 1963); "Theology of Fellowship," Mo. Syn. *Proceedings* 1965, pp. 264–291 (adopted, *Proceedings* 1967, p. 91).

Fellowship Following Buddha, The. Group supporting efforts of Dwight Goddard of Thetford, Vt., to circulate Buddhist scriptures and enable "homeless brothers" (Buddhist monks) to follow the path of Buddha. See also *Buddhism.*

Fellowship of Divine Truth, The. Founded 1934 by "Hilarion, The Master of Wisdom," in Philadelphia; assoc. with New* Thought Alliance.

Fellowship of St. Alban and St. Sergius. Soc. chiefly of Anglicans and exiled Orthodox; founded 1928 to cultivate cordial relations among denominations represented by its mems.

Fellowship of the Order of Christian Mystics, The. Founded by F. Homer Curtis and wife; awaits the appearance of Avatar, a great spiritual world teacher. See also *Hinduism,* 4.

Fendt, Leonhard (1881–1957). B. Baiershofen, Swabia; prof. RC dogmatics Dillingen; became Luth.

1918; prof. practical theol. Berlin 1934. Wrote on liturgics, catechetics, and practical theol.

Fénelon, Francois de Salignac de la Mothe (1651–1715). B. château Fenelon, Perigord. Fr.; miss. to Huguenots* 1685–87; adopted ideas of Madame Guyon*; abp. Cambrai 1695. Works include *Les Avantures de Télémaque, fils d'Ulysse.* See also *Bossuet, Jacques Bénigne.*

Ferdinand I. See *Reformed Confessions,* E 3.

Ferdinand II (1578–1637). Grandson of Ferdinand I (see *Reformed Confessions,* E 3). King of Boh. 1617–19, 1620–37; of Hung. 1621–37. Holy Roman emp. 1619–37; educ. by Jesuits to hate Protestantism; whole reign occupied in 1st part of Thirty* Years' War, beginning with persecution of Prots. 1617.

Ferdinand V of Castile (Ferdinand II of Aragon). See *Inquisition,* 6.

Ferghil. See *Celtic Church,* 6.

Ferguson, Samuel David (1842–1916). B. Charleston, S. C.; Negro pastor Prot. Episc. Ch., Liberia (see *Africa,* C 7); bp. 1884; est. educ. system including village and ch. schools; developed a trained nat. ministry.

Feria. Classical Lat. "feast day; holiday." Ecclesiastical usage applies the term to days (other than Sat. [Sabbatum*] and Sun. [Dies* dominica]) on which no feast falls; this practice perhaps originated in the custom of calling the day after Easter "Easter Mon.," regarding it as the 2d feria or feast day of that week. Since every Sun. is a little Easter, every Mon. is a "feria secunda," Tue. "feria tertia," etc.

Ferrandus, Fulgentius (d. ca. 546). Deacon of Carthage; opposed condemnation of Three Chapters (see *Three Chapters, Controversy of*). Works include *Breviatio canonum;* a life of Fulgentius* of Ruspe is ascribed to him. *MPL,* 67,877–962.

Ferrara-Florence Council. See *Basel, Council of; Florence, Council of.*

Ferrer, Vincent. See *Vincent Ferrer.*

Ferry, Paul (1591–1669). B. Metz, Fr.; Huguenot preacher and defender of the Ref. faith in Fr.; worked for union of Prots. and for fusion of RCs and Prots.

Fesch, Joseph (1763-1839). B. Ajaccio, Corsica; half-brother of Napoleon I's mother; representative of Napoleon I at the Vatican; abp. Lyon 1802; cardinal 1803; served on Ecclesiastical Commission, on which his activity was not always satisfactory to Napoleon I.

Fessler, Ignaz Aurelius (1756–1839). B. Zurány (Zurndorf; Zürndorf; Czurendorf), Hung. (Burgenland); orientalist; historian; converted from RCm to Lutheranism 1791; gen. supt. St. Petersburg 1833; interested in moral* philos., Kantianism (see *Kant, Immanuel*), panentheism.*

Festivals. See *Church Year.*

Feth, John Henry Frederick (Feb. 10, 1861–July 29, 1927). B. Cleveland, Ohio; educ. Fort Wayne and Conc. Sem., St. Louis; asst. pastor St. Matthew, NYC, 1883–85; pastor New Haven, Conn., and miss. at large 1885–88; prof. Conc. Collegiate Inst., Bronxville, N. Y., 1888–1927, pres. 1895–1918.

Fetishism (from Port. *feitiço,* "something artificial, done or made by art; sorcery"; Lat. *facticious,* "factitious"). Term used variously by anthropologists, e.g., to denote rivers, springs and other objects of nature; often understood to mean belief that a spirit may dwell temporarily or permanently in some material object, making it an object of reverence or worship; connected with animism. A fetish may be any object (e.g., claws, teeth, horns, bones, or other parts of animals; shells, stones, leaves, pieces of wood or metal, rags, refuse) thought to be inhabited by a spirit or endowed with preternatural power and which its possessor therefore tries to use for his own purposes. A savage will pray to it, anoint it with oil, and sprinkle it with blood. If he has great success with it, it may become the fetish of an entire tribe and the owner its priest. If it does not serve, it may be scolded, punished, and finally discarded. Fetishes may be found by chance, or certain objects may become fetishes by incantation or by simple invitation extended to a spirit to dwell in the object. Fetishism is found around the world, esp. in W Afr. See also *Primitive Religion.*

Feudalism. See *Western Christianity 500–1500,* 5.

Feuerbach, Ludwig Andreas (1804–72). B. Landshut, Bavaria; philos.; pupil of G. W. F. Hegel*; abandoned Hegelian idealism*; adopted atheism*; explained religion anthropologically; God, heaven, eternal life, are merely human desires; propagated sensualism. Works include *Das Wesen des Christentums; Grundsätze der Philosophie der Zukunft; Das Wesen der Religion.* See also *Ethics,* 4.

Feuerborn, Justus (Feurborn; 1587–1656). B. Herford, Ger.; ev. theol.; prof. Giessen 1617, Marburg ca. 1624; supt. Marburg 1650; supported B. Mentzer* against Tübingen theologians in Cryptokenotic Controversy.

Fiangona Loterana Malagasy. See *Africa,* B 9.

Fichte, Immanuel Hermann von (originally Hartmann instead of Hermann; 1796–1879). B. Jena; son of J. G. Fichte*; philos.; prof. Bonn 1836, Tübingen 1842; held that philos. must return to the view of personality in its conception of God; founded *Zeitschrift für Philosophie und spekulative Theologie* (changed 1847 to *Zeitschrift für Philosophie und philosophische Kritik*).

Fichte, Johann Gottlieb (1762–1814). B. Rammenau, Upper Lusatia, E cen. Ger.; philos. and metaphysician; prof. Jena, Erlangen, Königsberg, and Berlin; ardent patriot *(Reden an die deutsche Nation);* in earlier writings he stressed the pure ego in individuality; later held that individuality is of slight importance and is to be sacrificed in active striving for the highest good; the individual can become conscious of union with God through love in this life; rejected deity of Christ, atonement. See also *Philosophy.*

Ficino, Marsilio (Marsiglio; Marsilius Ficinus; 1433–99). It. humanist and Platonic philos.; tr. Plato and several Neo-Platonists into Lat.; taught hierarchical system of the universe (God, angelic mind, rational soul, quality, body) and gave many arguments for immortality of soul. Works include *Theologia Platonica.* See also *Florentine Academy.*

Fick, Carl Johann Hermann (Feb. 2, 1822–Apr. 30, 1885). B. Dönhausen, Hannover, Ger.; educ. Göttingen; private tutor Mecklenburg; to Am. 1846 with A. G. G. Francke* and C. L. A. Wolter*; charter mem. Mo. Syn.; pastor New Melle, Mo., 1847, Bremen, Mo., 1850, Detroit, Mich., 1854, Collinsville, Ill., 1859, and Boston, Mass., 1872. Works include *Das Geheimniss der Bosheit; Das Lutherbuch; Die Märtyrer der Evangelisch-Lutherischen Kirche; Es ist ein Gott; Geschichten aus Kirche und Welt;* poems, including the hymn "Gehe auf, du Trost der Heiden" ("Rise, Thou Light of Gentile Nations").

Ficker, Johannes Paul (1861–1944). B. Leipzig; prof. Strasbourg 1900, Halle 1919; ed. early lectures of M. Luther(WA 56–57).

Fideism. Term coined by E. Ménégoz*; used also by L. A. Sabatier* et al. in treating the problem of relation bet. faith* and reason; emphasizes predominant or exlusive role of faith (Lat. *fides*) in attaining certitude. Also called symbolism by Sabatier. Often called symbolofideism.

Fides acquisita (Lat. "acquired faith"). So-called faith acquired by man by his own efforts, in distinction from true faith. See also *fides historica.* WA *39* I, 44–48; Ap IV 48, 249–250.

Fides Damasi (Lat. "faith of Damasus"). Drawn up ca. 380 by Damasus I (ca. 304–384; pope [bp. Rome]

366–384); Lat. version of Nicene Creed and 24 anathemas against heretics and schismatics.

Fides explicita (Lat. "explicit faith"). RC term for faith based on knowledge of divine truth. See also *Fides implicita.*

Fides formata; fides informis. RCs distinguish bet. *fides informis* (mere faith; dead faith; unformed faith; lacking life because it lacks works, esp. love) and *fides caritate formata* (faith permeated by formative love; faith with works).

Fides generalis; fides specialis. Luth. distinction bet. gen. faith (acceptance, e.g., of God and sin) and the special, saving faith of an individual who believes his sins are forgiven for Christ's sake.

Ap IV 43–45; XII 45, 59; XIII 21.

Fides Hieronymi. Early form of Apostles' Creed; often attributed to Jerome.*

Fides historica (Lat. "historical faith"). Term used by P. Melanchthon* before 1521 for *fides informis* (see *Fides formata*), *fides* acquisita;* after 1521 he used only the terms *historica opinio, notitia historica.* But other Luth. dogmaticians continued to use the term *fides historica.*

AC XX 23; Ap IV 48.

Fides implicita *(fides velata; fides in mysterio; fides in universali).* Term for belief of that which is bound up with or implied by that which is explicitly known. Used variously in classic RC theol.: OT saints believed many things implicitly that we in the NT believe explicitly. Doctrines of the ch. are to be believed implicitly, though they may not be explicitly known. All the faithful of the RC Ch. believe the whole content of revelation; some believe it explicitly, others implicitly. Proclamation of dogma does not add to the content of revelation (believed implicitly by the ch.), but deepens knowledge of its truth, thus making possible explicit faith. RCs, together with other Christians, hold that something must be believed explicitly in any act of faith; e. g., in the OT, faith in an explicit promise led to implicit faith in Christ's redemption; explicit faith in the teaching function of the ch. leads to implicit faith in all its dogmas. See also *Fides explicita.*

Fides informis. See *Fides formata.*

Fides qua (quae) creditur. See *Faith.*

Fides quaerens intellectum. See *Christian Faith and the Intellectual,* 3.

Fides specialis. See *Fides generalis.*

Fiducia cordis. See *Certainty, Religious.*

Fiesole, Giovanni da. See *Angelico, Fra.*

Fifth Monarchy Men. Eng. fanatic millenarian sect ca. 1650–61; at first held that the Commonwealth was a preparation for the Fifth Monarchy of Dn 2:44; then turned against O. Cromwell.*

Figenbocz, Chunradus (Feigenbutz; Figenbotz; Konrad; Kunrad; d. after 1540). Pastor Halberstadt and Goslar, later Zerbst; represented Anhalt-Zerbst at Schmalkalden 1537; signed SA.

Figueras Evangelistic Mission. Est. 1877 at Figueras, Gerona province, Sp., to spread the Gospel in Sp.

Figulus. See *Jablonski.*

Fiji Islands. In SW Pacific Ocean; annexed by Brit. 1874; independent parliamentary democracy 1970; *Area:* ca. 7,095 sq. mi.; pop. (1973; est.); 567,520. Christianity first came to the Fijis from Tahiti ca. 1830. In 1834 native Christians from Tonga began work among the Fijis, followed 1835 by Eng. Wesleyans William Cross and David Cargill. RC miss. began 1863. Others active there include Anglicans and Assemblies of God. See also *Melanesia.*

Filiae Mariae. See *Marianists.*

Filioque Controversy. A major dispute in the ch.; became a chief point of difference bet. the E and the W Ch. The Nicene Creed had as the Third Article: "And in the Holy Spirit"; to this the Constantinopolitan Creed added: "The Lord and Giver of Life, Who proceeds from the Father." The belief that the Spirit proceeds *also from the Son* (Lat. *filioque*) is found in the 4th c. (e. g., in Ambrose*), was taught by Augustine* of Hippo, and probably first appeared in creeds in Sp. in the 5th c. The term *filioque* was adopted at Toledo* 589, probably against Arianism.* Thereafter it was gen. accepted in the W and was adopted at Rome soon after 1000. The E Ch., which made the Father alone the fountainhead of deity, rejected the *filioque,* but gen. found no difficulty in saying that the Spirit proceeds from the Father *through* the Son. See also *Eastern Orthodox Churches,* 3; *Ecumenical Creeds,* B 1; *Father, God the Fatherhood of God; Florence, Council of,* 2; *God; Lyons, Councils of; Procession of the Holy Spirit; Schism,* 4, 6; *Trinity.*

Fillmore, Charles (1854–1948). B. Minn. Cofounded with wife Myrtle (1845–1931) Unity* School of Christianity. Both originally Meth.; in search of healing for Myrtle, they came under influence of Christian Science (see *Church of Christ, Scientist*) 1887 but differed with it regarding reality of matter, the world, sin, and sickness. Works include *Talks on Faith; Christian Healing; The Twelve Powers of Man.*

Final Cause. See *Cause,* 3.

Final Judgment. See *Last Things.*

Final Perseverance of the Saints. Scripture teaches that God's elect saints will not be lost, but obtain everlasting salvation (Mt 24:22-24; Ro 8:28-39; 1 Co 1:8-9; 10:13). This does not mean that the elect saints cannot fall from grace and so temporarily lose their faith (David; Peter); but it does mean that God's saving grace, without any merit on their part, will restore them to the state of faith, so that in Christ they finally die a blessed death. The doctrine of final perseverance of the saints is pure Gospel, designed to comfort anxious and doubting believers; it should not be misused in the interest of carnal security. Those inclined to fleshly security and sinning against grace should be warned by such earnest Law preaching as is found Ro 11:20; 1 Co 10:12. The doctrine of final perseverance glorifies divine grace, not human merit. The Ref. doctrine that the elect saints, once called, may lose the exercise of faith, but not faith itself, even if they commit enormous sins, is opposed to Scripture. See also *Predestination.*

Finalism. The belief that ends or goals are present in all events. Hence it explains events not in terms of the past but of the future. See also *Teleology.*

Finan (d. ca. 661). Succeeded Aidan* as bp. Lindisfarne ca. 651; upheld Celtic ecclesiastical traditions; instrumental in conversion of Mercia and Essex.

Finances in the Church. 1. Christians must learn that the word of God teaches that giving for the support of the ch. is a Christian duty. Paul admonishes Christians to be lavish in the grace of giving and thereby prove their love to Christ and His ch., 2 Co 8:1-9. The Lord asks Christians to give financial support to their pastors, 1 Cor 9:7-14; 1 Ti 5:17-18 The Lord took His people severely to task when they were remiss in supporting His work, Hg 1:2-11; Ml 3:8-10. The poor widow and the chs. of Macedonia were praised because they gave liberally despite their poverty, Mk 12:41-44; 2 Co 8:1-5. When the tabernacle in the OT was built, the people brought "much more than enough" and had to be "restrained from bringing," Ex 36:5-7. The Lord promises to reward Christian giving, Pr 19:17; Ml 3:10; Lk 6:38. Christian giving is an act of worship enjoined by the Lord. It is therefore proper that giving money be part of worship services. In the OT the Lord said: "They shall not appear before the Lord empty; every man shall give as he is able, according to the blessing of the Lord, thy God, which He hath given thee," Dt 16:16-17. The NT says: "Upon the first day of the week let every one of you lay by him in store as God hath prospered him, that there be no gatherings when I come," 1 Co 16:2.

2. Christians must be duly informed regarding needs of the ch. This should be done, e.g., by sermons, in various meetings, and in ch. schools. Mems. should also be urged to read ch. papers and other ch. literature.

3. A cong. budget is a financial estimate of moneys needed. A budget is desirable in order that needs of the ch. and proportionate amounts needed by each treasury may be known. Pledging for support of the ch. is an old custom and is not contrary to the Scriptural method of freewill offerings if the individual is free to determine whether or not to pledge, the amount of his pledge, to give more if the Lord increases his ability to give, and to give less if circumstances prevent fulfillment of his pledge.

4. The weekly envelope system is successful in many congs. It is essentially the same system that Paul suggested 1 Co. 16:2. Some congs. use the single envelope system, the cong. deciding how much to use for its own needs and how much for the ch. at large. Some congs. use the duplex envelope system, one pocket used for home purposes and the other for outside purposes. The duplex system is preferred by some because it keeps needs of the ch. at large in the minds of mems. Scripture enjoins Christians to support the ch. by freewill offerings, to be given as the fruit of their faith and in accord with individual ability, Ex 35:5; 1 Ch 29:5; 1 Co 16:2; 2 Co 8:12.

5. Christians should support their ch. and not solicit contributions from people of other denominations or of the world. But if gifts are offered, they may be accepted, provided they are not ill-gotten gains. Raising money by bazaars and the like is not regarded good practice; the buyer is not giving a freewill offering, but is paying for something he gets in return. Often less money is secured in this way than when Christians are trained to bring freewill offerings out of love to Christ and His ch.

6. Tithing, giving a tenth, was commanded by God in the OT, Lv 27:30. There were several sorts of tithes: that paid to the Levites and priests (Nm 18:21-31); that paid for the Lord's feast (Dt 14:22-26); that given every 3d yr. for the poor (Dt 14:28-29). In times of religious depression the people neglected to pay tithes, Ml 3:7-9. In the NT tithing is not enjoined (Mt 23:23 and Lk 11:42 refer to past necessity); it would be contrary to Christian liberty. That does not mean that Christians should not give tithes; but if they do, it should be voluntarily.

7. A ch. extension fund provides a revolving system of financing bldg. projects. Money given to this fund by congs., through the budget, and by direct gifts, loans, or legacies, is lent to needy congs.

8. Some chs. have pension and relief, or welfare, systems to provide funds for retired workers and their widows and orphans. JHCF

See also *Stewardship*.

Finbar. See *Celtic Church,* 6.

Finck, Heinrich (ca. 1445–1527). Ger. composer; kapellmeister Stuttgart; admired by M. Luther. Works include hymns, motets, and part songs.

Findlater, Sarah. See *Borthwick, Jane.*

Finitum (non) est capax infiniti (Lat. "the finite is [not] capable of the infinite"). By asserting that "the finite is capable of the infinite" Luth. theologians tried to express the true deity and manhood of Christ* Jesus and the mystery* of the incarnation* and Word,* esp. in the true communion of natures in Christ. With the formula "the finite is not capable of the infinite" Ref. theologians denied the true communion of natures in Christ.

Finland (Fin.: Suomi). Indep. rep. in N Eur.; pop. (1968 est.): ca. 5 million. Christianity came to Fin. before 1000 probably through traders, merchants, or missionaries. The monastery at Valamo, in N Lake Ladoga, claims to have been founded 992. At least by the 12th c. Finland had received Christianity from Russ. and Sweden. Henry (d. ca. 1156; b. Eng.; according to legend, bp. Uppsala; martyr) came to Fin. ca. 1155 with crusaders under Eric IX of Sweden. Thomas (d. 1248; b. Eng.), a Dominican, believed to have been canon of Uppsala, was the 1st bp. of Finland ca. 1220–45. Under him Fin. became a RC protectorate. Fin. churchmen were educ. in cen. Eur. univs. The nat. ch. is Ev. Luth.; other religious communities include Baps., RCs, Jews, E. Orthodox, Meths., Adventists and the Confessional Ev. Luth. Ch. of Fin. (formerly Luth. Free Ch.). See also *Sweden, Conversion of, to Christianity.*

Finland, Lutheranism in. 1. Fin. was comparatively untouched by corruption common elsewhere before the Reformation. Lutheranism entered the country early in the Reformation.

2. Pietari Särkilahti (Peter Särkilax; d. ca. 1529), pastor and educator, converted to Lutheranism during studies at Rostock 1516–ca. 1522, labored diligently to abolish evils of RCm and to est. the Luth. faith. Martin (or Martti) Skytte (ca. 1458 [some say 1480] – 1550; consecrated bp. by Petrus Magni, bp. Strangnas, who had received canonical consecration; bp. Turku [Aabo] ca. 1527, but not confirmed by the pope) favored the Reformation and sent 8 men to study at Wittenberg 1532–50. Of these, M. Agricola* is most prominent. Paavali (or Paulus) Juusten (1516–76) was ordained bp. of Viipuri by bp. of Strangnas, Swed., 1554. The AC was adopted by the ch. of Sweden-Fin. 1593. See also *Sorolainen, Erik.*

3. A university was est. at Turku 1640. A fire destroyed much of Turku 1827. The university was moved to Helsinki 1828. Strict orthodoxy prevailed in the 17th c. Enevald Svenonius 1627–88) was its chief proponent. In 1663 the Swed. govt. encouraged clergy to study entire Book of Concord. The Ch. Law of 1686 made the Book of Concord the confession of the Swed.-Fin. Ch.

4. Pietism, introd. by revivalists at the end of the 17th c., soon took a conservative form. Noted representatives of this earlier awakening: Johan Wegelius Sr. (ca. 1660–1725), Johan Wegelius Jr. (1693–1764), and Abraham Achrenius (1706–69). But ch. leaders in the 1st half of the 18th c. were influenced by the Enlightenment.* A later awakening after the end of the 18th c. had several outstanding leaders. Many joined the peasant leader Paavo Ruotsalainen* (1777–1852); an inner feeling of grace and proportionate lack of assurance of salvation marked his pietism. Fredrik Gabriel Hedberg 1811–93) broke away from the pietists and became leader of the ev. movement. "Evangelical" pastors, influenced by J. T. Beck,* represented the "Scriptural movement." Evangelicals, under pressure for criticizing doctrinal indifference in the ch., organized the Lutheran* Ev. Assoc. of Fin. 1873 to carry on their work. The assoc, has tr. and pub. many writings of Luther* and the Book of Concord. Henrik Renqvist* (1789–1866), emphasizing prayer, became leader of the "praying ones." In N Fin. a new movement was begun by Lars Levi Laestadius* (1800–61) and developed by the lay preacher Juhani Raattama(a) (1811–99). Laestadians teach that the spoken word is the proper medium of the Holy Ghost and that confession and absolution are necessary for conversion. See also *Finnish Lutherans in America,* 4.

5. A new and more liberal Church Law was enacted 1869. Reaction against lack of confessionalism in the state ch. led to formation 1928 of a Luth. free ch. that est. fellowship with the Mo. Syn.; in 1967 it adopted the name Confessional Luth. Ch. of Finland.

6. Fin. was acquired by Russ. 1809; became indep. 1917.

7. Ca. 92% of the pop. is Luth. First complete Fin. Bible pub. 1642, rev. in the 1930s. A Fin. hymnal appeared ca. 1585. The official Fin. hymnal, derived from the Swed. period, traced its origin to the beginning of the 18th c. The Ch. Assem. approved a new liturgy and hymnal 1886; this hymnal was revised 1938. There are 8 dioceses, including the archdiocese of Turku. Each diocese is headed by a Chapter composed of bp., dean, and several additional mems. Freedom of religion obtains; efforts continue for complete separation of ch. and state. GAA

See also *Dogmatics,* B 9.

E. Bergroth, *Suomen Kirkko,* 2 vols. (Borgaa [Porvoo], Fin., 1902); L. Takala, *Suomen Evankelisen Liikkeen Historia,* vols. I and II (Helsinki, 1929, 1933); I. Salomies, *Suomen kirkon historia,* vols. I–III (Helsinki, 1944–62); W. Schmidt, *Finland's kyrka genom tiderna* (Stockholm, 1940); The Board of Directors of The Free Evangelical Lutheran Church of Finland, *The Free Evangelical Lutheran Church of Finland,* tr. J. Hirsto (Hämeenlinna, Fin., 1948); *Finnish Theology Past and Present,* ed. L. Pinomaa (Helsinki, 1963); G. Sentzke, *Finland: Its Church and Its People* (Helsinki, 1963); *Scandinavian Churches,* ed. L. S. Hunter (Minneapolis, 1965).

Finney, Charles Grandison (1792–1875). B. Warren, Conn.; pastor Second Free Presb. Ch., NYC, 1832; pastor Broadway Tabernacle, NYC, 1834–37; withdrew from Presb. Ch. and the Tabernacle became Cong. in polity 1836; prof. Oberlin (Ohio) Coll. 1837–75, pres. 1851–66; as revivalist emphasized "the *anxious seat.*" See also *Oberlin Theology; Revivals,* 2.

Finnian of Clonard (d. ca. 549). B. Leinster, Ireland; abbot; founded monastery at Clonard ca. 515; probably teacher of Columba (see *Celtic Church,* 7).

Finnian of Moville (ca. 495–579 [some say 576]). Irish abbot; b. N of Ireland; studied at Whithorn (see *Celtic Church,* 3); founded monastery at Moville ca. 540.

Finnish Apostolic Lutheran Church. See *Finnish Lutherans in America,* 4.

Finnish Evangelical Lutheran Church of America (Suomi Syn.). See *Finnish Lutherans in America,* 2.

Finnish Lutherans in America. 1. Finns first came to Am. in the early 1860's. Pioneer pastors: Alfred Elieser Backman (1844–1909; in Mich. 1876–83); J. J. Hoikka (1854–1917; ordained 1883); J. K. Nikander*; K. L. Tolonen (1845–1902; to Am. 1888); J. W. Eloheimo.*

2. Under leadership of J. K. Nikander The Finnish Evangelical Lutheran Church of America (Suomi Synod) was organized at Calumet, Mich., March 25, 1890. Other founding mems. included J. J. Hoikka, K. L. Tolonen, J. W. Eloheimo, and 17 laymen representing 9 congs. In 1896 this syn. founded Suomi Coll. and Theol. Sem., Hancock, Mich. Publications included *Paimen-Sanomia* (founded 1889) and *Amerikan Suometar* (founded 1899). A plan of cooperation with the ULC through its Immigrant Mission Board was adopted 1920. It supported the work of the Finnish* Missionary Soc. and theologically stood close to the state ch. of Finland. Pres.: J. K. Nikander 1890–98, 1902–19; K. L. Tolonen 1898–1902; John Wargelin, Jan.–June 1919, 1950–55; Alvar Rautalahti 1919–22; Alfred Haapanen 1922–50; Raymond Waldemar Wargelin 1955–62. Suomi Theol. Sem. affiliated with Chicago Luth. Sem., Maywood, Ill., 1958. The Suomi Syn. became part of the LCA Jan. 1, 1963. Later in 1963 the Suomi Conf. consisting of pastors and congs. of the former Suomi Syn., was organized at Wakefield, Mich., to assist in spiritual ministration to the Fin.-speaking constituency of the LCA. 1961 statistics: 77 pastors, 153 congs., 36,274 bap. mems.

3. The National Evangelical Lutheran Church was organized 1898 at Rock Springs, Wyo. Official publications: *Auttaja* 1907–1967); *The Lutheran Voice* (founded 1936). Home mission work was carried on in several states and Can. Support of the Gospel Assoc. of Fin. (see *Finland, Lutheranism in,* 4) was replaced by interest in the Mo. Syn. (see *Lutheran Church – Missouri Synod, The*) and The Ev. Luth. Synodical* Conference of North America. Pres.: J. W. Eloheimo 1898–1900; Wilhelm Adrian Mandellöf (1848–1916; to Am. 1899; returned to Fin. 1905) 1900–05; William Williamson (1854–1916) 1905–08; Karl Gustaf Rissanen (1871–1924) 1908–13; Peter Wuori (1869–1921) 1913–18; Arne Wasunta (b. 1891) 1918–22; Karl E. Salonen (b. 1883) 1922–23; Matti Wiskari (b. 1887) 1923–31; Gustaf A. Aho (b. 1897) 1931–53; Jalo E. Nopola (b. 1907) 1953–59; Emil A. Heino (b. 1908) 1959–63; Vilho V. Latvala (b. 1923) 1963–64.

After ca. 40 yrs. of close cooperation with the Mo. Syn., during which time all her ministerial students were trained at Conc. Sem., Springfield, Ill., the NELC merged with the LCMS Jan. 1, 1964. In accord with the *Merger Agreement,* a Bd. for Fin. Affairs was set up, consisting of 4 mems. of the former NELC and 4 from the LCMS, to study problems connected with ch. work among Fin.-speaking people and suggest ways in which the ch. might best serve these people. 1962 statistics: 43 pastors, 61 congs., 12,560 bap. mems.

4. Laestadians (followers of L. L. Laestadius*; see *Finland, Lutheranism in,* 4; also known as Apostolic Luths.) are represented by (a) Apostolic Luth. Ch. of Am. (name adopted 1962; organized 1872 at Calumet, Mich.; called Salomon Korteniemi Lutheran Society after their leader; inc. 1929 as Finnish Apostolic Lutheran Church of America); pres.: Johan Daniel Oberg (b. 1862) 1929–43, Andrew Mickelsen (b. 1897) 1943–; 1961 statistics: 24 ordained pastors with charges; 58 cong.; 6,994 mems.; (b) Heidemanians, named after their leader Arthur Leopold Heideman (May, 1862–Nov. 7, 1928) and his son Paul Arthur Heideman (ordained 1916); (c) Firstborn, a branch of the "Ch. of the Firstborn" of Gellivaara, N Swed., which came into existence ca. 1900; (d) New Awakenists, who reflect the contemporary New Awakening of Finland; (e) "Evangelicals," also called "Pollarites" after John Pollari (d. 1945), one of their leaders. Laestadians in gen. insist on conversion by auricular confession and absolution; they have no colleges or sems.; the Firstborn and the "Evangelicals" do not deem it advisable to have trained and ordained ministers. EL, GA

J. L. Neve, *History of the Lutheran Church in America,* 3d rev. ed. W. D. Allbeck (Burlington, Iowa, 1934); J. I. Kolehmainen, *The Finns in America: A Bibliographical Guide to Their History* (Hancock, Mich., 1947); A. Haapanen, *Our Church, Suomi Synod: The Finnish Evangelical Lutheran Church of America* (Hancock, Mich., n. d.); U. Saarnivaara, *The History of the Laestadian or Apostolic-Lutheran Movement in America* (Ironwood, Mich., 1947).

Finnish Missionary Council. Organized 1919 in Finland to promote interest in missions and provide a forum for discussing miss. problems. Membership open to all Christian miss. organizations.

Finnish Missionary Society (Finland Miss. Soc.). Founded 1859; organ of the Ev. Luth. Ch. of Fin., the nat. ch.; headquarters Helsinki. See also *Africa,* B 8; *Missionary Institutes; Ovamboland.*

Finnish Pentecostal Friends Mission. Integral part of the Pent. movement in Fin. that began 1911. Early miss. in E Afr., N China, N India.

Finschhafen, Lutheran Mission. See *New Guinea,* 5, 6.

Fioretti (It. "little flowers"). It. translation of Fra Ugolino Boniscambi, *Actus beati Francisci et sociorum eius,* written ca. 1325. See also *Francis of Assisi.*

Fire Baptized Holiness Church. See *Evangelistic Associations,* 18; *Holiness Churches,* 2.

Fire Baptized Holiness Church, The (Wesleyan). See *Evangelistic Associations,* 19; *Holiness Churches,* 2.

Fire Worshipers. Reverence for fire was an element in some primitive religions, esp. Zoroastrianism.* See also *Brahmanism,* 2; *Parsi.*

Firmelung. Ger. word for confirmation.*

Firmianus Lactantius. See *Lactantius Firmianus.*

Firmicus Maternus, Julius (d. after 350). B. Syracuse, Sicily; converted to Christianity as adult. Wrote an attack on paganism that led to some measures against heathen.

Firmilian (d. ca. 268). Bp. Caesarea in Cappadocia ca. 230; disciple of Origen*; opposed heretical baptism and supremacy of the pope; d. Tarsus on way to a council at Antioch in Syria (see *Antioch, Synods of*).

Firmung. Ger. word for confirmation.*

First Book of Discipline. See *Presbyterian Churches,* 1.

First Cause. See *Causa Secunda.*

First Century Christian Fellowship. See *Buchmanism.*

First Colored Methodist Protestant Church, African Union. See *Methodist Churches,* 4 c.

First Congregational Methodist Church of the U. S. A. See *Methodist Churches,* 4 b.

First Dogmatic Constitution of the Church of Christ. See *Vatican Councils,* 1.

First General Conference of Lutherans in America. See *Diets, Lutheran, in America.*

Fisch, Georges (1814–81). B. Nyon, Switz.; succeeded A. Monod* as leader of Free Ch., Lyons Fr.; leader of Evangelical* Alliance.

Fischa(e)rt, Johann (Fischer; Mainzer; Mentzer; ca. 1546–ca. 1590). B. probably Strasbourg (or Mainz); Ger. jurist, poet, satirist; Prot.; used various pen names; works include *Bienenkorb des heyligen römischen Immenschwarms; Das vierhörnige Jesuitenhütlein.*

Fischer, Albert Friedrich Wilhelm (1829–96). B. Ziesar, Brandenburg, Ger.; educ. Halle; pastor at Gross-Ottersleben, near Magdeburg; ed. *Kirchenlieder-Lexicon;* founded *Blätter für Hymnologie.*

Fischer, Christoph. See *Vischer, Christoph.*

Fischer, Ernst Kuno Berthold (1824–1907). B. Sandewalde, Silesia; educ. Leipzig and Halle; Ger. historian of philos. and literary critic; prof. Jena and Heidelberg; promoted revival of philos. of I. Kant*; works include *Geschichte der neueren Philosophie.*

Fischer, Johannes (ca. 1636–1705). B. Lübeck, Ger.; educ. Rostock and Altdorf; pastor Hamburg; supt. Sulzbach; called to Livonia by Charles* XI of Sweden; supt. there 1673, gen. supt. 1678; prominent in tr. Bible into Latvian and Estonian; worked for gen. education; prorector Dorpat; pietist; opposed centralization in Sweden.

Fish. Used extensively in early Christian symbolism. The letters of the Gk. word *ichthus* (fish) are the first letters of Gk. words for "Jesus Christ, God's Son, Savior."

Fisher, Clarence Stanley. See *Geography, Christian,* 6.

Fisher, George Park (1827–1909). B. Wrentham, Mass.; Cong.; prof. of divinity and coll. preacher, Yale Coll., 1854–61; prof. ecclesiastical hist., Yale Divinity School, 1861–1901; pres. Am. Hist. Assoc. 1898. Works include *History of the Reformation; History of the Christian Church; History of Christian Doctrine.*

Fisher, John (Roffensis [Lat. "of Rochester"]; ca. 1459 [or ca. 1469]–1535). B. Beverley, Yorkshire, Eng.; prof. Cambridge 1503, chancellor 1504; humanist; bp. Rochester 1504; opposed M. Luther*; opposed divorce of Henry* VIII and his efforts to make himself head of ch.; cardinal 1535; executed.

Fisherman's Ring. See *Ring of the Fisherman.*

Fiske, Fidelia (1816—64). B. Shelburne, Mass.; educ. and taught at Mount Holyoke Coll., South Hadley, Mass.; to Nestorian Miss., Iran, 1843; became a leading educator there.

Fiske, John (originally Edmund Fisk Green; John Fisk 1855; Fiske ca. 1860; 1842–1901). B. Hartford, Conn.; lecturer on philos. and hist.; asst. librarian Harvard; prof. Washington U., St. Louis, Mo., 1884; conceived of evolution as caused by immanent God and tending toward the highest spirituality of man, with human soul related to God. Works include *Outlines of Cosmic Philosophy.*

Fisk(e), Pliny. See *Middle East,* B, C.

Fitch, Eleazer Thompson (1791–1871). Educ. Yale Coll., New Haven Conn., and Andover (Mass.) Theol. Sem.; prof. Yale 1817; helped shape New* Haven theol. Works include *Two Discourses on the Nature of Sin.*

Five Mile Act. See *Presbyterian Churches,* 2.

Five Points of Arminianism. See *Arminianism.*

Five Points of Calvinism. See *Calvinism.*

Five Points of Fundamentalism. Formulated by the 1895 Niagara Bible Conference as necessary standards of belief: 1. Inerrancy of Scripture; 2. Virgin birth of Jesus Christ; 3. Substitutionary theory of the atonement; 4. Physical resurrection of Christ; 5. Christ's imminent bodily return to earth. See also *Fundamentalism.*

Five Years Meeting of Friends. See *Friends, Society of,* 4.

Fjellstedt, Peter (1802–81). Swed. pastor; miss. to India and Turkey 1828–40; after some time in Leipzig he returned to Swed. ca. 1843 and promoted miss. work. Works include devotional works and a Bible commentary.

Fjellström, Pehr. See *Lapland.*

Flabellum (Lat. "small fan"). Ceremonial fan; often made of silk, parchment, or peacocks' feathers; used in early ch. and in some RC and E Orthodox Chs. to keep insects away from sacred vessels; fans made of, or adorned with, peacocks' feathers are carried before the pope in solemn procession and displayed on special occasions.

Flacius Illyricus, Matthias (Croatian: Matija Vlacic Ilir; Serbian: Matija Frankovic Ilir; 1520–75). B. Labin (It.: Albona), Istria (Illyria); studied in Venice under Baptista Egnatius (humanist; d. 1553); Baldo Lupetino (Baldus Lupetinus; relative of M. Flacius Illyricus) pointed him to M. Luther*; went to Augsburg 1539, then Basel, where he lived in the home of S. Grynäus (see *Grynäus,* 1); his 3-yr. "soul struggle" began at Basel; spent some time at Tübingen, where he lived with Matthias Garbitius, prof. Gk.; came to Wittenberg and into close contact with P. Melanchthon* and M. Luther 1541; cured of "soul struggle" ca. 1543 (in own opinion by ev. doctrine of justification); prof. Heb., Wittenberg, 1544.

After Augsburg Interim* (see also *Lutheran Confessions,* C 1) he wrote 3 tracts using pseudonyms Joannes Waremund (attacked emp.), Theodor Henetus (criticizes Interim itself), and Christian Lauterwar (attacked canon of mass and J. Agricola*). After Leipzig Interim* (see also *Lutheran Confessions,* C 1) he pub. *Wider den schnöden Teuffel* under pseudonym Carolus Azarias (against the Interim). Left Wittenberg for Magdeburg 1549 and the Interimistic or Adiaphoristic Controversy (see *Adiaphoristic Controversies,* 1) began in earnest. Writings included *Apologia ad scholam Vitebergensem in adiaphorum causa* and *De veris et falsis adiaphoris.* Held interim introduced not only ceremonial but also doctrinal errors (see *Adiaphoristic Controversies*). At Magdeburg he began *Ecclesiastica historia* ("Magdeburg* Centuries"). His *Catalogus testium veritatis* appeared 1556. At Magdeburg he was also involved in other controversies that grew out of the Interimistic controversy. Against G. Major* and J. Menius* he contended that good works are not necessary to salvation (see *Majoristic Controversy*). Against A. Osiander* the Elder he urged that though the essential, eternal righteousness of Christ is not idle in redemption, it is not the righteousness that justifies (see *Osiandrian Controversy*). Against K. Schwenkfeld* he concentrated on the fact that the Holy Spirit employs the human word. While at Magdeburg he took part in attempts to reconcile warring parties within Lutheranism.

Prof. Jena 1557. Sharply criticized the Frankfurt* Recess 1558. At his prompting Duke John* Frederick II (Johann Friedrich der Mittlere; 1529–95) of Saxony had the *Konfutationsbuch** (polemical doctrinal statement upholding views of M. Flacius Illyricus and opposing G. Major, V. Strigel,* adiaphorists [see *Adiaphoristic Controversies*], and others) drafted 1558–59. With his *Refutatio propositionum Pfeffingeri de libero arbitrio* 1558 he involved himself in the Synergistic* Controversy against J. Pfeffinger* and V: Strigel.* Opposed Strigel's views on free will in Weimar Disputation 1560; held that original sin is *substantia,* not *accidens.* The unevangelical methods of the Flacian Supt. Balthasar Winter at Jena and Flacius' uncharitable attitude led to his dismissal at Jena 1561. To Regensburg 1562; involved in further controversies; worked on "Magdeburg Centuries" and *Clavis scripturae.* Regensburg withdrew asylum for Flacius 1566; with 5 others he was called to Antwerp to organize ch. life. Opposed union formula with Ref.; insisted on disputation. Wrote *Confessio ministrorum Jesu Christi, in ecclesia Antverpiensi, quae Augustanae Confessioni adsentitur.* On arrival of Duke of Alba went to Frankfurt 1567, then Strasbourg; refused to sign J. Andreä's articles for proposed union of Ger. chs. Gnesio-Luths. (including T. Hesshus* and J. Wigand*) and Andreä attacked Flacius' assertion that original sin is *substantia.* Forced to leave Strasbourg 1573; spent last yrs. in a former convent of White Ladies (also called Magdalens, or Penitents) at Frankfurt administered as a haven of refuge by Prot. prioress Katharina von Meerfeld. HR

See also *Lexicons,* B; *Synergiatic Controversy.*

J. W. Preger, *Matthias Flacius Illyricus und seine Zeit,* 2 vols. (Erlangen, 1859–61); M. Mirkovic, *Matija Vlacic Ilirik* (Zagreb, 1960;) *K. Heussi, Geschichte der Theologischen Fakultät zu Jena* (Weimar, 1954); H. W. Reimann, "Matthias Flacius Illyricus," *CTM, XXXV* (Feb. 1964), 69–93.

Flack, J. V. B. See *Christian Union.*

Flagellants. People who, inspired by fanatic religious zeal, practice castigation, often self-inflicted, e. g., by whipping, believing that they are thereby earning some form of merit. There were Christian flagellants at least as early as the 4th c., but the movement assumed internat. epidemic proportions in the 13th c., when it swept from Perugia through N It. into Alsace, Bavaria, Hungary, Bohemia, and Poland. In 1348–49, during the black death, the movement revived throughout Eur., including England. Flagellants formed fraternities and bound themselves to a penitential season. Movements of this kind recur periodically.

Flagon. Vessel for liquid; used when necessary besides chalice* to hold eucharistic wine; usually made of precious metal or glass.

Flatt, Johann Friedrich (1759–1821). B. Tübingen; brother of K. C. Flatt*; educ. Tübingen; prof. philos. Tübingen 1785, theol. 1792. Enthusiastic Kantian (see *Kant, Immanuel*); exponent of the Biblical supranaturalism (see *Rationalism*) of the older Tübingen* school, together with G. C. Storr,* F. G. Süskind,* and K. C. Flatt.

Flatt, Karl Christian (1772–1843). B. Stuttgart; brother of J. F. Flatt*; educ. Tübingen; prof. theol. Tübingen 1804; collegiate preacher and supreme consistorial councillor Stuttgart 1812; gen. supt. Ulm 1829. Held that forgiveness of sins depends on moral improvement; regarded the death of Christ as symbolic assurance of God's grace. Translated G. C. Storr,* *Doctrinae christianae pars theoretica e sacris litteris repetita,* into Ger. as *Lehrbuch der christlichen Dogmatik;* other works include *Philosophisch-exegetische Untersuchungen über die Lehre von der Versöhnung.*

Flattich, Johann Friedrich (1713–97). B. Beihingen, near Ludwigsburg, Ger.; educ. Tübingen; pastor and pedagogue Asperg 1742, Metterzimmern 1747, Münchingen 1760. Pupil and disciple of J. A. Bengel.*

Flavian. 1. *Flavian I* (ca. 320–ca. 404). B. probably Antioch, Syria; bp. or patriarch Antioch 381–404 but appointment not recognized by bp. Rome and bps. Egypt; opposed Arianism,* Eustathians (see *Eustathius of Antioch*), Euchites.* 2. *Flavian II* (d. 518 AD). Bp. or patriarch Antioch, Syria, ca. 498–512; accepted the Henoticon*; anathematized by patriarch of Constantinople; deposed and banished to Petra by Anastasius I (ca. 430–518; emp. 491–518). 3. *Flavian* (ca. 390–449). Bp. or patriarch Constantinople 447–449; opposed Eutyches*; deposed by "Robber Syn." of Ephesus.*

Fleischmann, Philipp (Jan. 22, 1815–Sept. 11, 1878). B. Regensburg, Bavaria; itinerant minister among Luths. in Pomerania and Nassau; pastor Walkers Point (suburban Milwaukee), Wis.; helped found and conduct Mo. Syn. teachers sem., Milwaukee, 1855 (see also *Lochner, Friedrich Johann Carl*); prof. and dir. teachers sem. Fort Wayne, Ind., 1857; resigned 1864 because of eye trouble; pastor Soest and Kendallville, Ind. See aslo *Ministry, Education of,* VIII C 2 f.

Fleming, John (1807–94). B. Mifflin Co., Pa.; educ. Princeton (N. J.) Theol. Sem.; Presb. ABCFM miss. to Creek Indians; devised Creek, or Muskogee, alphabet; miss. Grand Traverse Bay, Mich.; pastor Westmoreland Co., Pa.; home miss. La Salle Co., Ill.; settled at Ayr, Nebr. Works include primary Creek textbooks; translations of hymns into Creek.

Flemming, Paul (Fleming; 1606[1609?]–1640). Poet; b. Hartenstein, Ger.; studied medicine Leipzig; attached to embassy to Russ. 1633–35, Persia 1635–39. Hymns include "In allen meinen Taten "

Flesh. In some Scripture passages "flesh" stands for the material part of a human being (Job 33:21; Ps 78:39; Lk 24:39; 1 Ptr 2:24). In other passages it denotes man's incapacity for good, the total depravity of his whole nature (Ro 6:19; 7:18; 8:3). This sinful flesh remains with the Christian even after conversion and hinders the efficacy of the Law. The Law gains the assent of the new man (Eph 4:24; Cl 3:10), but it is not fulfllled because of the tendency of the flesh toward what is forbidden. The fleshly (carnal) mind is enmity against God (Ro 8:3-9); it is the source and seat of all evil passions and leads to death (Ro 6:21-23; 7:5). The lusts and works of the flesh are opposed to holy, divine impulses (Gl 5:16; Eph 2:1-3). The flesh can be crucified only through the Spirit of Christ, who dwells in the regenerate (Gl 5:24-25; Ro 8:13). In some passages "flesh" is used in a positive sense, connoting good character (Ez 11:19; 36:26). See also *Sanctification.*

Fletcher, John William (originally Jean Guillaume de la Fléchère; 1729–85). B. Nyon, Switz.; to Eng. ca. 1752; ordained 1757; vicar of Madeley, Yorkshire; assoc. of J. Wesley.* Works include *Five Checks to Antinomianism.*

Fleury, Claude (1640–1723). B. Paris; educ. by Jesuits; lawyer; ordained ca. 1672; friend of J. B. Bossuet,* L. Bourdaloue,* F. de S. de la M. Fenelon*; tutor to the princes of Conti, to the son of Louis XIV and Louise de la Vallière, and to the grandsons of Louis XIV. Works include *Histoire ecclésiastique.*

Fliedner, Fritz (1845–1901). B. Kaiserswerth, Ger.; son of T. Fliedner*; educ. Halle and Tübingen; chaplain to legation of Germany in Sp. 1870; tried to evangelize Sp. Works include Sp. biography of D. Livingstone,* M. Luther,* T. Fliedner,* J. Howard,* and E. Fry*; a Sp. hymnal. See also *Spain,* 6.

Fliedner, Theodor (1800–64). B. Eppstein, Ger.; educ. Giessen, Göttingen, and Herborn; pastor Kaiserswerth 1821–49. Organizations and institutions founded include Rheinisch-Westfälische Gefängnisgesellschaft 1826; refuge home for discharged female prisoners 1833; nursery school and deaconess institute that served as hosp. and training center at Kaiserswerth 1836 (see *Deaconesses,* 5); orphanage for girls 1842; deaconess house at Dresden and institute for training pastors' assistants at Duisburg 1844; sem. for women teachers for folk schools 1844; institution for female mental cases 1847; hospitals at Jerusalem, Constantinople, and Alexandria; training schools at Smyrna, Jerusalem, and Beirut. He brought 4 deaconesses to Pittsburgh, Pa., on request of W. A. Passavant* (see also *Deaconesses,* 7). Issued *Armen- und Krankenfreund* beginning 1849.

M. Gerhardt, *Theodor Fliedner: Ein Lebensbild,* I (Düsseldorf-Kaiserswerth, 1933); A. R. Wentz, *Fliedner the Faithful* (Philadelphia, 1936); A. Sticker, *Theodor und Friederike Fliedner: Von den Anfängen der Frauendiakonie* (Neukirchen, 1965).

Flierl, Johan(nes) (Apr. 16, 1858–Sept. 30, 1947). "Senior Flierl." B. Oberpfalz, Ger.; educ. Miss. Inst., Neuendettelsau; served in Australia at Bethesda Miss. Station 1878–85, Elim 1885–86; arrived at Finschhafen, New Guinea, July 12, 1886; est. miss. near Simbang; moved to Sattelberg, NW of Finschhafen; served 44 yrs. in New Guinea; retired to Australia 1930; returned to Eur. 1937. Senior Flierl Sem. est. 1957 at Finschhafen.

G. Pilhofer, *Johann Flierl, der Bahnbrecher des Evangeliums unter den Papua* (Neuendettelsau, 1953).

Fliesteden, Peter (Flysteden; d. 1529). Rhenish martyr; b. perhaps Fliesteden, near Cologne, Ger.; probably not assoc. with Anabap. movement as at times alleged; to Cologne in Dec. 1527; rejected "idolatrous worship" of mass and other features of RCm; tried to gain converts to Lutheranism; arrested in 1527 Christmas season; imprisoned nearly 2 yrs., last 9 mo. with A. Clarenbach*; their religious convictions given in pamphlets circulated by friends 1528 and after execution; refused to recant under torture; burned at Cologne Sept. 28.

Flittner, David (1796–1869). Ger. Luth. clergyman in Russ.; educ. Dorpat; pastor in Volga region and St. Petersburg; gen. supt. and vice-pres. of gen. consistory 1840–61.

Flit(t)ner, Johann (1618–78). B. Suhl, Ger.; educ. Wittenberg, Jena, Leipzig, and Rostock; precentor 1644, deacon 1646 at Grimmen, near Greifswald; hymnist. Hymns include "Jesu, meines Herzens Freud'."

Flodoard (Frodoard; ca. 894–966). B. probably Épernay, Fr.; educ. Reims; archivist cathedral ch. Reims. Works include *Historia Remensis ecclesiae; Annales* (919–966).

Flood, The. The deluge sent in the time of Noah as punishment for the sins of antediluvians. Described Gn 6–8.

Florence, Council of (1438–45). 1. Tried to reunite Gk. and Lat. chs. The Gk. Ch. was seeking support against Turks, who were approaching Constantinople. The council began Jan. 8, 1438, at Ferrara, It., with a session of W representatives, Cardinal Niccolò Albergati presiding. The combined E-W council opened Apr. 9 with over 500 dignitaries present. Important Gk. representatives included E Roman Emp. John* VIII Palaeologus, his brother Demetrius, Joseph* II (patriarch of Constantinople), Mark Eugenicus* (metropolitan of Ephesus), Isidore* of Kiev, G. Scholarios (see *Gennadius* II), and J. Bessarion.* Roman representatives included J. Cesarini,* J. de Torquemada,* Giovanni di Montenero (John of Montenero; Dominican provincial of Lombardy; scholastic), and Ambrogio* Traversari.

2. Discussions about purgatory, begun in June, were unresolved when interrupted by the plague. Debate about *filioque* (see *Filioque Controversy*), begun Oct. 8, raged partly around legitimacy of adding the term to the Nicene Creed. Little was accomplished in sessions Oct. 8–Dec. 13. Various factors, including financial and military, brought about the 1439 move to Florence. It was agreed that the Holy Spirit is eternally from the Father and the Son, that the essence and being of the Holy Spirit have existence from the Father together with the Son, and that the Holy Spirit proceeds from both Father and Son eternally as from one principle *(principium)* and by a single spiration; but differences in expression (e. g., "from the Father through the Son") were also allowed. Other agreements included: that both leavened and unleavened bread are valid in the Lord's Supper; that some souls go to purgatory after death and that they might be aided by prayers and gifts of the pious. The Gks. accepted the supremacy of the Roman pope; that this pope is a successor of Peter, true vicar of Christ, head of the whole ch., father and teacher of all Christians; that his rule does not infringe on the rights of patriarchs, with the Gk. patriarch of Constantinople 2d after the pope, followed in order by the patriarchs of Alexandria, Antioch, and Jerusalem. The agreement was signed July 5, promulgated July 6 in the decree *Laetentur caeli* by Eugenius* IV. Mark* of Ephesus refused to sign.

3. The council also made agreements with other non-Lat. chs. On Nov. 22, 1439, the bull *Exultate Deo* (often called *Decretum pro Armenis*) announced agreement bet. the Armenians* and the Latins. On Feb. 4, 1442, the bull *Cantate Domino* expressed agreement with Copts (see *Coptic Church*). In 1443 the council began sessions at the Lateran,* Rome. Union with Mesopotamian Syrians was proclaimed Sept. 30, 1444, and with Cypriots Aug. 7, 1445 (the last known session of the council). In Constantinople there was hostility to union with the W. But continuing Turkish threat led to continued pressure for support from the W. The decree of E-W union was officially promulgated in Constantinople Dec. 12, 1452, by Isidore of Kiev as papal legate. On May 29, 1453, the Turks captured Constantinople; that nullified the union. The Council of Florence did not achieve the aim of E-W union. But it gained a victory for the pope in the struggle bet. pope and council over primacy. CSM

See also *Basel, Council of.*

Concilium Florentinum: Documenta et scriptores (Rome, 1940–); *Sacrorum conciliorum nova, et amplissima collectio,* ed. J. D. Mansi et al. (Venice [1767]); *Conciliorum collectio,* ed. J. Hardouin, IX (Paris, 1715); *The Cambridge Medieval History,* ed. J. R. Tanner et al., IV, VII, VIII (Cambridge, 1923, 1932, 1936); L. Pastor, *History of the Popes,*

I–II, 5th ed. F. I. Antrobus (St. Louis, Mo., 1923); J. Gill, *The Council of Florence* (Cambridge, 1959) and *Personalities of the Council of Florence* (New York, 1964).

Florentine Academy. Circle of scholars assoc. with M. Ficino* at Careggi, near Florence, It., 1462–94. Also called Platonic Academy of Florence.

Florentius Radewijns (ca. 1350–1400). B. Leerdam, near Utrecht, Neth.; adherent of G. Groote*; head of the community of the Brethren* of the Common Life at Deventer 1384; founded monastery at Windesheim, but did not become monk himself.

Florian(us) (d. ca. 303 AD). Patron saint of Upper Austria; *princeps officii praesidis* in the Roman province Noricum ripense (along the Danube); martyred under Diocletian by having a millstone tied around his neck and being drowned in the Enns R.

Florida, Colonial Church in. See *United States, Religious History,* 2.

Florida, Synod of. See *United Lutheran Church, Synods of,* 4.

Florilegium (pl. *florilegia;* Lat. "gathering of flowers"). Anthology. Collections from patristic commentaries and dogmatics from early centuries are extant. Basil the Great and Gregory of Nazianzus (see *Cappadocian Theologians,* 1–2) made a collection from Origen* called Philocalia ca. 362. See also *Catena; Patristics,* 7.

Florinus. See *Gnosticism,* 7 g.

Florus (d. ca. 860). B. probably Sp.; deacon Lyons, Fr.; defended rights of the ch.; opposed Gottschalk in predestinarian* controversy. Works include commentaries; poems; liturgical works.

MPL 119, 9–424.

Flügel, Otto (1842–1914). B. Lützen, Ger.; educ. Schulpforte and Halle; Herbartian philos. and theol.; opposed monism*; held that God is finite. See also *Herbart, Johann Friedrich.*

Flysteden. See *Fliesteden.*

Föderaltheologie. See *Federal Theology.*

Foerster, Erich (1865–1945). B. Greifswald, Ger.; educ. Schulpforte, Marburg, and Berlin; pastor Hirschberg 1893, Frankfurt am Main 1895; honorary prof. ch. hist. Frankfurt 1915; adherent of Bekennende Kirche (see *Kirchenkampf*).

Fogazzaro, Antonio (1842–1911). B. Vicenza, It.; liberal RC; poet; novelist; philos.

Foliot, Gilbert (ca. 1110–ca. 1187). Bp. London; opposed T. à Becket.*

Font. Receptacle for water used at baptism.

Fontainebleau, Edict of. See *France,* 8.

Foot Washing (Lat. *pedilavium;* called *mandatum* by RCs, from *mandatum novum* [Lat. "a new commandment"], Jn 13:34). In Bible times it was a required courtesy to give a guest water to wash his dusty feet (Gn 18:4; Lk 7:44); to wash the feet of others was servants' work (1 Sm 25:41). Foot washing was invested with spiritual meaning by Christ when He washed the feet of His diciples (Jn 13:4-20). This act of Jesus led to development of a ceremony in the ancient ch. (1 Ti 5:10; *MPL* 33, 220). It is mentioned as a liturgical rite by the 694 Syn. of Toledo. By the 11th c. the custom had come to Rome.

The ceremony is preserved in RC and E Orthodox chs., performed on Maundy Thu. by bp. on 12 or 13 poor or in monasteries by abbot on monks accompanied by singing of antiphons from Jn 13. See also *Church Year,* 8.

Luther held that the physical washing is unimportant and that the original act is repeated in our acts of humility, kindness, love, and service toward fellowmen (WA 52, 216–226). Anabaps. (esp. Mennonites) and early Angl. Ch. practiced it. Called "kleine Taufe" by Brethren.*

Foot washing is practiced by some Baps. (e. g., Regular Baps.), some Holiness chs. (e. g., the Ch. of the Living God), Gen. Eldership of the Chs. of God in N. Am., and others. By some (e. g., Amana Ch. Soc.) it was observed in connection with the Lord's Supper. EL

Forbes, Alexander Penrose (1817–75). The "Scottish Pusey" (see *Pusey, Edward Bouverie*); b. Edinburgh, Scot.; studied at Glasgow U., Scot., and Haileybury Coll., Hertford, Eng.; in civil service in India; returned to Eng.; studied at Brasenose Coll., Oxford; influenced by Oxford Movement; Scot. Episc. bp. Brechin, Scot.; moved episc. residence to Dundee; defended doctrine of Real Presence; supported Tractarianism* and Old* Catholics. Works include *A Short Explanation of the Nicene Creed; An Explanation of the Thirty-nine Articles.*

Forbes, Anderson Oliver (1833–88). B. Hawaii; son of C. Forbes*; educ. Princeton Theol. Sem.; ABCFM miss. to Sandwich Islands (Hawaii) 1858.

Forbes, Cochran (1805–80). B. Goshen, Pa.; educ. Princeton Theol. Sem.; ABCFM miss. to Sandwich Islands (Hawaii) 1833–47.

Forbidden Degrees. See *Prohibited Degrees.*

Ford, Joshua Edwards (Aug. 3, 1825–Apr. 3, 1866). B. Ogdensburg, N. Y.; educ. Union Theol. Sem., N. Y.; arrived Beirut 1848 to join Syria Mission; returned to US 1865.

Foreign Christian Missionary Society. Organized by Disciples* of Christ at Louisville, Ky., 1875. Fields included Eng., Scand., Fr., Turkey, India, Japan, China, Afr.

Foreign Mission Societies in the United States, Early Lutheran. See *Lutheran Foreign Mission Societies in the United States, Early.*

Foreign Mission Society of the Evanglical Lutheran Church of the United State, The. See *Heyer, Johann Christian Friedrich; Lutheran Foreign Mission Endeavors in the United States, Early.*

Foreign Missions Conference of North America, The. See *Union Movements,* 13.

Foreign Missions, History of. See entries for the various countries.

Foreign-Tongue Missions (Ger. *Fremdsprachige Missionen*). Technical term denoting home miss. work carried on in their native tongue in the US among persons of for. origin and their descendants.

Foreknowledge, Divine. See *Prescience, Divine.*

Forensic Justification. Act of God by which He judicially declares a sinner righteous for the sake of Christ. See *Justification,* 7.

Foreordination. See *Predestination.*

Foreseen Faith. See *Intuitu fidei.*

Foresters (Canadian Order of Foresters; Independent Order of Foresters). These 2 organizations, indep. of each other, are similar in purpose and structure. Both maintain local lodges with initiation and other rituals containing religious significance. The Canadian order offers a funeral service. Emphasis in both organizations is on life insurance, which they offer without participation in the local lodge. Insurance is issued on application for membership in the lodge and is not canceled if the applicant does not submit to initiation. PHL

Forged Decretals. See *Pseudo-Isidorian Decretals.*

Forgiveness of Sins. The act of divine grace by which, in virtue of the merits of Christ's atonement, appropriated by faith, God frees the sinner from the guilt and penalties of his sins. The Law is vindicated by the atonement of Christ, and the penalty of sin is paid. God offers free and full forgiveness to all (Jn 3:16), and such forgiveness is received by all who believe in Christ as their Mediator and Redeemer (Is 1:18; 55:1-2; Acts 5:31; Ro 3:24, 28; 1 Jn 2:12). Viewed from another angle, this act is called justification, not in the sense that the person justified is morally just, but just with respect to the Law and the Lawgiver, i. e., one who has received pardon is justified in the sense that he is declared innocent, being placed in a position of not having broken the Law and not deserving punishment. See *Justification.* Such forgiveness is granted believers as a free gift, not because of any merit of their own (Eph 2:8). The whole pattern is one of mercy, to which the sinner makes his appeal. This mercy provided a Redeemer who reconciled men to God (2 Co 5:19).

R. C. Rein, "Forgiveness of Sin," *The Abiding Word,* I, ed. T. Laetsch (St. Louis, 1946), 146–167.

Form Criticism. See *Isagogics,* 3.

Formal Cause. See *Cause,* 3.

Formal Principle. The *principium cognoscendi* or formal principle of the Luth. Ch. is Holy Scripture, source and norm of all doctrine. See *Grace, Means of,* I 4; *Sola Scriptura.*

W. H. T. Dau, "The Heritage of Lutheranism," *What Lutherans Are Thinking,* ed. E. C. Fendt (Columbus, Ohio, 1947), pp. 9–25.

Formalism. Exernalism. The term has been applied to 1. overemphasis of outward observances of religion or rules of morality combined with neglect of inner spirit or value; 2. support of religious body in power (17th c. Eng.; now obsolete); 3. theories holding that the form of the moral law alone is ground for moral action without reference to purpose or value.

Forman, Charles William (d. Aug. 27, 1894). B. Kentucky; educ. Princeton Theol. Sem.; sailed for India Aug. 11, 1847, as miss. of Am. Presb. Bd. (N); worked at Lahore; organized and supervised system of miss. schools.

Formgeschichtliche Schule. See *Isagogics,* 3.

Formosa. See *Taiwan.*

Formula missae. See *Chant; Liturgics; Luther, Liturgies of.*

Formula of Concord. See *Lutheran Confessions,* C 2.

Formula of Government and Discipline. S. S. Schmucker* drafted *Formula for the Government and Discipline of the Lutheran Church in Maryland and Virginia* for the Syn. of Md. and Va. (see *United Lutheran Church, Synods of,* 11, 29). This *Formula* was adopted by that syn. 1822 and, with alterations, by The Ev. Luth. General* Synod of the United States of North Am. 1823. In 1827 Schmucker was on a committee instructed to draw up a const. for the govt. of dist. syns. In 1829 this committee presented such a const. to the Gen. Synod. After being amended, this const. was recommended by the Gen. Syn. to its constituent syns. for adoption. These 2 documents and the 1820 const. of the Gen. Syn. constitute the *Formula for the Government and Discipline of the Evangelical Lutheran Church (General Synod).*

Minutes of the Proceedings of the [*Second*] *General Synod, of the Evang. Luth. Church in the United States; Convened at Fredericktown (Md.) Oct. 1823* (York, Pa., 1823); *Minutes of the Proceedings of the* [*Fourth*] *General Synod of the Ev. Lutheran Church in the United States. Convened at Gettysburg, Pa., Oct. 1827* (Gettysburg, 1827); *Minutes of the Proceedings of the Fifth General Synod of the Ev. Luth. Church, in the United States. Convened at Hagerstown, Md., October 1829* (Gettysburg, 1829); P. Anstadt, *Life and Times of Rev. S. S. Schmucker, D. D.* (York, Pa., 1896); A. R. Wentz, *Pioneer in Christian Unity: Samuel Simon Schmucker* (Philadelphia, 1967).

Formula pii consensus. See *Lutheran Confessions,* A 5.

Fornication. See *Marriage,* III.

Forsander, Nils (Sept. 11, 1846–Aug. 21, 1926). B. Gladsax, Swed.; educ. Augustana Coll. and Theol. Sem., Paxton, Ill.; pastor in Ill. and Iowa; prof. Augustana Theol. Sem.; ed. *Augustana Theological Quarterly* 1900–12; contributed to *Korsbaneret* and other Swed. Luth. periodicals. Works include *Augsburgiska Bekännelsen; Life Pictures from Swedish Church History; Olavus Petri; The Marburg Colloquy; Lifsbilder ur Augustana Synodens historia.*

Forster, Johann (Förster; Forsthemius; Vorster; 1496–1558). B. Augsburg, Ger.; educ. Ingolstadt and Leipzig; taught Heb. at Zwickau 1522–23; preacher Wittenberg and Augsburg; prof. Heb. Tübingen 1539; provost St. Lawrence, Nürnberg, 1542; supt. Merseburg 1548; prof. Heb. Wittenberg 1549; involved in Leipzig Interim.*

Forster, Wilhelm Georg (William George). See *Ohio and Other States, Evangelical Lutheran Joint Synod of,* 1.

Forsyth, Peter Taylor (1848–1921). Brit. Cong.; liberal in early life through influence of G. W. F. Hegel* and A. Ritschl*; later stressed need of atonement and cross.

Fortress Press. See *Publication Houses, Lutheran.*

Fortunatus, Venantius Honorius Clementianus (ca. 530–ca. 610). Poet; b. near Ceneda and Treviso, It.; to Gaul 565; bp. Poitiers ca. 600. Hymns include "Vexilla regis prodeunt"; "Agnoscat omne saeculum"; "Salve, festa dies."

Fortune-telling. Pseudoscience of predicting the future. Various alleged signs or indications have been used, e. g., the flight of birds, the position of the intestines in a slaughtered sacrificial animal, the coincidence of minor happenings in a person's life, the appearance of water or other liquids in sacred cups and other vessels, the manner in which a deck of cards falls when dealt, the configuration of the lines in a person's hands, crystal globes. Divination is forbidden in the OT (Lv 19:26; Dt 18:10-11). When Saul became king, he cast all that had familiar spirits and the wizards out of the land (1 Sm 28:9), the witch at Endor being apparently the only person of that kind left in the country. Later the prophets reprimanded the people for practicing divination (Is 44:24-25; Mi 3:7). Compare 2 K 21:6 and 23:24. Christianity takes an unequivocal stand against fortune-telling.

Forty-four. See *Statement, A.*

Forty Hours Devotion. RC service in honor of the Eucharist; performed in the presence of the host; lasts 40 hrs.

Forty-two Articles. See *Anglican Confessions,* 5.

Fosdick, Harry Emerson (1878–1969). B. Buffalo, N. Y.; educ. Colgate U., Hamilton, N. Y., and Union Theol. Sem., NYC; ordained Bap. 1903. Pastor Montclair, N. J., 1904–15; 1st Presb. Ch., NYC, 1918–25; Park Ave. Bap. Ch., NYC, 1925 (it developed into Riverside Ch., which he served till 1946). Taught at Union Theol. Sem. 1908–46. Liberal. Works include *The Modern Use of the Bible; A Guide to Understanding the Bible; The Manhood of the Master; The Meaning of Faith; The Man from Nazareth; The Living of These Days; Riverside Sermons.*

Fossarians. Grave diggers in early ch.

Fossum, Ludvig Olsen (June 5, 1879–Oct. 10, 1920). B. Wallingford, Iowa; educ. St. Ansgar (Iowa) Sem. and, the United Ch. Sem. (St. Paul, Minn.) of the United Norw. Luth. Ch.; ordained 1902; pastor Slayton, Minn., 1902–05; miss. to Nestorian Chaldeans, Urmia, Persia, 1906–09; pastor Chicago, Ill., 1909–10; emissary Luth. Orient(al) Miss. Soc. 1910–11; miss. Missions to Mohammedan Kurds, Sonjbulak, Kurdistan, 1911–16; mem. Am. Red Cross in Armenia 1916–19; Dist. Commander of the Near East Relief at Erivan (Erevan; Yerevan), Armenia, 1919–20. Reduced Kurdish language to writing; works include a Kurdish grammar, Kurdish Luth. hymnal, tr. of Luther's SC into Kurdish.

Foster, Frank Hugh (1851–1935). B. Springfield, Mass.; educ. Andover Theol. Sem., Harvard U.,

Leipzig U.; ordained Cong. clergyman 1877; prof. Middlebury (Vt.) Coll., Oberlin (Ohio) Theol. Sem., Pacific Theol. Sem. (Berkeley, Calif.); pastor Olivet, Mich.; prof. Olivet (Mich.) Coll. Works include *Christian Life and Theology; A Genetic History of the New England Theology.*

Foster, George Burman (1858–1918). B. Alderson, W. Va.; educ. U. of W. Va., Rochester (N. Y.) Theol. Sem., Göttingen U., Berlin U.; pastor First Bap. Ch., Saratoga Springs, N. Y.; prof. McMaster U., Toronto, and Divinity School of U. of Chicago. Works include *The Finality of the Christian Religion; The Function of Religion in Man's Struggle for Existence; Christianity in Its Modern Expression.*

Foundation, The Lutheran Church — Missouri Synod. Est. 1959 by the LCMS to carry on religious, benevolent, educ., and miss. work in agreement with the principles of the LCMS.

Channels through the Foundation include 1. gifts, benefactions, and donations of money; 2. gifts of real estate and similar property; 3. bequests through wills; 4. annuities; 5. life income gifts; 6. life insurance; 7. stocks and bonds; 8. foundations; 9. revocable and irrevocable trusts; 10. special arrangements; 11. miscellaneous.

Causes and objects served by the Foundation include 1. missions; 2. education; 3. auxiliary agencies; 4. Christian literature; 5. research.

The Foundation has been inc. in Mo. as of Jan. 1, 1959. Its affairs are administered by Bd. of Trustees elected by the LCMS Bd. of Dir. Offices: 210 N Broadway, St. Louis, Mo. 63102. ERB

Foundation, Religious. A nongovernmental, nonprofit organization with a principal fund of its own managed by trustees or directors, est. to maintain or aid religious activities serving the common welfare. Both charitable trusts and corporations are included. Foundations are a phenomenon of the 20th c. There was mushroom growth of foundations in the 1940s and even faster growth in the 1950s. By 1964 there were ca. 15,000 philanthropic foundations in the US. Some support only religious endeavors; others administer religious grants as part of a more comprehensive philanthropic program.

In 1962, $46 million was granted for religious purposes by US foundations, totaling 6% of foundational philanthropy. Larger foundations granted a proportionately smaller percentage of total endowment to religious endeavors than did smaller foundations. Larger foundations (assets exceeding $10 million) administered 2% of total grants for religious work; smaller foundations (assets under $1 million) contributed ca. 20% to religion.

Religious grants vary widely in nature and purpose. In 1962 the larger foundations contributed ca. $5 million to religious causes. 36% of this total went to theol. sems., 27% to religious welfare agencies, 14% to religious educ., 11% to ch. and temple support, 12% to other agencies. Smaller foundations contributed ca. $41 million in a parallel pattern but including theol. scholarships, miss. support, religious hospitals, and other religious causes.

Foundations include *Prot.*: Cook, Elgin, Ill.; Christian, Columbus, Ind.; Lilly, Indianapolis, Ind.; Luce, New York, N. Y.; Mabee, Tulsa, Okla.; Davis, Pittsburgh, Pa.; Jarman, Nashville, Tenn.; Oldham Little Church, Houston, Tex.; Sealantic, New York, N. Y.; Moody, Galveston, Tex. *Meth.*: Duke, New York, N. Y. *Presb.:* Campbell, Atlanta, Ga. *Mennonite*: Schowalter, Newton, Kans. *Gk. Orthodox*: Taylor, New York, N. Y. *RC*: Doheny, Los Angeles, Calif.; Dorum, San Francisco, Calif.; Raskob, Wilmington, Del.; Cuneo, Chicago, Ill.; Murray-Macdonald, New York, N. Y. *Jewish:* Fischel, New York, N. Y. *Unspecified*: Merrill, Ithaca, N. Y.; Atkinson, San Francisco, Calif.; Hazen, New Haven, Conn.; Danforth, St. Louis, Mo.; McDonald, Hastings, Nebr.; Anglican, Garden City, N. Y.; Booth Ferris, New York, N. Y.; James, New York, N. Y.; Teagle, New York, N. Y.; Kresge, Detroit, Mich. JEG

See also *Foundation, The Lutheran Church – Missouri Synod; Foundation for Reformation Research.*

Foundation for Reformation Research. Organized 1957 under leadership of Herbert W. Knopp and Alfred O. Fuerbringer by a group of faculty and bd. mems. of Conc. Sem., St. Louis, Mo., who secured a charter from the State of Mo. to found a nonprofit corporation 1. to collect and preserve historical source material pertaining to the Protestant Reformation and related areas of the history of the Christian Church; 2. to make such material available to interested students and scholars through the establishment of a library and research center; 3. to stimulate historical research concerning the Protestant Reformation and to publish the results of such historical research; 4. to accept gifts, bequests, and devises of real and personal property, which property or the income therefrom shall be used solely to carry out the purposes set forth above and to hold, invest, and administer funds held by the Foundation for such purposes.

The 1st bd. of dir.: Roland H. Bainton, John A. Fleischli, Alfred O. Fuerbringer, Harold John Grimm, Herbert W. Knopp, Edgar M. Krentz, John T. McNeill, Carl S. Meyer, Frederic Niedner, Jaroslav J. Pelikan, Theodore G. Tappert. Ex. dirs. have been Ernest G. Schwiebert, William Toth (d. before assuming office), Carl S. Meyer (acting), Alfred O. Fuerbringer (acting), Ronald E. Diener.

Sponsors of the Foundation include Aid Assoc. for Luths., Appleton, Wis.; CPH; The Wis. Ev. Luth. Syn.; Lilly Foundation; Family Films; LCA; The ALC; Syn. of Ev. Luth. Chs. (Duda Foundation); individual donors.

The library bldg. is at 6477 San Bonita, Clayton, Mo. 63105. Micro-duplicated holdings cover a broad representation of 15th and 16th c. titles and many MSS. Most materials are Lat. and Ger., with a growing percentage of Fr., Eng., It., and Scand. languages. Special collections include works of 16th c. figures whose complete works have not appeared in modern critical eds. (e.g., J. Brenz,* J. H. Bullinger,* M. Bucer,* M. Flacius* Illyricus) and hist. collections (e. g., Political Archives of Philip* of Hesse and parts of the Sammlung of J. J. Simler*).

The Foundation is the nat. office of the Am. Soc. for Reformation Research.

The Foundation conducts an institute each summer to give special instructions in historiographical skills, e. g., paleography, bibliography, and philology as related to the Reformation. AOF

Foundation of Faith. See *Fundamental Doctrines.*

Four Elements. Fire, air, water, earth; recognized as primary bodies by some Gk. thinkers.

Four Points. C. Porterfield Krauth* in "Fraternal* Address" invited all syns., pastors, and congs. in US and Can. confessing the UAC to meet and form a new gen. body. After the organization of the General* Council of the Ev. Luth. Ch. in (North) America, misgivings led the Ohio Syn. (see also *Ohio and Other States, Evangelical Lutheran Joint Synod of,* 5) to ask the Gen. Council at its 1st Regular Convention 1867 to declare its stand on 4 points: chiliasm, mixed communion (altar fellowship), exchange of pulpits with sectarians (pulpit fellowship), and secret or unchurchly societies. The 1867 answer of the Gen. Council did not satisfy the Ohio Syn. The 1868 "Pittsburgh Declaration" of the Gen. Council declared: "I. AS REGARDS 'CHILIASM.' . . . 2. The General Council has neither had, nor would consent to have, fellowship with any

Synod which tolerates the 'Jewish opinions' or 'Chiliastic opinions' condemned in the XVII Article of the Augsburg Confession. . . . II. AS REGARDS 'SECRET SOCIETIES.' . . . 2. Any and all societies for moral and religious ends which do not rest on the supreme authority of God's Holy Word, as contained in the Old and New Testaments – which do not recognize our Lord Jesus Christ as the true God and the only Mediator between God and man – which teach doctrines or have usages or forms of worship condemned in God's Word and in the Confessions of His Church – which assume to themselves what God has given to His Church and its Ministers – which require undefined obligations to be assumed by oath, are unChristian, . . . III. AS REGARDS 'EXCHANGE OF PULPITS.' We hold: 1. That . . . no man shall be admitted to our pulpits, whether of the Lutheran name or any other, of whom there is just reason to doubt whether he will preach the pure truth of God's Word as taught in the Confessions of our Church. 2. Lutheran Ministers may properly preach wherever there is an opening in the pulpit of other Churches, unless the circumstances imply, or seem to imply, a fellowship with error or schism, or a restriction on the unreserved expression of the whole counsel of God. IV. AS REGARDS THE 'COMMUNION WITH THOSE NOT OF OUR CHURCH.' We hold: 1. That the principle of a discriminating as over against an indiscriminate Communion is to be firmly maintained. Heretics and fundamental errorists are to be excluded from the Lord's Table. The responsibility for an unworthy approach to the Lord's Table does not rest alone upon him who makes that approach, but also upon him who invites it. 2. It is the right and duty of every Pastor to make such examination as is necessary to determine the Scriptural fitness, in doctrine and life, of persons applying for admission to the Communion."

Because the Declaration of the Gen. Council regarding the "Four Points" was regarded unsatisfactory, the Ohio Syn. refused to join, the Iowa Syn. decided it could not enter into full membership, Wisconsin left 1869, Minn. and Ill. Syns. left 1871, Mich. left 1888. Tex. joined the Iowa Syn. as a dist. 1896. WGP

Fourah Bay College. See *Africa,* C 6.

Fourier, François Marie Charles. See *Communistic Societies,* 5.

Foursquare Gospel, The. Aimee Semple McPherson (1890–1944) organized Echo Park Evangelistic Association (see *Evangelistic Associations,* 20), Angelus Temple, Los Angeles, Cal., 1923, and the Internat. Ch. of the Foursquare Gospel, as evangelistic body with missions in many lands, 1927; Pentecostal. The name points to 4 basic articles of faith: conversion, divine healing,* baptism of the Holy Ghost (including gift of tongues*), premillennial advent of Christ (see *Millennium,* 7). A fuller statement of teaching is in *Declaration of Faith,* by Mrs. McPherson. Her son, Rolf Kennedy McPherson (b. 1913), continued the work.

Fowler, Charles Henry (1837–1908). B. Burford (later Clarendon), Ont., Can.; Meth. cleric; pastor Chicago; pres. Northwestern U. (Evanston, Ill.) 1873–76; ed. *Christian Advocate* 1876–80; corresponding secy. Meth. Episc. Miss. Soc. 1880–84; bp. 1884; founded univs. in Peking and Nanking 1888.

Fox, George (1624–1691). Mystic; founded Soc. of Friends.* B. Drayton, Leicestershire, Eng.; in late teens grieved at sham and insincerity in ch.; experienced "new light" 1647; convinced that Spirit of God dwells in heart of man; emphasized direct fellowship with God and disparaged external ordinances because he felt that they led to formalism and hypocrisy; at first opposed organizing his followers, but a const. was written 1660 and chs. organized. Visited W. Indies and Am. 1671–72.

Fox, Margaret (1833–93). Most prominent of "The Fox Sisters." B. Bath, Can.; moved to Hydesville, N. Y.; claimed to have heard supernatural rappings with her sister Catherine (Kate) 1848; moved to Rochester, N. Y., with Mrs. Leah Fish, an older sister (or aunt), who took Margaret and Kate to NYC, where the last 2 acted as mediums and held séances; also appeared in other parts of US and in London, Eng.; became RC 1888 and declared spiritism* a fraud; later retracted her confession and returned to rappings for a living.

Fox(e), John (1516–87). B. Boston, Lincolnshire, Eng.; martyrologist; fled persecutions of Mary* I; tr. *A Fruitfull Sermon of the Moost Evangelicall wryter M. Luther, made of the Angelles upon the xviii Chapi. of Mathew;* other works include *Rerum in ecclesia gestarum . . . commentarii,* popularly called *The Book of Martyrs.*

Fra Angelico. See *Angelico, Fra.*

Fragment Theory. See *Higher Criticism,* 13.

Fragmente eines Ungenamten. See *Lessing, Gotthold Ephraim; Reimarus, Hermann Samuel.*

France. 1. *Area:* ca. 212,000 sq. mi. *Pop.:* ca. 52,000,000 (1973 est.). Fr. (ancient Gaul) was one of the 1st countries of Eur. in which Christian chs. were est. A Christian community formed at Lyons ca. 150. At Lyons and Vienne Christians suffered persecution in 177 (see *Persecutions of Christians,* 3). There were ca. 30 episcopal sees by 250, ca. 70 by 350. A syn. was held at Arles* 314. Monasteries were est. in the 2d half of the 4th c. Christians among Goths, Franks, Huns, and others that overran Gaul in the 5th c. were mostly Arian. With conversion of Clovis* I to Cath. (as distinguished from Arian) Christianity (496) miss. work of monks (e. g., Columban*) increased. The Merovingian (from Mérovée, 2d Frankish king 448–458) king Dagobert I (b. ca. 605; king ca. 629–639) put all Fr. under one scepter. The Carolingian rulers (beginning with Pepin the Short [ca. 714–768; king of the Franks 751–768; helped pope against the Lombards and gave him sovereignty over the exarchate of Ravenna], son of Charles Martel [ca. 689–741; Frankish ruler of Austrasia 715–741; defeated Muslim at Tours, near Poitiers, 732] and father of Charlemagne*) assoc. themselves with the pope.

2. In the 11th and 12th c. the nobility gained greater control of the ch. and abuses multiplied. In the 12th and 13th c. extensive reforms were inaugurated; new orders and monasteries were founded; Fr. played a leading role in the crusades* (Peter* the Hermit, Bernard* of Clairvaux, Louis* VII, Louis* IX) and contributed outstanding scholars (e. g., Roscellinus,* P. Abelard,* Peter* the Lombard, Alexander* of Hales) to the scholastic movement (see *Scholasticism*).

3. In the 14th and 15th c. the struggle bet. Fr. and the papacy became acute. Philip IV (the Fair; 1268–1314; king 1285–1314) engaged in a long controversy with popes. The bull* *Clericis laicos* (1296) forbade him to tax the clergy; royal authority was challenged by *Ausculta fili* (1301) and *Unam sanctam* (1302). The first States-General (1302) supported the king against the pope. Clement* V (pope 1305–14) resided in Fr. (see *Babylonian Captivity,* 2). Charles VII (1403–1461; king 1422–61) issued the Pragmatic* Sanction of Bourges (1438), which upheld right of Fr. ch. to administer its temporal property and disallowed papal nominations to vacant benefices. During the papal schism (see *Schism,* 8) Fr. kings supported the popes that resided at Avignon.

4. Fr. took a prominent part in all great ch. movements of the Middle Ages. Reformatory movements were repeatedly inaugurated in the Fr. ch. to

restore purer Christianity or overthrow the papacy. See also *Albigenses; Huguenots; Waldenses.*

5. Under Louis* XIV (the Great; le Grand Monarque; 1638–1715; king 1643–1715) Fr. reached the zenith of its power and splendor. The Fr. Revolution, which broke out 1789, for a time seemed to sweep away the whole Fr. ch.; the Nat. Assem. decreed that all ecclesiastical officers, under penalty of losing office, should submit under oath to the Civil Constitution of the Clergy, which ordered priests and bps. to be chosen by civil elections and paid by the govt.* Napoleon, I, See also *Roman* paid by the govt. See also *Roman Catholic Church,* D7. Napoleon* I, on the contrary, regarded est. of RCM as state religion necessary; in 1801 he concluded a Concordat with Pius VII (see *Popes,* 27) and in 1802 enacted the Organic Articles, which preserved principles of Gallicanism* and were promulgated as supplementary and explanatory part of the 1801 Concordat (see *Concordat,* 5). In 1813 he concluded a new Concordat with the captive pope Pius VII at Fontainebleau; it dealt mainly with official confirmation of bps.; when the pope revoked his action, Napoleon pub. the Concordat as imperial law.

6. Louis XVIII (1755–1824; king 1814–15, 1815–24) and Charles X (1757–1836; king 1824–30) recognized RCm as state religion but granted toleration also to every other rel. The 1830 revolution revealed popular indignation against RCm; under Louis Philippe (Citizen King; 1773–1850; king 1830–48) RCm lost the privilege of a state religion. Repeal of the 1801 Concordat in 1905 and legal separation of ch. and state (in force since Jan. 1, 1906) radically changed the situation of the RC Ch. The separation law, e. g., repealed all state and municipal appropriations for pub. worship, abrogated all establishments of worship, and permitted use of chs. for divine service only by virtue of annual notifications to the civil authorities pending the term of their use. But the ch. retained freedom in organization, hierarchy, discipline, and liturgical arrangement.

7. The hist. of Protestantism is a long record of conflicts with RCm. Early stages of the Reformation in Fr. are assoc. with J. Lefèvre* d'Étaples. The center of the Fr. Reformation was J. Calvin.* The Geneva Academy, whose first rector was T. Beza,* trained many pastors and teachers for Fr.

8. Francis I (1494–1547; king, 1515–47) was originally mild toward the Reformation, but posting by extreme Prots. of placards against the mass 1534 led to severe reaction against them. In 1521 the Sorbonne (U. of Paris) had declared itself against the Reformation; but beginning the same yr. G. Briçonnet* gathered Lefèvre, G. Farel,* and others at Meaux and arranged for ev. preaching and for dissemination among the people of the Gospels and Epistles of the ch. yr. in a Fr. translation. The Jan. Edict (Jan. 25, 1535) was restated in severer form in the Edict of Fontainebleau (1540) and was a law against heresy aimed esp. at Evangelicals of Meaux and the Waldenses.* See also *Speyer, Diets of,* 1–2, 4. Prots. were persecuted as "Luths." under Henry II (1519–59; king 1547–59). But Prots. increased in number. A Prot. syn. assembled secretly in Paris 1559 and adopted a confession of faith, Calvinistic in content, called Gallican Confession (see also *Reformed Confessions,* B).

9. Catherine* de Médicis (Caterina de' Medici*; 1519–89), regent 1560–63 for her son Charles IX (1550–74; king 1560–74), at first tried to hold a mediating course bet. Evangelicals and RCs with Michel de L'Hospital (1507–73; chancellor 1560) and G. de Coligny* among her counselors. The Jan. 1562 Edict of Saint-Germain granted Prots. the right to assemble for worship outside the towns; but their activities sparked opposition and the 2d Duke of Guise (François de Lorraine; le Balafré, i. e. the Scarred; 1519–63) began hostilities by ordering an attack that led to the massacre of a number of Huguenots at Vassy (later spelled Wassy; also called Washy-sur-Blaise; in the Haute-Marne dept., NE Fr.) Mar. 1, 1562. Bloody civil wars followed. Prots., led by Louis I de Bourbon (Prince de Conde*) and Coligny,* suffered heavy losses. The 1st war ended with the 1563 Edict of Amboise, which left some places of worship in Huguenot hands. The 2d war (1567–68) ended with the Peace of Longjumeau; the govt. put large garrisons in Huguenot cities. The 3d war (1568–70) ended with the Peace of Saint-Germain, in which the govt. gave the Huguenots 4 fortified towns. The Huguenots gained further hope when their chief, Henry of Navarre (see *Henry IV*), married the king's sister Margaret* of Valois Aug. 18, 1572. But at the instigation of Catherine de Médicis, Margaret's mother, thousands of Prots. were massacred (sec *Bartholomew's Day Massacre*). Henry III (1551–89) succeeded Charles IX 1574. The Huguenots, under arms, obtained concessions in the Edict of Boulogne 1573, the Peace of Monsieur (Peace of Beaulieu) 1576, and the peace treaty of Bergerac (terms of which were pub. in the Edict of Poitiers) 1577. But a Holy* League, organized by the 3d Duke of Guise (Henri I de Lorraine; also called le Balafré; 1550–88) and others 1576, forced stringent action against Prots. In the treaty of Nemours 1585 Protestantism was suppressed.

10. The assassination of the Duke of Guise and his brother by order of the king 1588 led to the king's own assassination 1589. Henry of Navarre ascended the throne 1589 as Henry IV; became RC 1593. By the Edict of Nantes 1598, freedom of faith and limited pub. worship, civil rights, and pol. privileges were granted to the Huguenots. After the assassination of Henry IV 1610 the Prots. again took up arms to defend their rights. Cardinal Richelieu,* 1524–42 chief minister of Louis XIII (1601–43; king, 1610–43), disarmed them as a pol. party. Ecclesiastical concessions, granted by the Edict of Nantes, were granted again by the Amnesty (Gnadenedikt) of Nîmes (Peace of Alès, or Alais) 1629, but pol. power was denied. Louis XIV used rigorous legislation and dragonnades* 1683–86 to break the power of Protestantism in the state and revoked the Edict of Nantes 1685. Thousands of Prots. fled from Fr. Those that stayed were without organization and houses of worship. Huguenot preachers met 1715 under leadership of A. Court,* who gradually organized what has been called the "Ch. of the Desert." Louis XV (the Well-Beloved; Fr.: le Bien-Aimé; 1710–74; king 1715–74) again prohibited the Ref. religion 1724. But by 1744 Huguenots were holding meteings of 10,000. See also *Roman Catholic Church,* D 6.

11. A. Court opened a school of theol. at Lausanne that continued to supply the Prot. Ch. with pastors till the time of Napoleon I. After 1762 toleration began to be practiced. The 1789 Declaration of the Rights of Man and of the Citizen stated that there should be no discrimination against a person for his convictions (including religious) provided they do not militate against state laws.

12. Fr. remained a RC country, with Prots. widely scattered and gravitating toward the cities.

13. In 1848 F. J. J. G. Monod (see *Monod,* 1) and others seceded from the state ch. and 1849 formed the Union des Églises évangéliques libres de France (Free Ch.). Lutheranism also found early adherents in Fr. But Calvinism soon prevailed. Part of Alsace and other districts and towns were ceded to Fr. by the Peace of Westphalia* 1648 (Fr. took control of the rest of Alsace toward the end of the c.); religious toleration was secured for RCs, Luths.,

and Ref. The Peace of Westphalia was in gen. confirmed by the Peace of Nijmegen (Nimwegen; Nimeguen; ancient Noviomagus) 1678–79.

14. Since WW II RC's and Prots. seek so far as possible to conform to the principle of neutrality for the state. RC theologians and leaders concern themselves with biblical and liturgical renewal and development of a new form of Gallicanism.* Prots. form a small minority divided into several groups and concern themselves with new forms of witnessing and ecumenical movements. Theol. differences are disappearing.

15. The Ev. Luth. Ch. of the AC, composed of Luths. in Alsace and Lorraine, was formed in the early part of the 19th c. Orphaned after WW I, it became a miss. of LCMS. The Ev. Luth Ch.–Syn. of Fr. and Belgium is also assoc. with the LCMS. See also *Lutheran Confessions,* A 5; *Robert II.*

Histoire de l'Église depuis les origines jusqu'à nos jours, ed. A. Fliche and V. Martin (Paris, 1934–); C. S. Phillips, *The Church in France, 1789–1848* (New York, 1966) and *The Church in France, 1848–1907* (New York, 1936); A. Dansette, *Religious History of Modern France,* tr. J. Dingle, 2 vols. (New York, 1961).

Francis I. See *France,* 8.

Francis, Benjamin (1734–99). B. Wales; clergyman and poet; studied at Bristol Bap. Coll.; pastor at Sodbury and (1757–99) at Horsley (later called Shortwood), Gloucestershire. Hymns include "In Loud, Exalted Strains."

Francis of Assisi (Giovanni Francesco Bernardone; ca. 1182–1226). B. Assisi, It.; resolved to imitate Christ's voluntary poverty ca. 1208; preached repentance and brotherly love; gathered followers; received papal approval; when the order was constituted in the technical sense, he resigned as minister-gen. 1221 and founded a tertiary order. Lover of nature; often pictured with birds. Regarded as one of the most lovable figures in the medieval ch. See also *Barefooted Monks; Clare of Assisi; Franciscans; Stigmatization; Tertiaries.*

L. Salvatorelli, *The Life of St. Francis of Assisi,* tr. E. Sutton (New York, 1928); P. Sabatier, *Life of St. Francis of Assisi,* tr. L. S. Houghton (New York, 1894); O. Englebert, *Saint Francis of Assisi,* tr. E. M. Cooper, 2d Eng. ed. (Chicago, 1965); popular legends about Francis of Assisi are in *Fioretti.**

Francis Lüneburg. See *Lutheran Confessions,* A 2.

Francis of Paola (Francis of Paula; 1416–1507). B. Paola, Calabria, It.; Franciscan (see *Franciscans*) monk; founded Order of Minims* 1436.

Francis of Sales (François de Sales; 1567–1622). B. Thorens, Savoy, Fr.; nobleman and cleric; bp. Geneva 1602; helped found Order of the Visitation of Mary (Visitation* Nuns). Works include *Introduction à la vie dévote; Traite de l'amour de Dieu.*

Franciscan Crown. See *Seven Joys of Mary.*

Franciscans. Order founded 1209 by Francis* of Assisi. Their early yrs. were marked by strict poverty, limited use of property, begging, humble service to all, and miss. endeavors; but the order was wracked for more than a c. by disputes about the question of poverty. They produced such theologians as Bonaventura,* J. Duns* Scotus, and W. of Ockham.* Some of its mems. felt the arm of the Inquisition* 1318 for challenging the pope's authority. In 1517 a split took place bet. the stricter faction (Friars Minor proper [Observant]) and the moderate faction (Friars Minor Conventual). The Friars Minor Capuchins* were founded ca. 1528 by an Observant priest; they became one of the most powerful agencies of the Counter* Reformation. The Second Order (Poor Clares; see also Clare of Assisi) was founded 1212. There is also a Third Order (Tertiaries*). See also *Conventuals; Mendicant Friars; Observants; Recollects; Sisterhoods; Spirituals, Franciscan.*

Franck, César Auguste (1822–90). B. Liège, Belgium; organist Ste. Clotilde, Paris, 1858; prof. organ Paris Conservatory 1872; pioneer of modern Fr. instrumental school. Works include oratorios *(Ruth; Rédemption; Les Béatitudes; Rébecca); Symphony in D Minor; Masses.*

N. Demuth, *César Franck* (London, 1949); H. Andriessen, *César Franck* (New York, 1947); V. d'Indy, *César Franck,* tr. R. H. Newmarch (New York, 1910); L. Vallas, *César Franck,* tr. H. Foss (London, 1951).

Franck, Johann (1618–77). B. Guben, Ger.; studied at Königsberg; friend of S. Dach* and H. Held*; lawyer 1645; burgomaster Guben 1661; poet; firm faith, deep earnestness, finished form, simplicity of expression, and a personal, individual tone are evident in his hymns, which include "Herr Jesu, Licht der Heiden"; "Schmücke dich, o liebe Seele"; "Jesu, meine Freude"; "Herr, ich habe missgehandelt."

Franck, Johann Wolfgang (ca. 1644–ca. 1710). B. Unterschwaningen, Bavaria; court Kapellmeister at Anspach 1673–78. Works include operas and spiritual songs.

W. B. Squire, *Johann Wolfgang Franck* (London, 1912).

Franck, Melchior (ca. 1580–1639). B. Zittau, Ger.; Kapellmeister to Duke of Coburg 1603–39; among the first to write instrumental accompaniment of songs. Works include *Melodiae sacrae; Paradisus.*

Franck, Michael (1609–67). B. Schleusingen, Ger.; hymnist; studies interrupted by father's death; master-baker at Schleusingen, then at Coburg, where he was appointed master of the lower classes in the town school. Hymns include "Sei Gott getreu."

Franck, Salomo (1659–1725). Poet; probably b. Weimar; educ. Jena; secy. Schwarzburg ducal administration at Arnstadt 1689, of the Saxon administration and of the consistory at Jena 1697; secy. of the consistory, librarian, and curator of the ducal medal and coin collection, Weimar, 1702. Prepared texts for some of J. S. Bach's* cantatas and ca. 330 hymns, including "Ach Gott, verlass mich nicht"; "Ich halte Gott in allem stille."

Franck, Sebastian (Frank; Francus; Franck von Wörd; ca. 1499–ca. 1543). B. Donauwörth, Ger.; freethinker.* RC priest; Prot. 1525; indep. mystic 1528; opposed by M. Luther* and P. Melanchthon.* Works include *Chronica.* See also *Schwenkfelders,* 4.

Francke, Adolph Gustav Gottlieb (Jan. 21, 1821–Jan. 3, 1879). B. Meinersen, Hannover; educ. Göttingen and Jena; with C. J. H. Fick* and C. L. A. Wolter* to Am. 1846: ordained 1846; pastor Dover, Lafayette Co., Mo., 1846–51, 1853–57, Buffalo, N. Y., 1851–52, Addison, Ill., 1857; pres. of the bd. (Praeses der Anstalt) of the Ev. Luth. Teachers Sem., Addison, Ill.; pres. Ev. Luth. Orphan Asylum Assoc. of N. Ill.

Francke, August Hermann (1663–1727). B. Lübeck, Ger.; philanthropist, preacher, educator, leader of Pietism*; studied philos., theol., and languages, esp. Heb., at Erfurt, Kiel, and Leipzig; lectured at Leipzig; with P. Anton* founded the *Collegium philobiblicum* 1686 for closer, devotional Bible study. After spending some time at Lüneburg as student, at Hamburg as student and teacher, and with P. J. Spener* at Dresden, he returned 1689 to Leipzig, where his lectures aroused great interest, but also violent opposition as leading to pietistic self-complacency. Called as pastor to Erfurt 1690; his sermons awakened deep interest, but his opponents brought about his banishment Sept. 1691. Through Spener's influence he became pastor in Glaucha, near Halle, and prof. at Halle 1692. Here he developed a strenuous and successful activity as pastor, prof., educator, and organizer of charitable institutions; his school for poor, underprivileged children, founded 1695, expanded into a cluster of educ. and charitable institutions. Under him Halle became the center of the Dan.-Halle miss. to India (see also *Missions,* 7); B. Ziegenbalg,* H. Plütschau,* and C. F. Schwartz* were among those trained at Halle. Francke also corresponded with individuals and societies throughout Ger. and in other countries. Works include hermeneutical, practical, and exegetical treatises, and a few hymns. See also *Molinos, Miguel de; Pietism.*

G. Kramer, *August Hermann Francke,* 2 vols. (Halle, 1880–82); E. Beyreuther, *August Hermann Francke, 1663–1727: Zeuge des lebendigen Gottes* (Marburg, 1956) and *August Hermann Francke und die Anfänge der ökumenischen Bewegung* (Hamburg, 1957); *August Hermann Francke, Wort und Tat,* ed. D. Jungklaus (Berlin, 1966); E. Peschke, *Studien zur Theologie August Hermann Franckes* (Berlin, 1964–).

Francke, Gotthilf August (1696–1769). B. Glaucha, near Halle; son of A. H. Francke*; educ. Halle and Jena; prof. Halle; with J. A. Freylinghausen* he headed institutions est. by his father; Am. Lutheranism is indebted to him for supplying early Luth. pastors, esp. for the ch. in Pa.

Franckean Synod. Organized May 25, 1837, in Minden, N. Y., by a number of men of W Conf. of Hartwick* Syn. The Franckean Syn. did not only fail to adopt the AC but also failed to declare its belief in some fundamental doctrines of the Bible, e. g., the Trinity and the deity of Christ. It held aloof from all other Luth. syns. until it was admitted to the General* Synod of the Ev. Luth. Ch. in the US 1864. Its admission contributed to the disruption of the Gen. Syn. and the founding of the General* Council of the Ev. Luth. Ch. in N. Am. The Franckean Syn., Hartwick Syn., and the N. Y. and N. J. Syn. merged to form the N. Y. Syn. of the Gen. Syn. 1908. See also *Slavery and Lutheranism in America; United Lutheran Church, Synods of,* 15.

For Franckean Syn. II see *West, Missionary Synod of the* (Franckean Syn. II).

Franckenberg. See *Frankenberg.*

Frank. See also *Franck.*

Frank, Carl Adolf (Feb. 28, 1846–Jan.18, 1922). B. Wimpfen, Ger.; to Am. ca. 1854; grad. Conc. Sem., St. Louis, Mo., 1868; pastor Freedom, Beaver Co., Pa., Pittsburgh, Pa., Lancaster, Ohio, New Orleans, La., Zanesville, Ohio, Evansville, Ind.; prof. Columbus, Ohio, 1878–81; ed. *Lutheran Witness* 1882–91.

A. R. Suelflow, "The Father's Faith – The Children's Language," *CHIQ,* XXX (Fall 1957), 130–141; (Winter 1958), 182–188; XXXI (Apr. 1958), 7–26.

Frank, Franz Hermann Reinhold von (1827–94). B. Altenburg, Ger.; studied at Leipzig, where under G. C. A. v. Harless* he turned from rationalism to Lutheranism; prof. ch. hist. and systematic theol. Erlangen 1857. Works include *Theologie der Concordienformel.* See also *Lutheran Theology After 1580,* 11.

Frankenberg, Abraham von (Franckenberg; 1593–1652). Leader of a mystical, spiritualistic group in Silesia; biographer of J. Böhme.*

Frankfort; Frankfurt. 1. Frankfurt am Main; Eng.: Frankfort on the Main; Ger. city; notable bldgs. include cathedral; seat of syn., or council, 794 (see *Adoptionism*). 2. Frankfurt an der Oder; Eng.: Frankfort on the Oder; Ger. city; university founded 1506, moved to Breslau 1811.

Frankfurt Declaration. Statements on mission adopted Mar. 4, 1970, Frankfurt, Ger., by Ger. confession-minded theologians. Holds 1. Christian mission discovers its foundation, goals, tasks, and the content of its proclamation solely in the commission of the resurrected Christ and His saving acts; 2. The first and supreme goal of mission is glorification of the name of the one God throughout the world and proclamation of the lordship of Christ, His Son; 3. Christ our Savior, true God and true man, is the basis, content, and authority of our mission; 4. Mission is the witness and presentation of eternal salvation performed in the name of Christ by His ch. and fully authorized messengers by preaching, the sacraments, and service; 5. The primary visible task of mission is to call out the messianic, saved community from among all people; 6. The offer of salvation is directed to all who are not yet bound to Christ in faith; 7. The Christian world mission is the decisive, continuous saving activity of God among men bet. the resurrection and the final coming of Christ.

Frankfurt Recess (Frankfort Agreement; Frankfort Book; *Formula pacis Francofordianae*). Document based on a recommendation of P. Melanchthon* and intended to settle dispute bet. Gnesio-Lutherans* led by M. Flacius* Illyricus and followers of Melanchthon. Signed Mar. 18, 1558, by Elector Otto Henry (Ottheinrich) of the Palatinate, Elector Augustus I of Saxony, Elector Joachim II of Brandenburg, Count Palatine Wolfgang of Zweibrücken, Duke Christopher of Württemberg, and Philip* of Hesse.

In the document the signers confess adherence to the Scriptures, ecumenical creeds, AC, and Ap.; treat the doctrines of justification, good works, Lord's Supper, and adiaphora; state resolutions not to divulge new controversies but present them to consistories and supts., not to pub. new theol. treatises without censorship, to prohibit pub. of libelous treatises, to forgive and forget old differences, to depose anyone who taught or practiced contrary to the confession, and to invite other estates to adopt the Frankfurt Recess. N. v. Amsdorf,* at Weimar, and M. Flacius Illyricus, at Jena, opposed the document; P. Melanchthon defended it. See also *Lutheran Confessions,* C 1.

Frankfurter, The. See *German Theology.*

Frankl, Viktor E. See *Psychotherapy,* 13.

Franks, Saxons, and Other Germanic Nations, Conversion of. See *Celtic Church; France; Germany.*

Franson, Fredrik (1852–1908). B. Swed.; to Am. ca. 1869; religious experience during illness 1871–72 led him to join Bap. Ch.; to Chicago ca. 1875; joined Moody Ch.; ordained 1881 in Ev. Free Ch., Phelps Center, Nebr.; revivalist and world miss.; founded miss. socs., including Evangelical* Alliance Mission.

Franz, Wolfgang (1564–1628). B. Plauen, Ger.; prof. hist. Wittenberg; exegete; Luth. apologist.

Franz von Sickingen. See *Sickengen Franz von.*

Franzelin, Johannes Baptist (1816–86). B. Aldein, Tyrol; Jesuit; cardinal; prof. Gregorian U., Rome; papal theol. at Vatican Council I. Works include *De divina traditione et Scriptura.*

Franzén, Frans Mikael. See *Sweden, Lutheranism in,* 4.

Fraternal Address. Popular name (from expression in Pa. Ministerium resolution authorizing it) of an invitation to all syns., pastors, and congs. pledged to the UAC to meet and form a syn. The address held that the General* Synod of the Ev. Luth. Ch. in the US could no longer serve the purpose of uniting all Luths. and that a syn. should be founded on a solid Luth. basis. The Fraternal Address is dated Aug. 10, 1866. Names appended: G. F. Krotel,* C. Porterfield Krauth,* W. J. Mann,* C. W. Schäffer,* J. A. Seiss.* See also *General Council of the Lutheran Church in North America,* 2.

Verhandlungen der Kirchenversammlung bestehend aus Delegaten verschiedener Evangelisch Lu-

therischen Synoden in den Vereinigten Staaten und Canada, welche sich zur Ungeänderten Augsburgischen Confession bekennen. Gehalten in Reading, Pa., vom 12. bis 14. Dec. 1866 (Allentown, Pa., 1867).

Fraternal Appeal to the American Churches, with a Plan for Catholic Union, on Apostolic Principles. Plan for union among Am. Prots. issued 1838 by S. S. Schmucker.* It included a proposed new creed called "Apostolic Protestant Confession," which consisted of 2 parts: the Apostles' Creed and United Protestant Confession. The latter contained 12 articles: I. Of the Scriptures; II. Of God and the Trinity; III. Of the Son of God and the Atonement; IV. Of Human Depravity; V. Of Justification; VI. Of the Church; VII. Of the Sacraments, Baptism and the Lord's Supper; VIII. Of Purgatory, etc.; IX. Liberty of Conscience; X. Of Civil Government; XI. Communion of Saints; XII. Of the Future Judgment and Retribution. Approved 1839 by the General* Synod of the Ev. Luth. Ch. in the US.

S. S. Schmucker, *Fraternal Appeal to the American Churches, with a Plan for Catholic Union, on Apostolic Principles,* 2d ed., enl. (Philadelphia, [1839]); V. Ferm, *The Crisis in American Lutheran Theology* (New York, 1927), pp. 113–16, 345–350. EL

Fraternities, Student. Students' societies at univs., colleges, and high schools; Gk. letters standing for Gk. words or phrases are commonly used to designate different fraternities. They usually have individual badges, coats of arms, flags, etc. Some have rituals based on Christian and pagan sources. Many are organized on a nat. basis with chaps. at individual institutions. Sororities are the female counterparts. See also *Students, Spiritual Care of,* A 3, C 9.

W. R. Baird, *Manual of American College Fraternities,* ed. H. J. Baily, 15th ed. (Menasha, Wis., 1949); A. M. Lee, *Fraternities Without Brotherhood* (Boston, 1955).

Fratres militiae Christi. See *Estonia,* 1.

Frazer, Edward (b. 1798). B. Barbados, W. Indies; Negro slave; joined Meth. Ch. 1819; freed and became miss. of Wesleyan Meth. Miss. Soc. to Dominica 1828.

Frazer, James George (1854–1941). Scot. anthropologist; b. Glasgow; educ. Glasgow and Cambridge; prof. Liverpool 1907. Held 3 stages in mental development of man: 1. Magic; man seeks to help himself through occult means; 2. Religion; religion is attempt to propitiate powers superior to man which are believed to direct and control the course of nature and of human life; 3. Science; man seeks to help himself through rational processes and careful observation. Works include *The Golden Bough; The Belief in Immortality and the Worship of the Dead; Folk-lore in the Old Testament; Aftermath: A Supplement to the Golden Bough.*

Frecht, Martin (1492–1556). B. Ulm, Ger.; educ. Heidelberg: heard M. Luther's* Heidelberg* disputation 1518; leader of ch. in Ulm and its reformer; opposed Sebastian Franck* and K. Schwenkfeld*; participant at 1536 Wittenberg* Concord, 1540 Colloquy of Worms,* and 1541 Regensburg* Conf.

Freder(us), Johannes (Fret[h]er; Fretther; Irenaeus; 1510 [or perhaps 1507]–1562). B. Köslin, Pomerania; educ. Wittenberg; vice-principal of school and cathedral pastor Hamburg; prof. theol. Greifswald; supt. Rügen and Wismar; visitor Mecklenburg. Regarded laying on of hands at ordination an adiaphoron and thereby became involved in controversy with J. Knipstro.*

Frederick I (Dan.: Frederik; ca. 1471–1533). King of Den. 1523–33, of Norw. 1524–33. See also *Denmark, Lutheranism in,* 2; *Norway, Lutheranism in,* 1.

Frederick III (Dan.: Frederik; 1609–70). King of Den. and Norw. 1648–70; held positions in the ch. 1623–34.

Frederick IV (Dan.: Frederik; 1671–1730). King of Den. and Norw. 1699–1730; patron of missions; sponsored Dan.-Halle miss. at Tranquebar, India, 1705–06 and a coll. for promoting the spread of the Gospel 1714 at Copenhagen, Den. See also *Plütschau, Heinrich; Ziegenbalg, Bartholomäus.*

Frederick I (Barbarossa; "Redbeard"; ca. 1122–90). Holy Roman emp. 1152–90, crowned 1155. Son of Duke Frederick II of Swabia; as Frederick III, duke of Swabia; king of Ger. 1152–90, It. 1155–90; one of the leaders of the 3d crusade (see *Crusades,* 4); led repeated campaigns against It. cities; engaged in struggles with Adrian IV (see *Popes,* 8), Alexander III (see *Popes,* 9), Lucius III (ca. 1097–1185; pope 1181–85), Urban III (pope 1185–Oct. 1187), and Clement III (pope Dec. 1187–91); by Peace of Constance 1183 granted indep. to Lombard cities. See also *Church and State,* 6.

Frederick II (1194–1250). Holy Roman emp. 1215–50, crowned 1220; as Frederick I, king of Sicily 1198–1212; king of Ger. 1215–50. Tried to unite It. and Ger.; excommunicated 3 times; leader of 6th crusade (see *Crusades,* 7).

Frederick III (1415–93). Holy Roman emp. 1440–93, crowned 1452; as Frederick IV, king of Ger.; as Frederick V, archduke of Austria. Concluded Concordat of Vienna with Nicholas V 1448. See also *Concordat,* 3.

Frederick II (1485–1556). "The Wise." Elector of the Palatinate 1544–56; became Prot. under influence of P. Melanchthon.*

Frederick III (1515–76). "The Pious." Father of Louis* VI of the Palatinate. Elector of the Palatinate 1559–76; educ. RC; became Luth. 1546, Calvinist 1561. Had Heidelberg Catechism drawn up 1563. See also *Reformed Confessions,* D 2.

Frederick III (1463–1525). "The Wise." Duke and elector of Ernestine Saxony 1486–1525. He never married but had 2 sons and a daughter by Anna Weller, whom he deeply loved. He was a devout, if sometimes misled, Christian prince. He went on a pilgrimage to Palestine 1493 and began collecting relics,* finally assembling the largest collection in Ger. (19,013 by 1520). He founded the U. of Wittenberg 1502 and engaged outstanding scholars (e. g., J. v. Staupitz,* Karstadt,* and the Schurff* brothers). He defrayed the expenses for the doctoral promotion of M. Luther* 1512. Though he never met Luther, he protected him. He did not permit Luther to follow a summons to Rome 1518 and arranged for him to be heard and defend himself (see *Augsburg Diet* [1518]; *Altenburg Conference; Worms, Diet of*). When Maximilian* I died, the crown was offered to Frederick; he declined it. But Leo X (see *Popes,* 20) and Charles* V were anxious to win his support and did not immediately press charges against Luther. When Luther was in danger after the Diet of Worms, Frederick saw to it that he was "kidnapped" and taken to the Wartburg.* Communion under 2 kinds was introd. 1521–22. Frederick abandoned veneration of relics 1523. Most of his lands became Luth. For pol. reasons he did not declare himself either for or against the Reformation until the day of his death, when he took Communion under both kinds.

I. Höss, *Georg Spalatin,* 1484–1545 (Weimar, 1956); E. O. Borkowsky, *Das Leben Friedrichs des Weisen, Kurfürsten zu Sachsen* (Jena, 1929); W. G. Tillmanns, *The World and Men Around Luther* (Minneapolis, 1959), pp. 296–298. WGT

Frederick Augustus I (elector of Saxony). See *Augustus II.*

Frederick Francis II (Ger.: Friedrich Franz; 1823–83). Grand duke of Mecklenburg-Schwerin 1842–83;

gen.; advanced cause of Lutheranism; supported T. F. D. Kliefoth.*

Frederick William III (Ger.: Friedrich Wilhelm; 1770–1840). King of Prussia 1797–1840; b. Potsdam. After the defeat of Prussia by Napoleon 1801–05, Frederick was roused by nation to oppose France, but was defeated at Jena and Auerstedt 1806; his kingdom dismembered by Treaty of Tilsit 1807; Prussia restored by victory at Leipzig 1813 and Blücher's victories. Joined Holy* Alliance 1815; issued order for common agenda 1798; decreed Prussian* Union 1817. See also *Agenda Controversy.*

Frederick William IV (Ger.: Friedrich Wilhelm; 1795–1861). King of Prussia 1840–61; son of Frederick* William III; forced to grant constitution by 1848 revolution. Issued the "Generalkonzession" July 23, 1845; it permitted Luths. who remained separate from the Prussian* Union to organize free chs. See also *Germany, Lutheran Free Churches in,* 1; *Old Lutherans.*

Frederick William of Brandenburg (Ger.: Friedrich Wilhelm; 1620–88). The "Great Elector"; elector 1640–88. See also *Cassel, Colloquy of; Gerhardt, Paul; Syncretism.*

Free Apostolic Christian Congregations. See *Lammers, Gustav Adolph.*

Free Association. See *Psychotherapy,* 11.

Free Christian Zion Church of Christ. See *Evangelistic Associations,* 15.

Free Church Federal Council. Formed 1940 in Eng. by merger of the National* Council of the Ev. Free Chs. and the Federal Council of Ev. Free Chs. (organized 1919 by J. H. Shakespeare.* Provides machinery for joint action by free chs.

Free Church of England. See *England, Free Church of.*

Free Church of Scotland. Formed under leadership of T. Chalmers* at the time of the disruption of the Est. Ch. of Scot., May 18, 1843, and the pub. signing of the Act of Separation and Deed of Demission, May 23, 1843. Result of failure of Veto Law (proposed by Chalmers 1833, passed 1834; intended to allow effective protest against calling a pastor disapproved by a majority of male family heads in a cong.) and civil court decisions declaring the ch., so far as it is established, a creation of the state and under state control. Ca. a third of pastors and people of the Est. Ch. joined the Free Ch.

The Declaratory Act of 1892 modified the Calvinistic doctrine of the Free Ch. (emphasized divine love, extended God's mercy to those beyond the means of grace, modified doctrine of total depravity, rejected intolerance, endorsed Ref. faith in substance).

With the United Presb. Ch. (see *Presbyterian Churches,* 1) it formed the United* Free Ch. of Scot. 1900.

See also *Presbyterian Churches,* 1; *Scotland, Reformation in,* 2.

T. Brown, *Annals of the Disruption,* new ed. (Edinburgh, 1893); J. Barr, *The United Free Church of Scotland* (London, 1934).

Free Churches (Germany). See *Germany, Lutheran Free Churches in.*

Free Evangelical Lutheran Synod in South Africa. See *Mission of the Evangelical Lutheran Free Churches.*

Free Lutheran Conferences. 1. Series of confs. attended by pastors and laymen at Columbus, Ohio, Oct. 1–7, 1856; Pittsburgh, Pa., Oct. 29–Nov. 4, 1857; Cleveland, Ohio, Aug. 5–11, 1858; Fort Wayne, Ind., July 14–20, 1859. Invitations to attend were extended to all who subscribed to the AC without reservation. The AC was discussed. The Ev. Luth. Synodical* Conf. was a fruit of the discussions.

2. The free Luth. confs. of 1903–06 tried to heal the rift in the Syn. Conf. caused by the predestinarian controversy of the 1880s (see *Predestinarian Controversy,* 2). Mems. of many Luth. bodies attended, but not as official representatives.

3. After a preliminary meeting of pastors in Beloit, Wis., May 14, 1902, confs. were held at Watertown, Wis., Apr. 29–30, 1903; Milwaukee, Wis., Sept. 9–11, 1903; Detroit, Mich., April 6–8, 1904; Fort Wayne, Ind., Aug. 8–10, 1905; Fort Wayne, Ind., Oct. 24–25, 1906. Participants included H. A. Allwardt,* G. J. Fritschel,* M. Fritschel,* A. L. Gräbner,* A. Hönecke,* J. P. Köhler,* F. Pfotenhauer,* A. Pieper,* F. A. O. Pieper,* J. M. Reu,* F. A. Schmidt,* F. W. Stellhorn,* G. Stoeckhardt.*

4. The Watertown meeting initiated a dialog, but the situation deteriorated from that point on, as mutual polemics and a deepening awareness of the extent of the rift took their toll.

5. Mo. Syn. (see *Lutheran Church – Missouri Synod, The*) men held that God's election of some in Christ is in no way caused by their future faith. Ohio Syn. (see *Ohio and Other States, Evangelical Lutheran Joint Synod of*) men taught election *intuitu* fidei.* But a deeper conflict became apparent already at the Milwaukee conference. Mo. Syn. men sought to operate with a specific, limited set of proof texts for election; mems. of the Ohio Syn. and of the Iowa Syn. (see *Iowa and Other States, Evangelical Lutheran Synod of*) took recourse to a broader use of Scripture on the basis of the "analogy* of faith." This difference in approach was spelled out further at 2 committee meetings prior to the Detroit conf. Both sides agreed to understand election on the basis of FC XI. But after the Detroit conf. further polemics embittered both sides.

6. Toward the middle of the 20th c. local free Luth. confs. were initiated. In May 1949 the Mo. Syn. Coll. of Presidents called for free confs. involving all Luth. bodies in America. Free Luth. confs. were also held in Japan and at Bad* Boll, Ger., ca. the middle of the 20th c.

See also *Diets, Lutheran, in America; England,* 17; *Lutheran Church – Missouri Synod, The,* V 13; *United Lutheran Church in America, The,* I.

E. L. Lueker, "Walther and the Free Lutheran Conferences," *CTM,* XV (Aug. 1944), 529–563; W. G. Polack, "Lutheran Unity: The Present Status," *Lutheran Witness,* LXVIII (June 14, 1949), 194–196.

Free Lutheran Diets. See *Diets, Lutheran, in America; United Lutheran Church in America, The,* I.

Free Magyar Reformed Church in America. See *Reformed Churches,* 4 d.

Free Methodist Church of North America. See *Methodist Churches,* 4 b.

Free Methodist Youth. See *Young People's Organizations, Christian,* III 13.

Free Presbyterian Church of Scotland. See *Presbyterian Churches,* 1.

"Free Salvation." See *Methodist Churches,* 2.

Free Spirit, Brothers and Sisters of the. Name given to various religious organizations of the Middle Ages that practiced personal piety and held that they were free from clerical authority. Their theol., quietistic and pantheistic mysticism, seems to have developed from the Victorines.*

Free Will. The Scriptural doctrine of the freedom of the human will is closely connected with the doctrine of original sin (see *Sin, Original*). The doctrine of the freedom of the human will after the fall* of man must be studied from the viewpoint of original sin. Scripture emphatically declares that man, also after the fall, continues to be a responsible moral agent, who in earthly matters, to some extent, may exercise freedom of will; but it asserts that "natural man receiveth not the things of the

Spirit of God, . . . neither can he know them" (1 Co 2:14); that man, by nature, is "dead in trespasses and sins" (Eph 2:1); that "the carnal mind is enmity against God" (Ro 8:7); and that "no man can say that Jesus is the Lord, but by the Holy Ghost" (1 Co 12:3). Accordingly, Scripture denies to man after the fall and before conversion* freedom of will in spiritual matters, and asserts that conversion is accomplished entirely through the Holy Ghost by the Gospel. God "hath saved us, . . . not according to our works, but according to His own purpose and grace" (2 Ti 1:9); "Turn Thou me, and I shall be turned" (Jer. 31:18).

Augustine* of Hippo taught that by the sin of Adam the whole human race, of which Adam was the root, was corrupted and subjected to death and eternal punishment. By this sin human nature is both physically and morally corrupted. By it also the freedom to do right has been lost and fallen man is free only to sin (*Enchiridion,* XXV–XXX, in *MPL,* 40:244–247; *De gratia et libero arbitrio,* in *MPL,* 44:881–912). This view of Augustine is in accord with Scripture, which declares that "it is God which worketh in you both to will and to do of His good pleasure" (Phil 2:13); it has been substantially adopted by the Luth. Ch., which, at the same time, rejects fatalism (FC Ep II 8, SD II 74).

Opposed to the Scriptural doctrine, Pelagianism has held that by his transgression Adam injured only himself, not his posterity; that in respect to his moral nature every man is born in precisely the same condition in which Adam was created; that there is, therefore, no original sin; that man's will is free, every man having the power to will and to do good as well as the opposite; hence it depends on himself whether he be good or evil. This extreme view of Pelagianists was modified by semi-Pelagianists and later by Arminians who denied total corruption and depravity of human nature by the fall and admitted only partial corruption.

The Belgic Confession, which states the strictly Reformed doctrine, says: "We believe that, through the disobedience of Adam, original sin is extended to all mankind; which is a corruption of the whole nature, and an hereditary disease, wherewith infants themselves are infected even in their mother's womb, and which produceth in man all sorts of sin, being in him as a root thereof; and therefore is so vile and abominable in the sight of God that it is sufficient to condemn all mankind."

RC theologians define original sin as a state and as a cause. Thus the term designates 1. a condition of guilt, weakness, or debility found in human beings prior to their own free option for good or evil *(peccatum originale originatum);* 2. the origin, cause, or source of that state *(peccatum originale originans).* Free will is defined as the freedom of the will either to act or not to act. Those who have attained the use of reason are saved only by cooperating freely with the saving grace of God. In the fall man did not lose *dona naturalia* (natural gifts, e. g., freedom of the will; immortality of the soul) but *dona supernaturalia* (supernatural gifts, e. g., perfect control over concupiscence; immortality of the body), esp. sanctifying grace.

Opposed to Pelagianism and semi-Pelagianism, Arminianism,* and synergism,* the Luth. Confessions emphasize the total depravity of human nature by the fall and man's utter lack of freedom in spiritual matters since the fall.

A. Augustinus [Augustine of Hippo], *The Problem of Free Choice,* tr. and annotated by M. Pontifex (Westminster, Md., 1955); *Martin Luther on the Bondage of the Will,* tr. J. I. Packer and O. R. Johnston (London, 1957); P. A. Bertocci, *Free Will, Responsibility, and Grace* (New York, 1957); A. M. Farrer, *The Freedom of the Will* (New York, 1960); *Discourse on Free Will [by] Erasmus [and] Luther,* ed. and tr. E. F. Winter (New York, 1961).

Freedom, Christian. In gen., there are 2 views of Christian freedom. One tries to express individual rights as defined and stimulated by the Renaissance* and 18th c. liberal thought in Christian terms; it describes man's self-expression and achievement of highest self-realization as a dynamic imparted by the Christian religion. The other adheres more closely to the NT view. It regards man innately subject to the forces of death and the devil. His Christian freedom is that he has been liberated by Christ Jesus and freed to serve God. Parallel to this is his freedom from the Law as an obligation he must fulfill in order to be godly and the gift of the Holy Spirit to desire what God wills. This freedom does not imply license to be ungodly or selfish, but is simply the will to concur with the will of God and to devote oneself completely to the welfare of man (Ro 14:15; 1 Co 8; Gl 5). This concept was given a fresh and classic expression by M. Luther,* *Von der Freiheit eines Christenmenschen.*

H. Thielicke, *The Freedom of the Christian Man,* tr. J. W. Doberstein (New York, 1963).

Freedom of the Will. See *Free Will.*

Freedom, John Edgar (Dec. 27, 1809–June 13, 1857). B. NYC; educ. Princeton Coll. and Sem.; sent as miss. to India by Presb. Bd. of For. Miss. 1838; at Allahabad till 1849; in US 1850–51; returned to India 1851; worked at Mainpuri; to Fategarh (Farrukhabad) 1856; killed by Sepoys at Cawnpore.

Freeman, Thomas Birch (1809–90). Brit. Wesleyan Meth. miss. to Ghana (Gold Coast). B. Twyford, Eng., of Negro father, white mother; arrived Cape Coast, Ghana, 1838; obtained friendship of king of Kumasi, "the city of blood," among the Ashantis; est. miss. work in Gold Coast, Nigeria, and areas bet.; resigned 1857 but returned to ministry 1873; retired 1885.

Freemasonry. 1. Ancient Free and Accepted Masons. This order traces its hist. to guilds of stone masons of the Middle Ages. The words "free and accepted" first appear 1722 in the name of the order. Membership in masonic associations was highly prized by men who traveled, because it offered assurance of assistance, hospitality, and good service. Operative masonry consisted of the total number of workmen that designed and erected bldgs.; they included freemasons, who worked in free stone, carved free hand, and used geometry. Operative Freemasonry descended from freemasons. Speculative (i. e. symbolic, theoretical) Freemasonry arose within Operative Freemasonry. Modern Speculative Freemasonry began in London 1717, when 4 lodges formed the Grand Lodge of England. Antiquity dating to Bible times is sometimes claimed for Masonic organizations, but such traditions are only legendary and cannot be substantiated. Masonic rituals have often been printed in code to assist the initiate in memorizing them; many deciphered versions have also appeared, as well as manuals and periodicals containing the symbols, ceremonies, and philos. of Masonry.

2. Speculative Freemasonry put deism in place of the Christian elements of former guild rituals. The name of Christ was eliminated from all prayers and Scripture passages. The fatherhood of God and the brotherhood of man became the dominant religious emphasis; a system of doctrines and symbolism was adopted. Masonry regards the Bible only as one of many valuable sacred books. It teaches resurrection of the body and immortality as religious doctrines, promising eternal bliss to all who follow Masonic ethics. Jesus Christ is not regarded as man's Redeemer.

3. The Blue Lodge, in which the first 3 degrees (Entered Apprentice, Fellow Craft, and Master

Mason) are conferred, constituted the essence of Freemasonry. Higher degrees are arranged for those who wish to pursue Masonic philos. farther.

4. Freemasonry at times adapts its program and philos. to the religious convictions of an area or country. In Eng. and Am., Freemasonry occasionally appears to support Prot. Christianity; but the "Christian" degrees of the Scot. Rite and the "Christian" Am. Rite contain nothing that would distinguish Christian from Muslim, Buddhist, or unitarian. The anti-Christian character of the ritual is recognized by those who make an indep. study of the ritual and of its interpretation by spokesmen of the order. The lambskin is a badge of Freemasonry; it is to remind the Mason of purity of life, essential for admission into the Celestial Lodge above, where the Supreme Architect of the Universe presides.

5. Order of the Eastern Star. Am. Rite of Adoption organized 1876 at Indianapolis, Ind.; membership limited to Master Masons and most of their female relatives. The ritual borrows heavily from Masonic philos.; includes references to Jesus but is deistic.

6. Order of the Rainbow. Organized 1922 at McAlester, Okla.; membership limited to girls who are children or close friends of mems. of the Masonic Lodge or Eastern Star. Each local lodge is sponsored by a Masonic or Eastern Star lodge. Religious emphasis centers in good deeds.

7. Order of Job's Daughters. Organized 1920 at Omaha, Nebr.; similar to the Order of the Rainbow, but its membership is somewhat broader, including more girls of families unaffiliated with Masonry. The ritual revolves around the faithfulness of Job and emphasizes righteous service.

8. Order of DeMolay. Organized 1919 at Kansas City, Mo.; membership limited to boys with close Masonic relatives; strives to teach patriotism, reverence and related virtues; functions as a preparation for Masonic membership; ritual approaches God apart from Jesus Christ and promises eternal life to those that abide by the philos. of the order.

9. Ancient Arabic Order of Nobles of the Mystic Shrine ("Shriners"). Organized 1876 at NYC; related to Masonry inasmuch as it admits into membership only Masons of the Knights Templar degree (York Rite) and 32d degree (Scot. Rite); it is a playground of the Masonic Lodge. The order has performed notable service in treatment and rehabilitation of crippled children regardless of color, creed, or nationality.

10. Membership. 1964 est.: 4,100,000 in the US; 5,887,000 worldwide; plus 1,000,000 in ca. 50 assoc. orders.

W. Hannah, *Darkness Visible* (London, 1952) and *Christian by Degrees* (London, 1954); W. J. Whalen, *Christianity and American Freemasonry* (Milwaukee, 1958); T. F. Nickel and J. G. Manz, *A Christian View of Freemasonry* (St. Louis, 1957); references under *Lodges.* TG, TFN, PHL

Freemasonry and the Church. The Masonic Order gen. maintains a friendly and tolerant attitude toward many Christian chs. Adherents of any ch. are eligible for membership. Charitable and hosp. services of Masonic organizations are available to all, regardless of religious affiliation. Strong humanitarianism is characteristic of the order.

Great antiquity has been claimed for Masonry. OT and NT saints are regarded by some as included in the antecedents of Masonry. Modern alignment with Protestantism has been accompanied by speculation that relates M. Luther* to the Craft of his day. A religious and pol. part in the work of the Reformation is claimed for allegedly Masonic 16th c. groups. All statements about ancient, medieval, and Reformation connections with Masonry are tenuous.

The definite and universal form of Freemasonry first appeared 1717 with the organization of the Grand Lodge in London. Christians then began to note its secrecy and basic deistic principle. The constitution (or bull) *In Eminenti,* issued 1738 by Clement XII (1652–1740; pope 1730–40), condemned Freemasonry on grounds of naturalism, required oaths, religious indifference, and potential threat to ch. and state. The RC Ch. is committed to definite ecclesiastical judgments concerning the religious and moral implications of membership in the order. Documents issued by later popes, esp. the encyclical *Humanum Genus,* issued 1884 by Leo XIII (see *Popes,* 29), have dealt with the Masonic question. The RC Ch. regards Deism,* naturalism,* liberalism,* and anticlericalism* as typical of Masonic religion and influence. Membership in Masonic and certain related orders results in excommunication (CIC 1399; 2335). E. Orthodox chs. also forbid Masonic membership to clergy and laity.

Luth. parishes and syns. have expressed themselves on the issue. A "lodge par." is found in the constitutions of many Luth. congs. Representative sentiment of Luths. in Am. is given in the 1925 Minneapolis* Theses. This statement was incorporated in the 1952 United Testimony on Faith and Life and is part of the Articles of Union of The ALC: "These synods agree that all such organizations or societies, secret or open, as are either avowedly religious or practice the forms of religion without confessing as a matter of principle the Triune God or Jesus Christ as the Son of God, come into the flesh, and our Savior from sin, or teach, instead of the Gospel, salvation by human works or morality, are anti-Christian and destructive of the best interests of the Church and the individual soul, and that, therefore, the Church of Christ and its congregations can have no fellowship with them." Major Luth. bodies in Am. agree regarding the basic religion of Freemasonry, but practices and procedures in dealing with Freemasons differ. Syn. Conf. Lutheranism was comparatively strict in practice. The *Handbook* (1967 ed., p. 213) of the LCMS contains the following: "It is the solemn, sacred, and God-given duty of every pastor properly to instruct his people on the sinfulness of such lodges as deny the Holy Trinity, the Deity of Christ, the Vicarious Atonement, and other Scriptural doctrines, and to induce his congregation(s) to take action against all members who after thorough instruction refuse to leave such a lodge." Masonry is not named specifically in these declarations. Orders related to and orders similar to Masonry are included. Genuine lodgery is held to be in conflict with the First Table of the Law, esp. the first 2 commandments.

Many Prot. chs. had rules forbidding Masonic membership. Some Ref. chs. still enforce such rules, but many allow Masonic membership. Masonic services, including funeral rites, have been held in Ref. chs. Many mems. of these chs. see in Masonic affiliation a connection that concerns only soc. and civic life.

Questions about Freemasonry and related orders are raised when ch. unity negotiations take place. The issue is also a source of some of the most vexing problems that arise in parish life. Full discussion of all factors involved raises vital issues that must be considered in the area of pastoral theol. JGM

W. Hannah, *Darkness Visible* (London, 1952) and *Christian by Degrees* (London, 1954); *Interseminary Series, II: The Church and Organized Movements,* ed. R. C. Miller (New York, 1946); W. J. Whalen, "Freemasonry," *New Catholic Encyclopedia,* VI (New York, 1967), 132–139, and *Christianity and American Freemasonry* (Milwaukee, 1958); *Doctrinal Declarations: A Collection of Official Statements on the Doctrinal Position of Various Lutheran Synods in America* (St. Louis, 1957);

Lutheranism and Lodgery (n. p., n. d.); T. F. Nickel and J. G. Manz, *A Christian View of Freemasonry* (St. Louis, 1957); J. W. Constable, "Lodge Practice Within the Missouri Synod," *CTM,* XXXIX, No. 7 (July–Aug. 1968), 476–496.

Freethinker. In gen., one who recognizes no other authority in religion than his own reason. In Eng. the term was applied to deists. Fr. freethinkers (e. g., Rousseau,* Voltaire,* and other Encyclopedists*) were usually agnostics, at times atheists. Ger. free thought led to organization of Freie Gemeinden (Free Congregations). Free thought is reflected in the 1789 Declaration of the Rights of Man and of the Citizen, which held that no one should be interfered with because of his views, also in religion, provided these views do not lead to disturbance of public order. See also *Agnosticism; Atheism; Collins, Anthony; Darwin, Charles Robert; Deism; Diderot, Denis; Lichtfreunde; Paine, Thomas; Shaftesburg, Anthony Ashley Cooper, Third Earl of; Spencer, Herbert.*

Free Will Baptist Foreign Missions. The Bd. of For. Missions of the Nat. Assoc. of Free Will Baptists was founded 1936. First missionaries were sent to India and Cuba. Later fields included Brazil, Ecuador, France, Ivory Coast, Panama, and Uruguay.

Freewill Baptist Foreign Missionary Society. Organized 1832 at N. Parsonsfield, Maine; inc. 1833. Its first missionaries were sent to India 1835.

Freewill Baptists. See *Baptist Churches,* 26.

Frege, Friedrich Ludwig Gottlob (1848–1925). B. Wismar, Ger.; mathematician and logician; prof. Jena; one of the founders of symbolic logic.* Works include *Grundgesetze der Arithmetik.*

Freie Gemeinden. See *Lichtfreunde.*

Freifeldt, Konrad Raimund (1847–1923). B. Dorpat (Tartu); entered Ger. Luth. ch. work in St. Petersburg (Leningrad) 1871; pres. gen. consistory Ev. Luth. Ch. in Russ. 1902, bp. 1918.

Frelinghuysen, Theodore Jacob (Theodorus Jacobus; 1691–ca. 1748; b. Lingen, Ger.; ordained Ref. Dutch Ch. 1717; served in Neth.; to N. Y. 1720; miss. N. J. Valley. See also *Great Awakening in England and America; Reformed Churches,* 4 b.

French, Thomas Valpy (1825—91). B. Burton on Trent, Eng.; educ. Rugby School and U. Coll., Oxford; miss. to Muslim in N India 1850; bp. Lahore 1877. See also *Middle East,* L 7.

French Catechism. See *Reformed Confessions,* A 7.

French Equatorial Africa. Former Fr. territory, NW Afr.; included Chad, Gabon, Middle Congo, and Ubangi-Shari. See also *Africa,* F 3–6.

French Guiana. See *South America,* 14.

French Indochina. Before 1946 consisted of Annam, Cambodia, Cochin China, Kwangchowan, Laos, and Tonkin. Annam, Tonkin, and Cochin China now form Vietnam. Kwangchowan was returned to China 1946. See also *Asia,* C 5–7.

French Protestant Synod (1559). See *France,* 8.

French Revolution. See *Church and State,* 15; *France,* 5; *Voltaire.*

French Somaliland. See *Africa,* E 4.

French Territory of the Afars and the Issas. See *Africa,* E 4.

French West Africa. Former Fr. territory; included Dahomey, Fr. Guinea, Fr. Sudan (Mali), Ivory Coast, Mauritania, Niger, Senegal, and Upper Volta. See also *Africa,* C 1–4, 8–10, 12.

French West Indies. See *Caribbean Islands,* E 6.

Frescobaldi, Girolamo (1583–ca. 1643). B. Ferrara, It.; organist at St. Peter's, Rome; court organist at Florence 1628–ca. 1633; influenced Ger. music esp. through his pupil J. J. Froberger.* Works include canzoni, caprices, hymns, madrigals,* motets, and toccatas.*

Handbuch der Musikgeschichte, ed. G. Adler (Frankfurt am Main, 1924); G. Frotscher, *Geschichte des Orgelspiels und der Orgelkomposition,* 2 vols. (Berlin, 1935–[36]); P. H. Láng, *Music in Western Civilization* (New York, 1941).

Fresenius, Johann Philip (1705–61). B. Niederwiesen, Ger.; pietist; Luth. pastor Niederwiesen, Giessen, Darmstadt, and Frankfurt am Main; interested in Am. missions; aided J. C. Stoever* Sr. and Jr. Works include *Evangelische Predigten.*

Freud, Sigmund (1856–1939). B. Freiberg, Moravia, of Jewish extraction; educ. U. of Vienna; studied in Paris under Fr. neurologist Jean Martin Charcot (1825–93); founded psychoanalysis; developed technique for treating hysteria and neuroses. In *Die Zukunft einer Illusion* he describes religion as a neurosis of mankind in which the concept of God is a fictitious extension of the human father ideal as a refuge from fear. See also *Psychology,* J 6; *Psychotherapy,* 10, 11.

E. Jones, *The Life and Work of Sigmund Freud,* 3 vols. (New York, 1953–57).

Freund(t), Cornelius (ca. 1535–91). Ger. hymnist; b. Plauen; precentor in Borna, near Leipzig, later in Zwickau. Wrote "Freut euch, ihr Menschenkinder all'."

Freylinghausen, Johann Anastasius (1670–1739). Theol., composer, and poet; b. Gandersheim, Brunswick, Ger.; educ. Jena, Erfurt, and Halle; A. H. Francke's* asst. at Glaucha; married his daughter; later was his colleague at St. Ulrich's, Halle; succeeded Francke to that pastorate; with G. A. Francke* he headed institutions est. by A. H. Francke; ed. collections of hymns, including *Geistreiches Gesangbuch* and *Neues Geistreiches Gesangbuch;* composed 22 hymn tunes, including one for "Macht hoch die Tür."

Freystein, Johann Burkhard (1671–1718). B. Weissenfels, Ger.; educ. Leipzig and Jena; lawyer, principally at Dresden; influenced by P. J. Spener.* Hymnist; hymns include "Mache dich, mein Geist, bereit."

Friar (from Lat. *frater,* "brother"). Mem. of a RC mendicant* order.

Friars Minor. See *Franciscans.*

Frick, Heinrich (1893–1952). B. Darmstadt, Ger.; prof. Giessen and Marburg. Coed. *Einführung in das Studium der Evangelischen Theologie.* Other works include *Die Kirchen und der Krieg; Vergleichende Religionswissenschaft; Die evangelische Mission: Ursprung, Geschichte, Ziel.*

Frick, William Keller (Feb. 1, 1850–Aug. 20, 1918). Luth. clergyman; b. Lancaster, Pa.; educ. Muhlenberg Coll., Allentown, Pa.; ordained 1873; pastor Philadelphia 1873–83; prof. Gustavus Adolphus Coll., Saint Peter, Minn., 1883–89; miss. in Wash. and Oreg. 1889; helped found Eng. Luth. work in Wis.; pastor Ch. of the Redeemer, Milwaukee, 1889–1918. Pres. Eng. Ev. Luth. Syn. of the Northwest 1894–1901. Wrote *Henry Melchior Muhlenberg.*

Fricke. See *Frincke.*

Fridolin. See *Germany,* A 1.

Fridrichsen, Anton Johnson (1888–1953). B. Meraker, Norw.; prof. Oslo and Uppsala; espoused "realistic" theol. that made concept of ch. central. Works include *The Apostle and His Message; Johannesevangeliet; Markusevangeliet.*

Friedrich. Ger. form of Frederick (q. v.).

Friedrich, Gerhard. See *Lexicons,* B.

Friedrich, Johann(es) (1836–1917). Theol. and hist.; b. Poxdorf, Upper Franconia, Ger.; educ. Bamberg and Munich; RC priest 1859; prof. Munich; opposed papal infallibility at Vatican Council I; excommunicated 1872; leader of Old* Catholics; helped est. Old Cath. theol. faculty at U. of Bern 1874.

Friendly Islands. See *Tonga Islands.*

Friends, Society of. 1. Commonly called Quakers; religious body founded ca. 1652 in Eng. by G. Fox.* Followers first called themselves Children of Truth, or Children of Light; finally adopted the name Religious Society of Friends. Their number grew rapidly, including many of the higher classes, ministers, army officers, justices. Converts included W. Penn* and R. Barclay.* During the first decades Friends suffered much persecution, largely because they held pub. meetings (other nonconformists met in secret); they also disparaged clergy, sacraments, and chs., interrupted services, and refused to take oaths, pay tithes, and take off hats as a show of deference. By 1656 Quakerism reached New Eng., where it encountered persecution esp. by Puritans* in Mass., who hanged 4 Quakers in Boston. Pa. offered Quakers an asylum where they prospered and became known for their kind treatment of Indians and their efforts toward abolition of slavery.

2. The Soc. of Friends as a whole recognizes the hist. value of the ecumenical creeds but does not regard them as binding; some declarations of faith have been issued (e. g., those of 1658, 1663, 1671, 1693, and 1887) in self-defense or for the information of non-Quakers. The declaration adopted 1879 in Ohio ran counter to conservative Quaker teaching in holding that God saves through preaching. Barclay and his followers acknowledged the Father, Son, and Holy Ghost, but Quakers often moved in thought-patterns of dynamic monarchianism (see *Monarchianism,* A) and anti-Trinitarianism. Other teachings result from the "inner light" theory. This theory, not agreed on in detail by all Quakers, holds in gen. that God communicates with man, that He does not leave Himself without witness in man's heart, and that the measure of light thus given grows by obedience. The redemption of Christ is not sufficient, but gives man the power to complete it; an inward redemption must follow, accomplished when the capacity for justification becomes active. Justification is not a declaratory act, but a moral change enabling the believer to acquire righteousness by works. God gives His Spirit also without the means of His Word; it is possible to be saved without knowledge of the hist. Christ. All who are illumined by the "inner light" and are obedient to it are mems. of the ch. Baptism and the Lord's Supper are regarded as mere rites without intrinsic value. Services are completely nonliturgical. Assembled worshipers sit silently until someone is called by the "inner light" to speak. If no one is so moved the meeting ends in silence. God did not institute a special ministry. But ministers are employed, though not ordained; most of them do not receive salary.

3. Quakers believe that the dignity and essential worth of the individual rest on the measure of the Spirit that he possesses. They believe in the brotherhood of man and respect for human rights. They advocate broad humanitarianism and are active in many phases of philanthropy. They are opposed in principle to participation in war, capital punishment, and litigation. Ch. organization is simple, including Monthly, Quarterly, and Yearly Meetings. 1963: 1,100 Friends socs. in US; 128,630 mems.

4. Friends United Meeting (formerly Five Years Meeting of Friends). Organized 1902; largest Friends body in US; composed of 14 Yearly Meetings, including 3 outside the US; belongs to NCC. 1967: 502 chs.; 70,673 mems.

5. Oregon Yearly Meeting of Friends Church. Withdrew from Five Years Meeting 1926. 1967: 63 chs.; 6,055 mems.

6. Religious Society of Friends, Kansas Yearly Meeting. Withdrew from Five Years Meeting 1937. 1966: 89 chs.; 8,227 mems.

7. Religious Society of Friends (Conservative). "Wilburites"; founded 1845 by John Wilbur (1774–1856) of R. I.; separated from main body of Friends to maintain primitive teachings. 1961: 21 chs.; 1,696 mems.

8. Religious Society of Friends (General Conference). "Hicksites"; followers of Elias Hicks (1748–1830), who led the most liberal elements of Friends into separation 1827–28; composed of 8 Yearly Meetings and 1 Quarterly Meeting. 1967: 292 chs.; 31,670 mems., including Philadelphia Yearly Meeting of the Religious Society of Friends, which is a mem. of the NCC.

9. Central Yearly Meeting of Friends. Ev. and fundamental group with chs. in Ohio, Ark., Mich., Ind., and missions in Bolivia. 1963: 12 chs.; 534 mems.

10. Ohio Yearly Meeting of Friends Church (Evangelical Friends Alliance). Name changed 1971 to Ev. Friends Ch., Eastern Region. Cen. office in Damascus, Ohio. 1971; 85 chs.; 7,874 mems.

11. Pacific Yearly Meeting of Friends. Est. 1947 at Palo Alto, California. 1967: 36 chs.; 2,227 mems.

See also *Keith, George; Perfectionism,* 3; *Scotland, Reformation in,* 5; *Shakers.*

Friends Foreign Missionary Association. Organized in Eng. 1865; early miss. work in India, Madagascar, and China; later fields include Pemba (Zanzibar) and Syria.

Friends of Augsburg. See *Lutheran Free Church.*

Friends of God (Gottesfreunde). Group of 14th c. Rhenish and Swiss mystics who drew this name probably from such passages as Ex 33:11; Is 41:8; Jn 15:14-15; Ja 2:23 to express freedom from servitude through Christ and elevation to true friendship with God. Most had no organization, but some extremes formed separate societies. Teachers included J. Eckhart,* Henry* of Nördlingen, H. Suso,* J. Tauler.* Rulman* Merswin, their chief author, refers to an unidentified and probably fictitious "Great Friend," who, after sudden conversion among worldly pleasures, allegedly withdrew to a mountain in Austria. C. and M. Ebner* were prominent in the movement.

Friends Service Council. Organized 1918 as Friends Council for Internat. Service to help relieve postwar human distress and promote peace and internat. understanding. Awarded 1947 Nobel Peace Prize jointly with Am. Friends Service Committee.

Friends Syrian Mission. Organized 1874 to support schools and other institutions in the Middle* East. United with Friends* For. Miss. Assoc. 1898.

Friends Youth Fellowship. See *Young People's Organizations, Christian,* III, 19.

Fries, Jakob Friedrich (1773–1843). Ger. philos.; b. Barby, Saxony; educ. Leipzig and Jena; prof. Heidelberg 1805, Jena 1816. Favored doctrines of I. Kant,* but held that the mind can directly grasp transcendental truth through "Ahn(d)ung." Works include *System der Logik; System der Metaphysik; Neue oder anthropologische Kritik der Vernunft; Wissen, Glaube und Ahndung.*

Frincke, Carl Heinrich Friedrich (Karl Fricke; July 13, 1824–June 5, 1905). B. Brunswick, Ger.; through influence of F. C. D. Wyneken,* he studied theol. under W. Sihler*; grad. Luth. Nothelferseminar (emergency sem.), Fort Wayne, Ind., 1847; present at the organization meeting of the Mo. Syn. 1847 (see *Lutheran Church – Missouri Synod, The,* I 8); commissioned May 6, 1847, Mo. Syn. traveling miss. to Luth. settlements in the Midwest (Ohio, Ind., Ill., and Wis.) that had no pastor; ordained Fort Wayne, Ind., Nov. 7, 1847; pastor White Creek, Ind., Nov. 1847, Indianapolis, Ind., 1851, Baltimore, Md., 1868.

Frith, John (Fryth; 1503–33). Eng. Prot. martyr; b. Westerham, near Sevenoaks, Kent; educ. Eton and King's Coll., Cambridge; made jr. canon of Cardinal Coll. (later Christ Ch.), Oxford, by T. Wolsey* 1525; acquainted with W. Tyndale*; imprisoned for reformation views; released at request of Wolsey; to Marburg, Ger., where he met P. Hamilton* and assisted Tyndale; wrote against T. More* and J.

Fisher*; returned to Eng. 1532; imprisoned 1532; burned at the stake at Smithfield July 4, 1533. Learned and pious. Denied purgatory, transubstantiation, and papal infallibility.

Fritsch, Ahasverus (Ahasuerus; 1629–1701). B. Mücheln, Ger.; tutor to Count Albert Anton of Schwarzburg-Rudolstadt 1657; university chancellor and pres. of the consistory, Rudolstadt; poet; hymnist; ed. *Himmelslust und Welt-Unlust.*

Fritschel. Mems. of the Fritschel family have been prominent in the Ev. Luth. Syn. of Iowa* and Other States and in the ALC.

1. Conrad Sigmund (Dec. 2, 1833–Apr. 26, 1900). B. Nürnberg, Ger.; attended miss. inst. founded by J. K. W. Löhe* at Nürnberg and relocated as a sem. 1853 at Neuendettelsau*; commissioned for work in Iowa 1854; arrived at Dubuque, Iowa, July 1854; helped organize the Ev. Luth. Syn. of Iowa*; pastor in Wis. and Mich.; prof. Wartburg Theol. Sem. (see *Ministry, Education of,* X P) 1858–1900; taught OT exegesis,* dogmatics,* and pastoral* theol.; collected funds in Eur. for the sem.; mem. of the commission of the General* Council of the Luth. Ch. in N. Am. that issued the *Kirchenbuch für Evangelisch-Lutherische Gemeinden.* Sigmund and his brother Gottfried (see par. 2 below), called *par nobile fratrum* (Lat. "a noble pair of brothers"), were leading theologians of the Iowa Syn. They issued *Kirchen-Blatt* (Ger. ch. paper) and *Kirchliche Zeitschrift* (theol. monthly). In many cases it is impossible to ascertain which of the two is author of a specific art.; as a rule, they discussed every phase of an art. before pub. it. Polemical articles were often against theologians of the Mo. Syn. (see *Lutheran Church – Missouri Synod, The*), with whom they differed chiefly on "open* questions," predestination,* unionism,* and eschatology.* They are often described as having been sincere in their desire for sound and united Lutheranism in Am. but of a somewhat milder type than the strict orthodoxy* of the Mo. Syn.

2. Gottfried Leonhard Wilhelm (Dec. 19, 1836–July 13, 1889). Brother of Sigmund (see par. 1 above); b. Nürnberg, Ger.; studied at Neuendettelsau inst. of Löhe and U. of Erlangen; commissioned 1856 to be prof. at the theol. sem., Dubuque, Iowa; ordained at Dubuque 1857; miss. in Ill. and Iowa; prof. 1857–89; taught NT exegesis, ch. hist., dogmatics, symbolics; ed. *Kirchen-Blatt* and *Kirchliche Zeitschrift;* learned Eng. and Scand. languages. Works include *Passionsbetrachtungen; Theophilus.*

3. Maximilian Christopher Immanuel (Feb. 21, 1868–Jan. 1, 1940). Son of Sigmund (see par. 1 above); b. St. Sebald, Iowa; educ. Wartburg Coll., Mendota, Ill., Thiel Coll., Greenville, Pa., and the univs. of Rostock, Erlangen, and Leipzig; prof. Wartburg Sem. 1891; pres. 1906.

4. Karl August Johannes (June 24, 1863–Aug. 23, 1943). Son of Sigmund (see par. 1 above); b. St. Sebald, Iowa; educ. Wartburg Coll. and Sem., Mendota, Ill., Thiel Coll., Greenville, Pa., and the univs. of Leipzig and Erlangen; ordained 1885; pastor Butler Center, Iowa; prof. Wartburg Coll. (see *Ministry, Education of,* VIII B 28) over 50 yrs.

5. George John (May 24, 1867–Oct. 5, 1941). Son of Gottfried (see par. 2 above); b. St. Sebald, Iowa; studied at Wartburg Coll. and Sem., Mendota, Ill., Thiel Coll., Greenville, Pa., and later in life at univs. of Rostock, Erlangen, and Leipzig; asst. prof. Wartburg Sem., Mendota, Ill.; pastor West Superior, Wis.; prof. Tex. Luth. Coll., Brenham, Tex., 1892, Wartburg Sem. 1906. Worked for unity with Mo. Syn. Works include *Aus den Tagen der Väter; Geschichte der Lutherischen Kirche in Amerika auf Grund von Prof. Dr. H. E. Jacobs "History of the Evang. Luth. Church in the United States"; Die Lehre von der Bekehrung nach D. Hoeneckes Dogmatik; Quellen und Dokumente zur Geschichte und Lehrstellung der ev.-luth. Synode von Iowa u. a. Staaten; The Formula of Concord.*

6. Herman Lawrence (May 15, 1869–Nov. 23, 1957). Son of Gottfried (see par. 2 above); b. St. Sebald, Iowa; educ. Wartburg Sem. and univs. of Leipzig and Erlangen; ordained 1892; parish pastor 10 yrs.; pres. and gen. dir. Passavant Institutions in W Pa., Wis., and Ill.; dir. Milwaukee Hospital; rector Luth. Deaconess Motherhouse, Milwaukee.

A. Spaeth, *S. Fritschel, D. D.: A Short Biography* (Waverly, Iowa, 1901); H. L. Fritschel, *Biography of Professor Dr. Conrad Sigmund Fritschel . . . And of Professor Dr. Gottfried Leonhard Wilhelm Fritschel* (Milwaukee, 1951). JHB

Fritz, John Henry Charles (July 30, 1874–Apr. 12, 1953). B. Martins Ferry, Ohio; grad. Conc. Coll., Fort Wayne, Ind., 1894, Conc. Sem., St. Louis, Mo., 1897; pastor Bismarck and Pilot Knob, Mo., 1897–1901, Our Savior, Brooklyn, N. Y., 1901–14, Bethlehem, St. Louis, Mo., 1914–20; pres. Western Dist., Mo. Syn., 1919–20; prof. ch. hist. and pastoral theol., Conc. Sem., St. Louis, 1920–53; dean Conc. Sem., St. Louis, 1920–40; coorganizer St. Louis Noonday Lenten Services; cofounder LCMS radio and TV miss. Noted for loyalty to Word of God, insistence that all the content and words of the Bible are inspired, and interest in Bible class and pastoral work. Contributed to *The Lutheran Witness* and *CTM;* ed. *Der Lutheraner* 1949–53; other works include *The Practical Missionary; Pastoral Theology; The Essentials of Preaching; The Preacher's Manual.*

Fritzsche, Gotthard Daniel (July 20, 1797–Oct. 26, 1863). B. Liebenwerde, Ger.; student of J. G. Scheibel* at Breslau; invited by J. A. A. Grabau* to immigrate to US; declined; invited by A. L. C. Kavel,* he led a band of emigrants to Australia 1841 and founded Bethany and Lobethal 1842. See also *Australia, Lutheranism in,* A 1.

Fritzsche, Karl Friedrich August (1801–46). B. Steinbach, Ger.; brother of O. F. Fritzsche*; prof. Leipzig 1825, Rostock 1826, Giessen 1841; chiefly interested in textual criticism and in the linguistic element in exegesis; rationalistic theol. Works include *De nonnullis posterioris Pauli ad Corinthios epistolae locis dissertationes duae;* commentaries on Mt, Mk, and Ro.

Fritzsche, Otto Fridolin (1812–96). B. Dobrilugk, Ger.; brother of K. F. A. Fritzsche*; prof. Zurich 1837. Works include writing on NT exegesis, ch. hist., OT apocrypha, and textual criticism.

Fröbel. See *Froebel.*

Frodoard. See *Flodoard.*

Froebel, Friedrich Wilhelm August (Fröbel; 1782–1852). B. Oberweissbach, Thuringia; founded kindergarten 1837 at Blankenburg, Thuringia; held that the work of the educator is primarily guidance; education permits, stimulates, leads, and directs self-activity and expression of a child's inner nature.

Froeschel. See *Fröschel.*

Frohschammer, Jakob (1821–93). B. Illkofen, near Regensburg, Ger.; philos. and theol.; priest 1847; prof. philos. Munich 1855; conceived of the world as resulting from the imagination of God. Many early writings placed on the Index* of Prohibited Books. Attacked the view of Thomas* Aquinas that philos. is the handmaid of theol. and upheld the indep. of philos. from the authority of the ch. Excommunicated 1871. Works include *Einleitung in die Philosophie und Grundriss der Metaphysik; Über die Freiheit der Wissenschaft.*

Frommel, Emil Wilhelm (1826–96). B. Karlsruhe, Ger.; brother of M. Frommel*; educ. Halle, Erlangen, and Heidelberg; pastor Karlsruhe 1855, Barmen 1862; military chaplain Berlin 1869; court preacher 1872. Works include *Das Gebet des Herrn.*

Frommel, Gaston (1862–1906). B. Altkirch, Alsace;

prof. theol. Geneva; follower of A. R. Vinet*; tried to construct doctrine by reference to moral consciousness.

Frommel, Max (1830–90). B. Karlsruhe, Ger.; brother of E. W. Frommel*; through G. C. A. von Harless* a decided Luth.; for a time in Breslau* Syn.; gen. supt. Celle. Works include *Kirche der Zukunft, oder: Zukunft der Kirche; Der Kampf der deutschen Freikirche in der Gegenwart und seine Bedeutung für die Zukunft; Hauspostille; Herzpostille.*

Fronius, Marcus (Markus; 1659–1713). B. Kronstadt, Transylvania (Siebenbürgen); Luth. pastor in Transylvania; pedagogical reformer in sense of J. A. Comenius*; influenced by pietism.*

Frontal. Covering of the front of an altar; often embroidered cloth; sometimes ornamented wood or metal panel; usually changeable, its color agreeing with the liturgical season (see *Colors, Liturgical*).

Frosch, Johann(es) (ca. 1480–1533). B. Bamberg, Ger.; Carmelite*; studied at Wittenberg; prior of Carmelites at Augsburg; Luth. preacher; opposed Zwinglians; expelled from Augsburg 1531; pastor Nürnberg; poet; composer. Tracts on music include *Rerum musicarum opusculum rarum ac insigne.*

Fröschel, Sebastian (1497–1570). B. Amberg, Ger.; intimate friend of M. Luther* and P. Melanchthon*; present at disputation bet. Luther and J. Eck* at Leipzig 1519; asst. of J. Bugenhagen* at Wittenberg 1525. Works include *Catechismus wie der in der Kirchen zu Witteberg nu viel jar, auch bey Leben D. M. Lutheri ist gepredigt worden; Von den heiligen Engeln, Vom Teuffel, und des Menschen Seele: Drey Sermon, mit des Herrn P. Melanchthon Definition und Erklerung.*

Frothingham, Nathaniel Langdon (1793–1870). B. Boston, Mass.; educ. Harvard; Unitarian pastor Boston 1815–50; poet. *Metrical Pieces* pub. in 2 vols. Hymns include "O Lord of Life and Truth and Grace."

Froude, Richard Hurrell (1803–36). B. Dartington, Eng.; educ. Oxford; close friend of J. H. Newman*; cofounded Oxford Movement (see *Tractarianism*).

Frühwirth, Franz Andreas (1845–1933). B. St. Anna, Styria, Austria; Dominican*; gen. of the order 1891–1904; cardinal 1915. Promoted the writing of the hist. of his order and pub. of works of Thomas* Aquinas and Albertus* Magnus.

Fruits of Islam. See *Lost-Found Nation of Islam in the Wilderness of North America, The.*

Fruits of the Spirit. Effects produced in man by the indwelling Spirit: love, joy, peace, longsuffering (patience), gentleness (kindness), goodness, faith (fidelity), meekness (gentleness), temperance (self-control). Called "harvest of the Spirit" in *The New English Bible.* Gl 5:22-23.

Frumentius (ca. 300–ca. 380). "Apostle of the Abyssinians." B. Tyre, Phoenicia; of Gk. extraction; captured on a voyage, he and a companion became assistants of the Ethiopian king and carried on miss. work; consecrated bp. of Aksum by Athanasius*; called *abuna* ("our father") and Abba Salamah ("father of peace").

Fry, Charles Luther (Mar. 16, 1894–Apr. 12, 1938). B. Philadelphia, Pa.; educ. Muhlenberg Coll. (Allentown, Pa.) and Columbia U. (NYC); prof. U. of Rochester (N. Y.) 1933; made numerous studies and surveys in sociology and religion. Works include *Diagnosing the Rural Church; The U. S. Looks at Its Churches:* text of the summary vol. of 1926 Fed. Census of Religious Bodies.

Fry, Elizabeth (nee Gurney; 1780–1845). B. Norwich, Eng.; "The Female Howard" (see *Howard, John*); sister of J. J. Gurney; Quaker minister 1811; began to visit prisons 1813. As a result, societies for prison reform were organized in Gt. Brit. and many continental countries.

Fry, Franklin Clark (Aug. 30, 1900–June 6, 1968). Luth. clergyman; b. Bethlehem, Pa.; educ. Hamilton Coll. (Clinton, N. Y.), Philadelphia (Pa.) Luth. Sem., Am. School for Classical Studies (Athens, Greece), and Muhlenberg Coll. (Allentown, Pa.); ordained ULC 1925; pastor Yonkers, N. Y., 1925–29, Akron, Ohio, 1929–44; pres. ULC 1945–62, LCA 1962–68, LWF 1957–63; pres. Luth. World Relief, Inc., 1946–68; dir. Ch. World Service, Inc., 1946–50; dir. Wittenberg Coll., Springfield, Ohio, 1934–38; chm. WCC Cen. Committee and Ex. Committee 1954–68. Noted for parliamentary skill, aggressive leadership, organizational ability, unity efforts, philanthropic interests. Ed. *Geschichtswirklichkeit und Glaubensbewährung: Festschrift für Bischof D. Friedrich Müller.*

E. W. Modean, "A Giant in the Land," *The Lutheran Standard,* VIII, 13 (June 25, 1968), 17, 30 (reprint. *CHIQ,* XLI, 3 [Aug. 1968], 117–119).

Fry, Franklin Foster (Nov. 1, 1864–Dec. 13, 1933). Luth. clergyman; b. Carlisle, Pa.; son of J. Fry*; educ. Muhlenberg Coll. (Allentown, Pa.) and Philadelphia (Pa.) Luth. Sem.; ordained 1888; acting pastor Reading and Easton, Pa., 1890; pastor Bethlehem, Pa., 1890–1901, Rochester, N. Y., 1901–27; leader in organizing ULC; mem. ULC Ex. Bd.; delegate to 1st World Convention of Luths., Eisenach, 1923; ex. secy. ULC Bd. of Am. Missions 1927; pres. N. Y. and New Eng. Syn.

Fry, Jacob (Feb. 9, 1834–Feb. 19, 1920). B. Trappe, Pa.; educ. Union Coll. (Schenectady, N. Y.) and Luth. Theol. Sem., Gettysburg, Pa.; ordained 1853; prof. Philadelphia (Pa.) Luth. Sem. 1891. Works include *Elementary Homiletics; The Pastor's Guide.*

Fryth. See *Frith.*

Fuerbringer, Ludwig Ern(e)st (Fürbringer; Mar. 29, 1864–May 6, 1947). Son of O. Fuerbringer*; b. Frankenmuth, Mich.; grad. Conc. Sem., St. Louis, Mo., 1885; pastor Frankenmuth, Mich., 1885–93; prof. Conc. Sem., St. Louis, 1893–1947; pres. 1931–43; pres. Synodical* Conf. 1927–44.

Combined strong pastoral sense with fluent literary activity and scholarship across a broad front, esp. in Biblical exegesis. Strongly conservative in some respects of the latter (repudiation of source hypothesis [see *Higher Criticism,* 6], simplified view of the Bible canon,* Messianic prophecy understood in terms of E. W. Hengstenberg*), but his exegetical lectures also revealed mastery of contemporary, esp. Ger., scholarship (influenced by T. Zahn*) and moved ahead of his time in stress on unity of the Testaments, salvation hist., and the eschatological tension bet. the present and the Parousia.* Displayed remarkable alertness to cultural values of his ch. and community and phenomenal memory for the 2 generations of his students and their families. Free and open in discussion, but cautious in establishing policy. Often progressive in educ., soc., and pol. areas.

Works include *80 Eventful Years; Persons and Events; The Eternal Why; Theologische Hermeneutik; Einleitung in das Alte Testament; Einleitung in das Neue Testament; Liturgik.* Ed. *Der Lutheraner* 1896–1912, 1917–47; *Synodalhandbuch* and *Statistisches Jahrbuch* of the Mo. Syn.; *Briefe von C. F. W. Walther;* the *Men and Missions* series; sermons: *The Thomasius Gospel Selections; Die Evangelischen Perikopen des Kirchenjahres;* rev. eds. of M. Günther's* *Populäre Symbolik.* RRC

Fuerbringer, Ottomar (Fürbringer; June 30, 1810–July 12, 1892). B. Gera, Thuringia; studied theol. at Leipzig 1828–30 with C. F. Walther,* T. J. Brohm,* J. F. Bünger,* and others of the circle led by an elderly candidate named Kühn. Instructor 1831–38 in an institute for boys at Eichenberg, conducted by G. H. Löber; to Am. 1839 in the Saxon immigration (see *Lutheran Church – Missouri Synod,* I 1-2); with

Brohm and Bünger founded Conc. Coll., Perry Co., Mo.; 1st instructor in classic languages and hist. Pastor Venedy, Ill., 1840. Helped draw up Mo. Syn. const.; present 1847 at the 1st meeting of the Syn.; became a voting mem. 1848 at the 2d meeting. Pastor of the congs. in Freistadt and Kirchhayn, Wis., 1851 and was drawn into the controversy with the Buffalo* Syn.; his articles appeared in *Der Lutheraner.* Pres. N. Dist., Mo. Syn., 1854–72, 1875–82. Pastor Frankenmuth, Mich., 1858–92. At the beginning of the Civil War he called together unmarried men in his parish and persuaded them voluntarily to fill the quota of men demanded from their county in order that husbands and fathers might be exempted from military service. Pastoral wisdom combined with Luth. soundness characterized his pastoral work; his deep learning and simple, popular style made him an effective preacher and catechist; regarded by some as the profoundest thinker among the fathers of the Mo. Syn.

W. G. Polack, "Ottomar Fuerbringer," *CTM,* V (1934), 211–217 (reprint in *CHIQ,* VII [1934], 42–50).

Fugue (from It. *fuga,* "flight"). Contrapuntal musical composition in which 1 or more themes flee, as it were, pursued, so to say, by repetition or imitation in voices entering successively. Most fully developed by J. S. Bach.* See also *Canon,* 3.

Führich, Joseph von (1800–76). B. Kratzau, Bohemia; Austrian romantic painter assoc. with the Nazarenes (see *Nazarenes,* 3); revived style of earlier ages, esp. that of A. Dürer*; master of distribution, form, movement, and expression, but inferior in feeling for color. Works include "The Incarnation"; "The Prodigal Son"; etchings; designs for woodcuts and steel engravings.

Fulbert de Chartres (ca. 960–1028). Probably of Fr. extraction; studied at Reims under Gerbert (see *Popes,* 6); founded school at Chartres 990; propagated secular learning; upheld ch. against nobles; distinguished bet. human knowledge and divine revelation. Bp. Chartres 1006.

Fulgentius Ferrandus. See *Ferrandus, Fulgentius.*

Fulgentius, Claudius Gordianus (ca. 467–533). Bp. Ruspe, N Afr., ca. 507; opposed Arianism* and semi-Pelagianism; championed Augustinianism.* See also *Pelagian Controversy.*

Full Gospel. See *Pentecostalism.*

Full Gospel Assembly. See *Pentecostalism.*

Full Gospel Business Men's Fellowship International. Founded 1953 in Calif. by mems. of Pentecostal chs.: membership includes mems. of many denominations; tries to make speaking in tongues (see *Tongues, Gift of*) an added dimension in mainstream chs. Purposes: 1. Provide basis of fellowship among all full gospel men everywhere; 2. Reach men everywhere for Christ; 3. Bring about more unity in the body of Christ. Publications include *Voice; Vision; Charisma Digest.*

"Full Salvation." See *Methodist Churches,* 2.

Fuller, Andrew (1754–1815). B. Wicken, Eng.; Bap.; pastor Soham 1775, Kettering 1782. Works include *The Gospel of Christ Worthy of All Acceptation; The Gospel Its Own Witness.*

Fuller, Charles Edward (1887–1968). Radio evangelist; b. Los Angeles, Calif.; ordained Bap. 1925; pastor Placentia, Calif., 1925–32; taught at Los Angeles Bap. Sem. 1927–28; founded The Old Fashioned Revival Hour 1925.

Fuller, Thomas (1608–61). B. Aldwincle, Eng.; Angl. clergyman; antiquary; historian; royalist. Works include *The History of the Holy Warre; A Pisgah-Sight of Palestine; The Church-History of Britain.*

Fullerton, Robert Steward (1821–65). B. Bloomington, Ohio; educ. Miami (Ohio) U., and Western Theol. Sem., Allegheny (now part of Pittsburgh), Pa.; Presb. Bd. miss. to India 1850; stationed at Agra and Fatehgarh.

Funck, Johann(es) (1518–66). Luth. clergyman; b. Wöhrd, near Nürnberg; educ. Wittenberg; court preacher Königsberg. Sided with A. Osiander* the elder and his son-in-law A. Aurifaber,* focusing wrath of Osiander's opponents on himself. Accused of opposing ecclesiastical and pol. measures of the govt.; beheaded at Königsberg. See also *Osiandrian Controversy.*

Funcke, Friedrich (1642–99). B. Nossen, Ger.; cantor Perleberg, later at Lüneburg; pastor Römstedt; hymnist; musician. Hymns include "Zeuch uns nach dir, so laufen wir."

Funcke, Otto Julius (1836–1910). Ev. clergyman; b. Wülfrath, near Düsseldorf, Ger.; pastor Holpe; inner mission inspector Bremen. Works include *Reisebilder und Heimatklänge; Die Welt des Glaubens und die Alltagswelt; Wie man glücklich wird und glücklich macht; Alltagsfragen im Ewigkeitslicht.*

Functional Psychology. See *Functionalism.*

Functionalism (Functional Psychology). Theory of W. James,* J. Dewey,* and others; holds that perception, emotion, and will are functions of the biological organism aimed at adapting to and controlling environment. See also *Educational Psychology,* D 6; *Psychology,* J 3.

Fundamental Doctrines. 1. J. Gerhard,* following scholastic theol., distinguished bet. "fundamental and principal" and "less principal" doctrines. But a fully developed distinction bet. fundamental and nonfundamental doctrines first appeared 1626 in N. Hunnius'* *Diaskepsis theologica de fundamentali dissensu doctrinae Evangelicae Lutheranae et Calvinianae seu Reformatae;* it was intended to show that there were fundamental doctrinal differences bet. Luths. and Ref. Later Luth. dogmaticians, esp. J. Hülsemann* and B. Meisner,* continued to elaborate the distinction, sometimes with differing classifications of doctrines.

2. Fundamental doctrines pertain to the "fundamentum" or foundation of saving faith, forgiveness of sin in Christ* Jesus. Primary fundamental articles (e. g., person and work of Christ) are constitutive for saving faith and can be neither unknown nor denied without loss of salvation. Secondary fundamental articles (e. g., Holy Baptism, Lord's Supper) are related to the foundation of faith, but in such a way that one may be ignorant of them, yet have saving faith.

3. Nonfundamental doctrines do not deal directly with the foundation of faith; therefore they may be unknown, even denied, without destroying saving faith, provided such a denial does not result from conscious opposition to Holy Scripture. Luth. dogmaticians gen. included in them such doctrines as the unpardonable sin against the Holy Ghost, immortality of man before the fall, eternal rejection of the evil angels, and the Antichrist.

4. Both fundamental and nonfundamental doctrines are Scriptural doctrines. Questions not answered conclusively by Scripture are "open questions" or "theol. problems." This classification of doctrines serves primarily to emphasize the greater importance of certain doctrines for the faith of the believer.

5. The question of fundamental and nonfundamental doctrines was much discussed after C. F. W. Walther* stated (*Der Lutheraner,* XXVII [May 1, 1871], 131) that he considered taking interest to be forbidden in Scripture, but regarded this teaching as nonfundamental: "Let everyone know, who desires to know, that we are certainly able to distinguish between articles of faith and Scripture doctrines that are not articles of faith. We indeed insist that no clear Scripture doctrine, may it appear great or

small, may be regarded as an 'open question'; but though we consider it necessary to contend most strenuously for every article of faith, on each of which our faith and hope depend, to condemn the error that opposed it, and to deny fellowship to those who stubbornly contradict the article in question, we on the other hand by no means believe it necessary under all circumstances to contend to the utmost for other Scripture teachings that are not articles of faith, much less to pronounce sentence of condemnation on the opposing error, though we reject it, and to deny fellowship to those who err only in this point. If the issue in a doctrinal controversy concerns teachings that do not belong to the articles of faith, then it is of greatest concern to us to see whether the opponents show that they contradict because they refuse to obey the Word of God, that is, whether they, while apparently not attacking the fundamental doctrines of the Word of God, nevertheless destroy the foundation itself on which these teachings rest, the Word of God." Here Walther evidently uses the term "articles of faith" in the sense of fundamental doctrines. It should be noted that he does not declare nonfundamental doctrines to be a matter of indifference, but holds that an error in such doctrines does not necessarily terminate fellowship. WA, RAB

F. Pieper, *Christliche Dogmatik,* I (St. Louis, 1924), 89–108, tr. and ed. T. Engelder et al., *Christian Dogmatics,* I (St. Louis, 1950), 80–96; H. Schmid, *The Doctrinal Theology of the Evangelical Lutheran Church,* 3d ed., rev., tr. C. A. Hay and H. E. Jacobs (Minneapolis, 1961), 92–99; A. Hoenecke, *Ev.-Luth. Dogmatik,* I (Milwaukee, 1909), 450–458; J. G. [W.] Baier, *Compendium Theologiae Positivae,* ed. C. F. G. [W.] Walther, I (St. Louis, 1879), 49–68; T. Graebner and P. E. Kretzmann, *Toward Lutheran Union* (St. Louis, 1943).

Fundamentalist Methodist Church, Inc. See *Methodist Churches,* 4 b.

Fundamental Principles of Faith and Church Polity. Theses prepared by C. Porterfield Krauth,* read to representatives of various Luth. syns. at Reading, Pa., and adopted Dec. 12–14, 1866. The 1st part, of Faith, contained 9 theses. These theses taught that the true unity of a particular ch. is unity in faith and confession. The unity of the ch. is witnessed to the world by a formal confession subscribed to in its original sense. The unity of the Luth. Ch., as a part of the holy Christian ch., depends on its adherence to the confession to which it owes its name, its distinctiveness, its political recognition, and its history, namely the UAC. The doctrines of this confession are acknowledged as being throughout in harmony with the Word of God. Subscription to the UAC indicates acknowledgment of the other Luth. confessions (Ap., SC, LC, SA, and FC) as true, Scriptural, and in complete agreement with the UAC. The 2d part, of Ch. Power and Polity, contained 11 theses. It held that all power in the ch. belongs to Christ and is transferred to no person or group. The ch., as servant of Christ, exercises power in accord with the Word of God. The primary bodies through which this power is normally exercised are congs. The normal cong. is neither pastor without people nor people without pastor. The cong. has the right to exercise its power not only through the pastor but also through representatives elected by it from its midst to act under constitutional limits approved by the cong. Representatives thus elected to meet in a gen. council or syn. are congs. themselves in representative form. The syn. is, representatively, the ch. of the congs. represented. There is a higher moral probability that decisions of syns. are true and right than decisions in conflict with them made by single congs. or persons. Among the purposes of a syn. the document lists the preservation of pure doctrine. See also *General Council of the Evangelical Lutheran Church in North America,* 2.

Verhandlungen der Kirchenversammlung bestehend aus Delegaten verschiedener Evangelisch Lutherischen Synoden in den Vereinigten Staaten und Canada, welche sich zur Ungeänderten Augsburgischen Confession bekennen. Gehalten in Reading, Pa., vom 12. bis 14. Dec. 1866 (Allentown, Pa., 1867); *Proceedings of the Convention Held by Representatives from Various Evangelical Lutheran Synods in the United States and Canada accepting the Unaltered Augsburg Confession, at Reading, Pa., Dec. 12, 13 and 14, A.D. 1866* (Pittsburgh, 1867). EL

Fundamentalism. Religious position opposed to liberalism* and Modernism* in 20th-c. Am. Protestantism. Adheres to the inspiration of the Bible and to its cardinal doctrines, but many of its protagonists have been assoc. with premillennialism (see *Millennium,* 7). Fundamentalism is polemic, attacking liberalism in sems. and chs. and causing sharp cleavages esp. among Baps. and Presbyterians. It is distinguished from Lutheranism in this, that the latter uses the Bible not as code but source of faith and emphasizes culture of spiritual life by the means of grace rather than by controversy. See also *Five Points of Fundamentalism; United States, Religious History of the,* 17.

M. L. Rudnick, *Fundamentalism and the Missouri Synod* (St. Louis, 1966).

Funeral. See *Burial.*

Fürbringer. See *Fuerbringer.*

Furlough. Leave of absence granted to governmental or institutional employee; often used of leave of absence granted to missionaries.

Future Reward and Punishment. See *Hereafter.*

Fux, Johann Joseph (ca. 1660–1741). "The Austrian Palestrina"; b. Hirtenfeld, near Gras, Styria; composer; organist Vienna. Works include *Gradus ad Parnassum* (a manual on counterpoint).

G

Gabirol (ibn-Gabirol [or ben-Gabirol], Solomon ben Judah). See *Avicebrón.*

Gabler, Johann Philipp (1753–1826). B. Frankfurt am Main; prof. Altdorf 1785, Jena 1804; studied under J. G. Eichhorn (see *Eichhorn,* 2); demanded separation of Biblical theol. and dogmatics; applied a myth concept to the OT in which myth is considered a form of thought and expression of primitive man.

Gabon Republic. See *Africa,* F 5.

Gabriel (Heb. "hero, man, or champion of God"). Heavenly messenger sent to Daniel to interpret the vision of the ram and the he-goat (Dn 8) and to communicate the prophecy of the 70 weeks (Dn 9). Announced the birth of John the Bap. to Zacharias and to Mary and that of the Savior to Mary (Lk 1: 11-37). Ordinarily spoken of as an archangel, his superior dignity being deduced both from the august nature of his messages and from the phrase "stand in the presence of God" (Lk 1:19). See also *Angels, Good.*

Gabriel Severus (1541–1616). B. Monemvasia, Greece; Orthodox metropolitan of Philadelphia, Asia Minor; exarch of It.; defended doctrines of his ch., esp. on Lord's Supper, against R. Bellarmine.*

Gabrieli, Andrea (Gabrielli; ca. 1510–86). B. Venice, It.; organist, composer; taught his nephew G. Gabrieli* and H. L. Hassler*; organist St. Mark's, Venice; master of polyphony; representative of Venetim* school of ch. music. Works include madrigals, motets, and compositions for organ and instrumental ensembles. See also *Toccata.*

Gabrieli, Giovanni (Gabrielli; 1557–ca. 1612). B. Venice; nephew of A. Gabrieli*; taught M. Praetorius* and H. Schütz*; organist St. Mark's, Venice; pioneer composer of baroque ch. music and of independent orchestrated instrumental music; master of polyphony.

Gaelic Society. See *Celtic Church,* 13.

Gaetano. See *Cajetan.*

Gagarin, Ivan Sergeevich (1814–82). Russ. nobleman; RC 1842; Jesuit 1843; tried to unite Russian and RC Ch.

Gaidheals, Church of the. See *Celtic Church,* 12.

Gairdner, William Henry Temple (1873–1928). B. Ardrossan, Scot.; educ. Oxford; to Cairo, Egypt, ca. 1899 as CMS miss. to Muslim. Works include *Christianity and Islam; Egyptian Colloquial Arabic; The Muslim Idea of God; The Reproach of Islam; The Phonetics of Arabic.*

Galateo, Fra Girolamo (1490–1541). B. Venice, It.; Franciscan; teacher of theol. Padua and Venice; condemned to death 1530 for ev. teaching; Senate refused to endorse verdict; d. in prison.

Galen, Claudius. See *Psychology,* B 2.

Galen, Clemens August(inus) (1878–1946). B. Dinklage, Oldenburg, Ger.; bp. Münster 1933; cardinal 1946; outspoken opponent of Nazism.

Galerius (Gaius Galerius Valerius Maximianus; d. 311). Son-in-law of Diocletian*; father-in-law of Maxentius*; uncle of Galerius Valerius Maximinus*; b. near Sardica, Thrace (or Serdica, Dacia), now Sofia, Bulgaria; Roman emp. 305–310/311. See also *Persecutions of Christians,* 4.

Galesburg Rule. 1875 ruling at Galesburg, Ill., of the General* Council of the Ev. Luth. Ch. in Am. regarding pulpit and altar fellowship. The words "fundamental errorists" in the 1868 "Pittsburgh* Declaration" were explained 1870 in answer to a question of the Minn. Syn.: "In employing the terms *'fundamental errorists,'* in the declarations made at Pittsburgh, it [the Council] understands, not those who are the victims of involuntary mistake, but those who wilfully, wickedly, and persistently desert, in whole or in part, the Christian faith, especially as embodied in the Confessions of the Church Catholic, in the purest form in which it now exists on earth, to wit: the Evangelical Lutheran Church, and thus overturn or destroy the *Foundation* in them confessed; and who hold, defend and extend these errors in the face of the admonitions of the Church, and to the leading away of men from the path of life."

At Lancaster, Ohio, 1870, C. Porterfield Krauth* made a verbal statement on the meaning of the "Pittsburgh Declaration." At Akron, Ohio, 1872, he was asked to put his explanation into writing. The result was the Akron Rule, adopted by the 1872 convention: "I. THE RULE is: Lutheran pulpits are for Lutheran ministers only. Lutheran altars are for Lutheran communicants only. II. *The Exceptions* to the rule belong to the sphere of *privilege,* not of *right.* III. *The Determination* of the *exceptions* is to be made in consonance with these principles by the conscientious judgment of pastors, as the cases arise."

At Galesburg 1875 the Council declared: "The rule, which accords with the word of God and with the confessions of our Church, is: 'Lutheran pulpits for Lutheran ministers only – Lutheran altars for Lutheran communicants only.' " The question, raised by the N. Y. Ministerium, whether the 1875 Galesburg addition to the 1872 Akron Rule (viz., "which accords with the word of God and with the confessions of our Church") did not practically annul points II and III of the Akron Rule regarding exceptions was answered by the Council at Pittsburgh, Pa., 1889: "Inasmuch as the General Council has never annulled, rescinded or reconsidered the declarations made at Akron, Ohio, in the year 1872, they still remain, in all their parts and provisions, the action and rule of the General Council."

S. E. Ochsenford, *Documentary History of the General Council of the Evangelical Lutheran Church in North America* (Philadelphia, 1912); J. Deindörfer, *Geschichte der Evangel.-Luth. Synode von Iowa und anderen Staaten* (Chicago, 1897).

Galilei, Galileo (1564–1642). B. Pisa, It.; astronomer, physicist. His views brought him under the suspicion of the Inquisition* 1611 and 1632; condemned 1633; recanted under threat of torture. Tried to harmonize Scripture with the findings of science*; made many discoveries in astronomy and physics.

Gall (Cellach; Caillech; probably ca. 560–probably ca. 645). B. Ireland; trained by Columban* at Bangor*; accompanied Columban to Gaul ca. 590; miss. to Suevians and Alemanni. Est. a hermitage ca. 613 on the Steinach R., Switz., where the Benedictine Monastery of St. Gall was est. ca. 720. See also *Notken, Ratpert.*

Gallaudet, Thomas Hopkins (1787–1851). B. Philadelphia, Pa.; educ. Yale Coll., New Haven, Conn., and Andover (Mass.) Theol. Sem.; studied in Fr.; brought Laurent Clerc (1785–1869; b. near Lyons,

Fr.; deaf teacher of deaf*) to Am. 1816. Founded (Hartford) Connecticut Asylum (later called Am. Asylum, now Am. School for the Deaf) 1817; principal of this school 1817–30; chief objective was to bring Gospel to deaf.

Gallican Articles. See *Gallicanism.*

Gallican Chants. Liturgical chants used 5th–9th c. in Fr. Gaul; suppressed in favor of RC chants; examples preserved by absorption into RC rite, e. g., in the Good Friday liturgy: *improperia, Crux fidelis, Pange lingua . . . certaminis,* and *Vexilla regis.* See also *Chant.*

Gallican Confession. See *Christian Church, History of,* III 6; *Reformed Confessions,* B.

Gallican Rite. See *Liturgies.*

Gallicanism. Term applied to the polity in certain areas of the RC Ch., e. g., Ger. (see *Febronianism*) and esp. France. Gallicanism includes 2 primary principles: 1. Secular govt. is supreme in its own sphere; 2. papal jurisdiction, even in the sphere of religion, is subordinate to the collective episcopate. These principles were gen. maintained against papal absolutism 13th–19th c. The Pragmatic* Sanction of Bourges, issued 1438, embodied, with modifications, 23 reformatory decrees of the Council of Basel* directed against extortionary and other arbitrary proceedings of the papacy. In particular, it declared the supremacy of the nat. ch. as against the papal ideal of universal rule. A prominent phase of Gallicanism grew out of the quarrel bet. Louis* XIV and Innocent* XI; the Fr. clergy supported the king and in 1682 issued 4 Gallican Articles drawn up by J. B. Bossuet*: 1. The authority of the pope is limited to spiritual matters; 2. the authority of a council is above that of the pope; 3. the authority of the pope is restricted by the laws, institutions, and usages of the Fr. Ch.; 4. doctrinal pronouncements of the pope are final and authoritative only with concurrence of the whole ch. in council. See also *Church and State,* 8; *Concordat,* 4, 5; France, 1–3; *Roman Catholic Church,* D 2; *ultramontanism.*

Gallien. See *Psychology,* B 2.

Gallitzin, Adelheid Amalia (1748–1806). B. Berlin; countess von Schmettau; m. Russ. Prince Dimitri Alexeyevich Gallitzin; prominent mem. of Münster* Circle.

Gallus, Jacobus. See *Handl, Jakob.*

Gallus, Nikolaus (real family name: Han, or Hahn; ca. 1516–70). B. Köthen, Ger.; pastor and Reformation leader in Regensburg; opposed Interim* 1548; co-worker of M. Flacius* Illyricus in Magdeburg 1549; opposed adiaphorism of Wittenberg theologians and Reformed leanings of P. Melanchthon*; gave Flacius refuge 1562–66. Works include *Disputation von Mitteldingen.*

Galton, Francis. See *Eugenics.*

Gambia, The. *Area:* ca. 4000 sq. mi. *Pop.:* ca. 343,000 (1967 est.). Former Brit. Colony and Protectorate, W Afr.; the colony (ca. 69 sq. mi.) included Georgetown and Bathurst; indep. mem. of the Commonwealth of Nations 1965. Miss. organizations that worked in The Gambia include RC Ch., Angl. Ch. (United* Soc. for the Propagation of the Gospel), Meth. Ch., and Seventh-day Adventists; ca. 12,000 Christians, 220,000 Muslim.

See *Missions, Bibliography.*

Gambling. Gambling has been defined as playing a game for money or other stakes. It involves a hazard or wager and unnecessary risk. Concern is not with unavoidable uncertainties of life but with calculated attempts to secure a stake at the expense of others. Gambling in this sense was practiced in most of the world since earliest times, though comparatively unknown in some areas, e. g., among native Australians, Papuo-Melanesians, Siberians, and SE Africans. The practice or prohibition of gambling does not correlate with either surplus or scarcity of property. Legal codes reflect influential thought and practice at various times and places and vary widely on gambling.

Scripture does not speak directly to the matter of gambling but speaks of stewardship of life and possessions, which come from God. 1 Co 10:31 shows that God expects His gifts to be used to His glory. For Christians the problem of gambling does not lie in objects or amount involved but in motivation prompting one to seek gain at the expense of others in contrast to imperatives of Christian love in all things toward all men. The sinfulness of gambling is rooted in the sinfulness of man. Examination of soc. ethics of gambling must be conditioned by confrontation of man by God in Christ.

A. L. Kroeber, *Anthropology,* rev. ed. (New York, 1948), pp. 552–553; C. Stocking, "Gambling," *Encyclopaedia of the Social Sciences,* ed. E. R. A. Seligman and A. Johnson, VI (New York, 1931), 555–558; R. Sommerfeld, "What's Wrong with Gambling?" (St. Louis, n. d.); G. W. Forell, *Faith Active in Love: An Investigation of Principles Underlying Luther's Social Ethics* (New York, 1954); E. C. Devereux, Jr., "Gambling," *International Encyclopedia of the Social Sciences,* ed. D. L. Sills, VI (New York, 1968), 53–62. RS

Gambold, John (1711–71). B. Puncheston, Pembrokeshire, Eng.; educ. Oxford; vicar Stanton, Harcourt, Oxfordshire; resigned 1742; joined Moravian* Ch.; bp. 1754. Ed. *A Collection of Hymns of the Children of God in all Ages, from the Beginning till now.*

Gamma Delta. See *Students, Spiritual Care of,* A 3, C 9.

Gandhi, Mohandas Karamchand (1869–1948). "Father of the Nation." Called Mahatma ("Great-souled"). B. Porbandar, Kathiawar, W India; educ. in India and London; lawyer in India; to S Afr. 1893; worked for liberties of S Afr. Indians against white rulers; developed concept of nonviolent resistance which he called *satyagraha* ("soul-force" or "truth-force"); helped found *Indian Opinion,* a weekly journal pub. at Phoenix Farm (small settlement he est. near Durban), center of his activity in Natal, S Afr.; to Eng. 1914; to India, arriving Bombay Jan. 9, 1915; applied organized *satyagraha* repeatedly in home rule movement; elected "sole executive authority" by Indian Nat. Congress 1921; tried to integrate the untouchables; worked for understanding bet. Hindus and Muslim; opposed partition of India; taught that happiness for all was to be achieved through fearlessness, truth, and nonviolence; assassinated on way to prayer. Works include *Hind Swaraj; An Autobiography.* Ed. *Young India; Navajivan; Harijan.*

Gangra, Council of. Syn., variously dated from ca. 340 to ca. 379, held at Gangra (Gankiri; Kangri; Kankari; Changra), Paphlagonia; its 21 canons included vindication of the sacredness of marriage and condemnation of clerical celibacy.*

Ganse, Hervey Doddridge (1822–91). B. near Fishkill, N. Y.; educ. Columbia Coll., NYC, and New Brunswick (N. J.) Theol. Sem.; pastor Ref. Dutch and Presb. chs. Hymnist; wrote 3 new stanzas for "Nearer, My God, to Thee."

Gansfort, Wessel. See *Wessel.*

Gapon, Georgi Apollonovich (ca. 1870–1906). "Father Gapon"; b. Poltava govt.; Russ. priest; influenced by L. N. Tolstoi*; tried to introd. soc. reforms through laws; planned, as leader of 200,000, to hand demands for reforms to czar; this march of workers to the Winter Palace was ruthlessly suppressed on Bloody Sun., Jan. 22, 1905; Gapon escaped to London; later returned; hanged at Terioki, Fin.

Garampi, Giuseppe (1725–92). B. Rimini, It.; RC theol.; hist.; diplomat; archivist; cardinal 1785.

Gardiner, Allen Francis (1794–1851). B. Basildon, Berkshire, Eng.; captain in Royal Navy; resigned;

miss. in Natal, S Afr.; later in S Am.; founded the Patagonian Miss. Soc. 1844, later called The South Am. Miss. Soc.; unsuccessfully attempted miss. in Tierra del Fuego, perishing of hunger on its coast.

Gardiner, Robert Hallowell (1855–1924). B. Fort Tejon, Calif.; studied law at Harvard; lawyer in Boston 1880; Episc.; pres. Brotherhood* of St. Andrew 1904–10; worked for organizational unity of ch.; mem. of the ex. committee FCC; secy. (1910) of commission that arranged the 1920 Geneva Preparatory Conf. on Faith and Order (see also *Ecumenical Movement, The,* 7).

Garlichs, Hermann (1807–65). B. Ger.; educ. Göttingen, Leipzig, Bonn, Munich; to Mo. 1833 with a group of Ref. Westphalians; settled as farmer on Femme Osage Creek, St. Charles Co.; began serving as pastor 1834/35; to Ger. in fall 1835; passed theol. examaination at Bielefeld; ordained 1835; retnrned to Mo. Jan. 1836; served various congs. See also *German Evangelical Church Society of the West, The.*

Garnier, Jean (1612–81). B. Paris, Fr.; Jesuit; patristic scholar. Works include treatises on Pelagianism* and Nestorianism*; ed. works of Marius* Mercator and the last vol. of J. Sirmond's ed. of Theodoret.*

Garstang, John (1876–1956). B. Blackburn, Lancashire, Eng.; archaeol.; excavated Roman sites in Britain, and sites in Egypt, Asia Minor, N Syria, Sudan, Palestine, and other places. Works include *The Foundations of Bible History; The Hittite Empire; The Burial Customs of Ancient Egypt as Illustrated by Tombs of the Middle Kingdom; The Heritage of Solomon;* coauthor with J. B. E. Garstang, *The Story of Jericho.*

Gartenhaus, Jacob. See *International Board of Jewish Missions, Inc.*

Garve, Karl Bernhard (1763–1841). B. Jeinsen, near Hannover, Ger.; teacher at Moravian (see *Moravian Church*) school at Barby and Niesky; pastor Amsterdam, Ebersdorf, Norden, Berlin, and Neusalz an der Oder; his attempt to construct a philos. basis for Moravian theol., beginning with I. Kant's* criticism, proved a failure; hymnist. Hymns include "Christus lebt" (tr. J. Borthwick,* "Hallelujah! Jesus Lives!").

Garvey, Marcus Moziah, Jr. (Aug. 17, 1887–June 10, 1940). Negro leader; b. St. Ann's Bay, Jamaica; printer's apprentice at age 14; worked in Costa Rica, Panama, and London; influenced by Duse Mohammed Ali (half-Negro Egyptian nationalist) and by B. T. Washington's* *Up from Slavery;* returned to Jamaica 1914; organized the Universal* Negro Improvement Assoc. Aug. 1, 1914; to NYC 1916; est. a Harlem branch of UNIA 1917; pub. *Negro World;* est. Negro Factories Corp. and Black Star Steamship Line; convicted 1923 of using mails to defraud after collapse of Black Star Line; imprisoned; sentence commuted 1927; deported to Jamaica; moved to London 1934.

E. D. Cronon, *Black Moses: The Story of Marcus Garvey and the Universal Negro Improvement Association* (Madison, Wis. 1955).

Garvie, Alfred Ernest (1861–1945). Brit. Cong. theol.; b. Zurardow, Russ. Poland; educ. Edinburgh, Glasgow, and Oxford; lecturer Mansfield Coll., Oxford, 1892; pastor Macduff, Scot., 1893, Montrose, Scot., 1895; active in union and ecumenical movements. Works include *The Ritschlian Theology, Critical and Constructive; A Guide to Preachers; Studies in the Inner Life of Jesus; Christian Life and Belief; The Christian Doctrine of the Godhead; The Christian Ideal for Human Society; The Christian Belief in God, in Relation to Religion and Philosophy.*

Gascoigne, Thomas (1403–58). B. Hunslet, near Leeds, Eng.; theol.; educ. Oxford; ordained 1427; spent time in scholarly pursuits at Oxford, often as chancellor or vice-chancellor; opposed abuses in ch., but also Wycliffite movement (see *Wycliffe, John; Lollards*). Works include a theol. dictionary.

Gasparri, Pietro (1852–1934). B. Ussita (Macerata), It.; RC canonist and diplomat; cardinal 1907. Works include introduction to *Codex iuris canonici.*

Gass, Friedrich Wilhelm Joachim Heinrich (1813–89). B. Breslau; educ. Breslau and Halle; prof. Breslau, Greifswald, Giessen, and Heidelberg; strong advocate of *Evangelischer* Bund.* Made valuable contributions to the study of the Gk. Ch.; other works include *Geschichte der protestantischen Dogmatik; Geschichte der Ethik.*

Gassend(i), Pierre (1592–1655). B. Champtercier, near Digne, Fr.; philos.; opposed philos. of R. Descartes* and scholastic Aristotelianism (see *Aristotle*); revived Epicureanism*; emphasized modified empiricism.*

Gates, Theophilus Ransom (1787–1846). B. Hartland, Conn.; early experienced strange, disturbing visions; in Philadelphia 1810–35; criticized existing religions; pub. the monthly *Reformer;* unhappy home life led him to adopt perfectionism*; influenced by J. H. Noyes*; launched "Battle-Axe Experiment" 1837, advocating free love based on a "principle of holiness" leading to union of "soul mates"; his colony in "Free Love Valley" near Philadelphia, Pa., disappeared after he left in reaction against excesses.

Gattinara, Mercurino Arborio di (1465–1530). B. Castello di Arborio, Vercelli (Piedmont), It.; prof. of law at Dôle; emissary of Maximilian I (1459–1519; king of Ger. 1486–1519; Holy Roman emp. 1493–1519); grand chancellor of Charles* V; cardinal 1529.

Gaudentius (d. after 406). Bp. Brescia, It.; friend of Ambrose*; unsuccessfully helped try to persuade E emp. Arcadius to return J. Crysostom* from exile. Works include sermons and other treatises. *MPL,* 20, 795–1006; *MPG,* 52, 715–716.

Gauger, Joseph (1866–1939). B. Winnenden, Württemberg; dir. *Evangelische Gesellschaft für Deutschland;* opposed *Deutsche Christen* (see *Barmen Theses*); championed the *Bekennende Kirche* (see *Kirchenkampf*).

Gaume, Jean Joseph (1802–79). B. Fuans, Doubs, Fr.; RC priest 1825; vicar-gen. of Reims and Montauban; advocated excluding pagan classics from Christian schools and substituting patristic writings.

Gaunilo(n) (d. ca. 1080). Benedictine monk of noble birth; criticized Anselm* of Canterbury's ontological argument in *Pro insipiente* (*In Behalf of the Fool;* the title is a reference to Ps 14:1).

Gausewitz, Carl F. W. (Aug. 29, 1861–Sept. 4, 1928). B. Reedsville, Wis.; educ. Northwestern Coll., Watertown, Wis., and Luth. Sem., Milwaukee, Wis.; pastor (Minn. Syn.) East Farmington, Minn., 1882–85; St. Paul, Minn., 1885–1906; (Wis. Syn.) Milwaukee, Wis., 1906–28. Pres. Minn. Syn. 1894–1906; helped organize Joint Syn. of Wis.; its pres. 1901–07, 1913–17; pres. Synodical* Conf. 1912–27. Wrote official Wis. Syn. catechism.

Gaussen, François Samuel Robert Louis (1790–1863). B. Geneva, Switz.; Ref. theol.; at first inclined to rationalism*; became strictly orthodox; deposed 1831; prof. systematics of theol. school of Société* évangélique de Genève.

Gautama Buddha (Sanskrit; Pali: Gotama; ca. 563–ca. 483 B. C). According to tradition, Siddhartha ("he who has accomplished his aim"), b. Lumbini Grove, near Kapilavastu, NE India, was a son of Sakya raja Suddhodana Gautama; proclaimed Sakyamuni ("sage of the Sakyas"), Tathagata ("he who has arrived at the truth"), and Buddha ("the enlightened"). Founded Buddhism.* Prompted by reflections on the frailty of human life, he at 29 renounced succession to the throne, left wife and infant child (act called by Buddhists "The Great Renunciation"), and became a wandering mendicant.

After yrs. of study of Brahmanism* and practice of severe asceticism* failed to satisfy him, he attained the enlightenment that made him Buddha. After his enlightenment he organized a mendicant order for his followers, traveled, and taught.

In Buddhist thought a Buddha is one who through knowledge of truth and conquest of sin has escaped the burdens and pains of existence and who then teaches the true doctrine. There have been and will be many Buddhas. The last historic one was Gautama.

Gavanti, Bartolom(m)eo (1569–1638). B. Monza, It.; Barnabite* liturgical scholar.

Gavazzi, Alessandro (1809–89). B. Bologna, It.; Barnabite*; at first supported by Pius IX (see *Popes,* 28); to Eng. 1849; evangelical 1850; leader of It. Ev. Ch., London; chaplain of Garibaldi; helped found *Chiesa libera cristiana in Italia* 1870.

Gay, John (1699–1745). Eng. moral philos.; vicar Wilsham(p)stead, Bedfordshire, 1732–45; utilitarian (see *Utilitarianism*). Works include writing on the fundamental principle of virtue or morality.

Gebhard (1547–1601). B. Heiligenberg, near Pfullendorf, S Baden, Ger.; Frhr. zu Waldburg; abp. and elector of Cologne; elected Dec. 1577; ordained priest Mar. 1578; Prot. 1582; granted Protestantism and RCm equal rights; married 1583. His defection and marriage led to the War of Cologne, which devastated Westphalia and ended with Romanists as victors.

Gebhardi, Heinrich Brandanus (Brandanus Henricus; 1657–1729). B. Brunswick, Ger.; prof. oriental languages and theol. Greifswald; furthered pietism.*

Gebhardt Eduard Karl Franz von (1838–1925). B. St. Johann(is), Estonia; Ger. Luth. realist painter following style of the old Nürnberg and Flemish schools. Works include mural paintings in the monastery at Loccum, Ger.; *The Crucifixion; The Last Supper; The Ascension.*

Geddes, Alexander. See *Higher Criticism,* 13.

Geddie, John (1815–72). B. Banff, Scot.; Presb. miss.; evangelical Aneityum, ca. 35 mi. in circumference, at the S end of the New* Hebrides islands.

Geert Zerbolt van Zutphen. See *Gerhard of Zutphen.*

Gehenna. See *Hereafter,* C 5.

Gehrke, George. See *Canada,* 19.

Geibel, Johannes (1776–1853). B. Hanau, Ger.; Ref. pastor in Lübeck; preached Bible-centered sermons in opposition to rationalism.*

Geier, Martin, Jr. (1614–80). B. Leipzig; prof. and pastor Leipzig; court preacher Dresden. Works include commentaries and hymns.

Geiger, Abraham (1810–74). B. Frankfurt am Main; rabbi, philos., and orientalist.

Geijer, Erik Gustaf (1783–1847). Poet, philos., hist., hymnist; b. Ransäter, Värmland, Swed.; educ. Uppsala; prof. hist. Uppsala. Influenced by I. Kant* and Ger. idealists (e. g., F. W. J. von Schelling* and G. W. F. Hegel*), but remained conservative till ca. 1838, when influenced by Eur. revolutions, industrialism, and the changing Am. scene to become a pol. and soc. liberal. Deeply religious throughout life. Works include *Svenska folkets historia (History of the Swedes); Thorild; Föreläsningar öfver menniskans historia.* See also *Sweden, Lutheranism in,* 4.

Geiler von Kaysersberg, Johann(es) (Geyler von Kaisersberg; 1445–1510). "The Ger. Savonarola"; b. Schaffhausen, Switz.; to Kaysersberg, Upper Alsace, 1448; educ. Freiburg U.; lectured there on Aristotle* and grammar; studied theol. in Basel 1471; influenced by J. de Gerson*; preacher at Strasbourg. Criticized civil and ecclesiastical corruption; suggested reforms to council, but remained in theol. of Middle Ages; criticized humanism; upheld indulgences, good works; works placed on Index* of Prohibited Books by Paul* IV.

Geiseman, Otto Albert Ferdinand (Aug. 8, 1893–Nov. 7, 1962). B. Sioux City, Iowa; grad. Conc. Sem., St. Louis, Mo., 1915; pastor, Wenona, Pekin, and River Forest, Ill.; occasional speaker Internat. Luth. Hour (see *Radio and Television Evangelism, Network,* 6). Contributed to *(The) American Lutheran* and *This Day;* other works include *Make Yours a Happy Marriage; Horizons of Hope; Where God Meets Man; Old Truths for a New Day; God's Answer.*

Geismar, Eduard Osvald (1871–1939). B. Randers, Jutland; Dan. theol.; prof. Copenhagen 1921; influenced by R. C. Eucken*; popularized S. Kierkegaard* in the 1920s.

Gelasian Sacramentary. RC missal with feasts arranged acc. to ch. yr.; erroneously ascribed to Gelasius* I.

Gelasius I (d. 496). Pope 492–496. Asserted papal supremacy (see *Church and State,* 5). Works include treatise on the natures of Christ. *MPL,* 59, 9–190.

Gelasius of Caesarea (ca. 335–ca. 395). Bp. Caesarea ca. 367; nephew of Cyril* of Jerusalem. Works include continuation of Eusebius* of Caesarea's *Historia ecclesiastica; Expositio symboli;* treatise against Anomoeans.*

F. Diekamp, *Analecta patristica* (Rome, 1938).

Geldenhauer, Gerhard (1482–1542). B. Nijmegen, Neth.; hist. and theol.; became Luth. in Wittenberg 1525; reformer of Neth.; prof. Marburg 1532.

Gellert, Christian Fürchtegott (1715–69). B. Hainichen, Saxony; studied theol. at Leipzig; asst. to his father; ill health and shyness combined to redirect his life; after further studies at Leipzig he became prof. at Leipzig. Works include *Leben der schwedischen Gräfin von G.;* comedies; songs, fables. Hymns include "Jesus lebt, mit ihm auch ich."

Gemara. See *Talmud.*

Gemistos Pletho(n), Georgios (Georgius Gemistus; ca. 1355–ca. 1450). Renaissance scholar from Constantinople; Neoplatonist; influenced It. humanists at Council of Florence.*

General Assembly. See *Polity, Ecclesiastical,* 7.

General Assembly of the Presbyterian Church in Ireland. See *Presbyterian Churches,* 3.

General Associate Synod. See *Presbyterian Churches,* 1.

General Association of Regular Baptist Churches. See *Baptist Churches,* 15.

General Baptist Foreign Mission Society. Organized 1903; represents Gen. Assoc. of Gen. Baps.; works in Guam, Philippines, Jamaica, Saipan.

General Baptist. See *Baptist Churches,* 2, 18, 20–33.

General Church of the New Jerusalem. See *Swedenborgians,* 5.

General Conference Mennonite Church. See *Mennonite Churches,* 3.

General Conference of Lutherans in America, First. See *Diets, Lutheran, in America.*

General Conference [Synod] of the Evangelical Lutheran Preachers in Ohio and the Adjacent States. See *Ohio and Other States, Evangelical Lutheran Joint Synod of,* 2.

General Confession. In Luth. terminology, a pub. confession* of sins made by an assem. with the pastor. In RC terminology, conf. made by an individual in which he surveys his entire life, or a considerable part of it, confessing also sins previously confessed.

General Convention. See *Protestant Episcopal Church,* 8.

General Convention of the Christian Church. See *United Church of Christ, The,* I.

General Convention of the New Jerusalem in the United States of America. See *Swedenborgians,* 4.

General Council of Congregational Christian Churches. See *United Church of Christ, The,* I.

General Council of the Evangelical Lutheran Church in (North) America ("North" inserted 1876). 1. This body owed its existence to the 1866 disruption of The Ev. Luth. Gen. Syn. of the US of N Am. (see *General Synod of the Evangelical Lutheran Church in the United States of America, The*). In the face of the rising tide of confessionalism (see *United States, Lutheran Theology in,* 6–10) the Gen. Syn. had received into membership the Melanchthon* Synod 1859 and the Franckean* Synod 1864. The delegates of the Ministerium of Pa. protested the admission of the Franckean Syn., withdrew from the sessions of the Gen. Syn., and founded the Philadelphia Sem. in opposition to lax confessionalism at the Gettysburg Sem. (see also *Ministry, Education of,* XI B 2, 5; *United Lutheran Church, Synods of,* 22).

2. At the 1866 conv. the Gen. Syn. refused to seat the Pa. Ministerium delegates, whereupon the Ministerium severed its connection with the Gen. Syn. and a few weeks later issued a "fraternal* address." In response, a conv. was held at Reading, Pa., Dec. 12–14, 1866, with delegates present from 5 groups hitherto mems. of the Gen. Syn.: Ministerium of N. Y., Eng. Syn. of Ohio, Ministerium of Pa., Pittsburgh Syn., and Minnesota* Syn. (see also *United Lutheran Church, Synods of,* 15, 22, 24), and from the Joint Syn. of Ohio (see *Ohio and Other States, Ev. Luth. Joint Synod of,* 4–5), Eng. Dist. Syn. of Ohio (see *United Lutheran Church, Synods of,* 19), Syn. of Wis. (see *Wisconsin Synod*), Michigan* Syn., Iowa Syn. (see *Iowa and Other States, The Ev. Luth. Joint Synod,* 4–5), of Can. (see *Canada,* A 7; *United Lutheran Church, Synods of,* 1), Norw. Syn. (see *Evangelical Lutheran Church, The,* 8), and Mo. Syn. (see *Lutheran Church – Missouri Synod, The*). At this convention C. Porterfield Krauth's* *Fundamental* Principles of Faith and Church Polity* were unanimously adopted. Of the 13 groups represented by delegates at the 1866 conv., 11 were represented at the organization meeting at Fort Wayne, Ind., Nov. 20–26, 1867: Ministerium of Pa., Ministerium of N. Y., Pittsburgh Syn., Eng. Syn. of Ohio, Syn. of Wis., Eng. Dist. Syn. of Ohio, Mich. Syn., Minn. Syn., Syn. of Can., Iowa Syn., and the Joint Syn. of Ohio. Of these, the Iowa Syn. and the Joint Syn. of Ohio did not enter into voting membership of the Gen. Council (see *Four Points*). The Norw. Syn. and the Mo. Syn. had withdrawn from the movement. The Ev. Luth. Syn. of Ill. and Other [Adjacent] States (see *Illinois, Evangelical Lutheran Synod of,* b), organized 1867, also joined the Gen. Council 1867.

3. The Syn. of Wis. left the Gen. Council 1869 because of disagreement regarding the Four Points. The Swed. Augustana Syn. (see *Augustana Evangelical Lutheran Church,* 10) joined the Gen. Council 1870. The Minn. Syn. and the Ill. Syn. left the Gen. Council 1871 and helped form the Synodical* Conference 1872. The Mich. Syn. left the Gen. Council 1887 because of disagreement regarding the Four Points. Most of the Tex. Syn., admitted 1868, withdrew 1894 and joined the Iowa Syn. as a dist. 1896; the minority ultimately became part of the ULC (see *United Lutheran Church, Synods of,* 28). By 1872 the Eng. Syn. of Ohio had disbanded.

Following syns. also joined the Gen. Council: Ind. Syn. of the Ev. Luth. Ch. 1872 (see also *Indiana Synod* [II]); Holston Syn. 1874 (requested approval to withdraw 1884 to help form the United* Syn. of the Ev. Luth. Ch. in the South; see also *United Lutheran Church, Synods of,* 29); Eng. Ev. Luth. Syn. of the Northwest 1893 (see also *United Lutheran Church, Synods of,* 17); Man. Syn. 1897 (see also *Canada,* A 14); Pacific Syn. 1901 (see also *United Lutheran Church,. Synods of,* 20); N. Y. and New Eng. Syn. 1903 (see also *United Lutheran Church, Synods of,* 15); Nova Scotia Syn. 1903 (see also *United Lutheran Church, Synods of,* 18); Cen. Can. Syn. 1909 (see also *Canada,* A 4).

Leading men in the Gen. Council: G. H. Gerberding,* J. A. W. Haas,* H. E. Jacobs,* C. Porterfield Krauth,* G. F. Krotel,* W. J. Mann,* W. A. Passavant,* T. E. Schmauk,* B. M. Schmucker,* J. A. Seiss,* A. Spaeth,* C. A. Swensson.*

4. Doctrinal basis of the Gen. Council: "the Unaltered Augsburg Confession in its original sense as throughout in conformity with the pure truth of which God's Word is the only rule"; the other Luth. Confessions "are, with the Unaltered Augsburg Confession, in the perfect harmony of one and the same scriptural faith" (Const. of the Gen. Council of the Ev. Luth. Ch. in Am. Principles of Faith and Church Polity. Of Faith, VIII, IX). In relation to congs. the Gen. Council was a legislative body and considered conformity to its decisions a moral obligation. But despite its strictly Luth. confessional basis the Gen. Council never issued a declaration satisfactory to strict Luths. regarding the Four Points. According to the Akron-Galesburg Rule (see *Galesburg Rule*), non-Luths. may under certain circumstances be admitted to the Lord's Supper, and there were exceptions to the rule "Lutheran pulpits for Lutheran ministers only." Its declaration on chiliasm (see *Millennialism*) left room for the finer kind, and, though its declaration on secret societies agreed with Luth. principles, its practice did not agree with its principles. The teachings of some leaders of the Gen. Council on ordination, the ministerial office, conversion, predestination, the inspiration of Scripture, evolution, etc., were not always in harmony with the Bible and the Luth. Confessions; yet the Gen. Council did not take such men to task.

5. Home miss. work of the Gen. Council was carried on throughout the US, esp. in the Northwest and Can., and reached even to Alaska. The theol. sem. of J. Paulsen* at Kropp, Ger., furnished many Ger. pastors (see *Kropp Seminary*).

6. The Gen. Council conducted a miss. among the Telugus in India and, with the United* Syn. of the Ev. Luth. Ch. in the South, also in Japan. The Augustana Syn. had an indep. miss. in China; other Augustana Syn. for. miss. fields included Puerto Rico and Afr.

Sems. of the Gen. Council and its syns. included Mount Airy, Philadelphia, Pa.; Maywood (first at Lake View), Chicago, Ill.; Waterloo, Ont., Can.; Portland, Oreg. (moved to Seattle, Wash.); Rock Island, Ill. See also *Ministry, Education of,* XI B, E.

Classical institutions of collegiate grade of the Gen. Council and its syns. included Muhlenberg, Allentown, Pa.; Thiel, Greenville, Pa.; Wagner, Rochester (moved to Staten Is.), N. Y.; Waterloo, Waterloo, Ont.; Augustana, Rock Island, Ill.; Bethany, Lindsborg, Kans.; Gustavus Adolphus, St. Peter, Minn.; Uppsala, E. Orange, N. J.; Weidner Institute, Mulberry, Ind.; Ev. Luth. Coll., Saskatoon, Sask. See also *Ministry, Education of,* VIII A, B.

Within the Gen. Council there were many orphanages and other charitable institutions maintained either by dist. syns. or private assocs. Many of them owed their existence to the labors of W. A. Passavant.* The Gen. Council also conducted an immigrant and seamen's miss. (see *Immigrant and Emigrant Missions; Seamen's Homes*). J. D. Lankenau* est. the Mary J. Drexel Home in Philadelphia 1888.

7. At its conv. Oct. 24–29, 1917, the Gen. Council approved the plan to merge with the Gen. Syn. and the United Syn. of the Ev. Luth. Ch. in the South into The United* Luth. Ch. in Am. The merger was consummated Nov. 1918, but the Swed. Augustana Syn. did not enter it. In 1917 the Gen. Council, including the Augustana Syn., numbered 14

syns., 1,680 pastors, 2,564 congs., and 524,259 conf. mems.

See also *Students, Spiritual Care of,* B 1. *United Lutheran Church, Synods of; United Lutheran Church in America.*

Die Synode von Pennsylvanien und die letzte Versammlung der General-Synode zu Fort Wayne, Indiana (Philadelphia, 1866); *Proceedings of the Convention Held by Representatives from Various Evangelical Lutheran Synods in the United States and Canada Accepting the Unaltered Augsburg Confession, at Reading, Pa., Dec. 12, 13, and 14, A. D. 1866* (Pittsburgh, 1867); *Verhandlungen der Kirchenversammlung bestehend aus Delegaten verschiedener Evangelisch Lutherischen Synoden in den Vereinigten Staaten und Canada, welche sich zur Ungeänderten Augsburgischen Confession bekennen. Gehalten in Reading, Pa., vom 12. bis 14. Dec. 1866* (Allentown, Pa., 1867); H. E. Jacobs, "The General Council," *The Distinctive Doctrines and Usages of the General Bodies of the Evangelical Lutheran Church in the United States,* 4th ed., rev. and enl. (Philadelphia, 1914), pp. 93–126; A. Spaeth, "The General Council of the Evangelical Lutheran Church in North America," *The Lutheran Church Review,* IV (Apr. 1885), 81–126; S. E. Ochsenford, *Documentary History of the General Council of the Evangelical Lutheran Church in North America* (Philadelphia, 1912).

General Council of the Italian Pentecostal Assemblies of God. See *Christian Church of North America, General Council.*

General Eldership of the Church(es) of God (in North America). See *Churches of God in North America.*

General English Evangelical Lutheran Conference of Missouri and Other States, The. See *Missouri and Other States, The English Evangelical Lutheran Synod of.*

General Semantics. See *Semantics General.*

General Six-Principle Baptists. See *Baptist Churches,* 3, 21.

General Synod of the Evangelical Lutheran Church in the United States of America, The. 1. Organized at the Oct. 22–24, 1820, conv. at Hagerstown, Md.; 1820 constitutional name: "The Evangelical Lutheran General Synod of the United States of North America," changed 1869 to "The General Synod of the Evangelical Lutheran Church in the United States of America." Other names used include Gen. Syn. of the Ev. Luth. Ch. in the US; Gen. Syn. of the Ev. Luth. Ch. in the US of Am.; Gen. Syn. of the Ev. Luth. Ch. in the US of N Am. It was the 1st fed. of Luth. syns. in America. Syns. participating in the organization of the gen. body: Md.-Va. Syn., N. Y. Ministerium, N. C. Syn., and Pa. Ministerium (see also *United Lutheran Church, Synods of,* 11, 15, 16, 22, 23, 29).

2. The idea of a gen. body, apparently first suggested 1807 by J. H. C. Helmuth,* was promoted since ca. 1812 esp. by G. Schober* and C. A. G. Stork* of the N. C. Syn. and took definite shape in the *Planentwurf* adopted 1819 in Baltimore by the Pa. Ministerium (sometimes called the "mother syn.") and representatives of other syns. The Tenn. Syn. (see also *Henkels, The; United Lutheran Church, Synods of,* 16) objected to the organization on doctrinal grounds; the Ohio Syn. (see *Ohio and Other States, Evangelical Lutheran Joint Synod of*) did not join the movement for practical reasons. Eleven pastors and 4 lay delegates attended the organization meeting. The N. Y. Ministerium withdrew after the 1st meeting because of lack of interest and was not again represented till 1837.

3. The Pa. Ministerium receded from the Gen. Syn. 1823 because it feared centralized authority and because some of its congs. feared infringement of their liberties; it did not return till 1853. It was due chiefly to efforts of S. S. Schmucker* that the Gen. Syn. survived its critical initial yrs. When the Pa. Ministerium withdrew, a new syn. was formed W of the Susquehanna R., the Syn. of W Pa. (see also *United Lutheran Church, Synods of,* 22, 23; abbreviated *ULC, Syns. of* in rest of this par.), which joined the Gen. Syn. 1825. The Hartwick* Syn. joined 1831; the S. C. Syn. (see also *ULC, Syns. of,* 27) joined 1835; the N. Y. Ministerium returned 1837; the Va. Syn (see also *ULC, Syns. of,* 29) joined 1839. Other syns. joined as follows: Syn. of the West* 1841; Eng. Dist. Syn. of Ohio 1843 (called East Ohio Syn. of the Evangelical Lutheran Ch. beginning 1857; see also *Ohio and Other States Evangelical Lutheran Joint Synod of,* 4, and *ULC, Syns. of,* 19); E Pa. Syn. 1843 (see also *ULC, Syns. of,* 22, 23); Allegheny Syn. 1843 (see also *ULC, Syns. of,* 23); Western Va. Syn. 1843 (see also *Synods, Extinct; ULC, Syns. of,* 29); Miami* (Ohio) Syn. 1845 (see also *ULC, Syns. of,* 8, 19); Ill. Syn. 1848 (see also *ULC, Syns. of,* 7); Wittenberg* Syn. 1848 (see also *ULC, Syns. of,* 19); Ev. Luth. Syn. of the Southwest* 1848 (see also *Kentucky Synod,* 2; *Synods, Extinct*); Olive Branch Syn. 1850 (see also *ULC, Syn. of,* 8); Pittsburgh Syn. 1853 (see also *ULC, Syns. of,* 24); Tex. Syn. 1853 (see also *ULC, Syns. of,* 28); N Ill. Syn. 1853 (see also *ULC, Syns. of,* 7); Pa. Ministerium returned 1853; Cen. Pa. Syn. joined 1855 (see also *ULC, Syns. of,* 23); Eng. Dist. Syn. of Ohio 1855 (the minority group that continued as a dist. 1840 when the majority of the dist., which was organized 1836, resolved to become indep.; see also *Ohio and Other States, Evangelical Lutheran Joint Synod of,* 4; *ULC, Syns. of,* 19); Kentucky* Syn. 1855; N Indiana* Syn. 1857 (see also *ULC, Syns. of,* 8); Iowa Syn. 1857 (see also *ULC, Syns. of,* 9); S Ill. Syn. 1857 (see also *Illinois, Evangelical Lutheran Synod of Southern; ULC, Syns. of,* 7); Melanchthon* Syn. 1859; Ev. Luth. Syn. of New* Jersey (I) 1862; Franckean* Syn. 1864 (see also *ULC, Syns. of,* 15); Minn. Syn. 1864 (see also *Minnesota Synod,* 1); Susquehanna Syn. 1866 (see also *ULC, Syns. of,* 23); Ev. Luth. Syn. of New* York 1868 (see also *ULC, Syns, of,* 15); Cen. Ill. Syn. 1868 (see also *Illinois, Evangelical Lutheran Synod of Central*); Kans. Syn. 1869 (see also *ULC, Syns. of,* 3); Nebr. Syn. 1875 (see also *ULC, Syns, of,* 3); Ger. Ev. Luth. Syn. of Maryland* and Adjacent States 1875; Swed. Ansgarius Syn. 1875 (see also *Evangelical Covenant Church of America*); Wartburg Syn. 1877 (see also *ULC, Syns. of,* 30); Middle Tennessee* Syn. 1879; Calif. Syn. 1891 (see also *ULC, Syns. of,* 21); Rocky Mountain Syn. 1891 (see also *ULC, Syns. of,* 25); Ger. Nebr. Syn. 1893 (see also *ULC, Syns. of,* 3); Syn. of N. Y. 1909 (see also *ULC, Syns. of,* 15; W. Va. Syn. 1913 (see also *ULC, Syns. of,* 31).

4. Admission of the liberal Melanchthon Syn. 1859 contributed to reasons for withdrawal of conservative Scands. (Swedes) from the N Ill. Syn. 1860 (see also *Augustana Evangelical Lutheran Church,* 8). In 1863, because of the Civil War, the S syns. (N. C., S. C., Va., and Southwestern Va.) withdrew and the Ga. Syn. (see also *United Lutheran Church Synods of,* 5), organized The Gen. Syn. of the Ev. Luth. Ch. in the Confederate* States of Am. Reception of the un-Luth. Franckean Syn. 1864 led to disruption of the Gen. Syn. The Pa. Ministerium withdrew 1866 and helped form the Gen. Council 1867. See also *General Council of the Evangelical Lutheran Church in (North) America,* 2.

5. From its beginning the Gen. Syn. did not adhere to strict Luth. confessionalism (see *Fellowship,* B; *Lutheran Confessions,* D 2). The Bible and the Confessions of the Luth. Ch. were not mentioned in its const.; that the omission was intentional is evident from the fact that the Gen. Syn. remained

silent in regard to its confession despite vigorous protests of the Tenn. Syn. and its refusal to join the Gen. Syn. on that account. Yet the Gen. Syn. served as a rallying point for those who wanted to be Luth.; it fostered a Luth. self-consciousness and helped prevent submergence of Lutheranism in Am. sectarianism. In opposition to rationalism in the NY Ministerium it confessed Jesus Christ as "the Son of God, and ground of our faith and hope," thus acting as check on inroads of Socinianism.*

6. On the other hand, the platform of the Gen. Syn. was so broadly "evangelical" that it lost sight of some essentials of Lutheranism. The AC was recognized as a Luth. Conf., but distinction was made bet. "fundamental" and "non-fundamental" doctrines. S. S. Schmucker, theol. leader of the Gen. Syn. for ca. 40 yrs., repeatedly said that the AC was not to be followed unconditionally; its binding force was limited expressly to fundamentals. The confessional statements of the Gen. Syn. from 1820 till 1864, when the disruption of the Gen. Syn. began, may be summarized: The fundamental doctrines of the Bible, i. e., the doctrines in which all evangelical (non-Socinian) Christians agree, are taught in a manner substantially correct in the AC. The doctrines concerning baptismal regeneration and the real presence of the body and blood of Christ in the Lord's Supper, e. g., were rejected. The Ref. view of the Christian Sabbath was gen. adopted. See also *American Lutheranism.*

7. Those who defended the Confessions were decried as "Henkelites" (after the Henkels*) and "Symbolists.*" In 1855 S. S. Schmucker prepared the "Definite* Synodical Platform," which included a substitute for the AC. B. Kurtz* sponsored it in the *Lutheran Observer.* But a confessional reaction that had begun to set in ca. 10 yrs. earlier (see *United States, Lutheran Theology in,* 6) prevented gen. adoption of this document and even induced the Gen. Syn. 1864 to propose a constitutional amendment (see *York Amendment*) requiring syns. applying for membership to receive and hold "the Augsburg Confession, as a correct exhibition of the fundamental doctrines of the Divine Word, and of the faith of our Church founded upon that Word"; this amendment became part of the const. 1869. In course of time the official doctrinal basis of the Gen. Syn. conformed more and more to that of the Luth. Ch. In 1895, at Hagerstown, Md., the Gen. Syn. defined "the unaltered Augsburg Confession as throughout in perfect consistence with" the Word of God. In 1901, at Des Moines, Iowa, the Gen. Syn. resolved "that to make any distinction between fundamental and so-called non-fundamental doctrines in the Augsburg Confession is contrary to that basis as set forth in our formula of confessional subscription." In 1909, at Richmond, Ind., the Gen. Syn. resolved that "the General Synod in no wise means to imply that she ignores, rejects, repudiates or antagonizes the Secondary Symbols of the Book of Concord, . . . On the contrary, she holds those Symbols in high esteem, regards them as a most valuable body of Lutheran belief, explaining and unfolding the doctrines of the Augsburg Confession, . . ." In 1913, at Atchison, Kans., all Symbols of the Luth. Ch. were formally and officially adopted, thus paving the way for merger with the Gen. Council. Still there remained a wide gap bet. formal adoption and actual recognition of the Confessions; un-Luth. doctrine and practice were tolerated without official censure. Freemasons among clergy and laity occupied positions of trust and honor in the Gen. Syn. Leading men of the Gen. Syn. included D. H. Bauslin,* J. A. Brown,* J. G. Butler (see *Butler,* 2), F. W. Conrad,* L. A. Gotwald,* C. Philip Krauth,* C. Porterfield Krauth* (until 1866), B. Kurtz.* F. P. Manhart,* J. G. Morris,* W. M. Reynolds,* J. W. Richard,* D. F. Schaeffer,* S. S. Schmucker,* J. A. Singmaster,* S. Sprecher,* V. G. A. Tressler,* M. Valentine,* G. U. Wenner,* E. J. Wolf.*

8. Besides Home Miss. work carried on chiefly through dist. syns., the Gen. Syn. conducted a miss. at Guntur, India, and another in Liberia, Afr. Educational institutions included Carthage* Coll., Pa. Coll. (see *Gettysburg Coll.*), Gettysburg* Sem., Hamma* Divinity School, Hartwick* Sem., Martin* Luther Sem. (Lincoln, Nebr.), Midland* Coll., Susquehanna* U., Arthur G. Watts* Mem. Coll., Western* Sem., Wittenberg Coll. (see *Universities in the United States, Lutheran,* 6). Other institutions included a number of homes for orphans and the aged, and a deaconess motherhouse at Baltimore, Md.

9. In 1918 the Gen. Syn. entered the merger of various Luth. bodies, which had its origin in the movement for a joint celebration of the 1917 Reformation Quadricentennial. Largely as a result of action by laymen the planning committee resolved Apr. 18, 1917, to issue a call for union of "the General Synod, the General Council and the United Synod of the South, together with all other bodies one with" them in their Luth. faith. The Gen. Syn. approved this plan in Chicago June 23, 1917. The merger was consummated in NYC Nov. 14–18, 1918. At the time of this merger the Gen. Syn. consisted of 24 dist. syns., ca. 1,440 pastors, ca. 1,850 congs., ca. 370,300 confirmed mems. See also *United Lutheran Church in America, The.*

See also *Lutheran Foreign Mission Endeavors in the United States, Early; Sunday School,* 5; *Union and Unity Movements in the United States, Lutheran; United States Lutheranism in the.*

E. L. Hazelius, *History of the American Lutheran Church, from Its Commencement in the Year of Our Lord 1685, to the Year 1842* (Zanesville, Ohio, 1846); S. S. Schmucker, *The American Lutheran Church, Historically, Doctrinally, and Practically Delineated, in Several Occasional Discourses,* 5th ed. (Philadelphia, 1852); J. L. Neve, *The Formulation of the General Synod's Confessional Basis* (Burlington, Iowa, 1911); J. A. Singmaster, "The General Synod," *The Distinctive Doctrines and Usages of the General Bodies of the Evangelical Lutheran Church,* 4th ed., rev. and enl. (Philadelphia, 1914), pp. 36–68; V. Ferm, *The Crisis in American Lutheran Theology* (New York, 1927); E. J. Wolf, "History of the General Synod" and "Lutheranism in the General Synod," *The Quarterly Review of the Evangelical Lutheran Church,* XIX (July 1889), 420–458, and XXI (April 1891), 285–303; "Our General Synod," *The Evangelical Review,* V, No. 18 (Oct. 1853), 239–280.

General Synod of the Evangelical Lutheran Church in the Confederate States of America, The. See *General Synod of the Evangelical Lutheran Church in the United States of America, The,* 4; *United Lutheran Church, Synods of,* 5; *United Synod of the Evangelical Lutheran Church in the South.*

General Synod South, The Evangelical Lutheran. See *United Synod of the Evangelical Lutheran Church in the South,* 1.

Generalists. Advocates of The General* Syn. of the Ev. Luth. Ch. in the USA.

See also *Indiana Synod* (I).

Generalkonzession. See *Frederick William IV.*

Genesis, The Little. See *Jubilees, Book of.*

Geneva, Academy of. See *Calvin, John,* 7.

Geneva Bands. See *Vestments, Clerical,* 3.

Geneva Bible. See *Bible Versions,* K.

Geneva Catechism. See *Reformed Confessions,* A 7.

Geneva, Consensus of. See *Reformed Confessions,* A 9.

Geneva Gown. See *Vestments, Clerical,* 3.

Genevan Theocracy. See *Calvin, John,* 5.

Geneviève (Genovefa; ca. 422–ca. 500). Venerated by RCs as patron saint of Paris for her benevolence and alleged prophetic gift when Attila (ca. 406–453; king of the Huns ca. 433–453) attacked Paris 451.

Genizah. Repository in synagog for sacred objects and discarded or defective books and papers.

Gennadius I (d. 471). Patriarch Constantinople 458–471; opposed monophysitism. Works include commentaries on books of the Bible.

MPG, 85, 1611–1734.

Gennadius II (Georgios Scholarios; ca. 1405–ca. 1472). Byzantine scholar; lay theol.; patriarch Constantinople 1453–ca. 1466. Present at Council of Florence, where he advocated reuniting E and W Chs. After returning E he became leader of the opponents of union. See also *Eastern Orthodox Standards of Doctrine,* B 1; *Florence, Council of,* 1; *Russia,* 2.

MPG, 160, 249–774.

Gennadius of Marseilles (d. ca. 500 AD). Presbyter; hist.; semi-Pelagian. Works include *De viris illustribus* (continuation of a similar work by Jerome).

MPL, 58, 979–1120.

Gennadius of Novgorod (Gennadij; d. ca. 1505 AD). Archimandrite Moscow; abp. Novgorod ca. 1484; deposed ca. 1505; collected Slavic Bible translations.

Gennep, Arnold van. See *Dynamism.*

Gentile. Term used in the Vulgate for non-Jews. Non-Jews were admitted gradually into the ch., Acts 10:44-48. Miss. work was first done among gentiles at Antioch, Acts 11:19-20. Thereafter gentile Christianity soon exceeded Jewish converts in numbers.

Gentile, Giovanni (1875–1944). B. Castelvetrano, Sicily; It. philos.; prof. Naples, Palermo, Pisa, Rome; reformed It. educ. system; founded *Giornale critico della filosofia italiana.* Held reality is pure act of thinking in which 3 moments are distinguishable: subject, object, synthesis of these. Art is subjectivity and religion objectivity.

Gentile, Giovanni Valentino (ca. 1520–66). B. Cosenza, Calabria, It.; anti-Trinitarian; to Geneva ca. 1556 but left under pressure to subscribe to a confession emphasizing the Trinity*; attacked J. Calvin's* doctrine of the Trin. in *Antidota;* charges against him of blasphemy and mocking the Ref. Ch. led to his execution. See also *Socinianism,* 1.

Genuflectentes. Class of penitents (see *Penitential Discipline*) in the early ch. that were permitted to be present and kneel in the 1st part of worship services but were dismissed before the *Missa* fidelium.* See also *Missa catechumenorum.*

Genus idiomaticum, maiestaticum, apotelesmaticum. See *Christ Jesus,* I D.

Geoffrey of Monmouth (ca. 1100–54). B. probably at or near Monmouth, Eng.; bp. St. Asaph, Wales, Gt. Brit. Works include *Historia Britonum* (largely fiction; source of stories of King Arthur, King Lear, etc.).

Geography, Christian. 1. Christian geog. deals with geog., life, and hist. of Bible lands, esp. Palestine; furnishes the setting for Bible hist.; esp. its archaeol. aspect brings to life the domestic, soc., pol., and religious life of past ages.

2. Chronology of Christian geog. may be divided into 4 periods. The 1st begins with Constantine* I granting Christianity legal standing and imperial support and continues through the 18th c. To satisfy the stream of pilgrims visiting holy sites and places in Palestine, legends and traditions were developed.

3. In the 4th c. Eusebius* of Caesarea prepared a Gk. onomasticon* of Bible place names; Jerome* tr. it into Lat.

4. The 2d period, ca. 1800–ca. 1890, continued topographical interest. Journeys of E. Robinson* in 1838 and 1852 and his writings began the scientific approach. In the 2d half of the 19th c. the Palestine* Exploration Fund (inc. London, Eng., 1865) sponsored surveys and explorations of Palestine. Claude Reignier Condor (1848–1910) and Horatio Herbert Kitchener (1850–1916) were important participants. Achievements of Robinson and the Fund formed the basis of all later topographical work.

5. Various excavations were carried on in this period. Charles Warren (1840–1927; Brit. archaeol.), Selah Merrill (1837–1909; Am. Cong. clergyman; archaeol.), Charles Clermont-Ganneau (1846–1923; Fr. orientalist), and Hermann Guthe (1849–1936; Ger. geographer; archaeol.) were among those active in topographical and excavational exploration.

6. The 3d period covered ca. 1890–1914. It saw the beginning of the development of 2 basic principles of modern scientific archaeol.: stratigraphy and typology. The former is the study of the physical relationships of man-made objects in light of the strata in which they are found; the latter is classification of these objects based on comparative study of types. In the excavation of Tell el-Hesi (perhaps Eglon), F. Petrie* developed and applied these principles by setting up a chronological scheme for dating objects and strata. Among excavations of this period were those at Gezer (Robert Alexander Stewart Macalister [1870–1950; Irish archaeol.]) and Samaria (George Andrew Reisner [1867–1942; Am. Egyptologist] and Clarence Stanley Fisher [1876–1941; Am. hist. architect]). Frederick Jones Bliss (1859–1937; Am. archaeol.), Duncan Mackenzie (1859–1935; Scot. archaeol.), Charles Leonard Woolley (1880–1960; Eng. archaeol.), Thomas Edward Lawrence (1888–1935; Brit. archaeol.), E. F. M. Sellin,* Nathaniel Schmidt (1862–1939; Am. orientalist), Carl Watzinger (1877–1948; Ger. archaeol.), Warren Joseph Moulton (1865–1947; Am. archaeol.), and others explored and excavated in this period.

7. The 4th period began 1920. It has seen development of stratigraphy and typology. Aside from educ. institutions, the Am. and Brit. Schools of Oriental Research have contributed much to archaeol. development.

8. Important excavations were made at Megiddo, Beth-shan, Tell Beit Mirsim, Jericho, Lachish, Jerash (Gerasa), and Mounts Ophel and Zion. An increasing number of minor excavations were made. Nelson Glueck* (b. 1900; Am. archaeol.) made an extensive survey of Biblical sites in E Palestine. Other archaeologists of this period include Félix Marie Abel (1878–1953; Fr. Biblical scholar and Palestinian geographer), William Foxwell Albright* (b. 1891; Am. orientalist and archaeol.), J. Garstang,* Elihu Grant (1873–1942; Am. archaeol.), M. G. Kyle,* Louis Hugues Vincent (1872–1960; Fr. Biblical scholar and Palestinian archaeol.), and George Ernest Wright (b. 1919; Am. educator and archaeol.; Presb. clergyman). EHK

See also *Archaeology, Biblical; Dead Sea Scrolls.*

The Westminster Historical Atlas to the Bible, rev. ed. G. E. Wright and F. V. Filson (Philadelphia, 1956), pp. 9–14, 111—117; G. A. Barton, *Archaeology and the Bible,* 5th ed. (Philadelphia, 1927), pp. 89–117; W. F. Albright, "The Present State of Syro-Palestinian Archaeology," *The Haverford Symposium on Archaeology and the Bible,* ed. E. Grant (New Haven, Conn., 1938), pp. 1–46; C. C. McCown, *The Ladder of Progress in Palestine* (New York, 1943); D. Baly, *The Geography of the Bible* (New York, 1957) and *Geographical Companion to the Bible* (New York, 1963).

George (d. ca. 303 AD). Patron saint of Eng. and of the Order of the Garter; legendary figure allegedly of noble Cappadocian descent; perhaps a Christian martyr; development of his cult in the E led to inclusion of his effigy in the Russ. czars' coat of arms; legend of his combat with a dragon to liberate a princess arose ca. 12th c., possibly founded on the myths of Perseus and Siegfried.

George (ca. 640–ca. 724). B. in the lower Afrine valley, in the diocese of Antioch, Syria; bp. of Arab nomads in Mesopotamia. Writings are sources for hist. of Syrian Christianity.

George, Duke of Saxony. See *George the Bearded.*

George, Margrave of Brandenburg. See *George of Brandenburg-Ansbach.*

George, St., Church. See *Canada,* A 1.

George III of Anhalt (1507–53). B. Dessau, Ger.; canon at Merseburg 1518; studied at Leipzig; priest 1524; became Luth. after his mother's death June 1530; "coadjutor in spiritual affairs" at Merseburg 1544; did not join Schmalkaldic* League; favored Leipzig Interim*; known for piety, love of peace, gentleness, and benevolence.

George Ernst of Henneberg-Schleusingen (1511–83). Count of Henneberg-Schleusingen 1559–83; helped write Maulbronn Formula (see *Lutheran Confessions,* C 2); instituted a ch. order of Ref. character; signed Book* of Concord Oct. 17, 1579.

George Hamartolos (9th c. AD). "George the Monk"; Byzantine chronicler; opposed iconoclasm.

MPG, 110.

George of Brandenburg-Ansbach (1484–1543). Called The Pious and The Confessor. B. Ansbach (formerly Onolzbach), Ger.; margrove of Brandenburg; helped his brother Albert* of Prussia Lutheranize Prussia; aided the Reformation in Silesia and Ansbach; protested at Speyer 1529. See also *Lutheran Confessions,* A 2.

George of Denmark (1653–1708). Consort of Queen Anne (1665–1714; m. 1683; queen of Gt. Brit. and Ireland 1702–14); consistent Luth.; founded court chapel of St. James.

George Scholarius. See *Gennadius II.*

George the Bearded (1471–1539). B. Dresden, Ger.; duke of Albertine Saxony; welcomed M. Luther's* Ninety-five Theses* and attacked the corruptions of the ch.; fiercely opposed Luther's doctrine of grace and rejection of the Council of Constance*; persecuted Luths.; sponsored Leipzig* Debate 1519; banned Luth. publications; pub. a NT. See also *Pack, Otto von.*

Georgia Synod. See *United Lutheran Church, Synods of,* 4, 5.

Georgia-Alabama Synod. See *United Lutheran Church, Synods of,* 5.

Gerardus Magnus. See *Groote, Gerhard.*

Gerberding, George Henry (Aug. 21, 1847–Mar. 27. 1927). B. Pittsburgh, Pa.; educ. Thiel Coll. and Muhlenberg Coll. (see *Ministry, Education of,* VIII A 7, 11); ordained 1876; pastor and miss. in Pa., Ohio, and N. Dak.; founder and 1st pres. Syn. of the Northwest, pres. Chicago Syn. (see *United Lutheran Church, Synods of,* 20, 8); prof. Chicago Luth. Sem. and Northwestern Luth. Sem. (see *Ministry, Education of,* XI B 6, 10). Works include *The Way of Salvation in the Lutheran Church; Life and Letters of W. A. Passavant, D.D.; The Lutheran Pastor; The Lutheran Catechist; The Lutheran Church in the Country; Lutheran Fundamentals; R. F. Weidner.*

G. H. Gerberding, *Reminiscent Reflections of a Youthful Octogenarian* (Minneapolis, Minn., 1928).

Gerbert of Aurillac. See *Popes,* 6.

Gerdtell, Ludwig von (b. 1872; d. during period of nat. socialism). B. Brunswick, Ger.; Bap. traveling evangelist; espoused unitarian pacifistic Christianity.

Gerhard, Johann (Oct. 17, 1582–Aug. 17, 1637). "Archtheologian of Lutheranism"; b. Quedlinburg, Ger.; attended school at Quedlinburg till 1598. At the age of 15 he went through a critical illness and severe depression, during which he expected to die. This experience permanently deepened his piety and increased his understanding of Christian tribulation. His pastoral adviser, J. Arnd(t),* persuaded him to study theol.; throughout life Gerhard regarded him as his father in God.

When the plague swept through Quedlinburg, Gerhard entered school at Halberstadt 1598; attended univs. at Wittenberg (1599, philos., theol.; 1601, medicine), Jena (1603, theol.), and Marburg (1604, theol.); returned 1605 as student and lecturer to Jena, where he received his doctorate in theol. Nov. 13, 1606. In summer 1606 he had been made supt. at Heldburg under duke Johann* Kasimir of Coburg; ordained Aug. 14, 1606; gen. supt. Coburg 1615; prof. Jena; advisor to churchmen and statesmen.

Gerhard was the most influential of 17th c. Luth. theologians. He was an early participant in the renewal of Aristotelian metaphysics that began in Ger. univs. ca. 1600. He decisively influenced Prot. theologians to study the ev. character of pre-Reformation Christianity. In the doctrine of Scripture he made a significant advance by treating Scripture not as the object of faith but as the principium (basis) of theol. knowledge. The doctrine of justification is treated (as it was by the Reformers) as the *articulus stantis et cadentis ecclesiae* (the article with which the ch. stands or falls).

Works include *Patrologia; Loci theologici,* in which he combined the pattern of P. Melanchthon's* topical ("local") arrangement with methodology developed by J. Zabarella*; *Meditationes sacrae,* his most popular work, which, tr. into all major Eur. languages, attained a circulation next in order to the Bible and Thomas* a Kempis' *Imitatio Christi; Confessio catholica,* a model for ev. studies of pre-Reformation RC thought; *Schola pietatis.* RPS

See also *Quenstedt Johann(es) Andreas; Weimarische Bibelwerk, Das.*

E. R. Fischer, *Vita I. Gerhardi* (Leipzig, 1723); B. V. Hägglund, *Die heilige Schrift und ihre Deutung in der Theologie Johann Gerhards* (Lund, 1951); R. P. Scharlemann, *Thomas Aquinas and John Gerhard* (New Haven, Conn., 1964); E. Troeltsch, *Vernunft und Offenbarung bei Johann Gerhard und Melanchthon* (Göttingen, 1891); J. Wallmann, *Der Theologiebegriff bei Johann Gerhard und Georg Calixt* (Tübingen, 1961).

Gerhard, Johann Ernst. 1. (1621–68). B. Jena, Ger.; son of J. Gerhard*; prof. theol. Jena. Works include oriental and theol. studies; ed. his father's *Patrologia* and *Schola pietatis.* 2. (1662–1707). B. Jena, Ger.; son of 1; prof. Giessen. Works include *Kurtze Untersuchung eines unlängst herausgekommenen Büchleins unter dem Titul Der Luterisch- und Reformirten Religion Einigkeit.*

Gerhard of Zutphen (Geert Zerbolt van Zutphen; Gerhard Zerbolt, 1367–98). B. Zutphen, Neth.; priest and librarian of Brethren* of the Common Life at Deventer. His *De reformatione virium animae* and *De spiritualibus ascensionibus* influenced *Spiritual* Exercises* of Ignatius of Loyola.*

Gerhardt, Paul(us) (1607–76). B. Gräfenhainichen, bet. Wittenberg and Halle, Ger.; studied theol. in Wittenberg 1628–42; candidate of theol. and tutor in Berlin 1643–51; provost Mittenwalde 1651; pastor Berlin 1657; dismissed 1666 for refusal to sign syncretistic (see *Syncretism*) edicts of Frederick William ("Great Elector") of Brandenburg (1620–88; elector 1640–88); declined opportunity to return 1667; archdeacon Lübben 1669; hymnist.

Outward circumstances of his life are gloomy (wife and 4 children preceded him in death), but his hymns are full of cheerful trust, sincerely and unaffectedly pious, benign and amiable, reflecting firm grasp of objective realities but also transition to modern subjectivism.

Wrote 14 Lat. and 134 Ger. hymns; many have been tr., including "I Will Sing My Maker's Praises"; "O Lord, How Shall I Meet Thee"; "All My Heart

This Night Rejoices"; "Now Let Us Come Before Him"; "A Lamb Goes Uncomplaining Forth"; "Upon the Cross Extended"; "O Sacred Head, Now Wounded"; "Awake, My Heart, with Gladness"; "Oh, Enter, Lord, Thy Temple"; "Jesus, Thy Boundless Love to Me"; "Commit Whatever Grieves Thee"; "Now Rest Beneath Night's Shadow."

E. Kochs, *Paul Gerhardt* (Leipzig, 1926); T. B. Hewitt, *Paul Gerhardt as a Hymn Writer and his Influence on English Hymnody* (New Haven, Conn., 1918); H. Petrich, *Paul Gerhardt* (Gütersloh, 1907); W. Nelle, *Paul Gerhardt: Der Dichter und seine Dichtung* (Leipzig, [1940]); *Paul Gerhardt, sein Leben – seine Lieder: Karl Hesselbachers Paul Gerhardt – Der Sänger fröhlichen Glaubens,* ed. S. Heinzelmann (Neuffen, Ger., 1963).

Gerho(c)h of Reichersberg (Gerhohus; ca. 1093–1169). B. Polling, Bavaria; provost of Canons Regular of St. Augustine at Reichersberg 1132; a leading Gregorian (see *Popes,* 7) reformer in Ger.; banned by Emp. Frederick* I 1166.

MPL, 193, 461–1814.

Gericke, Christian Wilhelm (Apr. 5, 1742–ca. Oct. 2/3, 1803). B. Kolberg, Prussia; Luth. miss. in India; worked in Cuddalore 1767–82, Negapatam 1783–88, Madras 1788–1803; traveled extensively in S India.

Gerlach, Karl Friedrich Otto von (1801–49). B. Berlin, Ger.; studied theol. in Berlin 1834; court preacher 1847. Works include a 6-vol. Bible commentary.

Gerlach, Peters (Gerlac Peters; Gerlach Petersz; Gerlacus Petri; 1378–1411). B. Deventer, Neth.; lay theol. of the Brethren* of the Common Life; sent by Florentius* Radewijns into Windesheim monastery ca. 1400; exponent of *devotio* moderna* in Neth. Wrote *Soliloquium* and *Breviloquium.*

Gerlach, Stephan (1546–1612). B. Knittlingen, Württemberg; studied at Tübingen; Luth. embassy pastor at Constantinople 1573–78; active in unity efforts of Tübingen theologians with Jeremiah II (see also *Crusius, Martin*). Works include *De contemplatione coenae Domini* and polemical works against Reformed and RC theologians. See also *Schweigger, Solomon.*

Germain (Germanus; ca. 378–ca. 448). B. Auxerre, Fr.; bp. Auxerre; to Brit. 429 to combat Pelagianism (see *Pelagian Controversy*); allegedly led Brit. troops to victory over Picts and Saxons 447.

Germain (ca. 496–576). B. Autun, Fr.; bp. Paris 555; took part in councils at Paris (557, 573) and Tours (566); adviser of Frankish king Childebert I (son of Clovis* I; reigned 511–558); legendary elements gathered around his life.

MPL, 72, 55–111.

German Baptist Brethren. See *Brethren.*

German Catholics. Sect formed 1844 in Ger.; grew out of reform movement within RC Ch. caused by veneration of the Holy* Coat of Treves, against which J. Ronge* protested.

German Evangelical Church Society of the West, The (Der Deutsche Evangelische Kirchenverein des Westens; "Verein" is variously tr. in contemporary documents, e. g., "society," "association," "conference," "synod," "union"). Founded Oct. 1840 by H. Garlichs,* L. E. Nollau,* G. W. Wall,* and others at Gravois Settlement, near St. Louis, Mo. The constitutional assem. was held near St. Charles, Mo., May 1841.

The Kirchenverein considered itself related to the Ev. Ch. est. by the Prussian* Union. Its mems. acknowledged the Holy Scriptures of the Old and New Testaments as the Word of God and the only norm of faith, and the interpretation of the Holy Scriptures found in the symbolical books of the Ev. Luth. and the Ev. Ref. Ch. of Ger. "insofar as they agree." Confessional statements mention Augsburg Confession, Luther's and Heidelberg Catechisms. Where the Confessions disagree, mems. were to adhere to "the passages of Holy Scripture bearing on the subject" and retain freedom of conscience. The 1st issue of *Friedensbote,* organ of the Kirchenverein, appeared Jan. 1850. In 1866 the name of the Kirchenverein was changed to Deutsche Evangelische Synode des Westens (German Evangelical Synod of the West). Increasing favorable use of the term "synod" made inappropriate the old name, which was changed 1877 to Deutsche Evangelische Synode von Nord-Amerika (German Evangelical Synod of North America).

See also *United Church of Christ, The,* II B.

A. Schory, *Geschichte der Deutschen Evangelischen Synode von Nord-Amerika* (St. Charles, Mo., 1889); C. E. Schneider, *The German Church on the American Frontier* (St. Louis, 1939). EL

German Evangelical Lutheran Central Bible Society of Missouri, Illinois, and Iowa, in St. Louis, Missouri. Organized Apr. 1853 to promulgate Ger. Bibles and NTs in complete and correct eds. Held quarterly meetings and a Bible festival Sept. 22. Only Luths. in good standing were admitted to membership.

German Evangelical Lutheran Synod of Indianapolis. See *Indianapolis, German Evangelical Lutheran Synod of.*

German Evangelical Lutheran Synod of Maryland and Adjacent States. See *Maryland and Adjacent States, German Evangelical Lutheran Synod of.*

German Evangelical Lutheran Synod of New York and Other States. See *New York and Other States, German Evangelical Lutheran Synod of.*

German Evangelical Synod of North America. See *German Evangelical Church Society of the West, The; United Church of Christ, The,* II B.

German Evangelical Synod of the West. See *German Evangelical Church Society of the West, The.*

German Foreign Missionary Society, The. See *Lutheran Foreign Mission Endeavors in the United States, Early,* 2.

German Mass. See *Liturgics; Luther, Lituriges of.*

German Nebraska Synod. See *United Lutheran Church, Synods of,* 3.

German Protestant Union. See *Protestant Union, German.*

German Reformed Churches. See *Reformed Churches,* 3.

German Seventh-Day Baptists. See *Brethren,* 1; *Baptist Churches,* 17.

German Southwest Africa. See *Africa,* B 8.

German Theological Seminary of the General Synod. Est. in the early 1880s at Chicago, Ill., by The General* Syn. of the Ev. Luth. Ch. in the USA; discontinued 1898; became a Ger. dept. in Western* Theol. Sem., Atchison, Kans., 1898. See also *Neve, Juergen Ludwig; Severinghaus, John Dietrich.*

German Theology *(Deutsche Theologie; Theologia deutsch).* Book written ca. the end of the 14th or beginning of the 15th c. and containing a summary of fundamentals of Christian religion, "a noble booklet of the right understanding concerning Adam and Christ, and how Adam should die and Christ arise in us," as Luther puts it, who pub. the tract as a fragment 1516 and in complete form 1518. It is a product of Ger. mysticism.* Its unknown author, apparently active at Frankfurt, is often referred to as the Frankfurter (or Frankforter).

Germanos I (Germanus I; ca. 634–ca. 733). B. Constantinople; patriarch Constantinople 715–ca. 730; promoted Quinisext* Synod; opopsed Emp. Leo* III's iconoclasm; supported veneration of icons; promoted cult of Mary. Works include *De haeresibus et synodis.* See *also Acathistus.*

MPG, 98, 9–454.

Germanos, Lukas Pantaleon (family name Strenopoulos; 1872–1951). B. Eastern Thrace; educ. Constantinople; Gk. Orthodox metropolitan Thyatira;

leader of E Orthodox ecumenical delegations; held that all chs. compose the one body of Christ.

Germanus. See *Germain; Germanos.*

Germany. A. *Early Christian Hist.* 1. Christianity entered Ger. possibly as early as the 2d c. and spread in the Roman provinces of Ger. in the 3d c.; Gothic invasions 3d–6th c. led to a return to paganism. Subsequent missionaries to the Alemanni include Fridolin (largely a shadowy figure, said to have been an Irish Celt of the 6th or 7th c.), Columban* (see also *Celtic Church,* 8; preached among the Alemanni ca. 610), Gall,* and Pirmin.* Christianity entered the Roman provinces of Raetia and Noricum before the time of Constantine* I and spread after Constantine I and Theodosius* I. Agil(us)* and Eustace* came soon after 615 but had little success. Emmeram* was active in the 7th or 8th c., Rupert* and Kilian* of Würzburg ca. the end of the 7th c., and Corbinian* in the 1st part of the 8th c. Amandus* helped introd. Christianity among the Frisians. Wilfrid* evangelized south Saxons. Willibrord* is said to have been active throughout N Ger. Boniface* was active in Bavaria, Hesse, and Thuringia in the 8th c.

2. Two Anglo-Saxon monks, apparently both called Hewald (or Herwald) and distinguished as "the fair" and "the dark," engaged in unsuccessful miss. work among the Saxons near the end of the 7th c. Charlemagne* imposed Christianity on the Saxons in ca. 33 yrs. of military campaigns 772–ca. 805; the spiritual work was done by representatives of the ch. in bishoprics at Bremen, Verden, Minden, Münster, Paderborn, and Osnabrück, and later at Hildesheim and Halberstadt. Christianity was spread 919–973 by Henry* I and Otto* I among Wends in Holstein, Mecklenburg, Pomerania, and parts of Saxony and Lusatia chiefly by conquest, compulsion, and colonization. Pomerania submitted 1121 to Boleslav III (1086–1138; "Wry-mouthed"; king of Poland 1102–38) and Otto* of Bamberg est. the ch. 1124–28. The Gospel was first brought to the Prussians (Letts) 997 by Adalbert* of Prague; ca. 1209 the monk Christian* came to the Prussians. The crusade of the Teutonic Knights (see *Military Religious Orders,* c) and their allies ended 1283, with most of the Prussians slain and Christianity est. by real missionaries.

B. *Germany and the Luth. Ch.* Orders that supplied followers of M. Luther* include Augustinian* Hermits, Benedictines,* Carmelites,* Dominicans,* Franciscans,* and Premonstratensians.* M. Zell began ev. preaching in Strasbourg 1521; a 1523 resolution of the city council permitted only ev. preaching. Heinrich* von Zutphen began ev. preaching in Bremen 1522. Melchior Mirisch, an Augustinian prior who had studied at Wittenberg, began ev. preaching at Magdeburg 1522, and N. v. Amsdorf* with C. Cruciger* organized the Reformation there 1524. By 1535 Bremen, Brunswick, Goslar, Göttingen, Rostock, Hamburg, Lüneburg, and Hanover had declared for the Reformation. John* the Constant issued a directive Aug. 16, 1525, making Ernestine Saxony ev. The ch. in Hesse adopted the principles of the Saxon* ch. visitation 1528. George* of Brandenburg-Ansbach successfully undertook the Reformation in his Franconian territories. Other Ger. provincial chs. that followed the same or a similar pattern include those of Nürnberg, Brunswick-Lüneburg, Ostfriesland, Schleswig, Holstein, and Silesia. Albert* of Prussia introd. the Reformation in Prussia. Other areas won for the Reformation included Württemberg, Augsburg, Anhalt, Pomerania, Westphalia, Albertine Saxony, Brandenburg, Mecklenburg, Quedlinburg, Naumburg, Brunswick, the Palatinate, and Cologne. By 1555 Prots. were as strong as RCs. See also *Augsburg, Religious Peace of; Reformation.*

C. *Later Developments.* 1. RCs tried hard to halt the spread of Lutheranism and reconquer lost ground. Activity of Jesuits and of the courts of Austria and Bavaria, virulent persecution and suppression of Protestantism, and the Thirty* Years' War saved a large portion of Ger., esp. S Ger., for Rome. (See also *Counter Reformation.*) Areas that became Calvinistic in the 2d half of the 16th c. and early in the 17th c. include the Palatinate, Bremen, Nassau, Anhalt, Lippe-Detmold, and Hesse-Cassel. John* Sigismund, Elector of Brandenburg, turned Ref. 1613, but the people remained Luth.

2. Union bet. Luths. and Ref. in Prussia was decreed and effected 1817 by Frederick* William III, with gen. approval; Luths. and Ref. united also in Nassau, Baden, the Palatinate, Anhalt, and to some extent in Hesse. The new ch. thus brought into existence was called Evangelical. But some Luths. and some Ref. refused to have anything to do with it. See also *Germany, Lutheran Free Churches in; Prussian Union.*

The 1870s and 1880s were marked by the *Kulturkampf.** See also *May Laws.*

3. Prior to WW I the Luth., Ref., and Ev. Chs. in Ger. were organized as state chs., their govt. gen. being in the hands of consistories (see *Consistory*) and supts. appointed by the secular governing body, which provided, in greater part, for the support of the congs. out of the nat. revenues and more or less controlled ch. affairs. The const. of the Ger. Rep., adopted at Weimar Aug. 1919 by the Nat. Assem., declared ch. and state separate and all religious denominations equal (religious freedom having been est. already during the time of the Empire by the several state constitutions and by imperial law). There is no longer a state ch. But many among the clergy and laity seem to desire some kind of state support and control and a Volkskirche (People's Ch., Nat. Ch.), which the masses would regard as their ch.

4. Paul von Hindenburg (1847–1934; field marshall; pres. of the Rep. 1925–34) protected the rights of the ch. Adolf Hitler (1889–1945) came to power as chancellor Jan. 1933. It was at first felt that the rights of chs. would be protected also by him. A wave of religious revival followed. Ludwig Müller (1883–1945; a leader of *Deutsche Christen*) was elected Bp. of the Reich Sept. 1933. His attempt to unite the Ger. Prot. chs. in harmony with Nazi (National Socialist) party principles led to opposition by Martin Niemöller (b. 1892; leader of *Pfarrernotbund*) and others. Opposition to Nazi control of the ch. led to surveillance by police, arrests, imprisonment, and execution. Activities of chs., schools, and military ministries were curtailed. By the end of WW II the chs. were exhausted. See also *Barmen Theses; Kirchenkampf; Socialism,* 3.

5. Hardships endured during WW II drew Prot. groups closer together. Efforts were made to unite all Ger. Prots. The EKD (Evangelische Kirche in Deutschland) was organized July 13, 1948, as a fed. of Luth., Ref., and Ev. (or United) chs. The VELKD (Vereinigte Evangelisch-Lutherische Kirche Deutschlands) was organized July 8, 1948; its purpose is to strengthen Luth. consciousness through an organic union of all Luths. Of the 27 chs. in EKD (as of 1962), 13 are Luth.: the chs. of Saxony, Hanover, Bavaria, Schleswig-Holstein, Thuringia, Mecklenburg, Hamburg, Braunschweig, Lübeck, Schaumburg-Lippe, Württemberg, Eutin, and Oldenburg (all except the last 3 belong to VELKD); 12 Union (or United) chs.: Berlin-Brandenburg, Province of Saxony, Pomerania, Silesia, Westphalia, Rhineland, Hesse-Nassau, Kurhessen-Waldeck, Baden, the Palatinate, Anhalt, and Bremen (Luths. predominate in Pomerania, Berlin-Brandenburg, Crown Province of Saxony, Rhineland, Silesia, West-

phalia, Hesse-Nassau, Kurhessen-Waldeck, Anhalt, and Bremen); 2 Ref.: NW Ger. and Lippe. See also *Union Movements,* 8–9.

6. Free conferences at Bad Boll, Ger., were arranged 1948 by representatives of the LCMS and Luth. chs. in Ger. These conferences were a *Begegnung* (meeting of minds). The conferences were enlarged for 1949 to include representatives of additional Luth. groups in Eur. and Am.

See also *Roman Catholic Church, History of, Since the Reformation,* 9; *Germany, Lutheran Free Churches in.*

A. Hauck, *Kirchengeschichte Deutschlands.* 5 vols. in 6, 8th ed. (Berlin, 1954); K. Brandi, *Deutsche Reformation und Gegenreformation,* 2 vols. (Leipzig, [1927–30]); J. Lortz, *Die Reformation in Deutschland,* 2 vols., 3d ed. (Freiburg, 1949); R. Seeberg, *Die Kirche Deutschlands im neunzehnten Jahrhundert,* 2d ed. (Leipzig, 1904); *Die evangelische Christenheit in Deutschland: Gestalt und Auftrag,* ed. G. Jacob (Stuttgart, [1958]).

Germany, Catholic Church in. See *Counter Reformation,* 8; *Roman Catholic Church, History of, Since the Reformation,* 9.

Germany, Lutheran Free Churches in. 1. Before the monarchy in Ger. was abolished 1918, the state ch. was controlled by the govt.. One result was much interference by the state in the ch. Confessionalism was destroyed in many chs. by rationalism* and unionism.* In the 19th c. some Luths. organized free chs. for the sake of confessionalism and to avoid state control. The oldest of these chs. is the *Ev. Luth. (Old Luth.) Ch.* (also called Breslau Syn.), which originated 1830 in Prussia when Frederick* William III ordered enforcement of the union decreed 1817 and use of a unified *Agende* (see also *Prussian Union*). In Breslau, J. G. Scheibel* refused to conform. Many ch. mems. and some pastors in Silesia joined him. Among those that joined were G. P. E. Huschke* and H. Steffens.* For more than 10 yrs. the Old Luths. were persecuted by the state. Many went overseas (see *Australia, Lutheranism in; Buffalo Synod,* 1). In 1845 they were granted toleration by the "Generalkonzession" (see *Frederick William IV*). See also *Huschke, Georg Philipp Edward; Scheibel, Johann Gottfried.*

2. The movement spread steadily. By 1860 it numbered over 50,000, by 1918 over 60,000, with ca. 80 ministers serving ca. 180 congs. Its inner buildup was guided by Huschke. He created a const. according to which directive power is in the hands of the gen. ch. council, responsible to the gen. syn., the highest ecclesiastical authority. Cong. regulations are concerned with ev. ch.-discipline alongside doctrinal discipline. Elders are to aid pastors in spiritual care. A theol. sem. (1883–1945), a deaconess motherhouse, and support of the Leipzig* Ev. Luth. Miss. gave witness of active spiritual life.

3. Due to controversy about ch. polity, a number of individuals withdrew 1861–62 and formed the Immanuel Syn. 1864; reunion was achieved 1904. Soon after the end of WW II half of the congs. were dissolved, mainly the old original parishes in E Ger. provinces. The Ev. Luth. (Old Luth.) Ch. in 1968 numbered ca. 37,000 mems. Since the Luth. territorial chs. of Ger. joined the EKD (see *Germany,* C 5; *Union Movements,* 8–9) after WW II, the Ev. Luth. (Old Luth.) Ch. broke off ch. relations with them and allied more closely with other Free Churches. Church fellowship was est. Jan. 1948 with the Ev.-Luth. Free Ch. and the Mo. Syn. In place of the abandoned Breslau Sem. a new theol. school was est.; it was dedicated at Oberursel June 13, 1948; it is operated by the Ev. Luth. (Old Luth.) Ch. and the Ev.-Luth. Free Ch.

4. The *Ev.-Luth. Free Ch.* has a double root. F. A. Brunn* left the Nassau Ch. 1846 with 26 families and in nearby Steeden founded a Free Luth. Ch. that was severely persecuted by the govt. But the 1848 revolution brought toleration. More Luth. congs. formed in Nassau. They joined the Ev. Luth. (Old Luth.) Ch. of Prussia, but after the withdrawal that led to formation of the Immanuel Syn. (see par. 3 above), they also withdrew. Brunn had est. contact with C. F. W. Walther* in the 1850s. After Walther's 1860 visit in Ger., Brunn founded a "Proseminar" in Steeden which sent 235 candidates to the Mo. Syn.

5. In Saxony 2 Luth. laymen est. "Lutheranervereine" (Luth. socs.) in Dresden, Planitz, and Zwickau. These socs. strengthened their mems. spiritually by studying the Luth. Confessions and writings of Walther, Brunn, et al. When the state ch. abolished the old confessional subscription of the clergy 1871, the socs. lost all hope of improving ch. circumstances. They withdrew from the state ch., united with Free Luth. congs., and called F. C. T. Ruhland,* of the Mo. Syn., to be their pastor. Soon other pastors were found in Ger., including H. Z. Stallmann,* O. H. T. Willkomm,* and K. G. Stöckhardt.* The Syn. of the Ev.-Luth. Free Ch. in Saxony was formed 1876; the words "and Other States" were added to the name when congs. at Steeden, Wiesbaden, Frankfurt, and Ansbach joined 1877.

6. Ruhland was the 1st pres. of this syn. According to its const., all spiritual power lay in the parish, but with syn., advisory, not legislative, exercising spiritual influence in overseeing doctrine and life. A conflict about predestination, beginning ca. 1880, and a 1906 conflict about justifying faith led to painful separations from the syn. In syn. convs. and pastoral confs., doctrinal discussions are of prime importance.

7. Free Luth. parishes in Hanover, E. Prussia, Den., and S Ger. joined. In 1968 the Ev. Luth Free Ch. numbered ca. 15,000 mems. Like the Ev. Luth. (Old Luth.) Ch., the Ev.-Luth Free Ch. suffers under the division of Ger. The ch. press in the E was suppressed. Importing ch. leaflets from the W was prohibited. The parish school system had been abolished under the Nazis. But unity of faith and confession remained. The theol. sem. at Leipzig became the educational center for students of the E part of the ch.

8. The *Indep. Ev. Luth. Ch.* has its parishes in W. Ger. It came into being 1947–50 and is an alliance of 5 Luth. Free Chs., formerly indep., that exist as dioceses in the new church. 1968 membership ca. 21,000.

9. The oldest of the 5 chs. in the Indep. Ev. Luth. Ch. is the Ev. Luth. Free Ch. of Baden, where Karl Eichhorn (b. 1810 at Kembach, Baden; educ. Halle; pastor Bofsheim; left Baden Est. Ch. and joined Luth. Free Ch. 1850; active in Ihringen and Waldeck) led the struggle for the awakening of the Luth. Ch. Despite yrs. of persecution by the state, he succeeded in gathering a number of congs. The diocese of Baden has ca. 5,500 mems.

10. Two Luth. Free Chs. developed in Hesse against a complicated hist. background as Hessian and Lower Hessian dioceses. They contended for freedom of the ch. from the state and defended themselves against the unionistic ch. policy of the state ch. In 1873–75 they were separated from the state ch. and founded an indep. free ch. 1877. The Hessian Diocese has ca. 3,800 mems., the Lower Hessian Diocese ca. 1,600 mems.

11. The roots of the Hanover and the Hermannsburg-Hamburg-dioceses lie in the awakening movement connected with G. L. D. T. Harms.* His followers watched rationalistic and unionistic influences in the Luth. state ch. of the province of hannover with growing anxiety, esp. after the land was an-

nexed by Prussia in 1866. When a new marriage rite was introd. 1875, several pastors refused to adopt it; among them was T. Harms,* brother and follower of G. L. D. T. Harms. They were dismissed from office and forsook the state ch., taking a large segment of their congs. with them. Unfortunately questions about ch. organization soon divided this Free Ch. The split became deeper when the Hermannsburg* Miss. resumed closer relations with the state ch. 1890. The Hermannsburg-Hamburg Free Ch. continued to support the Hermannsburg Miss.; the Hanover Free Ch. est. its own miss. 1892 with headquarters in Bleckmar (see also *Mission of the Evangelical Lutheran Free Churches*). The Hanover Diocese has ca. 5,400 mems., the Hermannsburg-Hamburg Diocese ca. 4,600 mems.

12. The Indep. Ev. Luth. Ch. is headed by the gen. supt. and the supts. of dioceses, assisted by an advisory council. All decisions of the leadership are subject to diocesan approval.

13. The *Ev. Luth. Confessional Ch.* (Ev.-luth. Bekenntnis-Kirche in der Diaspora) began 1946 as Ev. Luth. Refugee Miss. Ch. (Ev.-luth. Flüchtlingsmissions-Kirche) and changed to its present name 1951. It consists of mems. of the former Ev. Luth. Free Ch. of Poland, founded 1924 in Lodz; made contact with the Wisconsin* Ev. Luth. Syn.; has ca. 3,400 mems.

14. The Luth. Free Chs. of Ger. are in pulpit and altar fellowship with each other. The Ev. Luth. (Old Luth.) Ch., the Ev. Luth. Free Ch., and the Indep. Ev. Luth. Ch. united 1958 to form the Work Union of Free Ev. Luth. Chs. in Ger. (Arbeitsgemeinschaft freier ev.-luth. Kirchen in Deutschland). These 3 chs. merged 1972/73 to form the Indep. Ev. Luth. Ch. (Selbständige Evangelisch-Lutherische Kirche); the Ev. Luth. Confessional Ch. (see 13) did not enter the merger.

E. Bingmann, *Geschichte der hannoverschen evang-luth. Freikirche* (Celle, 1924); F. Brunn, *Mitteilungen aus meinem Leben* (Zwickau, n. d.); G. Froböss, *Drei Lutheraner an der Universität Breslau* (Breslau, 1911) and *Die Evangelisch-lutherischen Freikirchen in Deutschland,* 2d ed. (Leipzig, 1913); G. Herrmann, "Vorgeschichte und Anfänge der Evangelisch-Lutherischen Freikirche in Sachsen und anderen Staaten," *Lutherischer Rundblick,* VIII (1960), 12–31; A. Lückhoff, *Die lutherischen Freikirchenverfassungen in Deutschland* (Lüchow, 1960); G. Malschner-Maliszewski, "Die evangelisch-lutherische Bekenntniskirche in der Diaspora," *Viele Glieder – Ein Leib,* ed. U. Kunz (Stuttgart, 1953), pp. 40–43; A. Mie, *Die lutherischen Freikirchen in Deutschland* (Molzen, n. d.); K. Müller, *Die selbständige evangelisch-lutherische Kirche in den hessischen Landen* (Elberfeld, 1906); G. J. S. Nagel, *Unsere Heimatkirche,* 2d ed. (Breslau, 1924); J. Nagel, *Die evangelisch-lutherische Kirche in Preussen und der Staat* (Stuttgart, 1869) and *Die Errettung der evang-luth. Kirche in Preussen* (Erlangen, 1869); J. G. Scheibel, *Actenmässige Geschichte der neuesten Unternehmung einer Union zwischen der reformirten und lutherischen Kirche, vorzüglich durch gemeinschaftliche Agende in Deutschland, und besonders in dem preussischen Staate,* 2 vols. (Leipzig, 1834); K. Wicke, *Die hessische Renitenz* (Kassel, 1930); *Eine kleine Kraft,* ed. M. Willkomm (Zwickau, 1921); W. Wöhling, *Geschichte der Evangelisch-Lutherischen Freikirche in Sachsen u. a. St.* (Zwickau, 1925); *Continuing in His Word* (Milwaukee, 1951), pp. 251–260. GR (tr. EH)

Gernler, Lukas (1625–75). Pastor Basel, Switz., 1653, prof. 1656; helped write *Formula consensus ecclesiarum helveticarum reformatarum* (see also *Reformed Confessions,* A 10).

Gerok, Karl Friedrich von (1815–90). B. Vaihingen, Württemberg, Ger.; educ. Tübingen; held positions in state ch. at Stuttgart beginning 1849, finally as chief court preacher and mem. high consistory; eloquent preacher; poet. Works include spiritual lyrics (e. g., *Palmblätter; Pfingstrosen*).

Gerretsen, Jan Hendrik (1867–1923). B. Nijmegen, Neth.; court preacher in Holland; pub. of his *Liturgy* contributed to liturgical revival in the Nederlandse Hervormde Kerk; he tried to develop a new approach to justification and Christology; considered material world not creation of God but the result of error in the originally created ethical world.

Gerrits(z), Lubbert (official family name: Yserman; 1534–1612). B. Amersfoort, Dutch province of Utrecht; weaver; joined Mennonite movement ca. 1556; persecuted at Amersfoort 1559; fled to Hoorn, Dutch province of N. Holland, 1559; ordained 1559. Leader of less strict Frisian Mennonites. Works include *Verantwoordinghe op die seven Artyckelen.*

Gerson, Jean de (Jean Charlier; Johannes Arnaudi de Gersonio; ca. 1363–ca. 1429). B. Gerson (Jarson), near Rethel, Fr.; educ. Reims and Paris; influenced by P. d'Ailly (see *Ailly, Pierre d'*); chancellor U. of Paris 1395.

Drawn to the problem of papal schism, Gerson influenced the Councils of Pisa* and Constance.* Pol. turmoil in Fr. and hostility of Jean sans Peur (John the Fearless; 1371–1419; duke of Burgundy 1404–19), whose theory of tyrannicide Gerson dared to oppose, kept Gerson from returning to Fr. He spent some time in Bavaria and Austria and concluded his life in pastoral and literary activities at Lyons, Fr.

Gerson was equally at home in ecclesiastical politics, philos., and the cure of souls, and was a renowned orator. His chief concern was that the people, both educated and simple, would live truly pious lives. He sought to blend his nominalism* with a simple mysticism,* in an attempt to achieve a kind of religious experience in which all could participate. A moderate conciliarist (see *Councils and Synods,* 7), he supported the Gallican way in the papal schism and called for the abdication of the incumbents. He has with some reason been spoken of as a prereformer, but he held that for salvation man must "do what is in him."

Works include sermons; ecclesiastical, mystical and pastoral treatises; devotional writings. Editions include *Opera Omnia,* ed. L. E. Dupin, 5 vols. (Antwerp, 1706); *Oeuvres Complètes,* ed. P. Glorieux (Paris, 1960–).

J. L. Connolly, *John Gerson: Reformer and Mystic* (Louvain, 1928); W. Dress, *Die Theologie Gersons* (Gütersloh, 1931) and "Gerson und Luther," *ZKG,* LII (1933), 122–161. DGS

Gersonides. See *Levi ben Gershon.*

Gertrude. 1. the Great (1256–perhaps ca. 1302). Ger. mystic; placed in convent of Helfta, near Eisleben, at age 5; famed for visions; exponent of devotion to Sacred* Heart of Jesus. Works include *Legatus divinae pietatis; Exercitia spiritualia.* See also *Mechthild of Hackeborn.* 2. of Hackeborn (ca. 1232–92). Abbess of convent at Rodersdorf, Ger. (convent moved to Helfta 1258); sister of Mechthild* of Hackeborn. 3. of Nivelles (ca. 626–659). Abbess of convent at Nivelles, Belg.; regarded as patroness of travelers.

Gervase and Protase (Gervasius and Protasius). Traditional martyrs; patrons of Milan, It.; nothing definite is known about them; even their existence has been questioned; said to have suffered under Nero (see *Persecutions of Christians,* 3); Ambrose* discovered their alleged bodies in the ch. of SS. Nabor and Felix, Milan, and transferred them to the Basilica of St. Ambrose, Milan.

Gesellschaft für innere (und äussere) Mission im Sinne der Kirche. See *Neuendettelsau Mission Society.*

Gesenius, Heinrich Friedrich Wilhelm (1786–1842). B. Nordhausen, Ger.; educ. Helmstedt and Göttingen; Prot.; Hebraist; rationalist; prof. Halle 1810; attacked by K. F. O. v. Gerlach* and E. W. Hengstenberg* in *Evangelische Kirchenzeitung.* Works include *Hebräische Grammatik; Thesaurus philologicus criticus linguae Hebraeae et Chaldaeae Veteris Testamenti; Der Prophet Jesaia. See also Buhl, Frants Peder William; Lexicons,* A.

Gesenius, Justus (1601–73). B. Esbeck, Ger.; educ. Helmstedt and Jena; pastor Brunswick 1629; court chaplain Hildesheim 1636; chief court preacher and gen. supt. Hanover 1642; accomplished theologian; hymnist; with D. Denicke* ed. Hanoverian hymnal; adapted old hymns to the style of M. Opitz.* Hymns include "Wenn meine Sünd' mich kränken."

Gesius, Bartholomäus (Gese; Göse; Göss; perhaps ca. 1560–ca. 1614). Luth. choral composer; b. Müncheberg, Ger.; studied theol. at Frankfurt an der Oder; cantor Müncheberg 1582, Frankfurt an der Oder 1593. Works include *Johannes-Passion.*

Gess, Wolfgang Heinrich Christian Friedrich (1819–91). B. Kirchheim unter Teck, Ger.; educ. Tübingen; pastor Grossaspach 1847; prof. systematic theol. and exegesis Göttingen 1864, Breslau 1871; mem. Silesian consistory; gen. supt. province of Posen; kenoticist (see *Kenosis*). Works include *Die Lehre von der Person Christi.*

Gestalt Psychology. See *Educational Psychology,* D 5; *Psychology,* J 5.

Gettysburg College. Beginnings date to gymnasium or academy classes taught at Gettysburg, Pa., 1827 by D. Jacobs,* a student at Gettysburg* Sem.; inc. 1832 as Pa. Coll.; name changed 1921 to Gettysburg Coll. See also *General Synod of the Evangelical Lutheran Church in the United States of America, The,* 8; *Lutheran Church in America,* V; *Ministry, Education of,* VIII B 13; *United Lutheran Church, Synods of,* 23.

Gettysburg Seminary. Founded 1826 at Gettysburg, Pa., by the Gen. Syn. See also *General Synod of the Evangelical Lutheran Church in the United States of America, The,* 8; *Lutheran Church in America,* V; *Ministry, Education of,* VI C, X J; *United Lutheran Church, Synods of,* 23.

A. R. Wentz, *History of the Gettysburg Theological Seminary . . . 1826–1926* (Philadelphia, [1926]).

Geulincx, Arnold (Aernout; Geulingx; Geulings; 1624–69). B. Antwerp, Belg.; Cartesian (see *Descartes, René*) philos.; educ. Louvain; prof. Louvain 1641–58; became Prot. (Calvinist) 1658; prof. Leiden 1665. Developed theory of occasionalism.* Works include *Ethica; Metaphysica vera.*

Geyer, Carl Ludwig (Mar. 16, 1812–Mar. 6, 1892). B. Zwickau, Saxony; educ. Zwickau and Leipzig; private tutor; joined Saxon Emigration 1838 (see *Lutheran Church – Missouri Synod,* I 1–2); teacher Old Trinity, St. Louis, Mo., till 1840, Johannesberg, Cape Girardeau Co., Mo., 1840–44. Ordained Oct. 23, 1844; pastor Lebanon, Wis., 1844–60, Carlinville, Ill., 1860–76, Serbin, Tex., 1876–92. Wrote Ger. primer used widely in Mo. Syn.

A. C. Stellhorn, "Carl Ludwig Geyer," *CHIQ,* XII (1939), 3–12.

Geyer, Christian Karl Ludwig (1862–1929). B. Manau, Unterfranken; chief preacher St. Sebald Ch., Nürnberg, 1902; leader of liberal theol. with F. Rittelmeyer*; with Rittelmeyer founded journal *Christentum und Gegenwart* 1910 (it took the name *Christentum und Wirklichkeit* 1923); later turned from Rittelmeyer; emphasized God's forgiveness.

Geyer, Florian (ca. 1490–1525). B. Giebelstadt, near Würzburg, Ger.: knight; leader of peasants; adherent of M. Luther.*

Geyler von Kaisersberg. See *Geiler von Kaysersberg.*

Geyser, Gerhard Josef Anton Maria (1869–1948). B. Erkelenz, Ger.; RC philos.; taught at Münster, Freiburg, and Munich. Criticized materialistic tendencies in psychology; espoused Aristotelian causality.

Gezelius. 1. *Johan(nes) the Elder* (1615–90). B. Romfartuna, Västmanland, Swed.; orthodox Fin. Luth. theol.; prof. Dorpat 1641–49; gen. supt. Livonia 1661–64; bp. Aabo 1664–90; advanced educ. of clergy and laity. 2. *Johan(nes) the Younger* (1647–1718). B. Dorpat; son of 1, whose work he continued; bp. Aabo 1690–1718; opposed pietism.* 3. *Johan(nes) Nepos* (1686–1733). B. Narva; son of 2; prof. Aabo 1710–21; bp. Borgaa 1721–33.

Ghana. See *Africa,* C 11.

Ghazzali, al- (Ghazali; Lat.: Algazel; Arab.: Abu-Hamid Muhammad al-Ghazzali). See *Arabic Philosophy.*

Ghiberti, Lorenzo (1378–1455). B. Florence, It.; painter, goldsmith, and sculptor. Works include N and E portals of San Giovanni baptistery, Florence.

Ghirlandajo, Domenico (Ghirlandaio; Grillandajo; Domenico do Tommaso Bigordi; 1449–94). B. Florence, It.; painter; teacher of Michelangelo.* Works include frescoes in Florence; helped decorate Sistine Chapel, Rome.

Ghost. 1. Immortal spirit in man (soul). 2. Phantom or apparition. 3. Used in the name of the 3d Person of the Trinity.* See also *Holy Ghost.*

Ghost, Holy. See *Holy Ghost.*

GI Gospel Crusade. See *Far Eastern Gospel Crusade.*

Gibbon, Edward (1737–94). B. London, Eng.; historian; RC for a short time. Works include *The History of the Decline and Fall of the Roman Empire.*

Gibbons, James (1834–1921). B. Baltimore, Md.; educ. Baltimore; RC priest 1861; titular bp. Adramyttium and vicar bp. N. C.; bp. Richmond, Va., 1872; abp. Baltimore 1877; presided over 3d plenary council of Baltimore 1884 (see also *Councils and Synods,* 6); cardinal 1886. Works include *The Faith of Our Fathers.* See also *Roman Catholic Church,* E 9.

J. T. Ellis, *The Life of Cardinal Gibbons,* 2 vols. (Milwaukee, 1952).

Gibbons, Orlando (1583–1625). B. Cambridge, Eng.; organist and composer; used only Eng. in the text of his music.

Giberti, Gian Matteo (1495–1543). B. Palermo, Sicily; bp. Verona; advocated reform; prepared way for Council of Trent.*

Gibson, Edmund (1669–1748). B. Hampton, Eng.; bp. Lincoln and London; orthodox theol.; opposed Latitudinarians* and Deism*; expert on ecclesiastical law. Works include *Codex juris ecclesiastici Anglicani.*

Gichtel, Johann Georg (1638–1710). B. Regensburg, Ger.; to the Neth. with J. E. v. Wel(t)z*; influenced by F. Breckling*; in Amsterdam from 1668; mystic and visionary; eccentric follower of J. Böhme*; attacked Luth. Ch. and doctrine of justification; followers called Gichtelians.*

Gichtelians. Followers of J. G. Gichtel*; also called Angelic Brethren or Brethren of the Angels (Ger.: Engelsbrüder) because they rejected marriage (cf. Mt 22:30). The movement spread to Altona, Berlin, Hamburg, Magdeburg, and Nordhausen.

Gideons. See *Bible Societies,* 5.

Gieseler, Johann Karl Ludwig (pseudonym: Irenäus; 1792–1854). B. Petershagen, near Minden, Ger.; ch. hist.; prof. Bonn 1819, Göttingen 1831; active in social work. Works include *Lehrbuch der Kirchengeschichte.* See also *Mediating Theology.*

Gifford Lectures. Lectures for Scot. univs.; endowed by Adam Gifford (1820–87) "for promoting, advancing, teaching, and diffusing the study of natural theology."

Gifftheil, Ludwig Friedrich (1595–1661). B. Böhringen, Ger.; apocalyptic writer; traveled in Scand.; spent last yrs. in Holland; pacifist.

Gift of Tongues. See *Tongues, Gift of.*

Gifts of the Spirit (charismata). 1. The gift of justifying faith* is the Holy* Ghost's primary gift (1 Co 12:3; Eph 1:19).

2. In Ro 12, 1 Co 12, and Gl 5 many other, supplementary, gifts are listed which, according to His purposes, the Spirit gives in varying measure; they are called fruits and represent qualities that every Christian may attain to some degree; some have gifts in greater degree than others. The fruits include love, joy, peace, longsuffering, gentleness, goodness, faith, meekness, and temperance (Gl 5: 22-23).

3. Gifts of the Spirit are nurtured in Christian lives through reverent use of Word and Sacraments. These fruits of the Spirit stand in marked contrast to the "works of the flesh" (Gl 5:19-21).

4. Gifts of the Spirit not intended for all believers are enumerated 1 Co 12:8-10: the word of wisdom, the word of knowledge, faith, gifts of healing, working of miracles, prophecy, discerning of spirits, tongues (glossolalia; from Gk. for "tongue" and "speaking"), and interpretation of tongues. Some will have one of these gifts, others another, or one person may have several in various measure. Such gifts may in some cases be directed to special use or bestowed on persons weak in faith.

5. Various offices by which mems. of the body of Christ serve one another in special ways are also gifts of the Spirit. God gives the ch. apostles, prophets, teachers, miracles and workers of miracles, gifts of healings, helps, governments, diversities of tongues and the interpretation of tongues (1 Co 12:28-30). The list in 1 Co 12:8-10 overlaps with that in 1 Co 12:28-30 and the counterparts are not all clear.

6. The role which gifts of the Spirit are to play in the Christian community is stated 1 Co 12:7 ("to profit withal") and 1 Ptr 4:10 ("minister the same one to another"). The extent and range of special gifts seem to have been greater in apostolic times than now.

7. In Ro 12:5-6 the origin of specific gifts is stated in gen. terms ("having then gifts differing according to the grace that is given to us") and their use is related to the grand truth that "we, being many, are one body in Christ, and every one members one of another."

8. The classic chap. on the gift of tongues,* 1 Co 14, follows immediately after the chapter in which Paul says that apart from "charity," or "Christian love," other gifts and endeavors are nothing.

9. After an admonition to follow charity and desire spiritual gifts (1 Co 14:1) Paul speaks about the gift of tongues. He recognizes the gift of tongues as a valid and important spiritual gift but also points out how easily this gift can be abused and cautions against unwholesome use.

10. According to Acts 2 the apostles received ability to speak (at least for the occasion) in languages they had never learned, but the gift of tongues referred to 1 Co 14 seems to be another type of utterance granted by the Spirit. These tongues are gen. called "ecstatic utterances" and involve use of Spirit-motivated sounds that are not intelligible in terms of known language. They do have meaning that can be stated by one who has the gift of interpretation.

11. Other references to gifts of the Spirit include Mt 10:1, 8; Lk 10:9, 17, 19; Acts 10:44-46; 1 Co 7:7. OS

See also *Seven Gifts of the Holy Spirit.*

Gigas. See *Heune, Johann.*

Gilbert de la Porrée (Gilbert[us] Porreta[nus]; Gilbert of Poitiers; ca. 1070s–1154). B. Poitiers, Fr.; scholastic theol.; bp. Poitiers 1142; differentiated bet. class essence *(subsistentia)* and substance *(substantia);* accused of tritheism* by Bernard* of Clairvaux. *MPL,* 64, 1255–1300, 1301–10, 1313–34, 1353 to 1412; 188, 1247–70.

Gilbert Islands. Group of 16 atolls in W Pacific SSE of Marshall Is. and NE of Solomon Is.; ca. 2,800 mi. NE of Australia. *Land area:* ca. 102/105 sq. mi.; *pop.* (mixed Malay and Polynesian): ca. 44,000. Brit. protectorate 1892; made part of Gilbert and Ellice Is. Colony 1915; occupied by Jap. Dec. 1941–Nov. 1943. ABCFM began work 1857, LCMS 1870. After WW I the ABCFM turned its work over to the LMS.

Gilbertines. Eng. order of nuns founded ca. 1135 by Gilbert of Sempringham (ca. 1083–1189; Eng. priest; b. Sempringham); dissolved by Henry* VIII.

Gildas (ca. 500–ca. 570). Called "Sapiens" and "Badonicus;" Brit. monk and hist.; wrote *Gildae Sapientis de excidio et conquestu Britanniae,* which includes description of the battle of Mons Badonicus, which, he seems to say, occurred in the yr. of his birth.

Giles. Eng. form of Aegidius.*

Gilgamesh Epic. See *Babylonians, Religion of the,* 6.

Gill, John (1697–1771). B. Kettering, Northamptonshire, Eng.; joined Particular Baps. 1716; ordained 1720; pastor Horselydown [Horsley Down], Southwark, London, 1720–71; strict Calvinist. Works include *A Body of Doctrinal Divinity;* commentary on the Bible.

Gill, William (1813–78). B. Totness, Eng.; LMS miss. to Rarotonga 1838; visited Mangaia, Loyalty Islands, New Hebrides, New Caledonia, and Samoa; returned to Eng. 1853. Works include rev. of the Rarotongan Bible.

Gillespie, Thomas (1708–74). B. Clearburn, near Edinburgh, Scot.; educ. Edinburgh and Doddridge's academy, Northampton, Eng.; Presb. pastor Carnock, Scot.; deposed by Gen. Assem. 1752 for refusal to conform; with other indeps. he founded a presbytery 1761 for relief of Christians deprived of ch. privileges; this grew into the Relief* Ch., which 1847 joined with the United* Secession Ch. to form the United* Presb. Ch. of Scotland. See also *Presbyterian Churches,* 1.

Gilman, Samuel (1791–1858). B. Gloucester, Mass.; hymnist; educ. Harvard; Unitarian pastor Charleston, S. C. Hymns include "This Child We Dedicate to Thee," perhaps a tr. of a Ger. hymn.

Gingrich, Felix Wilbur. See *Lexicons,* B.

Ginsburg, Christian David (1831–1914). B. Warsaw, Poland; Jewish grammarian and Massorete; educ. Warsaw; became Christian ca. 1846; to Eng.; mem. OT Rev. Committee 1870.

Gioberti, Vincenzo (1801–52). It. pol. and philos.; b. and educ. Turin; priest 1825; held that God is the only true being *(ens)*; all other things are only existences, the universal idea in God individualized and become finite; attacked Jesuits; tried to reform the papacy.

Giotto (Giotto di Bondone; ca. 1267–ca. 1337). B. Vespignano, near Florence, It.; painter, sculptor, and architect. Works include many religious frescoes.

Giovanni da Fiesole. See *Angelico, Fra.*

Girard, Stephen (1750–1831). B. Bordeaux, Fr.; settled in Philadelphia, Pa., ca. 1776; philanthropist; freethinker; admired Voltaire* and J. J. Rousseau.*

Girdle. In liturgical attire, a cincture. See also *Vestments, Clerical.*

Girgensohn, Karl Gustav (1875–1925). B. Carmel, on the island Oesel, Latvia; conservative Ger. Luth. theol.; prof. Dorpat, Greifswald, and Leipzig; used findings of experimental psychology in attempts to explain psychological aspects of faith.

Girl Guides. Originated in Eng. as a spontaneous movement of girls; similar to Girl* Scouts; organized by R. Baden-Powell and his sister Agnes; given royal charter 1923; purpose: to promote good citizenship and a sense of service to others. The Girl Guide pledges duty to God and country; to help others; to obey the Guide law. The movement includes Brownies (8–11), Guides (11–15), Rangers 15–21).

Girl Scouts. There is no community of organization and administration bet. Girl Scouts and Boy* Scouts. Like scouting for boys, the Girl Scout movement has these features: 1. a pledge and a law; 2. uniforms and insignia; 3. degrees of advancement; 4. ch. troops and non-ch. troops; 5. program of indoor and outdoor activities; 6. regular organization; 7. trained leaders. Supervision is exercised by headquarters to maintain uniform prescribed standards for advancement in degrees, but no attempt is made to encroach on the duties and prerogatives of ch. and home. See also *Girl Guides.*

Given, James F. See *Christian Union.*

Giving, Christian. See *Finances in the Church.*

Gjerset, Knut (Sept. 15, 1865–Oct. 29, 1936). B. Romsdal, Nor.; to Am. 1871; educ. U. of Minn., Johns Hopkins, Heidelberg, Oslo, and Berlin; prof. St. Ansgar (Iowa) Sem. 1893–95, Glenwood (Minn.) Academy 1900–02, Luther Coll., Decorah, Iowa 1902–16, 1917–36; pres. Park Region Luther Coll., Fergus Falls, Minn., 1916–17; helped found Norw.-Am. Hist. Assoc.; curator Norw. Am. Hist. Museum; vice-pres., later pres., Iowa Hist. Assoc. Works include histories of Scand. countries and people.

Gjevre, Anders Haldorsen (June 9, 1852–Apr. 29, 1930). B. Vang, Valdres, Norw.; to Am. 1871; Luth. clergyman, ordained Norw. Syn. 1881 (see *Evangelical Lutheran Church, The,* 8–13); studied Heb. by correspondence under W. R. Harper*; attended Columbia U. 1902–03; pastor of various parishes in S. Dak., Minn., and Wis. 1881–1913; prof. Heb., United Ch. Sem., 1897–98; miss. to Jews, N. Y., 1900–03, Minneapolis, Minn., 1913–30. Works include *The Jewish Problem and Its Solution.*

Gladden, Washington (1836–1918). Cong. clergyman; author, hymnist; b. Pottsgrove, Pa.; educ. Williams Coll., Williamstown, Mass.; pastor Brooklyn, N. Y., 1860, Morrisania, N. Y., 1861, North Adams, Mass., 1866, Springfield, Mass., 1874, Columbus, Ohio, 1882. Studied writings of F. W. Robertson* and H. Bushnell*; at North Adams began applying Christian principles to soc. problems; early apostle of the social* gospel; held that govt. should bring about soc. adjustments not by force or by endorsing an economic program, but by inspiring individuals with love of justice and the spirit of service; acknowledged the right of labor to organize; organized Christian League of Connecticut 1883; active in civic leagues; his poetry reveals mystical elements.

E. T. Thompson, "Washington Gladden and the development of the 'New Theology,'" *Changing Emphases in American Preaching* (Philadelphia, 1943), pp. 137–180.

Gladstone, William Ewart (1809–98). Eng. statesman; b. Liverpool; educ. Oxford; supported Oxford* Movement. Favored establishment of ch. in *The State in its relations with the Church* (1838); upheld visibility of the ch. in *Church Principles considered in their results* (1840); defended disestablishment of the ch. in *A Chapter of Autobiography* (1868). In *Ritual and Ritualism* (1874) and *The Vatican Decrees in their Bearing on Civil Allegiance* (1874) he opposed the dogma of papal infallibility (see *Vatican Councils,* 16) and held that henceforth a person could not join the RC ch. without placing his civil allegiance at the mercy of another. See also *Metaphysical Society, The.*

A. R. Vidler, *The Orb and the Cross: A Normative Study in the Relations of Church and State with Reference to Gladstone's Early Writings* (London, 1945).

Glasgow Bible Society. See *Bible Societies,* 4.

Glas(s), John. See *Disciples of Christ,* 1.

Glas(s)ites. See *Disciples of Christ,* 1.

Glass(ius), Salomo(n) (1593–1656). B. Sondershausen, Ger.; educ. Jena and Wittenberg; prof. Heb. and Gk. at Jena 1621; supt. Sondershausen 1625; prof. theol. at Jena as J. Gerhard's successor 1638; gen. supt. and court preacher Gotha 1640–56. Works include *Philologia sacra* (1623–36), a biblico-philol. encyclopedia widely used for ca. 2 centuries. See also *Weimarische Bibelwerk, Das.*

Glaubensbekenntnis der wahren Inspirationsgemeinde. See *Amana Society.*

Gleason, Anson (May 2, 1797–Feb. 24, 1885). B. Manchester, Conn.; ABCFM miss. to Choctaw, Mohegan, and Seneca Indians.

Glinka, Mikhail Ivanovich (ca. 1804–57). B. Novopassky, Smolensk, Russ.; composer; called by F. Liszt* the "prophet-patriarch of Russ. music." Impressed in early youth by Russ. folk music; later studied works of L. v. Beethoven,* W. A. Mozart,* and other classical masters; studied in Milan, Rome, Naples; acquainted with It. composers Gaetano Donizetti (1797–1848) and Vincenzo Bellini (1801–35); choirmaster of Imperial Chapel 1837–39. Works include operatic, orchestral, and ch. music.

Gloege, Gerhard. See *Dogmatics,* B 13.

Gloria in excelsis. See *Canticles; Doxology; Worship, Parts of,* 6.

Gloria Patri. See *Canticles; Doxology; Rosary; Worship, Parts of,* 4.

Glory. The Bible speaks of (1) the glory of God, the manifestation of His attributes, esp. holiness and majesty (e. g., Ex 33:18-22; Is 6:3; Ps 63:2; 104:31; 138:5; Jn 1:14; 2 Ptr 1:17); (2) the glory of Christ* Jesus; (3) the glory of the church* militant and triumphant, which is also the glory of the individual believers, veiled and hidden to mortal eyes in this world, but to be fully revealed on the Last Day (see *Last Things*), culminating in the beatific vision (Ps 17:15; 1 Co 13:12; 1 Jn 3:2; Rv 22:4). Believers partake of spiritual glory (Jn 17:22; 1 Co 2:7; 2 Co 3:18) and of eternal glory (Ro 8:18; 1 Co 15:43; Ph 3:21; 2 Th 2:14; 2 Ti 2:10; 1 Ptr 5:10). In heaven they will have glorified bodies (Ph 3:21). Doctrines of degrees of glory in heaven are usually based on Dn 12:3; Lk 19:12-26; 1 Co 15:41-42 (see also *Hereafter,* A 6). Christians are not to seek glory from men (Mt 6:2; 1 Th 2:6), they are to seek only God's glory (1 Co 10:31; 2 Co 10:17).

E. C. Pautsch, "Eternal Life," *The Abiding Word,* I, ed. T. Laetsch (St. Louis, 1946), 561–582. JMW

Glory, Kingdom of. See *King, Christ as.*

Glosses and Glossarists. The practice of supplying MSS with glosses, i. e., marginal notes to explain certain words in the text, dates back to classical times. Glosses were also inserted in Bible MSS, both in the margin and bet. the lines. In the course of time they were extended to include a variety of explanatory material. Glossing was carried to great length in canon* law by glossarists, canonists of the 12th–15th c., esp. in Bologna, It. By successive additions of masters a running comment was est. that explained, illustrated, and reconciled the various provisions. These glosses were highly regarded.

Glossolalia. See *Gifts of the Spirit; Tongues, Gift of.*

Glover, Jose (Josse; Joss; d. 1638). Eng. nonconformist clergyman; visited New Eng. ca. 1634; instrumental in bringing a printing press to Am.; regarded by many as the father of printing in the Eng. colonies of the US.

Gloves, Liturgical. Worn in RC Ch. at pontifical mass, ordinarily by pope, cardinals, and bps.; sometimes allowed for abbotts and others.

Gluck, Christoph Willibald (1714–87). B. in the Upper Palatinate; studied music in Prague and Milan;

distinguished principally as operatic writer. Works include *De profundis.*

Glück, Ernst Johann (ca. 1652–1705). B. Wettin, Ger.; pastor and provost Marienburg; founded secondary school in Moscow; tr. Bible into Latvian and Russ. (latter MS lost). See also *Latvia.*

Glueck, Nelson (1900–71). B. Cincinnati, Ohio; educ. U. Cincinnati; prof., later pres., Heb. Union Coll., Cincinnati; pres. combined Heb. Union Coll.–Jewish Institute of Religion (Cincinnati, NYC, Los Angeles, Jerusalem); prof. Am. School of Oriental Research, Baghdad; dir. Am. School of Oriental Research, Jerusalem; involved in archaeol. expeditions in Palestine and neighboring countries. Works include *Explorations in Eastern Palestine; The River Jordan; The Other Side of the Jordan; Hesed in the Bible,* tr. A. Gottschalk, ed. E. L. Epstein. See also *Geography, Christian,* 8.

Gluttony. See *Sins, Venial and Mortal.*

Gnesio-Lutherans ("Genuine Luths."; from Gk. *gnesios,* "genuine"). After the death of M. Luther,* so-called genuine Lutheranism was represented by such men as N. v. Amsdorf,* M. Flacius* Illyricus, J. Wigand,* N. Gallus,* M. Judex,* J. Mörlin,* T. Hesshus,* J. Timann,* J. Westphal* of Hamburg, A. Hunnius,* A. Poach,* and E. Sarcerius.* Headquarters were at Jena beginning 1557. Their opponents were called Philippists.*

Gnosticism (from Gk. *gnosis,* "knowledge"). 1. Syncretistic movement with roots in pre-Christian times; flowered in 2d–3d c. AD; continued to the 7th c.; involved occult lore, magic watchwords, and secret names; claimed to have a divinely-given secret message that held the key for a higher life.

2. The beginnings of gnosticism may be found in the fusion of religious beliefs and cultures that arose as a result of Persian power and the conquests of Alexander III (the Great; 356–323 BC; king of Macedonia 336). Scholars do not agree as to what makes religious symbols "gnostic." Elements of gnosticism have been traced to Gk. philos., movements in Judaism, Hellenism, Orphic cults, and religious thought in such countries as Babylonia, Iran, Egypt, and India. Some, on the basis of such literature as the Dead* Sea Scrolls and Jewish apocalyptic writing, regard Judaism as a channel through which gnosticism entered the Graeco-Roman world.

3. In contrast to the rational insight of the classical mind, the basic theme of gnosticism was redemption from the material world (matter considered evil; ordered cosmos had malevolent purpose) and escape into a world of freedom, thus achieving the liberty implied in human spirit. The soul, escaping from matter, is to be reunited with the *pleroma,* or fullness, of God.

4. While this redemption took place through initiations, rites, mysteries, magic (each sect having its own peculiarities), the more speculative adherents needed philosophical basis. Hence the dualism* inherent in the doctrine of redemption was expanded (supreme God – demiurge; good–evil; light–darkness; cosmic fall–historic fall; spirit–matter; *pleroma–hysterema*) and synthesized in the good God.

5. The following reflects elements of gnosticism in Christian times: God is pure abstraction, a fathomless abyss. From Him emanate divine potencies *(aeons)* which in their totality constitute the *pleroma* (fullness, ideal world of light opposed to *kenoma,* or emptiness of matter). *Sophia* (wisdom) disturbed the harmony of the *pleroma* and fell into the formless chaos beyond *(hysterema).* Through matter *sophia* gave birth to a demiurge (identified with the OT Jehovah). Redemption takes place through the restoration of the harmony of the *pleroma* and rescue of the seeds of divine light scattered in darkness. This is done by the most perfect aeon *(Soter),* who entered Jesus at baptism and left Him before Calvary. Christ accomplishes His work by teaching knowledge *(gnosis),* which is received only by a select few (*pneumatikoi,* spirituals). The next class of men (*psychikoi,* psychics) must be content with faith; the lowest (*hylics,* material) are preoccupied with worldly cares. (See also par. 7 g below.) The ethical system tried to overcome flesh (matter) and developed into both strict asceticism* and extreme libertinism.

6. Some recent studies see relationship bet. gnosticism, nihilism,* and existentialism.*

7. a. Simon* Magus. Samaritan sorcerer (Acts 8:9-24); regarded in patristic literature as the originator of gnosticism. According to Irenaeus* (*Adversus haereses,* I, xxiii, 5), Menander, another Samaritan, was his successor.

b. Cerinthus (ca. 100). Active at Ephesus; reputed opponent of John (Jn; 1 Jn); no writings survive; accounts in patristics vague and contradictory.

c. Saturninus (Satornilus; 2d c.). Said to have been a disciple of Menander (see par. a); flourished in Antioch, Syria (Irenaeus, *Adversus haereses,* I, xxiv).

d. Elkesaites promulgated their doctrine (all receive forgiveness of sins who accept their form of baptism and receive their doctrines) in the trans-Jordanic regions ca. 101; teachings still influential in Arab. in 10th c.

e. Basilides (2d c.). Allegedly claimed to be a disciple of the apostle Matthias and of Glaucias, an interpreter of Peter; perhaps a disciple of Menander; divergent accounts of his theories are in Clement* of Alexandria, Epiphanius,* Eusebius* of Caesarea, Hippolytus,* Irenaeus,* and Origen.* His system, variously explained, holds that God did not directly create the world; Christ* Jesus human in appearance only; Simon of Cyrene died in His stead on the cross. Isidorus (2d c.) was a son or disciple of Basilides.

f. Carpocrates (2d c.). Alexandrian; antinomian; followers called Carpocratians. His son Epiphanes (2d c.) wrote *De iustitia* advocating communism (Clement* of Alexandria, *Stromata,* III, ii).

g. Valentinus (2d c.). B. Egypt; educ. Alexandria; at Rome ca. 138–ca. 160. It is hard to glean facts from the few details (often inconsistent) of his life preserved by ancients. Followers formed 2 schools, It. and Oriental, with divergent tendencies. Distinguished a phenomenal and spiritual *(pleroma)* sphere. In the latter there are emanations including the Holy Spirit and Christ, who united with the man Jesus. One aeon, Sophia, fell into passion and disgrace and caused emission of matter which Demiurge (God of OT) shaped into world. Classified people as pneumatics (Valentinians), psychics (other Christians), hylics (unsaved), whereas other gnostic systems divide men into children of light and children of darkness (see also pars. 4 and 5 above). Fragments of his writings are preserved in the *Stromata* of Clement* of Alexandria and other patristic writers. Followers include Heracleon (probably fl. 170–180 in It.), Ptolemy (Ptolemaeus; d. ca. 180), Florinus, Axionicus, Marcus, Secundus, Theodotus* the Fuller. (See also par. h.) Works include letters, sermons, hymns.

h. Bardesanes (Bar-Daisan; ca. 154–ca. 222). B. Edessa* on the Daisan; believed in a number of lesser gods subordinate to the supreme God; he and his son Harmonius* wrote many hymns. Hippolytus,* *The Refutation of All Heresies,* VI, xxx, calls Bardesanes a Valentinian, but some disagree.

i. Ophites (Ophians; from Gk. *ophis,* "serpent"). Early ch. fathers grouped under this name such sects as the Barbelo Gnostics (Barbelo derived by some from 2 Syrian words meaning "God in a Tetrad," by others from 2 Heb. words meaning "Daughter of the

Lord"; Irenaeus, *Adversus haereses* I xxix), Naasenes (from Heb., *nahash,* "serpent"), Perates, Sethites (or Sethians), Cainites, Archontics, and Severians; Justin the Gnostic is also included. The serpent plays various parts in the doctrine or worship of many of these. See also par. j.

j. Also included among Ophites: Antitactes (Clement of Alexandria, *Stromata,* III, iv); Nicolaitans (Rv 2:6, 15; Irenaeus, *Adversus haereses,* I, 26; Clement of Alexandria, *Stromata,* III, iv); Prodicians (Clement of Alexandria, *Stromata,* III, iv).

k. Marcion (ca. 100–ca. 160). B. Sinope, Pontus; excommunicated by father, bp. Sinope; repudiated by Polycarp* as the first-born of Satan; to Rome ca. 139; excommunicated there 144. Marcion's primary purpose was to free Christianity from Jewish influences by rejecting the OT entirely and purging the NT of all Judaistic elements. Jehovah was a just God (Demiurge); Jesus revealed the good God.

8. Recent important Gnostic discoveries include the finding of Manichean writings in Egypt by C. Schmidt* and the uncovering of 49 Coptic treatises at Chenoboskion, near Nag Hammadi, near Luxor, Egypt, by peasants in the 1940s.

9. Prominent anti-Gnostic writers include Irenaeus,* Tertullian,* and Hippolytus.*

See also *Docetism; Paulicians; Philosophy; Tatian.*

S. Angus, *The Mystery-Religions and Christianity* (New York, 1925); A. Hilgenfeld, *Die Ketzergeschichte des Urchristentums* (Leipzig, 1884); E. F. Scott, "Gnosticism," *Encyclopedia of Religion and Ethics,* ed. J. Hastings, VI (New York, 1913), 231–242; J. Knox, *Marcion and the New Testament* (Chicago, 1942); H. Jonas, *The Gnostic Religion,* 2d ed. rev. (Boston, 1963); R. K. Bultmann, *Primitive Christianity in its Contemporary Setting,* tr. R. H. Fuller (London, 1956), *Theology of the New Testament,* tr. K. Grobel, 2 vols. (New York, 1951, 1955), and "Gnosis," tr. R. H. Lightfoot, *The Journal of Theological Studies,* New Series, III, Part 1 (Apr. 1952), 10–26; R. M. Grant, *Gnosticism and Early Christianity* (New York, 1959); *Gnosticism,* ed. R. M. Grant (New York, 1961); R. M. Grant and D. N. Freedman, *The Secret Sayings of Jesus,* with an Eng. tr. of the Gospel of Thomas by W. R. Schoedel (New York, 1960); G. G. Scholem, *Jewish Gnosticism, Merkabah Mysticism, and Talmudic Tradition* (New York, 1960); *The Gospel of Truth,* ed. and tr. K. Grobel (New York, 1960); *The Gospel According to Thomas,* tr. A. Guillaumont et al. (New York, 1959); J. Doresse, *The Secret Books of the Egyptian Gnostics,* tr. P. Mairet, with an Eng. tr. and critical evaluation of the Gospel According to Thomas (New York, 1960); W. C. van Unnik, *Newly Discovered Gnostic Writings* (Naperville, Ill., 1960); W. R. Schoedel, "The Rediscovery of Gnosis," *Interpretation,* XVI, No. 4 (Oct. 1962), 387–401. EL, WG.

Go-Ye Fellowship. Interdenom. miss. organization inc. 1944 Calif.; traces its beginings to a 1932 S. S. class. Fields have included South Afr., Brazil, Haiti, Hong Kong, India, Indonesia, Jap., Malaysia, Puerto Rico, Taiwan, Trinidad.

Goar. 1. Reputed priest and hermit; said to have come from Aquitania and done miss. work along the Rhine; some make him contemporary with Childebert I (son and successor of Clovis* I; king 511–558), some place him as late as the 8th c. 2. Jacques (1601–ca. 1653). B. Paris, Fr.; Dominican liturgical scholar; tried to unite Gk. and Roman Ch. Works include *Euchologion sive Rituale Graecorum,* a classic for Gk. liturgical study.

Gobat, Samuel (Jan. 26, 1799–May 11, 1879). B. Crémine, Bern, Switz.; educ. Basel Miss. Inst. and at Paris; ordained Luth.; CMS miss. in Abyssinia and Malta; ordained Angl. deacon 1845; bp. Jerusalem 1846; supervised tr. of Bible into Arabic.

Gobel, Jean Baptiste Joseph (1727–94). B. Thann, Fr.; bp. Paris 1791; sided with radicals in controversy regarding the Civil Constitution of the Clergy (see *France,* 5); abdicated priesthood 1793; espoused religion of reason; executed.

Goch. See *Johannes von Goch.*

God. The Being who made the world and man and to whom man is responsible. Man's knowledge of God falls into 2 broad categories: (1) God is known to man through power and design in the natural world and through pattern in the forces of hist. (Ps 19; Acts 17:22-31; Ro 1:18–2:16); man is thereby enabled to construct a mental picture of a supremely powerful Force working out man's destiny with a heavy hand, confronting mankind with continual challenge. Human reactions to this understanding of God result in reverence for nature and idolatry, in attempts to rationalize God into abstract natural law and to remove man's responsibility to Him (2 Ptr 3:3-4), or in despair and fear. This natural knowledge of God, basic to every human system of religion and to most philos., is insufficient for a satisfying and adequate faith in God, who still remains *Deus incognitus* (the unknown God). Insight into God is not within range of human endowment (Jn 1:18). (2) God revealed Himself to man more clearly and completely by the incarnation* of Christ* Jesus *(Deus incarnatus)* as a Being infinitely pained by man's deviation from His holiness, yet infinitely desirous to repair the breach, to the point of Himself assuming responsibility for this repair at the cost of His own sacrifice. Thus God is revealed as perfect and holy, as personal and driven by love to conform man to the image of His Son (Ro 8:29). This revelation* of God in His Son is communicated through the written Word (see *Word of God).* This Word presents more data about His nature, which are intelligible and credible to us, however, only in the light of the central revelation in Christ Jesus, the Word of God *(Deus revelatus).* God is eternal, not subject to time (Ps 90:1-4; 2 Ptr 3:8). God is neither confined to space or time nor limited in power, knowledge, or wisdom. He is benevolent, inasmuch as He desires to bless the objects to His love. All resources of God are at the disposal of man in Christ (Ph 4:13) and are recognized by him to work for his good (Ro 8:24-39). A Chirstian's insight into God and his power to grasp and to trust in God as his forgiving and enabling Father is the work of God Himself, the gift of His Spirit (see *Holy Ghost*). The Christian Church* summarized the nature of God and a Christian's knowledge of God in the concept of the Trinity.* RRC

See also *Father, God the; Fatherhood of God; Filioque Controversy; Immutability of God; Infinity of God; Justice of God; Procession of the Holy Spirit.*

R. R. Caemmerer, "The Nature and Attributes of God," *The Abiding Word,* II, ed. T. Laetsch (St. Louis, 1947), 59–77.

God, Arguments for the Existence of. The *natural,* or gen. argument for God's existence rests on the fact that man knows that there is a God* even without the special revelation in the Bible, because God Himself inscribed this knowledge in his heart at creation (Ro 2:14-15). Hence the existence of God need not be proved to anyone of morally sound mind. The *theological* argument is this, that the Bible, without explanation, confronts man with the fact of God's being and sovereignty, which is at once acknowledged. Other arguments for God's existence are reasonably deduced from His self-manifestation in the universe, human hist., and conscience (Ro 1.19-20; Acts 14:17; 17:24-28): the *cosmological* argument reasons from the effect to the cause that this orderly world cannot be the effect of chance, but must have for its Creator an intelligent and omnipotent God; the *teleological* argument demonstrates God's existence from the evidences of design, purpose, and adaptation in the world; the *moral* argument is based on man's moral nature and the moral order traceable throughout the world; the *esthetic* argument is founded on beauty and comeliness in the universe, which must have as its Maker a loving God; the *ontological* argument reasons that the concept of a perfect and absolute divine Being must be founded on fact since it cannot exist in a vacuum. Atheism* denies the validity of all arguments for God's existence; unbiased reason must admit that they supply cumulative proof. See also *Anselm of Canterbury; Apologetics (Christian),* 4 I A; *Philosophy of Religion.* JTM

The Existence of God, ed. J. H. Hick (New York, 1964).

God-breathed. See *Theopneustia.*

God, Love of. See *Love; Loving-kindness; Lund, Theology of.*

God, Names of. See *Revelation,* 6.

Godehard (Gotahard; Gothard; Gotthard; ca. 960–1038). B. Reichersdorf (Ritenbach), near Niederaltaich, Bavaria; bp. Hildesheim; reformed monasteries in Ger.

Godet, Frédéric Louis (1812–1900). B. Neuchâtel, Switz.; Ref. theol.; prof. in the theol. school of the est. ch. at Neuchâtel 1850; pastor Neuchâtel 1851; prof. Ev. Free Ch. theol. academy 1873; gen. conservative in theol. Works include commentaries on Lk, Jn, Ro, and 1 Co.

Godfather; Godmother. See *Sponsors.*

Godfrey of Fontaines (ca. 1250–ca. 1306). Declined bishopric of Tournai 1300. *Quodlibeta* develop thoughts of Thomas* Aquinas.

Godhead. 1. The nature of God, esp. as triune. 2. Deity; divinity.

Godparents See *Sponsors.*

Gods. See *Idolatry.*

Goebel, Max (1811–57). B. Solingen, Ger.; theol. and hist.; espoused union of Luths. and Ref.; ed. *Bonner Monatsschrift.*

Goering, Jacob (1755–1807). B. York Co., Pa.; studied theol. under J. H. C. Helmuth*; pastor in and near Carlisle and York, Pa.; wrote against Anabaptists (see *Baptist Churches,* 2; *Mennonite Churches*) and Methodists (see *Methodist Churches*).

C. A. Hay, *Memoirs of Rev. Jacob Goering, Rev. George Lochmann, D. D., and Rev. Benjamin Kurtz., D. D., LL. D.* (Philadelphia, 1887).

Goethe, Johann Wolfgang von (1749–1832). B. Frankfurt am Main, Ger.; poet. In early life instructed in the Bible by his mother; later inclined toward pantheistic (see *Pantheism*) view of nature; his high regard for classical antiquity resulted mainly from his It. journey 1786–88. He had no true conception of the character of sin, no appreciation of the Christian doctrine of redemption. Self-redemption is achieved by striving to comprehend the secrets of nature and penetrating the essence of things. That is salvation by works, as he says in *Faust* (II, v, 11936-7): "Whoe'er aspires unendingly is not beyond redeeming" ("Wer immer strebend sich bemüht, den können wir erlösen"). Goethe was essentially a rationalist given to syncretism* in religion. See also *Schiller, Johann Christoph Friedrich von.*

Goethe, Matthias. See *Australia, Lutheranism in,* B 1.

Goetwasser, John Ernst (Johannis Ernestus Goetwater). See *Gutwasser, John Ernst.*

Goeze, Johan(n) Melchior (1717–86). B. Halberstadt, Ger.; educ. Jena and Halle; pastor Aschersleben, Magdeburg, and Hamburg. Defended orthodox Lutheranism; opposed Enlightenment*; opponents included K. Alberti,* K. F. Bahrdt,* J. B. Basedow,* G. E. Lessing,* and J. S. Semler.*

Goforth, Jonathan (Feb. 10, 1859–Oct. 8, 1936). B. near Thorndale, W Ont., Can.; educ. Knox Coll., Toronto; ordained 1887; Presb. miss. in China, esp. at Honan and Changte; noted for evangelistic work and training native evangelists and preachers.

Gogarten, Friedrich (1887–1967). B. Dortmund, Ger.; educ. Berlin, Jena, Heidelberg; vicar Stolberg, Rhineland; asst. pastor Bremen; pastor Stelzendorf in Thuringia and Dorndorf on the Saale; prof. Breslau 1931, Göttingen 1935. Works include *Entmythologisierung und Kirche; Der Mensch zwischen Gott und Welt; Verhängnis und Hoffnung der Neuzeit; Jesus Christus: Wende der Welt; Luthers Theologie.*

Goguel, Maurice (1880–1955). B. Paris, Fr.; prof. NT on free faculty for Prot. theol., Paris, 1906; at École des Hautes Études 1927. Exponent of historicocritical method.

Göhre, Paul (1864–1928). B. Wurzen, Ger.; ev. theol.; as student interested in soc. problems; worked 3 mo. in a factory and wrote of the experience; gen. secy. of Ev. Soc. Congress 1891–94; wrote with M. Weber* a study on condition of farm hands 1894; helped found Nat. Socialist Union but later withdrew; joined Soc. Democratic Party of Ger.: broke with ch. 1906 and encouraged masses to follow; wrote on problems of socialism, materialism, and religion.

Gold Coast. Now Ghana (see *Africa,* C 11).

Golden Bull. Charter decorated with golden bulla as seal. Esp. the bull* of Charles IV (1316–78; king of Ger. and Boh. and Holy Roman emp. 1347–78, crowned 1355); promulgated at Diet of Nürnberg, Jan. 10, 1356; gives details of ceremonies to be observed in imperial election; fixed the number of electors at 7 (abps. Mainz, Trier, Cologne; king of Boh.; count palatine of Rhine, duke of Saxony, margrave of Brandenburg); outlined procedures for convocating electors and crowning the emp.; arranged for administration of empire during vacancy; gave added rights to electors.

Golden Legend *(Legenda aurea; Legenda sanctorum; Historia Lombardica* or *Langobardica).* Manual containing chiefly lives of saints (often legendary) uncritically compiled by Jacob* of Voragine 1255–66 from MSS and oral tradition. Popular book of edification in the W Ch. of the Middle Ages.

Golden Number. See *Sunday Letter.*

Golden Rose. Rose of gold, sometimes embellished with gems, blessed by pope on 4th Sun. in Lent (hence sometimes called Rose Sun. by RCs); sent as special favor to a person or place; custom probably originated in 11th c. Henry* VIII received 3; Frederick* III ("The Wise") was offered one in an effort to get his support against M. Luther.*

Golden Rule. Modern name for precept in Mt 7:12 and Lk 6:31. The negative form is found in some texts of Acts 15:29, *Didache* 1:2 (see *Apostolic Fathers,* 8), and other cultures and religions. See also *Confucianism,* 5.

G. B. King, "The 'Negative' Golden Rule," *The Journal of Religion,* VIII (Apr. 1928), 268–279.

Golden Sequence. Lat. hymn *Veni Sancte Spiritus,* sequence* for Pentecost (see *Church Year,* 10).

Goldziher, Ignaz (Isaak Jehuda; 1850–1921). B. Stuhlweissenburg, Hung.; prof. Budapest; noted for Islamic studies. Works include *Die islamische und die jüdische Philosophie; The Influence of Parsism on Islam; Der Mythos bei den Hebräern und seine geschichtliche Entwickelung.*

Golubinsky, Evgeny Evsigneevich (1834–1912). Prof.

ch. hist. Moscow 1860. Works include *Geschichte der russischen Kirche.*

Gomarus, Francis(cus) (Franz Gommer; 1563–1641). B. Brugge, Belgium; prof. theol. Leiden 1594; opposed Arminius (see *Arminianism*); held double predestination (see *Predestination,* 4); resigned when K. Vorst* was called to Leiden; prof. Saumur, Fr., 1615, and Groningen, Neth., 1618. Supported strict supralapsarianism at Dort 1618–19 (see also *Dordrecht, Synods of,* 3; *Predestination,* 4; *Reformed Confessions,* C 2).

Gompe, Nikolaus (1524 [or 1525]–1595). B. Rauenthal, Ger.; Luth. pastor Erbenheim, near Wiesbaden, 1546; banished 1548 for opposition to Interim*; court preacher Wiesbaden 1553; helped formulate a ch. order.

Gonesius, Petrus (Goniadzki; Conyza; 1525–81). B. Goniadz, Poland; antitrinitarian; opposed infant baptism and service by Christians in army and govt.

Gönner, Johann Jakob (May 11, 1807–June 25, 1864). One of the Saxon pilgrims of 1839 (see *Lutheran Church – Missouri Synod,* I 1); 1st full-time prof. Conc. Coll., Altenburg, Mo.; moved with the school to St. Louis 1849; on leave to ed. *Altenburger* Bibelwerk* 1857; resigned 1861.

Good Friday. See *Church Year,* 4, 7, 8.

Good Shepherd, Sisters of the. See *Sisterhoods.*

Good Works. 1. In Biblical and proper use of the term, the outflow and fruit of faith, esp. in outward deeds of believers, performed for love of Christ and God in agreement with the Word and will of God. Every good thing a Christian says and does, every act by which he omits something evil as an evidence of the divine life of faith in his heart, is a good work (Eph. 2:10; Tts 2:14; Heb 13:20-21). Good works, properly speaking, are not the believer's own performance, but the works of God in and through him; God gives both the incentive and the power for the performance of works that are well-pleasing in His sight (Mt 5:16; Jn 15:5; 2 Co 9:8; Ph 2:12-13). It is true, of course, that because of sin the works of believers are not in themselves perfect, neither in their inception nor in their fruition (Ro 7:18-19). But these flaws, imperfections, and frailties connected with the good works of the believers have been atoned for by Christ* Jesus, for whose sake God regards these works and those who perform them as perfect (Ro 8:1).

2. In direct contrast to the spiritually good works of believers *(iustitia spiritualis)* there are fictitious good works of men who have no faith, but whose outward behavior in many cases resembles that of Christians. If these works are an outflow of an attempt to merit righteousness before God, as in the penances of RCm and in all other self-appointed forms of religion, they defeat their own end. Such works are the basis of every false religion. "People outside of Christ and without faith and the Holy Spirit are in the power of the devil. He drives them into many kinds of manifest sin" (FC SD II 29). One can distinguish a certain form of civil righteousness *(iustitia civilis, opera externa),* in which certain virtues are connected with outward maintenance of civil authority in the world (e. g., obedience to laws, honesty in business). Man is free to choose such outward manifestations and civil virtues. But they are not necessarily connected with a regenerated heart. They may be the outflow of natural altruism and even of extreme selfishness and as such are not truly good works.

3. That good works merit no reward is evident from passages adduced above. Where the Bible speaks of such rewards it is evident that a reward of mercy is meant. God regards the imperfect good works of believers on account of the perfect obedience of Christ as though they were in themselves good and perfect. In this sense good works will also serve as evidence on the Last Day to prove the presence of faith. Good works are not necessary to salvation, as G. Major* taught, but they are a necessary fruit and proof of faith; the Luth. Ch. has been unjustly accused of setting aside good works and a life of sanctification. See also *Majoristic Controversy; Sanctification.*

Goodell, William (1792–1867). B. Templeton, Mass.; educ. Dartmouth Coll., Hanover, N. H., and Andover (Mass.) Theol. Sem.; arrived Beirut 1823; est. mission; to Malta 1828, Constantinople 1831. Tr. Bible into Armeno-Turkish. See also *Dwight, Harrison Gray Otis.*

Goodenough, Erwin Ramsdell (1893–1965). B. Brooklyn, N. Y.; educ. Hamilton Coll., Clinton, N. Y., Drew Theol. Sem., Madison, N. J., Garrett Biblical Institute, Evanston, Ill., Harvard, and Oxford; instr. hist. Yale 1923–26, prof. 1926–62; Jacob Ziskind prof. Medit. studies Brandeis U., Waltham, Mass., 1962–63; mem. Soc. of Biblical Literature and Exegesis; pres. Am. Soc. for Study of Religion; specialized in study of hellenized Judaism. Ed. *Journal of Biblical Literature* 1934–42; other works include *The Church in the Roman Empire; Religious Tradition and Myth; An Introduction to Philo Judaeus; Jewish Symbols in the Greco-Roman Period; Toward a Mature Faith.*

Goodness. 1. The goodness of God is exhibited in Scripture in 4 aspects: love, benevolence, grace, and mercy. "God is Love, inasmuch as He longs for and delights in union and communion with the objects of His holy desire" (A. L. Graebner, *Outlines of Doctrinal Theology* [St. Louis, 1910 ed.], p. 38). The world that is the object of His love was a lost world; yet God would not have His creatures perish, and He longs for reunion with them, Jn 3:16. He yearns in bitter anguish for the children that have gone astray, Is 1:2-5; 49:15-16. Yet it is a holy desire; God cannot have communion with those who are separated from Him by sin. To make them His own and unite them with Himself, He wrought a redemption, Is 43:1. – The benevolence of God is that kindness by which He provides for the wants of His creatures, Ps 104:27-28. Esp. does He desire to promote the happiness of men; hence He formed the plan of salvation. – "God is gracious, inasmuch as He offers and confers His blessings regardless of the merits or demerits of the objects of His benevolence" (A. L. Graebner, op. cit., p. 40), Ro 6:23; Eph 2:8-9. – That aspect of goodness by which He has compassion with the afflicted and bestows His benefits on the miserable is called mercy. His mercy is abundant and extends over all who suffer trouble and affliction, whether physical, mental, or spiritual, Ps 68:5; Is 49:13.

2. In a relative sense the creatures of God are also good (Gn 1:31) even after the Fall (1 Ti 4:4). But the goodness of the creature is not perfection (essential goodness); it is a dependent goodness, i. e., the creatures are good only as God's handiwork.

Goodrich, Chauncey Allen (1790–1860). B. New Haven, Conn.; educ. Yale Coll.; Cong. clergyman, educator, lexicographer; studied under T. Dwight* (b. 1752); pastor Middletown, Conn.; prof. rhetoric Yale 1817, pastoral theol. Yale Divinity School 1839; supported N. W. Taylor*; promulgated ideas of the New* Haven Theology.

Goodspeed, Edgar Johnson (1871–1962). Bap. theol.; b. Quincy, Ill., educ. Denison U., Granville, Ohio, Yale U., Chicago U., and U. of Berlin: taught Biblical and Patristic Gk. at Chicago U. 1902–37; chm. NT dept. 1923–37; mem. of committee that produced the RSV. Works include *The New Testament: An American Translation; An Introduction to the New Testament; The Apocrypha: An American*

Translation; How to Read the Bible; The Apostolic Fathers: An American Translation; A Life of Jesus.

Gooszen, Maurits Albrecht (1837–1916). Pastor Nederlandse Hervormde Kerk 1861; prof. Leiden 1878; theologian of Groningen* School. Held that in addition to the emphases of M. Luther* and J. Calvin* there was a 3d type of reformation (biblico-theol., practico-ethical) represented by J. H. Bullinger* and the Heidelberg Catechism (see *Reformed Confessions,* D 2).

Gorchakov, Mikhail Ivanovich (Gorčakov; 1838–1910). Priest of Russ. Orthodox Ch. Became acquainted with W theol. when cantor at Orthodox ch., Stuttgart; prof. ch. law U. of Saint Petersburg.

Gorcum Martyrs. See *Gorkum Martyrs.*

Gordon, Adoniram Judson (1836–95). Bap. minister; b. New Hampton, N. H.; educ. Brown U., Providence, R. I., and Newton (Mass.) Theol. Sem.; pastor Jamaica Plain and Boston, Mass.; noted for support of miss. and soc. work. Works include *The Ministry of Healings; The Ministry of the Spirit.*

Gordon, Andrew (Sept. 17, 1828–Aug. 13, 1887). B. Putnam, N. Y.; studied theol. at the sem of the Assoc. Presbytery of Pa. (see *Associate Reformed Church*) at Jefferson Coll., Canonsburg, Pa.; miss. to Sialkot, Punjab, N India, (later W. Pakistan); founded miss. there. Wrote *Our India Mission.*

Gordon, Charles William (pseudonym Ralph Connor; 1860–1937). B. Indian Lands, Glengarry Co., Ont., Can.; Presb. pastor; miss. to miners and loggers in SW Alberta, Can., 1890–93; pastor Winnipeg 1894–1924; army chaplain; moderator Gen. Assem. of Presb. Ch. of Canada. Works include *Black Rock; The Sky Pilot; The Man from Glengarry; The Girl from Glengarry; Glengarry School Days.*

Gordon, George Angier (1853–1929). B. Scot.; to US 1871; Cong. pastor Temple, Maine, 1877–78, Greenwich, Conn., 1881–83, Old South Ch., Boston, Mass., 1884–1929; university preacher Harvard and Yale. Works include *The Christ of To-Day; The New Epoch for Faith; Religion and Miracle; Revelation and the Ideal; Through Man to God; The Witness to Immortality in Literature, Philosophy, and Life.*

Gore, Charles (1853–1932). B. Wimbledon, Eng.; bp. Worcester 1902, Birmingham 1905, Oxford 1911; under his influence the Oxford* Movement underwent changes opposed by old school Tractarians (see *Tractarianism*); held kenotic view that the Lord so restrained His deity as to become subject to all human limitations. *Lux mundi,* ed. by him, tried to bring the Christian creed "into its right relation to the modern growth of knowledge, scientific, historic, critical; and to modern problems of politics and ethics"; it helped the High Ch. movement develop along modernistic lines. See also *Christian Social Union; Kenosis.*

Gorgonia (d. ca. 370). Sister of Gregory of Nazianzus (see *Cappadocian Theologians*); he praises her in *Oratio VIII.*

Gorham, George Cornelius (1787–1857). B. St. Neots, Huntingdonshire, Eng.; Angl. cleric rejected for the vicarage of Brampford Speke by H. Phillpotts* and the Court of Arches* for denying rebirth in baptism, but upheld by the Judicial Committee of the Privy Council and instituted by J. B. Sumner.*

Gorkum Martyrs. 19 RC religious and secular priests slain by Calvinists (see *Calvinism*) July 9, 1572, after Gorkum (Gorcum; Gorinchem; town in S Holland) was captured by the Gueux* de mer June 26, 1572.

Görres, Johann Joseph von (1776–1848). B. Koblenz, Ger.; supported Fr. Revolution in his youth; turned from RCm to rationalism and pantheism, then back to RCm; championed ultramontanism.* Works include *Glauben und Wissen; Die Wallfahrt nach Trier.*

Görres-Gesellschaft. Est. 1876 in Ger. on the 100th anniversary of the birth of J. J. v. Görres* to foster sciences. Areas of concern: philos., pedagogy, psychol. and psychotherapy, hist., archaeol., language and literature, oriental study, law and pol. science, business and soc. science, art, folklore, natural science and technology.

Gorton, Samuel (ca. 1592–1677). B. Gorton, Eng.; clothier in London; to Am. 1637; founded Gortonites (or Gortonians); antitrinitarian; espoused conditional immortality dependent on the character of the individual.

Göschel, Karl Friedrich (1784–1861). Jurist, philos.; b. Langensalza, Ger.; educ. Gotha and Leipzig; held judicial positions at Langensalza, Naumburg, Berlin, Magdeburg; tried to harmonize Christianity with modern culture.

Gospel. See *Grace, Means of.*

Gospel Association. See *Finland, Lutheranism in,* 4.

Gospel Mission Corps, The. See *Evangelistic Associations,* 16.

Gospel Mission of South America. Formerly Soldiers' and Gospel Mission of S. Am.; founded 1923; present name adopted 1963. Began with work among the military in Tacna, Chile (now in Peru). Service Cen. for soldiers opened in Concepcion 1926, closed after a few yrs. Work begun 1971 in Argentina and Uruguay.

Gospel Missionary Union. Organized 1892 Topeka, Kans., as World's Gospel Union; present name adopted 1901. Fileds have included Morocco, Ecuador, Colombia, Fr. Sudan, It., Panama, Brit. Honduras, Bahama Is., Mex., Greece, Fr., Ger., Switz., Mali Rep.

Gospel of Egyptians, Hebrews, Ebionites, Peter, James, etc. See *Apocrypha,* B 2.

Gospel Reductionism. Defined by LCMS Commission on Theology and Ch. Relations as use of the Gospel as the norm of theol. in such a way as to suggest that considerable freedom should be allowed within the ch. in matters that are not an explicit part of the Gospel.

Gospel and Scripture: The Interrelationship of the Material and Formal Principles in Lutheran Theology (n. p., Nov. 1972), p. 4.

Gospel Side of Altar. Liturgical north*; left as one faces the altar. See also *Church Furniture,* 1.

Gospels, Harmony of. See *Harmony of the Gospels.*

Gossner, Johannes Evangelista (1773–1858). B. Hausen (near Ober-Wallstädt), near Augsburg, Ger.; educ. Dillingen and Ingolstadt; RC priest 1796; renounced RCm; pastor Dirlewang 1803–11; beneficiary Munich; pastor St. Petersburg 1820–24, Berlin 1829; founded Gossner* Missionary Society. Works include *Schatzkästchen.*

Gossner Missionary Society (Gossnersche Missionsgesellschaft; Berlin II). Founded 1836 in Berlin by J. E. Gossner,* who withdrew from Berlin* Missionary Society I because of policy differences. Berlin I stressed a mission as a thoroughly organized institution; Gossner emphasized the missionary as an apostle driven by faith and casting all his cares on God. His soc. received royal sanction 1842. Sent missionaries to Australia, New Guinea, South Sea Islands, Indonesia, India (with special success among the Kols), Afr., and Am.

Gotahard. See *Godehard.*

Gotama Buddha. See *Gautama Buddha.*

Gotha Covenant. Agreement of Feb. 1526 bet. John* the Constant of Saxony and Philip* of Hesse to defend ev. faith and worship.

Gothaische Bibel. See *Weimarische Bibelwerk, Das.*

Gothard. See *Godehard.*

Gothic Architecture. See *Church Architecture,* 8-11.

Gothic Bible Version. See *Bible Versions,* I.

Gothic Style. See *Church Architecture,* 8-11.

Goths, Conversion of. The Goths, Germanic (or Teutonic) people, may have come from Scandinavia to live along the lower Vistula near the Baltic Sea. Thence they moved, beginning ca. 150 AD, to Silesia and then to the N shore of the Black Sea, where they came into conflict with the decadent power of the Roman Empire. They were in touch with Christianity at least as early as 276, when captives they took in Cappadocia included Christians. Audius (see *Audians*) was miss. among the Goths in the 4th c. but it was not till the time of Ulfilas* that Christianity was formally est. among them. Tr. of the Bible into Gothic was an important factor in their conversion (see *Bible Versions,* I). Arianism* got a foothold among the Goths, since Ulfila(s) was consecrated bp. among them by Arian Eusebius* of Nicomedia; their subsequent westward migration (Visigoths in Fr., Ostrogoths in It.) spread the error far and wide. Narses,* Byzantine gen. of Justinian I, defeated the last Gothic army in It. 553. The end of Visigothic power came in 711 when they were overwhelmed by Arabs.

Gotter, Ludwig Andreas (1661–1735). B. Gotha, Ger.; privy secy., later *Hofrat* at Gotha; pietistic; hymnist. Hymns include "Herr Jesu, Gnadensonne."

Gottesfreunde. See *Friends of God.*

Gotteskasten. In 1840 a soc. *(Verein zur Unterstützung der lutherischen Kirche in Nordamerika)* was organized in Dresden, Ger.; active only a few yrs. As a result of pleas for help by F. C. D. Wyneken,* L. A. Petri* and others est. a *Gotteskasten* in Hannover 1853, primarily to help provide spiritual care for Luths. in N. America. Other similar organizations followed. A fed. of *Gotteskastenvereine* was est. 1880. Preachers, teachers, and religious literature were provided for diaspora Luths. In 1932 the name *Martin-Luther-Bund* with subtitle *Lutherisches Hilfswerk der Gotteskasten und Martin-Luther-Vereine* was adopted. Since 1947 it is called *Diasporawerk der ev. luth. Kirche Deutschlands.* Areas served have included N. Am., Brazil, Australia, S. Afr., and predominantly RC, Ref., and Ev. territories in Eur. See also *Diaspora,* 3.

Gottfried. 1. Brother Gottfried (ca. 1373–1453). Lay preacher of Brethren* of the Common Life; helped found settlements at Herford and Hildesheim. 2. von Clairvaux (von Auxerre; ca. 1115/20–after 1188). B. Auxerre; pupil of P. Abelard*; companion and biographer of Bernard* of Clairvaux; abbot Clairvaux 1162. 3. von Strassburg (fl. ca. 1210). Well-versed in theol. Wrote *Tristan und Isolde.*

Gotthard. See *Godehard.*

Gotthelf, Jeremias (pseudonym of Albert [or Albrecht] Bitzius; 1797–1854). B. Morat, Switz.; author; son of Zwinglian pastor; Ref. pastor in Switz.; influenced by J. H. Pestalozzi.* Opposed materialism; worked for religious education. Held that man can only prosper when he has love (sustained by love for God) for his fellowmen; God is the Greatest that can enter the life of man; the family is the first temple of God.

Gottschalk of Orbais (Godescal[c]us; Gottescale; Gottschalck; Gottschalk of Fulda; ca. 803-ca. 868). B. near Mainz; son of Saxon nobleman; Benedictine monk and priest; placed in Fulda monastery as a child; moved to Orbais monastery, where he studied Augustine* of Hippo and C. G. Fulgentius*; involved in predestinarian* controversy.

Gottschick, Johannes Friedrich (1847–1907). B. Rochau, Ger.; educ. Erlangen and Halle; prof. practical theol. Giessen 1882, Tübingen 1892; adherent of A. Ritschl.*

Gottskalksson, Oddur (ca. 1500 [or perhaps as late as 1514] – 1556). Son of Norw. bp. in Holar, Iceland. Tr. NT into Icelandic; tr. Luth. classics.

Gotwald, Luther Alexander (Jan. 31, 1833–Sept. 15, 1900). Am. Luth. theol. and educator; educ. Gettysburg, Pa.; pastor Pa. and Ohio 1859–88; then prof. practical theol. Wittenberg Sem., Springfield, Ohio, till 1895; charges brought against him for conservative position; acquitted by unanimous vote of the sem. bd. of dirs. 1893.

Goudimel, Claude (ca. 1505 [or perhaps as late as 1514]–1572). B. probably Besançon, Fr.; composer and music ed.; joined Huguenots* probably ca. 1557; killed in Bartholomew's* Day Massacre.

Gouge. 1. Thomas (1609–81). B. London, Eng.; vicar St. Sepulchre's, London, 1638; noted for catechetics and care of poor. 2. William (1578[1575?]–1653). B. Bow, E London, Eng.; teacher of logic and Hebraist, Cambridge; Presb.; espoused Puritanism*; participated in Westminster Assem. 1643–48.

Goulart, Simon (1543–1628). B. Senlis, Fr.; pastor Geneva; leader of pastors there after death of T. Beza*; poet, ed., hist., and tr.

Gounelle, Elie Joel (1865–1950). B. Sauve, Fr.; pastor and military chaplain; championed Christian* socialism and the ecumenical* movement.

Gounod, Charles François (1818–93). B. Paris, Fr.; composer; organist; studied music at Paris and Rome; studied theol. 2 yrs. at Paris. His religious music is not churchly in the best sense of the term but mystical and sensuous, with dramatic and operatic elements in oratorios. *Ave Maria,* originally called *Méditation,* is based on J. S. Bach's* 1st prelude. Other works include operas *Faust* and *Roméo and Juliette;* oratorios *La Rédemption* and *Mors et vita;* several Masses; a Te Deum; motets; hymns.

Government. The action of governing, ruling with authority, directing, controlling, regulating the affairs of the body politic. Govt. is ordained by God for punishment of evildoers and for common welfare (Pr 8:15; Ro 13:1; 1 Ptr 2:14). Obedience, payment of taxes, and prayers for rulers (Ro 13:1-7; 1 Ti 2:1-2) belong to duties of citizens, who are to render to the govt. what is due to it and to God what is due to Him (Mt 22:21).

Monarchical govts. have usually been hereditary; they have been absolute, as that of Louis* XIV, or limited (constitutionalism), as that of the Brit. monarchy after 1688. Govts. may be autocratic (1 person having unlimited power), benevolent or tyrannical, with or without a strong undergirding of bureaucracy. They may be aristocratic or plutocratic (rule of the "best" or favored few regarded as superior, e. g., in rank, intellect, or wealth). Totalitarian govts. in the 20th c. have claimed total control over all their subjects for the benefit of the state; they have furthered a 1-party system and rule of 1 person. Democratic govts. allow direct or representative voices of the people to function ("of the people, by the people, for the people"). J. J. Rousseau* popularized the social contract theory of govt.; it holds that govts. are based on agreement bet. the ruled and the rulers. See also *Hobbes, Thomas.*

The powers of govt. have gen. been classified as legislative (making of laws), administrative (enforcing or carrying out laws), and judicial (interpreting laws and fixing penalties for lawbreakers). Exercise of governmental functions through commissions and agencies has extended the police powers of govt. CSM

See also *Church and State.*

Governmental Theory. See *Atonement, Theories of,* 5.

Grabau, Johannes Andreas August (1804–79). B. Olvenstedt, near Magdeburg, Ger.; studied theol. at Halle; pastor St. Andreas, Erfurt; imprisoned twice for refusal to use official Agenda (opposed its Ref. tendencies); permitted to emigrate with mems. of congs. at Erfurt, Magdeburg, and elsewhere; to Am. 1839; settled at Buffalo, N. Y.; pastor there ca. 40 yrs.; founded Martin Luther Coll., Buffalo, N. Y., and The Syn. of the Luth. Ch. Emigrated from Prussia (see *Buffalo Synod*). Ed. *Die Wachende Kirche*.

J. A. Grabau, *Lebenslauf des Ehrwürdigen J. An. A. Grabau* (Buffalo, N. Y., 1879).

Grabe, Johann(es) Ernst (1666–1711). B. Königsberg, Ger.; to Eng. 1697; Angl. priest 1700; engaged in textual studies of NT and patristics; issued an ed. of the LXX.

Grabmann, Martin (1875–1949). RC hist. of medieval philos.; b. Winterzhofen, near Berching, Bavaria; priest 1898; prof. theol. Eichstätt 1906, philos. Vienna 1913, theol. Munich 1918. Works include *Thomas Aquinas; Die Geschichte der scholastischen Methode; Mittelalterliches Geistesleben.*

Gräbner. See *Graebner.*

Grace. Good will and favor shown to one who can plead no merit*; particularly, the love of God in relation to the sinner as such. There may be love, but not grace, bet. equals or bet. a judge and an innocent person. Grace implies mercy or compassion for one who has by every right forfeited his claim on love. Such is the grace of God to the sinner. It is "free" because it is not grounded in any worthiness of man (Ro 11:6). Any admixture of merit or deserts, as constituting a claim on mercy, destroys the very essence of grace. Merit and grace are mutually exclusive.

Grace is universal. The entire world is its object. God became incarnate in Christ for the benefit of all men; He died for the atonement of the sins of all; all have been pronounced righteous through His resurrection; the invitation or call of grace is intended for all. No one is excluded from the salvation which grace has provided.

The grace of God is revealed (1) in the sending of His Son into the flesh, (2) in the justification of the sinner who accepts Jesus Christ as his Substitute in Judgment, and in the conversion of the sinner, and (3) in his glorification (resurrection, eternal life). This doctrine of grace gives assurance to Christian faith. Its promises are certain.

Grace is resistible, since it is offered to us through certain means (see *Grace, Means of*). Scripture constantly warns not to reject salvation.

Saving grace, in Christian theol., has been distinguished in its various operations as "prevenient," inasmuch as by means of outward circumstances and associations, particularly through the outward hearing of the Word, the Holy Spirit would prepare the heart for conversion; as "operative," inasmuch as it generates faith; as "cooperative," inasmuch as it is active in the Christian, jointly with the regenerated will, to produce good works.

Scripture also uses the word "grace" in the sense of a gift possessed by man, 1 Ptr 4:10. This, properly a result of divine grace and not, as in its original sense, a divine quality or attitude, has been called "infused grace." The RC Ch. teaches justification by "infused grace" *(gratia* infusa)*; see also *Grace, Means of*, I 8.

See also entries beginning with the word *Gratia.*

E. Jauncey, *The Doctrine of Grace, up to the End of the Pelagian Controversy, Historically and Dogmatically Considered* (London, 1925); J. Moffat, *Grace in the New Testament* (New York, 1931); T. Hoyer, "The Grace of God," *The Abiding Word*, II, ed T. Laetsch (St. Louis, Mo., 1947), 200–234; O. Hardman, *The Christian Doctrine of Grace* (London, 1937); T. F. Torrance, *The Doctrine of Grace in the Apostolic Fathers* (Edinburgh and London, 1948); C. Moeller and G. Philips, *The Theology of Grace and the Oecumenical Movement*, tr. R. A. Wilson (London, 1961); K. Rahner, *Nature and Grace: Dilemmas in the Modern Church* (New York, 1964).

Grace, Kingdom of. See *King, Christ as.*

Grace, Means of. I. *Doctrine in gen.* 1. *Definition.* The term "means of grace" denotes the divinely instituted means by which God offers, bestows, and seals to men forgiveness of sins, life, and salvation. Properly speaking, there is but 1 means of grace: the Gospel of Christ (Ro 1:16-17); but since in the Sacraments* the Gospel appears as the *verbum visibile* (visible Word; Ap XIII 5; Augustine* of Hippo, *Tract 80* on Jn 15:3; see also par. 6 below) in distinction from the *verbum audibile* (audible Word), it is rightly said that the means of grace are the Gospel and the Sacraments. The Law, though also a divine Word and used by the Holy Spirit in a preparatory way to work contrition,* without which there can be no saving faith (see *Faith,* 2), is not, properly speaking, a means of grace (see *Law and Gospel*). It is the very opposite of a means of grace, namely a "ministration of death," 2 Co 3:7. Prayer is not a means of grace, but faith in action.

2. *Basis of the means of grace.* There are means of grace because there is, 1st, Christ's objective justification (see *Justification,* 5) or reconciliation* (2 Co 5:19-21) and, 2d, Christ's institution. In other words, there is forgiveness for all through Christ's active and passive obedience. Christ wants this forgiveness to be offered and conveyed to all men through the Gospel and the Sacraments (Mt 28:19-20; Mk 16:15; AC V, VIII).

3. *Twofold power of the means of grace.* The means of grace have an offering or conferring power, by which God offers to all men forgiveness of sins, life, and salvation (Mt 18:20; 26:28; Acts 2:38; 20:24; FC SD II 57), and an operative or effective power, by which the Holy Spirit works, strengthens, and preserves saving faith (Ro 1:16; 10:17; 1 Co 4:15; 2 Co 2:14-17; 3:5-6; 1 Th 2:13; 1 Ptr 1:23; FC SD II 56).

4. *Importance of the means of grace.* The doctrine of the means of grace, part of the doctrine of the Word, is a fundamental doctrine (see *Fundamental Doctrines*). God bestows His saving grace "only through the Word and with the external and preceding Word" (*nisi per verbum et cum verbo externo et praecedente,* SA-III VIII 3; Jn 8:31-32; Ro 10:14-17). Therefore the Bible inculcates faithful adherence to the Gospel and the Sacraments administered according to Christ's institution (Mt 28:19-20; Jn 8:31-32; Acts 17:11; Tts 1:9). Because of the strong emphasis on the Word in the Luth. Confessions, Holy Scripture has rightly been called the Formal* Principle of the Reformation.

5. *Means of grace and the Luth. Ch.* The doctrine of the means of grace is a distinctive feature of Luth. theol., which owes to this cen. teaching its soundness, strong appeal, freedom from sectarian tendencies and morbid fanaticism, coherence, practicality, and adaptation to men of every race and degree of culture. Acc. to Luth. doctrine the means of grace are unchanging, sufficient, and efficacious. The efficacy of the means of grace does not depend on the faith, ordination, gifts, or intention of the administrator. Hearers of the Word, communicants, and subjects of Baptism derive no benefit from the means of grace unless they have faith (the receiving means; the hand reached out to accept blessings offered in the conferring means); but it does not follow that faith makes the means of grace effective. The Word is effective per se; the Sacraments are Sacraments by virtue of Christ's institu-

tion. Faith does not belong to the essence of the means of grace; it is itself a blessed work through the means of grace by the power of the Holy Ghost (Ro 10:14-17; Eph 1:19-20).

The Luth. Confessions gen. speak of the Word and the Sacraments as the means of grace (Ap VII-VIII 36; SA-III VIII 10; FC SD II 48), specifically denoting the Gospel as the means of grace (AC V).

The Luth. Confessions take a decisive stand against "enthusiasts," who teach that the Holy Spirit works in the hearts of men without the Word and Sacraments (SA-III VIII 3–13; LC II 34–62; FC Ep II 13). See also *Enthusiasm.*

6. *Means of grace have the same effect.* The Sacraments have the same effect as the spoken or written Word because they are nothing else than the visible Word (see par. 1 above), that is, the Gospel applied in sacred action in connection with the visible signs. For this reason the Sacraments offer, convey, and seal to the recipients forgiveness of sins, life, and salvation just as the Gospel does when it is spoken, contemplated, or read. It is therefore not in agreement with Scripture to ascribe to Baptism (see III below) regeneration exclusively and to the Lord's Supper (see IV below), as a special function, the implanting of the germ of the resurrection body. Also the Gospel regenerates when it is read, preached, or contemplated in the heart (1 Ptr 1:23).

7. *Calvinism* and the means of grace.* Calvinism rejects the means of grace as unnecessary; it holds that the Holy Spirit requires no escort or vehicle by which to enter human hearts. The Ref. doctrine of predestination* excludes the idea of means which impart the Spirit and His gifts to men, the Holy Spirit working effectively only on the elect. Acc. to Ref. teaching, the office of the Word is to point out the way of life without imparting that of which it conveys the idea. Ref. theol. regards Word and Sacraments as necessary because of divine institution. They are symbols of what the Holy Spirit does within as He works immediately (i. e. without means) and irresistibly. "Enthusiast" doctrine of the Anabaptists* and of the many sects since their day regarding the "inner light," gen. identified with the "baptism of the Holy Spirit" and the "2d conversion," has its root in this specifically Ref. doctrine of the immediate working of the Holy Spirit. See also *Enthusiasm.*

8. *RCm and the means of grace.* RCm emphasizes 7 sacraments as means of grace. The Council of Trent* (Sess. VII, Canons on the sacraments in gen., 6 and 8) taught that these sacraments confer grace *ex opere operato* (see *Opus operatum*) on those who do not put an obstacle in the way. RC theologians differ on questions pertaining to sacramental grace, e. g., some regard it as identical with sanctifying grace, others hold that it is a special type of sanctifying grace. Grace bestowed by the sacraments is often described in RCm as a spiritual quality infused by God into the soul (see also *Gratia infusa*). Baptism, acc. to RCm, wipes out original sin* in the baptized. See also *Sacraments, Roman Catholic.*

9. *Necessity of the means of grace.* The means of grace are necessary because of Christ's command and because they offer God's grace. God has not bound Himself to the means of grace (Lk 1:15, 41), but He has bound His ch. to them. Christians dare not regard as unnecessary the Sacraments and the preaching of the Word (Mt 28:19-20; Lk 22:19; 1 Co 11:23-28), as some "enthusiasts" do. But Luth. theol. does not assert an absolute necessity of the Sacraments, since faith and regeneration can be worked by the Holy Spirit in the hearts of men through the Word without the Sacraments. Mere lack of the Sacraments does not condemn, but contempt for them does (Lk 7:29-30).

II. *Law and Gospel.* 1. *Distinction bet. Law and Gospel.* The terms Law and Gospel are used at times in a wide sense for the entire body of Bible doctrine (Ps. 1:2; Mk 1:1). But in a narrow sense Law and Gospel are contradictory or opposite, one threatening and condemning, the other promising and forgiving (Ro 3:19-31). The Law, in its proper sense, is the Word "which reproves all sins" (FC SD V 2). The Gospel is the joyous message of God's grace in Christ Jesus toward all sinners (Jn 3:16). This "distinction between law and Gospel is an especially glorious light that is to be maintained with great diligence in the church so that, according to St. Paul's admonition, the Word of God may be divided rightly" (FC Ep V 2).

2. *Moral Law and ceremonial laws.* The ceremonial laws of the OT have been abolished (Cl 2:16-17), but the Moral Law (see *Decalog*) is in force to the end of time (Mt 5:18). The Moral Law, however, determined by the law of love (Mt 22:35-40), must not simply be identified with the Decalog as given in the OT (Ex 20; Dt 5), since that contains ceremonial elements, meant only for the Jews (e. g., Dt 5:15). The "Ten Commandments" (Ex 34:28; Dt 4:13; 10:4) must direct our conduct inasmuch as they serve the principle of love (Ro 13:8) and are restated in the NT (Mt 19:18-19; Ro 13:9). The 3d Commandment, "Remember the Sabbath day, to keep it holy," is omitted in the NT; this shows that emphasis no longer rests on the day, but on sanctifying through the Word (LC I 78–102).

3. *Use of the Law and the Gospel.* The use of the Law is 3-fold. The Luth. Ch., in accord with Holy Scripture, confesses: "The law of God serves (1) not only to maintain external discipline and decency against dissolute and disobedient people, (2) and to bring people to a knowledge of their sin through the law, (3) but those who have been born anew through the Holy Spirit, who have been converted to the Lord and from whom the veil of Moses has been taken away, learn from the law to live and walk in the law" (FC SD VI 1). H. C. Schwan,* *A Short Exposition of Dr. Martin Luther's Small Catechism* (see also *Catechetics,* 11), question 91: "What purposes does the Law, then, serve? First, it checks, in a measure, the coarse outbursts of sin, and thereby helps to maintain outward discipline and decency in the world. *(A curb.)* Secondly, and chiefly, it teaches man the due knowledge of his sin. *(A mirror.)* Thirdly, it leads the regenerate to know what are truly good works. *(A rule.)*" From the hour when Adam and Eve fell into sin to the end of this present world there never was, nor is, nor will be a man conceived and born in the natural way who could by his own efforts satisfy the demands of the Law and stand in the presence of God by virtue of his own righteousness. All are guilty, under condemnation, deserving of, and liable to punishment at the hands of God, whose Law they have broken and whose sovereign majesty they have offended (Ro 3:22-23). That is the last word the Law has to say to the sinner. It leaves him with the threat of divine retribution.

The Gospel of Jesus Christ, in its proper sense, is the glad tidings of forgiveness, peace, life, and joy, the eternal divine counsel of redemption, of which Christ Himself ever was, is, and will be the living center, the very heart and soul. The Gospel, just as the Law, though in a different and opposite way, has a 3-fold use: (1) The Law teaches the knowledge of sin; the Gospel imparts forgiveness of sin; (2) the Law teaches what good works are; the Gospel produces true joy and zeal to do good works; (3) the Law checks sin outwardly, but increases sin inwardly; the Gospel destroys sin both outwardly and inwardly. The difference bet. the Law and Gospel may be put thus: "The Law prescribes; the Gospel inscribes," and "The Law kills the sinner, but not sin; the Gospel kills sin, but not the sinner." See also *Law and Gospel.*

III. *Baptism as a means of grace.* 1. *Baptism instituted by Christ.* Baptism was instituted by Christ (Mt 28:18-19) and is to be used as a means to impart forgiveness of sins, life, and salvation till the end of time. Its visible element is water (1 Ptr 3:20-21); nothing else may be substituted. The mode of applying water is an adiaphoron (see *Adiaphora*), the Gk. term *baptizein* meaning not only immersing but also washing, sprinkling, and pouring (Mk 7:3-4; Acts 1:5 cf. 2:16-17; Eph. 5:25-26; Heb 9:10 ["washings," literally "baptisms"] cf. Nm 19:13, 19; *Didache* 7:1-3).

2. *Purpose of Baptism.* "It works forgiveness of sins, delivers from death and the devil, and gives eternal salvation to all who believe this, as the words and promises of God declare" (SC IV 6). Acc. to Scripture, Christ sanctifies His ch. with the washing of water by the Word (Eph 5:25-26). Baptism makes disciples of men (Mt 28:19); it saves (1 Ptr 3:21); it is a washing of regeneration (Tts 3:5) by which men are born again (Jn 3:5-6). Through Baptism we put on Christ, that is, His merits and righteousness, by the very faith which, by application of the Gospel, it creates in the heart (Gl 3:26-27); for Baptism is pure Gospel, not Law, and hence it does not save mechanically (see *Opus operatum*), but by faith, which receives the blessings Baptism offers and which is worked by this Sacrament; the Gospel is both the means of creating faith and the foundation of faith. Baptism also unites the baptized with the Triune God, for we are baptized into communion with the Father, Son, and Holy Ghost (Mt 28:19) as also into communion with Christ (Gl 3:27). And by Baptism we are buried with Christ into death, that is, through Baptism we partake of the merits which Christ procured for the whole world by His vicarious suffering and death (Ro 6:3-5). Baptism, as the application of the saving Gospel, is, therefore, a true means of grace. "How can water do such great things? It is not the water indeed that does them, but the word of God which is in and with the water, and faith, which trusts such word of God in the water" (SC IV 9–10). Baptism is a means of grace because it "is not simple water only, but it is the water comprehended in God's command and connected with God's word" (SC IV 2), the Gospel promise of salvation. Those who have fallen from baptismal grace should remember that God's promises of forgiveness, life, and salvation remain unshaken; they should return penitently to the Gospel covenant est. by God with the baptized in and through Baptism.

3. *Meaning of Baptism.* By Baptism we are buried with Christ into death and arise with Him to newness of life (Ro 6:4). "What does such baptizing with water signify? It signifies that the Old Adam in us should, by daily contrition and repentance, be drowned and die with all sins and evil lusts and, again, a new man daily come forth and arise, who shall live before God in righteousness and purity forever" (SC IV 11–12).

4. *Infant Baptism.* Baptism in the NT is the counterpart of circumcision in the OT (Cl 2:11-12), and in the OT infants were circumcised (Gn 17:12; Lv 12:3). In the NT families were baptized (Acts 16:15, 33; 18:8; 1 Co 1:16); in Acts 2:38-41 Baptism is connected with the promise "to your children." Christ's command to baptize all nations certainly also included infants (Mt 28:19-20). The need for infant regeneration is clear (Ps 51:5; Jn 3:6; Eph 2:3). Baptism is the washing of regeneration and renewing of the Holy Ghost (Jn 3:3-7; Tts 3:5). Christ desires to have also little children brought to Him for the blessings of His grace (Mk 10:14). Little children can believe (Mt 18:2-6).

See also *Baptism, Liturgical; Sponsors.*

IV. *Lord's Supper as a means of grace.* 1. *Names of this Sacrament.* Names by which this Sacrament is known are derived partly from Scripture (Breaking of Bread, Mt 26:26 and 1 Co 10:16; Holy Communion, 1 Co 10:16-17; Lord's Table, 1 Co 10:21; Lord's* Supper, 1 Co 11:20; Eucharist [from Gk. *eucharistesas,* "when He had given thanks"], 1 Co 11:24), partly from ch. usage (e. g., Sacrament of the Altar). See also *Mass.*

2. *Institution of the Lord's Supper:* Mt 26:17-28; Mk 14:22-24; Lk 22:19-20; 1 Co 11:23-25. These accounts agree in all essentials, but supplement each other in details. All quote Christ's words: "This is My body." With regard to the cup, Mt and Mk emphasize the blood of the NT, given with the cup; Lk and Paul stress the blessing given with the cup, the forgiveness of the new covenant, procured by the blood of Christ, which is offered to the communicant in the Sacrament.

3. *Real Presence.* The words of institution, "Take, eat; this is My body," clearly state: "With this bread I give you My body." So these words are explained 1 Co 10:16. There is no transubstantiation* of the bread and wine into the body and blood of Christ, nor any consubstantiation* or impanation.* In, with, and under the bread and wine a communicant, also an unbelieving communicant (1 Co 11:27-29), receives Christ's true body, given into death, and His true blood, shed for sins. This is the point of controversy bet. Luths. and Ref. The question is not whether Christ is present acc. to His divine nature in the Sacrament, or whether the soul by faith is united with Christ (spiritual eating and drinking), or whether the believing communicant receives the merits of Christ's shed blood by faith (all of which is acknowledged as true by both Luths. and Ref.). In Luth. terminology the eating and drinking of Christ's body and blood in, with, and under the bread and wine is called sacramental* eating and drinking. The Ref. deny that the words of instit. should be taken in a literal sense, or that in, with, and under the bread and wine the true body and blood of Christ are really present (Real Presence, a mystery). The Ref. teach instead the real absence of Christ's body and blood in the Sacrament by resorting to a figurative, or symbolical, interpretation. Karlstadt* sought the figure in "this," H. Zwingli* in "is" (making "is" mean "represents"), J. Calvin* and others in "body" (making "body" mean "the sign of My body"), and others (e. g., W. Bucanus,* B. Keckermann,* and H. Zanchi*) in the entire statement. The multifarious attempts to pervert the proper sense of the words are but so many evidences of the persistent refusal of the words to yield to perversion. See also *Lutheran Confessions,* A 2 (b); *Sacramental Union.*

4. *Elements in the Sacrament.* The heavenly elements in the Sacrament are the true body and the true blood of Christ; the earthly elements are true bread and true wine, for which no substitutes should be used, since the use of any substitute makes void, or at least renders uncertain, the Sacrament (Mt 26:29; Mk 14:25; Lk 22:18; 1 Co 11:21). Jesus used not unfermented grape juice but wine, used in the OT on festive occasions (Gn 14:18; Jb 1:13; Is 5:12). Bread and wine are received in a natural manner; the body and blood of Christ, though received orally, are received in an incomprehensible, supernatural manner (no Capernaitic* eating; FC SD VII 64). The Sacrament should be received by

all communicants *sub utraque specie* ("under both kinds"), acc. to Christ's instit. In RC practice the celebrating priest receives the bread and wine, other communicants usually only bread (*sub una specie,* "under 1 kind").

5. *Purpose of the Lord's Supper.* The Lord's Supper is essentially an application of the Gospel, with all its spiritual blessings, in a sacred act. It offers, conveys, and seals to the communicant forgiveness of sins, life, and salvation; strengthens faith; promotes sanctification through strengthening of faith; increases love toward God and the neighbor; affords patience in tribulation; confirms hope of eternal life; and deepens union with Christ and His mystical body, the ch. (1 Co 10:17). It also serves a confessional purpose (Acts 2:42; 1 Co 10:20-21; 11:26). All these blessings are mediated through the Gospel-promise in the Sacrament ("Given and shed for you for the remission of sins") and are apprehended by faith in the divine promise. The words "This do in remembrance of Me" do not mean merely that the communicant is to remember the absent Christ, who atoned for his sins; they invite the communicant to accept the forgiveness offered in the Sacrament ("Do this in remembrance of Me" means: remember Christ's blessings and accept them by faith; cf. Ap XXIV 72). The Lord's Supper differs from the preaching of the Gospel, which is addressed to all hearers, believers and unbelievers, and from Absolution,* which is individually addressed to believers, to the believers as a penitent group, in that the Sacrament offers forgiveness of sins, life, and salvation individually to each communicant under pledge of Christ's body and blood, received with the bread and wine. Since the Sacrament may be received unto damnation (or judgment; 1 Co 11:29), close* Communion should be observed, the pastor as the steward of the mysteries of God (1 Co 4:1) admitting only such as are able to examine themselves (1 Co 11:28). JTM

See also *Grace; Law and Gospel; Remanence; Sacraments; Word of God.*

J. T. Mueller, "The Means of Grace," *What Lutherans Are Thinking,* ed. E. C. Fendt (Columbus, Ohio, 1947), pp. 265–288, *Christian Dogmatics* (St. Louis, 1934), and "Holy Baptism," *The Abiding Word,* II, ed. T. Laetsch (St. Louis, 1947), 394–422; C. F. W. Walther, *The Proper Distinction Between Law and Gospel,* tr. W. H. T. Dau (St. Louis, 1929); J. M. Reu, *Die Gnadenmittellehre* (Chicago, 1917); F. R. Zucker, "Circumcision and Baptism," *CTM,* XV (Apr. 1944), 245–259; W. Geihsler, "The Law and the Gospel," *The Abiding Word,* I, ed. T. Laetsch (St. Louis, 1946), 105–123; E. E. Pieplow, "The Means of Grace," *The Abiding Word,* II, ed. T. Laetsch (St. Louis, 1947), 322–346; S. W. Becker, "The Gospel," *The Abiding Word,* II, ed. T. Laetsch (St. Louis, 1947), 347–366; A. E. Neitzel, "The Sacraments," *The Abiding Word,* II, ed. T. Laetsch (St. Louis, 1947), 367–393; R. Prenter, "Luther on Word and Sacrament," *More About Luther,* ed. G. L. Belgum, D. T. Nelson, and J. C. Bale (Decorah, Iowa, 1958); E. B. Koenker, *Worship in Word and Sacrament* (St. Louis, 1959); H. Sasse, *This Is My Body: Luther's Contention for the Real Presence in the Sacrament of the Altar* (Minneapolis, 1959); *Meaning and Practice of the Lord's Supper,* ed. H. T. Lehmann (Philadelphia, 1961); K. Aland, *Did the Early Church Baptize Infants?* tr. G. R. Beasley-Murray (London, 1963); J. Jeremias, *Infant Baptism in the First Four Centuries,* tr. D. Cairns (Philadelphia, 1961), *The Origins of Infant Baptism,* tr. D. M. Barton (Naperville, 1963), and *The Eucharistic Words of Jesus,* tr. N. Perrin (New York, 1966); *A Short Exposition of Dr. Martin Luther's Small Catechism* (St. Louis, 1912); E. J. Kilmartin, *The Eucharist in the Primitive Church* (Englewood Cliffs, N. J., 1965); bibliography under *Dogmatics.*

Grace at Meals. Prayers asking blessing before or giving thanks after eating (Jn 6:11; Acts 27:35).

Gracián y Morales, Balt(h)asar (pen name Lorenzo Gracián; 1601–58). B. Belmonte, near Calatayud, Sp.; author; Jesuit 1619; influenced F. W. Nietzsche* and A. Schopenhauer.* Works include *El criticón,* a philos. novel that evaluates civilization on basis of its effects on a savage.

Gradine (from Fr. *gradin,* "step"). Ledge above and behind altar on which cross, candlesticks, and other ornaments may be placed.

Gradual. Part of traditional Christian worship service, bet. Epistle and Gospel readings; originally called *responsorium* or *responsorium graduale;* it was intoned by the precentor (see *Cantor*) on the steps (Lat. *gradus*) of the altar* or ambo* from which the Epistle was read. Texts of the graduals are from Scripture, usually from Ps. In Luth. chs. the gradual may be replaced by a hymn or other fitting music. In many chs. only the Hallelujah* is used.

The Graduals for the Church Year, ed. E. Kurth and W. E. Buszin (St. Louis, 1944); G. Reese, *Music in the Middle Ages* (New York, 1940).

Graebner, August(us) Lawrence (Gräbner; July 10, 1849–Dec. 7, 1904). Son of J. H. P. Graebner*; b. Frankentrost, Mich.; educ. Conc. Coll., Fort Wayne, Ind., and Conc. Sem., St. Louis, Mo.; instructor Lutheran High School (later called Walther* Coll.), St. Louis, 1872; prof. Northwestern* Coll., Watertown, Wis., 1875; prof. Wis. Syn. theol. sem., Milwaukee, 1878; prof. Conc. Sem., St. Louis, 1887. Visited Australia, New Zealand, and Europe 1902. Works include *Dr. Martin Luther; Half a Century of Sound Lutheranism in America; Geschichte der Lutherischen Kirche in America; Outlines of Doctrinal Theology.* Ed. *Evangelisch-Lutherisches Gemeinde-Blatt* (see *Wisconsin Synod,* 3); *Der Lutheraner; Theological Quarterly.*

K. Kretzmann, "The Reverend Doctor Augustus Lawrence Graebner, 1849–1904," *CHIQ,* XX (July 1947), 79–93.

Graebner, Carl Frederick (Friedrich; Gräbner; Oct. 8, 1862–June 5, 1949). Son of J. H. P. Graebner*; b. St. Charles, Mo.; educ. Northwestern* Coll., Watertown, Wis., and Conc. Sem., St. Louis, Mo.; pastor Sedalia, Mo., 1885, Topeka, Kans., 1889, Bay City, Mich., 1897; to Australia 1903; dir. Conc. Coll. and Sem., Murtoa, 1904, (Unley-Malvern) Adelaide 1905; resigned as dir. 1939 but continued as pres. of the theol. faculty and as teacher till the end of 1941.

Graebner, Johann Heinrich Philip (Gräbner; July 7, 1819–May 27, 1898). B. Burghaig, near Kulmbach, Bavaria; studied theol. under J. K. W. Löhe*; under Löhe's direction he led a group of emigrants to Am. 1847 and founded Frankentrost, Mich.; pastor Roseville, Mich., 1853; founded a cong. at Mount Clemens, Mich.; pastor St. Charles, Mo., 1859.

Graebner, Martin Adolph Henry (Gräbner; Sept. 22, 1879–Nov. 13, 1950). Son of A. L. Graebner*; b. Milwaukee, Wis.; educ. Conc. Coll., Fort Wayne, Ind., and Conc. Sem., St. Louis, Mo.; ordained at St. Charles, Mo., Apr. 7, 1901; miss. at large Okla.; pastor Cushing, Okla., 1901, Oklahoma City, Okla., 1902; prof. St. John's Coll., Winfield, Kans., 1910–22; lawyer 1914; prof. Conc. Coll., Milwaukee, Wis., 1922–27; pres. Conc. Coll., St. Paul, Minn., 1927–46. Works include *The Lord's Prayer and the Christian Life.*

Graebner, Theodore Conrad (Gräbner; Nov. 23, 1876–Nov. 14, 1950). Son of A. L. Graebner*; b. Watertown, Wis.; educ. Conc. Coll., Fort Wayne,

Ind., and Conc. Sem., St. Louis, Mo.; instructor Walther* Coll., St. Louis, Mo., 1897–1900; instructor Lutheran Ladies' Sem., Red Wing, Minn., 1900–06; ordained 1902 as mem. of The Syn. for the Norw. Ev. Luth. Ch. in Am. (Synoden for den Ev. Luth. Kirke i Amerika; see *Norwegian Evangelical Lutheran Synod of America*); asst. pastor Trin. Ch., Red Wing, Minn., 1902–06; miss. for Norw. Syn. in Irving Park, Chicago, Ill., 1906–08; pastor Jehovah Ch. (Mo. Syn.), Chicago, 1908–13; prof. Conc. Sem., St. Louis, Mo., 1913–50; active in many religious, civic, and cultural organizations. Works include *The Borderland of Right and Wrong; Church Bells in the Forest; Concordia Seminary; The Dark Ages; A Dictionary of Bible Topics; Essays on Evolution; The Expository Preacher; God and the Cosmos; Handbook for Congregational Officers; A Handbook of Organizations; The Historic Lutheran Position in Non-Fundamentals; Inductive Homiletics; Is Masonry a Religion?; Letters to a Masonic Friend; Pastor and People; The People; The Pastor as Student and Literary Worker; Dr. Francis Pieper; The Pope and Temporal Power; Prayer Fellowship; The Problem of Lutheran Union, and Other Essays; Prophecy and the War; The Secret Empire; Spiritism; The Story of the Augsburg Confession; The Story of the Catechism; Touring with God; A Treatise on Freemasonry; War in the Light of Prophecy.* Coauthor *Popular Symbolics; Toward Lutheran Union.* Ed. *The Annotated Pocket New Testament; Illustrated Home Journal; Lutheran Herald; Der Lutheraner; The Lutheran Witness; The Bible Student.* Coed. *What Lutherans Are Thinking.* Assoc. ed. *CHIQ; The Cresset.* Dept. ed. *L. u. W.; Homiletic Magazine.* ARS

Graf, Karl Heinrich (1815–69). B. Mühlhausen, Alsace; educ. Strasbourg; pupil of E. G. E. Reuss*; teacher 1847, prof. Heb. and Fr. 1852 Meissen; helped develop documentary hypothesis (see *Higher Criticism,* 6–16).

Grail, Holy. See *Holy Grail.*

Gramann, Johann(es) (Graumann; Poliander; 1487–1541). B. Neustadt an der Aisch, Middle Franconia, W Bavaria, Ger.; educ. Leipzig; rector Thomasschule, Leipzig; secy of J. Eck* at Leipzig* Debate, but adopted the cause of the Reformation because of M. Luther's* appeal to Scripture and conscience; preacher Würzburg, Nürnberg, and Mansfeld; pastor Königsberg 1525–41. Wrote "Nun lob', mein' Seel', den Herren," the oldest Luth. hymn of praise, based on Ps 103.

Grammars. A. *Old Testament.* The hist. of Heb. grammar begins roughly with the 9th c. AD, when Saadia* (or Saadja) ben Joseph (ca. 882–942) laid the foundation for a science indep. of the Masoretes (see *Masorah*). The prince among his successors was David ben Joseph Kimchi (ca. 1160 – ca. 1235), who paved the way for hist. and critical study of the Heb. language. The father of Christian Heb. grammarians is J. Reuchlin* (1455–1522); A. Schultens* (1686–1750) and Nikolaus Wilhelm Schröder (1721–98) laid the foundations for comparative grammatical methodology. Their most illustrious successor is H. F. W. Gesenius*; the 1st ed. of his *Hebräische Grammatik* was pub. 1813; the 28th appeared 1909; a beginning of the 29th was issued by G. Bergsträsser* 1918, 1926–29. The 2d ed. of George Wolseley Collins' (ca. 1846–95) Eng. tr., *Gesenius' Hebrew Grammar,* rev. by Arthur Ernest Cowley (1861–1931) appeared 1910, with corrections in reprints since 1946. Other works include G. H. A. Ewald,* *Ausführliches Lehrbuch der hebräischen Sprache des Alten Bundes,* 8th ed. (1870); B. Stade,* *Lehrbuch der hebräischen Grammatik* (1879); F. E. König,* *Historisch-kritisches Lehrgebäude der hebräischen Sprache,* 3 vols. (1881 to 89); A. B. Davidson,* *An Introductory Hebrew Grammar* (1884; 25th ed. rev. John Mauchline 1962); Jacob Weingreen, *A Practical Grammar for Classical Hebrew* (1939); Alexander Sperber, *A Historical Grammar of Biblical Hebrew* (1966).

B. *New Testament.* S. Glass(ius)* in *Philologia sacra* (1623–36) pioneered in undertaking a systematic description of the peculiarities of NT diction. G. Pasor* broke fresh ground 1655 with *Grammatica graeca sacra Novi Testamenti domini nostri Jesu Christi,* but NT Gk. grammar remained fettered in Heb. associations until J. G. B. Winer,* whose *Grammatik des neutestamentlichen Sprachidioms* (1822) saw 7 eds. and was tr. into Eng. 1825. Papyri discoveries moved G. A. Deissmann* to write *Bibelstudien* (1895) and *Neue Bibelstudien* (1897). A new era broke for NT interpretation. Much literature on the NT written before 1900 became obsolete. A grammar was begun by J. H. Moulton.* The 1st vol. appeared 1906; a 2d, ed. Wilbert Francis Howard, appeared in 3 parts 1919–29; the 3d vol., ed. Nigel Turner, appeared 1963. A. T. Robertson* issued *A Grammar of the Greek New Testament in the Light of Historical Research* (the "Big Grammar"). It has largely been superseded by J. A. Debrunner's* eds. of F. W. Blass,* *Grammatik des neutestamentlichen Griechisch* (1896; 9th ed. 1954), available in Robert W. Funk's 1961 rev. and tr., *A Greek Grammar of the New Testament, and Other Early Christian Literature.* For special problems of syntax Ernest De Witt Burton, *Syntax of the Moods and Tenses in New Testament Greek* (1888; 3d ed. 1898) and Charles Francis D. Moule, *An Idiom Book of New Testament Greek* (1953; 2d ed. 1959) should be consulted. See also *Robinson, Edward; Thayer, Joseph Henry.*

F. Danker, *Multipurpose Tools for Bible Study,* 2d, rev. ed. (St. Louis, 1966), pp. 97–132. FWD

Grammaticohistorical Method (historicogrammatical method). Term used to designate a variety of methods of exegesis that give attention to grammar and hist. Popularized by J. A. Ernesti.* See also *Schools, Early Christian,* 4.

Granada, Luis de. See *Luis de Granada.*

Grand View College, Des Moines, Iowa. See *Ministry, Education of.* VIII C 1 b.

Grand View Theological Seminary. See *Ministry, Education of,* X I.

Granfelt, Axel Fredrik (1815–92). B. Hausjärvi, Fin.; educ. Helsinki (Helsingfors); prof. ethics and dogmatics Helsinki 1854–75; credited with initiating the modern period of systematic theol. in Fin. Works include *Den kristliga dogmatiken; Den kristliga sedeläran.* See also *Dogmatics,* B 9.

Grant, Asahel (Aug. 17, 1807–Apr. 24, 1844). B. Marshall, N. Y.; studied medicine Pittsfield, Mass.; pioneer ABCFM medical miss. among Nestorians in Persia.

Grant, Elihu. See *Geography, Christian,* 8.

Grant, Robert (1779 [some say 1785]–1838). B. Bengal, India [some say Inverness, Scot.]; educ. Cambridge; lawyer 1807; MP 1818; supported emancipation of Jews; Privy Councillor 1831; Judge Advocate Gen. 1832; Gov. of Bombay 1834. Hymnist; hymns include "Oh, Worship the King" and "Savior, When in Dust to Thee."

Granth. See *Adi Granth.*

Grassman, Andrew (Feb. 23, 1704–Mar. 25, 1783). B. Senftleben, Moravia; to Count N. L. v. Zinzendorf's* estate at Berthelsdorf, later called Herrnhut, 1728; traveling miss. in Ger., Swed., Lapland, Greenland; bp. Moravian Ch. 1756.

Gräter, Kaspar (Gret[t]er; Greth; ca. 1501–57). B. Gundelsheim, near Heilbronn, Ger.; schoolmaster at Heilbronn 1527 on recommendation of J. Brenz*;

pastor Herrenberg, later at Cannstatt; court preacher of Duke Ulrich*; influential reformer.

Gratia. For all entries beginning with the word *Gratia* see also *Grace.*

Gratia actualis (actual grace). RC term for supernatural assistance from God which helps man perform acts leading to salvation; identified with *gratia adjuvans.* See also *Gratia infusa; Gratia praeveniens.*

Gratia adjuvans (helping grace). Identified by RCs with *gratia* actualis.*

Gratia concomitans (accompanying grace). Grace which accompanies free will.

Gratia cooperans. See *Gratia operans.*

Gratia creata. See *Gratia increata.*

Gratia gratis data; gratia gratum faciens (grace freely given; grace rendering acceptable). Acc. to RC theol., the supernatural grace of Christ, existing invisibly in the soul, tends either to the salvation of the person in whom it inheres or, through him, to the sanctification of others. The former is "grace which makes acceptable" *(gratia gratum faciens);* the latter is "grace freely given" *(gratia gratis data),* the term based on Mt 10:8: "Freely ye have received, freely give." *Gratia gratum faciens* is intended for all; *gratia gratis data* is ordinarily the charism of prophets, apostles, and priests, though it occurs also in others.

Gratia habitualis (habitual grace). Called habitual because it inheres in the soul; identified by RCs with sanctifying grace (see *Gratia infusa*).

Gratia increata; gratia creata (uncreated grace; created grace). Acc. to RC theol., uncreated grace is God Himself, inasmuch as He gives Himself to man. God is Love toward us, His creatures, so that from eternity He loves us, the Son of God became incarnate, and the Holy Ghost was poured out. Created grace is distinguished from God, who essentially is Grace, as the created gift of grace *(donum gratiae)* given to man as actual grace (see *Gratia actualis*) or as habitual grace (see *Gratia habitualis*).

Gratia infusa (infused grace). Acc. to RC theol., grace is a supernatural quality infused by God into the soul for salvation through the merits of Jesus Christ. This grace is of 2 kinds: 1. Sanctifying grace confers on the soul a sharing in the life of God; makes men holy, adopted children of God and temples of the Holy Ghost; gives the right to heaven. See also *Gratia habitualis.* 2. Actual grace enlightens the mind and strengthens the will to do good and avoid evil. See also *Gratia actualis.*

Gratia irresistibilis. See *Gratia resistibilis.*

Gratia naturalis (natural grace). Grace which comes to man from creation. Distinguished from *gratia supernaturalis* (supernatural grace) which comes to man in a supernatural way through the redemption.

Gratia operans (operating grace). Grace which generates faith; distinguished from *gratia cooperans* (cooperating grace) which is active in believers to produce good* works jointly with the regenerated will.

Gratia particularis. See *Gratia universalis.*

Gratia praeveniens (prevenient grace). Grace which precedes conversion. Referred by Luths. to outward circumstances (e. g., hearing of the Word) by which the Holy Ghost prepares the heart for conversion. In RCm it is often *gratia* actualis.* Distinguished from *gratia subsequens* (subsequent grace) which follows conversion.

Gratia resistibilis (resistible grace). Luths. are among those who teach that saving grace is resistible because it is offered through means. Others (e. g., Ref.) teach that God imparts grace without means and that such grace is irresistible *(gratia irresistibilis).* See also *Pelagian Controversy,* 3.

Gratia subsequens. See *Gratia praeveniens.*

Gratia supernaturalis. See *Gratia naturalis.*

Gratia universalis (universal grace). Term used to describe the belief (e. g., of Luths. and Arminians) that God's grace embraces all men, i. e., that He earnestly wills the salvation of all; distinguished from *gratia particularis* (particular grace), the belief (e. g., of Ref.) that God's grace does not embrace all but only some.

Gratian (Flavius Gratianus; 359–383). B. Sirmium, Pannonia; Roman emp. 375–383; E emp. 378; in his reign orthodox Christianity became dominant throughout the Roman Empire; severe in dealing with heathen and heretics. See also *Theodosius I.*

Gratian (12th c.). Camaldolese* monk; taught at Bologna, It.; founded science of canon law; wrote *Concordantia discordantium canonum (Decretum Gratiani).* See also *Canon Law,* 3; *Decrees.*

Gratius, Ortwin. See *Letters of Obscure Men.*

Gratry, Auguste Joseph Alphonse (1805–72). B. Lille, Fr.; RC priest, philos., and educ.; prof. Sorbonne 1863; opposed papal infallibility (see *Roman Catholic Confessions,* E 3), but accepted the dogma when it was promulgated; sought God through feeling rather than reason. See also *Oratorians,* 3.

Grau, Rudolf Friedrich (1835–93). B. Heringen on the Werra, Ger.; educ. Leipzig, Erlangen, and Marburg; Luth. theol.; prof. Königsberg. Works include *Ursprünge und Ziele unserer Kulturentwicklung; Entwicklungsgeschichte des neutestamentlichen Schrifttums; Biblische Theologie des Neuen Testaments; Das Selbstbewusstsein Jesu;* coed. *Beweis des Glaubens.*

Graul, Karl Friedrich Leberecht (Feb. 6, 1814–Nov. 10, 1864). B. Wörlitz, Ger.; Luth. theol.; educ. Leipzig; dir. Dresden-Leipzig Miss. Soc. 1844–60 (see *Leipzig Evangelical Lutheran Mission*); in India 1849–53; advocated considerate toleration of the caste system. Works include *Bibliotheca tamulica; Unterscheidungslehren der verschiedenen Christlichen Bekenntnisse.*

Graumann. See *Gramann.*

Graun, Karl Heinrich (ca. 1703 [some say 1701]–1759). Tenor singer; composer; b. Wahrenbrück, Ger.; educ. Kreuzschule, Dresden; Brunswick Opera tenor 1725; asst. conductor there 1726; entered service of Crown Prince Frederick of Prussia at Rheinsberg 1735; conductor Berlin Royal Opera 1740. Works include *Der Tod Jesu;* operas; concertos; motets. See also *Passion, The.*

Gray, Robert (1809–72). B. Bishop's Wearmouth [Sunderland], Eng.; educ. Eton and Oxford; consecrated Angl. bp. Cape Town, Afr., 1847, arrived Cape Town 1848; metropolitan S. Afr. 1853. See also *Colenso, John William; Hottentots.*

Gray Friars. See *Grey Friars.*

Great Avowal. Declaration ratified 1935 by Universalists, who believe in God as eternal and all-conquering Love, spiritual leadership of Jesus, supreme worth of human personality, authority of truth, power of men to overcome evil and est. the Kingdom of God.

Great Awakening in England and America. Widespread religious revival resulting chiefly from work of C. and J. Wesley* and G. Whitefield* in Eng. (the movement there is also called Evangelical Awakening) and of T. J. Frelinghuysen,* J. Edwards,* and Whitefield in Am. The revivals* ran ca. 1725–ca. 1750 in Am. and ca. 1740–ca. 1815 in Eng.

Great Bible. See *Bible Versions,* L 5.

Great Britain. Chief is. of United Kingdom of Gt. Brit. and N. Ireland; comprises England,* Scotland,* and Wales.* See also *Celtic Church.*

Great Renunciation. See *Gautama Buddha.*

Great Sabbath. See *Church Year,* 4.

Great Schism. See *Schism,* 6, 8.

Great Spirit. See *Indians, American,* 1, 3.

Great Week. See *Church Year,* 4, 8.

Greater Antilles. See *Caribbean Islands.*

Greater Doxology. See *Canticles; Doxology; Worship, Parts of,* 6.

Greater Europe Mission. Inc. 1949 as Eur. Bible Institute. Est. Bible institute at Paris, Fr., 1950, one in Ger. 1955, and one later in Rome. Besides providing religious literature it stresses use of radio and posters.

Greater Sunda Isles (Soenda). See *Indonesia,* 1, 3–6.

Grebel, Konrad (ca. 1498–1526). B. Zurich, Switz.; patrician; scholar; educ. Basel, Vienna, Paris; follower of H. Zwingli.* Mennonites originated in Switz. and the Neth.; Grebel founded the Swiss group at Zurich 1525. See also *Mennonite Churches.*

Grechaninov, Aleksandr Tikhonovich (Gretchaninoff; 1864–1956). Russ. composer; b. Moscow; studied music at Moscow and St. Petersburg; prof. Moscow conservatory; to Paris 1925; to US 1939; US citizen 1946; known esp. for ch. music. Works include *Missa oecumenica; Domestic Liturgy; Samson; Lullaby.*

Greco-Slav Church. See *Eastern Orthodox Churches,* 1.

Greece. *Area:* ca. 51,000 sq. mi. *Pop.* (1967 est.): 8,716,000. S part of Balkan peninsula, with the Peloponnesus peninsula as its S tip; ca. 5th c. BC–2d c. AD the seat of advanced classical civilization but marked by heathenism esp. in Corinth at the beginning of the Christian era. Paul first preached the Gospel in Eur. at Philippi (Acts 16: 9-40). Official ch.: Gk. Orthodox. Other religions: Islam 2%; Jewish 1.1%; others .9%. See also *Eastern Orthodox Churches.*

Greek Church. See *Eastern Orthodox Churches.*

Greek Letter Fraternities. See *Fraternities.*

Greek Orthodox Archdiocese of North and South America. See *Eastern Orthodox Churches,* 6.

Greek Religion. 1. The origins of Gk. religion are largely still obscure. Three tendencies: personification of natural forces (e. g., Naiads, dryads), survival of primitive magic and taboo, and the continuity of a primitive cult of the dead (hero worship). Gk. religion throughout its hist. was concerned with sanctity of places and of human life and purification of men.

2. By the time of Homer, if not earlier, Gk. religion was fairly well fixed in the form of the Olympic pantheon. Traditional gods: Zeus (god of the sky; supreme god), Poseidon (god of the sea), Hades (god of death and the underworld), Hera (sister and wife of Zeus), Athena (virgin goddess; patroness of cities; goddess of war), Ares (god of battle), Apollo (god of music and prophecy), Hephaestus (god of fire), Aphrodite (goddess of love and beauty), Demeter (goddess of vegetation), Hermes (god of flocks; messenger of gods), and Artemis (goddess of hunting and virginity). This "state religion" was a rationalizing of religious feeling, primarily ritualistic, not moral.

3. As time went on, religion underwent modifications and additions; most were completed by the end of the OT. (a) Philosophic religion, emphasizing ethics, challenged the anthropomorphic nature of the gods (e. g., Xenophanes,* Stoicism,* Euhemerus*). Epicureanism* tried to show that gods were not concerned with men. (b) Religious accretions, more or less official, came in. Gods such as Dionysus (god of wine) and Bendis (similar to Artemis) had come in early. Prior to the NT many E religions gradually made their way into the Gk. world, e. g., Isis* worship from Egypt, Mithraism* from Persia. These religions emphasized immortality and afterlife. (c) These more or less gen. religious beliefs involved countless folk beliefs, many of which survived longer than the official religion.

See also *Mystery Religions.*

M. P. Nilsson, *A History of Greek Religion,* tr. F. J. Fielden, 2d ed. (New York, 1949) and *Geschichte der griechischen Religion,* I, 3d ed. (Munich, 1967), II (Munich, 1950); A. M. J. Festugiere, *Personal Religion among the Greeks* (Berkeley, Calif., 1954); G. Murray, *Five Stages of Greek Religion* (London, 1935). EK

Greeley, Horace (1811–72). Am. journalist and pol. leader. See also *Communistic Societies,* 5.

Green, Samuel Fisk (Oct. 10, 1822–May 28, 1884). B. Worcester, Mass.; ABCFM medical miss. to Ceylon 1847–73; wrote medical works in Tamil.

Green, Thomas Hill (1836–82). B. Birkin, Yorkshire, Eng.; educ. Oxford; prof. philos. Oxford 1878; idealist; opposed agnosticism*; held that self-consciousness cannot be derived from material forces; explained consciousness of being part of a larger whole as evidence that the whole was created by absolute mind.

Green, William Henry (1825–1900). B. Groveville, N. J.; educ. Lafayette Coll. (Easton, Pa.) and Princeton (N. J.) Theol. Sem.; conservative Presb.; pastor Philadelphia 1849; prof. Princeton 1851–96; ch. Am. OT Company of Anglo-Am. Bible Rev. Committee. Works include *Moses and the Prophets; General Introduction to the Old Testament; The Unity of the Book of Genesis; A Grammar of the Hebrew Language.*

Green Thursday. See *Gründonnerstag.*

Greenland. *Area:* ca. 840,000 sq. mi. *Pop.* (1966 est.): 41,000. World's largest is.; since 1953 an integral part of Den. Discovered 9th or 10th c.; rediscovered and explored 16th and 17th c. H. P. Egede (see *Egede,* 1) est. miss. 1721 near Godthaab on the W coast; the Ev. Luth. Ch. (ca. 35,000 mems.) is connected with the Ev. Luth. Ch. of Den.; other chs. include Swed. Free Missions, Seventh-day Adventists, and Jehovah's witnesses. See also *Eskimos; Missions, Bibliography.*

Greenwald, Emanuel (Jan. 13, 1811–Dec. 21, 1885). B. Frederick, Md.; studied theol. under D. F. Schaeffer*; Luth. pastor in Ohio and Pa.; leader in early Luth. syns. in both states; 1st ed. *Lutheran Standard.*

Greenwood, John (d. 1593). Eng. Puritan (see *Puritans*) and nonconformist (see *Nonconformists*) leader; led unauthorized services at Rochford, Essex; hanged with H. Barrow(e).*

Grégoire, Henri (1750–1831). B. Vého, near Lunéville, Fr.; bp. Blois 1791–1802; worked for removal of special privileges of the nobles and the ch., for civil rights of Jews and colored people, and for freedom of Negro slaves; supported Civil Constitution of the Clergy (see *France,* 5).

Gregorian Calendar. Gregory* XIII ordered the Julian* calendar revised. The revision (also called New Style) reckoned Oct. 5, 1582, as Oct. 15 and c. yrs. as leap yrs. only when divisible by 400. It followed the system developed by Aloysius Lilius (or Luigi Lilio Ghiraldi), astronomer and physician of Naples, and verified and completed by Christopher Clavius (1537–1612), Bavarian Jesuit astronomer and mathematician. See also *Easter Dates.*

Gregorian Music. A. 1. Gregorian chant, also called plainsong, plainchant *(cantus planus),* choral chant *(cantus choralis),* is the unisonous, diatonic, worship music developed in the Christian Ch. for the Lat. liturgy, assoc. by tradition with Gregory I (see *Popes,* 4), under whom existing melodies were collected and ed. by ch. musicians, esp. the *schola cantorum,* which he is said to have founded or reorganized. The term *cantus firmus,* sometimes used in reference to Gregorian chant, denotes an unchanged melody to which a harmonic setting of one or more voices may be added. As the chant spread through Eur. and to Eng., schools were est. acc. to the Roman model at various places, e. g., Metz, Fr., and St. Gall, Switz. The golden era of the chant, the high point of Gregorian, dates ca. 600–ca. 1100. Then followed a period of preservation and transition. Measurable decadence began ca. 1300. Mensurable music, polyphony, harmony, instrumental music, and the operatic style, all in turn contributed to decay of the chant. Changes in method of chanting and simplification of melodies robbed the chant of its characteristic rhythm. Restoration began ca. 1850. Benedictine monks at Solesmes, Fr., tried to recapture the original melodies and method of chanting, but the Solesmes theory was gen. rejected in Ger. toward the end of the 19th c.

2. Gregorian chant is used in varying degrees in Luth. and Angl. chs. It was adapted for use in the Ger. Mass* (see also *Chant; Mass* [Music]); many later Ger. ch. orders followed suit, weathering pietistic and rationalistic movements. In the 19th c. renewed interest in the chant was manifested in Ger. and America. F. J. C. Lochner* wrote *Der Hauptgottesdienst der Evangelisch-Lutherischen Kirche* to restore it in Am. Plainsong settings were used in *The Psalter and Canticles Pointed for Chanting to the Gregorian Psalm Tones* (1897) and *The Choral Service Book* (1901), ed. H. G. Archer and L. D. Reed. Some Luth. chs. use plainsong for certain parts of the service; some have issued special eds. of Gregorian chant for the complete service. Scand. Luth. chs. also adopted Gregorian chant for the vernacular. The Swed. plainsong service is esp. noteworthy.

3. The Angl. Ch. and the Prot. Episc. Ch. followed J. Marbeck's* example of *The Booke of Common Praier Noted* (1550) and have adapted plainsong to the Eng. language extensively since 1850, chiefly as a result of work done by the Plainsong and Mediaeval Soc. (founded London, Eng., 1888) and such men as C. W. Douglas,* T. Helmore,* and Anselm Hughes (originally Humphrey Vaughan Hughes; b. London, Eng., 1889; musicologist; educ. Oxford; ed. *New Oxford History of Music, II: Early Medieval Music up to 1300*). CaB

B. The present repertoire of Gregorian chant includes ca. 3,000 melodies. Rhythmically free, Gregorian chants are based largely on prose texts taken from Ps. Some are simple and syllabic, others melismatic and involved. Tonalities used are modal, not major or minor. The claim formerly made that Gregorian chant is pure and absolute ch. music has been gen. discarded. Gregorian chant has elements akin to the music of various religious and pagan cultures. It is the finest chant music the world has ever known. WEB

See also *Modes, Ecclesiastical; Psalm Tones.*

G. M. Suñol, *Text Book of Gregorian Chant According to the Solesmes Method,* tr. G. M. Durnford (Tournai, Belgium, 1930); A. F. Klarmann, *Gregorian Chant* (Toledo, Ohio, 1945); D. [Franz] Johner, *A New School of Gregorian Chant,* tr. H. S. Butterfield (New York, 1906); A. Mocquereau, *Le nombre musical Grégorien,* 2 vols. (Rome, 1908, 1927); O. Brodde, "Evangelische Choralkunde," *Leiturgia,* ed. K. F. Müller and W. Blankenburg, IV (Kassel, 1961), 343–557; W. Apel, *Gregorian Chant* (Bloomington, Ind., 1958); E. J. Wellesz, *Eastern Elements in Western Chant,* 2d ed. (Copenhagen, 1968).

Gregorian Sacramentary. An early form of the Roman liturgy; probably based on a book written at the time of Gregory I (see *Popes,* 4); sent by Adrian I (Hadrian; b. Rome; pope 772–795) to Charlemagne* ca. 790.

Gregorian Tones. See *Modes, Ecclesiastical.*

Gregorius Palamas. See *Hesychasm.*

Gregory (Gregorios; b. ca. 559; d. after 603). B. near Agrigentum, Sicily; bp. Agrigentum. Works include commentary on Ec.

MPG, 98, 525–1228.

Gregory I. See *Church Year,* 17; *Popes,* 4.

Gregory II. See *Pseudo-Isidorian Decretals.*

Gregory III (d. 741). B. Syria; priest; pope 731–741; last pope to ask and receive approval of E emp. for election.

Gregory VII. See *Popes,* 7

Gregory IX. See *Popes,* 11.

Gregory XI. See *Popes,* 14.

Gregory XII (Angelo Corrario or Correr; ca. 1327–1417). B. Venice; pope 1406–15; elected by Roman cardinals in opposition to Benedict XIII (see *Benedict XIII,* 1); deposed at council of Pisa,* but refused to step aside; abdicated at council of Constance.* See also *Schism,* 8.

Gregory XIII (Ugo Buoncompagni; 1502–85). B. Bologna, It.; pope 1572–85; introd. Gregorian* Calendar. See also *Curia,* 2 d.

Gregory XV (Alessandro Ludovisi; 1554–1623). B. Bologna, It.; pope 1621–23. See also *Curia,* 2 d.

Gregory, Caspar René (1846–1917). B. Philadelphia, Pa.; educ. Philadelphia, Pa., Princeton, N. J., and Leipzig, Ger.; moved to Leipzig 1873; pastor of Am. Chapel, Leipzig, 1878–79; Ger. citizen 1881; prof. U. of Leipzig 1889; joined Ger. army WW I; killed in Fr. Works include *Canon and Text of the New Testament.*

Gregory of Elvira (ca. 320–ca. 392). B. Baetica, Sp.; bp. Elvira; opposed Arianism*; claimed as leader by Luciferians* after Lucifer's death.

Gregory of Nazianzus (Gregory Nazianzen; ca. 330–ca. 390). "Theologus." Bp. Constantinople 381; one of Cappadocian* theologians; leader in orthodox cause.

Gregory of Nyssa (ca. 331–ca. 396). Bp. Nyssa 371; one of Cappadocian* theologians; leader in orthodox cause.

Gregory of Rimini (ca. 1300–1358). B. Rimini, It.; vicar gen. of Augustinian order 1536, prior gen. 1537; outstanding exponent of nominalism.*

Gregory of Tours (ca. 538–594). B. Clermont-Ferrand, Fr.; Frankish bp. Tours 573. Works include *Historia Francorum;* books of miracles; biographies.

Gregory of Utrecht (ca. 707–ca. 775). B. near Trier; companion of Boniface*; abbot of Utrecht 754; leader of Frisian miss. after death of Boniface.

Gregory of Valencia (ca. 1549–1603). B. Medina del Campo, Sp.; Jesuit dogmatician; wrote extensively in confessional struggle in Germany. Works include *Analysis fidei catholicae; Commentarii theologici.*

Gregory Thaumaturgus (Gregorios Thaumaturgos, i. e., Gregory the Wonder-worker; ca. 213–ca. 270). B. Neocaesarea (modern Niksar, Turkey); bp. Neocaesarea; pupil and admirer of Origen*; zealous and successful miss.; attended syn. at Antioch ca. 264 which condemned Paul* of Samosata; in the course of time a wealth of legends attributed miracles to him. Works include *Exposition of Faith,* a statement of Trinitarianism.

Gregory the Great. See *Popes,* 4.

Gregory the Illuminator (Gregor[ius] Illuminator; Phoster; der Erleuchter; Armenian: Lusaworitsch; estimates of the yr. of his birth range from ca. 240 to ca. 257 and of his death from ca. 325 to ca. 337). B. Valarshapat, or perhaps Caesarea in Cappadocia; reputed founder of Armenian Ch. (see *Armenia*); several forms of Christianity had already entered Armenia and it remained for Gregory to be largely instrumental in making Christianity the national religion; bp. (catholicos*) Armenia.

Greif. See *Gryphius.*

Grell, Eduard August (1800–86). B. Berlin, Ger.; organist Nikolaikirche, Berlin, 1817, court cathedral

1839; dir. Singakademie; prof. Royal Academy of Arts. Works include oratorio *Die Israeliten in der Wüste.*

Grenada. See *Caribbean Islands,* E 5.

Grenfell, Bernard Pyne (1869–1926). B. Birmingham, Eng.; educ. Oxford; prof. Oxford; discovered, ed., and pub. many papyri* MSS. Assoc. with A. S. Hunt*; their pub. findings include *Fragments of an Uncanonical Gospel from Oxyrhynchus; New Sayings of Jesus and Fragment of a Lost Gospel from Oxyrhynchus.*

Grenfell, George (1849–1906). B. Sancreed, Cornwall, Eng.; educ. Birmingham; spent several yrs. in the Cameroons, W Afr., in the 1870s; explored rivers in the Congo basin; with others est. stations at Musuko, Vivi, Isangila, and Manyanga 1881.

Grenfell, Wilfred Thomason (1865–1940). B. Parkgate, Cheshire, Eng.; joined Royal Nat. Miss. to [or for] Deep-Sea Fishermen 1889; med. miss. in Labrador 1892. Works include *A Labrador Doctor; Forty Years for Labrador; Labrador: the Country and the People.* See also *International Grenfell Association.*

W. M. Comber, *Wilfred Grenfell, the Labrador Doctor* (London, 1950); B. W. Miller, *Wilfred Grenfell* (Grand Rapids, Mich., 1965); J. T. Rowland, *North to Adventure* (New York, 1963).

Grenfell Mission, The. See *International Grenfell Association.*

Gressmann, Hugo Ernst Friedrich Wilhelm (1877–1927). B. Mölln, Ger.; Prot. OT scholar and archaeologist; prof. Berlin; sided with H. Gunkel* in many literary-critical questions. Works include *Der Messias; Mose und seine Zeit; Forschungen zur Religion und Literatur des Alten und Neuen Testaments; Der Ursprung der israelitsch-jüdischen Eschatologie.* Prepared with others *Altorientalische Texte und Bilder zum Alten Testamente,* 2 vols.; *Handbuch zum Neuen Testament.* Ed. *Zeitschrift für die alttestamentliche Wissenschaft* 1924–27. See also *Lutheran Theology After 1580,* 13.

Gretchaninoff. See *Grechaninov.*

Gret[t]er; Greth. See *Gräter.*

Greving, Joseph (1868–1919). B. Aachen, Ger.; educ. Bonn and Munich; RC ch. hist.; prof. Münster 1909, Bonn 1917; specialized in Reformation era; organized Corpus* Catholicorum.

Grey Friars. Franciscans* whose habit was formerly gray (now brown).

Grey Nuns. RC Sisters* of Charity, esp. the cong. founded by Marie Marguerite d'Youville in Montreal, Can., 1738.

Gribaldi, Matteo (d. 1564). B. perhaps Padua; It. antitrinitarian leader; resided at Farges, near Geneva, after persecution at Padua and brief stays in a restless, vagrant life at Zurich, Geneva, Tübingen, Farges, and Bern. See also *Socinianism,* 1.

Griesbach, Johann Jakob (1745–1812). B. Butzbach, Ger.; educ. Tübingen, Halle, and Leipzig; prof. Halle and Jena. Issued several critically annotated eds. of the NT; other works include *Commentatio de imaginibus Judaicis; Historia editionum Novi Testamenti Graeci; Synopsis Evangeliorum Matthaei, Marci, et Lucae.* See also *Textual Criticism,* 3.

Griesinger, Georg Friedrich (1734–1828). B. Marschalkenzimmern, near Sulz am Neckar, Ger.; pastor Stuttgart; mem. Stuttgart consistory; supranaturalist.* Ed. hymnbook; other works include *Theologia dogmatica,* which expresses a deistic conception of God.

Griffiths, Davis (Dec. 20, 1792–Mar. 21, 1863). B. Wales; LMS miss. to Madagascar. Tr. Bible into Malagasy; other works include *History of Madagascar* in Welsh.

Grigg, Joseph (ca. 1720–68). B. probably London, Eng.; mechanic in earlier yrs.; minister at age 25 till retirement 1747; hymnist. Hymns include "Jesus, and Shall It Ever Be."

Grimm, Karl Ludwig Wilibald (1807–91). B. Jena; educ. Jena; prof. and ch. councillor Jena; supranaturalist.* Works include *Lexicon graeco-latinum in libros Novi Testamenti,* based on Christian Gottlob Wilke (1786–1854), *Clavis Novi Testamenti philological* (2d ed., 1851) and tr., rev., and enl. by J. H. Thayer.* See also *Lexicons,* B.

Grinbergs, Teodors (Gruenbergs; 1870–1962). B. Windau, Latvia; educ. Dorpat (Tartu); ordained 1899; pastor Lutrini and Windau; mem. Latvian parliament 1922; exiled by Nazis 1944; organized Latvian Luth. Ch. in Exile in Ger.; spent last yrs. at Esslingen, Ger.

Groenning. See *Grönning.*

Groete, Gerhard. See *Groote, Gerhard.*

Gronau, Israel Christian (d. Jan. 11, 1745). B. Ger.; tutor at orphanage in Halle, Ger.; accompanied J. M. Boltzius* to Am. as asst. pastor to Salzburgers (see *Salzburgers, Banishment of*).

Groningen School. School of Dutch theologians with center at U. of Groningen, Neth.; for a time dominated thinking in Ref. Ch. of Holland.

The movement originated at U. of Utrecht under influence of Philip Willem van Heusde (1778–1839), a platonist, who held that Christianity is essentially love, which through fear of God tends to reconcile men with men as children of God. At Groningen there was a similar group that met for study of the NT. This group was influenced by such men as L. Usteri,* A. D. C. Twesten,* K. Ullmann,* F. D. E. Schleiermacher,* G. E. Lessing,* and J. G. v. Herder.* Leaders included P. Hofstede* de Groot, Louis Gerlach Pareau (1800–66), and Johan Frederik van Oordt (1794–1852).

The Groningen school was reaction against intellectual systems of theol. It centered attention on the personality, work, and example of Christ. In Christology it approached Arian views: Christ is not God and man at the same time; His divine or spiritual nature is shared by God and man. It denied the doctrine of the Trinity. Christ did not die to atone for man's sin, but His death shows God's love and hence impels man to crucify sensual life. While Christianity is the highest religion, it is not the only true religion. The school denied the infallibility of the Bible and ascribed higher authority to NT than to OT. Liberty in theol. matters was emphasized.

See also *Mallinckrodt, Willem.*

A. Köhler, *Die Niederländische Reformirte Kirche* (Erlangen, 1856); P. Hofstede de Groot, *De Groninger Godgeleerden in hun eigenaardigheid* (Groningen, 1855); periodicals: *Waarheid in Liefde* (1837–72); *Geloof en Vrijheid* (1867–1919); *Nieuw Evangelisch Tijdschrift* (1919–).

Grönning, Carl Wilhelm (Nov. 22, 1813–Feb. 7, 1898). B. Fredericia, Den.; North* Ger. Miss. Soc. miss. to India 1845; active in Rajahmundry, Ellore, Guntur, and the Palnaud; transferred 1850 to For. Miss. Soc. of the Ev. Luth. Ch. of the US (connected with The Ev. Luth. Gen. Syn. of the US of N. Am. [see *General Synod of the Evangelical Lutheran Church in the United States of America, The*]); returned to Eur. 1865; pastor Hadersleben and Apenrade, Ger.

Grönning, Wilhelm (Sept. 29, 1852–July 9, 1889). B. Guntur, India; son of C. W. Grönning*; educ. Leipzig, Erlangen, and Kiel; inspector Breklum* Miss. Soc. 1879; ordained 1885; to India 1885 as miss. of The General* Syn. of the Ev. Luth. Ch. in the US of Am.

Groot(e), Gerhard (Groet[e]; de Groot[e]; de Groet[e]; Geert; Gerrit; Gerardus Magnus; 1340–84). B. Deventer, Neth.; educ. at cathedral school of Deventer and at U. of Paris; evangelizing preacher in

Holland and the Neth.; helped found Brethren* of the Common Life; leader of *Devotio* moderna.*

Gropper, Johann (1503–59). B. Soest, Westphalia, Ger.; studied law and theol. at Cologne; wrote *Enchiridion Christianae institutionis,* regarded by some RC theologians and cardinals as a suitable basis for reconciliation with Prots., but later placed on Index* of Prohibited Books; carried out Interim* at Soest and Bonn; active at Council of Trent* 1551-52. See also *Regensburg Book; Regensburg Conference.*

Gross, Carl (Sept. 26, 1834–July 10, 1906). B. Frankfurt am Main, Ger.; educ. Conc. Coll. and Sem., Altenburg and St. Louis, Mo.; pastor Richmond, Va., 1856, Buffalo, N. Y., 1867, Fort Wayne, Ind., 1880; pres. E. Dist., Mo. Syn.; vice-pres. Mo. Syn.

Grosseteste, Robert (nickname Greathead; ca. 1175–1253). B. Suffolk, Eng.; educ. Oxford and perhaps Paris; lecturer and chancellor Oxford; bp. Lincoln; called a "harbinger of the Reformation"; outstanding scholar; emphasized Scripture and preaching; like M. Luther,* he first expected help from the pope to correct abuses, but found that the papacy was a source of abuses. Known for open rebukes of both pope and king and for reform efforts.

Grossgebauer, Theophil (1627–61). B. Ilmenau, Ger.; educ Rostock; prof. Rostock; under Brit. puritan and Presb. influences he advocated thorough reform of Luth. orthodox ch. Works include *Wächterstimme aus dem verwüsteten Zion.*

Grossmann, Adolf Arthur (Feb. 18, 1890–Feb. 19, 1941). B. Fairfield, Minn.; educ. Conc. Coll., Saint Paul, Minn., and the teachers' sem., Addison, Ill.; teacher Milwaukee, Wis., 1908–20; 1st supt. of schools of S. Wis. Dist., Mo. Syn., 1920–24; asst. manager CPH 1924–31; active in Walther League (see *Young People's Organizations,* II 3) and Lutheran* Laymen's League. Works include "Present-Day Tendencies and Their Influence on Our Schools" (Concordia Teachers' Library, VIII, Part III).

Grossmann, Christian Gottlob Leberecht (1783–1857). B. Priessnitz, near Naumburg, Ger.; educ. Jena; pastor, supt., and prof. Leipzig; exponent of presbyteral and synodical ch. govt.; loyal to Lutheranism; 1st pres. Gustav-Adolf* Soc. Works include *Quaestiones Philoneae; Über eine Reformation der protestantischen Kirchenverfassung im Königreich Sachsen.*

Grossmann, Georg Martin (Oct. 18, 1823–Aug. 24, 1897). Luth. clergyman, educ., organizer. B. Gross-bieberau, Hesse-Darmstadt, Ger.; studied at normal school, Friedberg; taught at Friedberg, Rottheim, and Lollar; became interested in J. K. W. Löhe's* work in Am.; studied theol. at Erlangen and Nürnberg; sent by Löhe to Mich. 1852; conducted training school for teachers at Saginaw 1852; because of controversies with pastors of the Mo. Syn. (see *Lutheran Church – Missouri Synod, The*) he went to Iowa with J. A. Deindörfer* and reopened his school at Dubuque 1853; soon turned the school into a sem.; pres. of it till ca. 1874; helped organize Iowa* Syn. 1854; 1st pres. Iowa Syn. 1854–93; resumed training of teachers at orphanage at Andrew, Jackson Co., Iowa, 1878; this school was moved 1879 to Waverly, Iowa, where it was combined 1885 with the coll. that had been maintained in connection with the sem. at Mendota, Ill.; head of this school 1878–94. Wrote *Die christliche Gemeindeschule.*

Grotius, Hugo (Huigh de Groot; Huig van Groot; 1583–1645). "Father of International Law." B. Delft, Neth.; scholar, lawyer, politician; sided with Arminianism*; sentenced to life imprisonment 1619; escaped to Fr. 1621; Swed. ambassador to Fr. 1635–45. Tried to unite all chs. in Holland; used historico-philological methodology in Bible interpretation; originated governmental theory of atonement (see *Atonement, Theories of,* 5). Works include *De jure ac pacis; Votum pro pace ecclesiastica; Annotate ad Vetus Testamentum.*

Gruber, Eberhard. See *Amana Society.*

Gruber, Franz Xaver (1787–1863). B. Upper Austria; RC teacher and organist; composed music for "Stille Nacht, heilige Nacht" (see *Mohr, Joseph*).

Gruber, Levi Franklin (May 13, 1870–Dec. 5, 1941). Luth. pastor, prof., lecturer. B. near Reading, Pa.; educ. Neff Coll., Philadelphia, Keystone State Normal School [called Kutztown State Coll. since 1927], Muhlenberg Coll., Allentown, and Luth. Theol. Sem., Mount Airy, Philadelphia; pastor Utica, N. Y., and Minneapolis and St. Paul, Minn.; pres. Chicago Luth. Theol. Sem., Maywood, Ill., 1926–41. Works include *The Wittenberg Originals of the Luther Bible; Whence Came the Universe?; The Six Creative Days; What After Death?; The First English New Testament and Luther; Documentary Sketch of the Reformation; The Einstein Theory.*

Gruber, Theodor Carl Friedrich (Aug. 28, 1795–Sept. 2, 1858). B. Ger.; pastor Reust, Ger., 1825; with G. H. Löber,* E. G. W. Keyl,* O. Fuerbringer,* and others he joined the new orthodox movement of M. Stephan* (1777–1846), though suspicious of Stephan; led contingent of Ger. immigrants 1839 to join Saxons in Perry Co., Mo. (see *Lutheran Church — Missouri Synod, The,* II); pastor Paitzdorf (now Uniontown), Mo., 1840–57; together with G. A. Schieferdecker* became involved in chiliastic controversy; resigned from ministry.

Grubermann, Barbara. See *Communistic Societies,* 5.

Gruen, Olive Dorothy (Grün, Oliva Dorothea; June 20, 1883–May 11, 1963). "Chiao shih" (Chinese for "teacher"). B. St. Louis, Mo.; educ. St. Louis and Moody Bible Institute, Chicago, Ill.; taught in St. Louis; taught in Hankow, China, school for girls and women 1921–26; supervisor of girls' dept. of orphanage at Enshih; taught religion in high school at Wanhsien; active in preparation of S. S. literature and other materials; denied reentry to China after 1949–50 furlough; worked alone in Taiwan* among displaced Christians from 1951; after Missouri* Syn. missionaries arrived, she worked with them to organize Sun. schools and women's Bible classes; to US 1960.

Gruenbergs. See *Grinbergs.*

Gruendler. See *Gründler.*

Grueneisen. See *Grüneisen.*

Gruenewald. See *Grünewald.*

Grumbach, Argula von (von Stauff; ca. 1490–1554). B. Seefeld, Upper Bavaria; friend of M. Luther; wrote Reformation pamphlets; denounced attacks on Lutheranism; zealous student of Bible. See also *Seehofer, Arsacius.*

Grundemann, Peter Reinhold (1836–1924). B. Bärwalde, Neumark, Ger.; educ. Tübingen, Halle, Berlin; pastor Mörz, near Belzig, 1869–1913; founded Brandenburg miss. conf. 1879; missiologist. Works include *Allgemeiner Missionsatlas.*

Gründler, Johann Ernst (Apr. 7, 1677–Mar. 19, 1720). B. Weissensee, Thuringia, Ger.; educ. Leipzig and Wittenberg; taught in A. H. Francke's* institutions at Halle; miss. to India; supported by Dan. miss. soc.; arrived Tranquebar 1709; co-worker of B. Ziegenbalg.*

Gründonnerstag (Green Thursday). Ger. name for Maundy Thursday (see *Church Year,* 4, 8, 16). Origin of name is obscure. Suggested explanations include: 1. assoc. with a custom of giving penitents green branches on that day; 2. ref. to penitents readmitted that day as "green"; 3. eating green herbs that day to guard against disease; 4. use of green paraments in Ger. on that day, in contrast to other colors used on other days of that week. Because Rome used white paraments, the day was also called White Thu.

Grundtvig, Frederik Lange (May 1854–Mar. 21, 1903). Son of N. F. S. Grundtvig*; b. Den.; educ. Copenhagen as ornithologist; to Wis. 1881; influenced by T. Helveg* for ministry; ordained by The Dan. Ev. Luth. Ch. in Am. 1883; pastor Clinton, Iowa, 1883; led in organizing Dan Folk Soc. (Dansk Folkesamfund) 1887; returned to Den. 1900. Compiled *Sangbog for det danske Folk i Amerika;* other works include ornithological papers.

Grundtvig, Nikolai Frederik Severin (1783–1872). B. Udby, Zealand, Den.; Luth. bp.; poet; educator; 1810 trial sermon attacked rationalism and espoused Luth. orthodoxy; asst. to his father; pastor Praestö 1821, Vartov Hosp. Ch., Copenhagen, 1839; bp. 1861 but without see. Held that the Word *heard* in the ch. through the ages, esp. the Apostles' Creed, rather than *written* Scripture, was the "Living Word" given to the ch. by Christ Himself. By this Word and in the sacraments God meets the individual in the ch. Grundtvig's system of govt. stressed autonomy of the local cong.; est. Folk High School. Hymns tr. into Eng. include "Built on the Rock the Church Doth Stand" and "God's Word Is Our Great Heritage"; other works include *Decline of the Heroic Life in the North; Rhyme of Roskilde; Songs for the Danish Church.* His son Svend Hersleb (1824–83) was noted philologist and folklorist. See also *Denmark, Lutheranism in,* 8.

H. Koch, *Grundtvig* [Danish], (Copenhagen, 1943); P. G. Lindhardt, *Grundtvig: An Introduction* (London, 1951); E. D. Nielsen, *N. F. S. Grundtvig: An American Study* (Rock Island, Ill., 1955); J. Knudsen, *Danish Rebel: A Study of N. F. S. Grundtvig* (Philadelphia, 1955).

Grundtvigianism. See *Denmark, Lutheranism in,* 8; *Grundtvig, Nikolai Frederik Severin.*

Grüneisen, Carl (1802–78). B. Stuttgart, Ger.; educ. Stuttgart and Tübingen; influenced by F. D. E. Schleiermacher*; court chaplain, court preacher, prelate Stuttgart; active in reforms of liturgy, hymnal, and ch. const.: ed. *Christliches Kunstblatt für Kirche, Schule und Haus;* other works include *Niklaus Manuel, Leben und Werke eines Malers und Dichters, Kriegers, Staatsmanns und Reformators im 16. Jahrhundert.*

Grünewald, Matthias (Mathis [Mathes; Mathias; Matthäus] Gothar[d]t Nithar[d]t [Neithardt]; opinions on yr. of birth range from 1455 to 1480; d. 1528). B. probably Würzburg, Ger.; painter. Works include Isenheim altarpiece; *Mocking of Christ;* various Crucifixions.

Grunnet, Niels Pedersen (Feb. 19, 1827–Jan. 13, 1897). B. North Bjert, near Kolding, Den.; joined the Staerke jyder (Strong Jutlanders) movement formed ca. 1800 in opposition to rationalism; taught school at Hedensted and Egtved; soldier 1848; studied theol. at the school of the Basel* Miss. Soc. 1851–54; dismissed because of his refusal to embrace a compromising confessional position; plans to become a miss. did not materialize; travels in Den. 1855 led him to conclude that basic Christian doctrine was neglected in the est. ch.; organized the Ev. Luth. Free Ch. of Denmark* Nov. 4, 1855. Ed. *En Röst i Örken* 1856–79, *Evangelisk-luthersk Maanedsskrift* 1879–95; *Sandhed til Gudfrytighed* (E. Pontoppidan's* explanation of the SC); other works include *Psalmebog for Den evang.-luth. Frikirke i Danmark; Hvad laerer den evang.-luth. Frikirke.*

Grynäus (Grynaeus; Gryner). 1. *Simon* (1493–1541). B. Ve(h)ringen, Sigmaringen, Ger.; prof. Gk. 1524, Lat. 1526 Heidelberg; prof. Gk. Basel 1529, later also NT; helped reform Württemberg and the U. of Tübingen (see also *Blarer, Ambrosius; Schnepf[f], Erhard);* helped draw up the First Helvetic Confession 1536 (see *Reformed Confessions,* A 6); took part in Wittenberg* Concord discussions and Colloquy of Worms.* 2. *Thomas* (1512–64). Nephew of 1; teacher Bern; secretly espoused Luth. cause. 3. *Johann Jakob* (1540–1617). Son of 2; originally adherent of S. Sulzer* and J. Andreä,* he repudiated the FC and the Luth. doctrine of the Lord's Supper; with son-in-law A. Polanus* von Polansdorf gave Basel Ref. character.

Gryphius, Andreas (Greif; 1616–64). B. Glogau, Silesia; educ. Leiden; private tutor; settled in Fraustadt; syndic Glogau 1650; poet; playwright. Hymns include "Erhalt uns deine Lehre" and "Es ist vollbracht!"

Guadalupe, Shrine of. See Mexico, D.

Gualther, Rudolf (Gwalther; Walter; Walther; 1519–86). Received as orphan into family of J. H. Bullinger*; married daughter of H. Zwingli*; participated in Regensburg Conference 1541. Ed. Zwingli's works; other works include religious poetry, including Bible passages in verse form.

Guam (Guahan). Organized unincorporated US territory. Southernmost is. of Mariana* Is. *Area:* ca. 212 sq. mi.; *pop.* (1973 est.): ca. 87,000 (natives basically of Indonesian stock). Probably discovered 1521 by Ferdinand Magellan (ca. 1480–1521; Port. navigator sailing for the Spanish), who is said to have named it Ladrones ("thieves," perhaps in reference to behavior of natives); formally claimed by Sp. 1565; ceded to US 1898 at end of Sp.-Am. War, occupied 1899; occupied by Jap. 1941; retaken by US 1944. Official language: English. RC (now ca. 95%) since 1668; others have included Assemblies of God, Prot. Episc. Ch., Seventh-day Adv., S. Bap. Convention. The LCA began work in the early 1970s.

Guaranty Theory. See *Atonement, Theories of,* 6.

Guardian Angels. Belief in guardian angels is found in some form in Jewish and other cultures. It is stated in the NT (Mt 18:10; Acts 12:15) and referred to in patristic literature (e. g., Hermas, *Shepherd:* Mandate VI ii 1–3).

Guatemala. See *Central America,* A, D 3, E.

Guenther. See *Günther.*

Guericke, Heinrich Ernst Ferdinand (1803–78). B. Wettin, Ger.; Luth. theol.; educ. Halle; prof. Halle 1829; deposed from professorship 1834 because of his opposition to the Prussian* Union; served scattered Luths. until forbidden; reinstated ca. 1840 as prof.; in 1840, with A. G. Rudelbach,* he founded the *Zeitschrift für die gesammte lutherische Theologie und Kirche;* other works include *Neutestamentliche Isagogik; Handbuch der Kirchengeschichte.*

Guérinets. See *Illuminati.*

Guetzlaff. See *Gützlaff.*

Gueux de mer (Fr. "beggars of the sea"). Malcontents and desperadoes of Eur. who took to the sea in the late 1560s; opposed Sp. tyranny and RCm in the Neth. Called "beggars" because they were ready to become beggars for their cause. See also *Gorkum Martyrs.*

Guidetti, Giovanni Domenico (1530–92). B. Bologne, It.; pupil of G. P. da Palestrina*; chorister in papal choir; worked with teacher on rev. ed. of Gradual and Antiphonary; pub. Passion* based on harmony of gospels.

Guido de Pietro. See *Angelico, Fra.*

Guido d'Arezzo (Guido Aretino; Fra Guittone; Guy of Arezzo; ca. 990–ca. 1050). B. Arezzo, It. (or near Paris, Fr.); called the father of modern music; credited with introd. 4-line staff, F clef; predecessors used 2 lines; popularized standard set of syllables to designate individual notes; the syllables were the 1st in 6 lines of an ancient Sapphic hymn addressed to John the Baptist; thus originated the sol-fa system.

Guild, Women's. See *Woman in Christian Society.*

Guild of Saint Matthew. Founded in Eng. 1877 by Stewart Duckworth Headlam (1847–1924; Angl. priest); its 1st declared object: "to get rid, by every possible means, of the existing prejudices, especially on the part of Secularists, against the Church, her sacraments and doctrines, and to endeavor to 'justify God to the people.'" The last phrase is C. Kingsley's.* Called for more equitable distribution of wealth by progressive taxation and for eventual abolition of private ownership of land. See also *Christian Socialism; Secularism.*

Guillaume d'Auvergne. See *William of Auvergne.*

Guillaume de Champeaux. See *William of Champeaux.*

Guillaume de Paris. See *William of Auvergne.*

Guilmant, Félix Alexandre (1837–1911). B. Boulogne-sur-Mer, Fr.; organist, composer, teacher. Works include 2 symphonies for organ and orchestra; 8 sonatas; liturgical music. See also *Offertory.*

Guinness, Henry Grattan (1835–1910). B. Montpelier House, near Kingstown, Ireland; traveled in Mex. and West Indies at age 17; converted 1853; educ. New Coll., St. John's Wood, London; ordained as evangelist; preached in Eng., Fr., Am., Near East; founded East* London Institute for Home and For. Missions in the 1870s; dir. Livingstone* Inland Miss. 1880; united the latter with East London Institute for Home and For. Missions to form The Regions* Beyond Missionary Union 1899/1900.

Guiscard, Robert (ca. 1015–85). "The Resourceful." Norman adventurer and conqueror in It.; became vassal of the pope and duke of Calabria and Apulia 1059; excommunicated 1074 for attacking a papal fief; reinvested 1080; captured Rome 1084 and delivered Gregory VII (see *Popes,* 7) from Henry* IV of Ger.

Guise, Dukes of. See *France,* 9, 10.

Guizot, François Pierre Guillaume (1787–1874). B. Nîmes, Fr.; prof. hist. Sorbonne, Paris; Fr. premier 1840–48; supported orthodoxy in Fr. Ref. Ch. Works include *Histoire générale de la civilisation en Europe; Histoire de la civilisation en France; Méditations sur la religion chrétienne.*

Gullixson, Thaddeus Frank (Sept. 4, 1882–Apr. 2, 1969). B. Bode, Iowa; educ. Luther Theol. Sem., St. Paul, Minn., and Johns Hopkins U.; pastor Pierre, S. Dak., and Minot, N. Dak.; pres. Luther Theol. Sem. 1930–54; pres. American* Luth. Conf. 1944–55. Works include *Down into the Arena; In the Face of the West Wind; The Valley Waits; Christ for a World Like This; Christus Emptor.*

Gummerus, Jaakko (1870–1933). B. Sääminki, Fin.; Luth. theol.; prof. ch. hist. Helsinki 1900; bp. 1920; influenced by A. Hauck* and F. Loofs*; active in ecumenical movement and soc. work.

Gumpel(t)zhaimer, Adam (1559–1625). B. Bavaria, Ger.; Luth. composer; active as cantor in Augsburg ca. 40 yrs. Wrote *Compendium musicae;* compositions include *Neue teutsche geistliche Lieder.*

Gundert, Hermann (Feb. 4, 1814–Apr. 25, 1893). B. Stuttgart, Ger.; to India 1835; assoc. 1836 with K. T. E. Rhenius*; on Rhenius' death he entered the work of the Basel miss. in Malabar 1838; returned to Ger. because of illness 1859. Works include Malayalam dictionary; tr. of most of the Bible into Malayalam.

Gundeson, J. G. See *Canada,* A 22.

Gundisalvi, Dominic. See *Dominic Gundisalvi.*

Gunkel, Johann Friedrich Hermann (1862–1932). B. Springe, Ger.; Prot. theol.; prof. OT Giessen 1907, Halle 1920; early exponent of form criticism (see *Isagogics,* 3); adherent of Religionsgeschichtliche* Schule; his emphasis on *Sitz* im Leben* (origin in life situation) was at times complementary to, at times in opposition to, the works of literary critics. Works include commentaries on Gn and Ps. See also *Higher Criticism,* 16.

Gunnerus, Johan(nes) Ernst (1718–73). B. Christiania (Oslo), Norw.; Luth. bp. Trondheim 1758; botanist; cultural leader; espoused supranaturalism.*

Gunning, Peter (1614–84). B. Hoo, Kent, Eng.; educ. Canterbury and Cambridge; Angl.; prof. Cambridge; bp. Chichester 1669, Ely 1674; opposed both Puritans and RCs; had leading role at Savoy* Conf.

Gunpowder Plot. Conspiracy by RCs to destroy the Prot. govt. of Eng. by blowing up the Houses of Parliament Nov. 5, 1605, opening day of the session, when the king, Lords, and Commons would be present. The plot was discovered; ringleaders executed, including Guy Fawkes (1570–1606; b. Yorkshire, Eng.; Prot. turned RC), most famous mem. of the conspiracy.

Günther, Martin (Dec. 4, 1831–May 22, 1893). B. Dresden, Ger.; to Am. 1839 in the Saxon Immigration (see *Lutheran Church — Missouri Synod, The,* II); educ. Conc. Coll. and Sem., Altenburg and St. Louis, Mo.; pastor 1853 Grafton and Cedarburg, Wis., 1857 Mequon, Wis., 1860 Saginaw, Mich., 1872 Chicago, Ill.; prof. Conc. Sem., St. Louis, 1873–93. Ed. *Der Lutheraner; Magazin für Ev.-Luth. Homiletik;* other works include *Populäre Symbolik; Dr. C. F. W. Walther.* JA

L. E. Fuerbringer, *80 Eventful Years* (St. Louis, 1944); A. G[raebner], "Professor Martin Günther," *Der Lutheraner,* XLIX (June 6, 1893), 89; G. St[oeckhardt], "Prof. M. Günther," *L. u. W.,* XXXIX (May 1893), 149–150; J. W. Albers, *Martin Guenther: Life and Work* (STM Thesis, Conc. Sem., St. Louis, 1964).

Gurney, Mrs. Gerald. See *Blomfield, Dorothy Frances.*

Gurney, Joseph John (1788–1847). B. Earlham Hall, near Norwich, Eng.; brother of E. Fry*; Quaker; well educ.; wealthy; minister 1818; advocated prison reform, end of capital punishment, abolition of slavery; visited US, Can., and W. Indies 1837–40; followers called Gurneyites. See also *Friends, Society of.*

Gurneyites. See *Gurney, Joseph John.*

Gury, Jean Pierre (1801–66). B. Mailleroncourt, Haute-Saône, Fr.; Jesuit; prof. moral theol. Roman Coll Works include *Compendium theologiae moralis; Casus conscientiae in praecipuas quaestiones theologiae moralis.*

Gustav-Adolf Society. C. G. L. Grossmann* issued a call 1832 for the est. of an institution to aid needy Prots. in and outside Ger., esp. in RC countries. An assoc. was formed by committees in Leipzig and Dresden; received royal confirmation 1834. K. Zimmermann* of Darmstadt created a similar organization 1841. The 2 movements joined 1842 to form the *Evangelischer Verein der Gustav-Adolf-Stiftung.* Enlarged by receiving Prussian miss. socs. 1844. Dist. socs. were organized in Bav., Austria, Hung., Switz., Fr., Russ., Swed., Romania, It., Holland, Belg. Name changed 1946 to *Gustav-Adolf-Werk der Evangelischen Kirche in Deutschland.* Since 1948 the work in the *Bundesrepublik Deutschland* and the *Deutsche Demokratische Republik* is carried on separately. Publications include *Die Evangelische Diaspora; Gustav-Adolf-Kalender; Gustav-Adolf-Kinderkalender; Gustav-Adolf-Blatt.*

Gustavus I (Gustavus Vasa; Gustavus Erikson; 1496–1560). King of Swed. 1523–60; perhaps gained first favorable impressions of Lutheranism as exile in Lübeck 1519; freed Swed. from Den. by defeating Christian* II; favored Lutheranism; secularized RC wealth; corresponded with M. Luther*; made O. Petri* preacher at Stockholm and L. Petri* teacher at Uppsala; had Bible tr. into Swed. The Diet of Västeraas 1527 est. preaching and teaching of the Word of God; the Syn. of Örebro 1529 adopted Reformation principles. Gustavus I sent the 1st Luth. missionaries to the Lapps 1559. See also *Lapland.*

Gustavus II (Gustavus Adolphus; 1594–1632). "Lion of the North; Snow King." King of Swed. 1611–32; b. Stockholm; grandson of Gustavus* I; father of Christina.* Championed Prot. cause in Ger. in Thirty* Years' War. Landed in Pomerania 1630; conquered much of Ger.; killed in the Battle of Lützen, Nov. 16, 1632.

Gustavus Adolphus College, St. Peter, Minn. See *Lutheran Church in America,* V; *Ministry, Education of,* VIII B 14; *Norelius, Eric.*

Gutenberg, Johann(es) (Father's name Gensfleisch or Ganzfleisch; Gutenberg was probably his mother's maiden name or the name of her birthplace; 1394/99 –ca. 1468). B. probably Mainz, Ger.; printer; invented or perfected modern art of printing; believed by some to have printed the 1282-page Lat. Mazarin Bible (found ca. 1760 in the library of J. Mazarin*).

Guthe, Hermann. See *Geography, Christian,* 5.

Guthrie, Thomas (1803–73). B. Brechin, Forfar (Angus), Scot.; Presb. clergyman; joined Free Ch. 1843; philanthropist; soc. reformer; est. "Ragged Schools." Ed. Sunday Magazine; other works include *The Gospel in Ezekiel.*

Gutwasser, John Ernst (Goetwater, etc.; at least 16 different spellings of the name). Dutch; 1st pastor of the oldest Luth. ch. in Am.; called Apr. 3, 1657, by the Luth. Consistory, Amsterdam; ordained Apr. 10; sent to New Amsterdam (later NYC); Ref. pastors protested his presence and work; arrested several times; sent back to Holland June 19, 1659.

Gützlaff, Karl Friedrich August (July 8, 1803–Aug. 9, 1851). "Apostle of China; Apostle of Chinese." B. Pyritz, Prussian Pomerania; educ. *Pädagogium* est. by A. H. Francke* at Halle and at the miss. institute of J. Jänicke* at Berlin; to Eng. and gathered material for hist. of ev. missions (*Geschiedenis der uitbreiding van Christus Koningryk of Aarde, sedert de dagen der Kerkhervorming tot den tegenwoordigen tyd; inzonderheid met betrekking tot de Zendelingen en Zendelings-Genootschappen,* pub. Rotterdam 1828); met R. Morrison* in Eng.; sailed for Batavia 1826 under auspices of Netherlands* Miss. Soc.; arrived 1827; to Singapore Feb. 1828; severed connections with Neth. Miss. Soc. 1828; to Bangkok, Siam (now Thailand); helped tr. Bible into native languages; to Macao, China, 1831; made 3 miss. voyages along coast of China, Siam, Korea (see also *Korea,* 5), and Ryukyu Is.; interpreter and secy. to Brit. ambassador; supt. of trade; continued miss. work to end of life; d. Victoria, Hong Kong.

Guyana. See *South America,* 12.

Guyau, Marie Jean (1854–88). B. Laval, Fr.; poet; philos.; he opposed evolutionary theory of H. Spencer*; tried to build a religious system by harmonizing individual and soc. ideals.

Guyon (Jeanne Marie, nee Bouvier; Madame Guyon; 1648–1717). B. Montargis, Fr.; quietist (see *Quietism*); influenced F. Fénelon*; imprisoned; banished from Paris to Blois. Works include *Les Torrens spirituels; Le Cantique de cantiques.*

Gwalther. See *Gualther.*

H

Haakanson, Magnus Fredrik (Frederick; Hokanson; Sept. 7 [some say 11], 1811–Jan. 2, 1893). B. Ronneby, Blekinge, Swed.; shoemaker; tried unsuccessfully to become a miss.; to Am. 1847; est. a ch. at New Swed. (W of Burlington), Iowa, 1848, and served as pastor; ordained by Ev. Luth. Syn. of N Illinois* 1853. His cong. disturbed by Gustaf Unonius (Episc.), Jonas Hedstrom (Meth.), Gustaf Palmquist, and F. O. Nilssen (Bap.). Espoused Bap. views for short time and was rebaptized 1854. Resigned at New Swed. 1856; pastor Bergholm (later Munterville), Iowa, 1856–59, 1867–90, Swede Point (later Madrid), Iowa (serving also Swede Bend [later Stratford]), 1859–67. See also *Augustana Evangelical Lutheran Church,* 2.

Haarbeck, Theodor (1846–1923). B. Neukirchen, near Mörs, Rhineland, Ger.; became inspector Pilgermission St. Chrischona* 1883, dir. Johanneum* 1890; active in fellowship movement.

Haas, Hans (Dec. 3, 1868–Sept. 10, 1934). B. Donndorf, near Bayreuth, Ger.; miss. in Jap.; prof. comparative religion Jena 1913, Leipzig 1915. Wrote on missions in Jap. and on oriental religions.

Haas, John Augustus William (Aug. 31, 1862–July 22, 1937). B. Philadelphia, Pa.; educ. U. of Pa., Luth. Sem. at Philadelphia, and Leipzig; ordained 1888; pastor NYC; pres. Muhlenberg Coll., Allentown, Pa., 1904. Leader in the General* Council of the Ev. Luth. Ch. in N. Am. Works include *Trends of Thought and Christian Truth; In the Light of Faith; Freedom and Christian Conduct; The Unity of Faith and Knowledge; The Truth of Faith; What Ought I to Believe: A Moral Test; The Christian Way of Liberty; Christianity and Its Contrasts; Annotations on the Gospel According to St. Mark; Bible Literature.* Coed. *The Lutheran Cyclopedia* (1899).

Haas, Nicolas (1665–1715). B. Wunsiedel, Bav.; Luth. pastor Saxony; voluminous ascetic writer. Works include *Der getreue Seelen-Hirte; Des in Gott andächtigen Priesters Gottgeheiligte Beth-Andachten;* annotated ed. of M. Luther's Ger. Bible.

Haase, Theodor Karl (1834–1909). B. Lemberg, Ger.; ev. theol.; pres. Ev. Gen. Syn. in Vienna; noted for expanding the ev. ch. in Silesia.

Haberkorn, Peter (1604–76). B. Butzbach, Ger.; educ. Marburg, Leipzig, and Strasbourg; prof. physics Marburg 1632; court preacher Darmstadt 1633; supt. 1643 and prof. 1650 Giessen; defended Luth. orthodoxy against RCs and Calvinists (e. g., G. Calixtus*).

Habermann, Johann(es) (Avenarius; 1516–90). B. Eger, Boh.; pastor; prof. Jena and Wittenberg; supt. Naumburg-Zeitz; Hebraist. Works include *Christliche gebet;* Heb. grammar and lexicon.

Habit. Distinctive external sign (e. g., tunic, hood) of religious state.

Habitual Grace. See *Gratia increata.*

Hackenschmidt, Karl (1839–1915). B. Strasbourg, Fr.; Luth. pastor Jägerthal 1870, Strasbourg 1882; influenced by A. Ritschl.*

Hackett, Horatio Balch (1808–75). B. Salisbury, Mass.; educ. Phillips Academy (Andover, Mass.), Amherst (Mass.) Coll., and Andover Theol. Sem.; instructor Mount Hope Coll., Baltimore, Md., 1834–35; became Bap. 1835; prof. Brown U., Providence, R. I., 1835–39, Newton (Mass.) Theol. Institution 1839–68, Rochester (N. Y.) Theol. Sem. 1870–75. Coed. Am. ed. *Smith's Bible Dictionary;* other works include *Exercises in Hebrew Grammar and Selections from the Greek Scriptures to be Translated into Hebrew;* commentary on Acts.

Hades. See *Greek Religion,* 2; *Hereafter,* C 4.

Hades Gospel. Term designating belief that heathen to whom the Gospel was not preached and those who heard the Gospel but did not accept it will have another opportunity to be saved after death. Main passages quoted for this view: 1 Ptr 3:18-20; 4:6; others: Gn 3:15; Eze 33:11; Mt 5:25-26; 11:20-24; 12:31-32; Jn 14:2; Ro 2:4; 1 Ti 2:4; 2 Ti 1:12; 2 Ptr 3:9; 1 Jn 3:8. Scripture teaches that judgment follows death without a 2d chance, Mt 7:13-14; 2 Co 6:2; Heb 9:27.

T. Engelder, "The Hades Gospel," *CTM,* XVI (May 1945), 293–300, "The Argument in Support of the Hades Gospel," *CTM,* XVI (June 1945), 374–396, "The Evil of the Hades Gospel," *CTM,* XVI (Sept. 1945), 591–615, and "The Hades Gospel and the Apocatastasis Gospel," *CTM,* XVII (Sept. 1946), 641–676.

Had(h)ramaut. See *Middle East,* L 3.

Hadorn, Wilhelm (1869–1929). B. Bern, Switz.; prof. NT and Swiss ch. hist. Bern 1912.

Hadrian. See *Adrian.*

Haeckel, Ernst Heinrich Philipp August (1834–1919). B. Potsdam, Ger.; zoologist; philos.; prof. Jena 1865. Popularized and expanded Darwinism (see *Darwin, Charles Robert*). Adopted view of "biogenetic law," which antedated him, that development of an individual is a recapitulation* of the hist. of the race. Acc. to his carbon-theory, organic life evolved from albuminoid compounds of carbon. He regarded the seat of the soul as located in "phronetal cells" ("thought-cells"). Denied existence of personal God and immortality; exerted great influence, esp. on freethinkers; championed monism*; coined words "ecology," "ontogeny," "protozoa," and "metazoa." Works include *Natürliche Schöpfungsgeschichte; Die Welträtsel; Der Monismus als Band zwischen Religion und Wissenschaft; Die Lebenswunder.* See also *Loofs, Friedrich.*

Haentzschel, Adolph Theodore Esaias (Häntzschel; Dec. 24, 1881–June 5, 1971). Son of C. E. Häntzschel*; b. Addison, Ill.; educ. Conc. Sem., St. Louis, Mo.; pastor Ohio. Prof. Conc. Coll., Conover, N. C., 1907–17; St. Paul's Coll., Concordia, Mo., 1917–20; U. of Wis., Madison, 1920–37; Valparaiso (Ind.) U. 1937–57. Works include *Learning to Know the Child; The Great Paradox; The Great Quest; How About Christianity?*

Haentzschel, Clemens Esaias. See *Häntzschel, Clemens Esaias.*

Haering, Theodor von (Häring; 1848–1928). B. Stuttgart, Ger.; educ. Tübingen and Berlin; lectured at The Tübingen Ev. theol. sem. 1873–76; pastor Calw 1876, Stuttgart 1881; prof. Zurich 1886, Göttingen 1889, Tübingen 1895; modified Ritschlianism (see *Ritschl, Albrecht*) in the direction of conservative theol.; ascribed strong ethical significance to life of Jesus.

Haering, Theodor Lorenz (1884–1964). B. Stuttgart, Ger.; son of T. v. Haering*; educ. Halle, Tübingen,

Berlin, Bonn; prof. philos. Tübingen. Works include *Hegel: Sein Wollen und sein Werk; Über Individualität in Natur- und Geisteswelt; Die Struktur der Weltgeschichte; Schwabenspiegel; Der Mond braust durch das Neckartal.*

Haerter, Franz Heinrich (1797–1874). B. Strasbourg; educ. Strasbourg; pastor Ittenheim 1823, Strasbourg 1829; founded deaconess house in Strasbourg 1842.

Haetzer. See *Hetzer.*

Haevernick. See *Hävernick.*

Hafenreffer, Matthias (1561–1619). B. Lorch, Ger.; educ. Tübingen; pastor Ehningen 1588; court preacher Stuttgart 1590; prof. theol. Tübingen 1592; also taught mathematics and natural science; teacher and friend of J. Kepler.* Works include *Loci theologici; Templum Ezechielis.*

Haffner, Isaac (1751–1831). B. Strasbourg; educ. Strasbourg, Göttingen, Leipzig, Paris; pastor Strasbourg; prof. Prot. academy, Strasbourg, 1803; 1st dean of Prot. faculty of U. of Strasbourg; theol. mediated bet. rationalism* and strict Lutheranism.

Hafnica, Confessio (Hafniensis). See *Denmark, Lutheranism in,* 2.

Hagen, Carl Friedrich Wilhelm (Sept. 30, 1859–Nov. 21, 1938). B. Sterley, Lauenburg, Ger.; to Am. 1883; educ. Conc. Sem., St. Louis, Mo.; pastor Ludington, Riverton, and Detroit, Mich.; mem. Gen. Bd. of Control and Bd. of Dir., Mo. Syn.; proponent of confessional Lutheranism.

Hagen, Peter (Hagius; 1569–1620). B. Henneberg, near Heiligenbeil, E. Prussia; educ. Königsberg, Helmstedt, Wittenberg; rector Lyck, Prussia, and at the cathedral school, Königsberg; hymnist. Hymns include "Freu' dich, du werte Christenheit."

Hagenau Colloquy (Conference). Summoned by Charles* V; met 1540; purpose: to reach understanding bet. RCs and evangelicals. RC participants included Ferdinand I (1503–64; younger brother of Charles V; king of Ger. 1531–64; Holy Roman Emp. 1556–64), G. Morone,* Johannes Faber,* J. Cochlaeus,* J. Eck*; evangelicals present included J. Brenz,* M. Bucer,* J. Calvin,* W. Capito,* C. Cruciger,* F. Myconius,* A. Osiander* The Elder, U. Rhegius.* Differences were emphasized. Initial goals were not reached, but it was resolved to try again (see *Worms, Colloquy of*).

Hagenbach, Karl Rudolf (1801–74). Ger. ch. hist. and theol.; b. Basel, Switz.; educ. Basel; prof. Basel; exponent of mediating* theol.; emphasized imitation of Christ in life; influenced by G. C. F. Lücke,* F. D. E. Schleiermacher,* and J. A. W. Neander.* Works include *Encyklopädie und Methodologie der theologischen Wissenschaften; Lehrbuch der Dogmengeschichte; Grundlinien der Liturgik und Homiletik;* contributed to J. J. Herzog's* *Realencyklopädie.*

Hägerström, Axel Anders Theodor (1868–1939). Swed. philos.; prof. Uppsala. His analysis of metaphysics and dogmatics and his opposition to idealism influenced A. T. S. Nygren (b. Göteborg, Swed., 1890; see also *Lund, Theology of; Sweden, Lutheran Church in,* 6). Works include *Kants Ethik im Verhältnis zu seinen erkenntnistheoretischen Grundgedanken; Religionsfilosofi.*

Haggada(h). See *Talmud.*

Hagia Sofia. See *Church Architecture,* 6.

Hagiographa (Gk. "sacred writings"). Equivalent to Heb. *kethubim* ("writings"); denotes OT books other than "Law" and "Prophets"; includes Ps, Pr, Jb, Ru, Lm, SS, Ec, Est, Dn, 1 and 2 Ch, Ez, Neh.

Hahn, August (1792–1863). B. Grossosterhausen, near Querfurt, Ger.; educ. Leipzig and Wittenberg; prof., pastor, and supt. Königsberg; prof. Leipzig; opposed rationalism; prof. Breslau; gen. supt. Silesia; gained Silesian ch. for stricter Lutheranism; tried unsuccessfully to preserve the use of the Luth. agenda* for strict Luths. and keep them in the Prussian* Union. Works include *Über die Lage des Christentums in unserer Zeit; Lehrbuch des christlichen Glaubens; Bibliothek der Symbole und Glaubensregeln der apostolisch-katholischen* [*alten*] *Kirche.*

Hahn, Elieser Traugott (1848–1939). Son of K. H. Hahn* (1818–95); b. Komachas, South-West Afr.; grew up at Gütersloh, Ger.; Ger. Luth. theol.; pastor Estonia; forced to leave 1918; evangelist esp. in NW Ger.

Hahn, Gotthilf Traugott (1875–1919). Son of E. T. Hahn*; b. Rauge, Livonia; Ger. Luth. theol.; prof. Dorpat (Tartu) 1908; arrested and shot by Bolsheviks.

Hahn, Johann Michael (1758–1819). Ger. biblicistic mystic; theosophist; theol. centers in Christology; spiritual father of Hahn Soc. (also called Michelians) founded 1876.

Hahn, Karl Hugo (Oct. 18, 1818–Nov. 24, 1895). B. Riga, Latvia; Luth.; sent by Rhenish* Miss. Soc. to Afr. 1841; est. Herero* missions; severed connections with Rhenish Miss. Soc. 1873; pastor Cape Town 1874–84. Works include Herero grammar. See also *Africa,* B 8.

Hahn, Karl Hugo (1886–1957). Son of E. T. Hahn*; b. Reval (Tallin), Estonia; pastor Dorpat, Worbis, and Leipzig; pastor and supt. Dresden; banished from Saxony by Nazis 1938 (see *Germany,* C 4; *Socialism,* 3); chm. Confessing* Ch. of Saxony; pastor near Stuttgart; bp. Luth. Ch. of Saxony 1947–53.

Hahn, Philipp Matthäus (1739–90). B. Scharnhausen, near Esslingen, Ger.; theosophist; pietist; regarded the kingdom of Jesus as fundamental idea from which all else is derived; Godhead is conscious only in Christ. Emphasized humanity of Christ and divine spark in man. Works include *Die Lehre Jesu und seiner Gesandten.*

Hahn Society. See *Hahn, Johann Michael.*

Hail Mary. See *Ave Maria.*

Haimo. Exegetical writings, chiefly catena,* widely circulated 9th–12th c., were ascribed to a Haimo. They are regarded by some as in part collections by monk Haimo of Auxerre (d. ca. 855); some have been ascribed by some to Haimo (Haymo; Heimo; Aimo; Aymo; Hemmo) of Halberstadt (probably ca. 778–853; bp. Halberstadt 840–853); others have been ascribed by some to Remigius* of Auxerre.

Haimrham(m). See *Emmeram.*

Haiti. See *Caribbean Islands,* A, C, E 3; *Hispaniola.*

Hajj. See *Islam,* 3.

Halakah. See *Talmud.*

Haldane, James Alexander and Robert. See *Disciples of Christ,* 1.

Hale, Edward Everett (1822–1909). B. Boston, Mass.; pastor Ch. of the Unity, Worcester, Mass., 1846, South Congregational Ch., Boston, 1856; chaplain US Senate 1903–09. Works include poetry, short stories, essays, magazine articles, and more than 60 books, including *The Man Without a Country.*

Hales, John (1584–1656). B. Bath, Eng.; educ. Oxford; chaplain to W. Laud*; canon Windsor; supported latitudinarians.* Works include *A Tract Concerning Schisme and Schismaticks; Golden Remains.*

ha-Levi, Judah (Halevi). See *Judah ha-Levi.*

Halevy, Joseph (1827–1917). B. Adrianople, Turkey; of Jewish parentage; naturalized Frenchman; Orientalist; explorer; prof. Paris; made researches in Abyssinia and Arabia; held that Sumerians were the invention of the Babylonian priesthood. Works include *Documents religieux de l'Assyrie et de la Babylonie; Recherchez bibliques; Le Sumérisme et l'histoire babylonienne.*

Half-Way Covenant. Originally New Eng. Congregationalists (see *United Church of Christ, The,* I A) held that the ch. is a fellowship of believers who professed conversion, and that only such had the right to privileges of the ch., including baptism of children. The Half-Way Covenant was an expedient initiated early in the 2d half of the 17th c. allowing 2d-gen. parents who did not profess conversion to have their children baptized, provided they themselves were baptized and of correct life, acknowledged the justice of God's claims upon them, and promised to submit to the discipline of the ch. S. Stoddard* later advocated admitting baptized people to Communion without examination and evidence of conversion. The Half-Way Covenant was opposed by J. Edwards.*

Halfdánarson, Helgi (1826–94). B. N Iceland; Luth.; prof. and pres. of the theol. sem. at Reykjavík; hymnist. Works include a catechism; hist. and ethical studies; treatise on homiletics.

Halifax, Charles Lindley Wood (1839–1934). B. London, Eng.; 2d Viscount Halifax; Angl. High Churchman; pres. Eng. Ch. Union (soc. formed 1859 as Ch. of Eng. Protection Soc. [renamed 1860] to promote and defend High Ch. principles and practices); advocated reunion with the RC Ch.

Halitgar. See *Denmark.*

Hall, Gordon (Apr. 8, 1784–Mar. 20, 1826). B. near Tolland, Mass.; educ. Williams Coll., Williamstown, Mass., and Andover (Mass.) Theol. Sem.; ABCFM miss. to India 1812; 13 yrs. in Bombay. Works include *The Conversion of the World, or the Claims of Six Hundred Millions;* tr. of NT into Marathi. See also *Haystack Group.*

Hall, Granville Stanley (1846–1924). B. Ashfield, Mass.; psychol., philos., and educ.; taught at Antioch Coll. (Yellow Springs, Ohio), Harvard U., Johns Hopkins U., Clark U.; 1st pres. Clark U.; 1st pres. Am. Psychol. Assoc.; founded and ed. *American Journal of Psychology.* Works include *Adolescence; Jesus, the Christ, in the Light of Psychology; Morale: The Supreme Standard of Life and Conduct; Aspects of Child Life and Education.* See also *Psychology,* G 4.

Hall, Joseph (1574–1656). B. near Ashby de la Zouch, Leicestershire, Eng.; Angl. bp. Exeter and Norwich; helped James* I introd. Anglicanism in Scot.; advocated moderation at Syn. of Dordrecht* 1618. Works include *Meditations and Vowes, Divine and Morall.*

Hall, Robert (1764–1831). B. Arnesby, near Leicester, Eng.; Bap. preacher Bristol, Cambridge, Leicester; outstanding orator. Works include *An Apology for the Freedom of the Press, and for General Liberty; Modern Infidelity Considered with Respect to Its Influence on Society.*

Hall, Thomas (1610–65). B. Worcester, Eng.; educ. Oxford; at first Angl.; became Presb. under Puritan influence; pastor King's Norton, Warwick, Eng. Works include *The Pulpit Guarded with XVII Arguments; The Beauty of Holiness; The Font Guarded with XX Arguments.*

Hall, William Nelthorpe (Apr. 19, 1829–May 21, 1878). B. Sheffield, Yorkshire, Eng.; miss. of Methodist* New Connection at Soochow (Wuhsien), then at Tientsin, China; founded training coll. at Tientsin.

Halle Reports. See *Hallesche Nachrichten.*

Halle Resolutions. Resolutions adopted 1937 at Halle, Ger., by the Confessing* Ch.; concerns included the principle of confessing, confessions, ordination, and the Lord's Supper. On the Lord's Supper, it was emphasized that Jesus Christ Himself is the gracious gift in the sacrament; altar fellowship bet. Luths., Ref., and Evangelicals is not justified by the situation created by the Prussian* Union; separate altars for Luths., Ref., and Evangelicals are not justified in the light of 16th-c. controversies; altar fellowship has its foundation not in our understanding of the Lord's Supper, but in the grace of Him who is the Lord of it.

Hallel (Heb. "praise"). Psalms or hymns of praise were used in the OT (Ez 3:11; 2 Ch 7:6). In the course of time the name Hallel came to denote various groups of Psalms, e. g., 104–107, 111–117 (or 118), 135–136, 146–150; the word Hallelujah* occurs at the beginning and/or end of most of these. The name Great Hallel has been attached to Ps 113–118, or 119–136, or 136 alone. Ps 113–118 are also called Egyptian Hallel because of special assoc. with Passover. Hallel Psalms are used in connection with the celebration of Passover, Hanukkah, Pentecost (see *Church Year,* 10), and Tabernacles; see also *Judaism,* 4.

Hallelujah (alleluia; alleluiah; alleluja; Heb. "praise ye the Lord"). Occurs at the beginning of Ps 106, 111–113, 117, 135, 146–150, at the end of Ps 104–106, 113, 115–17, 135, 146–150, and in Rv 19:1, 3, 4, 6. In Christian liturgies it is often used after invitatories, antiphons, Ps., versicles, responsories, Graduals, and Sentences for the Seasons; may be omitted in penitential* seasons. See also *Jahweh; Response; Schism,* 6.

Haller, Albrecht von (1708–77). B. Bern, Switz.; physician in Bern 1729–36; prof. Göttingen 1737–53; regarded by some as the most learned man of the 18th c. in Ger. next to G. W. v. Leibniz*; tried to find synthesis of faith and knowledge.

Haller, Berchtold (1492–1536). B. Aldigen, near Rottweil, Ger.; reformer of Bern; studied theol. at Cologne; took part in conferences at Baden 1526, Bern 1528; helped compose a Prot. liturgy and the 1528 reformation edict. See also *Reformed Confessions,* A 2; *Switzerland,* 2.

Haller, Johannes (1523–75). B. Amsoldingen, Bern, Switz.; Ref. theol.; educ. Zurich, Tübingen, Marburg, and the Neth.; visited M. Luther and P. Melanchthon at Wittenberg; pastor Zurich, Augsburg, and Bern.

Hallesby, Ole Kristian (1879–1961). B. Aremark, Norw.; Luth. theol.; studied in Ger., esp. Erlangen; prof. systematic theol., free faculty, Oslo, 1909–51; leader of free faculty and conservative theologians; opposed Ger. occupation; arrested and placed in concentration camp 1943. Works include a dogmatics *(Den kristelige troslaere)* and ethics *(Den kristelige sedelaere);* works tr. into Eng. include *Infant Baptism and Adult Conversion; Temperament and the Christian Faith; Under His Wings; Religious or Christian; Prayer; Conscience; The Christian Life in the Light of the Cross.* See also *Dogmatics,* B 10.

Hallesche Nachrichten. Series of reports sent to Halle by early Luth. pastors in Am. (H. M. Mühlenberg,* P. Brunnholtz,* J. F. Handschuh,* et al.).

The Journals of Henry Melchior Muhlenberg, tr. T. G. Tappert and J. W. Doberstein, 3 vols. (Philadelphia, 1942, 1945, 1958).

Halyburton, Thomas (1674–1712). B. Dupplin, near Perth, Scot.; Ref. theol.; opposed deism.*

Hamann, Johann Georg (1730–88). "Magus in the North"; noted for his learning; devoted student of the Bible and M. Luther's* writings; brilliant defender of Christian faith in an age of rationalism; espoused a form of Christian existentialism; mem. Münster* Circle.

Hamartiology (from Gk. for "sin" and "account"). That part of doctrine which deals with sin.* See also *Ponerology.*

Hamelmann, Hermann (1525–95). B. Osnabrück, Ger.; as priest, first opposed M. Luther*; converted 1553; promoted Lutheranism at Bielefeld, Lemgo, Rostock, Antwerp, Gandersheim, and Oldenburg.

Hamestakan (Hamestagan). See *Zoroastrianism,* 6.

Hamilton, James (1819–96). B. Glendollar, Scot.; educ. Cambridge; held various charges, the last at

Bath and Wells; hymnist. Hymns include "Across the Sky the Shades of Night."

Hamilton, John (ca. 1511–71). Abp. St. Andrews and primate Scot. 1546; called syns. 1548, 1549, 1552, 1559 to reform clergy; opposed Protestantism; advisor of Mary, Queen of Scots (Mary Stuart; 1542–87).

Hamilton, Patrick (ca. 1504–28). Scot. Prot. martyr; educ. Paris and Louvain; began openly to promote Luth. doctrine in Scot. 1526; charged with heresy 1527, he fled to Ger., where he became acquainted with M. Luther* and P. Melanchthon*; matriculated at the U. of Marburg in spring 1527; returned to Scot. after 6 mo.; preached in various places; probably ordained; married; taught at St. Andrews U. 1528; executed for heresy by burning Feb. 29, 1528. Works include *Loci Communes* (also called *Patrick's Pleas* and *Patrick's Places*), an epigrammatic discussion of the doctrine of justification and the distinction bet. Law and Gospel; it influenced Eng. and Scot. theol.

P. Lorimer, *Precursors of Knox: or, Memoirs of P. Hamilton . . . A. Alane . . . and Sir D. Lindsay* (Edinburgh, 1857). NST

Hamilton, William (1788–1856). B. Glasgow, Scot.; philos.; prof. Edinburgh 1821; believed that the existence of a Supreme Being is at least a natural inference, but that this Being cannot be rationally known; influenced H. L. Mansel.*

Hamistagan. See *Zoroastrianism,* 6.

Hamma, Michael Wolf (Dec. 25, 1836–June 3, 1913). B. Richland Co., Ohio; educ. Wittenberg Coll. and sem. (see *Wittenberg University*); ministry included charges at Euphemia, Bucyrus, and Springfield, Ohio, Reading and Altoona, Pa., Baltimore, Md., Brooklyn, N. Y., and San Francisco, Cal.; pres. The General* Syn. of the Ev. Luth. Ch. in the USA 1897–99. See also *Hamma Divinity School.*

Hamma Divinity School. Began 1845 as the theol. dept. of Wittenberg Coll., Springfield, Ohio; name changed 1907 to Hamma Divinity School in recognition of bequests by M. W. Hamma*; name changed 1964 to Hamma School of Theol. See also *in the United States of America, The,* 8; *Lutheran Church in America,* V; *Ministry, Education of,* X F; *Wittenberg University.*

Hammerschmidt, Andreas (ca. 1611–75). B. Brüx (Most), Boh.; organist Weesenstein 1633–34, Freiberg 1634, Zittau 1639–75; one of the most distinguished composers of the 17th c. Works include *Dialogi oder Gespräche zwischen Gott und einer gläubigen Seele; Musikalische Andachten; Fest-, Buss- und Danklieder.*

Hammond, Henry (1605–60). B. Chertsey, Eng.; educ. Eton and Oxford; Angl. canon Christ Ch., Oxford; chaplain to Charles I (1600–49; king of Gt. Brit. and Ireland 1625–49). In the 1642–45 civil war he remained loyal to the king; subdean Christ Ch.; deprived of subdeanship by parliamentary visitors; imprisoned 1648. Works include *A Paraphrase and Annotations upon . . . the New Testament; Of the Reasonableness of the Christian Religion; A practical Catechisme; A Defence of the Church of England against the Objections of the Romanists; A View of the New Directory and a Vindication of the Ancient Liturgy of the Church of England.*

Hammond, William (1719–83). B. Battle, Sussex, Eng.; educ. Cambridge; joined Calvinistic Meths. 1743, Moravians 1745; hymnist. Hymns include "Lord, We Come Before Thee Now"; tr. of Lat. hymns.

Hammurabi, Code of. Legal code of Hammurabi, king of Babylon; promulgated perhaps ca. 1800 BC. See also *Law Codes.*

Hampton Court Conference. Meeting called by James* I and held Jan. 12–18, 1604, at Hampton Court Palace, near Hampton, Eng., to discuss differences bet. Puritans* and the High* Church. Puritan hope for reform was disappointed, but one important result of the conf. was the KJV (see *Bible Versions,* 10).

Handel, George Frederick (Georg Friedrich Händel; 1685–1759). B. Halle, Ger.; naturalized Brit. subject 1726; pupil of F. W. Zachow*; to Berlin ca. 1698; studied law at the U. of Halle and served as organist at the cathedral ch. 1702–03; devoted himself entirely to music 1703, when he went to Hamburg and became a musician in the opera house orchestra; traveled in It. 1706/07–10; kapellmeister Hanover 1710; visited Eng. 1710; settled in Eng. 1712, but traveled repeatedly and extensively in Eur.; kapellmeister to the duke of Chandos at Edgware, near London, ca. 1718–20. Works include 46 operas; 100 cantatas; 20 duets; 11 Chandos anthems; *Water Music, Forest Music, Fire Music;* 32 oratorios, of which *Messiah* (1742) is the best known. See also *Passion, The; Steffani, Agostino.* WEB

N. Flower, *George Frideric Handel: His Personality and His Times,* rev. ed. (London, 1947); O. E. Deutsch, *Handel: A Documentary Biography* (New York, 1955); W. Dean, *Handel's Dramatic Oratorios and Masques* (New York, 1959); P. H. Lang, *George Frideric Handel* (New York, 1966).

Handl, Jakob (Händl; Hähnel; Jacobus Gallus; 1550–91). Cistercian composer; b. Reifnitz, Carniola (Krain); kapellmeister to bp. of Olomouc (Olmütz), Moravia; cantor Prague. Works include *Opus musicum* (motets for the ch. yr.). See also *Passion, The.*

Handmann, Richard (Feb. 27, 1840–Dec. 7, 1912). B. Oschitz, near Schleiz, Ger.; educ. Leipzig and Erlangen; miss. to India 1862; returned to Ger. ca. 1887; mem. Mission Collegium, Leipzig. Ed. *Leipziger Missionsblatt;* wrote *Die Evangelisch-lutherische Tamulen-Mission in der Zeit ihrer Neubegründung.*

Hands, Imposition of. Ceremony used in OT to place sins on scapegoat (Lv 16:21-22); to convey blessings (Gn 48:14); at the installation of Joshua (Dt 34:9); in connection with sacrifices (Lv 1:4; 3:2, 8; 4:4, 24, 29). Used in NT in connection with healing (Mk 6:5); imparting blessing (Mk 10:13-16); blessing or ordaining ministers (Acts 13:1-3; 6:1-6; 1 Ti 4:14; 5:22; 2 Ti 1:6). Included in rites of baptism, confirmation, and ordination in E and W Chs.

Hands, John (Dec. 5, 1780–June 30, 1864). B. Roade, Northamptonshire, Eng.; LMS miss. to India 1809; tr. Bible into Kanarese; LMS agent in Dublin, Ireland, 1843.

Handschuh, John Frederick (1714–64). Educ. Halle, Ger.; to Am. 1748; Luth. pastor Lancaster, Germantown, and Philadelphia, Pa.; helped found Pa. Ministerium (see *United Lutheran Church, Synods of,* 22). See also *Liturgics.*

Hanneken, Philip Ludwig (1637–1706). B. Marburg, Ger.; educ. Giessen, Leipzig, Wittenberg, and Rostock; Luth. theol.; prof. Giessen; opposed Pietism*; defended Luth. Confessions.

Hannington, James (Sept. 3, 1847–Oct. 29, 1885). B. Hurstpierpoint, near Brighton, Eng.; educ. Oxford; CMS miss. to Cen. Afr. 1882; bp. 1884; murdered by natives of Uganda.

Hanover Free Church. See *Germany, Lutheran Free Churches in,* 11.

Hanover Evangelical Lutheran Free Church Mission. See *Mission of the Evangelical Lutheran Free Churches.*

Hansen, Heinrich (1861–1940). B. Klockries, N Friesland; Luth. theol.; pastor N Friesland and Schleswig-Holstein; advocated "ev. Catholicism"; issued 95 theses 1917 which criticized Protestantism; active in High Ch. movement.

Hanser, Carl Johann Otto (Sept. 7, 1832–Jan. 10,

1910). B. Schopflohe, Bav.; to Am. 1851; educ. Conc. Sem., St. Louis, Mo.; pastor Carondelet, Mo., 1860, Boston, Mass, 1863; dir. Conc. Coll., Fort Wayne, Ind., 1872–79; pastor Trin. Luth Ch., St. Louis, Mo., 1879, resigned 1906. Coed. *Missions-Taube* 1885–1900; other works include autobiography *Irrfahrten und Heimfahrten.*

Hanson, Minne. See *Evangelistic Associations,* 3.

Hanson, Östen (July 8, 1836–Aug. 4, 1898). B. Telemarken, Norw.; to Am. 1851; lay preacher; ordained 1861 by ELC; pastor Goodhue Co., Minn.; pres. Hauge* Syn. 1875–76, 1887–93; helped rev. const. of Hauge Syn. 1875; one of founders of Red Wing Sem. and soc. that organized Norw. Luth. Miss. in China.

Häntzschel, Clemens Esaias (Feb. 27, 1837–Oct. 21, 1890). Father of A. T. E. Haentzschel*; b. Meissen, Saxony; studied law in Leipzig; to Am.; served with the 74th Pa. Infantry Regiment in Civil War; parochial school teacher Sheboygan, Wis., and Fort Wayne, Ind.; prof. Ev. Luth. Teachers Sem., Addison, Ill., 1874–90.

Hanukkah (Hanukah). See *Judaism,* 4.

Harbaugh, Henry (1817–67). B. Washington Township, Franklin Co., Pa.; of Swiss descent; educ. Marshall Coll., Mercersburg, Pa.; Ger. Ref. pastor Lewisburg, Lancaster, and Lebanon, Pa.; prof. Mercersburg Sem.; defended "Mercersburg theology"; hymnist. Hymns include "Christ, by Heavenly Hosts Adored" and "Jesus, I Live to Thee"; ed. *Guardian* and *Mercersburg Review;* other works include *The Sainted Dead; The Heavenly Home; The True Glory of Woman; Christological Theology.*

Hard Shell Baptists. See *Baptist Churches,* 11.

Hardeland, August (Sept. 30, 1814–June 27, 1891. B. Hanover, Ger.; brother of J. Hardeland*; Rhenish* Miss. Soc. miss. to Borneo 1839; supt. Hermannsburg Miss.; in Afr. 1859–63; ret. to Ger. Works include tr. of Bible into Dayak, a language of Borneo.

Hardeland, Julius (Jan. 7, 1828–Oct. 11, 1903). B. Hanover, Ger.; brother of A. Hardeland*; educ. Göttingen; pastor Lauenburg 1854–60; dir. Leipzig* Ev. Luth. Miss. 1860–91; supt. Doberan, Mecklenburg, 1891–94.

Hardenberg, Albert (family name Rizaeus; ca. 1510–74). B. Hardenberg, Overijssel, Neth.; zealous advocate of the Reformation; active at Louvain, Aduard (monastery of the Brethren of the Common Life), Cologne, Einbeck, Bremen, Sengwarden, Emden; held un-Luth. view in a controversy at Bremen about the nature of the presence of Christ in the Lord's Supper.

Hardenberg, Friedrich von (Georg Friedrich Philipp; Leopold; Ludwig; pseudonym Novalis; 1772–1801). Romantic poet and thinker; b. Wiederstedt (or Oberwiederstedt), near Eisleben, Ger., of Moravian parents; educ. Jena, Leipzig, Wittenberg. Works include *Hymnen an die Nacht; Die Christenheit oder Europa; Heinrich von Ofterdingen.*

Harders, Johann Friedrich Gustav (Dec. 18, 1863–Apr. 13, 1917). B. Kiel, Ger.; educ. Kiel; taught in boys' institutions at Riga and Libau (Lepaya); to Am.; studied at Milwaukee, Wis., sem. of Wisconsin* Ev. Luth. Syn.; pastor Milwaukee 1889; miss. to Am. Indians at Globe, Ariz., 1907–17. Works include *"Ich auch!"; Wohin?: Ein Geleitswort auf den Lebensweg für die konfirmierte Jugend; Die heutigen Apachen; Jaalahn; La Paloma; Wille wider Wille.*

Hare, Julius Charles (1795–1855). B. Valdagno, near Vicenza, It.; Eng. theol. Works include *Vindication of Luther against his recent English Assailants.*

Hare, William Hobart (1838–1909). "Apostle to the Sioux." B. Princeton, N. J.; educ. Prot. Episc. Academy and U. of Pa., both at Philadelphia; ordained Episc. priest 1862; served chs. in Philadelphia; consecrated bp. Niobrara 1873, later bp. S. Dak.; supervised work among Sioux; worked in China and Jap. 1891, 1892.

Harijans. See *India,* 3.

Häring. See *Haering.*

Harless, Gottlieb Christoph Adolf von (Adolf Gottlieb Christoph; 1806–79). Conservative Luth. theol.; b. Nürnberg, Ger.; educ. Erlangen and Halle; prof. Erlangen 1833, Leipzig 1845; court preacher Dresden 1850; pres. supreme consistory Munich 1852. Works include *Commentar über den Brief Pauli an die Ephesier; Theologische Encyklopädie und Methodologie vom Standpunkte der protestantischen Kirche; Christliche Ethik.*

Harmensen, Jacob. See *Arminianism.*

Harmonists (Harmonites). See *Rappists.*

Harmonius (fl. 1st half 3d c. AD). Syrian hymnist; son of Bardesanes. See also *Gnosticism,* 7 h.

Harmony of the Gospels. 1. Work that combines into a continuous narrative the accounts of the 4 Gospels (see also *Diatessaron*). Works of this kind include that of Tatian*; Augustine* of Hippo, *De consensu euangelistarum;* J. de Gerson,* *Monotessaron;* A. Osiander* the Elder, *Harmoniae evangelicae libri iiii;* J. Calvin,* *Harmonia ex tribus Euangelistis composita, Matthaeo, Marco et Luca;* M. Chemnitz,* P. Leyser* the Elder, and J. Gerhard,* *Harmonia quatuor evangelistarum.*

2. Work exhibiting the text of the Gospels in parallel columns to show agreement or differences. Works of this kind include the tables, or canons, of Eusebius* of Caesarea; J. J. Griesbach,* *Synopsis Evangeliorum Matthaei, Marci et Lucae;* R. Anger, *Synopsis evangeliorum Matthaei, Marci, Lucae, cum locis qui supersunt parallelis litterarum et traditionum evangeliorum Irenaeo antiquiorum;* W. M. L. De Wette* and G. C. F. Lücke,* *Synopsis evangeliorum Matthaei, Marci et Lucae cum parallelis Joannis pericopis* (based on Griesbach); L. F. C. v. Tischendorf,* *Synopsis Evangelica;* W. G. Rushbrooke, *Synopticon;* E. Robinson, *A Harmony of the Gospels in Greek* and *A Harmony of the Four Gospels* (Eng.); A. Huck, *A Synopsis of the First Three Gospels,* rev. H. Lietzmann and F. L. Cross; *Synopsis quattuor evangeliorum locis parallelis evangeliorum apocryphorum et patrum adhibitis,* ed. K. Aland; E. D. Burton and E. J. Goodspeed, *A Harmony of the Synoptic Gospels for Historical and Critical Study;* A. Fahling, *A Harmony of the Gospels.*

Harmony, Preestablished. Theory of G. W. v. Leibniz* acc. to which God created each substance in such a way that everything that happens to any substance arises spontaneously from its own nature, yet in harmony with what happens to every other substance. With this theory v. Leibnitz hoped to solve the problem of the relation bet. mind and body.

Harmony of the Spheres. See *Pythagoreanism.*

Harms, Christian. See *Harms, Georg Ludwig Detlev Theodor.*

Harms, Claus (1778–1855). B. Fahrstedt, Schleswig-Holstein, Ger.; Luth. theol.; educ. Meldorf and Kiel; impressed by F. D. E. Schleiermacher's* *Über die Religion;* turned from rationalism to Lutheranism at Kiel; deacon Lunden 1806; archdeacon St. Nikolai Ch., Kiel, 1816; chief pastor and provost 1835; counselor of the high consistory 1841. In 1817 he issued M. Luther's* 95 Theses together with 95 of his own (see *Theses, Ninety-five, of Harms; Theses, Ninety-five, of Luther*) against rationalism* and the proposed Prussian* Union. Other works include *Pastoral-Theologie; Winter- und Sommer-Postille; Dr. Claus Harms, gewesenen Predigers in Kiel, Lebensbeschreibung verfasset von ihm selber; Das sind die*

95 theses *oder Streitsätze Dr. Luthers, theuren Andenkens. Zum besondern Abdruck besorgt und mit andern 95 Sätzen als mit einer Uebersetzung aus* Ao. *1517 in 1817 begleitet; Briefe zu einer nähern Verständigung über verschiedene meine Thesen betreffende Puncte. Nebst Einem namhaften Briefe, an den Herrn* Dr. *Schleiermacher.* See also *Theses, Ninety-five, of Harms.*

V. Ferm, *The Crisis in American Lutheran Theology* (New York, 1927), pp. 118–123.

Harms, Georg Ludwig Detlev Theodor (Louis; 1808–65). B. Walsrode, Hannover, Ger.; brother of T. Harms*; educ. Göttingen; asst. and successor to his father, Christian Harms (1773–1848), as pastor Hermannsburg; leader in spiritual awakening in N Ger.; founded Hermannsburg* Miss.

T. Harms, *Life Work of Pastor Louis Harms,* tr. M. E. Ireland (Philadelphia, 1900).

Harms, Theodor (1819–85). B. Hermannsburg, Ger.; Luth. pastor; called by his brother, G. L. D. T. Harms,* as teacher of theol. to the Hermannsburg* Miss. 1849; succeeded his brother as pastor and as leader of the Hermannsburg Miss. 1865; suspended for opposition to liberalism; founded Hannover Luth. Free Ch. (Selbständige Ev.-Luth. Kirche). See also *Germany, Lutheran Free Churches in,* 11.

Harnack, Karl Gustav Adolf von (1851–1930). Son of T. A. Harnack*; b. Dorpat (Tartu); educ. Dorpat and Leipzig; prof. Leipzig, Giessen, Marburg, Berlin; influenced by A. Ritschl*; teacher of K. Barth.* Stressed ethical side of Christianity. Held religion is practical and concerned with power (traced in Christianity to hist. revelation of God in Christ) to live holy life. Regarded rise of dogma as influenced by Gk. spirit and as perversion of primitive Christianity. Believed that the life and teaching of Jesus is adequately revealed in the NT and that Christ was an outstanding religious genius who taught the Fatherhood of God, value of human soul, advent of Kingdom of God. With E. Schürer* founded *Theologische Literaturzeitung* 1876; coed. 1881–1910; other works include *Dogmengeschichte; Das Apostolische Glaubensbekenntnis; Das Wesen des Christentums; Beiträge zur Einleitung in das Neue Testament; Geschichte der altchristlichen Literatur bis Eusebius; Die Mission und Ausbreitung des Christentums in den ersten drei Jahrhunderten.* See also *Switzerland, Contemporary Theology in,* 1–3.

Harnack, Theodosius Andreas (1817–89). Father of K. G. A. v. Harnack*; b. St. Petersburg, Russ.; orthodox Luth. theol.; prof. Dorpat (Tartu) 1847, Erlangen 1853; returned to Dorpat 1866; exerted influence for Lutheranism in Baltic provinces.

Harold Bluetooth. See *Denmark.*

Harold Klak. See *Denmark.*

Harper, William Rainey (1856–1906). B. New Concord, Ohio; 1st pres. new U. of Chicago 1891; founded Am. Institute of Heb. 1884. Works include *A Critical and Exegetical Commentary on Amos and Hosea; Elements of Hebrew by an Inductive Method; The Priestly Element in the Old Testament; The Prophetic Element in the Old Tetsament; Religion and the Higher Life.* See also *Religious Education Association of the United States and Canada.*

Harpster, John Henry (Apr. 27, 1844–Feb. 1, 1911). B. Centerhall, Pa.; Union soldier in Civil War; educ. Missionary Institute, Selinsgrove, Pa., Gettysburg (Pa.) Theol. Sem.; ordained 1871; miss. at Guntur, India, 1872–76 for The General* Syn. of the Ev. Luth. Ch. in the USA; pastor Ellsworth and Hays, Kans., Trenton, N. J., and Canton, Ohio; Gen. Syn. miss. Guntur, India, 1893–1901; miss. at Rajahmundry, India, 1902–09 for the General* Council of the Ev. Luth. Ch. in N. Am.

Harris, Howel (1714–73). B. Talgarth, Breconshire, S. Wales; miss. preacher in Wales; est. Christian community at Trevecca; often called the 1st lay preacher of the Calvinistic Meth. ch.

Harris, James Rendel (1852–1941). Biblical scholar, orientalist, archaeol.; b. Plymouth, Eng.; at first Cong.; joined Soc. of Friends* 1880; curator E MSS, John Rylands Library, Manchester, Eng.; prof. and lecturer in Am. and Eng. univs. and colls.; traveled in the E looking for ancient MSS. Works include *The Diatessaron* of Tatian; Four Lectures on the Western Text of the New Testament; Aaron's Breastplate, and Other Addresses; The Codex Sangallensis; The Annotators of the Codex Bezae; Memoranda sacra; Further Researches into the History of the Ferrar-group; The Newly-discovered Gospel of St. Peter, with a Full Account of the Same.*

Harris, Samuel. 1. (1724–ca. 1794). "Apostle of Va." Bap. cleric; b. Hanover Co., Va.; converted 1758; ordained 1769; designated "apostle" 1774 by Va. Gen. Assoc. of Separate Baps. (see *Baptist Churches,* 24); devoted his fortune to religious and charitable work. 2. (1814–99). B. East Machias, Maine; educ. Bowdoin Coll., Brunswick, Maine, and Andover (Mass.) Theol. Sem.; Cong. cleric; prof. systematic theol. Bangor (Maine) Theol. Sem. 1855–67; pres. Bowdoin Coll. 1867–71; prof. Divinity School, Yale U., New Haven, Conn., 1871–96. Works include *Zaccheus; The Philosophical Basis of Theism.*

Harris, William Wada (Wadé; b. ca. 1853). Called "Prophet." Liberian of Brebo tribe; converted in youth; to Ivory Coast 1913; barefoot; wore long white robe and turban; carried high bamboo cross, Bible, and calabash of water; converts estimated up to 100,000; fetishism* disappeared; arrested 1915 by Fr.; deported to Liberia. See also *Africa,* C 9.

Harrsch, Josua. See *Kocherthal, Josua.*

Hart, Joseph (ca. 1712–68). B. London; spiritually unsettled till converted 1757 under Moravian influence; pastor Indep. Chapel, London; hymnist. Hymns include "Come, Holy Spirit, Come"; "Lamb of God, We Fall Before Thee."

Hartenstein, Karl (1894–1952). B. Stuttgart, Ger.; ev. theol.; influenced by Pietism*; became increasingly heilsgeschichtlich (see *Heilsgeschichte*); esp. active in miss. and ecumenical work; dir. Basel* Miss. Soc. 1926–39; mem. International* Miss. Council 1938; mem. Council of EKD 1948.

Hartford Seminary Foundation. See *Tyler, Bennet.*

Hartmann, Karl Robert Eduard von (1842–1906). B. Berlin; held that Christianity exhausted its possibilities in the Middle Ages. In his philos. system the Absolute is the Unconscious; world process results from the struggle of ideas to free themselves from Universal Will, thereby causing consciousness to emerge from the Unconscious. His earlier pessimism rejected attempts to find hapiness in this world, in a future world, or in evolution. Later he modified his pessimism by positing 5 criteria of value: pleasure, purposiveness, beauty, morality, religiosity; he referred his pessimism primarily to the 1st. Works include *Philosophie des Unbewussten.*

Hartmann, Nicolai (1882–1950). B. Riga, Latvia; educ. St. Petersburg, Dorpat (Tartu), Marburg; Ger. realist philos.; prof. Marburg 1920, Cologne 1926, Berlin 1931, Göttingen 1945. Held that the object of knowledge exists indep. of thought and is given to thought; epistemology is based on ontology. Held that there are 4 strata of being, namely, in ascending order, matter, life, consciousness, spirit. Some categories of the lower penetrate the upper, but not vice versa. Emphasized importance of unraveling problems (aporias) into strands. Directed sentiments of love, faith, reverence, and gratitude not to a personal, transcendent God but to the sum of being. Works include *Der philosophische Gedanke* *und seine Geschichte; Ethik; Zur Grundlegung der Ontologie; Möglichkeit und Wirklichkeit; Grundzüge einer Metaphysik der Erkenntnis.*

Hartmann von Aue (Hartman von Ouwe; b. ca. 1165; d. after 1210). Ger. author; introd. stories of King Arthur in Ger.; some works emphasize moral themes (e. g., *Der arme Heinrich*).

Hartmuth von Kronberg (Cronberg; 1488–1549). Ger. knight; sided with M. Luther* early; wrote in the interest of the Reformation, beginning 1521; relative of Franz von Sickingen* and lost castle for standing by him; received it back 1541.

Hartwick, John Christopher (Johannes Christophorus; Jan. 6, 1714–July 17, 1796). Luth. cleric; b. Saxe-Gotha, Ger.; received theol. educ. in Ger.; ordained London, Eng.; to Am. as chaplain of a Ger. regiment in the service of Eng.; held various pastorates in the US and Nova Scotia; helped organize Pa. Ministerium (see *United Lutheran Church, Synods of,* 22); willed estate for endowment of Hartwick* Sem. See also *Ministry, Education of,* VI C.

Hartwick College. Outgrowth of Hartwick* Sem.; separate existence as standard liberal arts coll. at Oneonta, N. Y., began 1928. By 1970 it had withdrawn from the LCA to qualify for greater state support. See also *General Synod of the Evangelical Lutheran Church in the United States of America, The,* 8; *Ministry, Education of,* VIII B 15; *United Lutheran Church, Synods of,* 15.

Hartwick Seminary. Founded 1797 in NYC, funded by income from the J. C. Hartwick* estate; moved 1815 to new location soon named Hartwick, near Cooperstown, Otsego Co., N. Y.; moved back to NYC 1930; closed 1940. See also *General Synod of the Evangelical Lutheran Church in the United States of America, The,* 8; *Ministry, Education of,* VI C.

Hartwick Synod. Organized Oct. 26, 1830, in Schoharie, N. Y., by the W Conf. of the N. Y. ministerium (see *United Lutheran Church, Synods of,* 15); joined General* Syn. of the Ev. Luth. Ch. in the USA 1831; merged 1908 with the Franckean* Syn. and the N. Y. and N. J. Syn. into the Syn. of N. Y. (see also *New York, Synod of* [*II*]). At the time of this merger the Hartwick Syn. numbered 36 chs., 4 stations, 5,443 communicants. See also *Lintner, George Ames; United Lutheran Church, Synods of,* 15.

Harvard, John (1607–38). B. London, Eng.; educ. Cambridge; to Am. 1637 as pastor at Charlestown on Mass. Bay; Harvard U. (founded 1636 at New Towne, near Cambridge, Mass.) named after him in gratitude for his library and half his estate.

Harvest, Feast of (Jewish). See *Judaism,* 4.

Harvest, Festival of. See *Church Year,* 17; *Thanksgiving Day.*

Hase, Karl August von (1800–90). B. Niedersteinbach, near Penig, Saxony, Ger.; educ. Leipzig and Erlangen; prof. Jena 1829–83. Held mediating position bet. rationalistic and orthodox theologians; interpreted 17th-c. Luth. orthodoxy in terms of idealism. Works include *Das Leben Jesu* (expanded 1875 as *Geschichte Jesu*); *Evangelisch-protestantische Dogmatik; Hutterus redivivus; Kirchengeschichte; Handbuch der protestantischen Polemik gegen die römisch-katholische Kirche.* See also *Lutheran Theology After 1580,* 9.

Hasenkamp, Johann Gerhard (1736–77). B. Wechte, near Lengerich, Westphalia, Ger.; pietistic mystic; prominent in a group at Duisburg that included S. Collenbusch,* G. Tersteegen,* J. H. Jung-Stilling,* J. K. Lavater,* G. D. Krummacher, and F. W. Krummacher (see *Krummacher,* 2, 3). Tried to est. a unity of nature and grace. Influenced by J. Cocceius,* J. A. Bengel,* G. W. v. Leibnitz,* and J. Böhme.*

Hashemite Kingdom of Jordan. See *Middle East,* G.

Hasidism (Chasidism; from Heb. *hasid,* "pious one"). Ancient Hasidism was a Jewish movement ca. 200 BC that opposed Hellenization. Modern Hasidism, which fostered Jewish culture, began ca. 1740 in Poland under leadership of Baal* Shem-Tob; spread among Jews of E Eur. and to Israel, US, and Can.; emphasized joyful worship of Israel's God in the here and now.

Haskalah (Heb. "enlightenment"). Jewish enlightenment movement of maskilim (Heb. "intellectuals"); began as a movement in Ger. ca. the middle of the 18th c. with M. Mendelssohn* as protagonist; fostered knowledge of Jewish literature and philos. and encouraged interest in and adaptation to surroundings; spread to Austria and Russ.

Hasse, Johann Adolf (1699–1783). B. Bergedorf, near Hamburg, Ger.; composer; friend of J. S. Bach*; pupil of N. A. Porpora* and A. Scarlatti.* Works include operas, cantatas, oratorios, and masses.

Hasse, Zacharias. See *Estonia,* 2.

Hasselquist, Tuve Nilsson (Tufve; Mar. 2, 1816–Feb. 4, 1891). Luth. cleric; b. Osby (Ousby; or Hasslarod), Swed.; educ. Lund; ordained 1839; to Am. 1852; pastor and home miss. Galesburg, Ill., 1852–63; pres. Scand. Ev. Luth. Aug. Syn. in N. Am. 1860–70 (see *Augustana Evangelical Lutheran Church,* 8–9); head of Augustana Sem. and Coll., Paxton (1863–75) and Rock Island (1875–91), Ill. Founded and ed. *Det Rätta Hemlandet* (called *Augustana* beginning 1869); other works include a commentary on Eph. See also *Publication Houses, Lutheran.*

E. Norelius, *T. N. Hasselquist* (Rock Island, Ill., 1900); *Augustana Library Publications No. 14,* ed. I. O. Nothstein: O. F. Ander, *T. N. Hasselquist.*

Hassler, Hans Leo (von) (Hasler; 1564–1612). B. Nürnberg, Ger.; Luth. composer; pupil of A. Gabrieli*; fellow student of G. Gabrieli,* with whom he est. intimate and lasting friendship; organist Augsburg 1585, Nürnberg 1601, Dresden 1608. Wrote the melody now commonly used for the hymn "O Sacred Head, Now Wounded"; other works include *Psalmen und christliche Gesäng; Sacri concentus;* masses.

Hassold, Friedrich. See *New Zealand,* 3.

Hastings, Eurotas Parmelee (Apr. 17, 1821–July 31, 1890). B. Clinton, N. Y.; ABCFM miss. to Ceylon 1846; taught at Batticotta (Ceylon) Sem.; pres. of coll. at Jaffna, Ceylon.

Hastings, James (ca. 1852–1922). B. Huntly, Aberdeen, Scot.; educ. Aberdeen; ordained Presb. 1884; served Free Ch. parishes at Kincardineshire and Dundee. Founded *Expository Times;* ed. *Encyclopedia of Religion and Ethics; A Dictionary of Christ and the Gospels; Dictionary of the Apostolic Church; A Dictionary of the Bible; The Literature and Religion of Israel; The Speaker's Bible.*

Hastings, Selina (1707–91). Countess of Huntingdon; wife of Theophilus Hastings (1696–1746), 9th Earl of Huntingdon; b. Stanton Harold, near Ashby-de-la-Zouch, Leicestershire, Eng.; founded Calvinistic Meth. sect called Countess of Huntingdon's Connexion; assoc. with J. and C. Wesley* and G. Whitefield*; sided with Whitefield and Calvinism against the Wesleys; became sole trustee of Whitefield's institutions in Ga. at his death.

Hastings, Thomas (1784–1872). B. Litchfield Co., Conn.; music teacher, choirmaster, hymnist, composer. Hymns include "Delay Not"; composed Toplady, the tune commonly used for "Rock of Ages."

Hatch, Edwin (1835–89). Theol. and educator; b. Derby, Eng.; educ. Oxford; prof. in Can. 1859, in Eng. beginning 1867. Works include *The Organization of the Early Christian Churches; The Influence* *of Greek Ideas and Usages upon the Christian Church.*

Hatlestad, Ole Jensen (Hattlestad; Sept. 30, 1823–Sept. 7, 1892). Norw. Luth. cleric; to Am. 1846; pastor Leland, Ill., Milwaukee, Wis., and Decorah, Iowa; pres. Norwegian-Danish* Augustana Synod. Coed. *Nordlyset* (later called *Democraten*); ed. *Luthersk kirketidende;* other works include *Historiske meddelelser om den lutherske kirke i Amerika.*

Hattem, Pontiaen van (1645–1706). B. Bergen op Zoom, Neth.; separatist; declared antinomian, libertine, and socinian by the ch.; deposed 1683; founder and leader of quietist-perfectionist movement; followers, called Hattemists, disappeared by 1760. See also *Hebraeans.*

Hattstädt, Otto Frederick (Dec. 31, 1862–Nov. 29, 1950). B. Monroe, Mich.; educ. Conc. Coll., Fort Wayne, Ind., and Conc. Sem., St. Louis, Mo.; prof. Conc. Coll., Milwaukee, Wis., 1884–1938. Ed. *Handbuch der deutschen Nationalliteratur;* other works include *Deutsche Grammatik; Geschichte des Süd-Wisconsin-Distrikts der ev.-luth. Synode von Missouri, Ohio und andern Staaten.*

Hattstädt, Georg Wilhelm Christoph (Wilhelm Georg; Aug. 29, 1811–Mar. 22, 1884). B. Langenzenn, Bavaria; sent to Am. by J. K. W. Löhe* 1844; pastor Monroe, Mich.; founded congs. in S Mich.; mem. Michigan* Syn. 1844–46; charter advisory mem. Missouri* Syn. (received *in absentia* 1847). See also *Lutheran Church – Missouri Synod, The,* I, 3.

Hätzer, Ludwig. See *Hetzer, Ludwig.*

Hauck, Albert (1845–1918). Luth. theol.; b. Wassertrüdingen, Ger.; educ. Erlangen and Berlin; vicar and pastor 8 yrs.; prof. Erlangen 1882, Leipzig 1889; coed. with J. J. Herzog* *Realencyklopädie für protestantische Theologie und Kirche;* other works include *Kirchengeschichte Deutschlands.*

Hauge, Hans Nielsen (1771–1824). B. Tune, Norw.; influenced by M. Luther,* J. Arnd(t),* E. Pontoppidan,* H. Müller,* H. A. Brorson*; interpreted a 1796 religious experience as call to evangelize fellow countrymen; traversed much of Norw. on foot and sailed from port to port to preach; also tried to raise standard of living; often arrested and imprisoned for itinerant lay preaching; emphasized conversion and sanctification; classified himself as orthodox Luth., but his orthodoxy was challenged; warned against separatism; urged ch. attendance and use of sacraments administered by pastors. Works include *Reiser og vigtigste Hendelser; Religiöse Fölelser; Testament til hans Venner.* See also *Norway, Lutheranism in,* 10; *Evangelical Lutheran Church, The,* 4.

A. C. Bang, *Hans Nielsen Hauge og hans Samtid,* 4th ed. (Christiania [Oslo], 1924); J. B. Bull, *Hans Nielsen Hauge, der Erwecker Norwegens,* tr. P. Klaiber-Gottschau, 2d ed. (Stuttgart, 1929); J. M. Shaw, *Pulpit Under the Sky* (Minneapolis, Minn., 1955); M. Nodtvedt, *Rebirth of Norway's Peasantry* (Tacoma, Wash., 1965).

Hauge Synod (Hauges norsk lutherske Synode i Amerika). Title of 1850 Constitution (as pub. later): *Kirkekonstitution for den evangelisk-lutherske Kirke i Jefferson Prairie etc. i Nord Amerika.* See *Eielsen Synod; Evangelical Lutheran Church, The,* 12, 13.

Hauge's Seminary. See *Red Wing Seminary.*

Haupt, Paul (1858–1926). B. Görlitz, Ger.; educ. Leipzig and Berlin; prof. Göttingen, Ger., and John Hopkins U., Baltimore, Md.; mem. Soc. of Friends*; engaged in radical attempts to restore OT text. Ed. Polychrome* Bible; other works include *The Burning Bush and the Origin of Judaism; The Ethnology of Galilee or Was Jesus a Jew by Race?; The Ship of the Babylonian Noah; Akkadische und sumerische Keilschrifttexte; Das Babylonische Nimrodepos; Die Sumerischen Familiengesetze.*

Hauptmann, Gerhart (1862–1946). B. Salzbrunn, Silesia; Ger. poet and dramatist; style influenced by M. Luther*; opposed clericalism and religious compulsion in every form; over the yrs. his ideas became more and more eclectic, often seeking synthesis of Christian, Gk., and oriental thought.

Hausihl, Bernard Michael (Houseal; 1727–99). B. Strasbourg, Fr.; to Am. 1752; pastor Frederick, Md., Reading, Pa., and NYC; loyalist in Revolution; his house and ch. in NYC were burned 1776; to Halifax, N. S., 1783 to minister to Luths. in their native tongue; to Eng. 1784 for reordination by the bp. of London; returned to Can., where he served 16 yrs., gradually leading the cong. into the Ch. of England. See also *Canada,* A 1.

Hausknecht, Johann Peter (1799–1870). Founded Ger. sect; ascetic (opposed marriage, alcohol, medicine), separatistic, chiliastic.

Hausmann, Nicolaus (ca. 1478–1538). Close friend of M. Luther*; reformer of Zwickau and Dessau; opposed Zwickau* prophets.

Hausrath, Adolf (1837–1909). B. Karlsruhe, Ger.; educ. Jena, Göttingen, Berlin, and Heidelberg; Ref. liberal theol.; moderate adherent of Tübingen school (see *Isagogics,* 3; *Lutheran Theology After 1580,* 12); prof. ch. hist. Heidelberg 1867.

Haussleiter, Johannes (1581–1928). B. Löpsingen, Ries, Ger.; educ. Erlangen, Tübingen, Leipzig; prof. Dorpat and Greifswald. Works include *Die vier Evangelisten; Paulus; Jesus; Aus der Schule Melanchthons; Melanchthon-Kompendium; Trinitarischer Glaube und Christusbekenntnis in der alten Kirche.*

Haustafel. Statement of ethics, or table of duties. The form found at the close of M. Luther's* SC, compiled from ethical portions of the NT, is probably not altogether Luther's own. Useful for review and in forming habits of morality.

Havergal, Frances Ridley (1836–79). B. Astley, Worcestershire, Eng.; daughter of W. H. Havergal*; hymnist. Hymns include "O Savior, Precious Savior"; "Take My Life and Let It Be"; "I Gave My Life for Thee"; "I Am Trusting Thee, Lord Jesus"; "Now the Light Has Gone Away."

Havergal, William Henry (1793–1870). B. Wycombe, Buckinghamshire, Eng.; educ. Oxford; ordained 1816; rector Astley (Worcestershire), Worcester, and Shareshill (near Wolverhampton). Tried to restore metrical psalmody to original purity. Works include *Old Church Psalmody; A Hundred Psalms and Hymn Tunes; Fireside Music; Evening Service in A.*

Hävernick, Heinrich Andreas Christoph (1811–45). B. Kröpelin, Ger.; educ. Leipzig, Halle, and Berlin; taught at Geneva, Rostock, and Königsberg; adopted theol. views of E. W. Hengstenberg*; defended traditional views concerning origin of OT books.

Hawaii. *Area:* ca. 6,425 sq. mi.; 1970 *pop.:* ca. 770,000; formerly Sandwich Islands (so named by Capt. James Cook of Eng. [who discovered them 1778] in honor of the Earl of Sandwich, 1st Lord of the Admiralty); annexed to US 1898; US territory 1900; US state (except Midway Is.) 1959; ca. 2,100 mi. WSW of San Francisco; 8 major and many minor islands, most of the latter uninhabited, form a chain ca. 1,600 mi. long; capital: Honolulu, on the is. Hawaii; aborigines Polynesian; now many races freely intermingle. In the late 18th c. natives practiced crude and sanguinary idolatry, including human sacrifices; cannibalism was rare. A request for Christian teachers sent to Eng. 1794 by Kamehameha I (Nui, i. e., the Great; ca. 1737–1819; king 1795–1819) went unanswered. Miss. efforts began when ABCFM missionaries, including H. Bingham* and A. Thurston,* arrived 1820. In the 1860s the

ABCFM gradually turned over its work to the native ch. The work was taken over by the Hawaiian Ev. Assoc. (also known as Hawaiian Bd. of Missions; organized under ABCFM supervision). An Angl. bp. and 2 SPG missionaries were sent to Honolulu 1861; 1st person bap. by them (1862) was the queen. This miss. was transferred to the Am. Prot. Episc. Ch. 1902. RC miss. efforts in Hawaii began 1827, but the priests were banished 1831. Another RC miss. was est. 1839. A leper colony was est. on Molokai Is. in the 1860s. The 1st Missouri* Syn. cong., a result of chaplains' work, was organized 1945. 1967 LCMS statistics: ca. 2,100 bap. mems.; 9 stations; 9 pastors. Other ventures include those of Assemblies of God; Christian Science; Methodists; Miss. Ch. Assoc.; Mormons; Pent. Holiness Ch.; Prot. Episc. Ch.; Seventh-day Adventists; S. Bap. Conv.; Theosophy. OHS

See *Missions, Bibliography.*

Haweis, Hugh Reginald (1838 [1839?]–1901). B. Egham, Surrey, Eng.; educ. Cambridge; pastor London 1866–1901; Broad* Ch. leader. Works include *The Broad Church; Arrows in the Air; Christ and Christianity; Music and Morals.*

Haweis, Thomas (1734–1820). B. Truro, Cornwall, Eng.; physician; studied theol. at Cambridge; asst. chaplain Lock Chapel, London; rector All Saints, Aldwinkle; composer; hymnist. Composed the tune "Chesterfield"; hymns include "O Thou from Whom All Goodness Flows"; other works include *The Communicant's Spiritual Companion; Carmina Christo.*

Hawkins, Edward (1789–1882). Prof. Oxford; sermon on tradition influenced J. H. Newman*; opposed Tractarianism.*

Hawthorne, Nathaniel (1804–64). B. Salem, Mass.; fiction writer; occupied with man's struggle with sin. Works include *The Scarlet Letter,* an intensive study of psychological effects of adultery.

Hay, Charles Augustus (Feb. 11, 1821–June 26, 1893). Luth. cleric; b. York, Pa.; educ. Pa. Coll. (later called Gettysburg Coll.), Gettysburg Theol. Sem., Berlin and Halle, Ger.; licensed to preach 1843; served at Middletown, Md.; prof. Biblical literature and Ger. at Gettysburg 1844–48; pastor Hanover, Pa., 1848, Harrisburg, Pa., 1849–65; withdrew his ch. from the Pa. Ministerium and joined the East Pa. Syn. 1857 (see *United Lutheran Church, Synods of,* 22, 23); prof. Gettysburg 1865–93; pres. East Pa. Syn. 1860, 1874, The General* Syn. of the Ev. Luth. Ch. in the USA 1881. Works include tr. of M. Luther's* *Wochenpredigten über Matth. 5–7 (Commentary on the Sermon on the Mount);* with H. E. Jacobs* tr. H. Schmid,* *The Doctrinal Theology of the Evangelical Lutheran Church* from Ger. and Lat.; *Memoirs of Rev. Jacob Goering, Rev. George Lochman, D. D., and Rev. Benjamin Kurtz, D. D., LL. D.*

Haydn, Franz Joseph (1732–1809). RC composer; brother of J. M. Haydn*; b. Rohrau, Austria; choirboy St. Stephen's, Vienna, 1740–49; kapellmeister to the Esterházy family 1761–90; visited London 1791–92, 1794–95; lived in Vienna 1795–1809. Works include oratorio *The Creation;* Austrian nat. anthem; masses; operas; symphonies; sonatas; *Stabat mater.* See also *Passion, The.*

K. Geiringer, *Haydn,* 2d ed. (New York, 1963); R. Hughes, *Haydn* (London, 1950); H. E. Jacob, *Joseph Haydn,* tr. R. and C. Winston (New York, 1950); G. A. Griesinger, *Joseph Haydn* (Madison, Wis., 1963).

Haydn, Johann Michael (1737–1806). Brother of F. J. Haydn*; b. Rohrau, Austria; choirboy St. Stephen's, Vienna, 1745–55; composer; kapellmeister at Grosswardein 1757; music dir. and konzertmeister to abp. of Salzburg 1762. Works include masses, graduals, offertories, symphonies.

Hayn, Henriette Louise von (1724–82). B. Idstein, Hesse-Nassau; Moravian; taught at Herrnhaag, Grosshennersdorf, and Herrnhut; hymnist. Hymns include "Weil ich Jesu Schäflein bin."

Haystack Group. Group of students (including G. Hall,* S. J. Mills,* and L. Rice*) at Williams Coll., Williamstown, Mass., unified by an impromptu prayer meeting in a storm, under shelter of a haystack, in the early 1800s; those who joined later, at Andover (Mass.) Theol. Sem., included A. Judson* and S. Newell*; efforts of the group led to organization of the American* Bd. of Commissioners for For. Missions.

Hayunga, Herman. See *Canada,* A 4; *Danish Lutherans in America,* 1.

Hazelius, Ernest Lewis (Sept. 6, 1777–Feb. 20, 1853). B. Neusalz, Silesia; educ. in Moravian schools; to Am. 1800; taught Lat., Gk., and theol. in Moravian school, Nazareth, Pa., 1800–09; ordained Luth. pastor 1809 by N. Y. Ministerium (see *United Lutheran Church, Synods* of, 15); pastor in Hunterdon and Morris Cos., N. J., 1809–15; prof. Hartwick* Sem. 1815–30, Gettysburg* Sem. 1830–33, Classical and Theol. Institute of the Syn. of S. C. (see *United Lutheran Church, Synods of,* 27), Lexington, 1834–53. Works include *Materials for Catechisation on Passages of the Scripture; History of the American Lutheran Church from Its Commencement in the Year of Our Lord 1685, to the Year 1842.*

Hazlitt, William (1811–93). B. Mitre Lane, Maidstone, Eng.; son of William Hazlitt (1778–1830), Brit. literary critic. Works include tr. of M. Luther's* *Table-Talk.*

Headlam, Arthur Cayley (1862–1947). B. Wharlton, Durham, Eng.; educ. Oxford; prof. King's Coll., London, and Oxford; bp. Gloucester; classified as enlightened conservative; adhered to hist. episcopacy while emphasizing validity of nonconformist ministry; prominent in Oxford* Movement; favored rev. of Book* of Common Prayer. Ed. *Church Quarterly Review* 1901–21; other works include *The Doctrine of the Church and Christian Reunion; Christian Theology.*

Heads of Agreement Assented to by the United Ministers in and about London, formerly called Presbyterian and Congregational. Unsuccessful formula intended to bind Cong. and Presb. pastors but not unite chs.; signed 1691 by most Cong. and Presb. pastors in the London area; the "Happy Union" was plagued by theol. controversy from the outset and completely disrupted by 1699.

Healing. For "healing" the NT uses the Gk. words *iaomai* (e. g., Mt 8:8; Mk 5:29; Lk 9:11) and *sozein,* which also means "to save" (e. g., Mt 9:22; Mk 6:56; Lk 8:48). The object of God's redemptive intent is man as a whole. The healing miracles of Jesus are part of His proclamation that in Him the kingdom of God had come. He therefore sent His disciples out both to proclaim the kingdom and to heal the sick (Mk 6:7, 13). Man was not created to be ill but to serve God in the full vigor of all his faculties. The power of physical healing is present in the ch. when persons are endowed by the Spirit with this special charism (1 Co 12:9, 28). The very possibility of such healing bears testimony to the grace of God. The medical profession enjoys the privilege of manifesting such divine grace in a special measure. Healing is a reminder of the presence of God's Spirit at work in His children to prepare them for the resurrection (Ro 8:11). Much of what passes for faith healing ("divine healing") distorts Biblical truth by offering health as an ultimate gift [end in itself] rather than a penultimate gift of God; this approach does not regard illness as a chastisement of God (Heb 12:6-11). MHS

W. H. Boggs Jr., *Faith Healing and the Christian Faith* (Richmond, Va., 1956); P. L. Garlick, *Man's Search for Health* (London, 1952); R. A. Lambourne, *Community, Church, and Healing* (London, 1963); M. H. Scharlemann, *Healing and Redemption* (St. Louis, Mo., 1965).

Hearing the Word. See *Worship,* 2, 3.

Hearne, Thomas (1678–1735). B. Berkshire, Eng.; educ. Oxford; antiquary. Works include eds. of classical writers and Eng. chroniclers. See also *Nonjurors.*

Heart. In nearly all passages in which the Hebrew word *leb* (or *lebab*) and the Gk. word *kardia* occur they are used of a man's heart and usually in a psychological sense as the organ of feeling, thinking, and willing. The heart is the seat of life (Gn 18:5; Ju 19:5, 8; Lk 21:34).

The spirit is the life principle of the heart and acts through it (heart and spirit paralleled Ps. 34: 18). With the heart man approaches God (Heb 10: 22); Christ dwells in the hearts of believers (Eph 3:17); estrangement from God is of the heart (Eph 4:18; Is 1:5). The heart determines the character of man (Lk 8:15; Acts 7:51; Ro 1:21; 2:5). It is the treasury of good and evil (Mt 12:34-35), receives God's Word and the Holy Spirit (Mt 13:19), is the organ of faith (Ro 10:9-10) and unbelief (Acts 7: 39), decision (Acts 5:4), and thought (Is 10:7). It is the object of Satan's activity (Jn 13:2). It resists God and becomes hardened (Acts 28:27). The work of the Law is written in the heart (Ro 2:15).

Heart of Jesus. See *Sacred Heart of Jesus, Devotion to.*

Heart of Mary, Immaculate. RC devotion to the Immaculate Heart of Mary is closely assoc. with devotion to the Sacred* Heart of Jesus; its material object is Mary's heart; 1st widely propagated in the 16th–17th c.

Heath, George (ca. 1745–ca. 1822). Educ. Exeter, Eng.; Presb. pastor Honiton, Devonshire; later apparently Unitarian; hymnist. Hymns include "My Soul, Be on Thy Guard."

Heathenism. Term gen. used to designate religious system or rites outside the Judeo-Christian tradition. Derivation of the word "heathen" uncertain; scope of its meaning variously defined. Of special interest to Christians is the heathenism that prevailed in the Roman Empire in the 1st cents. AD. There were "gods many and lords many" (1 Co 8:5), temples and shrines, cults and worships, including an imperial cult (see *Persecutions of Christians,* 1), in bewildering confusion. The world was losing confidence in its gods. Xenophanes* scoffed at man-made gods. Aristophanes (ca. 448–ca. 380 BC; Gk. playright) ridiculed them in his comedies. Epicurus relegated them to a state of innocuous irrelevance. Stoics (see *Stoicism*) reduced them to pantheistic abstraction. Lucretius* proclaimed a gospel of irreligion. The carpenter in Horace (65–8 BC; Roman poet and satirist) deliberates whether he should make a rude log into a bench or a god (*Satire,* I, viii). Pliny* the Elder is openly atheistic. Yet heathenism had not spent its force. The religion of the cultured classes did not reflect the religion of the masses, nor were all the cultured irreligious. There was much ambivalence among the most advanced thinkers; in deference to tradition or to the beliefs of the masses, they observed, and even championed, superstitious rites and ceremonies that they inwardly despised. There was some superstition even among the most cultivated and enlightened. But neither heathenism nor philosophy satisfied the soul. It remained for Christ* Jesus to bring "life and immortality to light" (2 Ti 1:10). See also *Pagan.*

Heaven. See *Hereafter,* A, C 1–2.

Heavenly Elements. See *Grace, Means of,* IV, 4.

Heavenly Prophets. See *Zwickau Prophets.*

Hebenstreit, Johann Christian (1686–1756). B. Neuenhof [Neuenhofen], near Neustadt on the Orla, Ger.; educ. Leipzig; began academic career Leipzig 1715; Sat. preacher Thomaskirche, Leipzig, 1721; conrector Thomasschule 1725; prof. Heb. 1731, theol. 1740 Leipzig. Works include *De corporis humani machina, divinae sapientiae ac providentiae teste; Disputationes I–IX in prophetam Malachiam; De sabbato ante legem Mosis existente.*

Hebenstreit, Johann Friedrich (d. bet. 1760 and 1770). Son of J. P. Hebenstreit*; educ. Jena and Wittenberg; supt. Buttstädt, Thuringia, Ger. Works include *De magorum messiam exosculantium nomine, patria, et statu.*

Hebenstreit, Johann Paul (1664–1718). B. Neustadt on the Orla, Ger.; educ. Jena; prof. theol. Jena; pastor and inspector Dornburg; mem. Weimar consistory. Works include *De praedestinatione; De theologiae exegeticae natura et constitutione; Theologia naturalis; Systema theologicum; De summa scriptura sacrae auctoritate; De legis ecclesiasticae natura, causis, et affectionibus.*

Heber, Reginald (1783–1826). Angl. cleric and hymnist; b. Malpas, Cheshire, Eng.; educ. Oxford; vicar Hodnet, Shropshire; bp. Calcutta, India. Hymns include "Hosanna to the Living Lord"; "Brightest and Best of the Sons of the Morning"; "Holy, Holy, Holy! Lord God Almighty"; "The Son of God Goes Forth to War"; "From Greenland's Icy Mountains."

Hébert, Marcel (1851–1916). RC philos.; b. Bar-le-duc, Fr.; dir. École Fenelon, Paris; friend of L. M. O. Duchesne*; removed from office 1903 on charge of modernism.*

Hebler, Matthias (d. 1571). B. Zips [Szepes], Hung.; teacher and pastor Hermannstadt; bp. ev. Saxons 1556; est. staunch Lutheranism in Transylvania.*

Hebraeans. Followers of J. Verschoor*; held it indispensably necessary to read the Bible in the original (hence their name, derived from "Hebrew"). United with followers of P. v. Hattem.*

Heck, Barbara (nee Ruckle; 1734–1804). "Mother of Methodism in Am." B. Ballingrane, Co. Limerick, Ireland; m. Paul Heck; to N. Y. 1760; enraged against cardplaying, she urged P. Embury* to preach 1766; some date beginning of Methodism in Am. from this; helped erect 1st Wesleyan chapel in Am. (in NYC) 1768; moved to Salem in present Washington Co., N. Y., 1770; being loyalist, the Heck family moved to Montreal, Can., shortly before beginning of Revolutionary War; later moved to Augusta, upper Can.

Hecker, Heinrich Cornelius (1699–1743). B. Hamburg, Ger.; pastor Meuselwitz; hymnist. Hymns include "Gottlob! ein neues Kirchenjahr."

Hecker, Isaac Thomas (1819–88). B. NYC; at first Prot.; RC 1844; joined Redemptorists* 1845; founded Soc. of Missionary Priests of St. Paul the Apostle (see *Paulists*); active in RC publicity work; founded and ed. *The Catholic World* and *Young Catholic* (later *Leader*).

Hedberg, Fredrik Gabriel. See *Finland, Lutheranism in,* 4.

Hedinger, Johann Reinhard (1664–1704). B. Stuttgart, Ger.; educ. Tübingen; court preacher and confessor to Duke Eberhard Ludwig of Württemberg; influenced by P. J. Spener.* Works include NT tr.; Bible commentary; hymns.

Hedio, Caspar (Heid; 1494–1552). B. Ettlingen, Baden, Ger.; educ. Freiburg and Basel; influenced by W. F. Capito*; court preacher Mainz 1520; pastor Strasbourg 1523; "1st Prot. ch. historian." Works include history of the ancient ch.; hist. of the world to 1543. See also *Reformed Confessions,* D 1.

Hedonism (from Gk. *hedone,* "pleasure"). Ethical hedonism holds that only pleasure (or enjoyment, or happiness) or pleasant states of mind are intrinsically desirable and that only displeasure (pain) or unpleasant states of mind are undesirable. But pleasure is not to be equated with sensory enjoyment. Hedonists are not agreed on a single definition or description of pleasure. Psychological hedonism seeks pleasure in goals to be achieved, pleasant contemplation or thought, or conditioning by pleasant experiences. See also *Aristippus; Epicureanism; Eudaemonism; Sensationalism.*

Hedwig of Anjou. See *Lithuania,* 1.

Heerbrand, Jakob (1521–1600). B. Giengen, Ger.; educ. Tübingen and Wittenberg; deacon Tübingen 1543; deposed 1548 for opposing Interim*; pastor Herrenberg 1550; signed Confessio Virtembergica (see *Lutheran Confessions,* A 5) 1551; one of Christoph* of Württemberg's delegates to Council of Trent 1552; helped reform Baden 1556; prof. Tübingen 1557; resigned 1599. Works include *Compendium theologiae methodi quaestionibus tractatum.*

Heermann, Johann (1585–1647). B. Raudten, Ger.; educ. Fraustadt, Breslau, Brieg; tutor Brieg and Strasbourg; returned to Raudten 1610; pastor Köben 1611; retired to Lissa, Posen, 1638; suffered in Thirty* Years' War, but bore trials with courage and patience; hymnist. Hymns include "Ach Jesu, dessen Treu' "; "Frühmorgens, da die Sonn' aufgeht"; "O Jesu Christe, wahres Licht"; "O Jesu, du mein Bräutigam"; "Herzliebster Jesu, was hast du verbrochen"; "O Gott, du frommer Gott"; "Gottlob, die Stund' ist kommen."

Johann Heermanns geistliche Lieder, ed. P. Wackernagel (Stuttgart, 1856); K. F. Ledderhose, *Christliche Biographien, V: Das Leben Johann Heermann's von Köben* (Heidelberg, 1857).

Hefele, Karl Joseph von (1809–93). B. Unterkocken, Württemberg, Ger.; RC prelate; prof. Tübingen; bp. Rottenburg; opposed doctrine of papal infallibility. Works include *Conciliengeschichte.* See also *Vatican Councils,* 1 b.

Hefenträger (Hefentreger). See *Trygophorus.*

Hegel, Georg Wilhelm Friedrich (1770–1831). 1. Ger. philos.; b. Stuttgart; educ. Tübingen; prof. Jena, Heidelberg, and (1818–31) Berlin.

2. Hegel viewed the task of philos. as comprehending what is, a task that is possible because what is, is reason; the structure of mind and reality is one. Language, the medium of knowledge, is conceptual: words always refer beyond particulars to universals. Since all words are concepts and all concepts are universal terms, it follows that truth is likewise universal; the individual self who grasps this discovers that the process of realization of the content of the universal-as-Spirit is the very process by which Spirit comes to Self-consciousness as the universal Self of Reason. In the attainment of ablsolute knowledge, the Self recognizes its own unity and its objects as Absolute Spirit. Philos. traces the structure of the Absolute (God) by investigating the structure of Idea (Mind) and Nature, which are integral parts of the singular process of the Absolute's Self-manifestation, apart from which there is no Absolute.

3. I. Kant* tried to end inconclusive philos. speculation, but his efforts gave way to absolute idealism. Hegel's philos. was in this stream of idealism.

4. Hegel's entire system rests on the triad Idea-Nature-Spirit. (1) *Idea-in-itself* (God in His eternal essence before Creation of Nature and finite mind) is the dynamic reality that gives rise to all that exists. All existence is the manifestation (actualization) of *Idea-in-itself,* which receives full reality only by being so manifested. In this state God does not yet "exist," but in Creation God passes out of Himself into Nature. (2) *Idea-outside-of-itself* (the antithesis of *Idea-in-itself*) is Creation, the divine manifestation in space as Nature. Essence assumes existence. Logic (thesis) is externalized as Nature (antithesis). The triadic structure of Nature emerges as mechanics, physics, and organics – developing from mineral and vegetable stages to man, in whose consciousness Idea becomes Self-conscious. The highest synthesis of organics is the free ego; Nature passes back into Spirit as mind awakens to the realization of the unity of Idea (logic) and Nature (space) in the free ego (Self), conscious of itself as Spirit. (3) *Idea-in-and-for-itself* (Self-conscious or Spirit) is the antithesis of *Idea-in-itself* and *Idea-outside-of-itself,* whose development in time is history.

5. History, as the Self-developing movement of Spirit, is embedded in a metaphysical flow of universal scope; universal hist. is a dialectical process of actualization of the divine Idea. Hence it is hist., not Nature, that is divine, for hist. is the unfolding of the divine plan, a theodicy. The philos. of Spirit is the emergence of the divine mind as Reason in hist. Tension bet. Spirit and its own hist. phases in world-historical individuals and nations constitutes the dialectic of history. The State as the cultural whole, the totality of all the artistic, pol., economic, moral, and religious ideas and institutions of a people who uniquely express Spirit, is the march of God on earth. Spirit is also the unfolding of mind as Reason in philos., which is the divine Idea knowing itself, and in religion, wherein the Idea-Nature-Spirit triad is seen as the Kingdom of the Father, the Son, and the Holy Ghost. Thus, in this vast dialectical structure of triads and triads-within-triads, God's infinitude is realized by the mind of man.

6. Kant's postulate of the external, unknowable "thing-in-itself" (see *Ding an sich*) was regarded by Hegel as an untenable contradiction in terms, for to say that anything is unknowable and exists is to know something about it, namely that it exists. Hence there is no reason to assume there is anything intrinsically unknowable behind appearances. What appears to us (phenomena) is not an appearance of an underlying, unknowable "thing-in-itself" beyond thought, but Reality itself. Thought and things-processes-events are dialectically interrelated.

7. Hegel found the clue to the nature of reality in the dialectical process by which mind proceeds in its logical operations. Examination shows that our mind fastens upon some idea (thesis) as true; then, in the face of difficulties, the opposite (antithesis) is held to be true. It is subsequently seen that though each alternative taken in abstraction is false, the whole truth is found in a synthesis of the two alternatives that takes up, reconciles, and preserves (aufheben) what is worthwhile and necessary in each partial, contradictory thesis. This synthesis serves as a new thesis for another train of thought ad infinitum; the whole world is enveloped in this dialectical chain until the attainment of the ultimate synthesis: God, or Absolute Spirit.

8. Since what is real in existence is only that which is divine in it, everything else is contingent and must perish. Thus the dialectical process is not only logical and ontological, but also chronological in nature and in significance; the temporal is but an aspect of the eternal in its ontological structure. The eternal Idea is affected by its actualization in the world, for man's spirit (the synthesis of the divine Idea and Nature) makes the indeterminate reality of Idea become determinate in existence. Hence by developing his own consciousness more fully, man makes Idea (the divine mind) more conscious of Himself. This process goes on throughout the course of human generations in the hist. of states and nations. History is thus the progressive Self-determination and Self-development of concrete Idea (Spirit), and the sequence of hist. events is both temporal (as Self-development of Spirit) and logical (as Self-devel-

opment of Idea). Temporal process thus follows dialectically after the logical process of *Idea-in-itself* (*God*) and *Idea-outside-of-itself* (spatial Nature). Since Spirit, or the synthesis of Idea and Nature, is in essence free, hist. is the progress of freedom, the development of Spirit in time. Real freedom is found neither in anarchy nor in despotism, but in that which accepts the limitations imposed by reasonable law; real law is that which is accepted by its subjects as what they will because it is seen to be reasonable. Thus hist. is not a mere catalog of events (some good, some evil), but the dialectical unfolding of the nature of Mind or Spirit in which one-sided principles conflict with their contradictories and are reconciled in a solution that does justice to both. Universal Reason, acting through men (citizens, persons, heroes, victims), thus providently shapes history.

9. Aside from the impetus his thought gave to historicism, Romanticism, and later absolute idealism, as well as the reaction of Kierkegaardian existentialism,* 3 streams may be noted as arising in Hegel's thought: (1) K. H. Marx* used Hegel's dialectical method, in union with a dynamic of economic determinism and the materialism of P. H. D. Holbach,* to formulate a scientific system of dialectical materialism, the revolutionary "Hegelian Left" of communism (see *Socialism*); (2) Hegel's conservatism (what is logically must be, and is both rational and right) was adopted by the authoritarian voices of the "Hegelian Right" of fascism (see *Socialism,* 3); J. Dewey's* philos. is largely a tr. of Hegel's method into terms of experimental science deemed necessary in the modern industrialized, urbanized, and democratized order, a philos. in which dualisms of all sorts are "overcome" in the unity of "experience" and "nature." Dewey replaces the notion of Absolute Mind with that of Society and naturalizes Hegel's thought in light of Darwinism.

Works include *Phänomenologie des Geistes; Wissenschaft der Logik; Enzyklopädie der philosophischen Wissenschaften im Grundrisse; Grundlinien der Philosophie des Rechts; Vorlesungen über die Philosophie der Geschichte; Vorlesungen über die Geschichte der Philosophie.* RVS

See also *Dualism; Lutheran Theology After 1580,* 10; *Monism; Philosophy.*

J. N. Findley, *Hegel: A Re-examination* (London, 1958); W. T. Stace, *The Philosophy of Hegel* (London, 1924); F. Wiedmann, *Hegel,* tr. J. Neugroschel (New York, 1968).

Hegelund, Peder Jensen (1542–1614). B. Ribe, Den.; exponent of Philippism (see *Philippists*); bp. Ribe; fostered schools.

Hegesippus. Probably a Hellenistic Jew who visited Rome bet. 155 and 189 AD; wrote *Memoirs* (Gk. *Hypomnemata*) as refutation of gnosticism*; fragments of it survive in Eusebius* of Caesarea, *HE.*

Hegira (from Arab. *hijrah,* "flight"). Flight of Muhammad* from Mecca to Medina 622 AD. Adherents of Islam* date their 354- or 355-day yrs. from this event.

Hegius, Alexander (ca. 1433–98). B. near Ahaus, Ger.; humanist; opposed Scholasticism*; taught in Wesel, Emmerich, Deventer; pupils included D. Erasmus.*

Hegler, Alfred (1863–1902). B. Stuttgart, Ger.; ch. hist.; taught at Tübingen. Works include *Geist und Schrift by Sebastian Franck: Eine Studie zur Geschichte des Spiritualismus in der Reformationszeit; Beiträge zur Geschichte der Mystik in der Reformationszeit; Die Psychologie in Kants Ethik.*

Hegumen (from Gk. *hegoumenos,* "leader"). Leader of monastery in E Ch.

Heiberg, Johan Alfred (1848–1936). B. Copenhagen, Den.; educ. Copenhagen; to Am. 1873; pastor Chicago, Ill., 1873–79; pres. The Dan. Ev. Luth. Ch. in Am. 1874–79; returned to Den. 1879. See also *Danish Lutherans in America,* 3, 4.

Heidanus (van der Heyden). 1. *Abraham* (1597–1678). B. Frankenthal, Ger.; prof. Leiden; held modified form of federal* theol. of J. Cocceius.* 2. *Caspar* (1530–86). Calvinist theol.; active in Antwerp, Frankfurt am Main, Frankenthal, Middelburg, and Bacharach; with P. v. Marnix* helped form Ref. syns. in Neth. and W Ger.

Heidegger, Johann Heinrich (1633–98). Prof. Heidelberg, Steinfurth, Zurich. Combined federal* theol. of J. Cocceius* with Ref. orthodoxy. See also *Reformed Confessions,* A 10.

Heidegger, Martin. See *Existentialism.*

Heidelberg Catechism. See *Reformed Confessions,* D 2.

Heidelberg Conference. See *Erastus, Thomas.*

Heidelberg Disputation (Heidelberg Meeting). Discussion, arranged by J. v. Staupitz,* at a meeting of the Gen. Chap. of the Augustinian Order held at Heidelberg, Ger., Apr. 1518. Opponents of M. Luther* hoped to silence him at this meeting. But Staupitz tried to give Luther's position a fair hearing. In his theses Luther opposed the *theologia gloriae* of W. of Ockham* with his own *theologia* crucis,* the philos. of Aristotle* with the theol. of Paul.

Heidelberg Polyglot. See *Polyglot Bibles.*

Heilbrunner, Jakob (1548–1618). Luth. theol.; exponent of the Book of Concord; court preacher of the duke of Zweibrücken. Wrote many polemical works against the Ref. and Jesuits.

Heiling, Peter. See *Africa,* E 2.

Heilsgeschichte (Ger. "hist. of salvation"). God's activity on behalf of man, understood on the one hand as salvation and grace, and on the other as its effect on man's spiritual development. In its larger sense the term refers to the unfolding of God's entire plan of salvation for man, from creation* to the hereafter.* OT prophecies and NT fulfillments are important in the basis for the theol. method of exponents of Heilsgeschichte. Recapitulation* formed the basis of the conception of Irenaeus.* The covenant approach is prominent in federal* theol. Augustine* of Hippo, Joachim* of Floris, and J. Cocceius* are also prominent in the hist. of Heilsgeschichte as a concept.

Heim, Karl (1874–1958). Luth. theol.; b. Frauenzimmern, Ger.; prof. Münster 1914, Tübingen 1920; influenced by Swabian pietism of J. A. Bengel,* F. C. Oetinger,* J. C. Blumhardt (see *Blumhardt,* 2), L. Hofacker.* Tried to present Gospel on scientific-philos. level and lead thought to choose bet. skepticism and despair or faith.

Heimonen, Juho. See *Canada,* A 15.

Hein, Carl Christian (Aug. 31, 1868–Apr. 30, 1937). B. Wiesbaden, Ger.; to US 1884; educ. Capital U. and Sem., Columbus, Ohio; pastor Marion, Wis., 1889–91, Detroit, Mich., 1891–1902, Columbus, Ohio, 1902–25; elected pres. Ev. Luth. Joint Syn. of Ohio* and Other States 1924, ALC 1930; active in LWC.

Hein, Johannes. See *Cassel, Colloquy of.*

Heine, Heinrich (originally Chaim Harry; 1797 [or 1799]–1856). Poet and critic; b. Düsseldorf, Ger.; of Jewish descent; Prot. 1825; moved to Paris 1831; d. there after ca. 8 yrs. disability; attacked religious order; preached "the rehabilitation of the flesh"; in later yrs. tempered his cynicism.

Heinemann, Barbara. See *Amana Society.*

Heinemann, Isaak (1876–1957). B. Frankfurt am Main, Ger.; lecturer Jewish theol. sem., Breslau, 1919–39; honorary prof. Breslau U. 1930–33; prof. Heb. U., Jerusalem, 1939. Ed. *Monatsschrift für die Geschichte und Wissenschaft des Judentums;* other works include *Altjüdische Allegoristik; Philons griechische und jüdische Bildung.*

Heinrich II (The Younger). See *John Frederick.*

Heinrich von Nördlingen. See *Henry of Nördlingen.*

Heinrich von Zütphen. See *Henry of Zutphen.*

Heinrici, Carl Friedrich Georg (1844–1915). Prot. theol.; b. Karkeln, E Prussia; educ. Halle and Berlin; prof. Marburg and Leipzig; interested esp. in the influence of Hellenism on early Christianity. Works include *Theologische Enzyklopädie; Hellenismus und Christentum.*

Heintz, Philipp Casimir (1771–1835). B. Konken, near Kusel, Ger.; Prot. pastor Zweibrücken and Munich; exponent of palatine union; historian of Palatinate.

Heintze, Richard William (Nov. 11, 1868–Mar. 23, 1937). B. Berlin, Ger.; educ. Conc. Sem., St. Louis, Mo.; pastor W. Hoboken, N. J., 1890–94; prof. Conc. Collegiate Institute, Bronxville, N. Y., 1894–1926; librarian Conc. Sem., St. Louis, 1926–36.

Heintzen, Erich Hugo (Feb. 17, 1908–Sept. 27, 1971). B. New Orleans, La.; educ. Conc. Sem., St. Louis, Mo.; ordained 1934; pastor Coal Valley, Ill., 1934; student pastor U of Ill., Champaign, 1941; prof. Conc. Sem., Springfield, Ill., 1958. Works include *With This Ring; Practical Christianity; Were You There?*

Heinzelmann, Gerhard (1884–1951). B. Coswig, Ger.; prof. Basel 1918, Halle 1931. Works include *Animismus und Religion; Philipperbrief.*

Heitmüller, Wilhelm (1869–1926). NT scholar; b. Döteberg, Ger.; taught at Göttingen, Marburg, Bonn, Tübingen; leader of Religionsgeschichtliche* Schule. Works include *Das Johannesevangelium; Taufe und Abendmahl bei Paulus; Taufe und Abendmahl im Urchristentum.*

Hejaz, Kingdom of (Hedjaz). *Area:* 150,000 sq. mi.; *pop.* (1965 est.): 2,000,000. Formerly part of Turkish Empire; indep. since June 1916; part of Saudi Arabia (see *Middle East,* L 1) since 1925/26. Contains chief Islamic sacred cities, Mecca (capital of Hejaz and Saudi Arabia) and Medina; Islam* is prevailing religion.

Held, Heinrich (1620–59). B. Guhrau, Silesia; educ. Königsberg, Frankfurt an der Oder, and Leiden; lawyer at Rostock, Guhrau, and Altdamm; hymnist. Hymns include "Gott sei Dank durch alle Welt"; "Komm, o komm, du Geist des Lebens."

Held, Heinrich (1897–1957). B. Saarbrücken, Ger.; pastor Essen-Rüttenscheid; cofounder Bekennende Kirche in Rhineland; also active in Bekennende Kirche der Altpreussischen Union; often imprisoned; pres. Ev. Ch. in Rhineland. See also *Kirchenkampf.*

Helder, Bartholomaeus (ca. 1585–1635). B. Gotha, Ger.; schoolmaster Friemar, near Gotha, 1607; pastor Remstädt, near Gotha, 1616; hymnist; composer. Works include *Cymbalum Genethliacum; Cymbalum Davidicum;* hymns include "O Lämmlein Gottes, Jesu Christ."

Helding, Michael (Michael von Merseburg; Sidonius; 1506–61). RC theol.; b. Langenenslingen, Hohenzollern, Ger.; titular bp. Sidon; bp. Merseburg 1549; active at Council of Trent*; noted for efforts in behalf of Augsburg Interim*; writings opposed by M. Flacius* Illyricus and J. Wigand.*

Heldring, Otto Gerhard(t) (1804–76). B. Zevenaar, Neth.; pastor Holland; leader in Awakening* and Inner* Mission.

Helena (b. perhaps as early as 247 or as late as 260 AD; d. at the age of ca. 80). Mother of Constantine* I. See also *Pilgrimages,* 1.

Helgason, Arni (1777–1869). Pastor Gardar, Iceland; rationalist of Enlightenment.*

Helgason, Jon (1866–1942). B. Gardar, Iceland; Luth. liberal theol.; educ. Copenhagen and in Ger.; taught theol. at Rejkjavík sem. 1894–1908; pres. of sem. 1908–10; prof. theol. U. of Iceland 1910; bp. Iceland 1917–38. Works include a gen. ch. hist. and a ch. hist. of Iceland.

Helgesen, Poul. See *Denmark, Lutheranism in,* 1.

Heliand ("Savior"; OE *haeland;* Ger. *Heiland*). 9th c. poetic presentation of the life of Christ in ca. 6,000 lines based on pseudo-Tatian's harmony of the Gospels; depicts Christ as a Germanic chief and the apostles as warriors; acc. to tradition, Louis* I commanded that the poem be written.

Hell. See *Hereafter,* B, C.

Hellinck, Joannes Lupus (Hellingk; ca. 1495–1541). B. Brugge, Belg.; priest; composer. Works include masses and Ger. sacred songs.

Hellmund, Egidius Günther (1678–1749). Pietistic theol.; b. Nordhausen, Ger.; educ. Jena and Halle; pupil and friend of A. H. Francke*; pastor Daaden 1708, Wetzlar 1711; involved in controversies with orthodox pastors because of his conventicles; est. orphanage at Wiesbaden; tried to create pietistic image of M. Luther* for laity. See also *Pietism.*

Helmbold, Ludwig (1532–98). "The Ger. Asaph"; theol.; hymnist; b. Mühlhausen, Thuringia; educ. Leipzig and Erfurt; lecturer Erfurt U.; crowned poet laureate 1566; became deacon 1571, pastor and supt. Mühlhausen 1586. Wrote metrical version of AC; hymns include "Herr Gott, erhalt uns für und für"; "Von Gott will ich nicht lassen"; "Ihr Eltern, hört, was Christus spricht."

Helmholtz, Hermann Ludwig Ferdinand von. See *Psychology,* G 3.

Helmold (ca. 1120–after 1177). B. Harz region, Ger.; pastor Bosau; his *Chronica Slavorum* is source material on Christianizing of E Holstein.

Helmont, Jan Baptista van (1577–1644). B. Brussels, Belg.; educ. Louvain; RC physician, scientist, philos., mystic; followed P. A. Paracelsus*; later made significant contributions in areas of psychol., physiol., and chemistry; rejected pantheism* for personal God; held interaction of spiritual and material.

Helmore, Thomas (1811–90). B. Kidderminster, Eng.; cleric; musical theorist. Works include *A Manual of Plain Song.*

Helmuth, Justus Henry Christian (May 16, 1745–Feb. 5, 1825). Luth. cleric; b. Helmstedt, Ger.; educ. Halle; influenced by G. A. Francke*; to Philadelphia, Pa., Apr. 1769; pastor Lancaster 1769–79, Philadelphia 1779–1820; trained J. Goering,* J. G. Butler,* F. L. Endress,* J. G. Lochman,* J. G. Schmucker,* S. S. Schmucker,* J. Steck*; noted for pastoral care during yellow fever epidemic 1793. Founded *Evangelisches Magazin;* other works include *Empfindungen des Herzens in einigen Liedern; Denkmal der Liebe und Achtung, welches seiner Hochwürden dem Herrn D. Heinrich Melchior Mühlenberg . . . ist gesetzet worden; Betrachtung der Evangelischen Lehre von der Heiligen Schrift und Taufe; Kurze Nachricht von dem sogenannten Gelben Fieber in Philadelphia; Kurze Andachten einer Gottsuchenden Seele; Plan einer Anstalt zur Erziehung der Jungen Prediger; Etliche Kirchenlieder.*

Help for Brazil Mission. Organized by Robert Reid Kalley (1809–88; Brit. miss.), who arrived in Brazil 1855; joined the Evangelical* Union of S. Am. 1913.

Heltai, Kaspar (Helth; Caspar; Gaspar; ca. 1500 [some think as late as ca. 1520]–ca. 1574). Reformer in Klausenburg; b. probably Heltau, Transylvania; educ. Wittenberg; first followed M. Luther* and P. Melanchthon,* later J. Calvin,* then Socinianism.* Works include Bible, catechism, poems, and theol. writings in Hungarian.

Helt, Georg (ca. 1485–1545). B. Forchheim, Ger.; advisor of George* III of Anhalt; present at the Feb. 1537 meeting of the Schmalkaldic League at Schmalkalden; signed SA and Tractatus (see *Lutheran Confessions,* B 2).

Helveg, Thorvald (1855–1917). B. Den.; educ. Copenhagen; pastor Neenah, Wis., 1881, West Denmark, Wis., 1887; pres. The Dan. Ev. Luth. Ch. in Am. (see *Danish Lutherans in America,* 3) 1883–85; pres. West Denmark Sem. 1887; returned to Den. 1895.

Helvetic Confessions. See *Reformed Confessions,* A 6.

Helvetic Consensus Formula. See *Reformed Confessions,* A 10.

Helvidius (4th c. AD). Lat. lay theol.; denied perpetual virginity of Mary ca. 380; Jerome* replied ca. 383.

MPL, 23, 193–216.

Helwys, Thomas. See *Baptist Churches,* 2.

Hemerobaptists (from Gk. *hemera,* "day," and *baptistes,* "baptizer"). Jewish sect named after its practice of daily ablution. Epiphanius* (*Panarion* i 17) describes them as similar to the Pharisees in gen. doctrine, but different from them, and like the Sadducees, in denying the resurrection. Mentioned by Hegesippus* (in Eusebius* of Caesarea, *HE,* IV, xxii, 6) and Justin* Martyr (*Dialogue with Trypho the Jew* 80). John the Baptist is called a Hemerobaptist in *Clementine Homilies* ii 23 (see *Clementines*).

Hemmerli(n), Felix (Lat. Malleolus; ca. 1388–ca. 1458). B. Zurich, Switz.; educ. Erfurt and Bologna; doctor of canon law 1424; worked for reform at Councils of Constance* and Basel*; opposed celibacy* and mendicancy (see *Mendicant Monks*); castigated immorality of clergy; advocated decreasing of feast days.

Hemmeter, Henry Bernard (Dec. 24, 1869–July 22, 1948). B. Baltimore, Md.; educ. Conc. Sem., St. Louis, Mo.; pastor Baltimore 1892–95, Pittsburgh, Pa., 1895–1902; prof. Conc. Coll., Conover, N. C., 1902–05; pastor Pittsburgh 1905–08, St. Louis 1908–14; pres. Conc. Coll., Conover, 1914–18, 1928–35; pastor Rochester, N. Y., 1918–28; pres. Conc. Sem., Springfield, Ill., 1936–45.

Hemming(sen), Niels (Nicolaus Hemmingii; 1513–1600). Dan. theol.; b. Errindlev, on the is. of Lolland; educ. Roskilde, Den., and Wittenberg, Ger.; follower of P. Melanchthon*; prof. U. of Copenhagen; accused of Crypto-Calvinism (see *Crypto-Calvinistic Controversy*); dismissed from the U. 1579; canon Roskilde. See also *Denmark, Lutheranism in,* 4.

Henderson, Alexander (ca. 1583–1646). B. Criech, Fifeshire, Scot.; educ. St. Andrews; leader of Scot. Presbyterians against Anglicans; leader at Westminster* Assembly; drafted Solemn League and Covenant (see *Presbyterian Confessions,* 1) for Eng. Covenant (see *Presbyterian Confessions,* 1) for Eng. and Scot. Directory* for the Public Worship of God.

J. Aiton, *The Life and Times of Alexander Henderson* (Edinburgh, 1836).

Hendrik van Zutphen. See *Henry of Zutphen.*

Henetus, Theodor. See *Flacius Illyricus, Matthias.*

Hengstenberg, Ernst Wilhelm (1802–69). B. Fröndenberg, Westphalia, Ger.; son of Ref. pastor; educ. Bonn; tutor in Basel 1823; privatdocent Berlin 1824, licentiate of theol. 1825, extraordinary prof. 1826, prof. 1828; through private study found Christ in Bible; became Luth.; opposed rationalism,* unionism,* and mediating* theol. Founded *Evangelische Kirchen-Zeitung* 1827; other works include *Christologie des Alten Testaments und Commentar über die Messianischen Weissagungen der Propheten; Beiträge zur Einleitung ins Alte Testament; Das Evangelium des heiligen Johannes; Die Offenbarung des heiligen Johannes; Commentar über die Psalmen.* See also *Vatke, Johann Karl Wilhelm.*

Ernst Wilhelm Hengstenberg, vols. 1–2 by J. F. J. Bachmann, vol. 3 by T. Schmalenbach (Gütersloh, 1876–92).

Henhöfer, Aloys (Alois; Henhoefer; 1789–1862). B. Völkersbach, near Karlsruhe, Ger., of RC parents; educ. Freiburg and Meersburg; priest; read M. Boos* and Scripture; began preaching justification by faith; excommunicated; joined Ev. Ch. 1823; exerted beneficial influence in Baden.

Henke, Heinrich Philipp Konrad (1752–1809). B. Hehlen, Brunswick, Ger.; educ. Helmstedt; prof. Helmstedt; rationalist; saw divinity and deeds of God in human hist. of Christ; held that doctrinal development in early cents. was perversion of primitive faith.

Henkel, Wilhelm Friedrich (July 2, 1868–July 5, 1929). B. Brandenburg, Ger.; to Am. 1882; educ. Watertown and Milwaukee, Wis.; pastor Wauwatosa, Maple Creek, and Morrison, Wis.; prof. Watertown 1912–20, Wauwatosa 1920–29.

Henkelites. See *General Synod of the Evangelical Lutheran Church in the United States of America, The,* 7.

Henkels, The. 1. This family, which gave a large number of pastors and educators to Am. Lutheranism, descended from Anthony Jacob Henkel (Henckel; formerly known as Gerhard, Gerhardt, or Gerhart), perhaps a descendant of the Henckel von Donnersmarck family. A Johann Henkel was chaplain to Mary* of Hung., who selected him on recommendation of M. Luther* ca. 1526; he was present with Mary at the Diet of Augsburg 1530 (see *Lutheran Confessions,* A). Count Erdman Henkel, a pious Luth., was a benefactor of the Halle institution of A. H. Francke*; helped H. M. Mühlenberg,* who is said to have been a blood relative of the Henkels.

Anthony Jacob Henkel (Henckel; 1663–1728). B. Me(h)renberg, Nassau, Ger.; educ. Giessen; ordained 1692; to Am. 1717 with his family and others; helped form a colony at New Hanover (also known as Falckner's Swamp), now in Montgomery Co., Pa.; pastor there; also served Luths. at Philadelphia and elsewhere; fatally injured in fall from horse Aug. 12, 1728.

2. Jacob Henkel (Mar. 14, 1733–Feb. 14, 1779), son of John (or Johann) Justus Sr. (Feb. 10, 1706–Aug. 1778; son of Anthony Jacob), was the father of Paul, Benjamin (ca. 1765–Feb. 4, 1794), Isaac (b. ca. 1767), Joseph (b. ca. 1770), John (ca. May 21, 1774–Dec. 30, 1803), all of whom became Luth. ministers, and of Moses (Sept. 18, 1757–July 28, 1827), who became a Meth. minister. Paul (Dec. 15, 1754–Nov. 27, 1825), b. near Salisbury, N. C., was educ. by J. A. Krug* and C. Streit*; licensed 1783 by Ministerium of Pa. (see *United Lutheran Church, Synods of,* 22); ordained 1792 by same body; active in areas including Va., N. C., S. C., Ky., Tenn., and Ohio; helped organize N. C. Syn. 1803, Ger. Ev. Luth. Ministerium in Ohio and the Neighboring States 1818, and Ev. Luth. Tenn. Syn. 1820 (see *United Lutheran Church, Synods of,* 16); fostered theol. studies of his brothers and sons; encouraged sons Solomon and Ambrose to est. a printery at New Market, Va. The Book of Concord was pub. in Eng. by the Henkel press 1851.

3. Solomon Henkel (Nov. 10, 1777–Aug. 31, 1847), Philip Augustus Henkel (Sept. 23, 1779–Oct. 9, 1833), Ambrose Henkel (July 11, 1786–Jan. 6, 1870), Andrew Henkel (Oct. 21, 1790–Apr. 23, 1870), David Henkel (May 4, 1795–June 15, 1831), and Charles Henkel (May 17 [or 18], 1798–Feb. 2, 1841), sons of Paul Henkel, became Luth. ministers, except Solomon, who was a doctor and main organizer, later owner, of the printery. Philip, b. Hampshire, Va., pastor N. C., opened a sem. 1817 which was short-lived; helped organize Ev. Luth. Tenn. Syn. (see *United Luth. Church, Synods of,* 16). David, b. Staunton, Va., gen. regarded as the most gifted

mem. of the Henkel family, was pastor N. C.; his miss. journeys extended into Ky. and Indiana. Andrew and Charles were pastors in Ohio; Charles tr. AC into Eng. in the early 1830s. Ambrose learned the printing trade as a young man; one of the founders of the Henkel Press ca. 1805; its first publisher and ed.; tr. SC into English. Polycarp C. Henkel (Aug. 23, 1820–Sept. 29, 1889), b. near Conover, N. C., son of David, was pastor in N. C. and at Gravelton, Mo.; 1st pres. Concordia* Coll., Conover. Socrates Henkel (Mar. 22, 1823–June 20, 1901), b. near Conover, N. C., son of David; was Tenn. Syn. pastor New Market, Va., 1850–95; prominent in connection with pub. of Luth. books. Eusebius Schultz Henkel (July 26, 1811–Dec. 17, 1874), b. near Lincolnton, Lincoln Co., N. C., son of Philip Augustus, was ordained 1831; mem. Tenn. Syn.; settled in Ind.; traveling miss.; helped organize Indiana* Syn. (I); helped form Union* Syn. of the Evangelic Luth. Ch. and became its pres. 1860.

The Henckel Family Records, ed. E. O. Henkel (New Market, Va., 1926–39); *The Henckel Genealogy, 1500–1960: Ancestry and Descendants of Reverend Anthony Jacob Henckel,* comp. W. S. Junkin and M. W. Junkin (Spokane, Wash., 1964); *The Henkel Memorial,* ed. A. Stapleton and E. O. Henkel (York, Pa., and New Market, Va., 1910–19); *History of the Lutheran Church in Virginia and East Tennessee,* ed. C. W. Cassell, W. J. Finck, and E. O. Henkel (Strasburg, Va., 1930); B. H. Pershing, "Paul Henkel: Frontier Missionary, Organizer, and Author," *Lutheran Church Quarterly,* VII (Apr. 1934), 125–151, also in *CHIQ,* VII (Jan. 1935), 97–120; W. J. Finck, "Paul Henkel, the Lutheran Pioneer," *LQ,* LVI (July 1926), 307–334; T. Graebner, "Diary of Paul Henkel," *CHIQ,* I (Apr. 1928), 16–20 (July 1928), 43–47, and "Paul Henkel, an American Lutheran Pioneer in Missions, Organization, and Publicity," *CHIQ,* V (July 1932), 58–63; W. E. Eisenberg, *The Lutheran Church in Virginia, 1717–1926* (Roanoke, Va., 1967). HGC

Hennepin, Louis (bap. Johannes; 1640–ca. 1701). B. Ath, Belg.; Fr. RC explorer and miss.; accompanied Robert Cavalier de La Salle (1643–87; Fr. explorer) to Can. 1675; traversed Great Lakes region; explored Upper Mississippi region; returned to Fr. 1682.

Henotheism (from Gk. *heis, henos,* "one," and *theos,* "God"). Term coined by F. M. Müller* (who used it as a synonym for kathenotheism*) to designate a sort of monotheistic polytheism* that recognizes the existence of many gods, but emphasizes the worship of one of them. See also *Monolatry.*

Henoticon (Gk. "instrument of union"). Formula probably drawn up by Acacius* of Constantinople; issued 482 by Emp. Zeno(n)* in unsuccessful attempt to settle the Monophysite* controversy.

Henricians. Followers of Henry* of Lausanne.

Henry. Eng. form of Ger. Heinrich.

Henry (Heinrich; 1473–1541). "The Pious." Duke of Albertine Saxony 1539–41; b. Dresden, Ger.; brother of George* the Bearded; introd. the Reformation in Freiberg ca. 1536, Albertine Saxony 1539.

Henry I (Heinrich; ca. 876–936). "The Fowler." Duke of Saxony 912–936; king of Ger. 919–936; reckoned as Holy Roman Emp. but never crowned as such.

Henry II (1133–89). Called Curtmantle because of his short mantle. King of Eng. 1154–89. Convened the council 1164 that adopted the Constitutions of Clarendon.* Engaged in controversy with Thomas à Becket.* See also *Popes,* 9.

Henry II (of Fr.). See *France,* 8.

Henry III (of Fr.). See *Poland,* 3.

Henry IV (Henry of Navarre; Henri de Navarre; Henry the Great; 1553–1610). King of Navarre as Henry III 1572–89; king of Fr. 1589–1610, 1st of Bourbon line; brought up as Calvinist; joined Huguenots* in religious war 1568–70; ended war with Holy League (see *Holy League,* 3) by renouncing Protestantism for RCm 1593; signed Edict of Nantes* 1598. See also *France,* 9, 10.

Henry IV (1050–1106). King of Ger. and Holy Roman emp. 1056–1106; engaged with Gregory VII (see *Popes,* 7) in struggle about investiture*; excommunicated and declared deposed by Gregory 1076; absolved after penance at Canossa 1077; excommunicated again 1080; declared Gregory deposed; crowned emp. 1084 by Clement III (Guibert, or Wibert, of Ravenna; ca. 1030–1100; b. Parma, It.; antipope 1080–1100).

Henry VIII (1491–1547). Tudor king of Eng. (1509–47); joined Holy League against Fr. 1511; appointed T. Wolsey* lord chancellor 1515; received title "Defender of the Faith" from pope 1521 for *Assertio septem sacramentorum,* directed against M. Luther*; in conflict with pope because latter refused to grant him divorce from Catherine of Aragon; dismissed Wolsey 1529; appointed T. More* chancellor 1529; secured from Parliament the Act of Supremacy 1534 (see *Church and State,* 9), creating a nat. ch. with king as head; closed monasteries and confiscated their property. See also *Anglican Confessions,* 1; *Clement VII,* 2; *England,* B 1–4; *Holy Leagues and Alliance,* 3; *King's Book, The; Luther Controversies of,* c.

Henry, Matthew (1662–1714). B. Broad Oak, Flintshire, Wales; Presb. pastor at Chester and Hackney; nonconformist. Works include *An Exposition of the Old and New Testament* (his work to Acts inclusive).

Henry Henderson Institute. See *Africa,* B 2.

Henry of Ahaus (Heinrich von Ahaus; ca. 1369–1439). B. Schöppingen, near Ahaus, Ger.; cathedral vicar Münster; est. Brethren* of the Common Life in W Ger.

Henry of Blois (d. 1171). Son of Stephen, count of Blois; abbot Glastonbury 1126; bp. Winchester 1129; founded hospital of St. Cross at Winchester; friend of Peter* the Venerable, T. à Becket,* John* of Salisbury.

Henry of Ghent (Henricus de Gandavo; ca. 1217–93). "Doctor solemnis; Summus doctorum; Doctor reverendus; Doctor digressivus." B. probably near Ghent, Neth.; scholastic philos.; canon Tournai 1267; archdeacon Bruges (Brugge) 1276, Tournai 1278; taught theol. at Paris. Works include *Quodlibeta; Summa theologica* (unfinished).

Henry of Langenstein (Henry of Hesse the elder; ca. 1325 [some say 1340]–1397). "Doctor conscientiosus." B. perhaps Hainbach, near Langenstein, Hesse; outstanding scholar; lectured on nominalist philos. at Paris 1363; supported council over pope (see *Councils and Synods,* 7); driven from Paris; became mystic-ascetic writer and defender of papacy; prof. Vienna 1384. Wrote encyclopedic, soc., exegetic, and dogmatic works.

Henry of Laufenberg (ca. 1390–1460). B. probably Laufenburg, Ger. or Switz.; priest; musician; outstanding hymnist.

Henry of Lausanne (12th c.). Inveighed first in Lausanne and Le Mans, later in Albi and Toulouse, Fr., against corruption and abuses in the ch.; denied original sin; emphasized personal responsibility and simple, ev. life; promoted teachings of Pierre de Bruys*; arrested twice; followers called Henricians.

Henry of Livonia (Heinrich von Lettland; Henricus de Lettis; d. 1529 or later). Priest at Papendorf, NE of Riga; missionary in N Livonia. Wrote *Chronicon Livoniae,* important source for Baltic hist.

Henry of Navarre. See *Henry IV* (of Fr.).

Henry of Nördlingen (d. 1379). B. perhaps Nördlingen, Ger.; secular priest; preacher; leader of Friends* of God: at Basel 1339–49; assoc. with J.

Tauler* and Rulman* Merswin. Tr. of Mechthild* of Magdeburg's *Das fliessende Licht der Gottheit* from Low Ger. into High Ger. ascribed to him; noted for correspondence with M. Ebner.*

Henry of Susa (Heinrich von Segusia; b. before 1200; d. ca. 1271). B. Susa (ancient Segusia, or Segusio), It.; studied law at Bologna; taught at Paris, Fr.; abp. Embrun, Fr., 1250; cardinal-bp. Ostia, It., ca. 1262.

Henry of Valois (king of Poland). See *Poland,* 3.

Henry of Zutphen (Hendrik van Zutphen; Heinrich von Zütphen; [Moller? Muller? Müller?]; Henricus Zutphaniensis; Supphenus; 1488–1524). Early Luth. martyr.* Augustinian monk; studied at Wittenberg 1508; lived in same monastery bldg. as M. Luther*; prior Augustinian monastery Dort 1516; went to Wittenberg 1520; prior Antwerp 1522; imprisoned 1522; forcibly freed by the people; to Bremen Nov. 1522; captured and burned at Meldorf, Dithmarschen, Dec. 11.

Henry Suso. See *Suso, Heinrich.*

Henschen, Gottfried. See *Bolland, Jean de.*

Hensel, Luise (1798–1876). B. Linum, Brandenburg, Ger.; daughter of a Prot. pastor; poet; became RC 1818. Hymns include "Immer muss ich wieder lesen" (1815); "Müde bin ich, geh' zur Ruh'" (1816).

Hensman, Charles John Grace (1862–1938). Organized The Berean Band. See also *Bereans,* 2.

Heortology (from Gk. *heorte,* "feast"). Science of the feasts and festivals of the Christian Ch.; concerned with origin, meaning, observance, and hist. of festivals and seasons of the church* year.

Hephaestus. See *Greek Religion,* 2.

Hephzibah Faith Missionary Association. See *Evangelistic Associations,* 8; *Holiness Churches,* 2.

Heppe, Heinrich Ludwig Julius (1820–79). B. Kassel, Ger.; prof. Marburg; upheld a "Melanchthonian" Ref. theol. as proper heritage of Hesse in opposition to A. F. C. Vilmar's* confessional Lutheranism; follower of F. D. E. Schleiermacher.*

Hera. See *Greek Religion,* 2.

Heracleon. See *Gnosticism,* 7 g.

Heraclides, Jacob Basilicus (ca. 1520–63). Probably of Gk. ancestry; scholar and adventurer; failed in effort to introd. Reformation in Moldavia.

Heraclitus (ca. 540–ca. 470 BC). "The Obscure; the Weeping Philosopher." B. probably Ephesus; metaphysician; held that the world order is an eternal changing fire; *panta rhei* (Gk. "all things flow"). See also *Dialectic; Philosophy; Time.*

Heraclius (ca. 575–641). B. Cappadocia; E Roman emp. 610–641; defeated by Persians who took Syria 613–614, Palestine 615, Egypt 616; Constantinople besieged. Defeated Persians 623–628; lost Syria, Palestine, Mesopotamia, and Egypt to Mohammedans 635–641. His efforts for reform were opposed by nobles and the ch. See also *Ecthesis;* Serbia.

Herbart, Johann Friedrich (1776–1841). B. Oldenburg, Ger.; educ. Jena; tutor Interlaken, Switz.; prof. Königsberg and Göttingen; developed and systematized J. H. Pestalozzi's* idea of "psychologizing" education. Held that the end and aim of education is to develop moral character. Character depends on knowledge; ideas act as forces; will, desire, interest, and feeling are grounded in intellectual activity; content of the mind largely regulates behavior; hence the teacher's duty to supply dominant thoughts and ideas in educative instruction. Absorption and reflection make the mind many-sided; necessary steps: clearness, association, system, method; "clearness" was later divided into "preparation" and "presentation" and "system" and "method" were renamed "generalization" and "application"; this resulted in "Five Formal Steps." In these steps the teacher first prepares the pupil by recalling such ideas as will make the mind receptive for new material, which is then presented; new material is assoc. with other ideas that may suggest themselves; then gen. conceptions are formed and applied. Works include *Allgemeine Pädagogik; Psychologische Untersuchungen.*

Herberger, Valerius (1562–1627). B. Fraustadt, Poland; educ. Frankfurt an der Oder and Leipzig; asst., later pastor Fraustadt; called "the little Luther" because of his outstanding preaching; hymnist. Works include *Evangelische Herz-Postille;* hymns include "Valet will ich dir geben," an acrostic on his given name.

Herbert, Edward (ca. 1583–1648). B. Eyton-on-Severn, Eng.; brother of G. Herbert*; educ. Oxford; 1st Baron Herbert of Cherbury; diplomat, soldier, hist., philos. Held that there are 5 innate religious Common Notions: there is a God; He ought to be worshiped; virtue and piety are essential to worship; man should repent of his sins; there are rewards and punishments in this life and in the future life. Works include *De veritate; De causis errorum; De religione gentilium.* See also *Deism,* III 1.

Herbert, George (1593–1633). B. Montgomery, Wales; brother of E. Herbert*; educ. Westminster School and Cambridge; rector Fugglestone and Bemerton; devotional poet; main theme was metaphysical love and glorification of God. Works include *The Temple: Sacred Poems and Private Ejaculations; A Priest to the Temple.*

Herbert, Peter (Petrus Hubertus; ca. 1535–71). B. Fulneck, Moravia; hymnist. Hymns include "Die Nacht ist kommen."

Herbst, Hans (ca. 1470–1540). City magistrate Schwabach, Ger.; active in Reformation of Franconia.

Herder, Johann Gottfried von (1744–1803). B. Mohrungen, E Prussia; critic, philos., educ., and preacher; gen. supt., court preacher, and pres. of high consistory Weimar; raised to the rank of a noble ca. 1802; influenced by I. Kant* (his teacher) and J. G. Hamann*; influenced J. W. v. Goethe,* J. P. F. Richter,* and other romantic writers; moving spirit in Sturm und Drang. Saw beauty and character in 16th-c. chorales and sought to preserve purity and antiquity of texts; regarded ch. hymns as true folk songs that deepened religious feeling. Prepared the way for the science of comparative philol. and modern comparative religion*; influenced developing Ger. nationalism and historiography; evolutionist after the manner of G. W. Leibniz,* but approached views of C. Darwin.* Ed. *Volkslieder;* other works include *Abhandlung über den Ursprung der Sprache; Ideen zur Philosophie der Geschichte der Menschheit; Lieder der Liebe; Vom Geist der Ebräischen Poesie.* See also *Historicism,* 2; *Philiosophy.* HFB

R. T. Clark, Jr., *Herder: His Life and Thought* (Berkeley, Calif., 1955); B. v. Wiese, *Herder: Grundzüge seines Weltbildes* (Leipzig, 1939); R. R. Ergang, *Herder and the Foundations of German Nationalism* (New York, 1966); J. K. Fugate, *The Psychological Basis of Herder's Aesthetics* (The Hague, Neth., 1966).

Hereafter. A. *Heaven (Eternal Life).* 1. Eternal, or everlasting, life, the gift of God through Christ* Jesus, is the end of faith, the ultimate object of a Christian's hope and striving (Ph 3:13-14; 2 Ti 4:6-8). The Bible describes eternal life as a kingdom (Lk 12:32), a paradise (Lk 23:43), an unfading inheritance (1 Ptr 1:4), a rest for the people of God (Heb 4:9), Abraham's bosom (Lk 16:22), a marriage supper (Rv 19:9), a crown of life (Rv 2:10), to picture under earthly symbols the ineffable joys and pleasures of heaven.

2. Scripture represents heaven as a place, a house with many mansions (Jn 14:2), everlasting habitations (Lk 16:9), a city (Heb 11:10), a new heaven and a new earth (2 Ptr 3:13; Rv 21:1). It makes no

attempt to locate heaven. All human efforts to do so must fail.

3. Essentially eternal life is immediate, uninterrupted fellowship with God. To be with God is to be in heaven (Ps 16:11; Lk 23:43). The saints in light are with God and with His Son (Jn 17:24). They see God face to face, as He is, and know God even as they are known; their knowledge of God and His wonderful works will no longer be partial, but perfect and complete (1 Co 13:9-12; 1 Jn 3:2).

4. This blissful fellowship is unbroken by time, unmarred and undisturbed by sin or any of its disrupting consequences (Ps 16:11; Jn 3:16). Pain, sorrow, tears, tribulation, hunger, thirst, and death will be no more (Rv 7:16-17; 21:4). In heaven the elect will sing the praises of God and their exalted Redeemer (Rv 5:9-13). The divine image will be fully restored (Ps 17:15; Heb 12:23). The glory that will be revealed surpasses human understanding (2 Co 12:4) and far outweighs the suffering of this present time (Ro 8:19). It is a blessedness beyond compare (2 Co 4:17).

5. The body of believers will share in the glory of everlasting life. Transformed to resemble the glorified body of their Redeemer, the body will be free from weakness, dishonor, and corruption (Ph 3:21; 1 Co 15:42-54). The white robes mentioned Rv 7:9-14 are symbols of the sinlessness effected through the cleansing power of Christ's blood. The institution of marriage will be abolished (Mt 22:30). In glory the believers will be equal to the angels of God (Lk 20:36). Whether the redeemed will recognize each other in heaven is not stated explicitly but may be inferred from the story of the Transfiguration, which says that the disciples recognized Moses and Elijah (Mt 17:3-4).

6. Though Scripture ascribes full salvation to all believers (Jn 3:16), there will be degrees of glory in accord with the difference of the works that the believers performed on earth (1 Co 3:8; 2 Co 9:6). It is futile and needless to speculate in what this difference of glory consists. This we know, that a believer enjoying a greater measure of glory will not be envied by those who have less. It is inherent in eternal life with its absolute perfection that the difference in glory will not give rise to any evil thoughts.

B. *Hell (Eternal Punishment).* 1. The doctrine of eternal punishment, repugnant to natural man, has been repudiated by errorists (e. g., Origen,* Universalists*) but is clearly revealed in Scripture. To deny this doctrine is to reject the authority of Scripture.

2. Acc. to the Bible, the unbelievers will be damned (Mk 16:16). They will be punished with everlasting destruction (2 Th 1:9), the damnation of hell (Mt 23:33). This punishment is variously described as unquenchable fire (Mk 9:43-48), outer darkness, where there will be weeping and gnashing of teeth (Mt 8:12), a prison from which there is no escape (Mt 5:25-26).

3. As regards the question whether the fire of hell (Mt 25:41 et al.) is a material fire or not, restraint is in order. Since other expressions are used to depict the suffering of the lost (e. g., "their worm does not die," Mk 9:48; they "shall be cast out into outer darkness," Mt 8:12), all of them may well be understood figuratively. The description that the Bible gives of hell is to express in terms taken from human experience the unspeakable torments of body and soul of the damned. Whatever has been said about the awful doom of the wicked is intended to call sinners to repentance and warn them of the wrath to come.

4. As the essence of heaven is fellowship with God, so the essence of hell is exclusion from this fellowship. Deprived of the blissful presence of God and the glory bestowed on the believers (2 Th 1:9; Mt 25:41), the unbelievers will languish in the company of the evil spirits to bemoan, in abject despair, their willful impenitence during the time of grace and their unalterable condemnation (Mt 8:12). This punishment, which is never alleviated, will be eternal in the 2-fold sense that it suffers no interruption (Lk 16:24-26) and has no end (Mk 9:48). Degrees of punishment are clearly taught Mt 11:22-24; Lk 12:47-48. Those who spurned the proffered grace and knew the Lord's will, will be punished more severely than those who never heard the Gospel. Hypocrites who devour widows' houses and for a pretense make long prayer shall receive the greater damnation (Mt 23:14). Wherein this difference consists has not been revealed, and we should not presume to know.

5. To identify the destruction of the wicked with annihilation (see *Annihilationism*) has no warrant in Scripture. If the punishment of the wicked consisted in their outright annihilation, the Bible could not speak of it as *everlasting* destruction (2 Th 1:9). Acc. to Ro 2:8-9 tribulation and anguish await those who do not obey the truth; acc. to Jn 3:36 the wrath of God abides on those who do not believe the Son. Neither could be predicated of men who cease to have a conscious existence. Destruction or perdition, when contrasted with life, denote not cessation of existence, but eternal misery, the loss of everlasting blessedness (Ph. 1:28).

6. The meaning of "eternal" has been called into question on the ground that the Gk. word *aionios,* tr. by "eternal" or "everlasting," does not denote "endlessness." *Aionios* (from *aion,* "age") is a relative term and may mean "age-long," "enduring for a time only," but it can also mean "everlasting," "endless," and it clearly has this meaning in all passages that speak of the destiny of men in the hereafter. The *temporal* is contrasted with the *eternal (aionios)* 2 Co 4:18; 1 Ptr 1:23-25. When judgment is pronounced, the wicked will go into *everlasting* punishment, but the righteous into life *eternal* (Mt 25:46). The same Gk. word is used in both sentences. If *aionios* denotes endlessness in the one, it must have the same meaning in the other. The punishment of the wicked is unending misery and woe (Mk 3:29).

7. The same passages that unequivocally teach the eternity of punishment rule out as unscriptural the teaching of the ultimate salvation of all men. 1 Co 15:22, Eph 1:10, and Rv 21:5 cannot be adduced as proof for the final salvation of all, for when the Scriptures speak of the ultimate goal of the world's hist., they refer only to the blessed perfection of the faithful. 1 Co 15:28 and related passages teach the final victory of the kingdom of God, the subjugation of all the enemies of Christ; they do not state that all these enemies will be converted to God.

8. No physical location of hell is intended by what Scripture says of the habitation of the wicked. Hell is where God reveals Himself in His vindictive justice to the finally impenitent.

9. One of the objections raised to the doctrine of eternal punishment is that it is inconsistent with the love of God to condemn men to unending perdition. But it must be remembered that while God is a God of love, His love is only one of His attributes. Justice is also one of His attributes. Since God is a perfect being, we find in Him the perfect and harmonious expression of all His attributes. It is significant, too, that the most solemn and explicit declarations of eternal punishment recorded in Scripture were spoken by the forgiving and compassionate Savior (Mt 25:41, 46; Mk 9:43-48). Some hold that it is unworthy of a just God to punish men with everlasting condemnation. But how can man presume to

determine the justice of the infinite God acc. to human conceptions of justice? (Ps. 19:9; Is 55:9; Ro 11:33).

C. *Definition of Biblical Terms.* 1. *Heaven* is (1) the vaulted expanse of the sky with all things in it (Heb 1:10), the aerial heavens or sky where clouds and tempests gather (Mt 16:2), the starry heavens (Heb 11:12); (2) the dwelling place of God (Mt 5:34; 23:22; Acts 7:49) and His holy angels (Mt 18:10; 24:36), to which Christ ascended (Acts 1: 9-11), the eternal home of all believers (Mt 5:12; 1 Ptr 1:4).

2. *Paradise.* This word, perhaps of Persian origin, denotes (1) a garden or park, e. g., the Garden of Eden (Gn 2:8-17); (2) the heavenly Paradise, home of the saints of God (Lk 23:43; 2 Co 12:4 [RSV 3]; Rv 2:7).

3. *Sheol.* The etymology of this word, occuring 65 times in the Heb OT, is still obscure. M. Luther* tr. it *Hölle* in all places except Gn 37:35; 42:38; 44:29, 31; in these passages he tr. it with *Grube.* The KJV tr. it with "grave," "hell," and "pit." Since the derivation of the word is uncertain, the context must determine the meaning in each case.

(a) Sheol may mean the resting place of man's mortal remains (Jb 17:16; Is 38:10).

(b) Sheol may mean realm of the dead, into which all enter who depart this life, righteous as well as wicked (e. g., Gn 37:35; Jb 7:9; Ps 16:10; 31:17; 89:48). In this sense it is a gen. term used very much like Eng. "the hereafter" or "the beyond." The phrase "to go down into Sheol" means "to die, to depart from the land of the living." But it should be noted that when the righteous are said to descend into Sheol, their fate beyond is never taken into account. The hope of the pious in the OT is expressed differently, e. g., Ps 73:24.

(c) Sheol may mean the place where God's judgment overtakes evildoers. In this sense Sheol receives such as are taken away in God's anger. Korah's rebel band went down to Sheol because they had provoked the Lord (Nm 16:30, 33). Harlots go to Sheol (Pr 5:5). The anger of the Lord burns to the depths of Sheol (Dt 32:22). Acc. to Ps 49 all men die physically, righteous as well as ungodly (v. 10), but there is a difference in their existence in the hereafter. The confidence of the Psalmist is exressed in the words "They (i. e. the wicked) are laid in Sheol (KJV the grave), death shall feed on them, but God will redeem my soul from the power of Sheol (KJV the grave); for He shall receive me" (vv. 14-15). Clearly there is a sharp contrast bet. the doom of the ungodly and the glorious hope of the believer, who hopes to rest securely in the hands of God; cp. Ps 73.

4. *Hades* (perhaps derived from the Gk. word for "unseen"). In non-Biblical Gk. literature this term denotes the realm of the dead. In the LXX Hades is used almost exclusively for Sheol. In the NT it means "realm of the dead" (Acts 2:27, 31; Rv 20: 13-14) or (e. g., Lk 16:23) a place where unbelievers suffer. When the rich man found himself in Hades, he was not in an intermediate state, but "in torments."

5. *Gehenna* was the Gk. name of a deep, narrow valley SW and S of Jerusalem; the Heb. name was *ge hinnom,* "valley of Hinnom"; the meaning of Hinnom is obscure. It was the scene of the sacrifice of children to the idol Moloch (2 K 23:10). Later it was used for disposal of refuse by fire. By transfer of thought the name Gehenna came to denote the abode of the wicked after death (e. g., Mt 5:22, 29; 10:28; Mk 9:43, 45; Lk 12:5; Ja 3:6).

6. *Abyssos.* A Gk. word derived from an adjective meaning bottomless, unbounded, denotes (1) the "deep," or primeval waters (LXX Gn 1:2); (2) the depths of the earth as a symbol of great distress and anguish of soul (Ps 71:20); (3) the abode of the dead (Ro 10:7); (4) hell, as the abode of evil spirits presided over by Apollyon, identified by many with Satan (Rv 9:1-2, 11; 11:7; 17:8; 20:1, 3).

7. *Tartaros.* This Gk. word is not in the Bible, but a related verb form occurs 2 Ptr 2:4. In Gk. mythology Tartaros is an underground prison, regarded as the abode of the wicked dead where they suffer punishment for their evil deeds; its corresponds to Gehenna (see par. 5 above) as a name for hell.

CAH

H. Ebeling, *Der Menschheit Zukunft,* 2d ed. (Zwickau, 1913); T. Kliefoth, *Christliche Eschatologie* (Leipzig, 1886); C. E. Luthardt, *Die Lehre von den letzten Dingen,* 2d ed. (Leipzig, 1870); R. Seeberg, *Ewiges Leben?* (Leipzig, 1915); A. Althaus, *Die letzten Dinge* (Verden, 1858); P. Althaus, *Unsterblichkeit und ewiges Sterben bei Luther* (Gütersloh, 1930) and *Die letzten Dinge,* 4th ed. (Gütersloh, 1933); J. A. West, *What the Bible Teaches About the World Beyond* (Burlington, Iowa, 1939); L. F. Gruber, *What After Death?* (Burlington, Iowa, 1925); E. C. Pautsch, "Eternal Life," *The Abiding Word,* I, ed. T. Laetsch (St. Louis, 1946); W. F. Wolbrecht, "The Doctrine of the Last Things," *The Abiding Word,* I, ed. T. Laetsch (St. Louis, 1946); E. C. Fendt, "The Life Everlasting," *What Lutherans Are Thinking* (Columbus, Ohio, 1947), pp. 307–322; G. Beiderwieden, *Heaven* (St. Louis, 1937); *That Unknown Country, or What Living Men Believe Concerning Punishment After Death* (Springfield, Mass., 1891).

Hereditary Sin. See *Sin, Original.*

Heredity. See *Educational Psychology,* B 3.

Hereford, Nicholas. See *Nicholas of Hereford.*

Herero. Bantu tribe (ca. 50,000) in cen. South-West Afr. and NW Bechuanaland Protectorate; evangelized in the 19th c. by the Rhenish* Miss. Soc. and the Finnish* Miss. Soc. See also *Africa,* B 8; *Hahn, Karl Hugo.*

Heresiarch. Originator of a heresy*; leader of a heretical sect.

Heresimach. Heresy hunter; opponent of heretics.

Heresiologist. Student of heresy; opponent of heresy.

Heresy (from Gk. *hairesis,* "act of choosing," then "chosen opinion; sect"). 1. Used in the LXX for choices that are either good or bad (e. g., Gn 49:5; Lv 22:18, 21). In F. Josephus,* *Jewish War,* II viii 2, it is used of either a party or a sect (cf. Acts 5:17; 15:5; 24:5, 14; 26:5). The term is used in the NT in a condemnatory sense; heretics are contentious (1 Co 11:16-19), deny the Lord, are pernicious, covetous, deceivers for gain, false teachers (2 Ptr 2:1-3), are subverted, sinners, and self-condemned (Tts 3:10-11; cf. schism in 1 Co 1:10; 11:18; 12:25).

2. The term "heresy" occurs in Ignatius (see *Apostolic Fathers,* 2), *Epistle to the Trallians,* shorter version, vi, and *Epistle to the Ephesians,* vi. Justin* Martyr, *Dialog with Trypho the Jew,* LXXX, speaks of "godless, impious heretics" and their "blasphemous, atheistical, and foolish" doctrines. The later Fathers often use the term "heresy." In earliest Christian times Jewish sects and Gk. schools were regarded heretics. In the 2d and 3d c. Gnostics (see *Gnosticism*) were the great heretics. Then came Monarchianism,* Montanism,* and Manichaeism.* Arianism,* Apollinarianism,* Pelagianism,* Nestorianism,* Monophysitism,* and Monothelitism* were outstanding heresies of the Nicene and post-Nicene era (see *Christian Church, History of,* 3, 4).

3. In early Christian times charges of heresy were used in pol. maneuvering. As ch. organization developed into a pol. system, heresy was outlawed and suppressed. From ca. the end of the 4th c. into the 16th c. heresy was a capital crime. In the Middle

Ages, heresies became in part protests of individuals against an est. order and included speculative thinkers (Cathari,* Amalricians*), mystics (J. Tauler,* H. Suso,* J. v. Ruysbroeck,* Thomas* a Kempis), enthusiasts (Franciscan Spirituals*), antisacerdotalists (Pierre de Bruys,* Henry* of Lausanne). J. Wycliffe* and J. Hus* were also considered heretics.

4. M. Luther* restored the term to its original meaning: Heresy is stubborn error in an article of faith in opposition to Scripture (WA 54, 288; 30 II, 422, 426); is an individually made doctrine and mode of living (WA 8, 389); springs from pride (WA 31 I, 333); cannot endure grace (WA 28, 574) and substitutes other works for those commanded by God (WA 32, 516); is not evolved from Scripture, but from perverted minds (WA 45, 647–648; 18, 701); pretends to be Scriptural (WA 17 I, 363); refuses to listen or be opposed (WA 19, 610); sins against Holy Ghost (WA 19, 610; 2, 184); errs in a fundamental doctrine (WA 1, 391); errorists strive against recognized truth and their own conscience (WA 50, 545). (Cf. Ap IV 232, 242; SA II iv 7, III viii 9; Tractatus 38, 72; FC Ep XII, SD VIII 17, XII 39).

5. J. Gerhard,* *Loci theologici,* XIII, pp. 222–223: "For one to be properly called a heretic, it is required (1) that he be a person received by the Sacrament of Baptism into the visible church; (2) that he err in faith . . . ; (3) that the error conflict directly with the very foundation of faith; (4) that to the error be added malice and obstinacy, in which he stubbornly defends his error, though repeatedly admonished; (5) that he stir up dissensions and scandals in the church and rend its unity. C. F. W. Walther* summarized the teaching of Luther and the Luth. dogmaticians: A heretic (1) errs in a fundamental article; (2) brings about divisions; (3) continues in his perverse ways despite repeated admonitions and contrary to his own better knowledge and conscience. EL

See also *Inquisition.*

G. Arnold, *Unparteyische Kirchen- und Ketzer-Historie, von Anfang des Neuen Testaments biss auff das Jahr Christi 1688,* 4 parts (Frankfurt, 1699–1700); A. Hilgenfeld, *Die Ketzergeschichte des Urchristenthums* (Leipzig, 1884); C. F. W. Walther, *Die Stimme unserer Kirche in der Frage von Kirche und Amt,* jubilee ed. (Zwickau, Ger., 1911), pp. 10–14, and *Die Evangelisch-Lutherische Kirche, die wahre sichtbare Kirche Gottes auf Erden* (St. Louis, Mo., 1867), pp. 24–25, 151–152, tr. J. T. Mueller, *The True Visible Church* (St. Louis, Mo., 1961), pp. 20–29, 134; *Studia Friburgensia,* New Series, 10, ed. H. O. Lüthi: J. Cahill, *The Development of the Theological Censures After the Council of Trent (1563–1709)* (Fribourg, Switz., 1955); *Beiträge zur historischen Theologie,* ed. G. Ebeling, 10: W. Bauer, *Rechtgläubigkeit und Ketzerei im ältesten Christentum,* 2d ed. G. Strecker (Tübingen, 1964); K. Rahner, *On Heresy,* tr. W. J. O'Hara (New York, 1964); J. Guitton, *Great Heresies and Church Councils,* tr. F. D. Wieck (New York, 1965); G. Leff, *Heresy in the Later Middle Ages,* 2 vols. (New York, 1967).

Heretical Baptism. Baptism (see *Grace, Means of,* III) performed by heretics was a subject of controversy in the 3d–4th c. ch. The question was: Is heretical baptism, even if administered in the right form, true Baptism, or is it a mere ceremony? Cyprian* of Carthage held the latter view (Epistles 69–74), which was shared by the Afr. Ch. Heretical baptism was rejected by several syns. at Carthage (e. g., 255–256; see also *Carthage, Synods and Councils of*) and in Asia Minor. Stephen* I of Rome defended the validity of heretical baptism administered in the name of the Trinity.* This view prevailed. The Syn. of Arles* declared Trinitarian baptism by heretics valid; the Council of Nicaea* recognized baptism of Novatians (see *Novatianism*) but rejected that of followers of Paul* of Samosata; the Syn. of Laodicea* did not require rebaptism of converts from Novatians and some other sects; a syn. at Carthage 348 sanctioned heretical baptism properly performed. Augustine* of Hippo defended the validity of heretical baptism as to form but denied it saving efficacy until the baptized person joined the true ch. If there is no absolute certainty on the validity of previous baptism, RCs gen. rebaptize conditionally. Luths. and most Prots. recognize Trinitarian baptism of other chs.

Hergenröther, Joseph (1824–90). B. Würzburg, Ger.; RC theol.; defended papal infallibility; opposed J. J. I. v. Döllinger*; ch. hist.; cardinal 1879. Works include *Handbuch der allgemeinen Kirchengeschichte;* vols. 8–9 of K. J. v. Hefele's* *Conciliengeschichte.*

Herimannus Augiensis. See *Hermann von Reichenau.*

Hering, Hermann Julius (1838–1920). Luth. theol.; b. Dallmin, Brandenburg, Ger.; educ. Halle; prof. practical theol. Halle 1878–1908.

Herlitz, Herman. See *Australia, Lutheranism in,* B 1.

Herman, Nikolaus (Nicolaus Hermann; estimates of the yr. of his birth range from ca. 1480 to near the end of the 15th c.; d. 1561). B. Altdorf near Nürnberg, Ger.; teacher and organist Joachimstal ca. 1518; hymnist; composer. Works include text of "Erschienen ist der herrlich' Tag"; text and music of "Lobt Gott, ihr Christen" and "Die helle Sonn' leucht't jetzt herfür."

Hermann, Rudolf (1887–1962). B. Barmen, Ger.; prof. Breslau 1919, Greifswald 1926, Berlin 1953. Works include *Gesammelte Studien zur Theologie Luthers und der Reformation; Luthers Theologie; Von der Klarheit der Heiligen Schrift.*

Hermann, Zacharias (1643–1716). B. Namslau, Silesia; pastor and inspector Lissa, Posen; hymnist. Hymns include "Wie kurz ist doch der Menschen Leben."

Hermann von Reichenau (1013–54). "Hermann der Lahme (i. e. the Lame); Hermannus Contractus (i. e. the Cripple); Herimannus Augiensis." B. Saulgau, Ger.; monk of the Benedictine abbey at Reichenau (Lat. *Augia dives*); hist., poet, polymath. Works include *Chronicon,* a hist. of the Christian era to 1054; some sequences (see *Sequence*) have been ascribed to him.

Hermann von Wied (1477–1552). B. Wied, Ger.; count of Wied; abp. and elector Cologne; at first supported papacy* against M. Luther*; tried to correct abuses in Cologne beginning ca. 1536; called in M. Bucer* 1542, P. Melanchthon* 1543. His thoughts on reform are given in *Von Gottes genaden unser Hermans Ertzbischoffs zu Cöln, unnd Churfürsten . . . einfaltigs bedencken, warauff ein Christliche, in dem wort Gottes gegrünte Reformation . . . anzurichten seye* (drafted by Bucer and Melanchthon; pub. 1543). Some of his proposals found their way into the Book* of Common Prayer. Deposed and excommunicated 1546 by Charles* V and Paul* III.

Hermannsburg-Hamburg Free Church. See *Germany, Lutheran Free Churches in,* 11.

Hermannsburg Mission. Founded 1849 by G. L. D. T. Harms* at Hermannsburg, Ger.; candidates given religious and vocational training; first missionaries sent out 1853 to Afr., the most important field of this soc. See also *Harms, Theodor; India,* 13; *Michigan Synod,* 4.

Hermannus Contractus. See *Hermann von Reichenau.*

Hermansz, Jacob. See *Arminianism.*

Hermas, Shepherd of. See *Apostolic Fathers,* 5.

Hermeneutics. 1. Branch of theology* which deals with the study of the principles of interpretation; the theory of exegesis.* The term is derived from Gk. *hermeneuein,* used, with variations, for "translate" (Jn 1:38, 42; Heb 7:2) and "explain" (Lk 24:27). The Gk. word, in turn, probably goes back to the name of the god Hermes, who was credited with inventing language and had the task of communicating the things of heaven to men. In the days of Aristotle* the art of hermeneutics dealt with matters of rhetoric and translation. In the ancient ch. *hermeneia* included commentary on a text. The term was used by J. K. Dannhauer* and others to denote *ars interpretandi* ("the art of interpretation"). F. D. E. Schleiermacher* and W. C. L. Dilthey* limited the study of the theory of exegesis almost entirely to analysis of the problem of understanding.

2. Hermeneutics tries to point the way to removing distance bet. author and reader. The rules and principles are not a matter of caprice, but are determined by (a) the gen. laws of human thought and expression; (b) the nature, origin, form, and purpose of a book. Biblical hermeneutics tries to show how the meaning of the Bible may be determined and communicated.

3. Since gen. rules of expression and understanding are affected to some extent by the cultural situation in which the interpreter lives, interpretation has, in the course of its hist., been marked by various presuppositions and emphases. When the Gospel made contact with the Graeco-Roman Empire, it adjusted itself to the Platonic world view, a vertical distinction bet. the material and the realm of ideas (cf. "letter" and "spirit," 2 Co 3:6). This situation gave rise to development of the allegorical method (see *Exegesis,* 3–5; *Schools, Early Christian,* 1, 4). See also *Catena.*

4. The Luth. Reformation included reformation in the art of Biblical interpretation. It proceeded from assumption of the perspicuity* of Scripture to application of 2 revolutionary principles: (a) the sense of a passage is a single one *(sensus literalis unus est);* (b) Scripture is its own interpreter *(scriptura sacra sui ipsius interpres).* M. Flacius* Illyricus formalized these principles 1567 in *Clavis scripturae sacrae.* The period of Luth. orthodoxy (see *Lutheran Theology After 1580,* 3–5) has been characterized as a time of "dogmatic exegesis," i. e., of interpreting the Bible in terms of doctrinal definitions and distinctions. Pietism* reacted to Luth. orthodoxy by a desire to provide a devotional spirit for interpretation. The Enlightenment* was characterized by interest in textual investigation and literary analysis, philos., and hist., and contributed to comparative religion. These trends influenced Biblical hermeneutics.

5. The 20th c. opened with a burst of activity that provided new translations, commentaries, dictionaries, grammars, and lexicons (see *Bible Versions,* 12–16; *Commentaries, Biblical; Encyclopedias and Dictionaries; Grammars).* The yrs. beyond the middle of the 20th c. found interpreters engaged in contest bet. those who follow the existential approach of R. Bultmann (see *Demythologization; Existentialism)* and others who see in his method of "demythologizing" a threat to the content and hist. base of Scripture. Most hermeneutical studies today are built on an awareness of the uniqueness of the Bible; an appreciation of its theol. aspects; a recognition of the needs of Israel and the early ch. in terms of worship, teaching, and preaching as providing occasion for creation of oral tradition and various literary materials which were used by the sacred writers in preparing the Biblical documents; and a strong desire to study the Scriptural materials in the light of their original milieu (Sitz* im Leben). This last emphasis has given rise to an interest in the life and practices of Judaism. MHS

See also *Tychonius.*

F. W. Danker, *Multipurpose Tools for Bible Study,* 2d ed. (St. Louis, Mo., 1966); K. Frör, *Biblische Hermeneutik,* 2d ed. (Munich, 1964); *Biblical Authority for Today: A World Council of Churches Symposium on "The Biblical Authority for the Churches' Social and Political Message Today,"* ed. A. Richardson and W. Schweitzer (London, 1951); J. D. Smart, *The Interpretation of Scripture* (Philadelphia, 1961).

Hermes. See *Greek Religion,* 2.

Hermes, Georg (1775–1831). B. Dreierwalde, Westphalia; RC philos. and theol. See also *Hermesianism.*

Hermes, Hermann Daniel (1734–1807). B. Petznick, Pomerania; brother of J. T. Hermes*; Luth. ch. leader in Berlin.

Hermes, Johann August (1736–1822). B. Magdeburg, Ger.; nephew of H. D. Hermes* and J. T. Hermes*; pastor Quedlinburg; poet. Works include *Handbuch der Religion.*

Hermes, Johann Timotheus (1738–1821). B. Petznick, Pomerania; brother of H. D. Hermes*; prof. Breslau; influenced by pietism.* Works include moral-sentimental novels.

Hermesianism. Philos. and theol. system which tried to reconcile RC theol. with the philos. of I. Kant.* Basically anthropocentric, it holds that the only sure knowledge is that of ideas in the mind. System received its name from G. Hermes,* who, in opposition to Kant, held that the existence of God and supernatural revelation could be rationally proved. Popular among RCs for a time. Some of Hermes' works were put on the Index* of Prohibited Books 1835.

Hermetic Books. Group of non-Christian religious writings of 2d and 3d (and possibly 1st) c. AD; syncretistic; aim at deifying man through knowledge. See also *Poimandres.*

Hermits (from Gk. eremites, "living in the desert"). Religious orders whose mems. lead solitary lives. "Anchorite" often synonymous with "hermit"; when distinguished, a hermit is one who has retired from human society, an anchorite is close to a religious community. Cenobites,* in contrast to anchorites and hermits, live in secluded communities. Hermits include Augustinian* Hermits, Camaldolese,* early Carmelites,* Carthusians,* Celestines (see *Celestines,* 1). See also *Anthony; Paul of Thebes; Recluse.*

Hermits of St. Augustine. See *Augustinian Hermits.*

Hermits of St. Damian. See *Celestines,* 1.

Hermits of Murone (Morone). See *Celestines,* 1.

Hernaman, Claudia Frances (1838–98). B. Addlestone, Surrey, Eng. Wrote over 150 hymns, many for children; also tr. Lat. hymns. Works include *The Child's Book of Praise.*

Herrenmoral (Ger. "morality of masters"). Term applied to F. W. Nietzsche's* ruthless aristocratic morality, which emphasized will to power, superman, primacy of strong-willed.

Herrmann, Ewald. See *Canada,* A 12.

Herrmann, Johann Wilhelm (1846–1922). B. Melkow, Ger.; prof. systematic theol. Marburg 1879; followed philos. of I. Kant* and theol. of A. Ritschl*; held that the ch. should teach only those things which influence man. Works include *Der Verkehr des Christen mit Gott.*

Herrnhut. See *Moravian Church,* 3.

Herrnschmidt, Johann Daniel (1675–1723). B. Bopfingen, Swabia (later Württemberg); educ. Altdorf and Halle; asst. to his father at Bopfingen; supt., preacher, mem. of consistory Idstein; prof. Halle; hymnist. Hymns include "Lobe den Herren, o meine Seele."

Hersleb, Svend Borchmann (1784–1836). Luth. theol.; prof. Oslo; exponent of mild biblicism.

Hertzog, Johann Friedrich (1647–99). B. Dresden, Ger.; educ. Wittenberg; tutor; practiced law at Dresden; musician; poet. Wrote "Nun sich der Tag geendet hat."

Hervet, Gentian (Gentianus Hervetus; 1499–1584). B. Olivet, near Orléans, Fr.; RC patristic scholar; active at Council of Trent.*

Herneus Natalis. See *Natalis Herneus.*

Herwald. See *Germany,* A 2.

Herzberger, Frederick William (Friedrich Wilhelm; Oct. 23, 1859–Aug. 26, 1930). B. Baltimore, Md.; educ. Conc. Sem., St. Louis, Mo.; pioneer miss. in Ark.; pastor Carson, Kans., Chicago, Ill., Hammond, Ind.; 1st city miss. (St. Louis) of Mo. Syn. 1899; championed many miss. and charitable endeavors. Works include *The Family Altar.*

Herzer, John Henry (Johann Heinrich; initial A. also occurs; Nov. 3, 1840–May 2, 1930). B. Louisville, Ky.; educ. Conc. Sem., St. Louis, Mo.; pastor Aurora, Steele Co., Minn., 1865–68, Minneapolis, Minn., 1868–79, Plymouth, Wis., 1879–92, Athens, Ill., 1899–1922; prof. Conc. Theol. Sem., Springfield, Ill., 1892–1914; pres. Wis. Dist., Mo. Syn., 1891. Author: *Evangelisch-Lutherische Katechetik.*

Herzl, Theodor. See *Zionism.*

Herzog, Eduard (1841–1924). B. Schongau, Switz.; educ. Tübingen, Freiburg, Bonn; joined Old* Catholics; pastor Crefeld, Prussia, and Olten and Bern, Switz.; 1st bp. The Christian* Cath. Ch. of Switz. 1876.

Herzog, Johann Georg (1822–1909). B. Hummendorf, near Kronach, Bav.; educ. Altdorf near Nürnberg; organist Munich 1843, cantor 1848, Conservatory prof. 1850; prof. Erlangen 1854. Works include *Orgelschule; Die gebräuchlichsten Choräle der evangelischen Kirche; Evangelisches Choralbuch.*

Herzog, Johann Jakob (1805–82). Ref. theol.; b. Basel, Switz.; educ. Basel and Berlin; began to teach at Lausanne, Switz., 1835; prof. there 1838, Halle 1847, Erlangen 1854. Ed. *Realencyklopädie für protestantische Theologie und Kirche;* other works include *Das Leben Ökolampadius' und die Reformation der Kirche zu Basel; Die romanischen Waldenser.*

Heshusius, Tilemann. See *Hesshus, Tilemann.*

Hess, Johann (Hesse; Hessus; 1490–1547). Reformer of Silesia; b. Nürnberg, Ger.; educ. Leipzig and Wittenberg; friend of M. Luther* and P. Melanchthon*; pastor Breslau 1523; founded All Saints Hosp., Breslau, 1526; hymnist. See also *Moiban(us), Ambrosius.*

Hess, Johann Jakob (1741–1828). B. Zurich, Switz.; urged by F. G. Klopstock* and C. M. Wieland* to devote himself to poetry; 1760 asst. to uncle, Kaspar Hess, pastor Neftenbach; influenced by J. K. Lavater*; deacon Zurich 1777; pastor Zurich and supt. Canton Zurich 1795. Emphasized spiritual brotherhood of believers. Works include *Geschichte der drey letzten Lebensjahre Jesu, sammt dessen Jugendgeschichte; Von dem Reiche Gottes.*

Hesse, Hermann Albert (1877–1957). Pastor Meiderich, Bremen, and Elberfeld, Ger.; mem. Bekennende Kirche (see *Kirchenkampf*); opposed Nazism (see *Socialism,* 3).

Hesse, Lutheran Free Churches in. See *Germany, Lutheran Free Churches in,* 10.

Hesse, Philip of. See *Philip of Hesse.*

Hesselius, Andreas (1677–1733). B. Swed.; nephew of J. Swedberg*; left Swed. for Am. 1711; Luth. pastor Christina (Wilmington) in the Swed. settlement on the Del. 1713–23; returned to Swed. 1723–24; pastor Gaguäf, Västeraas, Swed. Works include *Disertatio historica de Vandalis; Kort Berettelse Om Then Swenska Kyrkios närwarande Tilstaand i America Samt ofögripeliga tankar om thess widare förkofring.* His brother Samuel came to Am. 1719; served chs. in Montgomery Co., Pa., 1719–23 and was Andreas' successor at Wilmington 1723–31; returned to Swed. 1731; pastor Romfertuna, Västeraas, Swed. See also *Provost.*

Hessels, Jan (Johann Heinrich; Hesselinus; 1522–66). B. Louvain (or Arras), Fr.; RC theol.; active at Council of Trent*; probably helped prepare *Catechismus Romanus* (see *Roman Catholic Confessions,* A 3).

Hesshus, Tilemann (Hesshusius; Heshusius; Hesshusen; 1527–88). Ev. theol.; educ. Wittenberg, Oxford, and Paris; supt. Goslar 1553; prof. Rostock 1556, expelled for opposing worldliness 1557; prof. Heidelberg 1557, deposed 1559 for refusing to subscribe to the Variata (see *Lutheran Confessions,* B 1); pastor Magdeburg 1560; deposed 1562 for opposing edict forbidding polemics; active in Wesel, Frankfurt am Main, and Strasbourg; court preacher Neuburg 1565; prof. Jena 1569; exiled 1573 by Elector August* of Saxony; bp. Samland (peninsula of former E Prussia) 1573; deposed 1577 on charges of false doctrine in Christology; prof. Helmstedt 1577; helped to deter Brunswick from accepting FC. Works include *Vom Ampt und gewalt der Pfarrherr; Adsertio sacrosancti Testamenti Iesu Christi: contra blasphemam Calvinistarum exegesin* [*Exegesis perspicua et ferme integra controversiae de Sacra Coena*]; commentaries See also *Propst, Jakob.*

Hessus, Helius Eobanus (Eoban Koch; 1488–1540). B. Hesse; humanist; poet; active at Erfurt, Nürnberg, and Marburg; supported the Reformation.

Hesychasm (from Gk. *hesychos,* "quiet"). System of mysticism* in Eastern* Orthodox Ch.; propagated by monks of Mount Athos, Greece. Held that man, esp. through quiet of body and mind, could attain a vision of the Uncreated Light of deity (beatific vision) which was God's "energy," but not His essence. When the system was attacked by the Calabrian monk Barlaam (ca. 1290–1350; b. Seminara, Calabria), it was vigourously defended by Gregorius Palamas (ca. 1296–1359; Gk. theol.; b. probably Constantinople) and ultimately accepted by the E ch.

MPG, 148; 150, 771–1372; 151, 9–678; 153.

Hesychius (fl. perhaps ca. 300 AD). Jerome* (*MPL,* 23, 471; 29, 559) says that Hesychius prepared a revision of the LXX and the Gospels. Decretum Gelasianum (*MPL,* 59, 162 and 175): *Evangelia quae falsavit Hesychius; apoc.* May be the Hesychius who died as martyr under Diocletian* (Eusebius* of Caesarea, *HE,* VIII, xiii, 7).

Heterius of Libana. See *Adoptionism.*

Heterodoxy. Teachings or beliefs differing from a position held to be orthodox.*

Hetzer, Ludwig (Haetzer; Hätzer; ca. 1500–29). B. Bischofszell, Switz.; educ. Basel and Freiburg; chaplain Wädenswil; also active in Zurich; Anabaptist; joined H. Zwingli* but broke with him; opposed doctrines of justification and infant baptism and Luth. doctrine of Lord's Supper; became spiritualist and opposed the ev. doctrine of Scripture and the deity of Christ. See also *Socinianism,* 1.

Heubner, Heinrich Leonhard (1780–1853). B. Lauterbach, Ger.; educ. Wittenberg; lectured at Wittenberg; supt. and 1st dir. Wittenberg theol. sem. 1832; loyal to Luth. Confessions; opposed Prussian* Union.

Heuch, Johan Christian (1838–1904). B. Kragerö, Norw.; influenced as student by S. A. Kierkegaard,* C. P. Caspari,* and G. Johnson*; educ. Leipzig and Erlangen; pastor Christiania (Oslo); bp. Kristiansand 1889. Championed orthodoxy. Coed. *Luthersk Kirketidende* 1875–77, *Luthersk Ugeskrift* 1877–89; other works include *Vantroens Vaesen; Kirken og*

Vantroen; Mod Strömmen; Svar; Sjaelesorg hos de Syge.

Heumann, Christoph August (1681–1764). B. Alstädt, Thuringia; prof. literature and theol. Göttingen; defended Ref. doctrine of Lord's Supper.

Heune, Johann (Gigas; 1514–81). B. Nordhausen, Thuringia; friend of J. Jonas*; rector court school Pforta, near Naumburg, 1543–46; pastor Freystadt 1546–73, Schweidnitz 1573–81; hymnist. Hymns include "Ach, lieben Christen! seid getrost!"

Heungshan. See *China,* 6.

Heusde, Philip Willem van. See *Groningen School.*

Hewald. See *Germany,* A 2.

Hewitt. See *Huet, Heinrich.*

Hexaemeron (from Gk. *hexaemeros,* "six-day" [sc. *periodos,* "period"]). 6 days of creation,* Gn 1.

Hexaglot. See *Polyglot Bibles.*

Hexapla. See *Polyglot Bibles.*

Hexateuch (from Gk. *hex,* "six," and *teuchos,* "roll of writing material"). Name given 1876 by J. Wellhausen* to 1st 6 OT books; his theory that they were compiled from the same sources has since been questioned.

Hey, Wilhelm (1789–1854). B. Leina, near Gotha, Ger.; pastor Töttelstädt 1818–27; court preacher Gotha 1827–32; supt. Ichtershausen 1832–54; poet. Works include songs for children, e.g., "Weisst du, wieviel Sternlein stehen."

Heydenreich, August Ludwig Christian (1773–1858). Prof. and dir. of the ev. sem. at Herborn, Ger.; supernaturalist (see *Supernaturalism*). Issued 1841 Nassau hymnal.

Heyer, Johann Christian Friedrich (John Christian Frederick; [Carl?]; July 10, 1793–Nov. 7, 1873). B. Helmstedt, Ger.; to Philadelphia, Pa., ca. 1807; studied theol. under J. H. C. Helmuth* and F. D. Schaeffer*; taught Zion School, Southwark, Philadelphia, 1813–15; attended U. of Göttingen 1815–16; licensed 1817 by Pa. Ministerium (see *United Lutheran Church, Synods of,* 22); itinerant preacher Crawford and Erie Cos., Pa., 1817–18; preacher Cumberland, Md., 1818–24; ordained Lancaster, Pa., 1820; pastor Somerset, Pa., 1824–27, 1832–37; Carlisle, Pa., 1827–28; pres. West Pa. Syn. (see *United Lutheran Church, Synods of,* 22, 23) 1831. In 1837 the Central* Miss. Soc. of the Ev. Luth. Ch. in the US sent him to explore the miss. possibilities in the Mississippi Valley. In 1840 the For. Miss. Soc. of the Gen. Syn. (see *Lutheran Foreign Mission Endeavors in the United States, Early,* 2–4) asked him to consider foreign miss. work. He consented; studied medicine and Skt. at Baltimore, Md., 1840–41; to India as agent of Pa. Ministerium; worked at Guntur 1842–45; home miss. Baltimore 1847. For. Miss. Soc. of the Gen. Syn. assumed Guntur miss. 1846. Heyer left for India Dec. 1847; arrived Guntur 1848; in the Palnad 1849–53; at Guntur 1853–55; to Rajahmundry 1855; miss. in Minn. 1857–68; helped found Minnesota* Syn. 1860; in Ger. 1868–69; to India again 1869; chaplain, housefather Luth. Theol. Sem., Philadelphia, Pa., 1872–73. See also *Missions,* 10.

E. T. Bachmann, *They Called Him Father: The Life Story of John Christian Frederick Heyer* (Philadelphia, 1942); A. R. Wentz, "Father Heyer Planted a Church," *The Lutheran Church Quarterly,* XVI (1943), 39–49; G. Drach, "Father Heyer, the Pioneer," *The Lutheran Church Quarterly,* XI (1938), 187–193.

Hickes, George (1642–1715). B. Newsham, Yorkshire, Eng.; dean Worcester 1683; nonjuror (see *Nonjurors*); bp. Thetford 1694. Works include theol. treatises and linguistic works.

Hicks, Elias. See *Friends, Society of,* 8.

Hicksites. See *Friends, Society of,* 8.

Hieracas (Hierax; ca. 270–ca. 360). Learned ascetic of Leontópolis, Egypt; influenced by Origen*; denied bodily resurrection; followers called Hieracites or Hieracians.

Hierarchy (from Gk. *hieros,* "holy," and *arche,* "rule"). The word "hierarchy" may refer to the graded organization of angels (see *Dionysius the Areopagite*), but usually denotes the organization of the clergy.* Since pre-Reformation times the RC Ch. has had a hierarchy of order (or orders) and a hierarchy of jurisdiction. The hierarchy of order consists of 3 orders usually considered of divine origin (bishop,* priest,* deacon*) and 5 orders usually considered of ecclesiastical origin (subdeacon, acolyte, exorcist, lector, doorkeeper [also called ostiary or porter]); the 1st 4 are major, or holy, orders; the last 4 are minor. The hierarchy of jurisdiction, charged with the gen. guidance and control of the ch., consists of 2 degrees claimed to be of divine origin (primacy of the Roman Pontiff and the episcopate) and many other degrees of ecclesiastical origin (e. g., that of cardinal, patriarch, primate, metropolitan, vicar, apostolic, and prefect apostolic).

The Angl. Ch. retained only the hierarchical order of bp., priest, and deacon as of divine origin.

In Lutheranism a hierarchy is not considered necessary for the existence of the ch. The Luth. Ch. does not recognize the pope as head of the ch. by divine right. Luths. believe that the ch. can exist without bps. (as distinct from other pastors). The power of order (to preach the Gospel, remit sins, and administer the Sacraments) and the power of jurisdiction (to excommunicate) belongs by divine right to all who preside over the chs., whether they are called pastors, presbyters, or bps., and all pastors may administer ordination by divine right (Tractatus, 60, 61, 65, 74; AC XXVIII 20–22; Ap XXVIII 13). There is no essential, divinely-appointed difference in rank bet. pastor and bp. But Luths. recognize the value of ordered ranks in the clergy. "It is not our intention that the bishops give up their power to govern, but we ask . . . that they allow the Gospel to be taught purely" (AC XXVIII 77); "[it is] our deep desire to maintain the church polity and various ranks of the ecclesiastical hierarchy, although they were created by human authority [and] to keep the ecclesiastical and canonical polity" (Ap XIV 1, 5). Luths. also regard the distinction bet. bp. (or pastor) and deacon as Biblical (AC XXIII 10; Ap XIII 12 Ger. tr.).

The Swed. Ch. maintains hist. episcopacy, though admitting that it is not of the essence of the ch. EFP

See also *Apostolic Succession; Clergy; Gallicanism; Ministerial Office; Polity, Ecclesiastical; Ultramontanism.*

Hierocles (4th c. AD). Probably the Sossianus Hierocles of an inscription from Palmyra; gov. or proconsul Bythinia 303; prefect Egypt 308; Lactantius* calls him *auctor et consiliarius* of Diocletian* persecution (see *Persecutions of Christians,* 4).

Hieronymites. RC congs. in 14th–15th-c. Sp. and It. (1) Span. Cong. of Hermits* of St. Jerome*; organized ca. 1373 by Pedro Fernandez Pecha (d. 1374); suppressed 1835 by the Span. govt.; reest. in the 20th c. (2) Poor Hermits of St. Jerome; est. 1377 near Montebello, It., by Peter Gambacorta of Pisa (d. 1435); dissolved 1953. (3) The cong. est. 1406 at Fiesole, It., by Carlo de Montegranelli (d. 1417); dissolved 1668. (4) The Observants or cong. of Lombardy; est. 1424 by Lope de Olmedo (d. 1433), former gen. of the Span. cong.; the Span. branch joined the Span. cong. 1595.

Hieronymus de Angelis. See *Ainu.*

High Church. Term applied to 1 of 3 tendencies in the Ch. of Eng. and in The Protestant* Episc. Ch.

The High Ch. movement has been traced to such men as R. Bancroft* and R. Hooker,* includes L.

Andrewes,* J. Butler,* S. Johnson,* and W. Laud,* but the name dates from the end of the 17th c.; "Anglo-Catholicism" is a corresponding 20th-c. term. High churchmen stress hist. continuity; they wish to be neither RCs nor Prots. but claim to perpetuate non-Roman ("pre-Roman") Western Catholicism; gen. emphasize authority of ch., episc. succession, and use of sacraments. The "high ch." movement in Am. stresses spiritual life developed within the ch. through the sacraments.

The term "Low Ch." was coined in contrast to "High Ch." at beginning of 18th c. Low churchmen (also called "evangelicals") emphasize Gospel preaching, accept apostolic succession of episcopacy without rejecting validity of nonepiscopal ministry and give secondary position to sacraments and orders; often also emphasize justification* and conversion.* Many low churchmen identified with Latitudinarians,* Methodists (see *Methodist Churches*), nonconformists,* and similar groups.

The term "Broad Ch." became prominent in 2d half of 19th c. Broad churchmen opposed requiring adherence to definite theol. definitions, emphasized intellectual approach to Christianity, and advocated liberal interpretation of Angl. formularies and rubrics. Broad Ch. principles are often identified with liberalism* and Modernism.* See also *Stanley, Arthur Penrhyn.*

See also *England,* B, C; *Protestant Episcopal Church,* 7.

High Mass. See *Missa solemnis.*

High School, Lutheran. See *Parish Education,* G.

Higher Criticism. 1. Biblical higher criticism is an investigation of the origin of the books of the Bible. In distinction from lower criticism (see *Textual Criticism*) it deals with such questions as authorship, hist. background, authenticity, integrity, and unity of the books. It is profitable to evaluate properly the hist. and literary data supplied by the Bible and other hist. sources.

2. Conservative scholars have come to regard the work of most higher critics negatively, pointing out that most conclusions of higher critics make it impossible to accept at face value what Scripture itself says about the origin and authorship of a book or parts of it.

3. Theories of higher critics about the origin and composition of the Pentateuch* and other books reveal their methodology and its results.

4. Critical views regarding the Pentateuch are not all of recent origin. Origen* refuted Celsus* (*Contra Celsum,* IV, 33–55). Sporadic doubts about the authorship of the Pentateuch rose in the Middle Ages. Sweeping attacks were made by T. Hobbes* and B. Spinoza,* but their views were not gen. accepted. Higher criticism as a systematic and gen. method with specific criteria of investigation began in the latter part of the 18th c.

5. Most higher critics hold that the Pentateuch is not the earliest book of the Bible but is the product of oral and literary activity completed toward the end of the OT period, after the return from Babylonian captivity; the substance of some parts may derive from the Mosaic age, but the present structure of the Pentateuch resulted from development spanning a millennium of literary activity.

6. There is a growing tendency to recognize the problem as complex. But most higher critics regard the Pentateuch as the result of literary activity in 4 major stages producing 4 main strands of materials or sources (Ger. *Quellen**).

7. This "source hypothesis" or "documentary hypothesis" labels the 4 strands J, E, D, P (Jahwist, Elohist, Deuteronomist, and Priestly writers).

8. There is some variety of opinion, but higher critics are agreed in gen. on a timetable for the origin and fusion of these sources. J is dated no earlier than the time of David (11th c. BC). Since E reflects traditions current in the N Kingdom, its origin is dated prior to the fall of Samaria ca. 722 BC. About 100 yrs. later the fused J-E document was supplemented by a strand produced by D. The Priestly writer or writers flourished after the destruction of Jerusalem 586 BC. After the Babylonian exile these accumulated and interwoven materials were edited into Pentateuch form by an unknown writer or writers.

9. The 4 main strands have been identified and isolated according to literary criteria held to be valid in the study of any documents. Intense study, great ingenuity, and vast learning have gone into this dissection and linguistic analysis. It is held that the Pentateuch must be of composite origin because certain accounts (e. g., the creation story) and laws (e. g., the Decalog) appear more than once in slightly different versions. These "doublets" appear in various stages of fusion. Some parallel accounts have been left almost unchanged and have merely been set down side by side; others have been woven together so skillfully that only the seam and an occasional spot of color appears here and there to identify the original material. Further proof that the Pentateuch is the work of many hands is sought in vocabulary and style; e. g., J uses Jahweh (Jehovah), E uses Elohim (God) as a name of the Supreme Being and each source has many words that appear almost exclusively in its strand. A distinct style is predicated for each source; J is *volkstümlich,* popular; P is pedantic and statistically dry; D is highly historical.

10. The documentary hypothesis finds each strand marked also by varying points of view. Each writer is said to reflect a stage in the development of Israel's concept of God, J speaking of God in strikingly anthropomorphic terms that do not occur to so marked a degree in E. Later sources give further evidence of growing stress on the monotheistic and transcendental nature of God not found in the earlier writer. Each source also differs in treating Israel's hist., and its choice of materials is dictated by the aim of the writer.

11. Critics admit that it may be difficult to apply these criteria consistently. But they say there is enough validity to make the cumulative evidence conclusive.

12. This view of the origin of the Pentateuch, called the Graf-Wellhausen theory because it was developed esp. by K. H. Graf* and J. Wellhausen,* appeared in rudimentary form ca. a c. earlier. J. Astruc* concluded that Moses incorporated into Gn at least 2 main sources, one of which uses Elohim, the other Jahweh, to denote God. J. G. Eichhorn (see *Eichhorn,* 2) is regarded by many as the father of modern higher criticism; he elaborated Astruc's documentary hypotheses by applying and broadening its principles to the whole Pentateuch; in the last ed. of *Einleitung in das Alte Testament* (1823–24) he concluded that the Pentateuch was a compilation of sources later than Moses, though he conceded that some of the sources may have been of Mosaic origin.

13. But development of the documentary theory did not proceed in a straight line. A rival theory of the origin of the Pentateuch was introd. by Alexander Geddes (1737–1802; Scot. RC) and later championed by W. M. L. De* Wette. Their view that the Pentateuch resulted from fusion of many indep. strands and pieces was called the "fragment theory." Acc. to it the final ed. was not Moses, but the compiling took place at the time of the Exile, though some material may be traced to Moses' time. The main thesis of this theory was later discarded, but its

defenders contributed one of the permanent features of modern documentary theory: identification of the core of Dt, now called the Deuteronomic code, as part of the reform movement of Josiah and attributed to Moses as a literary device.

14. Another rival view that found favor for a time was the "supplement theory," which posits one initial document *(Grundschrift)* supplanted by additions of later writers. The core document was regarded as appearing in the 11th or 10th c. BC; Mosaic authorship was considered impossible. The most influential sponsor of this theory was G. H. A. Ewald.*

15. Neither the fragment theory nor the supplement theory survived for many yrs. H. C. K. F. Hupfeld* revived the documentary hypothesis 1853 in *Die Quellen der Genesis und die Art ihrer Zusammensetzung von neuem untersucht,* and it emerged dominant (see pars. 5–12 above).

16. During the last 50 yrs. some scholars have sought to supplement and even displace the documentary hypothesis by stressing the part that oral transmission rather than written sources played in the development. J. F. H. Gunkel* stressed the need of recognizing the oral beginnings of ancient literature which have their origin in definite settings of their presentation (Sitz* im Leben) and which are still recognizable in certain literary forms *(Gattungen).* Constant recital at various times and occasions modified and enlarged the first short and simple narratives and resulted in more complex and variegated composition in literary form. This attempt to find antecedents of the written form is known as "traditio-historical" research. A more radical rejection of the literary source hypothesis in favor of a long and reliable oral transmission is advanced by a group of Scand. scholars such as Johannes Peder Ejler Pedersen (b. 1883 in Illebölle, Den.; orientalist; prof. Copenhagen) and K. I. A. Engnell.* They and the followers of Gunkel also repudiate Mosaic authorship of the Pentateuch.

17. Conclusions of higher criticism were contested from the outset by conservative scholars. Investigations have been made to disprove the validity of the linguistic canons on which higher critical theories rest.

18. Opposing literature has also pointed to divergence in higher critical theories. No 2 critics agree on a detailed analysis of literature in question. They differ even in major issues. The same book or sections of a book are distributed by various scholars over many cents. and are assigned to many different hands. Multiplicity of theories, often mutually contradictory, does not preclude possibility that 1 theory may be correct, but it indicates the highly subjective character of the investigation and its lack of scientific checks and criteria.

19. Modern archaeol. has also had a sobering effect on the claims of higher criticism. Results of excavations have had direct bearing on some literary questions, as in the case of the Ras Shamra inscriptions. But it is above all in the hist. field that archaeol. has shown some higher critical theories to be unreliable. WR

See also *"Q."*

O. T. Allis, *The Five Books of Moses* (Philadelphia, 1943); G. W. Anderson, *A Critical Introduction to the Old Testament* (London, 1959); A. Bentzen, *Introduction to the Old Testament,* 5th ed., 2 vols. in 1 (Copenhagen, 1959); U. Cassuto, *The Documentary Hypothesis and the Composition of the Pentateuch,* tr. I. Abrahams (Jerusalem, 1961); J. Orr, *The Problem of the Old Testament* (New York, 1926); R. H. Pfeiffer, *Introduction to the Old Testament* (New York, 1948), abridged ed. *The Books of the Old Testament* (New York, 1957); J. E. Steinmueller, *A Companion to Scripture Studies,* 2d ed., II (New York, 1942); E. J. Young, *An Introduction to the Old Testament,* rev. ed. (London, 1964).

Higher Education. 1. Higher educ. is educ. on the coll. or university level. When the Christian era began, the pagan world had many schools of advanced learning. Alexandria was for cents. the intellectual cen. of the world. Many early ch. fathers were educ. there. But as the danger of pagan learning and philos. was more keenly realized, catechumenal schools developed into catechetical schools designed for higher educ. of leaders in the ch.

2. Pantaenus,* Clement* of Alexandria, and Origen* taught at Alexandria (see also *Exegesis,* 3). Origen est. a school at Caesarea in Palestine ca. 231. A school in Rome is dated from the 2d c. These schools, where literature, hist., and science were studied, were attended by scholars of all classes but were planned esp. for clergy training under direction of a bp. Later called episc. or cathedral schools, they spread over all Eur. and continued throughout the Middle Ages. Their importance increased as clergy promotion came to depend somewhat on studies pursued.

3. Ch. councils in the 5th and 6th c. ordered that boys destined for the priesthood be placed in these schools. As attendance increased, appropriate bldgs. were erected, teaching staffs were enlarged, courses of study regulated, and the life of teachers and pupils subjected to regular rules and canons. With the overthrow of Roman culture by the barbarians, higher educ. fell completely into the hands of the ch. From the 8th to the 12th c., monastic schools were of greater importance, but with expansion of knowledge and greater tolerance of inquiry the rigidity and narrowness of these schools resulted in renewed growth and revived importance of cathedral schools. The study of dialectics was emphasized; this stimulated interest in intellectual activity and in logical formulation and statement of religious beliefs. Plato* and Aristotle* dominated in these schools; the method was logical analysis of the subject with little observation and research; knowledge was mainly theol. and sophistic.

4. Because of the scholastic movement and the new intellectual and educ. interest, stimulated during the Crusades* by contact with E and Saracen learning, some cathedral schools developed into univs. The schools at Naples (est. ca. 1224), Bologna (11th c.), and Paris (2d half of 12th c.) became prominent. Many additional schools were est. in the 13th, 14th, and 15th cents. Univs. varied from place to place. Usually the organization was patterned after guilds. In some early univs., students controlled curriculum and faculty and were not under local govt.

5. Chivalry represents the educ. that upper secular soc. received. Training in knightly ideals and activities formed the educ. of the nobility. This educ. was divided into 2 periods: that of a page, which covered ca. the 7th–14th yr., and that of a squire, 14th–21st yr., when the squire was knighted. This educ. was a discipline both for the individual and for the soc. class to which he belonged; the intellectual element was slight. In addition to physical training, educ. emphasized manners and morals. Under chivalry, the ideals constituting the character of a gentleman were more definitely formulated than in modern ages.

6. The Renaissance* vitally affected educ. ideals. The "new learning," the study of classical antiquity, wedged its way into all schools and univs. The most important phase of this revival was restoration of the idea of a liberal educ. as formulated by the Gks. and adapted to the Romans by M. T. Cicero,* Quintilian,* C. Tacitus,* et al. Renaissance educ.

emphasized the physical element and tried to influence conduct and behavior. It was practical and tried to train for effective citizenship and to produce practical judgment in everyday affairs. Its aesthetic element found expression in the study of literature and became the dominant feature in the work of the schools.

7. This broad content and scope of Renaissance educ. was later restricted to the study of the languages and literatures of the ancients, which study, formerly but a means to the end, became the chief end in humanistic educ. Classics were studied chiefly for the sake of language and less for the sake of educ. value. The "new learning" found a permanent home in It. and spread from there through the rest of Eur.; it soon reached Oxford and Cambridge. The hostility of univs., the ch., and monastic schools led to the est. of many schools embodying the new spirit under patronage of monarchs and nobility, e. g., court schools in It. and *Fürstenschulen* (schools for princes) in Ger. The term "gymnasium" (from Gk. *gymnazein,* "to train naked; to exercise") became popular as a name for a humanistic secondary school. The gymnasium at Strasbourg, organized 1537–38 by Johannes and Jakob Sturm,* exerted great influence. St. Paul's School, London, founded ca. 1509, influenced educ. in Eng. Grammar schools of the Am. colonies were fashioned after Eng. schools as to scope and method. The Boston Lat. School was founded 1635. But in Am. the humanistic school gave place to a new type earlier than in any Eur. country.

8. The Reformation deeply affected educ. ideas and aims. Renaissance interests were mainly literary and aesthetic; the Reformation emphasized religious and moral interests. It made the "new learning" serve the Word of God. Lat., Gk., Heb., logic, math, hist., science, and music were studied besides the vernacular. The work of carrying out the ideas of M. Luther* was largely left to his co-workers. P. Melanchthon* became *Praeceptor Germaniae;* he was to Ger. as to educ. reform what Luther was with respect to religious reform. Wittenberg, from which all these influences radiated, was remodeled along humanistic-Prot. lines and became the model of many new univs.

9. At the death of Melanchthon there was scarcely a city in all Ger. that had not modified its schools acc. to his direct advice or his gen. suggestions. Many univs. and other schools threw off allegiance to the pope and transferred it to princes and the state. But even under state control the dominant motive was a religious one, and the school plan was strongly humanistic. These schools were organized into a system in Saxony in the 1520s, in Wüerttemberg 1559. Effectiveness of Prot. schools in reforming soc. and ecclesiastical evils and est. chs. moved the RC Ch. to use the same means. Teaching orders, esp. Jesuits, adopting many Prot. ideas and methods, made educ. their chief aim and controlled RC institutions. From a modern viewpoint their educ. was not broad, but it was thorough and effective.

10. Nearly all colleges est. in Am. before the end of the colonial period grew out of religious motives. Puritans controlled Harvard Coll., Cambridge, Mass., est. 1636. The Coll. of William and Mary, Williamsburg, Va., est. 1693, was a sem. for Angl. ministers; Yale Coll., New Haven, Conn., est. 1701, was under Puritan auspices; Princeton (N. J.) U., founded 1746 at Elizabethtown (now Elizabeth) as the Coll. of New Jersey, was Presb. The Academy and Coll. of Philadelphia, chartered 1753, owed its origin to Benjamin Franklin and was not under denominational control; Columbia U., NYC, was est. 1754 under predominantly Angl. direction as King's Coll.; Brown U., Providence, R. I., was est. 1764 under Bap. influence as R. I. Coll. in Warren, R. I.; Rutgers U., New Brunswick, N. J., was est. 1766 on initiative of leaders of the Dutch Ref. Ch.; Dartmouth Coll., Hanover, N. H., est. 1769, was Cong. See also *Ministry, Education of,* VI A; *Protestant Education in the United States.*

11. After the War of Am. Indep. (Revolutionary War; 1775–83) some States sought control of colleges in their territory. But the 1819 Dartmouth Coll. Case decision of the US Supreme Court protected educ. corporations against pol. interference and roused greater denominational interest in erection of colleges. Since then the no. of colleges has grown rapidly.

12. Development of pub. colleges and univs. was slow. The U. of Ga., Athens, Ga., was chartered 1785, opened ca. 1800; the U. of N. C. was chartered 1789, opened 1795; the U. of Vt., Burlington, Vt., was founded 1791, opened 1800; the U. of Va., Charlottesville, Va., was founded 1819, opened 1825; Ind. U. was est. 1820, the U. of Ala. 1831.

13. Rensselaer Polytechnic Institute, Troy, N. Y., was est. 1824. Emma Willard (nee Hart; 1787–1870) est. Troy (N. Y.) Female Sem. (later called Emma Willard School) 1821. Mount Holyoke Female Sem., South Hadley, Mass., was chartered 1836, opened 1837, called Mount Holyoke Coll. beginning 1893. Other early women's colleges: Wesleyan Coll. (Macon, Ga.), founded 1836; Rockford (Ill.) Coll., est. 1847; Elmira (N. Y.) Coll., est. 1855; Vassar Coll. (Poughkeepsie, N. Y.), chartered 1861. Oberlin (Ohio) Coll., coeducational, was founded 1833. Johns Hopkins U. (Baltimore, Md.), founded 1876, emphasized graduate study.

14. From ca. the middle of the 19th c., efforts to broaden curricular offerings became a prominent trend among colleges and univs. In the 20th c., financial support given univs. by state appropriations, individuals, foundations, and organizations greatly increased.

15. Standards for colleges and univs. have been set by state depts., colleges and univs., and voluntary organizations.

16. The Am. Assoc. of Theol. Schools is concerned with the curriculum and accreditation of theol. schools.

17. In the 20th c., enrollment rivalries and greater demands for higher educ. caused new studies of standards, curricular offerings, and teaching methods.

See also *Ministry, Education of; Universities in the United States, Lutheran.*

P. Monroe, *A Brief Course in the History of Education* (New York, 1915); *A Cyclopedia of Education,* ed. P. Monroe (Detroit, Mich., 1968); W. Boyd, *The History of Western Education,* 3d ed. (London, 1932); E. P. Cubberley, *Public Education in the United States,* rev. and enl. ed. (New York, 1934); S. G. Noble, *A History of American Education* (New York, 1938); F. Eby and C. F. Arrowood, *The History and Philosophy of Education Ancient and Medieval* (Englewood Cliffs, N. J., 1940) and *The Development of Modern Education* (New York, 1934); E. W. Knight, *Education in the United States,* 2d rev. ed. (New York, 1941); H. G. Good, *A History of American Education* (New York, 1956).

Hilarion of Gaza (ca. 291–371). Founder of Palestinian monasticism; b. Tabatha, near Gaza; converted at Alexandria, Egypt; influenced by Anthony.*

MPL, 23, 29–54.

Hilary of Arles (ca. 401–449). Abp. Arles, Fr.; leader of semi-Pelagians.

MPL, 50, 1213–92.

Hilary of Poitiers (ca. 315–367). "Athanasius of the West"; b. Poitiers, Fr. (Gaul), of pagan parentage; bp., though married, ca. 350; opposed Arianism*;

banished 356 to Phrygia, in Asia Minor, an Arian stronghold; returning ca. 361, he purged Gaul of the heresy, but was less successful in It.; outstanding Lat. theol.; hymnist. Works include *De Trinitate.*

Hildebert of Lavardin (ca. 1056–ca. 1133). B. Lavardin, Fr.; educ. at cathedral school of Le Mans; archdeacon Le Mans ca. 1091; bp. Le Mans ca. 1096; abp. Tours 1125; hymnist. Hymns include "De mysterio missae"; "De sacra eucharistia"; "De operibus sex dierum." Other works include *Tractatus theologicus; De sacramento altaris; De expositione missae.*

MPL, 171, 9–1458.

Hildebrand. See *Popes,* 7.

Hildebrand, Joachim (1623–91). B. Walkenried Monastery, Brunswick, Ger.; educ. Jena, Leipzig, Helmstedt; conrector Wolfenbüttel; prof. theol. and sacred antiquities Helmstedt; supt. Grubenhagen and Celle-Lüneburg. Works include *Sacra publica veteris ecclesiae; Theologia dogmatica cum praecipuis controversiis sacris; De nuptiis veterum Christianorum; Immortalitas animae rationalis ex solo lumine naturae ostensa.*

Hildegard of Bingen (ca. 1098–1179). B. probably Bermersheim, near Alzey, Ger. (some say Böckelheim, on the Nahe R., Ger.); one of the most influential women of Middle Ages; abbess Disibodenberg and Rupertsberg, near Bingen. Wrote visions *(Scivias),* letters, sermons, medical treatises, and theol. works.

MPL, 197.

Hilgendorf, Johannes Gottlieb Michael (1847–1928). B. Freistadt, near Milwaukee, Wis.; educ. Conc. Sem., St. Louis, Mo. Pastor Omaha, Nebr.; Arlington, Nebr.; Cheyenne, Wyo.; San Francisco, Calif.; Hood River and Portland, Oreg. First pres. Nebr. Dist., Mo. Syn.; helped found Conc. Teachers Coll., Seward, Nebr., and Luth. Orphanage, Fremont, Nebr.; Mo. Syn. vice-pres.

Hilgenfeld, Adolf Bernhard Christoph Christian (1823–1907). B. Stappenbeck, near Salzwedel, Ger.; prof. Jena; ed. *Zeitschrift für wissenschaftliche Theologie;* adopted theol. of Later Tübingen* School; wrote on Judaism, Biblical criticism, patristics.

Hill, John Henry (1791–July 1, 1882). Educ. Columbia Coll., NYC, and Prot. Episc. Theol. Sem., Alexandria, Va.; Am. Episc. Missionary Soc. miss. to Greece 1830; est. schools for boys and girls in Greece; these schools became models for municipal and nat. schools; chaplain of Brit. legation at Athens 1845.

Hillel I (ca. 70 BC–ca. 10 AD). "The Elder." Rabbi; Babylonian by birth; allegedly a descendant of David; to Palestine; pres. Sanhedrin*; in opposition to Shammai,* he advocated lenient interpretation of the Law.

Hillel II (ca. 330–365). Jewish patriarch ca. 350–365; said to be a descendant of Hillel* I; friend of Julian* the Apostate. To make it possible for Jews outside Palestine to determine festival days, he revealed the rules by which the Jewish calendar is calculated.

Hillel Ben Samuel of Barcelona ("of Verona": ca. 1220–ca. 1295). Grandson of Eleazar ben Samuel of Verona; Jewish physician, philos., Talmudist; practiced medicine at Rome, Capua, Ferrara, and Forli, It.; tr. Lat. scholastic writings into Heb. Works include *Tagmule hanephesh* (Rewards of the Soul).

Hillel Foundations. See *Students, Spiritual Care of,* A 3.

Hiller, Johann Adam (real name Hüller; 1728–1804). B. Wendisch-Ossig, near Görlitz, Silesia; educ. Görlitz, Dresden, and Leipzig; founder and conductor (1781–85) Gewandhaus concerts, Leipzig; cantor and dir. Thomasschule, Leipzig, 1789; originated Singspiel. Works include *Fünfzig geistliche Lieder für Kinder; Allgemeines-Choral-Melodien-Buch.*

Hiller, Philipp Friedrich (1699–1769). B. Mühlhausen on the Enz, Ger.; educ. Denkendorf, Maulbronn, and Tübingen; pastor; hymnist. Works include *Kurze und erbauliche Andachten; Beiträge zur Anbetung Gottes im Geist und in der Wahrheit, oder Morgen- und Abend-andachten nach dem Gebet des Herrn; Geistliches Liederkästlein.*

Hilprecht, Hermann Vollrat (Herman Volrath; Hermann Volrath; 1859–1925). Assyriologist; b. Hohenersleben, Ger.; educ. Leipzig; to U. of Pa., at Philadelphia, 1886; dir. several expeditions to Nippur, Babylonia, and made scientific explorations in Syria and Asia Minor. Works include *Explorations in Bible Lands During the 19th Century; The Excavations in Assyria and Babylonia;* ed. *The Babylonian Expedition of the University of Pennsylvania.*

Hilten, Johann(es) (ca. 1425–ca. 1500). B. perhaps Ilten, near Hanover, Ger.; Franciscan apocalyptic writer; said to have foretold the Reformation (Ap XXVII 1–4).

Hilton, Walter (ca. 1330–ca. 1395). Eng. mystic; Augustinian canon Thurgarton Priory, Nottinghamshire, Eng. Works include *Scala perfectionis.*

Hinayana. See *Buddhism,* 6.

Hinckelmann, Abraham (1652–95). B. Döbeln, Saxony; educ. Wittenberg; rector Gardelegen 1672, Lübeck 1675; deacon Hamburg 1685; court preacher to the landgrave of Hesse-Darmstadt and honorary prof. Giessen 1687; preacher Hamburg 1689; poet; orientalist; accused of millennialism* and pietism.* Works include *Sylloge vocum et phrasum rabbinicarum obscuriorum; De sacrificiis Ebraeorum.*

Hincmar (ca. 806–882). B. probably N Fr.; abp. Reims 845; adviser of Charles* II; strong in statesmanship and ch. govt.; upheld right of nat. ch. against papacy and nat. ruler; also ably defended his rights as metropolitan over bps. See also *Eucharistic Controversies; Predestinarian Controversy.*

Hindemith, Paul (1895–1963). Composer, violist; b. Hanau, Ger.; concertmeister Frankfurt am Main 1915–23; prof. Berlin 1927–33; to US 1933; taught at the Berkshire Music Cen., Tanglewood, an estate in Lenox, Mass., 1940; prof. Yale U., New Haven, Conn., till 1953; prof. U. Zurich, Switz., 1953; identified with ultramodern school. Works include *Das Unaufhörliche* (oratorio).

Hindenburg, Paul von. See *Germany,* C 4.

Hinderer, August Hermann (1877–1945). B. Weilheim an der Teck, Württemberg, Ger.; educ. Tübingen, Greifswald, Halle; dir. Ev. Press. Assoc. of Ger.; chm. Internat. Christian Press Commission 1926 (see *World Council of Churches*); initiated modern concepts of ch. publicity. Works include *Was zur Tat wurde; Bilder aus der inneren Mission in Württemberg; Das ökumenische Schrifttum.*

Hinduism. 1. Major religious and soc. system of India.* Hinduism as a religion began with Vedic* religion and developed through Brahmanism* and philosophic Hinduism into its modern forms. It survived the influences of Buddhism* and Jainism.* In its conglomeration of beliefs and cults, including some of non-Aryans, there is much compromise. It has been able to absorb, but not necessarily assimilate, almost every system of religious and philos. thought except Christianity. Its levels vary from metaphysical speculation to degraded nature worship.

2. Popular manifestations of Hinduism include gross and subtle pantheism,* worship of celestial bodies, trees, rocks, rivers (e. g., the Ganges), the sea, and animals (esp. the cow). Phallicism* and prostitution in temples is being eliminated, modified, or given abstract significance.

3. Hinduism includes the basically pantheistic concept that individual souls begin in the universal soul,

have many forms and incarnations, and finally rejoin the universal soul. Its ideas of creation, God, and man are self-contradictory. Constant themes include karma,* caste (see *Brahmanism,* 3), transmigration* of souls, and essential monism.* According to the doctrine of karma a present life is determined by a previous life. Transmigration of souls continues the soul's purification till all sins are expiated and the soul joins the Absolute or Infinite, like a drop of water falling into the sea. Besides the 4 traditional castes there are many subcastes. Pariahs (untouchables; mems. of the lowest subcastes) were given the name harijans ("children of God"; from Skt. *harijana,* "person belonging to Vishnu"; from *Hari,* "Vishnu," and *jana,* "person") by M. K. Gandhi.* Gen. speaking, marriage is permitted only within caste or subcaste; severe restrictions apply to eating and drinking across caste lines. New castes and subcastes arise along with new occupations; occupations are usually hereditary. The Caste Disabilities Removal Act of 1850 and later legislation tried to remove caste disabilities from the laws of marriage and inheritance.

4. The Hindu Trimurti, or triad, consisting of the gods Brahma, Vishnu, and S(h)iva, reflects Brahman, the neuter, impersonal, supreme, philosophic Absolute (see also *Brahmanism,* 3). The term Brahmanism is derived from Brahman, not from Brahma. Brahma (see also *Brahmanism,* 2) has no large following. Vishnu and Siva early became prominent; Hinduism divides roughly into their followers: Vishnuites and Sivaites. Vishnu, a Vedic celestial god (probably sun-god), regarded as Preserver, is not worshiped in his own person, but in his avatars, i. e., incarnations in animal, human, or superhuman forms. Siva, also a Vedic god (see also *Brahmanism,* 2) is regarded as Destroyer; the phallic aspect of his worship, apparently of non-Aryan origin, has found expression in indulgence or asceticism.

5. The ritualism and emphasis on knowledge of Brahmanism proper (see *Brahmanism,* 3) gave way to the bhakti (personal faith and devotion) of the followers of Vishnu and Siva, esp. in S India. Excessive devotion to a deity included "marriage to the god" by females, who became prostitutes. Vishnu was worshiped in one or more avatars, e. g., Krishna; Siva's emblem was the lingam (phallic symbol), often combined in temple architecture with the yoni (symbol of female genitals), in a stylized form repeated in rows of stone sculptures venerated with prayers and offerings.

6. Important sources for Hindu hist. are the great epic poems *Mahabharata* ("Great Bharata" story) and *Ramayana* ("the Career of Rama," an alleged incarnation of Vishnu). The *Mahabharata* may have begun to take form ca. the 4th c. BC; it was developed and enlarged till ca. 400 AD. It consists of ca. 100,000 stanzas, partly narrative, partly didactic, which tell of the struggle bet. the 2 branches of the house of Bhrata, legendary monarch of India. One of the heroes is Krishna, an alleged incarnation of Vishnu. The Bhagavad* Gita ("Song of the Lord [or of the Blessed One]"), a popular book of devotion in the form of dialog bet. the warrior Arjuna and Krishna, is part of the *Mahabharata.* The *Ramayana,* which also originated several cents. BC but in its present form is later than the Mahabharata, treats of one of Vishnu's avatars. Significant developments leading away from traditional Hinduism occurred with the rise of the Sikhs* in the 16th c. Increasing influence of Christianity and W civilization led to reform movements directed against polytheism and the abuses of the old religion. A theistic soc., the Brahma (or Brahmo) Samaj (or Sabha) (Bengali "Soc. of Brahman"), founded 1828 by a Brahmin, Ram* Mohan Roy (or Ray, or Rai) in cooperation with Wm. Adam* (Eng. Bap. miss. to India 1817; became Unitarian May 1821; d. 1883), was much influenced by Islam and Christianity; it returned to the monotheism of the Upanishads. Ram Mohan Roy was followed 1841 by Debendra Nath Tagore (1817–1905), father of the poet Rabindrâ Nath Tagore (1861–1941). Under Debendra's leadership the movement became more Hindu in character. Religious dispute led to a split 1865–66, when the Bharatvarshiya Brahma Samaj (Brahman Soc. of India; called Naba Bidhan, or Nava Vidhana, "New Dispenation," Jan. 1881) with emphasis on soc. reform, was formed by Keshab Chandra Sen (1838–84). Thereafter Debendra's organization was known as Adi Brahma Samaj (Original Brahman Soc.). Further fragmentation followed, with unsuccessful attempts at Hindu-Christian syncretism; decline of influence resulted. The Arya Samaj (Aryan Soc.) was founded 1875 by Mul Sankar (Dayananda Sarasvati*; 1824–83) to reform Indian religion. It regards the Vedas as divine revelation and is hostile to Christianity.

7. Gadadhar Chatterji (Ramakrishna* Paramahamsa; 1834–86), mystic, devotee of the goddess Kali, emphasized soc. service. Some of his followers, esp. Swami Vivekananda* (Narendranath Datta: ca. 1862–1902), devoted themselves to the spread of his teaching through the Ramakrishna mission (see also *Vedanta Society*). Gandhi, though more of a pol. than religious leader, effected reforms in matters with ancient religious sanction. Aurobindo Ghose (Yoga* philos.; 1872–1950) tried to combine Vedanta ideas with evolution theories in his ashram (religious community) est. 1910 in Pondicherry, India; his movement spread to other countries. GVS AJB

See also *Sacred Literature; Shastras; Theosophy.*

G. G. Atkins and C. S. Braden, *Procession of the Gods,* rev. ed. (New York, 1936); R. C. Dutt, *The Civilization of India* (London, 1900); J. A. Dubois, *Hindu Manners, Customs and Ceremonies,* 3d ed. (Oxford, Eng., 1906), ed. and tr. H. K. Beauchamp; J. N. Farquhar, *A Primer of Hinduism,* 2d ed. (London, 1914); H. Ringgren and A. V. Ström, *Religions of Mankind Today and Yesterday,* ed. J. C. G. Greig, tr. N. L. Jensen (Philadelphia, 1967).

Hinschius, Paul (1835–98). B. Berlin, Ger.; educ. Heidelberg and Berlin; taught canon law at Halle, Kiel, Berlin. Works include critical ed. of the pseudo-Isidorian* Decretals.

Hintze, Otto Charles, Jr. See *New Guinea,* 7.

Hippo Regius, Council of. See *Carthage, Synods and Councils of.*

Hippolytus (ca. 170–ca. 235). Scholars differ in attempts to identify him and on details of his life. Photius* calls him a pupil of Irenaeus*; opposed patripassianism* (see *Monarchianism,* B); accused Calixtus I (see *Monarchianism,* B 2) of Sabellianism (see *Monarchianism,* B 6) and lax discipline; elected bp. by his followers, thus causing so-called schism of Hippolytus, which lasted till 235; called 1st antipope. Works include *Philosophumena* (Exposition of Philosophical Teachings; also known as Refutation of All Heresies); *Syntagma* (Against All Heresies); *Demonstratio de Christo et Antichristo;* chronicle; commentaries. See also *Schools, Early Christian,* 2.

Hirah. See *Middle East,* L.

Hiranyagarbha. See *Brahmanism,* 2.

Hirschberger Bibel. M. Luther's* Ger. Bible, with annotations and parallel references, issued by E. Liebich* and J. F. Burg,* 3 vols., Hirschberg, Silesia, 1756–63.

Hirscher, Johann Baptist von (1788–1865). B. Altergarten, near Ravensburg, Ger.; RC prof. Tübingen 1817, Freiburg 1837; theology Biblical-Augustinian;

exponent of reform; advocated lay participation in diocesan syns.

Hirtenbrief. See *Buffalo Synod,* 3, 6.

Hispaniola (Sp. Española; Haiti, perhaps from a native word for "land of mountains"). Is. of cen. W. Indies; W third is rep. of Haiti, rest is Dominican Rep. Discovered 1492 by Christopher Columbus (1451–1506). See also *Caribbean Islands,* A; C; E 2, 3.

Historia Langobardica (Lombardica). See *Golden Legend.*

Historical Apologetics. See *Apologetics, Christian,* II.

Historical Criticism. See *Historicocritical Method.*

Historical Depositories in America, Lutheran. See *Archives.*

Historical Institute, Concordia. See *Archives.*

Historical Materialism. See *Marx, Karl Heinrich.*

Historical Societies. See *Archives.*

Historical Theology. See *Theology.*

Historicism. 1. One definition of historicism calls it "a theory that all sociocultural phenomena are historically determined, that all truths are relative, . . . and that the student of the past must enter into the mind and attitudes of past periods, accept their point of view, and avoid all intrusion of his own standards or preconceptions" (*Webster's Third New International Dictionary,* p. 1073).

2. J. G. v. Herder* in *Ideen zur Philosophie der Geschichte der Menschheit* (4 parts, 1784–91) stressed the organic unity of the historical process. He believed in an evolutionary process: every culture building on the basis of the preceding and striving for a higher humanity. History is a result of the interplay of environment and an internal force which can be described as the spirit of man; it is the scene of God's activity, the fulfillment of God's plan, the revelation of God in nature. Man exists solely to advance humanity (Humanität), the ideal which dominated Herder's later life.

3. G. W. F. Hegel* in *Vorlesungen über die Philosophie der Geschichte* viewed history as a logical process and felt that history could be explained dialectically (thesis, antithesis, synthesis). His philos. of history is part of his philos. of spirit. Historical phenomena are manifestations of the Weltgeist (World Spirit), which is opposed to nature and manifests itself in the spirit of the nation (Volksgeist), which in turn creates the total culture of the nation. The freedom (clue to history) towards which history moves is the freedom of the community as a whole.

4. Ultimately world history supplants Heilsgeschichte* in Herder's and Hegel's speculative philos. of history. C. L. Dilthey,* who rejected positivistic, naturalistic adaptations to history of A. Comte* and others, proclaimed the "autonomy of history," in which man and the principle of relativity were prominent. E. Troeltsch* in *Der Historismus und seine Probleme* (pub. 1922) preferred F. W. Nietzsche's* hist. philos. to that of K. H. Marx.* Troeltsch tried to overcome historicism by a formula in which history was to overcome history, by a cultural synthesis of the worthy past with the worthy present, by metaphysics. Historicism, which leaves no room for Heilsgeschichte and converts world history into revelation, has been called "Christian" heresy because it grew out of Christian soil. Progressivistic theories of history have received much criticism in recent yrs., and Heilsgeschichte has been used to overcome the predicament into which historicism brought theologians.

R. G. Collingwood, *The Idea of History,* ed. T. M. Knox (Oxford, 1946); H. Butterfield, *Christianity and History* (London, 1949); H. W. Krumwiede, *Glaube und Geschichte in der Theologie Luthers* (Göttingen, 1952); E. Fülling, *Geschichte als Offenbarung* (Berlin, 1956); *Theories of History,* ed. P. Gardiner (Glencoe, Ill., 1959); K. R. Popper, *The Poverty of Historicism* (London, 1957); W. H. Walsh, *An Introduction to Philosophy of History,* rev. ed. (London, 1958); *Philosophy & History: Essays Presented to Ernst Cassirer,* ed. R. Klibansky and H. J. Paton (Oxford, 1936). HFB

Historicocritical Method (Historical Criticism). Term used to designate a variety of methods using historical research in interpreting a document. See also *Exegesis,* 9; *Higher Criticism; Isagogics; Vitringa, Campegius.*

Historicogrammatical Method. See *Grammaticohistorical Method.*

Historicoreligious School. See *Religionsgeschichtliche Schule.*

History, Biblical. See *Biblical History.*

History, Dialectic of. See *Hegel, Georg Wilhelm Friedrich.*

History, Philosophy of. The pessimistic philos. of hist. presumes that human events have no pattern and reveal no control or concern of God. The humanistic philos. of hist. concerns itself with human events as reflections of human personality and/or groups (the hero dominant; sociological theories of hist.). The Christian philos. of hist. views God as dominant in human affairs, controlling and moving all things for His purposes. On the material level, God is concerned with preservation of the human race, with dispersion of peoples over the globe, with their protection by govt., and with human institutions. On the spiritual level, God uses hist. to keep man aware of his need for God; its misfortunes and disasters can be regarded as chastisements designed to turn man to God. Thus the Christian sees not only the pleasurable and beneficent events and trends of hist. but also, in its disasters and horrors, the hand of God seeking out man that He might glorify him by humbling him. In this philos. of hist. the greatest event is that in which God has intervened most directly to reveal His love to man, namely, the incarnation and redemption of Jesus Christ. All other events of hist., in the economy of God's design, have only the function of turning men to Christ before the end of time. RRC

See also *Apologetica, Christian,* III C; *Historicism.*

O. Piper, *God in History* (New York, 1939); *Philosophy and History: A Symposium,* ed. S. Hook (New York, 1963); J. Maritain, *On the Philosophy of History,* ed. J. W. Evans (New York, 1957); E. Kahler, *The Meaning of History* (New York, 1964); W. H. Dray, *Philosophy of History* (Englewood Cliffs, N. J., 1964); A. C. Danto, *Analytical Philosophy of History* (Cambridge, 1965); S. Kracauer, *History: The Last Things Before the Last* (New York, 1969); P. Gardiner, *The Nature of Historical Explanation* (New York, 1968).

History of Doctrine. See *Doctrine, Christian, History of; Dogmatics.*

History of Religion. See *Religion, Comparative; Religion, Science of.*

History of Susanna. See *Apocrypha,* A 3.

Hitchcock, Harvey Rexford (Mar. 13, 1799–Aug. 29, 1855). B. Great Barrington, Mass.; educ. Williams Coll., Williamstown, Mass., and Auburn (N. Y.) Theol. Sem.; ABCFM miss. to Sandwich Islands (Hawaii), arriving Honolulu 1832.

Hitler, Adolf. See *Germany,* C 4; *Kirchenkampf.*

Hittites. People in Asia Minor whose empire in the 2d millennium BC rivaled and threatened the power of Babylonia and Egypt. The name is derived from Heth (Gn 10:15), occurs repeatedly in the OT (e. g., Gn 23:1-20; 26:34; Jos 9:1; 2 Sm 11), and is assoc. with Khatti (Hatti), a city or region in E Asia Minor. Much information about the Hittites was gained from archaeol. finds at Bogazköy (Boghazkeui; Khatti; Hattushash; Hattusa; Gk. Pteria), N cen. Turkey, where ruins of a probable capital of a Hittite dynasty (ca. 16th–ca. 12th c. BC) were found.

The Hittite empire began with people who spoke an Indo-Eur. language and who founded city-states in Asia Minor ca. 2,000 BC. Consolidation of power into an empire dates from ca. 1,800 BC. Hittites engaged in war with Babylonia and Egypt. Hittites had settled in Palestine by the time of the patriarchs.

The Hittite religion was anthropomorphic. The gods were immortal, possessed a numinous ethical power *(para handandatar),* were masters of men, and were worshiped in temples or at open air sanctuaries. They were derived from many sources including the Hattic (e. g., Katahzipuris [Hittite: Kamrusipas]: goddess of healing; Wurusemu: sun-goddess; Taru: storm-god; Telepinus: vegetation god) and Hurrian (e. g., Hebat and Teshub, identified by many with Wurusemu and Taru; Shaushka, identified with Ishtar [see *Babylonians, Religion of the,* 1]).

Prominent elements in Hittite religion included concepts of sin, magic, prophecy, divination, myth. EL

Hjärne, Harald Gabriel (1848–1922). B. Klastorp, Västergötland, Swed.; prof. Uppsala 1885–1913. Wrote secular and ch. histories. Works include *Stat och kyrka; Gustaf Adolf, protestantismens förkämpe; Reformationsriksdagen i Västeraas; Kyrkliga inflytelser inom Sveriges äldre statsrätt.*

Hobart, John Henry (1775–1830). B. Philadelphia, Pa.; educ. Coll. of Philadelphia (now the U. of Pa.) and Coll. of N. J. (now Princeton); ordained Prot. Episc. deacon 1798, priest 1801; asst. bp. Diocese of N. Y. 1811, bp. 1816. Championed conservatism. Supported S. S. Founded Prot. Episc. Theol. Soc., NYC, 1806 (became Gen. Theol. Sem. 1817), N. Y. Sun. School Soc. 1817. Works include *A Companion for the Altar; The Clergyman's Companion; A Collection of Essays on the Subject of Episcopacy; An Apology for Apostolic Order and Its Advocates; The Christian's Manual of Faith and Devotion; The State of the Departed.*

Hobbes, Thomas (1588–1679). Philos.; b. Westport (Malmesbury), Wiltshire, Eng.; educ. Oxford. Rationalist (see *Rationalism*); held that sensation is the only source of knowledge; held that man emerges from a state of nature in which he is free, but exchanges his freedom for security by social contract (see *Government*). Best statement of his pol. and soc. philos. is in *Leviathan;* other works include *Behemoth; The Art of Rhetoric; The Elements of Law; Elementa philosophica de cive.* See also *Deism,* III 1.

Hobson, Benjamin (Jan. 2, 1816–July 28, 1839). B. Welford, Eng.; LMS med. miss. in China 1839; worked at Macao, Hong Kong, Canton, and Shanghai. Wrote and tr. into Chinese treatises on natural philos. and medical subjects. Works include *A Medical Vocabulary in English and Chinese.*

Hoburg, Christian (Hohburg; pseudonyms Elias Praetorius, Bernhard Baumann, Christianus Montaltus, Andreas Seuberlich; 1607–75). Ev. theol. and spiritualist; b. Lüneburg, Ger.; educ. Königsberg; in ch. and school work at various places; proofreader Lüneburg; Mennonite preacher Altona (now part of Hamburg). Works include *Der unbekannte Christus; Theologia mystica.* See also *Breckling, Friedrich.*

Hochmann von Ho(c)henau, Ernst Christoph. See *Brethren,* 1.

Hochstetter, Andreas Adam (1668–1718). Luth. theol.; pietist; b. Tübingen; son of J. A. Hochstetter*; educ. Maulbronn and Tübingen; prof. eloquence and poetry 1697, moral philos. 1698, theol. 1705 Tübingen; mem. of consistory and court preacher Stuttgart 1711; returned to Tübingen ca. 1715.

Hochstetter, Christian Friedrich (W.) (Apr. 1, 1828–June 12, 1905). B. Lorch, Württemberg, Ger.; educ. Tübingen; to US 1853; served Ohio Syn. (see *Ohio and Other States, Evangelical Lutheran Joint Synod of*) congs. in Fort Wayne, Ind., and Toledo, Ohio; asst. to J. A. A. Grabau* and joined Buffalo* Syn. 1857; present on side of Buffalo Syn. at Buffalo* colloquy Nov.–Dec. 1866; joined Missouri* Syn. ch. in Buffalo, N. Y., 1867. Pastor Pittsburgh, Pa., 1867; Indianapolis, Ind., 1868; Frohna, Mo., 1877; Humberstone and Stonebridge, Welland Co., Ont., Can., 1879; Wolcottsville, N. Y., 1883; Jordan, Lincoln Co., Ont., Can., 1900. Writings show interest in doctrinal discussion; emphasized unity through purity of doctrine. Ed. *Lutherisches Volksblatt* 1882–83; other works include *"Werdet nicht der Menschen Knechte!"; Erinnerungen an D. C. F. W. Walther, aus dessen hinterlassenen Briefen und anderweitigen vorliegenden Urkunden* (in *Lutherisches Volksblatt,* XXVIII, 7 [Apr. 7, 1898], 52–XXIX, 26 [Dec. 28, 1899], 205, and *Zeuge und Anzeiger,* IV, 51 [May 22, 1904], 399–VI, 18 [Oct. 1, 1905], 140); *Die Geschichte der Evangelisch-lutherischen Missouri-Synode in Nord-Amerika, und ihrer Lehrkämpfe von der sächsischen Auswanderung im Jahre 1838 an biz zum Jahre 1884.* See also *Lutheran Church – Missouri Synod Districts of The,* A 9.

Hochstetter, Friedrich (1870–1935). Ger. ev. theol.; active in Württemberg 1892–1900; pastor in Austria 1900, Berlin 1917. Works include *Fünfundzwanzig Jahre evangelischer Bewegung in Österreich.*

Hochstetter, Johann Andreas (1637–1720). B. Kirchheim unter Teck, Ger.; educ. Tübingen; pastor Wahlen, Böblingen, and Tübingen; prof. Tübingen; prelate Maulbronn and Bebenhausen; pietist. Works include *Disputationes.*

Hocking, William Ernest (1873–1966). B. Cleveland, Ohio; educ. Harvard, Göttingen, Berlin, Heidelberg; taught at Andover (Mass.) Theol. Sem., U. of Calif., Yale, Harvard. Tried to bring philos. out of the academy into the surrounding world; his system is classified as objective idealism and affirms the "other mind" or God; Cong. Works include *Science and the Idea of God; The Meaning of God in Human Experience; Strength of Men and Nations; Thoughts on Death and Life; Types of Philosophy.* See also *I-Thou.*

Hodge, Archibald Alexander (1823–86). Son of C. Hodge*; b. Princeton, N. J.; educ. Princeton; miss. in India 1847–50; pastor Md., Va., and Pa.; prof. theol. Western Theol. Sem., Allegheny (Pittsburgh), Pa.; assoc. and successor of his father at Princeton; helped found *Presbyterian Review.*

Hodge, Charles (1797–1878). Conservative Presb. theol.; father of A. A. Hodge*; b. Philadelphia, Pa.; educ. Princeton, N. J.; prof. Princeton Theol. Sem. Founded and ed. *Biblical Repertory* (later called *Biblical Repertory and Theological Review,* and after 1836 *Biblical Repertory and Princeton Review*); other works include *A Commentary on the Epistle to the Ephesians; Commentary on the Epistle to the Romans; Systematic Theology.*

Hodgkin, Henry Theodore. See *World Alliance for Promoting International Friendship Through the Churches.*

Hodgson, Shadworth Hollway (1832–1912). B. Boston, Lincolnshire, Eng.; 1st pres. Aristotelian Soc. (founded 1880 for systematic study of philos.); claimed to continue and expand the philos. of D. Hume* and I. Kant*; held that experience is both consciousness and content. Works include *The Metaphysic of Experience; Time and Space; The Philosophy of Reflection.* See also *Automatism; Metaphysical Society, The.*

Hodza, Michal Miloslav (1811–70). Slovak Lutheran pastor; educ. Bratislava and Vienna; pastor Vrbicko-Svätomikuláš; with Ludevít (L'udovít) Štúr (1815–56; Slovak writer, philos., pol.) and J. M. Hurban* unsuccessfully opposed union of Slovakia with Hung. See also *Slovakia, Lutheran Theology in*, 2.

Höe von Höenegg, Matthias (Hohenegg) (1580–1645). B. Vienna, Austria; educ. Wittenberg; 3d court preacher Dresden 1602; supt. Plauen 1603; dir. ev. chs. and schools Prague 1611; 1st court preacher Dresden 1613; active politically in Thirty* Years' War. Works include *Evangelisches Handbüchlein.* See also *Decisio Saxonica.*

Hoeck, Johann (Johannes Aepinus; 1499–1553). B. Ziesar, Mark Brandenburg, Ger.; educ. Wittenberg; pastor Hamburg 1529; supt. and cathedral pastor 1532; signed Schmalkaldic Articles (see *Lutheran Confessions,* B 2). Involved in controversy on Christ's descent into hell. See also *Westphal, Joachim* (of Hamburg).

Hoedemaker, Philippus Jacobus (1839–1910). Dutch theol.; in Am. 1851–63; pastor 1868; prof. Amsterdam 1880–88; held that offices and syns. are the organs through which Christ is active in the ch. and that reform is to be sought in reorganization from within.

Hoefling. See *Höfling.*

Hoelemann. See *Hölemann.*

Hoelscher. See *Hölscher.*

Hoen, Cornelisz Hendricxz (Cornelius; Hoon; Honius; Honnius; d. 1524). Dutch theol.; b. probably Gouda, near Rotterdam. On basis of a treatise by J. Wessel* he developed theory that in the words of institution of the Lord's Supper "is" means "signifies"; this view found favor with H. Zwingli* and his followers (see also *Grace, Means of,* IV 3).

Hoenecke. See *Hönecke.*

Höenegg, Höe von. See *Höe von Höenegg.*

Hoepfner. See *Höpfner.*

Hofacker, Ludwig (1798–1828). B. Wildbad, Württemberg, Ger.; brother of W. Hofacker*; educ. Tübingen, where he had conversion experience; vicar Stuttgart; pastor Rielingshausen. Influenced by N. L. v. Zinzendorf's* writings; powerful preacher of an awakening in Württemberg. Works include *Predigten für alle Sonn-, Fest-, und Feiertage.*

Hofacker, Wilhelm (1805–48). B. Gärtringen, near Herrenberg, Württemberg, Ger.; brother of L. Hofacker*; educ. Tübingen; pastor Waiblingen and Stuttgart; with his brother, leader in awakening. Ed. *Wilhelmsdorfer Predigtbuch;* other works include *Predigten für alle Sonn- und Festtage.*

Hofbauer, Johannes Clemens Maria (Hoffbauer; 1751–1820). B. Tasswitz, Moravia; vicar-gen. Redemptorists* N of Alps; opposed Josephinism (see *Joseph II and Josephinism*) and Enlightenment* in Vienna.

Höffding, Harald (1843–1931). Dan. positivist philos.; b. Copenhagen; educ. Copenhagen; prof. Copenhagen; influenced by S. A. Kierkegaard*; sought essence of religion in "conservation of value"; denied basic Christian tenets.

Hoffman, Emil (Mar. 1, 1862–Apr. 11, 1926). B. Oebisfelde, Ger.; educ. Halle and at the theol. sem. of J. Paulsen* at Kropp, Ger. (see also *Kropp Seminary*); pastor first at North Easthope-Wellesley-Gadshill, Ont., Can., then at Hamilton 1888–1904, Berlin 1904–12, Toronto 1912–20, all in Ont.; pres. Waterloo (Ont.) Theol. Sem. 1920–26 and pastor St. James Luth. Ch., St. Jacobs, Ont.; pres. Can. Syn. (see *Canada,* A 7–9; *United Lutheran Church, Synods* of, 1).

Hoffman, Melchior. See *Hofmann, Melchior.*

Hoffmann, August Heinrich (Hoffmann von Fallersleben; 1798–1874). Poet; philologist; b. Fallersleben, Ger.; educ. Helmstedt, Brunswick, and Göttingen; prof. Ger. language and literature Breslau 1835; banished 1843–48 for liberal pol. views; librarian Corvey (Höxter), Ger., 1860. Works include *Geschichte des deutschen Kirchenliedes bis auf Luthers Zeit.*

Hoffmann, Daniel (ca. 1538–1611). B. Halle, Ger.; educ. Jena; prof. ethics, dialectics, and theol. Helmstedt; opposed Philippists* and humanists; rejected a ubiquity which he alleged was in the FC; persuaded Brunswick not to subscribe to the FC; influenced by P. Ramus,* he opposed Aristotelianism (see *Aristotle*).

Hoffmann, Francis Arnold (June 5, 1822–Jan. 23, 1903). B. Herford, Kreis Minden, Westphalia, Prussia; to Chicago, Ill., 1840; taught school at Addison 1840; prepared for ministry probably under F. Schmid* in Mich.; pastor Addison till 1847, Schaumburg 1847–51; helped give Luth. character to several Ger. congs. in N Ill.; ordained E. Eielsen*; joined Missouri* Syn. 1849; resigned from ministry 1851 because of illness; lawyer; banker; statesman; cofounder Rep. party; lt. gov. Ill. 1861–65; retired from pub. life 1875; agricultural writer and ed. under pseudonym Hans Buschbauer; ed. *Haus- und Bauernfreund.*

K. Kretzmann, "Francis Arnold Hoffmann," *CHIQ,* XVIII (July 1945), 37–54.

Hoffmann, Gottfried (1658–1712). B. Löwenberg, Silesia; educ. Leipzig; conrector, then rector, Lauban; rector Zittau; hymnist. Hymns include "Hilf, Jesu, dass ich meinen Nächsten liebe."

Hoffmann, John Martin Theodore Ernst (1823–87). B. Treppeln, Prussia; educ. Berlin* Miss. Soc. I training school; to Am. 1850; served congs. in N. Y. state and Albany; ardently supported N. Y. Ministerium (see *United Lutheran Church, Synods of,* 15).

Hoffmann, Melchior. See *Hofmann, Melchior.*

Hoffmann von Fallersleben. See *Hoffmann, August Heinrich.*

Hoffmeister, Johann(es) (ca. 1509–47). B. Oberndorf am Neckar, Ger.; Augustinian hermit; prior at Colmar 1533; vicar-gen. of Ger. 1546; devoted life to defending his order against Lutheranism. See also *Regensburg Confernce.*

Hofhaimer, Paulus von (1459–1537). B. Radstadt, Austria; court organist to Maximilian* I. Works include choral works and songs.

Höfling, Johann Wilhelm Friedrich (1802–53). Conservative Luth. theol.; b. near Bayreuth, Ger.; educ. Erlangen; pastor Nürnberg 1827; prof. practical theol. Erlangen 1833; mem. high consistory Munich 1852. Helped found *Zeitschrift für Protestantismus und Kirche* (also known as *Erlanger Zeitschrift);* other works include *Grundsätze evangelisch-lutherischer Kirchenverfassung; Das Sakrament der Taufe nebst den andern damit zusammenhängenden Akten der Initiation; Von den Festen oder heiligen Zeiten der christlichen Kirche.*

Hofmann, Carl Gottlob (1703–74). B. Schneeberg, Ger.; educ. Leipzig; lectured on philos. and philol., served as preacher, Leipzig; prof. theol. Wittenberg; held various offices, including that of gen. supt. Ed. *Das privilegirte Vollständige und vermehrte Leipziger Gesangbuch;* other works include *De discrimine fidei divinae et humanae; Gegründete Anzeige derer Herrnhuthischen Grund-Irrthümer in der Lehre von der heiligen Dreyeinigkeit und von Christo; Institutiones theologiae exegeticae in usum academicarum praelectionum adornatae; Introductio in lectionem Novi Testamenti; Die in der Evangelischen Kirche gewöhnlichen Sonn- und Festtäglichen Episteln und Evangelia, mit . . . Betrachtungen.*

Hofmann, Johann Michael Ferdinand Heinrich (1824–1911). Painter; b. Darmstadt, Ger.; prof. Dresden 1870–92. Works include scenes from the life of Christ.

Hofmann, Johann Christian Konrad von (1810–77).

B. Nürnberg, Ger.; educ. Erlangen and Berlin; prof. Erlangen (see *Lutheran Theology After 1580,* 11) and Rostock; influenced by F. D. E. Schleiermacher,* G. W. F. Hegel,* and F. W. J. v. Schelling.* Unfolded theol. from consciousness of believer; held that Christianity is communion of God and man as mediated by the Spirit of Christ present in the ch. and that Christ suffered on our behalf, not in our stead. Works include *Weissagung und Erfüllung im alten und im neuen Testamente; Der Schriftbeweis; Die heilige Schrift neuen Testaments zusammenhängend untersucht; Biblische Hermeneutik,* Eng. tr. C. Preus, *Interpreting the Bible; Encyclopädie der Theologie; Theologische Ethik.* See also *Kenosis.*

P. Wapler, *Johannes v. Hofmann: Ein Beitrag zur Geschichte der theologischen Grundprobleme, der kirchlichen und der politischen Bewegungen im 19. Jahrhundert* (Leipzig, 1914); E. Hübner, *Schrift und Theologie: Eine Untersuchung zur Theologie Joh. Chr. K. von Hofmanns* (Munich, 1956).

Hofmann, Melchior (Hoffman; Hoffmann; ca.1500–ca. 1544). B. Schwäbisch Hall, Ger.; Anabap. mystic. Lay preacher; traveled in Livonia, Estonia, Swed., and N Ger.; denied Luth. doctrine of Lord's Supper; involved in controversy with J. Bugenhagen*; proclaimed advent of New Jerusalem to be located at Strasbourg; later imprisoned there; followers known as Hofmannites or Melchiorites. See also *Münster Kingdom.*

Hofmeister, Sebastian (1476–1533). B. Schaffhausen, Switz.; barefooted monk; educ. Paris; corresponded with M. Luther,* H. Zwingli,* F. Myconius,* and G. Farel*; reformer in Zofingen, Switz.; prof. Bern.

Hofstede, Petrus (1716–1803). B. Zuidlaren, Drenthe, Neth.; educ. Groningen and Franeker; honorary prof. ch. hist. and archaeol. Rotterdam; orthodox Calvinist.

Hofstede de Groot, Petrus (1802–86). B. Leer, Ostfriesland, Ger.; educ. Groningen; Ref. pastor Ulrum, Groningen, Neth., 1826–29; prof. Groningen 1829; helped found Groningen* School. Ed. *Waarheid in Liefde;* other works include *De moderne theologie in Nederland.*

Högström, Per. See *Lapland.*

Hohburg. See *Hoburg.*

Hohenegg. See *Höe von Hönegg.*

Hohenstein, Herman Hugo (Jan. 26, 1894–May 8, 1961). B. Peoria, Ill.; educ. Conc. Coll., Milwaukee, Wis., and Conc. Sem., St. Louis, Mo.; pastor Immanuel Luth. Ch. 1916, Christ Luth. Ch. 1919, both in St. Louis; installed as Program Dir. of Station KFUO (see *Radio Stations, Religious,* 2–4) Oct. 11, 1925; pioneered in religious broadcasting. Ed. *The Gospel Voice.*

Hoikka, J. J. See *Finnish Lutherans in America,* 1.

Hokanson, Magnus Fredrik. See *Haakanson, Magnus Fredrik.*

Hokkes. See *Nichiren.*

Holbach, Paul Henri Dietrich d' (1723–89). Fr. philos.; b. Edesheim, Palatinate, Ger., of Ger. parents; educ. Leiden; to Paris 1749; home became meeting place of prominent freethinkers (see *Freethinker*); one of the Encyclopedists*; attacked Christian religion as based on fraud and ignorance. Works include *Système de la nature,* which tries to combine materialism,* sensualism (see *Sensationalism*), determinism,* and atheism.*

Holbein, Hans. 1. The Elder (ca. 1460–1524). Painter; father of 2; b. Augsburg, Ger.; works include altar of St. Sebastian, Munich. 2. The Younger (ca. 1497–1543). Painter and engraver; son of 1; b. Augsburg, Ger.; court painter to Henry* VIII ca. 1536; works include OT illustrations.

Holberg, Ludwig (1684–1754. Poet, hist., philos.; b. Bergen, Norw.; educ. Copenhagen; prof. Copenhagen; traveled in Eng. and on the Continent; called founder of Dan. literature; writings emphasize tolerance. Works include *Almindelig Kirke-Historie fra Christendommens förste Begyndelse til Lutheri Reformation; Jödisk Historie fra Verdens Begyndelse fortsat til disse Tider; Religion, Love, Videnskab og Handel; Moralske Tanker.*

Holcot, Robert. See *Robert Holcot.*

Holdeman, John (1832–1900). B. New Pittsburg, Wayne Co., Ohio; began indep. preaching 1859; founded Church of God in Christ, Mennonite. See also *Mennonite Churches,* 3 a.

Hölderlin, Johann Christian Friedrich (1770–1843). Poet and novelist; b. Lauffen, Ger.; studied theol. at Tübingen; influenced by F. G. Klopstock,* J. C. F. v. Schiller,* J. W. v. Goethe,* J. G. v. Herder.* His earliest poetry shows influence of pietism; 2d period emphasized nature and the Kingdom of God on earth; in his prime, the spirit of nature became the spirit of hist. and he became concerned with problems of individual existence and yearning for the all. Works include *Hyperion; Der Tod des Empedokles; Die Verfahrensweise des poetischen Geistes; An die Hoffnung; Heimkunft.*

Hölemann, Hermann Gustav (1809–86). B. Baude, near Grossenhain, Ger.; educ. Meissen and Leipzig; taught at Zwickau and Leipzig; conservative Luth. theol. Works include *Bibelstudien; Die Reden des Satan in der Heiligen Schrift.*

Holiness (related to Anglo-Saxon *hal,* "whole, well"). 1. "Holiness is the absolute purity of God, according to which His affections, thoughts, will, and acts are in perfect consistency and harmony with His own nature, and in energetic opposition to everything that is not in conformity therewith" (A. L. Graebner,* *Outlines of Doctrinal Theology,* par. 36). In OT God is holy and stands utterly above the created world; He is the wholly other, the transcendent God (Ex 3:5; 19:12-13, 20-24). The holy God imparts Himself; He wishes men to share in His divine life within the scope of His judgment and mercy (Dt 7:6; Lv 11:44). His holiness is dynamic, manifested when He executes judgment (Ezek 28:22). The Holy One of Israel is man's Redeemer (Is. 43:14). The holiness of the Lord is assoc. with the glory of the Lord and with fire (e. g., Ex 3:2-5; 19:18-22).

2. NT understanding of holiness is built on the OT (1 Ptr 3:15; cf. Ps 99:9). Jesus is called "the Holy One of God" (Mk 1:24). The NT ch. is successor to the OT community of God's holy people (Ex 19:6; 1 Ptr 2:9-10); Christians are called to be saints, holy ones (Ro 1:7; 1 Co 1:2); the vocabulary of holiness appears, e. g., in NT statements regarding the work of the Holy* Spirit and the life and conduct of "the saints" and in references to "holy prophets" (Acts 3:21), "holy apostles" (Eph. 3:5), "holy calling" (2 Ti 1:9), "holy scriptures" (Ro 1:2), "holy covenant" (Lk 1:72).

3. In the hist. of theol. the classical view associates God's holiness with His righteousness and law. The theol. of F. D. E. Schleiermacher* and A. Ritschl* reduced the content of the concept of holiness, the former saying that God's holiness in effect was His approval and disapproval of man by His law and man's conscience, the latter suggesting that holiness is of no concern to man. Current theol. is trying to grasp the Biblical idea of holiness. God's love is holy love. Holiness is more than an ethical quality; there is also an ontological aspect (see *Ontology*). For some this means God's opposition to sin (K. Barth*), for others, God's transcendence (H. E. Brunner; see *Switzerland, Contemporary Theology in,* 6–8); for others, the Holy One is unapproachable (P. Tillich*).

4. Holiness is joined with love, yet is distinct from it. Holiness creates distance; love conquers distance. The holy God conquers distance. He reveals Him-

self as both exclusive and inclusive, unapproachable and approachable, transcendent and condescending.

R. K. Asting, *Die Heiligkeit im Urchristum* (Göttingen, 1930); R. Otto, *The Idea of the Holy*, tr. J. W. Harvey, 2d ed. (London, 1950); S. C. Neill, *Christian Holiness* (New York, 1960); O. R. Jones, *The Concept of Holiness* (New York, 1961). LDH

See also *Stockmayer, Otto.*

Holiness Churches. 1. *History.* To counteract the wave of immorality and spiritual indifference that swept over the US after the end of the Civil War, a number of Meths. and others began a holiness movement. They held that camp meetings, the class system, etc. were necessary. A number of evangelistic* assocs. were formed 1880–1900 to propagate the doctrine of entire sanctification and related views. Pentecostals (see also *Church of God; Pentecostalism*), often grouped with holiness chs., gained a foothold.

2. Following are among those that have been included among holiness bodies: Apostolic Overcoming Holy Ch. of God (inc. 1919 in Alabama); Christian Nation Ch. U. S. A. (organized 1895 Marion, Ohio, as "equality evangelists"; later formed Christian Nation Ch.; reinc. 1961); Christ's* Sanctified Holy Ch.; Church* of Christ (Holiness) U. S. A.; Church* of God; Church of God in Christ; Ch. of the Living God (Motto: Christian Workers for Fellowship) (see *Church of the Living God,* 1); Church* of the Nazarene; Churches* of God, Holiness; Congregational* Holiness Ch.; Gen. Conf. of the Ev. Bap. Ch., Inc. (see *Baptist Churches,* 32); Holiness Ch. of God, Inc. (est. 1920 Madison, N. C.; inc. 1928 Winston-Salem, N. C.); House of God, Which Is the Church of the Living God, the Pillar and Ground of the Truth, Inc. (see *Church of the Living God,* 2); Internat. Ch. of the Foursquare Gospel (see *Foursquare Gospel, The*); International* Pent. Assemblies; Kodesh* Ch. of Immanuel; National* David Spiritual Temple of Christ Ch. Union (Inc.), U. S. A.; Pentecostal* Assemblies of the World, Inc.; Pentecostal* Ch. of God of Am., Inc.; Pentecostal* Fire-Baptized Holiness Ch.; Pent. Holiness Ch., Inc. (formed by bodies organized in S and Midwest US beginning 1898); Triumph the Ch. and Kingdom of God in Christ (organized 1902 in Ga.); United* Holy Ch. of Am., Inc.; The Wesleyan* Ch.

Following evangelistic assocs. have all the marks of holiness chs.: Apostolic Christian Ch. (Nazarean); Apostolic Christian Chs. of Am.; Apostolic Faith Miss.; The Christian and Miss. Alliance; The Christian Cong.; Ch. of Daniel's Band; The Ch. of God (Apostolic); Ch. of God as Organized by Christ; Fire Bap. Holiness Ch.; The Fire Bap. Holiness Ch. (Wesleyan); Hephzibah Faith Miss. Assoc.; The Metropolitan Ch. Assoc.; Miss. Bands of the World; Miss. Ch. Assoc.; Pillar of Fire.

3. *Doctrine.* Holiness bodies subscribe to the fundamental doctrines of the Bible but differ greatly concerning points of interpretation. Some hold that all forms of luxury are forbidden, others that the charismatic gifts of the apostolic ch. must be present in the ch. today, others that it is contrary to Christ's injunction to salary the ministry. All are millennialists (see *Millennialism*). Claiming loyalty to Wesleyan-Arminian theol., holiness bodies believe in free will, human responsibility, and man's ability to reach entire satisfaction. They hold that Christ freed man not only from the curse and guilt of sin, but also from its power, for Christ is said to have prepared a "full salvation" for mankind. J. Wesley* believed that Christian perfection is obtained gradually; holiness bodies teach that the Holy Spirit bestows entire sanctification instantaneously. This is known as the "second* blessing," the Holy Spirit's work subsequent to and different from the work of conversion; after waiting, the "Spirit-baptized" believer is freed completely from inclinations to sin that come from within. The theory of entire sanctification rests on such false premises as these: only conscious sins are truly sins; God requires only relative holiness, i. e., holiness according to individual ability; God would not command holiness if He did not also enable man to be holy. FEM

See also *Perfectionism.*

See *Religious Bodies (US), Bibliography.*

Holiness Code. See *Law Codes.*

Holiness Methodist Church. See *Methodist Churches,* 4 b.

Holiness Methodist Church (N. C.). See *Evangelistic Associations,* 9.

Holl, Karl (1866–1926). B. and educ. Tübingen, Ger.; prof. ch. hist. Tübingen 1900, Berlin 1907; eminent Luther scholar. Works include *Gesammelte Aufsätze zur Kirchengeschichte.*

Holland. See *Netherlands.*

Holland, Henry Scott (1847–1918). B. Ledbury, Herefordshire, Eng.; educ. Eton and Oxford; prof. divinity Oxford 1910–18; tried to relate Christian principles to soc. and economic problems (see also *Christian Social Union*); hymnist. Ed. *Commonwealth* (organ of the CSU) 1895–1912; contributed to *Lux* mundi;* hymns include "Judge Eternal, Throned in Splendor."

Holland Christian Reformed Church in America. See *Reformed Churches,* 4 c.

Holland Reformed Church. See *Reformed Churches,* 4 c.

Hollaz, David [Friedrich] (Hollatz; Hollatius; 1648–1713). Outstanding Luth. dogmatician of the classical period. B. Wulkow, near Stargard, Pomerania; educ. Erfurt and Wittenberg; preacher Pützerlin 1670, preacher 1681 and conrector Stargard, rector Kolberg (Kolobrzeg) 1684, provost Jacobshagen (Dobrzany) 1692. Works include *Examen theologicum acroamaticum.*

J. J. Pelikan, "Natural Theology in David Hollaz," *CTM,* XVIII (Apr. 1947), 253–263.

Holmquist, Hjalmar Fredrik (1873–1945). B. near Sunne, Swed.; prof. ch. hist. and symbolics Lund 1909–38; wrote extensively on gen., Luth., and Swed. ch. hist.

Hölscher, Gustav (1877–1955). B. Norden, Ostfriesland, Ger.; prof. Halle, Giessen, Marburg, Bonn, Heidelberg; wrote extensively on the OT. Works include *Geschichte der israelitischen und jüdischen Religion; Geschichtsschreibung in Israel; Hezekiel; Die Propheten.*

Holst, Maria. See *Asia,* B 2.

Holste(nius), Lukas (1596–1661). B. Hamburg, Ger.; Vatican librarian; wrote on many classical and ecclesiastical writings, e. g., those of Porphyry* and Benedict* of Aniane. Works include *Graecorum Geographorum catalogus.*

Holston Synod. See *General Council of the Evangelical Lutheran Church in (North) America,* 3; *United Lutheran Church, Synods of,* 29.

Holtzmann, Heinrich Julius (1832–1910). B. Karlsruhe, Ger.; educ. Heidelberg and Berlin; taught at Heidelberg and Strasbourg; used historicocritical* method. Works include *Lehrbuch der historisch-kritischen Einleitung in das Neue Testament; Die synoptischen Evangelien; Lehrbuch der neutestamentlichen Theologie.*

Holy Alliance. Agreement signed Sept. 26, 1815, by Alexander I (1777–1825; emp. of Russ. 1801–25), Francis I (1768–1835; last Holy Roman emp. as Francis II 1792–1806; emp. of Austria as Francis I 1804–35), and Frederick* William III. It was an attempt to make Christianity basic in relations bet. nations and bet. rulers and subjects. Other nations of Eur. joined the Holy Alliance. It was regarded esp. by Russ. rulers as expressing the divine* right of kings. See also *Holy Leagues and Alliances.*

Holy Child Jesus, Society of the. See *Sisterhoods.*

Holy Church of North Carolina (and Virginia). See *United Holy Church of America, Inc.*

Holy Club. Formed at Oxford 1729 by C. Wesley* and a few others for systematic exercise in Christian worship. J. Wesley* and G. Whitefield* joined later. Mems. of the club were referred to as methodists (see also *Methodist Churches,* 1). Dispersed 1735.

Holy Coat of Treves. Famous RC relic; kept since the Middle Ages at Treves, W Ger.; accounts vary as to when and how it got there; said to be the seamless garment of Jn 19:23; said to have been woven by Mary for Christ in His infancy and to have increased in size as He grew; first made an object of pub. veneration and pilgrimage 1512; exhibited repeatedly, e. g., 1515, 1531, 1545, 1653, 1810, 1844, 1891, 1933; ca. 20 other coats also are claimed to be the original. *See also Ronge, Johannes.*

Holy Communion. Name for Lord's* Supper. See also *Grace, Means of,* IV.

Holy Communion, Consensus on the. Ten theses on the Lord's Supper adopted 1956 by Syn. of the Nederlandse Hervormde Kerk and the Ev. Luth. Ch. in the Kingdom of the Neth. See also *Netherlands.*
Lutheran World, III (Mar. 1957), 383–385.

Holy Cross Day. See *Church Year,* 17.

Holy Days. See *Church Year.*

Holy Family. Jesus, Mary, and Joseph. Cult of Holy Family became popular in RCm in 17th c.

Holy Feasts and Festivals. See *Church Year.*

Holy Ghost. Alternate name for Holy* Spirit.

Holy Ghost Fathers. See *Holy Ghost Under the Protection of the Immaculate Heart of Mary, Congregation of the.*

Holy Ghost Under the Protection of the Immaculate Heart of Mary, Congregation of the. Also known as Holy Ghost Fathers and as Spiritans. RC soc. founded 1703 as a group that became known as the Sem. and the Cong. of the Holy Ghost; noted esp. for its work in Afr.; other fields include S Am., W Indies, US, India, China.

Holy Grail (derivation of "grail" uncertain). Term applied to a dish, possibly the chalice, used at the institution of the Lord's Supper. Origins of legends about it are lost in the midst of the mists of mystery. Many romances have been woven about the quest of the grail and about the hist. of the vessel.

Holy Innocents. Children massacred at Bethlehem (Mt 2:16-18). See also *Church Year,* 1, 16.

Holy Island. See *Lindisfarne.*

Holy Leagues and Alliances. 1. RC holy leagues were formed in the 16th and 17th c. in continuation of the Crusades.* Such a league was organized in It. 1470 after the is. Negropont (Euboea) fell to the Turks. Another retook Otranto, It., 1481, which had fallen to the Turks 1480. Under leadership of Alexander VI (see *Popes,* 18) an alliance of Fr., Poland, Boh., and Hung. was formed 1500 and a Franco-Venetian fleet sailed the Aegean. In 1538 Charles* V, Paul* III, and Venice formed a holy league that ended the same yr., when the Venetian fleet was defeated by the Turks at the Gk. seaport Preveza. Another league against the Turks, formed 1570 by Pius V (see *Popes,* 21), Venice, and Philip II (1527–98; king of Sp. 1556–98), won a naval battle against the Turks at the Gulf of Lepanto (Gulf of Corinth), Greece, 1571. The Holy League formed 1683/84 under leadership of Innocent* XI joined Austria, Venice, and, for a short time, Poland against the Turks; helped liberate most of Turkish-occupied Hung. by 1700.

2. Charles VIII (1470–98; king of Fr. 1483–98) invaded It. to claim rights of house of Anjou to Naples, but was repulsed 1495 by Holy League of Ferdinand II (1469–96; king of Naples 1495–96) and Sp. gen. Gonzalo de Córdoba (1453–1515).

3. A Holy League was formed Oct. 1511 against Fr. by Julius II (see *Popes,* 19), Ferdinand of Aragon (1452–1516; "the Catholic"; b. Sos, Aragon, Sp.; king of Sicily 1468–1516; as Ferdinand V, joint ruler of Castile 1474–1504 with Isabella [1451–1504]; as Ferdinand II, king of Aragon 1479–1516), and Venice. Henry* VIII joined this league Nov. 1511; Maximilian I (1459–1519; king of Ger. 1486–1519; Holy Roman emp. 1439–1519) joined 1513.

4. In Sp., Toledo and other cities formed a Holy League (Santa Junta) at Avila 1520; opposed the govt.; disintegrated when radical tendencies appeared and upper elements withdrew.

5. The Holy League of Cognac was formed 1526 at Cognac, Fr., against Charles* V by Clement* VII, Francis I (see *France,* 8), Florence, Venice, and the duke of Milan (Francesco Sforza II). See also *Speyer, Diets of,* 1, 2.

6. In 1538 a RC Holy Alliance (or league) was formed at Nürnberg, Ger., against the Schmalkaldic* League.

7. The Holy League (Sainte Ligue) formed against Prots. 1576 under leadership of Henri I de Lorraine and his two brothers, Charles, duke of Mayenne, and Louis, abp. Reims and cardinal, aimed to destroy Calvinism and reest. RC unity. See also *France,* 9.

8. Maximilian I (1573–1651; "the Great"; duke of Bav. 1597–1651; elector 1623–51) led forces 1607 against Prot. Donauwörth; Prot. princes joined hands to resist; in reply, Maximilian became head of a RC holy league 1609.

See also *Dessau, League of; Holy Alliance; League and Covenant, Solemn; Regensburg, League of; Schmalkaldic League; Torgau, League of.* LP

Holy Maid of Kent. See *Barton, Elizabeth.*

Holy Myron. See *Myron.*

Holy Office. See *Curia,* 2 d; *Inquisition.*

Holy Ones. See *Angels, Good,* 4.

Holy Orders. See *Hierarchy.*

Holy Orthodox Catholic Apostolic Eastern Church. See *Eastern Orthodox Churches.*

Holy Orthodox Church in America. See *Eastern Orthodox Churches,* 6.

Holy Rollers. Name given (at times derisively) to mems. of some holiness* chs. because of the emotional nature of their services; worshipers sometimes fell to the ground in trances. But rolling was very rare, though leaping, shouting, and other manifestations were common. In 1915 the Church* of God (Cleveland, Tenn.) officially gave notice that reference to the Ch. of God as "Holy Rollers" would be considered and treated as a slanderous and malignant offense.

Holy Roman Empire. Former territory coextensive with the RC Ch. Crowning of Charlemagne* marks its formal beginning. This empire of W and cen. Eur. (Fr., Ger., Austria, N Sp., most of It.) perished when the Frankish state broke up in the 9th c. as a result of quarrels over succession to the throne and of barbarian invasions. But the idea of such an empire was revived with Otto I (912–973; "the Great"; king of Ger. 936; crowned Holy Roman emp. 962 by John XI [ca. 936–964; pope 955–964]), whose realm, however, was essentially an empire of the Ger. and It. nations and did not include Fr. or Sp. At its greatest extent this new Holy Roman Empire included Ger., the Neth., Boh. [Czechoslovakia], Austria, Switz., Burgundy, and most of It.; Frederick* I (Barbarossa) claimed Den., Poland, and Hung. Conflicts bet. emps. and popes, empire and ch., contributed to decay (see *Investiture Struggle; Frederick I* [Barbarossa]; *Fred-*

erick II). Loss of It. and struggle for the crown led to an interregnum 1254–73, in which the Ger. kingdom and the Holy Roman empire had no real head. With the accession of Rudolf I of Hapsburg (1218–91; king of Ger. 1273; Holy Roman emp. 1273–91) the empire became in effect a Ger. state. Sp. and the empire were joined under Charles* V. The rise of Napoleon I (1769–1821) led to the end of the empire with the resignation of Francis II (1768–1835; Holy Roman emp. 1792–1806; emp. of Austria as Francis I 1804–35).

Holy Saturday. See *Church Year,* 4, 16.

Holy Scripture (Bible; Holy Bible; [the] Scripture[s]; [the] Holy Scripture[s]; [the] Sacred Scripture[s]). Collection of writings (or part thereof) regarded by many Christians as inspired by God and of divine authority. See also *Apologetics,* II B; *Bible Societies; Canon, Bible; Commentaries, Biblical; Grace, Means of; Hermeneutics; Inspiration; Textual Criticism.*

Holy See. See *Apostolic See.*

Holy Spirit. The Holy Spirit (Spirit of God; Spirit of Christ; Spirit; Holy Ghost) is identified with God (Ps 139:7-8; Acts 5:3-4; Ro 8:9; 1 Co 3:16; 2 Co 3:17). In part He is described as a person distinct from Father and Son and proceeding from them (Mt 28:19; Jn 14:26; 15:26; Gl 4:6). Also called Paraclete on basis of the Gk., e. g., in Jn 14:16; 16:7.

The work of creation, ascribed to the Father (e. g., 1 Co 8:6) and to the Son (e. g., Jn 1:3), is also ascribed to the Holy Spirit (e. g., Jb 33:4); sanctification, ascribed to the Holy Spirit (e. g., Ro 8:14; Gl 5:17-25), is also ascribed to the Father and the Son (e. g., Eph 3:14-19). Acts assigned specifically to the Spirit: revealing of the truth and grace of God to man (1 Co 2:10-11); converting man and putting new life and spirit into him (Jn 3:5; 1 Co 12:3); preserving saving faith (1 Jn 4:13); enabling the believer to resist the flesh and produce fruits of faith in love (Gl 5:16-18, 22-25; Eph 4:22-24; 1 Ptr 1:22).

In one sense the Holy Spirit is wholly beyond reach of man; man makes no contribution to Him or to his grasp of Him (Jn 3:8). But the Christian has received the Holy Spirit and His power through Baptism (Tts 3:5) and can continually reinforce His presence through the Word of the Gospel (1 Ptr 1:22-25). Man is equipped with the Holy Spirit to communicate the grace of God in Christ Jesus, the forgiveness of sins, and the life of the Spirit to others (Mt. 28:19-20; Lk 24:45-49; Jn 20:21-23). RRC

Holy Supper. Name for Lord's Supper. See also *Grace, Means of,* IV.

Holy Synod. Governing body, usually composed of bps., in an autocephalous E Orthodox Ch.; in Russia formerly a coll. of bps. and monks, attended by a lay procurator as the emperor's representative, est. 1721 by Peter I ("the Great"; 1672–1725; coruler of Russ. 1682–89; sole ruler 1689–1725), abolished 1917.

Holy Thursday. Maundy Thu.; in older Eng. usage Ascension Day. See also *Church Year,* 4, 8, 16.

Holy Ukrainian Autocephalic Orthodox Church in Exile. See *Eastern Orthodox Churches,* 6.

Holy Unction. See *Unction.*

Holy Water. In RC Ch., water exorcised and blessed by a priest in the name of the ch.; used in various combinations with holy oil, salt, ashes, and wine for baptism, lustration, and other functions.

Holy Week. See *Church Year,* 4, 8, 16.

Holy Years. See *Jubilees.*

Holyoake, George Jacob (1817–1906). B. Birmingham, Eng.; soc. reformer; influenced by R. Owen*; minister to Owenites at Worcester 1840; turned rationailst; first promulgated secularism* ca. 1846, coined the term itself 1851. Ed. *Oracle of Reason* and *Reasoner;* other works include *Sixty Years of an Agitator's Life.*

Homann, Ernst. See *Australia,* A 2.

Homburg, Ernst Christoph (1605–81). B. Mihla, near Eisenach, Ger.; court clerk and legal adviser Naumburg; hymnist. Hymns include "Jesu, meines Lebens Leben"; "Ach wundergrosser Siegesheld"; "Kommst du, kommst du, Licht der Heiden?"

Home Finding Societies. See *Child and Family Service Agencies.*

Home Missions Council of North America. See *Union Movements,* 13.

Home of Onesiphorus. Miss. organization; began 1916; originally worked in China; mem. IFMA; 1966 fields: Hong Kong, Jordan, Lebanon. Headquarters Chicago, Ill.

Homer. Traditional Gk. poet to whom the *Iliad* (on Trojan War) and *Odyssey* (wanderings of Odysseus [Ulysses]) are assigned. Dates have been assigned to him ranging from 1200 to 850 BC. The 2 epic poems, sometimes called "the Bible of the Greeks," are probably composite products of many poets.

Homes for Convalescents and Chronically Ill. See *Hospitals.*

Homiletics. 1. Homiletics is the science of preaching. The term comes from the Gk. for being together, as in a crowd or conversation. The term "homily" came to signify an address to a Christian cong., in contrast to evangelizing non-Christians. The term has been applied either exclusively to the sermon in the parish service or more broadly to all preaching of the Christian religion. As a science, homiletics includes a formal theory: gathering preaching materials from the Word of God, from experience and observation, and from literature; arranging the materials in logical and psychological sequence; expressing the material in apt language; directing the material to the hearer by means of speech and bodily movement. Homiletics also includes a body of insights into the source and function of the Christian religion and its impact on the human mind, and into human nature as it responds to the spoken word.

2. The Jewish synagog developed a standard form of worship that included a sermon (e. g., Lk 4:16-32). Any competent mem. of the cong. was eligible to deliver such a discourse, but, if possible, the task was assigned to itinerant religious teachers. They learned the science of their craft by simple conference with, or imitation of, other rabbis or at the great rabbinical schools.

3. The NT provides no homiletical theory. Christ emphasized the content and purpose of the preaching message (e. g., Lk 24:45-48). The apostles stressed the sincerity and urgency of the message (e. g., 2 Co 2–5; 1 Th 4; 2 Ti 2:3; 1 Ptr 4:5). The early ch. soon developed a standard service in which teaching and preaching had a part (Acts 2; 6:4).

4. Under influence of rhetorical theory, standards and principles of homiletics were crystallized. Augustine* provided a summary of them in *De doctrina christiana.* Under influence of Aristotelian philos., principles of rhetoric and dialectic were applied to preaching. The influence of this method was curtailed by the fact that most clerics were poorly trained and that the preaching which most stirred the people was the direct and popular message of the preaching friars.

5. The Prot. Reformation vitalized the message of the parish minister by enhancing the place of the sermon in the service, by making the pastor the responsible shepherd, and by putting the Bible in the vernacular into the center of the sermon and the hearer's interest. M. Luther* was a direct and profuse preacher who used little theoretical form in his

approach to preaching. But the Luth. Ch. early emphasized a humanistically trained clergy. Thus principles of rhetoric and dialectic resumed a formal position in Luth. preaching and in training Luth. preachers. Theol. disputes and emphasis on doctrinal formulations of the 16th and 17th cents. gave more emphasis to the argumentative polemical method in Ger. Luth. preaching than elsewhere. The prestige and position of theol. faculties in Lutheranism produced a theoretical scaffolding for preaching that withstood Pietism,* rationalism,* and the Enlightenment.*

6. In Am., homiletical theory was produced also by dissenting communions that set up strong ch. organizations and sems. In the past, Prot. homiletical theory largely emphasized traditional forms and related the sermon to the parish service. This process has been reinforced by the trend in much of Protestantism to a more adequate attention to the service as a whole.

7. Homiletic theory is under review in light of audience and persuasion psychol. The impetus for this emphasis has come in part from new channels for evangelism in radio and publicity; in part from the effort to reach the pub. mind, which is not habituated to the authority of the Word of God. This emphasis has begun with rethinking of the "delivery" of the message and of the speaker's total participation in his message. The principles of persuasion as applied to the intrinsic message of the Gospel and expressed to the audience by every means at the preacher's disposal are subjects of current scrutiny. The result is homiletic theory that not merely concerns itself with the preacher's address to the Christian audience, but concentrates on the individual responding to analysis of his need and sympathy for his problem. RRC

See also *Preaching, History of; Theology.*

J. H. C. Fritz, *The Preacher's Manual* (St. Louis, 1941); J. M. Reu, *Homiletics,* tr. A. Steinhaeuser, 5th ed. (Columbus, Ohio, 1944); R. W. Kirkpatrick, *The Creative Delivery of Sermons* (New York, 1944); R. R. Caemmerer, *Preaching for the Church* (St. Louis, 1959); G. M. Bass, *The Renewal of Liturgical Preaching* (Minneapolis, 1967).

Homilius, Gottfried August (1714–85). B. Rosenthal, Saxony, Ger.; organist; composer; pupil of J. S. Bach,* but followed more closely the style of K. H. Graun*; cantor Kreuzschule and music dir. in 3 chief chs. Dresden. Works include *Passions-Cantate; Die Freude der Hirten über die Geburt Jesu;* motets.

Homme, Even Johannes (1843–1903). Pastor in the Norw. Syn. (see *Evangelical Lutheran Church, The,* 8–13); b. Telemark, Norw.; to Am. 1854; educ. Conc. Sem., St. Louis, Mo.; began pastoral work in Shawano Co., Wis., 1881, founding Wittenberg and there est. an academy, normal school, orphanage, old people's home, and printshop; active in founding Bethany Indian Miss., Wittenberg, ca. 1884. Ed. *For Gammel og Ung; Söndagsskolebladet; Weisenhus Kalendar; Christian Youth; Sunday School Helper.* See also *Wittenberg Academy.*

Hommel, Friderich Erdmann (1813–92). B. Fürth, Bav., Ger.; educ. Munich, Bonn, Erlangen; assessor and legal adviser; composer of hymn tunes; through acquaintance with J. K. W. Löhe* and others he learned to appreciate Luth. music. Works include *Liturgie lutherischer Gemeindegottesdienste; Der Psalter nach der deutschen Uebersetzung D. Martin Luthers für den Gesang eingerichtet; Geistliche Volkslieder.*

Hommel, Fritz (1854–1936). B. Ansbach, Ger.; orientalist; prof. Munich 1877–1924; authority on cuneiform and early Arab. poetry.

Hommius, Festus (1576–1642). B. Jelsum, Neth.; Calvinist theol.; active at 1618–19 Syn. of Dordrecht.*

Homoios (Gk. "like, similar"). Term used in stating the view of some of Arian (see *Arianism*) inclination in the early ch. that the Son is like the Father, without saying anything specifically about the *ousia* ("substance"). See also *Homoiousios; Homoousios.*

Homoiousios (Gk. "of like substance"). Term used in stating the view of some in the early ch. that the Son is of like substance with the Father. See also *Arianism,* 2, 3; *Homoios; Homoousios.*

Homologoumena. See *Antilegomena; Canon, Bible,* 5, 6.

Homoousios (Gk. "of one substance"). Term used in the Nicene Creed (see *Ecumenical Creeds,* B) to state Christian faith that the Son is of one substance with the Father. See also *Arianism,* 2, 3; *Athanasius; Homoios; Homoiousios; Nicaea, Councils of,* 1.

Homosexual Marriage. See *Marriage,* III.

Honduras. See *Central America,* A, D 2, G.

Hönecke, Gustav Adolf Theodor Felix (Feb. 25, 1835–Jan. 3, 1908). B. Brandenburg, Ger.; educ. Halle; influenced esp. by F. A. G. Tholuck*; tutor in the home of a certain Herr von Wattenwyl near Bern, Switz.; spent some time in Wittenberg; passed examination *pro ministerio* in Magdeburg; ordained there for Wisconsin* Syn. cong. at La Crosse, Wis.; to Am. Feb. 1863; the La Crosse cong. had meanwhile received a pastor; Hönecke spent a little time at Racine, Wis.; then pastor Farmington, near Watertown, Wis.; prof. at the newly-founded sem. at Watertown 1866–70 (see *Ministry, Education of,* X R). Acc. to an 1868/69 arrangement whereby the Wis. Syn. was to place a prof. at Conc. Sem., St. Louis, Mo., Hönecke was to teach at St. Louis, but financial difficulties in the Wis. Syn. and lack of a dwelling in St. Louis prevented execution of the plan. Pastor Milwaukee 1870–90. The sem. at Watertown, which had been closed 1870, was reopened 1878. Hönecke became dir. and prof. dogmatics while continuing his pastorate; full-time prof. 1890; taught dogmatics, ethics, homiletics, pastoral theol., and lectured on Ro. Ed. *Ev.-Luth. Gemeinde-Blatt;* helped found and ed. *Theologische Quartalschrift;* other works include *Predigt-Entwürfe über die altkirchlichen Evangelien und Episteln nebst einigen Freitexten; Wenn ich nur dich habe; "Ein Lämmlein geht und trägt die Schuld"; Ev.-Luth. Dogmatik.*

"Dr. Adolf Hönecke," *Ev.-Luth. Gemeinde-Blatt,* XLIII, 2 (Jan. 15, 1908), 17–26; A. Pieper, "Dr. Höneckes Bedeutung für die Wisconsinsynode und die amerikanisch-lutherische Kirche," *Theologische Quartalschrift,* XXXII, 3 (July 1935), 161–174; 4 (Oct. 1935), 225–244; XXXIII, 1 (Jan. 1936), 1–19; 2 (Apr. 1936), 81–101.

Honegger, Arthur (1892–1955). Composer; b. Le Havre, Fr., of Swiss descent; identified with ultramodern school. Works include *King David* and *Nicolas de Flue* (oratorios); *Judith* (Biblical drama).

Honesty. Term which includes, or is related to, such virtues as integrity, fairness, straightforwardness, truthfulness, adherence to facts, sincerity; opposite of duplicity and subterfuge. Pr 11:1; Lk 3:13; 12:47-48; 16:10; Ph 4:8; 1 Ti 2:2; Heb 13:18; 1 Ptr 2:12.

Hong Kong (Hongkong). Brit. crown colony SE China. *Area:* ca. 400 sq. mi.; *pop.* (1973 est.): ca. 4,200,000 (mostly Chinese). Official language: Eng. Came under Brit. control in 19th c.; occupied by Jap. 1941; reoccupied by Brit. 1945. Christian groups have included RCs (claim more than 200,000) and many Prots. See also *Lutheran Church – Missouri Synod, The,* VII 14.

Hon(n)ius. See *Hoen.*

Honoratus (ca. 350–ca. 429). Founded monastery of

Lérins ca. 410 on an is. in the Mediterranean, SE Fr.; bp. Arles ca. 427. See also *Wales.*

Honorius I. See *Constantinople, Councils of,* 3; *Monothelitism.*

Honter(us), Johann(es) (Gras; Gross; 1498–1549). B. Kronstadt (Brasov), Transylvania*; educ. Vienna; opened printshop in Kronstadt ca. 1535; preacher Kronstadt 1544; pub. M. Luther's* SC 1545; Luther called him "the Lord's evangelist in Kronstadt in Hung." (WA-Br 10, 565).

Hontheim, Johann Nikolaus von (1701–90). B. Treves (Trier), Ger.; RC hist. and canonist. See also *Febronianism.*

Hooker, Richard (ca. 1554–1600). Moderate Angl. defender of episcopacy; b. Heavitree, near Exeter, Devonshire, Eng.; educ. Oxford; ordained 1581; held livings in Buckinghamshire, Wiltshire, and Kent. Works include *Of the Laws of Ecclesiasical Polity.*

Hooker, Thomas (ca. 1586–1647). B. Leicestershire, Eng.; Cong. pastor Eng. 1620–30; fled to Holland 1530; to Am. with J. Cotton* and S. Stone* 1633; pastor 1633 New Towne, Mass., 1636 Hartford, Conn.; active in writing "Fundamental Orders" of Conn. and organizing "United Colonies of New England." See also *United States, Religious History,* 4.

Hoon. See *Hoen.*

Hooper, John (ca. 1495–1555). "Father of the Puritans"; b. Somersetshire, Eng.; educ. Oxford; probably Cistercian; became Zwinglian; fled to Continent 1539; returned to Eng. 1549; bp. Gloucester 1550 (consecrated 1551); objected to prescribed vestments and form of the oath (by the saints), but yielded on the vestments and the king yielded on the oath; the see of Worcester was given him 1552 to hold *in commendam* (revenues granted him temporarily during vacancy) with Gloucester; later Gloucester was made an archdeanery and he was termed bp. Worcester; imprisoned 1553 by Mary I (Mary Tudor; "Bloody Mary"; 1516–58; queen of Eng. and Ireland 1553–58); deprived of bishopric as a married man 1554; charged with heresy; burned at the stake. See also *Vestiarian Controversy.*

Hoornbeck, Johannes (1617–66). B. Haarlem, Neth.; Ref. theol.; educ. Leiden and Utrecht; pastor Mühlheim am Rhein 1639; prof. Utrecht 1644, Leiden 1654; OT scholar; wrote textbooks for all theol. disciplines.

Hope. The well-grounded expectation of things desired. The ground of Christian hope is the Word of divine promise. Christian hope is essentially faith concerning things to come; faith looks into the heart of God for a promised hope which is sure and final, the crowning glory of all faith. In heaven hope will be translated into joyous experience (Ro 8:24-25; 1 Co 13:13; Tts 3:7; Heb 11:1; 13:14; 1 Ptr 1:3-5, 13). The hope of the Christian is the fruit of justification (Ro 5:4-5), the anchor of his soul (Heb 6:19); it inspires to clean living (1 Jn 3:3), makes glad in trials (Ps 43:5; 146:5; Ro 12:12; Heb 3:6), and provides comfort and support in death (Pr 14:32; 2 Ti 4:18).

Höpfner, Heinrich (Höpffner; Heinricus Hoepffnerus; 1582–1642). Ger. Luth. theol.; b. Leipzig; educ. Leipzig, Jena, Wittenberg; prof. Leipzig; took part in Leipzig Colloquy (see *Reformed Confessions,* D 3 b) 1631. Works include treatise on justification; commentaries.

Hopkins, John. See *Psalter, English.*

Hopkins, Mark (1802–87). Cong. theol. and educ.; b. Stockbridge, Mass.; physician; prof. Williams Coll., Williamstown, Mass., 1830–37, pres. 1836–72; pres. ABCFM 1857–87. Works include *Exclusive Traits of Christianity; Influence of the Gospel in Liberalizing the Mind; Lectures on Moral Science; The Scriptural Idea of Man.*

Hopkins, Samuel (1721–1803). Cong. theol.; b. Waterbury, Conn.; pupil of J. Edwards* the Elder; pastor Newport, R. I.; prominent in "New* England theol."; developed modified Calvinism called Hopkinsianism.

Hopkinsianism. See *Hopkins, Samuel.*

Hoppe, Albert Friedrich (July 24, 1828–May 31, 1911). B. Rostock, Mecklenburg, Ger.; d. St. Louis, Mo.; educ. Erlangen and Dorpat (Tartu); private tutor 1853–55; to Am. 1855; pastor New Orleans, La., 1856–68; taught in New Orleans at Lutheran academy 1868, Select School ca. 1878, Progymnasium 1881–86; to St. Louis, Mo., 1886; edited Saint Louis ed. of M. Luther's* works 1886–1911.

Horarik, John. See *Canada,* A 25.

Horb, Johann(es) Heinrich (Horbe; Horbius; 1645–95). B. Colmar, Alsace; educ. Strasbourg; ev. theol.; influenced by J. K. Dannhauer* and P. J. Spener*; pietist; court preacher Bischwiller, Fr.; inspector Trarbach, Ger.; supt. Windsheim; pastor Hamburg; removed from office because of his opposition to orthodoxy.

Horebites. See *Hussites.*

Hormisdas. Pope 514–523; brought about reunion of E and W chs. 519, healing the Acacian* Schism.

Horn, Edward Traill (June 10, 1850–Mar. 4, 1915). B. Easton, Pa.; educ. Lutheran Theol. Sem., Philadelphia, Pa.; pastor Philadelphia, Pa., Charleston, S. C., and Reading, Pa.; prof. Philadelphia Luth. Theol. Sem. (Mount Airy), 1911–15. Pres. Pa Ministerium 1909–11. Works include *Outlines of Liturgics; Summer Sermons.*

Horn, Johann (Jan Roh; ca. 1490–1547). B. Taus (Domazlice), Boh.; met M. Luther* 1522–24; leader among Bohemian* Brethren; comp. *Ein Gesangbuch der Brüder inn Behemen unnd Merherrn.*

Horneck, Anthony (Anton; 1641–97). B. Bacharach, Ger.; studied at Heidelberg; to Eng. ca. 1660; became Ang.; pastor Doulton (Devonshire) and London; founded religious societies ca. 1678; wrote devotional works.

Horn(ejus), Konrad (Conrad; 1590–1649). Prof. Helmstedt; exponent of Melanchthonian tradition in Luth. orthodoxy; sided with G. Calixtus* in syncretistic controversy (see *Syncretism*).

Horning, Friedrich Theodore (1809–82). B. Eckwersheim, Alsace; educ. Strasbourg; pastor Grafenstaden and Strasbourg; pres. Strasbourg consistory 1865: changed from rationalism* to strict confessional Lutheranism ca. 1845.

Horrible Decree. See *Calvin, John,* 11.

Horsch, John (1867–1941). Mennonite hist. and theo.; b. Giebelstadt, near Würzburg, Ger.; studied at Bav. State Agricultural School, Würzburg: arrived N. Y. 1887; attended Indian Miss. School, Halstead, Kans ; worked at Mennonite Pub. Co., Elkhart, Ind.; studied at Ev. Theol. Sem., Naperville, Ill., Valparaiso U., Valparaiso, Ind., Baldwin-Wallace Coll., Berea, Ohio, U. of Wis., Madison, Wis.; pub. monthly *Farm und Haus;* Ger. ed. of Mennonite Pub. House, Scottdale, Pa. Works include *Modern Religious Liberalism; Mennonites in Europe; Menno Simons; Infant Baptism; Communism; The Failure of Modernism.*

Horsley, Samuel (1733–1806). B. London; educ. Cambridge; Angl. bp. 1788 St. David's (Wales), 1793 Rochester (Kent), 1802 St. Asaph (Wales), Eng.; opposed J. Priestley* on doctrines of the Trin. and of Christ. Wrote extensively in area of science and philology.

Horst, Henry W. (May 3, 1864–Aug. 26, 1949). B. Rendsburg, Ger.; to US at age 17; contractor; co-founder Lutheran* Laymen's League; made comprehensive survey of Missouri* Syn. S Am. missions 1928.

Hort, Fenton John Anthony (1828–92). B. Dublin,

Ireland; educ. Cambridge; Brit. NT scholar; mem. NT rev. committee 1870–80; prof. Cambridge 1878; with B. F. Westcott* pub. critical ed. of Gk. NT 1881.

Hosanna (Heb. *hoshiah nnah,* "Save now!" Ps 118:25). Part of great Hallel*; assoc. with Palm Sun. (Mt 21:9; see also *Church Year,* 4, 16); part of the Sanctus (see *Worship, Parts of,* 11). See also *Response.*

Hosius (Osius; Ossius; ca. 256–ca. 358). B. probably Cordova, Sp.; bp. Cordova ca. 295; friend and counselor of Constantine* I; prominent at Council of Nicaea* I 325 as defender of orthodoxy; subscribed an Arian creed under duress at Sirmium 357 which he abjured on his deathbed.

Hosius, Stanislaus (Hos[s]; 1504–79). B. Cracow, Poland; leader of Counter* Reformation; cardinal 1561. Works include *Confessio Catholicae Fidei Christiana.*

Hoskins, Joseph (1745–88). Cong. minister at Bristol, Gloucestershire, Eng., 10 yrs.; during last 3 yrs. of life wrote 384 hymns, including "Let Thoughtless Thousands Choose the Road."

Hospitalers (Hospitallers). Name of various RC nursing orders. See also *Brothers Hospitallers of Saint John of God; Military Religious Orders; Schwebel, Johannes.*

Hospitality. Kind reception and courteous entertainment of strangers or guests. In the orient it was regarded a sacred duty to receive, feed, lodge, and protect travelers who come to one's door. There are many instances of hospitality in Scripture (e. g., Gn 18:1-8; 19:1-15; 1 K 17:10-24; Jb 31:32; Lk 19:1-10; Acts 16:15; 2 Ti 1:16). It is commanded in the Mosaic law (Lv 19:34) and encouraged in the NT (Lk 14:12-14; Ro 12:13; 1 Ptr 4:9).

Hospitals (including sanatoria, homes for convalescents and chronically ill). Ca. 1800 the growth of such cities as Boston, NYC, Philadelphia, Newport, Charleston began to demand community action to provide pub. health services. Isolation hosps. were created in cities of the E coast of the US. Nearly all were est. under govt. auspices; most rendered basic service. Services soon improved in new hosps. est. under voluntary (ch. and community) auspices. The 1st ch. related hosps. in the US were under control of RC sisterhoods.

W. A. Passavant* est. a Luth. hosp. in Pittsburgh, Pa., 1849. Under his leadership hosps. were est. also in Milwaukee, Wis., and Chicago and Jacksonville, Ill.

The 1st hosp. in the Missouri* Syn. (the 1st Prot. hosp. W of Pittsburgh, Pa.) was the Luth. Hosp. at St. Louis, Mo., founded 1858 by J. F. Bünger.*

Luth. sponsorship of hosps. varies, including (1) operation of a group of indep.-owned hosps. over a broad geogr. area by a Luth. administrative organization; (2) operation of a group of hosps. owned by a single ch.-related entity serving a limited geogr. area; (3) ownership and operation of single hosp. units by an assoc. of Luth. congs, jurisdictional units of a Luth. body, or a Luth. body as such; (4) ownership and operation of single hosp. units by a corporation whose membership, by definition in the charter, consists of at least a majority of Luths.

Some Luth. hosps. have evolved into community hosps. in terms of orientation, perspective, and/or auspices. But most retain true and essential ev. Luth. characteristics: (1) interest and participation of the membership of the Luth. ch.; (2) well-oriented management by Christian people; (3) Christian administration; (4) ministry to the total personality of the patient; (5) chaplaincy services to administration, staff, and patients; (6) worship facilities in large hosps.

Most Luth. hosps. in the US are mems. of the Luth. Hosp. Assoc. of Am. There are about 130 Luth. hosps. in the US; nearly all of them are gen. hosps.

Luths. est. hosps. because the healing ministry was an important and integral aspect of the total ministry of Christ and His apostles and because the ch. patterns its work after His ministry. JCC

Host. Wafer, or bread, of the Lord's Supper (see *Grace, Means of,* IV).

Hotman, François (Hotmannus; Hotomanus; de Villiers Saint-Paul; 1524–90). B. Paris, Fr.; Huguenot jurist; urged Fr. to declare indep. from Rome; fled to Switz. after Bartholomew's* Day Massacre. Works include *De re numaria populi romani liber; De statu primitivae ecclesiae ejusque sacerdotiis; Francogallia; Jurisconsultus.*

Hottentots. Afr. people allied at least in physical resemblance to Bushmen; formerly lived as far S as Cape of Good Hope; 1967 est.: ca. 42,000. Most Hottentots now live in Eur. settlements or on reservations. George Schmidt* (1709–85), a Moravian (see *Moravian Church*) sent from Herrnhut, Ger., arrived Cape Town 1737, worked till 1743, when he returned to Eur. because of disagreement with the Dutch; further Moravian work has been done beginning 1792. The LMS sent J. T. Vanderkemp* 1799 and later R. Moffat* and D. Livingstone.* Meths. began work 1816. Rhenish* Mission Soc. workers arrived S Afr. 1829, their 1st station 1830. The Paris* Ev. Missionary Soc. began work 1829. The Berlin* Miss. Soc. I followed a few yrs. later. R. Gray* arrived Cape Town 1848.

Hottinger, Johann Heinrich (1620–67). B. Zurich, Switz.; educ. Geneva, Switz., and Groningen and Leiden, Neth.; orientalist; prof. Zurich and Heidelberg. See also *Lexicons,* A.

Hours, Canonical. Hours of special prayer and devotion growing out of the custom of the early ch. based on suggestions in Ps (e. g., 55:17; 119:164) and Acts 3:1; 10:9; 16:25. The Apostolic* Constitutions (VIII iv 34) name morning, 3d, 6th, and 9th hour, evening, and cockcrowing. The rule of Benedict of Nursia included (1) nocturna vigilia (matins*), 2 a. m.; (2) lauds* at daybreak; (3) prime*; (4) terce (tierce; from Lat. for "3d"); (5) sext; (6) none*; (7) vespers*; (8) compline.* Lauds, usually sung at dawn, may either be combined with matins or follow as the 2d canonical hour counting matins as the 1st). Matins may be said at any time of the day.

The Luth. Confessions speak of "useless, bothersome babbling of the Seven Hours" (LC, Longer Pref. 3; cf. AC XXVIII 41). "Seven" (based on Ps 118:164) is arrived at variously; the "day" hours may be listed: 1. matins with lauds; 2. prime; 3. terce; 4. sext; 5. none; 6. vespers; 7. compline. The hours survived in monasteries that became ev.; they provided content for the Luth. form of matins and vespers.

The divine office (*officium divinum;* daily office for canonical hours) is formal vocal prayer as developed in the W Ch. Its fixed form includes Psalms; hymns; scriptural, patristic, and hagiographic readings; prayers. It is recited in RC and other chs. by those commissioned to do so (e. g., priests, religious) as official prayer of the ch.

See also *Breviary; Worship.*

House of Bishops. See *England,* C 9; *Protestant Episcopal Church,* 8.

House of Clergy. See *England,* C 9.

House of David. Communal religious colony (see also *Communistic Societies*) est. 1903 by B. Purnell* at Benton Harbor, Mich. Purnell claimed to have received a revelation 1895 designating him the 7th messenger in Rv 8:6; 10:7; 11:15. He allegedly called himself "Son of Man" and "Younger Brother of Christ." He and his followers considered themselves the remnant of the 12 tribes of Israel, of whom 144,000 are to be gathered body, soul, and spirit and restored to their proper position as rulers and judges of God's kingdom est. on this earth; all others would at best receive immortality only for the soul and their bodies would return to dust.

Purnell taught that the glory of Christ's transfigured body consisted in immortality; there is no damnation; the 144,000 must keep the law of Christ, conform their bodies to His, refrain from all killing; communism of goods, vegetarianism, and wearing long hair were to be strictly observed by all mems.

House of Deputies. *See Protestant Episcopal Church,* 8 c.

House of God, Which Is the Church of the Living God, The Pillar and Ground of the Truth, Inc. See *Church of the Living God,* 2.

House of Laity. See *England,* C 9.

Houseal. See *Hausihl.*

Houtin, Albert (1867–1926). B. La Flèche, Fr.; RC priest 1891; exponent of Fr. modernism (see *Modernism,* 1); quit the priesthood 1912. Works include *Histoire du modernisme catholique; Courte histoire du Christianisme; Un vie de prêtre; Le Père Hyacinthe.*

Hove, Elling (Mar. 25, 1863–Dec. 17, 1927). B. Northwood, Iowa; educ. Luther Coll., Decorah, Iowa, and Conc. Sem., St. Louis, Mo.; Norw. Luth. pastor Portland, Oreg., Astoria, Oreg., Decorah, Iowa., Mankato, Minn.; prof. Luther Sem., Saint Paul, Minn. (later dissolved and reest. as Luther Theol. Sem.) 1901. Works include *Christian Doctrine* (pub. posthumously as completed by his son, Olaf Hjalmar Hove, b. Nov. 30, 1906).

How, William Walsham (1823–97). B. Shrewsbury, Shropshire, Eng.; educ. Oxford; held a number of positions as clergyman; bp. Wakefield; hymnist. Hymns include "For All the Saints Who from Their Labors Rest"; "Jesus! Name of Wondrous Love"; "O Word of God Incarnate"; "Soldiers of the Cross, Arise!"; "This Day at Thy Creating Word"; "To Thee, Our God, We Fly"; "We Give Thee But Thine Own."

Howard, John (ca. 1726–90). B. Hackney, London, Eng.; prison reformer; studied nature and treatment of plague. Works include *The State of the Prisons in England and Wales, with Preliminary Observations, and an Account of Some Foreign Prisons; An Account of the Principal Lazarettos in Europe.*

Howard, Thomas. See *Norfolk, Thomas Howard, 3d duke of.*

Howe, John (1630–1705). B. Loughborough, Leicestershire, Eng.; educ. Cambridge and Oxford; curate Great Torrington, Devonshire; chaplain of O. Cromwell* and his son Richard; took part in reed. Westminster Confession at Savoy (Oct. 1658); ejected 1662 from Torrington for nonconformity; chaplain at Antrim 1670; Presb. pastor London 1675; to Utrecht 1686; returned to London 1687; promoted union of Presbs. and Congs. Works include *The Blessedness of the Righteous; The Carnality of Christian Contention; The Living Temple.*

Howison, George Holmes (1834–1916). B. Montgomery Co., Md.; educ. Lane Theol. Sem. (Presb.), Cincinnati, Ohio, and Berlin, Ger.; taught at Washington U., St. Louis, Mo., Massachusetts Institute of Technology (at Boston), Harvard U., Concord (Mass.) School of Philos., U. of Mich., and U. of Calif.; opposed monism*; held philos. system which he called personal* idealism and which allowed for personal freedom, yet maintained the individual's relationship to other persons, supersonal beings, and God.

Howland, Frederick I. See *Communistic Societies,* 5.

Howson, John Saul (1816–85). B. Giggleswick-in-Craven, Yorkshire, Eng.; educ. Cambridge; deacon 1845; priest 1846; taught at Liverpool Coll.; vicar Wisbech 1866; dean of Chester 1867–85. Wrote *The Life and Epistles of St. Paul* with W. J. Conybeare*; other works include *The Character of St. Paul; The Metaphors of St. Paul; The Companions of St. Paul.*

Hoyer, Otto Daniel August (Nov. 17, 1849–Nov. 8, 1905). B. Hamburg, Ger.; to Am. at age 16; educ. Northwestern U. (see *Northwestern College*), Watertown, Wis., and Conc. Sem., St. Louis, Mo.; Wisconsin* Syn. pastor Neenah, Wis., 1875; Minnesota* Syn. pastor St. Paul, Minn., 1880; prof. and dir. Dr. Martin Luther Coll. (see *Ministry, Education of,* VIII B; *Minnesota Synod,* 3), New Ulm, Minn., 1885; dir. Saginaw, Mich., sem. of the Michigan* Syn. 1893; prof. and inspector Northwestern U., Watertown, Wis., ca. 1896.

Hoyer, Theodore (Aug. 22, 1883–Oct. 24, 1963). B. Spring Valley, Kans.; educ. Conc. Coll., Fort Wayne, Ind., and Conc. Sem., St. Louis, Mo.; pastor 1905–12 Natoma, Kans., 1912–27 Denver, Colo.; prof. 1927–30 St. John's Luth. Coll., Winfield, Kans., 1930–63 Conc. Sem., St. Louis. Works include *Missionary Forward Endeavor in the Light of the Book of Acts; The Story of the Church; The Christian View of Life.*

Hoyme, Gjermund (Oct. 8, 1847–June 9, 1902). B. Valdres, Norw.; to Am. 1851; educ. Augsburg Sem., Minneapolis, Minn. (see *Ministry, Education of,* XI G); pastor Duluth, Minn., Menomonie and Eau Claire, Wis.; pres. Norw.-Dan. Luth. conf. 1886–90, United* Norw. Luth. Ch. 1890–1902.

Hrabanus Maurus. See *Rabanus Maurus.*

Hrodbert. See *Rupert(us).*

Hromadka, Josef L. See *Czechoslovakia,* 9.

Hsin I Hui. Hsin I (Chinese "faith, righteousness") is the name that was used by many Luth. chs. in China. The Missouri* Syn. and some others transliterated "Lutheran" with "Lu-deh" and used that name. Hsin I Hui was the Chinese name for the United Lutheran Church in China (the ULC in Am. was one body connected with it). Hsin I Hui was organized 1920 by (1) Bd. of For. Missions of the ULC; (2) Augustana Syn. Mission; (3) Bd. of For. Missions of the Norw. Luth. Ch. of Am.; (4) Berliner Missionsgesellschaft; (5) Dan. Luth. Mission; (6) Fin. Mission; (7) Norw. Missionary Soc.; (8) Schleswig-Holsteinische Ev.-Luth. Missionsgesellschaft zu Breklum; (9) Ch. of Swed. Mission; (10) Ostasien-Mission, Allgemeiner Evangelisch-Protestantischer Missionsverein (Weimar Mission), Berlin. 1–3 were US-based. See also *China.*

M. Zschiegner, "Revival Movement of the Hsin I Church," *CTM,* VI, 3 (Mar. 1935), 184–192.

Hsün-Tzu (fl. 3d c. BC). Chinese philos.; held that man is evil by nature but can acquire goodness. See also *Chinese Philosophy,* 3.

Huai-nan Tzu. See *Chinese Philosophy,* 5.

Huber(inus), Kaspar (Hubel; 1500–53). B. near Aichach, Ger.; monk; Luth. 1525; active in ch. work in Augsburg and Öhringen. Wrote devotional literature.

Huber, Samuel (ca. 1547–1624). B. Burgdorf, near Bern, Switz.; Ref. pastor Switz.; opposed Ref. doctrine of predestination as presented 1586 at the Colloquy of Montbéliard*; deposed 1588; subscribed FC at Tübingen 1588; pastor Derendingen; prof. Wittenberg 1592; adopted view that man must make universal election and calling sure by repentance and faith; dismissed 1594; exiled 1595.

Hubert, Konrad (Conrad Huober; 1507–77). B. Bergzabern, Ger.; educ. Heidelberg and Basel; asst. to M. Bucer* at Strasbourg 1531; followed middle course bet. Luth. and Ref. theol.; relieved of all duties except occasional preaching 1563 by ascendant Luth.

powers; hymnist. Ed. some of Bucer's works; hymns include "Allein zu dir, Herr Jesu Christ."

Hubmaier, Balthasar (Huebmaier; Friedberger; Pacimontanus; ca. 1485–1528). B. Friedberg, near Augsburg, Ger.; educ. Freiburg; RC priest; became Ref. 1522/23; Anabap. 1524/25; est. Anabap. community 1526 at Nikolsburg, Moravia; burned at Vienna under RC condemnation.

Hübner, Johann(es) (1668–1731). B. Türchau, near Zittau, Ger.; educ. Leipzig; rector of the gymnasium at Merseburg 1694, of the Johanneum at Hamburg 1711. Works include *Zweimal zwei und funfzig biblische Historien; Genealogische Tabellen; Reales Staats- Zeitungs- und Conversations-Lexicon.*

Hucbald (Hubald; Hugbaldus; Ubaldus; Ugubaldus; ca. 840–ca. 930). B. probably near Tournai, Belg.; Benedictine monk at St. Amand (Nord), Fr. Works ascribed to him include *De institutione harmonica; Ecloga de calvis.*

Huegli, See *Hügli.*

Hueschen, Otto Raphael (Hüschen; May 25, 1856–Mar. 20, 1931). B. Kiel, Ger.; to Am. 1874; educ. Conc. Sem., Springfield, Ill.; pastor first at Drake, then at Hanover and Egypt Mills, then at Uniontown, all in Mo.; poet. Works include *Wo Gottes Brünlein rauschen.*

Huet, Heinrich (John Henry; descendants spell name Hewitt; Feb. 14, 1772–Feb. 16, 1855). B. near Hagerstown, Md.; granted ministerial license by Pa. Ministerium (see *United Lutheran Church, Synods of,* 22) 1812; attended 1812 Special Conference of the W Dist. of the Pa. Ministerium and the organization meeting of the Ev. Luth. Joint Syn. of Ohio* and Other States 1818; ordained by Ohio Syn. 1818; served congs. in Pa. and Ohio.

Huet, Pierre Daniel (Huetius; 1630–1721). B. Caen, Fr.; RC scholar; bp. Avranches. Ed. *Delphin Classics* (Lat. classics); other works include *Demonstratio evangelica.*

Huetter. See *Hutter.*

Hügel, Friedrich von (1852–1925). B. Florence, It.; to Eng. 1873; naturalized Brit. subject 1914; RC theol.; founded London Soc. for the Study of Religion. Works include *The Mystical Element of Religion as Studied in Saint Catherine of Genoa and Her Friends.*

Hugh of St. Cher (Hugo a [or de] Sancto Caro; ca. 1200–63). B. St. Cher, suburb of Vienne, Fr.; educ. Paris; Dominican 1225; cardinal 1244. Works include Lat. concordance of the Bible.

Hugh of St. Victor (Hugo; ca. 1096–1141). B. Flanders (or Saxony?); spent most of adult life in abbey of St. Victor, Paris, Fr.; combined mysticism and dialectics in treatment of theol. Works include *De arca Noe mystica; De unione spiritus et corporis; De vanitate mundi.*

Hugh the Great (Hugo of Cluny; 1024–1109). B. Burgundy; Fr. Benedictine monk; abbot of Cluny 1049–1109; supported papal reform efforts.

Hughes, Thomas (1822–96). B. Uffington, Berkshire, Eng.; educ. Oxford; jurist, soc. reformer; helped found Christian* Socialism; active in founding Working Men's Coll., London, 1854, and was its principal 1872–83; founded Rugby, an unsuccessful cooperative community, in Tenn. 1879. Works include *Tom Brown's School Days; Tom Brown at Oxford;* biographies of D. Livingstone and Alfred the Great.

Hügli, Johann Adam (Jan. 23, 1831–Apr. 12, 1904). B. Hassloch, Rhenish Palatinate, Ger.; educ. Conc. Sem., St. Louis, Mo.; ordained 1856; served in Jonesboro, Ill., Frankenmuth, Saginaw, and Detroit, Mich.; helped found Luth. School for the Deaf at Detroit (see *Deaf,* 10); pres. N Dist. of Mo. Syn. 1872–75.

Hugo a [or de] Sancto Caro. See *Hugh of St. Cher.*

Hugo of Cluny. See *Hugh the Great.*

Hugo of St. Victor. See *Hugh of St. Victor.*

Hugo of Strasbourg. See *Ripelin, Hugo.*

Hugo the Great. See *Hugh the Great.*

Huguenots. Term of unknown origin; applied ca. 1560 to Fr. adherents of the Reformation. Fr. Prots. had received support of Margaret* of Navarre, a lukewarm RC. G. Roussel* and J. Lefevre* d'Étaples were leaders in reform movement. Circulation of Lefevre's Bible tr. throughout Fr. helped gain followers. Efforts of J. Calvin* furthered the success of Fr. Prots. Soon persecution began (see *France,* 8). Huguenots, reckoned by some as one-third of the pop., resisted under leadership of Anthony of Bourbon (Antoine de Bourbon; 1518–62; b. Picardy; king of Navarre 1555–62; vacillating in religion; finally joined RC Ch.), Louis I de Bourbon (Prince de Condé*), and Gaspard (II) de Coligny.* Exile, imprisonment, execution, prohibition of worship, and other forms of persecution caused many Huguenots to emigrate to Holland, Eng., Ireland, Am., Switz., Ger., and other countries. Wars and unrest continued till 1789. See also *France,* 9–11; *United States, Religious History of the.*

The Huguenot Wars, comp. and ed. J. Coudy, tr. J. Kernan (Philadelphia, Pa., 1969); A. J. Grant, *The Huguenots* (Toronto, 1934); G. E. Reaman, *The Train of the Huguenots in Europe, the United States, South Africa, and Canada* (Toronto, 1963); S. Smiles, *The Huguenots: Their Settlements, Churches, and Industries in England and Ireland* (New York, 1874); H. M. Baird, *History of the Rise of the Huguenots of France,* 2 vols. (New York, 1879), *The Huguenots and Henry of Navarre,* 2 vols. (New York, 1886), and *The Huguenots and the Revocation of the Edict of Nantes,* 2 vols. (New York, 1895).

Huizinga, Johan (1872–1945). Dutch hist.; b. Groningen, Neth.; prof. Groningen 1905, Leiden 1915; exponent of a philos. of culture in which there is a harmonious balance of material and spiritual values. Works include *Homo ludens: A Study of the Play-Element in Culture; The Waning of the Middle Ages; Erasmus.*

Hülsemann, Johann (1602–61). B. Esens, Ostfriesland, Ger.; prof. Wittenberg 1629; represented Lutheranism at colloquy of Thorn* 1645; prof. and pastor Leipzig 1646. Works include *Extensio breviarii theologici; Dialysis apologetica problematis Calixtini; Manuale Augustanae Confessionis.*

Human Development. See *Educational Psychology,* C.

Human Nature of Christ. See *Christ Jesus,* I.

Humani generis. Encyclical of Pius XII (see *Popes,* 33), Aug. 12, 1950; directed RC scholars to study evolution,* existentialism,* and historicism* with a view to refuting the errors and determining the truth in them. Among other things it reaffirmed the importance of analogy* of faith and of ch. tradition in Scriptural interpretation; demonstration of the existence of God; doctrine of creation,* predestination,* existence of angels,* original sin,* transubstantiation (see *Grace, Means of,* IV 3); membership in the ch.; approval of Thomism (see *Thomas Aquinas*).

Humanism. Term used in various ways with different emphases for philosophies which center on man. It usually designates a philos. and literary movement which began in It. in the 14th c. and permeated W culture. The movement originally centered on Gk. and Lat. classics but soon influenced concepts of freedom, religion, hist., science, and other areas. *Christian humanism* stresses the values of human culture but subordinates them to Christian faith. *Devout humanism,* traced to L. Lessius,* tried to mitigate harsh concepts of man resulting from teachings on original sin by emphasizing man's goodness. *Secular humanism* emphasizes one or more of man's intellectual, cultural, or soc. achievements to the exclusion of religion. *New humanism* is common to several contemporary movements with varying emphases; it deals with the human as distinguished from the impersonal and the human as distinguished from the inhuman (the 1st pertains to attempts to humanize life by refusing to make people into things and by liberating them for human potential; the 2d pertains to emphasis on humanization, i. e., on ethical awareness of human nature and its possibilities as distinguished from a merely empirical measurement of man).

See also *Enlightenment,* 2; *Humanism, Sixteenth-Century German; Reformation, Lutheran,* 3; *Religious Humanism; Renaissance.*

Humanism, Sixteenth-Century German. 16th-c. Ger. humanism tried to correct decay of Lt. and Gk. style which resulted from scholasticism*; it was related in some ways to the humanism of D. Erasmus,* J. Colet,* and T. Moore.* The movement coincided with a revival of interest in classical literature, Scripture in the original languages, and ancient MSS. Initiator of the movement was R. Agricola.* Many humanists despised scholastic studies and degrees, some courted the favor of Ger. princes through their verses. Significant in the movement was a dispute regarding validity of Heb. studies; the dispute resulted in *Letters* of Obscure Men.* In the Luth. Reformation,* humanism was assoc. esp. with P. Melanchthon,* who founded the system of humanistic intermediate schools and classical coll. studies which became traditional in Ger. Lutheranism for higher educ. in gen. and ministerial training in particular. Humanism emphasized graceful and apt style patterned after classical models, and ethics reflecting natural* law. It provided linguistic tools for Scriptural studies and additional philos. methods for organizing thought. Humanists were interested in sources, literature, philos., and aesthetics. Humanism as such was neutral, without theol. or religious implications. RRC

F. Paulsen, *Geschichte des gelehrten Unterrichts,* 3d ed., 2 vols. (Leipzig, 1919–21); P. Petersen, *Geschichte der aristotelischen Philosophie im protestantischen Deutschland* (Leipzig, 1921); H. A. E. v. Gelder, *The Two Reformations in the 16th Century: A Study of the Religious Aspects and Consequences of Renaissance and Humanism* (The Hague, 1961); L. W. Spitz, *The Religious Renaissance of the German Humanists* (Cambridge, Mass., 1963); J. E. Seigel, *Rhetoric and Philosophy in Renaissance Humanism* (Princeton, 1968).

Humanitarianism. See *Social Work.*

Hume, David (1711–76). Scot. philos. and hist.; b. Edinburgh; studied law; tutor to George Johnstone, 3d marquess of Annandale; secy. to Gen. James Sinclair (d. 1762); keeper of Advocates' Library, Edinburgh; mem. Brit. embassy in Paris; undersecy. of state for the N dept.

Developed a philos. of skepticism (Humism) which restricted knowledge to experience of ideas and impressions; denied ultimate verification of truth.

According to Hume, cognition results from impressions of sensation and reflection, simple ideas come from simple impressions, complex ideas are either copies of complex impressions or mental combinations of simple ones. Knowledge is comparison of ideas.

Held that the "necessary connection" on which theory of cause-effect is based is not demonstrable (see also *Cause,* 5). Against the cosmological (or causal) argument for the existence of God, Hume argued that causal connections hold only bet. observable states, thus excluding God. He used Epicurean arguments of atomic materialism against teleological (or design) proofs for God's existence. This led defenders of theism (e. g., I. Kant*) to use moral arguments. In the 20th c. some philosophers have found contradictions in Hume's arguments on cause.

Works include *A Treatise of Human Nature; Essays, Moral and Political; Philosophical Essays Concerning Human Understanding* (later called *An Enquiry Concerning Human Understanding*); *An Enquiry Concerning the Principles of Morals; The Natural History of Religion; Dialogues Concerning Natural Religion.*

R. F. Anderson, *Hume's First Principles* (Lincoln, Nebr., 1966); A. H. Basson, *David Hume* (Harmondsworth, Middlesex, Eng., 1958); A. G. N. Flew, *Hume's Philosophy of Belief* (New York, 1961); R. H. Hurlbutt III, *Hume, Newton, and the Design Argument* (Lincoln, Nebr., 1965); R. Metz, *David Hume: Leben und Philosophie* (Stuttgart, 1968). EL

Hume, Robert Wilson (Nov. 9, 1809–Nov. 26, 1854). B. Stamford, Conn.; educ. Union Coll. (Schenectady, N. Y.), Andover, Mass., and Princeton, N. J.; ABCFM miss. to Bombay, India; secy. Bombay Tract and Book Soc.; ed. periodical *Dnyanodaya* ("Rise of Knowledge").

Humeral Veil (from Lat. *humerus,* "shoulder"). RC subdeacon's veil; worn around shoulders and covering hands, so that it, not hands, touches the monstrance* at high mass; used by priest and deacon in other eucharistic functions.

Humiliati (Berettini). Adherents of RC lay-poverty movement; originated 12th c. in Lombardy; practiced communal poverty as manual laborers; women cared for sick; men helped poor and engaged in soc. activity; refused to bear arms; preached against heresy and abuses in ch.; excommunicated by Lucius III (ca. 1097–1185; pope 1181–85) with Waldenses 1184; Innocent III (see *Popes,* 10) restored them 1201; involvement in wool industry brought them wealth and decline; male branch suppressed 1571; several It. convents survived.

Humiliation and Prayer, Day of. See *Church Year,* 17.

Humiliation of Christ. See *Christ Jesus,* II 1.

Humility. Theologically, recognition of human unworthiness in presence of transcendent God; ethically, in love valuing others above self. Non-Christian religions, including Islam,* define humility either in terms of approach to numinous power (esp. in prayer) or in terms of mystical relationship that emphasizes insignificance of man. In OT, concept of humility gen. little concerned with self-valuation apart from soc. context. A humble man depends on God, who requires humility of man (Mi 6:8). In NT, humility is not often assoc. with low soc. status, though it is part of Jesus' messianic character (Mt 11:29; 21:4-5). Included in NT catalogs of virtues (Cl 3:12; Eph 4:2; Ph 2:3). Humility involves man's relationship to God (2 Co 10:1, 12-18). Augustine* of Hippo posited humility as basic (Sermon 19 [69 in Benedictine ed.], 2 and 4, on Mt 11:28-29). Thomas* Aquinas viewed it as part of the cardinal virtue temperance, basic to Christian life. Mystical literature of the Middle Ages dealt at great length with humility. M. Luther* early defined humility as man's qualifying disposition (the deeper the humility, the greater God's mercy) which gave God honor, following Bernard* of Clairvaux (e. g., WA 1, 63–65). In many instances in the Ps Luther interprets humility as meaning nothingness of man before God, the crucifying of self, the will to hear God's Word (e. g., WA 40 II, 315–470). Humility assumes the character of God's work in man in Luther's lectures on Ro (e. g., WA 56, 408–409). In sermons of 1518 Christocentric humility appears in faith (e. g., WA 1, 329–334).

K. Thieme, *Die christliche Demut* (Giessen, 1906); W. C. v. Unnik, "Zur Bedeutung von Ταπεινοῦν τὴν ψυχήν bei den Apostolischen Vätern," *Zeitschrift für die neutestamentliche Wissenschaft,* XLIV (1952–53), 250–255; L. Pinomaa, *Der existenzielle Charakter der Theologie Luthers* (Helsinki, 1940); R. Damerau, *Die Demut in der Theologie Luthers* (Giessen, Ger., [1967]). JEG

Humism. See *Hume, David.*

Humoral Doctrine. See *Psychology,* B 2.

Humphreys, Joseph (b. 1720). B. Burford, Oxfordshire, Eng.; educ. at a ministerial school in London; assoc. with J. and C. Wesley,* later with G. Whitefield*; preached at Bristol, London, and Deptford; hymnist. Hymns include "Blessed Are the Sons of God."

Hungarian Confessions. See *Hungary; Reformed Confessions,* E 6.

Hungarian Reformed Church in America. See *Reformed Churches,* 4 d-e.

Hungary. Hungary was part of the Roman provinces of Pannonia and Dacia. Invading Magyars* founded a kingdom ca. 896. Stephen I (ca. 975–1038; "Apostle of Hung.; Apostolic King"; duke of Hung. 997; crowned 1st king of Árpád dynasty 1001; continued Christianizing policy of his father, Duke Geza; suppressed paganism; patron saint of Hung.) attached the ch. of Hung. closely to Rome. Hung. hist. is checkered. The monarchy, defeated in WW I, was replaced by a rep., followed 1919 by short communist rule that ended with Rumanian occupation. Shifting fortunes of war and peace led to a Hung. rep. 1946, a Soviet "People's Rep." 1949, and an unsuccessful uprising 1956.

Lutheranism (introd. by traveling merchants and returning students) and Calvinism* spread rapidly through Hung. in the 16th century. P. Melanchthon* was called "Preceptor of Hung." Reformation leaders included M. B. Dévay,* J. Honter(us),* and L. Stöckel.* A Luth. confession was adopted at Erdöd 1545; the *Confessio Pentapolitana* (see also *Lutheran Confessions,* A 5) was drafted 1548 at Medias, made legal 1555. The Hung. Confession (see also *Reformed Confessions,* E 6), adopted at Czenger 1557 (1558?), was printed 1570 at Debrecen.* In the Counter* Reformation, Hung. Prots. were severely persecuted. Joseph* II granted Prots. tolerance 1781. Further adjustments were made 1848, 1867, and 1948–49.

In A. Hitler's time (see *Germany,* C 4), Hung. chs. tried to help Jews.

After WW II, the Soviets allowed religious freedom in principle. After the fall of pol. parties, the Soviets regarded chs. as offering the chief surviving ideological opposition to communism. Through land reforms the chs. lost endowments by which they had supported and controlled educ. In 1948 Ref. and Luth. chs. accepted an arrangement by which schools were taken over by the state, but 2 hrs. of religious instruction allowed. The RC Ch. under leadership of Cardinal Primate J. Mindszenty opposed the move. Mindszenty was imprisoned, RC schools laicized, and many RC orders dissolved. A concordat advantageous to communist govt. (organized as People's Rep. by the 1949 const.) was imposed on the chs. and signed 1948 by Ref. and Luths., 1950 by RCs. In following yrs. the state assumed increasing control of ch. affairs. A 1957 decree with retroactive force required civil approval of nominations and elections to higher ch. offices. A 1958 decree made it possible for the secular govt. to fill certain ch. offices without consulting the ch. Mindszenty, who lived in refuge in US embassy Budapest 1956–71, was retired from the Hung. episcopate against his will by the pope and stripped of his title as RC primate of Hung. Feb. 1974.

Hunnius, Aegidius (Giles; Hunn; 1550–1603). Father of N. Hunnius*; b. Winnenden, Württemberg, Ger.; educ. Tübingen; asst. pastor Tübingen 1574; prof. Marburg 1576; tried unsuccessfully to win the U. of Marburg and the ch. of Hesse for the FC; prof. Wittenberg 1592; opposed Calvinism; was called to other Ger. territories (e. g., Silesia) to oppose Calvinism. Helped compose Saxon Visitation Articles (see *Articles of Visitation*); other works include *Tractatus de majestate, autoritate fide, ac certitudine sacrae scripturae propheticae et apostolicae veteris et novi testamenti; Articulus de providentia dei et aeterna praedestinatione; De peccato originali; Thesaurus apostolicus; Thesaurus evangelicus.*

Hunnius, Nikolas (1585–1643). Son of A. Hunnius*; b. Marburg, Ger.; educ. Wittenberg; instructor philos. and theol. Wittenberg 1609; supt. Eilenburg 1612–17; prof. Wittenberg 1617–23; pastor Lübeck 1623, supt. 1624. Defended orthodox Lutheranism against Calvinism and RCm.

Hunt, Arthur Surridge (1871–1934). B. Romford, Essex, Eng.; educ. Eastbourne Coll. and Oxford U.; excavated in Faiyûm province, N Egypt, with B. P. Grenfell* and David George Hogarth (1862–1927; b. Barton-on-Humber, Lincolnshire, Eng.; archaeologist); prof. Oxford; ed. with Grenfell papyrus texts issued by Egypt Exploration Soc.

Hunt, John (June 13, 1812–Oct. 4, 1848). B. Hykeham Moor, near Lincoln, Eng.; farm laborer; Meth. at ca. 16; educ. theol. coll. Hoxton; miss. to Fiji 1838. Helped tr. Bible into Fiji; other works include *Memoir of the Rev. W. Cross; Entire Sanctification, in Letters to a Friend.*

Hunt, Phineas R. (Jan. 30, 1816–May 29, 1878). B. Arlington, Vt.; ABCFM missionary printer Madras, India, 1839, and Peking, China, 1868.

Hunt, Robert (ca. 1568–1608). B. Eng.; Angl. cleric; chaplain of expedition which founded Jamestown, Va. See also *Protestant Episcopal Church,* 1 a.

Hunt, William Holman (1827–1910. B. London, Eng.; painter; mem. Pre-Raphaelite* Brotherhood; aimed at detail and truth to nature. Works include *Light of the World; The Finding of the Saviour in the Temple.*

Huntingdon, Countess of. See *Hastings, Selina.*

Hunton, William Lee (Feb. 16, 1864–Oct. 12, 1930). Luth. pastor and ed.; b. Morrisburg, Ont., Can.; educ. Thiel Coll., Greenville, Pa., and Philadelphia (Pa.) Theol. Sem.; pastor Amanda, Ohio, Rochester and Buffalo, N. Y., Wilkes-Barre, Pa., Chicago, Ill.; instr. Chicago Luth. Theol. Sem. 1902–06; mgr. Gen. Council Pub. House; literature mgr. United Luth. Pub. House. Ed. *The Lutheran* 1907–20; other works include *Favorite Hymns; I Believe; Facts of Our Faith.*

Hunzinger, August Wilhelm (1871–1920). B. Dreilützow, Mecklenburg, Ger.; prof. Leipzig and Erlangen; pastor Hamburg 1912. Works include *Probleme und Aufgaben der gegenwärtigen systematischen Theologie; Die religiöse Krisis der Gegenwart.*

Hupfeld, Hermann Christian Karl Friedrich (1796–1866). B. Marburg, Ger.; educ. Marburg; prof. Marburg and Halle; championed documentary hypothesis. See also *Higher Criticism,* 15.

Hurban, Josef Miloslav (1817–88). Luth. patriot and writer; b. Beckov, Slovakia; educ. Bratislava; chaplain Brezova 1840; pastor Hluboka 1843–88; opposed efforts toward Ref.-Luth. union. His *Unia* states position of Luth. confessionalism; ed. periodical *Cirkevní Listy,* which became rallying point for Slovak Luth. Ch. See also *Slovakia, Lutheran Theology in,* 2.

Huria Kristen Batak Protestant. See *Batak Protestant Christian Church.*

Hus, John (Huss; Johannes Hus von Husinetz; Czech: Jan Hus; ca. 1370–1415). 1. Reformer and martyr; b. Husinec, Boh.; educ. Prague; lecturer U. of Prague 1398; priest 1401; rector U. of Prague 1402; preacher Bethlehem Chapel, Prague, founded for the preaching of the Word of God in the language of the people. Hus tried to restore true devotion among Christians and fearlessly attacked corruption (e. g., simony* and indulgences*) on all levels in the ch.; supported Wenceslaus'* position in the Great Schism (see *Schism,* 8). His defense of J. Wycliffe's* reform ideas made him suspect of heresy.

2. Hus was forbidden to preach 1409, put under lesser excommunication 1410, under greater excommunication 1412 (see *Keys, Office of,* 9); went into hiding 1412 and turned to writing. His stress on the ch. as the body of the elect and on the need for doctrine and decrees to be in harmony with Scripture in order to be binding on conscience challenged the importance and authority of the hierarchy. Though Hus may not have accepted all of Wycliffe's views, he was accused of Wycliffite errors and cited to appear before the Council of Constance* 1414. Emp. Sigismund* promised him safe-conduct.

3. Hus hoped to defend his cause before the council. But he was thrown into prison and was only asked to recant his "errors." He insisted on the need to distinguish bet. what was true and what was heretical in Wycliffe. He also requested reasons for recanting. The council, anxious to assert its authority and accomplish its purpose to restore unity and pure doctrine in the ch. (see *Councils and Synods,* 7), was not inclined to argue with a man accused of heresy. And Hus's old enemies did their best to represent him as a heretic. July 6, 1415, he was condemned, stripped of clerical status, handed over to the secular arm, and burned at the stake. His ashes were cast into the Rhine.

4. Hus's inability to accept the authority of the ch. where it went against his conscience and his understanding of Scripture foreshadowed the advent of modern man and of the Reformation.

5. Works include *De ecclesia; De causa boemica; Determinatio de ablatione temporalium a clericis; Disputatio Joannis Hus;* letters; sermons.

See also *Hussites.*

The Cambridge Medieval History, ed. C. W. Previté-Orton and Z. N. Brooke, VIII (New York, 1936), 1–115; J. Hus, *De ecclesia: The Church,* tr. D. S. Schaff (New York, 1915); *The Library of Christian Classics,* ed. J. Baillie, J. T. McNeill, H. P. Van Dusen, XIV: *Advocates of Reform From Wyclif to Erasmus,* ed. M. Spinka (Philadelphia, 1953), 185–278; M. Spinka, *John Hus* (Princeton, N. J., 1968). MSF

Hüschen. See *Hueschen.*

Huschke, Georg Philipp Eduard (1801–86). B. Münden, Ger.; prof. law Rostock 1824, Breslau 1827; leader of Breslau indep. Luths.; held that the ch. is formed by the means of grace and hence separate from the state. Works include *Wort und Sakramente die Faktoren der Kirche* (pub. 1849 in *Zeitschrift für lutherische Theologie und Kirche*).

Husmann, Friedrich Wilhelm (Nov. 9, 1807–May 4, 1881). B. Nordel, Hannover, Ger.; teacher in Bremen; responded to call of F. C. D. Wyneken* for ch. workers in Am. by going to Fort Wayne, Ind., 1840; miss. teacher and pastor in and near Fort Wayne and elsewhere in N Ind. and Ohio; 1st secy. Mo. Syn. 1847–60; pastor South Euclid, near Cleveland, Ohio, 1863–81.

Husserl, Edmund (1859–1938). B. Prossnitz, Moravia; Ger. philos.; gave eidetic* science and phenomenology* 20th-c. connotation. Works include *Logische Untersuchungen.*

Hussites. Gen. name for followers of J. Hus.* Fierce indignation aroused throughout Boh. by execution of Hus and Jerome* of Prague, rejection by the Council of Constance* of the use of the cup – introd. during the imprisonment of Hus with his approval – as heretical, and determination of Hussites to defend their faith to the utmost resulted in grave disorders and civil war. A favorable setting for the Hussite movement had been prepared by *Devotio* moderna.* Wycliffism* furnished Hussites with a theoretical basis for revolt. Refusal of the estates to have Sigismund* as king brought on the Hussite Wars. Martin* V organized a crusade against the dissidents 1420. Hussite moderates (called Calixtines [from their demand for the use of the chalice (Lat. *calix*) in communing the laity] or Utraquists [from Lat. *sub utraque specie,* "under both kinds"]) were conservative in demands for reform. Taborites,* a more radical group, gathered around Jan (Johann) Zizka (Ziska; ca. 1360–1424), rejected transubstantiation,* adoration of saints, intercession for dead, and ecclesiastical customs not commanded in the Bible; they demanded that the state regulate its affairs by the Bible, and had chiliastic and communistic tendencies. Horebites (from a mountain which they called Horeb and to which they retired), another radical group, also gathered around Zizka. These 3 groups adopted the Articles of Prague 1420: 1. Freedom of preaching; 2. Communion under both kinds; 3. Reduction of clergy to apostolic poverty; 4. Severe punishment for mortal sin. Hussites were repeatedly victorious and carried the war into neighboring countries. Crushing defeat of the RC army 1431 blighted all hopes of emp. and pope of subjecting the Bohemians by force. The driving force of the Hussites was religious zeal nourished by Biblical preaching, frequent partaking of the Eucharist, and rich vernacular hymnody. Negotiations bet. the Council of Basel* and the Hussites resulted in the acceptance 1433 by the war-weary Utraquists of the *Compactata* of Prague, which granted the administration of Communion under both kinds. Taborites rejected the agreement and were well-nigh annihilated 1434 by moderate Hussites and RCs in a battle near Lipan. Hussite zeal and religious creativity came to an end but found new expression in the Bohemian* Brethren. Utraquists continued in an uneasy peace with RCs till the time of M. Luther* (see *Bohemia, Lutheran Theology in*). Most then became Luth. or neo-Utraquist; Old Utraquists merged with the RC Ch. See also *Poland,* 1.

F. G. Heymann, "The Hussite-Utraquist Church in the Fifteenth and Sixteenth Centuries," *Archiv für Reformationsgeschichte,* LII (1961), 1–16, and *John Zizka and the Hussite Revolution* (Princeton, N. J., 1955); F. H. H. V. v. Lützow, *A History of Bohemian Literature* (New York, 1900); *The Cambridge Medieval History,* ed. C. W. Previté-Orton and Z. N. Brooke, VIII (New York, 1936), 65–115. MSF

Hut, Hans (Hutt; ca. 1490–1527). Anabap.; b. Hain, near Grimmenthal, Franconia; sexton, bookbinder, book peddler; traveled in Ger. and Austria; influenced by T. Münzer*; won for the Anabap. cause by J. Denk*; influential in Bavaria, Franconia, Swabia, and Austria; defeated in disputation with B. Hubmaier*; d. in prison at Augsburg.

Hutchinson, John (1674–1737). B. Spennithorne, Yorkshire, Eng.; theol. writer; followers called Hutchinsonians. Works include *Moses's Principia,* written in opposition to I. Newton's* *Principia.*

Huter, Jakob (Hutter; d. 1536). Founded Huterites (Hutterian Brethren; Hutterites). B. Moos, S Tirol; itinerant hatmaker; leader of Anabaps. in Tirol after death of G. Blaurock*; reorganized some Anabaps.

into collective farms in Moravia; arrested in Tirol; burned at stake. See also *Mennonite Churches,* 3 a.

Huth, Carl Frederick Emil (Nov. 30, 1857–Apr. 23, 1926). B. Nieden, Brandenburg, Ger.; educ. Northwestern U. (later called Northwestern Coll.), Watertown, Wis. (see *Ministry, Education of,* VIII B), and Conc. Sem., St. Louis, Mo.; prof. Conc. Coll., Milwaukee, Wis., 1881–1926.

Huther, Johann Eduard (1807–80). B. Hamburg, Ger.; educ. Bonn, Göttingen, and Berlin; teacher Schwerin 1842–55; pastor Wittenförden 1855–80. Works include commentaries on NT pastoral and gen. Epistles and on Cl.

Hutten, Ulrich von (1488–1523). Humanist; b. Steckelberg Castle, near Fulda, Franconia, Ger.; studied at Benedictine monastery at Fulda and various univs. in Ger. and It.; joined imperial army 1513; joined Swabian League against duke Ulrich of Württemberg 1519; joined F. v. Sickingen* in struggle of nobles against spiritual principalities 1522; fled to Switz., where H. Zwingli* befriended him. Satirist; wrote part of *Letters* of Obscure Men;* vigorously defended M. Luther*; writings appealed to sympathies and patriotism of nobility; had dispute with D. Erasmus*; ed. L. Valla's* work on "Donation* of Constantine."

Hutter, Elias (b. 1553; d. bet. 1605 and 1609). B. Görlitz, Ger.; orientalist and Biblical scholar; prof. Leipzig; produced the Nürnberg polyglot (see *Polyglot Bibles*); founded school of languages at Nürnberg.

Hutter, Jakob. See *Huter, Jakob.*

Hutter, Leonhard (Leonard Hütter; Hutterus; 1563–1616). B. Nellingen, near Ulm, Ger.; educ. Strasbourg, Leipzig, Heidelberg, and Jena; prof. Wittenberg 1596; champion of Luth. orthodoxy (see *Lutheran Theology After 1580*); called *redonatus Lutherus* (Lat. "Luther given back"), by anagrammatic rearrangement of the letters in *Leonardus Hutterus.* Works include *Compendium locorum theologicorum; Concordia concors.*

Hutterian Brethren (Hutterites; Huterites). See *Huter, Jakob; Mennonite Churches,* 3 a.

Huxley, Thomas Henry (1825–95). Biologist; b. Ealing, near London, Eng.; lectured on biology and related subjects at various London institutions; held several govt. positions; embraced Darwinism (see *Darwin, Charles Robert*) and became skeptic, rejecting Christianity completely; engaged in warfare against Christian beliefs; promoted agnosticism.* Works include *Man's Place in Nature; Lessons in Elementary Physiology.* See also *Metaphysical Society, The.*

Huyck, Jan. See *Reformed Churches,* 4 b.

Hyacinthe, Père. See *Loyson, Charles.*

Hyde, William Dewitt (1858–1917). B. Winchendon, Mass.; educ. Harvard U. (Cambridge, Mass.), Union Theol. Sem. (NYC), Andover (Mass.) Theol. Sem.; Cong. pastor Paterson, N. J., 1883; pres. Bowdoin Coll. (Brunswick, Maine) 1885. Works include *Practical Ethics; Practical Idealism; From Epicurus to Christ; Self-Measurement.*

Hylemorphism. See *Hylomorphism.*

Hylics. See *Gnosticism,* 5.

Hylomorphism (hylemorphism). Theory that all things are constituted of 2 principles: *hyle* (Gk. "matter") remains the same; *morphe* (Gk. "form") changes.

Hylotheism (from Gk. *hyle,* "matter," and *theos,* "God"). Theory equating matter with God or merging one into the other. Synonym for pantheism* and materialism.*

Hymnody, Christian. 1. Ps, hymns, and spiritual songs were used by the Christian Ch. from its beginning (Eph. 5:19; Cl 3:16). But there is no direct evidence of hymns used in pub. worship until the 2d c.

2. Earliest known Christian hymns emphasized praise of God. "Shepherd of Tender Youth" (Gk. *Stomion polon adion,* literally "Bridle of Steeds Untamed,") is ascribed to Clement* of Alexandria. In the 2d and 3d c. Bardesanes (see *Gnosticism,* 7 h) and son Harmonius* tried to spread Gnostic speculation through hymns. To counteract heresies, Ephraem* wrote many hymns. Other early hymnists of the E Ch. include Methodius* of Olympus, Gregory* of Nazianzus, Synesius,* Andrew* of Crete, John* of Damascus, Theodore* of Studion. Gk. hymnody is characterized by objectivity and pure worship.

3. The Lat., or W Ch., from the 4th c. to the Reformation, produced hymnists including Hilary* of Poitiers (*Lucis Largitor splendide,* "Thou Splendid Giver of the Light"), Ambrose* (*O Lux beata Trinitas,* "O Trinity, Most Blessed Light"), C. Sedulius* (*Hostis Herodes impie,* "The Star Proclaims the King Is Here"), V. H. C. Fortunatus* (*Vexilla Regis prodeunt,* "The Royal Banners Forward Go"), Gregory I (see *Popes,* 4; hymns include *Rex Christe, factor omnium,* "O Christ, Our King, Creator Lord").

4. Hymnists of the Middle Ages include Bede* (*Hymnum canamus gloriae,* "A Hymn of Glory Let Us Sing"), Bernard* of Clairvaux, Adam* of St. Victor, Thomas* of Celano, Thomas* Aquinas (*Lauda Sion Salvatorem*). *Veni Creator Spiritus* was probably written by Ambrose, Gregory I, or Rabanus* Maurus; *Dies irae, dies illa* was probably written by Thomas of Celano; other hymns of the Middle Ages include *Veni, Sancte Spiritus; Salve caput cruentatum; Stabat mater dolorosa; Quem pastores laudavere* (the "Quempas Carol").

5. Lat. was the official language of the ch. in the Middle Ages, but hymns in the vernacular were in use in Ger. and surrounding countries at least as early as the 12th c. ("Christ ist erstanden"); "Nun bitten wir den Heiligen Geist" was in use in the 13th c., "Gelobet seist du, Jesu Christ" in the 14th c. Hymns such as these which ended with "Kyrieleis" ("Lord, have mercy") were called Leisen. Their use was limited seasonally or otherwise. Under leadership of M. Luther* the Reformation brought cong. singing in the vernacular to full development. The first Luth. hymnals were pub. 1524. Other Luth. hymnists to ca. 1560 include J. Agricola,* E. Alber* (Margrave of Brandenburg-Kulmbach), H. Bonnus,* E. Cruciger,* N. Decius,* V. Dietrich,* P. Eber,* J. Freder(us),* J. Frosch,* George* of Brandenburg-Ansbach, J. Gramann,* Henry* of Zutphen, N. Herman,* J. Hess,* J. Heune,* J. Jonas,* A. Knöpken,* W. Link,* Joachim and Johann Magdeburg,* J. Mathesius,* A. Moibanus,* W. Musculus,* H. Sachs,* J. Spangenberg,* L. Spengler,* P. Speratus,* J. Walther.*

Luth. hymnists ca. 1560–ca. 1618 include J. Arnd(t),* C. Becker,* M. Behm,* B. Bidembach,* J. Ebert,* J. Fischa(e)rt,* P. Hagen,* V. Herberger,* C. Knoll,* M. Moller,* P. Nicolai,* A. Osiander* (the Younger), B. Ringwaldt,* M. Schalling,* C. Schneegass,* N. Selnecker,* C. Spangenberg,* J. Steuerlein,* C. Vischer,* S. Weingärtner.*

6. Luth. hymnists ca. 1618–ca. 1648 include H. Alberti,* J. M. Altenburg,* J. V. Andreä,* L. Bacmeister,* A. H. Bucholtz,* S. Dach,* D. Denicke,* B. Derschau,* Z. Faber,* J. Gesenius,* A. Gryphius,* J. Heermann,* H. Held,* B. Helder,* M. A. v. Löwenstern,* J. M. Meyfart,* M. Opitz,* M. Rinckart,* J. Rist,* J. Saubert* the Elder, J. H. Schein,* J. Stegmann,* A. Thebesius,* C. Tietze,* J. Wegelin,* G. Weissel,* G. Werner,* S. Zehner,* K. Ziegler.*

Luth. hymnists ca. 1648–ca. 1680 include Aemilie*

Juliane, J. R. Ahle,* J. G. Albinus,* H. v. Assig,* S. v. Birken,* T. Clausnitzer,* W. C. Dessler,* J. M. Dilherr,* J. Flit(t)ner,* J. Franck,* Michael Franck,* S. Franck,* A. Fritsch,* M. Geier* Jr., P. Gerhardt,* J. F. Hertzog,* E. C. Homburg,* C. Keimann,* C. Knorr,* S. Liscow,* Ludämilia* Elisabeth, H. Müller,* K. F. Nachtenhöfer,* G. Neumark,* G. Olearius* (b. 1604), J. Olearius* (b. 1611), J. G. Olearius* (b. 1635), G. M. Pfefferkorn,* B. Praetorius,* S. Rodigast,* G. W. Sacer,* J. Saubert* the Younger, J. Scheffler,* H. Schenk,* M. Schirmer,* J. B. Schupp,* C. Scriver,* E. Stockmann,* B. Wiesenmeyer.*

With the rise of Pietism* the golden age of Luth. hymnody had passed. Luth. hymnists ca. 1680–1756 (beginning of the Seven Years' War) include J. L. C. Allendorf,* K. H. v. Bogatzky,* J. J. Breithaupt,* F. R. L. v. Canitz, B. Crasselius,* A. Drese,* J. Falckner,* A. H. Francke,* J. A. Freylinghausen,* J. B. Freystein,* L. A. Gotter* J. D. Herrnschmidt,* J. Lange,* L. Laurenti,* L. F. F. Lehr,* J. J. Rambach,* C. F. Richter,* J. C. Schade,* C. L. Scheidt,* J. E. Schmidt,* J. H. Schröder,* J. J. Schütz,* V. L. v. Seckendorf,* P. J. Spener,* J. F. Starck,* E. G. Woltersdorf.*

7. Hymnists in Eng., Ireland, and Scot. include S. Adams,* J. Addison,* H. Alford,* H. W. Baker,* S. Baring-Gould,* R. Baxter,* E. Bickersteth,* H. Bonar,* J. L. Borthwick,* J. Bowring,* M. Bridges,* S. A. Brooke,* J. Bunyan,* E. Caswall,* E. Charles,* G. K. Chesterton,* W. Cowper,* F. E. Cox,* W. C. Dix,* P. Doddridge,* J. Edmeston,* J. Ellerton,* E. Elliott,* C. Elven,* E. Hatch,* F. R. Havergal,* W. H. Havergal,* R. Heber,* G. Herbert,* W. W. How,* J. Keble,* T. Kelly,* T. Ken,* C. Kingsley,* J. E. Leeson,* H. F. Lyte,* R. Massie,* J. Milton,* J. S. B. Monsell,* J. Montgomery,* E. Mote,* J. M. Neale,* J. H. Newman,* J. Newton,* E. Osler,* E. Perronet,* H. J. Pye,* J. Rippon,* A. T. Russell,* A. Steele,* S. J. Stone,* G. Thring,* A. M. Toplady,* I. Watts,* C. Wesley,* J. Wesley,* S. Wesley,* C. Winkworth,* C. Wordsworth.*

8. Am. and Can. hymnists include L. F. Benson,* G. W. Bethune,* P. Brooks,* W. C. Bryant,* A. and P. Cary,* A. C. Coxe,* H. M. Dexter,* G. W. Doane,* G. Duffield* Jr. and son S. A. W. Duffield, T. Dwight,* N. L. Frothingham,* W. Gladden,* H. Harbaugh,* T. Hastings,* H. W. Longfellow,* D. March,* W. A. Muhlenberg (see *Mühlenberg, Heinrich Melchior, and Family,* 6), R. Palmer,* S. D. Phelps,* J. Schriven,* S. F. Smith,* F. J. Van* Alstyne.

Luth. hymnists in Am. include A. Crull,* C. J. H. Fick,* C. P. Krauth,* M. Loy,* W. G. Polack,* C. W. Schäffer,* C. H. L. Schuette,* J. A. Seiss,* C. F. W. Walther.*

9. Scand. hymnists include H. A. Brorson,* J. N. Brun (see *Norway, Lutheranism in,* 10), N. F. S. Grundtvig,* T. H. Kingo,* U. V. Koren,* H. Spegel,* J. O. Wallin.*

10. Other hymnists include H. A. C. Malan* (Fr.), G. Savonarola* (It.), W. Williams* (Welsh). See also *Theology.*

J. Julian, *A Dictionary of Hymnology,* 2d rev. ed. with new supplement (London, 1907); L. F. Benson, *The Hymnody of the Christian Church* (New York, 1927); C. W. Douglas, *Church Music in History and Practice,* rev. ed. (New York, 1962); F. Blume, *Geschichte der evangelischen Kirchenmusik* (New York, 1965); C. Blume and G. M. Dreves, *Hymnologische Beiträge,* 4 vols. (Leipzig, 1897–1930); W. G. Polack, *The Handbook to the Lutheran Hymnal,* 2d ed. (St. Louis, 1942); A. H. Hoffmann v. Fallersleben, *Geschichte des deutschen Kirchenliedes bis auf Luthers Zeit,* 3d ed. (Hanover, 1861); A. F. W. Fischer, *Das deutsche evangelische Kirchenlied des 17. Jahrhunderts,* 6 vols. (Gütersloh, 1904–16) and *Kirchenlieder-Lexicon* (Gotha, 1878–79); F. J. E. Raby, *A History of Christian-Latin Poetry from the Beginnings to the Close of the Middle Ages,* 2d ed. (Oxford, Eng., 1953); F. Spitta, *Das deutsche Kirchenlied in seinen charakteristischen Erscheinungen* (Berlin, 1912); E. Schmidt, *Führer durch das Gesangbuch der Evangel.-Luth. Kirche in Bayern rechts des Rheins* (Erlangen, 1936); K. E. P. Wackernagel, *Das deutsche Kirchenlied,* 5 vols. (Leipzig, 1864–77); J. Westphal, *Das evangelische Kirchenlied nach seiner Geschichtlichen Entwicklung,* 6th ed. (Berlin, 1925); C. G. A. V. v. Winterfeld, *Der evangelische Kirchengesang,* 3 parts (Leipzig, 1843–47); *Geschichte des Kirchenlieds und Kirchengesangs der christlichen, insbesondere der deutschen evangelischen Kirche,* ed. E. E. Koch, 3d ed. (Stuttgart, 1866–76); E. E. Ryden, *The Story of Christian Hymnody* (Rock Island, Ill., 1959); *Historical Companion to Hymns Ancient & Modern,* ed. M. Frost (London, 1962).

Hypatia (ca. 375–415). Neoplatonic (see Neoplatonism) philos. at Alexandria, Egypt; murdered by Christian fanatics; heroine of C. Kingsley's* *Hypatia.* See also *Synesius.*

Hyperdulia. See *Latria.*

Hyperius, Andreas Gerhard (1511–64). B. Ypres, Belg. (hence "Hyperius"); prof. theol. Marburg, Ger., 1542; tried to follow middle course bet. Lutheranism and Calvinism; regarded as founder of practical theol. as a theol. science. See also *Thamer, Theobald.*

Hypocrisy (from Gk. *hypokrisis,* "playing a part on a stage"). Dissimulating one's real character or belief, professing and pretending to be what one is not. Pr 21:27; Is 1:13-15; 29:13; Ml 1:6-14; Mt 6:1-5, 16; 7:5, 21; 15:1-9; 16:3; 22:18; 23; 26:25; Lk 11:39-52; 20:19-23; Jn 18:28; Acts 5:1-10; 2 Ti 3:5; Jude 12. Hypocrites are found in visible chs. but are not mems. of the invisible ch. They are counterfeit Christians. Their punishment is indicated Mt 24:51.

Hypostasis. See *Arianism,* 2; *Hypostatic Union.*

Hypostatic Union (from Gk. *hypostasis,* "person"). Personal union, specifically the union of Christ's 2 natures (divine and human) in His person. See also *Christ Jesus,* I; *Idiomata.*

Hypothetical Imperative. See *Categorical Imperative.*

Hypsistarians (from Gk. *hypsistos,* "highest"). 4th-c. sect in Cappadocia; included Jewish and Gk. elements; worshiped God only as "All Ruler and Highest," not as Father.

Hysterema. See *Gnosticism,* 4–5.

I

I. See *Buber, Martin; Corporate Personality; Ego.*

I Am. Movement organized in Chicago 1934 by Guy Warren Ballard (pseudonym Godfré Ray King; 1878–1939) and his wife Edna (nee Wheeler; pseudonyms: Chanera; Lotus Ray King). Ballard claimed to be an accredited messenger of a group of spirits called "The Ascended Masters," who included Christ, Moses, and esp. St. Germain. The movement is a conglomeration of elements including Hinduism,* Mazdaism (see *Zoroastrianism*), theosophy,* Spiritism,* and New* Thought.

I-Thou and I-It. Terms popularized by M. Buber* to emphasize the relationship as cen. in existential meaning. Subject-subject attitude (I-Thou) tends to give relational value; subject-object attitude (I-It) tends to reduce both parties to things. See also *Brunner, Heinrich Emil; Ebner, Ferdinand.*

Iamblichus (ca. 250–ca. 330). B. Chalcis, Coele-Syria; Gk. Neoplatonist; held elaborate system of mediation bet. spiritual and physical worlds.

Ibas (d. 457). Bp. Edessa 435–457; held mediating position bet. Nestorians and Cyril* of Alexandria in Christological* controversies; deposed at "Robber* Syn." of Ephesus 449; vindicated at Chalcedon* 451; views condemned at Constantinople* by the 5th ecumenical council 553. See also *Three Chapters, Controversy of.*

Ibn Daud, Abraham (Abraham ben David; ca. 1110–80). B. Toledo, Sp.; 1st prominent Jewish exponent of Aristotelianism. Works include *Sefer ha-Qabbalah* (Book of Tradition); *Emunah Ramah* (Exalted Faith).

Ibn Ezra. 1. *Abraham ben Meir* (1092–1167). B. Toledo, Sp.; outstanding medieval Jewish scholar; poet; also wrote on various sciences; other works include Biblical commentaries. 2. *Moses ben Jacob* (ca. 1070-ca. 1139). B. Granada, Sp.; Jewish profane and spiritual poet; philos.

ibn-Gabirol, Solomon ben Judah (ben-Gabirol). See *Avicebrón.*

ibn-Janah, Abul Walid Merwan. See *Jonah.*

Iceland. 1. *Area:* ca. 39,750 sq. mi. *Pop.:* ca. 200,000. N Atlantic is. S of the Arctic Circle, E of S Greenland, W of Norw. Settled in 9th c. or earlier by Irish hermits; they left when Norw. Vikings, chiefly heathen, arrived ca. 875, bringing with them some settlers. presumably Christian, from the Orkney Is., the Hebrides, Ireland, Scot., and Eng.

2. Thorvald* Kodransson came as miss. to Iceland ca. 981. Olaf* I sent to Iceland a number of missionaries, including Thangbrand*; all of them had some success. In 1000 Christianity was made the official religion of Iceland; freedom of religion was decreed 1874. The new ch. was served by foreigners. The country became a bishopric ca. 1056; Isleifur Gissurarson, a native, was bp. ca. 1056–82, with see at his ancestral estate at Skalholt; succeeded by son Gissur Isleifsson (bp. 1082–1118), who endowed the bishopric with the estate and founded for N Iceland the bishopric of Holar ca. 1106. The ch. in Iceland was first subordinate to the archdiocese of Bremen-Hamburg, then Lund (ca. 1104), then Nidaros (Trondheim; 1152). Scholars attended major institutions of learning in Eur. In the 12th–14th cents. the Icelandic Sagas were written.

3. Iceland was conquered by Norw. 1262–64; when Norw. came under Den., Iceland followed 1380. The Reformation was imposed by Christian* III of Den. in 1540 in Skalholt diocese, when G. Einarsson* became bp., and 1550 in Holar diocese, when the Cath. bp. Jon Arason (b. ca. 1484; bp. 1524) was executed. The causes of the Reformation in Iceland were largely political. The ev. ch. system was made the state ch. 1551.

4. The theol. foundation for Lutheranism in Iceland was consolidated by Gudbrandur Thorlaksson* (ca. 1541–1627; called to be bp. Holar 1570; ordained 1571), who obtained printing equipment and pub. many books, most of which were aimed at instruction in Lutheranism. His 1584 ed. of the Bible was the basis of every Bible issued for Iceland till 1826. Because the country was almost completely isolated, various movements in the ch. outside Iceland had little effect on the Icelandic ch. till the 19th c.

5. The external order of the ch. was little changed by the Reformation. Ch. operations were increasingly restricted as more and more ch. properties were appropriated by the state. The see of Skalholt was moved to Reykjavík 1785; the see of Holar was suppressed 1801.

A nat. renaissance began under leadership of Jón Sigurdsson (1811–79; statesman; man of letters). Iceland became an indep. kingdom 1918, but with Christian X (1870–1947; king of Den. 1912–47, Iceland 1918–44) king of both Den. and Iceland; a completely indep. rep. was est. 1944. SP

See also *Eddas; Pédursson, Hallgrémur; Pétursson, Pétur; Sveinson, Brynjuff.*

J. Helgason, *Islands Kirke fra dens Grundlaeggelse til Reformationen* (Copenhagen, 1925) and *Islands Kirke fra Reformation til vore Dage* (Copenhagen, 1922); K. Gjerset, *History of Iceland* (New York, 1925).

Icelandic Congregation in New Iceland, The. See *Canada,* A 13.

Icelandic Evangelical Lutheran Synod of (North) America. See *Canada,* A 13; *United Lutheran Church, Synods of,* 6.

Ichthus (Ichthys). See *Fish.*

Icons. Pictorial representations; images.* In Eastern* Orthodox Chs., flat-surface, or in very low relief, usually miniature, portrayals of Christ, saints, or sacred events; often richly ornamented; used as objects of veneration.

Iconoclastic Controversy. Controversy (726–842) in Eastern* Orthodox Chs.; concerned the role of icons* in the cultic life of the ch. First phase began when E emp. Leo III ("the Isaurian"; ca. 680–741; emp. 717–741), probably partly for pol. reasons and partly to remove an obstacle to conversion of Muslim and Jews, proscribed the use of icons. Constantine V (Copronymous; 717–775; son of Leo III; emp. 741–775) severely continued this policy. Leo IV (the Khazar; ca. 750–780; son of Constantine V; emp. 775–780) was milder. Under Irene (752–803; b. Athens; m. Leo IV 769; regent 780; abdicated 790; empress 792; sole ruler 797; dethroned 802; exiled) the 7th Ecumenical Council (Nicea* II; 787) reest. veneration of images. During this phase iconodules, represented mainly by monks, depended on John* of Damascus for theol. support.

Second phase began ca. 841 under Leo V ("the Armenian" [because Armenian by birth]; emp. 813–820) and continued under Michael II ("the Amorian"; emp. 820–829) and Theophilus (son of Michael II; emp. 829–842). Under Theodorea (d. ca. 867; 2d wife of Theophilus; regent 842; retired to a convent 858) the decisions of Nicea II were reaffirmed. Theodore* of Studion was a leading inconodule in this phase of the controversy.

Chief theol. questions in the controversy: (1) What is an image, and were iconodules guilty of idolatry? (2) Did veneration of images violate Chalcedonian formulations (see *Chalcedon, Council of*) on the nature and person of Christ? (3) Were arguments from tradition of either iconoclast or iconodule authentic? These arguments, based essentially on the same sources (OT, NT, tradition, and speculation) were also related to other soc., pol., and cultural issues. But the ultimate questions for the iconodules were hist. and theol.; though there may be no absolute identity bet. image and person represented, there is relative identity. Reverence offered to the icon passes to the prototype. To deny that Christ can be portrayed in an icon is to deny that Christ was man, part of hist. The incarnation lends justification to legitimate use of the icon. Icons preserve hist. continuity with the early ch. These "hist." arguments froze the style and form of the icon. Sculpture in the round disappeared in the E Ch. as a result of the controversy. WGR

See also *Luther, Martin,* 15; *Luther, Controversies of,* d; *Reformation, Lutheran,* 8.

E. W. Benz, *The Eastern Orthodox Church,* tr. R. and C. Winston (Chicago, 1963); E. J. Martin, *A History of the Iconoclastic Controversy* (New York, 1930); E. R. Bevan, *Holy Images* (London, 1940); G. Ostrogorski, *Studien zur Geschichte des byzantinischen Bilderstreites* (Breslau, 1929); *Der byzantinische Bilderstreit,* comp. H.-J. Geischer (Gütersloh, 1968).

Iconostasis (from Gk. *eikon,* from *eikenai,* "to resemble," and *histanai,* "to stand"). In Eastern* Orthodox Ch., screen ornamented with icons*; separates bema (see *Church Architecture,* 3) from nave.*

Id. See *Ego,* 3; *Psychology,* J 7.

Idealism. System of philosophy* which ascribes existence to ideas or thought perceptions rather than to material objects; i. e., the essence of the world as a whole and of its various parts does not consist in phenomena that can be perceived with senses, but in "ideas" of external perceptions. The metaphysical idealism of Plato* holds that there existed in the divine mind ideas, patterns, according to which individual things are formed. Reality belongs to the idea rather than to the phenomenon. The degree of reality attributed to any phenomenal form is to be measured on the scale in which it embodies the original idea. Modern psychological idealism tries to answer the question: Do things exist in themselves (realism*), or do only the ideas we have of them exist? It holds that there is no reality indep. of consciousness. A person cannot be sure of the reality of a tree, but only of his personal perception, mental picture, idea, of a tree.

Modern idealism was developed esp. by such Ger. philosophers as G. W. v. Leibniz* (ideas are innate; there is disparity bet. mind and matter), I. Kant* (critical or transcendental idealism), J. G. Fichte* (subjective idealism), F. W. J. v. Schelling* (transcendental idealism), G. W. F. Hegel* (absolute idealism), R. H. Lotze* (teleological idealism).

More recent idealists include F. H. Bradley,* B. Bosanquet,* J. Caird,* Maine de Biran,* B. Croce,* J. Royce,* W. E. Hocking,* G. H. Howison,* J. M. E. McTaggart,* H. Rashdall.*

Sometimes the term "idealism" is used in reference to the formation of ideals as goals.

See also *Monism; Nominalism; Realism.*

J. Royce, *The Religious Aspect of Philosophy* (New York, 1885); N. Hartmann, *Die Philosophie des deutchen Idealismus,* 2 vols. (Berlin, 1923, 1929); W. Lütgert, *Die Religion des deutschen Idealismus und ihr Ende,* 4 vols. (Gütersloh, 1923–30); N. K. Smith, *Prolegomena to an Idealist Theory of Knowledge* (London, 1924); J. H. Muirhead, *The Platonic Tradition in Anglo-Saxon Philosophy: Studies in the History of Idealism in England and America* (London, 1931); G. W. Cunningham, *The Idealistic Argument in Recent British and American Philosophy* (New York, 1933); W. E. Hocking, *Types of Philosophy,* rev. ed. (New York, 1939); A. C. Ewing, *Idealism: A Critical Survey* (London, 1933).

Ideas, Innate. See *Innate Ideas.*

Identity-Philosophy (Identitätsphilosophie). Term applied to monistic philos. (as of F. W. J. v. Schelling*) which fails to distinguish bet. subject and object and holds that spirit and nature are fundamentally identical, namely, the Absolute.

Idiomata (pl. of Gk. *idioma,* "peculiarity"). Attributes, or properties. In Christology *communicatio idiomatum* refers to the communication of attributes resulting from the communion of natures *(communio naturarum)* in Christ by virtue of the personal union. See also *Christ Jesus,* I; *Hypostatic Union.*

Idolatry (from Gk. *eidolon,* "image of a god," and *latreia,* "worship"). 1. Idol worship; worship of a false god instead of, or besides, the true God.* It may take various forms.

One may commit idolatry without really knowing the true God (Gl 4:8), or knowing Him, turning from Him to idolatry (2 K 17:7-18; gross, or coarse, idolatry).

2. Some presume to know and worship the true God but at the same time to worship 1 or more other gods (2 K 17:33; Is 42:8; 48:11).

3. The least apparent form of idolatry (fine idolatry) is to fear, love, or trust in anyone or anything else as we should fear, love, and trust in God alone, Mt 10:28, 37; Pr 3:5.

Ignatius of Antioch. See *Apostolic Fathers,* 2.

Ifni. See *Africa,* D 7.

Ignatius of Constantinople. See *Schism,* 5.

Ignatius (of) Loyola. See *Loyola.*

Ignorance, Spiritual. See *Knowledge,* 2.

IHC. See *Symbolism, Christian,* 6.

Ihlen, Christian (1868–1958). B. Holmestrand, Norw.; prof. systematic theol. Oslo 1906; moderate conservative.

Ihmels, Ludwig Heinrich (1858–1933). B. Middels, E Friesland; educ. Leipzig, Erlangen, Göttingen, Berlin; held pastorates in E Friesland; dir. studies at monastery of Loccum, Ger.; prof. systematic theol. Erlangen and Leipzig; bp. Saxony; inclined towards orthodox Lutheranism; chm. 1st Luth. World Conference.

Ikhnaton (14th c. BC). King of Egypt ca. 1375–1358; tried unsuccessfully to est. a religion of solar monotheism.*

Ildefonso (Ildefonsus; Ildephonsus; Hildefonsus; ca. 607–ca. 667). B. probably Toledo, Sp.; abp. Toledo 657. Works include *De virginitate sanctae Mariae; De cognitione baptismi; De viris illustribus* (hist. of the 7th-c. Sp. ch.).

MPL, 96, 9–330.

Ilgen, Karl David (1764–1834). B. near Eckartsberga, Ger.; educ. Leipzig; rector Naumburg 1789; prof. oriental languages 1794 and theol. 1799 Jena; rector Schulpforte (Bad Kösen) 1802–31. Works include

Die Urkunden des Jerusalemischen Tempelarchivs in ihrer Urgestalt.

Illingworth, John Richardson (1848–1915). B. London, Eng.; Angl. cleric; educ. Oxford; rector Longworth, Berkshire; mem. *Lux* mundi* group. Works include *The Church and Human Thought in the Present Day; Divine Immanence; Reason & Revelation; The Doctrine of the Trinity Apologetically Considered; The Problem of Pain.*

Illinois, Evangelical Lutheran Synod of (Ill. Syn.; Syn. of Ill.). a) 1846–67. The Syn. of the West* divided June 1846. One of the resultant syns. was the Ev. Luth. Syn. of Ill., which held its 1st conv. in Hillsboro, Ill., Oct. 15, 1846. Joined Gen. Syn. 1848 (see *General Synod of the Evangelical Lutheran Church in the United States of America, The*).

b) 1867–80. When the Ev. Luth. Syn. of Ill. decided to withdraw from the Gen. Syn. and join the Gen. Council (see *General Council of the Evangelical Lutheran Church in [North] America*), it divided at Mount Pulaski, Ill., Aug. 1867. The minority formed the Ev. Luth. Syn. of Cen. Illinois* and remained with the Gen. Syn. The majority formed the Ev. Luth. Syn. of Ill. and Other [Adjacent] States (also known as Ill. Syn.) and joined the Gen. Council 1867. When the Gen. Council took no definite stand on the Four* Points, this Ill. Syn. left the Gen. Council 1871 and helped organize the Ev. Luth. Synodical* Conf. 1872. In May 1880 this Ill. Syn. merged with the Ill. Dist. of the Mo. Syn. and expressed the expectation that its pastors and congs. in Mo. would join the W Dist. of the Mo. Syn., adding that no pastor or cong. was under any obligation to do so. Membership at time of merger: 23 pastors, 26 congs., 6,004 communicants. See also *Lutheran Church – Missouri Synod, The,* V 15.

Illinois and Other [Adjacent] States, Evangelical Lutheran Synod of. See *Illinois, Evangelical Lutheran Synod of,* b.

Illinois, Evangelical Lutheran Synod of Central (Cen. Ill. Syn.) (1867–97; 1901–20). Organized Aug. 1867 (see *Illinois, Evangelical Lutheran Synod of,* b). In 1875 Ger. ministers withdrew and organized the Wartburg Syn. (see *United Lutheran Church, Synods of,* 30). The Ev. Luth. Syn. of Cen. Ill. was combined with the Ev. Luth. Syn. of S Illinois* 1897–1901 as the Ev. Luth. Syn. of Cen. and S Illinois.* The latter syn. divided again 1901 into the Ev. Luth. Syn. of Cen. Ill. and the Ev. Luth. Syn. of Southern Ill. In 1918 the Cen. Ill. Syn. helped form the ULC. In June 1920 it merged with the Ev. Luth. Syn. of N Illinois,* the Ev. Luth. Syn. of S Illinois,* and part of the Chicago* Syn. of the Ev. Luth. Ch. into the Ill. Syn. of the ULC (see *United Lutheran Church, Synods of,* 7). Membership at time of merger: 25 pastors, 29 congs., 6,535 communicants. HT

Illinois, Evangelical Lutheran Synod of Central and Southern (1897–1901). Formed by union of the Ev. Luth. Syn. of Cen. Illinois* and the Ev. Luth. Syn. of S Illinois* in Oct. 1897. In 1901 the 2 syns. resumed separate existence. HT

Illinois, Evangelical Lutheran Synod of Northern (N Ill. Syn.) (1851–1920). Organized Sept. 8, 1851, at Cedarville, Ill. Joined The General* Syn. of The Ev. Luth. Ch. in the USA 1853. The Scands. withdrew 1860 and formed the Scand. Ev. Luth. Augustana Syn. in N Am. (see also *Augustana Evangelical Lutheran Church,* 8). In 1918 the Ev. Luth. Syn. of N Ill. helped form the ULC. In June 1920 it merged with the Ev. Luth. Syn. of Cen. Illinois,* the Ev. Luth. Syn. of S Illinois,* and part of the Chicago* Syn. of the Ev. Luth. Ch. into the Ill. Syn. of the ULC (see *United Lutheran Church, Synods of,* 7). Membership at time of merger: 54 pastors, 60 congs., 6,575 communicants. HT

Illinois, Evangelical Lutheran Synod of Southern (S Ill. Syn.) (1856–97; 1901–20). Organized Nov. 7, 1856, near Jonesboro, Ill., by 8 pastors and 4 laymen formerly mems. of the Syn. of the Southwest.* Joined Gen. Syn. 1857 (see *General Synod of the Evangelical Lutheran Church in the United States of America, The*). Area included S Ill., SE Mo., and W Tenn. Its pastors in Tenn. formed the Ev. Luth. Syn. of Middle Tennessee* 1878. The S Ill. Syn. was combined with the Ev. Luth. Syn. of Cen. Illinois* 1897–1901 as the Ev. Luth. Syn. of Cen. and S Illinois.* The latter syn. divided again 1901 into the Cen. Ill. Syn. and the S Ill. Syn. The S Ill. Syn. helped form the ULC 1918 and June 1920 merged with the Cen. Ill. Syn., the Ev. Luth. Syn. of N Illinois,* and part of the Chicago* Syn. of the Ev. Luth. Ch. into the Ill. Syn. of the ULC (see *United Lutheran Church, Synods of,* 7). Membership at time of merger: 10 pastors, 17 congs., 3,518 communicants. HT

Illinois State University. See *Carthage College.*

Illinois Synod (1846–67). See *Illinois, Evangelical Lutheran Synod of,* a.

Illinois Synod (1867–80). See *Illinois, Evangelical Lutheran Synod of,* b.

Illinois Synod (of the ULC). See *United Lutheran Church, Synods of,* 7.

Illness. See *Healing.*

Illuminati. Term designating several groups of religious enthusiasts who claimed illuminism (unusual enlightenment) by communication with deity or from higher reason. Gnostics (see *Gnosticism*) advocated some form of illuminism. Later Illuminati included Rosicrucians,* Alumbrados (16th-c. sect in Sp. which claimed direct illumination from the Holy Spirit), Illuminés (also called Guérinets; 17th-c. sect in S Fr. similar to Alumbrados), Illuminaten (Perfectibilists; Ger. secret soc. modeled after Society* of Jesus but diametrically opposed to Jesuits; founded by A. Weishaupt*; promoted pol. freedom and natural religion; anticlerical; later leaders included Adolf von Knigge [1752–96; Ger. author]).

Illumination (MSS). See *Miniatures and Illumination.*

Illumination (spiritual). See *Conversion,* II 1.

Illuminism. See *Illuminati.*

Illustris. See *Bishop,* 2.

Image of God. 1. God created man in His image, and man was "very good" (Gn 1:27, 31). Man was distinguished from other creatures by an excellence all his own, for he was made in the image of God. This image was not of the essence of man's nature, nor was it a gift to man after creation; it was a concreated quality.

2. Luth. theologians gen. hold that the image of God, which consists in the knowledge of God and holiness of the will, is lacking in man after the Fall (Cl 3:10; Eph 4:24). Some hold that Gn 9:6 and Ja 3:9 ascribe a divine image to man after the Fall, namely that the intellect and will of man constitute a similitude with God; those who reject this view (e. g., F. A. Philippi,* G. Hoffmann*) interpret Gn 9:6 and Ja 3:9 as referring to the image that is to be restored again in Christ.

3. Some theologians speak of the image of God in a wider sense, namely, inasmuch as man, even after the Fall, is still an intellectual, self-determining, rational being who feebly rules over other creatures. Others use the term only in the narrow sense; they point out that the upright body and the rational soul with its human understanding, affections, and will, woefully corrupt as a result of sin, are still the constituent elements of the human nature and therefore must not be considered as being the divine image or parts thereof. Conscience* and the Moral Law, whereby man is distinguished from

brutes in his present state, cannot be subsumed under the image of God.

4. "In his original state, man was not only sound in body and soul, without a germ of disease or death, or a taint of sin, but endowed with concreated spiritual wisdom and knowledge, and with perfect natural righteousness, goodness, and holiness, in the image and likeness of the Triune God. . . .

"While Christ's obedience imputed to us constitutes a perfect righteousness in the sight of God, our own obedience, or the righteousness inherent in us, must, on account of the residue of sinful flesh still active within us, remain imperfect in this life – *justitia inchoata* –, the beginning only of the restitution of the divine image in the regenerate being made in this temporal life." A. L. Graebner,* *Outlines of Doctrinal Theology,* pars. 70, 156.

Images. In broad sense, an image is any representation of men, animals, plants, etc. (pictures, statues, paintings, photographs, mosaics). In religious context "image" gen. refers to representations of Christ or of saints. Improper use (i. e. worship) of images is forbidden Ex 20:4-5. But the Bible nowhere forbids proper use of images, i. e. as reminders of Christ and saints, and so as aesthetic aids to devotion.

Paintings in the catacombs* at Rome dating back to the 2d c. include some of the earliest Christian images still extant. Later both pictures and statues began to play an integral part in Christian art and devotion. As a result of the 8th-9th c. Iconoclastic* Controversy, the E Ch. has restricted its use of images to icons.* The W Ch. has not restricted the forms that an image may take. Luth. reformers retained proper use of images. See also *Reformation, Lutheran,* 8.

Many Luth. and RC chs., esp. in Eur., are rich in statues, paintings, and other forms of religious art. Luths. have retained use of the crucifix*; many sectarian chs. use only the simple cross* or no cross at all. Luth. Confessions condemn abuse of images (Ap XXI 34–39). EFP

Imam (Arab. "leader"). Muslim term for person or thing serving as model, leader, pattern, guide. The Koran* (II 118) applies it to Abraham. Muhammad* is an "imam"; by constitutional law a caliph* is "supreme imam." The first 4 caliphs are "imams" of Sunnites.* Shi'ites* regard their imams as divinely appointed, illumined, and preserved from sin. The term also designates a leader in prayer or a religious functionary and is applied as honorary title to outstanding theologians.

Imitation of Christ. Classic manual of spiritual devotion; summarizes the religious attitude of the *Devotio* moderna* and gives it expression. Divided into 4 parts: admonitions useful for spiritual life; admonitions to promote interior life; discussion of interior dispositions of the soul; discussion of Holy Communion. Authorship disputed for centuries. Inseparably connected with Thomas* à Kempis; probably best traced to 4 of his 13 indep. treatises. Content derived esp. from *Devotio moderna* literature.

Immaculate Conception. RC dogma "that the most Blessed Virgin Mary was preserved from all stain of original sin in the first instant of her conception, by a singular grace and privilege of almighty God, in consideration of the merits of Jesus Christ, savior of the human race" (Pius IX, bull [or encyclical letter] *Ineffabilis Deus,* Dec. 8, 1854). The bull continues that this has been revealed by God and must, therefore, firmly and constantly be believed by all the faithful.

See also *Mariolatry; Roman Catholic Confessions,* C.

Immaculate Heart of Mary. See *Heart of Mary, Immaculate.*

Immanence (from Lat. *immanere,* "to remain in"). (1) In medieval scholasticism an immanent cause is one whose effects are exclusively in the agent. (2) In I. Kant* the immanent is experiential as opposed to transcendent. (3) In contemporary metaphysics immanence means presence as opposed to absence (see also *Immanence of God*). (4) Ernst Julius Wilhelm Schuppe (1836–1913; Ger. philos.; b. Brieg, Silesia; educ. Breslau, Bonn, and Berlin; taught in Silesia; prof. Greifswald 1873–1910) identified consciousness, an inseparable union of "I" and its objects, with the real.

Immanence of God. God is present in all creatures but is never part of them. All creatures live, move, and have their being in God (Acts 17:28; Cl 1:17); one difference bet. God and His creatures is that bet. infinite and finite (Nu 23:19; 1 Sm 15:29); God remains transmundane, transcendent. See also *Transcendence of God.*

Immanuel Lutheran College (Eau Claire, Wis.). Organized by a private assoc. of mems. of Immanuel Luth. Ch., Mankato, Minn., 1959. Became property of the Church* of the Luth. Confession 1961. Moved to Eau Claire, Wis., 1963. Courses of study are on the high school, coll., and sem. levels. Primary purpose: to prepare teachers and pastors for the Ch. of the Luth. Confession. See also *Ministry, Education of,* VIII C 2 k.

Immanuel Lutheran College (Greensboro, N. C). Preparatory school est. 1903 to train Negro preachers and teachers for the Ev. Luth. Synodical* Conf. of N Am. Closed June 30, 1961.

Immanuel Lutheran Seminary (Eau Claire, Wis.). See *Immanuel Lutheran College* (Eau Claire, Wis.).

Immanuel Synod. See *Germany, Lutheran Free Churches in,* 3.

Immanuel Synod auf alter Grundlage. See *Australia, Lutheranism in,* B 1.

Immanuel Synod of the Evangelical Lutheran Church in North America. Founded 1885 in Wall Rose, Pa., by Luths. desiring greater freedom in ch. life than they found in other Luth. syns. Dissolved 1917 by formal resolution. A remnant retained the name but disbanded ca. 1921.

Immaterial Concepts. See *Psychology,* C.

Immediate Working of the Holy Spirit. See *Grace, Means of,* I 7.

Immensa (RC constitution). See *Curia,* 2 b.

Immer, Karl (1888–1944). B. Manslagt, near Emden, Ger.; Ref. pastor Barmen-Gemarke; active in Kirchenkampf; leader among those who convoked the 1934 free syn. at Barmen-Gemarke (see *Barmen Theses*).

Immersion. Mode of baptism in which the baptized is submerged completely; some Baps. and others hold it to be the only correct mode. See also *Grace, Means of,* III 1.

Immigrant and Emigrant Missions. This kind of miss. did much to orient Luths. during 19th-c. mass immigrations. A conf. held in connection with the 1861 conv. of the N. Y. Ministerium discussed ways of protecting Luth. immigrants. The Pa. Ministerium resolved 1862 to investigate the possibility of helping to place a miss. for immigrants at Castle Garden, NYC, and the N. Y. Ministerium est. a committee to work with the miss. committee of the Pa. Ministerium in the placement of such a miss. Robert Neumann (formerly Gen. Syn. miss. to China) began work 1865, W. H. Berkemeier* 1867. The Gen. Council accepted care of the miss. 1869.

The N. Y. pastoral conf. of the Mo. Syn. opened an emigrant miss. 1869, with S. Keyl* directing the work; the same yr. the Mo. Syn. assumed the work which Keyl had begun. The *Lutherisches Pilgerhaus,*

8 State Street, NYC, was bought 1885, sold 1917. Emigrant miss. work was conducted also in Baltimore, Md.

Scands. also undertook immigrant miss. work in the 19th c. See also *Andersen, Rasmus.*

Immoralism. Ethic which tries to est. a new morality in place of a traditional one. See also *Nietzsche, Friedrich Wilhelm.*

Immortality (from Lat. *immortalis,* "undying; imperishable"). Exemption from death; in Christian thought such exemption is attained through Christ (Jn 11:25-26; 1 Ti 6:15-16; 2 Ti 1:10).

Belief in immortality is common in non-Christian thought. Plato assoc. the soul *(psyche)* with reason and on that basis urged the immortality of the soul, asserting that the soul exists before its embodiment. Some Gk. thinkers hinted at repeated incarnations of the same soul. Epicurus* and Lucretius* denied immortality. Many exponents of deism* taught the immortality of the soul as rationally implied in natural theol. In some Christian thought the body is considered an encumbrance or prison of the soul.

In the Bible, immortality pertains to the entire man, including the body, after the resurrection to eternal life. Some OT statements about the future world involve reference to a shadowy existence (e. g., Jb 10:20-22; Ps 88:10-12). The resurrection of the body is mentioned, e. g., Is 25:8; Dn 12:2. Acc. to Ec 12:7 the spirit of man returns to God at death, but this may simply mean for judgment; cf. Heb 9:27. Joy and pleasure are assoc. with eternal life Ps. 16:11.

In the NT immortality is assoc. with Jesus Christ (Jn 1:4; 3:36; 14:19; Ro 5:17; 1 Jn 5:12), esp. with His resurrection (Ro 6:4-23; 1 Co 15; Ph 3:8-21).

The early fathers continued to assoc. immortality and resurrection with Christ's redemptive work. Over against a one-sided emphasis on the soul, they often stressed the resurrection of the body in their creeds.

According to the NT, believers are with Christ after death (Lk 23:43; Ph 1:23; cp. 2 Co 5:1; 2 Ti 4:6-8). Unbelievers face judgment, damnation, and eternal death (Mt 25:41-46; 2 Ptr 2:9; Rv 20:14).

See also *Hereafter; Immortality, Arguments for; Last Things,* 4, 5. EL

Immortality, Arguments for. Arguments for immortality include (1) the *ethical,* which rests on the premise that evil is not adequately punished or virtue adequately rewarded in this world and that God's justice must be satisfied in some other world; (2) the *hist.*: since all nations at all times have believed in immortality, the idea of immortality must be founded on fact; the testimony of man's conscience to immortality is the witness of Him who gave man a conscience and a moral nature; or, we may say, man's belief in immortality is part of the divine Law written in man's heart; (3) the *metaphysical,* which operates with the thought that since man's soul is absolutely simple, and not compounded or material, it cannot be destroyed by death, which essentially is separation of body and soul; the soul, pure spirit, cannot be annihilated, as the body perishes, returning to dust; hence the soul must live on in some other world; (4) the *teleological:* since man, as a religious, moral being does not attain the goal of his existence on earth, his development here being imperfect, there must be a greater and better world, where man's religious and moral being may come into its own. JTM

Immortality, Medicine of. Term occasionally used in ancient times for Holy Communion to indicate that it gives eternal life in fellowship with God.

Immutability of God. In God's essence and attributes there never has been and never will be or can be division, increase, decrease, mutation, development, or any other change. Nm 23:19; Pr 19:21; Ml 3:6; Ro 1:23; 1 Ti 1:17; 6:16; Ja 1:17. See also *God.*

Impanation. Theory of local inclusion of Christ's body and blood in eucharistic elements without change in substances. The Wittenberg* Concord and FC SD VII 14-15, 64 reject impanation.

Impediments. Factors that prevent marriage* from being properly constituted.

Luths. have recognized impediments based on degrees of relationship either of consanguinity or of affinity (Lv 18:6-20; 20:10-23; Dt 27:20-23; Mt 14:3-4; 1 Co 5:1). Impotence and incurable disease were usually considered natural impediments.

In RC theol. 2 types of impediments are distinguished: (1) prohibitory, which make marriage unlawful but not invalid (e. g., vows of virginity; differences in religion); (2) diriment, which make marriage invalid and unlawful (e. g., when man is under 16 and woman under 14; permanent impotence prior to marriage; existing marriage; disparity bet. a RC and one who is unbaptized; sacred orders; certain blood relationships; affinity resulting from valid marriage; spiritual relationship). Bps. can dispense from many impediments; some are reserved for the diocese of the pope.

See also *Prohibited Degrees.*

Imperative, Categorical and Hypothetical. See *Categorical Imperative.*

Imperial Cathedral (Speyer). See *Church Architecture,* 7.

Imperium and Sacerdotium. See *Church and State,* 7.

Implicit Faith. See *Fides implicita.*

Imprimatur (Lat. "let it be printed"). Term used for license given by proper authority to print the book or item to which it is applied.

Improperia (Lat. "reproaches"). Part of W liturgy of Good Friday (see *Church Year,* 4, 7, 8); based on Lm 1:12. See also *Trisagion.*

Imputation. Term used by some dogmaticians with reference to Adam's sin and Christ's righteousness. Accordingly, Adam's sin is described as so attributed to every man as to be considered, in the divine counsels, each man's own and rendering him guilty; the righteousness of Christ is so attributed to a believer as to be considered his own and to justify him.

In coena Domini (Lat. "On the Lord's Supper"). Bulls of excommunication of offenders against faith and morals. Originally read also on Ascension Day (see *Church Year,* 5, 9) and the feast of the Chair* of Peter (Jan. 18) but later confined to Maundy Thursday (see Church Year, 8; *Gründonnerstag*). Practice dates from 13th c. Issue of the bull suspended 1773 by Clement XIV (see *Popes,* 25), abrogated 1869 by Pius IX (see *Popes,* 28).

In partibus infidelium. See *Titular Bishop.*

In View of Faith. See *Intuitu fidei.*

Incarnation. 1. The Incarnation of the Son of God consists in His assumption of a human body and soul (Mt 22:42-45; Lk 1:35; Jn 1:14; Ro 1:3; Ph 2:7; Cl 2:9; 1 Ti 3:16). It is commemorated Mar. 25.

2. The Incarnation was foretold (e. g., Gn 3:15; Is. 7:14 [Immanuel, Heb. "God with us"]).

3. By this mysterious union, Jesus Christ was Mediator bet. God and man, 1 Ti 2:5. "Though the 2 natures personally united in Christ are and remain essentially distinct, each retaining its own essential properties or attributes, its own intelligence and will, so that His divinity is not His humanity nor a part of the same, nor His humanity His divinity: yet there is in Christ a *communion* of natures, so that the divine nature is the nature of the Son of Man, and the human nature the nature of the Son of God" (A. L. Graebner,* *Outlines of Doctrinal Theology,* par. 101).

4. Inseparably connected with the doctrine of the

Incarnation is the doctrine of the Virgin Birth (Is 7:14; Mt 1:18-25; Lk 1:34-35).

5. Ebionites* and some Gnostics (e. g., early Ophites and adherents of Carpocrates and Cerinthus; see *Gnosticism,* 6 b, f, i) denied the Virgin Birth. The gen. belief of the early ch. in the Virgin Birth is reflected, e. g., in Irenaeus,* Ignatius of Antioch (see *Apostolic Fathers,* 2), Aristides (see *Apologists,* 3), and Justin* Martyr.

6. The Incarnation is a mystery beyond human understanding. Rationalists hold that incarnation involved change that would have destroyed the Godhead. Christian apologists reply: In the Incarnation the divine nature is the active, as the human nature is the passive, factor; any change resulting from the act will affect the human nature, not the divine (see also *Immutability of God*). The Logos* did not cease to be God when He became flesh; He was made man, not changed into man. Scripture continued to speak of the Logos incarnate in such a way that each nature must be understood as retaining all its essential characteristics. In Christ 2 complete natures are united in the personality of 1 of them (the relation bet. body and soul is esp. weak as analogy). Generation of the man Jesus and union of the 2 natures were simultaneous. The human nature of Christ never existed by itself; it was not produced from the essence of the Holy Spirit, but, by His creative energy, from the body of Mary. "Conceived by the Holy Ghost" denotes the efficient energy. "Born of the Virgin Mary" denotes the material.

J. G. Machen, *The Virgin Birth of Christ,* rev. ed. (New York, 1932); D. M. Baillie, *God Was in Christ* (London, 1948); A. Koeberle, "The Incarnation of Christ," *Journal of Theology of the American Lutheran Conference,* VII (Jan. 1942), 1–13.

Incense. Smoke or perfume of burning gums and spices; used in sacrifices (e. g., Ex 30:7-8; 37:29); assoc. esp. with prayer (Ps 141:2; Lk 1:10; Rv 8:3-4); used in some chs.

Incipit. See *Intonation.*

Indefectibility. Immunity to defect, failure, or decay. In RC theol. a property or quality of the ch., esp. the Roman see.

Indelible Character. See *Character Indelebilis.*

Independent Baptist Church of America. See *Baptist Churches,* 30.

Independent Churches. 1. Chs. not identified with any ecclesiastical body or denomination. See also *United Church of Christ,* I A 1. 2. Chs. variously called union, federated, community, etc., which represent the movement toward denominational fellowship and consolidation of ch. life for more effective work.

Independent Evangelical Lutheran Church. See *Germany, Lutheran Free Churches in,* 8–12, 14.

Independent Fundamental Churches of America. Organized Cicero, Ill., 1930 by chs. that had left their denominations because of modernism* in the latter. Requires mems. to sever all denominational ties. Its 16 articles of faith include inerrancy of Scripture, verbal inspiration, authority of Scripture; divine-human person of Christ; total depravity of man; vicarious atonement; regeneration by the Spirit; dispensationalism and premillennialism. They reject entire holiness and speaking in tongues. See also *Fundamentalism.*

Independent Methodists. See *Methodist Churches,* 1.

Independent Order of Foresters. See *Foresters.*

Independent Order of Odd Fellows. See *Odd Fellows, Independent Order of.*

Independents. See *United Church of Christ, The,* I A 1.

Indeterminism. Theory that certain decisions are indep. of physiol., psychol., or other causes; opposed to determinism.*

Index of Prohibited Books. RC list of books proscribed for the faithful. Its hist. begins with a list promulgated 405 by Innocent I (d. 417; pope 401–417). Many individual works were condemned by popes or councils, e. g., "Three Chapters" (see *Three Chapters, Controversy of*); works of Photius,* J. S. Erigena,* J. Wycliffe,* J. Hus.* The Council of Trent,* 4th Session, decreed that no religious books should be pub. without ch. approval.

Paul* IV gave the task of cataloging forbidden books 1557 to a cong. of cardinals that had been appointed 1542 (see *Inquisition,* 5) and that pub. a list 1559. A commission appointed by the Council of Trent drafted a list ratified 1564 by Pius* IV (Sess. XVII at the beginning; XXV, Concerning the index of books etc.; Ten rules concerning prohibited books, appended to the Confirmation of the Council). Various rules and lists were drafted thereafter. Leo XIII (see *Popes,* 29) drafted a new Index and gen. rules governing censorship and prohibition of books. The norms were promulgated 1897 and a new Index pub. 1900. Several eds. were pub. later.

Alfredo Ottaviani (b. Rome 1890; cardinal 1953), head of Cong. for the Doctrine of the Faith, announced 1966 that no more eds. of the Index would be pub. But the RC Ch. still claims the right to prohibit books it regards dangerous to faith and morals.

India. 1. Country in S Asia, S of the Himalayas, bet. Bay of Bengal and Arab. Sea. *Area:* ca. 1,261,600 sq. mi. *Pop.* (1973 est.): 584,704,000. Earliest evidences of civilization date back to the 3d and 2d millenniums BC. Aryans or Hindus invaded 2400 to 1500 BC. Alexander III (the Great; 356–323 BC; king of Macedonia 336) invaded ca. 327–326, withdrew 325–324; Muslim invaders founded the Mogul empire 1526 AD. Port. practically monopolized trade with India in the 16th c., followed by Dutch, Fr., and Eng. in the 1st half of the 17th century. Eng. est. a beachhead through the Eng. E India Company. Brit. supremacy was secured by defeat of Fr. and Muslim forces in the 1760s and by subsequent pacification or conquest of Indian kingdoms by war or treaty. India became a mem. of the Brit. Commonwealth of Nations 1947 (when India became indep. and was divided into India and Pakistan [see *Asia,* B 2], a partition marked by much bloodshed and massive migrations), a sovereign democratic rep. in the Commonwealth 1950.

2. Religions of India: Hinduism* (ca. 85%); Islam* (ca. 9.9%); Christianity (ca. 2.3%); Sikhism (see *Sikhs;* ca. 1.7%); Jainism,* Buddhism,* Zoroastrianism,* Judaism,* etc. (ca. 1.1%).

3. Indian soc. is divided into castes (see *Brahmanism,* 3; *Hinduism,* 3); the system is slowly losing rigidity.

4. Christianity may have come to India as early as the 1st c. An archaeological find indicates that Pallivaanavar, a Christian, was king in Kerala in the middle of the 2d c.

5. The Syrian Christians (reason for "Syrian" hard to determine), or Thomas Christians, of Kerala claim that the apostle Thomas arrived in that area at Malankara, near Cranganur (Cranganore), ca. the middle of the 1st c. and converted their ancestors. Other possibilities for the origin of Syrian Christians in India include a 4th or 7th c. (or later) immigration by Christians from Syria under a Thomas (of) Cana (or Thomas Cannaneo) and Nestorian influence of the patriarch of Seleucia; Eusebius* of Caesarea (*HE,* V, x, 2–3) connects the apostle Bartholomew and Pantaenus* with India.

6. The first Christians in India may have been converted by missionaries from Antioch or Edessa; in course of time they accepted Nestorian bps., perhaps from Seleucia. Port. RC missionaries came to

them ca. the beginning of the 16th c., initiating a period of transition. The Syrian Christians in India were forced 1599 (see *Diamper, Synod of*) to accede to many RC teachings and practices (including celibacy of priests and Communion under one kind) and to destroy E Syrian MSS. Many revolted against Rome and seceded, esp. 1653, going back to the Antioch patriarchate, which was now Monophysitic (see *Monophysitism*). Dutch influence abetted separation from RCm. Later Brit. influence attracted some. Further schisms are a tragic commentary on this ancient ch. and on problems of a religious group which had become in effect a caste of its own. The Mar* Thoma Ch. sent missionaries to the Tibetan border 1954. See also *Nonchalcedonian Churches,* 2.

7. There are more than 2 million Syrian Christians in India, chiefly in Kerala, which includes Malabar Coast: ca. 1,200,000 RCs of the Syro-Malabar rite (called Malabars), a uniate ch. (see *Uniate Churches*) using a Syriac liturgy; ca. 130,000 RCs of the Syro-Malankara rite (called Malankars), using a Malayalam (Dravidian language of Kerala) liturgy; ca. 700,000 Jacobites or Syrian Orthodox Christians whose allegiance is to the patriarch of Antioch and to the catholicos* in Kottayam, Kerala (after yrs. of litigation over the relative authority of the patriarch and the catholicos this group composed its differences 1959, the suit finally decided by the Supreme Court of India); ca. 300,000 Mar Thoma Christians, a reforming group which broke away from the Jacobites in the 1870s, maintaining an E Cath. type of episcopacy, though with local consecration; ca. 100,000 former Angls. who have joined the CSI; a group of ca. 5,000 mems. which has reest. a Nestorian connection; the Thozhiyur diocese, small but important for supplying a consecrating bp. for the Mar Thoma Ch. See also *Malabar Christians; Nonchalcedonian Churches,* 2.

8. Syrian Christians have been influential in Christian circles in India and in the WCC.

9. The 1497–98 discovery of a sea route to India by Vasco da Gama (ca. 1469–1524; Port. navigator) gave impetus to RC missions. Goa became a bishopric in the 1530s, archbishopric ca. 1558. RC missionaries include F. Xavier* and Robert(o) de Nobili.* Sp. lent govt. support to missions in India in the 16th and 17th c.

10. Prot. missions in India were initiated 1706 by Frederick* IV of Den. Prominent missionaries included B. Ziegenbalg,* H. Plütschau,* J. P. Fabricius,* C. W. Gericke,* C. F. Schwartz.* Ger. rationalism, the Napoleonic wars, and disease and poverty in the Tranquebar area wrought havoc in the miss. All stations except Tranquebar were turned over 1825 to the SPCK, which later gave them to the SPG. A. F. Kemmerer's* work in Tranquebar was curtailed by royal resolution 1825 but renewed by J. H. K. Cordes.* Work of the Ev. Luth. Miss. of Leipzig* and of the Church of Swed. Missions resulted 1919 in the Tamil Ev. Luth. Ch. See also *Missions,* 5–6.

W. Carey,* J. Marshman,* and W. Ward* est. an effective miss. base at Serampore (see also *Serampore Trio*). Other missionaries sponsored by Eng. socs. include W. T. Ringeltaube,* K. T. E. Rhenius.*

11. ABCFM missionaries 1812: A. Judson,* S. Newell,* G. Hall,* L. Rice,* S. Nott.* Judson and Rice became Bap. en route to India. Rice returned to Am. 1813 and helped organize the Am. Bap. Miss. Union, which supported Judson, began work 1840 among Telugu around Nellore, S Andhra Pradesh, S India, and 1841 in Assam, NE Indian Union.

12. A. Duff's* emphasis on secondary and higher educ. encouraged other miss. socs. and the Indian govt.; schools, colleges, and univs. were est., with govt. grants in many cases covering the operating costs of miss. schools.

Zenana (Hindi "belonging to women") work and med. miss. are distinct branches of miss. work in India. Zenanas are quarters for seclusion of women, who can usually be reached there with physical and spiritual ministry only by trained women workers. An assoc. for zenana work was formed 1852.

13. The Basel* Miss. Soc. entered India at Mangalore, S. Kanara, 1834. The Gossner* Miss. Soc. worked chiefly among Kols in Chota Nagpur. The autonomous Gossner Ev. Luth. Ch. in Chota Nagpur and Assam was est. 1919. J. C. F. Heyer* arrived Ceylon 1842.

K. G. T. Näther* and F. E. Mohn* began the work of the Mo. Ev. Luth. India Miss. in N. Arcot 1895. Work spread into the Salem, Mysore, and Tinnevelly Dists. and was begun in Travancore (present Kerala) 1907. Ceylon was entered 1927 (see also *Asia,* B 3). Wandoor has been served since 1950, Bombay since 1954. The India Ev. Luth. Ch. was organized 1958, accepted 1959 as a sister ch. of the LCMS. Work is done in Eng., Tamil, Malayalam, Telugu, Urdu, Kanarese, Marathi, and Gujerati and includes educ., med., pub., and radio activities.

The Hermannsburg* Miss. began work in the middle 1860s at Nellore. Two stations were sold 1912 to the Ev. Luth. Joint Syn. of Ohio* and Other States, which took over the whole field 1916. In 1930 the miss. came under the ALC Bd. of For. Miss. The S Andhra Luth. Ch. was organized for autonomy and self-support 1945. For Luth. Ch. in the Audhra Country of India see *United Lutheran Church in America, The,* III.

14. The Church* of S India was formed 1947. It observes an episcopate in practice, but no specific doctrine of apostolic succession is accepted. The Ch. of S India and Luths. have been in conversation since 1947.

15. See *Church of North India.*

16. In 1968 the India Ev. Luth. Ch. (see section 13 above) joined The Fed. of Ev. Luth. Chs. in India, formed 1926 and granting its mems. autonomy. All Luth. chs. in India are mems. of the Fed., which helps maintain contact among ca. 800,000 Luths. in India spread chiefly along the E coast. Chs. of considerable strength work in 6 different language areas, and at least 6 other languages are used. BHJ, HMZ, AJB.

See also *Accommodation,* 5; *Brahmanism; Buddhism; Hinduism.*

India Evangelical Lutheran Church. See *India,* 13.

India Mission, The. See *International Missions, Inc.*

Indian Home Mission to the Santals. See *Norwegian Foreign Missions,* 3.

Indian Mission, Mexican. See *Mexican Indian Mission.*

Indian Philosophy. See *Brahmanism; Buddhism; Hinduism.*

Indian Shaker Church. In 1881 a Skokomish Indian, John Slocum (reportedly a bap. RC), allegedly received teachings from God. Two syncretistic groups, both called Indian Shaker Ch., resulted among Indians of the Pacific NW from claims to represent continuation of a group organized 1910 to perpetuate the teachings.

Indiana Synod (I). Conflict bet. "Generalists"* and "Henkelites" (see *General Synod of the Evangelical Lutheran Church in the United States of America, The,* 7) was carried W beyond the Alleghenies in the 1820s. The Ev. Luth. Syn. of Ind. was organized Aug. 15, 1835, at St. John's Ch., Johnson Co., Ind., by 6 pastors (3 ordained pastors and 3 ordained deacons, the latter ordained as pastors at the conv.) and 7 laymen, representing ca. 10 congs., in opposition to the "Generalists," who had banded together 1834 in Ky. and organized 1835 as a syn. (see also *West, Synod of the*). Three generations of Henkels (see *Henkels, The*) had visited Ind. on miss. tours: Paul, his sons David and Philip, and his grandson Eusebius (who helped found this Ind. Syn.). This Ind. Syn. adopted the same doctrinal basis as the Tenn. Syn. (see *United Lutheran Church, Synods of,* 10), but in course of time was affected by infidelity, Universalism, revivalism, and annihilationism. A division came 1849, the "Miller Faction" (so called after 2 of its leaders, pastors Abraham and David Miller), which courts adjudged the real Syn. of Ind., opposing liberal leaders. But this faction soon disbanded, having exhausted its strength in lawsuits. The others continued under the old name till disbanding 1859. At the time of its greatest strength this Ind. Syn. probably had ca. 2,500 communicants. Its immediate successor was the Union* Syn. of the Evangelic Luth. Ch.

M. L. Wagner, *The Chicago Synod and Its Antecedents* (Waverly, Iowa, [1909?]).

Indiana Synod (II). The Ind. Syn. of the Ev. Luth. Ch. was organized Oct. 23, 1871, at East Germantown, Ind., by men formerly belonging to the Union* Syn. of the Ev. Luth. Ch. and the Eng. Dist. of the Joint Ohio Syn. (see *Ohio and Other States, Evangelical Lutheran Joint Synod of*) who desired union with the General* Council of the Ev. Luth. Ch. in (N) Am.; this Ind. Syn. joined the Gen. Council 1872. When the Ev. Luth. Syn. of Illinois* left the Gen. Council 1871, the Ind. Syn. branched out into Ill. Its interest centered in the Chicago Sem. est. 1891 by the Gen. Council; in 1895 it adopted the name Chicago* Syn. of the Ev. Luth. Ch.

Indiana Synod (ULC). See *United Lutheran Church, Synods of,* 8.

Indiana Synod, Northern. Organized Oct. 27, 1855, at Columbia City, Ind., by former mems. of the Olive Branch Syn. (see *United Lutheran Church, Synods of,* 8) and Wittenberg* Syn. Its territory included Mich. It united with The General* Syn. of the Ev. Luth. Ch. in the US of Am. 1857 and with it entered the ULC 1918. In 1920 it helped organize the Mich. Syn. of the ULC (see *United Lutheran Church, Synods of,* 12). At the time of this merger it numbered 53 pastors, 77 congs., and ca. 9,415 confirmed mems.

Indianapolis, German Evangelical Lutheran Synod of. Began to take shape 1846 when a few left the Syn. of the West*; J. F. Isensee pres., J. G. Kunz secy., W. Wier treas., J. J. Meissner miss. at large; formal organization completed 1847–48; received 1858 into the Ohio Syn. (see *Ohio and Other States, Evangelical Lutheran Joint Synod of*) as the Southern Dist.

H. M. Zorn, "Beginnings in Indianapolis," *CTM,* V, 1 (Jan. 1934), 19–29.

Indians, American. 1. The primitive* religion of Am. Indians was diverse. Discovery of original Indian beliefs is complicated by the fact that Indians quickly annexed white men's ideas of religion, e. g., the "Great Spirit" concept may be more non-Indian than Indian in origin. The belief that all natural forces are either spirits or expressions of spirits was apparently basic in Indian religion. It showed itself, e. g., in forms of veneration of sun, moon, stars, sacred trees, animals, reptiles, and fire; in religious actions (dances) and sacrifices (e. g., of animals); in beliefs in magic attributes of certain things (orenda: pervasive energy; otkon [or otgon]: malevolent orenda), in a life beyond the grave (happy hunting ground), and in shamans (medicine men, who allegedly possessed ability to converse with invisible spirits). Indians constantly tried to lay hold of orenda and expel otkon. See also *Primitive Religion.*

2. The hist. of Christian missions in N Am. began when Columbus held the cross before the natives. White men's subsequent mass invasion of Am. carried the Gospel with it.

3. Persuading Indians to accept the Gospel was made difficult, as B. de Las* Casas and others found, by inconsistent practice on the part of white professing Christians. The conversion of Pocahontas,* the search of the Nez Percé (Indians of cen. Idaho, Wash., and Oreg.) for the white man's "Book of the Great Spirit," early journeys of white men across the Rockies, the miss. hist. of Calif. and the SW under Sp. rule, heartbreaking journeys of missionaries to Indians as homes and families were broken up and tribes moved to strange lands show how some brought the Gospel to the Indians, others subjugated and deprived them of their natural heritage.

4. Brit. colonists stationed at Roanoke 1585–86 preached the Gospel to Indians, one of whom was bap. 1587. R. Williams* was an early Prot. miss. to Am. Indians. His work was reinforced and extended by J. Eliot,* E. Mayhew,* and others. An Indian ch. was formed 1660 at Natick, Mass.; 18th-c. Indian converts include S. Occam.*

5. Groups that pioneered in sponsoring missions to the Indians include Moravians, who worked in New Eng. and other areas (see also *Moravian Church,* 4), and the Soc. of Friends,* which began work 1796 in N. Y. and expanded it to other areas. The ABCFM sent missionaries (T. S. Williamson,* S. R. Riggs,* and others) to the Dakota (in Minn. and N. and S. Dak.). Cong. and Presb. missions were est. 1800–75 among many tribes, including Chippewa, Osage, Omaha, and Oto. See also *Spangenberg, Augustus Gottlieb.*

6. John Stewart (d. 1823; Meth.; freeborn mulatto; "Apostle to the Wyandottes") began preaching ca. 1816 among Wyandot in Ohio; the work was later extended to Potawatomi, Shawnee, Kickapoo, and other tribes. Other early Meth. missionaries to Indians include J. Lee.*

7. Moravians, Congs., and Presbs. engaged in miss. work in Indian Territory (now in Okla.), esp. among the "Five Civilized Tribes" (Creek, Cherokee, Choctaw, Chickasaw, Seminole).

8. Bap. miss. I. McCoy* began work 1817 among Indians in the Wabash valley.

9. The early hist. of New Eng. states includes instances of miss. work by Episcopalians; they began work in the interior in the 1st part of the 19th century. Indians ministered to by Episcopalians include Iroquois in N. Y., Oneida (an Iroquois people who moved to Wis. 1822), Arapaho and Shoshoni of Wyo., Chippewa of Minn., Sioux, and Dakota. Missionaries included E. Williams,* H. B. Whipple,* and W. H. Hare.*

10. In 1847 the Ev. Luth. Miss. Soc. of Dresden* began work among Chippewa in lower Mich.; other Luth. miss. areas included Wis. and Ariz. See also *Indians, Lutheran Missions to North Amercian.*

11. Mennonites (see *Mennonite Churches*) opened a miss. 1880 among Arapaho, later extended work to the Cheyenne.

12. Dutch Ref. miss. work among Am. Indians began in N. Y. in the 17th c. and expanded W beyond the Miss. R.

13. M. Whitman* and H. H. Spalding* journeyed as far as Walla Walla (Wash.) and est. missions worked later also by Meths.

14. J. Serra* est. RC missions in Calif.

15. Aggression against Indian lands, subjugation of Indians by military force, and graft in admin-

istering Indian affairs have helped to make miss. work among Indians difficult.

16. More than 30 Prot. denominations are doing miss. work among ca. 525,000 Indians in the US, most of whom are W of the Miss. River. There probably are ca. 143,000 RCs and bet. 39,000 and 100,000 Prots. among US Indians.

17. RCs and Prots. do miss. work among Indians in Alaska and Can. Work in Can. once done by Presbs. and Meths. is now largely under control of the United Ch. of Can. (see *Canada,* B).

18. Indian miss. work is carried on through such mediums as miss. stations, miss. schools, Christian centers, hospitals, and est. chs. in reservation areas.

19. Efforts to help Indians achieve self-determination in residence and vocation and become integral parts of urban soc. have been successful. Thousands annually migrate to metropolitan centers. Many urban chs. are including them in their outreach.

See also *Central America,* B. D; *Mexico.*

G. E. E. Lindquist, *The Red Man in the United States* (New York, 1923) and *The Indian in American Life* (New York, 1944); G. W. Hinman, *The Amerian Indian and Christian Missions* (New York, 1933) and *Christian Activities Among American Indians* (Boston, 1933); D. M. Cory, *Within Two Worlds* (New York, 1955); J. W. Clark, "Indians of North America, Missions to the," *The New Schaff-Herzog Encyclopedia of Religious Knowledge,* ed. S. M. Jackson (Grand Rapids, Mich., 1953 reprint), V, 480–485; R. P. Beaver, *Church, State, and the American Indians* (St. Louis, 1966); W. J. Mann, *Ein Aufgang im Abendlande: Mittheilungen aus der Geschichte der früheren evangelischen Missionsversuche unter den Indianern Amerikas* (Reading, Pa., 1883). RJS

Indians, Lutheran Missions to North American. Luth. work among Indians in the eastern US began soon after Swed. Luths. settled on the Delaware River. J. Campanius* tr. the SC into the language of the Indians. At the instigation of F. Schmid(t)* miss. work began 1845 near Sebewaing, Mich. At Frankenmuth, Mich., F. A. Craemer* worked among Chippewa. The work was taken over 1849 by the Mo. Synod. E. O. Clöter* was Mo. Syn. miss. to Chippewa in Minn. 1857–68. The Iowa Syn. (see *Iowa and Other States, Evangelical Lutheran Synod of*) made several attempts to est. missions among Indians in the NW (see also *Braeuninger, Moritz*). In Okla. a miss. was est. 1892 among Cherokee by the Dan. Ev. Luth. Ch. in Am. (see *Danish Lutherans in America,* 3). The Mo. Syn. also did miss. work among Indians in Okla. In 1892 the Wisconsin* Syn. est. a miss. among Apache in Ariz. (see also *Harders, Johann Friedrich Gustav*). The Mo. Syn. began work 1899 among Stockbridge Indians (named after Stockbridge, Mass., where they were first gathered into a miss. town in the 1730s by J. Sergeant*) in Wis. The Syn. for the Norw. Luth. Ch. in Am. (see *Norwegian Evangelical Lutheran Church in America*) founded Bethany Indian Miss. and Industrial School among Winnebago at Wittenberg, W cen. Wis.; it was dedicated July 4, 1887. The Eielsen* Syn. began miss. work near Wittenberg, Wis., among Potawatomi in the 1890s. See also *Indians, American,* 10; *Mexican Indian Mission; Michigan Synod,* 1.

A. Keiser, *Lutheran Mission Work Among the American Indians* (Minneapolis, Minn., 1922); T. Graebner, *Church Bells in the Forest* (St. Louis, 1944); C. F. Luckhard, *Faith in the Forest* (Sebewaing, Mich., 1952).

Indifferentism. 1. Attitude of indifference toward religion. 2. View that one religious belief is as good as another. 3. View that some things are neither commanded nor forbidden in the Bible; see also *Adiaphora.*

Individual and Collective. See *Corporate Personality.*

Individualism. Concept which places high value on individual freedom. *Philosophic* individualism holds that individuals exist independently; the universe is a collection of individuals. *Political* individualism holds that the state exists for the individual. *Economic* individualism calls for free enterprise, personal initiative, competition, and survival of the fittest. *Ethical* individualism holds that each man's ideals are the measure of his morality; everything is right that the individual believes to be right; sin is not transgression of God's law, but violation of one's own conviction and character. For Bap. view of theol. individualism see *Baptist Churches,* 5.

Indochina. 1. Peninsula SE Asia including Burma, Fed. of Malaya, Thailand, Cambodia,* Laos, and Vietnam; see also *Asia,* C. 2. See *French Indochina.*

Indonesia. 1. Name used in a wide sense for the Malay Archipelago ("The Islands of India") and by extension for all areas of Malay-related people, and in a narrow sense for the Rep. of Indonesia; former names of the latter: Dutch E Indies; E Indies; Neth. E Indies; Neth. Indies. *Area:* ca. 782,000 sq. mi. consisting of ca. 3,000 islands of SE Asia, N and NW of Australia; chief islands: the Greater Sundas (Soendas; include Java [which includes Madoera (Madura) since 1885], Sumatra, Borneo [Kalimantan], and Celebes [Sulawesi]), West Irian (West [or Neth., or Dutch] New Guinea), Moluccas (Maluku; Molukken; Spice Islands), and the Lesser Sundas (Soendas; renamed Nusa Tenggara 1954; include Bali, Lombok, Soembawa [Sumbawa], and Timor). *Pop.* (1971 census): 119,000,000, including Atjehnese (Achinese), Bataks, Menangkabaus, Javanese, Sundanese, Madurese, Balinese, Sasaks, Menadonese, Buginese, Dayaks, Papuans. Capital: Djakarta (Jakarta; formerly called Batavia). Neth. territory till Mar. 1942; occupied by Jap. 1942–45; proclaimed a rep. by nationalists 1945 (recognized by Neth. 1949); West Irian transferred by Neth. to UN 1962, given to Indonesia 1963. Indonesia withdrew from UN 1965. Religions: Islam* ca. 90%; Buddhism,* Hinduism,* and Christianity are important minorities. See also *New Guinea,* 1, 2.

2. Christians may have reached Indonesia in the 14th century. Port. (arrived 1511) and Spaniards brought RC missionaries in the 16th century. Dutch brought Protestantism ca. 1600. In the 17th c. the United E India Co. sponsored miss. work. The work of W. Carey* and A. Judson* stimulated formation of miss. socs. which sponsored work in Indonesia. H. Kraemer* and J. H. Bavinck* promoted indigenization of Indonesian chs.

3. *Java and Madoera. Area:* ca. 51,000 sq. mi.; *pop.* (1971 census): 71,527,000, ca. 90% Islamic. Ca. the middle of the 19th c. Mennonites sent workers to Sumatra and Java. The outstanding soc. is the Netherlands* Miss. Society. Baps. began work 1951 in Bandung (Bandoeng). The CIM (now OMF) began work among Mandarin-speaking Chinese after WW II. Other groups include Salvation* Army, Worldwide* Evangelization Crusade, Assemblies* of God, and Pentecostals. Indigenous Prot. chs.: E Java Ch., Middle Java Ch., and W Java Ch.

4. *Sumatra. Area:* ca. 182,800 sq. mi. including islands along W and SE coasts; *pop.:* ca. 19,171,000 (Malays, Hindus, and Chinese). Hindus arrived early in the Christian era; Arabs invaded 13th c.; Dutch est. settlements on SW coast 1663–64. H. Lyman* and S. Munson* were pioneer ABCFM missionaries; mistaken for Muslim spies, killed, eaten by Bataks (see also *Batak Protestant Christian Church*). Basel* Miss. Soc. began work in W Sumatra 1858. L. Nommensen* of Rhenish* Miss. Soc. was very

successful. Batak Ch. and Nias Ch. resulted from work of the Basel and Rhenish societies. Meths. sent permanent miss. to Chinese 1912. Other groups include Worldwide Evangelization Crusade and OMF.

5. *Kalimantan. Area:* ca. 208,300 sq. mi.; *pop.:* ca. 5,123,000. RMS began work 1835 among Dayak in SE Borneo. Field given to Basel Miss. Soc. 1925. The Christian and Miss. Alliance (see *Evangelistic Associations,* 5) began work in Borneo ca. 1929. Other groups include Regions* Beyond Miss. Union since 1932; Worldwide Evangelization Crusade since 1950; OMF; New* Tribes Miss.; Go-Ye* Fellowship; Dutch Ref. Ch.; Pentecostals.

6. *Celebes* (Sulawesi). *Area:* ca. 73,000 sq. mi.; *pop.:* ca. 8,535,000; Neth. Miss. Soc. began 1822 and est. strong native church. CMA began work in Makassar 1928.

7. *West Irian. Area:* ca. 159,300 sq. mi.; *pop.:* ca. 923,000. The Evangelical* Alliance Miss. is carrying on work in Anggi Lakes and Manokwari region. It est. the Erickson-Tritt Bible Institute 1959 (named after 2 miss. murdered 1952 by natives). The Australian Baps. began 1954 in Baliem Valley and Regions Beyond Miss. Union in Swaart Valley 1955. A Dutch group began work 1957. The Missionary* Aviation Fellowship serves all missions. See also *New Guinea,* 1, 2.

8. *Moluccas. Area:* ca. 32,300 sq. mi.; *pop.:* ca. 1,089,000. Dutch ministers assoc. with United E India Co. pioneered here. J. Kamm* of Neth. Miss. Soc. arrived 1815. The Molucca Protestant Church has several hundred thousand mems.

9. *Bali. Area:* ca. 2,150 sq. mi.; *pop.:* ca. 2,120,-000, mostly Hindu. The Ch. of E Java works in Bali. The CMA sent a Chinese miss. 1932. Closed by govt. to miss. work 1935; later reopened.

10. *Lombok. Area:* ca. 1,825 sq. mi.; *pop.* (1961): 1,300,000, ca. 70% Muslim. CMA began work 1929.

11. *Soembawa* (Sumbawa). *Area:* ca. 5,700 sq. mi.; *pop.* (1961): 407,600. The Nat. Bible Soc. of Scot. has distributed much literature. The CMA began work in the 1930s. Work temporarily halted by WW II.

12. *Timor. Area:* (Indonesian part of island plus large nearby islands): ca. 18,876 sq. mi.; *pop.:* 2,295,000. Dutch Prots. arrived 1612. Neth. Miss. Soc. began work 1819. Churches affiliated with the Prot. Ch. of the Neth. Indies 1870. The Ev. Ch. of Timor became autonomous 1947. EL

See also *New Guinea.*

Indra. See *Brahmanism,* 2.

Indulgences. 1. Roots of the RC doctrine of indulgences reach back to the ancient practice of penitential* discipline. As the penitential system changed its character and the RC sacrament of penance* evolved, penance was no longer regarded as a mere expression of sorrow for sin or even as the discharge of ch. penalties, but as pleasing to God, meritorious, and compensatory for sin. It was held to remove, acc. to the degree of its merit, a portion of that temporal punishment of sin (chiefly purgatory*) which could not be removed by absolution.* Commutations* of penance, or indulgences, became commutations of divine punishment and were gained by giving money to chs. and monasteries, by pilgrimages,* sometimes by direct payment to the priest. Contrition,* or at least attrition,* was in theory necessary to gain indulgence.

2. The Crusades* marked an epoch in the hist. of indulgences, for each crusader received plenary indulgence (see par. 5). In the later Middle Ages plenary indulgences were offered in gen. for opposition against various "heretics" and their followers.

3. Boniface VIII (see *Popes,* 12) instituted special plenary indulgences connected with jubilees* beginning 1300.

4. Sixtus IV (see *Popes,* 16) introd. indulgences for souls in purgatory* 1476.

5. M. Luther's* exposure of the indulgence traffic convinced many of the corruption of the RC Ch. and prepared them to welcome the restored Gospel. The Council of Trent* made quaestors of alms (indulgence preachers) scapegoats, "absolutely [Lat. *penitus*] abolished" their name and service [Lat. *usus*], but decreed "that the use of indulgences, most salutary for Christian people and approved by authority of holy councils, is to be retained in the Church," that "moderation be observed," and "that all evil traffic in them . . . be absolutely [Lat. *omnino*] abolished" (Sess. XXI, Decree Concerning Reform, chap. ix; XXV, Decree Concerning Reform, chap. xxi, Decree Concerning Indulgences). Indulgences are called plenary (remitting all temporal punishment due to sin) or partial (e. g., for 40 days, which means the equivalent of that period of canonical penance). Some indulgences can be gained only at particular places or at certain times; others are attached to objects, e. g., crosses, medals. To gain some indulgences, prayers must be said.

See also *Opera supererogationis; Treasury of Merits.*

Indult (from Lat. *indultum,* "privilege, grant"). Special favor permitting bps. and others to act beyond or contrary to common ecclesiastical laws; may be positive (e. g., benefice*) or negative (e. g., dispensation*).

Industry and the Church. 20th-c. industry has presented new problems to the ch. in the application of moral principles to a complex economic structure. Rapid industrialization and urbanization, increase of large corporations and holding companies, impersonal control of industry, absentee ownership, managerial direction of the capitalist system, concentration of wealth, and increasing use of natural resources have created human and moral problems which concern the ch. Areas of strain are to be found not only in labor-management relations, but also in the degree of interest and control by industry and its leaders of civic welfare, philanthropy, production and consumption of goods, and the ownership of property in the manufacturing and financial colossus which governs industry. These, as well as benefactions of industrial giants, are to be viewed in light of Lv 19:13; Jer 22:13; Ja 5:1-6.

Papal encyclicals have warned against abuse of wealth and power as fertile ground for radical economic and pol. ideologies. Prots. are increasingly interested and active in Christian industrial reconstruction. The ch. ministers to industrialist and laborer and applies the ethical teachings of Scripture to both. JD

See also *Capital and Labor; Foundation, Religious; Labor and the Church.*

A. I. Abell, *The Urban Impact on American Protestantism 1865–1900* (Cambridge, Mass., 1943); E. B. Chaffee, *The Protestant Churches and the Industrial Crisis* (New York, 1933); J. Daniel, *The Church and Labor-Management Problems of Our Day* (Bethlehem, Pa., 1947) and *Labor, Industry, and the Church* (St. Louis, 1957); T. C. Graebner, *The Business Man and the Church* (Clinton, S. C., 1942); F. H. Knight and T. W. Merriam, *The Economic Order and Religion* (New York, 1945); H. F. May, *Protestant Churches and Industrial America* (New York, 1949); S. Miller and J. F. Fletcher, *The Church and Industry* (New York, 1930); R. H. Tawney, *Religion and the Rise of Capitalism* (New York, 1926); A. W. Taylor, *Christianity and Industry in America* (New York, 1933).

Ineffabilis Deus. See *Immaculate Conception.*

Inerrancy of the Bible. See *Inspiration,* B 2, 7.

Infallibility, Papal. RC doctrine that the pope is infallible when he speaks ex* cathedra. See also *Old Catholics; Vatican Councils,* 1 b.

Infant Communion. Eastern* Orthodox Chs. regard the Lord's Supper as necessary for salvation and therefore admit also infants to it.

Infant Salvation. J. Calvin* held that all elect infants are saved. Luths. hold that, if infant children of Christians die without Baptism (see *Grace, Means of,* III), it is best to commend them to the mercy of God, who has power to work faith also without ordained means (Lk 1:15, 44).

Infants (children). A. *Scripture.* 1. God's people in the OT and NT viewed children as a blessing (Gn 21:1-8; 22:17; Ps 127:3-5; 128:3) and barrenness as a deprivation and, at times, reproach (Gn 15:2; 30:1; 1 Sm 1:11, 20; Lk 1:7, 24-25). After the Fall, God promised the Woman's Seed to crush the Serpent's head. This first Gospel promise provided the message of hope. Longing for the coming of the Messiah grew in the heart of God's people (Gn 3:15; 4:1; 49:10; Is 7:14; 9:6, 7; Lk 2:25-26).

2. Children were involved in worship life from infancy. Ceremonial acts after childbirth were prescribed (Lv 12; Lk 2:22-27). The firstborn son belonged to God; redeemed after Levites became priestly tribe (Ex 13:2, 13, 15; 22:29; Nm 3:12-15; 18:15-16; Lk 2:23). Sons were circumcised on the 8th day (Gn 17:12-13); those not receiving circumcision were rejected (Gn 17:14). Children were involved in religious observances (Ex 12:26; 1 Sm 1:24-28; Lk 2:21-51) and given religious instruction (Dt 4:9; 6:6; Pr 22:6; Eph 6:4; 2 Ti 3:15).

3. Children were at times received into special relationship with God (1 Sm 3:1-18). Jesus loved children and praised their faith (Mt 18:1-6; Mk 9:36-37; 10:13-16). Children are mems. of the kingdom of God (Lk 18:15-16). Many see a reference to little children in Acts 2:38-39.

4. After the Fall, all men are born in sin and hence separate from God (Gn 3:1-19; 8:21; Ps 51:5; Ro 5:12-19; see also *Sin, Original*). This alienation is overcome by Christ's work of redemption and reconciliation (2 Co 5:19; Eph 2:13, 16; Heb 2:17; see also *Justification*). Connection with Christ (Ro 6:3-8; Gl 3:27), sanctification and cleansing (Eph 5:25-27), regeneration (Tts 3:5), salvation are est. through Baptism. In the NT, believers are described as circumcised in Christ by Baptism (Cl 2:11-13).

5. The requirement of baptism applies to all, since the NT makes no distinction bet. adult and infant baptism and mentions no age for baptism. Evidence suggests that infants were baptized from the very beginning. The NT term *oikos* derives from OT usage (e. g., Jos 24:15) and indicates that entire families were baptized (1 Co 1:16; Acts 16:15, 33-34; 18:8).

B. *Patristics.* 1. Earliest known direct patristic evidence for infant baptism is in Tertullian (*De baptismo* XVIII 4–5). Indirect evidence includes: Polycarp* was probably baptized in infancy (*Martyrium* IX 3); Irenaeus* mentions infants, children, boys, youths, and adults as being born again (*renascuntur*) in the Lord (*Adversus haereses* II xxii 4). Apparently there was no age limitation in the first 2 cents.

2. Hippolytus* (Order of Service for the rite of baptism, 21) regarded infant baptism as the rule and instructed parents or other mems. of the family to speak for them. Origen* (Commentary on Romans, V, 9, on 6:5-7) held that the tradition of baptizing infants came from the apostles. Cyprian* (Epistle LVIII [LXIV]) held that, because of original sin, baptism should not be postponed till the 8th day, but that infants should be baptized on one of the first days immediately after birth.

3. Augustine* of Hippo (*De peccatorum meritis et remissione et de baptismo parvulorum,* III [vi] 12) and Pelagius* (in Augustine, *De gratia Christi et de peccato originali, II* [xviii] 20) said they had not heard of a heretic or schismatic who renounced infant baptism.

C. *Middle Ages.* In the Middle Ages the objective nature of baptism was stressed.

D. *Reformation Era.* 1. In the 1520s Anabaps. rejected infant baptism, insisted on "believer's baptism," and denied that infants can have real faith.

2. M. Luther* fostered instruction and tried to involve infants and other children in the life of the ch. He advocated baptism for infants and other children because it is God's will. He granted that Scripture does not explicitly command infant baptism, but pointed out (1) that Scripture does not say "You are to baptize adults and not children" and (2) that "nations" (Mt 28:19) includes infants (WA 26, 158 and 166). LC IV 57 holds that infants should be baptized because of God's gen. command. Later catechisms hold that infants should be baptized because they can believe (Mt 18:6; Mk 10:13-16) and because Baptism is the only means whereby they can ordinarily be regenerated.

3. Ap IX 1 states that Baptism is necessary for salvation, but the Luth. Confessions and Luther do not say that the unbaptized are damned. In Baptism children are committed to God and become acceptable to Him (AC IX). Ap IX 2: "It is most certain that the promise of salvation also applies to little children. . . . Therefore it is necessary to baptize children, so that the promise of salvation might be applied to them according to Christ's command (Mt 28:19)." SA-III V 4: "children should be baptized, for they, too, are included in the promise of redemption which Christ made. . . ." Infants are in need of regeneration because they are born in sin (AC II; Ap II; FC I). By Baptism a child is received into the Christian community, receives the promise, and enters Christ's kingdom (LC IV 2, 39, 67).

E. *Since the Reformation.* 1. Emphasis on form under state ch. influence tended to externalize baptism.

2. Pietism* tended to minimize infant baptism and the role of children in the ch. Rationalism* reduced baptism to an initiation ceremony, a view held also by some Luths. in Am. in the 1st half of the 19th c. (see also *Definite Synodical Platform*).

3. Many denominations in Am. followed Anabaps. in rejecting the right of infants to receive baptism for various reasons: denial of inherited sin; a child's inability to believe; faith ought be in evidence before baptism; an age of accountability must first be reached. Baptism is gen. viewed by these as merely a sign or symbol. CML

See also *Grace, Means of,* III 4.

O. C. Hallesby, *Infant Baptism and Adult Conversion,* tr. C. J. Carlsen (Minneapolis, 1924); *Die Bekenntnisschriften der evangelisch-lutherischen Kirche,* 6th ed. (Göttingen, 1967); F. Pieper, *Christliche Dogmatik,* III (St. Louis, 1920), 297–339, Eng. tr. *Christian Dogmatics,* ed. W. W. F. Albrecht (St. Louis, 1953), 253–289; *Christian Baptism,* ed. A. Gilmore (Chicago, 1959); *The Book of Concord,* tr. and ed. T. G. Tappert (St. Louis, 1959); J. Jeremias, *Infant Baptism in the First Four Centuries,* tr. D. Cairns (London, 1960) and *The Origins of Infant Baptism: A Further Study in Reply to Kurt Aland,* tr. D. M. Barton (London, 1963); O. Cullmann, *Baptism in the New Testament,* tr. J. K. S. Reid (London, 1950); E. Schlink, *Theology of the Lutheran Confessions,* tr. P. F. Koehneke and H. J. A. Bouman (Philadelphia, 1961); M. E. Marty, *Bap-*

tism (Philadelphia, 1962); K. Aland, *Did the Early Church Baptize Infants?* tr. and introd. G. R. Beasley-Murray, pref. J. F. Jansen (London, 1963); H. Fagerberg, *Die Theologie der lutherischen Bekenntnisschriften von 1529 bis 1537,* tr. G. Klose (Göttingen, 1965); R. Jungkuntz, *The Gospel of Baptism* (St. Louis, 1968); J. H. Elliott, *The Christ Life* (Chicago, 1968).

Infidelity. (1) Lack of faith or belief in a religion; (2) lack of faithfulness to an obligation, esp. marriage.*

Infinity of God. Attribute acc. to which God* is not contained within bounds of time or space. Scripture ascribes to God infinity in essence (Ps 145:3) and attributes (Ps 147:5).

Infinitum capax finiti (Lat. "the infinite [is] capable of grasping, or holding, the finite"). Term used in stating that God enters into fellowship with man through revelation in hist. See also *Finitum (non) est capax infiniti.*

Infralapsarianism. View that God permitted man to fall into sin and that predestination* followed the fall. Adherents called infralapsarians or sublapsarians. See also *Supralapsarianism.*

Infused Grace. See *Gratia infusa.*

Inge, William Ralph (1860–1954). B. Crayke, Yorkshire, Eng.; educ. Cambridge; Angl.; dean St. Paul's, London; influenced by Platonic spirituality. Works include *Christian Mysticism; Personal Idealism and Mysticism; Christian Ethics and Modern Problems.*

Ingersoll, Robert Green (1833–99). Lawyer and lecturer; b. Dresden, N. Y.; Union colonel in Civil War; agnostic; attacked Christian beliefs in pub. lectures.

Ingressa. See *Ambrosian Music.*

Inini. See *South America,* 14.

Innate Ideas. 1. Ideas alleged to be inborn, e. g., belief in God and immortality. 2. Power of understanding given with mind. 3. Ideas which all men as human and rational have.

Inner Light. See *Friends, Society of,* 2; *Grace, Means of,* 1, 7; *Mennonite Churches,* 2; *Münzer, Thomas; Pentecostalism.*

Inner Mission. 1. Modern Christian soc. service began in Ger. in the 1st part of the 19th c. See also *Fliedner, Theodor; Wichern, Johann Hinrich.*

2. Objectives of Inner Miss. are soc. and spiritual, Christian soc. services in the fullest sense of the term.

3. A. Stoecker* exerted strong influence in later Inner Miss. developments. Nazism and WW II combined to undo many soc. gains achieved by Inner Miss. in Ger. Late in Kirchenkampf* the Inner Miss. saved many lives by opposing euthanasia. The Hilfswerk (relief work) of EKD was organized 1945; in 1957 it united with Inner Miss. as Innere Mission und Hilfswerk der EKD. In Am. the term "Inner Mission" fell into disuse by the middle of the 20th c. and was replaced by such terms as "soc. miss.," "soc. service," and "soc. welfare work." Responsibility for much soc. work was assumed by govts. of various countries. HFW

See also *Aging and Infirm, Homes and Services for; Associated Lutheran Charities; Charities, Christian; Child and Family Service Agencies; Hospitals; Social Work.*

Inner Mission, Church Society for. See *Denmark, Lutheranism in,* 10.

Innocence. Man was created in the image of God (Gn 1:27). Through the Fall, man became sinful (Gn 3; Ro 5:12). Justified by faith in Christ, man becomes righteous before God (Ro 3:21-28; cp. Ps. 19:12-13). A man may be innocent with respect to demands and judgments of civil laws, e. g., not guilty of a gross moral offense (Ps 18:26), without fault in the eyes of human judges and soc. in gen. (Gn 20:5; Job 33:9; Ps 26:6; Jer 2:35; Dn 6:22). God regards believers innocent when He sees them clothed in Christ's righteousness and cleansed by His blood. JMW

Innocent II. See *"Stabat mater."*

Innocent III. See *Popes,* 10.

Innocent IV (Sinibaldo Fieschi; ca. 1200–1254). B. Genoa; pope 1243–54; convoked 1st Council of Lyons (see *Lyons, Councils of*). Works include a commentary on decretals.

Innocent VI. See *Babylonian Captivity,* 2.

Innocent VII. See *Schism,* 8.

Innocent VIII. See *Popes,* 17; *Schism,* 8.

Innocent X. See *Popes,* 23.

Innocent XI (Benedetto Odescalchi; 1611–89). Pope 1676–89; b. Como, It.; educ. Naples; cardinal 1645; bp. Novara 1650; championed moral and administrative reform; engaged in controversy with Louis* XIV over royal prerogatives in ecclesiastical appointments. See also *Gallicanism.*

Innocents, Feast of the. See *Church Year,* 1.

Innuit. See *Eskimos.*

Inorganic Evolution. See *Evolution,* I.

Inquisition (from Lat. *inquiro,* "inquire; search for"). 1. Special permanent RC tribunal est. ca. 1231 to detect and punish those guilty of dissent from accepted teachings and rites of the ch. Called Cong. of the Holy Office by Pius X (see *Popes,* 30). Directed by Gregory IX (see *Popes,* 11) to combat Cathari* and Waldenses,* its activity was later extended to others (e. g., Beguines [see *Beghards and Beguines*], witches, diviners, blasphemers, and sacrilegious people). Its name is derived from its power to make inquiries in search of heresy. Inquisitors became known as severe oppressors.

2. Historical antecedents. Theodosius* I persecuted heathen and deprived heretics of civil rights. Intolerance appears in the codes of Theodosius* II and Justinian* I. Charlemagne* "converted" the Saxons by force.

3. In the later Middle Ages an organized inquisitorial system to guard against inroads of heresy was developed. Popes, councils, syns., and secular rulers provided legislative and administrative machinery. Lateran* Council II (1139) required secular princes to prosecute heretics. Alexander III (see *Popes,* 9) ordered imprisonment and confiscation of property of convicted heretics 1162–63. At the 1229 Syn. of Toulouse (see also *Toulouse, Synods of*) bps. were ordered to appoint a priest and 2 or more laymen to hunt heretics in their sees and bring them to trial before the episcopal tribunal (hence called Episcopal Inquisition). Gregory IX ordered life imprisonment for repentant heretics and capital punishment by state for obstinate heretics 1231 (Constitution *Excommunicamus*).

4. Because he felt that bps. were lax in enforcing these regulations, Gregory IX entrusted trial and punishment of heretics to Konrad* von Marburg, who used esp. Dominicans* for this purpose. This inquisition was first limited primarily to Ger., extended to Aragon 1232, made gen. 1233.

5. Thereafter inquisitors or judges were selected almost exclusively from Dominicans and Franciscans.* Each tribunal was to have 2 inquisitors who received their power directly from the pope. Responsible only to the pope, many inquisitors were cruel and ruthless. At times there was lawless retaliation against them; K. v. Marburg was murdered 1233.

6. The Sp. Inquisition was peculiar to Sp. and its colonies. It was est. at the request of Ferdinand V of Castile (Ferdinand II of Aragon; "the Catholic"; 1452–1516; b. Sos, Aragon; king of Sicily 1468–1516, of Castile as Ferdinand V with Isabella 1474–1504, of Aragon as Ferdinand II 1479–1516) and Isabella I (Sp.: Isabel; "the Catholic"; 1451–1504;

m. Ferdinand II of Aragon 1469; ruled with him as Ferdinand V of Castile and Aragon 1479–1504) to eradicate heresy, to deal with *conversos* or *Marranos* (Jews and Moors who professed Christianity, but in some cases only halfheartedly or to escape persecution), to consolidate their realm, to share in spoils. Sixtus IV (see *Popes,* 16) gave RC kings right to appoint 2 or 3 doctors of theol. as inquisitors 1478. Inquisitors were appointed 1480, installed 1481; in 1483 Ferdinand raised this tribunal to the dignity of the 5th council of the state and called it Concejo de la Suprema y General Inquisicion (Council of the Supreme and Gen. Inquisition). The whole Sp. Inquisition was put under T. de Torquemada,* who became known as a cruel, uncouth persecutor. Suppressed 1808, reest. 1813, it was abolished 1834.

7. A permanent cong. of cardinals with headquarters at Rome and supreme and universal competence in matters concerning heretics and suspected heretics was est. 1542 by Paul* III and further defined by subsequent popes. Paul VI (see *Popes,* 35) reorganized it 1965 into the Sacred Cong. for the Doctrine of the Faith, which is to condemn error and promote orthodox doctrine. EL

H. C. Lea, *A History of the Inquisition of the Middle Ages,* 3 vols. (London, 1888), *A History of the Inquisition of Spain,* 4 vols. (New York, 1906–07), and *The Inquisition in the Spanish Dependencies* (New York, 1908); A. H. Verrill, *The Inquisition* (New York, 1931); E. van der Vekené, *Bibliographie der Inquisition* (Hildesheim, Ger., 1963); A. S. Turberville, *Mediaeval Heresy & the Inquisition* (London, 1920) and *The Spanish Inquisition* (Hamden, Conn., 1968).

In-Service Training of Teachers. See *Teachers,* 7.

Inspiration, Doctrine of. A. 1. The NT does not use the Gk. word *empneo* ("inspire") used by Philo* Judaeus and other classical and Hellenistic authors in reference to an ecstatic and often impersonal relationship bet. a person and a source of "inspiration." In 2 Ptr 1:21 a verb is used ("Prophecy did not ever come [*enechthe*] by the will of man, but men moved by [*pheromenoi*] the Holy Ghost spoke from God") which occurs 2 Ptr 1:17-18 with reference to the voice heard at the Transfiguration ("Such a voice came [*enechtheises*] to Him. . . . This voice . . . came [*enechtheisan*] from heaven"). In 2 Ti 3:16 a word (*theopneustos,* "God-breathed"; see also *Theopneustia*) is used which echoes the thought of Gn 2:7 ("God . . . breathed"), suggesting that Scripture may be the product of God's creative work in much the same way as that in which man was made a living being. The Luth. Confessions cite 2 Ti 3:16 only in reference to the effectiveness of the Bible and cite 2 Ptr 1:21 to prove the fact of inspiration.

2. To say that the Bible is the work of the Holy Spirit as Author does not imply suspension or extinction of the personality or individuality of the writers. God's Spirit used each writer with his endowments and his background of grammar, style, knowledge of nature and hist., etc.

3. That the Holy Spirit suggested to the writers the whole content and the words (plenary and verbal inspiration) is est., e. g., by Is 59:21; 1 Co 2:13; Gl 3:16; 1 Th 2:13. Accordingly, inspiration is a special, potent activity of the Holy Spirit which He exercised on those whom He chose as His instruments for writing the Biblical documents.

4. The fact of inspiration is taught in various passages of the OT and NT. What is written in the Bible is at times attributed to "the Holy Spirit" or "God," at other times to persons, e. g., David and Moses (2 Sm 23:1-2; Mt 15:4; 22:43; Mk 7:10; cp. Mt 19:4-5 and Gn 2:24).

5. Inspiration differs from revelation* in the sense that the latter term is used more broadly of all the methods by which God has made Himself known to men, including oral utterances of prophets, whereas the former refers, in its narrow sense, to specific guidance provided by the Holy Spirit to the writers. The word "inspiration" occurs in a broader sense 2 Ti 3:16; there it indicates that the individual books of the Bible are an end-product of God's power at work among His people (Lk 1:1-4; Jos 10:13; 1 Co 15:3), resulting in documents accepted by the ch. as canonical (see *Canon, Bible*).

6. The relation bet. God as Author and the men whom He used to transmit His Word is expressed in the Nicene Creed (see *Ecumenical Creeds,* B) by the phrase, "*Who* spake *by* the prophets," which not only exactly summarizes the comparison bet. such texts as 1 Co 5:9 and 1 Jn 1:4 with that group represented by Mt 2:17 and 24:15, but is found as to its very terms Ro 1:2: "Which *He* had promised . . . *by* His prophets in the holy scriptures." MHS

B. 1. *M. Luther* and Inspiration.* Through Luther the Bible was restored as sole authority in the ch. In his 1st lectures on Ps (1513–16) he showed that he held Scripture to be the Word of God, regarding such expressions as "God speaks" and "Scripture speaks" as interchangeable. But as late as 1516 he still surrendered to the fathers and to the ch. his own right to understand and explain Scripture. In controversy with J. Eck,* Luther divorced himself from the authority of councils. By the time of the Diet of Worms* he had concluded that Scripture is far above the authority of the whole human race. Thereafter Scripture remained his sole authority. Though many things in the Bible puzzled and amazed him, he admitted no error in its original MSS. At the same time he emphasized the human part in its writing.

2. The Luth. Confessions do not include a separate systematic treatment of inspiration; they take for granted that the Bible is God's Word and the only infallible guide and authority.

3. a. *Early Luth. Dogmaticians.* M. Chemnitz* regarded Scripture as the inspired Word of God. N. Selnecker* held that since Scripture is throughout the Word of God, its content throughout is heavenly, divine, and spiritual. He maintained that the real meaning is not in the "dead letter," but comes through the enlightenment of the Spirit. J. Gerhard* emphasized that Scripture is *autopistos* (Gk. "trustworthy on its own authority"; it needs no testimony except that of God, its Author) and held that the energy of Scripture which leads us to Christ also convinces us that God is the Author of the Bible.

b. G. Calixtus* held that only doctrinal matter of Scripture is inspired, but writers kept from error also in other matters. Over against this view, A. Calov(ius)* held that the Bible forms a whole: *forma revelationis divinae est theopneustia,* per quam revelatio divina est, quod est* ("The form of divine revelation is divine inspiration, by which divine revelation is what it is"). He also distinguished bet. the act of the revealing God and the form of the revealed Word. Feeling that Calov had gone too far toward a mechanical theory, J. Musaeus* sought to analyze human activity in the act of inspiration and emphasized the divine direction voiced by Calixtus.

c. J. A. Quenstedt's* presentation of inspiration is noteworthy because of the hist. evidence he marshals. He held that Apostolic writing is the same as preaching since both serve the purpose of awakening faith in Christ. He differentiated bet. the need of the whole ch. and the immediate need of the writing. He distinguished an enlightenment *(irradiatio)* which preceded the impulse *(impulsus)* to write. Inspiration itself he characterized as the descent of the Holy Spirit to the capabilities of the agent. J. K. Dannhauer* distinguished (1) *aspiratio* (the activity of the penman in obedience to divine will, such as study, comparison of OT, investigations, etc.); (2) *postspiratio* (the quiet influence of the Holy Spirit on the penman); (3) *inspiratio* (the culmination of inspiration); (4) *respiratio* (the working of the Holy Spirit in the hearts of those who read the Word).

d. Later dogmaticians of the classical period concerned themselves with problems given above and developed certain phases of them. One of the important problems which concerned earlier and later dogmaticians was the relation bet. revelation and inspiration.

4. *Reformed.* Early Ref. writers and confessions adhered to a strict view of inspiration. Many Ref. theologians tried to harmonize reason and revelation. Ref. fundamentalism* emphasized association of inspiration with inerrancy.

5. *Roman Catholicism.* RCm upholds the inspiration of Scripture. The Council of Trent* held that Scripture and unwritten traditions are the source of all saving truth and rules of conduct (Sess. IV). RC scholars disagree on the meaning of this. The *Dogmatic Constitution on Divine Revelation* of Vatican II (see *Vatican Councils,* 2) states: "8. And so the apostolic preaching, which is expressed in a special way in the inspired books, was to be preserved by a continuous succession of preachers until the end of time. . . . 9. . . . Thus, led by the light of the Spirit of truth, these successors can in their preaching preserve this word of God faithfully, explain it, and make it more widely known. Consequently, it is not from sacred Scripture alone that the Church draws her certainty about everything which has been revealed." Many scholars explain this to mean that Scripture is the only source, and tradition the Spirit-guided explanation, unfolding, and teaching of that source by the ch.

6. Pietism* and rationalism* influenced later conceptions of inspiration. A popular theory in the 1st part of the 20th c. held that the Bible is a human account of divine revelation and hence not without error. Others held that there were degrees of inspiration. Thoughts on inspiration in the middle of the c. ranged from mechanical theories to total rejection of inspiration. Since the 1950s, scholars have emphasized the mystery of Scripture, i. e., the relation of the divine to the human.

7. *Lutheranism in America.* Constitutions of major Luth. chs. in Am. and that of LCUSA pledge these bodies to Scripture as the Word of God and only infallible guide of doctrine and life. Other syn. statements affirm the inspiration of Scripture:

a. *Pittsburgh* Agreement* (adopted by the ALC and the ULC 1940): "2. The Bible consists of a number of separate books, written at various times, on various occasions, and for various purposes. Their authors were living, thinking personalities, each endowed by the Creator with an individuality of his own and each having his peculiar style, his own manner of presentation, even at times using such sources of information as were at hand. Nevertheless, by virtue of a unique operation of the Holy Ghost (2 Tim. 3:16; 2 Pet. 1:21) by which He supplied to the holy writers content and fitting word (2 Pet. 1:21; 1 Cor. 2:12, 13) the separate books of the Bible are related to one another and, taken together, constitute a complete, errorless unbreakable whole, of which Christ is the Center (John 10:35). They are rightly called the Word of God. This unique operation of the Holy Spirit upon the writers is named inspiration. We do not venture to define its mode or manner, but accept it as a fact."

b. *Common* Confession,* Part I, V (adopted by LCMS and ALC 1950): "Through the Holy Scriptures, which God caused to be written by men chosen and inspired by Him, God instructs and assures us regarding His will for us. The Holy Scriptures constitute His Word to men, centering in the revelation of Himself in the person and work of Jesus Christ for our salvation. Through the Holy Scriptures God continues to speak to men in all ages until the end of time. He speaks as the infallible and unchanging God, whose message to mankind never changes. Since the Holy Spirit by divine inspiration supplied to the holy writers content and fitting word, therefore we acknowledge the Holy Scriptures in their entirety as the inspired Word of God. His Holy Spirit testifies in our hearts that His Word is true, that He will keep all His promises to us, and that our faith in Him is not in vain.

"We therefore recognize the Holy Scriptures as God's inerrant Word, and this Word of God alone shall establish articles of faith (cf. Smalcald Articles, Part II, Art. II). We pledge ourselves to teach all things taught in the Holy Scriptures, and nothing but that which is taught us by God in the Holy Scriptures."

c. *Brief Statement of the Doctrinal Position of the Missouri Synod* (adopted 1932): "We teach that the Holy Scriptures differ from all other books in the world in that they are the Word of God. They are the Word of God because the holy men of God who wrote the Scriptures wrote only that which the Holy Ghost communicated to them by inspiration, 2 Tim. 3:16; 2 Peter 1:21. We teach also that the verbal inspiration of the Scriptures is not a so-called 'theological deduction,' but that it is taught by direct statements of the Scriptures, 2 Tim. 3:16; John 10:35; Rom. 3:2; 1 Cor. 2:13. Since the Holy Scriptures are the Word of God, it goes without saying that they contain no errors or contradictions, but that they are in all their parts and words the infallible truth, also in those parts which treat of historical, geographical, and other secular matters, John 10:35. . . .

"We reject the doctrine, which under the name of science has gained wide popularity in the Church of our day, that Holy Scripture is not in all its parts the Word of God, but in part the Word of God and in part the word of man and hence does, or at least might, contain errors." EL

J. M. Reu, *Luther and the Scriptures* (Columbus, Ohio, 1944); T. E. W. Engelder, *Scripture Cannot Be Broken* (St. Louis, 1944) and "Haec Dixit Dominus," *CTM,* XVIII (July 1947), 484–499, (Aug. 1947), 561–572, reprint. ([St. Louis], n. d.) with tr. of Lat. and Ger. quotations; P. E. Kretzmann, "The Christocentric Theory of Inspiration," *CTM,* XV (Mar. 1944), 187–192; W. Dallmann, *Why Do I Believe the Bible Is God's Word?* 5th print. (St. Louis, 1943); W. Arndt, "Die Lehre von der Inspiration nach 1 Petr. 1, 10–12," *CTM,* V (Mar. 1934), 192–198; W. W. F. Albrecht, "Holy Scripture the Word of God," *The Abiding Word,* II, ed. T. Laetsch (St. Louis, 1947), 1–34; C. Eberhard, "Geography of the Bible in Relation to Inspiration," *CTM,* XV (Nov. 1944), 736–747; J. A. Dell, "The Word of God," *What Lutherans Are Thinking,* ed. E. C. Fendt (Columbus, Ohio, 1947), pp. 26–47; P. Schumm, "The Clearness and Sufficiency of Scripture," *The Abiding Word,* I, ed. T. Laetsch (St. Louis, 1946), 58–66; W. Elert, *Morphologie des Luthertums,* I, improved print. (Munich, 1952), 157–176, tr. W. Hansen, *The Structure of Lutheranism,* I (St. Louis, 1962), 179–191; W. Walther, *Das Erbe der Reformation im Kampfe der Gegenwart,* I: *Der Glaube an das Wort Gottes* (Leipzig, 1903); W. Rohnert, *Die Inspiration der heiligen Schrift und ihre Bestreiter* (Leipzig, 1889); *The Infallible Word: A Symposium* by the mems. of the faculty of Westminster Theol. Sem. (Philadelphia, 1946); R. R.

Caemmerer, A. C. Piepkorn, M. H. Franzmann, W. R. Roehrs, "Essays on the Inspiration of Scripture," *CTM,* XXV (Oct. 1954), 738–753; R. Preus, *The Inspiration of Scripture,* 2d ed. (London, 1957); B. Baepler, "Scripture and Tradition in the Council of Trent," *CTM,* XXXI (June 1960), 341–362; Faculty of Concordia Seminary, St. Louis, Mo., "A Statement on the Form and Function of the Holy Scriptures," *CTM,* XXXI (Oct. 1960), 626–627; K. Rahner, *Inspiration in the Bible,* tr. C. H. Henkey (New York, 1961); P. Lengsfeld, *Überlieferung: Tradition und Schrift in der evangelischen und katholischen Theologie der Gegenwart* (Paderborn, 1960); D. M. Beegle, *The Inspiration of Scripture* (Philadelphia, 1963); B. B. Warfield, *The Inspiration and Authority of the Bible,* ed. S. G. Craig (Philadelphia, 1948); H. W. Robinson, *Inspiration and Revelation in the Old Testament* (Oxford, 1946); *Report of the Commission on Theology and Church Relations: A Study Document on Revelation, Inspiration,* [*and*] *Inerrancy,* pub. by LCMS ([St. Louis], n. d.). See also documentation under related articles, e. g., *Dogmatics; Reformed Confessions.*

Inspirationists. See *Amana Society.*

Inspirationsgemeinden. See *Amana Society.*

Institute of Religious Science and School of Philosophy, The. Theosophist cult with headquarters at Los Angeles, Calif. Claims to give understanding of man's physical, mental, and spiritual nature.

Institute of (the) Brothers of the Christian Schools. See *Jean Baptiste de la Salle.*

Institutes, Missionary. See *Missionary Institutes.*

Institutes of the Christian Religion. See *Calvin, John.*

Institution of a Christian Man. See *Anglican Confessions,* 2.

Institutional Church. Name given at beginning of 20th c. to Am. Prot. ch. which undertook a program of recreation and soc. service besides functions of worship and soul-care. Theologically it was a product of the Social* Gospel and socially of pop. shifts. As ch. plants came to be surrounded by underprivileged, transient, and foreign-born groups, emphasis shifted to an approach to physical need and provision for leisure time. The designation has largely fallen into disuse for various reasons.

G. Hodges and J. Reichert, *The Administration of an Institutional Church* (New York, 1906); H. P. Douglass, *Protestant Cooperation in American Cities* (New York, 1930); H. P. Douglass and E. de S. Brunner, *The Protestant Church as a Social Institution* (New York, 1935); M. H. Leiffer, *City and Church in Transition* (Chicago, 1938).

Instituto Concordia, Sao Paulo, Brazil. See *Lutheran Church — Missouri Synod, Districts of,* B 1.

Institutum Judaicum. Institute dedicated to the study of Heb. language and Jewish literature, esp. for miss. purposes. The first such inst., founded 1728 by J. H. Callenberg* in Halle, continued till 1792. H. L. Strack* est. one 1883 in Berlin; closed 1933. Franz Delitzsch (see *Delitzsch,* 1) est. one 1886 in Leipzig; later called Delitzschianum; to Vienna 1935; closed 1938; reopened 1948 in Münster by Karl Heinrich Rengstorf (b. 1903 at Jembke, near Gifhorn, Ger.). Another was est. 1956 in Tübingen by Otto Michel (b. 1903 at Elberfeld [now in Wuppertal], Ger.).

Instrumentalism. See *Dewey, John; Pragmatism.*

Integral Humanism. Term used by neo-Thomists; considers man in the wholeness of his being.

Integrity. Completeness; term used to designate that quality of the books of the Bible acc. to which no part of the original MSS is lacking and all parts now included in the Bible belong to it as first drafted.

Intellectual, The. See *Christian Faith and the Intellectual.*

Intellectualism, Philosophical. System teaching that we learn to know the essence of things not through the senses (sensationalism*) but through pure concepts inherent in the very nature of the mind. Learning is a recollection of inborn ideas suggested by their imperfect copies in the phenomenal world. Principles of ethics are grounded in reason, not in feeling. In theol. the term is sometimes used to distinguish intellectual knowledge of Bible doctrines from mysticism.* See also *Idealism.*

Intelligence, Creative. Term denoting presence of purpose, self-direction, and self-consciousness in creative world processes. In personalism,* a synonym for God or *élan vital* (see *Bergson, Henri*).

Intemperance. Lack of moderation; includes all abuse of God's gifts by excess; assoc. esp. with excessive drinking of intoxicants. Lk 21:34; Ro 13:13; 1 Co 6:10; Gl 5:21; Eph 5:18; 1 Ti 3:8; 2 Ptr 1:6. Cp. WA 47, 757–771.

Intention of Priest. See *Sacraments, Roman Catholic.*

Inter mirifica. See *Vatican Councils,* 2.

Intercession. See *Prayer.*

Interchurch World Movement of North America. Grew out of a Dec. 17, 1918, meeting in NYC of representatives of various Prot. home and for. miss. bds.; object: to coordinate various enterprises in home and for. miss., soc. services, and Christian educ.; collapsed in less than 2 yrs. for lack of unity and financial support.

Interdenominational Cooperation. See *Ecumenical Movement, The; Federal Council of the Churches of Christ in America; Union Movements; World Council of Churches.*

Interdenominational Foreign Mission Association of North America. Founded 1917 to strengthen "faith missions." Requires mems. to subscribe to a Statement of Faith which includes belief in Bible as divinely inspired Word of God; Trinity; personality of Satan; total depravity; deity, virgin birth, death, bodily resurrection, exaltation, personal and imminent return of Christ; substitutionary atonement; resurrection of saved and unsaved; church as body of Christ consisting of believers; Christ's Great Commission. It is a fellowship of miss. socs. which functions as a service agency and accrediting assoc.

Applicants for full membership must be governed by a properly constituted bd. of dirs., be a soc. with at least 10 N Am. missionaries supported by N Am. funds, or a service organization which contributes to effectiveness of mem. missions, evangelize, and form or further indigenous chs., demonstrate necessity and purpose of its existence, issue annual audited financial reports, rely on God through prayer and faith, be approved as to its policies and practices by mem. missions.

Official pub.: *IFMA News.* The *Evangelical Missions Quarterly* is pub. under joint sponsorship with the Evangelical* Foreign Missions Association.

J. H. Kane, *Faith Mighty Faith* (New York, 1956).

Interdenominational Missionary Fellowship (Vic.). Organized 1945; fosters joint prayer and mutual help among miss. agencies; headquarters Melbourne, Victoria, Australia.

Interdict (from Lat. *interdicere,* "forbid"). RC censure or penalty by which divine services and sacred rites are suspended. Interdicts may be personal or local, and each of these may be particular or gen.; a particular personal interdict is imposed on a person or persons specifically mentioned; a gen. personal interdict is imposed on persons mentioned only as a group; a particular local interdict is imposed on a specific individual place; a gen. local interdict is imposed on a larger area (e. g., diocese, province, state, or nation). Gen. interdicts may be imposed only by the Roman see. Interdicts have often been used effectively against recalcitrants since the 6th c. See also *Western Christianity 500–1500,* 8.

Interest, Monetary. See *Fundamental Doctrines,* 5.

Interim (from Lat. *interim,* "meanwhile"). Provisional agreement in religious matters until the next ch. council.

I. *Augsburg Interim* (June 30, 1548). Charles* V proposed a temporary armistice bet. RCs and Luths. and in Feb. 1548 appointed a commission including J. v. Pflug,* M. Helding* (suffragan bp. Mainz 1537), and J. Agricola* to draft the terms. The draft, rev. by some Sp. monks, consisted of 26 articles: (1–2) Man before and after the fall; (3) Redemption; (4–6) Justification; (7) Love and good works; (8) Forgiveness of sins; (9–12) The church; (13) Bishops; (14–21) The sacraments; (22) Sacrifice of the mass; (23) Saints; (24) Commemoration of the dead; (25) Communion at mass; (26) Ceremonies of sacraments. Joachim II Hektor of Brandenburg (see *Joachim,* 2) and Frederick* II of the Palatinate approved; Ulrich of Württemberg (1487–1550) approved under pressure; Philip* of Hesse approved in hope of gaining release from prison thereby; John* Frederick of Saxony rejected it. Maurice* of Saxony and others were dissatisfied but did not protest. The emp. succeeded in enforcing the Interim in parts of S Ger., where many pastors, including J. Brenz* and M. Bucer,* were driven out. But there was vehement and successful opposition to it in the Palatinate, Brandenburg, Hesse, Saxony, Mecklenburg, Pomerania, and N Ger. cities led by Magdeburg.

II. *Leipzig Interim.* After his return from Augsburg, Maurice of Saxony consulted with his theologians and councillors, including C. Cruciger the Elder (see *Cruciger,* 1), J. v. Pflug, P. Melanchthon,* Johann VIII von Maltitz (bp. Meissen 1537–1549), George* III of Anhalt, J. Forster,* and P. Eber.* Proposals drafted and modified at inconclusive meetings in Aug. at Pegau and Oct. at Torgau were further considered in Nov. at Altzella, near Nossen, Saxony, at a meeting attended also by J. Bugenhagen,* G. Major,* J. Camerarius,* H. Weller,* and A. Lauterbach*; an interim was drawn up which compromised the doctrine of justification and some other points, and which regarded as adiaphora* such things as extreme unction, confirmation, lights, vestments, images, fasts, and festivals. Maurice of Saxony and Joachim II of Brandenburg came to an agreement in Dec. on the points they would be willing to accept and follow. Saxony accepted the Altzella terms at Leipzig Dec. 1548 (hence the name Leipzig Interim); the bps. of Naumburg and Meissen dissented. The Brandenburg diet met Jan. 1549.

Reaction was immediate. N. v. Amsdorf* and M. Flacius* Illyricus opposed the Interim. Charles V made Maurice of Saxony head of an army to enforce a renewed ban imposed on Magdeburg, where M. Flacius Illyricus, N. v. Amsdorf, and other Luths. had found refuge. Maurice turned his forces against Charles V, forced temporary suspension of the Council of Trent* 1552, and secured the convention of Passau* 1552, which recognized the Luth. faith as among the ecclesiastical institutions of the empire. See also *Augsburg, Religious Peace of.*

See also *Synergistic Controversy.*

III. *Regensburg (Ratisbon) Interim.* See *Regensburg Conference.*

See also *Lutheran Confessions,* C 1.

Interimistic Controversy. See *Flacius Illyricus, Matthias; Interim.*

Interior India United World Mission. Mission based in Bahraich, India; begun 1930 by A. E. Rassmann of Indianapolis, Ind.; first called Rassmanns Mission Bahraich, then Interior India Mission; present name adopted 1962.

Interlude. Instrumental musical passage bet. hymn stanzas or parts of liturgy.

Intermediate State. Belief in an interval bet. death and the world to come has given rise to various speculations which assume an intermediate state, e. g., a state of sleep or insensibility (see *Soul Sleep*), and purgatory.*

Internal Works of God. See *Father, God the.*

International, The. See *Marx, Karl Heinrich.*

International Apostolic Holiness Union. Organized 1897 in Cincinnati, Ohio, to unite Pent. and holiness groups; movement resulted in Pilgrim Holiness Ch. 1922, which merged 1968 with Wesleyan Meth. Ch. of Am. (see *Methodist Churches,* 4 b) to form The Wesleyan* Ch.

International Association for Liberal Christianity and Religious Freedom. Organized 1900 to provide a common forum for liberal chs. and promote religious freedom.

International Association of Lutheran Students. See *Students, Spiritual Care of,* A 3.

International Bible Reading Association. Founded 1882 as a ministry of the Nat. Christian Educ. Council (formerly the Nat. S. S. Union). Encourages Bible reading and publishes helps.

International Bible Students Association. See *Jehovah's witnesses.*

International Board of Jewish Missions, Inc. Founded 1949 by Jacob Gartenhaus (assoc. with S Bap. Conv.) to work among Jews in all lands.

International Christian Leprosy Missions, International Council, Inc. The Internat. Christian Leprosy Miss. was organized 1944, the Internat. Council 1961. It seeks to complement programs of other missions. US-based.

The Internat. Christian Leprosy Miss. of Can., formed 1955, has operated as a separate unit since 1956.

International Christian Youth Exchange. Organized 1957; sponsored by 12 US Prot. denominations to arrange for internat. exchange of high school students and to provide exchange students with Christian environment.

International Church of the Foursquare Gospel. See *Foursquare Gospel, The.*

Inter-National Constitutional Church. Spiritualist ch. founded 1937 at Los Angeles, Calif. Believes in tolerance, divine gifts of God listed 1 Co 12–13, Sermon on the Mount.

International Convention of Christian Churches (Disciples of Christ). See *Disciples of Christ.*

International Council of Christian Churches, The. Organization of Prot. chs. from various parts of the world formed Aug. 11–19, 1948, in the Eng. Ref. Ch., Amsterdam, Neth. The doctrinal statement of the const. includes plenary inspiration and inerrancy of Scripture; Trinity; essential, absolute, eternal deity, and the real and proper, but sinless, humanity of Jesus Christ; virgin birth; substitutionary, expiatory death of Christ; bodily resurrection of Jesus; total depravity of man; salvation, the effect of regeneration by the Spirit and the Word, not by works but by grace through faith; everlasting bliss of the saved, and everlasting suffering of the lost; real spiritual unity in Christ of those redeemed by His precious blood; necessity of maintaining purity of doctrine and life; acceptance of Apostles' Creed.

C. McIntire, *Servants of Apostasy* (Collingswood, N. J., 1955).

International Council of Religious Education, The. Rapid spread of the Sunday* school beginning in the 1780s led to formation of S. S. unions to meet the need for cooperation. The 1st S. S. Conv. was held 1832 in NYC. Internat. convs. began in the 1870s. The 1905 internat. conv. adopted the name "The International Sunday School Association." The S. S. Council of Ev. Denominations was organized 1910. These 2 organizations united 1922 to form

The Internat. S. S. Council of Religious Educ., later called The Internat. Council of Religious Educ., which in Nov. 1950 became the Division of Christian Education of the National* Council of Chs. of Christ in the USA. ACM

See also *Protestant Education in the United States; Union Movements,* 13.

International Fellowship of Evangelical Students, The. Fellowship of student movements; grew out of Inter-Varsity Fellowship of Gt. Brit.; organized 1947 at Harvard U., Cambridge, Mass.

International General Assembly of Spiritualists. Organized 1936 at Buffalo, N. Y.; charters spiritualist groups. See also *Spiritualism.*

International Gospel League. Founded 1906 to give material and spiritual aid to people in stricken areas of the world; opposes atheistic communism; headquarters Pasadena, Calif.

International Grenfell Association. Founded 1892 by W. T. Grenfell* (hence known as The Grenfell Miss.) to give med. and soc. aid; headquarters St. Anthony, Newfoundland, Can.

International Hebrew Christian Alliance. Organized 1925 at London, Eng., to provide aid to Jews.

International Humanist and Ethical Union. See *Ethical Culture.*

International Jews Society. See *International Society for the Evangelization of the Jews.*

International Lutheran Hour. See *Radio and Television Evangelism, Network,* 6.

International Medical Missionary Society. Organized 1881 in NYC; objects included support of med. students sent to miss. fields by other miss. agencies.

International Missionary Alliance. See *Evangelistic Associations,* 5.

International Missionary Council. Formed Oct. 1921 at Lake Mohonk, N. Y., integrated 1961 at New Delhi, India, with the World* Council of Chs. and became the WCC Commission on World Mission and Evangelism. Official organ: *International Review of Missions.* See also *Ecumenical Movement, The,* 6.

International Missionary Union. Organized 1884 at Niagara Falls, Ont., Can.; interdenom.; membership composed of ev. for. missionaries.

International Missions, Inc. Founded 1930 as The India Mission; first missionaries sent to Hyderabad, India, 1932. 1966 fields included E. Afr., India, Iran, Philippines. Surinam, E and W Pakistan. The Oriental Boat Miss. (first called South China Boat Mission), which worked in Hong Kong, Japan, and Thailand, merged 1966 with Internat. Missions, Inc.; mem. IFMA; headquarters Wayne, N. J.

International New Thought Alliance. See *New Thought.*

International Order of the King's Daughters and Sons. See *King's Daughters.*

International Pentecostal Assemblies. Successor of Association* of Pent. Assemblies (founded 1921) and National* and Internat. Pent. Missionary Union (founded 1914). See also *Holiness Churches,* 2; *Pentecostalism.*

International Religious Liberty Association. Organized 1888 to work for the religious rights and freedom of all men.

International Society for the Evangelization of the Jews. Founded 1842 in London, Eng., as the Brit. Soc. for the Propagation of the Gospel Among the Jews; became known as Brit. Jews Soc.; name changed in mid-1960s; also known as Internat. Jews Soc.; worked first primarily in Eng. and on the Continent, then also in other countries including Can., Israel, S Afr., Rhodesia, Australia, India, New Zealand, and Tasmania.

International Society of Christian Endeavor. See *Christian Endeavor.*

International Student Service. Founded 1910 under leadership of J. R. Mott* as the Committee on Friendly Relations Among Foreign Students by various chs. and religious socs. to give spiritual aid to for. students; headquarters NYC.

International Sunday School Association, The. See *International Council of Religious Education.*

International Sunday School Convention. See *International Council of Religious Education.*

International Uniform Bible Lessons. See *Sunday School,* 6.

International Workingmen's Association. See *Marx, Karl Heinrich.*

Internuncio. See *Legates.*

Interpretation, Biblical. See *Exegesis; Hermeneutics.*

Interseminary Committee. See *National Council of the Churches of Christ in the United States of America.*

Interstice. In RCm, required interval bet. promotions.

Intersynodical Theses. See *Chicago Theses.*

Intertestamental. Term applied to period bet. the OT and NT. These yrs. witnessed diffusion of Gk. culture through conquests of Alexander III of Macedonia (356–323 BC; "the Great"; succeeded his father, Philip II of Macedon, 336) and his successors, and conflict of Gk. (Hellenistic) and Jewish cultures. The life and thought of Jewish people, changed significantly (see *Judaism,* 2), formed the background for much of the NT. See also *Apocrypha.*

D. S. Russell, *Between the Testaments* (Philadelphia, 1960), *The Method and Message of Jewish Apocalyptic* (London, 1964), and *The Jews from Alexander to Herod* (London, 1967); N. H. Snaith, *The Jews from Cyrus to Herod* (New York, n. d.); R. H. Pfeiffer, *History of New Testament Times, With an Introduction to the Apocrypha* (New York, 1949). HTM

Inter-Varsity Christian Fellowship. See *Students, Spiritual Care of,* A 5.

Intinction. Dipping bread of the Lord's Supper into the wine prior to distribution. An early instance is noted in Eusebius* of Caesarea, *HE,* VI xliii. The practice often includes use of a spoon. It is common in the E Ch. and observed in some parts of the W Ch.

Intonation. In chanting, the *incipit* (Lat. "it begins"), i. e., notes leading to reciting tone, and act of intoning after such an introduction, indicating proper pitch.

Introduction, Biblical. See *Isagogics.*

Introit (from Lat. *introitus,* "entrance"). The initial proper* of the Common Service (see *Liturgics*); marks the entrance of clergy into the sanctuary in the beginning of the service and expresses the thought of the day. Texts are usually from OT. The introit consists of antiphon, Ps, and Gloria Patri (addition of the latter assures a NT element). It is traditionally sung in plainsong settings. Hist. of the introit goes back at least to the 1st half of the 6th c. Several Sundays of the ch. yr. are named after the 1st word of the Lat. text of the introit for the day (see also *Church Year,* 14).

The Introits for the Church Year, with introd. by W. E. Buszin (St. Louis, 1942).

Intuition of Right and Wrong. See *Conscience.*

Intuitionism. Philos. view that truth is immediate, i. e., self-verifying in character; esp. applied in ethics to the view that right and wrong are known by direct intuition, without consideration of results.

Intuitu fidei (Lat. "in view of faith"). Phrase often used in the Predestinarian* Controversy that burst upon conservative Lutheranism in Am. ca. 1880. The expression had been adopted by Luth. theologians chiefly through influence of A. Hunnius.* In opposing the Calvinistic view that the election of

God is absolute, Hunnius and others taught that divine election is not absolute, but that God chose people for eternal life "in view of faith." The term may have the meaning that God, in electing people to salvation, included faith in the decree of election, resolving to lead men to heaven through faith. But it came to mean that God chose certain people for salvation because of the faith which He foresaw they would have; in this view, faith is a cause of election, the factor which "explains" the mystery of predestination*; this contradicts complete and free grace. The term fell into disuse in the Mo. Synod as a result of the Predestinarian Controversy. There is no Scripture warrant for it, and though the phrase is capable of correct interpretation, it can be seriously misunderstood. The Chicago* Theses, in the 1928 revision, opposed use of the term, as did the 1938 Declaration of the Representatives of the Am. Luth. Church (see *American Lutheran Church,* V). The *Brief* Statement of the Doctrinal Position of the Missouri Synod,* par. 36: "Nor does Holy Scripture know of an election 'by foreseen faith,' 'in view of faith,' as though the faith of the elect were to be placed before their election; but according to Scripture the faith which the elect have in time belongs to the spiritual blessings with which God has endowed them by His eternal election." WA

F. Pieper, *Die Grunddifferenz in der Lehre von der Bekehrung und Gnadenwahl* (St. Louis, 1903); T. C. Graebner, "The Missouri Synod's Attitude Towards the Doctrine of Election 'Intuitu Fidei,'" *CTM,* XV (Sept. 1944), 616–621.

Inuit. See *Eskimos.*

Invention of the Cross, The. Acc. to legend (e. g., Ambrose* in *Oratio de obitu Theodosii*), Helena,* mother of Constantine* I, discovered the 3 crosses of Golgotha, with the cross* of Christ identified by miracle. Cyril* of Jerusalem says the cross was found in the days of Constantine I. *MPG,* 33, 1167.

Investigative Judgment. See *Adventist Bodies,* 4.

Investiture, Struggle About. Investiture is the conferring of symbols of office. The rite of investiture applied to abbots and bps. provoked a controversy in the Middle Ages bet. the papacy and various secular rulers. Before the fall of the Roman Empire, imperial influence prevailed. No important office was filled without direct sanction of the emp., often not without nomination by him. When papal power increased, traditions respecting emps. were often set aside. The struggle was esp. severe in Germany. The matter was formally adjusted in a compromise, the Concordat of Worms. See also *Concordat,* 2; *Eigenkirche; Popes,* 7; *Simony; Western Christianity 500–1500,* 5.

Invincibilis, Doctor. See *Ockham, William of.*

Invisible Church. See *Church,* 3.

Invitatory. Exhortation "Oh, come, let us worship the Lord, for He is our Maker" (cf. Ps 95:6) chanted responsively in the Matin* service immediately before the Venite.*

Invocation. (1) Prayer at opening of service or special occasion, usually imploring divine presence. (2) "In the name of the Father and of the Son and of the Holy Ghost" spoken at opening of service or special occasion.

Invocavit. See *Church Year,* 14, 16.

Inward Works of God. See *Father, God the.*

Iona. Small is. of Inner Hebrides, off W coast of Scot.; *area:* ca. 6 sq. mi.; noted for monastery founded by Columba (see *Celtic Church,* 7) ca. 563. See also *Lindisfarne.*

Iowa and Other States, Evangelical Lutheran Synod of. 1. Organized Aug. 24, 1854, at St. Sebald (named after the patron saint of Nürnberg, Ger.), near Strawberry Point, Clayton Co., Iowa, ca. 45 mi WNW of Dubuque, by G. M. Grossmann,* J. Deindörfer,* C. S. Fritschel,* and Michael Schüller (ordained at the meeting). Grossmann was made pres., Fritschel secy. There was no formal constitution till 1864, when the name "Die deutsche ev. luth. Synode von Iowa" was used. At the request of J. A. A. Grabau,* who visited Dubuque 1855, the syn. took charge of Buffalo* Syn. congs. in Wisconsin. Iowa Syn. pastors went to serve Buffalo Syn. congs. in Detroit, Mich., and Toledo, Ohio, and joined the Buffalo Syn. Beginning 1858, doctrinal tensions developed bet. the Iowa and Buffalo Syns., esp. regarding chiliasm (see *Millennialism*).

2. The Iowa Syn. was in a strategic position to meet the spiritual needs of Luth. immigrants who poured into the NW in 2d half of 19th c. Its home missionaries were scattered bet. the Alleghenies and the Pacific Coast. It also attempted several missions to Indians in the NW. The larger part of the Tex. Syn. (see *United Lutheran Church, Synods of,* 28) joined the Iowa Syn. 1896 as a district. See also *Lutheran Foreign Mission Societies in the United States, Early,* 5.

3. Wartburg Sem., founded 1853 as a teachers sem. at Dubuque, moved 1857 to St. Sebald, 1874 to Mendota, Ill., 1889 back to Dubuque. A normal school opened 1878 at Andrew, Iowa, moved 1879 to Waverly, combined 1885 at Waverly with the coll. that had opened 1854, connected with the theol. sem. at Dubuque and St. Sebald, was separately est. 1868 at Galena, Ill., and had been maintained since 1875 in connection with the sem. at Mendota. The coll. moved 1894 to Clinton, Iowa, and combined 1935 with jr. colls. of the former Ohio and Iowa Syns. to form Wartburg Coll., Waverly. The Iowa Syn. operated Wartburg Pub. House, Chicago, Ill. (later absorbed by Wartburg Press, Columbus, Ohio, which in turn was absorbed by Augsburg Pub. House, Minneapolis, Minn.). Publications included *Kirchen-Blatt* and *Kirchliche Zeitschrift.*

4. Leading men of the Iowa Syn. included the Fritschels,* G. M. Grossmann,* J. A. Deindörfer,* F. Richter,* and J. M. Reu.*

5. By 1930 the Iowa Syn. had 654 pastors, 934 congs., 216,000 mems.

6. During its entire hist. the Iowa Syn. was involved in controversy with the Mo. Syn. See *Lutheran Church – Missouri Synod, The,* V 12; *Sunday; Walther, Carl Ferdinand Wilhelm,* 5.

7. When intersyn. confs. 1903–07 failed to solve differences on predestination and conversion, the Iowa Syn. suggested gen. and open confs. for discussion of points at issue. See also *Chicago Theses* (Intersynodical Theses; Theses for Union).

8. After disruption of the Gen. Syn. 1866 (see *General Synod of the Evangelical Lutheran Church in the United States of America, The,* 4), the Iowa Syn. took part in meetings that led to founding of the General* Council of the Ev. Luth. Ch. in (N) Am., approved that body's doctrinal basis, but did not join because it regarded the Gen. Council's answer on the Four* Points unsatisfactory. Iowa maintained friendly relations with the Council and was represented in an advisory capacity at its meetings. See also *Klindworth, John; Schieferdecker, Georg Albert.*

9. A private conf. was arranged 1883 bet. leaders of the Iowa Syn. and those of the Ev. Luth. Syn. of Ohio* and Adjacent States. The Ohio Syn. initiated action 1886 for discussion with the Iowa Syn. on an official level. Resultant theses drawn up 1893 by representatives of both syns. in Michigan City, Ind., proved inconclusive. The Toledo* Theses were drawn up by representatives of both syns. 1907, adopted by the Iowa Syn. 1907, by the Ohio Syn. 1914. The Iowa Syn. helped organize the National*

Lutheran Council 1918, the American* Lutheran Church 1930.

See also *Davenport Theses; Madison Theses; Michigan City Theses.*

J. Deindörfer, *Geschichte der Evangel.-Luth. Synode von Iowa und anderen Staaten* (Chicago, 1897); G. J. Fritschel, *Quellen und Dokumente zur Geschichte und Lehrstellung der ev.-luth. Synode von Iowa u. a. Staaten* (Chicago, n.d.) and *Aus den Tagen der Väter* (Chicago, 1930); G. J. Zeilinger, *A Missionary Synod with a Mission: A Memoir for the Seventy-fifth Anniversary of the Evangelical Lutheran Synod of Iowa and Other States* (Chicago, 1929); S. Fritschel, "The German Iowa Synod," *Lutheran Church in the United States,* 4th ed., rev. and enlarged (Philadelphia, 1914), pp. 69–92; F. W. Meuser, *The Formation of the American Lutheran Church* (Columbus, Ohio, 1958).

Iowa, Evangelical Lutheran Synod of (Iowa Syn.). See *United Lutheran Church, Synods of,* 9.

Iran. See *Middle East,* I.

Iraq. See *Middle East,* H.

Irbe, Karlis (1861–1934). B. Lielsatini, Kurland (Courland; later in Latvia); educ. Dorpat (Tartu); pastor Moscow 1887, Livonia 1888–1905; dir. Lettish Gymnasium in Riga 1905–15; pres. Lettish Ev. Luth. consistory in Russ. 1917–20; bp. 1922–31; organized ch. in Latvia.*

Ireland (Erin; Emerald Isle; Lat.: Hibernia). 1. One of the Brit. Isles; W of Eng. and Wales; includes Eire (Ireland; Irish Free State; Republic of Ireland) and Northern* Ireland. *Area:* Eire ca. 27,140 sq. mi.; N Ireland ca. 5,460 sq. mi. *Pop:* Eire ca. 2,975,000; N Ireland ca. 1,525,000.

2. For the early hist. of Christianity in Ireland see *Celtic Church; Palladius* (5th c.); *Patrick.*

3. The RC date of Easter was gen. adopted in Ireland by the end of the 7th c. Adrian IV (see *Popes,* 8) "gave" Ireland to Henry* II of Eng. ca. 1155, provided he secure the rights of the ch. and render tribute to Rome. Henry invaded Ireland and was acknowledged sovereign 1171. By 1172 the Romanization of the Irish Ch. in internal affairs was complete.

4. In the Reformation period the Eng. govt. tried to enforce a form of Protestantism (see *Henry VIII*). But the loyalty of many to Rome made it impossible to secure dominance of state over ch. The Irish Articles (1615; see *Anglican Confessions,* 8) yielded ca. 1635 to the Thirty-nine Articles (see *Anglican Confessions,* 6), which were less Calvinistic. The 1829 Catholic Emancipation Act restored civil rights to RCs. See also *England.*

The est. Irish Episc. Ch. was dissolved 1869, effective 1871.

5. The 1920 Government of Ireland Act offered Home Rule to all Ireland. S Ireland refused and, after the 1919–21 Anglo-Irish War, became the Irish Free State (Gaelic: Saorstat Eireann; called Eire beginning 1937), a dominion of the Brit. Empire, effective 1922; declared complete independence 1948; officially proclaimed the Republic of Ireland 1949.

6. See *Northern Ireland.*

7. The 1st Luth. service in Ireland was probably that conducted ca. 1690 by Iver Didericksen Brink (b. 1665 Norway; pastor London, Eng., 1691–1702), chaplain of a Dan. regiment supporting William III (Dutch: Willem; 1650–1702; count of Nassau [prince of Orange]; stadtholder of Holland 1672–1702; king of Eng. 1689–1702) against James II (1633–1701; of the house of Stuart; king of Eng., Scot., and Ireland 1685–88; father-in-law of William III) A Luth. ch. was est. at Dublin ca. 1697, with services in Scand. languages and Ger.; this ch. lost its Luth. character and vanished ca. 1850. After WW II many Luths. came to Ireland; the LWF est. a ch. at Dublin (pastor installed 1955).

J. Lanigan, *An Ecclesiastical History of Ireland,* 4 vols. (Dublin, 1822); G. T. Stokes, *Ireland and the Anglo-Norman Church,* 2d ed. (London, 1892); *History of the Church of Ireland,* ed. W. A. Phillips, 3 vols. (London, 1933–34); F. R. Webber, *A History of Preaching in Britain and America,* 3 vols. (Milwaukee, Wis., 1952–57).

Ireland, John (1838–1918). Am. RC prelate; b. Burnchurch, Co. Kilkenny, Ireland; to Am. in the late 1840s; to St. Paul, Minn., in the early 1850s; educ. France; ordained St. Paul 1861; abp. St. Paul 1888; opposed Cahenslyism.*

Irenaeus (Gk. "the Peaceful"; d. ca. 200 AD). Gk. ch. father; b. probably Smyrna (modern Izmir), Asia Minor; saw and heard Polycarp*; presbyter Lyons, Gaul, 177; succeeded Pothinus* as bp. Lyons 178; opposed gnosticism and other heresies; worked zealously for the spread of Christianity and defense of its doctrines; developed a concept of recapitulation*; emphasized apostolic succession and tradition. Works include *Detection and Overthrow of the False Gnosis* (also known as *Adversus haereses*); *Demonstration of the Apostolic Teaching.* See also *Tradition.*

F. R. M. Hitchcock, *Irenaeus of Lugdunum* (Cambridge, Eng., 1914); J. Lawson, *The Biblical Theology of Saint Irenaeus* (London, 1948); G. Aulén, *Christus Victor,* tr. A. G. Hebert (London, 1931), pp. 32–51.

Irenaeus, Christoph (ca. 1522–ca.1595). B. Scheidnitz, Silesia, Ger.; probably studied in Wittenberg; rector Bernburg and Ascherleben 1545; pastor Eisleben 1562; court preacher Koburg and Weimar; supported M. Flacius* Illyricus and opposed J. Andreä.*

Irenics (irenic theol.). Theol. which tries to arrive at Christian peace. Irenics presupposes polemics,* which in its true character should have no other aim than irenics. The "bond of peace," Eph 4:3, embraces all Christians, and "speaking the truth in love," Eph 4:15, deserves to be emphasized at all times. But he who truly seeks ecclesiastical peace well-pleasing to God will find himself compelled to engage in controversy. True irenics does not exclude polemics, but is another way of gaining the same end. The danger of polemics lies in the direction of separatism and magnification of unessential differences; irenic efforts are prone to degenerate into syncretism and unionism; love of revealed truth guards against both dangers.

Irenicus, Franciscus (Friedlieb; 1495–1559 [or 1565?]; educ. Tübingen; won for Reformation by Heidelberg* Disputation 1518; court preacher of Philipp I (1479–1533) of Baden-Baden; present at 1526 Diet of Speyer*; pastor and leader Lat. School at Gemmingen 1531.

Irish Articles. See *Anglican Confessions,* 8.

Irish Free State. See *Ireland,* 1 and 3.

Iro-Pictish Church. See *Celtic Church,* 12.

Iron Age. See *Time.*

Irons, William Josiah (1812–83). B. Hoddesdon, Hertfordshire, Eng.; educ. Oxford; Angl. cleric; lecturer; hymnist. Tr. "Dies* irae" into "Day of Wrath, O Day of Mourning."

Iroquois. See *Indians, American,* 9; *Primitive Religion.*

Irresistible Grace. See *Common Grace.*

Irving, Edward (1792–1834). B. Annan, Dumfriesshire, Scot.; educ. Edinburgh; asst. to T. Chalmers*; pastor Hatton Garden Caledonian Chapel, London, 1822, and of a new ch. in Regent Square, London, 1829; charged with heresy in doctrine of Trin.; accepted Pentecostal phenomena, esp. speaking in tongues; charged with heresy regarding sinlessness of

Christ; deposed from ranks of clergy 1833 by presbytery of Annan. Followers, known as Irvingites, formed the Catholic* Apostolic Ch. (sometimes called Holy Catholic Apostolic Ch.).

Irvingites. See *Irving, Edward.*

Isaac Nathan ben Kalonymus. See *Nathan ben Kalonymus, Isaac.*

Isaac of Antioch (d. ca. 460 AD). Syrian theol., author, poet.

Isaak, Heinrich (variants of name include Henricus; Isaac; Isac; Izac; Yzac; Yzaac; Yzach; ca. 1450–1517). B. perhaps Brabant or E Flanders; contrapuntist composer; pioneered in giving melody to soprano; organist at court of Lorenzo the Magnificent (see *Medici*) and Maximilian* I. Composed sacred and secular music. See also *Senfl, Ludwig.*

Isaak, Stephan (1542–97). Polemical preacher; b. Wetzlar, Ger.; bap. Luth. 1546; became RC 1548, Ref. 1584.

Isaak Levita, Johannes (Jochanan Isaak ha-Levi Germanus; Johann Isaac Levi; 1515–77). Jewish scholar; b. Wetzlar, Ger.; rabbi; converted to Christianity 1546; RC 1547; prof. Heb. at Cologne 1551.

Isabella I. See *Inquisition,* 6.

Isagogics (from Gk. *eisagoge,* "introduction"). 1. Introductory studies. Applied to the Bible and its individual books (Biblical introduction), it deals, e. g., with authorship, time and place of composition, people addressed, occasion and purpose, chief parts, and attacks on genuineness (authenticity); it treats of the assembling of the books into 1 collection and recognition of the latter as the canon of inspired Scripture (see *Canon, Bible*). The hist. of the sacred books to our time is included. Because the books of the Bible were composed in antiquity, because they were written in languages for. to us, and because conditions under which the first readers lived were different from ours, an introd. to the various books is desirable for the ordinary reader. The Bible is a clear book; but one better understands Gl, e. g., if he learns that it was written by Paul to oppose the false notion that the old Jewish Ceremonial Law is still binding for the children of God in the NT. See also *Antilegomena; Theology.*

2. Eusebius* of Caesarea, Jerome,* and M. Luther* devoted much attention to isagogics. It began to flourish unprecedentedly in the 18th c. See also *Higher Criticism; Semler, Johann Salomo.*

3. Negative NT criticism reached a high in the Tübingen* school, followed by a more moderate school of liberal theol. (see also *Harnack, Karl Gustav Adolf von; Jülicher, Gustav Adolf*). The school of form criticism *(formgeschichtliche Schule),* which includes Charles Harold Dodd (b. 1884 Wrexham, N Wales; Cong.; taught at Oxford, Manchester, and Cambridge, Eng.), Joachim Jeremias (b. 1900 Dresden, Ger.; prof. Berlin, Greifswald, and Göttingen), and Charles Francis Digby Moule (b. 1908; prof. Cambridge, Eng.), arose after WW I; it tries to determine the nature of the original documents which, so it is held, existed before composition of the gospels in Gk. as we have them. Eng. introductions that incline in this direction include those of B. W. Bacon,* J. Moffatt,* and E. J. Goodspeed.* Conservative views accepting the genuineness of NT books have been defended esp. by G. Salmon,* T. Zahn,* and J. H. Snowden.* See also *Schmidt, Karl Ludwig.* WA

T. Zahn, *Einleitung in das Neue Testament,* 2 vols., 3d ed. (Leipzig, 1906–07), Eng. tr. *Introduction to the New Testament,* by J. M. Trout et al., 3 vols. (Edinburgh, Scot., 1909); G. Salmon, *An Historical Introduction to the Study of the Books of the New Testament,* 10th ed., new impression (London, 1913); E. J. Goodspeed, *An Introduction to the New Testament* (Chicago, 1937).

Ishtar. See *Babylonians, Religion of the,* 1.

Isidore of Kiev (ca. 1385–1464). B. Monemvasia, Greece; humanist; metropolitan of Kiev and all Russia 1436; cardinal 1439; attended Council of Florence*; favored union of E and W chs.; invested with the temporalities of the Lat. patriarchate of Constantinople 1452; Gk. patriarch 1459.

Isidore of Pelusium (fl. 1st half of 5th c. AD). Ascetic; exegete; abbot of monastery near Pelusium, NW Sinai, on the Nile; followed J. Chrysostom*; opposed Nestorius* and Eutyches.*

MPG, 78.

Isidore of Seville (ca. 560–636). Brother of Leander.* Abp. Seville, Sp., ca. 600; encyclopedist. Works include *Etymologiae; Sententiae.* See also *Pseudo-Isidorian Decretals.*

Isidorus. See *Gnosticism,* 7 e.

Isis. Moon goddess of the Egyptians. See also *Greek Religions,* 3 b.

Islam (Arab. "submission"). 1. Islam (Muhammadanism; Mohammedanism) is the only major religion est. after Christianity, to which it claims to be superior. It began in Arabia (see *Middle East,* L), under leadership of Muhammad.* It emphasizes submission to God (Allah). One who submits to God is said to be a Muslim (Moslem). The short creed of Islam is the *shahadah:* "There is no deity (god) but God, and Muhammad is his apostle." It is perhaps best to regard the word "Allah" not as the Arab. *name* of God but as the *word* for "God." Muslims object to being called Muhammadans; to them, Muhammad is the finest example of manhood, but only a man.

2. The sacred book of Islam is the Koran,* regarded as God's "uncreated Speech" revealed to man through Muhammad. The basic guide to Muslim daily life is the Koran. Where it is silent, the accepted tradition called *sunna* is used. Where this is silent, the custom *(adat)* of an Islamic community provides the answer.

3. Main tenets of Islam concern God, Holy Scriptures, angels, prophets, resurrection and final judgment, and predestination, with decisive differences from Christian doctrine. The "five pillars" of Islamic religious practice (required at least once in a lifetime, if possible): *shahadah;* 5 daily prescribed prayers *(salat);* annual month of fasting *(Ramadan*);* pilgrimage to sacred places in and near Mecca *(hajj);* giving alms to poor (legal, *zakat;* voluntary, *sadakat*).

4. Islam recognizes 6 great prophets: Adam, Noah, Abraham, Moses, Jesus, and Muhammad. Muhammad is said to have thought he would be accepted by Christians and Jews in Arab. because they were also "people of the book." When he failed to win them, he directed his hostility first against Jews, later against Christians. Within 100 yrs. after Muhammad's death, Islam spread over Christian areas in N Afr., Spain,* and Fr. (see *France,* 1) to claim half of the former Roman Empire. Islam later spread toward the E to India,* Malaya, Indonesia* and was halted in the Philippine* Islands by the Span. In the 15th c. Islam entered Eur. under leadership of Ottoman Turks, who threatened the Holy* Roman Empire at the time of the Luth. Reformation* (see also *Holy Leagues and Alliances,* 1).

5. The largest of many Muslim sects include Sunnites* and Shi'ites.* Others include Wahhabis* (18th-c. reform group founded by Muhammad ibn-Abdul Wahhab; revived in the 20th c. by Ibn Sa'ud); Kharijites (Khawarij; from Arab. khariji, "dissenter"; radically puritanical and democratic), and the Ahmadiya miss. movement founded ca. 1879 by Mirza Ghulam Ahmad and centered in W Pakistan. Despite differences, there is an under-

lying unity and brotherhood in these sects. Black Muslims (see *Lost-Found Nation of Islam in the Wilderness of North America, The*) in the US began as a radical Negro group, not as part of worldwide Islam.

6. Muslim pop. (1968 est.): ca. 493,000,000 (ca. 13,848,000 in Eur., ca. 374,167,000 in Asia, ca. 104,297,000 in Africa,* ca. 118,000 in Oceania, ca. 416,000 in S Am., ca. 166,000 in N Am.).

See also *Arabic Philosophy; Asia,* B 2; *Crusades; Indonesia; Kaaba; Middle East,* A 3.

H. A. R. Gibb, *Mohammendanism: An Historical Survey* (New York, 1949); *A Reader on Islam,* ed. A. Jeffery (The Hague, Neth., 1962); P. S. R. Payne, *The Holy Sword* (New York, 1959). RDM

Isle of Pines. See *Caribbean Islands,* E 1.

Isleifsson, Gissur. See *Iceland,* 2.

Ismailis. See *Shi'ites.*

Israel. See *Middle East,* F.

Israel, Conversion of. See *Dispensationalism; Jews, Conversion of; Millennium,* 7 and 8.

Israel ben Eliezer. See *Baal Shem-Tob.*

Israelite House of David. See *House of David.*

Istrian. See *Consul, Stipan.*

Itala. See *Bible Version,* J 1.

Italian Christian Churches of North America. See *Christian Church of North America, General Council.*

Italian Pentecostal Assemblies of God, General Council of the. See *Christian Church of North America, General Council.*

Italy, Religious History of, Before the Reformation. Christianity reached Italy at an early date. The ch. at Rome was widely known ca. 57 (Ro 1:8); in 64 the Christians in Rome were a "vast multitude" (Tacitus, *Annales,* XV, 44). At the time of Constantine* I Christianity had taken firm root; paganism was losing its hold. During this 1st stage the religious hist. of It. did not differ essentially from that of the Roman Empire in gen., though the commanding position and influence of the ch. at Rome and the beginnings of the papacy lend it a somewhat distinctive character and indicate its subsequent trend.

From the time that Constantine I transferred the seat of empire to Byzantium and esp. after barbarian invasions, the religious his. of It. became virtually the hist. of the papacy. The papacy alone gives a semblance of unity to the story of It. during the Middle Ages. Arian (see *Arianism*) Teutonic invaders gen. did not try to force their creed on their new subjects. Odoacer (Odovacar; Odovakar; ca. 434–493; ruled It. 476–493) and Theodoric* were tolerant. The Lombards entered It. 568, est. a kingdom, combined martial despotism with religious intolerance, eventually adopted the religion of Rome and succumbed to the diplomacy of the popes and the weapons of the Frankish allies of the papacy (see also *Charlemagne*). From Otto* I to the time of Gregory VII (see *Popes,* 7), the emps. gen. had the upper hand. From Gregory VII to the overthrow and end of the Hohenstaufens 1268 the popes asserted supremacy. From ca. the beginning of the 14th c. the papacy began to decline. Its dependence on Fr. kings during the "Babylonian* captivity" 1309–77, the papal schism 1378–1418 (see *Schism,* 8), and authority assumed by councils (see *Councils and Synods,* 7) show papal power on the wane.

I-Thou. Term used in philos. to emphasize value of personal being as developed by M. Buber,* F. Ebner,* W. E. Hocking,* et al. See also *Corporate Personality.*

Itinerancy. A characteristic feature of Methodism (see *Methodist Churches*) acc. to which pastorates are limited in time. Itinerancy was est. in Eng. to help meet the need of pastoral service in districts where pastoral supply was limited. Itinerancy was also adopted in Am., with variations in the length of pastorates.

Itinerarium. Travel prayer in breviary*; may have originated in blessing pilgrims leaving for Palestine.

Iu-. See also *Ju-.*

Ius antiquam. See *Canon Law,* 3.

Ius divinum (Lat. "divine right"). God's right and authority over man; His principles, laws, or orders for man. *Iure divino* (or *iuris divini*) means by (or of) divine law or arrangement, hence unalterable; *iure humano* (or *iuris humani;* from *ius* humanum, "human right") means by (or of) human arrangement, hence alterable. Cf. AC XXVIII 19, 21, 22, 29, 63.

Ius gentium. Laws governing aliens subject to Rome and international intercourse bet. Roman citizens and aliens. Sometimes a synonym for natural* law.

Ius naturae. See *Natural Law.*

Ius naturale. See *Natural Law.*

Ius novissimum. See *Canon Law,* 3.

Ius novum. See *Canon Law,* 3.

Iustitia aliena (Lat. "for. righteousness"). Term used to refer not to our righteousness but that of another, Christ.

Iustitia inchoata. See *Image of God,* 4.

Iustitia originalis (Lat. "original righteousness"). Righteousness of Adam and Eve before the fall* of man.

Ivo (Yvo Carnotensis [i. e., of Chartres]; ca. 1040–1116). B. Beauvais, Fr.; educ. Paris and Bec*; bp. Chartres 1090; canonist. Works include *Collectio tripartita; Decretum; Panormia.*

MPL, 161; 162, 9–616.

Ivory Coast. See *Africa,* C 9.

J

"J." In Biblical criticism, the letter "J" is the symbol for one of the alleged sources of the Pentateuch. See also *Higher Criticism,* 6–13.

Jäbker, Gerhard Heinrich (Nov. 13, 1821–June 20, 1877). B. Wimmern, Hannover, Ger.; to Am. ca. 1841; taught school at Friedheim, near Decatur, Ind., 1841; prepared for ministry by F. C. D. Wyneken* and W. Sihler*; pastor Friedheim 1846–77; charter mem. Mo. Syn.

Jablonski. (1) *Peter Figulus* (took the name Jablonski from the city of his birth; 1618–70). Father of 2; b. Jablunkov, Silesia; pastor Danzig 1654, Nassenhuben (near Danzig) 1657; joined Bohemian* Brethren 1659; pastor Memel 1667. (2) *Daniel Ernst* (resumed name Figulus 1688; 1660–1741). Son of 1; b. Nassenhuben; educ. Frankfurt an der Oder and Oxford; Ref. preacher Magdeburg 1683; pastor Polish cong. and rector of Gymnasium at Lissa (Leazno), Poland, 1686; court preacher Königsberg 1691, Berlin 1693, bp. 1699; tried to est. Luth. and Ref. union; ordained D. Nitschmann* and N. L. v. Zinzendorf.*

Jackson, Samuel Macauley (1851–1912). B. NYC; educ. Princeton (N. J.) Theol. Sem., Union Theol. Sem. (NYC), and Berlin; Presb. pastor Norwood, N. J., 1876–80; prof. ch. hist. NYU 1895–1912. Ed. many reference works; ed. in chief *The New Schaff-Herzog Encyclopedia of Religious Knowledge.*

Jackson, Sheldon (May 18, 1834–1909). B. Minaville, N. Y.; educ. Union Coll., Schenectady, N. Y., and Princeton (N. J.) Theol. Sem.; miss. to Choctaw Indians 1858, to Indians and Anglo-Americans in Wis. and Minn. 1859–69; miss. supt. Iowa, Nebr., and Rocky Mountain areas 1869–70, Colo., Wyo., Ariz., N. Mex., Mont., and Utah 1870–82, Alaska 1877–1907. Ed. *Presbyterian Home Missionary* 1882–84; other works include *Alaska and Missions on the North Pacific Coast.*

Jackson, Thomas (1579–1640). B. Willowing, Durham, Eng.; educ. Oxford; Angl. dean Peterborough ca. 1639; first inclined to Puritanism (see *Puritans*), later to High* Ch. Works include *Commentaries Upon the Apostles' Creed.*

Jacob Baradaeus (from Syrian for "ragged," because he usually wore ragged clothes; ca. 500–578). B. Tella, near Edessa (Urfa), Turkey in Asia; educ. in monastery as Phesilta, near Nisibis (Nusaybin); bp. Edessa ca. 542; championed Monophysitism; reputed founder of Jacobites. Influenced the Ethiopic* Ch. See also *Jacobites,* 1.

Jacob ben Asher (ca. 1269–ca. 1343). Jewish scholar; b. Ger.; lived in Sp.; outstanding systematician of Talmud. Works include *Arba Turim.*

Jacob of Edessa (James; ca. 640–708). B. En-debha (Indeba; Indaba), province of Antioch; Monophysite bp. Edessa perhaps ca. 684; after a few yrs. withdrew to monasteries; returned to bishopric of Edessa 708; Gk. and Heb. scholar. Works include Syriac grammar; scholia on the Bible.

Jacob of Jüterbog (1381–1465). B. near Jüterbog, Brandenburg, Ger.; RC reformer; at first Cistercian; Carthusian 1443; held that infallible presence of the Holy Spirit is promised to the ch., not to the pope.

Jacob of Nisibis (James; Jacob of Mygdonia; Jacob the Great; d. 338). Bp. Nisibis, SE Turkey in Asia; attended 325 Council of Nicaea*; championed orthodoxy; teacher of Ephraem.*

Jacob of Sarug (Serugh; 451–521). B. Kurtam, on the Euphrates; Syriac ecclesiastical writer; Monophysitic bp. Batnae (Batnan), in Sarug, Mesopotamia, 519. Wrote metrical homilies and hymns.

Jacob of Vitry. See *Jacques de Vitry.*

Jacob of Voragine (James; Jacobus de Varagine; ca. 1230–ca. 1298). B. Varazze (Viraggio), near Genoa, It.; Dominican; abp. Genoa 1292. Works include a chronicle of Genoa; the *Golden* Legend.*

Jacobi, Friedrich Heinrich (1743–1819). B. Düsseldorf, Ger.; opposed subjective idealism* of I. Kant* and dogmatic rationalism of B. Spinoza*; held that truth is known through faith, i. e. through revelation in consciousness.

Jacobi, John Christian (1670 [1679?]–1750). B. Thuringia, Ger.; keeper of Royal Ger. Chapel, St. James's Palace, London, Eng. Works include *Psalmodia germanica.*

Jacobins. Name given Dominicans* because James (Jacobus) was patron of their 1st house in Paris.

Jacobites. 1. Mems. of chs. which resulted from activities of Jacob* Baradaeus. See also *Monophysite Controversy; Nonchalcedonian Churches.* 2. Adherents of a movement to restore the Stuart dynasty following the flight of James II (Jacobus; 1633–1701; king of Eng., Scot., and Ireland 1685–88) after the revolution of 1688. See also *England,* C 1.

Jacobs, Aletta. See *Family Planning,* 3.

Jacobs, Charles Michael (Dec. 5, 1875–Mar. 30, 1938). Son of H. E. Jacobs*; b. Gettysburg, Pa.; educ. Luth. Theol. Sem., Mt. Airy, Philadelphia, Pa., U. of Pa., and U. of Leipzig; pastor North Wales, Pa., 1899–1904, Allentown, Pa., 1904–13; prof. ch. hist. Luth. Theol. Sem., Mt. Airy, 1913–38. Coed. 6-vol. *Works of Martin Luther;* mem. bd. of eds. *Lutheran Church Quarterly;* other works include *The Way; The Story of the Church; Helps on the Road; The Faith of the Church; What Then Is Christianity?*

Jacobs, David (1805–Nov. 30, 1830). Brother of M. Jacobs*; 1st teacher in Classical School (est. 1827; connected with Gettysburg [Pa.] Sem.), renamed Gettysburg Gymnasium 1829, reorganized 1832 as Pa. Coll., later called Gettysburg* Coll.

Jacobs, Henry Eyster (Nov. 10, 1844–July 7, 1932). Son of M. Jacobs*; father of C. M. Jacobs*; b. Gettysburg, Pa.; educ. Pa. Coll. (see *Gettysburg College*) and Luth. Theol. Sem., Gettysburg. Tutor Pa. Coll.; miss. Pittsburgh, Pa.; principal Thiel Hall (later called Thiel Coll.); pastor W Pa.; prof. Pa. Coll., Gettysburg, and Luth. Theol. Sem., Mount Airy, Philadelphia. Coed. *The Lutheran Cyclopedia;* asst. ed. *Universal Cyclopaedia and Atlas;* ed. *The Lutheran Commentary* and *The Lutheran Church Review;* other works include *The Lutheran Movement in England During the Reigns of Henry VIII. and Edward VI.; The American Church History Series,* IV: *A History of the Evangelical Lutheran Church in the United States; Martin Luther: The Hero the Reformation; A Summary of the Christian Faith; The Doctrine of the Ministry as Taught by the Dogmaticians of the Lutheran Church; Elements of Religion; The Four Hundred and Four Theses of Dr. John Eck.* RDL

Jacobs, Michael (Jan. 18, 1808–July 22, 1871). B. Waynesboro, Pa.; helped brother D. Jacobs* at Gettysburg Gymnasium 1829; prof. math. and natural science Gettysburg 1832. Works include *Notes on the (Rebel) Invasion of Maryland and Pennsylvania, and the Battle of Gettysburg.*

Jacobsen, John Christian. See *Danish Lutherans in America,* 1.

Jacobus de Varagine (Voragine). See *Jacob of Voragine.*

Jacopone da Todi (Jacobus de Benedictis; Jacopo [de] Benedetti; ca. 1230 [1240?]–1306). Hymnist; b. Todi, Umbria, It.; after death of wife in an accident 1268 he withdrew from world; Franciscan lay brother; fearlessly attacked abuses of the ch. Hymns ascribed to him include "Cur mundus militat" and "Stabat mater dolorosa."

Jacques de Vitry (Jacob of Vitry; ca. 1170 [1180?]–ca. 1240). B. probably Vitry near Reims, Fr.; bp. Acre 1216; cardinal bp. Tusculum ca. 1228; elected patriarch Jerusalem ca. 1239 but not instated by pope; active in Crusades.* Works include *Historia orientalis.*

Jadwiga. See *Lithuania,* 1.

Jaenicke. See *Jänicke.*

Jaeschke. See *Jäschke.*

Jagello (Lith.: Jagela). See *Lithuania,* 1.

Jäger, Johannes. See *Crotus Rubianus.*

Jagiello. See *Lithuania,* 1.

Jahiz, al-. See *Arabic Philosophy.*

Jahweh (Yahweh; Jehovah). The Heb. consonants of this name of God are JHWH. Because of its sacredness, this name was usually not pronounced in ancient times; *adonai* (Heb. "Lord") was substituted. Early Gk. versions of the OT use *kyrios* ("Lord") for this name. Many Eng. translations use "the Lord." Masoretes (see *Masorah*) added vowels to the Heb. text. The vowels of *adonai* were added to JHWH, resulting in *JaHoWaH,* "Jehovah."

The name was revealed to Moses, Ex 3. Three consonants of *'eHJeH* (Heb. "I will be," Ex 3:12, where God's saving presence is promised; "I am," Ex 3:14), namely HJH (older root form of the verb: HWH), run parallel to HWH in JHWH (Ex 3:15).

To call on the name of Jahweh (e. g., Jl 2:32) is to call on God Himself. To speak in the name of Jahweh or to bless or curse in His name is to invoke Him and His power. The 2d Commandment forbids taking the name "Jahweh" lightly or in vain. Men should rather use this name in praise (hallelu-jah, Heb. "praise-Jah[weh]") and hallow it (cf. 1st Petition of the Lord's Prayer).

See also *Hallelujah.*

O. Grether, *Name und Wort Gottes im Alten Testament* (Giessen, 1934); J. A. Motyer, *The Revelation of the Divine Name* (London, 1959); A. Murtonen, *A Philological and Literary Treatise on the Old Testament Divine Names* (Helsinki, 1952); E. C. B. MacLaurin, "YHWH: The Origin of the Tetragrammaton," *Vetus Testamentum,* XII (1962), 439–463. JHS

Jahwist (Jahvist). See *Higher Criticism,* 7–13.

Jainism. Religion of India founded 6th c. BC by Nigantha Nataputta, later called Vardhamana Jnatiputra Mahavira (Mahavira means "Great Hero"). His followers also called him Jina ("Conqueror"). Arose in opposition to Brahmanism,* as did Buddhism,* but, unlike the latter, prescribed asceticism* as a means of attaining salvation, i. e., release of the soul from reincarnation.* Regards the universe as eternal. Denies divine authority of the Vedas.* Noteworthy is the Jain doctrine of ahimsa, i. e., of refraining from harming or killing any living thing. Schism created 2 sects: the Svetambara (Skt. "white-clad") and the Digambara (Skt. "sky-clad," nude). Adherents may become mems. of monastic orders or remain laymen. Latter include wealthy tradesmen. Costly and beautiful temples include one at Mount Abu. See also *Theosophy.*

Jajus, Claudius (Jay; Claude le Jay; ca. 1500 [1504?]–1552). B. Mieussy, near Bonneville, Upper Savoy, Fr.; RC priest; studied in Paris; assoc. with I. Loyola*; participated in founding Society* of Jesus; present at Council of Trent* 1545–47. See also *Counter Reformation,* 8.

Jakob. See *Jacob.*

Jamaica. See *Caribbean Islands,* E 5.

James. See also *Jacob.*

James, Liturgy of St. See *Divine Liturgy.*

James I (1566–1625). King of Scot. as James VI 1567–1625, of Gt. Brit. as James I 1603–25; promoted pub. of 1611 rev. of Eng. Bible known as King James Version. See also *Bible Versions,* L 10–11; *Roman Catholic Church,* D 9.

James VI. See *James I.*

James, Henry, Sr. (1811–82). Philos.; father of H. James* Jr. and W. James*; b. Albany, N. Y.; educ. Union Coll. (Albany, N. Y.) and Princeton (N. J.) Theol. Sem.; dissatisfied with what he called "professional religion"; to Eng. 1837; influenced by R. Sandeman (see *Disciples of Christ,* 1) and E. Swedenborg*; held that selfhood is the sin of sins and that religion and morality turn man to God through sociality. Works include *Society the Redeemed Form of Man, and the Earnest of God's Omnipotence in Human Nature; Substance and Shadow.*

James, Henry, Jr. (1843–1916). Novelist; son of H. James* Sr.; born NYC; naturalized Brit. citizen 1915; interested in spiritual and mystic phenomena. Works include *The American; Confidence; A Passionate Pilgrim, and Other Tales; The Portrait of a Lady.*

James, John Angell (1785–1859). B. Blandford, Dorsetshire, Eng.; educ. Gosport academy, Hampshire; qualified as dissenting preacher 1803; pastor Birmingham 1805; helped found Evangelical* Alliance. Works include *The Anxious Enquirer After Salvation Directed and Encouraged.*

James, William (1842–1910). Psychol. and philos.; son of H. James* Sr.; b. NYC; prof. Harvard U., Cambridge, Mass. Works include *The Principles of Psychology; Pragmatism; The Varieties of Religious Experience.* See also *Pragmatism; Psychical Research; Psychology,* H.

James of Edessa. See *Jacob of Edessa.*

James the Elder, St. See *Church Year,* 16.

Jamestown. See *United States, Religious History, of the,* 3.

Jamnia, Synod of (Jabneh; Biblical Jabneel; ca. 4 mi. inland, ca. 13 mi. S of Jaffa). Meeting of rabbis (ca. 100 AD) at which extent of OT canon was probably settled. See also *Canon, Bible,* 2.

Jan van Brugge. See *Joris, David.*

Jan van Ruysbroeck. See *Ruysbroeck, Jan van.*

Janah, ibn-, Abul Walid Merwan. See *Jonah.*

Jane Frances de Chantel. See *Chantel, Jeanne Françoise Fremiot de.*

Jänicke, Johann(es) (Jenjk; 1748–1827). B. Berlin, Ger.; educ. Berlin, Dresden, and Leipzig; pastor Rixdorf and Berlin; in 1800 founded in Berlin a training school, from which ca. 80 missionaries, including K. F. A. Gützlaff* and K. T. E. Rhenius,* were sent out. See also *Berlin Missionary Society I; Schmelen, Johann Heinrich.*

Jánosi, Zoltán (1868–1942). B. Nagyleta, Hung.; educ. Debrecen, Zurich, and Budapest; Ref. pastor; worked for universal suffrage and educ., and for introd. of the principle of Christian brotherhood into economic and soc. structure.

Janow, Matthias von (ca. 1350 [1355?]–1394). B. probably Prague or Brüx (Most), Boh. (now

Czechoslovakia); son of knight Wenzel of Janow; educ. Prague and Paris; precursor of J. Hus*; emphasized apostolic Christianity, frequent Communion, universal priesthood of believers.

Jansen, Cornelis (Cornelius Jansenius; 1585–1638). RC theol.; b. near Leerdam, Neth.; educ. Louvain and Paris; prof. Louvain; bp. Ypres 1636. Works include *Augustinus,* pub. posthumously; it led to Jansenism.*

Jansenism. Reformatory movement in Fr. RCm inaugurated by C. Jansen* and supported by such men as J. Du Vergier* de Hauranne, B. Pascal,* A. Arnauld,* P. Quesnel.*

The movement tried to revive the Augustinian doctrine of sin and grace as a means of counteracting Jesuitism (see *Society of Jesus*) and of quickening spiritual life. Jansen's book *Augustinus* was attacked by Jesuits, condemned 1641 by the Inquisition,* and by Urban VIII (Maffeo Barberini; 1568–1644; b. Florence, It.; pope 1623–44) in the bull *In eminenti* (signed 1642, promulgated 1643). Arnauld's attack on the *opus* operatum* theory and the lax moral theol. of the Jesuits was met 1653 by Innocent X (see *Popes,* 23) with the bull *Cum occasione,* which explicitly condemned 5 propositions which Arnauld said could be favorably understood. When Jansenists protested that the propositions were not taught by Jansen in the sense in which they were condemned, Alexander VII (Fabio Chigi; 1599–1667; b. Siena, It.; pope 1655–67) said they contained the meaning which Jansen intended and condemned them in the bull *Ad sanctam beati Petri sedem* (1656; released in Fr. 1657). He also demanded that Jansenists accept the papal pronouncements of 1642, 1653, and 1656. Refusal of Jansenists to comply led to repressive measures against them by pope and king (see also *Port Royal*). Many fled or were banished. Temporary cessation of the Jausenist conflict was effected ca. 1668.

The 2d stage of Fr. Jansenism began 1693 with pub. of Quesnel's NT with devotional comments, which provoked another outburst of Jesuit wrath and the bull *Unigenitus.** The ensuing quarrel rent the Fr. clergy into Acceptants (who accepted the bull) and Appellants (who appealed from the pope to a gen. council). Appellants were excommunicated 1718. Dutch Jansenists separated from the RC Ch. 1723/24, later joined the Old* Catholics.

See also *Baius, Michael; Ultramontanism.*

N. J. Abercrombie, *The Origins of Jansenism* (Oxford, 1936); A. Gazier, *Histoire générale du mouvement janséniste depuis ses origines jusqu'à nos jours* (Paris, 1922).

Janson, Eric (Erik Jansson). See *Communistic Societies,* 5; *Sweden, Lutheranism in,* 5.

Janssen, Johannes (1829–91). B. Xanten, Ger.; educ. Münster, Ger., Louvain, Belg., and Bonn and Berlin, Ger.; RC prof. hist. Frankfurt am Main; his hist. of Ger. since the Middle Ages strongly influenced RC attitudes toward Reformation; championed ultramontanism.*

Jansson, Erik (Eric Janson). See *Communistic Societies,* 5; *Sweden, Lutheranism in,* 5.

Januarius (Gennaro; fl. 3d c.). Bp. Beneventum, It.; allegedly martyred at Pozzuoli, near Naples, in Diocletian-Maximian persecution (see *Persecution of Christians,* 4); since ca. the 14th c., relics of his blood are said to liquify a number of times a yr.

January Edict. See *France,* 8.

January Edict of Saint-Germain. See *France,* 9.

Janzow, John William Carl (Mar. 7, 1875–July 20, 1949). B. Lewiston, Minn.; educ. Conc. Sem., St. Louis, Mo.; pastor St. Ansgar, Iowa, 1900–06, and Adelaide, Australia, 1906–45; pres. S. Australian Dist. 1913–23; pres. ELCA 1923–41.

Japan. *Area:* ca. 142,725 sq. mi., ca. one-sixth arable. *Pop.* (1973): 107,070,000. Major religions: Buddhism,* Shinto,* and Christianity. Shinto is indigenous and the oldest. Acc. to tradition, Buddhism, now dominant, was introd. AD 552 and Confucianism* about the same time. Jesuits under leadership of F. Xavier* introd. Christianity 1549. By 1600 Christians totaled hundreds of thousands. Suspicion of ultimate designs of proponents of Christianity led to prohibition (in effect till 1873) of the profession and practice of Christianity.

A commercial treaty bet. Japan and the US was signed July 29, 1858. In 1859 Episc., Presb., and Dutch Ref. missionaries reached Japan from the US. Outstanding missionaries of the years that followed include S. R. Brown,* J. H. Neesima,* and G. F. Verbeck.* Their work helped give direction to soc. reform, govt. policies, and educ. Beginning in the early 1930s nationalism combined with Shinto, the state religion, dampened Japanese interest in Christianity, but a new period of Christian miss. began after WW II.

The United* Syn. of the Ev. Luth. Ch. in the S began work on Kyushu 1892. The United Dan. Ev. Luth. Ch. (see *Danish Lutherans in America,* 5) sent its 1st miss. 1898, the Lutheran* Ev. Assoc. of Fin. 1900, the General* Council of the Ev. Luth. Ch. in N Am. 1908, the Icelandic Syn. (see *Canada,* A 13; *United Lutheran Church, Synods of,* 6) 1916 (worked in connection with the for. miss. bd. of the Gen. Council of the Ev. Luth. Ch. in N Am.). Luth. missionaries in Jap. formed The Japan Ev. Luth. Ch. 1920. Largely as a result of govt. pressure in the early 1940s, this ch. joined the Nihon [or Nippon] Kirisuto Kyodan ("Ch. of Christ in Jap."), a union of Prot. denominations; withdrew 1947. See also *United Lutheran Church, The,* III. The LCMS began work in Jap. 1948; the resultant Missionary Conf. was absorbed into the Japan Luth. Ch. (organized 1968), which was accepted 1971 as a sister ch. of LCMS. The Evangelical* Luth. Ch., the Church* of the Luth. Brethren of Am., the Norw. Luth. Miss. and The Norw. Miss. Soc. (the last 2 Norway-based) began work 1949; the Augustana* Ev. Luth. Ch., the Suomi Syn. (see *Finnish Lutherans in America*), and the Norwegian* Luth. Free Ch. 1950; the Lutheran* Free Ch. 1951; the Wisconsin* Ev. Luth. Syn. in the early 1950s.

The Japan* Ev. Luth. Ch. and the Tokai* Ev. Luth. Ch. were united May 3, 1963, to form a new Japan Ev. Luth. Ch.

By 1970 there were ca. 20,000 Luths. in Japan. TAG

T. Fukuyama, *Nihon Fukuin Ruteru Kyokai Shi* ("History of the Ev. Luth. Ch. in Jap."; Tokyo, 1954); B. P. Huddle, *History of the Lutheran Church in Japan* (New York, 1958).

Japan Evangelical Lutheran Church. The United* Syn. of the Ev. Luth. Ch. in the S began work in Japan 1892. The Japan Ev. Luth. Ch. was organized 1920. It maintained the Japan Luth. Theol. Sem. in Tokyo, a boys school and girls school (middle and high) in Kyushu, and soc. welfare institutions in Kyushu and the Tokyo area. Merged 1963 with the Tokai* Ev. Luth. Ch. to form a new Japan Ev. Luth. Church. See also *Japan.*

Japan Evangelical Mission. Organized after WW II; first called Bible Institute Miss. of Jap.; interdenom.; headquarters Seattle, Wash.; Three Hills, Alta., Can.; mem. IFMA.

Japan Evangelistic Band. Founded 1903. Concentrates on village evangelism and Bible school work. Mem. IFMA. Helped form the autonomous, indigenous Nihon Iesu Kirisuto Kyodan ("Japan Ch. of Jesus Christ") as a sister organization 1935.

Japan Lutheran Church. See *Japan.*

Jaroslav. Alternate form of Yaroslav. See *Estonia,* 1.

Jäschke, Heinrich August (May 17, 1817–Sept. 24, 1883). Moravian miss. and linguist; b. Herrnhut, Saxony, Ger.; educ. and taught at Paedagogium at Niesky; in 1856 he went to Kyelang (Kailing), Lahul province, India, near Tibet, to prepare for work among Chinese Mongols. Works include Ger.-Tibetan lexicon; Eng.-Tibetan lexicon; Tibetan grammar.

Jaspers, Karl (1883–1969). Philos.; b. Oldenburg, Ger.; studied law at Heidelberg and Munich, medicine at Berlin, Göttingen, and Heidelberg; asst. in psychiatry Heidelberg; prof. psychology Heidelberg 1916; prof. philos. Heidelberg 1921; deposed by Nazis 1937; reinstated 1945; taught at Basel 1948. Emphasized subjectivity of thought. Method distinguished 3 levels of interpretation: philos. orientation in world (based on physical, psychol., and soc. sciences); illumination of existence (i. e. of human reality; *Existenzerhellung*); metaphysics (concern with transcendence). Held that *Existenz* (experience of infinity of possibilities in man) is the eternal, *Dasein* (the observable and describable) the temporal in man. *Existenz* is limited by boundaries which authentic existence explores and accepts. God is beyond all metaphysical conceptualization. Works include *Allgemeine Psychopathologie; Philosophie; Existenzphilosophie; Die Schuldfrage; Der philosophische Glaube.*

Jaspis, Albert Sigismund (1809–85). B. Nossen, Saxony, Ger.; pastor Lugau, Rödlitz, Elberfeld; gen. supt. Pomerania 1855; confessional pietist. Wrote devotional literature.

Jataka ([Buddhist] "birth story"). In Buddhism,* a story in which the Bodhisattva, i. e. the Buddha in a former birth, plays a role.

Jatho, Carl (1851–1913). B. Kassel, Ger.; pastor in Bucharest (Romania), and Boppard and Cologne, Ger.; developed mystic-pantheistic religion in opposition to classical Christology; removed from office 1911.

Java. See *Indonesia,* 1, 3.

Jaworskij, Stephan (Javorskij; Jaworsky; original name Simeon changed to monastic name Stephan [Stefan]; 1658–1722). Russ. Orthodox prelate; made pres. of Holy Syn. 1721 by Peter I (1672–1725; coruler of Russ. with half brother Ivan 1682–89, thereafter alone; "the Great"). Works include *Kamen very* ("Rock of Faith"), which shows Jesuit influence.

Jay. See *Jajus.*

Jealousy. God is jealous of His divine honor (Ex 20:5; 34:14; Nm 25:11; Dt 29:20; 32:16, 21; Ps 79:5; Is 42:8; 48:11; Zch 1:14; 8:2; 1 Co 10:22). It is God-pleasing when believers show holy zeal for God's honor, are indignant over wickedness, or are moved by intense interest for the welfare of others. All jealousy of men that is equivalent to suspicion and envy* is sinful. Examples: Gn 4:5-8; 37.3-11; Ps 37:1; 73:3; Pr 24:1, 19; Mt 27:18; Ro 13:13; 1 Ptr 2:1-2. Cp. LC I 184.

Jean Baptiste de la Salle (John Baptist de la Salle; 1651–1719). B. Reims, Fr.; RC priest; founded Institute of (the) Brothers of the Christian Schools (see *Christian Brothers*).

Jean de Matha (John of Matha; 1160–1213). B. Faucon, Provence, Fr.; priest; founded Trinitarians.*

Jean Paul. See *Richter, Johann Paul Friedrich.*

Jeanne d'Arc. See *Joan of Arc.*

Jeanne de Valois. See *Annunciation, Orders of,* 1.

Jeans, James Hopwood. See *Evolution,* I.

Jeep, Johann(es) (Jepp; ca. 1582–1644). B. Dransfeld, Hannover, Ger.; Luth. composer of ch. music; kapellmeister Weikersheim 1613. Works include *Studentengärtlein.*

Jefferson, Thomas. See *Deism,* III, 1; V.

Jeffreys, Harold A. See *Evolution,* I.

Jehovah. See *Jahweh.*

Jehovah Conference. Organized 1886 [1893?] by a small group of men who came from the Missionshaus founded by W. Vilmar* at Melsungen, Ger. Prominent among them was Wilhelm C. F. Hartwig (Oct. 30, 1854–May 31, 1927; b. Cassdorf, Hesse-Cassel, Ger.). The conf. held the AC to be the only true Confession of the Luth. Ch. as such. Mostly located in and near Detroit, Mich. Disappeared from statistical lists toward the end of the 1920s.

Jehovah's witnesses (note lower case "w"). 1. Adv. group founded ca. 1872 in Pittsburgh, Pa., by C. T. Russell*; name based on Is 43:10; known also as Millennial Dawnists (after a book by Russell entitled *Millennial Dawn,* pub. in the 1880s), Russellites, and Internat. Bible Students Assoc.; several local groups were known as Watch Tower (or Watchtower) Bible and Tract Soc. Russell claimed to be the 7th messenger of Rv 11:25, rejected the Scriptural teaching on hell, Trin., and immortality of the soul; denounced chs. and the contemporary soc. order, and promised a "3d world," the golden age of mankind. J. F. Rutherford* succeeded Russell. Jehovah's witnesses engage in worldwide preaching and in propaganda through literature, radio, and colporteurs.

2. The cen. idea of Jehovah's witnesses is belief in the complete reorganization of the soc. order through establishment of Jehovah's theocracy. Adherents consider themselves to be faithful witnesses of Jehovah who must proclaim that the present "world" will be destroyed in the final war of Armageddon; that Jehovah is now gathering His faithful witnesses to est. His theocracy, which will be the only form of govt. in the "world to come," and will offer the only refuge for distressed humanity. The "divine plan of the ages," acc. to Russell and Rutherford: The hist. of the world falls into 3 great dispensations, in each of which man is given an opportunity to merit for himself the right to live in this world "for ages to come" by obedience to God's law. Good angels were in charge of the 1st dispensation, but they were unable to control the counter govt. which Satan est. Satan misled Adam and Eve by teaching them the lie of the immortality of the soul. Through disobedience of God's laws, man forfeited the right to live. In the 2d dispensation, beginning with Noah and ending with Armageddon, Satan used as allies the capitalistic system, human govts., and chs., to prevent man from being obedient to God's theocracy. Only few can withstand the onslaughts of Satan's allies and merit the right to live. Chs. are singled out as allies of Satan because organized chs. have undermined Jehovah's authority through the lie of the Trinity. Jehovah's witnesses speak of Christ as God's Son, but deny the eternal preexistence of the 2d Person in the Trin. and speak of the Logos only as God's chief administrator. Hell is said to be a place of entire destruction or annihilation. Jesus is said to have voluntarily given up His right to live and to have deposited it with God; thus He made it possible for God to restore the right to live to all men. Besides Christ, also the 144,000 of Rv 7:4-8, by perfect obedience to God's theocracy, earned the right to live. But they also give up the right to life; with Jesus they constitute "the Christ." They alone will receive immortality. The rest of mankind will be resurrected; that is, new bodies will be created for them and their right to life will be restored to them. They will be given opportunity for 100 yrs. to be obedient to God's theocracy in the "new world." Those who at the end of the probationary period are not obedient will be annihilated. The obedient will live under God's theocracy for ages to come. FEM

1972 statistics: 1,658,990 mems. in 208 countries; 431,179 mems. in 5,794 congs. in US.

See *Religious Bodies (US), Bibliography.*

Jehuda(h). Variant form of "Judah."

Jehuda, Isaak. See *Goldziher, Ignaz.*

Jehuda ben Samuel Ha-Levi. See *Judah ha-Levi.*

Jehuda von Regensburg. See *Judah ben Samuel.*

Jelke, Robert (1882–1952). B. Frose, Anhalt, Ger.; prof. systematic theol. Rostock 1919, Heidelberg 1920. Exponent of neo-Lutheranism.

Jellinek, Adolf (ca. 1821–93). B. Drslawitz, near Ungarisch-Brod, Moravia; educ. Prague and Leipzig; rabbi and preacher Leipzig and Vienna. Wrote a hist. of Cabala.*

Jellinghaus, Theodor (1841–1913). B. Schlüsselburg on the Weser, Ger.; Gossner* Miss. Soc. miss. in India; pastor Prussia; influenced by the perfectionism and holiness views of R. P. Smith.* Works include *Das völlige, gegenwärtige Heil durch Christum.*

Jen. See *Chinese Philosophy,* 3.

Jensen, Alfred (Jan. 6, 1893–Sept. 1, 1966). B. Brenderup, Den.; educ. Grand View Coll. and Sem., Des Moines, Iowa; ordained by The Dan. Ev. Luth. Ch. in Am. 1920. Pastor Cordova, Nebr. (twice); Tyler, Minn.; Kimballton, Iowa. Pres. AELC 1936–60.

Jensen, Christian (1839–1900). B. Lütjenswarf, Schleswig; Luth. pastor Breklum; est. Breklum* Miss. Soc. 1876; est. school 1878 for training pastors for Am.

Jensen, Rasmus. See *Canada,* A 1; *Danish Lutherans in America,* 1.

Jensson, Jens Christian. See *Roseland, Jens Christian.*

Jepp. See *Jeep.*

Jepsen, Aage. See *Denmark, Lutheranism in,* 1.

Jeremias II (Jeremiah; Tranos; ca. 1530–95). B. Anchialos, on the Black Sea; metropolitan of Larissa 1565; patriarch Constantinople ca. 1572–79, 1580–84, 1586–ca. 1595. See also *Eastern Orthodox Churches,* 5; *Eastern Orthodox Standards of Doctrine,* A 5.

Jeremias, Alfred (1864–1935). Luth. theol.; b. Markersdorf, near Chemnitz, Ger.; pastor Leipzig; lectured at Leipzig U. Works include *Allgemeine Religions-Geschichte; Das Alte Testament im Lichte des Alten Orients* (tr. *The Old Testament in the Light of the Ancient East*); *Die Panbabylonisten: Der Alte Orient und die Aegyptische Religion.*

Jeremias, Joachim. See *Isagogics,* 3.

Jerome (Sophronius Eusebius Hieronymus; b. probably in the 340s; d. 419 or 420). Ch. father; b. Stridon (probably in Dalmatia, near Aquileia, It.) of Christian parents; bap. at 19 in Rome, where he had gone to study rhetoric and philos.; journeyed through Gaul; then lived at Aquileia till ca. 373; traveled, living in and near Syrian Antioch, then in Constantinople, Rome, Antioch, Palestine, Egypt, settling finally at Bethlehem. Turned from secular studies to the things of God during his 1st stay at Antioch; secy. to Damasus I (see *Fides Damasi*). Works include rev. of the Lat. Bible (see *Bible Versions,* J 1-2); commentaries on books of the Bible; *De viris illustribus;* polemical writings. See also *Geography, Christian,* 3; *Millennium,* 3; *Origenistic Controversy.*

MPL, 22-30; R. and M. Pernoud, *Saint Jerome,* tr. R. Sheed (New York, 1962); D. S. Wiesen, *St. Jerome As a Satirist* (Ithaca, N. Y., 1964).

Jerome of Prague (b. probably in the 1360s; d. 1416). B. Prague; friend of J. Hus*; educ. Prague, Oxford, Paris, Cologne, Heidelberg; copied *Dialogus* and *Trialogus* of J. Wycliffe*; championed Wycliffism; burned at Constance.

Jerusalem, Synods of. The 1st Christian syn. or council was held at Jerusalem, Acts 15. Later syns. at Jerusalem include: one in 335, which restored Arius to fellowship in an attempt to settle the Arian controversy (see *Arianism*); one in the 340s, which acknowledged fellowship with Athanasius, who had been deposed 335 by a council at Tyre, restored in the 340s by a council at Sardica (later called Sofia); an indecisive diocesan syn. in 415 called to deal with the Pelagian* Controversy; one in 634 against Monothelitism,* in favor of Dyothelitism*; one in 1672 against Calvinism. See also *Eastern Orthodox Standards of Doctrine,* A 2.

Jerusalemsverein. See *Middle East,* G.

Jessup, Henry Harris (Apr. 19, 1832–Apr. 28, 1910). B. Montrose, Pa.; educ. Yale U. (New Haven, Conn.) and Union Theol. Sem. (NYC); ABCFM Presb. miss. to Tripoli and Beirut; transferred to Presb. Bd. of For. Miss. 1870; prof. Syrian Theol. Sem., Beirut. Works include *Syrian Home Life; The Greek Church and Protestant Missions.*

Jesuitism. See *Society of Jesus.*

Jesuits. Mems. of the Society* of Jesus.

Jesus, Lives of. Since about 1775 an immense literature has grown up which concerns itself with the life of Jesus. A survey chiefly of critical, negative works in this field is furnished in A. Schweitzer,* *Von Reimarus zu Wrede* (1906), 2d ed. 1913 entitled *Geschichte der Leben-Jesu-Forschung,* Eng. tr. of 1st ed. entitled *The Quest of the Historical Jesus.* A similar book bringing Schweitzer up to date and introd. several new viewpoints: C. C. McCown, *The Search for the Real Jesus* (1940); like Schweitzer's book, it is written from the viewpoint of the negative critic, but it is valuable because it acquaints one with the productions of radical and skeptical scholarship in this field. Some deny that Jesus ever lived; they speak of the story of His life as the Christ-myth (e. g., B. Bauer,* A. Kalthoff,* C. H. A. Drews*). They were refuted by S. J. Case,* *The Historicity of Jesus.* D. F. Strauss* advocated the "mythical" theory: Jesus was a hist. person, but we know few facts of His life; the Gospel accounts are results of mythical development. J. E. Renan,* *Vie de Jésus,* treated hist. facts more like a novelist than a historian. The "liberal" portrait of Jesus was drawn by J. F. W. Bousset,* K. G. A. v. Harnack,* and others who held that Jesus taught chiefly the Fatherhood of God, the brotherhood of man, and the value of human personality. The "eschatological" Jesus (the view that Jesus taught that the end of the world was coming very soon and that He would then be revealed as the Messiah) was the conception of Schweitzer and J. Weiss.* A. Edersheim,* F. W. Farrar,* J. Stalker,* A. Fahling,* et al. uphold the Scriptural presentation of the life of Jesus.

Form criticism (see *Isagogics,* 3) has tended to discourage attempts to write on the life of Jesus; many form critics hold that the chronological framework in the Bible accounts is hist. untrustworthy. Most Eng. critics have been conservative on this point, as witness accounts of the life of Jesus by Archibald Macbride Hunter (b. 1906), Vincent Taylor (b. 1887), John William Charles Wand (b. 1885) et al. Some words of Eur. RCs (e. g., Louis Claude Fillion [1843–1927], Léonce Loizeau de Grandmaison [1868–1927], Marie Joseph [or Joseph Marie; Albert] Lagrange [1855–1938], Jules Lebreton [1873–1956], Ferdinand Prat [1857–1938], Giuseppe Ricciotti [1890–1964]) are available in Eng. tr. Some students of R. Bultmann (see *Demythologization; Existentialism,* 1) have tried to break with his extreme hist. skepticism. This has led to a "new quest" of the hist. Jesus, with widely varying results. Best-known treatment is Günther Bornkamm (b. Görlitz, Ger., 1905; pastor; prof. Göttingen and Heidelberg), *Jesus von Nazareth* (1956; Eng. tr. 1960). Others include Ethelbert Stauffer (b. 1902), *Jesus: Gestalt und Geschichte* (1957; Eng. tr. 1960: *Jesus and His Story*); Walter Grundmann

(b. 1906), *Die Geschichte Jesu Christi* (1957). WA, VAB

C. C. McCown, *The Search for the Real Jesus* (New York, 1940) and "Jesus, Son of Man: A Survey of Recent Discussion," *The Journal of Religion,* XXVIII, No. 1 (Jan. 1948), 1–12; J. M. Robinson, *A New Quest of the Historical Jesus* (London, 1959); *Der historische Jesus und der kerygmatische Christus,* ed. H. Ristow and K. Matthiae, 2d ed. (Berlin, 1961); H. Conzelmann, "Jesus Christus," *Die Religion in Geschichte und Gegenwart,* ed. K. Galling, 3d ed. (Tübingen, 1959), III, col. 619–653; F. C. Grant, "Jesus Christ," *The Interpreter's Dictionary of the Bible,* ed. G. A. Buttrick et al. (New York, 1962), II, 869–896.

Jesus, Portrayals of. Pictures of Jesus are found in the catacombs. One of the oldest extant statues of the Good Shepherd is held to be of 3d-c. origin. Mosaic representations of Jesus are common and include the Baptism of Jesus in the dome of the Orthodox baptistery at Ravenna, It., Christ Dividing the Sheep from the Goats in the ch. of St. Apollinare Nuovo, Ravenna, and Christ Enthroned in the ch. of St. Pudenziana, Rome. In the Middle Ages representations of Jesus relegated His character as Redeemer to the background and featured such subjects as Christ in the Glory of the New Jerusalem, Christ in His Majesty as Teacher, Christ on the Clouds of Heaven, Christ on the Globe of the World. Renaissance art was more concerned with Mary than with Jesus, though Andrea Mantegna (1431–1506; b. near Padua, It.; printer and engraver) painted a Crucifixion of Christ, Leonardo* da Vinci His Last Supper, and Guido Reni (1575–1642; b. near Bologna, It.) an Ecce Homo. Reformation and post-Reformation artists portraying Jesus as Savior include A. Dürer,* J. M. F. H. Hofmann,* B. Plockhorst,* H. Thoma,* E. K. F. v. Gebhardt,* F. v. Uhde,* and J. Schnorr* v. Carolsfeld.

Jesus, Society of. See *Society of Jesus.*

Jesus, the Son of Sirach. Author of Ecclesiasticus (see *Apocrypha,* A 2, 3).

Jewel, John (1522–71). B. Buden, Devonshire, Eng.; educ. Oxford; bp. Salisbury 1560; friend and assoc. of Peter* Martyr; supported Angl. Ch. against Romanists and Puritans. Works include *Apologia ecclesia Anglicanae.*

Jewish Calendar. See *Judaism,* 4.

Jewish Missions. The number of Jews is ca. 14,000,000 (1969 est.), with ca. 6,000,000 in N Am. (ca. 1,836,000 in NYC). Luth. interest in miss. work among Jews dates back to M. Luther.* Modern Luth. missions to Jews include the work of the Zion* Soc. for Israel (known since 1964 as The Church's Ministry to the Jewish People) and that of the National* Luth. Council. See also *International Board of Jewish Missions, Inc.; International Society for the Evangelization of the Jews; Landsmann, Daniel.*

Jewish Philosophy. Jewish philosophers include J. Albo,* Avicebrón,* M. Buber,* H. Cohen,* C. ben A. Crescas,* U. da Costa (see *Da Costa,* 2), A. Ibn* Daud, Levi* ben Gershon, Maimonides,* M. Mendelssohn,* Philo* Judaeus, B. Spinoza.* See also *Cabala; Karaites; Talmud.*

Jewish Student Organizations, Federation of. Organized 1937 to promote Jewish student activities. Headquarters NYC.

Jewish War. War resulting from revolt of Jews against Romans 66 AD. Nero sent Vespasian* to quell revolt. Vespasian was joined in 67 by son Titus* Flavius Sabinus Vespasianus, whom he left in charge of Roman forces in Palestine 68. Jerusalem fell 70 AD. The war and fall of Jerusalem was described by F. Josephus.* See also *John of Galilee.*

Jews. See *Jews, Conversion of; Jewish Missions; Judaism.*

Jews, Conversion of. Conversion of Jews as a nation has been taught in connection with millenarian hopes (see *Millennium*). The claim is based on Ro 11:15-29. Advocates of the theory hold that Paul asserts and proves from OT prophecies that a final and universal conversion of the Jews will occur; that such OT prophecies as Is 11:11-12; 59:20; Jer 3:17; 16:14-15; 31:31; Eze 20:40-44; Hos 3:4-5; Jl 3:1-17; Am 9:11-15; Zch 10:6-10; 12:10; 14 must be taken literally; that the entire territory promised to Abraham has not been fully possessed by his descendants (hence the prophecies in Gn 15:18-21; Nm 34:6-12; Eze 47 must refer to the millenial reign of Christ, with Jews occupying the land described); and that the Jews, though scattered among the nations, have been preserved as a separate people for the purpose of constituting a distinct people during Christ's reign on earth.

Opponents of the theory hold that literal interpretation of the OT prophecies cited is untenable, since such interpretation, to be consistent, must be literal in all its parts. This literalism would imply that David will reign in person in Jerusalem, Eze 37:24; that the Levitical priesthood will be restored and bloody sacrifices offered to God, Jer 17:25-26; that Jerusalem must be the center of govt., and all worshipers must come monthly and from Sabbath to Sabbath, from the ends of the earth, to worship at the Holy City, Is 2:3; Zch 14:16-21. The literal interpretation leads to a complete revival of the Jewish ritual which was abrogated by Christ and which is opposed to clear NT teaching. Most important, Is 10:22-23; Ro 9:27-28; 11:3-8, 25-32 refer to the elect saints in Israel, Israel acc. to the spirit, spiritual Israel. As in OT Israel only those called by grace were saved, so in NT times the chosen ones will be brought in only through the preaching of the Gospel (Ro 11:1-7). Thus such NT expressions as "Abraham's seed" and "Israel of God" (Gl 3:29; 6:16) apply to all believers in Christ, not only reconverted Jews.

Jiménez de Cisneros, Francisco (Ximenes; Ximenez; 1437–1517). B. Torrelaguna, Sp.; Observant* prelate; statesman; at times anchorite (see *Hermits*); in 1492 became confessor to Isabella I (see *Inquisition,* 6); Franciscan* provincial in Castile 1494; primate of Sp. 1495; cardinal 1507; inquisitor gen. of Castile and León; in 1516 became regent of Castile for Charles I (see *Charles V*). See also *Counter Reformation,* 3; *Polyglot Bibles.*

Jina. See *Jainism.*

Joachim. Acc. to *The Protevangelium of James* (2d c.), Joachim was the husband of Anne and father of Mary, mother of Jesus.

Joachim. Name of 3 electors of Brandenburg. 1. *Joachim I Nestor* (Cicero Teutonicus; 1484–1535). Elector 1499–1535; father of 2; founded U. of Frankfurt an der Oder 1506; opposed M. Luther; helped organize League of Dessau.* See also *Pack, Otto von.* 2. *Joachim II Hektor* (1505–71). Elector 1535–71; son of 1; Prot. 1539. See also *Interim,* I. 3. *Joachim Friedrich* (1546–1608). Elector 1598–1608; son of John* George, elector of Brandenburg; bp. Havelberg 1553, Lebus 1555; 1st ev. abp. Magdeburg 1566–98; disbanded cloisters; removed RC ceremonies; unwillingly yielded to requests of Magdeburg nobility to introd. FC; desired union bet. Luths. and Ref.

Joachim of Floris (de Floris; of Fiore [or Flora]; ca. 1130 [1145?]–ca. 1202). B. Celico, near Cosenza, Calabria; mystic; Cistercian*; founded monastery of St. John in Fiore, on Montenero, in La Sila mountains, S It. Best known for dividing hist. into 3 ages, of the Father (OT), of the Son (from Christ to ca. 1260), and of the Holy Ghost (beginning ca. 1260), the latter the time of the eternal Gospel, of prayer, song, and contemplation, the monastic age *par excellence.* Followers called Joachimites. Influence declined when 1260 failed to usher in the age of the Holy Ghost. See also *Spirituals, Franciscan.*

Joachimites. See *Joachim of Floris.*

Joan of Arc (Jeanne d'Arc; 1412–31). "The Maid of Orleans"; Fr. "La Pucelle (d'Orleans)"; b. Domremy-la-Pucelle, Fr., of peasant parents. On the basis of alleged visions she led a Fr. army against the Eng.; raised the siege of Orléans 1429; captured by Burgundians 1430; sold to English, who persuaded Fr. to join in convicting her of witchcraft and heresy; burned at the stake at Rouen on May 30, made a Fr. nat. holiday 1920.

Joasaph. See *Eastern Orthodox Churches,* 5.

Job's Daughters, Order of. See *Freemasonry,* 7.

Jochanan ben Zakkai. See *Johanan ben Zakkai.*

Jocists. Assoc. of RC factory workers (*Jeunesse Ouvrière Chrétienne;* acronym JOC; hence the terms Jocist and Jocism; Eng.: Young Christian Workers) formed in Belgium beginning 1912 and esp. after WW I; spread to Fr. and in various forms throughout the world.

Jodl, Friedrich (1849–1914). B. Munich, Ger.; positivist philos.; developed naturalistic ethic.

Jogaila. See *Lithuania,* 1.

Johanan ben Zakkai (Johanan; ca. 1–80 AD). B. Palestine; Jewish savant; escaped to Romans during siege of Jerusalem; with Vespasian's permission he est. a school at Jamnia (see *Jamnia, Synod of*).

Johann(es). See also *John.*

Johann Albrecht I (1525–76). Duke of Mecklenburg, Ger., 1547–76; consolidated Luth. Ch. in Mecklenburg; est. the 1552 ch. order; reorganized the U. of Rostock; favored FC.

Johann Georg. See *John George.*

Johanna. Legendary female pope; supposedly reigned for ca. 2½ yrs. after Leo IV (d. 855); legend became popular in 13th c. but was disproved in 17th c.

Johannes III Scholasticus (d. 577). B. Sirimis, near Antioch; patriarch Constantinople 565; made collection of canons (see also *Canon Law,* 2).

Johannes IV Jejunator (Lat. "one who fasts"; Gk. *Nesteutes;* Ger. *der Faster;* d. 595). B. probably Cappadocia; patriarch Constantinople 582–595; made his see supreme in E and equal to Rome.

Johannes XI Bekkos (Beccos; Beccus; Veccus; b. early in the 13th c.; d. ca. 1293). B. Constantinople; patriarch Constantinople 1275–82; convinced of validity of W Church's position on procession of the Holy Spirit (see also *Filioque Controversy*), he worked for union.

Johannes Damascenus. See *John of Damascus.*

Johannes Scotus Erigena. See *Erigena, Johannes Scotus.*

Johannes von Goch (Johann Pupper; Capupper; ca. 1400–ca. 1475). B. Goch (Geldern), Lower Rhine; adherent of Brethren* of the Common Life; Augustinian in theol.; opposed Scholasticism; theol. convictions summarized: from God, through God, to God. Works include *De libertate christiana; Dialogus de quatuor erroribus circa legem evangelicam exortis, et de votis et de religionibus facticiis.*

Johanneum. Est. 1886 at Bonn, Ger., by T. Christlieb* to train men 20–30 yrs. old, who already had a vocation, for miss. work and evangelism; moved to Wuppertal-Barmen 1893 by T. Haarbeck.*

The name Johanneum is also applied to an older institution at Hamburg which combined a Gymnasium and Realschule, and to schools elsewhere, e. g., Breslau and Lüneburg.

An advanced school (Hoch Schule) called Johannes was est. at Herborn 1584. enl. to a U. 1654, changed to a sem. 1817.

Johannine Comma (Comma Johanneum; "Three Witnesses"; *comma* is Lat. for "phrase"). That part of 1 Jn 5:7-8 which is regarded by many as interpolation, namely the italicized words in the following (KJV): "For there are three that bear record *in heaven, the Father, the Word, and the Holy Ghost; and these three are one. And there are three that bear witness in earth,* the spirit, and the water, and the blood: and these three agree in one."

Johannitius. See *Arabic Philosophy.*

Johansson, Gustaf (1844–1930). B. Ylvieska, Fin.; educ. Helsinki and in Ger. and Switz.; prof. ethics and dogmatics Helsinki 1877–85; abp. Fin. 1899. Works include *Pyhä Uskomme* (Swed.: *Vaar heliga tro*). See also *Dogmatics,* B 9.

John. See also *Johann; Johannes.*

John (king of Eng.). See *Church and State,* 6; *England,* A 3.

John, called *Nauclerus.* See *Nauclerus, Ioannes.*

John VIII (pope). See *Schism,* 5.

John VIII Palaeologus (ca. 1391–1448). E Roman emp. 1425–48; attended Council of Florence.*

John XXII. See *Popes,* 13.

John XXIII. 1. *Baldassare Cossa* (d. 1419). Neapolitan; elected pope (now gen. regarded antipope) 1410 at Bologna by cardinals who honored the action of the Council of Pisa*; convoked the Council of Constance*; promised to resign if Gregory* XII and Benedict* XIII would do likewise; fled Mar. 1415 when his sincerity became suspect; suspended, imprisoned, and deposed May 1415; released ca. 1418; bp. Tusculum (Frascati), It., 1419.

2. *Angelo Giuseppe Roncalli.* See *Popes,* 34.

John Baptist de la Salle. See *Jean Baptiste de la Salle.*

John Buridan. See *Buridan, Jean.*

John Casimir (Johann Kasimir; 1564–1633). Son of John* Frederick II; duke of Saxe-Coburg; est. Gymnasium at Coburg; befriended J. Gerhard.*

John Chrysostom. See *Chrysostom, John.*

John Climacus (ca. 570 [579?]–649). Also known as Sinaites and Scholasticus; abbott Sinai; ascetic. Works include *Ladder of Paradise* (Gk. *Klimax tou paradeisou,* whence his cognomen).

MPG, 88, 579–1248.

John Damascene. See *John of Damascus.*

John Frederick (Johann Friedrich; 1503–54). Called "the Magnanimous" (Ger. *der Grossmütige*) because of his spirit and bearing under misfortune. B. Torgau, Prussia; son of John* the Constant; educ. by G. Spalatin*; early supporter of M. Luther*; went with his father to Diet of Augsburg 1530 (see *Lutheran Confessions,* A). Elector of Ernestine Saxony 1532–47. Impulsive; not a far-sighted politician. Unity of the Schmalkaldic* League suffered from disagreements bet. John Frederick and Philip* of Hesse, leaders of the League; e. g., John Frederick took a strict Luth. position, Philip favored union with other evangelicals; John Frederick disliked Philip's bigamy. He set aside the 1541 election of RC J. v. Pflug* as bp. Naumburg and substituted N. v. Amsdorf,* an avowed Luth. He antagonized Maurice,* duke of Saxony, 1542, by unilaterally trying to introd. the Reformation into the city of Wurzen, whose see was under joint protection of electoral and ducal Saxony; war bet. the 2 Saxonies was averted only by efforts of Luther and Philip. He was suspicious of colloquies and rejected papal overtures for a council. Helped drive Heinrich II (the Younger; 1514–68; duke of Braunschweig-Wolfenbüttel; RC) from his duchy 1542. Failed to support the Cologne Reformation (see *Hermann von Wied*). Did not attend diets and similar meetings from the diet (or convention) of the ev. states at Schmalkald 1537 (he had asked Luther for a positional paper; result: the Schmalkaldic Articles [see *Lutheran Confessions,* B 2]) to the 1544 Diet of Speyer.* When Charles* V prepared to attack the Schmalkaldic League, John Frederick was duped and was slow in taking countermeasures. With the outbreak of the Schmalkaldic* War July 1546, John Frederick left his realm with an army to engage the imperial forces, but returned when Maurice, who had joined the cause of Charles V, invaded electoral Saxony. John Frederick reconquered most of his land, repelling Maurice, but was defeated and captured by imperial forces at Mühlberg Apr. 24, 1547. Condemned to death by Charles V; sentence commuted to life imprisonment when Wittenberg surrendered; released 1552 by Maurice (who had defeated and almost captured Charles V and forced him to conclude the convention of Passau*) but did not regain title.

Reorganized the U. of Wittenberg 1535–36; benefactor of U. of Leipzig; laid the plans for the U. of Jena (founded 1558). WGT, LP

B. Rogge, *Johann Friedrich, Kurfürst von Sachsen, genannt "der Grossmütige"* (Halle, 1902); W. G. Tillmanns, *The World and Men Around Luther* (Minneapolis, 1959), pp. 300–302.

John Frederick II (1529–95). Called "der Mittlere." Father of John* Casimir; b. Torgau, Prussia; son of John* Frederick the Magnanimous; allowed to rule small part of his father's land by Charles* V after 1547; deposed 1566; imprisoned 1567. See also *Konfutationsbuch, Synergistic Controversy.*

John George (Johann Georg; 1525–98). Elector of Brandenburg 1571–98; son of Joachim II Hektor (see *Joachim,* 2); father of Joachim Friedrich (see *Joachim,* 3).

John George I (Johann Georg I; 1585–1656). Elector of Saxony of the Albertine line 1611–56; son of Christian* I; b. Dresden; in Thirty* Years' War first sided with Ferdinand II (1578–1637; king Boh. 1617–19 and 1620–37; Holy Roman emp. 1619–37), later with Gustavus* II; concluded treaty with emp. 1635; fought Swed. 1636; defeated at Wittstock. Promoted culture.

John Gualbert (ca. 990 [995?]–1073). B. Florence, It.; founded Vallombrosans.*

John Knox's Liturgy. See *Presbyterian Churches,* 1.

John Lackland. King of Eng. See also *Church and State,* 6; *England,* 3.

John Malalas (John Rhetor; Scholasticus; 6th c.). B. probably Antioch in Syria; wrote *Chronography* (Books 1–17 are Monophysite, 18 is orthodox).

MPG, 97, 9–790.

John Milton Society. See *Blind,* 3.

John Moschus (Moschos). See *Moschus, John.*

John of Amida. See *John of Ephesus.*

John of Antioch (d. ca. 441). Bp. Antioch ca. 429; leader of moderate Nestorians. See also *Exegesis,* 4.

MPG, 77, cols. 131–132, 163–166, 167–174, 247–250, 329–332, 1449–62; 84, 550–864.

John of Asia. See *John of Ephesus.*

John of Ávila (Juan de Ávila; ca. 1500–69). "Apostle of Andalusia"; b. Almodóvar del Campo, Sp.; mystic. Works include *Audi Filia.*

John of Beverley (d. 721). Anglo-Saxon bp. Hexham, Eng., 687, York 705; disciple of Hilda (614–680; founded double monastery 657 at Streoneshalh [later called Whitby]) at Whitby (where the famous Syn. of Whitby* was held); ordained Bede* deacon 692, priest 703; resigned 720 and retired to abbey at Inderawood (later Beverley), which he had founded and where he died.

John of Damascus (Johannes Damascenus; John Damascene; b. perhaps ca. 675 [as early as 645? as late as 700?]; d. ca. 750). Called *Chrysorrhoas* (Gk. "Golden Speaker"). B. Damascus; monk in a monastery near Jerusalem; priest; hymnist. Involved in iconoclastic* controversy. Works include *De haeresibus; Expositio accurata fidei orthodoxae; De sacris imaginibus; Sacra parallela;* hymns "Come, Ye Faithful, Raise the Strain" and "The Day of Resurrection."

MPG, 94–96.

John of Ephesus (John of Asia; John of Amida; ca. 507–ca. 586). B. near Amida (later Diyarbekir, or Diarbekr, Turkey in Asia); precursor of Monophysites. Works include a ch. hist. and biographies of E saints.

John of Freiburg (ca. 1250–1314). B. Haslach (which?); teacher of theol. and (ca. 1294) prior Freiburg, Ger.; prepared a practical system of pastoral casuistry widely used in Middle Ages.

John of Galilee (Gischala; Giscala). Leader of Jewish rebels in Galilee and Jerusalem 66–70; hostile to policy of F. Josephus*; imprisoned in Rome. See also *Jewish War.*

John of God (Juan Ciudad; Juan de Dios; Joao de Deo; 1495–1550). B. Montemor-o-Novo, Port.; Sp. religious; after life of dissipation he devoted himself to caring for sick (see *Brothers Hospitallers of St. John of God*).

John of Jandun (Johannes de Janduno; ca. 1275–1328). B. Jandun, Fr.; educ. Paris; taught at U. of Paris; proponent of philos. of Averroes (see *Arabic Philosophy*); championed king's claims against papacy's. Helped Marsilius* of Padua write *Defensor pacis.*

John of Kronstadt (Iwan Il'jitsch Sergiev; b. 1820s; d. ca. 1908). B. probably Sura, Archangel govt., Russ.; Orthodox priest; allegedly performed miracles; cared for sick and needy.

John of Leiden (Jan Beuckelszoon; Bockelson; Beuckels; Ger.: Johann Bockholdt; other variant spellings; (1509–36). B. near Leiden, Neth.; tailor; merchant, innkeeper; Anabap. fanatic; leader at Münster; proclaimed himself king; introd. polygamy and community of goods; imprisoned 1535 by bp. of Münster; executed. See also *Münster Kingdom.*

John of Matha. See *Jean de Matha.*

John of Montecorvino (1247–ca. 1330). B. Montecorvino (Salerno), It.; RC miss. to Orient; founder and 1st abp. of RC Ch. in China.

John of Montenero. See *Florence, Council of,* 1.

John of Nepomuk (Pomuk; Welflin, or Wölflin; ca. 1340–ca. 1393). B. Nepomuk (or Pomuk), Boh.; martyr; patron saint of Boh.; vicar-gen. Prague; opposed attempts of Wenceslaus IV (Wenzel [1361–1419]; king of Ger. and Holy Rom. emp. 1378–1400; king of Boh. as Wenceslaus IV 1378–1419) to suppress an abbey and create a see for a favorite; drowned in Moldau.

John of Paris (Jean de Paris; Joannes Parisiensis; Quidort; ca. 1269 [or as early as 1240?]–1306). B. Paris, Fr.; Dominican; promoted conciliar* movement; formed theory of consubstantiation or impanation. Works include *Tractatus de potestate regia et papali; Determinatio . . . de modo existendi corporis* [or *corpus*] *Christi in sacramento altaris.*

John of Salisbury (ca. 1115/20–1180). B. near Salisbury, Eng.; philos.; hist.; bp. Chartres 1176; held that a secular prince in effect receives authority from the ch. Works include *Polycraticus.*

MPL, 199, 1–1040.

John of the Cross (Juan de la Cruz; Juan de Yepis y Alvarez; 1542–91). B. Fontiveros, Ávila, Sp.; mystic; poet; with Teresa* founded discalced (reformed) Carmelites* ca. 1568. Works include *The Ascent of Mount Carmel – The Dark Night; The Spiritual Canticle; The Living Flame of Love.*

John Philoponus (6th c.). Alexandrian theol.; held a form of tritheism: the 3 persons of the Trin. have unity of concept but not of nature. Works include commentaries on Aristotle.

John Scholasticus. 1. See *Johannes III Scholasticus.* 2. See *John Climacus.* 3. See *John Malalas.*

John Sigismund (1572–1619). Elector Brandenburg

1608–19; b. Halle, Ger.; educ. as Luth. but became Ref. 1613; 1st duke Duchy of Prussia 1618–19. As a result of his conversion to Calvinism and his reluctance to est. it by force, his successors followed a union ch. policy.

John the Baptist, Beheading of. See *Church Year,* 17.

John the Baptist, Birth of. See *Church Year,* 16.

John the Constant (the Steadfast; 1468–1532). B. Meissen, Ger.; brother of Frederick* III ("the Wise"); father of John* Frederick; received scholarly educ.; knight; elector Saxony 1525; early partisan of M. Luther.* After pub. of Luther's NT 1522, John read the Bible daily. Luther preached at his court in Weimar Oct. 1522 and wrote for him the treatise *Von weltlicher Obrigkeit* 1523. John was tolerant toward T. Münzer* and A. R. B. v. Karlstadt,* did not interfere with abolition of the Corpus* Christi procession, and permitted Prot. observance of the Lord's Supper. After becoming elector he refused to make common cause against Luths. with his cousin, George* the Bearded. Issued a directive on Aug. 16, 1525, making Ernestine Saxony evangelical. Signed treaty with Philip* of Hesse Feb. 27, 1526 (see *Gotha Covenant*), and led Luth. party at 1526 Diet of Speyer*; approved ch. visitations suggested by N. Hausmann*; at 1529 Diet of Speyer* he defended the ev. interpretation of the recess of the 1526 diet and protested with others the resolution of the RC majority; at the 1530 Augsburg Diet (see *Lutheran Confessions,* A) he took a heroic stand against Charles* V; led Schmalkaldic* League 1531. His motto: *Verbum Dei manet in aeternum* (Lat. "The Word of God abides forever"). See also *Pack, Otto von; Visitations, Church.* WGT

John the Evangelist and Apostle. See *Church Year,* 1, 16.

Johnsen, Erik Kristian (Sept. 20, 1863–Jan. 21, 1923). B. Stavanger, Norw.; educ. U. of Oslo (Christiania); private instructor in theol. at Christiania 1888–91; to US 1892; prof. theol. Red Wing (Minn.) Norw. Ev. Luth. Sem. 1892–97; pastor Hudson, Wis., 1897–1900; prof. theol. at the sem. of The United Norw. Luth. Ch. in Am. 1900–17, Luther Theol. Sem. 1917–23, both in St. Paul, Minn. Works include *En kort udredning; Paulus; I kirke.*

Johnson, Edward (1813–Sept. 1867). B. Hollis, N. H.; ABCFM miss. to Sandwich Islands (Hawaii) 1836; 30 yrs. on island of Kauai.

Johnson, Gisle Christian (1822–94). B. Fredrikshald, Norw.; educ. Christiania (Oslo); engaged in further studies and travel in Eur.; prof. systematics and ch. hist. Christiania. Influenced by S. A. Kierkegaard*; held that the function of dogmatics is to analyze the Christian's self-consciousness. Loyal to Luth. Confessions. Revival preacher. Ed. *Luthersk Kirketidende;* other works include *Grundrids af den systematiske Theologi; Dogmehistorie; Kristelig Ethik.* See also *Norway, Lutheranism in,* 11.

Johnson, John (1662–1725). Eng. theol.; educ. Cambridge. Works include *The Unbloody Sacrifice, and Altar, Unvailed and Supported; The Propitiatory Oblation; The Clergyman's Vade-Mecum.*

Johnson, Oscar John (Oct. 8, 1870–Mar. 9, 1946). B. Cleburne, Kans.; educ. Augustana Coll. and Theol. Sem., Rock Island, Ill.; pastor McKeesport, Pa., 1899–1901; pres. Luther Coll. and pastor Wahoo, Nebr., 1901–13; pres. Gustavus Adolphus Coll., St. Peter, Minn., 1913–42.

Johnson, Samuel (1709–84). B. Lichfield, Eng.; lexicographer, essayist, critic, conversationalist, romancer. Some of his writings reflect the theol. of the Ch. of Eng. Works include *A Dictionary of the English Language; Prayers and Meditations; The Lives of the English Poets.* See also *High Church.* EEF

Johnson, William A. B. See *Africa,* C 6.

Joint Synod of Ohio and Other States, Evangelical Lutheran. See *Ohio and Other States, Evangelical Lutheran Joint Synod of.*

Joint Synod of Wisconsin. See *Wisconsin Evangelical Lutheran Synod.*

Jommelli, Nicoolò (Jomelli; Nicola; 1714–74). B. Aversa, It.; composer; director; 15 yrs. kapellmeister to Duke of Württemberg at Stuttgart; mem. Neapolitan school. Works include oratorios and cantatas.

Jonah (Arab.: Abul Walid Merwan ibn-Janah; Abulwalid; ibn Ganach; R. [Rabbi; Rab] Marinus; ca. 990–ca. 1050). Heb. grammarian and philol.; physician; b. Córdoba, Sp.; later settled in Saragossa. Works include *Sefer Harikmah; Sefer Hashorashim.* See also *Lexicons,* A.

Jonas, Justus (originally Jodocus [or Jodokus] Koch; "Jodocus" became "Justus" and he adopted his father's given name as family name; 1493–1555). B. Nordhausen, Ger.; educ. Erfurt and Wittenberg; prof. and canon at Erfurt 1518, rector of U. of Erfurt 1519; provost Castle Ch. and prof. canon law U. of Wittenberg 1521; colaborer of M. Luther*; supt. Halle 1541–47, Eisfeld 1553–55. Hymnist; wrote "Wo Gott der Herr nicht bei uns hält"; stanzas 4 and 5 of "Erhalt uns, Herr, bei deinem Wort." See also *Lutheran Confessions,* B 1.

M. E. Lehmann, *Justus Jonas: Loyal Reformer* (Minneapolis, 1964); T. Pressel, *Justus Jonas* (Elberfeld, 1862).

Jones, Abner. See *United Church of Christ, The,* I B.

Jones, Absalom. See *African Methodist Episcopal Church.*

Jones, Edward. See *Africa,* C 6.

Jones, Eli Stanley (1884–1973). B. Clarksville, near Baltimore, Md.; educ. Asbury Coll.; taught at Asbury Coll.; Meth. evangelist to high castes of India 1907; bp. 1928, resigned to continue miss. work; exponent of social* gospel. Works include *The Christ of the Indian Road; Victory Through Surrender.*

Jones, John Taylor. See *Asia,* C 4.

Jones, Rufus Matthew (1863–1948). B. South China, Maine; Quaker; educ. Haverford (Pa.) Coll., U. of Heidelberg, Ger., and U. of Pa.; principal Oak Grove Sem., Vassalboro, Maine, 1889–93; prof. Haverford Coll. 1904–34. Wrote extensively on the Quaker religion.

Jones, Samuel Porter (Sam Jones; 1847–1906). B. Oak Bowery, Chambers Co., Ala.; Confederate soldier in Civil War; lawyer, drunkard; converted and became Meth. Episc., S., pastor 1872; agent of N. Ga. Orphanage 1880–92; revivalist.

Jónsson, Finnur (1704–89). Bp. Skalholt, Iceland, 1754. Wrote *Historia ecclesiastica Islandiae.*

Jordan. See *Middle East,* G.

Jordanes (Jordanis; Jordannis; Jornandes; Jornandez; 6th c.). Goth; notary; after conversion probably priest or monk; wrote hist. of Goths (condensed from F. M. A. Cassiodorus* and extended to 551) and a universal hist.

Jörgensen. 1. *Alfred Theodor* (1874–1953). B. Vejle, Den.; churchman; gen. secy. LWC Copenhagen 1929; active in ecumenical movement; helped form cong. welfare projects. Works include Luther studies. 2. *Jens Johannes* (1866–1956). B. Svendborg, Den.; poet, naturalist, symbolist; first Luth., then atheist, then (1896) RC. Works include biographies of Francis of Assisi and Catherine of Siena.

Joris, David (Jan Jorisz; Joriszoon; ca. 1501–56). B. Flanders; Anabap.; spiritualist; self-styled "prophet"; advocated ascetic practices; lived under pseudonym Jan van Brugge in Basel after 1522. Followers called Davidists or Jorists.

Josenhans, Friedrich Joseph (1812–84). B. Stuttgart, Ger.; inspector Basel* Miss. Soc. 1849–79; visited India 1851/52; reorganized the work of the Basel Miss. Soc. along centralized lines.

Joseph, Sisters of St. Name of many RC communities of women, including those that derive from the foundation made 1648 at the Le Puy, Velay, Fr., by Bp. Henry de Maupas (1606–80) and John Peter Médaille (Jesuit; 1610–69); specialize in educ. and hosp. work.

Joseph II (ca. 1360–1439). Metropolitan Ephesus ca. 1393; patriarch Constantinople 1416; attended Council of Florence.*

Joseph II and Josephinism (Josephism). Joseph II (1741–90; king of Ger. 1764–90; Holy Roman emp. 1765–90; coregent of Austria with his mother 1765–80, sole ruler 1780–90) tried to make the ch. subordinate and subservient to the state and to separate the ch. from Roman authority. Issued an edict of toleration 1781; it granted a large measure of freedom of religion to Prots., imposed restrictions on RC activities, and removed religious bars to civil offices. These and other similar measures raised RC protest. Pius VI (see *Popes,* 26) visited Joseph II in vain 1782. But disturbances gradually induced Joseph II to revoke his legislation. After his death the old constitution and privileges were restored. See also *Church and State; Josephinism; Roman Catholic Church,* D 2.

Joseph Calasanctius. See *Piarists.*

Joseph of Studion. See *Joseph of Thessalonica.*

Joseph of Thessalonica (ca. 762–ca. 832). Known in Gk. hymnody as Joseph of Studion. Younger brother of Theodore* of Studion, with whom he was at the monastery Studion at Constantinople since 798. Abp. Thessalonica 807; exiled ca. 809 in controversy concerning the adulterous marriage of Constantine VI (771–ca. 797; E Roman emp. 780–797).

Joseph the Hymnographer (ca. 810–86). B. Syracuse, Sicily, It.; Gk. hymnist; ca. 830 to Thessalonica, where he became monk and priest; later to Constantinople; captured by pirates and enslaved on way to Rome 841; ransomed; est. monastery ca. 850 at Constantinople.

MPG, 105, 925–1426.

Josephinism (Josephism). Ecclesiastical policy of Joseph II (see *Joseph II and Josephinism*). See also *Ultramontanism.*

Josephites. 1. See Latter Day Saints, g 2. 2. Name attached to various RC groups, including St.* Joseph's Soc. of the Sacred Heart.

Josephus, Flavius (Joseph ben Matthias; ca. 37–ca. 100). B. Jerusalem; of Jewish royal and priestly descent; joined Pharisees; commander in Galilee during Jewish* War; policy clash aroused hostility of John* of Galilee; captured by Romans; freed by Vespasian*; to Rome after war. Works include *De Maccabeis; De bello Judaico; Antiquitates Judaicae; Contra Apionem; Vita Flavii Josephi.*

L. Bernstein, *Flavius Josephus* (New York, 1938); A. H. Tamarin, *Revolt in Judea* (New York, 1968); G. A. Williamson, *The World of Josephus* (London, 1964).

Josquin Deprès (variants include Després; des Prés; Despréz; Jodocus Pratensis; a Prato; a Pratis; del Prato; ca. 1440–ca. 1521). Leading Franco-Flemish composer in the transition from the Middle Ages to the Renaissance; precursor of G. P. de Palestrina*; regarded by some as having been a pupil of J. d' Okeghem,* with whom he holds common ground in counterpoint.

Journals, Theological. See *Theological Journals.*

Jovinian (fl. 4th c. AD). It. "heretic" known only from writings of his opponents, including Jerome.* His views developed from his opposition to E monasticism and included: married people have equal merit with unmarried and widows; fasting not better than thankful feasting; Mary conceived, but did not bear Christ as a virgin, since childbearing ends virginity; the regenerate are essentially sinless. Excommunicated by Siricius (b. Rome; pope [bp. Rome] 384–ca. 399) and a syn. at Rome and by Ambrose* and a syn. at Milan, all in 390.

Jowett, Benjamin (1817–93). B. Camberwell (London), Eng.; educ. Oxford; master Balliol Coll. 1870; regius prof. Gk. 1855 and vice-chancellor 1882–86 Oxford; exponent of Broad* Ch. theol.; best known for tr. of Plato's* *Dialogues.*

Jowett, John Henry (1864–1923). B. Halifax, Yorkshire, Eng.; Cong. pastor New Castle upon Tyne 1889, Birmingham 1895, NYC 1911, London 1918. Works include *The High Calling; The Transfigured Church; Things That Matter Most; The Passion for Souls.*

Jube. See *Road Screen.*

Jubilate. See *Church Year,* 14, 16.

Jubilatio. See *Jubilus.*

Jubilees. Also called Holy Years. In 1300 Boniface VIII (see *Popes,* 12) offered plenary indulgence to all the faithful who, in 1300 and every 100th yr. thereafter, would make a stated number of daily visits to the chs. of Peter and Paul in Rome with pious prayer and penitent confession. A yr. of Jubilee was celebrated again 1350 (by a 1342 decree of Clement VI [Pierre Roger; 1291–1352; b. Correze, Fr.; pope 1342–52]) and 1390 (by direction of Urban VI [Bartolommeo Prignani; 1318–89; b. Naples, It.; pope 1378–89], who set the cycle at 33 yrs. on the analogy of the length of Christ's life). Further adjustments were made in the 15th c.; in 1470 Paul II (Pietro Barbo; 1417–71; b. Venice, It.; pope 1464–71), in view of the shortness of human life, reduced the time to 25 yrs. beginning 1475. Jubilees usually begin with opening of the "holy doors" of the basilicas of Peter, Paul, John Lateran, and Mary Major at Vespers Dec. 24. Essential modern ceremonies were specified by Alexander VI (see *Popes,* 18).

Jubilees, Book of. Also called The Little Genesis. Reinterpretation of Genesis. See also *Apocrypha,* A 4.

Jubilus (jubilatio; jubilum). Melismatic rendition of the final syllable of the 2d alleluia (see *Hallelujah*) before and of the alleluia after the alleluiatic verse in the gradual.* The sequence* grew out of the jubilus.

Jud, Leo (Judae; Keller; 1482–1542). "Meister Leu." B. Gemar, Alsace; educ. Basel, Switz., and Freiburg im Breisgau, Ger.; pastor Alsace and Switz.; assoc. with H. Zwingli* and J. H. Bullinger.* Helped formulate the First Helvetic Confession (see *Reformed Confessions,* A 6) and made its official Ger. tr.; helped make the (Ger.) Zurich Bible tr.; tr. OT books into Lat.; other works include a Lat. and 2 Ger. catechisms.

Judah ben Samuel (Jehuda von Regensburg; ca. 1150–1217). B. Speyer, Ger.; Jewish mystic and moralist; founded a school at Regensburg 1195.

Judah ha-Levi (Judah ben Samuel Halevi; Arab.: Abu'l Hasan; ca. 1085–ca. 1140). B. Toledo, Sp.; rabbi, physician, poet, and philos.; tried to show superiority of revealed religion over rational and philos. belief.

Judaism. 1. Religion and religious practices of the Jews. Term is of Gk. origin (2 Mac 2:21; 8:1; 14:38; 4 Mac 4:26; Gl 1:13, 14). The foundation of all forms of Judaism is the Pentateuch,* which records how God made the Jews His people and how He gave ordinances for faith and life. Judaism was unique in the ancient world in its doctrines that Jahweh* is one God, the Creator and Ruler of the universe; that He is a spirit; that He is holy and demands holiness from His followers, yet is ready to forgive repentant sinners who seek His mercy in faith; that He would provide a Messiah* who would redeem His people and extend His kingdom over all the earth; and that in the world to come the righteous are eternally blessed, but the wicked are eternally punished for their sins. Unique was also the observance of the Sabbath.* Characteristic rite of Judaism is circumcision as the sign of the covenant* bet. God and His people. Sacrifices at the nat. sanctuary held a cen. position before the destruction of the temple (2 K 25:9, 13-17; 2 Ch 36:18-19).

2. During the cents. after the return from the Babylonian Captivity (see *Babylonian Captivity,* 1) the voice of prophecy became silent. But loss of pol. indep., trials of the Babylonian Captivity, and difficulties under for. rule centered attention on spiritual heritage. Much study was spent on the Torah* and its interpretation in light of the prophets and oral tradition. The sect of the Pharisees sprang up, added its regulations to those of the Torah, and developed a system of obedience to the letter of the Law without true service of God. Another contemporary sect was that of the Sadducees; they were liberals or freethinkers. Many Jews, esp. among the common people, adhered to the OT hope and faith. With the conquest of Jerusalem and destruction of the temple by Romans 70 AD, the period of Judaism characterized by the Talmud* began; it is marked by extreme legalism and ritualism, but no unified system of doctrine resulted till Maimonides* in the 12th c. codified the teachings of Judaism under 13 principles: (1) Existence of God, source of all creation; (2) His unity; (3) His spirituality; (4) His unity has no beginning; (5) worship of Him alone; (6) prophecy; (7) Moses the supreme prophet; (8) revelation of the Torah to Moses; (9) Torah the only and unchangeable Law; (10) Creator knows thoughts and deeds of man; (11) God rewards and punishes; (12) coming of the Messiah; (13) resurrection of the dead.

3. In modern times Jews have been able to play a large part in the soc., economic, and pol. world. Many still adhere to Orthodox Judaism despite difficulties in adjusting religious practices to prevailing conditions. Others, called Conservative, regard the Torah and traditional laws of Judaism as basic, but have made concessions by being less strict in observing religious regulations. A 3d group, Reform Judaism, originated in Ger. as a lay movement in the late 18th c.; it tries to adjust Judaism to modern needs; services are in the vernacular and are modernized. Reform Judaism aims to retain elements of Jewish tradition regarded as permanent, but allows changes in all other respects. It stresses the principle that the Jew must make a contribution toward enlightening mankind. Reform Judaism is prominent in the struggle against anti-Semitism.* Despite differences, all Jews recognize each other as mems. of one family; variations in belief and practice are viewed as expressions of different schools of Judaism. See also *Schechter, Solomon.*

4. Besides observing Sabbaths, new moons, special fast days, and minor festivals, Judaism keeps as major festivals: Passover (Ex 12:21-51; Mt 26:1-30 and parallel passages) and Pentecost (from Gk. *pentekoste* sc. *hemera,* "fiftieth day"; Feast of Weeks [Heb. *Shabuoth,* "weeks"]; Dt 16:9-13; Acts 2:1) in spring; New Year (Heb. *Rosh Hashanah,* "head of the year"; beginning of the 1st mo. of the Jewish civil [7th mo. of the religious] yr.; Feast of Trumpets; Lv 23:24; Nm 29:1), Day of Atonement (Heb. *Yom Kippur;* Lv 16; 23:26-32; Nm 29:7-11; Acts 27:9), and Feast of Tabernacles (Heb. *Sukkoth,* "booths; tabernacles"; Feast of Harvest; Ex 23:16; Lv 23:39-43) in fall. To these Mosaic festivals were added later Purim (Heb. "lots"; Feast of Esther; commemorates rescue of Jews from Haman's plot; Est, esp. 9:20-28) and Hanukkah (Heb. "dedication"; commemorates victory of Maccabees over Syrians and the rededication of the defiled temple at Jerusalem; 1 Mac 1:41-64; 2 Mac 1:18; 6:2; Feast of Lights; falls near Christmas). Up to AD 70, pilgrimages to the temple at Jerusalem were required in connection with observance of Passover, Pentecost, and Feast of Tabernacles. GVS

See also *Church Year; Middle East; Pasch; Zionism.*

Judd, Gerrit Parmele (Apr. 23, 1803–Jan. 12, 1873). B. Paris, N. Y.; ABCFM med. miss. to Sandwich Islands (Hawaii) 1828; interpreter and recorder of Kamehameha III (Kauikeaouli; 1813–54; king of Sandwich Islands 1825–54); organized 1st Hawaiian cabinet 1843; minister of finance 1844.

Judex, Matthäus (Richter; 1528–64). B. Dippoldiswalde, Ger.; educ. Wittenberg; vice-principal (Konrektor) of Gymnasium and deacon Magdeburg; prof. theol. Jena 1560; deposed and banned 1561; to Magdeburg, Wismar, and Rostock. Gnesio-Lutheran.* Contributed to *Magdeburg* Centuries.* See also *Synergistic Controversy.*

Judgment, Final. See *Hereafter; Last Things,* 5.

Judgment of Conscience. See *Conscience.*

Judica. Passion Sun. See also *Church Year,* 14, 16.

Judith. See *Apocrypha,* A 3.

Judson, Adoniram (Aug. 9, 1788–Apr. 12, 1850). B. Malden, Mass.; educ. Brown U. (Providence, R. I.) and Andover (Mass.) Theol. Sem.; Cong. ABCFM miss. to India or Burma 1812; became Bap. on way and separated from ABCFM; from Calcutta, Ind., to Rangoon, Burma, 1812–13, via the is. Mauritius and Madras, Ind.; suffered hardships during war bet. Eng. and Burma; miss. headquarters moved to Amherst 1826, to Moulmain 1827. Judson returned to the US 1845; back to Burma 1846. Tr. Bible and other books into Burmese. Other literary efforts include a Burmese-Eng., Eng.-Burmese dictionary; a Burmese grammar; a Pali dictionary. See also *India,* 11; *Judson, Ann Hasseltine; Judson, Emily Chubbuck; Judson, Sarah Hall, Haystack Group.*

Judson, Ann Hasseltine (Dec. 22, 1789–Oct. 24, 1826). B. Bradford, Mass.; school teacher; married A. Judson*; with him to Burma. Tr. Gospel of Matthew and a catechism into Siamese; other works include a history of the Burman mission.

Judson, Emily Chubbuck (pseudonym Fanny Forester; Aug. 22, 1817–June 1, 1854). B. Eaton, N. Y.; taught at Utica; married A. Judson*; with him to Burma 1846. Works collected under titles including *Olio; Kathayan Slave; My Two Sisters.*

Judson, Sarah Hall (Boardman; Nov. 4, 1803–Sept. 1, 1845). B. Alstead, N. H.; married G. D. Boardman*; with him to Burma; after Boardman's death, married A. Judson.* Tr. tracts, hymns, part of J. Bunyan's* *Pilgrim's Progress,* and other Christian literature into Burmese; helped tr. tracts and the NT into the language of the Peguans.

Jugoslavia. See *Yugoslavia.*

Julian (Flavius Claudius Julianus; ca. 331–363). "The Apostate." Roman emp. 361–363. B. Constantinople; reared Christian; embraced paganism; developed strong anti-Christian policy.

Julian, John (1839–1913). B. St. Agnes, Cornwall, Eng.; vicar Wincobank and Topcliffe; canon York; hymnist; hymnographer. Works include *A Dictionary of Hymnology.*

Julian Calendar. Roman calendar as reformed ca. 46 BC under Julius Caesar (from whom it takes its name); days were added to the year of adjustment to restore the vernal equinox to Mar. 25; the normal yr. then had 365 days; leap yrs. (every 4th yr.) had a day inserted after Feb. 24. Called Old Style. See also *Gregorian Calendar.*

Julian of Eclanum (ca. 380–ca. 455). B. Eclanum, It.;

bp. Eclanum; deposed and exiled 418 with 17 other bps. for refusing to subscribe to a papal condemnation of Pelagianism; opposed Augustine* of Hippo's doctrine of the total depravity of fallen man; held that sin is a matter of the will, not of inheritance or nature.

Julian of Halicarnassus (d. after 527). Bp. Halicarnassus (modern Bodrum), Caria, Asia Minor; Monophysitic; expelled 518; adopted view that Jesus was incorruptible, immortal in death, without pain in suffering.

Julian(a) of Norwich (ca. 1342–probably ca. 1416/23). Eng. mystic. Works include *(Sixteen) Revelations of Divine Love.*

Jülicher, Gustav Adolf (1857–1938). B. Falkenberg (Berlin), Ger.; orphanage chaplain Rummelsberg (Berlin) 1882–88; taught at univs. of Berlin and Marburg; prof. Marburg 1889; liberal. Initiated critical ed. of Old Latin NT (see *Bible Versions,* J 1); other works include *Die Gleichnisreden Jesu* and *Einleitung in das Neue Testament.*

Julius (1528–89). B. Wolfenbüttel, Ger.; duke of Brunswick 1568–89; introd. the Reformation there. See also *Chemnitz, Martin; Kirchner, Timotheus.*

Julius II. See *Popes,* 19.

Julius III (Giammaria [or Giovanni Maria] Ciocchi del Monte; 1487–1555). B. Rome; cardinal 1536; Council of Trent's* 1st pres. and papal legate 1545; pope 1550–55; confirmed Society* of Jesus 1550 and increased its privileges; sent R. Pole* to reunite Eng. with RC Ch. 1554; patron of Michelangelo.*

Julius Africanus, Sextus (ca. 160–ca. 240). B. probably Jerusalem (some say Libya); lived at Emmaus; traveled through Asia Minor; Christian author. Works include a hist. of the world up to ca. AD 221, which was quoted by Eusebius* of Caesarea and became the foundation of medieval historiography.

Julius Caesar. See *Augustus.*

Jumpers. Derisive name given ca. 1760 to followers of G. Whitefield* in S Wales because they leaped in religious enthusiasm; justification for leaping was sought in 2 Sm 6:16; Lk 6:23; Acts 3:8.

Jung, Carl Gustav (1875–1961). B. Switz.; lectured U. of Zurich 1905–13; assoc. with S. Freud*; held that all people have introvert and extrovert characteristics, with classification determined by dominance; explained religious and mythical symbols through the collective unconscious; stressed man's strong need for religious experiences and belief.

Jung-Stilling, Johann Heinrich (Heinrich Jung; Heinrich Stilling; 1740–1817). B. Grund, near Hilchenbach, Westphalia; prof. Kaiserslautern, Heidelberg, and Marburg; friend of J. W. v. Goethe* and J. G. v. Herder*; mystic; theosophist. Adopted name Stilling because of sympathy with Pietists of the Lower Rhine, who were called "die Stillen im Lande" (cf. Ps 35:20 in Ger.).

Jungreformatorische Bewegung. See *Kirchenkampf.*

Junilius Africanus (Junillus; d. ca. AD 550). State official under Justinian* I. Tr. into Lat. *Instituta regularia divinae legis.*

MPL, 68, 11–42.

Junior Colleges, Lutheran. See *Ministry, Education of,* VIII C.

Junius, Franciscus (Franz; François du Jon; 1545–1602). B. Bourges, Fr.; studied under T. Beza* in Geneva, Switz.; preacher to the Walloon cong., Antwerp, Belg.; helped his father-in-law J. I. Tremellius* tr. OT into Lat.

Jupiter. See *Roman Religion,* 1.

Jure divino; jure humano. See *Ius divinum.*

Juri(j). See *Dalmatin, George.*

Jurieu, Pierre (1637–1713). B. Mer, near Blois, Fr.; educ. Saumur and Sedan, and in the Neth. and Eng.; Ref. pastor; prof. Sedan 1674, Rotterdam 1681; controversialist.

Juris divini; juris humani. See *Ius divinum.*

Jurisdiction, Spiritual. See *Keys, Office of,* 8.

Jus divinum. See *Ius divinum.*

Jus gentium. See *Ius gentium.*

Jus humanum. See *Ius divinum.*

Jus naturae; jus naturale. See *Natural Law.*

Jus novissimum; jus novum. See *Canon Law.*

Justice of God. The justice of God* is that quality in God by reason of which He legislates justly, His laws being the perfect expression of His holy will. He is true to His promises and will execute judgment acc. to the principles of right. He is His own perfect ethical norm and, consistent with Himself, He and His judgments are just and righteous, Dt 32:4; Ps 19:9. In His justice He gave laws which are perfect. When they are transgressed, His justice demands punishment; if vicarious atonement is made, it must be full satisfaction. His justice considers the manner and measure of sin committed, Mt 11:21-24; Lk 12: 47-48. Just punishments are inflicted in retribution, Heb 2:2. Fulfillment of divine promises, credited in one respect to grace,* is also right, Is 54:10; 2 Ti 4:8.

Justification. 1. Judicial act of God which consists of non-imputation of sin and imputation of Christ's righteousness.

2. The Luth. Confessions (Ap, esp. the Ger. version, IV 2, 3; FC SD III 6) and renowned teachers, e. g., M. Luther* (WA 30 II, 650; 43, 178; 40 III, 739), M. Chemnitz,* B. Meisner,* and C. F. W. Walther* call the doctrine of justification the most important teaching of divine revelation. The apprehension of this doctrine by Luther made him the divinely equipped Reformer of the ch.

3. The doctrine of justification presupposes that man, through his natural condition and his thoughts, words, and deeds, is a transgressor of God's Law, subject to His wrath, condemned to eternal death, Ec 7:20; Is 64:6; Mt 25:41; Ro 1–3. See also *Sin; Sin, Original.*

4. The doctrine includes, as one of its chief elements, that God is moved to justify us by grace,* a special kind of love, directed toward those who are undeserving or unworthy, Jn 3:16; Ro 3:23; 5:20.

5. God's grace accomplished its purpose through the redemption of Christ. God sent His holy, innocent Son to become man and made Him man's Substitute. This Substitute fulfilled all requirements of the Law in our place (active obedience). He also suffered the pangs and woes which we had deserved (passive obedience). Divine justice is satisfied and love triumphs. Through Christ God reconciled the world unto Himself, 2 Co 5:19. This act of God is called objective justification; it is not the same as redemption, justification being judicial, redemption sacrificial. See also *Priest, Christ as.*

6. The righteousness of Christ is given us by God in the Gospel and sacraments. These means of grace (see *Grace, Means of*) offer, give, and seal to us God's forgiveness, Jn 15:3; Ro 1:16; Gl 3:27. We receive this righteousness through faith.* The moment we accept the righteousness which Christ won, God pronounces us justified, free from sin, acquitted (subjective justification, Gn 15:6; Lk 15; Gl 2:16). ". . . the forgiveness of sins is a thing promised for Christ's sake. Therefore it can be accepted only by faith, since a promise can be accepted only on faith. In Rom. 4:16 Paul says, 'That is why it depends on faith, in order that the promise may rest on grace and be guaranteed,' as though he were to say, 'If it depended on our merits, the promise would be uncertain and useless inasmuch as we could never determine whether we had merited enough.' Experienced consciences can readily understand this. Therefore Paul says (Gal. 3:22), 'God consigned

all things to sin, that what was promised to faith in Jesus Christ might be given to those who believe.' Here he denies us any merit, for he says that all are guilty and consigned to sin. Then he adds that the promise of the forgiveness of sins and justification is a gift, and further that the promise can be accepted by faith. Based upon the nature of a promise, this is Paul's chief argument, which he often repeats (Rom. 4:16; Gal. 3:18). Nothing one can devise or imagine will refute Paul's argument. So pious men should not let themselves be diverted from this declaration, that we receive the forgiveness of sins for Christ's sake only by faith; here they have a certain and firm consolation against the terrors of sin, against eternal death, and against all the gates of hell (Matt. 16:18)." (Ap IV 84–85).

7. Since justification is brought about by God's grace through the sacrifice of Christ and we become possessors of it through faith, all human merit is excluded, Ro 3:27-31. Faith is not merit, since we are not justified on account of, but through, faith (J. Gerhard,* *Locus XVII. De justificatione per fidem,* CLXXX). Justification takes place outside of us, at the tribunal of God, Ro 8:33-39.

8. When a sinner is justified, he has peace with God, enjoys Christian liberty, does good works, and is filled with hope of eternal life, Jn 8:36; Ro 7:25; 8:1-2, 17.

9. Justification is not a long-drawn-out process, but occurs in a moment; it is never partial, but always perfect and complete; it is alike in all who are justified; it puts one into a state of righteousness which continues as long as one believes; it can be lost; it can be obtained anew when it has been lost. WA

See also *Atonement; Material Principle.*

See bibliography under *Dogmatics;* T. Engelder, "Objective Justification," *CTM,* IV, Nos. 7–9 (July–Sept. 1933), 507–517, 564–577, 664–675; W. Arndt, "The Doctrine of Justification," *The Abiding Word,* II (St. Louis, 1947), 235–257; T. Hoyer, "Through Justification unto Sanctification," *CTM,* XIII, No. 2 (Feb. 1942), 81–111; E. W. A. Koehler, "Objective Justification," *CTM,* XVI, No. 4 (Apr. 1945), 217–235; W. Elert, Morphologie des Luthertums, I (Munich, 1931; improved print. 1952), 64–123, tr. W. A. Hansen, *The Structure of Lutheranism,* I (St. Louis, 1962), 73–140; A. Köberle, *The Quest for Holiness,* tr. J. C. Mattes (New York, 1936); F. R. E. Preuss, *Die Rechtfertigung des Sünders vor Gott,* 2d ed. (Berlin, 1871); C. P. Krauth, *The Conservative Reformation and Its Theology* (Philadelphia, 1871); G. Aulén, *Christus Victor,* tr. A. G. Hebert (London, 1931); E. L. Lueker, "Justification in the Theology of Walther," *CTM,* XXXII, No. 10 (Oct. 1961), 598–605.

Justin Martyr (Justin the Philosopher; ca. 100–ca. 165). B. Flavia Neapolis (Nablus; ancient Shechem), Samaria, of heathen parents; Platonist; converted ca. 130; est. Christian school at Rome. See also *Apologists,* 4.

Justinian I (Flavius Petrus Sabbatius Justinianus; Flavius Anicius Justinianus; 483–565). "Justinian the Great." B. Tauresium, Illyricum, Macedonia; consul 521; E Roman emp. 527–565; brilliant ruler; tried to restore the religious and pol. unity of the empire, but failed to prevent increased estrangement bet. the E and the W Ch.; efforts to codify Roman law resulted in *Corpus iuris civilis* (Code of Justinian), a revision and updating of the Code of Theodosius* II; it decreed the destruction of Hellenism. Closed the philos. school at Athens 529; promoted Christian missions; restricted civil rights and religious affairs of Jews; made Niceno-Constantinopolitan Creed the sole symbol of the ch.; accorded legal force to the canons of the first 4 ecumenical councils. See also *Constantinople, Councils of,* 2; *Natural Law; Popes,* 3.

Justinian II (Rhinotmetus [Gk. "with the nose cut off"]; 669–711). Son of Constantine* IV; E Roman emp. 685–695; 705–711; convened Quinisext* Synod; cruel; defeated 695 by his gen., Leontius, who cut off his nose.

Justitia aliena. See *Iustitia aliena.*

Justitia inchoata. See *Image of God,* 4.

Juusten, Paavali. See *Finland, Lutheranism in,* 2.

Juvenal (d. 458). Bp. Jerusalem ca. 422. Tried to make Jerusalem one of the important sees of Christendom.

Juvencus, Caius Vettius Aquilinus (Gaius; Aquilius; 4th c.). Sp. presbyter. Wrote Lat. poetry, including a metrical form of the 4 gospels.

K

Kaaba (Kaabeh; Kaba[h]; Caaba; Arab. "cube"). Ancient Arab. shrine in the form of an irregular cube in the heart of Mecca. Muhammad* retained it as chief sanctuary of Islam,* prescribed pilgrimages to it, and appointed it as qibla(h) (kibla[h]), the point toward which Muslim* turn to pray. Set in masonry in its SE corner, at a height convenient for kissing, is the sacred Black Stone, main object of veneration in the Kaaba. Every devout Muslim is supposed to visit the shrine at least once.

Kaas, Ludwig (1881–1952). B. Trier, Ger.; educ. Rome; RC priest, prof., and prelate; mem. Weimar Nat. Assem. 1919, Ger. Diet 1920–33; moved to Rome 1933; participated in 1933 concordat bet. Ger. and Rome (see *Concordat,* 8).

Kaba(h). See *Kaaba.*

Kabala (Kabbala[h]). See *Cabala.*

Kabisch, Richard (1868–1914). B. Kemnitz, near Greifswald, Ger.; ev. theol. of religionsgeschichtliche* Schule; educator; advocated culture-religion in state education. Works include *Die Eschatologie des Paulus in ihren Zusammenhängen mit dem Gesamtbegriff des Paulinismus; Das neue Geschlecht: Ein Erziehungsbuch; Wie lehren wir Religion?* (with H. Tögel).

Kaehler. See *Kähler.*

Kaeppel. See *Käppel.*

Kaffir (Kafir; Caffer; Caffre; Arab. "infidel"). Term sometimes applied to Bantu tribes (see *Africa,* A 1).

Kaftan, Julius Wilhelm Martin (1848–1926). B. Loit, near Apenrade, Schleswig, Ger.; brother of T. Kaftan*; theol.; educ. Erlangen, Berlin, Kiel; prof. theol. Basel 1874, Berlin 1883–1920; representative of Ritschlian theol. (see *Ritschl, Albrecht*); emphasized mystic element in Christianity; regarded the Christian religion as the only satisfying religion. Works include *Die Wahrheit der christlichen Religion; Das Wesen der christlichen Religion.*

Kaftan, Theodor (1847–1932). B. Loit, near Apenrade, Schleswig, Ger.; brother of J. W. M. Kaftan*; Prot. theol.; educ. Erlangen, Berlin, and Kiel; asst. pastor Kappeln; pastor Dan. cong. Apenrade 1873; govt. and school councillor Schleswig 1880; provost Tönder, Den., 1885; gen. supt. Schleswig 1886; pastor Luth. cong. Baden-Baden. Works include *Moderne Theologie des alten Glaubens; Zur Verständigung über moderne Theologie des alten Glaubens.*

Kagawa, Toyohiko (1888–1960). B. Kobe, Jap.; Presb. evangelist and soc. reformer; studied theol. in Jap., sociol. in US; founded 1st Labor Federation in Jap. 1918, also Peasant Union 1921, Anti-War League 1928, Kingdom of God Movement 1930. Works include *The Religion of Jesus; Christ and Japan; Songs from the Slums; The Two Kingdoms.*

Kähler, Karl Martin August (1835–1912). B. Neuhausen, near Königsberg, Ger.; educ. Königsberg, Heidelberg, Halle, Tübingen; taught at Halle and Bonn. In opposition to quest for hist. Jesus (see *Jesus, Lives of*), Kähler held that the gospels were not primarily sources for hist. research, but records of apostolic proclamation. Faith is related to hist. events. Kähler distinguished mission, which emphasizes that the ch. exists where Christ and His Spirit are active through His Word, from propaganda, which is egocentric and seeks to proselytize for one's own views and interests. Works include *Der sogenannte historische Jesus und der geschichtliche Christus; Theologe und Christ; Gott in der Geschichte; Die Wissenschaft der christlichen Lehre von dem evangelischen Grundartikel aus im Abrisse dargestellt.* See also *Biblicism.*

Kahnis, Karl Friedrich August (1814–88). Luth. theol.; b. Greiz, Ger.; educ. Halle; taught at Berlin 1842; prof. Breslau 1844, Leipzig 1850. At first defended confessional Lutheranism; joined Old* Lutherans 1848. Later adopted a subordinationist view (see *Subordinationism*) and divergent views on Scripture and the Lord's Supper. Works include *Der innere Gang des deutschen Protestantismus; Die lutherische Dogmatik historisch-genetisch dargestellt.* See also *Kenosis.*

Kairis, Theophilos (Kaires; 1784–1853). B. on the is. Andros, Greece; Orthodox priest and liberal theol.; educ. Pisa and Paris; imbibed philos. of Fr. Revolution; took part in Gk. War of Indep. (1821–30); founded orphanage on Andros 1835; opposed and imprisoned by ch. authorities for theophilanthropism* and ideas derived from Enlightenment.* His system came to be called theosebism.

Kaiser, Jakob (Kayser; Schlosser; d. 1529). Pastor Zurich; burned at stake.

Kaiser, Leonhard (Käser; Kayser; ca. 1480–1527). B. Raab, near Schärding, Bav.; educ. Leipzig; vicar Waizenkirchen ca. 1517; endorsed M. Luther*; imprisoned; recanted; to Wittenberg 1525; returned home 1527 to visit dying father; fell ill; imprisoned; burned at stake.

Kaiser-Wilhelmsland. See *New Guinea,* 1, 5.

Kaiserswerth. See *Charities, Christian,* 5.

Káldi, György (1570/72–1634). B. Trnava (Hung.: Nagyszombat; Ger.: Tyrnau); Hung. Jesuit; educ. Rome; preacher Transylvania and Vienna; prof. Olomouc (Ger.: Olmütz) and Brno (Ger.: Brünn); dir. Trnava 1615, Bratislava (Ger.: Pressburg; Hung.: Pozsony) 1625. Works include Bible tr. into Hungarian.

Kalevala (Kalewala; Fin. "dwelling place of Kaleva [Kalewa]"). Collection of Fin. epic poems containing myths, legends, and hist. Kaleva is a mythological hero.

Kalimantan. See *Indonesia,* 1, 5.

Kalkar, Christian Andreas Herman(n) (1803 [1802?]–86). B. Stockholm; rabbi's son; became Christian in Den. 1823; pastor Seeland (Zealand; Sjaelland). Works include OT commentary; hist. of the Bible.

Kalley, Robert Reid. See *Africa,* C 16; *Help for Brazil Mission.*

Kalm, Peter (1716–79). B. Aangermanland, Swed.; educ. Aabo and Uppsala; prof. Aabo; naturalist; account of his Am. travels sheds light on early Am. Luth. hist.

Kálmáncsehi Sánta, Márton (ca. 1500–57). B. Kálmáncsa, Hung.; RC till the late 1530s; ev. pastor in the 1540s; apologist; organizer; influenced by H. Zwingli,* J. H. Bullinger,* and the Consensus Tigurinus (see *Calvin, John,* 12; *Reformed Confessions,* A 8).

Kalthoff, Albert (1850–1906). B. Barmen, Ger.; pastor Bremen 1888–1906; helped est. "Bremen radicalism"; held an idealistic monism; contended that

"Christ myth" developed out of soc. and ethic situations.

Kam. See *Kamm.*

Kamehameha I. See *Hawaii.*

Kamehameha II and III. See *Thurston, Asa.*

Kamerun (Cameroons; Port.: Camarões; Cameroun). Former Ger. protectorate in W Afr. Divided 1920 into Brit. and Fr. mandate; UN trust territory 1946; Fr. territory became indep. 1960, annexed Southern Cameroons (part of Brit. territory) 1961 (Northern Cameroons, the other part of Brit. territory, remained part of Nigeria). See also *Africa,* F 7.

Kami. See *Shinto.*

Kamm, Joseph Carel (Jozef Kam; ca. 1769–1833). "Apostle to the Moluccas"; b. 's Hertogenbosch (Fr.: Bois-le-Duc), Neth.; influenced as child by Moravian Brethren (see *Moravian Church,* 3); educ. Netherlands* Miss. Soc. institute at Berkel, near Rotterdam, and LMS sem. at Gosport, Eng.; sent by Neth. Miss. Soc. with help of LMS to Indonesia; active there ca. 1814–33. Effected renewal of the ch. by emphasizing its native character and the training of native ministers.

Kamphausen, Adolf Hermann Heinrich (1829–1909). B. Solingen, Ger.; educ. Bonn; private secy. of C. K. J. v. Bunsen*; taught at Heidelberg 1856–59; returned to Bonn; prof. Bonn 1863–1901; mem. of committee for revising M. Luther's* OT tr. Works include *Das Buch Daniel und die neuere Geschichtsforschung; Die Chronologie der hebräischen Könige.*

K'ang-hsi. See *China,* 6.

Kankan Mission Press. See *Africa,* C 4.

Kansas, Evangelical Lutheran Synod of. See *United Lutheran Church, Synods of,* 3.

Kansas City Platform. Statement adopted 1913 at Kansas City, Mo., by the Nat. Council of Cong. Chs. Reaffirms democratic principles; confesses God the Father, Jesus Christ, and the Holy Spirit; states that it is the miss. of the ch. to proclaim the Gospel and work for progress in knowledge, justice, peace, and brotherhood; asserts the freedom and responsibility of the individual soul and the right of private judgment; affirms autonomy of local chs.; holds to fellowship of chs. for counsel and cooperation in matters of common concern. See also *United Church of Christ, The,* I A 3.

Kansas Synod. See *United Lutheran Church, Synods of,* 3.

Kant, Immanuel (1724–1804). 1. B. Königsberg, E. Prussia, in a pietistic home; educ. at the Collegium Fredericianum in Königsberg and the U. of Königsberg; prof. logic and metaphysics Königsberg 1770; never married; academic life rigorously disciplined.

2. Kant concerned himself esp. with the problem of knowledge. He tried to overcome the limitations and contradictions of empiricism* and rationalism.*

3. Kant detected in the "new" physical science: a scientist is active, not passive or "discovering" laws in nature; he (a) thrusts laws upon nature (b) in accord with characteristics of the human mind. The clue for Kant came in an analysis of the concept of causality. The notion of cause is not deduced by reason or gained inductively or disposed by mere mental habit of associated ideas (D. Hume*), but springs a priori from pure understanding. This led Kant to affirm: (a) reason has insight into that only which it produces after a plan of its own; accidental observations can never be made to yield *necessary* laws, which reason alone is concerned to discover; (b) using its own principles and experiments, reason must approach nature to learn from it not as a pupil, passively, but as an appointed judge who compels the witness to answer questions which the judge himself formulates.

4. Kant affirmed that space and time are subjective, a priori forms of possible perception and that judgment (the fundamental unit of thought) must conform to basic, a priori categories of understanding (i. e., connective concepts which are basic forms of the elaboration in thought of the material of cognition, e. g., unity, multiplicity, substance, causality, possibility). Experience is the product of the joint operation of forms of perception and categories of understanding, which the mind uses spontaneously in accord with the inherent laws of its being, in the very act of experiencing, as essential preconditions of significant experience.

5. The upshot is that all significant experience is in part a mental construction, for there is no significant experience unless the mind itself is at work in it, decisively determining what it is as assimilated to the laws of its own nature. The categories are applicable only to phenomena within our consciousness, hence *we* prescribe laws to nature. Our constructive understanding builds up the world from the sum total of impressions, acc. to its own laws of thought. Our world picture is not an image of reality mirroring the "original." In fact, we can never learn the nature of the world in itself, but only as it appears to us. But neither is it purely a subjective fiction, for that there is a connection of our sensibility and understanding with the "outer" world is verified by experimentation in science.

6. Human beings, then, can never transcend the limits of possible experience, hence there can be no rational metaphysics of being as it is "in itself" (beyond experience), but only knowledge of appearances as constituted in the mind. A priori knowledge has to do only with the appearances (phenonmena) in our experience; the thing-in-itself (noumenon; see also *Ding an sich*) is always beyond our forms of perception and categories of understanding. Causality, e. g., applies only to phenomenal objects, hence the will in its invisible, phenomenal acts cannot appear free, but in itself (as noumenal) is *not* bound by our category of understanding and hence is free. The attempt to "prove" the existence of God, human freedom, and immortality is doomed to failure as beyond the scope of pure reason, but such beliefs (regulative ideals) are necessarily postulated in faith by practical reason as essential conditions of the possibility of our moral experience of duty and obligation.

7. Kant's formalistic ethic centered in the notion of moral autonomy: man as giving moral laws to himself. The only thing intrinsically good is "good will." Kant's test of the morality of an act: Can the maxim of the act be universalized? Religion is the recognition of our duties as enjoined by divine commands; the clue to the purpose of the world is thus found in moral experience, the realm of the "ought." See also *Categorical Imperative.*

8. Kant's influence was tremendous. (a) His notion that all experience is a mental construction, riddled with reason, had led him to postulate the unknown thing-in-itself (see par. 6). Absolute idealism* (see also *Hegel, Georg Wilhelm Friedrich*) rejected noumena (see par. 6). Experienced phenomena *are* reality. The real is the rational. All reality is theoretically knowable. (b) Because reason is a tool for interpreting phenomena only, its range coincides with physical science; metaphysics and theol. are cognitively meaningless, beyond our mental powers. Not only categories of thought but also human language is inadequate for expressing anything meaningful about the transempirical. Conscious of the limitations of reason, we must concentrate on natural science, renouncing more ambitious but unattainable intellectual projects. (c) Reason can deal only with phenomena, but in intense moral experience we approach ultimate being, – not in thought about being, but in the *act* of being, of self-

consciousness; for self-consciousness implies, paradoxically, both self-transcendence and an abiding self. Rational metaphysics is impossible, but it is by being ourselves and discovering within ourselves that which transcends the world of phenomena that we grasp our kinship with Ultimate Being. The proper task of philos. is plumbing man as he knows and experiences himself in the depths of his personality, and how he apprehends God, freedom, and human destiny. (d) Laws and theories of physics are not "laws of nature" but laws of the physicists; such laws are not "discovered" in nature but are imposed on nature. The aim of physics is to forge a practical instrument for coordinating and predicting phenomena. Modern atomic theory is not of "the real nature of things" but belongs to the categorical and conventional order. (e) The necessity, authority, and certainty of propositions of logic and mathematics reside in language, not in the constitution of the world. Logical propositions, like categories, are imposed on the world by the mind, arising from customary and conventional categories of language. The world lying behind the logico-lingual categorical frame is beyond our intellectual reach, hence metaphysics, ethics, theol., and other nonempirical enterprises are not cognitively but only emotively meaningful. (f) Theol. assertions about the Godhead and divine Persons are not to be taken as metaphysical statements but as value judgments of the believing community. Thus ethical rather than metaphysical categories are the foundation of theol. discourse. The hist. Jesus is taken as (has the value of) God because of His moral perfection. The goal of Christianity is establishment of the morally ideal "kingdom of God." The essence of religion is the human feeling of absolute dependence. The essence of theol. is the phenomenology of religious experience of "the holy."

See also *Lutheran Theology After 1580,* 9; *Philosophy.*

Works include *Kritik der reinen Vernunft; Kritik der praktischen Vernunft; Kritik der Urtheilskraft; Grundlegung zur Metaphysik der Sitten; Prolegomena zu einer jeden künftigen Metaphysik die als Wissenschaft wird auftreten können.* RVS

H. J. Paton, *The Categorical Imperative* (London, 1936) and *Kant's Metaphysic of Experience* (London, 1936); S. Körner, *Kant* (Harmondsworth, Middlesex, Eng., 1955); E. Hirsch, "Luthers Rechtfertigungslehre bei Kant," *Lutherstudien,* II (Gütersloh, 1954), 104–121; W. Pannenberg, "Theologische Motive im Denken Immanuel Kants," *Theologische Literaturzeitung,* LXXXIX, No. 12 (Dec. 1964), cols. 897–906.

Kantionale. See *Cantionale.*

Kantorei. Choral group usually identified with a ch., school, court, or municipality; provides music (often choral-instrumental) for religious, cultural, or soc. occasions. Kantorei hist. begins in the early Middle Ages. The Kantorei led by J. Walther* became a model for others.

Kanzel. See *Cancelli.*

Kapff, Sixt Karl (von) (1805–79). B. Güglingen, Württemberg, Ger.; educ. Tübingen; Pietist; pastor Korntal, near Stuttgart, 1833; dean Münsingen 1843, Herrenberg 1847; to Reutlingen 1850; preacher Stuttgart 1852. Works include *Der religiöse Zustand des evangelischen Deutschlands nach Licht und Schatten.*

Kapler, Hermann (1867–1941). B. Oels (Olesnica), Silesia; led in reshaping the ch. and its relationship to the state after 1918; led Ger. delegation at Universal Christian Conference on Life and Work (see *Ecumenical Movement,* 9) 1925; pres. Ger. Ev. High Consistory 1925–33.

Käppel, Georg Christoph Albert (George Christopher Albert Kaeppel; Apr. 19, 1862–Jan. 11, 1934). B. Indianapolis, Ind.; educ. Ev. Luth. Teachers Sem. (Mo. Syn.), Addison, Ill. Parish school teacher Wittenberg, Mo., 1881–83; St. Louis, Mo., 1883–97. Prof. Addison, Ill., 1897; River Forest, Ill., 1913. Organist; composer. Works include contatas *Unto Us, Agnus Dei,* and *Soli Deo Gloria;* organ compositions; *Die Orgel im Gottesdienst.*

Käppel, Johann Heinrich Christian (John Henry Christian Kaeppel; Sept. 15, 1853–Feb. 3, 1925). B. Cleveland, Ohio; educ. Fort Wayne, Ind., and St. Louis, Mo.; Mo. Syn. parish school teacher St. Louis; instructor Walther Coll., St. Louis; pastor Jefferson City, Mo., 1887–88; dir. St. Paul's Coll., Concordia, Mo., 1888–1925.

Karadzic, Vuk Stefanovic (1787–1864). Serbian scholar. Works include Serbian-Ger.-Lat. lexicon; Serbian grammar; Serbo-Croatian NT.

Karaites (Qaraites). Heb. *Bene miqra,* "sons of the Scripture." Jewish sect founded ca. 765 in Baghdad by Anan* ben David; spread to Jerusalem, Syria, Egypt, S Russ., W Eur., and US; rejects rabbinism and Talmudism; accepts OT as sole authority. In 1910 there were ca. 13,000, nearly all in S Russ.

Karen. See *Asia,* C 1.

Karfreitag. See *Church Year,* 8.

Karg, Georg. See *Parsimonius, Georg.*

Karg-Elert, Sigfrid (originally Karg; added wife's maiden name). B. Oberndorf am Neckar, Ger.; organist, pianist, composer. Works include *Passacaglia and Fugue on B-A-C-H;* chorale improvisations.

Karlstadt, Andreas Rudolf Bodenstein von (Carlstadt; Karolstadt; ca. 1480–1541). Revolutionist of the Reformation; b. Karlstadt, Lower Franconia, NW Bav., Ger.; educ. Erfurt and Cologne; prof. Wittenberg; supported M. Luther's* 95 theses*; tangled with J. Eck* at the Leipzig* Debate 1519; introd. Reformation at Wittenberg 1521, but forced the issue; preacher at Orlamünde 1523/24; rejected Baptism and the Lord's Supper as sacraments and abolished ceremonies in undue haste; expelled 1524 by Saxon authorities; wandered from place to place; assoc. with H. Zwingli* at Zurich and finally with J. H. Bullinger* at Basel.

H. Barge, *Andreas Bodenstein von Karlstadt* (Leipzig, 1905); F. Kriechbaum, *Grundzüge der Theologie Karlstadts* (Hamburg, 1967).

Karma (Skt. "deed, action, work"). Term used in Hindu doctrine of reward and punishment, combined with the doctrine of reincarnation*; designed to explain inequalities in human conditions. Brahmanic in origin. Souls have been transmigrating for ages; whatever happiness or sorrow an individual experiences is the unalterable recompense for good or evil deeds in former incarnations; whatever good or evil an individual does will result in happiness or sorrow in future existences. Reincarnations continue till all acts of the present and past have worked out their consequences. All ways to release from karma suggested by Indian religions amount to salvation by works. See also *Brahmanism,* 3, 4; *Buddhism,* 2, 3; *Jainism; Transmigration of Souls.*

Károlyi, Gáspár (1520/30–91). B. Nagykároly (now Carei, Romania); Hung. Ref. theol.; opposed Unitarians; his Bible tr. of 1590 was adopted by all Hung. Prots.

Karsavin, Lev Platonovich (1882–1952). B. St. Petersburg (Leningrad), Russ.; philos.; prof. St. Petersburg 1912; exiled 1922; prof. Kaunas, Lith., 1928; held that God and cosmos form one unity; cosmos is the absolute becoming or the completion of the being of divinity; all existence is theophany.

Käser. See *Kaiser, Leonhard.*

Kastenbauer. See *Agricola, Stephan.*

Katar. See *Middle East,* L 8.

Kathenotheism (from Gk. *kath' hena,* "one at a time,"

and *theos,* "God"). Worship of 1 god at a time without denying existence of other gods; usually includes tendency to change from one god to another. See also *Henotheism; Monolatry.*

Katholisches Bibelwerk. See *Bible Societies,* 6.

Katona von Geleji, István (1589–1649). Preeminent Ref. theol. in Hung.; opposed Unitarians, Sabbatarians, Puritans, and Presbs. Works include *Canones.*

Kattenbusch, Ferdinand (1851–1935). B. Kettwig, Ger.; educ. Bonn, Berlin, Halle; prof. Giessen, Göttingen, Halle; follower of A. Ritschl.* Works include *Das apostolische Symbol; Lehrbuch der vergleichenden Confessionskunde; Von Schleiermacher zu Ritschl.*

Kautz, Jakob (Cucius; ca. 1500–after 1532). B. Grossbokkenheim, in The Palatinate; preacher Worms 1524; became Anabap.; dismissed; became wandering preacher. With J. Denk* and L. Hetzer* wrote 7 theses for disputation with Luth. preachers; other works include Bible tr. See also *Socinianism,* 1.

Kautzsch, Emil Friedrich (1841–1910). Prot. theol.; b. Plauen, Ger.; educ. Leipzig; prof. Basel, Tübingen, Halle; Hebraist and grammarian. Tr. and ed. OT (see also *Bible Versions,* M), including apocryphal and pseudepigraphic books; other works include *Wilhelm Gesenius' hebräische Grammatik völlig umgearbeitet.*

Kavel, August Ludwig Christian (Sept. 3, 1798–Feb. 11, 1860). B. Berlin, Ger.; educ. Berlin; private tutor 1821–26; ordained Berlin 1826; pastor Klemzig, Harthe, and Goltzen 1826; influenced by work and writings of J. G. Scheibel*; resigned pastorate; joined Old* Luths. at Posen; early in 1836 began to explore possibility of emigration to Am. or Australia; while negotiating for financial support, he served Ger. seamen and the Ger. community in London, Eng. After many negotiations in the face of opposition from the Prussian govt. to emigration, conditional approval was obtained and ca. 250 persons under Kavel's leadership left Ger. June 8, 1838, and arrived Port Adelaide, Australia, Jan. 27, 1839. They named their new community in S. Australia Klemzig. The 1st Luth. syn. (conv.) in Australia was held 1839 at Glen Osmond under Kavel's leadership. Later other immigrants joined them. Additional colonies were est. A rupture occurred 1846 as a result of differences regarding polity and chiliasm. This breach was not healed till the Luth. Ch. in Australia was formed 1966. See also *Australia, Lutheranism in,* A 1, B 1. ARS

Kawerau, (Peter) Gustav (1847–1918). B. Bunzlau, Silesia; educ. Berlin; pastor; prof. Kiel 1886, Breslau 1893; provost, mem. supreme ch. council, and honorary prof. Berlin 1907. Ed. several vols. of WA; *Der Briefwechsel des Justus Jonas.* Other works include *Hieronymus Emser; Johann Agricola von Eisleben; Luther in katholischer Beleuchtung.*

Kayser. See *Kaiser.*

Keach, Benjamin (1640–1704). B. Stoke-Hammond, Buckinghamshire, Eng.; Calvinistic Bap.; introd. cong. singing into Bap. congs. Works include *The Progress of Sin; Spiritual Melody; The Travels of True Godliness; War with the Devil; Tropologia.*

Keble, John (1792–1866). Angl. cleric and poet; b. Fairford, Gloucestershire, Eng.; educ. Oxford; prof. Oxford 1831–41; vicar (priest) Hursley 1836–66. Launched Oxford* Movement (see also *Tractarianism*). Hymns include "Word Supreme, Before Creation"; "Sun of My Soul, Thou Savior Dear"; "The Voice that Breathed O'er Eden"; "One Thy Light, the Temple Filling."

Keckermann, Bartholomäus (ca. 1571–1609). B. Danzig; educ. Wittenberg, Leipzig, and Heidelberg; Ref. philos.; prof. Heb. Heidelberg; rector and prof. philos. Ref. Gymnasium, Danzig, 1601. Works include *Systema theologiae.* See also *Dogmatics,* B 5; *Grace, Means of,* IV 3.

Keffer, Adam. See *Canada,* A 5.

Keil, Johann Friedrich Karl (1807–88). B. Lauterbach, near Ölsnitz, Saxony; educ. Dorpat (Tartu) and Berlin; prof. OT and NT exegesis Dorpat 1833–58; moved to Leipzig 1859; concentrated on literary work and on practical affairs of the Luth. Ch.; belonged to the orthodox conservative school of E. W. Hengstenberg*; regarded so-called scientific theol. as a passing phase. With Franz Delitzsch (see *Delitzsch,* 1) he wrote an OT commentary; other works include *Lehrbuch der historisch-kritischen Einleitung in die kanonischen und apokryphischen Schriften des Alten Testaments.*

Keil, Wilhelm. See *Communistic Societies,* 5.

Keim, Karl Theodor (1825–78). B. Stuttgart, Ger.; educ. Tübingen; prof. Zurich 1860, Giessen 1873. Works include *Geschichte Jesu von Nazara; Rom und das Christenthum.*

Keimann, Christian (1607–62). B. Pankratz, near Gabel, Boh.; educ. Wittenberg; conrector, then rector, at Zittau Gymnasium; hymnist. Hymns include "Freuet euch, ihr Christen alle"; "Meinen Jesum lass' ich nicht."

Keinath, Herman Ottoman Alfred (Dec. 27, 1894–June 13, 1952). B. Richville, Mich.; educ. Conc. Sem., St. Louis, Mo.; asst. pastor Immanuel Luth. Ch., Grand Rapids, Mich., 1918–26. Prof. Conc. Teachers Coll., Seward, Nebr., 1926–43; Conc. Teachers Coll., River Forest, Ill., 1943–52. Works include *My Church: A History of the Missouri Synod for Young People.*

Keith, George (ca. 1639–1716). B. Peterhead, Aberdeen, Scot.; educ. Aberdeen; became Quaker in the early 1660s; to Eng. ca. 1682 for several yrs.; to Am.; denied sufficiency of "light" within; founded Christian Quakers; to Eng. ca. 1694; joined Angl. Ch. 1700; SPG miss. to Am. 1702. See also *Friends, Society of.*

Keith-Falconer, Ion Grant Neville (1856–87). B. Edinburgh, Scot.; educ. Harrow and Cambridge; interested in evangelistic work in Cambridge and London; studied Arabic and Koran*; to Aden 1885 and 1886; est. Keith-Falconer miss. See also *Middle East,* L.

Keller, Ezra (1812–48). B. near Middletown, Md.; educ. Pa. Coll. (later called Gettysburg Coll.) and Gettysburg Sem.; traveling miss. of Ministerium of Pa. (see *United Lutheran Church, Synods of,* 22); 1st pres. Wittenberg Coll., Springfield, Ohio (see *Ministry, Education of,* VIII A 6). See also *Miami Synod.*

Keller, Helen Adams (1880–1968). Author and lecturer; b. Tuscumbia, Ala.; became blind and deaf at 19 mo.; learned to "hear" by touch and to speak. See also *Blind,* 2.

Keller, Samuel (1856–1924). B. St. Petersburg (Leningrad), Russ.; educ. Dorpat (Tartu); Luth. pastor S Russ.; revivalist; supported miss. work; fled to Ger. 1891; pastor Düsseldorf 1892. Works include devotional literature.

Kelly, Thomas (1769–1855). B. Kellyville, near Athy, Queen's Co. (later called Laoighis, or Leix), Ireland; educ. Dublin; studied law in London, Eng.; developed deep consciousness of sin; became ascetic; ordained Angl. 1792; seceded, after assoc. with ev. movement in Dublin; built chapels at Athy, Portarlington, Wexford, Waterford, and elsewhere; hymnist. Hymns include "Stricken, Smitten, and Afflicted"; "Who Is This that Comes from Edom"; "Zion Stands by Hills Surrounded."

Kelpius, Johann. See *Communistic Societies,* 4.

Kelso, James Anderson (1873–1951). B. Rawalpindi, India; educ. Washington and Allegheny (Pittsburgh), Pa., Berlin, and Leipzig; Presb. cleric 1898;

prof. Heb. at Western Theol. Sem., Allegheny, Pa., 1901, pres. 1909–43; lecturer Am. School of Oriental Research at Jerusalem 1922–23. Works include *Hebrew-English Vocabulary to the Book of Genesis; The Hebrew Prophet and His Message.*

Kemmerer, August Friedrich (Cämmerer; June 22, 1767–Oct. 22, 1837). B. Wusterhausen, Brandenburg, Ger.; educ. Halle; ordained Copenhagen, Den., 1789; miss. to Tranquebar, India, arriving 1791. See also *India,* 10.

Kemp, Johannes Theodorus van der. See *Vanderkemp, Johannes Theodorus.*

Kempis, Thomas a. See *Thomas a Kempis.*

Ken, Thomas (1637–1711). B. Little Berkhampstead, Hertfordshire, Eng.; educ. Winchester and Oxford; bp. Bath and Wells; was 1 of 7 bps. imprisoned in Tower of London 1688 on charges of disloyalty; acquitted; among nonjurors*; deprived of see 1891; hymnist. Hymns include "Awake, My Soul, and with the Sun" and "All Praise to Thee, My God, This Night," each of which ends with "Praise God, from Whom All Blessings Flow."

Kennett, Robert Hatch (1864–1932). Angl. OT and Semitic scholar; prof. Heb. Cambridge; held late date for Dt, Maccabean date for the Psalms and other parts of the OT.

Kennet(t), White (1660–1728). B. Dover, Eng.; Angl. bp. Peterborough; Low Churchman (see *High Church*); antiquary. Works include *The Christian Scholar; The History of England from the Commencement of the Reign of Charles I. to the End of the Reign of William III.,* in *A Complete History of England,* III.

Kennicott, Benjamin (1718–83). B. Totnes, Devonshire, Eng.; educ. Oxford; canon Christ Ch., Oxford. OT scholar. Ed. *Vetus Testamentum hebraicum cum variis lectionibus;* other works include *The State of the Collation of the Hebrew Manuscripts of the Old Testament.*

Kenoma. See *Gnosticism,* 5.

Kenosis (Gk. "an emptying," from *kenos,* "empty"). Term based on Ph. 2:7: Christ "emptied" *(ekenosen)* Himself; applied esp. to the view (e. g., of G. Thomasius,* K. F. A. Kahnis*) that the Son of God in His incarnation emptied Himself of such operative, or relative divine attributes as omnipotence, omnipresence, and omniscience, and to the view (e. g., of W. H. C. F. Gess,* J. C. K. v. Hofmann*) that He emptied Himself of all divine attributes, or that a human personality replaced His divine personality. Orthodox Luths. hold that Christ in His state of humiliation did not always and fully use the divine properties communicated to His human nature by virtue of the personal union (see *Christ Jesus*). See also *Crypto-Kenotic Controversy; Decisio Saxonica.*

Kensit, John (1853–1902). B. London, Eng.; Angl.; opponent of High* Ch. movement; founded Prot. Truth Soc. 1890.

Kent, (Holy) Maid of (Nun of Kent). See *Barton, Elizabeth.*

Kentigern. See *Celtic Church,* 6.

Kentucky Revival. See *Presbyterian Churches,* 4 b.

Kentucky Synod. 1. Pastors in Ky. who favored the strict confessionalism of the Henkels* held conventions 1822 and 1823; no permanent syn. was organized, but the name Ky. Syn. (or Ev. Luth. Syn. of Ky.) is sometimes used in connection with this venture.

2. Pastors favoring the modified confessionalism of The General* Syn. of the Ev. Luth. Ch. in the USA held a conv. 1834 at Jeffersontown, Ky. This venture also has been called Ky. Syn. (or Ev. Luth. Syn. of Ky.); adopted the name Ev. Luth. Syn. of the West* 1835. See also *Indiana Synod* (I).

3. A Ky. Syn. (Ev. Luth. Syn. of Ky.) was formed 1854, joined The General* Syn. of the Ev. Luth. Ch. in the USA 1855, and was absorbed 1865 by the Olive Branch Ev. Luth. Syn. of Ind. (see *United Lutheran Church, Synods of,* 8). See also *Southwest, Synod of the.*

Kentucky-Tennessee Synod. See *United Lutheran Church, Synods of,* 10.

Kenya. See *Africa,* E 6.

Kepler, Johann(es) (Keppler; 1571–1630). B. Weil der Stadt, near Stuttgart, Württemberg, Ger.; astronomer and mathematician; educ. Tübingen; pupil of M. Hafenreffer*; held Copernican theory (see *Copernicus, Nicolaus*); discovered 3 laws of planetary motion; held that the conjunction of Jupiter and Saturn 747 A. U. C. indicated the birth of Christ to the Magi, and that a new celestial sign ca. 748 A. U. C. guided them to Christ; denied Luth. doctrine of ubiquity*; opposed Calvinistic doctrine of predestination (see *Predestination,* 4); held that God created world in accord with a Pythagorean pattern of harmony (see *Pythagoreanism*).

Ker, John (1819–86). B. Bield farm, Tweedsmuir parish, Peeblesshire, Scot.; educ. Edinburg, Halle, Berlin; United Presb. pastor Alnwick, Eng., and Barrhead and Glasgow, Scot.; prof. Edinburgh theol. sem. 1876. Works include *Lectures on the History of Preaching; The Psalms in History and Biography.*

Kerala. See *India,* 4, 5, 7.

Kerll, Johann Kaspar (von) (Kerl; Kherl; Cherle; 1627–93). B. Adorf, Saxony, Ger.; RC composer; organist Munich and Vienna.

Kerr, Hugh Thomson (1871–1950). B. Elora, Ont., Can.; educ. Toronto, Ont., and Western Theol. Sem., Allegheny (Pittsburgh), Pa.; pastor Pittsburgh, Pa., Hutchinson, Kans., Chicago, Ill., Pittsburgh, Pa.; moderator Gen. Assem. of Presb. Ch. in the USA 1920–31. Works include *Children's Story-Sermons; Old Things New; A God-Centered Faith.*

Kerygma (*kerugma;* Gk. "proclamation"). Term for Gospel, esp. that of the first apostles. Also used for proclamation of Gospel. See also *Grace, Means of.*

Kerygmatic Theology. Also known as "theol. of the Word"; points to the content of theol. as proclamation of the saving and revelatory acts of God; assoc. esp. with K. Barth.*

Keswick Conventions. Annual interdenominational meetings held at Keswick, Eng., since 1875 to promote "practical holiness" by prayer, Bible study, discussion, and personal conversation.

Kessler, Johann (Johannes Chesselius; Ahenarius; ca. 1502–74). Pupil of D. Erasmus,* M. Luther,* and P. Melanchthon*; reformer in Saint Gall, Switz.

Kethubim. See *Hagiographa.*

Ketteler, Wilhelm Emmanuel (von) (Emanuel; 1811–77). B. Münster (Harkotten), Westphalia; RC priest 1844; bp. Mainz 1850; ultramontanist (see *Ultramontanism*); tried to strengthen the ch. in Ger. and free it from state control; opposed dogma of papal infallibility* but submitted after its promulgation.

Kettenbach, Heinrich von (d. apparently ca. 1525). B. perhaps Kettenbach, Ger.; Franciscan preacher at Ulm. Denounced corruption of the ch.; praised M. Luther,* P. Melanchthon,* and A. R. B. v. Karlstadt.*

Kettler, Gotthard (ca. 1517 [or 1511?]–87). B. Westphalia; last grand master of Teutonic Knights (see *Military Religious Orders,* c) in Livonia 1559–62; 1st duke of Kurland 1562; favored Reformation.

Kettner, Elmer Arthur (Apr. 22, 1906–Sept. 24, 1964). B. Elgin, Ill.; educ. Conc. Sem., St. Louis, Mo.; Mo. Syn. pastor Wollaston, near Boston, Mass. Ed. *Advance* 1954–64; other works include *Evangelism in the Sunday School; Adventures in Evangelism; A Closer Walk with God; Living with My Lord; Elders at Work.*

Key to Theosophy. See *Theosophy,* 5.

Keyl, Ernst Gerhard Wilhelm (May 22, 1804–Aug. 4,

1872). Father of S. Keyl*; b. Leipzig, Ger.; educ. Leipzig; pastor Niederfrohna, near Penig, 1829; adherent of M. Stephan* the elder; to US 1839 (see *Lutheran Church – Missouri Synod, The,* II, 1). Pastor Frohna, Mo., 1839–47; Freistadt and Milwaukee, Wis., 1847–50; Baltimore, Md., 1850–69; Willshire, Van Wert Co., Ohio, 1869–71. Indefatigable student of M. Luther.* Works include *Katechismusauslegung; Predigt-Entwürfe über die Sonn- und Festtags-Evangelien.*

J. F. Köstering, *Leben und Wirken des Ernst Gerhard Wilh. Keyl* (St. Louis, 1882).

Keyl, Stephanus (June 27, 1838–Dec. 15, 1905). Son of E. G. W. Keyl*; b. Niederfrohna, near Penig, Saxony, Ger.; to US 1839 with his father and other Saxons (see *Lutheran Church–Missouri Synod, The,* II, 1); educ. Conc. Sem., St. Louis, Mo.; pastor Philadelphia, Pa., 1862–67; immigrant* and emigrant miss. 1869–1905.

P. Rösener, *Unser erster Emigrantenmissionar, Pastor Stephanus Keyl* (St. Louis, 1908); T. S. Keyl, "The Life and Activities of Pastor Stephanus Keyl," *CHIQ,* XXII, No. 2 (July 1949), 65–77.

Keys, Office of. 1. The Office of the Keys (Mt 16:19; 18:15-20; Jn 20:22-23; Rv 1:18) is a peculiar, special, unique, spiritual power given by Christ to the ch.

2. Christ is Master (Mt 23:8-10), Head of the ch. (Eph 1:22; 4:15; 5:23; Cl 1:13, 18); His Word is authoritative (Jn 12:48-50; 1 Ti 6:3-5). The ch. should not go beyond His Word or allow other authority to est. its doctrine and creeds (Gl 1:8-9; Cl 2:8).

3. The Office of the Keys is spiritual (Mt. 20:25-26; Jn 18:36; 2 Co 10:4; Eph 6:10-17); it includes all spiritual rights, duties, and privileges necessary for the welfare of the ch. on earth, e. g., the conveying of grace to mankind through preaching, administering Baptism and Lord's Supper, and through mutual conversation and consolation. In particular, the Office of the Keys gives power to forgive and retain sins (loosing and binding), i. e., not merely to announce and to declare to men the remission or retention of sins, but actually to give forgiveness to penitent sinners and to deny forgiveness to impenitent sinners (Jn 20:23; 2 Co 2:10). See also *Justification,* 6.

4. The whole Gospel of Christ is an absolution.* Absolution does not exist outside the Gospel, but is a special form of administering the Gospel in which a minister or other Christian forgives the sins of others. It is not a better or more powerful forgiveness, but a special application which conveys reassurance (Lk 7:47-48).

5. Only God can forgive sins (Is 43:25; Mk 2:7). Christ gave the Office of the Keys to the ch. on earth; the ch. delegates and transfers the pub. exercise of the Office of the Keys to called servants of the Word (Acts 20:28; 1 Co 4:1; 2 Co 2:10; Eph 4:10-12). See also *Ministerial Office,* 5.

6. When the Office of the Keys is properly administered, the act is as valid and effective in the sight of God as though Christ Himself had performed it (Jn 20:23). The validity does not depend on faith, repentance, worthiness, good works, satisfaction of the one who pronounces absolution. Unbelief does not annul validity of forgiveness (Ro 3:3), but forgiveness is received through faith (Acts 10:43).

7. Possession of the Office of the Keys obligates Christians to observe all corresponding duties, e. g., to proclaim the Word publicly (Mt 28:18-20) and privately (Cl 3:16), to maintain purity of the Word (Jn 8:31-47; 1 Ti 6:20), to express faith (Ro 10:9), to forgive sins (Mt 18:21-35; Eph 4:32), to practice discipline (Mt 18:17; 1 Co 5:2-5; 1 Ti 1:20; Tts 3:10-11), to judge doctrine (Mt 7:15; 1 Jn 4:1; Acts 17:10-11).

8. RC interpretation refers the Office of the Keys to supremacy of spiritual jurisdiction vested in the pope and including unqualified executive power, universal legislative power, supreme judicial power, infallibility,* primacy (see *Vatican Councils,* 1 b). RCm holds that this supremacy originally belonged to Peter (but see, e.g., Mt 18:1-4; Lk 22:24-26; Acts 15:6-31; Gl 2:7-11; Eph 2:20; 1 Ptr 5:1; 2 Ptr 1:19) and that the popes are Peter's successors. CCS

9. Ban, or excommunication, is the process whereby impenitent sinners are excluded from Communion and other fellowship of the ch. In the Middle Ages a distinction was made bet. lesser ban, which excluded from the Sacraments, and greater ban, or interdict, which included civil penalties and excluded from all blessings and graces of the ch. The Luth. Confessions recognize only lesser ban as truly Christian and of concern to ministers (SA-III IX; cf. AC XXVIII 2; Ap VII–VIII 3; XI 4; XXVIII 12; Tractatus 60, 74). The RC Ch. distinguishes bet. *tolerati* (tolerated) and *vitandi* (to be avoided) excommunicates. The faithful need not shun the *tolerati* either in profane or religious matters. The *vitandi* are to be avoided as much as possible. The *vitandi* are excommunicated by being named in a pub. decree of the papal see. In 1971 a papal-appointed commission recommended dropping the *vitanti* category.

See also *Priesthood.*

C. C. Stephan, "The Office of the Keys," *The Abiding Word,* I, ed. T. Laetsch (St. Louis, 1946), 342–365; W. H. Bouman, "The Practical Application of Matthew 18:15-18," *CTM,* XVIII (Mar. 1947), 178–204; O. Cullmann, *Peter: Disciple–Apostle–Martyr,* tr. F. V. Filson, 2d ed. (Philadelphia, 1962); H. Frhr. v. Campenhausen, *Kirchliches Amt und geistliche Vollmacht in den ersten drei Jahrhunderten,* 2d ed. (Tübingen, 1963), tr. J. A. Baker, *Ecclesiastical Authority and Spiritual Power in the Church of the First Three Centuries* (Stanford, Cal., 1969); G. Ebeling, *Kirchenzucht* (Stuttgart, 1947); R. Bohren, *Das Problem der Kirchenzucht im Neuen Testament* (Zurich, 1952).

Keyser, Leander Sylvester (Mar. 13, 1856–Oct. 18, 1937). Leading theol. in The General* Syn. of the Ev. Luth. Ch. in the USA; b. Tuscarawas Co., Ohio; educ. Wittenberg Coll. (Sem.), Springfield, Ohio (see *Hamma Divinity School*). Pastor La Grange, Ind., 1879–81; Elkhart, Ind., 1883–89; Springfield, Ohio, 1889–95; Atchison, Kans., 1897–1903; Dover, Ohio, 1903–11. Prof. systematic theol. Hamma Divinity School 1911. Works include *A System of Natural Theism; A System of Christian Evidence; In the Redeemer's Footsteps; In the Apostles' Footsteps; Contending for the Faith; The Problem of Origins; Our Bird Comrades.*

Keyserling, Hermann Alexander (1800–1946). B. Könno, Livonia (now Estonia); philos.; beginning with free, spiritual Christianity, he tried to est. an ecumenical basis for all religions, esp. RCm and Buddhism; called religious forms human; held that God reveals Himself in human religious presuppositions and errors.

Keysser, Christian (Keyszer; Mar. 7, 1877–Dec. 14, 1961). B. Geroldsgrün, Bav., Ger.; Neuendettelsau* Miss. Soc. miss. at Sattelberg, near Finschhafen, New Guinea, ca. 1900–20; proposed evangelization of tribes, rather than making first approach to individuals. Works include *Wörterbuch der Kâte-Sprache; Eine Papuagemeinde.*

KFUO. See *Radio Stations, Religious,* 3.

Khama, King. See *Africa,* B 3.

Khmer Republic. See *Cambodia.*

Khomyakov, Aleksei Stepanovich (Khomiakov; Khomiakoff; 1804–60). B. Moscow, Russ.; lay theol., philos., Slavophile; opposed scholastic rationalism* and idealism*; held that the Orthodox Ch. has Christ as Head and the Holy Spirit as Soul and that its essence is freedom in the spirit at one with itself. See also *Christian Socialism,* 3; *Sobornost.*

Kickapoo. See *Indians, American,* 6.

Kidd, Benjamin (1858–1916). B. Croydon, Eng.; sociol.; held that progress in animal and human realms comes only at great sacrifice in kind. Works include *Social Evolution; Principles of Western Civilisation.*

Kiddush (Heb. "sanctification"). Jewish rite consisting of the ordinary benediction over wine or bread and a benediction proclaiming the holiness of the occasion; some hold that the Eucharist (see *Grace, Means of,* IV) may have the Kiddush as its background.

Kieffer, George Linn (Nov. 25, 1883–Apr. 25, 1937). B. near Millersburg, Pa.; educ. Gettysburg* Coll. and Sem., Union Theol. Sem. (NYC), Columbia U. (NYC); pastor Rosedale, in Queens borough, W Long Is., N. Y., 1916–26; NLC statistician and reference librarian 1918–37. Assoc. ed. *Lutheran World Almanac.*

Kierkegaard, Sören Aaby(e) (1813–55). B. Copenhagen, Den.; religious philos. and author; marked by deep-seated melancholy; broken engagement affected his writings; tried to adhere to Luth. Confessions; studied theol., but never took office; attacked Est. Ch. for worldliness; held that a Christian is an isolated individual alone with God, in contact with the world only through suffering; made important contributions through self-analyses. Works include *Either/Or; Philosophical Fragments; Concluding Unscientific Postscript; Edifying Discourses; Fear and Trembling.* See also *Existentialism.*

E. Geismar, *Sören Kierkegaard: Seine Lebensentwicklung und seine Wirksamkeit als Schriftsteller* (Göttingen, 1929); D. F. Swenson, *Something About Kierkegaard,* 2d ed. (Minneapolis, 1945); W. Lowrie, *A Short Life of Kierkegaard* (Princeton, N. J., 1942); J. E. Hohlenberg, *Sören Kierkegaard,* tr. T. H. Croxall (London, 1954); L. Shestov, *Kierkegaard and the Existential Philosophy,* tr. E. Hewitt (Athens, Ohio, 1969).

Kiessling, Johann Tobias (Kieszling; 1742–1824). Merchant in Nürnberg, Ger.; helped found Deutsche Christentumsgesellschaft.*

Kildahl, John Nathan (Jan. 4, 1857–Sept. 25, 1920). B. Beitstaden (Namdalseidet), Norw.; educ. Luther Coll., Decorah, Iowa, and Luther Sem., Madison, Wis.; pastor Minn. and Ill.; pres. Red Wing (Minn.) Norw. Ev. Luth. Sem. 1885–86 and St. Olaf Coll., Northfield, Minn., 1899–1914; prof. Luther Sem., St. Paul, Minn., 1914.

Kilian, Johann (Jan; Mar. 22, 1811–Sept. 12, 1884). B. of Wendish parents in Dahlen, Saxony, Ger.; educ. Leipzig; pastor Kotitz, Saxony, 1837–48; to Texas with Wendish (Serbian) Luths. 1854, settled with them at Serbin, near Giddings, and was their pastor 1854–84; joined Mo. Syn. 1855. Works include tr. of AC and LC into Wendish.

Kilian of Aubigny (Chillen; d. 670). Irish monk; allegedly made pilgrimage to Rome and was given site for hermitage at Aubigny, near Arras, by Faro, bp. Meaux, Fr.

Kilian of Würzburg (Killena; Kyllena; Kyllina; Killian; Cilian; Chilian; ca. 640–ca. 689). B. probably Mullagh, Co. Cavan, Ireland; bp.; to court of Gozbert, Thuringian duke at Würzburg; did miss. work in Franconia and Thuringia; converted Gozbert and persuaded him to separate from Geilana, his brother's widow; in revenge, Geilana had Kilian murdered. See also *Celtic Church,* 9; *Germany,* A 1.

Kilimanjaro Christian Medical Center. See *Africa,* E 7.

Kilwardby, Robert (d. 1279). Eng. Dominican (see *Dominicans*); abp. Canterbury 1272–78; took Canterbury registers and judicial records to It.; opposed Thomas* Aquinas. Works include *De natura theologiae.*

Kimchi, David ben Joseph (Kimhi; Redak [from initials of Rabbi David Kimchi]; ca. 1160–1235). Jewish philol. and exegete; b. Narbonne, Fr. Works include Heb. grammar and lexicon; OT commentaries. See also *Grammars,* A.

Kinder, Ernst. See *Dogmatics,* B 13.

Kindergarten. See *Froebel, Friedrich Wilhelm August.*

Kindi, al-. See *Arabic Philosophy.*

Kindness. Two words commonly tr. "kindness" in the Bible are *chesed* (Heb.; OT) and *chrestotes* (Gk.; NT). Both refer to kindness as a quality of God and man, 2 Sm 9:1; Neh 9:17; Cl 3:12; Tts 3:4. Kindness is akin to love, goodness, friendliness, generosity, mercy, gentleness, meekness, patience, forgiveness, and tenderheartedness; anger, crudeness, and harshness are usually excluded.

Chesed used in reference to a quality in God has been variously tr., e.g., "lovingkindness," "kindness," "mercy," "steadfast love." It is used in connection with the covenant* relationship bet. God and His people, Ps 106:45. God's kindness is intertwined with His everlasting faithfulness, Is 54:10. We praise Him for His kindness, Ps 138:2.

Chrestotes and related words used in reference to a quality in God involve His grace (Eph 2:7), love (Tts 3:4), and kindness to the unthankful and wicked (Lk 6:35). Christ not only was the vehicle of God's kindness, He is also the pattern for our kindness. His kindness appears in His dealings with the penitent, Lk 7:37-50. So common was *chrestotes* in the ministry of Christ, that in the early ch. the word Christ was sometimes written *chrestos,* "the Friendly." So prominent was it among early Christians that they were sometimes called *chrestiani.*

Kindness is commanded by God (Eph 4:32), is an essential mark of *agape* (Christian love; 1 Co 13:4), a vital factor in the ministry (2 Co 6:6), and a fruit of the Spirit (Gl 5:22; KJV "gentleness"). LEZ

King, Christ as. 1. When Christ is called *kyrios* (*kurios,* Gk. "lord"; e.g., Lk 7:13) or *basileus* (Gk. "king"; e.g., Jn 1:49), fulfillment of OT promise and prophecy is indicated (2 Sm 7:11-13; Ps 8; 89; 110:1-2; Dn 7:13-27).

2. Divine adoration is due Christ also acc. to His human nature (Jn 5:23; Ph 2:9-11). Christ was King in the state of humiliation. His miracles and such passages as Mt 11:27; Jn 5:17; 12:15 make this clear. His royal powers, hidden in His humiliation, were used fully and continually bet. His resurrection and ascension and became esp. manifest with His ascension and session at the right hand of God (Mt 28:18), His human nature participating fully in all the functions of the Godhead as King of the world and of the ch.

3. Christ is Prophet, Priest, and King. If stress is laid on one office to the exclusion of the others, justice is not done to the fullness of the Gospel.

4. Scripture exempts no part of creation from the rule of Christ (Mt 11:27; 1 Co 15:27; Eph 1:22; Heb 2:8).

5. The universal realm of Christ may be divided: kingdom of power, kingdom of grace, kingdom of glory. In His kingdom of power Christ rules over all creatures by almighty power, Mt 28:18. In His kingdom of grace He rules and protects His church* on earth, whose mems. are "in the world but not of the world" (Jn 17:11, 15). His kingdom of glory is the ch. in heaven, 2 Ti 4:18. See also *Church Militant; Church Triumphant.*

6. The 3 kingdoms are under 1 Lord. His will and purpose direct, and His power controls, all things. All in heaven and earth serves the purpose of gathering and preserving the ch.

7. For Christians the choice is not bet. ecclesiastical power-politics and withdrawal of the ch. from the world. The 3d way: by Christian life and example, by participation in civil affairs, and by Christian witness to help prepare the way of Christ the King. HFB

O. C. J. Hoffmann, "Office, or Work, of Christ," *The Abiding Word,* II, ed. T. Laetsch (St. Louis, 1947), 112–144; F. A. O. Pieper, *Christliche Dogmatik,* II (St. Louis, 1917), 461–472, Eng. tr. *Christian Dogmatics,* II (St. Louis, 1951), 385-394; W. A. Visser 't Hooft, *The Kingship of Christ: An Interpretation of Recent European Theology* (New York, 1948).

King, Henry. See *Catholic Apostolic Church,* 1.

King, Henry Churchill (1858–1934). B. Hillsdale, Mich.; educ. Oberlin (Ohio) Coll., a Cong. school with a theol. department; prof. and pres. Oberlin Coll.; philos. Works include *The Ethics of Jesus; Reconstruction in Theology.*

King, Jonas (July 29, 1792–May 22, 1869). B. Hawley, Mass.; educ. Williams Coll., Williamstown, Mass., and Andover (Mass.) Theol. Sem.; noted linguist; miss. in Syria, Egypt, Greece. See also *Paris Evangelical Missionary Society.*

King, Martin Luther, Jr. (1929–1968). Bap. cleric; b. Atlanta, Ga.; educ. Crozer Theol. Sem. (Chester, Pa.), and Boston (Mass.) U.; pastor Montgomery, Ala.; organizer and pres. Southern* Christian Leadership Conference; pres. Montgomery Improvement Assn.; recipient of Nobel Peace Prize 1964; leader of nonviolent movements and demonstrations aimed at achieving civil rights for all races. Tried to relate Christian faith to hope for oppressed. Assassinated. Works include *Stride Toward Freedom; The Measure of a Man; Strength to Love; Why We Can't Wait; Where Do We Go from Here: Chaos or Community?*

King James Version. See *Bible Versions,* L 10.

Kingdom of Glory. See *King, Christ as,* 5.

Kingdom of God. Term prominent in proclamation of John the Baptist, Jesus, and apostles; evidently synonymous with "kingdom of heaven." Formerly it was taken for granted that "kingdom of God" is equivalent to "Christian ch."; contemporary scholars hold that "kingdom" usually means dominion or rule, and that only in a derived way, by figure of speech, does it in some passages designate subjects in God's kingdom. When John said that the kingdom of God had come near (Mk 1:15), he announced that God was, through the Messiah, laying the foundation for His gracious rule in human hearts. This rule presupposes that forgiveness of sins has been procured and that people accept it in faith. Where there is such acceptance, God has entered the heart and governs human thoughts and actions. Those who heard the message of John and of Christ were informed that God was preparing something special, that the fullness of the time had come (Gl 4:4), and that the plan of God for man's salvation was now to be carried out. The term did not point to an external kingdom like that of David or Solomon or the Roman Empire, but to something spiritual, the gentle rule of God through the Holy Spirit in the hearts of men. Passages which speak of the rule of God include Mt 12:28; Mk 4:11; Lk 9:27; 11:20. Passages which speak of the sum total of the subjects include Mt 13:41; 16:19. The kingdom is at times spoken of as a future blessing (Mt 7:21; 8:11), at times as a present reality (Lk 16:16; 17:20; Jn 3:3-5). It should be our heart's desire to be under the gracious rule of God (Mt 13:44-46). WA

Kingdom of Grace. See *King, Christ as,* 5.

Kingdom of Power. See *King, Christ as,* 5.

Kingo, Thomas Hansen (1634–1703). "Poet of Eastertide"; b. Slangerup, Den., perhaps of Scot. descent; Luth. pastor Slangerup; bp. Fyn 1677; composer; hymnist. Hymns include "On My Heart Imprint Thine Image"; "Like the Golden Sun Ascending"; "The Sun Arises Now."

King's Book, The. See *Anglican Confessions,* 2.

King's Confession, The. Drawn up 1581 for Scot. by John Craig (ca. 1512–1600; Scot. reformer; coworker of J. Knox*; Dominican friar; held Prot. tenets), signed by James VI (see *James I*). See also *Presbyterian Confessions,* 1.

King's Daughters (International Order of the King's Daughters and Sons). Founded 1886 by Margaret McDonald Bottome (1827–1906; b. NYC; married clergyman; assoc. ed. *Ladies' Home Journal*); interdenom.; object: to develop spiritual life and stimulate Christian activities; pub. periodical *Silver Cross;* membership over 50,000 in the 1960s.

Kings, Divine Right of. See *Divine Right.*

Kingsbury, Cyrus (Nov. 22, 1786–June 27, 1870). B. Alstead, N. H.; educ. Brown U., Providence, R. I., and Andover (Mass.) Theol. Sem.; ABCFM miss. to Choctaw Indians. See also *Indians, American,* 7.

Kingsley, Charles (1819–75). B. Holne, Devonshire, Eng.; educ. London and Cambridge; Angl. rector; prof. modern hist. Cambridge 1860–69; canon Westminster 1873; promoted Christian* Socialism; engaged in controversy with J. H. Newman*; hymnist. Works include *Hypatia.** See also *Guild of Saint Matthew.*

Kinner, Samuel (1603–68). B. Breslau, Ger.; court physician of Duke of Liegnitz-Brieg. Wrote the hymn "Herr Jesu Christ, du hast bereit't."

Kirchen-Blatt. See *Iowa and Other States, Evangelical Lutheran Synod of,* 3; *Fritschel,* 1, 2.

Kirchenbuch für Evangelisch-Lutherische Gemeinden. See *Fritschel,* 1.

Kirchenbund. See *Australia, Lutheranism in,* B 1.

Kirchenkampf (Ger. "ch. struggle"). Struggle in Ger. bet. ch. and the nat. socialism (abbr. Nazism, from Ger. *Nationalsozialismus*) of Adolf Hitler (Schick'lgruber? 1889–1945; cofounder Nat. Socialist Ger. Workers' Party 1919–20; Ger. chancellor [called "Führer" (leader)] with dictatorial powers 1933). See also *Socialism,* 3.

First stage in the Kirchenkampf was Hitler's attempt to incorporate the ch. into nat. socialism as a cultural factor (spring to fall 1933). A concordat was concluded July 20, 1933, with the RCs (see *Concordat,* 8). In the ev. chs., elections brought the Deutsche Christen (see *Barmen Theses*) notable victories, but many opposed Nazism and under leadership of W. Künneth (see *Dogmatics,* B 13), M. Niemöller (pres. WCC 1961–68; see also *Germany,* C 4), Hanns Lilje (b. Hanover, Ger., 1899; gen. secy. Ger. Christian Student Movement, vice-pres. World Student Christian Movement 1927–34; bp. VELKD), et al. formed the Jungreformatorische Bewegung May 1933. This became the Pfarrernotbund (Pastors' Emergency League) Sept. 1933.

In the 2d stage (fall 1933–fall 1934), Hitler tried to complete the assimilation of the ch. into the Nazi state. This led to opposition and the adoption of the Barmen Theses, which mark the beginning of the Bekennende Kirche (Confessing Ch.), which tried to unite evangelicals who opposed Nazism. Thereafter Hitler was no longer interested in using the ch. and increasingly opposed it.

In the 3d stage (fall 1934–Feb. 1937), the state tried to restrict activities of the ch. by controlling its finances. The Bekennende Kirche tried to maintain its own govt. It became clear that the ch. could be destroyed neither by internal nor by external forces because pastors and chs. continued to use Word and sacraments. On the other hand, the ch. found it difficult to maintain a govt. without state sanction.

In the 4th stage (Feb. 1937–1939), the opponent of the ch. was no longer primarily the Deutsche Christen, but Nazism itself and its anti-Christian worldviews. Some pastors resisted the state and were imprisoned; others tried to avoid conflict with the state in their ministry.

In the 5th stage (WW II; 1939–1945), increasingly serious attacks were made on the ch. Niemöller was imprisoned, D. Bonhoeffer* imprisoned and executed. Pastors were called into the army, ch. publications suppressed, ch. services and functions curtailed or suppressed. Though hampered also by internal strife, the chs. tried to continue working.

Nazism collapsed 1945. God's grace preserved the Christian chs. of Ger. despite their weaknesses and failures.

See also *Altona Confession.*

F. Zipfel, *Kirchenkampf in Deutschland 1933–1945* (Berlin, 1965); J. S. Conway, *The Nazi Persecution of the Churches 1933–45* (New York, 1968); *Arbeiten zur Geschichte des Kirchenkampfes 1933–1945,* ed. K. D. Schmidt, H. Brunotte, E. Wolf (Göttingen, 1958–). EL

Kirchenordnungen. See *Church Orders.*

Kirchliche Mitteilungen aus und über Nordamerika. See *Löhe, Johann Konrad Wilhelm.*

Kirchliche Zeitschrift. See *Fritschel,* 1, 2; *Iowa and Other States, Evangelical Lutheran Synod of,* 3.

Kirchliches Informatorium. See *Buffalo Synod,* 6.

Kirchner, Timotheus (1533–87). B. Döllstädt, Thuringia, Ger.; Luth. pastor; deposed 1561 at Herbsleben for opposing V. Strigel's* Melanchthonianism; prof. Jena 1572; supt. Wolfenbüttel and Gandersheim; prof. Helmstedt 1576; criticized Julius* of Brunswick-Wolfenbüttel for Romanizing; deposed 1579; helped prepare *Apology of the Book of Concord;* prof. Heidelberg 1580; deposed 1583; supt. Weimar 1584. Made the index to the Jena ed. of M. Luther's works. See also *Chemnitz, Martin; Selnecker, Nikolaus; Neistadiensium admonitio.*

Kirk. Scot. for "church."

Kirk of Scotland. See *Presbyterian Churches,* 1.

Kirk-session. See *Consistory.*

Kirkeberg, Olav L. (Oct. 11, 1849–Feb. 16, 1925). B. Valdres, Norw.; to Am. 1874; pastor The Dan. Ev. Luth. Ch. in Am. 1874–1900, pres. Feb.–Sept. 1893; supt. Elk Horn (Iowa) Folk School. Founded and ed. *Dannevirke* (periodical named after a 10th c. earthen wall built by Dan. Queen Thyra for protection against invaders); ed. *Kirkelig Samler;* helped comp. *Nordisk Folke-Sangbog.*

Kirkelig Samler. See *Danish Lutherans in America,* 3; *Kirkeberg, Olav L.*

Kirn, Otto (1857–1911). B. Heslach, near Stuttgart, Ger.; educ. Maulbronn, Blaubeuren, and Tübingen; prof. Basel and Leipzig. See also *Atonement, Theories of,* 6.

Kiss of Peace (*pax* [Lat. "peace"]). Originally actual kiss (e. g., Ro 16:16; 1 Ptr 5:14); early assoc. with Lord's Supper (Justin* Martyr, *Apologia* I lxv). Form has been modified in all rites. See also *Agnus Dei.*

Kitchener, Horatio Herbert. See *Geography, Christian,* 4.

Kittel, Gerhard (1888–1948). Luth. NT scholar; son of R. Kittel*; b. Breslau, Ger.; educ. Leipzig, Tübingen, Berlin, Halle; taught at Kiel, Leipzig, Greifswald, Tübingen, and Vienna; studied unique character of Christianity in its environment; traced Oriental and Jewish influences on early Christian cong. Works include *Theologisches Wörterbuch zum Neuen Testament; Christus und Imperator; Die Probleme des palästinischen Spätjudentums und das Urchristentum; Die Judenfrage; Urchristentum, Spätjudentum und Hellenismus; Die Religionsgeschichte und das Urchristentum.* See also *Lexicons,* B.

Kittel, Johann Christian (1732–1809). B. Erfurt, Ger.; pupil of J. S. Bach*; organist Langensalza and Erfurt; composer. Issued *Neues Choralbuch für Schleswig-Holstein;* other works include organ preludes.

Kittel, Rudolf (1853–1929). Luth. OT scholar; father of G. Kittel*; educ. Tübingen; prof. Breslau 1888, Leipzig 1898. Ed. Heb. OT; other works include *Geschichte des Volkes Israel; Die Religion des Volkes Israel.*

Kitto, John (1804–54). B. Plymouth, Eng.; deaf ca. 1817; trained as printer at Islington (London) Miss. Coll.; CMS miss. printer Malta 1827–29; tutor in miss. group to Persia 1829–33. Ed. *The Cyclopaedia of Biblical Literature;* other works include *The Pictorial Bible; Daily Bible Illustrations.*

Kiwanis Club International. Organized 1915 in Detroit, Mich., for practical application of the Golden* Rule to modern life, esp. in business and professional relations.

Klauder, Charles Zeller (1872–1938). B. Philadelphia, Pa.; executive architect for projects including buildings at Princeton (N. J.) U., U. of Pittsburgh (Pa.), Brown U. (Providence, R. I.), and Conc. Sem., St. Louis, Mo.

Klaveness, Thorvald (Thorwald; 1844–1915). Norw. pastor; originally exponent of conservative theol. with pietistic inclinations. After involvement in problems of ch. and culture, soc. justice, and the nature of Scripture, he was at times regarded as a liberal leader. Held Scripture is eternal truth in earthly thoughts and words. Cofounded *Kirke og Kultur; Norsk Kirkeblad;* other works include *Evangeliet forkyndt for nutiden.*

Klein, Bernhard Joseph (1793–1832). B. Cologne, Ger.; composer; conductor at Cologne Cathedral; taught at Berlin U. and Institute for Church Music, Berlin. Works include oratorios *Jephtha* and *David.*

Klein, Henry Adam (Feb. 17, 1869–Dec. 21, 1935). B. Spring, Tex.; educ. Conc. Sem., St. Louis, Mo.; pastor Chattanooga, Tenn., 1892–1902; miss. Brazil 1902–07; pastor Wittenberg, Mo., 1907–10, St. Joseph, Mo., 1910–15, Collinsville, Ill., 1915–22; pres. Conc. Sem., Springfield, Ill., 1922–35.

Kleine Gemeinde. See *Mennonite Churches,* 3 a.

Kleinert, Hugo Wilhelm Paul (1837–1920). B. Vielguth, Silesia; educ. Breslau and Halle; prof. Berlin; mem. Brandenburg consistory. Works include *Musik und Religion, Gottesdienst und Volksfeier; Die Revidierte Lutherbibel;* commentaries on Minor Prophets.

Kleinpolen. See *Lutheran Confessions,* A 5.

Klemme, Pankratius (ca. 1475–1547). B. Hirschberg, Silesia; reformer of Danzig; Dominican; preacher Danzig 1526; met M. Luther* at Wittenberg 1539.

Klemmer, Conrad. See *Estonian Lutherans in the US,* 1.

Klenovsky, Johann (ca. 1431–98). B. Prossnitz, Moravia; lay preacher in Moravian* ch.

Klesl, Melchior (Klesel; 1552 [or 1553]–1630). B. Vienna; bp. Vienna 1598; cardinal ca. 1615; leader of Counter* Reformation in lower Austria.

Kleuker, Johann Friedrich (1749–1827). Prot. apologete; b. Osterode, Ger.; educ. Göttingen; prorector Gymnasium in Lemgo 1775; rector Osnabrück 1778; prof. OT, NT, and symbolics Kiel 1798; exponent of Biblical supranaturalism* in opposition to rationalism.*

Kleutgen, Joseph (Jesuit name: Peters; 1811–83). B. Dortmund, Ger.; taught at Freiburg; prof. and prefect Gregorian U., Rome; helped promote rise of neo-scholasticism.*

Kliefoth, Theodor Friedrich Dethlof (1810–95). Luth. theol.; b. Körchow, near Wittenberg, Mecklenburg, Ger.; educ. Schwerin, Berlin, and Rostock; tutored Mecklenburg princes 1833–39; pastor Ludwigslust

1840; supt. and cathedral preacher Schwerin 1844; pres. supreme ch. council 1886; promoted ecclesiastical and liturgical reforms. Works include *Liturgische Abhandlungen; Christliche Eschatologie;* commentaries on Eze, Dn, Zch, Rv.

Klinck, Arthur William (Jan. 19, 1900–Aug. 9, 1959). B. Elmira, Ont., Can.; educ. Conc. Coll., Fort Wayne, Ind., and Conc. Sem., St. Louis, Mo.; miss. North Platte (1925–28) and Lincoln (1928–39), Nebr.; pres. Conc. Teachers Coll., River Forest, Ill., 1939–53; prof. Conc. Sem., St. Louis, 1954–59. Assoc. ed. *Lutheran School Journal* 1939–47, *Lutheran Education* 1947–53, *The Lutheran Witness* 1957–59; other works include *Home Life in Bible Times* and *Old Testament History.*

Klindworth, John (Aug. 9, 1833–Dec. 5, 1907). B. Stade, Hannover, Ger.; educ. Neuendettelsau; to Am. 1858; pastor Galena, Ill., 1858–1907; excluded from Ev. Luth. Syn. of Iowa* and Other States 1876 because of dissident views; joined Ev. Luth. Syn. of Wisconsin* and Other States and later Ev. Luth. Joint Syn. of Ohio* and Other States.

Klingelbeutel. Open cloth bag on long rod, originally with bell attached; used for gathering offerings in ch.

Klingmann, Stephan (Sept. 3, 1833–Apr. 17, 1891). B. Gau Angelloch, Baden; educ. Basel; commissioned for Am. 1860; pastor Mich.; helped organize the 2d Mich. Syn. (see *Michigan Synod,* 2) and was its pres. 1867–81.

Klopfer, Balthasar Christoph (1659–1703). B. Jüdenberg, near Bitterfeld, Ger.; harpist and scribe of count of Hanau; secy. in Greifenstein; lived in Giessen 1697–99, then in Laubach; influenced by J. Tauler*; radical mystic individualist; influential in Hesse.

Klopriss, Johann (Klopreis; Kloprys; d. 1535). B. Bottrop, Ger.; influenced by Reformation; later joined Anabaps. in Münster; burned at the stake.

Klopstock, Friedrich Gottlieb (1724–1803). B. Quedlinburg, Ger.; educ. Jena and Leipzig; Christian poet. Works include *Messias.*

Klotsche, Ernst Heinrich (Ernest; Aug. 7, 1875–Feb. 11, 1937). B. Elstra, near Kamenz, Saxony, Ger.; educ. at the training school of the Leipzig* Ev. Luth. Miss.; miss. India 1900–03; to Am. 1903; joined General* Syn. of the Ev. Luth. Ch. in the USA; pastor S. Dak. ca. 1903–13; to Nebr. 1913; taught Martin Luther Sem., Lincoln, Nebr.; taught Western Theol. Sem. (at Midland Coll.), Fremont, Nebr., 1919–30, as mem. of the Ger. Ev. Luth. Syn. of Nebr. (see *United Lutheran Church, Synods of,* 3) and Chicago (Ill.) Luth. Theol. Sem. 1930–37 as mem. of the Wartburg Syn. (see *United Lutheran Church, Synods of,* 30). Works include *An Outline of the History of Doctrines; Christian Symbolism; The Supernatural in the Tragedies of Euripides as Illustrated in Prayers, Curses, Oaths, Oracles, Prophecies, Dreams, and Visions.*

Kluepfel. See *Klüpfel.*

Klug, Joseph (Klöck; Clug; Sophos; d. ca. 1552). Printer in Wittenberg. Pub. *Geystliche gesangk Buchleyn* (1524; ed. M. Luther); *Geistliche Lieder* (1529); other works of Luther,* M. Aurogallus,* J. Bugenhagen,* J. Jonas,* P. Melanchthon,* U. Rhegius,* C. Cruciger the Elder (see *Cruciger,* 1), et al.

Klüpfel, Andreas (monastic name Engelbert; Kluepfel; 1733–1811). B. Wipfeld, near Würzburg, Ger.; Augustinian monk 1750 (1751?); priest 1756; prof. Freiburg; opposed scholasticism* and rationalism.* Works include *Institutiones theologiae dogmaticae.*

Knaake, Joachim Karl Friedrich (1835–1905). Ger. Luther scholar; cadet pastor Potsdam 1865; pastor Drakenstedt, Saxony 1883; initiator and 1st ed. of WA.

Knak, Gustav Friedrich Ludwig (1806–78). B. Berlin, Ger.; educ. Berlin; pastor Berlin; friend of missions; hymnist. Hymns include "Lasst mich gehn."

Knapp, Albert (1798–1864). B. Tübingen, Ger.; educ. Maulbronn and Tübingen; held various secondary positions in Feuerbach near Stuttgart, Gaisburg, Sulz, Kirchheim, and Stuttgart; pastor Stuttgart 1845; poet. Ed. *Christoterpe;* comp. *Evangelischer Liederschatz;* hymns include "O Vaterherz, das Erd und Himmel schuf."

Knapp, Georg Christian (1753–1825). B. Glaucha, near Halle, Ger.; educ. Halle and Göttingen; prof. Halle; exponent of pietism* and moderate supranaturalism.* Ed. Gk. NT; other works include *Beiträge zur Lebensgeschichte August Gottlieb Spangenbergs.*

Knapp, Johann Georg (1705–71). B. Öhringen, Ger.; prof. Halle; pietist; dir. Halle institution (see *Francke, August Hermann*) 1769.

Kneelers. 1. See *Genuflectentes.* 2. Cushion or other provision for kneeling.

Knights, Teutonic. See *Military Religious Orders,* c.

Knights Hospitallers (of St. John of Jerusalem). See *Military Religious Orders,* a.

Knights of Columbus. RC fraternal insurance benefit soc.; philanthropic; promotes RC publicity and publications.

Knights of Malta. See *Military Religious Orders,* a.

Knights of the Sword. See *Estonia,* 1.

Knights' Revolt. Uprising of knights in Ger. 1522–23 for religious, economic, and pol. reasons. Led by F. v. Sickingen* and U. v. Hutten,* the knights attacked the ecclesiastical princes and principalities, who, with the help of Philip* of Hesse and Elector Ludwig of The Palatinate, defeated the knights.

Knights Templars. See *Military Religious Orders,* b.

Knipperdolling, Bernt (Berend; Bernhard[t]; Knipperdollinck; Knipperdollink; ca. 1490 [or 1500?]–1536). Cloth-merchant at Münster, Ger.; became Anabap. leader; pol. motivated; imprisoned; tortured; executed. See also *Münster Kingdom.*

Knipstro, Johann(es) (Knipstrov[ius]; Knipstrow; Kniepstroh; 1497–1556). B. Sandow, near Havelberg, Ger.; legend from end of 17th c. says he defeated J. Tetzel* in debate on indulgences Jan. 1518; preached M. Luther's* doctrine; fled to Stettin; preacher Stralsund; supt. Wolgast; prof. Greifswald; helped found Prot. Ch. in Pomerania. Works include *Antwort der Theologen und Pastorn in Pommern auff die Confession A. Osiandri, wie der Mensch gerecht wird durch den Glauben an den Herrn Christum.*

Knoke, Hans Georg Wilhelm Karl (1841–1920). B. Schmedenstedt, Hannover, Ger.; educ. Göttingen and Erlangen; Luth. theol. and pedagog; dir. sem. at Wunstorf; prof. theol. Göttingen 1882. Ed. *D. Martin Luthers Kleiner Katechismus nach den ältesten Ausgaben hochdeutscher, niederdeutscher und lateinischer Sprache;* other works include *Praktisch-theologischer Kommentar zu den Pastoralbriefen des Apostels Paulus; Der Christ und das politische Gepräge der Zeit.*

Knoll, Cristoph (Cnollius; 1563–1621). B. Bunzlau, Silesia, Ger.; interested in mathematics and astronomy; held various positions at Sprottau beginning 1586; hymnist. Hymns include "Herzlich tut mich verlangen."

Knoll, Michael Christian (b. Aug. 27, 1696). B. Rendsburg, Holstein, Ger.; ordained 1732 by Luth. pastors in London, Eng.; pastor Trin. Luth. Ch., NYC, 1732–50, Loonenburg (later called Athens) and related congs. 1751–65 as successor to W. C. Berkenmeyer,* and 1773–74.

Knolle, Theodor (1885–1955). B. Hildesheim, Ger.; pastor Wittenberg and Hamburg; bp. Hamburg territory 1954; cofounder Luther-Gesellschaft; leader Luth. Liturgical Conf. in Ger.

Knoodt, Franz Peter (1811–89). Old Cath. (see *Old Catholics*) philos. and theol.; believed that free research and doctrinal norms could be maintained and that Christendom could be reunited.

Knöpken, Andreas (Knopken; Knop; Knopke; Knopf; Knophius; Knoppe; Cnophius; perhaps ca. 1493–1539). B. in or near Küstrin (Cüstrin; Kostrzyn), Brandenburg; assoc. with J. Bugenhagen* at Treptow on the Rega, Poland; to Riga, Latvia, 1521, with some Livonian scholars; enjoyed protection of civil authorities; with J. Briesmann* prepared ch. order for Riga based largely on M. Luther's* *Formula missae* (see *Chant; Liturgics; Luther, Liturgies of*); gained Riga for Reformation* by successfully defending 15 theses in disputation with Romanists; hymnist. Works include commentary on Ro. See also *Estonia,* 2; *Latvia.*

Knorr von Rosenroth, Christian (1636–89). B. Alt-Raudten, near Raudten, Upper Silesia; educ. Leipzig and Wittenberg; high official at court of Christian August, Count Palatine, at Sulzbach; mystic; hymnist. Hymns include "Morgenglanz der Ewigkeit"; other works include *Kabbala denudata.*

Knowledge. 1. *Divine.* God is a God of knowledge (1 Sm 2:3). His is an ever-present knowledge, one that directly knows things that exist and come to pass; not progressive knowledge, but total and perfect (Ps 139:1-4; Jn 21:17). He and His knowledge had no beginning (Ps 90:2; Eph 1:4). He is omniscient. See also *Prescience, Divine.*

2. *Human.* Man's knowledge was darkened by the fall. He can still know God and do natural acts of righteousness; but, under delusion of being wise, he becomes a fool and changes the truth of God into a lie (Ro 1:19-23, 25; 2:14-16). Man cannot by his own powers understand God and believe the Gospel and so save himself (1 Co 2:14-16). By faith he conforms to God through Christ and tries to bring his thoughts into harmony with the Gospel (2 Co 10:5). See also *God; God, Arguments for the Existence of.*

Knowlton, Charles. See *Family Planning,* 2.

Knox, John (ca. 1505 [or ca. 1514]–1572). Reformer; b. in or near Haddington (perhaps Giffordgate), E. Lothian, Scot.; perhaps educ. U. of Glasgow and/or St. Andrews; priest by 1540; tutor; assoc. with G. Wishart*; Prot. preacher St. Andrews 1547; captured when French, summoned by the Scot. queen regent, took St. Andrews castle 1547; galley prisoner 19 mo.; released 1549; preacher in Eng.; chaplain to Edward VI (see *England,* B 4); to Fr. 1554; to Switz. 1554, where he met J. Calvin*; pastor of Eng. refugee cong. Frankfurt, Ger., and Geneva, Switz.; to Scot. 1559, where he vigorously opposed RCm and promoted the establishment of Protestantism in Presb. form as the nat. religion; pastor Edinburgh. Politics and religion intertwined in his work. Helped revise Book* of Common Prayer 1552 and was apparently chiefly responsible for Black* Rubric; other works include *The Appellation of John Knox from the Cruell . . . Sentence Pronounced Against Him by the False Bishoppes and Clergy of Scotland; The Book of Common Order; The First Blast of the Trumpet Against the Monstrous Regiment of Women; The First Book of Discipline; The First Booke of the History of the Reformation of Religioun Within the Realme of Scotland.* See also *Calvinism; Scotland, Reformation in,* 1; *Sunday School,* 2.

T. M'Crie, *Life of John Knox,* 5th ed., 1st complete Am. ed. (Philadelphia, [1831?]); *The Works of John Knox,* ed. D. Laing (Edinburgh, 1846–48); A. Lang, *John Knox and the Reformation* (London, 1905); F. A. MacCunn, *John Knox,* 2d and rev. ed. (London, 1908); J. G. Ridley, *John Knox* (New York, 1968).

Knox's Liturgy. See *Presbyterian Churches,* 1.

Knubel, Frederick Hermann (May 22, 1870–Oct. 16, 1945). B. NYC; educ. Gettysburg (Pa.) Theol. Sem. and U. of Leipzig; pastor N. Y. 1896–1918; 1st pres. ULC 1918–44.

Knud. See *Canute.*

Knudsen, Hans (Knudson; Jan. 11, 1813–Feb. 16, 1886). B. Copenhagen, Den.; miss. Tranquebar, India, 1838; sick, returned to Eur. May 1843, leaving the station in charge of J. H. K. Cordes*; pastor Jutland, then on Zealand, then at Deaconess Institute, Copenhagen; resigned latter position 1872; founded Soc. for Care and Educ. of Crippled Children, pioneering in that work.

Knutson, Kent Sigvart (Aug. 7, 1924–Mar. 12, 1973). B. Goldfield, Iowa; educ. Iowa State U., at Ames, and Luther Sem., St. Paul, Minn.; ordained 1954 by the ELC (now part of The ALC); pastor Staten Is., N. Y., 1954–58; prof. Luther Sem. 1958–69; pres. Wartburg Sem., Dubuque, Iowa, 1969–70; pres. The ALC 1970–73. Ed. *Dialog* 1965–68; other works include *His Only Son, Our Lord* and *The Shape of the Question.*

Ko Tha Byu (Ko-Thah-Byu; d. 1840). Karen (Burmese) native; robber and murderer in early life; slave of Burman Buddhist; redeemed and became servant in family of A. Judson*; bap. by G. D. Boardman (see *Boardman,* 2) 1828; miss. to Burmese. See also *Asia,* C 1.

Koch, Eduard Emil (1809–71). B. Castle Solitude, near Stuttgart, Ger.; educ. Tübingen; pastor Ehningen (near Böblingen), Gross-Aspach (near Marbach), Heilbronn, and Erdmannhausen (near Marbach). Wrote *Geschichte des Kirchenlieds und Kirchengesangs der christlichen, insbesondere der deutschen evangelischen Kirche.*

Koch, Hal (Hans Harald; 1904–63) Luth. hist.; b. Hellerup, suburb of Copenhagen, Den.; prof. Copenhagen 1937. With B. S. Kornerup ed. *Den danske Kirkes Historie;* other works include *Pronoia und paideusis; Grundtvig; Det danske Folk, 1042–1241.*

Koch, Hugo (1869–1940). B. Andelfingen, Württemberg, Ger.; RC prof. ch. hist. and law Braunsberg; through study of Cyprian came into conflict with RC Ch.

Koch, Johannes. See *Cocceius, Johannes.*

Koch, Karl (1876–1951). B. Witten, Ger.; pastor Westphalia; active in ch. administration and state politics; leader in the Confessing* Ch.

Koch, Peter (Kock; d. 1749). Swed. merchant in Philadelphia, Pa.; helped P. Brunnholtz* tr. SC into Eng.; advocated union of Ger. and Swed. chs.

Kocherthal, Josua (von) (Joshua; original name: Harrsch; ca. 1669/70–Dec. 27, 1719). B. in or near Bretten, Ger.; pastor Landau, Palatinate; after Fr. invasion 1703, visited London 1704 to investigate feasibility of emigration to Am.; reached N. Y. Dec. 31, 1708, with ca. 50 followers; he returned to Eur. 1709; led ca. 10 shiploads of Palatines to Am. 1710; settled them along Hudson.

Kochhafe, David. See *Chytraeus, David.*

Kodesh Church of Immanuel (*kodesh* is Heb. for "holy"). Formed 1929 mainly by a group that withdrew from the Afr. Meth. Episc. Zion Ch. (see *Methodist Churches,* 4 c). See also *Holiness Churches,* 2.

Kodransson. See *Thorvald Kodransson.*

Kodratos. See *Quadratus.*

Koe-. See also as if spelled without this e.

Koelle, Sigismund Wilhelm (1822–1902). CMS miss. Afr. and Constantinople.

Koelman, Jacobus (1632–95). B. Utrecht, Neth.; Ref. theol.; pastor Sluis 1662; deposed 1675 because of his opposition to fixed liturgical formulas, multiplicity of ch. festivals, and assoc. of ch. and state; became traveling preacher; opposed separatism.

Koerner. See *Cornerus.*

Koetsveld, Cornelis Eliza van (1807–93). B. Rotterdam, Neth.; ev. pastor The Hague; noted for sermons, soc. work, interpretations of parables.

Kö-. See also *Koe-*.

Koffka, Kurt (Curt; 1886–1941). Psychol.; b. Berlin, Ger.; educ. Berlin and Edinburgh; asst. to Oswald Külpe (1862–1915; Ger. philos. and psychol.; b. Kandava, Latvia) and Karl Marbe (1869–1953; Ger. philos. and psychol.; b. Paris, Fr.) at Würzburg, Ger.; taught at academy Frankfurt am Main 1910–11; prof. Giessen 1911, Smith Coll., Northhampton, Mass., 1927; helped popularize Gestalt psychol. (see *Educational Psychology,* D 5; *Psychology,* J 5). Ed. journal *Psychologische Forschung;* other works include *The Growth of the Mind* (tr. R. M. Ogden); *Principles of Gestalt Psychology.*

Kögel, Julius (1871–1928). B. Berlin, Ger.; prof. Greifswald and Kiel. Ed. H. Cremer's *Biblisch-theologisches Wörterbuch der Neutestamentlichen Gräzität;* other works include *Christus der Herr; Die Gedankeneinheit des Ersten Briefes Petri; Der Sohn und die Söhne.* See also *Lexicons,* B.

Kögel, Theodor Johannes Rudolf (1829–96). B. Birnbaum, Posen, Prussia; educ. Halle and Berlin; gymnasial teacher Dresden 1852–54; supply pastor Nakel (near Bromberg) ca. 1854–57, The Hague 1857–63; court preacher Berlin. Championed Prussian* Union and orthodoxy as opposed to liberalism; founded Positive Union 1876; opposed syn. principle.

Kohlbrügge, Hermann Friedrich (Kohlbrugge; 1803–75). B. Amsterdam, Neth.; first Luth., later Ref.; pastor Elberfeld, Ger. Works include *Das alte Testament nach seinem wahren Sinne gewürdigt aus den Schriften der Evangelisten und Apostel; Opleiding tot recht verstand der Schrift voor eenvoudigen die Gods woord onderzoeken;* sermons.

Köhler, Edward William August (Koehler; Eduard; Oct. 31, 1875–May 12, 1951). B. Wolfenbüttel, Brunswick, Ger.; educ. Conc. Coll., Fort Wayne, Ind., and Conc. Sem., St. Louis, Mo.; pastor Billings, Christian Co., Mo., 1899–1902; Knoxville, Tenn., 1903–09. Prof. Mosheim* Coll., Mosheim, Tenn., 1902–03; Conc. Teachers Coll., Addison and River Forest, Ill., 1909–51. Works include *A Short Explanation of Dr. Martin Luther's Small Catechism . . . with Additional Notes; A Christian Pedagogy; Summary of Christian Doctrine; Conscience.*

Köhler, Johann Philipp (Jan. 17, 1859–Sept. 30, 1951). B. Manitowoc, Wis.; son of P. Köhler.* Educ. Northwestern Coll., Watertown, Wis., and Conc. Sem., St. Louis, Mo. Vicared for G. A. T. F. Hönecke* 1878; asst. pastor to his father at Hustisford, Wis., 1880–82; pastor Two Rivers, Wis., 1882–88. Prof. Northwestern Coll. 1888–1900; Wis. Syn. sem. at Wauwatosa and Thiensville (near Mequon), Wis., 1900–30 (pres. 1920–30). Taught NT exegesis, ch. hist., hermeneutics, ch. music, liturgics, Ger., and Lat. Deposed from professorship 1930 as a result of intrafaculty tensions. Works include *Der Brief Pauli an die Galater,* tr. E. E. Sauer, *The Epistle of Paul to the Galatians; Lehrbuch der Kirchengeschichte; Geschichte der Allgemeinen Evangelisch-Lutherischen Synode von Wisconsin und andern Staaten* (tr., rev., and updated by author, "The History of the Wisconsin Synod," *Faith-Life,* XI, 2–XVII, 1 [Feb. 1938–Jan. 1944]; ed. L. D. Jordahl and pub. in book form 1970). See also *Protes'tant Conference; Wauwatosa Theology.* WJH

Kohler, John (1820–98). B. Juniata Co., Pa.; educ. Pa. Coll. and Gettysburg Sem., both at Gettysburg, Pa.; pastor Williamsport 1844–49, New Holland 1850–64, Trappe 1864–73, Stroudsburg 1873–82, and Leacock 1884–93, all in Pa.; principal of academic dept. Muhlenberg Coll., Allentown, Pa., 1882–84; mem. Ministerium of Pennsylvania* and Other States; advocated episcopate.

Köhler, Ludwig Hugo (1880–1956). Nephew of P. Köhler*; b. Neuwied, Ger.; educ. Zurich, Switz.; prof. OT Zurich; criticoliberal; noted for word studies, lexicography, grammatical studies. Coauthor (with Walter Baumgartner *Lexicon in Veteris Testamenti libros;* other works include *Theologie des Alten Testaments.*

Köhler, Philipp (Oct. 8, 1828–Sept. 3/4, 1895). Father of J. P. Köher*; uncle of L. H. Köhler*; b. Neuwied, Ger.; educ. Barmen; to Milwaukee, Wis., 1854; ordained Milwaukee at the 1855 Wis. Syn. conv.; pastor Wis.; championed confessional Lutheranism.

Köhler, Philipp August (1835–97). Luth. theol.; b. Schmalenberg, Rhine Palatinate; educ. Bonn, Erlangen, and Utrecht; prof. Erlangen, Jena, and Bonn. Works include *Lehrbuch der Biblischen Geschichte Alten Testamentes.*

Köhler, Walther Erich (Koehler; 1870–1946). Luth. theol.; b. Elberfeld, Ger.; educ. Halle, Heidelberg, Strasbourg, Bonn, and Tübingen; prof. Giessen, Zurich, Heidelberg. Outstanding hist. of Reformation, M. Luther,* H. Zwingli,* Anabaps. (see *Mennonite Churches; Baptist Churches,* 2). Works include *Zwingli und Luther; Die Geisteswelt Ulrich Zwinglis; Huldrych Zwingli; Luther und die Kirchengeschichte nach seinen Schriften.*

Köhler, Wolfgang (1887–1967). Psychologist and educ.; b. Reval (Tallin), Estonia; educ. Tübingen, Bonn, Berlin; privatdocent Frankfurt am Main; dir. anthropoid experiment station, Tenerife, Canary Is., 1913–20; helped found journal *Psychologische Forschung;* prof. Berlin 1922; visited Am. several times; prof. Swarthmore (Pa.) Coll. 1935; research prof. Dartmouth Coll., Hanover, N. H., 1958; exponent of Gestalt psychology (see *Educational Psychology,* D 5; *Psychology,* J 5). Works include *Intelligenzprüfungen an Anthropoiden; Die physischen Gestalten in Ruhe und im stationären Zustand; Gestalt Psychology; The Place of Value in a World of Fact; Dynamics in Psychology.*

Kohlhoff, Johann Balthasar (Nov. 15, 1711–Dec. 17, 1790). Father of J. C. Kohlhoff*; b. Neuwarp, W Pomerania; educ. Rostock and Halle; Danish-Halle miss. Tranquebar, India, 1737–90.

Kohlhoff, Johann Caspar (Kaspar; 1762–Mar. 27, 1844). Son of J. B. Kohlhoff*; b. Tranquebar, India; miss. at Tanjore 1787–1844.

Kohn, William Christian (June 2, 1865–Mar. 13, 1943). B. Ger.; to US 1865; educ. Conc. Sem., St. Louis, Mo.; asst. pastor St. James Luth. Ch., Chicago, Ill., 1887–88; pastor St. Andrew Luth. Ch., Chicago, 1888–1913; pres. N. Ill. Dist. of Mo. Syn. 1909–13; pres. Conc. Teachers Coll., River Forest, Ill., 1913–39; continued to teach.

Koine (Gk. "common"). Language used in E Mediterranean countries by those who spoke Gk. in the Hellenistic and Roman periods; language of the Gk. NT.

Koinonia. Gk. for "fellowship."* See also *Communio sanctorum.*

Kojiki (Jap. "chronicle of ancient events"). Jap. collection of source material of Shinto* up to 628; oldest extant document on the subject; compiled 712.

Kol. Collective name for non-Hindu aboriginal tribes in Chota Nagpur, Bihar, India; missions begun 1845 by Gossner* Miss. Soc.; CMS granted financial aid 1858; SPG entered field 1869; RC Ch. came 1880; Dublin U. Miss. est. 1891; Gossner missions became autonomous after WWI.

Kol Nidre (Aramaic "all vows"). Opening prayer (named after its first words) of Jewish service on eve of Day of Atonement (see *Judaism,* 4); speaks of annulment of vows. Entire service is also called Kol Nidre. Connection with Day of Atonement is not clear.

Kölbing, Paul (1843–1925). Instructor at theol. sem. of Herrnhuters (see *Moravian Church,* 3) at Gnadenfeld, Upper Silesia, 1868; under influence of A. Ritschl* he clashed with prevailing theology and left the school; returned 1886 after change of administration; dir. sem. 1894–1907; prominent esp. 1895–97 in his ch.'s controversy regarding the hist.-critical method; a working solution of the controversy was based on common "faith of the heart"; preacher Strasbourg 1907.

Kolde, Hermann Friedrich Theodor (von) (1850–1913). B. Friedland, Silesia; educ. Breslau and Leipzig; Luth. prof. Marburg and Erlangen. Works include *Luther und der Reichstag zu Worms; Martin Luther; Das religiöse Leben in Erfurt beim Ausgange des Mittelalters.*

Kollár, Jan. See *Slovakia, Lutheran Theology in,* 2.

Komander, Johann(es) ("Komander" is formed from Gk. *kome,* "village," and *aner, andros,* "man," and is equivalent to Ger. Dorfmann; also called Hutmacher; ca. 1484–1557). Reformer of Swiss canton Graubünden (Fr. Grisons); b. Maienfeld, Switz.; educ. Saint Gall and Basel, Switz. Works include a catechism.

Konfessionskundliches Institut. See *Evangelischer Bund.*

Konfutationsbuch. Doctrinal norm for realm of John* Frederick II, who had it drafted 1558–59 at the prompting of M. Flacius* Illyricus; upheld views of Flacius; opposed G. Major,* V. Strigel,* adiaphorists (see *Adiaphoristic Controversies*), and others. See also *Weimar, Colloquies and Conventions of; Synergistic Controversy.*

König, Friedrich Eduard (1846–1936). B. Reichenbach, Ger.; educ. Leipzig; privatdocent 1879, assoc. prof. OT exegesis 1885 Leipzig; prof. Rostock 1888, Bonn 1900; conservative in theol.; opposed extreme higher criticism. Works include *Historisch-kritisches Lehrgebäude der hebräischen Sprache; Hebräisches und aramäisches Wörterbuch.*

König, Georg Friedrich Justus (Sept. 23, 1825–Nov. 17, 1891). B. Haynholtz, Hannover, Ger.; educ. Göttingen; to Am. 1852; joined Mo. Syn. Pastor Lafayette, Ind., 1852–58; Cincinnati, Ohio, 1858–72; NYC 1872–91.

König, Johann Friedrich (1619–64). B. Dresden, Ger.; prof. Greifswald and Rostock. Works include *Theologia positivo-acromatica,* basis of many 17th c. dogmatic lectures, esp. J. A. Quenstedt's* *Theologia didactico-polemica.*

König, Samuel (1670–1750). B. Gerzensee, Switz.; pietistic theol.; deposed because of mystic chiliasm and insistence that a pastor must show evidence of having been converted; banned 1699; prof. Bern 1730.

Konrad von Gelnhausen (ca. 1320–90). Taught at Paris 1344, Heidelberg 1387; canon Mainz 1359; provost Worms ca. 1380. Advocated conciliar* movement. Urged calling a gen. council without papal convocation, to settle the papal schism* which began 1378. See also *Councils and Synods,* 7.

Konrad von Marburg (ca. 1180–1233). 1st papal inquisitor in Ger.; known for severity.

Konsul, Stephan. See *Consul, Stipan.*

Kooiman, Willem Jan (1903–68). Luth. theol.; b. Barneveld, Neth.; pastor Veendam 1927, Deventer 1929, Amsterdam 1935; prof. ch. hist. Amsterdam 1945. Works include *Luthers kerklied in de Nederlanden; Maarten Luther, Doctor der Heilige Schrift, Reformator der Kerk* (tr. B. L. Woolf, *By Faith Alone: The Life of Martin Luther*); *De Nederlandsche Luthersche gemeenten in Noord-Amerika 1649–1772; Philippus Melanchthon; Luther en de Bijbel* (tr. J. Schmidt, *Luther and the Bible*).

Koolhaas (Koolhaes). See *Coolhaes.*

Koopmann, Wilhelm Heinrich (1814–71). Luth. theol.; b. Tönning, Ger.; educ. Kiel; pastor Lauenburg 1845, Ottensen (near Altona) 1854; gen. supt. Altona 1855; opposed rationalism*; defended confessionalism. Works include *Das evangelische Christenthum in seinem Verhältnisse zu der modernen Cultur; Die Rechtfertigung allein durch den Glauben an Christum im Lichte der neueren Theologie.*

Köpfel, Wolfgang (Köpphel; Köphel; Köfl; Wolff; 16th c.). Printer in Strasbourg at time of Reformation. Works printed include *Teutsch Kirchen ampt; Psalmen und geystliche Lieder; Psalmen, Gebet und Kirchenübung; Ein New Auserlesen Gesang büchlin; Enchiridion geistlicher gesenge.*

Köpfel, Wolfgang Fabricius. See *Capito, Wolfgang.*

Koran (Qur'an; Quran; Qoran; Arab. "book; reading; recitation"). Sacred book of Islam*; source of Muslim* religious, soc., civil, commercial, military, and legal regulations; regarded by Muslim as revealed by Allah to Muhammad* through an angel. Text was compiled after Muhammad's death. The present common text consists of 114 suras (surahs; Arab. "that which opens, or begins"); the last 2 are imprecations against evil spirits and enchantments; the others are arranged acc. to length, from the longest (nearly 700 lines) to the shortest (2 lines). Includes Arab. legendary matter and distorted echoes of the Bible. See also *Ramadan.*

Korea (Corea; N. Korean and official Jap. name: Chosen [see par. 2], "Land of Morning Calm"; S. Korean: Hangook, or Han-kuk; name used within Korea after WW II by Rep. of Korea: Tae Han. The name Korea is said to derive from Koryo [see par. 2]). 1. Peninsula S from Manchuria bet. Yellow Sea and Sea of Jap.; ca. 550 mi. long; ca. 125–ca. 200 mi. wide; more mountainous in N than in S; thousands of islands along the coast. *Area:* ca. 85,250 sq. mi. (N. Korea [People's Democratic Rep. of Korea] ca. 46,663 sq. mi., S. Korea [Rep. of Korea] ca. 38,100 sq. mi., demilitarized since 1953 [see par. 2] ca. 487 sq. mi.); *pop.* (1973 est.): N. Korea ca. 14,643,000, S. Korea ca. 36,864,000. Climate gen. hot and wet in summer, cold and dry in winter. Han people (Tungusic or Mongoloid) invaded the land perhaps ca. the 3d millennium BC, formed the dominant racial stock, and originated the Korean language, which resembles Japanese in grammar.

2. Korea's legendary past begins 2333 BC. Recorded hist. begins ca. 57 BC with the Period of Three Kingdoms (Silla, Koguryu, Pakche), followed by the Koryo dynasty (ca. 918–1392) and the Li (or Yi) dynasty (1392–1910), under which the land was named Chosen by the emp. of China. Jap. protectorate 1907, province 1910–45; divided at 38th parallel into zones of Russ. (N) and Am. (S) occupation; N. Korean People's Rep. and S. Korean Rep. est. 1948; Korean War 1950–53.

3. The 6-3-3-4-grade educ. system is in popular use, with compulsory educ. on the elementary level. The literacy rate is high.

4. Shamanism,* oldest indigenous religion, began in prehistoric times. Confucianism* was introd. from China before the Christian era. Buddhism* entered Korea 4th c. AD, reached its zenith 12th–14th c. Chondokyo (ch'ondogyo ["Religion of the Heavenly Way"]; first called Tonghak ["Eastern Learning"]), indigenous and eclectic, was founded ca. 1860 by Ch'oe Che-u (Suun [honorific title]; 1824–64). Shinto,* introd. from Jap., virtually disappeared after 1945.

5. First contact with Christianity apparently was with Jap. RCs who came 1592 with invaders. There were Korean Christians at least as early as 1784. Severe persecution, intermittent since 1785, started anew 1801, continued till 1881; total martyrs est. ca. 10,000. Three Fr. RC missionaries arrived in

the 1830s, were martyred. K. F. A. Gützlaff* explored the coast 1832, spent ca. a mo. there. Robert J. Thomas, LMS miss. to China, visited Korea 1865 as agent of the Nat. Bible Soc. of Scot., was martyred 1866. J. Ross* helped tr. Scripture into Korean, baptized Koreans in Manchuria 1881 and 1884. Other miss. ventures include those of H. N. Allen,* Presb., 1884; other Presbs. and N. Meths. in the middle 1880s; Australian Presb. Ch. and Ch. of Eng. near the turn of the decade; S. Presbs. 1892; S. Meths. in middle 1890s; Can. Presbs. 1898; Advs. and the Oriental* Miss. Soc. in the 1st decade of the 20th c.; Salv. Army 1908; LCMS 1958. Hankuk Rutu Kyohoe (Korea Luth. Ch.) grew out of LCMS efforts; organized 1971; accepted as a sister ch. of LCMS 1971. After WW II many schisms occurred, resulting in many sects. Ca. 1,500,000 Christians in S. Korea; figures for N. Korea not available. Luth. theol. training program began in the middle 1960s in Seoul. See also *Nevius Method.*

G. M. McCune, E. McCune, and A. L. Grey Jr., *Korea Today* (Cambridge, Mass., 1950); C. B. Osgood, *The Koreans and Their Culture* (New York, 1951); Chae Kyung Oh, *Handbook of Korea* (New York, 1958); *Korea: Its Land, People and Culture of All Ages* (pub. by Hakwon-sa, Seoul, 1960); S. H. Moffett, *The Christians of Korea* (New York, 1962); R. E. Shearer, *Wildfire: Church Growth in Korea* (Grand Rapids, Mich., 1966); *Korea Struggles for Christ,* ed. H. S. Hong, Won Yong Ji, and Chung Choon Kim (Seoul, 1966); M. W. Dorow, *Developing a Ministry on Mission Fields in the Light of the New Testament Concepts of Church and Ministry* (Conc. Sem., St. Louis, Mo., STM Thesis, 1963); G. T. Brown, *Mission to Korea* (n.p., 1962); B. B. Weems, *Reform, Rebellion, and the Heavenly Way* (Tucson, Ariz., 1964). WYJ

Koren, Ulrik Vilhelm (Dec. 22, 1826–Dec. 19, 1910). Luth. clergyman; b. Bergen, Norw.; educ. Christiania (Oslo); taught Lat. School, Christiana, 1852–53; to US 1853; ordained 1853; pastor Little Iowa (later called Washington Prairie) and adjoining congs., near Decorah, Iowa, 1853–1910; taught at Luther Coll., Decorah, 1874–75; pres. Syn. for the Norw. Ev. Luth. Ch. in Am. (see *Evangelical Lutheran Church, The,* 8–13) 1894–1910. Works pub. under title *Samlede Skrifter.*

Koreshanity. See *Communistic Societies, 5.*

Korner (Körner; Kornerus). See *Cornerus.*

Kortholt, Christian (Cortholt; 1632 [1633?]–94). B. Burg, on is. Fehrmarn (Femern), Ger.; educ. Rostock, Jena, and Wittenberg; prof. Rostock 1662, Kiel 1666; opposed R. Bellarmine,* C. Baronius,* B. Spinoza,* T. Hobbes,* E. Herbert.*

Korum, Michael Felix (1840–1921). B. near Colmar, Fr.; RC bp. Trier 1881; defended clericalism*; founded a community of Sisters of Joseph 1891 (they do soc. work in Trier, Freiburg, and Cologne).

Korzybski, Alfred Habdank Skarbek (1879–1950). B. Warsaw, Poland; to US 1916, naturalized 1940; pres. and dir. Institute of Gen. Semantics, Chicago, Ill., from 1938. Works include *Manhood of Humanity; Science and Sanity: An Introduction to Non-Aristotelian Systems and General Semantics.* See also *Semantics, General.*

Köster, Heinrich Bernhard (Henrich; Küster; 1662-1749). B. Blumenberg, Lippe, Westphalia; studied law in Bremen; hofmeister of Baron Otto von Schwerin; drawn to Lutheranism by baron's father; to Germantown, Pa., 1694; conducted Luth. services; opposed Quakers; mystic pietist; returned to Eur., arriving London near the end of Jan. 1700. Works include *Ein Bericht an alle Bekenner und Schrifftsteller.*

CHIQ, XXII (Jan. 1950), 158–166.

Köstering, Johann Friedrich (Feb. 20, 1830–Jan. 20/21, 1908). B. Hannover, Ger.; educ. Fort Wayne, Ind. Pastor Adams Twp., near Fort Wayne, Allen Co., Ind., 1853–58; Frankenthal, Spencer Co., Ind., 1858–61; Arcadia, Hamilton Co., Ind., 1861–64; Altenburg, Perry Co., Mo., 1864–87; St. Louis, Mo., 1887–1904. Wrote *Auswanderung der sächsischen Lutheraner im Jahre 1838.*

Köstlin, Heinrich Adolf (1846–1907). B. Tübingen, Ger.; educ. Tübingen; taught in Paris 1869–70; military chaplain 1870–71; music tutor Tübingen 1872–73; pastor Maulbronn 1875–78, Friedrichshafen 1878–81, Stuttgart 1881–83; prof. theol. Friedberg, Hesse, 1883–91; supreme consistorial councillor and supt. of the province of Starkenburg 1891–95; privy ecclesiastical councillor and prof. theol. Giessen 1895–1901. Organized Württemberg Evangelischer Kirchengesangsverein; helped found Evangelischer Kirchengesangverein für Deutschland. Works include *Geschichte der Musik im Umriss; Die Tonkunst; Luther als der Vater des evangelischen Kirchengesanges; Geschichte des christlichen Gottesdienstes; Die Lehre von der Seelsorge nach evangelischen Grundsätzen.*

Köstlin, Julius Theodor (1826–1902). Prot. theol.; b. Stuttgart, Ger.; prof. Göttingen 1855, Breslau 1860, Halle 1870; introd. Presb. features into Ger. ch. govt. Works include *Christliche Ethik; Martin Luther; Luthers Theologie in ihrer geschichtlichen Entwicklung und ihrem inneren Zusammenhange,* tr. (from the 2d Ger. ed.) Charles Ebert Hay, *The Theology of Luther in Its Historical Development and Inner Harmony.*

Köthe, Friedrich August (1781–1850). B. Lübben, Ger.; prof. Jena 1810; supt. Allstedt 1819; opposed rationalism.* Issued an ed. of the Luth. Confessions and of some of P. Melanchthon's* works.

Kottwitz, Hans Ernst von (1757–1843). B. Tschepplau (Tepplau), near Glogau, Silesia; educ. Breslau; pietist; philanthropist; founded institution to provide work for poor.

Kowert, Wilhelm Hermann (July 7, 1842–Apr. 9, 1923). B. Neukirchen, near Melle, Hannover, Ger.; educ. Hermannsburg* Miss. school; miss. to Maori in New Zealand 1876; pastor of Ger. colonists at Upper Moutere, New Zealand, 1882; to Am. 1886. Mo. Syn. pastor Harvel, Ill., 1886–91; Orchard Farm, Mo., 1891–1908; Ontarioville, Ill., 1908–16. Later lived in Sheboygan, Wis., and Elgin, Ill.

Kozlowska, Felicja. See *Mariavites.*

Kraeft, Walter Otto (Kräft; Aug. 11, 1893–Mar. 30, 1960). B. Oregon City, Oreg.; educ. Ev. Luth. Teachers Sem., Addison, Ill., and Conc. Teachers Coll., River Forest, Ill.; taught school at Rock Island, Ill., and St. Louis, Mo.; prof. Conc. Teachers Coll., River Forest, 1926. Works include *Religion for Primary Grades in Units of Learning; The Lutheran Teacher's Handbook; Working Together;* ed. *Our Church at Work.*

Kraemer, Hendrik (1888–1965). Lay theol.; b. Amsterdam, Neth.; assoc. with Neth. Bible Soc. (see *Bible Societies,* 4) in Indonesia 1921–35; prof. Leiden 1937; dir. Ecumenical Institute of the Ecumenical Council, Bossey, Switz., 1948; emphasized community of Christians, missions, and role of laity in ch.; sought ways to build Christian way of life into secular callings; regarded relationship of young chs. to W chs. as partnership instead of dependence. Works include *The Christian Message in a Non-Christian World; A Theology of the Laity; The Communication of the Christian Faith; Religion and the Christian Faith; World Cultures and World Religions: The Coming Dialogue.*

Krafft, Adam (ca. 1460–ca. 1508). See *Kraft, Adam.*

Krafft, Adam (Kraft; Adam of Fulda; Crato Fuldensis; Vegetius; 1493–1558). B. Fulda, Ger.; educ. Erfurt; humanist; taught at Erfurt; became Luth.; court preacher of Philip* of Hesse; supt. Marburg 1526; prof. theol. Marburg 1527.

Krafft, Johann. See *Crato von Crafftheim.*

Krafft, Johann Christian Gottlieb Ludwig (1784–1845). Ref. clergyman; b. Duisburg, Ger.; educ. Duisburg; tutor Frankfort am Main; pastor Weeze, near Cleve, 1808; pastor Erlangen 1817; prof. Erlangen; helped revive Prot. ch. in Bav.

Kraft, Adam (Krafft; ca. 1460–ca. 1508). B. probably Nürnberg, Ger.; stone sculptor. Works include reliefs of scenes from the life of Christ.

Kraft, Adam (1493–1558). See *Krafft, Adam.*

Krakevitz, Albrecht Joachim von (1674–1732). B. Gevezin, Mecklenburg, Ger.; prof. oriental languages 1699, theol. 1713, Rostock; prof. theol. and Gen. Supt. Greifswald 1721; moderate orthodox pietist.

Krakewitz, Berthold von (Barthold; 1582–1642). Luth. theol.; educ. Wittenberg and other Ger. univs.; supt. and prof. Greifswald; responsible for inclusion of FC among Pomeranian confessions.

Kralice, Bible of. See *Bohemian Brethren,* 3; *Czechoslovakia,* 7.

Kranach. See *Cranach.*

Krapf, Johann Ludwig (Jan. 11, 1810–Nov. 26, 1881). B. Derendingen, near Tübingen, Ger.; educ. Basel and Tübingen; CMS miss. to Abyssinia 1837; expelled as a result of hostile RC influence; est. miss. at Mombasa 1844; traveled through E Afr. with J. Rebmann*; projected plan for miss. chain across Afr. from the N. Tr. NT and parts of OT into Galla; rev. Amharic OT; other works include *A Dictionary of the Suahili Language.* See also *Africa,* A 6.

Krasonicky, Laurentius (d. 1532). Priest of Unitas Fratrum (see *Bohemian Brethren*); developed doctrine in rational biblicistic direction.

Kraus, Franz Xaver (1840–1901). B. Trier, Ger.; RC priest; taught at Strasbourg 1872, Freiburg 1878; noted in field of archaeol. and hist. of art; opposed ultramontanism.* Works include *Lehrbuch der Kirchengeschichte.*

Krausert, Michael. See *Amana Society.*

Krauss, Elmer Frederick (Sept. 7, 1862–May 23, 1946). B. Kraussdale, Lehigh Co., Pa.; educ. Muhlenberg Coll., Allentown, Pa., and Lutheran Theol. Sem., Philadelphia, Pa. Pastor Homestead, Pa., 1887–92; Minneapolis, Minn., 1892–94; Leechburg, Pa., 1894–1900. Prof. Chicago Luth. Theol. Sem. 1900, pres. 1915–20.

Krauss, Eugen Adolf Wilhelm (June 4, 1851–Oct. 9, 1924). B. Nördlingen, Bav.; educ. Erlangen and Leipzig; severed connection with state ch. before graduation; to US 1873; Mo. Syn. pastor Cedarburg, Wis., 1874; returned to Ger. 1875 to serve a Free Ch. cong. at Sperlingshof, Baden; returned to US; rejoined Mo. Syn.; dir. Ev. Luth. Teachers Sem., Addison, Ill., 1880–1905; prof. Conc. Sem., St. Louis, Mo., 1905–24. Ed. *Lebensbilder aus der Geschichte der christlichen Kirche;* other works include *Meine Schuljahre.*

Kraussold, Lorenz (Ludwig; 1803–81). Luth. theol.; b. Mistelgau, near Bayreuth, Ger.; pastor Aufsess 1830, Fürth 1835; counsellor of the consistory and chief preacher Bayreuth 1854. Works include *Katechetik; Vom alten protestantischen Choral; Historisch-musicalisches Handbuch für den Kirchen- und Choralgesang; Amt und Gemeinde in der evangelisch-lutherischen Kirche; Musicalische Altaragende für den evangelisch-lutherischen Gottesdienst.*

Krauth, Charles Philip (May 7, 1797–May 30, 1867). Father of C. Porterfield Krauth*; b. New Goshenhoppen, Montgomery Co., Pa.; studied medicine at the U. of Md.; then studied for the Luth. ministry under D. F. Schaeffer*; asst. pastor Winchester, Va., 1818; licensed by Ministerium of Pennslyvania* 1819; pastor Martinsburg and Shepherdstown, both now in W. Va.; helped organize The Ev. Luth. Syn. of Md. and Va. (see *Synods, Extinct; United Lutheran Church, Synods of,* 11, 29) 1820; ordained by this syn. 1821; its pres. 1826; pastor Philadelphia, Pa., 1827–33; prof. Biblical and oriental literature Gettysburg (Pa.) Sem. 1833; also taught in Pa. Coll. (later called Gettysburg Coll.); 1st pres. Pa. Coll. 1834–50; also taught at the Sem. during this time; pres. The Ev. Luth. Gen. Syn. of the United States of North America (see *General Synod of the Evangelical Lutheran Church in the United States of America, The*) 1848; prof. Biblical philol. and ecclesiastical hist. Gettysburg Sem. 1850–67. Asst. ed. *The Evangelical Lutheran Intelligencer;* ed. *The Evangelical Review.* JW

Krauth, Charles Porterfield (March 17, 1823–Jan. 2, 1883). Son of C. Philip Krauth*; b. Martinsburg, now in W. Va.; educ. Pa. Coll. (later called Gettysburg Coll.) and Gettysburg Sem.; licensed by Md. Syn. (see *United Lutheran Church, Synods of,* 11) 1841; served a miss. at Canton, suburb of Baltimore, Md.; ordained 1842. Pastor Baltimore 1842–47; Martinsburg and Shepherdstown, both now in W. Va., 1847–48; Winchester, Va., 1848–55; Pittsburgh, Pa., 1855–59; Philadelphia, Pa., 1859–67. Prof. Luth. Theol. Sem. 1864–83, U. of Pa. 1868–83, both at Philadelphia. Opposed theology of Definite* Syn. Platform but advocated kindness toward its adherents. Helped organize The General* Council of the Ev. Luth. Ch. in (N.) Am.; its pres. 1870–80. C. F. W. Walther* described him as "without doubt the most eminent man in the Eng. Luth. Ch. of this country, a man of unusual learning, at home in modern as well as old theol., and, what is most important, heartily devoted to the pure doctrine of [the Luth.] Ch." (*L. u. W.*, XXIX, 1 [Jan. 1883], 32). Ed. *Lutheran and Missionary* and *The Lutheran Church Review;* other works include *The Conservative Reformation and Its Theology.* See also *Fraternal Address; Fundamental Principles of Faith and Church Polity; Galesburg Rule.* JW

A. Spaeth, *Charles Porterfield Krauth,* 2 vols. (New York, 1898; Philadelphia, 1909).

Krebs, Fritz. See *Catholic Apostolic Church,* 2.

Krebs, Johann Ludwig (1713–80). Son of J. T. Krebs*; b. Thuringia, Ger.; pupil of J. S. Bach,* who coined the double pun: "der einzige Krebs im Bache." Organist Zwickau, Zeitz, and Altenburg. Works include preludes; chorales with variations.

Krebs, Johann Tobias (1690–1762). Father of J. L. Krebs*; b. Heichelheim, near Weimar, Ger.; pupil of J. S. Bach*; Luth. organist Buttelstedt and Buttstädt. Works include *Prelude and Fugue in C Major; Trio in C Minor;* organ chorales.

Kreinheder, Oscar Carl (Nov. 10, 1877–Mar. 26, 1946). B. Buffalo, N. Y.; educ. Conc. Sem., St. Louis, Mo.; ordained by The Eng. Ev. Luth. Syn. of Missouri* and Other States. Pastor E. St. Louis, Ill., 1901–03; St. Paul, Minn., 1903–20; Detroit, Mich., 1920–30. Pres. Eng. Dist. (Mo. Syn.) 1918–27; pres. Valparaiso U. 1930–39.

Krell, Nikolaus. See *Crell, Nikolaus.*

Kremmer, Karl Friedrich (Sept. 8, 1817–July 24, 1887). B. Schmalkalden, Ger.; educ. Dresden Miss. Inst. (see *Leipzig Evangelical Lutheran Mission*); miss. to India 1846; served Madras 1848–58, 1865–75; Tamil scholar; founded Cuddalore and Madura stations; head of Leipzig Miss. in India 1884–87.

Kretzmann, Karl Gustave Henry (Feb. 23, 1877–Apr. 3, 1949). Brother of P. E. Kretzmann*; b. Dudleytown, near Seymour, Ind.; educ. Conc. Coll., Fort Wayne, Ind., and Conc. Sem., St. Louis, Mo. Pastor Stamford, Conn., 1899–1905; Baltimore, Md., 1905–06; NYC 1906–21; Orange, N. J., 1921–43. First full-time curator Conc. Hist. Institute, St. Louis, 1943–48. Works include *The Atlantic District of the Evangelical Lutheran Synod of Missouri, Ohio, and*

Other States and Its Antecedents; The Oldest Lutheran Church in America.

W. G. Polack, "Karl Kretzmann, D. D.," *CHIQ,* XXII (July 1949), 49–55.

Kretzmann, Paul Edward (Aug. 24, 1883–July 13, 1965). Brother of K. G. H. Kretzmann*; b. Farmers Retreat, Dearborn Co., Ind.; educ. Conc. Coll., Fort Wayne, Ind., and Conc. Sem., St. Louis, Mo.; pastor Shady Bend, Kans., 1906–07; Denver, Colo., 1907–12; prof. sciences and math. Conc. Coll., St. Paul, Minn., 1912–19; ed., later production manager, Conc. Pub. House, St. Louis, Mo., 1919–23; prof. Conc. Sem., St. Louis, Mo., 1924–46; pastor Forest Park, Ill., 1946–48; helped form Orthodox* Luth. Conference; pres. of its sem., Minneapolis, Minn. Works include *Education Among the Jews; The Liturgical Element in the Earliest Forms of the Medieval Drama, with Special Reference to the English and German Plays; Die Pastoralbriefe; Christian Art in the Place and in the Form of Lutheran Worship; Popular Commentary of the Bible; The Religion of the Child and Other Essays; The New Testament in the Light of a Believer's Research; The GOD OF THE BIBLE and other "GODS"; The Foundations Must Stand!* ARS

Kretzschmar, Richard Theodore (May 17, 1868–March 5, 1940). B. Hartha, Saxony, Ger.; to US as a child with his father (Friedrich Hermann Kretzschmar; Oct. 22, 1840–Nov. 14, 1930; b. Mittweida, Saxony; to US; educ. Wartburg Theol. Sem., St. Sebald, Iowa, grad. 1872. Iowa Syn. pastor Prairie du Chien, Wis.; Albert Lea, Minn. Joined Mo. Syn. 1875. Pastor Minn.); educ. Conc. Sem., St. Louis, Mo.; pastor St. Louis 1891–1940; pres. W. Dist., Mo. Syn., 1921–39. Ed. *Die Missions-Taube* 1900–08.

Kreuzer, Erwin (1878–1953). B. Berlin, Ger.; bp. Old* Cath. Ch. 1935. Ed. *Altkatholisches Volksblatt.*

Krieger, Adam (1634–66). B. Driesen (in the Neumark, Prussia); pupil of S. Scheidt*; organist Leipzig 1655, Dresden 1658; composer. Works include the cantata *An den Wassern zu Babel;* the melody of the hymn "Nun sich der Tag geendet hat."

Krieger, Johann Philipp (1649–1725). Luth. organist and composer; b. probably Nürnberg, Ger.; pupil of J. Rosenmüller*; forerunner of J. S. Bach*; kapellmeister Halle and Weissenfels. Works include cantatas and operas.

Krimmer Brüder-Gemeinde. See *Mennonite Churches,* 3 a.

Krishna. An alleged incarnation of Vishnu. See also *Hinduism,* 3–6.

Krishnamurti, Jiddu. See *Besant, Annie.*

Krispin, M. See *Reformed Confessions,* E 4.

Krist. Old High Ger. gospel harmony by Otfrid*; 5 books of metrical rhymed lines.

Kritopoulos, Metrophanes. See *Metrophanes Kritopoulos.*

Krol, Sebastian Jansen. See *Reformed Churches,* 4 b.

Kromayer, Hieronymus (1610–70). B. Zeitz, Ger.; educ. Leipzig, Wittenberg, and Jena. Works include *Theologia positivo-polemica* (against RCm, Calvinism, syncretism).

Kromayer, Johannes (1576–1643). Luth. theol.; b. Döbeln, Ger.; pastor Eisleben; court preacher 1613, gen. supt. 1627 Weimar; exponent of orthodoxy; active in liturgical reform.

Kromer, Martin (Cromer; 1512–89). B. Biecz, near Krakow, Poland; RC bp.; leader in Counter* Reformation in Poland. Works include a hist. of Poland.

Kronach. See *Cranach.*

Kronberg, Hartmuth von (Hartmut von Cronberg; 1488–1549). B. Franconia, Ger.; knight; early adherent of M. Luther*; leader of reform movement in Oppenheim; related to and shared defeat of F. v. Sickingen*; lost castle and city Kronberg to Philip* of Hesse 1522; lived in exile 19 yrs.; reconciled to Philip 1541.

Kropatscheck, Friedrich (Kropatschek; 1875–1917). B. Wismar, Ger.; educ. Greifswald, Basel, and Berlin; Luth. prof. Greifswald 1902, Breslau 1904. Ed. *Biblische Zeit- und Streitfragen;* other works include *Das Schriftprinzip der lutherischen Kirche.*

Kropf, Albert (1822–1910). Miss. of Berlin* Miss. Soc. 1 in Union of S. Afr.; exponent of strict Luth. confessionalism.

Kropp Seminary. Est. 1882 at Kropp, near Schleswig, Schleswig-Holstein, Ger., by J. Paulsen*; in ca. 40 yrs. trained ca. 400 pastors for Ger. Luths. in Am.. See also *General Council,* 5; *Michigan Synod,* 4.

Krotel, Gottlob Frederick (Feb. 4, 1826–May 17, 1907). B. Ilsfeld, Württemberg, Ger., to Philadelphia, Pa., 1830; educ. U. of Pa.; pastor Lebanon, Lancaster, and Philadelphia, Pa., and NYC; prof. Luth. Theol. Sem., Philadelphia, 1864–68; pres. Ministerium of N. Y. 1866–68, Ministerium of Pa. 1884–92. Helped found General* Council of the Ev. Luth. Ch. in (N.) Am.; its pres. 1869–70, 1888–93. Ed. in chief *The Lutheran;* ed. *Der lutherische Herold.*

Krüdener, Barbara Juliana von (nee von Vietinghoff; 1764–1824). Russ. Pietist and chiliast; b. Riga, Livonia; restless wife of Russ. diplomat; converted 1804; assoc. with J. H. Jung-Stilling* and other mystics; promoted formation of Holy* Alliance.

Krug, John Andrew (Kruch; Krugh; Mar. 19, 1732–Mar. 30, 1796). B. Saxony; instructor Halle; arrived Philadelphia, Pa., 1764; assisted H. M. Mühlenberg* and J. F. Handschuh.* Pastor Reading, Pa., 1764; Frederick, Md., 1771.

Krüger. See *Crüger.*

Krummacher. 1. *Friedrich Adolf* (1767–1845). Ref. theol.; poet; brother of 2, father of 3 and 4; b. Tecklenburg, Ger.; taught in Hamm, Mörs, and Duisburg; pastor Kettwig, Bernburg, and Bremen. Opposed rationalism.* Works include *Parabeln.*

2. *Gottfried Daniel* (1774–1837). Brother of 1, uncle of 3 and 4; b. Tecklenburg, Ger.; Ref. pastor Baerl, Wülfrath, and Elberfeld; opposed rationalism* and the Prussian* Union.

3. *Friedrich Wilhelm* (1796–1868). Son of 1, brother of 4, nephew of 2; b. Mörs, Ger.; educ. Halle and Jena; Ref. pastor Ruhrort, Middle Barmen (Barmen-Gemarke), Elberfeld, Berlin, and Potsdam; opposed rationalism*; endorsed Prussian* Union and Evangelical* Alliance. Works include *Salomo und Sulamith; Elias der Thisbiter.*

4. *Emil Wilhelm* (1798-1886). Son of 1, brother of 3, nephew of 2; b. Mörs, Ger.; educ. Jena and Tübingen; Ref. pastor Baerl, Langenberg, and Duisburg; endorsed Prussian* Union; vehemently opposed confessionalism; declined fellowship with rationalistic C. K. J. v. Bunsen.*

Kruyt, Albertus Christiaan (Oct. 10, 1869–Jan. 19, 1949). Netherlands* Miss. Soc. miss. to Celebes in the 1890s; tried to develop technique for bringing people into the ch. in soc. units rather than as individuals.

Kshatriya. See *Brahmanism,* 3.

Kübel, Robert Benjamin (1838–94). B. Kirchheim unter Teck, Ger.; educ. Schoenthal, in Württemberg, and Tübingen; prof. Herborn 1870; pastor Ellwangen 1874; prof. Tübingen 1879. Influenced by J. T. Beck* and F. D. E. Schleiermacher*; inclined to Lutheranism. Works include *Das christliche Lehrsystem nach der heiligen Schrift; Ueber den Unterschied zwischen der positiven und der liberalen Richtung in der modernen Theologie; Christliche Ethik; Exegetisch-homiletisches Handbuch zum Evangelium des Matthäus.*

Kuder, Calvin F. (Apr. 10, 1864–Sept. 8, 1935). B.

Laurys, Lehigh Co., Pa.; educ. Roanoke Coll., Salem, Va., and the Luth. Theol. Sem. at Philadelphia, Pa.; ordained by Ministerium of Pa. 1891; commissioned by General* Council of the Ev. Luth. Ch. in N. Am. as miss. to India 1891; given charge of the sem. at Rajahmundry 1892; returned to US 1898; sent to India again 1908; returned to US 1913. Coauthor (with J. G. P. Drach*), *The Telugu Mission of the General Council of the Evangelical Lutheran Church in North America.*

Kuegele, Frederick Gottlob (Apr. 16, 1846–Apr. 1, 1916). B. Columbiana, Columbiana Co., Ohio; educ. Conc. Sem., St. Louis, Mo.; Mo. Syn. pastor Omaha, Nebr., 1870, and Cumberland, Md., 1871; Ohio Syn. pastor of a 2-ch. cong. near Koiner's (or Coyner's) Store and near Waynesboro, Augusta Co., Va., 1879; resigned from Ohio Syn. in Predestinarian Controversy (see *Ohio and Other States, Evangelical Lutheran Joint Synod of,* 5); helped form Ev. Luth. Concordia* Syn. of Pa. and Other States 1882; when it disbanded 1886 he remained indep. till 1888, when he and his cong. joined with the Eng. (Ev.) Luth. Conference of Mo. to form the Gen. Eng. (Ev. Luth.) Conference of Mo. and Other States (see also *Missouri and Other States, The English Evangelical Lutheran Synod of*); he was elected pres. Works include *Country Sermons; Book of Devotion; Your Confirmation Vow.*

Kuenen, Abraham (1828–91). B. Haarlem, Neth.; educ. Leiden; prof. Leiden; exponent of moderate liberalism in religion. Works include *Historisch-kritisch onderzoek.*

Kugler, Anna Sarah (Apr. 18, 1856–July 26, 1930). B. Ardmore, near Philadelphia, Pa.; educ. Philadelphia; med. miss. of Woman's Home and For. Missionary Soc. of The Gen. Syn. of the Ev. Luth. Ch. in the USA to Guntur, India, 1883; founded hosp. at Guntur.

Kühl, Ernst Richard Theodor (1861–1918). B. Visbuhr (or Wisbuhr), near Köslin, Pomerania, Ger.; educ. Berlin; prof. NT exegesis Breslau 1887, Marburg 1893, Königsberg 1895. Works include *Der Brief des Paulus an die Römer; Die Gemeindeordnung in den Pastoralbriefen; Zur paulinischen Theodicee.*

Kuhn, Albert (Feb. 2, 1835–May 1, 1915). B. Saint Gallen canton, Switz.; educ. St. Chrischona*; to Trin. Luth. Ch. (mem. Ev. Luth. Syn. of Minn. and Other States; see *Minnesota Synod*), St. Paul, Minn., as asst., 1865; pastor Woodbury 1865, Mankato 1869, Greenwood (Hennepin Co.) 1882, all in Minn.; pres. Ev. Luth. Syn. of Minn. and Other States 1876–83; asst. to his son Gustave A. Kuhn at Lake Benton 1900, at Jordan 1907, both in Minn. Wrote "Geschichte der Synode von Minnesota und andern Staaten," in *Geschichte der Minnesota-Synode und ihrer einzelnen Gemeinden* (St. Louis, [1910]), pp. 1–50.

Kuhn, Johann(es) Evangelist (von) (1806–87). RC theol. and philos.; b. Wäschenbeuren, Württemberg, Ger.; educ. Tübingen; prof. Giessen and Tübingen; tried to maintain independence of philos., and harmony of faith and knowledge.

Kuhnau, Johann (1660–1722). Luth. organist and composer; b. Geising, Saxony, Ger.; cantor Thomaskirche, Leipzig, 1701. Works include *Markus-Passion;* cantatas. See also *Passion, The.*

Kuinöl, Christian Gottlieb (Kühnöl; Kuinoel[ius]; Kuehnoel; Theophilus; (1768–1841). B. Leipzig, Ger.; educ. Leipzig; prof. Leipzig and Giessen; philol. Works include *Commentarius in libros Novi Testamenti historicos.*

Kuiper, Gerard Peter. See *Evolution,* I.

Kukk, Jakob. See *Estonia,* 3.

Kulturkampf ("cultural struggle" or "struggle for civilization"). Term used Jan. 17, 1873, in the Prussian Landtag (diet) by Rudolf Virchow (1821–1902; Ger. pathologist, anthropologist, pol.; b. Schivelbein, Pomerania) in reference to the conflict bet. church* and state. RC power and influence had waned with the decline of Austria (marked by the fall of Sadowa [Königgrätz] to Prussia 1866) and Fr. (marked by the fall of Sedan to Prussia 1870); Protestantism came into ascendancy in Ger. with the founding of the Ger. empire under William I (Wilhelm Friedrich Ludwig; 1797–1888; king of Prussia 1861–88; Ger. emp. 1871–88) and Otto Eduard Leopold von Bismarck (1815–98; "Iron Chancellor" of Ger. 1871–90); papal infallibility* and authority was challenged. Resultant tension led to May* Laws. In the ensuing polarization, Prots. also came to resist the new policy. Basic realignment and relief of tension was effected by change in policy when Pius IX was succeeded by Leo XIII (see *Popes,* 28–29); most pertinent laws were modified or nullified; Falk resigned 1879; by 1887 the Kulturkampf was over.

Kulvietis, Abraham. See *Lithuania,* 2.

Künneth, Walter. See *Dogmatics,* B 13; *Kirchenkampf.*

Kunz, Johann Georg (Mar. 8, 1824–Aug. 30, 1889). B. Tringenstein, Nassau, Ger.; educ. Idstein; teacher Lochum; to US ca. 1855; joined Mo. Syn. 1857; teacher St. Louis, Mo., 1863–89; organist; composer. Ed. *Immanuels-Sängerbund; Vor- und Zwischenspiele zu den gangbarsten Choralmelodien aus "Kern des deutschen Kirchengesangs, von Dr. Fr. Layriz";* helped ed. and compile H. F. Hölter's *Choralbuch;* other works include *Zwischenspiele zu den gebräuchlichen Chorälen der evangelisch-lutherischen Kirche.*

Kunze, John Christopher (Johan[n]; Kuntze; Aug. 5, 1744–July 24, 1807). B. Artern, near Mansfeld, Saxony, Ger.; educ. Leipzig; to Philadelphia, Pa., 1770; coadjutor to H. M. Mühlenberg*; ordained 1770; est. pre-theol. school Philadelphia 1773, closed 1776 by Revolutionary War; succeeded Mühlenberg as chief pastor 1779; pastor NYC 1784; prof. Oriental languages Columbia Coll., NYC, 1784–87, 1792–99; official tr. of Congress 1785; prof. Hartwick Sem. 1797–1807. Works include *Einige Gedichte und Lieder; Von den Absichten und dem bisherigen Fortgang der privilegirten Deutschen Gesellschaft zu Philadelphia in Pennsylvanien; Ein Wort für den Verstand und das Herz vom Rechten und Gebanten Lebenswege.* See also *United Lutheran Church, Synods of,* 15.

Kurfürsten Bibel. See *Weimarische Bibelwerk, Das.*

Kurios. Variant of Kyrios. See *King, Christ as.*

Kurtz, Benjamin (Feb. 28, 1795–Dec. 29, 1865). Grandson of J. N. Kurtz*; b. Harrisburg, Pa.; studied theol. under J. G. Lochman*; asst. to his uncle, J. D. Kurtz,* Baltimore, Md., 1815. Pastor Hagerstown, Md., 1815–31; Chambersburg, Pa., 1831–33. Pres. The General* Syn. of the Ev. Luth. Ch. in the USA 1829, 1862; championed Definite* Synodical Platform; founded Missionary Institute, Selinsgrove, Pa., 1858; exponent of American* Lutheranism. Ed. *Lutheran Observer, and Weekly Religious Visiter;* other works include *Why Are You a Lutheran?* See also *New Measures; Universities in the United States, Lutheran,* 4.

E. W. Hutter, *Eulogy on the Life and Character of Rev. Benjamin Kurtz, D. D., LL. D.* (Philadelphia, 1866); C. A. Hay, *Memoirs of Rev. Jacob Goering, Rev. George Lochman, D. D., and Rev. Benjamin Kurtz, D. D., LL. D.* (Philadelphia, 1887).

Kurtz, Johann Heinrich (1809–90). Luth. ch. hist. and exegete; b. Montjoie, near Aachen, Rhenish Prussia; educ. Halle and Bonn; prof. Dorpat 1849–70. Works include *Lehrbuch der Kirchengeschichte für Studierende; Handbuch der allgemeinen Kirchengeschichte; Die Astronomie und die Bibel; Biblische Geschichte; Geschichte des Alten Bundes; Lehrbuch* *der heiligen Geschichte; Abriss der Kirchengeschichte.*

Kurtz, John Daniel (Mar. 30, 1764 [1763?]–June 30, 1856). Son of J. N. Kurtz*; uncle of B. Kurtz*; b. Germantown, Pa.; pastor Baltimore, Md., 1786–1832. Chm. organization meeting of The General* Syn. of the Ev. Luth. Ch. in the USA; pres. 1823, 1827.

Kurtz, John Nicolas (Nicholas; Oct. 12, 1720–May 12, 1794). Grandfather of B. Kurtz*; father of J. D. Kurtz*; b. Lutzenlinden, Nassau-Weilburg, Ger.; educ. Giessen and Halle; to Am. 1745; ordained Ministerium of Pa. 1748. Pastor Tulpehocken (near Reading) 1748, York 1773, both in Pa.

Küry, Adolf (1870–1956). B. Basel, Switz.; educ. Bern, Switz., and Bonn, Ger.; pastor Lucerne 1896, Basel 1906, both in Switz.; bp. The Christian* Cath. Ch. of Switz. 1924. Issued *Internationale Kirchliche Zeitschrift.*

Kutter, Hermann (1863–1931). B. Bern, Switz.; ev. theol.; pastor Zurich; advocated Religious Socialism (see *Christian Socialism,* 4); held God, in Christ, to be the only reality; his theocentric theol. was a precursor of dialectical* theol.

Kuwait. See *Middle East,* L 6.

Kuyper, Abraham (1837–1920). Calvinist theol. and statesman; b. Maassluis, Neth.; founded Free (Ref.) U. of Amsterdam 1880, Free Ref. Ch. (Ref. Free Ch.; Calvinistic Ref. Ch. Community) 1886; prime minister 1901–05; opposed modernism and liberalism. Works include *Het Calvinisme oorsprong en waarborg onzer constitutioneele vrijheden; Encyclopaedie der Heilige Godgeleerdheid* (tr. *Encyclopedia of Sacred Theology*); *Het Modernisme; Nabij God te zijn* (tr. J. H. de Vries, *To Be Near Unto God*).

Kuzmány, Karol. See *Slovakia, Lutheran Theology in,* 2.

Kvacala, Jan (Kvacsala; 1862–1934). B. Petrovac, Bosnia, Yugoslavia; ev. theol.; prof. Bratislava (Pressburg) 1888, Dorpat (Tartu) 1893–1918, Bratislava 1921; authority on J. A. Comenius.*

Kwei. See *Confucianism,* 3.

Kyle, Melvin Grove (1858–1933). United Presb. Egyptologist; b. near Cadiz, Ohio; educ. Muskingum Coll., New Concord, Ohio, and Allegheny (Pittsburgh, Pa.) Theol. Sem.; prof. Biblical theol. and archaeol. Xenia Theol. Sem. (later called Pittsburgh-Xenia Theol. Sem.) 1915, pres. 1922–30. Ed. in chief *Bibliotheca Sacra;* other works include *The Deciding Voice of the Monuments in Biblical Criticism; Moses and the Monuments; The Problem of the Pentateuch; Excavating Kirjath-Sepher's Ten Cities.*

Kynewulf. See *Cynewulf.*

Kyrie. See *Worship, Parts of,* 5.

Kyrillos Loukaris. See *Lucaris, Cyril.*

Kyrios. See *King, Christ as.*

L

Labadie, Jean de (la Badie; 1610–74). Mystic; b. Bourg, near Bordeaux, Fr.; Jesuit, priest, preacher; Prot. ca. 1650; preacher in various cities in Eur. Followers called Labadists. See also *Communistic Societies,* 4.

Labadists. Followers of J. de Labadie.*

Labarum. Standard of Constantine* I.

Laberthonnière, Lucien (1860–1932). RC theol. and philos.; b. Chazelet, Indre, Fr.; developed a theory of divine immanence (see *Immanence of God*). Works include *Essais de philosophie religieuse* and *Le Réalisme chrétien et l'idéalisme grec; Études sur Descartes.*

La Bigne, Marguerin de (1546 [1547?]–89). RC preacher; b. Bernieres-la-Patry, Normandy, Fr. Issued *Bibliotheca sanctorum patrum* in opposition to "Magdeburg* Centuries" (see also *Flacius Illyricus, Matthias*).

Labor and Capital. See *Capital and Labor; Industry and the Church; Labor and the Church; Social Ethics; Social Gospel; Socialism.*

Labor and the Church. Antipathy bet. organized labor and chs. was aroused by methods of Knights of Labor (organized as a secret organization 1869 in Philadelphia, Pa.; dropped secrecy early in 1880s; ended formal organization 1917) in 1880s and Industrial Workers of the World (organized 1905 in Chicago, Ill.) 1908–ca. 1917. In course of time, after organization of the American Federation of Labor 1886 and the Congress of Industrial Organizations 1938, demands of labor were oftener in harmony with Christian goals of love and justice. Arbitration of labor disputes by clerics and increasing activity of ch. mems. in unions have helped develop and widen areas of common interest. Application of Gl 6:2; Cl 3:22–4:1; 2 Th 3:10; 1 Ti 5:18 to collective bargaining, cooperatives, working conditions, wages, and overtime work has brought greater interest in the ch. to labor. See also *Capital and Labor; Industry and the Church.* JD

L. Pope, *Millhands & Preachers: A Study of Gastonia* (New Haven, Conn., 1942); *Labor's Relation to Church and Community,* ed. L. Pope (New York, 1947); *Labor Speaks for Itself on Religion,* ed. J. Davis (New York, 1929); J. Myers, *Do You Know Labor?* (Washington, D. C., 1940); W. H. Greever, *Human Relationships and the Church* (New York, 1939); C. Stelzle, *The Church and the Labor Movement* (Philadelphia, Pa., 1910); J. Daniel, *The Church and Labor-Management Problems of Our Day* (Bethlehem, Pa., 1947) and *Labor, Industry, and the Church* (St. Louis, 1957); R. C. Kwant, *Philosophy of Labor* (Pittsburgh, Pa., 1960); G. Siefer, *The Church and Industrial Society: A survey of the Worker-Priest Movement and its implications for the Christian Mission* (London, 1964).

Labrador (perhaps named after a Portuguese mariner). 1. Peninsula divided bet. Newfoundland and Quebec (see *Canada,* A 27; C). *Area:* ca. 530,000 sq. mi.

2. Mainland part of Newfoundland province, Can. *Area:* ca. 112,600 sq. mi. Moravian missions in Labrador began soon after the middle of the 18th c. Nearly all of pop. is Christian. See also *Canada,* C; *Grenfell, Wilfred Thomason.*

La Chaise, François d'Aix de (La Chaize; 1624–1709). B. Château d'Aix, Forez (Loire), Fr.; Jesuit; confessor of Louis* XIV.

Lachelier, Jules (Jules-Esprit-Nicolas; 1832–1918). RC philos.; b. Fontainbleau, Fr.; influenced E. Boutroux* and H. Bergson*; tried to found induction in a philos. of nature based on twin laws of efficient and final causes.

Lachmann, Johann (Lachamann; ca. 1491–1538). B. Heilbronn, Ger.; educ. Heidelberg; reformer of Heilbronn, of which he became vicar 1514, city preacher 1520.

Lachmann, Karl Konrad Friedrich Wilhelm (1793–1851). Philol.; b. Brunswick, Ger.; applied textual* criticism to NT. Produced Gk. NT based on ancient authorities and not on Textus* Receptus.

Lacordaire, Jean Baptiste Henri (1802–61). B. Recey-sur-Ource, Côte d'Or, Fr.; first followed J. J. Rousseau*; lawyer Paris; RC 1824; priest 1827; interpreted RCm acc. to slogans of the Revolution: liberty, equality, and fraternity; opposed free thought. See also *Church and State,* 15; *France,* 5.

Lactantius Firmianus (Firmianus Lactantius; first names Lucius Caelius [or Caecilius]; ca. 240/260–ca. 320/340). Christian apologist; b. probably N Afr. [or It.?] of heathen parents; pupil of Arnobius*; taught rhetoric at Nicomedia (modern Izmit, Turkey); became Christian perhaps ca. 300. Works include *De mortibus persecutorum; Epitome divinarum institutionum; De origine erroris; De justitia; De ira dei.*

Lacunza y Días, Manuel de (1731–1801). B. Santiago, Chile; Jesuit; when Jesuits were banished he moved to It. Wrote *Venida del mesías en gloria y majestad;* it influenced E. Irving* and Adventists.

Ladies' Aid Societies. See *Woman in Christian Society,* I 3.

Ladies' Peace. See *Cambrai, Peace of.*

Ladrone Islands. See *Mariana Islands.*

Lady Chapel. Chapel dedicated to Mary, in or with a larger ch.

Lady Day. Feast of the Annunciation, Mar. 25. See also *Church Year,* 13, 16.

Lady Huntingdon's Connection. See *Calvinistic Methodism.*

Laemmer. See *Lämmer.*

Laestadians. See *Finland, Lutheranism in,* 4; *Finnish Lutherans in America,* 4; *Laestadius, Lars Levi.*

Laestadius, Lars Levi (1800–61). B. Arjeplog, Norrbotten Co., N Swed.; educ. Uppsala; botanist; Luth. pastor Arjeplog 1825, Kaaresuvanto (Karesuando; Karesuanto) 1826, Pajala 1849; led pietistic movement that spread in N Swed., Norw., and esp. Fin. Adherents of the movement, called Laestadians, oppose luxury. See also *Finland, Lutheranism in,* 4; *Finnish Lutherans in America,* 4; *Lapland.* GH

Laestadius, Petrus. See *Lapland.*

Laetare. See *Church Year,* 14, 16.

Laetentur caeli. Papal decree. See *Florence, Council of,* 2.

Laetsch, Theodore Ferdinand Karl Feb. 11, 1877–Dec. 29, 1962). B. Milwaukee, Wis.; educ. Conc. Sem., St. Louis, Mo. Pastor Chippewa Falls, Deer Park, Eau Claire and Pleasant Valley, and Sheboygan, all in Wis.; St. Louis, Mo. Prof. Conc. Sem., St. Louis, 1927–47. Ed. *The Abiding Word.* Other works include *The Minor Prophets; Jeremiah.*

LaFaye, Antoine (d. 1615). Ref. theol.; prof. philos. and later (1581) theol. Geneva; participated in Colloquy of Montbéliard.* Works include a life of T. Beza.*

Lagarde, Paul Anton de (father's surname: Bötticher; 1854 adopted the surname of his grandaunt [de Lagarde] who reared him; 1827–91). Orientalist and philol.; b. Berlin, Ger.; educ. Berlin and Halle; prof. Göttingen; desired a new nat. ch. with a faith welling up out of the collective heart of the people. Works include *Arica; Gedichte; Über das Verhältnis des deutschen Staates zu Theologie, Kirche und Religion.*

Lagrange, Albert Marie-Henri (religious name: Marie Joseph; 1855–1938). B. Bourg, Fr.; Dominican; est. École Pratique d'Études Bibliques in Jerusalem 1890. Works include *Études sur les religions sémitiques; L'Évangile de Jésus-Christ* (tr. [L. Walker and R. Ginns] mems. of the Eng. Dominican Province, *The Gospel of Jesus Christ*); *Introduction a l'étude du Nouveau Testament;* commentaries.

La Iglesia Lutherana Mexicana. See *American Lutheran Church,* IV 2.

Lainez. See *Laynez.*

Laity. Division of ch. mems. into clergy and laity is valid if the words simply distinguish those who have been called into the ministry (see *Ministerial Office,* 5) from those who have not been so called. But with the rise of the sacerdotal system, which culminated in the papacy, the idea that the priesthood formed an intermediate class bet. God and man became prevalent, and the term "clergy" took on added, hierarchic meaning in that context.

The doctrine of justification by faith alone abolished human mediation bet. man and God. M. Luther* effectively proclaimed the priesthood of all believers (cf. 1 Ptr 2:9). As a result, the laity recovered its proper position and lay representation again became possible. See also *Laymen's Activity in the Lutheran Church; Priesthood; Priesthood, Universal.*

Lake, Kirsopp (1872–1946). Biblical and patristic scholar; b. Southampton, Eng.; educ. Oxford; prof. Leiden, Neth., 1904–13, and Harvard U., Cambridge, Mass., 1914–38; did research work on NT MSS; organized archaeol. expeditions. Works include *The Historical Evidence for the Resurrection of Jesus Christ; The Text of the New Testament; The Earlier Epistles of St. Paul;* coed. (with F. J. F. Jackson) *The Beginnings of Christianity;* tr. *The Apostolic Fathers.*

Lamaism (from Tibetan *lama* [or *blama*], "superior one"). Form of Mahayana Buddhism (see *Buddhism,* 1) first introd. into Tibet in the 7th c.; became distinctive Lamaism in the 8th c.; reintrod. in the 10th c.; reformed in the 14th c.; expanded to include temporal power; spread into Mongolia and Manchuria. The Dalai Lama was exiled from Lhasa, capital of Tibet, and fled to India 1959; est. an exile "capital" at Dharmsala, Punjab. The Tashi Lama (or Pan-ch'en Lama) was removed to Peking 1965 by Communist China.

Lamarck, Jean Baptiste Pierre Antoine de Monet, chevalier de (1744–1829). Naturalist; b. Bazantin, Picardy, Fr.; forerunner of C. R. Darwin.* See also *Evolution,* II.

Lambaréné Hospital. See *Africa,* F 5.

Lambert, Franz (François; Francis; Lambert of Avignon; Johannes Serranus; ca. 1486–1530). B. Avignon, Fr.; at first Franciscan (see *Franciscans*); Prot. 1522; met M. Luther* 1523; tr. Reformation pamphlets into Fr. and It.; promoted Reformation in Hesse 1526; prof. Marburg 1527; held Zwinglian view of Lord's Supper (see *Hoen, Cornelisz Hendricxz*).

Lambert von Hersfeld (Lampert von [or of]; probably ca. 1025–probably after 1080). B. probably Thuringia; educ. probably Bamberg; monk Hersfeld 1058; abbot at monastery Hasungen, near Kassel. Works include a life of Lullus*; world hist. up to 1077.

Lambeth Articles. See *Anglican Confessions,* 7.

Lambeth Conference. Assem. of Engl. bps. at Lambeth palace, London, Eng.; cen. consultative body of the Angl. communion. Meetings have been held 1867, 1878, 1888, 1897, 1908, 1920, 1930, 1948, 1958, 1968. See also *England,* C 11.

Lambeth Quadrilateral. See *England,* C 11.

Lambillotte, Louis (1796–1855). B. Lahamaide, near Charleroi, Hainaut, Belg.; RC organist Charleroi and Dinant, Belg., and Amiens, Fr.; Jesuit 1825; promoted revival of Gregorian chant (see *Gregorian Music*). Compositions include oratorios and cantatas.

Lamennais, Hugues Félicité Robert de (La Mennais; 1782–1854). B. Saint-Malo, Fr.; RC priest 1816; philos.; first supported ultramontanism,* later abandoned it; broke with the RC Ch. 1834; mem. Nat. Assem. 1848. Ed. *L'Avenir;* other works include *Essai sur l'indifférence en matière de religion* (tr. Lord Stanley of Alderley, *Essay on Indifference in Matters of Religion*). See also *Mirari vos.*

Lamentabili. See *Popes,* 30.

Lamentations. Lamentations of Jeremiah sung in the RC rite as lessons of the 1st nocturn of matins (Tenebrae*) on Thu., Fri., and Sat. of Holy Week.

La Mettrie, Julien Offroy de (1709–51). Physician and philos.; atheist; b. Saint-Malo, Fr.; forced to flee from Fr. and, later, Leiden, because of his materialism.* Held that the soul is produced by physical growth, that the brain has thought muscles, that psychical phenomena are caused by changes in brain and nervous system, and that sensual pleasures should be pursued. Works include *Histoire naturelle de l'âme; L'homme machine.*

Lämmer, Hugo (1835–1918). B. Allenstein, Ger.; at first ev. theol.; pupil of E. W. Hengstenberg*; RC 1858; priest 1859; prof. ch. hist. Breslau 1864–1905.

Lammers, Gustav Adolph (1802–78). Norw. Luth.; educ. Christiania (Oslo); pastor Skien; revivalist; founded local soc. for inner missions 1853; left state ch. and founded Free Apostolic Christian congs. 1856; rejoined state ch. 1860. Coauthor (with G. Johnson*) *Nogle Ord om Barnedaaben.*

Lampe, Friedrich Adolf (Adolph; 1683–1729). Ref. theol.; b. Detmold, Ger.; educ. Bremen, Ger., and Franeker, Neth.; pastor Weeze (near Cleve) 1703, Duisburg 1706, Bremen 1709; prof. dogmatics and ch. hist. Utrecht 1720; prof. and pastor Bremen 1727; exponent of federal* theol.

Lampert von Hersfeld. See *Lambert von Hersfeld.*

Lamp unto My feet. See *Radio and Television Evangelism, Network,* 5.

Lamprecht, Theodore Henry (Aug. 7, 1858–Apr. 30, 1928). Mo. Syn. Luth. businessman (woolen business), churchman, and philanthropist; b. NYC; educ. Conc. Coll., Fort Wayne, Ind., and Conc. Sem., St. Louis, Mo.; cofounder LLL, its pres. till 1926; pres. ALPB 1920–28; supported Luth. educ. for clergy and laity; promoted Luth. soc. and miss. work; instrumental in founding Luth. Theol. Sem. at Zehlendorf,* near Berlin, Ger.; helped est. endowment fund for Mo. Syn. retired pastors and teachers.

Lancelot, Claude (ca. 1615–95). B. Paris, Fr.; humanistic teacher at Port* Royal; Jansenist (see *Jansenism*).

Landesbischof. See *Bishop,* 8.

Landgraf, Artur Michael (1895–1958). B. Traunstein, Bav., Ger.; RC theol.; did research on early scholasticism.*

Landmark Baptists (Landmarkers). Mems. of the Am. Bap. Assoc. (see *Baptist Churches,* 14). "Landmarkism" is a term used in reference to their emphasis on what they regard as landmarks of the ch. and its practice: the ch. is only visible and local; valid baptism requires a proper administrator; other chs. are not recognized as Christian; true chs. are connected with NT times by "apostolic succession" or "succession of believer's* Baptism."

Landsberg(er), Johann(es) Justus (Landsperger; Lansperger; Gerecht; ca. 1490–1539). B. Landsberg am Lech, Bav., Ger.; Carthusian 1509; noted for sermons and devotional writings.

Landsmann, Daniel (June 18, 1836–May 13, 1896). B. Pinsk, Minsk, Russ., of Jewish parents; educ. as teacher; converted to Christianity in Jerusalem; was persecuted; wife divorced him; children taken from him; miss. to Constantinople; converted Elieser Bassin (Eliezer; Bessin), who became Scot. Free Ch. miss. Constantinople; to US; spent 9 mo. at Conc. Theol. Sem., Springfield, Ill.; miss. to Jews NYC July 1883.

Landstad, Magnus Brostrup (1802–80). B. Maasö, Finmarken, Norw.; educ. Christiania (Oslo); vicar Gausdal; pastor Kviteseid, Seljord, Frederikshald, and Sande; poet; interest in folk songs influenced his hymns. Hymns include "I Know of a Sleep in Jesus' Name"; "When Sinners See Their Lost Condition"; "O Blessed Home Where Man and Wife"; "Lo, Many Shall Come from the East and the West"; other works include *Kirkesalmebog*.

Lanfranc (ca. 1005–89). B. Pavia, It.; to Fr. ca. 1035; Benedictine (see *Benedictines*) at Bec*; involved in controversy with Bérenger* (see *Eucharistic Controversies*); abp. Canterbury* 1070–89. Works include *De corpore et sanguine domini*.

MPL, 150, 9–782.

Lang, August (1867–1945). B. Huppichteroth, near Gommersbach, Ger.; educ. Bonn and Berlin; Ref. cathedral preacher in Halle 1893; active in ecumenical movement. Works include *Johannes Calvin; Zwingli und Calvin*.

Lang, Heinrich (1826–76). B. Frommern, near Balingen, Württemberg, Ger.; educ. Tübingen; pastor Switz. at Wartau 1848, Meilen 1863, Zurich 1871; radical theol.; rejected hist. faith for "modern" philos. world view.

Lang, Johann (ca. 1487–1548). Reformer of Erfurt, Ger.; b. Erfurt; Augustinian* monk 1506; priest 1508; friend of M. Luther*; supported Luther at the 1519 Leipzig* Debate; introd. new order of service in Erfurt 1525.

Lang, Johann Michael. See *Lange, Johann Michael*.

Lang, Matthäus, (von Wellenburg) (ca. 1468–1540). B. Augsburg, Ger.; educ. Tübingen, Ingolstadt, and Vienna; imperial secy.; bp. Gurk 1505; cardinal 1511/12; abp. Salzburg 1519; first favorably inclined toward evangelicals; relapsed after receiving from Rome unqualified patronage of certain bishoprics in his diocese; demanded that J. von Staupitz* reject Luth. heresy 1521; drove P. Speratus* out of Salzburg; at the 1530 Augsburg Diet (see *Lutheran Confessions*, A) he declared himself a bitter foe of M. Luther.*

Langbein, Bernhard Adolph (Adolf; 1815–73). B. Wurzen, Saxony, Ger.; educ. Leipzig; deacon Meissen; pastor Chemnitz; court preacher Dresden; consistory mem.; exponent of confessional Lutheranism.

Lange, August (Jan. 5, 1864–Nov. 29, 1938). B. St. Louis, Mo.; educ. Conc. Coll., Fort Wayne, Ind., and Conc. Sem., St. Louis, Mo. Pastor Fremont, Nebr.; Chicago, Ill.; St. Louis, Mo.; Fort Wayne, Ind. Coed. *Die Rundschau;* ed. *Die Abendschule* and *Lutherisches Kinder- und Jugendblatt*.

Lange, Carl Heinrich Rudolf (Rudolph; Jan. 8, 1825–Oct. 2, 1892). B. Polish Wartenberg, Prussia; studied theol. privately; to US 1846; educ. at the practical sem. est. by J. K. W. Löhe* at Fort Wayne, Ind., and at the Mo. Syn. theoretical sem., Altenburg, Perry Co., Mo.; pastor St. Charles, Mo., 1848; prof. Conc. Coll. and Sem., St. Louis, Mo., 1858, and in Fort Wayne, Ind., 1861. Pastor Defiance, Ohio, Sep.–Dec. 1872; Chicago, Ill., Dec. 1872–78. Prof. theol. and philos. Conc. Sem., St. Louis, 1878–92; lectured in English. Coed. *Lehre und Wehre* 1861–64; ed. *The St. Louis Theological Monthly* 1881–82 (18 issues; pub. in connection with the predestinarian* controversy); other works include *Kleines Lehrbuch der Englischen Sprache*.

Lange, Friedrich Albert (1828–75). B. Wald, near Solingen, Ger.; son of J. P. Lange*; educ. Duisburg, Zurich, and Bonn; taught at various places; prof. Zurich; neo-Kantian philos., economist, sociol.; opposed materialistic metaphysics; held that materialism is valid only as a method; championed pol. freedom and the well-being of the working class. Works include *Geschichte des Materialismus und Kritik seiner Bedeutung in der Gegenwart* (tr. E. C. Thomas, *The History of Materialism and Criticism of Its Present Importance*); *Die Arbeiterfrage*.

Lange, Friedrich Theodor (Theodore; Oct. 26, 1866–May 27, 1934). B. St. Louis, Mo.; mgr. Louis Lange Pub. Co. (pub. *Die Abendschule*).

Lange, Joachim (1670–1744). B. Gardelegen, Altmark, Ger.; prof. Halle 1709; prominent Pietist; controversialist; opposed orthodox Luths. (esp. V. E. Löscher*), rationalists (C. Thomasius,* C. v. Wolff*), and the Wertheim* Bible; recommended B. Ziegenbalg* and H. Plütschau* as missionaires to India. See also *Millennium*, 5.

Lange, Johann. See *Estonia*, 2.

Lange, Johann Michael (Lang[ius]; 1664–1731). Luth. pietistic theol.; b. Etzelwang(en), near Sulzbach, in The Palatinate; educ. Altdorf (Altorf) and Jena; served several parishes as pastor; prof. Altdorf; chiliast. Wrote in various fields of theol.; works include *Kern des wahren Christentums; Tractatus de nuptiis et divortiis*.

Lange, Johann Peter (1802–84). Ref. theol.; father of F. A. Lange*; b. Sonnborn, near Elberfeld, Prussia, Ger.; educ. Düsseldorf and Bonn; asst. pastor Elberfeld, near Langenberg, 1825; pastor Wald, near Solingen, 1826, Langenberg 1828, Duisburg 1832; prof. theol. Zurich 1841, dogmatic theol. Bonn 1854; consistorial councillor 1860. Ed. *Theologisch-homiletisches Bibelwerk;* other works include *Das Leben Jesu nach den Evangelien* (refutation of D. F. Strauss*; ed. M. Dods, various translators, *The Life of the Lord Jesus Christ*).

Lange, Louis (see *Publishing Houses, Lutheran*.

Langhans, Urban(us) (ca. 1510–ca. 1570). B. Schneeberg, Saxony; cantor; deacon Glauchau and Schneeberg. The Christmas hymn "Lasst uns alle fröhlich sein" ("Let Us All with Gladsome Voice") has been ascribed to him, but his authorship of it is dubious.

Langmann, Adelheid (ca. 1312–75). B. Nürnberg, Ger.; Dominican; mystic.

Langton, Stephen (d. 1228). Abp. Canterbury; division of Vulgate into chaps. ascribed to him. See also *England*, A 3.

Language Question in the Lutheran Church (US). The Luth. Ch. was transplanted to Am. mainly by Germans and Scandinavians. Since Am. became an Eng.-speaking country, it was natural that Luths. adopted the Eng. language. The N. Y. Ministerium made Eng. its official language 1807. Failure to use Eng. had adverse effects in some cases.

Many feared that a change of language from Ger. would lead to loss of pure doctrine. In many places, strong opposition against language transition resulted in ch. membership losses. In some cases the problem was temporarily solved by organizing Eng. syns. Over the yrs. the change to Eng. was effected. Nearly all Luths. in the US now worship and transact syn. affairs in Eng. ARS

W. A. Baepler, *A Century of Grace* (St. Louis,

1947); *Documentary History of the Evangelical Lutheran Ministerium of Pennsylvania and Adjacent States* (Philadelphia, 1898); V. Ferm, *The Crisis in American Lutheran Theology* (New York, 1927); J. L. Neve, *History of the Lutheran Church in America,* 3d ed., prepared by W. D. Allbeck (Burlington, Iowa, 1934); J. Nicum, *Geschichte des Evangelisch-Lutherischen Ministeriums vom Staate New York und angrenzenden Staaten und Ländern* (Reading, Pa., 1888); W. G. Polack, *The Building of a Great Church,* 2d ed. (St. Louis, 1941); A. R. Wentz, *A Basic History of Lutheranism in America,* rev. ed. (Philadelphia, 1964).

Láni, Elias (1570–1618). Luth. supt. in Slovakia.

Lankenau, Franz Friedrich Wilhelm Jakob (Francis James; Apr. 26, 1868–July 15, 1939). B. Fort Wayne, Ind.; educ. Conc. Sem., Springfield, Ill.; pastor New Orleans, La., 1891; pres. Luther Coll., New Orleans, 1903–08; pastor Napoleon, Ohio, 1908–39. Works include *In Season — Out of Season; Occasional Addresses; Communion Counsel and Prayers;* ed. *The Lutheran Pioneer.*

Lankenau, John Diederich (Diedrich; Mar. 18, 1817–Aug. 30, 1901). Luth. businessman; philanthropist; b. Bremen, Ger.; to Philadelphia, Pa., 1836; helped expand Ger. Hosp. (later called Lankenau Hosp.), Philadelphia. Est. Mary J. Drexel Home (named in honor of his wife, nee Drexel, who died 1873) in Philadelphia and Philadelphia Deaconess Motherhouse 1888; also School for Girls (renamed Lankenau School for Girls 1910).

Lao-tzu (Lao Tzu; Lao-tse; Lao-tsze; sometimes identified with a Li Erh and Li An; perhaps ca. 604–ca. 531 BC). Details of his life and activity uncertain; b. perhaps Ch'u State, Honan Province, China; stressed mystic adherence to right conduct or the spirit of righteousness in opposition to Confucius' emphasis on proper form and ceremony. Traditionally, founder of Taoism* and author of Tao Tê Ching ("teaching of Tao"). See also *Chinese Philosophy,* 2.

Laodicea, Synod of. Syn. allegedly held perhaps ca. 360 in Laodicea in Phrygia (Laodicea ad Lycum); 60 canons ascribed to it (genuineness of at least the 60th is dubious). See also *Tempus clausum.*

Laos. See *Asia,* C 6.

La Peyère, Isaac de (Pereira; ca. 1594/1600–76). B. Bordeaux, Fr., of Port. New Christian, or converted Jewish, background; Calvinist; humanist; held that there were people on earth before Adam; became RC to escape persecution. Works include *Praeadamitae; Relation du Groenland; Relation de l'Islande.*

Laplace, Pierre Simon de. See *Evolution,* I.

Lapland. Region of N Norw., N Swed., N Fin., and the Kola Peninsula of NW Russ.; most of it is N of the Arctic Circle. Lapps (word of obscure origin; probably from Swed.), Finno-Ugrians who call themselves Samelats, were carried N to this their present homeland before the birth of Christ by migrations of Slavs, Goths, and other Finno-Ugrians, to whom they are linguistically related. Swedes and Russians influenced Lapps culturally and religiously by propagating the Luth. and Gk. Orthodox faith resp. Attempts to Christianize Lapps in the late Middle Ages yielded no large results. Effective miss. work began in the 17th and 18th cents. by Erik Bredal (d. 1617; bp. Trondheim, Norw.) after Swedes drove him out of Trondheim 1658 and by T. v. Westen.* After decline, miss. work again prospered mid-19th c. under leadership of N. J. C. V. Stockfleth.*

Lapps in Swed. were introd. to Christianity in the late Middle Ages. Several Vasa kings showed interest in them, esp. Charles* IX, who laid the foundation of an ecclesiastical organization in Lapland. A 1723 royal ordinance required all clergy in Lapland to know the native tongue and provided educ. facilities and printed matter in Lapp at pub. expense. An early Swed. miss. to Swed. Lapps was Pehr Högström (1714–84). Pehr Fjellström (1697–1764) issued a cat. 1738, ch. manual and hymnal 1744, and a Lapp NT 1755. A Lapp Bible appeared 1811. The work of L. L. Laestadius* and his brother Petrus Laestadius (d. 1841) is noteworthy. Important adjustments in ch. organization were made 1846 and 1896.

Lapps in the Kemi area of Fin. were under Swed. rule till 1809. Gk. Orthodox miss. work among Lapps in Russ. began in the 16th c. and won most Lapps there. HOK

See also *Gustavus I.*

E. Haller, *Svenska Kyrkans mission i Lappmarken under Frihetstiden* (Stockholm, 1896); *East Carelia and Kola Lapmark,* ed. V. T. Homén (New York, 1921).

Lapp, Paul Wilbert (Aug. 5, 1930–Apr. 26, 1970). B. Sacramento, Calif. Educ. Conc. Coll., Oakland, Calif.; Conc. Sem. and Washington U., St. Louis, Mo.; U. of Calif., Berkeley. Taught at Am. U., Washington, D. C.; Am. School of Oriental Research, Jerusalem; Pittsburgh (Pa.) Theol. Sem. Excavated many sites, including 'Araq el 'Emir, Tell el Ful, Wâdi Dâliyeh, Bâb edh-Dhrâ' (by the Dead Sea), Ta 'anach; planned excavations at Idalion. Works include *Palestinian Ceramic Chronology 200 B. C.–A. D. 70; The Dhar Mirzbâneh Tombs; Biblical Archaeology and History.*

Lapsed. See *Lapsi.*

Lapsi (Lat. "lapsed"). Term applied in early ch. to former mems. of Christian congs. who became weak in persecutions (see *Persecutions of Christians*) and (1) put incense on fire before image of emp. (*thurificati;* from Lat. *thurificare,* "burn incense"), (2) took part in heathen sacrifices (*sacrificati;* from Lat. *sacrificare,* "sacrifice"), (3) bought letters certifying that the bearer had returned to paganism (*libellatici,* from Lat. *libellum,* "letter; certificate"), (4) made some false depositions to save their lives (*acta facientes;* Lat., literally "those doing the acts"), or (5) gave up sacred books and/or vessels and/or revealed names of fellow Christians (*traditores;* from Lat. *tradere,* "hand over; deliver; betray," whence Eng. "traitor"). Some favored readmitting the lapsed to the ch. after they had done rigorous penitential acts; others, e. g. Tertullian* (e. g., *De pudicitia,* xx), opposed their readmission.

Lardner, Nathaniel (1684–1768). B. Hawkhurst, Kent, Eng.; educ. Utrecht and Leiden; asst. Presb. pastor London 1729–51; used historical criticism. Works include *The Credibility of the Gospel History.*

Lars Anderson (Andersson). See *Anderson, Lars.*

Larsen, Lauritz (Nov. 28, 1882–Jan. 28 [29?], 1923). Son of P. L. Larsen*; b. Decorah, Iowa; educ. Luther Coll., Decorah, Iowa, and Luther Theol. Sem., St. Paul, Minn.; ordained The United* Norw. Luth. Ch. in Am. 1907; pastor N. Dak., Iowa, N. Y.; pres. NLC 1920–23. Ed. *Our Friend; Children's Friend.*

Larsen, Morten (1851–1936). B. Vesterö, on is. Laesö, Den.; ev. theol.; pastor Dan.-Norw. ch. Paris 1881; teacher 1885, pastor 1887 Jutland; exponent of Grundtvigianism (see *Grundtvig, Nikolai Frederik Severin*).

Larsen, Peter Laurentius (Lauritz; Aug. 10, 1833–Mar. 1, 1915). Father of L. Larsen*; b. Kristiansand (Christiansand), Norw.; educ. Christiania (Oslo); ordained Christiania 1857; to US 1857 in response to call issued by Norw. Ev. Luth. Ch. of Am.; pastor near Rush River, Pierce Co., Wis., 1857–59; Norw. prof. Conc. Coll. and Sem., St. Louis, Mo., 1859–61; pres. Luther Coll., Halfway Creek, La Crosse, Wis., 1861–62, Decorah, Iowa, 1862–1902; prof. Heb. there till 1911; acting pres. Synodical* Conf. 1880–82. Helped ed. *Kirkelig Ma-*

anedstidende; ed. its successor, *Evangelisk Luthersk Kirketidende.*

K. Larsen, *Laur. Larsen* (Northfield, Minn., 1936).

Larvae dei (Lat. "masks of God"). Term used by M. Luther* (e. g., WA 40, 1, 174–177; cf. 31 I, 436; 45, 522) and others who held that God, because He cannot be viewed by man in His naked transcendence, wears a mask or veil (e. g., human form, word, sacraments) in all His dealings with men, to shield them from His unapproachable brightness.

La Salette. Village in Fr. Alps, near Grenoble, where a poor, uneducated, peasant boy and girl allegedly saw a vision of Mary Sept. 19, 1846. "Virgin of the Alps" shrine begun 1852.

La Salle, Jean Baptiste de. See *Jean Baptiste de la Salle.*

La Salle, René Robert Cavelier de (1643–87). B. Rouen, Fr.; explorer; settler, trader near Montreal, Can., 1666; made expedition to Lake Ontario region 1669; claimed to have discovered Ohio R.; went down Mississippi R. to Gulf of Mex., claiming the whole valley for Louis* XIV. RCs settled in regions he explored.

Las Casas, Bartolomé de (1474–1566). B. Seville, Sp.; priest 1510; miss. to natives of W Indies, Cen. Am., and Mex.; appointed their protector by F. Jiménez* de Cisneros; hostility of conquistadores put many obstructions in his way; bp. Chiapa(s), Mex., 1544–47; returned to Sp. Works include *Historia de las Indias.*

Lasco, Johannes a. See *Laski, Jan.*

Lasitius, Johann(es) (John Lasicius; Jan Lasicki; Lasiczky; 1534–1600). B. Grosspolen (NW Poland) or Lithuania; nobleman; joined Ref. Ch. 1557; friend of T. Beza,* Bohemian* Brethren, J. Calvin,* Philippists.* Works include *De origine et rebus gestis Fratrum Bohemicorum; De Russorum, Moscovitarum et Tartarorum religione, sacrificiis, nuptiarum, funerum ritu.*

Lasius, Christophorus (ca. 1500–72). Luth. theol.; b. Strasbourg; pastor; active in Görlitz, Greussen, Spandau, Lauingen, and Cottbus; opposed M. Flacius* Illyricus. Works include *Das güldene Kleinot vom verlornen Schaf; Grundfeste der reinen evangelischen Warheit.* See also *Religious Drama,* 3.

Laski, Jan. (Johannes a Lasco; John Laski, or Lasco; 1499–1560). B. probably Lask, near Lodz, Poland; nobleman; assoc. with D. Erasmus* and other reformers in the 1520s; became strict Calvinist theol.; supt. of ch. of for. Prots., London, Eng., 1550; influential at court of Edward VI (see *England,* B 4); returned to Poland 1556 to spread Reformation; tried to reconcile Ref. and Luths. Worked on Bible translations. See also *Poland; Trepka, Eustachy; Utenhove, Jan.*

Lassenius, Johann(es) (1636–92). B. Waldow, Pomerania; educ. Rostock; preacher 1676, prof. theol. 1678 Copenhagen; exponent of *Pektoraltheologie.** Works include treatises against Jesuits; devotional books, hymns.

Lasso, Orlando di (Orlandus; Roland de Lassus; originally Roland Delattre, or de Lattre; ca. 1532–94). RC composer; regarded by some as the greatest representative of the Flemish school; teacher of J. Eccard* (1553–1611) and L. Lechner*; active at court of dukes of Bav. beginning 1556; polyphonist. Works include motets, masses, madrigals, settings for Psalms.

Last Things. Eschatology is that part of dogmatics, or doctrinal theol., which treats of the last things in life and hist.: immortality, resurrection, life after death, last coming of Christ, final judgment, and end of the world.

1. *Signs of the Last Times.* Besides many promises to return (e. g., Mt 25:31; Mk 13:26; Lk 21:27), the Lord has placed a description of many signs into His Word by which believers are to recognize and be reminded that He shall come again.

a. Signs of the last times in the physical world are those which are in the universe itself, e. g., signs in the sun, moon, stars, planets, and constellations (Jl 2:31; Mt 24:29-30; Lk 21:25-32). All decline and alteration in the nature and operation of the universe indicates that heaven and earth shall pass away (Heb 8:13).

b. The 1st sign in human hist. is the gross and fine materialism which rules the inhabitants of the world (Lk 17:26-30; 1 Th 5:1-3; 2 Ti 3:1-5; Jude 17-19).

c. Another sign is the worldwide preaching of the Gospel of the kingdom of God for a witness unto all nations (Mt 24:14).

d. A 3d sign is the frequent appearance of unfaithful mems. within the ch., traitors to the truth of God, antichrists almost without number (Mt 24:11, 24-27; 2 Th 2:3-11; 1 Ti 4:1-3; 2 Ti 4:3-4; 2 Ptr 2:1-3; 3:3-4).

e. A 4th sign lies in perilous times (2 Ti 3:1).

f. A 5th sign is the continuing existence of the Jews (Lk 21:32).

g. A 6th sign lies in wars and rumors of wars (Mt 24:6-8; Rv 6:4).

h. A 7th sign is this, that men living in the last times will not read the signs or refuse to heed them (2 Ptr 3:3-4).

2. *Return of Christ.* It is a clear Bible doctrine that Christ's return will coincide with the end of the world. The Bible does not allow separation in time of these events (2 Ptr 3:7; 2 Ti 4:1). Christ's last coming will be visible (Mt 24:27, 30; Lk 17:24; Acts 1:11), in full divine glory and majesty, and with all the holy angels (Mt 25:31; Lk 9:26); it will be sudden and, despite all signs pointing to it, almost completely unexpected (Lk 17:24; 21:35; 1 Th 5:2-4). At His return (a) all dead will return to life (Jn 5:28-29); (b) the bodies of all believers will suddenly be glorified (1 Co 15:51-54); (c) He will judge the whole human race (Mt 25:31-32; Rv 20:12) and (d) carry out the verdict. These events will occur at a time set in eternity but unknown to men (Mt 24:36, 42; Mk 13:32; Lk 12:40; Acts 1:7). Christ's return is emphasized over against scoffers (2 Ptr 3:3-4) and the forgetfulness of believers (Mt 24:42-44; Mk 13:32-37).

3. *The end of the world* will coincide with Christ's last coming (see also par. 2). The world which God created (Gn 1:1) shall "pass away" (Ps 102:26; Lk 21:33; 1 Co 7:31; Heb. 1:10-12; 1 Jn 2:17). The earth and the works therein "shall be burned up" (2 Ptr 3:10). Luth. dogmaticians divide as to how this is to occur. Some hold with J. Gerhard* (*Loci theologici,* Locus XXX ["De consummatione seculi"], chap. V ["De forma consummationis seculi"; pars. xxxvii–lxiii]) a total destruction (annihilation) of the world; others hold with M. Luther* (WA 41, 309) that only the form of this world as it appears now will pass (cf. Ro 8:21; 2 Ptr 3:13).

4. *The Resurrection.* The bodily resurrection of all mankind (an essential point in the faith of Christendom) will occur immediately upon Christ's return at the end of the world (Mt 25:31-32). The resurrection is not a long process, nor does it include interruptions (cf. Jn 5:26; 6:40; 1 Co 15:51-52; 1 Th 4:16). The resurrection will be universal (2 Co 5:10; Rv 20:12), but there will be 2 distinct classes: They who have done evil will rise to damnation (Dn 12:2; Mt 25:41-46; Jn 5:29); they who died in saving faith will rise with a spiritual body (1 Co 15:44) fashioned like unto Christ's glorious body (Lk 24:39; 1 Co 15:51-52; Ph 3:21; 1 Jn 3:2). The body of believers, sown in corruption, will be raised in incorruption; sown in dishonor, it will be raised in glory;

sown in weakness, it will be raised in power; sown a natural body, it will be raised a spiritual body (1 Co 15:42-45).

5. *Last or Final Judgment.* There will be a final judgment (Mt 25:31-46; 2 Co 5:10). It does not decide the question of eternal life or eternal death; that is previously determined (conversion or nonconversion; Jn 3:18; 6:47). There will be no need of questions of evidence or law, but Christ the Judge, who knows all things, will proceed at once to pronounce sentence by judicial and final separation. Since faith and unbelief are invisible to created eyes, the outward fruits of both will bear witness. The works of love, by which the faith of the elect was active, are cited, not by the righteous, but by the Judge, to prove righteousness. The counterpart is true of the failures of unbelievers, cited by the Judge to prove unrighteousness. The Judge will award to believers the kingdom prepared for them by Himself, not as a remuneration, but as an inheritance (Gl 3:26-29). The wicked works of the wicked will testify that the wicked are of their father, the devil (Jn 8:41, 44), and that it is just for them to share his abode. The condemned will go away into everlasting punishment, the righteous into eternal life (Mt 25:24-46). WFW

See also *Dispensationalism; Millennium; Parousia; Particular Judgment.*

P. Althaus, *Die Letzten Dinge* (Gütersloh, 1933); L. Fuerbringer, "Leading Thoughts on Eschatology in the Epistles to the Thessalonians," *CTM,* XIII (1942), 183–192; 265–273; 321–329; 401–414: 511–518; 591–603: 641–654; W. F. Beck, "I Believe in the Resurrection of the Body," *CTM,* XVI (1945), 153–169; W. F. Wolbrecht, "The Doctrine of the Last Things," *The Abiding Word,* I, ed. T. Laetsch (St. Louis, 1946), 544–560; G. F. Hall, "Luther's Eschatology," *The Augustana Quarterly,* XXIII (1944), 13–21; T. F. D. Kliefoth, *Christliche Eschatologie* (Leipzig, 1886); J. A. Seiss, *The Last Times and the Great Consummation,* rev. and enl. ed. (Philadelphia, 1863); P. S. Minear, *Christian Hope and the Second Coming* (Philadelphia, 1954); T. A. Kantonen, *The Christian Hope* (Philadelphia, 1954) and *Life after Death* (Philadelphia, 1962); J. Moltmann, *Theology of Hope,* tr. J. W. Leitch (New York, 1967); U. Hedinger, *Hoffnung zwischen Kreuz und Reich* (Zurich, 1968); C. E. Braaten, *The Future of God* (New York, 1969).

Lateran. Bldg., or group of bldgs., on Monte Celio in Rome, named after the family of the Laterani, former owners of an ancient palace which stood on the site. Main bldgs.: 1. Basilica of St. John Lateran; originally called Ch. of the Savior; episc. seat of pope as bp. Rome; meeting place of many councils. 2. Baptistery; founding traced to Constantine* I. 3. Lateran Palace; occupied by popes in Middle Ages; the Scala Sancta (Lat. "holy steps"; Scala Pilati; 28 steps allegedly ascended by Christ to the praetorium of Pilate and climbed on his knees by M. Luther*) once led to one of its corridors, now leads to the old private papal chapel; largely destroyed by earthquake 896 and fires 1308 and 1360; museum est. on site 1843. See also *Lateran Councils; Pseudo-Isidorian Decretals,* 2.

Lateran Councils. Many RC councils were held at the Lateran* beginning 313. Those of 1123, 1139, 1179, 1215, and 1512–17 are traditionally called Lateran Councils.

412 abps. and bps. and 800 or more abbots and priors attended Lateran Council IV 1215; concerns included recovery of the Holy Land (see *Crusades,* 7), ch. reform, and condemnation of doctrines of Albigenses,* Cathari,* and Waldenses*; noteworthy also for definitive doctrine of transubstantiation* and for legislation on annual confession and Communion.

Average attendance at Lateran Council V 1512–17 was ca. 100–150; approved Leo X's (see *Popes,* 20) 1516 bull *Pastor aeternus,* which abolished the Pragmatic* Sanction of Bourges and declared the pope superior to councils; approved strict censorship of publications; confirmed *Unam* sanctam.* See also *Councils and Synods,* 4; *Inquisition,* 3.

Lateran Treaty. See *Concordat,* 7.

Latermann, Johann (1620–62). B. Zellershausen, near Coburg, Ger.; asst. prof. Königsberg 1647; gen. supt. Derenburg, near Halberstadt, 1654; suspended for immorality; Austrian chaplain. Disciple of G. Calixtus*; proposed a type of synergism* (Latermannianism) in which man converts himself by spiritual powers given by God.

Latimer, Hugh (ca. 1485–1555). B. Thurcaston, Leicestershire, Eng.; educ. Cambridge; priest ca. 1515; embraced Protestantism; bp. Worcester 1535; resigned 1539 because he opposed the Six Articles (see *Anglican Confessions,* 3); imprisoned in Tower of London 1546; released 1547 by Edward VI; burned at stake. See also *England,* B 3–5; *Parker, Matthew; Ridley, Nicholas.*

Latin America Mission. Organized 1921 by Harry and Susan Strachan et al. as The Latin America Evangelization Campaign with headquarters at San Jose, Costa Rica; present name adopted 1938; carried on evangelistic work in tents, theaters, pub. halls; experimented with attention-catching methods; first allowed existing missions to absorb converts. Mem. IFMA. 1966 fields included Colombia, Costa Rica, Dominican Rep., El Salvador, NYC, Panama. Cooperated with World* Radio Miss. Fellowship; active in other radio ventures. US headquarters Bogota, N. J. Publications include *El Mensajero Bíblico* 1924–61; *Latin America Evangelist.*

Latin American Lutheran Mission. See *Mexico,* D 3.

Latin Bible Versions. See *Bible Versions,* J.

Latin Christianity. Beliefs and practices developed in W Christianity (which used Lat. as its official language) in distinction from Gk., or E Christianity (see *Eastern Orthodox Churches*). See also *Western Christianity 500–1500.*

Latitudinarians. 17th c. Eng. churchmen who professed indifference to supposedly insignificant matters in dispute bet. Puritans* and the High* Ch.; stressed Christian fundamentals rather than any professed ecclesiastical system and were tolerant toward dissenters. Also called Cambridge Arminians. See also *Cambridge Platonists.*

Latomus, Bartholomaeus Heinrici (Steinmetz [father was stonemason]; ca. 1490–1570). RC humanist and controversialist; b. Arlon, Luxembourg, Belg.; educ. Freiburg im Breisgau, Ger.; taught at Cologne, Louvain, Paris; friend of D. Erasmus*; councillor of elector of Trier 1542; present at Hagenau* Colloquy 1540, Regensburg* Conf. 1546, Consultation of Worms* 1557; involved in controversy with M. Bucer,* P. Dathenus,* Jakob Andreä.*

Latomus, Jacobus (Jacques Masson; ca. 1475–1544). RC theol. and controversialist; b. Cambron, Hainaut, Belg.; educ. Paris and Louvain; prof. Louvain; opposed D. Erasmus,* M. Luther,* P. Melanchthon,* J. Oecolampadius,* W. Tyndale.*

Latourette, Kenneth Scott (1884–1968). Bap. cleric and Oriental scholar; b. Oregon City, Oreg.; educ. Yale U., New Haven, Conn.; traveling secy. Student Volunteer Movement For. Missions 1909–10; mem. faculty Coll. of Yale in China 1910; taught at Reed Coll., Portland, Oreg., 1915; prof. Denison U., Granville, Ohio, 1916; prof. Yale U. 1921–53; lecturer many univs.; pres. Am. Bap. Conv. 1951. Works include *The Development of Japan; The Development of China; China; The Chinese: Their His-*

tory and Culture; Beyond the Ranges: An Autobiography; Christianity in a Revolutionary Age; Christianity Through the Ages; A History of the Expansion of Christianity.

Latria. RC theologians distinguish 3 kinds of cultus: *latria, dulia,* and *hyperdulia. Latria* ("worship; adoration") is accorded only God; *dulia* ("honor; reverence; veneration; homage") is accorded saints and angels in gen.; *hyperdulia* ("higher *dulia*") is accorded Mary, gen. regarded in RCm as the noblest and holiest creature. Cultus involving a symbol is referred to the prototype, the cultus being regarded as applying only in a realtive way to the symbol. See also *Nicaea, Councils of,* 2; *Saints, Veneration of.*

Latrocinium. See *Ephesus, "Robber Synod" of.*

Latter Day Saints (Latter-Day; Latter-day; Latter day). a. The Ch. of Jesus Christ of Latter-day Saints (see also par. g 1) was founded 1830 with 6 mems. at Fayette, Seneca Co., N. Y., by Joseph Smith* Sr. He claimed that Moroni, son of Mormon (alleged 4th c. AD prophet in Am.; collected and revised the material later pub. in *The Book of Mormon*), repeatedly appeared to him and said that God had work for him (Smith) to do in the latter days to help restore the full Gospel in preparation for the premillennial coming of Christ. He claimed that in 1827, at the direction of Moroni, he found thin metal plates, ca. 6 inches by 7 inches, gold in appearance, which had been buried ca. 420 AD near the top of the W side of a hill (anciently called Cumorah) near Manchester, Ont. Co., N. Y.; the plates, he said, contained a record in "Reformed Egyptian" and 2 stones in silver bows, fastened to a breastplate (Urim and Thummim), by which he tr. part of the record; he pub. his tr. 1830 as *The Book of Mormon;* the plates, he said, were returned to Moroni when he called for them. *The Book of Mormon* includes a purported hist. of ancient Am., parts of the Bible (e. g., parts of Is; the Sermon on the Mount acc. to Mt; Pauline passages), and apparent reflections of some Ref. confessions of faith.

b. Smith and Oliver Cowdery claimed ordination to Aaronic priesthood by John the Baptist May 1829 and to Melchizedek priesthood by Peter, James, and John shortly thereafter. In 1831 the ch. numbered several hundred. It moved to Kirtland, Ohio, the same yr. and also began to settle in Jackson Co., Mo., where it hoped to build the city of Zion with a magnificent temple. It was driven from Jackson Co. 1833. Lillburn W. Boggs (1792–1860; b. Lexington, Ky.; gov. Mo. 1836–40) expelled the Mormons from Mo. by military force 1838–39. They moved to Ill. and immediately settled in Hancock Co. at Commerce, renaming the settlement Nauvoo ("Beautiful Place," acc. to Mormons from Heb. *naveh,* "pleasant"); Smith had civil and military control of it. Discontent arose when Smith claimed a revelation authorizing polygamy. Civil war became imminent. State militia intervened 1844. Joseph Smith and his brother Hyrum were imprisoned in Carthage, where a mob stormed the jail, killed both, and wounded other Mormons including John Taylor.*

c. B. Young* assumed leadership. When persecution again became fierce 1846, the Mormons moved from Ill. first to Iowa, then W of the Mo. R. near Omaha, and 1847 to Great Salt Lake, Utah, where they founded Salt Lake City and est. the "provisional govt. of the State of Deseret [which, Mormons say, means 'honeybee']" with Young as gov.; other settlements were scattered over the face of the entire region.

d. The Territory of Utah was created 1850. Young was appointed gov., reappointed 1854 when Colonel E. J. Steptoe declined to accept the appointment; succeeded 1857 under US military pressure by Alfred Cumming (1802–73; b. Augusta, Ga.; gov. Territory of Utah 1857–60). Peaceful relations were restored 1858.

e. Mormon Articles of Faith:

"1. We believe in God, the Eternal Father, and in His Son, Jesus Christ, and in the Holy Ghost. 2. We believe that men will be punished for their own sins, and not for Adam's transgression. 3. We believe that through the atonement of Christ, all mankind may be saved, by obedience to the laws and ordinances of the Gospel. 4. We believe that the first principles and ordinances of the Gospel are: – (1) Faith in the Lord Jesus Christ; (2) Repentance; (3) Baptism by immersion for the remission of sins; (4) Laying on of Hands for the Gift of the Holy Ghost. 5. We believe that a man must be called of God, by prophecy, and by the laying on of hands, by those who are in authority, to preach the Gospel and administer in the ordinances thereof. 6. We believe in the same organization that existed in the Primitive Church, viz: apostles, prophets, pastors, teachers, evangelists, etc. 7. We believe in the gift of tongues, prophecy, revelation, visions, healing, interpretation of tongues, etc. 8. We believe the Bible to be the word of God, as far as it is translated correctly; We also believe the Book of Mormon to be the word of God. 9. We believe all that God has revealed, all that He does now reveal, and we believe that He will yet reveal many great and important things pertaining to the Kingdom of God. 10. We believe in the literal gathering of Israel and in the restoration of the Ten Tribes; That Zion will be built upon this [the American] continent; That Christ will reign personally upon the earth; and, That the earth will be renewed and receive its paradisiacal glory. 11. We claim the privilege of worshiping Almighty God according to the dictates of our conscience, and allow all men the same privilege, let them worship how, where, or what they may. 12. We believe in being subject to kings, presidents, rulers, and magistrates, in obeying, honoring, and sustaining the law. 13. We believe in being honest, true, chaste, benevolent, virtuous, and in doing good to *all men;* indeed, we may say that we follow the admonition of Paul, We believe all things, we hope all things, we have endured many things, and hope to be able to endure all things. If there is anything virtuous, lovely, or of good report, we seek after these things." ("Articles of Faith . . ." by Joseph Smith, in J. E. Talmage, *The Articles of Faith* [Salt Lake City, 1899], p. iii)

f. Smith claimed sanction of polygamy by revelation, which Young openly promulgated first 1852. The practice of plural marriage, as it was called, was undergirded by the thought that it insured more inhabitants of heaven. Marriage rites took place in temples to which outsiders were not admitted. W. Woodruff* issued a "manifesto" against polygamy 1890: "I now publicly declare that my advice . . . is to refrain from contracting any marriage forbidden by the law of the land."

In baptism for the dead, performed only in temples, with only approved Mormons admitted, a living person is proxy for one who died without a chance to hear or accept the Gospel.

g. Latter Day Saints divided:

1. *The Church of Jesus Christ of Latter-day Saints.* 1970 membership ca. 2,200,000. See also pars. a–f.

2. *Reorganized Church of Jesus Christ of Latter Day Saints* (Josephites [after Joseph Smith* Jr.]). Formed as a result of division among Latter Day Saints after the death of Joseph Smith* Sr. Differences involved the question of succession of leadership, the doctrine of the Godhead, and polygamy. Joseph Smith Jr. became leader of the dissenters.

Reorganization began in Wis. 1852, was completed 1860. Headquarters were moved to Plano, Ill., 1865, Lamoni, Iowa, 1881, Independence, Mo., 1920. Membership 1970 ca. 150,000.

3. *Church of Christ.* Formed in Bloomington, Ill., as a result of division among Latter Day Saints after the death of Joseph Smith* Sr., by men who opposed baptism for dead, exaltation of men to be gods, and the idea that God was once man like other men, the doctrine of lineal right to office since the Christian era began, and the doctrine of polygamy; to Independence, Mo., 1867; bought "temple lot" there. Membership 1956 ca. 3,000. Headquarters: Temple Lot, Independence, Mo.

4. *Church of Jesus Christ* (Bickertonites). Organized 1862 at Greenock (Green Oak), Pa., by William Bickerton; opposed baptism for dead, polygamy, and other features of The Church of Jesus Christ of Latter-day Saints. Membership 1970 ca. 2,400.

5. *Church of Jesus Christ* (Cutlerites). Organized 1853 at Fisher Grove, Fremont Co., Iowa, by Alphaeus Cutler. 1957 membership: 22.

6. *Church of Jesus Christ* (Strangites). Organized 1844 near Burlington, Wis., at a place which was given the name Voree (said to mean "garden of peace"), by J. J. Strang* after the death of Joseph Smith* Sr. Denied virgin birth of Christ. 1965 membership ca. 250.

Latter Rain Movement. On basis of Jl 2:23-24 and Acts 2:16-21 some Pentecostals compare the "former rain" with the beginning of the 6th dispensation (NT era) and the "latter rain" with its end, beginning ca. 1890. The term Latter Rain Movement probably originated with the revival movement of R. G. Spurling* Sr. and Jr. (see also *Church of God,* 2).

Latvia. N Eur. country at E end of Baltic Sea; includes part of medieval Livonia (see *Estonia,* 1–2); *area:* ca. 25,000 sq. mi.; *pop.* (1970 est.): ca. 2,300,000; Latvian (or Lettish), akin to Lithuanian, belongs to Baltic branches of Indo-Eur. languages.

Acc. to Adam* of Bremen (*Gesta* IV 16), Sweyn II (Sweyn Estrithson; Sven Estridson; d. 1075; b. Eng.; king Den. 1047–75) helped a Dan. merchant build a ch. in Latvia ca. 1045. Some missionaries of the Russ. Orthodox Ch. appeared in tribal kingdoms; in the 12th c. a few Orthodox chs. were built at Gersika (Gerzike; Jersika) on the Dvina (Daugava; Düna; Southern Dvina; Western Dvina; Zapadnaya Dvina). For hist. of Ger. colonization see *Estonia,* 1.

For 7 cents. (13th–20th) Latvians lived under for. rulers (Ger., Poland, Swed., Russ.). Until the 16th c. the ruling class did not provide for popular educ. Few chs. and no schools for children were built in Latvia before the 16th c. In 1522 A. Knöpken* and S. Tegetmeyer* began preaching ev. sermons in Riga in the early 1520s. Walter (or Wolter) von Plettenberg (ca. 1450–1535), grand master Teutonic Knights (see *Military Religious Orders,* c), assured Lutheranism complete freedom 1525. E. J. Glück* promoted schools and pub. of religious and educ. books.

Ca. the end of the 19th c. Latvian teachers and pastors, educ. U. of Dorpat (Tartu), est. 1632 by Gustavus* II Adolphus, initiated religious revival among their own people. K. Irbe* was invested Luth. bp. Latvia by N. Söderblom* 1922; resigned 1931. T. Grinbergs* succeeded him 1932 and was immediately named abp. In 1935 the total no. of Ev. Luths. in Latvia was ca. 1,000,000 (including ca. 61,000 Ger. Luths.) or ca. 56% of the pop. Of the Luths., those of Latvian origin constituted ca. 93%.

Latvia, which became an indep. rep. 1918, was occupied by USSR 1940, by Ger. forces 1941–44; retaken by USSR 1944/45. Under subsequent severe strictures the ch. in Latvia declined. By the end of WW II the abp. and more than 100 Latvian Luth. pastors, followed by ca. 100,000 or more Latvian laymen, fled from their homeland, many to the US and Can. Other countries with Latvian congs. include Argentine, Australia, Brazil, Chile, Den., Fr., Gt. Brit., W. Ger., New Zealand, Norw., Swed., and Venezuela. Under leadership of abp. K. Kjundzins they formed a fed. of Latvian Luth. congs. AL

See also *Lutheran Confessions,* A 5.

A. Svabe, F. Balodis, E. Blese, O. Silis, and V. Korsts, *Latvia on the Baltic Sea* (n. p., 1946); A. Bilmanis, "The Church in Latvia," *The Augustana Quarterly,* XXIII (1944), 291–310.

Laud, William (1573–1645). B. Reading, Berkshire, Eng.; educ. Oxford; Angl. priest 1601; opposed Calvinism,* Puritanism (see *Puritans*), and RCm; high churchman (see *High Church*); abp. Canterbury 1633; failed in attempt to force ritualism on Scot. Ch.; persecuted nonconformists; committed to Tower of London 1641; beheaded on Tower Hill.

Lauds. Service of canonical hours*; either the 2d or, combined with matins,* the 1st; until the reform of Pius X (see *Popes,* 30) it always closed with Ps 148–150, in which *laudate* (Lat. "praise ye") and related words occur frequently.

Laura (Gk. "street"). Colony of anchorites or cenobites* (see also *Hermits*) whose separate monastic cells form a street, as it were; first est. early in the 4th c. in Palestine. See also *Sabas.*

Laurenti(i), Laurentius (Lorenz Lorenzen; 1660–1722). B. Husum, Schleswig-Holstein, Ger.; educ. Rostock and in music at Kiel; cantor and dir. at Luth. Cathedral Ch., Bremen; piestistic hymnist; based many hymns on Gospel pericopes* in application to Christian life. *Evangelia Melodica,* pub. 1700, contains ca. 150 of his hymns.

Laurentius. See *Lawrence.*

Laurentius Andreae. See *Anderson, Lars.*

Laurentius von Brindisi (Lawrence of Brindisi; Giulio Cesare Russo [Rossi]; 1559–1619). B. Brindisi, It.; Capuchin exegete and preacher; leader in Counter* Reformation in Boh., Austria, and Ger.

Lauterbach, Anton (1502–69). B. Stolpen, Ger.; educ. Wittenberg; deacon Leisnig and Wittenberg; supt. Pirna. Noted esp. for recording much of M. Luther's* table talk and for correspondence with Luther; helped draft Leipzig Interim.*

Lauterburg, Moritz (1862–1927). Prof. Bern, Switz. Works include *Der Begriff des Charisma und seine Bedeutung für die praktische Theologie; Die Bedeutung der Autorität im Glaubensleben; Recht und Sittlichkeit.*

Lauterwar, Christian. See *Flacius Illyricus, Matthias.*

Lauxmann, Richard (1834–90). B. Schönaich, Württemberg, Ger.; educ. Schöntal and Tübingen. Pastor Adolzfurt, near Öhringen, 1862; Heilbronn 1870; Stuttgart 1874. Hymnographer. Works include *Geschichte des Kirchenlieds und Kirchengesangs, VIII: Die Kernlieder unserer Kirche.*

Lavater, Johann Kaspar (Caspar; 1741–1801). Philos., mystic, poet, theol., physiognomist. B. Zurich, Switz.; pioneer in personal counseling and pastoral ministry; contributed to decline of rationalism and rise of idealism. Poetic works include *Christliche Lieder; Die Auferstehung der Gerechten; Jesus Messias;* other works include *Aussichten in die Ewigkeit.*

Lavigerie, Charles Martial Allemand (1825–92). B. Huire, near Bayonne, Fr.; abp. Algiers 1867; apostolic delegate of W. Sahara and Sudan 1868; cardinal 1882; abp. Carthage and primate of Afr. 1884; sought greater pol. freedom for natives and tried to est. Christian Arab villages; opposed slavery; founded Société des missionaires d'Algier.

Lavington, George (1684–1762). B. Mildenhall, W Suffolk, E Eng.; Angl. bp. Exeter 1747; opposed Methodism.

Law, Book of the. See *Canon, Bible,* 2.

Law, Canon. See *Canon Law.*

Law, Divine. See *Decalog; Grace, Means of,* II; *Law and Gospel.*

Law, Natural. See *Natural Law.*

Law, William (1686–1761). Angl. cleric; b. King's Cliffe, Northamptonshire, Eng.; educ. Cambridge; nonjuror*; mystic, ascetic, philanthropist. Works include *A Serious Call to a Devout and Holy Life.*

Law and Gospel. "The law is a divine doctrine which reveals the righteousness and immutable will of God, shows how man ought to be disposed in his nature, thoughts, words, and deeds in order to be pleasing and acceptable to God, and threatens the transgressors of the law with God's wrath and temporal and eternal punishment. For, as Luther says against the nomoclasts, 'Everything that rebukes sin is and belongs to the law, the proper function of which is to condemn sin and to lead to a knowledge of sin' (Rom. 3:20; 7:7). Since unbelief is a root and fountainhead of all culpable sin, the law reproves unbelief also." (FC SD V 17)

"The Gospel, strictly speaking, is the kind of doctrine that teaches what a man who has not kept the law and is condemned by it should believe, namely, that Christ has satisfied and paid for all guilt and without man's merit has obtained and won for him forgiveness of sins, the 'righteousness that avails before God' [Ro 1:17; 2 Co 5:21], and eternal life." (FC Ep V 4)

"The word 'Gospel' is not used in a single sense in Holy Scripture, and this was the original occasion of the controversy. Therefore we believe, teach, and confess that when the word 'Gospel' means the entire doctrine of Christ which he proclaimed personally in his teaching ministry and which his apostles also set forth (examples of this meaning occur in Mark 1:15 and Acts 20:24), then it is correct to say or write that the Gospel is a proclamation both of repentance and of forgiveness of sins." (FC Ep V 6)

Law and Gospel do not differ if Law is taken in a broad sense, as in Is 2:3, or if Gospel is taken in a broad sense, as in Mk 1:1. They do not contradict each other. Both are God's Word; both are in the OT and NT; both are to be applied to people everywhere, including Christians.

The fact that Law and Gospel differ in their narrow sense is suggested or indicated, e. g., Zch 11:7; Mt 13:52; Lk 12:42; Ro 10:4; Gl 3:24. The difference was used, e. g., 2 Sm 12:1-14; Lk 7:36-50; Acts 2:37-39; 16:27-31; 1 Co 5:1-5; 2 Co 2:6-8.

Differences: (a) The Law was written into man's heart; the Gospel is not known by nature, but was revealed through Jesus and the Word of God. (b) The Law contains commandments of what we are to do and not to do and how we are to be; the Gospel reveals what God has done and still does for our salvation. (c) The Law promises eternal life conditionally; the Gospel promises it freely. (d) The Law demands perfect fulfillment and pronounces curses and threats if there is no perfect fulfillment; the Gospel has only promises and comforting assurrances. (e) The purpose of the Law is to serve as a curb, mirror, and rule (see also FC VI); the purpose of the Gospel is to forgive sins and give heaven and salvation as a free gift.

Law and Gospel are both operative in conversion* (see also *Contrition*). But the very nature of justification excludes the Law and leaves the Gospel as the only means whereby God justifies the sinner. The incentive power of the Gospel and the criterion of the Law are operative in sanctification* (see also *Good Works*).

See also *Grace, Means of,* II; *Worship,* 2.

W. Geihsler, "The Law and the Gospel," *The Abiding Word,* I, ed. T. Laetsch (St. Louis, 1946), 105–123; C. F. W. Walther, *The Proper Distinction Between Law and Gospel,* reproduced from the Ger. ed. of 1897 by W. H. T. Dau (St. Louis, 1929); W. Elert, "Gesetz und Zorn Gottes," *Morphologie des Luthertums,* I (Munich, 1931; improved print., 1952), 31–39, tr. W. A. Hansen, "The Law and the Wrath of God," *The Structure of Lutheranism,* I (St. Louis, 1962), 35–43; T. M. McDonough, *The Law and the Gospel in Luther* (London, 1963).

Law Codes. 1. A law code is a collection of laws which has become authoritative for a specific community. The code of Sumerian king Ur-Nammu (sometimes called Ur-Engur) antedates 2000 BC; that of Lipit-Ishtar (Lipiteshtar) of Issin (Isin), Babylonia, stems from ca. 1870–1860 BC (the time of Abraham); that of Hammurabi* was promulgated perhaps ca. 1800 BC. Hittite codes probably stem from ca. the 15th c., Assyrian codes from the 14th c. BC. Many of these ancient laws are casuistic: hypothetical cases are based on common precedent. Ancient Near E codes gen. have no clear parallels to the Biblical practice of setting laws in the form of direct command or prohibition as in the Decalog.* But they have many parallels to Biblical Law. Law 195 of the Hammurabi code: "If a son has struck his father, they shall cut off his hand"; the parallel Biblical law Ex 21:15 sets the penalty at death.

2. The OT law codes are covenant law: law to which a community bound itself in covenant allegiance to God as its overlord (Ex 24:3-8; Jos 24:25). The 1st OT code law is Ex 20:2-17. Ex 20:ca. 21–23, sometimes called Covenant Code, includes civil, criminal, soc., and cultic laws. Lv 1–7 contains directions for offerings and sacrifices. Ex 34:ca. 10-26 (some add 22:29b-30; 23:12-19), sometimes called Ritual Decalog, including laws regarding Jewish festivals and cultus. Lv 17–26, sometimes called Holiness Code (or Law of Holiness) esp. because of such passages as Lv 19:2; 20:7-8, 26; 21:8, includes cultic, civic, ceremonial, dietary, and hygienic laws. Dt 12–26, sometimes called Deuteronomic Code, treats esp. of religious, agricultural, martial, soc., and ecclesiastical activities. Isolated laws are scattered through the rest of Scripture.

3. Theol. emphases of OT codes vary. Laws pertaining to the same subject appear in each of these codes presented in varying forms and divergent perspectives, e. g., Ex 12; 23:14-19; 34:18-26; Lv 23; Nm 28–29; Dt 16:1-17. This has led to the suggestion that original Mosaic laws were reformulated by later inspired leaders to make them relevant to changing conditions. Many therefore date the final formulation of the various codes at various times from Moses to Ezra. Some identify the book of the law found by Hilkiah (2 K 22:8) with some form of Dt. The codes are esp. significant for an appreciation of Jewish customs and of the way in which daily life of the community and of the individual was to be related to God. They were God's guide for living for the people of God under the OT dispensation. NH

See also *Higher Criticism.*

G. E. Mendenhall, *Law and Covenant in Israel and the Ancient Near East* (Pittsburgh, Pa., 1955); R. de Vaux, *Les Institutions de L'Ancien Testament,* tr. J. McHugh, *Ancient Israel: Its Life and Institutions* (New York, 1961); J. B. Pritchard, *Ancient Near Eastern Texts Relating to the Old Testament,* 3d ed. with supplement (Princeton, N. J., 1969); J. Bright, *A History of Israel* (Philadelphia, 1959); H. M. Buck, *People of the Lord* (New York, 1966); *The World History of the Jewish People, First Series:*

Ancient Times, I: At the Dawn of Civilization, ed. E. A. Speiser (New Brunswick, N. J., 1964).

Lawes, William George (July 1, 1839–Aug. 6, 1907). B. Aldermaston, Berkshire, Eng.; trained by LMS at Bedford; miss. to Niue (Savage Is.) 1861–72; home on furlough 1872; to New Guinea 1874; at Port Moresby 20 yrs., then at Vatorata. Completed the work (begun by others) of tr. NT into Niuean 1886; reduced Motu (language of a Melanesian people in Papua) to writing; other Motu works include selections from OT hist., a rev. NT, a grammar and dictionary, a manual of geogr. and arithmetic. See also *New Guinea,* 4.

Lawrence (Laurence; Laurentius; Lorenz; 3d c.). Deacon Rome; martyr; Ap IV ca. 377 (Ger.) cites him as example of a saint who did not trust in his works. See also *Symbolism, Christian,* 4–5.

Lawrence, Thomas Edward. See *Geography, Christian,* 6.

Lawrence of Brindisi. See *Laurentius von Brindisi.*

Lay Abbot. Layman in charge of an abbey and its income.

Lay Baptism. See *Baptism, Lay.*

Lay Brothers and Lay Sisters. Nonclerical religious in a RC monastic community; take precedence over laity. See also *Monasticism.*

Lay Delegates. See *Lutheran Church – Missouri Synod, The,* III 7; V 3; *Ministerium.*

Laying on of Hands. See *Hands, Imposition of.*

Laymen's Activity in the Lutheran Church. Cong. polity of Luth. chs. directs laymen's chief energies into parish administration and work. Membership assemblies, bds., etc., provide opportunities to contribute time and talent. Many parishes also organize groups for soc. and recreational purposes. These groups occasionally sponsor or promote direct service in the interest of the cong. budget or program of evangelism. They may form nat. or internat. assocs. Areas of interest and activity include Scouting and other parish youth programs and scholarships at colleges and univs. Unofficial groups engage in intersyn. contact. See also *Lutheran Laymen's League; Lutheran Women's Missionary League.*

Laymen's Missionary Movement. Organized 1906 in 5th Ave. Presb. Ch., NYC; incited new interest in for. missions; endorsed 1907 by annual conf. of for. miss. bds. of US and Can.; plan was not to send out missionaries or administer miss. funds, but to cooperate in enlargement of for. miss. work of affiliated chs.

Laynez, Diego (Laínez; Iago; Jakob; James; Giacomo; 1512–65). B. Almazán, Sp.; educ. Alcalá, Sp., and Paris, Fr.; Gen. of Jesuits* 1558–65; prominent at Council of Trent* and Colloquy of Poissy*; supported papal absolutism. Works include *Disputationes Tridentinae.* See also *Counter Reformation,* 8.

Layriz, Friedrich (Layritz; 1808–59). B. Nemmersdorf, Bav., Ger.; educ. Erlangen and Leipzig; pastor Hirschlag 1837, St. Georgen (near Bayreuth) 1842, Schwaningen 1846; advocated restoration of the original form of the Ger. rhythmical chorale. Works include *Kern des deutschen Kirchengesangs; Kern des deutschen Kirchenlieds von Luther bis auf Gellert; Die Liturgie eines vollständigen Hauptgottesdienstes nach lutherischem Typus;* music supplement to J. K. W. Löhe's* *Agende;* tune for the hymn "Eins ist Not" ["One Thing's Needful"].

Lazarists (Lazarites; Lazarians; so named after the priory of St. Lazare, which they received from the canons regular of St. Victor 1632. Also called Vincentians, and Cong. of the Mission). Community of priests, clerics, and brothers founded 1625 by Vincent* de Paul for miss. work among Fr. peasants; suffered severely in Fr. Revolution (see *Church and State,* 15; *France,* 5); engages in extensive miss. work in many countries; early bases in the US included Perryville and St. Louis, Mo.; dir. Kenrick Sem., St. Louis.

Lazarites. See *Lazarists; Military Religious Orders,* d.

Lea, Henry Charles (1825–1909). B. Philadelphia, Pa.; mem. of a Philadelphia pub. firm. Works include *History of Sacerdotal Celibacy in the Christian Church; A History of Auricular Confession and Indulgences in the Latin Church; A History of the Inquisition of Spain; A History of the Inquisition of the Middle Ages; The Inquisition in the Spanish Dependencies.*

Lead(e), Jane (nee Ward; 1623–1704). B. Norfolk, Eng.; mystic at ca. 16; m. William Lead 1654; influenced by writings of J. Böhme*; claimed prophetic visions; with T. Bromley,* J. Pordage,* and F. Lee* organized The Philadelphian* Soc. for the Advancement of Piety and Divine Philos.; Lee helped spread her doctrines in Eur. See also *Millennium,* 5.

League and Covenant, Solemn. Agreement drawn up 1643 in Edinburgh, Scot., bet. the Eng. Parliament and the Scots. Pledged subscribers to maintenance of Ref. Ch. of Scot., to Reformation in Eng. and Ireland, to common endeavor toward uniformity of discipline and doctrine, to loyalty to Parliament and crown, and to extirpation of popery and prelacy. Renewed in Scot. 1648. Signed 1650 and 1651 by Charles II ("Merry Monarch"; 1630–85; king of Eng., Ireland, and Scot.). See also *Covenanters; Presbyterian Confessions,* 1, 3.

Leagues and Alliances, Holy. See *Holy Leagues and Alliances.*

Leander (ca. 549 [early as 540?]–ca. 600). B. probably Cartagena, Sp.; bp. (or abp., or metropolitan) Seville ca. 577/578 [584?]; brother of Isidore* of Seville; friend of Gregory I (see *Popes,* 4); won Visigoths of Sp. from Arianism* for orthodoxy; presided at 589 Council of Toledo.*

Lebanon. See *Middle East,* D.

Lebanon Bible Institute. See *Middle East,* D.

Lebanon Evangelical Mission. Known 1860–81 as Ladies' Assoc. for Soc. and Religious Improvement of the Syrian Females, 1882–88 as Brit. Syrian Schools and Bible Miss., 1889–96 as Brit. Syrian Schools and Bible Work, 1897–1903 as Brit. Syrian Miss. and Bible Work, and in more recent yrs. simply as Brit. Syrian Miss. Est. 1860 to rehabilitate women and children widowed and orphaned by Druzes and Muslim (by massacres in Syrian hinterland). Interdenom., conservative, ev. Field was Syria, but 1959 legislation obliged move of its center of activity to Lebanon. Established village schools, larger institutions, and special schools (e. g., for blind); sends out miss. evangelists; relates groups of believers to existing nat. ev. chs. See also *Middle East,* C, D.

LeBouthillier de Rancé, Armand Jean. See *Rancé, Armand Jean Le Bouthillier de.*

Lebuin (Lebwin; Lebuinus; Libuinus; Liafwin[e] [OE "dear friend"]; d. perhaps ca. 780). Anglo-Saxon Benedictine priest; miss. in Frisia and Saxony.

Lecerf, Auguste (1872–1943). B. London, Eng.; pastor Lunéville, Fr., 1895; Ref. prof. dogmatics Paris 1938. Works include studies of Calvinism.*

Lechler, Gotthard Victor (Viktor; 1811–88). Brother of K. Lechler*; Luth. theol.; b. Reichenbach, near Freudenstadt, Württemberg, Ger.; educ. Tübingen; prof. Leipzig 1858. Works include *Geschichte des englischen Deismus; Das apostolische und das nachapostolische Zeitalter; Johann von Wiclif und die Vorgeschichte der Reformation.*

Lechler, Karl (1820–1903). Brother of G. V. Lechler*; Luth. pastor Württemberg; gen. supt. Ulm; in theory derived ministerial office from office of bp.; worked for union of Luth. and Ref. chs.

Lechler, Rudolf (1824–1908). With Knut Theodor Hamberg (1819–54) of Swed. to Hong Kong as co-workers of K. F. A. Gützlaff* 1846/47; Lechler and Hamberg est. the China miss. of the Basel* Miss. Soc.; Lechler led the miss. 1854–99.

Lechner, Leonhard (Lehner; Lehener; Athesinus [from Athesis, Lat. name of the Etsch]; ca. 1553–1606). Luth. composer; b. Etsch (Adige) valley, S Tirol; pupil of O. di Lasso*; held positions at Nürnberg, Hechingen, Tübingen, and Stuttgart. Works include *Deutsche Sprüche von Leben und Tod;* a Passion acc. to John. See also *Passion, The.*

Le Clerc, Jean (Leclerc). See *Arminianism.*

Leclercq, Henri (1869–1945). Benedictine scholar; b. Tournai, Belg.; became Fr. citizen; to Eng. 1896; priest 1898; in London 1914–45. Wrote extensively, esp. on Lat. Christianity; ed. with F. Cabrol,* *Monumenta ecclesiae liturgica* and *Dictionnaire d'archéologie chrétienne et de liturgie;* issued an enl. but somewhat unreliable Fr. ed. of K. J. v. Hefele,* *Conciliengeschichte;* other works include hist. of Christianity in Afr. and Sp.; manual of Christian archaeol. to 8th c.

Lecot, Victor Lucien Sulpice (1831–1908). B. Montescourt, near St. Quentin, Fr.; bp. Dijon 1886; abp. Bordeaux 1890; cardinal 1893; active in soc. reform and in behalf of the working class.

Lectern. See *Church Furniture,* 1.

Lectionary. Book containing Scripture readings as lessons for the ch. yr. Some lectionaries are elaborately embellished. The earliest Lat. lectionary (*comes,* "companion") has been ascribed to Jerome* but is probably of later origin; Gallican lectionaries are dated as early as the 5th or 6th c.; Gk. lectionaries are traced at least to the 6th c. See also *Pericope; Service Books.*

Lector. See *Clergy; Hierarchy.*

Ledesma. 1. *Martin de* (d. 1574). Sp. Dominican 1525; Thomist; prof. Coimbra, Port. 2. *Pedro de* (ca. 1550–1616). B. Salamanca, Sp.; Dominican 1563; strict Thomist; taught at Segovia, Ávila, and Salamanca; defended D. Báñez*; opposed Luis (de) Molina.*

Ledóchowski, Mieczyslaw Halka (Miecislaus Johann; 1822–1902). Uncle of W. Ledóchowski*; b. Klimontów, near Sandomierz, Poland; papal diplomat in Port. and S Am.; nuncio in Brussels; abp. Gnesen-Posen; imprisoned 1874 for opposing May* laws; cardinal 1875; spent last yrs. in Rome; supported papal infallibility.*

Ledóchowski, Wladimir (Wlodzimierz; 1866–1942). Nephew of M. H. Ledóchowski*; b. Loosdorf, Austria; Gen. of Society* of Jesus 1915; extended the order, esp. with a view toward the E Ch.

Lee, Ann (Lees; "Mother Ann"; "Ann the Word"; 1736–84). B. Manchester, Eng.; joined Shaking Quakers in Eng. Ca. 1758; their leader 1770; m. blacksmith Abraham Standerin (Stanley; Standley) 1762; to US 1774; settled with followers at present Watervliet, N. Y., founding 1st Shaker community in US 1776; arrested for treason 1780, soon released. See also *Shakers.*

Lee, Francis (1661–1719). B. Cobham, Surrey, Eng.; educ. Oxford; nonjuror (see *Nonjurors*); left Eng. 1691; studied medicine; entered U. Leiden, Neth., 1692; practiced medicine at Venice, It.; on way home 1694 became acquainted with writings of J. Lead(e)*; became her disciple in London; m. her daughter. Became head of The Philadelphian Soc. for the Advancement of Piety and Divine Philosophy. Works include *Horologium Christianum; The Labouring Person's Remembrancer; Considerations concerning Oaths.*

Lee, Frederick George (1832–1902). Angl. theol. writer; b. Thame, Oxfordshire, Eng.; educ. Oxford; helped found A. P. U. C. 1857; vicar All Saints', Lambeth, 1867–99; RC 1901; advocated reunion of RC Ch. and Ch. of Eng. Ed. *The Union Review* 1863–69; other works include *A Glossary of Liturgical and Ecclesiastical Terms; Historical Sketches of the Reformation.*

Lee, Jason (June 28, 1803–Mar. 12, 1845). Meth. miss.; b. near Stanstead, Quebec, then considered part of Vt.; conversion experience at 22; minister in and near Stanstead; ordained deacon 1832, later elder; miss. to Flathead country (Mont. and Brit. Columbia) 1833, but soon went instead to Williamette, 10 mi. NW of Salem, Oreg.; est. missions at The Dalles and elsewhere in Oreg. See also *Indians, American,* 6.

Leeson, Jane Elizabeth (1809–81). Hymnist; b. London, Eng.; active in Catholic* Apostolic Ch.; RC late in life. Hymns include "Gracious Savior, Gentle Shepherd"; tr. include "Christ the Lord Is Risen Today."

Leeward Islands. Part of the Lesser Antilles, E West Indies; name derived from their comparatively sheltered position from prevailing NE winds. Govt. division of W Indies Fed. (1958–62): Antigua, St. Christopher [Kitts]-Nevis-Anguilla, and Montserrat. See also *Carribean Islands,* E 5, 7, 8.

Lefèvre, Pierre. See *Favre, Pierre.*

Lefèvre d'Étaples, Jacques (Jacobus Faber; Fabri; surname Stapulensis; ca. 1450–ca. 1537). Reformer, humanist, and Aristotelian philos.; b. Étaples, Fr.; educ. Paris; settled near Paris; condemned for heresy; fled to Strasbourg because of Reformation sympathies; recalled; lived under royal protection. Works include tr. of Bible into Fr.; commentary on Paul's epistles. See also *France,* 7.

Legalism. (a) Seeking salvation through works rather than grace; (b) emphasis on the letter rather than the spirit of the law. See also *Luther, Chief Writings of,* 3.

Legates (from Lat. *legare,* "send as deputy"). Emissaries or deputies. Papal legates represent the pope. Legates *a latere* ("from the [pope's] side") are always cardinals. When their function pertains only to local chs. they are known as apostolic delegates. When to a legation of a religious or ecclesial nature there is added legation to states and govts., the title of nuncio, pronuncio, or internuncio is given to the legate.

Legenda aurea. See *Golden Legend.*

Legislation Pertaining to Christian Education. See *Christian Education,* J.

Lehmann, Gottfried Wilhelm (1799–1882). B. Hamburg, Ger.; leader of Bap. movement in Eur.; poet; active in miss., temperance, and soc. work.

Lehmann, Wilhelm Friedrich (Oct. 16, 1820–Dec. 1, 1880). B. Markgröningen, Württemberg, Ger.; to Am. 1824; educ. Theol. Sem. of the Ev. Luth. Joint Syn. of Ohio* and Other States, Columbus, Ohio; licensed 1839; ordained 1843; assumed duties as prof. Sem. at Columbus 1847; pastor Trin. Luth. Ch., Columbus, Ohio; pres. Capital U. 1857; pres. Joint Syn. of Ohio 1854–60, 1878–80; pres. The Ev. Luth. Synodical* Conf. of N. Am. 1873–76, 1877–80. Ed. in chief *Lutherische Kirchen-Zeitung* 1860.

Lehmus, Johann Adam (Lehms; 1707–88). B. Rothenburg ob der Tauber, Bav., Ger.; educ. Jena; Luth. pastor, active in Scheckenbach and Rothenburg; hymnist; grandfather of A. T. A. F. Lehmus.*

Lehmus, Adam Theodor Albert Franz (1777–1837). Grandson of J. A. Lehmus*; b. Soest, Ger.; Luth. theol. of Erlangen School (see *Lutheran Theology After 1580,* 11); influenced by J. G. Fichte*; moved from romantic idealism toward confessionalism; valued M. Luther* and Luth. Confessions highly; tried to maintain contact with philos. and contemporary sciences; helped reest. Luth. confessionalism in Bav.

Lehr, Leopold Franz Friedrich (1709–44). B. Cronenburg (Cronberg; Kronberg), near Frankfurt am Main; educ. Jena and Halle; tutor; served Halle orphanage; active in Köthen; hymnist. Hymns include "Mein Heiland nimmt die Sünder an" ("My Savior Sinners Doth Receive").

"Lehre und Wehre." See *Lutheran Church – Missouri Synod, The,* V 2.

Leibniz, Gottfried Wilhelm von (Leibnitz; Lubeniecz; 1646–1716). Prot. philos. and polymath; b. Leipzig, Ger.; educ. Leipzig, Jena, Altdorf; held various positions; held that the universe is made up of "monads," units endowed with physical and psychical properties, God being the Supreme Monad; tried to unite Prots. and RCs, Luths. and Ref. Works include *Hypothesis physica nova; De concursu corporum; De principio individui; Discours de métaphysique; Essais de Théodicée sur la bonté de Dieu, la liberté de l'homme, et l'origine du mal; La Monadologie; Nouveaux Essais sur l'entendement humain.* See also *Harmony, Pre-Established. Logic, Symbolic; Lutheran Theology After 1580,* 8; *Time.*

Leiden School. See *Scholten, Jan Hendrik.*

Leighton, Robert (1611–84). Scot. Presb. prelate; b. probably London, Eng. (or Edinburgh, Scot., or Ulishaven, Forfarshire, Scot.); educ. Edinburgh; prof. Edinburgh 1653; Angl. bp. Dunblane 1661, abp. Glasgow 1670, resigned 1674 after failing to harmonize Presbs. and Angls. Works include *Rules and Instructions for a Holy Life; A Practical Commentary upon the First Epistle of St. Peter.*

Leipzig Colloquy. Conference at Leipzig, Ger., 1631 bet. Luths. (John* George I and Saxon theologians M. Höe* v. Höenegg, P. Lyser,* and H. Höpfner*) and Calvinists (Georg Wilhelm [1595–1640; elector of Brandenburg 1620–40; son of John* Sigismund; father of Frederick* William of Brandenburg] and his court preacher J. Bergius*; Wilhelm V [1602–37; landgrave of Hesse-Cassel 1627–37], his court preacher T. Neuberger,* and J. Crocius*) to prevent execution of the Edict of Restitution.* The colloquents agreed on most of the AC but disagreed on the communication of attributes, Lord's Supper, and predestination.

Leipzig Debate. In 1518 J. Eck* challenged A. R. B. v. Karlstadt* to a pub. debate on matters involving Luth. doctrine. The debate was held 1519 in the great hall of castle Pleissenburg, Leipzig. Disputants: June 27–July 3, Eck and Karlstadt; July 4–13, Eck and M. Luther*; July 14–16, Eck and Karlstadt. Luther said that popes and councils were fallible and rested his case on Scripture alone. The univs. of Erfurt and Paris were to render a verdict on the debate, but Erfurt asked to be excused and Paris issued no statement till 1521, when it rendered a verdict adverse to Luther based on his writings, without mention of the Leipzig Debate.

W. H. T. Dau, *The Leipzig Debate in 1519* (St. Louis, 1919).

Leipzig Disputation. Disputation resulting from the inaugural address of A. Hahn* in Leipzig 1827; he held that rationalism* has no legitimate place in the ch.; he was opposed by K. A. v. Hase,* J. F. Röhr,* et al.

Leipzig Evangelical Lutheran Mission (Evangelisch-lutherische Mission zu Leipzig). Began 1819 as Dresden Ev. Luth. Miss. (Evangelisch-lutherische Mission zu Dresden), which was largely supported by pietists and sent money and missionaries to the Basel* Miss. Soc. Largely as a result of reaction against the Prussian* Union the Dresden soc. est. its own miss. school 1832, which developed into a sem. 1836. The soc. also became an indep. Luth. miss. soc. 1836. In 1848 its miss. bd. moved to Leipzig. Under K. F. L. Graul* it became the most important Luth. miss. in Eur.

The Leipzig Miss. was pledged to the Luth. confessions. Its purpose was not only to win converts but also to gather the converts into congs. loyal to the Luth. confessions and to develop indigenous, self-supporting chs. Missionaries were trained in the religious, scientific, literary, pol., and soc. aspects of their field.

Fields included India 1847, Kenya 1886, Tanganyika 1893, New Guinea 1955. It also est. a miss. at Station Bethany, St. Louis, Mich. (see also *Baierlein, Eduard Raimund*), which was given to the Mo. Syn. 1849.

See also *Hardeland, Julius.*

Leipzig Interim. See *Interim,* II; *Lutheran Confessions,* C 1.

Leisen. See *Hymnody, Christian,* 5.

Leist, Jacob (Jan. 8, 1788–Nov. 7, 1870). B. probably Snyder Co., Pa.; moved to Ohio; licensed by Ministerium of Pa. 1812; ordained 1818 at organization meeting of the Ohio Syn. (see *Ohio and Other States, Evangelical Lutheran Joint Synod of*); pastor in the area bet. Lancaster and Circleville, Ohio; pres. Ohio Syn. 1825–27; retired by 1854.

Le Jay. See *Jajus.*

Lela, Chundra (ca. 1825–1907). Indian evangelist; Brahman (see *Brahmanism*); married at 7; widowed at 9; learned Sanskrit and Shastra from her father; converted to Christianity after father's death; preached in gateways of native temples.

Leland, John (1691–1766). Presb. cleric, polemicist; b. Wigan, Lancashire, Eng.; wrote against M. Tindal,* T. Morgan,* H. Dodwell* Jr., H. St. J. Bolingbroke,* and other deists (see *Deism*). Works include *A View of the Principal Deistical Writers That Have Appeared in England in the Last and Present Century.*

Leland, John (1754–1841). Bap. cleric; hymnist; b. Grafton, Mass.; preacher from age 20, first in Va., then in Mass. (mostly at Cheshire); restless and eccentric. Hymns include "The Day Is Past and Gone."

Le Maister. Jansenist (see *Jansenism*) brothers at Port* Royal, Fr. 1. *Antoine* (1608–58). B. Paris, Fr.; lawyer; Bible translator. 2. *Issac Louis* (de Saci, or Sacy [anagrams of Isaac]; 1613–84). B. Paris, Fr.; priest; Bible translator; ed. *Heures du Port Royal.* 3. *Simon* (de Sericourt; 1611–58). Strict ascetic.

Le Maistre, Mattheus (Le Maitre; Meistre; Maystre; perhaps ca. 1505–ca. 1577). B. possbily Roclenge-sur-Geer, Liège, Belg.; composer; kapellmeister Dresden 1554. Works include *Catechesis* (settings of Lutheran catechism).

Lemme, Ludwig (1847–1927). Prot. theol.; b. Salzwedel, Ger.; educ. Berlin; prof. Breslau, Bonn, and Heidelberg; theol. position allied to that of I. A. Dorner* and R. Rothe.* Works include *Christliche Ethik; Christliche Glaubenslehre.*

Le Neve, John (1679–1741). Eng. antiquary. Works include *Fasti Ecclesiae Anglicanae; The Lives, Characters, . . . and . . . Benefactions of All the Protestant Bishops of the Church of England Since the Reformation.*

Lenker, John Nicholas (Nov. 28, 1858–May 16, 1929). B. Sunbury, Pa.; educ. Wittenberg Coll. and Hamma Divinity School, Springfield, Ohio, and Leipzig, Ger.; ordained 1880; pastor Grand Island, Nebr., 1882–86; with Bd. of Christian Extension of Gen. Syn. 1886–94; prof. Trin. Sem. of the United Dan. Ev. Luth. Ch. in Am. (see *Danish Lutherans in America,* 5), Blair, Nebr., 1900–04; settled in Minneapolis, Minn., 1904, and served as pastor and miss. in and near the city; founded Luther Press. Founded and ed. *Northern Review;* other works include *Lutherans in All Lands; Lutherans in All Lands, Supplement; Die Lutherische Kirche der Welt;* tr. of M. Luther's works into Eng.

Lenoir Rhyne College. Named after Col. W. W. Lenoir, who donated the grounds, and Daniel Rhyne, who richly endowed it 1922. See also *Lutheran Church in America,* V; *Ministry, Education of,* VIII B 16; *United Lutheran Church Synods of,* 16.

Le Nourry, Denis Nicholas (1647–1724). B. Dieppe, Fr.; Benedictine (see *Benedictines*); Maurist (see *Maurists*) hist. Helped prepare standard eds. of ch. fathers, esp. F. M. A. Cassiodorus* and Ambrose*; other works include *Apparatus ad bibliothecam maximam veterum patrum et antiquorum scriptorum ecclesiasticorum Lugduni editam.*

Lenski, Richard Charles Henry (Sept. 14, 1864–Aug. 14, 1936). Luth. cleric; b. Greifenberg, Prussia, Ger.; to Am. 1873; educ. Capital U. and its Theol. Dept., Columbus, Ohio; ordained 1887. Ev. Luth. Joint Syn. of Ohio* and Other States pastor successively at Baltimore, Md.; Trenton, Springfield, and Anna, all in Ohio, till 1911. Prof. Capital U. and its Theol. Dept. 1911. Ed. *Lutherische Kirchenzeitung* 1904–24; other works include *The Active Church Member; The Eisenach Gospel Selections; The Eisenach Old Testament Selections; The Epistle Selections of the Ancient Church; The Gospel Selections of the Ancient Church; The Sermon: Its Homiletical Construction; Saint Paul;* commentary on the NT.

Lent. See *Church Year,* 3, 4, 8, 14, 16; *Tempus clausum.*

Leo I. See *Popes,* 2.

Leo III (ca. 680–741). "The Isaurian"; b. perhaps N Syria, rather than Isauria, as formerly thought; E Roman emp. 717–741; forced Suleiman (Arab.: Sulayman; d. 717; Umayyad caliph 715–717) to give up siege (begun 716) of Constantinople 717; defeated Muslim 726 and 739; iconoclast; confiscated papal lands.

Leo IX (Bruno of Egisheim; 1002–1054). B. Egisheim, Alsace; pope 1048 (crowned 1049); enjoined clerical celibacy; declared war against Normans in S It. 1053; defeated 1053 at Civitate (Civitella del Tronto), on the Fortore R. and detained. See also *Schism,* 6.

Leo X. See *Popes,* 20.

Leo XIII. See *Popes,* 29.

Leo, Heinrich (1799–1878). Prot. hist.; b. Rudolstadt, Ger.; first influenced by G. W. F. Hegel,* later, in reaction against the "Hegelian Left," became conservative under influence of E. W. Hengstenberg,* F. J. Stahl,* et al.

Leonardo da Vinci (1452–1519). Florentine artist, scientist; b. Vinci, Tuscany, It. Architect of Milan cathedral; paintings include *Last Supper; Mona Lisa.*

Leonine City. Part of Rome, It., fortified 848–852 by Leo IV (ca. 800–855; b. Rome; pope 847–855); contains Vatican* and Castel Sant' Angelo (which includes Hadrian's tomb [see *Persecutions of Christians,* 3]).

Leonine Prayers. In RCm, prayers in vernacular at end of mass recited by priest and people.

Leontius of Byzantium (Byzantinus; Scholasticus; ca. 500–ca. 543). Anti-monophysite theol.; probably distinguished from Scythian monk of same name and from one Leontius of Jerusalem; probably the monk whom Sabas* took from the New Laura* in Palestine to Constantinople ca. 530; defended Chalcedonian Christology against Monophysites. Wrote against Nestorianism* and Eutychianism.*

MPG, 86, 1185–2100.

Leporius (fl. early 5th c.). B. probably Trier; monk in S Gaul; originally Nestorian and perhaps somewhat Pelagian; recanted under influence of Augustine* of Hippo.

MPL, 31, 1215–32.

Leprosy (Hansen's Disease). Bacterial disease which causes nodules to appear on body surface; nerves become involved; eventually paralysis results.

In the NT (except Lk 17:15) removal of leprosy is spoken of as cleansing. The Gk. word *lepra* (found in LXX and NT) was used also for psoriasis or similar ailment. Leprosy was known in India ca. 1400 BC. It is apparently mentioned in the Egyptian papyrus Ebers ca. 1550 BC. Leprosy of the body, and its symptoms, are alluded to Ex 4:6; Lv 13; Nm 12:10; 2 Sm 3:29; 2 K 5; 15:5; 2 Ch 26:23; leprosy in garments is mentioned Lv 13:47-59, in houses Lv 14:34-57.

Leprosariums were est. early. Sometimes lepers were banished into desert and outlying districts. Jesus' attitude toward lepers (Mk 1:40-45) led to humane treatment of them by Christians.

1970 est.: 10–15 million lepers in the world, most of them in Afr., India, and China. Since the early 1940s sulfone drugs have been used effectively against leprosy.

Socs. which have worked among lepers include Am. Leprosy Missions, Inc. (organized 1906 as Am. Committee of the Mission to Lepers, inc. 1917 as Am. Mission to Lepers; headquarters NYC); Internat. Christian Leprosy Missions (organized 1944; Internat. Council formed 1961; headquarters Portland, Oreg.); The Leprosy Mission (organized 1874; headquarters London, Eng. Also known as The Mission to Lepers in India; The Mission to Lepers in India and the East; Mission to Lepers).

Leps, Johan(n) Christian (Lepps). B. Den.; to Am. via W Indies 1770; studied theol. under J. C. Kunze*; prof. pre-theol. school est. by Kunze; pastor Loonenburg, N. Y.; mem. Pa. Ministerium, retired to a farm in Pa. 1782; attended 1783 conv. of the Pa. Ministerium. See also *Danish Lutherans in America,* 1.

Lepsius, Johannes (1858–1926). Pastor Jerusalem 1884; Friesdorf, Ger., 1887. Est. Dr. Lepsius' Deutsche Orient-Mission in Berlin for work among Muslim ca. 1895; this miss. was dissolved 1965 and its work integrated with Berlin* Miss. Soc. I. Persecution of Armenians in Turkey led him to est. agencies to aid Armenians in various countries.

Le Quien, Michel (1661–1733). B. Boulogne-sur-Mer, Fr.; patristic scholar; Dominican. Ed. works of John* of Damascus; other works include *Oriens christianus.*

Lercheimer, Augustin (Hermann Wilcken; Hermann Witekind; pseudonym A. L. v. Steinfelden; 1522–1603). Educ. Frankfurt an der Oder and Wittenberg; friend of P. Melanchthon*; rector Lat. school Riga; taught Gk. at Heidelberg 1551; taught at academy in Neustadt 1579–83.

Leslie, Charles (1650–1722). B. Dublin, Ireland; educ. Dublin; Angl. nonjuror (see *Nonjurors*); controversialist; wrote against deism,* RCm, Soc. of Friends,* Presbs., Jews, Socinians. Works include *The Snake in the Grass; The Wolf Stript of His Shepherd's Cloathing; A Short and Easie Method with the Deist; The Truth of Christianity Demonstrated.*

Leslie, John (Lesley; 1527–96). B. Kingussie, Invernesshire, Scot.; educ. Aberdeen, Scot., and Paris, Toulouse, and Poitiers, Fr.; ordained priest Scot. 1554; opposed Reformation in Scot.; disputed with J. Knox* at Edinburgh 1561; supported Mary (Queen of Scots; Mary Stuart; 1542–87; RC); bp. Ross 1566, Coutances, Normandy, Fr., 1593; hist. Works include *De origine, moribus, et rebus gestis Scotorum; The Historie of Scotland.*

Lesotho, Kingdom of. See *Africa,* B 6.

Lesser Antilles. See *Caribbean Islands.*

Lesser Doxology. See *Canticles; Doxology; Worship, Parts of,* 4.

Lesser Sundas (Soendas). See *Indonesia,* 1, 9–12.

Lessing, Gotthold Ephraim (1729–81). Critic and dramatist; b. Kamenz, Saxony; librarian Wolfenbüttel 1770; promoted Enlightenment*; criticized shallowness of rationalistic theol., but became one of the greatest promoters of rationalism; engaged in controversy with J. M. Goeze* over H. S. Reimarus'* *Fragmente eines Ungenannten;* gave a liberal, soc., and humanitarian interpretation to Christianity. Works include *Nathan der Weise; Minna von Barnhelm; Laokoon; Die Erziehung des Menschengeschlechts.* See also *Philosophy.* WS.

Lessius, Leonard(us) (Leys; Leonhard; 1554–1623). B. Brecht, near Antwerp; educ. Louvain; Jesuit; engaged in RC controversy on grace and inspiration. Works include *Theses theologicae; De iustitia et iure; De gratia efficaci.* See also *Humanism.*

Lessons (Liturgical). See *Lectionary; Pericope.*

Letters of Obscure Men *(Epistolae obscurorum virorum).* In 1514 J. Reuchlin* pub. *Clarorum virorum epistolae,* a collection of letters upholding his defense of Jewish literature and studies. In 1515–17 there appeared, in 2 parts, a series of satirical letters, *Epistolae obscurorum virorum,* lampooning Cologne Dominicans, esp. their leader Ortwin Gratius (van Graes; ca. 1480–1542; b. Holtwick, near Münster, Ger.; educ. Deventer, Neth.; prof. Cologne), to whom most of them were addressed, for attacks on Reuchlin. Crotus* Rubianus wrote most of the 1st part of *Epistolae obscurorum virorum.* U. v. Hutten* probably wrote most of the 2d part. A papal brief against authors, publishers, and possessors of *Epistolae obscurorum virorum* did little to dull the satire's cutting edge. See also *Humanism, Sixteenth-Century German.*

Leuba, James Henry (1868–1946). B. Neuchâtel, Switz.; educ. Neuchâtel, Clark U. (Worcester, Mass.), Leipzig, Halle, Heidelberg, Paris; prof. psychol. Bryn Mawr (Pa.) Coll. 1899–1933. Works include *A Psychological Study of Religion; The Psychology of Religious Mysticism; God or Man?: A Study of the Value of God to Man.*

Leube, Hans (1896–1947). B. Leipzig, Ger.; ch. hist.; prof. Leipzig, Breslau, Rostock; student of H. Böhmer*; interested in Ref. thought in Lutheran* theol. after 1580 and in humanistic ideas in the ch. of Fr. and Eng.

Leuchter, Heinrich (1558–1623). Luth. theol.; b. Melsungen, Ger.; studied under A. Hunnius* at Marburg; pastor Kirtorf 1586; preacher and supt. Marburg 1588; supt. Hesse-Darmstadt 1608; among those delegated 1621 to settle the Crypto-Kenotic* Controversy.

Leucippus (5th c. BC). Gk. philos.; held that being is infinity of homogeneous atoms in infinite variety of forms and in infinite space; becoming results from the motion of atoms and their combinations. See also *Deism,* 1; *Democritus.*

Leusden, Johann(es) (Jan; 1624–99). Hebraist; b. Utrecht, Neth.; prof. Oriental languages Utrecht; ed. Heb. OT and pub. it in collaboration with Joseph ben Abraham Athia(s) (Atia; d. 1700; Jewish printer at Amsterdam); other works include *Onomasticum sacrum; Philologus Hebraeus;* ed. Gk. NT.

Levellers. Faction in O. Cromwell's* army with radical ideas on govt. and religion. In religion they sought freedom of conscience and liberty for everyone to act acc. to his best knowledge; religion has 2 sides, or aspects: (a) right understanding of revelation (and this is a private matter), (b) works of righteousness and mercy (subject to approval by mankind, esp. authorities); all controversy about religious faith and practice is wrong. See also *Diggers.*

Levertoff, Paul (1878–1954). B. White Russ.; Jew trained in Hasidism* and Cabala*; Christian 1895; taught in Institutum* Judaicum Delitzschianum 1911–19; dir. East London Fund for the Jews 1922–54; tried to est. Jewish branch of universal ch. in which Christian faith would be expressed in Jewish forms.

Levi ben Gershon (Gerson[ides]; Leo de Bagnolas; Maestro Leon; Leo Hebraeus; called Ralbag from the initials of "rabbi" and of his name [though he may not have been a rabbi]; ca. 1288–ca. 1344). B. Bagnols, Languedoc, Fr.; Jewish Bible commentator, astronomer, mathematician, Aristotelian philos.; held that that part of the soul which contains the sum of exalted thoughts is immortal; God knows things in gen. but not in particular. Works include *Milhamot Adonai* ("Wars of the Lord"); commentaries on Bible and Talmud; treatises on astronomy and trigonometry.

Levirate Marriage. OT requirement under which the widow of a man without male descendants marry her husband's brother; the 1st son of this union was reckoned as the son of the deceased (Dt 25:5-10). Under other circumstances Lv 18:16 and 20:21 applied.

Levita, Elijah (Elias; Elijah ben Asher ha-Levi; also called Ashkenazi ["the German"], Bachur, or Bahur ["the youth" or "student"], and Tishbi; ca. 1469–1549). B. Neustadt an der Aisch, Middle Franconia, W Bav., near Nürnberg and Erlangen, Ger.; Jewish scholar; active esp. in Padua, Venice, and Rome, It.; proved post-talmudic origin of Heb. vowel points; teacher of J. Eck*; collaborator of P. Fagius.* Works include *Sefer ha-bahur; Tishbi* (a talmudic lexicon); *Massoret ha-massoret.*

Levitical Degrees. See *Prohibited Degrees.*

Levshin, Peter. See *Platon.*

Lévy-Bruhl, Lucien (1857–1939). Comtian philos.; b. Paris, Fr.; educ. Paris; prof. Paris; investigated primitive mentality of non-literate peoples. See also *Primitive Religion.*

Lewis, Clive Staples (1898–1963). B. Belfast, N. Ireland; educ. Oxford; in military in WW I; classical scholar Oxford; fellow and tutor Oxford 1925–54; prof. Medieval and Renaissance English at Cambridge 1954–63. Works include *The Screwtape Letters; The Problem of Pain; Mere Christianity; The Last Battle; Poems; Studies in Words; Of Other Worlds: Essays and Stories.*

Lex naturalis. See *Natural Law.*

Lex talionis. OT law that punishment should be the same in kind as the offense (Ex 21:23-25).

Lexicons. A. *Old Testament.* Earliest known Heb. lexicon is *Agron* (or *Egron;* from Heb. *agar,* "to collect"), now lost, of Saadia(h)* ben Joseph. *Mahbereth,* compiled by Menahem ben Saruk (ca. 910–ca. 970; Sp. Jew) is a complete lexicon. Rabbi Jonah's* *Sepher ha-dikduk* ("Book of Grammar") includes enterprising use of Arab. and Talmudic materials and an alphabetic list of Heb. roots. 17th c. Christian scholars include Valentin Schindler (d. 1604 [1610?]; b. Meissen, Ger.; prof. Wittenberg and Helmstedt), J. Hottinger,* and Edmund Castell (1606–85; b. Cambridgeshire, Eng.; educ. Cambridge; prof. Cambridge 1667). H. F. W. Gesenius'* *Hebräisch-Deutsches Handwörterbuch über die Schriften des Alten Testaments* appeared 1810–12; its "ed. altera," *Thesaurus philologicus criticus linguae Hebraeae et Chaldaeae veteris testamenti,* became a standard reference work. *Neues hebräisch-deutsches Handwörterbuch über das Alte Testament* mit *Einschluss des biblischen Chaldäismus: Ein Auszug aus dem grösseren Werke* [of 1810–12] appeared 1815; its 17th ed., prepared by F. P. W. Buhl,* appeared 1921 under the title *Wilhelm Gesenius' hebräisches und aramäisches Handwörterbuch über das Alte Testament.* The 1st Eng. tr. of Gesenius' *Handwörterbuch:* C. Leo, *A Hebrew Lexicon to the Books of the Old Testament* (1825–28). S. P. Tregelles,* *Gesenius' Hebrew and Chaldee Lexicon to the Old Testament Scriptures, Translated with Additions and Corrections from the Author's Thesaurus and Other Works,* designed to combat rationalistic and neologistic tendencies, appeared London 1847. E. Robinson,* *A Hebrew and English Lexicon of the Old Testament, including the Biblical Chaldee,* tr. of Gesenius' 1833 *Lexicon manuale Hebraeicum et Chaldaeicum in Veteris Testamenti libros,* became basis of *A Hebrew and English Lexicon of the Old Testament* (Part I 1891; complete ed. 1907), ed. F. Brown,* S. R. Driver,* and C. A. Briggs.* L. H. Köhler* and Walter Baumgartner (b. 1887), *Lexicon in Veteris Testamenti libros,* appeared 1948–53, suppl. 1958; 3d ed., W. Baumgartner et al., *Hebräisches und aramäisches Lexikon zum Alten Testament* (197–). See also *Pagninus, Santes.*

B. *New Testament.* Vol. 1 of the Complutensian Polyglot (see *Polyglot Bibles*) includes a rudimentary Gk.-Lat. glossary of words of the NT, Ecclus, and Wis. M. Flacius* Illyricus issued *Clavis scripturae s. seu de sermone sacrarum literarum* 1567. G. Pasor's* *Lexicon* appeared 1619. Modern NT lexicography begins with C. A. Wahl,* *Clavis Novi Testamenti philologica* (1822), superseded 1840–41 by C. G. Wilke,* *Clavis Novi Testamenti philologica,* which K. L. W. Grimm* ed. and reissued beginning 1862 and called *Lexicon graeco-latinum in libros Novi Testamenti* beginning 1868. J. H. Thayer's* 1886 Eng. tr. of Wilke-Grimm's 2d ed. (1879) added material reflecting new emphasis on etymology. Thayer's 1889 corrected ed. became a standard tool. Papyri discoveries stimulated fresh lexicographical studies. E. F. W. F. Preuschen,* *Vollständiges Griechisch-Deutsches Handwörterbuch zu den Schriften des Neuen Testaments und der übrigen urchristlichen Literatur* (1910), was thoroughly revised by W. Bauer* (5th ed. 1963). Bauer's 4th ed. (1952) was tr. with modifications by W. F. Arndt* and Felix Wilbur Gingrich (b. 1901 Annville, Pa.; educ. Lafayette Coll., Easton, Pa., and U. of Chicago; prof. Albright Coll., Reading, Pa.; mem. The Ev. United Brethren Ch.) and appeared 1957 as *A Greek-English Lexicon of the New Testament and Other Early Christian Literature.* J. H. Moulton* and G. Milligan,* *The Vocabulary of the Greek Testament Illustrated from the Papyri and Other Non-Literary Sources* (1914–29; 1-vol. ed. 1930) offers a fascinating picture of life in NT times. A. H. Cremer,* *Biblisch-theologisches Wörterbuch der neutestamentlichen Gräcität* (1868; tr. W. Urwick from the latest Ger. ed., *Biblico-Theological Lexicon of New Testament Greek,* 4th Eng. ed., with supplement, 1895), rev. J. Kögel* (11th ed. 1923), is basis of *Theologisches Wörterbuch zum Neuen Testament;* the latter work, first ed. by G. Kittel,* then Gerhard Friedrich (b. 1908 Jodszen, E Prussia; prof. Kiel 1953, Erlangen 1954), is useful for its discussion of selected words with theol. significance and for its extensive reference to Heb., LXX, and classical usage; some articles have appeared in *Bible Key Words* (1949–; various editors and translators); an unabridged Eng. version, *Theological Dictionary of the New Testament,* ed. and tr. G. W. Bromiley, is in progress since 1964.

Beginners in NT Gk. will benefit from Bruce Manning Metzger (Presb. cleric and educator; b. 1914 Middletown, Pa.; educ. Lebanon Valley Coll., Annville, Pa., and Princeton [N. J.] Theol. Sem.; prof. Princeton Theol. Sem.), *Lexical Aids for Students of New Testament Greek* (1946; new ed. 1969).

See also *Encyclopedias and Dictionaries; Grammars.*

F. W. Danker, *Multipurpose Tools for Bible Study,* 3d ed. (St. Louis, Mo., 1970), pp. 97–132. FWD

Leyser, Polykarp (Leiser; Lyser; Polycarp[us]; 1552–1610). The Elder; father of P. Leyser* the Younger; Luth. theol.; b. Winnenden, Württemberg, Ger.; pastor Göllersdorf (Gellersdorf), NE Lower Austria, 1573; prof. and gen. supt. Wittenberg 1577–87; helped restore sound Lutheranism in Wittenberg after 1st stage of Crypto-Calvinistic* Controversy; coadjutor and supt. Brunswick 1587–93; court preacher Dresden 1594. Ed. M. Chemnitz,* *Loci theologici.* See also *Harmony of the Gospels,* 1.

Leyser, Polykarp (Leiser; Lyser; Polycarp[us]; 1586–1633). The Younger; son of P. Leyser* the Elder; b. Wittenberg, Ger.; prof. Wittenberg and Leipzig. Works include *Disputationes theologicae de aeterna Dei electione credentium et reprobatione incredulorum;* commentaries on Gl, AC, and FC.

Lhotzky, Heinrich (1859–1930). Theol. and philos.; b. Klausnitz (Claussnitz), Saxony, Ger.; studied under F. Delitzsch (see *Delitzsch,* 1); pastor of Ger. colonists in Bessarabia 1888. Works include *Das Buch der Ehe; Die Seele deines Kindes* (tr. A. Barwell, *The Soul of Your Child*). See also *Müller, Johannes.*

Libanius (Libanios; 314–ca. 393 [or 404?]). Gk. Sophist; b. Antioch, Syria; educ. Athens; head Antioch rhetoric school ca. 354; students included J. Chrysostom,* Amphilochius,* and perhaps the Cappadocian* theologians; tried to reest. Gk. culture; opposed Christianity. Works include orations; life of Demosthenes.

Libellatici. See *Lapsi.*

Liber censuum. Official RC register drawn up 1192 by Cencio Savelli (b. Rome, It.; pope Honorius III 1216–27); recorded dues payable by various institutions to Roman see.

Liber pontificalis (Lat. "book of popes"). Collection of lives of popes from Peter to Pius II (see *Popes,* 15); its origin traced to 6th or 7th c.; continued by various hands to 886; then continued by catalog of popes to the time of Gregory VII (see *Popes,* 7), when biographies were resumed.

L. Duchesne, *Le Liber pontificalis: Texte, introduction et commentaire,* 2 vols. (Paris, 1886, 1892); T. Mommsen, *Gesta pontificum romanorum* (Berlin, 1898).

Liberal Arts, Seven. See *Quadrivium; Trivium.*

Liberal Catholic Church. Formed ca. 1916–18 by theosophist mems. of the Old* Cath. Ch. in Gt. Brit.; Charles Webster Leadbeater (1847–1934) was consecrated bp. 1916 by an Old Cath. bp. Holds that there are various paths to truth; claims apostolic succession through Old Caths. and has 7 sacraments: baptism, confirmation, eucharist, absolution, unction, matrimony, orders. Am. branch est. 1917.

Liberal Evangelicalism. View held by some in Ch. of Eng. who try to restate classic doctrines (e. g., atonement) in harmony with modern thought. Promoted by Anglican* Evangelical Group Movement.

"Liberal" Jesus. See *Jesus, Lives of.*

Liberalism. See *Modernism.*

Liberia. See *Africa,* C 7.

Libertines. 1. Mems. of a synagog at Jerusalem who opposed Stephen (Acts 6:9). 2. Antinomian, pantheistic party in the Neth. and Fr. ca. the time of the Reformation. See also *Spirituels.* 3. Perrinists; pol. party in Geneva which, under leadership of Ami Perrin (Amy Pierre; d. 1561; condemned to death 1554; fled to Berne), opposed moral reforms of J. Calvin.* 4. Those who indulge appetites without restraint. 5. Disparaging term for freethinkers, usually religious.

Liberty, Religious. See *Church and State.*

Liberty of Conscience. See *Baptist Churches,* 1, 2.

Libido. See *Lust; Psychology,* J 7.

Libri Carolini. See *Caroline Books.*

Libya. See *Africa,* D 1.

Licentiate. One licensed to practice a profession. In early Luth. chs. in Am., e. g., many candidates were licensed for interim service before ordination (see *Ministerial Office,* I 5).

Lichtenberg, Karl Wilhelm Franz (1816–83). B. Hanover, Ger.; pres. Hannoverian Consistory; est. syn. form of ch. govt.; furthered missions; introd. new hymnal.

Lichtenberger, Frédéric Auguste (Friedrich August; 1832–99). B. Strasbourg, Fr.; educ. Strasbourg and various Ger. univs.; Prot. prof. systematic and practical theol. Strasbourg 1864–70; first orthodox, later liberal; to Paris after Franco-Ger. war of 1870–71; cofounder theol. faculty Paris 1877; active in S. S. movement. Ed. *Encyclopédie des sciences religieuses;* other works include *Histoire des idées religieuses en Allemagne* (tr. and ed. W. Hastie, *History of German Theology in the nineteenth century*).

Lichtenstein, Friedrich Wilhelm Jacob (1826–75). B. Munich, Ger.; son of a Jew; Luth. 1842; educ. Erlangen and Halle; pastor Pegnitz 1856, Kulmbach 1863. Wrote *Lebensgeschichte des Herrn Jesu Christi in chronologischer Uebersicht.*

Lichtfreunde (Ger. "friends of light"). Popular name of Protestantische Freunde, organized 1841 at Gnadau, Ger., by liberal theologians; gained support of many schoolteachers; objective: to defend the Enlightenment.*

Licinius (Valerius Licinianus Licinius; ca. 270–325 AD). Roman emp. 308–324; b. Dacia; made Augustus in E 308 by Galerius (see *Persecutions of Christians,* 4); sole E emp. 311; married Constantia, half sister of Constantine* I; issued so-called Edict of Milan* with Constantine I; defeated 324 by Constantine I; executed.

Liddon, Henry Parry (1829–90). High Ch. Angl. theol.; b. N Stoneham, Hampshire, Eng.; educ. Oxford; prof. exegesis Oxford 1870–82, canon St. Paul's, London, 1870–90, chancellor St. Paul's 1886; defended Nicene Christology; opposed *Lux* Mundi.* Works include *The Divinity of Our Lord and Saviour Jesus Christ; Life of Edward Bouverie Pusey.*

Lidenius, John Abraham (Johan[n]; b. 1714 or '15; d. ca. 1765). B. near Raccoon Creek (a river and settlement), N. J.; to Swed. ca. 1724 with his father, who had come from Swed. 1712; educ. and ordained Swed.; returned to US 1751; pastor Raccoon Creek (later called Swedesboro) and Pennsneck (later called Pennsville) 1756–62.

Lidgett, John Scott (1854–1953). Meth. divine; b. Lewisham, London, Eng.; est. a settlement (see *Settlements*) of cultured people 1891–92 in Bermondsey, S London, to help underprivileged by friendship, cooperation, and educ.; 1st pres. newly united Meth. Ch. (see *Methodist Churches,* 1) 1932; advisor of several abps. of Canterbury; influenced by theol. of J. F. D. Maurice.*

Lidman, Jonas. B. Swed.; ordained Skara, SW Swed., 1719; to US 1719 with S. Hesselius (see *Hesselius, Andreas*); pastor Gloria Dei Ch., Wicaco (Philadelphia) 1719–30; provost* (or supt.) ca. 1723; returned to Swed.

Lie. Statement or act made to deceive, often to benefit the deceiver. The Bible condemns lying (Ps 40:4; 62:4; Pr 14:5, 25; 19:5; Is 59:4; Eph 4:25).

Liebenzeller Mission. Organized 1899 in Hamburg, Ger., by H. Coerper* as branch of CIM; moved to Bad Liebenzell, Württemberg, S Ger., ca. 1902; called Liebenzeller Mission since 1906; Am. branch organized 1941 on Schooley's Mountain, N. J.: Mission Home Eben-Ezer (name changed 1951 to Liebenzell Miss. of USA, Inc.); fields included China, Japan, Taiwan, New Guinea, Admiralty Islands, Caroline Islands.

Lieberkühn, Samuel (1710–77). Moravian theol.; b. Berlin, Ger.; educ. Halle and Jena; with Salzburgers to Prussia 1733 (see *Salzburgers, Banishment of*) returned to Jena 1733; worked as Herrnhut miss. among Jews in Holland and Eng. 1739–42. Works include *Geschichte unsers Herrn und Heilandes Jesu Christi; Der Hauptinhalt der Lehre Jesu Christi.*

Liebermann, Bruno Franz Leopold (1759–1844). Jesuit theol.; b. Molsheim, Alsace; head 1st Mainz School of Theol.; forerunner of neo-scholasticism. Works include *Institutiones theologiae.*

Liebich, Ehrenfried (1713–80). B. Probsthain, near Goldberg, Liegnitz, Silesia, Prussia, Ger.; educ. Schweidnitz, Breslau, and Leipzig; pastor Lomnitz and Erdmannsdorf, near Hirschberg. Issued (with J. F. Burg*) Hirschberger* Bibel; hymnist.

Liebich, George Sigismund. See *Canada,* A 5.

Liebner, Karl Theodor Albert (1806–71). Luth. mediating theol. (see *Mediating Theology*); b. Schkölen, near Naumburg, Ger.; educ. Leipzig, Berlin, and the Wittenberg Theol. Sem.; prof. and U. preacher Göttingen 1835; prof. Kiel 1844, Leipzig 1851; court preacher and vice-pres. high consistory of Saxony 1855. Works include *Die christliche Dogmatik aus dem christologischen Princip dargestellt.*

Lietzmann, Hans (1875–1942). Prot. theol.; b. Düsseldorf, Ger.; educ. Jena and Bonn; prof. Jena 1905, Berlin 1924. Ed. *Handbuch zum Neuen Testament; Zeitschrift für die neutestamentliche Wissenschaft und die Kunde der älteren Kirche; Die Bekenntnisschriften der evangelisch-lutherischen Kirche;* other works include *Catenen; Catenenstudien; Apollinaris von Laodicea und seine Schule: Texte und Untersuchungen; Petrus und Paulus in Rom: Liturgische und archäologische Studien; Messe und Herrenmahl; Geschichte der Alten Kirche.*

Life and Advent Union. See *Adventist Bodies,* 8.

Life and Work. Branch of the ecumenical* movement concerned with implications of the Gospel for daily life and work. See also *Christian Socialism,* 5; *Union Movements,* 15.

Ligarius, Johannes (1529–96). Luth. theol.; b. Nesse, Ostfriesland; educ. Wittenberg; pastor Uphusen, Norden, and Wolthusen; helped M. Flacius* Illyricus, C. Spangenberg, et al. est. Lutheranism in Antwerp; army chaplain; pastor Wertherbruch, then in Nesse (1569–77); court preacher Aurich 1577–85; pastor Woerden, Neth., 1586–91. Issued a hymnal and 2 catechisms.

Light and Darkness (symbolic). The Bible uses both terms not only in a physical sense (e.g., Gn 1) but also metaphorically or symbolically. It refers to God as Light, the Source of light, or as dwelling in light (Ps 27:1; 104:2; 1 Ti 6:16; Ja 1:17; 1 Jn 1:5; Rv 21:23). Christ is called "the Light of the world" (Jn 1:4-9; 8:12; 9:5; 12:35-36, 46). The Word of God, esp. the Gospel, is given to man to serve him as a light unto salvation (Ps 119:105, 130; Pr 6:23; Is 8:20; Mt 4:16; 2 Ptr 1:19). All believers are to function as lights in the world (Mt 5:14-16; Lk 16:8; Eph 5:8; Ph 2:15; 1 Th 5:5; 1 Ptr 2:9). "Light" figuratively designates holiness and purity (Pr 6:23; Is 5:20; Ro 13:12), spiritual illumination (2 Co 4:6; Eph 5:14), the heavenly state (Is 60:19-20; Cl 1:12; Rv 21:23; 22:5).

"Darkness" is opposed to "light" (Jn 3:19-21; 12:35-36; Acts 26:18; Eph 5:8), esp. in reference to ignorance and spiritual blindness (Is 9:2; Jn 1:5; 1 Jn 1:6; 2:8), powers of evil (Lk 22:53; Eph 6:12; Cl 1:13; 1 Th 5:5; Rv 16:10), love of sin (Ro 13:12), sphere of evil deeds (Eph 5:11), despair and misery of the lost in hell (Mt 8:12; 22:13; 25:30), sorrow and distress (Jl 2:2). JMW

Lightfoot, John (1602–75). Hebraist; b. Stoke on Trent, Staffordshire, Eng.; educ. Cambridge; vice-chancellor Cambridge U. 1654; prebendary Ely 1668. Works include *Horae hebraicae et talmudicae.*

Lightfoot, Joseph Barber (1828–89). Angl. theol.; b. Liverpool, Lancashire, Eng.; educ. Birmingham and Cambridge; ordained 1858; prof. Cambridge 1861; canon St. Paul's, London, 1871; bp. Durham 1879;

mem. committee for rev. of Eng. NT 1870–80. Ed. *The Apostolic Fathers;* coauthor *The Fourth Gospel;* other works include commentaries on Paul's Epistles.

Liguori, Alfonso Maria de' (Alphonsus Liguori; 1696–1787). RC moralist; b. Marianella, near Naples, It.; priest 1726; bp. Sant' Agata de' Goti 1762–75. Founded Redemptorists*; developed theory of equiprobabilism.* Works include *Theologia moralis; Le Glorie de Maria.*

Liliencron, Rochus von (1820–1912). Luth. scholar and musicologist; b. Plön, E Schleswig-Holstein, N Ger.; educ. Kiel and Berlin; prof. Kiel 1851, Jena 1852; supt. ducal chapel and library, Meiningen, 1855. Coed. *Allgemeine Deutsche Biographie;* other works include *Deutsches Leben im Volkslied um 1530; Über den Chorgesang in der evangelischen Kirche.*

Lilienthal, Theodor Christoph (1717–82). Luth. theol.; b. Königsberg, E Prussia, Ger.; educ. Königsberg, Jena, and Tübingen; prof. and pastor Königsberg. Works include *Die gute Sache der in der heiligen Schrift alten und neuen Testaments enthaltenen Göttlichen Offenbarung.*

Lilje, Hanns. See *Kirchenkampf.*

Limbo (from Lat. *limbus,* "border; hem; fringe"). In RCm, region on border of hell. *Limbus patrum* ("fathers' limbo"): place and/or state of souls of OT saints while they awaited redemption and release by Christ. *Limbus infantum* (*infantium; puerorum;* "infants' limbo; children's limbo"): everlasting place and/or state of unregenerate, unbaptized infants (or children).

Limborch, Philip(pus) van (Philipp von). See *Arminianism.*

Lindberg, Conrad Emil (June 6, 1852—Aug. 2, 1930). B. Jönköping, Swed.; to US 1871; educ. Augustana Coll. and Theol. Sem., Paxton, Ill., and Lutheran Theol. Sem., Philadelphia, Pa.; ord. 1874 Augustana Syn. (see *Augustana Ev. Luth. Ch.*); pastor Philadelphia 1874—80; New York 1880—84. Prof. and dean Augustana Sem., Rock Island, Ill., 1884—1930. Works include *Apologetics; Chr. Dogmatics and Notes on the Hist. of Dogma,* tr. C. E. Hoffsten.

Lindberg, Jakob Christian (Jacob; 1797–1857). B. Ribe (Ripen), Jutland, Den.; follower of N. F. S. Grundtvig*; opposed H. N. Clausen.* Helped est. *Theologisk maanedsskrift.*

Lindemann, Friedrich (Frederick; Jan. 12, 1851–Dec. 13, 1907). Son of J. C. W. Lindemann*; b. Baltimore, Md.; educ. Conc. Sem., St. Louis, Mo. Pastor Decorah, Iowa, 1874; Champaign, Ill., 1875; Pittsburgh, Pa., 1878; Boston, Mass., 1885; Fort Wayne, Ind., 1890. Prof. Ev. Luth. Teachers Sem., Addison, Ill., 1893–1907. Works include *Was sagen die Worte?* (Eng. tr. *Scholia*).

Lindemann, Johann Christoph Wilhelm (Jan. 6, 1827–Jan. 15, 1879). Father of F. Lindemann*; b. Göttingen, Hannover, Ger.; educ. privately and at the Hanover teachers' sem.; to US 1848; teacher Baltimore, Md., 1848; studied theol. at the Luth. Sem. in Fort Wayne, Ind., 1852–53; asst. to H. C. Schwan* in Cleveland, Ohio, 1853; later pastor Trin. Luth. Ch., Cleveland; pres. Ev. Luth. Teachers Sem., Addison, Ill., 1864–79. Coed. *Evangelisch-Lutherisches Schulblatt;* ed. *Amerikanischer Kalender für deutsche Lutheraner* and *Dr. Martin Luther als Erzieher der Jugend.* Other works include *Amerikanisch-Lutherische Schul-Praxis; Evangelisch-Lutherische Katechismus-Milch.*

A. C. Stellhorn, "J. C. W. Lindemann," *CHIQ,* XIV (Oct. 1941), pp. 65–92.

Lindenau, Paul (1489–1544). B. Chemnitz, Ger.; educ. Leipzig; entered Benedictine cloister; left it 1522. Pastor Ehrenfriedersdorf, and then (1523) Zwickau; at Zwickau he helped further Reformation and, for a time, from 1526, with his wife, supervised a Ger. school for girls; resigned 1529. Pastor Werdau, Elsterberg, Neumark, and Auerbach; court preacher Freiberg (1537), where he opposed J. Schen(c)k*; court preacher Dresden; fostered Reformation in Annaberg, Meissen, and Sagan.

Linderholm, Johannes Emanuel (1872–1937). B. Hakarp, Swed.; theologian of *Religionsgeschichtliche* Schule.* Ed. *Religion och kultur;* other works include *Fraan dogmat till evangeliet.*

Lindisfarne. Also called Holy Is.; peninsula (is. at high water) off NE coast of Northumberland, Eng.; miss. center est. there by Aidan,* who arrived there from Iona* 635 AD.

Lindsay. 1. *Thomas Martin* (1843–1914). Father of 2; cleric, ch. hist., and educ.; b. Lesmahagow, Lanark, Scot.; educ. Glasgow and Edinburgh; prof. ch. hist. Free* Ch. of Scot. Coll., Glasgow, 1872; principal United* Free Ch. of Scot. Coll., Glasgow, 1902. Works include *Luther and The German Reformation; A History of the Reformation; The Church and the Ministry in the Early Centuries.*

2. *Alexander* (1879–1952). Son of 1; Master of Balliol Coll., Oxford, 1924–49. Wrote on personal, soc., pol. ethics.

Lindsey, Theophilus (1723–1808). B. Middlewich, Cheshire, Eng.; educ. Leeds and Cambridge; vicar Catterick; favored latitudinarianism (see *Latitudinarians*); friend of J. Priestley*; participated in petition to Parliament against subscription to Thirty-nine Articles (see *Anglican Confessions,* 6); Unitarian (see *Unitarianism*) 1773/74. Works include *An Historical View of the State of the Unitarian Doctrine and Worship from the Reformation to Our Own Times.*

Lingard, John (1771–1851). RC hist. Works include *A History of England, from the First Invasion by the Romans* (to 1688); *A New Version of the Four Gospels.*

Link, Georg (Mar. 19, 1829–Sept. 21, 1908). B. Thalmessing, Bav.; educ. Luth. Sem. at Fort Wayne, Ind.; excellent preacher. Pastor Neu-Bielefeld (Black Jack), St. Louis Co., Mo., 1851; Pleasant Ridge, Madison Co., Ill., 1856; Lebanon, near Watertown, Wis., 1860; St. Louis, Mo., 1873. Compiled *Luthers Tägliche Hausandacht;* other works include sermons.

Link, John Thomas (Nov. 23, 1873–Dec. 20, 1936). B. Chicago, Ill.; educ. Ev. Luth. Teachers Sem., Addison, Ill.; teacher St. John Luth. School, Decatur, Ill., 1895; prof. Conc. Teachers Coll., Seward, Nebr., 1908. Works include *Outlines in Geography; A Short Course in Physiology; Origin of the Place Names of Nebraska.*

Link, Wenzeslaus (Wenceslaus; Wentzeslaus; Wenzel, Vincilaus; Linck; 1483–1547). B. Colditz, near Leipzig, Saxony, Ger.; educ. Leipzig and Wittenberg; Augustinian at Waldheim; to Wittenberg perhaps ca. 1503; dean Wittenberg faculty 1512; preacher Nürnberg 1517; zealous friend of M. Luther*; succeeded J. v. Staupitz* 1520 as vicar-gen. of Ger. Augustinians; hymnist.

Linsenmann, Franz Xaver von (1835–98). RC theol.; b. Rottweil, Ger.; prof. moral and pastoral theol. Tübingen 1867; elected bp. Rottenburg 1898; emphasized freedom of children of God. Works include *Der ethische Charakter der Lehre Meister Eckhardt's; Lehrbuch der Moraltheologie.*

Lintner, George Ames (Lintener; Feb. 15, 1796–Dec. 21, 1871). B. Minden, Montgomery Co., N. Y., educ. Union Coll. (of The Dutch Ref. Ch. in N Am. (see *Reformed Churches,* 4 b), Schenectady, N. Y.; licensed 1818, ordained 1819, Ministerium of N. Y.; pastor Schoharie and Cobleskill (one parish), N. Y., 1819; helped organize Hartwick* Syn.; its pres. 1830; pres. Gen. Syn. 1841. Ed. *The Lutheran Magazine;* issued a liturgy.

Linus (d. ca. 79 AD). In RC lists, successor of Peter

as pope (bp. Rome) perhaps ca. 67–ca. 79.

Linzner, Georg (fl. ca. 1680). B. Kamenz, Saxony, Ger.; private teacher Breslau ca. 1680. Hymnist: "Meinen Jesum lass' ich nicht, denn er ist allein mein Leben."

Lioba (Leoba; Leobgyth[a]; Leobgyta; Truthgeba; ca. 710–ca. 782). B. Wessex, Eng.; to Ger. to help Boniface,* to whom she was related; ca. 735 abbess Tauberbischofsheim, which became center for training women missionaries.

Lion. In Christian symbolism,* type of God's redemption of His people (cf. Dn 6); also symbol of Mark (cf. Eze 1:10; Rv 4:7).

Lipit-Ishtar (Lipiteshtar). See *Law Codes,* 1.

Lippi, Fra Filippo (Lippo; Filippo del Carmine; ca. 1406–69). Painter; b. Florence, It.; Carmelite ca. 1421; released from vows ca. 1461. Works include frescoes and canvases portraying many religious subjects.

Lippomano, Luigi. See *Counter Reformation,* 4.

Lipsius, Richard Adelbert (1830–92). Prot. theol.; b. Gera, Thuringia, Ger.; educ. Leipzig; taught at Leipzig 1855, Vienna 1861, Kiel 1865; prof. systematic theol. Jena 1871; tried to create speculative theol. which rejected both old orthodoxy and Ritschlianism (see *Ritschl, Albrecht*); moved toward idealism* of I. Kant*; held that "Christian principle" existed in Christ. Wrote on early Christian apocryphal literature; other works include commentaries on Ro, Gl, and Ph; *Lehrbuch der evangelisch-protestantischen Dogmatik; Philosophie und Religion.*

Liquor. See *Alcoholism; Intemperance; Temperance Movements and the Lutheran Church.*

Liscow, Salomo (Lischkow; Liscovius; 1640–89). B. Niemitsch, near Guben (or Gubin), Lower Lusatia, Ger.; educ. Leipzig and Wittenberg; pastor Otterwisch, near Grimma and Bad Lausick (or Lausigk) 1644; Diakonus (2d pastor) Wurzen 1685; hymnist. Hymns include "Nun freue dich, o Christenheit"; "O Jesu, treuer Hirte"; "Schatz über alle Schätze"; "Bedenke, Mensch, das Ende."

Lismanini, Franz (d. ca. 1566). B. Corfu; educ. It.; Franciscan provincial in Krakow, Poland; court preacher of Polish Queen Bona Sforza (1493–1557; m. Polish King Sigismund 1518) 1546; won for Protestantism by writings of J. Calvin* and Bohemian* Brethren; to Geneva 1553; became Calvinist; served ch. in SE Poland; helped draw it closer to Calvinism; rejected error of F. Stancarus*; accused of Arianism.*

Lismore, The Book of. Collection of lives of Irish saints; found at Lismore, Scot., 1814.

Liszt, Franz (1811–86). Piano virtuoso, conductor, composer; b. Raiding (Dobotjan), near Sopron, Sopron Co., W Hung.; Franciscan 1865. Works include oratorios "Die Legende von der heiligen Elisabeth" and "Christus"; masses.

Litany (Gk. *litaneia,* Lat. *litania,* "entreaty; supplication"). Liturgical prayer consisting of petitions and supplications spoken or sung, usually alternately, by worship leader and cong. OT background in such passages as Ps 136. 1st NT use traced to early ch.

Literal Interpretation. See *Exegesis,* 4–5.

Literary Criticism. See *Higher Criticism; Isagogics; Literature and Theology.*

Literature, Lutheran. 1. The Luth. Reformation* began as a literary movement, to capitalize on the invention of printing. M. Luther* was the most widely read publicist of his time (see *Luther, Chief Writings of*). His Bible tr. standardized the Ger. language for centuries. The Luth. movement stirred all levels of literature esp. in Ger. and Scand. It produced works for professionals and for the common people.

2. Luther's style was concrete and idiomatic. His preaching was in the tradition of late 15th c. folk preachers, his polemic in the manner of satire current at that time.

3. Some outstanding Ger. literary figures were sons of Luth. pastors. But the influence of popular Luth. literature reached out into the masses. Luther's SC and selected Bible stories formed Ger. and Scand. primers. Standard devotional vols. were the average household library's nucleus. They included prayer books (some large and used for many occasions in family and community life), a hymnal, used for daily and Sun. worship, postils (see *Postil*) beginning with Luther's, and devotional material written for family use. Beginning in the 17th c., romances with religious content competed for the reading interest of Christian families. In the 19th c., family magazines with religious emphases were developed in Eur. and Am. They often provided pol. comment, fiction, devotional material, and features of gen. interest. With the beginning of special activity in missions and charity fostered by Pietism,* popular books and magazines tried to stimulate interest in and support for these projects.

4. Since Luther's time the chief religious vernacular literature to achieve a high degree of excellence has been the hymn (see *Hymnody, Christian*). Vernacular worship helped make this possible.

5. The Luth. Ch. has always been aggressive in publishing professional literature. 16th c. doctrinal controversies climaxing in the Confessions (see *Lutheran Confessions*) produced many doctrinal, exegetic, and polemic writings. In keeping with the humanist emphasis, early literature was predominantly Latin. Ger. and Scand. univs. provided more and more technical material. Orthodoxy (see *Lutheran Theology After 1580*), Pietism,* Rationalism,* Enlightenment,* and various 19th c. trends produced much exposition, propaganda, and debate. Beginning in the late 18th c., technical journals provided special studies, usually pub. under auspices of theol. faculties.

6. By the middle of the 20th c., theol. literature of Scand. influenced the theol. of Luths. and many other chs.

7. Since the middle of the 19th c. a literature of critical review and restudy of Luth. origins has emerged, stimulated by critical eds. of works of the reformers and scientific hist. studies and resulting in heightened appreciation of the Luth. Reformation (see *Luther Renaissance; Luther, Works of, Editions of*) extending also through Ref. circles. Stress and questions connected with 20th c. wars and their aftermath led to further reexamination of Luth. thought. RRC

Literature and Theology. Literature of the day is of concern to a Christian theologian. M. Luther*: "I am persuaded that without knowledge of literature pure theology cannot at all endure, just as heretofore, when letters have declined and lain prostrate, it [theology] too has very wretchedly fallen and lain prostrate; on the other hand, I see that there has never been a great revelation of the Word of God unless He has first prepared the way by the rise and flowering of languages and letters, as though they were forerunner [John the] Baptists. . . . Certainly it is my desire that there be as many poets and rhetoricians as possible, because I see that by these studies, as by no other means, people are wonderfully fitted for grasping sacred truth and for handling it skillfully and effectively. . . . Therefore I beg you that at my request (if that has any weight) you will urge your young people to study poetry and rhetoric diligently" (cf. WA-Br 3, 50).

Many problems arise as a Christian examines a work of literary artistry. The author's intention and the work's integrity must be considered. A critic must beware of the "heresy of paraphrase" and observe the rules of literary criticism. The besetting question is when, if at all, a statement of Christian "judgment" should be made on the *Weltanschauung* of an artist or of his protagonists.

Major concerns involved include the inherent quality of the work itself. In contrast to most contemporary writing, which only mirrors life as some authors see it, are those works which some call "great." For purposes of analysis, "great" literature is sometimes regarded as that which honestly comes to grips with man's existential problems (see *Existentialism*) and which, if written by a Christian, does not ignore tension and struggle in the life of one who is both saint and sinner (Lat. *simul justus et peccator*).

Literature dealing with man's ultimate destiny and responsibility to the Creator is sometimes called religious writing. It may be held that though the question of a God is raised and His existence *denied*, an author's coping with the issue makes his writing "religious." Some authors hold that they need not deal with man's responsibility to any being extrinsic to his world.

Much ostensibly Christian writing is not great, and in a sense not "religious" or "Christian," because it does not come to grips with life; some of it depicts an unreal, saccharine world.

Another issue is the question whether a theol. can be a writer, and vice versa. A theol. may be tempted to sit in judgment on literature and be inclined to be didactic. But some hold that the more veiled a literary work is, the "greater" it is.

Those who feel constrained to make a Christian judgment on literature raise such questions as whether man's problems are seen in relation to his Creator and whether evil and guilt are simply seen as "the state of us all" or an adequate picture is drawn of personal guilt and of one's radical, individual rebellion against God. Others hold that though some writers do not do justice to ethical questions, they may perform a service in grappling with the question of existence itself. An increasing number of students of the interrelationship of literature and theol. hold that Christ-man (one who claims assoc. with Christ) must begin his dialogue with pagan man in the realm of the ontological and ethical.

Despite disagreement as to meaning, such terms as "truths," "values," "law-affirmations," and "Biblical insights" are often used in discussing "great" writing. At what point an author's statements on the nature of man and his condition become "Christian" truths is debatable; but Christian ideas and insights may appear in works of one who is not a professed Christian.

Another concern is that of a possible "Christ-figure" (character with qualities of Christ) in an author's work and the concomitant need to distinguish bet. imitation of Christ and substitution for Him, bet. reflection of Christ-like qualities and replacement of the need for Christ and His work, bet. a follower of Christ and a substitute for Him.

Theologians are increasingly interested in contemporary writing. More and more literature is being viewed as a "prophetic voice," a "handwriting on the wall," indicating what our culture is and may become. Besides gaining rich insights into internal struggles of man, Christians have also seen enlightening images of themselves in writings of perceptive contemporary authors, esp. in depictions of the Old Adam plaguing the Christian in this life. Many hold that lack of a full portrayal of the "new man" (Eph 4:24; Cl 3:10) drives one back to the Christ of the Gospels where one finds the true Christ-figure, who is at once the person like whom man is to be, and in whom one finds the power to *become* Christian man. DLD

E. Fuller, *Man in Modern Fiction* (New York, 1949); R. M. Frye, *Perspective on Man: Literature and the Christian Tradition* (Philadelphia, 1961); R. W. B. Lewis, *The Picaresque Saint: Representative Figures in Contemporary Fiction* (Philadelphia, 1958); N. A. Scott Jr., *Modern Literature and the Religious Frontier* (New York, 1958); R. Stewart, *American Literature & Christian Doctrine* (Baton Rouge, La., 1958).

Lithuania. 1. *Christianity before Reformation.* Grand Duke Mindaugas (crowned king 1253; d. 1263), his family, and many of his people were bap. RC 1251. Jagela (Jagello; Jagiello; Jogaila; ca. 1350–1434; Grand Duke; bap. RC Feb. 15, 1386; m. Jadwiga [Ger.: Hedwig (von Anjou) 1370(1374?)–99; queen Poland 1384–99] Feb. 18, 1386) was crowned king of Poland (including Lith. and Ruthenia) Mar. 4, 1386, as Ladislas II (or V; Ladislaus; Vladislav; Wladislaus; Wladislaw; Wladyslaw). Many other Lithuanians became Christian 1387. Christianization of the country continued under RC influence.

2. *Reformation and subsequent history.* During the Reformation nearly all Lith. became Protestant. Ev. ideas penetrated the country from Prussia, Poland, Czechoslovakia, and Switzerland. Among those who helped the ev. cause: Abraomas (Abraham) Kulvietis (ca. 1510–45; 1st rector of academy at Vilnius) and Martynas Mazvydas (Martin[as] Mosvidius; issued SC 1547). The 1st Lith. Bible tr. (by Jonas Bretkunas; 1536–1602) remained unpub. The NT was pub. 1701, the whole Bible 1735. In Königsberg (in Prussia; later called Kaliningrad) a sem. for training Lith. Luth. pastors was est.

Jesuits carried the Counter* Reformation to Lith. in the 2d half of the 16th c. and recaptured most of the Prots. for RCm. Princes, nobles, and the small minority under their influence remained Prot.

Lith. came under Russ. control in the 2d and 3d partition of Poland (1793, 1795). The Congress of Vienna recognized the Czar as Grand Duke of Lith. and King of Poland. After the unsuccessful Polish revolution of 1863–64 Russification was extended to every aspect of pub. life, including worship. RCs were persecuted.

The *Lietuvos taryba* (Council of Lith.) renounced all previous foreign ties and proclaimed independence 1918. A brief Russ. occupation was followed 1919–23 by an extensive border dispute with Poland. In 1925 a Prot. theol. faculty was est. in Kaunas; it functioned till 1936. The liturgy of Liths. is that used by E Prussian and Baltic Luths.

The 1st Prot. Conf. of Liths. in exile after WW II met at Hanau, Ger., May 30, 1946. The 1st Lith. Prot. Syn. for W. Ger. met at Lebenstedt, near Brunswick, Nov. 10, 1946, and elected a Lith. Ev. Ch. Council. Since 1948 the Lith. Luth. Ch. Council and the Ref. Ch. of Lith. have maintained a brotherly but separate existence. The Lith. Ev. Luth. Ch. in Exile is a mem. of LWF. It published *Tiesos Balsas* ("The Voice of Truth"), *Evangeliku Kelias* ("The Evangelical Way"), and *Sandora* ("Unity"). HOK

See also *Lutheran Confessions,* A 5.

C. R. Jurgela, *History of the Lithuanian Nation* (New York, 1948); F. W. Pick, *The Baltic Nations* (London, 1945).

Lithuanian National Catholic Church. Organized Scranton, Pa., 1914, under guidance of Francis Hodur, bp. Polish Nat. Cath. Ch., with which it is connected since ca. the early 1960s.

Litterae apostolicae sub plumbo. See *Bull.*

Litterae annuae. See *Aquaviva, Claudio.*

Little Canon. See *Offertory.*

Little Sisters of the Poor, Congregation of the. See *Sisterhoods.*

Littmann, Enno (1875–1958). Semitist; b. Oldenburg, Ger.; prof. Strasbourg, Göttingen, Bonn, Tübingen; participated in archaeological expeditions to Syria and Abyssinia. Works include *Geschichte der äthiopischen Litteratur; Semitic Inscriptions; Morgenländische Wörter im Deutschen.*

Liturgics (from Gk. *leitourgia,* "pub. service; divine service"). Study of liturgy, i. e., of the hist. and practice of pub. worship.* "Liturgy" in a narrow sense denotes the order of service for celebration of Communion. In a wider sense the term denotes the whole system of formal worship.

Types of worship distinguished in the NT: (1) Jerusalem type (Acts 2:42, 46; 5:42; 6:2-4; preserved certain Jewish forms; added Christian features); (2) Gentile-Christian type (Acts 20:7; 1 Co 16:2; emphasized Lord's Day and Eucharist; developed esp. in Asia Minor and Corinth). For elements of worship cf. Cl 3:16; 1 Ti 2:1. The agape (see *Agape,* 2) usually preceded the Eucharist.

2d c. writings show a connection bet. the service of the Word and the Eucharistic service. The former included readings from the OT and the gospels, homily, common prayers, kiss* of peace. The Eucharistic service included a prayer of thanksgiving and consecration (including words of institution). The liturgy was essentially congregational and included spontaneous responses. The agape and prophecy disappeared. At the beginning of the 3d c. a formal ritual pattern for the Eucharist was recognized.

E liturgies, marked by objectivity and repetition, are of 2 main types: Syrian and Egyptian. Egyptian includes Coptic and Abyssinian. Syrian (Antiochene) includes W Syrian (Antioch and Jerusalem), E Syrian (Persia and Mesopotamia), and Cappadocian-Byzantine (Armenian and Byzantine). The Byzantine rite became the rite of Eastern* Orthodox Chs.

In the W, Rome (esp. under Gregory I [see *Popes,* 4]) and Carthage developed a liturgy called Roman. Another form, called Gallican and influenced by E liturgies, developed in Sp., Fr., Ger., Brit., Swed., and elsewhere. The Roman, marked by simplicity and strength, finally prevailed in the W.

In the Middle Ages the Eucharist became the most important part of worship as it came to be regarded as a sacrifice rather than a sacrament (see also *Mass,* 4).

M. Luther* stressed the importance of the Word in the service 1516 (WA 1, 444–445). *Von Ordnung Gottesdiensts in der Gemeine* (WA 12, 31–37), issued 1523, criticized the silencing of God's Word, unscriptural material, the idea that a service is a meritorious work. On *Formula missae* 1523 and *Deutsche Messe* 1526 see *Luther, Liturgies of.*

16th c. Luth. liturgies have been classified as Saxo-Luth. (to which Luther's belonged), ultraconservative, and mediating or radical.

The Thirty* Years' War, Pietism,* and rationalism* affected liturgical development adversely. Frederick* William III, C. F. v. Böckh,* and J. K. W. Löhe* worked for a return to hist. types of liturgies.

The 1st Am. Luth. liturgy of note was prepared by H. M. Mühlenberg,* P. Brunnholtz,* and J. F. Handschuh* and adopted 1748 by the Pa. Ministerium. It was in gen. the hist. Luth. liturgy.

By the 1780s liturgical decline had begun, largely as a result of close relation bet. Luths. and Ref. In 1855 the Pa. Ministerium, N. Y. Ministerium, Joint Syn. of Ohio, and The Ev. Luth. Gen. Syn. of the US of N. Am. issued a liturgy which in gen. restored old Luth. forms. The 1868 *Church Book* of the Gen. Council of the Ev. Luth. Ch. in (N.) Am. made further improvements.

Mems. of the Gen. Council, Gen. Syn., and The Ev. Luth. Gen. Syn. S. met 1884 to initiate work toward a "Common Service." Liturgies based on work of a joint committee, which first met 1885, were pub. 1888 by The United* Syn. of the Ev. Luth. Ch. in the S. and the Gen. Syn., 1892 by the Gen. Council. The *Common Service Book of the Lutheran Church,* authorized by the Gen. Syn., the Gen. Council, and the United Syn., appeared 1917, was authorized without delay by the ULC. The *Service Book and Hymnal of the Lutheran Church in America,* authorized by AELC, The ALC, Augustana Ev. Luth. Ch., ELC, Finnish Ev. Luth. Ch. in Am., LFC, UELC, and ULC, appeared 1958.

The Mo. Syn. first used orders of service brought from Ger., adopted the Common Service 1914, approved production of a common service book and hymnal to unify the worship of all Luths. in N. Am. 1971.

J. Calvin* was more conservative than H. Zwingli.* Both greatly modified the hist. liturgy.

The Book* of Common Prayer benefited from Luth. liturgies. Some of its translations were used in liturgies of Am. Luths. EL

See also *Chant; Divine Liturgy; Mark, Liturgy of Saint; Theology; Worship, Orders of; Worship, Parts of.*

L. D. Reed, *The Lutheran Liturgy,* rev. ed. (Philadelphia, [1960]); F. Lochner, *Der Hauptgottesdienst der Evangelisch-Lutherischen Kirche* (St. Louis, 1895); Y. T. Brilioth, *Eucharistic Faith & Practice, Evangelical and Catholic* (London, 1930); G. Dix, *The Shape of the Liturgy* (Westminster, 1945); W. D. Maxwell, *An Outline of Christian Worship: Its Development and Forms* (London, 1936); J. A. Jungmann, *The Mass of the Roman Rite,* tr. F. A. Brunner, 2 vols. (New York, 1951–55); *Liturgy and Worship,* ed. W. K. L. Clarke and C. Harris (New York, 1932); G. Rietschel, *Lehrbuch der Liturgik,* 2d ed. P. Graff (Göttingen, 1951); *Leiturgia,* ed. K. F. Müller and W. Blankenburg (Kassel, 1954–); O. Cullmann, *Early Christian Worship* (Chicago, 1953); A. O. T. Hellerström, *Liturgik* (Stockholm, 1954); L. D. Reed, *Worship* (Philadelphia, 1959); P. H. D. Lang, *Ceremony and Celebration* (St. Louis, 1965). Periodicals and serials: *Monatschrift für Gottesdienst und kirchliche Kunst* (1896–); *Jahrbuch für Liturgiewissenschaft* (1921–); *Liturgiegeschichtliche Quellen* (1918–); *Liturgiegeschichtliche Forschungen* (1918–); *Liturgiewissenschaftliche Quellen und Forschungen* (1928–); *Pro Ecclesia Lutherana* (1933–); *Sursum Corda* (1939–); *Una Sancta* (1940–); *Jahrbuch für Liturgik und Hymnologie* (1955–).

Liturgy. See *Chant; Divine Liturgy; Liturgics; Mark, Liturgy of Saint; Worship, Orders of; Worship, Parts of.*

Liu An. See *Chinese Philosophy,* 5.

Liudger (Ludger; probably ca. 742–809). B. Suecsnon (now Zuilen, on the Vecht, near Utrecht, Frisia) of Christian parentage; pupil of Gregory* of Utrecht and Alcuin*; miss. Neth., Frisia, and Westphalia; 1st bp. Münster, Westphalia, ca. 804; est. monastery of Werden. Works include a life of Gregory of Utrecht.

Liutprand (Liudprand; Luitprand; ca. 922–ca. 972). B. perhaps Pavia, Lombardy, N It.; deacon Pavia; chancellor of Berengar II (d. 966; king of It. 950–961; overthrown by Otto I [912–973; "the Great"; king of Ger. and Holy Roman emp. 936–973; crowned 962]); made bp. Cremona by Otto I 961. Works include *Antapodosis* ("Retribution").

MPL, 136, 769–1180.

Livingston, John Henry (1746–1825). Dutch Ref. cleric and educ.; b. near Poughkeepsie; educ. Yale U. (New Haven, Conn.) and U. of Utrecht, Neth.; pastor NYC 1770; left NYC in Revolution and served chs. at Kingston, Albany, Livingston Manor, Poughkeepsie, and Red Hook; returned to NYC 1783; prof. theol. Gen. Syn. of Dutch Ref. Ch.

1784–1825; pres. Queen's Coll. (now Rutgers U.) 1810–25.

Livingstone, David (Livingston; 1813–73). Scot. miss. and explorer; b. Blantyre, Lanark, Scot.; d. Chitambo's Village, on the Lulimala, in Ilala, N. Rhodesia, Afr.; studied med. and theol. at Glasgow; volunteered to LMS 1838; left Eng. for Bechuanaland, S Afr., Dec. 1840; arrived Cape Town Mar. 14, Kuruman July 31, 1841; traveled 2 yrs.; miss. 9 yrs.; exploration predominated 1852–73; in Eng. 1856–58; severed connection with LMS 1857; Brit. consul 1858. Lost contact with outside world 1868 while exploring cen. Afr.; found Nov. 1871 by Henry Morton Stanley (original name John Rowlands; 1841–1904; b. Denbigh, Wales; adopted name of New Orleans merchant who adopted him; newspaper correspondent from 1865; commissioned 1869 by James Gordon Bennett Jr. [1841–1918; ed. N. Y. *Herald*] to find Livingstone). Buried in Westminster Abbey, London. Works include *Missionary Travels and Researches in South Africa.* See also *Africa,* B 2; *Susi.*

Livingstone Inland Mission. See *Africa,* F 2; *Regions Beyond Missionary Union, The.*

Livingstonia Mission. See *Africa,* B 2.

Livonia. See *Estonia,* 1; *Latvia; Lohmüller, Johann.*

Livonian Knights. See *Estonia,* 1.

Lloyd, Elizabeth Maria. See *Middle East,* C.

Löber, Christian (1683–1747). B. Orlamünde, Thuringia, Ger.; educ. Jena; gen. supt. Altenburg. Contributed to the 1736 ed. *Das Weimarische* Bibelwerk;* other works include *Die Lehre der Wahrheit zur Gottseligkeit, d. i. Theologia positiva, deutsch,* new ed. entitled *Evangelisch-Lutherische Dogmatik,* with preface by C. F. W. Walther.*

Löber, Christoph Heinrich (Oct. 11, 1828–Mar. 18, 1897). Son of G. H. Löber*; b. Eichenberg, near Kahla, Saxe-Altenburg, Ger.; to US 1839 (see *Lutheran Church – Missouri Synod, The,* II 1); educ. Conc. Sem., Altenburg, Mo. Pastor Frohna, Mo., 1850; Thornton (Thornton Station; Coopers Grove), Cook Co., Ill., 1862; Milwaukee, Wis., 1869. Dir. Conc. Coll., Milwaukee, 1885–93. Chaplain Luth. Hosp. and Wartburg Old Folks Home, Brooklyn, N. Y. 1894.

Löber, Gotthold Heinrich (Jan. 5, 1797–Aug. 19, 1849). Father of C. H. Löber*; b. Kahla, Saxe-Altenburg, Ger.; educ. Jena; tutor 1819–24; pastor Eichenberg and Bibra, near Kahla, 1824; to US 1839 (see *Lutheran Church – Missouri Synod, The,* II 1); pastor Altenburg, Mo., and served neighboring congs.; instructor at the Luth. elementary and high school, Altenburg; attended 1846 meetings in St. Louis, Mo., and Fort Wayne, Ind., preliminary to organization of the Mo. Syn.; helped organize Mo. Syn. 1847 as advisory mem. and, with W. Sihler,* was elected examiner.

R. O. Rupprecht, "Gotthold Heinrich Loeber," *CHIQ* (1938), 48–54.

Lobstein, Paul (1850–1922). Prot. theol.; b. Épinal, Fr.; educ. Strasbourg, Tübingen, and Göttingen; prof. Strasbourg; theol. position related to that of E. G. E. Reuss,* L. A. Sabatier,* and A. Ritschl.* Works include *An Introduction to Protestant Dogmatics; The Virgin Birth of Christ.*

Lobwasser, Ambrosius (1515–85). Luth. theol., poet, and educ.; b. Schneeberg, Saxony, E cen. Ger., in the Erzgebirge; educ. Leipzig; lecturer till 1550; tutor 1550–57; court councilor and chancellor Meissen 1557; prof. law Königsberg 1563–80. Works include *Der Psalter dess Königlichen Propheten Davids* (the so-called "Lobwasser Psalter"), a tr. into Ger. which he based on the Ref. Fr. metrical Psalter of C. Marot* and T. Beza* in order to retain the musical settings of C. Goudimel.*

Loccum. See *Molanus, Gerard Walter.*

Lochman, John George (Johann Georg; Dec. 2, 1773–July 10, 1826). B. Philadelphia, Pa.; educ. U. of Pa.; tutored for ministry by J. H. C. Helmuth. Pa. Ministerium pastor Lebanon, Pa., 1794–1815; Harrisburg, Pa., 1815–26. Pres. The Ev. Luth. Gen. Syn. of the US of N. Am. 1821. Works include *The History, Doctrine and Discipline of the Evangelical Lutheran Church; Principles of the Christian Religion.*

C. A. Hay, *Memoirs of Rev. Jacob Goering, Rev. George Lochmann, D. D., and Rev. Benjamin Kurtz, D. D., LL. D.* (Philadelphia, 1887).

Lochner, Friedrich Johann Carl (Sept. 23, 1822–Feb. 14, 1902). B. Nürnberg, Middle Franconia, Bav., Ger.; studied drawing, engraving, and music; failing eyesight and advice of J. K. W. Löhe* prompted him to change career and study for Luth. ministry at Preparatory School in Nürnberg, sem. at Schwabach, and sem. at Neuendettelsau, where he studied liturgical singing under F. E. Hommel*; to Am. 1845. Pastor Salem United Luth. and Ref. Cong., Toledo, Ohio, 1845–46; failed in efforts to have cong. constitute itself a Luth. cong. Served parishes in Madison and Macoupin Cos., Ill., 1846–50; Milwaukee, Wis., 1850–76; pastor Springfield, Ill., and instructor at Conc. Sem. there 1876–87; asst. pastor Trin. Luth. Ch., Milwaukee, 1889. With P. Fleischmann* et al. est. a training school for teachers in Milwaukee 1855; this school later moved to Fort Wayne, Ind., then to Addison, Ill., then to River Forest, Ill. (see *Lutheran Church – Missouri Synod, The,* V 6). Issued *Notwehrblatt* to counteract the influence of J. A. A. Grabau*; other works include *Feste und Gebräuche in der lutherischen und katholischen Kirche; Der Hauptgottesdienst der Evangelisch-Lutherischen Kirche; Liturgie für einen Kinder-Gottesdienst zur Feier der heil. Weihnacht; Liturgische Formulare; Osterbuch; Passionsbuch; Predigten über die Episteln der Sonn- und Festtage des Kirchenjahres nebst ein paar Gelegenheitspredigten.* See also *Detzer, John Adam; Michigan Synod,* 2. FLP

"Friedrich Johann Carl Lochner: An Autobiography," tr. W. Lochner, *CHIQ,* VI (1934), 110–117; O. F. Hattstädt, "The Life and Works of Pastor Frederick Lochner," *CHIQ,* XXI (1949), 166–174.

Lochner, Karl Friedrich (1634–97). B. Nürnberg, Ger.; educ. Breslau, Altdorf, and Rostock; vicar Fürth 1659; pastor Fürth 1663. Hymn "Was gibst du denn, o meine Seele" ascribed to him.

Lochner, Louis (Apr. 7, 1842–Nov. 9, 1909). B. Nürnberg, Ger.; educ. Conc. Sem., St. Louis, Mo.; vicar Milwaukee, Wis., 1864. Pastor Rich, near Matteson, Cook Co., Ill., 1864; Richmond, Va., 1867; Chicago, Ill., 1877. Active promoter of home and for. miss.

Lochner, Martin (Feb. 7, 1883–Feb. 6, 1945). Son of F. J. C. Lochner*; Luth. pastor, educ., organist. B. Springfield, Ill.; educ. Conc. Coll., Milwaukee, Wis., and Conc. Sem., St. Louis, Mo.; prof. Immanuel Coll., Greensboro, N. C., and pastor of a Negro ch. at Meherrin, Va.; prof. Addison (Ill.) Teachers Sem. and Conc. Teachers Coll., River Forest, Ill., 1912–45; taught Eng., Ger., music, hymnology, liturgics; organist 20 yrs. Grace Luth. Ch., River Forest. Ed. music dept. *Lutheran School Journal;* other works include *Handbook for Organists.*

Lochner, Stephan (Lochener; Loechener; formerly misread Loethener; Stephen; Stefan; perhaps ca. 1405/15–1451/52). Ger. painter; b. Meersburg, S Baden, Ger., on Überlinger See, a branch of Lake Constance; active in Cologne 1442–51; combined strong realism with excellent perspective. Works include *Altar of the Patron Saints; Last Judgment; Adoration of the Magi; Presentation in the Temple.*

Loci (short for Lat. *loci classici,* literally "classical places," i. e. passages). Passages standard for elucidating a subject or word. Theol. works entitled *Loci*

were produced in the 16th and 17th cents. by P. Melanchthon,* M. Chemnitz,* J. Gerhard,* A. Praetorius,* V. Strigel,* M. Hafenreffer,* L. Hutter,* et al. In course of time the term *loci communes* ("common places") came to connote any work dealing with the sum of Christian doctrine, *loci theologici* ("theological places [or passages]") came to denote the content, and thus the main passages of Scripture as included in individual *loci*.

Lock, Lars Carlson (Laurentius Carolus Lokenius; d. 1688). B. Fin.; to US from Swed. 1647; Luth. pastor New Swed.

Locke, John (1632–1704). Philos.; b. Wrington, Somersetshire, Eng.; exponent of empirical psychol.; held that all knowledge is acquired by experience through senses and through reflection on sense experience; denied existence of innate ideas, even moral and religious, and believed mind initially to be *tabula* rasa* (Lat. "blank slate"); held that faith is above, but not contrary to, reason; advocated tolerance in religious matters and unity among Christians; held Godhead as Supreme Being, virgin birth and Messiahship of Jesus, miracles, need of living a Christian life, resurrection; some of his concepts were developed by later adherents of deism.* Works include *An Essay Concerning Human Understanding; The Reasonableness of Christianity, as Delivered in the Scriptures; Some Thoughts Concerning Education; Two Treatises of Government; Elements of Natural Philosophy*. See also *Deism*, III 3.

R. I. Aaron, *John Locke*, 2d ed. (Oxford, 1955); J. Gibson, *Locke's Theory of Knowledge and Its Historical Relations* (Cambridge, Eng., 1917); S. G. Hefelbower, *The Relation of John Locke to English Deism* (Chicago, 1918).

Loculi. Tombs in catacombs* in form of horizontal rectangular niches.

Lodenstein, Jodocus von (Joost van Lodensteijn; Lodensteyn; 1620–77). Ref. theol., Pietist, ascetic, poet; b. Delft, Neth.; educ. Utrecht under influence of G. Voetius* and Franeker under influence of J. Cocceius.* Pastor Zoetermeer, near Delft, 1644; Sluis, Flanders, 1650; Utrecht 1653. Works include *Bloemlezing uit de Gedichten van J. van Lodensteyn; De Heerlykheyd van een waar Christelyk Leven.*

Lodges. (1) Halls or meeting places of local branches of Masons and other secret socs.; (2) groups of persons composing such branches; (3) fraternal orders or secret socs.

Modern lodges have no hist. connection with secret socs. of ancient times or of primitive, savage tribes. They are gen. patterned after Freemasonry.*

Common to all fraternal orders properly designated as lodges: (1) ritual: dialog, pantomime, and play acting to illustrate importance and teachings of the order; (2) ritualistic initiation, almost always religious or semireligious, and usually including 1 or more of the following: prayers, Scripture readings, lessons inculcating some moral principle, an altar, chaplain, and oaths in which God is invoked as witness; (3) aims: moral and spiritual advancement and mutual aid, the latter sometimes in sick benefits and death benefits. Many lodges use a burial ritual in which the hope of a blessed hereafter is offered on basis of good moral ideals and conduct.

Am. has been a fertile field for lodges; several thousand were organized in the eighties and nineties of the 19th c., each with its own ritual and most with some insurance feature. Many lodges ignored mortality tables, defaulted on payments, and passed out of existence; losses ran into billions of dollars.

Ritualistic features of men's lodges are losing drawing power because of a soc. tendency toward ready-made entertainment and emphasis on family activities. Women's organizations still tend strongly toward ceremony and ritualism. Some local lodges have instituted memberships without initiation, but this is discouraged by the governing bodies and often forbidden by lodge statute.

To provide information, literature, and advice concerning fraternal organizations, The Lutheran Church – Missouri Synod maintains a Commission on Fraternal Organizations and has engaged the services of a full-time ex. secy. Objectives of the Commission include meeting and negotiating with officials of fraternal organizations in hope of having removed from their rituals and philos. all things that are contrary to the Gospel or that require compromise of Christian convictions. The Commission also is working in the field of audio-visual aids and issues releases on fraternal organizations. TG, PHL

Lods, Adolphe (1867–1948). OT scholar; b. Courbevoie, suburb of Paris, Fr.; prof. OT on ev. theol. faculty Paris; prof. Heb. literature on Faculté des Lettres, Sorbonne, Paris, 1906–37; used literary-critical methods of J. Wellhausen*; applied principles of archaeol. and sociol. to Biblical material.

Loe-. See also as if spelled without this e.

Loesche, Georg Karl David (1855–1932). B. Berlin, Ger.; educ. Bonn, Tübingen, and Berlin; prof. ch. hist. Vienna, Austria; active in Gesellschaft für die Geschichte des Protestantismus in Österreich, founded 1879, and ed. its yearbook beginning 1889.

Loewenthal, Isidor (ca. 1827–64). B. Posen (Poznan), Prussian Poland, of Jewish parents; to US 1846; converted to Christianity; educ. Princeton (N. J.) Theol. Sem.; Presb. miss. to N India 1856. Tr NT into Pashto, language of the Afghans.

Löffler, Josias Friedrich Christian (Loeffler; 1752–1816). Rationalist theol.; b. Saalfeld, Ger.; prof. Frankfurt an der Oder; gen. supt. and mem. of high consistory Gotha. Works include *Kleine Schriften; Bonifacius;* sermons.

Loftis, Zenas Sanford (May 11, 1881–Aug. 12, 1909). B. Gainesboro, Tenn.; educ. Vanderbilt U., Nashville, Tenn.; active in retail drug business, manufacturing laboratories, slum miss. work, and teaching in a Chinese S. S. in St. Louis, Mo.; volunteered for med. miss. work; sent by For. Christian Missionary Soc., Cincinnati, Ohio, to Tibet 1908; d. Batang, China. Wrote *Message from Batang*.

A. McLean, *Epoch Makers of Modern Missions* (New York, 1912), pp. 282–296.

Logia. See *Apocrypha*, B 2.

Logic, Symbolic (logistic; mathematical logic; algebra of logic). System of logic traced to G. W. v. Leibniz* and developed by F. L. G. Frege* et al.; characterized by use of symbols similar to those of mathematics and by careful deductions.

Logical Positivism (logical neopositivism; consistent empiricism; logical empiricism; scientific empiricism). Philos. movement which fl. in the 1930s, with roots in Eng. and Austria; primarily concerned with language and epistemology; exponents tried to achieve empirical and scientific accuracy in all philos. thought. Held that a sentence is significant only if it can be empirically verified in principle; mathematical and logical propositions are tautological and do not contribute to knowledge; statements not empirical, and tautological statements, are "meaningless"; metaphysical and theol. propositions are rejected as lacking cognitive meaning. Prominent representatives of the movement include L. Wittgenstein* (in his early writings) and B. A. W. Russell.* See also *Scientism*.

A. J. Ayer, *Language, Truth and Logic*, 2d ed. (London, 1946); R. Carnap, *Philosophy and Logical Syntax* (London, 1935).

Logo-Tigiac. See *Celtic Church*, 2.

Logos (Gk. "word"). Jn 1:1, 14 the term designates the 2d Person of the Trinity* (see also *Christ Jesus*). When one speaks a word, it comes from within and reveals his thoughts. The 2d Person of the Trin. is called Word because He is the Son of God, begotten of the Father from eternity; He reveals thoughts of God about us, e. g., His love and gracious plan of salvation. John's use of the term rests on divine inspiration, the teaching of Christ, and the OT. Pr 8:22-30 wisdom (term parallel to "Word") is personified and said to have been before the earth came into existence. *Logos* connotes thought, understanding, principle. The assumption that John borrowed the term from Philo* Judaeus or Stoicism* is gratuitous.

Logotherapy. See *Psychotherapy,* 13.

Löhe, Johann Konrad Wilhelm (Feb. 21, 1808–Jan. 2, 1872). B. Fürth, near Nürnberg, Ger.; educ. Nürnberg, Erlangen, and Berlin; pastor Neuendettelsau 1837; mem. of the State Ch.; bore testimony against its rationalism and laxity and against state control of the ch.

Lohe responded to F. C. D. Wyneken's* appeals for help in support of Luth. ch. work in Am. He pub. a plea for workers 1841 and with J. F. Wucherer pub. a paper 1843 in behalf of America's need: *Kirchliche Mittheilungen aus und über Nord-Amerika.* He supported a theol. school for training emergency helpers *(Nothelferseminar),* est. 1846 at Fort Wayne, Ind., with W. Sihler* at its head and 11 students enrolled, including C. H. R. Lange,* H. Wunder,* and C. J. A. Strasen.* The school opened in rented quarters; soon land and bldgs. were bought with money collected largely by Löhe and friends (see also *Lutheran Church – Missouri Synod, The,* I; Teachers, 4).

On request of the Mo. Syn., Löhe turned the school over to it 1847 (see also *Ministry, Education of,* VIII C 2 f; X D), though he did not fully agree with the Mo. Syn. const. on the doctrine of the ministry. Differences increased (to include the doctrine of the ch. and ownership of the teacher training school at Saginaw, Mich.; see also *Grossmann, Georg Martin*), intensified, and led to a break 1853 bet. Löhe and the Mo. Synod. Löhe and his followers taught the oneness of the visible and invisible ch., but distinguished bet. them, holding that there is a visible assem. of the called, within which is an invisible assem. of the elect (cf. Mt 22:14); these 2 assemblies are related much like body and soul; pure confession and faithfulness to Scripture are marks of that denomination which has the most truth or the complete truth, the church par excellence.

Contrary to the Mo. Syn., Löhe held that the office of the ministry is a divine institution in its own right and does not derive its right and authority from the local cong.; a cong. does not transfer its powers to bearers of the ministry but is simply the instrument of Christ for conferring the ministry; ch. governance is part of the office of the ministry. Löhe feared that C. F. W. Walther* and other Saxons placed too much power into the hands of the cong. and that chaos would result. After the split bet. Löhe and Walther, Löhe men in Am. founded the Iowa Syn. (see *Iowa and Other States, Evangelical Lutheran Synod of*).

In 1849 Löhe est. the Neuendettelsau* Miss. Soc.; in 1854 he est. a deaconess soc. in Bav. The Deaconess Home at Neuendettelsau opened 1854; chapel was added 1858–59, *Rettungshaus* 1862, *Blödenanstalt* 1864, *Magdalenium* 1865, hosp. for men 1867, hosp. for women 1869. Construction continued except during WW I and II, resulting in many bldgs., including old folks homes, a new and greatly expanded hosp., a secondary school (Augustana-Hochschule), a pub. house (Freimund-Verlag), and a sem. to train pastors for N. Am., Australia, New Guinea, and Brazil. Löhe missioners include E. A. Brauer,* J. G. Burger,* E. O. Clöter,* F. A. Crämer,* J. A. Detzer,* J. A. Ernst,* C. J. H. Fick,* A. G. G. Francke,* J. H. P. Graebner,* G. W. C. Hattstädt,* F. W. Husmann,* C. H. R. Lange,* F. J. C. Lochner,* C. A. W. Röbbelen,* J. A. Saupert,* J. M. G. Schaller,* G. E. C. F. Sievers,* W. Sihler,* W. S. Stubnatzy,* P. J. Trautmann,* C. L. A. Wolter,* H. Wunder.* See also *Lutheran Church – Missouri Synod, The,* I 2.

Liturgical life of Lutheranism in Am. was greatly influenced by Löhe's *Agende für christliche Gemeinden des lutherischen Bekenntnisses* (1844; 2d enl. ed. 1853–59), esp. prepared for Luths. in N. Am. In the foreword to the 1st ed., directed to F. C. D. Wyneken, Löhe says that he examined ca. 200 old agendas (see *Agenda*) in search of best usage. The Order of Communion (also called *Hauptgottesdienst,* i. e., main service) contains specific and complete rubrics.* Also included among other things in *Agende:* orders for matins* and vespers*; preces for lauds,* vespers, prime, compline (see also *Hours, Canonical*); litany*; gen. prayers; orders for ordination and installation of pastors, for baptism, confirmation, confession and absolution, weddings, churching of women, communion of the sick, consecration of the dying. It was gradually supplanted by *Kirchen-Agende* issued 1856 by the Mo. Syn.

Other works include *Einfältiger Beichtunterricht; Beicht- und Communion-Büchlein für evangelische Christen; Samenkörner des Gebetes,* tr. H. A. Weller, *Seed-Grains of Prayer; Haus-, Schul- und Kirchenbuch; Evangelien-Postille; Epistel-Postille; Martyrologium; Hausbedarf christlicher Gebete; Der Kleine Katechismus Dr. Martin Luthers, in Fragen und Antworten erklärt; Von der weiblichen Einfalt; Drei Bücher von der Kirche,* tr. E. T. Horn,* *Three Books Concerning the Church; Vom christlichen Hausgottesdienst; Erinnerungen aus der Reformationsgeschichte von Franken.* FLP

J. Deinzer, *Wilhelm Löhes Leben,* 4th ed., 3 vols. in 2 (Neuendettelsau, 1935); T. Schäfer, *Wilhelm Löhe* (Gütersloh, 1909); H. Kressel, "Löhe als Künstler," *Allgemeine Evangelisch-Lutherische Kirchenzeitung,* LX (1927), col. 1195–97; 1220–25; 1242–45, *Wilhelm Löhe als Prediger* (Gütersloh, 1929), *Wilhelm Löhe als Liturg und Liturgiker* (Neuendettelsau, 1952), and *Wilhelm Löhe als Katechet und als Seelsorger* (Neuendettelsau, 1955); S. Hebart, *Wilhelm Löhes Lehre von der Kirche, ihrem Amt und Regiment* (Neuendettelsau, 1939); *Wilhelm Löhe: Gesammelte Werke,* ed. K. Ganzert (Neuendettelsau, 1951–; vols. III–VII in 10 by 1966); E. H. Heintzen, "Wilhelm Loehe and the Missouri Synod, 1841–1853" (unpub. doctoral thesis, U. of Ill., Urbana, 1964); J. L. Schaaf, "Wilhelm Löhe's Relation to the American Lutheran Church" (unpub. doctoral thesis, U. Heidelberg, Ger., 1962).

Lohman, Alexander Frederik de Savornin (1837–1924). Neth. statesman; prof. Free U. Amsterdam 1884–96; with A. Kuyper* opposed liberalism; later broke with Kuyper.

Lohmann, Rudolf (1825–79). Luth. theol.; b. Winsen an der Aller, near Celle, Ger.; educ. Halle and Göttingen; pastor Fürstenwalde 1853–65, Müden an der Örtze (near Hermannsburg) 1866; favored Immanuel Syn. against the Breslau Syn. in the controversy about ch. polity (see also *Germany, Lutheran Free Churches in,* 1–3). Works include *Lutherische und unierte Kirche; Von Luther's Tode bis zur Concordienformel.*

Lohmeyer, Ernst (1890–1946). Prot. NT scholar; b. Dorsten, Westphalia, Ger.; taught at Breslau and Greifswald; was nominated rector Greifswald 1945; applied form criticism (see *Isagogics,* 3) to Pauline Epistles; opposed Nazism (see *Germany,* C 4; *Socialism,* 3); arrested for unknown reasons; day and place of death unknown. Works include *Galiläa und Jerusalem; Das Vater-unser;* commentaries on NT books.

Lohmüller, Johann (Lomoller; ca. 1500–60). City

secy. Riga; won for Lutheranism by A. Knöpken*; Reformer of Livonia; M. Luther,* *Den auserwählten lieben Freunden Gottes, allen Christen zu Riga, Reval und Dorpat in Livland* (WA 12, 143–150) replied to his letters.

Löhner. See *Löner.*

Loisy, Alfred Firmin (1857–1940). RC theol.; b. Ambrières, Fr.; priest 1879; prof. Heb. and exegesis Institut Catholique, Paris; influenced by L. M. O. Duchesne* and J. E. Renan*; exponent of modernism*; dismissed from Institut 1893 as result of controversy about Biblical inerrancy; 5 works placed on Index* of Prohibited Books 1903; excommunicated 1908 as *vitandus* (see *Keys, Office of,* 9); prof. ch. hist. Collège de France 1909–26, École des Hautes Études 1924–27. Works include *L'Évangile et l'Église; Les Évangiles synoptiques; La Naissance du Christianisme;* tr. of Acts.

Lollards. Term of uncertain origin designating (1) a 14th c. Neth. sect related to Beghards* and Beguines; (2) followers of J. Wycliffe.*

Loman, Abraham Dirk (1823–97). Dutch Prot. theol.; b. The Hague, Neth.; educ. Luth. and Mennonite sems. Amsterdam; pastor of Luth. congs. Maastricht 1848–49, Deventer 1849–56; prof. Luth. sem. Amsterdam 1856, U. Amsterdam 1877–93. In 1881 he held that Christ was not a hist. person but the incorporation of thoughts and principles developed in the 2d c.; His death and resurrection are the death of Israel and its revival in Christianity. In 1882 he admitted the historicity of Christ but denied that He founded Christianity. Works include *Symbool en werkelijkheid in de Evangelische geschiedenis; Het Vierde Evangelie.*

Lombard, Peter. See *Peter the Lombard.*

Lombok. See *Indonesia,* 10.

London Charity Organization Society. See *Social Work,* B 4.

London Confession. Several Bap. confessions are called London Confession. See *Democratic Declarations of Faith,* 3.

London Jews' Society. Organized 1809 as London Soc. for Promoting Christianity amongst the Jews, commonly called London Jews' Soc.; later called Church Missions to Jews, and then (1962) The Church's Ministry among the Jews. Mission fields included Egypt, Syria, Iran, Iraq, Israel, Tunisia, Algeria, Morocco, Ethiopia. Headquarters London, Eng.

London Missionary Society, The. Founded London, Eng., 1795 by Congs., Angls., Presbs., Wesleyans. Fundamental principle was to be interdenominational, and "not to send Presbyterianism, Independency, Episcopacy, or any other form of church order and government (about which there may be difference of opinion among serious persons), but the glorious Gospel of the blessed God, to the heathen, and that it shall be left (as it ought to be left) to the minds of the persons whom God may call into the fellowship of His Son from among them, to assume for themselves such form of church government as to them shall appear most agreeable to the Word of God." In recent times the soc. has been maintained chiefly by Congregationalists. Fields have included S. Pacific, India, S. Afr., Madagascar, China, Papua.

London Polyglot. See *Polyglot Bibles.*

London Presbytery in Communion with the Church of Scotland, The. See *Presbyterian Churches,* 2.

Löner, Josua (Löhner; Lohner; Loner[us]; Lonnerus; 1535–95). Son of K. Löner*; b. Ölsnitz im Vogtland, Saxony, Ger.; Luth. theol.; educ. Wittenberg; positions included supt. at Altenburg. Coauthor 1593 *Saxon Visitation Articles* (see *Articles of Visitation*); other works include sermons on Daniel and Jonah.

Löner, Kaspar (Löhner; Lohner; Loner[us]; Lonnerus; Caspar; 1493–1546). Father of J. Löner*; Ger. priest, reformer, and poet; b. (Markt) Erlbach, Middle Franconia, Ger.; educ. in monastery at Heilsbronn and at U. Erfurt; served at Nesselbach 1520, Hof 1524; removed for preaching Luth. doctrine; at Wittenberg 1526; pastor Ölsnitz im Vogtland, Saxony, 1527, Hof 1527–28, Ölsnitz 1531; preacher Naumburg 1542; pastor Nördlingen 1544. Ed. hymnals; other works include *Unterricht des Glaubens.*

Long, Ralph Herman (Dec. 3, 1882–Feb. 19, 1948). B. Loudonville, Ohio; educ. Capital U. (coll. and Ev. Luth. Theol. Sem.), Columbus, Ohio. Joint Syn. of Ohio pastor Newton Falls-Warren, Ohio, 1909–13; Coraopolis, Pa., 1913–21; Pittsburgh, Pa., 1921–27. Ex. dir. NLC 1930–48.

Long, Simon Peter (Oct. 7, 1860–Jan. 3, 1929). B. McZena, near Loudonville, Ashland Co., Ohio; educ. Capital U. (coll. and Ev. Luth. Theol. Sem.), Columbus, Ohio, and Luth. Theol. Sem., Philadelphia, Pa. Served congs. in Ohio and Ill. 1886–1929. Pres. Lima Coll., Lima, Ohio, 1898–1903. Prof. Chicago Luth. Bible School 1921–29; its pres. in the later 1920s. Works include *The Wounded Word; The Eternal Epistle; The Crime Against Christ.*

Long Parliament. See *Presbyterian Confessions,* 3; *Westminster Assembly.*

Longfellow, Henry Wadsworth (1807–82). Poet; b. Portland, Maine; educ. Bowdoin Coll., Brunswick, Maine; prof. modern languages Bowdoin 1829–35, Harvard 1835–54. Tr. S. Dach's* "O wie selig seid ihr doch, ihr Frommen" ("Oh, How Blest Are Ye Whose Toils are Ended"); other works include *Evangeline: A Tale of Acadie; The Song of Hiawatha; The Courtship of Miles Standish; Tales of a Wayside Inn.*

Longinus. Traditional name of soldier who pierced the side of Jesus (Jn 19:34) and of the centurion who confessed Christ (Mt 27:54; Mk 15:39; Lk 23:47).

Longjumeau, Peace of. See *France,* 9.

Longobardi, Niccolò (Longobardo). See *Chinese Term Question.*

Loofs, Friedrich (1858–1928). Luth. ch. hist.; b. Hildesheim, Ger.; educ. Leipzig, Tübingen, and Göttingen; influenced by K. G. A. v. Harnack; and A. Ritschl*; taught at Leipzig 1882–87, Halle 1887–1926. Mem. Saxon Consistory; opposed E. H. P. A. Haeckel's* materialism.* Works include *Symbolik; Wer war Jesus Christus?; Leitfaden zum Studium der Dogmengeschichte;* patristic studies.

Look Up and Live. See *Radio and Television Evangelism, Network,* 5.

Lope de Vega. See *Vega, Lope de.*

Lopez, Gregor (Lopes; Gregorio; 1542–96). Mystic and hermit; b. Madrid, Sp.; to Mex. 1567; influenced by Teresa,* John* of the Cross, and John* of Ávila; emphasized inner love to God.

Lopez, Gregory (native name Lo, or A-lu, Wen-tsao; 1611–ca. 1690). 1st RC native Chinese bp.; b. Fogan, Fukien, China, of heathen parents; bap. as adult by Franciscans; educ. Manila, Philippine Is.; Dominican 1651; ordained 1656; vicar apostolic Nanking, China, 1674; bp. 1685.

Lord's Day. Sunday.* Rv 1:10 is commonly understood as referring to the 1st day of the week; the assoc. is based primarily on the resurrection of Christ (Lk 24:13-49; Jn 20:1-25). The outpouring of the Spirit apparently also took place on that day (Acts 20:7; 1 Co 16:1-2). The name is often used when the sacred character of the day is stressed. In Christian terminology also called sabbath,* or sabbath day.

Lord's Prayer. Cf. Mt 6:9-13; Lk 11:2-4. Divided into Invocation, Petitions, Doxology. The Invocation summarizes the Gospel, for "Father" presupposes that the one who prays is a child of God by faith in Christ; the 7 Petitions include all spiritual and bodily needs; the Doxology states reasons for the prayer. See also *Amen.*

Liturgical use of the Lord's Prayer is traceable to the 2d or 3d c.

Lord's Supper. The 1st part of a service of Holy Communion, or Eucharist, in Luth. chs. usually follows fairly closely the orders of service (Morning, Matins, or Vespers); main points of variation occur in the form of the Confession of Sins, Absolution, Creed, and music for the Offertory. The 2d part, or Communion Service proper, begins with Salutation and Prefatory Sentences. See also *Worship, Parts of.*

For other aspects of the Lord's Supper in doctrine and hist. see also *Covenant,* 7; *Eucharistic Controversies; Grace, Means of,* I, IV.

Lord's Table. See *Church Furniture,* 1; *Grace, Means of,* IV.

Lorenz. See Lawrence.

Lorenzen, Lorenz. See *Laurenti(i), Laurentius.*

Loreto (formerly also spelled Loretto). Town near Ancona, It., with RC shrine of the Holy House (Santa Casa), in which, acc. to legend, Mary lived at the time of the Annunciation*; the house is said to have been carried by angels from Nazareth first to Dalmatia 1291, then to It. 1294, where it was miraculously relocated twice 1295. The name Loreto is said to be derived either (1) from Laureto, the woman who owned the wooded spot near Recanati, where the house was brought from Dalmatia; or (2) from the woods (Lat. *lauretum*) itself.

Lorichius, Jodocus (Lurkäs; Jodokus; Justus; ca. 1542–1613). B. Trarbach, on the Mosel, Ger.; RC prof. poetry 1568, theol. 1574–1605 Freiburg im Breisgau; opposed introd. of Jesuits and assoc. of profs. with a religious order. Wrote in area of dogmatics, polemics, moral theol., mysticism.

Los von Rom (Ger. "away from Rome" or "free from Rome"). Movement away from Rome. The term (said to have been coined 1897 by a student in Vienna) designates various attempts to effect widespread defections from RCm, esp. in the Ger. provinces of the Austrian empire. The latter form began as a pol. movement but soon drew in religious elements to serve its purposes of nationalism and spread to countries including Belg., Ceylon, Fr., Mex., Poland; its effects are still in evidence.

Löscher, Valentin Ernst (1673–1749). Luth. theol. and poet; b. Sondershausen, N Thuringia, Ger.; educ. Wittenberg and Jena; pastor and supt. Jüterbog 1698; supt. Delitzsch 1701–07; prof. Wittenberg 1707–09; supt. Dresden 1709. Opposed Pietism,* syncretism,* unionism.* Works include *Vollständige Reformations-Acta und Documenta; Catalogus bibliothecae viri summi; Praenotiones theologicae contra naturalistarum et fanaticorum omne genus atheos, deistas, indifferentistas, antiscripturarios, etc.; Breviarium theologiae exegeticae, regulas de legitima scripturae interpretatione succincte atque solide tradens.*

Lossius, Lucas (Loss; Lotze; 1508–82). Luth. musicologist; b. Vacha, Hesse, Ger.; educ. at schools in various cities, including Wittenberg; rector or conrector Lüneburg 1533. Works include *Psalmodia, hoc est Cantica sacra veteris Ecclesiae selecta.*

Lost-Found Nation of Islam in the Wilderness of North America (Black Muslims; Nation of Islam). In 1930 a peddler, perhaps Arab., known as Farrad Mohammad (or Fard Mohammed [Muhammad]; F. Mohammad Ali; Elijah Mohammed [Muhammad]; Wallace Fard Muhammad; Wali [or Walli] Farrad; W. D. Fard; Ford) began teaching the Bible to Negroes in Detroit, Mich., but came to oppose Scripture in favor of Islam.* The meeting hall was called Temple of Islam; later called Muhammad's Temple of Islam, No. 1; later ones were called Temple 2 (Chicago, Ill.), etc. Farrad Mohammad lived in Detroit till 1933 or 1934, when he disappeared and Elijah Muhammad (Elijah Poole; Robert Poole; Paul Poole; Karriem; Ghulam Bogam) became the leader.

Black Muslims hold that the solution of the Negro problem in Am. is separation and that the US owes them land. They reject the white race, soc., Christianity, and the term "Negro," and regard North America as a cultural and moral wilderness. They accept modified Islam. Am. Negroes, they hold, are descendants of original man ("people of the moon") and part of the ancient lost tribe of Shabazz, which allegedly lived in the region of Mecca. F. Mohammad is regarded by some of his followers as the incarnation of Allah; E. Muhammad is regarded as the Messenger of Allah. Muslim claim ca. 80 temples in the US (1963). The "Fruits of Islam" are young Muslim men who act as guards. The "Moslem Girls' Training and General Civilization Class" teaches women to be wives and mothers and prepares them for various work in the movement.

E. U. Essien-Udom, *Black Nationalism* (Chicago, 1962); C. E. Lincoln, *The Black Muslims in America* (Boston, 1961); W. H. Burns, *The Voices of Negro Protest in America* (New York, 1963); W. J. Brink and L. Harris, *The Negro Revolution in America* (New York, 1964). EL

Lotteries. Schemes for distributing prizes or making selections on the basis of lots (involving, e. g., numbers, pieces of wood, pebbles, dies, straws, wheels). Used in gambling.* Casting lots was common also in ancient times and is often mentioned in Scripture (e. g., Nm 26:55; Jos 18:10; Est 3:7; Jon 1:7; Mt 27:35; Lk 1:5-9; Acts 1:24-26).

Lotti, Antonio (1667–1740). RC composer and organist; b. Venice, It., or Hanover, Ger.; wrote in both old contrapuntal (or polyphonic) and modern style. Works include operas, oratorios, and ch. choral works.

Lotze, Lucas. See *Lossius.*

Lotze, Rudolph Hermann (1817–81). Ger. philos.; b. Bautzen, Saxony, Ger.; held system of teleological idealism: ultimate substance is God, good and personal, of whom all beings are parts without losing their selfhood.

Lotzer, Sebastian (b. ca. 1490). Lay theol.; b. Horb, S Württemberg, Ger.; influenced by C. Schappeler* and J. Eberlin*; defended lay right to speak and write about the Word of God. His *Zwölf Artikel,* written during Peasants'* War, based demands of peasants on the Bible, but advocated peaceful solution. After the war he fled to Saint Gall, Switz.

Louis I (778–840). Called "le Debonnaire" and "le Pieux" ("the Pious"): king of Fr. and Ger. and emp. of the W 814–840; crowned 816.

Louis II. See *Stolzer, Thomas.*

Louis IV (of Bav.; ca. 1282/87–1347). B. Munich, Ger.; duke of Bav. 1294–1347; king of Ger. and Holy Roman emp. 1314–47 (crowned 1328): in conflict with John XXII (see *Babylonian Captivity,* 2; *Popes,* 13) over his disputed election as emp.; invaded It. 1327–30 and arranged for election of antipope Nicholas* V. See also *Michael of Cesena.*

Louis VI (Ludwig; 1539–83). Son of Frederick* III of the Palatinate, whom he succeeded as elector of the Palatinate 1576; favored FC; tried to restore Lutheranism in the Palatinate.

Louis VII (le Jeune ["the Young"]; ca. 1121–80). King of Fr. 1137–80; engaged in struggle ca. 1157–80 with Henry* II of Eng. over parts of Fr.; a leader in 2d Crusade (see *Crusades,* 3). See also *Philip II.*

Louis IX (1214–70). "Saint Louis"; b. Poissy, Fr.; king of Fr. 1226–70; took crusader's vow 1244; engaged in Crusades (see *Crusades,* 8); noted for long and gen. peaceful reign. See also *France,* 2.

Louis XIII. See *France,* 10.

Louis XIV (1638–1715). "The Great"; "le Grand

Monarque"; "le Roi Soleil," "the sun king"; b. Saint Germain-en-Laye, Fr.; king of Fr. 1643–1715; assumed power 1661 on death of J. Mazarin.* See also *France, 5; Gallicanism: Government; Utrecht, Treaty of.*

Louis XV. See *France,* 10.

Louis of Granada. See *Luis de Granada.*

Louis Philippe. See *France,* 6.

Louisville Resolution. Resolution adopted Oct. 1942 at Louisville, Ky., by the ULC in reply to a resolution adopted Oct. 1942 at Mendota, Ill., by the ALC (see *Mendota Resolutions,* 1): "Resolved that: 1. We receive with appreciation and deep gratitude to God the resolution of the American Lutheran Church in convention assembled at Mendota, Ill., which recognizes our fundamental agreement and proclaims their readiness to establish full pulpit and altar fellowship with The United Lutheran Church in America. 2. We instruct the President of our Church, in conjunction with the President of the American Lutheran Church, to consummate and declare at the earliest possible date the establishment of pulpit and altar fellowship."

Loukaris. See *Lucaris.*

Lourdes. Town SW Fr., with RC shrine marking the alleged 1858 appearance of Mary to a peasant girl.

Love. Love is more easily described than defined. It usually involves intimate knowledge, kindness, loyalty, and responsibility. In its basic Biblical sense love is not only an emotion but a deep expression of the total personality; it is not caused by any goodness in its object but is the free, creative, and unmerited response of the one who loves.

Basic OT Heb. words for love (*ahabah,* "love"; *ahab* and *aheb,* "to love") denote sexual, family, soc., and divine love. Hosea brings these words into focus as God's love for His covenant people. OT Heb. words related in meaning to love include *rachamim* ("tender mercies") and *chesed* ("loving-kindness"). The LXX rather consistently tr. *ahab* and *aheb* with *agapao.* Most frequent NT Gk. words for love: *agapao* and the related noun *agape;* e.g., Jn 3:16, 35; Ro 13:8; 1 Co 13; 1 Jn 3:18. Christian love is unique in that it extends also to the unworthy. This love is not mere aspiration or desire but God's love active in the Christian. It is often distinguished from *eros,* a word for love in non-Biblical Gk. which usually implies egocentricity also in the approach to the divine. Divine love found fullest expression in the life and death of Christ, who loved not the righteous but the sinner, Mt 9:10-13. The word *phileo* is also common in the NT. It usually means brotherly love and affection (e.g., Mt 10:37), though it is also used of God's love to man (e.g., Jn 16:27) and expresses close relationship bet. Father and Son (Jn 5:20).

Love described in the Bible: God's love for man, man's love for God, man's love for man. In the OT God's love was directed esp. toward the community. It is His covenant action toward Israel by which He chose and sustained His people, Dt 4:37. This love is personal, selective, spontaneous, serving in judgment and forgiveness, Dt 7:6; Hos 3:1; Am 3:2; Is 54:8. In the NT God's love is expressed in Jesus Christ, who, by His sacrificial and willing death on the cross demonstrated that God is love and revealed the true nature of love, Ro 5:8; 1 Jn 3:16; 4:8. Christ's love was never a mere emotion; it was always connected with His work of redemption, Mt 20:28. God's love to man demands response. The proper response is love that shows itself in willing and worshipful obedience, Dt 6:5; Mt 22:27-29; Jn 21:15-17; 1 Jn 5:3. Love to one's fellowman is a proper expression of love to God, Eph 5:2; 1 Jn 4:20. Love to God is never abstract; it always centers in worship of God and service to man, Mt 25:45; Jn 14:15. Not only is love commanded (Jn 15:17); it is also a gift of the Spirit (Gl 5:22), a mark of discipleship (Jn 13:35), a sign that the believer has passed from death to life, 1 Jn 3:14. LEZ

See also *Grace; Loving-kindness; Lund, Theology of; Mercy.*

C. E. B. Cranfield, "Love," *A Theological Word Book of the Bible,* ed. A. Richardson (New York, 1951), pp. 131–136; E. M. Good, "Love in the OT," *The Interpreter's Dictionary of the Bible,* ed. G. A. Buttrick, et al., III (New York, 1962), 168–178; A. Nygren, *Agape and Eros,* 2 vols. in 3 parts; rev., and in part retranslated, and pub. in 1 vol. (London, 1953).

Love Feast. See *Agape.*

Lovedale School. See *Africa,* B 5.

Loving-kindness. Term expressing God's love to man, acc. to which He bestows favors of His grace and mercy on sinners, who are His enemies by nature and unworthy of His kindness (Ps 17:7; 26:3; 36:7, 10; 89:33; 103:4; Jer 31:3). See also *Grace; Love; Mercy.*

Low Church. Term originating in the early 18th c.; originally denoted latitudinarianism*; later applied to Angl. Evangelicals (see *Evangelical*). See also *England,* C 8; *High Church; Protestant Episcopal Church,* 7.

Low Mass. See *Missa lecta.*

Low Sunday. 1st Sun. after Easter. Name probably originated in contrast to the "high" feast of Easter. Also called Quasimodogeniti and Dominica* in albis. See also *Church Year,* 14, 16.

Löwenstern, Matthäus Appelles von (1594–1648). B. Neustadt, Silesia; hymnist and musician; privy councillor Oels. Hymns include "Christe, du Beistand deiner Kreuzgemeine"; "Nun preiset alle Gottes Barmherzigkeit!"

Lower Criticism. See *Textual Criticism.*

Lowrie, Walter (1868–1959). Prot. Episc. cleric; b. Philadelphia, Pa.; educ. Princeton (N. J.) U., Princeton Theol. Sem., Greifswald U., Berlin U., Am. Academy in Rome; rector Trin., Newport, R. I., and St. Paul's Am. Ch., Rome. Works include *Christian Art and Archaeology* (later issued under the title *Monuments of the Early Church*); *Art in the Early Church; Kierkegaard; Problems of Church Unity.*

Lowth, Robert (Louth; 1710–87). B. Winchester, Hampshire, Eng.; educ. Winchester Coll. and Oxford U.; prof. poetry Oxford 1741–50; bp. St. Davids (Pembrokeshire, Wales) 1766, Oxford 1766, London 1777; pointed out parallelism (*parallelismus membrorum;* synonymous, synthetic, or antithetic) of 2 or 3 rows of a period as basic structure of Heb. poetry. Treated OT from aesthetic viewpoint. Works include *De sacra Poesi Hebraeorum praelectiones academicae Oxonii habitae.*

Loy, Matthias (Mar. 17, 1828–Jan. 26, 1915). B. Cumberland Co., Pa.; educ. Luth. Theol. Sem. at Columbus, Ohio; Joint Syn. of Ohio pastor Delaware, Ohio, 1849–65; prof. theol. Capital U., Columbus, 1865–1902; pres. Capital U. 1881–90; pres. Ev. Luth. Joint Syn. of Ohio* and Other States 1860–78, 1880–94; leader at free Luth. Conferences of the 1850s (see *Free Lutheran Conferences,* 1); hymnist. Ed. *Lutheran Standard* 1864–91, *Columbus Theological Magazine* 1881–88; other works include *The Augsburg Confession; The Doctrine of Justification; Sermons on the Gospels; Sermons on the Epistles; Essay on the Ministerial Office;* hymns include "The Law of God is Good and Wise," "The Gospel Shows the Father's Grace," "An Awe-full Mystery Is Here," "Jesus, Thou Art Mine Forever."

M. Loy, *Story of My Life,* 2d ed. (Columbus, Ohio, 1905).

Loyal Order of Moose. See *Moose, Loyal Order of.*

Loyalty: Christ and Country. See *Armed Services Commission,* 2.

Loyalty Islands. See *Melanesia.*

Loyola, Ignatius (of) (1491–1556). Founder Society* of Jesus; b. Loyola, near Azpeitia, N Sp.; injured 1521 as soldier in defense of Pampeluna (present Pamplona) against the French; converted during convalescence; ascetic and pilgrim for several yrs.; educ. 1524–35 in Spain at Barcelona, Alcalá de Henares, and Salamanca, and at Paris, Fr.; at Paris, beginning 1529, he and 6 others (P. Favre,* F. Xavier,* D. Laynez,* A. Salmeron,* S. Rodriguez* de Azevedo, and N. A. de Bobadilla*) formed a group which developed into the Soc. of Jesus; Loyola was the 1st gen. of the order. See also *"Spiritual Exercises."*

Loyson, Charles (1827–1912). "Père Hyacinthe"; b. Orléans, Fr.; RC prof. philos. Avignon 1851, dogmatics Nantes 1854; curate Paris 1856; preacher Notre Dame; 1868 Advent sermons led to breach with RC Ch.; opposed papal infallibility and was excommunicated 1869; pastor Old Cath. Ch. (see *Old Catholics*), Geneva, 1873–74.

Lubbertus, Sibrandus (ca. 1556–1625). B. Langwarden, Ostfriesland; Ref. theol.; educ. Wittenberg, Marburg, Geneva; preacher Friesland; prof. dogmatics Franeker. Upheld orthodox Calvinism* in Holland against Arminianism*; took part in 1618–19 Syn. of Dordrecht.* Works include *De principiis Christianorum dogmatum; Episolica disceptatio de fide justificante, deque nostra coram Deo justificatione; Declaratio responsionis D. C. Vorstii.*

Lübeck, Peace or Treaty of. See *Thirty Years' War.*

Lübeck, Vincent (ca. 1654–1740). B. probably Padingbüttel, near Dorum, Hannover, Ger.; composer; organist Stade 1675, Hamburg 1702–40. Works include cantatas and choral-preludes.

Lubin, Eilhard (Eilhardus; 1565–1621). B. Westerstede in Ammerland, Oldenburg, Ger.; educ. Leipzig, Cologne, Helmstedt, Strasbourg, Jena, Marburg, Rostock. Traced evil to *non-ens.* Works include *Clavis graecae linguae; Phosphorus, de prima causa & natura mali;* commentaries on poets and Pauline epistles.

Lucaris, Cyril (Lukaris; Kyrillos Loukaris; 1572–1638). Eastern* Orthodox prelate; b. Crete; educ. Padua; ordained; opposed union of E and W Chs.; condemned by several E Orthodox syns.; opposed by E prelates and theologians and by Jesuits; murdered by Turkish soldiers because he was suspected of rousing the Cossacks. Works include *Confessio fidei,* which shows strong Ref. influence. See also *Eastern Orthodox Standards of Doctrine,* C.

G. A. Hadjiantoniou(s) (Chatzeantoniou), *Protestant Patriarch* (Richmond, Va., 1961).

Lucian of Antioch (ca. 240–312). Mem. of Antioch School (see *Exegesis,* 4; *Schools, Early Christian,* 4); martyr; b. probably Antioch or Samosata; educ. Edessa; presbyter Antioch. His theol. traces all to creation; everything, including Logos,* is created out of nothing by an act of God's will. Emphasized literal meaning of Scriptures; his rev. of the LXX and the 4 gospels (called Lucianic text, or Byzantine [or Syrian] text) conflated variants and removed crudities and obscurities and became standard in Syria, Asia Minor, and Constantinople; most surviving MSS of the 4 gospels (thus Textus* Receptus and KJV) embody his text.

G. Bardy, *Recherches sur saint Lucien d'Antioche et son école* (Paris, 1936).

Lucian of Samosata (ca. 115–ca. 200). Pagan satirist. Apart from literary significance, important for cultural and religious information; treatment of philos. superficial; regarded Christians with contemptuous indifference and depicted them as kind but credulous. Works include *De morte Peregrini; Alexander seu Pseudomantis.*

Lucianic Text. See *Lucian of Antioch.*

Luciferians. Schismatic followers of Lucifer (d. ca. 371), anti-Arian bp. Calaris (Caralis; Carales; now Cagliari), Sardinia; organized on Novatian principles (see *Novatianism*); returned to ch. ca. beginning of 5th c. See also *Gregory of Elvira.*

Lucius, Paul Ernst (Ernest; 1852–1902). Alsatian Luth. theol.; b. Ernolsheim, near Strasbourg; educ. Strasbourg, Zurich, Paris, Jena, Berlin; prof. ch. hist. and miss. hist. Strasbourg; liberal. Works include *Bonaparte und die protestantischen Kirchen Frankreichs; Der Essenismus in seinem Verhältnis zum Judentum; Die Therapeuten und ihre Stellung in der Geschichte der Askese; Die Anfänge des Heiligenkults in der christlichen Kirche.*

Lücke. See also *Luecke.*

Lücke, Gottfried Christian Friedrich (1791–1855). B. Egeln, near Magdeburg, Ger.; educ. Halle and Göttingen; prof. Bonn 1818, Göttingen 1827; mediating theol. (see *Mediating Theology*); assoc. closely with F. D. E. Schleiermacher*; NT exegete. Works include *Commentar über die Schriften des Evangelisten Johannes; Grundriss der neutestamentlichen Hermeneutik und ihrer Geschichte.*

Lucretius (Titus Lucretius Carus; ca. 97–55 BC). B. perhaps Rome; poet; adopted atomism* of Democritus* and Epicurus*; held that all things, including gods (who take no concern in human affairs) and the soul, consist of fine particles; envisioned a kind of steady state, in which nothing is created out of nothing, and the universe does not change. Works include the poem *De rerum natura.* See also *Secularism.*

Ludämilia Elisabeth (Ludämilie; Ludomilla; 1640–72). Cousin of Aemilie* Juliane; b. Heidecksburg, Rudolstadt, Ger.; lived for some yrs. at castle of Friedensburg, near Leutenberg; hymnist. Hymns include "Jesus, Jesus, nichts als Jesus"; "Sorge, Vater, sorge du"; "Wo ist ein solcher Gott zu finden."

Lüdemann, Hermann Karl (1842–1933). B. Kiel, Ger.; educ. Kiel, Heidelberg, and Berlin; prof. Kiel 1878, Bern, Switz., 1884; his Christian ideas were influenced by his philos. and psychol. thought. Works include *Christliche Dogmatik.*

Ludger. See *Liudger.*

Lüdke, Friedrich Germanus (1730–92). B. Stendal, Prussia, Ger.; chaplain; pastor Berlin; exponent of biblicistic (see *Biblicism*) neology* against authority of confessions; contributed to spread of Enlightenment*; differentiated bet. fundamental and non-fundamental arts. of faith; favored tolerance and freedom of conscience.

Ludlow, John Malcolm Forbes (1821–1911). Angl. soc. reformer; b. Nimach, India; educ. Fr.; to London 1838; helped found Christian* Socialism; promoted 1852 Industrial and Provident Societies Act; with J. F. D. Maurice* and T. Hughes* founded Working Men's Coll., London; founded and ed. *Christian Socialist* 1850.

Ludolf, Hiob (Ludolph; Leutholf; 1624–1704). Orientalist; b. Erfurt, Ger.; educ. Erfurt and Leiden; learned Ethiopic from Abyssinian scholar in It. Ed. *Psalterium Davidis Aethiopice et Latine;* other works include *Historia aethiopica* (Eng. tr. *A New History of Ethiopia*); Ethiopic-Lat. lexicon; Ethiopic grammar.

Ludolf of Saxony (Ludolph; ca. 1300–78). "The Carthusian"; Dominican (see *Dominicans*) for ca. 30 yrs.; joined Carthusians* at Strasbourg 1340; prior of charterhouse at Koblenz 1343; resumed status as ordinary monk 1348. Works include commentary on Ps; *Meditationes vitae Jesu Christi.*

Ludwig VI. See *Louis VI.*

Ludwig von Württemberg (1554–93). Duke of Württemberg 1568–93; fostered Luth. confessionalism; hymnist. See also *Africa,* A 5.

Luecke. See also *Lücke.*

Luecke, Martin Louis Ernest (Lücke: June 22, 1859–Apr. 13, 1926). B. Sheboygan Co., Wis.; educ. Conc. Coll., Fort Wayne, Ind., and Conc. Sem., St. Louis,

Mo. Pastor Bethalto, Ill., 1881–84; Troy Ill., 1884–92; Springfield, Ill., 1892–1903; pres. Conc. Coll., Fort Wayne, 1903–26. Works include *Der Bürgerkrieg der Vereinigten Staaten, 1861–'65; Tabellen für die heilige Geschichte; Biblische Symbole: oder, Bibelblätter in Bildern; Outlines of The Sacred History of The Old and New Testaments.*

Lufft, Hans (1495–1584). Printer Wittenberg, Ger.; printed 1st complete ed. of M. Luther's* Ger. Bible and other works of Luther.

Luger, Friedrich Paul (1813–90). B. Lübeck, Ger.; Luth. pastor. Works include *Über Zweck, Inhalt und Eigenthümlichkeit der Rede des Stephanus; Heinrich Pestalozzi;* sermons.

Lugo, Juan de (1583–1660). B. Madrid, Sp.; Jesuit; taught philos. and theol. at several Jesuit schools in Sp.; to Rome ca. 1621; cardinal 1643. Taught that God gives enough light for salvation to every soul; emphasized destruction as distinctive factor in sacrificial worship of Eucharist. Works include *De incarnatione Domini; Disputationes scholasticae et morales; Tractatus de venerabili Eucharistiae Sacramento; Responsorum moralium libri sex.*

Luis de Granada (Louis of Granada; 1504–88). B. Granada, Sp.; Dominican; famous preacher; influenced by humanism*; provincial for Port.: confessor of Port. queen regent. Wrote ascetic treatises.

Luitprand. See *Liutprand.*

Lukaris. See *Lucaris.*

Luke of Prague (Lukas Prazsky; ca. 1458–1528). B. probably Prague; educ. Prague; joined Bohemian* Brethren ca. 1480; bp. 1500. Guided the Brethren to maturity as an autonomous reform ch. Corresponded with D. Erasmus* and M. Luther.*

Luke was an Augustinian in his understanding of justification. He tried to clarify what is "essential" ("substantial"), "ministerial," and "accidental" to salvation, and the relationship of these 3 in the church's life. Works include *Zprávy knezské (Directives to Priests).*

See also *Bohemia, Lutheran Theology* in, 2.

M. S. Fousek, "The Second-Generation Soteriology of the Unitas Fratrum," *Zeitschrift für Kirchengeschichte* (1965), 41–63; A. Molnar, *Bratr Lukás* (Prague, 1948); J. T. Müller, *Geschichte der Böhmischen Brüder,* 3 vols. (Herrnhut, 1922–31); E. Peschke, *Die Theologie der Böhmischen Brüder in ihrer Frühzeit,* I (Stuttgart, 1935), *Die Böhmischen Brüder im Urteil ihrer Zeit* (Stuttgart, 1964), and "Der Kirchenbegriff des Bruder Lukas von Prag," *Wissenschaftliche Zeitschrift der Univ. Rostock,* V (1955/56), Gesellschaftliche u. Sprach. Reihe, Heft 2, p. 274. MSF

Lullus (ca. 710–786). Anglo-Saxon; b. Wessex, S Brit.; Benedictine; companion of Boniface*; bp. Mainz 754; est. monastery Hersfeld ca. 769; noted for learning.

Lully, Raymond (Ramón Lull; Raimundus Lullus; Raimond Lulle; Raimundo Lulio; ca. 1235–1315). "Doctor Illuminatus"; b. Palma, Majorca (Mallorca), Balearic Islands; well-educ. RC nobleman; converted 1265 after dissolute life; devoted self to study of Arabic and miss. work to Muslim; taught Arabic in Franciscan monastery at Miramar, Majorca; preached crusade for conversion of Muslim; miss. to Muslim of Tunis, Cyprus, and Asiatic Turkey; acc. to legend, stoned at Bougie, Afr., and died on board ship in sight of Majorca. See also *Cabala.*

Lumber River Annual Conference of the Holiness Methodist Church (Lumber Miss. Conf. of the Holiness Meth. Ch.). See *Evangelistic Associations,* 9.

Lumen Gentium. See *Vatican Councils,* 2.

Luna, Pedro de. See *Benedict XIII,* 1.

Lund, Theology of (Swed. *lundateologi*). Theol. of Lundensian School, which includes Gustaf Emanuel Hildebrand Aulén (b. 1879 Ljungby, Kalmar, Swed.; prof. dogmatics U. of Lund 1913–33; bp. Strängnäs 1933–52), Anders Teodor Samuel Nygren (b. 1890 Göteborg, Swed.; prof. systematic theol. U. of Lund 1924; pres. LWF 1947–52; bp. Lund 1949–58), and Ragnar Bring (b. 1895 Skara, Swed.; Aulén's successor at U. of Lund).

The Lundensian School has tried to set forth a strictly scientific methodology to be used in systematic theol. Bring and esp. Nygren have tried to demonstrate positive relationships bet. theol. and other branches of scientific research. Nygren's objective in earlier writings (e. g., *Religiöst apriori,* 1921; *Dogmatikens vetenskapliga grundläggning,* 1922; *Filosofisk och kristen etik,* 1923) was to lay a solid foundation of dogmatics and ethics by means of a philos. of religion that can guarantee not only them but, on the whole, all kinds of science. The keynote of this speculation is the concept of eternity. It belongs, Nygren claims, to the religious sphere, but secures the validity of all other knowledge as well, since that which is true cannot be true or valid if it is not true always and everywhere, i.e., has the characteristics of that which is eternal.

After trying to show a religious a priori, Nygren turned to the study of the hist. of ideas, to show how religion, or the religious a priori, is realized. He began the "motif research," to which Aulén, Bring, et al. have made valuable contributions. Aulén broke with K. G. A. v. Harnack's* interpretation of ch. hist. and showed that the Luth. Reformation* went back to the early ch. The best examples of the theol. approach of "motif research" are perhaps Nygren's *Agape and Eros* and Aulén's *Christus Victor,* the former a study of religious ideas of Gk. philos. and the NT that follows the hist. of religious motives until the Reformation, the latter an analysis and evaluation of the most influential ideas about the essential meaning of the atonement. Nygren sharply contrasts the Platonic idea of love* *(eros)* and the Christian *agape.* Whereas *eros* is a desire of good for self (man's effort to ascend to God and, primarily, human love), *agape* is God's way to man: free, spontaneous, unselfish, and self-giving love. Aulén emphasizes the "classical" theory of the atonement held, e. g., by Irenaeus* and Luther: the atonement is primarily God's action taken in Jesus Christ to set man free from death, sin, and all destructive powers (see also *Atonement, Theories of,* 7; *Christus Crucifixus*). This classical theory is contrasted with more anthropocentric and legalistic views, e. g., of Anselm* of Canterbury. Similar ideas are set forth by Aulén* in *The Faith of the Christian Church.*

The Lundensian School strongly emphasized Luther's theol. as the legitimate renewal of NT thoughts. Bring has contributed works on Luther (e. g., *Förhaallandet mellan tro och gärningar inom luthersk teologi*) which have stimulated further Luther research (see also *Luther Renaissance*). As to evaluation of Luther and Lutheranism, there is a marked tendency to stress that P. Melanchthon* differed from Luther and that the orthodox period (see *Lutheran Theology After 1580*) did not always grasp the depths of Luther's thought.

The foremost representatives of the Lundensian School have played an important role in contemporary ecumenical debates. Aulén's and Nygren's books have been studied as textbooks at theol. schools outside Swed. and outside Lutheranism. The Lundensian School has also met opposition, e. g., in the criticism of Gustav Wingren (b. 1910 Tryserum, Swed.; taught in Lund, Aabo, and Basel; prof. dogmatics U. of Lund 1951). GH

See also *Sweden, Lutheran Church in,* 6.

A. T. S. Nygren, *Agape and Eros,* tr. P. S. Watson, 2 vols. in 3 parts, rev., and in part retranslated, and pub. in 1 vol. (London, 1953); G. E. H. Aulén,

Christus Victor, tr. A. G. Hebert (New York, 1931) and *The Faith of the Christian Church,* 2d ed., tr. E. Wahlstrom from the 5th Swed. ed. (Philadelphia, 1960); P. S. Watson, *Let God be God!* (Philadelphia, 1947); E. M. Carlson, *The Reinterpretation of Luther* (Philadelphia, 1948); G. Hillerdal, "La théologie de Lund," *Positions luthériennes,* V (1957), 49–61; G. Wingren, *Theology in Conflict,* tr. E. H. Wahlstrom (Philadelphia, 1958).

Lund Missionary Society. See *Swedish Missionary Societies,* 1.

Lundateologi. See *Lund, Theology of.*

Lundensian School. See Lund, Theology of.

Lundeberg, Knut Olafson (Jan. 23, 1859–June 6, 1942). B. Kviteseid, Telemark, Norw.; studied at normal school there; to US 1879; educ. Luther Coll. and Breckenridge Institute (Decorah, Iowa), Milton (Wis.) Coll., U. of N. Dak. (at Grand Forks), and at Northfield, Minn. Pastor Kenyon, Minn.; Portland, Oreg.; Minneapolis, Minn.; Deer Park, Wis.; Ellsworth, Iowa. Helped organize Church* of the Lutheran Brethren of America; taught at their Bible school at Wahpeton, N. Dak.; pres. Ch. of the Luth. Brethren of Am. 1900–03. Ed. *Broderbaandet;* other works include *The Church of the Living Lord.*

Lund-Quist, Carl Elof (Sept. 19, 1908–Aug. 26, 1965). B. Lindsborg, Kans.; educ. Bethany Coll., Lindsborg, Kans., and Augustana Sem., Rock Island, Ill.; pres. Luth. Student Assoc. of Am. 1931–33; pastor Chicago, Ill., 1936–41; student pastor U. of Minn., Minneapolis, 1941–46; asst. exec. dir. NLC 1946–51; ex. secy LWF 1951–60.

Lundström, Anders Herman (1858–1917). B. Filipstad, Swed.; prof. ch. hist. Uppsala; pioneer of ch. hist. research in Swed.

Lüpke, Hans von (1866–1934). B. Müden an der Aller, Ger.; pastor; given position 1933 at Göttingen U. to teach village ch. work; founded Dorf-Kirchenbewegung (Village Ch. Movement).

Lupus (ca. 383–ca. 478). B. Toul, Fr.; married Pimeniola, sister of Hilary* of Arles; separated and devoted themselves to religious life; bp. Troyes ca. 426.

Lupus Servatus (Loup de Ferriéres; ca. 805–862 or later). B. Diocese of Sens, Fr.; studied under Rabanus* Maurus; humanist; abbot Ferriéres ca. 846; leader in revival of learning under Charlemagne*; made Ferriéres a center of learning. Held double* predestination and that fallen man on his own is capable only of evil. See also *Predestinarian Controversy.*

MPL, 119, 423–700.

Luria, Isaac ben Solomon (surnamed Ashkenazi, Heb. "the German"; 1534–72). Jewish cabalist (see *Cabala*) and mystic; b. Jerusalem of Ger. descent; founded school of mystics.

Lust. Desire, craving, longing, passion (e. g., Ex 15:9; Nm 11:34; Dt 12:15; Ro 7:7; Ja 1:14; 4:1-5). "Lusts of the flesh" are evil (e. g., Ro 13:14; Gl 5:17; Eph 2:1-3; 1 Jn 2:16) and "war against the soul" (1 Ptr 2:11); Christians are to flee them (e. g., 2 Ti 2:22; Tts 2:12). Gk. *epithymia* is used in a neutral (e. g., Mk 4:19), good (e. g., Lk 22:15; Ph 1:23; 1 Th 2:17), and bad (e. g., 1 Th 4:5; 1 Ptr 4:3) sense. "Libido" refers mainly to the sexual urge. See also *Concupiscence; Sensuality; Sin; Sins, Venial and Mortal.*

Luthardt, Christoph Ernst (1823–1902). Luth. theol.; b. Maroldsweisach, Lower Franconia, Bav., Ger.; educ. Erlangen and Berlin; taught at Gymnasium at Munich 1847–51, at Erlangen 1851–54; prof. Marburg 1854–56; prof. dogmatics and NT exegesis Leipzig 1856–1902; mem. Erlangen School (see *Lutheran Theology After 1580,* 11). Ed. *Allgemeine Evangelisch-Lutherische Kirchenzeitung;* other works include *Apologetische Vorträge über die Grundwahrheiten des Christenthums; Die Ethik Luthers in ihren Grundzügen; Geschichte der christlichen Ethik.*

Luther, Martin (Nov. 10, 1483–Feb. 18, 1546). Father of Protestantism; founder of Lutheranism; b. and d. Eisleben, Ger.

1. Information on ancestry is limited. Family name variously spelled, e. g., Chlotar, Luder, Ludher, Luder, Lauther, Lutter. The ancestral lands were at Möhra, near Eisenach, Thuringia. Luther's grandparents, Heine and Margareth (nee Lindemann) Luder, had 4 sons. The oldest, Gross-Hans ("Big Hans"), married Margareth Ziegler (some say Lindemann) and moved to Eisleben, at the E foot of the lower Harz mountains, to become a miner. Their oldest son was bap. Martin on Nov. 11, St. Martin's Day, in nearby St. Peter's Ch. The family moved to Mansfeld 1484; industry and thrift improved their circumstances; by 1491 Hans Luther had become an influential citizen.

2. M. Luther's childhood was that of a normal RC boy in a burgher home. His father wanted him to become a lawyer and sent him to 3 preparatory schools (in Mansfeld, Magdeburg, and Eisenach). In Mansfeld he received training preparatory to academy work. It was probably in Magdeburg, under instruction of the Brethren* of the Common Life at the Cathedral School, that he first saw a (Lat.) Bible. In Eisenach he fortunately moved in the Schalbe-Cotta family circles, where he seems to have roomed at the Cottas (see *Cotta, Ursula*) and boarded at the Schalbes, whose son he tutored. Both families were very devout. A frequent guest was Johann Braun, vicar at St. Mary's Ch. and in charge of the Franciscan monastery at the foot of the Wartburg, a castle near Eisenach; around him gathered a group of young people interested in music and poetry.

3. In spring 1501 Luther entered the U. of Erfurt, which had ca. 2,000 students (see also *Trutvetter, Jodocus*). In May 1505 he entered the Erfurt Law School; obtained a copy of *Corpus* iuris canonici* to aid his studies. Then, quite unexpectedly, July 17, 1505, he entered the Black Cloister of the local Augustinian* Hermits (their black garb gave it its name). Later he often spoke of a severe thunderstorm which had wrung from him a prayer to St. Anne and a vow to become a monk.

4. Luther did not find peace of mind and soul in the monastery, but he determined to keep his vows. He was ordained priest in spring 1507, celebrated his 1st mass May 2, 1507, in presence of his father, other relatives, and many friends. He continued his studies 1507–12, acquiring the degrees of *Biblicus* (or *lector*), *Formatus, Sententiarius,* and ThD. The more he studied medieval theol. and the more he became involved in the labyrinth of scholasticism,* the more confused be became. The main problem which disturbed him: How may I render God gracious to my soul?

5. Luther was called to Wittenberg 1508 to teach moral philos. He was recalled to Erfurt 1509, perhaps to assist his old Augustinian teacher Johannes Nathin (15th–16th c.) instruct novitiates. In Nov. 1510 Luther and another monk set out on foot for Rome to help settle some matters pertaining to the Augustinian Order. They reached Rome Jan. 1511. The pope was in Romagna. All cardinals except 2 were absent. Few relic chambers were open. Luther was shocked by the worldliness of some of the It. clergy. He climbed the Scala Sancta (see *Lateran*), praying for his grandparents.

6. Shortly after his return to Ger. he was recalled to the U. of Wittenberg, where he was trained to succeed John Staupitz in the chair of *lectura in Biblia* as soon as he had earned the doctorate, which was awarded Oct. 18–19, 1512 (see also *Frederick III* [1463–1525]). While lecturing on Gn, Ps, Rm,

Gl, and Heb 1512–18, Luther evolved from a scholastic theol. to a Biblical humanist. Probably in fall 1514, while lecturing on Ps 71, he discovered the key to the entire Bible in the principle of "justification by faith." He did not fully understand all its implications but realized that he had found the "Gate to Paradise" (WA 54, 186). In course of time he won the whole U. faculty to his point of view. By 1517 the school was becoming a center of Biblical humanism.

7. The "New Theol.," which was Christocentric and stressed *sola* Scriptura,* was too dynamic to leave the RC Ch. unaffected. Conflict with traditional scholastic theol. was unavoidable; it began in connection with sale of indulgences.* Luther posted notice of a debate on the school bulletin board (N door of the Castle Ch.) Oct. 31, 1517, listing 95 theses (see *Theses, Ninety-Five, of Luther*) for discussion. He hoped that an academic debate would clarify the subject of indulgences and determine the position the U. should adopt toward the practice. The theses were in Lat. because that was the academic language of the day. For some unknown reason the debate was never held. But the subject was timely. The theses rapidly spread through Ger. Many agreed with Luther's stand. Financial returns from indulgence sales in Ger. were greatly reduced.

8. This financial loss brought immediate reaction from J. Tetzel,* indulgence salesman in Luther's territory, from Tetzel's fellow Dominicans, and from Albert* of Brandenburg, who was hoping thus to pay his "fee" for appointment as abp. Mainz, which made him holder of 3 ch. positions simultaneously. All these brought pressure to bear on the pope to silence Luther.

9. The *processus inhibitorius* (Lat. "process of inhibiting"), the RC church's way of silencing its critics, was set in motion. The Augustinian Order was instructed to discipline its recalcitrant mem. But at the Heidelberg* Disputation, Apr. 1518, Luther won many new friends; instead of reprimanding him, the Order asked him to write an elaboration of his original 95 theses.

10. Under influence of the Saxon Dominican provincial, the fiscal procurator of Rome opened Luther's case, charging "suspicion of heresy." In Sept. 1518 Luther was summoned to appear at Augsburg before the papal legate Cajetan* (see also *Augsburg Diet* [1518]). Luther was willing to be convinced on the basis of Scripture that indulgences were Biblical. But the differences could not be reconciled. J. v. Stanpitz* absolved Luther of the vow of obedience ca. the middle of Oct. 1518. Cajetan recommended to Frederick III that Luther be either banished or surrendered to Rome.

11. On Luther's initiative the Wittenberg U. faculty sent a letter dated Nov. 22, 1518, to Frederick III, attesting complete agreement with Luther's views. Upon this statement of Luther's case and the advice of his court, Frederick III refused to surrender Luther to Rome before he had been proved a heretic by a neutral tribunal. Luther hoped for solution by a gen. council.

12. RCs connected with the case include K. v. Miltitz* and J. Eck,* the latter known esp. for his part in the Leipzig* Debate 1519. First hopeful of cleansing the ch. of error, Luther began to realize that no reformation of the existing body, permeated with error in head and mems., was possible.

13. After election of Charles* V 1519 Rome again turned its attention to the Luther case. The univs. of Louvain and Cologne had issued condemnations of Luther's theol. 1519. The bull *Exsurge, Domine* was drafted June 15, 1520: it gave Luther 60 days to recant and required all his writings to be burned. Tension mounted. At Wittenberg, Luther retaliated by burning the Canon* Law and the bull. Rome's reply was the bull of excommunication, *Decet Romanum Pontificem,* issued Jan. 3, 1521. Considerable pressure was exerted on Charles to condemn Luther. After much pol. maneuvering, Charles summoned Luther to appear at the Diet of Worms* 1521. Luther resisted all efforts to persuade him to recant and privately and pub. reiterated that he could not recant unless convinced of error by Scripture. Lacking necessary support of Ger. princes to secure Luther's condemnation, Charles waited till the Diet had been dismissed, then in a rump session declared Luther a heretic and outlaw who could be killed on sight. Luther's prince, who left the Diet earlier because of illness, anticipated the outcome and arranged to have Luther placed in "protective custody" at the Wartburg.*

14. At the Wartburg Luther reexamined his position and clearly realized that reform of the existing ch. was impossible, that the only solution was a return to the practices and tenets of early Christianity. His Wartburg works include a Ger. NT (see *Bible Versions,* M).

15. In Mar. 1522 Luther returned to Wittenberg against the wishes of his prince to quiet the confused situation which had developed there under the ill-considered leadership of A. R. B. v. Karlstadt* and G. Zwilling* (see also *Luther, Controversies of,* d). He preached a series of 8 sermons and began to reorganize ch. services. Hymn singing was introd. and the liturgy revised, providing greater participation by the cong. (see also *Luther, Hymns of; Luther, Liturgies of*).

16. Other works include the Large and Small Catechisms (see *Catechisms, Luther's*); postils (see *Postil*) providing sermon materials for the "emergency preachers" who filled pulpits made vacant by conversion of many congs from RCm to Lutheranism: a Ger. Bible (see *Bible Versions,* M); tracts; letters; treatises (see also *Luther, Chief Writings of*).

17. The pol. situation that followed the Diet of Worms was confused. The Edict of Worms* could not be enforced. New economic forces brought on other disturbances culminating in the Knights* Revolt and the Peasants* War. In both cases Luther's writings were misconstrued. When he called on forces of law and order to quell the revolt, he was accused by his enemies of turning against the peasants.

18. When the 1529 Diet of Speyer* nullified an earlier pronouncement permitting a prince to control religious affairs in his realm both factions prepared for violence. The rift which had developed among followers of Luther and those of H. Zwingli* divided Prot. forces. An attempt to resolve their differences at the Marburg Colloquy 1529 (see *Luther, Controversies of,* g; *Lutheran Confessions,* A 2) ended in agreement on all points but the Real Presence (see *Grace, Means of,* IV 3; *Lutheran Confessions,* A 2 [b]). Other attempts at reconciliation bet. RCs and Prots, include the 1530 Diet of Augsburg (see *Lutheran Confessions,* A). See also *Lutheran Confessions,* B 1–2.

19. Never a robust man and beset by many attacks of illness, Luther led an amazingly active and productive life. Late in 1545 he was asked to arbitrate a family quarrel among the princes of Mansfeld. Though old, ill, and loath to undertake an arduous journey of ca. 80 mi. from Wittenberg in winter, Luther went to Eisleben. Adjusting the family quarrel proved hard. Besides, Luther preached 4 times and helped conduct several services. The quarrel was settled Feb. 17, 1546. That evening Luther felt severe pains in the chest. Despite treatment he died early the following morning in presence of sons Martin and Paul (see *Luther, Family Life of*), 2 doctors, et al.

20. Testimony of the love and esteem with which he was regarded by the people was the homage given his mortal remains as the funeral cortege returned to Wittenberg, where his body was laid to rest in the Castle Ch. Feb. 22, 1546. EGS

See also other entries beginning *Luther . . . ; Christian Church, History of,* III, 1; *Pack, Otto von; Philip of Hesse; Psychology,* F.; *Reformation, Lutheran; Sachs, Hans.*

A. H. Böhmer, *Road to Reformation,* tr. J. W. Doberstein and T. G. Tappert (Philadelphia, 1946) and *Luther in Light of Recent Research,* tr. C. F. Huth Jr. (New York, 1916); J. Mackinnon, *Luther and the Reformation,* 4 vols. (London, 1925–30); M. Reu, *Luther's German Bible* (Columbus, Ohio, 1934); P. Nettl, *Luther and Music,* tr. F. Best and R. Woods (Philadelphia, 1948); E. M. Plass, *This Is Luther* (St. Louis, 1948); E. G. Schwiebert, *Luther and His Times* (St. Louis, 1950); R. H. Bainton, *Here I Stand: A Life of Martin Luther* (New York, 1950); W. Dallmann, *Martin Luther,* rev. ed. (Saint Louis, 1951); P. Althaus, *The Theology of Martin Luther,* tr. R. C. Schultz (Philadelphia, 1966).

Luther, Bible Translations of. See *Bible Versions,* M.

Luther, Catechisms of. See *Catechetics,* 1, 7, 9, 11; *Catechisms, Luther's.*

Luther, Chief Writings of. 1. The loving care of M. Luther's* contemporaries and followers and the industry of modern Luther research (see *Luther Renaissance*) have made it possible to trace the development of his thought in his chief writings.

2. Among Luther's early writings, his 1515–16 lectures on Ro have attracted much attention. In these lectures, discovered and pub. in the 20th c., the Reformer's growing insight into the true meaning of the Gospel is evident. Present, too, is testimony to his keen interest in the problems of individual and soc. ethics. Like the lectures on Ro, those on Heb (1517–18) show the eschatological bent of his theol. and his intense effort to assert his faith in the context of RC theol.

3. By 1519 Luther's thought had progressed considerably. That progress is reflected esp. in his 1519 commentary on Gl (rev. 1523; a longer one appeared 1535). From this charter of ev. freedom against legalistic tyranny, Luther derived his incisive analysis of the distinction bet. Law and Gospel and his realization of the work of Christ as that of victorious liberation from Law and sin.

4. Perhaps best-known of Luther's works are the trilogy issued 1520: *An Open Letter to the Christian Nobility of the German Nation Concerning the Reform of the Christian Estate* refutes 3 basic assumptions of the medieval ch.: the supremacy of the spiritual over the secular arm; the absolute right of the pope to interpret Holy Scripture; and the exclusive authority of the pope to convoke a council. The sacramentalism and sacerdotalism of the RC Ch. is subjected to close scrutiny in *The Babylonian Captivity of the Church.* And against the whole authoritarian structure of the ch., *On the Freedom of a Christian Man* asserted the spiritual freedom of a Christian, but his bondage under Christ to serve all men.

5. But the freedom of a Christian cannot be construed as the freedom of man as such in relation to God. Luther made his position on this clear in *On the Bondage of the Will* (1525), directed against D. Erasmus.* This is one of the most difficult and perhaps most profound of Luther's writings. God, not man, is the directing agent in the divine-human relationship; man does not choose, but is chosen. But yrs. later Luther warned that he had meant this treatise to be understood soteriologically, not as an abstract philos. discussion.

6. For the old Luther, probably no work is as revealing as his 1535–45 lectures on Gn. Despite his insistence on the literal meaning of the text, he often went far beyond its explicit and implicit meaning. This commentary contains some of his best theol. work, combined with sections of deep devotion and much practical pastoral counsel. Few theol. problems are untouched in this his last great work.

7. In 1539 he issued *On Councils and the Church,* a work of profound hist. and theol. scholarship, written to overthrow hist. claims of the papacy. The treatise also reveals Luther's thought on the nature of the ch., to which he devotes the 3d section, a clear and systematic definition of the relationship bet. the empirical ch. and the hidden, or invisible, ch. See also *Church,* 3. JP

Luther, Coat of Arms or Seal of. Described by M. Luther* in a letter to L. Spengler* July 8, 1530: "There is first to be a cross, black [and placed] in a heart, which should be of its natural color, so that I myself would be reminded that faith in the Crucified saves us. . . . Even though it is a black cross, [which] mortifies and [which] also should hurt us, yet it leaves the heart in its [natural] color [and] does not ruin nature; that is, [the cross] does not kill but keeps [man] alive. . . . Such a heart is to be in the midst of a white rose, to symbolize that faith gives joy, comfort, and peace; in a word it places the believer into a white joyful rose; for [this faith] does not give peace and joy as the world gives and, therefore, the rose is to be white and not red, for white is the color of the spirits and of all the angels. Such a rose is to be in a sky-blue field, [symbolizing] that such joy in the Spirit and in faith is a beginning of the future heavenly joy; it is already a part [of faith], and is grasped through hope, even though not yet manifest. And around this field is a golden ring, [symbolizing] that in heaven such blessedness lasts forever and has no end, and in addition is precious beyond all joy and goods, just as gold is the most valuable and precious metal." Cf. WA-Br 5, 445.

Luther, Confessions of. See *Lutheran Confessions.*

Luther, Controversies of. a. With the *papacy.** See *Luther, Martin,* 7–14.

b. With *J. Eck.** See *Leipzig Debate.*

c. With *Henry* VIII* et al. Luther's *The Babylonian Captivity of the Church* (see *Babylonian Captivity,* 3; *Luther, Chief Writings of,* 4) encountered widespread opposition. Henry VIII issued *Assertio septem sacramentorum* July 1521. Luther replied to Henry VIII July 1522. To this Henry VIII did not reply personally but was defended by writings of T. Murner,* J. Fisher,* and T. More.* Further correspondence bet. Luther and Henry VIII 1525–28 failed to settle the issues in controversy.

Luther and Henry VIII clashed for the 2d time when Henry VIII proposed divorce from Catherine of Aragon. Luther held that the marriage had taken place under a dispensation which should not have been granted, but that the marriage should not be broken.

d. With *Anabaptists.* While Luther was at the Wartburg (see *Luther, Martin,* 13–15), G. Zwilling* and A. R. B. v. Karlstadt* with their radical reforms caused disturbance in Wittenberg. Luther came secretly to the city Dec. 1521 to restore quiet. But the Zwickau* prophets came Dec. 1521 and fanned the sparks into a blaze. Luther was asked to return and bring order out of chaos. This he did Mar. 1522 with 8 sermons. Karlstadt and the Zwickau prophets went elsewhere. See also *Münster Kingdom.*

e. With the *Peasants.* See *Peasants' War.*

f. With *Erasmus.* At first D. Erasmus* favored Luther, but finally, under threat of losing pension, he wrote *De libero arbitrio* against Luther 1524. Luther replied with *De servo arbitrio* 1525, in which he showed from the NT that salvation does not depend on man's free will, but on God's free grace; many regard this as his most profound work. Erasmus wrote *Hyperaspistes* 1526, but Luther did not reply.

g. With *Zwingli.* H. Zwingli* read Luther 1518, received religious power and moral depth from him, received his doctrine of the Lord's Supper from C. H. Hoen* ca. 1523, attacked Luther's position 1524. Union of pope and emp. against evangelicals was in evidence at the 1529 Diet of Speyer.* In defense, Philip* of Hesse and Zwingli tried to build a pol. alliance bet. Swiss and Saxon ev. forces and to that end to remove doctrinal differences at the Colloquy of Marburg (see also *Lutheran Confessions,* A 2). Luther there gave Zwingli and his followers "the hand of peace and charity" but could not agree with them on the question of the Real Presence (see also *Grace, Means of,* IV 3).

Luther, Descendants of. Contemporary descendants of M. Luther* (called Lutherides, or Lutherids) are traced through his son Paul and daughter Margaret; see also *Luther, Family Life of.* Many are in the US. With great-great-grandson Martin Gottlob Luther, attorney in Dresden, the family name died out Nov. 3, 1759.

O. Sartorius, *Die Nachkommenschaft D. Martin Luthers in vier Jahrhunderten* (Verlag der Lutheriden-Vereinigung, Göttingen, 1926).

Luther, Family Life of. Leon[h]ard Koppe of Torgau helped some nuns escape from the cloister of Marienthron at Nimbschen, near Grimma, and brought 9 to Wittenberg in spring 1523. M. Luther* returned some to their former homes, placed the rest in good families; married 1 of them, Katharina von Bora (Katherine; 1499–1552; b. Saxony; Cistercian nun 1515–23), June 13, 1525. Katharina was a good wife and capable manager. Their children: (1) Johannes (Hans; June 7, 1526–Oct. 27, 1575; studied law; employed in Weimar chancellory as adviser); (2) Elisabeth (Elizabeth; Dec. 10, 1527–Aug. 3, 1528); (3) Magdalene (Magdalena; May 4, 1529–Sept. 20, 1542); (4) Martin (Nov. 9, 1531 – Mar. 2[3?], 1565; studied theol. but never occupied a pulpit); (5) Paul (Jan. 28, 1533–Mar. 8, 1593; physician in several courts); (6) Margaret(a) (Margarethe; Dec. 17, 1534–1570; m. Georg von Kuhnheim [or Kunheim] Aug. 5, 1555). The letter Luther wrote 1530 from the Coburg to his oldest son ("Hänsichen") is unique in literature (see also *Richter, Adrian Ludwig*).

Luther was an extremely fond father, but a strict disciplinarian. As a rule he fared frugally. On festivals he enjoyed a good dinner. He took relatives into his home; students and many others enjoyed his hospitality. His table talk (see *Luther, Table Talk of*) was recorded by various guests and later pub.

Luther, Hymns of. When the Luth. Reformation* began, corporate worship included no singing by the common people. In harmony with M. Luther's* enunciation of the doctrine of spiritual priesthood, a need for hymn texts and tunes for cong. singing arose. The Luth. chorale* is one of Luther's gifts to Christendom. It is hard to say with final authority which hymn texts Luther wrote and for which he composed the music. Some of his hymns are apparently wholly original. As to text, some are original additions to 1 or more existing stanzas; some are poetic forms of Bible passages; some are translations or adaptations of extant material. As to music, some melodies are ascribed to him, e. g., the one for "Jesaia, dem Propheten" ("Isaiah, Mighty Seer") and "Ein feste Burg" ("A Mighty Fortress"); in other cases he adopted and/or adapted extant melodies; for others he requested contributions of other composers. Early Luth. hymnals appeared 1524: *Etlich christlich lider,* also known as *Achtliederbuch,* ascribes the hymn "Nun freut euch, lieben Christen gmein" to Luther; *Enchiridion* (2 eds.) includes 18 hymns ascribed by many to Luther; *Geystliche gesangk Buchleyn,* designed for choir use, includes 24 hymns ascribed by many to Luther.

Hymns ascribed to Luther include "Ach Gott vom Himmel, sieh darein" ("O Lord, Look Down from Heaven, Behold"); "All Ehr' und Lob soll Gottes sein" ("All Glory Be to God Alone"); "Aus tiefer Not schrei ich zu dir" ("From Depths of Woe I Cry to Thee"); "Christ lag in Todesbanden" ("Christ Jesus Lay in Death's Strong Bands"); "Dies sind die heil'gen zehn Gebot" ("That Man a Godly Life Might Live"); "Ein feste Burg ist unser Gott" ("A Mighty Fortress Is Our God"); "Erhalt uns, Herr, bei deinem Wort" ("Lord, Keep Us Steadfast in Thy Word"); "Es woll' uns Gott genädig sein" ("May God Bestow on Us His Grace"); "Gelobet sei'st du, Jesu Christ" ("All Praise to Thee, Eternal God"); "Gott der Vater wohn' uns bei" ("God the Father, Be Our Stay"); "Gott sei gelobet und gebenedeiet" ("O Lord, We Praise Thee"); "Jesaia, dem Propheten, das geschah" ("Isaiah, Mighty Seer, in Days of Old"); "Komm, Heiliger Geist, Herre Gott" ("Come, Holy Ghost, God and Lord"); "Mit Fried' und Freud' ich fahr dahin" ("In Peace and Joy I Now Depart"); "Mitten wir im Leben sind" ("In the Midst of Earthly Life"); "Nun bitten wir den Heiligen Geist" ("We Now Implore God the Holy Ghost"); "Vater unser im Himmelreich" ("Our Father, Thou in Heaven Above"); "Vom Himmel hoch, da komm' ich her" ("From Heaven Above to Earth I Come"); "Vom Himmel kam der Engel Schar" ("To Shepherds as They Watched by Night"); "Wär Gott nicht mit uns diese Zeit" ("If God Had Not Been on Our Side"); "Wir glauben all' an einen Gott" ("We All Believe in One True God").

See also *Music, Church.*

Martin Luthers geistliche Lieder, ed. K. E. P. Wackernagel (Stuttgart, 1848); F. Spitta, *"Ein feste Burg ist unser Gott": Die Lieder Luthers in ihrer Bedeutung für das evangelische Kirchenlied* (Göttingen, 1905); W. E. Buszin, "Luther on Music," *The Musical Quarterly,* XXXII (Jan. 1946), 80–97; P. Nettl, *Luther and Music,* tr. F. Best and R. Wood (Philadelphia, 1948); *Dr. Martin Luther's deutsche geistliche Lieder,* Ger. and Eng., ed. L. W. Bacon and N. H. Allen (New York, 1883); B. Pick, *Luther's Battle Song* (New York, 1917); G. K. Wolfram, *Ein feste Burg ist unser Gott* (Berlin, 1936); *Luther's Works,* Am. ed., LIII, ed. H. T. Lehmann and U. S. Leupold (Philadelphia, 1965), 189–334.

Luther, Liturgies of. At the urging of N. Hausmann,* M. Luther* in Dec. 1523 pub. *Formula missae et communionis pro ecclesia Vuittembergensi,* an account of the ev. mass which omitted the sacrifice of the mass. It included Introit; Kyrie; Gloria in excelsis; Collect; Epistle; Gradual and/or Hallelujah; Gospel; Nicene Creed; Sermon; Preface; Consecration; Sanctus (including elevation of the elements during the Benedictus for the sake of the weak); Lord's Prayer; Pax; Distribution during Agnus Dei (the pastor communicating first himself and then the cong.); Collect; Benedicamus; Benediction; all in Lat., except sermon in the vernacular; vernacular hymns also to be included.

Multiplication of Ger. masses led to demand for a standard order of service. On Oct. 29, 1525, Luther's 1st completely Ger. mass was held in Wittenberg; it was fully introd. Dec. 25, 1525, and appeared in print 1526 as *Deudsche Messe und ordnung Gottis diensts.* Included: Hymn or Ps, Kyrie, Collect, Epistle, Hymn, Gospel, versified Creed, Sermon, paraphrase of the Lord's Prayer and admonition to communicants, Consecration and distribution of bread, Ger. Sanctus ("Jesaia, dem Propheten, das geschah") or Hymn, Consecration and distribution of wine, Ger. Agnus Dei ("Christe, du Lamm Gottes") or Hymn, Collects, Aaronic benediction.

Luther also prepared liturgies for occasional services (see *Baptism, Liturgical,* 3; *Marriage Liturgy*).

See also *Chant; Liturgics.*

Luther's Works, Am. ed., LIII, ed. H. T. Lehmann and U. S. Leupold (Philadelphia, 1965), 3–188; WA 12, 31–37; 19, 44–113.

Luther, Music of. See *Luther, Hymns of; Luther, Liturgies of; Music, Church.*

Luther, Reformation of. See *Luther, Martin; Reformation, Lutheran.*

Luther, Table Talk of (Tischreden). Many eds. have appeared. Those who recorded M. Luther's* table talk include J. Aurifaber* (1519–75), H. Besold,* C. Cordatus,* V. Dietrich,* A. Lauterbach,* J. Mathesius,* G. Rörer,* J. Schlaginhaufen,* H. Weller.*

Luther, Works of, Editions of. *Ger. and Lat.* (1) Wittenberg 1539–59, ed. G. Rörer, C. Cruciger the Elder, G. Major, C. Walther; 19 vols. (12 Ger., 7 Lat.) plus index vol.; reprint. repeatedly up to 1603. (2) Jena 1555–58, ed. G. Rörer et al.; 12 vols. (8 Ger., 4 Lat.) plus index vol. for the Ger. vols. by T. Kirchner 1564; reprint. several times in whole or in part up to 1615; Eisleben Supplement to Wittenberg and Jena eds., ed. J. Aurifaber, 2 vols. 1564–65, reprint. Leipzig 1603. (3) Altenburg 1661–64. ed. J. C. Sagittarius; 9 vols. (Ger.) plus index vol.; Halle Supplement vol. 1702, ed. J. G. Zeidler. (4) Leipzig 1729–34 and 1740, ed. J. G. Pfeiffer, C. F. Borner, and J. J. Greiff, 22 parts in 11 vols. plus appendix and index in 1 vol. (5) Walch 1 (Halle, 1740–53), ed. J. G. Walch; 22 vols. (Ger.) plus Luther biography and indexes, 2 vols.; enl. and repub. as St. Louis ed. (Walch 2; 1880–1910), 22 vols. plus index vol. (6) Erlangen (1826–86), ed. J. K. Irmischer and J. G. Plochmann; 65 vols. (Ger.) plus 2 index vols. and 38 vols. (Lat. in 3 series); vols. 1–20 and 24–26 repub. as Erlangen-Frankfurt ed. (1862–85), ed. E. L. Enders (Ger.). (7) Weimar (1883–), begun by J. K. F. Knaake; pub. in 4 sections: Works, vols. 1–54 and 56–58 I (in 68 parts; vol. 55 projected for 2 parts); Tabletalk, 6 vols. (complete); Ger. Bible, vols. 1–12 (in 15 parts); Correspondence, vols. 1–11. (8) Editions of selected works: a. Braunschweig (1889–93), 3d ed. Leipzig 10 vols; b. Bonn [Berlin] students' ed. (1912–33), vols. 1–4 6th ed. 1966–68, vols. 5–8 3d ed. 1962–66, ed. O. Clemen et al.; c. Munich eds. (1914–27; 1934–39; 1940 [suppl. vol. 1] and 1948–65); d. Luther Deutsch (Berlin, Stuttgart, and Göttingen, 1948–; some vols. in 2d and 3d ed.); e. Calwer (Stuttgart, 1930–40), 6 vols.; f. Volksbibliothek (St. Louis, 1859–76), 30 vols. in 15. *Bibliographic keys and indexes* comparing collation and contents of eds.: (1) and (2), S. Schwob, *Register* (Breslau, 1563; Wittenberg, 1564, 3d ed. 1573); (1)–(3), index of Altenburg ed.; (1)–(4), index of Leipzig ed.; (1)–(5), indexes of Walch 1; (5)–(6), index of Erlangen ed.; (5)–(8d), K. Aland et al., *Hilfsbuch zum Lutherstudium,* 3d ed. (Witten, Ger., 1970).

English. (1) Cole (London, 1826), ed. H. Cole; 4 vols. (2) Lenker (Minneapolis, 1903–10), ed. J. N. Lenker; 13 vols. (3) Holman (Philadelphia, 1915–32), ed. H. E. Jacobs; 6 vols. (reprint. 1943). (4) Am. (St. Louis and Philadelphia, 1955–), ed. J. Pelikan and H. T. Lehman; 55 vols, plus companion vol. (J. Pelikan, *Luther the Expositor: Introduction to the Reformer's Exegetical Writings*). *Bibliographic keys and indexes* comparing collation and contents of eds.: G. S. Robbert, "A Checklist of Luther's Writings in English," *CTM,* XXXVI (Dec. 1965), 772–792, and XLI (Apr. 1970), 214–220; for (3) and (4), K. Aland et al., *Hilfsbuch zum Lutherstudium,* 3d ed. (Witten, Ger. 1970).

French. Geneva (1957–). JAH

"Kurze Geschichte und Charakteristik aller Gesammtausgaben von Dr. M. Luther's Schriften," *Zeitschrift für Protestantismus und Kirche,* XIX (1850), 43–59; *Bibliotheca Lutherana* (Nördlingen, Ger., 1883).

Luther and Civil Authority. M. Luther* approached the concept of state as authority and power (Ger. *Obrigkeit*) rather than as community of citizens. He called such authority God's kingdom of the left hand (WA 36, 385), a realm in which God is at work, directing the rule for His purposes (WA 30 I, 136, 152; 42, 129). Powers in ch. and state are under God, who is the ultimate authority (WA 51, 240; cf. 2, 16; 6, 415; 19, 656–658). The authority of the state is est. in the 4th Commandment (LC, 141). To serve in govt. is a noble task. Citizens owe obedience to govt. except when it overreaches itself and tyranically interferes in matters of faith (cf. Jn 19:10-11; WA 28, 286, 359–363). The Luth. Confessions follow Luther in distinguishing bet. ch. and state on basis of function. The ch. operates with the Word, the state with the sword (AC XXVIII). See also *Church and State,* 10 and bibliography.

Luther and Councils. See *Councils and Synods,* 8–13.

Luther and Education. See *Christian Education,* D.

Luther and Inspiration. See *Inspiration, Doctrine of,* B 1.

Luther and Psychology. See *Psychology,* F.

Luther and the Reformation, Anniversaries of. In 1646 the centennial of M. Luther's* death was observed esp. in Wittenberg and Erfurt. In succeeding cents. the date was noted more widely. The anniversary of Luther's birth was not extensively celebrated till 1883, which saw the greatest celebration in honor of Luther which had thus far occurred.

For some time there was little agreement on a date commemorating the Luth. Reformation. In 1568 Pomerania marked the anniversary of Luther's birth. Other areas in Ger. observed the date on which Lutheranism was introd. The centennial of the pub. of Luther's 95 Theses* was observed 1617 and the centennial of the AC 1630. Annual commemorations of the Reformation were apparently observed first in Saxony 1668; Gotha followed 1717, Württemberg 1740, Hannover 1769, Schleswig 1770, Baden 1835; but the dates varied (e. g., Oct. 31, Nov. 18, June 25). Beginning ca. 1878, on initiative arising in Eisenach, the Sun. after Oct. 30 was gen. adopted as the anniversary date.

Other important Reformation events are also commemorated (e. g., Catechism anniversaries and anniversaries of the Bible tr.).

Important literature is often pub. on the anniversaries. Less frequently attempts are made to have important events take place (e. g., Prussian* Union 1817).

Luther College. 1. Luther Coll., Decorah, Iowa; est. by The Norw. Ev. Luth. Ch. in Am. (see *Evangelical Lutheran Church, The,* 8); founding resolution adopted 1857; 1st prof. P. L. Larsen*; the school was at Halfway Creek, La Crosse Co., Wis., 1861–62, moved to Decorah 1862; coed. 1936; The ALC. See also *Ministry, Education of,* VIII B 17; *Schmid(t), Friedrich August.*

2. Luther Jr. Coll., Wahoo, Nebr.; formerly Luther Academy; est. 1883 by Augustana Syn.; merged with Midland Coll., Fremont, 1962; LCA. See also *Ministry, Education of,* VIII C 1 d.

3. Dr. Martin Luther Coll., New Ulm, Minn.; est. 1883/84 by Ger. Ev. Luth. Syn. of Minn.; Wis. Syn. 1892. See also *Ministry, Education of,* VIII B 12.

4. Luther Coll., New Orleans, La. The Synodical* Conf. resolved 1902 to est. 1 or 2 schools to train Negro pastors and teachers. F. J. Lankenau* opened the New Orleans school 1903 and was pres. 1903–08. The school also served as a sem. but was reduced 1910 to a preparatory school for Imman-

uel* Luth. Coll., Greensboro, N. C.; closed 1925; in 1928 the Syn. Conf. resolved to reopen it; new beginning made 1929; closed 1932.

5. Luth. Coll., Regina, Sask., Can.; est. 1913 as Luther Academy at Melville, Sask.; classes began 1914; moved to Regina; affiliated with U. Sask.; coed.; jr. coll.; sponsored by ELCC; action taken 1966 to fed. the school with the U. of Sask. See also *Ministry, Education of,* VIII C 1 c.

Luther Leagues. See *Young People's Organizations, Christian,* II 1, 2, 4.

Luther Medals. See *Reformation Medals.*

Luther Monuments. Monuments of M. Luther* are found esp. in the cities where he was active. Among the earliest is that at Wittenberg created 1821 by Johann Gottfried Schadow (1764–1850; b. Berlin, Ger.; sculptor). The one at Worms, in a group of statues, was created 1868 by E. F. A. Rietschel*; a character study of the highest order, it shows Luther standing with his closed right hand resting on a closed Bible. He is surrounded by statues of other Reformation and pre-Reformation figures: G. Savonarola* seated at the front of the base, to Luther's right; J. Hus* similarly to Luther's left; P. Waldo (see *Waldenses*) and J. Wycliffe* similarly at the 2 rear corners of the base; Frederick* III ("the Wise") standing on a separate pedestal at Luther's right in the foreground; similarly J. Reuchlin* at Luther's right in the background, Philip* of Hesse at his left in the foreground, and P. Melanchthon* at his left in the background; on a separate pedestal, to Luther's right, bet. Frederick III and Reuchlin is a seated figure, facing Luther, with the palm of peace, representing the city of Augsburg; similarly a seated figure at Luther's left, bet. Philip of Hesse and Melanchthon, represents mourning Magdeburg, and a seated figure behind Luther, bet. Reuchlin and Melanchthon, represents protesting Speyer. On the wall framing the entire group to Luther's right, rear, and left are emblems (left to right as you face the monument) of 1. Brunswick, 2. Bremen, 3. Konstanz, 4. Eisenach, 5. Eisleben, 6. Emden, 7. Erfurt, 8. Frankfurt, 9. Schwäbisch-Hall, 10. Hamburg, 11. Heilbronn, 12. Jena, 13. Königsberg, 14. Leipzig, 15. Lindau, 16. Lübeck, 17. Marburg, 18. Memmingen, 19. Nördlingen, 20. Riga, 21. Schmalkalden, 22. Strasbourg, 23. Ulm, 24. Wittenberg.

Other important statues in Ger. include one in Eisleben created 1883 by Rudolf Siemering (1835–1905; b. Königsberg, Ger.; sculptor) and the Luther-Melanchthon memorial in Leipzig, designed 1883 by Johannes Schilling (1828–1910; b. Mittweida, Ger.; sculptor).

Replicas of the Worms statue in the US include (1) one dating from 1883 in front of Luther Place Memorial Luth. Ch., Washington, D. C.; (2) one dating from 1903 at Conc. Sem., St. Louis, Mo.; (3) one at Luther Coll., Decorah, Iowa; (4) one at Wartburg Sem., Dubuque, Iowa; (5) one at Conc. Coll., St. Paul, Minn.; (6) one in Luther Memorial Park, Detroit, Mich.

Other Luther statues in the US include (1) one by Hans Schuler (1874–1951; b. Morange, Lorraine, Ger.; to US 1880; sculptor) formerly (since 1936) in Druid Hill Park, since 1959 at 33d St. and Hillen Rd., near Lake Montebello, Baltimore, Md.; (2) one at Lutheran Theol. Sem., Gettysburg, Pa.; (3) one at Conc. Sem., Springfield, Ill.; (4) one by Walter Kirtland Hancock (b. 1901 St. Louis, Mo.; sculptor) in the "Washington Cathedral" (also known as National [Prot. Episc.] Cathedral; Cathedral of Saint Peter and St. Paul), Washington, D. C.

Luther Renaissance. The sterility of rationalism* and the theol. waywardness of Pietism* led, by the 19th c., to restudies of original Lutheranism. Revived interest in M. Luther* led to pub. of the Erlangen ed. of his works and to advocacy of confessional Lutheranism. Controversies and theol. currents engendered by these studies developed a huge literature on doctrinal and hist. themes dealing with Luther and climaxed in the definitive critical ed. of his works (Weimar, 1883–; see *Luther, Works of, Editions of*). A 2d period of the back-to-Luther movement began with the 20th c. and the effort to discern motives of primitive Luth. concepts introd. into the Ger. ch. by Luther's co-workers and successors. In Scand. the theol. of Lund* contributed to the Luther renaissance. Am. contributions include those of J. M. Reu, the Foundation* for Reformation Research, the St. Louis ed. (also called Walch 2) of Luther's works, and the Am. ed. of Luther's works in Eng. (see *Luther, Works of, Editions of*), development toward the Luth. parish ideal, and studies in the Luth. liturgy. The Luther renaissance played a part in Eur. and Am. neo-orthodoxy.* RRC

See also *Lutheran Theology After 1580,* 11–15; *Neo-Lutheranism.*

Luther Research. See *Luther Renaissance.*

Luther Society (Luther-Gesellschaft). Est. 1918 on initiative of R. C. Eucken* as a result of the 1917 Reformation Jubilee, to promote better knowledge and understanding of M. Luther* and his work. Headquarters Hamburg, Ger.

Luther Theological Seminary. 1. Luther Theol. Sem., St. Paul, Minn.; est. 1876 by the Norw. Syn. (see *Evangelical Lutheran Church, The,* 8–13) as a "practical" sem. at Madison, Wis.; "theoretical" dept. added 1878 (moved to Madison from St. Louis, Mo.); moved temporarily to Minneapolis, Minn., in the 1880s; to Robbinsdale, Minn., 1889; to the Hamline section of St. Paul 1899; merged 1917 with the United* Norw. Luth. Ch. in Am. sem. (see 4) and Hauge's Norw. Ev. Luth. Syn. (see *Eielsen Synod*) sem. to form Luther Theol. Sem., St. Anthony Park, St. Paul; since 1961 one of the 4 units of The ALC sem. See also *Ministry, Education of,* X G; *Red Wing Seminary.*

2. Luther Theol. Sem., Saskatoon, Sask., Can. See *Canada,* A 14, 20; *Ministry, Education of,* X L.

3. Luther Sem. of the Joint Ohio Syn., St. Paul, Minn. See *Ohio and Other States, Evangelical Lutheran Joint Synod of,* 8.

4. Luther Sem. (Norw.), St. Anthony Park, St. Paul, Minn. Founded 1890 in connection with formation of The United* Norw. Luth. Ch. in Am., by merger of the Anti-Missouri* Brotherhood sem., Northfield, Minn.; parts of Augsburg Sem., Minneapolis (organized 1869 Marshall, Wis., by the Scand. Ev. Luth. Augustana Syn. of N. Am. [see *Augustana Evangelical Lutheran Church,* 8]; moved to Minneapolis 1872 by The Conf. for the Norw.-Dan. Ev. Luth. Ch. in Am. [see *Norwegian-Danish Augustana Synod in America, The*]); and Augustana Sem., Beloit, Iowa (begun 1874 Springfield, near Decorah, Iowa, by the Scand. Ev. Luth. Augustana Syn. of N. Am., moved 1876 to Marshall, Wis., 1881 to Beloit, Iowa [across the state line from Canton, S. Dak.]). The United Ch. sem. was located 1890–93 in Augsburg Sem. bldgs., after that in temporary quarters, then in more permanent quarters in Minneapolis, and moved to St. Paul 1902.

See also *Ministry, Education of,* X–XI.

Lutheran. Term (adjective and noun) derived from the name M. Luther*; refers to his followers and to doctrines and practices of the Luth. Ch.; apparently 1st used ca. 1519 or in the early 1520s, but it may be impossible to determine exactly when and by whom (but first, apparently, by Luther's enemies). William Warham (ca. 1450–1532; b. Okeley, Hampshire, Eng.; educ. Winchester and Oxford; abp. Canterbury 1504) used the term of followers of Luther 1521. Luther wrote 1522: "True, by any consideration of body or soul you should never say: I am Lutheran, or Papist. For neither of them died for you, or is your master. . . . But if you are convinced that Luther's teaching is in accord with the Gospel and that the pope's is not, then you should not discard Luther so completely. . . . It is on account of the teaching that they attack you and ask you whether you are Lutheran" (WA 10 II, 40). Ap XV 44 (Ger.): "The saving doctrine, the precious, holy Gospel, they call Lutheran."

Lutheran Academy for Scholarship (Academia Lutherana Philosophiae; Gk. acronym Alpha Lamda Phi). Assoc. organized Mar. 1942 Chicago, Ill. Membership by invitation: patron, mem., fellow, award fellow. Purposes: to serve (1) as a means whereby professionally trained persons belonging to the Luth. Ch. may jointly confront and discuss the major problems of ch. and soc.; (2) as an instrument providing opportunity for the individual mem. of the Academy to contribute at his level of accomplishment to the thought and life of the Luth. Ch.; (3) as an instrument helping to preserve and develop the distinctive accents of Lutheranism within our pluralistic soc.; (4) as a means of creating opportunities to discuss and to formulate specific ethical concerns of the Luth. Ch. in various academic disciplines and in particular professions. Functions: (1) Pub. a quarterly journal, various symposia of proceedings from colloquies, institutes, assemblies, and conferences; (2) planning and implementation of nat. meetings designed to bring to the attention of selected groups of professional persons the nature and size of various issues of concern to both ch. and soc.; (3) joint work with appropriate bds. and commissions in raising and discussing matters of major concern to persons engaged in educ. coll. and grad. students; (4) selection of certain professions as areas meriting specific and concentrated investigation, analysis, and prescription.

R. Beese, "The First Quarter Century," *The Lutheran Scholar,* XXVI (1969), 28–32, 45–61.

Lutheran Bible Translators, Inc. See *Messengers of Christ, Inc.*

Lutheran Book Concern. See *Publication Houses, Lutheran.*

Lutheran Brethren. See *Church of the Lutheran Brethren of America.*

Lutheran Brethren Schools. See *Ministry, Education of,* VIII C 2 l.

Lutheran Bureau. See *National Lutheran Council.*

"Lutheran Chaplain, The." See *Armed Services Commission,* 3.

Lutheran Charities Association. See *Child and Family Service Agencies,* 4.

Lutheran Church. See *Luther, Martin; Lutheran Confessions; Lutheran Theology After 1580; Reformation, Lutheran.*

Lutheran Church – Canada. See *Canada,* A 28.

Lutheran Church – Missouri Synod, The. Name adopted 1947 by that body of Luths. in Am. which had first been called Die Deutsche Evangelisch-Lutherische Synode von Missouri, Ohio und andern Staaten, 1917 adopted the name Die Evangelisch-Lutherische Synode von Missouri, Ohio und andern Staaten (The Evangelical Lutheran Synod of Missouri, Ohio, and Other States), and was often called "Missouri Synod" or simply "Missouri."

I. *Löhe Men.* 1. The Mo. Syn. was organized Chicago, Ill., Mon., Apr. 26, 1847. Three meetings preceded: Cleveland, Ohio, Sept. 1845 (cf. par. I 2); St. Louis, Mo., May 1846 (cf. par. II 6); Fort Wayne, Ind., July 1846 (cf. par. III 1).

2. At the Cleveland meeting several Löhe missionaries (Ger.: *Sendlinge*) withdrew from the Ohio Syn. (see *Document of Separation*).

3. Löhe men in Mich. included G. W. C. Hattstädt,* F. A. Crämer,* and G. E. C. F. Sievers.*

4. Löhe men in Fort Wayne included C. A. W. Röbbelen,* W. Sihler,* and C. L. A. Wolter.*

5. Other Löhe men included F. J. C. Lochner,* J. H. P. Graebner,* J. M. G. Schaller,* C. J. H. Fick,* E. A. Brauer.*

6. Löhe men helped organize the Mo. Syn. and were a strong element in its early hist. The 1st suggestion for a syn. including Saxons seems to have been made by J. A. Ernst * in a letter to C. F. W. Walther* early in 1845.

II. *Saxons in Mo.* 1. Saxons under M. Stephan* the elder came to St. Louis and Perry Co., Mo., 1839. Other pastors in the group: E. M. Bürger,* E. G. W. Keyl,* G. H. Löber,* C. F. W. Walther,* O. H. Walther.* Candidates included T. J. Brohm,* J. F. Bürger,* O. Fuerbringer,* C. L. Geyer,* J. J. Gönner,* G. A. Schieferdecker.* There were more than 600 persons on the 4 ships that arrived (*Copernicus, Johann Georg, Republik, Olbers;* ca. 57 were lost at sea with the *Amalia*). They were soon joined by a group from N. Y. that had come to the US 1836 and by more than 100 from Saxe-Altenburg under T. C. F. Gruber.*

2. Within a few months after arrival in Mo., Stephan was found guilty of moral turpitude and exiled. His views on ch. and ministry also raised questions regarding status of the immigrant congs., validity of the pastoral office in their midst, and efficacy of sacraments as administered among them.

3. The Altenburg* Debate clarified matters for the Perry Co. settlers Apr. 1841. By that time, too, their physical conditions had improved.

4. Shortly after the Altenburg Debate, C. F. W. Walther became pastor of the St. Louis cong., which became the largest and dominant cong. among the Saxons. A log-cabin "college" was founded 1839 at Dresden, Perry Co., by J. F. Bünger, T. Brohm, O. Fuerbringer, and C. F. W. Walther; classes soon moved to Altenburg; became a preparatory school for pastors and a sem., with J. J. Gönner rector; see also *Ministry, Education of,* X C.

5. Under Walther's leadership the St. Louis cong. began pub. *Der Lutheraner* 1844, a medium of communication which brought the Saxons into contact with F. C. D. Wyneken* and Löhe men including W. Sihler and F. A. Crämer. The size and economic strength of this cong. contributed to the prominence it enjoyed.

6. The St. Louis cong. shared in preliminary drafting of the const. of the Mo. Syn. in the St. Louis meeting May 1846 (cf. par. I 1). Löhe men present: F. J. C. Lochner, W. Sihler, and J. A. Ernst. Saxons included C. F. W. Walther, O. Fuerbringer, J. F. Bünger, G. H. Löber, E. G. W. Keyl, T. C. F. Gruber.

III. *Organization of the Mo. Syn.* 1. The draft of the const. drawn up in St. Louis was discussed at a meeting in Fort Wayne in July 1846 (cf. par. I 1). 16 pastors and 5 candidates attended. Saxons included T. J. Brohm, G. H. Löber, C. F. W. Walther. Others included F. W. Husmann,* G. H. Jäbker,* and W. Sihler* from Ind.; J. G. Burger,* J. A. Detzer,* J. A. Ernst,* and P. J. Trautmann* from Ohio; F. A. Crämer* and G. W. C. Hattstädt* from Mich.; C. A. T. Selle* from Ill. The approved form of the const. was submitted to the congs. and pub. in *Der Lutheraner,* III, 1 (Sept. 5, 1846).

2. The organization meeting was held Sun., Apr. 25–Thu., May 6, 1847, in Chicago. 19 pastors attended; 12 (11 present, 1 absent) became voting mems.; 10 (6 present, 4 absent) became advisory mems.; 2 did not join. C. F. W. Walther was elected pres., W. Sihler vice-pres., F. W. Husmann secy., F. W. Barthel* (a St. Louis layman) treas. C. J. H.

Fick was elected miss. committee chm. *Der Lutheraner* became property and official organ of the syn., which elected a pub. committee; C. F. W. Walther continued as ed. Steps were taken with a view to acquiring the schools at Altenburg, Mo. (see par. II 4), and Fort Wayne, Ind. (see *Löhe, Johann Konrad Wilhelm*), and the Löhe miss. among Indians at Frankenmuth, Mich. (see *Crämer, Friedrich August; Indians, Lutheran Missions to North American*). C. H. F. Frincke* was appointed *Besucher* ("visitor"; traveling missionary) to look up Luth. settlers needing services of the ch. The syn. was divided into 6 pastoral conferences.

3. A notable feature already of the 1st const. is a statement of reasons for forming a syn. organization. See also par. IV 1.

4. The syn. adopted as its confessional basis Holy Scripture of the OT and NT as the written Word of God and only rule and norm of faith and life, and all the Luth. confessions as the pure and unadulterated explanation and presentation of the divine Word.

5. The advisory character of syn. in regard to self-government of the individual cong. became a concern of the syn. from the outset (cf. 1847 Proceedings, p. 7; see also par. IV 5 below).

6. Conducting missions, operating educ. institutions for preprofessional ch. workers, certifying pastors and teachers, expanding the syn. territories, publishing ch. periodicals, and carrying on relations with other ch. bodies were matters that belonged to syn.

7. Each cong. was allowed representation in conventions by pastor and elected lay delegate.

IV. *1854 Const. Rev.* 1. 1854 const. statement of reasons for forming a syn. organization: "(1) The example of the apostolic church (Acts 15:1-31). (2) The Lord's will that the diversities of gifts be used for the common profit (1 Co 12:4-31). (3) The joint extension of the kingdom of God and the establishment and promotion of special church enterprises (seminary, agenda, hymnal, Book of Concord, schoolbooks, Bible distribution, missionary endeavors within and without the church, etc.). (4) The conservation and promotion of the unity of the pure confession (Eph 4:3-6; 1 Co 1:10) and the common defense against schism and sectarianism. (Ro 16:17). (5) The protection and maintenance of the rights and duties of pastors and congregations. (6) The establishment of the largest possible uniformity in church government." (Cf. *Moving Frontiers,* ed. C. S. Meyer [St. Louis, 1964], p. 149)

Syn. was divided into 4 geog. and administrative districts. The dist. pres. was given some functions originally assigned to the syn. pres., esp. that of visiting individual congs. The districts were charged with direct responsibility of maintaining correct doctrine and acceptable practices; overall supervision of doctrine and practice still belonged to the syn. pres. See also *Lutheran Church – Missouri Synod, Districts of The,* A 1-5.

2. After 1854 the syn. conv. pattern was no longer annual but triennial. The districts met in each of the intervening yrs., and concurrently with the gen. conv. as necessary. Greater participation in gen. ch. matters and better administrative procedures were hoped for as results of the change.

3. Needs of spiritually neglected Luths. in its territory were made concerns of each dist. Conditions were specified under which a dist. could supply a pastor for a mixed cong., i.e., one consisting of Luths., Ref., and so-called Evangelicals or United (Ger. *Uniert*). (1854 Const., V A 10–11)

4. The 1854 const. continued arrangements for bds. of control of the 2 institutions of higher learning, 1 bd. of electors for choosing professors at these schools, and 2 examining commissions for colloquizing ministerial candidates not trained by the 2 schools.

5. Relation bet. syn. and mem. congs. was defined: "Synod is in respect to the self-government [*Selbstregierung*] of the individual congregations only an advisory body. Therefore no resolution of the former, when it imposes anything upon the individual congregation as a synodical resolution, has binding force for the latter. – Such a synodical resolution has binding force only when the individual congregation through a formal congregational resolution has voluntarily adopted and confirmed it. – Should a congregation find a synodical resolution not in conformity with the Word of God or unsuited for its circumstances, it has the right to disregard, that is, to reject it." (1854 Const., Chap. IV A 9; *Moving Frontiers,* p. 151)

V. *Planting, 1847–87.* 1. The 1st period of Mo. Syn. hist. extends from its founding 1847 to the death of C. F. W. Walther 1887.

2. This period was dominated by the personality of Walther, syn. pres. 1847–50, 1864–78. The *Gesamtgemeinde* ("whole parish") in St. Louis, of which Walther was chief pastor, grew to 4 congs. (Trinity 1839, Immanuel 1847, Holy Cross 1858, Zion 1860) and was the most influential parish in synod. Conc. Sem. moved to St. Louis 1849. Walther was its pres. 1854–87. He ed. *Der Lutheraner* 1844–65; ed. *Lehre und Wehre* (professional journal for pastors) from its beginning 1855 to 1860, coed. 1861–64. He was the outstanding preacher, writer, and theol. in the synod. F. C. D. Wyneken, syn. pres. 1850–64, was primarily concerned with planting new congs. During his tenure the syn. divided into 4 districts (see IV 1–3). See also *Stephan, Martin, Jr.*

3. In 1872 the syn. adopted the delegate pattern, acc. to which congs. in groups of 2–7 elected a pastor and a layman to represent them at the triennial conv.; the 1st delegate syn. met 1875. Growth continued. H. C. Schwan* was syn. pres. 1878–99.

4. The syn. gained many mems. by miss. work among immigrants. See also *Immigrant and Emigrant Missions.*

5. Many parochial schools, often taught by a pastor, were est. Esp. in large cities they attracted many non-Luths., usually Ger. The syn. produced textbooks. Part-time agencies (e. g., summer schools; Sat. schools) were also used. Instruction before confirmation* and Communion was emphasized (see also *Catechetics,* 11).

6. A private "teachers' sem." opened Milwaukee, Wis., 1855 by F. J. C. Lochner,* P. Fleischmann,* et al. In 1857 the syn. adopted it and moved it to Fort Wayne, Ind., and united it with the theol. sem. there (see *Löhe, Johann Konrad Wilhelm*). In 1864 it moved to Addison, Ill.; 1913 it moved to River Forest, Ill. See also *Ministry, Education of,* VIII B 9; *Stephan, Martin, Jr.*

7. The Fort Wayne theol. sem. moved to Saint Louis 1861, to Springfield, Ill., 1875. The Gymnasium conducted in conjunction with the St. Louis sem. (see *Ministry, Education of,* VI C; X C) moved to Fort Wayne 1861. In 1881 preparatory schools were begun in Milwaukee, Wis., and NYC. The NYC school moved to Hawthorne (other names: Sherman Park, Unionville, Neperan), N. Y. 1894, to Bronxville, N. Y., 1908–10. The Milwaukee school came under the control of the Mo. Syn. 1887, the Bronxville school 1896. In 1896 the syn. also assumed control of St. Paul's Coll., begun 1884 in Concordia, Mo. See also *Ministry, Education of,* VIII C 2 j.

8. Educational leaders included A. F. T. Bie-

wend,* J. C. W. Lindemann,* G. Schick,* C. A. T. Selle.*

9. F. A. Brunn* of Steeden, Nassau, Ger., sent students to reecive coll. and sem. training in the US 1862–86.

10. Efforts were directed also toward work in English. A. F. T. Biewend and C. H. R. Lange* lectured in English. The Eng. Ev. Luth. Conf. of Mo. was organized 1872, reorganized 1888, renamed 1891 The Eng. Ev. Luth. Syn. of Missouri* and Other States, became the Eng. Dist. of the Mo. Syn. 1911 (see *Lutheran Church – Missouri Synod, Districts of The,* A 26).

11. Syn. and dist. convs., the twice-yearly pastoral conferences, and more frequent smaller conferences gave doctrinal discussions priority. Walther's writings were largely doctrinal; his work on pastoral theol., e. g., was grounded in systematic theol. Doctrinal preaching was emphasized. Ch. periodicals featured doctrinal articles. C. Löber,* *Evangelisch-Lutherische Dogmatik,* and Walther's ed. of J. W. Baier,* *Compendium,* were widely used. C. F. (W.) Hochstetter,* *Die Geschichte der Evangelisch-lutherischen Missouri-Synode in Nord-Amerika, und ihrer Lehrkämpfe,* told chiefly about doctrinal controversies.

12. Beginning 1840 the Saxon theologians differed with J. A. A. Grabau* esp. on the doctrine of the ministry (see also *Buffalo Synod,* 2–5). Difference regarding ch. and ministry led to a break 1853 bet. the Mo. Syn. and Löhe and to controversy with the Ev. Luth. Syn. of Iowa* and Other States. Most severe was the Predestinarian* Controversy (see also VI 1). Polemics against W. Nast,* a Ger. Meth., were sustained.

13. Because of the movement known as American* Lutheranism, Walther issued a call for free* Luth. confs. Four were held: Columbus, Ohio, 1856; Pittsburgh, Pa., 1857; Cleveland, Ohio, 1858; Fort Wayne, Ind., 1859.

14. Fraternal relations were est. 1857 with The Norw. Ev. Luth. Ch. in Am. (see *Evangelical Lutheran Church, The,* 8) on the latter's initiative. P. L. Larsen* taught at Conc. Sem., St. Louis, 1859–61. Norw. students attended the St. Louis sem.

15. A colloquy was held with the Buffalo* Syn. 1866 (see *Buffalo Colloquy*). The Mo. Syn. was represented 1866 at the Reading, Pa., conv. which preceded organization of the General* Council of the Ev. Luth. Ch. in (N.) Am.; it did not join the Gen. Council. A colloquy was held 1868 with the Ev. Luth. Joint Syn. of Ohio* and Other States, on the latter's initiative, at Columbus, Ohio; it led to fellowship 1872. Agreement was reached with the Wisconsin* Syn. 1869, the Ev. Luth. Syn. of Illinois* 1872. See also *Synodical Conference,* 1.

16. A meeting was held 1871 in Fort Wayne, Ind., which led 1872 to organization of the Synodical* Conf., of which Walther was 1st pres.

VI. *Conservation, 1887–1932.* 1. The Syn. Conf. suffered severe losses as result of the predestinarian* controversy; the Ohio Syn. withdrew in bitter opposition to the Mo. Syn.; the Norw. Syn. withdrew to preserve its unity and for language reasons but remained in fellowship with the syns. of the Syn. Conf. The controversy seems to have made the Mo. Syn. even more concerned about correct doctrine and wary of entangling alliances. After Walther's death 1887 this concern and wariness became dominant.

2. F. Pieper* was pres. Conc. Sem., St. Louis, 1887–1911, syn. pres. 1899–1911; F. Pfotenhauer* was syn. pres. 1911–35. Both were conservative, emphasized confessionalism, and favored Ger. culture.

3. As a result of immigration, settlement, and expansion the Am. Frontier practically vanished 1890. In an endeavor to keep pace, the ch. used circuit riders. 1884–1935 the Mo. Syn. grew from 348,182 to 1,288,950 bap. mems., faster than the pop. growth rate to ca. 1900 and ca. the same as the pop. growth rate 1900–35.

4. Cultural isolation is reflected in the synod's stand on economic and soc. questions. Life insurance, dancing, and the theater were condemned. Pol. quietism, a rural outlook, and fear of defections became evident. Transition from Ger. to Eng. was resisted by many in fear that surrender to Eng. would mean sacrifice of doctrinal integrity. The language question was settled largely as a result of WW I. The war caused conflict in some communities, hostility against "Ger. Luths.," destruction of property, and bodily harm. See also *Language Question in the Lutheran Church [US].*

5. Legislation against parochial schools was successfully resisted in the late 1880s and early 1890s esp. in Wis., Ill., N. Y., S. Dak., Minn., Wyo., and Man., Can., and 1920–25 in Nebr., Mich., and Oreg.

6. School enrollments increased but did not keep pace with ch. membership growth. By 1900 attempts were made to raise scholastic standards; in many schools the school week was increased from 4 to 5 days; instructional materials were improved. A. C. Stellhorn* was Secy. of Schools 1921–60. Dist. supts. were appointed; the first: for N. Ill. 1918, Cen. 1918, Mich. 1919. Conc. Teachers Coll., Seward, Nebr., was founded 1894 as a preparatory dept. for the school at Addison, Ill. (see V 6).

7. The S. S. movement gained momentum in the syn. ca. 1910. First S. S. materials issued by CPH 1911. By 1935 enrollment was over 250,000. Other part-time agencies included Sat. schools, summer schools, and VBS (see also *Christian Education,* E 9). Walther* Coll., St. Louis, was founded 1887. Secondary schools were begun in Milwaukee 1903, Chicago 1909, Fort Wayne 1916. Ministerial preparatory schools were est. in St. Paul, Minn., 1893; Winfield, Kans., 1893; Portland, Oreg., 1905; Oakland, Calif., 1906; Edmonton, Alberta, Can., 1921; Austin, Tex., 1926. Conc. Sem., St. Louis, was relocated 1926 on a new campus in Clayton, Mo. An institute for training pastors and teachers was est. 1903 at Bom Jesus, São Lourenço, Rio Grande do Sul, Brazil (see also *Lutheran Church – Missouri Synod, Districts of The,* B 1). In 1924 a sem. opened at Nagercoil and a Gospel Training School and a Bible Women's Training School at Ambur, India; a teacher training school opened at Ambur 1926.

8. The syn. created a Bd. for For. Miss. 1893 and directed that work begin in Jap. But, under changing circumstances, the 1st missionaries, K. G. T. Näther* and F. E. Mohn,* were sent to India.

9. Miss. work began in Brazil 1901. A miss. to the Isle of Pines was called 1911. E. L. Arndt* organized the Ev. Luth. Miss. for China 1912, went to China under its auspices 1912/13; the syn. adopted this miss. 1917. F. Brand* became Dir. of For. Miss. 1920.

The syn. adopted E. Dist. missions to Latvians and Estonians 1899, Polish and Lith. miss. 1908, Fin. miss. 1911.

10. The period also saw considerable activity on the part of welfare and benevolent socs. The Am. Luth. Bd. for Relief in Eur. was appointed 1919. Miss. and charitable activities of the syn. show that it was not wholly isolationist.

In relations with other chs. the syn. seemed to stand aloof. It maintained fellowship with syns. of the Syn. Conf. (despite friction with the Wis. Syn.) and with the Norw. Syn. but made no move to unite with other Luths.

11. Free* Luth. conferences were held in the early 1900s in an endeavor to heal the rift in the Syn. Conf. caused by the predestinarian* controversy of the 1880s. In 1917 the Mo. Syn. created an Intersyn. Committee which met with representatives of the Wis., Buffalo, Iowa, and Ohio syns. The Chicago* Theses (Intersyn.) were adopted 1925 by representatives of the Buffalo, Iowa, Mo., Ohio, and Wis. syns., but the Mo. Syn. did not adopt them. The 1929 Mo. Syn. conv. authorized drafting another set of theses; this led to the 1932 *Brief* Statement.*

12. The syn. presidency became a full-time office 1911. A Bd. of Dirs. was created 1917. The Gen. School Bd. and the Gen. S. S. Bd. were combined 1929 into a Bd. of Christian Educ. (see also VII, 4).

VII. *Expansion, 1932–.* 1. Characterized by rapid growth, expansion of Christian educ., miss. outreach, greater lay activity, active efforts toward Luth. union, doctrinal tensions, and increase in syn. centralization and in administration.

2. Bap. syn. membership more than doubled (1932: 1,210,206; 1970: 3,045,668).

3. With an increase in dists. (see *Lutheran Church –Missouri Synod, Districts of The*), administrative functions and full-time ex. positions increased (e. g., full-time dist. presidents and ex. secretaries of educ., miss., evangelism, and stewardship, or combinations of some of these).

4. On the syn. level, bds. and executives were added. In 1959 the office of ex. dir. was est. The 1st vice-presidency became a full-time office 1950. The Bd. of Christian Educ. (see VI, 12) was renamed The Bd. for Parish Educ. 1944, Bd. of Parish Educ. 1959.

5. A 9-mem. committee on higher educ. authorized by the 1929 syn. conv. became a 13-mem. Committee on Higher Educ. 1932, Bd. for Higher Educ. 1938.

Reports (1959, 1962) of the Syn. Survey Commission created by the 1956 conv. led to divisional administrative structure.

6. Conc. Pub. House (see *Publication Houses, Lutheran*) was expanded from time to time. KFUO (see *Radio Stations, Religious,* 3) has provided program materials for stations in the US and abroad. "This Is the Life" TV programs have been produced since 1952 (see *Radio and Television Evangelism, Network*). Conc. Hist. Institute (see *Archives*) was designated as the Dept. of Archives and Hist. of LCMS 1959. A Dept. of Pub. Relations was created in 1947.

7. Auxiliary agencies in or related to syn. included (1) The Walther League (see *Young People's Organizations, Christian,* II 3); (2) The Luth. Deaconess Assoc. (see *Deaconesses,* 9–14); (3) Lutheran* Laymen's League; (4) Lutheran* Women's Missionary League; (5) Society* for the Promotion of Mohammedan Missions; (6) Lutheran* Med. Miss. Assoc.; (7) Lutheran* Educ. Assoc.; (8) Nat. Luth. Parent-Teacher League (see *Parish Education,* J).

8. Parish educ. was promoted vigorously, but parochial schools suffered esp. during the 1930s Great Depression; enrollment: (1932) 79,204; (1942) 70,647; (1965) 167,574; (1970) 150,980 (1,215 schools; 6,616 teachers, of whom 3,934 were women).

9. S. S. enrollment: (1932) 233,279; (1940) 281,572; (1942) 262,276; (1965) 899,103; (1970) 786,374. Summer schools became almost totally defunct; Sat. schools decreased sharply in no.; Vacation Bible School flourished.

10. The no. of high schools increased from 3 (1932) to 26 in 1970 in N. Am.

11. Valparaiso U. (see *Universities in the United States, Lutheran,* 5) also grew.

12. Conc. Sr. Coll., Fort Wayne, Ind., authorized. Depression: enrollment: (1932) 79,204; (1942) 1947, opened 1957/58 (see also *Ministry, Education of,* VIII B 8). Conc. Luth. (Jr.) Coll., Ann Arbor, Mich., authorized 1959, opened 1963. A jr. coll. was authorized for S Calif. 1962. Entrance requirements at Conc. Sem., St. Louis, were raised in the late 1950s to include a BA degree or its equivalent.

13. During the 1930s Great Depression the sems. produced more candidates than could be placed in ch. work. During WW II the syn. helped supply military chaplains. For. miss. expansion, a trend toward earlier retirement and est. of new congs. led to manpower shortage.

14. More extensive expansion followed WW II. New miss. fields included the Philippines 1946, Jap. and New Guinea 1948, Hong Kong 1950, Taiwan 1951, Venezuela 1951, Korea 1958, the Middle East 1959. Work in India (see VI 7–8) expanded (see also *India,* 13). A Bible institute at Tokyo, Jap., became a theol. school 1953. Sem. classes began 1952 in Taipei, Taiwan. A sem. est. 1955 in the Philippines at Manila moved to Baguio City 1960. A sem. was est. at Hong Kong 1959. The miss. program included elementary and secondary schools and various part-time agencies. Bible correspondence courses became prominent in for. miss. fields after the middle of the 20th c. Medical missions were fostered in India at Bethesda Hosp., Ambur (opened 1923), Malappuram (work begun 1955; dispensary [child welfare center] opened 1956), Wandoor (dispensary opened 1952; later became a hosp.), and elsewhere; in New Guinea at the Mambisanda Hosp. and related clinics; in the Philippines; in Afr. at Eket, Nigeria. In 1970 the LCMS was active in 11 for. fields. See also *Middle East Lutheran Ministry.*

15. H. F. Wind* was appointed ex. secy. of the dept. of soc. welfare 1953. "Cooperation in externals" led to est. of Luth. welfare councils, feds., and assocs. in NYC, Chicago, Ohio, Washington state, and elsewhere. The Armed Services Commission (called Armed Forces Commission beginning 1965) cooperated with the National* Luth. Council in maintaining service centers for military personnel.

16. Notable doctrinal statements include *A Statement** and *Common* Confession.* Doctrinal controversies may broadly be said to have revolved around the question of fellowship. Problems in the area of Biblical studies became prominent after the middle of the 20th c.

17. A Committee on Luth. Ch. Union was created 1935. In 1938 the syn. resolved to "declare that the *Brief Statement* of the Missouri Synod, together with the *Declaration* of the representatives of the American Lutheran Church and the provisions of this entire report of Committee No. 16 now being read and with Synod's actions thereupon, be regarded as the doctrinal basis for *future church-fellowship* between the Missouri Synod and the American Lutheran Church" (1938 LCMS *Proceedings,* p. 231). The 1940 *Pittsburgh* Agreement* was regarded as inadequate in its statement on Scripture. The *Common* Confession* was "recognized as a statement in harmony with the Sacred Scriptures and the Lutheran Confessions" but was not adopted "as a functioning basic document toward the establishment of altar and pulpit fellowship with other church bodies" (1956 LCMS *Proceedings,* p. 505). Realignment of Luth. bodies, esp. formation of The ALC 1960 and the LCA 1962 arrested the union movement.

18. The Norw. Syn. of the Am. Ev. Luth. Ch. (name changed 1958 to Ev. Luth. Syn.) suspended relations with LCMS 1955; the Wis. Ev. Luth. Syn. suspended fellowship with LCMS 1961.

VIII. In 1965 LCMS resolved to approve the proposed const. of the Lutheran* Council in the

USA and became a participating body in that agency. In 1969 LCMS entered altar and pulpit fellowship with The ALC.

IX. Pres.: C. F. W. Walther 1847–50, 1864–78; F. C. D. Wyneken 1850–64; H. C. Schwan 1878–99; F. A. O. Pieper 1899–1911; F. Pfotenhauer 1911–35; J. W. Behnken* 1935–62; Oliver R. Harms 1962–69; Jacob A. O. Preus 1969–. CSM

Lutheran Church – Missouri Synod, Districts of The. A. *North America.* Rapid growth soon called for division of the syn. into districts. Great distances, poor traveling facilities, and great expenses of annual conv. trips strained the resources of congs., pastors, and teachers and interfered with full attendance. The problem was noted already by the 1848 conv., but decision was deferred till the convs. of 1852–54, when the syn. was divided into 4 districts (Western, Central, Northern, and Eastern), these to meet 2 yrs. in succession separately and the 3d yr. in gen. conv. (districts 1855 and 1856, gen. conv. 1857, etc.), and dist. meetings as necessary concurrent with gen. convs.

Districts, with par. nos. in this section:

Alberta and British Columbia 30
Atlantic 20
California and Nevada 17
California and Oregon 16
Canada 9
Central 2
Central Illinois 23
Colorado 29
Eastern 4
English 26
Florida-Georgia 40
Illinois 5
Indiana 42
Iowa 8
Iowa East 36
Iowa West 37
Kansas 15
Manitoba and Saskatchewan 31
Michigan 10
Mid-South 46
Minnesota 12
Minnesota North 43
Minnesota South 44
Minnesota and Dakota 12
Missouri 45
Montana 39
Nebraska (old) 13
Nebraska (new) 47
New England 50
New Jersey 51
North Dakota 25
North Dakota and Montana 25
North Wisconsin 28
Northern 3, 6
Northern Illinois 22
Northern Nebraska 33
Northwest 18
Northwestern 7
Ohio 41
Oklahoma 34
Ontario 9
Oregon and Washington 18
SELC 49
South Dakota 21
South Wisconsin 27
Southeastern 38
Southern 14
Southern California 35
Southern Illinois 24
Southern Nebraska 32
Texas 19
Western 1
Wisconsin 11
Wyoming 48

1. *Western Dist.* (Mo., Ill., La.). Pres.: G. A. Schieferdecker* 1854–57, J. M. G. Schaller* 1857–63, J. F. Bünger* 1863–75, F. J. Biltz* 1875–91, C. C. Schmidt* 1891–98, Paul Theodore Roesener 1898–1901, John Jacob Bernthal 1901–19, J. H. C. Fritz* 1919–20, Ludwig Friedrich Brust (Acting Pres.) 1920–21, R. T. Kretzschmar* 1921–39, Paul F. Koenig 1939–45, Elfred L. Roschke 1945–51, T. A. Weinhold 1951–57, George W. Wittmer 1957–59, W. J. Stelling 1959–63, Kurt W. Biel 1963–66.

Out of the W. Dist. were carved the Ill. Dist. (see 5) 1874, the Iowa Dist. (see 8) 1878/79, the Nebr. Dist. (see 13) and the Southern Dist. (see 14) 1881/82, the Kans. Dist. (see 15) and the Calif. and Oreg. Dist. (see 16) 1887. The W. Dist. divided 1965/66 to form the Mo. Dist. (see 45) and the Mid-South Dist. (see 46).

2. *Central Dist.* (Ohio and Ind.). Pres.: W. Sihler* 1854–60, H. C. Schwan* 1860–78, W. S. Stubnatzy* 1878–80, J. H. Niemann* 1880–1909, John H. Wefel 1909–15, William E. Moll 1915–19, J. Adam Schmidt 1919–20, John Dietrich Matthius 1920–27, W. F. Lichtsinn 1927–47, J. H. Meyer 1947–51, Ottomar Krueger 1951–63. The dist. divided 1962/63 to form the Ind. Dist. (see 42) and the Ohio Dist. (see 41).

3. *Northern Dist.* (Mich. and Wis.). Pres.: O. Fuerbringer* 1854–72, J. A. Hügli 1872–75. The N. Dist. divided 1874/75; part retained the old name (see 6), the other part was called Northwestern Dist. (see 7).

4. *Eastern Dist.* (N. Y., Pa., Md., and D. C.; later Ont.). Pres.: E. G. W. Keyl* 1854–69, C. Gross* 1869–75, J. P. Beyer* 1875–88, P. Brand* 1888–99, Herman Henry Walker 1899–1915, Franz (Francis) Carl Verwiebe 1915–21 and 1931–38, William Broecker 1921–28, J. K. E. Horst 1928–31, Oscar Adelbert Sauer 1938–39, Paul Fretthold 1939–45, Charles A. Behnke 1944–55, Eric Carl Malte 1955–58, Gustav M. Karkau 1958–66, Herman R. Frincke 1966–. The Eastern Dist. transferred Ont. to the Northern Dist. (see 6) 1874, divided 1906 (part retained the old name, the other part was called Atlantic Dist. [see 20]).

5. The *Illinois Dist.,* carved out of the Western Dist. (see 1) 1874, held its 1st conv. 1875. Pres.: H. Wunder* 1875–91, H. H. Succop* 1891–1903, Herman Engelbrecht Sr. 1903–07. The dist. divided 1907/08 to form the N. Ill. Dist. (see 22), Cen. Ill. Dist. (see 23), and S. Ill. Dist. (see 24). See also *Illinois, Evangelical Lutheran Synod of,* b.

6. The reorganized Northern Dist. (see 3) included Mich. and Ont. (the latter transferred from the Eastern Dist.) and held its 1st conv. 1875. Pres.: O. Fuerbringer* 1875–82. The Can. Dist. (see 9) was carved out of the Northern Dist. 1878/79. The Northern Dist. changed name to Mich. Dist. (see 10) 1881.

7. *Northwestern Dist.* (not to be confused with the later Northwest Dist.; see 18), formed when the Northern Dist. divided (see 3), included Wis. and Minn. and held its 1st conv. 1875. Pres.: C. J. A. Strasen* 1875–82. The Northwestern Dist. divided 1882/82 to form the Wis. Dist. (see 11) and the Minn. and Dakota Dist. (see 12).

8. *Iowa Dist.,* carved out of the Western Dist. (see 1) 1878/79, held its 1st conv. 1879. Pres.: J. Lorenz Crämer 1879–88, Philipp Studt 1888–91, Ludwig Friedrich Brust 1891–94, Ernst Zürrer 1909–09, A. D. Greif 1909–14, Theodore Wolfram 1914–27, Herman A. Harms 1927–36. Then the dist. divided into Iowa East Dist. (see 36) and Iowa West Dist. (see 37).

9. *Canada Dist.* (name changed to *Ontario Dist.* 1923), carved out of the Northern Dist. (see 6) 1878/79, held its 1st conv. 1879. Pres.: J. A. Ernst* 1879–81, C. F. (W.) Hochstetter* 1881–83, Fred-

erick Dubpernell 1883–87, G. F. Bente* 1887–93, Johannes Wilhelm Weinbach 1893–1906, C. W. G. Eifrig* 1906–09, William Carl Boese 1909–18, Paul Karl Graupner 1918–19, Reinhard Eifert Sr. 1919–21, Frank Paul Edmund Malinsky 1921–48, Walter Oscar Rathke 1948–60, Philip Fiess 1960–70, Albin Stanfel 1970–.

10. The Northern Dist. (see 3 and 6) changed name to *Michigan Dist.* 1881. Pres.: M. J. Schmidt* 1882–91, Gustav Ernst Spiegel 1891–1912, T. E. W. Engelder* 1912–14, Emanuel August Mayer 1915–24, John Jacob Frederick Schinnerer 1924–42, Andrew Zeile 1942–57, W. Harry Krieger 1957–65, Edwin C. Weber 1965–69, Richard L. Schlecht 1969–.

11. The Minn. and Dak. Dist. (see 12) was carved out of the Northwestern Dist. (see 7) 1881/82. The remainder was called *Wisconsin Dist.* and held its 1st conv. as such 1882. Pres.: C. J. A. Strasen* 1882–85, Henry F. Sprengeler 1885–91, J. H. Herzer* 1891, Bernhard Carl Ludwig Sievers 1892–94, John Conrad Strasen (son of C. J. A. Strasen) 1894–1900, Claus (Klaus) Seuel 1900–06, Samuel William Herman Daib 1906–16. Then the dist. divided to form the N. Wis. Dist. (see 28) and S. Wis. Dist. (see 27).

12. *Minnesota and Dakota Dist.*, formed 1881/82, when the Northwestern Dist. divided (see 7), held its 1st conv. 1882. Pres.: E. O. Clöter* 1882–85, Frederick J. Sievers 1885–91, F. Pfotenhauer* 1891–1908, Henry Schulz 1908–12, Franz Robert Koehler 1912–18, J. H. W. Meyer* 1918–30, Henry Jansen Bouman 1931–33, Johann Christoph Ludwig Meyer 1933–42, Robert Gottfried Heyne 1942–48, Hugo A. Gamber 1948–57, Ernst H. Stahlke 1957–63.

The S. Dak. Dist (see 21) was carved out of the Minn. and Dak. Dist. 1905/06; the remainder continued using the name Minn. and Dak. District. The N. Dak. and Mont. Dist. (see 25) was carved out of the Minn. and Dak. Dist. 1910. The Minn. and Dak. Dist. changed name to *Minnesota Dist.* 1912. The Alta. and B. C. Dist. (see 30) and the Man. and Sask. Dist. (see 31) branched off of the Minn. Dist. 1920. The Minn. Dist. divided 1962/63 to form the Minn. N. Dist. (see 43) and the Minn. S. Dist. (see 44).

13. *Nebraska Dist.* (not to be confused with the later Nebr. Dist.; see 47), was carved out of the Western Dist. (see 1) 1881/82, held its 1st conv. 1882. Pres.: J. Hilgendorf* 1882–1900, Carl Henry Becker 1900–15, C. F. Brommer* 1915–22. Then the dist. divided to form the S. Nebr. Dist. (see 32) and the N. Nebr. Dist. (see 33).

14. *Southern Dist.* (Tex., La., and adjoining states), carved out of the W. Dist. (see 1) 1881/82, held its 1st conv. 1882. Pres.: Timotheus Stiemke 1882–88, Gotthilf Heinrich Wilhelm Birkmann 1888–91, Gottfried Johann Wegener 1891–1927, Martin W. H. Holls 1927–54, Paul W. Streufert 1954–57, Edgar Homrighausen 1957–69, Lothar Kleinhans 1969–70, John E. Ellermann 1970–.

The Tex. Dist. (see 19) was carved out of the S. Dist. 1905/06, the Fla.-Ga. Dist. (see 40) 1947/48.

15. *Kansas Dist.* (Kans. and Colo.), carved out of the W. Dist. (see 1) 1887/87, held its 1st conv. 1888. Pres.: Friedrich Pennekamp 1888–94, Carl (Karl: Charles) Hafner 1894–1906, Friedrich Christoph Droegemueller 1906–12, Theodore H. Juengel 1912–19, Carl Frederick Lehenbauer 1919–32, W. Mahler* 1932–39, Walter H. Meyer 1939–60, Arlen J. Bruns 1960–.

The Kans. Dist. divided 1920/21. Part retained the name Kans. Dist. and included Kans., Okla., and N. Mex. The other part was called Colo. Dist. (see 29). The Okla. Dist. (see 34) was carved out of the Kans. Dist. 1923/24.

16. The Pacific Coast had been part of the W. Dist. (see 1) since 1860, when J. M. Bühler* settled in San Francisco, Calif. The *California and Oregon Dist.*, carved out of the W. Dist. 1887, held its 1st conv. 1887. Pres.: J. M. Bühler 1887–99. Then the dist. divided to form the Calif. and Nev. Dist. (see 17) and the Oreg. and Wash. Dist. (see 18).

17. *California and Nevada Dist.*, formed when the Calif. and Oreg. Dist. (see 16) divided 1899, held its 1st conv. 1900. Pres.: J. M. Bühler 1899–1901, George P. Runkel 1901–05, George A. Bernthal 1905–20, J. W. Theiss* 1920–24, Arthur Clemens Henry Brohm 1924–45, C. Fickenscher 1945–54, Arthur C. Nitz 1954–59, Paul E. Jacobs 1959–.

The S. Calif. Dist. (see 35) was carved out of the Calif. and Nev. Dist. 1929/30.

18. *Oregon and Washington Dist.* (Oreg., Wash., and Idaho), formed when the Calif. and Oreg. Dist. (see 16) divided 1899, held its 1st conv. 1899. Pres.: Henry August Carl Paul 1899–1903, W. Lüssenhop 1903–06, W. H. Behrens* 1906–09, Ludwig Frederick Emil Stuebe 1909–18, Johann Adam Rimbach 1918–21, Weert J. Janssen 1921–36, Frederick Max Leopold Nitz 1936–48, Carl H. Bensene 1948–70, Emil G. Jaech 1970–.

The Oreg. and Wash. Dist. changed name 1948 to *Northwest Dist.* (not to be confused with Northwestern Dist.; see 7).

19. *Texas Dist.*, carved out of the S. Dist. (see 14) 1905/06, held its 1st conv. 1906. See also 29. Pres.: Adolf W. Kramer 1906–09, Charles A. Waech 1909–12, Gotthilf Heinrich Wilhelm Birkmann 1912–20, Henry Peter Studtmann 1920–26, J. W. Behnken* 1926–29, Constantin Martin Beyer 1929–42, Edwin A. Heckmann 1942–48, Oliver R. Harms 1948–50, Roland P. Wiederaenders 1950–59, Albert F. Jesse 1959–63, Carl A. Heckmann 1963–.

20. *Atlantic Dist.*, formed when the E. Dist. (see 4) divided 1906, included the territory of the N. Y. and New Eng. Conf., with the boundary line in N. Y. passing bet. Utica and Rome; 1st conv. 1907. Pres.: E. C. L. Schulze* 1906–18, H. P. L. Birkner* 1918–30, A. J. Brunn* 1930–41, George Charles Koenig 1941–42, Herman John Rippe 1942–60, Karl Frank Graesser 1960–67, Rudolph P. F. Ressmeyer 1967–. The Atlantic Dist. divided 1971/72; part retained the old name, part was called New Eng. Dist. (see 50), part was called New Jersey Dist. (see 51).

21. *South Dakota Dist.*, carved out of the Minn. and Dak. Dist. (see 12) 1905/06, held its 1st conv. 1906. Pres.: August Frederick Breihan 1906–12, Johann Dietrich Ehlen 1912–18, Ernst Gottlieb Jehn 1918–21, Friedrich W. Leyhe 1921–36, Walter Nitschke 1936–51, Philip H. Mueller 1951–60, Elmer O. Luessenhop 1960–68, Leonard Eberhard 1968–70, Arthur J. Crosmer 1970–.

22. *Northern Illinois Dist.*, formed when the Ill. Dist. (see 5) divided 1907/08, held its 1st conv. 1909. Pres.: Hermann Engelbrecht Sr. 1907–09, W. C. Kohn* 1909–13, Friedrich Heinrich Brunn 1913–27, Alex Ullrich 1927–36, Ernest Theodore Lams 1936–45, Arthur Henry Werfelmann 1945–60, Erwin L. Paul 1963–66, Edmund H. Happel 1966–.

23. *Central Illinois Dist.*, formed when the Ill. Dist. (see 5) divided 1907/08, held its 1st conv. 1909. Pres.: F. Brand* 1907–17, Fred William Brockmann 1917–18, August Friedrich Wilhelm Heyne 1918–27, P. Schulz 1927–32, Philip Wilhelm 1932–33, Walter Ernest Hohenstein 1933–35, John Carl Schuelke 1935–42, Albert Otto Carl Bernthal 1942–48, Emil Frederick Tonn 1948–54, Alvin W. Mueller 1954–63, Lewis C. Niemoeller 1963–70, Rudolph A. Haak 1970–74, Arthur Kuehnert 1974–.

24. *Southern Illinois Dist.*, formed when the Ill. Dist. (see 5) divided 1907/08, held its 1st conv.

1909. Pres.: Fred William Brockmann 1907–09, Ulfert Iben 1909–12, Johannes Gottlieb Frederick Kleinhans 1912–33, C. Thomas Spitz Sr. 1933–45, Erhard H. Bohrer 1945–46, Paul Juergensen 1946–47, Harry C. Welp 1947–57, Walter William Adolf Raedeke 1957–58, W. Theophil Janzow 1958–59, Alfred Buls 1959–67, Herman Neunaber 1967–.

25. *North Dakota and Montana Dist.*, carved out of the Minn. and Dak. Dist. (see 12) 1910, held its 1st conv. 1910. Pres.: Tietje Hinck 1910–24, Joseph Paul Klausler 1924–41, Albert Jordan 1941–42, Arnold Henry Grumm 1942–45.

The N. Dak. and Mont. Dist. divided 1944/45 to form the Mont. Dist. (see 39) and the *North Dakota Dist.* Pres. of the latter: Arnold Henry Grumm 1945–50, Walter Henry Theodore Cordts 1950–54, Bernhard G. Mueller 1954–57, Lothar Karl Meyer 1957–61, Harold V. Huber 1961–65, John D. Fritz 1965–67, Alwin M. Reimnitz 1967–.

26. *English Dist.* (see also *Missouri and Other States, The English Evangelical Lutheran Synod of*) held its 1st conv. 1912. Pres.: Henry Philip Eckhardt* 1911–12, M. S. Sommer* 1912–15, John Adam Detzer 1915–18, O. C. Kreinheder* 1918–27, Guido R. Schuessler 1927–36, Paul Lindemann 1936–38, M. F. Walker* 1938–45, Herman William Bartels 1945–51, Hugo G. Kleiner 1951–63, Bertwin L. Frey 1963–70, John H. Baumgaertner 1970–74, Harold L. Hecht 1974–.

27. *South Wisconsin Dist.*, formed when the Wis. Dist. (see 11) divided 1916, held its 1st conv. (25th in the Wis. Dist. series) 1918. Pres.: Edward Albrecht 1916–21, Henry John Andrew Grueber 1921–32, John Frederick Boerger 1932–36, Fred A. Schwertfeger 1936–48, Arthur H. Oswald 1948–53, Herbert W. Baxmann 1953–70, Karl L. Barth 1970–.

28. *North Wisconsin Dist.*, formed when the Wis. Dist. (see 11) divided 1916, held its 1st conv. 1918. Pres.: Johann Gotthilf Schliepsiek 1916–18, Samuel William Herman Daib 1918–36, William Louis Kohn 1936–54, Lloyd H. Goetz 1954–74, Henry E. Simon 1974–.

29. *Colorado Dist.*, formed 1920/21 when the Kans. Dist. (see 15) divided, included Colo. and Utah and held its 1st conv. 1921. In course of time the dist. came to include congs. in Page, Ariz.; Venango, Nebr.; El Paso, Texas. N. Mex. (see 15) and the Tex. Dist. congs. in southern N. Mex. became part of the Colo. Dist. 1941/42. Pres.: Otto Luessenhop 1921–30, Otto K. Hensel 1930–34, Frederick William Obermeier 1934–42, E. Julius Friedrich 1942–50, Henry G. Hartner 1950–54, Herbert H. Hellbusch 1954–60, Walter A. Enge 1960–66, Waldemar E. Meyer 1966–.

30. *Alberta and British Columbia Dist.* branched off of the Minn. Dist. (see 12) 1920 and held its 1st conv. 1921. Pres.: August J. Mueller 1921–30, William C. Eifert 1930–51, Carl F. Baase 1951–60, Alfred F. Miller 1960–66, George Rode 1966–.

31. *Manitoba and Saskatchewan Dist.* branched off of the Minn. Dist. (see 12) 1920 and held its 1st conv. 1922. Pres.: Paul E. Wiegner 1922–27, Christian T. Wetzstein 1927–30, John H. Lucht 1930–51, Leonard W. Koehler 1951–70, Philip Fry 1970–.

32. *Southern Nebraska Dist.*, formed when the Nebr. Dist. (see 13) divided 1922, held its 1st conv. 1924. Pres.: C. F. Brommer* 1922–24, Wilhelm Heinrich Ferdinand Cholcher 1924–30, Herman Ernst Meyer 1930–36, A. J. C. Moeller* 1936–38, Iddo Charles Heinicke 1938–49, Arthur Frederick Wegener 1949–56, Henry F. Krohn 1956–60, Henry W. Niermann Sr. 1960–70. The S. Nebr. Dist. and the N. Nebr. Dist. (see 33) combined 1969/70 to form the new Nebr. Dist. (see 47).

33. *Northern Nebraska Dist.*, formed when the Nebr. Dist. (see 13) divided 1922, included stations in Wyo. and held its 1st conv. 1924. Pres.: John Frederick William Harms 1922–33, Martin Eugene Mayer 1933–39, Walter E. Homann 1939–57, Frederick A. Niedner 1957–70. The N. Nebr. Dist. and the S. Nebr. Dist. (see 32) combined 1970 to form the new Nebr. Dist. (see 47).

34. *Oklahoma Dist.*, carved out of the Kans. Dist. (see 15) 1923/24, held its 1st conv. 1924. Pres.: Henry Mueller 1924–39, Carl R. Matthies 1939–40, Edward C. Hauer 1940–42, Paul J. Hartenberger 1942–43, Otto Henry Hoyer 1943–54, Alfred E. Behrend 1954–70, Harold Brockhoff 1970–.

35. *Southern California Dist.*, carved out of the Calif. and Nev. Dist. (see 17) 1929/30, held its 1st conv. 1930. Pres.: Gotthold Herman Friedrich Smukal 1930–42, Walter F. Troeger 1942–48, Armand Elmer T. Mueller 1948–55, Victor Louis Behnken 1955–69, Arnold G. Kuntz 1969–.

36. *Iowa East Dist.*, formed when the Iowa Dist. (see 8) divided 1936, held its 1st conv. 1937. Pres.: Herman A. Harms 1936–38, Carl John Henry Hesse 1938–49, Walter D. Oetting 1949–63, Fred H. Ilten 1963–70, John C. Zimmermann 1970–.

37. *Iowa West Dist.*, formed when the Iowa Dist. (see 8) divided 1936, held its 1st conv. 1937. Pres.: Adolph Schwidder 1936–45, Herbert W. Berner 1945–46, John Theodore Martin Hoemann 1946–48, Gustav W. Lobeck 1948–66, Ellis Nieting 1966–.

38. *Southeastern Dist.*, formed 1938/39 in an area involving esp. the Eastern Dist. (see 4) and the Eng. Dist. (see 26) and including in gen. S. C., N. C., Va., Md., Del., D. C., and part of Ga., held its 1st conv. 1939. Pres.: J. George Spilman 1939–45, Oscar Adelbert Sauer 1945–48, Rudolph Stang Ressmeyer 1948–54, William H. Kohn 1954–59, Leslie F. Frerking 1959–63, William H. Kohn 1963–67, Martin C. Poch 1967–70, Charles S. Mueller 1970–.

39. *Montana Dist.*, formed when the N. Dak. and Mont. Dist. (see 25) divided 1944/45, held its 1st conv. 1946. Pres.: Paul M. Freiburger 1945–66, August F. Droegemueller 1966–69, George F. Wollenburg 1969–.

40. *Florida-Georgia Dist.*, carved out of the Southern Dist. (see 14) 1947/48, held its 1st conv. 1948. Pres.: Conrad F. Kellermann 1948–57, Frederick W. Lorberg 1957–63, August Bernthal 1963–74, L. Lloyd Behnken, 1974–.

41. *Ohio Dist.*, formed when the Cen. Dist. (see 2) divided 1962/63, included part of Ky. and W. Va. and held its 1st conv. 1964. Pres.: Ottomar Krueger 1963–66, Paul G. Single 1966–69, Edgar M. Luecke 1969–70, Arthur H. Ziegler 1970–.

42. *Indiana Dist.*, formed when the Cen. Dist. (see 2) divided 1962/63, included part of Ky. and Ohio and held its 1st conv. 1964. Pres.: Edgar C. Rakow 1963–70, Elwood H. Zimmermann 1970–.

43. *Minnesota North Dist.*, formed when the Minn. Dist. (see 12) divided 1962/63, held its 1st conv. 1963. Pres.: Alfred C. Seltz 1963–70, August T. Mennicke 1970–.

44. *Minnesota South Dist.*, formed when the Minn. Dist. (see 12) divided 1962/63, held its 1st conv. 1963. Pres.: Ernest H. Stahlke 1963–66, Martin W. Lieske 1966–.

45. *Missouri Dist.*, formed when the W. Dist. (see 1) divided 1965/66, held its 1st conv. 1968. Pres.: Herman C. Scherer 1966–.

46. *Mid-South Dist.*, formed when the W. Dist. (see 1) divided 1965/66, includes Ark., Tenn., and part of Ky. and held its 1st conv. 1968. Pres.: Wilbert E. Griesse 1966–.

47. The new *Nebraska Dist.* (not to be confused with the earlier Nebr. Dist. [see 13]), formed 1969/70 by combination of the S. Nebr. Dist. (see 32) and the N. Nebr. Dist. (see 33), includes all Nebr. except the panhandle (the line of division ap-

proximately follows the 102d meridian); 1st conv. 1970. Pres.: Frederick A. Niedner 1970–.

48. *Wyoming Dist.* formed 1969 by realignment of the N. Nebr. Dist. (see 33) and the S. Nebr. Dist. (see 32), held its 1st conv. 1970. Pres.: Henry W. Niermann 1970–.

49. *SELC Dist.*, formerly Synod* of Ev. Luth. Chs., became a mem. of LCMS 1971, held its 1st conv. 1972. Pres.: Milan A. Ontko 1971–72, Albert M. Marcis 1972–.

50. *New England Dist.*, formed 1971/72 when the Atlantic Dist. (see 20) divided, held its 1st conv. 1972. Pres.: Robert J. Riedel 1972–.

51. *New Jersey Dist.*, formed 1971/72 when the Atlantic Dist. (see 20) divided, held its 1st conv. 1972. Pres.: Walter L. Zeile 1972–.

B. *South America.* 1. *Brazil District* (Igreja Luterana do Brasil). On invitation of a German Luth. missionary, the Mo. Syn. sent a miss., C. J. Broders,* to Brazil 1900; under his dir. a cong. was organized at Sâo Pedro, Rio Grande do Sul. W. Mahler* was sent 1901 as his successor and miss. dir. The Brazil Dist. held its 1st conv. 1904. Work expanded 1921 to the states of Santa Catarina and Paraná. Work was begun in the city of Rio de Janeiro 1929 and in the state of Espírito Santo 1931. Before WW II most work was done in Ger. War hysteria caused persecution in some areas. Port. replaced Ger. as the common language for ch. work.

Broders and others promoted parochial schools successfully. An institute for training pastors and teachers was est. 1903 at Bom Jesus, Sâo Lourenço, Rio Grande do Sul; it was closed 1905, reopened 1907 in Pôrto Alegre, where it was relocated 1921; now called Seminario Concordia. A teacher training school opened in S. Joâo Grande ca. 1947, moved to Baixo Guandu ca. 1951, closed ca. 1957. Instituto Conc. was est. for pretheological training at Rio de Janeiro 1957, moved to Sâo Paulo 1962; closed 1973.

Periodicals pub. by the Brazil Dist. include *Evangelisch-Lutherisches Kirchenblatt für Süd-Amerika* (since 1903); *Mensageiro Luterano* ("Lutheran Messenger"); *Igreja Luterana; Em Marcha; O Jovem Luterano; O Pequeno Luterano.* Pub. house: Casa Publicadora Concordia, Pôrto Alegre.

Pres.: W. Mahler* 1904–10, Adolph A. Vogel 1910–13, August Heinrich Hartwig Heine 1913–16, Emil Mueller 1916–21, Joh. Kunstmann 1921–22, John F. K. Busch 1922–25, Conrad Ferdinand Lehenbauer 1925–30, A. H. H. Heine 1930–42, Rudolph Friedrich Hasse 1942–57, Arnold W. Schneider 1957–63, Arnaldo J. Schmidt 1963–66, Elmer Reimnitz 1966–74, Johannes Gedrat 1974–.

The Brazil Dist. divided 1926/27; part kept the name Brazil Dist., the other part was called Argentine Dist. (see 2).

See also *South America,* 4.

2. *Argentine District* (Iglesia Evangelica Luterana Argentina). On invitation of a Ger. miss. who claimed to be Luth. and planned to return to Ger., W. Mahler* 1905 visited the area of Urdinarrain, a town with neighboring villages, in the province of Entre Ríos, ca. 250 mi. N of Buenos Aires. The Brazil Dist. served Luths. in Argentina from 1905 till the 1920s. The *Argentine Dist.*, formed when the Brazil Dist. (see 1) divided 1926/27, held its 1st conv. 1928.

A few parochial schools were est. but were closed because of adverse school legislation. Various other agencies for religious educ. of the young have been more successful. Colegio Conc., a pretheol. school, was est. 1926 at Crespo, Entre Ríos. Theo. training was given at Pôrto Alegre, Brazil, till 1942, when a seminary (now called Seminario Concordia) was established in rented quarters (moved 1948 to its own quarters) in Villa Ballester (José León Suárez since 1970), ca. 12 mi. NW of Buenos Aires. Colegio Conc., Crespo, was closed 1950 and its work amalgamated with the sem. in Villa Ballester. The facilities at Crespo were used 1950–63 for primary instruction, something on the order of a parochial school; then it closed. A preparatory school (called Colegio Conc. since ca. the early 1960s) was est. 1956 at Obera, Misiones.

Periodicals pub. by the Argentine Dist. include *Evangelisch-Lutherischer Kirchenbote; El Luterano.*

Pres.: Alfred Theodor Kramer 1927–28, Gerhard P. Huebner 1928–41, August C. Kroeger 1941–42, Samuel H. Beckmann 1942–57, Luis Martin 1957–60, Edgar A. Kroeger 1960–69, Jorge P. Horn 1969–. WED

See also *South America,* 1, 5, 8, 10.

Lutheran Church – Missouri Synod Foundation, The. See *Foundation, The Lutheran Church – Missouri Synod.*

Lutheran Church in America. I. *Constituent bodies and date of merger.* The LCA, result of merger of the AELC (see *Danish Lutherans in America,* 3–4), Augustana* Ev. Luth. Ch., the Suomi Syn. (see *Finnish Lutherans in America,* 2), and The United* Luth. Ch. in Am., was organized Detroit, Mich., June 28–July 1, 1962, in full operation Jan. 1, 1963.

II. *History.* Discussions leading to the merger were initiated by the ULC and the Augustana Ev. Luth. Ch. 1955; a joint letter dated Dec. 16 was sent by the presidents of these chs. inviting other Luth. bodies in Am. to designate duly authorized representatives to meet to consider organic union, draft a const., and devise organizational procedures to effect union. Favorable responses were received from the AELC and the Suomi Syn. A joint Commission on Luth. Unity was formed Dec. 1956. Negotiations proceeded on the stated assumption that common adherence to the hist. Luth. Confessions provided adequate agreement in doctrine for merger of the chs. In 1960 a proposed const. was drawn up and an Agreement of Consolidation was approved by the 4 chs.

ULC hist. background. The preamble of the 1918 ULC const. included a standing invitation to all Ev. Luth. congs. and syns. in Am. to unite in 1 gen. organization (see also *United Lutheran Church in America, The,* I). In 1920 the ULC recognized no doctrinal reasons against complete cooperation and organic union with chs. calling themselves Ev. Luth. and subscribing the hist. Luth. Confessions (see *Washington Declaration,* B). In 1928 the ULC created a Commission on Luth. Ch. Unity and in 1934 directed the ULC pres. to invite the other Luth. chs. in Am. to discussions with a view to closer relationships and set up a Special Commission on Relationships to Am. Luth. Ch. Bodies (see also *Savannah Declaration*). Discussions with the Mo. Syn. and the ALC (in connection with the latter see *Baltimore Declaration; Pittsburgh Agreement*) led to neither union nor altar and pulpit fellowship. In 1944 the ULC declared itself to be in fellowship with all other Luth. chs. in Am. which accepted the Luth. Confessions, and invited the other Luth. chs. to make the same declaration. Beginning 1948 discussions were held with The Dan. Ev. Luth. Ch. of Am. (see *Danish Lutherans in America,* 3) on the possibility of The Dan. Ev. Luth. Ch. of Am. becoming a syn. of the ULC.

Augustana Ev. Luth. Ch. hist. background. In 1948 both the Aug. Ev. Luth. Ch. and the ULC proposed a fed. and/or merger of the 8 NLC chs. On invitation of the Augustana Ev. Luth. Ch., issued by its ex. council through the pres. of the ch., 34 representatives (who became known as The Committee of 34) of most of the NLC chs. met in Minneapolis, Minn., Jan. 4, 1949, to consider the possibility of organic union or of steps possibly leading to it. A resolution presented by ALC pres. E. F.

Poppen,* to the effect that it was the sense of the group that a closer organizational affiliation of the participating bodies in the NLC was desirable and should be sought by all proper means, was unanimously adopted. A Committee of 15 was set up to prepare a structural plan for consideration by the Committee of 34. The Committee of 15 recommended (1) a referendum of the 8 NLC chs. on the question of immediate union; (2) est. of a Nat. Luth. Federation as an intermediate step toward union. But before the Sept. 27, 1949, meeting of the Committee of 34, which was to consider these proposals, representatives of the American* Luth. Ch., The Evangelical* Luth. Ch., and UELC (see *Danish Lutherans in America,* 5) met (Sept. 16, 1949) and proposed that these 3 chs. begin looking toward union. The Augustana Ev. Luth. Ch. entered into negotiations for this merger. But the following 1952 resolution of the Augustana Ev. Luth. Ch. was presented to the Committee of 45 (9 representatives of each of the ALC chs.) at Minneapolis Nov. 10, 1952: "The Augustana Lutheran Church expresses itself as being unwilling to continue in unity discussions which are not open to all Lutheran general bodies and which do not include the considerations of the subject of ecumenical relations." The representatives of the ALC, ELC, and UELC replied that they were without authority from their respective chs. to include all other Luth. chs., but that the question of ecumenical relations was still open. The representatives of the Augustana Ev. Luth. Ch. regarded the reply as unsatisfactory and withdrew from negotiations. In 1955 Augustana and the ULCA again sought to secure consideration of a merger of Luth. chs. in Am. Efforts toward union finally resulted in formation of the LCA.

III. *Doctrinal basis, theol. work, spirit, and tendency.*

LCA doctrinal basis: Const. "Art. II. Confession of Faith. Section 1. This church confesses Jesus Christ as Lord of the Church. The Holy Spirit creates and sustains the Church through the Gospel and thereby unites believers with their Lord and with one another in the fellowship of faith.

"Section 2. This church holds that the Gospel is the revelation of God's sovereign will and saving grace in Jesus Christ. In Him, the Word Incarnate, God imparts Himself to men.

"Section 3. This church acknowledges the Holy Scriptures as the norm for the faith and life of the Church. The Holy Scriptures are the divinely inspired record of God's redemptive act in Christ, for which the Old Testament prepared the way and which the New Testament proclaims. In the continuation of this proclamation in the Church, God still speaks through the Holy Scriptures and realizes His redemptive purpose generation after generation.

"Section 4. This church accepts the Apostles', the Nicene, and the Athanasian creeds as true declarations of the faith of the Church.

"Section 5. This church accepts the Unaltered Augsburg Confession and Luther's Small Catechism as true witnesses to the Gospel, and acknowledges as one with it in faith and doctrine all churches that likewise accept the teachings of these symbols.

"Section 6. This church accepts the other symbolical books of the evangelical Lutheran church, the Apology of the Augsburg Confession, the Smalcald Articles, Luther's Large Catechism, and the Formula of Concord as further valid interpretations of the confession of the Church.

"Section 7. This church affirms that the Gospel transmitted by the Holy Scriptures, to which the creeds and confessions bear witness, is the true treasure of the Church, the substance of its proclamation, and the basis of its unity and continuity. The Holy Spirit uses the proclamation of the Gospel and the administration of the Sacraments to create and sustain Christian faith and fellowship. As this occurs, the Church fulfills its divine mission and purpose."

This reflects the gen. theol. spirit and tendency of the LCA. Concentrated attention was given 1964–70 to a study of the doctrine of the ministry. Emphasis has also been laid on the church's responsibility in soc. work. Publications include M. J. Heinecken, *The Meaning of the Cross* and *Christian Teachings: Affirmations of Faith for Lay People;* W. H. Lazareth and R. O. Hjelm, *Helping Youth and Adults Know Doctrine;* G. W. Forell, *Understanding the Nicene Creed* and *The Augsburg Confession: A Contemporary Commentary;* J. Sittler, *The Anguish of Preaching;* J. H. P. Reumann and W. H. Lazareth, *Righteousness and Society: Ecumenical Dialog in a Revolutionary Age;* J. H. P. Reumann, *Jesus in the Church's Gospels;* J. A. Scherer, *Mission and Unity in Lutheranism: A Study in Confession and Ecumenicity.*

IV. *Size and organizational structure.*

As of Jan. 1, 1970, the LCA had ca. 3,258,000 bap., ca. 2,275,000 confirmed mems.; ca. 6,200 congs., ca. 5,400 pastoral charges, 33 syns., ca, 7,600 ordained ministers.

The biennial conv. is the highest legislative authority. All congs., ministers, syns., officers, the ex. council, bds., agencies (except common agencies), and auxiliaries are bound by all actions pertaining to them taken by a conv. in conformity with the const. A pres., secy., and treas. are elected to 4-yr. terms at a regular conv. The ex. council (the 3 officers, 15 ministerial, and 15 lay mems. elected by the conv.) carries forward the work and policies of the ch. and acts for the ch. bet. convs., subject to review of its action by the following conv.

Congs. retain authority in all matters not committed to the LCA or its syns. by const. provision or by later ch. action. Syns. are agents of the ch. in admitting congs. and ministers to the ch. and in supervising and furthering ch. work in designated areas. Delegates to the convs. are elected by the syns.

A 9-mem. Court of Adjudication deals with questions of principle or practice (including questions involving disputed jurisdiction or interpretation of powers claimed or conferred by the ch.) and questions of doctrine or conscience referred to it. Its decisions are binding unless reversed by a conv. A consultative and advisory Conference of Syn. Presidents meets at least annually with the officers of the ch. to discuss problems, program, and plans affecting the syns.

V. *Work.* Assistance and service is made available to mem. congs. by various bds., commissions, and agencies. The *Yearbook,* compiled and pub. by the Bd. of Pub., provides information on organizational structure, on officers, staff, and other personnel, and on the syns., institutions, and agencies. It includes a list of colleges, sems., univs., campus pastors, summer camps, health and welfare agencies, congs., pastors, and information on Am. and World Missions work.

Colleges and univs. related to the LCA and its syns.: Augustana Coll., Rock Island, Ill.; Bethany Coll., Lindsborg, Kans.; Calif. Lutheran Coll., Thousand Oaks, Calif.; Carthage* Coll., Kenosha, Wis.; Gettysburg Coll., Gettysburg, Pa.; Grand View Coll., Des Moines, Iowa (2-yr.); Gustavus Adolphus Coll., St. Peter, Minn.; Lenoir Rhyne Coll., Hickory, N. C.; Midland* Lutheran Coll., Fremont, Nebr.; Muhlenberg Coll., Allentown, Pa.; Newberry Coll., Newberry, S. C.; Roanoke Coll., Salem, Va.; Suomi Coll., Hancock, Mich. (2-yr.); Susquehanna* U., Selinsgrove, Pa.; Thiel Coll., Greenville, Pa.; Upsala Coll., E. Orange, N. J.; Wagner Coll., Staten Is.,

N. Y.; Waterloo Luth. U., Waterloo, Ont., Can.; Wittenberg* U., Springfield, Ohio.

Theol. sems. related to the LCA and its syns.: Hamma School of Theol., Springfield, Ohio; Lutheran School of Theol. at Chicago, Ill.; Lutheran Theol. Sem., Gettysburg, Pa.; Lutheran Theol. Sem., Philadelphia, Pa.; Lutheran Theol. Sem., Saskatoon, Sask., Can.; Lutheran Theol. Southern Sem., Columbia, S.C.; Northwestern* Luth. Theol. Sem., St. Paul, Minn.; Pacific Luth. Theol. Sem., Berkeley, Calif.; Waterloo Luth. Sem., Waterloo, Ont., Can.

Through its Bd. of World Missions the LCA shares in work of affiliated chs. overseas and on miss. fields. Financial assistance and necessary assisting personnel are supplied. Miss. fields have included Argentina, Chile, Ethiopia (radio), Guyana, Jamaica, Hong Kong, India, Jap., Liberia, Malaysia, Peru, Taiwan, Tanzania, Trinidad, Uruguay.

With guidance and assistance of the Bd. of Am. Miss., new congs. are organized in the US and Can. Ministries have been performed among migrants, Am. Indians, and several ethnic groups.

The Bd. of Soc. Ministry is related to soc. miss. institutions and agencies through the syns., which, through committees on soc. ministry, advise and exercise gen. supervision of institutions and agencies approved and supported, directly or indirectly, by the syns. The Bd. of Soc. Ministry supplies consultative services for institutions and agencies, aids in training and placing workers, undergirds ministries to persons or groups with special needs, and helps initiate new work.

VI. *Affiliations and relationships.* The LCA is a mem. of the Lutheran* Council in the USA (the LCA–Can. Section [see IX] is a mem. of the Can. Luth. Council [see *Canada,* A 30]), the Lutheran* World Fed., the National* Council of the Chs. of Christ in the USA (the LCA–Can. Section is a mem. of the Canadian* Council of Chs.), and of the World* Council of Chs. Any Luth. ch. fostered by the Bd. of World Miss. which concurs in the LCA Confession of Faith and in its art. on Assoc. Chs. (Const., Art. XXI) is recognized as in filial assoc. An assoc. ch. may send 2 representatives to regular convs., with privilege of seat and voice.

VII. *Official publications.* Official LCA organ: *The Lutheran. World Encounter* is pub. by the Bd. of World Miss., *Lutheran Women* by the Luth. Ch. Women (LCA auxiliary); *Resource* is sponsored by the Bd. of Parish Educ.

VIII. *Pres.:* F. C. Fry* 1962–68, Robert J. Marshall 1968–.

IX. A. *Function of syns. and relationship to gen. body.*

The LCA is divided into 33 syns., which serve as agents of the ch. in implementing its program. All syns. except the Slovak Zion Syn. (see IX B 26) are organized on a geographic basis. LCA syns. in Can. constitute the LCA–Can. Section.

Principal function of syns. is shepherding constituent congs. and ministers, including oversight to conserve unity in the true faith and to guard against any departure therefrom, encouragement to the fuller employment of resources, guidance in filling vacancies in pastorates, and intervention and mediation in times of strife and division. The syns. have primary responsibility for recruiting, preparing, and ordaining ministers, receiving congs., and disciplining congs. and ministers. Responsibility for ownership and administration of theol. sems., for provision of Christian higher educ. through ch.-related colleges, for stimulating cong. evangelism and works of mercy, and for maintaining and supporting soc. mission institutions and agencies rests in the syns. Each syn. has jurisdiction in its own affairs; when the LCA deals with internal matters of a syn., the cooperation and consent of the syn. must be secured. A syn. desiring to pub. books of devotion and instruction must first secure permission from a conv. or the ex. council. Syns. may memorialize a conv. on any subject affecting the welfare of the ch.

B. *Synods, with areas and presidents.*

1. *Caribbean* (Puerto Rico; Virgin Islands). Pres.: Arnold Adolph Wuertz 1963–64, Victor M. Rodriguez 1964–.

2. *Cen. Can.* (Sask.; Man.; W Ont). Pres.: Otto A. Olson Jr. 1963–.

3. *Cen. Pennsylvania.* Pres.: Dwight F. Putman 1963–66, Howard J. McCarney 1966–.

4. *Cen. States* (Ark.; Kans.; Okla.; W Mo.). Pres.: N. Everett Hedeen 1963–70, Harvey L. Prinz 1970–.

5. *E Can.* (N. B.; N. S.; Prince Edward Is.; Newf.; Quebec; E Ont.). Pres.: Albert W. Lotz 1963–70, Otto F. Reble 1970–.

6. *E Pennsylvania.* Pres.: Samuel E. Kidd 1963–68. Divided 1968 to form the NE Pa. Syn. (see 20) and the SE Pa. Syn. (see 29).

7. *Florida.* Pres.: Royall A. Yount 1963–.

8. *Ill.* (Ill.; E Mo.). Pres.: Robert J. Marshall 1963–68, Gerald K. Johnson 1968–.

9. *Ind.-Kentucky.* Pres.: Walter M. Wick 1963–.

10. *Iowa.* Pres.: Raynold J. Lingwall 1963–.

11. *Md.* (Del.; D. C.; Accomac and Northampton counties of Va.; E Md.). Pres.: J. Frank Fife 1963–68, Paul M. Orso 1968–.

12. *Metropolitan NY.* Organized 1966 when the NY Syn. (see 18) divided. Pres.: Alfred L. Beck 1966–69, James A. Graefe 1969–.

13. *Mich.* (lower peninsula of Mich., including adjacent islands). Pres.: Frank P. Madsen 1963–72, Howard A. Christensen 1972–.

14. *Minn.* (Minn., except the Red R. valley). Pres.: Leonard Kendall 1963–65, Melvin A. Hammarberg 1965–.

15. *Nebraska.* Pres.: Alfred W. Young 1963–64, Reuben T. Swanson 1964–.

16. *New Eng.* (Maine; N. H.; Vt.; Mass.; Conn.; R. I.). Pres.: O. Karl Olander 1963–70, Eugene A. Brodeen 1970–.

17. *New Jersey.* Pres.: Edwin H. Knudten 1963–70, Edwin L. Ehlers 1970–.

18. *New York.* Pres.: Alfred L. Beck 1963–66. Divided 1966 to form the Metropolitan NY Syn. (see 12) and the Upper NY Syn. (see 31).

19. *N. Carolina.* Pres.: George R. Whittecar 1963–.

20. *NE Pa.* Organized 1968 when E Pa. Syn. (see 6) divided. Pres.: Wilson E. Touhsaent 1968–.

21. *Ohio.* Pres.: Herbert W. Veler 1963–66, John W. Rilling 1966–72, Kenneth H. Sauer 1972–.

22. *Pacific NW* (Alaska; Idaho; Oreg.; Wash.; Mont.). Pres.: A. G. Fjellman 1963–.

23. *Pacific SW* (Ariz.; Calif.; Utah; Nev.; Hawaii). Pres.: Carl W. Segerhammer 1963–.

24. *Red R. valley* (N. Dak.; S. Dak.; Red R. valley of Minn.). Pres.: Walter E. Carlson 1963–68, Carl W. Larson 1968–.

25. *Rocky Mountain* (Wyo.; Colo.; N. Mex.; W Tex.). Pres.: Leeland C. Soker 1963–70, Franklin C. Heglund 1970–.

26. *Slovak Zion* (Syn. with distinctive linguistic characteristics organized on a nongeographic basis). Pres.: John Zornan 1963–.

27. *S. Carolina.* Pres.: Karl W. Kinard 1963–71, Herman W. Cauble 1971–.

28. *Southeastern* (Ga.; Ala.; Miss.; Tenn.). Pres.: Raymond D. Wood 1963–67, Harvey L. Huntley 1967–.

29. *SE Pa.* Organized 1968 when the E Pa. Syn. (see 6) divided. Pres.: William A. Janson Jr. 1968–.

30. *Tex.-La.* (La.; Tex., except the far W part). Pres.: Philip L. Wahlberg Jr. 1963–.

31. *Upper NY.* Organized 1966 when the NY

Syn. (see 18) divided. Pres.: Edward Kersten Perry 1966–.

32. *Va.* (Va., except Accomac and Northampton counties; eastern W. Va.). Pres.: J. Luther Mauney 1963–.

33. *W Can.* (B. C.; Alta.; Yukon Territory). Pres.: John M. Zimmerman 1963–70, Donald W. Sjoberg 1970–.

34. *W Pa.-W. Va.* (W Pa.; western W. Va.). Pres.: William C. Hankey 1963–.

35. *Wis.-Upper Mich.* (Wis.; upper peninsula of Mich., including adjacent islands). Pres.: Theodore E. Matson 1963–.

ULC *Minutes* 1918–62; Augustana Ev. Luth. Ch. *Minutes* 1918–62; LCA *Minutes* 1962–70; *The Lutheran* 1930–70; *The Lutheran Companion* 1930–62; *Lutheran Herald* 1930–60; ULC *Year Book* 1930–62; LCA *Yearbook* 1963–71; A. R. Wentz, *A Basic History of Lutheranism in America,* rev. ed. (Philadelphia, 1964); R. C. Wolf, *Documents of Lutheran Unity in America* (Philadelphia, 1966). DF

Lutheran Church in America – Canada Section. See *Canada,* A 27; *Lutheran Church in America,* VI.

Lutheran Church in the Philippines, The. See *Philippines, Republic of the,* 3.

Lutheran Church of Australia. See *Australia, Lutheranism in,* B 1; *Kavel, August Ludwig Christian.*

Lutheran Churches of the Reformation. Fed. organized Apr. 28-29, 1964, at Emmaus Luth. Ch., Chicago, Ill., by congs. which withdrew from LCMS. Adheres to the Book* of Concord of 1580 and the Brief* Statement of 1932. Cong. autonomy is emphasized in its const. The fed. holds annual delegate meetings and is governed in the interim by a council of 9 or more, one-third of which are pastors. Pub. *One Accord.*

Lutheran College and Seminary. See *Canada,* A 14, 20; *Ministry, Education of,* X L.

Lutheran Confessions. The Luth. Reformation* caused the confessional principle, which had been dead for many cents., to revive.

A. *General.* 1. During the early days of the Reformation, M. Luther* and his writings soon came to be rallying points for his followers. The 1st books to organize Luth. doctrines were the Catechisms of 1529, pub. for instructing congs. (see *Catechisms, Luther's*).

2. *Hist. Background of the Augsburg Confession.* (a) After the 1529 Diet of Speyer,* Philip* of Hesse took the initiative in trying to unite, in a *pol. fed.* for mutual defense, those who had protested the autocratic action of Charles* V. Philip of Hesse and Jakob Sturm* united Saxony and Hesse with certain S Ger. Ev. cities (with Ulm, Strasbourg, and Nürnberg as nucleus) in a fed. created Apr. 22, 1529, in a secret agreement at Speyer. To clear the way for possible inclusion of Swiss in the fed., Philip of Hesse initiated plans for settling the dispute bet. Luther and H. Zwingli* at a colloquy in Marburg (see [b]; *Luther, Controversies of,* g). (b) *Pol. disintegration.* After the Diet of Speyer, P. Melanchthon,* who had kept silent regarding differences bet. Ger. Luths. and Swiss, had a change of heart and tried to thwart the fed. Luther also opposed a fed. without confessional unity. Hans von Minckwitz, representative of John* the Constant at a meeting in Rotach June 7, 1529, which had been set at Speyer for final negotiations concerning the fed., succeeded in postponing action on the fed. to Schwabach Aug. 24; this meeting was later reset for Oct. 16, when the 17 *Schwabach Arts.,* prepared bet. ca. July 25 and Sept. 14 by Luther et al. and reflected in the Marburg Arts., were first presented, with another meeting set to consider them at Schmalkalden at the end of Nov. Meantime, at a meeting of representatives of John the Constant, George* of Brandenburg-Ansbach, and Philip of Hesse in Saalfeld July 8, the representatives of George of Brandenburg-Ansbach successfully demanded, as prerequisite for fed.: adoption of a uniform confession, uniform ch. order, and other practical regulations; this helped give direction to the Schwabach Arts. Meanwhile also, the Colloquy of Marburg (see [a]) had been held Oct. 1–4. *Marburg Arts.* 1–14 list the doctrines on which the Sacramentarians and the Luths. apparently agreed; agreement was in evidence also in the 1st part of the 15th, the last part of which, however, reads in part: "We are not agreed as to whether the true [real: Ger. *wahre*] body and blood of Christ are bodily [corporally, really; Ger. *leiblich*] present in the bread and wine." By 1530 Zwingli's writings showed that he had a spirit very different from that of Luther. The Colloquy of Marburg failed to provide a basis for including Swiss in the fed. (see [a]). Demand for confessional unity was asserting itself over demand for fed. This trend issued at Schmalkalden at the end of Nov. and beginning of Dec. in defeat of the fed. Nürnberg and Brandenburg accepted the Schwabach Arts.; Strasbourg and Ulm rejected them; all 4 refused to enter the fed., which thus was wrecked. (c) In Jan. 1530 Charles* V issued a summons for a Diet at Augsburg. John the Constant asked Luther, Melanchthon, J. Bugenhagen,* and J. Jonas* to deliberate regarding arts. of faith and usage. The result of their deliberations, in the hands of John the Constant at Torgau by Mar. 27: *Torgau Arts.* (MS discovered at Weimar 1830), divided into an introd. and 10 arts.: human doctrine and human order; marriage of priests; both forms; mass; confession; jurisdiction; ordination; vows; invocation of saints; Ger. song. Because Luther was under the ban,* he did not attend the Diet but spent the time at Coburg. Since the summons stated that "every man's opinions, thoughts, and notions" were to be heard, Melanchthon, using the Torgau Arts. as guide, prepared a statement of the Luth. position and a preface. Abusive arts. (404) by J. Eck* moved Melanchthon to include a summary of doctrine based on the Schwabach Arts. Melanchthon changed the Confession repeatedly before its presentation. John the Constant sent it to Luther May 11 for consideration and possible revisions; Luther returned it May 15. Various things (e. g., the harsh message of Charles V to John the Constant on May 27, which included a ban on ev. preaching in Augsburg [repeated June 15]; the demand of Charles V that the Luths. join the Corpus Christi procession June 16) led to a rewriting of the preface so as to indicate that it was being submitted by others besides John the Constant. The Ger. draft of the AC was read Sat. afternoon, June 25, 1530, "in the lower large room," by C. Beyer*; then the AC was given in both Ger. and Lat. to Charles V by G. Brück.* There are variants bet. the Lat. and Ger. texts; in some cases (e. g., VII 2, where the Lat. *doctrina* is rendered by the Ger. *gepredigt*) the one language elucidates the other. Following are listed as signatories in *Die Bekenntnisschriften der evangelisch-lutherischen Kirche,* 6th ed. (Göttingen, 1967), pp. 136–137, which notes that complete certainty in the listing has not been est.: John the Constant and John* Frederick of Saxony, George* of Brandenburg-Ansbach, Ernest* and Francis (younger brother of Ernest; d. 1549) of Lüneburg, Philip of Hesse, Wolfgang* of Anhalt, and representatives of Nürnberg and Reutlingen. Before the close of the Diet, representatives of Frankfurt am Main, Heilbronn, Kempten, Weissenburg, and Windsheim also signed.

3. *Defense of the Confession.* June 27 the RC estates resolved to answer the AC. Their reply tried to show that the matters that were true in the AC were taken from RCm, that the AC was not in harmony with statements of Ev. leaders, that the here-

sies in the AC had been condemned long ago, that other condemned heresies were held by Lutner and his followers, and that Luther was the cause of the Anabap. and Capernaitic* heresies. The RC estates rejected it July 15 because of its harshness, and the *Confutatio pontificia* (also known as *Responsio pontificia*) was prepared and read to the Diet Aug. 3. During the ensuing weeks, Luths. were subjected to tremendous pressure and intrigue. The *Confutatio* was not given to the Luths. Melanchthon prepared a reply (*Prima delineatio apologiae;* not the one in the Book* of Concord) based on notes taken by J. Camerarius* during the reading of the *Confutatio.* When the imperial recess Sept. 22 declared the AC "for good reasons answered and rejected by the Holy Scriptures and other writings," the Luths. through Brück presented the *Prima delineatio apologiae,* but it was refused by Charles V. After receiving a copy of the *Confutatio,* Melanchthon continued work and pub. *Apologia confessionis* as a private document. It was signed 1537 with the AC at Schmalkalden (see B 2). It is a refutation of the *Confutatio* and a defense and amplification of the AC. The sequence of arts. follows in gen. that of the AC (see A 4) and the *Confutatio.* Arts. not disputed were treated briefly; those dealing with similar subject matter were combined. The Ap has the double value of theol. thoroughness and the warmth of a living confession. Luther endorsed both the AC and the Ap.

4. Outstanding AC characteristics: objective universality, emphasis on personal salvation through justification by faith alone, air of reverent freedom, and spirit of catholic continuity. It claims to present nothing new but only to reemphasize the doctrines taught by the true ch. through the ages.

AC arts. I–XXI treat basic doctrine, XXII–XXVIII abuses corrected: I. God; II. Original Sin; III. The Son of God; IV. Justification; V. The Office of the Ministry; VI. The New Obedience; VII. The Church; VIII. What the Church Is; IX. Baptism; X. The Holy Supper of Our Lord; XI. Confession; XII. Repentance; XIII. The Use of the Sacraments; XIV. Order in the Church; XV. Church Usages; XVI. Civil Government; XVII. The Return of Christ to Judgment; XVIII. Freedom of the Will; XIX. The Cause of Sin; XX. Faith and Good Works; XXI. The Cult of Saints; XXII. Both Kinds in the Sacrament; XXIII. The Marriage of Priests; XXIV. The Mass; XXV. Confession; XXVI. The Distinction of Foods; XXVII. Monastic Vows; XXVIII. The Power of Bishops.

5. *Subsequent Hist. of the AC.* In *Germany** the AC became the confessional basis of the Schmalkaldic* League 1531 and was adopted by nearly all Ev. Ger. within ca. 15 yrs. after its presentation. In 1551 the Luths. asked Melanchthon and J. Brenz* to work out confessions supplementary to the AC for the Council of Trent* (*Confessio Saxonica* [Saxon Confession], also called *Repetitio confessionis Augustanae; Confessio Virtembergica* [Württemberg Confession]). In *Austria** the AC was early received by many; official toleration of its adherents was granted 1568. In *Boh.* many accepted the AC soon after 1530; it gained recognition among the Unitas Fratrum by way of the "Boh. Confession" (see *Bohemia, Lutheran Theology in,* 4). In *Silesia* official recognition of the AC was obtained 1609 by the Charter of Rudolf* II. In *Hungary** parts of the AC are reflected in the *Confessio Pentapolitana* (named after 5 free cities of Upper Hung.: Eperjes [Eperies; Presov], Bartfeld [Bardejov; Bártfa], Klein-Zeben [Kis-Szeben; Sabinov], Kaschau [Kosice; Kassa], and Leutschau [Levoca; Löcse]). In *Slovakia** and in *Yugoslavia** several groups accepted the AC. In *Transylvania** the AC was accepted mostly by Saxons. In 1572 Lucas Ungleich (1526–1600) presented a compilation of the AC (*Formula pii consensus inter pastores ecclesiarum Saxonicarum*) which was adopted in addition to the AC. *Kleinpolen* (Little Poland; SE, mountainous part of the former kingdom of Poland; included, e. g., Krakau, Sandomir, Zator, Oswiecim [Auschwitz], Lublin, Red Russ., Podolia, Belz, Kiev), dominated 1530–55 by Wittenberg, adhered to the AC till 1555, but with increasing Ref. tendencies; *Grosspolen* (Greater Poland; NW, plain part of the former kingdom of Poland; included, e. g., Posen and Gostyn) used 2 Polish translations of the AC: that which Albert* of Prussia had made and that pub. by Martin Florus Quiatkowski; the 1st Luth. syn. pledged itself to the AC 1565; see also *Poland; Reformation, Luth.,* 12. In *Lithuania** a small minority accepted the AC. In *Latvia** acceptance of the AC dates from the time of the Reformation. After the influence of N. Hemming(sen)* was overcome, loyalty to the AC and SC became strong in *Den.* (see *Denmark, Lutheranism in,* 5) and *Norw.* (see *Norway, Lutheranism in*) in the last part of the 16th c. *Iceland* also accepted the AC (see *Iceland,* 3). The AC was not formally accepted in *Swed.* until 1593, when it, with the Bible and the ecumenical symbols, became the confessional basis of the Swed. Ch. and the 1571 ch. order was confirmed (see also *Sweden, Lutheranism in,* 1, 2). In *Livonia* and *Estonia** the Diet of Reval 1524 decided for the Reformation, and use of the AC was a matter of course. In *Russia** the AC became known through the Baltic Provinces. An *Eng.* tr. of the AC and the Ap, by R. Taverner,* was printed in London 1536 under the title *The Confessyon of the Fayth of the Germaynes.* 16 arts. *(Wittenberg Articles; Repetitio Augustanae)* agreed on by a delegation of Henry* VIII and Luths. (Luther, Melanchthon, Bugenhagen, Jonas, Cruciger*) in spring 1536 exerted (with the AC) a lasting influence on Angl. confessions and demonstrated what concessions the Luths. were ready to make to win a country like Eng. (see also *England,* B 2–3). Lutheranism came to the *Netherlands** by 1518, but persecution beginning in the 1550s left only a few who adhered to the AC (1st Dutch version pub. 1543 in Wesel). Two *Fr.* translations were made at the time of the Augsburg Diet; others followed (see also *France,* 15). The AC may have been tr. in *Sp.* in the 16th c., but did not become somewhat gen. available in print till the 20th c. (see also *Spain,* 3). Two *It.* translations of the AC were made soon after the Augsburg Diet: one for the emp., the other for the pope; a 1562 It. tr. of the AC and the Ap was made for Dalmatia, Istria, and part of Carniola but made no lasting impression. The AC was pub. in *Gk.* 1559. See also *Eastern Orthodox Churches,* 5.

6. The AC is used in *N., Cen., and S. Am.* Luth. pastors who came to Am. in the 17th c. were pledged to the AC, and their congs. bound by it. The Pa. and N. Y. Ministeriums, which did not have the AC in their constitutions, required the pledge at ordination. In the 18th and 19th cents. this pledging became an empty form due to Pietism,* rationalism,* and sectarianism. Reaction to the Prussian* Union and the coming of Old* Luths. brought renewed emphasis on the AC. The Definite* Syn. Platform encountered decisive opposition. Free* Luth. Conferences led to formation of the Synodical* Conf. Emphasis on confessionalism was also felt in formation 1867 of the General* Council of the Ev. Luth. Ch. in (N.) Am., which pledged itself to the Book* of Concord. T. E. Schmauk,* H. E. Jacobs,* C. Porterfield Krauth* were esp. active in the interest of confessionalism. In The General* Syn. of the Ev. Luth. Ch. in the USA there was also a trend toward stricter confessionalism which made possible the formation of The United* Luth. Ch. in Am.

7. *Other Continents.* Luths. in *Afr.* use the AC

(tr., e. g., into Zulu, Twi, Shambala, Swahili). Various versions have been used in *India* (e. g., Tamil, Telugu, Eng., Hindi, Santali). *Chinese* translations include wen-li ca. 1914, Mandarin 1928. The AC has been tr. several times into *Jap.* The AC came to *Australia* 1836 (see *Australia, Lutheranism in,* A 1).

B. *1530–46.* 1. A conference was held 1536 in the home of Luther bet. Luths. and Reformed. As a result, the *Wittenberg* Concord* was signed by Reformed (M. Bucer,* W. F. Capito,* M. Alber,* M. Frecht,* J. Otter,* W. Musculus,* et al.) and Luths. (M. Luther, P. Melanchthon, J. Bugenhagen, J. Jonas, Cruciger,* J. Menius,* F. Myconius,* U. Rhegius,* G. Spalatin,* J. Otter,* et al.). See also *Union Movements,* 3.

2. June 2, 1536, Paul* III called a gen. council to meet at Mantua, It., on May 23, 1537, for the extirpation of heresy. In Dec. 1536 John* Frederick asked Luther to write a positional statement to be reviewed and approved also by other Luth. theologians. It was signed at Wittenberg by Luther, Jonas, Cruciger, Bugenhagen, N. v. Amsdorf,* Melanchthon (with the reservation that the pope might hold primacy *jure humano*), J. Agricola,* G. Spalatin; delivered to John Frederick Jan. 3, 1537. To help prepare for a possible gen. ch. council, John Frederick called for Luth. theologians to attend a meeting of the Schmalkaldic* League which had been considered for Jan. 8 but postponed to Feb. 7. Because of illness Luther could not attend this meeting, Feb. 7–23, 1537, at Schmalkalden, which reaffirmed AC and AP but did not act officially on Luther's arts., though most men present signed them. In lieu of Luther's arts., Melanchthon wrote *Tractatus* [Tract; Treatise], which was signed by all theologians present and which dealt with the power and primacy of the pope and with the power and jurisdiction of bps. Luther recd. his arts. and had them pub. in spring 1538; they grew in esteem, came to be known as *Schmalkaldic Arts.,* and were pub. 1580 in the Book of Concord, with Melanchthon's Tractatus appended. SA Part I treats "the sublime articles of the divine majesty." Part II: 1. Christ and Faith; 2. Mass and Invocation of Saints; 3. Chapters and Monasteries; 4. Papacy. Part III: 1. Sin; 2. Law; 3. Repentance; 4. Gospel; 5. Baptism; 6. The Sacrament of the Altar; 7. The Keys; 8. Confession; 9. Excommunication; 10. Ordination and Vocation; 11. The Marriage of Priests; 12. The Church; 13. How Man Is Justified before God, and His Good Works; 14. Monastic Vows; 15. Human Traditions. In Apr. 1537 the council set for Mantua was postponed to Nov. 1, 1537; later it was reset for May 1, 1538, Vicenza, It., and finally indefinitely suspended May 21, 1539. See also *Vergeris, Pietro Paolo* (2d entry).

3. While the AC was being est., Melanchthon made alterations in its wording. The 1540 *Variata* caused particular concern. See also *Union Movements.* 3. Agricola had jeopardized the Luth. position on Law and Gospel (see *Antinomian Controversy*). By 1543 Melanchthon had gone so far as to rework, for the reformation of Cologne, arts. in a document by Bucer, for which Bucer alone, however, wrote the art. on the Lord's Supper.

C. *1546–80.* 1. After Luther's death the storm broke over the Ev. Luth. chs. South Ger. and most of N Ger. were conquered by Charles V. The Augsburg Interim (see *Interim,* I), which sacrificed the doctrine of justification, recognized 7 sacraments and transubstantiation, and interpreted the mass as a thank offering, was accepted by most of the crushed Prot. princes. Melanchthon opposed the Augsburg Interim but soon became fearful and yielded. The Leipzig Interim (see *Interim,* II) compromised the doctrine of justification by faith; reintrod. RC ceremonies at Baptism, and Corpus Christi; and included other rules favoring RCm. Controversies which arose chiefly out of aberrations of Melanchthon's followers and the extremism of M. Flacius* Illyricus et al. include Adiaphoristic* 1548, Osiandrian* 1549, Majoristic* 1551, Crypto-Calvinistic* 1552, Synergistic* 1555, Second Antinomian* 1556. The attempt to adjust controversies by academic disputations, to fix religion by dogmatic formulations, and to restore peace by the Frankfurt* Recess 1558 and Naumburg* Diet 1561, together with conflict regarding the *Variata,* led to at least 20 Luth. Confessions bet. 1546 and the adoption of the FC. Best-known: *Corpus Philippicum* 1560 (doctrinal writings of Melanchthon), also called *Misnicum* (because it was to be used *in ecclesiis et scholis regionum Saxonicarum et Misnicarum, subditarum ditioni Principis Electoris Saxoniae*) and *Wittenbergense;* issued under the title *Corpus* doctrinae christianae.*

2. In 1567 Jakob Andreä* was commissioned to draw up a formula of harmony. 1574 Elector August* took sharp measures against the Philippists.* See also *Crypto-Calvinistic Controversy.* 1573 Andreä had published "Six Christian Sermons," which, at the suggestion of M. Chemnitz,* was rev. into the *Swabian Concordia* (11 arts.). Rev. by D. Chytraeus* and Chemnitz, it was known as the *Swabian-Saxon Concordia.* L. Osiander* the elder and B. Bidembach* prepared a formula adopted at Maulbronn Jan. 19, 1576. A meeting at Torgau May 28–June 7, 1576, attended by N. Selnecker,* Andreä,* Chemnitz,* Chytraeus,* A. Musculus,* C. Cornerus,* et al., formulated the *Torgau Book* on the basis of the *Swabian-Saxon Concordia* and the *Maulbronn Formula.* After Elector August had received criticisms of the work, final rev. was made 1577 at Bergen by Chemnitz, Andreä, Selnecker, Musculus, Cornerus, and Chytraeus. This *Bergen Book (Solid Declaration; Thorough Declaration),* together with Andreä's *Epitome,* was finished by May 28, 1577. These 2 works were brought together as the *Formula of Concord* in the *Book of Concord* (with a preface prepared by the theologians and signed by the princes), which appeared officially at Dresden June 25, 1580 (see *Book of Concord*). The *Epitome* (1) defines the state of controversy, (2) affirms the true doctrine, (3) rejects false doctrines. The *Solid Declaration* omits this division and discusses matters at length. Both have introductions. Contents of the FC: Introd. confesses the Scriptures as the only rule of faith and practice and also accepts the 3 ecumenical creeds and Luth. confessions previously adopted; Art. I: Original Sin; II: Free Will or Human Powers; III: The Righteousness of Faith before God; IV: Good Works; V: Law and Gospel; VI: The Third Function of the Law; VII: The Holy Supper; VIII: The Person of Chirst; IX: Christ's Descent into Hell; X: The Ecclesiastical Rites that Are Called Adiaphora or Things Indifferent; XI: Eternal Foreknowledge and Divine Election; XII: Other Factions and Sects which Never Accepted the Augsburg Confession. The FC was signed by 3 electors, 2 bps., 18 princes, 24 counts, 4 barons, 35 cities, and nearly 8,200 clerics, teachers, and others by 1580.

D. *Subscription.* 1. Speaking of the Sept. 22, 1530, Reichsabschied (imperial edict; recess), Luther expressed the view that all who hold the AC, whether openly or secretly, must be regarded and treated as brothers (St. L. ed., XVI, 1538). This view was reemphasized by C. F. W. Walther* (e. g., "Urtheil einer Conferenz," *Der Lutheraner,* XII [July 1, 1856], 181–182; cf. A. B., "Eine freie Conferenz," *L. u. W.,* II [Mar. 1856], 84–85, and ed. comment 85–86). Fellowship on basis of the Luth. Confessions was stressed also by C. Porterfield Krauth,* H. E. Jacobs,* T. E. Schmauk,* et al. Acceptance of the AC indicates that one has the Luth. attitude on the great fundamentals (sola Scriptura, sola gratia, sola fide) and by conscientious study will find himself in agreement with the doctrinal content of the other symbols. This does not imply that he reaches absolute and errorless perfection in exegesis, doctrine, life. Cf. "Von dem Namen 'Lutheraner,'" *Der Lutheraner,* I (Sept. 1, 1844), 2–4; "Antwort auf die neueste Vertheidigung der Union," *Der Lutheraner,* I (June 18, 1845), 82–84; "Vorwort der Redaktion zum dreizehnten Jahrgang des 'Lutheraner,'" *Der Lutheraner,* XIII (Aug. 26, 1856), 1–3; *Verhandlungen der dreizehnten Jahresversammlung des Westlichen Districts der Deutschen Ev.-Luth. Synode von Missouri, Ohio, u. a. Staaten im Jahre 1867* (at Chicago, Ill.) (St. Louis, Mo.), pp. 31–33.

2. In the 17th and 18th c. the Luth. symbols were not mentioned in some Luth. constitutions in the US. H. M. Mühlenberg* tried to rally Luths. around the AC and other Luth. symbols. After his death 1787, a trend away from confessionalism lasted into the 19th c. The Tenn. Syn. (see *Henkels, The,* 2, 3; *United Lutheran Church, Synods of,* 10, 16) insisted on strict confessionalism. As the symbols came into prominence, distinctions bet. fundamental* and nonfundamental doctrines were reemphasized. The Definite* Syn. Platform tried to eliminate certain doctrines which had been regarded as nonfundamental and rejected by some.

3. The distinction bet. arts. of faith by which the subscriber is bound and ordinary factual statements was prominently elaborated in Am. by C. F. Schaeffer,* "Symbolic Theology," *The Evangelical Review,* I (Apr. 1850), 457–483. For a Mo. Syn. statement that since the symbols are confessions of the faith or of the teaching of the ch., the subscriber binds himself to all the doctrine therein contained but not to hist. references, matters belonging to science, logic, method of presentation, adiaphora, etc. see [C. F. W. Walther; cf. *Der Lutheraner,* XXIII (May 1, 1867), 130, col. 2, footnote] "Referat über die Frage: Warum sind die symbolischen Bücher unserer Kirche von denen, welche Diener derselben werden wollen, nicht bedingt, sondern unbedingt zu unterschreiben?" in *Verhandlungen der Vierten Sitzungen des westlichen Distrikts der Deutschen Evang.-Luth. Synode von Missouri, Ohio und andern Staaten, im Jahre 1858* (St. Louis, 1858), pp. 7–25, reprint. without footnotes in *Der Lutheraner,* XIV (Aug. 10, 1858), 201–206, tr. and condensed by A. W. C. Guebert, "Why Should Our Pastors, Teachers and Professors Subscribe Unconditionally to the Symbolical Writings of Our Church," *CTM,* XVIII (1947), 241–253. In the same art. Walther indicates that the symbols should be accepted *quia* ("because"), not *quatenus* ("insofar as"), they agree with Scripture.

4. The major Luth. syns. in Am. require subscription to all Luth. symbols. Some Luths. subscribe only to the AC and SC. EL

Die Bekenntnisschriften der evangelisch-lutherischen Kirche, 6th rev. ed. (Göttingen, 1967); J. M. Reu, *The Augsburg Confession: A Collection of Sources with An Historical Introduction* (Chicago, 1930); *Die symbolischen Bücher der evangelisch-lutherischen Kirche,* ed. J. T. Müller, 11th ed. (Gütersloh, 1912); H. L. J. Heppe, *Die Bekenntnisschriften der altprotestantischen Kirche Deutschlands* (Kassel, 1855); T. G. Tappert, "The Symbols of the Church," *What Lutherans Are Thinking,* ed. E. C. Fendt (Columbus, 1947); M. Loy, *The Augsburg Confession* (Columbus, 1908); T. E. Schmauk and C. T. Benze, *The Confessional Principle and the Confessions of the Lutheran Church as Embodying the Evangelical Confession of the Christian Church* (Philadelphia, 1911); G. J. Fritschel, *The Formula of Concord: Its Origin and Contents* (Philadelphia, 1916); J. L. Neve, *Story and Significance of The Augsburg Confession on Its Four Hundredth Anniversary* (Burlington, Iowa, 1930); C. Bergendoff, *The Making and Meaning of the Augsburg Confession* (Rock Island, Ill., 1930); C. H. Little, *Lutheran Confessional Theology* (St. Louis, 1943); V. Ferm, *The Crisis in American Lutheran Theology* (New York, 1927); C. Mauelshagen, *American Lutheranism Surrenders to Forces of Conservatism* (Athens, Ga., 1936); E. Schlink, *Theology of the Lutheran Confessions,* tr. P. F. Koehneke and H. J. A. Bouman (Philadelphia, 1961); F. Brunstäd, *Theologie der lutherischen Bekenntnisschriften* (Gütersloh, 1951); H. Volz, *Luthers Schmalkaldische Artikel und Melanchthons Tractatus de potestate papae* (*Gotha,* [1931]); H. Fagerberg, *Die Theologie der lutherischen Bekenntnisschriften von 1529 bis 1537,* tr. from the Swed. MS by G. Klose (Göttingen, 1965), Eng. tr. from the Swed. MS by G. J. Lund, *A New Look at the Lutheran Confessions (1529–1537)* (St. Louis, 1972); J. Meyer *Historischer Kommentar zu Luthers Kleinem Katechismus* (Gütersloh, 1929); W. Arndt, "The Pertinency and Adequacy of the Lutheran Confessions," *CTM,* XX (Sept. 1949), 674–700; A. C. Piepkorn, "Suggested Principles for a Hermeneutics of the Lutheran Symbols," *CTM,* XXIX (Jan. 1958), 1–24; *The Church and the Confessions,* ed. V. Vajta and H. Weissgerber (Philadelphia, 1963).

Am. eds.: *The Christian Book of Concord,* tr. Ambrose and Socrates Henkel, J. Stirewalt, H. Wetzel, J. R. Moser, and D. Henkel (Solomon D. Henkel and Bros., New Market, Va., 1851); *The Book of Concord,* ed. H. E. Jacobs, 2 vols. (Philadelphia, 1882–83); *Concordia Triglotta* (St. Louis, 1921); *The Book of Concord,* tr. and ed. T. G. Tappert, J. Pelikan, R. H. Fischer, A. C. Piepkorn (Philadelphia, 1959).

Lutheran Congregation. Acc. to early leaders of the Mo. Syn., the local cong. of believers has all spiritual powers summed up under the term Office of the Keys.* The sphere of the ch. is exclusively spiritual, concerned solely with bldg. Christ's kingdom on earth; its governing principle is the Word of God. See also *Authority; Hierarchy; Polity, Ecclesiastical.*

Lutheran Council in Canada. 1. Inter-Luth. agency; became operative Jan. 1967, representing ca. 99% of Canada's ca. 300,000 Luths. Represents The Ev. Luth. Ch. of Can. (see *Canada,* A 26), the Luth. Ch.–Can. (see *Canada,* A 28), the LCA–Can. Section (see *Canada,* A 27). Headquarters Winnipeg 2, Man., Can.

2. The LCIC succeeded the Canadian Luth. Council. A Commission on War Service was organized Apr. 2, 1940, to represent the Luth. Ch. in appointment of chaplains and to help congs. keep in touch with service personnel. This commission was empowered by the fed. govt. Mar. 14, 1946, to organize Canadian Luth. World Relief to serve Luths. in matters of immigration and material relief. A home mission conf. convened 1944 by the Commission on Am. Missions of the Nat. Luth. Council at Saskatoon, Sask., favored establishing a council similar to the NLC and took steps toward that goal. The Canada Committee of the Lutheran* World Fed. was formed May 1948. The Canadian Luth. Council was organized Winnipeg, Man., Dec. 4, 1952. Charter mems.: American* Luth. Ch., Augustana* Ev. Luth. Ch., The Evangelical* Luth. Ch., Lutheran* Free Ch., United Ev. Luth. Ch. (see *Danish Lutherans in America,* 5), The United* Luth. Ch. in America. Divisions: Canadian Missions, Pub. Relations, Welfare, Student Service, War Service.

3. LCIC purposes and objectives:

"a. To further the witness, the work, and the interests of the participating bodies.

"b. To seek to achieve theological consensus in a systematic and continuing way on the basis of the

Scriptures and the witness of the Lutheran Confessions.

"c. To provide an instrumentality through which the participating bodies may work together in fulfilling their responsibility of Christian service where co-ordination or joint activity is deemed by them to be desirable and feasible" (*Constitution of Lutheran Council in Canada,* Art. IV). To achieve these objectives the council provides a forum for discussions; establishes procedures and provides resources for theol. study and discussion; promotes understanding and helpful relationships with other Luth. chs. in Can.; brings to the attention of participating bodies matters which may need action; represents the interests of the council, and of participating bodies so requesting, in matters requiring common action before the public in Can., the govt., and organized agencies and bodies outside the Luth. Ch.; makes studies and surveys; performs specific services for participating bodies; establishes liaison with inter-Luth. groups; takes necessary steps to meet emergencies. Additional functions may be undertaken upon approval by two-thirds of the participating bodies.

4. Clergy and lay representatives of participating chs. est. and supervise the program carried on through 6 divisions and 1 committee: a. Division of Theol. Studies; all participating bodies take part. b. Division of Soc. Services. c. Division of Canadian Missions. d. Division of Campus Foundation Activity. e. Division of Educational Services. f. Division of Pub. Relations. g. Committee on Youth Activities. WAS

See also *Canada,* A 30.

Lutheran Council in the United States of America. I. Organized at Cleveland, Ohio, Nov. 1966, by 43 delegates from The American* Luth. Ch., the Lutheran* Ch. in Am., The Lutheran* Ch.–Mo. Syn., and the Synod* of Ev. Luth. Churches. LCUSA began functioning Jan. 1967. Headquarters 315 Park Ave. S., New York, N. Y., 10010.

II. *History.* LCUSA grew out of a 1958 resolution of the National* Luth. Council calling for an examination of cooperative activities in Am. Lutheranism and possible extension of such activities. The LCMS hesitated to participate until assured 1959 that doctrinal implications would be examined.

Three major meetings 1960–61 of representatives of interested bodies led to the conclusion that there was basis for further exploration of possible establishment of a new cooperative agency whose functions would include (1) common theol. study with a view to consensus and (2) Christian service.

Meanwhile mergers decreased the participating bodies to 3: The ALC, LCA, LCMS, representing ca. 95% of ca. 8.6 million Luths. in the US and Can. Their 1962 convs. authorized further discussions.

Invitations were extended to other Luth. chs., but of them only the SELC sent observers to a meeting at Chicago, Ill., Jan. 22–23, 1963. The SELC became part of the Inter-Luth. Consultation (as the group constituted itself Jan. 1963) at the next meeting, in Chicago, Oct. 1963.

By Jan. 1964 the consultation had endorsed a proposed name and const. for the new agency, chosen NYC as the site for its headquarters, and selected Jan. 1, 1967, as target date for est. the agency. The const. was approved by The ALC 1964, LCMS 1965, SELC 1965, LCA 1966. The NLC held its 48th and final annual meeting Feb. 1–3, 1966.

III. *Concurrent Developments.* The NLC ceased operation Dec. 31, 1966. Nat. Luth. Campus Ministry was set up as an agency of the ALC and LCA, with LCUSA functioning only in a consultative capacity; in 1969 LCUSA accepted responsibility for administering the program on request of the 2 sponsoring bodies. See also *Students, Spiritual Care of,* B 4.

Several inter-Luth. agencies which previously had functioned separately were brought together by the organization of LCUSA: Publicaciones "El Escudo," which pub. Sp. materials; Luth. Film Associates; Luth. Immigration Services; Luth. Service Commission; Nat. Luth. Commission on Scouting; God-Home-Country Program Committee; World Brotherhood Exchange, a lay volunteer service program. The council also provides staff services for the Luth. Educational Conf. of N. Am. and the Luth. Soc. Welfare Conf. of Am.

IV. *Purposes and Constitutional Bases.* Const., Art. IV, Purposes and objectives: "a. To further the witness, the work, and the interests of the participating bodies.

"b. To seek to achieve theological consensus in a systematic and continuing way on the basis of the Scriptures and the witness of the Lutheran Confessions.

"c. To provide an instrumentality through which the participating bodies may work together in fulfilling their responsibility of Christian service where coordination or joint activity is deemed by them to be desirable and feasible."

Functions include providing a forum for discussing mutual concerns and planning common action; promoting understanding, amity, and helpful relationships with other US Luth. chs.; representing interests of participating bodies, upon request, before the public, govts., and other organized bodies and agencies; proposing new work; performing specific services in behalf of participating chs.; establishing liaison with voluntary or unofficial inter-Luth. groups.

V. *Structure and Administration.* LCUSA is an agency of its participating bodies. Its only authority is that delegated to it by the participants. Except for the constitutional requirement of participation in the program of ongoing theol. study, each body determines the extent of its cooperation in LCUSA activities.

Primary governing assem.: the annual meeting of representatives of the bodies. Each ch. is entitled to 1 representative for every 200,000 bap. mems. in the US or remaining major fraction thereof, with all participants entitled to a least 1 representative.

The annual meeting elects a pres., vice-pres., secy., and 7 other representatives, who together form the Ex. Committee, which acts for the council bet. annual or special meetings. A treas. is selected by the Ex. Committee.

A standing committee for each division, dept., and commission is appointed annually by the Ex. Committee upon nominations made by the participating bodies.

Regular financial support of the council is derived mainly from appropriations made by the participating bodies is proportion to their bap. membership. A current budget and projected needs for 2 additional yrs. are presented for approval to each annual meeting.

Work not provided for in the const. or bylaws cannot be initiated without two-thirds approval of the annual meeting and a majority of the participating bodies.

A gen. secy., elected for 4 yrs., is the chief ex.

VI. *Divisions and Functions.* Divisions: Educational Services, Mission Services, Pub. Relations, Service to Military Personnel, Theological Studies, Welfare Services.

Office of Research, Statistics, and Archives includes a reference library, archives of inter-Luth. cooperation, and information service and provides for coordination and correlation of research projects in the council and in the participating bodies.

Office of Nat. Youth Agency Relationships represents the interests of the participating bodies in matters relating to civic agencies, e.g., Boy Scouts of Am., Camp Fire Girls, 4-H Clubs; administers ch.-related programs recognized by the youth agencies; provides training opportunities for Luth. leaders assoc. with these youth groups.

Office of World Community Issues was added 1973.

VII. Publications include *Interchange,* a newsletter; *Circle,* a news and resource packet for Luth. campus ministers; *Challenger,* succeeded 1972 by *Volunteer,* pub. by World Brotherhood Exchange; *In Step,* for Luths. in the US armed forces; *The Lutheran Chaplain,* esp. for active duty Luth. military chaplains, chaplains in the reserve forces, and military contact pastors; *Focus on Public Affairs,* comment on and analysis of nat. and internat. issues; *The Lutheran Scouter.* HWD

Lutheran Danish Halle Missions. See *Missions,* 5–6.

Lutheran Deaconess Association. See *Deaconesses,* 10–14.

Lutheran Education Association. Assoc. of Luth. pastors, teachers, and laymen interested in promoting Christian educ.; organized July 1942 at River Forest, Ill.; endorsed 1944 by the Mo. Syn., which suggested that the Ex. Secy. of the synod's Bd. for Parish Educ. be advisory mem. of the Ex. Bd. of LEA. A research council, later called Research Committee, was created 1946 to identify broad areas of activity in Christian educ. requiring research. Research later came to be handled through the ex. board. LEA chaps. have been est. in all of the synod's teacher-training institutions. LEA publications include a yearbook, monographs on educ. subjects, minutes and essays of convs., and *Lutheran Education,* successor of *Evangelisch-Lutherisches Schulblatt* (1865–1920) and *Lutheran School Journal* (1921–47). ALA

Lutheran Evangelical Association of Finland (Luth. Gospel Assoc. of Fin.; Fin. *Luterilainen Evankeliumiyhdistys*). Organized 1873. Emphasized confessional Luth. theology. Miss. field: Japan. See also *Finland, Lutheranism in,* 4.

Lutheran Faculty of Theology. See *Canada,* A 14.

Lutheran Foreign Mission Endeavors in the United States, Early. 1. Early in the 19th c., Luths. in the US showed interest in for. missions by supporting various Eur. miss. socs. See also *Central Missionary Society of the Evangelical Lutheran Church in the United States.*

2. The General * Syn. of the Ev. Luth. Ch. in the USA lent support to K. T. E. Rhenius * in India. Die deutsche Auswärtige Missions-Gesellschaft (The Ger. For. Missionary Soc.) was organized 1837 to work for Ref. and Luths., but failed; its name in the const. as amended 1841: The Foreign Mission Society of the Evangelical Lutheran Church of the United States; engaged J. C. F. Heyer * as miss. 1840; fearing complications because of difference in policy bet. the Gen. Syn. and ABCFM, with which the Gen. Syn. had cooperated, Heyer resigned 1841; he was then engaged for the same field (India) by the Pa. Ministerium.

3. In 1867 the General * Council of the Ev. Luth. Ch. in (N.) Am. asked the Ex. Committee of Missions of the Pa. Ministerium to carry on the for. miss. work. In 1869 the Gen. Council accepted responsibility for for. missions and appointed the Ex. Committee of Missions of the Pa. Ministerium as the Ex. Committee on For. Missions of the Gen. Council.

4. The United * Syn. of the Ev. Luth. Ch. in the S. began work in Jap. 1892. All for. miss. work of the Gen. Syn., Gen. Council, and United Syn. of the Ev. Luth. Ch. in the S. was transferred 1918 to The United * Luth. Ch.

5. The Ev. Luth. Syn. of Iowa * and Other States carried on its for. miss. work in connection with the Gen. Council, the Neuendettelsau * Miss. Soc., the Hermannsburg * Miss., and the Leipzig * Ev. Luth. Miss.

6. The Ev. Luth. Joint Syn. of Ohio * and Other States supported the work of the Hermannsburg Miss. in India; 1912 it took over the Hermannsburg stations at Kodur and Puttur, among Telugu in E India. See also *India,* 13.

7. Norw. Luths. supported missions in Afr., China, India, and Madagascar.

8. The Augustana Syn. (see *Augustana Evangelical Lutheran Church*) supported miss. work in India beginning 1862, Afr. 1866, Persia 1888, Puerto Rico 1898.

See also *Lutheran Church – Missouri Synod, The,* VI, 8–9; *Lutheran Church – Missouri Synod, Districts of The,* B, 1–2; *Missions,* 9–10.

Lutheran Foreign Missions Conference of (North) America. See *Missions,* 11.

Lutheran Fraternity. See *Netherlands,* 3.

Lutheran Free Church. Assoc. of Norw. Luth. congs. organized Minneapolis, Minn., June 1897, as result of a dispute in the United * Norw. Luth. Ch. involving matters pertaining to union agreements and new trends in theol. thinking, cong. life, and sem. training. Known 1893–97 as Friends of Augsburg. (in reference to Augsburg Theol. Sem. [see *Ministry, Education of,* X G]).

The congs. participated in an annual conf. which had no authority over congs. The sovereignty of each cong. under the authority of the Word and Spirit of God was emphasized. All voting mems. and voting mems. of other Luth. congs. who were willing to sign a statement that they accepted the LFC's "Fundamental Principles and Rules for Work" and promised to work for the purpose stated in Art. 2 ("making Lutheran congregations free and living, so that, according to their calling and ability, they may work in spiritual freedom and autonomy for the cause of the Kingdom of God at home and abroad through such agencies and institutions as the congregations themselves may designate") were eligible to vote. The LFC helped form the NLC 1918. Until 1920 the pres. was only moderator of the annual conference.

Pres. Friends of Augsburg: Christian T. Sangstad 1893–94, G. Sverdrup * 1894–97.

Pres. LFC: Elias P. Harbo 1897–99, 1901–03, 1907–09; Endre E. Gynild 1899–1901, 1905–07, 1909–10, 1912–14, 1916–18, 1923–28; Christopher K. Ytrehus 1903–05; Paul Winther 1910–12; Johan Mattson 1914–16, 1918–20; Olai H. Sletten 1920–23; Hans J. Urdahl 1928–30; Thorvald Olsen Burntvedt 1930–58; John Stensvaag 1958–63.

The LFC merged with The ALC Feb. 1, 1963. LFC statistics 12-31-62: 260 ordained pastors; 328 congs.; 60,564 confirmed mems.; 92,900 bap. mems.

See also *Association of Free Lutheran Congregations, The; Lutheran Council in Canada,* 2.

E. L. Fevold, *The Lutheran Free Church* (Minneapolis, 1969).

Lutheran Friends of the Deaf. See *Deaf,* 13.

Lutheran Gospel Association of Finland. See *Lutheran Evangelical Association of Finland.*

Lutheran Hospital Association of America. See *Hospitals.*

Lutheran Hospitals. See *Hospitals.*

Lutheran Hour. See *Radio and Television Evangelism, Network,* 5–7.

Lutheran Human Relations Association of America. Founded 1953. Holds "it to be the responsibility of the Church to remove all restrictions on her fellowship based upon race or ethnic origin." Pub.: *The Vanguard.* HQ Valparaiso U., Valparaiso, Ind.

Lutheran Lay Training Institute. School for training

laymen for ch. work; est. 1961 on the campus of Conc. Coll., Milwaukee, Wis. The 1950 and 1953 LCMS convs. resolved to develop the training of laymen for ch. work. A planning commission was authorized 1956. This commission developed gen. objectives of an institute. Those who completed the program were to be well grounded in the Christian faith; possess a working knowledge of the Bible; be trained in teaching, witnessing, group work, family services, ch. administration, and miss. services. Establishment of the institute was authorized 1959. MAH

Lutheran Laymen's League. LCMS auxiliary organized June 22, 1917, in Milwaukee, Wis. Purpose: To aid LCMS in word and deed.

A $100,000 syn. debt led to organization of the LLL. A group including A. H. Ahlbrand,* J. W. Boehne,* B. Bosse,* A. G. Brauer,* H. W. Horst,* T. H. Lamprecht,* E. Seuel,* and F. C. Pritzlaff * met at the latter's home and launched a successful effort to liquidate the debt.

As a thankoffering at the close of WW I, the LLL began collecting a $3 million Endowment Fund to support superannuated and infirm pastors, teachers, profs., and their widows and orphans. By June 1923 the LLL gave the Mo. Syn. more than $2,300,000.

The LLL helped est. KFUO (see *Radio Stations, Religious,* 3) and the (Internat.) Luth. Hour (see *Radio and Television Evangelism, Network,* 5–7).

The LLL began pub. *Leader's Guide* 1943 (quarterly for LLL-affiliated clubs); inaugurated laymen's seminars 1943 (discontinued 1971); began providing scholarships to Valparaiso (Ind.) U., 1944; produced its 1st feature film, *Youth for the Kingdom,* 1944; initiated an LLL memorial campaign for classroom-administration bldg. at Valparaiso U. 1947; began operation of a Luth. hosp. at Vicksburg, Miss., 1949 (returned to doctor donors 1954).

A program of aid in placing Luth. workers began in the early 1950s. In 1952 *The Lutheran Layman,* official LLL pub. (begun July 1929 as *Lutheran Laymen's League Bulletin* [name changed Apr. 1933]), adopted newspaper format. In the 1950s the LLL also cooperated with LCMS in planning a program for enlisting and training the laity.

"The Family Worship Hour," a radio program, was produced by the LLL 1954–71. Grants to the Conc. Hist. Inst., St. Louis, Mo., for microfilming began 1954; summer study grants to pastors through Conc. Sem., St. Louis, Mo., 1955; cosponsorship of the Youth Leadership Training Program at Valparaiso U. 1956.

The LLL added a club services dept. 1956. In 1958 a full-time music dir. was employed. A field services dir. was added for "The Lutheran Hour" 1962, for the LLL 1963.

Having formerly rented space at CPH, the LLL dedicated its own headquarters in St. Louis in Apr. 1959; an expansion wing was dedicated Oct. 1971.

In 1961 the LLL initiated "Preaching Through the Press," advertisements in publications with wide circulation. EFK

See also *Laymen's Activity in the Lutheran Church.*

Lutheran Literature. See *Literature, Lutheran.*

Lutheran Medical Mission Association. Organized 1951 to support LCMS and Syn. Conf. miss. work. Pub. *Cross and Caduceus.* See also *Medical Missions.*

Lutheran Mission Finschhafen. See *New Guinea,* 5, 6.

Lutheran Mission Madang. See *New Guinea,* 5.

Lutheran Mission New Guinea. See *New Guinea,* 5.

Lutheran Orthodoxy. See *Lutheran Theology After 1580,* 1–5.

"Lutheran Outlook, The." See *American Lutheran Conference,* 10.

Lutheran Press. Dept. of American* Luth. Publicity Bureau, including its tract publishing operations.

Lutheran Publishing House. See *Publication Houses, Lutheran.*

Lutheran School of Theology at Chicago. See *Lutheran Church in America,* V; *Ministry, Education of,* X I.

Lutheran Seminary, Baguio City, Philippines. See *Lutheran Church – Missouri Synod, The,* VII 14; *Ministry, Education of,* XI B 22.

Lutheran Societies. See *Germany, Lutheran Free Churches in,* 5.

Lutheran Student Association of America. See *Students, Spiritual Care of,* A 3.

Lutheran Synod of Mexico, The. See *Mexico,* D 3.

Lutheran Theological Seminary, Gettysburg, Pa. See *General Synod of the Evangelical Lutheran Church of America, The,* 8; *Gettysburg Seminary; Lutheran Church in America,* V; *Ministry, Education of,* X J.

Lutheran Theological Seminary, Philadelphia, Pa. See *Lutheran Church in America,* V; *Ministry, Education of,* X K; *United Lutheran Church, Synods of,* 22.

Lutheran Theological Seminary, Saskatoon, Sask., Can. See *Canada,* A 14, 20; *Lutheran Church in America, V; Ministry, Education of,* X L.

Lutheran Theological Southern Seminary. See *Lutheran Church in America,* V; *Ministry, Education of,* VI C, X M; *United Luhteran Church, Synods of,* 27.

Lutheran Theology After 1580. 1. The Book * of Concord marked the beginning of ca. a c. of strict Luth. orthodoxy. After many controversies, Luths. achieved unity. (See *Lutheran Confessions,* C.) Determination to safeguard this blessing accounts for the large development of theol. literature which followed.

2. The theol. calm created by the FC was disturbed by 2 Christological * controversies (see *Crypto-Kenotic Controversy; Lütkemann, Joachim*) and syncretism.*

3. Luth. orthodoxy was not dead orthodoxy. It lived and flourished. Its useful productions include S. Glass(ius),* *Philologia sacra;* M. Walther,* *Officina biblica;* A. Pfeiffer,* *Critica sacra* and *Hermeneutica sacra* (later titled *Thesaurus hermeneuticus*); E. Schmidt,* Lat. tr. of the NT, with notes and *Tamieion* (Gk. "Treasury"; concordance of the Gk. NT); S. Schmidt,* commentaries on several OT and NT books; A. Calov(ius),* *Biblia illustrata;* L. Hutter,* *Compendium locorum theologicorum;* J. Gerhard, *Loci theologici;* J. A. Quenstedt,* *Theologia didactico-polemica, sive Systema theologicum.*

4. This activity was not merely of the head. Luth. orthodoxy produced J. Arnd(t),* *Bücher vom wahren Christentum* and *Paradies-Gärtlein;* J. Gerhard, *Meditationes sacrae* and *Schola pietatis;* C. Scriver,* devotional works; and such hymnists as H. Albert,* T. Clausnitzer,* S. Dach,* P. Flemming,* P. Gerhardt,* J. Hermann,* M. Meyfart,* M. Rinkart,* J. Rist,* G. Weissel.* See also *Hymnody, Christian,* 5–6.

5. Luth. orthodoxy is also reflected in such rulers as Ernest * I and Gustavus * II.

6. Pietism * spread through Ger., Scand., and Switz., preparing the way for rationalism.*

7. Notable works produced in the period of Pietism: J. G. Walch,* *Historische und theologische Einleitung in die Religions-Streitigkeiten* and an ed. of M. Luther's works (see *Luther, Works of, Editions of*); J. L. v. Mosheim,* *Institutiones historiae ecclesiasticae;* J. A. Bengel,* *Gnomon Novi Testamenti;* K. H. v. Bogatzky,* *Güldenes Schatz-Kästlein der Kinder Gottes.* The spirituality of the time found expression in A. H. Francke's * institutions, the works of such missionaries as B. Ziegenbalg,* H. Plütschau,* C. F. Schwartz,* H. P. Egede* and

his son Paul, and in hymns (see *Hymnody, Christian,* 6).

8. By about 1750 rationalism had appeared in Germany. G. W. v. Leibniz* and C. v. Wolff* had planted the seed. Frederick II (1712–86; "the Great"; king of Prussia 1740–86) cultivated the soil. Rationalism substituted dictates of human reason for authority of God's Word. Others connected with the development of rationalism include J. A. Ernesti,* J. D. Michaelis,* J. S. Semler,* J. G. Toellner.* Rationalists who made noteworthy contributions to theol. scholarship include H. F. W. Gesenius * and K. G. Bretschneider.*

9. Rationalism suffered a serious blow at the hand of 2 of its disciples: I. Kant * exalted reason but showed its limitations in spiritual matters; K. A. v. Hase * is credited with having dealt the deathblow to *rationalismus vulgaris* (common rationalism) with *Hutterus redivivus* (1828; an attempt to set forth Luth. dogmatics as L. Hutter * might have done had he lived in these days) and a series of pamphlets 1834–37. F. D. E. Schleiermacher * contributed to the decline of the old rationalism by making feeling rather than reason the seat of religion. Luth. orthodoxy never was dead; it continued to live, e. g., in C. Harms.* But neither did rationalism die.

10. Liberal theol. derived the pattern of its development largely from Kant, G. W. F. Hegel,* and Schleiermacher. For Kant not creeds but moral precepts are the important factor in religion. Hegel converted hist. religion into philos. and rational ideas and stimulated the tendency to pantheism; men influenced by Hegel include B. Bauer,* F. C. Baur,* L. A. Feuerbach,* O. Pfleiderer,* D. F. Strauss,* J. Wellhausen.* Schleiermacher gave the new rationalism an anthropocentric approach to theol.

11. Luth. confessionalism reappeared as neo-Lutheranism * in reaction against the Prussian * Union and divided into repristination theol. and the theol. of the Erlangen School. Repristination theol. tried to restore hist. Lutheranism and was represented by C. P. Caspari,* E. W. Hengstenberg,* G. A. T. F. Hönecke,* T. F. D. Kliefoth,* J. K. W. Löhe,* F. A. Philippi,* A. F. C. Vilmar,* C. F. W. Walther.* The Erlangen School tried to combine Reformation theol. with the new learning; confessionalism was not to be static but dynamic; representatives of the Erlangen School included F. Delitzsch (see *Delitzsch,* 1), F. H. R. v. Frank,* T. A. Harnack,* J. C. K. v. Hofmann,* K. F. A. Kahnis,* C. E. Luthardt,* G. Thomasius.*

12. A. B. Ritschl * broke with the theol. of F. C. Baur's* Tübingen* school and later est. a school of his own; men influenced by Ritschl included W. Baur's* Tübingen* school and later est. a school of J. W. Herrmann,* J. W. M. Kaftan,* F. Kattenbusch,* P. Lobstein,* F. Loofs,* H. H. Wendt.*

13. The hist.-religious school *(Religionsgeschichtliche* Schule)* stressed development of Christianity as seen in light of its hist. and geogr. environment. Christianity, like other religions, is considered a product of evolution. K. H. Graf* and J. Wellhausen* applied this theory to the study of the OT (see *Higher Criticism,* 12); those who applied it to the study of the NT include R. Otto,* J. Weiss,* W. Wrede.* Other mems. of this school include J. F. W. Bousset,* G. A. Deissmann,* A. Eichhorn,* H. E. F. W. Gressmann,* J. F. H. Gunkel,* W. Heitmüller,* A. Schweitzer,* E. P. W. Troeltsch,* A. Dietrich,* B. Duhm,* J. E. Linderholm,* R. Reitzenstein,* H. Windisch.*

14. More respectful of the creeds of Christianity: in Biblical studies T. v. Zahn,* A. Schlatter,* K. M. A. Kähler,* R. Kittel,* F. E. König*; in Luther research W. M. Walther,* K. Holl,* A. H. Boehmer,* H. Preuss*; in systematic theol. K. H. Ihmels,* O. K. Hallesby,* R. Seeberg,* T. Kaftan.* These represent various shades of theol. opinions and degrees of conservatism.

15. Other representatives of neo-Lutheranism include W. Elert,* P. Althaus* Jr., K. Heim,* G. Kittel,* and exponents of the theol. of Lund.* LWS

See also *Luther Renaissance.*

J. H. Kurtz, *Church History,* III, tr. J. MacPherson (London, 1890); J. L. Neve, *A History of Christian Thought,* II, by O. W. Heick, [rev. ed.] (Philadelphia, 1966); E. H. Klotsche and J. T. Mueller, *The History of Christian Doctrine* (Burlington, Iowa, 1945).

Lutheran Union and Unity Movements in the United States. See *Union and Unity Movements in the United States, Lutheran.*

"Lutheran Witness." Official periodical of LCMS. See also *Missouri and Other States, The English Evangelical Lutheran Synod of.*

Lutheran Women's Missionary League. See *Woman in Christian Society,* II C 11.

Lutheran World Conference. See *Lutheran World Federation.*

Lutheran World Convention. See *Lutheran World Federation.*

Lutheran World Federation, The. Conditions after WW I, relief work by Luths. of the US and other countries, and increased contact bet. Luths. in various parts of the world created desire for meetings in which all Luths. would be represented and where issues of common interest could be discussed. The Allgemeine* Evangelisch-Lutherische Konferenz and the NLC were among leaders whose efforts led to the 1st Luth. World Conference 1923 Eisenach, Ger., which est. the Luth. World Conv. (Lutherischer Weltkonvent); chm. L. H. Ihmels.* The 2d Luth. World Conv. met 1929 Copenhagen, Den.; the 3d 1935 Paris, Fr.; the 4th was to be held 1940 Philadelphia, Pa., but was postponed because of WW II and held 1947 in Lund, Swed. A const. was adopted and the name changed to The Luth. World Federation. 1964 Const.: Art. II: "The Lutheran World Federation acknowledges the Holy Scriptures of the Old and New Testaments as the only source and the infallible norm of all church doctrine and practice, and sees in the three Ecumenical Creeds and in the Confessions of the Lutheran Church, especially in the Unaltered Augsburg Confession and Luther's Catechism, a pure exposition of the Word of God." On the nature, functions, and scope of The LWF, Art. III of its const. says: "1. *Nature.* The Lutheran World Federation shall be a free association of Lutheran Churches. It shall act as their agent in such matters as they assign to it. It shall not exercise churchly functions on its own authority, nor shall it have power to legislate for the Churches belonging to it or to limit the autonomy of any Member Church. 2. *Functions.* In accordance with the preceding paragraphs, The Lutheran World Federation shall: (a) Further a united witness before the world to the Gospel of Jesus Christ as the power of God for salvation. (b) Cultivate unity of faith and confession among the Lutheran Churches of the world. (c) Develop fellowship and cooperation in study among Lutherans. (d) Foster Lutheran interest in, concern for, and participation in ecumenical movements. (e) Support Lutheran Churches and groups as they endeavor to meet the spiritual needs of other Lutherans and to extend the Gospel. (f) Provide a channel for Lutheran Churches and groups to help meet physical needs. 3. *Scope of Authority.* In accordance with its nature, function and structure, The Lutheran World Federation may take action on behalf of one or more Member Churches in such matters as they may commit to it." The 2d LWF assem. was held Hanover, Ger., 1952; the 3d Minneapolis, Minn., 1957; the 4th Helsinki, Fin., 1963; the 5th Évian-les-Bains, Fr., 1970.

See also *Lutheran World Services; Radio Voice of the Gospel.*

Lutheran World Relief. See *Lutheran World Service.*

Lutheran World Service. After WW II, interchurch aid and refugee service increased; Luth. chs. often carried on activities with little knowledge of each other's work. In the US, Luth. World Relief, Inc., was founded 1945 as an agency of the National* Luth. Council; it serves people regardless of race, creed, or pol. connection. The Lutheran* World Fed. resolved 1952 to create a Dept. of Luth. World Service. Luth. nat. organizations cooperate with this dept. See also *Canada,* A 29; *National Lutheran Council,* 4.

"Lutheraner, Der." See *Lutheran Church – Missouri Synod, The,* II 5; III 1–2; V 2.

Lutheranism, American. See *American Lutheranism.*

Lutherischer Verein. Founded 1848 in Pomerania to champion Lutheranism; similar socs. were organized in other parts of Ger.; a gen. assoc. was formed 1849 at Wittenberg.

Lutherischer Weltkonvent. See *Lutheran World Federation.*

Lutherisches Hilfswerk der Gotteskasten und Martin-Luther-Vereine. See *Gotteskasten.*

Lutherisches Pilgerhaus. See *Immigrant and Emigrant Missions.*

"Luthersk Ugeblad." See *Danish Lutherans in America,* 5.

Lütkemann, Joachim (1608–55). B. Demmin, Pomerania; educ. Griefswald, Strasbourg, Rostock; disputed the continuation of the true humanity of Jesus in death. Works include *Der Vorschmack göttlicher Güte,* a book of devotions.

"Lux mundi" (Lat. "light of the world"). Series of studies in the religion of the incarnation; pub. 1889 under editorship of C. Gore* by Oxford Angl. scholars including H. S. Holland,* J. R. Illingworth,* and F. Paget.*

Luzzatto, Samuel David (Heb. acronymic abbreviation Schedal; 1800–65). B. Trieste; conservative Jewish theol.; Heb. and Aramaic language scholar. Tr. parts of the Bible into It., with Heb. commentary; other works include studies in Targums.

Lycanthropy (from Gk. for "wolf" and "man"). 1. Form of insanity in which one believes that he is an animal, esp. a wolf. 2. Belief that one can transform himself and/or others into animal (esp. wolf) form (hence "werewolf," from OE *wer,* "man"). In the Middle Ages, as late as the 17th c., theologians regarded lycanthropy as a branch of sorcery.

Lydius. 1. *Balthasar* (ca. 1576–1629). "Palatinus." Son of 3, father of 2; b. (Gross) Umstadt, near Darmstadt, Ger.; Dutch Ref. theol.; preacher Dordrecht; delivered opening and closing sermon at 1618–19 Syn. of Dordrecht.* 2. *Jacob* (1610–79). Son of 1; b. Dordrecht, Neth.; exegete; archaeol.; pastor Dordrecht. 3. *Martin* (ca. 1539–1601). Father of 1; b. Lübeck, Ger.; Dutch Ref. pastor; preacher Amsterdam 1580, Leeuwarden 1585; prof. Franeker 1585; moderate Calvinist.

Lyman, Henry (Nov. 23, 1809 [1810?] – June 28, 1834). B. perhaps Northampton, Mass.; educ. Amherst (Mass.) Coll. and Andover (Mass.) Sem.; studied medicine; ABCFM miss. to Indian Archipelago (Malay Archipelago; Malaysia; East Indies; Indonesia) with S. Munson* 1833. See also *Indonesia,* 4.

Lyons, Councils of. Many councils were held at Lyons, Fr., beginning in the 470s. RC ecumenical council Lyons I 1245 tried unsuccessfully to unseat Frederick* II; enjoined preaching of crusade* against Saracens, but without effect. RC ecumenical council Lyons II 1274 tried to remove the schism of 1054 (see *Schism,* 6); Gk. representatives agreed to terms of union, including *filioque* (see *Filioque Controversy*), but union dissolved in the 1280s. See also *Councils and Synods,* 4.

Lyra, Justus Wilhelm (1822–82). B. Osnabrück, Ger.; theol.; hymnist; liturgist; composer.

Lyra, Nicolaus de (variants include Lyranus and Lyre; ca. 1270–1340). B. Lyre (Lire; la Neuve-Lyre), Fr.; exegete; Franciscan; provincial for Burgundy 1325; prof. Sorbonne, Paris. Works include commentaries on the Bible known for emphasis on literal sense and praised by M. Luther.

Lysius, Heinrich (1670–1731). B. Flensburg, Ger.; educ. Jena, Leipzig, Königsberg; pastor and prof. Königsberg; exponent of Pietism.*

Lyte, Henry Francis (1793–1847). Eng. Angl. cleric and hymnist; b. Ednam, near Kelso, Scot.; educ. Dublin, Ireland; ordained 1815; curate Lower Brixham, Devonshire, Eng., 1823–47; d. Nice, Fr. Hymns include "Abide with Me! Fast Falls the Eventide"; "God of Mercy, God of Grace"; "My Spirit on Thy Care"; "Jesus, I My Cross Have Taken."

Lyttelton, George (1709–73). 1st Baron Lyttelton of Frankley; statesman, author; b. Hagley, near Kidderminster, Worcestershire, Eng.; educ. Eton and Oxford; mem. parliament 1735; lord commissioner of treasury 1744–54, chancellor of exchequer 1755–56. Works include *Observations on the Conversion and Apostleship of Saint Paul.* See also *Deism,* IV.

Lyttleton, Raymond Arthur. See *Evolution,* I.

M

Maass, Clara Louise (1876–1901). B. East Orange, N. J.; educ. Newark (N. J.) Ger. Hosp., School of Nursing; Contract Nurse, US army in Cuba, during Span.-Am. War; in Philippines 1900–01; one of ca. 20 volunteers in Cuba bitten by mosquitoes carrying yellow fever and d. of the fever. Clara Maass Mem. Hosp., Belleville, N. J., named after her.

Maassen, Friedrich Bernhard Christian (1823–1900). Hist. of canon* law; b. Wismar, Ger.; lawyer N Ger.; RC 1851; prof. in Austria at Innsbruck, Graz, and Vienna. Opposed papal infallibility* but defended claims of RC Ch. in Kulturkampf.* Works include *Pseudoisidor-Studien* and the unfinished *Geschichte der Quellen und der Literatur des canonischen Rechts im Abendlande bis zum Ausgange des Mittelalters.*

Mabillon, Jean (1632–1707). B. Saint-Pierremont (Ardennes), near Reims; Benedictine historian. Coed. *Acta sanctorum ordinis S. Benedicti.*

Macalister, Robert Alexander Stewart. See *Geography, Christian,* 6.

Macarius. 1. *Of Alexandria* (4th c. AD). "Politicus"; Egyptian hermit; retired to desert of Cellia at 40; regarded as miracle worker. 2. *Of Egypt* (ca. 300–ca. 390). "The Elder; the Great"; native of Upper Egypt; at ca. 30 joined colony of monks in desert of Scete; ordained priest ca. 340; renowned as miracle worker. 3. *Of Jerusalem* (d. ca. 334 AD). Bp. Jerusalem ca. 312; opposed Arianism*; present at 325 Council of Nicaea.*

Maccabees, Books of. See *Apocrypha,* A 3.

McComb, William (1793–1873). B. Coleraine, Londonderry Co., Ireland; poet; teacher, then bookseller (1828) Belfast; est. *McComb's Presbyterian Almanac* 1840. Wrote the hymn "Chief of Sinners Though I Be."

McCoy, Isaac (June 13, 1784–June 21, 1846). B. near Uniontown, Fayette Co., Pa.; Bap. preacher, Clark Co., Ind.: miss. to Indians in Wabash valley 1817; helped arrange for westward removal of Indians. Works include *Remarks on the Practicability of Indian Reform; History of Baptist Indian Missions.* See also *Indians, American,* 8.

Macedonius (d. perhaps ca. 362 AD). Semi-Arian bp. Constantinople ca. 342; deposed 360 by a syn. at Constantinople (see also *Acacius of Caesarea*). Because he allegedly denied full deity of the Holy Spirit as well as of the Son, the Pneumatomachians* are called Macedonians, though Macedonius did not found the sect.

McGiffert, Arthur Cushman (1861–1933). B. Sauquoit, N. Y.; ordained Presb. 1888, became Cong. 1899. Instr. and prof. ch. hist. Lane Theol. Sem., Cincinnati, Ohio, 1888–93; prof. ch. hist. 1893–1927, pres. 1917–26 Union Theol. Sem., NYC. Tr. *Church History of Eusebius;* other works include *A History of Christianity; Martin Luther.*

McGilvary Theological Seminary. See *Asia,* C 4.

McGready, James. See *Presbyterian Churches,* 4 b.

Machen, John Gresham (1881–1937). Fundamentalist theol.; b. Baltimore, Md.; instr. 1906–14, asst. prof. 1914–29 Princeton (N. J.) Theol. Sem.; withdrew in protest against liberalism; helped found Westminster Theol. Sem., Philadelphia, Pa., 1929; helped form Indep. Bd. for Presb. For. Missions, Inc., 1933; suspended from ministry 1935/36; helped organize Presb. Ch. of Am. 1936 (name changed 1939 to Orthodox Presb. Ch.). Works include *The Origin of Paul's Religion; Christianity and Liberalism; The Virgin Birth of Christ.* See also *Presbyterian Churches,* 4 d.

Machiavelli, Niccolò (1469–1527). B. Florence, It.; statesman; pol. philos.; deprived of office by Medici.* Developed a theory of govt. and practical statecraft that involved unscrupulous methods and gave rise to the term Machiavellianism. Works include *Il Principe* ("The Prince").

McIntire, Carl. See *Union Movements,* 11.

Mack, Alexander. See *Brethren,* 1.

Mackay, Alexander Murdoch (1849–90). B. Rhynie, Scot.; d. Uganda, Afr.; sent by CMS to Zanzibar 1876; reached Uganda 1878; opposed by RCs and Muslim. Known for work in Bible tr. into the vernacular of Uganda. See also *Africa,* F 1.

Mackay, Margaret (1802 [1801?]–1887). Writer and poet; b. perhaps Hedgefield, Inverness, Scot. Hymns include "Asleep in Jesus! Blessed Sleep"; other works include *Sabbath Musings; The Wycliffites.*

McKendree, William (1757–1835). B. William City, Va.; served in Revolutionary War; Meth. 1787; traveled with F. Asbury* as itinerant preacher, evangelist; 1st Am.-born bp. M. E. Ch. 1808.

Mackenzie, Duncan (d. 1855). See *Catholic Apostolic Church,* 1.

Mackenzie, Duncan (1859–1935). See *Geography, Christian,* 6.

McKim, Randolph Harrison (1842–1921). B. Baltimore, Md.; served in Confederate Army; Prot. Episc. priest 1866; held various rectorates. Works include *Leo XIII at the Bar of History; The Problem of the Pentateuch; For God and Country.*

Maclaren, Alexander (McLaren; 1826–1910). B. Glasgow, Scot.; Eng. Bap. preacher. Works include sermons; *Expositions of Holy Scripture.*

Macleod, Norman (1812–72). B. Campbeltown, Argyll, Scot.; educ. Glasgow and Edinburgh; pastor Loudoun in Ayr, Dalkeith, Glasgow; chaplain to Queen Victoria 1857; cofounder Evangelical* Alliance; moderator Gen. Assem. of Ch. of Scotland. Ed. *Christian Instructor* and *Good Words;* other works include *Character Sketches; Daily Meditations: Deborah; The Gold Thread.*

Macmillan, John (1670–1753). B. Barncachla, Kirkcudbrightshire, Scot.; educ. Edinburgh U.; minister Balmaghie 1701–27; sympathetic to Cameronians*; successfully resisted deposition 1703; 1st Cameronian minister 1706; helped found Ref. Presb. Ch. (first called Reformed Presbytery) 1743. See also *Assoicate Reformed Church; Scotland, Reformation in,* 1.

McPherson, Aimee Semple. See *Foursquare Gospel, The.*

McPherson, Rolf Kennedy. See *Foursquare Gospel, The.*

Macrina. See *Cappadocian Theologians,* 1.

McTaggart, John McTaggart Ellis (M'Taggart; 1866–1925). Philos.; b. London, Eng.; disciple of G. W. F. Hegel*; held a theory of pluralistic personal idealism.* Works include *Some Dogmas of Religion.*

Madagascar. See *Africa,* B 9.

Madang, Lutheran Mission. See *New Guinea,* 5.

Madeira Islands. See *Africa,* C 16.

Madison, James (1749–1812). B. near Staunton, Va.;

educ. Coll. of William and Mary, Williamsburg, Va.; its pres. 1777–1812; Prot. Episc. bp. Va. 1790. See also *Protestant Episcopal Church,* 3.

Madison Settlement (Madison Agreement; Opgjör). As early as 1870 the Norw. Syn. (see *Evangelical Lutheran Church, The,* 8) sought unity through free conferences. In 1905 Hauge's Norw. Ev. Luth. Syn. (see *Eielsen Synod*) invited Norw. ch. bodies to hold discussions with possible union in view (see also *Evangelical Lutheran Church, The,* 13). Committees of the Norw. Syn., Hauge's Syn., and the United* Norw. Luth. Ch. agreed on the doctrine of absolution 1906, lay activity 1906, and the call and conversion 1907–08. Sharp disagreement developed beginning 1908 regarding the doctrine of election and predestination bet. the committees of the United Ch. and the Norw. Syn. In 1911 these 2 bodies elected new committees which adopted the "Settlement" at Madison, Wis., 1912. Content:

"1. The union committees of the Synod and the United Church, unanimously and without reservation, accept that doctrine of election which is set forth in Article XI of the Formula of Concord . . . and in Pontoppidan's *Sandhed til gudfrygtighed,* Question 548.

"2. Since both the conferring bodies acknowledge that Article XI of the Formula of Concord presents the pure and correct doctrine of the election of the children of God unto salvation as taught in the Word of God and the Confessions of the Lutheran Church, it is deemed unnecessary for church unity to set up new and more elaborate theses on this article of faith.

"3. However, since it is well known that in presenting the doctrine of election two forms of doctrine have been used, both of which have won acceptance and recognition within the orthodox Lutheran Church,

"some, in accordance with the Formula of Concord, include under the doctrine of election the whole order of salvation of the elect from the call to the glorification (Formula of Concord, Part II, Art. XI: 13-24 [the original has '10-20,' acc. to Norw. ed. of Book of Concord by Johnson and Caspari]), and teach an election 'unto salvation through the sanctification of the Spirit and belief of the truth,'

"while others, with Pontoppidan, in agreement with John Gerhard, Scriver, and other recognized teachers of the Church, define election more specifically as the decree concerning the final glorification, with faith and perseverance wrought by the Holy Spirit as its necessary presupposition, and teach that 'God has appointed all those to eternal life who He from eternity has foreseen would accept the offered grace, believe in Christ and remain constant in this faith unto the end'; and since neither of these two forms of doctrine, thus presented, contradicts any doctrine revealed in the Word of God, but does full justice to the order of salvation as presented in the Word of God and the confessions of the Church,

"we find that this should not be cause for schism within the Church or disturb that unity of the spirit in the bond of peace which God wills should prevail among us.

"4. Since, however, in the controversy over this question among us, there have appeared words and expressions – justly or unjustly attributed to the respective parties – which seemed to the opposite party to be a denial or to lead to a denial of the Confession,

"we have agreed to reject all errors which seek to explain away the mystery of election . . . either in a synergizing or a Calvinizing manner, in other words, every doctrine which either on the one hand would deprive God of His glory as only Savior or on the other hand would weaken man's sense of responsibility in relation to the acceptance or rejection of grace."

The "Settlement" rejected the doctrines (5 a) that the mercy of God and merit of Christ is not the only cause of election, (b) that election takes into account anything that man is or may do or omit to do "as of himself and by his own natural powers," (c) that faith is in whole or in part a product of or dependent on man's choosing, power, or ability, (d) that faith is the result of an ability and power imparted by the call of grace, which therefore now dwell within and belong to the unregenerate heart, (6 a) that God acts arbitrarily and unmotivated in election, (b) that God's will regarding salvation is of 2 kinds, one revealed in Scripture, the other unknown and concerning only the elect, (c) that when resistance is removed in those who are saved and not in those who are finally lost, the cause of this different result lies in God, (d) that a believer can and shall have an absolute assurance of his election and salvation instead of an assurance of faith, (e) all doctrines concerning election which directly or indirectly would conflict with the order of salvation, and would not give to all a full and equally great opportunity to be saved.

The 3 conferring bodies resolved 1912 "that the essential agreement concerning these doctrines which has been attained is sufficient for church union." Most of the Norw. Syn. agreed to the Madison Settlement. The minority, led by C. K. Preus* and I. B. Torrison,* requested 1. that Section 1 of the Madison Settlement be omitted; 2. that in Section 3 the reference to FC II [SD] XI read "1–20" instead of "10–20"; 3. that the end of Section 4 be changed from "or on the other hand [would] weaken man's sense of responsibility in relation to the acceptance or rejection of grace" to "or on the other hand [would] weaken man's sense of duty in relation to the acceptance of grace and blame for the rejection of grace." The Union Committee found a formula agreeable to the merging bodies and to most of the Norw. Syn. minority in this: ". . . there is nothing in the . . . request which is contrary to Scripture and the Confessions, and . . . we regard the position taken in that document as a sufficient expression of unity in faith. . . .

"Note. It is obvious that the above cited resolution must not be construed to mean that [the Madison] 'Agreement' as a basis for the union of the three contracting bodies thereby has been abridged or altered."

This "Austin Agreement" (Austin Settlement; 1916–17) takes its name from Austin, Minn., where agreement was reached. A minority of the minority disagreed with it and organized the Norw. Syn. of the Am. Ev. Luth. Ch. (see *Evangelical Lutheran Synod*).

The Union Documents of the Evangelical Lutheran Church, comp. and tr. G. M. Bruce (Minneapolis, Minn., 1948); *L. u. W.,* LVIII (1912), 222–223, 511–513, 562; *Documents of Lutheran Unity in America,* ed. R. C. Wolf (Philadelphia, Pa., 1966), pp. 232–235.

Madison Theses. Adopted 1875 by the majority of the Ev. Luth. Syn. of Iowa* and Other States, to clarify its doctrinal position in view of const. changes made 1873. Held (1) the Iowa Syn. does not follow any school, but declares itself loyal to the Luth. Confessions, permits differences in theol. views only as long as the views are within confessional bounds, and repudiates doctrinal development *(Fortentwicklung)* which militates against the confessional basis; (2) by making the doctrines of the Confessions binding it is not changing position, since it had formerly not excluded any doctrine; (3) it adheres to the amended form of the doctrinal par.

in the const. because it is simpler, less ambiguous, and less offensive; (4) it accepts the statements of the Luth. Confessions on the ministry, but regards the Mo. doctrine (without judging its correctness) neither as a confessional doctrine nor as a doctrine of faith and hence does not regard it as divisive; (5) it accepts the judgment of the Luth. Confessions regarding the antichristian character of the papacy but does not regard as an art. of faith the statement "the pope is the Antichrist" (as the final and complete fulfillment of the prophecy in 2 Th 2); (6) it acknowledges the doctrine of the Last Things as found in the AC but does not reject details from prophecy as long as they are in harmony with basic Luth. doctrines; (7) in the doctrine of Sun. the point concerning which the older Luth. dogmaticians disagreed (whether 1 day of the week must be selected for worship in harmony with the order of creation) is not an art. of faith; (8) "open questions" is synonymous with "nondivisive questions."

J. Deindörfer, *Geschichte der Evangel.-Luth. Synode von Iowa und anderen Staaten* (Chicago, 1897); G. J. Fritschel, *Quellen und Dokumente zur Geschichte und Lehrstellung der ev.-luth. Synode von Iowa u. a. Staaten* (Chicago, n. d.).

Madoera. See *Indonesia,* 1, 3.

Madonna (It. "my lady"). Term often used for picture, statue, or other artistic representation of Mary, mother of Jesus. In the earliest examples in the catacombs Mary has the Christ Child in her arms. In Byzantine art several types became prominent, including *Panagia Nikopoia* (Mary enthroned with Child seated on her knees), *Hodegetria* (Mary standing and holding Child in her left arm), *Blacherniotissa* (Mary praying, with Child on her breast), *Platytera* (variant of *Blacherniotissa*), *Pelagoneotissa* (Mary and Child seen from back).

In the Middle Ages the West developed greater freedom in portraying Mary in such types as *Glykophilousa* (Mary dressed as a noblewoman fondling Child); *Galaktotrophousa* (Mary nursing Child); *Deesis* (Mary, with John the Baptist, interceding at Last Judgment); Mother of Mercy (sheltering the faithful); Mother of 7 Sorrows (7 swords through heart); Mary of the Rose Garden; Virgin of Humility.

Later types include Madonna of the Rosary*; Immaculate* Conception; Annunciation (see *Annunciation, Feast of*); Nativity; Assumption (see *Assumption, Feast of*); Madonna of Lourdes*; Madonna of Fatima*; Pietà.*

Madrid, Peace (or Treaty) of. See *Speyer, Diets of,* 1.

Madrigal. 1. A kind of pastoral or love poem. 2. A type of secular choral music which originated in the 14th c. and fl. 16th–18th c. esp. in It., Fr., Eng., Ger., Neth., Den., and Sp. Early madrigals were motet-like, reflected contrapuntal skills, somewhat restricted freedom and spontaneity, helped pave the way for homophonic and harmonic music, and influenced development of the chorale* and Luth. ch. cantata.* Madrigals were written by Luths. such as L. Lechner,* H. L. v. Hassler,* Melchior Franck,* and T. Selle.*

Madsen, Peder (1843–1911). B. Toustrup, near Holstebro, Vinding parish, Den.; prof. theol. Copenhagen 1875; bp. Sjaelland (Zealand) 1909.

Madura (Madoera). See *Indonesia,* 1, 3.

Magdalen Homes. Institutions of refuge or reform for unwed mothers or fallen women. Several RC orders have been est. to support such institutions. T. Fliedner* et al. did similar work.

Magdeburg, Joachim (ca. 1525 – after ca. 1587). Brother of Johann Magdeburg*; b. Gardelegen, Ger.; educ. Wittenberg; held various ecclesiastical and educ. positions; banished for refusing to comply with Interim*; with M. Flacius* Illyricus worked on Magdeburg* Centuries; spent last yrs. in Ger., Austria, Hung.; hymnist; composer. Hymns include "Wer Gott vertraut, hat wohl gebaut." See also *Hymnody, Christian,* 5.

Magdeburg, Johann (ca. 1520–1560). Brother of Joachim Magdeburg.* Wrote rhymed Psalter. See also *Hymnody, Christian,* 5.

Magdeburg Centuries. Multivol. research by ev. scholars of Magdeburg and elsewhere, on initiative of M. Flacius* Illyricus, in sources of ch. hist. up to 1300 and its interpretation as a battle bet. truth and error. Called "Centuries" because of division of the work by centuries. First Lat. title: *Ecclesiastica historia, integram Ecclesiae Christi ideam quantum ad locum, propagationem, persecutionem, tranquillitatem, doctrinam, haereses, ceremonias, gubernationem, schismata, synodos, personas, miracula, martyria, religiones extra Ecclesiam, et statum Imperii politicum attinet, secundum singulas centurias . . . complectens . . . congesta per aliquot studiosos et pios viros in urbe Magdeburgicae.* A later title: *Centuriae Magdeburgenses, seu historia ecclesiastica Novi Testamenti, cum variorum theologorum continuationibus ad haec nostra tempora, quas excipient supplementa emendationum, defensionum, illustrationumque ad priores centurias XIII.* See also *Pseudo-Isidorian Decretals; Wigand, Johann(es).*

Magi. Originally 1 of 6 tribes or castes into which, acc. to Herodotus (I 101), Medes were divided. Magi came into ascendancy 1st among Medes, later among Persians, by assuming priestly functions (a development similar to that of Brahmans in India; see *Brahmanism*); invested with functions of Zoroastrianism.* Wise men of Mt 2 probably were magi. See also *Church Year,* 2.

Magic. Alleged art of bringing about supernatural results by means of occult agencies, conjurations, and malevolent or benevolent incantations. Among primitive races magic and superstition play a significant role, as in voodooism.* Magic was practiced from ancient times in many countries. The Bible opposes magic; e. g., Ex 22:18; Acts 19:13-19. See also *Primitive Religion.*

Magni, Petrus (Petrus Magni; Peder Maansson; Peter Magnusson; d. 1534). B. Jönköping, Swed.; rector Vadstena; monk of Brigittine order, Vadstena; head of order 1511; bp. Västeraas 1524; ordained 3 bps. not approved by Rome 1528; ordained L. Petri* abp. 1531.

Magnificat. See *Canticles.*

Magnus (d. AD 1550). Duke of Mecklenburg, Ger.; 1st ev. bp. Schwerin; attended 1530 Diet of Augsburg (see *Lutheran Confessions,* A 2).

Magnusson, Peter. See *Magni, Petrus.*

Magyars. Perhaps of Finno-Ugrian and Turkish stock; originally lived along Ural Mountains. Toward the end of the 9th c. they appeared at the Danube and eventually settled in Pannonia; extended campaigns to N. Sea and It. Christianity had gained a foothold among them by ca. 1000. Chief ethnic group in Hungary* today.

Mahabharata. See *Hinduism,* 6; *Sacred Literatures.*

Mahan, Asa (1799–1889). Cong. cleric and educ.; b. Vernon, N. Y.; school teacher; educ. Hamilton Coll., Clinton, N. Y., and Andover (Mass.) Theol. Seminary. Pastor Pittsford, N. Y.; Cincinnati, Ohio. Pres. Oberlin (Ohio) Coll. 1835; Cleveland U. 1850. Returned to pastoral work in Mich. 1855. Ed. periodical *The Divine Life;* other works include *Scripture Doctrine of Christian Perfection; Doctrine of the Will; The Science of Moral Philosophy; The System of Mental Philosophy.*

Mahatmas. See *Theosophy,* 2.

Mahavira. See *Jainism.*

Mahbereth. See *Lexicons,* A.

Mahler, William (Nov. 16, 1870–Jan. 22, 1966). B. Polkwitz, Ger.; educ. Conc. Sem., St. Louis, Mo.;

ordained 1893; pastor Ogallala and Stark, Nebr.; sent 1901 to Brazil as successor of C. J. Broders* and Miss. Dir.; pres. Brazil Dist. 1904–10; instructor Conc. Coll., Pôrto Alegre 1907; returned to US 1914; served congs. in Nebr. and Kans.; retired 1942. See also *Lutheran Church – Missouri Synod, Districts of The,* A 15; B 1.

Mahling, Friedrich (1865–1933). B. Frankfurt am Main, Ger.; theol. and soc. reformer. Pastor Frankfurt am Main 1904; prof. practical theol. Berlin 1909. As mem. of cen. committee for inner missions gave special attention to sex ethics, alcoholism, and other soc. problems.

Mahomet (Mahomed). See *Muhammad.*

Mahoning Baptist Association. See *Disciples of Christ,* 2 d.

Mahu, Stephan (Machu; 1480/90–ca. 1541). Composer; employed ca. 1520–ca. 1541 at court of Anna of Boh. and Hung. (1503–47; b. Prague; m. Ferdinand I 1521) and Ferdinand I (1503–64; b. Alcalá de Henares; king Hung. and Boh. 1526, Ger. 1531–64; Holy Roman emp. 1556–64); vice-kapellmeister under A. v. Bruck* 1529. Works, some pub. by G. Rhau,* include settings of "Christ ist erstanden" and "Ein feste Burg ist unser Gott."

Mai, Angelo (1782–1854). B. Schilpario, near Bergamo, It.; paleographer and philol.; educ. Rome; Jesuit 1799; prof. classics Naples 1804; custodian (or scriptor) Ambrosian Library, Milan, 1813; left Jesuits 1819; Vatican librarian 1819; cardinal 1838. Issued 4 collections of theol. and classical texts: *Classicorum auctorum e vaticanis codicibus editorum tomus I*[*–X*]; *Scriptorum veterum nova collectio; Spicilegium romanum; Novae patrum bibliothecae tomus primus*[*–decimus*].

Maid of Kent, (Holy). See *Barton, Elizabeth.*

Maier, Johann. See *Eck, Johann.*

Maier, Walter Arthur (Oct. 4, 1893–Jan. 11, 1950). Luth. radio preacher, writer, educ.; b. Boston, Mass. An appeal at a miss. festival helped dir. him into the ministry. Educ. at the Conc. academy which was in process of establishment at Bronxville, N. Y., and which was later called Conc. Collegiate Institute; Boston (Mass.) U.; Conc. Sem., St. Louis, Mo.; Harvard U., Cambridge, Mass.

First full-time ex. secy. The Walther League (see *Young People's Organizations, Christian,* II 3) 1920; prof. Conc. Sem., St. Louis, 1922–44; Luth. Hour speaker (see *Radio and Television Evangelism, Network,* 5–7).

Other activities included: dean Lutherland resort, near Pocono Pines, Pa.; cofounder Gamma Delta (see *Students, Spiritual Care of,* C 9); Luth. pastor for Ger. internees on Gallup's Is., Boston Harbor, for prisoners at Camp 1, Still River, Mass., and for Camp Gordon, Atlanta, Ga., in WW I; US Army consultant on educ. and religious affairs in Ger. 1947. Ed. *The Walther League Messenger;* other works include *Day by Day with Jesus; For Better Not for Worse; The Book of Nahum;* sermons; tracts. LEZ

The Dr. Walter A. Maier Memorial Booklet (issued by The Lutheran Laymen's League, St. Louis, Mo., n. d.); P. L. Maier, *A Man Spoke, a World Listened* (New York, 1963); L. E. Zeitler, "An Investigation of the Factors of Persuasion in the Sermons of Dr. W. A. Maier" (unpub. STM thesis, Conc. Sem., St. Louis, Mo., 1956).

Maimbourg, Louis (1610–86). B. Nancy, Fr.; Jesuit 1626–82; educ. Rome; opposed Protestantism* and Jansenism*; defended Gallicanism*; forced out of Jesuits* by Innocent* XI. Wrote chiefly on the hist. of heresies and schisms; many works put on Index* of Prohibited Books. See also *Sukendorf, Veit Ludwig von.*

Maimonides (Moses ben Maimon; also called Rambam by acronym of "Rabbi Moses ben Maimon"; 1135–1204). Jewish scholar and philos.; b. Córdoba, Sp.; fled under persecution after Córdoba fell to Muslim 1148; lived in Morocco, Palestine, Egypt; tried to reconcile Rabbinic, or talmudic, Judaism with Aristotelian philos. modified by Arab. interpretation. Works include expositions of the Jewish faith; commentary on the Mishnah (see *Talmud*).

Maistre, Joseph Marie de (1753 [1754?]–1821). RC philos., diplomat; b. Chambéry, Fr.; opposed Fr. Revolution (see *Church and State,* 15; *France,* 5) and its results; championed ultramontanism.* Works include *Du pape.*

Maistre, Mattheus Le. See *Le Maistre, Mattheus.*

Maitland. 1. *Samuel Roffey* (1792–1866). Grandfather of 2; b. London, Eng.; of Scot. descent. Works include monograph on Albigenses* and Waldenses*; *The Dark Ages; Essays on Subjects Connected with the Reformation in England.* 2. *Frederic William* (1850–1906). Grandson of 1; b. London, Eng.; prof. law Cambridge. Works include *Roman Canon Law in the Church of England;* "The Anglican Settlement and the Scottish Reformation," *Cambridge Modern History,* II, pp. 550–598; *The Constitutional History of England.*

Majolus (ca. 910–994). B. Valensolle or Avignon, Fr.; abbot Cluny*; led Cluniac* reform in Fr., Burgundy, It.

Major, Georg (1502–74). B. Nürnberg, Ger.; Luth. theol.; educ. Wittenberg; friend of M. Luther*; school rector Magdeburg 1529–36; preacher 1537, prof. 1545–52 and 1553–74 Wittenberg; supt. Eisleben 1552. His involvement in Leipzig Interim* incurred the wrath of M. Flacius* Illyricus, N. v. Amsdorf,* N. Gallus,* et al., who accused him of denying the Luth. doctrine of justification. He denied the charge but taught that good works are necessary for salvation, later that they are necessary to retain faith; his phrases are repudiated by FC IV. He lived to see the overthrow of Crypto-Calvinists in electoral Saxony; Torgau arts. signed for him by P. Crell.* Works include *Psalterium Davidis; Vitae patrum;* commentaries on epistles of Paul. See also *Majoristic Controversy; Regensburg Conference; Religious Drama,* 3. AHH

Major, Johann (Gross; 1564–1654). B. Reinstädt, near Orlamünde, Ger.; diaconus Weimar; pastor and supt. 1605, later prof. theol. Jena. Coed. *Das Weimarische* Bibelwerk,* contributing commentary on Acts and 1–3 Jn; the hymn "Ach Gott und Herr, wie gross und schwer," ascribed by some to M. Rutilius* or Johann Göldel (1556–1604; b. Altdorf, Ger.; pastor Dienstedt, near Kranichfeld, 1583), was 1st printed in a sermon by Major.

Major Orders. In RCm, orders of bps., priests, deacons, and subdeacons. See also *Hierarchy.*

Majoristic Controversy. Controversy 1551–74 among Luth. theologians; named after G. Major.* Shortly, before he became supt. Eisleben 1552, Major was accused by N. v. Amsdorf* of denying the Luth. doctrine of justification in the Leipzig Interim.* After suspension from office Major replied that he had never doubted the *sola* fide;* but he defended the phrase "good works are necessary for salvation," though he held that good works do not effect or merit forgiveness of sins, justification, the gift of the Holy Spirit, and eternal life. M. Flacius* Illyricus joined Amsdorf, N. Gallus,* et al. in opposing Major and holding that good works are not necessary for salvation, but are necessary for other reasons. Major modified his position 1553 to hold that good works are necessary not to obtain but to retain salvation.

J. Menius* came under suspicion of siding with Major 1554; in 1556 he held that beginning of new life in believers is necessary for salvation. He was attacked by M. Flacius Illyricus, suspended from office, and called before a syn. at Eisenach 1556, where he subscribed 7 propositions on good works which could be interpreted as a repudiation of his former position.

In 1558 Major tried to end controversy with a confession on justification which stated that he had ceased using the controversial phrase because of wrong interpretation placed on it; but he continued to hold that he had never erred in his teaching of the Gospel or his understanding of good works. M. Flacius Illyricus demanded of Major unqualified rejection of the phrase. Major refused.

Amsdorf attacked Menius 1559, stating that good works are harmful for salvation; he meant that trust in good works for salvation is injurious.

The controversy was settled by FC IV, which rejected both Major's and Amsdorf's terminology but held that believers, in so far as they are reborn, spontaneously do good works commanded by God. AHH

C. Schlüsselburg, "De Maioristis," *Catalogus haereticorum,* VII (Frankfurt, 1599); W. Preger, *Matthias Flacius Illyricus und seine Zeit,* I (Erlangen, 1859); G. L. Schmidt, *Justus Menius, der Reformator Thüringens,* II (Gotha, 1867).

Majus, Heinrich (1545–1607). Prof. Wittenberg; opposed FC.

Majus, Johann Heinrich. See *May, Johann Heinrich.*

Majuscules. See *Manuscripts of the Bible,* 2 a.

Makkai, Sándor (1890–1951). Hung. Ref. bp. Siebenbürgen 1926; prof. Debrecen 1936. Works include novels and theol. writings.

Makumira, Lutheran Theological College at. See *Africa,* E 7.

Malabar Christians. Also called Thomas Christians. Christians in SW India who trace origin to the apostle Thomas on basis of apocryphal Acts of Thomas; perhaps of E Syrian origin; maintained connection with Nestorians (see *Nestorianism*); connected with Rome at Syn. of Diamper* as Malabar Uniat Ch.; broke with Rome 1653; divided 1662, some realigning with Rome, others with Jacobites (see *Jacobites,* 1). In 1930 Metropolitan Mar Ivanios with ca. 10,000 followers, formerly Jacobite, formed the Malankarese Uniat Ch. See also *India,* 5–7; *Uniate Churches.*

Malabar Uniat Church. See *Diamper, Synod of; Malabar Christians.*

Malabars. See *India,* 7.

Malachy (1094–1148). B. Armagh, Ireland; abp. Armagh; friend of Bernard* of Clairvaux; introd. Cistercian* order into Ireland.

Malagasy Republic. See *Africa,* B 9.

Malan, Henri Abraham César (1787–1864). B. Geneva, Switz.; educ. Geneva; pastor in Nat. Ch. of Geneva and at first in accord with its near-Unitarian character; pastor of separatist group in Geneva ca. 1820; hymnist; founded movement for better hymns in Fr. Ref. Church. Hymns include "Non, ce n'est pas mourir" ("It Is Not Death to Die").

Malankarese Uniat Church. See *Malabar Christians.*

Malankars. See *India,* 7.

Malawi. See *Africa,* B 2.

Malaya, Federation of. See *Malaysia,* 1, 2.

Malayalam. 1. A Dravidian* language of Kerala (S India); closely related to Tamil.* 2. Script used in writing Malayalam.

Malaysia. 1. Fed. formed Sept. 16, 1963, by Fed. of Malaya, state of Singapore, Sarawak, and Sabah (formerly N. Borneo); mem. Brit. Commonwealth and UN. *Area:* ca. 130,000 sq. mi. *Pop.:* ca. 11,000,000; Malays, Chinese, Indians, Pakistanis, non-Malay indigenous peoples. Chief languages: Malay, Eng., Chinese, Tamil. Capital: Kuala Lumpur. Religious liberty granted; Islam dominant; other religions include Buddhism, Taoism, Confucianism, Hinduism, Christianity, animism.

2. The name *Malaya* has been used to designate the Malay Peninsula, Brit. Malaya, and the Fed. of Malaya. Acc. to legend, the hist. of Malacca, the 1st Malay kingdom, begins ca. the middle of the 14th c. Captured 1511 by Port., who introd. Christianity; F. Xavier* was miss. there in the 1540s. Fell 1641 to the Dutch, who introd. Ref. Christianity but without miss. thrust. Ceded to Brit. 1824. W. Milne* was the 1st Prot. miss. in Malaya. The SPG entered Malaya 1848; the Presb. Ch. of Eng. 1851; Am. Meths. 1885, concentrating on schools. WW II interrupted miss. work; postwar work concentrated on New Villages. The Malayan Christian Council was organized 1948. The Council on Christian Literature for Overseas Chinese was est. 1951 with headquarters in Hong Kong.

3. *Singapore, Rep. of. Area:* ca. 224 sq. mi. *Pop.* (1970 est.): ca. 2,100,000. Formerly Brit. crown colony; full internal self-govt. 1959. Joined in Fed. of Malaysia 1963; withdrew 1965 and became an indep. rep. in the Brit. Commonwealth. Missions closely related to those of Malaya (see 2). The Soc. for the Promotion of Female Educ. in the East sent a worker to Singapore 1843. Trin. Coll., a theol. school est. 1948, is supported by Angls., Eng. Presbs., and Am. Meths. Singapore Theol. Sem. was founded 1952 by Chinese Christians. See also *Asia,* C 3.

4. *Sarawak.* Brit. protectorate 1888, occupied by Jap. in WW II, crown colony 1946; joined in Fed. of Malaysia 1963. Religion was mostly animist. CMS began work 1848. Am. Meths. began work 1901, organized the Sarawak Provisional Annual Conf. 1952; a Batak pastor began work among Dyaks 1938.

5. *Sabah* (former North Borneo). Brit. protectorate 1881; occupied by Jap. 1942–45; Brit. crown colony 1946; joined in Fed. of Malaysia 1963 as Sabah. Miss. work closely connected with that of Sarawak (see 4). The Basel Miss. Soc. was in N. Borneo before WW I. The Conservative Bap. For. Miss. Soc. (organized 1943; headquarters Wheaton, Ill.) resolved 1959 to enter N. Borneo.

6. For Malaysia in the sense of Malay Archipelago see *Indonesia; New Guinea; Philippines.* EL

See *Missions Bibliography.*

Malche, Frauenmission. Est. in the Malchetal, near Bad Freienwalde, Ger., 1898, for work among persecuted Christians in Turkey; educates women for for. miss. work, inner miss., and cong. service.

Malcolm X (Malcolm Little; Big Red; Al Hajj Malik Shabazz; 1925–65). B. Omaha, Nebr.; his father was a Bp. preacher; to NYC; engaged in burglary; sentenced to 10 yrs. in prison 1946; used time for self-improvement; paroled after 6 yrs.; joined Black Muslims 1962; became prominent leader; suspended 1963; resigned 1964; founded Organization for Afro-American Unity 1964; conflict with Black Muslims resulted; assassinated.

Maldonatus, Johannes (Joannes; Juán [de] Maldonado; Maldonata; 1533 [1534?]–1583). RC theol. and exegete; b. [Las] Casas de [la] Reina, Estremadura, Sp.; Jesuit 1562; prof. Collège de Clermont, Paris, 1564; attacked unsuccessfully as heretic by profs. of the Sorbonne 1574. Works include *Commentarii in praecipuos sacrae scripturae libros Veteris Testamenti; Commentarii in quatuor Evangelistas.*

Male Émile (1862–1954). B. Commentry, Fr.; art hist.; prof. Sorbonne, Paris, 1906, noted for studies on art of Middle Ages.

Malebranche, Nicolas de (1638–1715). Metaphysician; b. Paris, Fr.; philos. based on that of R. Descartes.* Developed doctrine of occasionalism.* See also *Norris, John.*

Mali, Republic of. See *Africa,* C 3.

Malicious Abandonment (malicioius desertion). See *Marriage,* II; III.

Malines Conversations. Talks bet. Angl. and RC theologians at Malines (Mechelen; Mecheln; Mechlin[ia]), Belg. 1921–26. Agreed that the pope be given primacy of honor; that the Eucharist is a true mystical sacrifice; that Communion in both kinds is a matter of discipline, not dogma; that the body and blood of Christ are received in the Eucharist; that episcopacy is by divine right.

Malleolus haereticorum (from Lat. *malleus* [diminutive *malleolus*], "hammer," and LL *haereticus,* "heretic": "hammer of heretics"). Title given to vigorous opponents of heretics, e. g., Johannes Faber.*

Mallet, Friedrich Ludwig (1793–1865). B. Braunfels, near Wetzlar, Ger.; educ. Herborn and Tübingen; Ref. pastor Bremen; wrote against liberal tendencies and espoused spiritual and soc. needs of young laborers.

Mallinckrodt, Willem (1844–1925). Dutch pastor Holland 1869–72, 1892–1902; in Neth. E. Indies 1872–92; prof. dogmatics, ch. law, and Neth. ch. hist. Groningen 1902; exponent of Groningen* school.

Malmgren, Arthur (1860–1947). Luth. bp. in Russ.; b. Reval (Tallin), Estonia; pastor St. Petersburg (Leningrad) 1891–1931; gen. supt. St. Petersburg territory 1916; elected bp. by the 1st gen. syn. of Russ. Evangelicals at Moscow 1924; head of sem. at Leningrad till its closing 1935; lived in Mainz 1936–47.

Malta. See *Middle East,* A 5; *Military Religious Orders,* a.

Malta Bible Society. See *Bible Societies,* 4.

Malthus, Thomas Robert (1766–1834). B. near Guildford, Surrey, Eng.; Angl. cleric; economist; prof. Haileybury Coll., near Hertford; held that human pop. tends to increase in a geometric ratio, means of subsistence in an arithmetic ratio. His views, called Malthusianism, led to the conclusion that propagation of the human race should perhaps be made subject to preventive controls; influenced the practice of birth control. See also *Family Planning,* 2.

Malthusian League. Organized in Eng. 1861 by George R. Drysdale (1825–1904; physician; works include *The Elements of Social Science*) and Charles Bradlaugh (1833–91; ed. *National Reformer*) to advocate, defend, and provide information on birth control. Branches were est. in many countries. Disbanded 1927 because it considered its work completed.

Malthusianism. See *Malthus, Thomas Robert.*

Maltzew, Alexej Petrowitsch von (1854–1915). Russ. theol.; b. Jaroslaw, Galicia; active in ch. unity; pub. Russ. Ger. ed. of E Orthodox liturgy.

Maluku. See *Indonesia,* 1, 8.

Malvenda. 1. *Pedro de* (ca. 1500–60). B. Burgos, Sp.; Dominican theol.; present at 1540–41 Colloquy of Worms,* 1546 Regensburg* Conf., and Council of Trent* 1551–52; helped prepare Augsburg Interim.* 2. *Tomás* (1566–1628). B. Játiva, or Játiba (formerly Xátiva), Sp.; Dominican exegete, dogmatician, ch. hist.; belonged to Sp. cong. of the Index* of Prohibited Books.

Mamertine Prison (Tullianum). Ancient prison in Rome under Ch. of San Giuseppe dei Falegnami; tradition identifies it as the place of imprisonment of Paul and Peter. Called Mamertine perhaps because of nearby temple of Mars Ultor (*Mamertini:* "children of Mars") or from the name of an owner of the property; called Tullianum either by connection with Servius Tullius or from a non-extant Lat. word *tullus,* "spring," indicating a well-chamber.

Mamertus (d. ca. AD 475). Bp. Vienne, Gaul; older brother of Claudianus* Mamertus; ca. 470 he organized litanies in the Ascension season. See also *Rogation Days.*

Mamphrasius, Wolfgang (1557–1616). B. Wurzen, Ger.; educ. Wittenberg; pastor Nitzschwitz; supt. Wurzen; wrote polemical works; coauthor Saxon Articles* of Visitation.

Man. Science divides the study of man into *physical anthropology,* which deals with the essence and origin of physical (animal) characteristics, and *cultural anthropology,* which deals, e. g., with languages, inventions, customs.

Christian theol. studies man's origin (see *Creation*), 1st condition, probation, and apostasy (see *Fall of Man*), sin (see *Sin; Sin, Original*), and redemption (see *Conversion; Grace; Justification*), and related matters.

Luth. theol. begins the study of man with the study of God.* Proper and full understanding of man cannot be achieved through science, man's natural knowledge of God, or God apart from Christ. See also *Anthropology.*

E. T. Bachmann, "Man," in *What Lutherans Are Thinking,* ed. E. C. Fendt (Columbus, Ohio, 1947), pp. 148–173; *What, Then, Is Man?* (St. Louis, 1958).

Mana. See *Primitive Religion.*

Manasseh, Prayer of. See *Apocrypha,* A 3, 4.

Mandaeans (Mandeans; Mendaeans; from Mandaean Aramaic *mandayya,* "having knowledge" [reflecting Gk. *gnostikoi,* "gnostics"]. Sabians, Sabaeans, Sabeans, etc.; probably either from an Aramaic word meaning "baptize" or a Heb. word meaning "host," referring to ritual washings or worship of the stars. Nasoraeans, Mandaean for "observers" [of cult and code] or "true believers"; cf. "Nazarenes," Acts 24:5. St. John's Christians, so called because of veneration for John the Baptist). Gnostic sect; originated possibly as early as the 3d c.; remnants in Iraq and Iran. Sacred books include *Ginza* ("Treasure") or *Sidra rabba* (the "Great Book"); *Sidra d'Yahya* ("the Book of John") or *Drase d'malke* ("Recitations of the Kings"), also called *Drase d'Yahya* ("Recitations of John"); *Qolasta* (a hymnbook; cf. Syriac *kullasa,* "praise"). See also *Sabianism.*

Mandatum. See *Foot Washing.*

Mande, Hendrik (ca. 1360–1431). B. Dordrecht, Neth.; mystic of Brethren* of the Common Life; had visions; entered Windesheim monastery, near Zwolle, Neth. Works include *De tribus statibus hominis conversi.*

Mandel, Hermann (1882–1946). B. Holzwickede, Westphalia, Ger.; lecturer Greifswald 1906; prof. Rostock 1912; prof. systematic theol. Kiel 1918. Works inclue *Christliche Versöhnungslehre; Metapsychologie.*

Mandelkern, Salomon (1846–1902). Rabbi Odessa 1873; lived in Leipzig, Ger., since 1880. Works include *Hekhal ha-Kodesh* (Lat. title *Veteris testamenti concordantiae hebraicae atque chaldaicae*).

Manes. See *Ancestor Worship.*

Manhart, Franklin Pierce (Aug. 30, 1852–Sept. 13, 1933). Luth. theol.; b. Catawissa, Pa.; educ. Missionary Institute, Selinsgrove, Pa., and Pa. College (see *Gettysburg College*). Pastor Bloomsburg, Pa., 1881–89; Philadelphia, Pa., 1889–93. Supt. Missionary Institute and pres. Susquehanna U., Selinsgrove; head of deaconess motherhouse, Baltimore, Md.; dean theol. dept. Susquehanna* U. Pres. The General* Syn. of the Ev. Luth. Ch. in the USA 1922–26. Works include *Present-Day Lutheranism; Lutheranism and Episcopacy; History of Susquehanna Synod.*

Mani (Manes; Manichaeus; ca. 216–ca. 277). Founded Manichaeism.* Biographical details difficult to est.; b. perhaps Seleucia-Ctesiphon, Persia; allegedly received divine revelations; claimed to be the last and highest prophet; traveled probably to India and perhaps China; became acquainted with Buddhism*; returned to Persia; successfully opposed by Magi*; perhaps suffered a cruel death in prison.

Manichaeism (Manicheism; Manichaeanism; Manicheanism; Manicheeism). 1. Religion founded by Mani.*

2. Syncretistic, dualistic (see *Dualism*) philos. of nature, including Gnostic, Zoroastrian, and Christian elements. Held in gen. that the kingdom of light and kingdom of darkness were in conflict from eternity. Satan and his hosts, born of the kingdom of darkness, imprisoned elements of light that were later called *Jesus patibilis* ("Jesus capable of suffering"). This led to formation of the world by command of the God of light, in order to deliver the imprisoned light. *Jesus impatibilis* ("Jesus incapable of suffering") came from the kingdom of light to lead his followers into strict asceticism and completely effect separation bet. light and darkness. The souls of the saved reach final blessedness in light; men's bodies and the souls of the lost fall victim to darkness. Conflagration consumes the world.

3. Manichaeism spread over the Roman Empire and was a menace to the ch. Augustine* of Hippo was Manichaean in his youth. Manichaeans and Manichaeism are referred to AC I 5; Ap XVIII 1; FC Ep I 17, 19, 22; II 8; SD I 26, 27, 30, 45.

See also *Albigenses; Cathari.*

Maniple. See *Vestments, Clerical.*

Manism. See *Ancestor Worship.*

Manitoba. See *Canada,* A 11, 13, 14, 19, 20, 27, 28; *United Lutheran Church, Synods of,* 32.

Manitoba and Other Provinces, The German Evangelical Lutheran Synod of. See *Manitoba and the Northwest Territories, Synod of.*

Manitoba and the Northwest Territories, Synod of. A Ger. Ev. Luth. Syn. of Man. and the NW Territories was organized 1897; name changed 1907 to The Ger. Ev. Luth. Syn. of Man. and other Provinces. See also *Canada,* A 14; *United Lutheran Church, Synods of,* 32.

Manitou. See *Primitive Religion.*

Mann, Horace (1796–1859). B. Franklin, Mass.; educ. Brown U., Province, R. I.; admitted to bar 1823; mem. Mass. House of Representatives and Senate; then active in field of educ., developing widespread awareness of the need for training teachers; mem. US House of Representatives 1848–53; pres. Antioch Coll., Yellow Springs, Ohio.

Mann, Johann Carl Gottlieb (Karl; 1766–1826). B. Taucha, near Leipzig, Ger.; pastor Naumburg; rationalist; hymnist. Ed. *Neues Naumburgisches Gesangbuch.*

Mann, Wilhelm Julius (William; May 29, 1819–June 20, 1892). A leading theol. of the General* Council of the Ev. Luth. Ch. in (N.) Am. and one of its founders; b. Stuttgart, Ger.; educ. Tübingen; to Pa. 1845 on invitation of P. Schaff*; ordained 1846; asst. pastor of a Ger. Ref. cong.; asst. pastor Saint Michael's and Zion's Cong., Philadelphia, 1850–54, pastor 1854; pres. Pa. Ministerium 1860–62, 1880; opposed Definite* Syn. Platform; prof. Luth. Theol. Sem., Philadelphia, 1864. Works include *Heinrich Melchior Mühlenbergs Leben und Wirken* (Eng. title *Life and Times of Henry Melchior Mühlenberg*); *Lutheranism in America; Ein Aufgang im Abendland: Mittheilungen aus der Geschichte der früheren evangelischen Missionsversuche unter den Indianern Amerikas; Das Buch der Bücher und seine Geschichte; Leben und Wirken William Penn's; Heilsbotschaft; A Plea for the Augsburg Confession, in Answer to the Objections of the Definite Platform.*

See also *Fraternal Address.*

E. T. Mann, *Memoir of the Life and Work of William Julius Mann* (Philadelphia, 1839); A. Spaeth, *D. Wilhelm Julius Mann, ein deutsch-amerikanischer Theologe: Erinnerungsblätter* (Reading, Pa., 1895).

Manning, Henry Edward (1808–92). B. Totteridge, Hertfordshire, Eng.; educ. Oxford; ordained Angl. 1832; Tractarian; archdeacon Chichester; RC 1851 in reaction against the Privy Council judgment against G. C. Gorham*; priest 1851; ultramontanist; abp. Westminster 1865; advocated doctrine of papal infallibility* 1870; cardinal 1875; active in educ., soc., charitable work. Works include *The Rights and Dignity of Labour; The Eternal Priesthood; Sin and Its Consequences.* See also *Metaphysical Society, The; Tractarianism; Ultramontanism.*

Manning, James (1738–91). B. Piscataway, N. J.; educ. Coll. of N. J., Princeton (now Princeton U.); Bap. cleric and educ.; helped found R. I. Coll. at Warren (now Brown U., Providence, R. I.); helped organize Warren* Assoc.; urged adoption of fed. Const. by R. I. and other New Eng. states.

Manse (from Lat. manere, "to stay"). Dwelling of Presb. minister; used also of residences of other clergymen.

Mansel, Henry Longueville (1820–71). Metaphysician; b. Cosgrove, Northamptonshire, Eng.; influenced by W. Hamilton*; held that man cannot know God by reason or by intuitive approach. Works include *The Limits of Religious Thought; The Philosophy of the Conditioned; Prolegomena logica.*

Mansi, Giovanni Domenico (1692–1769). B. Lucca, It.; abp. Lucca. Ed. early vols. of *Sacrorum conciliorum nova et amplissima collectio;* other works include *Tractatus de casibus, et excommunicationibus episcopis reservatis, confectus ad normam Tabellae Lucanae.*

Manson, Thomas Walter (1893–1958). B. Tynemouth-North Shields, Northumberland, Eng.; NT scholar. Prof. Mansfield Coll. (Cong.), Oxford, 1932–36; Manchester U. 1936–58. Works include *The Teaching of Jesus; The Sayings of Jesus; The Old Testament in the Teaching of Jesus; The Church's Ministry; Ethics and the Gospel.* See also *Corporate Personality.*

Manson, William (1882–1958). B. Cambuslang, Scot. Prof. NT Knox Coll., Toronto, Can.; Edinburgh U. Works include *Jesus the Messiah; The Epistle to the Hebrews; The Gospel of Luke.*

Mant, Richard (1776–1848). B. Southampton, Eng.; educ. Winchester and Oxford; held various positions as cleric. Bp. Killaloe and Kilfenora, Ireland, 1820; Down and Connor 1823, and Dromore 1842. Hymnist. Coed. an ed. of the Bible with selected notes; other works include *The Book of Psalms in an English Metrical Version; The Happiness of the Blessed; Poems;* hymns include "For All Thy Saints, O Lord."

Mantegna, Andrea. See *Jesus, Portrayals of.*

Mantelletta. Short sleeveless mantle open in front; worn by cardinals, bps., and other RC prelates.

Mantellone. Long purple mantle worn by lesser prelates of the papal court.

Manton, Thomas (1620–77). B. Lydeard St. Lawrence, Somersetshire, Eng.; educ. Oxford; Presb. theol.; popular preacher London; scribe Westminster Assem. (see *Presbyterian Confessions,* 3); nonconformist*; imprisoned. Sermons influenced C. H. Spurgeon.*

Mantova, Benedetto da (16th c.). Benedictine connected with J. de Valdés* in Naples, It. Wrote *Del beneficio di Gesù Cristo crocifisso verso i cristiani* (suppressed by Inquisition*).

Mantua, Proposed Council at. See *Lutheran Confessions,* B 2.

Manu. In Hinduism, mythical 1st man; preserved from flood; father of postdiluvian people. The Code of Manu is a collection of Hindu laws, including rules for caste.

Manuel, Nikolaus (Niklaus; Niclaus; Nicolas; Deutsch; original name may have been Alleman, changed anagrammatically to Manuel; ca. 1484–1530). B. Bern, Switz.; painter; wood carver; poet; dramatist; supported Reformation; critized worldliness of the papacy. See also *Religious Drama,* 3.

Manuscripts of the Bible. 1. *Old Testament.* The

original OT MSS are lost. Copies (rolls or scrolls, Jer 36:2; Lk 4:17), handwritten on parchment derived from clean animals, were made for private individuals and religious services. One large book (e. g., Is) or a combination of several small ones was written on a single roll. OT Heb. was originally written with consonants only, no punctuation marks, and perhaps no spaces bet. words. Division into pars. seems ancient. Proper pronunciation was orally preserved. Loss of Jerusalem as religious center of Judaism* made it necessary to add vowel points and accents to indicate and fix, as far as possible, proper reading and intonation. Another mark indicated verse division. These marks were gradually introd. under guidance of Masoretes (see *Masora[h]*). Extraordinary care was exercised in copying. There are practically no important textual differences. MSS used in synagogs met esp. rigid standards. A complete copy of Is and fragments of other OT books were discovered 1947 among the Dead* Sea Scrolls. Chap. divisions were marginally indicated at least as early as the 14th c.

2. *New Testament.* a. NT autographs, written in nonliterary Hellenistic Gk. on parchment or papyrus* (2 Ti 4:13; 2 Jn 12), seem to have disappeared very early. But many copies were made. The writing was at first in majuscules (large letters [as capitals or uncials]), with no separation of words, no breathings, accents, or distinction of initial letters, and few, if any, punctuation marks.

b. There are many allusions to and quotations from Scripture in patristic writings beginning with the Apostolic* Fathers. The Muratorian* Fragment shows that there was an almost complete collection of apostolic writings ca. the middle of the 2d c.

c. The external hist. of the NT text for ca. 1,000 yrs. before the invention of printing can be traced by MSS. Some MSS from the 4th–5th c. include noncanonical writings. In course of time parchment (or vellum, a high-quality parchment) replaced papyrus and the book form replaced rolls. But since parchment was often scarce, old MSS were sometimes reused after the old writing was erased or washed off. Some Bible MSS were treated thus to make room for other writing. Such MSS are called *codices palimpsesti* (palimpsests) or *rescripti.* Chemicals and ultraviolet-ray photography have been used to determine the original text. See also *Codex.*

3. a. K. Aland, *Kurzgefasste Liste der griechischen Handschriften des Neuen Testaments* (Berlin, 1963), pp. 29–33, lists 76 papyrus MSS. Of these, P52, in the John Rylands Library, Manchester, Eng., is the oldest, dated by Aland beginning of the 2d c. Of the Chester Beatty papyri (named after Alfred Chester Beatty [1875–1968]; b. NYC; educ. Princeton U.; mining engineer; industrialist; collector of Oriental MSS; naturalized Englishman 1933) Aland assigns P46 to ca. 200, P45 to the 3d c., P47 to the end of the 3d c.; they contain large portions of the gospels, Acts, the Pauline epistles, and Rv. Of the Bodmer papyri (named after Martin Bodmer [b. 1899], Swiss industrialist, who secured them for his private library in Cologny, near Geneva, Switz.) Aland assigns P66 (large portions of Jn) to ca. 200, P75 (Lk and Jn) to the beginning of the 3d c.

There are ca. 250 4th–10th c. uncials. The most important: Codex Sinaiticus (א), complete NT, 4th c., discovered (1844 and 1859) by L. F. K. v. Tischendorf* in the monastery of St. Catherine on Mount Sinai, formerly in St. Petersburg (Leningrad), since 1933 in the Brit. Museum, London; Codex Vaticanus (B), 4th c., in Vatican Library, Rome; Codex Alexandrinus (A; called Alexandrinus from its supposed origin at Alexandria, Egypt), 5th c., in the Brit. Museum; Codex Ephraemi (C; called Ephraemi because some writings of Ephraem* were superimposed on the text), 5th c., rewritten upon probably in the 12th c., in Bibliothèque National, Paris, Fr.; Codex Bezae (D; named after T. Beza*), 5th or 6th c., in University Library, Cambridge, Eng.

b. Beginning in the 9th c. the uncial form of writing changed to the cursive, or minuscule, of which there are many MSS. There are perhaps ca. 200,000 variant readings in NT MSS, depending on how the count is made, but in nearly all cases the correct reading is not hard to est., and in nearly all other cases the variants are of no importance as affecting the sense. EL, FWD

See also *Chapters and Verses of the Bible.*

Manz, Felix (Mantz; ca. 1500–27). Anabap. leader in Zurich, Switz.; probably received humanist educ.; broke with H. Zwingli* in matters regarding the ch., infant baptism, and govt.; condemned, and drowned in the Limmat R.

Maori. See *New Zealand,* 2, 3.

Maphrian ("one who makes fruitful"). Title of bp. of Jacobite Syrians.

Mar. Syriac equivalent of Lat. *dominus,* "lord." May be tr. "St." in such connections as Mar Thoma and Mar Saba.

Mar Thoma Church (Mar Thomites). A Syrian ch. in India; broke away as a reforming group from the Jacobites (see *Jacobites,* 1) beginning in the 1870s, maintaining an episcopacy with local consecration. See also *India,* 6, 7; *Nonchalcedonian Churches,* 2.

Marahrens, August (1875–1950). Luth. theol., educ., ch. leader. B. Hanover, Ger.; educ. Göttingen and Erlangen; dir. Erichsburg theol. sem. 1909–20; supt. Einbeck 1920; gen. supt. Stade 1922; bp. Ev. Luth. nat. ch. (Landeskirche) Hannover 1925–47; chm. Allgemeine* Ev.-Luth. Konferenz 1933; pres. LWC 1935–45. Worked for ch. rights in Kirchenkampf*; popular as *pastor pastorum,* but criticized for yielding too much to the state, esp. in agreeing to exclude non-Aryans from cong. life of the Deutsche* Evangelische Kirche 1941.

Marbach, Franz Adolph (1798?–June 6, 1860). Lawyer at Dresden, Ger.; lay leader of Saxon Immigration (see *Lutheran Church – Missouri Synod, The,* II); returned to Ger. 1841. See also *Altenburg Debate.*

Marbach, Johannes (1521–81). B. Lindau, Bav., Ger.; educ. Strasbourg and Wittenberg; pastor Strasbourg 1545; championed Lutheranism; present at Council of Trent* 1551.

Marbeck, John (Marbecke; Merbeck[e]; ca. 1510–ca. 1585). Calvinist theol.; musician; b. probably Windsor, Eng.; organist St. George's Chapel, Windsor, 1541; condemned for heresy 1543; received royal pardon. Ed. *The Booke of Common Praier noted;* other works include a concordance to the Eng. Bible (see also *Concordances*).

Marbeck, Pilgrim (ca. 1495–1556). Mediating Anabap. leader in S Ger.; b. Rattenberg, Tyrol, Austria; first inclined toward Lutheranism; joined Anabaps. 1527; fled to Strasbourg 1528; worked there in connection with lumbering and mining till 1532; traveled extensively; engineer of wells in Augsburg 1544–56.

Marburg, Colloquy of. See *Lutheran Confessions,* A 2.

Marburg Articles. See *Lutheran Confessions,* A 2.

Marburger Mission. Indep. branch of *Deutscher Gemeinschafts-Diakonieverband;* worked in China 1909–51, Jap. since 1951, Taiwan since 1952, Thailand since 1953.

Marca, Pierre de (1594–1662). RC canonist; b. Gan, near Pau, Béarn, Fr.; bp. Conserans 1648; abp. Toulouse 1652, Paris 1662; defended Gallicanism.* Works include *De Concordia Sacerdotii et Imperii.*

Marcel, Gabriel. See *Existentialism.*

Marcella (ca. 325/335–410 or 411). Of noble Roman family; after death of husband devoted herself to charitable works, study, asceticism; her home on Aventine Hill, Rome, was a center of Christian influence. *MPL,* 22, 1087–95.

Marcellina (ca. 330–98). Sister of Ambrose*; ascetic; Ambrose dedicated *De virginibus* to her. *MPL,* 16, 197–244.

Marcellina, Sisters of St. See *Annunciation, Orders of,* 3.

Marcellus of Ancyra (Markellos; ca. 280–ca. 374). Bp. Ancyra (now Ankara, Turkey); repeatedly condemned by some, acquitted by others, of alleged Sabellianism (see *Monarchianism,* B 6), beginning with a council at Constantinople in the 330s; followers, called Marcellians, condemned by 2d ecumenical council of Constantinople.*

March, Daniel (1816–1909). B. Millbury, Mass.; educ. Yale Coll. and Divinity School, New Haven, Conn.; pastor Presb. and Cong. chs. in New Eng. and Pa.; hymnist. Hymns include "Hark! the Voice of Jesus Crying."

Marcianus, Flavius (Marcian; ca. 392–457). E Roman emp. 450–457; b. probably Thrace (Eur. Turkey); attended Council of Chalcedon 451 and enforced its decrees, repressing monophysitism (see *Monophysite Controversy*).

Marcion (2d. c.). Gnostic. See also *Cerdo; Gnosticism,* 7 k.

Marco Polo. See *China,* 6.

Marcus. See *Gnosticism,* 7 g.

Marcus Aurelius (original name Marcus Annius Verus; after 139 Marcus Aelius Aurelius Antoninus; 121–180). Roman emp. 161–180; Stoic philos.; b. Rome; adopted by Antoninus Pius (see *Persecutions of Christians,* 3); emp. with Lucius Aurelius Verus (original name Aelius Aurelius Commodus; son of Lucius Ceionius Commodus [d. 138]; 130–169; b. Rome; adopted by Hadrian [see *Persecutions of Christians,* 3] and by Antoninus Pius) 161–169; sole emp. 169; probably supported the persecutions of Christians that occurred in his reign. Works include *Meditations.* See also *Ethics,* 3; *Persecutions of Christians,* 3.

Marduk. See *Babylonians, Religion of the,* 1.

Marenzio, Luca (probably ca. 1553–90). RC composer; b. Coccaglio, near Brescia, It. Works include madrigals (see *Madrigal*); sacred choral music.

Maresius, Samuel (des Marets; Des Maret; Desmarets; 1599–1673). Ref. theol. and polemicist; b. Oisemont, Picardy, Fr.; educ. Paris, Saumur, Geneva; held various pastorates; prof. Sedan, 's Hertogenbosch, Groningen; defended infralapsarianism* against G. Voetius*; opposed Cartesianism* and federal* theol. Works include *Collegium theologicum, sive systema breve universae theologiae.*

Margaret of Navarre (Marguerite; Margaret of Angoulême [or of Orleans, or of Valois]; 1492–1549). Sister of Francis I (see *France,* 8); queen of Navarre 1544–49; supported Reformation.

Margaret of Valois (Margaret of Fr.; 1553–1615). Sister of Charles IX of Fr. (see also *France,* 9).

Margaret Sanger Research Bureau. See *Family Planning,* 3.

Marguerite Marie Alacoque. See *Alacoque, Marguerite Marie.*

Marheineke, Philipp Konrad (1780–1846). Prot. theol. and hist.; b. Hildesheim, Ger.; educ. Göttingen; prof. Erlangen, Heidelberg, Berlin; held the speculative view of K. Daub* and G. W. F. Hegel*; equidistant from orthodox Lutheranism, rationalism, and old supernaturalism.

Maria Vittoria Fornari. See *Annunciation, Orders of,* 2.

Mariana, Juan de (1536–ca. 1624). B. Talavera de la Reina, Sp.; Jesuit 1554; taught theol. in Rome, Sicily, Paris; held that royal authority derives from sovereignty of people, that bps. are also to dir. activities of the state, and that tyrants could be forced to obey laws and even be murdered.

Mariana Islands (Marianas; Ladrone Is.). Group of is. in Micronesia.* *Area* (including Guam*): ca. 450 sq. mi.; discovered 1521 by Ferdinand Magellan (ca. 1480–1521; Port. navigator); originally called Islas de los Ladrones ("Islands of the Robbers"); name changed to Las Marianas 1668 in honor of Mariana of Austria (1634–96), widow of Philip IV of Sp. (1605–65; king of Sp. 1621–65); sold (except Guam) by Sp. to Ger. 1899; Jap. mandate 1919; trust territory (except Guam) assigned by UN to US 1947. RCs were the first Christian missionaries on the islands (17th c.). ABCFM and Bap. missionaries came early in the 20th c.

Marianists (Societas Mariae; Society of Mary; not to be confused with Marists*). RC cong. founded Bordeaux, Fr., 1817/18 (recognized by pope 1865, 1891) by Guillaume Joseph Chaminade (1761–1850) to oppose religious indifference; besides vowing poverty, chastity, and obedience, mems. vow stability in service of Mary; devoted to educ. Daughters of Mary (Marianist Sisters; Cong. of the Daughters of Mary Immaculate; Filiae Mariae), a Marianist offshoot, was founded 1816 Agen, Fr.

Mariavites. Polish sect founded 1906 by priest Jan Kowalski and Felicja Kozlowska (Maria Franziska; Franciscan tertiary [see *Franciscans*]; 1862–1921) after excommunication from RC Ch.; assoc. with Old* Catholics 1909–24; emphasizes devotion to Mary, ascetic practices.

Marienland. See *Estonia,* 1.

Marillac, Louise de. See *Vincent de Paul.*

Mariolatry. Idolatrous worship of Mary, i. e., giving Mary the kind of worship that is due to God alone. See also *Mariology.*

Mariology. Teaching about Mary, mother of Jesus.

Many hold (on basis of Lk 1:32; 3:23-38; Ro 1:3; 2 Ti 2:8; Acts 2:30) that Mary was a descendant of David. Jesus was conceived in her by the miraculous power of the Holy Spirit and was born of her. The Bible does not say whether or not she had other children. She appears only briefly in accounts of her Son's later life (e. g., Lk 2:41-52: Jn 2:1-11; Mt 12: 46-50; Jn 19:25-27) and Acts 1:14.

In the early Christian cents. Mary received comparatively little attention. But as Christological* controversies developed, she was increasingly recognized, esp. in the E; the 431 Council of Ephesus* adopted a letter of Cyril* of Alexandria which calls her "mother of God." Many legends about her also arose. In the 4th and 5th cents. devotion to her increased rapidly. The 787 Council of Nicea* stated: "We honor and salute and reverently venerate . . . the image of . . . our spotless Lady the all-holy mother of God."

In the Middle Ages, P. Damiani,* Bernard* of Clairvaux, et al. promoted veneration of Mary. Ave* Maria became a popular form of devotion, esp. as used in the Angelus* and rosary.*

In the early Christian cents. only a few feast days honored Mary (e. g., Annunciation, Mar. 25; Purification [Presentation], Feb. 2); the Middle Ages saw a sharp increase in the number of days devoted to her.

Devotion to Mary was modified by the Luth. Reformation.* For many yrs. M. Luther* held that Mary had been conceived without sin (WA 4, 559; 17 II, 409; 31 II, 689). But later he held that it was at Christ's conception that she was totally purged of sin (WA 39 II, 107). He held that she remained a virgin in childbirth (WA 40 III, 680) and for the rest of her life (WA 48, 579). Throughout his life Luther insisted that she is the mother of God (WA 7, 545; 36, 60; 10 II, 407). In 1522 he urged that one pray the Ave Maria but omitted "Pray for us sinners now and at the hour of our death" (WA 10 II,

407–409). For Luther, Mary was "queen of Heaven," but he warns against making that name say too much (WA 7, 573).

The Book* of Concord refers to Mary as "blessed" (AC III 1), "pure, holy, and ever-virgin" (SA-I 4), who "is most worthy of the most ample honors" (Ap XXI 27) and "is rightly called and truly is the mother of God" (FC Ep VIII 12). "Granted that blessed Mary prays for the church" (Ap XXI 27), yet "Scripture does not teach the invocation of saints" (AC XXI 2). See also *Mariolatry; Theotokos.*

As a result of Pietism,* rationalism,* and Prot. sectarianism, the esteem in which 16th c. Luths. held Mary nearly disappeared in many areas, though she is commemorated in most Luth. service books on the Feasts of the Annunciation* (Mar. 25), Presentation of Our Lord and Purification of Mary (Feb. 2), and Visitation (July 2). See also *Church Year,* 13, 16.

M. Luther, "The Magnificat Translated and Expounded," tr. A. T. W. Steinhaeuser, *Luther's Works,* XXI, ed. J. Pelikan (St. Louis, 1956), 295–358; H. D. Preuss, *Maria bei Luther* (Gütersloh, 1954); M. Thurian, *Mary Mother of All Christians,* tr. N. B. Cryer (New York, 1963); W. Tappolet, *Das Marienlob der Reformatoren* (Tübingen, 1962); H. Asmussen, *Maria die Mutter Gottes* (Stuttgart, 1950); R. Laurentin, *The Question of Mary,* tr. I. G. Pidoux (New York, 1965); *Maria in Liturgie und Lehrwort,* ed. P. T. Bogler (Maria Laach, 1954). EFP

Marion (Jr.) College. See *Ministry, Education of,* VIII C 1 e; *United Lutheran Church, Synods of,* 29.

Marists (Society of Mary; Marist Fathers; not to be confused with Marianists*). RC cong. founded by Jean Claude Courveille (1787–1866) and Jean Claude Marie Colin (1790–1875). The first group formed 1816 at Lyons, Fr.; approved by Rome 1836. Mems. meditate on the personality of Mary and are devoted to missions. Colin's request for approval of a 4-branched soc. (priests, brothers, religious sisters, 3d order) was refused by Rome. As a result, 4 indep. congs. developed: Marist Fathers (with Marist 3d Order attached); Marist Brothers (Little Brothers of Mary; founded 1817 near Lyons); Marist Sisters (Sisters of the Cong. of Mary; founded 1817 Cerdon, Ain, Fr.); Marist Missionary Sisters (Miss. Sisters of the Soc. of Mary; founded 1845 Saint-Brieuc, Fr.).

Marital Impediments. See *Impediments.*

Maritimes. See *Canada,* A 27.

Marius Mercator (d. after AD 431). Lat. polemicist; b. probably Afr.; opposed Nestorianism* and Pelagianism.* *MPL,* 48.

Mark, Liturgy of Saint. Egyptian Melchite (see *Melchites*) liturgy attributed by some to St. Mark, by others to Cyril* of Alexandria. Abandoned by Egyptian Melchites in gen. ca. 12th/13th c. in favor of the liturgy of Constantinople. Survived in modified form among Coptic Monophysites* and Abyssinians (see *Ethiopic Church*).

Mark of Ephesus (Eugenicus; ca. 1391–1445). Pupil of G. Gemistos* Pletho(n); monk; metropolitan of Ephesus. Most of his works oppose doctrines of the Lat. ch. and 1439 resolutions of the Council of Florence.* *MPG,* 160, 1071–1104.

Mark the Hermit (d. after 430). Ascetic; pupil of J. Chrysostom*; abbot Ancyra (now Ankara, Turkey); hermit; opposed justification by works. Writings mostly practical. *MPG,* 65, 893–1140.

Markellos. See *Marcellus.*

Marks of the Church. See *Church,* 4.

Marlorat, Augustin (Marloratus; du Pasquier; 1506–62). Ref. theol.; b. Bar-le-Duc, Fr.; friend of T. Beza*; pastor in Crissier (near Lausanne and Vevey, Switz., and Rouen, Fr.; took part in Colloquy of Poissy*; executed when RCs conquered Rouen. Works include *Novi Testamenti catholica expositio ecclesiastica.*

Marnix, Philip van (Philipp; Philips; ca. 1538–98). Baron St. Aldegonde; b. Brussels; educ. Louvain, Paris, Dôle, and Geneva; friend of J. Calvin* and T. Beza*; statesman, soldier, theol.; played major role in advancing Ref. theol. in Neth.; resisted Inquisition*; advised William* I in struggle for Neth. indep. Tr. Psalms into Flemish.

Maro(n). See *Maronites.*

Maronites. Syrian Uniate ch., chiefly in Lebanon; name perhaps derived from Maro(n) (Maroon; d. ca. 410), a hermit to whom a monastery on the Orontes in N Syria was dedicated; probably originated in 7th c. controversy over Monothelitism*; in union with Rome since 13th c.; played a significant role in modern Lebanese politics.

Marot, Clément (ca. 1495–1544). B. Cahors, Fr.; poet; resided in court of Francis I (see *France,* 8). Cast selected Psalms into hymn form.

Marperger, Bernhard Walther (1682–1746). B. Hamburg, Ger.; court preacher Dresden; hymnist. Ed. 9th-11th eds. of the Dresden hymnbook (1727, 1734, 1738).

Marprelate Tracts (1588–89). Puritan tracts attacking episcopacy* under pseudonym Martin Marprelate; believed written by J. Penry*; occasioned great controversy.

Marquesas Islands. See *Polynesia.*

Marquette, Jacques (Père; 1637–75). Jesuit miss. and explorer; b. Laon, Fr.; d. near present Ludington, Mich.; sailed for Can. (then called New Fr.) 1666; reest. miss. Sault Sainte Marie 1668; accompanied Louis Jolliet (1645–1700) on voyage down Wis. and Miss. rivers to mouth of Ark. R. 1673.

Marriage. I. *History.* In the OT it is implied that marriage is an expression of the will of God (e. g., Gn 2:18-24). Religious instruction was a distinctive feature of the home (Dt 6:6-9). OT prophets abundantly defend sexual purity and domestic virtue. Blessings of marriage and evils of impurity are often used figuratively (e. g., Rv 21:2; Ex 34:15-16).

Monogamy was considered ideal in the OT (Gn 2:24; Pr 31:10-31), but there is no OT prohibition of polygamy.* It persisted well into the Christian era and is not forbidden in the NT but conflicts with the NT ideal of monogamy (1 Ti 3:2, 12; Tts 1:6; cf. Jn 4:18).

In the first Christian cents. the view developed that virginity and celibacy* were superior to marriage. Marriage had only a physical basis, and to marry was only to choose the lesser of 2 evils (wedlock or fornication). But by the 15th c. marriage was spoken of as a sacrament and was so confirmed by the Council of Trent* (Sess. XXIV, Doctrine of the Sacrament of Matrimony, Canon 1).

M. Luther's* views on marriage developed gradually and against varying backgrounds. Hence contradictory statements may be found in his writings. In gen., his earlier writings emphasize a strong naturalism in his approach to marriage; his later, more mature writings emphasize a spiritual conception. His cen. teaching, salvation by faith alone, was normative. In his approach to the subject he tried to be Scriptural. Freedom of the individual, faith, and conscience were vital considerations. Luther held that the normal sex urge is imperious and cannot be escaped, but he pleaded for self-control.

On the spiritual side Luther regarded marriage as an obedience of faith which lifts marriage above its gross naturalism. He wrote beautiful passages on marriage, and his home life is regarded as ideal (see *Luther, Family Life of*).

Marriage had been under ch. control. Luther held that it should be under state control, but that religious features might be connected with the wedding

(WA 30 III, 74). Luther also held that a Christian might marry an unbeliever, even a Turk.

These positions of Luther were developed in the Lutheran* Confessions (e. g., AC and Ap, XXIII).

Luth. dogmaticians fortified Luther's positions, tried to determine the church's proper role in marriage, and discussed such details as impediments* and causes for divorce (see III).

Lutheranism in Am. began to give widespread and concentrated attention to marriage problems in the 20th c.

Historically, several steps developed in marriage procedure. They often depended on soc. conditions and special circumstances (cf. Gn 2:18-25; 11:29; 24:61-67). Soon there were 2 steps: agreement (engagement) and consummation (assoc. with a marriage feast). After the exile the custom of drawing up and sealing a contract came into vogue (Tob 7:14).

At first the ch. did not concern itself with control of matrimony or its process. Gradually the RC Ch. took control, made marriage a sacrament (see above), and demanded that it must occur under RC auspices, restricted it, and regulated the process in various ways. Luther and the Luth. Confessions protested against this (Tractatus, 77; see also above). Usual acts of marriage: consent of 2 eligible persons to live in matrimony (the only step in common-law marriage); meeting legal requirements (license, etc.); legally recognized ceremony.

II. *Definition and Principles.* A. L. Graebner* defined the state of marriage, or wedlock, as "the joint status of one man and one woman, superinduced and sustained by their mutual consent to be and remain to each other husband and wife in a lifelong union for legitimate sexual intercourse, the procreation of children, and cohabitation for mutual care and assistance" (*TQ,* VIII, 1 [Jan. 1903], 34).

The marriage relationship is holy. Marriage is the usual state for the average adult, both from the soc. and from the hygienic standpoint. Children are a gift of God (Ps 127:3). The family is the fundamental unit of the nation.

Luths. in Am. have usually advocated engagement, as a rule with consent of parents, as prelude to marriage. Marriage is a natural right and therefore cannot be forbidden to those eligible. The real affection of married people is a creation and gift of God that cannot be set aside by absolute commands. Engagement has been regarded as a sacred promise that must not be lightly made or lightly broken.

Acc. to Scripture, marriage has a 3-fold purpose: companionship and mutual help; procreation; and, since the fall of man into sin, avoidance of fornication (Gn 1:28; 2:18-24; 1 Co 7:2). Refusal of sexual intercourse is denial of a right and neglect of a duty assumed by marriage acc. to Gn 2:24; 1 Co 7. It has been regarded as a form of malicious abandonment.

Marriage is intended by God to be lifelong (Mt 19:6; Mk 10:9; Ro 7:2; 1 Co 7:39). It is immaterial whether the one or the other spouse, acc. to the regular course of nature, later becomes impotent or, as result of disease, becomes incapable of performing the prime duties of marriage. Mutual care and assistance become more prominent in course of time.

III. *Incidentals. Clandestine engagements* are those made without parental knowledge. Marriage *banns* (pl. of ban, "authoritative proclamation") originated in medieval times and are still pub. in some chs.; they announce the intention of persons to marry, giving opportunity for anyone to show just cause why the marriage should not take place. *Common law marriage* is the living together of a man and a woman as husband and wife, and with such intent, without legal or ecclesiastical marriage ceremony (see also I). State laws now gen. demand a physical examination, marriage license, and legally recognized marriage ceremony. *Artificial insemination* with seed other than that of the husband is gen. opposed by Christians. On basis of Gn 1:27-28; 2:21-24; Ro 1:26-27 Christians oppose *homosexual marriage.*

Divorce. Acc. to Mt. 5:32; 19:9, a man who divorces his wife except for *porneia* (Gk. "fornication; unchastity") causes (Gk. *poiei,* Mt 5:32) her to be stigmatized as adulterous. Jesus does not say that failure in marriage, even because of fornication, must be followed by divorce; nor does He say that there may be no divorce for fornication. *Malicious abandonment* (1 Co 7:15) is the willful breaking of the marriage bond by deliberate separation. A Christian "is not bound" in such cases, 1 Co 7:15. This has been interpreted to mean that a Christian suffers a marriage break, i. e., he submits to it, when such circumstances make it impossible for him to keep his marriage intact. The NT ideal is that marriage should end only with death (Ro 7:2-3). Cf. also Mk 10:11-12; Lk 16:18. JHCF HGC

See also *Ring, Engagement and Wedding; Tempus Clausum.*

G. E. Howard, *A History of Matrimonial Institutions,* 3 vols. (Chicago, 1904); E. A. Westermarck, *The History of Human Marriage,* 5th ed., 3 vols. (New York, 1922); G. E. Lenski, *Marriage in the Lutheran Church* (Columbus, Ohio, 1936); W. A. Maier, *For Better, Not for Worse,* 3d, rev. ed. (Saint Louis, 1939); O. A. Geiseman, *Make Yours a Happy Marriage* (St. Louis, 1946); J. T. Landis and M. G. Landis, *The Marriage Handbook* (New York, 1948); L. M. Epstein, *Marriage Laws in the Bible and the Talmud* (Cambridge, Mass., 1942); E. R. Groves and G. H. Groves, *The Contemporary American Family* (Philadelphia, 1947); R. E. Baber, *Marriage and the Family,* 2d ed. (New York, 1953); E. W. Burgess and P. Wallin, *Engagement and Marriage* (Philadelphia, 1953); D. R. Mace, *Hebrew Marriage* (London, 1953); *Engagement and Marriage: A Sociological, Historical, and Theological Investigation of Engagement and Marriage,* ed. Family Life Committee of the Bd. for Parish Educ. of LCMS (St. Louis, 1959); O. A. Piper, *The Biblical View of Sex and Marriage* (New York, 1960); *Sex and the Church: A Sociological, Historical, and Theological Investigation of Sex Attitudes,* ed. Family Life Committee of the Bd. for Parish Educ. of LCMS (St. Louis, 1961); H. Thielicke, *The Ethics of Sex,* tr. J. W. Doberstein (New York, 1964); *Family Relationships and the Church: A Sociological, Historical, and Theological Study of Family Structures, Roles, and Relationships,* ed. Family Life Committee of the Bd. for Parish Educ. of LCMS (St. Louis, 1970).

Marriage Laws. There is no uniform marriage law in the US. Following is a summary of laws as they obtain in the US:

Marriage is often defined as a contract; but it is also more than a contract: it is a change of status, or condition. It is the complete performance of a prior contract to marry. For a valid contract of this kind, also called engagement, the parties must be competent, there must be agreement, the consent must be genuine, i. e., free from fraud, duress, or mistake, and the agreement must be free from illegality. The express contract, or promise to marry, is proved, like other contracts, by the express words of the parties or by circumstantial evidence from their conduct, though explicit words have not been spoken.

Formal requisites of marriage are fixed by law. They usually include marriage license, performance of a marriage ceremony by a magistrate or cleric, and return of the license with evidence that the marriage has been solemnized. Certain factors or conditions make a marriage voidable or void. A marriage before the age of consent, as fixed by law, is valid until voided. Persons below legal age must have consent of parents or guardians in a manner acknowledged by law in order to make their marriage valid. Marriage of insane persons is void. Impotence in itself is no bar to marriage, but if marital intercourse is impossible because of an incurable defect, marriage may be annulled.

Relationship of affinity or consanguinity (see also *Impediments*) is gen. regulated by law, each state specifying in which degrees of relationship marriage is prohibited. The tendency has been toward making regulations stricter (e. g., to require [1] a waiting period bet. application for and issuance of licenses and [2] blood tests and other examinations). AJCM

R. V. Mackay, *Law of Marriage and Divorce Simplified,* 2d ed. by I. Mandell (New York, 1954); J. W. Morland, *Keezer on the Law of Marriage and Divorce,* 3d ed. (Indianapolis, 1946); M. Weinberg, *1959 Cumulative Supplement to Keezer on the Law of Marriage and Divorce, Third Edition* (Indianapolis, 1959).

Marriage Liturgy. M. Luther* was influenced by Christian marriage ceremonies of the late Middle Ages. In *Ein Traubüchlein für die einfältigen Pfarrherr* (1529) he divided the rite into (1) pub. of banns (see *Marriage,* III), (2) marriage proper in front of the church, (3) benediction by God's Word and prayer before the altar. This order for solemnizing marriage was gen. accepted as fundamental. The text and basic order remained even when the whole ceremony took place at the altar. But many ch. orders then placed the lessons first, followed by the marriage ceremony proper, prayers, and benediction. Luths. in Am. use many different, but basically similar, marriage ceremonies.

Marriott, Charles (1811–58). B. Church Lawford, near Rugby, Eng.; Angl. cleric; disciple of J. H. Newman*; assoc. with Oxford* Movement; with E. B. Pusey* and J. Keble* produced *A Library of Fathers of the Holy Catholic Church.*

Mars. See *Roman Religion,* 1.

Marsay, Charles Hector de St. George, Marquis de (1688–1753). Descendant of noble Huguenot family in Paris, Fr.; became hermit at Schwarzenau and Berleburg, Ger.; contracted spiritual marriage with Clare Elisabeth von Callenberg (1675–1742); followed mysticism of Guyon.*

Marsden, Samuel (1764–1838). Angl. miss.; b. Horsforth, near Leeds, Yorkshire, Eng.; d. Windsor, New S. Wales, Australia; educ. Cambridge; ordained 1793; to Parramatte, near Sydney, Australia, as chaplain of penal colony, 1794; returned to Eng. 1807 to report and solicit aid; returned to New S. Wales 1809; sought miss. aid for New Zealand with little success; made 7 voyages to New Zealand 1814–37 to work among natives.

Marsh, Herbert (1757–1839). B. London, Eng.; educ. Cambridge, Eng., and Göttingen and Leipzig, Ger.; prof. Cambridge 1907; bp. Llandaff, Wales, 1816 and Peterborough, Eng., 1819; brought Ger. critical methods to Eng. by tr. J. D. Michaelis,* *Einleitung in die göttlichen Schriften des Neuen Bundes* (Eng. title *Introduction to the New Testament*); opposed Calvinism. Other works include *The History of the Politicks of Great Britain and France; A Comparative View of the Churches of England and Rome.*

Marsh, James (1794–1842). Cong. minister; b. Hartford, Vt.; educ. Dartmouth Coll., Hanover, N. H., and Andover (Mass.) Theol. Sem.; pres. U. Vt. 1826–33; romanticist; influenced transcendentalists. Ed. S. T. Coleridge,* *Aids to Reflection;* tr. J. G. Herder,* *Vom Geist der Ebräischen Poesie* (Eng. title *The Spirit of Hebrew Poetry*).

Marshall Islands. Archipelago of atolls and reefs in W Pacific Ocean; *area* (land): ca. 66 sq. mi.; formerly Ger., controlled by Jap. after WW I; US trust territory 1947. Early miss. work by ABCFM (1857) and Hawaiian Ev. Assoc. Predominant religion: Christianity. See also *Micronesia.*

Marshman, John Clark (1794–1877). Son of Joshua Marshman*; pub. 1st complete Chinese Bible.

Marshman, Joshua (1768–1837). Father of J. C. Marshman*; b. Westbury Leigh, Wiltshire, Eng.; d. Serampore, India; weaver till 1794; later studied Lat., Gk., Heb., Syriac; 1799 sent with others, including W. Ward,* by Baptist* Miss. Soc. to join W. Carey* in India; because of Brit. E. India Co. opposition, landed at Dan. Serampore, near Calcutta, 1799. Wrote on Chinese language and grammar; other works include tr. of parts of the Bible into Chinese. See also *Serampore Trio.*

Marsilius of Padua (Marsiglio dei Mainardini; ca. 1290 – ca. 1343). It. philos. and scholar. Prof. Paris 1311, rector 1313. With John* of Jandun wrote *Defensor pacis* 1324, a treatise against temporal power of papacy; excommunicated 1327 by John XXII (see *Popes,* 13). See also *Christian Church, History of,* II 3; *Councils and Synods,* 7.

Marsow, Hermann. See *Estonia,* 2.

Martène, Edmond (1654–1739). B. Saint-Jean-de-Losne, near Dijon, Fr.; Benedictine liturgist. Works include *De antiquis ecclesiae ritibus; Tractatus de antiqua ecclesiae disciplina in divinis celebrandis officiis.*

Martensen, Hans Lassen (1808–84). Dan. Luth. theol.; b. Flensburg, Ger., near Dan. border; prof. Copenhagen, then court preacher; bp. Zealand (Sjaelland) 1854; marked by speculative-mystic tendency. Works include *Den kristelige dogmatik; Den kristelige etik.* See also *Denmark, Lutheranism in,* 9.

Marti, Benedictus. See *Aretius, Benedictus.*

Marti Karl (1855–1925). B. Bubendorf, canton Basel, Switz.; OT scholar; pastor; prof. Bern; exponent of historicocritical* method of J. Wellhausen.* Ed. *Kurzer Hand-Commentar zum Alten Testament; Zeitschrift für die alttestamentliche Wissenschaft* 1907–23.

Martianay, Jean (1647–1717). Benedictine exegete, patrologist, textual critic. Wrote on life and works of Jerome; tried to reconstruct Heb. text used by Jerome for the Vulgate.

Martianus Capella (5th c.). Lat. writer of N Afr. Works include *Satyricon* (or *Satyra;* or *De nuptiis Philologiae et Mercurii et de septem artibus liberalibus*), an encyclopedia of contemporary culture which tried to classify human intellectual enterprise. See also *Quadrivium; Trivium.*

Martin (saint). See *Church Year,* 17.

Martin V (Ottone [Oddone; Oddo; Odo] [de] Colonna; 1368–1431). B. Genazzano, near Rome, It.; pope 1417–31 (elected at Council of Constance*); tried to heal papal schism of 1378. See also *Basel, Council of; Schism,* 8.

Martin, Adam (Aug. 9[8?], 1835–May 18, 1921). B. Budershausen, Bav., Ger.; educ. Hamilton Coll. (Clinton, N. Y.) and Hartwick* Sem.; pastor Middleburg, N. Y., 1861; 1st pres. of the Wis. Syn. coll. at Watertown, Wis., 1865–69; prof. Pa. Coll., Gettysburg, 1869.

Martin, Johann Nicolaus (ca. 1725–97). Pastor St. John Luth. Ch., Charleston, S. C., 1763–67, 1774–78, 1786–87; pastor Saluda Forks, S. C., at junction of Saluda R. and Broad R., 1767.

Martin, Paul See *Rade, Paul Martin.*

Martin-Luther-Bund. See *Gotteskasten.*

Martin Luther Seminary, Lincoln, Nebr. Founded 1913 by the Ger. Nebr. Syn.; merged 1932 with Western* Theol. Sem. and Northwestern Theol. Sem. (see *Ministry, Education of,* X N; *United Lu-*

theran Church, Synods of, 17); suspended operation June 1934. See also *General Synod of the Evangelical Lutheran Church in the United States of America,* 8; *United Lutheran Church, Synods of,* 3.

Martin-Luther-Vereine. See *Gotteskasten.*

Martin of Braga (ca. 510/520–ca. 579). B. Pannonia; monk in Palestine; abbot, bp. Dumio (Dumia; Dumium; Duma), near Braga (ancient Bracara [Braccara] Augusta; now in Port.); abp. Braga. Works include *De ira; De moribus; Formula honestae vitae.*

MPL, 72, 17–52; 74, 381–394.

Martin of Tours. See *Celtic Church,* 2.

Martineau, James (1805–1900). B. Norwich, Eng.; educ. Manchester Coll., York; Unitarian (see *Unitarianism*) theol.; prof. Manchester New Coll. 1840; apologist of theism* against materialism,* but rejected doctrines of Trin., incarnation of Christ, vicarious atonement. See also *Metaphysical Society, The.*

Martini, Cornelius (Corneille; 1568 [1567?]–1621). B. Antwerp, Belg.; educ. Rostock, Ger.; prof. philos. Helmstedt 1592; introd. Aristotelian metaphysics into Luth. thought; tried to determine the relationship bet. philos. and theol.; influenced J. Gerhard; followers included J. Martini* and G. Calixtus.* Works include *Commentarium in librum Aristotelis de interpretatione; Compendium theologiae; Tractatus de analysi logica.*

Martini, Jakob (1570–1649). B. Langenstein, near Halberstadt, Ger.; educ. Helmstedt and Wittenberg; prof. logic 1602, ethics 1613, theol. 1623 Wittenberg; exponent of (Prot.) Aristotelian metaphysics. Works include *Partitionum & quaestionum metaphysicarum libri VIII.*

Martini, Matthias (1572–1630). B. Freienhagen, Waldeck, Ger.; Ref. theol.; court preacher and prof. Herborn; pastor Emden; prof. and rector Bremen Gymnasium; exponent of federal* theol.; followers included J. Cocceius.* Works include *Christianae doctrinae summa capita; Lexicon philologicum.*

Martinson, Anna Hauge (Sept. 18, 1868–July 26, 1969). B. Huxley, Iowa; d. Hong Kong; wife of Andrew Martinson, United* Norw. Luth. Ch. in Am. miss. to China 1902; after his death 1913 she continued his work until forced to flee to Hong Kong 1948.

Martyn, Henry (1781–1812). Angl. miss.; b. Truro, Cornwall, Eng.; d. Tokat, Asia Minor. Educ. Cambridge; reached Calcutta, India, May 1806 as chaplain of E. India Co.; settled at Dinapur (Dinapore) Oct. 1806; ministered to natives; transferred to Cawnpore 1809; ill; in search of health to Persia 1811, then to Arabia and Asia Minor. Tr. NT into Hindustani, Persian, and Arab., the Ps into Persian, and the *Book of Common Prayer* into Hindustani. See also *Middle East,* I.

Martyr (from Gk. *martys, martyros,* "witness"). The disciples and apostles were "witnesses" of the life, death, and resurrection of Jesus; cf. Acts 1:8 "Ye shall be witnesses (Gk. *martyres*)." Clement of Rome (see *Apostolic Fathers,* 2) spoke of witness in the sense of giving one's life for one's faith. Tertullian* regarded martyrdom in this sense as a 2d baptism because it removed all sin and assured heavenly bliss. Augustine* of Hippo held that the reason for suffering, not suffering itself, makes a martyr.

Some regard the Holy Innocents of Bethlehem as the 1st Christian martyrs (see *Church Year,* 1). Other early Christian martyrs include Stephen (Acts 6:8–7:60), James (Acts 12:2), and Antipas (Rv 2:13); Peter and Paul are usually included on basis of tradition; others include Ignatius of Antioch and Polycarp (see *Apostolic Fathers,* 3) and others who perished in persecutions* of Christians.

Legendary accounts of martyrs began to be gathered in special books in the 4th c. See also *Acta martyrum; Acta sanctorum; Bolland, Jean de; Bollandists.*

Martyrs of the Reformation and post-Reformation age include L. de Berquin,* A. Clarenbach,* G. (II) de Coligny,* T. Cranmer,* J. Diaz,* J. Esch,* P. Fliesteden,* P. Hamilton,* Henry* of Zutphen, J. Hooper,* B. Hubmaier,* L. Kaiser,* H. Latimer,* N. Ridley,* J. Rogers,* H. Voes,* G. Wishart.*

In the 1st half of the 20th c. many Christians, esp. clerics, were killed in Russ. Many lost their lives in persecutions of RCs in Sp. 1936–37 and Mex. 1926–38. In Ger., RCs and Prots. were executed by Nazis (see also *Bonhoeffer, Dietrich; Kirchenkampf*). Armenian Christians were killed in Ottoman persecutions during and after WW I.

Missionaries were often killed by natives to whom they were bringing the Gospel.

In Am., some RC missionaries were killed by natives. Most prominent Luth. martyrs: Jean Ribault of Dieppe, Fr., and ca. 280 companions (mems. of a naval miss. sent by the king of Fr. to colonize the E coast of Fla.), killed by Spanish "because they were Lutherans and enemies of our holy Catholic faith," Sept. and Oct. 1565 near Saint Augustine, Fla.

See also *Saints, Veneration of,* 2, 3; *United States, Religious History of the,* 2.

L. E. Smith, *Heroes and Martyrs of the Modern Missionary Enterprise* (Providence, R. I., 1856); H. W. Surkau, *Martyrien in jüdischer und frühchristlicher Zeit* (Göttingen, 1938); B. H. Forck, *und folget ihrem Glauben nach: Gedenkbuch für die Blutzeugen der Bekennenden Kirche* (Stuttgart, 1949); D. Attwater, *Martyrs from St. Stephen to John Tung* (London, 1958); G. Ricciotti, *The Age of Martyrs: Christianity from Diocletian to Constantine,* tr. A. Bull (Milwaukee, 1959); N. Brox, *Zeuge und Märtyrer: Untersuchungen zur frühchristlichen Zeugnis-Terminologie* (Munich, 1961); K. Rahner, *On the Theology of Death,* tr. C. H. Henkey (New York, 1961); H. v. Campenhausen, *Die Idee des Martyriums in der alten Kirche,* 2d ed. (Göttingen, 1964); W. H. C. Frend, *Martyrdom and Persecution in the Early Church: A Study of a Conflict from the Maccabees to Donatus* (Oxford, 1965). EL

Martyr, Justin. See *Justin Martyr.*

Martyr, Peter. See *Peter Martyr.*

Martyr Theory. See *Atonement, Theories of,* 2.

Martyrdom of Isaiah. See *Apocrypha,* A 4.

Martyrium. Monument or memorial edifice commemorating the death of a Christian martyr or witness for Christ.

Martyrium Clementis. See *Apostolic Fathers,* 1.

Martyrology. Register, catalog, or list of Christian martyrs. See also *Acta martyrum.*

Marucchi, Orazio (1852–1931). B. Rome, It.; archaeol.; secy. pontifical commission of sacred archaeol.; known for research of Roman catacombs. Works include *Éléments d'Archéologie chrétienne; Le Catacombe romane.*

Marutas (Marut[h]a of Tag[h]rit[h]; ca. 565–649). Jacobite monk 605; 1st maphrian* of Jacobites in Persia ca. 629.

Marx, Karl Heinrich (1818–83). Pol. philos.; regarded by many as founder of modern socialism based on hist. materialism; b. Trier (Treves), Prussia; bapt. in Luth. ch. 1824; educ. Bonn and Berlin; joined "Hegelian Left" (see *Hegel, Georg Wilhelm Friedrich,* 9); ed. *Rheinische Zeitung* in Cologne 1842 (it was suppressed 1843); to Paris 1843; coed. the only issue of *Deutsch-Französische Jahrbücher;* influenced by Fr. socialists including C. H. de Rouvroy, Comte de Saint-Simon*; 1844 wrote, with F. Engels,* *Die heilige Familie,* an attack on B. Bauer*; 1845 contributed to *Vorwärts,* a radical Ger. paper pub. in Paris; expelled from Fr. 1845; to Brussels,

Belg., 1845, where he contacted the workingmen's movement; wrote *La Misère de la Philosophie* 1847; with Engels wrote *Communist Manifesto* 1847; expelled from Brussels 1848; to Cologne via Paris; 1849 via Paris to London; led in organizing Internat. Workingmen's Assoc. 1864 (known as "First International"; this and the 2 following Internationals [1889; 1919] gave rise to the shorter name "The International"); spent last days in illness and financial difficulties.

Communist Manifesto is divided: I. Bourgeois and Proletarians; II. Proletarians and Communists; III. Socialist and Communist Literature; IV. Position of the Communists in Relation to Various Existing Opposition Parties. Basic suppositions ordinarily regarded as underlying *Communist Manifesto:* 1. Marxian dialectics; 2. class struggle; 3. economic determinism (or hist. materialism); 4. labor theory of value and surplus value. Other works include *Das Kapital.*

See also *Socialism,* 4.

P. M. Bretscher, "The Communist Manifesto," *CTM,* XVII (Oct. 1946), 742–769.

Mary. See *Mariolatry; Mariology.*

Mary I (Mary Tudor; "Bloody Mary"; 1516–58). Daughter of Henry* VIII and Catherine of Aragon; queen of Eng. and Ireland 1553–58. Educ. strict RC; lived in comparative obscurity till 1553; ordered execution of Jane Grey, Prot. and potential rival to throne; married Philip II (1527–98; king of Sp. 1556–98) 1554; reest. RCm in Eng.; Prot. martyrs numbered ca. 300. See also *Cranmer, Thomas; England,* B 5; *Hooper, John; Latimer, Hugh; Ridley, Nicholas; Rogers, John.*

Mary, Assumption of. See *Munificentissimus Deus.*

Mary, Cult of. See *Mariolatry.*

Mary, Little Brothers of. See *Marists.*

Mary, Veneration of. See *Church Year,* 13; *Mariology.*

Mary Festivals. See *Church Year,* 13.

Mary Magdalene of Pazzi (de' Pazzi; 1566–1607). B. Florence, It.; entered Carmelite convent, Florence, 1582; first experienced great physical and spiritual suffering, later spiritual ecstasies in course of which she gave spiritual counsels which were recorded and pub. by fellow nuns after her death.

Mary of Egypt (probably 344–ca. 421). Penitent; subject of legends. After sinful life in Alexandria, allegedly converted at Jerusalem and lived 47 yrs. in isolation in desert E of Palestine.

Mary of Hungary (1505–58). B. Brussels, Brabant; queen of Hung. 1522–26; regent of Neth. 1531–52; sister of Charles* V; M. Luther* dedicated his interpretation of Ps 37, 62, 94, and 109 to her at her husband's death.

Maryland, Evangelical Lutheran Synod of (Md. Syn.; 1833–1962). See *United Lutheran Church, Synods of,* 11.

Maryland, German Synod of. Indep. syn. organized ca. 1876; disbanded ca. 1890.

Maryland, Virginia, and so forth, The Evangelical Lutheran Synod of. See *United Lutheran Church, Synods of,* 11, 29.

Maryland and Adjacent States, German Evangelical Lutheran Synod of (Ger. Syn. of Md. and the South; Ger. Syn. of Md.; Md. and the South Syn.; ca. 1874–ca. 1876). Joined The General* Syn. of the Ev. Luth. Ch. in the USA 1875; disbanded.

Maryland and Virginia, The Evangelical Lutheran Synod of (Md. and Va. Syn.; 1820–33). See *United Lutheran Church, Synods of,* 11, 29.

Maryland Colony. See *United States, Religious History of,* 5.

Maryland Synod. Name sometimes applied to various syns. whose territory included Md. See entries beginning *Maryland.* For Md. Syn. 1962 – see *Lutheran Church in America,* IX B 11.

Maryland Synod Question. Question debated in Md. Syn. beginning 1853 regarding status of a pastor who ceases to be a mem. of a syn.

Mashal. See *Revelation,* 7 c.

Masingo Bible School. See *Africa,* B 2.

Masjid. See *Mosque.*

Maskilim. See *Haskalah.*

Mason, Charles Harrison. See *Church of God in Christ.*

Mason, Lowell (1792–1872). B. Medfield, Mass.; cofounder Boston Academy of Music. Ed. *Church Psalmody* and *Manual of Christian Psalmody;* composed hymn tunes, including "Nearer, My God, to Thee," "From Greenland's Icy Mountains," and "My Faith Looks Up to Thee"; other works include *Manual of the Boston Academy of Music, for Instruction in the Elements of Vocal Music.*

Masonic Lodge. See *Freemasonry.*

Masonic Order. See *Freemasonry.*

Masonry. See *Freemasonry.*

Masora(h) (Massora[h]; from Heb. Mas[s]oreth, literal meaning uncertain, perhaps "tradition"). Jewish critical notes on (consonantal) OT text, esp. Pentateuch; compiled ca. 6th–ca. 10th c. by Mas(s)oretes (Masorites); tried to preserve OT text accurately; verses (traditionally 23,203), words, and letters were counted; peculiarities were noted and classified; explanations of difficulties were transmitted orally from generation to generation at least till the 7th c.; questions of spelling were discussed; systems of vowel points developed; textual-critical apparatus was included, as was also division of the text into larger (sidra) and smaller (parashah) sections. See also *Manuscripts of the Bible,* 1.

Masoretes (Masorites). See *Masora(h).*

Masoretic Hebrew Text. See *Manuscripts of the Bible; Masora(h).*

Masqat. See *Middle East,* L 7.

Mass (from Lat. *missa,* perhaps in its use in *"Ite, missa est,"* a formula of dismissal at end of *missa* catechumenorum* and *missa* fidelium;* Ger. *Messe*). 1. Old name for Lord's Supper (see *Grace, Means of,* IV). In the Middle Ages it became the most common name for the service.

2. RC doctrine made the mass more sacrificial than sacramental in people's minds.

3. At the time of the Reformation many Prot. leaders (e. g., H. Zwingli*) abolished the RC form of the mass and substituted a memorial Communion service. Luths. retained the mass but purged it of all misinterpretations.

4. The Luth. symbols object to certain medieval features of the mass, e. g., Communion under one kind; celebration by a solitary priest as a private devotion; understanding the mass as a propitiatory sacrifice for the sins of the living and the dead (see also *Liturgics*); buying and selling masses. Cf. SA, Part II, Art. II; AC XXII.

5. "We are unjustly accused of having abolished the Mass. Without boasting, it is manifest that the Mass is observed among us with greater devotion and more earnestness than among our opponents. Moreover, the people are instructed often and with great diligence concerning the holy sacrament, why it was instituted, and how it is to be used (namely, as a comfort for terrified consciences) in order that the people may be drawn to the Communion and Mass. . . . Since, therefore, no novelty has been introduced which did not exist in the church from ancient times, and since no conspicuous change has been made in the public ceremonies of the Mass except that other unnecessary Masses which were held in addition to the parochial Mass, probably through abuse, have been discontinued, this manner of holding Mass ought not in fairness be condemned as heretical or unchristian." (AC XXIV 1, 40)

6. "To begin with, we must repeat the prefatory

statement that we do not abolish the Mass but religiously keep and defend it. In our churches Mass is celebrated every Sunday and on other festivals, when the sacrament is offered to those who wish for it after they have been examined and absolved. We keep traditional liturgical forms, such as the order of the lessons, prayers, vestments, etc." (Ap XXIV 1)

7. The Luth. symbols call the mass a sacrifice, but eucharistic rather than propitiatory (Ap XXIV 20 ff.). Even so, they place the most important emphasis on the sacrament of the body and blood of Christ, not the eucharistic sacrifice.

8. M. Luther* said that the New Testament is the mass, for Christ said, "This is the cup of a new, everlasting testament in my blood." (WA 6, 358)

9. At the time of the Reformation there was great need for vernacular masses. Therefore in many Luth. parishes, esp. in rural areas, the mass was sung in the vernacular, often based on Luther's *Deudsche Messe* (see *Luther, Liturgies of*). In larger cities, esp. at univs., the Lat. mass was used by some Luths. as late as the 18th c.

10. In the 16th c. the ceremonies of the mass remained almost unchanged. In most Luth. chs. the canon of the mass was omitted, but the other parts of the service remained intact. Luther wrote to G. Brück* Apr. 4, 1541: "In our churches, thank God, the neutral things [common to both Luths. and RCs] are such that when a layman, Walloon, or Spaniard who could not understand our sermon, would see our mass, choir, organ, bells, chasubles, etc., he would have to say, 'This is indeed a Roman Catholic church.' There is no difference, or at least no more than they have among themselves." (WA-Br 9, 357)

11. Many Luths. in the US do not use the term "mass," but in some other countries (e. g., Norw.; Swed.) it is the common word for the Communion service.

See also *Missa brevis; Missa cantata; Missa lecta; Missa solemnis; Pontifical Mass.*

Y. Brilioth, *Eucharistic Faith and Practice,* tr. A. G. Hebert (New York, 1930); G. Aulén, *Eucharist and Sacrifice, tr.* E. H. Wahlstrom (Philadelphia, 1958); G. Dix, *The Shape of the Liturgy,* 2d ed. (London, 1945); F. Lindemann, *The Sermon and the Propers,* 4 vols. (St. Louis, 1958–59); L. D. Reed, *The Lutheran Liturgy,* rev. ed. (Philadelphia, 1959); H. Sasse, *This Is My Body* (Minneapolis, 1959); F. Lochner, *Der Hauptgottesdienst der Evangelisch-Lutherischen Kirche* (St. Louis, 1895); J. A. Jungmann, *The Mass of the Roman Rite,* tr. F. A. Brunner, 2 vols. (New York, 1951–55); *Leiturgia* (Kassel, 1954–70); G. Rietschel, *Lehrbuch der Liturgik,* 2d ed., ed. P. Graff (Göttingen, 1951); M. Luther, "The Blessed Sacrament of the Holy and True Body of Christ, and the Brotherhoods," tr. J. J. Schindel, rev. E. T. Bachmann, in *Luther's Works,* Am. ed., XXXV (Philadelphia, 1960), 45–73, "A Treatise on the New Testament, That Is, The Holy Mass," tr. J. J. Schindel, rev. E. T. Bachmann, in *Luther's Works,* Am. ed., XXXV (Philadelphia, 1960), 75–111, "The Adoration of the Sacrament," tr. A. R. Wentz, in *Luther's Works,* Am. ed., XXXVI (Philadelphia, 1959), 269–305, "Formula of Mass and Communion," tr. P. Z. Strodach, in *Works of Martin Luther,* Holman ed., VI (Philadelphia, 1932), 65–117, and "The German Mass and Order of Service," tr. and introd. A. Steimle, with special introd. by L. D. Reed, in *Works of Martin Luther,* Holman ed., VI (Philadelphia, 1932), 151–189. EFP

Mass (music). The mass has been set to music by many Luth., Angl., and RC composers. In musical setting it consists of Kyrie, Gloria in Excelsis, Credo, Sanctus, and Agnus Dei. Gregorian settings were used in the Middle Ages (see *Gregorian Music*); the polyphonic mass became prominent 1200–1400. In RC circles the golden age for the polyphonic mass began perhaps ca. 1450 and reached its climax in G. P. da Palestrina* and O. di Lasso.* Luth. composers of masses include H. L. Hassler* and A. Scandello.* Beginning ca. 1600, the character of mass music changed radically. The a cappella mass was replaced by the orchestrally accompanied mass, e. g., by J. S. Bach,* M. L. C. Z. S. Cherubini,* W. A. Mozart,* L. v. Beethoven,* F. S. P. Schubert,* F. Liszt,* G. Verdi,* C. A. Franck,* C. F. Gounod,* and A. Bruckner.*

Mass, High. See *Missa solemnis.*

Mass, Low. See *Missa lecta.*

Mass, Private. See *Missa lecta.*

Mass, Solemn. See *Missa solemnis.*

Mass, Sung. See *Missa cantata.*

Mass of Catechumens. See *Missa catechumenorum.*

Mass of Faithful. See *Missa fidelium.*

Massachusetts Bay Colony. See *United States, Religious History of,* 4.

Massacre of St. Bartholomew. See *Bartholomew's Day Massacre.*

Massarelli, Angelo. See *Roman Catholic Confessions,* A 1.

Massenet, Jules Émile Frédéric (1842–1912). B. Montaud, near Saint-Étienne, Fr.; composer; prof. Paris Conservatory; mem. Académie des Beaux-Arts. Works include oratorios (e. g., *Marie-Magdeleine*), operas (e. g., *Manon*), cantatas, ballets, songs.

Massie, Richard (1800–87). B. Chester, Cheshire, Eng.; tr. many hymns of M. Luther,* P. Gerhardt,* K. J. P. Spitta,* and other Ger. hymnists. Translations include "To Shepherds as They Watched by Night"; "Now Praise We Christ, the Holy One"; "Christ Jesus Lay in Death's Strong Bands"; "God the Father, Be Our Stay"; "That Man a Godly Life Might Live"; "Dear Christians, One and All, Rejoice"; "May God Bestow on Us His Grace"; "If God Himself Be for Me"; "Come, Thou Bright and Morning Star."

Massilians. See *Semi-Pelagianism.*

Massillon, Jean Baptiste (1663–1742). B. Hyères, Fr.; bp. Clermont 1717; delivered oration at funeral of Louis* XIV, who had said that he was pleased with other preachers but Massillon made him displeased with himself.

Massoretes. See *Masora(h).*

Master Mason. See *Freemasonry,* 3.

Masznyik, Endre (1857–1927). Hung. theol.; prof. NT and systematic theol. at Ev. Luth. Academy, Bratislava. Works include a life of M. Luther, dogmatics, life of Jesus, life and letters of Paul, Hung. tr. of NT and of selected writings of M. Luther.

Material Cause. See *Cause,* 3.

Material Principle. The material principle of the Luth. Ch. is the doctrine of justification* by faith alone *(sola* fide).* See also *Faith, Justifying.*

W. H. T. Dau, "The Heritage of Lutheranism," *What Lutherans Are Thinking,* ed. E. C. Fendt (Columbus, Ohio, 1947), pp. 9–25.

Materialism. Theory which originated in Gk. philosophy* and regards matter as the original cause of all, even psychic, phenomena. Asserting that all psychic processes are due to changes of material molecules, it denies the existence of the soul*; developed by Encyclopedists*; became prominent in Ger. in the 19th c. See also *Büchner, Friedrich Karl Christian Ludwig; Democritus; Dialectical Materialism; Loofs, Friedrich; Marx, Karl Heinrich; Naturalism; Vogt, Karl.*

Mather. Family name prominent in early New Eng. hist. 1. *Richard* (1596–1669). Father of 2; b. Lowton, Lancashire, Eng.; ordained in Angl. Ch. 1618; suspended 1633/34 for Puritanism; to Boston, Mass., 1635; Cong. pastor Dorchester, Mass., 1636–69. 2. *Increase* (1639–1723). Son of 1, father of 3; b.

Dorchester, Mass.; educ. Harvard U., Cambridge, Mass.; Cong. pastor Boston 1664–1723; pres. Harvard U. 1685–1701. 3. *Cotton* (1663–1728). Son of 2; b. Boston, Mass.; asst. to his father 1685–1723; his father's successor 1723; first supported witch-hunts, later regarded them as unfair. Works include *Magnalia Christi Americana: Or the Ecclesiastical History of New England from Its First Planting in the Year 1620 unto the Year of Our Lord 1698.*

Mathesius, Johann(es) (1504–65). B. Rochlitz, near Chemnitz, Ger.; studied at Ingolstadt; employed at Adelshausen, near Munich, where he became acquainted with writings of M. Luther*; attended Wittenberg U.; teacher Altenburg; rector Joachimsthal (Jáchymov) 1532; completed studies in theol. at Wittenberg; table companion of Luther; preacher (Diakonus) 1541, pastor 1545 Joachimsthal; hymnist. First biography of Luther imbedded in his sermons; hymns include "Herr Gott, der du mein Vater bist." See also *Luther, Table Talk of.*

Mathew, Arnold Harris (1853–1919). Ordained RC priest 1878; lost status because of marriage 1892; allowed to officiate in Angl. Ch.; consecrated abp. in Gt. Brit. at Utrecht, Neth., by Dutch Old Cath. Ch. 1908; repudiated 1910.

Mathews, Shailer (1863–1941). Bap. layman, educ.; b. Portland, Maine; prof. NT hist. and interpretation, and of systematic, hist., and comparative theol. U. of Chicago (Divinity School), dean 1908; pres. FCC 1912–16; pres. N. Bap. Conv. 1915; liberal theol. With G. B. Smith ed. *A Dictionary of Religion and Ethics;* other works include *The Social Teaching of Jesus: The Church and the Changing Order; The Spiritual Interpretation of History; The French Revolution; The Faith of Modernism; Creative Christianity.* See also *Social Gospel.*

Mathurins (Mathurines). See *Trinitarians.*

Matilda of Hackeborn (also of Helfta). See *Mechtild of Hackeborn.*

Matilda of Magdeburg. See *Mechtild of Magdeburg.*

Matins (Mattins; from Lat. matutinus, "pertaining to the morning"). One of the canonical hours (see *Hours, Canonical*).

Matrimony. See *Marriage.*

Matteo Serafini da Bascio (ca. 1495–1552). B. Bascio, near Pesaro, Pesaro e Urbino province, It.; 1st vicar-gen. Capuchins.*

Mattes, John Caspar (Nov. 8, 1876–Jan. 27, 1948). B. Easton, Pa.; educ. Lutheran Theol. Sem., Mount Airy, Philadelphia; Pa. Ministerium pastor Trenton, N. J., 1901–15, Scranton, Pa., 1915–38; ALC prof. theol. Wartburg Theol. Sem., Dubuque, Iowa, 1939–48. Hymn translations include stanza 5 of "Behold, a Branch Is Growing."

Mattheson, Johann (1681–1746). Musician, composer, writer, theorist, critic, controversialist; b. Hamburg, Ger., of Norw. parents; active in Hamburg; helped develop ch. cantata; supported more dramatic style; introd. female singers into his choir; deaf 1728. Works include oratorios; a Passion; a mass. See also *Passion, The.*

Matthew of Aquasparta (ca. 1238/40–1302). Franciscan philos.; b. Aquasparta, Umbria, It.; minister gen. of his order 1287; cardinal 1288; advisor of Boniface VIII (see *Popes,* 12); defended Augustinianism* against Aristotelianism (see *Aristotle*) of Thomas* Aquinas.

Matthew of Cracow (ca. 1330/35–1410). B. Cracow, Poland; prof. theol. Prague ca. 1384, Heidelberg 1395; bp. Worms 1405; worked for ch. reform. Works include *De squaloribus curiae Romanae.*

Matthew of Janov. See *Janow, Matthias von.*

Matthew (of) Paris (Parisiensis; ca. 1200–59). Eng. chronicler; Benedictine; monk at Monastery of Saint Albans, Eng. Works include *Historia maior;* lives of abbots of St. Albans.

Matthew's Bible. See *Bible Versions,* L 4.

Matthias von Janow. See *Janow, Matthias von.*

Matthys, Jan. See *Münster Kingdom.*

Mattson, Karl Evald (Oct. 9, 1905–Nov. 16, 1964). B. Warren, Minn.; educ. Augustana Theol. Sem., Rock Island, Ill. Pastor East Orange, N. J., 1930–39; New Haven, Conn., 1939–45. Pres. New Eng. Conf. of Ev. Luth. Augustana Syn. of N. Am., Worcester, Mass., 1945–48. Pres. Augustana Theol. Sem., Rock Island, Ill., 1948–62. Translated Y. T. Brilioth, *A Brief History of Preaching;* other works include *The Glory of Common Tasks.*

Mau Mau. See *Africa,* E 6.

Maude, Mary Fawler (nee Hooper; 1819–1913). B. Bloomsbury, London, Eng.; married Angl. cleric Joseph Maude 1841; hymnist. Hymns include "Thine Forever, God of Love!"

Maulbronn Colloquy. Unsuccessful colloquy held at Maulbronn, Ger., 1564, to heal dissension bet. Luths. of Württemberg and Calvinists of the Palatinate. Representatives of the Palatinate included Frederick* III, M. Diller,* P. Boquin,* C. Olevian(us),* Z. Ursinus,* P. Dathenus,* T. Erastus*; of Württemberg: J. Brenz,* Jakob Andreä,* B. Bidembach,* L. Osiander* the Elder.

Maulbronn Formula. See *Lutheran Confessions,* C 2.

Maundy Thursday. See *Church Year,* 4, 8, 16; *Gründonnerstag.*

Maur, Congregation of St. See *Maurists.*

Maurenbrecher, Max (1874–1930). B. Königsberg (Kaliningrad), Ger.; ev. theol.; socialist; mem. various parties which emphasized socialism and nationalism; forerunner of *Deutsche Christen* movement (see *Barmen Theses*).

Maurice. Legendary leader of Christian "Theban Legion" which is said to have been massacred by Maximian* when it refused to sacrifice.

Maurice, John Frederick Denison (1805–72). B. Normanstone, near Lowestoft, Suffolk, Eng.; son of a Unitarian cleric; Angl. priest 1834; tried to attract the educated and liberal to the ch., which ought to grapple with skepticism; emphasized Fatherhood of God and the ethical and spiritual influence of Christ's sacrifice; leader in Broad Ch.; with T. Hughes* and J. M. F. Ludlow* founded Working Men's Coll., London, 1854; with Hughes, Ludlow, and C. Kingsley* founded Christian* Socialism. Works include *The Kingdom of Christ; Theological Essays; Mediaeval Philosophy; Modern Philosophy; What Is Revelation?* See also *Metaphysical Society, The.*

Maurice of Saxony (Moritz; 1521–53). Duke of Saxony 1541–53; in return for guarantee of territory (protectorate of the bishoprics of Magdeburg and Halberstadt) and the title of elector, he helped Charles* V crush John* Frederick, his (Maurice's) cousin; tried to find common ground bet. Charles V and the Prot. states in the Leipzig Interim (see *Interim,* II); feared growing power of Charles V; angered at harsh treatment of his father-in-law, Philip* of Hesse; turned against Charles V, defeated him at Innsbruck, Austria, and forced him to agree to the terms of the convention of Passau*; died at Sievershausen, Ger., in battle against Albert,* Margrave of Brandenburg-Kulmbach, who had refused to agree to the convention of Passau.

Maurists. Fr. Benedictine Cong. of St. Maur; named after Maurus (or Maur; ca. 512–584; b. perhaps Rome, It.; legendary Fr. monk; disciple of Benedict* of Nursia); founded 1621 by L. Benard* as part of reform movement begun 1589 at the Benedictine abbey of Saint-Vanne, Verdun, Fr.; known for scholarship (see *Mabillon, Jean; Martène, Edmond; Montfaucon, Bernard de*); suppressed by Fr. Revolution (see *Church and State,* 15; *France,* 5); dissolved 1818 by Pius VII (see *Popes,* 27).

Mauritania. See *Africa,* C 2.

Mauritius (formerly Ile de France). Mem. Brit.

Commonwealth as indep. nation since 1968. Is. ca. 450/500 mi. E of Madagascar. *Area:* 720 sq. mi.; *pop.* (1973 est.): ca. 834,000. Religion: ca. 50% Hindu, ca. 33% Christian (ca. 240,000 RCs; ca. 11,000 Ch. of Eng.; ca. 3,000 other Prots.), ca. 14% Muslim, ca. 2% Buddhist, ca. 1% other. RCm introd. 1722 by Lazarists.*

Maurus, Rabanus. See *Rabanus Maurus.*

Mausbach, Joseph (1861–1931). B. Wipperfeld, near Wipperfürth, Ger.; RC prof. moral theol. and apologetics Münster. Works include *Katholische Moraltheologie.*

Max Müller, Friedrich. See *Müller, Friedrich Max(imilian).*

Maxentius, Marcus Aurelius Valerius (d. 312). Son of Maximian*; son-in-law of Galerius*; Roman emp. 306–312; proclaimed Caesar by praetorians; drove Galerius out of It.; defeated by Constantine* I.

Maximian (Marcus Aurelius Valerius Maximianus; surname Herculius; Maximianus I; d. 310). Father of Maxentius*; b. Pannonia, It.; Roman emp. with Diocletian* 286–305, with Maxentius 306–308; persecuted Christians. See also *Maurice; Persecutions of Christians,* 4.

Maximilian (Marmilian; ca. 274–295). B. Theveste, Numidia; martyr; allegedly executed at Theveste for refusing service in Roman army.

Maximilian I (1459–1519). King of Ger. 1486–1519; Holy Roman emp. 1493–1519.

Maximilla. See *Montanism.*

Maximinus, Gaius Julius Verus (Caius; Maximin; surnamed Thrax [i. e., the Thracian]; 173–238). Roman emp. 235–238. See also *Persecution of Christians,* 3.

Maximinus, Galerius Valerius (originally Daza; d. 314). Nephew of Galerius*; b. Illyria; Caesar 305; Roman emp. 308–314. See also *Persecution of Christians,* 4.

Maximus the Confessor (ca. 580–622). B. Constantinople; abbot of monastery of Scutari, near Chrysopolis (Üsküdar), in Asia, across the Bosporus from Constantinople; prominent opponent of Monothelitism* in Afr. and at Rome.

Maximus the Cynic (4th c.). Consecrated bp. Constantinople in opposition to Gregory* of Nazianzus; tried to combine Cynic philos. with Nicene Creed.

May, Johann Heinrich (Mayus; Majus; Mai; 1653–1719). Luth. theol.; b. Pforzheim, Ger.; pupil of A. Calov(ius)*; prof. Heb. Durlach 1684, orientalism and theol. Giessen 1688; supt. Giessen and Alsfeld 1690; follower of J. Cocceius* and P. J. Spener*; opposed orthodox scholasticism; favored a practical covenant theology. Pub. a Heb. Bible.

May Laws (Falk Laws). Drawn up by Paul Ludwig Adalbert Falk (1828–1900; Ger. Minister of Pub. Worship and Educ. 1872); enacted by the Prussian diet May 1873; condemned 1875 by Pius IX (see *Popes,* 28) in encyclical *Quod numquam;* an expression of Ger. nationalism aimed at RCm, but put all relations bet. ch. and state on a new basis. See also *Kulturkampf.*

Maya. See *Mexico,* B.

Mayer, Frederick Emanuel (Nov. 5, 1892–July 20, 1954). B. New Wells, Mo.; educ. Conc. Coll., Milwaukee, Wis., and Conc. Sem., St. Louis, Mo. Pastor Sherrard and Coal Valley, Ill., 1915–18; Kewanee, Ill., 1918–26. Prof. Conc. Theol. Sem., Springfield, Ill., 1926–37; Conc. Sem., St. Louis, Mo., 1937–54. Ed. *Concordia Theological Monthly;* coauthor *Popular Symbolics;* other works include *To Sign or Not to Sign the Catholic Prenuptial Contract; Jehovah's Witnesses; American Churches: Beliefs and Practices; The Proper Distinction Between Law and Gospel and the Terminology Visible and Invisible Church; The Religious Bodies of America; The Story of Bad Boll.*

Mayer, Johann. See *Eck, Johann.*

Mayer, Johann Friedrich (1650–1712). Luth. theol.; b. Leipzig, Ger.; educ. Leipzig and Strasbourg; pastor Leipzig; supt. Leisnig and Grimma; prof. Wittenberg 1684; pastor Hamburg 1686 and prof. Kiel 1687; gen. supt. and prof. Greifswald 1701; opposed Pietism* because it threatened *sola* fide;* worked for better hymnbook and better catechetical and homiletical training.

Mayflower Compact. Agreement adopted by Pilgrims (Plymouth colonists) at Cape Cod, Mass., Nov. 11, 1620; states that the purposes of the colony to be founded included the glory of God and advancement of the Christian faith.

Mayhew, Experience (1673–1758). B. Martha's Vineyard, Mass.; miss. Martha's Vineyard for the Society* for the Propagation of the Gospel in New England. Tr. Ps and Jn for Indians; other works include *Indian Converts; Grace Defended.*

Maywood Theological Seminary. See *Lutheran School of Theology at Chicago; Ministry, Education of,* X I; *United Lutheran Church, Synods of,* 7.

Mazarin, Jules (It.: Giulio Mazarini; 1602–61). Fr. cardinal and statesman; b. Pescina, It., of Sicilian parentage; educ. Rome (by Jesuits) and Alcalá de Henares, Sp.; infantry captain in army of the papal states; in papal diplomatic service; vice-legate at Avignon; naturalized Frenchman 1639; cardinal 1641; succeeded A. J. du P. de Richelieu* as prime minister 1642; enlarged Fr. territory at Peace of Westphalia* 1648; maintained conciliatory policy toward Huguenots*; sided with Innocent X (see *Popes,* 23) against Jansenists (see *Jansenism*). See also *Mazarin Bible.*

Mazarin Bible. Bible found in library of J. Mazarin*; believed by some to have been printed by J. Gutenberg* ca. 1455; the 1st important book produced with movable type in Eur.

Mazdaism. See *Zoroastrianism.*

Mazvydas, Martynas. See *Lithuania,* 2.

M'Taggart. Alphabetized as if spelled MacTaggart.

Mc-. Alphabetized as if spelled Mac-.

Mead, Joseph. See *Mede, Joseph.*

Means of Grace. See *Grace, Means of.*

Mecca. See *Islam,* 3; *Muhammad.*

Mechanism. Term used in philos., biology, physics, and psychol. to denote a theory which holds that natural processes, esp. those of life, are mechanically determined and are to be explained by laws of physics and chemistry; it has no fixed meaning; its meaning was often modified by its antithesis (e.g., supernaturalism,* teleology,* vitalism).

Mechitar (Mekhitar; other variant spellings; "Consoler"; name adopted 1691 when he became a monk; bap. name: Peter Manoug [Manug]; 1676–1749). B. Sivas (Sebaste), Turkey in Asia; RC priest 1696; founded Mechitarists 1701 at Constantinople; worked for educ. among Armenians* and union of Armenians and RCs. Works include a commentary on Mt; Armenian catechism, grammar, and dictionary; Armenian Bible tr.

Mechitarists. See *Mechitar.*

Mechthild of Hackeborn (Mechtild; Matilda; also "of Helfta"; ca. 1240–ca. 1298). Mem. of the family of the lords of Hackeborn; Cistercian nun and mystic; trained by her sister, Gertrude of Hackeborn (see *Gertrude,* 2); dir. cloister school at Helfta [Helpede], near Eisenach, Ger.; teacher of Gertrude the Great (see *Gertrude,* 1), who ed. *Liber specialis gratiae,* an account of Mechthild's alleged revelations emphasizing devotion to the sacred* heart of Jesus.

Mechthild of Magdeburg (ca. 1210–ca. 1282/94). Mystic; b. Saxony; became a Beguine (see *Beghards and Beguines*) at Magdeburg 1230; collected works, entitled *Das fliessende Licht der Gottheit,* exerted strong influence on Ger. mysticism.

Mecum. See *Myconius, Friedrich.*

Mede, Joseph (Mead; 1586–1638). Angl. Biblical scholar; b. Berden, Essex, Eng.; educ. Cambridge; fellow Christ's Coll., Cambridge, 1613. Works include *Clavis apocalyptica; The Apostasy of the Latter Times.*

Mediating Theology (mediation theol.; Vermittlungstheologie). Term occasionally used loosely for any theol. that tries to est. contact bet., or to fuse, diverging tendencies. In a specific sense the Ger. term is traced to *Theologische Studien und Kritiken,* a periodical est. 1828 by K. Ullmann* and F. W. K. Umbreit,* together with J. K. L. Gieseler,* G. C. F. Lücke,* and K. I. Nitzsch,* to mediate bet. modern science and concepts of Christianity, the free scientific spirit and the peculiarly Christian spirit. The philos. of G. W. F. Hegel* and theol. of F. D. E. Schleiermacher* were prominent in the early period. Mediating theol. was criticized for its support of the Prussian* Union and unsatisfactory conclusions, but it stimulated study in many areas and affected subsequent Ger. theol. See also *Dorner,* 1.

Medical Missions. 1. Med-evangelistic work is a fruit of faith (Gl 5:6; 6:10).

2. LCMS resolved 1965 to "affirm that the church is God's mission to the whole man. Wherever a Christian as God's witness encounters the man to whom God sends him, he meets someone whose body, soul, and mind are related in one totality. Therefore Christians, individually and corporately, prayerfully seek to serve the needs of the total man. Christians bring the Good News of the living Christ to dying men. They bring men instruction in all useful knowledge. They help and befriend their neighbor on our small planet in every bodily need. They help their neighbor to improve and protect his property and business by bringing him economic help and enabling him to earn his daily bread in dignity and self-respect. Christians minister to the needs of the whole man, not because they have forgotten the witness of the Gospel but because they remember it. They know that the demonstration of their faith in Christ adds power to its proclamation" (*Proceedings,* p. 81).

3. Med. missionaries hold that all good gifts and abilities are from God and that all believers are called into the work of the ch. Thus the ministry of healing can and should be practiced in many forms, e.g., through Christian physicians in private practice, in govt. service in overseas countries, in full-time ch. work as med. missionaries; through first aid work by wives of missionaries. The aim and purpose of med. miss. work is the same as that of any other special Christian ministry: witness to Christ (Acts 1:8).

4. The Tambaram report (see *Missionary Conferences*) of the section on the Christian Ministry of Health and Healing, dealing with the basis of the medical ministry, begins: "The sanction and compelling motive of this ministry are found in the very nature of God, which is revealed in Jesus Christ as redeeming love. God's redemptive purpose embraces the entire range of man's spiritual, mental and physical need, and offers the one sure hope for a world in which sin and suffering abound. Through the Church, which is His body, the living Christ ministers to the needs of men. . . . As He identified Himself with the need and suffering of the world, so must His disciples identify themselves with that need and suffering, that the redeeming love of God may be mediated through them to the lives of others. . . . The ministry of health and healing belongs to the essence of the Gospel and is, therefore, an integral part of the mission to which Christ has called and is calling His Church." (Quoted in P. V. Benjamin, "A New Outlook in Christian Medical Work," *The International Review of Missions,* XXVIII [1939], 562–563)

5. The Division of World Mission and Evangelism of the WCC held a consultation on the healing ministry in the mission of the ch., in Tübingen, Ger., 1964, at the request of the Dept. of World Mission of the LWF and with its collaboration. The *Report* of the consultation, p. 2, describes the relationship of Christian understanding of healing to salvation: "The Christian understanding of healing begins from its place in the ministry of Jesus. There it was a sign of the breaking into human life of the powers of the Kingdom of God, and of the de-throning of the powers of evil. The health which was its fruit was . . . an involvement with Jesus in the victorious encounter of the Kingdom of God with the powers of evil." (Quoted in C. H. Germany, "The Healing Ministry: Report on the Tübingen Consultation," *The International Review of Missions,* LIII [1964], 471)

6. Modern med. missions go back to 1730, when Dr. Caspar Gottlieb Schlegelmilch (b. Sagan [Zagan], Silesia) was sent by the Dan.-Halle Miss. (see *Missions,* 5-6) to Tranquebar, India; he died Aug. 30, 19 days after arrival. Other doctors followed. But the real upsurge came ca. 100 yrs. later under leadership of J. Scudder,* P. Parker,* D. Livingstone,* et al.

7. LCMS resolved 1911 to allow its For. Miss. Bd. to arrange for placing suitable doctors in med. missions, as means permit, and to exercise its judgment as to time and place (*Synodal-Bericht,* p. 128). Under sponsorship of LCMS women's socs. L. E. Ellermann* went to India 1913 and est. a dispensary at Bargur (Barugur), Madras. Other clinics and small hospitals in miss. fields have been made possible by special gifts from individuals, congs., et al., e. g., LWML and Wheat* Ridge Foundation.

8. Most LCMS med. miss. work has been done in New Guinea, S India, and Nigeria; other fields include the Philippine Islands, Hong Kong, Japan, and Guatemala.

9. Luth. chs. in the US give med. missions prominence in their work. WRB

See also *Lutheran Medical Mission Association.*

Medici. It. family active esp. 14th–18th c. in Florence, Tuscany; merchants, bankers, art patrons, civil and religious leaders. 1. *Cosimo* (Cosmo; 1389–1464). Father of 2; formed the library which later grew into the Biblioteca Mediceo-Laurenziana. 2. *Lorenzo* (1449–92). "The Magnificent"; father of Catherine* de Médicis (1533 m. Henry II; see also *France,* 8, 9) and Leo X (see *Popes,* 20); initiated movement for revival of nat. It. literature. 3. See *Clement VII.*

Medici, Giovanni Angelo. See *Pius IV.*

Medieval Church. See *Eastern Orthodox Churches,* 2–5; *Western Christianity 500–1500.*

Medina. See *Muhammad.*

Medler, Nikolaus (Nicolaus; Nicholas; 1502–51). B. Hof, Ger.; educ. Wittenberg; teacher Arnstadt and Hof; school rector Eger ca. 1524; teacher and preacher Hof ca. 1527/29–31; tutor and preacher Wittenberg 1531–36; pastor and reformer Naumburg 1536; supt. Brunswick 1545–51; court preacher Bernburg 1551. M. Luther* is said to have regarded him, V. Dietrich,* and J. Spangenberg* as his 3 true disciples.

Medley, Samuel (1738–99). Bap. cleric and hymnist; b. Cheshunt, Hertfordshire, Eng.; pastor Watford 1767 (ordained 1768), Liverpool 1772. Hymns include "I Know That My Redeemer Lives"; "Awake, My Soul, to Joyful Lays."

Mees, Theophilus Martin Konrad (July 13, 1848–July 25, 1923). Educator; mem. Ev. Luth. Joint Syn. of Ohio* and Other States; b. Columbus, Ohio. Educ. Conc. Coll., Fort Wayne, Ind.; Conc. Sem., St. Louis, Mo.; Berlin and Leipzig, Germany. Prof. Capital U., Columbus, 1875–88, 1903–23; Ev. Luth. Theol. Sem.,

Columbus, 1903–23. Pres. Teachers' Sem., Woodville, Ohio, 1888–1903. Asst. ed. *Theologische Zeitblätter–Theological Magazine;* other works include *Dogmengeschichtlicher Beitrag zur Entwickelung der Lehre von der Gnadenwahl innerhalb der lutherischen Kirche von 1522 bis 1580.*

Megander, Kaspar (Grossmann; 1495–1545). B. Zurich, Switz.; educ. Basel; Zwinglian; taught at the exegetical school founded by Zwingli; prof. Bern 1528; dismissed 1537; cathedral dean Zurich. Helped write 1st Helvetic Confession (see *Reformed Confessions,* A 6).

Megarian School of Philosophy. See *Euclid(es) of Megara.*

Megerle, Hans Ulrich. See *Abraham a Sancta Clara.*

Megingoz (d. not later than 768 AD). Co-worker of Boniface*; became bp. Würzburg ca. 751/754.

Meiganga, Lutheran Seminary at. See *Africa,* F 7.

Meinardus, Ludwig Siegfried (1827–96). Composer, teacher, musicologist; b. Hooksiel, Oldenburg, Ger.; teacher at Dresden Conservatory 1865; teacher and music critic Hamburg 1874; court organist Bielefeld 1887. Works include choral ballades, 2 symphonies, and oratorios: *Simon Petrus; Gideon; König Salomo; Luther in Worms; Emmaus.*

Meinhard (Meinhart). See *Estonia,* 1.

Meinhold, Johann Wilhelm (1797–1851). Half brother of K. Meinhold*; hymnist; b. Netzelkow, Usedom Is., off the coast of Pomerania, Ger.; educ. Greifswald; school rector Usedom 1820; pastor Coserow 1821, Crummin 1828, both on Usedom; pastor Rehwinkel, near Stargard, Pomerania, Ger.; resigned 1850, partly in protest against the 1848–49 revolution in Ger., partly because of his increasing leaning to RCm. Hymns include "Guter Hirt, du hast gestillt"; "O Bethlehem! O Bethlehem!"

Meinhold, Johann(es) Friedrich Hellmut (Hans; 1861–1937). Son of K. H. J. Meinhold*; b. Cammin (Kammin), Pomerania, Ger.; educ. Leipzig, Berlin, Greifswald, and Tübingen; prof. Greifswald and Bonn. Collaborator in *Kurzgefasster Kommentar,* ed. H. L. Strack* and O. Zöckler*; other works include *Die Weisheit Israels in Spruch, Sage und Dichtung.*

Meinhold, Karl Heinrich Joachim (1813–88). Half brother of J. W. Meinhold*; father of J. F. H. Meinhold*; b. Liepe, on Usedom Is., off the coast of Pomerania, Ger.; educ. Greifswald and Halle; pastor Kolzow, on the is. of Wollin, Pomerania, 1838; supt. Cammin (Kammin) 1851; helped strengthen Lutheranism in Prussia.

Meinrad (late 8th c.–861). Hermit; b. Sülichgau, Württemberg, Ger.; Benedictine monk and priest Reichenau, S. Baden, Ger.; eventually settled at the place where the abbey of Einsiedeln, Switz., of which he is patron, was founded 937.

Meiser, Hans (1881–1956). B. Nürnberg, Ger.; pastor Munich 1915; dir. Nürnberg sem. 1922; bp. Luth. ch. in Bav. 1933; took part in Kirchenkampf*; championed Luth. Confessions; leader of VELKD 1949.

Meisner, Balthasar (1587–1626). B. Dresden, Ger.; educ. Wittenberg, Giessen, Strasbourg, and Tübingen; prof. ethics 1611, theol. 1613 Wittenberg. Works include *Philosophia sobria.*

Meisner, Johann(es) (1615–84). B. Torgau, Ger.; educ. Wittenberg; rector Torgau; prof. theol. Wittenberg 1649; irenic theol.; his distinction of fundamental and nonfundamental arts. led to controversy with A. Calov(ius).*

Meister, Christoph Georg Ludwig (1738–1811). Poet; b. Halle, Ger.; educ. Halle; rector 1761, preacher 1763 Ballenstedt; Anhalt-Bernburg consistorial assessor, and pastor, Waldau, 1770; at Altenburg, Anhalt, near Bernburg, 1772; pastor 1774, prof. 1778 Duisburg; in Bremen as preacher and Gymnasium prof. theol. 1784, pastor 1796, Gymnasium rector 1802. Hymns include "Heil ihm, dem Todesüberwinder"; "Lass mir die Feier deiner Leiden."

Mekum. See *Myconius, Friedrich.*

Mel, Conrad (1666–1733). Ref. theol.; b. Gudensberg, Ger.; educ. Rinteln, Bremen, and Gröningen; preacher 1690 Mietau (Mitau; Mitava; Jelgava; Yelgava), Courland (Kurland), Latvia, and 1692 Memel, Lith.; court preacher 1697, prof. 1702 Königsberg (Kaliningrad), Prussia; followed pietistic methods of P. J. Spener*; noted as devotional writer.

Melanchthon, Philipp (Melancthon; Melanthon; Schwar(t)zerd; Schwarzert; Feb. 16, 1497–Apr. 19, 1560). B. Bretten, Lower Palatinate (Baden), Ger.; educ. Heidelberg and Tübingen; ed. classics and served as corrector in printery of Thomas Anshelm at Tübingen 1514; gained praise of D. Erasmus* for style 1515; became known as a humanist (see also *Humanism, Sixteenth-Century German*); wrote one of the prefaces to J. Reuchlin,* *Clarorum virorum epistolae,* engaged in subsequent controversy, and was cited in *Epistolae obscurorum virorum* (see *Letters of Obscure Men*); issued Gk. grammar 1518; recommended by Reuchlin for U. of Wittenberg and arrived there Aug. 25, 1518; won by M. Luther* for the cause of theol.; abandoned plans to issue an edition of Aristotle; studied and taught theol. and other subjects; his lectures were attended by hundreds and sometimes outstripped Luther's in popularity. The movement of the Zwickau* Prophets and the Peasants'* War emphasized the need for an educ. program to implement the Luth. Reformation.* Melanchthon was prominent in devising methods and planning an educ. process incorporating classic languages and philos. as basic for specialized vocational studies. The princes were the patrons of the organized program of instruction. Melanchthon was prominent in the preparation of *Articuli de quibus egerunt per visitatores in regione Saxoniae.* Every parish in electoral Saxony was surveyed and religious and moral life supervised. Melanchthon strongly opposed H. Zwingli's* doctrine of the Lord's Supper at Marburg 1529. Guided by Luther, Melanchthon prepared the AC and the Ap (see also *Lutheran Confessions,* A 2, 3; B 3; C 1; *Union Movements,* 3).

In 1521 Melanchthon issued *Loci communes rerum theologicarum seu Hypotyposes theologicae* (variant titles: *Loci communes theologici; Loci theologici; Loci praecipui theologici;* see also *Dogmatics,* A 3); the 1535 and later eds. increasingly reflected synergism.* Melanchthon had a prominent role in formulating the Wittenberg* Concord. The Colloquy of Worms* further revealed Melanchthon's trend to concession, evident also in his approval of the Leipzig Interim (see *Interim,* II). But he joined others against A. Osiander* (1498–1552) in the Osiandrian* Controversy. RRC

See also *Lutheran Confessions,* A 5; Pack, Otto von; *Philippists; Praeceptor Germaniae; Regensburg Conference; Synergistic Controversy; Visitations, Church.*

G. Ellinger, *Philipp Melanchthon* (Berlin, 1902); H. Engelland, *Melanchthon, Glauben und Handeln* (Munich, 1931); K. Hartfelder, *Philipp Melanchthon als Praeceptor Germaniae* (Berlin, 1889); P. F. Joachimsen (Joachimsohn), *Sozialethik des Luthertums* (Munich, 1927); C. L. Manschreck, *Melanchthon: The Quiet Reformer* (New York, 1958); *Melanchthon on Christian Doctrine: Loci communes 1555,* ed. and tr. C. L. Manschreck (New York, 1965); *Melanchthon: Selected Writings,* ed. E. E. Flack and L. J. Satre, tr. C. L. Hill (Minneapolis, 1962); W. Maurer, *Der junge Melanchthon zwischen Humanismus und Reformation,* 2 vols. (Göttingen, 1967, 1969); C. Schmidt, *Philipp Melanchthon* (Elberfeld, Ger., 1861); G. Kisch, *Melanchthons Rechts- und Soziallehre* (Berlin, 1967).

Melanchthon Synod. See *United Lutheran Church, Synods of,* 11.

Melanesia ("Black Islands," so called from the color of the natives). Islands NE of Australia, including Bismarck Archipelago, Solomon Islands, Santa Cruz Islands, Banks Islands, New Hebrides, New Caledonia, Loyalty Islands, Fiji Islands; New* Guinea sometimes included. Belief in *mana* (see *Primitive Religion*), animistic spirits, magic, ancestral ghosts, and sorcery dominates religious life. Meth. missionaries came to the area 1834. The Melanesian Miss. (Angl.) was founded 1849. Presbs., RCs, PEMS, et al. are also active.

Melania. 1. The Elder (ca. 345–ca. 410). Grandmother of 2; Roman aristocratic lady; adopted ascetic life; helped found monastery on Mount of Olives, near Jerusalem. See also *Rufinus, Tyrannius.* 2. The Younger (ca. 383-ca. 438). Granddaughter of 1; founded convents.

Melchiorites. See *Hofmann, Melchior.*

Melchites (Melkites; from Syriac *malka,* "king," and related form meaning "imperial"). Christians of Syria and Egypt who rejected Monophysitism* and remained in union with the imperial see of Constantinople. Gk. Uniate chs. of Syria, Egypt, and Palestine are also called Melchites.

Meletian Schisms (Melitian). 1. Egyptian; arose ca. 305; its effects lasted till the 8th c.; resulted from encroachments of Meletius of Lycopolis (Melitius; fl. 303–325; d. ca. 325; bp. Lycopolis, Egypt) on metropolitan rights of Peter* of Alexandria. 2. Antiochian (362–ca. 415). Originated when followers of Eustathius* of Antioch consecrated Paulinus (Paulinos; d. probably 388) counter-bp. to Meletius* of Antioch. See also *Mark, Liturgy of Saint.*

Meletius of Antioch (Melitius; d. 381). B. Melitene (Malatya; Malatia), Lesser Armenia (Cilicia), Turkey; at first Arian; after election as bp. Antioch ca. 361 professed Nicene orthodoxy; pres. Council of Constantinople* 381. See also *Meletian Schisms,* 2.

Meletius of Lycopolis. See *Meletian Schisms,* 1.

Melin, Hans Magnus (1805–77). B. Swed.; prof. theol. Lund; opposed D. F. Strauss.* Works include *Den Heliga Skrift, i en fraan grundtexten utförd, efter Lutherska Kirkobibeln lämpad öfwersättning; Föreläsninger öfwer Jesu befwerne.*

Meliorism. Belief that the world tends to become better and that man can contribute to the betterment; seeks a middle course bet. optimism and pessimism.

Melitian Schisms. See *Meletian Schisms.*

Melitius. See *Meletius.*

Melito (d. probably before AD 190). Bp. Sardis (Sardes); Gk. apologist. Most works lost, including an apology addressed to Marcus* Aurelius; remaining fragments include a homily on the passion of Christ. See also *Apologists,* 7.

Melius, Peter (grecized from Hung. Juhász, "shepherd"; ca. 1536–72). Ref. theol. and reformer; b. Horhi, Somogy Co., Hung.; educ. Wittenberg; supt. Debrecen 1558, which he made center of Ref. activity; active in exegesis, Bible tr., and writing of confessions.

Melkites. See *Melchites.*

Melville, Andrew (Melvill; Melvin[us]; 1545–1622). Presb. reformer; b. Baldovy, near Montrose, Forfarshire (Angus), Scot.; educ. Saint Andrews, Scot., and Paris and Poitiers, Fr.; taught at Geneva, Switz.; principal Glasgow U. 1574, St. Mary's Coll. (St. Andrews) 1580; prof. Biblical theol. Sedan, Fr., 1611. Helped reconstruct Aberdeen U. 1575 and encouraged study of languages, science, philos., and theol.; imprisoned 1607–11 for opposing Episcopalianism. Helped write 2d *Book of Discipline* (see *Discipline, Books of,* 2).

Melville, Herman (1819–91). Novelist; b. NYC; brought up in Dutch Ref. Ch. Works, which include *Moby Dick,* portray disillusionment and skepticism, ending in frustration.

Memling, Hans (Jean; Jan Memlinc; Jan van Memmelynghe; Hemling and Hemmelinck now gen. regarded as false forms; perhaps ca. 1430/40–ca. 1494). Flemish painter; b. probably Seligenstadt (some say Mainz; or Mömlingen, near Mainz and Seligenstadt [though that may be where the family came from]; or Constanz; or Bruges); reputation rests mainly on portraiture and on representations of Mary; his art is more one of religious conviction than earthly realism. Works include *Last Judgment: Adoration of the Magi.*

Menahem ben Saruk. See *Lexicons,* A.

Menaion (pl. Menaia; from Gk. *men,* "month"). In the E Orthodox Ch., the name given to all or each of 12 liturgical books (1 per mo.) containing the variable parts for immovable feasts, with the annual cycle beginning in Sept. See also *Menologion; Synaxarion.*

Menas (ca. 3d–4th c.). Egyptian martyr whose story was probably fused with that of a Phrygian soldier martyred 296 under Diocletian*; cult spread to Constantinople, Rome, Gaul, and Ger.

Mencel, Hieronymus (Menzel; 1517–90). Luth. theol.; b. Schweidnitz, Prussia (later Swidnica, Poland); supt. Mansfeld 1560; first supported M. Flacius* Illyricus; later, influenced by J. Wigand,* opposed Flacianism. Works include *Lehre von der Erb-Sünde; Hochzeit Predigten; Erklerung der Weinmarischen Bekentnis halben.*

Mencius (Chinese *Meng-tse* or *Mêng-tzu;* ca. 372–ca. 289 BC). Philos.; b. state of Lu (now Shantung province), China; studied under grandson of Confucius*; professional teacher; served briefly as govt. official; traveled ca. 40 yrs. from state to state advocating reform and expounding Confucianism.* Taught original goodness of human nature endowed with feeling of love, righteousness, propriety, and wisdom. Filial piety is basis of virtue. Govt. (which comes from God) should serve the people (most important element in nation). Works include *Meng Tsu Shu (Book of Mencius),* one of the Four Books of Chinese classics. See also *Chinese Philosophy,* 3.

Mendaeans. See *Mandaeans.*

Mendel, Gregor Johann (1822–84). B. Heinzendorf (Hyncice), near Odrau (Odry), Austrian Silesia (now Czechoslovakia); abbot of Augustinian monastery at Brünn, Austria (now Brno, Czechoslovakia); discovered Mendel's law, a principle in genetics.

Mendelssohn, Moses (Moses ben Menahem Mendel; Moses Dessau; 1729–86). Grandfather of J. L. F. Mendelssohn-Bartholdy*; b. Dessau, Ger.; Jewish philos.; friend of G. E. Lessing.* Tried to win the educated class among the people for rational religion, tolerance, and good taste; popularized the philos. of C. v. Wolff*; interpreted Judaism with Eur. philos. concepts; held that unity (as beauty) is only enjoyed in feeling and experience; developed "moral theol." proof for immortality of the soul; tried to show the rational character of Judaism; held that God gave the Jews only a law, not a religion, and demands works, not faith. See also *Haskalah.*

Mendelssohn-Bartholdy, Jakob Ludwig Felix (1809–47). Grandson of M. Mendelssohn*; composer; b. Hamburg, Ger.; his father's brother-in-law, Jakob Salomon, had adopted the name Bartholdy on acquiring land formerly owned by a man named Bartholdy; when J. L. F. Mendelssohn's father became Luth. and had his children bap., he, at the suggestion of Jakob Salomon Bartholdy, added Bartholdy to the name Mendelssohn, to distinguish the Christian Mendelssohns from those who adhered to Jewish belief. Child prodigy at 9. Led revival of works of J. S. Bach* 1829. Works include 5 symphonies, including *Reformation Symphony;* symphony cantata *Lob-*

gesang (Hymn of Praise); oratorios *St. Paul* and *Elijah;* organ sonatas.

Mendicant Friars (from Lat. *mendicare,* "to beg"). Religious orders (including Franciscans,* Dominicans,* Carmelites,* Augustinian* Hermits, Servites*) which originally renounced common as well as individual possessions. The Council of Trent* (Sess. XXV, Concerning Regulars and Nuns, chap. 3) permitted most mendicant orders to hold goods in common *("exceptis domibus fratrum sancti Francisci Capucinorum et eorum, qui Minorum de observantia vocantur":* "except the houses of the Capuchin brethren of St. Francis and [the houses] of those called Minor Observants"); papal concessions have been extended also to Franciscan conventuals.

Mendota Resolutions. Resolutions adopted by the ALC Oct. 1942 Mendota, Ill. 1. One reads in part: "Whereas, though these documents – the Pittsburgh Agreement on the one hand, and the Brief Statement and Declaration on the other – differ in wording, yet both express the true position of the American Lutheran Church; and

"Whereas, the United Lutheran Church in America has adopted the Pittsburgh Agreement; and the Declaration of our Commissioners in connection with the Brief Statement has found acceptance within the Missouri Synod . . .

"Therefore Be It Resolved, that the American Lutheran Church declare its readiness to establish pulpit and altar fellowship with either or both of these honorable church bodies on the basis of their full and wholehearted acceptance of and adherence to either of these documents, in the hope that the existing obstacles may be removed and that such pulpit and altar fellowship may be declared at an early date; and therefore that the Commission on Lutheran unity be continued."

2. Another supported formation of an All-Am. Luth. Conv. which would avoid the problems of pulpit and altar fellowship but would provide joint testimony "for the pure Gospel of Jesus Christ and for the true Christian faith as confessed by the Evangelical Lutheran Church"; foster Luth. unity; promote cooperative efforts in missions, higher educ., welfare and charity work, and pub. Christian literature: aid Luths. in distress; defend its mems. against encroachments on religious and civil liberties.

See also *Louisville Resolution.*

Ménégoz, Louis Eugène (1838–1921 [1920?]). Fr. Luth. theol.; b. Algolsheim, near Breisach, Alsace; educ. Strasbourg, Erlangen, Berlin, Halle, and Marburg; vice-pres. Luth. theol. Sem. Paris 1866; prof. dogmatics Sorbonne, Paris 1877; exponent of fideism.*

Meng-tse (Mêng-tzu). See *Mencius.*

Menge, Hermann (1841–1939). Philol.; b. Seesen, Brunswick, Ger.; educ. Brunswick and Göttingen; dir. Gymnasium Sangerhausen and Wittstock; tr. Bible into Ger.

Mengering, Arnold (1596–1647). B. Halle, Ger.; educ. Wittenberg and Jena; loyal and conscientious Luth. pastor; writings give insight into soc. and pol. conditions during Thirty* Years' War.

Mengs, Anton Raphael (1728–79). Artist and critic; b. Aussig (Ústí), Bohemia; neoclassicist; worked at Vatican 1769–72. Works include *Holy Family; Nativity; Annunciation.*

Menius, Justus (Jodocus [Jost] Menig; 1499 [1494?]–1558). Reformer of Thuringia; b. Fulda, Ger.; educ. Erfurt and Wittenberg; early follower of M. Luther*; supt. Eisenach 1529; took part in ch. visitations, the 1529 Colloquy of Marburg (see *Lutheran Confessions,* A 2), the Feb. 1537 meeting of the Schmalkaldic* League, and the 1540 Hagenau* Colloquy; signed the 1536 Wittenberg Concord and had F. Myconius* sign the Schmalkaldic Arts. for him; wrote extensively against Anabaps., his treatment becoming standard for Luth. polemics; defended G. Major* and taught that beginning of new life in believers is necessary for salvation. See also *Lutheran Confessions,* B 1.

G. L. Schmidt, *Justus Menius, Der Reformator Thüringens,* 2 vols. (Gotha, 1867).

Menken, Gottfried (1768–1831). B. Bremen, Ger.; educ. Jena and Duisburg; Prot. pastor Uedem (near Cleve), Frankfurt, Wetzlar, and (since 1802) Bremen; influenced by J. A. Bengel* et al.; developed a biblicism (Bible as hist. harmonious whole) in opposition to moralism of enlightenment* and ecclesiastical confessionalism of orthodoxy; kingdom of God was prominent in his theol.

Menno Simons (ca. 1492/96–ca. 1559/61). B. Wittmarsum, near Bolsward, Friesland, Neth.; father's first name: Simon, which became the son's patronymic: Simon's (zoon); RC priest Utrecht 1524; in doubt regarding transubstantiation and under reform influences; priest Witmarsum 1531–36; left RC Ch. 1536; joined Anabap. movement 1537 and became its leader in the Low Countries. See also *Mennonite Churches.*

Mennonite Churches. 1. Mennonites (named after Menno* Simons) are spiritual descendants of 16th c. Anabaps. (see also *Baptist Churches,* 2). Early Anabap. groups related to Mennonites were known by various names. Anabaps. in Switz. and S Ger. came to be called Swiss Brethren; leaders included G. Blaurock,* K. Grebel,* F. Manz,* P. Marbeck,* and M. Sattler.* Official name in the Neth.: Doopsgezind (Doopsgesinde; Doopsgesint; Doopsgezinden; Doopsghesinde). They have also been called Wederdoper (Wiedertäufer). Followers of J. Huter* are called Hutterian Brethren (Hutterites; Huterites). United Missionary Ch. is the name adopted 1947 by a US and Can. group called up to that time Mennonite Brethren in Christ Ch. Other groups have other names.

2. Mennonites entertain widely divergent doctrinal views but agree on theol. principles summarized in the 18 arts. of the 1632 Dordrecht* Confession.

Formal Principle: Acc. to Mennonite theol., the source of Christian knowledge is the Bible; but at the same time the true understanding of saving truth is said to come from a mystical experience of Christ.

Mennonites strongly emphasize the immediate operation of the Holy Spirit (enthusiasm*), who is said to "guide the saints into all truth." The Holy Spirit is viewed as "the inner word" enabling Christians to understand the Bible. Mennonites insist that without this inner word, or inner light, the Bible is a dead letter and a dark lantern.

Material Principle: The cen. doctrine can probably most appropriately be called "mystical pietism." The pronounced mystical spiritualism, which seems to dominate the whole doctrinal system, appears most clearly in emphasis on the outward purity of the ch. Mennonites often claim affinity to Novatians (see *Novatianism*), Paulicians,* Albigenses,* Waldenses,* and similar groups, because these stressed abstinence from the world and advocated a life of self-abnegation. Mennonites believe that the ch. must be a visible organization of regenerated persons and that it must be kept holy by the strict exercise of the ban.

Mystical pietism becomes the mother of a paradox: complete tolerance of conflicting and even mutually exclusive doctrinal views, and violent dissensions in matters of cultus. Mennonites offer shelter to "enthusiasts" of the Quaker type; to Socinians, who deny the doctrine of the Trin. and teach that personal piety is the essence of Christianity; to Pelagians and Arminians; to spiritualists and mystics; and to Quietists, who see in faith an intense consciousness of God without a definite knowledge about God.

3. The many schisms among Mennonites were occasioned largely by divergent views on discipline. But in recent yrs. the separate bodies or agencies have moved toward closer cooperation. Am. Mennonites may be grouped: conservatives, a cen. group, and liberals.

a. Conservatives are represented in Am. esp. by the *Old Order Amish Ch.,* named after J. Amman* and derived from Amish who came to Am. beginning ca. 1720; they use hooks and eyes instead of buttons, hold worship services in private houses, and use the Ger. language. The *Conservative Mennonite Conference* (called *Conservative Amish Mennonite Ch.* till 1954) separated gradually from the Old Order Amish Ch.; they introd. meetinghouses and the use of Eng. in worship. The *Church of God in Christ (Mennonite)* was organized 1859 in Ohio to reest. order and discipline. The *Old Order (Wisler) Mennonite Ch.* traces its origin to an 1870 separation of Mennonites in protest against use of Eng. in services and the introd. of Sun. schools. The *Reformed Mennonite Ch.,* organized 1812 Lancaster Co., Pa., tries to hold closely to the NT and believes that there is but one ch. of believers united in love and doctrine. The *Beachy Amish Mennonite Chs.* separated from the Old Order Amish Ch. over a period of yrs. The small *Stauffer Mennonite Ch.* was organized 1845 Lancaster, Pa. The *Ev. Mennonite Ch., Inc:* (formerly *Defenseless Mennonite Ch. of N. Am.*) separated from the Amish and organized ca. 1865 Adams Co., Ind. *Hutterian Brethren,* named after J. Huter,* have groups in S. Dak., Minn., Mont., Wash., Alask., Sask., and Man.

Mennonites settled in Eur. Russ. as early as 1789, in Crimea (Russ. *Krim*) beginning 1862. The *Ev. Mennonite Brethren* (formerly *Defenseless Mennonite Brethren of Christ in N. Am.*), organized 1889 Mountain Lake, Minn., are derived from 1873–74 Russ. immigrants. *Ev. Mennonite Ch.* is the name adopted 1952 by the *Kleine Gemeinde* Mennonite Ch. in Man., Can., derived from 1874 Russ. immigrants; another 1874 Russ. immigrant Kleine Gemeinde group settled at Jansen, Jefferson Co., Nebr., moved to Meade, Kans., 1906–08, dissolved 1944; many mems, of the Kleine Gemeinde in Can. moved to Mex. in the late 1940s. Two 1874 Russ. immigrant groups to Am. merged 1960: the *Gen. Conf. of Mennonite Brethren Chs.* and the *Krimmer Mennonite Brethren Conf. (Krimmer Mennoniten Brüdergemeinde).*

b. The cen. group is represented by the *Mennonite Ch.*, founded 1683, largest Mennonite body in N. Am. Many who seceded from it reunited with it. It engages in educ., philanthropic, and miss. work. The *Cen. Conf. Mennonite Ch.* (till 1914 the *Cen. Ill. Mennonite Conf.*) joined The Gen. Conf. of the Mennonite Ch. of N. Am. (see c) 1945, lost identity 1951 in merger with the Middle Dist. Conf. of the Gen. Conf. Ch.

c. Liberals are represented by the *Gen. Conf. Mennonite Ch.,* organized 1860 as *The Gen. Conf. of the Mennonite Ch. of N. Am.* (name changed 1953). FEM EEF

See also *Netherlands,* 4.

See *Religious Bodies (US), Bibliography of.*

Menologion (pl. Menologia; from Gk. *men,* "month," and *logos,* "word"). Term variously used usually in reference to E. Orthodox liturgy or cultus of saints. 1. Propers of saints in Menaion.* 2. Martyrology arranged acc. to calendar. 3. Lives of saints arranged acc. to calendar. A noted Menologion is that of Symeon* Metaphrastes (*MPG,* 114, 293 to 116, 1426). 4. Private nonliturgical collection of lives of saintly persons.

Mensa (Lat. "table"). Top or cen. slab of altar.* See also *Church Furniture,* 1.

"Mensageiro Luterano." See *Lutheran Church – Missouri Synod, Districts of The,* B 1.

Mensurius (d. ca. 311 or 307 AD). Bp. Carthage; during Diocletian persecution opposed voluntary and needless martyrdom. See also *Donatist Schism, The.*

Mentzer, Balthasar, I (1565–1627). Father of B. Mentzer* II; b. Allendorf, Hesse, Ger.; educ. Marburg; pastor Kirtorf; prof. Marburg and Giessen; rector Marburg; involved in Crypto-Kenotic* controversy; gained reputation as polemicist though more concerned about positive statements.

Mentzer, Balthasar, II (1614–79). Son of B. Mentzer* I; prof. theol. Marburg, Rinteln, and Giessen; court preacher and supt. Darmstadt; helped rebuild the ch. after the Thirty* Years' War.

Mentzer, Johann (1658–1734). B. Jahmen (or Jahma), near Rothenburg, Silesia; educ. Wittenberg; pastor Merzdorf, Hauswalde (near Bischofswerda), and Kemnitz (near Bernstadt); hymnist. Hymns include "O dass ich tausand Zungen hätte"; "O Jesu, einig wahres Haupt."

Merbeck(e), John. See *Marbeck, John.*

Mercadante, Giuseppe Saverio Raffaele (Raffaelo; 1795–1870). Composer; b. probably Altamura, It.; studied at Naples under N. A. Zingarelli*; lived in It., Austria, Sp., Fr., and Port. Works include masses, psalms, cantatas.

Mercedarians (from Lat. *Ordo Beatae Mariae de Mercede,* "Order of the Blessed Mary of Mercy"). 1. RC order for men said to have been founded by Peter* Nolasco (hence also called Nolascans) at Barcelona, Sp., to care for sick and rescue those taken captive by Moors; spread through W Eur.; est. houses in Lat. Am. 2. RC order for women founded 1568 at Seville, Sp.

Mercersburg Theology. 19th c. school of philos. and theol. developed at the Theol. Sem. of the Ger. Ref. Ch., Mercersburg, Pa.; leaders included P. Schaff* and J. W. Nevin*; tried to revivify Calvinistic doctrine by emphasizing the Christocentric idea. See also *United Church of Christ, The,* II A 2.

Mercier, Désiré Felicien François Joseph (1851–1926). B. Braine-l'Alleud, near Waterloo, Brabant province, Belg.; RC priest 1874; prof. Mechelen (Fr. Malines; Eng. Mechlin) 1877–82, Louvain 1882–1906; abp. 1906; cardinal 1907; founded Institut Supérieur de Philosophie, Louvain; played important role in neo-Thomism*; tried to unify Angl., Prot. Episc., RC chs.; presided over Malines* Conversations; founder and ed. *Revue Néo-Scolastique (de Philosophie).*

Mercy. Compassion, forbearance, clemency, kindness. God's mercy is abundant (Ps 103:17; 108:4; Is 49:13; Mi 7:18; Tts 3:5). Men should also be merciful (Mi 6:8; Mt 5:7; Lk 6:36). See also *Grace; Love; Loving-kindness.*

Merensky, Alexander (1837–1918). B. Panten, near Liegnitz, Silesia, Ger.; led miss. activity of Berlin* Miss. Soc. I in Transvaal, S. Afr., with headquarters at Botshabelo ("refuge") 1859–82; inspector Berlin city miss. 1883–86; supervisor of missions of the Berlin soc. 1886; led an expedition and began work in E Afr. 1891. Works include *Erinnerungen aus dem Missionsleben in Südostafrika [Transvaal]; Deutsche Arbeit am Njassa, Deutsch-Ostafrika.*

Merger Agreement. See *Finnish Lutherans in America,* 3.

Mergner, Adam Christoph Friedrich (1818–91). B. Regensburg, Ger.; educ. Erlangen; pastor Ditterswind (Lower Franconia) 1851, Erlangen 1874, Heilsbronn (Middle Franconia) 1880; supt. (Ger. *Dekan*) Muggendorf 1870; tried to restore the old Luth. liturgy and its music. Issued *Paul(us) Gerhardts geistliche Lieder in neuen Weisen; Choral-*

buch, zunächst zu dem Gesangbuche der ev.-luth. Kirche in Bayern.

Merici, Angela. See *Ursulines.*

Merit. RC theol. distinguishes bet. condign merit *(de condigno)* and congruent merit *(de congruo);* condign merit is merit to which reward is due in justice; congruent merit is based on the liberality of him who rewards. Accordingly, good works of the regenerate, in so far as they proceed from free will, are meritorious *de congruo;* in so far as they are done in the state of grace, they are meritorious *de condigno.* The Ap rejects this distinction as a screen for Pelagianism* (IV 19) and as a device which robs Christ of His honor and gives it to men (IV 316–318) and leads to doubt and despair (IV 321).

Merkel, Paul Johannes (1819–61). B. Nürnberg, Ger.; prof. Germanic jurisprudence Berlin, Königsberg (Kaliningrad), Halle; Luth.; opposed Prussian* Union.

Merkle, Sebastian (1862–1945). B. Ellwangen, Ger.; RC ch. historian. Ed. journals of Council of Trent*; other works include studies of Reformation period and 18th c. RC Enlightenment.

Merle. See *Merula, Angelus.*

Merle d'Aubigné, Jean Henri (1794–1872). Ref. Ch. hist.; b. near Geneva, Switz., of Fr. ancestry; pastor Fr. cong. Hamburg; court preacher Brussels; prof. Geneva 1831; helped organize Société* évanélique de Genève. Works include *Histoire de la réformation du seizième siècle* (various Eng. translations).

Merrill, Selah. See *Geography, Christian,* 5.

Merry del Val, Rafael (Raphael; Raffaele; Raffaelo; 1865–1930). B. London, Eng., of Sp. descent; educ. by Jesuits; priest 1888; apostolic delegate Can. 1897; titular abp. Nicaea 1900; secy. conclave 1903; secy. of state 1903 under Pius X (see *Popes,* 30); cardinal 1903; secy. Holy Office 1914–30; opposed modernism* and Angl. ordinations.

Mersch, Émile (Emil; 1890–1940). B. Marche, Belg.; Jesuit; priest 1917; prof. philos. Namur 1920–35; tried to fashion a synthesis of the doctrine of the mystical body of Christ. Wrote *Le Corps mystique du Christ* (tr. J. R. Kelly, *The Whole Christ*).

Mersenne, Marin (pseudonym Sieur de Sermes; 1588–1648). B. (La) Soultière, near Bourg-d'Oizé, Dept. Sarthe, Province (Le) Maine, W Fr.; philos., theol., scientist; friend of leading Fr. scientists and philosophers; fostered new scientific movement and helped keep it from becoming antireligious.

Merswin, Rulman. See *Rulman Merswin.*

Merula, Angelus (Engel de Merle; Engel Willemsz; van Merlen; 1482–1557). Reformer and martyr; b. Brielle (Den Briel; The Brill), Neth.; educ. U. of Paris; ordained priest 1511; accepted ev. doctrine of justification; opposed worship of Mary and saints, other abuses; arrested 1553; imprisoned at The Hague, Louvain, Bergen; d. as he knelt in prayer at the place of execution.

Merz, Georg (1892–1959). B. Walkersbrunn, Upper Franconia, Bav., Ger.; educ. Leipzig and Erlangen; pastor and educ.; contributed to development of dialectical* theol. Ed. *Zwischen den Zeiten.*

Mesopotamia. See *Middle East,* H.

Mesrob (Mesrop; Mastoc [Maschtotz]; probably ca. 345/361–ca. 440). B. Hasik (variously spelled), Taron, Armenia; educ. probably Antioch; monk; scholar; said to have invented Armenian and Georgian alphabet.

Messalians. See *Euchites.*

Messe. See *Mass.*

Messenger Press, The. See *Publication Houses, Lutheran.*

Messengers of Christ, Inc. Organized May 4, 1964, North Hollywood, Calif., primarily to recruit and train lay men and women for language analysis, literacy work, and Bible translation. The alternate name "Lutheran Bible Translators" was added 1968.

Messiah (Heb. *mashiach,* "anointed"). Word used in various forms in OT in reference to anointing with holy oil (e. g., Ex 28:41; 1 Sm 9:16; 1 K 19:16). The NT word is Christ (Gk. *christos;* e. g., Mt 16:16; Jn 1:41). See also *Judaism; Messianic Hope.*

Messianic Age. See *Messianic Hope.*

Messianic Hope. Distinguished from hope for the Messiah* in this, that it refers to *every* type of Jewish thought which looked for God's deliverance and salvation. The OT offers hope of a messiah-king after the image of David (e. g., Ps 2; 18; 20; 21; 45). It also refers to Messiah in such terms as the coming Judge (e. g., Is 42:1-4), Ruler of Israel (e. g., 2 Sm 7:13; Zch 9:9; Ps 2:6; Dn 9:25), Wonderful, Counselor, Mighty God, Everlasting Father, Prince of Peace (Is 9:6; cf. Ju 13:18). In the intertestamental* period, messianic hope developed and changed. By the time of Jesus' birth the average Jew had a messianic hope different from that sketched above. One form emphasized the messiah as the Son of Man, a heavenly, powerful figure in the spirit of Dn 7 (cf. pseudepigraphic Book of Enoch, esp. chs. 46 and 48). Another form pictured him as the mighty pol. king of Israel, in the image of David. Some looked for a messiah from the house of Aaron, others awaited him from the tribe of Judah. Some looked for 2 messiahs, 1 from the house of Aaron, 1 from Judah. Under Gk. and Persian influence the conviction grew that this world was totally evil and corrupt, beyond redemption. The function of the messiah then became that of announcing a new heaven and a new earth; or of serving as God's herald to announce the end of the present age; or of being the agent for ending the old and beginning the new age. For many the hope of the new age was nationalistic and materialistic: Jerusalem would be the cen. of the world; Palestine would yield fantastic crops. Intertestamental writers gen. excluded heathen from any share in the messianic age and do not speak of a messiah who would suffer *and* die in his mission. This probably explains the disciples' shock and confusion when Jesus announced that He was on the way to the cross (Mk 10:32-34; Lk 18:31-34). Is 53 was either changed in meaning or ignored. A personal messiah was not an essential part of the messianic hope for some. The age of the messiah would be preceded by great calamity, a cosmic struggle bet. forces of evil and of the messiah (some said at Armageddon). The intertestamental messianic hope might be expressed in summary form as the hope of restoring on a higher level the unity of nat. life broken at the exile.

O. Cullmann, *The Christology of the New Testament,* tr. S. C. Guthrie and C. A. M. Hall, 2d Eng. ed. (London, 1963); J. Klausner, *The Messianic Idea in Israel,* tr. W. F. Stinespring (New York, 1955); T. W. Manson, *The Servant-Messiah* (Cambridge, Eng., 1953); S. O. P. Mowinckel, *He That Cometh,* tr. G. W. Anderson (New York, [1956?]). HTM

Mestizos. See *Central America,* B; *Mexico,* B.

Metaphrastes. See *Simeon Metaphrastes.*

Metaphysical Argument. See *Immortality, Arguments for.*

Metaphysical Society, The. Organized 1869 by Sir James Thomas Knowles (1831–1908; b. London, Eng.; architect. Ed. *Contemporary Review;* founded and ed. *Nineteenth Century*) to foster debate bet. exponents of science and religion; last meeting held 1880; mems. included H. Alford,* A. B. Balfour,* W. K. Clifford,* W. E. Gladstone,* S. H. Hodgson,* T. H. Huxley,* H. E. Manning,* J. Martineau,* J. F. D. Maurice,* J. B. Mozley,* H. Sidgwick,* A. P. Stanley,* A. Tennyson,* J. Tyndall,* J. Ward.*

Metaphysics. See *Philosophy; Psychology,* E.

Metempsychosis. See *Transmigration of Souls.*

Methodist Church, The. Formed 1939 at Kansas City, Mo., by union of the M. E. Ch., the Meth. Prot. Ch., and the M. E. Ch., S, on basis of Plan of Union drafted 1934. Merged 1968 with the Evangelical* United Brethren Ch. to form The United Meth. Ch. See also *Methodist Churches,* 1.

Methodist Churches. 1. *History.* Meth. chs. owe their origin to the religious experiences of J. Wesley,* C. Wesley,* and their co-workers. Spiritual indifference prevailed in the Angl. Ch., but the Wesleys were concerned with personal piety. C. Wesley helped organize the Holy Club at Oxford, Eng., 1729. The miss. activity of the Wesleys and their co-workers resulted in great revival (see *Great Awakening in England and America*). Their unconventional methods, esp. field preaching, watch-night meetings, and use of lay preachers, did not appeal to Angl. clergy. At first the Wesleys did not intend to form a new ch., but Angl. opposition led to organization of "methodists" into socs. under tutorship of lay preachers. Several such congs. were placed under the care of 1 lay preacher. In 1744 J. Wesley called a conf. of lay preachers; later the conf. became an annual event. In 1784 the Conf. was legally defined in a deed of declaration. Secessions included Meth. New Connection 1797; in 1805 Meths. mainly in N Eng. who later became Indep. Meths.; 2 groups in 1810 who joined 1811 to form the Primitive Meths.; Bible* Christians 1815; Wesleyan Meth. Assoc. 1835; those excluded by the 1849 Manchester Conf. who then formed the Wesleyan Reformers. These groups gradually reunited into larger groups: the Wesleyan Meth. Assoc. and the Wesleyan Reformers united 1857 to form the United Meth. Free Chs.; the Meth. New Connection, Bible Christians, and United Meth. Free Chs. joined 1907 to form the United Meth. Ch. In 1932 the original ("Wesleyan") Meth. Ch., the Primitive Meths., and the United Meth. Ch. joined to form the United Conf. of Meth. Chs.

Methodism in Can. lost its identity in the United Ch. of Can. (see *Canada,* B). See also *Union Movements,* 5.

Methodism had its greatest expansion in the US. The 1st annual Am. Meth. Conf. was held Philadelphia 1773. At the 1784 Christmas Conf., regarded as founding the M. E. Ch. as an ecclesiastical organization, F. Asbury* was ordained supt. In the late 1780s the term "bp." came to replace "supt." This led to schisms: J. O'Kelly* organized the Rep. Meth. Ch. 1792; the Meth. Prot. Ch. was organized Baltimore, Md., 1830. Lay delegates were elected to the Gen. Conf. 1870 for the 1st time. J. Wesley opposed slavery; James Osgood Andrew (1794–1871; bp. 1832; worked chiefly in the S confs.) was a slaveholder; this led to crisis 1844 resulting in the M. E. Ch., S, organized Louisville, Ky., 1845 (1st Gen. Conf. at Petersburg, Va., 1846). The M. E. Ch., the Meth. Prot. Ch., and the M. E. Ch., S, united 1939 to form The Methodist* Ch., which merged 1968 Dallas, Tex., with The Evangelical* United Brethren Ch. to form The United Meth. Ch.

2. *Doctrine.* J. Wesley's theol. was a modified Arminianism.* He and his followers stressed Christian activity. The 25 arts. he prepared as a doctrinal guide are patterned after the Thirty-nine Arts. of the Angls. (see *Anglican Confessions,* 6). It is significant, however, that the real standards of Meth. doctrine are Wesley's "preached sermons," in which great emphasis is laid on sanctification (see *Democratic Declarations of Faith,* 6). Christian perfection may be viewed as the cen. doctrine of Methodism. Wesley differed from J. Calvin* in holding that Christ died for all (universal salvation). He held that all men who are obedient to the Gospel acc. to the measure of light given them are in God's kingdom. Man is free to reject or, by the grace of God, to accept salvation (free salvation). The Holy Spirit assures man of his salvation directly (sure salvation). The real heart of Wesley's theol. was the doctrine of the pure heart. Christian perfection in Meth. theol. is man's ability to overcome evil and reach perfection (full salvation). In the 1st quarter of the 20th c. large sections of Methodism became modernist (see *Modernism*). The transition from Wesley's individual perfection to modernism's soc. perfection was comparatively simple. The Meth. Fed. for Soc. Service was formed 1907. The Gen. Conf. of the M. E. Ch. adopted the Soc. Creed of Methodism 1908. *Doctrines and Discipline of The Methodist Church 1944* and *The Book of Discipline of The United Methodist Church 1968* make it the duty of the ch. to help soc. solve such problems as class tensions, racial inequality, agricultural problems, economic insecurity, industrial accidents, liquor traffic, internat. strife. See also *Democratic Declarations of Faith,* 6; *Social Gospel.*

3. *Polity.* The gen. lines laid down by J. Wesley developed in different directions in Eng. and Am. In Eng. the conf. remained supreme; in Am. the superintendency became an episcopacy. When the episc. form of govt. was adopted by the 1st Annual Conf. 1784, govt. by conferences was not abrogated, but actually made an integral part of the episc. system. The Meth. system operates under conferences: the Gen. Conf. for the whole ch.; Jurisdictional Confs. for the ch. in the US and Can.; Cen. Confs. for the ch. outside the US and Can.; Annual Confs. as the fundamental bodies of the ch. and, if necessary, Provisional Annual Confs.; a Charge Conf. for each ch. or charge. The ordained ministry of the United Meth. Ch. consists of elders and deacons; qualified laymen may be licensed to perform certain pastoral functions; bps. are elected by resp. Jurisdictional and Cen. Confs. and consecrated in the hist. manner. The Council of Bps. consists of all bps. of the United Meth. Ch.

4. *Separate Bodies.* (a) *The United Meth. Ch.* (see par. 1).

(b) *Ref. Meth. Ch.;* founded 1814 Readsboro, Vt., in protest against episcopacy; by the middle of the 19th c. most of its socs. merged with the Meth. Prot. Ch. (see par. 1); what remained in 1952 merged in that yr. with the Churches* of Christ in Christian Union. *The Wesleyan Meth. Ch. of Am.;* founded 1843 at Utica, N. Y., in protest against slavery and episcopacy; merged 1968 with Pilgrim Holiness Ch. to form The Wesleyan* Church. *Primitive Meth. Ch., U. S. A.;* est. 1812 in Eng. after Lorenzo Dow (1777–1834; b. Coventry, Conn.; M. E. Ch. preacher; on his own initiative made several trips to Ireland and Eng. beginning ca. 1799) introd. Am. type camp meetings; brought to Am. by immigrants by 1829; Gen. Conf. organized 1889. *Congregational Meth. Ch.;* organized 1852 in protest against polity and itinerancy of the M. E. Ch., South. *(First) Cong. Meth. Ch. of the USA;* organized Forsythe, Ga., 1852. *New Cong. Meth. Ch.;* separated from M. E. Ch., S, 1881, as result of conflict over consolidation of some rural chs. in Fla. and Ga.; includes footwashing. *Free Meth. Ch. of N. Am.;* organized 1860 Pekin, N. Y., by B. T. Roberts*; fundamentalist; emotional in worship. *Holiness Meth. Ch.;* organized 1909 Grand Forks, N. Dak., as Constitution Northwestern Holiness Assoc.; name changed 1920. *Fundamental Meth. Ch., Inc.;* withdrew from The Methodist* Ch. in protest against modernism; formed 1942 Ash Grove, Mo., as Indep. Fundamental Meth. Ch.; name changed 1956. *Southern Meth. Ch.;* organized 1939 by a small group in dissent against the merger that produced The Methodist* Ch. and as continuation of the M. E. Ch., South. *Cumberland Meth. Ch.;* withdrew from Cong. Meth. Ch. in protest against certain features of doctrine and polity; organized 1950 Laager, Grundy Co., Tennessee. *Ev. Meth. Ch.;* organized 1946 Memphis, Tenn., in protest against episcopacy and modernism. Bible Prot. Ch.; organized after some mems. of the E Conf. of the Meth. Prot. Ch. withdrew 1939 in protest against the merger that resulted in The Meth. Ch.; name adopted 1940.

(c) The *African* M. E. Ch.* was organized 1816. *A. M. E. Zion Ch.* is the name adopted 1848 by a ch. that traces its beginning to 1796 (when some Negroes withdrew from John St. Meth. Ch., NYC) and that held its 1st annual conf. 1821 under the name Afr. A. M. Zion Ch. in America. *Christian M. E. Ch.;* organized 1870 Jackson, Tenn., as Colored M. E. Ch. in Am.; parallel of M. E. Ch., S.; present name adopted 1954/56. *Union Am. M. E. Ch.;* traces its roots to the beginning of the 19th c., its organization to 1875. *Ref. Zion Union Apostolic Ch.;* broke from the A. M. E. Zion Ch.; organized 1869 Boydton, Va., as Zion Union Apostolic Ch.; disrupted 1874; reorganized 1881/82 under present name. *Ref. Meth. Union Episc. Ch.;* broke from A. M. E. Ch. over disputed elections of Gen. Conf. delegates; organized 1885 Georgetown, S. C.; adopted episc. and connectional polity 1896. *Afr. Union 1st Colored Meth. Prot. Ch., Inc.;* formed 1866. *The United Wesleyan Meth. Ch. of Am.;* founded 1905.

(d) *Lumber River Annual Conf. of the Holiness Meth. Ch.* See *Evangelistic Associations,* 9. FEM

See also *Holiness Churches; Itinerancy; Ranters,* 2; *Whitefield, George.*

See *Religious Bodies (US), Bibliography of.*

Methodist Episcopal Church. See *Methodist Churches,* 1.

Methodist Episcopal Church, South. See *Methodist Churches,* 1.

Methodist Protestant Church. See *Methodist Churches,* 1.

Methodist Student Movement. See *Students, Spiritual Care of,* A 3.

Methodius (Eubulus; Eubulius; d. ca. 300/311). E Ch. theol.; bp. Olympus in Lycia; probably martyred in persecution instituted by Diocletian*; opposed Origen*; held bodily resurrection. Works include *Symposium* (in praise of virginity; includes hymn to Christ as Bridegroom of the Ch.); *De resurrectione* (against Origen); *De libero arbitrio* (against *Gnosticism**).

Methodit Student Movement. See *Students, Spiritual Care of,* A 3.

Methodius (d. 885). See *Cyril and Methodius.*

Methodology, Theological. Practical application of theol. encyclopedia.*

Metrophanes Kritop(o)ulos (Critopoulos; Critopulus; 1589–1639). B. Beroea (Veroia), Macedonia; Gk. monk; sent by Cyril Lucaris* to study in Eng.; traveled in Eur.; metropolitan Memphis, Egypt, 1633; elected patriarch Alexandria 1636, enthroned 1637; signed anathemas against Cyril Lucaris for his Calvinism.* See also *Eastern Orthodox Standards of Doctrine,* B 2.

Metropolitan. 1. Title hist. borne by bps. of capital (mother) cities of Roman provinces or of fictional provinces; such bps. presided at provincial syns. and exercised gen. supervision over other bps. of the province; title first occurs in acts of the 325 Council of Nicaea (see *Nicaea, Councils of,* 1). 2. In E Orthodox Ch., head of an ecclesiastical province. 3. Abp. in Ch. of Eng.

See also *Archbishop; Polity, Ecclesiastical,* 3.

Metropolitan Church Association, The. See *Evangelistic Associations,* 10.

Metz, Christian (1794–1867). B. Neuwied, Prussia; sectarian leader; head of Amana* Soc.

Metzger, Bruce Manning. See *Lexicons,* B.

Metzger, Max Joseph (Josef; 1887–1944). RC theol.; b. Schopfheim (Schopfloch?), Ger.; after WW I devoted to cause of peace; active in soc. and ecumenical work; opposed Nazism (see *Socialism,* 3).

Meurer, Moritz (1806–77). B. Pretzsch, near Wittenberg, Ger.; educ. Leipzig; private tutor Wittenberg; taught at Weissenfels 1833; held various ministerial positions at Waldenburg 1834–41; pastor Callenberg, near Waldenburg, 1841–77. Works include *Altarschmuck; Der Kirchenbau vom Standpunkte und nach dem Brauche der lutherischen Kirche; Luthers Leben aus den Quellen erzählt;* ed. and coauthor, *Das Leben der Altväter der lutherischen Kirche.*

Meusel, Karl Heinrich (1837–89). B. Wiederau, Saxony; educ. Leipzig; vicar 1863, subdeacon 1865 Dresden; teacher Gymnasium at Bauzen 1867, Gymnasium at Dresden 1871; pastor Grosshennersdorf, near Herrnhut, 1873; supt. Rochlitz 1885. Ed. 2 vols. of *Kirchliches Handlexikon.*

Meusel, Wolfgang (Meusslin). See *Musculus, Wolfgang.*

Mexican Indian Mission. Founded 1930/31 by James Gary Dale (1870–1960) and his wife Katherine Neel Dale (1872–1941; med. doctor); he had been in Mex. since 1899, she since 1898, as missionaries of the Assoc. Ref. Presb. Bd. The 1st miss. station, opened 1931 at Tamazunchale in the heart of the Huastec country, E Mex., is the center of this work.

Mexican Lutheran Church. See *Mexico,* D 3.

Mexican Theological Community. See *Mexico,* D 3.

Mexico. A. *Historic Formation.* The arrival of Hernando Cortes (Cortez; Hernán Cortés; 1485–1547; b. Medellín, Estremadura, Sp.; conqueror of Mex.) in 1519 ushered into modern hist. that vast section of the W hemisphere mainland known today as Mex., but then called New Sp. by its conquerors. The fall of the Aztec empire 1521 sealed the conquest of the Indian civilizations and brought the entire area under Sp. colonial rule for 3 centuries. In 1821 Mex. became indep. of the Sp. empire. Its most southerly state: Chiapas, which broke away from Guatemala 1821 and became one of the original 19 states of Mex. 1824. Present N border est. after secession of Tex. 1836 and Mex. War 1846–48.

B. *Gen. Description. Area:* ca. 760,000 sq. mi. *Pop.* (1971 est.): ca. 52,500,000, mostly mestizos of mixed Sp. and Indian descent; pure Indian descendants of various peoples (e. g., Aztec, Maya, Olmec, Tlascala, Toltec, Zapotec), some of which had highly developed preconquest cultures, are now concentrated mostly in cen. highlands and S Pacific area; others include Creoles (of Sp. descent), N. Americans, Negroes, and Orientals.

C. *Soc. and Pol. Aspects.* Independence intensified inherent soc. problems, rooted in an agricultural economy largely based on communal land tenure, bequeathed by the colonial period, and complicated by vast landless Indian pop. The 1857 Reform and const. separated ch. and state, creating a secular, fed. govt. in which all ch. property was nationalized, religious orders dissolved, educ. secularized, and ch. tithes abolished. Land reform was also attempted. The Revolution that began 1910 led to the 1917 Constitution and full reform. Today Mexico's govt. is a blend of soc. and capitalist pragmatism under a one-party system. Principles of the Reform are applied and objectives of the Revolution are pursued through varying emphases by a strongly centralized govt. No religious organization can own real estate. Educ. is under state control. Businesses in the pub. interest are nationalized, but private investment, including for., is at a high level. See also D 1.

D. *Religion.* 1. Preconquest Indian cults still exist in remote interior regions, often blending with old Sp. forms of RCm. Acc. to tradition, Mary appeared to Indian Juan Diego 1531. A shrine to mark the event was erected ca. 1533; over the yrs.

it grew into the Basilica of Our Lady of Guadalupe in Guadalupe Hidalgo (Gustavo A. Madero), Fed. Dist., cen. Mex. The RC Ch. exercised strong pol. power in the colonial period and controlled much arable land; this led to reaction against ecclesiastical domination and privilege reflected in the constitutions of 1857 and 1917 (see C). Mex. is mainly RC, but for many the connection is only nominal. Evidence of spiritual awakening has followed Vatican II (see *Vatican Councils,* 2). With relaxation of some laws, the relationship bet. ch. and state has improved. Missions are still hindered by restrictions against for. clergy.

2. Protestantism entered Mex. in force after religious freedom was permitted by the 1857 const.

3. The 1st Ev. service in Mex. was held 1861 in German. Ger. immigration favored establishment of the Ger. Speaking Ev. Luth. Cong. This parish has Heilig Geist Kirche (Holy Spirit Ch.) in Mex. City with sister congs. and many preaching stations throughout the country. It is served by a multiple ministry. This parish also shares in the work of the Soc. Service Center erected with help of funds allocated by Ger., Swiss, and Austrian interests. The Mo. Syn. began Eng. work 1922, abandoned it 1931, began Sp. work 1940. This work, now assoc. with the Caribbean Miss. Dist. of LCMS, led to organization Apr. 1968 of The Luth. Syn. of Mexico. ALC Sp. work in Mex., begun in the middle 1940s, led to founding 1957 of Iglesia Luterana Mexicana, a mem. of LWF. Eng.-speaking Good Shepherd Ch. (LCMS), organized Mex. City 1949, and Ascension Ch. (ALC), organized 1958, united 1963 into a cong. recognized by both parent bodies. The Lat. Am. Luth. Miss., founded in the early 1930s by Myrtle Nordin, a mem. of the LFC of Lake Lillian, Minn., is supported by contributions of stateside chs. The World* Mission Prayer League began work in Lower Calif. ca. 1944, on the mainland of Mex. ca. 1950. The Scand. Luth. Cong., Mex. City, has operated with Swed. services. Augsburg Center, founded in the 1960s in Mex. City, trains pastors for Luth. groups in Mex. and elsewhere in Lat. Am. and is part of Mex. Theol. Community, formed in the late 1960s by sems. of various Prot. groups. RFG

Mexico, Roman Catholic Church in. See *Mexico,* D 1.

Meyenberg, Albert (1861–1934). RC theol.; b. Zug, Switz.; prof. in sem. at Lucerne 1891; apologist and homiletician. Works include *Homiletische und katechetische Studien.*

Meyer, Adolf William (Adolph[us] Wilhelm; July 20, 1860–May 26, 1937). B. Australia; educ. Conc. Coll., Fort Wayne, Ind., and Conc. Sem., St. Louis, Mo. Pastor Rader, Webster Co., Mo. (mem. The Eng. [Ev.] Luth. Conf. of Mo.) 1885; Winfield, Kans. (mem. The Gen. Eng. [Ev.] Luth. Conf. of Mo. and Other States) 1888; Pittsburgh, Pa. (mem. The Eng. Ev. Luth. Syn. of Mo. and Other States) 1891. Pres. St. John's Coll., Winfield, Kans., 1895–1927; The Eng. Ev. Luth. Syn. of Mo. and Other States 1901–05. Pastor Long Island, N. Y., 1927. Taught at Conc. Institute, Bronxville, N. Y. Ed. *The Lutheran Guide.*

Meyer, Carl Stamm (Mar. 12, 1907–Dec. 17, 1972). B. Wetaskiwin, Alta., Can.; educ. Conc. Sem., Saint Louis, Mo. Studied at State Teachers Coll., Mankato, Minn.; U. of Minn., Minneapolis; U. of Chicago; Washington U., St. Louis; U. of London. Pastor Rochester, Minn., 1931–34; instructor Bethany Lutheran Coll., Mankato, Minn., 1934–43; pres. Luther Institute, Chicago, 1943–54; acting supt. Luth. High School Assoc., Chicago, 1950–52; prof. Conc. Sem., St. Louis, 1954–72 (dir. of its School for Grad. Studies 1960–69); ex. dir. Foundation for Reformation Research 1969–72. Ed. *Sixteenth Century Journal; Concordia Historical Institute Quarterly; Cranmer's Selected Writings; The Lutheran High School; Moving Frontiers; Walther Speaks to the Church: Selected Letters; Lutheran Secondary and Higher Education for Effecitve Action; Luther for an Ecumenical Age.* Coed. *The Caring God.* Ed. and tr. *Letters of C. F. W. Walther: A Selection.* Coauthor *A History of Western Christianity.* Other works include *Elizabeth I and the Religious Settlement of 1559; Pioneers Find Friends; Log Cabin to Luther Tower; The Church: From Pentecost to the Present; A Brief Historical Sketch of The Lutheran Church – Missouri Synod; A Catholic President?*

Meyer, Heinrich August Wilhelm (1800–73). B. Gotha, Ger.; educ. Jena. Pastor Osthausen, near Kranichfeld, Thuringia, 1822; Harste, near Göttingen, 1831. Pastor and supt. Hoya, near Verden, 1837; Neustadt, Hannover, 1841. Mem. consistory 1841, high consistory 1861. Works include *Kritisch exegetischer Kommentar über das Neue Testament* (in collaboration with others).

Meyer, Herman Edward Ernest (June 30, 1881–Apr. 4, 1920). Brother of J. P. C. Meyer*; b. Caledonia, Racine Co., Wis. Educ. Northwestern U. (called Northwestern Coll. 1910), Watertown, Wis.; teacher-training school (Dr. Martin Luther Coll.), New Ulm, Minn.; Conc. Coll., Milwaukee, Wis.; Wis. Syn. sem., Wauwatosa, near Milwaukee, Wis. Pastor successively Eden Valley, Buffalo and Pelican Lake, and Goodhue, all in Minn., 1904–13. Principal Milwaukee Luth. High School 1913–15. Prof. sem. at Wauwatosa 1915–20.

Meyer, Johann Friedrich von (1772–1849). B. Frankfurt am Main, Ger.; theol., jurist, statesman, poet, Bible tr.; pres. Bible Soc. in Frankfurt 1816; first influenced by rationalism, later turned to mysticism and theosophy. Works include *Zur Aegyptologie; Inbegriff der christlichen Glaubenslehre.*

Meyer, Johannes Peter Carl (Feb. 27, 1873–Nov. 10, 1964). Brother of H. E. E. Meyer*; b. Zittau, Winnebago Co., Wis.; educ. Northwestern U. (called Northwestern Coll. 1910), Watertown, Wis., and at the Wis. Syn. sem. at Wauwatosa, near Milwaukee. Pastor Beaver Dam, Wis., 1896–1902; Oconomowoc, Wis., 1915–18. Prof. Northwestern U. 1902–03; Dr. Martin Luther Coll., New Ulm, Minn., 1903–15. Pres. Dr. Martin Luther Coll. 1918–20. Prof. Wis. Syn. sem. at Wauwatosa till 1929, then at Thiensville (Mequon) till 1964; acting pres. 1937, later pres., of this sem. till 1953. Works include *Ministers of Christ.*

Meyer, John Herman (Johann Hermann; May 25, 1866–May 7, 1949). B. Baltimore, Md.; educ. Conc. Sem., Springfield, Ill.; miss. Fresno, Calif., 1889–90. Pastor Canistota, S. Dak., 1890–93; Waltham, Minn., 1893–1900; St. Paul, Minn., 1900–06; St. Louis, Mo., 1906–11; Town Rost, near Lakefield, Minn., 1912–42. Pres. Minn. Dist. of Mo. Syn. 1918–30. Works include *Dein Reich komme!;* ed. *Die Missions-Taube* 1908–11.

Meyfart, Johann Matthäus (Mayfart; 1590–1642). B. Jena, Ger.; educ. Jena; prof. Gymnasium at Coburg 1616; dir. there 1623; prof. Erfurt 1633. Devotional works include *Tuba novissima,* which contains the hymn "Jerusalem, du hochgebaute Stadt."

Mezger, Johann Leonhard Georg (Metzger; Dec. 18, 1857–Nov. 3, 1931). B. Brunswick, Ger.; educ. Conc. Sem., St. Louis, Mo. Pastor Waterloo, Iowa, 1881–85; near Okawville, Ill., 1885–95; Decatur, Ill., 1895–96. Prof. Conc. Sem., St. Louis, 1896–1923; prof. at sem. in Zehlendorf, Berlin, Ger., 1923–31. Ed. *Denkstein zum fünfundsiebzigjährigen Jubiläum der Missourisynode;* other works include *Lessons in the Small Catechism of Dr. Martin Luther; Entwürfe zu Katechesen über Luthers Kleinen Katechismus.*

Miami Synod (Ev. Luth. Syn. of Miami). Named after the valley of the Great and Little Miami

Rivers. Organized Oct. 16, 1844, at Xenia, Ohio, under leadership of E. Keller*; joined Gen. Syn. 1845 (see *General Synod of the Evangelical Lutheran Church in the United States of America, The*), ULC 1918; merged Nov. 1920 with the Dist. Syn. of Ohio (formerly of the Gen. Council [see *General Council of the Evangelical Lutheran Church in (North) America*]), the East Ohio Syn. of the Ev. Luth. Ch., and the Wittenberg* Syn. of the Ev. Luth. Ch. of Ohio (of the Gen. Syn.) into the Syn. of Ohio of the ULC. See also *United Lutheran Church, Synods of,* 8, 19.

Michael. See *Angels, Good,* 3, 5.

Michael III (the Drunkard; 839–867). E Roman emp. 842–867; waged war with Saracens, Bulgarians, Russians; involved in Photian Schism (see *Schism,* 5).

Michael Caerularius (Cerularius). See *Caerularius, Michael.*

Michael of Cesena (probably ca. 1270/80–1342). B. Cesena, It.; Franciscan minister gen. 1316; when John XXII (see *Popes,* 13), beginning 1322, condemned the Franciscan ideal of poverty, Michael of Cesena led opposition to papal claims and supported Louis* IV.

Michaelis, Christian Benedikt (1680–1764). Nephew of J. H. Michaelis*; father of J. D. Michaelis*; b. Ellrich, near Nordhausen, Saxony, Ger.; educ. Halle; assoc. prof. Halle 1713–14; prof. philos. 1714–31, theol. 1731–38, Gk. and Oriental languages 1738–64 Halle. Contributed to J. H. Michaelis' ed. of the Heb. OT; issued Heb. OT with Gk. apocrypha and NT.

Michaelis, Johann David (1717–91). Son of C. B. Michaelis*; b. Halle, Ger.; educ. Halle; prof. philos. 1746–50, Oriental languages 1750–91 Göttingen; regarded as a founder of Syriac philol. Works include *Abhandlung von der Syrischen Sprache und ihrem Gebrauch.* See also *Lutheran Theology After 1580,* 8; *Marsh, Herbert.*

Michaelis, Johann Heinrich (1668–1738). Uncle of C. B. Michaelis*; b. Klettenberg, near Nordhausen, Saxony, Ger.; prof. Oriental languages 1699, theol. 1709 Halle; senior and inspector of the Halle theol. sem. 1732; exponent of Pietism. Issued partial Heb. O. T.

Michaelis, Walter (1866–1953). Ev. theol.; b. Frankfurt an der Oder, Ger.; pastor Bielefeld 1892 and leader in awakening there; inspector Miss. Soc. for Ger. E. Afr. 1901; returned to Bielefeld 1908. Works include *Erkenntnisse und Erfahrungen aus fünfzigjährem Dienst am Evangelium.*

Michaelius, Jonas. See *Reformed Churches,* 4 b.

Michaelmas. See *Church Year,* 16, 17.

Michelangelo (Michelagniolo di Lodovico di Lionardo di Buonarroto Simoni; Michael Angelo; Michelangelo [or Michelangiolo] Buonarroti; 1475–ca. 1564). Renaissance sculptor, painter, architect, poet; b. Caprese, Arezzo province, Tuscany, It.; pupil of D. Ghirlandajo*; assoc. with Lorenzo di Medici (see *Medici,* 2); influenced by RC reform movement. Sculptures include *David; Moses; Pieta* (1 in St. Peter's, 1 in the Rondanini Palace, Rome). Paintings include *Holy Family;* in Sistine Chapel: ceiling decorations, and *The Last Judgment* on the altar wall. Architectural works include plans for completion of St. Peter's. Poetry includes religious and philos. poems.

Michelfelder, Sylvester Clarence (Oct. 27, 1889–Sept. 30, 1951). Luth. cleric; b. New Washington, Ohio; educ. coll. and sem. of Capital U., Columbus, Ohio. Pastor Willard, Ohio, 1914–21; Pittsburgh, Pa., 1921–26; Toledo, Ohio, 1931–45. Supt. Luth. Inner Miss. Soc., Pittsburgh, Pa., 1926–31; Luth. representative of Am. section of LWC at WCC, Geneva, Switz., 1945–46; prominent in formation of LWF.

Michelians. See *Hahn, Johann Michael.*

Michigan City Theses. Theses on (1) Church, (2) Ministry, (3) Symbols, (4) Open Questions, (5) Chiliasm and Antichrist, (6) Predestination and Conversion. Agreed on July 1893 Michigan City, Ind., by representatives of the Ev. Luth. Syn. of Iowa* and Other States and the Ev. Luth. Joint Syn. of Ohio* and Other States. See also *Toledo Theses* (Ohio and Iowa, 1907).

F. W. Meuser, *The Formation of the American Lutheran Church* (Columbus, Ohio, 1958); *Documents of Lutheran Unity in America,* ed. R. C. Wolf (Philadelphia, 1966); C. S. Fritschel, "Die Thesen des Colloquiums von Michigan City," *Kirchliche Zeitschrift,* XVII (1893), 161–170; XVIII (1894), 33–48; F. P[ieper], "Das Colloquium der Synoden von Ohio und Iowa," *L. u. W.,* XXXIX (1893), 257–264.

Michigan Lutheran College. Est. 1937 at Detroit, Mich., as Great Lakes Coll., given to Luths. of the LCMS Mich. Dist. 1962 and name changed to Mich. Luth. Coll.; dedicated Feb. 6, 1966; taken over by Shaw U. 1970.

Michigan Lutheran Seminary. See *Michigan Synod* 4.

Michigan Synod. 1. Swabian immigrants settled 1830 in Washtenaw Co., Mich. They asked the Basel* Miss. Soc. for a pastor. F. Schmid(t)* was sent to them 1833. He est. ca. 20 congs. and helped found the 1st Luth. syn. in Mich. (called Missionary Syn. of the West, to indicate its interest in missions) 1840. It sent 3 miss. to Ojibwa at Sebewaing, Mich., in the mid-1840s. J. K. W. Löhe* put his Indian missions under supervision of the syn. on Schmid(t)'s pledge that confessional Lutheranism would prevail. Löhe men G. W. C. Hattstädt,* P. J. Trautmann,* F. J. C. Lochner,* and F. A. Crämer* joined the syn. They soon realized that Schmid(t)'s pledge was a paper promise and left the syn. 1846. The syn. disbanded. Schmid(t) joined the Ev. Luth. Joint Syn. of Ohio* and Other States, but soon became indep., served congs. in S Mich., trained some men himself, received some from Basel, and by 1860 was ready for a 2d venture in organizing a syn.

2. S. Klingmann* and C. L. Eberhardt* came to Mich. from Basel 1860 and the 2d Mich. Syn. ("Ev.-Luth. Synode von Michigan und andern Staaten") was organized Detroit Dec. 1860 with 8 pastors and 3 delegates. Schmid(t) was its pres. Klingmann and Eberhardt were leaders in successfully insisting that the confessional statement of the syn. be soundly Luth.; but practice in syn. began to diverge as miss. fields and manpower grew. Many pastors (some volunteers, some from Basel) were unionists; some withdrew with their congs. Those who remained in the syn. often lent financial support to the Basel Miss. Soc., to the eventual detriment of the Mich. Syn.

3. The Mich. Syn. joined the General* Council of the Ev. Luth. Ch. in (N.) Am. 1867 but persistently protested the Four* Points. The syn., represented by Klingmann, was put off from one meeting to the next, yet remained hopeful. When the Gen. Council met 1884 in Monroe, Mich., 2 Eng. pastors of the Gen. Council preached in a Presb. Church. A protest by the Mich. Syn. delegates was tabled and evaded; protests in 1885 and 1886 were also discounted. The Mich. Syn. sent no delegates to the 1887 Gen. Council conv. and withdrew from the Gen. Council 1888.

4. The Mich. Syn. had drawn pastors from various sources (e. g., Basel, St. Chrischona,* Hermannsburg* Miss., Kropp* Sem.). A theol. sem. was est. 1885 at Manchester with 6 students, moved to Saginaw 1887 (see also *Hoyer, Otto Daniel August*), discontinued 1907, reopened 1909/10, when it was est. as a high school (Progymnasium) by the Ev. Luth. Joint Syn. of Wis., Minn., Mich., and Other

States (see *Wisconsin Evangelical Lutheran Synod*); called Mich. Luth. Sem.

The Mich. Syn. joined the Synodical* Conf. and united with the Wisconsin* Syn. and the Minnesota* Syn. to form the Ev. Luth. Joint Syn. of Wis., Minn., Mich., and Other States 1892. The agreement with the other syns. required that the sem. be discontinued, but in 1895 the Mich. Dist. Syn. resolved to continue the sem. for those already enrolled. A minority lodged a successful protest against this resolution with the Ev. Luth. Joint Syn. of Wis., Minn., Mich., and Other States. This minority (10 pastors) was excluded by the Mich. Dist. 1896, organized the Ev. Luth. Dist. Syn. of Mich., and remained part of the Ev. Luth. Joint Syn of Wis., Minn., Mich., and Other States and of the Syn. Conf.; the majority, on the other hand, withdrew 1896 from the Ev. Luth. Joint Syn. of Wis., Minn., Mich., and Other States and from the Syn. Conf., joined the Augsburg* Syn. 1897 on a doctrinally shaky basis in a joint-syn., 2 dist. arrangement which dissolved 1900.

5. New leaders arose. Conferences with the Mo. Syn. (1904) and the Ev. Luth. Dist. Syn. of Mich. (1906) led to reconciliation. In 1909 the Mich. Syn. reunited with the Ev. Luth. Dist. Syn. of Mich. and rejoined the Ev. Luth. Joint Syn. of Wis., Minn., Mich., and Other States.

6. Official organ: *Evangelisch-Lutherischer Synodal-Freund.*

For further hist. see *Wisconsin Evangelical Lutheran Synod.* 3.

3. *Kurzgefasste Geschichte der Evangelisch-Lutherischen Synode von Michigan u. a. St.* (Saginaw, Mich., [1910?]).

Michigan Synod of The United Lutheran Church in America. See *United Lutheran Church, Synods of,* 12.

Micron, Marten (Martinus Micronius; Marten de Cleyne; 1523–59). Ref. theol.; b. probably Gent, Belg.; pastor Neth. refugee cong. London 1550; fled to Den. and Ger. 1553; debated with Menno Simons (see *Mennonite Churches,* 1) in Wismar, J. Westphal* in Hamburg.

Micronesia. Islands of W Pacific, E of Philippines. *Area:* ca. 1,335 sq. mi.; inhabitants of Melanesian, Polynesian, and Malaysian stock. Includes the Caroline,* Gilbert,* Mariana,* Marshall,* and Palau (formerly Pelew) Is.

Middle Age(s) (Lat. *medium aevum*). Term first used by late 15th c. humanists for Eur. hist. ca. 500–ca. 1500; now often used for 11th–15th cents.). See also *Dark Age(s); Western Christianity 500–1500.*

Middle East. A. 1. Area not exactly defined; gen. includes lands bet. Medit. basin and Indus R.; sometimes includes Balkan States and NE Afr.; often called Near East. Christianity, Judaism,* and Islam* began in the Middle E. Inhabitants include Turks, Armenians, Greeks, Kurds, Arabs, Assyrians, Jews, Persians.

2. Decline of Brit. influence, rise of nationalism, creation of the state of Israel 1948, formation of the United Arab Rep. 1958, Fed. of S. Arabia 1963, and Fed. of Arab Reps. 1971, and other more recent developments profoundly influenced the Middle E.

3. Islam claims 90–99% of the inhabitants of most of Middle E. countries. Most Middle E. countries signed the 1948 UN *Universal Declaration of Human Rights,* which granted freedom of thought, conscience, and religion; but in practice the community combination of family, clan, religion (often legally recognized) does not allow change of religion. Freedom of religion means that non-Muslim can minister to their own groups within their own precincts; it does not allow miss. work. In many areas the "millet" is the non-Muslim religious community organized as a legal entity in the state, with its own community court and community laws, with the provision to refrain from pol. agitation. Non-Muslim religious groups not in a "millet" have no rights. Islam identifies the statues and icons of Christian chs. with idolatry. It opposes the doctrine of the Trin. and associates Christians with imperialism and colonialism.

4. Christians in the Middle E. are mostly mems. of RC and E Cath. chs. These chs. strive to keep their community intact, fear change in their "working arrangement" with Muslim, are prejudiced against Muslim, and distrust Prots.

5. Brit. possession of Malta 1799 furthered miss. work there. The LMS, BFBS, ABCFM, CMS, SPCK, SPG, and the London Soc. for Promoting Christianity Among the Jews (Ch. Missions to Jews) were at work in the Middle E. early in the 19th c.

6. Since immediate effective contact with Muslim was impossible, Prot. missions tried to est. a working relationship with Cath. chs. (Roman and E.). Caths. who favored Prot. efforts were excluded by Cath. chs. and became the nucleus of nationalized Prot. chs. Their work was done through hosps., schools, clinics, orphanages, etc. By the late 1960s the Syrian Orthodox Ch. was a mem. of the Near* E. Council of Chs.; other Orthodox chs. sat on some committees and participated in some projects.

B. *Turkey. Area:* ca. 300,000 sq. mi. *Pop.* (1971 est.): ca. 36,500,000; ca. 98% Muslim. Modern pol. hist. dates from 1923, when Mustafa Kemal became 1st pres. of Rep. of Turkey. The teaching of Islam in jr. high schools throughout the country became compulsory 1956; a faculty of theol. was est. in state-controlled U. of Ankara. Evangelistic activity is sharply curtailed by law.

In 1820 Pliny Fisk(e) (1792–1825; Cong. miss.; b. Shelburne, Mass.; educ. Middlebury [Vt.] Coll. and Andover [Mass.] Theol. Sem.; preacher Wilmington, Vt.; miss. to Middle E.; works include Eng.-Arab. dictionary) and Levi Parsons (1792–1822; b. Goshen, Mass.; educ. Middlebury [Vt.] Coll. and Andover [Mass.] Theol. Sem.; worked under Vt. Miss. Soc.; miss. to Middle E.) explored the possibilities of miss. work in Asia Minor for the ABCFM. William Goodell (1792–1867; Cong. miss.; b. Templeton, Mass.; educ. Phillips Academy, Andover, Mass., Dartmouth Coll., Hanover, N. H., and Andover [Mass.] Theol. Sem.; studied medicine; miss. to Middle E.) began permanent work June 1831 with HQ at Constantinople; worked ca. 5 yrs. in Beirut (1823–28); tr. Bible into Armeno-Turkish. Most of his converts were from the Armenian Ch. Excommunicated by the Armenian Ch., they organized the 1st ev. ch. in the Middle E. in Constantinople 1846; it was officially recognized 1850. ABCFM missionaries est. Robert Coll. at Bebek 1863 (moved to Constantinople ca. 1871) and Am. Coll. for Girls, Constantinople (Istanbul). The Basel Miss. Soc. began work in the 1820s. The CMS began in Smyrna in the 1830s. Others included SPG, Am. Baps., Disciples of Christ, Ch. of the Brethren, Eng. Quakers, London Jews' Soc., Seventh-day Adventists. Nearly all withdrew in course of time, leaving the ABCFM as almost the only representative of Protestantism. The ABS est. a depository in Istanbul. See also *Anatolia; Malche, Frauenmission.*

C. *Syria* (Syrian Arab Rep.). *Area:* ca. 72,000 sq. mi. *Pop.:* ca. 6,400,000 (1971 est.), ca. 90% Arab (others include Kurd, Armenian, Turkish, Fr.); ca. 87% Sunni Muslim. Ca. 830,000 Christians: mostly RC, E Orthodox, and Nonchalcedonian; Prots. (ca. 17,000). Paul preached at Damascus (Acts 9:20). Antioch (now Antakya, or Antakiya) was an early Christian center. Since the

Arab conquest 636, Islam* has been the prevailing religion. Fr. mandate 1920; indep. in the mid-1940s; joined Egypt 1958 to form United Arab Rep., withdrew 1961; joined Egypt and Libya 1971 to form Fed. of Arab Republics.

Joseph Wolff (1795–1862; b. Weilersbach, near Bamberg, Ger.; Jew; converted 1812) of London Jews' Soc. (see also H and I) made exploratory visits to Syria 1822–23. L. Parsons and P. Fisk(e) (see B) arrived Smyrna 1819. In 1870 the field was transferred to Am. Presbs., who operate Aleppo College. Elizabeth Maria Thompson (nee Lloyd; d. Nov. 14, 1869) founded the work which became the Lebanon* Ev. Miss. By 1912 there were 38 Prot. groups in Syria; decreased to ca. 20 by withdrawal and combinations. Well-known Prot. hosps. in Syria: Deir-Ez-Zor Hosp.; Victoria Hosp. in Damascus (Edinburgh Med. Miss.); Luth. Hosp. at En Nebk (Dan. Orient Miss.). Larger Prot. groups: Nat. Ev. Syn. of Syria and Lebanon; Angl. Ch., Diocese of Jordan, Lebanon, and Syria. Smaller groups: Ch. of God; Ch. of the Nazarene; Assemblies of God; Seventh-day Adventist. Syria and Lebanon are often worked together.

D. *Lebanon. Area:* ca. 4,000 sq. mi. *Pop.:* ca. 2,900,000 (1971 est.), mostly Arab. Govt. structure is based on official (and approximate) 50-50 Muslim-Christian balance; pres. traditionally is Maronite (see *Maronites*), premier a Sunni Muslim. P. Fisk(e) (see B and C) began work in Beirut 1823. Am. Presbs. began 1835, took over much of the Middle E. work of the ABCFM 1870; they operate 2 boys' schools (Tripoli, Sidon), 4 girls' schools (Tripoli, Sidon, Beirut, En [or El] Nabatiye [or Al-Nabatiyah]), and 2 colleges in Lebanon (Beirut Coll. for Women; Near E. Coll. of Theol. in Beirut). Kennedy Mem. Hosp. (Tripoli) and Hamlin Mem. Sanatorium (near Beirut) are outstanding med. institutions. Syrian Prot. Coll., founded 1866 under Christian miss. sponsorship, became Am. U. of Beirut 1920. St. Joseph U. was founded 1846 at Ghazir by Jesuits as a sem.; moved to Beirut 1875; other faculties added to form U.

Other miss. include Lebanon* Ev. Miss.; Ch. of God (Anderson, Ind.); The Ev. Alliance Miss.; S. Baps.; Disciples of Christ; Home of Onesiphorus; Ref. Presb. Ch. of Scot.; Seventh-day Adventists; Dan. Ch.

Carl Leonard Folke Agerstrand (b. Aug. 14, 1900) of LCMS began a radio miss. on the state-operated radio station in Beirut in the early 1950s. It was extended to station ELWA, Monrovia, Liberia, 1957, and Radio Voice of the Gospel, Addis Ababa, 1963. This miss. also operates Bible correspondence courses since 1952 and has chapels in Beirut.

Beirut is a center of Christian missions to the Middle East. The Near* E. Council of Chs. has its headquarters there. The Am. Press, Arabic Christian Publishers (formerly Nile Mission Press), Tower Library, ABS, the Middle E. HQ of BFBS, and Union of Armenian Ev. Chs. in the Near E. are in Beirut. Miss. schools in Beirut include Near E. Coll. of Theol.

E. *Cyprus.* Is. ca. 60 mi. W of Syria. *Area:* 3,572 sq. mi. *Pop.:* ca. 600,000 (1971 est.). Visited by Paul and Barnabas (Acts 13). Most Gks. (ca. 78–80% of pop.) are E Orthodox; most Turks (ca. 18% of pop.) are Muslim. Angls., other Prots., and RCs are a small minority. Active socs. and chs. include Christian Missions in Many Lands; Jerusalem and the East Miss.; Ch. of God; Ref. Presb. Ch. of N. Am.

F. *Israel. Area:* ca. 7,992 sq. mi. *Pop.:* ca. 3,000,000 (1971 est.), perhaps ca. 85–88% Jews; ca. 7% Muslim; most Christians are RC and E Orthodox; several thousand Prots. The Balfour Declaration 1917 helped pave the way for Jews to est. a nat. homeland in Palestine. The Jewish Nat. Council proclaimed the Jewish state of Israel May 14, 1948. Official language: Heb. Religious courts are autonomous in the several religious communities. The League to Combat Apostasy obstructs miss. work. The OT is a standard textbook in schools. Christian shrines are preserved.

Prot. miss. work in Israel is confined almost exclusively to Jerusalem, Jaffa, Tel Aviv, Haifa, Lydda, Nazareth, and Tiberias. The London Jews' Soc. (Angl.) started in Jerusalem 1820, opened Jerusalem Hosp. 1848. Christ Ch. began 1833. An Angl. bishopric was est. 1840. The CMS started in Jerusalem 1851, built hosps. at Jaffa and Lydda, an orphanage at Nazareth. The Edinburgh Med. Miss. Soc. has a hosp. at Nazareth. Other socs. and chs. working in Israel include Jerusalem and the E. Miss.; Mildmay Miss. to Jews; United Free Ch. of Scot.; Christian and Miss. Alliance; Christian Missions in Many Lands, Ltd.; Wesleyan Meth. Miss. Soc.; Seventh-day Adventists; Assemblies of God; Mennonites; Ch. of the Nazarene; S. Baps. The 1948 Arab-Israeli War extensively damaged Christian missions.

BFBS and ABS have a joint agency in Haifa. See also *Judaism; Zionism.*

The Fin. Miss. Soc. has a children's home and school in Jerusalem. The Swed. Israel Miss. has a theol. research institute there. The Dan. Israel Miss. has workers in Carmel and Tel Aviv, and the Norw. Israel Miss. has workers in Haifa and Jaffa (part of Tel Aviv).

G. *Jordan* (called Transjordan [Trans-Jordan; Transjordania] till 1949; const. name since 1949 Hashemite Kingdom of Jordan). *Area:* ca. 37,000 sq. mi. *Pop.:* 2,400,000 (1971 est.), ca. 94% Arabs. Jordan was Brit. mandate 1923–46, indep. kingdom since 1946. Religion ca. 94% Muslim, ca. 6% Christian. Severe restrictions are placed on miss. work among Muslim.

The RC and E Orthodox chs. came to Jordan at an early date. Petra was the seat of a metropolitan bp. in the 4th c. Angls. were among earliest Prots. in Jordan. The CMS has a girls' school in Amman and relief work in Zerka and Salt. The Jerusalem and the East Miss. has the Bishop's School for Boys in Amman and St. George's School in Jerusalem. The Christian and Miss. Alliance has worked in Jerusalem and Hebron since the 1890s. Others at work in Jordan include S. Baps.; Seventh-day Adventists; Indep. Bd. for Presb. For. Miss.; Am. Friends; Ch. of the Nazarene; Assemblies of God.

Luths. have worked in Jerusalem since mid-19th c. Kaiserswerth deaconesses came to Jerusalem 1851 and est. the "Talitha Kumi" orphanage and a hosp. The Ger. *Jerusalemsverein* was est. 1852. J. L. Schneller* est. his "Syrian orphanage"; his work was continued by his son and grandson, and the Schneller schools were est. William II (Friedrich Wilhelm Viktor Albert; 1859–1941; emp. of Ger. and king of Prussia 1888–1918) built the Ch. of the Redeemer and the Augusta Victoria Institute (the latter on the Mount of Olives). After WW II the LWF carried on an extensive relief program and subsidized the cong. and educ. work of the Ger. missions *(Palästinawerk).* The Ev. Luth. Ch. in Jordan was organized in 1959.

H. *Iraq* (Rep. of Iraq; formerly Mesopotamia). *Area:* ca. 168,000 sq. mi. *Pop.:* ca. 10,000,000 (1971 est.), ca. 95% Arab Muslim, ca. 3.5% Christians, ca. 1.5% others (e. g., Yezedees [Yezidis] and Jews). Iraq freed from Turks in WW I; const. monarchy est. by Gt. Brit. 1921; sovereign state 1932. There is tension and strife bet. Kurds and Iraqis. Since the revolution of 1958 missions have been curtailed.

In the 1820s J. Wolff (see C and I) contacted Jewish colonies in Iraq. The Basel Miss. Soc. founded a school for Armenians in Baghdad 1830. Henry Aaron Stern (1820–85; b. Unterreichenbach, Hessen-Kassel, Ger.; Jew; converted 1840) made contacts with Jews at Baghdad and elsewhere in Mesopotamia beginning 1844. ABCFM est. a station at Mosul in the 1850s. CMS entered Iraq 1882; its missions were later given to the Jerusalem and the East Mission. The United Miss. in Iraq was formed in 1924 by Am. chs. of Ref. background; it has a school for girls in Baghdad. Others include Arabian Miss.; Ev. Alliance Miss.; Seventh-day Adventists; Assemblies of God. The Luth. Orient Miss. Soc. (Kurdistan Miss.), est. ca. 1910, works among Kurds.

I. *Iran* (called Persia till 1935). Area: ca. 636,000 sq. mi. *Pop.:* ca. 29,200,000 (1971 est.); Aryans descended of ancient Persians who speak Farsi (Persian); ca. 95% Shi'a Muslim. Islam, Judaism, Zoroastrianism, and Christianity are officially recognized. The govt. is a const. monarchy. The ev. chs. have complete freedom to conduct services; conversions from Islam are more numerous than in any other Middle E. country. See also *Fossum, Ludvig Olsen.*

H. Martyn* was the 1st modern miss. to Iran 1811; tr. NT into Persian. Ten yrs. later J. Wolff (see C and H) contacted Jews in Iran. The Basel Miss.. Soc. began at Tabriz 1831. Justin Perkins (1805–69; b. West Springfield, Mass.; miss. to Nestorian Christians in NW Persia) of the ABCFM began 1834, opened an important station at Urmia (now Rizaiyeh) 1835; this miss. was given to the Am. Presb. Bd. 1870. The Ev. Presb. Ch. emphasizes educ. and med. work, with hosps. in Tehran, Tabriz, Hamadan, Resht, Kermanshah, and Meshed; its schools were nationalized 1940; it operates a community school in Tehran for children of for. diplomats; its miss. numbers ca. 3,000 communicants. The CMS began 1869 and concentrated on evangelization of Muslim and Jews, and strengthening the older chs.; it has stations at Isfahan, Shiraz, and Abadan. Others include Iran Interior Miss. (work later taken over by Internat. Missions, Inc.); Assemblies of God; Seventh-day Adventists; BFBS; Ch. Miss. to Jews.

J. *Afghanistan. Area:* ca. 250,000 sq. mi. *Pop.:* 17,400,000 (1971 est.); perhaps ca. 95% Sunni Muslim; some Hindus, Sikhs, and Jews. Began 1747 as the indep. Durani Empire; became const. monarchy with Islam* as the state religion 1932. In 1973 the monarchy was overthrown and a rep. proclaimed. Miss work forbidden. CMS in Pakistan and the Presbs. USA in Iran have stations near the border.

K. *Pakistan.* See *Asia,* B 2.

L. *Arabia.* Peninsula SW Asia ca. 1,400 mi. long, ca. 1,250 mi. wide; pop. by Arab Muslim. Saudi Arabia and Yemen did not sign the *Universal Declaration of Human Rights* (see also A 3). Slavery is legalized.

Acc. to tradition, Bartholomew preached the Gospel in Arabia. Paul visited Arabia (Gl 1:17-18). When Persian Christians were persecuted by Shapur II (Lat. Sapor; reigned 309–379), many fled to Arabia. A Christian settlement was founded 380 AD in Hirah. Acc. to tradition, Abd-Kelal, Hamyarite (or Himyarite) king ca. 275 AD, was a Christian. Dzu-Nowas (Dunowas; king 490–525) embraced Judaism and persecuted the Christians. Arabia is the birthplace of Islam.*

I. G. N. Keith-Falconer * began modern Prot. missions in Arabia at Aden 1886. After his death, students of the Dutch Ref. Ch. in Am. continued the work and est. the Arabian Miss. 1888/89; its most famous miss. was S. M. Zwemer *; The Ref. Ch. in Am. lent support to this miss. beginning 1894. Other miss. include the Dan. Ch. Miss.; Ch. of Scot. Miss.; Indep. Bd. for Presb. For. Miss.; S. Baps.; and Sudan Interior Miss.

1. *Saudi Arabia.* 99% Muslim. Mecca and Medina are in this country. Islam * enforced by law.

2. *Aden.* Settlement on coast of SW Arabia; captured by Turks 1538; ruled by Sultan of San'a since 17th c.; held by Brit. and governed as part of India 1839–1937; Brit. colony since 1937; part of Fed. of S. Arabia 1963; helped form People's Rep. of Southern Yemen 1967 (name changed 1970 to People's Democratic Rep. of Yemen). CMS began work in middle 1880s, after I. G. N. Keith-Falconer (see above), but turned it over to the Ch. of Scot. a few yrs. later; Dan. Luth. Ch. entered 1904; Sudan Interior Miss. also did some work in Aden.

3. *Had(h)ramaut.* Coastal region of S Arabia. *Area:* ca. 58,500 sq. mi. Helped form People's Rep. of Southern Yemen 1967.

4. *Yemen Arab Rep.* (from Arab. *al Yemen,* "the right hand"; here refers to the direction of the land as one stands before the Kaaba *). *Area:* ca. 75,300 sq. mi. *Pop.* 5,900,000 (1971 est.), chiefly Muslim.

5. *Bahrein* (Bahrain). *Area:* ca. 231 sq. mi. *Pop.:* 222,000 (1970 est.), chiefly Muslim. Indep. sheikdom. The Arabian Miss. began work ca. 1892/93.

6. *Kuwait* (Kuweit; Koweit). *Area:* 6,178 sq. mi. *Pop.:* ca. 800,000 (1971 est.), ca. 95% Muslim. Former sheikdom under Brit. protection, indep. emirate 1961. The Arab. Miss. (see 5) entered 1903 and est. a hosp. and med. miss. RCs est. bishopric 1954.

7. *Oman* (called Muscat and Oman till 1970). *Area:* 82,000 sq. mi. *Pop.:* 700,000 (1971 est.); chiefly Arab; ca. 99% Muslim. Indep. sultanate. Angl. bp. T. V. French * began work in Muscat for CMS 1891.

8. *Qatar* (Katar). *Area:* ca. 8,000 sq. mi. *Pop.:* ca. 180,000 (1970 UN est.), largely Arab Muslim. Indep. sheikdom.

9. *Union of Arab Emirates.* Formed Dec. 2, 1971, by 6 of the Trucial States (also called Trucial Oman, or Trucial Coast; "Trucial" refers to truces with Gt. Brit. in the 1800s): Dubai (Debai; Dibai), Abu Dhabi, Fujairah, Sharjah, Umm al Qaiwan, and Ajman; Ras al Khaima did not join. Mostly Muslim.

M. Parts of Afr. are often included in the Middle E. See *Africa; Egypt; Ethiopia.* EL

See also *Lutheran Church – Missouri Synod, The,* VII, 14; *Middle East General Mission; Middle East Lutheran Ministry.*

Middle East General Mission (Egypt Gen. Miss.; formerly known as Egypt Mission Band). Organized 1897 Belfast, N. Ireland; worked in Egypt * till 1956; began work in Lebanon and Eritrea in the late 1950s.

Middle East Lutheran Ministry. Est. 1960 as Luth. Ch. – Middle E. Conf. (name changed 1963) by Bd. for World Missions of LCMS. HQ Beirut, Lebanon. Conducts radio work and a Bible Correspondence Course. See also *Lutheran Church – Missouri Synod, The,* VII, 14.

Middle Tennessee Synod. See *Tennessee, Evangelical Lutheran Synod of Middle; Illinois, Evangelical Lutheran Synod of Southern.*

Middleton, Conyers (1683–1750). Angl. theol.; b. York, or Richmond, Yorkshire, Eng.; educ. Cambridge; rector Coveney, on the Isle of Ely; librarian Cambridge U.; prof. Cambridge 1731–34; opposed some features of deism.*

Middleton, Thomas Fanshaw(e) (1769–1822). B. Kedleston, Derbyshire, Eng.; educ. Cambridge; ordained Angl. 1792; bp. Calcutta, India, 1814; diocese covered all territories of E. India Co.

Midland Association Confession. See *Democratic Declarations of Faith,* 3.

Midland Lutheran College. Founded 1887 at Atchison, Kans., by The General * Syn. of the Ev. Luth. Ch. in the USA; moved to Fremont, Nebr., 1919. See also *Lutheran Church in America,* V; *Ministry, Education of,* VIII B 18 and VIII C 1 d.

Midrash (Heb. "commentary"). 1. Jewish exegesis that tries to penetrate deeply into the Biblical text and find meaning in addition to the literal one. 2. Early Jewish exposition of Scripture; most flourishing period: ca. 100 BC to 200 AD. 3. In the widest sense, all noncanonical Jewish literature, including the Talmud,* to the 13th c.

Midwest Synod. See *United Lutheran Church, Synods of,* 3.

Miessler, Ernst Gustav Hermann (Jan. 12, 1826–Mar. 1, 1916). B. Reichenbach, Silesia; educ. for miss. work at Dresden and Leipzig; to US 1851 as miss. to Chippewa at Station Bethany, St. Louis, ca. 30 mi. W of Saginaw, Mich.; worked with E. R. Baierlein*; succeeded him 1853; mission was almost lost 1860 in govt. transfer of Indians to Isabella Co., Mich.; Miessler served them there till 1869; teacher Saginaw 1869–71; accepted temporary supply position at Saginaw; left ministry 1871 to study and practice medicine (1874–99) in Chicago, Ill.

Migne, Jacques Paul (1800–75). B. Saint-Flour, near Orléans, Fr.; RC priest Puiseaux, in the diocese of Orléans, 1824–33; to Paris 1833; founded pub. house; began ed. large collection of religious texts and encyclopedias; esp. significant: *MPL,* Lat. ecclesiastical writings up to 1216 (217 vols. text; 4 vols. indexes); *MPG,* Gk. ecclesiastical writings to ca. 1438 (161 vols. Gk. text with Lat. tr., and 81 vols. of the Lat. text only on Gk. fathers). Supplement vols. to *MPL* began to appear 1958, ed. A. Hamman. Indexes to *MPG* have appeared, ed. D. Scolarios (1879), F. Cavallera (1912), T. Hopfner (1928, 1936).

Mihrab. See *Mosque.*

Mikkelsen, Hans (d. 1532). Dan. theol.; b. Malmö (then under Dan. rule), Swed.; mayor Malmö; secy. of Christian* II; helped tr. NT into Flensburg-Dan. 1523/24 (Gospels and Acts from D. Erasmus'* Lat., remainder from M. Luther's* Ger.).

Milan, Edict of. Agreement issued 313 AD by Constantine* I and Licinius* after meeting at Milan; recognized Christianity. After many persecutions failed their purpose, Constantine and Licinius resolved "to grant both to the Christians and to all men freedom to follow the religion which they choose" and that "liberty is to be denied to no one, to choose and to follow the religious observances of the Christians . . . ." (Eusebius, *HE,* X, v, 4-5). Some question Eusebius' account.

Milanese Rite. See *Ambrosian Rite.*

Mildmay Institutions. Confs. on miss. enterprise were begun by William Pennefather (1816–73; b. Merrion Square, Dublin, Eire; educ. Dublin) at Barnet, Hertfordshire, Eng., in the middle 1850s; after he moved to Mildmay Park, London, 1864, the confs. were continued there on a much larger scale; the conf. hall became the center of many permanent miss. organizations.

Milíc, Jan (Milíc of Kremsier; Milicz; Militsch; Johann[es]; John; ca. 1325–74). Forerunner of Boh. Reformation; b. Kremsier, Moravia, Czechoslovakia; active in imperial chancery 1358–62; resigned benefices 1363; lived in poverty; preached repentance in vernacular at Prague; awaited end of world and coming of Antichrist 1365–67; to Rome 1367; imprisoned by Inquisition*; when released submitted document to pope listing faults of the ch. and pointing out the need for a gen. council and popular preaching; returned to Prague to preach repentance and oppose clerical abuses. Works include *Libellus de Antichristo* (or *Prophetia et revelatio de Antichristo*).

Military Religious Orders. Assocs. formed before and during Crusades*; combined military and monastic principles; originally est. to protect and aid pilgrims to the Holy Land; took part in Crusades and later struggles; included:

a. *Knights of Malta* (Knights Hospitallers [of Saint John of Jerusalem]; Knights of St. John; Sovereign Military Order of the Hosp. of St. John of Jerusalem, of Rhodes, and of Malta). Began in Jerusalem before the 1st Crusade in a hospice-infirmary; received papal approval 1113; built a network of *domus hospitales* ("guest houses") for pilgrims; driven from Jerusalem to Rhodes, then to Malta and Tripoli; survived as a religious community of chaplains and lay brothers dedicated to sanctification of its mems., service of the faith and of the papal see, and welfare work.

b. *Templars* (Poor Fellow-Soldiers of Christ and the Temple of Solomon; Knights Templars). Est. ca. 1119; originally devoted to protect and guide pilgrims; rule approved 1128 was a variation of the Benedictine. With strongholds throughout the E and W, mems. of the order became internat. bankers. Desiring their wealth, Philip IV (see *France,* 3) persuaded Clement* V to pressure the Council of Vienne* into supplying the order 1312.

c. *Teutonic Knights* (Ger. Knights; Knights of the Cross; Knights of St. Mary's Hosp. at Jerusalem; Der deutsche Orden; Deutsche Ritter). Originated ca. 1190 in efforts by merchants of Lübeck and Bremen to care for sick and poor Ger. pilgrims at Acre, Palestine; military order 1198. Under Hermann von Salza (ca. 1170–1239; grand master ca. 1210–39) the order conquered, and introd. Christianity into, large parts of the Baltic provinces and Russ.; declined from 15th c.; existence in Ger. dissolved by Napoleon 1809; revived 1840 in Austria as a semireligious knighthood; serves schools and hosps.; a Prot. branch of the order survived in the Neth.

d. *Hospitallers of St. Lazarus of Jerusalem* (Lazarites). Order of knights and nurses following the rule of Augustine* of Hippo; founded ca. 1120 in Jerusalem to operate hosps. (esp. for lepers), spread the faith, care for pilgrims; activities transferred to Eur. in 13th c.; suppressed during Fr. revolution; revived in It. and Fr. in 19th c.; now an honorific soc.

H. G. Prutz, *Die geistlichen Ritterorden* (Berlin, 1908).

Mill, John. See *Mills, John.*

Mill, John Stuart (1806–73). Eng. philos. and economist; precocious child; served with E. India Co. 1823–58; applied economic doctrine to soc. conditions; advocated women's suffrage. Works, which include *A System of Logic,* also treat *utilitarianism** and methods of inductive logic.

Mill, William Hodge (1792[1791?]–1853). B. Cambridge, Eng.; Angl. cleric; 1st principal Bishop's Coll., Calcutta, India, 1820–38; helped pub. Christian works in Indian vernaculars; prof. Heb. Cambridge 1848; supported Tractarianism.*

Mill Neck, New York, Lutheran School for the Deaf. See *Deaf,* 13.

Millais, John Everett (1829–96). B. Southampton, Eng.; painter; mem. Pre-Raphaelite* Brotherhood; distinguished in portraiture. Works include *Christ in the House of His Parents* (gen. called *The Carpenter's Shop*); *The Return of the Dove to the Ark; Jephthah; Young Men of Benjamin Seizing Their Brides.*

Millenarianism. See **Millennialism.**

Millennial Church, The. See *Shakers.*

Millennial Dawn. See *Jehovah's witnesses.*

Millennialism (from Lat. *mille,* "1,000," and *annus,* "yr."). Belief in a 1,000-yr. rule of the ch. on earth, at the beginning (premillennialism) or end (postmillennialism) of which Christ will return. Also called millenarianism and chiliasm (from Gk. *chilioi,* "1,000"). See also *Dispensationalism; Millennium.*

Millennium. 1. In theol., a period of 1,000 yrs. supposedly referred to Rv 20:1-7. See also *Millennialism.* Millenarians (or chiliasts) differ regarding the character of Christ's millennial kingdom; some view it as more, others as less spiritual in nature, extension, duration, and joys; they differ also in many other regards. But they agree in gen. on Christ's personal advent and a glorious period of peace and joy.

2. The OT does not mention a 1,000-yr period; yet chiliasm may be regarded as rooted in a Jewish view of an earthly messianic kingdom (cf. 2 Esd 7:28: "My son the Messiah shall appear with his companions and bring 400 yrs. of happiness to all who survive"). When the 1,000 yrs. of Rv 20:1-7 (one of the most misunderstood passages of the Bible) were superimposed on this view, the basic elements of chiliasm were complete.

3. The millennial theory is variously found in the Epistle of Barnabas; in the writings of Cerinthus, Hermas, Papias, Irenaeus, Justin Martyr, Tertullian; and in apocryphal books of Jews and Jewish Christians (Book of Enoch; Testament of the Twelve Patriarchs; Sibylline Books). The crass form in which chiliasm entered into the heresy of Montanism* helped strengthen opposition to chiliasm. It was opposed by the School of Alexandria, esp. Origen* (see also *Exegesis,* 3). Ca. the middle of the 3d c., Nepos* of Arsinoe wrote *Elengchos allegoriston* ("Refutation of Allegorists"; now lost) in defense of chiliasm. This work was refuted by Dionysius* of Alexandria. Jerome* opposed chiliasm. Gradually chiliasm became obnoxious and proscribed largely because the conditions and prospects of the ch. were altered.

4. In the Middle Ages the idea prevailed that the judgment and the end of the world would soon occur, i. e., that the *dies* irae* was at hand. "Apocalyptic parties" (individuals or groups of enthusiasts) looked for the miraculous advent of Jesus as the indispensable means of purifying and extending the ch.

5. At the Luth. Reformation* the traditional allegorical interpretation of Rv was abandoned. M. Luther* and other leading reformers, some of whom regarded the pope as Antichrist and as a sign of the end, looked for the speedy coming of Christ and the end of the world. Chiliasm prevailed among enthusiasts and sects. It was espoused esp. by Ger. Anabaps. in Münster (see *Münster Kingdom*). Chiliasm was condemned in AC XVII and the 2d Helvetic Confession XI but gained free play in the 17th c. when Eur. convulsions, revolutions in Eng., religious wars in Ger., and maltreatment of Prots. in Fr. spread it far and wide. Toward the end of the 17th c. the Luth. Ch. was influenced in this direction by Pietists, esp. P. J. Spener* (proponent of a refined chiliasm), Joachim Lange,* and J. Lead(e).* Luth. theols. who defended chiliasm include J. A. Bengel.* Chiliasm was championed by the Plymouth Brethren (see *Brethren, Plymouth*) and the Catholic* Apostolic Ch.

6. In Am., chiliasm was widely endorsed among Adventist* bodies, the Amana* Soc., Christadelphians,* the Christian* Cath. Ch., some elements of Fundamentalism,* the Holiness* chs., the House* of David, Jehovah's* witnesses, and Latter* Day Saints.

7. Millenarians may be divided into pre- and postmillenarians. *Premillenarians* hold that the millennium is a period of worldwide righteousness introd. by the sudden, unannounced visible advent of Christ; that before this coming, the Gospel will be proclaimed throughout the world as a witness to it; that the righteous will then rise and reign with Christ on earth; that the Lord and His saints will bring about a great tribulation, Rv 2:22; that Israel will acknowledge the crucified Savior as the Messiah, Zch 12:10; that through the outpouring of the Holy Spirit many sinners will be converted, while Satan will be bound and locked in the abyss; that Satan, after 1,000 yrs., will be loosed; that he will make a final vain effort to est. himself; that soon thereafter he, his angels, and all lost souls that have been raised from the dead will be judged and hurled into the lake of fire, there doomed to everlasting torment; that the earth will be renewed by fire and become the everlasting home of the redeemed. *Postmillenarians* have gen. defended the following views: that through Christian agencies the Gospel will gradually permeate the entire world; that this condition will continue 1,000 yrs.; that the Jews will be converted either at the beginning of or during this period; that after this period of universal Gospel-acceptance there will be a brief apostasy, followed by a dreadful conflict bet. Christian and evil forces; and that finally and simultaneously there will occur the advent of Christ, the gen. resurrection, and the judgment of all men, after which the world will be destroyed by fire and new heavens and a new earth will be revealed.

8. Chiliasts disagree as to time and place of the millennial reign. Some have tried, others have refused, to fix a definite date. Many regarded Jerusalem as the center of Christ's reign (see *Jews, Conversion of*). Millennial joys have been variously described, from intoxication of the senses to pure contemplation of Christ.

9. Chief proof text of chiliasts is Rv 20:1-7, which they interpret literally. Opponents hold that this passage does not treat of the final advent of Christ, and that, if the whole passage is interpreted literally, hopeless confusion and absurdities result.

Miller, Albert Herrman (Jan. 23, 1864–July 30, 1959). Luth. educ.; educ. Teachers Sem., Addison, Ill., and U. of Chicago; teacher and principal Danbury, Conn., 1889–1906; prof. Eng. and chemistry Addison and River Forest, Ill., 1906–47. Asst. ed. *Lutheran School Journal;* other works include *The Modern Grammar; The Modern Speller; Lessons in English and Busy Work for the Lower Grades; Science for the Grades.*

Miller, Charles Armand (Mar. 7, 1864–Sept. 10, 1917). B. Sheperdstown, W. Va. Educ. Roanoke (Va.) Coll.; Luth. Theol. Sem., Philadelphia, Pa.; Chicago (Ill.) Luth. Theol. Sem. Pastor Roanoke Coll. Ch. 1888–96; NYC 1896–1908; Charleston, S. C., 1908–12; Philadelphia 1912–17. Works include *The Way of the Cross; The Perfect Prayer and Its Lessons.*

Miller, George. See *Evangelical Church,* 3.

Miller, William. See *Adventist Bodies,* 1, 2.

Miller Faction. See *Indiana Synod* (1).

Millet. See *Middle East,* A 3.

Milligan, George (1860–1934). B. Kilconquhar, Fife, Scot.; educ. Aberdeen, Edinburgh, Göttingen, Bonn; pastor Morningside (suburb of Edinburgh) 1883–94 and Caputh, Perth, 1894–1910; prof. Glasgow U. 1910–32. Works include *The Vocabulary of the Greek Testament Illustrated from the Papyri and Other Non-Literary Sources* (parts 1 and 2 with J. H. Moulton*); *The New Testament Documents; Here & There Among the Papyri.* See also *Lexicons,* B.

Mills, Benjamin Fay. See *Revivals,* 2.

Mills, John (Mill; 1645–1707). Brit. NT textual scholar; fellow Queens Coll., Oxford; principal Saint Edmund Hall; formulated principles of NT textual* criticism; issued Gk. NT with variants of nearly 100 MSS 1707.

Mills, Samuel John (1783–1818). B. Torringford, Conn. Educ. Williams Coll., Williamstown, Mass.;

Andover (Mass.) Theol. Sem. Befriended H. Obookiah.* Made miss. tours through midwestern and southern states; ordained Cong. 1815; helped found United For. Miss. Soc. for Presb. and Ref. Chs. and the ABS; to W Afr. as agent of a colonization soc. Works include *Report of a Missionary Tour Through That Part of the United States Which Lies West of the Allegany Mountains.* See also *Haystack Group.*

Milman, Henry Hart (1791–1868). B. London, Eng.; educ. Eton and Oxford; priest 1816; vicar Reading 1818–35; rector and canon Westminster 1835–49; dean St. Paul's, London, 1849–68; prof. poetry Oxford 1821–31. Ed. E. Gibbon's* *The History of the Decline and Fall of the Roman Empire.* Other works include *The History of the Jews; The History of Christianity from the Birth of Christ to the Abolition of Paganism in the Roman Empire; History of Latin Christianity.* Hymns include "Ride On, Ride On in Majesty."

Milne, William (1785–1822). B. Kinnethmont, ca. 28 mi. NW of Aberdeen, Scot.; educ. at a miss. coll. of the LMS at Gosport, Eng.; miss. to China, arriving Macao 1813; to Malacca 1815, where he became chief founder of the Anglo-Chinese Coll. 1818, which was moved to Hong Kong 1843. Helped R. Morrison* tr. the Bible into Chinese; other works include a commentary on Eph. See also *Asia,* C 2; *Malaysia,* 2.

Miltiades (2d c.). Christian rhetorician; wrote against Montanists, Valentinians, Hellenes, Jews; said to have addressed *Apology* "to the rulers of the world," i. e., the emps.; works are lost; excerpts in Eusebius* of Caesarea's *HE.* See also *Apologists,* 9.

Miltiades (Melchiades; d. 314). B. perhaps Afr.; bp. (RCs: pope) Rome ca. 311–314; during his tenure the so-called Edict of Milan* was issued.

Miltitz, Karl von (ca. 1490–1529). B. Rabenau, near Dresden, Ger.; curial diplomat; papal notary and titular chamberlain; emissary of Leo X (see *Popes,* 20) to confer with M. Luther* after Cajetan's* defeat. See also *Luther, Martin,* 10–12.

Milton, John (1608–74). B. London, Eng.; educ. Cambridge; studied classics at home at Horton 1632 to 38; traveled in Fr. and It. 1638–39; assoc. with scholars including H. Grotius,* G. Galilei,* and Halste(nius)*; returned to Eng. 1639; supported *Morning of Christ's Nativity; L'Allegro; Il Pense-* civil and religious liberty; Lat. (or for.) secy. to O. Cromwell's* Council of State 1649; blind 1652; arrested, fined, and imprisoned several months at the Restoration 1660 (see also *England,* C 1); last yrs. spent in literary seclusion.

1st period (ca. 1626–37) works include *On the roso; Comus; Lycidas.* 2d period (ca. 1641–60) *Of Reformation Touching Church-Discipline in England; Of Prelatical Episcopacy; The Doctrine and Discipline of Divorce; Of Education; The Tenure of Kings; Areopagitica: for the Liberty of Unlicensed Printing; Treatise of Civil Power in Ecclesiastical Causes; De doctrina Christiana.* 3d period (ca. 1663–74) *Paradise Lost; Paradise Regained; Samson Agonistes.*

In *De doctrine Christiana* Milton spells out precisely the theol. operating in *Paradise Lost.* He insists on man's rational freedom and responsible power of choice; denied J. Calvin's* view of predestination; espouses Arminian and Arian theol.; asserts that God created the world out of His own substance, that the Trin. is not coequal but a descending order, and that the soul dies with the body until revived at the resurrection; favors polygamy. EEF

Milton Society, John. See *Blind,* 3.

Milwaukee Lutheran Teachers College. See *Ministry, Education of,* VIII C 1 f.

Milwaukee Lutheran Teachers Seminary. See *Lutheran Church – Missouri Synod, The,* V, 6.

Mimamsa. See *Brahmanism,* 4.

Minbar. See *Mosque.*

Mindaugas. See *Lithuania,* 1.

Miner, Alonzo Ames (1814–95). Universalist cleric; b. Lempster, N. H.; pastor Methuen 1839, Lowell 1842, Boston 1848–91, all in Mass.; pres. Tufts Coll., Medford, Mass., 1862; lectured on slavery and temperance. Ed. *Star of Bethlehem;* other works include *Bible Exercises* and *The Old Forts Taken.*

Ming Chia. See *Chinese Philosophy,* 4.

Miniatures and Illumination. Illumination (brightening, or illustration) of MSS is their artistic decoration with colors and/or gold (rarely silver); usually connected with ornamental letters, chap. openings, and page borders. "Miniatures" (from Lat. *minium,* "red lead") originally referred to illumination of MSS.

The earliest surviving illuminated papyrus roll is the Ramesseum Papyrus from Egypt ca. 1900 BC. Christian illumination arose in Constantinople ca. AD 500. E monasteries preserved the practice during the Iconoclastic* Controversy. Anglo-Saxon and Irish illumination flourished 7th-8th c. Noted scriptoriums (see *Scriptorium*) were founded in the Carolingian renaissance.

The 1st schools of illumination in S Fr. were est. in the 11th c. The It. renaissance revived the classical style. With the invention of printing the number of MSS copied by hand decreased, and the art of illumination disappeared, though Ger. was slow to give it up.

In the 16th-17th c. small portraits came to be called miniatures. JEG

Minims *(Ordo [Fratrum] Minimorum).* Franciscan order founded 1435 by Francis* of Paola; its 1st rule, confirmed 1493, was based on that of Francis* of Assisi; its 2d, sanctioned 1501, was more indep. and entailed abstention not only from meat and fish but also from eggs, cheese, butter, and milk.

Ministerial Office. 1. The office of the ministry is a divine institution. Scripture distinguishes bet. the office of the ministry and the universal* priesthood of believers. All Christians are priests (1 Ptr 2:9; Rv 1:6), but only some hold the office of the ministry. The Bible speaks of the latter in various terms (e.g., overseers, ministers, pastors, teachers, deacons, elders), indicating the scope of the office (Acts 20:28; 1 Co 4:1; 12:29; Eph 4:11-12; 1 Ti 3:1-2, 8-13; Tts 1:5). The office of a minister is not a continuation of the priesthood of the OT, nor does it consist in certain rights and powers vested in the Apostles which only they and their successors could and can confer on others, nor is it conferred indelibly on any individual by ordination (see *Character indelebilis*). Christ continues His prophetic office through the work of the ministry; those who are called by Christian congs. or groups of congs. are Christ's undershepherds, Christ Himself being the one Lord and Master (Mt 23:8; 1 Ptr 5:4). The means of grace (see *Grace, Means of*) were given by God to the ch. A Christian cong. calls certain men to administer them for the cong., thus making them *ministrantes inter Christianos* ("those who minister among Christians"). The ch. has the obligation to carry out the commission of Mt 28:19-20 and may create whatever other offices are necessary.

2. We may distinguish bet. the ministerial office *in abstracto* (*Predigtamt;* ministry) and *in concreto* (*Pfarramt;* pastorate). AC V speaks of the ministry *in abstracto:* "In order that we may obtain this faith, the ministry of teaching the Gospel and administering the sacraments was instituted. . . . Our churches condemn the Anabaptists and others who think that the Holy Spirit comes to men without the external Word, through their own preparations and works." AC XIV speaks of the ministerial office *in concreto:* "It is taught among us that nobody should publicly

teach or preach or administer the sacraments in the church without a regular call."

3. Pastors properly called by congs. are shepherds of their flock acc. to God's will (Acts 20:28; Tts 1:5).

4. God provided that His work be done through chs. (e. g., Acts 2:41-42, 47; 20:28). The apostles were inspired; ministers are not; but the apostles made no distinction bet. themselves and pastors *as far as the work of the ministry is concerned,* but spoke of pastors as having the same duties (2 Ti 2:2; 1 Ptr 5:2), the same authority (Heb 13:17), performing the same service (1 Co 3:5); and regarded them fully as their fellow ministers (1 Co 3:22; 4:1; Cl 1:7; 1 Ptr 5:1).

5. Two elements have been distinguished in the call to the ministry. One is the inward conviction urging the individual to enter the ministry. The other is the call, the invitation from God through the ch. to specific pub. ministry in the ch. Ordination usually follows the 1st call received and accepted. JHCF

See also *Pastor as Counselor; Teachers.*

P. G. Lindemann, *Ambassadors of Christ* (St. Louis, 1935); G. H. Gerberding, *The Lutheran Pastor,* 4th ed. (Philadelphia, 1902); C. F. W. Walther, *Die Stimme unserer Kirche in der Frage von Kirche und Amt,* 4th ed. (Zwickau, Ger., 1894); C. C. Stoughton, *Set Apart for the Gospel* (Philadelphia, 1946); W. H. Greever, *The Minister and the Ministry* (Philadelphia, 1945); P. F. Koehneke, "The Call into the Holy Ministry," *The Abiding Word,* I, ed. T. Laetsch (St. Louis, 1946), 366–388; M. J. Steege, "The Lutheran Pastor," *The Abiding Word,* I, ed. T. Laetsch (St. Louis, 1946), 389–409; E. E. Foelber, "The Office of the Public Ministry," *The Abiding Word,* II, ed. T. Laetsch (St. Louis, 1947), 474–492; T. F. Gullixson, "The Ministry," *What Lutherans Are Thinking,* ed. E. C. Fendt (Columbus, Ohio, 1947), pp. 289–306; R. R. Caemmerer and E. L. Lueker, *Church and Ministry in Transition* (St. Louis, 1964); *The Ministry in Historical Perspectives,* ed. H. R. Niebuhr and D. D. Williams (New York, 1956); E. L. Lueker, *Change and the Church* (St. Louis, 1969).

Ministerium. Term in Am. Lutheranism originally referring to a body of ordained ministers charged with certain responsibilities, e.g., to examine, license, and ordain candidates for the ministry; lay* delegates were included in meetings of the N. Y. Ministerium from its beginning, the Pa. Ministerium from 1792. See also *United Lutheran Church Synods of,* 5, 15, 22.

Ministerium in North America, An Evangelical Lutheran. See *United Lutheran Church, Synods of,* 22.

Ministry, Education of. I. Christ instructed His disciples before commissioning them to preach. Paul and other apostles trained colaborers by instruction. Facing gnostics and heathen philosophers demanded educ. leaders in the ch. In course of time, catechetical schools were est. for instruction in Christian doctrine preparatory to ch. membership; these schools came to prepare men for the ministry. See also *Catechetics,* 3; *Exegesis,* 3; *Schools, Early Christian.*

II. Standards declined in the Middle Ages. Students in urban areas were trained in monasteries and cathedral schools, those in rural areas were trained by local priests. In course of time, training became so deficient that even some who became bps. found it hard to preach a short sermon, and many priests had difficulty reading appointed Scripture lessons in pub. services. Charlemagne* gathered men of learning about him and encouraged better ministerial training (see also *Alcuin*).

III. The 13th c. brought great change. Theol. schools were united with univs.; those at Paris and Oxford became esp. famous. Peter* the Lombard's *Sententiarum libri quatuor* became the standard textbook. Both lecture and discussion methods were used. The Renaissance* left its mark on ministerial training.

IV. As the Luth. Reformation* conquered most of cen. Eur., it was hard to provide able ministers for the thousands of ev. congs. The average educ. of RC priests was minimal. In the preface to the SC M. Luther* says: "Many pastors are quite unfit and incompetent to teach." Leaders of the Reformation were gathered into a faculty at Wittenberg to train future ministers. But it took time to effect widespread and lasting improvement. During the 1st 25 yrs. most men ordained by M. Luther, J. Bugenhagen,* and their assistants were without university or coll. educ. Before the middle of the c., men with full university training had become the rule, and the standard of examinations before ordination was consistently raised. Scholastic theol. gave way to exegesis (study of the Bible on basis of its original languages), systematic theol. (study of Bible doctrines), and practical theol. (emphasizing preaching and teaching). So the foundation was laid for the 4 depts. of present-day Luth. theol. sems.: Exegetic, Systematic, Historical, Practical.

The Council of Trent* (Sess. V, Decree Concerning Reform, chap. 1) ordered provision for theol. educ. in every cathedral ch.; later it made each diocese responsible for the theol. educ. of its clerics and gave govt. of the sems. to the resp. bps. (Sess. XXIII, Decree Concerning Reform, chap. 18).

V. The beneficial influence of the Reformation was brief. Within a c., university training became mainly intellectual and philos. In the 18th c., rationalism* gained control even in theol. faculties, with devastating effect on the ministry. In the 19th c., scientific and liberal thinking dominated Prot. Eur. theol. and spread to other countries. The Kropp* Sem. trained hundreds of pastors for Luths. in Am.

VI. In the US, ministers are trained without interference by the state. Each denomination establishes its plan of educ., confessional basis, and schools for its own communion. Most Prot. ministers who came with early settlers or emigrated to the colonies before ca. 1700 were educ. in Eur. With the growth of an Am. ch. came the need for Am. theol. educ.

A. Colleges, patterned after Eur. schools, were established. Harvard (Cambridge, Mass.; 1636), William and Mary (Williamsburg, Va.; 1693), Yale (New Haven, Conn.; 1701), Princeton (Princeton, N. J.; 1746) were founded with ministerial educ. as one primary objective. In the early days, the Am. coll. of liberal arts was a distinctively religious institution, and the educ. offered was centered in equipping men for the ministry. The Bible was taught on basis of its original languages, and all students were held to learn its doctrines and precepts. Chairs of divinity were est. (Hollis professorship of divinity at Harvard 1721; Yale professorship of divinity 1755). These schools were inaccessible to candidates for the ministry living far away. Such candidates sought private instruction from a neighboring minister. J. Bellamy trained scores of students in his home, N. Emmons perhaps nearly 100 (see also *New England Theology,* 4). H. M. Mühlenberg* also tutored students. Private tutoring was not always of high quality. Am. chs. began to consider est. schools exclusively for ministerial training. The Dutch Ref. Ch. est. what is usually regarded as the 1st separate Prot. sem. in Am. at Flatbush, Long Island, N. Y., 1784, under J. H. Livingston.* RC St. Mary's Sem., Baltimore, Md., was est. 1791. Congregationalists est. Andover (Mass.) Theol. Sem. 1807/08. A divinity school was est. at Harvard 1819, Yale 1822. The Hartford (Conn.) Theol. Sem. was founded 1833/34. Other similar schools were est. in course of time, some ch.-controlled, some indep. See also *Higher Education,* 10; *Protestant Education in the United States.*

B. At the beginning of the 19th c. the Prot. chs. felt that each denomination could best train its own ministry by founding as many sems. as it considered necessary under direct denominational control, setting its own educ. standards and doctrinal position. Many sems. received many students without coll. preparation. Problems incident to WW I led to a 1918 gathering of a group of theol. educators at Cambridge, Mass. As a result, a conf. of theol. sems. and colleges was formed. In 1936 this conf. became The Am. Assoc. of Theol. Schools, which adopted standards for accreditation and placed theol. educ. at the graduate level, requiring an AB or its equivalent for admission to a 3-yr. course leading to the BD, and a faculty of at least 4 full-time profs., and setting standards for library, equipment, finances, etc. Schools which did not conform were not admitted. 1926 religious census figures for 17 of the largest white Prot. denominations in the US show that 2 in 5 of all ministers in these denominations were not grads. of a coll. or theol. sem.; only 1 in 3 was a grad. of both. The highest proportion of ministers who were both coll. and sem. grads. was in the Luth. Church.

C. Luths. in Am. also first looked to Eur. for ministers. Ca. the middle of the 18th c. it became evident that this source would be inadequate or cease entirely. A beginning of a native ministry was made by appointing certain men as theol. instructors authorized to prepare young men for the ministry. Candidates were then examined by the clergy in convention. Hartwick* Sem., the 1st Luth. school, was est. 1797, but was not an official ch. sem. The 1st official Luth. theol. sem. in Am. opened 1826 at Gettysburg, Pa. (see *Gettysburg Seminary*). The Ev. Luth. Theol. Sem., begun 1830 at Canton, Ohio, by the Ev. Luth. Joint Syn. of Ohio* and Other States, moved 1831 to Columbus; connected with Capital U. till 1959. Luth. Theol. Southern Sem., est. 1830 near Pomaria, S. C., by the Ev. Luth. Syn. of S. C. (see *United Lutheran Church, Synods of,* 16, 27), moved to various cities, finally to Columbia, S. C., 1911. In 1839 Luth. immigrants from Saxony founded, in Perry Co., Mo., the school which developed into Conc. Sem., St. Louis, Mo.

For a more complete listing of Luth. sems in Am. see X.

VII. *Pretheological Training.* A. *General.* The 1st colleges in the US were strictly religious institutions; all students were required to take theol. courses. But the attitude toward religion underwent a radical change. The old colleges became indep. and self-perpetuating. Increasing emphasis has been put on physical sciences. Rise of state univs. affected ministerial training. In these schools the demand for practical courses, designed to fit men for business or profession, has been crowding out the liberal arts coll. Credit courses in religion are offered in some state univs. The number of students of theol. sems. from state univs. and the old colleges is comparatively small.

B. These trends led to many ch.-related schools, listed in *Yearbook of American Churches.*

C. 1. When pub. schools became widespread ca. 1850, parish schools decreased in number. New impetus was given the parish schools by the Saxon Luth. immigrants and the Mo. Syn. (see *Lutheran Church – Missouri Synod, The,* V, 5–6; *Parish Education; Teachers*).

2. Luth. high schools (see *Parish Education,* D 1) link parish schools and ch.-related colleges.

VIII. *Feeder Schools for Luth. Sems.* A. *Luth. Univs. in Am.* include:

1. Capital U., Bexley (Columbus), Ohio, founded 1850; The ALC. See also VI C; X E; *Universities in the United States, Lutheran,* 2.

2. Pacific Luth. U., Tacoma, Wash., founded 1890; The ALC. See also *Universities in the United States, Lutheran,* 3.

3. Susquehanna* U., Selinsgrove, Pa., founded 1858; LCA.

4. Valparaiso U., Valparaiso, Ind., founded 1859. See also *Universities in the United States, Lutheran,* 5.

5. Waterloo Luth. U., Waterloo, Ont., Can. *United Lutheran Church, Synods of,* 1.

6. Wittenberg* U., Springfield, Ohio, founded 1845.

B. *Luth. 4-yr. Colleges* include:

1. Augsburg Coll., Minneapolis, Minn., founded 1869; sem. dept. eliminated 1963; The ALC.

2. Augustana Coll., Rock Island, Ill., founded 1860; LCA. See also *Augustana Evangelical Lutheran Church,* 14; *Lutheran Church in America,* V.

3. Augustana Coll., Sioux Falls, S. Dak., founded 1860; The ALC.

4. Bethany Coll., Lindsborg, Kans., founded 1881; LCA. See also *Lutheran Church in America,* V; *Swenson, Carl Aaron.*

5. Calif. Luth. Coll., Thousand Oaks, Calif., founded 1959; LCA and The ALC.

6. Carthage* Coll., Kenosha, Wis., founded 1847; LCA.

7. Conc. Coll., Moorhead, Minn., founded 1891; The ALC.

8. Conc. Sr. Coll., Fort Wayne, Ind., consecrated 1957, dedicated 1958; bridge bet. jr. colleges and Conc. Sem., St. Louis; LCMS. See also C 2 f; X C; *Lutheran Church – Missouri Synod, The,* VII, 12.

9. Conc. Teachers Coll., River Forest, Ill.; LCMS. See also *Lutheran Church – Missouri Synod, The,* V, 6.

10. Conc. Teachers Coll., Seward, Nebr., founded 1894; LCMS. See also *Lutheran Church – Missouri Synod, The,* VI 6.

11. Dana Coll., Blair, Nebr., founded 1884; The ALC.

12. Dr. Martin Luther Coll., New Ulm, Minn., est. 1883/84; Wis. Syn. See also *Luther College,* 3.

13. Gettysburg* Coll., Gettysburg, Pa., founded 1832; LCA.

14. Gustavus Adolphus Coll., St. Peter, Minn., founded 1862; LCA. See also *Norelius, Eric.*

15. Hartwick* Coll., Oneonta, N. Y., founded 1928; LCA. By 1970 it had withdrawn from the LCA to qualify for greater state support.

16. Lenoir Rhyne Coll., Hickory, N. C., founded 1891; LCA. See also *Lutheran Church in America,* V; *United Lutheran Church, Synods of,* 16.

17. Luther Coll., Decorah, Iowa, founded 1859; The ALC. See also *Luther College,* 1.

18. Midland* Luth. Coll., Fremont, Nebr., founded 1887; LCA.

19. Muhlenberg Coll., Allentown, Pa., founded 1848; LCA.

20. Newberry Coll., Newberry, S. C., founded 1856; LCA. See also *United Lutheran Church, Synods of,* 27.

21. Northwestern* Coll., Watertown, Wis., founded 1865; WELS.

22. Roanoke Coll., Salem, Va., founded 1842; LCA.

23. St. Olaf Coll., Northfield, Minn., founded 1874; The ALC.

24. Texas Luth. Coll., Seguin, Tex., founded 1891; The ALC.

25. Thiel Coll., Greenville, Pa., founded 1866; LCA. See also *United Lutheran Church, Synods of,* 24.

26. Upsala Coll., East Orange, N. J., founded 1893; LCA.

27. Wagner Coll., Staten Is., N. Y., founded 1883; LCA.

28. Wartburg Coll., Waverly, Iowa, founded 1852; The ALC.

C. *Luth. Jr. Colleges.* 1. *Without high school academy:*

a. Conc. Luth. Jr. Coll., Ann Arbor, Mich., founded 1963; LCMS. See also *Lutheran Church – Missouri Synod, The,* VII, 12.

b. Grand View Coll., Des Moines, Iowa, founded 1896; LCA.

c. Luther Coll., Regina, Sask., Can., est. 1913/14; The ALC. Action taken 1966 to fed. it with the U. of Sask. See also *Luther College,* 5.

d. Luther Jr. Coll., Wahoo, Nebr., founded 1883; merged with Midland Coll., Fremont, 1962. See also VIII B 18; *Luther College,* 2.

e. Marion Coll., Marion, Va., founded 1873; LCA. LCA recognition withdrawn 1966; school closed. See also *United Lutheran Church, Synods of,* 29.

f. Milwaukee Luth. Teachers Coll., Milwaukee, Wis., founded 1960; WELS. Name changed 1967 to Wis. Luth. Coll.; merged 1970 with Dr. Martin Luther Coll., New Ulm, Minn. See also VIII B 12.

g. Suomi Coll., Hancock, Mich., founded 1896; LCA.

h. Wis. Lutheran Coll., Milwaukee, Wis., inc. 1972; WELS.

2. *With high school academy:*

a. Alabama Luth. Academy and Coll., Selma, Ala., est. 1920/22 by the Synodical* Conf.; LCMS.

b. Bethany Luth. Coll. and High School, Mankato, Minn., founded 1911; ELS.

c. Calif. Conc. Coll., Oakland, Calif., founded 1906; LCMS.

d. Camrose Luth. Coll., Camrose, Alberta, Can., founded 1911 by Hauge's Norw. Ev. Luth. Syn. and The United Norw. Luth. Ch. in Am.; ALC/ELCC 1960; affiliated with U. of Alberta 1959. See also *Canada,* A 20.

e. Conc. Coll., Edmonton, Alberta, Can., founded 1921; LCMS.

f. Conc. Coll., Fort Wayne, Ind., founded 1846; deeded to Mo. Syn. 1847; P. Fleischmann* and 6 normal-school students moved 1857 from Milwaukee, Wis., to Fort Wayne and united with the theol. sem. (see also *Lutheran Church – Missouri Synod, The,* V, 6); an Eng. academy, under syn. discussion 1852, 1853, 1854, and 1857, opened 1857, closed 1858; the coll. section of the Mo. Syn. St. Louis sem. moved to Fort Wayne 1861. Closed when Conc. Sr. Coll. came into existence. See also VIII B 8; X D.

g. Conc. Coll., Milwaukee, Wis., founded 1881; LCMS. See also *Lutheran Church – Missouri Synod, The,* V, 7.

h. Conc. Coll., Portland, Oreg., founded 1905; LCMS.

i. Conc. Coll., St. Paul, Minn., founded 1893; LCMS. See also *Teachers,* 6.

j. Conc. Coll. (name changed 1969 from Conc. Collegiate Institute), Bronxville, N. Y., founded 1881; LCMS. See also *Lutheran Church – Missouri Synod, The,* V, 7.

k. Immanuel* Luth. Coll., Eau Claire, Wis., founded 1959.

l. Luth. Brethren Schools (formerly Luth. Bible School), Fergus Falls, Minn., founded 1903. See also *Church of the Lutheran Brethren of America.*

m. Conc. Luth. Coll. of Tex., Austin, Tex., founded 1926; LCMS.

n. St. John's Coll., Winfield, Kans., founded 1893; LCMS. See also *Missouri and Other States, The English Evangelical Lutheran Synod of.*

o. St. Paul's Coll., Concordia, Mo., founded 1884; LCMS.

For LCMS teachers colleges see also *Teachers,* 4–6.

IX. A. The LCA has a Bd. of Coll. Educ. and Ch. Vocations which works to recruit workers for ch. vocations.

B. Other Luth. bodies in Am. also recruit workers for the ministry.

C. Most Luth. sems. require graduation from a recognized coll., preferably Luth.

D. The syn. or group of syns. operating Luth. sems. writes the const. by which the respective sem. is governed. The syn. elects the Bd. of Control. In most cases the membership of the bd. is divided bet. clergy and laity.

Profs. at the sems. are selected either by the syn. in conv. or by the Bd. of Control or Bd. of Electors. Many syns. require an active parish ministry prior to sem. teaching. Regularly called Luth. teachers are pledged to Holy Scripture and the Lutheran* Confessions. Evidence that a teacher no longer holds the belief to which he is pledged makes him subject to discipline and possible dismissal.

X. *Luth. Theol. Sems. in the US.*

A. Bethany Luth. Sem., Mankato, Minn., est. 1946; ELS.

B. Cen. Luth. Theol. Sem., Fremont, Nebr., est. 1893 as Western* Theol. Sem.; LCA; merged 1966 with Luth. School of Theol. at Chicago (see X I).

C. Conc. Sem., St. Louis, Mo. Legal title: Conc. Coll. Founded 1839 Perry Co., Mo., as a classical coll. and school of theol. (see *Lutheran Church – Missouri Synod, The,* II, 4).

Ownership, control, and supervision of the school, which moved to temporary quarters in St. Louis 1849 and to a more permanent location on S. Jefferson Ave. 1850, passed into the hands of the Mo. Syn. 1849/50. C. F. W. Walther* was its 1st prof. theol. (by syn. designation 1849) and its leading teacher and pres. (the latter from 1854) until his death 1887. It received a formal charter from the state of Mo. 1853. In 1861 the classical (preparatory) dept. (Gymnasium) moved to Fort Wayne, Ind., and the practical sem. moved from Fort Wayne to St. Louis; the practical sem. moved to Springfield, Ill., 1875.

In 1882/83 a new bldg. replaced the one begun 1849. In 1907 an addition was built, increasing the capacity to ca. 300 resident students. In 1926 the sem. moved to a site (ca. 71 acres) at 801 De Mun Ave., Clayton (suburb of St. Louis), where an entirely new Tudor-Gothic plant had been erected for ca. $3,000,000. KFUO (see *Radio Stations, Religious,* 3) is on the W part of the campus. Later construction includes Sieck Hall, dormitories, Ludwig E. Fuerbringer Hall, and Luther Tower.

A "pretheological" yr. was part of the curriculum 1938—57 as bridge bet. jr. colleges and the sem. The BA was first awarded 1940 after the 2d yr. of study. In view of the est. of Conc. Sr. Coll., Fort Wayne, Ind. (see VIII B 8), entrance requirements were stated in terms of a BA. In 1959 the first grads. of Conc. Sr. Coll. entered under the rev. curriculum. The BD is awarded after the 4th yr. The sem. was fully accredited by the Am. Assoc. of Theol. Schools 1964.

The curriculum falls into the 4 traditional areas of exegetic, systematic, hist., and practical theol. Primary goals: to introd. each student to essential knowledge and skills in these 4 areas, to outline the course that future growth and use of the material can take, and to instill a desire to work with people in the application of the Gospel.

The sem. has an extensive field work program. Six students vicared 1903–04. The dept. of field work was officially est. 1945. In their first 2 yrs. students take part in local cong. and inst. field work. The 3d yr. is spent in a ministerial internship (or "vicarage") under supervision of a LCMS pastor and is followed by 4th-yr. academic courses.

A Correspondence School was founded 1920. One-week summer sessions began 1929 but encountered difficulty as a result of the Depression. A solid program of summer work began 1951.

The School for Grad. Studies began 1923 with 6 students. In 1944 a dir. of grad. studies was appointed, and a ThD program inaugurated. The MAR program was est. 1956.

Pres.: C. F. W. Walther* 1854–87, F. Pieper* 1887–1931, L. Fuerbringer* 1931–43, L. J. Sieck* 1943–52, Alfred Ottomar Fuerbringer (b. 1903) 1953–69, John Henry Tietjen (b. 1928) 1969–.

See also *Lutheran Church — Missouri Synod, The,* I, 4; V, 2; VI, 7.

D. Conc. Sem., Springfield, Ill., est. 1846 at Fort Wayne, Ind., as a practical sem. (see *Löhe, Johann Konrad Wilhelm*); deeded to Mo. Syn. 1847; moved to St. Louis, Mo., 1861, where it functioned with the theoretical sem. (see X C) till 1875, when it moved to Springfield, Ill., on grounds of the former Ill. State U. (see *Carthage College*).

The policy of the sem. is to train for the ministry men who have a BA. The MDiv degree is offered (first conferred on graduates of the 1972–73 class). Field work and a year's internship are integral elements of the program of study. The sem. is a mem. of the Am. Assoc. of Theol. Schools.

Pres.: W. Sihler* 1846–61, C. F. W. Walther* 1861–75, F. A. Crämer* 1878–91, R. Pieper* 1891–1914, R. D. Biedermann* 1914–21, H. A. Klein* 1922–35, H. B. Hemmeter* 1936–45, G. C. Barth* 1945–52, W. A. Baepler* 1953–58, George John Beto (b. 1916) 1959–62, Jacob A. O. Preus (b. 1920) 1962–69, Richard J. Schultz (b. 1920) 1970–74, Robert D. Preus (b. 1924) 1974–.

E. Ev. Luth. Theol. Sem. (Capital U. Sem.), Columbus, Ohio; est. 1830; indep. of Capital U. 1959; The ALC. See also VI C; *Ohio and Other States, Evangelical Lutheran Joint Synod of,* 3.

F. Hamma School of Theol., Springfield, Ohio; est. as Wittenberg Coll. 1845; named Hamma Divinity School 1907; indep. of Wittenberg U. 1964; name changed 1964 to Hamma Divinity School; LCA.

G. Luther Theol. Sem., St. Paul, Minn., est. 1876; ELC 1917–61, then The ALC; in 1963 merger Augsburg Theol. Sem., Minneapolis (est. 1869; after 1897 LFC), united with Luther Theol. Sem. on the latter's campus. See also *Luther Theological Seminary,* 1.

H. Lutheran Brethren Schools (formerly Luth. Bible School and Sem.), Fergus Falls, Minn., est. 1903; Church* of the Luth. Brethren of Am.

I. Lutheran School of Theol. at Chicago, Ill., formed 1962 by completion of consolidation of Augustana Theol. Sem., Rock Island, Ill. (est. 1860; Augustana Ev. Luth. Ch.), Chicago Luth. Theol. Sem., Maywood, Ill. (est. 1891; ULC), Grand View Sem., Des Moines, Iowa (est. 1896; AELC), and Suomi Theol. Sem., Hancock, Mich. (est. 1904; Suomi Syn.); LCA. Cen. Luth. Theol. Sem., Fremont, Nebr. (est. 1893; ULC/LCA) merged with the consolidated Chicago sem. 1966. Prior to summer 1967 the Chicago sem. operated on campuses at Chicago, Rock Island, and Fremont. Full operations in Chicago began in fall 1967. See also *Augustana Evangelical Lutheran Church,* 9, 14; *Lutheran Church in America,* V.

J. Lutheran Theol. Sem., Gettysburg, Pa.; est. 1826; LCA; joint administration with Luth. Theol. Sem., Philadelphia, since 1964. See also K; *Gettysburg Seminary.*

K. Lutheran Theol. Sem., Mount Airy, Philadelphia, Pa., est. 1864 in Philadelphia, moved 1889 to Mount Airy, NW cen. Philadelphia; LCA; joint administration with Lutheran Theol. Sem., Gettysburg, Pa., since 1964. See also J; *Lutheran Church in America,* V; *United Lutheran Church, Synods of,* 22.

L. Lutheran Theol. Sem., Saskatoon, Sask., created 1965 by merger of Lutheran Coll. and Sem. (est. 1913; LCA; see *Canada,* A 14) and Luther Theol. Sem. (est. 1939; The ALC; see *Canada,* A 20); LCA and The ALC. See also *Lutheran Church in America,* V.

M. Lutheran Theol. Southern Sem., Columbia, S. C., est. 1830; LCA. See also VI C; *Lutheran Church in America,* V; *United Lutheran Church, Synods of,* 27.

N. Northwestern* Luth. Theol. Sem., St. Paul, Minn., est. 1920; LCA. See also *United Lutheran Church, Synods of,* 17.

O. Pacific Luth. Theol. Sem., Berkeley, Calif., est. 1950; LCA. See also *United Lutheran Church, Synods of,* 20, 21.

P. Wartburg Theol. Sem., Dubuque, Iowa, est. 1854; originally the school of G. M. Grossmann*; moved from Dubuque to St. Sebald, Iowa, and called Wartburg 1857; to Mendota, Ill., 1874; to Dubuque, Iowa, 1889; The ALC. Trin. Sem., Blair, Nebr. (est. 1884; UELC), united with Wartburg 1961. See also *Ohio and Other States, Evangelical Lutheran Joint Synod of,* 8.

Q. Waterloo Luth. Sem., Waterloo, Ont., Can. See *United Lutheran Church, Synods of,* 1.

R. Wis. Luth. Sem., Mequon (Thiensville), Wis., est. 1863; WELS. See also *Wisconsin, Evangelical Lutheran Joint Synod of,* 2; *Wisconsin Synod,* 2.

S. Immanuel Luth. Sem., Eau Claire, Wis. See *Immanuel Lutheran College* (Eau Claire, Wis.).

XI. *For. Miss. Sems. Training Luth. Ministers.*

A. Africa.

1. École Biblique Centrale, Kaélé, Cameroon. Luth. Brethren Miss.

2. École de Théologie Évangélique, Meiganga, Cameroon. The ALC; Norw. Missionary Soc.

3. Fairview Theol. Sem., Port Elizabeth, Cape Province, Rep. of South Africa. The Moravian Ch. in South Afr. (Western Cape Province).

4. Mekane Yesus Sem., Addis Ababa, Ethiopia. The Ethiopian Ev. Ch.–Mekane Yesus (*Coptic,* "the place of Jesus").

5. Bible and Pastors' Training School, Dilla, Ethiopia. Norw. Luth. Miss.

6. Lutheran Training Institute, Monrovia, Liberia.

7. École Pastorale Luthérienne, Ivory, Fianarantsoa, Madagascar. Malagasy Luth. Ch.

8. Lutheran Sem., Obot Idim, Nigeria. Ev. Luth. Ch. of Nigeria and LCMS.

9. Theol. Coll., Bukuru, Northern Nigeria. Fellowship of Chs. of Christ in the Sudan.

10. Lutheran Theol. Sem., Enhlanhleni, Natal, Rep. of South Afr. The Mission of the Ev. Luth. Free Chs.

11. Hermannsburg Sem., Greytown, Natal, Rep. of South Afr.

12. Luth. Theol. Coll., Umpumulo, Natal, Rep. of South Africa. Ev. Luth. Ch. of South Afr., Southeastern Region.

13. Lutheran Theol. Sem., Marang, near Rustenburg, Transvaal, Rep. of South Africa. Ev. Luth. Ch. of South Afr. (Tswana Region) and the Hermannsburg Miss.

14. United Luth. Theol. Sem. Paulinum, Otjimbingwe, South-West Africa. Fin. Miss. Soc.

15. Lutheran Theol. Coll., Makumira, Tanzania (Tanganyika). Ev. Luth. Ch. of Tanzania.

16. École Biblique Centrale, Gouna Gaya, Chad. Luth. Brethren Miss.

B. Asia and Australia.

1–2. Formation 1966 of the Luth. Ch. of Australia (see *Australia, Lutheranism in,* B 1) led to merger of Conc. Sem. (see *Australia, Lutheranism in,* A 2) and Immanuel Sem., both in Adelaide, on the site of Immanuel Sem., North Adelaide. The resultant school, Luther Sem., was dedicated Mar. 3, 1968.

3. Conc. Theol. Sem., Kowloon, Hong Kong. LCMS.

4. Lok Yuk Theol. Sem., Hong Kong.

5. Lutheran Theol. Sem., Sha Tin (Shateen), Hong Kong. The ALC, LCA, Ch. of Swed. Miss., Fin. Miss. Soc., Norw. Miss. Soc., Ev. Luth. Ch. of Hong Kong.

6. Basel Mission Theol. Sem., Mangalore, India.

7. Conc. Theol. Sem., Nagercoil, India. The India Ev. Luth. Ch.

8. Gurukul Luth. Theol. Coll. and Research Institute, Kilpauk, Madras, India. The mem. chs. of the Fed. of Ev. Luth. Chs. in India.

9. Gurusala Divinity School, Tranquebar, India. Tamil Ev. Luth. Ch.

10. Jensen Theol. Coll. and Bible School, Kotapud, India. Jeypore Ev. Luth. Ch.

11. Lutheran Theol. Coll., Ranchi, India. Gossner Ev. Luth. Ch.

12. Luthergiri Theol. Coll., Rajahmundry, India. Andhra Ev. Luth. Ch. et al.

13. Nimasarai Bengali Divinity School, Old Malda, India. Dan. Luth.

14. Santal Theol. Sem., Santal Parganas, India. Northern Ev. Luth. Ch.

15. Universitas H. K. B. P. Nommensen, Pematangsiantar, Indonesia.

16. Japan Luth. Theol. Sem., Tokyo, Japan. Japan Ev. Luth. Ch.

17. Kobe Luth. Sem., Kobe, Japan. Norw. Luth. Miss.

18. Theol. Training Program, Tokyo, Japan. Japan Luth. Ch. and LCMS.

19. Trin. Theol. Coll., Singapore, Malaysia. Meth. et al.

20. Pakistani Luth. Ch. Sem., Mardan, (W.) Pakistan.

21. Senior Flierl Sem., Logaweng, Finschhafen, New Guinea. Ev. Luth. Ch. of New Guinea. See also *Flierl, Johan(nes).*

22. Lutheran Theol. Sem., Baguio City, Philippines. See also *Lutheran Church – Missouri Synod, The,* VII, 14.

23. Federated Luth. Sem., Taichung, Taiwan.* LCMS and The ALC.

C. Cen. and S. America.

1. Facultad Luterana de Teologia, José C. Paz, Argentina. United Ev. Luth. Ch. in Argentina.

2. Seminario Concordia, Libertad, Argentina. Argentina Ev. Luth. Ch.

3. Faculdade de Teologia, Sao Leopoldo, Brazil.

4. Seminário Concórdia, Pôrto Alegre, Brazil. The Ev. Luth. Ch. of Brazil.

5. Seminario Teológico Augsburgo, Mexico City, Mexico. Ev. Luth. Ch., Columbia Syn., et al.

XII. *Non-Luth. Prot. Theol. Sems. in US include:*

Anderson Coll. School of Theol., Anderson, Ind. (Ch. of God) 1917.

Andover Newton Theol. School, Newton Centre, Mass. (Baps. and United Ch. of Christ) 1807.

Asbury Theol. Sem., Wilmore, Ky. (Interdenom.) 1923.

Austin Presb. Theol. Sem., Austin, Tex. 1902.

Bangor Theol. Sem., Bangor, Maine (United Ch. of Christ) 1814.

Berkeley Divinity School, New Haven, Conn. (Episc.) 1854.

Bethany Theol. Sem., Oak Brook, Ill. (Ch. of Brethren) 1905.

Boston U. (School of Theol.), Boston, Mass. (Meth.) 1839.

Calvin Theol. Sem., Grand Rapids, Mich. (Christian Ref.) 1876.

Cen. Bap. Theol. Sem., Kansas City, Kansas (Bap.) 1901.

Chicago Theol. Sem., Chicago, Ill. (United Ch. of Christ) 1855.

Christian Theol. Sem., Indianapolis, Ind. (Christian Ch. [Disciples of Christ]) 1925.

Church Divinity School of the Pacific, Berkeley, Calif. (Episc.) 1893.

Colgate Rochester Divinity School/Bexley Hall, Rochester, N. Y. (Interdenom.) 1817.

Columbia Theol. Sem., Decatur, Ga. (Presb.) 1828.

Divinity School of the Prot. Episc. Ch., The, Philadelphia, Pa. 1857.

Drew U. (Theol. School), Madison, N. J. (Meth.) 1866/67.

Duke U., Durham, N. C. (Meth.) 1926.

Eastern Bap. Theol. Sem., Philadelphia, Pa. 1925.

Eden Theol. Sem., St. Louis, Mo. (United Ch. of Christ) 1850.

Emory U. (The Candler School of Theol.), Atlanta, Ga. (Meth.) 1914.

Episc. Theol. School, Cambridge, Mass. 1867.

Episc. Theol. Sem. of the Southwest, Austin, Tex. 1951.

Ev. Theol. Sem., Naperville, Ill. (Meth.) 1873.

Ev. Theol. Sem., Inc., Goldsboro, N. C. (Bap.) (1971?)

Fuller Theol. Sem., Pasadena, Calif. (Nondenom.) 1947.

Garrett Theol. Sem., Evanston, Ill. (Meth.) 1853.

Gen. Theol. Sem., NYC (Episc.) 1817.

Golden Gate Bap. Theol. Sem., Mill Valley, Calif. (Bap.) 1944.

Goshen Biblical Sem., Elkhart, Ind. (Mennonite) 1894.

Grace Theol. Sem. and Grace Coll., Winona Lake, Ind. (Brethren) 1937.

Hartford Seminary Foundation, The, Hartford, Conn. (Interdenom.) 1834.

Harvard U. (Divinity School), Cambridge, Mass. (Nondenom.) 1636.

Howard U. (School of Religion), Washington, D. C. (Interdenom.) 1867.

Iliff School of Theol., The, Denver, Colo. (Meth.) 1892.

Lancaster Theol. Sem. of the United Ch. of Christ, Lancaster, Pa. 1825.

Lexington Theol. Sem., Lexington, Ky. (Christian Ch. [Disciples of Christ]) 1865.

Louisville Presb. Theol. Sem., Louisville, Ky. 1853.

McCormick Theol. Sem., Chicago, Ill. (Presb.) 1829.

Meadville/Lombard Theol. School of Lombard Coll., Chicago, Ill. (Unitarian Universalist) 1844.

Moravian Theol. Sem., Bethlehem, Pa. 1885.

Nashotah House, Nashotah, Wis. (Episc.) 1842.

New Brunswick Theol. Sem., New Brunswick, N. J. (Ref. Ch. in Am.) 1874.

New Orleans Bap. Theol. Sem., New Orleans, La. 1917.

New York Theol. Sem., NYC (Interdenom.) 1900.

North Park Theol. Sem., Chicago. Ill. (Ev. Covenant Ch. of Am.) 1891.

Northern Bap. Theol. Sem., Chicago, Ill. 1913.

Pacific School of Religion, Berkeley, Calif. (Interdenom.) 1866.

Perkins School of Theol. (Southern Meth. U.), Dallas, Tex. 1913.

Phillips U., The Grad. Sem., Enid, Okla. (Christian Ch. [Disciples of Christ]) 1906.

Pittsburgh* Theol. Sem., Pittsburgh, Pa. (Presb.) 1794.

Princeton Theol. Sem., Princeton, N. J. (Presb.) 1812.

Prot. Episc. Theol. Sem. in Va., Alexandria, Va. 1823.

San Francisco Theol. Sem., San Anselmo, Calif. (Presb.) 1871.

School of Theol. at Claremont, Claremont, Calif. (Meth.; Christian Ch. [Disciples of Christ]) 1885.

Seabury-Western Theol. Sem., Evanston, Ill. (Episc.) 1858.

Southeastern Bap. Theol. Sem., Wake Forest, N. C. 1951.

Southern Bap. Theol. Sem., Louisville, Ky. 1859.

Southwestern Bap. Theol. Sem., Fort Worth, Tex. 1905.

Union Theol. Sem., NYC (Nondenom.) 1836.

Union Theol. Sem. in Va., Richmond, Va. (Presb.) 1812.

United Theol. Sem., Dayton, Ohio (Meth.) 1871.

U. of Chicago (Divinity School), Chicago, Ill. (Interdenom.) 1855.

U. of Dubuque (Theol. Sem.), Dubuque, Iowa (Presb.) 1852.

U. of the South (School of Theol.), Sewanee, Tenn. (Episc.) 1878.

Vanderbilt U. (Divinity School), Nashville, Tenn. (Interdenom.) 1875.

Wesley Theol. Sem., Washington, D. C. (Interdenom.) 1867.

Western Theol. Sem., Holland, Mich. (Ref. Ch. in Am.) 1866.

Yale U. (Divinity School), New Haven, Conn. (Nondenom.) 1701.

XIII. *RC Sems.* The Council of Trent* (Sess. 23, Decree Concerning Reform, ch. 18) ordered that episc. sems. be est. to train priests. The Cong. of Sems. and Univs. administers theol. educ. in the RC Ch. except where rights of the Cong. for the Propagation of the Faith take precedence. Each diocese should have its own sem. There are also sems. and houses of study of religious orders in Rome.

Important sees normally have a 6-yr. minor sem. for humanities and a 6-yr. major sem. for philos. and theol.

The Vatican II Decree on Priestly Formation (Oct. 28, 1965), ch. 5, reads in part: "Before beginning specifically ecclesiastical subjects seminarians should be equipped with that humanistic and scientific training which young men in their own countries are wont to have as a foundation for higher studies." It adds: "The students are to be formed with particular care in the study of the Bible, which ought to be the soul of all theology."

XIV. *The Future and Ministerial Educ.* The upsurge of Biblical theology,* the ecumenical* movement, and the return to confessional sources have made an impact on contemporary theol. educ. Many sems. are strengthening their grad. schools to handle the onrush on post-BD students. New forms of training, e. g., the Urban Training Center in Chicago, Ill., influence both the curriculum and institutional form of contemporary sems. Experimental methods of teaching have made inroads. Field work programs are expanding and entering new areas. Theol. sems will probably both mirror the life of the ch. and challenge the ch. with new forms of ministry.

R. L. Kelly, *Theological Education in America: A Study of One Hundred Sixty-One Theological Schools in the United States and Canada* (New York, 1924); O. A. Winfield, *The Control of Lutheran Theological Education in America* (Rock Island, Ill., 1933); F. G. Gotwald, "Theological Education in the Lutheran Church in the United States Prior to the Founding of Wittenberg College and Seminary in 1845," *The Lutheran Quarterly,* XLVI (1916), 82–100; A. R. Wentz, *History of the Gettysburg Theological Seminary* (Philadelphia, [1926]); C. F. Haussmann, *Kunze's Seminarium* (Philadelphia, 1917); T. C. Graebner, *Concordia Seminary* (St. Louis, [1927]); C. V. Sheatsley, *History of the First Lutheran Seminary of the West* (Columbus, [1930]); P. S. Vig, *Trinitatis Seminarium* (Blair, Nebr., 1911); *Zum 50jährigen Jubiläum des praktischen evang.-lutherischen Concordia-Seminars zu Springfield, Ill., 1846–96* (St. Louis, 1896); T. Coates, *The Making of a Minister* (mimeographed; Portland, Oreg., [1955]) and "The European Background of the Missouri Synod Program of Ministerial Training," *The American Lutheran,* XXXIV, No. 11 (Nov. 1951), 8–9, 18; C. S. Meyer, *Log Cabin to Luther Tower* (St. Louis, 1965); The Am. Assoc. of Theol. Schools, *AATS Directory 1964* (Dayton, Ohio, 1964); R. H. Bainton, *Yale and the Ministry* (New York, 1957); K. R. Bridston and D. W. Culver, *Pre-Seminary Education* (Minneapolis, 1965); G. E. Arden, *The School of the Prophets: The Background and History of Augustana Theological Seminary 1860–1960* (Rock Island, Ill., 1960); J. E. Roscoe, *A Short History of Theological Education* (London, [1948]); W. W. Sweet, *Religion in the Development of American Culture 1765–1840* (New York, 1952), pp. 173–183; G. H. Williams, *The Harvard Divinity School* (Boston, 1954); W. A. Brown et al., *The Education of American Ministers,* 4 vols. (New York, 1934); Y. Allen, *A Seminary Survey* (New York, 1960); S. Simpson, "Early Ministerial Training in America," *Papers of the American Society of Church History,* ed. S. M. Jackson, 2d Series, vol. 2 (New York, 1910), 117–129; H. R. Niebuhr et al., *The Advancement of Theological Education* (New York, 1957); *Toward a More Excellent Ministry,* ed. R. R. Caemmerer and A. O. Fuerbringer (St. Louis, 1964); M. Kruse, "Preparation for the Ministry: The Training of Pastors in Germany," *Lutheran World,* XI, No. 4 (Oct. 1964), 470–477; *Seminary Education in a Time of Change,* ed. J. M. Lee and L. J. Putz (Notre Dame, Ind. 1965). LJS, AMA, AOF, JEG.

Ministry, Walther's Theses on Church and. See *Church and Ministry, Walther's Theses on.*

Minneapolis Theses (1925). Theses adopted Minneapolis, Minn., Nov. 18, 1925, by representatives of the Ev. Luth. Joint Syn. of Ohio* and Other States, the Ev. Luth. Syn. of Iowa* and Other States, the Buffalo* Syn., and The Norw. Luth. Ch. of Am. (see *Evangelical Lutheran Church, The,* 13–14); they were adopted by the 4 bodies and were the doctrinal basis of the American* Luth. Ch. and of The American* Luth. Conf.

"Minneapolis Theses. I. *The Scriptures.* The synods signatory to these Articles of Agreement accept without exception all the canonical books of the Old and the New Testaments as a whole, and in all their parts, as the divinely inspired, revealed, and inerrant Word of God, and submit to this as the only infallible authority in all matters of faith and life.

"II. *The Lutheran Symbols.* 1. These synods also, without reservation, accept the symbolical books of the Evangelical Lutheran Church, not insofar as, but because they are the presentation and explanation of the pure doctrine of the Word of God and a summary of the faith of the Lutheran Church, as this has found expression in response to the exigencies arising from time to time.

"(The Norwegian Lutheran Church of America . . . has officially accepted only the three Ecumenical Creeds, the Unaltered Augsburg Confession, and Luther's Small Catechism. This position does not imply that the Norwegian Lutheran Church . . . rejects the remaining symbolical books of the Lutheran Church . . . but since the other symbolical books are not known to her constituency generally, it has not been deemed necessary to require formal subscription to the entire Book of Concord.)

"2. Adherence to our confessions pertains only to their doctrinal content, . . . but to these without exception or limitation. . . . All that pertains to the form of presentation (historical comments, questions purely exegetical, etc.) is not binding.

"III. *Church Fellowship.* 1. . . . presupposes unanimity in the pure doctrine of the Gospel and in the confession of the same in word and deed.

"Where the establishment and maintenance of church fellowship ignores present doctrinal differences or declares them a matter of indifference, there is unionism, pretense of union which does not exist.

"2. They agree that the rule, 'Lutheran pulpits for Lutheran pastors only, and Lutheran altars for Lutheran communicants only,' is not only in full accord with, but necessarily implied in, the teachings of the divine Word and the Confessions of the evangelical Lutheran Church. This rule, implying the rejection of all unionism and syncretism, must be observed as setting forth a principle elementary to sound and conservative Lutheranism."

IV. In *points of doctrine* the Minneapolis Theses endorse the Chicago* Theses.

"V. *The Lodge Question.* 1. These synods agree that all organizations or societies, secret or open, as are either avowedly religious or practise the forms of religion without confessing as a matter of principle the Triune God or Jesus Christ as the Son of God, come into the flesh, and our Savior from sin, or teach instead of the Gospel, salvation by human works or morality, are anti-Christian and destructive of the best interests of the church and the individual soul, and that, therefore, the Church of Christ and its congregations can have no fellowship with them.

"2. They agree that a Lutheran synod should not tolerate pastors who have affiliated themselves with any anti-Christian society. And they admonish their pastors and congregations to testify against the sin of lodgery and to put forth earnest efforts publicly and privately to enlighten and persuade persons who are members of anti-Christian societies, to sever their connection with such organizations." EL

Journal of Theology of the American Lutheran Conference, VI (1941), 13–15; *TM,* VII (1927), 112–114; *CTM,* I (1930), 688–690; XV (1944), 194–195; *Doctrinal Declarations: A Collection of Official Statements on the Doctrinal Position of Various Lutheran Synods in America* (St. Louis, Mo., 1957), pp. 107–108; *Documents of Lutheran Unity in America,* ed. R. C. Wolf (Philadelphia, 1966), pp. 340–342.

Minneapolis Theses (LWF). Theses adopted 1957 Minneapolis, Minn., by the 3d Assem. of the LWF; subjects: I. The Freedom We Have in Christ; II. The Unity of the Church in Christ; III. The Freedom to Reform the Church; IV. Free for Service in the World; V. Free and United in Hope.

Minnesota Synod. 1. Organized 1860 at St. Paul under leadership of J. C. F. Heyer* as Die [Deutsche] Evang.-Lutherische Synode von Minnesota und anderen Staaten, also known as the Ev. Luth. Syn. of Minn. and Other States; est. a working relationship with the Wisconsin* Syn. 1864; joined The General* Syn. of the Ev. Luth. Ch. in the USA 1864.

2. The Minn. Syn. left the Gen. Syn. and joined the General* Council of the Ev. Luth. Ch. in (N.) Am. 1866/67; left the Gen. Council 1871 (see *Four Points*); joined the Synodical* Conf. 1872 under leadership of J. H. Sieker.* See also *Synodical Conference,* 1.

3. A coll. was est. at New Ulm 1883/84 (see *Hoyer, Otto Daniel August; Luther College,* 3). The Minn. Syn. helped form the Ev. Luth. Joint Syn. of Wis., Minn., Mich., and Other States 1892 (see *Wisconsin Evangelical Lutheran Synod*). Official pub.: *Evangelisch-Lutherischer Synodal-Bote.*

4. Pres. till 1892, when the Minn. Syn. became the Minn. Dist. (or Minn. Dist. Syn.) of the Joint Syn. of Wis. and Other States: J. C. F. Heyer, J. H. Sieker, A. Kuhn,* C. J. Albrecht.*

E. Abbetmeyer-Selke, "The Beginnings of the German Lutheran Churches in Minnesota," *CHIQ,* II (1929–30), 75–81, 108–115; A. Kuhn, *Geschichte der Minnesota Synode und ihrer einzelnen Gemeinden, 1860–1910* (St. Louis, 1910); J. P. Köhler, *Geschichte der Allgemeinen Evangelisch-Lutherischen Synode von Wisconsin und andern Staaten* (Milwaukee, 1925), tr., rev. and updated by author, "The History of the Wisconsin Synod," *Faith-Life,* XI, 2–XVII, 1 (Feb. 1938–Jan. 1944), ed. L. D. Jordahl and pub. in book form 1970.

Minnesota Synod (LCA). See *Lutheran Church in America,* IX B 14.

Minocchi, Salvatore (1869–1943). RC modernist; b. Raggioli, It.; prof. Heb. Istituto Superiore, Florence, 1903; suspended 1908; prof. U. at Pisa. Ed. *Rivista bibliografica Italiana* 1896, *Studi religiosi* 1901; wrote in area of OT and on Francis of Assisi.

Minor, Friars. See *Franciscans.*

Minor Orders. See *Hierarchy.*

Minucius Felix, Marcus (2d and/or 3d c.). Lat. apologist; b. probably Afr. Wrote *Octavius* (Book VIII of Arnobius,* *Adversus nationes*), a dialog bet. Octavius (a Christian), Caecilius Natalis (a pagan, converted at the dialog's end), and Minucius. See also *Apologists,* 10.

Miracle. Unusual act of divine self-manifestation in the spiritual and natural world. In the OT, miracles are described as extraordinary manifestations of God's presence (Nm 16:30; Jos 10:10-14; 2 K 20:8-11) and recognized as being from God by faith (Ex 7–12; Ju 6:11-24; 1 K 18:38-39). They are involved in God's saving activity (Gen 18:14; Ex 15:11; Ps 72:18) and are signs of His overruling power (Ex 7:3; 11:9-10; Jos 24:17).

In the NT, miracles correspond to OT miracles and are described as acts of power (*dynameis,* Acts 19:11); signs (*semeia,* Lk 21:25; Jn 2:11) whose significance is perceived by faith (Jn 11:25-27, 38-40; 20:30-31); wonders beyond laws as known (Jn 4:48; Acts 2:19; 2 Co 12:12). The miracles of Christ show that the kingdom of God has come (Mt 12:28; Lk 11:20). Paul contrasted his preaching of the cross with the Jewish request for a sign (1 Co 1:22-23).

Various interpretations and conceptions of miracles have been held since ancient times. Miracles in the Bible were distinguished from magic. Miracles of Christ were used as evidence for His deity. The view that miracles demonstrated the authority of the OT and NT became prominent.

M. Luther* emphasized the faith-strengthening function of miracles and stressed the inner miracle of faith more than the external phenomena of miracles. He and J. Calvin* hesitated to acknowledge contemporary miracles.

Religionsgeschichtliche-Schule theologians try to trace Scriptural miracles to the Gk. or Jewish world. Rationalists look for natural explanations.

RCs hold that miracles still occur. Prots. gen. do not deny the possibility but hesitate to grant the fact. EL

Miracle Plays. See *Religious Drama,* 2.

Mirandola, Giovanni Pico della. See *Pico della Mirandola, Giovanni.*

Mirari vos. 1832 papal encyclical condemning soc. and pol. doctrines of H. F. R. de Lamennais* et al.

Mirbt, Carl Theodor (Karl; 1860–1929). Prot. ch. hist.; b. Gnadenfrei (32 mi. S of Breslau), Silesia; taught Marburg 1889, Göttingen 1912. Ed. *Quellen zur Geschichte des Papsttums und des römischen Katholizismus.*

Mirus, Martin(us) (1532–93). Luth. theol.; b. Weida, Ger.; educ. Jena; positions included court preacher Dresden, prof. and supt. Jena. Works include *Fest-Postille.*

Miserere. First word of Ps 51 (Vulgate 50) in Lat. The Ps played a prominent role in 16th c. musical hist.; set to music by Josquin* Deprès, O. di Lasso,* G. P. da Palestrina,* G. Gabrieli,* G. Allegri,* et al.

Misericordia(s) Domini. See *Church Year,* 14, 16.

Mishna. See *Talmud.*

Misnicum, Corpus. See *Lutheran Confessions,* C 1.

Misrule, Lord of (Abbot, or Master, of Misrule). Person chosen in Middle Ages to preside over Christmas games and revels.

Missa cantata (Lat. "sung mass"). Simplified form of *missa* solemnis,* without deacon and subdeacon.

Missa catechumenorum. Term in use since ca. the 11th c. to designate the 1st part of the mass,* preceding Communion; derived from the ancient practice of dismissing catechumens at the end of the 1st part. See also *Catechetics,* 3.

Missa fidelium (Lat. "mass of the faithful"). That part of the mass* which extends from the offertory* to the end; in the ancient ch. only the baptized (or "faithful") were allowed to attend this part.

Missa lecta (Lat. "spoken mass"). Low mass*; mass without music, celebrated by 1 priest and 1 acolyte; also called *missa privata* ("private mass").

Missa solemnis (sollemnis; Lat. "solemn mass"). High mass*; deacon chants Gospel and dismissal, subdeacon the Epistle.

Missal. In RCm, the liturgical book containing all that is said or sung at mass.* See also *Popes,* 21; *Service Books.*

Mission (of bp.). See *Bishop,* 3.

Mission, Congregation of the. See *Lazarists.*

Mission, Inner. See *Inner Mission.*

Mission Affirmations. Series of statements on missions based on "Report of Mission Self-Study and Survey" composed by Martin L. Kretzmann. The affirmations, adopted by LCMS at Detroit June 1965, are titled: "The Church Is God's Mission"; "The Church Is Christ's Mission to the Whole World"; "The Church Is Christ's Mission to the Church"; "The Church Is Christ's Mission to the Whole Society"; "The Church Is Christ's Mission to the Whole Man"; "The Whole Church Is Christ's Mission."

Convention Workbook, LCMS, 1965, pp. 113–123; *Proceedings,* LCMS, 1965, pp. 79–81.

Mission Covenant Church of America, (Swedish) Evangelical. See *Evangelical Covenant Church of America.*

Mission Festivals. Festivals observed to arouse and further interest in miss. work; miss. festivals in the US have been traced to the 1850s; the custom of annual miss. festivals began to wane in the LCMS in the 1950s in favor of more frequent emphasis on missions.

Mission of the Evangelical Lutheran Free Churches. Also called Bleckmar Miss.; est. 1892 as Hanover Ev. Luth. Free Ch. Miss.; supported since 1951 by 3 dioceses of the Indep. Luth. Ch., the Ev.-Luth. Free Ch., the Ev. Luth. (Old Luth.) Ch., and the Free Ev. Luth. Syn. in South Afr. (the latter consisting chiefly of congs. of Ger. descent); works chiefly in S. Afr.; has ca. 18,000 mems. See also *Germany, Lutheran Free Churches in,* 1–12.

Missionary Aviation Fellowship. Founded 1944; provides rapid and efficient transportation for many missions; operated by experienced and tested pilots. 1966 fields included Brazil, Congo, Ecuador, Ethiopia, Guyana, Honduras, Kenya, Mex., Philippines, Surinam, Venezuela, W. Irian. HQ Fullerton, Calif., London, Eng., and Box Hill (Melbourne), Australia. Mem. IFMA. Pub. *Missionary Aviation; Wings of Praise and Prayer.*

Missionary Bands of the World. See *Evangelistic Associations,* 13.

Missionary Baptists. Generic description of N (and later S) Baps. (see *Baptist Churches,* 8–9) because they favored organized efforts to raise miss. funds. Antimission Baps. (see *Baptist Churches,* 11) opposed such efforts, alleging that they were not by NT command.

Missionary Church Association. See *Evangelistic Associations,* 11; *Holiness Churches,* 2.

Missionary Conferences. Conferences for joint study and solution of miss. problems; denominational or interdenom.; constituted by voluntary participation of interested socs., administrators, and missionaries; advisory, without legislative power; most Am., Eur., and Asiatic countries have such confs., which have been held, e. g., NYC 1854, London 1854, Calcutta 1855, Benares (India) 1857, Liverpool 1860, Shanghai 1877 and 1890, London 1878 and 1888, NYC 1900, Edinburgh 1910, Jerusalem 1928, Tambaram, Madras, India, 1938, Whitby, Ont., Can., 1947, Willingen, Ger., 1952, Accra, Ghana, 1958. See also *International Missionary Council.*

Missionary Convention for Foreign Missions. See *Baptist Churches,* 9.

Missionary Education Movement of the United States and Canada. See *Union Movements,* 13.

Missionary Institute (Selinsgrove, Pa.). See *Susquehanna University; Universities in the United States, Lutheran,* 4.

Missionary Institutes. Jesuits est. a sem. for miss. training 1542 in Coimbra, Port., Carmelites in Rome 1613; the Collegium Urbanum, organ of the Sacred Cong. for the Propagation of the Faith (see *Curia*) was est. in Rome 1627; there was a Dutch Ref. miss. sem. in Leiden 1622–32; J. Jänicke* est. a school 1800 in Berlin in which ca. 80 missionaries were educ.; the Basel* Miss. Soc. opened a sem. 1816; the Barmen Miss. Soc. (see *Rhenish Mission Society*) est. a preseminary 1825, enlarged it to a full sem. 1827; the Dresden Ev. Luth. Miss. est. a school 1832, moved to Leipzig 1848 (see *Leipzig Evangelical Lutheran Mission*); the Gossner* Miss. Soc. opened a sem. 1836; the Norw. Miss. Soc. est. 1843 at Stavanger a school which was closed 1847, reopened 1858 (see also *Norwegian Foreign Missions*); a training institute was est. 1861 at Steeden, Ger., under leadership of F. A. Brunn*; a Dan. miss. school opened 1862 near Copenhagen, closed several yrs. later as a result of dissension; the Finnish* Miss. Soc. est. a school 1862; the Swed. Miss. Soc. est. a sem. at Johannelund 1863 (see also *Swedish Missionary Societies*); the Breklum* Miss. Soc. opened a sem. 1876, dedicated its Miss. House 1877; other institutes were est. later. See also *Walaeus, Antonius.*

Miss. institutes in Am. are gen. attached to theol. sems.; some chs. use univs. for preparation in such areas as anthropology. The ecumenical* movement has encouraged cooperation in training miss. personnel.

Missionary Societies. See *Missions.*

Missionary Synod of the West. See *Michigan Synod.*

Missions. 1. This term defines the activity of bringing the Gospel of salvation in Jesus Christ to people everywhere through word and deed, the obligation of the ch. collectively and of its mems. individually (Mt 28:18-20; Mk 16:15-16; Lk 24:46-48; Jn 20:21; Acts 1:8).

2. Many types of miss. expression have developed. The prime undertaking is the direct preaching of the Gospel. Other efforts include those in educ., health and medicine, agriculture, industry, economic development, concern for the handicapped, for the oppressed, for those experiencing discrimination, economic or soc. repression. Means used include mass communications, printed materials, audio-visual aids, radio, and TV.

3. Reasons for delay of Luth. world miss. efforts after the Reformation: (1) The seafaring and colonial govts. were RC; (2) Some held that the miss. command was limited to the apostles.

4. Gustavus* I sent pastors to Lapps (see *Lapland*) 1559. Swed. Luth. colonists in Am. supported efforts of J. Campanius* to reach Am. Indians 1643–48. Peter Heiling, a lawyer of Lübeck, Ger., was in Ethiopia 1634–54; tr. NT into Amharic. See also *Weltz, Justinian Ernst von.*

5. Miss. concerns of Frederick* IV of Den. and lack of miss. manpower in Den. combined to lead Frederick to contact A. H. Francke* at Halle, Ger., for missionaries to Dan. colonies in India. Pioneer work of the Dan.-Halle miss. was done by B. Ziegenbalg* and H. Plütschau.* See also *Medical Missions,* 6.

6. The work in India was supported by Eng. socs. with royal encouragement. For its further hist. see *India,* 10.

7. Frederick IV also founded a coll. for promoting the spread of the Gospel 1714. See also *Egede; Westen, Thomas von.*

8. Missions were encouraged esp. by C. Wesley* and J. Wesley* in Eng. and N. L. v. Zinzendorf* in Germany. Miss socs. est. as a result of miss. movements in the 18th and 19th cents. include Baptist* Miss. Soc. 1792, The London* Miss. Soc. 1795, Church* Miss. Soc. 1799, Wesleyan* Meth. Miss. Soc. 1813, Basel* Miss. Soc. 1815, Paris* Ev. Miss. Soc. 1822, Berlin* Miss. Soc. I 1824, Rhenish* Miss. Soc. 1828, Leipzig* Ev. Luth. Miss. 1836, Gossner* Miss. Soc. 1836, Neuendettelsau* Miss. Soc. 1849. Hermannsburg* Miss. 1849; other socs. were est. elsewhere (e. g., Scot. and Scand.).

9. When Luths. came to N. Am. they continued to show interest in missions of Eur. socs.; in various ways they often supported missions begun by Eur. groups.

10. As Luth. chs. in Am. grew they est. miss. socs. or bds. (see *Central Missionary Society of the Evangelical Lutheran Church in the United States*). "The Society of the Synod of Pennsylvania for the propagation of the Gospel," founded 1836, sent J. C. F. Heyer* to the E. Indies 1841 in search of a suitable miss. field; he chose India, arriving 1842. LCMS sent K. G. T. Näther* and F. E. Mohn* to India 1894. The Ev. Luth. Joint Syn. of Ohio* and Other States began work in India 1912, when it bought 2 stations of the Hermannsburg Miss. (see also *India,* 13). The Joint Ev. Luth. Syn. of Wis., Minn., Mich., and Other States (see *Wisconsin Evangelical Lutheran Synod*) did Miss. work among Apache Indians beginning 1892 (see also *Indians, Lutheran Missions to North American*). It joined the other chs. of the Ev. Luth. Synodical* Conf. of N. Am. in opening work in Nigeria 1936 and in 1953 began its own work in N. Rhodesia. Other missions have been est. in various countries by Luth. chs.

11. As a result of WW I, many missions related to Eur. chs. were orphaned because of internat. tensions. Already during the war much interch. help was given. To ensure that no miss. would be overlooked, various US bds. est. the Luth. For. Missions Conf. of (N.) Am. 1919; it disbanded at the end of 1966, when the Lutheran* Council in the USA became operative.

12. The Lutheran* World Fed., est. 1947, soon created an agency to help foster Luth. world miss. work.

13. More than 1,400 agencies, including at least 20 ecumenical and internat. organizations, are engaged in world missions. Ca. 600 miss. bds. or socs. or related groups in N. Am. send or support ca. 33,000 Prot. missionaries (ca. 70% of all missionaries). Of N. Am. Prot. missionaries, ca. 32% serve in Lat. Am., ca. 29% in Asia, ca. 29% in Afr., and ca. 10% elsewhere.

14. LCMS missions becoming chs. include India Ev. Luth. Ch. (see *India,* 13), Luth. Ch. of Nigeria (see *Africa,* C 14), The Ev. Luth. Ch. of Ghana (see *Africa,* C 11), The Luth. Ch. in the Philippines (see *Philippines,* 3), The China Ev. Luth. Ch. (see *Taiwan*), Wabag Luth. Ch. (see *New Guinea,* 7), The Luth. Syn. of Mex. (see *Mexico,* D 3), Japan Luth. Ch. (see *Japan*), Korea Luth. Ch. (see *Korea,* 5). Missionaries are at times loaned to or borrowed from other miss. and ch. related agencies.

Luth. chs. have been est. also in many other areas. HHK, MLK

See also *Bible Societies;* all entries beginning with the words *Mission, Missionary,* and *Missions; Theology.*

Missions Bibliography. *International Review of Mission* (called *The International Review of Missions* till Apr. 1969; pub. by the Commission on World Mission and Evangelism of the WCC); *Occasional Bulletin from the Missionary Research Library* (New York, N. Y.); *World Christian Handbook* (London, 1949, 1952, 1957, 1962, 1968); *North American Protestant Ministries Overseas* (former titles: *Directory of Foreign Missionary Agencies in North America* [1956], *Directory of North American Protestant Foreign Missionary Agencies* [1958], *North American Protestant Foreign Mission Agencies* [1962]; New York, 1968); minutes and reports of the International* Miss. Council.

Atlas der evangelischen Missions-Gesellschaft zu Basel, ed. J. Josenhans, 2d ed. (Basel, 1859); *The Encyclopedia of Missions,* ed. H. O. Dwight, H. A. Tupper Jr., E. M. Bliss, 2d ed. (New York, 1904); A. v. Harnack, *The Mission and Expansion of Christianity in the First Three Centuries,* tr. and ed. J. Moffatt, 2d enl. ed., 2 vols. (London, 1908); C. H. Robinson, *History of Christian Missions* (New York, 1915); *World Missionary Atlas,* ed. H. P. Beach and C. H. Fahs (New York, 1925); K. S. Latourette, *A History of the Expansion of Christianity,* 7 vols. (New York, 1937–45); *Interpretative Statistical Survey of the World Mission of the Christian Church,* ed. J. I. Parker (New York, 1938); J. C. Thiessen, *A Survey of World Missions,* rev. 3d ed. (Chicago, 1961); R. H. Glover, *The Progress of World-Wide Missions,* rev. and enl. J. H. Kane (New York, 1960); *Weltmission in ökumenischer Zeit,* ed. G. Brennecke et al. (Stuttgart, 1961); *Frontiers of the Christian World Mission since 1938,* ed. W. C. Harr (New York, 1962); B. G. M. Sundkler, *The World of Mission,* tr. E. J. Sharpe (Grand Rapids, Mich., 1965); G. F. Vicedom, *Mission im ökumenischen Zeitalter* (Gütersloh, 1967); *The Encyclopedia of Modern Christian Missions: The Agencies,* ed. B. L. Goddard et al. (Camden, N. J., 1967); R. Keen, *A Survey of the Archives of Selected Missionary Societies* (London, 1968); *Dictionary Catalog of the Missionary Research Library, New York,* 17 vols. (Boston, 1968); *Concise Dictionary of the Christian World Mission,* ed. S. Neill, G. H. Anderson, J. Goodwin (Nashville, Tenn., 1971).

L. B. Wolf, *Missionary Heroes of the Lutheran Church* (Philadelphia, 1911); *Ebenezer,* ed. W. H. T. Dau (St. Louis, 1922); *Men and Missions,* ed. L. Fuerbringer, 10 vols. (St. Louis, 1924–33); *Our Church Abroad,* ed. in chief G. Drach (Columbus, Ohio, 1926); F. J. Lankenau, *The World Is Our Field* (St. Louis, 1928); W. G. Polack, *Into All the World* (St. Louis, 1930); E. T. Bachmann, *They Called Him Father* (Philadelphia, 1942); O. A. Buntrock, "The History of American Lutheran Missions in Asia, Africa, and Oceania since World War I," *CHIQ,* XIX (Apr. 1946), 25–42; (July 1946), 57–62; (Oct. 1946), 129–141; (Jan. 1947), 178–191; XX (July 1947), 102–107; (Oct. 1947), 142–154;

(Jan. 1948), 188–192; XXI (Apr. 1948), 42–48; (July 1948), 88–96; (Oct. 1948), 114–128; (Jan. 1949), 187–192; XXII (July 1949), 84–89; (Oct. 1949), 127–142; R. Syrdahl, "Lutheran Missions," *What Lutherans Are Thinking,* ed. E. C. Fendt (Columbus, Ohio, 1947), pp. 556–588; C. E. Lund-Quist, H. Lilje, R. Askmark, L. Terray, S. Herman, E. T. Bachmann, R. B. Manikam, F. Birkeli, *Lutheran Churches of the World* (Minneapolis, Minn. [1957]); W. J. Danker, "Into All the World," *Moving Frontiers,* ed. C. S. Meyer (St. Louis, 1964), pp. 294–343, and *Two Worlds or None* (St. Louis, 1964); F. D. Lueking, *Mission in the Making* (St. Louis, 1964).

Mississippi Conference. See *Augustana Evangelical Lutheran Church,* 8.

Mississippi Synod. See *United Lutheran Church, Synods of,* 13, 16.

Missouri. Abbreviated name for The Lutheran* Church – Missouri Synod.

Missouri, Ohio, and Other States, The Evangelical Lutheran Synod of. See *Lutheran Church – Missouri Synod, The.*

Missouri and Other States, The English Evangelical Lutheran Synod of. Henkelite Luths. (see *General Synod of the Evangelical Lutheran Church in the United States of America, The,* 7) moved W from western N. C. and eastern Tenn. before 1839 and settled esp. in SE Mo. On invitation from mems. of this group, a free conf. was held 1872 at Gravelton, Wayne Co., Mo., in which mems. of the Ev. Luth. Tenn. Syn., Holston Syn., Mo. Syn., and Norw. Syn. took part. C. F. W. Walther* took the lead in guiding the Eng. group (3 pastors, including P. C. Henkel [see *Henkels, The,* 3]) toward immediate organization of The Eng. (Ev.) Luth. Conf. of Mo.; A. W. Meyer* joined 1885, C. F. W. Dallmann* 1886. On basis of an 1886 resolution the conf. applied to the 1887 Mo. Syn. conv. for admission as a dist. but was advised to organize an indep. syn.

A city miss. cong. was est. by C. F. W. Dallmann in Baltimore, Md., 1888. Similar ventures followed in St. Louis, Mo.; Pittsburgh, Pa.; Winfield, Kans.; Washington, D. C.; Chicago, Ill.; Detroit, Mich.; St. Paul, Minn.; Cleveland, Ohio; Buffalo and NYC, N. Y. In 1888 the conf. adopted a const. and a new name expressing broader vision: The Gen. Eng. (Ev.) Luth. Conf. of Mo. and Other States. The conf. joined the Ev. Luth. Synodical* Conf. of N. Am. 1890. In 1891 the conf. changed name to The Eng. Ev. Luth. Syn. of Mo. and Other States.

The Lutheran Witness, begun 1882 under auspices of the Cleveland Dist. Conf. and ed. by C. A. Frank,* was presented to the syn. 1888. In 1893 the syn. received Concordia* Coll., Conover, N. C., and St. John's Coll., Winfield, Kans. (see *Ministry, Education of,* VIII C 2 n); the latter was given to the Mo. Syn. 1908. *The Lutheran Guide* (a child's paper for Sunday Schools), founded by 1891 syn. resolution and ed. by A. W. Meyer,* began to appear 1893. In 1911 the syn. became the Eng. Dist. of the Mo. Syn. See also *Lutheran Church – Missouri Synod, The,* V. 10.

Pres.: F. G. Kuegele* 1888–1899; C. F. W. Dallmann* 1899–1901; A. W. Meyer 1901–05; H. P. Eckhardt* 1905–11.

H. P. Eckhardt, *The English District* (n.p., 1946).

Missouri Evangelical Lutheran India Mission. See *India,* 13.

Missouri Synod. Abbreviated name for The Lutheran* Ch. – Mo. Syn.

Miter (mitre). 1. Piece of headgear. 2. Liturgical headdress of ch. dignitaries, e.g., popes, abps., bps., and abbots.

Mithraism. Oriental mystery* religion named after Mithras, mythical Persian savior hero; includes features of Zoroastrianism* and Hellenism; rivaled Christianity in the Roman Empire 2–4 c. AD. See also *Greek Religion,* 3 b.

Mizpah Benediction. See *Benedictions.*

Mnene Station. See *Africa,* B 2.

Mo Ti (Mo-tzu). See *Chinese Philosophy,* 4.

Moabite Stone. Black basalt stele discovered 1868 at Dhiban (Biblical Dibon; Nm 21:30), E of the Dead Sea; 34-line inscription on it, Heb., tells of wars of Mesha (king of Moab) with Omri (king of Israel) and his successors, and with the Edomites.

Möckhel, Johann Friedrich (Möckel; 1661–1729). B. Kulmbach, Ger.; educ. Jena; private chaplain and pastor at various places; hymnist. Hymns include "Nun sich die Nacht geendet hat."

Modalistic Monarchianism. See *Monarchianism,* B.

Mode. See *Modes, Ecclesiastical.*

Moderates. Name applied to theologians in the Ch. of Scot. who favored patronage, held that civil courts were supreme in ecclesiastical matters, and defended a "moderate" orthodoxy; became prominent in the 2d half of the 18th c.; began to decline in the 1st part of the 19th c.

Moderation. See *Intemperance.*

Moderator. In Protestantism in gen., the officer presiding over assemblies or ch. meetings; in Presbyterianism, a presbyter appointed to preside over courts, presbyteries, syns., or gen. assemblies. See also *Polity, Ecclesiastical,* 7.

Modern Churchmen's Union. Angl. soc. founded 1898 as Churchmen's Union for the Advancement of Liberal Religious Thought (name changed 1928). Advocated liberal theol., restatement of doctrine, and alteration of liturgical forms. Included such men as E. W. Barnes,* W. R. Inge,* K. Lake,* H. Rashdall.*

Modern Translations of the Bible. See *Bible Versions.*

Modernism. 1. Designation applied to the liberal movement that arose in some quarters of the RC Ch. toward the end of the 19th c. Under leadership of G. Tyrrell,* A. F. Loisy,* A. Houtin,* et al. modernism made considerable progress. In 1907 it was curbed by Pius X (see *Popes,* 30), who condemned it as the "résumé of all the heresies." His 1910 motu* proprio *Sacrorum antistitum* required of clerics an oath for traditional RC belief and against modernism. See also *Roman Catholic Church,* 8.

2. Modernism in Protestantism has roots in the early 19th c. Its premise is that there is no revealed and absolute truth and that man is constantly in search of religious truth. It is a theol. method rather than a system of beliefs; it follows principles of Ger. schools of liberal theol. F. D. E. Schleiermacher* claimed to find the source of truth in a pious feeling of dependence on God; A. Ritschl* emphasized the kingdom of God and ethics; E. P. W. Troeltsch* sought truth in the comparative study of all religions. Modern presuppositions in philos., science, sociol., and psychol. are considered basic to discovery of religious truth. Modernism claimed that the basic religious truths are: the fatherhood of God, the immanence of God, the brotherhood of man, the perfectibility of man.

3. Liberal theol. held that the function of the ch. was to est. the kingdom of God as an ethical and moral community. Since such a kingdom could not be est. until the soc. ideals of Jesus had permeated all human soc., liberal theol. invented the social* gospel. Modernism may, therefore, be summarized as follows: (a) The religious experiences of the past and the present are the criterion and standard of truth. The Bible is viewed as a record of religious experiences of OT and NT times. All religious concepts (e. g., sin, grace, redemption, heaven) must be reinterpreted in light of current religious experience. (b) It assumes that man's moral growth toward a unified personality is possible if man follows the biological and psychol. laws of the universe. Man

must also have faith in his own inherent capability for his development for a good life. (c) The message of modernism is the soc. gospel. FEM

J. G. Machen, *Christianity and Liberalism* (New York, 1923); S. Mathews, *The Faith of Modernism* (New York, 1924); C. J. Södergren, *Fundamentalists and Modernists* (Rock Island, Ill., 1925); L. Berkhof, *Recent Trends in Theology* (Grand Rapids, Mich., 1944); N. F. Furniss, *The Fundamentalist Controversy, 1918–1931* (New Haven, Conn., 1954); *Controversy in the Twenties: Fundamentalism, Modernism, and Evolution,* ed. W. B. Gatewood, Jr. (Nashville, Tenn., 1969).

Modes, Ecclesiastical (Ch. Modes; Ch. Tones; Kirchentöne; Kirchentonarten). Medieval parent scales of our major and minor scales were used for all Gregorian* and polyphonic ch. music till ca. 1600, to a lesser degree thereafter. The octave range of the individual modes may be related to any major scale; they are most commonly related to C major. One can easily determine the character of the individual modes by using only the white keys in playing the following octaves as so-called authentic modes: Ionian (C–C), Dorian (D–D), Phrygian (E–E), Lydian (F–F; helped pave the way for F major by often using B flat instead of B natural to avoid the use of the tritone [an interval of 3 whole steps, or augmented 4th; here from F to B]), Mixolydian (G–G), Aeolian (A–A; same as a pure minor scale). The Hyperaeolian mode, beginning on the 7th degree, or leading tone, of the scale, was rejected, since this tone leans too heavily on the 1st degree. In relating to other major keys, one must use their key signature. Plagal (from Gk. *plagios,* "oblique") modes began half an octave lower (Gk. *hypo*) than the authentic modes and had their keynote on the 4th scale step; e. g., with Dorian beginning on D, Hypodorian begins on A. Many 16th and 17th c. chorales are modal hymns. Many are in the Dorian and Phrygian modes, the soft Lydian mode being gen. avoided. M. Luther's* chorale version of the Creed (*TLH,* 251, 2d tune) is in the Dorian mode; "From Depths of Woe I Cry to Thee" (*TLH,* 329) is in the Phrygian mode: "A Mighty Fortress" (*TLH,* 262) is in the Ionian mode. Ecclesiastical modes, also called Gregorian modes or tones, are the 8 groups of chants corresponding to the 8 modes to which the Psalms are sung in the Gregorian system: Dorian, Hypodorian, Phrygian, Hypophrygian, Lydian, Hypolydian, Mixolydian, Hypomixolydian. See also *Gregorian Music; Psalm Tones.* Sometimes, improperly, all modes are called ecclesiastical modes. WEB

Modimo. See *Africa,* B 6.

Modrzewski (Andrzej Frycz; 1503–72). Polish Prot.; educ. Kraków and Wittenberg (strongly influenced by P. Melanchthon*); called for ecclesiastical, pol., and soc. reform. Works include *De republica emendanda.*

Moeller, Albert John Charles (May 6, 1891–Nov. 21, 1950). B. Barnes, Kans.; educ. Conc. Sem., Saint Louis, Mo.; pastor Champion 1914–16, Ainsworth 1916–21, Walton 1921–27, Grand Island 1927–38, all in Nebraska. Pres. S. Nebr. Dist. of the Mo. Syn. 1936–38, St. Paul's Coll., Concordia, Mo., 1938–50.

Moempelgard. See *Montbéliard, Colloquy of.*

Moenkemoeller, J. F. William (Nov. 9, 1867–May 9, 1933). B. Westphalia, Ger.; educ. Conc. Sem., Saint Louis, Mo. Pastor Cairo, Ill., 1889–92; Springfield, Mass., 1892–99; New Britain, Conn., 1899–1905. Prof. Conc. Coll., St. Paul, Minn., 1905–33. Works include *The Festivals and Sacrifices of Israel; Word-Pictures of Bible Events.*

Moffat, Robert (Dec. 21, 1795–Aug. 9, 1883). B. Ormiston, W East Lothian, Scot.; LMS miss. 1816/17 to Bushmen, Hottentots, and Bechuanas in Afr.; won Afrikaner* for Christianity; organized a school for native helpers in Kuruman; on furlough to Eng. he met D. Livingstone* 1839 and influenced him for Afr. missions; tr. the Bible into Bechuana 1857; returned to Eng. 1870. See also *Africa,* A 6; B 2, 3, 5.

Moffatt, James (1870–1944). B. Glasgow, Scot.; educ. Glasgow Academy, Glasgow U., Glasgow Coll. of the Free Ch. of Scot.; ordained Free Ch. 1896; pastor United Free Ch. 1907–11. Prof. Mansfield Coll., Oxford, Eng., 1911–15; Glasgow Coll. 1915–27; Union Theol. Sem., NYC, 1927–44. Works include *An Introduction to the Literature of the New Testament; The First Five Centuries of the Church; The Thrill of Tradition;* Bible tr.; commentaries.

Mogila, Peter (Petr; Petrus; Piotr Simeonovitch; Moghila; Mohyla; ca. 1596– ca. 1647). Influential theol. of the E Orthodox Ch.; b. Moldavia, of a noble Wallachian family; metropolitan Kiev. Works include *Orthodox Confession of the Faith of the Catholic and Apostolic Eastern Church;* a catechism; liturgical writings. See also *Eastern Orthodox Standards of Doctrine,* A 1; *Russia,* 3.

Mohammed (Mohamed). See *Islam; Lost-Found Nation of Islam in the Wilderness of North America; Muhammad.*

Mohammedanism. See *Islam; Lost-Found Nation of Islam in the Wilderness of North America; Muhammad.*

Mohism (Moism). See *Chinese Philosophy,* 4.

Möhler, Johann Adam (1796–1838). RC theol.; b. Igersheim, Württemberg, Ger.; educ. Ellwangen; priest 1819; taught at RC sem. and U. of Tübingen; prof. Louis-Maximilian U., Munich, 1835; influenced by F. D. E. Schleiermacher* and F. W. J. v. Schelling.* Opposed theory of papal infallibility; worked for Christian unity: taught invisibility of the ch. Works include *Die Einheit in der Kirche; Athanasius der Grosse und die Kirche seiner Zeit, besonders im Kampfe mit dem Arianismus; Symbolik; Neue Untersuchungen der Lehrgegensätze zwischen den Katholiken und Protestanten.*

Mohn, Franz Edward (Theodor[e]? Edmund? Edmond? Nov. 4, 1867–June 18, 1925). B. Weisstropp [Weistoop?], near Dresden, Ger.; educ. Leipzig Miss. Sem.; miss. Negapatam, near Madras, India, 1889–94; commissioned by Mo. Syn. 1894: miss. Ambur, India, 1896–1913. Pastor Waubay, S. Dak., 1914–17; near Decatur, Ind., 1917–22. See also *India,* 13; *Lutheran Church – Missouri Synod, The,* VI, 8; *Missions,* 10.

Mohr, Joseph (1792–1848). B. Salzburg, Austria; priest 1815; held various positions in the diocese of Salzburg; hymnist. Hymns include "Stille Nacht, Heilige Nacht!" (music by F. X. Gruber*).

Moiban(us), Ambrosius (1494–1554). B. Breslau, Ger.; educ. Kraków; rector Breslau; studied under J. Reuchlin* at Ingolstadt; pastor Breslau; with J. Hess* introd. the Reformation in Breslau; hymnist.

Moism (Mohism). See *Chinese Philosophy,* 4.

Mokosh (Mkosh). See *Slavs, Primitive Religion of.*

Moksha. See *Brahmanism,* 3, 4.

Molanus, Gerard Walter (Gerhard; Walther; Wolter; van der Muelen; 1633–1722). Luth. theol.; b. Hameln, Ger.; educ. Helmstedt; prof. math 1659, theol. 1664 Rinteln; dir. Hannover consistory 1674; 1677 abbott Loccum (founded 1163 as a Cistercian monastery; reformed in the early 1590s); hymnist. Hymns include "Ich trete frisch zu Gottes Tisch" ("Thy Table I Approach").

Molay, Order of De. See *Freemasonry,* 8.

Moldehnke, Edward Frederick (Eduard; Aug. 10, 1836–June 25, 1904). B. Insterburg, East Prussia; educ. Halle; amanuensis of F. A. G. Tholuck*; rector Eckersberg; teacher Elk (Ger.: Lyck, or Lück); ordained Königsberg July 1861; to Am. 1861 to be traveling miss. of the Wis. Syn.; 1st prof. Wis. Syn. coll. and sem. at Watertown, Wis., 1863–66; returned to Ger.; pastor Johannisburg 1866; returned to Am. 1869; pastor NYC; mem. of the N. Y. Ministerium in the Gen. Council. Ed. *Evangelisch-Lutherisches Gemeinde-Blatt.*

Moldenhawr, Daniel Gotthilf (Moldenhauer? ca. 1753 to 1823). B. Königsberg, Germany. Prof. theol. and oriental and classical philol. Kiel 1777; ch. hist. and dogmatics Copenhagen, Den., 1784; advocated nationalistic supranaturalism.

Molina, Luis (de) (1535–1600). B. Cuenca, New Castile, Sp.; educ. Salamanca and Alcalá de Henares, Sp., and Coimbra, Port.; Jesuit 1553; prof. philos. Coimbra 1563–67; prof. theol. Évora, Port., 1568–83; prof. moral theol. Madrid, Sp., 1600. His teachings (Molinism) were widely accepted by Jesuits but disputed by Dominicans. Works include *Concordia liberi arbitrii cum gratiae donis, divina praescientia, providentia, praedestinatione, et reprobatione.*

Molinism. See *Molina, Luis (de).*

Molinos, Miguel de (Michael; 1628 [some say ca. 1640] – ca. 1696). Quietist; b. Muniesa, near Saragossa, Sp.; educ. Valencia, Sp.; to Rome 1663; friend of many prelates, including future Innocent* XI. Held that perfection consisted in union with and transformation into God; in this state external observances are a hindrance and means of grace unnecessary. Wrote *Guida spirituale* (tr. into Lat. by A. H. Francke,* into Ger. by A. Arnold*). See also *Quietism.*

Moller, Heinrich (Möller? Muller? Müller?). See *Henry of Zutphen.*

Möller, Johann Friedrich (1789–1861). B. Erfurt, Ger.; ev. theol.; gen. supt. Magdeburg 1843; involved in controversy with *Lichtfreunde.** Works include *Das Verhalten der christlichen Herrschaften gegen ihre Diener.*

Möller, Johann Joachim (1660–1733). B. Sommerfeld, Brandenburg, Ger.; archdeacon Krossen; hymnist. Hymns include "Ich habe g'nug"; "Das ist je gewisslich wahr."

Moller, Martin (1547–1606). B. Kropstädt, near Wittenberg, Ger.; educ. Görlitz; cantor 1568, diaconus 1569 Löwenberg; pastor Kesselsdorf 1572, Sprottau 1575, Görlitz 1600; used his initials as a reminder of the warning *memento mori* (Lat. "remember that you must die"); hymnist. Hymns include "Nimm von uns, Herr, du treuer Gott."

Moller von Hirsch, Heinrich (Möller; Müller; 1530–89). B. Hamburg, Ger.; educ. Wittenberg; prof. Heb. Wittenberg 1560–74; deposed because of Crypto-Calvinism. See also *Crypto-Calvinistic Controversy.*

Molucca Protestant Church. See *Indonesia,* 8.

Moluccas. See *Indonesia,* 1, 8.

Mombritius, Boninus (ca. 1424–ca. 1500). B. Milan, It.; humanist; prof. Lat. and Gk. Milan ca. 1460. Tr. and pub. classics and Eusebius* of Caesarea's *Chronicon;* other works include *Sanctuarium* (legends of saints).

Mommsen, Theodor (1817–1903). Ger. hist. of Rome; jurist; b. Garding, Schleswig; educ. Kiel; prof. Leipzig 1848, Zurich 1852, Breslau 1854, Berlin 1858. Works include *Römische Geschichte; Corpus Inscriptionum Latinarum.*

Mömpelgard. See *Montbéliard, Colloquy of.*

Monad. See *Arianism,* 1; *Leibniz, Gottfried Wilhelm von; Monarchianism,* B 6.

Monarchian Prologues. Brief accounts of evangelists prefixed to gospels in many Vulgate MSS. Formerly regarded as coming from Monarchians (see *Monarchianism*). Recent studies put them in the 4th c.

Monarchianism. View that developed esp. in the 2d and 3d c.; stressed that God is a single being, thereby trying to preserve monotheism and unity (monarchy) of the Godhead. Two divergent views arose:

A. *Dynamic Monarchianism.* Christ is a mere man (though conceived by the Holy Spirit and born in a wonderful way of the Virgin Mary) whom God endowed with His power (Gk. *dynamis*). See also *Adoptionism.*

1. *Alogi* (in Asia Minor ca. 170). Denied that Jesus was the Logos,* hence rejected the Gospel and Epistles of John; also rejected Rv as chiliastic.

2. *Theodotians.* Followers of Theodotus* the Fuller; 2 of his followers, a certain Asclepiodotus (apparently a Gk.) and Theodotus* the Money Changer, tried unsuccessfully to found their own ch. at Rome.

3. *Artemonites.* Followers of Artemon (Artemas; 3d c.), who taught at Rome and was excommunicated by Zephyrinus.* Sometimes classified with Modalistic Monarchians.

4. *Paul* of Samosata.* Held that Jesus was "from hence," and that the Logos worked in Him "from above."

B. *Modalistic Monarchianism.* View that Father, Son, and Holy Spirit are not 3 persons but 3 modes or forms of God's activity; God revealed Himself as Father in the work of creation, as Son in the work of redemption (Patripassianism*), and as the Holy Spirit in the work of sanctification.

1. *Noetus.**

2. *Calixtus I* (Callistus). Bp. Rome ca. 217–ca. 223.

3. *Beryllus* (3d c.). Bp. Bos(t)ra (Busra), ca. 70 mi. S of Damascus, ca. 230–244. Refuted in disputation by Origen* 238/244. Sometimes classified with Dynamic Monarchians.

4. *Praxeas.**

5. *Epigonus* (fl. ca. AD 200). Disciple of Noetus*; founded a sect at Rome later headed by Sabellius.

6. *Sabellius.** Modalistic Monarchianism as developed under him is known as Sabellianism: God, the absolute monad, reveals Himself successively in 3 *prosopa* (Gk. "faces"), each representing the entire monad (Father: Creator and Lawgiver; Son: Redeemer; Holy Spirit: Lifegiver). Opposed by Dionysius* of Alexandria.

See also *Unitarianism.*

K. G. A. v. Harnack, *History of Dogma,* tr. N. Buchanan et al. (London, 1894–99); J. N. D. Kelly, *Early Christian Doctrines,* 2d ed. (New York, 1960); F. Loofs, *Leitfaden zum Studium der Dogmengeschichte,* 4th rev. ed. (Halle, 1906); R. Seeberg, *Text-book of the History of Doctrines,* tr. C. E. Hay (Grand Rapids, Mich., 1952).

Monarchical Episcopate. See *Bishop,* 1.

Monastery. Residence for a group of persons living under religious vows in retirement or seclusion from the world. See also *Cloister; Monasticism.*

Monasticism. 1. The term monasticism covers a variety of phenomena and institutions that grow from the common root of asceticism.* Underlying the formations of monasticism is the consciousness of sin and the desire for reconciliation with God. The monastic seeks this reconciliation by renunciation, e. g., of (a) the everyday world; (b) family; (c) property; (d) pleasure and comfort; (e) will; by acts of self-mortification and by frequent repetition of set prayers, acts of devotion, and religious meditation. Fundamental vows* of the monastic are vows of poverty, celibacy, and obedience.

2. Monasticism in its essential features was highly developed in India* and other parts of Asia before the Christian era. Christian monasticism originated in Egypt. Its first exponents (perhaps refugees from the persecution of Decius [see *Persecutions of Christians,* 4]; perhaps others, who tried to attain moral perfection and everlasting happiness by escape from the sinful world) lived as hermits.*

3. Ca. 305 Anthony* began gathering hermits into colonies. Pachomius (ca. 290–346 [348?]; b. at or near Esneh [Esna; Isna], ca. 25/30 mi. S. of Thebes [Luxor], Upper Egypt; Christian monk ca. 314; see also *Origenistic Controversy*) founded the 1st ceno-

bitic monastery.* Thereafter the hermitic type of ascetic life rapidly yielded to the cenobitic type. Basil* the Great gave monasticism standing and drew up regulations for its guidance. Through Athanasius,* Jerome,* et al. the monastic idea found acceptance in the W. Many monasteries were founded under various rules. The rule of Benedict* of Nursia regulated monasticism in the W for many cents. (see *Benedictines*).

4. Boniface* and Ansgar* were Benedictines. Celtic* monks also played a significant role in miss. work. When growing wealth of monasteries and abbeys led to relaxation of the rule of Benedict, efforts at reform were made. In the 10th and 11th cents. Cluniacs (see *Cluniac Reform*) tried to reform monasticism. The beginning of the 12th c. saw a new effort at reform (see *Cistercians*). With the Crusades* arose military* religious orders. Mount Athos, Greece, came into prominence as a monastic center.

5. More radical than earlier reforms was the est. of the Franciscans* and Dominicans.* Other orders founded 11th–14th c. include Carthusians,* Camaldolese,* Vallumbrosans,* Celestines.* Monasticism exerts a great liturgical influence on contemporary RCm.

6. The Luth. Reformation* repudiated the excesses and errors of monasticism (see *Asceticism*). RC orders active in the Counter* Reformation include Barnabites,* Capuchins,* Clerks Regular of Somascha,* Oratorians,* Society* of Jesus, Theatines,* Ursulines.* Other RC orders include Brothers* Hospitallers of St. John of God, Congregation* of the Brothers of Charity, Lazarists,* Maurists,* Oblate* Fathers, Trappists. Monasticism is practiced also in Islam,* Buddhism,* Jainism,* and other religions, but not in Judaism. Though Christian monasticism in the W is fostered primarily among RCs, there are also some Prot. communities.

7. The Luth. Confessions concede that virginity is a higher gift than marriape (Ap XXIII 19, 38, 69; LC I 211). They hold, however, that it is un-Christian to require monastic vows of those who do not have the gift of continence (Ap XXVII 51). They advocate that associations and monasteries be restored to the useful purposes for which they had been founded (SA II III 1). Abuses in monastic life are frequently censured. See also *Asceticism*.

See also *Lay Brothers and Lay Sisters; Mendicant Friars*.

W. Bousset, *Apophthegmata: Studien zur Geschichte des ältesten Mönchtums,* ed. T. Hermann and G. Krüger (Tübingen, 1923); *The Library of Christian Classics,* XII: *Western Asceticism,* ed. O. Chadwick (Philadelphia, 1958); D. Bonhoeffer, *Life Together,* tr. J. W. Doberstein (New York, 1954); J. O. Hannay, *The Spirit and Origin of Christian Monasticism* (London, 1903).

Moncrieff, Alexander. See *Associate Reformed Church*.

Mone, Franz Joseph (1796–1871). RC hist. and liturgical scholar; b. Mingolsheim, near Bruchsal, Baden, Ger. Prof. Heidelberg 1819–27, 1831–35; Louvain, Belg., 1827–ca. 1830/31. Dir. Baden Archives 1835–68. Works include *Lateinische und griechische Messen aus dem zweiten bis sechsten Jahrhundert*.

Monergism. Theol. opposite of synergism*; holds that the grace of God is the only efficient cause in beginning and effecting conversion.*

Mongols. Chiefly pastoral people of Mongolia, mostly Lamaistic (see *Lamaism*) in religion. Probably had contact with Nestorians (see *Nestorianism*) by ca. the 10th c., but without great or lasting effect. RC miss. endeavors among Mongols began in the 13th c., Eng. and Scand. in the 19th c. No for. missionaries have been able to enter the Soviet Mongolian rep. est. in the 20th c. See also *Russia,* 2.

Monica (Monnica; ca. 332–387). Mother of Augustine* of Hippo; b. probably of Christian parents at Tagaste, Numidia, N Afr. (now Souk-Ahras, Algeria). Known for her prayers for her son.

Monism. Metaphysical theory that reduces all phenomena to 1 material or spiritual principle. It considers God and world, matter and spirit, body and soul to be modifications of 1 principle. Manifestations of monism include pantheism,* which identifies God and the world; materialism,* which regards matter as basic reality; and spiritualism or idealism,* which regards spiritual beings or ideas as the only basis of reality.

Metaphysical monism is opposed to Christianity. The Bible asserts essential difference bet. Creator and creation.

See also *Dualism; Haeckel, Ernst Heinrich Philipp August; Pluralism; Russell, Bertrand Arthur William; Thales; Wolff, Christian von*.

Monk. Male mem. of a monastic order or one who lives in solitary retirement from the world to practice asceticism.* See also *Monasticism*.

Monk, William Henry (1823–89). B. London, Eng.; organist, composer. Prof. Nat. Training School for Music, London, 1876; Bedford Coll., London, 1878. Helped ed. *Hymns Ancient and Modern;* hymn tunes include "Coronae," "Energy" (also called "St. Ethelwald"), and "Eventide."

Monod. Family of Fr. Ref. theologians. (1) *Frédéric Joel Jean Gérard* (1794–1863). Brother of 2 and 3; father of 4, 5, and 6; b. near Morges, Vaud, Switz.; educ. Geneva; pastor Paris, Fr.; helped found Union des Eglises évangéliques libres de France 1849. (2) *Guillaumé* (1800–96). Brother of 1 and 3; b. Copenhagen, Den.; educ. Geneva, Switz.; held various pastorates; succeeded 3 in Paris 1856; founded free cong. 1874; fell victim to messianic delusions. (3) *Adolphe Louis Frédéric Théodore* (1802–56). Brother of 1 and 2; b. Copenhagen, Den.; educ. Geneva, Switz.; pastor Naples, It., 1825(1826?), Lyons, Fr., 1827; dismissed 1832; est. a free ch. at Lyons 1832; prof. Montauban 1836; pastor Paris 1847; regarded as one of the greatest preachers of the Ref. ch. in Fr. (4) *Jean Paul Frédéric* (1822–1907). Son of 1, brother of 5 and 6; b. Paris, Fr.; preacher Marseille 1848, then at Nimes; prof. dogmatics Montauban 1864–94. (5) *Théodore* (1836–1921). Son of 1, brother of 4 and 6, father of 7; b. Paris 1864; joined nat. ch. 1874; agent of the inner miss. in Fr. 1875; pastor Paris 1878. (6) *Léopold* (1844–1922). Son of 1, brother of 4 and 5; pastor Free Ch. Lyons 1869–1909. (7) *Wilfred* (1867–1943). Son of 5; b. Paris; prof. theol. free Prot. faculty Paris 1909; revived principles of gnosticism* and Manichaeism.*

Monogenes (Gk. "only begotten"). Hymn to triumphant Redeemer in some liturgies, e. g., Byzantine (see *Liturgics*), St. James (see *Divine Liturgy*), and liturgy of St. Mark.*

Monograms of Christ. See *Symbolism, Christian,* 6.

Monolatry (from Gk. *monos,* "alone," and *latreia,* "worship"). Worship of 1 god.

See also *Henotheism; Kathenotheism*.

Monophysite Controversy. The Council of Chalcedon* declared that there are 2 natures in Christ, divine and human. In opposition, some taught Monophysitism.*

As a result of the controversy, some orthodox bps. were deposed. Much of Palestine was carried away by the movement. In Egypt, Dioscurus (d. 454) wielded powerful influence; his party elected a patriarch with Eutychian tendencies 457, who was in turn expelled but returned with even greater prestige until 460, when he was banished. Antioch and Jerusalem were occupied by Monophysite bps. The *Henoticon** failed to settle the controversy, which resulted in enduring schism. The Coptic* Ch., Syrian Jacobite Ch. (see *Jacobites,* 1), and Armenian Ch. (see *Armenia; Armenians*) hold Monophysite

Monophysites. Adherents of Monophysitism.* See also *Mark, Liturgy of Saint.*

Monophysitism (from Gk. *monos,* "single," and *physis,* "nature"). The view that there is only 1 nature in Christ, namely the divine, or 1 compounded nature. Opposed to dyophysitism (see *Dyophysites*). See also *Eutychianism; Monophysite Controversy.*

Monotheism (from Gk. *monos,* "single," and *theos,* "god"). Belief that there is only 1 God.

Monothelitism (Monotheletism; Monothelism; from Gk. *monos,* "single," and *thelema,* "will"). Belief that in Jesus Christ there was only 1 mode of activity (1 divine human energy; 1 volitional activity), or, as it came to be expressed, that Christ had only 1 divine human will. Opposed to Dyothelitism.*

In discussions aimed at healing the Monophysite* controversy, the terms "1 energy" and "1 will" or at least "1 state of will" first came into prominence in Alexandria, Egypt, as descriptive of Monophysitism.* Honorious I (see also *Constantinople, Councils of,* 3) sanctioned use of "1 will." Sophronius (ca. 560–638; b. Damascus; patriarch Jerusalem ca. 634) took exception to "1 nature." The 6th ecumenical council (see *Constantinople, Councils of,* 3) on Sept. 16, 681, sanctioned 2 natural wills and natural energies in Christ, holding that the wills are not opposed, but that the human will follows and is subordinate to the divine will. The Quinisext* Syn. homologated the condemnation of Monothelitism. Cf. Christ's human will, e. g., Mt 27:34; Jn 1:43; 17:24; 19:28; divine will Lk 13:24; Jn 5:21. See also *Ecthesis; Christological Controversies.*

Monsell, John Samuel Bewley (1811–75). Angl. cleric, hymnist; b. St. Columb's, Londonderry, Ireland; educ. Trin. Coll., Dublin. Hymns include "Fight the Good Fight with All Thy Might"; "Lord of the Living Harvest"; "O'er the Distant Mountains Breaking."

Monsieur, Peace of. See *France,* 9.

Monstrance. Vessel or receptacle used in Cath. chs. to hold relics or a consecrated host when exposed to view; also called ostensorium.

Montaigne, Michel Eyquem de (1533–92). B. Montaigne, near Bordeaux, Fr.; essayist; skeptical philos.; moralist; humanist; satirized the RC Ch. but did not leave it. Tr. Raymond* of Sabunde's *Theologia naturalis;* other works include *Essais.*

Montalembert, Charles René Forbes (Charles Forbes René de; 1810–70). Fr. RC hist.; b. London, Eng.; assoc. with H. F. R. de Lamennais* and J. B. H. Lacordaire*; worked for freedom of conscience, for separation of ch. and state, and for freedom of the press, assem., and instruction; submitted under papal condemnation for liberalism and became an outspoken exponent of RC principles in the Chamber of Deputies.

Montanism. In early NT times the immediate return of Christ was expected (2 Th 2:2). Fanciful hopes connected with that expected return led to chiliastic speculations, esp. among followers of Montanus.* Inveighing against increasing laxity and worldliness in the ch., he declared himself the instrument of the Paraclete promised by Christ (cf. Jn 14:16) and with 2 prophetesses (Prisca [or Priscilla] and Maximilla) announced the speedy est. of the millennium centered at Pepuza in Phrygia (hence Montanists have also been called Pepuzians and Cataphrygians). Adherents of the movement practiced asceticism. The movement spread through Asia Minor, Gaul, Sp., Rome, and N Afr.

Montanus (fl. 2d half of 2d c. AD). Schismatic of Phrygia, Asia Minor; founded Montanism.* Followers called Montanists.

Montanus, Jacobus (d. after 1534). B. Gernsbach, near Speyer, Ger.; educ. Deventer, Neth.; joined Brethren* of the Common Life in Münster, Ger.; carried on friendly correspondence with P. Melanchthon* and M. Luther.* Works include textbooks, hymns, and songs.

Montbéliard, Colloquy of (Moempelgard; Mömpelgard; Muempelgard; Mümpelgart). Held 1586 to compose differences bet. Luths. and Calvinists. J. Andreä* and T. Beza* discussed the Lord's Supper, person of Christ, images and ceremonies, Baptism, and election. Some agreement was reached, but deep differences remained. Those present included also L. Osiander* the Elder.

Monte Cassino. Monastery on site of ancient Casinum in cen. It.; est. ca. 529 by Benedict* of Nursia; cradle of Benedictine Order (see *Benedictines*); destroyed and rebuilt several times, most recently in and after WW II.

Montefiore, Claude Joseph Goldsmid (1858–1938). B. London, Eng.; educ. Oxford; exponent of liberal Judaism*; emphasized importance of rabbinic writing for understading NT. Works include *Outlines of Liberal Judaism; The Synoptic Gospels.*

Montenegro. See *Yugoslavia.*

Montes pietatis (from Lat. *mons,* "large mass," and *pietas,* "piety" and by transfer "kindness"). Medieval charitable institutions, or organizations, that lent money to the needy without interest or at comparatively low rates.

Montesquien, Charles Louis de Secondat (1689–1755). Jurist, pol. theorist and philos., philos. hist.; b. Labrède, near Bordeaux, Fr.; educ. Bordeaux; championed freedom, moderation, toleration, and constitutional govt.; advocated division of govt. power into executive, legislative, and judicial branches; deist; moralist; believed in free will and natural law. Works include *De l'Esprit des Loix; Lettres Persanes.*

Montessori, Maria (1870–1952). B. Chiaravalle, near Ancona, It.; received med. degree from U. of Rome; influenced by J. Locke,* J. R. Pereire,* Edouard Seguin (1812–80; b. Clamecy, Fr.; physician; specialist in mental disease), et al. Devised methods for educ. feebleminded, later applied to younger, normal children; gave special attention to the child, learning materials, and prepared environment. Works include *Il metodo della pedagogia scientifica* (Eng. tr. by A. E. George: *The Montessori Method*).

Monteverdi, Claudio Zuan [Giovanni] Antonio (1567–1643). Composer; b. probably Cremona, It.; master of both the old conservative style and of the new style of the Baroque* period; music dir. St. Mark's, Venice, 1613; priest ca. 1632; assoc. with early development of opera; popularized *arias da capo* (used by J. S. Bach* et al.); helped make accompanied music in chs. common. Works include masses, madrigals, and cantatas.

Montfaucon, Bernard de (1655–1741). B. château de Soulage, Languedoc, Fr.; joined Maurists.* Ed. patristic works. Other works include *Palaeographia graeca; Bibliotheca bibliothecarum.*

Montgomery, James (1771–1854). Brit. poet, hymnist, ed., journalist; b. Irvine, Ayrshire, Scot., son of John Montgomery, an Irish Moravian minister; educ. at Moravian school at Fulneck, near Leeds, Yorkshire, Eng., to prepare for the ministry; parents sent to W. Indies as missionaries 1783 and soon d. there; Montgomery then worked in Mirfield (near Wakefield), Wath (near Rotherham), and Sheffield; engaged in religious and philanthropic work. Ed. *Sheffield Iris* (formerly called *Sheffield Register*); wrote ca. 400 hymns, including "Angels from the Realms of Glory"; "Go to Dark Gethsemane"; "Forever with the Lord."

Montserrat. See *Caribbean Islands,* E 5.

Monuments of Luther. See *Luther Monuments.*

Moody, Dwight Lyman (1837–99). Indep. evangelist; b. Northfield, Mass.; received grade school educ.; shoe salesman Boston, Mass., 1854; originally Unitarian, became Cong. 1855; to Chicago, Ill., 1856; opened a S. S. 1858; organized a nondenominational ch. 1863; pres. Chicago YMCA; conducted preaching tours in Eng. and Am. with I. D. Sankey*; founded the Bible school later called Moody Bible Institute, Chicago, and other institutions. See also *Revivals,* 2.

Moore, George Foot (1851–1931). Presb. Semitic scholar; b. West Chester, Pa.; educ. Yale Coll. (New Haven, Conn.) and Union Theol. Sem. (NYC); pastor Zanesville, Ohio, 1878–83; prof. Andover (Mass.) Theol. Sem. 1883–1902; prof. Harvard 1902–28. Works include *A Critical and Exegetical Commentary on Judges; The Literature of the Old Testament; Judaism in the First Centuries of the Christian Era.*

Moore, Mrs. Stuart. See *Underhill, Evelyn.*

Moore, Thomas (pseudonyms Thomas Little and Thomas Brown the younger; 1779–1852). Poet; b. Dublin, Eire; educ. Trin. Coll., Dublin, and Middle Temple, London, Eng.; Admiralty registrar Bermuda 1803; traveled through US, Can., in Eng., and on the Continent. Tr. *Odes of Anacreon.* Other works include *Odes and Epistles;* lyrics in *Irish Melodies;* hymns include "Come, Ye Disconsolate."

Moore, Thomas E. See *American Rescue Workers.*

Moose, Loyal Order of. Founded 1888 at Louisville, Ky. (1st lodge organized Cincinnati, Ohio), as a secret fraternal and benevolent order. Institutions include Mooseheart ("child city"), near Aurora, Ill., and Moosehaven, Orange Park, Fla. (serves dependent old people). Profession of belief in a Supreme Being is required for membership. Religious features are deistic (see *Deism*). PHL

Moral Argument. See *Apologetics,* 4, I, A; *God, Arguments for the Existence of.*

Moral Feeling. See *Conscience.*

Moral-Influence Theory. See *Atonement, Theories of,* 4.

Moral Law. See *Decalog; Grace, Means of,* II, 2.

Moral Philosophy. Branch of philos. that investigates, without reference to supernaturalism, the rightness as A. A. C. Shaftesbury* and D. Hume* to develop of human actions. See also *Ethics; Theology.*

Moral Re-Armament. See *Buchmanism.*

Moral Sense. (1) Ability to distinguish bet. right and wrong; believed by such 18th-c. Brit. philosophers in the mind as a result of the assoc. of ideas; pleasure is felt when right is approved, displeasure when wrong is disapproved; (2) in common usage the term often implies some aspect of conscience*; (3) See *Exegesis,* 3.

Moral Theology. Science of Christian ethics.*

Moral Virtues. See *Cardinal Virtues.*

Morales, Cristóbal de (perhaps ca. 1500–53). B. Seville, Sp.; RC composer; priest; mem. papal choir 1535–45; held posts in Sp.; master of polyphony. Works include magnificats, masses, motets.

Morality Play. See *Religious Drama,* 2, 3.

Morata, Olympia Fulvia (Olimpia; father's name originally Pellegrini, then Moretto or Morato [also called Peregrino Fulvio Morata]; 1526–55). Scholar and devotee of humanistic culture; b. Ferrara, It.; at court of the duchess of Ferrara; inclined to Lutheranism; married Andrew Gruntler (Gründler; Grünthler; Gruntler), a Ger. student of philos. and medicine; with him to Schweinfurt and Heidelberg, Ger.; became Prot. at Schweinfurt. Works include Lat. treatises; religious poetry (esp. Gk.); *Prolegomena in Ciceronis Paradoxa.*

Moravia. Derives its name from the Morava R. (Ger.: March), a left-bank tributary of the Danube; crownland of Austria 1849; province of Czechoslovakia 1918; united with Silesia as 1 administrative unit 1927; suffered under the impact of WW II; came under Communist control after 1948; with abolition of historic provinces, Moravia was split up into the Brno and Gottwaldov administrative regions and other parts. Home of the Moravian* Ch.

Moravian Brethren. See *Bohemian Brethren; Moravian Church.*

Moravian Church. 1. The Moravian Ch. may be traced to the Bohemian* Brethren. At the beginning of the Luth. Reformation* the Brethren had ca. 400 chs. and ca. 200,000 mems. Relations were est. with Luths. and Ref. See also *Bohemia, Lutheran Theology in.*

2. In polity the Brethren were episc. Administration of the congs. was in the hands of elders. Communities were supervised and counseled by masters and matrons. One group in the community, regarded as the perfected, renounced private property, performed pastoral functions, and earned their living largely by the work of their hands; they were called priests, but there was no specially appointed priesthood till 1467, when a Waldensian apparently conferred on 3 of them orders which they regarded as being in the proper hist. succession. The name Brethren, already in unofficial use, was adopted. As a whole they called themselves Jednota Bratrska (Brüdergemeinschaft; later tr. *Unitas fratrum,* Lat. "Unity of Brethren"). They became active esp. in educ. and literature; their Czech Bible tr. (called Bible of Kralice [Ger. Kralitz] from the place of pub.) was completed 1593 and contains J. Blahoslav's* NT.

3. Moravians suffered severely during the Thirty* Years' War. Many fled to Hung., Saxony, Silesia, Poland, and elsewhere. See also *Comenius, John Amos.*

In 1722 two Hussite Bohemian families from Moravia found refuge on the estate of N. L. v. Zinzendorf* in Saxony; in course of yrs. they were joined by hundreds of others from Moravia, Bohemia, and elsewhere. The settlement, founded on the slope of Mount Hut, was called Herrnhut. An assoc. was formed on basis of common religious ground; order and discipline were est. A Communion service Aug. 13, 1727, helped unify the group; some regard it as the beginning of the Moravian Ch.. See also *Nitschmann, David.*

4. The 1st Moravian miss. came to Pa. 1734. Bethlehem, Pa., was settled 1740–41 by Moravians. Nearby Nazareth was bought by Moravians from G. Whitefield* 1740. At Bethlehem, Nazareth, and affiliated settlements there gradually arose, and prevailed ca. 1744–62, a system of life called Economy, Spartan in rigor and formed esp. to support miss. work, which included outreach to Indians. In 1749 the Brit. parliament recognized the Brethren as "an ancient Protestant Episcopal Church." Lititz, Pa. (named after an estate on which the Boh. Brethren found their 1st home 1456), was settled ca. 1740, laid out 1757, inc. 1759; Salem (now part of Winston-Salem), N. C., was founded 1766 by a Moravian colony. The exclusive community system was abandoned ca. the middle of the 19th c.

5. Doctrines of the Moravian Ch. are stated, e. g., in A. G. Spangenberg,* *Idea fidei fratrum, oder kurzer Begrif der Christlichen Lehre in den evangelischen Brüdergemeinen.* This statement was authorized, but not received as a pub. confession. In Luth. countries, Moravian doctrines were influenced by Lutheran* Confessions; in Eng. and Am., Ref. influence prevailed. Because Luth. and Ref. elements largely existed side by side, a strong and enduring tendency toward union developed. At first the Moravian Ch. was not free from fanaticism. The Trin. was thought of in a grossly offending way; the 1st person of the Godhead was called Papa, Grand-

father, or Father-in-law; the 3d person was called Mama and the eternal Spouse of God the Father. Elimination of such things is largely due to Spangenberg. In gen. the doctrine of the Moravan Ch. represents Calvinistic Protestantism. The Bible is accepted as an adequate rule of faith and practice. The Apostles' Creed is regarded as formulating the prime arts. of faith found in the Bible. Foot washing was discontinued 1818. Infant Baptism is practiced. Adult bap. mems. are confirmed on application after receiving instruction. Nonbaptized applicants are received as mems. through Baptism, usually by sprinkling. Communion is open to communicant mems. of other chs.

6. Moravian ch. govt. is presb. Each cong. has its own council but gen. supervision rests with the provincial syn. comprised of an equal no. of lay and cleric representatives. The syn. deals with all matters of faith and practice. Moravians recognize 3 orders of ministry: deacons, presbyters, and bps. Only bps. may ordain. Moravians have an elaborate liturgy.

7. Moravians are very active in miss. work, holding that Moravian colonies should be as leaven. Early Moravians did not try to gain mems. for their group but often advised converts to join other Protestants. Miss. fields include W. Indies, Greenland, Surinam, S. Afr., N. Am., Labrador, Nicaragua, Australia, Tanzania.

8. In the 1960s the Moravian Ch. had 5 provinces, each responsible for an area of miss. work: Eur. (HQ Herrnhut and Bad Boll), Czechoslovakia (HQ Prague), Brit. (HQ London), Am. N. (HQ Bethlehem, Pa.), Am. S. (HQ Winston-Salem, N. C.). Miss. membership ca. 222,000; total membership over 300,000.

9. In the US the Moravian Ch. is represented by the *Moravian Ch. in Am. (Unitas Fratrum)* with 2 provincial syns. The *Unity of the Brethren* (known as *Ev. Unity of the Czech-Moravian Brethren in N. Am.* till 1959) is mostly in Tex.

Moravian Church in America. See *Moravian Church,* 9.

More, Gertrude (1606–33). Eng. Benedictine nun of the cong. at Cambrai. Works include *The Holy Practices of a Divine Lover; Confessiones amantis.*

More, Hannah (1745–1833). Philanthropist, writer; b. Stapleton, near Bristol, Eng.; worked for moral reform, care for poor, abolition of slavery. Works include *Sacred Dramas; Coelebs in Search of a Wife; Practical Piety; Christian Morals.* See also *Religious Tracts.*

More, Paul Elmer (1864–1937). Philos., literary critic; b. St. Louis, Mo.; educ. Washington U. (St. Louis) and Harvard U. (Cambridge, Mass.); taught at Harvard and Bryn Mawr (Pa.) Coll.; lectured at Princeton (N. J.) U.; tried to defend Christianity on basis of Gk. dualism. Ed. *The Nation* 1909–14; other works include *The Greek Traditions; The Religion of Plato.*

More, Thomas (1478–1535). Statesman, humanist; b. London, Eng.; educ. Oxford and London; lived ca. 4 yrs. under discipline of Carthusian monks; opposed M. Luther* 1523; in controversy with W. Tyndale* 1528; lord chancellor of Eng. 1529–32; beheaded on charge of high treason. Works include *Utopia.*

Morehead, John Alfred (Feb. 4, 1867–June 1, 1936). B. Pulaski Co., Va.; educ. Roanoke Coll. (Salem, Va.), Luth. Theol. Sem. (Philadelphia, Pa.), and Berlin and Leipzig univs.; pastor Va. 1892–98; prof. and head Luth. Theol. S. Sem., Mt. Pleasant, S. C., 1898–1903; pres. Roanoke Coll. 1903–19; pres. 2d LWC Copenhagen, Den., 1929.

Morgan, Thomas (1680–1743). Eng. deist of Welsh descent; pastor of a Presb. ch. Marlborough, Wiltshire, 1716; became Arian; dismissed; practiced med. in Bristol; took up literary work in London; rejected Judaism as nat. religion; held that Christianity must be purged of all Jewish elements. Works include *The Moral Philosopher.*

Morin, Jean (Johannes Morinus; 1591–1659). B. Blois, Fr.; Oratorian theol.; studied patristics and texts.

Morin, Leopold Germain (1861–1946). RC patristic scholar; b. Caen, Fr.; Benedictine monk at Maredsous, Belg., 1891; to Munich 1907; in Switz. during WW I and ca. 1940–45.

Morison, James. See *Evangelical Union.*

Morison, John (1749–98). B. Aberdeenshire, Scot.; educ. U. Aberdeen; pastor Canisbay, Caithness, 1780–98; mem. committee to rev. 1745 *Translations and Paraphrases;* hymnist. Hymns include "The People That in Darkness Sat."

Mörlin, Joachim (1514–71). Older brother of M. Mörlin*; b. Wittenberg, Ger.; educ. Wittenberg; deacon Wittenberg and M. Luther's* chaplain 1539; supt. Arnstadt 1540–43; deposed 1543/44; supt. Göttingen 1544–50; opposed Interim*; dismissed; pastor and inspector Königsberg 1550–53; involved in Osiandrian* controversy; resigned supt. Brunswick 1553/54–1567; bp. Samland at Königsberg 1567.

Mörlin, Maximilian (1516–84). Younger brother of J. Mörlin*; b. Wittenberg, Ger.; educ. Wittenberg; court preacher Coburg 1544; with N. v. Amsdorf* opposed J. Menius* when the latter defended G. Major*; first agreed with M. Flacius* Illyricus, later helped depose him; deposed 1569 as a result of change of regents; restored 1573 under new regent; supported FC.

Mormon, The Book of. See *Latter Day Saints.*

Mormonism. See *Latter Day Saints.*

Mornay, Philippe de (du Plessis-Marley; Duplessis-Mornay; 1549–1623). "Huguenot pope"; Fr. Huguenot; adviser of Henry* IV (of Navarre) till the latter renounced Protestantism; withdrew from court; engaged in extensive writing. See also *Saumur Academy; Sidney, Philip.*

Morocco. See *Africa,* D. 4.

Morone, Giovanni (1509–80). B. Milan, It.; bp. Modena 1529; nuncio to Ger. 1536; present at Hagenau* Colloquy 1540, Regensburg* Conf. 1541; sympathetic to Reformers; cardinal 1542; imprisoned 1557 for supposed heresy; released by Pius* IV; active in final sessions of the Council of Trent.*

Moroni. See *Latter Day Saints,* a.

Morris, John Gottlieb (Nov. 14, 1803–Oct. 10, 1895). Luth. theol.; b. York, Pa.; educ. Dickinson Coll., Carlisle, Pa. (a Presb. school), Princeton (N. J.) Theol. Sem., and Luth. Theol. Sem., Gettysburg, Pa.; pastor Baltimore, Md., 1827–60; librarian Peabody Institute, Baltimore, 1860–65; pastor Baltimore 1864–73; pres. Gen. Syn. 1843, 1883; attended 1st conv. Evangelical* Alliance, London, Eng., 1846. Works include *Bibliotheca Lutherana; Life of John Arndt; Fifty Years in the Lutheran Ministry.*

Morrison, Charles Clayton (1874–1966). B. Harrison, Ohio; educ. Drake U., Des Moines, Iowa; ordained Disciples of Christ minister 1892; lecturer. Ed. *The Christian Century, The Christian Century Pulpit* (later called *The Pulpit*), *Christendom,* and *The American Pulpit;* other works include *The Meaning of Baptism; The Outlawry of War; The Social Gospel and the Christian Cultus; What Is Christianity?*

Morrison, Robert (1782–1834). B. Morpeth, Northumberland, Eng.; d. Canton, China; LMS miss. to China 1807; Brit. E. India Co. interpreter 1809–34. Works include Bible tr.; Chinese dictionary.

Mortal Sins. See *Sins, Venial and Mortal.*

Mortification (from Lat. for "a killing"). Subjection,

denial, and destruction of evil passions and appetites of the flesh. See also *Contrition; Conversion; Repentance; Sanctification.*

Mosaic Art. Art of using pieces of glass, stone, etc., to make a pattern or picture. See also *Art, Ecclesiastical and Religious,* 3.

Mosaic Law. See *Decalog.*

Moschus, John (Moschos; Eucratas; Eukratas; ca. 550–ca. 619). Entered monastery of St. Theodosius, near Jerusalem, perhaps ca. 575; later visited monastic centers in Egypt, Antioch, Cyprus, Rome, and at Mt. Sinai. Works include an account of monastic life and beliefs. *MPG,* 87, 2851–3112.

Mosellanus, Petrus (Peter Schade; Protegensis; 1493 – 1524). B. Bruttig (Proteg), on the Moselle R., Ger.; humanist; prof. Gk. Leipzig; friend of P. Melanchthon*; delivered opening address at Leipzig* Debate.

Moser, Johann Jakob (1701–85). B. Stuttgart, Ger.; educ. Tübingen; prof. Tübingen and Frankfurt an der Oder; arch-chancellor Hesse-Homburg 1747; inclined to Pietism*; hymnist. Wrote extensively on pol. science.

Moses, Assumption of. See *Apocrypha,* A 4.

Moses Ben Jacob Ibn Ezra. See *Ibn Ezra,* 2.

Moses Ben Maimon. See *Maimonides.*

Moses de Leon. See *Cabala.*

Moses of Chorene (probably 5th c. AD). Acc. to tradition a disciple, perhaps a nephew, of Mesrob.* Authenticity of the hist. of Armenia that is assoc. with him is disputed.

Mosheim, Johann Lorenz von (Lorentz; ca. 1694–1755). "Father of modern ch. hist." Luth. theol. and scholar; B. Lübeck, Ger.; educ. Kiel; prof. theol. Helmstedt 1723; prof. and chancellor U. at Göttingen, which he helped found, 1747. Works include *Institutiones historiae ecclesiasticate; De rebus Christianorum ante Constantinum Magnum commentarii.*
L. Spitz, Jr., "Johann Lorenz Mosheim's Philosophy of History," *CTM,* XX (May 1949), 321–339.

Mosheim College (Mosheim Institute). Male and female academy founded ca. 1870 at Mosheim, Greene Co., Tenn. Assoc. with Holston Syn. (see *United Lutheran Church, Synods of,* 10, 29) till ca. 1897; existed till ca. 1903/04; last pres. was mem. of the SW Va. Syn. (see *United Lutheran Church, Synods of,* 16, 29).

Moshesh, Chief. See *Africa,* B 6.

Moslem. See *Islam.*

Mosque (from Arab, *masjid,* "temple"). "Place of prostration" or pub. prayer in Islam*; in the middle of the open, rectangular court, which is surrounded by covered porticoes, is a fountain for ablutions; in a wall of the hall on the side facing Mecca is a niche called mihrab, which indicates the direction of Mecca and usually contains a copy of the Koran*; to its right is the minbar (mimbar), or pulpit; call to prayer is sounded from minarets attached to outside wall of bldg.

Mot. See *Canaanites, Religion of.*

Mote, Edward (1797–1874). B. London, Eng.; joined Bap. Ch. after wayward youth; later became Bap. minister; pastor Horsham, Sussex; hymnist. Hymns include "My Hope is Built on Nothing Less."

Motet. A type of sacred polyphonic choral music written esp. ca. 1250–ca. 1750 usually unaccompanied and based on a Lat. sacred text; similar music in the Angl. Ch., set to Eng. words and usually accompanied, came to be called anthem*; Luth. composers of motets include J. S. Bach,* D. Buxtehude,* J. Pachelbel,* J. A. Reinken,* H. Schütz,* Selle.*

Mother of God. See *Mariology; Theotokos.*

Motif Research. See *Lund, Theology of.*

Motions in Conversion, Inner. See Conversion, II 4.

Mott, John Raleigh (1865–1955). Meth. leader; b. Livingston Manor, N. Y.; student secy. Internat. Committee YMCA 1888–1915; chm. ex. com. Student Volunteer Movement 1888–1920; gen. secy. World's Student Christian Fed. 1895–1920, chm. 1920–28; chm. Continuation Committee, World Miss. Conf., Edinburgh, Scot., 1910–20; chm. Internat. Miss. Council 1921; honorary pres. World* Council of Chs. 1948. Works include *The Present Day Summons to the World Mission of Christianity.* See also *Ecumenical Movement, The,* 5, 6; *Missionary Conferences.*

Motu proprio (Lat. "by one's own impulse"). Document drawn up, signed, and issued by a pope on his own initiative.

Motus interni in Conversion. See *Conversion,* II 4.

Moule, Charles Francis Digby. See *Isagogics,* 3.

Moulton, Forest Ray. See *Evolution,* I.

Moulton, James Hope (1863–1917). Meth. theol.; b. Richmond, Surrey, Eng.; Tutor Wesleyan Coll., Didsbury, Manchester, Lancashire; prof. Hellenistic Gk. and Indo-Eur. philol. Manchester U. 1908. Works include *A Grammar of New Testament Greek;* with G. Milligan,* *The Vocabulary of the Greek Testament.* See also *Lexicons,* B.

Moulton, Warren Joseph. See *Geography, Christian,* 6.

Mounier, Emmanuel (1905–50). B. Grenoble, Fr.; developed a philos. of personalism*: man as a person is not merely an individual, but a spiritual being, a varied personality, separate, yet assoc. with humanity.

Mourners' Bench (anxious bench or seat). Bench or seat near the pulpit reserved in some revival services for those esp. concerned about their spiritual condition.

Mowinckel, Sigmund Olaf Plytt (1884–1965). B. Kjerringöy, Salten, Norw.; educ. Christiania (Oslo), Copenhagen, Marburg, Giessen; prof. Christiania. Works include *Psalmenstudien; Erwägungen zur Pentateuch Quellenfrage; Han som kommer* (Eng. tr. *He That Cometh*); *Offersang og sangoffer* (Eng. tr. *The Psalms as Israel's Worship*); *Det Gamle Testament som Guds Ord* (Eng. tr. *The Old Testament as Word of God*).

Mozambique. See *Africa,* B 4.

Mozarabic Chant. Chant* used in chs. in Sp. in the Middle Ages; named after Mozarabs: Sp. Christians during the Muslim rule of Sp. ca. 8th–15th c.

Mozart, Wolfgang Amadeus (Johannes Chrysostomus Wolfgangus Theophilus; 1756–91). RC musician, composer; b. Salzburg, Austria; educ. by his father, who was a violinist and composer; as a child prodigy, gave concerts in Munich, Vienna, Brussels, Paris, London, and in Holland, Belg., Switz., and It.; involvement in Freemasonry, beginning 1784, is reflected in some of his music. Works include *Mass in C Minor; Requiem.* WEB

Mozley, James Bowling (1813–78). Brother of T. Mozley*; b. Gainsborough, Lincolnshire, Eng.; educ. Oxford; fellow Magdalen Coll., Oxford, 1840; canon Worcester 1869; prof. divinity Oxford 1871; adherent of Tractarianism.* Works include *Essays Historical and Theological.* See also *Metaphysical Society, The.*

Mozley, Thomas (1806–93). Brother of J. B. Mozley*; b. Gainsborough, Lincolnshire, Eng.; educ. Oxford; pupil of J. H. Newman*; ordained 1831; supported Tractarianism.* Works include *Reminiscences, Chiefly of Oriel College and the Oxford Movement.*

Mozzetta (Mozetta). Nonliturgical short cape with small hood worn on occasion by some RC ecclesiastics; color depends on office of wearer and occasion.

Mtesa. See *Africa,* F 1.

Muehlenberg. See *Mühlenberg.*

Mueller, John Theodore (Apr. 5, 1885–Apr. 15, 1967). B. Town Freedom, Waseca Co., Minn.; educ.

Conc. Sem., St. Louis, Mo. Instructor Luther Coll., New Orleans, La., 1907–11; Wittenberg* Academy, Wittenberg, Wis., 1911–13; Pastor Hubbell, Mich., 1913–17; Ottawa and Marseilles, Ill., 1917–20. Prof. Conc. Sem., St. Louis, 1920–64. Ed. *Missionstaube;* other works include *My Church and Others; Faith of Our Fathers; Faith Unshaken; The Church at Corinth; Luther's Large Catechism; Christian Dogmatics; Problem Sermons for Young People.*

Mueller. See also *Müller.*

Mueller-Otfried, Paula (1865–1946). B. Hoya, Ger.; soc. worker; defended women's rights; tried to achieve for women a place in the ch. in harmony with the NT; helped est. Christian-social female sem. in Hannover 1905; demanded the right to vote in ch. for women 1918; mem. Reichstag 1920–32.

Muempelgard. See *Montbéliard, Colloquy of.*

Muffat, Georg (1653–1704). B. Mégève, Alsace; Ger. composer; organist Strasbourg, Salzburg, Passau. Works include *Armonico tributo cioé Sonate di camera commodissime a pocchi ò a molti stromenti; Apparatus musico-organisticus.*

Muggleton, Lodowicke (Lodowick; Ludowicke; Ludovic; 1609–98). B. London, Eng.; Puritan tailor; cofounder Muggletonians.*

Muggletonians. Sect founded ca. 1652 by L. Muggleton* and his cousin John Reeve (1608–58), who claimed to be the 2 witnesses of Rv 11:3-6; rejected the Trin.; held that Elijah ruled in heaven while God lived as Jesus on earth; became extinct ca. 1868.

Muhammad (Mahomet; Mahomed; Moham[m]ed; 570–632). Founder of Islam*; b. Mecca, Arab.; acc. to tradition, a caravan conductor; m. a rich widow merchant 595; engaged in religious contemplation; moved by alleged divine call, began reform movement in Mecca ca. 610; first taught openly ca. 613; opposed by Meccan leaders; fled 622 to Yathrib, later called Medina ("the City," i.e., of the prophet); this flight, called Hegira (from Arab. *hijrah,* "flight"), came to be regarded as the beginning of the Muhammadan era; Muhammad organized a military force; gained control of Mecca 628–630, which became the religious capital of Islam, with Medina the pol. capital. See also *Lost-Found Nation of Islam in the Wilderness of North America, The.* W. M. Watt, *Muhammad: Prophet and Statesman* (London, 1961).

Muhammadanism. See *Islam.*

Mühlberg, Battle of. See *John Frederick; Schmalkaldic War.*

Muhlenberg, Eve Elisabeth. See *Mühlenberg, Henry Melchior, and Family,* 8.

Muhlenberg, Frederick Augustus. See *Mühlenberg, Henry Melchior, and Family,* 14, 15.

Muhlenberg, Frederick Augustus Conrad. See *Mühlenberg, Henry Melchior, and Family,* 6.

Mühlenberg, Gotthilf Henry Ern(e)st. See *Mühlenberg, Henry Melchior, and Family,* 7.

Mühlenberg, Heinrich Melchior. See *Mühlenberg, Henry Melchior, and Family,* 1–4.

Muhlenberg, Henry. See *Mühlenberg, Henry Melchior, and Family,* 11.

Muhlenberg, Henry Augustus Philip. See *Mühlenberg, Henry Melchior, and Family,* 12.

Mühlenberg, Henry Melchior, and Family. 1. *Henry Melchior Mühlenberg* (Sept. 6, 1711–Oct. 7, 1787). B. Einbeck, Ger.; educ. Göttingen; teacher at Halle; ordained 1739; diaconus and inspector of an orphans' home at Grosshennersdorf, Upper Lusatia (Silesia) 1739–41; to Pa. 1742 as pastor of Luth. congs. at Philadelphia, New Providence (also called Providence; now called Trappe), and New Hanover (Falckner's Swamp, Montgomery Co.).

2. In course of time he extended his services to guide, advise, and organize other congs., esp. in N. Y., N. J., and Ga.; helped organize the Pa. Ministerium 1748 (see *United Lutheran Church, Synods of,* 22); semi-retired 1776.

3. His staunch Lutheranism was tinged with Pietism.*

4. In 1745 he married Anna Maria Weiser, daughter of J. C. Weiser* Jr.; their 11 children included the 6 in pars. 5–10.

5. *John Peter Gabriel Muhlenberg* (Oct. 1, 1746–Oct. 1, 1807). B. Trappe, Pa.; educ. Halle, Ger.; returned to Pa. 1767; ordained by Pa. Ministerium 1768; pastor Bedminster (Somerset Co.) and New Germantown (Hunterdon Co.), N. J., 1769–71; ordained Angl. priest London, Eng., 1772, to meet requirements for serving in Va.; pastor Woodstock, Va., till 1776; officer in the Continental Army 1776–83; political offices included mem. Supreme Ex. Council of Pa. 1784, vice-pres. Pa. 1785–87, mem. Pa. Const. Conv. 1790, repeatedly mem. US Congress 1789–1801, Pa. revenue officer 1801–07.

6. *Frederick Augustus Conrad Muhlenberg* (Jan. 1, 1750–June 4, 1801). Grandfather of W. A. Muhlenberg (see par. 11); b. Trappe, Pa.; educ. Halle, Ger.; returned to Pa. 1770; ordained by Pa. Ministerium 1770; pastor Pa. and N. Y. 1770–79; entered politics; mem. Continental Congress from Pa. 1779–80; mem. Pa. House of Representatives 1780–83; mem. US House of Representatives from Pa. 1789–97; 1st speaker of US House of Representatives and speaker in 3d Congress. See also *United Lutheran Church, Synods of,* 15.

7. *Gotthilf Henry Ern(e)st Mühlenberg* (Nov. 17, 1753–May 23, 1815). B. Trappe, Pa.; educ. Halle, Ger.; returned to Pa. 1770; ordained by Pa. Ministerium 1770; pastor Philadelphia 1774–79, New Hanover 1779–80, Lancaster 1780–1815; 1st pres. Franklin Coll., Lancaster, 1787; botanist.

8. *Eve Elisabeth Muhlenberg* (Eva; Betsy; Jan. 29, 1748–1808). Married Christopher Emanuel Schultze (Jan. 25, 1740–Mar. 9, 1809; b. Saxony, Ger.; educ. Halle; ordained 1765 at Wernigerode; to Philadelphia, Pa., 1765; pastor Philadelphia) 1766.

9. *Margaret(ta) Henrietta Muhlenberg* (Peggy; Sept. 17, 1751–Oct. 23, 1831). Married J. C. Kunze.*

10. *Maria Salome Muhlenberg* (Mary; Sally; July 13, 1766–Mar. 13, 1827). Married Matthias Richards (Reichard; Feb. 26, 1758–Aug. 4, 1830; b. near Pottstown, Pa.; in Berks Co. [Pa.] Militia 1777–78; mem. US House of Representatives from Pa. 1807–11) 1782; their son J. W. Richards* was prominent in the Pa. Ministerium.

11. *William Augustus Muhlenberg* (Sept. 16, 1796–Apr. 8, 1877). Son of Henry Muhlenberg, who was a son of F. A. C. Muhlenberg (see par. 6); b. Philadelphia, Pa.; educ. U. Pa.; ordained Episc. deacon 1817, priest 1820; in NYC 1852 he founded the Sisterhood of the Church of the Holy Communion, the 1st Am. order of Prot. Episc. deaconesses; hymnist. Hymns include "I Would Not Live Alway"; "Savior, Who Thy Flock Art Feeding." See also *Protestant Episcopal Church,* 4 b.

12. *Henry Augustus Philip Muhlenberg* (May 13, 1782–Aug. 11, 1844). Son of G. H. E. Mühlenberg (see par. 7), father of H. H. Muhlenberg (see par. 13); b. Lancaster, Pa.; m. Mary Hiester 1805, Rebecca Hiester 1808; licensed to preach 1802, ordained 1804; pastor Trin. Luth. Ch., Reading, Pa., 1803–28; mem. US House of Representatives from Pa. 1829–38; minister to Austria 1838–40.

13. *Hiester Henry Muhlenberg* (Jan. 15, 1812–May 5, 1886). Son of H. A. P. Muhlenberg (see par. 12); b. Reading, Pa.; trained for med. profession but abandoned that course 1842; cashier Farmers' Bank, Reading, 1842–86; 1st treas. General* Council of the Ev. Luth. Ch. in (N.) Am.

14. *Frederick Augustus Muhlenberg,* Sr. (1795–July 5, 1867). Son of G. H. E. Mühlenberg (see

par. 7), father of F. A. Muhlenberg (see par. 15); physician Lancaster, Pa.

15. *Frederick Augustus Muhlenberg,* Jr. (Aug. 25, 1818–Mar. 21, 1901). Luth. cleric; son of F. A. Muhlenberg Sr. (see par. 14); b. Lancaster, Pa.; educ. Princeton (N. J.) Theol. Sem.; ordained 1854. Prof. Franklin Coll., Lancaster; Pa. Coll., Gettysburg, Pa. First pres. Muhlenberg Coll., Allentown, Pa., 1867–76. Prof. U. Pa., Philadelphia, 1876–88; pres. Thiel Coll., Greenville, Pa., 1891–93.

The Journals of Henry Melchior Muhlenberg, tr. T. G. Tappert and J. W. Doberstein, 3 vols. (Philadelphia, 1942–58); *Hallesche Nachrichten;* W. J. Mann, *Life and Times of Henry Melchior Muhlenberg,* 2d ed. (Philadelphia, 1911); M. L. Stoever, *Memoir of the Life and Times of Henry Melchior Muhlenberg, D. D., Patriarch of the Evangelical Lutheran Church in America* (Philadelphia, 1856); W. Germann, *Heinrich Melchior Mühlenberg, Patriarch der Lutherischen Kirche Nordamerika's: Selbstbiographie, 1711–1743* (Allentown, Pa., 1881); W. K. Frick, *Henry Melchior Muhlenberg, "Patriarch of the Lutheran Church in America"* (Philadelphia, 1902); H. A. Muhlenberg, *The Life of Major General Peter Muhlenberg of the Revolutionary Army* (Philadelphia, 1849); P. A. W. Wallace, *The Muhlenbergs of Pennsylvania* (Philadelphia, 1950). RFM

Muhlenberg, Hiester Henry. See *Mühlenberg, Henry Melchior, and Family,* 13.

Muhlenberg, John Peter Gabriel. See *Mühlenberg, Henry Melchior, and Family,* 5.

Muhlenberg, Margaret(ta) Henrietta. See *Mühlenberg, Henry Melchior, and Family,* 9.

Muhlenberg, Maria Salome. See *Mühlenberg, Henry Melchior, and Family,* 10.

Muhlenberg, William Augustus. See *Mühlenberg, Henry Melchior, and Family,* 11; *Protestant Episcopal Church,* 4 b.

Muhlenberg College. See *Lutheran Church in America,* V; *Ministry, Education of,* VIII B 19.

Muhlenberg Press. See *Publication Houses, Lutheran.*

Mühlhäuser, Johannes (John Muehlhaeuser; Aug. 9, 1804–Sept. 15, 1868). "Father of the Wis. Syn."; b. Notzingen, Württemberg, Ger.; joined Christian young men's soc. Basel, Switz.; enlisted by C. F. Spittler* for a miss. trip to Austria, Hung., and Boh. 1829–32; imprisoned Mar.–Oct. 1832 on charge of proselytizing and organizing secret socs.; released; returned to Notzingen; entered Rhenish* miss. house Barmen 1835; sent to Am. 1837 as teacher NYC; unsuccessful; ordained by N. Y. Ministerium; pastor Rochester, N. Y., 1838–48; to Milwaukee, Wis., June 1848 as colporteur; founded Grace Luth. Ch., Milwaukee, 1849, of which he was pastor to his death; 1st pres. (1849–60) of what was later called Wisconsin* Syn.; elected "Senior" 1860, an office created for him.

Mühlmann, Johann(es) (Mülmann; Mulmannus; 1573 to 1613). Luth. hymnist; b. Pegau, near Leipzig, Saxony, Ger.; educ. Leipzig and Jena; held various clerical positions in Leipzig, Naumburg, and Laucha; prof. Leipzig 1607. Hymns include "Dank [or Lob] sei Gott in der Höhe" ("While Yet the Morn is Breaking").

Muinntir. See *Celtic Church,* 3, 11.

Müller, Adam Heinrich von (1779–1829). Pol. economist and soc. philos.; b. Berlin, Ger.; united traditional, romantic, and Christian thought: the Absolute, God, is the unitive factor in organic development; by his birth in time, Christ is the bearer of hist. life; he becomes the *restaurator generis humani* and consequently the ch. becomes the symbol for unity and the goal of hist. Works include *Die Elemente der Staatskunst in Vorlesungen.*

Müller, Frieda. See *Evangelisch-Johannische Kirche.*

Müller, Friedrich (1828–1915). B. Sighisoara (Schässburg), Romania; bp. of the ev. ch. of Transylvania (Siebenbürgen) 1893–1906; tried to develop the inner potential of the ch. through soc. and philanthropic organizations.

Müller, Friedrich (1884–1969). B. Langenthal, Transylvania, Romania; educ. Leipzig, Klausenburg, Vienna, Berlin; mem. educ. council Brasov (Kronstadt; renamed Stalin 1950), Romania, 1911; dir. of an ev. school for training lady teachers at Sighisoara (Schässburg), Romania, 1917; mem. Romanian school council 1922; pastor Sibiu (Hermannstadt) 1928; bp. Ev. Ch. of the AC in Romania 1945. Works include *Völkerentwicklung und Christentum; Geschichtswirksamkeit des Evangeliums in seinem lutherischen Verständnis.*

Müller, Friedrich Max(imilian) (1823–1900). Anglo-Ger. orientalist and philol.; b. Dessau, Ger.; educ. Leipzig and Berlin; prof. Oxford 1854–68; researched mythology and comparative religion; held existence of only 2 kinds of religion: religion of salvation by works (all pagan religions) and religion of salvation by faith in Christ. Ed. *Sacred Books of the East;* other works include *Science of Language; Chips from a German Workshop.*

Müller, Georg Friedrich (1805–98). B. Kroppenstedt (Croppenstedt), near Halberstadt, Ger.; educ. Halle; began to preach 1826; to London 1829; joined Plymouth Brethren*; pastor Teignmouth 1830, Bristol 1832; est. The Scriptural Knowledge Institution for Home and Abroad 1834, orphanage at Bristol 1836, building his work on faith and prayer; engaged in a preaching mission in Eur., Am., India, Australia, and China beginning 1875. Works include *A Narrative of Some of the Lord's Dealings with G. Müller.* See also *Primitive Religion.*

Müller, Heinrich (1631–75). Renowned Luth. devotional writer; b. Lübeck, Ger.; educ. Greifswald; archdeacon St. Mary's 1652, prof. Gk. 1659, theol. 1662, pastor St. Mary's 1662, supt. 1671, all in Rostock; exponent of orthodoxy; an example of living piety; popular preacher; hymnist. Works include *Himmlischer Liebeskuss; Geistliche Erquickstunden.*

Müller, Jakob Aurelius (1741–1806). B. Sibiu (Hermannstadt), Transylvania (Siebenbürgen), Romania; educ. Jena; bp. of ev. Saxons in Transylvania 1792–1806; mildly rationalistic; Freemason. Works include *Die Siebenbürger Sachsen.*

Müller, Johann Andreas Friedrich Wilhelm (Oct. 29, 1825–Dec. 26, 1900). B. Planena, near Halle, Ger.; to Am. with the 1839 Saxon immigration (see *Lutheran Church – Missouri Synod, The,* II); 1st grad. of the sem. at Altenburg, Mo. Pastor Manchester, Mo., 1847; Chicago, Ill., 1856; Pittsburgh, Pa., 1863; several congs. in Somerset Co., Pa., 1870; Chester, Ill., 1875. Vice-pres. E. Dist. 1867–73, Ill. Dist. 1885–1900, both of the Mo. Syn.

Müller, Johann Georg (1759–1819). B. Schaffhausen, Switz.; Ref. educator; prof. Gk. and Heb. Schaffhausen 1794; friend of J. G. v. Herder.* Works include *Philosophische Aufsätze.*

Müller, Johann Georg (1800–75). Ref. educator and student of comparative religion; b. Basel, Switz.; educ. Basel; ordained 1825; teacher Basel; prof. Basel 1835. Works include *Geschichte der amerikanischen Urreligionen.*

Müller, Johannes (1864–1949). B. Riesa, Saxony, Ger.; studied theol. under F. Delitzsch (see *Delitzsch,* 1) and F. H. R. v. Frank*; worked briefly in miss. to Jews; then initiated a miss. to the unchurched educated; est. a house for free development of personal life, with H. Lhotzky* as coworker for a short time; moved the venture 1916 to Elmau castle, bet. Garmisch and Mittenwald. Held that man must be true to his essence; emphasized

Sermon on the Mount; felt that national rebirth was at hand 1933, but admitted his error 1948.

Müller, Joseph Theodor (1854–1946). Theol. of Unitas fratrum (see *Moravian Church,* 3); hymnist; b. Niesky, Ger.; educ. at Moravian sem. Gnadenfeld. Ed. *Zeitschrift für Brüdergeschichte;* tr. *Acta unitatis fratrum;* other works include *Zinzendorf als Erneurer der alten Brüderkirche.*

Müller, Julius (1801–78). Mediating theol.; b. Brieg (Brzeg), Silesia, Ger.; educ. Göttingen, Breslau, and Berlin; defended the purpose of the Prussian* Union but refused to use the union ritual; prof. Göttingen, Marburg, and Halle. Works include *Die christliche Lehre von der Sünde.*

Müller, Karl Ferdinand Friedrich (1852–1940). Ch. hist.; b. Langenburg, Württemberg, Ger.; educ. Tübingen and Göttingen; prof. Halle, Giessen, Breslau, and Tübingen; held that ch. hist. is only a part of hist. in gen. and must be written in connection with the latter without preconceived views.

Müller, Ludwig. See *Germany,* C 4.

Müller. See also *Mueller.*

Mullins, Edgar Young (1860–1928). B. Franklin Co., Miss.; educ. S. Bap. Theol. Sem., Louisville, Ky., and Johns Hopkins U., Baltimore, Md.; Bap. pastor Ky., Md., and Mass.; pres. S. Bap. Theol. Sem. 1899, S. Bap. Conv. 1921–24, Bap. World Alliance 1923–28. Works include *The Axioms of Religion; Why is Christianity True?*

Mumford, Stephen. See *Baptist Churches,* 16.

Mumm, Reinhard (1873–1932). B. Düsseldorf, Ger.; Christian socialist; active in ecumenical movement; supported soc. legislation.

Mümpelgart. See *Montbéliard, Colloquy of.*

Münchmeyer, August Friedrich Otto (1807–82). Luth. theol.; b. Barskamp, Hannover, Ger.; educ. Göttingen, and at the preachers' sem. in Hanover; pastor Lamspringe, near Hildesheim, 1840; supt. Catlenburg (Katlenburg-Duhm), near Northeim, 1851; supt. and consistorial councillor Buer (now part of Gelsenkirchen) and mem. Osnabrück consistory 1855; advocated complete separation of ch. and state; with L. A. Petri* and R. Steinmetz* founded Gotteskasten.*

Munger, Theodore Thornton (1830–1910). Cong. cleric; b. Bainbridge, N. Y.; educ. Yale Coll. and Divinity School, New Haven, Conn.; pastor Mass., Calif., and Conn.; tried to relate New* Eng. Theol. to literature and educ. Works include *On the Threshold; The Freedom of Faith; Lamps and Paths; Essays for the Day; Horace Bushnell, Preacher and Theologian.*

Mungo. See *Celtic Church,* 6.

Munificentissimus Deus. 1950 apostolic const. (see *Constitutions*) of Pius XII (see *Popes,* 33) defining the RC doctrine of the Assumption of Mary into heaven.

Munk, Jens. See *Danish Lutherans in America,* 1.

Munk, Kaj Harald Leininger (1898–1944). B. Maribo, Den.; original family name: Petersen; adopted at age 6 by the Munk family after his parents died; educ. Copenhagen; ordained 1924; pastor Vederso, W. Jutland, Den.; poet, dramatist; killed for opposing Nazism (see *Socialism,* 3). Works include *En Idealist* (Eng. tr. *Herod the King*); *Cant* (on the rise and fall of Anne Boleyn); *Han sidder ved Smeltedligen* (Eng. tr. *He Sits at the Melting Pot;* portrays Hitler's Germany). See also *Denmark, Lutheranism in,* 12.

Munkácsy, Mihály von (Michael Lieb; 1844–1900). Hung. hist. and genre painter; b. Munkács, Ruthenia (Hung.; now Mukachevo, Ukraine); studied in Vienna, Munich, and Düsseldorf. Works include *Christ Before Pilate; Golgotha.*

Münkel, Kornelius Karl (1809–88). Luth. cleric; b. Hameln, Hannover, Ger.; tutor Hameln; teacher in Gymnasium at Hanover; pastor Oiste, near Verden, Hannover; prominent in the state ch.

Munson, Samuel (Mar. 23, 1804–June 28, 1834). B. New Sharon, Maine; educ. Bowdoin Coll., Brunswick, Maine, and Andover (Mass.) Theol. Sem.; ABCFM miss. to Indian Archipelago with H. Lyman.* See also *Indonesia,* 4.

Münster, Sebastian (1489–1552). B. Ingelheim, Ger.; Franciscan; supported the Luth. Reformation; became a pupil of J. Reuchlin*; taught Heb. in Heidelberg and Basel; made a rather literal tr. of the OT into Lat.; studied math, astronomy, geography; cosmographer.

Münster Circle. Group of intellectuals, chiefly RC, est. in Münster, Ger., in the latter part of the 18th c. to discuss philos., pedagogy, and Christian perfection. See also *Gallitzin, Adelheid Amalia; Hamann, Johann Georg; Stolberg, Friedrich Leopold von.*

Münster Kingdom (or Tragedy). Jan Matthys (many variant spellings; d. 1534), a baker of Haarlem, Neth., and disciple of M. Hofmann,* announced 1533 that he was the Enoch foretold by Hofmann and gained a following in Münster, Westphalia, Ger. Aided by Bernhard Rothmann (Bernard; Bernd; Bernt; Rottmann; ca. 1495–ca. 1535; cleric educ. at Deventer, Neth., in the school of the Brethren of the Common Life), B. Knipperdolling,* and John* of Leiden, Matthys tried to make Münster the New Jerusalem. Control of the city was taken by force. Knipperdolling became burgomaster 1534. Opponents of Anabaps. were driven out. Communism and polygamy were est. After Matthys' death, John of Leiden became leader and king. Bp. Franz von Waldeck (ca. 1492–1553) and others led the forces that captured Münster 1535. Many Anabaps. were massacred; their leaders were executed with savage torture. See also *Millennium,* 5.

Münter, Friedrich Christian Karl Heinrich (1761–1830). B. Gotha, Ger.; acquainted with J. W. v. Goethe,* F. G. Klopstock,* and F. L. v. Stolberg*; interested in poetry and archaeol.; led by C. W. F. Walch* and L. T. Spittler* to take up hist.; prof. Copenhagen, Den., 1788; bp. Sjaelland (Zealand; Seeland) 1808.

Münzer, Thomas (Müntzer; ca. 1489/91–1525). Ger. enthusiast; b. Stolberg, Saxony; educ. Leipzig and Frankfurt an der Oder; preacher Zwickau 1520; tried to surpass M. Luther as reformer; fanatical ascetic and Anabap.; built religion on direct revelation; claimed enlightenment by inner light through visions, dreams, etc.; leader in Peasants'* War; defeated at Frankenhausen; beheaded.

Muratori, Ludovico Antonio (1672–1750). Hist. and RC theol.; b. Vignola, It.; priest 1695; librarian and archivist at Modena; discovered Muratorian* fragment. Comp. and ed. collections of theol. and hist. sources, including *Rerum italicarum scriptores.*

Muratorian Fragment (Canon Muratori). 85-line fragment of a Lat. treatise (probably tr. from Gk.) on the Bible canon*; includes a list of NT books accepted as canonical in It. at the end of the 2d c.; does not mention Heb, Ja, 1–2 Ptr, and 1 of the epistles of Jn; mentions Apocalypse of Peter and Wis; writings rejected include Shepherd of Hermas. Discovered 1740 by L. A. Muratori* in the Ambrosian Library at Milan. Author unknown.

Murillo, Bartolomé Esteban (1617–82). Painter; b. Seville, Sp. Noted for paintings titled *Immaculate Conception.*

Murmellius, Johannes (1480–1517). B. Roermond, Neth.; humanist, poet, educ.; taught in Cologne and Münster, Ger., and Alkmaar, Neth.

Murner, Thomas (1475–1537). B. Oberehnheim (Obernai), Alsace; Franciscan; priest 1497; made poet laureate by Maximilian I; in Eng. 1523, supporting Henry VIII in conflict with M. Luther; returned to Ger. but was driven out by revolting peasants 1525; pastor Lucerne, Switz., 1526; driven out by Zwinglians. Satirist. Opposed Luth. Reformation.

Murray, Andrew (1828–1917). B. Graaff-Reinet, Union of S. Afr.; educ. Aberdeen, Scot., and Utrecht, Netherlands. Dutch-Ref. pastor Bloemfontein, Union of S. Afr., 1848; Worcester, Cape Province, Union of S. Afr., 1860–64; Cape Town 1864-71. Pastor of a Huguenot community at Wellington, Cape Province, 1871. Founded a Huguenot sem. and miss. training school at Wellington.

Murray, John (1741–1815). "Father of Am. Universalism"; b. Alton, Hampshire, Eng.; moved to Cork, Ireland, ca. 1752; joined Methodists ca. 1760; won for Universalism by James Relly* (see *Universalists*); excommunicated from the Meth. Ch.; to Am. 1770; itinerant preacher from New Eng. to Virginia; chaplain in Am. Revolution. Pastor Gloucester, Mass., 1779–93; Boston 1793–1809. See also *Ballou, Hosea.*

Murtoa College. See *Australia, Lutheranism in,* A 2.

Musa, Anton (Wesch; West; ca. 1485–1547). B. Wiehe, near the Unstrut R. and Naumburg, Ger.; pastor Erfurt 1521, Jena 1527; inspector E. Thuringia 1528–29; pastor and supt. Rochlitz 1537; reformer of Rochlitz and Merseburg.

Musäus, Johann(es) (1613–81). Great-grandson of S. Musäus*; brother of P. Musäus*; b. Langewiesen, near Arnstadt, Ger.; prof. Jena 1643; defended Lutheranism against RCs, Reformed, sectarians, deists, pantheists; charged with syncretism; signed a statement condemning all syncretism. See also *Synergistic Controversy.*

Musäus, Peter (1620–74). Great-grandson of S. Musäus*; brother of J. Musäus*; b. Langewiesen, near Arnstadt, Ger.; prof. Rinteln 1648, Helmstedt 1663, Kiel 1665; suspected of syncretism.

Musäus, Simon (1521–76). Great-grandfather of J. Musäus* and P. Musäeus*; b. Vetschau, near Cottbus, Ger.; prof. Jena; held many other positions; opposed synergism and Zwinglian doctrine of the Lord's Supper.

Muscat. See *Middle East,* L 7.

Musculus, Andreas (Latinized form of Meusel; 1514–81). B. Schneeberg, Saxony, Ger.; educ. Leipzig and Wittenberg; prof. Frankfurt an der Oder; polemic against the Interim,* A. Osiander* the Elder, F. Stancarus,* P. Melanchthon,* J. Calvin*; gen. supt. Brandenburg after J. Agricola* d. 1566; present at Torgau 1576, Bergen 1577 (see *Lutheran Confessions,* C 2). Works include *Thesaurus* (compilation of excerpts from M. Luther's writings).

Musculus, Wolfgang (Meusel; Meusslin; Mäusslin; Mösel; Mosel; Müsslin; 1497–1563). B. Dieuze, Lorraine; Benedictine till 1527, then ev. pastor; 1531–47 in Augsburg; signed Wittenberg* Concord; inclined to Confessio Tetrapolitana (see *Reformed Confessions,* D 1); attended Colloquy of Worms* and Regensburg* Conf. 1540–41; driven out of Augsburg by the Interim*; prof. Bern, Switz.; hymnist. Hymns include "Christe, der du bist Tag und Licht" (tr. of Lat. *Christe qui lux es et dies*).

Music, Church. Music is properly used (cf. e. g., Ps 96; Eph 5:19; Cl 3:16) by the Christian Ch. to worship God and spiritualize man; to that end it should be worthy, fitting, and reverent.

Christ, His disciples, and Paul and Silas used music in worship (Mt 26:30; Acts 16:25). Pliny* the Younger wrote to Trajan (see *Persecution of Christians,* 3) that the Christians sing a hymn to Christ as God. Ch. fathers speak of Christian song. Ambrose* helped develop ch. music. Gregorian* music became standard.

A. M. T. S. Boethius* regarded music as part of mathematics and an instrument of philos. with ethical influence. Polyphony developed throughout the Gothic Period (ca. 1200–ca. 1450). The Renaissance rejected some things in Boethius and F. M. A. Cassiodorus* but continued to stress the scientific aspects of music. As music flourished at courts it suffered in chs.

Under leadership of M. Luther good music flourished among his followers. In line with the doctrine of the universal priesthood of believers he encouraged singing of hymns by the cong. as well as the choir (see *Luther, Hymns of*). Luth. students of theol. were required to study liturgics, ch. music, and hymnology. Luther rated music next to theol. and made knowledge and appreciation of good music an important requirement for pastors and teachers. He regarded it as an aid to worship that helps present the Word and express reactions of the worshiper. In course of time the Luth. Ch. came to be known as the "singing ch." with a rich musical heritage. See also *Chant; Chorale; Chorale Prelude; Hymnody, Christian,* 5–6; *Luther, Liturgies of;* cf. WA 35; WA-Br 5, 639; WA-T 3, 636, No. 3815.

Other 16th-c. Luth. leaders (e. g., P. Melanchthon,* J. Bugenhagen,* N. Selnecker,* J. Walther,* G. Rhau*) also adopted attitudes toward ch. music that allowed for progress and helped prevent obsolescence.

The Luth. heritage of hymns includes versions of parts of the liturgy (e. g., *Agnus Dei*: "O Christ, Thou Lamb of God"; *Gloria in excelsis*: "All Glory be to God on High"; *Nunc dimittis*: "In Peace and Joy I Now Depart"; *Sanctus*: "Isaiah, Mighty Seer, in Days of Old").

Distinctions bet. ch., concert, secular, and folk music were rarely, if ever, made until the 16th c., when Reformed groups and the Council of Trent* raised points of difference. For hymn texts the Reformed (including Puritans and Pietists) required Bible texts (sometimes versified, e. g., by T. Beza* and C. Marot*). The E Orthodox Ch. and Angl. Ch. also have important schools of music.

Legislation of the Council of Trent was directed against the nonliturgical character of some ch. music, curtailment and unintelligibility of liturgical texts, and use of nonchurchly vernacular songs in ch. The 1903 motu proprio of Pius X (see *Popes,* 30) est. norms of holiness, true art, and universality for liturgical music and recommended Gregorian chant, classical polyphony, and approved modern compositions but disapproved the use of instruments, except the organ, in ch. In RCm choirs are a lower clergy; in the Luth. Ch., choirs are a part of the cong. Vatican II's *Constitution on the Sacred Liturgy,* ch. 6, contains a short code of sacred music.

Composers of Luth. ch. music include H. L. (v.) Hassler,* H. Schütz,* J. S. Bach,* J. L. F. Mendelssohn-Bartholdy,* H. A. Distler,* Ernst Pepping (b. Duisburg, Ger., 1901; works include *Spandauer Chorbuch; Choralbuch*). WEB

See also *Mass* (Music).

Muslim. Adherent of Islam.* See also *Africa; Middle East.*

Mutian, Konrad (Mutianus Rufus; Muth; Conrad(us); 1470–1526). Humanist; b. Homberg, Ger.; educ. Deventer, Neth., Erfurt, Ger., and in It.; Neoplatonist; held that there is divine revelation in every religion and that Christ is the universal spirit.

Myconius, Friedrich (Mecum; Mekum; 1490–1546). Luth. reformer of Thuringia; b. Lichtenfels, Upper Franconia, N Bav., Ger.; Franciscan priest 1516; follower of M. Luther 1517; preacher and pastor Gotha 1524/25; present at Colloquy of Marburg 1529 (see *Lutheran Confessions,* A 2), the 1537 meeting of the Schmalkaldic League (see *Lutheran Confessions,* B 2), Hagenau* Colloquy 1540; signed Wittenberg* Concord 1536; took part in visitation of

Thuringia 1528/29 and 1533; ducal Saxony 1539. Works include *Historia Reformationis.*

Myconius, Oswald (Geisshüssler; Molitoris; 1488–1552). B. Lucerne, Switz.; educ. Basel; taught in Basel and Zurich; co-worker of H. Zwingli.* Helped write 1st Basel Confession (see *Reformed Confessions,* A 5) and the 1st Helvetic Confession (see *Reformed Confessions,* A 6).

Mylius, Georg (Miller; Müller; Gering; ca. 1544/48–1607). B. Augsburg, Ger.; educ. Strasbourg, Marburg, Tübingen; pastor Augsburg 1571, later supt. and rector there; deposed 1584 for opposing Gregorian calendar; prof. Wittenberg and Jena. Coauthor Articles* of Visitation; other works include *Exodus evangelica; Send- und Trostbrieff; Bapstpredigten; Augustanae confessionis . . . explicatio; In epistolam D. Pauli ad Romanos.*

Mynster, Jacob Pier (Jakob Peter; 1775–1854). B. Copenhagen, Den.; educ. Copenhagen; pastor on Sjaelland (Zealand) 1802; chaplain Copenhagen 1812; tutor Copenhagen 1813; court preacher 1826; bp. Sjaelland (highest ch. office in Den.) 1834–54; opposed N. F. S. Grundtvig* and rationalism. Works include *Kleine theologische Schriften.*

Myron (Holy Myron; from Gk. *myron,* "ointment"). Name of holy oils* used in liturgical ceremonies of the E Ch.

Myslenta, Cölestin (1588–1653). Luth. leader; b. Kutten, East Prussia; prof. theol. (1616), preacher, inspector Königsberg (Kaliningrad); opposed syncretism* of G. Calixtus,* C. Dreier,* and J. Latermann.*

Mysos, Demetrius. See *Demetrius of Thessalonica.*

Mystagogical Theology (from Gk. *mystagogia,* "initiation into mysteries"). Theol. that interprets or involves religious mysticism* or mysteries.

Mysteries (Mystery plays). Plays performed in Middle Ages in chs. or in the streets for religious instruction by means of amusement. See also *Religious Drama.*

Mystery Religions. Ancient religions with secret rites of initiation. Most important: Gk., Phrygian, Syrian, Egyptian, Persian. See also *Cybele; Greek Religion; Isis; Mithraism.*

Mystic Shrine. See *Freemasonry,* 9.

Mystical Interpretation. See *Exegesis,* 3, 5.

Mystical Union. Spiritual relationship est. bet. a Christian and God by the indwelling of God, esp. the Holy Spirit (Jn 14:23; Ro 8:15; 1 Co 3:16; 6:15, 19; 2 Co 6:16; Gl 4:6; Eph 3:17); est. by the gift of justifying faith* (Gl 3:2); to be distinguished from false mysticism.* See also *Sacrament and the Sacraments,* F.

Mysticism (from Gk. *mystikos,* "mystical; secret"). A. Term applied to a wide range of phenomena (e. g., demonology,* magic,* dreaminess, weird experiences, occultism [see *Spiritism; Theosophy*], certain philosophies of life). Mysticism may be divided: (1) Contemplative (as in Augustine* of Hippo, J. Eckhart,* R. W. Emerson,* Plotinus*); (2) Personal, emphasizing personal communion with God (as in Thomas* à Kempis, Fra Angelico,* F. de S. de la M. Fénelon,* G. Fox,* T. Kagawa*); (3) Nature (as in Francis* of Assisi, W. Wordsworth*); (4) Practical, marked by sacrificial service prompted by love.

The goal of mysticism is the alleged intuitive and emotional contact with the Absolute ("that which is," "the Good," "God," and many other ultimate spiritual values). In its practical aspects, mysticism is the attempt to apperceive, use, and enjoy ultimate values.

Following steps may be distinguished in mysticism: (1) freeing oneself from wrong; (2) freeing oneself of the phantasmata of the world; (3) departure into the realm of the pure through contemplation and yearning; (4) mystic view or experience. Mysticism is not so much a doctrine as a method of thought, a reaching for the Infinite through methods of reasoning and attempted direct contemplation. The word "contemplation" is often used for mystic experience in pre-Renaissance W writers.

In his early period M. Luther* ed. *Deutsche Theologie* (see *"German Theology"*) and commended the work of J. Tauler* (St. L. ed., XXIa, 56). J. Staupitz* was a mystic. But Luther's system centered in the external Word of God and its doctrine of justification. He condemned the mysticism of S. Franck,* A. R. B. v. Karlstadt,* T. Münzer,* K. Schwenkfeld (see *Schwenkfelders*), N. Storch (see *Zwickau Prophets*).

B. Other mystics include Angela* de Foligno, J. Böhme,* Bernard* of Clairvaux, Bonaventura,* Catherine* of Sienna, Clement* of Alexandria, R. Crashaw,* Dionysius* the Areopagite, Gertrude the Great (see *Gertrude,* 1), Gregory* of Nyssa, Guyon,* Hildegard* of Bingen, W. Hilton,* F. v. Hügel,* Hugh* of St. Victor, W. R. Inge,* Jacopone* da Todi, W. James,* John* of the Cross, R. M. Jones,* Julian(a)* of Norwich, W. Law,* Luis* de Granada, Mechthild* of Hackeborn, Mechthild* of Magdeburg, M. de Molinos,* Richard* of St. Victor, R. Rolle* de Hampole, J. v. Ruysbroeck,* H. Suso,* Teresa* of Ávila, E. Underhill.* EL

See also *Mystical Union; Sufism; Taoism; Yoga.*

C. A. A. Bennett, *A Philosophical Study of Mysticism* (New Haven, Conn., 1923); W. K. Fleming, *Mysticism in Christianity* (London, 1913); E. C. Butler, *Western Mysticism,* 3d ed. (London, 1967); M. Smith, *An Introduction to the History of Mysticism* (New York, 1930) and *Studies in Early Mysticism in the Near and Middle East* (London, 1931); R. M. Jones, *New Studies in Mystical Religion* (New York, 1927); W. R. Inge, *Christian Mysticism* (London, 1899) and *The Philosophy of Plotinus,* 3d ed. (London, 1929); E. Underhill, *Mysticism,* 6th ed. (London, 1916) and *The Essentials of Mysticism and Other Essays* (London, 1920); R. Otto, *Mysticism East and West,* tr. B. L. Bracey and R. C. Payne (New York, 1932).

Myth (Gk. *mythos,* "talk; myth"). 1. Story ostensibly relating hist. events which usually explain some belief, custom, institution, or phenomenon. 2. Story in which deity acts in space and time. 3. Presentation of primitive, eschatological, or other-worldly truth in this-worldly language and form. 4. Story invented as veiled explanation of truth. 5. Imaginary person or thing either nonexistent or incapable of verification.

See also *Demythologization.*

N

Naasenes. See *Gnosticism,* 7 i.
Nabu. See *Babylonians, Religion of the,* 1.
Nachtenhöfer, Caspar Friedrich (Kaspar; 1624–85). B. Halle, Ger.; educ. Leipzig; diaconus 1651, pastor 1655 Meeder, near Coburg; pastor Coburg 1671; hymnist. Hymns include "Dies ist die Nacht, da mir erschienen"; "Kommst du nun, Jesu, vom Himmel herunter auf Erden"; "So gehst du nun, mein Jesu, hin."
Nagel, Julius (1809–84). Luth. theol.; b. Bahn (Stecklin?), Pomerania; influenced by F. D. E. Schleiermacher*; revival preacher on Wolin Is.; opposed Prussian* Union; formed separate Luth. ch.; supt. of Old* Luths. in Breslau; taught divine right of ch. govt. (see also *Huschke, Georg Philipp Eduard*).
Nägeli, Hans Georg (1773–1836). B. Wetzikon, Zurich canton, Switz.; composer, author, educ., pub.; issued many works for home, ch., and school; pub. works of old masters; founded Swiss Assoc. for Cultivation of Music.
Nairn(e), Thomas. See *Associate Reformed Church.*
Namaqualand (Namaland). Coastal SW Afr.; Great Namaqualand in South-West Afr.; Little Namaqualand in Rep. of S. Afr. See also *Africa* B 5, 8; *Schmelen, Johann Heinrich; Shaw, Barnabas.*
Name of God. See *Revelation,* 6.
Name of Jesus, Feast of the. In 1530 Franciscans* were given permission to celebrate the Feast of the Name of Jesus Jan. 14; 1721 it was made a gen. observance for the whole RC Ch. on the 2d Sun. after Epiphany*; Pius X (see *popes,* 30) reset the date for the RC ch. on the Sun. bet. Jan. 1 and 6, or, when there is no such Sun., Jan. 2. In the Luth. Ch. the Circumcision and the Name of Jesus are commemorated Jan. 1.
Namibia. See *Africa,* B 8.
Nanini, Giovanni Bernardino (Nanino; ca. 1560–1623). Brother of G. M. Nanini*; b. Vallerano, Viterbo, It.; RC composer; maestro di cappella S. Luigi de' Francesci 1599, later at S. Lorenzo in Damaso. Works include motets, psalms, and a *Venite, exultemus.*
Nanini, Giovanni Maria (Nanino; ca. 1545–1607). Brother of G. B. Nanini*; RC composer; b. Tivoli, It.; assoc. with G. P. da Palestrina.* Works include motets and psalms.
Nantes, Edict of. Issued 1598 by Henry* IV of Fr.; gave Fr. Prots. a measure of toleration, civil rights, and liberties; revoked 1685. See also *France,* 10.
Napoleon I (Fr.: Napoléon Bonaparte; It.: Napoleone Buonaparte; 1769–1821). "le Petit Caporal; the Corsican"; b. Ajaccio, Corsica; Fr. Consul 1799, emp. 1804–09, 1810–14; assumed title of king of It. 1805; became practical master of the Continent; put relatives on Eur. thrones; defeated at Waterloo 1815; d. in exile on St. Helena. See also *Concordat* 5; *France,* 5.
Narsai (Narses; 399–ca. 502/503). "The Leper"; b. 'Ain Dulbe, on the Tigris R., Persia; taught at Edessa* from ca. 437; deposed for his Nestorianism ca. 457; taught at Nisibis* ca. 457–ca. 497. See also *Barsumas; Schools, Early Christian,* 5.
Narses (ca. 478–ca. 573). Byzantine gen. under Justinian* I; defeated last Gothic army in It. 553; prefect of It. 554–567.
Narses of Nisibis. See *Narsai.*
Narthex. Vestibule leading to the nave of a ch.; originally a western porch used by persons not entering the ch. itself. See also *Church Architecture,* 3.
Näsman, Gabriel. Swed. Luth. pastor; served in and around Philadelphia, Pa., 1743–52; helped found Pa. Ministerium.
Nasmith, David (1799–1839). Philanthropist; b. Glasgow, Scot.; est. Glasgow city miss. 1826; est. missions in Eng., Ireland, Fr., Can., and US; est. the London (Eng.) City Miss. 1835.
Nast, William (1807–99). B. Stuttgart, Ger.; studied theol. at Tübingen; to US 1828; Meth. preacher in Ohio 1835. Ed. *Der Christliche Apologete.* See also *Lutheran Church – Missouri Synod, The,* V 12.
Natal. Province in Rep. of S. Afr. (see *Africa,* B 5).
Natalis Alexander (Noel Alexandre; 1639–1724). Dominican ch. hist.; b. Rouen, Fr.; sympathetic to Jansenism*; opposed *Unigenitus** 1714. Works include *Selecta historiae ecclesiasticae capita; Theologia dogmatica et moralis secundum ordinem Catechismi Concilii Tridentini.*
Natalis Herveus (Herveus Natalis; Hervaeus; Harvey Nedellec; 1250/60–1323). B. Brittany, Fr.; master gen. Dominicans 1318; leader of the Fr. school of Thomas* Aquinas.
Natalitia (from Lat. *natalis* [sc. *dies*], "birthday"). Term used in early ch. for death days of Christians, esp. martyrs, in the sense of birthday into everlasting life.
Nathan ben Kalonymus, Isaac (15th c.). Fr. rabbi and philos.; comp. Heb. Bible concordance pub. under name Mordecai Nathan. See also *Concordances, Bible.*
Näther, Karl Gustav Theodor (Sept. 14, 1866–Feb. 13, 1904). B. Bautzen, Saxony, Ger.; educ. Leipzig Miss. Sem.; miss. to India 1887; separated with F. E. Mohn* from Leipzig Miss. for reasons of conscience 1893; both joined the Mo. Syn., came to US via Ger., and were commissioned 1894 as the first Mo. Syn. missionaries to India; est. a miss. at Krishnagiri, Salem Dist., Madras Presidency, India; d. of bubonic plague at Krishnagiri. See also *India,* 13; *Lutheran Church – Missouri Synod, The,* VI 8; *Missions,* 10.
Nathin, Johannes. See *Luther, Martin,* 5.
Nation of Islam. See *Lost-Found Nation of Islam in the Wilderness of North America.*
National and International Pentecostal Missionary Union. Founded 1914 by Philip Wittich. See also *International Pentecostal Assemblies.*
National Association for the Advancement of Colored People. William Edward Burghardt Du Bois (1868–1963; b. Great Barrington, Mass., of mixed Fr., Dutch, and Afr. descent; educ. Fisk U., Nashville, Tenn., and Harvard U., Cambridge, Mass.; taught at Wilberforce [Ohio] U., U. of Pa., Philadelphia, and Atlanta [Ga.] U.; works include *Black Reconstruction; Color and Democracy*) and 28 other Negro professional men met 1905 at Niagara Falls, Ont., Can., to form a protest movement in behalf of Negroes. The "Niagara Movement," as it came to be known, held further meetings 1906, 1907, 1908, 1909. Its mems. joined white liberals. The NAACP was inc. 1910. Goal: soc., pol., and economic equality for Negroes. Organ: *The Crisis.*
F. L. Broderick, *W. E. B. DuBois: Negro Leader in a Time of Crisis* (Stanford, Calif., 1959); W. H. Burns, *The Voices of Negro Protest in America*

(New York, 1963); L. Hughes, *Fight for Freedom: The Story of the NAACP* (New York, 1962); *NAACP – An American Organization* (New York, 1960); W. D. St. James, *The National Association for the Advancement of Colored People: A Case Study in Pressure Groups* (New York, 1958); *International Library of Negro Life and History:* W. S. Robinson, *Historical Negro Biographies,* 2d ed., rev. (New York, 1969) and C. H. Wesley, *The Quest for Equality: From Civil War to Civil Rights* (New York, 1968/69). EL

National Association of Congregational Christian Churches. Organized 1955 Detroit, Mich., by mems. of Cong. Christian Chs. who did not wish to become part of the United* Church of Christ.

National Association of Evangelicals. See *Teachers,* 33; *Union Movements,* 12.

National Association of School Social Workers. See *National Association of Social Workers.*

National Association of Social Workers. Formed 1955 by merger of Am. Assoc. of Group Workers, Am. Assoc. of Med. Soc. Workers, Am. Assoc. of Psychiatric Soc. Workers, Am. Assoc. of Soc. Workers, Assoc. for the Study of Community Organization, Nat. Assoc. of School Soc. Workers, Soc. Work Research Group. Purposes include: strengthening and unifying the soc. work profession in gen.; developing soc. work practices in particular. Pub. *Social Work Year Book;* quarterly *Social Work.* HQ NYC.

"History, Status, and Trends Articles," *Social Work Year Book,* ed. R. H. Kurtz (New York, 1960), pp. 19–73.

National Baptist Convention of America. See *Baptist Churches,* 10.

National Baptist Convention, U. S. A., Inc. See *Baptist Churches,* 10.

National Baptist Evangelical Life and Soul Saving Assembly of the U. S. A. See *Baptist Churches,* 31.

National Bible Society of Scotland. See *Bible Societies,* 4.

National Christian Association. Organization opposed to secret socs.; organized 1868 Pittsburgh, Pa., as Nat. Assoc. of Christians Opposed to Secret Societies by representatives of 17 denominations; inc. 1874 as The Nat. Christian Association. Pub. *Christian Cynosure.* HQ Chicago, Ill. See also *Blanchard, Charles Albert.*

National Christian Education Council. See *International Bible Reading Association.*

National Conference of Charities and Correction. See *National Conference on Social Welfare.*

National Conference of Christians and Jews. Outgrowth of a committee formed by the FCC in response to anti-RC prejudice in the 1928 presidential campaign. HQ NYC.

National Conference of Social Work. See *National Conference on Social Welfare.*

National Conference on Social Welfare. Organized in the early 1870s as Conf. of Bds. of Pub. Charities; later known as Nat. Conf. of Charities and Correction and (till 1956) as Nat. Conf. of Soc. Work. HQ Columbus, Ohio.

National Council of Boston. See *Democratic Declarations of Faith,* 2.

National Council of Catholic Youth. See *Young People's Organizations, Christian,* V, 1.

National Council of the Churches of Christ in the United States of America. Formed 1950, Cleveland, Ohio, by merger of:

1. Federal* Council of the Chs. of Christ in Am.
2. For. Miss. Conf. of N. Am. (see *Union Movements,* 13).
3. Home Miss. Council of N. Am. (see *Union Movements,* 13).
4. The International* Council of Religious Educ.
5. Miss. Educ. Movement of the US and Can. (see *Union Movements,* 13).
6. Nat. Prot. Council on Higher Educ. (see *Union Movements,* 13).
7. United Council of Ch. Women (see *Union Movements,* 13).
8. United Stewardship Council (see *Union Movements,* 13).

Others joining later include:

1. Church* World Service.
2. Interseminary Committee (founded 1880). See also *Student Volunteer Movement,* 4.
3. Prot. Film Commission (founded 1947).
4. Prot. Radio Commission (est. 1947).
5. Student* Volunteer Movement.
6. United Student Christian Council (see *Young People's Organizations, Christian,* I, 6).

The NCC supports the ecumenical* movement and is known for radio, TV, and other mass media work. EL

National Council of the Congregational Churches of the United States. See *United Church of Christ,* I.

National Council of the Evangelical Free Churches. Assoc. of nonconforming chs. founded in Eng. in the mid-1890s for cooperation in religious, soc., and civil work. Merged 1940 in Free* Ch. Fed. Council.

National Council on Alcoholism. See *Alcoholism.*

National Councils. See *Councils and Synods,* 1, 5.

National Covenant. See *Presbyterian Confessions,* 1.

National David Spiritual Temple of Christ Church Union (Inc.), U. S. A. Organized 1932 Kansas City, Mo., as David Spiritual Temple of Christ Ch.; larger organization effected 1936; held that wisdom, knowledge, faith, healing, miracles, prophecy, discerning of spirits, divers kinds of tongues, and interpretation of tongues are spiritual gifts; claimed to be the true and universal ch. of Christ and not simply another denomination. See also *Holiness Churches,* 2.

National Evangelical Lutheran Church. See *Archives; Finnish Lutherans in America,* 3.

National Grange. See *Order of Patrons of Husbandry.*

National Holiness Association. Coordinating agency of religious bodies holding the Wesleyan-Arminian view; organized 1867; name changed in early 1970s to Christian Holiness Association.

National Lutheran Campus Ministry. See *Lutheran Council in the United States of America,* III.

National Lutheran Commission for Soldiers' and Sailors' Welfare. See *National Lutheran Council,* 1.

National Lutheran Council. 1. Organized 1918 as a common agency for The General* Syn. of the Ev. Luth. Ch. in the USA, the General* Council of the Ev. Luth. Ch. in N. Am., the Ev. Luth. Joint Syn. of Ohio* and Other States, the Ev. Luth. Syn. of Iowa* and Other States, the Augustana* Ev. Luth. Ch., The Norw. Luth. Ch. of Am. (see *Evangelical Lutheran Church, The,* 13, 15), the Lutheran* Free Ch., and The Dan. Ev. Luth. Ch. in Am. (see *Danish Lutherans in America,* 3). The United* Syn. of the Ev. Luth. Ch. in the S. joined soon thereafter.

Cooperative efforts to promote and publicize the celebration of the 400th anniversary of the Reformation in 1917 gave original incentive to its organization. The Nat. Luth. Commission for Soldiers' and Sailors' Welfare was organized Oct. 1917 to give spiritual ministration to men in the armed forces. The Luth. Bureau was est. Nov. 1917 to issue publicity.

2. On initiative of the Ex. Com. of the Nat. Luth. Commission for Soldiers' and Sailors' Welfare, 15 representatives of various Luth. bodies met in Harrisburg, Pa., July 17, 1918, and elected a planning committee of 8, which met in Pittsburgh Aug. 1, 1918. The NLC was organized at Chicago, Ill., Sept. 6, 1918.

3. No formal constitution was adopted, but stated purposes included: providing statistical information; publicity; pub. relations; coordinating Luth. activi-

ties and agencies; fostering Christian loyalty and a righteous relation bet. ch. and state.

4. Luth. World Service, launched after WW I to reconstruct Luth. chs. in Eur., continued till 1925 and helped prepare the way for the LWC (see *Lutheran World Federation, The*).

5. Rev. regulations for the conduct of the NLC were adopted 1926.

6. NLC work was departmentalized into Administration, Publicity, and Reference Library and Statistics. A Dept. of Welfare was est. 1939.

7. Scope and activity of the NLC were enlarged as a result of WW II. The Const. and By-Laws adopted 1945 recognized that the participating bodies accepted the Bible as the Word of God and the only source, norm, and guide of Christian faith and life, and the UAC and M. Luther's Catechism as the true exposition and presentation of the doctrine of the Bible.

8. Purposes and objectives stated in the 1945 Const. and later amendments:

a. To witness for the Luth. Ch. on matters which require an expression of common faith, ideals, and program.

b. To bring to the attention of the participating bodies matters which in its judgment may require utterance or action on their part.

c. To represent Luth. interests in Am. in matters which require common action, before

(1) Nat. and state govts.

(2) Organized bodies and movements outside the Luth. Ch.

d. To emphasize the continuing importance of a right relation bet. ch. and state.

e. To further the interests and the work of the Luth. chs. in Am.

f. To be the Nat. Committee for the LWF in the US.

g. To undertake and carry on such work as may be authorized by the participating bodies in fields where coordination or joint activity may be desirable and feasible, e. g., publicity, statistics, welfare work, missions, educ., student work.

h. To take the necessary steps to meet emergencies requiring common action, each participating body to determine the extent of its cooperation in emergency work.

i. To undertake additional work with the specific consent of the participating bodies.

9. Representation was on the basis of 1 for every 100,000 confirmed mems., or one-third fraction thereof, provided, however, that each participating body be entitled to at least 1 representative. Mem. bodies helped form The United* Luth. Ch. in America, the American* Luth. Ch., and the Lutheran* Ch. in Am.

10. The NLC was replaced at the end of 1966 by the Lutheran* Council in the USA. RHL HMK

National Lutheran Parent-Teacher League. See *Lutheran Church – Missouri Synod, The,* VII 7; *Parish Education,* J.

National Lutheran Radio and Television Week. See *Radio Stations, Religious,* 4.

National Primitive Baptist Convention, Inc. See *Baptist Churches,* 12.

National Primitive Baptist Convention in the U. S. A. See *Baptist Churches,* 12.

National Protestant Council on Higher Education. See *Union Movements,* 13.

National Red Cross. See *Red Cross.*

National Socialism. See *Germany,* C 4; *Kirchenkampf; Socialism,* 3.

National Society, The. Formed ca. 1809/11 to promote the educ. of the poor in the principles of the est. ch. in Eng. and Wales; operated on a voluntary basis.

National Student Christian Federation. See *Student Volunteer Movement,* 4; *Students, Spiritual Care of,* 5.

National Sunday School Union. See *International Bible Reading Association.*

National Synods. See *Councils and Synods,* 1, 5.

National Union of Christian Schools. See *Teachers,* 31.

Natorp, Paul Gerhard (1854–1924). B. Düsseldorf, Ger.; educ. Berlin, Bonn, Strasbourg; prof. Marburg; neo-Kantian philos.; composer, mainly of piano pieces and songs. Philos. works include *Platos Ideenlehre; Allgemeine Psychologie; Sozialidealismus; Johann Heinrich Pestalozzi.*

Natura naturans. Term used, with *natura naturata,* by Averroes (see *Arabic Philosophy*), F. G. Bruno,* Nicholas* of Cusa, and B. Spinoza.* *Natura naturans* designated the creative force, or God as the active power of nature; *natura naturata* designated the created substance.

Natural History of the Bible. Branch of knowledge or inquiry involving study, description, and classification of natural objects of Bible times (e. g., animals, plants, minerals).

Natural Knowledge of God. That which is known of God by observation of His creatures (Ro 1:19-21). See also *Apologetics; God; God, Arguments for the Existence of; Knowledge,* 2.

Natural Law (Lat. *lex naturalis*). 1. Term used in various senses and more or less synonymous with "natural justice" *(ius [jus] naturae, ius [jus] naturale),* the "law of nations" *(ius [jus] gentium),* and "natural rights."

2. The concept of natural law was first developed by early Stoics, but the term was coined by later (Roman) Stoics (see *Stoicism*). Over against those who held that all laws of men are but the product of utility and convention, the Stoics, following Socrates* and Aristotle,* asserted that behind all changing laws of man is the changeless law of nature. They believed that nature has a rational basis and that human reason is a reflection of this rationality. They concluded that, by thinking rationally, man can know not only what is but also what ought to be. The content of natural law, they believed, is deducible from those rules of conduct that are similar among widely separated peoples. This concept of natural law was further developed by Roman jurists and embodied in the Institutes of Justinian* I (supplements to the Code of Theodosius* II). Roman jurists considered natural law the basis of civil law but rarely put it into practice. They called on it to supplement civil law but never invoked it to invalidate laws in conflict with natural law (e. g., those governing property rights and slavery).

3. Ch. fathers, esp. Lat., some of whom were deeply influenced by Roman law, shared this concept of natural law but identified it with the primitive natural revelation of God in man's heart, the innate knowledge of right and wrong, and regarded it as evidence of the truth of Ro 2:14-15.

4. This concept was further developed, but not fundamentally modified, by medieval thinkers. Thomas* Aquinas divided all law into 4 classes: (1) eternal law (exists only in the mind of God); (2) divine law (part of eternal law and directly revealed to men); (3) natural law (discernible by human reason and the knowledge of which has been moving from the imperfect to the perfect); (4) human law (implementation of natural law within the changing situations of life). But such thinking remained essentially speculative and had little or no practical effect on the development of law and govt.

5. Not till modern times was the concept of natural law implemented by pol. action. In fact, this concept more than any other supplied philos. justification for the great revolutionary movements that have marked Western civilization since the 17th c.

The Prot. Reformation gen. accepted the patristic view of natural law. M. Luther* and P. Melanchthon* followed Augustine* of Hippo in regarding the decalog as the directly revealed codification of natural law. But the Renaissance, esp. in its humanistic aspects, deemphasized the divine and overemphasized the purely rational character of natural law. As a result, in the age of reason (see *Age of Reason,* 2) the concept of natural law was pressed into service as the ideological basis of "natural rights," the "social contract" (see *Government*), constitutional govt. based on the consent of the governed, and the right of revolution. In one form or another this is the view of T. Hobbes,* J. Locke,* T. Jefferson (see *Deism,* III, 1; V), T. Paine,* and J. J. Rousseau.* The most typical and pol. effective expressions of this view are the Am. Declaration of Independence and the Fr. Declaration of the Rights of Man and of the Citizen (see *France,* 11). Early 19th-c. individualistic, liberal, democratic thought and action were largely the fruits of this concept.

6. The concept of natural law has been under increasing attack, esp. from 2 quarters: (1) the hist. school of jurisprudence regards law as nothing more than a product of hist. development; (2) positive soc. scientists regard law as nothing more than a result of personal and soc. relationships. Writers who profess to have rediscovered the spiritual and teleological character of the universe support the concept of natural law.

7. In Luth. theol., natural law is a remnant of the knowledge with which man was created. Because man's awareness of natural law was obscured by sin, God gave man the decalog and elaborated on it in the Bible. Acc. to the principle of *sola* scriptura,* the law from within (subjective morality) must be interpreted in light of the law from without (objective morality). WB

G. W. Paton, *A Text-Book of Jurisprudence,* 2d ed. (Oxford, 1951); R. W. Carlyle and A. J. Carlyle, *A History of Medieval Political Theory in the West,* 6 vols. (New York, 1903–36); K. G. Stöckhardt, *Commentar über den Brief Pauli an die Römer* (St. Louis, 1907).

Natural Rights. See *Natural Law.*

Natural Theology. See *Natural Knowledge of God; Theology, Natural.*

Natural Virtues. See *Cardinal Virtues.*

Naturalism. Term with various meanings corresponding to the different senses in which "nature" and "natural" may be used.

In theol. and philos.: the teaching that religious truth is derived from nature (see also *Natural Theology*), that there is no reality except matter, that all, even psychical, phenomena may be explained through natural sciences, esp. chemistry and physics, and that their ultimate basis is matter and motion. Such a view leads to materialism* and atheism* and hardly differs from positivism.*

In ethics: the doctrine that nature and natural impulses are the highest guide of man in moral conduct; variously developed in Stoicism* and by J. J. Rousseau,* L. N. Tolstoi,* and F. W. Nietzsche*; may lead to elevation of every personal desire to a moral law, contempt of marriage, glorification of the nude.

In art: tendency to avoid all idealization and portray only reality.

In literature: tendency to picture men and circumstances true to reality, often emphasizing the immoral.

See also *Secularism.*

Nau, Heinrich (Henry; Sept. 21, 1881–May 17, 1956). B. Beltershausen, Marburg, Ger.; educ. Conc. Sem., St. Louis, Mo.; miss. to India 1905–14; hosp. chaplain Chemnitz, Ger., 1914–18; vacancy pastor Berlin 1918–19; prof. Luther Coll., New Orleans, La. (see *Luther College,* 4), 1921–25; pres. Immanuel* Luth. Coll., Greensboro, N. C., 1925–50; miss. in Calabar Province, Nigeria, Afr., 1936–37; explored Muslim miss. opportunities in Iran and India 1949; miss. to Muslim in India 1951–54. Ed. *The Minaret* 1945–51; other works include *Prolegomena zu Pattanattu Pillaiyars Padal: Inaugural-Dissertation zur Erlangung der Doktorwürde der hohen philosophischen Fakultät der Preussischen Vereinigten Friedrichs-Universität, Halle-Wittenberg* (hist. of Tamil literature); *Vanji Bhumi: Einiges über Travancore und seine Bewohner; We Move into Africa.* See also *Society for the Promotion of Mohammedan Missions.*

Nauclerus, Ioannes (Johannes; John; Verge; Vergenhans; ca. 1425/30–1510). Helped found U. of Tübingen 1477; its rector 1477–78; humanist. Works include *Memorabilium omnis aetatis et omnium gentium chronici commentarii.*

Naudé, Philipp (Naudäus; 1654–1729). Ref. theol.; b. Metz, Fr.; Huguenot refugee to Berlin 1687; mem. Berlin Academy 1701; prof. mathematics Berlin 1704. Defended sovereign grace of God and supralapsarianism.*

Naumann, Emil (1827–88). Luth. composer, musicologist; b. Berlin, Ger.; pupil of J. L. F. Mendelssohn-Bartholdy.* Works include *Illustrierte Musikgeschichte* (tr. F. Praeger, Ed. F. A. G. Ouseley, *The History of Music*); *Christus der Friedensbote* (oratorio); Psalms for the ch. yr.

Naumann, Justus Heinrich (Mar. 14, 1865–Feb. 5, 1917). B. Dresden, Ger.; attended Lat. school in Niederplanitz conducted by K. G. Stöckhardt*; to Am. 1878; educ. Conc. Coll., Fort Wayne, Ind., and Conc. Sem., St. Louis, Mo.; pastor in that part of Dakota Territory which became S. Dak. 1889; pastor Gibbon, Minn., 1895, simultaneously joining the Minnesota* Syn.; pastor Wood Lake, Minn., ca. 1904, and of the parish in and near Goodhue, Minn., 1913; moved to St. Paul 1915; pres. Minn. Syn. 1912–17.

Naumann, Martin Justus (Aug. 30, 1901–Mar. 30, 1972). B. Glenwood City, near Menomonie, Saint Croix Co., Wis.; educ. Conc. Coll., Milwaukee, Wis., and Conc. Sem., St. Louis, Mo.; Ev. Luth. Free Ch. of Saxony pastor at Chemnitz, Schoenfeld, Annaberg, and Hamburg, Ger.; pastor Altamont, Ill., 1941; prof. Conc. Sem., Springfield, Ill., 1948; participant in Bad* Boll conferences; originated Conc. Sem. Bible Lands Seminars 1965.

Naumburg Diet. Diet (convention; assembly; Fürstentag) at Naumburg, Ger., 1561, at which Luth. princes and theols. reaffirmed the AC, 1531 ed. Dissension among Luths. after P. Melanchthon's* death and the scheduled reopening of the Council of Trent* had made reunification of Luths. desirable. But some did not sign the statement drawn up at Naumburg on grounds that certain heresies were not mentioned and condemned and that disputed arts. had not been directly dealt with. The diet declined an invitation to participate in the Council of Trent (because the invitation addressed the princes as sons of the pope) and expressed desire for a nat. Ger. diet with vote as well as voice for the Ger. princes. See also *Lutheran Confessions,* C 1.

Nausea, Friedrich (Grau; Blancicampianus; ca. 1480 [1490?]–1552). RC theol.; b. Waischenfeld, Upper Franconia, Bav., Ger.; accompanied L. Campeggio* to Ger. 1524 with the assignment to lure P. Melanchthon* back to the RC Ch.; pastor Frankfurt am Main 1526 but forced to flee by the pro-Luth. cong.; preacher cathedral ch., Mainz; court preacher Vienna 1534; took part in Hagenau* Colloquy and Colloquy of Worms*; participated in Council of Trent* beginning 1551; favored Communion under both kinds and marriage of clergy.

Naval and Military Bible Society. See *Bible Societies,* 3.

Nave. Main part of the interior of a ch. See also *Church Architecture,* 3, 7.

Navigators Islands. See *Samoa.*

Naville, Édouard Henri (1844–1926). Egyptologist; b. Geneva, Switz.; visited Egypt for the 1st time 1869; prof. Geneva 1891. Works include *la Religion des anciens Egyptiens.*

Naylor, John (1838–97). Musician, composer; b. Stanningley, near Leeds, Eng.; organist Scarborough and York; conductor York Musical Soc. Works include 4 cantatas: *Jeremiah; The Brazen Serpent; Meribah; Manna.*

Nazarene, Church of the. See *Church of the Nazarene.*

Nazarene Young People's Society. See *Young People's Organizations, Christian,* III, 14.

Nazarenes. 1. Judaizing Christian sect that united belief in the Messiahship of Jesus with observance of the Mosaic Ceremonial Law but without rejecting the authority of Paul and the validity of Gentile Christianity.

2. Sect also known as Württemberg Pietists; founded by Johann Jakob Wirz (1778–1858; b. Basel, Switz.; silk-weaver), who claimed to have been made a priest by Jesus 1826; awaits the coming of the 3d period, that of the Holy Spirit, in the 3 "dispensations of God."

3. Assoc. of Ger. painters founded 1809 Vienna by J. F. Overbeck* et al.; moved to Rome 1809–11; others assoc. with the group in course of time included P. J. v. Cornelius,* J. Schnorr* v. Carolsfeld, F. W. v. Schadow-Godenhaus,* J. v. Führich,* and E. J. v. Steinle.* Called Nazarenes because of their long hair; also called Lukasbund (Guild of St. Luke) and Lukas-brüderschaft (Brotherhood of St. Luke).

Nazianzus, Gregory of. See *Gregory of Nazianzus.*

Nazism. See *Germany,* C 4; *Kirchenkampf; Socialism,* 3.

Ne temere. The Council of Trent* decreed: "Those who will try to contract marriage in another way than in the presence of a parish priest or of another priest authorized by that priest or by an ordinary, and with two or three witnesses, the holy synod declares altogether unable so to marry and decrees such contracts null and void, as by the present decree it makes them invalid and annuls them" (Sess. XXIV, Decree Concerning the Reform of Matrimony [called *Tametsi* decree after its 1st Lat. word], chap. I). The *Ne temere* decree of 1907 (named after its 1st Lat. words), effective 1908, exempted from this rule non-Catholics who marry among themselves and made certain other provisions. The chief points of this decree, with minor modifications, were later included in the Code of Canon Law, further rev. 1948/49.

Neale, John Mason, (1818–66). Angl. hymnist; b. London, Eng.; educ. Cambridge; warden Sackville Coll., E. Grinstead, 1846–66. Works include *Essays on Liturgiology and Church History.* Hymns include "Around the Throne of God a Band"; "Blessed Savior, Who Hast Taught Me"; "Art Thou Weary, Art Thou Troubled"; "O Lord of Hosts, Whose Glory Fills"; translations of Lat. and Gk. hymns.

A. G. Lough, *The Influence of John Mason Neale* (London, 1962); E. A. Towle, *John Mason Neale* (New York, 1906)

Neander, Joachim (grecized from Neumann, Niemann, or Nigemann by his grandfather; 1650–80). Ref. hymnist, composer; b. Bremen, Ger.; rector Lat. school Düsseldorf 1675; pietist. Neanderthal named after him. Hymns (collected in *Glaub- und Liebes-Übung*) include "Lobe den Herren, den mächtigen König der Ehren"; "Wunderbarer König." Hymn tunes include *Neander* (sometimes called *Unser Herrscher, Magdeburg,* or *Ephesus*).

Neander, Johann August Wilhelm (original name David Mendel; 1789–1850). Prot. ch. hist.; b. Göttingen, Ger., of Jewish descent; influenced by F. D. E. Schleiermacher; changed name when he became Christian 1806; prof. ch. hist. Berlin 1812/13; exponent of Pektoraltheologie.* Works include *Allgemeine Geschichte der christlichen Religion und Kirche.*

Neander, Michael (originally Neumann; 1525–95). Educator; b. Sorau (now Zary), Brandenburg, Ger. (now Poland); pupil of P. Melanchthon*; teacher, then rector, Ilfeld; ed. classical texts; wrote on principles of teaching; emphasized humanistic studies; also gave attention to natural sciences; antinomian. Works include *Graecae linguae erotemata* (preface by Melanchthon); *Theologia Christiana.*

Near East. See *Middle East.*

Near East Christian Council. See *Near East Council of Churches.*

Near East College of Theology. See *Middle East,* D.

Near East Council of Churches. Organized 1927 as mem. council of the International Missionary Council; mem. WCC 1961; called Near East Christian Council till 1964; has also been known as Council for W Asia and N Afr.

Nebraska, Evangelical Lutheran Synod of. See *United Lutheran Church, Synods of,* 3, 25.

Nebraska, German Evangelical Lutheran District Synod of. Johann M. Höckendorf (Hoeckendorf; Hökendorf; d. ca. 1877), former officer in the Prussian army and mem. of C. L. Geyer's* cong. at Lebanon, near Watertown, Wis., was a delegate to the meeting at which the Mo. Syn. was organized. He took exception to I, 1 of the Const., which gave as a reason for forming a syn. organization the example of the apostolic ch. (Acts 15:1-31). Eventually he divided his home cong. and became pastor of ca. 100 adherents, est. a cong. at Ixonia, Wis., ca. 3 mi. S of Lebanon. In 1866 a number of them moved to the site of the later city of Norfolk, Nebr. Höckendorf, their pastor till he died, was succeeded by Michael H. Pankow (May 26, 1852–July 11, 1936; b. Lebanon, Dodge Co., Wis.; educ. Northwestern U. [later called Northwestern Coll.], Watertown, Wis., and Conc. Sem., Springfield, Ill.; pastor Norfolk, Nebr., 1878–91, then in Wis. till 1917, when he retired), who joined the Wisconsin* Syn. 1881 and organized other congs. In course of time other pastors and congs. in Nebr. joined the Wis. Syn. In 1901 a Nebr. Dist. of the Wis. Syn. was tentatively organized; it was released from district membership in the Wis. Syn. and became the Ger. Ev. Luth. Dist. Syn. of Nebr. 1904; it joined The Ev. Luth. Joint Syn. of Wis., Minn., Mich., and other states 1905/06 and the Synodical* Conf. 1906/10; it became the Nebr. Dist. of the Ev. Luth. Joint Syn. of Wis., Minn., Mich., and Other States 1917. See also *Wisconsin Evangelical Lutheran Synod,* 2, 3.

Nebraska, German Evangelical Lutheran Synod of. See *United Lutheran Church, Synods of,* 3.

Nebraska Synod (1871). See *United Lutheran Church, Synods of,* 3.

Nebraska Synod (LCA; 1962–). See *Lutheran Church in America,* IX B 15.

Necrology. List of persons that have died; sometimes used in connection with prayers for the dead.

Necromancy (from Gk. *nekros,* "corpse," and *manteia,* "divination"). Consulting the spirits of the dead (cf. 1 Sm 28:3-20); forbidden Lv 19:31; Dt 18:10-11; Is 8:19-20. Cf. LC, Part I, 12.

Nectarius (Nektarios). 1. *of Jerusalem* (ca. 1602–ca. 1675). Patriarch of Jerusalem ca. 1661–69; opposed W theol.; supported confession of P. Mogila*; took part in 1672 Syn. of Jerusalem.* 2. *of Constantinople* (d. 397). Bp. (or patriarch) Constantinople 381; presided at 2d ecumenical council (see *Councils and Synods*). *MPG* 39, 1821–40.

Nederlandsch Zendeling-Genootschap. See *Netherlands,* 7.

Neesima, Joseph Hardy (Neeshima; Niishima; originally Neesima Shimeta; Feb. 12 [Jan. 14 Jap. old style], 1843–Jan. 23, 1890). B. Yedo (Tokyo), Jap.; by chance became acquainted with the Bible as a boy; contrived 1864 to get to Hakodate and smuggled himself on board a schooner to Shanghai, China; to US on a ship (the captain called him Joe) owned by Alpheus Hardy, of Boston, Mass., who sent him to Amherst (Mass.) Coll. and Andover (Mass.) Theol. Sem.; pardoned for leaving Jap. illegally and became interpreter of Jap. embassy to US 1871; ABCFM miss. to Jap. 1874; founded Doshisha coll. and theol. school (now a U.) at Kyoto 1875; taught there till 1890.

J. D. Davis, *A Sketch of the Life of Rev. Joseph Hardy Neesima* (New York, 1894); A. S. Hardy, *Life and Letters of Joseph Hardy Neesima* (Boston, 1891); W. F. McDowell et al., *Effective Workers in Needy Fields* (New York, 1902), pp. 153–183.

Neff, Félix (1797 [1798?]–1829). B. near Geneva, Switz.; Swiss army officer; resigned 1819; catechist (or parish miss.) in Switz. and at Grenoble, Fr.; ordained London, Eng., 1823; revival preacher in Swiss and Fr. Alps.

Negative Confession. 1. Chap. 125 of Egyptian *Book* of the Dead.* 2. See *Presbyterian Confessions,* 1.

Negro Missions. See *Africa; Missions; Synodical Conference,* 7.

Neitzel, Richard C. (Sept. 8, 1875–May 22, 1951). B. Gnevin, Pomerania, Ger.; educ. Conc. Coll., Milwaukee, Wis., and Conc. Sem., St. Louis, Mo.; miss. Oklahoma 1899–1901. Pastor Kansas City, Kans., 1901–13; Summit, Ill., 1913–18. Prof. Conc. Sem., Springfield, Ill., 1918–51. Secy. Mo. Syn. Wartime Bureau 1918; chm. Mo. Syn. Catechism Committee.

Nelle, Wilhelm (1849–1918). B. near Hameln, Ger.; educ. Halle and Tübingen; pastor Hamm 1886; prof. Münster 1916. Founded Evangelischer Kirchengesang-Verein für Westfalen. Works include *Geschichte des deutschen evangelischen Kirchenliedes; Unsere Kirchenliederdichter.*

Nelson, Robert (1656–1715). B. London, Eng.; pupil of G. Bull*; educ. Cambridge; nonjuring layman (see *Nonjurors*); supported charitable and miss. endeavors, including SPCK and SPG; returned to est. ch. 1710. Works include *A Companion for the Festivals and Fasts of the Church of England.*

Nemesius (4th or 5th c. AD). Bp. Emesa (Homs; Hims), Syria; Gk. Christian philos. Wrote *Peri physeos anthropou* (Lat. title *De natura hominis*), in which he tries to build on Platonic basis a doctrine of the soul agreeable to Christian revelation. *MPG,* 40, 479–844.

Nemours, Treaty of. See *France,* 9.

Neocaesarea, Council of. Cappadocian Council; probably early 4th c. AD, perhaps bet. 314 and 325; adopted canons on discipline and marriage that became canon law for E and W.

Neo-Calvinism. An awakening and restatement of Calvinism.*

Neology. In religion, a new doctrine, or new method of theol. interpretation; hence also called Modern Theol., or Transitional Theol. (Übergangstheologie). Hist. critical movement in theol. of 18th c.; embraced a number of theol. tendencies and such concepts as cosmic pluralism in opposition to a closed Ptolemaic universe, hierarchy of being from inanimate objects to angels, moral miracles (e. g., the redeemed life is a miraculous gift of grace), new Biblicism opposed to scholastic orthodox dogma, and emphasis on the incarnation and the cross.

Neo-Lutheranism. Revival of Luth. confessionalism. See also *Luther Renaissance; Lutheran Theology After 1580,* 11–15.

Neoorthodoxy. Movement in 20th-c. Prot. theol. that opposed modernism.* Proponents include S. A. Kierkegaard,* K. Barth,* and H. E. Brunner.* Reinhold Niebuhr's* dialectical concept of God (both transcendent and immanent), man, and hist. aroused widespread interest in Am. See also *Dialectical Theology; Switzerland, Contemporary Theology in.*

R. Niebuhr, *The Nature and Destiny of Man,* 2 vols. (New York, 1941–43), reviewed in *CTM,* XIII (1942), 156–158; XV (1944), 640–644.

Neophyte (Gk. "newly planted"; novice, 1 Ti 3:6). Term applied in the early ch. to newly converted or newly bap. Christians, esp. during the 8 days following baptism, when they wore white garments, and in some cases longer, up to a yr. after baptism. In RCm the neophyte status was considered an irregularity, or at least impediment, for the reception of orders; by extension the term came to describe one newly admitted to the clerical or monastic life.

Neoplatonism. Philos. school reputedly founded by Ammonius* Saccas; chief exponents included Plotinus,* Porphyry,* and Iamblichus.* Tried to develop new thoughts from Platonic ideas (see *Plato*). Speaks of the One (source of all being), of the Over-Mind (mind, spirit, intelligence; Gk. *nous*) which emanates from the One, and of the Over-Soul (or World-Soul; Gk. *psyche*), which emanates from the Over-Mind. The Over-Soul makes, produces, or generates individual souls and matter (the concrete, corporeal, or phenomenal world), which is evil. Man is part spirit, part matter; his soul is part of the World-Soul; he should strive to free himself as far as possible from the body and from sin and achieve communion with the One by avoiding what is sensual, but without excessive asceticism. The most important Neoplatonic contribution to Eur. thought and culture was the influence of a diluted and transformed Neoplatonism in such traditional Christian theol. as that of Augustine* of Hippo (cf. esp. his *Confessions,* Book VIII).

See also *Cambridge Platonists; Emanation; Ficino, Marsilio; Gemistos Pletho(n), Georgios; Proclus; Renaissance; Theosophy; Transmigration of Souls.*

Neo-scholasticism. Revival of scholasticism* in RCm beginning ca. the middle of the 19th c.

Neostadiensium admonitio. Short name for *De libro Concordiae quem vocant, a quibusdam Theologis, nomine quorundam Ordinum Augustanae Confessionis, edito, Admonitio Christiana,* issued 1581, written chiefly by Z. Ursinus* in the name of the Ref. group at Neustadt an der Hardt, Ger., in defense of their beliefs against Luth. doctrines; tried to refute FC, AC, and M. Luther*; discussed distinctive Ref. beliefs regarding Christology, communion, and predestination. T. Kirchner,* M. Chemnitz,* and N. Selnecker* drafted the *Erfurtsche Buch* in reply.

Neo-Thomism. Neoscholasticism* concerned with teachings of Thomas* Aquinas. Often described as "moderate realism." Distinguishes bet. *act* or *actuality* and *potency* or *potentiality* (all except God, who is pure act, is made up of act and potency); *existence* and *essence; substance* and *accident; form* and *matter.* Includes a doctrine of causes (material, formal, efficient, and final). Prominent neo-Thomists include P. Coffey* and D. F. F. J. Mercier.* See also *Popes,* 29.

R. G. Bandas, *Contemporary Philosophy and Thomistic Principles* (New York, 1932); E. H. Gilson, *Christianity and Philosophy,* tr. R. MacDonald (New York, 1939); J. Maritain, *On the Philosophy of History,* ed. J. W. Evans (New York, 1957); P. M. Bretscher, "Neo-Thomism Once More," *CTM,* XXII (1951), 357–364; W. Siegel, "The Revival of Thomist Pholosophy," *The Augustana Quarterly,* XIX (Jan. 1940), 38–45. See also references under *Thomas Aquinas* and writings of neo-Thomists mentioned above. EL

Neo-Utraquists. See *Hussites.*

Nepal. See *Asia,* B 5.

Nepomuk, John of. See *John of Nepomuk.*

Nepos of Arsinoe (3d c.). Bp. Arsinoe, in Cyrenaica, E Libya; his literal interpretation of Rv is chiliastic; his followers severed connection with the Alexandrian ch.; refuted by Dionysius* of Alexandria. See also *Millennium,* 3.

Eusebius of Caesarea, *HE,* VII, xxiv.

Nergal. See *Babylonians, Religion of the,* 5.

Neri, Filippo de' (Philip Neri; 1515–95). B. Florence, It.; tutor Rome 1533; studied philos. and theol.; said to have experienced ecstasy; cofounder Confraternitá di SS. Trinità 1548; ordained priest 1551; founded an Oratory (see also *Oratorians,* 2) that developed out of confessional and spiritual conferences beginning 1564 and was perhaps called Oratory after the oratory (place of prayer; chapel) where the meetings were held.

Nero (Nero Claudius Caesar Drusus Germanicus; originally Lucius Domitius Ahenobarbus; 37–68). Roman emp. 54–68; b. Antium (Anzio), Latium, S cen. It.; accused of starting the fire that burned much of Rome 64, he in turn accused the Christians and persecuted them; suicide. He is the emperor referred to in Acts 25:11-12, 21, 25; 26:32; Ph 4:22. See also *Persecutions of Christians,* 3.

Nerses (I) (ca. 310–ca. 373). "The Great." 6th catholicos* of Armenian Ch.; b. probably Vagarshapat, near Echmiadzin, Cappadocia (Armenian SSR); tried to reform the ch.; founded hosps. and orphanages; poisoned for censuring the immorality of the king.

Nerses (IV) (ca. 1102–73). "The Gracious" [*Snorhali*]. Catholicos* of the Armenian Ch. 1166–73; b. Cilicia; tried to unite Armenian and Gk. chs. against Monophysitism*; exegete, hist., poet.

Nesmelov, Victor Ivanovic (1863–ca. 1920). Russ. religious philos.; prof. at Kazan; tried to prove existence of God on basis of man's awareness of tension bet. his own free personality and his subservience to physical nature.

Nestle, Christoph Eberhard (Christof; 1851–1913). Luth. Bible scholar; b. Stuttgart, Ger.; educ. Blaubeuren, Tübingen, and Leipzig; prof. Ulm, Tübingen, and Maulbronn; mediating theol. (see *Mediating Theology*). Ed. Gk. NT; other works include *Einführung in das griechische Neue Testament.*

Nestorian Tablet. See *China,* 5.

Nestorianism. 1. Heresy* named after Nestorius.* Held that there is no communion of natures in the person of Christ (see also *Christology; Christ Jesus,* I), that Mary is not *theotokos** but *Christotokos* (mother of Christ), and that acc. to His human nature Christ is in effect the Son of God only by adoption. Condemned by the 431 Council of Ephesus,* but adherents spread its doctrine far and wide.

2. Nestorianism spread into Persia (see *Middle East,* I), Mesopotamia (see *Edessa; Nisibis; Middle East,* H), Arabia (see *Middle East,* L), China (see *China,* 5), and India (see *India,* 5, 6).

A. R. Vine, *The Nestorian Churches: A Concise History of Nestorian Christianity in Asia from the Persian Schism to the Modern Assyrians* (London, 1927); J. Joseph. *The Nestorians and Their Muslim Neighbors: A Study of Western Influence on Their Relations* (Princeton, 1961); J. P. Junglas, *Die Irrlehre des Nestorius* (Trier, 1912); F. Loofs, *Nestorius and His Place in the History of Christian Doctrine* (New York, 1914); R. V. Sellers, *Two Ancient Christologies* (London, 1940); M. Chemnitz, *De duabus naturis,* tr. J. A. O. Preus, *The Two Natures in Christ* (St. Louis, 1971).

Nestorius (d. ca. AD 451). B. Germanicia (modern Maras[h]; now in Turkey), Syria; studied at Antioch; monk; patriarch Constantinople 428; condemned by 431 Council of Ephesus* for false teaching in Christology and deposed; sent back to monastery at Antioch; banished to Upper Egypt 436. Wrote *Tragoedia* in defense of his views. See also *Nestorianism.*

Nethenus. 1. *Matthias* (1618–86). Brother of 2; Ref. pietistic theol.; b. Süchteln, Ger.; educ. Neth. at Harderwijk, Deventer, and Utrecht; pastor; prof. Utrecht 1654; deposed 1662 because of polemics against S. Maresius*; prof. Herborn 1669; influenced by W. Ames* and G. Voet*; opposed Arminianism,* Cartesianism,* RCm. 2. *Samuel* (1628–ca. 1700). Brother of 1; Ref. theol.; b. Rees, Ger.; pastor; won for ch. reform by puritanical writings and Voetians (see *Voet, Gisbert*); active in efforts at Christian instruction and edification.

Netherlands. 1. *Area:* ca. 13,000–14,000 sq. mi.; *pop.* (1971 est.): ca. 13,100,000; capital Amsterdam; seat of govt. The Hague ('s Gravenhage). Conversion, dated from ca. 630 under Dagobert I (see *France,* 1), was continued by Willibrord,* and completed under Charlemagne* toward the end of the 8th c. Protestantism came to prevail in the N, RCm in the S, with both well represented in the center.

Doctrines and polity of the *Ref. Ch.,* represented also in refugee groups in London, Eng., and Emden, Ger., took form at the 1619 Syn. of Dordrecht.* William I (1772–1844; b. The Hague, Neth.; driven into exile by French 1795; returned and was proclaimed prince sovereign 1813; assumed title of king of the Neth. 1814; Congress of Vienna 1815 provided for formation of the kingdom of the Neth. [former Rep. of Holland and the Austrian Neth. (Belg.)]) gave the ch. a const. modified to suit his views 1816, and assurance was given that the old confession ("Three Forms of Unity") would be maintained; this const. gave shape to the 1852 Gen. Regulations of the Ref. Ch. In 1954 the ch. became fully indep. of the state.

Under influence of liberals and Romanists the govt. banished religious instruction from schools 1857; 1876 it changed theol. faculties in univs. into faculties of comparative religion. But when rationalists secured these professorships, the orthodox party est. a Free Ref. U. at Amsterdam 1880 and secured free schools in which ev. religion is taught. Pub. schools are nonconfessional, but hundreds of parochial schools are supported by Prots. or RCs. Important assocs. were formed 1860 and 1877 to support and extend such schools.

2. A change in the form of subscription to confessions, introd. 1816 (see 1), which in effect substituted *quatenus* for *quia* (see also *Lutheran Confessions,* D 3), led to controversy, as did the larger and more gen. feeling of some that the doctrine and polity of the 1619 Syn. of Dordrecht were falling into neglect.

In 1834 a group under H. De Cock* seceded and organized the *Christian Ref. Ch.* (on common ground with the Ref. Ch. of Am. and the Christian Ref. Ch. [see *Reformed Churches,* 4 b and c]), which est. a theol. school at Kampen 1854 and united 1892 with a group called *Doleantie* (or *doleerende*) that had formed 1886 under A. Kuyper*; the united bodies call themselves *The Ref. Chs. in the Neth.*

3. The Luth. Ch. gained only minor importance (see also *Lutheran Confessions,* A 5). The 1st cong., est. at Woerden, adopted the AC 1566. A small union of congs. formed 1605 developed into a Fraternity (or Brotherhood) 1614. The last Luth. syn. under the Rep. met 1696. At first all ministers were educ. in Ger.; a Luth. sem. was founded in Amsterdam 1816. In 1818 William I gave the *Ev. Luth. Ch.* a new organization, modified twice in the 1850s to make the ch. indep. of the state. Reaction had begun ca. 1791 against rationalism in the ch. and led to formation of the *Restored Luth. Ch.* (or Old Luth. Ch.), with legal standing 1835, legal confirmation in the 1860s. An attempt at reunion in the 1870s was unsuccessful, but differences bet. the 2 bodies subsided in course of time; common ground for agreement and unity was found in the theol. statements

of the 1947 LWF Assem.; in 1952 the Ev. Luth. Ch. and the Restored Luth. Ch. reunited to form *The Ev. Luth. Ch. in the Kingdom of the Neth.*

4. *Mennonites* (see *Mennonite Churches*) est. a sem. in Amsterdam 1735. A Gen. Soc. was formed 1811 to encourage theol. educ. and support the ministry among poorer congs. All congs. are free in calling ministers and indep. in govt.

5. *Remonstrants** object to some of the doctrines of the 1619 Syn. of Dordrecht, hold fast to freedom and toleration. Contacts with the Dutch Ref. Ch. are being restored.

6. Since separation of ch. and state 1796, RCm tried to regain lost control. The hierarchy was reest. 1853 with a great increase of priests, the Neth. forming 1 province divided into 7 dioceses comprising ca. 40% of the pop.

7. Little miss. work was done by the Dutch in the 17th c. among natives of their colonies. Miss. work was regarded as a function of the E India Co., rather than as a concern of the ch., until separation of ch. and state 1796. Important miss. socs. organized toward the end of the 18th and beginning of the 19th c. include the Netherlands* Miss. Soc. WJK

See also *Holy Communion, Consensus on the; Reformed Churches,* 2; *William I* (1533–84).

J. S. Bartstra and W. Banning, *Nederland tussen de natien,* 2 vols. (Amsterdam, 1946–48); J. Reitsma, *Geschiedenis van de Hervorming en de Hervormde Kerk der Nederlanden,* 5th ed. J. Lindeboom (The Hague, 1949); J. Loosjes, *Geschiedenis der Luthersche Kerk in de Nederlanden* (The Hague, 1921).

Netherlands Antilles. See *Caribbean Islands,* C, E 7.

Netherlands Bible Society. See *Bible Societies,* 4.

Netherlands East Indies. See *Indonesia,* 1, 7.

Netherlands Lutheran Society for Home and Foreign Missions (Nederlandsch Luthers Genootschap voor in- en uitwendige Zending). Founded 1852; reorganized 1880; began work in Batoe (or Batu: Indonesian is. group) 1882.

Netherlands Missionary Council (Nederlandsche Zendings-Raad). Also known as Missionary Study Council (Zendings Studieraad). Founded 1929 as a dept. of the International* Miss. Council. Has a number of Dutch miss. bds. as mems.

Netherlands Missionary Society (Nederlandsch Zendeling-Genootschap). Est. 1797 Rotterdam, S. Holland, W Neth., through influence of J. T. Vanderkemp*; est. a school for training missionaries; collaborated with LMS early in 19th c.; fields included Ceylon, Java, Celebes, China, India, S. Am.; became part of the Netherlands* Ref. Ch., Bd. of For. Miss., 1951.

Netherlands Missionary Union (Nederlandsche Zendings-Vereeniging). Founded 1858 Rotterdam, S. Holland, W Neth.; became affiliated with the Dutch Ref. Ch.; fields included W. Java and Celebes (Sulawesi).

Netherlands New Guinea. See *Indonesia,* 1, 7.

Netherlands Reformed Church, Board of Foreign Missions (Nederlandse Hervormde Kerk, Raad voor de Zending). Founded 1951 by combination of various agencies including Netherlands* Miss. Soc.; fields include N Sumatra, Java, Bali, Celebes, Timor, and Afr. See also *Utrecht Missionary Society.*

Netherlands Reformed Missionary Association (Dutch Ref. Miss. Assoc.). Organized Amsterdam, Neth., 1861; worked in Java.

Netter, Thomas (Waldensis; ca. 1375–1430). B. Saffron Walden, Essex, Eng.; Carmelite; educ. Oxford; took part in Council of Pisa* and Constance*; confessor and privy councillor to Henry V (1387–1422; father of Henry VI; king of Eng. 1413–22), confessor and advisor to Henry VI (1421–71; son of Henry V; king of Eng. 1422–61, 1470–71). Works include *Doctrinale antiquitatum fidei catholicae ecclesiae* against J. Wycliffe* and the Hussites.*

Nettleton, Asahel. See *Revivals,* 2.

Neuberger, Theophilus (1593–1656). B. Jena, Ger.; Ref. theol.; educ. Jena; court preacher Güstrow 1623, Kassel 1628; took part in Leipzig* Colloquy. Works include devotional books; sermons; treatise on the Lord's Supper.

Neuchatel, Independent Evangelical Church of. Free ch. organized 1873 under G. Farel* in Neuchatel canton, Switz.; indep. of the state.

Neudecker, Johann Christian Gotthold (1807–66). B. Gotha, Ger.; educ. Jena; private scholar Gotha 1832–42; teacher, then conrector, Knabenbürgerschule at Gotha; 2d rector of the garrison and Erfurt Vorstadtschule 1855; dir. Gotha Bürgerschule 1860. Works include writings on the hist. of the Reformation.

Neuendettelsau Mission Society (Bav. For. Miss. Soc.). Est. as Gesellschaft für innere Mission im Sinne der lutherischen Kirche in Bayern 1849 (const. 1850) by J. K. W. Löhe.* Concerns included work among Ger. immigrants in Am.; in connection with this, a miss. to Am. Indians was carried on until the mid-1860s. In 1888 the Ger. name of the soc. became Gesellschaft für innere und äussere Mission im Sinne der lutherischen Kirche. Work among natives in Australia was begun in the 1870s, in New Guinea 1886 (see also *Flierl, Johan[nes]; Keysser, Christian*); for further developments in the latter field see *Australia, Lutheranism in,* B 1; *New Guinea.* Other fields included Brazil 1897.

Neukomm, Sigismund von (1778–1858). Composer; organist; pianist; b. Salzburg, Austria; pupil of F. J. Haydn*; friend of Cherubini.* Works include 7 oratorios (e. g., *Mount Sinai* and *David*), 15 masses, and cantatas *(Miriam; The Prophecy of Babylon; Absalom).*

Neumann, Kaspar (Caspar; 1648–1715). B. Breslau, Ger.; educ. Jena; court preacher Altenburg 1676; diaconus 1678, pastor 1689 Breslau; prof. Breslau 1697; hymnist. Hymns include "Gott, du hast in deinem Sohn"; "Herr, es ist von meinem Leben."

Neumann, Robert. See *Immigrant and Emigrant Missions.*

Neumark, Georg (1621–81). B. Langensalza, Thuringia, Ger.; studied law and poetry at Königsberg; court poet, librarian, and registrar at Weimar; musician; hymnist. Hymns include "Wer nur den lieben Gott lässt walten." Composed the tune *Wer nur den lieben Gott.*

Neumeister, Erdmann (1671–1756). B. Üchteritz, near Weissenfels, Ger.; educ. Leipzig; pastor Bibra and supt. Eckartsberge dist. 1698; court diaconus Weissenfels 1704; supt. Sorau 1706; pastor Hamburg 1715; opposed millennialism, unionism, and pietism; assoc. of J. S. Bach,* who set some of his texts to music; poet. Works include texts for cantatas; hymns include "Jesus nimmt die Sünder an"; "Ich weiss, an wen ich glaube."

Neuroses. See *Psychotherapy,* 9.

Neuser, Adam (d. 1576). B. Gunzenhausen, Middle Franconia, W Bav., Ger.; Luth. pastor Heidelberg; imprisoned for treason and unitarianism; fled to Constantinople; embraced Islam.

Neustädter Bibel. See *Pareus, David.*

Neve, Juergen Ludwig (June 7, 1865–Aug. 12, 1943). B. Silesia, Ger.; educ. Breklum and Kiel; to Am. 1887; ordained Luth. 1888; prof. ch. hist. German* Theol. Sem. of the General* Synod 1887–92; pastor Bremen, near Chester, Ill., and ed. *Zionsbote* 1892–98; prof. ch. hist. and symbolics Western Theol. Sem., Atchison, Kans., 1898–1909; prof. symbolics and hist. of doctrine Hamma Divinity School, Springfield, Ohio, 1909–43. Coauthor *A History of Christian Thought.* Other works include *Churches and Sects of Christendom; History of the Lutheran Church in America; The Lutherans in the Movements for Church Union; Story and Significance of* *the Augsburg Confession on Its Four Hundredth Anniversary.*

Nevin, John Williamson (1803–86). Ref. theol.; b. in or near Strasburg, Pa.; educ. Princeton (N. J.) Theol. Sem. Prof. Western Theol. Sem., Allegheny (near Pittsburgh), Pa., 1830–40; (Ger. Ref.) Theol. Sem., Mercersburg, Pa., 1840–53; acting pres. Marshall Coll., Mercersburg, 1841–53; prof. hist. and aesthetics Franklin and Marshall Coll., Lancaster, 1861–66; pres. Franklin and Marshall Coll. 1866–76; helped found Mercersburg* Theol. Ed. Mercersburg Review 1849–53. Other works include *The Anxious Bench; The Mystical Presence: A Vindication of the Reformed or Calvinistic Doctrine of the Holy Eucharist; History and Genius of the Heidelberg Catechism.*

T. Appel, *The Life and Work of John Williamson Nevin* (Philadelphia, 1889).

Nevius, John Livingston (Mar. 4, 1829–Oct. 19, 1893). Presb. miss to China; b. near Ovid, N. Y.; educ. Union Coll., Schenectady, N. Y., and Princeton (N. J.) Theol. Sem.; worked at Ningpo (now Ninghsien) 1854–59, Hangchow 1859, in Shantung Province 1861–64, 1871–93; in Japan 1859–61, in Am. 1864–68; developed Nevius* Methods. Works include *China and the Chinese; The Planting and Development of Missionary Churches.*

H. S. C. Nevius, *The Life of John Livingston Nevius* (New York, 1895).

Nevius Methods. Plan for miss. work developed by J. L. Nevius*; successfully used first in Korea; aims to est. self-propagating, self-supporting, self-governing indigenous chs. from the beginning. The methods have been summarized:

1. Let everyone stay in his calling and be an individual worker for Christ in his neighborhood, supporting himself by his trade.
2. Develop organization only as far as the native ch. can handle it.
3. Use the best qualified natives for evangelistic work.
4. Natives provide their own ch. bldg. in harmony with native architecture and economic standards.

Nevius emphasized extensive travel by missionaries, personal evangelism by all ch. mems., systematic Bible studies, strict discipline, cooperation and union with other chs., noninterference in lawsuits. WK

C. A. Clark, *The Nevius Plan for Mission Work, Illustrated in Korea* (Seoul, Korea, 1937); W. J. Kang, "The Nevius Methods: A Study and an Appraisal of Indigenous Mission Methods," *CTM,* XXXIV (1963), 335–342.

New Amsterdam. See *United States, Religious History of,* 6.

New Apostolic Church of North America. See *Catholic Apostolic Church,* 2.

New Birth. See *Conversion.*

New Brunswick. See *Canada,* A 27.

New Caledonia. See *Melanesia.*

New Church. See *Swedenborgians.*

New Congregational Methodist Church. See *Methodist Churches,* 4 b.

New Connection Methodist. See *Methodist Churches,* 1.

New-England Primer. See *Catechetics,* 13.

New England Theology. 1. Federal* theol. helped form the thought of New Eng. Puritanism. In 1648 the Cambridge (Mass.) Syn. (1646–48) approved in substance the doctrinal parts, but not the arts. on discipline, of the Westminster Confession, replaced in Mass. 1680, Conn. 1708, by a modified Savoy Declaration. See also *Democratic Declarations of Faith,* 2.

2. New Eng. Theol., which dominated New Eng. Congregationalism till ca. the middle of the 19th c. and may be dated from a 1734 sermon of J. Edwards* the Elder, developed in opposition against a decline in doctrine and morals.

3. J. Edwards* the Elder opposed Arminianism* with a modified Calvinism* that emphasized the unworthiness of man and his complete dependence on God.

4. Successors of J. Edwards* the Elder include J. Edwards* the Younger, who developed the New* Eng. Theory of Atonement; Joseph Bellamy (1719–90; exponent of the views of J. Edwards the Elder; works include *True Religion Delineated* and *The Wisdom of God in the Permission of Sin;* see also *Ministry, Education of,* VI A); S. Hopkins* (works include *The System of Doctrines, Contained in Divine Revelation, Explained and Defended*); Nathanael Emmons (Nathaniel; 1745 [1746?]–1840; held that all "exercises" of the will [holiness and sin] are caused by the divine efficiency of First Cause; see also *Ministry, Education of,* VI A); Edward(s) Amasa Park (1808–1900; b. Providence, R. I.; prof. Andover [Mass.] Theol. Sem.; ed. *Bibliotheca sacra;* other works include *Discourses on Some Theological Doctrines*). See also *Taylor, Nathaniel William.*

5. New Eng. Theol. spread rapidly in Cong. chs. in New Eng. and westward and was favored by many in other Calvinistic chs. The movement founded Andover (Mass.) Theol. Sem. (1807/08), the Theol. Dept. of Yale U., New Haven, Conn. (1822), and Hartford (Conn.) Theol. Sem. (1833/34).

Adherents of New Eng. Theol. deviated from the old Calvinistic system in holding, e. g., (1) Predestination secures the certainty of man's choices but not their necessity; (2) Adam's guilt is not imputed to his descendants but as a result of his transgression man is constituted to choose wrong instead of right; (3) Christ did not suffer the exact penalty of the Law but pains substituted for that penalty and designed to secure moral govt.; (4) justification does not involve transfer of Christ's righteousness to the believer but forgiveness for Christ's sake and treatment of man as if innocent or holy; (5) Regeneration is either active or passive, or both, and either instantaneous or gradual, a restoration of life-communion with God; (6) The elect can fall after regeneration but never will.

G. N. Boardman, *A History of New England Theology* (New York, 1899); F. H. Foster, *A Genetic History of the New England Theology* (Chicago, 1907); P. Y. De Jong, *The Covenant Idea in New England Theology, 1620–1847* (Grand Rapids, Mich., 1945).

New England Theory of Atonement. Governmental theory of atonement (see *Atonement, Theories of,* 5) of H. Grotius* as developed by J. Edwards* the Younger (hence also called Edwardean Theory): God is a moral governor rather than a sovereign; the work of Christ is universal, not particular; neither Adam's sin nor Christ's righteousness is imputed. See also *New England Theology,* 4.

New Guinea. 1. 2d-largest is. (after Greenland); part of Malay Archipelago; sometimes included in Melanesia*; N of Australia, S of equator. *Area:* more than 300,000 sq. mi. Divided into *Territory of Papua* (SE part; area perhaps ca. 90,000 sq. mi.; pop. ca. 700,000; Brit. colony from 1888; under control of Australia 1901; became Territory of Papua 1906), *Territory of New Guinea* (NE part; area perhaps ca. 93,000 sq. mi.; pop. ca. 2,000,000; Ger. colony called Kaiser Wilhelmsland from 1884; mandated to Australia 1920 by League of Nations; under UN trusteeship, Australian administration, 1946; administrative union of Papua and New Guinea promulgated 1949; "and" officially deleted from the combined name 1971; Papua New Guinea attained self-govt. Dec. 1, 1973), and *West Irian* (see *Indonesia,* 1, 7). Natives related to Negroes and Melanesians.

2. Luth. miss. work in West Irian, begun 1855 by the Gossner* Miss. Soc., was taken over 1862 by the Utrecht* Miss. Soc. Other missions in West Irian include The Christian and Missionary Alliance, Unevangelized Fields Mission, Baps., and RCs. See also *Indonesia,* 1, 7.

3–4. The LMS began work in what is now the Territory of Papua in the early 1870s (see also *Chalmers, James; Lawes, William George*), RCs in the mid-1880s, Angls. and the Overseas Mission of the Meth. Ch. in Australia in the early 1890s.

5. J. Flierl* began work 1886 near Finschhafen, in what is now the Territory of New Guinea; C. Keysser arrived ca. the turn of the c.; this miss. became known as the Luth. Miss. Finschhafen. Friedrich Eich (Jan. 20, 1843–Oct. 21, 1919; b. Dierdorf, Ger.) and J. I. Wilhelm Thomas (June 6, 1843–Dec. 30, 1900; b. Eilbach, Ger.) of the Rhenish* Miss. Soc. explored several fields, including the islands of New Brit. and New Ireland; Thomas abandoned the work because of illness; Eich opened a miss. 1887 at Bogadjim, near Madang; this miss. became known as the Luth. Miss. Madang. For further developments see *Australia, Lutheranism in,* B 1.

By 1940 the Luth. Miss. Finschhafen had ca. 40,000 bap. mems., Luth. Miss. Madang ca. 20,000. Missions and missionaries suffered severely in WW II. The UELCA, ALC, and NLC joined hands to rebuild. In 1953 the 2 missions merged to form the Lutheran Mission New Guinea. In 1956 the Ev. Luth. Ch. of New Guinea (ELCONG) was formed.

6. In 1936 the ELCA acquired the Neuendettelsau miss. on the Rooke-Siassi islands, bet. the is. of New Brit. and the Huon Peninsula of the Territory of New Guinea. In 1951 the ELCA expanded to the interior of the mainland, opening a station among the Kukukuku (Kukakuka) natives at Menyamya, W of Huon Gulf.

7. On appeal of the ELCA, the LCMS resolved 1947 to aid ELCA miss. work in the Territory of New Guinea with men and money. The ELCA est. a station at Yaramanda (Yaramunda) Aug. 1948. Otto Charles Hintze Jr. (b. Mar. 22, 1923, at El Paso, Tex.; educ. Conc. Sem., St. Louis, Mo.; LCMS miss. to New Guinea 1948; asst. prof. Conc. Sem., Springfield, Ill., 1966) and Willard Lewis Burce (b. Feb. 9, 1924, at Marshall, Mich.; educ. Conc. Sem., St. Louis, Mo.; LCMS miss. to New Guinea 1948) arrived there Nov. 1948. Work began under joint sponsorship of the ELCA and LCMS; the miss. took the name New Guinea Luth. Miss. ("Mo. Syn." was later added to the name). The Luth. missions of Rooke-Siassi and Finschhafen provided evangelists and teachers in the early yrs. of work. LCMS assumed full responsibility for this field 1949. First baptisms (79): Jan. 6, 1957. The const. of the Wabag Luth. Ch. was ratified 1961. VEH

New Hampshire Confession. The N. H. Bap. conv. appointed a committee 1830 to prepare a statement of faith to offset Arminianism; it was pub. 1833; moderately Calvinistic. See also *Baptist Churches,* 5, 14.

New Haven Theology (Taylorism). New Eng. Calvinism* (see also *New England Theology*) modified by a group of men chiefly of Yale U., New Haven, Conn., background, including L. Beecher,* T. Dwight,* E. T. Fitch,* C. A. Goodrich,* and N. W. Taylor*; held that freedom to choose as well as to do is the only possible basis for responsibility; defined sin as voluntary transgression of known law, and total depravity as the occasion but not the cause of sin.

New Hebrides. Group of islands and islets ca. 250 mi. NE of New Caledonia and ca. 500 mi. W of Fiji; Anglo-Fr. condominium since 1906. *Area:* ca. 5,700 sq. mi.; *pop.* (1970 est.): 84,000. Most natives are Melanesian. J. Williams,* 1st miss., was killed and eaten by cannibals on arrival 1839; many others suffered a similar death. More successful workers include J. Geddie* and J. G. Paton.* Missions include RCs, Angl. Ch. of New Zealand, Presbs. from Australia and New Zealand, Australian Chs. of Christ, Seventh-day Adventists, Apostolic Ch. Missionary Movement.

New Humanism. See *Humanism.*

New Icaria. See *Communistic Societies,* 5.

New Jersey, Evangelical Lutheran Synod of (I). Organized 1861 German Valley, N. J., by 6 pastors and 4 laymen who had withdrawn 1859 from the N. Y. Ministerium; consisted mainly of chs. in the Raritan valley; joined The General* Syn. of the Ev. Luth. Ch. in the USA 1862; merged 1872 with the Ev. Luth. Syn. of New* York. See also *United Lutheran Church, Synods of,* 15.

New Jersey, Evangelical Lutheran Synod of (II). See *United Lutheran Church, Synods of,* 14.

New Jersey Synod (LCA). See *Lutheran Church in America,* IX B 17.

New Jerusalem, Church of the. See *Swedenborgians.*

New Jerusalem, The General Church of the. See *Swedenborgians,* 4–5.

New Jerusalem Church. See *Swedenborgians.*

New Jerusalem in the USA, General Convention of the. See *Swedenborgians,* 4–5.

New Lichts (New Lights). Mems. Scottish Secession Chs. who supported the principle of voluntarism*; opposed the small minority Auld Lichts (Old Lights), who held to the principle of connection bet. ch. and state. See also *Presbyterian Churches,* 1.

New Lights. 1. Those among Baps., Congs., and Presbs. who favored revivals and emotionalism during and after the Great* Awakening in Am.; Old Lights opposed revivals and emotionalism in religion. 2. See *New Lichts.*

New Measures. Name given revivals and related practices that followed after rationalism in Am. had spent itself early in the 19th c.; prevalent from ca. 1830 in some areas; advocated, e. g., by B. Kurtz*; regarded by others as questionable Lutheranism.

New Morality. See *Situation(al) Ethics.*

New Netherlands. See *United States, Religious History of,* 6.

New School Presbyterians. The Presb. Ch. in the US began to divide internally ca. 1825 into a New School (advocated liberal interpretation of the confessions and cooperation with Congregationalists; opposed slavery) and a conservative Old School; schism occurred 1837; the New School adopted the Auburn* Declaration 1838; the Old School Gen. Assem. endorsed it 1868; the 2 groups reunited 1869.

New Side Presbyterians. See *Presbyterian Churches,* 4 a.

New Spain. See *Mexico,* A.

New Style Calendar. See *Gregorian Calendar.*

New Sweden. See *United States, Religious History of,* 6.

New Theology. 1. Term referring to the effort ca. 1880–ca. 1910 to restate Christian beliefs to harmonize with modern critical views and beliefs; proponents included R. J. Campbell* and T. T. Munger.* 2. See *England,* C 13.

New Thought. Movement beginning late in the 19th c. with roots in work of P. P. Quimby,* who influenced M. M. Eddy.* Quimby formed no organization, but many were formed on basis of his thought. Basic attitude is positive; emphasizes psychic control and faith healing; teachings vary from naturalism to mysticism and from Christianity to pantheism and atheism. The Nat. New Thought Alliance (1908 name) grew out of nat. annual convs. beginning 1894 and became the Internat. New Thought Alliance 1914. See also *Divine Science; Trine, Ralph Waldo; Unity School of Christianity.*

H. W. Dresser, *A History of the New Thought*

Movement (New York, 1919); E. S. Holmes, *New Thought Terms and Their Meanings* (New York, 1942).

New Tribes Mission. Organized in the 1940s as an indep. effort to work among tribes to whom the Gospel is not preached; emphasizes indigenous chs.; first missionaries sent to Bolivia 1942; other fields include Colombia, Paraguay, Venezuela, Brazil, New Guinea, Jap., the Philippines, Thailand, Panama, Senegal, Liberia, India; New Tribes Institute founded 1943 Chicago, Ill.

New Year (Jewish). See *Judaism,* 4.

New Year's Day. Beginning of the secular calendar yr.; as such not part of the ch. yr. See also *Church Year,* 16.

New Year's Eve. End of the secular calendar yr.; as such not part of the ch. yr. See also *Departed, Commemoration of; Silvesterabend.*

New York, Evangelical Lutheran Synod of. Organized Oct. 22, 1867, Red Hook, N. Y., under leadership of H. N. Pohlman,* by 17 pastors and 10 congs. who seceded from the N. Y. Ministerium 1866 in protest against its withdrawal from The General* Syn. of the Ev. Luth. Ch. in the USA; joined Gen. Syn. 1868; merged 1872 with the Ev. Luth. Syn. of New* Jersey. See also *Synods, Extinct; United Lutheran Church, Synods of,* 15.

New York, Ministerium of. See *United Lutheran Church, Synods of,* 15.

New York, Synod of, of the Evangelical Lutheran Church. See *United Lutheran Church, Synods of,* 15.

New York, United Lutheran Synod of. See *United Lutheran Church, Synods of,* 15.

New York and New England, Evangelical Lutheran Synod of. See *United Lutheran Church, Synods of,* 15.

New York and New England, United Lutheran Synod of. See *United Lutheran Church, Synods of,* 15.

New York and New Jersey, Evangelical Lutheran Synod of. See *United Lutheran Church, Synods of,* 15.

New York and Other States, German Evangelical Lutheran Synod of (Steimle Syn.; The Ger. Syn. of N. Y.). Founded 1866 by F. W. T. Steimle* and a few others who seceded from the N. Y. Ministerium because of the Ministerium's stand in regard to the Luth. confessions; the syn., but not Steimle, rejoined the Ministerium 1872. See also *United Lutheran Church, Synods of,* 15.

New Zealand. 1. Dominion in the Brit. Commonwealth of Nations, ca. 1,200 mi. SE of Australia; consists of 2 chief islands (North Is.; South Is.; separated by Cook Strait), Stewart Is. (off the S tip of South Is.), and the Chatham Islands (ca. 500 mi. E of South Is.). *Area:* ca. 103,735 sq. mi.; *pop.* (1971 est.): ca. 2,900,000. Maori natives (perhaps ca. 8% of the pop.) are Polynesian.

Miss. work began 1814 with S. Marsden.* Wesleyan Meths. of London, Eng., entered the field 1822, RCs 1838; many other groups followed.

2. There is no state ch. The Ang. Ch. is largest (more than 800,000), followed by Presbs. (more than 550,000, reflecting a large immigration from Scot.), RCs (ca. 365,000), Meths. (more than 170,000); others include Baps., Brethren, Latter Day Saints, Salv. Army, Seventh-day Adventists, Assoc. Chs. of Christ, Cong. Union, and Luths.

3. The first Luth. immigrants came from Ger. with missionaries 1843–44; some went on to Australia; the permanent settlers est. congs. at Nelson (on the N coast of South Is.) and elsewhere. Mo. Syn. missionaries to N. Z. include Martin Theodore Winkler (Nov. 24, 1880–May 13, 1942; b. Stratmann [Strathman], ca. 5 mi. W. of Clayton, Mo.; educ. Conc. Coll., Fort Wayne, Ind., and Conc. Sem., St. Louis, Mo.; miss. to N. Z. 1903; prof. Conc. Coll., Adelaide, Australia, 1908) and Frederick Henry Stephen Hassold (Jan. 22, 1882–Sept. 6, 1970; b. Huntington, Ind.; educ. Conc. Coll., Fort Wayne, Ind., and Conc. Sem., St. Louis, Mo.; miss. to N. Z. 1905). Hamuera Te Punga (Aug. 16, 1880–July 30, 1968; b. Lower Hutt, N. Z.), a native Maori, was educ. Conc. Sem., Springfield, Ill. (grad. 1912), returned to work among his people for ca. 10 yrs., with little success; then worked in other areas of the N. Z. ch. till retirement 1951. In 1914, N. Z. Luths. connected with the Mo. Syn. became part of the Ev. Luth. Syn. in Australia (now ELCA; see *Australia, Lutheranism in,* A). OHS

See also *Cook Islands; Graebner, August(us) Lawrence; Kowert, Wilhelm Hermann; Selwyn, George Augustus.*

Newberry College. See *Lutheran Church in America,* V; *Ministry, Education of,* VIII B 20; *United Lutheran Church, Synods of,* 27.

Newcomer, Christian (1749–1830). B. Lancaster Co., Pa., of Mennonite parents; helped found Ch. of the United* Brethren in Christ; active in miss. work W of the Alleghenies.

Newell, Samuel (July 25[24?], 1785[1784?]–May 30, 1821). B. Durham, Maine; educ. Harvard Coll., Cambridge, Mass., and Andover (Mass.) Theol. Sem.; ABCFM miss. to Calcutta, India, 1812; forbidden to disembark there, he went to Mauritius, then to Ceylon; joined G. Hall* and S. Nott* at Bombay, India, 1814. See also *Haystack Group.*

Newfoundland. See *Labrador.*

Newman, John Henry (1801–90). Theol., first Angl., then RC; b. London, Eng.; educ. Oxford; helped found Oxford* Movement; RC 1845; cardinal 1879. Engaged in controversy with C. Kingsley.* Coauthor *Tracts for the Times;* other works include *The Idea of a University; Apologia pro vita sua;* the hymn "Lead, Kindly Light."

Newman Club. See *Students, Spiritual Care of,* A.

Newton, Isaac (1642–1727). Mathematician, natural philos.; b. Woolsthorpe, near Grantham, Lincolnshire, Eng.; educ. Cambridge; prof. Cambridge 1669; some claim to find Arian views in his writings. Works include *Philosophiae naturalis principia mathematica.* See also *Deism,* I, 3; *Time.*

Newton, John (1725–1807). B. London, Eng.; sailor till 1755, the last 4 yrs. in Afr. slave trade; tide surveyor Liverpool 1755–60; studied Gk. and Heb.; ordained Angl. curate Olney, Buckinghamshire; produced *Olney Hymns* with W. Cowper.* Hymns include "Glorious Things of Thee Are Spoken"; "How Sweet the Name of Jesus Sounds."

Nez Percé. See *Indians, American,* 3.

Niagara Movement. See *National Association for the Advancement of Colored People.*

Nias. Is. in the Indian ocean W of Sumatra. See also *Indonesia,* 4; *Sundermann, Wilhelm Heinrich.*

Nicaea, Councils of (modern Iznik, NW Turkey in Asia). 1. *The 1st Ecumenical Council* (Nicaea I). Convened by Constantine* I; probably began May or June and ended ca. Aug. 25, 325; ca. 300 bps. present; chief concern: doctrinal issues, esp. Christology. Arians (see *Arianism*) proposed a creed that was rejected. Eusebius* of Caesarea proposed a creed, probably that which was used at baptism in his ch.; it found gen. approval but was found to lack necessary precision against Arianism; clauses were added (*ek tes ousias tou patros,* "of the substance of the Father"; *gennethenta, ou poiethenta,* "begotten, not made"; *homoousion to patri,* "of one substance with the Father"). The 3d art. has the statement "and in the Holy Spirit" and then anathematizes those who hold Arian propositions. The "Nicene Creed" as we know it is a later modification of the creed adopted 325 at Nicaea; see *Constantinople, Councils of,* 1; *Ecumenical Creeds,* B. See also

Homoousios. The Council also fixed the date of Easter (see *Easter Controversy*).

2. *The 7th Ecumenical Council* (Nicaea II). Convened by Byzantine Empress Irene (ca. 752–803; b. Athens, Greece; wife of Emp. Leo IV [the Khazar; ca. 750–780; m. Irene 769; E Roman emp. 775–780]; coruler with her son Constantine VI 780–797; sole ruler 797–802; deposed) in the name of Constantine VI; met Aug. 786–Oct. 787; opened in the basilica of the Holy Apostles, Constantinople; disrupted by iconoclastic soldiers; transferred to Nicaea, where it met Sept. 24–Oct. 23, 787; est. legitimacy of veneration of images as opposed to latria*; declared belief in efficacy of prayers of saints. See also *Mariology.*

See also *Councils and Synods; Doctrine, Christian, History of,* 3.

Nicaragua. See *Central America,* A, H.

Nicene Creed. See *Constantinople, Councils of,* 1; *Ecumenical Creeds,* B; *Nicaea, Councils of,* 1.

Nicephorus (ca. 750/758–ca. 828). Represented Leo IV at 2d Council of Nicaea*; patriarch Constantinople 806; founded monastery on the Propontis (Sea of Marmara); defended veneration of images; deposed 815. *MPG,* 100, 9–1068.

Nicephorus Callistus (Xanthopoulos; ca. 1256–ca. 1335). B. perhaps Constantinople; hist. Works include ch. hist. from time of Christ to death of Phocas (E Roman emp. 602 till his death 610). *MPG,* 145, 549–1332; 146; 147, 9–632.

Nicephorus Gregoras (ca. 1295–ca. 1359). B. Heraclea Pontica, NW Turkey in Asia, on Black Sea; hist.; opposed hesychasm.* Works include Roman hist. 1204–1359.

Niceta(s) (Nic[a]eus of Dacia; perhaps ca. 340–after 414). Bp. Remesiana (Civitas Romatiana; modern Bela Palanka, Yugoslavia) perhaps ca. 366/367. Works include *Explanatio symboli* (contains first known use of the term *communio* sanctorum*); *Competentibus ad baptismum instructionis libelli sex.*

A. E. Burn, *Niceta of Remesiana* (Cambridge, Eng., 1905).

Nicetas of Chonia (Khonae; Khonas; Nicetas Choniates; incorrectly called Akominatos [Acominatos; Acominatus]; perhaps ca. 1140/50–ca. 1212/13). Theol., hist.; b. Chonae (Khonae; Khonas; ancient Colossae), Phrygia; fled to Nicaea when Crusaders took Constantinople 1204 (see *Crusades,* 5). Works include a hist. covering 1118–1206.

MPG, 139, 287–1444; 140, 9–292.

Nichiren (1222–82). B. Kominato, prov. Awa, Jap.; founded Hokkes, a Buddhist sect.

Nicholas (fl. 1st half of 4th c.). Bp. Myra, in Lycia, Asia Minor; patron saint of Russia, sailors, and children; acc. to legend, provided dowries for 3 maidens; stories of his secret gifts to children on his feast, Dec. 6, came to be connected with Christmas and his name was corrupted in Am. into Santa Claus.

Nicholas (Nicolaus Kemph de Argentina; 1397–1497). B. Strasbourg, Ger.; studied in Vienna; Carthusian; mystic theol.

Nicholas I. See *Popes,* 5.

Nicholas V (Pietro Rainalducci; d. 1333). B. Corvaro, Rieti, It.; antipope to John XXII (see *Babylonian Captivity,* 2; *Popes,* 19) 1328 (see Louis IV); submitted to John XXII 1330.

Nicholas V (pope). See *Concordat,* 3.

Nicholas, Henry. See *Niclaes, Hendrik.*

Nicholas of Amiens (fl. 2d half of 12th c.). Probably wrote *De arte seu articulis catholica fidei,* formerly ascribed to Alain* de Lille.

MPL, 210, 595–618.

Nicholas of Basel (d. ca. 1395). Beghard (see *Beghards and Beguines*); claimed inspiration; became prominent through preaching in the area around Basel; held that his followers were sinless and need not obey any authority; at one time identified as the "Great Friend" of the Friends* of God; burned at stake under the Inquisition.*

Nicholas of Clémanges (Nicolas de Clémanges; Nikolaus von Clémanges; Clamenges; Clamanges; Nicolaus de Clemangiis; originally Nicholas Poillevillain; ca. 1360/67–1437). Theol; Christian humanist; b. Clémanges, Champagne, NE Fr.; educ. Paris; rector U. of Paris; tried to help heal the Western Schism (see *Schism,* 8); secy. to antipope Benedict XIII (see *Benedict XIII,* 1) 1397; resigned 1407; lived with Carthusians; later taught again in Paris. Works include *De corrupto ecclesiae statu; Disputatio super materia concilii generalis.*

Nicholas of Cusa (Nicolas; Cues; Nikolaus Cryftz; Khrypffs; Kryfts; Chrypffs; Nicolaus Cusanus; name originally Nicolaus Krebs of Cues or Cusa; 1401–64). B. Kues or Cusa, on the Moselle, in the archbishopric of Trier (Treves); educ. Deventer (?), Heidelberg, and Padua; mem. council of Basel; supported first the conciliar, then the papal party; cardinal 1448; bp. and reformer Brixen (Bressanone), NE It. Doubted scholastic proofs of theol. truths; extolled "learned ignorance"; held that God is the coincidence of opposites; tried to give intuition cognitive meaning in mathematical terms; anticipated Copernicus with a theory of the rotation of the earth on its axis; proposed calendar reform; said the world would end 1734. Works include *De docta ignorantia; De coniecturis; Apologia doctae ignorantiae; De visione Dei; De concordantia catholica; De auctoritate praesidendi in consilio generali; De pace fidei.* Works pub. Paris 1514, Basel 1565, Leipzig 1932–. See also *Pseudo-Isidorian Decretals.*

F. A. Scharpff, *Der Cardinal und Bischof Nicolaus von Cusa als Reformator in Kirche, Reich und Philosophie des fünfzehnten Jahrhunderts* (Tübingen, 1871); E. Vansteenberghe, *Le Cardinal Nicolas de Cues* (Paris, 1920); E. Cassirer, *Individuum und Kosmos in der Philosophie der Renaissance* (Leipzig, 1927), tr. with an introd. M. Domandi, *The Individual and the Cosmos in Renaissance Philosophy* (New York, 1963); H. Bett, *Nicholas of Cusa* (London, 1932); P. E. Sigmund, *Nicholas of Cusa and Medieval Political Thought* (Cambridge, Mass., 1963). PR

Nicholas of Flüe (Nikolaus von der Flüe; orig. Nikolaus Löwenbugger; 1417–87). "Bruder Klaus"; b. at what is now Flüeli, near Sachseln, cen. Switz.; farmer, soldier, councillor, judge; with wife's consent, left her and 10 children to be hermit in Ranft ravine, near Flüeli, ca. 19 yrs.; helped avert Swiss civil war 1481.

Nicholas of Hereford (Nicholas Hereford [Herford]; d. ca. 1420). Wycliffite; b. probably Hereford, Eng.; educ. Oxford; excommunicated 1382; in Rome appealed to pope; imprisoned; escaped 1385; returned to Eng.; resumed Wycliffite activity; recanted and repudiated Wycliffites in the early 1390s; Carthusian monk Coventry 1417. Helped J. Wycliffe* tr. Bible.

Nicholas of Lyra. See *Lyra, Nicolaus de.*

Nicholas of Strasbourg (fl. ca. 1323–29). Dominican mystic; lector at monastery at Cologne, Ger., ca. 1323–29. Works include sermons and a philos. *Summa.*

Nicholas of Tolentino (ca. 1245–ca. 1305). Augustinian friar; devoted to preaching and pastoral work among poor; fragments of his body at Tolentino, It., reputed to bleed in connection with unusual events in ch. hist.

Nicholites. Also called New Quakers. Sect founded by Joseph Nichols in latter half of 18th c. in Caroline Co., Md., with religious beliefs much like those of the Soc. of Friends,* with whom they united after ca. 20 yrs. of indep. existence.

Niclaes, Hendrik (Niclas; Henry Nicolas; ca. 1502–ca. 1580). B. probably Münster, Westphalia, of RC parents; believed he saw visions at an early age; to

Amsterdam, Neth., ca. 1529; in Emden, Ger., 1540–60; founded Familists*; before proceedings could be taken against his antinomianism at Emden he escaped; fugitive during his last yrs.

Nicolai, Christoph Friedrich (1733–1811). B. Berlin, Ger.; rationalistic author, critic, and bookseller. Founded and ed. *Allgemeine Deutsche Bibliothek*. See also *Enlightenment,* 3.

Nicolai, Melchior (Nikolai; 1578–1659). B. Schorndorf, Ger.; educ. Tübingen; held various positions; prof. Tübingen 1619. Works include polemical writings against RCs, Ref., Anabaps.; treatise on the kenosis of Christ (see also *Crypto-Kenotic Controversy*).

Nicolai, Philipp (1556–1608). Luth. preacher and hymnist; b. Mengeringhausen, Waldeck, Ger.; educ. Erfurt and Wittenberg; held various pastorates; helped sustain staunch Lutheranism during the Counter* Reformation. Credited with words and music of "Wie schön leucht's uns der Morgenstern" and "Wachet auf! ruft uns die Stimme," called resp. the Queen and King of Chorales.

Nicolaitans. See *Gnosticism,* 7 j.

Nicoll, William Robertson (1851–1923). B. Lumsden, Aberdeenshire, Scot.; educ. Aberdeen; Free Ch. minister Dufftown, Banffshire (1874–77), and Kelso, Roxburghshire (1877–85); resigned because of ill health and devoted himself to literary work; knighted 1909. Ed. *The Expositor's Greek Testament.*

Nicum, John (Jan. 6, 1851–Nov. 1, 1909). B. Winnenden, Württemberg, Ger.; educ. Muhlenberg Coll., Allentown, Pa., and Luth. Theol. Sem., Philadelphia, Pa. Pastor Frackville and Philadelphia, Pa., and Syracuse and Rochester, N. Y.; prof. and pres. Wagner Mem. Lutheran Coll., Staten Is., N. Y., 1894–1902. Works include *The Beginnings of the Lutheran Church on Manhattan Island; Geschichte des Evangelisch-Lutherischen Ministeriums vom Staate New York und angrenzenden Staaten und Ländern; Laws of the State of New York Relating to Churches; The Confessional History of the Lutheran Church in the United States.*

Niebuhr, Helmut Richard (1894–1962). Brother of R. Niebuhr*; b. Wright City, Mo.; educ. Elmhurst (Ill.) Coll. and Eden Theol. Sem., Webster Groves (St. Louis), Mo.; ordained Ev. Syn. of N. Am. 1916; pastor St. Louis 1916–18; prof. Eden Theol. Sem. 1919–22, 1927–31; pres. Elmhurst Coll. 1924–27. Works include *The Kingdom of God in America; The Meaning of Revelation; The Social Sources of Denominationalism; Christ and Culture.*

Niebuhr, Reinhold (1892–1971). Brother of H. R. Niebuhr*; b. Wright City, Mo.; educ. Elmhurst (Ill.) Coll. and Eden Theol. Sem., Webster Groves (St. Louis), Mo.; ordained Ev. Syn. of N. Am. 1915; pastor Detroit, Mich., 1915–28; prof. Union Theol. Sem., NYC, 1928–60. Favored labor movement and became interested in social* ethics; opposed theol. and pol. liberalism; exponent of dialectical* theol.; regarded pride as chief threat to mankind; emphasized original sin; held that human structures are limited and pol. visions should not be confounded with the kingdom of God. Works include *Moral Man and Immoral Society; The Nature and Destiny of Man; Faith and History; An Interpretation of Christian Ethics; Christian Realism and Political Problems.* See also *Encounter; Neoorthodoxy.*

Niedermünster. See *Odilia.*

Niedner, Christian Wilhelm (1797–1865). B. Oberwinkel, Saxony, Ger.; educ. Leipzig; prof. Leipzig 1829–50; resigned because of differences arising out of the 1848 revolution; prof. Berlin and mem. Brandenburg consistory 1859. Works include *Geschichte der christlichen Kirche.*

Niedner, Frederic H. (July 8, 1887–Nov. 13, 1974). B. Fredericktown, Mo.; educ. Conc. Sem., St. Louis, Mo., and U. of Minn.; ordained 1910 at St. Paul, Minn.; city miss. St. Paul-Minneapolis area; taught at Conc. Coll., St. Paul, Minn.; pastor Atchison, Kans., St. Charles, Mo., Pagedale, Mo.; served on bds. in the area of ch. extension, missions, ministerial training. Works include *The Great Physician;* numerous homiletic studies and sermon outlines.

Niehaus, Hermann. See *Catholic Apostolic Church,* 2.

Nielsen, Anders Sixtus (1832–Mar. 26, 1909). "Gamle Nielsen ('Old Nielsen')"; Dan. cleric; to Am. 1871; ordained 1871. Pastor Cedar Falls, Iowa, 1871; Chicago, Ill., 1879; Withee, Wis., 1893–1903. Pres. The Dan. Ev. Luth. Ch. in Am. 1879–83, 1885–87, 1891–93, 1893–94 (see also *Danish Lutherans in America,* 3); ordainer 1872–1901.

Nielsen, Jörgen Peter (Dec. 18, 1877–Aug. 1, 1963). B. Sludstrup, Parish Sjalland, Den.; to Am. 1879; educ. Dana Coll. and Trin. Sem., both at Blair, Nebr.; pastor Philadelphia, Pa., 1905–07; principal Brorson Folk High School, Kenmare, N. D., 1908–09; miss. to Jap. 1910–27; prof., then pres. (1932) Trin. Sem. 1927–46; supt. Good Shepherd Home for the Aged, Blair, 1949–56.

Nielsen, Rasmus (1809–84). B. on the is. of Fyn (Fünen), Den.; educ. Copenhagen; prof. Copenhagen; successively a follower of G. W. F. Hegel,* S. A. Kierkegaard,* and N. F. S. Grundtvig.* Opposed H. L. Martensen's* speculative theol.

Niem, Dietrich von (Nieheim; Nyem; Theodoricus; ca. 1340–ca. 1418). B. Nieheim, Westphalia; officer in papal chancellery under Gregory XI (see *Popes,* 14) at Avignon and Rome. Works include a life of antipope John XXIII (see *John XXIII,* 1) and a hist. of the papal schism that began 1378 (see *Schism,* 8).

Niemann, Johann Heinrich (Apr. 11, 1848–Mar. 15, 1910). B. Hoyel, near Melle, Hannover, Ger.; educ. Conc. Sem., St. Louis, Mo. Pastor Little Rock, Ark., 1869; Cleveland, Ohio, 1876. Pres. Cen. Dist. of the Mo. Syn. 1880–1909.

Niemeyer, August Hermann (1754–1828). Great-grandson of A. H. Francke*; father of H. A. Niemeyer*; b. Halle, Ger.; prof. (1779), chancellor (1808) of the U. at Halle; asst. dir. (1785), dir. (1789) of the Francke institutions.

Niemeyer, Herman Agathon (1802–51). Son of A. H. Niemeyer*; b. Halle, Ger.; educ. Halle and Göttingen; prof. Jena 1826, Halle 1829; dir. of the A. H. Francke* institutions. Works include *Collectio confessionum in ecclesiis reformatis publicatarum.*

Niemöller, Martin. See *Confessing Church; Germany,* C 4; *Kirchenkampf.*

Nietzsche, Friedrich Wilhelm (1844–1900). Philos.; b. Röcken, near Lützen, Ger.; educ. Bonn and Leipzig; prof. classical philol. Basel 1869–79; resigned and devoted himself to writing; declared incurably insane 1889.

First followed Wilhelm Richard Wagner (1813–83; composer) and A. Schopenhauer,* then turned against the former as the musician of decadent emotionalism and rejected the latter's pessimism. Developed an individualistic, antidemocratic, and bitterly anti-Christian atheistic philos.; its fundamental idea is the "will to power" (Ger.: *Wille zur Macht*) that underlies Herrenmoral,* opposed to Sklavenmoral (slave morality; represented by Christianity, which makes a virtue of humility and tends to weakness); held that Christianity is a stain on the hist. of mankind and that Herrenmoral produces the highest type of humanity, the Übermensch ("superman"), in contrast, or antithesis, to God. Works include *Also sprach Zarathustra; Jenseits von Gut und Böse; Zur Genealogie der Moral.* See also *Christian Faith and the Intellectual,* 4.

Niger. See *Africa,* C 10.

Nigeria. See *Africa,* C 14.

Nigeria, Christian Council of. See *Africa,* C 14.

Nightingale, Florence (1820–1910). Hospital reformer, philanthropist; "The Lady with the Lamp"; b. Florence, It., of Eng. parents and named after that city; trained at deaconess institute, Kaiserswerth, Ger. (see *Deaconesses,* 5), then studied the nursing system and management in hosps. of the Sisters of St. Vincent de Paul, Paris; with money raised in recognition of her services in the Crimea 1854–56 she est. the Nightingale Home for training nurses at St. Thomas's and King's Coll. Hosps., London. Works include *Notes on Nursing.*

Nigrinus, Georg (1530–1602). Luth. theol.; b. Battenberg, Ger.; educ. Marburg; pastor Homburg 1556, Giessen 1564; supt. Alsfeld and Nidda 1580; promoted FC. Works include tr. of M. Chemnitz's* *Examen Concilii Tridentini* into Ger.

Nigrinus, Theobald (d. 1566). B. Haguenau (Hagenau), Fr.; Dominican; won for the Reformation and advanced it in Strasbourg.

Nihil obstat (Lat. "nothing stands in the way"). In RCm, clearance for pub. issued by an official censor.

Nihilianism. The teaching that Christ's essential being is in His Godhead only, His human nature being nothing; held by some 12th-c. theologians.

Nihilism. In philos., the view that nothing exists and that knowledge is therefore impossible. In politics, the program of 19th and 20th c. Russians who opposed despotic absolutism and tried to destroy soc. and pol. institutions; fostered by materialism; developed terroristic methods (e. g., assassination of Russ. Romanov emp. [czar] Alexander II 1881).

Nihongi, See *Shinto,* 1.

Nijmegen, Peace of. See *France,* 13.

Nikander, Juho Kustaa (John; Sept. 3 [Mar. 9?], 1855–Jan. 13, 1919). B. Lammi, Fin.; educ. Lyceum and Theol. Dept., U. of Helsinki (Helsingfors); ordained 1879 by bp. of Porvoo; to US 1884 [1885?]; pastor Hancock, Calumet, and Allouez, Mich., 1885–97; pres. Suomi Coll. and Sem., Hancock; pres. Suomi Syn. 1890 (see *Finnish Lutherans in America,* 2). Works include a Bible hist. and a life of Luther, both in Finnish.

Nikolaus, Johann. See *Febronianism.*

Nikon (Nikita Minin [or Minov]; 1605–81). B. Valmanovo, near Nizhni Novgorod (modern Gorki), Russ.; received monastic educ.; became a married secular priest; children died; separated from wife, who entered a convent; withdrew to monastic life; metropolitan Novgorod; patriarch Moscow 1652; reformed the liturgy; deposed and banished 1666 (1667?); pardoned; d. on way back to Moscow; now regarded as a great bp.

Nilsen, Nils. See *Africa,* B 9.

Nilssøn, Jens (1538–1600). B. Christiana (Oslo), Norw.; educ. Copenhagen, Den.; bp. Oslo 1580; preached Reformation; espoused humanism.

Nilus the Ascetic (d. ca. 430 AD). B. probably Ancyra; acc. to doubtful legend, resigned from high court position in Constantinople and lived as ascetic on Mount Sinai; more probably founded a monastery near Ancyra. Works include letters and ascetic writings.

Nimbus. Halo, or circle of light, represented in art as surrounding heads of holy persons; found in Brahmanic, Buddhist, Christian, Greek, and Roman art.

Nimeguen. See *Nijmegen.*

Nimes, Amnesty (Edict) of. See *France,* 10.

Nimes, Synod of. See *Tempus clausum.*

Nimrod, Tower of. See *Babylonians, Religion of the,* 4.

Nimwegen. See *Nijmegen.*

Ninazu. See *Babylonians, Religion of the,* 5.

Ninety-five Theses. See *Theses, Ninety-five.*

Nineveh, Fast of. Two-week pre-Lenten fast observed by Nestorians, Jacobites (see *Jacobites,* 1), Copts, and Armenians.

Ninian. See *Celtic Church,* 3.

Nippold, Friedrich Wilhelm Franz (1838–1918). Prot. ch. hist.; b. Emmerich, Ger.; educ. Halle and Bonn; prof. Heidelberg, Ger., Bern, Switz., and Jena, Ger. Works include *Handbuch der neuesten Kirchengeschichte.*

Nirvana (Skt. "blowing out"). In Buddhism, the highest goal of spiritual discipline. See also *Buddhism,* 3.

Nisan. Apparently a Babylonian name used by Jews from the time of the Exile for the opening mo. of the ecclesiastical yr., 7th mo. of civil yr.; roughly Apr., in which the Passover was celebrated; older name: Abib.

Nisibis (Nisibin). Modern Nusaybin, SE Turkey in Asia; important on ancient trade routes; residence of Armenian kings ca. 150 BC–ca. 115, when it was captured by Trajan*; center of theol. studies ca. the middle of the 4th c.; when Nisibis came under Persian rule 363, the school moved to Edessa, where it became Nestorian after ca. 431; returned to Nisibis ca. 457 and flourished ca. 200 yrs. See also *Schools, Early Christian,* 4, 5.

Nissen, Rasmus Tönder (1822–82). Prof. ch. hist. Christiania (Oslo), Norw.; councillor of state and pres. Norw. Ch. Dept. 1874. Works include *De nordiske kirkers historie* and a gen. ch. hist.

Nitschmann, David. 1. (d. 1758 at Bethlehem, Pa.). B. Moravia; from Kunwald, Moravia, to Herrnhut, Ger., 1725; daughter Anna became N. L. v. Zinzendorf's 2d wife 1757. 2. *David I* (d. 1729 in prison in Moravia). "The Confessor." 3. *David II* (1696–1772). "The Bishop"; b. Zauchtenthal (Zauchtel), Moravia; imprisoned 1725 in Kremsier (Kromeríz) for religious reasons; to Herrnhut 1727; with J. L. Dober* to St. Thomas 1732; returned soon; active in Holland and Holstein in the interest of Herrnhut Moravians; consecrated bp. 1735 in Berlin by Jablonski (see *Jablonski,* 2); met C. and J. Wesley on a trip to Am. 1735/36; traveled extensively; d. Bethlehem, Pa. 4. *David III* (d. 1779). "The Syndic"; miss. to Ceylon 1739/40; succeeded Zinzendorf as leader; Moravian archivist.

See also *Moravian Church,* 3, 4.

Nitzsch, Friedrich August Berthold (1832–98). Son of K. I. Nitzsch*; Prot. theol.; b. Bonn, Ger.; educ. Berlin, Halle, and Bonn; prof. Giessen 1868, Kiel 1872; influenced by A. B. Ritschl.* Works include *Grundriss der christlichen Dogmengeschichte* (incomplete).

Nitzsch, Karl Immanuel (Carl; 1787–1868). Father of F. A. B. Nitzsch*; Prot. theol.; b. Borna, Ger.; educ. Wittenberg; mediating theol. (see *Mediating Theol.*); defended Prussian* Union; influenced by F. D. E. Schleiermacher.* Works include *System der christlichen Lehre; Praktische Theologie.* See also *Pericope,* 2.

Nobili, Robert(o) de (1577–1656). B. Montepulciano, Siena province, Tuscany, (or in Rome?), It.; Jesuit 1597; sent as miss. to India 1604, arrived Goa 1605; worked esp. in Madura; an exponent of missionary adaptation (see *Accommodations,* 5), he dressed and lived like a sannyasi (Hindu ascetic). Works include hymns; 2 catechisms; a book on doctrine; a life of Mary in Skt. verse. See also *India,* 9.

Nocturna vigilia. See *Hours, Canonical.*

Noesgen, Karl Friedrich. See *Nösgen, Karl Friedrich.*

Noetus (fl. ca 180–ca. 200). B. probably Smyrna (modern Izmir), W Turkey in Asia; Monarchian; teachings known chiefly from writings of Hippolytus*; allegedly taught patripassianism*; denied doctrine of Logos*; interpreted prologue of John's Gospel allegorically; condemned by syn. of presbyters at Smyrna ca. 200.

Nohrborg, Anders (1725–67). B. Swed.; educ. Västeraas and Uppsala; ordained 1754; pastor Stockholm 1754; court preacher Stockholm 1765; confessional Luth. influenced by Pietism.* Works include

Den fallna människans salighetsordning. See also *Sweden, Lutheran Church in,* 4.

Nolasco, Peter. See *Peter Nolasco.*

Nollau, Louis Eduard (1810–69). B. Prussia; educ. Barmen sem. (see *Missionary Institutes*); sent to Am. 1837 by Rhenish* Miss. Soc. to join other missionaries to Indians; assigned to work near St. Louis, Mo.; Indian project abandoned; served a cong. in Gravois Settlement, near St. Louis; to Afr. via Ger. 1846; returned to Gravois Settlement 1849/50; helped organize German* Ev. Ch. Soc. of the West.

Nominalism. As opposed to realism* and idealism,* it holds that only individual objects have real existence, that "universals" (gen. or abstract ideas) are but names (Lat. *nomina*); e. g., the gen. idea "tree" does not really exist in itself, only individual trees exist; all trees resemble each other; the mind can consider points of resemblance apart from points of difference, but the idea obtained by abstraction of all common points is only a name and has no indep. existence. Exponents of nominalism include Roscellinus,* P. Abelard,* and W. of Ockham.* See also *Philosophy.*

Nomism. Ethical or religious principle acc. to which moral conduct is based on observance of law.

Nommensen, Ludwig Ingwer (Feb. 6, 1834–May 23, 1918). "Apostle of the Batak." B. of poor parents on is. of Nordstrand, NW Ger.; at 12 vowed on sickbed to become miss.; educ. sem. of Rhenish* Miss. Soc.; to Sumatra 1861; trained missionaries, lay brothers, deaconesses; est. institutions for training teachers and pastors; developed ch. order suited for Asiatics. Works include tr. OT stories and the NT into the language of the natives. See also *Batak Protestant Christian Church.*

Nommensen University. See *Batak Protestant Christian Church.*

Nomocanon. In the E Ch., a collection of ecclesiastical canons and civil laws.

Non expedit (Lat. "it is not expedient"). 1868 papal decree named after its first words (cf. 1 Co 10:23); forbade It. RCs to vote in certain elections or hold office under the Kingdom of It., which was hostile to the papacy; modified considerably 1904/05.

Nonchalcedonian Churches. 1. Chs. that reject the Christological definition of the Council of Chalcedon*; sometimes called Oriental Orthodox in distinction from E. Orthodox. See also *Monophysitism.*

2. The Syrian Orthodox Ch. of Antioch (with an archdiocese of the US and Can. and 20 archdioceses in the Middle E) acknowledges the authority of the Orthodox patriarch of Antioch who resides at Damascus. It traces its beginning to 5th-c. Christians in Syria. After the 7th-c. Muslim conquest of Syria it engaged in extensive for. miss. work, as far as China. It reached its zenith in the 12th and 13th c. At the Council of Florence* it was united for several yrs. (1444-53) with the W Ch.

A Syrian Jacobite (see *Jacobites,* 1) bp. of Jerusalem came to the Malabar Coast of India 1665 and brought the Syrian Christians that had seceded from Rome (see *India,* 6) under the authority of the patriarch of Antioch. The Mar* Thoma Ch. separated from the Malabar Jacobite group beginning in the 1870s (final appellate court judgment 1889). The Malankarese Uniat Ch. was est. 1930 (see also *Malabar Christians*). In Syria a rival RC Syrian patriarchate was est. 1783.

In doctrine the Syrian Ch. is similar to the E Orthodox Ch. It accepts the dogmas of the 1st 3 ecumenical councils (see *Councils and Synods,* 4); believes in 9 choirs of angels, perpetual virginity of Mary, procession of the Holy Spirit from the Father, grace as a quality in the soul, 7 sacraments, baptism by triple immersion; divides the Decalog into 4 and 6 commandments. The honor paid saints is not regarded as worship.

3. The Syrian Orthodox Ch. of Malabar in the US; a small group, mainly in the E states.

4. Tradition links Armenians* with the apostles, esp. Thaddaeus-Lebbaeus (Mt 10:3) and Bartholomew. Mass conversion of Armenia took place probably late in the 3d c. Armenian Christians reject Nestorianism,* accept the dogmas of the 1st 3 ecumenical councils and the Henoticon.* RC and E Orthodox efforts to absorb the Armenians proved futile. The mother see is at Echmiadzin, cen. Armenian SSR. Armenians suffered cents. of persecution by Persians, Arabs, and Turks. Their creed reflects the E form of the Niceno-Constantinopolitan; the Holy Spirit proceeds only from the Father. 6 sacraments are recognized: baptism, chrismation, eucharist, penance, marriage, orders; anointing of sick has fallen into disuse, though retained in service books.

Armenian chs. in Am.: Diocese of the Armenian Ch. of N. Am. (under jurisdiction of the see of Echmiadzin); Armenian Apostolic Ch. of Am. (under jurisdiction of the see of Cilicia, Lebanon).

5. Coptic* Ch. immigrants organized the Coptic Assoc. of Am. in NYC 1962. The Diocese of N. Am. of the Coptic Orthodox Ch. was est. 1965; HQ Toronto, Ont., Can.

6. The Ethiopian Orthodox Ch. in the USA was est. 1959. See also *Ethiopic Church.* ACP, EL

Non-Church Movement. See *Uchimura, Kanzo.*

Nonconformist. In gen., one who does not conform to norms, esp. of an est. ch. See also *Dissenter.* Other terms: separatist, indep., *Congregationalist.* More specifically, 1 of many clerics who left the Ch. of Eng. rather than submit to the 1662 Act of Uniformity (see *United Church of Christ,* I A 1). Nonconformists of one kind or another include J. Bunyan,* O. Cromwell,* R. W. Dale,* P. T. Forsyth,* G. Fox,* J. Greenwood,* J. Milton,* C. H. Spurgeon,* I. Watts,* C. Wesley,* J. Wesley,* G. Whitefield, M. Poole.* See also *Recusant.*

None. One of the canonical hours*; the 9th hour (3 p. m. acc. to old reckoning, but often observed several hours earlier in the Middle Ages, possibly giving rise to the word "noon").

Nonfundamental Doctrines. See *Fundamental Doctrines.*

Nonjurors. More than 400 mems. of the Ch. of Eng. (including H. Dodwell, Sr. [see *Dodwell,* 1], T. Hearne,* G. Hickes,* T. Ken,* W. Law,* C. Leslie,* R. Nelson*) who refused to swear allegiance to William III and Mary II 1689 (see *England,* C 2) or their successors, because they (the nonjurors) refused to break their oath to James II. See also *Scotland, Reformation in,* 3.

Nonna. See *Cappadocian Theologians,* 2.

Nonnus of Panopolis (Nonnos; perhaps ca. 400–after 450). B. Panopolis (modern Akhmim [Ekhmim]), Upper Egypt. Regarded as author of *Dionysiaka* (legends about Dionysus [Dionysos]; see *Greek Religion,* 3) and of a paraphrase of John's Gospel. *MPG* 43, 749–920, 1227–84.

Noological Method. See *Eucken, Rudolf Christoph.*

Norbert (ca. 1080/85–1134). B. Xanten, Duchy of Cleves, Ger.; after worldly life, converted and became priest 1115; itinerant preacher France; founded Premonstratensians* 1120; abp. Magdeburg 1126, all Poland (1133?); chancellor for It. 1133 (1132?).

Nordin, Robert. See *Baptist Churches,* 22.

Norelius, Eric (Oct. 26, 1833–Mar. 15, 1916). B. Hassela, Helsingland, Swed.; to Am. 1850; educ. Capital U., Columbus, Ohio; ordained 1856 by the Ev. Luth. Syn. of N. Illinois; spent most of his ministry in Minn. (1859–60 Attica, Ind.); helped found Augustana* Ev. Luth. Ch. 1860 and was its pres. 1874–81, 1899–1911; founded Minnesota Elementar Läroverk in Red Wing 1862 (later moved to Carver, Minn., as Ansgar Academy; relocated 1875 in St.

Peter, Minn., as Gustavus Adolphus Coll.); founded orphanage Vasa, Minn., 1865 and served it 11 yrs. Founded and ed. *Minnesota Posten* 1857; ed. *Augustana;* other works include *T. N. Hasselquist* and *De svenska luterska församlingarnas och svenskarnes historia i Amerika.*

E. Johnson, *Eric Norelius* (Rock Island, Ill., 1954).

Norfolk, Thomas Howard, 3d duke of (1473–1554). 3d duke of Norfolk in the Howard line 1524; opposed T. Wolsey*; became Henry* VIII's most trusted adviser; favored divorce of Henry VIII from Catherine of Aragon; opposed Protestantism.

Norlie, Olaf Morgan (Jan. 11, 1876–June 22, 1962). B. Sioux City, Iowa. Educ. St. Olaf Coll., Northfield, Minn.; Milwaukee (Wis.) State Normal; U. of Wis., Madison, Wis.; United Norw. Luth. Ch. Sem., St. Paul, Minn.; U. of Minn., Minneapolis, Minn. Prof. Luther Coll., Decorah, Iowa, 1919–28, 1933–41; Hartwick Coll., Oneonta, N. Y., 1928–32. Dean Grad. School, Hartwick Sem., NYC, 1932–33. Codifier The Evangelical* Luth. Ch. 1951–54. Hist.; statistician. Ed. *The Translated Bible 1534–1934;* other works include *The Academy for Princes; An Elementary Christian Psychology; The Bible in a Thousand Tongues; Simplified New Testament.*

Norma normans (Lat. "the ruling rule"). Term applied to Scripture because it is the absolute norm of faith *(norma primaria, norma decisionis),* decisive by its own right. Scripture as the decisive norm is absolutely necessary, being the norm which decides whether doctrines are true or false. See also *Norma normata.*

Norma normata (Lat. "the ruled rule"). Term applied to a Confession, or body of Confessions, as secondary norm *(norma secundum quid; norma secondaria; norma discretionis),* determined by the *norma* normans.* The *norma normata* is only relatively necessary. It decides whether a person has clearly understood the true doctrines of Scripture.

Normal Schools. See *Teachers,* 4–6, 26–34.

Norris, John (1657–1711). B. Collingbourne-Kingston, Wiltshire, Eng.; educ. Winchester and Oxford. Rector Newton St. Loe, Somersetshire, 1689; Bemerton, near Salisburg, Wiltshire, 1691. Cambridge* Platonist; advocated theories of N. de Malebranche.* Works include *An Essay Towards the Theory of the Ideal or Intelligible World.*

North, Liturgical. Left, as one faces the altar in a ch.; Gospel* side. See also *Orientation of Churches.*

North Africa Mission. Est. London, Eng., 1881 for work in N Afr.; embraces mems. of all denominations; emphasizes evangelism; HQ Upper Darby, Pa.; mem. IFMA. See also *Africa,* D 3.

North America, An Evangelical Lutheran Ministerium in. See *United Lutheran Church, Synods of,* 22.

North American Baptist Association. See *Baptist Churches,* 33.

North American Baptist General Conference. See *Baptist Churches,* 34.

North American Old Roman Catholic Church. See *Old Catholics,* 4.

North American Phalanx. See *Communistic Societies,* 5.

North Borneo. See *Malaysia,* 1, 5.

North Carolina, United Evangelical Lutheran Synod of. See *United Lutheran Church, Synods of,* 16.

North Church (Dan.). See *Danish Lutherans in America,* 3.

North German Mission Society in Bremen (Norddeutsche Missionsgesellschaft in Bremen). Organized 1836 by merger of 7 miss. unions. A miss. school was est. 1837 Hamburg. The soc. was unionistic. Stricter Luth. elements withdrew in course of time. Missionaries were sent to India and New Zealand 1842, W Afr. 1847, Jap. 1953.

Northern Baptist Convention. See *Baptist Churches,* 8.

Northern Illinois Synod. See *Illinois, Evangelical Lutheran Synod of Northern.*

Northern Ireland. 6 of the 9 counties of the former province of Ulster, N Ireland (Antrim, Armagh, Down, Fermanagh, Londonderry, Tyrone). *Area:* ca. 5,238 sq. mi.; *pop.* (1969 est.): 1,513,000. A 1920 Govt. of Ireland Act offered home rule to both N and S Ireland. N. Ireland is part of the United Kingdom of Gt. Brit. and N. Ireland and has a semi-autonomous govt. Ca. two-thirds of the pop. is Prot., the rest RC. Violence marred the hist. of the country beginning 1966 and arising out of RC reaction against alleged discrimination and Prot. fear that RCs might attain local majority.

Beginning in the mid-1950s, Luths. in N. Ireland were served by the pastor at Dublin (see *Ireland,* 7). The ULC provided a pastor for a ch. at Belfast 1960; he returned to the US 1962.

Northern Presbyterians. See *Presbyterians,* 4.

Northern Rhodesia. See *Africa,* B 2.

Northwest Synod. See *United Lutheran Church, Synods of,* 17.

Northwest Territories. See *Canada,* A 14.

Northwestern College. Est. 1865 at Watertown, Wis., by the Wisconsin* Syn.; connected with Wisconsin* Luth. Sem.; the 1st pub. announcement of its opening called it "The Lutheran College in Watertown." The 2d announcement, 3 mo. later, called it "Wisconsin University and Grammar School." The name "Wisconsin University" was adopted, but the 1867 charter called it "Northwestern University." Called Northwestern Coll. since 1910. See also *Ministry, Education of,* VIII B 21.

Northwestern Lutheran Theological Seminary. Founded 1920 Chicago, Ill., by the Eng. Ev. Luth. Syn. of the Northwest (see *United Lutheran Church, Synods of,* 17) as Chicago Luth. Divinity School. Moved to Fargo, N. Dak., and name changed to Northwestern Luth. Theol. Sem. 1921. Moved to Minneapolis, Minn., 1922, to St. Paul, Minn., 1970. LCA. See also *Lutheran Church in America,* V; *Ministry, Education of,* X N.

Northwestern Publishing House. See *Publication Houses, Lutheran.*

Norton, John (1606–63). Puritan cleric; b. Bishop's Stortford, Hertfordshire, Eng.; educ. Cambridge; to Am. 1635; preached at Plymouth; teacher, then pastor, Cong. ch. Ipswich 1636–56; pastor Boston 1656–63; took part in persecution of Mass. Quakers. Works include *Responsio ad totam quaestionum syllogen* (Lat. treatise on New Eng. ch. govt.).

Norway, Early Christianity in. Norw. heard of Christianity through the Vikings (see also *Iceland,* 1), who made piratical raids on Eng., Scot., Ireland, Fr., and elsewhere and whose captives included Christians. Haakon I ("the Good"; ca. 914–961; king of Norw. 935–961), brought up as a Christian by Athelstan (Aethelstan; 895–940; king of West Saxons and Mercians ca. 924, of Eng. ca. 937), brought Christian influences to Norw. but failed in the attempt to persuade his people to embrace Christianity. Olaf* I and Thangbrand* used violence in trying to Christianize Norway. Olaf* II continued the task, which was completed toward the end of the 11th c. But king and hierarchy fought till late in the 13th c. Decay set in early in the 14th c. Much of the clergy perished in the Black Death 1349. Morals declined in the 15th and early 16th c.

Norway, Evangelical Lutheran Free Church of, The. See *Norwegian Lutheran Free Church, The.*

Norway, Lutheranism in. 1. The Luth. Reformation* reached Norw. through Denmark. Anton(ius), a Ger. monk, is said to have preached ev. doctrines in Bergen in the late 1520s. Two others followed, but without great success. Frederick* I is said to have counseled tolerance for both Luths. and RCs.

2. Christian* III attended the Diet of Worms*;

enforced the Reformation in Norw. beginning 1537, against considerable opposition. For a long time there was no Norw. but only a Dan. Bible, hymnal, and liturgy; the 1st Norw. Bible to achieve common use appeared ca. 1819. Torbjörn Olafssön Bratt (d. 1548), 1st Luth. bp. Trondheim (Drontheim) 1542, studied 2 yrs. in Wittenberg and lived in M. Luther's* house for a time. J. Erikssön gave great impetus to the Reformation. See also *Pederssön, Gjeble; Nilssön, Jens.* By 1600 Lutheranism was est. and organized in Norw.

3. More and more Norw. pastors studied in Ger. The 1607 "Ordinance," or Directory of Worship, required theol. candidates to spend some time at a for. university. A 1629 ordinance required theol. examination of every Norw. candidate at the U. of Copenhagen.

4. Luth. orthodoxy (see *Lutheran Theology After 1580,* 3–5) came to Norw. from Ger.

5. Orthodoxy est. theol. on the Bible and built a lasting reverence for the Word; its emphasis on catechetical instruction produced a notable literature.

6. In the 17th c. proper orthodoxy fell victim to cold insistence on doctrinal correctness, without Gospel warmth and spiritual fervor in Christian life and love.

7. The next wave was Pietism,* which combined with remnants of proper orthodoxy esp. among the laity and such influences as the spiritual hymns and songs of P. Dass* to avert the death of orthodoxy.

8. Ger. Pietism came into Norw. from Halle (see *Francke, August Hermann*). But it began in Norw. as a fanatical and separatistic sectarianism hostile to ch. and ministry, spiteful toward the sacraments, and extremely legalistic. Proper orthodoxy was rescued by such healthy elements as the "Syvstjernen," a pleiad of 7 pastors under leadership of T. v. Westen* in Romsdals Amt, near Molde and Kristiansund (Christiansund), W Norw. Confirmation was instituted 1736. See also *Pontoppidan, Erik.* By ca. 1750 Pietism had run its course and dissipated into subjectivism and recurrence of its early fanaticism.

9. Next came rationalism* tinged with the spirit of J. J. Rousseau* and Voltaire* and strongly impregnated with elements of the Enlightenment.* Revelation gave way to reason. God, virtue, immortality were the passwords. Science, culture, and art became the main concern.

10. Johan Norda(h)l Brun (1745–1816; bp. Bergen 1804; poet) opposed the theol. of the Enlightenment. H. N. Hauge* played a significant role in directing the ch. back to proper orthodoxy, but with possible overemphasis on sanctification, with resultant legalism.

11. Prominent theologians at the U. of Christiania (Oslo) include C. P. Caspari,* S. B. Hersleb,* G. C. Johnson,* S. J. Stenersen.* With resurgent orthodoxy arose an interest in missions (see *Missionary Institutes; Norwegian Foreign Missions*), but with a division of interest as bet. ch.-related socs. and schismatic groups. See also *Laestadius, Lars Levi.*

12. Modernism* and higher* criticism also came to Norw. from Ger. In response, a "free faculty," organized 1908, est. an indep. theol. sem. 1925/26 Oslo. Conservative profs. include Leiv Aalen (b. 1906 Rennesöy, Norw.), Sverre Aalen (b. 1909 Rennesöy, Norw.; educ. Tübingen, Halle, Marburg, Leipzig, Copenhagen, Lund), O. K. Hallesby,* Olaf Eedvard Moe (1876–1963; b. Modum, Norw.), Olav Guttorm Myklebust (b. 1905 Bergen, Norw.), John Nome (b. 1904 Öyslebö, Norw.), Sigurd Vilhelm Odland (1857–1937; b. Bergen, Norw.; cofounder "free faculty"; resigned 1916), Andreas Seierstad (b. 1890), Ivar P. Seierstad (b. 1901 Hedrum, Norw.).

The ch. suffered in WW II under Ger. occupation of Norw. (See *Berggrav, Eivind*). Its relation to the state was redefined, but it still is a state ch.

13. Norw. Lutheranism was transplanted to Am. by immigration in the middle of the 19th c. HAP

A. C. Bang, *Den norske kirkes historie* (Christiania, Norw., 1912); P. G. Lindhardt, *Den nordiske kirkes historie* (Copenhagen, Den., 1945); H. C. Christie, *Den norske kirke i kamp,* 2d ed. (Oslo, Norw., 1945); R. T. Nissen, *De nordiske kirkers historie* (Christiania [Oslo], Norw. 1884).

Norwegian and Danish Evangelical Free Church Association. See *Evangelical Free Church of America.*

Norwegian-Danish Augustana Synod in America, The ("Danish" and "in America" dropped 1878). Norwegians (O. J. Hatlestad* et al.) withdrew from the Scand. Ev. Luth. Augustana Syn. in Am. (see *Augustana Evangelical Lutheran Church,* 9–10) at Andover, Ill., June 1870. What followed is not entirely clear; it involves the question whether the action which the Norwegians immediately took toward organization was temporary. In this action, June 1870, Hatlestad was elected pres. of the "Norwegian-Danish Augustana Synod." But a const. was to be adopted later. In Aug. 1870 a conf. was held at St. Ansgar, Iowa, with Hatlestad chm., to discuss with C. L. Clausen* the possibility of having the latter and those assoc. with him join the new group. At this meeting the matter of a const. was also discussed; Hatlestad's const. (on which action had been postponed in June and which specified the whole Book* of Concord as confessional base) was rejected; a const. prepared by Clausen (which specified only the traditional Dan.-Norw. confessions [3 ecumenical* creeds, UAC, SC] as doctrinal base) was adopted with only minor changes, and with it the name The Conf. for the Norw.-Dan. Ev. Luth. Ch. in Am. (often shortened to Norw.-Dan. Conf., or simply the Conf.); it was also proposed to dissolve the Norw-Dan. Augustana Syn.; Hatlestad objected and went home; in his absence the conf. resolved to dissolve the Norw-Dan. Augustana Syn. so that its mems. might join The Conf. for the Norw.-Dan. Ev. Luth. Ch. in America. Hatlestad reacted by meeting with his followers Oct. 1870 at Jefferson Prairie (near Clinton), Wis.; at this meeting the "dissolution" action of the Aug. 1870 conf. was declared null and void. Continuity of organization was declared by (1) claiming validity for the const. of the Scand. Ev. Luth. Augustana Syn. till a new const. be approved; (2) adopting (a) the const. which Hatlestad had presented at Andover, Ill., June 1870, and at St. Ansgar, Iowa, Aug. 1870, and (b) the name The Norw.-Dan. Augustana Syn. in Am. Name changed 1878 to The Norw. Augustana Syn. See also *Danish Lutherans in America,* 3; *United Norwegian Lutheran Church in America, The.*

Norwegian-Danish Conference. See *Norwegian-Danish Augustana Synod in America, The.*

Norwegian Evangelical Lutheran Church in America, The. See *Evangelical Lutheran Church, The,* 8–10, 12–13; *Evangelical Lutheran Synod; Madison Settlement.*

Norwegian-Danish Evangelical Lutheran Church in America, The Conference for the. See *Clausen, Claus Laurits; Evangelical Lutheran Church,* 10; *Norwegian-Danish Augustana Synod in America, The; United Norwegian Lutheran Church in America, The.*

Norwegian Foreign Missions. These include (1) The Norw. Mission Soc. (Det Norske Misjonsselskap), founded 1842 Stavanger. Union of socs. that sprang up in Norw. beginning with one in Stavanger 1826; till 1842 they cooperated with the Basel* Miss. Soc. and the Rhenish* Miss. Society. The state ch. and clergy remained almost entirely aloof from it; this led to The Norw. Ch. Mission by Schreuder (see 4). A miss. school, founded 1843 Stavanger, closed 1847, reopened 1858 (see also *Missionary Institutes*). Fields have included Zululand, Madagascar, China, Cameroon, Jap., Hong Kong, Taiwan. (2) The Norw. Miss. to Israel (Den Norske Israelmisjon). Continuation of Israels Venner (The Friends of Israel), a Luth. organization founded 1844 Stavanger. Fields have included Romania, Hung., Israel. (3) Santal Miss. of the Northern Chs. (Nordiske Santalmision). Founded 1867 NE India as a self-supporting venture by H. P. Börresen* and L. O. Skrefsrud* (both left the Gossner* Miss. Soc. in the 1860s) as Indian Home Mission to the Santals; also known as Benegaria Miss. (Benagaria; Bengarhia; so called after the place in Bihar that was prominent in the beginning of the work). Received regular support from groups in Norw., Den., and Gt. Brit. beginning 1876, in course of time also from Swed., and since 1892 from the US. Reorganized 1958/59 as Northern Ev. Luth. Ch. After the 1947 division of India the E. Pakistan Ev. Luth. Ch. was organized. See also *Asia,* B 2; *Bodding, Paul Olaf.* (4) The Ch. of Norw. Miss. by Schreuder (Den Norske Kirkes Misjon ved Schreuder). Also known as Schreudermisjonen (Schreuder Miss.). Founded 1873 by H. P. S. Schreuder* as a mission of the Norw. state ch. (see 1) with Zululand, NE Natal, S Afr., as its field. The Norw. Luth. Ch. in Am. (ELC 1946; part of The ALC end of 1960) took over the miss. 1927, with Norway providing funds and manpower. Helped form the Ev. Luth. Ch. in S. Afr. – SE Region (or Syn.) 1960 (see also *Africa,* B 5). (5) The Ev. Luth. Free Ch. Miss. (Den evangelisk-lutherske Frikirkes Misjon). Fields have included China, Taiwan, and Jap. (6) Norw. Luth. Miss. (Norsk Luthersk Misjonssamband). Founded 1891. Fields have included China, N Manchuria, Jap., Taiwan, Hong Kong, Ethiopia, Tanganyika, Sumatra. (7) The Scand. Christian Miss. to Buddhists (Den Nordiske Kristne Buddhistmisjon). Founded in the 1920s. Supported by groups in Norw., Swed., and Den. Fields have included China and Jap. (8) The Norw. Miss. to Tibet (Den Norske Tibetmisjon). Founded 1938. Fields have included Tibet and Nepal. (9) The Norw. Miss. Among Muslims (Den Norske Muhammedanermisjon). Founded 1940. Fields have included India and W. Pakistan.

Norwegian Lutheran Church of America, The. See *Evangelical Lutheran Church, The,* 13–14.

Norwegian Lutheran Church of Canada. See *Canada,* A 20.

Norwegian Lutheran Free Church, The (The Ev. Luth. Free Ch. of Norw.). In 1877 and 1878 a number of Congs. seceded from the state ch. of Norw. to gain greater autonomy and doctrinal discipline. They formed an organization that operates several schools, including a Bible school and miss. school. Fields have included Jap. and Formosa (Taiwan). Pub.: *Budbaereren; Nuorttanaste.*

Norwegian Synod. See *Evangelical Lutheran Church, The,* 8; *Evangelical Lutheran Synod.*

Norwegian Synod of the American Evangelical Lutheran Church, The. See *Evangelical Lutheran Synod,* 2.

Nösgen, Karl Friedrich (1835–1913). Luth. scholar; b. Halberstadt, Ger.; educ. Halle and Berlin; vicar Schloppe, W Prussia, 1859; prison chaplain Graudenz, W Prussia, 1861; pastor Klein Furra, near Nordhausen, Saxony, Ger., 1873; prof. NT exegesis Rostock 1883. Works include *Geschichte der neutestamentlichen Offenbarung.*

Nösselt, Johann August (1734–1807). B. Halle, Ger.; educ. Halle; prof. theol. Halle; as exegete he followed the strict hist.-philol. method of J. A. Ernesti.*

Nostra aetate. See *Vatican Councils,* 2.

Noth, Martin (1902–68). B. Dresden, Ger.; educ. Erlangen, Rostock, Leipzig; lecturer Greifswald and Leipzig; prof. Königsberg 1930, Bonn 1945. Works include *Geschichte Israels; Die Gesetze im Pentateuch; Die Welt des Alten Testaments.*

Nothelferseminar. See *Löhe, Johann Konrad Wilhelm.*

Notitia historica. See *Fides historica.*

Notker (ca. 840–912). "Balbulus" ("the Stammerer," from Lat. *balbus,* "stammering"). B. Heiligau (now Elgg), near Zurich, or Jonschwil (near St. Gall), Switz.; monk at monastery of St. Gall (see *Gall*); known esp. for sequences (see *Sequence*).

E. Wellesz, *Eastern Elements in Western Chant* (Boston, 1947).

Notker (ca. 940–1008). Swabian; perhaps educ. at St. Gall (see *Gall*); bp. Liège 972 (969?); built many fine bldgs.; improved moral and intellectual standards.

Notker (ca. 950–1022). "Labeo" (Lat. "one who has large lips," from *labia,* "lip"); "Teutonicus" ("the German"); b. Thurgau, Switz.; monk at monastery of St. Gall (see *Gall*). Tr. Lat. classics and other writings into Ger.; helped fix the form of the Ger. language.

Notre Dame Cathedral of Paris, France. Example of early Fr. Gothic style; begun 1163; consecrated 1182; W front added 1200–20; desecrated in Fr. Revolution (see *Church and State,* 15; *France,* 5); reopened for Christian worship 1795; in restoration since 1845. See also *Church Architecture,* 10.

Notre-Dame-la-Grande Church of Poitiers, France. See *Church Architecture,* 7.

Nott, Henry (1774–May 2, 1844). B. Eng.; LMS miss. to Tahiti, Eimeo (Mooréa), and Huahiné 1796. Tr. Bible into Tahitian.

Nottrott, Alfred (1837–1924). Gossner* Miss. Soc. miss. to India 1867; pres. Gossner Miss. Soc. 1887–1913. Tr. the Herford Luth. Catechism of 1690 into Hindi; other works include a Mundari grammar and Bible tr.

"Notwehrblatt." See *Lochner, Friedrich Johann Carl.*

Notz, Eugen Adolf (Oct. 7, 1847–Feb. 5, 1903). Brother of F. W. A. Notz*; b. Haberschlacht, Württemberg, Ger. Educ. sem. at Blaubeuren, Ger.; Northwestern U., Watertown, Wis.; Conc. Sem., St. Louis, Mo. Instructor Northwestern U. 1874–75; ordained 1877; pastor Menomonie, Wis.; prof. Heb. and OT exegesis Wis. Syn. sem. Milwaukee 1878–1903.

Notz, Friedrich Wilhelm August (Frederick William Augustus; Feb. 2, 1841–Dec. 16, 1922). Brother of E. A. Notz*; b. Lehren-Steinsfeld, near Weinsberg, Württemberg, Ger.; educ. Maulbronn and Tübingen; private tutor; to Am. 1866; tutor Ga. 1866–68; prof. (Gettysburg) Pa. Coll. 1868, Muhlenberg Coll., Allentown, Pa., 1869–72; prof. Gk. and Heb., Northwestern U., Watertown, Wis., 1872–1912 (inspector 1874–81). Secy. Ger. Am. Press Assoc. 1870; pres. Ger. School Assoc. of Pa. 1871. Tr. J. K. Dietrich, *Institutiones catecheticae,* into Ger.; ed. *Schul-Zeitung* 1876–94 (title changed Mar. 1879 to *Lutherische Schul-Zeitung*).

Nous. See *Psychology,* G 1.

Nova Scotia. See *Canada,* A 1–3, 27; *United Lutheran Church, Synods of,* 18.

Novalis. See *Hardenberg, Friedrich von.*

Novatian (Lat.: Novatianus; b. probably ca. 200 AD). B. perhaps It., possibly Phrygia; priest in Rome; differences with Cornelius* regarding treatment of the lapsed (see *Lapsi*) led to his election as antipope (bp. of Rome) 251; excommunicated; followers called Novatians; martyr ca. 257/258. Works include *De Trinitate* (*MPL,* 3, 911–982; opposed Monarchianism*); *De cibis Judaicis.*

Novatianism. Named after Novatian,* who held that the lapsed (see *Lapsi*) should not be readmitted to the ch., which is to be a community of none but saints. The schism spread from Spain to Syria; disappeared by the end of the 7th c.

Novatus (3d c.). Presbyter of Carthage, N Afr.; ordained Felicissimus* deacon; fled to Rome to escape the wrath of Cyprian* of Carthage; assoc. of Novatian.*

Novena. In RCm, 9 days' devotion to obtain special graces or favors.

Novice. 1. One who is preparing in a formal period of probation for membership in a religious institute; the period of time is called novitiate and it usually follows a period of postulancy (see Postulant). 2. See *Neophyte.*

Noviomagus. See *France,* 13.

Nowell, Alexander (Nowel; Noel; ca. 1507–1602). Angl. cleric; b. Whalley, Lancashire, Eng.; educ. Oxford; dean St. Paul's, London, 1560. Works include *Large Catechism; Middle Catechism; Small Catechism* (very similar to that of the 1549 Book* of Common Prayer).

Noyes, John Humphrey (1811–86). B. Brattleboro, Vt.; educ. Dartmouth Coll. (Hanover, N. H.), Andover (Mass.) Theol. Sem., and Yale Coll. Theol. Dept., New Haven, Conn.; held perfectionism*; advocated free love and "Bible communism," which he promoted in the community he est. in the 1830s at Putney, Vt.; arrested 1846; fled to cen. N. Y. State, where he est. the Oneida* Community 1848; fled to Can. 1880 to escape prosecution for adultery. See also *Communistic Societies.*

Nuelsen, John Louis (1867–1946). B. Zurich, Switz. Educ. Drew Theol. Sem., Madison, N. J.; Cen. Wesleyan Coll., Warrenton, Mo.; Berlin and Halle, Ger. Pastor Sedalia, Mo., 1890. Prof. St. Paul's Coll., Minn., 1890–92; Cen. Wesleyan Sem., Warrenton, Mo., 1894–99; Nast Theol. Sem., Berea, Ohio, 1899–1908. M. E. bp. 1908; in charge of M. E. Ch. in Eur. 1912, retired 1940. Ecumenist. Works include *Some Recent Phases of German Theology; Kurzgefasste Geschichte des Methodismus; Das Heilserlebnis im Methodismus; Die Ordination im Methodismus; John Wesley und das deutsche Kirchenlied; Luther: The Leader.*

Numinous. Term popularized by R. Otto*; designates an inconceivable concept of God pointed to in the word "holy."

Nun of Canterbury (Nun of Kent). See *Barton, Elizabeth.*

Nunc dimittis. See *Canticles; Worship, Parts of,* 13.

Nuncio. See *Legates.*

Nuns. Women belonging to a religious order. In RCm the life of nuns is primarily one of contemplation and mortification.

Nürnberg Bible Society. See *Bible Societies,* 2.

Nürnberg Declaration, The. 1870 statement of Ger. RCs against the decree of papal infallibility.*

Nürnberg, Diet of. Several diets were held at Nürnberg, Ger., from 1522 to 1543, including one convened Mar. 1522, dismissed May 1522, reconvened Dec. 1522, closed 1523. At this diet, convened by Charles* V to devise means to defeat the Turks and to settle internal religious difficulties, the RCs acknowledged the need to reform the ch., declared willingness to reform, and demanded enforcement of the Edict of Worms.* The diet refused to enforce the Edict of Worms, demanded a free council within a yr., and stipulated that neither M. Luther* nor his followers should meanwhile give any occasion for disturbance.

Another diet, convened Nov. 1523, opened Jan. 1524, dissolved Apr. 1524. The RCs regarded the "100 grievances" (Lat. *gravamina;* actually there finally were 102 grievances of the Ger. nation against the papal court; they began accumulating esp. in the 2d half of the 15th c. and received official form at the 1518 Augsburg* Diet and were further crystallized as a result of the 1521 Diet of Worms*; they were presented at the 1522–23 Diet of Nürnberg) as the product of spiteful private individuals and advised enforcement of the Edict of Worms; political events prevented effective enforcement of the edict.

Nürnberg Normal Books. Writings accepted 1573 as norms by pastors of Nürnberg and Brandenburg-Ansbach: the ecumenical* creeds; M. Luther's* catechisms; AC; Ap; SA; P. Melanchthon's* *Loci communes* and *Examen ordinandorum* and *Definitiones appellationum; Confessio Saxonica* (see *Lutheran Confessions,* A 5); Answer to the Impious Bavarian Articles *(Responsio ad impios articulos Bavaricos);* Answer Concerning the Controversy of Stancarus* *(Responsio de controversia Stancari);* Brandenburg-Nürnberg ch. order.

Nürnberg Religious Peace. Temporary settlement 1532 at Nürnberg of difficulties bet. RC and Prot. states. In this peace (or truce) the emp. assured the Prots. that the status quo would be maintained until a council or diet met. See also *Schmalkaldic League.*

Nürnberger Bibel. See *Weimarische Bibelwerk, Das.*

Nursery Class. See *Parish Education,* B 4.

Nursery Roll. See *Parish Education,* B 2, 3.

Nusa Tenggara. See *Indonesia,* 1.

Nussmann, Adolph (Nüssmann; Nuessmann; Nussman; Aug. 1739–Nov. 3, 1794). B. Münster, Westphalia, Ger.; Franciscan priest; converted to Lutheranism; to Am. 1773; thorough scholar; laid foundations for the Luth. Ch. in N. C.

J. B. Moose, "Adolph Nussmann, Pioneer Lutheran Preacher in North Carolina," *The Lutheran Church Quarterly,* XIII (1940), 375–391.

Nyasaland. See *Africa,* B 2.

Nyaya. See *Brahmanism,* 4.

Nyberg, Lorenz Thorstonsen (Laurentius Theophilus; Lawrence; Thorstansen?; 1720–92). Luth. pastor of Swed. descent; educ. Uppsala; ordained in Swed.; to Am. 1744; served the Ger. cong. at Lancaster, Pa.; with some of his mems. he joined the Moravian Ch. 1746; caused disturbances in chs. in Pa., Md., and N. J.; returned to Eur. ca. 1750.

Nygren, Anders Teodor Samuel. See *Lund, Theology of; Sweden, Lutheranism in,* 6.

O

Oak, Synod of the. See *Quercum, Synodus ad.*

Oakeley, Frederick (1802–80). Tractarian; Margaret Chapel, London (where All Saints, Margaret Street, was later built), became a center of the Oxford* Movement under his ministry 1839–45; joined RC Ch. 1845; priest 1847. Works include *The Church of the Bible; Historical Notes on the Tractarian Movement.*

Oates, Titus (ca. 1649–1705). Son of Anabap. preacher; created panic of 1678–81 by spreading stories of RC intrigue (Popish Plot).

Oath. 1. Solemn appeal to God (Gn 21:23; Ex 22:11; 1 Sm 14:39, 44; 20:3; Mt 26:63, 64), a person (Gn 42:15; 2 Sm 11:11), or an object (Mt 5:34) as attestation of truth. Oaths of covenants were elaborate (Gn 21:28-31). A proper oath by God's name shows allegiance to Him (Dt 6:13). Lifting hands (Gn 14:22), putting a hand under a thigh (Gn 24:2), passing bet. a divided sacrificial animal (Jer 34:18), standing before an altar (1 K 8:31) may be connected with an oath.

2. Oaths have been connected with vows, covenants, wagers, or ordeals from early times. Primitive peoples believed that evil spells, even harm and destruction, could be magically imposed on persons and things by oaths.

3. In the OT, oaths by false gods were forbidden (Jer 5:7; Am 8:14), oaths by the true God enjoined (Dt 6:13; 10:20; Nm 30:2; Is 65:16). Some formulas: "as the Lord lives" (Ju 8:19), "as God lives" (2 Sm 2:27), "as thy soul lives" (1 Sm 1:26). In adjuration an oath is laid on a person, or he is caused to swear (1 K 8:31; Eze 17:13).

4. In the NT, Mt 5:34, 36 and Ja 5:12 are misunderstood by some as forbidding all oaths; cf. Mt 26:63-64; Ro 1:9; Ph 1:8; Gl 1:20; 2 Co 1:23; 1 Th 2:5; Heb 6:16. The ideal situation is pictured Mt 5:37.

5. Some early fathers held that oaths placed people in danger of perjury. The ch. in gen. has upheld proper use of oaths.

6. AC XVI 2: Christians may take required oaths; Ap XVI 1: Christians may take an oath when the government requires it. FC Ep XII 15, SD XII 20 condemns Anabaps. for teaching that a Christian cannot take an oath in good conscience nor pay oath-bound feudal homage to his territorial sovereign or liege lord. M. Luther (LC, I, 65-66): "If it is so understood, you have easily solved the question that has tormented so many teachers: why swearing is forbidden in the Gospel, and yet Christ, St. Paul, and other saints took oaths. The explanation is briefly this: We are not to swear in support of evil (that is, to a falsehood) or unnecessarily; but in support of the good and for the advantage of our neighbor we are to swear. This is a truly good work by which God is praised, truth and justice are established, falsehood is refuted, people are reconciled, obedience is rendered, and quarrels are settled. For here God himself intervenes and separates right from wrong, good from evil."

Obedience. Willing submission to proper restraint, control, or command. God demands (1) perfect obedience to His Law (Dt 27:26; Mi 6:8; Lk 10:28); (2) obedience of children to their parents (Eph 6:1-3); (3) submission of servants to their masters (Eph 6:5-8; Cl 3:22-24); (4) respect for, and obedience to civil authority (Ro 13:1-7; 1 Ptr 2:13-16). Cf. Gn 6:22; 12:1-4; Jos 11:15; 2 K 18:6; Lk 2:39; Acts 26:19; Heb 5:8.

Obedience of Christ, Active and Passive. See *Justification,* 5.

Obendiek, Harmannus (1894–1954). Ref. theol. of Ostfriesland, Ger.; instructor Elberfeld 1932–41; co-founder of Church Coll., Wuppertal, 1945; prof. practical theol. Works include *Satanismus und Dämonie in Geschichte und Gegenwart; Der Teufel bei Luther; Glauben oder Schauen; Die Obrigkeit nach dem Bekenntnis der reformierten Kirche.*

Oberammergau. Village in the Bavarian Alps; famous for performance, every 10 yrs., of a passion play by residents of the community, where it originated as result of a vow made in gratitude for cessation of a plague 1633. See also *Religious Drama,* 5.

Oberlin, Jean Fréderic (Johann Friedrich; 1740–1826). Pastor in the Steintal, a barren valley in the Vosges Mts. Through preaching, educ., soc. work, and economic endeavors he improved the Christian life of people and transformed the villages of the valleys into flourishing communities. His influence continues in the Oberlinhaus.*

Oberlin Theology. Doctrine of Christian perfection taught at Oberlin (Ohio) Coll. by C. G. Finney,* A. Mahan,* and assocs. Did not claim that a Christian could be absolutely perfect, but only that he could grow toward perfection. Held that all responsible character pertains to the will in its voluntary attitude and action and that each individual determines for himself, in exercise of his own freedom, under motives that gather about him, whatever is morally good or bad in his character and life; that sin is a voluntary failure to meet obligation; that righteousness is a voluntary conforming to obligation; that neither sin nor holiness can be transmitted, inherited, or imputed. Atonement cannot involve transfer of our guilt to Christ or of His righteousness or merit to us. The repentance required as a condition of salvation is the renunciation of sin, an obligation that rests on every sinner and that is always in his power. The power to sin involves the power to renounce sin, and this voluntary renunciation is the change required of every sinner in order for him to obtain acceptance with God. The work of the Holy Spirit in a sinner's conversion is a moral work, wrought by the presentation of motives that induce repentance; the subsequent work of sanctification and preservation in faith is essentially of the same nature and is wrought by the Holy Spirit through the truth. The sovereignty of God always works in harmony with the freedom and responsibility of the creature, so that one factor in man's salvation must always be his own voluntary cooperation. See also *Perfectionism,* 4.

H. S. Smith, R. T. Handy, and L. A. Loetscher, *American Christianity: An Historical Interpretation with Representative Documents,* II, 1820–1960 (New York, 1963). LJM

Oberlinhaus. Founded 1874 at Nowawes (Potsdam-Babelsberg), Ger., as a diaconate institution. Originally a school for small children, it became a deaconess motherhouse to which an institution for crippled, deaf, dumb, and blind was added.

Oberursel Seminary. See *Germany, Lutheran Free Churches in,* 3.

Objectivism. Movement inaugurated by Ayn Rand (b. Russ. 1905). Endorses selfishness (not greed) over against altruism and teaches the perfectibility of man. Denies faith and revelation; deifies reason; rejects Christianity and belief in the existence of God.

Oblate Fathers (Oblates of Mary Immaculate). Soc. of priests and laymen leading a common life, formed 1816 by Charles Joseph Eugène de Mazenod (1782–1861) to repair the havoc of the Fr. Revolution. Tries to influence rural and industrial populations through missions and retreats that inculcate devotion to the Sacred Heart and to Mary as a supernatural means of regeneration. Fosters young men's assocs., Cath. clubs, etc., and has many institutions of learning, including industrial and reform schools.

Oblations. Offerings; the term is used to designate bread and wine offered for consecration in the Eucharist and gifts presented at the Eucharist for the clergy, sick, and poor.

Obookiah, Henry (Obookaiah; ca. 1792–1818). B. Kau, Owhyhee (one of the Hawaiian Is.); parents slain when he was ca. 10 yrs. old; lived for a time with an uncle, a pagan priest; to Am. with a ship captain from New Haven, Conn.; with S. J. Mills* at Andover Sem.; converted and joined Cong. Ch.; studied at ABCFM school for Am. Indians, Pacific Islanders, and Orientals at Cornwall, Conn. Inspired zeal for work on Hawaiian Is.

Obrecht, Jakob (ca. 1450–1505). Flemish composer of the Neth. School; priest 1480; master of polyphony. See also *Passion, The.*

Obscurantism. Opposition to intellectual enlightenment.

Obscure Men, Letters of. See *Epistolae obscurorum virorum.*

Observants (Observantines). Franciscans* who observed the strict rule; existed as a separate body 15th–19th c.; inc. into the Order of Friars Minor 1897.

Occam, William of. See *Ockham, William of.*

Occasional Ceremonies. Ceremonies or offices serving certain special occasions; in the Angl. and E Orthodox Ch. they include, e. g., Baptism, Marriage, Burial.

Occasional Conformity Act. See *Corporation Act of 1661.*

Occasional Offices. See *Occasional Ceremonies.*

Occasionalism. View developed esp. by A. Geulincx* and N. de Malebranche*; denied possibility of mind-matter interaction; assumed that on occasion of each soul process God produces corresponding motion or sense-perception in the body.

Occom, Samson (Ockum; Occum; 1723–92). Mahican Presb. cleric; b. Mohegan, New London Co., Conn.; converted ca. 1740 in Great* Awakening; studied privately 1743–47; teacher and minister to Montauk Indians on Long Is. 1749–59, preaching for Congregationalists; ordained Presb. 1759; miss. to Oneida Indians 1761–63; solicited funds in Eng. for Indian charity school, inc. 1769 as Dartmouth Coll.; itinerant preacher in New Eng. 1768–89; pastor among Oneida in N. Y. during last yrs. of his life; hymnist. Issued *A Choice Collection* (or *Selection*) *of Hymns and Spiritual Songs.*

Occultism (from Lat. *occultus,* "hidden; concealed"). Belief in hidden or mysterious powers and the possibility of controlling them. See also *Theosophy; Spiritism.*

Ochino, Bernardino (1487–1564). B. dist. dell' Oca, Siena, It.; Observant Franciscan ca. 1504; Capuchin 1534; Prot. ca. 1541; fled to Geneva, Switz., 1542 to escape the Inquisition*; in Augsburg 1545–47, London 1547–53; pastor Zurich 1553–63; banished; made his way via Basel, Mulhouse in Alsace, and Nürnberg to Poland and finally to Moravia. Works include a catechism issued while he was in Zurich. See also *Socinianism,* 1.

Ochs, Carl Ernst Christoph (Feb. 10, 1812–Nov. 16, 1863). B. Greglineng, Württemberg, Ger.; miss. of the Dresden Ev. Luth. Miss. (see *Leipzig Evangelical Lutheran Mission*) to India 1842; engaged in indep. work 1859; joined Danish* Miss. Soc. 1863.

Ochsenford, Solomon Erb (Nov. 8, 1855–June 19, 1932). B. near New Hanover, Douglass Twp., Montgomery Co., Pa.; educ. Muhlenberg Coll., Allentown, Pa., and Lutheran Theol. Sem., Philadelphia, Pa.; ordained 1879 Pa. Ministerium; pastor in Pa. and N. Y.; prof. Muhlenberg Coll. 1899–1909. Ed. *Lutheran Church Almanac* 1883–1904; other works include *Documentary History of the General Council of the Evangelical Lutheran Church in North America.*

Ockham, William of (Occam; ca. 1280? [some say ca. 1300]–ca. 1349). "Doctor Invincibilis; Venerabilis Inceptor." Scholastic philos.; b. probably Ockham, Surrey, near London, Eng.; Franciscan; educ. Oxford; pupil, later rival, of J. Duns* Scotus; defended evangelical poverty against John XXII (see *Popes,* 13); imprisoned at Avignon, Fr.; escaped; excommunicated 1328; probably spent remainder of life at Munich, Ger. Advocated independence of civil rule. Nominalist; held that the real is always individual, universals are abstractions (a view also called terminism or Ockhamism). Works include *Quaestiones et decisiones in quattuor libros sententiarum; De sacramento altaris et de corpore Christi.* See also *Christian Faith and the Intellectual,* 3; *Franciscans; Nominalism; Philosophy; Via moderna.*

Octave. Originally the 8th day after a ch. feast or festival, beginning the count with the day of the feast or festival itself; later the term came to denote all 8 days.

Octavian(us). See *Augustus.*

Octoechos (from Gk. *oktoechos* [*sc. biblos*], "book of 8 tones"). Liturgical book of the E Orthodox Ch.; contains variable parts of the services from the 1st Sun. after Pent. to the 10th Sun. before Easter.

Oculi. See *Church Year,* 14, 16.

Odd Fellows, Independent Order of. Secret social and benevolent fraternal society. Originated in Eng. in the 18th c.; reason for the name is indeterminate. Introd. into the US 1819. Consists of 4 degrees: Initiatory (White), Friendship (Pink), Love (Blue), Truth (Scarlet). Deistic; moralistic; its God is not the Triune God but an indeterminate Supreme Being; salvation is not by faith in Christ but by a good moral life as taught in the order. The privilege of a burial ritual that asserts eternal rewards is extended to every mem. Rebekah lodges are an adjunct to the Indep. Order of Odd Fellows. PHL

Odilia (Othilia; ca. 660–ca. 720). Founded a convent (Niedermünster) before 710 in the Vosges Mountains, Alsace; it became a center of pilgrimages but died out 1542.

Odilo (ca. 962–Dec. 31, 1048 or Jan. 1, 1049). 5th abbot Cluny.* Under his leadership Cluniac monasteries grew in number and influence. Introd. commemoration of All Souls' Day (see *Church Year,* 14; *Departed, Commemoration of*).

Odo (ca. 879–942). 2d abbot Cluny,* succeeding Berno 927. Canon St. Martin of Tours. Entered monastery at Baume, in Burgundy, 909. Raised Cluny to high position and influence. Works include moral essays; a life of Gerald of Aurillac; sermons; an epic on the Redemption.

Odo (Oda; ca. 875–ca. 959). "Odo the Good." Abp. Canterbury 942; active in bldg. programs and in reform of the clergy.

Odo (Eudes; ca. 1036–97). B. Normandy; half brother of William the Conqueror (1027–87; king of Eng. 1066–87); bp. Bayeaux 1049; fought at Hastings 1066; involved in pol. affairs of Eng.; ruled Eng.

tyrannically during William's absence; supported the 1st Crusade (see *Crusades*).

Oecolampadius, Johannes (Oekolampadius; Grecized from Ger. *Huszgen,* or *Huschke,* changed to *Hausschein;* 1482–1531). B. Weinsberg, Württemberg, Ger.; educ. Heidelberg; helped D. Erasmus* issue his ed. of the Gk. NT; influenced by M. Luther*; to Basel 1522; influenced by H. Zwingli*; held that there is a figure of speech in "body" and "blood" in the words of institution of the Lord's Supper; attended the Colloquy of Marburg 1529 (see *Lutheran Confessions,* A 2). Works include commentaries on OT prophets; translations of early ch. fathers. See also *Reformed Confessions,* A 5; *Sickingen, Franz von; Switzerland,* 2.

Oehler, Gustav Friedrich (von) (1812–72). B. Ebingen, Württemberg, Ger.; educ. Tübingen; prof. Breslau 1845, Tübingen 1852; specialized in theol. of the OT.

Oekolampadius. See *Oecolampadius.*

Oemcken (Oemeken; Oemichen). See *Ömcken.*

Oepke, Albrecht (1881–1955). B. Arle, Ostfriesland; tutor at miss. sem. Leipzig 1914; prof. NT Leipzig U. 1922. Works include commentaries on epistles of Paul.

Oetinger, Conrad(us) (Konrad). See *Öttinger, Konrad.*

Oetinger, Friedrich Christoph (1702–82). B. Göppingen, Ger.; educ. Tübingen; private tutor there 1731–38; pastor Hirsau 1738, Schnaitheim 1743, Walddorf 1746; dean Weinsberg 1752, Herrenberg 1759; prelate Murrhardt 1766. Pietist, mystic, alchemist, theosophist.

Oetting, Walter Wayne (Apr. 25, 1929–Feb. 24, 1964). B. Davenport, Iowa; educ. Valparaiso (Ind.) U. and Conc. Sem., St. Louis, Mo. Pastor St. Joseph, Mich., 1955–59; prof. Conc. Sem., St. Louis, Mo., 1959–64. Wrote *The Church of the Catacombs.*

Oettingen. See *Öttingen.*

Oettli, Samuel (1846–1911). B. St. Gall, Switz.; educ. Basel, Göttingen, and Zurich; pastor at various places; prof. Bern 1879, Greifswald 1895. Collaborator in *Kurzgefasster Kommentar,* ed. H. L. Strack* and O. Zöckler*; other works include *Der Kampf um Babel und Bibel; Die revidierte Lutherbibel.*

Offense. In the Biblical sense, anything whereby one is led to sin or error or whereby he is encouraged to continue therein. The Gk. word *skandalon,* of which "offense" is a tr., is used to designate the trigger stick of a trap; a trap, snare, or impediment put in the way to cause one to stumble or fall; stumbling block. The seriousness of giving offense is evident from the fact that offense is an obstacle placed in the way of one's salvation (1 Co 8:11; Ro 14:15). Christ and the Gospel are an offense to some (cf., e. g., Mt 11:6; 13:57; 15:12; 17:27; Jn 6:61; Ro 9:33; 1 Co 1:23; Gl 5:11; 1 Ptr 2:8). A Christian's conduct may be an offense to some (cf., e. g., Ro 14:13-15, 19-21).

Offense is *given* by uncharitable use of Christian liberty, without consideration for the weak (1 Co 8:9), or unchristian life (Mt. 18:6; Ro 2:23-24). Offense may be unjustly *taken* on basis of a prejudiced, loveless judgment of a Christian's actions or words.

A Christian must give offense when avoiding offense would involve denial or yielding of a truth of God's Word (Gl 2:11-14). RGL

Offerings, Church. See *Finances in the Church.*

Offermann, Henry Frederick (July 11, 1866–May 21, 1953). B. Hanover, Ger.; educ. Kropp* Sem.; to US 1889; studied Semitics at U. Pa.; Ger. secy. Pa. Ministerium 1900–08; prof. NT Luth. Theol. Sem., Mount Airy, Philadelphia, Pa., 1910–44. Ed. *Lutherisches Kirchenblatt.* Other works include *The Jesus of the New Testament; Introduction to the Epistles and Gospels of the Church Year.*

Offertory (Lat. *offertorium*). Originally the offertory was the 1st liturgical act of the *missa* fidelium.* It was the offering of one's self through prayer and supplication, supplemented by placing on the altar gifts that might be used as sacramental elements (bread and wine), or used in the agape (see *Agape,* 2), or given to the poor. In the Middle Ages the offertory as an act of the people was replaced by sacerdotal ceremonies and prayers of different character. These anticipated the consecration and the sacrifice of the mass* and became the "Little Canon" by the 14th c. During the various ceremonies a choral group sang a Psalm and antiphon* in Gregorian chant (see *Gregorian Music*). Each Sun. and feast or festival day had its own offertory (see also *Propers*). Since these offertories were usually short, further musical settings were added later, including motets, songs, and organ compositions. In 1593 G. P. da Palestrina* issued 68 offertories for the whole yr. In the 18th and 19th c. organ offertories were written by F. A. Guilmant,* C. C. Saint-Saens,* C. M. Widor,* et al. In It. such organ music was called *elevazióne* in reference to the elevation.* The Luth. Ch. refused to adopt the RC view of the offertory. M. Luther* was willing to drop the offertory entirely and begin the liturgy of Holy Communion with the preface.* But many did not follow him in this. In the 17th c. Georg Winer's (1583–1651) "Schaffe in mir, Gott, ein reines Herze" became popular as an offertory. Some used penitential hymns, hymns of praise, and Lenten hymns as the offertory. Some used the exhortation in place of the offertory. But the exhortation and penitential and Lenten hymns were not readily accepted by those who stressed the joyful eucharistic nature of the service. "Create in Me a Clean Heart, O God," sung to a melody from hymns assoc. with J. A. Freylinghausen,* is widely used. Plain chant settings of Psalm texts are also used. WEB

Office, Congregation of the Holy. See *Curia,* 2 d.

Office of Christ. See *Christ Jesus,* III.

Office of the Dead. See *Burial.*

Office of the Holy Communion. See *Worship, Parts of,* 11–15.

Office of the Keys. See *Keys, Office of the.*

Office of the Word. See *Worship, Parts of,* 3–10.

Officer, Morris. See *Africa,* C 7.

Officium divinum. See *Hours, Canonical.*

Oftedal, Sven (Mar. 22, 1844–Mar. 30, 1911). B. Stavanger, Norw.; educ. Oslo (Norw.) U. and Paris, Fr.; to US 1873; pastor Minneapolis, Minn., 1873–81; prof. NT Augsburg Theol. Sem. (see *Ministry, Education of,* X G) 1873–1905; helped found LFC. Ed. *Kvartalskrift* and *Kirkebladet.* See also *Publication Houses, Lutheran.*

Ohio, District Synod of. See *United Lutheran Church, Synods of,* 19.

Ohio, East, Synod of the Evangelical Lutheran Church. See *General Synod of the Evangelical Lutheran Church in the United States of America, The,* 3.

Ohio, Synod of, of The United Lutheran Church in America. See *United Lutheran Church, Synods of,* 19.

Ohio and Other States, The Evangelical Lutheran Joint Synod of. 1. Names used by this body include Gen. Conf. of the Ev. Luth. Preachers in Ohio and the Adjacent States (General Conferenz Der Evangelisch-Lutherischen Prediger in Ohio und den angrenzenden Staaten) 1818–29; The Ger. Ev. Luth. Ministerium in Ohio and the Neighboring States (Das Deutsche Ev. Luth. Ministerium in Ohio und den benachbarten Staaten) 1818–49; Syn. and Ministerium of the Ev. Luth. Ch. in the State of Ohio 1830–43; Ev. Luth. Joint Syn. of Ohio and Other States 1844–; Ev. Luth. Syn. of Ohio and Adjacent States (1849 charter); The Ev. Luth. Joint Syn. of Ohio and Other States 1902–30.

In the last decades of the 18th c. many Luths. moved to the Northwest Territory, which included Ohio. The number increased after Ohio became a state 1802/03. Early Luth. pastors in Ohio include Wilhelm Georg Forster (William George; Foster; Foerster; d. 1815; licensed as candidate by Pa. Ministerium 1798, ordained 1802; pastor Shenandoah Co., Va.; to Fairfield Co., Ohio, ca. 1806), P. Henkel (see *Henkels, The,* 2), J. Steck,* and J. Stauch.* The 1st of 7 special conferences was held Oct. 17–19, 1812, Washington Co., Pa.; the 7th was held Sept. 20–24, 1817, New Philadelphia, Ohio.

2. Sept. 14, 1818, a conf., or syn. (the minutes use both terms), was formed at Somerset, Ohio, but without a specific name; the title page of the minutes uses the name Gen. Conference of the Ev. Luth. Preachers in Ohio and the Adjacent States; pres. J. Stauch, secy. P. Henkel, treas. G. H. Weygandt.* The body declined to join The General* Syn. of the Ev. Luth. Ch. in the USA 1820.

3. A sem. was est. 1830 at Canton, Ohio, transferred 1831 to Columbus, Ohio; 1st prof. W. Schmidt* (1803–39); see also *Ministry, Education of,* X E. In 1831 the body divided into an E Dist. of the Ohio Syn. and a W Dist. of the Ohio Syn. In course of time other districts were formed. By the mid-1840s it was commonly called a "Joint Syn." (Ger. "Allgemeine Synode"). The term arose out of the fact that its districts met together, or "joined," in the gen. conv. The body met biennially as a delegate syn. since 1854. The word "Joint" was officially included in the name 1902.

4. In Nov. 1836 the Syn. and Ministerium of the Eng. Ev. Luth. Chs. in Ohio and Adjacent States (later called The Eng. Ev. Luth. Syn. and Ministerium of Ohio and Adjacent States) was organized as an Eng. Dist., or Dist. Syn., at Somerset, Ohio, by mems. of the Joint Syn., which adopted a provision forbidding this new dist. to join any other body without approval of the Joint Syn. The majority of this dist. severed connection with the Joint Syn. 1840 and joined the Gen. Syn. 1843 (see *General Synod of the Evangelical Lutheran Church in the United States of America, The,* 3). The minority continued the Eng. Dist., which seceded from the Joint Syn. and joined the Gen. Syn. 1855 as the Eng. Syn. and Ministerium (see also *General Synod of the Evangelical Lutheran Church in the United States of America, The,* 3). A dissenting minority organized a new Eng. Dist. at Circleville, Ohio, 1857. It joined the Gen. Council 1867 as the Eng. Ev. Luth. Dist. Syn. of Ohio and Adjacent States without approval of the Joint Syn. and separated from the latter 1869. But a minority organized 1869 as an Eng. Dist. loyal to the Joint Syn.

5. The Joint Syn. of Ohio was influenced by the Pa. Ministerium and the Tenn. Syn.; it was also affected by unionism and New* Measures. The *Lutheran Standard* was est. 1842, *Lutherische Kirchen-Zeitung* 1860. Relations were est. through J. G. Burger* and J. A. Ernst* with J. K. W. Löhe.* Influx of Ger. candidates strengthened conservatism under leadership of W. Sihler* in the early 1840s. The conservatives withdrew 1845 (see *Document of Separation*); yet the Joint Syn. resolved 1848 to adhere to the Luth. Confessions and took an antilodge stand beginning 1854. Contact with the Mo. Syn. in the 1856–59 Free* Luth. Conferences deepened the confessionalism of the Joint Syn. For lack of a clear statement by the Gen. Council on the Four* Points the Joint Syn. did not join the Council. Fraternal relations were est. with the Mo. Syn. 1872 (see *Lutheran Church – Missouri Synod, The,* V, 15). The Joint Ohio Syn. helped organize the Synodical* Conf. As a result of the Predestinarian* Controversy beginning Jan. 1880, the Joint Syn. withdrew from the Syn. Conf. 1881; spokesmen for the position of the Joint Syn. included H. A. Allwardt,* F. A. Schmidt,* and F. W. Stellhorn.* Unsuccessful efforts were made at intersyn. conferences 1903–06 to heal the breach; see also *Chicago Theses* (Intersynodical Theses; Theses for Union).

6. On relations with the Iowa Syn. see *Iowa and Other States, Evangelical Lutheran Synod of,* 9. See also *National Lutheran Council; American Lutheran Church.*

7. The Joint Ohio Syn. engaged in home mission work; conducted a miss. among Negroes in Baltimore, Md., and in cen. Ala., and among Jews, esp. with Pittsburgh, Pa., as a center; in 1912 it took over the Hermannsburg stations at Kodur and Puttur, among Telugu in E India (see also *India,* 13).

8. Schools: a sem. at Columbus, Ohio (see par. 3); Capital U., Columbus (see *Ministry, Education of,* VIII A 1); Luther Sem. (the "Practical Dept." added 1881/82 to the sem. at Columbus moved 1884 to Afton, Minn., as Luther Sem., moved 1892/93 to St. Paul, Minn., united 1932 with Wartburg Sem., Dubuque, Iowa); Hebron Coll. and Academy, Hebron, Nebr. (opened 1911 as academy, expanded 1924 into a Jr. Coll.; closed 1942); Luther Coll., Regina, Sask., Can. (see *Luther College,* 5); St. John's Academy and Coll., Petersburg, W. Va. (opened 1921 as academy, enl. 1931 into a Jr. Coll.; closed 1933); Woodville (Ohio) Normal School (est. 1882, closed 1923); Pacific Sem., Olympia, Wash. (opened 1907; theol. dept. discontinued 1911; coll. dept. discontinued with the close of the school year 1917); practical sem., Hickory, N. C., 1887–1912.

C. Spielmann, *Abriss der Geschichte der evangelisch-lutherischen Synode von Ohio u. a. Staaten, in einfacher Darstellung, von ihren ersten Anfängen bis zum Jahre 1846* (Columbus, Ohio, 1880); P. A. Peter and W. Schmidt, *Geschichte der Allgemeinen Evang.-Lutherischen Synode von Ohio und anderen Staaten* (Columbus, Ohio, 1900); E. A. Boehme, *Handbuch der Evangelisch-Lutherischen Synode von Ohio und anderen Staaten: Manual of The Evangelical Lutheran Joint Synod of Ohio and Other States* (Columbus, Ohio, 1910); C. V. Sheatsley, *History of the Evangelical Lutheran Joint Synod of Ohio and Other States From the Earliest Beginnings to 1919* (Columbus, Ohio, 1919); M. Loy, "The Joint Synod of Ohio," *The Distinctive Doctrines and Usages of the General Bodies of the Evangelical Lutheran Church in the United States,* 4th ed., rev. and enl. (Philadelphia, Pa., 1914), pp. 5–35; B. H. Pershing, "Lutheran Synodical Organization in Ohio Before 1850," *The Lutheran Church Quarterly,* IX (1936), 402–418; G. W. Mechling, *History of the Evangelical Lutheran District Synod of Ohio Covering Fifty-three Years 1857–1910* (n. p., 1911); W. D. Allbeck, *A Century of Lutherans in Ohio* (Yellow Springs, Ohio, 1966).

Ohio Yearly Meeting of Friends Church (Evangelical Friends Alliance). See *Friends, Society of,* 10.

Ohl, Jeremiah Franklin (June 26, 1850–Jan. 21, 1941). B. Cherryville, Northampton Co., Pa.; educ. Lutheran Theol. Sem., Philadelphia; pastor Quakertown, Pa., 1874–93; organizer and rector Luth. Deaconess Motherhouse at Milwaukee, Wis., 1893–98; city miss. Philadelphia, Pa., 1899–1930, supt. 1903–30. Active in prison reform work. Hymnist; liturgist.

Ohly, Emil (1821–90). B. Buchenau, Grossherzogtum Hessen, Ger.; positive theol., though in the Prussian Union; pastor Ginsheim. Ed. *Vademecum pastorale* and homiletical works.

Oikonomos, Constantine (1780–1857). Gk. theol.; opposed W influences in Gk. religious life. Works include writings on philol. and on the hist. of literature.

Oils, Holy. Oils used in liturgical ceremonies. In RCm: oil of catechumens (olive oil applied before

Baptism), chrism (olive oil and balm applied after Baptism, at confirmation, at conferring holy orders [see *Hierarchy*]), and oil used at various consecrations and blessings. Blessed, or consecrated, on Maundy Thu. See also *Myron.*

Okeghem, Jean d' (Ockeghem; Jan van; Johannes Ockenheim; other variations occur; ca. 1430–ca. 1495). Composer; b. Flanders; at court of Charles VII (see *France,* 3) 1453, head of the chapel 1454; treas. St. Martin's at Tours 1459; regarded by many as founder of the 2d Netherlands school of contrapuntists, distinguished from the 1st by an easier and more imaginative use of counterpoint.

O'Kelly, James (O'Kelley; ca. 1757 [ca. 1735?]–1826). B. perhaps Ireland (or S Va.?); Meth. preacher Va. and N. C. 1778–84; elder and mem. ruling council M. E. Ch. 1784–92; withdrew; est. Rep. Meth. Church in the early 1790s. See also *Methodist Churches,* 1; *United Church of Christ,* I B.

Okinawa. Only large is. (ca. 454 sq. mi.; *pop.* [1974 est.]: 850,000) in is. group (also called Okinawa) in cen. chain of Ryukyu Is., bet. East China Sea and Pacific Ocean. Scene of heavy fighting in WW II; occupied by US forces 1945; came under US control by treaty 1951; N part of the is. group returned to Jap. 1954; Ryukyu Is. returned to Jap. administration 1972 under terms of a 1971 treaty, now form the Jap. prefecture of Okinawa. Buddhism and Confucianism have appealed successfully to upper classes. K. F. A. Gützlaff* visited the Ryukyus 1832; RC work began 1844; a Brit. miss. effort extended from 1845 to 1855; the Meth. Episc. Ch. began work ca. the end of the 19th c.; others included Bap., Presb., and Holiness groups. Chs. joined during WW II to form the Ch. of Christ on Okinawa. Post-WW II miss. endeavors include Luth. work initiated 1959 by LCMS.

Olaf I (Olaf Tryggvesson; Trygvason; 969–1000). King of Norw. 995–1000; b. while parents were in exile; brought up at court of Vladimir I (ca. 956–1015; "Vladimir the Great"; ruled Russ. 980–1015; converted to Christianity ca. 989); converted to Christianity in Scilly Islands; led Viking expedition 994 and ravaged coasts of Fr., Eng., and Ireland; to Norw.; brought bps. and priests from Eng. and tried to Christianize Norway. See also *Iceland; Norway, Early Christianity in.*

Olaf II (Olaf Haraldsson; Olave; ca. 995–1030). "The Fat"; patron saint of Norw.; king of Norw. 1016–1028/30; brought bps. and priests from Eng. and tried to complete the conversion of Norw. by force; rebellion resulted; fled to Russ. 1028; killed in battle at Stiklestad in attempt to reconquer Norw. See also *Norway, Early Christianity in.*

Olafsson, Stefan (ca. 1620–88). Educ. Copenhagen, Den.; dean Vallanes, Iceland; lyric poet. Tr. hymns of T. H. Kingo* into Icelandic.

Old Catholic Church in America. See *Old Catholics,* 4.

Old Catholics. 1. Some RCs rejected the decree of papal infallibility and absolutism (see *Nürnberg Declaration, The; Vatican Councils,* 1 b), seceded from the RC Ch., and est. an indep. organization known as Old Catholics.

2. Leaders included J. J. I. v. Döllinger,* J. Friedrich,* J. H. Reinkens,* F. H. Reusch,* and J. F. v. Schulte.*

3. The 1st Old Cath. Congress met Sept. 1871 Munich, the 2d in Sept. 1872 at Cologne. An electoral body chose Reinkens bp. June 1873; he was consecrated in Aug. The 3d Congress met Sept. 1873 Constance and adopted a const. Some Old Caths. considered themselves bound by the Council of Trent* until 1889, when the doctrinal basis of Old Caths. was formalized in the Declaration of Utrecht.* Old Caths. recognize doctrines accepted before 1054. The Bible and tradition are admitted as sources of revelation. But Old Caths. have been affected by Prot. influences. The clergy is permitted to marry. Bible reading is encouraged. The mass is celebrated in the vernacular.

4. Abortive miss. efforts in Am. early in the 20th c. resulted in Old Cath. chs. not recognized by those of Eur., e. g., N. Am. Old RC Ch. (formerly N. Am. Cath. Ch.); Old Cath. Ch. in Am.; Old Cath. Archdiocese of the Americas and Eur.; Ref. Cath. Ch. (Utrecht Confession), Province of N. Am.; Am. Cath. Ch., Archdiocese of N. Y.

5. The 1931 Bonn Agreement allowed intercommunion bet. the Angl. Ch. (including the Prot. Episc. Ch.) and the Old Cath. Church. Old Caths. have shown interest in ecumenical movements.

See also *Christian Catholic Church of Switzerland, The; Jansenism.*

Old Fashioned Revival Hour, The. See *Radio and Television Evangelism, Network,* 5.

Old German Baptist Brethren. See *Brethren,* 3.

Old High German Religious Poetry and Prose. Dates from the 8th c.; includes the Weissenburger Katechismus, the *Heliand,** and the eschatological poem *Muspilli.* See also *Otfrid.*

Old Lights. See *New Lichts; New Lights.*

Old Lutherans. Originally this name was applied to Luths. who refused to join in the Prussian* Union (see also *Germany, Lutheran Free Churches in,* 1). There was a similar reaction against unionism and rationalism in Saxony. Old Luths. continued in Ger. and Poland under various names including Altlutheraner; Breslauer Synode; Verein der evangelisch-altlutherischen Kirchengemeinden; Ev.-luth. Kirche in Westpolen; Ev.-luth. Kirche in Preussen, later Ev.-luth. Kirche in Altpreussen, and since 1945 Evangelisch-lutherische (altlutherische) Kirche.

The name Old Lutherans was also applied to confessional Luths. who emigrated to Am. 1838–48 under such men as J. A. A. Grabau* and M. Stephan* Sr. See also *Buffalo Synod; Lutheran Church – Missouri Synod, The,* II; *Symbolists.* ARS

V. Ferm, *The Crisis in American Lutheran Theology* (New York, 1927); C. Mauelshagen, *American Lutheranism Surrenders to Forces of Conservatism* (Athens, Ga., 1936); R. D. Owen, "The Old Lutherans Come," *CHIQ,* XX, No. 1 (Apr. 1947), 3–56; F. Lichtenberger, *History of German Theology in the Nineteenth Century,* tr. and ed. W. Hastie (Edinburgh, 1889).

Old Order Amish Church. See *Mennonite Churches,* 3 a.

Old Order (Wisler) Mennonite Church. See *Mennonite Churches,* 3 a.

Old Order, or Yorker, River Brethren. See *Brethren, River.*

Old People's Homes. See *Aging and Infirm, Homes and Services for.*

Old Roman Catholic Church, North American. See *Old Catholics.*

Old Roman Creed. See *Ecumenical Creeds,* A 4.

Old School Baptists. See *Baptist Churches,* 11.

Old School Presbyterians. See *New School Presbyterians.*

Old Side Presbyterians. See *Presbyterian Churches,* 4 a.

Old Style Calendar. See *Julian Calendar.*

Old Syriac Version. See *Bible Versions,* C.

Oldcastle, John (ca. 1377–1417). Lord, or Baron, Cobham; b. probably in the manor of Almeley, Herefordshire, Eng.; m. Joan, Lady Cobham, 1409; friend of Prince of Wales (later Henry V; 1387–1422; king of Eng. 1413–22); convicted of Lollardism (see *Lollards,* 2) and given 40 days to recant 1413; escaped; headed Lollard conspiracy; captured; hanged and burned as heretic and traitor. Thought by some to be the basis of Shakespeare's Falstaff in *Henry IV.*

R. Fiehler, "Sir John Oldcastle Reconsidered," *CTM*, XXVIII (1957), 579–594, and *The Strange History of Sir John Oldcastle* (New York, 1965).

Oldenberg, Hermann (1854–1920). Indologist; b. Hamburg, Ger.; prof. Kiel 1889, Göttingen 1908; engaged in research in early religions of India. Issued texts and translations.

Oldendorp, Johannes (ca. 1488–1567). Luth. jurist and canonist; b. Hamburg, Ger.; prof. law Greifswald, Rostock, and Frankfurt an der Oder; developed a Luth. concept of natural* law influenced by Aristotle,* humanism,* and P. Melanchthon.*

Olearius. 1. *Johann(es)* (1546–1623); b. Wesel, Ger.; educ. Marburg and Jena; rector Gymnasium at Königsberg 1574; prof. theol. Helmstedt 1578; pastor and supt. Halle 1581; son-in-law of T. Hesshus*; strict Lutheran. 2. *Gottfried* (1604–85); son of 1, brother of 3; Luth. pastor and supt. Halle; hymnist. Works include *Ideae dispositionum biblicarum; Annotationes biblicae; Aphorismi biblici; Halygraphia.* 3. *Johann(es)* (1611–84); son of 1, brother of 2; b. Halle; preacher and supt. Halle and Weissenfels; hymnist. Hymns include "Herr, öffne mir die Herzenstür"; "Gelobet sei der Herr"; "Tröstet, tröstet meine Lieben"; "Ach, wie gross ist deine Gnade"; "Jesus selbst, mein Licht, mein Leben." 4. *Johann Gottfried* (1635–1711); son of 2, brother of 5; b. Halle; educ. Leipzig and Jena; diaconus Halle; supt. and consistorial councillor Arnstadt; wrote in field of patristics; hymnist. Hymns include "Komm, du wertes Lösegeld"; "Es war die ganze Welt." 5. *Johann(es)* (1639–1713); son of 2, brother of 4; prof. Leipzig. Works include *De stylo Novi Testamenti; Hermeneutica sacra.* 6. *Johann Christian* (1646–99); son of 3; supt. and pastor Querfurt 1672, Halle 1685; consistorial councillor Halle; orthodox Lutheran; hymnist. 7. *Johann Christoph(orus)* (1668 [1669?]–1747); son of 4; b. Halle; polymath; held various ch. positions in Arnstadt; hymnologist. 8. *Gottfried* (1672–1715); son of 5; b. Leipzig; prof. theol. Leipzig 1708.

Olevian(us), Caspar (Kaspar; 1536–87). B. Trier, Ger.; prof. Heidelberg 1561; helped prepare Heidelberg Catechism (see *Reformed Confessions,* D 2); attended Maulbronn* Colloquy 1564; furthered Calvinism also in Berleburg and Herborn.

Olier, Jean Jacques (1608–57). B. Paris, Fr.; RC priest 1633; founded Sulpicians.*

Oive Branch Synod. See *Indiana Synod, Northern; United Lutheran Church, Synods of,* 8.

Olivétan, Pierre Robert (Petrus Robertus Olivetanus; Louis Olivier; ca. 1506–38). B. Noyon, Fr.; adopted Luth. doctrines 1528 during studies at Orléans; fled to Strasbourg; preached to Waldenses* in Piedmont 1532–35; tr. Bible into Fr.; said to have been called Olevitan (a reference to olive oil) because he burned the midnight oil.

Olivetans. Indep. branch of Benedictines*; est. 1313/19 at Accona, near Siena, It.; Accona came to be called Monte Oliveto, whence the name of the order.

Olmec. See *Mexico,* B.

Olshausen, Hermann (1796–1839). Brother of J. Olshausen*; b. Oldesloe, Holstein, near Hamburg, Ger.; educ. Kiel and Berlin; prof. Königsberg 1821, Erlangen 1834; upheld the genuineness of the 4 canonical gospels. Works include a commentary on the NT.

Olshausen, Justus (1800–82). Brother of H. Olshausen*; b. Hohenfelde, Holstein, Ger.; prof. oriental languages Kiel 1823, Königsberg 1853. Works include a Heb. grammar; commentary on the Psalms.

Olsson, Olof (Mar. 31, 1841–May 12, 1900). B. Karlskoga, Vaermland (Varmland; Värmland; Vermland), Swed.; educ. Uppsala, Swed., and Leipzig, Ger.; to Am. 1869; pastor Lindsborg, Kans., 1869; prof. Augustana Theol. Sem., Rock Island, Ill. (see *Ministry, Education of,* X I) 1876–88 [87?]; pastor Woodhull, Ill., 1890; pres. Augustana Coll. and Sem. 1891–1900; musician. Works include *Vid korset* (tr. *At the Cross*).

Oltramare, Paul (1854–1930). Swiss Indologist and historian of religions; held that progress of civilization made religion largely unnecessary and that religion results from ignorance and inability.

Olympic Pantheon. See *Greek Religion,* 2.

Omaha. See *Indians, American,* 5.

Oman. See *Middle East,* L 7.

Oman, John Wood (1860–1939). Presb. theol.; b. Orkney, Scot.; minister Alnwick, Northumberland, Eng., 1899–1907; prof. Westminster Coll., Cambridge, 1907–35. Rejected such concepts as grace, faith, and infallible revelation; emphasized sincerity.

Ömcken, Gerdt (Gerhard; Oemcken; Oemeke[n]; Oemichen; Omeken; Omich[ius]; Omken; ca. 1485 [1500?]–1562). B. Kamen, Westphalia, Ger.; spokesman for Lutheranism in the Rhine-Westphalia-Lippe territory; pastor Soest 1532, Lemgo 1533–35; supt. Minden 1535–40; present at the Feb. 1537 meeting of the Schmalkaldic* League and signed the SA.

Omnipotence. Attribute of God by reason of which He can and does perform whatever He pleases (Ps 115:3; 135:6).

Omnipresence. Attribute of God acc. to which He is present everywhere. See also *Immanence of God.*

Omniscience. See *Knowledge,* 1.

Omophorion. See *Vestments, Clerical,* 1.

Oncken, Johann Gerhard (1800–84). B. Varel, Ger.; influenced by Presbs. and Meths. in Leith (near Edinburgh), Scot., and in London, Eng.; joined the Continental Soc., whose object it was to oppose rationalism on the Continent; to Hamburg 1823; est. a S. S. 1824; agent Edinburgh Bible Soc. 1828; inclined to Bap. views 1829; immersed in Elbe 1834; est. Bap. congs. in Ger., Holland, Scand., and E Eur.

Onderdonk, Henry Ustick (Onderdonck; 1789–1858). Prot. Episc. cleric; b. NYC; ordained 1815; rector Brooklyn 1820; bp. Pa. 1836; hymnist.

Oneida. See *Indians, American,* 9.

Oneida Community. Communistic perfectionist settlement est. 1848 in Madison Co., N. Y., by J. H. Noyes*; reorganized 1880/81 as a joint stock company; became known for "Community" silverware. See also *Communistic Societies.*

Onkelos, Targum of. See *Bible Versions,* B.

Onomasticon (from Gk. *onomazo,* "to name"). List of names or words, esp. in a specialized field, in the form of an encyclopedic dictionary. See also *Geography, Christian,* 3.

Ontario. See *Canada,* A 4–6, 8–12, 15, 19, 20; 25–28; C.

Ontological Argument. See *Apologetics, Christian,* 4 I a; *God, Arguments for the Existence of.*

Ontology. 1. Study or theory of being or essence. 2. Theory regarding kinds of entities and abstract entities to be admitted to a language system.

Oordt, Johan Frederik van. See *Groningen School.*

Oosterzee, Johannes Jacobus van (Jan Jakob; 1817–82). Ref. theol.; b. Rotterdam, Neth.; educ. Utrecht; preacher Eemnes-Binnen (in the province of Utrecht) 1841, Alkmaar 1843, Rotterdam 1844; prof. theol. Utrecht 1863. Works include *De Theologie des Niewen Verbonds,* tr. *The Theology of the New Testament.*

Open Questions. In the 19th c. and 1st part of the 20th c. this term played an important role in Lutheranism in America. Attempts at definition affected relations bet. the Iowa Syn. and the Mo. Synod. In an 1867 colloquy bet. the 2 syns. it was agreed to regard the term as equivalent to "theol. problems" in this sense, that the Bible does not solve them; e. g., on which creation day were the angels created? See also *"Brief Statement"; Fundamental Doctrines,* 4; *Toledo Theses* (Ohio and Iowa), IV.

Opera supererogationis (Lat. "works paid in addition"). The RC Ch. teaches that by works of penance and charity saints gained more merit than was needed to meet the obligations of duty and the requirements of the Law for salvation; this excess of merit, with Christ's merit, is in the keeping and at the disposal of the ch. and can be applied by it to the needs of those who have not enough merit of their own to keep them out of purgatory. From this "treasury of the ch." the RC Ch. claims to impart in granting indulgences.*

Operationalism. See *Dewey, John.*

Operative Grace. See *Grace.*

Opere operantis, ex. See *Ex opere operantis.*

Opere operato, ex. See *Opus operatum.*

Opgjör. See *Madison Settlement.*

Ophites. See *Gnosticism,* 7 i, j.

Opinio, Historica. See *Fides Historica.*

Opitz, Martin (Obizo; Opitz von Boberfeld; 1597–1639). Poet, metrical reformer, critic; b. Bunzlau, on the Bob(e)r R., Ger.; educ. Frankfurt an der Oder and Heidelberg; prof. Weissenburg; held various pol. and diplomatic offices. Hymns include "Brich auf und werde lichte."

Opium War. See *China,* 7.

Optatam totius. See *Vatican Councils,* 2.

Optatus (4th c. AD). Bp. Milevis, Numidia, N Afr.; polemicist; opposed Donatists.

Optimism. In philos., the view that this world is the best possible, or even absolutely good.

Opus operatum. Term used to express RC doctrine that the 7 RC sacraments* confer grace by the act in itself, apart from faith. Canons and Decrees of the Council of Trent, Sess. VII, Canons on the Sacraments in General, Canon 8: "If anyone says that by the sacraments of the New Law grace is not conferred *ex opere operato,* but that faith alone in the divine promise is sufficient to obtain grace, let him be anathema." Ap XIII 18: "We condemn the whole crowd of scholastic doctors who teach that unless there is some obstacle, the sacraments confer grace *ex opere operato,* without a good disposition in the one using them." Cf. Ap IV 63; XII 12. Not to be confused with *ex* opere operantis.* See also *Grace, Means of,* I, 8.

Opzoomer, Cornelis Willem (1821–92). Philos. and jurist; b. Rotterdam, Neth.; educ. Leiden; prof. Utrecht 1846; positivistic empiricist; urged expulsion of the unscientific from religion; leader of Dutch liberal theol.

Oral Transmission Theory. See *Higher Criticism,* 16.

Orange, Second Synod of. See *Pelagian Controversy,* 11.

Orange Free State. See *Africa,* B 5.

Orarion (orarium). Stole worn over the left shoulder by deacons in Eastern* Orthodox chs. See also *Vestments, Clerical.*

Oratorians. 1. Mems. of the Oratory of Divine Love, founded ca. 1517. See also *Counter Reformation,* 4. 2. Mems. of the Oratory founded by F. de' Neri* and authorized 1575. See also *Counter Reformation,* 7. 3. Mems. of the Fr. Oratory (also called Oratory of Jesus), founded 1611 Paris, Fr.; dissolved in the Fr. Revolution (see *France,* 5); reest. 1852 by A. J. A. Gratry* et al.

Oratorio. Sacred or secular musical composition with libretto usually consisting of arias, recitatives, choruses, and orchestral music; sometimes includes spoken narration or dialog; action, costume, and scenery sometimes used till ca. 1730. The name oratorio seems derived from dramatic services of F. de' Neri* at an oratory in Rome.

A. Hammerschmidt* contributed to the early development of the oratorio. Oratorios in the more modern sense were written by A. Scarlatti,* A. Lotti,* J. A. Hasse,* and N. Jommelli. Luth. composers of oratorios include H. Schütz,* J. S. Bach* (whose *Christmas Oratorio* is a series of 6 cantatas integrated into a unit), and K. P. E. Bach.* Eng. composers of oratorios include G. F. Handel,* who influenced F. J. Haydn.* *Oedipus Rex,* a scenic oratorio by Igor Fedorovich Stravinsky (b. 1882 at Oranienbaum, near St. Petersburg, Russ.), has been accorded great acclaim.

See also *Elgar, Edward; Franck, César Auguste; Gounod, Charles François; Hindemith, Paul; Honegger, Arthur; Liszt, Franz; Massenet, Jules Émile Frédéric; Mendelssohn-Bartholdy, Jakob Ludwig Felix; Saint-Saens, Camille; Spohr, Ludwig.*

A. Schering, *Geschichte des Oratoriums* (Leipzig, 1911); A. W. Patterson, *The Story of Oratorio* (London, 1915).

Oratory. 1. Place of prayer. In RC canon law: a structure, other than a parish ch., set aside for prayer and mass; may be public (open to all), semipublic (principally for mems. of the religious community in whose house it is erected), or private (domestic; for a private family). 2. See *Oratorians.*

Order of Ancient Free and Accepted Masons. See *Freemasonry,* 1–4.

Order of DeMolay. See *Freemasonry,* 8.

Order of Patrons of Husbandry (Grange; Nat. Grange; originally Nat. Grange of the Patrons of Husbandry). Agricultural trades union or soc. based on occupational interests; has many features of a lodge but is not a lodge in the strict sense. Purposes: industrial benefits and soc. improvement of mems. Exercises considerable influence, esp. in promoting cooperation among farmers. Politics are kept out. Has a ritual and 7 degrees. Uses signs, pledges, and allegorical ceremonies characteristic of secret socs. A typical injunction: "Friends, your present condition is but an example of Faith, and emblematic of a higher confidence in a Supreme Being. We are constantly passing blindly along the pathway of life, events occurring that we do not understand, and often encountering difficulties and obstructions in our way; but we should press forward, having faith that God will ultimately bring us into the broad and pleasant fields of Paradise." In all degrees pledges are made to observe the precepts and injunctions and not to reveal the secrets. Initiation on application only, without ceremonial, has not been allowed. The order is more like a union than a secret fraternal order, but it has pan-religious and deistic features. The grange hall has an altar. Prayers are spoken. Officers of the Assem. of Demeter, which has charge of the secret work, are called priest or priestess. A burial service is provided. The ritual of the Nat. Grange is mandatory for all subordinate granges. But Grange law says: "A member cannot be required to do anything in conflict with his religious convictions, and entire freedom of conscience is assured to all members in matters of prayer . . . but so long as he holds a position in the Grange he must perform his duties thereof, in accordance with the laws and usages of the Order." TG, PHL

Order of the Eastern Star. See *Freemasonry,* 5.

Order of the Nobles of the Mystic Shrine, Ancient Arabic. See *Freemasonry,* 9.

Order of the Rainbow. See *Freemasonry,* 6.

Order of Worship. See *Worship, Orders of.*

Ordered Ranks. See *Hierarchy.*

Orders, Holy. See *Hierarchy.*

Orders, Major. See *Hierarchy.*

Orders, Minor. See *Hierarchy.*

Orders in the United States, Early Roman Catholic. Fr. and Sp. conquerors were accompanied by mems. of various orders, esp. Franciscans,* Dominicans,* Jesuits,* and Carmelites,* who est. their work in many places. Paulists* originated in Am.

Ordinance. See Norway, *Lutheranism in,* 3.

Ordinary. 1. In RCm, one who has jurisdiction in his

own right, as distinguished from one who has only delegated jurisdiction. 2. See *Propers.*

Ordination. See *Ministerial Office,* 1, 5.

Ording, Hans Nielsen Hauge (1884–1952). Norw. Luth. theol.; educ. Christiania (Oslo); prof. systematic theol. Oslo. Wrote in German and Norwegian; works include writings in the area of aesthetics and dogmatics.

Ording, Johannes (1869–1929). Liberal Luth. theol.; b. Drammen, Norw.; educ. Christiania (Oslo); prof. systematic theol. Oslo 1906; his appointment as prof. was preceded by controversy and followed by the founding of a "free faculty" (see *Norway, Lutheranism in,* 12). Works include *Den religiöse Erkjendelse, dens art og vished; Den kristelige tro; Teologien: En encyklopaedisk fremstilling; Kristelig ethik.*

Ordo (Fratrum) Minimorum. See *Minims.*

"Ordo Romanus." In the Middle Ages, one of a number of directories of ch. rites giving the order and arrangement of ceremonies but not the liturgical text. By the 13th c. the term "ordo" was replaced by "ceremoniale." "Ordo" now denotes an annual publication in the basic form of a calendar listing offices and feasts of the RC Ch. for every day of the yr.

Ordo Sanctissimi Salvatoris. See *Brigittines.*

Örebro, Synod of. See *Gustavus I.*

Oregon Yearly Meeting of Friends Church. See *Friends, Society of,* 5.

Orelli, Hans Konrad von (1846–1912). B. Zurich, Switz.; educ. Lausanne, Zurich, Erlangen, Tübingen, Leipzig; prof. theol. Basel. Works include commentaries on Is, Jer, Eze, and the 12 minor prophets (Hos to Ml).

Orenda. See *Indians, American,* 1; *Primitive Religion.*

Organic Evolution. See *Evolution,* II.

Oriental Boat Mission. See *International Missions, Inc.*

Oriental Church. See *Eastern Orthodox Churches,* 1.

Oriental Missionary Society. Founded 1901. Fields have included Jap., Korea, China, India, Colombia, Greece, Brazil, Formosa, Ecuador, Hong Kong, Haiti, Nigeria.

Oriental Research, Schools of. See *Geography, Christian,* 7.

"Orientalium Ecclesiarum." See *Vatican Councils,* 2.

Orientation of Churches. Placing chs. in such a way that the altar is in the E end, the main portal in the W end. The original basic concern may have been the direction in which the celebrant, rather than the people, faced; this would explain early chs. with the altar in the W end, but with the celebrant, officiating behind a freestanding altar, facing E. With the change to the altar in the E end (est. 5th–8th c), both celebrant and cong. face E.

Various reasons for facing E have been suggested, e. g., the orient was believed to be man's 1st home; Christ lived in the E and many believe that His final return will be from the E (cf. Mt 24:27); Christ is regarded as the Rising Sun. Imitation of pagan sun worship does not commend itself as a reason in light of Christian opposition to heathenism.

Regardless of geographic position, it is good form to speak of the altar end of any ch. as the E in a liturgical sense, the opposite end as the W, and N and S transepts.

See also *Church Architecture,* 3.

Origen (ca. 185–ca. 254). Gk. ch. father; b. probably Alexandria, Egypt, of Christian parents; taught school and instructed catechumens in Alexandria 202; mystic and ascetic; mutilated himself on basis of a misunderstanding of Mt 19:12. Travelled to Rome, Arabia, Palestine, and Greece. His ordination in Palestine 230 was not regarded as valid in Alexandria; exiled; taught school at Caesarea in Palestine 231–233; travelled to Arabia, Cappadocia, and Nicomedia; suffered in persecution under Decius (see *Persecutions of Christians,* 4). Doctrines held by, or attributed to, him are called Origenism.

Works include *Peri archon* ("On First Principles"); *Contra Celsum;* OT textual studies *(Hexapla; Tetrapla);* exegetical writings; sermons. EK

See also *Exegesis,* 3; *Millennium,* 3; *Origenistic Controversy; Philosophy; Preaching, Christian, History of,* 6. *Schools, Early Christian,* 1, 3.

E. R. Redepenning, *Origenes: Eine Darstellung seines Lebens und seiner Lehre,* 2 vols. (Bonn, 1841–46); J. Danielou, *Origen,* tr. W. Mitchell (New York, 1955); H. de Lubac, *Histoire et esprit* (Paris, 1950); R. P. C. Hanson, *Allegory and Event* (Richmond, Va., 1959).

Origenistic Controversy. Arose over the question of Origen's* orthodoxy; began when Methodius* (d. ca. 300/311) attacked Origen's teaching on preexistence of souls and denial of bodily resurrection; raged esp. in Egypt, Palestine, and Constantinople 394–438; Pachomius* and his followers opposed the mysticism and spiritualism of Origen's followers; Jerome* and Theophilus* of Alexandria first supported, then opposed Origen; Epiphanius* was one of the most zealous opponents of Origen. Origen was anathematized 553 by the 5th ecumenical council (see *Constantinople, Councils of,* 2). See also *Rufinus, Tyrranius.*

(Original) Church of God, Inc., The. See *Church of God, Inc., The (Original).*

Original Sin. See *Sin; Sin, Original.*

Orinoco River Mission, The. Founded 1920; inc. 1924 in Cal.; operates in E Venezuela.

Orléans, Councils of. A number of councils or syns. were held at Orléans, Fr. The 1st, called by Clovis* I, met 511. Matters treated in its 31 canons included inviolability of chs. as sanctuaries; ordination; jurisdiction of bps.; prohibition of remarriage of widows of priests or deacons; exclusion of monks who marry from orders; prescription of 40 days fast before Easter; use of income from ch. property; observation of Rogation Days. Councils in 533, 538, 541, and 549 gave considerable attention to soc. concerns. The council of 1022 was called against Manichaeism.* See also *Simony.*

Orosius (forename Paulus first occurs in 8th c.; perhaps ca. 380/390 – perhaps ca. 418). B. probably Sp. or Port., possibly Bracara Augusta (modern Braga), Galicia (or Tarragona); presbyter or priest; assoc. with Augustine* of Hippo beginning ca. 413/414; opposed Origenists (see *Origen*), Pelagius,* and Priscillianists.* Works include *Historiarum adversus paganos libri vii.*

Orphanages. See *Child and Family Service Agencies.*

Orr, James (1844–1913). B. Glasgow, Scot.; educ. Glasgow; United Presb. pastor Hawick 1874–91; prof. ch. hist. Theol. Coll. of the United Presb. Ch. of Scot. 1891–1901; prof. apologetics and theol. Glasgow Coll. of the U. F. C. of Scot. 1901–13; lectured in the US and Can. 1895–1909; helped form U. F. C. of Scot. 1900. Works include *Revelation and Inspiration; The Virgin Birth of Christ; The Problem of the Old Testament Considered with Reference to Recent Criticism; The Progress of Dogma;* ed. *The International Standard Bible Encyclopaedia.*

Ort, Samuel Alfred (Nov. 11, 1843–Jan. 6, 1911). Luth. theol.; b. Lewistown, Pa.; educ. Wittenberg Coll., Springfield, Ohio (see *Wittenberg University*); pastor Louisville, Ky., 1874–78, NYC 1878–80; prof. theol. Wittenberg Coll. 1880–1910, pres. 1882–1900; pres. The General* Syn. of the Ev. Luth. Ch. in the USA 1887.

Orthodox. The term orthodox (antonym: heterodox; see *Heterodoxy*) implies conformity to a certain standard; used esp. in a religious sense; often used in E Christendom of those in communion with Constantinople.

Orthodox Catholic Church (of the East). See *Eastern Orthodox Churches,* 1.

Orthodox Church in America, The. See *Eastern Orthodox Churches,* 6.

Orthodox Churches, Eastern. See *Eastern Orthodox Churches.*

Orthodox Confession of the Faith of the Catholic and Apostolic Eastern Church. See *Eastern Orthodox Standards of Doctrine,* A 1.

"Orthodox Creed, An." See *Democratic Declarations of Faith,* 3.

Orthodox Judaism. See *Judaism,* 3.

Orthodox Lutheran Conference, The. Organized at St. John's Ch., Okabena, Minn., Sept. 26, 1951, by a small group whose mems. then or soon withdrew from LCMS in protest against alleged doctrinal deviations. Invitations had been sent to all who had signed *Confession of Faith Professed and Practiced by All True Lutherans,* which had been adopted Nov. 19, 1950, at Manchester, Mo., by the St. Louis Study Club. The Conference accepted the Bible, the Luth. Confessions as contained in the *Book* of Concord,* and the Brief* Statement; it endorsed 12 points listed in Part II of its *Confession;* it took exception to LCMS action regarding the *Common* Confession.* The Orthodox Luth. Sem. opened Sept. 1952 Minneapolis, Minn., with P. E. Kretzmann* pres.; it was discontinued ca. 1962. Monthly pub.: *The Orthodox Lutheran* and *The Orthodox Lutheran Theologian.* Mems. of the Conference were received into WELS 1963 and the Conference ceased to exist. WHM

Orthodox Presbyterian Church. See *Presbyterian Churches,* 4 d.

Orthodoxy, Age of. See *Lutheran Theology After 1580,* 1–5.

Orthodoxy, Feast of. Observed on the 1st Sun. in Lent since 842 in the E Ch. to celebrate the end of iconoclasm (see *Iconoclastic Controversy*); later it included, by some, commemoration of the 869–870 Council of Constantinople (see *Constantinople, Councils of,* 4), which approved the use of icons, as the 8th ecumenical council.

Orthodoxy, Neo-. See *Neoorthodoxy.*

Orthros (orthron). E Orthodox name of the morning office similar to lauds.*

Ortlieb of Strasbourg (fl. early in the 13th c.). Founded an ascetic sect that emphasized the inner authority of the Spirit against the tenets of the ch.; rejected the hist. meaning of Scripture (e. g., Noah's ark, Christ's passion, and the Trinity were regarded only as symbols); his teaching was condemned by Innocent III (see *Popes,* 10).

Orzechowski, Stanislaus (Orichovius and other variants; Stanislaw; 1513–66). Humanist; b. Orzechowice, near Przemysl, Poland; RC priest; excommunicated for challenging the authority of the ch.; returned to RCm 1559. Works include *De lege coelibatus contra Siricium in concilio habita oratio.*

Osage. See *Indians, American,* 5.

Osiander, Andreas (the Elder; 1498–1552). Father of L. Osiander* the Elder; b. Gunzenhausen, Middle Franconia, W Bav., Ger.; educ. Ingolstadt; priest Nürnberg 1520; introd. the Reformation and opposed fanatics and Anabaps. there; sided with M. Luther* against H. Zwingli* at Marburg 1529 (see *Lutheran Confessions,* A 2) and with Luther in distinction from P. Melanchthon* at Augsburg 1530; helped crystallize a Brandenburg-Nürnberg ch. order 1530–32; present at the 1537 meeting of the Schmalkaldic League (see *Lutheran Confessions,* B 2), at the Hagenau* Colloquy 1540, and at the Colloquy of Worms* 1540–41; reformed the principality Pfalz-Neuburg 1542–43; opposed the Augsburg Interim*; prof. Königsberg 1549. Works include a gospel harmony (Gk. and Lat.); a polemic against J. Eck*; an edition of N. Copernicus,* *De revolutionibus orbium caelestium; Conjecturae de ultimis temporibus, ac de fine mundi, ex Sacris literis* (in which he calculated the end of the world for ca. 1656 and identified the papacy as the Antichrist). See also *Osiandrian Controversy.*

Leben und ausgewählte Schriften der Väter und Begründer der lutherischen Kirche, Part V: W. Möller, *Andreas Osiander* (Elberfeld, 1870).

Osiander, Andreas (the Younger; 1562–1617). Son of L. Osiander* the Elder; brother of L. Osiander* the Younger; uncle of J. A. Osiander*; b. Blaubeuren, N Württemberg, Ger.; pastor Güglingen 1587; court preacher 1590; abbot Adelberg 1598; prof. theol. and chancellor Tübingen 1605; defended FC; attended Colloquy of Montbéliard* 1586; hymnist. Works include a manual for communicants.

Osiander, Johann(es) (1657–1724). Son of J. A. Osiander*; b. Tübingen, Ger.; educ. Tübingen; prof. Tübingen 1686; abbot Königsbronn 1697, Hirsau 1699; dir. consistorium 1708; introd. confirmation 1721–23.

Osiander, Johann Adam (1622–97). Nephew of A. Osiander* the Younger and L. Osiander* the Younger; father of J. Osiander*; b. Vaihingen, N Württemberg, Ger.; prof. 1656, chancellor 1680 Tübingen; friend of P. J. Spener.*

Osiander, Lukas (the Elder; 1534–1604). Son of A. Osiander* the Elder; father of A. Osiander* the Younger and L. Osiander* the Younger; b. Nürnberg, Ger.; educ. Tübingen; supt. Blaubeuren and Stuttgart; court preacher and consistorial councillor; abbot Adelberg 1596; deposed and banished but permitted to return to Stuttgart; hymnist. With B. Bidembach* wrote the Maulbronn Formula (see *Lutheran Confessions,* C 2).

Osiander, Lukas (the Younger; 1571–1638). Son of L. Osiander* the Elder; brother of A. Osiander* the Younger; uncle of J. A. Osiander*; b. Stuttgart, Ger.; educ. Tübingen; held various ch. positions; prof. theol. 1619, provost and chancellor 1620 Tübingen; staunch Luth.

Osiandrian Controversy. Begun 1549 by A. Osiander* the Elder. Reacting against what he regarded as overemphasis on forensic justification, he taught that God does not declare the sinner just, but makes him just; does not impute Christ's obedience and righteousness to the sinner, but has Christ Himself dwell in the sinner for his justification; does not act as a judge but as a physician. M. Chemnitz,* M. Flacius* Illyricus, P. Melanchthon,* J. Mörlin,* et al. opposed him. Osiander also held that Christ is our righteousness only acc. to His divine nature (see also *Stancarus, Franciscus*). FC SD III 4: "Christ is our righteousness, not according to the divine nature alone or according to the human nature alone but according to both natures."

Osler, Edward (1798–1863). B. Falmouth, Cornwall, SW Eng.; educ. for the med. profession at Falmouth and London; later devoted himself to literary pursuits; hymnist. Ed. *Royal Cornwall Gazette;* hymns include "Lord of the Church, We Humbly Pray" and "May We Thy Precepts, Lord, Fulfil."

Ostensorium. See *Monstrance.*

Ostervald, Jean Frédéric (Johann Friedrich Osterwald; 1663–1747). Ref. theol.; b. Neuchâtel (Neuenburg), Switz.; deacon and pastor Neuchâtel; emphasized the Bible and personal piety. Works include a catechism; Bible tr. and commentary.

Ostiary. Doorkeeper. See also *Hierarchy.*

Ostrogoths. See *Goths, Conversion of.*

Otfrid (Otfried; perhaps ca. 790/800–875/880). Ger. monk; probably b. near Weissenburg (Wissembourg), NE Fr. (Alsace); pupil of Rabanus* Maurus. Works include *Liber evangeliorum* (formerly known as *Krist;* in Old High Ger. poetic form with end rhyme; stresses symbolic interpretation of Christ's acts rather than the acts themselves).

Otherworld. World beyond the present one. See also *Hereafter.*

Otkon. See *Indians, American,* 1.

Oto. See *Indians, American,* 5.

Otter, Jakob (Jacobus Otther; ca. 1485–1547). Reformer; b. Lauterburg, Alsace; educ. Heidelberg and Freiburg; pastor Wolfenweiler, near Freiburg, 1518; became Luth. 1520. Pastor Kenzingen, near Lahr, 1522; Neckarsteinach, near Heidelberg, 1524; Solothurn (Soleure), Switz., early 1529; Aarau, Switz., Aug. 1529; Esslingen, Ger., 1532. Signed Wittenberg* Concord. Works include a catechism and devotional writings.

Otterbein, Philip William. See *United Brethren,* 1; *United Church of Christ, The,* II A 2.

Ottesen, Jakob Aall (June 1, 1825–Oct. 30, 1904). B. Christiania (Oslo), Norw.; educ. Christiania; taught Lat. school Christiania; to Am. 1852. Pastor Manitowoc, Wis., 1852; Koshkonong, Wis., 1860; Decorah, Iowa, 1894–96. Helped organize The Norw. Ev. Luth. Ch. in Am. (see *Evangelical Lutheran Church, The,* 8). Coed. *Evangelisk Luthersk Maanedstidende.*

Öttingen, Alexander von (1827–1906). Luth. theol.; b. Wissust, near Dorpat (Tartu), Livonia; prof. systematic theol. Dorpat 1856; held that individual guilt must be viewed against the background of community guilt. Works include *Die Moralstatistik und die christliche Sittenlehre.*

Öttinger, Konrad (Ötinger; Conradus Öttingerus; d. 1540). B. Pforzheim, Ger.; court preacher of Philip* of Hesse and (1534) of Ulrich of Württemberg; signed SA.

Otto I (Otho; 912–973). "The Great." Son of Henry* I, the Fowler; king of Ger. and Holy Roman Emp. 936–973, crowned 962. See also *Germany,* A 2.

Otto, Anton (b. ca. 1505). B. Herzberg, Ger. (hence also called Herzberger); studied under M. Luther at Wittenberg; pastor Gräfenthal and Nordhausen; preached sermons 1565 rejecting the 3d use of the Law as source of Majorism (see *Majoristic Controversy*) and synergism.*

Otto, Rudolf (1869–1937). B. Peine, Ger.; educ. Erlangen and Göttingen; taught at Göttingen 1897, Breslau 1914, Marburg 1917. Works include *Das Leben und Wirken Jesu nach historisch-kritischer Auffassung,* tr. *Life and Ministry of Jesus According to the Historical and Critical Method; Das Heilige,* tr. *The Idea of the Holy.* See also *Numinous.*

Otto of Bamberg (ca. 1060/62–1139). "Father of the Monks"; b. Swabia; bp. Bamberg 1102; founded more than 20 monasteries; helped prepare Concordat of Worms (see *Concordat,* 2); made miss. journeys to Pomerania 1124–25, 1128.

Otto of Freising (ca. 1110/15–1158). B. perhaps Neuburg, near Vienna, Austria; studied at Paris, Fr.; Cistercian 1132; abbot Morimond, Fr., ca. 1137; abbot Freising, Bav., ca. 1138; active in politics; took part in 2d Crusade (see *Crusades,* 3). Works include a world chronicle.

Ouseley, Frederick Arthur Gore (1825–89). Composer; ed. of ch. music and related works; b. London, Eng.; educ. Oxford; ordained 1849; curate London; prof. music Oxford and priest and precentor Hereford cathedral 1855; vicar St. Michael's, Tenbury, and warden St. Michael's Coll. there 1856. Ed. sacred music of O. Gibbons.* Other works include *The Martyrdom of St. Polycarp* (cantata); *Hagar* (oratorio); anthems; hymn tunes include "Aberystwyth" (called "Tenbury" by some).

Outlook College. See *Canada,* A 20.

Outward Works of God. See *Father, God the.*

Ovambokavango Church. See *Africa,* B. 8.

Ovamboland (Amboland). Region in N part of South-West Afr.; name derived from the name of the dominant native race. The Finnish* Miss. Soc. worked among Ovambo in the 1870s as its 1st field. See also *Africa,* B 8.

Overbeck, Franz Camille (1837–1905). Hist. and philos.; b. St. Petersburg (Leningrad), Russ.; educ. Leipzig and Göttingen, Ger.; prof. Basel, Switz., 1870–97; criticized Christianity and its tension with culture as he saw it.

Overbeck, Johann Friedrich (1789–1869). Painter; b. Lübeck, Ger.; romantic idealist; RC 1813. Works include *Joseph Sold by His Brethren; The Seven Years of Famine; Adoration of the Magi; Christ's Entry into Jerusalem; Supper at Emmaus.* See also *Nazarenes,* 3.

Overseas Missionary Fellowship. Name adopted in the mid-1960s by the China* Inland Miss. The soc. tries to express Scriptural ecumenicity in an internat. and interdenom. fellowship. Emphases: evangelizing pioneer fields; shepherding emerging chs.; serving existing chs.; training potential leaders; extending vital auxiliaries. Fields have included Singapore, Malaya, Thailand, Vietnam, Laos, Indonesia, the Philippines, Taiwan, Hong Kong, and Japan. HQ Philadelphia, Pa. Mem. IFMA.

Overseer. See Bishop.

Oversoul (Ger. *Überseele*). Name adopted by R. W. Emerson* for the concept of absolute reality as a spiritual being that perfectly realizes man's ideal nature, imperfectly manifested in human beings. Analogous to various views of the absolute* and to the idealism* of Plato.*

Overture for Lutheran Unity. A 6-par. overture adopted by the ex. committee of the Am. Luth. Conf. Jan. 7, 1944, Chicago, Ill. Main thoughts: (1) The "Lutheran Church is rightly jealous of the integrity of its doctrine and practice, rightly wary of indifferentism or latitudinarianism, no matter what emergencies may arise." (2) The Luth. Ch. has always insisted on genuine acceptance by its mems. of its great hist. standards. (3) "Since some important points of doctrine and practice . . . were not issues in the sixteenth century . . . [but] have more recently become issues affecting inner unity, . . . Lutheran Church bodies have rightly required and provided supplementary statements . . . " (4) The Minneapolis* Theses (1925), Brief* Statement, Declaration (see *American Lutheran Church,* V, 1), and Pittsburgh* Agreement "have made sufficiently clear the position of the three major groups within American Lutheranism." (5) "We, the constituent synods of the American Lutheran Conference, severally and collectively reaffirm our sincere and wholehearted adherence to our mutual pledge as to doctrine and practice in the Minneapolis Theses. We as earnestly expect of those with whom we seek complete fellowship that their doctrine and practice shall conform to their respective declarations." (6) "We submit the above statements to other Lutheran bodies with a view to the establishment of pulpit and altar fellowship." Appended: the 1925 Minneapolis Theses and the parts of the Chicago Theses (formulated 1919) referred to in the Minneapolis Theses.

"An Overture for Lutheran Unity," *The Lutheran Outlook,* IX (1944), 10–12; "An Overture for Lutheran Unity," *CTM,* XV (1944), 193–197, 274–276.

Owen, John (1616–83). B. Stadham(pton), Oxfordshire, Eng.; educ. Oxford; private chaplain; Calvinistic Presb.; cleric Fordham, Essex; Indep. (Cong.) cleric Coggeshall, near Fordham, 1646; chaplain to O. Cromwell*; vice-chancellor Oxford 1652–58; pastor London.

Owen, Robert (1771–1858). Father of R. D. Owen*; socialist and philanthropist; b. Newtown, Wales; tried to improve soc. conditions of workingmen; founded communistic socs. (see also *Communistic Societies,* 2) in Eng. and one at New Harmony, Ind. (1825–28), all unsuccessful; tried to abolish private or individual property, systems of religion that he regarded as absurd and irrational, and marriage founded on individual property; turned from disbelief in all religions to belief in spiritualism ca. 1853; followers called Owenists. Works include *Discourses on a New System of Society.*

Owen, Robert Dale (1801–77). Son of R. Owen*; soc. reformer; b. Glasgow, Scot.; educ. Hofwyl, Switz.; to Am. with his father 1825; taught school New Harmony, Ind.; mem. Ind. legislature; Democrat mem. US House of Representatives 1843–47. Ed. *New Harmony Gazette* at New Harmony, Ind., and *Free Enquirer* (the *New Harmony Gazette* renamed) in N. Y. Other works include *The Policy of Emancipation; The Wrong of Slavery, the Right of Emancipation, and the Future of the African Race in the United States.*

Oxford Group Movement. See *Buchmanism.*

Oxford Movement. High* Ch. movement in the interest of Anglo-Catholicism; began 1833 at Oxford, Eng. Leaders: J. Keble,* J. H. Newman,* E. B. Pusey.* Adherents include F. W. Faber,* R. H. Froude,* H. E. Manning,* C. Marriott,* W. H. Mill,* F. Oakeley,* W. Palmer* (1803–85). See also *Anglo-Catholics; England,* C 7; *Tractarianism.*

P

"P." In Biblical criticism the letter "P" is the symbol for one of the alleged sources of the Pentateuch. See also *Higher Criticism,* 6–13.

P. E. O. Sisterhood. Philanthropic educ. organization formed 1869 by 7 coll. girls to be a campus sorority; no longer maintains campus chaps.; has become a women's community group interested primarily in "bringing to women greatly increased opportunities for higher education." To this end the P. E. O. Sisterhood maintains Cottey Coll., Nevada, Mo., a jr. coll. of liberal arts est. 1884. The Sisterhood has a religious framework and an optional funeral service which implies that every mem. passes "through the sunset gates into the Great Beyond" and there sparkles as a star "new-set in heaven."

Pacca, Bartolom(m)eo (1756–1844). B. Benevento, Campania, S It.; nuncio to Cologne 1785, Lisbon 1794–1801; cardinal 1801; led RC opposition against Napoleon* I; imprisoned by French from July 1809 to 1813; worked effectively for restoration of the Society* of Jesus.

Paccanari, Niccolo (1760 [1773?]–1810 or later). B. Valsugana, near Trent, NE It.; lacked formal educ.; ambitious of power; merchant; soldier; turned to RC interests; founded Paccanarists* 1797; priest 1800; disinclined to restore Society* of Jesus; imprisoned 1808; released 1809; imprisoned 1810; no further record of his life.

Paccanarists (Society of the Faith of Jesus; Fathers of the Faith of Jesus). Founded 1797 by N. Paccanari* to replace the suppressed Society* of Jesus; disappeared when the latter was restored.

Pacelli, Eugenio. See *Popes,* 33.

Pachelbel, Johann (Bachelbel; Pachelbell; 1653–1706). Luth. composer; organist; b. Nürnberg, Ger.; held many important positions; one of J. S. Bach's* early models. Works include cantatas *(Was Gott tut, das ist wohlgetan; Christ lag in Todesbanden);* chorale fugues and preludes; *Magnificat Fugues.* See also *Schwemmer, Heinrich; Toccata.*

Pachomius. See *Monasticism,* 3.

Pacian (ca. 310–ca. 391). B. Sp.; bp. Barcelona perhaps ca. 350/360. Works include *De Baptismo; Paraenesis sive exhortatorius libellus; Contra Novatianos* (3 letters, the 1st of which contains the phrase *Christianus mihi nomen est, catholicus vero cognomen* ("My name is Christian, but my surname Catholic").

MPL, 13, 1051–94.

Pacific Lutheran Theological Seminary. See *Lutheran Church in America,* V; *Ministry, Education of,* X O; *United Lutheran Church, Synods of,* 20, 21.

Pacific Lutheran University. See *Ministry, Education of,* VIII A 2; *Universities in the United States, Lutheran,* 3.

Pacific School of Religion. Founded 1866 by the Gen. Assoc. of the Cong. Chs. of Calif.; classes began 1869 in San Francisco; property bought in Oakland 1871; school moved to Berkeley 1901; coed.

Pacific Southwest Synod of the United Lutheran Church. See *United Lutheran Church, Synods of,* 21.

Pacific Synod. See *Canada,* A 18.

Pacific Synod of the Evangelical Lutheran Church. See *United Lutheran Church, Synods of,* 20.

Pacific Yearly Meeting of Friends. See *Friends, Society of,* 11.

Pacifism. A. Term coined apparently ca. 1905 in reference to attempts to settle internat. disputes by peaceful means; in wider definition it has more gen. reference to use of peaceful means rather than violence. Reasons for pacifism are usually given as either religious (e. g., Mt. 26:52) or humanitarian. Oriental philosophies contain elements of pacifism. See also *Buddhism; Gandhi, Mohondas Karamchand; Confucianism; Taoism.*

B. Pacifism seems to have been the accepted view in the early ch. Some early fathers opposed military service (e. g., Tertullian, *On Idolatry,* or *De Idololatria,* xix, and *The Chaplet,* or *De Corona,* xi; Lactantius, *The Divine Institutes,* or *Divinae Institutiones,* VI, xx).

After Christianity was given legal standing and imperial support (see *Constantine I*), Christians helped keep peace in the empire. Augustine* of Hippo (e. g., *The City of God,* or *De civitate dei,* XIX, vii) spoke of "just wars." Waldenses* first condemned war, finally fought in self-defense. Bohemian* Brethren first opposed, later permitted military service. Pacifism also played a part in the hist. of Dunkers (see *Brethren*), Dukhobors (see *Russian Sects*), the Soc. of Friends,* Shakers,* et al.

The 1st peace soc. was organized Aug. 1815 NYC; others soon followed in Am., including the Ohio Peace Soc., Mass. Peace Soc., Am. Peace Soc., and others, till ca. the 1850s, in Maine, Mass., R. I., Conn., N. Y., Pa., S. C., and some toward the interior of the country. In Gt. Brit. a similar movement ran parallel, beginning ca. the same time; ca. 1867 it spread to the Continent, later to Norw., Jap., S. Am., and elsewhere. Interrupted by the Civil War, the peace movement began anew in Am. with the organization of the Universal Peace Union 1866. After interruption by WW I, pacifism reemerged with renewed vigor. In WW II pacifists were silenced or liquidated in Ger. and Russ. In Eng. and Am. they were recognized and, if possible, assigned to civilian work or noncombatant service in the armed forces; some were imprisoned for refusal to perform any service.

C. Peace socs. in Am. include the Fellowship of Reconciliation, affiliated with the Internat. Fellowship of Reconciliation and the Internat. Confederation for Disarmament and Peace. AMR

A. L. Huxley, *Science, Liberty, and Peace* (New York, 1946); R. M. Jones, *The Church, the Gospel, and War* (New York, 1948); C. C. Morrison, *The Christian and the War* (Chicago, 1942); R. H. Bainton, *Christian Attitudes Toward War and Peace* (Nashville, Tenn., 1960); G. H. C. Macgregor, *The New Testament Basis of Pacifism* (new and rev. ed. 1954) and *The Relevance of an Impossible Ideal* (1941), both reprinted together in 1 vol. (Nyack. N. Y., 1960).

Pack, Otto von (ca. 1480–1537). Ger. conspirator; studied at Leipzig; counselor and vice-chancellor of George* the Bearded, duke of Albertine Saxony; early in 1528 he informed Philip* of Hesse (some think with Philip's own connivance) of an alleged plot by George the Bearded, Joachim I of Brandenburg (see *Joachim,* 1), and other RC leaders, secular and religious, to conquer Hung. and then suppress the Reformation in Ger. In response to the alleged impending attack, Philip of Hesse made an alliance with John* the Constant, elector of Saxony,

March 1528 with a view to defense and possible preemptive measures. But on the advice of M. Luther, P. Melanchthon, and J. Bugenhagen, the defensive (or preventive) attack was largely deferred and, instead, the RC leaders accused of the plot were confronted to explain the information that Pack had supplied. The plot was denied; the papers were called forgeries. Under examination in Kassel, Pack maintained that he had transmitted genuine documents bearing official seals; but then he fled, was apprehended in the Neth., admitted forgery under torture and was executed. Neither Luther nor Philip were convinced that the documents were forged. Philip and John came out ahead on balance by securing repayment of armament costs from the Frankish bishoprics (Bamberg and Würzburg) and surrender of jurisdiction over Hesse and Saxony by Mainz. Resultant distrust of Prots. by RCs helped consolidate the latter's position at the 1529 Diet of Speyer.*

Padre (Sp., It., or Port., "father"). Designation for chaplain; often used for all clerics.

Paedobaptism (pedobaptism). See *Grace, Means of,* III, 4.

Paenula, See *Vestments, Clerical,* 1.

Pagan (from Lat. *paganus,* "of the country," from *pagus,* "country; village; district"). 1. Since Christianity first came to *cities* of the Roman empire, those who lived in the country adhered longer to non-Christian religions; hence the assoc. of the word "pagan" with the concept "heathen." 2. One with little or no religion.

See also *Heathenism.*

Paget, Francis (1851–1911). Angl. theol.; b. London, Eng.; educ. Oxford; regius prof. pastoral theol. Oxford and canon Christ Ch. 1885–92; dean Christ Ch. 1892–1901; bp. Oxford 1901–11. Contributed to *Lux* mundi;* other works include *The Spirit of Discipline.*

Paget, William (1505–63). 1st Baron Paget of Beaudesert; Eng. statesman; one of Henry* VIII's chief advisers; comptroller of king's household on accession of Edward VI (see *England,* B 4); imprisoned 1551 on charges of conspiracy; restored to privy council by Mary* I 1553; lord privy seal 1556–58.

Pagi, Antoine (1624–99). RC ch. hist.; b. Rognes, Provence, Fr.; Franciscan. Works include *Critica historico-chronologica in universos annales ecclesiasticos eminentissimi & reverendissimi Caesaris Cardinalis Baronii.*

Pagninus, Santes (Pagnini; Pagnino; Sanctes; Xantes; 1470–1541). B. Lucca, Tuscany, It.; Dominican; Hebraist. His tr. of the Bible into Lat. was used by M. Coverdale* in preparing the Great Bible (see *Bible Versions,* L 5); other works include a Heb. lexicon.

Pagoda. Far East temple, memorial, or similar structure.

"Paimen-Sanomia." See *Finnish Lutherans in America,* 2.

Paine, John Knowles (1839–1906). Composer; organist; b. Portland, Maine; prof. Harvard U., Cambridge, Mass., 1875–1906 (the 1st prof. music in any Am. university). Works include cantatas (e. g., *The Nativity*); *St. Peter* (oratorio).

Paine, Thomas (1737–1809). Pol. philos. and writer; freethinker*; inventor of an iron bridge; b. Thetford, Norfolk, Eng.; to Am. 1774; took part in Am. Revolution: to Eur. 1787; involved in Fr. Revolution (see *France,* 5); returned to Am. 1802. Foe of Christianity. Pioneer opponent of slavery; agitator for emancipation of women. Works include *The Rights of Man; The Age of Reason; Crisis* (which begins: "These are the times that try men's souls." See also *Deism,* V.

Paix, Jakob (Jacob; 1556 [1550?] – probably after 1623). Luth. composer; b. Augsburg, Germany. Compiled and ed. an *Orgel-Tabulatur* and other collections.

Pajon, Claude (1626–85). Ref. theol.; b. Romorantin, Loir-et-Cher, Fr.; influenced by M. Amyraut* and J. Cameron*; influenced by occasionalism* in his explanation of conversion and by deism* in his view of double* predestination; founded theol. system called Pajonism; some followers became RC, others Socinian (see *Socinianism*); influenced G. W. v. Leibniz* and F. D. E. Schleiermacher.*

Pakistan. See *Asia,* B 2.

Pakistani Lutheran Church. See *Asia,* B 2.

Palace Chapel at Aachen. See *Church Architecture,* 7.

Palamas, Gregorius. See *Hesychasm.*

Palästinawerk. See *Middle East,* G.

Palau. See *Micronesia.*

Paleario, Aonio (Antonio della Paglia, or degli [or dei] Pagliaricci; Aonius Palearius; ca. 1503–70). Humanist; reformer; b. Veroli, Latium, It.; thrice accused of heresy, one of the last charges being that he taught justification by faith alone; he seems to have weakened under pressure for a time; died a martyr.

Palestine. The Holy Land (Zch 2:12) of Hebrews and Christians. The name is ultimately derived from "Philistine." Geog. boundaries have varied but have always included the region (ca. 140 mi. long, ca. 30–ca. 70 mi. wide) bet. the Mediterranean Sea and the Jordan R. and bordering SW on Egypt. Longitudinal sections in this area: (1) coastal plain; (2) mountains intersected by the Plain of Esdraelon (sometimes called "valley of Jezreel") immediately N of Carmel; (3) Jordan valley, from the Anti-Liban mountains S through the Waters of Merom and the Sea of Galilee (or Lake of Gennesaret) to the N end of the Dead Sea. See also *Middle East,* F; *Zionism.*

Palestine Exploration Fund. Founded 1864, inc. London, Eng., 1865 for excavations and cartography in Palestine for Biblical verification and illustration. See also *Geography, Christian,* 4.

Palestrina, Giovanni Pierluigi da (1525/26–94). Composer; b. Palestrina (ancient Praeneste), Roma prov., Latium, cen. Italy. Maestro di cappella, Capella Giulia, Rome, 1551; St. John Lateran 1555–61; Santa Maria Maggiore 1561. Composer to papal chapel 1565; master of music Cappella Giulia 1571. Works include masses, hymns, motets, litanies, magnificats. See also *Offertory.* WEB

P. H. Lang, *Music in Western Civilization* (New York, 1941); H. Leichtentritt, *Music, History, and Ideas* (Cambridge, Mass., 1938); *The New Oxford History of Music,* IV: *The Age of Humanism 1540–1630,* ed. G. Abraham (London, 1968); Z. K. Pyne, *Giovanni Pierluigi da Palestrina, His Life and Times* (London, 1922).

Paley, William (1743–1805). Angl. theol.; utilitarian philos.; apologist; b. Peterborough, Northamptonshire, Eng.; educ. Cambridge; ordained 1767; archdeacon Carlisle 1782; prebendary St. Paul's 1794; subdeacon Lincoln 1795; rector Bishop's Wearmouth (on S side of Wear R., now part of Sunderland) 1795. Opposed deism*; defended the reliability of the NT; supported the teleological argument for the existence of God. Works include *The Principles of Moral and Political Philosophy; A View of the Evidences of Christianity; Horae Paulinae; Natural Theology.*

Palimpsests. See *Beuron, Abbey of; Manuscripts of the Bible,* 2 c.

Pall. 1. White cloth, usually linen, enclosing a thin substance (e. g., cardboard), usually 6 to 9 in. square; used in Communion services to cover the chalice* before and after Communion or to cover the paten* if the latter is put on the chalice. See also *Corporal.*

2. Heavy cloth, often velvet (black, purple, or white), draped over a coffin or bier, tomb, or hearse;

hence, figuratively, a coffin; formerly pallbearers held up the corners of the cloth; now those who carry the coffin are called pallbearers.

Palladius (ca. 363/365–425). Probably b. Galatia, N cen. Asia Minor; influenced by Evagrius* Ponticus; monk in Jerusalem; monk in Egypt ca. 388; returned to Palestine ca. 399; bp. Helenopolis, Bithynia (in NW Asia Minor), 400; friend of J. Chrysostom*; accused of Origenism (see *Origen*) by Jerome* and Epiphanius*; banished ca. 406; returned to Asia Minor ca. 412; bp. Aspuna, Galatia, ca. 417. Works include a hist. of early monasticism.

MPG, 34, 991–1262.

Palladius (5th c.). Acc. to Prosper* of Aquitaine he was sent ca. 431 by Celestine I (pope 422–432) as 1st bp. to Christians in Ireland*; unsuccessful.

Palladius, Peder Esbernsen (1503–60). 1st Luth. bp. Zealand (Sjaelland), Den., 1537; prof. Copenhagen. Tr. SC into Dan.; helped C. Pedersen* tr. Bible into Dan. See also *Denmark, Lutheranism in*, 3.

Pallium. See *Vestments, Clerical*, 1.

Pallivaanavar. See *India*, 4.

Pallottine Fathers (Pallottini Fathers; Societas Apostolatus Catholici). Founded 1835 by Vincent Pallotti (1795–1850; b. Rome, It.); name changed 1854 to Pia Societas Missionum; original name restored 1947. Original aims resemble those of Catholic* Action. One special interest: return of Oriental Christians to the RC Ch.

Palm Sunday. Sun. before Easter; introd. Holy Week. The name is derived from the Gospel for the day (Mt 21:1-9) and in RCm is assoc. since the 6th c. with blessing the palms. Since 1955 RCm uses also the original Roman name, "2d Sun. of the Passion." The custom of the procession of the palms originated early (at least by the 4th c.) in Jerusalem. See also *Church Year*, 4, 8, 14, 16; *Feast of Asses*.

Palmer, Christian David Friedrich (1811–75). B. Winnenden, Württemberg, Ger.; educ. Schönt(h)al (Jagstkreis, near Künzelsau), Württemberg, and Tübingen; held various positions, esp. important at Tübingen and Marburg. Prof. Tübingen 1852; rector 1857. Works include writings on homiletics, catechetics, pedagogy, hymnology, and pastoral theol.

Palmer, George Herbert (1842–1933). Philos.; moralist; b. Boston, Mass.; educ. Harvard U., Cambridge, Mass.; prof. Harvard 1883–1913; championed Christian theism.

Palmer, Paul. See *Baptist Churches*, 26.

Palmer, Ray (1808–87). Cong. cleric; hymnist; b. Little Compton, R. I.; educ. Yale Coll., New Haven, Conn. Hymns include "Come, Jesus, from the Sapphire Throne"; "My Faith Looks Up to Thee"; "Thou Who Roll'st the Year Around."

Palmer, William (1803–85). Angl. theol.; b. Dublin, Eire; fellow Worcester Coll., Oxford, 1831; adherent of Oxford* Movement but expressed misgivings when it became less anti-Roman. Works include *Origines liturgicae; A Treatise on the Church of Christ.*

Palmer, William (1811–79). B. Mixbury, Oxfordshire, Eng.; educ. Oxford; High Churchman (see *High Church*) but not very active in Oxford* Movement; traveled repeatedly to Russ., Athens, and Constantinople in the interest of closer relations bet. the Angl. and E Orthodox chs.; opposed the plan for an Anglo-Luth. bishopric in Jerusalem. Works include *Dissertations on Subjects Relating to the "Orthodox" or "Eastern Catholic" Communion.*

Paltz, Johann Jenser von (Genser? Zenser? Jeuser? ca. 1445–1511). Perhaps b. Pfalzel, near Trier, Ger.; studied at Erfurt; Augustinian monk; prof. theol. Erfurt 1483; active in reforming Augustinians; emphasized cross of Christ, Eucharist, Bible reading; teacher of M. Luther* 1505/06. Works include *Coelifodina* (in defense of indulgences).

Pamperrien, Karl Heinrich Ferdinand Ludwig (Friedrich instead of Ferdinand? Aug. 11, 1845–1926). B. Crivitz (or Krakow?), Mecklenburg, Ger.; educ. Rostock and Berlin; ordained Rudolstadt 1877; miss. to India for the Leipzig* Ev. Luth. Miss. 1877. At Tranquebar 1878–80, Tanjore 1880–84; instructor at Leipzig Miss. Sem., India, since 1885; head of Leipzig Miss. in India provisionally 1887, definitively 1893; returned to Ger. 1920.

Pamphilus of Caesarea (ca. 240–ca. 309). B. Berytus (modern Beirut, Lebanon); studied at Alexandria, Egypt, under Pierius*; presbyter Caesarea, Palestine, ca. 290; martyr. See also *Schools, Early Christian*, 3; *Persecution of Christians*, 4.

Panagia (Gk. "all holy"). E Orthodox term for (1) Mary; (2) case enclosing an image of Mary and worn on the breast by bps. (see also *Encolpion*); (3) bread blessed in honor of Mary, esp. at the 1st morning meal.

Panama. See *Central America*, A, D 2, J.

Pancosmism. See *Pantheism*, 1.

Pancras (ca. 290–304). Legendary child martyr; perhaps a Phrygian; died at Rome under Diocletian.*

Pan-Ecclesiastical Ceremonies. In the E Orthodox Ch., ceremonies directly and collectively concerning the edification of the whole cong.: Evensong (Esperinos, Vespers), Matins (Orthros), the Hours, the Compline (Apodeipnon), the "Chairetismoi" or Salutations, the "Coming of the Bridegroom" (the Vigils of Passion Week), and the Divine Service.

Panentheism (from Gk. *pan*, "all"; *en*, "in"; *theos*, "God"). The view that all things are in God, who, by transcendence,* is more than the sum of them all.

Pannenberg, Wolfhart. See Dogmatics, B 13.

Panta rhei. See *Heraclitus.*

Pantaenus (d. perhaps ca. 190/200 AD). Christian philos.; b. perhaps Sicily, Athens, or Alexandria; convert from Stoicism*; head of catechetical school at Alexandria ca. 180 (see *Schools, Early Christian*, 1); taught Clement* of Alexandria; said to have been a miss. to "India" (probably S Arabia). EK

Pantaleon (from Gk. *panteleemon*, "all-merciful"). Legendary martyr; known for having helped the poor and forsaken; said to have been beheaded under Diocletian (see *Persecutions of Christians*, 4) as physician of Galerius (or Maximian?).

Pantheism. 1. Monistic religious and philos. view that God and the universe are one; denies the personality of God; ascribes to Him only an immanent existence in the universe and identifies Him with it.

One kind of pantheism, pancosmism, holds that God is merged in the universe; it emphasizes nature and its unity, almost loses sight of God, hence approaches atheism.* Another kind, acosmism, holds that the universe is merged in God. There is little practical difference bet. the 2 kinds; both are aspects of the same thing.

2. The concept of pantheism is older than the term. The word "pantheist" was apparently coined 1705 by J. Toland.* Pantheism is the fundamental doctrine of much ancient philos. (see, e. g., *Hinduism*, 2). True pantheistic ideas are rare in medieval literature. In modern times the pantheism of B. Spinoza* influenced J. G. Fichte,* J. W. v. Goethe,* G. W. F. Hegel,* J. G. v. Herder,* G. E. Lessing,* F. W. J. v. Schelling,* F. D. E. Schleiermacher,* et al.

3. Pantheism has occurred among Eng. and Am. thinkers only in a veiled or partial form. RCm has found pantheistic leanings linked more with mysticism than doctrine and has always opposed the basic notions of pantheism; pope and council have formally condemned pantheism repeatedly since 1861.

4. Besides destroying the personality of God and reducing Him to a lower object of worship, pantheism destroys the personality of man, who becomes merely a part of the Whole. Individual responsi-

bility and the moral world order are destroyed. Pantheism does not explain the existence of evil. Christ's redemptive work becomes an illusion.

See also *Atheism; Monism.*

Pantheon. 1. Temple dedicated to all the gods. 2. All the gods of a people, esp. major deities.

Pantocrator (Gk. "almighty ruler"). Term used of God 2 Co 6:18; Rv 1:8; 4:8; 11:17; 15:3; 16:7, 14; 19:6, 15; 21:22. Used in the E Orthodox Ch. also of Christ on His throne.

Papa Angelicus (Pastor Angelicus). Ideal pope(s) envisioned in utopian hope that arose in early 13th c. It., sparked by a desire for revival of apostolic simplicity and zeal.

Papacy. 1. Beginnings of the papacy are obscure; growth was gradual.

2. The ch. at Rome, the world's capital, became prominent early on as the oldest ch. in the West; Irenaeus* mentions its preeminence (*Adversus haereses,* III, iii, 2). As it and its bps. grew in honorary preeminence in the first 3 cents., its bps. began with increasing success to claim, though not without widespread dissent, supremacy of right, as successors of Peter. But the 325 Council of Nicaea* mentioned the bp. of Rome only incidentally; neither it nor the immediately following councils were convened by the bp. of Rome, nor did he or his legates preside. Despite protest of the bp. of Rome, the Council of Chalcedon (451) declared the patriarch of Constantinople his official equal.

3. The fall of the W Roman Empire 476 (when Odoacer deposed Romulus Augustulus), enabled Roman bps. to increase their power and enlarge the area of their spiritual sway, including superiority over earthly rulers (see also *Church and State,* 5). Monasticism became a useful tool. Gregory I (see *Popes,* 4) is a bridge bet. the ancient and medieval world. The spread of Islam put E rivals of the bp. of Rome into eclipse. Missionaries inculcated obedience to Rome among Germanic peoples. In return for papal favors Pepin* the Short and Charlemagne* laid the foundation of papal temporal power.

4. There followed a period of decline. Attempts were made to undergird the papacy with the Donation* of Constantine and the Pseudo-Isidorean* Decretals. It was a time of moral degradation, including rival popes. The emp. intervened 1046 and secured the election of a pope who crowned the emp., who gained the right to appoint popes. Gregory VII (see *Popes,* 7) raised the papacy to its peak. It rode the crest of this wave ca. 1073 – ca. 1303 (see *Popes,* 7–12). See also *Crusades.* Then decline set in, with Fr. and Eng. esp. in revolt against the papacy (see also *Babylonian Captivity,* 2; *England,* A 3–4; *France,* 3; *Schism,* 8.

5. The Council of Constance* ended the papal schism, but instead of meeting demands for true and complete reform it burned the reformer J. Hus.* By the end of the 15th c. the papacy had recovered much of its power. But through the Luth. Reformation its power was again reduced and it has not regained its former stature. In some countries nationalism opposes papal claims. Papal temporal power ended 1870, was restored 1929.

See also *Antichrist,* 5–8; *Popes; Vatican Councils.*

B. J. Kidd, *The Roman Primacy to A.D. 461* (London, 1936); W. d'Ormesson, *The Papacy,* tr. M. Derrick (New York, 1959); F. Gontard, *The Chair of Peter,* tr. A. J. and E. F. Peeler (New York, 1964).

Papadopoulos, Chrysostomos (1868–1938). Gk. Orthodox ch. hist.; b. Madyton, Thrace; prof. theol. School of the Cross, Jerusalem, 1895; prof. ch. hist. Athens 1914; abp. Athens and Greece 1923. Works include histories of the ch. in Jerusalem and Greece.

Papal Bull. See *Bull.*

Papal Household. Called papal court till 1932. In the narrow sense, the papal household *(fami[g]lia pontificia)* consists of clerics and laymen who have a function by protocol in the papal residence; its mems. live both in and outside Vatican City. In the broad sense, the papal household consists of the papal household in the narrow sense and the papal chapel *(capella pontificia),* whose mems. may take part in liturgical functions solemnly celebrated by the pope. Not to be confused with curia.*

Papal Legates. See *Legates.*

Papal Nuncio. See *Legates.*

Papal Pontifical Mass. See *Pontifical Mass.*

Papal Schism. See *Schism,* 8.

Papal States. See *States of the Church.*

Papal Syllabus. See *Roman Catholic Confessions,* D.

Papal System. See *Polity, Ecclesiastical,* 5.

Papamichail, Grigorios (Gregorios Papamichael; 1874 [1875?]–1956). Gk. Orthodox theol.; b. Ippion, on Lesbos (Mytilene); prof. School of the Cross, Jerusalem, 1905; head of a printery Alexandria 1907; prof. Athens 1918. Works include a book on socialism and Christianity; a life of Gregorius Palamas (see *Hesychasm*); apologetics.

Papebroch, Daniel van (Papebroeck; Papenbroeck; 1628–1714). B. Antwerp, Belg.; Bollandist*; denied that Carmelites* can be traced to OT times.

Paphnutius. Name of many monks in the Egyptian desert, including (1) bp. Upper Thebaid; fl. 4th c.; suffered severely in persecution; said to have helped persuade the 325 Council of Nicaea* to leave the question of continence to the discretion of clerics who had married before ordination; (2) abbot in Desert of Scete (Nitrian Valley ca. 50 mi. S of Alexandria, Egypt); friend of J. Cassianus*; noted for meditation.

Papiamento. See *Caribbean Islands,* E 7.

Papias. See *Apostolic Fathers,* 4.

Pappus, Johann(es) (1549–1610). Luth. theol.; b. Lindau, Bav., Ger.; educ. Strasbourg and Tübingen; prof. Strasbourg and pastor of the cathedral there; in controversy with Johannes Sturm*; opposed the Tetrapolitan Confession (see *Reformed Confessions,* D 1); successfully promoted adoption of a Luth. ch. order and the FC in Strasbourg 1598.

Papua. See *New Guinea,* 1, 3–4.

Papyrus. Tall sedge plant of the Nile valley; used ca. 5th c. BC to ca. 4th c. AD for making writing material often used for Bible MSS. The word "paper" is derived from the Gk. *papyros.* See also *Manuscripts of the Bible,* 2 a, c.

G. A. Deissmann, *Light from the Ancient East,* tr. L. R. M. Strachan, rev. ed. (New York, 1927); R. K. Harrison, *Archaeology of the New Testament* (New York, 1964); F. G. Kenyon, *Our Bible and the Ancient Manuscripts,* 5th ed., rev. A. W. Adams (New York, 1958); E. C. Malte, "Light from the Papyri on St. Paul's Terminology," *CTM,* XVIII (1947), 499–517.

Paracelsus, Philippus Aureolus (Theophrast[us] Bombast[us] [Baumbast] von Hohenheim; ca. 1493/94–1541). Alchemist; physician; b. near Einsiedeln, Switz.; may himself have invented the name Paracelsus to indicate equality with, or superiority to, Aulus Cornelius Celsus (early 1st c. AD; Roman writer; compiled an encyclopedia on agriculture, law, medicine, military science, and philos.); tried to recast med. science; proponent of iatrochemistry (chemistry combined with medicine; ca. 1525–ca. 1660); empiricist; emphasized nature study; Christian mystic philos. Lived a restless life; studied at several univs., esp. Padua and Ferrara, It.; army surgeon in It. and Den., probably also Moscow and Constantinople; lived at Strasbourg, Basel, Nürnberg, Vienna, and Salzburg. PR

F. Gundolf, *Paracelsus* (Berlin, 1928); W. E. Peuckert, *Pansophie,* 2 vols. (Stuttgart, 1936–67); F. Spunda, *Das Weltbild des Paracelsus* (Vienna, 1941/

42); H. M. Pachter, *Magic into Science* (New York, 1951).

Paraclete. See *Holy Spirit.*

Paradise. See *Hereafter,* A, C 2.

Paraguay. See *South America,* 8.

Paraments (from Lat. *parare,* "adorn, prepare, equip"). 1. Paraments in the wide sense include all liturgical vestments, coverings, and hangings; in the narrow sense paraments are distinguished from vestments.

2. Nondecorative altar paraments should be white in all seasons; some have found in this a symbol of unchanging doctrine. These paraments include a linen cloth covering the altar without front overhang and resting on 1 or 2 layers of linen that have no front or side overhang; corporal*; possibly a veil, of silk or linen, ca. 30 or 36 in. square. See also *Pall,* 1; *Purificator.*

3. The decorative paraments of altar, lectern, and pulpit are called antependia (sing.: antependium; from Lat. for "frontal hanging") and are properly in the liturgical color of the season (see *Colors, Liturgical*); the altar antependium is attached to a linen cloth under the white linen altar covering (see 2).

Pardieck, Edward (Eduard; Apr. 29, 1867–Mar. 21, 1926). B. Indianapolis, Ind.; educ. Conc. Coll., Fort Wayne, Ind., and Conc. Sem., St. Louis, Mo. Pastor Chicago, Ill., 1890–1902. Prof. St. Paul's Coll., Concordia, Mo., 1902–12; Conc. Sem., St. Louis, Mo., 1912–23. Ed. *Der Lutheraner* 1912–13; other works include *Logen und weltliche Unterstützungsvereine;* essays on the Trinity, the Priesthood of Believers, and other subjects for Mo. Syn. Dist. convs.

Pardons. Name used for indulgences* in Art. 22 of the Thirty-nine Arts. (see *Anglican Confessions,* 6).

Pareau, Louis Gerlach. See *Groningen School.*

Parent-Teacher Organizations, Lutheran. See *Parish Education,* H 3 e, J.

Parents and the Christian Education of Their Children. See *Christian Education,* D 3; *Parish Education.*

Pareto, Vilfredo (1848–1923). It. sociologist and economist; b. Paris, Fr.; prof. Lausanne; considered religion wishful thinking; despised democracy; Fascism (see *Socialism,* 3) based largely on his theories.

Pareus, David (1548–1622). Ref. theol.; b. Frankenstein in Schlesien (present Zabkowice, Poland); educ. Heidelberg; held various pastorates; prof. Heidelberg 1598–1622; tended to compromise with Luths. but not with RCs. Issued the *Neustädter Bibel* 1587; other works include exegetical writings.

Pariah. See *Hinduism,* 3.

Paris, Cathedral at. See *Church Architecture,* 10.

Paris, Matthew (of). See *Matthew (of) Paris.*

Paris Evangelical Missionary Society. Founded 1822 by Fr. Prots.; several similar groups previously organized in Fr. became auxiliaries; "Maison des Missions" (Mission House) opened 1823; its 1st student was J. King.* Began work in Bechuanaland 1829 (see *Africa,* B 3; soon abandoned), Basutoland 1833 (see *Africa,* B 6), Senegal 1862 (see *Africa,* C 1), Barotseland (in W Northern Rhodesia; see *Africa,* B 2) in the 1880s. The PEMS lent aid to miss. work in Madagascar (see *Africa,* B 9) in the late 1890s. The work of Am. Presbs. in Gabon (in W equatorial Afr.) was gradually transferred to the PEMS 1892–1913. As a result of WW I the work of Ger. missionaries in Togo (see *Africa,* C 13) and of Ger. and Swiss missionaries in Cameroon (see *Kamerun*) passed into the hands of the PEMS. Other fields have included Tahiti (see *Society Islands*) and the Loyalty Is. and New Caledonia (see *Melanesia*).

Paris Polyglot. See *Polyglot Bibles.*

Parish. Territory of a cong. in which it exercises its usual functions. See also *Western Christianity 500–1500,* 9.

Parish Centers. See *Armed Services Commission,* 5.

Parish Education. A. *Parish Educ. Defined.* 1. Responsibility for Christian educ. is shared by parents (Dt 6:6-7; Ps 78:1-6; Eph 6:4) and the ch. (Mt 28:19-20; Jn 21:15-17). The ch. emphasizes the importance of Christian training in the home and organizes an educ. program for all ch. mems. Dt 32:46; Acts 20:28; Cl 1:10; and 2 Ptr 3:18 show that parish educ. is to meet high standards set by God, continue through life, and provide for spiritual growth and regular opportunities for Christian education.

2. All parish educ. activities should try to achieve the 3-fold aim of Christian educ.: the glory of God, the temporal and eternal happiness of the individual, and the welfare of mankind. This art. concerns parish educ. esp. in LCMS.

B. *Parish Educ. at the Preschool Level.* 1. The ch. was slow in arranging programs for children too young for formal agencies.

2. The preschool program of the ch. includes the S. S. nursery (or cradle) roll (birth to age 3), the S. S. nursery class (ages 3–4), the S. S. kindergarten class (ages 4–5), and weekday kindergarten (age 5 up to 6).

3. *S. S. Nursery (or Cradle) Roll.* "Nursery Roll" and "Cradle Roll" are somewhat interchangeable designations for the dept. giving attention to infants and small children. Some use "Cradle Roll" for birth to age 1, "Nursery Roll" for 1–3. Aims:

a. To awaken in parents a sense of responsibility for the religious instruction and training of their little ones and to give them initial guidance;

b. To est. and maintain a bond of unity bet. parents, S. S., and ch.;

c. To give the ch. additional access to homes of unchurched who have prekindergarten children;

d. To provide basic materials for a head start in Christian nurture.

Children are entered on the Nursery (or Cradle) Roll either at birth or at Baptism. In 1970 ca. 3,150 congs. in the US and Can. enrolled more than 90,000 children in the Nursery (or Cradle) Roll.

4. *Nursery and Kindergarten Classes in the Sunday School.* 3-yr.-olds who attend S. S. comprise the Nursery Class; 4-to-5-yr.-olds comprise the Kindergarten Class. In 1970, congs. in the US and Can. enrolled ca. 48,700 in Nursery Classes and ca. 79,900 in Kindergarten Classes.

5. *Weekday Nursery School and Kindergarten.* The Nursery School aims to provide learning experiences in a Christian environment for 3- and 4-yr.-olds. Some congs. operate nursery schools as part of the elementary school or as part of a nursery school-kindergarten program. The Kindergarten promotes learning through work and play in a Christian environment; it helps the child adjust to school life, develops creative abilities, broadens interests, and helps develop skills in learning, language, and self-expression.

6. Instructional materials for the preschool level were developed by the Bd. of Parish Educ. The Mission:Life materials, which began to appear 1971, provide coordinated courses for nursery and kindergarten classes in various kinds of schools, including VBS.

7. *Dept. of Early Childhood Education.* Sponsored 1971 by the LEA. Aim: to share resource information on early childhood educ. and develop special materials.

C. For the hist. of parish educ. on the elementary level see *Christian Education.*

D. *Parochial, or Elementary, School.* 1. The Luth. parochial, or elementary, school is est., maintained, and controlled by a cong. or group of congs.

2. Objectives (cf. *A Curriculum Guide for Lu-*

theran Elementary Schools, ed. F. Nohl and F. A. Meyer [St. Louis, 1964], pp. 2.4–2.5):

a. That the child in relation to God develop (1) a growing knowledge of the Triune God, a growing trust in Jesus Christ as the Savior from sin, and an increasingly worshipful, sanctified life; (2) a growing knowledge of the Bible as the Word of Life, a proper understanding of Law and Gospel, and increased ability to apply God's Word to life situations, and a desire to gain the blessings of Holy Baptism and the Lord's Supper; (3) an understanding of the nature, function, and responsibility of the ch. as the body of Christ, plus a willingness and ability to serve as an active mem. of this body and as a priest of God.

b. That the child in relation to himself and his powers (1) develop knowledges, attitudes, and conducts needed to function effectively as God's child (spiritual powers); (2) understand his body and accept responsibility for its health, safety, and recreation (physical powers); (3) develop logical, scientific, and creative thinking habits, gain knowledge and communication tools, and acquire significant elements of his cultural heritage (mental powers); (4) develop soc. skills needed to live competently and creatively (soc. powers); (5) understand and control his emotions, find security and a true picture of himself through firm reliance on God and trust in Christ, and practice Christian love toward all men (emotional powers); (6) appreciate the beauties of nature and the fine arts and express himself in various fine-arts media (aesthetic powers).

c. That the child in relation to his fellowmen (1) recognize all men to be God's creation and show respect, courtesy, and consideration for the rights and welfare of others; (2) respect parents as God's representatives and appreciate his privileges and responsibilities as a mem. of an earthly family of which Christ is Head; (3) develop Christian soc. responsibility and cooperative skills; (4) develop concern for the spiritual and material welfare of all men and show this concern by witnessing and welfare activities; (5) respect govt. as God-ordained and appreciate his privileges and responsibilities as a mem. of the local, state, nat., and world community.

d. That the child in relation to nature (1) understand that God is the Creator, Ruler, and Preserver of nature; (2) thank and praise God for the gifts of nature; (3) develop knowledges, attitudes, and conducts needed to understand, use, and care for God's gifts in nature; (4) willingly use nature to glorify God and serve man.

3. The school stresses Christian growth opportunities in the whole school experience and provides for complete education in the curriculum.

4. See *Teachers.*

5. The *curriculum* may be defined as the sum of the experiences the child has in school. The teacher tries to provide a Bible-based, Christ-centered, and life-related curriculum. The Bible is frame of reference for all school activities.

6. At first special instructional materials were produced and promoted on a local or regional level. Production of such materials was assigned to the 1st Gen. School Bd., est. 1914. Materials have included textbooks in Bible Hist. and Catechism, the Concordia Primary Religion Series, Units in Religion for Lutheran Schools, and other textbooks. Mission: Life materials, which began to appear 1971, provide a coordinated religion program for all age-levels and all agencies of Christian educ. Materials for the teacher include (1) guides produced by the Bd. of Parish Educ., (2) *General Course of Study for Lutheran Elementary Schools* (1943), and (3) *A Curriculum Guide for Lutheran Elementary Schools* (3 vols. 1964; updated by annual supplements).

7. *LCMS statistics* covering US, Can., and S. America (figures for congs. usually include preaching stations). *1850:* 41 congs., 41 schools, 41 teachers, 1,342 pupils; *1860:* 155 congs., 129 schools, 129 teachers, 6,843 pupils; *1870:* 214 congs., 226 schools, 20,369 pupils; *1880:* 851 congs., 784 schools, 43,368 pupils; *1890:* 1,662 congs., 1,226 schools; 1,305 teachers, 78,061 pupils; *1900:* 2,147 congs., 1,767 schools, 1,907 teachers, 92,042 pupils; *1910:* 2,736 congs., 2,130 schools, 2,360 teachers, 93,890 pupils; *1920:* 3,283 congs., 1,310 schools, 1,954 teachers, 73,063 pupils; *1930:* 3,843 congs., 1,339 schools, 3,335 teachers, 79,956 pupils; *1940:* 4,358 congs., 1,259 schools, 2,247 teachers, 71,151 pupils; *1950:* 5,608 congs., 1,277 schools, 3,228 teachers, 98,136 pupils; *1960:* 6,610 congs., 1,413 schools, 5,501 teachers, 156,244 pupils; *1970:* 7,233 congs., 1,215 schools, 6,616 teachers, 150,980 pupils. See par. 8.

8. In par. 7, figures for 1900 and 1910 include many Sat. schools and summer schools. Loss in pupils 1930–40 was largely a result of economic depression. Declining birth rate, higher school standards, and increased costs brought a decline in the no. of schools and pupils 1960–70.

9. *Statistics for other Luth. bodies in America.* 1969 LCA: 19 schools, 153 teachers, 2,908 pupils. 1970 figures for WELS: 244 schools, 1,038 teachers, 26,070 pupils; SELC: 3 schools, 14 teachers, 368 pupils; Ch. of the Luth. Confession: 11 schools, 31 teachers, 453 pupils; The ALC: 52 schools, 389 teachers, 6,975 pupils (plus 156 teachers, 2,846 pupils in kindergartens of 93 additional congs.).

10. LCMS has promoted schools and textbooks from its founding 1847. A Gen. School Bd. was created by syn. 1914. Secretaries of Schools: A. C. Stellhorn* 1921–60, William Albert Kramer (b. 1900) 1960–70. Secy. of Elementary and Secondary Schools: Al H. Senske 1971–.

11. *Dept. of Luth. Elementary School Principals.* Created 1966; sponsored by LEA; provides special resources and conducts workshops for school administrators.

E. *Sun. School.* 1. S. S. is a special school that meets for ca. 1 hr., as a rule Sun. mornings; provides religious instruction for young and old and serves as a miss. agency.

2. Hist. of the S. S. See *Sunday School.*

3. Because of strong emphasis on the parochial school, little attention was given the S. S. in the early yrs. of the Mo. Syn.

4. As the Mo. Syn. grew, many congs. could not, or at least did not, maintain parochial schools. Instead, they organized part-time agencies of religious instruction, including the S. S. Some congs. with parochial schools also recognized the merits of the S. S. The S. S. is the most widespread educ. agency in the Mo. Syn.; few congs. are without one.

5. Materials used in early Sun. schools included esp. the Bible, catechisms, Bible histories, and hymnals. Ger. and Eng. S. S. lesson leaflets first appeared Jan. 1911, *Concordia Lesson Helps* Jan. 1916 (replaced Jan. 1923 by *Concordia Sunday-School Teachers' Quarterly*), *Interaction* Oct. 1960.

6. The *Life in Christ* series began Oct. 1951. Mission:Life materials, which first appeared 1971, coordinate S. S. and parochial school curricula.

7. Meetings to instruct and train teachers were soon held regularly. S. S. assocs. were formed in St. Louis, Mo., Chicago, Ill., and Cleveland, Ohio, in the 1920s. Many other assocs. were later formed elsewhere. The Bd. of Parish Educ. promoted circuit S. S. assocs. and provided programs for them through Dist. bds. Most Districts have sponsored S. S. convs. Nat. conventions were sponsored by the Bd. of Parish Educ. 1960, 1963, 1966, 1970.

8. LCMS est. the office of Gen. S. S. Secy. 1956; Allan Hart Jahsmann was its 1st incumbent 1959–

68. In 1968 the name of the office was changed (present name: Secy. of Sun., Weekday, and Summer Schools) and Dale E. Griffin appointed to it.

9. In 1938 LCMS approved appointment of a S. S. teacher training committee, which issued 16 courses first called Concordia Teacher Training Series, later changed to Concordia Leadership Training Series (more than 10,000,000 copies 1938–68).

10. *Approximate LCMS S. S. figures. 1910:* 53,343 pupils; *1920:* 1,587 Sun. schools, 108,133 pupils, 9,553 teachers; *1930:* 2,849 Sun. schools, 210,988 pupils, 20,174 teachers; *1940:* 3,635 Sun. schools, 281,572 pupils, 29,531 teachers; *1950:* 4,421 Sun. schools, 425,499 pupils, 48,514 teachers; *1960:* 5,439 Sun. schools, 802,980 pupils, 92,206 teachers; *1970:* 5,899 Sun. schools, 885,128 pupils, 98,754 teachers.

Approximate 1970 figures for other Luth. bodies in the US and Canada. LCA: 5,918 Sun. schools, 841,372 pupils, 119,837 teachers; The ALC: 4,596 Sun. schools, 672,461 pupils, 80,361 teachers; SELC: 55 Sun. schools, 4,566 pupils, 683 teachers; WELS: 899 Sun. schools, 53,002 pupils, 6,740 teachers; Ev. Luth. Ch. of Can.: 296 Sun. schools, 21,472 pupils, 3,159 teachers; ELS: 82 Sun. schools, 3,812 pupils, 534 teachers; Ch. of the Luth. Confession: 57 Sun. schools, 1,619 pupils, 256 teachers; Ch. of the Luth. Brethren: 87 Sun. schools, 7,450 pupils, 1,070 teachers.

F. *Other Agencies of Elementary Educ.* 1. These include weekday schools, vacation Bible (or summer) schools, and confirmation classes.

2. *Weekday Schools.* For children not attending Luth. elementary schools the weekday school offers 2 or 3 hrs. of Christian educ. in addition to S. S. In 1970, weekday after school classes had ca. 69,420 pupils, Sat. schools ca. 47,000 pupils, released time schools ca. 18,960 pupils. Weekday schools are taught by pastors, professional teachers, and volunteer teachers. Materials were issued in the early and mid-1940s under the series title Lessons in Religion for Part-Time Schools. The Concordia Weekday Series appeared in the 1960s. Mission:Life materials, which first appeared 1971, provide a complete weekday program from prekindergarten through grade 12, built on the same course outlines as the parochial school program.

3. Approximate *summer school* (later called VBS) figures. 1945: 1,043 schools, 36,168 pupils; 1950: 1,937 schools, 125,126 pupils; 1960: 3,475 schools, 338,435 pupils; 1970: 4,162 schools, 376,299 pupils. Special VBS materials were developed.

4. *Confirmation instruction,* usually a 1 to 3 yr. course taught by the pastor, is based mainly on the SC. See also *Confirmation.*

5. *Christenlehre* is catechetical instruction for all, formerly conducted sometimes only for children, in a ch. service usually Sun. morning or afternoon.

G. *Parish Educ. at the Secondary Level.* Agencies used for post-confirmation youth: high schools, Bible classes, and young people's socs.

1. A few high schools were est. 1857–77 in the Mo. Syn. but closed for lack of sufficient financial support. A few other ventures, e. g., in Milwaukee, Wis. (1903), Chicago, Ill. (1909), and Fort Wayne, Ind. (1935), were more successful. A large increase in the no. of high schools began in the mid-1940s.

As of 1971, LCMS high schools (with yr. founded) include Luther High School North, Chicago, Ill. (1909); Conc. Lutheran High School, Fort Wayne, Ind. (1935); Luth. High School West, Detroit, Mich. (1944); Luth. High School, Racine, Wis. (1944); Luth. High School North and Luth. High School South, St. Louis, Mo. (1946); Luth. High School, Houston, Tex. (1949); Luther High School South, Chicago, Ill. (1951); Walther Luth. High School, Melrose Park, Ill. (1953); Maier Memorial Luth. High School, Los Angeles, Calif. (1953); Luth. High School, Denver, Colo. (1955); Milwaukee (Wis.) Luth. High School (1955); Our Savior Luth. High School, Bronx, N. Y. (1955); Luth. High School East, Harper Woods (near Detroit), Mich. (1957); Luth. High School East, Cleveland Heights, Ohio (1958); Luth. High School West, Rocky River (near Cleveland), Ohio (1958); Long Is. Luth. High School, Brookville, N. Y. (1959); Luth. High School, St. Paul, Minn. (1959); Luth. High School, Mayer, Minn. (1960); Martin Luther High School, Maspeth, N. Y. (1960); Minneapolis (Minn.) Luth. High School (1963); Luth. High School, Baltimore, Md. (1965); Germantown Luth. Academy, Philadelphia, Pa. (1965); Luth. High School, Rockford, Ill. (1965); Martin Luther High School, Greendale (near Milwaukee), Wis. (1968); Luth. High School, New Orleans, La. (1970); Saint John Luth. High School, Ocala, Fla. (1970).

In 1970 WELS had 9 high schools, the Ch. of the Luth. Confession 1.

Some Mo. Syn. colleges maintain high school depts. Some congs. have added a 9th grade to their parochial schools.

2. Most congs. conduct Bible classes at the youth level; ca. 35% of the youth of high school age in these congs. are enrolled.

3. The Walther League (see *Young People's Organizations, Christian,* II 3) provided many youth programs. The LCMS Bd. of Youth Ministry provides a variety of programs.

H. *Parish Education at the Adult Level.* 1. Congs. found it desirable to provide for adult educ. in Bible classes and special classes, particularly for parent educ. Topic studies of the LLL and LWML were used in meetings of those organizations. In 1944 the Mo. Syn. assigned the sphere of adult educ. to its Bd. for Parish Education. Secretaries of Adult Educ.: Oscar E. Feucht 1946–end of 1968, Victor Constien Jan. 1, 1969–. The Bd. gave special attention to Bible classes, family life educ., adult school of religion, cottage Bible classes, and leadership training in Bible institutes.

2. In 1947 LCMS launched an intensive syn.-wide Bible study movement. The Train-Two program (aim: to train 2 persons as lay leaders for every existing and every prospective Bible class) began 1959. See also *Bible Study.*

3. A Family Life Committee was appointed. Dirs. of Family Life Educ.: Charles A. Reichert 1965–67, Evan J. Temple 1969–. Major projects in family life education have included:

a. Helping Dist. bds. of educ. provide leadership for family life educ.

b. Developing materials for annual observances of Christian Family Month.

c. Developing resources for the whole program of ministry to families.

d. Providing direction and aids for marriage educ. and counseling. An in-service training program in pastoral care to families was developed. An extensive seminar program was projected.

e. Materials in the Parent Guidance Series provided topic studies for Parent-Teacher groups.

f. The 6-vol. Conc. Sex Educ. Series was produced to provide a graded program of educ. for young and old.

g. Research projects resulted in several vols.: *Engagement and Marriage; Sex and the Church; Family Relationships and the Church.*

4. Congs. were urged to est. a weekday Adult School of Religion with these features: short-term (6 to 8 week) courses in spring and fall; 1½ to 2 hrs. per session; multiple choices based on needs and interests; teachers selected to teach a specific

course. Special short-term courses were also developed for this program.

5. In cottage Bible classes, groups meet in homes of mems.

6. A manual entitled *Leadership Training Through Bible Institutes* was issued (later reissued as *Adult Education Through Bible Institutes*) to guide development of intercong. or circuit schools offering advanced courses.

7. In 1962 ca. 100 Bible institutes were in operation, most with weekly sessions for 6 to 8 weeks, some conducted in spring and fall. Programs included courses on the Bible, Christian doctrine, and various areas of ch. work.

I. *Financing the Program of Parish Educ.* 1. The cong. finances the program in amounts varying with the type of program and size of the cong.

2. Sun. schools, weekday schools, and vacation Bible schools usually help to finance themselves, with the balance, if any, subscribed by the cong. or other sources.

3. Responsibility for financing a parochial school rests with the cong. (or congs., in the case of a cen. school). In some cases, mission bds. may finance new schools for a time.

A 1970–71 survey revealed annual tuition charges ranging from $1 to more than $400; decisions connected with tuition charges lie within cong. jurisdiction.

Annual operating cost is figured on 2 bases: (1) average daily membership (ADM); (2) average daily attendance (ADA). In the 1970–71 school yr. the average per pupil cost (ADM) in a survey of 702 schools was $359; on ADA basis it was $364.

4. The supporting organization for a high school may be 1 cong., or, in the case of a cen. school, an assoc. of congs., or an assoc. of individuals. 1970–71 tuition charges for Luth. mems. ranged from $250 to $1,220, for non-Luth. mems. from $450 to $1,300. In 1969 it was estimated that the capital investment required to est. a Luth. high school ranged from $2,500 to $3,000 per pupil. In 26 high schools the 1970–71 average operating cost per pupil (ADM) was $643, with the range extending from $472 to $1,261.

5. Government Aid for Lutheran Schools. See *Public Aid to Church-Related Elementary and Secondary Schools.*

J. *Luth. Parent-Teacher Organizations.* Gen. meet monthly; program usually planned jointly by parents and teachers. Aims: (1) mutual home-school understanding; (2) home-school cooperation and unity; (3) supplementing the cong. budget and providing instructional equipment. The Nat. Luth. Parent-Teacher League was formed 1953 as a dept. of LEA. Later it became a separate organization. It has provided helps to cong. parent-teacher groups in organization, program, and service projects. 671 groups were affiliated 1970–71.

K. *Educational Administration and Supervision in the Local Congregation.* 1. LCMS policy regards the cong. as the basic unit of administration and supervision. As a rule, the cong. exercises its authority and responsibility in this field through such officers as the pastor, bd. of educ., principal, S. S. supt., weekday school supt., VBS supt., and dir. of educ.

2. It is usually the function of the pastor to supervise directly, or through others, the entire educational program of the ch. See also *Ministerial Office.*

3. A bd. of educ. may be elected or appointed to supervise the educ. program and to assist the pastor and other leaders. Bd. activities usually include 1 or more of the following:

a. Provide a parish educ. program that meets the needs of the whole cong.

b. Study participation of cong. mems. in the program.

c. Provide lay leadership for the program.

d. Promote the agencies.

4. Professionally trained parochial school teachers are usually used in the entire program of the cong.

5. The principal of the school takes the lead in faculty meetings, setting up the curriculum, and evaluating accomplishments. He is also to carry out policies adopted by the bd. of educ. and represent the school in pub. relations. Luth. principals usually teach, but there were 60 full-time principals 1970–71. Full-time principals function as the educ. leaders of their schools in the administration and supervision of the whole program. Some full-time principals also serve as directors of Christian educ. for the whole parish educ. program.

6. The S. S. supt. is the leader in the S. S. His concerns include standards and needs, and ways and means of meeting both.

7. The supt. of the weekday school or of the VBS supervises the operation of the school and helps recruit and train the staff.

8. Some congs. find merit in having a dir. of Christian educ. to help administer the parish program. In 1970 there were more than 200 such dirs.

L. *Educ. Administration and Supervision in the Syn. Dist.* 1. Soon after the Mo. Syn. created a Gen. School Bd. 1914 (see also D 6), various Dists. created similar bds. or committees. Their area of concern grew from the parochial school to include all agencies of parish educ. Functions as defined in the 1971 LCMS *Handbook,* p. 160: "The District board shall cooperate with the Synod's Board of Parish Education and shall assist and advise the local congregation with regard to the whole range of Christian education on all age levels, helping the local congregation achieve the objectives . . . of Christian education." More detailed regulations on the Dist. level usually specify that the bd. shall consider itself advisory both to the Dist. and its officials and to the congs. and their pastors and teachers. See also 2.

2. Circuit Counselors share responsibility for supervision with the Dist. bd. Many Dist. bds. have appointed a circuit consultant in educ. resources.

3. Some Dists. have appointed full-time functionaries variously called Supt., Ex. Secy., Dir. of Christian Educ., or Counselor in Parish Educ. Development of this office was gradual: 3 Dists. 1918, 5 Dists. 1920/21, 1 Dist. in the 1930s, 6 Dists. in the 1940s, 7 Dists. in the 1950s, 5 Dists. in the 1960s. In 1972 two Dists. provided some service through other Dist. executives; the other 7 Dists. provided leadership through mems. of the Dist. Bd. of Parish Educ.

M. *Educ. Administration and Supervision by the Bd. of Parish Educ.* 1. The Mo. Syn. appointed a Gen. School Bd. 1914 (see also D 6). A S. S. Bd. was created 1923. In 1932 these 2 bds. were joined to form 1 Bd. of Christian Educ. In 1944 the Mo. Syn. enlarged the scope of this bd. and changed its name to Board for Parish Education (changed 1959 to Bd. of Parish Educ.). Functions as defined in the 1971 LCMS *Handbook,* pp. 155–156:

"a. assist in planning an effective program of parish education and especially seek to improve and extend the system of elementary and secondary schools in all congregations;

"b. watch for all movements and tendencies which might endanger the program of parish education and marshal all available resources to counteract such tendencies and movements;

"c. plan and direct the production of textbooks and other printed materials necessary to carry out an effective program of parish education;

"d. assist in coordinating and integrating the various educational agencies and activities intended to promote parish education;

"e. assist the District Boards of Parish Education in supervising and directing all formal educational activities of the congregations of the Synod, such as the Lutheran elementary and secondary schools, the Sunday school, summer school, vacation Bible school, and the part-time weekday religious school;

"f. initiate and direct research activities necessary to promote and improve parish education;

"g. advise the Synod, its Districts, and congregations concerning problems, needs, and possibilities in the field of parish education;

"h. arrange an educational conference of representatives of the Boards of Parish Education of the Synod and the Districts which, as a rule, shall meet every year;

"i. provide a comprehensive program of leadership training materials to train church school teachers and church officers and to integrate the program with other leadership training in Bible institutes and camps;

"j. conduct invitational meetings as needed with members of the departments of education of our colleges and seminaries to deal with basic problems of Christian education;

"k. assist our families in the development of Christian family life on all age levels;

"l. provide periodical literature such as story papers and devotional literature for children and periodicals for youth and adults."

2. In 1920 the Mo. Syn. empowered the Gen. School Bd. to engage a Gen. Secy.

3. The office of Ed. of S. S. Literature was created 1927 (changed 1929 to Secretary of Sunday-schools.)

4. In 1932 the Mo. Syn. resolved that the syn. Bd. of Christian Educ. elect "an executive secretary, whose field of activities shall be our entire work of Christian childhood-training under instruction of the Board." This resolution was reiterated 1938 and 1941. The office was filled 1943 by the election of Arthur C. Repp, who was succeeded by Arthur L. Miller 1946–72, Melvin Kieschnick 1972–.

5. Additional staff mems. were authorized from time to time. For many yrs. the staff was divided into 5 depts.: school, S. S., VBS, weekday school, and adult educ.

6. In 1965, to focus attention on the learner instead of the agencies, staff mems. were assigned to 1 of 3 divisions: children, youth, adults, so they were mems. of a dept. and a division. In 1968 the staff was reorganized into 3 divisions: editorial, field services, and research and development. In this reorganized staff structure Allan H. Jahsmann served as Ex. Dir., Martin F. Wessler as Dir. of Field Services (till 1971), Delbert O. Schulz as Dir. of Research and Development. ALM

See also *Schools, Church-Related.*

4th LEA Yearbook: *100 Years of Christian Education,* ed. A. C. Repp (River Forest, Ill., 1947); 8th LEA Yearbook: A. L. Miller, *Educational Administration and Supervision of the Lutheran Schools of the Missouri Synod, 1914–50* (River Forest, Ill., 1951); 13th LEA Yearbook: *Readings in the Lutheran Philosophy of Education,* ed., L. G. Bickel and R. F. Surburg (River Forest, Ill., 1956); 14th LEA Yearbook: *Tests and Measurements in Lutheran Education,* ed. A. L. Miller (River Forest, Ill., 1957); A. H. Jahsmann, *What's Lutheran in Education?* (St. Louis, 1960); *Lutheran Elementary Schools in Action,* ed. V. C. Krause (St. Louis, 1963); M. P. Strommen, *Profiles of Church Youth* (St. Louis, 1963); A. C. Stellhorn, *Schools of the Lutheran Church – Missouri Synod* (St. Louis, 1963); 20th LEA Yearbook: M. A. Haendschke, *The Sunday School Story* (River Forest, Ill., 1963); *Church and State Under God,* ed. A. G. Huegli (St. Louis, 1964); A. C. Repp, *Confirmation in the Lutheran Church* (St. Louis, 1964); W. H. Beck, *Lutheran Elementary Schools in the United States,* 2d ed. (St. Louis, 1965); 22d LEA Yearbook: *The Teaching of Religion,* ed. J. S. Damm (River Forest, Ill., 1965); H. J. Boettcher, *Three Philosophies of Education* (New York, 1966); F. W. Klos, *Confirmation and First Communion* (Leader's Guide and A Study Book) (St. Louis, 1968); 26th LEA Yearbook: *Christian Education – in Transit!* ed. J. F. Choitz (River Forest, Ill., 1969); F. A. Meyer and H. W. Rast, *Foundations for Christian Education* (mimeo; n. p., n. d.).

Park, Edward(s) Amasa. See *New England Theology,* 4.

Parker, H. P. See *Africa,* F 1.

Parker, Horatio William (1863–1919). Composer; b. Auburndale, Mass.; prof. music Yale 1894–1919; dean Yale Music School 1904–19. Works include the oratorio *Hora novissima: The Rhythm of Bernard de Morlaix on the Celestial Country Set to Music for Soli, Chorus, and Orchestra.*

Parker, Joseph (1830–1902). Cong. cleric; b. Hexham, Northumberland, Eng.; pastor at Banbury 1853, Manchester 1858, London 1869; visited Am. 5 times; eloquent orator. Works include *The People's Bible: Discourses upon Holy Scripture.*

Parker, Matthew (1504–75). B. Norwich, Eng.; educ. Cambridge; friend of T. Bilney* and H. Latimer*; chaplain to Anne Boleyn (1507–36; m. Henry* VIII 1533; mother of Elizabeth* I; beheaded); vice-chancellor Cambridge 1544; friend of M. Bucer*; lived in obscurity under Mary* I; abp. Canterbury 1559. Tried to uphold Elizabethan Settlement of 1559 (see *England,* B 6) and to est. a middle course bet. RCm and Puritanism. Issued *Thirty-nine Articles* (see *Anglican Confessions,* 6) and editions of medieval historians; helped issue Bishop's Bible (see *Bible Versions,* L 7).

Parker, Peter (June 18, 1804–Jan. 10, 1888). B. Framingham, Mass.; educ. Amherst (Mass.) Coll. and Yale Coll. and Divinity School, New Haven, Conn.; studied medicine; ABCFM med. miss. to China 1834; est. ophthalmic hosp. Canton 1835; secy. and interpreter to US legation to China 1844–55; returned to US; Am. commissioner, minister to China 1855–57; regent Smithsonian Institution 1868.

Parker, Theodore (1810–60). Unitarian cleric; b. Lexington, Mass.; educ. Harvard Coll. and Divinity School, Cambridge, Mass. Pastor West Roxbury, Mass., 1837; Boston, Mass., 1846. Developed new, liberal school of Unitarianism based on Ger. Biblical criticism and idealistic philos.; denied the authority of the Bible and the supernatural origin of Christianity.

Parker Society. Founded 1840 in Eng.; name taken from M. Parker*; purpose: to issue works of "the Fathers and early writers of the Reformed Church."

Parlin, Olaus (Olaf; Olof; Olavus; 1716–1757). Swed. pastor; ordained 1745; to Am. 1750; pastor Philadelphia 1750; succeeded I. Acrelius* as provost 1755/56 (official document dated 1755 in Swed. reached Philadelphia 1756).

Parmenides (6th-5th c. BC). Gk. philos. of the Eleatic* School; denied creation and change; held that reality is "being," not "becoming." See also *Philosophy; Time.*

Parochial Schools. See *Christian Education,* E–K; *Parish Education,* D, I, K.

Parousia (Gk. "presence"). Term applied to the final coming of Christ. See also *Last Things.*

Parry, Charles Hubert Hastings (1848–1918). Composer; b. Bournemouth, Eng.; prof. 1883, dir. 1894 Royal Coll. of Music, London; prof. Oxford 1899–1908. Compositions include oratorios *Job* and *King Saul;* hist. works include *The Evolution of the Art of Music.*

Parsi (Parsee). Zoroastrian (see *Zoroastrianism*) descended from Persians who fled 7th c. Muslim persecution and settled mainly at Bombay, India; gen. wealthy, prosperous, educated, and prominent in business and the professions; their dead are exposed on "towers of silence" to be eaten by vultures. See also *Fire Worshipers.*

Parsimonius, Georg (latinized from Ger. Karg; 1512–76). B. Heroldingen, near Harburg, Swabia, W Bav., Ger.; educ. Wittenberg; pastor Ottingen, Schwabach, and Ansbach; supt. Bayreuth; denied doctrine of vicarious active obedience of Christ; suspended from office; retracted 1570; reinstated.

Parsimonius, Johann (d. 1589). Pupil of M. Luther and P. Melanchthon; court preacher Stuttgart; ev. abbot Hirschau 1569–89; denied Christ's descent into hell.

Parsons, Levi. See *Middle East,* B.

Parsons, Robert (Persons; 1546–1610). B. Nether Stowey, Somersetshire, Eng.; educ. Oxford; RC 1574/75; Jesuit 1575; involved in RC plots against Elizabeth* I; founded Eng. RC schools in Fr. and Sp.

Particular Baptists. See *Baptist Churches,* 2, 7–19.

Particular Church. See *Presbyterian Churches,* 2.

Particular Judgment. Divine judgment pronounced at death (Lk 16:22-23; 23:43; Heb. 9:27); this judgment is final, not subject to change or review. See also *Last Things,* 5.

Pascal, Blaise (1623–62). Scientist, philos., mathematician; b. Clermont, Fr.; assoc. with Jansenists (see *Jansenism*) 1646; assoc, with Port-Royal* 1655. Stressed the Person of Christ as Savior; held that only faith can free man from the distracting situation bet. greatness and misery and that reason can be used to demonstrate the truth of faith. Works include *Les provinciales* (tr. *Provincial Letters*); *Pensées* (tr. *Thoughts*).

Pasch (Pascha; from Heb. *pasah,* "to pass over"). 1. Passover (see *Judaism,* 4). 2. Easter.*

Paschal Candle. Large sanctuary candle first lit in a service in the evening before Easter; a symbol of the risen Christ, it is used at liturgical functions throughout the Easter season and extinguished for the last time after the Gospel on Ascension Day.

Paschal Controversy. See *Easter Controversy.*

Paschal Season. Easter* season. See also *Church Year,* 5–7.

Paschasius Radbertus. See *Radbertus, Paschasius.*

Pasor, Georg (1570–1637). B. Ellar, Nassau, Ger.; prof. Herborn, Ger., and Franeker, Neth. Works include *Grammatica Graeca Sacra Novi Testamenti; Lexicon Graeco-Latinum in Novum Domini nostri Jesu Christi Testamentum; Manuale Graecarum vocum N. Testamenti.* See also *Lexicons,* B.

Passau, Convention of. 1552 treaty bet. Maurice* of Saxony and Charles* V; signed at Passau, Bav.; granted Luths. freedom of religion till the next diet, which was to reconsider and possibly decide the question. See also *Augsburg, Religious Peace of; Interim,* II; *John Frederick.*

Passavant, William Alfred (Oct. 9, 1821–June 3, 1894). B. Zelienople, Pa.; educ. Luth. Theol. Sem., Gettysburg, Pa.; licensed 1842; ordained 1843. Pastor Baltimore, Md., and Pittsburgh, Pa. Helped organize Pittsburgh Syn. of the Ev. Luth. Ch. (see *United Lutheran Church, Synods of,* 24) and the General* Council of the Ev. Luth. Ch. in (N.) Am. Introd. the diaconate in Am. (see *Deaconesses,* 7); helped est. several hospitals* and orphanages and Thiel Coll., Greenville, Pa. (see *Ministry, Education of,* VIII B 25). Ed. *The Missionary; The Lutheran and Missionary; The Workman.* See also *Charities, Christian,* 6.

G. H. Gerberding, *Life and Letters of W. A. Passavant, D. D.* (Greenville, Pa., 1906); O. N. Olson, "William Alfred Passavant and the Augustana Synod," *The Augustana Quarterly,* XXIV (1945), 224–241.

Passion. See *Lust.*

Passion, The (from Lat. *passio,* "suffering"). The suffering of Christ. Passion harmonies used in the Luth. Ch. in commemorating the suffering and death of Christ date back to the 16th c.; dramatic forms of portrayal have been traced to the 12th c. (see also *Religious Drama,* 2, 5); roots of the choral Passion may be traced to the 4th c.

There are many musical settings of the Passion. In the Middle Ages the words of Christ were assigned to bass, evangelists to baritone, others to tenor. At first all parts were sung by priests; later the parts of the mob were sung from the choir loft by other choral groups.

Musical Passions became more dramatic when polyphony was introd. ca. the end of the 9th c. But in Luth. circles the dramatic element was at first absent. Luths. who began to use greater freedom include J. à Burck,* J. C. Demantius,* A. Scandello,* N. Selnecker,* and M. Vulpius.*

The motet type of Passion began to flourish with J. Obrecht* and was perpetuated by J. Handl,* L. Lechner,* and C. de Rore.*

In the 17th c., Passions continued to become more dramatic; baroque influence made itself felt (e. g., in the works of T. Selle*); a close relationship bet. Passion and oratorio developed. As of old, a St. Matthew Passion was often presented on Palm Sun., St. Mark on the following Tue., St. Luke on Wed., and St. John on Good Fri. Where elaborate presentations were impossible, the hymn "O Mensch, bewein dein Sünde(n) gross," regarded as the chorale version of the Passion, was often substituted.

The most famous Luth. Passions of the pre-Bach era are those of H. Schütz.* His St. Mark Passion is largely in the old recitative style, but his St. Luke and St. John Passions are more polyphonic. His St. Matthew Passion is his most dramatic, hence most popular. In his *Sieben Worte Christi am Kreuz* he uses an instrumental accompaniment for the words of Christ.

The Oratorio Passion (which used the Bible text) developed beginning in the 1st part of the 17th c. in works, e. g., of T. Selle* and J. Sebastiani.* The Passion Oratorio (which replaced the Bible text with a metrical rhymed paraphrase) developed late in the 17th c. Reaction, which combined Oratorio Passion and Passion Oratorio, began with G. F. Handel* and included, e. g., J. S. Bach,* J. Mattheson,* and G. P. Telemann.* Because of their proportions, some Passions (e. g., J. S. Bach's St. Matthew and St. John) are usually presented on a concert stage. Other 18th c. composers of Passion music include K. P. E. Bach,* F. J. Haydn,* J. Kuhnau,* G. Pergolesi,* and K. H. Graun* (the popularity of whose *Der Tod Jesu* helped keep the Passions of J. S. Bach obscure for a c.). 19th c. composers include L. v. Beethoven,* L. Spohr,* and J. Stainer.* 20th c. composers include H. A. Distler* and Kurt Thomas (b. 1904 Tönning, Ger.; works include *Passionsmusik nach dem Evangelisten Markus*).

See also *Porpora, Nicola Antonio; Walther, Johann.*

O. Kade, *Die ältere Passionskomposition bis zum Jahre 1631* (Gütersloh, 1893); H. Kretzschmar, *Führer durch den Koncertsaal,* II (Leipzig, 1899).

Passion Plays. See *Religious Drama,* 2, 5.

Passion Sunday. Name that originated in 19th-c. Anglicanism for Judica (5th Sun. in Lent). See also *Church Year,* 14, 16.

Passion Week. See *Church Year,* 4.

Passionists. RC order founded in It. 1720 by Paul* of the Cross; official name: Cong. of the Discalced

Clerics of the Most Holy Cross and Passion of Our Lord Jesus Christ; 1st US house est. 1852 Pittsburgh, Pa. The order is marked by prayer, penance, and solitude; besides the 3 usual vows* its mems. vow to promote devotion to the Passion of Christ; active in missions and retreats.

Passiontide. See *Church Year,* 4.

"Passiusalmar." See *Pétursson, Hallgrímur.*

Passive Obedience of Christ. See *Justification,* 5.

Passover. See *Judaism,* 4; *Pasch.*

Passy, Paul Édouard (1859–1940). Phonetician; evangelist; b. Versailles, Fr.; fundamentalist Christian; soc. reformer; founded Société des Volontaires évangélistes and Union des Socialistes chrétiens.

Pastor. See *Ministerial Office.*

Pastor, Ludwig von (1854–1928). RC hist.; b. Aachen, Ger.; prof. Innsbruck 1886; dir. Austrian Hist. Institute, Rome, 1901; Austrian representative at the Vatican 1920. Works include *Geschichte der Päpste seit dem Ausgang des Mittelalters.*

Pastor aeternus (1516). See *Lateran Councils.*

Pastor aeternus (1870). See Bull; *Vatican Councils,* 1 b.

Pastor and Education. See *Parish Education,* K 2.

Pastor as Counselor. 1. A pastor's main work is to give helpful guidance and support to disturbed and perplexed souls; this work is called cure of souls, soul care, pastoral care, or poimenics. Basically it is soul-winning, soul-reclaiming, and soul-keeping. His field is his flock and the unchurched; mems. of other Christian chs. are usually referred to their pastors. His goals are mainly spiritual, but by his ministration he also brings relief in physical, mental, and emotional ills. Pastoral counseling is eschatological; its goal: to prepare men to meet their God.

2. Pastoral counseling is receiving more specialized and intensive recognition and attention than ever before. Psychology and psychiatry often come to be involved, but the true basis of proper pastoral counseling remains the Word, which is able to save souls (Ja. 1:21). Exceptional cases may be referred to a Christian psychiatrist, though the ministries are distinct from each other. A psychiatrist is concerned mainly with the mental and emotional restoration of a client; a pastor is concerned mainly with spiritual welfare. Spiritual ministration often exerts a psychosomatic influence. In every case it is God who heals (Ex 15:26; Mt 4:4).

3. Pastoral counseling has application also to marriage,* family* life, and family* planning.

4. Effective pastoral counseling requires Christian faith, familiarity with the Bible, perseverance in prayer, and the ability to apply the Word of God properly (2 Ti 2:15); it also requires consecration, loyalty to the Bible, love for people, and confidence of success (Is 55:10-11; Ro 1:16). Depending on circumstances, laymen may assist in counseling.

5. A pastoral counselor should draw on the experiences of others and have respect to the times. He should be familiar with problems connected, e. g., with sickness and suffering, marriage, divorce, alcoholism,* drug addiction.

6. Pastoral counseling began with Christ and the apostles (Mt 10:5-15; Jn 20:21-23; 21:15-17; Acts 20:20, 31; Ro 12; 1 Co 12 and 14; Ja 5:13-20). The apostles took steps for training other pastors (2 Ti 2:2) and apostolic fathers continued the work.

7. Doctrinal and practical aberrations soon became disturbing problems for many. Some said that postbaptismal sins require special works of penance; fasting and almsgiving were stressed as necessary for salvation, and some added the keeping of the commandments. Some ruled out all chance for repentance after Baptism; some allowed 1 chance, but not in cases of idolatry, unchastity, or homicide. As a result, many postponed Baptism till late in life. In course of time asceticism* began to flourish. Martyrdom came to be regarded as a guarantee of salvation and became life's highest hope for many. But fanatical seeking after martyrdom was condemned.

8. With the rise of Christian monasticism,* monks and esp. parish priests became the chief pastoral counselors, controlling confession, absolution, and meting out penances.

9. The Luth. Reformation* revived proper pastoral counseling.

10. Pietism* emphasized Christian life and spiritual exercises. Rationalism* ran counter to Christian faith and led to decline in pastoral counseling.

11. Luth. pastoral counseling in the US owes much to H. M. Mühlenberg* and C. F. W. Walther.*

12. In the 2d half of the 20th c., lay participation in counseling has increased considerably. OES

See also *Ministerial Office; Seelsorge.*

J. T. McNeill, *A History of the Cure of Souls* (New York, 1951); J. H. C. Fritz, *Pastoral Theology* (St. Louis, 1932); S. Hiltner, *Religion and Health* (New York, 1943) and *Pastoral Counseling* (New York, 1949); J. C. Heuch, *Pastoral Care of the Sick* (Minneapolis, 1949); J. S. Bonnell, *Psychology for Pastor and People: A Book on Spiritual Counseling,* rev. ed. (New York, 1960); G. Bergsten, *Pastoral Psychology: A Study in the Care of Souls* (New York, 1951); W. E. Hulme, *Counseling and Theology* (Philadelphia, 1956) and *The Pastoral Care of Families: Its Theology and Practice* (New York, 1962); A. W. Blackwood, *The Growing Minister: His Opportunities and Obstacles* (New York, 1960); F. Greeves, *Theology and the Cure of Souls* (London, 1960); E. Thurneysen, *A Theology of Pastoral Care,* basic tr. J. A. Worthington and T. Wieser (Richmond, Va., 1962); D. R. Belgum, *The Church and Its Ministry* (Englewood Cliffs, N. J., 1963); T. Bovet, *That They May Have Life: A Handbook on Pastoral Care for the Use of Christian Ministers and Laymen,* tr. J. A. Baker (London, 1964), printed in US under the title *The Road to Salvation: A Handbook on the Christian Care of Persons* (New York, 1964).

Pastoral Care. See *Pastor as Counselor.*

Pastoral Constitution on the Church in the Modern World. See *Vatican Councils,* 2.

Pastoral Office. See *Ministerial Office.*

Pastoral Theology. Theology,* or the doctrine of the knowledge of God and of divine things, applied by a pastor to the spiritual needs of his flock. C. F. W. Walther,* *Americanisch-Lutherische Pastoraltheologie,* par. 1, defines it as a God-given practical aptitude of the soul, acquired by means of certain aids whereby a pastor is enabled validly and legitimately, for the glory of God and his own and his hearers' salvation, to perform all functions incumbent on him by virtue of his office. It has also been defined as the art of applying the truth.

C. F. W. Walther, *Americanisch-Lutherische Pastoraltheologie* (St. Louis, 1872) and *The Proper Distinction Between Law and Gospel,* reproduced from the Ger. ed. of 1897 by W. H. T. Dau (Saint Louis, 1929); J. H. C. Fritz, *Pastoral Theology,* 2d ed. (St. Louis, 1945); J. Schaller, *Pastorale Praxis in der Ev.-Luth. Freikirche Amerikas* (Milwaukee, 1913); T. C. Graebner, *The Borderland of Right and Wrong,* rev. (St. Louis, 1956) and *Pastor and People* (St. Louis, 1932); *The Abiding Word,* I–II, ed. T. Laetsch (St. Louis, 1946–47), III (St. Louis, 1960); C. M. Zorn, *Questions on Christian Topics,* tr. J. A. Rimbach, 3d ed. (Milwaukee, 1931); A. W. Blackwood, *Pastoral Work* (Philadelphia, 1945); A. Vinet, *Pastoral Theology* (Edinburgh, 1855); R. F. Weidner, *Theological Encyclopaedia and Methodology,* 2 vols. (Chicago, 1898–1910); F. Schulze, *A Manual of Pastoral Theology,* 3d ed. (St. Louis,

1923); J. M. Wilson, *Six Lectures on Pastoral Theology* (New York, 1903).

Pastors' Emergency League. See *Confessing Church.*

Patagonian Missionary Society. See *Gardiner, Allen Francis.*

Patarines (Patarenes). Adherents of a partly ecclesiastical, partly soc. movement est. Milan, It., ca. 1057; opposed wealthy, worldly clergy, esp. concubinage and simony.*

Paten. Dish, usually of precious metal, for the bread in a Communion service. See also *Church Furniture,* 3; *Pall,* 1.

Paternoster. Name for Lord's Prayer derived from its first 2 words in Lat.

Patience. Calm, unruffled temper in facing the evils of life; ability to meet duties and conflicts with fortitude; manifested in humble submission to God's ruling providence; synonyms include long-suffering, long-sufferance, longanimity, forbearance, resignation; cf. 2 Sm 16:10-13; Lk 8:15; Ro 5:3-4; 12:12; Cl 3:12-13; 1 Th 5:14; 2 Th 1:4; 2 Ti 2:10; 3:10-11; Ja 5:11; 1 Ptr 2:20; Rv 1:9. Patience is also a quality of God (Ex 34:6; Ro 2:4; 15:5; 1 Ptr 3:20). JMW

Paton, John Gibson (1824–1907). Presb. miss.; b. Kirkmahoe, Dumfriesshire, Scot.; educ. Glasgow; city miss. Glasgow 1847–57; miss. to New* Hebrides 1858. Tr. parts of the Bible into the language of natives of the is. of Aniwa.

Paton, William (1886–1943). Presb. minister; b. London, Eng.; educ. Oxford and Cambridge; Miss. Secy. of Student Christian Movement 1911; Gen. Secy. Nat. Christian Council of India, Burma, and Ceylon 1922–27; Secy. Internat. Miss. Council 1927 – 43. Ed. *The International Review of Missions.* Other works include *The Faiths of Mankind; The Message of the World-Wide Church; The Church and the New Order.*

Patres. See *Ancestor Worship.*

Patriarch. Highest dignitary in the ecclesiastical hierarchy as it developed from the 4th c. on. E patriarchates: Constantinople, Alexandria, Antioch, Jerusalem. RCm did not perpetuate the term in this sense but only as an honorary title without special jurisdiction (CIC 271; e. g., the bp. of Goa is patriarch of the East Indies). The title is also used of the spiritual head of various other E chs., e. g., the Russ. Orthodox Ch. and the Syrian and Coptic chs., as well as of the head of the Sanhedrin in Palestine, sometimes of the head of the Jewish Coll. at Babylon, and of certain functionaries in the Mormon ch.

Patriarchal Council. See *Councils and Synods,* 1.

Patrick (Sucat; Patricius; perhaps ca. 385/389 – ca. 461). Apostle and patron saint of Ireland; possibly b. Bannavem (Bannauenta? Banwen?), perhaps near the Severn, in Roman Britain (or near Kilpatrick, Scot.?); kidnaped at ca. 16 and taken as a slave to Ireland; herded swine; escaped at ca. 22; trained on the Continent to be a miss.; returned to Ireland. See also *Celtic Church,* 5; *England,* A 2.

Patrick, Simon (Symon; 1625[1626?]–1707). B. Gainsborough, Lincolnshire, Eng.; educ. Cambridge; ordained Presb. 1648, Angl. 1654; bp. Chichester 1689[1688?], Ely 1691. Works include *The Parable of the Pilgrim;* paraphrases of Gn to SS; controversial writings against RCs and nonconformists.*

Patrimony of the Church. Landed possessions and revenues of the Roman see up to ca. the 8th c. Sometimes applied to the States* of the Ch. 754–1870.

Patripassianism (from Lat. *pater,* "father," and *passus,* "having suffered"). A form of Monarchianism; the view (died out ca. the 5th c.) that in the work of redemption God the Father became incarnate and suffered. See also *Monarchianism,* B; *Noetus; Praxeas; Sabellius; Theopaschitism.*

Patristics. 1. Branch of theol. knowledge that deals with the lives and writings of the ch. fathers. The term "patrology" is often applied to the hist. side; "patristics" is then the formal side. The patristic era is often divided into ante-Nicene on the one hand and Nicene and post-Nicene on the other, with subdivisions of each.

2. Much patristic literature, esp. of the first 3 cents., is fragmentary. Eusebius* of Caesarea's *Historia ecclesiastica* contains important quotations and biographical facts. Photius's* *Bibliotheca* summarizes 280 works of classical writers. Patristic quotations are found also in heretical writings.

3. Earliest writers and writings are called Apostolic* Fathers (subapostolic teachers, some of whom had personal contact with the apostles).

4. The 2d and 3d cents. form the era of Apologists.*

5. Patristic writings in the 3d c. show a trend toward giving systematized expression to convictions. Controversies resulted, extending into the 4th c. See also *Arianism; Gnosticism.*

6. Golden age of patristic literature: 4th–5th cents. Change in the status of the ch. under Constantine* I gave Christian writers greater liberty. Questions concerning the Trin. and Christological* controversies led to many works. See also *Donatist Schism, The; Manichaeism; Pelagian Controversy.* Writers included Ambrose,* Aphraates,* Athanasius,* Augustine* of Hippo, Basil* the Great, J. Cassianus,* J. Chrysostom,* Diodorus* of Tarsus, Ephraem,* Eusebius* of Caesarea, Eustathius* of Antioch, Gregory* of Nazianzus, Hilary* of Poitiers, Jerome,* Ulfilas.*

7. Patristic literature declined beginning in the 5th c. Interest in polemics waned. Barbarian invasions in the W spread ruin. Centralization of power in the ch. stifled indep. investigation. There followed the age of the catena* and florilegium.*

8. Sometimes the patristic era is regarded as extending to the 14th c. Sometimes all respected theologians of the past are spoken of as "fathers."

9. The Luth. Ch. respects the writings of the fathers but realizes that none of them was infallible and that all are to be judged by the Bible. EL

See also *Theology.*

F. W. Farrar, *Lives of the Fathers* (Edinburgh, 1889); *The Fathers of the Church* (New York, 1947–); *Patrologiae cursus completus,* ed. J. P. Migne: Lat., 221 vols. in 223 (Paris, 1844–55), Gk., 161 vols. in 167 (Paris, 1857–66); *Patrologia orientalis,* ed. R. Griffin and F. Nau (Paris, 1903–); *Corpus Christianorum,* series Latina (Turnhout, Belg., 1953–); *The Ante-Nicene Fathers,* ed. A. Roberts and J. Donaldson (Edinburgh, 1885–97; reprinted with supplements, New York 1890–99); *A Select Library of Nicene and Post-Nicene Fathers of the Christian Church,* 1st series, 14 vols., ed. P. Schaff (New York, 1886–89), 2d series, 14 vols., ed. P. Schaff and H. Wace (New York, 1890–1925); G. Krüger, *History of Early Christian Literature in the First Three Centuries,* tr. C. R. Gillett (New York, 1897); E. J. Goodspeed, *A History of Early Christian Literature* (Chicago, 1942); J. N. D. Kelly, *Early Christian Doctrines,* 2d ed. (New York, 1960); F. L. Cross, *The Early Christian Fathers* (London, 1960); J. Quasten, *Patrology,* 3 vols. (Westminster, Md., 1950–60).

Patron Covenant. See *Covenant,* 2.

Patron Saint. In RCm, heavenly protector (saint or angel) of individuals, institutions, or activities. The example of a patron saint's life is proposed to those under his care. Chs. are often named after patron saints. Many countries, trades, professions, cities, towns, and illnesses also have patron saints. Celebration of patronal feasts of chs. was revived in the Angl. Ch. ca. the middle of the 19th c.

Patronage. Right of presentation to an ecclesiastical

benefice. In the early ch. a bp. had the right to place a priest in a parish. Later, when landowners built chs., the right of patronage was gradually yielded to them. Beginning toward the end of the 12th c. the RC Ch. tried to regain the right of patronage; Eng. took the lead in resisting this move. The system has been repeatedly modified.

Patrons of Husbandry. See *Order of Patrons of Husbandry.*

Patteson, John Coleridge (Apr. 1[2?], 1827–Sept. 20, 1871). Miss. bp.; b. London, Eng.; educ. Eton and Oxford; to New Zealand with G. A. Selwyn* 1855; bp. Melanesia 1861; cruised among the islands in the *Southern Cross.* Tr. Bible; reduced native languages to writing. Probably slain by natives on a visit to Nukapu (Nikapu) in the Santa Cruz islands.

Patton, Francis Landey (Jan. 22, 1843–Nov. 25, 1932). Presb. cleric and educ.; b. Warwick, Bermuda; educ. Toronto, Can., and Princeton (N. J.) Theol. Sem.; pastor NYC and at Nyack and Brooklyn, N. Y.; prof. Theol. Sem. of the NW (name changed 1886 to McCormick Theol. Sem.), Chicago, Ill., 1872–81; also pastor Jefferson Park Ch., Chicago, 1874–81; prof. Princeton Theol. Sem. 1881–88; prof. Princeton U. 1886–1913, pres. 1888–1902; pres. Princeton Theol. Sem. 1902–13. Works include *The Inspiration of the Scriptures; A Summary of Christian Doctrine; Fundamental Christianity.*

Paul, Jean. See *Richter, Johann Paul Friedrich.*

Paul, Lives of. Books on the life of the apostle Paul have been grouped as conservative and critical to middling. Prominent conservative works include those of W. J. Conybeare* and J. S. Howson,* F. W. Farrar,* A. T. Robertson,* C. F. W. Dallmann.* Of critical works (e. g., of W. Wrede*) some say Paul derived his message not from Christ but from Judaism, esp. so-called Jewish apocalyptic writings like the Book of Enoch. Others say Paul derived his distinctive religious teachings from mystery religions. Some say he was strongly influenced by Stoicism. Some try to destroy the divine character of his conversion by holding that lightning struck near him when he approached Damascus or that he suffered a sunstroke. Some say he had an epileptic seizure with hallucinations. Some (e. g., F. C. Baur*) say his conversion must be explained psychologically.

Paul III (Alessandro Farnese; 1468–1549). B. cen. It.; cardinal 1493; pope 1534–49; approved Society* of Jesus 1540; reorganized Inquisition* with HQ at Rome 1542; convened Council of Trent* 1545; patron of Michelangelo.* See also *Roman Catholic Confessions,* A 1.

Paul IV (Giovanni Pietro Caraffa; 1476–1559). B. near Benevento, It.; mem. of commission appointed to deal with the affair of M. Luther* 1520; cofounder of Theatines* 1524; cardinal 1536; pope 1555–59; opposed Protestantism esp. in It. See also *Counter Reformation,* 4, 5, 9.

Paul VI. See *Curia,* 2 d; *Popes,* 35.

Paul and Peter, Feasts of. See *Church Year,* 14, 16.

Paul of Burgos (ca. 1351–1435). Wealthy, educ. Jew; embraced Christianity; bp. Cartagena; abp. Burgos; active in Jewish missions; tried to show that Christ is a literal fulfillment of the OT.

Paul of Callinicum (6th c.). Monophysite; deprived of his bishopric, he lived in Edessa; tr. Monophysite writings into Syriac.

Paul of Constantinople (d. 350 AD). Bp. Constantinople 336; displaced by Macedonius; regained, then again lost, his see; friend of Athanasius*; strangled in Armenia.

Paul of Rhodes (Paulus Rhodius; 1489–1563). Ev. pastor Stettin 1523; supt. Stettin 1535; supt. Lüneburg 1537–38; supt. Stettin 1538; reformer of Pomerania; signed SA.

Paul of Samosata (3d c. AD). Bp. Antioch 260–272; dynamic monarchian; followers called Paulianists. See also *Dionysius of Alexandria; Exegesis,* 4; *Gregory Thaumaturgus; Monarchianism,* A 4.

Paul of Tella. See *Bible Versions,* C 2.

Paul of the Cross (Paolo Francesco Danei; 1694–1775). Son of poor It. parents; an alleged vision 1720 inspired him to found Passionists*; priest 1727; celebrated preacher.

Paul of Thebes (d. ca. 340 AD). "The Hermit"; acc. to tradition, the 1st Christian hermit; said to have fled into the desert during the Decian persecution and lived there for ca. 100 yrs.

MPL, 23, 17–30.

Paul the Deacon (Levita; Warnefridi; Diaconus; ca. 720–ca. 800). Benedictine; to Monte Cassino; visited Charlemagne 782–ca. 787. Works include *De ordine episcoporum Metensium; Gesta episcoporum Metensium; De gestis Longobardorum; Historia Romana;* liturgical writings; homilies; life of Gregory the Great et al. See also *Preaching, Christian, History of,* 7.

MPL, 95, 413–1710.

Paula (347–404). Roman lady; followed Jerome to Palestine 385; est. a convent for nuns and one for monks in Bethlehem.

MPL, 22, 878–906.

Paulianists. See *Paul of Samosata.*

Paulicians. Gnostic-Marcionite (and possibly Manichaean) sect traced to mid-7th c. Armenia, where they stayed, despite persecution, till their removal to Thrace ca. 970. In the 11th c. some returned to the ch., others joined various sects. Held a dualism in which a demiurge made the material world and man's body and a good god made heaven and man's soul; Christ saves humanity from the former for the latter. See also *Gnosticism.*

Pauline Privilege (Lat. *privilegium Paulinum; privilegium fidei,* "privilege of the faith"). Derives its name from Paul's statement 1 Co 7:12-15. Acc. to RC interpretation and conditions (CIC 1120–27) a legitimate marriage bet. unbaptized persons, even after consummation, may be dissolved in favor of RCm if 1 of the parties to the marriage becomes RC.

Paulinus of Antioch (d. 388 AD). Bp. Antioch 362; supported by Rome and Alexandria against Meletius.

Paulinus of Aquileia (ca. 730–ca. 802). It. grammarian; at court of Charlemagne 776; friend of Alcuin; patriarch of Aquileia 787. Opposed Adoptionism.*

MPL, 99, 9–684.

Paulinus of Milan (5th c. AD). Deacon and secy. with Ambrose; to Afr.; friend of Augustine of Hippo. His complaint against Celestius* 411 started the Pelagian* controversy. Works include a life of Ambrose.

MPL, 14, 27–46.

Paulinus of Nola (ca. 353–431). B. Bordeaux, Fr.; son of wealthy parents; bap. 390; gave his wealth to the ch. and the poor; priest 394; settled with wife at Nola, It.; bp. 409; friend of Augustine* of Hippo, Martin of Tours (see *Celtic Church,* 2), Ambrose.* Works include letters and poetic writings.

MPL, 61.

Paulinus of York (d. 644 AD). Sent to Eng. by Greggory I (see *Popes,* 4); worked with Augustine* of Canterbury in Kent; bp. York 625, Rochester 633. Influenced King Edwin of Northumbria and his chiefs to accept Christianity.

Paulists. The Soc. of Missionary Priests of St. Paul the Apostle (Paulist Fathers) was founded 1858 New York by I. T. Hecker* to further RC interests and work in the US.

Paulsen, Johannes (1847–1916). B. Witzhave, Holstein, Ger.; educ. Kiel, Tübingen, and Berlin; private tutor Kropp, Holstein, 1870; founded institutions at Kropp, including a deaconess house, normal school, orphanage, hosp., printshop, and sem. See also *General Council of the Evangelical Lutheran Church in*

(North) America, 5; *Hoffman, Emil; Kropp Seminary.*

Paulsen, Paul Christian (Mar. 26, 1881–July 26, 1948). B. Alstrup, Jutland, Den.; to Am. 1904; ordained 1911; UELC pastor in Minn., Wis., Ill., Calif., and Alta., Canada. Tr. Dan. hymns.

Paulus, Heinrich Eberhard Gottlob (1761–1851). Ger. orientalist and theol.; prof. Jena, Würzburg, Heidelberg. Rationalist; influenced by J. S. Semler* and J. D. Michaelis; opposed F. W. J. v. Schelling.* Tried to harmonize acceptance of the Gospel narrative as accurate with rejection of miracles. Works include *Das Leben Jesu als Grundlage einer reinen Geschichte des Urchristentums; Exegetisches Handbuch über die drei ersten Evangelien.*

Paumann, Konrad (Pawman; ca. 1409/15–1473). "Father of Ger. organ music"; b. Nürnberg, Ger.; born blind, but became a noted organist; active in Nürnberg; instrumentalist. Works include *Fundamentum organisandi.*

Pax. See *Kiss of Peace.*

Pax Brede (Pax board; Pax; Osculatorium). Plate, or board, with projecting handle on back, used, e. g., by Dominicans* and Carthusians* to convey the kiss* of peace esp. to laity and mems. of the choir at mass.*

Pax Christi. RC movement aimed at peace bet. nations, originally bet. Ger. and Fr. Began 1944 by a Fr. bp. who was imprisoned by Germans at Compiègne; internat. structure est. 1951.

Pax dissidentium. See *Poland,* 3.

Pax Romana. See *Students, Spiritual Care of,* A 3.

Pax vobiscum (Lat. "peace [be] with you"). Benediction bet. the consecration of the elements and the Agnus* Dei; common Eng. equivalent: "The peace of the Lord be with you alway!"

Pázmány, Péter (1570–1637). B. Nagyvárad (Oradea, or Oradea Mare; Ger.: Grosswardein), Rumania, of Ref. parents; RC at 13; Jesuit 1587/88; priest 1596; prof. Graz 1597; abp. Esztergom (Ger.: Gran), Hung., 1616; cardinal 1629. Opposed Prots. in sermons and writings; won the 30 leading noble families for RCm; leader of the Counter* Reformation in Hung.

Peabody, Francis Greenwood (1847–1936). Unitarian theol.; b. Boston, Mass.; pastor Cambridge, Mass., 1874; prof. Harvard 1881–1913; exchange prof. Berlin 1905/06; exponent of Social* Gospel. Works include *Jesus Christ and the Social Question; The Approach to the Social Question.*

Peace, Ladies'. See *Cambria, Peace of.*

Peace Mission Movement of Father Divine. Movement centering in Father* Divine; strongly marked by New Thought and theosophy; its followers were led to believe that heaven is here and now and that the interracial character of the movement expressed the atonement.

Peace Movements. See *Pacifism.*

Peace of Ales (Peace of Alais). See *France,* 10.

Peace of Augsburg. See *Augsburg, Religious Peace of.*

Peace of Beaulieu. See *France,* 9.

Peace of Bergerac. See *France,* 9.

Peace of Cambrai. See *Cambrai, Peace of.*

Peace of Constance. See *Frederick I* (Holy Roman emp.).

Peace of Longjumeau. See *France,* 9.

Peace of Lübeck. See *Thirty Year's War.*

Peace of Madrid (1526). See *Speyer, Diets of,* 1.

Peace of Monsieur. See *France,* 9.

Peace of Nijmegen. See *France,* 13.

Peace of Nürnberg. See *Nürnberg Religious Peace.*

Peace of Poitiers. See *France,* 9.

Peace of Prague. See *Thirty Years' War.*

Peace of Saint-Germain. See *France,* 9.

Peace of the Church. 1. State of the ch. after the Edict of Milan* 313.

2. Temporary cessation of the Jansenist conflict ca. 1668 (see *Jansenism*).

Peace of the Dissidents. See Poland, 3.

Peace of Utrecht. See *Utrecht, Treaty of.*

Peace of Westphalia. See *France,* 13; *Westphalia, Peace of.*

Peake, Arthur Samuel (1865–1929). Biblical scholar; b. Leek, Staffordshire, Eng.; educ. Oxford; taught at Hartley Primitive Meth. Coll., Manchester; prof. Biblical criticism and exegesis Manchester U. Works include *The Bible: Its Origin, Its Significance, and Its Abiding Worth; The Problem of Suffering in the Old Testament;* a 1-vol. commentary on the Bible.

Pearse, Mark Guy (1842–1930). Meth. theol.; hymnist; b. Camborne, Cornwall, Eng.; pastor Leeds, Bristol, and London. Hymns pub. in a collection entitled *The Child Jesus.*

Pearson, John (1613–86). Prelate and theol.; b. Great Snoring, Norfolk, Eng.; educ. Eton and Cambridge; pastor Thorington, Suffolk, 1640; supported Royalists in the Civil War of the 1640s; under the Commonwealth (1649–60) he lived in semi-retirement in London; prof. Cambridge 1661; bp. Chester 1673; Arminian. Works include *An Exposition of the Creed; Vindiciae epistolarum S. Ignatii.*

Peasants' War. Uprising of Ger. peasants 1525 brought on by oppression under wealthy and powerful landowners operating under the feudal system; establishment of codified Roman law in Ger. had given the lords advantages over the peasants. M. Luther* first sided with the peasants, but when they refused to refrain from violence and murder he called on the govt. to take necessary countermeasures. The authorities overreacted, disregarding Luther's admonition for mercy to innocent peasants. T. Münzer was among the slain. See also *Philip of Hesse; Schilling, Johann.*

E. Baumgartner, *Der grosse Bauernkrieg* (Vienna, n. d.); E. B. Bax, *The Peasants War in Germany 1525–1526* (London, 1899; reprint. New York, 1968); E. Bohnenblust, *Luther und der Bauernkrieg* (Bern, 1929); G. Franz, *Der deutsche Bauernkrieg,* 2 vols. (Munich, 1933–35) and *Quellen zur Geschichte des Bauernkrieges,* in *Ausgewählte Quellen zur deutschen Geschichte der Neuzeit,* II (Darmstadt, 1963); P. Althaus, *Luthers Haltung im Bauernkrieg(e)* in *Luther-Jahrbuch* VII (Wittenberg, 1925; repub. separately Basel, n. d.); H. J. Grimm, "Luther, Luther's Critics, and the Peasant Revolt," *The Lutheran Church Quarterly,* XIX (1946), 115–132.

Pécaut, Felix (1827[8?]–1898). Cofounder of the Free Ch. in Neuchâtel, Switz.; advocated humanization of the Bible, divesting it of supernatural elements.

Pecci, Gioacchino Vincenzo. See *Popes,* 29.

Peck, John Mason (1789–1858). Bap. cleric; b. Litchfield, Conn.; pastor N. Y.; itinerant miss. Ill., Ind., and Mo.; est. a sem. 1827 at Rock Spring, Ill., which moved to upper Alton after several yrs., where it was renamed Shurtleff Coll. 1835; helped found Am. Bap. Home Mission Soc. 1832.

Peckham, John (Pecham; ca. 1225–92). B. Patcham (formerly Pecham), Sussex, Eng.; Franciscan ca. 1250; educ. Oxford and Paris; pupil of Bonaventura*; *lector sacri palatii* Rome 1276; abp. Canterbury 1279; supported the papacy and worked for correction of abuses in the ch.

Pecock, Reginald (ca. 1390/95–ca. 1460/61). B. Wales; educ. Oxford; master Whittington Coll., London, 1431; bp. St. Asaph 1444, Chichester 1450; opposed what he regarded as uncritical biblicism of Lollards with the "law of kind" written in men's souls by God; critical of authority of Apostles' Creed, Decalog, ch. fathers; questioned Mosaic authorship of Pentateuch.

Pectoral Cross. Cross, usually of precious metal,

worn by ch. dignitaries on the breast and suspended from a chain around the neck.

Pectoral Theology. See *Pektoraltheologie.*

Pedersen, Christiern (ca. 1480–1554). B. Helsingör (or Svendborg?), Den.; educ. Paris; chancellor of the abp. of Lund; fled to his fugitive king, Christian* II, in the Neth. 1526, where he supported the Reformation; after imprisonment of Christian II in the early 1530s, Pedersen returned to Den. 1532 and became a printer at Malmö. Founded modern Dan. literature. Tr. NT and Ps; helped produce the Dan. Bible issued by Christian* III 1550. See also *Palladius, Peder Esbernsen.*

Pedersen, Johannes Peder Ejler. See *Higher Criticism,* 16.

Pederssön, Gjeble (ca. 1490–1557). Norw. theol.; teacher, priest, archdeacon Bergen; supported Christian* III in Reformation of Den.; ordained by J. Bugenhagen* as Norw. supt. 1537.

Pedilavium. See *Foot Washing.*

Pedobaptism (infant Baptism). See *Grace, Means of,* III, 4.

Péguy, Charles Pierre (1873-1914). Fr. poet and author; at first socialist and Dreyfusard, later a mystic nationalist and leader of Cath. renewal movement; founded *Cahiers de la Quinzaine,* organ of religious, patriotic, indep. socialists; anticlerical.

Peirce, Charles Santiago Sanders (1839–1914). Physicist; mathematician; logician; b. Cambridge, Mass.; educ. Harvard U., Cambridge; lectured at Harvard 1903; influenced by George Boole's *The Mathematical Analysis of Logic* and *An Investigation of the Laws of Thought;* laid foundation in logic of relations; founded pragmatism,* later developed by W. James,* and pragmaticism, which he differentiated from James's system.

Pektoraltheologie (Pectoral theol.). Term derived from the statement of J. A. W. Neander*: *"Pectus est, quod facit theologum"* (Lat. "the heart makes the theologian"); pectoral theol. emphasized emotion, esp. in opposition to rational supernaturalism and neoorthodoxy; other exponents include J. Lasenius.*

Pelagia (d. ca. 311 AD). 1. Virgin and martyr of Antioch; said to have preserved her virginity, when her house was surrounded by soldiers during a persecution, by leaping from a window into the sea.

2. Legends of other virgins named Pelagia (e. g., a converted actress of Antioch; a martyr of Tarsus) became interwoven with the story of the martyr of Antioch.

Pelagian Controversy. 1. Named after Pelagius.* For the beginning of the controversy ca. 411 see 5.

2. There had been no full agreement among ch. fathers on justification.* In gen. they agreed that man's nature was depraved by the Fall and that man thereafter needs God's grace and a rebirth. Some (e. g., Ambrose,* Cyprian,* Hilary* of Poitiers, Tertullian*) taught a total depravity; others (e. g., the Cappadocian* Theologians, J. Chrysostom,* Clement* of Alexandria, Didymus* of Alexandria) held that man retained a remnant of free will, which is active toward good independently of grace.

3. In his early writings, Augustine* of Hippo did not exclude free will from conversion; later he excluded it emphatically, but rationalism misled him to a false view of election. He held that all men since Adam's fall (which ruined human nature physically and morally) are essentially in the same state of estrangement from God and of condemnation, in which they can do only what displeases God. From this state they can be rescued only by God's grace in Christ. This grace attracts man's depraved will with inner conquering necessity *(gratia irresistibilis),* and whoever receives it is saved. Not all receive it. Out of lost mankind *(massa perditionis),* God, acc. to His compassion in Christ, elects some to salvation, fitting them thereto by kindling faith in them by His grace *(gratia praeveniens, operans, et cooperans);* all others God, acc. to His justice, leaves in depravity and consigns to merited damnation. The reason why grace is accorded only to part of mankind lies in an eternal, holy, inexplicable, absolutely free decree *(decretum absolutum)* of God. Cf. H. E. F. Guericke,* *Handbuch der Kirchengeschichte,* I (Leipzig, 1866), 351–352.

4. Pelagius and his followers held that man's nature is not depraved since the fall but is still in its original state of moral indifference and depends on the individual will to develop the moral germ of his nature and be saved. Irresistible grace and absolute predestination do not fit this system. But acc. to the view of Pelagius, neither was grace or salvation by Christ necessary (a view incompatible with the essence of Christianity).

5. Pelagius first taught his view in a commentary on Paul's epistles ca. 400; then he spread them personally at Rome ca. 409/410. He went to Carthage with Celestius* ca. 410/411. When the latter applied for the office of presbyter, he (Celestius) was accused of heresy by Paulinus* of Milan and had to defend himself before a syn. at Carthage, probably 411. Views of which he was accused included: (1) Adam would have died even if he had not sinned; (2) his sin affected only himself, not his progeny; (3) newborn children are in the same state in which Adam was before the fall; (4) it is not true that all men die in Adam and rise in Christ; (5) the Law leads to salvation as much as the Gospel; (6) before the Lord's coming there were people without sin. Celestius is reported to have been excommunicated when he refused to recant.

6. Meanwhile Pelagius had gone to Palestine and the controversy continued. Augustine of Hippo wrote *De natura et gratia* ("Of Nature and Grace") against Pelagius. At the syns. of Milevis and Carthage (both 416) Afr. bps. condemned Pelagianism; pope Innocent I confirmed the judgment and excommunication, but his successor Zosimus declared Pelagius and Celestius orthodox 417. The Afr. bps. repeated their condemnations 417/418. Emp. Flavius Honorius also opposed Pelagianism. Then Zosimus concurred with the judgment of the Afr. bps. and issued a statement widely circulated for subscription; the 18 bps. who refused to sign, including Julian* of Eclanum, were deposed. Pelagius was expelled from Palestine and disappeared from hist.

7. Esp. through the influence of Marius* Mercator, probably a layman, also the E condemned Pelagianism at the 431 council of Ephesus.* But the E did not fully accept Augustinian theol.; e. g., Theodore* of Mopsuestia and Isidore of Pelusium stood midway bet. Augustinianism and Pelagianism.

8. In the W, Augustinianism found new foes in semi-Pelagianism,* which held that free will was only partly impaired by the fall and needs the help of grace. The question why not all are saved, since grace alone saves and is universal, and since all are in equal corruption and guilt (a question that the Bible leaves unanswered) was discussed. Both parties erred. Augustinianism looked for the answer in God, who does not treat all alike; semi-Pelagianism looked for the answer in man (some using their natural powers aright, others not). Augustine refuted extreme misconstructions of his view (e.g., that all moral effort is unnecessary and all punishment of sin unjust).

9. Early semi-Pelagian leaders include J. Cassianus, who held that man, despite inclination to evil after the fall, could by free choice turn to good but needed grace to grow in sanctification. Augustine wrote *De praedestinatione sanctorum* and *De dono perseverantia* (both 428/429) to justify his system. After his death his friend Prosper* of Aquitaine also

wrote against semi-Pelagianism. But the movement continued. Prosper induced pope Celestine I to issue a statement, albeit somewhat indeterminate, condemning bps. of Gaul for opposing Augustine. Vincent* of Lerins supported semi-Pelagianism as in harmony with monastic belief in human merit.

10. After Augustine's death some of his followers, including Prosper, tried to reduce the harshness of his system. They distinguished bet. gen. and special grace; only reception of the latter would save. But they left unsolved the mystery why not all received special grace. Other followers of Augustine continued to stress the harshness of his system. Semi-Pelagians charged them with going beyond Augustine and gained some victories, including a semi-Pelagian work written on assignment given by a syn. at Arles in the 470s to Faustus of Riez (Faustus Reiensis; Rhegiensis; of Rhegium, or Regium, or Reji, in Provence, SE Fr.; ca. 408–490; abbot Lérins; bp. Rhegium 454) in which he compared the relation of grace and free will to that of Christ's 2 natures and held that free will was not destroyed by the fall but that an indestructible germ of good remained. But these victories were only in Gaul.

11. Augustinianism was championed in Afr. and Italy. C. G. Fulgentius* refuted Faustus. Through the influence of Caesarius* of Arles the 2d syn. of Orange 529 restated Augustinianism, albeit modified, over against Pelagianism and semi-Pelagianism; its position was confirmed 530 by Boniface II (pope 530–532).

12. The W had thus taken a stand for the essence of Augustine's doctrine of sin and grace, decisively anti-Pelagian; but the speculative dialectic predestinarian matter was not resolved.

Pelagianism. Doctrinal position of Pelagius.* See also *Pelagian Controversy,* 4–5.

Pelagius (ca. 354/360–ca. 418/420). B. probably Brit. or Ireland; to Rome ca. 400; ascetic; to Carthage ca. 410/411; then to Palestine; expelled ca. 418; disappeared from hist. Works include commentaries on 13 epistles of Paul; a book on faith; treatises on Christian life, virginity, and on the divine law; letters. HTM

See also *Pelagian Controversy; Pelagianism.*

Pellicanus, Conradus (latinized from Ger. Kürschner, "furrier"; 1478–1556). Hebraist; b. Ruffach, Alsace; Franciscan 1493; supported the Reformation in Basel and esp. Zurich, Switz.; prof. theol. Basel 1523, Zurich 1525/26. Works include *Commentaria bibliorum.*

Penance. Fourth of the 7 RC sacraments*; molded from the Office of the Keys,* and the ancient practice of pub. penance for grave offenses (see *Penitential Discipline*), under influence of RC teaching of the merit of works and with aid of the monastic spirit.

"Those who by sin have fallen from the grace of justification which they had received can be justified again when, moved by God, they shall have taken steps, through the sacrament of penance, to recover, by Christ's merit, the grace which they lost. For this manner of justification is restoration of the fallen, which the holy fathers have aptly called a second plank after the shipwreck of grace lost" (Baptism being the 1st).

"The acts of the penitent himself, namely contrition,* confession,* and satisfaction, constitute, as it were, the matter of this sacrament."

"So great is the liberality of divine munificence that we can, through Jesus Christ, make satisfaction to God the Father, not only by punishments voluntarily undertaken by ourselves to atone for sin, or by those imposed at the priest's discretion according to the measure of the offense, but also (and this is the greatest proof of love) by temporal afflictions imposed by God and borne patiently by us." See also *Indulgences; Merit.*

"If anyone says . . . that there are only two parts of penance, namely the terrors with which a conscience convinced of sin is stricken and faith generated [or conceived] by the Gospel or by absolution, whereby one believes that sin is forgiven him through Christ, let him be anathema."

"If anyone says that the whole punishment is always remitted by God together with the guilt and that the satisfaction of penitents is nothing else than faith, by which they grasp the fact that Christ has made satisfaction for them, let him be anathema."

*Canons and Decrees of the Council of Trent,** Sess. VI, Decree Concerning Justification, chap. 14; Sess. XIV, The Most Holy Sacraments of Penance and Extreme Unction, chaps. 3 and 9, and Canons Concerning the Most Holy Sacrament of Penance, canons 4 and 12.

Acc. to RC doctrine, faith must precede penance but can in no sense be properly called part of penance (*Catechismus Romanus,* II, v, 5).

AC XII: "It is taught among us that those who sin after Baptism receive forgiveness of sin whenever they come to repentance, and absolution should not be denied them by the church. Properly speaking, true repentance is nothing else than to have contrition and sorrow, or terror, on account of sin, and yet at the same time to believe the Gospel and absolution (namely, that sin has been forgiven and grace has been obtained through Christ), and this faith will comfort the heart and again set it at rest. Amendment of life and the forsaking of sin should then follow, for these must be the fruits of repentance, as John says, 'Bear fruit that befits repentance' (Matt. 3:8). . . . Rejected . . . are those who teach that forgiveness of sin is not obtained through faith but through the satisfactions made by man."

See also *Repentance.*

Penington, Isaac (Pennington; . 1619–79). "The Younger"; son of a Lord Mayor of London, Eng.; educ. Cambridge; Quaker ca. 1657/58; distinguished preacher; repeatedly imprisoned. Works include *The Fundamental Right, Safety, and Liberty of the People Briefly Asserted.*

Penitential Days and Seasons. Various days of penance, repentance, or penitence, have been proclaimed and observed from time to time at various places, to the extent that it is difficult to distinguish anything near a common long-standing pattern. In the early ch., Wednesdays and Fridays of every week were thought of as penitential days. The 1st of M. Luther's* 95 Theses* reads: "Our Lord and Master Jesus Christ, in saying: 'Repent ye,' etc., intended that the whole life of believers should be penitence." In modern times, esp. under Ref. influence (e. g., in Kassel, Hesse, and Württemberg) quarterly and even monthly penitential days were appointed. After 1893 many Luths. in Ger. observed the Wed. before the last Sun. after Trin. as a penitential day. Luth. liturgical books provide for a Day of Humiliation and Prayer without setting a specific date. Advent and Lent are gen. observed as penitential seasons. See also *Hallelujah.*

Penitential Discipline. Procedure in the early ch. by which one guilty of wrongdoing was subjected to punishment intended to restore him to membership, usually by a series of steps: (1) *Prosklausis* (Gk.), or *fletus* (Lat.); both terms refer to weeping. Penitents (*cheimazomenoi* [Gk.], or *hiemantes* [Lat.], "troubled, distressed," or *lugentes* [Lat.], "mourning"), in mourning, admitted only to the ch. vestibule, wept and requested prayers of the assembling cong.; usually 1 yr. (2) *Akroasis* (Gk.), or *auditio* (Lat.); both terms refer to hearing. Penitents admitted into ch. for Bible readings and sermon, but restricted to the background, near the entrance;

constrained to leave before *missa* fidelium;* usually 3 yrs. (3) *Hypoptosis* (Gk.), or *genuflexio* or *substratio* (Lat.); reference is to gestures of humble obedience and respect. Penitents admitted farther into the ch. to kneel at prayer and receive special assignments, e. g., burial of the dead in times of pestilence; time indeterminate. (4) *Systasis* (Gk.), or *consistentia* (Lat.), lit. "a standing together." Penitents permitted to stand with the cong. to the end of the service; time indeterminate. At the end of this step full membership, including admission to Communion, was restored in a special ceremony by the bp. Advancement from step to step was usually in Lent, restoration to membership usually on Maundy Thu. See also *Discipline, Church; Genuflectentes.*

Penitential Psalms. See *Seven Penitential Psalms, The.*

Penitentiary. 1. RC officer in charge of the sacrament of penance in a given area. 2. See *Curia,* 2 e.

Penn, William (1644–1718). B. Tower Hill, London, Eng.; studied at Oxford, where he was dismissed 1661 for refusal to conform to Anglicanism; Quaker; anti-Trinitarian; imprisoned for nonconformity 1667, 1669, 1670; received grant of lands now constituting Del. and Pa. in satisfaction of his father's claims against the king; in Am. 1682–84, 1699-1701; made the colony a refuge for Quakers and others in search of liberty of conscience; developed good relations with Indians. See also *Friends, Society of.*

Pennefather, William. See *Mildmay Institutions.*

Pennington. See *Penington.*

Pennsylvania. See *United States, Religious History of,* 5–7.

Pennsylvania, Evangelical Lutheran Synod of Central (Cen. Pa. Syn.). See *United Lutheran Church, Synods of,* 23.

Pennsylvania, Evangelical Lutheran Synod of East (East Pa. Syn.). See *United Lutheran Church, Synods of,* 23.

Pennsylvania, Evangelical Lutheran Synod of West (West Pa. Syn.). See *United Lutheran Church, Synods of,* 22, 23.

Pennsylvania, Ministerium of. See *United Lutheran Church, Synods of,* 22.

Pennsylvania and Adjacent States, Ministerium of. See *United Lutheran Church, Synods of,* 22.

Pennsylvania College. See *Gettysburg College.*

Penry, John (Penri; Ap-Henry; 1559–93). B. Brecknockshire, Wales; educ. Cambridge and Oxford; Puritan; fled to Scot. 1590 under suspicion of having written the Marprelate* tracts; to Eng. 1592; Brownist (see *United Church of Christ,* I A 1); hanged on charge of treason.

Pension System, Ministerial. System in which a minister and/or those who employ him pay a percentage of the minister's salary into a fund that provides income for him when he retires.

Pentapolitana, Confessio. See *Lutheran Confessions,* A 5.

Pentateuch (Gk. "five scrolls"). Title for the 5 Books of Moses: Gn, Ex, Lv, Nm, Dt.

Pentateuch, Unity of. See *Higher Criticism.*

Pentecost. See *Church Year,* 5, 10, 16; *Judaism,* 4.

Pentecostal Assemblies of Jesus Christ. See *United Pentecostal Church, Inc.*

Pentecostal Assemblies of the USA. See *Pentecostal Church of God of America, Inc.*

Pentecostal Assemblies of the World, Inc. Organized ca. 1914 in midwest US; practice baptism in the name of Jesus; other requirements for membership include baptism of the Holy Ghost evidenced by speaking in tongues as the Spirit gives utterance; similar to Meths. in organization. HQ Indianapolis, Ind. See also *Pentecostalism.*

Pentecostal Church, Inc. See *United Pentecostal Church, Inc.*

Pentecostal Church of God of America, Inc. Organized 1919 Chicago, Ill., as Pentecostal Assemblies of the USA (called Pentecostal Church of God 1922; "of Am." added later). 1st conv. 1933; inc. 1936 in Mo.; Gen. Conv., highest ruling body, meets biennially; practices gen. coincide with those of other Pent. groups; noted for work among Am. Indians. See also *Pentecostalism.*

Pentecostal Church of the Nazarene. See *Church of the Nazarene.*

Pentecostal Fire-Baptized Holiness Church. Organized 1918 Nicholson, Ga.; consolidated ca. 1919/20 with Pent. Free Will Baps. Stresses sanctification as a 2d work of grace subsequent to regeneration and baptism by the Holy Spirit evidenced by speaking in tongues. See also *Pentecostalism.*

Pentecostal Free-Will Baptist Church. Formed 1959 by 3 Free-Will Bap. conferences in N. C. Other Free Will Bap. Chs. that had embraced Pentecostalism in the 1st half of the 20th c., but had remained indep., joined the movement. See also *Pentecostalism.*

Pentecostal Holiness Church, Inc. See *Holiness Churches,* 2; *Pentecostalism.*

Pentecostalism. Modern Pentecostalism in the US and Can. drew most of its first strength from the revivalism of the end of the 19th and beginning of the 20th c. (see *Latter Rain Movement*). It spread through Tenn., N. C., Minn., New Eng., Ohio, Kans., Calif., other states, and elsewhere in the world, e. g., Swed., Switz., Fr., Eng., Fin. Pentecostalists believe that speaking in tongues, the gift of healing, and prophecy are normal for every truly converted believer. Meetings of "spirit-baptized" Pentecostals also include testifying and other features said to be evidence of the Holy Spirit's immediate presence. The psychological phenomena of Pentecostalism resemble the ecstatic experiences of Montanism* and the Camisards,* the tongues movement under E. Irving,* and features of revivals in Ky. (see *Presbyterian Churches,* 4 b) and under leadership of G. Whitefield.* The theol. of modern Pentecostalism is a fusion of the Bap. "inner light" theory and Arminian perfectionism.* Pentecostals usually claim to proclaim the "Full Gospel" or "Foursquare* Gospel" (terms often imbedded in names of their chs.), referring to special emphasis on conversion, entire sanctification, divine healing,* and the premillennial coming of Christ (see *Millennialism*). Their preaching centers in the necessity of being baptized with the Holy Spirit; some classify their membership as converted, saved, and Spirit-baptized. Typical Pent. beliefs: that Jesus Christ shed His blood for the remission of sins that are past, for the regeneration of penitent sinners, and for salvation from sin and sinning; the Scriptural doctrine of justification by faith alone; that Jesus Christ shed His blood for the complete cleansing of the justified believer from all indwelling sin and from its pollution, subsequent to regeneration; that entire sanctification is an instantaneous, definite 2d work of grace, obtainable by faith on the part of the fully justified believer; that the Pentecostal baptism of the Holy Spirit and fire is obtainable by a definite act of appropriating faith on the part of the fully cleansed believer, and that the 1st evidence of the reception of this experience is speaking with other tongues as the Spirit gives utterance. Pent. groups include The Church* of God in Christ; The Church* of God in Christ, Internat.; Internat. Ch. of the Foursquare* Gospel; International* Pent. Assemblies; Pentecostal* Assemblies of the World, Inc.; Pentecostal* Ch. of God of Am., Inc.; Pentecostal* Fire-Baptized Holiness Ch.; Pentecostal* Free-Will Bap. Ch.; Pent. Holiness Ch., Inc. (see *Holiness Churches,* 2); United* Pent. Ch., Inc. FEM

See *Religious Bodies (US), Bibliography.*

Pepin the Short (Pépin le Bref; ca. 714–768). Son of Charles Martel; father of Charlemagne*; king of the Franks 751-768; called Pepin III as king of Ger.; with papal blessing he deposed the last of the Merovingian kings 751 and founded the Carolingian dynasty; in return, by the "Donation of Pepin," he gave the pope sovereignty over the exarchate of Ravenna. See also *Papacy,* 3.

Pepuzians. See *Montanism.*

Perates. See *Gnosticism,* 7 i.

Perceval, Spencer. See *Catholic Apostolic Church,* 1.

Perdition. See *Hereafter,* B.

Pereire, Jacob Rodrigue (Pereira; Giacobbo Rodriguez; 1715–80). B. Berlanga, Badajoz prov., in Estremadura, W Sp.; developed sign language for deaf-mutes in Fr. and taught there.

Peretti, Felice. See *Popes,* 22.

Perfectae caritatis. See *Vatican Councils,* 2.

Perfectibilists. See *Illuminati.*

Perfectionism. 1. Under this term is understood the doctrine acc. to which freedom from sin is possible in this life. That such perfection is attainable was claimed by Franciscans, Jesuits, and Molinists, largely on basis of distinguishing bet. mortal and venial sin; Dominicans and Jansenists denied the claim.

2. Perfectionism was denied by M. Luther* and J. Calvin.* But "Christian perfection" of sanctification is part of Meth. doctrine. J. Wesley* based his view mainly on commandments and promises of Scripture concerning sanctification, but said he held neither an angelic nor an Adamic perfection but one which does not exclude ignorance and error of judgment, with consequent wrong affections; i. e., not perfection acc. to the absolute Moral Law, but acc. to the special remedial economy introd. by the atonement,* in which the sanctified heart fulfills the Law by love; its involuntary imperfections are provided for, by that economy, without the imputation of guilt, as in the case of infancy and irresponsible persons.

3. Wesley was influenced by Jeremy Taylor,* Thomas* à Kempis, and W. Law.* Perfectionism is found also in other writers, RC and Prot. The Soc. of Friends* holds a perfectionism that still admits of growth and leaves room for possible sin "where the mind doth not most diligently and watchfully attend unto the Lord" (The Confession of the Soc. of Friends, 1675, 8th Proposition).

4. Oberlin* theol. held that as virtue and sin belong only to voluntary action, and are contradictory in their nature, they cannot coexist in the soul; the soul is either wholly consecrated to Christ or has none of His Spirit; the 2 states may alternate: a man may be a Christian at one moment and a sinner the next, but he cannot be at any one moment a sinful or imperfect Christian.

5. A holiness movement developed in the US in the latter part of the 19th c. in reaction against the wave of immorality and spiritual indifference that followed the Civil War. See also *Holiness Churches.*

6. Perfectionism implies (a) that Jesus can keep from sin those who trust in Him; (b) that if one trusts Him completely he will be preserved from all deliberate sin; and (c) that unintentional wrongdoings will be regarded as error rather than sin. Some claim to have so lived in the presence of Christ as to have been unconscious of sin for weeks and months. But most who hold perfectionism admit more frequent failures. Opponents of perfectionism hold that it rests (a) on misinterpretation of the Bible regarding sanctification and justification; (b) on defective ethical standards; (c) on antinomianism (see *Antinomian Controversy*). Cf. Mt 26:41; 1 Ptr 5:8; 1 Jn 1:8.

See also *Victorious Life.*

W. E. Sangster, *The Path to Perfection* (New York, 1943); R. N. Flew, *The Idea of Perfection in Christian Theology* (London, 1934); H. G. A. Lindström, *Wesley and Sanctification* (Stockholm, 1946); L. G. Cox, *John Wesley's Concept of Perfection* (Kansas City, Mo., 1964).

Performative Theory. See *Truth.*

Pergolesi, Giovanni Battista (Pergolese; 1710–36). Composer; b. Iesi, near Ancona, It.; family may have come from Pergola, It. Works include *Stabat Mater.* See also *Passion, The.*

Perichoresis (Gk. "a surrounding"). Theol. term for the union, communion, and interpenetration (1) of the 3 Persons of the Trinity,* (2) of the 2 natures of Christ (see *Christ Jesus,* I C), (2) of the 2 natures of Christ. The word was first used as a technical term for both (1) and (2) by John* of Damascus (e. g., *Expositio accurata fidei orthodoxae,* I, viii; IV, xviii).

Pericope (Gk. "section"). 1. Section of the Bible appointed to be read in ch. It is not possible to trace a clear connecting pattern bet. readings in the ancient synagog and those in Christian chs.

2. The oldest known pericopal system of the W ch. is ascribed to Jerome.* It was variously modified till ca. the time of Charlemagne,* when the selections became standardized. But further changes occurred in course of time, e. g., when RCm introd. Corpus* Christi in the 13th c. on the Thu. after Trin. and the festival of the Sacred Heart of Jesus in the 18th c. on the Fri. after the octave of Corpus Christi; this resulted in the hist. gospel pericope being read in Luth. and Angl. chs. 1 week ahead of the RC pattern, though the epistle pericopes are usually the same. More modern times have seen the appearance of many more pericopal systems, e. g., those of Eisenach, Württemberg, Nassau, G. Thomasius,* K. I. Nitzsch,* and the Synodical* Conf. See also *Lectionary.*

Perkins, Justin. See *Middle East,* I.

Perkins, William (1558–1602). Puritan theol.; b. Marston Jabbet, Warwickshire, Eng.; educ. Cambridge; emphasized Biblicism, conscience, rebirth, casuistry. Works include *Armilla Aurea; Reformed Catholike; An Exposition of the Lord's Prayer; An Exposition of the Symbol or Creed of the Apostles.*

Perpetua, Vibia (d. ca. 202 AD). Noblewoman; martyr with Felicity,* her slave, at Carthage, Afr.

Perrin, Ami. See *Libertines,* 3.

Perrinists. See *Libertines,* 3.

Perrone, Giovanni (1794–1876). B. Chieri, near Turin, It.; Jesuit 1815; prof. dogmatic theol. Collegio Romano, Rome, 1824–30, 1834–48; coll. rector Ferrara 1830–34; taught theol. at the Jesuit school Benhart, Wales, 1848–51; returned to Collegio Romano. Neoscholastic leader; helped formulate doctrine of Immaculate* Conception. Works include *Praelectiones theologicae.*

Perronet, Edward (1726–92). B. Sundridge, Kent. Eng., of Fr. parents; brought up Angl.; joined Meths. by 1746 and became an itinerant preacher; sided with the Countess of Huntingdon's Connexion (see *Hastings, Salina*) against the Wesleys; left the Connexion and became pastor of an indep. ch. Canterbury; hymnist. Hymns include "All Hail the Power of Jesus' Name."

Perrot, Charles (1541–1608). Ref. theol.; b. Paris, Fr.; pastor Geneva, Switz., 1567; prof. Geneva 1572; exponent of religious tolerance.

Persecution by Christians. 1. Persecution, or infliction of penalties for deviation from an acknowledged standard of religious belief, is an invasion of man's original rights that are his as an individual personally accountable to God. Wrong in principle, it is foolish as a policy. M. Luther*: "We neither should nor can force anyone to faith" (WA 30 II, 400). Persecution is rooted in mistaken religious zeal, ignorant fanaticism, the natural malice of the human heart, and sometimes also in the idea that uniformity in religion is essential to the welfare of the state. Constantine* I, who with Licinius* issued the Edict of Milan,* granting equal toleration to all religions, banished Arius (see *Arianism*) and Athanasius.* Theodosius* I made certain religious deviations capital crimes. Priscillian and 6 supporters were executed at Trier 385 (see *Priscillianists*).

2. Jerome* (appealing to Dt 13:6-10) and Augustine* of Hippo (appealing to Lk 14:23) advocated physical measures against errorists and heretics. Leo I (see *Popes,* 2) approved the execution of the Priscillianists *(Epistola xv ad Turribium)* and advocated the death penalty for heresy, as did Thomas* Aquinas (*Summa Theologiae,* II, ii, q. xi, art. 3). The 33d of 41 alleged heresies of M. Luther condemned by Leo X (see *Popes,* 20) was that it is against the will of the Spirit to burn heretics.

Persecution of Christians. 1. For a gen. statement on persecution see *Persecution by Christians,* 1.

Persecution was practically inevitable for early Christianity because of the sharp antithesis bet. it and the Roman empire. Christianity was spiritual, worshiped the King of kings, and looked for the ultimate triumph of His kingdom; the Roman empire was carnal, worshiped the emp., and made the welfare of his realm their goal. As a result, Christians came under suspicion and were charged with treason, atheism, etc. Pub. calamities (e. g., floods, earthquakes) were regarded as signs of divine wrath against them. Heathen priests, artisans, and tradesmen, whose living depended on maintaining the traditional faith, stirred up the masses against them. Extreme charges included incest and cannibalism, based on warped reports of love feasts (see *Agape,* 2) and Communion.

2. At first, indeed, Christianity was only regarded as a sect of Judaism (cf. Acts 18:12-17). But when it became clear that it was not anchored to Jerusalem but was a community knit by distinctive beliefs and practices, it was regarded as a menace and proscribed. This change of imperial policy probably occurred under the Flavian emps. 69–96 (Titus Flavius Sabinus Vespasianus [see *Vespasian*], emp. 69–79; Titus* Flavius Sabinus Vespasianus, emp. 79–81; Titus Flavius Domitianus Augustus [see *Domitian*], emp. 81–96).

3. Orosius* popularized the concept of 10 persecutions, but their numbering and identification are not altogether simple. They may be listed as under (1) Nero*; (2) Domitian*; (3) Trajan*; (4) Marcus* Aurelius; (5) Lucius Septimius Severus*; (6) G. J. V. Maximinus*; (7) Decius*; (8) Valerian*; (9) Aurelian*; (10) Diocletian* and successors to 313.

The persecution under Nero 64 did not result from est. imperial policy. Nero, suspected of burning Rome, apparently used Christians as scapegoats. C. Tacitus* describes the scene: "A vast multitude was convicted, not so much of arson as of hatred of the human race. And they were not only put to death, but subjected to insults, in that they were either dressed up in the skins of wild beasts and perished by the cruel mangling of dogs, or else put on crosses to be set on fire, and, as day declined, to be burned, being used as lights by night."

In the persecution under Domitian 96, who called himself "Lord and God," many were executed on charge of atheism.

In the persecution under Trajan 112–113, which extended over Asia Minor, Syria, and Palestine, Christians were not to be sought out, but if accused and convicted they were to be punished. Ignatius of Antioch (see *Apostolic Fathers,* 2) died in this persecution. Polycarp (see *Apostolic Fathers,* 3) suffered martyrdom ca. 156 under the reign of Antoninus Pius, but at the hands of the people rather than by will of the authorities.

Marcus Aurelius probably supported the persecutions that occurred in his reign, esp. 177 at Vienne and Lyons, S Fr. Martyrs included Pothinus* and Justin* Martyr.

Violent persecutions erupted in Egypt and N Afr. under Septimius Severus 202. Martyrs included V. Perpetua* and Felicity.*

G. J. V. Maximinus reversed the policy of his immediate predecessor, Alexander Severus, who was apparently well disposed toward Christians. Legends assign the martyrdom of Ursula* to persecution under Maximinus ca. 235.

4. Martyrs in the persecution under Decius 249–251 include Babylas.* See also *Seven Sleepers of Ephesus.*

Martyrs in the persecution under Valerian 257 include Cyprian.*

The edict of persecution issued by Aurelian ca. 274 was voided by his assassination.

The persecution 303–313 under Diocletian and his successors Galerius* and Galerius Valerius Maximinus* was most violent. Goaded by Galerius, Diocletian issued 3 edicts against Christians 303; Maximian (subordinate coregent; suicide 310) added a 4th 304. Christian chs. were to be destroyed, all Bibles burned, all Christians deprived of pub. office and civil rights, and all were to sacrifice to the gods on pain of death. A 5th edict 308 required all provisions in markets to be sprinkled with sacrificial wine. Eusebius* of Caesarea: "Large crowds [were executed] in one day, some suffering decapitation, others tortured by fire, so that the murderous sword was blunted, and becoming weak, was broken, and the very executioners grew weary and relieved each other" (*HE,* VIII, ix, 4). Martyrs assigned by hist. or legend to this persecution include Agnes,* Alban,* Januarius,* Pamphilus* of Caesarea, Peter* of Alexandria, and Phileas.*

The Edict of Milan* granted equal toleration to all religions 313.

See also *Lapsi.*

Perseverance. See *Final Perseverance of the Saints.*

Persia. See *Middle East,* I.

Personal Union in Christ. See *Christ Jesus,* C.

Personalism and Personalistic Psychology. Personalism is the philosophic view which holds that person is the ontological ultimate and personality the basic explanatory principle. Personalism in the generic sense connotes all data of self-conscious life. Acc. to this view, characteristic personal values and experiences are the final tests of truth and reality; in the metaphysics of personalistic psychology, conscious personality is the ultimate nature of all reality. Religious personalism regards the real framework of reality as spiritual and makes the active, living God both the immanent reason and the power of the life of the world and all beings in the world. One might perhaps harmonize this with Acts 17:28. See also *Bowne, Borden Parker.*

Persons, Robert. See *Parsons, Robert.*

Perspicuity of Scripture. Quality of Scripture acc. to which the doctrine of salvation is clearly set forth in Scripture. See also *Exegesis,* 1; *Hermeneutics,* 4.

Persuasion. See *Homiletics,* 7.

Perth, Articles of. Five arts. (requiring kneeling at Communion, observance of Christmas and Easter, confirmation, Communion at home for the dying, baptism on Sun. after birth), forced on the ch. in Scot. at Perth 1618 by James* I.

Perthes, Friedrich Christoph (1772–1843). B. Rudolstadt, Ger.; apprentice at ca. 15 to a Leipzig bookseller; to a similar position Hamburg 1793; est. his own bookshop Hamburg 1796, later expanded it to a pub. house; founded nat. museum Hamburg

1810; to Gotha 1822, where he specialized in pub. hist. and theol. works.

Peru. See *South America,* 9.

Perun. See *Slavs, Primitive Religion of.*

Peshitta. See *Bible Versions,* C.

Pessimism. Philos. view that regards this world the worst possible and man's lot hopeless; evil triumphs, good is defeated. Pessimism is found, e. g., Ec 1:2, 14; 3:19; 11:8; 12:8; in the Gk. poet Hesiod (perhaps ca. 8th–7th c. BC); in A. Schopenhauer,* who tried to expound pessimism philosophically.

Pestalozzi, Johann Heinrich (1746–1827). Educ. reformer; b. Zurich, Switz.; studied theol. and law; est. a school for poor children ca. 1774/75 on his estate Neuhof, near Brugg, Aargau canton; it failed ca. 1779/80; conducted a school for orphans at Stans, Nidwalden, 1798–99; helped develop a school at Burgdorf 1799–1804; connected with a school at Münchenbuchsee 1804, which was moved to Yverdon 1805, where he taught till 1825. Engaged in educ. experiments and investigation; tried to "psychologize" educ.; held that all proper educ. processes start from "nature," i. e., a child's own interests and activities; educ. must be essentially religious, develop man as a whole, stimulate and guide self-activity, and be based on "Anschauung" (intuition; perception; cognition; internalized apperception) and exercise. Works include *Lienhard und Gertrud.*

Petavius Dionysius (Denis Pétau; Denys; 1583–1652 [54?]). Jesuit hist.; b. Orléans, Fr.; prof. Reims, La Flèche, and Paris. Works include *Opus de doctrina temporum; De theologicis dogmatibus; Uranologion.*

Peter, Acts of. See *Apocrypha,* B 3.

Peter, Chair of. See *Chair of Peter*

Peter and Paul, Feast of. See *Church Year,* 14, 16.

Peter Chelcicky. See *Chelcicky, Peter.*

Peter Chrysologus (perhaps as late as 406 [or as early as 380?] – ca. 450). B. Forum Cornelii, near Imola, It.; bp. Ravenna perhaps ca. 431; famed as orator (hence Gk. Chrysologos, "golden-worded"); opposed Monophysitism.

MPL, 52, 9–680.

Peter Claver (ca. 1580/81–1654). "Apostle of Cartagena; Apostle of the Negroes"; b. Verdu, Catalonia, Sp.; desired to convert heathen in the New World; to Cartagena (in what is now Colombia) 1610; worked among slaves brought from W Afr.; priest 1615/16.

Peter Comestor (Petrus; ca. 1100–ca. 1179/80). B. Troyes, Fr.; chancellor cathedral school Paris 1164–68. Works include *Historia scholastica* (hist. from creation to the end of Acts); sermons; commentaries; doctrinal treatises.

MPL, 198, 1045–1844.

Peter Damian. See *Damiani, Pietro.*

Peter Lombard. See *Peter the Lombard.*

Peter Martyr (Pietro Martire Vermigli; 1500–62). B. Florence, It.; Augustinian at ca. 16; abbot Spoleto 1530; prior Naples 1533; championed Calvinism; prof. Oxford, Strasbourg, Zurich. Works include *Tractatio de sacramento Eucharistiae* and *Disputatio de eodem Eucharistiae sacramento.*

Peter Mogila. See *Mogila, Peter.*

Peter Mongo (from Gk. for "stammerer"; d. 490). Patriarch of Alexandria; Monophysite; supported Acacius* of Constantinople.

Peter Nolasco (ca. 1182–1249[1256?]). B. probably Barcelona, perhaps Languedoc; life legendary; probably helped found Mercedarians.*

Peter of Alcántara (Garavito; 1499–1562). B. Alcántara, Estremadura, Sp.; Franciscan; priest 1524; provincial of province of St. Gabriel 1538–41; retired to hermitage near Lisbon, Port.; returned to Sp.; founded Alcantarines (Sp. Discalced Franciscans). Works include *Tratado de la oración y meditación.*

Peter of Alexandria (d. 311). Head of school of Alexandria; bp. Alexandria 300–311; advocated mild treatment of *lapsi**; when he went into hiding under persecution 306, Meletius of Lycopolis claimed his position (see also *Meletian Schisms,* 1); beheaded in persecution under Galerius Valerius Maximinus.* See also *Persecution of Christians,* 4.

MPG, 18, 449–522.

Peter of Bruys. See *Bruys, Pierre de.*

Peter of Laodicea (ca. 7th–8th c.). Gk. Patristic writer; little known of his life.

MPG, 86, 3321–36.

Peter the Fuller (d. 488). Monophysite*; backed by emp. Zeno(n),* he became bp. Antioch 470; deposed and reinstated twice; endorsed the "Henoticon.*"

Peter the Hermit (Peter of Amiens; ca. 1050–ca. 1115). Fr. hermit and monk; one of the leaders of the 1st Crusade (see *Crusades*). See also *Preaching, Christian, History of,* 8.

Peter the Lombard (Petrus Lombardus; ca. 1100–ca. 1160/64). "Magister sententiarum"; Scholastic (see *Scholasticism);* b. near Novara, Lombardy, It.; taught at Paris ca. 1139; bp. Paris 1159; helped blend mysticism and scholasticism. Works include *Sententiarum libri quatuor,* a collection of doctrinal statements of the fathers, with contradictions resolved dialectically; long used as a textbook.

Peter the Venerable (Peter of Montboissier; ca. 1092 to 1156). B. Auvergne, Fr.; monk at Cluny 1109; abbot Cluny 1122; friend of Bernard* of Clairvaux; gave shelter to P. Abelard*; preferred literal sense of Scripture, avoiding allegorical speculation. Works include writings against Jews and Saracens.

MPL, 189, 9–1072.

Peters, Gerlach. See *Gerlach, Peters.*

Peter's Pence ("pence" is a pl. of "penny"). Tax formerly paid in Eng. to the pope; originated in the 8th c.; extended to Scand. countries; attempts to introduce it in other countries were not successful; abolished in Eng. 1534; gen. abandoned as a result of the Reformation. Revived 1860 as a freewill offering to compensate for loss of income from states* of the ch.

Petersen, Fredrik (1839–1903). Luth. theol.; b. Stavanger, Norw.; prof. Oslo 1875. Works include writings concerned with problems in theol. occasioned by modern science.

Petersen, Johann Wilhelm (1649–1727). Luth. theol., poet, mystic, chiliast; b. Osnabrück, Ger.; educ. Giessen and Rostock; held various teaching positions and pastorates. Works include commentaries and hymns.

Petra. See *Middle East,* G.

Petrarch (Francesco Petrarca; originally Petracco; 1304–74). Poet; humanist; b. Arezzo, It.; studied at Montpellier and Bologna; traveled extensively; devoted himself to study of classics. Works include *De contemptu mundi; De otio religiosorum; De vera sapientia.*

Petri, Laurentius (1499–1573). Brother of O. Petri*; b. Örebro, Swed.; educ. Wittenberg, Ger.; 1531 Prot. abp. Swed.; opposed Calvinism; promoted Lutheranism. Helped tr. Bible into Swed.

Petri, Ludwig Adolf (1803–73). Luth. theol; b. Lüthorst, Hannover, Ger.; educ. Göttingen; pastor Hanover 1829; opposed rationalism and the Prussian* Union; with A. F. O. Münchmeyer* and R. Steinmetz* founded *Gotteskasten.**

Petri, Olaus (Olavus; ca. 1493–1552). Brother of L. Petri*; b. Örebro, Swed.; educ. Leipzig and Wittenberg; promoted the Reformation in Swed. after 1520; imperial chancellor 1531–33; fell into disfavor and was condemned to die, but was pardoned; pastor Stockholm 1543–52; hymnist. Helped tr. the Bible into Swed. Other works include a minister's manual; catechism; postil.

Samlade Skrifter af Olavus Petri, ed. B. Hesselman, 4 vols. (Uppsala, 1914–17).

Petrie, William Matthew Flinders (1853–1942). Egyptologist; b. Charlton, Kent, Eng.; prof. Egyptology, Univ. Coll., London, 1892–1933; founded Brit. School of Archaeology in Egypt 1894; excavated in Palestine 1927–38. Excavation sites include Abydos, Am, Daphne, Hawara, Kahun, Medum, Memphis, Nagada, Naucratis, Tanis, Tarkhan, Thebes, Lachish, Tell el-Amarna, and Tell el-Hesi. Works include *Methods & Aims in Archaeology; Seventy Years in Archaeology.* See also *Geography, Christian,* 6.

Petrobrusians. Followers of Pierre de Bruys.*

Petrock. See *Celtic Church,* 6.

Petronius (early 5th c.). Said to have made a pilgrimage to Palestine in early life; bp. Bologna, It., ca. 432; built a ch. in Bologna modeled after structures in Jerusalem; a ch. begun 1390, finished in the 17th c., was named in his honor.

Petrus Magni. See *Magni, Petrus.*

Pettazzoni, Raffaele (1883–1959). Hist.; b. S. Giovanni Persiceto, Bologna, It.; prof. Bologna 1914, Rome 1924–58; chm. Internat. Assoc. for the Study of the Hist. of Religions 1950–59. Contributed esp. to phenomenology of religion.

Pétursson, Hallgrímur (ca. 1614–74). Poet; parish priest Saurbaer, Iceland. Works include 50 Passion hymns (collection known as "Passiusalmar," one of the greatest literary works in Icelandic). SP

Pétursson, Pétur (1808–91). Educ. Copenhagen; pastor in Iceland 1838; sem. pres. Reykjavík 1847–66; bp. Iceland 1866. Continued Finn(u)r Jónsson's *Historia ecclesiastica Islandiae* from 1740 to 1840.

Peucer, Kaspar (1525–1602). Son-in-law of P. Melanchthon*; b. Bautzen, Ger.; studied math and medicine Wittenberg; prof. Wittenberg 1554; gen. supt. Lat. schools; physician to elector August* of Saxony; furthered Crypto-Calvinism (see *Crypto-Calvinistic Controversy*); arrested 1574; imprisoned; released 1586; physician and councillor Dessau.

Peutinger, Konrad (1465–1547). Humanist and antiquary; b. Augsburg, Ger.; educ. It.; interested esp. in hist. and Ger. antiquities; sympathetic to Reformation but never broke with RCm.

Pezel, Christoph (1539–1604). B. Plauen, Ger.; educ. Jena and Wittenberg; prof. 1567, preacher 1569 Wittenberg; banished 1576 for Crypto-Calvinism; teacher Siegen, then preacher Dillenburg 1577; openly accepted Calvinism; pastor Herborn 1578; to Bremen 1581. Works include *Argumenta et objectiones de praecipuis articulis doctrinae Christianae;* catechisms of Bremen and Wittenberg.

Pfaff, Christoph Matthäus (1686–1760). B. Stuttgart, Ger.; educ. Tübingen; chancellor Tübingen U. ca. 1720/21; chancellor and supt. Giessen 1756; inclined to pietism. Works include writings in nearly all depts. of theol.; directed publication of a new Ger. Bible tr., the so-called Tübinger Bibelwerk. See also *Collegialism.*

Pfander, Karl Gottlieb (1803–65). B. Waiblingen, Württemberg, Ger.; Basel* Miss. Soc. miss. to Muslim in Armenia, Mesopotamia, and Persia 1825–37; CMS miss. India and Pakistan 1841–57; in Constantinople 1858–65. Works include writings on Islam.

Pfarramt. See *Ministerial Office,* 2.

Pfarrernotbund. See *Barmen Theses; Germany,* C 4; *Kirchenkampf.*

Pfeffer, Paul (1651–1710). B. Neustadt, Glogau, Ger.; mayor Bautzen; hymnist. Wrote the hymn "Ach, jawohl bin ich nunmehr entgangen" (to be sung antiphonally with S. Dach's* "O wie selig seid ihr doch, ihr Frommen").

Pfefferkorn, Georg Michael (1645[6?]–1732). B. Ifta, near Kreuzburg, Ger.; educ. Jena and Leipzig; private tutor Altenburg; held various positions; consistorial assessor and supt. Gräfen-Tonna 1682; hymnist. Hymns include "Was frag ich nach der Welt" (tr. A. Crull* "What Is the World to Me").

Pfeffinger, Johann (1493–1573). B. Wasserburg, Ger.; held several positions and became priest; preacher Passau 1521, where he heard of M. Luther; fled threatened arrest; studied at Wittenberg 1524; pastor Sonnenwalde 1527, Eicha 1530, Belgern 1532; pastor and 1st Luth. supt. Leipzig 1540[1541?]; helped introd. Reformation in Schönburg; prof. Leipzig 1544; connected with developments that led to the Leipzig Interim (see *Interim,* II); Philippist (see *Philippists*). Works include moral, ascetic, and polemic writings. See also *Synergistic Controversy.*

Pfeiffer, August (1640–98). Orientalist; pastor Meissen 1675; archdeacon and prof. Leipzig 1681; supt. Lübeck 1689. Works include *Dubia vexata Scripturae Sacrae; Critica sacra; Thesaurus hermeneuticus.*

Pfeiffer, Edward (Nov. 23, 1857–Dec. 19, 1926). B. Columbus, Ohio; educ. Capital U. and Luth. sem., Columbus, Ohio; pastor Pa. and Ohio 1881–99; sem. prof. Capital U. 1899–1926. Ed. *The Little Missionary* 1886–91; ed. miss. dept. *Lutheran Standard* 1891 to 1925; other works include *Mission Studies.*

Pfeil, Christian (or **Christoph**) **Karl Ludwig** (1712–84). B. Grünstadt, near Worms, Ger.; educ. Halle and Tübingen; held several pol. offices; influenced by N. L. v. Zinzendorf* and J. A. Bengel*; pietist; hymnist. Hymns include "Wohl einem Haus, da Jesus Christ" (tr. C. Winkworth* "Oh, Blest the House, Whate'er Befall").

Pfenninger, Johann Konrad (1747–92). B. Zurich, Switz.; educ. Zurich; chaplain Zurich orphanage 1775; pastor Zurich 1786; friend and co-worker of J. K. Lavater, poet. Works include apologetic and exegetic writings.

Pfleiderer, Otto (1839–1908). B. Stetten, Württemberg, Ger.; educ. Tübingen; held various positions; pastor Heilbronn 1868; pastor and prof. Jena 1870; prof. Berlin 1875. Denied miraculous origin of Christianity. See also *Lutheran Theology After 1580,* 10.

Pflug, Julius von (1499–1564). B. Eyt(h)ra (or Pegau?), near Leipzig, Ger.; educ. Leipzig, Bologna, and Padua; cathedral provost Zeitz 1522; cathedral dean Meissen 1537; elected RC bp. Naumburg-Zeitz 1541, accepted and confirmed 1542, est. 1547. Humanistic; interested in peace with Prots.; took part in 1541 Regensburg* Conf. Helped draft Augsburg and Leipzig Interim.*

Pfotenhauer, Johann Friedrich (Apr. 22, 1859–Oct. 9, 1939). B. Altencelle, Hannover, Ger.; to Am. 1875; educ. Conc. Coll., Fort Wayne, Ind., and Conc. Sem., St. Louis, Mo.; traveling miss. Minn. and territories of Dak. and Mont. (base Odessa, Minn.) 1880–87. Pastor Lewiston, Minn., 1887–94; Hamburg, Minn., 1894–1911; pres. Minn. and Dak. Dist. of the Mo. Syn. 1891–1908; pres. Mo. Syn. 1911–35, honorary pres. 1935–39.

E. A. Mayer, "Dr. Friedrich Pfotenhauer (1859–1939)," tr. F. A. Hertwig *CHIQ,* XIII, 1 (Apr. 1940), 1–22; H. A. Grueber, "F. Pfotenhauer: The Man and the Leader," *CHIQ,* XIII, 1 (Apr. 1940), 22–25.

Phallicism (phallism). Type of nature worship in which generative powers as symbolized in the male organ, or phallus, are worshiped; common among primitive peoples and usually assoc. with fertility cults, but found also among such more advanced peoples as Phoenicians and Greeks; in many cases assoc. ceremonies are orgiastic.

Phanar. Residence and court of the patriarch of Constantinople.

Pharisees. See *Judaism,* 2.

Phelps, Sylvanus Dryden (1816–95). B. Suffield, Conn.; educ. Brown U., Providence, R. I.; Bap. pastor New Haven, Conn., 1846; hymnist. Hymns include "Savior, Thy Dying Love."

Phelps, William Lyon (1865–1943). B. New Haven, Conn.; educ. Yale Coll. (now Yale U.), New Haven, Conn., and Harvard U., Cambridge, Mass.; instructor English at Harvard 1891–92; instructor Yale 1892–96, asst. prof. 1896–1901, prof. 1901–33. Works include *Reading the Bible; Human Nature in the Bible; Human Nature and the Gospel.*

Phenomenology. Philos. term used in various senses. I. Kant* called subjects and events as they are in experience "phenomena." G. W. F. Hegel* regarded phenomenology as the science in which we come to know mind as it is itself through the ways in which it appears to us.

In the 19th c., phenomenology came to mean descriptive study. In E. Husserl's* philos. it is used for the assertion of the intentional structure of consciousness, the analysis of the ontological ground of that structure, and the classification of the types of intentionality.

M. Heidegger, Jean-Paul Sartre, et al. (see *Existentialism*) used the term in descriptions of their own work.

The expression "phenomenology of religion" is used in various ways, including (1) that part of phenomenology developed by thinkers beginning with E. Husserl which is devoted to the study of religion; (2) hist. studies that use methods related in a gen. way to those of phenomenology in the study of religions; (3) gen. phenomenological methods applied to the study of the whole spectrum of religious ideas, activities, institutions, customs, and symbols. EL

Philadelphia Association. See *Baptist Churches,* 4, 26.

Philadelphia Confession. See *Baptist Churches,* 4; *Democratic Declarations of Faith,* 3.

Philadelphia Yearly Meeting for the Religious Society of Friends. See *Friends, Society of,* 8.

Philadelphian Society for the Advancement of Piety and Divine Philosophy, The. Organized in Eng. ca. 1670 by T. Bromley,* J. Lead(e),* and J. Pordage,* who professed a kind of mystic pantheism and held that their souls were immediately illumined by the Holy Spirit. See also *Lee, Francis.*

Philanthropinism. Pedagogical reform movement in Ger. 1770–1800 named after J. B. Basedow's* school called Philanthropinum. Philanthropinists included K. F. Bahrdt* and C. G. Salzmann.*

Philaret (lay name Vasili Mikhailovich Drozdov; 1782–1867). B. Kolomna, near Moscow, Russ.; monk 1808; prof. St. Petersburg (now Leningrad) 1808; mem. Holy Syn. 1818; bp. Jaroslav 1820; abp. Moscow 1821; metropolitan of Moscow 1825. Proponent of syn. state ch. See also *Eastern Orthodox Standards of Doctrine,* A 4.

Philaster (Filaster; d. ca. 396). Bp. Brescia, Lombardy, N It.; opposed Arians.

MPL, 12, 1111-1302.

Phileas (d. ca. 307). Bp. Thmuis, in the Nile Delta, Egypt; martyr at Alexandria. See also *Persecution of Christians,* 4.

Philip II (Philip Augustus; 1165–1223). Son of Louis* VII; king of Fr. 1180–1223; engaged in various wars, including war with Eng. 1187–89; built many chs. and institutions; a leader of the 3d Crusade (see *Crusades,* 4).

Philip IV. See *France,* 3.

Philip, John (Apr. 14, 1775–Aug. 27, 1851). B. Kirkcaldy, Fife, Scot.; educ. Hoxton theol. school, London, Eng.; preached at Newbury Cong. Ch., Berkshire, 1802; pastor Aberdeen, Scot., 1814–18; helped inspect LMS miss. stations in S. Afr. 1818; pastor Cape Town 1822; supt. LMS miss. stations in S. Afr.; tried to protect natives from abuse and exploitation. Works include *Researches in South Africa.*

Philip and James the Less, Saints. See *Church Year,* 16.

Philip Augustus. See *Philip II.*

Philip Neri. See *Neri, Filippo de'.*

Philip of Hesse. (Philip the Magnanimous; 1504–67). Son-in-law of George* the Bearded; father-in-law of Maurice* of Saxony; b. Marburg, Ger.; landgrave of Hesse 1509–67; declared of age 1518; met M. Luther at the Diet of Worms 1521; successfully opposed F. v. Sickingen* and the knights'* revolt; helped suppress rebellious peasants (see *Peasants' War*); introd. reforms; founded the U. of Marburg 1527 (1st Prot. U.). For his part in union maneuvers after the 1529 Diet of Speyer see *Luther, Controversies of,* g; *Lutheran Confessions,* A 2. Signed the AC but felt the art. on the Lord's Supper should have been milder. Helped form Schmalkaldic* League 1531. Entered bigamous marriage 1540 with private consent of M. Luther and P. Melanchthon, who did not have full knowledge of the facts; scandal resulted; for further results see *Schmalkaldic War.* After his defeat at Mühlberg 1547 (see also *John Frederick*), Philip was imprisoned; approved the Interim*; released 1552 after the Convention of Passau.* Engaged in further unsuccessful efforts to unite Prots. See also *Gotha Covenant; Pack, Otto von.*

Philip of Swabia (Philipp; ca. 1177/80–1208). Son of emp. Frederick* I; bp. Würzburg 1190 [1191?]; resigned his see 1192; duke Tuscany 1195, Swabia 1196; Holy Roman emp. 1198–1208 but never crowned. See also *Crusades,* 5.

Philip the Arabian (Marcus Julius Philippus; d. 249). Roman emp. 244–249; said to have been barred from ch. by Babylas* until he confessed his sins; killed in struggle with Decius.*

Philip the Magnanimous. See *Philip of Hesse.*

Philippi, Ferdinand (1840–90). Son of F. A. Philippi*; b. Berlin, Ger.; pastor Hohenkirchen. Contributed to K. H. Meusel's* *Kirchliches Handlexikon.* Other works include *Der Knecht Gottes; Das Buch Henoch, sein Zeitalter und sein Verhältnis zum Judasbrief; Die biblische und kirchliche Lehre vom Antichrist; Über die Notwendigkeit und Verbindlichkeit des kirchlichen Bekenntnisses.*

Philippi, Friedrich Adolf (1809–1882). Father of F. Philippi*; b. Berlin, Ger.; of Jewish descent; became Christian and was bap. 1829 while a student at Leipzig; induced by E. W. Hengstenberg to study theol.; private tutor Berlin 1837–40; prof. Dorpat (Tartu) 1841/42, Rostock 1851/52; proponent of confessional Lutheranism; upheld verbal inspiration. Works include *Commentar über den Brief Pauli an die Römer; Kirchliche Glaubenslehre.*

Philippicum, Corpus. See *Lutheran Confessions,* C 1.

Philippines, Republic of the. 1. *Area:* ca. 115,800 sq. mi.; *pop.* (1971 est.): 39,400,000. Consists of ca. 7,100 islands; ca. 2,773 are named; ca. 462 are larger than 1 sq. mi.; part of Malay Archipelago. Legal capital: Quezon City (pop. ca. 545,500), in the Greater Manila area (pop. ca. 2,500,000; Manila, pop. ca. 1,500,000, is the administrative capital). Ferdinand Magellan (ca. 1480–1521; Port. navigator), exploring for Sp., discovered the islands 1521 and was slain during a tribal feud. The islands came under dominion and control of Sp. 1564–84. Intermittent native rebellions led to revolution 1896. At the end of the Sp.-Am. war the islands were ceded to the US 1898; indep. 1946. Filipinos are basically Malayan and Indonesian, but strongly influenced by Sp., Am., and Chinese cultures. Heavy W influence is evident in cities. Civilization is highly developed, but some animistic groups remain, e. g., on Luzon and Mindanao. Languages include 87 dialects; Tagalog is the nat. tongue; Eng. is in gen. use; Sp. is the language of the elite.

2. Ca. 83% is RC. As a result of schism ca. the time of the Sp.-Am. war, the Philippine Indep. Ch. (Iglesia Filipina Independiente) was formed 1902. As a result of factionalism, part of the Philippine Indep. Ch. entered into full communion with the Prot. Episc. Ch. of the US 1961; the other part, Unitarian, broke into several sects. Other Christian bodies total less than 5% of the pop. Other religious groups include Muslim (ca. 2,000,000), animists (ca. 400,000), and Buddhists (ca. 43,000, mostly Chinese).

3. The Mo. Syn. entered the Philippines 1946. Under leadership of Alvaro A. Carino, a native, educ. Conc. Sem., St. Louis, Mo., work expanded from Manila to Pangasinan and Ilocos Sur provinces 1948, to Mountain province 1949. Missionaries also entered Mindanao is. 1949, the Visayas 1959, Cebu and Leyte 1960. 1962 saw the beginning of miss. work among Muslim on Mindanao and est. of the Dept. of Mass Communications and the Dept. of Lay Training (later called Dept. of Parish Educ.). Other ventures include a med. program among highlanders and a theol. sem. (see *Lutheran Church – Missouri Synod, The,* VII, 14). The Luth. Ch. in the Philippines (1966 constitutional name) adopted new bylaws 1968; reorganized 1970; joined Nat. Christian Council in the Philippines; was accepted 1971 as a sister ch. of LCMS; pres: Alvaro A. Carino 1968–72, David Schneider 1972–. JJJ

Philippists (Interimists; synergists). Called Philippists because they favored the synergistic tendencies of Philipp Melanchthon* and his compromising statements of the Lord's Supper. Called Interimists because, with Melanchthon, they agreed to the Leipzig Interim (see *Interim,* 2), holding that it yielded to RCm only in matters that were adiaphora.* Included J. Bugenhagen,* J. Camerarius,* N. Crell,* C. Cruciger the Younger (see *Cruciger,* 2), P. Eber,* G. Major,* P. Melanchthon,* K. Peucer,* J. Pfeffinger,* V. Strigel.* Opponents called Gnesio-Lutherans.* See also *Synergism; Synergistic Controversy.*

Phillimore, Greville (1821–84). Eng. hymnist; educ. Westminster, The Charterhouse (London), and Oxford. Vicar Downe-Ampney, Cricklade, Gloucestershire, 1851; rector Henley-on-Thames 1867, Ewelme 1883. Hymns include "Every Morning Mercies New."

Phillpotts, Henry (1778–1869). B. Bridgewater, Somersetshire, Eng.; educ. Oxford; prebendary Durham 1809; dean Chester 1828; bp. Exeter 1830–69. See also *England, Free Church of; Gorham, George Cornelius.*

Philo Judaeus (Lat. "the Jew"; Philo of Alexandria; ca. 20/30 BC to ca. 50 AD). Hellenistic Jewish philos. of Alexandria; tried to fuse Judaism and Gk. thought by showing that the latter was contained in the OT; regarded this world as imperfect; held that God's contact with it was through the Logos; by allegory he transforms OT persons and events into abstractions. See also *Therapentae.*

Philology, Biblical. Study of the original languages of the Bible.

Philosophical Realism. See *Realism.*

Philosophy (from Gk. *philein,* "to love," and *sophia,* "wisdom"). Search for wisdom, and the resulting body of knowledge of gen. principles explaining facts and existences, elements, powers or causes, and laws.

Philos. may be regarded as the science of the principles and methods that underlie all knowledge and existence. It tries to think methodically and clearly about notions that occur in thinking but are not solved by special sciences. It tries to present a harmonious and comprehensive world view.

Main divisions of philos.: 1. epistemology, or study of knowledge, dealing with limitations and grounds of knowledge; 2. metaphysics, dealing with principles at the basis of all phenomena; 3. natural philos., dealing with the origin and nature of the world; 4. psychol.; 5. logic; 6. ethics; 7. aesthetics.

The term "philos." has been used in a popular way for private wisdom or consolation. Philos. and religion have in common a concern with the nature of God and His relation to the world. Philos. of hist. tries to find meaning in the course of hist. Exponents of a philos. of hist. include Augustine* of Hippo, W. C. L. Dilthey,* J. G. Fichte,* G. W. F. Hegel,* J. G. v. Herder,* I. Kant,* G. E. Lessing,* Origen,* F. W. J. v. Schelling,* Tertullian,* G. B. Vico.* Philosophy* of religion tries to investigate religions generally and impartially.

Philos. may be divided into formal philos. (science of knowledge) and material philos., which tries to grasp the truth and essence of the universe. In this division, formal philos. includes logic (which deals with the science of the intellect or mind) and metaphysics (which deals with reason and the domain of ideas); material (or real) philos. tries to understand and explain the universe: nature, spirit, God. As regards the last 3: The philos. of nature deals with matter and energy as expressed in the organism; the philos. of spirit treats of the individual spirit in the science of psychol., organized community life in pol. science, and of beauty in its various forms in the science of art; the philos. of God takes up the idea and reality of religion in the philos. of religion, morality in the science of ethics, and the development and progress or retrogression of humanity in the philos. of hist.

We are here concerned mainly with philos. as it appears in the philos. of religion, in ethics, and in the philos. of hist. We want to know how near the intellect and reason of man has come to understand God and things divine and explain the relation bet. God and the universe.

The human mind can arrive at some knowledge of God (Ro 1:18-25). Philosophers even before Christ drew a picture of a Supreme Being, one in essence, Father of all, omnipotent, omnipresent, omniscient, eternal, holy, just, wise, truthful.

If the science of philos., esp. philos. of religion, had continued along lines of the last remnant of the natural knowledge of God (Ro 1–2), there would have been no need of debates bet. Paul and philosophers (Acts 17:18-34) or of such warnings as in Cl 2:8.

Pre-Christian Gk. philosophers performed a propaedeutic service to Christianity. They sought the 1 permanent element (Anaxagoras,* Anaximander,* Anaximenes* of Miletus, Democritus,* Thales*), the Being (Parmenides,* Xenophanes*), the law of change (Heraclitus*), the mathematics of the universe (Pythagoras; see *Pythagoreanism*) unsuccessfully. Sophists made man the measure of all things, gave language precision, and introd. skepticism.* Socrates* and Plato* introd. inductive reasoning and gen. definitions, developed the doctrines of ideas and recollections (which played a prominent part in later struggles bet. realism* and nominalism*), and turned philos. into a study of ethics. After Aristotle* the followers of Pyrrho revived skepticism.* In a period of corruption the Epicureanism* and Stoicism* made happiness the goal.

Philo* Judaeus influenced Jewish philos.

The apostolic ch. opposed philosophy. Ro 12:2 was followed literally. The wisdom of this world was largely ignored. Christians considered themselves strangers and pilgrims who had no continuing city here (Heb 11:13; 13:14). For E speculation in the early ch. see, e. g., *Gnosticism.*

Change began with est. of catechetical schools

(see *Schools, Early Christian*). Neoplatonism* left a lasting mark on the ch.

A. M. T. S. Boethius* was the last true philos., except J. S. Erigena,* before nominalism and realism. The theol. of the ch. in the Middle Ages was governed by the philos. of Aristotle; scholasticism* dominated (see, e. g., *Abelard, Peter; Albertus Magnus; Alexander of Hales; Anselm of Canterbury; Duns Scotus, John; Gilbert de la Porrée; Peter the Lombard; Roscellinus; Thomas Aquinas*). As a result, theol. degenerated and ch. life decayed.

M. Luther was influenced in his youth by nominalist philos. He thought highly of W. of Ockham* because he saw traces of the influence of the Gospel in him. But he repudiated medieval philos. in its rejection of free grace and spoke harshly of Aristotle. His position may be summarized: he "maintained an ambivalent attitude toward the place of philosophy in the Church. . . . In general he regarded philosophy as dangerous; and yet, when the occasion seemed to demand it, he was not at all averse to philosophical speculation. . . . Luther saw . . . that philosophy and theology differ as to method, content, purpose, and result . . . [and that] the work of the theologian . . . is to describe the workings of faith, and to do so in faith's own terms. . . . Nevertheless [Luther] was competent in the use of Aristotelian logic and . . . acknowledged it as valid" (J. Pelikan, *From Luther to Kierkegaard,* pp. 10, 12, 13).

Through P. Melanchthon* the influence of ancient philosophies came to bear on construction of Luth. thought. His description of faith in mental or intellectual terms has been called "the Melanchthonian blight" (R. C. Caemmerer, "The Melanchthonian Blight," *CTM,* XVIII [1947], 321–338); its influence has not entirely disappeared.

On the influence of philos. in theol. in the 18th–20th cents. see, e. g., *Deism; Doctrine, Christian, History of,* 5; *Dogmatics; Existentialism; Fichte, Johann Gottlieb; Hegel, Georg Wilhelm Friedrich; Kant, Immanuel; Leibniz, Gottfried Wilhelm von; Rationalism; Schelling, Friedrich Wilhelm Joseph von; Schleiermacher, Friedrich Daniel Ernst; Semler, Johann Salomo; Wolff, Christian von.*

All movements against the pure and complete doctrine of the Bible are efforts of philos. in decay to replace the revealed truth of the Word. Proper philos. serves theol.

T. Gomperz, *Greek Thinkers,* vol. 1 tr. L. Magnus, vols. 2–4 tr. G. G. Berry (New York, 1901–12); H. O. Taylor, *The Classical Heritage of the Middle Ages,* 3d ed. (New York, 1925); T. Whittaker, *The Neo-Platonists,* 2d ed. (New York, 1928); M. M. C. J. de Wulf, *History of Mediaeval Philosophy,* 2 vols. (New York, 1925–26); J. Pelikan, *From Luther to Kierkegaard* (St. Louis, 1950); D. D. Runes, *The Dictionary of Philosophy* (New York, [1942]); V. Ferm, *An Encyclopedia of Religion* (New York, 1945); *The Encyclopedia of Philosophy,* ed.-in-chief P. Edwards, 8 vols. (New York, 1967).

Philosophy of History. See *Apologetics, Christian,* III C; *History, Philosophy of.*

Philosophy of Lutheran Education. See *Christian Education, G.*

Philosophy of Religion. The term "philos. of religion" was apparently first used in Ger. near the end of the 18th c. in connection with the Enlightenment.* It refers to the application of philosophy* to the world of religion; see, e. g., *God, Arguments for the Existence of.* Some read Scripture in the light of philos.; others, including some followers of K. Barth,* question the validity of the very notion of philos. of religion. See also *Apologetics,* III B; *Religion, Comparative.*

Philostorgius (ca. 368–ca. 430/440). Arian hist.; b. Borissus, near Nazianzus, Cappadocia, Asia Minor; follower of Eunomius*; spent most of his active life in Constantinople. Wrote a ch. hist. covering ca. 300–ca. 430.

MPG, 65, 455–638.

Philostratus (ca. 170–245). Gk. Sophist; taught at Athens and Rome. Works include *The Lives of the Sophists;* life of Apollonius* of Tyana. See also *Deism,* I, 1.

Philoxenus (ca. 440/450–523). B. Tahal, Persia; bp. Mab(b)ug(h) (Hierapolis) 485–519; Monophysite (see *Monophysitism*). Contributed to tr. of the Bible into Syriac; other works include dogmatic, exegetical, and liturgical writings. See also *Bible Versions,* C 2, 5.

Phocas. The name Phocas bobs up at various times and places and in various connections in the mingled stream of ancient legend and tradition; e. g., he is said to have been a gardener at Sinope in Pontus, bp. Sinope, martyr in Trajan or Diocletian persecution, a martyr of unspecified time at Antioch; there probably were 2 or more men named Phocas; in the E the patron saint of mariners is called Phocas.

Photian Schism. See *Schism,* 5.

Photinianism. Christology of Photinus (d. ca. 376; b. probably Ancyra, Galatia (now Ankara, Turkey); bp. Sirmium, Pannonia ca. 343/344; exiled 351; returned yrs. later; exiled again perhaps ca. 364); it has been variously described and seems to have been a form of Monarchianism*; some call it Sabellianism; others assoc. it more closely with the views of Paul of Samosata.

Photius (ca. 810/820–ca. 891/898). Lay scholar; patriarch Constantinople 858(857?)–867 and 878 (877?)–886; twice deposed and excommunicated. Works include *De Spiritus Sancti mystagogia.* See also *Eastern Orthodox Standards of Doctrine; Patristics,* 2; *Schism,* 5.

Phrygian Religion. See *Cybele; Mystery Religions.*

Phytolatry. Worship of plants.

Pia desideria. See *Spener, Philipp Jacob.*

Pia Società San Girolamo. See *Bible Societies,* 6.

Pia Società San Paolo. See *Bible Societies,* 6.

Piarists. Order of Poor Clerics Regular of the Mother of God of the Pious Schools; founded 1597 in Rome by Joseph Calasanctius (Jose Calasanzio; Joseph of Calasanza; 1556–1648; b. Peralta de la Sal [or Calasanza], Sp.) for educ. of the young.

Piccolomini, Enea Silvio. See *Popes,* 15.

Pick, Bernhard (Dec. 19, 1842–Apr. 10, 1917). B. Kempen, Prussia; educ. Breslau, Berlin, and Union Theol. Sem., NYC. Presb. pastor NYC 1868–69; N. Buffalo, N. Y., 1869–70; Syracuse, N. Y., 1870–74; Rochester, N. Y., 1874–81. Pastor Luth. chs. Allegheny, Pa., 1881–95; Albany, N. Y., 1895–1903. Occasional supply, NYC, 1903–05; pastor Newark, N. J., 1905. Works include *Luther as a Hymnist; The Life of Jesus According to Extra-Canonical Sources; Hymns and Poetry of the Eastern Church; Jesus in the Talmud; Dr. Martin Luther's "Ein feste Burg ist unser Gott" in 21 Sprachen; Das Lutherlied Ein feste Burg ist unser Gott und seine Geschichte; Luther's Battle Song "Ein feste Burg ist unser Gott": Its History and Translations.*

Pickett, Clarence Evan (1884–1965). B. Cissna Park, Ill. Educ. Penn Coll., Oskaloosa, Iowa; Hartford (Conn.) Theol. Sem.; Harvard Divinity School, Cambridge, Mass. Soc. of Friends pastor Toronto, Ont., Can., 1913–17; Oskaloosa, Iowa, 1917–19. Prof. Earlham Coll., Richmond, Ind., 1923–29. Mem. Pres.'s Commission on Immigration and Naturalization 1952; mem. Quaker Team at UN Assem. 1950–55 and Peace Corps Nat. Advisory Council 1961. Works include *For More Than Bread.*

Pico della Mirandola, Giovanni (1463–94). Humanist philos.; theol.; b. Mirandola, near Ferrara, It.;

educ. It.; traveled in It. and Fr.; in Rome 1486 he issued 900 theses, some of which were regarded as heretical by Innocent VIII (see *Popes,* 17); absolved 1493 by Alexander VI (see *Popes,* 18). Works include *Apologia; Heptaplus.* See also *Cabala; Renaissance.*

Picpus Congregation *(Congregatio Sacrorum Cordium Jesu et Mariae necnon adorationis perpetuae Sacrosancti Sacramenti Altaris).* Founded 1797/1800 by Pierre Marie-Joseph Coudrin (1768–1837; priest) and countess Henriette Aymer de la Chevalerie (1767–1834) at Poitiers; received papal sanction 1817; name derived from location of motherhouse on Rue de Picpus in Paris till 1966. Cultivates worship of the heart of Jesus and Mary, practice of love, perpetual prayer to the eucharist, discipleship, and missions.

Pictet, Bénédict (1655–1724). Ref. theol.; b. Geneva, Switz.; pastor and prof. Geneva; tried to revive orthodoxy. Works include *La Morale chretienne; Theologia christiana.*

Piderit, Johann Rudolf Anton (1720–91). B. Pyrmont, Ger.; prof. Marburg 1747, Kassel 1766; disciple of C. v. Wolff.* Opposed neology* and naturalism. Tried to demonstrate the integrity of the Biblical text, including vowel points. Envisioned reunion of Prots. and RCs.

Pieper, August Otto Wilhelm (Sept. 27, 1857–Dec. 23, 1946). Brother of F. A. O. Pieper* and R. Pieper*; b. Carwitz, Pomerania, Ger.; after his father's death, his mother emigrated with the family to Am. 1870, settling at Watertown, Wis.; educ. Northwestern U., Watertown, Wis., and Conc. Sem., St. Louis, Mo. Pastor Kewaunee, Wis., 1879–85, Menomonie, Wis., 1885–90; ill; pastor Milwaukee, Wis., 1891–1902; prof. Wis. Syn. sem. Wauwatosa, near Milwaukee, Wis., 1902. Works include *Biblische Hausandachten; Jesaias II.* WJH

Pieper, Franz August Otto (June 27, 1852–June 3, 1931). Brother of A. O. W. Pieper* and R. Pieper*; b. Carwitz, Pomerania, Ger.; educ. Northwestern U., Watertown, Wis., and Conc. Sem., St. Louis, Missouri. Wis. Syn. pastor Centerville, later called Hika, Wis., 1875–76; Manitowoc, Wis., 1876–78. Prof. Conc. Sem., St. Louis, Mo., 1878–1931; pres. 1887–1931. Pres. Mo. Syn. 1899–1911.

F. A. O. Pieper's most outstanding theol. contributions were in the field of dogmatics; he presented doctrines in such a way as to appeal not only to the mind but also to the heart; the doctrines of grace and inspiration received special attention. His exceptional abilities were brought into play also as preacher and syn. pres.

Works include *Christliche Dogmatik; Zur Einigung der amerikanisch-lutherischen Kirche in der Lehre von der Bekehrung und Gnadenwahl; Die Grunddifferenz in der Lehre von der Bekehrung und Gnadenwahl; Unsere Stellung in Lehre und Praxis.* EL

L. Fuerbringer, "Dr. F. Pieper als Theolog," *CTM,* II (1931), 721–729, 801–807; W. H. T. Dau, "Dr. Francis Pieper the Churchman," *CTM,* II (1931), 729–736; T. Laetsch, "Dr. Pieper als Prediger," *CTM,* II (1931), 761–771.

Pieper, Reinhold (Mar. 2, 1850–Apr. 3, 1920). Brother of A. O. W. Pieper* and F. A. O. Pieper*; b. Carwitz, Pomerania, Ger.; educ. Northwestern U., Watertown, Wis., and Conc. Sem., St. Louis, Missouri. Wis. Syn. pastor Wrightstown, Wis., 1876–78; Manitowoc, Wis., 1878–91. Prof. Conc. Sem., Springfield, Ill., 1891–1914. Pastor Chatham, Ill., 1914–18; Riverton, Ill., till 1920. Works include sermons; lectures on the SC.

Piepkorn, Arthur Carl (June 21, 1907–Dec. 13, 1973.) B. Milwaukee, Wis.; educ. Conc. Sem., St. Louis, Mo. Studied at U. of Chicago (Ill.); Am. School of Oriental Research, Baghdad, Iraq; Western Reserve U., Cleveland, Ohio; The Chaplain School of the U. S. Army, Cambridge, Mass.; The Command and Gen. Staff School of the U. S. Army, Fort Leavenworth, Kans.; Washington U., St. Louis; St. Louis (Mo.) U.; U. of Geneva, Switz. Ordained Mo. Syn. 1930. Served congs. in St. Louis, Mo.; Chisholm, Minn.; Cleveland, Ohio. Army chaplain 1940–51. Ed. 2d–4th eds. of F. E. Mayer, *The Religious Bodies of America.* Other works include *The Historical Prism Inscriptions of Ashurbanipal; Education for Realities; What the Symbolical Books of the Lutheran Church Have to Say About Worship and the Sacraments; The Survival of the Historic Vestments in the Lutheran Church After 1555.*

Pierius (d. ca. 312 AD). Presbyter Alexandria; disciple of Origen*; probably head of the catechetical school at Alexandria; teacher of Pamphilus* of Caesarea; confessor in Diocletian persecution. Works include homiletical and exegetical writings. *MPG,* 10, 241–246.

Pierre de Bruys. See *Bruys, Pierre de.*

Pierson, Allard (1831–96). B. Amsterdam, Neth. Preacher Louvain, Belg., 1854; Rotterdam, Neth., 1857; resigned 1865 because of unbelief; humanist; taught at Heidelberg, then at Amsterdam; doubted that Jesus and Paul ever lived.

Pierson, Arthur Tappan (1837–1911). B. NYC; educ. Hamilton Coll., Clinton, N. Y., and Union Theol. Sem., NYC. Presb. pastor Conn., N. Y., Mich., Ind., Pa., and London, England. Ed. *Missionary Review of the World.* Other works include *Keys to the Word; Seed Thoughts for Public Speakers; George Müller of Bristol; Knowing the Scriptures.*

Piers Plowman (in full: The Vision of William Concerning Piers the Plowman). 14th-c. Eng. allegorical poem attributed to William Langland (Langley; ca. 1332–ca. 1400; a shadowy figure; supposedly a native of the W Midlands); criticizes corruption in ch. and state; tries to create love of truth and appreciation of the dignity of labor.

Pietà. Representation (painting or sculpture) of Mary lamenting over the dead Christ (usually held on her knees); favorite subject of artists in the Middle Ages.

Pietilä, Antti Jaakko (1878–1932). Fin. Luth. theol.; b. Oulu, Fin.; educ. Helsinki; instr. U. of Helsinki 1911; prof. Helsinki 1919. Ed. periodical *Vartija;* other works include writings on ethics and dogmatics.

Pietism. 17th–18th c. movement in Ger. Protestantism; it regarded prevailing orthodoxy as spiritually unproductive. Origin of the movement is gen. traced to P. J. Spener,* who urged pastors to become curates, theol. students educated, nobility true administrators, and the commonalty to avoid secular amusements. Others Pietists in Ger. included A. H. Francke,* G. Arnold,* J. J. Rambach,* J. J. Schütz,* E. G. Woltersdorf,* L. v. Zinzendorf.* Others affected by Pietism include H. M. Mühlenberg* and J. Wesley.* See also *Lutheran Theology After 1580,* 6, 7. PJS

A. Ritschl, *Geschichte des Pietismus* (Bonn, 1880–86); J. G. Walch, *Historische und theologische Einleitung in die Religions-Streitigkeiten* (Jena, 1730–39); J. T. McNeil, *Modern Christian Movements* (Philadelphia, 1954).

Pighius, Albert (Pighi; Pigge; ca. 1490–1542). B. Kampen, Holland; educ. Louvain and Cologne; called to Rome by the pope 1523; took part in Colloquy of Worms* and Regensburg* Conf. 1540–41; emphasized free will in opposition to J. Calvin* and M. Luther*; his formulation of the doctrine of justification, related to Luther's, was rejected at the Council of Trent.* See also *Reformed Confessions,* A 9.

Pike, James Albert (1913–69). B. Oklahoma City, Okla. Educ. U. of Santa Clara, Santa Clara, Calif.; U. Cal. at Los Angeles; U. of S Cal., Los Angeles;

Yale U., New Haven, Conn.; Va. Theol. Sem., Lynchburg; Union Theol. Sem., NYC; Trin. Coll., Hartford, Conn.; U. King's Coll., Halifax, N. S., Canada. Taught Cath. U. of Am., Washington, D. C., 1938–39; George Washington U., Washington, D. C., 1938–42. Ordained Prot. Episc. deacon 1944, priest 1946; held various positions in Washington, D. C., NYC, and Poughkeepsie, N. Y., 1944–49. Assoc. with Columbia U., NYC, 1949–58; dean Cathedral of St. John the Divine, NYC, 1952–58; bp. coadjutor diocese of Calif. 1958; bp. Calif. 1958–66; theol.-in-residence Center for Study of Democratic Institutions, Santa Barbara, Calif., 1966. Works include *The Next Day; Beyond the Law; Doing the Truth; If This Be Heresy; If You Marry Outside Your Faith; You and the New Morality.*

Pilate, Acts of. See *Apocrypha,* B 2.

Pilgerhaus, Lutherisches. See *Immigrant and Emigrant Missions.*

Pilgermission St. Chrischona. See *Chrischona.*

Pilgrim Fathers. See *United Church of Christ,* I, A, 1 and 2.

Pilgrim Holiness Church. See *International Apostolic Holiness Union; Methodist Churches,* 4 b; *Wesleyan Church, The.*

Pilgrimages. 1. Pilgrimages are assoc. with many religions (see, e. g., *Islam,* 3). From earliest times Christians visited places assoc. with Christ's earthly life; such pilgrimages increased after Helena,* mother of Constantine* I, made an exploratory pilgrimage and built basilicas in Palestine. Motives for pilgrimages include penance, thanksgiving, and a desire to obtain supernatural help. In course of time Christian pilgrimages expanded to include such goals as Rome and graves of martyrs and various other holy places elsewhere. Legend and tradition helped build a complex structure connected with pilgrimages in the Middle Ages, including travel in organized companies under armed protection, hospices, esp. in the Alps, and special observance of jubilee yrs. Pilgrims came to be given special consideration by other Christians. Some made pilgrimage a way of life.

2. Outrages committed against pilgrims by Muslim led to Crusades* and military* religious orders.

3. The Luth. Reformation opposed abuses assoc. with pilgrimages (AC XX 3; XXV 5; Ap XII 14, 144; SA II ii 16, 18).

4. Pilgrimages revived in the 19th c., with new centers of attraction, e. g., at Loreto,* It.; Einsiedeln, Switz. (with a famous image of Mary; see also *Meinrad*); Fátima,* Port.; Lourdes,* Fr.; Auriesville, N. Y. (where Fr. RC missionaries were killed in the 1640s by Iroquois).

The Library of the Palestine Pilgrims' Text Society, 13 vols. and index (London, [1885]–97); E. R. Barker, *Rome of the Pilgrims and Martyrs* (London, 1913); H. Lamb, *The Crusades,* 2 vols. (New York, 1930–31); S. H. Heath, *Pilgrim Life in the Middle Ages* (London, 1911); B. Kötting, *Peregrinatio religiosa* (Munich, 1950); E. A. Moore, *The Ancient Churches of Old Jerusalem: The Evidence of the Pilgrims* (London, 1961).

Pilgrim's Progress. See *Bunyan, John.*

Pillar of Fire. See *Evangelistic Associations,* 14.

Pillar Saints. See *Stylites.*

Pionios (Pionius; d. probably ca. 250 [or 180?] AD). Presbyter Smyrna; martyr.

Pious Society of St. Jerome. See *Bible Societies,* 6.

Pious Society of St. Paul. See *Bible Societies,* 6.

Piran. See *Celtic Church,* 4.

Pir(c)kheimer, Willibald (1470–1530). Humanist; b. Eichstätt, Bav., Ger.; educ. Padua and Pavia, It.; at first he favored M. Luther, later he completely abandoned him. Works include *Eccius dedolatus.* See also *Religious Drama,* 3.

Pirmin (Pirminius; Permin; Primin?; d. ca. 755 AD). Ancestry obscure; perhaps a Visigoth from Aquitaine or Sp.; Benedictine; promoted monasticism in S Ger. and Alsace.

Pisa, Cathedral at. See *Church Architecture,* 7.

Pisa, Council of. Councils were held at Pisa ca. 1135, 1409, and 1511. That of 1409, 1st of 3 reform councils (see *Councils and Synods,* 7), was the most important of the councils at Pisa. It was called to solve the papal schism of 1378 (see *Schism,* 8), but failed. See also *Gerson, Jean de.*

Piscator, Johannes (Fischer; 1546–1625). Ref. theol.; b. Strasbourg, Ger.; educ. Tübingen; prof. Strasbourg 1573, Heidelberg 1574; rector Siegen 1577; prof. Neustadt 1578; rector Moers 1581; prof. Herborn 1584–1625. Denied redeeming power of Christ's active obedience. Works include Bible tr.; commentaries.

Piscina (from Lat. *piscis,* "fish"). Originally, an artificial reservoir for fish or swimming; by adaptation the term is used for a basin or niche in the sanctuary well near the altar, with drain, for liturgical ablutions and disposal of water used in ceremonies; some use it also for disposal of wine left in chalice after Communion.

Pistis Sophia. See *Apocrypha,* B 5.

Pistorius. 1. See *De Bakker, Jan.* 2. *Johannes* (d. 1583); father of 3; ev. theol.; supt. Alsfeld 1541; took part in Hagenau* Colloquy 1540, Colloquy of Worms* 1540–41, Regensburg* Conf. 1541 and 1546, and Consultation of Worms* 1557; supported reform efforts of Hermann* von Wied; defended AC as explained in Wittenberg* Concord; adherent of P. Melanchthon* and M. Bucer.* 3. *Johann* (1546–1608); son of 2; b. Nidda, Ger.; inclined to Calvinism; joined RC Ch. 1588; held religious colloquy with J. Andreä* and J. Heerbrand* at Baden 1589 and with J. Pappus* at Emmendingen 1590; works include polemical and hist. writings. 4. *Hermann Alexander* (1811–77); b. Walbeck, near Eisleben, Ger.; educ. Halle; Luth. pastor Süpplingen; opposed Prussian* Union and Lichtfreunde*; joined Breslau* Syn.; active in Wernigerode, Wollin, Breslau, and in Basedow, Mecklenburg.

Pithou, Pierre (1539–96). B. Troyes, Fr.; Calvinist; RC 1573; defended Gallicanism. Ed. ancient and medieval hist. and legal source materials.

Pitris. See *Ancestor Worship.*

Pittsburgh Agreement (Articles of Agreement). Agreement adopted 1940 by the ALC and the ULC: "I. That all persons affiliated with any of the societies or organizations designated in the Washington Declaration of the U. L. C. A. as 'organizations injurious to the Christian faith' should sever their connections with such society or organization and shall be so admonished; and members of our churches not now affiliated with such organizations shall be warned against such affiliation. Especially shall the shepherds of the flocks be admonished to refuse adherence and support to such organizations. II. That pastors and congregations shall not practice indiscriminate pulpit and altar fellowship with pastors and churches of other denominations, whereby doctrinal differences are ignored or virtually made matters of indifference. Especially shall no religious fellowship whatsoever be practiced with such individuals and groups as are not basically evangelical. III. 1. The Bible (that is, the canonical books of the Old and New Testaments) is primarily not a code of doctrines, still less a code of morals, but the history of God's revelation, for the salvation of mankind, and of man's reaction to it. It preserves for all generations and presents, ever anew, this revelation of God, which culminated and centers in Christ, the Crucified and Risen One. It is itself the Word of God, His permanent revelation, aside from which, until Christ's return in glory, no other is to be expected. 2. The Bible consists of a number of separate books, written at various times, on various occasions, and for various purposes. Their authors were living, thinking personalities, each endowed by the Creator with an individuality of his own and each having his peculiar style, his own manner of presentation, even at times using such sources of information as were at hand. Nevertheless, by virtue of the unique operation of the Holy Spirit (2 Tim. 3:16; 2 Peter 1:21), by which He supplied to the holy writers content and fitting word (2 Peter 1:21; 1 Cor. 2:12, 13), the separate books of the Bible are related to one another and, taken together, constitute a complete, errorless, unbreakable whole, of which Christ is the Center (John 10:35). They are rightly called the Word of God. This unique operation of the Holy Spirit upon the writers is named inspiration. We do not venture to define its mode, or manner, but accept it as a fact. 3. Believing, therefore, that the Bible came into existence by this unique co-operation of the Holy Spirit and the human writers, we accept it (as a whole and in all its parts) as the permanent divine revelation, as the Word of God, the only source, rule, and norm for faith and life, and as the ever fresh and inexhaustible fountain of all comfort, strength, wisdom, and guidance for mankind." Both ALC and ULC had serious misgivings regarding the Pittsburgh Agreement.

Documents of Lutheran Unity in America, ed. R. C. Wolf (Philadelphia, 1966), pp. 378–379; *The Lutheran Church Quarterly,* XIII (1940), 346–347; *Doctrinal Declarations* (St. Louis, 1957), pp. 69–70.

Pittsburgh Declaration. Declaration adopted 1868 at Pittsburgh, Pa., by the General* Council of the Ev. Luth. Ch. in (North) Am. defining positions on the Four* Points. See also *Galesburg Rule.*

S. E. Ochsenford, *Documentary History of the General Council of the Evangelical Lutheran Church in North America* (Philadelphia, 1912), pp. 207–210; *Documents of Lutheran Unity in America,* ed. R. C. Wolf (Philadelphia, 1966), pp. 162–165.

Pittsburgh Infirmary. See *Deaconesses,* 7.

Pittsburgh Synod. See *Synods, Extinct; United Lutheran Church, Synods of,* 24.

Pittsburgh Theological Seminary. Created 1959 by consolidation of Pittsburgh-Xenia Theol. Sem. (United Presb. Ch. of N. Am.) and Western Theol. Sem. (Presb. Ch., USA), following 1958 merger of the 2 bodies (see *Presbyterian Churches,* 4 a).

Pittsburgh-Xenia Theol. Sem. was formed 1930 by union of Pittsburgh and Xenia Sems. The Xenia branch was founded 1794 at Service, Pa.; moved 1821 to Canonsburg, Pa.; consolidated with another sem. 1830; moved 1855 to Xenia, Ohio; name changed 1858; absorbed Monmouth, formerly Oxford, Sem. 1874; charter received 1877; moved 1920 to St. Louis, Mo. The Pittsburgh branch was est. 1825 as Allegheny Theol. Sem., in Allegheny (now part of Pittsburgh); charter granted 1868. Both branches were later augmented by resources of Newburgh Sem., founded NYC 1805.

Western Theol. Sem., Allegheny, est. 1825 by the Gen. Assem. of the Presb. Ch., USA, began with classical academies founded 1785 and 1787 in Washington, Pa.

Pius II. See *Popes,* 15.

Pius IV (Giovanni Angelo Medici; 1499–1565). B. Milan, It.; cardinal 1549; pope 1559–65; reassembled and concluded the Council of Trent* 1562–63; confirmed its decrees, but granted the chalice to the laity in Ger., Austria, Hung., and several other countries 1564; forbade laymen to read Scripture except by special permission; not related to the famous Medici* of Florence. See also *Counter Reformation,* 9.

Pius V. See *Counter Reformation,* 9; *Popes,* 21.

Pius VI. See *Popes,* 26.

Pius VII. See *Popes,* 27.

Piux IX. See *Popes,* 28.

Pius X. See *Popes,* 30.

Pius XI. See *Popes,* 32.

Piux XII. See *Popes,* 33.

Place, Francis. See *Family Planning,* 2.

Place, Josué de la (Placeus; Placaeus; Josua; ca. 1596 to ca. 1655/65). Ref. theol.; b. Saumur, Fr.; pastor Nantes 1625; prof. Saumur 1633; held modified Calvinism, rejecting direct imputation of Adam's sin on mankind in favor of indirect imputation as a result of hereditary corruption. See also *Reformed Confessions,* A 10.

Placebo (Lat. "I will please"). Traditional name for Vespers of the Dead (see *Burial,* 4); derived from 1st word of the opening antiphon in Lat. (Ps. 116:9 [Vulgate 114:9] *Placebo Domino in regione vivorum*).

Placement of Teachers. See *Teachers,* 15.

Plainchant. See *Gregorian Music.*

Plainsong. See *Gregorian Music.*

Plan of Union. See *Methodist Church, The; Presbyterian Churches,* 4 a; *United Church of Christ,* I A 3; *United States, Religious History of,* 13.

Planck, Gottlieb Jakob (1751–1833). Ev. theol.; hist.; b. Nürtingen, Württemberg, Ger.; educ. Tübingen; taught at Tübingen and Stuttgart; prof. Göttingen; rational supernaturalist; works marred by subjectivism.

Planentwurf. See *General Synod of the Evangelical Lutheran Church in the United States of America, The,* 2.

Planned Parenthood. See *Family Planning.*

Planned Parenthood Federation of America, Inc. See *Family Planning,* 3.

Plath, Karl Heinrich Christian (1829–1901). Ger. Luth. promoter of for. miss.; educ. Halle, Bonn, and theol. sem. at Wittenberg; preacher and instr. Halle 1856–63; inspector Berlin* Miss. Soc. I 1863–71, Gossner* Miss. Soc. 1871–77; lecturer U. of Berlin 1867, prof. 1882; 1st inspection visit to India 1877–78, 2d to India and Palestine 1887–88, 3d to India 1895–96.

Platner, Tileman (1490–1551). B. Stolberg, Ger.; friend of M. Luther, P. Melanchthon, and J. Jonas; supt. Stolberg, where he introd. the Reformation.

Plato (ca. 428/427–347 BC). Gk. philos.; b. perhaps on the island Aegina (or Athens?); of aristocratic Athenian descent; saw Athens decline politically and commercially as a result of the Peloponnesian War 431–404 BC; founded the Academy (perhaps ca. 386 BC), which became the 1st endowed university (it flourished till closed by Justinian 529 AD). Originally named Aristocles, he was popularly called Plato (from the Gk. for "broad"), probably either because of the breadth of his forehead or chest and shoulders or because of the breadth of his literary treatises. Influenced by the posit of Socrates (virtue is knowledge, which includes the ability to define abstract terms and to maintain definitions against dialectic questioning) and with a propensity for mathematics, Plato held that the material sensible world is merely a temporary copy of permanent unchanging Forms, which are the object of all real knowledge. The theorems of geometry, e. g., hold true not for the symbols which humans construct and which are necessarily faulty, but only of the perfect triangle, circle, etc., which exist in the suprasensible world of Forms (Ideas). The link bet. such a dualistic universe is the immortal soul, which has had contact with the Forms before its incarnation, and which, during its human existence, relearns as best possible its prenatal knowledge by dialectic recollection. True ethical values are attained only by those individuals who have the proper perspective of soul or mind as more important than physical bodies and possessions, and who place reason above the high-spirited and appetitive elements of their personality. Moreover, the best govt. is possible only when philosophers (the rational element of the state) attain adequate concept of the perfect Forms and become rulers. Plato's influence on Aristotle, the Stoics, Cicero, Plutarch, the Neoplatonists, and early ch. fathers (esp. Augustine of Hippo and Origen) is inestimable; his influence on psychol., ethics, and aesthetics is increasing. See also *Socrates.*

Works include (1) Socratic dialogues, e. g., *Charmides* (on temperance), *Laches* (on courage), *Lysis* (on friendship), *Euthyphro* (on piety), *Apology* (of Socrates), *Protagoras* and *Meno* (on the teachableness of virtue), *Gorgias* (on rhetoric); (2) highly literary writings that develop his views more extensively, e. g., *Symposium* (on the good), *Phaedo* (on the soul), *Republic* (on the just), *Phaedrus* (on love); (3) less literary writings on more abstruse questions of ontology *(Parmenides),* epistemology *(Theaetetus),* logic *(Sophist),* cosmology *(Timaeus),* ethics *(Philebus),* and politics *(Statesman* [or *Politicus*] and *Laws).* RGH

See also *Jowett, Benjamin; Philosophy; Psychology, C; Transmigration of Souls.*

P. Shorey, *What Plato Said* (Chicago, 1933); A. E. Taylor, *Plato: The Man and His Work,* 6th ed. (London, 1949).

Platon (original name Peter Levshin; 1737–1812). B. near Moscow, Russ.; adopted name Platon on becoming monk; bp. Tver (Kalinin) 1770; abp. Moscow 1775; metropolitan Moscow 1787. See also *Eastern Orthodox Standards of Doctrine,* A 4.

Platonic Academy of Florence. See *Florentine Academy.*

Platytera. Representation of Mary standing in prayer, with the boy Jesus in a medallion on her breast; common in E Orthodox Chs.; found occasionally in the W.

Platz, Ludwig (Placenta; d. 1547). Ev. theol.; educ. Erfurt; taught at Erfurt; Prot. ca. 1530; withdrew from the U. 1536; pastor Walschleben, near Erfurt; signed SA.

Plautus, Titus Maccius. See *Religious Drama,* 2.

Pledge of Allegiance. 1. *To the flag:* I pledge allegiance to the flag of the United States of America and to the republic for which it stands, one nation under God, indivisible, with liberty and justice for all. 2. *To the cross:* I pledge allegiance to the cross of the Lord Jesus Christ and to the faith for which it stands, one Savior eternal, with mercy and grace for all. So help me God.

Pledging for Church Support. See *Finances in the Church,* 3.

Plenary Council. See *Councils and Synods,* 1.

Plenary Indulgence. See *Indulgences,* 2, 3, 5.

Plenary Inspiration. See *Inspiration, Doctrine of,* A 3.

Plenitudo potestatis. Term of Leo I (see *Popes,* 2) referring to unrestricted papal power over a metropolitan bp.

Pleroma. See *Gnosticism,* 3–5.

Pletho(n). See *Gemistos Pletho(n), Georgios.*

Plettenberg, Walter von (Wolter). See *Latvia.*

Pliny (Gaius Plinius Secundus; 23–79). "The Elder"; uncle of Pliny* the Younger; b. Como, It.; Roman procurator in Sp. ca. 70–72. See also *Essenes; Heathenism.*

Pliny (Gaius Plinius Caecilius Secundus; 62–113). "The Younger"; nephew of Pliny* the Elder; b. Novum Comum (Como) in Cisalpine Gaul or in N It.; studied under Quintilian*; Roman proconsul (gov.) Bithynia and Pontus 111(112?). See also *Music, Church.*

Plitt, Gustav Leopold (1836–80). B. Genin, near Lübeck, Ger.; educ. Erlangen and Berlin; instr. Erlangen 1862, prof. 1867. Ed. P. Melanchthon's *Loci;* coed. with J. J. Herzog* 2d ed. *Real-Encyklopädie für protestantische Theologie und Kirche.* Other works include *Einleitung in die Augustana; Die Apologie der Augustana, geschichtlich erklärt.*

Plockhorst, Bernhard (1825–95). Painter; b. Brunswick, Ger. Works include "Christ Taking Leave of His Mother"; "The Consoling Christ"; "The Flight into Egypt"; "The Good Shepherd"; "Christ Walking on the Water"; "Christ's Triumphal Entry into Jerusalem"; "He is Risen."

Plotinus (ca. 205–270). Neoplatonic philos.; b. possibly Lycopolis, Egypt; of Gk., Roman, or Egyptian descent; taught in Rome from 244. See also *Neoplatonism.*

Plummer, Alfred (1841–1926). B. Heworth, county borough Gateshead, Durham, Eng.; educ. Oxford; ordained deacon 1866; taught at Oxford; master U. Coll., Durham 1874–1902. Coed. *The International Critical Commentary.* Other works include *The Church of the Early Fathers; The Church of England in the Eighteenth Century;* commentaries on NT books.

Pluralism. Belief that there are many ultimate substances, not only 1 (see *Monism*) or 2 (see *Dualism*). Empedocles* held that there are 4 elements; M. E. de Montaigne* felt that diversity is the rule of nature; G. W. v. Leibniz* advocated pluralism in his system of monads; C. S. S. Peirce,* W. James,* and J. Dewey* rejected monism in favor of pluralism; ideas of diversity are also found in the Gen. Semantics* movement.

Plutarch (ca. 46–ca. 120). B. Chaeronea, Boeotia; educ. Athens; traveled; taught at Rome. Works include *Moralia; Parallel Lives.* See also *Deism,* I, 1.

Plütschau, Heinrich (1678[7?]–1747[6?]). B. Wesenberg, Mecklenburg-Strelitz, Ger.; educ. Halle; taught at the A. H. Francke* institutions, Halle, from 1703; commissioned 1705 at Copenhagen, Den., with B. Ziegenbalg* as miss. to India; arrived Tranquebar 1706; his chief work consisted in serving the Port. cong.; returned to Ger. 1711; pastor in Holstein. See also *Frederick IV; India,* 10; *Missions,* 5.

Pluvial. See *Vestments, Clerical,* 1.

Plymouth Brethren. See *Brethren, Plymouth.*

Plymouth Colony. See *United States, Religious History of,* 4.

Plymouth Separatists. See *United Church of Christ,* I A 1, 2.

Pneumatikoi. See *Gnosticism,* 5.

Pneumatology. Doctrine of spiritual beings, esp. the Holy* Spirit.

Pneumatomachians (Gk. "adversaries of the Spirit"). Term applied to all who hold false views of the Holy Spirit; originally used of 4th-c. heretics who denied the deity or personality of the Holy Spirit; condemned by the 381 council at Constantinople.* See also *Macedonius.*

Poach, Andreas (1516–85). Gnesio-Lutheran*; b. Eilenburg, Ger.; educ. Wittenberg; pastor Halle, Nordhausen, and Erfurt; deposed 1572 in antinomian* controversy; pastor Utenbach, near Apolda, 1573. Ed. sermons of M. Luther.

POAU. See *Church and State,* 14.

Pocahontas (Mataoha; Matoaka; ca. 1595–1617). Am. Indian princess; b. Virginia; daughter of Powhatan, Algonquian chief; allegedly saved life of John Smith (1580–1631; pres. Jamestown, Va., colony 1608–09); bap. name Rebecca; married John Rolfe 1614; d. Eng. See also *Indians, American,* 3.

Pococke, Edward (1604–91). Orientalist; b. Oxford, Eng.; educ. Oxford; chaplain to the Eng. factory Aleppo, Syria, 1630–36; prof. Arabic Oxford 1636–40; rector Childrey, Berkshire, 1642–47; prof. Heb. Oxford 1648. Helped prepare B. Walton's* polyglot Bible; other works include commentaries.

Pohlman, Henry Newman (Mar. 8, 1800–Jan. 20, 1874). B. Albany, N.Y.; licensed by N.Y. Ministerium 1819; served congs. at Saddle River, Ramapo, New Germantown, German Valley, Spruce

Run, and Albany; pres. N. Y. Ministerium, N. Y. Syn., N. Y. and N. J. Syn., The Gen. Syn. of the Ev. Luth. Ch. in the USA.

Poimandres (from Gk.; "shepherd of men"). First Hermetic* book (named after Hermes Trismegistus ["Hermes the Thrice-Greatest"], later name of Egyptian god Thoth, believed to be father and protector of all knowledge); perhaps 2d c. AD.

Poimenics. Study or application of pastoral* theol. See also *Pastor as Counselor.*

Poiret, Pierre (1646–1719). Fr. Prot. mystic; pastor in The Palatinate; companion of A. Bourignon.* Works include *Bibliotheca mysticorum;* studies of mystics.

Poissy, Colloquy of (Disputatio Pussicena). Religious colloquy, or conference, at Poissy, near Paris, Fr., 1561; called by Catherine de Médicis; dealt with differences, esp. on the Lord's Supper, bet. Ref. led by T. Beza* and RCs; D. Laynez,* Peter* Martyr, and A. Marlorat* were among those present. No dogmatic agreement was reached, but the way was paved for recognition of and greater freedom for Prots.

Poitiers, Peace and Edict of. See *France,* 9.

Polack, William Gustave (Dec. 7, 1890–June 5, 1950). B. Wausau, Wis.; educ. Conc. Coll., Fort Wayne, Ind., and Conc. Sem., St. Louis, Mo.; pastor Evansville, Ind., 1914–25; prof. ch. hist., hymnology, and liturgics Conc. Sem., St. Louis, 1925–50; minister Clear Lake Chapel, Clear Lake, Ind., 1938–50; chm. Intersyn. Committee on Hymnology and Liturgics 1929–49; charter mem. Conc. Hist. Institute. Ed. *Concordia Junior Messenger* 1928–39, *Concordia Historical Institute Quarterly* 1928–50, and *Martin Luther in English Poetry;* assoc. ed. *The Cresset* 1937–50. Other works include *Beauty for Ashes; Beside Still Waters; The Building of a Great Church; Choice Morsels; David Livingstone; Famous Hymns and Their Story; Fathers and Founders; Favorite Christian Hymns; The Handbook to the Lutheran Hymnal; Hymns from the Harps of God; Into All the World; John Eliot; The Story of C. F. W. Walther; The Story of Luther.*

Poland. E Eur. country. *Area:* ca. 120,756 sq. mi.; *pop.* (1973 est.): 33,869,000.

1. The beginnings of Christianity in Poland are traced to the 2d half of the 9th c. and are apparently connected with Boh. and/or Moravia (see *Czechoslovakia,* 2). The land soon came under RC influence but was receptive to anti-RC movements (e. g., that of the Hussites*).

2. The Luth. Reformation reached Poland early, esp. through Polish students at Wittenberg and through M. Luther's* writings (see also *Reformation, Lutheran,* 10, 12). Reformed movements included that of J. Laski.* Many Bohemian* Brethren under persecution fled to Poland. These 3 ev. groups effected a union of sorts in the Consensus of Sandomierz 1570 (see *Reformed Confessions,* E 5), which Luth. objections against its lack of precise definition, esp. in connection with the Lord's Supper, soon made ineffective.

3. In the 1573 *Pax dissidentium* (Peace of the Dissident) the Prot. nobles insisted that every new king vow equal protection for Prots. and RCs. But the intended effect was not secured. Henry of Valois (1551–89; b. Fontainebleau, Fr.; king of Poland 1573–74; king Henry III of Fr. 1574–89) took the oath reluctantly. Stephen Báthory (István Báthory; 1533–86; king of Poland 1575–86) took the oath but supported the Counter* Reformation. Sigismund III (Sigismund Vasa; 1566–1632; king of Poland 1587–1632, of Swed. 1592–1604 [crowned 1594]), educ. by Jesuits, also supported the Counter Reformation.

4. The 1645 Colloquy (Conf., Syn.) of Thorn not only failed to restore unity bet. RCs and Prots. but divided Luths. and Calvinists. In 1717 the Prots. lost the right to build chs. In 1733 they were barred from civil offices and the diet. Ca. 1767, on insistence of Russ. and Prussia, Prots. and Gk. Orthodox Caths. regained equal rights with RCs. 1772–95 Poland underwent 3 partitions, with territories going to Russ., Austria, and Prussia. Strictures against the RC Ch. were imposed in retaliation against the 1830–31 revolution and Russification began. The 2d Polish Revolution (1863–64) was followed by further strictures. With regard to the use of the Russ. language in the life and work of the ch. a compromise was agreed on in the early 1880s.

5. The const. of the rep. of Poland (indep. proclaimed 1918) gave preeminence to RCm, equal rights to all. Poland was torn in WW II by Ger. and Russia. Christians and Jews suffered severely. But a 1949 decree specified that no disadvantages accrue to anyone because of ch. membership, and the 1952 Const. of the Polish People's Rep. says that the ch. is separate from the state, that all citizens have liberty of conscience and faith, and that the ch. and other religious assocs. are free to engage in religious activities. JP, LP

See also *Crusades,* 9; *Lutheran Confessions,* A 5; *Skarga, Piotr.*

Polanus, Robertus. See *Pullus, Robert.*

Polanus von Polansdorf, Amandus (1561–1610). B. Troppau (Opava), Silesia; educ. Tübingen; became Ref. and went to Basel and Geneva 1583; prof. OT Basel 1596; with his father-in-law, J. J. Grynäus (see *Grynäus,* 3), led orthodox Calvinism in Basel. Tr. NT into Ger.; other works include *Syntagma theologiae Christianae;* commentaries on OT books. See also *Dogmatics,* B 5.

Pole, Reginald (1500–58). RC theol.; b. Stourton Castle, Staffordshire, Eng.; educ. Oxford, Rome, Padua, Paris; Paul* III summoned him to confer on a gen. council, appointed him to a committee on reform, and made him cardinal 1536; opposed Henry* VIII's divorce proceedings against Catherine of Aragon; with G. Contarini* tried to conciliate the Prots.; one of 3 legates appointed to preside at the Council of Trent*; legate to Eng. 1553; abp. Canterbury 1557. See also *Counter Reformation,* 4, 5.

Polemics (from Gk. *polemos,* "battle"). Controversial discussions or arguments involving attack and/or refutation. See also *Apologetics; Irenics; Theology.*

Poliander. See *Gramann.*

Polish National Catholic Church of America. Organized 1897 at Scranton, Pa., as a result of dissatisfaction with RC ideology and administration, coupled with desire for religious freedom; 1st syn. held 1904 Scranton, Pa. See also *Polish National Catholic Church of Canada.*

Polish National Catholic Church of Canada. Diocese created 1967 by the Polish* Nat. Cath. Ch. of Am.

Politiques. Fr. pol. party that advocated religious toleration, esp. after Bartholomew's* Day Massacre; made alliance with Huguenots*; many supported Henry* IV of Fr.

Politus, Ambrosius Catharinus (Lancellotto de'Politi; 1484–1553). B. Siena, It.; Dominican theol.; early opposed Reformation in It. Works include *Apologia pro veritate catholicae et apostolicae fidei; Excusatio disputationis contra Lutherum.*

Polity, Ecclesiastical. 1. Principles, form, or constitution for ch. organization, administration, and discipline.* The local ch., the cong. of believers locally circumscribed, is the seat of authority; e. g., it was the business of the cong. at Colossae to provide for ample preaching (Cl 3:16) and to admonish Archippus to be faithful (Cl 4:17); the admonitions of Rv 2–3 are addressed to local chs.; the various chs. in Galatia, Macedonia, and Achaia were asked to give toward the collection for needy (1 Co 16:1;

2 Co 8–9). There were elders or bps. (overseers) in the early ch.; at the election of Matthias (Acts 1) the whole cong. selected the candidates, and choice was made by lot; in Acts 6 the cong. elected 7 deacons; cf. Acts 20:28.

2. Ecclesiastical polity deals also with relations bet. congs. At first the apostles were the main external bond; the apostolate was undivided; every apostle belonged to each cong. Communication and common concerns helped knit the congs. together; cf. Acts 11:19-30; 15; 18:27; Ro 16:5; 2 Co 3:1; 8:19, 23.

3. Outward organization was gradually effected. Congs. united into dioceses,* dioceses grouped together under metropolitans.* This process of pyramiding centralization led finally to the papacy with its unwarranted claims of power and authority. The other extreme, that of complete fragmentation into cong. units, should also be avoided. Eph 4:3-6 indicates assoc. of those who are one in faith, e. g., in syns. that are not legislative but advisory in relation to mem. congs.; valid acts of any cong. should be honored by all others; erring congs. should be properly dealt with by other congs., within the syn. framework (1 Co 12:25–26).

4. The cong. system is different from others, e. g., papal, presb., and episc.; see also *Collegialism; Territorial System.* Most syns. in Am. have the cong. system, in which, e. g., also the right to call, elect, and install ministers, teachers, and ch. officers rests with the local ch. See also *Authority; Keys, Office of the; Lutheran Congregation.*

5. On the monarchical, or papal, system see *Bishop,* 1–3, 5, 11; *Hierarchy.*

6. In the episc. system, bps. are regarded as successors of the apostles. Apostolic* succession is held in Anglicanism (esp. the High* Ch.), RCm, and others on the unwarranted assumption that episcopal consecration can be traced unbroken to the apostles. See also *Episcopacy.*

7. In the presb. system, ch. govt. is exercised by presbyters, or elders,* elected by the people. The Gen. Assem. covers the nation; the Syn. covers the state; the presbytery* covers the next division of territory assigned to it; the session* deals with the local cong.

See also *Theology.*

W. Elert, "Kirchenverfassung," *Morphologie des Luthertums,* I (Munich, 1931; improved print., 1952), 320–335, tr. W. A. Hansen, "Church Government," *The Structure of Lutheranism,* I (St. Louis, 1962), 367–385; C. S. Mundinger, *Government in the Missouri Synod* (St. Louis, 1947); J. L. Neve, *Die Freikirche im Vergleich mit der Staatskirche* (Burlington, Iowa, n.d.), tr. C. E. Hay, *The Free Church System Compared with the German State Church* (Burlington, Iowa, 1903); J. L. Schaver, *The Polity of the Churches* (Chicago, 1947); *Episcopacy Ancient and Modern,* ed. C. Jenkins and K. D. Mackenzie (London, 1930); A. Brunn, *The Polity of a Lutheran Congregation* (St. Louis, 1940).

Pollich, Martin von Mellrichstadt (Mellerstadt [Lower Franconia, Upper Bav., Ger.]; d. 1513). "Dr. Mellerstadt"; Dr. of Medicine, Philos., and Theol.; physician of Frederick* III of Saxony; helped est. U. of Wittenberg, where he was the 1st rector and taught scholastic theol. and medicine; spoke disparagingly of theol., but is said to have had a presentiment of the coming importance of the monk M. Luther as reformer of the ch. Works include *Laconismus.*

Polyander à Kerckhoven, Johannes (1568–1646). B. Metz; educ. Bremen, Heidelberg, and Geneva; pastor Walloon cong. Dordrecht, Neth., 1591; prof. U. of Leiden 1611; took part in 1618–19 Syn. of Dordrecht*; infralapsarian.

Polyandry. See *Polygamy.*

Polycarp (ca. 69–ca. 156). Bp. Smyrna; martyr. Works include letter to the Philippians. See also *Apostolic Fathers,* 3; *Infants,* B 1; *Persecution of Christians,* 3.

Polychrome Bible. Ed. of parts of Scripture in which higher critical opinions were reflected in colors used to identify various sections; ed. P. Haupt*; 16 vols. of the Heb. text and 6 vols. of the Eng. tr. appeared from 1894. Also called rainbow Bible.

Polychronius (d. ca. 430). Brother of Theodore* of Mopsuestia; bp. Apamea (Dinar), Syria (or Phrygia). Works include commentaries on OT books. *MPG,* 93, 13–468.

Polycrates (2d c. AD). Bp. Ephesus; Quartodeciman. See also *Easter Controversy.*

Polycraticus. See *John of Salisbury.*

Polygamy (from Gk.; "multiple marriage"). Forms of polygamy include polygyny (marriage of 2 or more women to the same man at the same time) and polyandry (marriage of 2 or more men to the same woman at the same time). The fact that polygamy was (e. g., in the OT) and is practiced does not justify it. Scripture does not present it as God's intent, or as God-pleasing, or as an example to follow. God made 1 man and 1 woman to live together in wedlock. That pattern is underscored by the singular "a man" and "his wife" (Gn 2:24) and by the reference to "the beginning" (cf. Mt 19:4-9). Man (Lamech, Gn 4:19) departed from God's pattern. Cf. Mk 10:2-12 (v. 8 "they twain"); Eph 5:22-33 (v. 31 "they two"); 1 Th 4:4; 1 Ti 3:2, 12; 5:9; 1 Ptr 3:1-7.

Polyglot Bibles. The *Tetrapla* (texts of the LXX, Aquila, Symmachus, Theodotion) and *Hexapla* (Heb., Heb. in Gk. characters, Aquila, Symmachus, LXX, Theodotion) of Origen were the earliest known polyglot Scriptures; extant in fragments of excerpts. One page of a projected polyglot was printed in the 15th or 16th c. by the Aldine press, founded by Aldus Manutius (1450–1515). The 1st complete printed polyglot was the Biblia Sacra *Polyglotta,* 600 copies printed in 1517 at Complutum (Alcalá de Henares), Sp. (hence called *Complutensian Polyglot*), under patronage of F. Jimenez* de Cisneros at cost of 50,000 ducats; pub. ca. 1522; see also *Lexicons,* B. The *Antwerp Polyglot,* 8 vols., 1569–72, also called *Biblia Regia* because it was printed under patronage of Philip II of Sp. (1527–98; king of Sp. 1556–98), contains the Complutensian texts, a Chaldee paraphrase, the Syriac version, and a Lat. tr. by B. Arias* Montano. The *Paris Polyglot,* 10 vols., was pub. 1645; additions to former polyglots include the Samaritan Pentateuch and an Arab. version of both Testaments. The *London Polyglot,* 6 vols., ed. B. Walton,* pub. 1657, is much more comprehensive than previous polyglots. The *Leipzig Polyglot (Biblia Sacra Quadrilinguia,* ed. C. Reineccius*), 3 vols. 1713–51, includes M. Luther's Ger. tr. The *Heidelberg Polyglot* (probably ed. Bonaventura Cornelius Bertram [1531–94; b. Thouars, Fr.; prof. Heb. Geneva, Switz.]), 3 vols., was pub. 1586; the *Hamburg Polyglot* (ed. D. Wolder*) 1596; the *Nürnberg Polyglot* of E. Hutter* (OT to Ruth, Ps, and NT) 1599–1602; Bagster's *Polyglot* 1831; the 4-vol. *Polyglotten-Bibel,* ed. E. R. Stier and K. G. W. Theile, was pub. from the mid-1840s to 1855; *The Hexaglot Bible, Comprising the Holy Scriptures of the Old and New Testaments in the Original Tongues, Together with the Septuagint, the Syriac (of the New Testament), the Vulgate, the Authorized English, and German, and the Most Approved French Versions,* 6 vols., 1876; *Biblia Polyglotta Matritensia,* Madrid, 1957–.

Historical Catalogue of the Printed Editions of Holy Scripture in the Library of the British and Foreign Bible Society, comp. T. H. Darlow and H. F. Moule, 2 vols. in 4 (New York, 1903–11).

Polygyny. See *Polygamy.*

Polynesia. Includes Hawaiian Is., New Zealand, and Easter Is., and the islands lying within the triangle formed by these (e. g., Samoa, Line Is., Cook Is., Phoenix Is., Ellice Is., Tonga, Tahiti, Marquesas Is., the Tuamotu Archipelago, Mangareva [Gambier] Is., Tubuai [Austral] Is.). Groups that have done miss. work in Polynesia include Australasian socs.; LMS; Assemblies of God; Paris Ev. Miss. Soc.; Seventh-day Adv.; LCMS; Methodist; Missionary Ch. Assoc.; Pent. Holiness Ch., Inc.; S. Bap. Conv.

Polytheism. Belief in, or worship of, more than 1 god; may include deification of man and/or natural forces and phenomena; sometimes taken to include animism (see *Primitive Religion*); opposed to monotheism.* See also *Confucianism; Hinduism; Shinto.*

Pomeranian Confessions. See *Krakewitz, Berthold von.*

Pomeranus. See *Bugenhagen, Johann.*

Pommer. See *Bugenhagen, Johann.*

Pomponazzi, Pietro (Petrus Pomponatius; ca. 1462/64–ca. 1524/25). Philos.; b. Mantua, It.; educ. Padua; taught at Padua, Ferrara, and Bologna; held that immortality of the soul is a matter of faith, not of reason. Works include *De immortalitate animae.*

Pond, Enoch (1791–1882). Cong. cleric; b. Wrentham, Mass.; educ. Brown U., Providence, R. I.; pastor Ward (now called Auburn), Mass. 1815; opposed Unitarianism; prof. 1832, pres. 1858 Bangor (Maine) Theol. Sem. Works include *The Mather Family; Lectures on Christian Theology.*

Ponerology. Branch of theol. dealing with the doctrine of evil. See also *Hamartiology.*

Pontifex maximus (Lat. "greatest priest"). Originally the title of the pagan chief priest at Rome; used satirically by Tertullian* of the pope; regular title of the pope from the 5th c.

Pontifical Book. See *Liber pontificalis.*

Pontifical College. Originally the close advisers of the pagan pontifex* maximus at Rome; in RCm, from the 16th c., the term designated any coll. or sem. founded by, or under direct jurisdiction of, the papacy; later it came to mean such institutions for training for. missionaries; since 1931 it refers to all RC colleges and univs. granting academic degrees.

Pontifical Mass. Mass celebrated by a bp. or higher prelate; if celebrated by the pope it is called papal pontifical mass.

Pontificals. Episcopal attire; specifically episcopal insignia including miter* and crosier* (CIC 337).

Pontius (d. ca. 260 AD). Deacon and biographer of Cyprian* of Carthage.

Pontoppidan, Erik (the family name is perhaps a Latinization, by one of his ancestors, of the Ger. equivalent [Brückenstadt] for Brody, on the is. Fyn; 1698–1764). Luth. theol.; b. Aarhus, Jutland; royal chaplain 1735, prof. 1738 Copenhagen; bp. Bergen, Norw., 1748; vice-chancellor U. Copenhagen 1755. Works include *Sandhed til gudfrygtighed* ("Truth unto Piety"), an explanation of the SC (1737), written for use in school and confirmation instruction (see also *Norway, Lutheranism in,* 8).

Poole (Elijah, or Robert, or Paul). See *Lost-Found Nation of Islam in the Wilderness of North America.*

Poole, Matthew (1624–79). B. York, Eng.; educ. Cambridge; Presb. rector London ca. 1648/49; nonconformist* 1662. Works include *Synopsis; Vox clamantis in deserto; The Nullity of the Romish Faith.*

Poor Clares. See *Clare of Assisi; Franciscans.*

Pope (From Lat. *papa,* "father"). 1. Bp. of Rome as head of the RC Ch. Elected by Coll. of Cardinals.* During the election the cardinals are secluded. Election may be by acclamation, ballot, or compromise (election by a committee). Two-thirds majority is required for election. The winner announces what name he will bear as pope, is given a fisherman's ring,* is robed in papal vestments, and the cardinals adore him. The news is pub. If the new pope is not a bp., he must be consecrated such.

2. Pontificate is reckoned from the day of coronation. Papal titles include Pontifex* maximus, Vicar* of Christ, Servant of the servants of God. Acceptable form of address: Your Holiness.

3. Nonliturgical (prelatial) vestments are simple and include white cassock, small humeral cape, oversleeves, sash, zucchetto, white stockings, pectoral cross; mozzetta, camauro, shoes, mantello, and hat are red except in Eastertide. Liturgical vestments are much more elaborate. Other traditional insignia include the *falda* (white flowing robe with a train), *subcinctorium* (in the form of a maniple [see *Vestments, Clerical*], pendent from the girdle on the right side), fanon (similar to a short cape), *sedia gestatoria* (portable chair), and tiara (triple crown; not a liturgical insignia). The Swiss Guard, whose principal function is to protect the pope, was est. 1505/06; other papal guard corps include the Noble Guard, est. 1801, and the Palatine Guard, est. 1850.

See also *Curia; Papal Household; Vatican.*

Pope, Alexander (1688–1744). Poet; b. London, Eng.; illness at 12 resulted in deformity; health undermined by overstudy. Works include *Messiah; Essay on Man; Moral Essays;* hymns include "Rise, Crowned with Light, Imperial Salem, Rise."

Pope, Primacy of. See *Vatican Councils,* 1 b.

Pope, William Burt (1822–1903). Meth. theol.; b. Horton, N. S.; minister in several cities in Eng.; tutor Didsbury Coll., Manchester. Ed. *London Quarterly Review;* other works include *A Compendium of Christian Theology.*

Popes. Some others, not included in the following list, are entered under their names (e. g., see *Linus*).

1. *Sylvester I* (Silvester; d. 335). B. Perhaps Rome; pope 314–335; reputed recipient of Donation* of Constantine. See also *Pseudo-Isidorian Decretals,* 1 a, 2; *Silvesterabend.*

2. *Leo I* (ca. 390–461). B. probably Tuscany; pope 440–461; opposed Pelagianism,* Manichaeism,* and Priscillianists*; pressed claims to jurisdiction in Sp., Gaul, and Afr.; persuaded Attila to spare Rome 452; first bp. of Rome to achieve recognition of claim to supremacy as successor of Peter (hence regarded by many as the 1st pope in distinction from preceding bps. of Rome); Valentinian III (419–455; W Roman emp. 425–455) proclaimed his jurisdiction in the W; his definition of the person of Christ was adopted by the Council of Chalcedon.* See also *Plenitudo potestatis.*

3. *Vigilius* (b. before 500). B. Rome; pope 537(8?)–555; probably elected pope at instigation of Theodora (ca. 508–548; m. Justinian* I 523); changed position several times regarding the Three* Chapters, finally condemning them 554.

4. *Gregory I* (ca. 540–604). "The Great, father of medieval papacy"; b. Rome; pope 590–604; followed the teaching of Augustine* of Hippo; extended papal power into the realm of politics; sent Augustine* (of Canterbury) to Eng. 597; rejected title *Papa universalis* claimed by patriarch at Constantinople. Works are pervaded by superstitions, including mythological reflections about angels and demons. Writings include *Moralia* (exposition of Jb); *Regula pastoralis;* homilies. See also *Church Year,* 17; *Gregorian Music; Hymnody, Christian,* 3.

5. *Nicholas I* (ca. 800–867). "The Great"; b. Rome; pope 858–867. See also *Schism,* 5.

6. *Sylvester II* (Silvester; Gerbert; ca. 940–1003). Pope 999–1003; b. near Aurillac, Auvergne, Fr.; educ. Aurillac, Barcelona, Rome, Reims; eminent scholar; taught at Reims; abp. Reims 991, Ravenna 998; dialectic philos. Works include writings on theol., mathematics, music, and the sciences.

7. *Gregory VII* (Hildebrand; ca. 1020–85). Pope

1073–85; b. perhaps near Siena, Tuscany, It.; regarded by many as the most noteworthy character of the Middle Ages after Charlemagne*; closely associated with previous popes from Leo* IX; instituted reforms directed against clerical concubinage, simony,* and lay investiture*; compelled emp. Henry* IV to humble penance at Canossa 1077; Henry besieged Gregory at Rome; Gregory was freed by R. Guiscard* but forced into exile. See also *England,* 3.

8. *Adrian IV* (Hadrian; Nicholas Breakspear; ca. 1100–59). Pope 1154–59; b. near St. Albans, Eng.; the only Englishman to become pope; known for insistence on papal supremacy in conflict with emp. Frederick* I.

9. *Alexander III* (Orlando Bandinelli; ca. 1105–81). Pope 1159–81; b. Siena, It.; in conflict with emp. Frederick* I; opposed by 4 antipopes: Victor IV, Paschal III, Calixtus III, Innocent III (not to be confused with 10); successful in conflict with Henry* II of Eng. See also *Becket, Thomas à.*

10. *Innocent III* (Lothar of Segni; Giovanni Lotario de' Conti [di Segni]; 1161–1216). Pope 1198–1216; b. Anagni, It.; educ. Bologna and Paris; brought papacy to its pinnacle; Eng., Aragon, Port., and other kingdoms became papal fiefs; promoted the 4th Crusade (see *Crusades,* 5). See also *England,* 3; *Vicar of Christ.*

11. *Gregory IX* (Hugo [lino]; Ugolino; ca. 1170–1241). Pope 1227–41; b. Anagni, It.; excommunicated Frederick* II 1227 for abandoning the idea of a crusade, and again 1239; entrusted Inquisition* largely to Dominicans* 1232. Pub. decretals 1234 (see *Decrees*). See also *Raymond of Peñafort; Stedingers.*

12. *Boniface VIII* (Benedetto Caetani; Benedict Gaetani; ca. 1235–1303). Pope 1294–1303; b. Anagni, It.; issued *Sext* 1298, which contains decretals (see *Decrees*) after those compiled by Gregory IX. See also *Bull; Canon Law,* 3; *Church and State,* 7; *Two Swords.*

13. *John XXII* (Jacques d'Euse [or Deuse] [of Cahors]; ca. 1245/49–1334). Pope 1316–34; b. Cahors, Fr.; had long conflict with the emp.; opposed Franciscan Spirituals* (see also *Franciscans*); enl. and reorganized the curia.* See also *Babylonian Captivity,* 2.

14. *Gregory XI* (Pierre Roger de Beaufort; ca. 1329/31–1378). Pope 1370–78; b. near Limoges, Fr.; condemned teachings of J. Wycliffe; ended the Babylonian Captivity (see *Babylonian Captivity,* 2) by returning to Rome 1377.

15. *Pius II* (Enea Silvio [Aeneas Sylvius (Silvius)] Piccolomini; 1405–64). Pope 1458–64; b. near Siena, It.; bp. Siena 1449; took name Pius as pope in reference to Vergil's "pious Aeneas"; before he became pope he supported the conciliar* movement, but 1460 he condemned it in his bull *Execrabilis* (see *Execrabilis,* 2).

16. *Sixtus IV* (Francesco della Rovere; 1414–84). Pope 1471–84; b. Celle Ligure, near Savona, It.; Gen. of the Franciscans 1464; cardinal 1467; erected Sistine Chapel and Sistine Bridge, whose heavy cost helped make him unpopular; rearranged and enl. the Vatican library; promoted doctrine of the immaculate* conception; addicted to avarice, nepotism, and simony.* See also *Indulgences,* 4; *Inquisition,* 6.

17. *Innocent VIII* (Giovanni Battista Cibo; 1432–92). Pope 1484–92; b. Genoa, It.; educ. Rome and Padua; bp. Savona 1467; cardinal 1473; interfered in Eng. politics; appointed T. de Torquemada* grand inquisitor of Sp.

18. *Alexander VI* (Rodrigo Lanzol y Borja [Borgia]; ca. 1431–1503). Pope 1492–1503; b. Játiva [Xátiva], Valencia, Sp.; known for mental gifts and moral defects; opposed by G. Savonarola.* See also *Holy Leagues and Alliances,* 1.

19. *Julius II* (Giuliano della Rovere; 1443–1513). Pope 1503–13; b. Albisola Superiore, near Savona, It.; joined Sp., Fr., and Ger. in League of Cambrai against Venice 1508; joined Aragon and Venice against Fr. 1511 (see *Holy Leagues and Alliances,* 3); convened 5th Lateran* Council 1512; patron of art; pope at the time of M. Luther's visit (see *Luther, Martin,* 5). See also *States of the Church,* 3.

20. *Leo X* (Giovanni de' Medici; 1475–1521). Pope 1513–21; b. Florence, It.; cardinal 1488; used his influence in the interest of his family; est. a concordat with Francis I of Fr. (see *France,* 8); misunderstood the importance of M. Luther 1519, excommunicated him 1521 (see *Luther, Martin,* 13). See also *Lateran Councils.*

21. *Pius V* (Michele [Antonio?] Ghislieri; 1504–72). Pope 1566–72; b. Bosco Marengo, near Alessandria, It.; Dominican; tried to enforce reform decrees of the Council of Trent*; ordered pub. of *Catechismus Romanus* 1566 (see also *Roman Catholic Confessions,* A 3), *Breviarium Romanum* 1568 (see also *Breviary*), and *Missale Romanum* 1570 (see also *Missal*); excommunicated Elizabeth* I 1570. See also *Counter Reformation,* 9.

22. *Sixtus V* (Felice Peretti; ca. 1520/21–1590). Pope 1585–90; b. Grotammare, near Montalto, in the March of Ancona, It.; tried to enforce reforms of the Council of Trent*; ordered all bps. to report to Rome at stated intervals; fixed the number of cardinals* at 70 in 1586; aided Sp. in war against Eng. 1587–88; sanctioned the Sixtine ed. of the Vulgate (see *Bible Versions,* J 2) in the bull *Aeternus ille* 1590 (the ed. was so poor that it was withdrawn after Sixtus' death).

23. *Innocent X* (Giovanni Battista Pamphili; ca. 1572/74–1655). Pope 1644–55; b. Rome, It.; in a 1648 breve* he repeated previous protests against certain terms of the Peace of Westphalia*; condemned Jansenism.*

24. *Benedict XIV* (Prospero Lorenzo Lambertini; 1675–1758). Pope 1740–58; b. Bologna, It.; educ. Rome; cardinal 1728; abp. Bologna 1731; settled the accommodation controversy (see *Accommodation,* 5) by bulls issued 1742 and 1744; promoted education, science, and literature; followed a liberal for. policy.

25. *Clement XIV* (Giovanni Vincenzo Antonio Ganganelli; 1705–74). Pope 1769–74; b. Sant' Arcangelo di Romagna, near Rimini, It.; cardinal 1759; cultivated good relations with secular powers; suppressed Society* of Jesus 1773.

26. *Pius VI* (Giovanni Angelo Braschi; 1717–99). Pope 1775–99; b. Cesena, It.; opposed Febronianism,* Josephinism,* and Gallicanism*; took part in First Eur. Coalition against Fr. (formed 1792/93); defeated by Napoleon* I; d. a prisoner at Valence, Fr.

27. *Pius VII* (Luigi Barnaba Chiaramonti; 1742–1823). Pope 1800–23; b. Cesena, It., made concordat with Fr. 1801 (see *Concordat,* 5; *France,* 5); crowned Napoleon* I 1804; papacy declined; Holy* Roman Empire ended 1806; the Congress of Vienna 1814/15 restored much papal power. See also *States of the Church,* 3.

28. *Pius IX* (Giovanni Maria Mastai Ferretti; 1792–1878). Pope 1846–78; b. Senigallia, It.; lost papal states 1870 to Victor Emmanuel II (1820–78; 1st king of It. 1861–78), thus creating the "Roman Question" (settled under Pius XI [see 32]); defined the doctrine of the Immaculate* Conception 1854; convened Vatican* Council I, which promulgated the dogma of papal infallibility; created many new dioceses, notably also in the US. See also *Kulturkampf.* See also *States of the Church,* 3; *Syllabus of Errors.*

29. *Leo XIII* (Gioacchino Vincenzo Pecci; 1810–1903). Pope 1878–1903; b. Carpineto, It.; cardinal

1853; statesman and scholar; favored renewal of Thomist scholasticism*; founded the Cath. U. of Am., Washington, D. C., 1889. See also *Commission, Biblical; Kulturkampf.*

30. *Pius X* (Giuseppe Melchiorre Sarto; 1835–1914). Pope 1903–14; b. Riese, It.; bp. Mantua 1884; cardinal 1893; issued the decree *Lamentabili* and the encyclical *Pascendi* against Modernism (see *Modernism,* 1); reorganized the curia 1908 (see *Curia,* 2 b); est. the Pontifical Biblical Institute, Rome; est. *Acta* apostolicae sedis.* See also *Roman Catholic Confessions,* D.

31. *Benedict XV* (Giacomo della Chiesa; 1854–1922). Pope 1914–22; b. Pegli, near Genoa, It.; abp. Bologna 1907; cardinal 1914; known for peace efforts during WW I; opposed Modernism*; pub. CIC 1917.

32. *Pius XI* (Ambrogio Damiano Achille Ratti; 1857–1939). Pope 1922–39; b. Desio, near Milan, It.; known for many encyclicals (e. g., the marriage encyclical *Casti connubii;* see also *Family Planning,* 6); promoted art and science (e. g., with the apostolic* constitution *Deus scientiarum Dominus* 1931); gave specific content and worldwide significance to Catholic* Action; est. Roman Institute for Christian Archaeol. 1925, Russ. Coll. 1929, and Rumanian Coll. 1930; made the Ethiopian Coll. a pontifical coll. 1930. See also *Concordat,* 7.

33. *Pius XII* (Eugenio Maria Giuseppe Giovanni Pacelli; 1876–1958). Pope 1939–58; b. Rome, It.; abp. Sardi 1917; signed concordat with Bav. 1924, Prussia 1929; cardinal 1929; papal secy. of state 1930; concluded concordat with Baden 1932; traveled widely (also to US 1936); during WW II he favored peace, but not at any price; opposed communism.

34. *John XXIII* (Angelo Giuseppe Roncalli; 1881–1963). Pope 1958–63; b. Sotto il Monte, near Bergamo, It.; cardinal 1953; raised the number of cardinals above 70 1958; convened Vatican* Council II; approved liturgical reforms; authorized use of vernacular in services; created a pontifical commission to revise CIC; made all E rite patriarchs mems. of the Cong. for the Oriental Ch.; initiated cordial relations with the patriarch of Constantinople; promoted missions and a better climate in interfaith relations; encyclicals include *Mater et Magistra* and *Pacem in terris.*

35. *Paul VI* (Giovanni Battista Montini; b. 1897). Pope 1963–; b. Concesio, Lombardy, It.; abp. Milan 1954; cardinal 1958; continued the program of John XXIII and Vatican* Council II; instituted the Pontifical Commission for the Media of Social Communication; est. Secretariat for Non-Christians and Secretariat for Non-Believers; fostered ecumenical relations; est. a commission to implement liturgical renewal; promoted world peace. EL

H. K. Mann, *Lives of the Popes in the (Early) Middle Ages,* 18 vols. in 19 (London, 1902–32); L. v. Pastor, *Geschichte der Päpste seit dem Ausgang des Mittelalters,* Eng. title *History of the Popes from the Close of the Middle Ages,* various editors and translators, 40 vols. (London, 1891–1953); L. v. Ranke, *The History of the Popes,* tr. E. Foster, 3 vols. (London, 1896).

Popes, Captivity of. See *Babylonian Captivity,* 2, 3.

Poppen, Emmanuel Frederick (Emanuel; Oct. 14, 1874–Feb. 13, 1961). B. New Dundee, Ont., Can.; educ. Capital U. and Luth. Sem., Columbus, Ohio. Pastor Versailles 1895–97, St. Marys 1897–1905, Sidney 1905–15, Grove City 1915–30, all in Ohio. Pres. ALC 1937–50; chm. Intersyn. Luth. Hymnal Committee 1922–30. Ed. *Lutherische Kirchenzeitung;* coed. *American Lutheran Hymnal.*

Poppen, Hermann Meinhardt (1885–1956). Luth. musician and composer; b. Heidelberg, Ger.; educ. Berlin, Kiel, and Heidelberg; assoc. with P. Wolfrum* and M. Reger*; dir. music U. of Jena 1914; soldier in WW I; dir. music U. of Heidelberg and dir. Bach Soc. 1919; instigated founding of Heidelberg Institute of Ch. Music 1931.

Population Explosion. See *Family Planning.*

Pordage, John (1607–81). Angl. astrologer and mystic; b. London, Eng.; educ. Oxford; influenced by J. Böhme. Works include *Theologia mystica.* See also *Philadelphian Society for the Advancement of Piety and Divine Philosophy, The.*

Porphyry (Porphyrius; original name Malchus; ca. 232/233–ca. 304). Neoplatonist; b. Syria; studied under Plotinus.* Works include *Adversus Christianos* (extant in fragments).

Porpora, Nicola Antonio (Niccolò; 1686–ca. 1768). Baroque Neapolitan composer; b. Naples, It.; educ. Naples; music dir. to Port. ambassador at Naples; chamber virtuoso to the prince of Hesse-Darmstadt; conductor to the king of Poland; est. a school of singing at Naples ca. 1712. Works include oratorios, cantatas, masses, duets on the Passion* in Lat.

Porrée, Gilbert de la. See *Gilbert de la Porrée.*

Porst, Johann (1668–1728). B. Kotzau, near Bayreuth, Ger.; educ. Leipzig; tutor; pastor Malchow and Hohen-Schönhausen 1698, Berlin 1704; chaplain to the queen 1709; provost Berlin 1713; consistorial councillor 1716. Strongly influenced by P. J. Spener. Ed. *Geistliche liebliche Lieder,* marked by pietism and subjectivism.

Port-Royal (Port-Royal-des-Champs). Cistercian convent near Trappes, Versailles, and Paris, Fr.; est. 1204; mainstay of Jansenism*; suppressed 1709; destroyed 1711.

H. Reuchlin, *Geschichte von Port-Royal,* 2 vols. (Hamburg, 1839–44).

Porta, Konrad (Conrad; 1541–85). B. Osterwieck, near Halberstadt, Ger.; rector Osterwieck 1566; conrector Eisleben 1567; deacon, finally pastor Eisleben. Issued *Pastorale Lutheri* 1582 (selection of passages from M. Luther on pastoral theol.).

Porter. Doorkeeper. See also *Hierarchy.*

Portugal (ancient Lusitania). W part of Iberian peninsula, W Eur.; *area:* more than 35,300 sq. mi.; *pop.* (1973 est.) 9,780,000. Indep. kingdom in 12th c.; Sp. dependency 1580–1640; dependent ally of Gt. Brit. in late 17th c.; occupied by Fr. 1807–14; rep. 1910; new const. adopted 1933, amended 1959; govt. overthrown by military coup 1974. More than 70% nominally RC; others have included Assemblies of God, Brethren, Baps., Presbs., Meths., Pents., Seventh-day Adventists. Effects of the Reformation were felt early in Port. Organized Luth. work began soon after the middle of the 20th c. LCMS granted its Brazil Dist. permission to regard miss. work in Port. as its project 1962.

Portuguese East Africa. See *Africa,* B 4.

Portuguese Guinea. See *Africa,* C 15.

Portuguese West Africa. See *Africa,* B 1.

Poseidon. See *Greek Religion,* 2.

Positivism. Philos. system of A. Comte*; called positivism because it deals only with "positive" knowledge arrived at by experience and observation. Comte classified the sciences in a series beginning with consideration of attributes of objects that are most gen. and proceeding to other attributes combined in greater complexity: (1) mathematics, (2) astronomy, (3) physics, (4) chemistry, (5) biology, (6) sociology; from the 2d on, each is more special than the one before it and depends on the facts of all that precede it. Later he tried to construct a "religion of humanity," in which humanity takes the place of God as the object of worship. See also *Dewey, John; Dühring, Karl Eugen; Durkheim, Emile; Lévy-Bruhl, Lucien; Naturalism.*

Positivism, Logical. See *Logical Positivism.*

Positivism, Sociological. Type of sociological realism held, e. g., by É. Durkheim; held that society is a reality and the group-mind a fact.

Possidius (ca. 370–ca. 440). Bp. Calama, in Numidia, 397. Works include a life of Augustine* of Hippo. *MPL*, XXXII, 31–66.

Postel, Guillaume (1510–81). Humanist; mystic; b. near Barenton, Fr.; studied oriental languages; sought union of all religions in a universal ch. based on a Christian-catholic world mission; Jesuit 1544, expelled 1546; rejected by Prots. and RCs. Works include *De orbis terrae concordia.*

Postil (from Lat. *postilla,* probably from *post illa* [*verba textus*], "after those words of the text"). Explanation of a Biblical text; originally perhaps a gloss, later a homily, then a collection of homilies.

Postlude (Lat. *postludium;* Ger. *Nachspiel*). Music played at the end of a worship service. Should be in the spirit of the service.

Postmillenarians. See *Millennium,* 7.

Post-Nicene Fathers. Patristic writers after the 325 Council of Nicaea. See also *Patristics.*

Post-Pentecost Season. Some chs. use this term and calculation instead of post-Trinity. Trin. Sun. is the 1st Sun. after Pent., and 1st Sun. after Trin. is the 2d Sun. after Pent., etc.

Post-Trinity Season. See *Church Year,* 6.

Postulant. 1. In RC terminology, an applicant for admission to an order; the period of time in which a postulant prepares for the novitiate (see *Novice*) is called postulancy. 2. In Episc. terminology, an applicant for ordination.

Postulator. See *Canonization.*

Potawatomi. See *Indians, American,* 6.

Pothinus (ca. 87–ca. 177/178). Bp. Lyons, Fr.; probably b. Asia Minor; probably pupil of Polycarp*; martyr. See also *Persecution of Christians,* 3.

Poullain, Valérand (Valerandus Polanus; ca. 1520–57). Ordained by M. Luther* 1540; influenced by M. Bucer* and J. Calvin*; served Fr. cong. Strasbourg; after Interim* went with Bucer to Eng.; supt. Walloons in Glastonbury 1552; emigrated with them to Frankfurt am Main; opposed Gnesio-Lutherans,* T. Beza,* and G. Farel.*

Powell, Thomas Edward (1823–1901). B. Hampstead, Middlesex, Eng.; educ. Oxford; curate Cookham-Dean, near Maidenhead, 1846; vicar Bisham 1848; hymnist. Issued a book of hymns, anthems, etc. for pub. worship. Hymns include "Bow Down Thine Ear, Almighty Lord."

Power, Kingdom of. See *King, Christ as.*

Power of Jurisdiction. See *Hierarchy.*

Power of Order. See *Hierarchy.*

Practical Realism. See *Realism.*

Practical Seminary. See *Löhe, Johann Konrad Wilhelm; Ministry, Education of,* X C and D; *Sihler, Wilhelm; Wyneken, Friedrich Conrad Dietrich.*

Practical Theology. Branches of theol.* that deal with the practical work of the ministry, e.g., catechetics,* homiletics,* liturgics,* pastoral* theol., casuistry,* ch. polity.*

Praeceptor Germaniae (Lat. "teacher of Germany"). Title often given P. Melanchthon* because of his influence on educ. and humanism in Ger.

Praemunire, Statutes of. Eng. statutes named after the Lat. word *praemunire* ("to warn"), prominent in the writ issued under the statutes, which were first passed 1353, 1365, and 1393, preventing encroachment of papal jurisdiction and upholding the indep. of royal courts; used by Henry* VIII (against T. Wolsey*), Elizabeth* I, and by courts under James* I.

Praetorius, Abdias (Gottschalk Schulze; 1524–73). B. Salzwedel, Ger.; educ. Frankfurt an der Oder and Wittenberg; pupil of P. Melanchthon*; taught at Salzwedel 1544, Magdeburg 1553; taught Heb. at Frankfurt an der Oder 1558–63; engaged in controversy with A. Musculus* on the necessity of good works; joined the philos. faculty at Wittenberg 1563. Works include *Loci.*

Praetorius, Benjamin (1636–probably ca. 1674). B. near Weissenfels, Ger.; studied theol., probably at Leipzig; pastor Gross-Lissa, near Delitzsch, Saxony; hymnist. Hymns include "Sei getreu bis an das Ende."

Praetorius, Hieronymus (1560–1629). Luth. composer; father of J. Praetorius*; b. Hamburg, Ger.; cantor Erfurt 1580; organist Hamburg; follower of the Venetian* school of ch. music. Issued *Melodeyen Gesangbuch* (to which he contributed harmonizations of 21 chorales); most of his works pub. in a collection titled *Opus Musicum.*

Praetorius, Jacob (1586–1651). Luth. composer; son of H. Praetorius*; b. Hamburg, Ger.; studied under J. P. Sweelinck*; organist Hamburg 1603–51. Works include motets, wedding songs, and contrapuntal settings of chorales.

Praetorius, Michael (real surname Schultheiss, or Schulz [with variants]; ca. 1571/72–1621). Luth. composer; musicologist; b. Creuzburg, Thuringia, Ger.; studied at Frankfurt an der Oder; in service of duke of Brunswick-Wolfenbüttel. Compositions include *Musae Sioniae; Hymnodia Sionia; Terpsichore; Polhymnia; Puericinium; Urainia.* Writings include *Leiturgodia; Syntagma musicum.*

Pragmatic Sanction (Lat. *pragmatica sanctio*). In Roman law (Theodosian and Justinian codes), a govt. decision in a matter (Gk. *pragma*) involving community or pub. interest. Later, an expression of will by a sovereign defining the limits of his own power or regulating the succession. The Pragmatic Sanction of Bourges 1438 upheld the right of the Fr. Ch. to administer its temporal property and disallowed papal nominations to vacant benefices. See also *Church and State,* 8; *Concordat,* 4; *France,* 3; *Gallicanism; Lateran Councils.*

Pragmatic Theory. See *Truth.*

Pragmaticism. See *Peirce, Charles Santiago Sanders.*

Pragmatism. In philos., a logical process intended to help make ideas clear. It proposes that the meaning of an idea should be determined by the practical, or pragmatic, difference it would make if it were assumed to be true. As bet. 2 ideas, if there were no difference in effect, it would be concluded that either the difference was purely verbal or that the 2 ideas meant the same. First developed by C. S. S. Peirce* in the 1870s; revived and reformulated 1898 by W. James,* who proposed the pragmatic test for the nature of truth itself. Ideas were to be held true if they worked; i.e., if the practical consequences of acting on an idea brought to the individual concerned personal satisfaction, the idea was to be regarded as acceptable, or true, at least in a sense or up to a point. James wanted to confine the application of pragmatism to problems not otherwise verifiable; others felt that the test might be made in any instance. J. Dewey,* sometimes called a pragmatist, preferred his philos. to be called instrumentalism, later experimentalism. Pragmatism has stressed use of interest in learning, because the pragmatic test of truth is affected by the interest of the learner. Pragmatism has no proper application to the transcendental, where divine revelation is the deciding factor.

Prague, Peace or Treaty of. See *Thirty Years' War.*

Prajapati. See *Brahmanism,* 2.

Pratensis, Felix (a Prato; ca. 1460–1558). Jew; Augustinian hermit in Prato, It., 1506; to Rome 1514/15; active in miss. to Jews; M. Luther used his tr. of Psalms. Ed. the Heb. Bible printed 1516/17 by D. Bomberg.*

Praxeas (fl. toward end of 2d and beginning of 3d c.). Exponent of patripassianism*; opposed by Tertullian.* See also *Monarchianism,* B 4.

Praxedes (1st–2d c.). Martyr at Rome.

Prayer. 1. In the narrow sense, a request, or petition, for benefits or mercies; in the wide sense, any communion of a soul with God. May be divided into adoration, expressing a sense of God's goodness and greatness; confession, acknowledging unworthiness; supplication, asking pardon, grace, or any other blessing; intercession (praying for others); thanksgiving. Private prayer includes spontaneous ejaculations, wishes, or appeals and deliberate prayer (cf. Mt 6:6). Family prayer (as at mealtime and in family worship ["family altar"]) and social prayer in pub. worship are forms of corporate prayer.

2. Prayer is commanded by God (1 Ch 16:11; Ps 50:15; Mt 7:7; Ph 4:6), has His promises (Ps 91: 15-16; Jn 16:23; Ja 5:16b), and hence is a vital part of Christian life. To be valid, prayer must be made to the true God (1 Sm 7:3; Is 42:8); Ap XXI 8–10 grants that saints and angels pray for us but adds: "it does not follow that they should be invoked"; cf. AC XXI 2, which quotes 1 Ti 2:5. It must proceed from faith (Mt 21:22; Ja 1:6-7), which is created by the Holy Spirit (1 Co 12:3), who assists and guides in prayer (Ro 8:26); faith excludes willful sin, which invalidates prayer (Ps 66:18; Pr 28:9; Is 1:15; 59:2; Jn 9:31). It must be conditioned by the will of God (1 Jn 5:14; cf. Ro 8:28) and be as broad as living mankind (1 Ti 2:1; Heb 9:27).

3. Prayer must be more than an emergency measure in time of trouble; it must constantly reach out for the more abundant life promised by God (Ro 12:12; Ph 4:6-7; 1 Th 5:17). Prayer must be an integral part of the home that is to function acc. to God's plan (Jos 24:15) and is essential to the ch. in its life and functions (Mt 18:19-20; Lk 11:13). A cong. prays the Lord to give its pastor "utterance" (Eph 6:19) and open doors to him (Cl 4:3). The pastor prays that God may strengthen his cong. "with might by His Spirit in the inner man" (Eph 3:16). Pastor and people present special needs of individual mems. and families to God.

4. Kinds and forms of prayer are indicated, e. g., in the OT by such words as *tephillah* (in heading of Ps 17, 86, 90, 102, 142 and in Hab 3:1; prayer, intercession, supplication), *sheelah* (e.g., 1 Sm 2:20; Est 5:6, 7; prayer in gen., request, petition), *todah* (e.g., Ps 26:7; 42:5; Is 51:3; thanksgiving, praise). For kinds and forms of prayer mentioned in the NT cf., e.g., 1 Ti 2:1.

5. Jesus was in constant prayer communication with His heavenly Father (e.g., Mt 14:19; 26:39, 42, 44; Mk 1:35; 6:46; Lk 23:46; Jn 17; cf. Mt 6:9-13).

Incentives to prayer: God's command and promise and our own and our neighbor's need (Ps 122:6; Jer 29:7; Mt 5:44; 6:6; 9:38; 24:20; 26:41; Lk 6:28; 18:1-7; Ro 8:26; 1 Th 5:17, 25; 1 Ti 2:1, 8; Ja 5:13).

6. Other examples include Abraham, Moses, David, Solomon, Hezekiah, Ezra, Daniel, Zacharias, Paul, John, Chrysostom, Augustine of Hippo, M. Luther, J. F. Starck, C. F. W. Walther.

See also *Grace, Means of,* I, 1; *Saints, Veneration of,* 6–8; *Worship.*

Prayer, Liturgical. The sacrificial part of pub. worship, including, e.g., hymns, collects, prayers, Preface, Sanctus, Agnus Dei, canticles; antiphonal chanting may be regarded sacrificial if it does not include proclamation of the Word. Set or fixed prayers reflect the life, work, and worship of the ch. through the ages. Specific postures are not essential to prayer; standing and kneeling are common, usually with head bowed and hands folded. See also *Worship, Parts of.*

Prayer Books. Name given by some liturgical chs. to their service books, e.g., Book* of Common Prayer; Scottish Prayer Book (see *Covenanters*).

Prayer Meeting (prayer service). Meeting or service, common in Ref. chs., usually held ca. the middle of the week, featuring extempore prayers by worshipers, hymns, and relation of religious experiences, with or without evangelistic or revivalistic preaching; prayer is regarded as a means of grace. But see *Grace, Means of,* I, 1.

Prayers for the Dead. See *Dead, Prayers for.*

Preaching. See *Homiletics; Worship,* 2.

Preaching, Christian, History of. 1. Christian preaching has as its content the Word of God (2 Ti 4:2), esp. the Gospel (1 Co 2:2). Purposes of Christian preaching: to bring the sinner to a knowledge of his sins (Ro 3:20) and to repentance and faith (Mk 1:14-15; 16:15-16); to strengthen the Christian (2 Ptr 3:18; Ro 12; 15:4); to give glory to God (2 Ptr 3:18).

2. Great OT preachers include Isaiah, Amos, Ezekiel, Jeremiah, Jonah.

3. The great preacher was Jesus Christ (Mt 4:17; Mk 1:14-15; Lk 4:43-44).

4. Jesus ordained, or appointed, the 12 disciples to preach (Mk 3:14). The 70 were sent with the message: "The kingdom of God is come nigh" (Lk 10: 1-16). The ch. was commissioned to preach (Mk 16:15; Lk 24:47).

5. Those who were scattered in the persecution by Saul "went everywhere preaching the Word" (Acts 8:4). In course of time, and largely spearheaded by Paul, Christian preaching spread throughout the Roman empire.

6. We know little of the preaching of the first 2 cents.; it was informal and by men who had no special training but whose heart was aflame with love of Christ. Origen* allegorized too much, as did many others after him. Theol. schools were est. Preaching expanded tremendously from Constantine* I to J. Chrysostom* and Augustine* of Hippo (whose *De doctrina Christiana,* Book IV, often called the 1st book on homiletics, influenced preaching at least till ca. 600).

7. Ceremonialism and the mass overshadowed preaching 600–1100. When sermons were preached they were in Lat., not the vernacular. Most lower clergy were ignorant and irreligious. Charlemagne* directed Paul* the Deacon to compile homilies; the collection, *Homiliarium,* was long in use.

8. Preaching improved from the 12th c. Peter* the Hermit was fanatic but eloquent; Bernard* of Clairvaux, regarded as the greatest preacher of his age, preached 86 sermons on the SS, but did not get beyond chap. 3, verse 1. The Dominicans* were founded to counteract defection from RCm in S France. Anthony* of Padua, who is said to have preached to 30,000 on at least 1 occasion, divided his sermons into several parts (an innovation), used illustrations, and went to the extreme in allegorizing. Thomas* Aquinas combined profound studies with practical preaching. Berthold von Regensburg, "The Chrysostom of the Middle Ages" (perhaps ca. 1210 –72; perhaps b. Regensburg, Ger.), preached in German to audiences est. 60,000–200,000 against indulgences and dependence on intercessory prayers of Mary and other saints. Other Ger. preachers of the 13th and 14th c. include Albertus* Magnus, J. Eckhart,* H. Suso,* and J. Tauler.*

9. Preachers also called Prereformers include J. Hus,* G. Savonarola,* and J. Wycliffe.* J. Colet* was a well-known pre-Reformation preacher in Eng.

10. The Reformation reemphasized (1) the purpose of Christian preaching: to proclaim the Gospel; (2) the source of Christian preaching: the Bible; (3) the proper place of Christian preaching in pub. worship: 1st place, with sacrificial parts in 2d place. Preachers of the Reformation and post-Reformation period include in Germany: M. Luther,* J. Brenz,* J. Bugenhagen,* V. Herberger*; in England: J. Knox.* 17th-c. preachers include in Germany: C. Scriver,* H. Müller,* V. E. Löscher,* P. J. Spener,* A. H. Francke*; in England: J. Tillotson,* R. Bax-

ter*; RCs in France: J. B. Bossuet,* J. B. Massilon*; Ref. in France: J. Claude.* 18th-c. preachers include in Germany: J. A. Bengel,* J. L. v. Mosheim,* N. L. v. Zinzendorf*; in Holland: J. Saurin*; in England: R. Hall,* T. Chalmers*; in England and Am.: J. Wesley,* G. Whitefield.*

11. The Enlightenment,* deism,* materialism,* and rationalism* affected preaching adversely. On the other hand, J. H. Jung-Stilling,* J. K. Lavater,* and F. C. Oetinger* exerted a good influence.

12. F. D. E. Schleiermacher,* who attacked rationalism, yet based his theol. on the inner consciousness of the individual, held that the purpose of preaching is to awaken religious feeling, not to instruct or incite to action; his preaching was topical; he did not write his sermons, but carefully prepared them. In contrast, L. Hofacker* said: "I have but 1 sermon: I preach the Lamb that was slain." C. Harms* reacted against the rationalistic influences under which he grew up, adopted a positive Bible-based theol., and used the topical method in forceful preaching. E. R. Stier* said the sermon should be Scriptural and applied to the hearer. F. W. Krummacher (see *Krummacher,* 3) was one of the most popular preachers of his day. G. L. D. T. Harms* exerted great influence by his preaching. T. J. R. Kögel,* brilliant preacher, said the sermon must be a battle. Other Ger. preachers of the 19th c. include J. T. Beck,* K. F. v. Gerok,* C. E. Luthardt,* Julius Müller,* F. K. L. Steinmeyer,* and J. G. W. Uhlhorn.*

13. 19th and early 20th c. preachers in Eng. and Scot. include H. Alford,* J. Caird,* T. Guthrie,* J. H. Jowett,* J. Ker,* H. P. Liddon,* A. Maclaren,* F. W. Robertson,* C. H. Spurgeon.*

14. Luth. preachers of the past in Am. include C. F. W. Walther,* J. A. Seiss,* W. A. Maier.*

15. Non-Luth. Prot. preachers of the past in Am. include H. W. Beecher,* P. Brooks,* C. G. Finney,* H. E. Fosdick,* D. L. Moody.* JHCF

J. A. Broadus, *Lectures on the History of Preaching* (New York, 1876); E. C. Dargan, *The Art of Preaching in the Light of Its History* (New York, 1922); J. H. C. Fritz, *The Preacher's Manual* (St. Louis, 1941); H. C. Howard, *Princes of the Christian Pulpit and Pastorate,* 2 series (Nashville, Tenn., 1927–28); E. R. Kiesow, *Dialektisches Denken und Reden in der Predigt: an Beispielen aus der Predigtliteratur der Gegenwart untersucht* (Berlin, 1957); C. H. Dodd, *The Apostolic Preaching and Its Development: Three Lectures* (New York, 1936); D. W. Lehmann, *Das Wort der Propheten in der Predigt der evangelischen Kirchen von Luther bis zum Beginn des 20. Jahrhunderts* (Frankfurt am Main, 1963); Y. T. Brilioth, *Predikans historia* (Lund, 1945), tr. K. E. Mattson, *A Brief History of Preaching* (Philadelphia, 1965); H. Davies, *Varieties of English Preaching 1900–1960* (London, 1963); F. R. Webber, *A History of Preaching in Britain and America,* 3 vols. (Milwaukee, Wis., 1952–57).

Preadamites. 1. Term referring to human beings conceived of as living before the Adam of Gn; assoc. esp. with Isaac de la Peyrère (1594–1676; Bordeaux Huguenot), who held that Ro 5:12-14 meant that human beings before Adam sinned, that they were the ancestors of the Gentiles, and that the Jews sprang from Adam; Peyrère later renounced the theory and became RC ca. 1657. 2. Followers of Peyrère.

Prebend. In Eng., stipend from the estate of a cathedral or collegiate ch. for a canon or chapter member; land or tithe that provides the stipend. Holder of a prebend is called prebendary.

Precentor. See *Cantor.*

Predella. 1. Step or platform on which an altar is placed. 2. Sculpture or painting along front of superaltar or at foot of altarpiece.

Predestinarian Controversy. 1. 847–ca. 868. Began when Gottschalk* of Orbais began spreading his views on predestination in It., ended with his death. Rediscussion of the stricter and laxer view of the Augustinian doctrine of predestination (see *Pelagian Controversy*). Gottschalk, who held an absolute predestination, was immediately opposed by Rabanus* Maurus and condemned by a syn. at Mainz 848. Hincmar* was instructed to take necessary measures against him. Gottschalk was condemned again 849 by a syn. at Crécy (Chiersy; Quierzy; other variants), Fr., and imprisoned for the rest of his life in the convent at Hautvilliers.

Gottschalk's view was defended by Ratramnus,* Lupus* Servatus, Remigius* of Lyons, Florus,* et al. and was confirmed by a syn. at Valence 855 and Langres 859. But a syn. at Crécy 853 adopted a different view. J. S. Erigena* set forth a 3d theory. A syn. at Savonnières, near Toul, postponed final decision to the 860 syn. at Toucy, near Toul, which expressed only the common ground among parties to the controversy. Finally, Gottschalk appealed to Nicholas I (see *Popes,* 5) 866, might have been successful, but was outmaneuvered by Hincmar, who refused him Communion and Christian burial unless he would recant. Gottschalk refused, died in his belief, and was buried in unconsecrated soil.

At the time of the Reformation the two main streams in the controversy stood revealed in RC semi-Pelagianism and Ref. predestinarianism. Lutheranism found the golden mean bet. them.

2. The name "Predestinarian Controversy" is also applied to a controversy over conversion and election bet. mems. of the Mo. Syn., the Ohio Syn., and other Luth. bodies in Am. in the 1880s. See also *Evangelical Lutheran Church, The,* 10; *Intuitu fidei; Lutheran Church – Missouri Synod, The,* V, 12; VI, 1; *Ohio and Other States, Evangelical Lutheran Joint Synod of,* 5; *Thirteen Theses.*

See also *Double Predestination; Preterition.*

Predestination. I. Acc. to the Bible, all that God does in time for our conversion, justification, and final glorification is based on, and flows from, an eternal decree of election or predestination, acc. to which God, before the foundation of the world, chose us in His Son Jesus Christ out of the mass of sinful mankind unto faith, the adoption of sons, and everlasting life; this election is not based on any good quality or act of the elect, nor is it *intuitu* fidei,* but is based solely on God's grace, the good pleasure of His will in Christ Jesus. The Bible does not teach reprobation, i. e., an election of wrath for those who are lost; God earnestly desires the salvation of all; the lost are lost by their own fault. The Bible does not solve the problem that exists for the human mind that tries to harmonize the doctrine of universal grace and the doctrines of election and salvation by grace alone. The doctrine of election by grace, properly used, will not foster carnal security, but will make the believer conscious of the matchless glory of the grace of God, serve as a constant incentive to sanctification, comfort him in the ills and tribulations of this life, and give him the blessed assurance of final salvation. Since the doctrine of election by grace is clearly taught in the Bible, it is written for all Christians to learn. FK

II. The decree of predestination is an eternal act of God (Eph 1:4; 3:11; 2 Th 2:13; 2 Ti 1:9), who, for His goodness' sake (Ro 9:11; 11:5; 2 Ti 1:9), and because of the merit of the foreordained Redeemer of all mankind (Eph 1:4; 3:11; 2 Ti 1:9), proposed to lead into everlasting life (Acts 13:48; Ro 8:28-29; 2 Ti 1:9; 2:10), by the way and means of salvation designated for all mankind (Ro 8:29-30; Eph 1:4-5; 1 Ptr 1:2), a certain number (Mt 20:16; 22:14; Acts 13:48) of certain persons (Jn 13:18; 2 Ti 2:19; 1 Ptr 1:2), and to procure, work, and promote what would pertain to their final salvation (Mk 13:20, 22; Ro 8:30; Eph 1:11; 3:10-11). Cf. A. L. Graebner, *Outlines of Doctrinal Theology*, par. 51.

III. FC Ep XI 5–7: "Predestination or the eternal election of God . . . is concerned only with the pious children of God in whom He is well pleased. It is a cause of their salvation, for He alone brings it about and ordains everything that belongs to it. Our salvation is so firmly established upon it that the 'gates of Hades cannot prevail against' it (John 10: 28; Matt. 16:18).

"We are not to investigate this predestination in the secret counsel of God, but it is to be looked for in His Word, where He has revealed it.

"The Word of God, however, leads us to Christ, who is 'the book of life' in which all who are to be eternally saved are inscribed and elected, as it is written, 'He chose us in Him before the foundation of the world' (Eph. 1:4)."

FC SD XI 14–23: "This means that we must always take as one unit the entire doctrine of God's purpose, counsel, will, and ordinance concerning our redemption, call, justification, and salvation, as Paul treats and explains this article (Rom. 8:28 ff.; Eph. 1:4 ff.) and as Christ likewise does in the parable (Matt. 20:2-14), namely, that in his purpose and counsel God has ordained the following:

"1. That through Christ the human race has truly been redeemed and reconciled with God and that by His innocent obedience, suffering, and death Christ has earned for us 'the righteousness which avails before God' and eternal life.

"2. That his merit and these benefits of Christ are to be offered, given, and distributed to us through His Word and sacraments.

"3. That He would be effective and active in us by His Holy Spirit through the Word when it is preached, heard, and meditated on, would convert hearts to true repentance, and would enlighten them in the true faith.

"4. That He would justify and graciously accept into the adoption of children and into the inheritance of eternal life all who in sincere repentance and true faith accept Christ.

"5. That He also would sanctify in love all who are thus justified, as St. Paul says (Eph. 1:4).

"6. That He also would protect them in their great weakness against the devil, the world, and the flesh, guide and lead them in His ways, raise them up when they stumble, and comfort and preserve them in tribulation and temptation.

"7. That He would also strengthen and increase in them the good work which He has begun, and preserve them unto the end, if they cling to God's Word, pray diligently, persevere in the grace of God, and use faithfully the gifts that they have received.

"8. That, finally, He would eternally save and glorify in eternal life those whom He has elected, called, and justified.

"In this His eternal counsel, purpose, and ordinance God has not only prepared salvation in general, but He has also graciously considered and elected to salvation each and every individual among the elect who are to be saved through Christ, and also ordained that in the manner just recounted He wills by His grace, gifts, and effective working to bring them to salvation and to help, further, strengthen, and preserve them to this end."

See also *Analogy of Faith; Double Predestination; Infralapsarianism; Supralapsarianism; Thirteen Theses.*

A. Hunnius, *Articulus de providentia Dei et aeterna praedestinatione seu electione filiorum Dei ad salutem* (Frankfurt, 1603); W. Elert, "Versöhnung und Prädestination bei Luther in Disjunktion" and "Versöhnung und Prädestination in den Bekenntnissen in Konjunktion," *Morphologie des Luthertums,* I (Munich, 1931; improved print., 1952), 103–123, tr. W. A Hansen, "Reconciliation and Predestination in Luther in Disjunction" and "Reconciliation and Predestination in the Confessions in Conjunction," *The Structure of Lutheranism,* I (St. Louis, 1962), 117–140; *Verhandlungen der Allgemeinen Pastoralconferenz der Synode von Missouri, Ohio u. a. Staaten über die Lehre von der Gnadenwahl* (St. Louis, 1880); *Einundzwanzigster Synodal-Bericht des Westlichen Districts der deutschen ev.-luth. Synode von Missouri, Ohio und anderen Staaten* (St. Louis, 1877), pp. 21–109 (C. F. W. Walther essayist); *Zweiundzwanzigster Synodal-Bericht des Westlichen Districts der deutschen ev.-luth. Synode von Missouri, Ohio und anderen Staaten* (St. Louis, 1879), pp. 22–120 (C. F. Walther essayist); *Zeugniss wieder die neue, falsche Gnadenwahlslehre der Missouri Synode auf Grund der hl. Schrift und des lutherischen Bekenntnisses abgelegt von einigen ehemaligen Gliedern genannter Synode* (Milwaukee, 1882); G. J. Fritschel, *Die Schriftlehre von der Gnadenwahl* (Chicago, 1906) and *Zur Einigung der amerikanisch-lutherischen Kirche in der Lehre von der Bekehrung und Gnadenwahl,* 2d ed. (Chicago, 1914); C. W. Schaeffer, W. J. Mann, A. Spaeth, and H. E. Jacobs, "Concerning the Dogma of Predestination," *The Lutheran Church Review,* III (1884), 223–236; C. F. W. Walther, *The Controversy Concerning Predestination,* tr. A. Crull (St. Louis, 1881); F. Pieper, *Zur Einigung der amerikanisch-lutherischen Kirche in der Lehre von der Bekehrung und Gnadenwahl,* 2d ed., enl. (St. Louis, 1913), tr. *Conversion and Election: A Plea for a United Lutheranism in America* (St. Louis, 1913); L. S. Keyser, *Election and Conversion: A Frank Discussion of Dr. Pieper's Book on "Conversion and Election," with Suggestions for Lutheran Concord and Union on Another Basis* (Burlington, Iowa, 1914); A. L. Graebner, "The Doctrine of Predestination as Taught in Ephesians 1, 3–6," *TQ,* V (1901), 25–46; T. Engelder, "Let Us Get Together on the Doctrines of Conversion and Election," *CTM,* VI (1935), 539–543; T. Graebner, "Predestination and Human Responsibility," *CTM,* V (1934), 164–171; J. T. Mueller, "Die Gnadenwahl nach Ewigkeit und Zeit," *CTM,* V (1934), 748–757; F. Kramer, "The Doctrine of Election, or Predestination," *The Abiding Word,* I, ed. T. Laetsch (St. Louis, 1946), 522–543; 3 arts., each headed "Predestination," 1 each by A. L. Graebner, S. Fritschel, and H. E. Jacobs in *The Lutheran Cyclopedia,* ed. H. E. Jacobs and J. A. W. Haas (New York, 1899), pp. 388–393; L. Poellet, "The Doctrine of Predestination in Romans 8:28-39," *CTM,* XXIII (1952), 342–353.

Predigtamt. See *Ministerial Office,* 2.

Preestablished Harmony. See *Harmony, Preestablished.*

Preexistence of Christ. See *Christ Jesus.*

Preexistence of the Soul. See *Transmigration of Souls.*

Preface. In Christian worship, the beginning of the Communion service proper. Includes the *Salutation* ("The Lord be with you") and response ("And with thy spirit"), the *Sursum Corda* ("Lift up your hearts") and response ("We lift them up unto the Lord"), the *Eucharistia* ("Let us give thanks unto the Lord our God") and response ("It is meet and right so to do") and the *Common Preface* and *Proper Preface.* The Common Preface consists of the *Thanksgiving* ("It is truly meet, right, and salutary, that we should at all times, and in all places, give thanks unto Thee, O Lord, Holy Father, Almighty, Everlasting God") and the *Ascription* of praise ("Therefore with angels and archangels, and with all the company of heaven, we laud and magnify Thy glorious name, evermore praising Thee and saying:"); it is called "common" because it is always (i. e. commonly) used. The Proper Preface is inserted bet. the Thanksgiving and the Ascription; it is called "proper" because it varies with the seasons of the ch. year, with the one that is proper for the occasion used in a given service. In the Gallican liturgy, the preface is of the nature of an attestation and is called *Contestation.*

Prefect Apostolic. In RCm, a prelate with ordinary jurisdiction over a miss. territory.

Preger, Johann Wilhelm (1827–96). Luth. theol.; b. Schweinfurt, Bav., Ger.; educ. Erlangen and Berlin; active in various capacities in Munich. Issued an ed. of M. Luther's 1531–32 Table Talk. Other works include a life of M. Flacius Illyricus; a hist. of Ger. mysticism in the Middle Ages.

Prelate. High ranking ch. official.

Pre-Lent. See *Church Year,* 3.

Prelude (Lat. *praeludium;* Ger. *Vorspiel*). Musical composition used in a worship service to introd. the service itself and/or hymn singing. Should be in the spirit of the occasion for which it is used. The chorale preludes of the Luth. masters of the 17th and 18th cents. are among the finest organ music extant.

Premillenarians. See *Millennium,* 7.

Premonstratensians (Norbertines; Canons Regular of Prémontré; in England also called White Canons). Order founded 1120 at Prémontré, near, Laon, Fr., by Norbert*; objects include personal holiness and preaching. Various factors, including secularization, plagues, the Reformation, and the Fr. Revolution, helped keep the order small, but it has grown measurably, esp. in Belg., and is represented in the US with a coll. at West De Pere, Wis.

Prenter, Regin. See *Dogmatics,* B 11.

Pre-Raphaelite Brotherhood. Brotherhood of artists including W. H. Hunt,* J. E. Millais,* D. G. Rossetti*; formed 1848 in Eng. to restore in painting and promote in criticism the principles and practices that marked It. art before Raphael.*

Presanctified, Liturgy of the. See *Divine Liturgy.*

Presbyter. See *Elders; Polity, Ecclesiastical,* 7.

Presbyterian. For distinction bet. "Presb." and "Ref." see *Reformed Churches,* 1.

Presbyterian Church in the United States of America, The. See *Presbyterian Churches,* 4 a.

Presbyterian Church in the United States of America, The Board of Foreign Missions of the. Committee of the Gen. Assem. of the Presb. Ch. that traced its hist. to a "Bd. of Correspondents" est. 1741 in N. Y. by the Soc. in Scot. for Propagating Christian Knowledge (see *Bible Societies,* 3) to work among Am. Indians. The work of the Bd. of Correspondents was largely abandoned ca. 1781 after the death of J. Brainerd.* The N. Y. Miss. Soc. (indep.) was est. 1796 to resume the work. It was succeeded 1797–ca. 1800 by the Northern Miss. Soc. The Gen. Assem. of the Presb. Ch. carried on the work ca. 1800–18. The United For. Miss. Soc., active 1818–1826, transferred its work to the ABCFM. The Western For. Miss. Soc., formed 1831, was replaced 1837 by a Bd. of For. Missions, which was in turn discontinued 1958, when the Commission on Ecumenical Mission and Relations, Inc., of the United* Presb. Ch. in the USA was est.

Presbyterian Churches. Presbyterians helped perpetuate the doctrinal and governmental features that J. Calvin* emphasized. See also *Polity, Ecclesiastical,* 7.

1. *Presbyterianism in Scotland.* Calvin's doctrinal and ecclesiastical system was brought to Scot. by J. Knox.* The Reformation had found early root in Scot. See *Hamilton, Patrick.* The martyrdom of G. Wishart* was avenged by assassination of D. Beaton.* RCs sought help from France, Prots. from England. The assassins and others, including Knox, were captured and taken to Fr.

1560 saw the consolidation, nat. recognition, and est. of the Ref. Church. The Scotch Confession of Faith was ratified August. The 1st Gen. Assem. met December. The 1st *Book of Discipline* was drafted 1560, signed by some nobles 1561 (see *Discipline, Books of,* 1). The govt. of the ch. was vested in supts., ministers, doctors, elders, and deacons. Communion was to be celebrated 4 times a yr. In towns there were to be daily services. Marriages were to be performed "in open face and public audience of the Kirk." *The Book of Common Order* (drawn up 1556 by Knox for the Eng. Prot. congs. in Geneva and also known as "The Order of Geneva" and "John Knox's Liturgy") was appointed for use in Scot. by the Gen. Assem. 1562, rev. and enl. 1564 and was in gen., but not exclusive, use for ca. 80 yrs. The Reformation in Scot. was effected by presbyters, and the govt. of the ch. naturally became Presb. The ch. was est. by Parliament 1567. The Scotch Confession of Faith was superseded 1647 by the Westminster Confession (see *Presbyterian Confessions,* 3, 4).

The 1st formal division arose 1688, when the Cameronians,* dissatisfied with the compromising spirit of the ch., refused to concur in the Revolution settlement and remained an isolated body till 1876, when they joined the Free Ch. (see next par.). Next came 2 secessions that eventually coalesced in the United Presb. Church. E. Erskine* led a secession 1733. The seceders divided into Burghers and Antiburghers 1747 over the question of taking the Burgess oath: "I profess and allow with my heart the true religion presently professed within this realm and authorized by the Laws thereof; I shall abide thereat and defend the same to my life's end, renouncing the Roman religion called Papistry." The Burghers were known as the Associate Syn. (later called Associate Presbytery), the Antiburghers as the Gen. Associate Syn. Both Burghers and Antiburghers threw off small minorities of Auld Lichts (see New Lichts). The Auld Licht Burghers returned to the Est. Ch. shortly before the 1843 Disruption, when they left it again; most Auld Licht Antiburghers joined the Free Ch. 1852, the rest remained separate. Burghers and Antiburghers reunited 1820 to form the United* Secession Ch. This ch. was known for for. miss. enthusiasm. The next secession was the Relief* Ch., which began with T. Gillespie* and was known for its liberal spirit. The Relief Ch. and the United Secession Ch. joined to form the United Presb. Ch. 1847.

The Free* Ch. of Scot., largest and most influential, came into being on a nat. scale 1843. Those who left (or "came out" of) the Est. Ch. in what is called The Disruption claimed to be the true Ch. of Scot. and made their organization indep. of the state, holding that the spiritual liberty and indep. of the ch. were at stake.

The Free Ch. of Scot. and the United Presb. Ch. united 1900 to form the United Free Ch. of Scot., which united with the Est. Ch. of Scot. 1929.

Other indep. chs. were organized: *Free Presb. Ch. of Scot.* (formed 1893 as Free Ch. Presbytery of Scot., in reaction against the 1892 Declaratory* Act; name changed later to avoid legal complications), *Ref. Presb. Ch.* (see also *Macmillan, John*), legitimate descendant and representative of the Covenanted Ch. of Scot. in its period of greatest purity 1638–49 (see also *Covenanters*), and *United Original Secession Ch.,* dated from 1733 and Erskine (see above).

See also *Scotland, Reformation in,* 1–3.

2. *Presbyterian Ch. of Eng.* Under oppression, a considerable number of persons left the Est. Ch.

and held services acc. to the Presb. order. Others still in the ch., who were likeminded, held conferences or "ministers' meetings," one of which in London 1572 deputed 2 mems. to visit nearby Wandsworth and organize a Particular Ch. in acc. with Presb. order, the 1st open formation in Eng. of a ch. different from the Est. Church. W. Laud* took severe measures against nonconformists.* Tension developed bet. the king, who held to the Est. Ch., and Parliament. Presbs. felt driven to join the parliamentarians. Subsequent alliance of Parliament with the Scot. army, and decisions of the 1647 Westminster Assem., resulted in replacement of the episc. form in the Est. Ch. by presbytery. The Westminster Assem. drew up a *Directory for the Pub. Worship of God* 1643 and the *Westminster Confession*. The *Directory of Church Government*, an Eng. tr. of a Lat. work by W. Travers,* was circulated in support of the presb. system.

The Establishment was now Presb., but Presb. polity was accepted largely only in London and Lancashire. O. Cromwell* replaced presbytery by independency. The 1662 Act of Uniformity required (1) every minister not episcopally ordained to be reordained; (2) adherence to everything in the Book* of Common Prayer; (3) obedience to the ordinary (bp.); (4) abjuration of the Solemn League* and Covenant; (5) an oath declaring it unlawful to take up arms against the king. Many clerics refused obedience and left their charge. The Conventicle Act (passed 1664, modified and reenacted 1670) made it practically impossible for them to preach to any sizeable group; the Five Mile Act of 1665 was designed to keep them away from centers of population. The Revolution of 1688 brought in its wake the "Happy Union" arrangement of 1691, acc. to which all branches of nonconformity acted as practically a single community with little authority or doctrinal clarity. See also *Puritans; United Church of Christ*, I A 1.

Many nonconformist groups had provided chapels. In course of time nearly all these groups joined Scotch Presb. congs. that formed in London and elsewhere, but had no official connection with the Scottish gen. assem. By 1772 the ministers of the 7 such congs. in London formed The Scots Presbytery of London. It claimed "communion" with the Ch. of Scot., but had no ecclesiastical connection with it and was little more than a "ministers' meeting." In 1836 it changed name to The London Presbytery in Communion with the Ch. of Scot. In 1839 the Scottish Assem. counseled it to organize as The Presb. Syn. in Eng. The 1843 Disruption (see 1) divided also The Presb. Syn. in Eng. The majority sided with the Free Ch. of Scot. and kept the name Presb. Syn. in Eng.; the minority stayed with the Est. Ch. of Scot. and formed The Scottish Presbytery in London in Connection with the Ch. of Scot. In 1850 this presbytery and 2 others formed The Syn. of the Ch. of Scot. in Eng. In 1863 the United Presb. Ch. in Scot. (see 1) formed its congs. in Eng. into the Eng. Syn. In 1876 this syn. united with the Presb. Syn. in Eng. to form the Presb. Ch. of Eng.

3. *Presb. Ch. in Ireland.* When Ulster was extensively colonized by Scot. and Eng. Prot. settlers under James* I, beginning 1610, Presbs. gained a permanent footing in Ireland. Presb. ministers began to come from Scot. 1613 and for a time they were appointed without reordination to vacant charges in the Est. Ch. In 1641 there was a rebellion in Ireland; perhaps ca. 30,000 Prots. were massacred. In 1642 a Scot. army was sent to quell the rebellion; each regiment had a chaplain and a regular kirk session selected from the officers; the 1st presbytery consisted of 5 chaplains and 4 elders. Ministers came from Scot.; new presbyteries were formed; at the time of O. Cromwell* there was a gen. syn. with 80 congs. and 70 ministers. In 1661, 64 ministers were dismissed for nonconforming; many Presbs. went to Am.

William III (1650–1702; king of Eng., Scot., Ireland 1689–1702) authorized a payment to the Presb. ministers of Ireland in recognition of the loyal support of Presbs. on his arrival in Ireland 1690. This was the beginning of the Irish *regium donum* (Lat. "royal gift"), later increased, and paid almost continuously till the disestablishment of the Irish Ch. 1869. Toward the end of the 1st half of the 18th c. some ministers were influenced by modernism. A cong. of seceders formed 1741; in time there came to be a Secession Syn. as well as a Syn. of Ulster. Ministers of secession congs. also received a *regium donum.* Arian views of some Syn. of Ulster ministers ca. 1825 led to reaction in which the Syn. of Ulster, by overwhelming majority, declared in favor of the doctrine of the Trin. In 1829 seventeen ministers withdrew from the syn. and later formed The Remonstrant Syn. of Ulster. In 1840 the Syn. of Ulster and most of the Secession Syn. united to form the Gen. Assem. of the Presb. Ch. in Ireland.

There were Presbs. in S Ireland before 1610. Presbs. in S Ireland outside the Syn. of Ulster and the Secession Syn. belonged to the Southern Assoc., which became the Syn. of Munster 1809. In 1840 the orthodox mems. of this syn. withdrew and formed the Presbytery of Munster, which joined the Gen. Assem. of the Presb. Ch. in Ireland 1854.

The Ref. Presb. or Covenanting Ch. of Ireland traces its origin to the Covenanters* of Scot. ("Society people"), who had fled persecution and settled in the NE part of the island. A presbytery was organized 1792, a syn. 1811. In 1840 a number of ministers and congs. withdrew as a result of controversy about the power of the civil ruler. Some of the congs. returned, others joined the Presb. Ch. of Ireland. Standards: the Westminster Confession and Catechisms, together with the *Testimony,* which sets forth the church's distinctive position.

Some seceders did not enter the Gen. Assem. of the Presb. Ch. in Ireland 1840 but formed the Associate Syn. of Ireland or the Presb. Syn. of Ireland distinguished by the name Seceder.

4. *Presbyterianism in Am.* Presbs. in the US number more than 4,000,000; most are of Eng. extraction.

a. *The United Presb. Ch. in the USA* was formed 1958 by merger of *The Presb. Ch. in the USA* ("Northern Presbs.") and *The United Presb. Ch. of N. Am.*

The Presb. Ch. in the USA traces its hist. to colonial days. The 1st presbytery was organized 1706 Philadelphia, Pa. In New Eng., Presbyterianism yielded to Congregationalism. The Great* Awakening deeply affected Presb. ch. life. G. Tennent* and W. Tennent,* leaders of the progressive or New Side party (Syn. of N. Y.), endorsed the revival system of G. Whitefield* and held that only such should be admitted to the ministry as had "experienced" conversion. W. Tennent est. a "log coll." 1782 in a log house on his estate at Neshaminy, Bucks Co., Pa., near Philadelphia, to train candidates whose chief requisite was a religious "experience"; the coll. was a predecessor of Princeton (N. J.) U. The conservative or Old Side party (Syn. of Philadelphia) held that Calvinism was theol. opposed to revivalism and that only coll.-bred men should become ministers. The 2 parties reunited 1758.

In the 1st part of the 19th c. the Presb. Ch. and the Cong. assocs. of New Eng. operated under the Plan of Union (based on 1801–10 agreements bet. the gen. assem. and the assocs. of Conn. and other states), which allowed Cong. ministers to serve Presb. congs. and vice versa. The Plan of Union was abandoned 1837 largely as a result of conservative or Old School party pressure against interdenom. miss. agencies. Progressive or New School party leaders included A. Barnes.*

The New School took a stand against slavery 1850. In 1857 some of its syns. and presbyteries (ca. 15,000 communicant mems.) in the south withdrew; in 1858 they organized the United Syn. of the Presb. Ch. In 1861 southern presbyteries withdrew from the Old School and formed the Gen. Assem. of the Presb. Ch. in the Confederate States of Am. In the 1860s this Gen. Assem., the United Syn., and the Indep. Presb. Ch. of S. C. united and adopted the name Gen. Assem. of the Presb. Ch. in the US (later known as Presb. Ch. in the US; see also c); other bodies joined it 1867–74. This is the so-called Southern Presbyterian group.

The United Presb. Ch. of N. Am. was formed 1858 by union of the Assoc. Ref. Presb. Ch. and the Assoc. Presb. Ch. See also *Associate Reformed Church.*

Towards the end of the 19th c. liberalism began to affect Presbyterianism. The confessions were revised to bring the doctrine of God's decree into harmony with His universal grace. The Welsh Calvinistic Meth. Ch. (Presb. in polity) united with the Presb. Ch. in the USA 1920. See also *Auburn Affirmation; Briggs, Charles Augustus; Coffin, Henry Sloane; Union Movements,* 7.

b. *Cumberland Presb. Ch.* Organized 1810 Dickson Co., Tenn., as a result of the Ky. Revival at the close of the 18th c. led by James McGready (ca. 1758–1817) and in opposition to indifferentism, fatalism, and formalism. Its Confession of Faith and Discipline is a modified version of the Westminster Confession and Catechisms (see *Presbyterian Confessions,* 3, 4). Operates Memphis (Tenn.) Theol. Sem. and Bethel Coll., McKenzie, Tenn. Membership more than 90,000.

In 1869 the gen. assem. approved est. of a separate organization for Negro chs. called Colored Cumberland Presb. Ch. In 1940 the latter group received a Presbytery in Liberia, Afr., into membership and changed name to Cumberland Presb. Ch. in the US and Afr. In the mid-1960s the name was changed to 2d Cumberland Presb. Ch. in US and connection with the Liberia Presbytery severed. 1949 membership ca. 30,000.

c. *Presb. Ch. in the US* (Southern Presbyterians). Beginning traced to 1861 (see a). Theologically more conservative than Northern Presbs., though in 1939 the Gen. Assem. deleted from the Westminster Confession the par. on the decree of election and the par. in which the pope is called the Antichrist.

d. *The Orthodox Presb. Ch.* (called Presb. Ch. of Am. 1936–39). Founded 1936 by J. G. Machen* and followers, who opposed modernism in the Northern Presb. Ch. (see a), were suspended for insubordination, and withdrew.

e. *Bible Presb. Ch.* Founded by men suspended with Machen (see d) but who were more rigid on abstinence and premillennialism. Name changed 1961 to Ev. Presb. Church. United 1965 with Ref. Presb. Ch. in N. Am. (Gen. Syn.) to form the Ref. Presb. Ch., Ev. Syn.

f. Scotch Presbs. are often called Covenanters.* Many regarded convenanting as both pol. and religious in function: a pub. testimony to one's belief that the Bible must be followed also in soc. relations. Covenanters observe Sun. and the NT Sabbath, practice close Communion, do not take part in affairs of a govt. that does not recognize the Triune God, and do not permit membership in secret socs. Some Covenanters oppose singing hymns not in the Bible. Scotch Presbs. are conservatively Calvinistic and champion the inerrancy of the Bible. Representatives in Am. include Ref. Presb. Ch. of N. Am.; Assoc. Ref. Presb. Ch. (Gen. Syn.).

g. *Ref. Presb. Ch., Ev. Syn.* See e.

h. *Associate Ref. Presb. Ch. (Gen. Syn.).* A syn. (Gen. Syn. from 1935) of the former Associate Ref. Presb. Ch. (the latter helped form The United Presb. Ch. of N. Am. 1858; see *Associate Reformed Church*); result of realignments among Covenanters.

i. 2d Cumberland Presb. Ch. in US. See b.

Presbyterian Confessions. 1. Early Prot. statements in Scot. took the form of "covenants." In 1557 a number of Prot. nobles and gentlemen signed a covenant at Edinburgh to maintain, nourish, and defend to the death "the whole Congregation of Christ and every member thereof." Early covenants opposed RCm (e. g., the Nat. Covenant, subscribed by James* I [James VI of Scot.] 1581; also called 2d Scotch Confession, King's Confession, and Negative Confession; endorsed the 1560 Scotch Confession of Faith [see 2]), later ones opposed episcopacy. The 1638 Nat. Covenant repeats the 1581 Nat. Covenant and adds statements against bps. and royal measures that "do sensibly tend to the re-establishment of the Popish religion and tyranny, and to the subversion and ruin of the true Reformed religion, and of our liberties, laws, and estates." The 1643 Solemn League* and Covenant (see also *Covenanters*) was used by Puritans in an attempt to force Presbyterianism on the Est. Ch. of Eng. as a reward to Scots for help against Charles I (1600–49; son of James I of Eng. [James VI of Scot.]; father of Charles II [see *Roman Catholic Church,* D 9]; king of Gt. Brit. and Ireland 1625–49; tried unsuccessfully to impose episcopacy).

2. The 1560 Scotch Confession of Faith *(Confessio fidei Scoticana I),* decidedly Calvinistic, was drawn up by J. Knox* and associates and ratified by the 3 estates. It holds that the ch. is one from the beginning to the end of the world and exists where the Gospel is preached, the sacraments administered, and discipline exercised.

3. Westminster Confession 1647. The Long Parliament (1640–60) in 1643 called for an assem. at Westminster beginning July 1, 1643, to draw up arts. for the Ch. of Eng. to bring it into more agreement with the Ch. of Scot. and the Ref. Chs. on the Continent. The 121 clerical mems. of the assem. included 9 Episcopalians, who seldom attended; a few Independents and Erastians (see *Erastianism*), who withdrew before final adoption of the Book of Discipline; Presbs. formed the great majority. There were also 30 lay assessors. And 5 clerical and 3 lay Scotch commissioners came in after adoption of the Solemn League* and Covenant.

Documents drawn up by the Assem. include "Propositions Concerning Church Government and Ordination of Ministers," which led to adoption of the Presb. form of govt.; "Directory for the Public Worship of God"; "Larger Catechism"; "Shorter Catechism"; Westminster Confession of Faith.

The Apostles' Creed is omitted from the Larger Catechism and annexed to the Smaller Catechism with the note: "not as though it were composed by the Apostles, or ought to be esteemed Canonical Scripture"; at "He descended into hell" the footnote is added: "i. e., Continued in the state of the dead, and under the power of death, until the third day." The Shorter Catechism begins: "*Question.* 1. What is the chief end of man? *Answer.* Man's chief end is to glorify God, and to enjoy Him forever."

The Westminster Confession presents mature Calvinism. It starts from God's sovereignty and justice and makes the predestinarian scheme control the historical and Christological scheme. Chap. III, iii–vii: "By the decree of God, for the manifestation of his glory, some men and angels are predestinated unto everlasting life, and others foreordained to everlasting death . . . to the praise of his glorious grace . . . [and] justice." VII, ii–vi: "The first covenant made [by God] with man was a covenant of works, wherein life was promised to Adam, and in him to his posterity, upon condition of perfect and personal obedience. iii. Man by his fall having made himself incapable of life by that covenant, the Lord was pleased to make a second, commonly called the covenant of grace. . . . v. This covenant was differently administered in the time of the Law [OT] and in the time of the Gospel [NT]. . . . There are not, therefore, two covenants of grace differing in substance, but one and the same under various dispensations." See also *Federal Theology.* XVII, i: "They whom God hath accepted in His Beloved, effectually called and sanctified by His Spirit, can neither totally nor finally fall away from the state of grace; but shall certainly persevere therein to the end, and be eternally saved." XXI, vii–viii: ". . . [God] hath particularly appointed one day in seven for a Sabbath, to be kept holy unto Him: which, from the beginning of the world to the resurrection of Christ, was the last day of the week; and, from the resurrection of Christ, was changed into the first day of the week . . . viii. This Sabbath is then kept holy unto the Lord, when men, after a due preparing of their hearts, and ordering of their common affairs beforehand, do not only observe an holy rest all the day from their own works, words, and thoughts, about their worldly employments and recreations; but also are taken up the whole time in the public and private exercises of His worship, and in the duties of necessity and mercy." XXIII, iii: "The civil magistrate may not assume to himself the administration of the Word and Sacraments, or the power of the keys of the kingdom of heaven: yet he hath authority, and it is his duty to take order, that unity and peace be preserved in the Church, that the truth of God be kept pure and entire, that all blasphemies and heresies be suppressed, all corruptions and abuses in worship and discipline prevented or reformed, and all the ordinances of God duly settled, administered, and observed." XXIX, vii–viii: "Worthy receivers, outwardly partaking of the visible elements in this sacrament, do then also inwardly by faith, really and indeed, yet not carnally and corporally, but spiritually, receive and feed upon Christ crucified, and all benefits of His death . . . viii. Although ignorant and wicked men receive the outward elements in this sacrament, yet they receive not the thing signified thereby. . . ."

4. In 1659 the Westminster Confession (except chaps. 30–31) was endorsed again by the Long Parliament but was set aside when episcopacy was restored 1660 with the 39 Arts. (see *Anglican Confessions,* 6) and the Book* of Common Prayer. In Scot. the Gen. Assem. ratified the Westminster Confession 1647 (see *Presbyterian Churches,* 1) and required all ministers and probationers of the Gospel with license to preach, and all ruling elders to subscribe to it without amendment 1690, 1699, 1700, 1704, etc. This remained law in the chs. of Scot. till the 1879 Declaratory* Act modified some of the extreme Calvinistic statements; the Free Ch. adopted a similar Declaratory Act 1892 (see also *Presbyterian Churches,* 1). In 1890 the Eng. Presb. Ch. adopted The Articles of the Faith, 24 in number, which emphasize the love of God. In 1892 the Eng. Presb. Ch. decided that acceptance of the Westminster standards by office-bearers should be modified by reference to these 24 arts. The Savoy Declaration 1658 included a revision of the Westminster Confession (see also *Democratic Declarations of Faith,* 2). The 2d London Confession of Eng. Baps. 1677 was based on the Westminster Confession (see also *Democratic Declarations of Faith,* 3).

5. Presbs. in Am. adhered in a gen. way to the Westminster Confession and Catechisms in accord with the 1729 Adopting Act. In 1967 The United Presb. Ch. in the USA (see *Presbyterian Churches,* 4 a) adopted a Book of Confessions that includes the Apostles' Creed, Nicene Creed, Westminster Confession, and Confession of 1967 (irenic). EL

See also *Scotland, Reformation in,* 1.

P. Schaff, *The Creeds of Christendom,* 3 vols., rev. and enl. (New York, c1919); *Creeds of the Churches,* ed. J. H. Leith (Chicago, 1963); *The Faith of Christendom,* ed. B. A. Gerrish (Cleveland, Ohio, 1963); *Reformed Confessions of the 16th Century,* ed. A. C. Cochrane (Philadelphia, 1966); J. A. Hardon, *The Spirit and Origins of American Protestantism: A Source Book in Its Creeds* (Dayton, Ohio, 1968).

Presbyterian Synod in England. See *Presbyterian Churches,* 2.

Presbyterian System. See *Polity, Ecclesiastical,* 7.

Presbyterian Youth Fellowship. See *Young People's Organizations, Christian,* III, 5.

Presbyterorum ordinis. See *Vatican Councils,* 2.

Presbytery. Body of presbyters (see *Elders; Polity, Ecclesiastical,* 7). The word occurs 1 Ti 4:14. In Presb. polity: the ministers of a region and elders representing the chs., with authority over chs. and ministers, under the superior judicatories. See also *Reformed Churches,* 1.

Preschool Education. See *Parish Education,* B.

Prescience, Divine. An attribute of God; also called foreknowledge; beholds all things as if present; comprehends all events, however contingent on human activity or freedom (Is 48:8; Mt 24:36; Jn 21:17; 1 Jn 3:20). God knows the acts of men as acts of rational and responsible beings who have a will of their own and act acc. to the counsels of their hearts; thus the foreknowledge of God includes the agency of the human will and the causality of human counsels. "God's foreknowledge of His own acts, especially of the rulings of His providence . . . includes the prayers of His children, which He in His counsel has answered before they were uttered (Is 65:24), permitting them to enter as a powerful factor (Ja 5:16-18) into the government of the universe (Ps 33:10-22; 145:13-19)" (A. L. Graebner, in "Theology," *TQ,* II [1898], 139).

Presence, Divine. See *Holy Spirit.*

Presentation of Our Lord. See *Church Year,* 13, 16.

Presentation of the Augsburg Confession. See *Church Year,* 17.

Preservation of the World. See *Providence.*

Presiding Elder. In the Meth. Ch., an elder appointed by a bp. as dist. supt.

Press, Religious. See *Publication Houses, Lutheran; Religious Press.*

Pressensé, Edmond Dehault de (Dehaut; 1824–91). B. Paris, Fr.; educ. Lausanne, Halle, and Berlin; influenced esp. by A. R. Vinet*; pastor of an ev. free ch. cong. Paris. Founded and ed. *Revue chretienne;* other works include a life of Christ and a hist. of the Christian ch. in the 1st 3 cents.

Pressius, Paul. See *Reformed Confessions,* E 4.

Preston, John (1587–1628). B. Upper Heyford, Northamptonshire, Eng.; educ. Cambridge; won for Puritanism by J. Cotton*; befriended by L. Andrewes*; court preacher to crown prince Charles (who became Charles I; see *Presbyterian Confessions,* I) 1620.

Preterition (from Lat. for "pass by"). Doctrine of election held by Calvinists, acc. to which God "passed by" a portion of mankind and retained it to dishonor and wrath. 1647 Westminster Confession of Faith (see *Presbyterian Confessions,* 3, 4), III, vii: "The rest of mankind God was pleased, according to the unsearchable counsel of His will, whereby He extendeth or withholdeth mercy as He pleaseth, for the glory of His sovereign power over His creatures, to pass by [Lat. *praeterire*], and to ordain them to dishonor and wrath for their sin, to the praise of His glorious justice." See also *Double Predestination; Predestinarian Controversy.*

Preternatural. Existing outside of nature or beyond nature; unnatural.

Pretheological Schools. See *Ministry, Education of,* VII.

Preus, Adolph Carl (1814–78). B. Norw.; educ. Christiania (Oslo) U.; asst. pastor Gjerpen 1848; to Am. 1850. Pastor Koshkonong Prairie, Wis., 1850–60; Chicago, Ill., 1860–63; Coon Prairie, Wis., 1863–72. Pres. The Norw. Ev. Luth. Ch. in Am. 1853–62 (see *Evangelical Lutheran Church, The,* 8); returned to Norw. 1872; pastor Holt and Tvedestrand; dean East Nedenäs.

Preus, Christian Keyser (1852–1921). Son of H. A. Preus*; educ. Luther Coll., Decorah, Iowa, and Conc. Sem., St. Louis, Mo.; pastor; involved in predestination controversy (see *Evangelical Lutheran Church, The,* 10); prof. Luther Coll. (its pres. 1902–21). See also *Madison Settlement.*

Preus, Herman Amberg (June 16, 1825–July 2, 1894). Father of C. K. Preus*; b. Kristiansand (Christiansand), Norw.; educ. Christiania (Oslo) U.; to Am. 1851; served Luths. in Wis.; helped organize The Norw. Ev. Luth. Ch. in Am. (see *Evangelical Lutheran Church, The,* 8) and was its pres. 1862–94; pres. Synodical* Conf. 1876–77; proposed Negro and Am. Indian miss. 1877. Coed. *Maanedstidende* 1859–68.

Preuschen, Erwin Friedrich Wilhelm Ferdinand (1867–1920). B. Lissberg, near Frankfurt am Main, Ger.; educ. Giessen; held various pastorates in Hesse-Darmstadt; teacher in a Gymnasium at Darmstadt 1897–1907; prof. Darmstadt 1907; noted for work on NT canon and text in early Christianity. Founded and ed. *Zeitschrift für die neutestamentliche Wissenschaft.* Other works include *Analekta: kürzere Texte zur Geschichte der alten Kirche und des Kanons; Vollständiges Griechisch-Deutsches Handwörterbuch zu den Schriften des Neuen Testaments und der übrigen urchristlichen Literatur.* See also *Lexicons,* B.

Preuss, Friedrich Reinhold Eduard (July 10, 1834–July 17, 1904). B. Königsberg, Prussia; educ. Königsberg; tutor Lichterfelde; prof. Berlin till 1868; prof. Conc. Sem., St. Louis, Mo., 1869–71; RC (bap. Jan. 22, 1872). Edited M. Chemnitz, *Examen Concilii Tridentini; Amerika* (RC). Other works include *Die Römische Lehre von der unbefleckten Empfängniss, aus den Quellen dargestellt und aus Gottes Wort widerlegt; Die Rechtfertigung des Sünders vor Gott; Zum Lobe der unbefleckten Empfängniss der Allerseligsten Jungfrau* (a recantation); *Die Zeitrechnung der Septuaginta vor dem vierten Jahr Salomo's.*

Preuss, Hans (1876–1951). B. Leipzig; educ. Leipzig and Halle; prof. Erlangen. Works include *Das Bild Christi im Wandel der Zeiten; Die Entwicklung des Schriftprinzips bei Luther bis zur Leipziger Disputation; Martin Luther: Der Künstler; Von den Katakomben bis zu den Zeichen der Zeit.*

Prevenient Grace. See *Grace.*

Preyer, Wilhelm Thierry. See *Psychology,* G 4.

Pride. Inordinate self-esteem; considered one of the 7 deadly sins (see *Sins, Venial and Mortal*); represented in the Bible as a vice (Pr 16:18; 21:4; 29:23; 1 Ptr 5:5; 1 Jn 2:16); may manifest itself (1) with respect to God, as spiritual arrogance and self-assertion or self-righteousness (Mt 23:5-12; Lk 18:11-12; Rv 3:17), (2) with respect to other people, as haughtiness, feeling of superiority, boasting, vainglory (Jb 12:2; Ps 101:5; Pr 14:21; Jer 9:23). God will punish the proud (Dt 8:11-20; Pr 8:13; Jn 5:44; Ja 4:6).

Prierias, Silvester (Sylvester; originally Maz[z]olini; de Prierio; ca. 1456–1523). B. Prierio, Asti province, 40 mi. W of Genoa, near Montferrat, SE Piedmont, N It.; Dominican; Thomist; taught at Bologna and Venice; vicar gen. Lombardy 1508–10; prior Cremona; prof. theol. Gymnasium Romanum 1514; *magister sacri palatii* 1515. Works include *Dialogus* (against M. Luther).

Priest (derived ultimately from Gk. *presbyteros,* "elder"). Title of ordained or authorized religious functionary who performs mediatorial, interpretative, ministerial, sacrificial, and ritualistic functions. Sometimes used as a synonym for pastor. Designation for a mem. of the clergy in RC, Angl., Scand. Luth., E Orthodox, and some other chs. See also *Hierarchy; Priesthood; Western Christianity 500–1500,* 9.

Priest, Christ as. The priestly office of Christ is the heart of the Christian faith. This topic takes us back to the climax of OT worship and the silence of the multitude in the moment of reconciliation with God through the hands of a mediator.

In Heb. conceptions the priest was the representative of the people (Heb 5:1). Christ was given by God to be man's representative (Heb 2:14-17).

The priestly work of Christ was foretold and foreshadowed in OT prophecy and types (Ps 110:1, 4; the whole OT priestly cult pointed forward to Christ). OT priests and sacrifices were imperfect, but Christ, His work, and His sacrifice were perfect (Heb 9:11-14; 1 Ptr 1:18-19).

The active obedience of Christ consists in His substitutionary work of freeing us from the demands of the Law and obtaining perfect righteousness for us by perfectly fulfilling, as our Substitute, the entire Law in all its demands, so that His righteousness may be made our own by faith (Mt 5:17; Ro 10:4; Gl 4:4-5). His passive obedience consists in His substitutionary work of freeing us from the penalties provided by the Law for all sinners; He did this by taking our sins on Himself and suffering our punishment in our stead (Is 53; Gl 3:13; Eph 5:2; Cl 1:14; 1 Ptr 2:21-24; 1 Jn 1:7).

Christ's priesthood continued after His ascension (Heb 7:24; 8); He continues to intercede for us as our High Priest (Ro 8:34; Heb 7:25; 1 Jn 2:1-2).

O. C. J. Hoffmann, in "Office, or Work, of Christ," *The Abiding Word,* II, ed. T. Laetsch (St. Louis, 1947), 135–144.

Priesthood. There is no need of a NT priesthood to offer sacrifice for sin as did the OT priesthood (Heb 7:20-28; Heb 10:8-14). All believers constitute a universal spiritual priesthood (Eph 2:14, 18; Heb 10:19-22; 1 Ptr 2:9; Rv 1:6; 5:10), which is to offer itself to God (Ro 12:1; Heb 13:15) and into whose charge Christ has given all rights and powers of His kingdom (Mt 18:18-20; 1 Co 3:21-23). To all believers belongs the right to select and call ministers (Acts 1:15-26; 6:1-6), whom God has chosen and appointed (Acts 13:2-4; 1 Co 12:28; Eph 4:11-12), and to set them apart through ordination (Acts 14:23) to be servants of Christ and His ch. (2 Co 4:5) in preaching the Word and administering the sacraments (1 Co 4:1; 2 Ti 4:2; Tts 1:9). See also *Keys, Office of the.*

L. W. Spitz, "The Universal Priesthood of Believers," *The Abiding Word,* I, ed. T. Laetsch (St. Louis, 1946), 321–341.

Priestley, Joseph (1733–1804). Cleric; scientist; b. Fieldhead, near Leeds, Yorkshire, Eng.; studied for Presb. ministry at Daventry Academy; became a dissenting minister at 22; opposed positive Christian doctrines; Unitarian; to Am. 1794; organized several Unitarian congs. See also *Unitarianism.*

Priestly Writer. See *Higher Criticism,* 7–13.

Prima delineatio apologiae. See *Lutheran Confessions,* A 3.

Primacy of the Pope. See *Vatican Councils,* 1 b.

Primasius (d. ca. the middle of the 6th c.). Bp. Hadrumetum, N Afr. Works include a commentary on Rv.

MPL, 68, 407–936.

Primate. See Hierarchy.

Prime (from Lat. *prima* [*hora*], "1st hour"). 1. Religious office constituting the 1st of the daytime canonical hours.* 2. See *Sunday Letter.*

Primer. See *Anglican Confessions,* 9.

Primitive Baptists. See *Baptist Churches,* 11–12.

Primitive Methodist Church, U. S. A. See *Methodist Churches,* 4 b.

Primitive Methodists (Eng.). See *Methodist Churches,* 1.

Primitive Religion. Both words, "primitive" and "religion," have been variously interpreted. "Primitive culture" was gen. regarded in the 19th c. as referring to 1st stages of an evolutionary development. Some used the term to include such advanced people as Chinese who were not in the Indo-Eur. development.

Many studies have been made of the mentality of primitive people; conclusions range from views that regard primitives mentally retarded and wholly superstitious to views that regard primitive ratiocinations as parallel to those of civilized peoples. Esp. after 1950 have scholars emphasized that values, ideas, judgments, and actions of "civilized peoples" are often as irrational as those of primitives.

Definitions and descriptions of religion vary. Edward Burnett Tylor (1832–1917; Eng. anthropologist) defined religion as "the belief in spiritual beings" (*Primitive Culture,* I, 383). Scholars soon pointed out that he excluded magic and religious actions. J. G. Frazer* described religion as a propitiation or conciliation of powers superior to man that are believed to direct and control the course of nature and human life. Some despair of precise definitions and describe magico-religious phenomena as the whole area of the sacred.

Attempts to explain the origin of religion may be classified as psychol. and sociological. Psychol. explanations include the theory of Charles de Brosses (1709–77; b. Dijon, Fr.; called *le Président de Brosses* because he was pres. of the parliament of Burgundy 1740–77; scholar; works include *Du Culte des dieux fétiches*), who held that religion originated in fetishism.* Adherents of the nature-myth school (e. g., F. M. Müller*) believe that gods are personified nat. phenomena. Psychol. explanations trace the origin of religion to such experiences as dreams, visions (e.g., of ghosts), diseases, death, and to magic, ideas of luck and of power, etc. Others find the origin of religion in such feelings as awe, amazement, mystery, fear.

Sociol. theories trace the origin of religion to institutions and practices of a community and hold that religion contributes to community cohesion. E. Durkheim* advanced the theory that primitive religion is a totemic clan cult. The totemic god of a clan is the clan itself divinized. Totemism,* he held, is the most elementary form of religion. The totem is symbol of the good and of society. In the totem the individual expresses his identity with the community.

L. Lévy-Bruhl* and other philosophers combined psychol. and sociol. aspects in studies of primitive mentality, holding that beings and objects are all involved in a network of mystical participations and exclusions.

Ca. the middle of the 20th c. interest in studies of primitive religion waned. Anthropologists pointed out that few writers on primitive religion had field experience; they were simply projecting rationalizations on cultures regarded as primitive; their theories could be neither proven nor disproven and were of little value to anthropologists working in the field.

Recent studies deal with phenomenological analyses and comparisons of psychol. and sociol. aspects of religion.

Terms used in the study of primitive religion include *mana* (Melanesian word designating mysterious power residing in persons because of birth, soc. status, or ability; animals such as tribal totems; inanimate things); *taboo**; *manitou* (*manitu; manito;* used by Algonquian Indians for spirits or objects that arouse awe and reverence because of their power for good or evil); *animism* (used by E. B. Tylor, *Primitive Culture,* chaps. xi–xvii, to describe gen. belief in spirit; began with belief in soul; core of religion; in opposition to Tylor, Robert Ranulph Marett [1866–1943; Eng. anthropologist; works include *The Threshold of Religion*] held that belief in animation [animatism] of nonphysiological things precede soul ideas; see also *Polytheism*); *animatism* (term coined by R. R. Marett to describe a tendency of primitives to regard and treat inanimate things, when considered sacred, as having life, feeling, will); *baraka* (Berber term for holiness of people or things; prophets and sultans have baraka); *wakan* (wakanda; wakon; wakonda; Sioux Indian term for power similar to mana believed to pervade animate and inanimate objects); *orenda* (Iroquois Indian term for power believed present in animate and inanimate objects as a kind of spiritual energy; see also *Indians, American,* 1).

Some characteristics of the primitive sacred: forbidden, mysterious, secret, potent, animate, ancient.

See also *Ancestor Worship.*

Primus. Presiding bp. in Scot. Episc. Ch.

Prince Edward Island. See *Canada,* A 27.

Principal. See *Parish Education,* K 5.

Principle, Formal. See *Formal Principle.*

Principle, Material. See *Material Principle.*

Printz, Johan Bjornsson. See *Campanius, Johan.*

Prior. Monastic official next in rank to an abbot and acting either as asst. to an abbot or as superior of a monastic house without abbot.

Prisca (Priscilla). See *Montanism.*

Priscillianists. 4th–6th c. sect with Gnostic-Manichaean tendencies in Sp. and Gaul; religious system involved dualism and emanationism; carnal pleasures and marriage forbidden. Founded by Priscillian (ca. 345–385; b. probably Mérida, Lusitania, of distinguished parents; layman; bp. Ávila ca. 380). Condemned ca. 380 by a syn. at Saragossa. Ca. 384 Priscillian was charged with heresy, sorcery, and immorality; beheaded with some followers at Trier. See also *Crosius; Popes,* 2.

Prithivi Matar. See *Brahmanism,* 2.

Pritzlaff, Fred C. (May 1, 1861–Nov. 9, 1951). B. Milwaukee, Wis.; educ. at a business coll., Valparaiso, Ind.; cofounder Lutheran* Laymen's League.

Private Confession. See *Confession.*

Private Judgment. The right of an individual Christian to decide matters pertaining to faith and morals for himself on the basis of divine revelation, to search Scripture and judge doctrine for himself, is a right that God has given and that the Christian is required to exercise (Mt 7:15; Acts 17:11; 1 Co 10:15; 1 Th 5:21; 1 Jn 4:1. WA 10 II, 180–222, 227–262; 11, 408–416). This right does not place the individual in the seat of authority, since the norm remains the Word of God (Is 8:20; Acts 17:11; 1 Ti 6:3-5; 2 Ti 3:15-17. WA 7, 429–430, 640; 12, 360–361; 24, 565. St. L. ed. 15, 1565).

Those who remove the right of private judgment (e.g., RCs, who emphasize the voice of the ch. as though it were the final criterion) prevent Christians from performing a duty imposed on them by God and enslave conscience and faith.

The right of private judgment is abused when a departure from Scripture as norm occurs or when the human mind is made judge over Scripture (Dt 4:2; Ps 19:7; 2 Co 2:17; 10:5; Eph 2:20; 1 Th 2:13;

1 Ti 6:3-5; 2 Ti 3:16-17; 2 Ptr 1:20-21; Rv 22:18-19). RGL

T. Engelder, "The Right and Wrong of Private Judgment," *CTM,* XV (1944), 217–236, 289–314, 385–402, 433–459.

Private Mass. See *Missa lecta.*

Privilegium canonis (Lat. "privilege of the canon"). In RCm, acc. to this privilege they are guilty of sacrilege who inflict a real injury on clerics and religious, including novices and mems. of socs. without vows. Cf. CIC 119.

Privilegium Paulinum *(privilegium fidei).* See *Pauline Privilege.*

Probabilism. See *Carneades.*

Probst. See *Provost.*

Probst, Jakob. See *Propst, Jakob.*

Process Philosophy. Theistic philos. that emphasizes emergent evolution, regards being as primarily relational, and rejects or criticizes nonreligious naturalism.

Procession of the Holy Spirit. The Holy Spirit proceeds from the Father and the Son (Jn 14:26; 15: 26; 20:22; Gl 4:6). This doctrine of procession is emphasized in the Confessions of the W ch. The essential nature of this procession cannot be grasped by reason. See also *Father, God the; Filioque Controversy.*

Processional. Hymn sung during a procession; also a collection of hymns for processions, or a procession itself, or the part of a service in which a procession occurs.

Processions. Processions are prominent in RCm. The clergy form a procession when they approach the altar for mass and other services, and when they return to the sacristy. Solemn pub. processions are held in certain places on Palm* Sun., Corpus* Christi, and other festivals or as an expression of thanksgiving, penitence, or honor to a dignitary. They are also held in times of calamity, or to plead for rain or fair weather, etc. Music, candles, statues, and relics may be used. Those lowest in rank march first, those highest in dignity last. Greatest magnificence in processions was reached in the Middle Ages.

Proclus (d. ca. 446/447). Abp. Cyzicus, Asia Minor, 426; patriarch Constantinople 434; noted preacher; opposed Nestorius.*

MPG, 65, 651–887.

Proclus (ca. 410–485). Gk. Neoplatonic philos.; b. Constantinople; taught at Athens, Greece, ca. 450; defended paganism; opposed Christianity. Works include *The Nature of Evil; Providence and Fate; Doubts About Providence;* a work on Platonic theol.

Procopius of Gaza (ca. 465/475–ca. 528/538). Christian sophist and rhetorician; b. Gaza; compiled catena* on OT.

Procurator. One authorized to manage the affairs of another. In RCm, a diocesan official who initiates criminal proceedings in ch. courts. As procurator of Judea, Pontius Pilate was a Roman official under the legate of Syria.

Prodicians. See *Gnosticism,* 7 j.

Professio fidei Tridentina. See *Roman Catholic Confessions,* A 2.

Profession of Monks and Nuns. The ceremony by which a novice,* having completed the novitiate, enters a religious order or cong. Cf. CIC 572–586. See also *Vows.*

Profession of the Tridentine Faith. See *Roman Catholic Confessions,* A 2.

Professional Literature. See *Literature, Lutheran,* 5.

Progressive National Baptist Convention, Inc. See *Baptist Churches,* 35.

Progressive Orthodoxy. Title of papers pub. ca. 1884–85 by the Andover (Mass.) Theol. Sem. faculty as a statement of Andover theol., which modified Calvinistic orthodoxy.

Prohászka, Ottokár (1858–1927). B. Neutra (Nitra; Nyitra), S Slovakia province, E cen. Czechoslovakia; educ. Gran (Esztergom) and Rome; prof. Gran 1882, Budapest 1904; bp. Stuhlweissenburg (Székesfehérvár) 1905. His aesthetic sermons, Scriptural discussions, and other edifying works contributed to inner Christian renewal. See also *Christian Socialism,* 3.

Prohibited Degrees (forbidden degrees). Degrees of relationship, of either consanguinity or affinity, within which marriage is forbidden by Scripture or by the state. Degrees prohibited Lv 18 and called Levitical degrees. See also *Impediments.*

Prohibition. See *Temperance Movements and the Lutheran Church.*

Prokopovich, Feofan (Theofan; Teofan; 1681–1736). B. Kiev; Russ. Orthodox theol.; bp. Pskov; abp. Novgorod; a leader in the Holy* Syn. Wrote the spiritual regulation for the reform of the Russ. ch.

Proles, Andreas (1429–1503). B. Dresden; predecessor of J. v. Staupitz*; priest 1453; prof. theol. Magdeburg; vicar of monasteries at Himmelpfort(e), Magdeburg, Dresden, Waldheim, Königsberg; reformed monasteries; praised by M. Luther for sermons.

Promissory Covenant. See *Covenant,* 2.

Promotor fidei. See *Canonization.*

Proof Passages. See *Sedes doctrinae.*

Prooimiakos (from Gk. for "opening hymn"). In E Orthodox Ch., Ps 104 chanted as a gen. introd. to evensong.

Propaedeutic, Theological. Title of a work by P. Schaff* in which he uses the term propaedeutic (from Gk. for "teach beforehand") to designate an introduction to the whole field of theol. The pl. "propaedeutics" is construed as a singular.

Propagation of the Faith, Sacred Congregation of the. See *Curia,* 2 d.

Propagation of the Gospel. See *Evangelism; Missions.*

Propagation of the Gospel in Foreign Parts, Society for the. See *Bible Societies,* 3; *Society for the Propagation of the Gospel in New England.*

Propers. Variable parts of the Communion service that are fixed as to content (hence not including sermon and hymns) but which change with the Sundays and seasons of the church* yr.: Introit,* Collect,* OT Lesson, Epistle, Gradual* (Tract,* Hallelujah,* Sequence*), and Gospel. In some rites the Offertory,* Communion, and Post-Communion are also variable. Though it does not change with every Sun. and Feast Day, the variable part of the Preface,* which changes with the seasons, is called Proper Preface. Invariable parts of the service are called the Ordinary. EFP

Prophecy. Work, vocation, or utterance of a prophet. OT Heb. words: *nabi'* (probably from a root meaning "to announce"), *ro'eh* (seer), and *chozeh* (seer). NT Gk.: *prophetes* (forth-teller). In classical Gk. thought prophecy is related to divining, but in Scripture a prophet is a divinely inspired forth-teller (1 Sm 10:6; Jer 1:2; Eze 1:1; Hos 1:1; 1 Ptr 1:11; 2 Ptr 1:21) who rebukes sin (2 Sm 12; Is 58:1; Eze 3:17; Mi 3:8), shows God's mercy (Is 40; 53), and in gen., proclaims messages of God (Ex 4:14-15; 7:1-2; Eze 11; Heb 1:1-2). He does this in assoc. with events of the past, present, and future, with constant emphasis on God's acts; hence the Messiah has a prominent place in prophecy.

Moses was the great prophet of the OT (Dt 18: 15-18; 34:10-12), Jesus Christ of the NT (Jn 1: 1-18).

The Heb. canon speaks of former prophets (Jos, Ju, 1–2 Sam, 1–2 K) and latter prophets (Is to Malachi), not with reference to time, but to the place of the books in the canon. The latter prophets include the 4 major (Is, Jer, Eze, Dn; called major because of the great range they cover and the large size of their books; Is, Jer, and Eze are each larger than all 12 minor prophets together; Dn is ca. the size of the 2 largest minor prophets, Hos and Zech, together) and the 12 minor (Hos, Jl, Am, Ob, Jon, Mi, Nah, Hab, Zeph, Hg, Zch, Ml; called minor because of the comparatively small size of their books and their much smaller spheres of activity; cf. Ecclus 49:10 [12]).

The vague and possibly misleading phrase "schools of the prophets" (not used in Scripture) came into use in reference to prophetic assocs., companies, communities, or bands or prophets with which Samuel, Elijah, and Elisha were connected (1 Sm 19:18-20; 2 K 2:1-7; 4:38).

In the NT the proclamation of the Gospel is the chief function of prophets. In course of time "prophesy" came to be largely a synonym of "foretell."

Prophet, Christ as. Christ often mentioned His prophetic mission (e. g., Lk. 4:16-27; Jn 18:37). He was anointed to be a prophet (Acts 3:22; 10:38). Some recognized Him as a prophet (Mt 21:46; Lk 7:16; 24:19; Jn 4:19; 6:14; 7:40-41). Terms applied to Him reveal an awareness of His prophetic office (e.g., teacher Jn 3:2; apostle Heb 3:1; witness Rv 1:5).

Christ regularly pointed to the OT (e.g., Mt 22: 29, 31; Lk 10:26; 24:27; Jn 5:39). He preached Law (e.g., Mt 5–7; 23) and Gospel (Jn 1:17). His miracles, signs, and wonders were intended to make it easier for people to believe (Mk 1:27; 9:24). The theme of His prophecy was the proclamation of Himself as the long-promised Messiah (Jn 4:25-26).

At His ascension Christ entrusted the preaching and teaching of His Word to the ch. (Mk 16:15; Acts 1:8).

See also *Angel of the Lord.*

O. C. J. Hoffmann, in "Office, or Work, of Christ," *The Abiding Word,* II, ed. T. Laetsch (St. Louis, 1947), 127–135.

Prophetic Religion. See *Switzerland, Contemporary Theology in,* 3.

Prophets, Former and Latter. See *Prophecy.*

Prophets, Major and Minor. See *Prophecy.*

Propitiation. The Gk. word *(hilasterion)* tr. "propitiation" Ro 3:25 is tr. "mercy seat" Heb. 9:5; the Heb. equivalent *(kapporeth)* Ex 25:17 denotes the cover, or lid, of the ark of the covenant. Once a yr. the high priest sprinkled the blood of sacrifice on this lid to make propitiation for the sins of the people. This was a type of the propitiatory sacrifice of Christ. See also *Atonement; Reconciliation.*

Propst. See *Provost.*

Propst, Jakob (Praepositus; 1486–1562). B. Ieper (Ypres), W Flanders, NW Belg.; prior Augustinian monastery Antwerp 1519; studied in Wittenberg 1521; preached against indulgences in Antwerp 1521; imprisoned; recanted 1522; resumed ev. preaching; arrested; escaped to Ger.; in Wittenberg 1523; pastor (1524) later supt. Bremen; friend of M. Luther; involved in A. Hardenberg* controversy on Lord's Supper; replaced by T. Hesshus* 1559.

Proselytes (from Gk. *proselytos,* "alien resident"). Strangers, or foreigners, who live in the midst of a people and enjoy its hospitality; then, by extension, converts to Judaism (Mt 23:15; Acts 2:10[11]; 13: 43). Now: converts from one religion to another.

Prosopa. See *Monarchianism,* B 6.

Prosper of Aquitaine (Prosper Tiro [or Tyro]; Lusentius? ca. 390–ca. 455/463). B. perhaps Limoges, Aquitaine; follower of Augustine* of Hippo; assoc. with Leo I (see *Popes,* 2). Wrote against semi-Pelagians, in defense of Augustine, and against the 13th *collatio* of J. Cassianus* (on free will); other works include a synthesis of the chronicles of Jerome* (to AD 378), Sulpicius* Severus, and Orosius* (to 433), with possible reflections of his own experience 433–455.

Prostration. See *Worship,* 4.

Protase. See *Gervase and Protase.*

Protestant. See *Speyer, Diet of, 1529.*

Protes'tant Conference, The. Organized 1927 by perhaps ca. 30/40 pastors and teachers and some congs. suspended for various reasons, mainly for supporting the hist. and exegetical emphasis in Wauwatosa* theol., from membership in the Ev. Luth. Joint Syn. of Wisconsin* and Other States. The conference is not organized as a syn. It suffered a rupture 1964. In 1972 it had 7 congs. Since 1928 it pub. the periodical *Faith–Life* to perpetuate the specific emphasis of Luth. theol. for which its mems. stood. WJH

Protestant Confession of Faith, A. See *Democratic Declarations of Faith,* 3.

Protestant Education in the United States. Educ. in the colonial period of Am. was basically Christian. The major task of Christian educ. was assumed by the home, but schools were also agencies for religious educ. In New Eng., ch. and state combined to administer schools. Heterogeneous pop. in the middle colonies led to various kinds of schools, most of them under religious sponsorship. Angl. influence dominated educ. in S colonies. Religious influence continued till ca. 1750, when a more secular spirit reflected growing economic and pol. interests. Except for the Coll. and Academy of Philadelphia (1755; U. of Pa. 1791), the 9 colleges and univs. founded before the Revolution were est. under ch. control: (1) Harvard coll. 1636; called U. at Cambridge in the 1780 Mass. const.; (2) Coll. of William and Mary, Williamsburg, Va., 1693; (3) Yale coll., New Haven, Conn., 1701; Yale U. 1887; (4) Coll. of N. J. 1746; Princeton U. 1896; (5) King's coll., NYC, 1754; Columbia coll. 1784: Columbia U. 1912; (6) R. I. coll., Providence, 1764; Brown U. 1804; (7) Queen's coll., New Brunswick, N. J., 1766 (see also *Reformed Churches,* 4 b); Rutgers coll. 1825: Rutgers U. 1924; the state univ. of N. J. 1945; (8) Dartmouth coll., Hanover, N. H., 1770. See also *Higher Education,* 10; *Ministry, Education of,* VI A; *Protestant Episcopal Church, The.*

In a number of places a form of catechetical instruction was given by pastors to children on Sun. morning in early colonial times. Sunday* schools appeared beginning ca. 1786, mainly in the middle states; they were more closely assoc. with the ch. than those in Eng., which were part of a lay movement. As the pub. school system grew, gen. educ. came to be eliminated from the S. S. Public schools were at first strongly influenced by religious thought, later less so. Chs. were forced to depend increasingly on Sun. schools for religious educ. outside the home.

The First Day, or S. S. Soc. was organized 1790 Philadelphia. The Am. S. S. Union was formed 1824. First nat. conventions: 1832 NYC; 1833 Philadelphia, 1859 Philadelphia, 1869 Newark, N. J., 1872 Indianapolis, Ind. A Gen. Conv. was held 1862 London, England. The 1872 conv. resolved to invite Can. to full participation and approved a system of internat. lessons. Internat. convs. were held beginning 1875.

In course of time the scope of the S. S. came to include preschool children, young people, and adults.

By 1905, conv. meetings had lost all but nominal control over policy to a bd. of officials called (1905) Internat. S. S. Association. Reaction led 1910 to formation of the S. S. Council of Ev. Denominations. The Assoc. and the Council united 1922 to form the Internat. S. S. Council of Religious Educ. (changed name 1924 to The International* Council of Religious Educ.), which in Nov. 1950 became the Division of Christian Educ. of the National* Council of Chs. of Christ in the USA. In 1905 G. U. Wenner* proposed a plan for teaching religion in co-operation with pub. schools under a released time plan, which was inaugurated with modifications at Gary, Ind., ca. 1913 and spread to other states. In 1948 the US Supreme Court ruled in favor of Mrs. Vashti McCollum of Champaign, Ill., self-styled "rationalist," and held that use by religious groups of the state's compulsory pub. school machinery is not separation of ch. and state; but in 1952 the Supreme Court pronounced religion classes outside school bldgs. on school time constitutional.

Prot. chs. that conduct nonpublic schools include Assem. of God, Bap., Episc., Luth., Mennonite, Seventh-day Adv.

Thought has been given to the possibility of including in pub. educ. some form of instruction on religion that would satisfy Christians and non-Christians. ACR

See also *Christian Education; Parish Education; Schools, Church-Related.*

A. A. Brown, *A History of Religious Education in Recent Times* (New York, 1923); M. C. Brown, *Sunday-School Movements in America* (New York, 1901); E. M. Fergusson, *Historic Chapters in Christian Education in America* (New York, 1935); C. L. Hay, *The Blind Spot in American Public Education* (New York, 1950); J. M. Reu, *Catechetics,* 3d ed. (Chicago, 1931); E. H. Rian, *Christianity and American Education* (San Antonio, Tex., 1949); *The Church and Christian Education,* ed. P. H. Vieth (St. Louis, 1947).

Protestant Episcopal Church, The (alternate name since 1967: The Episc. Ch.). 1. a. Began 1789 (see 3).

The 1st permanent Angl. ch. in Am. was built 1607 Jamestown, Va.; see also *Hunt, Robert.* Unfortunate conditions, arising mainly out of distance from ch. authorities and out of a growing practice of hiring local ministers temporarily, were corrected by J. Blair.* The harsh tone of the Angl. Ch. was echoed also in Va. in rigid laws regarding Puritans and Quakers.

b. In New Eng., Puritans applied to Angls. the same proscriptions from which they themselves had fled, hence only isolated attempts at ch. organization were made. In 1698 an Episc. ch. was est. Newport, R. I., and Trin. Ch., NYC, was dedicated. In Md. the ch. grew slowly till T. Bray* arrived 1700. The SPG, organized partly in response to a petition by Bray to the king of Eng., sent a delegation to visit the chs. in Am. 1702. Result: the no. of chs. greatly increased and a better grade of ministers was secured for them.

c. G. Berkeley,* who came to Newport, R. I., 1729, gave large financial support to Yale coll.; after his return to Eng. 1731 he was instrumental in forming the charters and directing the course of King's coll. and of the Academy and Coll. of Philadelphia. See also *Protestant Education in the United States.*

2. The Revolutionary War left the Angl. chs. in Am. disorganized. First move toward effecting organization was made by W. White,* who wrote the pamphlet *The Case of the Episcopal Churches in the United States Considered,* pub. anonymously 1782; he urged that, without waiting for a bp., the chs. should unite in some form of assoc. and common govt., and he outlined a plan that embodied most of the essential characteristics of the diocesan and gen. convs. as adopted later.

Meantime the Md. Legislature had (1779) passed an act committing to certain vestries as trustees the property of the parishes, but also prohibiting gen. assessments. In 1780 a conference was called and a petition sent to the legislature asking that the vestries be empowered to use money obtained by pew rents and other means of parish purposes; the name Prot. Episc. Ch., suggested for the organization, was formally approved by a conference at Annapolis 1783, definitely adopted by the 1789 Gen. Conv.

A movement to constitute an Episc. Ch. for the whole US was inaugurated, largely by White, May 1784 at a meeting at which N. Y., N. J., and Pa. were represented. Delegates from 8 states attended a conv. Oct. 1784. Seven of the 13 States (but not New Eng.) were represented at a 1785 conv., which, despite protests against the proposed plan of organization, adopted, with modifications, principles recommended 1784 and drew up a const. and liturgy.

3. Request for affiliation with the Ch. of Eng. was granted. In 1787 the abp. Canterbury consecrated White abp. Pa., S. Provoost* abp. N. Y.; S. Seabury* had been consecrated abp. by nonjuring Scot. prelates 1784. Thus there were 3, the canonical no. required for consecrating other bps. Two houses (Bps. and Deputies; see also 8 c) were constituted in the 1789 Gen. Conv., which also adopted a const. and Book of Common Prayer. To obviate any possible objection to the Scot. consecration of Seabury, J. Madison* was elected bp Va. 1790 and consecrated in Eng.

For more than 20 yrs. the ch. had to combat various hostile influences, since it was widely distrusted, being regarded as an Eng. institution. Loss of Meths., who chose to form an indep. ch., deprived the Episc. Ch. of some strength, and growth was slow.

4. a. A change came in the 2d decade of the 19th c., with new bps. for newly settled areas, esp. in the W. The Domestic and For. Missionary Soc. was organized 1820/21 ("For." included Indians within the states). Effects of the Oxford* Movement were felt in Am.

b. Ca. 1845 W. A. Muhlenberg (see *Mühlenberg, Henry Melchior and Family,* 11) came into prominence. He founded a system of ch. schools, organized the 1st free ch. of any importance in NYC, introd. the male choir, sisterhoods, and the fresh-air movement (providing rural and outdoor facilities for health and recreation for the poor and underprivileged). The Memorial Movement began 1853, when a memorial, drawn up mainly by Muhlenberg but signed also by other prominent clerics, was addessed to the House of Bps., asking "whether the Protestant Episcopal Church, with only her present canonical means and appliances, her fixed and invariable modes of public worship, and her traditional customs and usages, is competent to the work of preaching and dispensing the Gospel to all sorts and conditions of men, and so adequate to do the work of the Lord in this land and in this age." In partial answer the memorial said: ". . . a wider door must be opened for admission to the Gospel ministry than that through which her candidates for holy orders are now obliged to enter. Besides such candidates among her own members, it is believed that men can be found among the other bodies of Christians around us, who would gladly receive ordination at your hands, could they obtain it, without that entire surrender which would now be required of them, of *all* the liberty in public worship to which they have been accustomed – men who could not bring themselves to conform in all particulars to our prescriptions and customs, but yet sound in the faith, and who, having the gifts of preachers and pastors, would be able ministers of the New Testament." This memorial helped prepare the way for the Lambeth Quadrilateral 1888 (see *England,* C 11) and the movement for the rev. of the Am. prayer book, completed 1892 (but rev. again 1928).

c. Outbreak of the Civil War led to organization 1861 of the Prot. Episc. Ch. in the Confederate

States, with close ties to the ch. in the N; the end of the war brought reunion.

Further effects of the Oxford Movement led to a serious rift. G. D. Cummins* organized the Reformed* Episc. Ch. 1873.

The Brotherhood* of St. Andrew was organized 1886. Parochial, diocesan, and provincial bds. and commissions were formed for soc. service throughout the country. The Prot. Episc. Ch. played a prominent part in interfaith movements.

5. As to doctrine, some events in the yrs. immediately preceding est. of the Prot. Episc. Ch. are enlightening. At the 1785 conv. the Nicene and Athanasian creeds were omitted from a proposed revision of the Book of Common Prayer and the reference to Christ's descent into hell deleted from the Apostles' Creed. The 1786 conv. included the Nicene Creed and restored the Apostles' Creed to integrity; the Athanasian Creed was again omitted, mainly because of its damnatory clauses.

The Athanasian Creed was again rejected 1789. In 1801 the Thirty-nine Articles (see *Anglican Confessions,* 6), except the 21st, relating to the authority of the Gen. Council, and with some modifications of the 8th, 35th, and 36th arts., were accepted as a gen. statement of doctrine and are appended to the Book of Common Prayer, but adherence to them as a creed is not gen. required.

6. The Prot. Episc. Ch. expects of its mems. loyalty to the doctrine, discipline, and worship of the one holy catholic apostolic ch. in all essentials but allows great liberty in what it regards as nonessentials. Its proposed basis for the unity of Christendom is the Lambeth Quadrilateral. In baptizing children either immersion or pouring is allowed. Participation in Communion is technically limited to the confirmed, but is practically open to all baptized.

7. The High* Ch., Broad Ch., and Low Ch. tendencies of the Angl. Ch. are in evidence also in the Prot. Episc. Ch.

8. a. The system of ch. govt. includes the parish or cong., the diocese, the province, and the Gen. Convention. A cong. is "required, in its constitution or plan or articles of organization, to recognize and accede to the constitution, canons, doctrine, discipline, and worship of the church, and to agree to submit to and obey such directions as may be from time to time received from the bishop in charge, and council of advice."

Officers of the parish are the rector, who must be a priest; wardens (usually 2), representing the body of the parish and usually having charge of records, collection of alms, and ch. repair; vestrymen: trustees who hold the property for the corporation.

b. Direction of spiritual affairs is exclusively in the hands of the rector. Govt. of the diocese is vested in the bp. and the diocesan conv., the latter consisting of all the clergy, and of at least 1 lay delegate from each parish or cong. This conv. meets annually; election of delegates to it is governed by the specific canons of each diocese. Sections of states and territories not organized into dioceses are est. by the House of Bps. and the Gen. Conv. as miss. districts. Dioceses and miss. dists. are grouped into 8 provinces, to procure unity and cooperation in dealing with regional interests, esp. in the fields of missions, religious educ., soc. service, and judicial proceedings.

c. The Gen. Conv., highest ecclesiastical authority in the ch., consists of 2 houses: House of Bps and House of Deputies (see also 3). The House of Bps. includes every bp. having jurisdiction, every bp. coadjutor, and every bp. who by reason of advanced age or bodily infirmity or disability has resigned his jurisdiction. The House of Deputies is composed of delegates elected from the dioceses, including for each diocese not more than 4 presbyters canonically resident in the diocese, and not more than 4 laymen, communicants of the ch., resident in the diocese. The 2 houses sit and deliberate separately. Ecclesiastical head of the ch. is the presiding bp., elected by the House of Bps. Three orders are recognized in the ministry: bps., priests, deacons. A bp. must be consecrated by at least 3 bps. He is the administrative head and spiritual leader of his diocese; duties include presiding over the diocesan conv., ordaining deacons and priests, instituting rectors. If a bp. is unable to perform all his duties, a bp. coadjutor or a suffragan bp. may be elected. Election of a rector is acc. to diocesan law; notice of election is sent to the ecclesiastical authority of the diocese. Lay readers and deaconesses are appointed by the bp. or ch. authority of a diocese or miss. dist. to assist in pub. services, in the care of the poor and sick, and in religious training. Support of the rector and gen. expenses of each local cong. (parish) are in the care of the vestry; the bishop's salary is fixed by the diocesan conv., with the amount apportioned among the chs. of his diocese.

9. The Prot. Episc. Ch. engages in miss. work at home and abroad, supports a number of institutions of higher educ., has many orders, and fosters "brotherhoods" for men and boys.

See also *Teachers,* 32.

See *Religious Bodies (US), Bibliography of.*

Protestant Evangelical Church. See *Belgium.*

Protestant Film Commission. See *National Council of the Churches of Christ in the United States of America.*

Protestant Radio Commission. See *National Council of the Churches of Christ in the United States of America.*

Protestant Seminaries. See *Ministry, Education of,* VI–XII.

Protestant Truth Society. See *Kensit, John.*

Protestant Union, German. The *Deutscher Protestantenverein* was organized 1863 Frankfurt am Main by representatives of Prot. chs. in Ger.; object: creation of a Ger. nat. Prot. Ch.; opposed divisions created by theol. differences and urged chs. to proclaim divine love and the fact that Christians are children of God as taught by Christ. See also *Ewald, Georg Heinrich August; Rothe, Richard; Schenkel, Daniel; Schwarz, Karl; Sydow, Karl Leopold Adolf.*

Protestantische Freunde. See *Lichtfreunde.*

Protestantism. Term derived from the protest submitted by the ev. party at the 1529 Diet of Speyer.* Issues involved (1) the authority of Scripture, to be explained by itself; (2) freedom of conscience. Protestantism stands for religious liberty based on obedience to God and His Word. RCm: where good works are, there are faith and justification; Protestantism: where faith is, there are justification and good works. See also *Formal Principle; Material Principle.*

Protestantism is favorable to civil and religious freedom, to the rights of the individual, and to development of those inventive capacities that have led to achievements called civilization. It favors universal education, since all should read the Bible and help do the work of the ch. intelligently. Freedom of thought, speech, and press are involved in the freedom and responsibility of the individual emphasized by Protestantism.

See also *United States, Religious History of.*

Prothesis (from Gk. for "to place before"). In the E Orthodox Ch., a side table on which eucharistic elements are prepared. See also *Divine Liturgy.*

Protocanonical. Term describing books accepted early into the Bible canon* without serious controversy. Distinguished from deuterocanonical, a term used esp. by RCs of books accepted into the canon later and with more controversy. See also *Apocrypha,* A 4.

Protonotarius apostolicus (prothonotary apostolic). In RCm, a mem. of the Coll. of Prothonotaries Apostolic. There are 4 categories of prothonotaries apostolic, with varying functions. Prothonotaries apostolic are created by papal brief and are addressed as right reverend monsignor.

Providence. Divine providence is that activity of God whereby He uninterruptedly upholds (preserves), governs, and directs lifeless creation (Jb 9:5-6; 28:25-26; Ps 89:9; 148:8), plant life (Ps 104:13-14; 147:9), animal life (Ps 145:15; Jon 4:11), the world of men (Ps 139:13, 15-16; Jer. 1:5; Mt 4:4; 5:45; 6:26-28; 18:14; Acts 17:24-28) and all that concerns men (Ps 31:15; 91:1, 3; 121; Pr 20:24; 21:1; Lk 12:7), heaven, hell, everything (Lk 12:6-7; Cl 1:16-17; Heb 1:1-3).

Divine providence normally expresses itself in definite laws (Gn 8:22) that represent inner urges and drives implanted by God in His creatures. These laws proclaim the benignity of the Creator (Acts 14:17).

Divine providence is ordinarily exercised through secondary causes; but these are operative only so long as God works through them. Scripture teaches that both God and the means are operative (Ps 69:9-11; 127:1; Is 55:10; 1 Co 12:6); this cannot be completely explained by the human mind.

Divine providence deprives men neither of their liberty nor of their responsibility; it neither reduces men to automata nor makes God responsible for sin (Ro 1:18-32). God is operative in men and acts through men also when their deeds are evil (2 Sm 16:10; 24:1; Acts 17:28), but He is not the author of sin (Ps 50:16-21).

From the viewpoint of God all is predetermined and immutably fixed (Jb 14:5; Acts 4:27-28); from the human viewpoint things happen contingently, events cān be modified and depend on circumstances and decisions that men make and for which they are responsible (Ps 55:23; Is 38:1-5).

Ultimate goals of divine providence: (1) the temporal and eternal welfare of man, esp. the salvation of the elect; (2) the spreading of the Gospel; (3) the promotion of the glory of God (Ro 11:36).

P. F. Bente, "The Providence of God," *The Abiding Word,* II, ed. T. Laetsch (St. Louis, 1947), 78–111; E. W. Hinrichs, "God's Direction in Our Lives and the Element of Chance," *CTM,* XVII (1946), 425–439.

Providence Plantations. See *United States, Religious History of,* 4.

Province. See *Protestant Episcopal Church, The,* 8.

Provincial. In RCm, a religious superior, under the gen. of an order, over all religious houses in a province of the order.

Provincial Council or Synod. See *Councils and Synods,* 1, 3.

Provincial Letters. See *Pascal, Blaise.*

Provinciale. See *Canon Law,* 5.

Provoost, Samuel (ca. 1742–1815). B. NYC; educ. King's coll. (now Columbia U.), NYC; ordained deacon by Prot. Episc. Ch. 1766, priest 1776; held various positions; elected bp. N.Y. 1786, consecrated by abp. Canterbury 1787. See also *Protestant Episcopal Church, The,* 3.

Provost (Ger.: *Probst* or *Propst*). Ecclesiastical dignitary in various positions, including: head of a cathedral or collegiate chap.; Prot. cleric in charge of the main ch. in a region of Ger.; ecclesiastic with duties similar to those of a dean or prior but sometimes second in authority. The head of some religious orders is called provost general. Supts. of Swed. chs. on the Delaware R. were called provosts and included I. Acrelius,* E. T. Björk,* A. Hesselius,* J. Lidman,* A. Rudman,* A. Sandel,* J. Sandin,* C. M. Wrangel.*

Prudentius Clemens, Aurelius (Aurelius Clemens Prudentius; Aurelius Prudentius Clemens; 348–after 404/405, perhaps ca. 410/413). B. probably Calahorra, N Sp.; practiced law; abandoned secular work at age 56/57; entered a monastery and wrote hymns, which include *Corde natus ex parentis* ("Of the Father's Love Begotten") and *Salvete, flores martyrum* ("Sweet flowerets of the martyr band").

Prussian Bible Society. See *Bible Societies,* 2.

Prussian Union. Sept. 27, 1817, Frederick* William III announced the union of the Luths. and Ref. into 1 ev. Christian cong. at the court and among the military in Potsdam in celebration of the 300th anniversary of the Reformation and appealed for voluntary union of Luths. and Ref. in all of Prussia and elsewhere. Several smaller Ger. states followed suit. But Luths., led by C. Harms,* objected. In the resulting controversy the issues were muddied and compulsory measures adopted: in 1821 candidates were required at their examination to pledge loyalty to the union; the *Kirchenagende für die Hof- und Domkirche in Berlin* (drawn up 1821, pub. 1822 on personal initiative of the king) gave rise to the Agenda* Controversy (F. D. E. Schleiermacher* was among those who challenged the right of the king to act with authority in the area of liturgics); in 1823 ministers were pledged to the confessional writings of the united ev. ch. insofar as these confessions were in harmony; in 1830 it was decreed that "Evangelical" be substituted for the distinctive names "Luth." and "Ref."; in 1832 the union was enforced in the army and the Bonn faculty; the new agenda was prescribed 1834.

Reaction against the union had found practical expression beginning 1830 in formation of the Ev. Luth (Old Luth.) Ch. (see *Germany, Lutheran Free Churches in,* 1), which led to an 1834 cabinet order recognizing both Luth. and Ref. confessions and to Frederick* William IV's "Generalkonzession" 1845; an 1852 cabinet order said the union was not doctrinal but administrative. But enactments 1853 and later reenforced the Prussian Union so as to make it practically also doctrinal.

See also *Germany,* C 2.

Psalm Tones (Ger. *Psalmtöne*). Psalmody holds an intermediate position bet. accentus* and concentus. There are 8 traditional psalm tones, corresponding to the 8 kinds of octaves (Ger. *Oktavengattungen*) in ancient music. In course of time a 9th, for. *(tonus peregrinus),* or "irregular," tone was added, which is usually treated as a separate tone since opinions regarding it differ. It occurs in the antiphons *Nos qui vivimus, Martyres domini,* and *Angeli domini* and found Luth. use for the *Magnificat* and Benediction. Each psalm tone is individually determined (1) by the reciting tone (see *Intonation*) of the psalm, which is always the dominant note of the scale; (2) by the inflection that ends the 1st half of the verse; (3) by the inflection at the end of the 2d half of the verse, which need not end on the tonic note. Each psalm tone has a festal and a ferial form. In the ferial form the initial notes leading to the reciting tone *(initium; inchoatio; intonatio; incipit)* are omitted, and the middle part *(mediante; medium; mediatio;* Ger. *Mitte)* is simplified by resolving the ligatures and substituting syllabic chanting. The ferial form is used, e. g., on ordinary Sundays and during the week; the festal form, e. g., on festivals and for the *Magnificat* and *Benedictus.* See also *Gregorian Music; Intonation; Modes, Ecclesiastical.*

Psalmellus. See *Ambrosian Music.*

Psalms, The Seven Penitential. See *Seven Penitential Psalms, The.*

Psalms as Hymns. Many Psalms were written for use

in pub. worship, as their superscriptions and dedications show. The Hallel (Ps 113–118) is assoc. with Passover and other Jewish festivals; some think the hymn mentioned Mt 26:30 and Mk 14:26 was Ps 115–118, others Ps 136 (which rabbis called Great Hallel). Various assocs. have been suggested for the Psalms of Degrees, including the annual festivals in Jerusalem.

Christians probably used OT Psalms from the beginning. The "psalm" mentioned 1 Co 14:26 is not necessarily from the OT. The psalms mentioned Eph 5:19 and Cl 3:16 may refer (but not necessarily exclusively) to OT psalms. The noun "psalms" in Ja 5:13 KJV is not in the original (cf. RSV "sing praise"). Scripture does not require exclusive use of OT Psalms in their original form. Metrical versions of Psalms include "The Lord's My Shepherd, I'll Not Want" (Ps 23); "The Man Is Ever Blest" (Ps 1).

Psalms of Solomon. See *Apocrypha,* A 4.

Psalter, English. When other hymns were frowned on by some Ref., esp. in Gt. Brit., metrical versions of Psalms began to come into their own. Robert Crowley (ca. 1518–88; b. Gloucestershire, Eng.; educ. Oxford; printer; exiled under Mary* I; returned to Eng. under Elizabeth* I; held several positions as vicar and prebendary) is gen. regarded as the 1st to render the whole Psalter into Eng. verse (1549). Ca. the same time, perhaps as early as 1548, appeared the 1st ed. of 19 Psalms versified by Thomas Sternhold (ca. 1500–49; b. Southampton or near Blakeney, Eng.; educ. Oxford; groom of the chambers to Henry* VIII and Edward* VI); 2d ed. ca. 1549/51, with 18 more Psalms versified by Sternhold and 7 by John Hopkins (d. 1570); enlargement continued at Geneva during the reign of Mary I; this Genevan Psalter was put into use in Eng. on accession of Elizabeth I. Partial and complete versions of Psalms versified multiplied in Eng. and Scot. The 1st book pub. by Puritans in New Eng. was the "Bay Psalm Book" (1640), characterized by rigorous literalism. *A New Version of the Psalms of David Fitted to the Tunes Used in Churches,* by Nahum Tate (1652–1715; b. and educ. Ireland; hymns include "While Shepherds Watched Their Flocks by Night") and Nicholas Brady (1659–1726; b. Bandon, Eng.; educ. Oxford and Dublin; held various positions) appeared 1696. Others who have versified Psalms include J. Addison,* T. Dwight* (1752–1817), J. Keble,* H. F. Lyte,* J. Montgomery,* I. Watts.*

Psellus, Michael Constantine (Psellos; ca. 1018/20–ca. 1078). B. Constantinople or Nicomedia; Byzantine statesman, hist., philos., theol.; Imperial secy. and secy. of state; helped reest. U. of Constantinople; prof. philos. there; favored unity at time of 1054 schism (see *Schism,* 6) and was forced out; became monk, adopting the name Michael; soon returned to serve at court till 1072. Exponent of Neoplatonism* and Christian humanism.*

Pseudepigrapha. See *Apocrypha.*

Pseudo-Christs. See *Christs, False.*

Pseudo-Dionysius. See *Dionysius the Areopagite,* 2.

Pseudo-Isidorian Decretals (False Decretals; Forged Decretals). 1. a. Collection of ecclesiastical documents, some genuine, some forged, made probably in Franconia in the 1st half of the 9th c. An earlier collection, based on that of Dionysius* Exiguus, had been erroneously attributed to Isidore* of Seville. The Frankish fraud also appeared under Isidore's name.

The Pseudo-Isidorian Decretals are divided into 3 parts: I. 50 apostolic canons; ca. 59/60 spurious decretals of Roman bps. (popes) from Clement I (see *Apostolic Fathers,* 1) to Miltiades* (Melchiades). II. The Donation* of Constantine (see also 2); tracts on the council of Nicaea; canons of the Gk., Afr., Gallic, and Sp. councils to 683. III. Decretals (including 35 spurious ones) of popes from Sylvester I (see *Popes,* 1) to Gregory II (ca. 669–731; b. Rome, It.; pope 715–731).

b. The spurious decretals are for the most part not complete forgeries but are rather based on the literature of theol. and canon law then existing, amplified or altered, and so formulated as to serve the purposes of the compiler(s) (see c). But the fraud is clumsy: (1) 2d-3d c. Roman bps. are made to write in the Frankish Lat. of the 9th c.; (2) they write in the spirit of post-Nicene orthodoxy; (3) they write on medieval relations of ch. and state; (4) they quote Scripture from post-Jerome translations; (5) a 3d-c. bp. writes to a 5th-c. bp. about the celebration of Easter.

c. Purpose of the Pseudo-Isidorian fraud was to extend into antiquity the papal claim of temporal power (see *Pepin the Short*) and to est. the pope as unquestioned ruling head of the ch. and its hierarchy. The fraud was perpetrated in an uncritical age. It was questioned by Nicholas* of Cusa, L. Valla,* M. Luther,* and J. Calvin* (*Institutio religionis christianae,* IV, vii, xi, xx), then unmasked by the authors of the Magdeburg* Centuries, finally revealed so clearly by D. Blondel* that RCs have also been openly convinced.

2. In the Donation of Constantine, Constantine* I is portrayed as confessing his faith and telling how he was converted and cured of leprosy by Sylvester I, as recognizing the primacy of the Roman bp., and as giving him the Lateran* palace, with imperial power in the W. That far exceeds donations by Constantine I to Sylvester I related in *Acta Sylvestri* and in a letter by Adrian I (Hadrian; d. 795; b. Rome; pope 772–795) to Charlemagne* perhaps ca. 778/780.

Psilanthropy (psilanthropism; from Gk. *psilos,* "mere," and *anthropos,* "man"). Doctrine that Christ was only man. See also *Monarchianism,* A.

Psyche. See *Psychology,* B 3.

Psychiana. Religious cult, promoted mainly by mail; founded 1929 Moscow, Idaho, by F. B. Robinson*; mystical; opposed chs.; denied sin, atonement, future life, inspiration of the Bible; ridiculed all Christianity; emphasized health, happiness, prosperity.

Psychiatrists. See *Psychotherapy,* 14 a.

Psychical Research. Investigation of such phenomena as apparent telepathy, visions and apparitions, dowsing, automatism* (e. g., automatic writing), clairvoyance and clairaudience, coincidental dreams, monitions, physical phenomena of mediumship (e. g., materialization, rapping, telekinesis), precognition, predictions, psychokinesis, psychometry, extrasensory perception. The Soc. for Psychical Research was est. in Eng. 1882 by H. Sidgwick* et al. A similar soc. was est. in Am. 1885 through influence of W. James*; this society later adopted the name Am. Soc. for Psychical Research; membership stands only for investigation of alleged phenomena.

Psychoanalysis. Method of investigating psychic content and mechanisms not readily accessible to voluntary exploration by the conscious mind. See also *Psychotherapy,* 14 a.

Psychological Realism. See *Realism.*

Psychology. A. *Definition.* The word "psychology" is derived from Gk. *psyche,* "soul; mind," and *logos,* "discourse; theory; science." The word *psyche* was from early times also used in other senses, e. g., spirit, breath, and principle of life. The tendency now is to define psychology broadly as the science of experience and behavior. More specifically, it tries to understand, predict, and control human behavior.

The term "psychology" apparently was 1st used by Ger. scholars of the 16th c. Its 1st form seems to have been the Lat. *psychologia.* P. Melanchthon is said to have used the term as title of a prelection. It appears in 17th-c. med. writings: *psychologia* and *somatotomia* (or *somatologia*) were spoken of as the 2 parts of *anthropologia*. The term continued to appear in technical works but was not gen. used in modern languages till the 19th c.

B. *Early Developments*. Roots of naturalistic psychol. lie in early forms of mythology, not as a separate system of thought, but combined with, and woven into, a primitive culture. Attempts were made to explain life, including mental life, in a world that often appeared as more chaos than cosmos to the primitive mind. Man soon noted that human life is more than body, bone, muscle, and tissue. His dreams and imaginary flights, with the body asleep or at rest, required explanation. But concepts involving immaterial and incorporeal forms and substances are hard to grasp. Hence a double materialism developed. Soul or mind was thought of as vapor, air, blood, or some other material substance.

2. As in mythology, mental powers and forces came to be closely assoc. with the elements: air, fire, earth, water. The early form of the temperament theory is an example. Air was thought to be related to the sanguinary temperament, earth to the melancholic, fire to the choleric, water to the phlegmatic (see also *Empedocles*). Later the temperaments were thought to be based on the body fluids or humors. From these came through Claudius Galen(us) (Gallien; ca. 130/131 – perhaps ca. 200/201; Gk. physician; b. Pergamum, Asia Minor; settled in Rome, It., 164) the names of the main temperaments: sanguine, phlegmatic, choleric, melancholic. The elemental basis and "humoral doctrine" were gradually abandoned.

3. The relation of psychol. to mythology is indicated by the personification of the soul as a princess named Psyche, so beautiful that even Venus became jealous of her and imposed many hardships on her.

C. *Approach to Immaterial Concepts*. 1. In Gk. philos. writings the explanation of soul, mind, reason, intelligence, and will was approached with a new vigor and placed on a higher intellectual level. In this period the philosophies of Plato* and Aristotle* were epochal. But here too soul, mind, intellective powers, and will were discussed as aspects of a broader philos. that took in a wide range of cosmological factors and human experiences.

2. Plato and Aristotle put psychical forces and forms on an immaterial basis, at least in part. Plato elevated consciousness into the realm of the spiritual. He considered the soul immortal and incapable of dissolution. To him the idea in its purest form was the ultimate in mental life, and matter was of secondary importance. God was the supreme mind. Apparently, man's soul was thought to be closely attached to, or part of, an immortal god or gods.

3. Aristotle also sought the ultimate of man's existence. He disagreed with Plato that ideas were the ultimate. He considered soul the actuality of the body and distinguished bet. souls of plants and animals, on the one hand, and the soul of man, on the other, the main difference being man's intellective capacity. Besides the 5 senses (sight, hearing, smell, taste, touch) he spoke of a common sense that is conscious and classifies and coordinates the sensory experiences. He distinguished bet. passive reason, which acts as a receptor for the senses, and active reason, which provides forms of thought, may exist apart from soul and body, and is immortal.

4. Plato and Aristotle lifted mental life from the material to the immaterial and systematized psychological thought in a cosmological frame. The influence of their philosophies on later movements of thought is little short of phenomenal.

D. *Relationship to Christianity*. 1. The basis for the Christian approach to psychology is laid in Gn. Man was created a being consisting of body and soul (Gn 2:7). Man was created in the image of God with the command and ability to be fruitful and rule over every living thing (Gn 1:27-28). Thus man's preeminent position in the order of creation was est. However, man is not a god, nor part of God, but a being separate from God, a creature. That Adam was an intellective being is evident from his ability to name every creature that passed before him (Gn 2:19-20). Man had a free will, subject only to the will of God. Knowledge of right and wrong was implanted in him, that he might subdue the earth and enjoy its fruits, but he was forbidden to eat "of the tree of the knowledge of good and evil" (Gn 2:17). With the fall into sin came a stricken conscience, conflicts, a sense of guilt, even a projection of guilt, and with the promise of a Savior came faith and hope. Thus the basic concepts (soul, intellect, knowledge, free will, conscience, sense of guilt, conflicts, heredity, environment, emotion) were est.

2. Psychol. is not treated as a separate subject in the Bible. It is no more than an essential part of the framework of the Bible. Psychol. as a separate and distinct field of systematic activity is a development esp. of the 20th c. But many words and expressions in the Bible have a psychol. meaning or connotation. Psalms speak of the effects of emotions on man. Solomon pointed to the need of divine wisdom in a godly personality. Christ emphasized the need of translating knowledge into action. Paul speaks of the Christian's need to devote his whole being to the Lord's work, and he recognized individual differences (cf. Ro 12). The very essence of Christianity, man's possessing a soul, the immortality of the soul, the inspiration of the Bible, sin, forgiveness of sin and eternal life by grace through faith, regeneration and the miraculous work of the Holy Spirit in and through Word and Sacraments, all have been stumbling blocks to philosophies, systems of logic, and psychologies based solely on naturalistic thought and effort.

3. It has been the determined and conscious purpose of Christians to guard these and other values against all encroachments. Not every effort of psychological thought and experimentation was condemned. Many Christians became properly interested in the study and explanation of mental phenomena.

E. *Confluence of Theol. and Philos. in the Middle Ages*. 1. After the apostolic age the cen. movement of thought was dominated by (1) the Christian religion; (2) the heritage of philos. and the classics; (3) current thought as represented by sects, cults, and ethnic groups. Theol. gradually assumed the leading role and held it through the Middle Ages, with philos., poetry, psychol., and logic playing ancillary roles.

2. Augustine* of Hippo was perhaps the greatest metaphysician of his age. He markedly influenced later thought. His writings cover many areas of theol. and human thought and experience. His *Confessions,* X, presents his psychological ideas in some detail. He considered soul the life-giving force. Apparently he separated soul and mind, the latter being a functional power. Both are immaterial. Man is superior to animals because of his reason and understanding. Augustine dealt with such concepts as sensation, reason, memory (or the act of remembering), learning, thinking, conscience, free will, dreams. He recognized 4 "perturbations of the mind": desire, joy, fear, sorrow; in this he came close to the emotional theory of the modern behaviorists. He dwelt at length on memory, exalting its function and usefulness and calling it "the belly of the mind."

3. Augustine was well acquainted with the philosophies of Plato and Aristotle and classical literature.

He learned much from them but rejects them all as valid sources of information in spiritual matters. In the latter he gradually learned to depend on Scripture alone. He completely rejected astrology and similar practices.

4. Thomas* Aquinas, "the Christian Aristotle," was first of all a theol. and churchman, but also a logician, philos., and psychol. His explanations of soul, mind, and emotions and systematic, encyclopedia, and metaphysical. His rigid logic and ideological conclusions have been called more metalogical (beyond or outside the scope of logic) than metaphysical.

5. Though greatly devoted to logic and inference, Thomas Aquinas held that in spiritual matters revelation is the only reliable source. But the line bet. revelation and reason had been blurred; Scripture no longer stood alone as accepted authority; ecclesiastical pronouncements, traditions, and legends had made deep inroads into all religious matters.

F. *The Reformation and Psychology.* 1. M. Luther* was educ. in the traditional materials and schools of thought of his era. He was acquainted with Gk. philos., the poetry and literature of the classics, the mixture of religion and reason in the ch. fathers, the systematized and finespun logic of the Scholastics, the creative efforts of the Renaissance, and the secular interests of humanism. He had a deep interest in the dignity and welfare of man and in est. the rights of the individual but was not concerned with developing a new system of philos. or psychol. He was dedicated to a return to Scripture as the sole basis for Christian faith and life. All human knowledge and activity was judged in light of God's Word. The simplest statement of God's natural gifts to man is summarized SC II, 2: ". . . I believe that God has . . . given me and still sustains my body and soul, all my limbs and senses. . . ."

2. Speculative philosophies, ecclesiastical fiats and legends, the black arts, horoscopy, and superstitions were critically examined and denounced in rugged terms as so much nonsense or the work of the devil. Adiaphora* were left open. Reasonable and sensible laws, decrees, and explanations were evaluated properly and given support.

3. Not all contemporary reformers and supporters of the Reformation followed Luther's pattern; some fell victim to humanistic philosophies or other schools of thought from which Luther remained free.

G. *The Philos.-Experimental Approach to Modern Psychol.* 1. After the Reformation the trend of thought fell increasingly under the spell of a confluence of philos. and science. The concept of *nous* (Gk. "mind; intellect") rose to prominence at the expense of Christian theol. Philosophy flourished; philosophies multiplied. Modern psychol. draws heavily on 17th–19th c. speculations. Various forms of dualism, materialism, idealism, innate intelligence, psycho-physical parallelism, influence of the environment *(tabula* rasa),* associationism, sensation, perception, phrenology, and biological determinism were proposed and defended by some philosophy.

2. Psychology was influenced also by scientific developments and experimental techniques but held its ground, for scientific experiment is often preceded and followed by speculation.

3. The earlier experiments of the 19th c. drew heavily on physics and physiology and were more psychophysics than psychology. Examples: experiments in sensation by Ernst Heinrich Weber (1795–1878; b. Wittenberg, Ger.; physiologist; anatomist); investigations of mechanisms of sight and hearing by Hermann Ludwig Ferdinand von Helmholtz (1821–94; b. Potsdam; physicist; anatomist; physiologist); the work of G. T. Fechner.*

4. W. M. Wundt* est. the 1st laboratory for experimental psychology 1879 Leipzig, Ger. Analysis of conscious processes, memory experiments, esp. by Hermann Ebbinghaus (1850–1909; b. Barmen, Ger.), experiments in reaction time, introspection, analysis of the learning process, systematic observation of child development (e. g., by Wilhelm Thierry Preyer [1841–97; b. Moss Side, near Manchester, Eng.; Ger. physiol. and psychol.; advocated Darwinism; works include *Die Seele des Kindes*] and G. S. Hall*) contributed to early 20th-c. psychol.

H. *Nature and Scope of Modern Psychol.* By the beginning of the 20th c. psychol. had emerged as a separate branch of learning. Contributions of W. James* had broken the close attachment to philos. and given psychol. thought a wide range of materials. Since 1900, psychol. materials, methods, and principles have been further clarified. By 1940 large univs. were offering more than 50 courses in various aspects of psychol. Individuals and "schools of psychol." created crosscurrents of thought resulting in "psychologies." But the attempt to est. facts by rigid experimentation remained uppermost.

In the middle decades of the 20th c. there was a shift away from a more or less exclusive interest in empirical studies. The influence of psychoanalysis, existential philos., and related soc. sciences led to growing interest in clinical, longitudinal, and sociocultural studies.

I. *Sources from Which Psychol. Draws Material.* Sources other than philos. and scientific investigation include biology, physiol., anatomy, roentgenology. Observations of physical growth and changes from conception to death are correlated with growth and changes in emotion, learning, and personality as a whole. Extensive use of statistics is necessary for accuracy in experiments. Refinements of psychometrics have led to a more precise concept of individual differences, intelligence, achievement, aptitude, special ability, interests, emotions, and other aspects of human behavior. Nature study has led to animal experimentation, brain extirpation, and induction of abnormal behavior under controlled conditions. Ontological and phylogenetic surmises led to specific experiments and observations in the relative influence of heredity and environment. Cell twins, fraternal twins, siblings, foster children, and parent-child relationships in similar and different environments have been minutely studied. Observation of abnormal behavior is essential to gen. psychol. thought. Study of the learning process shifted from an introspective approach to objective observation of the whole life span. Study of perception, thinking, imagination, and growth of language continues.

J. *Schools and Systems.* 1. The "quest for certainty" of which J. Dewey* spoke is not satisfied with mere atomistic experimentation. A theoretical description of phenomena of experience and behavior is a natural by-product of experimentation. The points of departure that have grown up with experimentation and observation have come to be known as systems or schools of psychology. But the grouping of fellow workers with a somewhat similar viewpoint as a school is not entirely accurate. Each school has subcurrents and divergent positions as clear as differences bet. "schools."

2. Structuralism, which flourished at the beginning of the 20th c., tried to analyze sensation, images, and affections as elements of consciousness. Its main method was introspection. It tried to find the pure elements of the mind. It did not concern itself with meaning directly because meaning is more than an elementary mental process. It emphasized the elements rather than the reaction of the

organism as a whole. Exponents include E. B. Titchener.*

3. Functionalists are more concerned with activities of the mind than its structure. Mind and behavior are considered inseparable. Functionalism* therefore deals with feelings, impulses, behavior, habits. It makes controlled observation a major part of investigative technique. Its main contributions are in learning and education. See also 5, 6.

4. Behaviorism has little faith in analysis of consciousness by introspection or any other method. It operates mainly with the stimulus response theory of simple behavior situations, because it believes that only in that way is observation accurate and objective. Reflexes and mechanistic responses are described in great detail, scant attention is given to motivation by thought and reason. The conditioned response, or substitute stimulus, is highly regarded in the method of investigation. Behaviorism has helped make psychol. investigation more objective, but it has not given enough attention to motivation; and it makes inferences from outward behavior without taking into consideration inner thoughts that might be discovered by introspection or some form of projection. See also 5; *Educational Psychology,* D 4.

5. The Gestalt (or Configuration) school emphasizes the whole pattern of the learning act, taking issue with the piecemeal theories of behaviorists (see 4). It operates with the concept of insight as basis for an intelligent response and does not accept the trial-and-error pattern of learning proposed by functionalists (see 3). It supports its position by experimentation in human and animal learning. Gestalt theories exerted great influence on psychol. and educ. thought in Am. See also *Educational Psychology,* D 5; *Ehrenfels, Maria Christian Julius Leopold Karl von.*

6. Psychoanalysis (or Freudianism), founded by S. Freud,* has been a prolific source of psychol. thought. Its crosscurrents are strong, literature vast.

Dynamic psychol. incorporates some theories of psychoanalysis; in a broad sense Am. functionalism (see 3) is dynamic. See also *Psychology, Dynamic.*

7. Freudianism makes much of the libido, defined as a sex instinct or the urge to life (see also *Lust*); "id," "ego,*" and "superego" are terms used in psychoanalysis to describe the stream of life resulting from the trauma and frustrations that interfere with impulses of the libido. The school is mainly interested in behavioral disorders and forms the disorders may take in psychic life. Its therapeutic technique through abreaction or catharsis (see also *Psychotherapy,* 2) finds widespread use in psychiatry, literature, the arts.

8. Adherence to 1 school or system by current psychologies is rare; contemporary psychologists lean toward eclecticism.

K. *Influence of Psychol.* 1. Psychol. has developed a field of materials of its own, though the method of investigation is largely that of natural sciences. Many specialties have developed.

2. Psychol. has invaded many fields of endeavor, including educ., medicine, industrial management, art, advertising, salesmanship, vocational guidance.

L. *Contribution of Christianity to Psychol.* 1. The attitude of Christianity toward psychol. is indicated in D–F. Psychol. could hardly have reached its present state of development without contributions of Christianity, which holds certain sacred values and has forced psychol. into a field of its own in the study of psychic phenomena, where it applies itself to psychic materials amenable to methods of natural science.

2. It is questionable whether psychol. would have achieved rigid technique in experimentation if Christianity had not insisted on seeking the truth.

3. Christianity holds that man is dichotomous (body-soul) structurally, but for all practical ends here on earth he acts as 1 being, a single self, under normal circumstances. Functionally, man is a monistic being; the study of his functional mental life is as important as the study of his bodily functions. The structure of the body, but not the structure of the soul, is subject to investigation by natural science. Speculation about the soul, beyond or contrary to revelation, is futile.

4. In its judgment of and attitude toward psychol. theories and findings Christianity must be guided by the Word of God. Al S, AHJ

See also *Psychotherapy,* 14 b.

Psychology, Dynamic. Psychology emphasizing motivation (conation). See also *Educational Psychology,* D 6; *Psychology,* J 6.

Psychology, Functional. See *Functionalism; Psychology,* J 3.

Psychology and Education. See *Educational Psychology.*

Psychology of Religion. Application of psychol. to the field of religion; tries to collect facts of religious consciousness, systematize them, est. relation bet. them, and explain them on basis of gen. psychol. principles. The only proper function of psychol. of religion in the field of conservative theol. is to explain the phenomena connected with the remnant of the natural knowledge of God and of the Law written in the hearts of all (Ro 2:14-15). See also *Apologetics, Christian,* III D.

Psychopannychism. See *Soul Sleep.*

Psychoses. See *Psychotherapy,* 9.

Psychotherapy. 1. As pastors become increasingly involved in pastoral counseling, they are showing more and more interest in methods and findings of psychotherapy. The pastoral counseling movement, developed esp. in the middle decades of the 20th c., used psychotherapeutic techniques and insights.

2. Psychotherapy is not a substitute for Christian faith, but it may be used to help solve emotional and mental problems. As gen. practiced, it does not harm Christian faith; rather, some aspects, e. g., catharsis (see also 6; *Psychology,* J 7), may lead to a stronger spiritual life.

3. "Psychotherapy" comes from Gk. *psyche,* "soul; mind" and *therapeia,* "healing."

4. Psychotherapy involves a relationship bet. therapist and patient or interrelationships in a group (group or multiple therapy). It is essentially treatment through words and actions; drugs may also be used in some cases. It deals with emotions and motivation; it is not primarily information-giving.

5. Basic thesis underlying psychotherapy: Emotional problems often result from chronic anxiety and frustration, repressed fears and guilt, or inadequate ways of relating to others. In the therapeutic relationship, the patient explores these hidden feelings; when he feels free to express anger or guilt, their tyrannical hold on him is removed; he feels more comfortable and is free to act more appropriately in relationships with mems. of his family, fellow employees, friends, and others. From the therapist the patient learns more adequate ways of relating to people. He tries his new discoveries and is supported throughout by the therapist.

6. Important ingredients of psychotherapy: A strong bond bet. patient and therapist in which the therapist expresses basic confidence in the patient and allows him almost complete freedom to speak, act, and make decisions as he wishes. The therapist does not condemn the patient for any feelings expressed, leaving the patient free to pour out pent-up emotions (catharsis). The patient benefits from the experience of being accepted by the therapist, learning that not all will reject him and that not all are

harsh and unforgiving (reeducation, desensitization, redirection).

7. Goals of psychotherapy: reduction of emotional tensions, greater maturity, willingness to face reality, acquisition of better techniques for coping with problems, self-understanding.

8. The need for psychotherapy exceeds the supply of available help; the gap seems to be widening.

9. Psychotherapy is used most commonly in treating psychoses, neuroses, other forms of mental illness, children's behavioral problems, stuttering, sexual problems, alcoholism.

10. Approaches to psychotherapy vary. In gen. there are 2 kinds of therapists: (1) Those who are more directive, give more advice, and tend more to tell the patient what to do. These therapists often include use of drugs and/or other physical treatments in therapy. They tend to see patients for a shorter period of time and seem to be closer to other med. specialties in orientation, attitude, appearance of their offices, etc. (2) Those who tend to emphasize psychological aspects of problems, are more analytic in approach, see the patient for longer periods at a time and for more sessions. Psychoanalysts form a subdivision of this group.

11. Psychoanalysis was founded by S. Freud,* but many psychoanalysts have abandoned orthodox Freudian viewpoints and formed systems of their own. Psychoanalysis is most often used for neurotic disorders but is not limited to them. It is the most intensive of the therapies and usually involves several sessions a week over months, sometimes years. Psychoanalysts typically use a couch to help a patient relax and become more spontaneous in saying whatever comes to mind (free association).

12. Another approach under the more analytic category is the client-centered (formerly called nondirective) school of Carl Ransom Rogers (b. 1902 Oak Park, Ill.; psychologist). In the accepting and permissive atmosphere encouraged by the counselor, the client is expected to verbalize his feelings and gain insight into his problems. Insight leaves him more mature, freer, and more capable of indep. action (self-actualization).

13. The Eur. school of logotherapy (or existential analysis) has developed special interest for clerics. It emphasizes the importance of working toward an understanding of the meaning of life. It holds that other therapies, in treating the will to pleasure or the will to power, miss the fundamental ingredient of a satisfying therapeutic solution, i. e., what life actually means. It seems to be more compatible with Christianity but is not a religious therapy. Exponents include Viktor E. Frankl (b. 1905 Vienna, Austria; psychiatrist; works include *The Doctor and the Soul: An Introduction to Logotherapy* and *Man's Search for Meaning*).

14. Psychotherapy, as differentiated from counseling, is practiced by:

a. *Psychiatrists.* Psychiatrists must have an MD degree; are qualified to use physical treatments (e. g., shock therapy) besides psychotherapy; must meet legal requirements in order to practice. Bona fide psychoanalysts meet the same requirements as psychiatrists and have further special training; but since the term "psychoanalyst" is not protected by law, anyone may call himself a psychoanalyst.

b. *Psychologists.* Reputable psychologists who practice psychotherapy usually have a PhD degree from an accredited university. Training includes supervised experience in psychotherapy. Since the term "psychologist" is not protected by law, anyone may call himself a psychol.

c. *Psychiatric soc. workers.* Some soc. workers, with an MA degree from an accredited university, are qualified to practice psychotherapy. The term "soc. worker" is not defined by law.

15. The relative effectiveness of the various schools of psychotherapy is hard to determine. In any given case, success is probably determined more by the function of the therapist, the qualities of the patient, and the type of problem than by the therapist's theoretical orientation. KHB

P. E. Meehl, *What, Then, Is Man?* (St. Louis, 1958); A. C. Outler, *Psychotherapy and the Christian Message* (New York, 1954); C. R. Rogers, *Client-Centered Therapy* (Boston, 1951).

Ptolemy (Gnostic). See *Gnosticism,* 7 g.

Ptolemy (Lat.: Ptolemaeus). Name of kings of Egypt, the Ptolemies (323–30 BC), comprising the 31st (or Macedonian) dynasty, which included *Ptolemy I* (Ptolemy Soter [Gk. "savior"]; ca. 367–283; reputed son of Lagos [or Lagus]; king 323–285); *Ptolemy II* (Ptolemy Philadelphus; son of Ptolemy I; 309–ca. 247/246; king 285–ca. 247/246; acc. to tradition the LXX resulted from his initiative); *Ptolemy III* (Ptolemy Euergetes [Gk. "benefactor"]; son of Ptolemy II; ca. 282–ca. 222/221; king ca. 247/246 – ca. 222/221); *Ptolemy IV* (Ptolemy Philopator [or Philopater; from Gk. for "loving (his) father"]; son of Ptolemy III; ca. 244 – ca. 205/203; king ca. 222/221 – ca. 205/203; Jews probably less in favor at court than under previous reigns); *Ptolemy V* (Ptolemy Epiphanes [Gk. "illustrious"]; son of Ptolemy IV; ca. 210 – probably ca. 181/180; king ca. 205/203 – probably ca. 181/180); *Ptolemy VI* (or Ptolemy VII; Ptolemy Philometor [from Gk. for "loving (his) mother"]; son of Ptolemy V; ca. 186 – ca. 146/145; king probably ca. 181/180–146/145; cf. 1 Mac 10:51-60; 11:1-18; 2 Mac 1:10; 4:21); *Ptolemy VII* (or Ptolemy IX; Ptolemy Euergetes II; nicknamed Physcon [or Physkon; from Gk. for "fat paunch"]; brother of Ptolemy VI; ca. 184–117/116; king ca. 146/145 – ca. 117/116). Prophecies in Dn 9:9-12; 11 have been assoc. with the Ptolemies.

Public Aid to Church-Related Elementary and Secondary Schools. The question whether or not ch.-related elementary and secondary schools in the US should receive govt. aid became an issue in the late 1950s–1960s. The US Congress, many state legislatures, and courts wrestled with constitutional and practical problems. The 1965 Elementary and Secondary Educ. Act provides minimal aid to children in nonpublic schools under certain conditions. Under the child benefit theory, which holds that aid to the child is permissible but aid to the institution is not, the aid under this Act normally flows to the child through pub.-school channels. Benefits were broadened 1972.

The fed. lunch program was made available to all schools 1946; children and teachers in ch.-related schools have benefited also from other services.

In 1970, sixteen states provided bus transportation for children in nonpublic schools; 13 others authorized such transportation under various restrictions. A number of states provided textbook loans, and med., dental, psychiatric, testing, speech correction, reading and/or other services.

In the 1960s the "purchase of services" concept gained momentum. Several states authorized purchase of services from nonpublic schools, including ch.-related schools, in specified curriculum areas. Pa. pioneered in introd. this concept and several other states followed suit.

The debate about aid to ch.-related schools deals partly with constitutionality, on which the courts will have to rule, partly with "pub. service" performed by nonpublic schools. The US Supreme Court has ruled that incidental aid to a ch.-related school is not unconstitutional so long as the education serves the "secular purpose" of the state; further rulings are necessary in the interest of constitutional clarity.

Aid for direct religious instruction, for worship activities, and for special efforts in training for ch. membership is clearly out of the question. Perhaps more attention will be given to the "permeation issue": whether or not a ch.-related school may in its gen. educ. program accept aid and still refer to God or use religious motivation in so-called secular subjects for which aid is provided. A distinction bet. "secular purpose" and "secular instruction" will have to be made.

Various organizations of interested citizens and ch.-related groups seek aid to ch.-related schools on state and nat. levels. Citizens for Educational Freedom was perhaps the 1st. The Nat. Cath. Educational Assoc. and the Nat. Union of Christian Schools favor it. LCMS favors aid so long as it does not interfere with the distinctive purpose of ch.-related schools; it encourages its officials to help shape acceptable legislation.

Organized opponents of aid to ch.-related schools include the Am. Civil Liberties Union, Americans United for Separation of Ch. and State, the Am. Jewish Congress, and various groups representing pub. schools.

Important issues for chs. maintaining schools: (1) who will control their educ. enterprise; (2) how to maintain willing support for their schools by their mems. if the secular govt. contributes much to meet nonpublic school costs. These issues involve risks. WAK

See also *Church and State,* 14; *Schools, Church-Related.*

Public Relations. 1. Christians have pub. relations as a matter of fact and principle. Christianity and isolationism are a contradiction in terms. The ties that bind believers to Christ connect them to one another. Christians are not of this world, yet in this world; they are to be salt and light and by good works to invite unbelievers to give glory to the believers' Father who is in heaven.

2. In pub. relations the ch. tries to let the world know what the ch. is and does; sometimes that calls for correction of distorted information and impressions.

3. The ch. speaks as God's agent to the world. It echoes His judgment on sin and proclaims the mercy by which He forgives sin. The ch. also acts for Him in ministering His love and concern for men suffering under the burden which sin's curse brings.

4. In pub. relations terminology: the ch. by word and work creates a climate designed to make unbelievers receptive to the message and ministry of God. In doing so, reflecting in its own life the blessings of God, the ch. carries out God's plan. When Christians identify themselves with Christ and His Gospel, they by word and act convey God's judgment and forgiveness.

5. There are 2 audiences in the church's public. One is its own membership. Through internal pub. relations the ch. strives for the goals outlined Eph. 4:13: "to attain to the unity of the faith and of the knowledge of the Son of God, to mature manhood, to the measure of the stature of the fulness of Christ." To this end, congs. need to keep lines of communication open. Bonds of Christian fellowship can be strengthened, e. g., by personal contact, telephone calls, mail, various publications.

6. The other audience in the church's pub. is on the outside: all who are without Christ. The individual Christian touches part of this audience. The cong., denomination, and Christendom touch millions more.

7. The many channels through which the ch. can reach out to its audience at large include radio, TV, and the printed page. The overriding concern is for insistence reflecting God's saving purposes with integrity and dignity.

8. Christian stewardship requires time and effort devoted to programs for effective witness through all available means. Workshops, conferences, manuals, and professional books help all who lend themselves to meet the challenges and opportunities of the pub. relations of the church. AAW

Public Schools, Bible Reading in. See *Christian Education,* J 5.

Public Schools, Religion in. See *Christian Education,* J 5.

Public Worship. See *Worship, Orders of; Worship, Parts of.*

Publication Houses, Lutheran. By the time M. Luther* posted his 95 Theses* 1517 (see *Christian Church, History of,* III, 1) printing was widespread; Luther made extensive use of it. See also *Gutenberg, Johann(es).*

In the US, Luth. immigrants immediately printed periodicals and other literature, some before organizing into ch. bodies. Luth. pub. houses in Am. include:

Augsburg Publishing House. Minneapolis, Minn. Beginning traced to 1873, when a periodical committee was elected by the Conference (see *Norwegian-Danish Augustana Synod in America, The*). In 1890 the Conf., helped form The United* Norw. Luth. Ch. in Am., which est. Augsburg Pub. House 1891. The business changed quarters several times till it moved to its present location 1908.

When The Norw. Luth. Ch. of Am. was formed 1917, Augsburg Pub. House absorbed the pub. business of Hauge's Norw. Ev. Luth. Syn. in Am. (see *Eielsen Synod*) and the Norw. Syn. (see *Evangelical Lutheran Church, The,* 8–13); The Norw. Luth. Ch. of Am. changed name to The Ev. Luth. Ch. 1946. A new bldg. was erected 1953 for gen. offices and some production operations.

When the ELC, ALC, and UELC formed The ALC 1960/61, the pub. operations of the 3 uniting bodies (Augsburg Pub. House, Minneapolis; Lutheran Pub. House, Blair, Nebr. [UELC]; Wartburg Press, Columbus, Ohio [ALC]) were merged under the Bd. of Publication of The ALC, with the name Augsburg Pub. House. Main offices were est. Minneapolis, branch offices Columbus, Ohio; Omaha, Nebr.; Seattle, Wash.; Calgary, Alta., Can. The Messenger Press (see below) of the LFC, which merged with The ALC 1963, was inc. into Augsburg Pub. House.

Augustana Book Concern. Publishing activities of the Augustana Syn. began 1851 when L. P. Esbjorn* issued a tract for immigrants. T. N. Hasselquist* set up a printing press in his home in Galesburg, Ill., 1855 and issued various books, pamphlets, and periodicals.

The Swed. Luth. Publication Soc. was organized 1858 to take over the periodicals and conduct a printing business in the basement of Immanuel Ch., Chicago, Ill. The Augustana Syn. took over this business 1860. When the est. was lost in the 1871 Chicago Fire, Augustana Coll. (see *Augustana Evangelical Lutheran Church,* 14) was asked to take up the work. The school sold the business 1874 to Engberg-Hohnberg & Lindell, Chicago, who served the syn. 15 yrs. Then a new publication soc., Ungdomens Vänner, was est. at Augustana Coll. This soc. was later reorganized as Augustana Tract Soc. and secured interest in the printing plant of Thulin and Anderson, Moline, Ill. Another reorganization took place 1884, when the Augustana Book Concern was est. "for the benefit of Augustana Coll.," Rock Island, Ill. This was a venture without syn. sanction; there were other publishing ventures; gen. confusion resulted.

The Augustana Syn. resolved 1889 to est. a Bd. of Publication, which took over the affairs of the Augustana Book Concern and formed a new corporation, Luth. Augustana Book Concern, which also absorbed other ventures and was in turn absorbed in The Bd. of Publication of the LCA (see below).

Concordia Publishing House. In 1844 mems. of Trin. Luth. Ch., St. Louis, Mo., acted on their conviction that their leaders should reach out through the printed word to more people. C. F. W. Walther* became mgr. of printing activities and ed. Funds came from individual contributions and from appropriations by the cong. In 1849 the Mo. Syn. created a publication society. From 1854 the basement of Trin. Luth. Ch. was used by August Wiebusch and Son as a syn. printery (Synodal-Druckerei). Several yrs. later the syn. elected a publication committee.

In the late 1860s a successful effort was made under leadership of Louis Lange (1829–93; b. Hesse, Ger.; to Am. ca. 1846; worked in printeries in NYC, Detroit, and St. Louis; became pub. of *Die Abendschule* [previously pub. Buffalo, N. Y.] 1857) to est. a Synodal-Druckerei that was approved by the Mo. Syn. and came to be housed on the campus of Conc. Sem., with the composing room in operation by Dec. 27, 1869, and the plant dedicated Feb. 28, 1870. The name "Lutherischer Concordia-Verlag" was adopted 1878; the Eng. counterpart, "Concordia Publishing House," came into use at least as early as 1889.

New property was acquired on the NW corner of the intersection of Miami and Indiana 1872, the new bldg. completed 1874; units were added 1887 and 1892/93 (the latter on Jefferson); other bldgs. were added 1911, 1925, and 1941; pressroom and bindery were enlarged 1948; another large bldg. was added 1951; a 4th floor for offices was added to the 1925 bldg. 1955; the 1874 bldg. was replaced by a 5-story structure 1963/64.

M. C. Barthel was made Gen. Agent in charge of production and sales 1874; Martin Tirmenstein replaced him as Manager 1891 and was succeeded by E. Seuel* 1907; O. A. Dorn succeeded E. Seuel as Gen. Manager 1944 and was succeeded 1971 by Ralph L. Reinke as Pres.

One of the early major projects was *Der Lutheraner.* 1st issue dated Sept. 7, 1844. Another project was *Evangelisch-Lutherisches Schulblatt* (1865–1920; *Lutheran School Journal* 1921–47; *Lutheran Education* from Sept. 1947). *Lehre und Wehre* (1855–1929), *Magazin für ev.-luth. Homiletik* (1877–1929), and *Theological Monthly* (1921–29; successor of *Theological Quarterly* 1897–1920) merged into *Concordia Theological Monthly* (1930–). CPH pub. *The Lutheran Witness* (formerly organ of the [Eng.] Ev. Luth. Syn. of Mo. and Other States) from 1912. *This Day,* a Christian family magazine, was pub. 1949 to Jan. 1971, *Spirit,* a magazine for Christian teen-agers, Oct. 1963 to Aug. 1971.

Dr. Martin Luthers Sämmtliche Schriften, 23 vols. in 25, including index, was pub. 1880–1910. A 56-vol. Am. ed. of Luther's works in Eng. (joint project with Fortress Press [see below]) was begun 1955. Various eds. of Luther's SC have been pub.

F. A. O. Pieper,* *Christliche Dogmatik,* 3 vols. plus index vol., was pub. 1917–28, an Eng. version 1950–57. *Concordia Triglotta* was pub. 1921.

The Concordia Cyclopedia was pub. 1927, *Lutheran Cyclopedia* 1954, both predecessors of the present vol.

Publications cover a wide range of vocal and instrumental music. The audiovisual dept. produces and distributes many religious films and filmstrips and acquired Family Films 1959. There is a large ecclesiastical arts dept.

Lutheran Publishing House. Pub. activities of the UELC are traced back to the 1st issue of *Dansk luthersk Kirkeblad* Aug. 1877 (see *Danish Lutherans in America,* 5). A committee was appointed 1884 to plan establishment of a pub. plant. Pub. activity was taken over officially by the ch. 1891, to be dir. by a publication committee. In 1893 it was resolved to est. Dan. Luth. Publishing House at Blair, Nebr. At first nearly all publications were Danish, but use of Eng. increased to meet growing demands. The organization was controlled by a bd. elected by the convention of the church. LPH merged into Augsburg Publishing House (see above) 1961.

The Messenger Press. Beginning may be traced to Folkebladet Publishing Co. (organized 1877 by S. Oftedal*), which merged 1922 with the Free Ch. Book Concern (formed 1896 by Friends of Augsburg [see *Lutheran Free Church*]); a new corporation, the Luth. Free Ch. Publishing Co., was formed; name changed 1946 to The Messenger Press; merged with Augsburg Pub. House (see above) 1963.

Northwestern Publishing House. The Wisconsin* Syn. resolved 1876 to est., a syn. bookstore; it opened in Milwaukee 1876. In 1891 the syn. resolved to est. a bookstore-printshop; the venture was inc. 1891 as Northwestern Pub. House. Early publications included *Evangelisch-Lutherisches Gemeinde-Blatt* (est. 1865). *Church Hymnal for Lutheran Services* appeared 1910. *The Northwestern Lutheran* first appeared 1914, *The Junior Northwestern* 1919. The plant was housed successively in 4 downtown locations (1891–97, 1897–1902, 1902–14, 1914–48) before moving late 1948 into its present W North Ave. home, dedicated 1949.

The United Lutheran Publication House. The Bd. of Publication of the ULC, chartered 1919, resulted from merger of the corresponding bds. of the bodies that merged to form the ULC. Beginning traced to organization 1855 of the Publication Soc. of The General* Syn. of the Ev. Luth. Ch. in the USA. Trade name: Muhlenberg Press. Merged into The Bd. of Publication of the LCA (see below).

The Bd. of Publication of the LCA resulted 1963 from merger of pub. activities of the AELC, the Augustana Ev. Luth. Ch., the Fin. Ev. Luth. Ch. in Am. (Suomi Syn.), and the ULC; property and business of the Fin. Book Concern were sold by the Bd. later in 1963. Printing plants are in Philadelphia, Pa., and Rock Island, Ill. Publications include *The Lutheran;* curricular materials; books on theol.; devotional material; fiction. Trade name: Fortress Press; London, Eng., subsidiary: Lutheran Books Ltd. Operations include an ecclesiastical arts dept.

The Wartburg Press traced its beginning to an 1880 resolution of a committee of the Ev. Luth. Joint Syn. of Ohio* and Other States; operations were est. 1881 in Columbus, Ohio, under the name Lutheran Book Concern. Became HQ of ALC pub. activities 1930. Wartburg Publishing House, Chicago, Ill. (see *Iowa and Other States, Evangelical Lutheran Synod of*), was closed 1944 and the name Wartburg Press given to the Luth. Book Concern; a branch store and office opened in Omaha, Nebr. Merged into Augsburg Pub. House 1961 (see above). OAD GT

Publicity, Church. Christ's miss. command Mt 28:19-20 calls for all-out efforts, including publicity, in the interest of worldwide missions; cf. Lk 14:23.

Publicity was part of early NT ch. work (Acts 2:1-11; 8:4; Ro 1:8). Paul was untiring in efforts to make the Gospel known far and wide.

Ch. publicity was mainly by the spoken and written word for many cents. The Reformation used the printing press as an instrument for publicity.

A Ger. Bible was printed 1743 Germantown, Pa., by Christopher Saur (Sauer; Sower; 1693–1758; b. Laasphe, Wittgenstein, Westphalia, Ger.; educ. Marburg and Halle; joined Ger. Bap. Brethren*; to Pa. 1724; tailor, then farmer, then printer [1738]).

Luths. in Am. made early use of printing. The

Henkel Press was est. at New Market, Va., ca. 1805 (see also *Henkels, The,* 2, 3). The Saxon forebears of the Mo. Syn. began issuing *Der Lutheraner* 1844. See also *Lutheran Church – Missouri Synod, The,* V, 2; *Publication Houses, Lutheran.*

Other types of publicity include ch. bulletin bds.; highway bulletin bds. and other kinds of signs; banners; flags; emblems; statues; distinctive dress; special events; posters; window displays; radio; TV. Practically all denominations have made effective use of publicity. EWG

See also *American Lutheran Publicity Bureau; Radio and Television Evangelism, Network; Religious Press; Religious Tract Movement.*

Puerto Rico. See *Caribbean Islands,* A, C, E 4.

Pufendorf, Samuel von (1632–94). B. Dorf-Chemnitz, Saxony, Ger.; educ. Leipzig and Jena; prof. natural and internat. law Heidelberg 1661, Lund, Swed., 1670; held that natural law rests on the instinct of soc., moral law is revealed, civil law enacted by govt.

Pullus, Robert (Robertus; Bullen; Polanus; Pulby; Pulein; Puley; Pullan[us]; Pullein; Pullen; Pulley; Pulleyn; Pully; ca. 1080–ca. 1146/50). B. SW Eng.; taught at Oxford and Paris; cardinal 1144; helped develop doctrine of repentance; held that forgiveness of sin depends on a sacramental system. Works include 8 books of Sentences.

Pulpit. See *Church Furniture,* 1.

Pulpit Fellowship. See *Fellowship,* B.

Punishment, Eternal. See *Hereafter,* B, C; *Last Things,* 5.

Pupper. See *Johannes von Goch.*

Purana. See *Sacred Literature.*

Purcell, Henry (ca. 1658/59–1695). Organist; composer; b. probably London (Westminster?), Eng.; organist Westminster Abbey 1679, Chapel Royal 1682. Works include 2 settings for "Thou Knowest, Lord, the Secrets of Our Hearts"; *Te Deum; Magnificat; Nunc Dimittis; Jubilate.* The popular Trumpet Tune commonly ascribed to him may be of other origin. See also *Blow, John.*

Purgatory. *Catechismus Romanus,* I, vi, 3: "Besides [hell] there is a purging fire, by which the souls of the pious, tormented for a set time, are purified, so that they might enter the eternal fatherland, into which nothing defiled enters." *Canons and Decrees of the Council of Trent,* Sess. XXV, Decree Concerning Purgatory: "There is a purgatory, and . . . the souls there detained are aided by the suffrages of the faithful and chiefly by the acceptable sacrifice of the altar. . . . The more difficult and subtle questions . . . are to be excluded from popular instructions to uneducated people. Likewise, things that are uncertain or have the appearance of falsehood they shall not permit to be made known publicly and discussed." RCm refers to 2 Mac 12:43-45.

C. N. Callinicos, *The Greek Orthodox Catechism* (New York, 1960), p. 48: "Scripture . . . has never expressed anything whatever concerning a third state, such as a temporary Purgatory."

The idea of purgatory entered the Ch. of Eng. through the Oxford* Movement (see also *England,* C 7) in the form of an intermediate* state but without developing into a gen. accepted teaching. Common opinion makes it less a process of purification than of development and growth, ending only at the Last Judgment.

Luths. regard purgatory as unscriptural, insulting to Christ, indefensible, mercenary. WA 7, 452; 30 III, 309; 44, 812; WA-T 3, 539.

See also *Florence, Council of,* 2; *Indulgences.*

Purification of Mary. See *Church Year,* 13, 16.

Purificator. White cloth (usually linen, ca. 11 in. to 13 in. square) used to remove impurities from chalice and paten during Communion.

Purim. See *Judaism,* 4.

Puritans. Term in use since ca. the middle 1560s; designates a faction in the Angl. Ch. (see also *England,* B 7) that sought continued purification of the ch. to the point of perfection. The movement began with J. Hooper* and the Vestiarian* controversy 1550. When the Angl. Ch. renewed emphasis on vestments 1559, the movement responded by objecting to episcopacy and opted for Presbyterianism. But assemblies could not operate effectively under est. nat. policy. In the 1580s some Puritans advocated independency or congregationalism (see also *Conventicle; Dissenter; Nonconformist; United Church of Christ,* I A 1). Finally royal supremacy in the ch. came under attack, intensified by pol. enemies of the royal policy of the "divine* right of kings." Puritanism became practically a pol. party; for a time Puritans were in majority in the House of Commons.

Puritans did not want to separate from the est. ch. But oppression under James* I and Charles I (see *Presbyterian Confessions,* 1) led many to flee, esp. to Holland, whence the Pilgrim Fathers (see *United Church of Christ,* I A 1 and 2) came to Am. 1620 (see also *United States, Religious History of,* 4). TH

W. Haller, *The Rise of Puritanism* (New York, 1938); M. M. Knappen, *Tudor Puritanism* (Chicago, 1939); D. C. Neal, *The History of the Puritans,* 5 vols. (Portsmouth, N. H., 1816–17); *The Presbyterian Movement in the Reign of Queen Elizabeth,* ed. R. G. Usher (London, 1905); R. G. Usher, *The Reconstruction of the English Church,* I (New York, 1910); T. Hoyer, "The Historical Background of the Westminster Assembly," *CTM,* XVIII (1947), 572–591.

Purnell, Benjamin (1861–1927). B. Ky.; married 1877; deserted his wife; appeared before a justice of the peace in Ohio and acknowledged that he and Mary Stollard were husband and wife; lived as broom maker with Mary at Richmond, Ind.; joined a Southcottian (see *Southcottians*) colony at Detroit, Mich.; one of the Four Pillars of that colony 1892; expelled ca. 1895 for claiming to be the angel of Rv 10:7 (practical treason to the founder of the colony); roving evangelist and street preacher in various states; settled 1903 with a small group of friends from Ohio at Benton Harbor, Mich.; founded House* of David; charged with dishonesty and immorality; died at the height of the scandal.

Purposivism. Term denoting any of various theories of animal and human behavior or of nature that regard purpose or conscious intent as a basal fact. See also *Educational Psychology,* D 6.

Purusha. See *Brahmanism,* 2.

Purvey, John (ca. 1353/54 – ca. 1427/28). Educ. probably Oxford; assoc. with J. Wycliffe*; rev. Bible tr. of Wycliffe and Nicholas* of Hereford; imprisoned 1390; recanted under pressure but continued to spread Wycliffite views.

Pusey, Edward Bouverie (1800–82). B. Pusey, near Oxford, Eng.; educ. Oxford; assoc. with J. Keble* and J. H. Newman*; studied in Ger.; prof. Heb. and canon Christ Ch., Oxford; resolved to reform Angl. Ch. and unite Eng. and Roman chs.; head of Oxford* Movement after Newman's defection to RCm; suspended from preaching 1843 for 2 yrs. for a moderately RC sermon on the Eucharist; because of his prominence in the movement, Tractarianism* is also called Puseyism. Coed. *A Library of Fathers of the Holy Catholic Church;* other works include *Eirenikon* and 8 Tracts for the Times (18, 66–69, 76, 77, 81).

Puseyism. See *Pusey, Edward Bouverie.*

Pye, Henry John (ca. 1825–1903). Educ. Cambridge, Eng.; rector Clifton-Campville, Staffordshire 1851; RC 1868; hymnist. Hymns include "In His Temple Now Behold Him."

Pygmies. See *Africa,* A 1, E 6, F 1, 2, 5, 7.
Pyrrho. See *Skepticism.*
Pythagoreanism. Pol. movement and philos. named after Pythagoras (perhaps ca. 585/565 – perhaps ca. 495/475 BC; b. Samos, in the Aegean Sea; probably traveled in Greece, Egypt, and Asia in quest of wisdom; founded a school at Croton [modern Crotone], Catanzaro province, Calabria, S It.; little authentic about his life is known).

Developed some basic principles of astronomy and mathematics; held a theory of metempsychosis (see *Transmigration of Souls*); believed the earth to be round and originated the doctrine of the harmony of the spheres. The Pythagorean proposition is the theorem in geometry that the square on the hypotenuse of a right triangle equals the sum of the squares on the other sides. Developed dualism* into a table of opposites based on the proposition that the universe is composed of 10 pairs of contradictories (e. g., one/many; limited; unlimited; light/darkness; good/evil). Applied a theory of numbers to music, medicine, etc. sometimes in semimystical speculation, holding in effect that the world is made of numbers. When mems. of the Croton school expressed doubt or ventured to suggest departure from school rules they were told: *"Ipse dixit"* (Lat. "He himself said it").

See also *Philosophy.*

Q

"Q." First letter of the Ger. word *Quelle* ("source"). In Biblical criticism the letter "Q" is the symbol of an alleged source of Mt and Lk.

Qabbala(h). See *Cabala.*

Qaraites. See *Karaites.*

Qatar. See *Middle East,* L 8.

Qua Iboe Mission. See *Africa,* C 14.

Quadragesima (Lat. "fortieth"). 1. The 40 days of Lent (Ash Wed. to Holy Sat., excluding Sundays); 2. Ancient name of the 1st Sun. in Lent (with preceding Sundays named by analogy: Quinquagesima, Sexagesima, Septuagesima); 3. The 40th day after Easter: Ascension (cf. Acts 1:3).

See also *Church Year,* 3–5, 8, 9, 14, 16; *Tempus clausum.*

Quadragesimo Anno. See *Encyclicals.*

Quadratus (Kodratos; early 2d c.). Christian apologist; a fragment of his apology to emp. Hadrian ca. 124/129 preserved by Eusebius* of Caesarea (*HE,* IV, iii, 1–2); erroneously identified by Jerome with Quadratus, early bp. Athens (perhaps under Marcus Aurelius or Antoninus Pius) and by others with bp. Quadratus of Utica (martyr in Valerian persecution; see *Persecution of Christians,* 4). See also *Apologists,* 2; *Christian Church, History of,* I, 2.

Quadrilateral, Lambeth. See *England,* C 11; *Protestant Episcopal Church, The,* 4 b.

Quadrivium (Lat. "crossroads; place where 4 roads meet"). In the Middle Ages, the group of studies consisting of arithmetic, music, geometry, astronomy. Quadrivium was the higher group of the 7 liberal arts, trivium* the lower. The concept of the quadrivium is ascribed by some to A. M. T. S. Boethius.* See also *Cassiodorus, Flavius Magnus Aurelius; Martianus Capella.*

Quakers. Common name for mems. of Soc. of Friends.*

Quandt, Johann Jakob (1686–1772). B. Königsberg, Prussia, Ger.; educ. Halle and in the Neth.; prof., pastor, court preacher Königsberg; exponent of orthodox Lutheranism. Issued *Neue Sammlung alter und neuer Lieder.*

Quartodeciman Controversy. See *Church Year,* 7; *Easter Controversy.*

Quasimodogeniti. See *Church Year,* 14, 16; *Low Sunday.*

Quatember ("4 ember periods," from Lat. for "4" and OE *ymbren,* perhaps a corruption of *ymbryne,* "period; revolution of time; cycle," from *ymb,* "about; round" and *ryne,* "course; running"; or from Lat. *quatuor tempora,* "4 periods"). Four periods, of 3 ember days each, set aside for fasting,* prayer, and almsgiving in the 4 seasons (Lat. *ieiunia* ["fasts"] *quatuor temporum*). The pattern followed in modern times was est. in the 11th c.: Wed., Fri., and Sat. after (1) 1st Sun. in Lent; (2) Pentecost; (3) Holy Cross Day, Sept. 14; (4) St. Lucia's Day, Dec. 13.

Quatenus and Quia Subscriptions. See *Lutheran Confessions,* D 3.

Quattuor Coronati. 4 saints (identity indefinite) commemorated Nov. 8 since the 6th c. in a ch. dedicated to them in Rome, It.

Quebec. See *Canada,* A 27, C.

Queen Anne's Bounty. Fund est. 1704 by Queen Anne of Eng., from first fruits (annates*) and tenths confiscated by Henry* VIII, to augment livings of poorer Angl. clergy.

Queensland, Evangelical Lutheran Synod of. See *Australia, Lutheranism in,* B 1.

Queirós. See *Quirós.*

Queiss, Erhard von (d. 1529). B. Storkow, Lusatia, Ger.; chancellor of duke Frederick II of Liegnitz till 1523; then bp. Pomesania (later called Marienwerder; now Kwidzyn, Poland); joined Reformation movement 1524.

Quellen. See *Higher Criticism,* 6; *"Q."*

Quempas Carol. See *Hymnody, Christian,* 4.

Quenstedt, Johann(es) Andreas (1617–88). Nephew of J. Gerhard*; Luth. dogmatician; b. Quedlinburg, Ger.; educ. Helmstedt and Wittenberg; prof. logic, metaphysics, and theol. Wittenberg; noted for mild, irenic spirit and retiring, pious disposition. Works include *Theologia didactico-polemica, sive Systema theologicum,* a standard of Luth. orthodoxy. See also *König, Johann Friedrich.*

Quercum, Synodus ad (Syn. at The Oak). Held 403 on the imperial estate called The Oak (Lat. *Quercus*), in a suburb of Chalcedon (modern Kadiköy, opposite Istanbul, on E side of entrance to Bosporus); attended by perhaps ca. 36 bps.; condemned and deposed J. Chrysostom* in his absence on charges that were for the most part of no importance and showed nothing but the enmity of his accusers.

Quesnel, Pasquier (Paschasius; 1634–1719). B. Paris, Fr.; mem. Fr. Oratory (see *Oratorians,* 3) 1657; exiled to Brussels, Belg., 1685 for not condemning Jansenism.* Works include *Réflexions morales,* which reflected also his extreme Gallicanism*; the book was condemned by *Unigenitus** 1713. Quesnel was arrested 1703 in Brussels; escaped; fled to Amsterdam; est. a Jansenist ch. in the Neth.; died RC.

Quia and Quatenus Subscriptions. See *Lutheran Confessions,* D 3.

Quick, Oliver Chase (1885–1944). Angl. theol.; educ. Harrow and Oxford; priest 1912; held various positions, including regius prof. divinity Oxford; upheld orthodox Anglicanism. Works include *Essays in Orthodoxy; Catholic and Protestant Elements in Christianity; Doctrines of the Creed.*

Quicunque, Symbolum. See *Ecumenical Creeds,* C.

Quidditas (ML, "whatness"). Scholastic term for essence.

Quidditative Cognition. See *Cognition.*

Quietism. Form of mysticism; holds that spiritual exaltation is reached by self-abnegation and by withdrawing the soul from outward activities and fixing it in passive religious contemplation; representatives included A. Bourignon,* F. de S. de la M. Fénelon,* Guyon,* M. de Molinos.*

Quimby, Phineas Parkhurst (1802–66). Mental healer; b. Lebanon, N. H.; clockmaker; hypnotist; office Portland, Maine; tried to formulate a religious philos. and a science of happiness and health; consultants included M. M. Eddy*; followers developed New* Thought. See also *Church of Christ, Scientist.*

Quinisext Synod (2d Trullan, from ML *trullus,* "dome"; so called from the domed hall in the imperial palace where it was held; the 1st Trullan syn. or council was held here 680–681). Convened by Justinian* II; held ca. 691/692 Constantinople;

adopted 102 disciplinary canons (including one reasserting canon 28 of Chalcedon) to complete the work of the 5th and 6th (hence called Quinisext; Gk.: *penthekte*) Ecumenical Councils (see *Councils and Synods,* 4); there were no duly-appointed W legates; its acts were rejected by Sergius* 1. See also *Eastern Orthodox Standards of Doctrine; Germanos I; Monothelitism; Schism,* 4.

Quiñones, Francisco de (perhaps ca. 1475/80–1540). B. León, Sp.; Franciscan 1498; minister gen. Observants* 1523–28; mediated bet. Clement* VII and Charles* V from 1526; cardinal 1527 (1528?); defended the interests of the queen in the question of the divorce of Henry* VIII. Compiled a breviary that influenced the Book* of Common Prayer. See also *Counter Reformation,* 3.

Quinquagesima Sunday. See *Church Year,* 3; *Esto mihi; Quadragesima.*

Quinquesaecularis, Consensus. See *Consensus Quinquesaecularis.*

Quintilian (Marcus Fabius Quintilianus; 1st c. AD). Roman rhetorician; b. Calagurris (modern Calahorra), Logroño prov., N Sp.; educ. Rome, It.; in Sp. ca. 57–68; taught rhetoric in Rome; pupils included Pliny* the Younger. Works include *Institutio oratoria.* See also *Higher Education,* 6.

Quirós, Pedro Fernandes de (Queirós; Fernandez; perhaps ca. 1560/65–ca. 1614/15). B. Évora, Port.; explored Pacific; envisioned a "city of God" there; est. "New Jerusalem" as miss. base on the New Hebrides island Espíritu Santo; tried to est. a new soc. order. See also *Society Islands.*

Quistorp. Name of several Luth. theologians, including (1) *Johann* (1584–1648). Grandfather of 2; b. Rostock, Ger.; educ. Frankfurt an der Oder and Rostock; prof. theol. 1614, archdeacon 1616, supt. 1644, all at Rostock; firmly confessional; practical in preaching; zealous for educ. of the young; indefatigable. Works include *Articuli Formulae concordiae illustrati; Manducatio ad studium theologicum;* commentaries on books of the Bible. (2) *Johann Nikolaus* (1651–1715). Grandson of 1; b. Rostock, Ger.; educ. Rostock and Konigsberg; traveled through Ger., Holland, and Den.; deacon 1676, then successively pastor, supt., prof. theol., all in Rostock. Works include *De sanctissima et omni tempore sufficientissima Christi satisfactione; De Bellarmini in ecclesiam notis non notis; De principio theologiae cognoscendae unico; De privata confessione; De poenitentia; De quaestione, an peccatum originis formaliter sit mere privativum an positivum simul.*

Quitman, Frederick Henry (Aug. 7, 1760–June 26, 1832). Luth. theol.; b. Iserlohn, Duchy of Cleves, Westphalia, near the lower Rhine; educ. Halle, where he was influenced by J. S. Semler*; private tutor 2 yrs.; ordained 1783 by Luth. consistory Amsterdam; pastor Curaçao, W. Indies; pol. unrest caused him to sail with his family for home via N. Y. 1795; decided to stay in Am.; pastor at various places in N. Y. more than 30 yrs.; pres. N. Y. Ministerium 1807–25. Rationalism* and Socinianism* increased under his leadership; he denied the doctrine of original sin; the doctrines of the Trin., deity of Christ, Baptism, Lord's Supper, wrath of God, and Christ's priestly office are either not mentioned or are not clearly taught in his writings. Works include a catechism; a treatise on magic; 3 sermons on the Luth. Reformation.

H. J. Kreider, *History of The United Lutheran Synod of New York and New England* (Philadelphia, 1954); J. Nicum, "The Doctrinal Development of the New York Ministerium," *The Lutheran Church Review,* VI (1887), 140–152; *Annals of the American Pulpit,* issued also as part of *Annals of the American Pulpit,* ed. W. B. Sprague, IX (New York, 1869), 115–121. WWW

Qumran. See *Dead Sea Scrolls.*

Qur'an. See *Koran.*

R

Raabe, Wilhelm Karl (Carl; pseudonym Jakob Corvinus; 1831–1910). Poet and novelist; b. Eschershausen, Ger.; his trilogy *Der Hungerpastor, Abu Telfan,* and *Der Schüdderump* has been called Christian symbolic realism. Other works include *Deutscher Mondschein; Nach dem grossen Kriege; Unruhige Gäste.*

Raattama(a), Juhani. See *Finland, Lutheranism in,* 4.

Rabanus Maurus (Hrabanus; Rhabanus; originally Rabanus Magnentius; called Maurus by Alcuin, after St. Maur [see *Maurists*]; ca. 776–856). Frankish theol., scholar, teacher; b. Mainz, Ger.; educ. Fulda and Tours (under Alcuin*); head of Fulda school 803; priest 814; abbot Fulda 822–842; abp. Mainz 847. Works include *De institutione clericorum; De laudibus sanctae crucis; Poenitentiale.* See also *Predestinarian Controversy,* 1.

MPL, 107–112.

Rabaut, Paul (1718–94). B. Bédarieux, Hérault dept., in Languedoc, S Fr.; vicar Nimes 1738; studied under A. Court* from 1740; pastor Nimes 1742; severely persecuted; withdrew from active ministry 1785; imprisoned; died soon after release.

Rabbi (Heb. "my master"; from *rabh,* "great one; chief"). Title of authoritative teacher of Judaism (cf., e. g., Jn 3:2).

Rabbinism. Traditions and teachings of rabbis (see *Rabbi*). See also *Talmud.*

Rabbula (Rabbulas; Rabula[s]; ca. 350–ca. 435/436). B. Qennesrin, near Aleppo, NW Syria; monk ca. 400; bp. Edessa 411 [412?]; opposed Nestorianism,* esp. Theodore* of Mopsuestia; Peshitta (see *Bible Versions,* C) ascribed to him; succeeded by Ibas.*

Rabe, Antonius. See *Corvinus, Antonius.*

Rabelais, François (perhaps ca. 1483/95–1553). Satirist; humorist; b. near Chinon, Indre-et-Loire dept., NW cen. Fr., on the Vienne R.; Franciscan, then Benedictine, then secular priest; taught at U. of Montpelier; physician; traveled, held various positions, finally a parish at Meudon from 1552. Works include *Pantagruel* and *Gargantua,* issued under pseudonym Alcofribas Nasier (anagram of his name) and satirizing the monastic ideal, superstitious veneration of saints, old-fashioned educ., and university theology.

Rabinówitsch, Joseph (1837–99). Founder Jewish-Christian movement in Kishinev, Bessarabia, S Russ., on a tributary of the Dniester R., 90 mi. NW of Odessa; b. Resina, on the Dniester, Bessarabia; reared in strict Judaism; visited Palestine in the early 1880s; became Christian; studied NT; est. a cong. in Kishinev called Israelites of the New Covenant; bap. 1885. Works include apologetic writings.

Rabula(s). See *Rabbula.*

Race Relations. See *Social Action.*

Rachmaninoff, Sergei Wassilievitch (1873–1943). Composer, pianist, conductor; b. Oneg estate, near Ilmen Lake, Novgorod govt., Russ.; US resident 1918. Works include symphonies; piano concertos; sonatas; *Liturgy of St. John Chrysostomus* for mixed chorus.

Racovian Catechism. See *Rakau Catechism; Socinianism.*

Rad, Gerhard von (1901–71). B. Nürnberg, Ger.; educ. Friedrich-Alexander-U. (Erlangen-Nürnberg) and Tübingen; prof. Jena, Göttingen, Heidelberg; investigated peculiarities of individual Biblical witnesses; gave special attention to the relationship bet. theol. and philos. in wisdom literature; influenced exegesis and systematics. Works include *Das erste Buch Mose; Das fünfte Buch Mose; Theologie des Alten Testaments; Gesammelte Studien zum Alten Testament.*

Radama I. See *Africa,* B 9.

Radbertus, Paschasius (Paschase Radbert; ca. 785/786–ca. 860/865). Benedictine theol.; b. Soissons, Fr.; monk at Corbie; abbot there ca. 842/843–ca. 851/853. Works include *De corpore et sanguine Domini.* See also *Eucharistic Controversies; Ratramnus.*

MPL, 120.

Rade, Paul Martin (pseudonym Paul Martin; 1857–1940). B. Rennersdorf, Upper Lusatia, Ger.; educ. Leipzig; pastor Schönbach and Frankfurt am Main; prof. Marburg. Cofounder and ed. *Die christliche Welt.*

Radegunde (Radegunda; Radegundis; 518–587). Pious Frankish queen; wife of Clotaire I (Clothaire; Ger.: Clothar; also Lothar and Lothaire; king Soissons 511–588, of all Franks 558–561); after Clotaire murdered her brother, she fled from court, was ordained deaconess, and est. a nunnery near Poitiers.

Radewijns, Florentius. See *Florentius Radewijns.*

Radio and Television Evangelism, Network. 1. Religious broadcasting began Jan. 2, 1921, when Edwin Jan van Etten (1884–1956), rector Calvary Episc. Ch., Pittsburgh, Pa., conducted an Epiphany service over Station KDKA, Pittsburgh.

2. Religious broadcasts over networks were common by the 1950s.

3. Policies of the various radio and TV networks differ and have been changed repeatedly. NBC and ABC gave free time to Prots. (but not, as a rule, to individual denominations), RCs, and Jews. CBS est. the Columbia Ch. of the Air, giving time on successive Suns. to representatives of various denominations in approximate proportion to their numerical strength in the US. MBS also gave considerable time for religious programs.

4. NBC, ABC, and MBS also made time available for purchase.

5. Sponsored network radio religious broadcasts have included The Lutheran Hour, Bringing Christ to the Nations (Oswald C. J. Hoffmann, b. 1913; see also 6 and 7); The Hour of Decision (Billy Graham, b. 1918); The Old Fashioned Revival Hour (founded 1925 by Charles Edward Fuller,* 1887–1968; Bap. evangelist; b. Los Angeles, Calif.); The Voice of Prophecy (Harold Marshall Sylvester Richards, 1894–).

Religious network TV programs (sustaining) have included Frontiers of Faith (NBC); Lamp unto My Feet (CBS); Look Up and Live (CBS); Direction '63. Nationally distributed TV filmed programs have included This Is the Life (Lutheran TV Productions Bd.; see also 8); Talk Back and Breakthru (TV, Radio, and Film Commission, The Meth. Ch.), Davey and Goliath (children's puppet program, LCA).

6. The Luth. Hour began 1930, was suspended 1931–35 (partly because of uncertain financial support), was heard in the 1970s in 125 lands over more than 1,500 stations.

7. Luth. Hour speakers: W. A. Maier* 1930–31,

1935–50; Lawrence Acker 1950–51; Armin C. Oldsen 1951–53; O. C. J. Hoffmann 1955–.

8. This Is the Life (TV program), sponsored by LCMS, began 1952, spread to other countries including Can., Australia, the Philippines, Bermuda, Nigeria, and to Gibraltar. ERB

C. T. Griswold and C. H. Schmitz, compilers, *How You Can Broadcast Religion,* ed. L. J. Anderson (New York, 1957); H. E. Luccock, *Communicating the Gospel* (New York, 1954); E. C. Parker et al., *Religious Radio: What to Do and How* (New York, 1948); J. W. Bachman, *The Church in the World of Radio-Television* (New York, 1960); E. A. Nida, *Message and Mission* (New York, 1960); E. C. Parker, *Religious Television: What to Do and How* (New York, 1961).

Radio Stations, Religious. 1. Christian chs. in gen. were slow to realize the vast potential of owning and operating a radio station. In the early days of radio, facilities were available in abundance. The fed. govt. would have gladly assigned desirable frequencies to stations owned by denominations. But nearly all frequencies were soon assigned to commercial interests. Only a few denominations or congregations began to operate stations. Some of these soon discontinued operation; some became completely commercial; some became largely commercial, reserving only a small amount of time for religious broadcasts. It became nearly impossible for chs. to est. new AM stations. The advent of FM offered chs. a 2d chance.

2. Religious radio stations est. in the US include:

Ark.: KRLW–S. Bap. Coll., Walnut Ridge.

Calif.: KFSG (FM: KKLA)–Echo Park Evangelistic Assoc., Los Angeles; KPPC–Pasadena Presb. Ch., Pasadena.

Colo.: KPOF–Pillar of Fire, Inc., Denver.

Ill.: WMBI (FM: WMBI-FM)–Moody Bible Institute, Chicago; WCBD–Christian Cath. Ch. Chicago.

Ind.: WGRE (FM)–DePauw U., Greencastle.

Iowa: KFGQ (FM: KFGQ-FM)–Boone Biblical Coll., Boone; KWLC–Luther Coll., Decorah.

Ky.: WMTC–Ky. Mountain Holiness Assoc., Van Cleve; WSDX (FM)–S. Bap. Theol. Sem., Louisville.

La.: KVOB (FM: KVOB-FM)–Cen. La. Broadcasting Corp. (La. Bap. Assoc.), Alexandria; WWL (FM: WWLH)–Loyola U., New Orleans.

Mich.: WMRP–Meth. Radio Parish, Inc., Flint; WMPC–Liberty Street Gospel Ch. of Lapeer, Lapeer.

Minn.: KTIS (FM: KTIS-FM)–Northwestern Theol. Sem. and Bible Training School, Minneapolis; WCAL (FM: WCAL-FM)–St. Olaf Coll., Northfield.

Mo.: KFUO (FM: KFUO-FM)–The Luth. Ch.–Mo. Syn., Clayton. See also 3.

N. J.: WSOU (FM)–Seton Hall Coll., South Orange; WAWZ–Pillar of Fire, Zarephath.

N. Y.: WKBW–WKBW, Inc. (Churchill Tabernacle), Buffalo; WBBR–Watch Tower Bible and Tract Soc., Inc., N. Y.

R. I.: WPTL–Providence Bible Institute, Providence.

Tex.: KMHB (FM)–Mary Hardin-Baylor Coll., Belton; KWBU–Baylor U. (Bap. Gen. Conv. of Tex.), Corpus Christi; KYBS (FM)–Bap. Gen. Conv. of Tex., Dallas; KSMU (FM)–Southern Meth. U., Dallas; KELP–Paso Broadcasting Co., Inc. (Richey Evangelistic Assoc.), El Paso; KHBL (FM)–Wayland Bap. Coll., Plainview; KFTW–Southwestern Bap. Theol. Sem., Fort Worth.

Va.: WBBL–Grace Covenant Presb. Ch., Richmond.

Wash.: KTW–1st Presb. Ch., Seattle; KGA–Gonzaga U., Spokane.

3. KFUO, "The Gospel Voice," St. Louis, Mo., was dedicated Dec. 14, 1924. It had a 500-watt transmitter. Control room and studio were in the attic of Conc. Sem. on S. Jefferson Ave. The cost of $14,000 was covered by sem. students and mems. of the LLL, Walther League, and others. 1st radio committee: J. H. C. Fritz* and W. A. Maier.* The St. Louis Luth. Publicity Organization appropriated an annual sum toward maintenance of the station. At first the station broadcast 2 hrs. a week. H. H. Hohenstein* became full-time dir. 1925. In 1927 the station moved to the new campus, 801 De Mun Ave., Clayton (suburb of St. Louis), and was rebuilt for $50,000 contributed by the LLL. The new plant was dedicated May 29, 1927, and given to the Mo. Syn. It had a 1,000-watt transmitter; broadcast hrs. were increased to ca. 30 a week. In 1940 the Fed. Communications Commission granted KFUO a new frequency, with full daytime broadcasting privileges, from 80½ to 102½ hrs. a week; this led to erection of a new tower and antenna system, enlargement and renovation of the radio bldg., and installation of a 5,000-watt transmitter; later the bldg. was enlarged and FM added.

4. KFUO helps promote religious broadcasting over other stations. It also promotes Nat. Luth. Radio and TV Week. HHH

See also *Radio Voice of the Gospel.*

Radio Voice of the Gospel (RVOG). Radio station ETLF, Addis Ababa, Ethiopia; owned and operated by LWF; affiliated with the Coordinating Committee for Christian Broadcasting, which represents the All Afr. Conf. of Chs., the East Asia Christian Conf., and the Near East Council of Chs. The franchise to build and operate the station was granted by the Ethiopian govt. 1959. The station began operations 1963. Purposes: proclaim the Gospel; strengthen the life of Christian chs.; promote culture and educ. It broadcasts in English, Fr., and a variety of Asiatic and Afr. tongues.

Radziwill, Nicholas (Nikolaus; Mikolaj; 1515–65). "The Black"; b. Nieswiez; military head Vilnyus (Vilna); chancellor Lithuania; joined Reformation movement 1553; Calvinist; J. Laski* was his house guest 1557; sponsored Polish Bible tr. pub. 1563.

Rafael (Raffael; Raffaello; Raffaelo). See *Raphael.*

Raffay, Sándor (Alexander; 1866–1947). Educ. Pozsony (Bratislava), Jena, Leipzig, and Basel; prof. Pozsony 1896; pastor Budapest 1908; bp. 1918–45. Noted preacher and organizer; helped arrange 1st LWC. Tr. NT into Hung.; helped prepare an order of service.

Ragaz, Leonhard (1868–1945). B. Tamins, Graubünden, Switz.; cathedral pastor Basel 1902; became socialist; prof. Zurich 1908; resigned in the early 1920s to devote himself to soc. work. Influenced by C. F. Blumhardt's (see *Blumhardt,* 3) concept of the kingdom of God, he worked for its realization through democratic soc. order, discipleship of Christ, Franciscan poverty, and peace movements.

Ragged Schools. See *Guthrie, Thomas.*

Rahamägi, Hugo Bernhard. See *Estonia,* 3.

Rahlfs, Otto Gustav Alfred (1865–1935). B. Linden, near Hanover, Ger.; prof. OT Göttingen; devoted his life to textual study of the LXX and preparation of a critical ed.

Rahtmann, Hermann (Rathmann; 1585–1628). B. Lübeck, Ger.; diaconus 1612, pastor 1626 Danzig. His *Jesu Christi: des Königs aller Könige und Herrn aller Herren Gnadenreich* led to widespread controversy in Lutheranism on the relationship bet. Word and Spirit and to a fuller systematic statement of the doctrine of the Word as means of grace, esp. of the efficacy of Scripture.

Raikes, Robert (1735–1811). B. Gloucester, Eng.; in 1757 he inherited the *Gloucester Journal* (est. 1732) and issued it 40 yrs.; philanthropist; interested in soc. problems, esp. prison reform; saw the chief cause of degradation in inadequate training of children; in 1780 he engaged a woman to teach a Sun. school. See also *Sunday School,* 2.

Raimund. Variant spelling of Raymond.*

Rainbow, Order of the. See *Freemasonry,* 6.

Rainbow Bible. See *Polychrome Bible.*

Rainolds, John (Reynolds; 1549–1607). B. Pinhoe, near Exeter, Devonshire, Eng.; educ. Oxford; pres. Corpus Christi Coll., Oxford, 1598–1607; Aristotelian scholar; Calvinist; chief representative of Puritans* at Hampton* Court Conf.

Rainy, Robert (1826–1906). B. Glasgow, Scot.; educ. Glasgow and Edinburgh; pastor Free* Ch. of Scot.; prof. ch. hist. 1862, principal 1874 New Coll., Edinburgh; helped form United* Free Ch. of Scot. 1900.

Rakau Catechism (Racovian Catechism). First statement of Socinian principles; begun by F. P. Socinus*; pub. in Polish 1605, Ger. 1608; Lat. 1609; takes its name from Raków, Kielce dept., Poland, on a tributary of the Vistula; not a formal confessional creed. See also *Smalcius, Valentinus; Socinianism.*

Ram Mohan Roy (Ram Mohan Rai; Ram Mohan Ray; Ramamohana Rai; Rammohun Roy; ca. 1772/74–1833). B. Radhanagar, Hugli dist., near Murshidabad, Bengal; Hindu religious reformer; founded Brahma (or Brahmo) Samaj (see *Hinduism,* 6); sometimes credited with founding comparative religion.* See also *Adam, William.*

Ramabai Mukti Mission, American Council. Founded 1889 by P. Ramabai*; mem. IFMA.

Ramabai, Pandita (1858–1922). Hindu educator; b. S India; father Brahmin; because of her gifts and learning and the esteem in which she came to be held she was called "Pandita" (related to Eng. "pundit"), highest title possible for a native woman in India; known in full as Pandita Sarasvati Ramabai or Pandita Ramabai Sarasvati (sarasvati: "divine embodiment of language, literary expression, and learning"); bap. 1883 in England; visited Am. 1886 and with resultant gifts est. Sarada Sadan ("House" [or "Home"] of Wisdom"), a nonsectarian school for high caste Hindu girls, esp. child widows, at Bombay 1889; this school moved to Poona 1890/91. At Khedgaon (Kedgoan), ca. 30 mi. from Poona, an additional institution called Mukti Sadan ("House" [or "Home"] of Salvation") was est., largely for girls of low caste; it included a farm, ch., hosp., and printing press. Tr. Bible into Marathi.

Ramadan. 9th mo. of the Muhammadan yr.; observed by Muslim with fasting; commemorates the giving of the Koran.* See also *Islam,* 3.

Ramakrishna Paramahamsa (1834–86). Hindu mystic, yogi; b. Kamarpukur, Hooghly dist., W Bengal; tried to grasp the divine also in Islam* and Christianity; held that the Absolute transcends all appearances of deity. See also *Hinduism,* 7.

Ramanuja (perhaps ca. 1017?/50–perhaps ca. 1137/50). Hindu philos.; b. perhaps Bhutapuri or Conjeeveram, S India; founded Vaishnava sect; held 3 eternal principles: God (the highest soul), the world (without soul), the individual soul.

Ramayana. See *Hinduism,* 6; *Sacred Literature.*

Rambach, August Jakob (1777–1851). B. Quedlinburg, Ger.; educ. Halle; diaconus 1802, pastor 1818, senior of the ministerium 1834, all at Hamburg; hymnologist.

Rambach, Johann Jakob (1693–1735). B. Halle, Ger.; educ. Halle and Jena; helped J. H. Michaelis* prepare his Heb. Bible; pietist; taught at Halle from 1723; prof. theol. and supt. Giessen 1731; dir. Giessen Paedagogium 1732; hymnist. Hymns include "Gesetz und Evangelium sind beide Gottesgaben"; "Ich ben getauft auf deinen Namen"; "Mein Schöpfer, steh mir bei."

Rambam. See *Maimonides.*

Rambaud, Jules. See *Evangelisch-christliche Einheit.*

Rampolla del Tindaro, Mariano (1843–1913). B. Polizzi, near Palermo, Sicily; entered diplomatic service of Roman Curia* 1869; cardinal 1887; exponent of temporal power of pope.

Ramsay, William Mitchell (1851–1939). Classicist, archaeol., NT scholar; b. Glasgow, Scot.; taught at Oxford and Aberdeen; traveled extensively in Asiatic Turkey. Works include *The Church in the Roman Empire; St. Paul the Traveller and the Roman Citizen; The Christ of the Earliest Christians; The Bearing of Recent Discovery on the Trustworthiness of the New Testament; The Cities of St. Paul; A Historical Commentary on St. Paul's Epistle to the Galatians; Luke, the Physician; The Historical Geography of Asia Minor; The Cities and Bishoprics of Phrygia; Was Christ Born at Bethlehem?*

Ramus, Petrus (Pierre [de] la Ramée; 1515–72). Philos. and mathematician; b. Cuth (or Cuts), Vermandois, in Picardy, near Soissons and Noyon, in Oise, Fr.; opposed Aristotelianism; Prot. 1561 (1562?); to Switz. 1568, Ger. 1569; returned to Fr. 1570(1571?); perished in Bartholomew's* Day Massacre.

Ranavalona I and II. See *Africa,* B 9.

Rancé, Armand Jean Le Bouthillier de (1626–1700). B. Paris, Fr.; priest 1651; abbot La Trappe monastery, Normandy, 1664 till retirement 1695; founded Trappists.*

Randall, John. See *Baptist Churches,* 26.

Ranke, Leopold von (1795–1886). Hist.; b. Wiehe, Thuringia, Ger.; founded the modern school of history; prof. Berlin 1825–71. Works include *Die römischen Päpste, ihre Kirche und ihr Staat in 16. und 17. Jahrhundert; Deutsche Geschichte im Zeitalter der Reformation.*

Rankin, Melinda (1811–88). Presb. miss.; began a school, mainly for Mexicans, at Brownsville, Tex., 1852; to Monterrey, Mex., 1855, where she est. a school 1865.

Ranters. 1. Name of reproach given to an antinomian and spiritualistic sect in mid-17th c. Eng. 2. Term applied colloquially to 19th-c. Primitive Meths. (see *Methodist Churches,* 1, 4 b) because of the loud tones of their preaching and responses.

Raphael (Raffaello [in full Raffaello Santi, or Sanzio]; Raffael; Raffaelo; Rafael; 1483–1520). Painter; b. Urbino, It.; to Florence 1504; to Rome after 1508; in service of Julius II (see *Popes,* 19); protege of Leo X (see *Popes,* 20); chief architect of St. Peter's, Rome, 1514; conservator of Roman excavations 1515. Works include *St. George and the Dragon; Coronation of the Virgin; Sistine Madonna.*

Rapoport, Solomon Judah Löb (Jehuda; 1790–1867). B. Lvov, Galicia; rabbi Tarnopol 1837, Prague 1840. Works include biographies and vol. 1 of an encyclopedia on the Talmud.

Rapp, Johann Georg (1757–1847). B. Iptingen, near Vaihingen, Württemberg, Ger.; linen weaver; mystic; separatist; est. a sect; persecuted; to US. Est. Harmony, Butler Co., Pa., ca. 1803/05; New Harmony, Posey Co., Ind., 1814; Economy, Beaver Co., Pa., ca. 1825. Followers called Rappists.*

Rappists (Rappites; Harmonists; Harmonites). Followers of J. G. Rapp*; extinct by ca. 1900 because of celibacy.

Ras Shamra. See *Canaanites, Religion of.*

Raselius, Andreas (Rasel; ca. 1562/64–1602). Luth. composer; b. Hahnbach, near Amberg, Upper Palatinate, Ger.; educ. Heidelberg; active in Regensburg and Heidelberg. Arranged chorales so that the cong. could sing the melody in the upper part, while the choir provided the harmonies, but not always simply note-for-note.

Rashdall, Hastings (1858–1924). Theol. and philos.; b. London, Eng.; educ. Oxford; held various teaching and preaching positions; tried to combine features of idealism* and utilitarianism.* Works include *The Theory of Good and Evil.*

Rashi (acrostic of Heb. name Rabbi Shelomoh [Solomon] Yitzhaki [= ben Isaac]; 1040–1105). B. Troyes, Fr.; educ. Mainz and Worms. Works include a commentary on the OT and on the Babylonian Talmud.*

Raskolniks (Raskolniki). See *Russian Sects.*

Rasmussen, Peder Andreas (Jan. 9, 1829–Aug. 15, 1898). B. Stavanger, Norw.; to Am. 1850; teacher Lisbon, Kendall Co., NE Ill.; attended the Mo. Syn. practical sem. at Fort Wayne, Ind. (see *Ministry, Education of,* X D) 1853–54; ordained 1854; pastor Lisbon, Ill.; mem. Norw. Syn.; helped promote the movement that resulted in the United* Norw. Luth. Ch. in Am. (see also *Evangelical Lutheran Church, The,* 8–10).

Rasputin, Grigori Efimovich (ca. 1871–1916). Monk, mystic, adventurer; b. Pokrovskoe, near Tyumen, Tobolsk, Siberia; left his family 1904 and devoted himself to religion; gained influence over czar and czarina; interfered in ch. and secular affairs; noted for debauchery; murdered by nobles.

Rassmanns Mission Bahraich. See *Interior India United World Mission.*

Ratherius (Rathier; ca. 890–974). Benedictine; b. near Liège. Bp. Verona, It., 931–934, 946–948, 962–968; Liège 953–955. Involved in many controversies; supported eucharistic views of P. Radbertus.* Works include *Excerptum exdialogo confessionali; De proprio lapsu.*

Rathmann. See *Rahtmann.*

Ratichius, Wolfgang (Ratich; Ratke; 1571–1635). B. Wilster, Holstein, Ger.; educ. at Hamburg Johanneum* and Rostock; educ. adviser in various parts of Ger.; considered a practical failure, but helped achieve recognized standing for the vernacular and for psychol. principles in educ.

Ratio atque institutio studiorum. See *Aquaviva, Claudio.*

Rationalism. The term "rationalism" has been used in many different ways; care must be exercised to avoid misrepresentation and misunderstanding. Lucretius* ascribed to Greeks leadership in investigating the essence of things on basis of reason. Rationalism in philos. is usually traced to the Eleatic* School, Pythagoreans (see *Pythagoreanism*), and Plato.* Systems called rationalistic include those which are deductive; which hold that reason, apart from sense, is the highest criterion; which apply mathematical methods; which make coherence a criterion of truth. Contrasted with empiricism, rationalism has been described as being abstract, supernatural, absolute, certain, peaceful, authoritative, eternal, religious.

Religious use of the term "rationalism" does not correspond completely to philos. use. The term "rationalistic" applied to scholasticism implied application of dialectics to theol.; scholastic rationalism and Aristotelianism (see *Aristotle*) have been identified. Applied to the theol. of H. Zwingli* or J. Calvin,* the term "rationalistic" often means to say that they interpreted revelation in such a way as to render it harmonious with deductive reasoning, logic, and/or phenomena.

Attempts were made in the 17th c. to show that Christianity is reasonable (see *Cambridge Platonists; Locke, John*). Revelation was not rejected but was regarded as in harmony with reason (rational supernaturalism).

When reason gained the upper hand in the 17th c., the transition to deism* followed. The rationalism of deism rejected revelation but was tempered by assumption of 5 principles common to all religions.

The next stage, which also began in the 17th c., was rejection of all dogmatic assertions, thus leading to the rationalism of skepticism; leaders included P. Bayle,* D. Diderot,* T. Hobbes,* D. Hume,* Voltaire.*

Rationalistic skepticism led to atheism* and mechanistic philosophies (see *Mechanism*). See also *Holbach, Paul Henri Dietrich d'; La Mettrie, Julien Offroy de.*

Four types of attitudes toward rationalism in the religious realm: (1) Revelation is above reason; (2) Revelation and reason are in harmony; (3) Revelation and reason conflict but may be held in compartments; (4) Revelation is to be discarded in favor of reason.

Antiauthoritarian rationalists must be distinguished from those who are antisupernaturalists. EL

See also *Lutheran Theology After 1580,* 6, 8–10; *Ministry, Education of, V; Norway, Lutheranism in,* 9; *Quitman, Frederick Henry.*

A. Tholuck, *Geschichte des Rationalismus* (Berlin, 1865); J. F. Hurst, *History of Rationalism* (New York, 1866); W. E. H. Lecky, *History of the Rise and Influence of the Spirit of Rationalism in Europe,* rev. ed., 2 vols. (New York, 1914); J. B. Bury, *A History of Freedom of Thought* (New York, 1913); H. R. Mackintosh, *Types of Modern Theology: Schleiermacher to Barth* (London, 1937); T. E. W. Engelder, *Reason or Revelation?* (St. Louis, 1941); H. Martin, *The Inquiring Mind* (New York, 1947); E. Bizer, *Frühorthodoxie und Rationalismus* (Zurich, 1963); K. Aner, *Die Theologie der Lessingzeit* (Hildesheim, 1964).

Ratisbon. Alternate name for Regensburg.*

Ratke. See *Ratichius, Wolfgang.*

Ratpert (d. perhaps ca. 884/890). B. Zurich, Switz.; monk and teacher with Notker* at St. Gall. Works include poems; a history of the St. Gall monastery.

Ratramnus (Rathramnus; d. after 868). Benedictine monk Corbie, Somme, Fr., from ca. 825/830. Requested by Charles* II (when he was Charles I as king of Fr.) to evaluate P. Radbertus'* *De corpore et sanguine Domini,* he wrote a treatise with the same title. See also *Eucharistic Controversies; Predestinarian Controversy.*

Ratzeberger, Matthäus (Ratzenberger; 1501–59). B. Wangen, near Stuttgart, S Württemberg, Ger.; educ. Wittenberg; friend of M. Luther; city physician Brandenburg 1525; physician of the count of Mansfeld and 1538–46 of Elector John* Frederick; medical adviser of Luther; opposed Philippists.* Works include a hist. of Luther and his times.

Rauh, Frédéric (1861–1909). Philos.; b. Saint-Martin-le-Vinoux, Isère, Fr.; prof. Toulouse and Paris; advocated experimental morality.

Rauhes Haus. See *Charities, Christian,* 5; *Wichern, Johann Hinrich.*

Raumer, Karl Georg von (1783–1865). Geologist; educator; b. Wörlitz, Anhalt, Ger.; educ. Göttingen, Halle, Paris; prof. Breslau 1811–19, Halle 1819–23; tutor Nürnberg; prof. Erlangen 1827. Issued *Sammlung geistlicher Lieder.* Other works include *Geschichte der Pädagogik; Palästina.*

Rausch, Emil Friedrich (1807–84). B. Kassel, Ger.; educ. Marburg, Halle, Berlin; pastor Kassel; opposed rationalism; driven out of Kassel; pastor Rengshausen, where he est. a home for neglected children and a printery. Works include sermons.

Rauschen, Gerhard (1854–1917). RC hist.; b. Heinsberg, in the Rhineland, Ger.; prof. ch. hist. Bonn 1902. Founded (1904) and ed. *Florilegium patristicum.*

Rauschenbusch, Walter (1861–1918). Bap. cleric; b. Rochester, N. Y.; educ. Rochester; pastor Louisville, Ky., and (1886–97) NYC, where he engaged in religious work among Ger. immigrants; taught in Ger. dept. Rochester Theol. Sem. 1897–1902; prof. ch. hist. Rochester Theol. Sem. 1902–18. Exponent of the social* gospel; identified the kingdom of God with soc. evolution. Works include *Christianity and the Social Crisis; Prayers of the Social Awakening; Christianizing the Social Order; The Social Principles of Jesus; A Theology for the Social Gospel; Dare We Be Christians?* JD

A. M. Singer, *Walter Rauschenbusch and His Contribution to Social Christianity* (Boston, 1926); D. R. Sharpe, *Walter Rauschenbusch* (New York, 1942); V. P. Bodein, *The Social Gospel of Walter Rauschenbusch and Its Relation to Religious Education* (New Haven, Conn., 1944).

Rauscher, Joseph Othmar von (1797–1875). B. Vienna, Austria; priest 1823; prof. theol. Salzburg 1825; prince bp. Vienna 1853; cardinal 1855; opposed Josephinism*; voted against dogma of papal infallibility but soon submitted to it.

Rautanen, Martin. See *Africa,* B 8.

Rautenberg, Johann Wilhelm (1791–1865). Luth. theol.; b. Moorfleth, near Hamburg, Ger.; educ. Kiel and Berlin; pastor Hamburg 1820; exponent of orthodoxy. Works include *Denkblätter.*

Rautenstrauch, Franz Stephan (1734–85). B. Platten (Blottendorf), near Böhmisch-Leipa, Boh.; Benedictine 1750; prelate of united monasteries of Braunau and Brewnow 1773; dir. theol. faculty Prague 1774 and later Vienna; exponent of modified Josephinism*; favored laying more stress on exegesis, ch. hist., and practical theol. in educ. of clergy.

Ravalli, Antonio (May 16, 1812–Oct. 2, 1884). RC miss.; b. Ferrara, It.; Jesuit 1827; taught at various places in It.; studied medicine; to Oregon Country 1843/44; worked among Indians in Mont.

Raymond IV (ca. 1043–1105). Marquis of Provence, Fr., 1066; count of Toulouse 1093; a leader of the 1st Crusade (see *Crusades,* 2).

Raymond Martin(i) (ca. 1220–ca. 1285/86). Dominican; b. Subirats, Catalonia, Sp.; miss. to Muslim; taught at Tunis and Barcelona; Heb., Aramaic, and Arabic scholar. Works include *Explanatio symboli apostolorum; Capistrum Iudaeorum; Pugio fidei adversus Mauros et Iudaeos; Summa contra gentiles.*

Raymond of Agiles (Aguilers; fl. late 11th c.). Canon Le Puy; chaplain of Raymond* IV on 1st Crusade. His *Historia Francorum qui ceperunt Ierusalem* describes alleged finding of the lance that pierced Jesus' side.

Raymond of Capua (delle Vigne; de Vineis; ca. 1330–99). B. Capua, It., of the royal Delle Vigne family; educ. Bologna; Dominican ca. 1347; dir. monastery Montepulciano 1363; prior Santa Maria sopra Minerva, Rome, 1367; spiritual dir. Catherine* of Siena 1374; master gen. Dominicans 1380; promoted prestige of pope.

Raymond of Peñafort (ca. 1175–1275). B. Vilefranca de Penades, near Barcelona, Sp.; educ. Barcelona; confessor of Gregory IX (see *Popes,* 11); chaplain and penitentiary collected papal letters for *Decretales Gregorii IX;* master gen. Dominicans; helped est. Inquisition* in Aragon. Works include *Summa iuris canonici* (unfinished); *Summa de casibus poenitentiae.*

Raymond of Sabunde (Sabiende; Sebonde; Sibiuda; d. 1436). B. Barcelona, Sp.; taught at Toulouse, Fr.; held that nature and Scripture cannot conflict since both come from God. Wrote *Theologia naturalis* (or *Liber creaturarum*).

Raymund. Variant spelling of Raymond.*

Real Presence. See *Grace, Means of,* IV, 3; *Lutheran Confessions,* A 2 (b).

Realism. Practical realism is the attitude to take things as they really are in life and to make the best of them. The realist deals with facts and is seldom swayed by high ideals; he tries less to improve the world than to make use of it. Philos. realism is the theory that gen. abstract ideas have real existence, indep. of individual objects; e. g., the idea of a circle exists apart from round things. Psychol. realism holds that things have real existence, indep. of our conscious experience; e. g., the tree I see exists not merely in my consciousness, as a concept of my mind, but there really is a tree in the yard, also when no eyes are looking at it. Common sense is realistic as it assumes that objects we perceive really exist. But in hallucinations we see things that are not real. In literature and art, realism as opposed to romanticism and idealism, pictures life not as it should be, but as it is. See also *Critical Realism; Idealism; Nominalism; Philosophy.*

Realism, Biblical. See *Switzerland, Contemporary Theology in,* 7.

Realism, Critical. See *Critical Realism.*

Realism, Sociological. See *Positivism, Sociological.*

Reason. See *Rationalism.*

Rebekah Lodges. See *Odd Fellows, Independent Order of.*

Rebling, Gustav (1821–1902). Composer; b. Barby, Ger.; studied under J. C. F. Schneider* at Dessau 1836–39; organist Magdeburg. Works include Psalms and motets.

Rebmann, Johann(es) (Jan. 16, 1820–Oct. 4, 1876). Miss.; b. Gerlingen, N. Württemberg, Ger.; educ. Basel, Switz.; sent 1846 by CMS to work with J. L. Krapf* in E Afr.; discovered Mt. Kilimanjaro and Mt. Kenya; studied Swahili and other native languages. Tr. Lk into a native tongue; helped prepare dictionaries for 3 native tongues. See also *Africa,* E 6.

Recapitulation. In theol., the theory (drawn from Eph. 1:10, "gather together," literally "recapitulate") that the Logos* in His state of humiliation went through all experiences of the life of a sinner in order to purge man's sinfulness by His sinlessness; see also *Irenaeus.* In pedagogy, the theory that a human being must grow through all biological and social experiences of the human race, acc. to the theory of evolution, in order to reach maturity. See also *Haeckel, Ernst Heinrich Philipp August.*

Received Text. See *Textual Criticism,* 2.

"Rechenschafft unserer Religion, Leer und Glaubens." See *Democratic Declarations of Faith,* 1.

Rechlin, Friedrich (Feb. 16, 1851–Dec. 9, 1915). B. Bergen, cen. Rügen is., in the Baltic Sea, 16 mi. ENE of Stralsund, in former Prussian Pomerania prov., N Ger.; to Am. 1867; educ. at the Ev. Luth. Teachers Sem., Addison, Ill.; taught at Davenport, Iowa, Albany, N. Y., and Cleveland, Ohio; prof. Addison, Ill., 1893, and later at River Forest, Ill., till his death. Works include *Erstes Übungsbuch; Zweites Übungsbuch.*

Reciting Tone. See *Intonation; Psalm Tones.*

Recluse. One who lives in seclusion, e. g., a hermit,* esp. for religious reasons.

Recollects (from Lat. for "to gather again"). Branches of Augustinians (see *Augustinian Hermits*) and Franciscans*; called recollects beause their mems. returned to the early strict rule. Franciscan recollects began as a reform movement in Fr. ca. 1570; spread to Belg., Ger., Ireland, and Eng. Friars on the Continent; were inc. with other Observants* 1897. Augustinian recollects began in Sp. in the late 1580s; engaged in miss. work esp. in Peru and the Philippines; were constituted an indep. order 1912.

Reconciliation. Synonymous with atonement* in the sense of the act of reconciling and so restoring friendly relations. In the sense of state of being reconciled it is the result of atonement.

Recreation. Refreshment of body and mind through natural expression of human interests during leisure time, e. g., by diversion, agreeable exercise, play. Play activities date from ancient times. The Gk. educ. theory and practice emphasized adequate training of the young in mind, spirit, and body.

The importance of the human body is reflected, e. g., Gn 2:7 ("God . . . breathed into his nostrils the breath of life"), Jn 1:14 (assumed by Christ in incarnation), 1 Cor 3:17; 6:19 (temple of God), 1 Co 15:12; Ph 3:21 (shares in resurrection). Kinds of recreation mentioned in Scripture include storytelling and riddles (Ju 14:12-19; Eze 17:2), archery (1 Sm 20:35-40), "mirth making" (Neh 8:12), dancing (Jb 21:11; see also *Dance*), racing (Ps 19:5; Ec 9:11; 1 Co 9:24-27; 2 Ti 4:7; Heb 12:1); feasting (Am 8:10), children playing (Zch 8:5), children making music and dancing (Mt 11:17), feasting, merrymaking, music, and dancing (Lk 15:23-25). Recreation under sinful circumstances: Ex 32:6; Ju 16:25; 1 Sm 25:36; Am 6:4-6; Mt 14:6. Attempts to introd. nat. games similar to those of the Gks. were made in the reigns of Antiochus Epiphanes and Herod the Great (1 Mac 1:10-14; Josephus, *Antiquitates Judaicae,* XV, viii, 1).

In the Middle Ages, Teutonic influence caused interest in physical and military games. The monastic view that the body should be degraded to glorify the soul caused a negative attitude toward pleasurable bodily recreation. In the Renaissance,* humanistic interests fostered ideals opposed to monastic asceticism.

M. Luther* restored a positive attitude toward recreation: God created body and soul, and He wants recreation allowed to both, but with moderation and purpose (WA 43, 331). He emphasized the importance of the body (WA 28, 208–209; 36, 666–667). Not to care for the body, or abuse it, as was done in monasteries, he considered a mortal sin (WA 52, 415–416). The pleasing things at hand should be enjoyed (WA 20, 189–193), but recreation should be sanctified by prayer (WA 19, 313–314).

Sports developed comparatively early in Eng., but it was Puritanism (see *Puritans*) that was brought to New Eng. and fostered the idea that recreation and leisure were sin.

Forms of recreation in America included husking bees and ch. socials. Concentration of population in cities and shortened working hrs. led to development of parks, playgrounds, camps, etc. for recreation. First activities were gen. sports, games, etc. for the young; then came arts, crafts, hobbies, music, dramatics; finally all legitimate leisure interests of all were included.

In planning activities, chs. have recognized the need for recreation on all age levels. LFW

Rector. Title of a leader, e. g., (1) head of a school or university; (2) Prot. Episc. clergyman in charge of a parish; (3) incumbent of an Angl. benefice in full possession of its rights; (4) RC priest dir. a ch. without a pastor or a ch. whose pastor has other duties.

Recusant (from Lat. for "refusing"). One who refuses to submit to authority; specifically one who refuses to submit to the Angl or RC Ch.; a wider term than nonconformist.*

Red Cross. Founded by J. H. Dunant,* who was influenced by F. Nightingale's* service in the Crimean War (1854–56) and his own witness of carnage at Solferino, N It., the day after battle bet. Fr. and It. on one side and Austria on the other (1859; ca. 40,000 lay dead or wounded; described in his *Un Souvenir de Solférino*). The Société genovoise d'Utilité publique, a Swiss welfare agency, named a committee of 5 (including Dunant) that arranged a conf. of 36 delegates from 16 nations at Geneva Oct. 1863 to consider ways of implementing Dunant's ideas. A diplomatic conf. 1864 drew up the 1st Geneva convention, signed by 12 govts., arranging for care of sick and wounded in war; a red cross on a white field (similar to the Swiss flag, but with colors reversed) was adopted as emblem. Thus the 1863 committee of 5 was the beginning of the Internat. Committee of the Red Cross. The convention, repeatedly updated, has been ratified by most nations.

The Am. Red Cross traces its hist. to the US Sanitary Commission, which was organized mainly through efforts of H. W. Bellows* and functioned in the Civil War. The Am. Red Cross itself was founded 1881 as the Am. Assoc. of the Red Cross under leadership of Clarissa (or Clara) Harlowe Barton (1821–1912; b. Oxford, Mass.; schoolteacher 1836–54; patent office clerk, Washington, D. C., 1854–61; interested in war relief; 1st pres. Am. Red Cross), who had extended volunteer care to wounded in the Civil War and worked with the Red Cross in the Franco-Prussian War. The Am. Red Cross introd. peacetime services in times of disaster and presented the "Am." amendment regarding such work to the Internat. Red Cross 1884.

Red Pope, The. Nickname for cardinal prefect of the Sacred Cong. for the Propagation of the Faith (see *Curia,* 2 d) because of the importance and widespread jurisdiction of that cong.; red, because that is the color distinctive of both cardinals and missionaries.

Red Wing Seminary. Sem. of the Hauge* Syn. founded 1879 at Red Wing, Minn., as Hauge's Sem.; renamed 1883 Red Wing Norw. Ev. Luth. Sem. In 1917 the theol. dept. united with the United* Norw. Luth. Ch. in Am. sem. and Luther Theol. Sem., St. Paul, to form Luther* Theol. Sem., St. Anthony Park, St. Paul; the coll. dept. merged with St. Olaf Coll. (see *Ministry, Education of,* VIII B 23). An academy under the name "Luther Sem." continued at Red Wing till consolidation with Saint Olaf Coll. 1932.

Redemption (from Lat. for "buy back"). The concept is found in classical Gk. and the NT for setting a captive free by paying a ransom. In Christian theol. the term stands for recovery from sin and death by the obedience and sacrifice of Christ, who is therefore called the Redeemer (Jb 19:25; Is 59:20. Cf. Mt 20:28; Ro 3:24; 1 Co 6:20; Gl 3:13; 4:4-5; Eph 1:7; 1 Ti 2:5-6; 1 Ptr 1:18). The subject is sinful mankind, under guilt and the curse of the Law and the power and dominion of the devil, servants of sin, liable to death and eternal punishment. Redemption applies to all, but is not gratuitous; the ransom was paid and divinely sealed by the resurrection (1 Co 15:3-20).

Redemptorists. Community of priests and lay brothers founded 1732 at Scala, near Naples, It., by A. M. de' Liguori* for miss. work among the poor. Mems. add to the 3 usual vows* a vow not to accept any dignity or benefice outside the cong. except by express command of the pope or superior gen. and to remain in the cong. till death unless dispensed by the pope.

Redenbacher, Christian Wilhelm Adolf (1800–76). B. Pappenheim, on the Altmühl, Bav.; educ. Erlangen; private tutor; vicar; pastor; opposed rationalism* and the order of the Bav. ministry of war requiring all soldiers, also Prots., to genuflect to the host when carried in procession; suspended; sentenced to prison, but appeals by Prots. led the king to remit this penalty; after a pastorate in Saxony he returned to Bavaria. Works include *Lesebuch der Weltgeschichte;* sermons; devotional writings; a hist. of the Reformation.

Redpath, Henry Adeney (1848–1908). B. Sydenham (or Forest Hill?), London, Eng.; educ. Oxford; Angl. deacon 1872, priest 1874; held various positions. Collaborated with E. Hatch* on a concordance to the LXX (see also *Concordances, Bible*).

Redstone Baptist Association of Pennsylvania. See *Disciples of Christ,* 2 b.

Reed, Andrew (1787[1788?]–1862). Philanthropist;

hymnist; b. London, Eng.; educ. London; Cong. pastor London; founded several orphan asylums, an asylum for idiots, and a hosp. for incurables. Hymns include "Holy Ghost, with Light Divine."

Reed, Luther Dotterer (Mar. 21, 1873–Apr. 3, 1972). B. North Wales, Pa.; educ. Franklin and Marshall Coll., Lancaster, Pa., and Lutheran Theol. Sem., Mount Airy, Philadelphia, Pa. Pastor Pittsburgh, Pa., 1895–1903; Jeannette, Pa., 1904–05. Librarian 1906–50, prof. 1911–45, pres. 1938–45 Lutheran Theol. Sem., Philadelphia. Works include *The Lutheran Liturgy; Worship.*

Reeve, John. See *Muggletonians.*

Reform Councils. See *Councils and Synods,* 7.

Reform Judaism. See *Judaism,* 3.

Reformation, Anglican. See *Anglican Confessions; England,* B.

Reformation, Anniversaries of the. See *Luther and the Reformation, Anniversaries of.*

Reformation, Lutheran. 1. Reformation in this sense involves improvement by correction and presupposes formation and deformation.

2. In ch. hist., the Reformation is the 16th-c. movement to restore the ch. (founded and formed by Christ; deformed mainly by the papacy) to its early condition; it resulted in separation of a great part of the W ch. from the medieval ch. of Rome.

3. Before the Reformation, *humanism** provided freedom of thought and learning; to some extent it absorbed the pagan philos. of the ancient classics; where it fostered study of Scripture it promoted only moral and ethical reformation. *Univs.* led in demanding reform but were only intellectual centers. *Mysticism* demanded inwardness of religion and a personal relationship bet. creature and Creator (in contrast to the externalism and institutionalism of the ch.), but became wholly subjective. Growing *nationalism* helped prepare for the Reformation by arousing (a) violent criticism of, and opposition to, the arrogant claims and demands of the pope as a "for. prince"; (b) willingness to protect a fellow citizen against attacks from abroad.

But more was needed, because the root of corruption was not recognized.

4. The doctrine of the merit of good works denied the Gospel and made necessary such a thorough reformation as had been attempted by such "reformers before the Reformation" as P. Waldo (see *Waldenses*), J. Wycliffe,* J. Hus.* See also *Brethren of the Common Life; Jerome of Prague; Wessel; Savonarola, Girolamo.*

5. The ch. used the interdict* effectively against reform efforts.

6. The Reform Councils (see *Councils and Synods,* 7) failed to recognize the root of corruption; the hierarchy* wanted no reform.

7. The man of the Reformation was M. Luther.* The beginning of the Reformation may be traced to his question, "How do I obtain a gracious God?" and the answer he found ca. 1514 in Ps 31:1; 71:2; Ro 1:17.

8. When Luther found that through indulgences the people were taught a false way of salvation, he posted 95 Theses (see *Theses, Ninety-five, of Luther*) on the door of the Wittenberg Castle Ch. Oct. 31, 1517. There followed the Leipzig* Debate 1519 and the trilogy 1520: *An Open Letter to the Christian Nobility of the German Nation Concerning the Reform of the Christian Estate; The Babylonian Captivity of the Church; On the Freedom of a Christian Man.* The Diet of Worms* 1521 was a bench mark in hist. Scripture was Luther's standard also in dealing 1522 with inconoclastic radicals (Ger.: Bilderstürmer) who, among other things, sought to remove images and organs from chs. in Wittenberg.

9. Papal action against Luther began soon after Oct. 31, 1517, culminated in the bulls *Exsurge, Domine* (1520; threatened excommunication) and *Decet Romanum Pontificem* (1521; excommunicated him). The emp. added his condemnation of Luther in the Edict of Worms.*

10. The Reformation spread rapidly, entering various lands mainly through Luther's writings. The only attempt to impose the Reformation by force was made in Den. by Christian* II for pol. reasons and proved unsuccessful; but by 1530 Den. was gained for the Reformation by preaching (see also *Denmark, Lutheranism in,* 2).

11. At times pol. and personal reasons helped motivate efforts to introd. the Reformation in some lands. But occasional use of Prot. force was usually in defense against RC attacks or in suppression of RC plots against govt. authority.

12. By 1540 RCm had lost all N and most of cen. Ger. and all Scand.; in Poland, Boh., Moravia, Hung., and Transylvania nine-tenths of the pop. was said to be Luth.; Luth. influence was strong in S Germany. Eng. had separated from Rome and, though still Cath., was beginning to lean toward Protestantism.

RC response was first partly conciliatory (see *Hagenau Colloquy; Regensburg Conference; Colloquy of Worms*), then turned to open and violent attack, led by the Society* of Jesus and resulting in wars of religion in most of W Eur. (see *France,* 9–10; *Huguenots; Schmalkaldic War; Switzerland,* 2, 4-6; *Thirty Years' War; William I*).

Calvinism began to supplant Lutheranism in some Ger. states partly because Calvinism was more aggressive against RCm.

13. The Luth. Reformation led to all other true modern reform efforts. Divisions in Protestantism are not a result of the Reformation but of replacing Scripture with rationalism and/or subjectivism.

14. The Reformation is justified by the higher moral life and culture of its followers and by resultant improvement in the RC Ch. TH

See also *Denmark, Lutheranism in; Formal Principle; Germany,* B; entries beginning *Luther . . . ; Material Principle; Norway, Lutheranism in,* 1–3; *Sweden, Lutheranism in,* 1.

J. Mackinnon, *Luther and the Reformation,* 4 vols. (London, 1925–30) and *The Origins of the Reformation* (London, 1939); P. Smith, *The Age of the Reformation* (New York, 1920) and *The Life and Letters of Martin Luther* (Boston, 1911); T. M. Lindsay, *A History of the Reformation,* 2 vols. (New York, 1906–07); J. T. Köstlin, *The Theology of Luther in Its Historical Development and Inner Harmony,* 2 vols., tr. C. E. Hay from the 2d Ger. ed. (Philadelphia, 1897); T. v. Kolde, *Martin Luther,* 2 vols. (Gotha, 1884–93); publications of Verein für Reformationsgeschichte; A. C. McGiffert, *Martin Luther: The Man and His Work* (New York, 1910); A. H. Böhmer, *Road to Reformation,* tr. J. W. Doberstein and T. G. Tappert (Philadelphia, 1946); B. K. Kuiper, *Martin Luther: The Formative Years* (Grand Rapids, Mich., 1933) and a shorter version under the same title (Grand Rapids, 1943); *The Cambridge Modern History,* II–IV, ed. A. W. Ward et al. (Cambridge, Eng., 1903–06); E. G. Schwiebert, *Luther and His Times* (St. Louis, 1950); R. H. Bainton, *The Reformation of the Sixteenth Century* (Boston, 1952); H. J. Grimm, *The Reformation Era 1500–1650,* rev. ed. (New York, 1965); H. Bornkamm, *Luther's World of Thought,* tr. M. H. Bertram (St. Louis, 1958); C. L. Manschreck, *Melanchthon: The Quiet Reformer* (New York, 1958); É. G. Léonard, *A History of Protestantism, I: The Reformation,* ed. H. H. Rowley, tr. J. M. H. Reid (London, 1965); *Illustrated History of the Reformation,* ed. O. Thulin, tr. J. E. Nopola, H. C. Oswald, P. D. Pahl, and O. E. Sohn (St. Louis,

1967); G. Rupp, *Patterns of Reformation* (Philadelphia, 1969).

Reformation, Reformed. See *Calvin, John; Presbyterian Confessions; Reformed Churches; Reformed Confessions; Scotland, Reformation in; Zwingli, Huldreich.*

Reformation, Roman Catholic. See *Counter Reformation.*

Reformation Coins and Medals. Conc. Hist. Institute, St. Louis, Mo., has a collection of Luther and Reformation coins and medals. Literature on the subject includes C. Juncker, *Vita D. Martini Lutheri et successuum Evangelicae Reformationis jubilaeorumque evangelicorum historia nummis cxlv atque iconibus . . . illustrata* (Frankfurt and Leipzig, 1699), 1706 title of enl. Ger. ed. *Das Guldene und Silberne Ehren-Gedächtniss Des Theuren Gottes-Lehrers D. Martini Lutheri;* F. C. Lesser, *Besondere Müntzen* (Frankfurt and Leipzig, 1739); H. G. Kreussler, *D. Martin Luthers Andenken in Münzen nebst Lebensbeschreibung merkwürdiger Zeitgenossen desselben* (Leipzig, 1818); M. Bernhart, "Reformatorenbildnisse aud Medaillen der Renaissance," *Numismatik* (Dec. 1933).

Reformed. For origin of "Ref." in distinction from "Luth." and "Presb." see *Reformed Churches,* 1.

Reformed Church, General Regulations of the. See *Netherlands,* 1.

Reformed Church in America. See *Reformed Churches,* 4 b.

Reformed Church in the United States. See *Reformed Churches,* 4 e; *United Church of Christ, The,* II A and C.

Reformed Churches. 1. Beginnings of Ref. chs. may be traced to Switz., Fr., Holland, Scot., and Eng. The name "Ref.," in gen. use by the end of the 16th c., was given esp. to followers of J. Calvin,* H. Zwingli,* M. Bucer,* J. H. Bullinger,* and J. Oecolampadius,* to help distinguish them from followers of M. Luther,* who came to be called Lutheran* in the 1520s, esp. after the Colloquy of Marburg 1529 (see also 3; *Lutheran Confessions,* A 2). Since the Arminian controversy (see *Arminianism*) the Ref. are divided into Calvinistic (see *Calvinism*) and Arminian Ref. The term "Ref." is used commonly of Calvinists, rarely of Arminians. Calvinists are commonly known in Scot. and Eng. as Presbyterians (see *Presbyterian Churches,* 1–2), on the Continent (esp. Switz., Holland, Fr., and parts of Ger.) as Ref. In its stricter sense, then, "Ref." denotes continental Calvinistic chs. The main difference bet. Presb. and Ref. chs. is in nomenclature: Presbs. speak of session*, presbytery,* assembly (see also *Polity, Ecclesiastical,* 7); Ref. speak of consistory,* classis,* synod. See also *Presbyterian Churches,* 3; *Switzerland,* 2–6.

2. *Ref. Ch. in the Netherlands.** Forerunners of the Reformation in the Neth. include R. Agricola* and Wessel.* See also *Erasmus, Desiderius.* Some of M. Luther's early writings were well received in the Neth., but the main Reformation movement followed Ref. lines, often under severe persecution. The congs. worshiped at first as "The Chs. of the Neth. under the Cross." Organization began under leadership of Menno* Simons. Tr. hymns of T. Beza* and C. Marot* became popular. The Belgic Confession (see also *Reformed Confessions,* C 1) was adopted by a syn. at Antwerp 1566 and later syns. (see also *Dordrecht, Synods of*). Her scholars and theologians, schools and univs., zeal and martyr spirit gave the Ref. ch. in the Neth. a lead position among Ref. chs. on the Continent and the religious liberty that she achieved attracted many who were persecuted in other lands (see also *Robinson, John; United Church of Christ,* I A 1). See also *Marnix, Philip van.*

3. *Ref. Ch. in Ger.* The Ref. Ch. was est. in Ger. largely as a result of the controversy concerning the Lord's Supper (see 1). During the Crypto-Calvinistic* Controversy the Palatinate became Ref. (see also *Frederick III* [1515–76]. Brandenburg became Ref. under John* Sigismund. For developments from 1817 see *Prussian Union.*

4. *Ref. Chs. in Am.* a. *Ref. Ch. in the US.* See e; *United Church of Christ,* II A and C.

b. *Ref. Ch. in Am.* (also called The Ref. Prot. Dutch Ch. in N. Am.; The Prot. Dutch Ch. in N. Am.; Dutch Ref. Ch.). Est. as Ref. Prot. Dutch Ch. by immigrants from the Neth., who formed the colony of New Netherland. Its first Comforters of the Sick included Sebastian Jansen Krol (Bastiaen Crol) and Jan Huyck. First minister: Jonas Michaelius (1584 – after 1637; b. Grootebroek, Holland; educ. Leiden; minister Brabant and Holland 1605–25; miss. W. Afr. 1625–27; to New Amsterdam, New Neth., via Holland 1628; founded Collegiate Ch., NYC, and Ref. Prot. Dutch Ch. ca. 1628; returned to Holland 1632). The cong. consisted of Walloons and Dutch and was organized with at least 50 communicant mems. The 1st ch. was built at New Amsterdam 1633. At first the work was in charge of the Syn. of Holland. But the question of authority led to controversy ca. the middle of the 17th c. and independence became the issue in the latter part of the c. Under leadership of Theodorus Jacobus Frelinghuysen* Queen's Coll. (see also *Protestant Education in the United States*) was founded 1766 at New Brunswick, N. J. The Ref. Dutch Ch. in the USA (or The Dutch Ref. Ch. in N. Am.; both names were in use 1792) expanded in N. Y. and N. J. It was inc. 1819 as The Ref. Prot. Dutch Church. Ca. the middle of the 19th c. there was a large Dutch immigration, including whole congs. with their pastors, who settled in the North and Midwest, beginning in Mich. and Iowa. In 1867 the name of the ch. was changed to The Reformed Church in America. "The doctrinal standards of the Reformed Church in America are the Belgic Confession, the Heidelberg Catechism, and the Canons of the Synod of Dort. The church is thus a distinctively Calvinistic body. It has a liturgy for optional use in public worship, with forms of prayer. Some parts of the liturgy, as those for the administration of baptism and the Lord's Supper and for the ordination of ministers, elders, and deacons, are obligatory; the forms of prayer, the marriage service, etc., are not obligatory. Children are 'baptized as heirs of the Kingdom of God and of His Covenant'; adults are baptized (by sprinkling or immersion, as preferred) on profession of repentance for sin and faith in Christ. All baptized persons are considered members of the church, are under its care, and are subject to its government and discipline. No subscription to a specific form of words being required, admission to communion and full membership is on confession of faith before the elders and minister" (U. S. Dept. of Commerce, *Religious Bodies: 1936,* II, Part 2 [Washington, 1941], 1506).

c. *Christian Ref. Ch.* Organized 1857 Holland Mich., by congs. and ministers who withdrew from the Ref. Prot. Dutch Ch. for reasons of doctrine and discipline. Names adopted: 1859 Holland Ref. Ch.; 1861 True Dutch Ref.; 1880 Holland Christian Ref. Ch. in Am.; 1890 Christian Ref. Ch. in Am.; 1904 Christian Ref. Ch. Creeds: Belgic Confession, Heidelberg Catechism, Canons of Dordrecht (see *Reformed Confessions,* C 1–2, D 2). Besides Calvin Coll. and Theol. Sem., Grand Rapids, Mich., and Dordt Coll., Sioux Center, Iowa, it supports a system of Christian elementary schools.

d. *Hung. Ref. Ch. in Am.* The Ref. Ch. of Hung. organized a Hung. Ref. Ch. in N. Y. 1904. Work among Hung. Ref. in US had been begun by others 1891. The Ref. Ch. in Hung. transferred jurisdiction of its US chs. to the Ref. Ch. in the US by 1921 agreement at Tiffin, Ohio; but some congs. refused to accept the agreement and organized the Free Magyar Ref. Ch. in Am. at Duquesne, Pa., 1924. Name changed 1958 to Hung. Ref. Ch. in Am. See also *Union Movements,* 7.

e. *Ref. Ch. in the US.* The Eureka Classis, organized S. Dak. 1910, continued as the Ref. Ch. in the US when most of the parent body (Hung. Ref. Ch. in Am.; see d) merged into the Ev. and Ref. Ch. 1934 (see *United Church of Christ,* II A and C).

f. *Prot. Ref. Chs. in Am.* Organized 1926 Grand Rapids, Mich., by a group that separated from the Christian Ref. Ch. (see c); creeds: Belgic Conf., Heidelberg Catechism, Canons of Dordrecht (see *Reformed Confessions,* C 1–2, D 2). They stand for particular grace, for the elect only. FEM

Reformed Churches in the Netherlands, The. See *Netherlands,* 2.

Reformed Confessions. A. *Swiss Reformed.* 1. The *67 Arts.* of H. Zwingli* were prepared for, and maintained at, a pub. disputation in Zurich 1523 that practically decided the repudiation of RCm. Art. 15: he that believes the Gospel will be saved; 17: Christ is the only eternal and highest priest; 18: the mass is not a sacrifice, but a commemoration of the sacrifice offered once on the cross and, as it were, a seal of the redemption procured by Christ; 49: I know no greater and more serious offense than to forbid priests to marry; 57: Holy Scripture knows no purgatory after this life.

2. *10 Theses of Bern (10 Conclusions of Bern; Theses Bernenses).* Rev. by H. Zwingli* (written by others, including B. Haller*) for a 1528 discussion at Bern, Switzerland. Thesis 1: The holy Christian ch. is born of the Word of God; 4: The essential and corporeal presence of the body and blood of Christ can not be demonstrated from the Holy Scripture; 6: It is contrary to the Word of God to propose and invoke other mediators than Christ; 7: Scripture knows nothing of a purgatory after this life, hence all masses and other offices for the dead are useless; 8: Image worship is contrary to Scripture; 9: Matrimony is not forbidden in the Scripture to any class of men, but permitted to all.

3. H. Zwingli* tried, perhaps unsuccessfully, to get a confession of faith into the hands of Charles* V at Augsburg 1530; it differed from the AC mainly on original sin, the unbaptized, and the Sacraments.

4. The *Exposition of the Christian Faith,* which H. Zwingli* sent 1531 to Francis I (see *France,* 8), embodies statements of Zwingli's beliefs regarding, e. g., God; saints; Sacraments; Mary; the person and work of Christ; ch.; magistrates; forgiveness; faith and works; eternal life.

5. *1st Confession of Basel (Confessio fidei Basileensis prior;* 12 arts.). Drafted 1531 by J. Oecolampadius*; put into final form 1532 by O. Myconius; pub. Basel 1534; adopted at Mühlhausen 2 or 3 yrs. later, hence also called Confessio Mühlhusana (or Mylhusiana); essentially agrees with confessions of H. Zwingli.*

6. The *Helvetic Confessions* are the most important documents of the Swiss Prot. chs. The *1st Helvetic Confession* (Confessio Helvetica prior; also called *2d Confession of Basel* [*Confessio Basileensis posterior*] because it was written there [see 5]) consisted of 27 arts. in the Ger. version (27 or 28 in the Lat.) and was drawn up 1536, (1) as a result of M. Bucer's* and W. F. Capito's* efforts to unite Luths. and Ref. and (2) in hope of a gen. council, by J. H. Bullinger,* S. Grynäus (see *Grynäus,* 1), L. Jud,* K. Megander,* O. Myconius.* Treats of Scripture, the ancient fathers, and human traditions (I–V); God, man, sin, free will, and salvation (VI–XIII); faith, ch., Word, ministry, holy assemblies, adiaphora, heretics and schismatics, civil govt., marriage (XIV–end).

In course of time this confession was deemed too short and was replaced by the *2d Helvetic Confession (Confessio Helvetica Posterior),* which consists of 30 arts., was originally drawn up 1562 by Bullinger for his own use, and pub. at Zurich 1566. Treats Scripture, traditions, etc. (I–II); God (III); idols, and worship through Christ (IV–V); divine providence (VI); creation (VII); sin (VIII); free will (IX); predestination and election (X); Christ (XI); Law and Gospel (XII–XIII); repentance and justification by faith (XIV–XVI); ch., ministry, Sacraments, and holy assemblies (XVII–XXII); various other matters of doctrine and polity (XXIII–XXX). Adopted in Switz., Scot., Hung., Fr., Poland.

7. During his 1st stay at Geneva, Switz. (1536), J. Calvin* prepared a Fr. catechism *(Geneva Catechism; Catechism of Geneva)* consisting of 58 sections treating the religious constitution of man, the distinction bet. true and false religion, the knowledge of God, the original state of man, free will, sin, death, the way of salvation, the Law, faith, election and predestination, justification, sanctification, repentance, regeneration, good works, an exposition of the Apostles' Creed, the Lord's Prayer, Sacraments, ch., traditions, excommunication, and the civil magistrate. It appeared in French 1541 or 1542, Lat. 1545, was tr. into It. (1551 and 1556), Sp. (1550), Eng. (1556), Ger., Dutch, Hung., Gk., and Heb., and prepared the way and furnished material for a number of similar works that gradually superseded it (e. g., A. Nowell's,* the Heidelberg [see D 2] and Westminster* Confessions). See also *Dordrecht, Synods of,* 2.

8. Continued debates bet. Luths. and Ref. regarding the Lord's Supper led to the *Consensus of Zurich (Consensus Tigurinus; Zurich Consensus),* consisting of 24 propositions in the 1st draft (1548) drawn up by J. Calvin* and annotated by J. H. Bullinger,* 26 arts. in the final form (1549). Adopted by various Swiss centers, creating unity. Contains Calvinistic doctrine adjusted to the Zwinglian; asserts that we receive Christ's body and blood in the Lord's Supper by the power of the Spirit and the lifting of our souls to heaven, but that the internal effect of the Sacraments appears only in the elect.

9. The *Consensus of Geneva (Consensus Genevensis; Geneva Consensus),* pub. 1552 (written 1551?), is an elaborate argument by J. Calvin* defending absolute predestination; occasioned by attacks of A. Pighius* and Jérôme Hermès Bolsec (d. ca. 1585; b. Paris, Fr.; Carmelite, then Prot.; in Geneva he differed with Calvin on predestination; banished from Geneva and Bern; rejected in Fr.; RC again; wrote libel against Calvin 1577, 1588).

10. *Helvetic Consensus Formula (Formula Consensus Helvetica);* 1675; 26 arts. After adoption (1620, 1623) of the canons of the 1618–19 Syn. of Dordrecht* by the Ref. Ch. in Fr., a more liberal school arose at Saumur, France. See *Amyraut, Moïse; Cappel, Louis; Place, Josue de la.* In defense against the theol. of Saumur, J. H. Heidegger,* L. Gernler,* and F. Turrettini* wrote the *Formula consensus ecclesiarum helveticarum reformatarum,* which defended, e. g., inspiration (even of vowel points), absolute predestination, immediate imputation of Adam's sin.

B. *Ref. Confessions in France.* The *Gallican Confession (Confessio Gallicana; Confession of Rochelle; French Confession of Faith),* 40 arts., was drawn up by J. Calvin,* rev. by A de la R. Chandieu* and adopted 1559 by a syn. at Paris, rev. and ratified at a syn. at La Rochelle 1571. Summarizes Calvin's doctrines. See also *Waldenses.*

For the subsequent hist. of Protestantism in Fr., including the Fr. Revolution, which for a time seemed to sweep away the whole Fr. ch., see *France,* 5, 7–13.

The *Declaration of Faith of the Ref. Ch. in Fr.,* proposed by C. Bois (see *Bois,* 1), was adopted by a syn. at Paris 1872.

C. *Ref. Confessions in the Neth.* 1. The *Belgic Conf.;* 37 arts.; with the Heidelberg Catechism (see D 2) the recognized symbol of the Ref. chs. in Holland and Belg. and of the Ref. (Dutch) in Am.; prepared 1561 by G. de Bres*; adopted by syns. at Antwerp 1566, Wesel 1568, Emden 1571, Dordrecht 1574, Middelburg 1581, Dordrecht 1619; contents follow the order of the Gallican Conf. (see B) but are less polemical and more elaborate, esp. on the Trin., incarnation, ch., and Sacraments.

2. Opposition of Arminians (see *Arminianism*) to Calvinistic doctrines on predestination led the Neth. States Gen. to convene the 1618–19 Syn. of Dordrecht,* attended by representatives of the provinces, the States Gen., the academies, and for. countries including the Palatinate, Nassau, Hesse, E. Friesland, Switz., Eng., and Scot.; Luths. were not represented. Calvinism* triumphed. See also *Remonstrants.* Canons were adopted, confined to 5 points or "Heads of Doctrine" that summarize the Calvinistic system both positively and negatively (rejecting Arminian errors): I. Predestination (18 arts.); II. Christ's death and man's redemption (9); III–IV. Man's corruption and conversion (17); V. Perseverance (15).

See also *Reformed Churches,* 2.

D. *Ref. Confessions in Germany.* 1. *Tetrapolitan Confession (Confessio Tetrapolitana; Confessio Suevica; Swabian Confession; Strasbourg Confession; Confessio Argentinensis [Argentorati]; Confessio Quatuor Civitatum; Confession der Vier Städte; Vierstädte-Bekenntniss);* 23 arts.; oldest Ref. symbol in Ger.; prepared in haste by M. Bucer,* W. F. Capito,* C. Hedio,* and Jakob Sturm* at the Diet of Augsburg 1530 (see *Lutheran Confessions,* A 2) for Konstanz, Lindau, Memmingen, Strasbourg; tried to effect a compromise bet. Luths. and Ref., esp. on the Lord's Supper.

2. *Heidelberg Catechism (Palatinate Catechism);* drawn up 1562 by Z. Ursinus* and C. Olevianus* by order of Frederick* III (1515–76), who professed the Ref. faith as distinct from the Luth. It mentions election to holiness and salvation in Christ but says nothing of double predestination and is polemic on the mass. Its 129 questions are divided: I. Man's misery; II. Man's redemption; III. Thankfulness.

3. *Brandenburg Confessions.* a. John* Sigismund, though pledged 1593 to Lutheranism by his father, prepared his own confession 1614 endorsing Ref. doctrine, but with the reservation that God is not the author of damnation.

b. Efforts were made at the 1631 Leipzig* Colloquy to unite Luths. and Ref. to present a common front against the enemy; but differences persisted on the omnipresence of Christ's human nature, Eucharist, and election.

c. *Declaration of Thorn;* 1645; careful statement of the Ref. faith drawn up for a colloquy (conf., syn.) at Thorn*; divided into a gen. part and a special declaration; signed by noblemen and clergy from Poland, Lithuania, and Brandenburg. See also *Poland,* 4.

d. Less important confessions: *Catechism of Emden,* 1554; *Confession of Elector Frederick* III* (1515–76), pub. 1577; *Confession of Nassau,* 1578; *Confession of Anhalt* (*Repetitio Anhaltina,* i. e., Repetition of the AC), 1581; *Bremen Confession (Consensus Ministerii Bremensis),* 1598; *Hessian Confession,* adopted at Cassel 1607, pub. 1608; *Confession of the Heidelberg Theologians,* 1607.

E. *Ref. Confessions of Boh., Poland, and Hung.* 1. A catechism called *The Smaller Questions* (51 questions for children; 3 divisions: Faith, Hope, and Love), probably written before 1500, served confessional purposes among Waldenses* in Boh.

2. *Boh. Catechism,* 1521; 75 questions; follows *The Smaller Questions* (see 1) in gen. arrangement, but also treats the Beatitudes and has more on idolatry, Mariolatry, saints and martyrs, and the Lord's Supper.

3. The Bohemian* Brethren wrote 34 confessions 1467–1671. The 1st, *Bohemian Confession of 1535,* was presented at Vienna to Ferdinand (1503–64; brother of Charles* V; b. Alcalá de Henares, Sp.; king of Hung. and Boh. 1526, Ger. 1531; Holy Roman emp. as Ferdinand I 1556–64); resembles the AC in form and content; Luther disapproved the arts. on celibacy and justification, but after changes had been made he pub. it with a favorable preface. See also *Bohemia, Lutheran Theology in,* 3; Speyer, *Diets of,* 1–3.

4. Maximilian II (1527–76; son of Ferdinand I [see 3]; b. Vienna, Austria; king of Boh. and of the Romans [i. e. Germans] 1562, of Hung. 1563; Holy Roman emp. 1564–76) allowed the Prots. to submit their own confession of faith to a diet at Prague; Utraquists, Luths., Calvinists, and Boh. Brethren agreed on a moderate statement prepared by Paul Pressius and M. Krispin; it was adopted with some changes by the diet and presented to the emp. 1575. This *2d Boh. Confession* (25 arts.) agrees essentially with the AC and the older Boh. Confession but conforms to P. Melanchthon's* later view of the Lord's Supper.

5. The 1570 *Consensus of Sandomierz* (Sandomir; Sendomir; *Consensus Sendomiriensis*) is the only important confessional document of the ev. chs. in Poland. It states that the 3 ev. chs. (Luths., Calvinists, and Boh. Brethren) agree on the doctrines of God, Trin., incarnation, person of Christ, justification by faith, and other fundamental doctrines; in the Lord's Supper it distinguishes bet. the earthly form and the heavenly substance. See also *Poland,* 2.

6. *Hung. Confessions* include the *Hung. Confession (Confessio Czengerina),* prepared and adopted at a syn. in Czenger 1557 (1558?), printed 1570 at Debrecen. It opposes the "sacramentarian" view of a purely symbolic presence of Christ in the Lord's Supper; holds that Christ is truly though spiritually present; defends infant baptism; teaches free election; is silent on reprobation; denies that God is the author of sin; has only secondary hist. importance; was practically superseded by the 2d Helvetic Confession (see A 6). The Heidelberg Catechism (see D 2) was also introd. See also *Hungary.* EL

See also *Presbyterian Confessions.*

Die Bekenntnisschriften der reformierten Kirche, ed. E. F. K. Müller (Leipzig, 1903); *Schriften zur reformirten Theologie,* I: *Die Bekenntnisschriften der reformirten Kirchen Deutschlands,* ed. H. L. J. Heppe (Elberfeld, 1860); P. Schaff, *Bibliotheca symbolica ecclesiae universalis: The Creeds of Christendom,* I. *The History of Creeds* and III. *The Evangelical Protestant Creeds,* with translations, 4th ed., rev. and enl. (New York, 1919); *Reformed Confessions of the 16th Century,* ed. A. C. Cochrane (Philadelphia, 1966).

Reformed Dutch. See *Netherlands; Reformed Churches,* 1, 2, and 4 b, c, f; *Reformed Confessions,* C; *United Church of Christ,* II A 2.

Reformed Ecumenical Synod, First. Grand Rapids, Mich., 1946. First suggested 1924 to the Ref. Ch. in S. Afr., which made overtures for syns. to the Ref. Ch. of the Neth. 1927. These 2, with the Christian Ref. Ch. in Am. (see *Reformed Churches,* 4 c), arranged the syn. It adopted as bases for future similar syns. the OT and NT (both regarded as infallible) as interpreted in Ref. confessions (1st Helvetic

Conf., Gallican Conf., Belgic Conf., Canons of Dordrecht, Heidelberg Catechism [see *Reformed Confessions,* A 6; B; C 1, 2; D 2]; Scotch Conf., Westminster Conf. [see *Presbyterian Confessions,* 2 and 3]; Thirty-nine Arts. [see *Anglican Confessions,* 6]).

Reformed Episcopal Church. Organized 1873 NYC under leadership of G. D. Cummins.* Regards Scripture as the Word of God and sole rule of faith and practice; accepts the Apostles' Creed (but omits "He descended into hell") and Nicene Creed, Baptism and the Lord's Supper, and the doctrines of grace substantially as set forth in the 39 Arts. (see *Anglican Confessions,* 6), but Art. III, of the descent of Christ into Hades, is omitted; rejects the doctrine that the presence of Christ in the Lord's Supper is a presence in the elements of bread and wine and that regeneration is inseparably connected with Baptism; "minister" and "Lord's Table" are substituted for "priest" and "altar" in the liturgy. Polity agrees with that of the Prot. Episc. Ch. For worship the ch. uses the Book* of Common Prayer as rev. by the Gen. Conv. of the Prot. Episc. Ch. 1785, but holds that no liturgy should be imperative and reserves full right to alter, abridge, enlarge, and amend the same as may seem best, "provided that the substance of the faith be kept entire."

Reformed Mennonite Church. See *Mennonite Churches,* 3 a.

Reformed Methodist Church. See *Methodist Churches,* 4 b.

Reformed Methodist Union Episcopal Church. See *Methodist Churches,* 4 c.

Reformed Presbyterian Church. See *Presbyterian Churches,* 1.

Reformed Presbyterian Church, Evangelical Synod. See *Presbyterian Churches,* 4 e.

Reformed Presbyterian Church of North America. See *Presbyterian Churches,* 4 f.

Reformed Presbyterians. See *Associate Reformed Church;* entries beginning *Reformed Presbyterian . . . .*

Reformed Presbytery. See *Associate Reformed Church.*

Reformed Protestant Dutch Church, The. See *Reformed Churches,* 4 b.

Reformed Youth Fellowship. See *Young People's Organizations, Christian,* III, 11.

Reformed Zion Union Apostolic Church. See *Methodist Churches,* 4 c.

Reformers Before the Reformation. See *Reformation, Lutheran,* 4.

Regalia Petri. Various rights and high prerogatives which, acc. to RCm, belong to the pope as a kind of universal sovereign and king of kings.

Regalism. Doctrine of royal supremacy, esp. in ch. matters. See also *England,* B 1; *Roman Catholic Church,* D 2.

Regeneration. See *Conversion,* II, 1.

Regensburg, League of. Formed 1524 by Rhineland and S Ger RC princes and bps. under leadership of L. Campeggio* against Lutheranism; ineffectual, but an official step in the direction of reform; inaugurated denominational leagues (see *Dessau, League of*).

Regensburg Book. Basis for discussion at Regensburg* Conference. Developed from secret discussions bet. RCs J. Gropper* and G. Veltwick* and Evangelicals M. Bucer* and W. F. Capito.* Draft of the conclusions was approved Jan. 1541 by Philip* of Hesse as preliminary to agreement and sent to Joachim II Hektor (see *Joachim,* 2) to show to M. Luther* and other Prot. princes. The document used at Regensburg had 23 arts.

Regensburg Conference (also called colloquy and diet). Continuation of Colloquy of Worms*; held Apr. 1541 to restore religious unity in Germany. RC discussants: J. Gropper,* J. v. Pflug,* J. Eck*; evangelicals: M. Bucer,* J. Pistorius the elder (see *Pistorius,* 2), and P. Melanchthon.* Papal legates G. Contarini* and G. Morone* were also present. Discussions were based on the Regensburg* Book. There was agreement on the first 4 arts. (man before the Fall, free will, cause of sin, original sin); partial agreement on justification; no agreement on doctrinal authority, hierarchy, discipline, sacraments. Charles* V tried in vain to induce the Prots. to accept the disputed arts. Mutual agreement to refer settlement of remaining differences to a gen. council was included in the imperial summation of the conf. (Reichstagsabschied) as Regensburg Interim.

Another conf. was held at Regensburg early 1546 in an unsuccessful effort to overcome differences. RCs present included E. Billick,* J. Cochlaeus,* J. Hoffmeister,* Malvenda*; Prots.: J. Brenz,* M. Bucer,* G. Major,* E. Schnepf.* Failure of the conf. was soon followed by the Schmalkaldic* War. See also *Diaz, Juan; Dietrich, Veit; Draconites, Johann(es); Gualther, Rudolf; Pistorius,* 2.

A conf. at Regensburg 1601 dealt with the question whether Scripture alone, without tradition, is the source and norm of faith and theol.; Prots. said Yes, RCs No. The gap was not bridged. See also *Tradition; Trent, Council of.*

Regensburg Interim. See *Regensburg Conference.*

Regensburg Synod (792). See *Adoptionism.*

Reger, Max (1873–1916). Composer, conductor, pianist; b. Brand, Bav., Ger.; pupil of H. Riemann*; organist Weiden RC ch. 1886–89; taught at Wiesbaden Conservatory 1895–96; held various other positions. Works include chorale arrangements; Ger. motets; sacred songs for small choir; a setting of Ps 100 for chorus, organ, and orchestra.

Regino (ca. 840–915). B. probably Altrip, near Speyer; Benedictine; abbot Prüm 892, St. Martin at Trier 899. Works include *Libri duo de synodalibus causis et disciplinis ecclesiasticis; De harmonica institutione; Chronicon.*

Regions Beyond Missionary Union, The. Organized 1873 by H. G. Guinness* as East* London Institute for Home and For. Missions; interdenom. from the beginning; led to est. of the Livingstone Inland Miss. 1878 (see also *Africa,* F 2), whose name changed 1888 to Congo Balolo Mission; the latter united 1899/1900 with the East London Institute for Home and For. Missions to form The Regions Beyond Missionary Union. Fields have included Indonesia; Congo; India; Nepal; Peru.

Regium donum. See *Presbyterian Churches,* 3.

Regius, Urbanus. See *Rhegius, Urbanus.*

Regula Chrodegangi. Rule of 34 canons and a preface drawn up 760 by Chrodegang* for the clergy of his cathedral ch. on basis of the rule of Benedict* of Nursia; made obligatory for the whole empire 817.

Regula fidei. See *Rule of Faith.*

Regular Baptists. See *Baptist Churches,* 4, 23.

Regular Clergy. See *Clergy; Secular Clergy.*

Rehmke, Johannes (1848–1930). B. Elmshorn, Schleswig-Holstein, Ger.; prof. philos. Greifswald 1885–1921; sought a philos. outside of materialism and idealism; tried to determine the essence of consciousness; held that God is the real as such, but that there is also something real outside of God.

Reichenau, Hermann von. See *Hermann von Reichenau.*

Reichert, G. Adam (1795–Sept. 18, 1877). Traveling miss. in W Pa. till 1837; pastor Philadelphia 18 yrs., then at Kittaning, Pa.

Reid, Thomas (1710–96). B. Strachan, Kincardine, Scot.; licensed to preach 1731; librarian Marischal coll., Aberdeen, 1733–36; pastor New Machar, near Aberdeen, 1737; prof. philos. King's coll., Aberdeen, 1751; prof. moral philos. Glasgow 1764; founded Scot. or common* sense realism school. Works include *An Inquiry into the Human Mind, on the*

Principles of Common Sense; Essays on the Intellectual Powers of Man; Essays on the Active Powers of Man.

Reid, William. See *Africa,* D 1.

Reimann, Georg (1570–1615). B. Leobschütz (now Glubczyce, Poland), Upper Silesia; prof. rhetoric Königsberg; hymnist. Hymns include "Wir singen all' mit Freudenschall"; "Aus Lieb' lässt Gott der Christenheit."

Reimann, Henry William (Jan. 4, 1926–Jan. 6, 1963). B. Oak Park, Ill.; educ. Conc. Coll., Milwaukee, Wis., and Conc. Sem., St. Louis, Mo.; pastor Charleston, S. C., 1951; asst. prof. Conc. Sem., St. Louis, 1955. Works include *Let's Study Theology.*

Reimarus, Hermann Samuel (1694–1768). B. Hamburg, Ger.; rationalistic philos.; taught at Wittenberg from 1719; rector Wismar 1723; prof. Hamburg from ca. 1727/29. Works include *Apologie oder Schutzschrift für die vernünftigen Verehrer Gottes,* parts of which became better known as *Fragmente eines Ungenannten* or *Wolfenbüttel Fragments* under the hands of G. E. Lessing.*

Reims, Cathedral at. See *Church Architecture,* 10.

Reina, Cassiodoro de (Reyna; Reinius; ca. 1520–94). B. Montemolin, Sp.; entered monastery at Seville; fled from Sp. ca. 1557; to Frankfurt am Main, Ger., via Eng. and Holland; became Ref.; preached to ev. Spaniards in London ca. 1559; returned to Frankfurt ca. 1563/64; Luth. preacher Antwerp ca. 1578; est. a Dutch ch. of the AC at Frankfurt 1585, became its pastor 1593. Tr. Bible into Sp.

Reinbeck, Johann Gustav (1683–1741). B. Celle, Ger.; educ. Halle; asst. 1709, then pastor (preacher) Berlin; provost Berlin-Cologne 1717; consistorial councillor there 1729; exponent of C. v. Wolff's* rationalistic theol.; tried to show that faith and reason agree.

Reincarnation. Belief that a soul may reenter some body, or succession of bodies, thus leading a continued existence. See also *Transmigration of Souls.*

Reineccius, Christian (1668–1752). Luth. scholar; b. Grossmühlingen, Zerbst, Ger.; rector of the academy at Weissenfels. Ed. *Biblia Sacra Quadrilinguia.* See also *Polyglot Bibles.*

Reineccius, Jakob (Reneccius; 1572–1613). B. Salzwedel, Ger.; educ. Wittenberg; pastor Tangermünde, Berlin, and Hamburg; inspector Gymnasium at Hamburg 1612. Works include *Panoplia sive armatura theologica; Clavis sacrae theologiae.*

Reinhard, Franz Volkmar (1753–1812). Luth. theol.; b. Vohenstrauss, in The Palatinate, Ger.; educ. Wittenberg; prof. philos. 1780, theol. 1782, Wittenberg; chief court preacher and mem. high consistory Dresden; at first a supernaturalist (see *Supernaturalism*), holding necessity of revelation over against rationalists (who denied the need of revelation), but practically left little as a matter of revelation; later more orthodox Luth.; his 1800 Reformation sermon led to revival of Luther studies in Saxony. Works include *System der christlichen Moral; Vorlesungen über die Dogmatik.*

Reinhard, Johannes (John Rinehart; Reinhart; Mar. 14, 1776–June 7, 1861). Moved as farmer from Washington Co., Pa., to Jefferson Co., Ohio, 1804; cong. officer Is. Creek Twp.; encouraged by J. Staunch,* he became a mem. Pa. Ministerium; helped organize Gen. Conf. of the Ev. Luth. Preachers in Ohio and the Adjacent States (see *Ohio and Other States, The Evangelical Lutheran Joint Synod of,* 1) and was ordained by it 1818; pastor Jefferson Co., Ohio; name disappears from syn. roll after 1833 without explanation.

Reinhart, Lucas Friedrich (Lukas; 1623–88). B. Nürnberg; educ. Altorf, Helmstedt, Jena; prof. theol. and archdeacon Altorf. Works include *Synopsis theologiae dogmaticae.*

Reinke, August (Sept. 29, 1841–Nov. 18, 1899). B. Winsen, Hannover, Ger.; educ. Conc. Sem., St. Louis, Mo.; pastor Blue Island and Chicago, Ill.; pioneer in Mo. Synod work among deaf (see also *Deaf,* 10); helped found Old Folks' Home, Arlington Heights, Ill.

Reinken, Jan (Reincken; Reinike; Jan Adams Reincken; Johann Adam; 1623–1722). Organist; composer; b. probably Wilshausen, Alsace; pupil of H. Scheidemann,* whom he succeeded in Hamburg; helped found opera in Hamburg; J. S. Bach* went several times to hear him play. Works include compositions for organ and for other instruments.

Reinkens, Joseph Hubert (1821–96). B. Burtscheid (now part of Aachen), Ger.; opposed dogma of papal infallibility*; suspended 1870; excommunicated 1872; Old* Cath. bp. Ger. 1873.

Reiser, Friedrich (Fridericus Danubianus; ca. 1400/01–1458). Hussite; b. Swabia; priest 1432; attended Council of Basel*; noted preacher; reorganized Waldensian congs. in Ger., Austria, and Switz.; captured and burned in Strasbourg by Inquisition.*

Reisner, Adam (Reissner). See *Reusner, Adam.*

Reisner, George Andrew. See *Geography, Christian,* 6.

Reiterated Conversion. See *Conversion,* II, 8.

Reitz, Johann Heinrich (1655–1720). Ref. mystic; b. Oberdiebach, near Bacharach, Ger.; educ. Leiden, Bremen, Heidelberg; held various pastoral and educ. positions; changed from Ref. orthodoxy to enthusiasm (see *Ecstasy*) when he tried to convert B. C. Klopfer* to orthodoxy; returned to orthodoxy ca. 1711. Works include *Historie der Wiedergebohrnen; Der geöffnete Himmel; Die Nachfolge Jesu Christi.*

Reitzenstein, Richard (1861–1931). B. Breslau, Ger.; taught at Breslau, Rostock, Giessen, Strasbourg, Freiburg, Göttingen; exponent of Religionsgechichtliche* Schule. Works include *Poimandres; Die hellenistischen Mysterienreligionen; Studien zum antiken Synkretismus aus Iran und Griechenland.*

Relativism. The view that truth is relative and may vary from individual to individual, from time to time, or from group to group.

Relativity. See *Einstein, Albert.*

Released-Time Classes. See *Christian Education,* E 9, J 5; *Parish Education,* F 2; *Protestant Education in the United States.*

Relics (from Lat. *reliquiae,* "remains" [sc. of a martyr or other saint]). Ex. 13:19; 2 K 2:13-14; 13:21; Acts 19:11-12 do not support any cult of relics.

In the 2d c. the remains of Polycarp* were honored. Veneration of relics spread under persecution. From the 4th c. the Lord's Supper was celebrated over martyrs' tombs in Roman catacombs.* Belief that relics are instruments of miracles developed gradually. The 787 Council of Nicaea* forbade consecration of chs. without relics. Council of Trent*: "The holy bodies of holy martyrs and of others living with Christ . . . are to be venerated by the faithful, through which [bodies] many benefits are bestowed by God on men" (Sess. XXV, "On the Invocation, Veneration, and Relics of Saints, and on Sacred Images").

SA II ii 22–23: "Even if there were some good in them, relics should long since have been condemned. They are neither commanded nor commended. They are utterly unnecessary and useless. Worst of all, however, is the claim that relics effect indulgences and the forgiveness of sin and that, like the Mass, etc., their use is a good work and a service of God."

See also *Frederick III* (1463–1525); *Holy Coat of Treves.*

Relief Church. Began in Scot. 1761 under leadership of T. Gillespie* as a presbytery for the relief of Christians oppressed in their Christian privileges; helped form United Presb. Ch. 1847 at Edinburgh.

See also *Presbyterian Churches,* 1; *Scotland, Reformation in,* 1.

Religio illicita. See *Church and State,* 2.

Religion, Comparative. Comparative study of religions and religious systems; regarded by some as equivalent to the science of religion,* by others as the latter's 2d phase (bet. hist. of religion and philos. of religion).

L. H. Jordan, *Comparative Religion: Its Genesis and Growth* (Edinburgh, 1905); *Sacred Books of the East,* various translators, ed. F. M. Müller, Am. ed., 12 vols. (New York, 1897–1901); *The Evolution of Ethics as Revealed in the Great Religions* (New Haven, 1927); J. G. Frazer, *The Golden Bough,* 3d ed., 12 vols. (London, 1911–15), abridged ed., 1 vol. (New York, 1922); M. Fitch, *Their Search for God* (New York, 1947); S. H. Kellogg, *A Handbook of Comparative Religion* (Philadelphia, 1899); E. D. Soper, *Religions of Mankind,* 3d ed. rev. (New York, 1951); W. Holsten, *Christentum und nichtchristliche Religion nach der Auffassung Luthers* (Gütersloh, 1932); P. E. Kretzmann, *The GOD OF THE BIBLE and other "GODS"* (St. Louis, 1943); N. Söderblom, *The Living God: Basal Forms of Personal Religion* (London, 1933); M. Eliade, *The Quest: History and Meaning in Religion* (Chicago, 1969); C. H. Toy, *Introduction to the History of Religions* (New York, 1970).

Religion, History of. See *Religion, Comparative; Religion, Science of.*

Religion, Philosophy of. See *Apologetics, Christian,* III B; *Philosophy of Religion; Religion, Comparative.*

Religion, Psychology of. See *Apologetics, Christian,* III D; *Psychology of Religion.*

Religion, Requisites of. See *Buddhism,* 2.

Religion, Science of. Science that aims to investigate the psychological, physiological, and ethnological bases of religion, the primitive popular ideas that underlie all hist. religions, and the alleged development of religion from that of primitive man upward; as it aims to present a hist. of the development of the forms of religious thinking and concerns itself with the origin of Christianity, which it regards not as an absolute religion but as a stage in an evolutionary process, it opposes the Biblical concept of revealed religion. Regarded by some as equivalent to the hist. of religion, by others as equivalent to comparative religion.*

Religion and Higher Education. See *Students, Spiritual Care of.*

Religionsgeschichtliche Schule (Historicoreligious School). Term coined 1904 by A. Jeremias*; denotes a 19th and 20th c. theol. school of thought that studied the development of Christianity in light of its hist. and geog. environment. See also *Lutheran Theology After 1580,* 13.

Religious Bodies (US), Bibliography of. M. Günther, *Populäre Symbolik,* 4th enl. ed. L. E. Fuerbringer (St. Louis, 1913); T. E. W. Engelder, W. F. Arndt, T. C. Graebner, F. E. Mayer, *Popular Symbolics* (St. Louis, 1934); *The American Church History Series,* ed. P. Schaff et al., 13 vols. (New York, 1893–97; some vols. revised later); *Yearbook of American Churches,* ed. C. H. Jacquet, Jr. (New York, 1972; issued since 1916 at various places and under various titles and editors); H. K. Rowe, *The History of Religion in the United States* (New York, 1924); T. C. Hall, *The Religious Background of American Culture* (Boston, 1930); W. W. Sweet, *The Story of Religion in America,* enl. ed. (New York, 1939; pub. 1930 as *The Story of Religions in America*); J. L. Neve, *Churches and Sects of Christendom* (Burlington, Iowa, 1940); E. H. Klotsche, *Christian Symbolics* (Burlington, Iowa, 1929); W. L. Sperry, *Religion in America* (Cambridge, Eng., 1946); E. T. Clark, *The Small Sects in America,* rev. ed. (New York, 1949); C. S. Braden, *These Also Believe* (New York, 1949); A. L. Drummond, *Story of American Protestantism* (Edinburgh, 1949); W. S. Hudson, *American Protestantism* (Chicago, 1961); F. E. Mayer, *The Religious Bodies of America,* 4th ed., rev. A. C. Piepkorn (St. Louis, 1961); C. E. Olmstead, *History of Religion in the United States* (Englewood Cliffs, N. J., 1960) and *Religion in America* (Englewood Cliffs, N. J., 1961); G. Weigel, *Churches in North America* (Baltimore, 1961); E. Routley, *Creeds and Confessions* (Philadelphia, 1962); *The Faith of Christendom,* ed. B. A. Gerrish (Cleveland, 1963); *Creeds of the Churches,* ed. J. H. Leith (Chicago, 1963); S. E. Mead, *The Lively Experiment* (New York, 1963); E. S. Gaustad, *A Religious History of America* (New York, 1966); W. A. Clebsch, *From Sacred to Profane America* (New York, 1968); J. A. Hardon, *The Spirit and Origins of American Protestantism* (Dayton, Ohio, 1968); *Issues in American Protestantism,* ed. R. L. Ferm (Garden City, N. Y., 1969); M. E. Marty, *The Modern Schism* (New York, 1969) and *Protestantism* (New York, 1972); R. Baird, *Religion in America* (New York, 1970); F. S. Mead, *Handbook of Denominations in the United States, 5th ed.* (Nashville, Tenn., 1970). See also references under *Statistics, Ecclesiastical.*

Religious Drama. The Gk. word *drama* means "deed, act," then "action represented on a stage." In a wider sense: any demonstration in action as opposed to abstraction; cf. Jer 19; 27; 28; Eze 4.

Natural instinct for imitation and rhythm in man led to imitative action. Dramatic action (e. g., dancing, pantomime) early played a prominent part in worship (e. g., at funerals).

1. *Classical.* Dramas of Gk. tragedians (e. g., Aeschylus [525–456 BC], Sophocles [ca. 496–406 BC], Euripides [5th c. BC]) were performed at the feast of Dionysus (see *Greek Religion,* 3 b). Plays of Aeschylus were deeply religious and dealt, e. g., with the power of gods and their relation to men, nemesis, and future life. Sophocles dealt with faith and moral issues (esp. in human relations). Euripides (the "liberal" in the trio) tried to show psychol. reasons for action. Under Roman influence, drama lost religious character. Christians opposed theater because of its idolatry and obscenity. Classical drama was crushed for ca. 1,000 yrs.

2. *Medieval.* Spiritual dramas of the Middle Ages originated in the ch. The first, in Lat., were performed at chief ch. festivals (e. g., Corpus* Christi). Guilds, nobility, city fathers, and common folk took part. Secular and diverting features were added (see *Feast of Asses*). In course of time the liturgy offered opportunity for dramatic action, which in turn led to Passion plays (dramas developed from responses and readings of Lent, esp. Holy Week). Saints' plays, developed from processions and other festival celebrations in honor of saints, led to miracle plays, which used mainly material connected with legends of saints and their intercession for those who venerate them. Mystery plays (or mysteries) originally were enactments of events from the life of Christ and later of the whole Bible; but distinction bet. mysteries and miracle plays disappeared and the terms were used interchangeably. Morality plays (or moralities), allegorical presentations popular esp. in the 15th and 16th cents., tried to teach a moral lesson by personifying vices and virtues (as in *Everyman*).

Secularization of plays resulted from influence of guildmen as actors, from increasing appeal of Fastnachtsspiele (drolleries of itinerant actors performed at Shrovetide*), and from revival of classicism with renewed interest in dramas of L. A. Seneca,* Titus Maccius Plautus (ca. 254–184 BC; Roman playwright), and Terence (Publius Terentius Afer; 185–159 BC; Roman playwright).

3. *Reformation.* M. Luther* took a positive attitude toward secular drama (see *Theater*) and encouraged religious drama. His praise of drama in his 1534 Bible (WA-DB 12, pp. 7, 109, 493) sparked use of the stage for the Reformation. The whole plan of salvation was dramatized, though Luther discouraged Passion plays (WA 2, 141). *Die Parabel vom Verlorenen Sohn* by B. Waldis* is one of the most outstanding 16th-c. dramas. Other authors include C. Lasius,* G. Major,* H. Sachs.*

Drama was used by evangelicals (e. g., N. Manuel,* W. Pir[c]kheimer*) also for polemics (e. g., to portray the pope as Antichrist). *Radtschlag des allerheiligsten Vaters Bapsts Pauli des Dritten, mit dem Collegio Cardinalium gehalten, wie das angesetzte Concilium zu Trient fürzunemen sey, Anno 1545* has a woodcut entitled DAS CONCILIUM ZUTRENT (the last word [1] indicating the place of assem. [Trent] and [2] being a play on the Ger. word *zertrennt,* "divided"). Some opposition dramas were directed against Luther's marriage.

Often borrowing from classical material, 16th-c. dramatists (e. g., J. H. Bullinger,* J. Camerarius,* B. Ringwaldt*) also wrote historiconovelistic and didacticosatirical works.

M. Rinckart* was one of several ev. dramatists who wrote on Luther's life.

4. *Jesuits,* noting the influence of dramas, soon produced plays of fixed form, with great pomp, and for pedagogical purposes and continued doing so till the gen. suppression of the order 1773.

5. *Modern.* The Passion play of Oberammergau,* Upper Bav., Ger., first presented 1634 by inhabitants of the RC village in fulfillment of a 1633 vow in gratitude for cessation of the Black Death; performed once every decade.

Gen. interest in religious drama was revived ca. the beginning of the 20th c. Pageants, dramas, and dramatized stories came to be widely used in ch. work via radio (various radio plays), motion pictures (e. g., *Martin Luther*), and TV (e. g., "This Is the Life" series [see *Radio and Television Evangelism, Network,* 8]).

Religious novelistic dramas of the 20th c. include M. Anderson, *Journey to Jerusalem;* C. R. Kennedy, *The Terrible Meek;* A. MacLeish, *J. B.;* J. Masefield, *The Trial of Jesus.* Dramas with religious themes include M. Connelly, *The Green Pastures.* EL

K. Young, *The Drama of the Medieval Church,* 2 vols. (Oxford, 1933); N. C. Brooks, "Processional Drama and Dramatic Procession in Germany in the Late Middle Ages," *Journal of English and Germanic Philology,* XXXII (1933), 141–171; H. Holstein, *Die Reformation im Spiegelbilde der dramatischen Litteratur des sechzehnten Jahrhunderts* (Halle, 1886); H. A. Ehrensperger, *Conscience on Stage* (New York, 1947); *The Questing Spirit,* ed. H. E. Luccock and F. Brentano (New York, 1947); P. E. Kretzmann, *The Liturgical Element in the Earliest Forms of the Medieval Drama, with Special Reference to the English and German Plays* (Minneapolis, 1916); O. B. Hardison, Jr., *Christian Rite and Christian Drama in the Middle Ages* (Baltimore, 1965); A. G. Loomis, *Guide for Drama Workshops in the Church Prepared for Leaders and Instructors* (New York, 1964); K. M. Baxter, *Contemporary Theatre and the Christian Faith* (New York, 1965; pub. London 1964 as *Speak What We Feel*); C. J. Stratman, *Bibliography of Medieval Drama* (Berkeley, Calif., 1954).

Religious Education. See *Christian Education; Ministry, Education of; Parish Education; Schools, Church-Related.*

Religious Education Association of the United States and Canada. Organization of Prot., Cath., and Jewish professional leaders of educ. and religion; beginning traced to organization effected 1903 Chicago, Ill., mainly through influence of W. R. Harper.* Pub. *Religious Education; The Religious Educator.* HQ NYC.

Religious Enthusiasm. See *Ecstasy.*

Religious Humanism. Am. movement, mainly of left-wing Unitarians, which holds that scientific advance removed distinctions bet. secular and sacred and that man must seek salvation through control of the physical and soc. world; doctrines pub. 1933 in Humanist Manifesto. See also *Humanism.*

Religious Journalism. See *Publication Houses, Lutheran; Religious Press in America; Religious Tract Movement.*

Religious Liberty. Freedom of religious profession, worship, and propaganda. US Constitution: "No religious test shall ever be required as a qualification to any office or public trust under the United States" (Art. VI); "Congress shall make no law respecting an establishment of religion, or prohibiting the free exercise thereof" (1st Amendment); the 14th Amendment ("No State . . . shall deprive any person of life, liberty, or property without due process of law") was interpreted 1922 by the US Supreme Court to assure "the right of the individual . . . to worship God according to the dictates of his own conscience."

Religious Press in America (Journalism). The 1st exclusively religious journal in Am. was the weekly *Christian History* (Boston, 1743–45), devoted to promoting the Great* Awakening. From 1745 to 1772 three religious papers were attempted in New York and 2 magazines in the Philadelphia area; only 1 survived its 1st yr.

More than 500 religious journals were founded 1789–1830; in 1830 ca. 175 were still alive. Circulation figures of 5,000–10,000 were common. In 1829 the Meth. *Christian Advocate* (est. 1826) had the world's largest subscription list: ca. 25,000.

1830–80 was a golden age. By 1880 there were more than 500 journals, with ca. 3 copies per inhabitant. The no. of journals continued to increase after 1880, but denominational interest waned; journals of broader interest flourished.

Most RC dioceses have weeklies. Other RC periodicals include *Catholic World; Ave Maria; America; Commonweal.*

Prot. denominational journals have included *Christian Advocate; Baptist Leader; A.D.* (beginning Sept. 1972 and including the former *Presbyterian Life* and *United Church Herald* in separate editions); *The Church Herald.* Prot. nondenom. journals have included *The Christian Century; Christian Herald; Christianity Today.*

Luth. periodicals have included *The Lutheran; The Lutheran Standard; Lutheran Herald; Lutheran Companion; The Lutheran Messenger; Lutheran Sentinel; The Lutheran Synod Quarterly; The Lutheran Voice; The Lutheran Witness; Der Lutheraner.* Various areas produce local publications.

See also *Missouri and Other States, The English Evangelical Lutheran Synod of; Publication Houses, Lutheran; Theological Journals.*

Religious Socialism. See *Christian Socialism,* 4.

Religious Society of Friends (Conservative). See *Friends, Society of,* 7.

Religious Society of Friends (Gen. Conf.). See *Friends, Society of,* 8.

Religious Society of Friends Kansas Yearly Meeting. See *Friends, Society of,* 6.

Religious Tracts. Widespread use of religious tracts began with the Reformation. The Meth. movement in Eng. made extensive use of tracts. A Soc. for the Distribution of Religious Tracts Among the Poor was est. 1782. In proposing this soc. J. Wesley* said: "Men wholly unawakened will not take the pains to read the Bible. They have no relish for it. But a small tract may engage their attention for half an hour and may, by the blessing of God, prepare them for going forward." Tracts pub. by this soc. include *Ten Short Sermons; Tokens for Children; A Word to a Swearer; A Word to a Drunkard.* H. More* wrote the tract *William Chip* and *The Cheap Repository Tracts* and distributed 2 million copies the 1st yr. See also *Simeon, Charles.*

The Religious Tract Soc. of London was organized 1799; its work led to organization of the BFBS. Other tract socs, of Gt. Brit. include The Religious Tract and Book Soc. of Scot. (1793), The Stirling Tract Enterprise (1848), The Dublin Tract Soc., The Monthly Tract Soc. (London, 1837). Many other tract socs. were est. in Eur., India, China, Australia, New Zealand, S. Afr., West Indies, Can., and elsewhere.

Tract socs. in the US included Mass. Soc. for the Promotion of Christian Knowledge (1803), Conn. Religious Tract Soc. (1807), Vt. Religious Tract Soc. (1808), The Prot. Episc. Tract Soc. (1809), N. Y. Religious Tract Soc. (1812), Ev. Tract Soc., Boston (1813), Albany Religious Tract Soc. (1813), New Eng. Tract Soc. (1814; became the Am. Tract Soc., Boston, 1823), Religious Tract Soc. of Philadelphia (1815), Religious Tract Soc. of Baltimore (1816), N. Y. Meth. Tract Soc. (1817), Am. Tract Soc., Boston (1823), Bap. Gen. Tract Soc. (1824), Am. Tract Soc., N. Y. (1825), NYC Tract Soc. (1827), NYC Mission and Tract Soc. (1864), Willard Tract Soc., Boston (1866), Monthly Tract Soc. of the US, N. Y. (1874).

The Am. Tract Soc., Boston, merged with the Am. Tract Soc., N. Y., 1878. The Bap. Gen. Tract Soc., organized Washington, moved to Philadelphia and became the Am. Bap. Publication Soc. 1840. The N. Y. Meth. Tract Soc. later was inc. as Tract Soc. of the Meth. Episc. Ch.

Other tract distributors in the US have included Good News Publishers, Lutheran Press (a dept. of ALPB), Moody Literature Mission, Pilgrim Tract Soc. OCH

See also *Tractarianism.*

Religious Wars. See *Reformation, Lutheran,* 12.

Relly, James (ca. 1722–78). B. Jeffreston, Pembrokeshire, Wales; Meth. preacher; Universalist ca. 1756; active in London. See also *Murray, John.*

Remanence (from Lat. *remanere,* "to remain"). Doctrine that in the Lord's Supper the substance of bread and wine remains after consecration coexistent with the body and blood of Christ. See also *Grace, Means of,* IV, 3–4.

Rembrandt Harmensz van Rijn (Harmenszoon; Ryn; other variants; probably 1606–69). Painter, etcher; b. Leiden, Neth.; moved to Amsterdam ca. 1631/32. Works include *Abraham's Sacrifice; Woman Taken in Adultery; Descent from the Cross.* See also *Art, Ecclesiastical and Religious,* 7.

Remensnyder, Junius Benjamin (Feb. 24, 1841–Jan. 2, 1927). B. near Staunton, Va.; served with 131st Pa. Volunteers 1862–63; educ. Luth. Theol. Sem., Gettysburg, Pa.; pastor Pa., Ga., N. Y.; pres. The General* Syn. of the Ev. Luth. Ch. in the USA 1911–13. Works include *The Lutheran Manual; What the World Owes Luther.*

Remigius of Auxerre (Remi; ca. 841–ca. 908). B. Burgundy; Benedictine at Auxerre; taught at Reims and Paris. Works include commentaries on OT and NT. See also *Haimo.*

Remigius of Lyons (Remi; d. 875). Abp. Lyons 852. See also *Predestinarian Controversy,* 1.

Remigius of Reims (Remi; Remy; ca. 436/438–ca. 533). "Apostle of the Franks"; abp. Reims ca. 459; bap. Clovis* I.

Remonstrant Synod of Ulster. See *Presbyterian Churches,* 3.

Remonstrants. Ca. 45 Arminian ministers who 1610 addressed a 5-art. remonstrance to the States Gen. of Holland and W. Friesland stating their differences from Calvinism. Calvinists presented a counter-address and were called Counter-Remonstrants. The remonstrant arts. were condemned at the Syn. of Dordrecht* 1619; remonstrants, whose leaders included S. Episcopius* and H. Grotius,* were deposed, imprisoned, banished, but permitted to return 1630. See also *Arminianism; Netherlands,* 5.

Renaissance. The concept of the Renaissance as a distinct period is largely the creation of J. C. Burckhardt,* who held that the Renaissance marked a rebirth of culture and, with the Reformation, gave rise to the modern world. The Renaissance began in It. in the 14th c., came to affect the rest of Eur. in varying degrees, and was marked by a change in the style of living, a greater degree of individualism, a more secular direction, a new appreciation of the world of nature, and a renewed emphasis on classical antiquity as form and norm for culture and way of life.

One feature of the Renaissance was an increase of learning assoc. with the renewal of classical culture. Humanists, many of whom served as profs. of poetry and rhetoric or as secretaries in city-states characteristic of It. pol. organization in this period, were men of letters mainly responsible for the revival of interest in Lat. and Gk. antiquity. A variety of types and a certain progression in Renaissance humanism is discernible. Literary humanists, e. g., Petrarch* and G. Boccaccio,* felt a sense of distance from the ancient past and tagged the cents. just preceding as the "dark* ages." Civic humanists, e. g., Lino Coluccio di Piero dei Salutati (1331–1406; b, Stignano, It.; chancellor Florence 1375) and Leonardo Bruni (Bruno; also called Leonardo Aretino; 1369–1444; b. Arezzo, It.; chancellor Florence 1427) helped develop republican consciousness. Metaphysical humanist, e. g., M. Ficino* and G. Pico* della Mirandola introd. revival of Neoplatonism. The Gk. revival, begun, e. g., by M. Chrysoloras* and J. Bessarion,* centered in Florence under Medici patronage and was the most important single element in the gen. expansion of the It. intellectual horizon.

The change from Gothic to neoclassic is indisputable in architecture and other visual art; but the significance of the Renaissance for science, economic hist., and the Reformation is not completely clear. Humanism, e. g., in criticism of abuse, interest in religious enlightenment, rediscovery of important texts, development of critical method, and cultivation of Gk. and Heb. helped prepare the way for the Reformation; but the reformers went beyond humanist emphasis on moral philos. to basic and distinctively Christian affirmations.

J. C. Burckhardt, *Die Cultur der Renaissance in Italien* (Leipzig, 1860), tr. S. G. C. Middlemore, *The Civilization of the Renaissance in Italy,* rev. and ed. I. Gorcon (New York, 1960); W. K. Ferguson, *The Renaissance in Historical Thought* (New York, 1948); *The Rise of Modern Europe,* ed. W. L. Langer, II: M. P. Gilmore, *The World of Humanism 1453–1517* (New York, 1952); D. Hay, *The Italian Renaissance in Its Historical Background* (Cambridge, Eng., 1961); *The New Cambridge Modern History,* I: *The Renaissance,* ed. G. R. Potter (Cambridge, Eng., 1957). LWSj

Renan, Joseph Ernest (1823–92). Orientalist, philos., philol.; b. Tréguier, Fr.; studied for the priesthood till 1845; studied Semitic philol.; prof. Coll. de Fr., Paris, 1862. His *Vie de Jésus* (pub. 1863) describes Jesus as ambitious, vain, sensuous, half-consciously deceiving himself and others. Renan was suspended 1862 for his views; reinstated 1870/71; mem. Fr. Academy 1878/79. Other works include *Les*

Apôtres; Saint Paul; L'Antéchrist; Histoire de peuple d'Israel.

Renata of Ferrara (Renée de France; 1510-75). Daughter of Louis XII (1463–1515; king of Fr. 1498–1515); b. Blois, Fr.; duchess Ferrara, It., 1528; patron of the Reformation; temporarily imprisoned by her husband; threatened with banishment by her son; to Fr.; died Huguenot.

Renato, Camillo (d. after 1570). It. Anabap.; b. Sicily; private tutor in the Valtellina valley, N. It.; in controversy with Zwinglian preacher at Chiavenna 1545; friend of L. Socinus* after 1547. See also *Rhaetian Confession.*

Rendtorff, Franz (1860–1937). Father of H. Rendtorff*; b. Gütergotz, near Potsdam, Ger.; educ. Kiel, Erlangen, Leipzig; held various pastoral positions; taught at Kiel and Leipzig; pers. Gustav-Adolf Soc. 1916; main academic interest: hist. roots of Prot. pub. worship and of religious educ.

Rendtorff, Heinrich (1888–1960). Son of F. Rendtorff*; b. Westerland, on the island of Sylt, in the North Sea, off W coast of Schleswig-Holstein, Ger.; educ. Tübingen, Halle, Kiel, Leipzig; pastor 1919; home miss. 1921; dir. sem. Preetz, Holstein, 1924; prof. Kiel 1926; bp. Mecklenburg-Schwerin and prof. Rostock 1930; deposed by Nazis 1933; pastor Stettin; prof. Kiel 1945. Inaugurated "Bible Weeks"; prepared NT study guides.

Reneccius. See *Reineccius.*

Reni, Guido (1575–1642). Painter and etcher; b. Bologna, It.; devoted to "ideal" beauty.

Works include *Holy Family* (etching); *Samson Victorious.*

Renouvier, Charles Bernard (1815–1903). B. Montpellier, Fr.; idealistic philos.; influenced by I. Kant* and G. W. v. Leibniz.* Founded *Critique philosophique* (1872) and *Critique religieuse* (1878). Held that reality consists of subjects as experienced. Works include *Les Dilemmes de la metaphysique; Le Personnalisme.*

Renqvist, Henrik (original name Kukkonen; changed to Renqvist, from Swed. for "pure branch"; 1789–1866). B. Ilomantsi, Fin.; educ. Turku; ordained 1817; pastor Liperi and Sortavala; held that repentance and faith are valid only if followed by pure life; opposed use of alcohol and tobacco; imprisoned 10 yrs. for harsh measures. See also *Finland, Lutheranism in,* 4.

Renunciation of the Devil. Formal repudiation of the devil and all his works, pomp, and ways; observed in the ch. since ancient times in connection with Baptism.

Renunciation, The Great. See *Gautama Buddha.*

Reorganized Church of Jesus Christ of Latter Day Saints. See *Latter Day Saints,* g 2.

Repass, Stephan Abion (Nov. 25, 1838–June 2, 1906). B. Wytheville, Va.; educ. Roanoke Coll., Salem, Va., and Lutheran Theol. Sem., Philadelphia, Pa. Pastor Salem (1869–72) and Staunton (1884–85), Va.; Allentown, Pa., 1885–1906. Served in army during Civil War; pres. theol. sem, Salem, Va., 1873–84 (see *United Lutheran Church, Synods of,* 27); pres. Ev. Luth. Gen. Syn. in N. Am. (later known as Gen. Syn. South; see *United Synod of the Evangelical Lutheran Church in the South, The,* 1) 1871–72. Ed. *The Church Messenger.*

Repentance. In the wide sense, change from a rebellious state to one of harmony with the will of God, from trusting in human merit to trusting in the merit of Christ; embraces contrition* and justifying faith*; sometimes the fruits of repentance are included (Ap XII 28). In the narrow sense, faith and fruits are not included. The means to repentance is the Word of God. Cf. Jer 31:18; Acts 5:31. Sometimes taken as equivalent to penance* and penitence. See also *Conversion.*

K. H. Ehlers, "Repentance," *The Abiding Word,* II, ed. T. Laetsch (St. Louis, 1947), 258–274.

Repetitio Augustanae. See *Lutheran Confessions,* A 5.

Repetitio confessionis Augustanae. See *Lutheran Confessions,* A 5.

Repression. See *Psychotherapy.*

Repristination Theology. See *Lutheran Theology After 1580,* 11.

Reprobation. See *Predestination,* I.

Republican Methodist Church. See *Methodist Churches,* 1.

Requiem *(missa pro defunctis; Totenmesse).* Mass for the dead; named after the 1st word of the 1st antiphon in the RC rite ("Requiem aeternam dona eis, Domine": "Grant them eternal rest, O Lord"). There are 4 such RC masses: 1. for commemoration of all dead (Nov. 2); 2. for the day of death or burial; 3. for anniversary of death; 4. for daily (i. e., unspecified) use. See also *Brahms, Johannes.* EFP

Requiescat in pace. Lat. "May he (or she) rest in peace." Often used as tombstone inscription. Sometimes abbreviated "R. i. p."

Reredos. See *Church Furniture,* 1.

Rerum Novarum. See *Encyclicals.*

Rescript. Written reply by an ecclesiastical superior regarding a question or request; binding only on concerned parties. Papal dispensations take the form of rescripts.

Rosen, Hans Poulsen (1561–1638). B. Resen, Jutland; educ. Copenhagen and Wittenberg; prof. Copenhagen. Tr. Bible into Dan.

Reservation. 1. Retention by the pope of the right to appoint to a certain benefice; see also *Execrabilis,* 1. 2. Retention of tithes. 3. Retention of certain powers (e. g., of absolution of certain sins) by an ecclesiastical superior from an inferior; see also *Reserved Cases.* 4. In RC, E Orthodox, and Angl. chs., retention of a portion of the consecrated species after Communion to communicate those unable to attend (e. g., sick and dying).

Reservatum ecclesiasticum. See *Augsburg, Religious Peace of.*

Reserved Cases. Power of absolution of "certain more atrocious and grace crimes" is reserved by bps. and popes to themselves; if absolution is pronounced by an unauthorized inferior, it is declared invalid also in God's sight; but there is no reservation at the point of death; cf. *Canons and Decrees of the Council of Trent,* Sess. XIV, Sacrament of Penance, chap. vii. See also *Reservation,* 3.

Resheph. See *Canaanites, Religion of.*

Resinarius, Balthasar (probably the same as Balthasar Harzer, or Hartzer; ca. 1485–1544). Composer; b. Tetschen (or Jessen?), Boh.; chorister in Hofkapelle of Maximilian* I; pupil of H. Isaak*; educ. Leipzig; priest; Luth. pastor Leipa, Boh., 1534. Works include *Responsoriorum numero octoginta . . . libri duo.*

Resistible Grace. See *Common Grace.*

Response (respond; responsory). In liturgics, something sung or said in reply to the officiant. See also *Amen; Antiphon; Hallelujah; Hosanna; Versicle; Worship, Parts of.*

Restitution (apocatastasis; apokatastasis; restoration). Doctrine of the final salvation of all sinful beings; held by Origen* and many others; opposed by Augustine* of Hippo and many others; not supported by Acts 3:21. See also *Hereafter,* B 7; *Unitarians; Universalists.*

Restitution, Edict of. Imperial edict secured 1629 by RCs; provided (1) all former RC property that had become Prot. since the convention of Passau* 1552 to become RC; (2) Prots. to be excluded from RC territories; (3) among Prots., only those adhering to the AC to have freedom of religion.

Restoration. See *Restitution.*

Restoration Period in English History. See *England,* C 1; *Steele, Richard.*

Restored Lutheran Church. See *Netherlands,* 3.

Resurrection of the Body. See *Last Things,* 4.

Retable. Raised ledge or shelf at the rear of an altar on which altar lights, cross, and flower vases may be placed; or: framework arising from the rear of an altar and enclosing a decorated panel.

Retention of sins. See *Keys, Office of the.*

Reu, Johann Michael (Nov. 16, 1869–Oct. 14, 1943). Luth. theol.; b. Diebach, near Rothenburg ob der Tauber, Bav.; educ. Neuendettelsau; to Am. 1889; asst. pastor (Ev. Luth. Syn. of Iowa* and Other States), Mendota, Ill., 1889; pastor Rock Falls, Ill., 1890; prof. Wartburg Theol. Sem., Dubuque, Iowa, 1899. Prominent in efforts toward Luth. unity at home and abroad. Ed. *Kirchliche Zeitschrift.* Other works include *Die Alttestamentlichen Perikopen nach der Auswahl von Professor Dr. Thomasius; Quellen zur Geschichte des kirchlichen Unterrichts in der evangelischen Kirche Deutschlands zwischen 1530 und 1600; Homiletics: A Manual of the Theory and Practice of Preaching,* tr. A. Steinhaeuser; *Dr. Martin Luther's Small Catechism: A History of Its Origin, Its Distribution and Its Use; The Augsburg Confession: A Collection of Sources with An Historical Introduction; Catechetics: Or Theory and Practise of Religious Instruction; Luther's German Bible: An Historical Presentation Together with a Collection of Sources; Luther and the Scriptures.*

Johann Michael Reu: A Book of Remembrance: Kirchliche Zeitschrift 1876–1943 (Columbus, Ohio, 1945); *A Bibliography of the Writings of Johann Michael Reu, 1869–1943,* comp. J. K. Burritt (Dubuque, Iowa, 1969, unpub.); R. C. Wiederaenders, *The Manuscripts of J. Michael Reu in the Archives of The A. L. C. Wartburg Theological Seminary, Dubuque, Iowa* (Dubuque, Iowa, 1970, unpub.); L. C. Green, "J. M. Reu and Reformation Studies," *CHIQ,* XLII (1969), 147–156, and "Introduction and Index to the *Quellen* of J. M. Reu," Bulletin of the Library, Foundation for Reformation Research, VI (1971), 9–11, 17–24, 25–32; VII (1972), 1–7. LCG

Reubke, Julius (1834–58). Pianist, composer; b. Hausneindorf, near Halberstadt, Ger.; pupil of F. Liszt.* Works include an organ sonata on Ps 94.

Reublin, Wilhelm (Roeubli; Raebl; many other variants; ca. 1480/84–after 1559). Anabap.; b. Rottenburg on the Neckar, S Württemberg, Ger.; educ. Freiburg and Tübingen; pastor Griessen, near Schaffhausen; people's priest Basel 1521; banished 1522; preacher Zurich and Witikon; opposed infant baptism; helped introd. believer's* baptism ca. 1525; banished from Zurich; applied believer's baptism to B. Hubmaier*; active in Strasbourg (where he was imprisoned Oct. 1528–Jan. 1529), Austerlitz and Auspitz (expelled from both), Rottenburg (1531); renounced Anabaptism; spent last yrs. as a restless figure in various cities.

Reuchlin, Johann (Johannes; Grecized Kapnio or Capnio; 1455–1522). Humanist; granduncle of P. Melanchthon*; b. Pforzheim, Ger.; educ. Freiburg im Breisgau, Paris, Basel, Orleans, and Poitiers; 1481 in service of Duke Eberhard of Württemberg (im Bart; mit dem Bart; Barbatus; 1445–96); in similar work at Heidelberg 1497; continued study of Gk. and Heb. in connection with a journey to Rome; returned to Stuttgart; judge in Swabian League 1502–13; in controversy with the U. and Dominicans at Cologne; prof. Gk. and Heb. Ingolstadt and Tübingen. Works include writings on Lat., Gk. and Heb. See also *Cabala; Letters of Obscure Men.*

Reusch, Franz Heinrich (1825–1900). Old* Catholic; b. Brilon, Westphalia, Ger.; educ. Bonn, Tübingen, Munich, Cologne; priest 1849; prof. Bonn 1858; rejected papal infallibility.* Scholarly interest included exegesis and ch. hist.

Reusner, Adam (Reussner; Reisner; Reissner; ca. 1496/1500 to ca. 1575/82). B. Mündelsheim (now Mindelheim), Bav. Swabia; educ. Wittenberg and Ingolstadt; private secy. to Georg von Frundsberg (Frondsberg; Fronsperg; 1473–1528; Ger. gen.; b. Swabia; met M. Luther at Diet of Worms 1521); adherent of K. Schwenkfeld*; hymnist. Hymns include "In dich hab ich gehoffet, Herr."

Reuss, Édouard Guillaume Eugène (1804–91). Alsatian-Fr. Prot. theol.; b. Strasbourg; prof. Strasbourg; exponent of historicocritical* method of Bible interpretation. Works include *Histoire de la théologie chrétienne au siècle apostolique; La Bible: Traduction nouvelle avec introductions et commentaires.*

Reuter, Hermann Ferdinand (1817–89). B. Hildesheim, Ger.; educ. Göttingen and Berlin; private tutor Berlin 1843; prof. Breslau, Greifswald, and Göttingen; cofounder *Zeitschrift für Kirchengeschichte.* Other works include *Geschichte der religiösen Aufklärung im Mittelalter vom Ende des achten Jahrhunderts bis zum Anfange des vierzehnten; Abhandlungen zur systematischen Theologie; Augustinische Studien.*

Reuter, Quirinus (1558–1613). B. Mosbach, Ger.; educ. at the Sapienzkollegium, a theol. institution in Heidelberg; to Neustadt 1578; tutor Breslau 1580–82; to Neustadt as teacher and preacher 1583; preacher Bensheim 1584; Neuhausen 1587; prof. Sapienzkollegium, Heidelberg, 1589; pastor Speyer 1593; ephor* Sapienzkollegium, Heidelberg, 1598; prof. OT theol. Heidelberg 1602. Ed. works of Z. Ursinus.* Other works include *De cultu dei naturali; De lege morali non abrogata; De reformatione ecclesiae.*

Reuterdahl, Henrik (1795–1870). B. Malmö, SW Swed.; educ. Lund; tutor at the theol. sem., Lund, 1817; assoc. adjunct in the theol. faculty 1824; prefect in the sem. 1826; 1st adjunct of theol.; chief librarian of the university 1838; prof. theol. 1844; deputy to the diet for the theol. sem. 1844; provost of the cathedral at Lund 1845; minister of religion 1852–55; bp. Lund 1855; abp. 1856. Helped found *Theologisk Quartalskrift;* other works include *Svenska kyrkans historia.*

Reval, Diet of. See *Lutheran Confessions,* A 5.

Revel, Albert (1837–88). Waldensian; b. Torre Pellice, Torino prov., Piedmont, NW It.; educ. Torre Pellice, Florence, and Edinburgh; ordained 1861; prof. Torre Pellice and Florence. Works include *Letteratura ebraica; Le origini del Papato; Teoria del culto.*

Revelation. 1. In revelation God Himself takes the initiative in bridging the gap bet. Himself and His creatures; for He is a hidden God (Is 45:15). In disclosing Himself to men in ways of judgment and grace, God always remains both subject and object of revelation. The knowledge that God grants is unified as regards its object but variable in the matter of means.

2. There is a revelation of God *in nature* (Ro 1:19-20); but there is a difference from other ancient religions in this, that in Scripture nature is only the garment, not the body, of God. The revelation of God in nature is part of gen. revelation, whose evidence is also found in man's capacity, e. g., for soc. institutions, pol. order, artistic creation.

3. Scripture is more concerned with special revelation, which takes place in various ways, e. g., in a theophany,* as when God appeared *personally* to Abraham and Lot (Gn 18–19). In gen., such direct assocs. with God are reserved for persons esp. chosen to this end (e. g., Moses; other prophets).

4. A *dream* can also be a medium of revelation (Gn 20:3; 28:12; 41:1-40; 46:2). Prophets criticized

the illusory character of this kind of revelation when claimed by lying prophets (Jer 23:25-32; 27:9; Zch 10:2).

5. God reveals Himself by *angels* (e. g., Gn 16:7-13; Ex 23:20-21; Mt 2:13). See also *Christ Jesus,* I A.

6. God's *name* constitutes a revelation (Ex 3:14; Is 30:27).

7. God reveals Himself most completely and precisely in the *Word** of God. That Word is, above all, God's Son (the incarnate Word; Jn 1:1-14). The Word may also take the form of the spoken or written Word (Jn 20:31; 1 Co 2:13).

a. The most ancient laws are known as words. The preamble to the 10 Commandments (Ex 20:1-2) recalls God's revelation to Moses and God's deliverance of His people. The laws of the holiness code (Lv 17–26; see also *Law Codes,* 2) are motivated, e. g., Lv 19:32, 34, 36.

b. The Word is characteristic of the prophetic office (Jer 18:18). The prophet is subordinate to his message. The formula "Thus saith the Lord" designates the Word as a royal message to be delivered faithfully and fully. The divine Word is placed into the prophet's mouth (Jer 1:9) or spoken in his ears (Is 5:9). Having been present in the council of God (Jer 23:18, 22), the prophet delivers what has been confided to him. At times the Word seized a prophet with such power that it cast him into an abnormal state of mind (e. g., Eze 3:15). By means of symbolic action or unusual dress a prophet sometimes illustrated his message (e. g., nakedness, Is 20; yoke, Jer 28; belt, or girdle, Acts 21:11).

c. The term *mashal* (Heb. "discourse; parable"), applied to the maxims of Wisdom literature, is also used of mysterious oracles (Nm 23:7; 24:3). This suggests that the element of revelation is the primary feature of these materials, at whose heart lies the statement that the fear of the Lord is the beginning of wisdom (Pr 1:7).

8. The distinctive mark of Biblical religion is the revelation of God *in hist.* God calls Abraham to go from his land to one that God would show him. God delivers His people from bondage in Egypt and reveals His power and purpose in the crucial events of Israel's hist., including the crucifixion and resurrection of Christ and the creation of the ch. But essential to the full fact of revelation is the sending of prophets, apostles, and evangelists as proclaimers and interpreters of these events. Through the confusion that characterizes man's hist., God accomplishes His saving purpose (Is 5:12, 19; 10:12; 28:21) acc. to a plan conceived in eternity (Mt 25:34; Eph 1:3-6; 1 Ptr 1:2).

9. Revelation deals with the event in which God breaks through to man; inspiration (see *Inspiration, Doctrine of*), as the term is used in theol., deals with the coming into being of the written Word (2 Ti 3:16) under special guidance of the Holy Spirit. The doctrine of inspiration deals with the way in which God, who reveals Himself in word and deed, is active in the process by which the message is committed to writing. The unique significance of the Bible is that it is to this book that we go for knowledge of the revelation that God has given of Himself in hist.

10. Since the knowledge of God transcends reason, the truth of revelation cannot be reached by the human mind left to its own devices. Yet the content of revelation is not irrational. Paul spoke to Festus and Agrippa of a proclamation that included his witness to the resurrection; but Paul insists that he is not beside himself (Acts 26:24-25). It is the province of God's gift of human reason to take God's revelation of Himself as given in Scripture and formulate and articulate it in such a way as to relate it to the particular situation of the ch. in a given age (systematic* theol.). MHS

J. Baillie, *The Idea of Revelation in Recent Thought* (New York, 1956); H. E. Brunner, *Revelation and Reason,* tr. O. Wyon (Philadelphia, 1946); *Revelation and the Bible,* ed. C. F. H. Henry (Philadelphia, 1958); J. McIntyre, *The Christian Doctrine of History* (Grand Rapids, Mich., 1957).

Reverence for Life. See *Schweitzer, Albert.*

Révész, Imre (1826–81). B. Debrecen, Hung.; educ. Debrecen, Vienna, Berlin, and in Switz.; pastor Debrecen 1856; resisted Austrian invasions of rights of Hung. Prots.

Réville, Albert (1826–1906). Father of J. Réville*; b. Dieppe, Fr.; educ. Dieppe, Geneva, Strasbourg; pastor Nimes, Luneray (in N Fr.), Rotterdam; prof. Paris. Works include *Lectures on the Origin and Growth of Religion as Illustrated by the Native Religions of Mexico and Peru,* tr. P. H. Wicksteed; *Histoire de dogme de la divinite de Jesus-Christ.*

Réville, Jean (1854–1908). Son of A. Réville*; b. Rotterdam, Holland; educ. Geneva, Paris, Berlin, Heidelberg; pastor Sainte-Suzanne, Fr.; teacher and prof. Paris. Works include *Les Origines de l'épiscopat; Le Protestantisme libéral: ses origines, sa nature, sa mission.*

Revised Standard Version. See *Bible Versions,* L 14.

Revised Version. See *Bible Versions,* L 12.

Revius, Jacobus (1586–1658). B. Deventer, Neth.; educ. Leiden and Franeker; pastor Zeddam, Winterswijk, Aalten, Deventer; regent of state coll. Leiden; helped est. Athenaeum at Deventer 1630. Active in Bible tr. Tr. Belgic Conf. (see *Reformed Confessions,* C 1) into Lat. and Gk. (approved by C. Lucaris*). Other works include *Libertas Christiana, circa usum capillitii, defensa; Over-ysselsche sangen en dichten; Daventriae illustratae.*

Revival of Confessional Lutheranism. See *Lutheran Confessions,* D.

Revival of Learning. See *Renaissance.*

Revivals (from Lat. *revivo,* "to live again"). 1. The phrase "revivals of religion" commonly indicates renewed interest in religious subjects or, more gen., religious awakenings. In its best sense it may be applied to the work of Christ and the apostles and to the 16th c. Reformation. But the term is often applied also to excitements that can hardly be assoc. with true religion since they do not revive spiritual life by preaching the Word but are mere enthusiastic outbursts of emotion. The term "revival" is gen. confined to an increase of spiritual activity in Eng.-speaking Prot. chs.

2. There were revivals in Scot. beginning at Stewarton 1625, extending north to Shotts 1630, and at Cambuslang and Kilsyth in the early 1740s. See also *Great Awakening in England and America.* There was a revival at Northhampton, Mass., beginning 1734 and throughout New Eng. in the early 1740s (see also *Edwards, Jonathan,* the Elder). From the close of the Great Awakening (ca. 1750 in Am.) there were no gen. revivals in Am. till ca. 1800, when L. Beecher* and T. Dwight* (1752–1817) began their remarkable work. A revival began in Ky. in the 1790s, spread to Pa. and Ohio, and was accompanied by violent physical phenomena called "the jerks." See also *Presbyterian Churches,* 4 b.

Other revivalists include Asahel Nettleton (1783–1844; b. North Killingworth, Conn.; educ. Yale; Cong. evangelist Mass., Conn., N. Y.), C. G. Finney,* D. L. Moody,* Benjamin Fay Mills (1857–1916; b. Rahway, N. J.; Cong. minister Cannon Falls, Minn., and Rutland, Vt.; Presbyterian minister Albany, N. Y.; evangelist; indep. 1897; Unitarian pastor Oakland, Calif.; Presb. 1915), R. A. Torrey,* John Wilbur Chapman (1859–1918; b. Richmond, Ind.; Presb. pastor Ohio, Ind., N. Y., and Pa.; assoc.

with D. L. Moody), Rodney Smith,* and W. A. Sunday.* The 1859 Irish revival was an import from the 1857–58 US revival (a movement directed mainly by laymen). The Great Welsh Revival occurred 1904–06.

See also *Jones, Samuel Porter; Radio and Television Evangelism Network,* 5; *Sankey, Ira David.*

F. G. Beardsley, *A History of American Revivals* (New York, 1904); W. W. Sweet, *Revivalism in America: Its Origin, Growth and Decline* (New York, 1944).

Revolution, American. See *United States, Religious History of,* 10–12.

Reynolds, John. See *Rainolds, John.*

Reynolds, William Morton (Mar. 4, 1812–Sept. 5, 1876). B. Little Falls Forge, Fayette Co., Pa.; educ. at Jefferson Coll., Canonsburg, Pa., and at Luth. Theol. Sem., Gettysburg, Pa.; prof. Pa. Coll., Gettysburg, Pa.; pres. of Capital U., Columbus, Ohio, and of Ill. State U. (see *Carthage College*); Prot. Episc. cleric 1864. Founded *Evangelical Review;* other works include tr. of I. Acrelius'* hist. of New Swed.

Rhabanus Maurus. See *Rabanus Maurus.*

Rhaetian Confession *(Confessio Rhaetica).* Drawn up, after several conferences, in fall 1552 by a syn. in Graubünden (Grisons canton, Switz.; formed largest part of ancient Roman province of Rhaetia) against antitrinitarian heresies and to resolve problems caused esp. by teachings of C. Renato* on conversion and the Sacraments; approved by J. H. Bullinger* and signed by most pastors involved in the matter.

Rhau, Georg (Rau; Rhaw; Raw; Hirsutus; Jörg; 1488–1548). B. Eisfeld, Ger.; cantor Thomasschule, Leipzig, 1519; teacher Eisleben and Hildburghausen 1520–22; printer Wittenberg ca. 1523/25. Printed. e. g., *Neue deudsche geistliche Gesenge;* LC; AC; books of devotion illustrated by L. Cranach the Elder (see *Cranach,* 1).

Rhegius, Urbanus (Regius; Rieger; 1489–1541). B. Langenargen, near Friedrichshafen, Ger.; educ. Freiburg and Ingolstadt; priest 1519; preacher Augsburg; sided with M. Luther against Rome and H. Zwingli; preacher Celle 1530; supt. Lüneburg 1531; signed Wittenberg* Concord 1536, Schmalkaldic Arts. 1537 (see *Lutheran Confessions,* B 2).

Rheims-Douai Version. See *Bible Versions,* L 9.

Rheinberger, Joseph Gabriel von (1839–1901). Organist, composer; b. Vaduz, Liechtenstein; pupil of J. G. Herzog*; dir. court ch. music Munich 1877. Works include choral works: *Jairus's Daughter; Christophorus; The Star of Bethlehem; Easter Hymn.*

Rheinbott, Friedrich (1781–1837). Son of T. Rheinbott*; Luth. pastor Moscow 1801, Saint Petersburg 1813; gen. supt. Saint Petersburg consistory 1832.

Rheinbott, Thomas (1750–1813). Father of F. Rheinbott*; b. Soest; Luth. pastor Saint Petersburg, Russ., 1778; principal of his congregation's school 1780; supt. Saint Petersburg 1800; gen. supt. Saint Petersburg and vicinity 1804.

Rhenanus, Beatus (1485–1547). Ger. humanist; b. Alsace; friend of D. Erasmus*; pub. classical texts; other works include *Rerum Germanicarum libri tres.*

Rhenish Mission Society (Rheinische Missionsgesellschaft). A small miss. soc. was formed 1799 at Elberfeld; the Berg Bible Soc. was formed at Elberfeld 1814; the Tract Soc. of the Wuppertal was formed at Barmen 1814. Another miss. soc., which cooperated with the miss. institute at Basel (see *Basel Missionary Society*), soon formed at Barmen. The 2 miss. socs. (at Elberfeld and Barmen), with a soc. at Cologne and one at Wesel, merged into the Rhenish Miss. Soc. 1828 with HQ at Barmen. Missionaries were sent to South Afr. 1829, Borneo 1834, South-West Afr. 1839, China in the mid-1840s, Sumatra in the early 1860s, Nias 1865, New Guinea 1887. See also *Missionary Institutes; New Guinea,* 5; *Schmelen, Johann Heinrich; Schreiber, August Wilhelm; Warneck, Johannes.*

Rhenius, Karl Theophil Ewald ("Theophil" occurs also as "Gottlieb"; Nov. 5, 1790–June 5, 1838). B. at the fortress of Graudenz (Grudziadz), West Prussia; educ. J. Jänicke's* miss. training school, Berlin; ordained 1812; CMS miss. to India 1814; at Tranquebar for several mos., then Madras till 1820; in the Tinnevelly dist. 1820–35; severed connection with CMS 1835; formed the Ger. miss. in Tinnevelly and led it 1835–38. See also *Lutheran Foreign Mission Endeavors in the United States, Early,* 2.

Rhetoric. See *Homiletics,* 4; *Trivium.*

Rhodesia. See *Africa,* B 2.

Ricci, Lorenzo (1703–75). B. Florence, It.; Jesuit 1718; gen. of order 1758; his refusal to change the const. of the order led to suppression of the order 1773.

Ricci, Matteo (1552–1610). B. Macerata, It.; Jesuit 1571; miss. to India 1578, China 1583; became a favorite of the Chinese emp. Works include writings on Chinese geog. and hist.; Christian works in Chinese, including *T'ien-chu-she-i* ("The True Doctrine of God").

Ricci, Scipione de' (1741–1810 [1809?]). B. Florence, It.; priest 1766; vicar-gen. to abp. Florence 1775; bp. Pistoia and Prato 1780; favored Jansenism; worked for reforms.

Rice, David (1733–1816). B. Hanover Co., Va.; educ. Coll. of N. J. (now Princeton U.); ordained Presb. 1763; pastor Hanover, Va., 1763–68; miss. Bedford Co., Va., 1769–83; itinerant preacher Ky. and Ohio 1783–98; helped found Hampden-Sydney Coll. (at Hampden Sydney, Va.) and Transylvania U. (at Lexington, Ky.); mem. Ky. Const. Conv. 1792; largely responsible for est. Presbyterianism in Ky. Works include *An Essay on Baptism; Slavery Inconsistent with Justice and Good Policy.*

Rice, Edwin Wilbur (1831–1929). B. Kingsboro (or Kingsborough; now Gloversville), N. Y.; educ. Union Theol. Sem., NYC; ordained Cong. 1860; miss. of Am. S. S. Union. Ed. periodicals and other publications of the Am. S. S. Union. Other works include *Our Sixty-Six Sacred Books; The Sunday-School Movement, 1780–1917, and the American Sunday-School Union, 1817–1917.*

Rice, Luther (Mar. 25, 1783–Sept. 25, 1836). B. Northborough, Mass.; educ. Andover (Mass.) Theol. Sem.; ordained Cong. 1812; ABCFM miss. to India 1812; became Bap. en route; returned to Am. 1813; helped organize Am. Bap. Miss. Union and Columbian Coll. (later George Washington U.), Washington, D. C. Pub. *The Latter Day Luminary; The Columbian Star.* See also *Haystack Group; India,* 11.

Rice, Nathan Lewis (1807–77). B. Garrard Co., Ky.; educ. Princeton (N. J.) Theol. Sem.; ordained Presb. 1833; pastor Ky., Ohio, Mo., Ill., N. Y.; prof. Presby. Theol. Sem. of the Northwest (later McCormick Theol. Sem.), Chicago, Ill.; pres. Westminster Coll., Fulton, Mo., 1869–74; prof. Danville (Ky.) Theol. Sem. 1874–77. Ed. *Western Protestant; St. Louis Presbyterian.* Other works include *Baptism: The Design, Mode and Subjects; Lectures on Slavery; The Pulpit: Its Relations to Our National Crisis; Immortality.*

Ricercar(e) (ricercata; from It. for "to search out"). Instrumental piece written in imitation of the motet,* canzone,* or similar technique; helped pave the way for the fugue; for J. S. Bach* a ricercar was practically a type of fugue.

Richard I (1157–99). Surnamed Coeur de Lion, "Lion-Hearted"; son of Henry* II (1133–89); fought twice against his father; king of Eng. 1189–99; a leader of the 3d Crusade (see *Crusades,* 4);

captured on return in Austria 1192; ransomed and returned to Eng. 1194.

Richard, James William (Feb. 14, 1843–Mar. 7, 1909). B. near Winchester, Va.; educ. Pa. Coll. and Luth. Theol. Sem., both at Gettysburg, Pa.; prof. Carthage* Coll. 1873, Wittenberg Sem. 1885 (see *Wittenberg University*), Gettysburg* Sem. 1889. Works include *Philip Melanchthon: The Protestant Preceptor of Germany, 1497–1560; The Confessional History of the Lutheran Church.*

Richard of Cornwall. See *Crusades,* 7.

Richard of St. Victor (d. 1173). B. Scot.; entered abbey of St. Victor, Paris, at an early age; pupil of Hugh* of St. Victor; prominent in struggle of Thomas à Becket* with Henry* II of Eng.; his theol. was influenced by mysticism; much of his expository work is along allegorical lines.

Richards, John William (Apr. 18, 1803–Jan. 24, 1854). Grandson of H. M. Mühlenberg*; father of M. H. Richards*; b. Reading, Pa.; licensed by Pa. Ministerium; pastor New Holland, Trappe, Germantown, Easton, and Reading, Pa.; prof. Lafayette Coll., Easton. Pub. works include sermons and contributions to *The Evangelical Review.*

Richards, Matthias Henry (June 17, 1841–Dec. 12, 1898). Son of J. W. Richards*; b. Philadelphia, Pa.; educ. Pa. Coll. (Gettysburg) and Gettysburg* Sem.; ordained by Pa. Ministerium; pastor Greenwich, N. J., Phillipsburg, N. J., and Indianapolis, Ind., prof. Muhlenberg Coll., Allentown, Pa., 1868–74, 1876–98. Ed. *The Helper;* coed. *The Lutheran.*

Richelieu, Armand Jean du Plessis de (1585–1642). Statesman; b. Paris, Fr.; cardinal 1622; chief minister of Louis XIII 1624–42 (see also *France,* 10); virtual ruler of Fr. to the end of his life. In for. policy he supported Prots. against the Hapsburgs; in domestic policy he opposed Huguenots in the interest of monarchical absolutism.

Richmond, Mary Ellen. See *Social Work,* B 5.

Richmond Resolution. Resolution adopted 1909 at Richmond, Ind., by The General* Syn. of the Ev. Luth. Ch. in the USA in response to a charge by the General* Council of the Ev. Luth. Ch. in (North) Am. that there were ambiguities in the doctrinal basis of the Gen. Syn. In this resolution the Gen. Syn. held that it had "never subscribed to any edition of the confession save the 'unaltered' form . . . known as the *Editio Princeps* of 1530–31, . . . precisely the edition from which a translation was prepared by a joint committee of the General Synod, the General Council, the United Synod in the South, and the Joint Synod of Ohio, 'as a Common Standard of the Augsburg Confession in English' " and hence the identical one subscribed by the Gen. Council. "When the General Synod says, in her formula of confessional subscription, that she accepts 'the Augsburg Confession as a correct exhibition of the fundamental doctrines of the divine word and of the faith of our Church founded upon that word,' she means . . . that the fundamental doctrines of God's word are correctly set forth in the Confession. She does not mean that some of the doctrines . . . are nonfundamental and, therefore, may be accepted or rejected; she means that they are all fundamental." The resolution calls the other symbols "Secondary Confessions" which the Gen. Syn. "holds . . . in high esteem" because they explain and unfold "the doctrines of the Augsburg Confession." Regarding the phrase "as contained in the canonical Scriptures of the Old and New Testament" in the Gen. Synod's formula of confessional subscription, the resolution explains: "When our fathers framed this language, the theological distinction between the two statements, 'The Bible *is* the word of God' and 'the Bible *contains* the word of God' had not yet been made, or at least, was not yet in vogue." The resolution declares "adherence to the statement, 'The Bible *is* the word of God,' " and rejects "the error implied in the statement, 'The Bible *contains* the word of God.' "

Richmond Theses. Theses proposed by G. L. Fritschel (see *Fritschel,* 2) and adopted 1883 at Richmond, Ind., by representatives of the Ev. Luth. Syn. of Iowa* and Other States and of the Ev. Luth. Joint Syn. of Ohio* and Other States. Since these theses were only presented by official representatives, they are not on a par with theses adopted by the syns. themselves.

Richter, Adrian Ludwig (1803–84). Painter, illustrator, graphic artist; b. Dresden, Ger. Though RC, he lent his talents to provide illustration for M. Luther's letter to his son "Hänsichen" (see *Luther, Family Life of*). Other works include *Vaterunser; Sonntag; Unser täglich Brot; Christnacht.*

Richter, Ämilius Ludwig (Aemilius; 1808–64). B. Stolpen, near Dresden, Saxony, Ger.; educ. Leipzig; prof. Leipzig, Marburg, Berlin; authority on Prot. ch. polity. Coed. an ed. of *Canones et decreta concilii Tridentini.* Other works include *Lehrbuch des katholischen und evangelischen Kirchenrechts; Geschichte der evangelischen Kirchenverfassung in Deutschland; Die evangelischen Kirchenordnungen des sechszehnten Jahrhunderts.*

Richter, Christian Friedrich (1676–1711). B. Sorau, Ger. (now Zary, Poland); educ. Halle; inspector of A. H. Francke's* Paedagogium (academy) at Halle 1698; physician to Francke's institutions 1699; Pietist; hymnist. Hymns include "Es glänzet der Christen inwendiges Leben."

Richter, Friedrich (Oct. 24, 1852–Oct. 18, 1934). B. Riesa, Saxony, Ger.; to Am. 1872; educ. at the sem. of the Ev. Luth. Syn. of Iowa* and Other States at St. Sebald, Iowa, and at Leipzig and Erlangen, Ger.; pastor Mendota, Ill., and teacher at the Iowa Syn. coll. and sem. there 1876; pres. Wartburg Coll., Clinton, Iowa, 1894; pres. Iowa Syn. 1904–26; prominent in merger of Buffalo, Iowa, and Ohio syns. Ed. *Kirchen-Blatt.*

Richter, Johann Paul Friedrich (pseudonym Jean Paul; 1763–1825). Ger. humorist and prose writer; b. Wunsiedel, near Bayreuth, Bav., Ger.; educ. Leipzig; indigent; tutor near Hof 1787–94; settled at Bayreuth 1804; received govt. pension 1808; held that visible things are symbols of the invisible. Works include *Blumen-, Frucht- und Dornenstücke; Titan; Levana oder Erziehungslehre; Vorschule der Ästhetik.*

Ridley, Nicholas (ca. 1500–55). B. Northumberland; Prot. ca. the mid-1530s; bp. Rochester 1547. London 1550; influential under Edward VI (see *England,* B 4); suffered martyrdom with H. Latimer.*

Riedel, Erhardt Albert Henry (June 12, 1889–Dec. 26, 1971). B. Lincoln, Ill.; educ. Conc. Sem., Springfield, Ill.; miss. to China 1916–27 as coworker of E. L. Arndt* (see also *China,* 8); pastor Casper, Wyo. Prof. Conc. Sem., Hankow, China, 1930–37; Conc. Sem., Wanhsien, China, 1939–41. Pastor Santa Ana, Calif.; White City, Kans.; Davenport, Nebr.; Summerfield, Kans. Taught at sem. in Chia Yi, Taiwan,* 1956–63; after a short furlough in the US he returned to Taiwan till 1971, then returned to the US. Ed. Chinese *Lutheran Witness* 1936–37. Translations into Chinese include FC; some of R. Pieper's sermons; hymns.

Riedel, Johann Friedrich (1798–Oct. 12, 1860). B. Erfurt, Ger.; educ. J. Jänicke's* training school Berlin; lived in Rotterdam 1827–29; miss. of the Netherlands* Miss. Soc. to Batavia 1830, Celebes 1831.

Riedel, Carl (Karl; 1827–88). Luth. composer; b. Cronenberg (or Kronenberg), near Elberfeld, Ger.; studied music at Leipzig; organized a male quartet 1854 that developed into the Riedel-Verein, which became famous esp. by a performance of J. S. Bach's *Mass in B Minor* 1859; helped found Beethoven Stiftung; championed music of Wilhelm Richard Wagner (1813–83).

Riedemann, Peter (1506–56). B. Hirschberg, Silesia; prominent Huterite elder and theol. (see *Huter, Jakob*); probably traveling preacher; imprisoned several times. Works include *Rechenschafft unserer Religion, Leer und Glaubens.* See also *Democratic Declarations of Faith,* 1.

Rieger, Georg Konrad (1687–1743). Father of K. H. Rieger*; b. Cannstatt (or Kannstatt), near Stuttgart, Ger.; held various positions, including that of preacher Stuttgart; Pietist. Works include *Herzens-Postille.*

Rieger, Karl Heinrich (1726–91). Son of G. K. Rieger*; b. Stuttgart, Ger.; court preacher and consistorial councillor Stuttgart; helped found *Die deutsche Christentumsgesellschaft.**

Rieger. See also *Rhegius.*

Riemann, Karl Wilhelm Julius Hugo (1849–1919). Music critic and hist.; b. Grossmehlra, near Sondershausen, Thuringia, Ger.; prof. Leipzig. Works include *Musik-Lexikon.*

Rietschel, Christian Georg (or Georg Christian; 1842–1914). Son of E. F. A. Rietschel*; b. Dresden, Ger.; educ. Erlangen, Berlin, and Leipzig; held various positions, e. g., at Rüdigsdorf (near Borna), Wittenberg, and Leipzig; prof. practical theol. Leipzig 1889. Works include *Die Aufgabe der Orgel im Gottesdienst bis in das 18. Jahrhundert; Der evangelische Gemeindegottesdienst; Lehrbuch der Liturgik.*

Rietschel, Ernst Friedrich August (1804–61). Father of C. G. Rietschel*; sculptor; b. Pulsnitz, Saxony, Ger.; prof. Dresden. Works include a pietà*; statues of M. Luther and J. Wycliffe in the Worms Luther Memorial that he projected, but which was finished by his pupils Karl Adolf Donndorf (1835–1916; b. Weimar, Ger.; prof. Stuttgart 1877; works include a bronze statue of J. S. Bach at Eisenach) and Gustav Kietz (1824–1908; b. Leipzig, Ger.; works include a madonna). See also *Luther Monuments.*

Riggenbach, Christoph Johannes (1818–90). Ref. theol.; b. Basel, Switz.; educ. Berlin and Bonn, Ger.; prof. Basel 1851. At first liberal, but soon conservative. Hymnologist. Contributed to J. P. Lange's *Theologisch-homiletisches Bibelwerk.*

Riggs, Stephen Return (Mar. 23, 1812–Aug. 24, 1883). B. Steubenville, Ohio; educ. Jefferson Coll., Canonsburg, Pa., and Western Theol. Sem., Allegheny (now part of Pittsburgh), Pa.; ABCFM miss. to Dakota Indians 1837–83. Reduced Dakota language to writing; prepared a Dakota dictionary; tr. nearly all Scripture into Dakota; prepared many books (some original, some translations) for Dakotas.

Righteousness. The righteousness of God* is the essential perfection of His nature. The term "righteousness" is applied to Christ not only in view of His essential righteousness, but also in view of the righteousness that He gained for mankind (Jer. 23:6; see also *Justification*). The righteousness of the Law is that righteousness which obedience to the Law requires (see *Decalog; Law and Gospel*). The righteousness of the Christian is the righteousness of faith (see *Conversion; Faith; Justification*).

Rights of Man and of the Citizen, Declaration of the. See *France,* 11.

Rig-Veda. See *Veda.*

Rijssen, Leonard van (Rijssenius; ca. 1636–ca. 1700). Dutch Ref. theol.; b. Doesburg, Neth.; pastor Tull en 't Waal, Heusden, and Deventer; exponent of theol. of G. Voet.* Works include *Synopsis impurae theologiae Remonstrantium.*

Rilke, Rainer Maria (René; 1875–1926). Lyric poet; b. Prague; educ. Prague, Munich, and Berlin; traveled in Russ., Swed., It., N Afr., Fr.; lived in Paris, It., Scand., Austria, and Switz.; intuitive religious philos. and mystic; regarded artistic work as religious activity; stressed immanence of God. Works include *Geschichten vom lieben Gott; Das Marienleben; Duineser Elegien; Sonette an Orpheus.*

Rimski-Korsakov, Nikolai Andreevich (1844–1908). B. Tikhvin, near Novgorod, Russ.; grad. Naval Academy, St. Petersburg; served in Russ. navy; prof. St. Petersburg Conservatory of Music. Works include *Easter Overture.*

Rinck, Johann Christian Heinrich (Rink; 1770–1846). Composer; b. Elgersburg, Thuringia, Ger.; pupil of J. C. Kittel; organist Giessen 1790; municipal organist Darmstadt 1805, court organist there 1813. Works include *Praktische Orgel-Schule;* motets; chorale preludes for male voices.

Rinck, Melchior. See *Rink, Melchior.*

Rinckart, Martin (Rinkart; Rinckhart; 1586–1649). B. Eilenburg, near Leipzig, Ger.; educ. Leipzig; cantor 1609, diaconus 1611 Eisleben; pastor Erdeborn, near Eisleben, 1613; archidiaconus Eilenburg 1617; hymnist. Hymns include "Nun danket alle Gott." See also *Religious Drama,* 3.

Rincker, Leroy Carl (Aug. 20, 1896–Jan. 28, 1953). B. Crete, Ill.; educ. Conc. Coll., Milwaukee, Wis., and Conc. Sem., St. Louis, Mo.; prof. Conc. Coll., Milwaukee, 1923, pres. 1936.

Rinckhart. See *Rinckart.*

Ring, Engagement and Wedding. A circle is an emblem of eternity; hence a ring serves as a symbol of faithfulness. An engagement ring is given as a token of betrothal by a man to his fiancée. A wedding ring is given by the groom to the bride in the wedding service; the bride may also give the groom a wedding ring. The rings may have, but need not have, precious stones. A ring is not essential to either engagement or marriage.

Ring of the Fisherman (Lat. *anulus piscatoris*). Papal signet ring that has an image of Peter casting out or drawing in a net, with the name of the current pope above it or around the edge; used from the 13th to the 15th c. to seal private papal letters, from the 15th to the 19th c. to seal papal briefs (see *Breve*); hence the formula *datum sub anulo piscatoris* ("given under the ring of the fisherman").

Ringeltaube, Wilhelm Tobias (Aug. 8, 1770–1816 or later). B. Scheidelwitz, near Brieg, Lower Silesia; educ. Halle; SPCK miss. to Calcutta, India, 1797; LMS miss. to India, active in Tranquebar and Tinnevelly 1804–06, in the Travancore region 1806–16. His end is shrouded in mystery.

Ringwaldt, Bartholomäus (Ringwald; Ringwalt; 1530 [1532?] – ca. 1599). B. Frankfurt an der Oder, Ger.; teacher; pastor of 2 congs. before becoming pastor Langfeld (or Langenfeld), near Sonnenburg, Neumark, 1566; staunch Luth.; hymnist. Hymns include "O heil'ger Geist, du höchstes Gut"; "Es ist gewisslich an der Zeit"; "Herr Jesu Christ, du höchstes Gut." Other poems include "Christliche Warnung des trewen Eckarts"; "Die lauter Wahrheit." See also *Religious Drama,* 3.

Rink, Johann Christian Heinrich. See *Rinck, Johann Christian Heinrich.*

Rink, Melchior (Rinck; Ring; Ringk; Grink; ca. 1493–1551 or later). Anabap.; b. Hesse; educ. Leipzig and Erfurt; influenced by T. Münzer*; took part in Peasants'* War; active in Landau, Worms, Hersfeld; his preaching led to an indeterminate discussion with the Marburg faculty 1528; exiled; twice imprisoned.

Rinkart. See *Rinckart.*

Rio de Oro. See *Africa,* D 6.

Ripelin, Hugo (Hugo of Strasbourg; d. ca. 1270). Ger. Dominican; prior Zurich and Strasbourg. Works include *Compendium theologicae veritatis.*

Rippon, John (1751–1836). B. Tiverton, Devonshire, Eng.; educ. Bap. Coll., Bristol; pastor London 1773–

1836; hymnist. Hymns include "The Day has Dawned, Jehovah Comes."

Rist, Johann von (1607–67). B. Ottensen, near Hamburg, Ger.; educ. Bremen, Rinteln, Rostock, Leiden, Utrecht, Leipzig; influenced by J. Stegmann*; pastor Wedel, near Hamburg, 1635. Wrote perhaps ca. 680 hymns, including "Auf, auf, ihr Reichsgenossen"; "Hilf, Herr Jesu, lass gelingen"; "Du Lebensbrod, Herr Jesu Christ"; "Wie wohl hast du gelabet"; "O Ewigkeit, du Donnerwort." See also *Schop, Johann.*

Ritschl, Albrecht Benjamin (1822–89). B. Berlin, Ger.; educ. Bonn, Halle, Heidelberg, Tübingen; prof. Bonn 1852, Göttingen 1864; consistorial councillor Göttingen 1874; pupil of K. I. Nitzsch,* F. A. G. Tholuck,* Julius Müller,* K. Schwarz,* and R. Rothe*; for a time a Hegelian of the later Tübingen* school of F. C. Baur*; since 1856 he became more and more the founder of a school of his own, influenced by I. Kant,* F. D. E. Schleiermacher,* and R. H. Lotze.* Ritschl claimed to be evangelical but based his theol. on the consciousness of the believer as presented esp. in the NT, which, in turn, the theologian makes his own by actual experience of the power of Christ working in His church. Acc. to Ritschl, religion is faith in high spiritual powers that elevated man. The preexistence of Christ is denied. There is no original sin; sin is mistrust in God and its punishment is the feeling of guilt; God regards it as ignorance. There is no wrath of God against sin and no vicarious atonement of Christ. God is love; as soon as man realizes this he is redeemed and justified. From this follows the new life of love toward God, faith, prayer, humility, and patience. Value judgments are important in theol. and its application. The influence of Ritschl is widespread. Works include *Die christliche Lehre von der Rechtfertigung und Versöhnung.* See also *Lutheran Theology After 1580,* 12; *Modernism,* 2; *Social Gospel; Subordinationism; Switzerland, Contemporary Theology in,* 1–2.

O. Ritschl, *Albrecht Ritschls Leben,* 2 vols. (Freiburg, 1892–96).

Rittelmeyer, Friedrich (1872–1938). B. Dillingen, on the Danube, Bav., Ger.; pastor Nürnberg 1902–16, Berlin 1916–22; moved from liberal theol. emphasizing "Jesus" to anthroposophy (see *Steiner, Rudolf*) emphasizing "Christ"; stressed religious freedom, religious experience, and the religious development and evolvement of self. With C. K. L. Geyer* wrote *Leben aus Gott.* Other works include *Jesus; Christus.*

Ritter, August Gottfried (1811–85). Luth. composer; b. Erfurt, Ger.; studied music at Erfurt, Weimar, and Berlin; organist Erfurt, Merseburg, Magdeburg. Works include *Die Kunst des Orgelspiels; Zur Geschichte des Orgelspiels.*

Ritter, Erasmus (d. 1546). B. Bav., Ger.; preacher in Ger. and Switz.; Zwinglian ca. 1523; tried to be nominally Luth.; sided with J. Calvin* and G. Farel* when Calvin and Farel were banished from Geneva 1538.

Ritual. See *Liturgics.*

Ritual Decalog. See *Law Codes.*

Rituale Romanum. Lat. title of official RC service book; first pub. 1614; rev. several times.

River Brethren. See *Brethren, River.*

Roanoke College. See *Lutheran Church in America,* V; *Ministry, Education of,* VIII B 22.

Röbbelen, Carl August Wilhelm (July 13, 1817–Sept. 20, 1866). B. Föhrste (Förste), near Alfeld, Hanover, Ger.; educ. Göttingen; private tutor Ohrdorf 1841; preacher Sack, near Alfeld, 1842–43; private tutor Scharnebeck 1843–44, Dohnsen till 1846; to Neuendettelsau; ordained 1846; sent to Am. 1846 by J. K. W. Löhe* as miss. at head of 11 students (including C. H. R. Lange,* H. Wunder,* and C. J. A. Strasen*) who enrolled in the Fort Wayne, Ind., *Nothelferseminar;* teacher at the *Nothelferseminar;* pastor Liverpool (later called Valley City), Ohio, 1846; joined Mo. Syn. 1849; pastor Frankenmuth, Mich., 1851; resigned because of failing health 1858; to Ger. 1858; to Staten Is., N. Y., 1859; to Ger. 1860; d. Kandern, Baden, Ger.

"Robber Synod" of Ephesus. See *Ephesus, "Robber Synod" of.*

Robbia, Andrea della (1437–1528). Nephew and pupil of L. della Robbia*; father of G. della Robbia*; b. Florence, It.; terra-cotta sculptor. Works include *Assumption of the Virgin;* a madonna.

Robbia, Giovanni della (ca. 1469–ca. 1529). Son of A. della Robbia*; b. Florence, It.; terra-cotta sculptor. Works include *Seven Works of Mercy; Resurrection.*

Robbia, Luca della (ca. 1399/1400–1482). Uncle and teacher of A. della Robbia*; b. Florence, It.; sculptor. Works include *Resurrection; Ascension;* many madonnas.

Röber, Paul (Paulus; 1587–1651). B. Wurzen, Ger.; educ. Leipzig and Wittenberg; archidiaconus and court preacher Halle 1614; prof. theol. Wittenberg 1627; city pastor and gen. supt.; noted as exegete and preacher.

Robert II (ca. 970–1031). "The Pious" (Fr. "le Pieux"); regarded by some as Robert I; king of Fr. 996–1031; regarded by some as a hymnist, but the claim is not clearly est.

Robert College (Istanbul). See *Armenia.*

Robert de Molesme. See *Cistercians.*

Robert Guiscard. See *Guiscard, Robert.*

Robert Holcot (ca. 1290–1349). B. Holcot, Northamptonshire, Eng.; Dominican; taught at Cambridge and Oxford; influenced by nominalism.*

Robert of Sorbonne. See *Sorbon, Robert de.*

Roberts, Benjamin Titus (1823–93). B. Leon, N. Y.; educ. Wesleyan U., Middletown, Conn.; M. E. pastor; criticized "new school" Methodism; expelled from ch. 1858; organized (The) Free Meth. Ch. (of N. Am.) 1860 (see also *Methodist Churches,* 4 b); gen. supt. 1860–93.

Roberts, Brigham Henry (1857–1933). Mormon; b. Warrington, Eng.; to US 1866; miss. in US 1880–86, Eng. 1886–88; was refused seat in US House of Representatives because of his plural marriages. Works include *A Comprehensive History of the Church of Jesus Christ of Latter Day Saints, Century I.*

Robertson, Archibald Thomas (1863–1934). B. near Chatham, Va.; educ. Wake Forest (N. C.) Coll. and Southern Bap. Theol. Sem., Louisville, Ky.; prof. Southern Bap. Theol. Sem. 1892. Works include *Word Pictures in the New Testament; Epochs in the Life of Paul; A Grammar of the Greek New Testament in the Light of Historical Research.*

E. Gill, *A. T. Robertson* (New York, 1943).

Robertson, Frederick William (1816–53). B. London, Eng.; educ. Edinburgh and Oxford; pastor Cheltenham 1843; resigned 1846; pastor of the Eng. Ch. at Heidelberg, Ger., 1846; pastor Oxford and (1847) Brighton; outstanding preacher.

Robinson, Charles Seymore (1829–99). B. Bennington, Vt.; educ. Williams Coll., Williamstown, Mass., Union Theo. Sem., NYC, and Princeton (N. J.) Theol. Sem.; Presb. pastor; hymnist. Hymns include "Savior, I Follow On."

Robinson, Edward (1794–1863). B. Southington, Conn.; educ. Hamilton Coll., Clinton, N. Y., and at Hudson, N. Y.; prof. Andover (Mass.) Theol Sem. 1830–33, Union Theol. Sem., NYC, 1837–63. Tr. J. G. B. Winer's* *Grammatik des neutestamentlichen Sprachidioms* (Eng. title *Grammar of New Testament Greek*) and H. F. W. Gesenius's* *Lexicon* (see *Lexicons,* A); other works include *Biblical Researches in Palestine, Mount Sinai, and Arabia*

Petraea. See also *Geography, Christian,* 4; *Grammars,* B.

Robinson, Frank Bruce (1886–1948). Son of an Eng. Bap. minister; pharmacist Moscow, Idaho; influenced by New* Thought; est. Psychiana*; ordained by an Old* Cath. bp.; assumed title abp. Moscow (Idaho); succeeded by son Alfred W. Robinson.

Robinson, Henry Wheeler (1872–1945). Bap. theol.; b. Northampton, Eng.; educ. Edinburgh, Oxford, Marburg, Strasbourg; pastor Pitlochry and Coventry; taught at Leeds, London, and Oxford. Works include *The Religious Ideas of the Old Testament; The Cross in the Old Testament; The Old Testament: Its Making and Meaning; The History of Israel: Its Facts and Factors; Redemption and Revelation.* See also *Corporate Personality.*

Robinson, John (ca. 1576–1625). Pastor to the Pilgrim Fathers (see United Church of Christ, I, A, 1 and 2); b. probably in or near Gainsborough, Lincolnshire (or in Nottinghamshire?), Eng.; probably educ. Cambridge; ordained Ch. of Eng.; probably curate Norwich ca. 1602; became Puritan; joined separatist cong. at Gainsborough; apparently assoc. with separatist cong. at Scrooby Manor 1607; to Amsterdam, Holland, 1608; pastor of separatists at Leiden 1609 with W. Brewster* as ruling elder; d. Leiden.

Roch (Rochus; It.: Rocco; ca. 1295–ca. 1327 [or ca. 1350–ca. 1378/79?]). Shadowy legendary figure; said to have been b. Montpellier, Fr.; Franciscans claim him as a tertiary; allegedly made a pilgrimage to Rome, curing many sick on the way.

Rochelle, Confession of. See *Reformed Confessions,* B.

Rochet. White linen vestment; similar to surplice, but with tight sleeves, which are wide on the upper part and narrow at the wrist and, like the hem, are embroidered or trimmed; reaches perhaps a little below the knees; worn by bps. and occasionally by other prelates.

Rochlitz, Johann Friedrich (1769–1842). Luth. musician and theol.; b. Leipzig, Ger.; educ. Leipzig. Ed. *Allgemeine musikalische Zeitung.* Other works include *Für Freunde der Tonkunst; Sammlung vorzüglicher Gesangstücke.*

Rocholl, Rudolf (1822–1905). Luth. theol.; b. Rhoden, in Waldeck principality, Ger.; pastor Sachsenberg; joined ch. of Hannover for confessional reasons; supt. Göttingen; left ch. of Hannover 1877; joined Old* Luths. 1878; pastor Radevormwald and Breslau; supt. and ch. councillor Breslau. Works include *Die Realpräsenz; Philosophie der Geschichte.*

Rock, Johann. See *Amana Society.*

Rockefeller, John Davison (1839–1937). Oil magnate; b. Richford, N. Y.; est. Rockefeller Foundation, Gen. Educ. Bd., Laura Spelman Rockefeller Memorial, and Rockefeller Institute for Med. Research; supported Bap. ch. work generously. Son John Davison Rockefeller Jr. (1874–1960; b. Cleveland, Ohio; educ. Brown U., Province, R. I.) continued and expanded the philanthropies and gave large sums of money for various religious projects.

Rock Mountain Synod. See *United Lutheran Church, Synods of,* 25.

Rococo. See *Church Architecture,* 13.

Rodigast, Samuel (1649–1708). B. Gröben, near Jena, Ger.; educ. Jena; adjunct of the philos. faculty Jena 1676; conrector Grey* Friars' Gymnasium Berlin 1680, rector 1698; hymnist. Wrote "Was Gott tut, das ist wohlgetan" (not to be confused with B. Schmolck's* hymn with the same 1st line).

Rodríguez, Alfonso (Alphonsus; ca. 1531/32–1617). B. Segovia, Sp.; educ. Jesuit coll. at Alcalá de Henares; businessman; after death of wife, children, and mother, became Jesuit 1571. Wrote mystic literature.

Rodríguez, Alonso (Alfonso; 1537–1616). B. Valladolid, Sp.; Jesuit 1557; teacher of moral theol. Wrote *Ejercicio de perfección y virtudes cristianas.*

Rodríguez de Azevedo, Simon (d. 1579). Companion of I. (of) Loyola*; rector Coimbra, Port., 1542.

Roeber, Paul(us). See *Röber, Paul.*

Roell, Hermann Alexander (1653–1718). Ref. theol.; b. Dolberg, Westphalia, Ger.; court preacher in Ger. and Neth.; pastor and prof. Deventer; prof. Franeker 1686, Utrecht 1704; influenced by J. Cocceius* and R. Descartes.*

Roerer. See *Rörer.*

Roffensis. See *Fisher, John.*

Rogall, Georg Friedrich (1701–33). B. Königsberg, Prussia, Ger.; prof., consistorial councillor, and cathedral preacher Königsberg; influenced by A. H. Francke* and C. v. Wolff.* Issued *Kern alter und neuer Lieder.*

Rogate. See *Church Year,* 14, 16; *Rogation Days.*

Rogation Days. Ca. 470 Mamertus* organized litanies in the Ascension season; the immediate reason may have been an earthquake, pestilence, or barbarian invasion. Rogation days are now observed by RCs and many Prots. on the 3 days before the Festival of the Ascension (see *Church Year,* 9) and in RCm on Apr. 25, the Feast of St. Mark, though neither the origin nor the theme of the rogation observance has anything to do with him. The Sun. before Ascension Day is called *Rogate* (after the Rogation days in that week) or *Vocem iucunditatis* (after the 1st words of the Introit in Lat.); but Rogate is a festival in its own right, not a penitential day; the fact that its propers lend themselves to the rogation theme is coincidental; the character of the rogation days is in traditional practice not made retroactive to Rogate. See also *Tempus clausum.*

Roger Williams Club. See *Students, Spiritual Care of,* A 3.

Rogers, Carl Ransom. See *Psychotherapy,* 12.

Rogers, John (ca. 1500–55). Martyr; b. Deritend, near Birmingham, Eng.; became Prot. through influence of W. Tyndale*; burned at Smithfield. See also *Bile Versions,* L 4.

Rohr, Heinrich Karl Georg von (Henry Carl George; 1797–May 15, 1874). Father of P. A. v. Rohr*; b. Billerbeck, Pomerania, Ger.; captain in Prussian army; joined Old* Luths. and was deprived of army commission in the mid-1830s; organized J. A. A. Grabau's* emigration group; to Am. 1839; led settlement of fellow immigrants in Milwaukee and near Cedarburg, Wis.; helped found Freistadt, ca. 15–20 mi. N of Milwaukee; farmer there; taught school ca. 1 yr.; studied theol. at Buffalo, N. Y., ca. 4 yrs.; pastor Humberstone, Ont., and (1846–74) Bergholz, Walmore, and Martinsville, N. Y.; helped found Buffalo* Syn. 1845; sided with C. F. (W.) Hochstetter* against Grabau in the 1866 schism of the Buffalo Syn., but led a protest group against Hochstetter when the latter became Missourian in docrtine.

Röhr, Johann Friedrich (1777–1848). B. Rossbach, near Naumburg, Ger.; educ. Leipzig; pastor; held various positions; influenced by I. Kant*; exponent of rationalism. See also *Dogmatics,* B 7.

Rohr, Philip Andreas von (Philipp; Feb. 13, 1843–Dec. 22, 1908). Son of H. K. G. v. Rohr*; b. Buffalo, N. Y.; educ. Buffalo* Syn. sem., Buffalo, N. Y.; pastor Toledo, Ohio, 1863–66, and Winona, Minn., 1866–1908; sided with his father in the 1866 divisions of the Buffalo Syn. and led his group after his father's death until it dissolved; joined Wisconsin* Syn. 1877 and was its pres. 1889–1908.

Rohrlack, August (Dec. 27, 1835–Nov. 26, 1913). B. Neu-Ruppin, Brandenburg, Prussia, Ger.; joined Breslau* Syn. ca. 1852; studied at Leipzig miss. school; J. K. W. Löhe* arranged for his coming to Am. 1858; asst. preacher near Detroit, Mich.; ordained 1858; itinerant preacher Wis.; then pastor successively in Portage and Loganville, Wis.; itinerant preacher along Lake Superior; pastor Oshkosh 1865, Reedsburg 1869–1909; many yrs. Mo. Syn. secy.

Rokycana, John. See *Bohemian Brethren.*

Rolf, Ernst Heinrich (d. Aug. 20, 1900). See *Canada,* A 11.

Rolle, Johann Heinrich (1716–1875). Luth. composer; b. Quedlinburg, Ger.; educ. Leipzig; active in Berlin and Magdeburg. Works include cantatas, motets, 5 Passions, and many choral compositions, including *The Death of Abel; Abraham on Moriah; Samson; Saul; David and Jonathan.*

Rolle de Hampole, Richard (ca. 1290/1300–1349). "The Hermit of Hampole"; mystic; b. N Yorkshire, Eng.; led contemplative life at Dalton, later at Hampole; opposed papal supremacy. Works include *De emendatione vitae; De incendio amoris.*

Roman Catechism *(Catechismus Romanus).* See *Catechetics,* 8; *Roman Catholic Confessions,* A 3.

Roman Catholic Church. A. *Name.* 1. The name, which designates the Christian ch. with a hierarchy* headed by the pope,* was popularized by reformers who denied that Rome had exclusive claim to catholicity. Many reformers, including M. Luther,* regarded themselves as catholic* and held that the Roman, or W, ch. was only part of the catholic ch. (see also *Western Christianity 500–1500*).

2. RC scholars regard the name as appropriate since they hold that Peter was given the primacy (see *Vatican Councils,* 1 b) and that subsequent bps. of Rome were his successors. They debate whether the connection of Rome with the primacy was divinely intended from the beginning or an accident of hist. resulting from a disposition of providence but changeable in the future.

3. In a narrower sense, the name is applied to a local ch. at Rome whose bp. is also a primate of the universal ch.

B. *Doctrine.* 1. The RC ch. traces its origin to the apostles. Its doctrine is derived from Scripture and tradition.* Some RC theologians make Scripture and tradition joint sources; others regard Scripture as the only source and tradition as Spirit-guided interpretation and application. Differences on this point have produced significant differences in emphases in RC doctrine.

2. The canons and decrees of the Council of Trent* are usually regarded as definitive and basic for RC doctrine. But some modern RC theologians regard Trent as an overreaction to Luther. The council accepted the canonical books of the OT and NT with apocrypha. It asserted that apostolic traditions on faith and customs were to be received with the same feeling of piety and reverence *(pari pietatis affectu ac reverentia)* as Scripture. It rejected Pelagian denial of original sin and Luther's assertion that original sin remained after baptism.

3. The council spent much time on the doctrine of justification. It concluded that God's grace is necessary for the whole process of salvation. It developed 3 points: a. Justification is remission of sins. b. Justification involves inner renewal through infusion of grace. c. Justification assumes man's voluntary acceptance of grace. In RC dogmatics, point 1 is interpreted as referring to divine restoration of grace and gifts. Infusion of grace implies habitual orientation to God. Man's voluntary cooperation in his justification involves awareness on his part of his movement against sin and toward God.

4. The sacraments (baptism, confirmation, Eucharist, penance, extreme unction, order, and matrimony) are efficacious signs, est. by Christ to give grace by the rite itself *(ex opere operato;* see *Grace, Means of,* I, 8, and *Opus operatum).* The council affirmed the real presence (see *Grace, Means of,* IV, 3; *Lutheran Confessions,* A 2 [b]) in the Lord's Supper against H. Zwingli* and transubstantiation* against Luther. It held that the entire Christ is received under either species (bread or wine). The mass is the center of the mystery of salvation, is propitiatory, and is a commemoration and a rendering present of the sacrifice of the cross; it may be offered for the living or dead.

5. The council declared the existence of a hierarchy based on divine ordinance and est. by sacerdotal ordination.

6. The sacraments are at the center of spiritual life in RCm. All give sanctifying grace; each gives special grace.

7. Only a priest* can change bread and wine into the body and blood of Christ and pronounce absolution in the sacrament of penance. The sacrament of marriage is performed by the participants in the presence of a priest. But baptism may be administered in crises by anyone, including heretics.

8. Toward the end of the 19th and early in the 20th c. so-called modernism* became a concern of the papacy and led to *Lamentabili* (a 1907 decree of the Holy Office), *Pascendi dominici gregis* (a 1907 encyclical of Pius X [see *Popes,* 30]), and *Sacrorum antistitum* (a 1910 *motu* proprio* of Pius X).

9. At the same time the popes took interest in soc. questions, e. g., capital and labor, educ., and the family. Leo XIII (see *Popes,* 29) issued the encyclical *Rerum novarum* 1891 on the condition of labor. Pius XI (see *Popes,* 32) issued encyclicals on Christian educ., marriage, the Christian soc. order, and atheistic communism. RC leaders in the US gave increasing attention to soc. problems. The Nat. Cath. Welfare Conf., organized 1919, became the U. S. Cath. Conf., Inc., 1966, active in civic-religious work.

10. Vatican Council II (see *Vatican Councils,* 2), 1962–65, began a new era for RCs and to some extent for Christendom. It neither set aside traditional doctrine nor resolved many doctrinal debates (e. g., on Scripture and tradition and on collegiality), but it did open a door for new interpretations. Its importance probably results more from emphases than from basic changes. It brought new insights into the doctrine of the ch.; encouraged dialog with non-RC Christians and adherents of non-Christian religions; discouraged judgmental approaches in such dialogs; provided for flexibility in liturgy; made significant pronouncements on religious freedom. It lagged behind some of the best contemporary RC theology, but opened doors for spiritual renewal and made possible some needed reform. See also *Popes,* 34, 35.

C. *Structure.* 1. Leadership in the RC Ch. centers in the papacy.* The pope has the sole and final authority in all matters of RC faith and life. He is aided in the administration of his office by cardinals,* who, in turn, lead the various congs. of the curia (see *Curia,* 2).

2. The ecumenical council, highest deliberative body, is rarely convened. Mems. with deliberative vote include cardinals, residential patriarchs, primates, abps. and residential bps., even if not yet consecrated; abbots or prelates *nullius* or exarchs, the abbot primate, abbott superiors of monastic congs., and heads of exempt clerical religious; titular bps. on invitation. An ecumenical council is convened by the pope, who determines matters to be treated and the order of business. The pope or his personal legate presides. Conciliar decrees obtain binding force only on papal ratification and may be promulgated only at the pope's word.

3. The RC Ch. is divided into jurisdictional areas. Jurisdiction is the power to rule, in distinction from the power to sanctify. Jurisdiction is divided into ordinary and delegated. Ordinary jurisdiction is attached to an office; delegated jurisdiction is attached

to a person. The area is usually a diocese* and the ordinary a bishop.* Dioceses are usually autonomous except for limited cases reserved for curia or pope. Dioceses are grouped into provinces under an archbishop.*

4. Indep. abbeys comprise communities ruled by abbots. RCs not included in a diocese are usually ruled by a prelate *nullius* (see also *Abbot*). Sometimes such areas are under an apostolic administrator. Miss. territories are under authority of the Sacred Cong. for the Propagation of the Faith (see *Curia,* 2 d). A miss. area in the initial stage of ecclesiastical organization is called a prefecture apostolic. A miss. area over which a vicar apostolic exercises jurisdiction is called a vicariate apostolic. The head is usually a titular bp.

5. Early archdioceses in the US include Baltimore, Md., 1808; Portland (originally Oregon City), Oreg., 1846; Saint Louis, Mo., 1847; Cincinnati, Ohio, 1850; New Orleans, La., 1850; New York, N.Y., 1850; San Francisco, Calif., 1853; Boston, Mass., 1875; Milwaukee, Wis., 1875; Santa Fe, N. Mex., 1875; Saint Paul, Minn., 1888; Dubuque, Iowa, 1893.

D. *Hist. in Eur. after the Council of Trent.* 1. The Council of Trent aimed at unifying RC doctrine and correcting abuses within the structure of the ch. A long struggle involving RCs, Luths., and Ref., and including wars, persecution, and intrigues, ensued.

2. Rome opposed emerging nationalism. The papacy lost pol. power and gradually shifted emphasis to supremacy in spiritual matters. Nationalism stressed the divine* right of kings (called Gallicanism* in Fr., Josephinism in Austria [see *Joseph II and Josephinism*], Febronianism* in Ger., regalism* in It.).

3. RC reform movements after the Reformation concentrated on the extirpation of Protestantism (see *Counter Reformation*). The Society* of Jesus gave special attention to the suppression of the Reformation. The Inquisition* was used against Prots. in RC countries. Both sides were guilty of cruelty.

4. In It. the Inquisition readily suppressed the Reformation. See also *Italy, Religious History of, Before the Reformation.*

5. In Spain,* which had also seen reform efforts before the Luth. Reformation,* Protestantism gained little ground and was readily suppressed.

6. In Fr., Huguenots* suffered bitter persecution that climaxed 1572 in the Bartholomew's* Day Massacre. The Edict of Nantes* granted some freedom of conscience to Prots. 1589, but it was revoked 1685. Laws were enacted against Prots. Thousands were expatriated. But by 1744 Huguenots were holding meetings of 10,000, and a 1787 edict reest. equality of rights (except the right to hold pub. office) and Prot. baptisms and marriages were declared valid. See also *France,* 10.

7. RCm suffered in the Fr. Revolution (see *France,* 5). The 1789 Assembly nationalized the ch. and its property and forbade religious discrimination (see *France,* 10). Dechristianization resulted in abolition of the Gregorian calendar 1793.

8. Reaction soon set in. The Directory permitted pub. worship 1795–97 but was repressive 1797–99. Napoleon* I forced the pope to sign the humiliating treaty of Tolentino 1797 and est. a concordat with the pope 1801 (see *Concordat,* 5), which included in its provisions: the state nominates bps., the pope appoints them; bps. appoint lower clergy, subject to govt. approval.

9. In England,* Henry* VIII broke with the pope and nationalized the ch. on basis of the 1534 Act. of Supremacy, passed by parliament (see also *Church and State,* 9); 1535 he declared himself to be *in terra supremum caput Anglicanae ecclesiae* ("on earth the supreme head of the Angl. Ch."). He persecuted Prots. for disagreeing with traditional doctrine and RCs for denying his supremacy and opposing his confiscation of ch. lands. Protestantism became prominent under Edward VI (see *England,* B 4). RC reaction came under Mary* I. Elizabeth* I favored Protestantism. The 1559 Act of Supremacy called her "Supreme Governor of this realm, and of all other her highness's dominions and countries, as well in all spiritual or ecclesiastical things or causes as temporal." The 1559 Act of Uniformity restored, and commanded to be used, the 2d Prayer Book of Edward VI (with some alterations) and made failure to attend ch. subject to fine. Some intractables were put to death. Attempts by RCs to put Mary Stuart, Queen of Scots (1542–87; next heir to Eng. throne after children of Henry VIII) on the Eng. throne led Elizabeth to have Mary executed. Failure of Philip II (1527–98; son of Charles* V; king of Sp. 1556–98) to conquer Eng. with the "Invincible Armada" 1588 ended serious threats by the papacy to gain Eng. See also *Elizabethan Settlement.* James* I first used mild measures against RCs; but when the latter increased, parliament confirmed Elizabethan anti-RC laws, which James enforced. This led to the Gunpowder* Plot, which, in turn, led to increased oppression of RCs. Charles I (see *Presbyterian Confessions,* 1), whose wife was RC, rarely enforced anti-RC laws. Charles II (1630–85; son of Charles I; king 1660–85) tried to assure restoration of RCm in Eng. by the 1670 treaty of Dover with Louis XIV* of Fr. This led the Eng. parliament to pass the Test* Act 1673 and the Papists' Disabling Act (excluded RCs from parliament; repealed 1829). James II (1633–1701; king of Eng., Scot., and Ireland 1685–88) became RC (probably before 1672) and ignored anti-RC laws; his attempts to restore RCm led to yrs. of subjection and degradation of RCs in England. William III (1650–1702; count of Nassau; prince of Orange; stadtholder of Holland 1672–1702; king of Eng. 1689–1702) was reared a Calvinist but broad in sympathies; the 1689 Act of Toleration suspended certain laws against Prots. (but RCs and disbelievers in the Trinity were excluded from benefits of this Act). The RC Emancipation Act was passed 1829.

10. In Germany,* M. Luther* and his supporters were put under the ban by the Edict of Worms.* Charles* V tried unsuccessfully to conquer the Prots. by force. See also *Augsburg, Religious Peace of; Passau, Convention of; Thirty Years' War; Westphalia, Peace of.*

11. The abps. of Mainz, Cologne, and Trier (who were also secular princes; Ger.: *geistliche Kurfürsten*) led unsuccessful attempts to achieve indep. from Rome.

12. Vatican Council I (see *Vatican Councils,* 1) est. papal supremacy. See also *Old Catholics.*

13. In Scand., practically the whole ch. became Luth. Legal restrictions against RCs were removed in the 19th and 20th c.

14. In Austria the Counter* Reformation almost extinguished Protestantism, which was also suppressed in Bohemia, Silesia, Livonia, and Carniola. Joseph II issued an edict of toleration 1781 (see also *Joseph II and Josephinism*).

15. In recent yrs. the laity has played a more active role in the RC Ch., which is trying (a) to indoctrinate its mems. on the church's position in soc. and moral issues, (b) to use the lay apostolate to disseminate RC principles on moral philos., (c) to involve the laity in governing processes of the ch.

E. *Hist. in the US.* 1. Juan Ponce de León (ca. 1460–1521; explorer; b. León, Sp.) discovered Fla. 1513; a mass conducted there 1521 is regarded as probably the 1st in the US. Franciscans came to Fla. 1528; 12 missionaries came with Hernando de Soto (ca. 1500–42; explorer; b. Barcarrota, Sp.) to Tampa

Bay 1539. City of Saint Augustine was founded and the oldest RC miss. in the US est. 1565. Regarding Luths. martyred 1565 near Saint Augustine see *Martyr.* RC missionaries accompanied various Sp. and Fr. explorers. By 1600 they had entered what is now Ala., Ariz., Ark., Calif., Fla., Ga., Kans., Miss., Nebr., N. Mex., N. Y., N. C., Okla., S. C., Tenn., Tex., Va. Early RC missionaries in US include Claude Jean Allouez (1622–89; Fr. Jesuit), John Altham (1589–1640; Eng. Jesuit), Louis Cancer de Barbastro (1500–49; Sp. Dominican), Jacques Gravier (1651–1708; Fr. Jesuit), Isaac Jogues (1607–46; Fr. Jesuit), Eusebio Francisco Kino (Chini; ca. 1645–1711; It. Jesuit), John Lalande (d. 1646; Fr. Jesuit brother), Antonio Margil (1657–1726; Sp. Franciscan), J. Marquette,* Zenobius Membre (1645–87; Fr. Franciscan), Juan de Padilla (d. 1542; Sp. Franciscan), Charles Raymbaut (1602–43; Fr. Jesuit), Junípero Serra (originally Miguel José; 1713–84; Franciscan; b. Majorca, Sp.), Andrew White (Eng. Jesuit; 1579–1656).

2. Two Jesuits were among first colonists of Md. 1634. In Mass., New Eng. was made a prefecture in charge of Fr. Capuchins 1630; the Mass Bay Co. enacted an anti-priest law 1647. The N. J. const. practically excluded RCs from office 1776. The N. H. const. barred RCs from office 1784. Md. adopted a religious toleration act 1649, but it was repealed 1654 as a result of Puritan influence. Pa. extended toleration to all faiths 1682. R. I. granted freedom of conscience 1663 but barred RCs from office 1719.

3. J. Carroll* was appointed head of US missions 1784, when there were ca. 25,000 RCs in a US pop. of ca. 4 million. Some RCs were prominent in the Revolutionary War.

4. J. Carroll was appointed bp. Baltimore (diocese coextensive with the US) 1789, consecrated 1790. Sulpicians* est. the 1st RC sem. in the US at Baltimore 1791. A school (which grew into Georgetown U.) opened at Georgetown, Md., 1791; a secondary school for girls opened at Georgetown 1792. By the 1840s RCs operated more than 200 elementary schools in the US.

5. Lack of organization, nationalism (e. g., on the part of Germans and Irish), and other factors led to schisms in US RCm late in the 18th and early in the 19th c.

6. In the 19th and 20th c., opposition to RCm took on various forms and was reflected, e. g., in the Know-Nothings in the 1850s, the Ku Klux Klan from 1866, the Am. Protective Assoc. from 1887. Non-RCs feared that a vow of obedience to Rome endangered secular govt. Pol. opposition became pronounced during the A. E. Smith presidential campaign 1928 and was intensified over the so-called Roman Question, occasioned by the 1929 Lateran Agreement (see also *Concordat,* 7; *Popes,* 28). Election of RC J. F. Kennedy as US Pres. 1960 and actions of Vatican Council II (see *Vatican Councils,* 2), e. g., in its *Declaration on Religious Freedom,* helped decrease soc. and pol. opposition to RCm.

7. Many RCs came to the US from Ireland, Ger., Fr., and E and S Eur. 1830–1900, raising the RC pop. in the US to ca. 12 million and presenting probems of acculturation.

8. US bps. met at Baltimore, Md., for 7 provincial councils 1829–49. They proclaimed Mary patroness of the US 1846. Three plenary councils at Baltimore: (a) 1852, drafted rules for parochial life, matters of ritual and ceremonies, financial matters, and teaching of doctrine; (b) 1866, condemned some current doctrinal errors and adopted rules regarding organization of dioceses, educ. and conduct of clergy, property management, parish duties, and gen. educ.; (c) 1884, prepared the Baltimore catechisms, required est. of parish schools, initiated action to est. Cath. U. of Am. in Washington, D. C., fixed 6 holy days of obligation to be observed in the US. See also *Councils and Synods,* 6.

9. In the Civil War RCs fought on both sides, but none were prominent in the movement for abolishing slavery. In the 19th c. the RC Ch. became known as a friend of labor. J. Gibbons* went to Rome to defend the Knights of Labor. The 1891 encyclical *Rerum Novarum* included rejection of the theory that the govt. should not interfere in soc. and economic matters and held that poverty should be alleviated by charity and justice.

10. Near the end of the 19th c., Am. RCs were accused of neglecting contemplative virtues in favor of practical virtues and of watering down doctrine to gain converts. In *Testem Benevolentiae* (1899 apostolic letter of Leo XIII [see *Popes,* 29] to J. Gibbons) doctrine is described as a divine deposit to be adhered to at all times, though adaptations may be made in Christian life to suit time, place, and nat. customs.

11. The RC Ch. in the US was removed from mission status 1908 by the apostolic constitution *Sapienti Consilio* of Pius X (see *Popes,* 30).

12. Vatican Council II spelled out the doctrine of collegiality of bps. Other phenomena of change in the 2d half of the 20th c. include differences in trends and emphases in theol.; variations in interpretation and implementation of Vatican Council II directives; changes in the spiritual formation and life-style of the clergy. Much attention is given to race relations, poverty, peace, and ecumenism.

13. Many sisterhoods are active in the US, e. g., in educ. and hosp. work.

14. The RC parish school system has been threatened by decline in the no. of priests and nuns to staff them and by various financial pressures. Institutions of higher education are also fighting for survival. Problems arising out of celibacy require solution. Liturgical reforms have created divisions that portend serious long-term aftereffects. The larger role played by laity may require revamping of the pol. structure of the ch. Soc. and ethical issues relating to birth control are proving to be difficult and disturbing. EL, JWC, MAM, ACP

New Catholic Encyclopedia, prepared by an ed. staff at The Cath. U. of Am., Washington, D. C., 14 vols. plus index (New York, 1967); *1972 Catholic Almanac,* ed. F. A. Foy (Huntington, Ind., 1971). See also *Religious Bodies (US), Bibliography of.*

Roman Catholic Confessions. A. 1. Besides the ecumenical* creeds, the RC Ch. accepts the pronouncements of its councils (see *Councils and Synods*) and papal decrees.*

Principal source and highest standard of the RC Ch.: *Canons and Decrees of the Council of Trent.* Doctrinal sessions of the Council of Trent*: III. Symbol of faith; IV. Scriptural canon (apocrypha* included); V. Original sin; VI. Justification (justification by faith alone condemned); VII. Sacraments in gen., Baptism in particular; XIII. Eucharist; XIV. Penance and extreme unction; XXI. Communion; XXII. Mass; XXIII. Ordination; XXIV. Marriage; XXV. Purgatory; invocation, veneration, and relics of saints; sacred images; indulgences*; fasting; index* of prohibited books; etc. Disciplinary measures dealt, e. g., with residence of bps. and priests, training of clerics, reformation of religious orders, finances. 255 signed. The original acts and debates of the council, recorded by Angelo Massarelli (1510–66; b. Sanseverino, Mark Ancona, It.; secy. Council of Trent) are in the Vatican. Interpretation is reserved to the pope alone.

2. The Council of Trent 1563 declared the need for a profession of faith (Sess. XXIV, Reform, Chaps. i and xii). Under direction of Pius* IV the Profession of the Tridentine Faith (*Professio fidei Tridentina;* also called Creed of Pius IV) was drawn

up 1564; it consisted of 12 arts. (1. Nicene Creed; 2–11. Summary of the doctrines of the Council of Trent; 12. Solemn adjuration) and soon became obligatory for all RC priests and pub. teachers and for converts from Protestantism; 2 arts. were added 1877 (one on the immaculate conception of Mary, the other on papal infallibility). In 1910 it was ordered that the profession be signed and confirmed by oath.

3. The Council of Trent also proposed a catechism (Sess. XXIV, Reform, Chap. vii; Sess. XXV, Reform, Concerning the Index of Books and the Catechism, Breviary, and Missal). The resultant Roman Catechism (*Catechismus Romanus;* also called Catechism of the Council of Trent) had been projected 1546 and was pub. in Lat. 1566; it was for teachers, not pupils, and deals with the Apostles' Creed, Sacraments, Decalogue, and Lord's Prayer. Other catechisms were written by P. Canisius,* R. Bellarmine,* J. B. Bossuet,* et al. See also *Popes,* 21; *Roman Catholic Church,* B 2–5.

B. *Papal bulls against Jansenism.**

C. *Papal definition of the Immaculate* Conception.* In 1849 Pius IX (see *Popes,* 28) invited opinions of bps. regarding definition of the immaculate conception. 600 replied; 4 dissented; 4 regarded the time inopportune. Pius IX proclaimed the dogma of the immaculate conception 1854.

D. *Papal Syllabus.* In 1864 Pius IX issued the Syllabus* of Errors. In 1907 Pius X (see *Popes,* 30) issued *Lamentabili,* which condemned Modernism (see *Modernism,* 1) in 65 theses directed esp. against A. F. Loisy.* EL

See also *Vatican Councils.*

H. Jedin, *A History of the Council of Trent,* tr. E. Graf, 2 vols. (St. Louis, 1957); *Canons and Decrees of the Council of Trent: Original Text with English Translation,* ed. and tr. H. J. Schroeder (St. Louis, 1941).

Roman Catholic Modernism. See *Modernism,* 1.

Roman Catholic Reformation. See *Counter Reformation.*

Roman Congregations. See *Curia.*

Roman Creed, Old. See *Ecumenical Creeds,* A 4.

Roman Missal. See *Missal.*

Roman Question. See *Concordat,* 7; *Popes,* 28; *Roman Catholic Church,* E 6.

Roman Religion. 1. Originally, Roman religion was quite different from the Gk. religion that later overwhelmed it. Its basic element was awe and anxiety felt before the divine (or numen), expressed in religious observances, mainly agricultural, without myth, theology, temples, or statues of gods. Its oldest gods were Jupiter and Mars. It survived mainly in the religious festivals of the Roman calendar.

2. Under the Roman kings, Etruscan (Gk.?) influence led to construction of temples and other anthropomorphic features. Under guidance of the Sibylline (from Gk. *Sibylla,* a prophetess) oracle at Cumae, It., a series of Gk. cults were introd., some not without opposition. At the same time, many earlier deities survived, with reassigned functions, so that Roman religion had many minor deities. See also *Sibylline Books and Oracles.*

3. By the time of the NT, Roman religion was thoroughly hellenized; it had philos. elements, many mystery cults and E cults, and a certain skepticism about things religious (cf. M. T. Cicero,* *De natura deorum*). In the period of the empire there is also a growth of ruler worship (esp. in the E Roman empire), the conflict of which with Christianity is reflected in Rv.

C. Bailey, *Phases in the Religion of Ancient Rome* (Berkeley, Calif., 1932); F. Altheim, *A History of Roman Religion,* tr. H. Mattingly (New York, [1937?]); *Ancient Roman Religion,* ed. and tr. F. C. Grant (New York, 1957). EK

Roman Rite. See *Liturgics.*

Roman See. See *Apostolic See.*

Romanesque Churches. See *Church Architecture,* 7.

Romania (Roumania; Rumania). One of the Balkan States, E Eur.; *area:* ca. 91,699 sq. mi.; *pop.* (1972 est.): 20,800,000; enl. 1918–20 to include Banat, Bessarabia, Bucovina, Transylvania; signed Balkan Pact 1934; forced to cede Bessarabia and N Bucovina to Russ., part of N Transylvania to Hung., S Dobruja to Bulgaria 1940; fought on side of Ger. in WW II; overrun by Russ. 1944; N Transylvania returned to Romania 1947; declared a people's rep. 1947, a socialist rep. 1965.

Most Romanians are mems. of the Gk. Orthodox Ch., which 1948 gained control of the Gk. Cath. Uniate churches. RCs: perhaps ca. 7–9%. Others include Armenians, Jews, and various Prots.

The Ref. Ch. is Hung. Headed by a bp., it has a const. since 1950 and (with Luths. and Unitarians) operates a theol. institute at Klausenburg.

Luther's catechism was printed in Romania 1543. A Luth. Ch. is said to have been est. at Bucharest by 1550. Luths. are mostly Hung. and Ger. Six groups merged 1926 to form the Ev. Ch. of the Augsburg Confession. Luths. numbered ca. 20,000 in Bucovina in the early 1920s; many were deported by Nazis 1940. Luths. (mostly Ger.) numbered ca. 100,000 in Bessarabia 1940. Most Luths. here and in Dobruja were deported by Nazis 1940.

Romanian Orthodox Episcopate of America, The. See *Eastern Orthodox Churches,* 6.

Romanticism. Movement in literature, art, religion, and theol. in the last half of the 18th and 1st part of the 19th c. Developed on background of classicism, humanism,* and the Enlightenment.* Characterized by subjectivity, appeal to imagination and fancy, emphasis on beauty of the natural world, mystery, idealizing pantheism or its counterpart as an explanation of the relation bet. the inner and outer world, freedom for each personality. See also *Christian Church, History of,* III 14; *Secularism.*

Romoser, George August (Dec. 14, 1870–July 9, 1936). B. Baltimore, Md.; educ. Conc. Sem., St. Louis, Mo.; prof. Conc. Coll., Conover, N. C., 1892–99; pastor Detroit, Mich.; pres. Conc. Coll., Conover, 1900–11; pastor Cleveland, Ohio, 1911–14; prof. Conc. Collegiate Institute, Bronxville, N. Y., 1915 (pres. 1918–36). Ed. *The Lutheran Witness.*

Romuald. See *Camaldolese.*

Roncalli, Angelo Giuseppe. See *Popes,* 34.

Ronge, Johannes (1813–87). B. Bischofswalde, Silesia; educ. Breslau; priest 1840; suspended 1843 for attacking RCm; excommunicated and degraded from priesthood 1844 for protesting against display of the Holy* Coat of Treves; founded German* Catholics.

Ronsdorf Sect. See *Ellerians.*

Rood. Cross or crucifix, esp. at entrance of chancel or choir.

Rood Screen. Screen separating chancel or choir from nave; often surmounted by a cross or crucifix. The screen or the gallery above it is also called jube.

Rooke-Siassi Islands. See *New Guinea,* 6.

Roos, Magnus Friedrich (1727–1803). B. Sulz, S Württemberg, Ger.; educ. Tübingen; diaconus Göppingen 1757; pastor Lustnau and dean of the diocese of Bebenhausen 1767; lectured on theol. at Tübingen; prelate Anhausen 1784. Moderate pietist; influenced by J. A. Bengel.* Works include *Christliche Gedanken von der Verschiedenheit und Einigkeit der Kinder Gottes.*

Rorate Masses. Masses named after the 1st word of the Introit in Lat. for the Wed. after the 3d Sun. in Advent, for the 4th Sun. in Advent, and for Dec. 18; celebrated in honor of Mary; in some places read daily Dec. 17–24.

Rore, Cyprien de (Cipriano da; 1516–65). Composer; b. Antwerp or Mechelen (Mechlin; Mecheln), Belg.; pupil and successor of A. Willaert* as choirmaster St. Mark's, Venice, It. Works include motets, masses, psalms. See also *Passion, The.*

Rörer, Georg (Rorarius; 1492–1557). B. Deggendorf, Bav., Ger.; educ. Leipzig and Wittenberg; diaconus Wittenberg 1525; devoted full time to helping Luther from 1537; proofreader; to Copenhagen 1551, Jena 1553. Ed. Luther's works. See also *Luther, Table Talk of.*

Rosary. RC string of prayer beads and the devotion for which it is used. 150 smaller beads are divided into 15 groups, called decades, by insertion of 15 larger beads. The devotion is begun and ended in various ways. As the beads are fingered, an Ave* Maria is said for each small one and a Lord's Prayer for each larger one. During the recital of each decade a "mystery" is to be contemplated, there being 5 joyful mysteries (Annunciation, Visitation, Nativity, Presentation, and finding of Jesus in the temple), 5 sorrowful mysteries (agony in Gethsemane, scourging, crowning with thorns, carrying the cross, crucifixion), and 5 glorious mysteries (resurrection, ascension, descent of the Holy Sprit, assumption of Mary, coronation of Mary). Indulgences are traditionally connected with recitation of the rosary.

See also *Seven Joys of Mary.*

Roscelin de Compiègne. See *Roscellinus.*

Roscellinus (Rucelinus; Roscellin; Roscelin de Compiègne; d. after 1120). Probably b. Compiègne, Fr.; scholastic philos.; canon Loches; teacher of P. Abelard.* Defended nominalism* in opposition to realism*; accused of tritheism,* he postulated a unity of will and power.

Roscher, Wilhelm Heinrich (1845–1923). B. Göttingen, Ger.; taught at Meissen and Wurzen; classical scholar. Works include *Ausführliches Lexikon der griechischen und römischen Mythologie.*

Rose Sunday. See *Golden Rose.*

Rosegger, Peter (Rossegger; Petri Kettenfeier; pseudonym till 1894: P. K.; 1843–1918). Poet and novelist; b. Alpl, near Krieglach, Styria, Austria; RC with ev. tendencies. Works include *Der Gottsucher; Das ewige Licht.*

Roseland, Jens Christian (changed name from Jensson to Roseland 1900; Mar. 25, 1859–Dec. 17, 1930). B. Sandnes, Jaederen (later spelled Jaeren), Norw.; to Am. 1861; educ. Augustana Sem. of The Norwegian-Danish* Augustana Syn. in Am., Marshall, Wis.; held various pastorates and syn. offices. Works include *Et Varsko; American Lutheran Biographies; Kvindens Stemmeret.*

Rosenius, Carl Olof (Karl; 1816–68). Luth. lay revivalist; hymnist; b. Nysätra, Västerbotten, Swed.; influenced by G. Scott*; opposed separatism; emphasized M. Luther's* teaching of justification by faith alone and stressed virtues as proofs of the indwelling Holy Spirit; helped found Evangeliska Fosterlands-Stiftelsen ("The Ev. Fatherland's Foundation": Ev. Nat. Missionary Soc.). Contributed to *Pietisten* ("The Pietist"). Other works include *Bref i andliga ämnen; Om de hemska twiflen paa allt heligt;* commentary on Ro; hymns. See also *Sweden, Lutheranism in,* 5.

Rosenmüller, Johann (Giovanni Rosenmiller; ca. 1619–84). Luth. organist, composer; b. Ölsnitz, Vogtland, Saxony, Ger.; educ. Leipzig; taught in Venice, It., nearly 20 yrs.; kapellmeister Wolfenbüttel, Ger. Works include motets; cantatas.

Rosenqvist, Georg Gustaf Alexander (1855–1931). Fin. theol.; taught at U. of Helsinki 1886–1917, prof. dogmatics 1894. See also *Dogmatics,* B 9.

Rosenzweig, Franz (1886–1929). Jewish philos.; b. Cassel, Ger.; educ. Göttingen, Munich, Freiburg, Berlin; soldier in WW I; appointed lecturer at Frankfurt but could not accept because of onset of paralysis; religious existentialist. Works include *Hegel und der Staat; Der Stern der Erlösung; Die Schrift und Luther.*

Rosh Hashanah. See *Judaism,* 4.

Rosicrucians (Brothers of the Rosy-Cross; Rosy-Cross Knights; Rosicrucian Fraternity). Became known in Ger. ca. 1614 through 2 anonymous pamphlets: *Fama Fraternitatis Roseae-Crucis* and *Die chymische Hochzeit Christiani Rosenkreutz* (both now gen. ascribed to J. V. Andreä and regarded as satire). Christianus Rosenkreutz, a shadowy lengendary figure, is alleged to have been born 1378, to have spent his last days in a cave in Morocco, and to have died there 1484 after giving his esoteric lore to disciples under vow of secrecy. In course of time, charlatans and imposters arose, claiming to be mems. of the alleged soc. with knowledge of its secrets (including that of alchemy and the elixir of life).

Rosicrucians claim access to all knowledge of man, including that deposited on the lost continents of Atlantis and Lemuria, and that they have the key whereby all can choose a life leading to perfection. They hold that the kingdom of God is within everyone and that therefore everyone has the powers of the universe in his body.

AMORC is acronym for Ancient Mystical Order of the Rosy Cross. FEM

See also *Illuminati.*

Rosinus, Bartholomäus (1520–86). Luth. theol.; b. Pössneck, Ger.; educ. Wittenberg; schoolmaster (1544) and diaconus (1551) Eisenach; pastor and supt. Weimar 1559; supt. Waldenburg 1562; returned to Weimar 1567; dismissed and called to Regensburg 1573. Works include *Fragstücke zu Luthers Katechismus.*

Ross, John (Aug. 6, 1842–1915). B. Easter Rarichie, Nigg, Scot.; educ. Glasgow and Edinburg; Presb. miss. Manchuria 1872. Tr. NT into Korean; contributed to a commentary on the Bible in Chinese. Other works include *History of Corea; Mission Methods in Manchuria; The Original Religion of China.*

Rossetti, Dante Gabriel (originally Gabriel Charles Dante; 1828–82). Painter and poet; b. London, Eng.; mem. Pre-Raphaelite* Brotherhood. Paintings include *Annunciation; The Girlhood of Mary Virgin.*

Rossi, Giovanni Battista de' (1822–94). RC archaeologist; b. Rome, It.; excavated and studied Roman catacombs.* Works include *Inscriptiones christianae urbis Romae septimo saeculo antiquiores; Roma sotteranea cristiana.*

Rosweyde, Heribert (1569–1629). Jesuit; b. Utrecht, Neth.; planned *Acta* sanctorum.* See also *Bolland, Jean de.*

Roswitha (Hrotsvitha; Hrotswitha; 10th c.). Ger. Benedictine nun and poet. Wrote chronicles of Otto* I in verse.

Rota, Sacred Roman. See *Curia,* 2 e.

Rotach, Meeting in. See *Lutheran Confessions,* A 2.

Roth, Karl Johann Friedrich von (1780–1852). Luth. jurist and statesman; b. Vaihingen, Württemberg, Ger.; educ. Tübingen; held various govt. positions; pres. of Bav. supreme consistory 1828–48; criticized for not giving strong support to Prots. in the genuflection controversy (see *Redenbacher, Christian Wilhelm Adolf*). Ed. selections from Luther's writings.

Roth, Stephan Ludwig (1796–1849). B. Mediasch, Transylvania; studied at Tübingen; pupil and coworker of J. H. Pestalozzi* in Switz.; applied the latter's method at Mediasch; instituted soc. reforms; became pastor; tried to lead people back to Luther's childlike faith.

Rothe, Johann Andreas (1688–1758). Luth. Pietist; b. Lissa, near Görlitz, Ger.; educ. Leipzig; pastor Berthelsdorf (see *Zinzendorf, Nikolaus Ludwig von*)

1722; broke with Zinzendorf 1737; pastor Hermsdorf (near Görlitz) 1737, Thommendorf (near Bunzlau) 1739; hymnist. Hymns include "Ich habe nun den Grund gefunden."

Rothe, Richard (1799–1867). Mediating theol.; b. Posen; educ. Heidelberg, Berlin, Wittenberg; influenced by F. D. E. Schleiermacher,* G. W. F. Hegel,* J. A. W. Neander,* and F. A. G. Tholuck*; cofounder Protestantenverein (Protestant* Union); prof. Wittenberg, Heidelberg, Bonn, Heidelberg. Works include *Zur Dogmatik; Die Anfänge der christlichen Kirche und ihrer Verfassung.*

Rothmann, Bernhard (Bernard; Bernd; Bernt; Rottmann). See *Münster Kingdom.*

Rothovius, Iisak (1572–1652). B. Angelstad, Swed.; educ. Uppsala and Wittenberg; Luth. pastor Nyköping, Swed.; bp. Turku, Fin., 1627; urged Finns to fight under Gustavus* II in Thirty* Years' War.

Rouen, Cathedral at. See *Church Architecture,* 10.

Rous, Francis (Rouse; 1579–1659). Puritan, hymnist; b. Dittisham, Devonshire [or Halton, Cornwall?], Eng.; educ. Oxford and Leiden; mem. Parliament. Hymns include "The Lord's My Shepherd, I'll Not Want."

Rousseau, Jean Jacques (1712–78). Fr. philos.; b. Geneva, Switz.; lived mainly in Fr. Works include *Du Contrat social; Julie, ou la Nouvelle Héloïse; Émile, ou Traité de l'éducation;* contributions to the *Encyclopédie* (see *Encyclopedists*). See also *Government; Natural Law,* 5; *Naturalism.*

Roussel, Gérard (ca. 1500–50). Reformer; b. Vaquerie, near Amiens, Fr.; to Paris 1520; co-worker of J. Lefèvre* d'Étaples; pastor and canon Meaux; bp. Oloron 1536; reformed the liturgy. See also *Huguenots.*

Rovere, Giuliano della. See *Popes,* 19.

Rowland, Daniel (Rowlands; 1713–90). B. Panty-y-beudy, Llancwnlle, near Llangeitho, Cardiganshire, Wales; ordained Angl. deacon 1733, priest 1735; held several curates; organized Calvinistic Methodistic socs.; suspended from clerical functions, but continued in an outstanding preaching career.

Roy, Ram Mohan. See *Ram Mohan Roy.*

Royce, Josiah (1855–1916). B. Grass Valley, Calif.; taught philos. at Harvard U., Cambridge, Mass., 1882–1916; influenced by W. James.* Advocated idealism* with emphasis on individuality and will; ultimate reality is the career of the absolute mind, of which human minds are fragmentary manifestations; perfection of the absolute includes victory over sin and suffering; though involved in process, the absolute grasps past, present, and future in a single act; virtue springs from loyalty that manifests itself in community. Royce's concept of a beloved and redemptive community influenced theol. descriptions of the ch. Works include *The Spirit of Modern Philosophy; The World and the Individual; The Sources of Religious Insight; The Problem of Christianity; The Hope of the Great Community.*

Rubens, Peter Paul (1577–1640). Flemish painter; b. Siegen, Westphalia, Ger. Works include *Raising of the Cross; Descent from the Cross; Holy Family; Return of the Holy Family from Egypt;* portraits.

Rubrics. Directions for conducting services; the name is derived from the red ink often used for them, in distinction from the text of the service, in black ink.

Rudbeck, Johannes (Rudbeckius; 1581–1646). B. Almby parish, near Örebro, Swed.; educ. Uppsala and Wittenberg; prof. Uppsala; court preacher and spiritual adviser of Gustavus* II; bp. Västeraas 1619–46. Est. schools, hospitals, and institutions for poor; worked for soc. reform.

Rudelbach, Andreas Gottlob (1792–1862). B. Copenhagen, Den.; educ. Copenhagen; pastor and supt. Glauchau, Saxony, Ger., 1829; staunch Luth.; opposed the separatist movement led by M. Stephan* (1777–1846); resigned pastorate 1845 in protest against state ch. unionism; returned to Den.; lectured at U. of Copenhagen 1846–48; pastor Slagelse 1848. With H. E. F. Guericke* he founded *Zeitschrift fuer die gesammte lutherische Theologie und Kirche* 1839. Other works include *Die Grundveste der Lutherischen Kirchenlehre und Friedenspraxis; Reformation, Lutherthum und Union.*

Rudman, Anders (Andreas; Andrew; 1668–1708). Studied under J. Swedberg* at the U. of Uppsala, Swed.; to Am. 1697; pastor Wicaco(a) (now in S Philadelphia) 1697–1702; Gloria Dei Ch. built there 1700 under his supervision; pastor Dutch Luth. ch., N. Y.; 1st provost* of the Swed. chs. on the Delaware 1704.

Rudolf II (1552–1612). Holy Roman emp. 1576–1612; educ. at Sp. court by Jesuits; intolerant toward Prots.; granted Bohemians religious freedom 1609. See also *Lutheran Confessions,* A 5.

Rudra. See *Brahmanism,* 2.

Ruet, Francisco de Paula (1826–78). Reformer; b. Barcelona, Sp.; came into contact with Waldensians in Turin, It.; ev. preacher Barcelona 1855; imprisoned and banished; returned to Sp. 1868; est. an ev. cong. at Madrid.

Ruff. See *Vestments, Clinical,* 3.

Rufinus, Tyrannius (ca. 345–ca. 410). Lat. theol.; b. probably Concordia, near Aquileia, It.; lived as monk in Egypt, on the Mount of Olives, where he founded a monastery in assoc. with Melania the Elder (see *Melania,* 1), and at Aquileia; friend of Jerome,* but bitterly opposed him over doctrines of Origen. Tr. Gk. Christian writers into Lat. See also *Ecumenical Creeds,* A 2.

Ruhland, Friedrich Carl Theodor (given names also occur in the order Carl Friedrich Theodor; Apr. 26, 1836–June 3, 1879). B. Grohnde, near Hameln, Hannover, Ger.; studied at Loccum; to Am. 1857; educ. practical sem., Fort Wayne, Ind. (see *Ministry, Education of,* X C and D). Pastor Oshkosh, Wis.; Wolcottsville and Buffalo, N. Y.; Pleasant Ridge, Ill. In 1872 he accepted a call to chs. in Dresden and Planitz, near Zwickau, Saxony, Ger., which had left the state ch. for reasons of conscience. See also *Germany, Lutheran Free Churches in,* 5–6.

H. Ruhland, "Friedrich Carl Theodor Ruhland," tr. and condensed by R. W. Heintze, *CHIQ,* VIII, 1 (Apr. 1935), 25–31, and 2 (July 1935), 57–62.

Rule of Augustine (Augustinian Rule). See *Augustinian Hermits.*

Rule of Benedict. See *Benedictines.*

Rule of Faith. Some 2d and 3d c. ch. fathers (e. g., Irenaeus,* Tertullian,* Dionysius* of Corinth, Clement* of Alexandria, Hippolytus,* Novatian*) and the Clementine Homilies (see *Clementines*) refer to the "rule of faith" (Lat. *regula fidei*); other terms for it: canon (or rule) of truth (Gk. *kanon tes aletheias*), canon (or rule) of the ch. (Gk. *kanon ekklesiastikos*), authority of the ch. (Lat. *auctoritas ecclesiae*), or, simply, the faith (Lat. *fides*).

The precise dimensions of the rule of faith have been considerably debated. Some include all Scripture; others include only the formulated creed. The term "rule of faith" experienced development and meant different things at different times.

Initially "rule of faith" was understood as the apostolic faith orally transmitted; Tertullian and Irenaeus present it in a variety of forms and with considerable fluctuation in content. What the apostles had preached and what had been received and preserved as apostolic tradition became the rule, or norm, of faith, the church's doctrine, as well as the guide to the right interpretation of apostolic Scripture.

From the beginning, the rule of faith and Baptism were closely related. Content of instruction given catechumens in preparation for Baptism: basic elements of apostolic doctrine (e. g., teaching concerning the triune God, the person and work of Christ, the meaning of Baptism, Christian life, the ch., and the final coming of Christ). Often a concisely worded summary was given catechumens to be memorized and spoken as a baptismal confession of faith. By the time of Augustine* of Hippo the rule of faith and the baptismal creed were regarded as identical. HJAB

See also *Analogy of Faith; Ecumenical Creeds,* A 3.

Rulman Merswin (1307–82). Mystic; b. Strasbourg, Ger.; banker Strasbourg; he and his 2d wife renounced the world; follower of J. Tauler*; obtained from Benedictines the monastery Grüner Wörth, on an island in the Ill. R., near Strasbourg, 1367; gave it to the Knights of St. John and retired to it 1371. See also *Friends of God.*

Rumania. See *Romania.*

Runeberg, Johan Ludvig (1804–77). Luth. pastor, hymnist; b. Pietarsaari, Fin.; educ. Turku; teacher Porvoo; wrote in Swedish. Works include *Hanna; Elgskyttarne* ("Elk Hunters"); *Julkvällen* ("Christmas Eve"); *Fänrik Staals sägner* ("Tales of Ensign Stal"); *Kung Fjalar* ("King Fjalar"); the Fin. nat. anthem "Vaart Land" ("Our Land"); hymns.

Ruotsalainen, Paavo Henrik (Paavo = Paul; 1777–1852). Lay preacher, revivalist, pietist; b. near Tolvaniemi, Iisalmi parish, Fin.; spent most of his life on a farm in Nilsiä; at 22 a blacksmith directed him to seek inner awareness of Christ; he soon came to a deep Christ-centered inwardness and a consciousness of human sinfulness; traveled through most of Fin. as leader and coordinator of a revival movement; harassed by ch. and state authorities, but maintained a following; exponent of *theologia* crucis;* held that Christianity is not essentially a set of regulations, rules, or formulations, but experience of God's forgiving grace in Christ; emphasized daily repentance and renewal. Wrote the tract *Naagra ord till väckta av bondestaandet* ("A Word to the Awakened Peasants"). See also *Finland, Lutheranism in,* 4.

Rupert (Rupertus; Ruprecht; Hrodbert; ca. 650–perhaps ca. 715/720). "Apostle of the Bavarians"; presumably of royal Frankish descent; founder and 1st bp. Salzburg; reputedly bp. Worms. See also *Germany,* A 1.

Ruperti, Hans Heinrich Justus Philipp (last 2 given names also occur in sequence Philipp Justus; Dec. 21, 1833–May 16, 1899). B. Kirch-Osten, near Stade, Hannover, Ger.; educ. Erlangen and Göttingen; pastor Emigrant House, Bremerhaven, 1856; pastor Geestendorf (part of Geestemünde) 1871–73, NYC 1873–76; mem. N. Y. Ministerium; returned to Ger. 1876; mem. of consistory and supt. Lübeck 1876–91; gen. supt. Holstein 1891. Works include *Christenlehre nach dem kleinen Katechismus Dr. Martin Luthers, als Leitfaden für den Konfirmanden-Unterricht; Licht und Schatten aus der Geschichte des Alten Bundes; Luther in seiner religiösen Bedeutung;* sermons.

Rupff, Conrad (Ruppich; Rupsch; Rupzsch; Konrad; perhaps ca. 1475 [or earlier]–1530). B. Kahla, Thuringia, Ger.; parish priest Kahla 1505; kapellmeister at court of Frederick* III (1463–1525). Helped prepare M. Luther's* *Deutsche Messe* (see *Chant*).

Rupprecht, Philip Martin Ferdinand (Nov. 10, 1861–July 5, 1942). B. North Dover, Ohio; educ. Conc. Sem., St. Louis, Mo. Pastor near Cole Camp, Mo., 1884; Detroit, Mich., 1889. Asst. ed. and proofreader Louis Lange Pub. Co., St. Louis, 1896; chief proofreader and house ed. Conc. Pub. House, St. Louis, 1900–42. Works include *Bible History References.*

Ruprecht. See *Rupert.*

Rural Church in America. 1. "Rural ch." is a distinctive and descriptive term. Its thrust is geog. and demographic; denotes a nonurban ch. or group of chs. The term was coined early in the 20th c. as Am. began to move from an agricultural and rural to an industrial and urban soc. As definition and lines of demarcation became clear, so also the distinction bet. urban and rural ch. The census definition of "rural," which included communities of less than 2,500 pop., was followed for many yrs. (at least into the 1930s) by many chs.

2. After WW II, "rural ch." came to be replaced by "Ch. in Town and Country," the latter term counteracting the implicaton that "rural" chs. were only in open country and removing the 2,500 pop. limit. Some chs. in communities as large as 5,000–25,000 were more rural than urban. Today there is no uniformity of definition or demarcation bet. rural and urban chs.

3. Luth. and most other Prot. chs. in Am. were predominantly rural till the 20th c.

4. As industrialization and urbanization grew, rural chs. supplied urban and suburban chs. with mems. and the denominations with ministers.

5. To meet new problems that arose when immigration and homesteading practically ceased early in the 20th c., rural ch. commissions were appointed and some schools offered courses in rural sociol. for ch. leadership.

6. Since ca. 1940, revolutionary methods in farming resulted in larger farms and less farmers. Rural to urban migration increased, leaving many rural areas with a static or declining pop. and ch. membership. Rural chs. sought strength by various measures, e. g., mergers.

7. Modern transportation eliminated the need for many rural chs.; more than 1,000 disbanded.

8. Urban sprawl surrounded some rural chs., which mushroomed as a result.

9. The challenge of reaching many unreached in low density but widely scattered pop. areas has not been completely met. But rural ch. work has been effective and promises to continue as an important part of the contemporary scene. RJS

C. De Vries, *Inside Rural America: A Lutheran View* (Chicago, 1962); E. W. Mueller and G. C. Ekola, *The Silent Struggle for Mid-America* (Minneapolis, Minn., 1963); V. Obenhaus, *The Church and Faith in Mid-America* (Philadelphia, Pa., 1963); *New Thousands in Town and Country* (Chicago, 1962).

Rurer, Johann (ca. 1480–1542). B. Bamberg, Ger.; pastor Ansbach; coreformer Brandenburg-Ansbach; celebrated Communion in German under both kinds 1525; expelled 1527; preacher Liegnitz; returned to Ansbach 1528. Works include *Christliche unterrichtung eines pfarhern an seinen hern.*

Rurik (Ryurik; d. 879 AD). Alleged Scand. chief said to have conquered Novgorod in the early 860s and to have founded the Russ. emp. See also *Russia.*

Russell, Arthur Tozer (1806–74). B. Northampton, Eng.; educ. Cambridge; held several pastorates, the last (1874) at Southwick, near Brighton. Began as an extreme high churchman; studied Augustine* of Hippo; became moderate Calvinist. Author; hymnist. Hymn translations include "Now Sing We, Now Rejoice"; "In Thee Alone, O Christ, My Lord."

Russell, Bertrand Arthur William (1872–1970). Brit. philos., mathematician, educator, soc. reformer; b. Trelleck, Wales; educ. Cambridge; lectured at Cambridge 1910–16; dismissed because of pacifist activities; founded experimental Beacon Hill School 1927; to US 1938. Taught at U. of Chicago; U. of Calif. at Los Angeles; Barnes Foundation, Philadelphia. Returned to Cambridge 1944.

Russell thrice ran unsuccessfully for parliament; was jailed twice for pacifist activities; became 3d earl Russell 1931; received Nobel Prize for Literature 1950; often in conflict with moralists and religious conservatives; pacifist in WW I, but in WW II held that defeat of Nazis was necessary if human life was to be tolerable.

Russell is known for contributions to logic and his attempt to identify methods of philos. with those of science. He espoused various systems at different times (idealism, realism, monism, pluralism), but atomism runs through all (nonmental facts exist apart from our awareness; propositions can be true in isolation; analysis is useful as a method in philos.). His basic system may be defined as logical constructionism (formulation of a body of knowledge in terms of relations bet. simpler, more intelligible, more undeniable entities). He formulated some principles for an ideal language and tried to show that mathematics is an extension of logic.

Russell advocated certain moral and political ideals; first he held that "good" and "bad" are qualities in objects regardless of opinion; later he rejected this view for a doctrine of the subjectivity of values.

After breaking with Platonic idealism, Russell called himself an agnostic or atheist. He granted possibility of God's existence, but regarded religious tenets as intellectually indefensible and religion (which he said was based primarily and mainly on fear) as harmful. He expected religion to disappear when man's soc. problems are solved.

Works include *Marriage and Morals; Education and the Social Order; The Principles of Mathematics; Introduction to Mathematical Philosophy; The Problems of Philosophy; A History of Western Philosophy; An Outline of Philosophy; The Analysis of Mind; The Practice and Theory of Bolshevism; Why I Am Not a Christian.* EL

See also *Logical Positivism.*

Russell, Charles Taze (1852–1916). "Pastor Russell"; b. Pittsburgh, Pa.; at first Cong.; pastor indep. ch. Pittsburgh 1878; held that Christ came invisibly 1874, at the beginning of the "Millennial Age," which would end 1914 and be followed by soc. revolution, chaos, resurrection of dead, and est. of Christ's kingdom on earth. Founded Jehovah's* witnesses.

Russell, Henry Norris. See *Evolution,* I.

Russia. 1. Reputed founder of the Russ. emp. was Rurik.* Princess Olga (d. 969) was bap. at Constantinople ca. 955; Vladimir* I, grandson of Olga, was bap. ca. 989.

2. Vladimir I and his successors promoted Christianity, but the masses remained largely pagan. The Mongol invasion (13th c.) was a blow to the ch. Gennadius* II allowed the Russ. Ch. to choose and consecrate its own metropolitans, but the ch. came under state control.

3. Moscow became a 3d Rome (Constantinople was the 2d). Christianity took deep root in Russia. Monasteries multiplied. But even the bps. remained ignorant. Contact with W learning was est. in the 17th c. P. Mogila* est. an influential coll. at Kiev 1631.

4. For a while, in the 18th and early part of the 19th c., the Enlightenment was favorably received, but Alexander I (Aleksandr Pavlovich; 1777–1825; emp. Russ. 1801–25) gradually turned toward mysticism. During most of the 19th c. anti-Protestantism predominated. Sems. were at St. Petersburg, Moscow, Kiev, and Kazan. Up until the USSR (est. 1922) the Gk. (or E) Orthodox Ch. was the state ch.; its membership grew to nearly 100,000,000. Bolsheviks, who came to power Oct./Nov. 1917, took strong measures against the ch. When the Soviet Fed. was recast 1936, Russ. became 1 of 11 states (later expanded to 15 reps.).

5. RCm became fairly strong in Russ. Poland. Ref. chs. in Russ. enjoyed some freedom till the anti-Ger. pressures in WW I and the ascendancy of Communism (beginning 1917) but remained comparatively small (see also *Russian Sects*).

6. Beginning ca. 1558, Estonian, Latvian, and Livonian peasants were resettled in Russ.; some of them were Luth. The 1st Luth. ch. in Moscow was built ca. 1575/76; the cong. was well est. by 1600. But Luths. were hampered by restriction and opposition till ca. 1700, when a new policy encouraged immigration and offered religious freedom. In 1832 the Luth. Ch. obtained, for the Baltic provinces and the congs. in cen. Russ., a ch. const. and service book. But ch. work was repressed under the ascendancy of Communism. Beginning 1929 most Luth. pastors were exiled. Cong. life and activity practically stopped after 1937. From ca. 1939/40 relations bet. state and ch. improved, but mainly, apparently, for the sake of unity in the face of invasion. Even so, in WW II large Luth. settlements suffered under a policy of deportation. In 1957 it became legally possible again to organize congs.

See also *Lutheran Confessions,* A 5.

Russian Bible Society. See *Bible Societies,* 4.

Russian Gospel Association. See *Slavic Gospel Association, Inc.*

Russian Orthodox Church Outside Russia, The. See *Eastern Orthodox Churches,* 6.

Russian Sects. Have been divided into 2 groups: 1. Raskolniks (Raskolniki; Russ. "schismatics") par excellence, who dissent from liturgical reforms of Nikon; divided into Popovtsy (who maintain the hierarchical structure of episcopate and priesthood) and Bezpopovtsy (Russ. "priestless"). 2. Schismatics for other reasons; e. g., (a) Khlysty; originated in the 17th c. or earlier; held that God becomes incarnate in many Christs through their suffering; followed ascetic and ecstatic practices. (b) Skoptsy (Russ. "eunuchs"); originated probably 18th c.; stress Mt 19:12; women usually have their breasts amputated. (c) Doukhobors (Dukhobors); originated 18th c.; follow those as prophets and leaders in whom they believe the Spirit is embodied; emphasize supreme authority of inner experience; reject external ecclesiastical and civil authority (e. g., refusing to pay taxes and do military service). (d) Molokans (or Molokani); offshoot of Doukhobors; antiritualistic; stress authority of the Bible; also called Spiritual Christians. (e) Stundists; originated ca. 1860/64, primarily in S Russ.; probably named after devotional hours (Ger. *Stunden*) at the colony of Rohrbach, visited by Russians; influenced by Baps.; hostile toward ritual, sacraments, and icons.

In pattern of repression and religious freedom they followed in gen. that of other religious groups in Russia.*

See also *Verígin, Peter Vasilich.*

Ruthenian Rite. Byzantine rite (see *Liturgics*) as used in the Galician Ch.

Ruthenians. See *Skarga, Piotr.*

Rutherford, Joseph Franklin (1869–1942). "Judge Rutherford"; b. Boonville, Mo.; joined Jehovah's* witnesses; became their legal adviser ca. 1907; succeeded C. T. Russell*; opposed military service; encouraged conscientious objectors; imprisoned 1917-19.

Ruysbroeck, Jan van (Ruysbroek; Ruusbroec; Rusbroek; Ruisbroeck; 1293–1381). Mystic; b. Ruisbroek, Belg.; priest and vicar Brussels; retired to Augustinian monastery of Groenendael, near Brussels and Waterloo, for a life of contemplation; prior of the monastery; developed a mystical system that borders on pantheism; influenced G. Groote.*

RVOG. See *Radio Voice of the Gospel.*

Rydelius, Andreas (1671–1738). Swed. Luth. philos., theol., bp.; educ. Uppsala; instructor 1699, prof. 1710 Lund; ordained 1725; bp. Lund 1734; influenced by R. Descartes.* Works include *Svenska vitterhets-arbeten; Sensus internus och sensus intimus.*

Rygh, George Alfred Taylor (Mar. 21, 1860–July 16, 1942). B. Chicago, Ill. Educ. Luth. Coll., Decorah, Iowa; Capital U., Columbus, Ohio; Luther Theol. Sem., St. Paul, Minn. Held various teaching positions. Pastor Maine, N. Dak., Wis., Ill., Minn. Hymnist. Tr. Scand. hymns into Eng., including "He is Arisen! Glorious Word!"; "Like the Golden Sun Ascending"; "Holy Spirit, God of Love"; "Speak, O Lord, Thy Servant Heareth"; "He that Believes and is Baptized." Other works include *Morgenrödens Vinger; Sangkor; The Shadow of a Wrong; The Pioneers; John Harding.*

Ryukyu Islands. See *Gützlaff, Karl Friedrich August; Okinawa.*

S

Saadia(h) ben Joseph (Seadiah; Saadja; Arab.: Sa'id al-Fayyumi; ca. 882/892–942). Jewish scholar and commentator; b. Dilaz, Faiyum, Egypt; gaon (head) of Talmudic academy at Sura, Babylonia. Tr. most of the Bible into Arabic. Other works include poetry; a grammatical treatise; polemical writings. See also *Bible Versions,* F; *Grammars,* A; *Lexicons,* A.

Saba. See *Caribbean Islands,* E 7.

Sabah. See *Malaysia,* 1, 5.

Sabaism. See *Sabianism.*

Sabas (439–ca. 531/532). B. Cappadocia; anchorite; founder and cofounder of lauras* in Palestine, including the Great Laura (called Mar Saba) 483, SE of Jerusalem, and the New Laura (see also *Leontius of Byzantium*) 507.

Sabatier, Louis Auguste (1839–1901). Prot. theol.; b. Vallon, Ardèche dept., S Fr.; educ. at the Prot. theol. faculty of Montauban and at Tübingen and Heidelberg; pastor 4 yrs.; prof. Ref. dogmatics Strasbourg ca. 1867/68–ca. 1872/73; expelled for his Fr. sympathies; taught in École libre des sciences religieuses, Paris, 1873; prof. in the Prot. theol. faculty Paris 1877; joined the religious science dept. of the École des Hautes Etudes at the Sorbonne, Paris, 1886; dean of the theol. faculty 1895. Conservative at first, later liberal. Works include *Esquisse d'une philosophie de la religion d'après la psychologie et l'histoire; Les Religions d'autorite et la religion de l'esprit.* See also *Fideism.*

Sabbatarianism. 1. Belief that the Sabbath* must be observed on Saturday (see, e. g., *Adventist Bodies,* 4; *Baptist Churches,* 16–17).

2. Belief that all enjoyment and unnecessary work should be avoided on Sun., in order to enforce sobriety and pious devotion. In Eng. a controversy on the observance of the Sabbath arose in the last part of the reign of Elizabeth* I. To counteract Puritanism (see *Puritans*), James* I issued a Declaration for Sports on the Lord's Day (known as The Book of Sports) 1617/18, defining recreation permissible on Sun. (e. g., archery and dancing). But the controversy continued and the book was publicly burned 1643 by order of parliament.

Sabbath. 1. Day of rest corresponding to the day of rest after creation (Gn 2:3; Ex 20:8, 11; 31:17).

2. When God gave the Israelites manna in double portion on the 6th day, they asked Moses what it meant; Moses said that half of the double portion was for the Sabbath on the 7th day (Ex 16:22-30). This has been regarded as the beginning of Sabbath observance. Cf. Dt 5:12-15.

3. God gave the Israelites Sabbath laws requiring, e. g., cessation from work (Ex 20:10) and increased offerings (Nm 28:9-10). The Sabbath was to be a reminder of creation (Ex 20:8, 11) and of the exodus from Egypt (Dt 5:15).

4. Most Christians regard the OT Sabbath laws as not binding in the NT (see also *Sabbatarianism*). Jesus defended a breach of the Sabbath commandment (Mk 2:23-28): (a) David broke a ceremonial law by eating showbread (1 Sm 21:1-6); (b) "The Sabbath was made for man, and not man for the Sabbath"; (c) "The Son of Man is Lord also of the Sabbath."

5. Some OT observances, including the Sabbath, were only foreshadows of Christ (Cl 2:16-17).

6. Jewish Christians continued to observe the 7th day as Sabbath for a time, but Sunday* soon emerged, by choice of Christians, as the day of worship because Christ had risen on that day (Mt 28:1-10); Christ's appearance on the following Sun. (Jn. 20:26-29) and Pentecost (see *Church Year,* 10) helped mark the day. Cf. Acts 20:7; Rv 1:10. Civil regulations for Sun. observance were added at the time of Constantine* I and later. The view developed in 17th-c. Eng. that Sun. is the NT Sabbath (see also *Presbyterian Confessions,* 3).

7. There is no divinely appointed day of rest in the NT.

8. AC XXVIII 55–64: "It is proper for the Christian assembly to keep such ordinances [e. g., regarding Sun.] for the sake of love and peace, to be obedient to the bishops and parish ministers in such matters, and to observe the regulations in such a way that one does not give offense to another and so that there may be no disorder or unbecoming conduct in the church. However, consciences should not be burdened by contending that such things are necessary for salvation or that it is a sin to omit them, even when no offense is given to others, just as no one would say that a woman commits a sin if without offense to others she goes out with uncovered head.

"Of like character is the observance of Sunday, Easter, Pentecost, and similar holy days and usages. Those who consider the appointment of Sunday in place of the Sabbath as a necessary institution are very much mistaken, for the Holy Scriptures have abrogated the Sabbath and teach that after the revelation of the Gospel all ceremonies of the old law may be omitted. Nevertheless, because it was necessary to appoint a certain day so that the people might know when they ought to assemble, the Christian church appointed Sunday for this purpose, and it was the more inclined and pleased to do this in order that the people might have an example of Christian liberty and might know that the keeping neither of the Sabbath nor of any other day is necessary.

"There are many faculty discussions of the transformation of the law, of the ceremonies of the New Testament, and of the change of the Sabbath, all of which have arisen from the false and erroneous opinion that in Christendom one must have services of God like the Levitical or Jewish services and that Christ commanded the apostles and bishops to devise new ceremonies which would be necessary for salvation. Such errors were introduced into Christendom when the righteousness of faith was no longer taught and preached with clarity and purity. Some argue that although Sunday must not be kept as of divine obligation, it must nevertheless be kept as almost of divine obligation, and they prescribe the kind and amount of work that may be done on the day of rest. What are such discussions but snares of conscience? For although they undertake to lighten and mitigate human regulations, yet there can be no moderation or mitigation as long as the opinion remains and prevails that their observance is necessary. And this opinion will remain as long as there is no understanding of the righteousness of faith and Christian liberty."

Cf. SC I 5–6; LC I 78–102.

Sabbath School. See *Sunday School.*

Sabbatine Privilege. In RCm, privilege granted Carmelites* and related confraternities: special intercession of Mary and early release from purgatory, provided certain conditions have been fulfilled. The name is drawn from the fact that Sat. (the Sabbath*) is regarded as Mary's day.

Sabbatum (Lat. "Sabbath"). Ecclesiastical term for Sat.

Sabellius (fl. early 3d c. AD). Leader of modalistic monarchians at Rome; excommunicated by Calixtus I ca. 220; his view, which included patripassianism,* was called Sabellianism, his followers Sabellians. See also *Monarchianism,* B 2, 6.

Sabianism (Sabaism). Religion of the Sabians (see *Mandaeans*).

Sacer, Gottfried Wilhelm (1635–99). B. Naumburg, Saxony, Ger.; educ. Jena; entered military service 1665; toured Holland and Den.; lawyer Brunswick and Wolfenbüttel; hymnist. Hymns include "Gott fähret auf gen Himmel."

Sacerdotalism. View acc. to which the laity can est. relation with God only through priests.

Sachs, Hans (1494–1576). Poet, dramatist; b. Nürnberg, Ger.; trained to be shoemaker; became Meistersinger; cen. figure in W. R. Wagner's* *Die Meistersinger von Nürnberg.* Works include "Die Wittenbergisch Nachtigall," written in M. Luther's honor. See also *Religious Drama,* 3.

Sack, August Friedrich Wilhelm (1703–86). Father of F. S. G. Sack*; Ref. theol.; b. Harzgerode, Ger.; educ. Frankfurt an der Oder and Leiden; pastor Magdeburg 1731; court preacher Berlin 1740. Works include *Vertheidigter Glaube der Christen.*

Sack, Friedrich Samuel Gottfried (1738–1817). Son of A. F. W. Sack*; father of K. H. Sack*; b. Magdeburg, Ger.; educ. Frankfurt an der Oder and in Eng.; tutor; preacher Magdeburg 1769–77; court and cathedral preacher Berlin 1777; mem. high consistory 1786; bp. of the Ev. Ch. 1816; advocated Prussian* Union. Works include *Über die Vereinigung der beiden protestantischen Kirchenparteien in der Preussischen Monarchie.*

Sack, Karl Heinrich (ca. 1789/90-1875). Son of F. S. G. Sack*; b. Berlin, Ger.; educ. Göttingen; soldier and chaplain; toured Ger., Holland, and Eng.; taught at Berlin and Bonn; also became pastor Bonn. Works include *Die christliche Apologetik; Die christliche Polemik.*

Sacrament and the Sacraments. A. In ecclesiastical and late Lat., *sacramentum* ("something to be kept sacred") has various meanings, e. g., (1) a secret; (2) the gospel revelation; (3) a mystery; (4) a sacrament (in the sense of ch. rites, e. g., Baptism and Communion); (5) the office of the ministry.

The term has been traced to the time of Tertullian, when it was applied, e. g., to Christian rites. The Vulgate uses *sacramentum* for the Gk. word *mysterion* Eph 1:9; 3:3, 9; 5:32; Cl 1:26-27; 1 Ti 3:16; Rv 1:20; 17:7. In all these passages the KJV and RSV use the word "mystery."

B. M. Luther: "The sacred writings have only 1 *sacramentum,* i. e., Christ Jesus" (WA 6, 97); he explains this by references to OT and NT passages in which he uses the word *Geheimnis* ("mystery") in his Ger. Bible tr. He compares the "great *sacramentum* of the incarnation of the Son of God" with Jacob's ladder (WA 43, 582); here too *sacramentum* is tr. *Geheimnis* in the Walch eds. But when, in the same passage, he uses the pl. *sacramenta,* the Walch eds. tr. *Sacramente* (Eng.: "He descends to us through the Word and the sacraments").

C. Luther (WA 56, 321–322) quotes Augustine of Hippo (*De trinitate,* IV iii 6 and IV xx 27): "To cause both our resurrections, He [Christ] appointed beforehand and set forth in *sacramentum* and type His own one resurrection. . . . In it was wrought a *sacramentum* as regards the inner man." In this passage, *sacramentum* has been tr. "mystery."

D. Without the mystery of the incarnation we would not have our liturgical sacraments. We are baptized into the death of the incarnate Son of God (Ro 6:3) and in Communion receive His body and blood (Mt 26:26-28).

E. The doer, or agent (Lat. *agens*), in the sacraments is Christ Himself. The act performed by a minister is not simply a *signum significans* ("sign that means something") but a *signum efficax* ("creative sign"). Hence Luther not only asks: "What does such baptizing with water signify?" but also says: "It effects forgiveness of sins, delivers from death and the devil, and grants eternal salvation to all who believe, as the Word and promise of God declare. . . . Baptism [is] a gracious water of life and a washing of regeneration in the Holy Spirit, as St. Paul wrote to Titus (3:5-8)." And: "Forgiveness of sins, life, and salvation are given to us in the sacrament [of the altar]." (SC IV 6, 10; VI 6)

The "community" in which the sacraments are administered is the ch., the body of Christ. Luther: "In the sacrament [of the altar] we are all, as it were, baked into 1 cake. For there is 1 [Ger. *einerlei*] faith, 1 confession, love, and hope. . . . Christ instituted this sacrament to keep the Christians together." (WA 52, 209 and 210)

Irenaeus: "Those . . . who do not partake of [Christ] are neither nourished into life from the mother's breasts nor do they enjoy that most limpid fountain which issues from the body of Christ." (*Adversus haereses,* III xxiv 1)

F. The union effected by faith bet. Christ and the believer is called mystical union. We are "baptized into Christ Jesus" (Ro 6:3). In Communion, "the cup of blessing which we bless, is it not a participation in the blood of Christ? The bread which we break, is it not a participation in the body of Christ? Because there is one bread, we who are many are one body, for we all partake of the one bread" (1 Co 10:16-17). But it is not the mere performance of a sacrament, nor even the reception of the body and blood of Christ, that creates the mystical union. For an unbeliever also receives the body and blood of Christ in Communion, but not to salvation; he does not thereby enter into the mystical union (1 Co 11:27-29). Faith alone joins one to Christ and so effects the mystical union.

G. These sacraments have been called holy mysteries of sublime purity and awesome mysteries of trembling (not of fear, but of joy).

H. Proper observance of the sacraments follows the directions of Christ's institution. Communion is observed in remembrance of Him. "To remember Christ is to remember His benefits and realize that they are truly offered to us" (AC XXIV 31 [Lat.]). "The remembrance of Christ is . . . the remembrance of Christ's blessings and the acceptance of them by faith, so that they make us alive" (Ap XXIV 72). "The command of Christ, 'Do this,' which comprehends the whole action or administration of this sacrament (namely, that in a Christian assembly we take bread and wine, consecrate it, distribute it, receive it, eat and drink it, and therewith proclaim the Lord's death), must be kept integrally and inviolately." (FC SD VII 84)

I. Luther calls Baptism not only important and precious, but a priceless medicine, an inexpressible, infinite, divine treasure (LC IV 26, 34, 37, 43) and the Lord's Supper a great and precious treasure, gift, and blessing, "a pure, wholesome, soothing medicine which aids and quickens us in both soul and body." (LC V 22, 29, 36, 56, 68, 78)

J. The miracles of Christ happened at a certain time for certain persons; the sacraments are for the universal ch. of all time. Cf. J. Gerhard, *Locus de sacramentis,* 10.

K. Fellowship with Christ involves fellowship

with one another (1 Jn 1:6-7; cf. Ro 12:4-5; Eph 4:25). Luther: "Disharmony and discord conflict with the Sacrament of the Altar. . . . The name is 'Communion,' the reality [Lat. *res*] [is] the unity of hearts, as [there is] 1 faith, 1 Baptism, 1 Lord, 1 hope." (WA 1, 329)

L. The no. of sacraments depends either on arbitrary listing or on definition of "sacrament." RCs list 7 sacraments, without defining "sacrament." Ap XII 41: "Absolution* may properly be called a sacrament of penitence"; this must be understood in the sense of LC IV 74: "Baptism . . . comprehends also the 3d sacrament, formerly called Penance, which is really nothing else than Baptism." "If we define sacraments as 'rites which have the command of God and to which the promise of grace has been added,' we can easily determine which are sacraments in the strict sense. . . . The genuine sacraments, therefore, are Baptism, the Lord's Supper, and absolution (which is the sacrament of penitence). . . . If ordination is interpreted this way, we shall not object either to calling the laying on of hands a sacrament. . . . Ultimately, if we should list as sacraments all the things that have God's command and a promise added to them, then why not prayer, which can most truly be called a sacrament?" (Ap XIII 3, 4, 12, 16). Luther: "A sacrament must have 2 things for sure: God's Word and the instituted external sign [or means, or element; Ger. *Zeichen*]; these we find only in the 2 sacraments [Baptism and Communion]." (WA 11, 454) ES

See also *Grace, Means of,* I, III, IV; *Roman Catholic Church,* B 4, 6, 7; *Sacraments, Roman Catholic; Worship.*

A. C. Piepkorn, *What the Symbolical Books of the Lutheran Church Have to Say About Worship and the Sacraments* (St. Louis, 1952).

Sacramental Eating and Drinking. Eating and drinking that takes place only in the Lord's Supper: by it Christ's body and blood are received in, with, and under the bread and wine. See also *Grace, Means of,* IV, 3.

Sacramental Union (Lat. *unio sacramentalis*). Union of bread and body, wine and blood in the Sacrament of the Altar. See also *Grace, Means of,* IV 3; *Ubiquity.*

Sacramentalism. 1. View and practice that assigns to sacraments a higher inherent saving power than the Word. 2. Belief that sacraments are inherently efficacious and necessary to salvation and can bestow grace on the soul. 3. Belief that nature and life have spiritual meaning and are symbols of the divine.

See also *Sacramentarian.*

Sacramentals. In RCm, holy signs, similar to sacraments, but instituted by the ch., that signify effects, esp. spiritual, obtained not directly, but through the intercession of the ch.; they dispose men to receive the main effect of sacraments and make various occasions holy. Sacramentals include priestly blessings and the prayers and ceremonies of the RC ritual. Blessed objects (e. g., palms, candles, holy water, medals, scapulars) are not sacramentals in the strict sense but only in a derived sense.

Sacramentarian. Term applied by M. Luther to H. Zwingli,* J. Oecolampadius,* and others (cf. St. L. ed., XVII, 2176) who held that in Communion bread and wine are Christ's body and blood only in a "sacramental" (i. e., metaphorical) sense. The term has also been used to denote sacramentalists (see *Sacramentalism*).

Sacramentary. Service book of the early W ch., containing the celebrant's part of the mass, prayers for baptism, ordination, blessing, and consecration.

See also *Service Books.*

Sacraments, Roman Catholic. The Council of Trent* fixed the no. of sacraments at 7 (baptism, confirmation, eucharist, penance, extreme unction, order, matrimony) and called them necessary for salvation (Sess. VII, Canons 1 and 4). Baptism and penance are called sacraments of the dead, because they are administered to those dead in sin; the others, sacraments of the living. Baptism, confirmation, and order are held to imprint an indelible character (see *Character indelebilis*) on the soul and therefore cannot be repeated. The validity of a sacrament is not made dependent on the personal worthiness of the officiating priest, provided he has the intention of doing, in the sacrament, what the ch. does. See also *Grace, Means of,* I 8; *Opus operatum; Roman Catholic Church,* B 4, 6, 7; *Sacrament and the Sacraments; William of Auxerre.*

Sacred Heart of Jesus, Devotion to the. Devotion paid in the RC Ch. to the physical heart of Jesus. An early exponent was Gertrude the Great (see *Gertrude,* 1). M. M. Alacoque* claimed private revelations in the matter 1673–75. Jesuits supported her claims with increasing success. Leo XIII (see *Popes,* 29) consecrated the world to the Sacred Heart 1899. See also *Heart of Mary, Immaculate.*

Sacred Literature. The Hinayana school of Buddhism* has its sacred canon in Pali, mainly in *Tipitaka.* The Mahayana school of Buddhism has its sacred literature in Skt.; it includes *Saddharmapundarika* ("Lotus of Good Religion" [or "of the Good Law"; or "of the True Doctrine"]), *Sukhavativyuha* ("Detailed Account of the Land of Bliss"), *Prajnaparamita* ("Perfection of Wisdom"), and *Lankavatara Sutra* ("Narrative of an incarnation [of Buddha] in Ceylon"; recognized text of the Zen school). Hinduism* began under influence of the Veda,* the *Rig-Veda* alone consisting of ca. 1,000 hymns addressed to the gods during sacrifice. Later Hindu religious literature includes the *Ramayana, Mahabharata,* and 18 *Puranas* (which deal with cosmogony, hist., and religious philos.). See also *Church of Christ, Scientist; Confucianism,* 2; *Holy Scripture; Islam,* 2; *Judaism; Latter Day Saints; Shastras.*

Sacrifice for Sin. See *Atonement.*

Sacrilege. All desecration, or profanation, of holy things by despising, polluting, or misusing things consecrated; cf. Lv 10:1-7; 19:8; Nm 3:4; 2 Sm 6:6-7; 2 Ch 26:16-21; Mt 21:12-13; Ro 2:22; 1 Co 3:17.

Sacristan. One in charge of sacred vessels, vestments, and whatever else is needed for sacred functions; in gen., one charged with the care of a ch. and its sacristy and furnishings; sometimes equivalent to sexton.* See also *Verger.*

Sacristy. Room in, or attached to, a ch. (and usually near the altar), where vestments, sacred vessels, altar linen and hangings, and sometimes ch. records are kept. Often used by officiants to prepare for a service. Often called vestry.*

Sacrosanctum concilium. See *Vatican Councils,* 2.

Sadakat. See *Islam,* 3.

Saddharma-pundarika. See *Sacred Literature.*

Sadducees. See *Judaism,* 2.

Sadoleto, Jacopo (1477–1547). B. Modena, It.; bp. Carpentras, Fr., 1517; cardinal 1536; mem. Paul* III's commission for reform (see also *Contarini, Gasparo*); papal legate to Fr. 1542; active at Council of Trent.* See also *Counter Reformation,* 4.

Saeculum obscurum. Term coined by C. Baronius* for ca. 880–ca. 1046 (last yrs. of the Carolingians to the beginning of the Gregorian reform [named after Gregory VII (see *Popes,* 7) but begun under Clement II (Suidger; Suitger; pope 1046–47)]), a period darkened esp. in Fr. and more esp. It. by inner decay and outer threats by Saracens, Vikings, and Hung., which adversely affected morals, civil order, and cultural development.

Sagittarius, Caspar (Kaspar; Schütze; 1643–94). Nephew of T. Sagittarius*; b. Lüneburg, Ger.; educ. Helmstedt, Leipzig, Wittenberg, Jena, and Altdorf;

rector Saalfeld 1668; prof. Jena 1671; specialized in ch. hist. of Saxony and Thuringia. Works include *Dissertatio de praecipuis scriptoribus historiae Germanicae.*

Sagittarius, Thomas (1577–1621). Uncle of C. Sagittarius*; poet; b. Stendal, Ger.; prof. Gk. and metaphysics Jena; rector Breslau. Works include *Horatius christianus; Horatius profanus; Disputationes politicae extraordinariae.*

Sahidic Bible Version. See *Bible Versions,* D.

Sailer, Johann Michael (1751–1832). RC theol.; b. Aresing, near Augsburg, Upper Bav., Ger.; prof. dogmatics Ingolstadt 1780; prof. ethics Dillingen 1784; prof. Ingolstadt 1799, Landshut 1800; bp. Regensburg 1829. Influenced by RC enlightenment movement; avoided scholastic concepts; based his pastoral theol. on Scripture and primitive Christianity. Works include *Vernunftlehre für Menschen wie sie sind; Vorlesungen aus der Pastoraltheologie.*

St. Andrew, Brotherhood of. See *Brotherhood of St. Andrew.*

St. Ansgar Academy. Founded at St. Ansgar, Iowa, 1878; supported by St. Ansgar circuit of The Conf. for the Norw.-Dan. Ev. Luth. Ch. in Am. (see *Danish Lutherans in America,* 3); became school of The United* Norw. Luth. Ch. in Am.; discontinued 1910.

St. Chrischona Pilgrim Mission. See *Chrischona.*

St. Christopher (is.). See *Caribbean Islands,* E 5.

St. Croix (is.). See *Caribbean Islands,* E 8.

St. Elizabeth. See *Elizabeth.*

St. Eustatius (is.). See *Caribbean Islands,* E 7.

St. Gall. See *Gall.*

St. George Lutheran Church, Halifax, N. S. See *Canada,* A 1.

Saint-Germain, Edict of. See *France,* 9.

Saint-Germain, Peace of. See *France,* 9.

St. John (is.). *See Caribbean Islands,* E 8.

St. John's College, Winfield, Kans. See *Ministry, Education of,* VIII C 2 n; *Missouri and Other States, The Evangelical Lutheran Synod of.*

St. Joseph Institute for the Deaf, St. Louis, Mo. See *Deaf,* 4.

St. Joseph's Society of the Sacred Heart (Josephites; Josephite Fathers; Josephite Missionaries). RC miss. soc. founded 1866 Mill Hill (now in Hendon, suburb of London), Eng., as St. Joseph's Soc. for For. Missions by Herbert Alfred Vaughan (1832–1903; b. Gloucester, Eng.; 2d bp. Salford 1872; abp. Westminster 1892; cardinal 1893); chief work among Negroes. St. Joseph's Sem., Baltimore, Md., was est. 1888. The Am. community formed the new Soc. of St. Joseph, est. 1932.

St. Lucia (is.). See *Caribbean Islands,* E 5.

St. Martin (is.). See *Caribbean Islands,* E 7.

St. Maur, Congregation of. See *Maurists.*

St. Olaf College, Northfield, Minn. See *Ministry, Education of,* VIII B 23.

St. Paul's College, Concordia, Mo. See *Ministry, Education of,* VIII C 2 o.

Saint-Riquier, Abbey Church of. See *Church Architecture,* 7.

Saint-Saens, Charles Camille (1835–1921). Composer, organist, poet; b. Paris, Fr.; organist Paris; influenced by F. Liszt.* Works include *Oratorio de Noel; Samson et Dalila* (opera); *Le Déluge* (oratario). See also *Offertory.*

Saint-Simon, Comte de, Claude Henri de Rouvroy (1760–1825). Philos.; b. Paris, Fr.; fought with Fr. army in Am. Revolution; regarded as founder of Fr. socialism; his views distorted by his followers.

St. Thomas (is.). See *Caribbean Islands,* E 8.

St. Victor, Order of. See *Victorines.*

Saints. The word "saints" has been used by the ch. in several ways. In Scripture it refers to believers on earth (e. g., Ro 1:7; Acts 9:32) and in heaven (e. g., Mt 27:52).

In current ecclesiastical language, "saints" refers to the faithful departed who have been recognized by the ch. as deserving the title. In RCm this is done by canonization. Luths. have no rite of canonization and ordinarily do not grant the title "saint" to anyone except those who were canonized before the Reformation.

For saints who have been included in Luth. calendars and service books see *Church Year,* 16–17. EFP

Saints (Plymouth Brethren). See *Brethren, Plymouth.*

Saints, Communion of. See *Church.*

Saints, Veneration of. 1. Paying special honor to departed ones (esp. those noted for holy life). In many religions a saint is a superhuman character who mediates bet. divine power and human beings. Cults of such saints existed in Gk. religion, Buddhism, Taoism, Confucianism, and other religions, sometimes with stress on ethical life.

2. Early Christian saints were martyrs (see *Martyr*), honored in their community and soon elsewhere. Services were held above their graves and altars and chs. erected. This developed into the custom of placing relics of saints under or in altars. By the 3d c., belief in the efficacy of the intercession of saints was est.

3. In the early ch., those who had suffered (e. g., imprisonment, torture, exile) for their faith were regarded as martyrs. By ca. the end of the 2d c., confessor* (one who suffered for the faith) and martyr (one who died for the faith) were distinguished. After the Roman persecutions (see *Persecution of Christians*), a confessor was a Christian noted for virtuous life. Confessors and ascetics were added to saints, making it possible to include Mary and John.

4. In the Middle Ages, pilgrimages* to shrines of saints, honoring relics, creation of patron saints and feasts for saints, etc. lent added impetus to veneration of saints.

5. In Eastern* Orthodox Chs. the creation of saints is a proclamation rather than a process and is less formal than in the RC Ch. Moral perfection and miraculous acts are prerequisites for sainthood. Veneration of saints is incorporated into the liturgy. See also *Menologion; Synaxarion.*

6. As the Roman see extended its power it assumed right of canonization. The 1st canonization was that of Ulrich von Augsburg 993 (d. 973; bp. Augsburg 923). Alexander III (see *Popes,* 9) forbade honoring anyone as saint without permission of the Roman see. Acc. to CIC 1277, 1, only those canonized by the RC Ch. may be publicly venerated. CIC 1999–2141 prescribe the process of canonization. Acc. to RCm, works of saints add to the treasury* of merits. CIC 1255, 1, distinguishes latria,* hyperdulia, and dulia. But the distinction bet. worship and veneration has not always been observed (e. g., D. Attwater, *A Catholic Dictionary,* 2d ed., rev. [New York, 1956], p. 512, speaks of veneration as worship). Some contemporary RCs affirm the all-sufficient mediation of Christ and try to justify veneration of saints and prayer for their intercession on basis of the doctrine of mystical body of Christ and the communion of saints.

7. Veneration of saints was influenced by pre-Christian cults of the dead. At times Christian saints replaced heathen gods. Cathari* and Waldenses* rejected prayers to saints.

8. The Luth. confessions assume the existence of saints and include them in the *communio* sanctorum.* Saints pray for the ch. in gen. (Ap XXI 9) but are not mediators of redemption (Ap XXI 14–30). Gen. the saints are given the same attributes they had on earth. Prayers to saints are prohibited. (SA-II II 25)

9. The Luth. confessions approve honoring the saints (AC XXI 1). They are honored in 3 ways: 1. By thanking God for examples of His mercy;

2. By using the saints as example for strengthening our faith; 3. By imitating their faith and other virtues. (Ap XXI 4–7) EL

Saints' Days. See *Church Year,* 13, 14, 16, 17.

Saints' Plays. See *Religious Drama,* 2.

Saker, Alfred. See *Africa,* F 7.

Saladin. See *Coptic Church,* 2.

Salat. *Islam,* 3.

Saldenus, Guilielmus (Seldenus; Willem Salden; pseudonym Christianus Liberinus; 1627–94). Ref. theol.; b. Utrecht, Neth.; educ. Utrecht; pastor at various places in the Neth.; worked for peace in the ch. Works include *Neerlands interest, tot vrede der Kercke.*

Salesians. RC soc. founded in the 19th c. by Giovanni (or John) Bosco (1815–88; b. Becchi, near Turin, It.; priest 1841); named after Francis* of Sales; devoted mainly to educ.

Salig, Christian August (1691 [1692?]–1738). B. Domersleben, near Magdeburg, Ger.; educ. Halle and Jena; taught at Halle and Wolfenbüttel. Works include a hist. of the AC and of the Council of Trent.*

Salmasius, Claudius (Claude de Saumaise; 1588–1653). Huguenot scholar; b. Sémur-en-Auxois, E cen. Fr.; educ. Paris and Heidelberg; prof. Leiden. Works include *Defensio regia pro Carolo I.*

Salmerón, Alfonso (1515–85). B. Toledo, Sp.; helped found Society* of Jesus; influential at Council of Trent.*

Salmon, George (1819–1904). B. Dublin, Ireland; educ. Trin. Coll. (=U. of Dublin); deacon 1844; priest 1845; regius prof. divinity 1866–88, provost 1888–1904 Dublin; chancellor St. Patrick's Cathedral, Dublin, 1871–1904. Works include *A Historical Introduction to the Study of the Books of the New Testament; The Infallibility of the Church.* See also *Isagogics,* 3.

Salt, Tasting of. See *Baptism, Liturgical,* 3.

Saltmarsh, John (d. 1647). Eng. mystic; educ. Cambridge; Angl. pastor Heslerton, Yorkshire; later espoused freedom of faith and conscience. Works include *Dawnings of Light; Groanes for Liberty; Reasons for Unity.*

Saltonstall, Gurdon (1666–1724). B. Haverhill, Mass.; educ. Harvard Coll., Cambridge, Mass.; ordained Cong. minister New London, Conn., 1691; gov. Conn. 1707; suggested the Syn. of Saybrook (Conn.); influential in chartering Yale Coll. and in its removal from Saybrook to New Haven.

Salutation. See *Worship, Parts of,* 10.

Salvador, El. See *Central America,* F.

Salvation. See *Predestination; Redemption.*

Salvation Army. 1. Founded 1865 in London, Eng., by William Booth (1829–1912; "General Booth"; b. Nottingham, Eng.; began revival preaching when he was ca. 16; regular preacher of the Meth. New Connection [see *Methodist Churches,* 1] 1852); the Salv. Army movement began in a series of informal open air and tent meetings designed to reach the unreached. The 1st name, Christian Mission, was changed to the present name 1878. The movement soon spread to the US, Can., and elsewhere.

2. The Salv. Army has no formal creed and gives little attention to doctrinal differences. In gen., it is Arminian (see *Arminianism*) and regards sacraments as unessential. Admission to membership is based on pledges to Christian conduct, understood to include total abstinence from intoxicating liquors and harmful drugs. Services are largely informal and include preaching by women, junior meetings, and S. S.

3. Govt. of the Salv. Army is administered by its Gen., assisted by other officers. Internat. HQ are in London; US HQ NYC; Can. and Bermuda HQ Toronto.

4. Work is divided into field work (spiritual regeneration) and soc. work.

See also *American Rescue Workers; Volunteers of America.*

Salvatorians. See *Societas Divini Salvatoris.*

Salvianus (ca. 400–ca. 480). B. Trier, Ger.; he and his wife vowed continence; monk at Lérins, Fr.; priest ca. 428; presbyter Marseille ca. 439. Works include *De gubernatione Dei.*

MPL, 53.

Salza, Hermann von. See *Military Religious Orders,* c.

Salzburgers, Banishment of. The hist. of Protestantism in Salzburg, long ruled by abps., is largely a hist. of oppression and persecution. In 1588 Prots. in the city of Salzburg were ordered to recant or abandon their property and leave the country; many went to Austria, Swabia, and elsewhere. The strictures were extended to the entire region of Salzburg 1613–15. Some Prots. went underground. In the 1680s J. Schaitberger* led a group that tried unsuccessfully to gain legal recognition under terms of the Peace of Westphalia.* The last edict of banishment was issued 1731. Many thousands went to Prussia 1732–33. A small group settled 1734 near Savannah, Ga., at a place they called Ebenezer. See also *Bergmann, Christopher; Bergmann, John Ernest; Boltzius, Johann Martin; Child and Family Service Agencies,* 3; *Gronau, Israel Christian; Urlsperger, Samuel.*

G. G. G. Göcking, *Vollkommene Emigrations-Geschichte von denen aus dem Ertz-Bissthum Saltzburg vertriebenen . . . Lutheranern,* 2 vols. (Frankfurt and Leipzig, 1734–37); W. J. Finck, *Lutheran Landmarks and Pioneers in America* (Philadelphia, 1913); P. A. Strobel, *The Salzburgers and Their Descendants* (Baltimore, 1855); C. Mauelshagen, *Salzburg Lutheran Expulsion and Its Impact* (New York, 1962).

Salzmann, Christian Gotthilf (1744–1811). B. Sömmerda, Ger.; pastor, later teacher, Dessau; founded school at Schnepfenthal, Thuringia; emphasized the role of nature and family in educ. Works include *Über die wirksamsten Mittel, Kindern Religion beyzubringen; Conrad Kiefer.* See also *Philanthropinism.*

Sam, Konrad (1483–1533). B. Rottenacker, near Ehingen, Ger.; educ. Freiburg and Tübingen; preacher Brackenheim, near Heilbronn; adherent of M. Luther; dismissed from office; preacher and reformer Ulm; sided with H. Zwingli on the Lord's Supper.

Samelats. See *Lapland.*

Samoa (Samoa Islands; formerly Navigators Islands). Fertile volcanic islands in SW cen. Pacific Ocean; formerly ruled by native chiefs. Divided: Am. Samoa (Eastern Samoa; *area:* ca. 76 sq. mi.; administered by US, Brit., and Ger. 1889–99; granted to US 1899) and Territory of Western Samoa (*area:* ca. 1,133 sq. mi.; granted 1879 to Ger. by treaty with native ruler; ruled by US, Brit., and Ger. 1889–99; recognized as Ger. 1899–1900; mandate of New Zealand 1920; UN trust territory 1947; indep. mem. Brit. Commonwealth 1962.

A Samoan visited Tonga 1828, learned Christianity from Meths. and brought it to Samoa. J. Williams* visited Samoa 1830 and left some Cong. Tahitian teachers. LMS entered the field in the 1830s. Most of the pop. is Christian. RCs began work 1845. Assemblies of God and Seventh-day Adventists also have missions.

Samson, Hermann (1579–1643). Luth. theol.; b. Riga, Latvia; educ. Rostock and Wittenberg; preacher Riga 1608; supt. Livonia 1622; prof. Riga 1631; mem. Dorpat 1633. Est. chs. and schools.

San Salvador. See *Central America,* A.

Sanatoria. See *Hospitals.*

Sanchez, Thomas (1550–1610). B. Córdoba, Sp.; Jesuit 1567. His *De sancto matrimonii sacramento* includes explicit discussion of sexual immorality.

Sanctification. In a wide sense, sanctification includes all effects of God's Word in man (cf., e. g., Acts

26:18; Eph 5:26; 2 Th 2:13; Heb 10:14; 1 Ptr 1:2). See also *Conversion,* III; *Good Works.*

In a narrow sense, sanctification is the spiritual growth (1 Co 3:9; 9:24; Eph 4:15; Ph 3:12) that follows justification (Mt 7:16-18; Jn 3:6; Eph 2:10). By God's grace (Gl 5:22-23; Ph 2:13) a Christian cooperates in this work (2 Co 6:1; 7:1; Ph 2:12; 1 Ti 4:14; FC SD II 65–66); through the Holy Spirit's work faith is increased daily, love strengthened, and the image of God renewed (cf., e. g., Jn 14:26; 16:13-14; Ro 6:15-23; 8:15-16, 26; 14:17; 15:13; 1 Co 12:7-11; Gl 5:16-18; 2 Ptr 3:18). A believer's good works are not perfect; but sins of weakness are forgiven (Jn 15:3). Sanctification differs in the same Christian at different times (Ro 7:14-19; Gl 2:11; 5:17; 1 Jn 1:8).

God works sanctification only through the means of grace.*

The most comforting part of the doctrine of sanctification is that which speaks of the completion of sanctification in heaven (Ps 17:15; 1 Co 13:12; 15:20-57; Rv 7:9-17; 21:4-7). RLS

R. L. Sommer, "Sanctification," *The Abiding Word,* II, ed. T. Laetsch (St. Louis, 1947), 275–298; A. Köberle, *The Quest for Holiness,* tr. J. C. Mattes (Minneapolis, 1936); C. G. Carlfelt, "The Work of the Holy Spirit," *What Lutherans Are Thinking,* ed. E. C. Fendt (Columbus, Ohio, 1947); C. J. I. Bergendoff, *The Secular Idea of Progress and the Christian Doctrine of Sanctification* (Rock Island, 1933); R. Hermann, *Luthers These "Gerecht und Sünder zugleich"* (Gütersloh, 1960); K. Barth, *The Christian Life,* tr. J. S. McNab (London, 1930); W. E. Hulme, *The Dynamics of Sanctification* (Minneapolis, 1966).

Sanctifying grace. See *Gratia habitualis.*

Sanctorum communio. See *Communio sanctorum.*

Sanctus. See *Worship, Parts of,* 11.

Sanday, William (1843–1920). Angl. scholar; b. Holme Pierrepont, near Nottingham, Eng.; educ. Oxford; priest 1869; prof. Oxford; canon Christ Ch., Oxford. Works include *The Authorship and Historical Character of the Fourth Gospel; An Examination of Harnack's "What Is Christianity?"; The Criticism of the Fourth Gospel; The Gospels in the Second Century.*

Sandecki-Malecki, Jan (Maletius; ca. 1482/90–1567). Educ. Kraków, Poland; pub. Polish tracts and books; ev. pastor Elk, Prussia, 1537. Works include a tr. of M. Luther's SC.

Sandegren, Johannes (Nov. 20, 1883–Nov. 15, 1962). B. Madura, S India; son of a Swed. Luth. miss.; educ. Uppsala, Swed.; ordained 1906; miss. to India 1907; pres. The Fed. of Ev. Luth. Chs. in India 1926; bp. Tamil Ev. Luth. Ch. (see *India,* 10) 1933; taught at Tranquebar (see *Ministry, Education of,* XI B 9). Works include *The Suffering God.*

Sandel, Andrew (Nov. 30, 1671–May 11, 1744). B. Hallnas parish, Roslagen, Swed.; Luth. pastor; to Am. 1702 at request of A. Rudman*; pastor in and around Philadelphia, Pa.; returned to Swed. 1719; pastor Hedemora. See also *Provost.*

Sandell-Berg, Lina (Carolina Vilhelmina nee Sandell; 1832–1903). Swed. hymnist; daughter of Luth. pastor at Fröderyd. Many of her hymns were pub. in *Ahnfelts Sanger.*

Sandeman, Robert. See *Disciples of Christ,* 1.

Sandemanians. See *Disciples of Christ,* 1.

Sanders, Henry Arthur (1868–1956). Philol.; b. Livermore, Maine; educ. Mich., Berlin, and Munich univs.; taught at U. of Mich., U. of Minn., U. of Ill.; noted for studies of Biblical MSS. Works include *The New Testament Manuscripts in the Freer Collection; A Third-Century Papyrus Codex of the Epistles of Paul.*

Sandin, John (d. Sept. 22, 1748). B. Swed.; pastor Racoon (or Raccoon), N. J.; helped found Pa. Ministerium. See also *Provost.*

Sandomierz, Consensus of. See *Poland,* 2; *Reformed Confessions,* E 5.

Sandt, George Washington (Feb. 22, 1854–Jan. 8, 1931). B. Belfast, Pa.; educ. Luth. Theol. Sem., Philadelphia; pastor of several congs. in Pa.; prof. Augustana Coll., Rock Island, Ill., 1884–89; dir. Luth. Theol. Sem., Philadelphia, 1904–31. Ed. *The Lutheran.* Other works include *How to Become a Christian; Ninety-five Theses for Protestant Church Doors; Should Lutherans Get Together?*

Sandusky Resolutions. Adopted by the ALC assembled in conv. Oct. 14–20, 1938, Sandusky, Ohio; read in part: "Resolved, . . . 2. That we declare the Brief Statement of the Missouri Synod, together with the Declaration of our Commission, a sufficient doctrinal basis for Church fellowship between the Missouri Synod and the American Lutheran Church.

"3. That . . . we are firmly convinced that it is neither necessary nor possible to agree in all nonfundamental doctrines. Nevertheless, we are willing to continue the negotiations concerning the points termed in our Declaration as 'not divisive of Church-fellowship,' and recognized as such by the Missouri Synod's resolutions . . . .

"4. . . . We . . . expect that henceforth by both sides the erection of opposition altars shall be carefully avoided and that just coordination of mission work shall earnestly be sought.

"5. . . . We believe that the brief statement viewed in the light of our Declaration is not in contradiction to the Minneapolis Theses which are the basis of our membership in the American Lutheran Conference. We are not willing to give up this membership."

The resolutions also reported progress in negotiations with the ULC.

Official Minutes, Fifth Convention of the American Lutheran Church (Columbus, Ohio, 1938), pp. 255–257; "Resolutions of the American Lutheran Church," *The Lutheran Witness,* LVII (1938), 373; "The Resolutions of the American Lutheran Church with Reference to Lutheran Union," *CTM,* X (1939), 59–61; "The Fellowship Convention," *Lutheran Standard,* XCV, No. 46 (Nov. 12, 1938), 3–13; *Documents of Lutheran Unity in America,* ed. R. C. Wolf (Philadelphia, 1966), pp. 400–401.

Sandwich Islands. See *Hawaii.*

Sanger, Margaret. See *Family Planning,* 1, 3.

Sangstad, Christian. See *Canada,* A 24.

Sanhedrin. Ancient Jewish supreme council and tribunal.

Sankey, Ira David (1840–1908). Meth. lay evangelist; b. Edinburgh, Pa.; choir leader; S. S. supt.; assoc. with D. L. Moody* from 1870. Compiled *Gospel Hymns; Sacred Songs.*

Sankhya. See *Brahmanism,* 4.

Sansovino, Andrea (Contucci; 1460–1529). B. Monte San Savino, near Arezzo, It.; Sculptor, architect. Works include *Baptism of Christ; Annunciation; Madonna, Child, and St. Anne; John the Baptist.*

Santa Claus. See *Nicholas* (fl. 1st half of 4th c. AD).

Santa Cruz. See *Caribbean Islands,* E 8.

Santal Mission of the Northern Churches. See *Norwegian Foreign Missions,* 3.

Santayana, George Agustin Nicolas de (1863–1952). Poet, philos.; b. Madrid, Sp.; to US 1872; educ. Harvard (Cambridge, Mass.) and Berlin, Ger.; taught at Harvard 1889–1912; lived in Eng., Paris, and Rome. Baptized RC; professed agnostic; tried to justify religious myth on intellectual grounds. Works include *The Sense of Beauty; The Life of Reason; Realms of Being; The Idea of Christ in the Gospels, or God in Man; Sonnets and Other Verses.*

Santo Domingo. 1. Early name of Hispaniola.* 2.

Former name of Dominican Rep. (see *Caribbean Islands,* A, E 2).

Sapienti consilio. See *Curia,* 2 b.

Sapor II. See *Middle East,* L.

Sapper, Karl Friedrich Wilhelm (Aug. 6, 1833–July 23, 1911). B. Wolfenbüttel, Brunswick, Ger.; educ. Hermannsburg (see *Hermannsburg Mission*); ordained in Ger.; to Am. 1866; pastor Carondelet, near St. Louis, Mo., and Bloomington, Ill. Coed. *(Die) Missions-Taube.*

Sarasvati, Dayananda (1827–83). Brahman; founded Arya Samaj (see *Hinduism,* 6); held that there are 3 eternal substances: God, spirit, matter. See also *Ramabai, Pandita.*

Sarawak. See *Malaysia,* 1, 4.

Sarcerius, Erasmus (Sorck; 1501–59). B. Annaberg, near Chemnitz, Ger.; educ. Leipzig and Wittenberg; taught at Lübeck, Graz, Vienna, and Siegen; supt. and chaplain to Count William the Rich (1516–59) of Nassau-Katzenelnbogen 1537; promoted the Reformation in Nassau; supt. of the county (Grafschaft) and (1541) court chaplain and preacher Dillenburg; compelled by the Augsburg Interim (see *Interim,* I) to leave Nassau, he went to Annaberg, then as pastor to Leipzig 1548; supt. Eisleben 1554 as G. Major's* successor; pastor Magdeburg 1559; gnesio-Lutheran.* Writings include a catechism, commentaries, sermons, and other theol. works.

Sarcophagus (from Gk. for "flesh-eating"). Originally, limestone used for coffins and held to disintegrate entombed bodies. Then, coffin in gen., often adorned with bas-reliefs, with OT and NT designs common from the 4th c.; examples at Arls, Fr., at Ravenna, It., and in the Lateran Museum, Rome.

Särkilathi, Pietari (Peter Särkilax). See *Finland, Lutheranism in,* 2.

Sarpi, Paolo (Pietro; Fra Paolo; Paulus Venetus; Paulus Servita; Brother Paul; 1552–1623). Prelate, hist., scientist, statesman; b. Venice, It.; Servite (see *Servites*); opposed Jesuits and temporal power of pope; counselor of state to Venice in conflict with papacy; suspected of heresy by the Inquisition. Works include a hist. of the Council of Trent.

Sartorius, Ernst Wilhelm Christian (1797–1859). B. Darmstadt, Ger.; educ. Göttingen; prof. Marburg and Dorpat (Tartu); supt. Prussia 1835–59. Works include *Die Lehre von der heiligen Liebe.*

Sartre, Jean-Paul. See *Existentialism,* 1.

Sarum Rite. Medieval modification at Salisbury (Lat. *Sarisburia*), Eng., of the RC rite. See also *Book of Common Prayer,* 2.

Saskatchewan. See Canada, A 11, 12, 14, 15, 19–21.

Sastras. See *Shastras.*

Satan. See *Devil.*

Sati. See *Suttee.*

Satisfaction, Vicarious. See *Atonement; Atonement, Theories of.*

Satispassion. Adequate suffering. In RCm: suffering in purgatory.

Satornilus (Saturninus). See *Gnosticism,* 7 c.

Sattler, Michael (ca. 1490–1527). B. Staufen, S Baden, Ger.; Benedictine prior Freiburg; converted by reading epistles of Paul; active in Zurich 1525; banished; in conflict with M. Bucer* and W. F. Capito*; to Austria; helped formulate basic tenets of Anabaps. in 7 arts.; martyred at Rottenburg.

Saturday Schools. See *Christian Education,* E 9; *Parish Education,* F 2.

Saturninus (Satornilus). See *Gnosticism,* 7 c.

Satyagraha. See *Gandhi, Mohandas Karamchand.*

Saubert, Johann (1592–1646). Father of J. Saubert* 1638–88); b. Altdorf, Nürnberg, Ger.; educ. Altdorf, Tübingen, Giessen, and Jena; preacher 1617, prof. 1618 Altdorf; preacher 1622, pastor 1627 Nürnberg; head of Nürnberg clergy 1637; loyal to Luth. confessions; hymnist. Works include *Miracula Augustanae confessionis; Zuchtbüchlein der evangelischen Kirche; Psychopharmakum.* See also *Hymnody, Christian,* 6.

Saubert, Johann (1638–88). Son of J. Saubert* (1592–1646); b. Nürnberg, Ger.; educ. Altdorf, Leipzig, and Helmstädt (Helmstedt); taught at Helmstedt; became syncretistic (see *Syncretism*); prof. theol. and supt. Altdorf 1673; hymnist. Issued *Nürnbergisches Gesangbuch;* hymns include "Es donnert sehr, o lieber Gott."

Saudi Arabia. See *Middle East,* L 1.

Sauer, Christopher. See *Publicity, Church.*

Saumur Academy. Prot. (Ref.; Huguenot) school founded in the 1590s or early in the 17th c. under leadership of P. de Mornay.* Strongly influenced Ref. orthodoxy in the 17th c. Closed 1685 with revocation of the Edict of Nantes.*

Saupert, J. Andreas (1822–July 6, 1893). B. Haag, near Wunsiedel, Upper Franconia, NE Bav., Ger.; attended teachers' sem. Altdorf; sent by J. K. W. Löhe* to Am. 1844; completed training at the sem. of the Ev. Luth. Joint Syn. of Ohio and Other States, in Columbus, Ohio; pastor Evansville, Ind., 1845–93; ordained Mo. Syn. 1847; founded many congs. in the Evansville area.

Saur, Christopher. See *Publicity, Church.*

Saurin, Elias (1639–1703). Ref. theol.; b. Usseau(x), Dauphiné, Fr.; pastor Venterol and Embrun; banished; served Walloons at Delft and Utrecht, Neth.; theol. influenced by mysticism and rationalism. Works include *Réflexions sur les droits de la conscience; Défense de la véritable doctrine de l'Eglise réformée.*

Saurin, Jacques (1677–1730). Prot. pulpit orator; b. Nimes, Fr.; educ. Geneva, Switz.; pastor London, Eng., and The Hague, Neth. Works include *Discours historiques, critiques, théologiques, et moraux, sur les événemens les plus mémorables du Vieux, et du Nouveau Testament; Sermons.*

Sava (Sabas; Rastko; ca. 1169/76–ca. 1235/36). Serbian nat. saint; fled to Mount Athos, Greece, 1193 and est. the Serbian monastery Chilandar(iu) (or Hilandar); organized autocephalous ch. of Serbia with Sava as abp. 1219.

Savannah Declaration. Adopted by the ULC at Savannah, Ga., 1934; reads in part: "We recognize as Evangelical Lutheran all Christian groups which accept the Holy Scriptures as the only rule and standard for faith and life, by which all doctrines are to be judged, and who sincerely receive the historic Confessions of the Lutheran Church (especially the Unaltered Augsburg Confession and Luther's Small Catechism) 'as a witness of the truth and a presentation of the correct understanding of our predecessors' (Formula of Concord, Part II, Intro.; ed. Jacobs, p. 538); and we set up no other standards or tests of Lutheranism apart from them or alongside of them.

"We believe that these Confessions are to be interpreted in their historical context, not as a law or as a system of theology, but as 'a witness and declaration of faith as to how the Holy Scriptures were understood and explained on the matters in controversy within the Church of God by those who then lived' (Formula of Concord, Part I, Intro.; ed. Jacobs, p. 492)."

The ULC reiterated this position at Minneapolis, 1944, declaring: "in addition to [the hist. Confessions of the Luth. Ch. (esp. the UAC and SC)] we will impose no tests of Lutheranism and beyond [these Confessions] we will submit to no tests of Lutheranism. . . . We regard ourselves as in full fellowship with all those other Lutheran Church bodies in America which with us accept the established Confessions."

See also *Lutheran Church in America,* II.

Minutes of the Ninth Biennial Convention of The United Lutheran Church in America, Savannah, Ga.,

Oct. 17–24, 1934 (Philadelphia, [1934]), p. 416; *Minutes of the Fourteenth Biennial Convention of The United Lutheran Church in America,* Minneapolis, Minn., Oct. 11–17, 1944 (Philadelphia, [1944]), pp. 241–242; *Documents of Lutheran Unity in America,* ed. R. C. Wolf (Philadelphia, 1966), pp. 355–357; *Doctrinal Declarations* (St. Louis, 1957), p. 59; E. Rinderknecht, "Lutheran Unity and Union from the Point of View of the United Lutheran Church," *The Lutheran Church Quarterly,* XIX (1946), 13–34.

Saving Faith. See *Faith,* 2.

Savior. See *Christ Jesus.*

Savonarola, Girolamo (Hieronymus; 1452–98). Dominican monk, reformer; b. Ferrara, It.; studied Augustine of Hippo, Thomas Aquinas, and the Bible; eloquent, passionate, and bold preacher of repentance at Florence; rebuked the sins of the people and of the rulers, including the pope, and insisted on clean living. Held that men are not saved by their own good works or by indulgences, but by the grace of God, through Christ, and that really good works are found only where the heart has been regenerated by faith. Held that he was a divinely inspired prophet and believed himself chosen to reform not only the ch. but also the state. Many of his predictions proved true. Became the idol of Florence and vicinity; people began to put into practice his moral, religious, and pol. ideals of a democratic theocracy. But pol. rancor developed against him; popular favor began to waver when some of his predictions failed; and fires of repressed youthful passion began to break out. He was excommunicated 1497; Florence was threatened with interdict.* Savonarola appealed to Eur. rulers for a council to depose the pope. In Florence an ordeal by fire was arranged; when circumstances combined to cancel it, a mob took Savonarola prisoner. Records of his trial are confused, but he was condemned to be hanged and burned. Writings include an exposition of Ps 51 and the first part of Ps 31, issued by M. Luther with a preface by the latter (cf. WA 12, 245–248); other works include *Trionfo della croce.*

W. H. Crawford, *Girolamo Savonarola* (Cincinnati, Ohio, 1907); P. Misciattelli, *Savonarola,* tr. M. Peters-Roberts (New York, 1930); A. G. Rudelbach, *Hieronymus Savonarola und seine Zeit* (Hamburg, 1835). J. Schnitzer, *Savonarola,* 2 vols. (Munich, 1924).

Savoy Conference. Meeting of 12 bps., 12 Presb. clerics, and 9 assistants on each side, at the Savoy Palace, London, Eng., 1661, to revise the Book* of Common Prayer, which was unsatisfactory to Puritans,* who hoped to delete elements they regarded as RC. Only minor changes were made; may Presb. clerics were deprived of office for not accepting the 1662 ed.

Savoy Declaration. See *Democratic Declarations of Faith,* 2.

Saxon Confession. See *Lutheran Confessions,* A 5.

Saxon Immigration. See *Lutheran Church–Missouri Synod, The,* II.

Saxon Visitation. See *Articles of Visitation; Melanchthon, Philipp; Visitations, Church.*

Saxons, Conversion of. See *Germany,* A.

Saxony and Other States, Synod of the Evangelical Lutheran Free Church in. See *Germany, Lutheran Free Churches in,* 4–7.

Saybrook, Synod of. See *Democratic Declarations of Faith,* 2.

Saybrook Platform. Adopted 1708 by Congs. at Saybrook, Conn.; as to doctrine, it reffirmed the Savoy Declaration and doctrinal parts of the Westminster Confession; abrogated 1784. See also *Democratic Declarations of Faith,* 2.

Sayce, Archibald Henry (1845 [1846?]–1933). Angl., orientalist; b. Shirehampton, near Bristol, Gloucestershire, Eng.; educ. Oxford; priest 1871; prof. Assyriology at Oxford 1891; mem. OT Revision Company 1874–84. Works include *The Monuments of the Hittites; The "Higher Criticism" and the Verdict of the Monuments.*

Sayings of Jesus. See *Apocrypha,* B 2.

Scaer, Charles (Oct. 11, 1857–June 9, 1928). B. Convoy, near Van Wert, Ohio. Educ. Ohio Northern U., Ada, Ohio; Hiram (Ohio) Coll.; Tri-State Normal Coll., Angola, Ind. Prof. Lat. at Tri-State Normal Coll.; prof. Eng. at St. John's Coll., Winfield, Kans., 1894–1927; admitted to ministry 1900 after private study in theol. Works include *A Treatise on Conscience.*

Scala sancta (Scala Pilati). See *Lateran.*

Scaliger, Joseph Justus (1540–1609). Hist., philol.; b. Agen, Fr.; joined Ref. ch. 1562. Prof. Geneva, Switz., 1572–74; Leiden, Neth., 1593. Founded scientific chronology. Works include *De emendatione temporum.*

Scandello, Antonio (Scandelli; Antonius Scandellus, or Scandellius; 1517–80). Composer; b. Bergamo, It.; originally RC; became Prot. at Dresden, Ger., where he was mem. of the court orchestra, asst. conductor 1566, 1st conductor 1568. Works include masses; Passion acc. to John.

Scandinavia. See *Denmark; Iceland; Norway, Early Christianity in; Norway, Lutheranism in; Norwegian Foreign Missions; Norwegian Lutheran Free Church, The; Sweden, Conversion of, to Christianity; Sweden, Lutheranism in; Swedish Missionary Societies.*

Scandinavian Ecumenical Institute. See *Sigtuna Foundation.*

Scandinavian Evangelical Lutheran Augustana Synod of North America. See *Augustana Evangelical Lutheran Church,* 1, 8–20.

Scandinavian Lutheran Congregation (Mexico City). See *Mexico,* D 3.

Scapular. Straight piece of cloth, ca. 14 to 18 in. wide, with a hole in the middle so that it can pass over the the head and hang down from the shoulders before and behind; various additions were made to the basic pattern; it became symbolic of Christ's cross and yoke; by ca. the end of the 11th c. it was worn by some orders of monks; later worn also by some lay persons assoc. with communities of monks or friars.

Scarlatti, Alessandro (ca. 1658/60–1725). Composer; b. Palermo, Sicily; regarded as founder of modern opera; said to have invented *da capo* (It. "from the beginning"; a part to be repeated). Works include oratorios (e. g., *Agar et Ismaele esiliati; Christmas Oratorio*); *Stabat mater;* masses; cantatas.

Scepticism. See *Skepticism.*

Schack, Tage. See *Denmark, Lutheranism in,* 12.

Schade, Johann Caspar (Kaspar; 1666–98). B. Kühndorf (or Kündorf), near Suhl and Meiningen, Thuringia, Ger.; educ. Leipzig and Wittenberg; diaconus Berlin, with P. J. Spener* as provost; hymnist. Hymns include "Meine Seel', ermuntre dich"; "Meine Seel' ist stille."

Schade, Peter. See *Mosellanus, Petrus.*

Schadow, Johann Gottfried. See *Luther Monuments.*

Schadow-Godenhaus, Friedrich Wilhelm von (ca. 1788/89–1862). Son of J. G. Schadow (see *Luther Monuments*); painter; b. Berlin, Ger.; RC 1814; prof. Academy of Art, Berlin, 1819; dir. Academy of Art, Düsseldorf, 1826. Works include "The Wise and the Foolish Virgins"; "Christ on the Mount of Olives"; "Christ and the Disciples of Emmasus." See also *Nazarenes,* 3.

Schaeder, Erich (1861–1936). Ev. theol.; b. Clausthal, Ger.; taught at Greifswald, Königsberg, Göttingen, Kiel, Breslau; exponent of theocentric Biblical theol. as opposed to the anthropocentric system of F. D. E. Schleiermacher* and others. Works include *Theozentrische Theologie.*

Schaefer. See *Schäfer.*

Schaeffer, Charles Frederick (Sept. 3, 1807–Nov. 23, 1879). Son of F. D. Schaeffer*; brother of D. F. Schaeffer*; b. Germantown, Pa.; educ. U. of Pa., Philadelphia; studied theol. under his father and brother-in-law, K. R. Demme*; licensed to preach 1829 by The Ev. Luth. Syn. of Md. and Va. (see *United Lutheran Church, Synods of,* 11, 29); ordained 1831 by the Ev. Luth. Syn. of West Pa. (see *United Lutheran Church, Synods of,* 22, 23); pastor Pa., Md., Ohio, N. Y. Prof. Ohio Syn. sem., Columbus, 1840–43; Pa. Coll., Gettysburg, 1855–64; Luth. Theol. Sem., Philadelphia, 1864–79. Tr. various Ger. theol. works; other writings include a commentary on Mt.

Schaeffer, Charles William. See *Schäffer, Charles William.*

Schaeffer, David Frederick (July 22, 1787–May 5, 1837). Son of F. D. Schaeffer*; brother of C. F. Schaeffer*; b. Carlisle, Pa.; educ. U. of Pa., Philadelphia; learned theol. from his father and other Luth. pastors; licensed 1808; served a cong. in Frederick, Md.; ordained 1812; pres. The General* Syn. of the Ev. Luth. Ch. in the USA 1831, 1833; trained E. Greenwald,* C. Philip Krauth,* and others for the ministry.

Schaeffer, Frederick David (Friedrich David Schäffer; Nov. 15, 1760–Jan. 27, 1836). B. Frankfurt am Main, Ger.; to Am. 1774; licensed by Pa. Ministerium 1786; ordained 1788; served congs. in Pa. Wrote *Antwort auf eine Vertheidigung der Methodisten.*

Schäfer, Philipp Heinrich Wilhelm Theodor (1846–1914). B. Friedberg, Hesse, Ger.; educ. Giessen, Erlangen, Leipzig, Friedberg; pastor Paris; inspector of an institution for epileptics and feebleminded at Alsterdorf, near Hamburg; dir. deaconess institute at Altona 1872–1911. Works include *Die weibliche Diakonie; Leitfaden der inneren Mission; Praktisches Christentum.*

Schäfer, Rudolf Siegfried Otto (1878–1961). Luth. artist; b. Altona, near Hamburg, Ger.; educ. Munich Academy of Arts, and Düsseldorf; settled at Rotenburg, Hannover. Illustrated hymns, folk songs, NT; noted esp. for illustrations in the so-called Schäfer-Bibel.

Schaff, Philip (1819–93). B. Chur, Switz.; educ. Tübingen, Halle, Berlin; traveled through It. and Sicily as tutor; tutor Berlin 1842; to Am. 1843; prof. Mercersburg, Pa., 1844 (see also *Mercersburg Theology*); prof. Union Theol. Sem., NYC, 1870; prominent in Evangelical* Alliance and in the production of the RV. Works include *Christliche Glaubens- und Sittenlehre; The Creeds of Christendom; Theological Propaedeutic; History of the Christian Church; A Companion to the Greek Testament and the English Version;* helped tr. and ed. *The Schaff-Herzog Encyclopaedia of Religious Knowledge;* tr. and ed. J. P. Lange, *A Commentary on the Holy Scriptures;* helped ed. *A Select Library of the Nicene and Post-Nicene Fathers of the Christian Church.* See also *Propaedeutic, Theological.*

Schäffer, Charles William (May 5, 1813–Mar. 15, 1896). B. Hagerstown, Md.; educ. U. of Pa., Philadelphia, and the Luth. Theol. Sem. at Gettysburg, Pa. Pastor Montgomery Co., Pa, 1835–41; Harrisburg, Pa., 1841–49; Germantown, Pa., 1849–75. Prof. Luth. Theol. Sem., Philadelphia. Pres. The General* Syn. of the Ev. Luth. Ch. in the USA 1859; Pa. Ministerium many yrs.; General* Council of the Ev. Luth. Ch. in (North) Am. 1868. Hymnist. Ed. *The Lutheran; The Foreign Missionary; The Philadelphian.* Tr. H. Sachs's "Die Wittenbergisch Nachtigall"; *Halle Reports;* W. Wackernagel's life of M. Luther. Other works include *Family Prayer for Morning and Evening and the Festivals of the Church Year; Early History of the Lutheran Church in America.* See also *Fraternal Address; Hymnody, Christian,* 8.

Schäffer, Friedrich David. See *Schaeffer, Frederick David.*

Schaitberger, Joseph (1658–1733). B. Dürnberg, near Hallein, Salzburg, W Austria, near Ger. border; miner; banished 1685 (see *Salzburgers, Banishment of*); settled at Nürnberg. Works include tracts and the hymn "Ich bin ein armer Exulant."

Schaller, Friedrich Fürchtegott Wilhelm (Mar. 23, 1868–Dec. 3, 1955). Son of J. M. G. Schaller*; brother of J. Schaller*; b. St. Louis, Mo.; educ. Conc. Sem., St. Louis. Pastor Baltimore, Md., 1889–1901; Quincy, Ill., 1901–06. Prof. Ger. St. Paul's Coll., Concordia, Mo., 1906–42; ed. CPH 1942–55; philol.; lexicographer. Contributor to J. and W. Grimm's *Deutsche Wörterbuch* for more than 50 yrs.

Schaller, Johann Michael Gottlieb (Feb. 12, 1819–Nov. 19, 1887). Father of F. F. W. Schaller* and J. Schaller*; b. Kirchenlamitz, Upper Franconia, NE Bav., Ger.; educ. Nürnberg and Erlangen; vicar Windsbach (near Nürnberg) and (1847) Kattenhochstädt (near Weissenburg, Middle Franconia, Bav.); to Am. 1848, largely on encouragement by J. K. W. Löhe*; pastor Philadelphia 1849; joined Mo. Syn. 1849; vicar Baltimore, Md., 1850; won over from Löhe's view to C. F. W. Walther's* view on the Office of the Keys at the 1850 Mo. Syn. conv.; pastor Detroit, Mich., 1850; vicar, then pastor, Trin. Luth. Ch., St. Louis, Mo., 1854–72; pres. Western Dist. of the Mo. Syn. 1857–63; prof. Conc Sem., St. Louis, 1872.

W. Schaller, "Gottlieb Schaller," *CHIQ,* XVI, No. 2 (July 1943), 34–48; No. 3 (Oct. 1943), 65–96.

Schaller, Johannes (Dec. 10, 1859–Feb. 7, 1920). Son of J. M. G. Schaller*; brother of F. F. W. Schaller*; b. St. Louis, Mo.; educ. Northwestern Coll. (also called Northwestern U.), Watertown, Wis., and Conc. Sem., St. Louis, Mo. Pastor Little Rock, Ark., 1881–85; Cape Girardeau, Mo., 1885–89. Prof. theol. dept. Dr. Martin Luther Coll., New Ulm, Minn. 1889–1908; pres. 1893–1908 of the school as a normal school and preparatory school for the coll. dept. at Watertown, Wis.; pres. of the (Wis. Syn.) theol. sem. at Wauwatosa 1908–19. Works include Kurze Bibelkunde (tr. *The Book of Books*); *Pastorale Praxis in der Ev.-Luth. Freikirche Amerikas; Biblical Christology.*

Schalling, Martin (1532–1608). B. Strasbourg, Ger.; educ. Wittenberg; diaconus Regensburg 1554, Amberg (Upper Palatinate, Bav.) 1558; pastor Vilseck, near Amberg, 1568; court preacher and supt. Amberg 1576; gen. supt. Upper Palatinate and court preacher Heidelberg; deprived of office 1583 for refusing to sign FC; pastor Nürnberg 1585; hymnist. Wrote "Herzlich lieb hab' ich dich, o Herr."

Schappeler, Christoph (1472–1551). B. St. Gall, Switz.; teacher St. Gall ca. 1503; preacher Memmingen, Swabia, SW Bav., Ger., 1513; follower of H. Zwingli*; opposed mass, claims of papacy, RC orders, oral confession, prayer to saints, tithing, purgatory; upheld Communion in both kinds and the universal priesthood of believers; supported peasant organization but opposed violence; fled Memmingen and in later yrs. was preacher elsewhere.

Scharschmidt, Justus Samuel (1664–1742). Ger. Luth. pastor; extended A. H. Francke's* influence to Russ., where he was pastor Moscow and Astrakhan; returned to Ger. 1717.

Schartau, Henric (1757–1825). B. Malmö, Swed.; educ. Lund; ordained 1780; served parishes in S Swed.; influenced by Ger. Pietism; noted preacher and catechist; emphasized psychology; held that an enlightened intellect affects the will; stressed the need to interpret the Word of God correctly. Students at Lund started a movement called Schartauanism; it spread through Lund and into Gothenburg. See also *Sweden, Lutheranism in,* 4.

Schauman, Frans Ludvig (Franz Ludwig; 1810 [1811?]–77). B. Maaria (or Niuskala?); Fin.; educ. Helsinki; instructor, then prof. Helsinki 1838–65; bp. Porvoo 1865–77; helped bring about reforms included in 1869 ch. law; helped est. pub. schools. Works include *Handbok i Finlands kyrkorätt; Praktiska theologin.*

Schechter, Solomon (1850 [1847?]–1915). Hebraist; b. Focsani, Rumania; educ. Lemberg, Vienna, Berlin; reader (or lecturer) in Talmud and rabbinical literature Cambridge 1890; prof. Heb., U. of London, 1899; pres. Jewish Theol. Sem. of Am., N. Y., 1901/02–15; helped found Conservative Judaism (see *Judaism,* 3). See also *Damascus Fragments.*

Scheeben, Matthias Joseph (1835–88). RC theol.; b. Meckenheim, near Bonn, Ger.; rector and teacher of religion in Ursuline convent at Münstereifel; prof. dogmatics Cologne. Exponent of neo-scholasticism; defended papal infallibility.

Scheel, Jürgen Otto Einar Immanuel (1876–1954). B. Tondern, Schleswig-Holstein, Ger.; educ. Halle and Kiel; prof. Kiel and Tübingen. Works include *Martin Luther.*

Schéele, Knut Henning Gezelius von (1838–1920). Luth. theol.; b. Stockholm, Swed.; educ. Uppsala; prof. Uppsala; bp. Visby (Wisby), on Gotland Is., in the Baltic Sea, 1885. Collaborator on O. Zöckler's* *Handbuch der theologischen Wissenschaften;* other works include writings on catechetics and symbolics.

Scheffler, Johann (also called Angelus Silesius; 1624–77). B. Breslau, Silesia, Prussia, Ger.; studied medicine at Strasbourg, and in Holland and Padua, It.; interested in mysticism; private physician to the Duke of Wurttemberg-Öls 1649; RC 1653, assuming the name Angelus from a 16th-c. Sp. mystic; imperial court physician 1654; RC priest 1661; spent most of his last yrs. in a monastery at Breslau; hymnist. Issued *Heilige Seelenlust,* which includes many of his hymns, which include "Jesu, komm doch selbst zu mir"; "Mir nach! spricht Christus, unser Held"; "Liebe, die du mich zum Bilde"; "Ich will dich lieben, meine Stärke."

Schegk, Jakob (Schegkius; Degen; 1511–87). B. Schorndorf, Ger.; educ. Tübingen; prof. philos. and medicine Tübingen; humanist; tried to avoid metaphysical questions closely related to theol.; attacked by P. Ramus*; finally defended the theol. position of the Luth. faculty at Tübingen. Works include *Ein collegium logicum im XVI. Jahrhundert; De causa continente; Philosophiae naturalis (quae Acroamata solitus fuit appellare Aristoteles) omnes disputationes, ac universa tractatio, duobus libris comprehensa; Tractationum physicarum et medicarum tomus unus.*

Scheibel, Johann Gottfried (1783–1843). B. Breslau, Ger.; educ. Halle; preacher, then prof. Breslau; wrote against rationalism* and the Prussian* Union; suspended from office 1830; to Dresden 1832; ordered to leave because of a polemical sermon, he went to Hermsdorf, then to Glauchau, finally to Nürnberg. See also *Germany, Lutheran Free Churches in,* 1.

Scheidemann, Heinrich (ca. 1596–1663). B. Wöhrden, near Heide, Dithmarschen, Ger.; organist Hamburg; pupil of J. P. Sweelinck*; composer. See also *Reinken, Jan; Toccata; Weckmann, Matthias.*

Scheidt, Christian Ludwig (1709–61). B. Waldenburg, near Schwäbisch Hall, Württemberg, Ger.; educ. Altdorf, Strasbourg, Halle, Göttingen; taught at the U. of Copenhagen; Hofrat and librarian Hanover; hymnist. Wrote the hymn "Aus Gnaden soll ich selig werden."

Scheidt, Samuel (1587–1654). B. Halle, Ger.; pupil of J. P. Sweelinck*; organist Halle. Wrote settings of Luth. chorales for organ. His *Tabulatura nova* includes psalms, hymns, chorales, a mass, magnificats. See also *Toccata.*

Schein, Johann Hermann (1586–1630). B. Grünhain, Saxony, E cen. Ger., in the Erzgebirge; educ. Leipzig; succeeded S. Calvisius* as cantor Saint Thomas, Leipzig; composer. Works include both text and music of hymns. See also *Hymnody, Christian,* 6.

Scheler, Max Ferdinand (1874–1928). B. Munich, Ger.; educ. Munich, Berlin, Heidelberg, Jena; taught at Jena and Munich; prof. Cologne 1919, Frankfurt am Main 1928. Influenced by F. Brentano,* R. C. Eucken,* and E. Husserl.* Investigated psychol. and sociol. aspects of phenomenology.*

Schellenecker. See *Selnecker.*

Schelling, Friedrich Wilhelm Joseph von (1775–1854). B. Leonberg, near Stuttgart, Ger.; educ. Tübingen and Leipzig; taught at Jena, Würzburg, Munich, Berlin. At first he developed an *Identitätsphilosophie* (the ideal and the real are absolutely identical) and a pantheism opposed to rationalistic theol.; later, influenced by J. Böhme,* he became a theist; still later he approached Christianity. See also *Philosophy.*

Schelwig, Samuel (Schelgwi[n]g; 1643–1715). Luth. theol.; b. Lissa, Poland; educ. Wittenberg; opposed Pietism*; conrector Gymnasium, Thorn, 1668; prof. Danzig 1673; pastor St. Catharine's, Danzig 1681; pastor Trin. Ch. and rector Athenaeum, Danzig, 1685.

Schemelli, Georg Christian (ca. 1676/80–1762). B. Herzberg, Ger.; pupil of the Thomasschule, Leipzig, from 1695; cantor of Zeitz castle. Comp. *Musicalisches Gesang-Buch,* ed. and partly composed by J. S. Bach.*

Schenk, Hartmann (Schenck; 1634–81). B. Ruhla, near Eisenach, Ger.; educ. Helmstädt and Jena; pastor Bibra 1662; diaconus Ostheim and pastor Völkershausen 1669; hymnist. Hymns include "Nun Gott Lob, es ist vollbracht."

Schenk, Jakob (Schenck; ca. 1508–46). Court preacher of Henry,* brother of George* the Bearded, at Freiberg, 1536; suspected of, and examined for, antinomianism; court preacher Weimar 1538; preacher and prof. Leipzig 1541; court preacher of Joachim II (see *Joachim,* 2) at Berlin 1544–46.

Schenkel, Daniel (1813–85). B. Dägerlen, Switz.; educ. Göttingen; preacher Schaffhausen 1841; prof. Basel 1850, Heidelberg 1851; helped found German Protestant* Union.

Scherer, Daniel (Sept. 12, 1790–Apr. 5, 1852). Luth. pastor; ordained 1821; pastor N. C. and served scattered Luths. in Ky., Ind., Ill., and Mo.

Scherer, Jacob (Feb. 7, 1785–Mar. 2, 1860). Luth. pastor; licensed by N. C. Syn. (see *United Lutheran Church, Synods of,* 16) 1810, ordained 1812; traveled extensively as missionary; helped organize Southwestern Va. Syn. (see *United Lutheran Church, Synods of,* 29).

Scherer, Melanchthon Gideon Groseclose (Mar. 16, 1861–Mar. 9, 1932). Educ. Roanoke Coll., Salem, Va.; licensed 1881, ordained 1883, by Ev. Luth. Syn. of Va. (see *United Lutheran Church, Synods of,* 29); pastor W. Va., Pa., N. C., S. C.; pres. N. C. Coll., at Mt. Pleasant, 1896–99; prof. Theol. Sem. of the United Syn. in the S., at Mt. Pleasant, near Charleston, S. C., 1901–05; pres. United* Syn. of the Ev. Luth. Ch. in the S. 1914–18; secy. ULC 1918–32. With F. H. Knubel* ed. *Our Church;* other works include *Christian Liberty and Church Unity.*

Schertzer, Johann Adam (Scherzer; 1628–83). B. Eger, Boh.; prof. Leipzig. Works include *Breviarium Eustachianum; Breviculus theologicus; Systema theologiae; Collegium Anti-Calvinianum.*

Scheurl, Christoph Gottlieb Adolf von (1811–93). B. Nürnberg, Ger.; educ. Erlangen and Munich; prof. Erlangen. Coed. *Zeitschrift für Protestantismus und*

Kirche; other works include *Über die lutherische Kirche in Bayern.*

Schicht, Johann Gottfried (1753–1823). Conductor, composer; b. Reichenau, near Zittau, Ger.; trained in piano, organ, and vocal music in Zittau; studied law at Leipzig; pianist 1781–85 at Gewandhaus concerts, Leipzig; conductor Gewandhaus concerts 1785; cantor Thomaskirche, Leipzig, from 1810. Comp. *Choralbuch.* Other works include oratorios (e. g., *Das Ende des Gerechten*) and other sacred music.

Schick, Georg (Feb. 25, 1831–Jan. 3, 1915). B. Homburg vor der Höhe, Hessen-Homburg, Ger.; educ. Erlangen, Berlin, Heidelberg, Paris; private tutor Leschnian, near Neuenburg and Marienwerder, Poland; asst. pastor Frankfurt am Main and vicar Kaiserslautern; differed with unionistic policy at Frankfurt; to Am. 1854; joined Mo. Syn. 1854; pastor Chicago, Ill., 1854; prof. ancient languages Conc. Coll., St. Louis, Mo., 1856, first as conrector, later rector; moved with the school to Fort Wayne, Ind., 1861; resigned 1914.

L. E. Fuerbringer, "Rector George Schick," *80 Eventful Years* (St. Louis, 1944), pp. 41–54.

Schick, George Victor (Feb. 3, 1886–Dec. 31, 1964). B. Chicago, Ill.; educ. Conc. Coll., Fort Wayne, Ind., and Conc. Sem., St. Louis, Mo.; studied at the Oriental Sem. of Johns Hopkins U., Baltimore, Md.; studied in Germany; instructor Johns Hopkins U.; prof. Conc. Coll., Fort Wayne, 1914–38, and Conc. Sem., St. Louis, 1938–64. Works include *Fundamentals of Biblical Hebrew* (mimeo); *The stems dum and damám in Hebrew;* tr. M. Luther's *Lectures on Genesis,* chap. 1 – nearly the end of chap. 27.

Schieferdecker, Georg Albert (Mar. 12, 1815–Nov. 23, 1891). B. Leipzig, Ger.; educ. Leipzig; taught in various places; to Am. 1838 with the Saxon Immigration (see *Lutheran Church – Missouri Synod, The,* II); taught school in Perry Co., Mo., and in Saint Louis; ordained pastor Monroe Co., Ill., 1841; also pastor Centreville, St. Clair Co., Ill., 1849; accepted a call to Altenburg, Perry Co., Mo., 1849 and was installed there early in 1850; pres. Western Dist. of the Mo. Syn. 1854. Divested 1857 first of membership in the Mo. Syn., and then of the pastorate of his cong., for his chiliasm, he joined the Ev. Luth. Syn. of Iowa* and Other States; renounced chiliasm (cf. *Der Lutheraner,* Aug. 1, 1875); pastor Hillsdale and Coldwater, Mich. (installed Sept. 12, 1875); rejoined the Mo. Syn. (Northern Dist.) 1876; pastor Neu Gehlenbeck, Madison Co., Ill., 1877. Works include *Geschichte der ersten deutschen lutherischen Ansiedlung in Altenburg, Perry Co., Mo.*

A. R. Suelflow, *Georg Albert Schieferdecker and His Relation to Chiliasm in the Iowa Synod* (unpub. BD thesis in Conc. Sem., St. Louis, library), 1946.

Schiller, Johann Christoph Friedrich von (1759–1805). Poet, playright; b. Marbach, Württemberg, Ger.; military surgeon; went without leave to see performance of his *Die Räuber* 1781; arrested and forbidden to pub. anything except med. writings; escaped; in Mannheim 1783–85, Weimar 1787; prof. hist. Jena 1789; friend of J. W. v. Goethe*; in Weimar 1799–1805. Regarded as greatest Ger. dramatist and 2d only to Goethe in Ger. literature. Combined art, morality, and religion in his writing. His ideal was the "schöne Seele" ("beautiful soul"). Cofounder of the literary journal *Die Horen;* founded *Musenalmanach.* Other works include *Geschichte des dreissigjährigen Krieges; Das Lied von der Glocke; Wallenstein; Wilhelm Tell; Maria Stuart; Die Jungfrau von Orleans.*

Schilling, Johann. Active in monastery at Augsburg, Ger. in the early 1520s; restless, rebellious preacher who laid bare abuses in ch. and state; held that the cong. has supreme authority, also to act if civil govt. fails; gathered a large following; championed the cause of peasants; probably died in Peasants'* War.

Schilling, Johannes. See *Luther Monuments.*

Schindler, Valentin. See *Lexicons,* A.

Schinkel, Karl Friedrich (Carl; 1781–1841). Architect, painter; b. Neuruppin, Brandenburg, Ger.; studied in Berlin and It.; mem. Royal Academy, Berlin, 1811. Designed many pub. bldgs., including chs.; known also for paintings of romantic landscape scenes.

Schirmer, Michael (1606–73). B. Leipzig, Ger.; educ. Leipzig; subrector 1636, conrector 1651 Grey* Friars Gymnasium, Berlin; had many domestic and personal afflictions; hymnist. Hymns include "Nun jauchzet all, ihr Frommen"; "Nun lieg' ich armes Würmelein"; "O heil'ger Geist, kehr bei uns ein."

Schism (from Gk. *schizein,* "to divide, tear, cleave asunder, open, cut apart"). 1. Used in the NT of the tearing of the temple veil (Mt 27:51; Mk 15:38; Lk 23:45), the heavens opening (Mk 1:10), tearing a garment (Mt 9:16; Lk 5:36), divergent opinions (Jn 7:43; Acts 14:4). The ch. uses the term in the sense of dissension, division, discord (1 Co 1:10; 11:18; 12:25). Schismatics disrupt ch. harmony and unity.

2. Irenaeus* used the term in a technical sense (*Adversus haereses,* IV, xxxiii, 7). Jerome* distinguished bet. heresy* and schism, the former being perversion of doctrine, the latter rebellion against authority (*In Epist. ad Titum,* iii, 10). Augustine* of Hippo held that heretics wound faith, schismatics deviate from charity (*De fide et symbolo,* x). It is sometimes hard to distinguish bet. heresy and schism, since heresy leads to schism and schism presupposes heresy.

3. The early ch. suffered several schisms (e. g., Hippolytan [see *Hippolytus*]; see also *Donatist Schism, The; Meletian Schisms; Novatian*). The Easter* controversy included the element of liturgical practice. Some schisms included elements of nationalism or economics (see, e. g., *Monophysite Controversy*); others resulted from patriarchal rivalries (see, e. g., *Nestorianism*). In most of these schisms there was also an accompanying heresy.

4. Basis for the pol. separation of the Roman empire into E and W was laid when Diocletian* reorganized it (ca. 285–ca. 293 AD). Pol., cultural, and linguistic differences accentuated the cleavage. Tensions arose in the ch. bet. Rome and Constantinople over pretensions of the latter to primacy (either equality with Rome or at least preeminence after Rome [the thrust is not altogether clear], Council of Constantinople,* 381 AD, canon 3; clear equality with Rome, Council of Chalcedon,* 451 AD, canon 28). Alexandria, Antioch, and Jerusalem tended to follow the lead of Constantinople. Later factors affecting relations bet. E and W included the Filioque* Controversy and the Quinisext* Syn. By crowning Charlemagne* 800 the pope declared his separation from the E emp. and looked henceforth to the W emp. for pol. support.

5. *Photian schism.* In 858(857?) Michael* III made Photius* patriarch of Constantinople in place of Ignatius (ca. 798–877; patriarch Constantinople 847–858 [857?], 867–877), who resigned in tension with the state. Legates of pope Nicholas I (see *Popes,* 5) confirmed the patriarchate of Photius 861, but Nicholas I anathematized Photius and restored Ignatius 863. Michael III continued to support Photius as patriarch. In 867 Photius excommunicated and anathematized the pope, but fell from power and was imprisoned in a convent when Michael III was murdered Sept. 867. Michael III was succeeded by Basil I ("the Macedonian"; ca. 812–886; caused death of Michael III; E Roman emp. 867–886), who restored Ignatius as patriarch. Ignatius, who alienated the pope by consecrating bps. for Bulgaria, was succeeded 878(877?) by Photius, apparently with approval of John VIII (ca. 820–882; pope 872–

882). In 886 Leo VI ("the Wise; the Philosopher"; son of Michael* III; 866–912; E Roman emp. 886–912) deposed Photius, who disappeared from hist.

6. *Schism of 1054* (sometimes called Great Schism). M. Caerularius* closed all Lat. chs. in Constantinople 1053. His main charge against the W was use of unleavened bread (Gk. *azyma;* see also *Azymite Controversy*) in Communion. Other charges included: omitting Hallelujah* in Lent; observing Saturdays in Lent in Jewish fashion; violating the rule regarding things strangled and blood (cf. Acts 15:20, 29). Leo* IX replied through legates with countercharges. Relations deteriorated. July 16, 1054, the papal representative laid a writ of excommunication on the altar of St. Sophia Ch., Constantinople (see also *Church Architecture,* 6). This, in effect, sealed the schism, regardless of the reaction of Caerularius, which is variously reported. Antipathy bet. E and W was heightened by the Crusades,* which included capture and sack of Constantinople 1204. See also *Florence, Council of; Lyons, Councils of.*

7. Vatican Council II (see *Vatican Councils,* 2) addressed itself to the schism bet. E and W in the Decree on E Cath. Chs., evaluated by the E with reservations because of its W orientation and because Uniate* chs. are an obstacle to harmony. Dec. 7, 1965, in ceremonies at Rome and Istanbul, pope and patriarch expressed desire to nullify the schismatic events of 1054.

8. *Papal schism* (also called Great schism; Western schism): schism in the W ch. at the end of the 14th and beginning of the 15th c. After the death of Gregory XI (see *Popes,* 14) 1378, 16 cardinals at Rome elected Urban VI (see *Jubilees*) Apr. 1378. Alienation soon developed among his electors. The Fr. cardinals among them joined others at Avignon, SE Fr., in electing Clement VII antipope (see *Clement VII,* 1) Sept. 1378. Urban VI was supported by It., Ger., Eng., Den., and Swed., Clement VII by Fr., Scot., Savoy, Castile, Aragon, and Navarre. Urban VI was followed by Boniface IX (Pietro Tomacelli; ca. 1355–1404; b. Naples, It.; pope 1389–1404), Innocent VII (Cosimo de' Migliorati; ca. 1336–1406; b. Sulmona, It.; pope 1404–06), and Gregory* XII. Clement VII was followed by Benedict XIII (see *Benedict XIII,* 1). The 1409 Council of Pisa* tried to depose Gregory XII and Benedict XIII and elected Alexander V (Petros Philargos; Pietro di Candia; ca. 1340–1410; cardinal 1405; pope 1409–10), who was followed by John* XXIII. But Gregory XII and Benedict XIII refused to submit to the council, with the result that 3 claimed to be pope. The Council of Constance* declared Apr. 6, 1415, that the pope must also obey an ecumenical council. It deposed John XXIII 1415; like the 1409 Council of Pisa, it tried to depose Benedict XIII 1417, but Benedict XIII, though almost wholly forsaken, defied all attempts to depose him till he died. The council elected Martin* V Nov. 11, 1417, practically ending the schism. It ended completely 1429 when Clement VIII (Gil [or Aegyd] Sánchez Muñoz; d. 1446; antipope 1423; bp. of the is. Mallorca [Majorca], Sp. 1429), nominal successor of Benedict XIII, resigned. See also *Babylonian Captivity,* 2. CAV

S. L. Greenslade, *Schism in the Early Church* (New York, n. d.); T. A. Lacey, *Unity and Schism* (London, 1917); F. Dvornik, *The Photian Schism* (Cambridge, Eng., 1948); W. Ullmann, *The Origins of the Great Schism* (London, 1948); S. Runciman, *The Eastern Schism* (Oxford, 1955).

Schism Act. See *Corporation Act of 1661.*

Schlaginhaufen, Johann(es) (Schlaginhauff; Schlachinhauffen; d. ca. 1560). Probably b. Neunburg, Upper Palatinate; recorded M. Luther's table talk 1531/32 (see also *Luther, Table Talk of*); pastor Zahna 1532; pastor 1533, later supt. Köthen; signed SA.

Schlatter, Adolf von (1852–1938). Ref. theol.; b. St. Gall, Switz.; educ. Basel and Tübingen; influenced by J. T. Beck*; taught at Bern, Greifswald, Berlin, Tübingen. Works include *Die Theologie des Neuen Testaments; Erläuterungen zum Neuen Testament.* See also *Bible Version,* M; *Biblicism.*

Schlatter, Michael (1716–90). B. St. Gall, Switz.; probably educ. Helmstedt (Helmstädt); ordained Holland; sent by Holland syns. as miss. to Ger. Ref. in Am. in the 1740s; pastor Philadelphia and Germantown 1747; active in organizing chs. in Pa., Md., Va., and N. J.; resigned Philadelphia pastorate 1755 to become supt. of proposed Eng. charity schools, but unpopularity of the schools among Germans led to his resignation 1757; chaplain Royal Am. Regt. 1757; pastor Philadelphia 1759; chaplain 2d Pa. Battalion 1764; captured and imprisoned by British 1777.

Schlegel, Johann Adolf (1721–93). Father of K. W. F. v. Schlegel*; b. Meissen, Ger.; diaconus and teacher Schulpforte, near Naumburg, 1751; head minister, and prof. theol. Gymnasium, Zerbst, 1754; at Hanover from 1759 in various capacities; hymnist.

Schlegel, Karl Wilhelm Friedrich von (1772–1829). Son of J. A. Schlegel*; b. Hanover, Ger.; educ. Göttingen and Leipzig; studied Persian and Indian at Paris 1802–04; held Austrian govt. offices. In his early period he emphasized Gk. and Lat. classics; this led him to neo-humanism and J. C. F. v. Schiller*; later developed a secular mysticism of nature and spirit. Held that nature is supreme in ancient culture, spirit in later culture. After conversion to RCm in the 1st decade of the 19th c. he emphasized Christian culture. Works include *Geschichte der alten und neuen Literatur; Philosophie des Lebens; Philosophie der Geschichte.*

Schleiermacher, Friedrich Daniel Ernst (1768–1834). 1. Founded modern Prot. theol.; b. Breslau, Ger.; entered Moravian sem. at Barby 1785; dissatisfied, he left 1787 for Halle, where he studied I. Kant* and Gk. philos.; engaged in private study at Drossen, near Frankfurt an der Oder; private tutor Schlobitten, West Prussia; taught at Berlin 1793; asst. pastor Landsberg an der Warthe 1794; Ref. preacher Berlin 1796. Wrote *Über die Religion, Reden an die Gebildeten unter ihren Verächtern* 1799 against the Enlightenment*; in it he sets forth his concept of religion ("taste and feeling for the infinite") and the ch. and lays the foundation for his view of subjectivism in religion; it shows traces of the influence of Kant, G. W. v. Leibniz,* F. W. J. v. Schelling,* and B. Spinoza.*

2. Schleiermacher became court preacher Stolpe 1802; prof. Halle 1804, Berlin 1807; also preacher Berlin 1809; dean of the theol. faculty U. of Berlin 1810. In 1811 he wrote *Kurze Darstellung des theologischen Studiums,* which presents theology as a positive science directed to the solution of a practical problem. His chief work is *Der christliche Glaube nach den Grundsätzen der evangelischen Kirche im Zusammenhang dargestellt* (1821–22), which defines piety as the feeling of gen. dependence, since man becomes aware that the whole world and his own freedom depend on God. The divine attributes of omnipotence, eternity, omnipresence, and omniscience are derived from application of the absolute feeling of dependence to God. To Schleiermacher, redemption is the transition from restricted to unrestricted consciousness of God realized in a new soc. life regarded by the community as divinely founded and based on the activity of Christ; redemption involves the communication of the power of His consciousness of God to man. The Holy Spirit is regarded as the spirit pervading the whole community founded by Christ.

3. Though Schleiermacher attacked rationalism, he based his own theol. on inner consciousness rather than revelation.

See also *Lutheran Theology After 1580,* 9, 10; *Modernism,* 2; *Prussian Union; Social Gospel; Switzerland, Contemporary Theology in,* 1.

Schleitheim Confession. See *Democratic Declarations of Faith,* 1.

Schleswig-Holsteinische evangelisch-lutherische Missionsgesellschaft zu Breklum (Schleswig-Holstein Ev. Luth. Mission Soc. at Breklum). See *Breklum Missionary Society.*

Schletterer, Hans Michael (Michel; 1824–93). Conductor and writer on music; b. Ansbach, Ger.; taught at the U. of Heidelberg 1854–58; founded Augsburger Musikschule 1873. Works that he issued include *Musica sacra* (2 vols. of Luth. ch. music).

Schlick, Arnolt (perhaps ca. 1455–perhaps ca. 1525). Musicologist; b. perhaps Heidelberg, Ger., or in Boh.; blind, apparently at least as early as 1486; noted organist. Works include *Spiegel der Orgelmacher und Organisten; Tabulaturen etlicher Lobgesang und Liedlein.*

Schlink, Edmund. See *Dogmatics,* B 13.

Schlosser, Jakob. See *Kaiser, Jakob.*

Schlunk, Martin (1874–1958). B. Calicut (now also called Kozhikode), cen. Kerala, S India, on the Malabar Coast; pastor Bottschow, near Frankfurt an der Oder; head North* Ger. Miss. Soc. in Bremen 1908–28; prof. Tübingen 1928; chm. Ger. Ev. Miss. Council. Works include *Die Weltreligionen und das Christentum; Die Weltmission des Christentums.*

Schlüter, Edwin Albert Benjamin (Schlueter; Aug. 28, 1880–Mar. 9, 1952). B. Watertown, Wis.; educ. Wauwatosa, Wis. Wisconsin* Syn. pastor Kingston, Wis., 1903, also serving neighboring congs.; Markesan, Green Lake Co., Wis., 1909; Oshkosh, Wis., 1921. Pres. Synodical* Conf. 1944–50.

Schmalkaldic Articles. See *Lutheran Confessions,* B 2.

Schmalkaldic Convention (1540). See *Schwenkfelders,* 4.

Schmalkaldic League. Defensive league of ev. princes organized 1531 at Schmalkalden, Hesse-Nassau, Prussia, Ger.

After the 1529 Diet of Speyer* the future looked dark for Prots. For subsequent events up to the 1530 Diet of Augsburg see *Luther, Controversies of,* g; *Lutheran Confessions,* A 2.

The Imperial Recess of Augsburg, pub. Nov. 19, 1530, gave Prots. 6 mo. grace. Prot. leaders met at Schmalkalden late in Dec. 1530 to protest terms of the recess, request modification of the terms, and prepare for the formation of a league. The protest fell on deaf ears; the request was not granted; the league was organized Feb. 1531 for defense against attacks threatened by emp., diet, and the leagues of Dessau* and Regensburg.* Temporary relaxation of RC-Prot. tension was arranged 1532 in the Nürnberg* Religious Peace by the emp., who needed national unity over against advancing Turks. A meeting of Luth. theologians was held in connection with the Feb. 1537 meeting of the league (see *Lutheran Confessions,* B 2).

For later hist. of the league see *Charles V; Schmalkaldic War.*

Schmalkaldic War. Charles* V was ready, when necessary or desirable, to follow a policy of reconciliation toward Prots. (see also *Regensburg Conference*). But when the Council of Trent* made reconciliation impossible, he moved to destroy the Schmalkaldic* League. John* Frederick ("the Magnanimous") and Philip* of Hesse were put under the ban 1546 and defeated at Mühlberg 1547. The league was dissolved and the Augsburg and Leipzig Interim* imposed. But the purpose of the league was attained as follows: The Interim was to be enforced by Maurice* of Saxony, who turned against Charles V 1552 and, with help of Fr., forced him to sign the convention of Passau.* TH

Schmalz. See *Smalcius.*

Schmauk, Theodore Emanuel (May 30, 1860–Mar. 23, 1920). B. Lancaster, Pa., where his father was Luth. pastor; educ. U. of Pa., Philadelphia, and Luth. Theol. Sem., Philadelphia; ordained Pa. Ministerium 1883; first asst. to his father, then pastor Lebanon, Pa.; pres. General* Council of the Ev. Luth. Ch. in N. Am. 1903–18; championed confessional Lutheranism; prof. Christian faith, apologetics, and ethics Luth. Theol. Sem., Mount Airy, Philadelphia, 1911–20; helped organize ULC. Ed. *The Lutheran; The Lutheran Church Review.* Other works include *A History of The Lutheran Church in Pennsylvania (1638–1820) from the Original Sources;* with C. T. Benze, *The Confessional Principle and the Confessions of the Lutheran Church; The Christian Kindergarten; Bible Readings: Precepts and Outlines; How to Teach in Sunday School.* JW

G. W. Sandt, *Theodore Emanuel Schmauk,* D. D., *LL.D.* (Philadelphia, 1921).

Schmelen, Johann Heinrich (1777–1848). B. Cassebruch, on the Weser, Hannover, Ger.; fled to London to escape the Fr. 1803; converted; resolved to be a miss.; studied in Berlin under J. Jänicke* 1807–10; returned to London; LMS miss. to S Afr. 1811–48; pioneer in Namaqualand*; m. a Hottentot and tr. the 4 gospels with her help; his work was taken over 1842 by the Rhenish* Miss. Soc.

Schmid, Christian Friedrich (1794–1852). B. Bickelsberg, near Sulz, Württemberg, Ger.; educ. Denkendorf, Maulbronn, and Tübingen; taught at Tübingen; conservative Luth. Works include *Biblische Theologie des Neuen Testaments; Christliche Sittenlehre.*

Schmid, Christoph Daniel von (Johann Nepomuk Christoph Friedrich; 1768–1854. "Canon Schmid"; b. Dinkelsbühl, Bav., Ger.; RC theol. and teacher; tried to teach children religion in stories suited to their feeling and world view. Works include *Biblische Geschichte.*

Schmid(t), Friedrich (Frederick; Sept. 6, 1807–Aug. 30, 1883). B. Dalddorf, Württemberg, Ger.; educ. Basel; ordained Lorrach, Baden, 1833; sent by Basel* Miss. Soc. to Am. 1833; pioneer pastor and miss. in and around Ann Arbor, Mich. See also *Indians, Lutheran Missions to North American; Michigan Synod,* 1, 2.

Schmid(t), Friedrich August (Frederick Augustus; Jan. 3, 1837–May 15, 1928). B. Leutenberg, principality of Schwarzburg-Rudolstadt, Thuringia, Ger.; to Am. as a child; educ. Conc. Sem., St. Louis, Mo. Pastor Eden, N. Y., 1857–59; Baltimore, Md., 1859–61. Taught at Luther Coll. (see *Luther College,* 1) 1861–72. Norw. Syn. prof. Conc. Sem., St. Louis, 1872–76. Prof. Luther Theol. Sem. (see *Luther Theological Seminary,* 1) 1876–85; Anti-Missouri* Brotherhood sem., Northfield, Minn., 1886–90; Luther Sem. (see *Luther Theological Seminary,* 4) 1890–1912. Prominent opponent of C. F. W. Walther* in predestinarian* controversy. Ed. *The Lutheran Watchman; Altes und Neues; Lutherske Vidnesbyrd; Luthersk Kirkeblad.* Other works include *Naadevalgsstriden; Intuitu fidei; Sandhed og Fred; Die Iowaischen Missverständnisse und Bemäntelungen.* See also *Evangelical Lutheran Church, The,* 8–13.

Schmid, Heinrich Friedrich Ferdinand (1811–85). B. Harburg, on the Wörnitz, near Nördlingen, W Bav., Ger.; educ. Tübingen, Halle, Berlin, Erlangen; prof. Erlangen. Coed. *Zeitschrift für Protestantismus und Kirche.* Other works include *Lehrbuch der Kirchengeschichte; Lehrbuch der Dogmengeschichte; Die Dogmatik der evangelisch-lutherischen Kirche dargestellt und aus den Quellen belegt* (tr. C. A. Hay and H. E. Jacobs, *The Doctrinal Theology of the Evangelical Lutheran Church, Exhibited, and Verified from the Original Sources*).

Schmidt, Carl (1868–1938). B. Hagenow, Mecklenburg, Ger.; educ. Leipzig and Berlin; prof. ch. hist. Berlin. Ed. *Koptisch-gnostische Schriften; Manichäische Handschriften der staatlichen Museen.* See also *Gnosticism,* 8.

Schmidt, Carl Christoph (Nov. 8, 1843–Oct. 14, 1925). B. Bonfeld, Württemberg, Ger.; to Am. 1852; educ. Conc. Sem., St. Louis, Mo. Pastor NYC 1868; Elyria, Ohio, 1872; Indianapolis, Ind., 1877; St. Louis, Mo., 1887. Pres. Western Dist. of the Mo. Syn. 1891–98; held other dist. and syn. offices. Works include *Erkenntnis des Heils; Glaube und Liebe; Katechismuspredigten; Leichenreden; Weg des Lebens; Lasst euch versöhnen mit Gott!*

Schmidt, Erasmus (Schmied; Schmid; 1570[1560?]–1637). B. Delitzsch, Ger.; adjunct philos. Wittenberg 1596, then prof. Gk. and math. Works include an improved ed. of T. Beza's* Lat. NT. See also *Concordances, Bible; Lutheran Theology After 1580,* 3.

Schmidt, Georg (Sept. 30, 1709–Aug. 2, 1785). B. Kunewalde, Moravia; sent from Herrnhut by Moravians (see *Moravian Church,* 3) as miss. to S Afr. 1736/37; worked among Hottentots. See also *Africa,* A 5, B 5.

Schmidt, Hans (1877–1953). B. Wolmirstedt, near Magdeburg, Ger.; co-worker of G. H. Dalman* at Ger. Ev. Inst. for Archaeology of the Holy Land in Jerusalem 1910–11; prof. Tübingen, Giessen, Halle; influenced by J. F. H. Gunkel.* Works include *Die Grossen Propheten und ihre Zeit; Der Mythos vom wiederkehrenden König im Alten Testament; Hiob: Das Buch vom Sinn des Leidens; Das Gebet der Angeklagten im Alten Testament; Gott und das Leid im Alten Testament; Der heilige Fels in Jerusalem; Jona; Luther und das Buch der Psalmen; Die religiöse Lyrik im Alten Testament; Die Thronfart Jahves am Fest der Jahreswende im alten Israel.*

Schmidt, Hans Christian (Heinrich? May 25, 1840–Mar. 6, 1911). B. Flensburg, Den.; spent some time with Herrnhuters at Christianfeld; soldier 1863; brought to Am. by J. C. F. Heyer* 1869; ordained Pa. Ministerium 1869; pastor Carlisle, Pa.; miss. to Rajahmundry, India, 1870; retired 1902. Completed Telugu ch. book begun by Heyer; helped rev. Telugu Bible. Interested in industrial missions.

Schmidt, Johann Eusebius (1669[1670?]–1745). B. Hohenfelden, near Erfurt, Thuringia, Ger.; educ. Jena, Erfurt, Leipzig; curate 1697, then pastor Siebleben, near Gotha; hymnist. Hymns include "Fahre fort, fahre fort, Zion, fahre fort im Licht."

Schmidt, Karl Ludwig (1891–1956). B. Frankfurt am Main; taught Berlin, Giessen, Jena, Bonn, Basel; exponent of *Formgeschichte* (see *Isagogics,* 3). Works include *Der Rahmen der Geschichte Jesu; Die Polis in Kirche und Welt.*

Schmidt, Martin Joseph (Mar. 25, 1846–May 1, 1931). B. Altenburg, Perry Co., Mo.; educ. Conc. Sem., St. Louis. Pastor Weston, Platte Co., Mo., 1868; served congs. in Town Dallas and at and near St. Johns, Clinton Co., Mich., 1869–72; pastor Saginaw, Mich., 1872–94; pres. Mich. Dist. of the Mo. Syn. 1882–91; prof. Conc. Coll., Fort Wayne, Ind., 1894–1917, dir. 1894–1903.

W. F. Kruse, "Prof. Martin Joseph Schmidt, D. D.," *CHIQ,* V, No. 1 (April 1932), 35–46.

Schmidt, Michael Ignaz (1736–94). B. Arnstein, Lower Franconia, NW Bav., Ger.; trained by Jesuits; separated from them and joined RC enlightenment movement; taught at Würzburg; imperial councillor and archivist Vienna. Works include *Geschichte der Deutschen.*

Schmidt, Nathaniel. See *Geography, Christian,* 6.

Schmidt, Sebastian (Schmid; 1617–96). B. Lampertheim, Alsace; rector and preacher Lindau; prof. theol. Strasbourg. Works include *Collegium biblicum;* Lat. tr. of the Bible. See also *Lutheran Theology After 1580,* 3; *Spencer, Philipp Jacob.*

Schmidt, Wilhelm (1839–1912). B. Erfurt, Ger.; pastor Schönstedt, Henschleben, and Cürtow (Neumark); prof. Breslau 1894. Works include *Zur Inspirationsfrage; Der alte Glaube und die Wahrheit des Christentums.*

Schmidt, Wilhelm (1868–1954). Philol., ethnographer; b. Hörde, near Dortmund, Westphalia, Ger.; RC priest 1892; prof. Mödling, near Vienna, later in Vienna; dir. Vatican miss. exhibit 1924; dir. papal miss. museum in the Lateran Palace 1926; prof. Fribourg, Switz. Works include *Der Ursprung der Gottesidee.*

Schmidt, William (Dec. 11, 1803–Nov. 3, 1839). B. Dunsbach (or Dünsbach), Württemberg, Ger.; educ. Halle; tutor in family of Brit. consul Teneriffe, Canary Islands, 1826; to Am. 1826. Luth. pastor near Weinsberg, Holmes Co., Ohio, 1827–28; joined The Ev. Luth. Joint Syn. of Ohio* and Other States 1828; pastor Canton, Ohio, 1828–30; prof. and pres. the Ev. Luth. Theol. Sem. that was begun 1830 at Canton, Ohio (see *Ministry, Education of,* VI C) 1830–37.

Schmidt, William (July 26, 1855–May 31, 1931). B. Hermannsburg, Hannover, Ger.; to Am. 1871; educ. Capital U., Columbus, Ohio. Pastor Hopewell Twp., Mercer Co., Ohio, 1878–81; Pomeroy, Ohio, 1881–86. Prof. hist. Luther Sem., Afton and St. Paul, Minn., 1886–1927 (see also *Ohio and Other States, The Evangelical Lutheran Joint Synod of,* 8). Assoc. ed. *Lutherische Kirchenzeitung;* with P. A. Peter wrote *Geschichte der Allgemeinen Evang.-Lutherischen Synode von Ohio und anderen Staaten;* with W. Schuette wrote *Sighard: The Tale of a Centurion;* with L. Schuh wrote *Through Luther to Liberty: A Story of the Reformation Period.* Other works include *Sri Ramuldu.*

Schmiedel, Paul Wilhelm (1851–1935). B. Zaukeroda (Zauckeroda; Zauckerode; Zaukerode), Saxony, Ger.; taught Jena and Zurich. Works include commentaries on 1 and 2 Co and 1 and 2 Th; arts. in *Encyclopaedia Biblica;* partial rev. of J. G. B. Winer's* NT grammar.

Schmieder, Heinrich C. See *Canada,* A 14.

Schmieder, Heinrich Eduard (1794–1893). B. Schulpforte (Schulpforta; Pforta), Hesse, Ger.; educ. Leipzig; embassy preacher Rome 1819; prof. and preacher Schulpforte 1824; at the Wittenberg theol. sem. from 1839; also mem. high consistory 1879; influenced by theosophy and mysticism of J. Böhme.* Contributed work on the prophets and apocrypha to K. F. O. v. Gerlach's* Bible commentary; other works include a devotional exposition of Jn 17.

Schmieding, Alfred August Friedrich (Alfried; Fred; Apr. 3, 1888–May 4, 1963). B. Malcolm, near Lincoln, Lancaster Co., Nebr.; educ. Conc. Teachers Coll., Seward, Nebr. Teacher at Newton, Kans.; Mount Olive, Ill.; North Saginaw, Mich. Prof. Conc. Teachers Coll., River Forest, Ill., 1922–58. Works include *Curriculum in Language for Lutheran Schools; Teaching the Bible Story; Reading in the Primary School; Understanding the Child; Sex in Childhood and Youth.*

Schmolck, Benjamin (1672–1737). B. Brauchitschdorf, near Liegnitz, Ger.; educ. Leipzig; asst. to his father at Brauchitschdorf 1701; diaconus 1702, archidiaconus 1708, senior 1712, pastor primarius and inspector 1714 Schweidnitz. Author; hymnist. Hymns include "Liebster Jesu, wir sind hier"; "Der beste Freund ist in dem Himmel"; "Wer nur mit seinem Gott verreiset"; "Tut mir auf die schöne Pforte"; "Jesus soll die Losung sein"; "Was Gott tut, das ist wohlgetan" (not to be confused with S. Rodigast's* hymn with the same 1st line).

Schmucker, Beale Melanchthon (Aug. 26, 1827–Oct. 15, 1888). Son of S. S. Schmucker*; b. Gettysburg, Pa.; educ. Luth. theol. sem. Gettysburg. Pastor Martinsburg and Shepherdstown, Va., 1847–51; Allentown, Pa., 1852; Easton, Pa., 1862; Reading, Pa., 1867; Pottstown, Pa., 1881–88. Conservative. Mem. Pa. Ministerium and General* Council of the Ev. Luth. Ch. in N. Am. Coed. *Hallesche Nachrichten.*

A. Spaeth, "Memorial of Beale Melanchthon Schmucker, D. D.," *The Lutheran Church Review,* VIII (1889), 105–127.

Schmucker, John George (Aug. 18, 1771–Oct. 7, 1854). Father of S. S. Schmucker*; b. Michelstadt, Ger.; to Am. 1785; prepared for ministry by Paul Henkel (see *Henkels, The,* 2); attended U. of Pa., Philadelphia; joined Pa. Ministerium in the early 1790s; ordained 1800. Served congs. in York Co., Pa.; Hagerstown, Md., 1794–1809; York, Pa., 1809–36; again in York Co., 1836–52; helped found The General* Syn. of the Ev. Luth. Ch. in the USA and the Luth. Theol. Sem., Gettysburg, Pa.

Schmucker, Samuel Simon (Feb. 28, 1799–July 26, 1873). Son of J. G. Schmucker*; father of B. M. Schmucker*; b. Hagerstown, Md.; educ. U. of Pa., Philadelphia, and Princeton (N. J.) Theol. Sem.; ordained 1821 The Ev. Luth. Syn. of Md., Va., and so forth (see *United Lutheran Church, Synods of,* 11, 29); served the parish in and around New Market, Va., up to 1826; began to prepare students for the ministry in the early 1820s; 1st prof. Luth. Theol. Sem., Gettysburg, Pa., from 1825/26; resigned 1864; helped found Gettysburg* Coll.

Works include *Kurzgefasste Geschichte der Christlichen Kirche, auf der Grundlage des vortreflichen Busch'en Werks; Elements of Popular Theology; Fraternal Appeal to the American Churches, with a Plan for Catholic Union, on Apostolic Principles; The American Lutheran Church, Historically, Doctrinally, and Practically Delineated; Definite Platform, Doctrinal and Disciplinarian, for Evangelical Lutheran District Synods, Constructed in Accordance with the Principles of the General Synod; American Lutheranism Vindicated; The Church of the Redeemer, as Developed in the General Synod of the Lutheran Church in America; The True Unity of Christ's Church: Being a Renewed Appeal to the Friends of the Redeemer, on Primitive Christian Union, and the History of its Corruption; A Plea for the Sabbath-School System; A Tract for the Times, or Elemental Contrast Between the Religion of Forms and of the Spirit; The Peace of Zion; Discourse on the Spiritual Worship of God; Evangelical Lutheran Catechism; Lutheran Manual on Scriptural Principles.* LEZ

See also *American Lutheranism; Definite Synodical Platform; Fraternal Appeal to the American Churches, with a Plan for Catholic Union, on Apostolic Principles.*

P. Anstadt, *Life and Times of Rev. S. S. Schmucker, D. D.* (York, Pa., 1896); V. Ferm, *The Crisis in American Lutheran Theology* (New York, 1927); L. Schmucker, *The Schmucker Family and the Lutheran Church in America* (n. p., 1937); K. Koch, *Influences that Contributed to the Theology of Samuel S. Schmucker* (STM Thesis, Conc. Sem., St. Louis, 1960); A. R. Wentz, *Pioneer in Christian Unity: Samuel Simon Schmucker* (Philadelphia, 1967).

Schnabel, Tilemann (ca. 1475–1559). Augustinian monk Alsfeld, Upper Hesse, Ger.; M. Luther's companion Erfurt and Wittenberg; joined ev. movement in Hesse 1521; forbidden to preach; left monastery and went 1523 to Luther, who sent him as preacher to Leisnig, on the Freiberger Mulde, near Döbeln; recalled to Hesse 1526 by Philip* of Hesse; leader in Reformation of Hesse.

Schneckenburger, Matthias (1804–48). B. Thalheim, near Tuttlingen, Württemberg, Ger.; educ. Tübingen and Berlin; prof. Bern, Switz. Works include *Vergleichende Darstellung des lutherischen und reformirten Lehrbegriffs.*

Schnedermann, Georg Hermann (1852–1917). Luth. theol.; b. Chemnitz, Ger.; educ. Leipzig and Erlangen; taught in Switz., Westphalia, and Leipzig; interested in the background of the life of Jesus. Works include exposition of 1 and 2 Co, Eph, Cl, Phmn, and Ph in *Kurzgefasster Kommentar,* ed. H. Strack and O. Zöckler.

Schneegass, Cyriacus (Cyriakus; 1546–97). B. Buffleben, near Gotha, Thuringia, Ger.; educ. Jena; pastor Friedrichroda, near Reinhardsbrunn and Gotha 1573; also adjunct to the supt. of Weimar; hymnist. Hymns include "Das neugeborne Kindelein"; "Herr Gott, Vater, wir preisen dich"; "Gib Fried, o frommer, treuer Gott."

Schneeweiss, Simon (fl. 16th c.). B. Znaim (Znojmo), S Moravia, Czechoslovakia; court preacher of George* of Brandenburg-Ansbach; pastor Creilsheim (Crailsheim), N Württemberg, Ger., 1534; took part in Hagenau* Colloquy, Colloquy of Worms,* and Regensburg* Conference 1540–41; signed SA.

Schneider, Johann. See *Agricola, Johann.*

Schneider, Johann Christian Friedrich (1786–1853). Composer; b. Altwaltersdorf (now Waltersdorf), near Zittau, Ger.; educ. Leipzig; organist and music dir. Leipzig; music dir. at the Dessau royal chapel 1821. Works include oratorios (e. g., *Die Höllenfart des Messias; Das Weltgericht; Die Sündflut; Das verlorene Paradies; Jesu Geburt; Christus der Meister; Christus das Kind; Pharao; Gideon; Absalon; Das befreite Jerusalem; Salomonis Tempelbau; Gethsemane und Golgatha; Christus der Erlöser*); cantatas; masses; hymns.

Schneider, Johannes (1857–1930). B. Höxter, on the Weser, Westphalia, NW Ger.; educ. Greifswald, Leipzig, and Bonn; pastor Warburg 1882, Lichtenau 1883, Elberfeld 1891; held various other positions. Ed. *Kirchliches Jahrbuch für die evangelischen Landeskirchen Deutschlands* from 1894; other works include *Was leistet die Kirche dem Staat und dem Volk?*

Schneider, Paul (1897–1939). "Prediger von Buchenwald"; ev. theol.; b. Pferdsfeld, near Kreuznach, Ger.; pastor 1926; his support of the Bekennende Kirche (see *Kirchenkampf*) led to conflict with Nazis; imprisoned 1937 at Buchenwald, where he died.

Schneider, Reinhold (1903–58). RC writer; b. Baden-Baden, Ger.; merchant; influenced by F. W. Nietzsche,* A. Schopenhauer,* S. A. Kierkegaard,* and M. de Unamuno* y Jugo; concerned with question of power and manifestation of God's activity in the world. Works include *Philipp der Zweite; Die Hohenzollern; Das Inselreich; Innozenz der Dritte.*

Schneller, Johann Ludwig (1820–96). B. Erpfingen, S Württemberg, Ger.; school teacher 1838; housefather and teacher at the boys' training school at Vaihingen 1843; head of Pilgermission St. Chrischona* 1847; transferred 1854 to Jerusalem. See also *Middle East,* G.

Schnepf, Erhard (Schnepff; Erhardus Schnepfius; Schnepffius; Snepfius; Sunipes; 1495–1558). B. Heilbronn, Ger.; educ. Erfurt and Heidelberg; preacher 1520; helped reform Nassau and Württemberg (see also *Blarer, Ambrosius; Grynäus,* 1); signed SA; prof. Tübingen 1544; forced to leave 1548 for opposing Interim*; prof. Jena 1549; opposed Philippists* at Consultation of Worms* 1557. See also *Regensburg Conference.*

Schniewind, Julius (1883–1948). B. Elberfeld, Ger.; educ. Bonn, Halle, Berlin, Marburg; prof. NT Halle 1914, Greifswald 1927, Königsberg 1929, Kiel 1935, Halle 1936; dismissed from office in Kirchenkampf*; opposed R. Bultmann's demythologization.* Works include commentaries on Mt and Mk in *Das Neue Testament Deutsch.*

Schnitger, Arp (1648–1719 [1720?]). B. Schmalenfleth, Oldenburg, Ger.; organ builder with factory at Neuenfelde and later at Hamburg.

Schnitzer, Josef (1859–1939). RC theol.; b. Lauingen, on the Danube, Swabia, W Bav., Ger.; prof. Dillingen 1893, Munich 1902; advocated reform; opposed encyclical *Pascendi* (see *Encyclicals*). Works include *Quellen und Forschungen zur Geschichte Savonarolas; Savonarola; Hat Jesus das Papsttum gestiftet?* (original title *Das Papsttum eine Stiftung Jesu?*).

Schnorr van Carolsfeld, Julius (1794 [1795?]–1872). Painter; b. Leipzig, Ger.; trained in Vienna; joined Nazarenes (see *Nazarenes,* 3) in Rome. Known for the pictures he contributed to an ed. of M. Luther's Ger. Bible; other works include *Luther at the Diet of Worms.*

Schober, Gottlieb (Shober; Nov. 1, 1756–June 27, 1838). B. Bethlehem, Pa.; trained in the Moravian faith; lawyer; N. C. Syn. pastor Salem (now part of Winston-Salem), N. C., 1810; helped form The General* Syn. of the Ev. Luth. Ch. in the USA and was its pres. 1825; rationalist.

Schöberlein, Ludwig Friedrich (Schoeberlein; 1813–81). Ev. theol.; b. Colmberg (or Kolmberg), near Ansbach, Ger.; prof. Heidelberg 1850, Göttingen 1855; consistorial councillor Göttingen 1862; abbot Bursfelde 1878. Works include *Schatz des liturgischen Chor- und Gemeindegesangs nebst den Altarweisen in der deutschen evangelischen Kirche; Ueber den liturgischen Ausbau des Gemeindegottesdienstes in der deutschen evangelischen Kirche.*

Schodde George Henry (Apr. 15, 1854–Sept. 15, 1917). B. Allegheny (now part of Pittsburgh); educ. Ev. Luth. Theol. Sem., Columbus, Ohio, and Tübingen and Leipzig; specialized in Heb. and allied Semitic languages. Pastor Canal Winchester, Ohio, 1877; Martin's Ferry, Ohio, 1878. Prof. Capital U., Columbus, Ohio, 1880. Tr. Book of Enoch from Ethiopic. Other works include *Outlines of Biblical Hermeneutics; The Protestant Church in Germany.*

Schoeneich, Aleksander Edward (1861–1939). Luth. pastor; b. Warsaw, Poland; educ. U. of Dorpat (called Tartu 1918); vicar Warsaw 1886; pastor Lublin 1888; supt. Warsaw diocese 1903, E diocese 1921.

Schöffel, Johann Simon (1880–1959). Luth. theol.; b. Nürnberg, Ger.; educ. Erlangen and Leipzig; pastor Schweinfurt 1909, Hamburg 1922; syn. pres. 1929; territorial bp. Ch. of Hamburg 1933; founded divinity school Hamburg (later dept. of theol. U. of Hamburg) 1949; prof. systematic theol.

Schola cantorum (Lat. "school of singers"). See *Choir* (musical); *Gregorian Music,* A 1.

Scholarios, Georgios Kurteses. See *Gennadius* II.

Scholasticism (from Gk. for "school"). 1. Occidental philos. movement dominant in the later Middle Ages; concerned with dogmatics; accepted the body of doctrine then current as complete; used dialectics (see *Dialectic*) and speculation in discussing and trying to comprehend, harmonize, and prove doctrines rationally; reasoning came to be patterned largely after that of Aristotle.*

2. Two schools of realism* (divided bet. followers of Aristotle and those of Plato*) and a school of nominalism* developed. See also *Anselm of Canterbury; Conceptualism.*

3. Other exponents of Scholasticism include P. Abelard,* Albertus* Magnus, Alexander* of Hales, G. Biel,* J. Duns* Scotus, Gilbert* de la Porree, W. of Ockham,* Peter* the Lombard, Roscellinus,* Thomas* Aquinas.

4. In the 12th c. Scholasticism fought for recognition; in the 13th it reached its zenith; in the 14th and 15th it declined.

5. Some mystics (e. g., Bernard* of Clairvaux) opposed Scholasticism, some (e. g., Bonaventura*) blended mysticism* and Scholasticism. Other opponents of Scholasticism include R. Bacon.*

Scholten, Jan Hendrik (Johann Heinrichs; 1811–85). Ref. theol.; b. Vleuten, Neth.; prof. NT, dogmatics, practical theol., and philos. of religion Leiden; at first exponent of Groningen* school, later leader of the modernism* of the "Leiden School." Works include *De leer der Hervormde Kerk en hare grondbeginselen; Symboliek en werkelijkheid.*

Scholz, Heinrich (1884–1956). B. Berlin, Ger.; student of K. G. A. v. Harnack*; prof. Breslau 1917, Kiel 1919, Münster 1928; at first conceived of religion in the sense of R. Otto*; later influenced by K. Barth,* B. A. W. Russell,* and A. N. Whitehead.*

Schongauer, Martin (Schöngauer; also called Martin Schön; or Hipsch, and Hübsch Martin; Bel Martino; Martinus Bellus; [le] Beau Martin; ca. 1425/53 [probably ca. 1450]–1491). Painter, draftsman, engraver; b. Colmar, Alsace; influenced A. Dürer.* Works include *Madonna of the Rose Bower* (variously entitled).

Schönherr, Johann Heinrich (Schoenherr; 1770–1826). Theosophist; b. Memel, Prussia; tried to develop a dualistic system (which posited 2 primitive potencies [named fire and water, or light and darkness], one male and active, the other female and passive, both personal and having intellect, will, form, and color; from their union resulted the universe, including God) in harmony with revelation.

Schönherr, Karl Gottlob (Schoenherr; Schonherr; 1824–1906). Painter; b. Lengefeld, Saxony, Ger.; prof. Academy of Arts, Dresden. Works include *The Good Shepherd; Christ Knocking at the Door.*

Schools, Church-Related. Some denominations maintain their own schools, with instruction directed toward faith as a motive for all of life. Most ch.-related schools are Christian, some Heb.

In 1970, RC elementary schools enrolled 3½ million students, secondary schools more than 1 million. Prot. chs. and ch.-related school assocs. enrolled 380,000 elementary, 55,000 secondary school students; of these, 190,000 elementary and 16,000 secondary school students attended Luth. schools. Heb. schools enrolled 58,000 elementary, 15,000 high school students. There are also some unaffiliated Christian schools. WAK

See also *Christian Education; Ministry, Education of; Parish Education; Protestant Education in the United States; Public Aid to Church-Related Elementary Schools; Teachers.*

Schools, Early Christian. In this art., "school" is used in the theol. as well as physical sense; Tertullian called Christianity a philos. (*De pallio,* 6).

1. *Alexandrian.* At Alexandria, Egypt, a university developed out of the catechumenate school. Leaders: Pantaenus,* Clement* of Alexandria, Origen.* Chief characteristics: allegorical exegesis and speculative theol. influenced by Gk. philos., esp. Philo* Judaeus.

2. *Roman.* Leader: Hippolytus.* Method: allegorical.

3. *Caesarean.* Begun by Origen,* discontinued at his death; his books formed the nucleus of the library of Pamphilus* of Caesarea, who reopened the school ca. 290. The school influenced the Cappadocian* Theologians.

4. *Antiochene.* Begun perhaps by Lucian* of Antioch. Used grammaticohistorical* method in opposition to allegorical method. After condemnation of Nestorius,* the school moved to Edessa,* later to Nisibis* (see 5 and 6).

5. *Nisibis.** Flourished esp. under Narsai.* See also 4 and 6.

6. *Edessa.** Begun by Ephraem.* See also 4 and 5.

See also *Exegesis.*

Schop, Johann (Schopp; ca. 1590–ca. 1660/67 [probably 1667]). Composer, instrumentalist; b. Lower Saxony, Ger.; mem. Dan. court orchestra 1615; in Hamburg 1621, first as dir. Ratsmusik, later city conductor and organist St. James. Works include melodies for hymns of J. v. Rist.*

Schopenhauer, Arthur (1788–1860). Ger. philos.; b. Danzig; to Hamburg 1793; educ. Göttingen and Berlin. His egotism and individualism made him unhappy. He rejected the moralism, philos. of religion, and idealism of his contemporaries in favor of aesthetics. He emphasized the transcendental aesthetic in the 1st section of I. Kant's *Critik der reinen Vernunft.* An examination of sensuous experience shows that man is driven by a will to live, an inner urge for sensations. This Schopenhauer regarded as part of a universal will, the process of becoming, a blind, irrational force that leads to desire, pain, and suffering. The indicated course for man is to negate the will by overcoming desire. Compassion is the highest moral principle. See also *Pessimism.*

Schoppe. See *Scioppius, Gaspar.*

Schornbaum, Karl (1875–1953). Catechist Nürnberg 1899; pastor Alfeld 1907; dean (or supt.; Ger.: Dekan) Roth 1917; dir. state ch. archives Nürnberg 1933; lectured at Erlangen. Ed. *Zeitschrift für bayerische Kirchengeschichte; Quellen zur Geschichte der Wiedertäufer.* Coed. *Die fränkischen Bekenntnisse.*

Schortinghuis, Willem (1700–50). Ref. theol.; b. Winschoten, Groningen prov., NE Neth.; educ. Groningen, Groningen prov. Pastor Weener, Ostfriesland, 1723; Midwolda, Groningen prov. Critical of institutional ch.; tried to awaken true Christianity. Works include *Het innige christendom; De geborene Christus.*

Schott, Heinrich August (Augustus; 1780–1835). B. Leipzig, Ger.; educ. Leipzig; prof. Leipzig and Jena; held a mediating position bet. rationalism and supernaturalism. Writings include an epitome of Christian theol.; a work on eloquence; a historicocritical introd. to the NT.

Schreiber, August Wilhelm (Nov. 8, 1839–Mar. 22, 1903). B. Bielefeld, Westphalia, Ger.; educ. Halle and Erlangen; trained for miss. work in London and Edinburgh; Rhenish* Miss. Soc. miss. to Sumatra 1866; returned to Ger. 1873 because of failing health of his wife; continued in Rhenish Miss. Soc. and was its head 1889–1903. Tr. NT into Batta.

Schreuder, Hans Paludan Smith (1817–82). Luth. miss.; b. Sogndal, Norw.; formed his own miss. committee; mem. The Norw. Miss. Soc. 1844–73; failed 1844 to gain admission to Zululand, NE Natal, E Union of S. Afr.; turned to China, but was discouraged by K. F. A. Gützlaff* because of his light hair; returned to Afr. and was admitted to Zululand; bp. of the miss. 1866; founded The Ch. of Norw. Miss. by Schreuder 1873. See also *Africa,* B 5; *Norwegian Foreign Missions,* 1, 4.

Schriftganze. See *Sedes doctrinae.*

Schröckh, Johann Matthias (1733–1808). B. Vienna, Austria; prof. Leipzig and Wittenberg, Ger.; moderate supernaturalist (see *Supernaturalism*). Works include *Christliche Kirchengeschichte* (35 vols.); Christliche Kirchengeschichte seit der Reformation (10 vols.; 9–10 by H. G. Tzschirner*).

Schrödel, Andreas (Jan. 29, 1851–Nov. 21, 1909). B. Neustadt, Bav., Ger.; to Am. 1853; educ. Northwestern Coll. (Northwestern U.), Watertown, Wis., and Conc. Sem., St. Louis, Mo. Pastor Naugart (Marathon Co.) 1876 and Ridgeville 1881 (serving also Norwalk and Tomah), all in Wis. Prof. Northwestern Coll. 1889. Pastor St. Paul, Minn., 1893. Pres. Minn. Dist. Syn. of the Joint Syn. of Wis. and Other States 1906–09.

Schröder, Joachim (1613–77). Luth. pastor Rostock 1637; exponent of reform through repentance, sanctification, and ch. discipline.

Schröder, Johann Heinrich (1667–99). B. Hallerspringe (later called Springe), Hannover, Ger.; educ. Leipzig; influenced by A. H. Francke*; pastor Meseberg, near Wolmirstedt (Wolmirstädt), which is near Magdeburg, 1696; inclined toward Pietism; hymnist. Hymns include "Eins ist not, ach Herr, dies eine."

Schröder, Nikolaus Wilhelm. See *Grammars,* A.

Schroeter, Leonhardt (Schröter, Leonhart; Leonard; ca. 1532/40–ca. 1595/1600). Composer; b. probably Torgau, Ger.; city cantor Saalfeld 1561–76; succeeded D. Dressler* as Lat. school cantor Magdeburg. Works include many hymns (e. g., the tune "Freut euch, ihr lieben").

Schubart, Johann Martin (1690–1721). Ger. Luth. musician; pupil of J. S. Bach,* whom he succeeded as court organist and chamber musician at Weimar.

Schubert, Franz Seraph Peter (1797–1828). Composer; b. Vienna, Austria; music teacher in Vienna; noted for songs. Works include *Erlkönig; Stabat Mater; Kyrie; Salve Regina; Magnificat;* masses; *Hark, Hark, the Lark; Who Is Sylvia?*

Schubert, Gotthilf Heinrich von (1780–1860). Luth. philos. and naturalist; b. Hohenstein, Saxony, Ger.; studied theol. at Leipzig, medicine and natural sciences at Jena; physician Altenburg 1803; dir. Realinstitut Nürnberg 1809; prof. Erlangen 1819, Munich 1827. Works include *Die Geschichte der Seele.*

Schubert, Hans Georg Wilhelm von (1859–1931). B. Dresden, Ger.; educ. Leipzig, Bonn, Strasbourg, Zurich, Tübingen, Halle; taught at Rauhe Haus, Hamburg (see *Wichern, Johann Hinrich*); prof. ch. hist. Strasbourg, Kiel, Heidelberg. Works include *Geschichte der christlichen Kirche im Frühmittelalter; Lazarus Spengler und die Reformation in Nürnberg.*

Schuette, Conrad Herman Louis (Hermann; June 17, 1843–Aug. 11, 1926). B. Varrel, Hannover, Ger.; to Am. 1854; educ. Ev. Luth. Theol. Sem., Columbus, Ohio; pastor Delaware, Ohio, 1865–72. Prof. Capital U., Columbus, 1872; sem. prof. 1880; U. pres. 1890. Pres. The Ev. Luth. Joint Syn. of Ohio* and Other States 1894, National* Luth. Council 1923. Hymnist. Hymn translations include "O Holy, Blessed Trinity" (sometimes altered to "O Blessed, Holy Trinity"). Other works include *Zeugnisse zur Einigung und zum Frieden in der Wahrheit; Die Lehre von der Gnadenwahl in Fragen und Antworten gestellt* (Eng. *The Doctrine of Predestination in the Form of Questions and Answers*); *Church Members' Manual.*

Schuh, Henry Frederick (May 30, 1890–Dec. 21, 1965). Son of L. H. Schuh*; b. Tacoma, Wash.; educ. Capital U. and Ev. Luth. Theol. Sem., Columbus, Ohio; pastor Ashland, Ohio, 1915–16; asst. pastor Toledo, Ohio, 1916–31; dir. stewardship and finance ALC 1930–50; pres. ALC 1951–60 (elected 1950, took office Jan. 1, 1951); honorary pres. The ALC 1961–65.

Schuh, Henry Jacob (Dec. 29, 1851–Sept. 7, 1934). B. Bauernhoff of Maisbach, Ger.; to Am. 1853; educ. Capital U. and Ev. Luth. Theol. Sem., Columbus, Ohio. Pastor Canal Winchester, Ohio, 1874; Detroit, Mich., 1882; Pittsburgh, Pa., 1885; Anna, Ohio, 1912–23. Pres. Western Dist. of The Ev. Luth. Joint Syn. of Ohio* and Other States 1923. Works include *The Life of Louis Harms; Catechisations on Luther's Small Catechism; Lakeside Lectures on the Gospel Ministry; Sixteenth Century Reformation and the Lodge.*

Schuh, Lewis Herman (July 7, 1858–Sept. 29, 1936). Father of H. F. Schuh*; b. Galion, Ohio; educ. Capital U. and Ev. Luth. Theol. Sem., Columbus, Ohio. Pastor Tacoma, Wash., 1890–95; Grove City, Ohio, 1912–14; Toledo, Ohio, 1914–35. Pres. Capital U. 1901–12. Works include *Enjoying Church Work; How to Make Marriage a Success; The Happy Family; Life's Morning; Saved to Serve; The Hidden Life;* with W. Schmidt (1855–1931), *Through Luther to Liberty.* Comp. and ed. *Funeral Sermons; Missionary Sermons; Occasional Sermons.*

Schulte, Johann Friedrich von (1827–1914). B. Winterberg, Sauerland, Westphalia, W. Ger.; prof.

Prague; authority on canon law; Old Catholic (see *Old Catholics*); opposed doctrine of papal infallibility.

Schultens, Albert (1686–1750). B. Groningen, Neth.; educ. Groningen, Leiden, and Utrecht; Heb. and Arab. scholar; prof. Franeker and Leiden; stressed comparative study of Semitic tongues; noted for work in Heb. grammar. Works include *Origines Hebraeae;* commentaries on Jb and Pr.

Schultz, Clemens (1862–1914). Ev. theol.; b. Hamburg, Ger.; pastor Hamburg 1896; noted for soc. and youth work; tried to combine freedom with fellowship. Works include *Die Halbstarken.*

Schultz, Frederick. See *Canada,* A 2.

Schultze, Christopher Emanuel. See *Mühlenberg, Henry Melchior, and Family,* 8.

Schultze, John Andrew (1775–1852). Son of C. E. Schultze (see *Mühlenberg, Henry Melchior, and Family,* 8); b. Tulpehocken, Pa.; Luth. pastor 1796–1804 (assist to his father); representative and state senator for several yrs.; gov. Pa. 1823–29.

Schultze, Maximilian Victor (Viktor; 1851–1937). B. Fürstenberg, near Corbach [Korbach], Waldeck, Ger.; educ. Basel, Strasbourg, Jena [Bonn?], Göttingen; taught Leipzig 1879; prof. ch. hist. and archaeol. Greifswald 1884. Works include *Das evangelische Kirchengebäude. Archäologie der altchristlichen Kunst; Die altchristlichen Bildwerke und die wissenschaftliche Forschung; Alchristliche Städte und Landschaften; Geschichte des Untergangs des griechisch-römischen Heidentums; Grundriss der christlichen Archäologie.*

Schulz, David (1779–1854). B. Pürben, near Freystadt, Silesia; educ. Halle, Ger.; taught Halle 1806, Leipzig 1807; prof. Halle 1809, Frankfurt an der Oder 1809, Breslau 1811; mem. royal consistory Silesia; dismissed from consistory for signing 1845 declaration against conservatives; rationalist; opposed Pietism,* F. D. E. Schleiermacher,* E. W. Hengstenberg.*

Schulz, Johann Abraham Peter (Schultz; 1747–1800). Musicologist; b. probably Lüneburg, Ger.; dir. of music Fr. Theater, Berlin, 1776–78; later active at Rheinsberg, and then at Copenhagen for ca. 7 yrs., then in Ger. again. Works include *Lieder im Volkston;* perhaps known best for his melody for "Ihr Kinderlein, kommet."

Schulz, Paul (Mar. 23, 1879–Jan. 30, 1950). B. Lindenau, West Prussia, Ger.; to Am. 1879; educ. Conc. Coll., Fort Wayne, Ind., and Conc. Sem., St. Louis, Mo. Pastor Bradford, New Albany, and Brownstown, Ind., 1900–04; Cincinnati, Ohio, 1904–21; Springfield, Ill., 1921. Pres. Cen. Ill. Dist. of the Mo. Syn. 1927–32; mem. Mo. Syn. Bd. of Dirs. 1932–50.

Schulze, Ernst Carl Ludwig (Ernest Carl Louis; Jan. 29, 1854–Oct. 9 [10?], 1918). B. Hüllhorst, Rheinberg, Westphalia, Ger.; to Am. ca. 1856; educ. Conc. Coll., Fort Wayne, Ind., and Conc. Sem., St. Louis, Mo. Pastor NYC 1878–80; Schenectady, N. Y., 1880–1918. Pres. Atlantic Dist. of the Mo. Syn. 1906–18. Works include *The Real Truth about Socialism; The Lodge Problem; Lebensversicherung.*

Schulze, Ludwig Theodor (1833–1918). B. Berlin, Ger.; educ. Berlin; taught NT exegesis and Biblical theol. at Berlin 1859; assoc. prof. theol. Königsberg 1863; head of theol. sem. Magdeburg 1866–74; prof. Rostock 1874. Works include *August Neander; Friede im Herrn; Luther und die evangelische Kirche; Vom Menschensohn und vom Logos; Friedrich Adolf Philippi.*

Schumann, Robert Alexander (1810–56). Composer; b. Zwickau, Ger.; educ. Leipzig. Founded and ed. *Neue Leipziger Zeitschrift für Musik;* other works include an opera; symphonies; overtures; piano pieces; songs; a Mass; a Requiem.

Schupp, Johann Balthasar (Schuppe; Schuppius; 1610–61). B. Giessen, Ger.; studied philos. and theol. at Marburg; prof. Marburg 1635, also preacher 1643; court preacher, consistorial councillor, and inspector at Braubach 1646; pastor Hamburg 1649; advocated ch. reform, but his writings displeased many. Hymnist.

Schuppe, Ernst Julius Wilhelm. See *Immanence.*

Schurff, Augustin (Schiurff; Schurpf; ca. 1495–1548). Brother of J. Schurff*; b. Saint Gall, Switz.; taught medicine at Wittenberg, Ger. Works include *Consilia medica.* See also *Frederick III.*

Schurff, Jerome (Schurf; Schürpf; Hieronymus; ca. 1480–1554). Brother of A. Schurff*; b. Saint Gall, Switz.; educ. Basel and Tübingen; prof. law Wittenberg; accompanied M. Luther to Worms; prof. Frankfurt an der Oder. Works include *Consiliorum centurias tres.* See also *Frederick III.*

Schütz, Heinrich (Sagittarius; 1585–1672). Luth. composer; b. Köstritz, Saxony, Ger. Works include 4 Passions (see *Passion, The*); oratorios (see *Oratorio*); psalms; sacred songs.

H. J. Moser, *Heinrich Schütz: His Life and Work,* tr. C. F. Pfatteicher (St. Louis, 1959); E. H. Müller von Asow, *Heinrich Schütz* (Leipzig, 1925); F. Spitta, *Heinrich Schütz, ein Meister der musica sacra* (Halle, 1925).

Schütz, Johann Jakob (1640–90). B. Frankfurt am Main; educ. Tübingen; lawyer Frankfurt; friend of P. J. Spener* (see also *Pietism*); later, under influence of J. W. Petersen,* he became a separatist. Hymnist; wrote "Sei Lob und Ehr' dem höchsten Gut."

Schuurman, Anna Maria van (1607–78). B. Cologne, Ger.; lived in Utrecht from 1623; linguist and artist; joined Labadists at 60 (see *Labadie, Jean de*). Works include *Pensées sur la Réformation nécessaire à présent à l'Eglise de Christ.*

Schwab, Johann Baptist (1811–72). RC hist.; b. Hassfurt, Lower Franconia, N Bav., Ger.; priest 1834; prof. ch. hist. and canon law Würzburg 1840. Tried to reconcile RC consciousness with scientific world view. Retired 1851.

Schwabach Articles. See *Lutheran Confessions,* A 2.

Schwan, Heinrich Christian (Apr. 5 [4?], 1819–May 29, 1905). B. Horneburg, Hannover, Ger.; educ. Göttingen and Jena; private tutor Dorum, Hannover; ordained 1843; miss. Leopoldina, Bahia, Brazil; to US 1850; pastor Neu-Bielefeld (now Black Jack), St. Louis Co., Mo., Sept. 1850; joined Mo. Syn. Oct. 1850; pastor 1851–81, asst. 1881–99 Cleveland, Ohio; helped popularize use of Christmas tree in Am. chs. Pres. Cen. Dist. of the Mo. Syn. 1860–78; pres. Mo. Syn. 1878–99. Commissioned by the Mo. Syn. 1890 to prepare a catechism; it appeared 1896 and became known as the Schwan Catechism.

E. W. Meier, "The Life and Work of Henry C. Schwan As Pastor and Missionary," *CHIQ,* XXIV, No. 3 (Oct. 1951), 132–139; No. 4 (Jan. 1952), 145–172; XXV, No. 2 (July 1952), 72–85; No. 3 (Oct. 1952), 97–121; K. Niermann, "Did Schwan Do Mission Work in Brazil?" *CHIQ,* XXV, No. 3 (Oct. 1952), 122–124.

Schwärmerei. See *Enthusiasm.*

Schwartz, Christian Friedrich (Oct. 22, 1726–Feb. 13, 1798). B. Sonnenburg, near Küstrin (Cüstrin), Brandenburg, Prussia; educ. Halle; ordained Copenhagen 1749; miss. to Tranquebar 1750; to Trichinopoly 1762; severed connection with the Dan.-Halle Miss. 1767 and became a miss. of the Ch. of Eng.; moved to Tanjore in the late 1770s and d. there.

Schwartz, F. W. See *Catholic Apostolic Church,* 2.

Schwarz, Gottfried (1845–1920). B. Kornmünster, Württemberg, Ger.; taught in Jaffa 1869, Beirut 1880; pastor Rosenberg and Binau, Baden, 1887. Held that Jesus is the ideal of humanity; rejected Trin., sacraments, justification, ministry, and ch. organization. Works include *60 Sätze gegen die Irrlehren der Christenheit.*

Schwarz, Johann Michael Nikolaus (Mar. 21, 1813–June 21, 1887). B. Hagenbüchach, near Langenzenn, Bav., Ger.; educ. Dresden miss. sem. (see *Leipzig Evangelical Lutheran Mission*); ordained 1842; miss. to India 1843; 1845–49 dir. of sem. founded 1842 by J. H. K. Cordes*; head of miss. station Poreiar 1850–51; based at Trichinopoly 1852–59, Mayavaram (called Mayuram since 1949) 1859–69, Tranquebar 1870–84; resigned because of eye trouble; d. Tranquebar.

Schwarz, Karl (1812–85). Ev. theol.; b. Wiek, on Rügen is., Ger.; educ. Halle, Berlin, and Greifswald; taught at Halle; court preacher Gotha 1856; gen. supt. in state ch. 1877; advocated freedom for ch. in doctrine, cultus, and govt.; cofounder Deutscher Protestantenverein (Ger. Protestant* Union); rationalist. Works include *Das Wesen der Religion.*

Schwarzenberg, Friedrich Johann Josef Cölestin von (1809–85). RC theol.; b. Vienna, Austria; abp. Salzburg 1836; cardinal 1842; prince abp. Prague 1850. Opposed liberalism and Protestantism; championed ultramontanism*; opposed doctrine of papal infallibility.*

Schwebel, Johannes (Schweblin; ca. 1490–1540). B. Pforzheim, Ger.; educ. Tübingen and Heidelberg; mem. Hospitallers of the Holy Spirit (brotherhood of knights that received papal sanction 1198); ev. preacher 1519; left Hospitallers 1521. Reformer of Zweibrücken. Works include *Form und Maass, wie es von den Predigern des Fürstentums Zweibrücken in nachfolgenden Mängeln soll gehalten werden.*

Schwegler, Friedrich Carl Albert (Karl; 1819–57). B. Michelbach, near Schwäbisch-Hall, Ger.; educ. Tübingen; student of F. C. Baur*; prof. Tübingen. Works include *Das nachapostolische Zeitalter in den Hauptmomenten seiner Entwicklung; Geschichte der Philosophie im Umriss; Römische Geschichte.*

Schweigger, Solomon (1551–1622). Successor of S. Gerlach* at the Ger. embassy at Constantinople; continued efforts to unite E Orthodox Ch. and Luth. Ch. See also *Crusius, Martin.*

Schweitzer, Albert (1875–1965). Cleric, philos., physician, musician; b. Kaysersberg, Upper Alsace; educ. Strasbourg; med. miss to Lambaréné, Fr. Equatorial Afr., 1913; emphasized apocalyptic element in the teaching of Jesus; did not adhere to fundamental Christian doctrines, e. g., deity of Christ; held that all world views based on nature are pessimistic, since nature is ultimately life-denying, and hence man must affirm his will to live, developing a philosophy of love; his ethics stressed reverence for life. Works include *Kulturphilosophie; Geschichte der Leben-Jesu-Forschung; Geschichte der Paulinischen Forschung von der Reformation bis auf die Gegenwart; Das Christentum und die Weltreligionen; Das Problem des Friedens in der heutigen Welt; Johann Sebastian Bach.* See also *Lutheran Theology After 1580,* 13; *Widor, Charles Marie Jean Albert.*

Schweizer, Alexander (1808–88). Ref. dogmatician; b. Murten (Morat), Switz.; educ. Zurich and Berlin; prof. 1840, pastor 1844 Zurich; influenced by F. D. E. Schleiermacher.* Works include *Homiletik der evangelisch-protestantischen Kirche systematisch dargestellt; Die Glaubenslehre der evangelisch-reformirten Kirche dargestellt und aus den Quellen belegt; Pastoraltheologie, oder Lehre von der Seelsorge des evangelischen Pfarrers.*

Schwemmer, Heinrich (1621–96). Luth. musician; b. Gumpertshausen, near Hallburg, Lower Franconia, NW Bav., Ger.; taught school at Nürnberg from 1650; dir. music Frauenkirche, Nürnberg, 1656–96; teacher of J. Pachelbel.*

Schwenkfeld, Kasper von (Schwenckfeld; Schwenkfeldt; Kaspar Schwenkfeld von Ossig; Casper; Caspar; ca. 1489/90–1561). Prot. mystic; b. Ossig (Ossigk; Ossing), near Liegnitz, Silesia; educ. Cologne and Frankfurt an der Oder; not ordained; Hofrat Liegnitz 1518–23; supported the Reformation from probably 1517/18, helped introd. it in Silesia, but was soon estranged from it; rejected justification, Scripture as the only source and norm of faith, efficacy of sacraments as means of grace, pedobaptism, and the AC; fled persecution from place to place; followers called Schwenkfelders* or Schwenkfeldians. See also *Flacius Illyricus, Matthias; Frecht, Martin.*

Schwenkfelders. 1. Followers of K. v. Schwenkfeld.*

2. After Schwenkfeld's death they met occasionally, called themselves "Confessors of the Glory of Christ," but did not organize. Ca. 200 of them emigrated to Pa. 1734 to escape persecution, settling esp. in Montgomery, Bucks, Berks, and Lehigh Cos.; by 1782 they organized a ch.; 1st ch. built 1790.

3. They hold a Eutychian monophysite theory of deification of Christ's human nature. The Lord's Supper, symbol of Christ's humanity and divinity, is regarded as a means of spiritual nourishment, but without change of elements. The mode of baptism is regarded as unimportant; the sacrament's efficacy as a means of grace is denied. Since 1895 they no longer object to war, secret societies, and oaths.

4. The 1540 Schmalkaldic Convention of Prot. theologians condemned S. Franck* and Schwenkfeld (CR 3, 985); the FC rejected 8 errors of Schwenkfeld (Ep XII 20–27; SD XII 28–35).

Schwerdtfeger, Johann Samuel Wilhelm (Schwerdfeger; June 4, 1734–1803). B. Burgbernheim, Bav., Ger.; educ. Erlangen; to Am. 1753 or 1754; served congs. in Pa., Md., and N. Y.; joined Pa. Ministerium 1762; helped organize N. Y. Ministerium 1786; served congs. in Dundas Co., Ont., Can., from ca. 1790/91. See also *Canada,* A 4.

Science. Originally designating all knowledge or learning, the term science has come to be limited to the systematized knowledge and study of the physical world. Logic and math are sometimes called abstract sciences. Concrete sciences are either physical science (astronomy, physics, chemistry, geology) or biological science (zoology, botany, bacteriology, paleontology), or cut across both (biochemistry, biophysics).

The distinguishing characteristic of science compared to other fields of accurate knowledge is emphasis on the method used, i. e., the scientific method. In the early hist. of science, authority was held supreme, and for cents. the supreme authority was Aristotle.* The type of reasoning followed was deduction almost without exception. The generalized principle was cited, based on authority, and the specific point in question was settled by application of this gen. principle.

Revolting against this often unfruitful and inaccurate method, F. Bacon* gave impetus to the inductive method applied by G. Galilei* in his demonstration of laws governing falling bodies. Bacon's extreme view that only the inductive method should be allowed has been supplanted by a compromise. The scientific method in modern science involves observation, formulation of a hypothesis, directed and controlled experimentation, drawing of conclusions. Conclusions thus reached are tentative, subject to review and possible revision and/or change on discovery of new facts. The deductive method is used in visualizing possible results expected from experimentation after a hypothesis has been formulated.

Science tries to understand completely the nature of matter and the laws relating to its forms and manifestations. It assumes the principle of causality.*

Gen. reluctance to allow or consider nonphysical or nonmaterial evidence is perhaps part of the reason for so-called conflicts bet. science and religion. The Christian religion concerns itself with matters outside the realm of physical measurement. OTW

O. T. Walle, "Toward an Evangelical Philosophy of Science," *CTM,* XXX (1959), 803–823.

Science, Christian. See *Church of Christ, Scientist.*

"Science and Health." See *Church of Christ, Scientist.*

Science of Religion. See *Religion, Comparative; Religion, Science of.*

Science, Philosophy, and Religion, The Conference on. Organized 1939 "to face the crisis in our culture by an experiment in corporate thinking, to build more secure foundations for democracy, and to explore the possibilities of collaboration between the various disciplines it represents." Sponsors various seminars, small group conferences, and publications. HQ NYC.

Scientific Empiricism. See *Logical Positivism.*

Scientific Method. See *Science; Semantics, General.*

Scientism. Thesis that factual knowledge based on rational interpretation of sensory evidence is the only valid knowledge. On a broader base it includes some nonsensory data drawn, e. g., from introspective observation. Excludes moral, aesthetic, and religious experience. Proponents include representatives of logical* positivism.

Scillitan Martyrs. Several Christian men and women from Scilla (or Scillium, or Sila, or Silli), an unidentified city in Numidia, N Afr., who were beheaded at Carthage 180.

Scioppius, Gaspar (Gasparus; Gaspar Sciopus; Kaspar [or Caspar] Schoppe; Schoppius; pseudonym Christoph von Ungersdorf[f], or Ungerssdorff; 1576–1649). B. Neumarkt, Upper Palatinate; educ. Heidelberg, Altdorf, Ingolstadt; RC 1598; worked in curia (see *Curia,* 2); conflict with Jesuits led to his retirement. Works include *Commentatio de arte critica; Pro auctoritate ecclesiae; De variis fidei controversiis.*

Scofield, Cyrus Ingerson (1843–1921). B. Lenawee Co., Mich.; lawyer in Kans. 1869; converted in St. Louis, Mo., 1879; ordained Cong. 1882. Pastor Dallas, Tex. 1882–95, 1902–07; Northfield, Mass. 1895–1902. Spent later yrs. writing and lecturing. Held that there were 7 dispensations in each of which God's relation to man was different. Ed. *The Scofield Reference Bible.* Other works include *Rightly Dividing the Word of Truth; Plain Papers on the Doctrine of the Holy Spirit; What Do The Prophets Say?*

Scotch Confession of Faith. See *Presbyterian Churches,* 1; *Presbyterian Confessions,* 2.

Scotists. See *Duns Scotus, John.*

Scotland, Free Church of. See Chalmers, Thomas; *Presbyterian Churches,* 1; *Scotland, Reformation in,* 2.

Scotland, Pre-Reformation Church History of. See *Celtic Church,* 3, 7.

Scotland, Reformation in. 1. The 1st wave of the Reformation was Luth. (see *Hamilton, Patrick*). Calvinism was est. largely through the influence of J. Knox.* The struggle bet. Presbyterianism and Episcopalianism lasted more than a c. In 1560 parliament adopted the confession of faith drawn up by Knox et al. and the Ref. Ch. was est. on Presb. lines. Knox's confession was replaced 1647 by the Westminster Confession 1647 (see *Presbyterian Confessions,* 3) and the Westminster* Catechisms 1648. With the revolution of 1688 and the fall of James II (see *England,* C 1) Scot. became overwhelmingly Presb. Union with Eng. 1707 (see *Great Britain*) brought the ch. in Scot. no share in the pol. and industrial prosperity that followed. Religious indifference reflected in deism* and the claim of the crown and landed aristocracy to clerical patronage* conflicted with Presb. concepts. Resultant dissatisfaction led to secession (see *Erskine, Ebenezer; Presbyterian Churches,* 1) and organization of the Ref. Presb. Ch. (see *Macmillan, John; Presbyterian Churches,* 1) and the Relief* Ch. In course of a c. the no. of separatist organizations had grown to ca. 500 congs. The United Secession Ch. was formed 1820, the United Presb. Ch. 1847 (see *Presbyterian Churches,* 1).

2. At the beginning of the 19th c. a reawakening took place under T. Chalmers* et al. The patronage struggle resumed and led to The Disruption and the organization of the Free* Ch. of Scot. 1843 (see also *Presbyterian Churches,* 1). The Free Ch. doubled its membership in the next 60 yrs. The right of patronage was removed by parliament 1874. Subsequently the Est. Ch. gained in popularity.

At the end of the 19th c. there were 3 large Presb. chs.: the Est. Ch., the Free Ch., and the United Presb. Ch. The difference bet. them principally involved the relation bet. ch. and state. Negotiations for union of the Free and United chs. opened 1863, broke off 1873, resumed 1896, resulted 1900 in organization of the United* Free Ch. of Scot. A small minority in the Free Ch. opposed union, declared itself to be the only true and legitimate Free Ch., and claimed all property of the Free Ch. Settlement was reached 1904.

Three small Presb. chs. had emerged: (1) Free Presb. Ch. of Scot.; (2) Ref. Presb. Ch.; (3) United Original Secession Ch. See *Presbyterian Churches,* 1.

3. *Scotch Episc. Ch.* (Scottish Episc. Ch.; Episc. Ch. of Scot.). Restoration of Charles II 1660 (crowned king Scot. Jan. 1, 1651; defeated by O. Cromwell* at Worcester Sept. 1, 1651; see also *England,* C 1) was followed by imposition of episcopacy on Scot. The Episc. Ch. came to rival the Presb. Ch. But after the death of Anne (1665–1714; Stuart queen Gt. Brit. and Ireland 1702–14) the Episcopalians were supposed to favor James, the Pretender, were regarded with distrust, and suffered repression under The House of Hanover, beginning with George I (George Louis; 1660–1727; king Gt. Brit. and Ireland 1714–27). Episcopal clerics regained some freedom 1719 after taking the oath of allegiance; many mems. continued to be nonjurors. The 2d Jacobite Rebellion 1745–46 nearly completed the destruction of Scotch Episcopalianism, which was regarded with renewed suspicion by The House of Hanover. But at the time of George III (George William Frederick; 1738–1820; king Gt. Brit. and Ireland 1760–1820) Episcopalianism clearly ceased to be a nonjuring ch. Restrictive measures were nearly all successively removed 1792, 1840, 1864.

4. *Congregationalists.* J. Glas(s), deposed from the Presb. ministry for indep. views 1728, formed an indep. ch. at Dundee ca. 1730. Other indep. chs. were organized later. See also *Disciples of Christ,* 1. The Evangelical* Union was formed 1843, the Cong. Union 1863. The Cong. and Ev. Unions (except for a minority of the latter) united 1896 to form the Cong. Union of Scot. The Bap. Union formed ca. 1750/65 and was comparatively small, Calvinistic in doctrine, simple in worship, and cong. in organization.

5. Other Prot. bodies include Meths. (Wesleyan and Primitive; J. Wesley* made the 1st of 22 visits to Scot. 1751), Soc. of Friends,* Catholic* Apostolic Ch., Unitarians,* Swedenborgians.*

6. When the Scot. parliament abrogated papal authority 1560 (see also 1), the RC Ch. in Scot. foundered almost completely. It survived only as a minority, esp. among Highlanders of Gaelic tongue. Its hierarchy was reorganized 1878.

Scott, George (1804–74). Eng. Wesleyan miss. to Stockholm, Swed., 1830; helped found Svenska Missionssällskapet 1835. Ed. *Nykterhets-Härold* (replaced 1836 by *Fosterlandsvännen*) and *Pietisten.*

Scott, Peter Cameron (1867–96). B. near Glasgow, Scot.; to Am. 1879; Internat. Miss. Alliance (see *Evangelistic Associations,* 5) miss. to Banana, Congo, 1891; returned to US because of failing health; helped found the Afr. Inland Miss. (see *Africa,* E 6) 1895; helped found miss. at Nzawi (Nzawe), in Kenya Colony, which after his death spread to Tanganyika, Uganda, Congo (Kinshasa), Chad, and Sudan.

Scott, Thomas (1705–75). B. Norwich, Eng.; teacher; preacher and pastor at several places; finally sole pastor Ipswich 1740; hymnist. Hymns include "Hasten, O Sinner, to Be Wise."

Scott, Walter (various pseudonyms; 1772–1832). B. Edinburgh, Scot.; lawyer, poet, novelist, historian, biographer. Poetic works as hymnist include a condensed rendering of "Dies* irae" ("That Day of Wrath, That Dreadful Day"); "When Israel of the Lord Beloved" (from *Ivanhoe*).

Scott, Walter (1796–1861). B. Moffat, Dumfriesshire, Scot.; educ. Edinburgh; to Am. 1818; helped found Disciples* of Christ. Works include *The Gospel Restored; The Messiahship, or the Great Demonstration.*

Scottish Prayer Book. See *Convenanters.*

Scottish Presbytery in London in Connection with the Church of Scotland, The. See *Presbyterian Churches,* 2.

Scottish Rite (Masonic). See *Freemasonry,* 4.

Scotus, John Duns. See *Duns Scotus, John; Scholasticism,* 3.

Scotus Erigena, Johannes. See *Erigena, Johannes Scotus.*

Scougal, Henry (1650–78). B. probably Leuchars, NE Fifeshire, Scot.; prof. Aberdeen; influenced early Meths. Works include *The Life of God in the Soul of Man.*

Scouting. See *Boy Scouts; Girl Scouts.*

Scriptorium. Workroom in medieval monasteries where MSS and books were written and copied.

Scriptura scripturam interpretatur (Lat. "Scripture interprets Scripture"). The hermeneutical principle that Scripture interprets itself, i. e., the meaning of a passage is to be understood in the context and light of other passages. The principle has also been stated: *Scriptura sacra sui ipsius interpres* (Lat. "Sacred Scripture [is] its own interpreter").

Scripture(s). See *Holy Scripture.*

Scriven, Joseph (1820–86). B. Dublin, Ireland; educ. Dublin; to Ont., Can. at 25. Wrote "What a Friend We Have in Jesus."

Scrivener, Frederick Henry Ambrose (1813–91). Angl. NT textual critic; b. Bermondsey, borough of London, Eng.; educ. Cambridge; held various positions; mem. NT rev. committee. Ed. a Gk. NT.

Scriver, Christian (pseudonym Gotthold; 1629–93). B. Rendsburg, Schleswig-Holstein, NW Ger.; educ. Rostock; archdeacon Stendal 1653; pastor Magdeburg 1667, where he also held other positions; court preacher Quedlinburg 1690; hymnist. Works include *Seelen-Schatz* and *Gottholds Zufälliger Andachten Vier Hundert;* hymns include "Der lieben Sonne Licht und Pracht."

Scrutiny (from Lat. for "search, investigate, examine"). 1. In the early ch., examination of the faith and life of candidates for baptism; made on 7 days ending Ash Wed. 2. In RCm, a mode of election (esp. of a pope by ballots of cardinals); also the examination of candidates for holy orders.

Scudder, John (1793–1855). B. Freehold, N. J.; educ. coll. of N. J. (later called Princeton U.) and Coll. of Physicians and Surgeons, NYC; Dutch Ref. Ch. miss. sent by ABCFM to Ceylon 1819; transferred to Madras 1836 for literary work; in the US 1842–46; from Madras to the Cape of Good Hope 1854 because of failing health.

Sculpture. See *Art, Ecclesiastical and Religious,* 4.

Seabury, Samuel (1729–96). B. Groton, Conn.; educ. Yale coll., New Haven, Conn.; ordained Prot. Episc. deacon 1753; miss. New Brunswick, Can., 1754–57; held various positions in N. Y.; guide to Brit. army 1776; consecrated 1st Prot. Episc. bp. in Am. by nonjuring Scot. prelates 1784. See also *Protestant Episcopal Church, The,* 3.

Seal, Luther's. See *Luther, Coat of Arms or Seal of.*

Seal, Sacramental. See *Character indelebilis.*

Seal of Confession. Seal of silence placed on one who hears private confession; places him under obligation not to reveal any sin confessed to him.

Seamen's Homes. Since seamen spend much time away from home, exposed to many temptations, institutions have been est. to provide for them a home away from home; in connection with these homes various Luth. chs. do miss. work in various ports.

Sebald. Legendary hermit and preacher near Nürnberg, Ger.; variously dated 8th–11th c.; patron saint Nürnberg; St. Sebald, Iowa, where the Ev. Luth. Syn. of Iowa* and Other States was organized, was named after him. See also *Church Architecture,* 11.

Se-Baptists. See *Smith, John.*

Sebastian. Acc. to tradition, a martyr, pierced by arrows, perhaps then beaten to death, under Diocletian* probably near the end of the 3d c.; b. perhaps Milan, It.; said to have been an army officer.

Sebastiani, Johann (1622–83). Luth. composer; b. Weimar, Ger.; in Königsberg from 1650. Works include *Das Leyden und Sterben unsers Herrn und Heylandes Jesu Christi nach dem heiligen Matthaeo,* which used chorale stanzas assigned to solo voice accompanied by strings. See also *Passion, The.*

Secession Church (Scot.). See *Erskine, Ebenezer.*

Secession Synod (Ireland). See *Presbyterian Churches,* 3.

Seckendorf, Veit Ludwig von (1626–92). The name Seckendorf is taken from the village of Seckendorf, bet. Nürnberg and Langenzenn. B. Herzogenaurach, near Erlangen, Ger.; educ. Strasbourg; held various positions, esp. in the service of Ernest* I; chancellor U. of Halle 1692; friend of P. J. Spener,* but himself not a Pietist; reconciled Pietists and Halle clergy 1692; hymnist. Works include *Commentarius historicus et apologeticus de Lutheranismo,* essentially a refutation of L. Maimbourg,* *Histoire du Luthéranisme.*

L. W. Spitz, "Veit Ludwig von Seckendorf: Statesman and Scholar," *CTM,* XVI (1945), 672–684.

Secker, Thomas (1693–1768). B. Sibthorpe, Nottinghamshire, Eng.; studied medicine London, Paris, Leiden; won from Dissent (see *Dissenter*) for the Ch. of Eng. by J. Butler* 1720; studied theol. Oxford; pastor at various places; bp. Bristol 1735, Oxford 1737; dean St. Paul's, London; abp. Canterbury 1758.

Second Advent of Christ. More properly called last, or final, coming, or advent of Christ, since He is spoken of as coming to us also in Word and Sacrament. See also *Last Things.*

Second Birth. See *Conversion.*

Second Blessing. Teaching of holiness* chs. that the Holy Spirit bestows entire sanctification (pure love of God, and a desire to do holy works, filling a clean heart) instantaneously. Justification, by which sins are forgiven, is regarded as the 1st blessing.

Second Cause. See *Causa secunda.*

Second Cumberland Presbyterian Church in US. See *Presbyterian Churches,* 4 b.

Second London Confession. See *Democratic Declarations of Faith,* 3.

Second Order. Order of nuns with common founder and spirit, and similar rules, of a corresponding order of men. See also *Dominicans.*

Secondary Education. See *Parish Education,* G.

Secret Societies. See *Lodges.*

Secretariat of Briefs to Princes. See *Curia,* 2 f.

Secretariat of Latin Letters. See *Curia,* 2 f.

Secretariat of State. See *Curia,* 2 f.

Sect (derived more probably from Lat. *sequi,* "to follow," than from *secare,* "to cut"). The following of some leader. In a narrow sense, a group that has separated from an older group by following another leader; or a group within a group (in this sense the Pharisees and Sadducees are called sects within Judaism; Acts 5:17; 26:5). In a wide sense, all religious bodies are sometimes referred to as sects.

Sectarianism. That which is characteristic of sects (see *Sect*). Usually defined as exclusive or narrow-minded adherence to a sect, denomination, party, or school of thought.

Secular Clergy. Mems. of the RC clergy* who live in the world (Lat. *saeculum*), in distinction from those who have withdrawn from the world, live under a rule (Lat. *regula*), and are called regular clergy; take precedence of regular clergy of equal rank; sometimes also called diocesan and parochial clergy.

Secularism (from Lat. *saeculum,* "race; generation; age; spirit of the age; world"). View based on the premise that this-worldly concepts are a sufficient framework and that religion and religious considerations may be ignored. Secularism is found in ancient (e. g., Lucretius*) and modern (e. g., F. Bacon*) philosophers and in various movements (e. g., Enlightenment,* naturalism,* romanticism,* modern technology, nationalism). When D. Bonhoeffer* spoke of a world that has come of age ("'mündig' gewordene Welt") he doubtless had in mind the fact that modern methods and insights have solved many problems formerly assigned to religious areas. The secularist feels that he no longer needs God, or at least lives as though there were no God.

Cleavage bet. secular and sacred leads to partial secularism. People worship God at fixed times and in fixed ways but live in their business, professional, educ., nat., and soc. world as though there were no God.

The term "secularism" is also applied to a system of ethics which holds that norms should be determined exclusively with reference to this world, i. e., atheistically. EL

See also *Bradlaugh, Charles; Holyoake, George Jacob; Ultramontanism.*

Secundus. See *Gnosticism,* 7 g.

Sedalia. Pastor's seat by side of and facing altar in chancel.

Sedes doctrinae (Lat. "seat [or base] of doctrine"). Term applied to clear passages of Scripture that treat individual doctrines and hence are proof passages (Lat. *dicta probantia*) for that doctrine. The view that doctrine is to be based on such individual passages is often opposed to the view that doctrine is to be determined by the entirety of Scripture (Ger. *Schriftganze*).

Sedulius, Coelius (Caelius; 5th c.). B. probably Rome, It.; probably teacher of heathen literature; Christian late in life. Works include *Carmen paschale; Hymnus de Christo,* from which the hymns *A solis ortus cardine* and *Hostis Herodes impie* have been drawn.

See. The seat (i. e., center of power or authority) of a bp.; the jurisdiction (e. g., province or diocese) of a bp. See also *Apostolic See.*

Seeberg, Erich (1888–1945). Son of R. Seeberg*; ev. theol.; b. Dorpat (Tartu); educ. Tübingen and Berlin; taught Greifswald 1913; army chaplain 1914–18. Prof. Breslau 1919, 1924; Königsberg 1920; Halle 1926; Berlin 1927. Works include *Luthers Theologie: Motive und Ideen; Luthers Theologie in ihren Grundzügen; Gottfried Arnold: die Wissenschaft und die Mystik seiner Zeit.*

Seeberg, Oskar Theodor Alfred (1863–1915). Brother of R. Seeberg*; ev. theol.; b. Pedua, Estonia; educ. Dorpat (Tartu), Erlangen, Leipzig; prof. Dorpat, Rostock, Kiel.

Seeberg, Reinhold (1859–1935). Father of E. Seeberg*; b. Pörrafer, near Pernau, Livonia; educ. Dorpat (Tartu) and Erlangen; taught Dorpat 1884, Erlangen 1889, Berlin 1898. Works include *Lehrbuch der Dogmengeschichte.* See also *Lutheran Theology After 1580,* 14.

Seehofer, Arsacius (d. 1545). B. Munich, Ger.; educ. Wittenberg; renounced Lutheranism; taught Ingolstadt; accused of using notes on P. Melanchthon's lectures in lectures on Paul's epistles; forced to retract 17 statements in his writings; imprisoned; excluded from the U.; A. v. Grumbach* et al., including M. Luther, protested the punishment; Seehofer escaped from prison, went to Wittenberg, was active for the Reformation in Prussia, taught in Augsburg, and became pastor in Württemberg, where he helped introd. the Reformation. Works were put on the Index* of Prohibited Books.

Seelsorge. Cure of souls. See also *Pastor as Counselor.*

Segura y Sáenz, Pedro (1880–1957). B. Carazo, Burgos, Sp.; priest 1906; bp. Coria 1920; abp. Burgos 1926; abp. Toledo, cardinal, and primate Sp. 1927; driven out by the govt. of the 2d rep. 1931; abp. Seville 1937; in conflict with pope and state; opposed 1953 concordat (see *Concordat,* 9); opposed tolerance toward Prots. advocated by US RCs.

Seiffert, Max (1868–1948). Musicologist; b. Beeskow, on the Spree, Ger.; studied at U. of Berlin under J. A. P. Spitta; prof. Berlin 1909. Ed. works of G. F. Handel,* J. P. Sweelinck,* et al.; *Sammelbände der Internationalen Musikgesellschaft.* Helped prepare *Denkmäler deutscher Tonkunst.* Comp. *Organum,* a collection of old music. Other works include Geschichte der *Klavier-Musik.*

Seiss, Joseph Augustus (Mar. 18, 1823–June 20, 1904). B. in (or near) Graceham, Frederick Co., Md., of Moravian parents; studied at Pa. Coll. (later called Gettysburg Coll.), Gettysburg, Pa., 1839–41, without graduating; studied theol. privately; licensed Ev. Luth. Syn. of Va. 1842. Pastor Martinsburg and Shepherdstown, Va., ca. 1843/44; Cumberland, Md., 1847; Baltimore, Md., 1852; Philadelphia, Pa., 1858–1904. Pres. Pa. Ministerium. Helped found Gen. Council* of the Ev. Luth. Ch. in (N.) Am. Ed. *The Lutheran.* Other works include *Ecclesia Lutherana; Lectures on the Gospels for the Sundays and Chief Festivals of the Church Year; Lectures on the Epistles for Sundays and the Chief Festivals; The Last Times and the Great Consummation; The Apocalypse.* See also *Fraternal Address.*

Seklucjan, Jan (Seklucyan; Johann Seklucian; Seclucianus; ca. 1500/10–ca. 1570/78). B. Siekluki, Radom Co., Poland; educ. Leipzig, Ger.; book dealer and customs collector Poznan; won for Reformation and championed it at Poznan 1541–44; forced to flee; pastor Königsberg-Steindamm; tr. arts. and books into Polish; pub. devotional Polish literature; helped pub. Polish NT.

Selbständige Evangelisch-Lutherische Kirche. See *Germany, Lutheran Free Churches in,* 14.

Selective Fellowship. Principle whereby the exercise of Christian fellowship* (e. g., pulpit, altar, prayer) is determined by an individual or by a local ch. See also *American Lutheran Church,* V.

Seleucid Era. See *Time.*

Self-Denial. To have fellowship with Christ involves denying oneself, crucifying the flesh, taking up the cross, and following Jesus in complete self-surrender (Lk 9:23; 14:27; Ro 8:13; Gl 5:24). It means, not to follow one's own will, but to do the will of Christ (1 Co 6:20), give up everything that is sinful, forego one's own comfort and pleasure in order to serve God and promote the welfare of others (Ph 3:7-8; 4:11-13). It is the opposite of self-will and self-indulgence. See also *Asceticism.*

Self-Righteousness. See *Pride.*

Selfishness. Concern for one's own welfare at the expense of or with disregard for that of others. Scripture admonishes against selfishness (e. g., Pr

11:26; Hg 1:4-6; Zch 7:6; Lk 6:32) and exhorts to care for others (e. g., Is 58:7; Ph 2:4; Ja 2:15-16; 1 Jn 3:17).

Selle, Christian August Thomas (Feb. 21, 1819–Apr. 3, 1898). B. Gelting, Angeln province, Schleswig, Ger.; teacher at 14; to Am. 1837; printer's apprentice and factory worker; studied theol. privately; licensed by what later was called The Ev. Luth. Joint Syn. of Ohio* and Other States. Pastor West Newton (then sometimes also called Robstown), Westmoreland Co., Pa.; New Lisbon, Columbiana Co., Ohio; withdrew from Ohio Syn. 1845 (see *Document of Separation*). Pastor Chicago, Ill., 1846. Charter mem. of the Mo. Syn. Pastor Crete, Ill., 1851; Rock Island, Ill., 1858. Prof. teachers sem., Fort Wayne, Ind., and Addison, Ill., 1861–93. Coed. *Evangelisch-Lutherisches Schulblatt.*

Selle, Thomas (1599–1663). Composer; b. Zörbig, near Bitterfeld, Saxony, Ger.; entered U. of Leipzig 1622; taught at Heide, Holstein, 1624; rector and dir. ch. music Wesselburen 1625; cantor Itzehoe 1634; cantor at the Johanneum,* Hamburg, 1641 (also worked at 5 chs.). Works include Passions, motets, ch. concertos, madrigals. See also *Madrigal; Motet; Passion, The.*

Sellin, Ernst Friedrich Max (1867–Dec. 31, 1945 [Jan. 1, 1946?]). B. Altschwerin, Mecklenburg, Ger.; taught at Erlangen, Vienna, Rostock, Kiel, Berlin. Conservative exegete. Works include *Der alttestamentliche Prophetismus; Jericho; Mose und seine Bedeutung für die israelitisch-jüdische Religionsgeschichte; Das Problem des Hiobbuches; Geschichte des israelitisch-jüdischen Volkes; Alttestamentliche Theologie auf religionsgeschichtlicher Grundlage; Einleitung in das Alte Testament.*

Selnecker, Nikolaus (Selneccer; Schellenecker; Selneccerus; Seleneccer; ca. 1528/30–1592). B. Hersbruck, near Nürnberg, Ger.; organist Nürnberg at ca. 12; studied in Wittenberg from ca. 1549 under P. Melanchthon; lectured on philol., philos., and theol.; court preacher Dresden ca. 1558; prof. theol. Jena 1565; prof. and pastor Leipzig 1568; court preacher Wolfenbüttel 1570; later active at Halle, Magdeburg, and Hildesheim, changing theol. circumstances largely determining his movements. Helped develop Thomas Choir, Leipzig. Helped prepare and promote FC (see *Lutheran Confessions,* C 2) and *Apologia oder Verantwortung des christlichen Concordienbuchs* 1582 (see also *Chemnitz, Martin; Kirchner, Timotheus*). Other works include *Christliche Psalmen, Lieder, und Kirchengesenge;* Lat. verse; theol. works in Lat. and Ger. See also *Neostadiensium admonitio; Passion, The.*

Selwyn, George Augustus (1809–78). Angl. churchman and miss.; b. Church Row, Hampstead, London, Eng.; educ. Eton and Cambridge; ordained deacon 1833; priest 1834; curate Windsor 1839; bp. New Zealand 1841. Est. a coll. to train candidates for the ministry 1843; a site for it near Auckland was selected 1844. Extended miss. work to the South Seas. Bp. Lichfield, Staffordshire, Eng., 1868. See also *Patteson, John Coleridge.*

Semantics, General. Discipline intended to train men in efficient methods of evaluation and better use of words and other symbols; formulated by A. H. S. Korzybski.*

Though described as non-Aristotelian, the system preserves the aims of Aristotle,* trying to update scientific methods of his day which, it claims, are reflected in the structure of Indo-European languages and have thus been retained in human evaluations, leading to serious results, many of which are said to be derived from an absolutistic, 2-valued, either-or orientation. It opposes ethical statements that classify behavior as only either good or bad, either right or wrong. Gen. semantics evaluates behavior on basis of a scale of many degrees bet. extremes by considering time, place, and context of actions. Its morality (a matter of self-control) aims at accumulating knowledge and making progress in civilization. Cooperation and freedom in the use of language for these purposes would demand elimination of assumptions, premises, creeds, prejudices, etc., that do not correspond to known scientific facts, in the estimation of gen. semanticists cause inadequate evaluations and lead to insanity, and otherwise impede progress.

Gen. semanticists reject belief in beings, events, or places whose reality or existence cannot be, or has not been, scientifically observed or determined. Statements involving a deity or "hereafter" are considered non-sense statements, which cannot be checked to determine correspondence to, or conflict with, scientific facts.

Gen. semantics is based on distinction bet. the chemistry-binding class of life (plants, which take in and use energies of sun, soil, water, and air), the space-binding class of life (animals, which appropriate basic energies and move about in space), and the time-binding class of life (man, who binds energies and space and, through the mechanism of recorded and spoken symbols, can start where the previous generation left off and continue accumulating knowledge for proper evaluation and guidance of his actions).

Gen. semanticists apply the scientific method (see *Science*) to all areas of human endeavor because it is considered to be the most accurate of all evaluative and predictive systems that have been used. Its use is regarded as essential to sane living in the present stage of man's development. AHN

A. H. S. Korzybski, *Science and Sanity: An Introduction to Non-Aristotelian Systems and General Semantics,* 3d ed. (Lakeville, Conn., 1948) and *Manhood of Humanity* (New York, 1921); C. Keyser, "Korzybski's Concept of Man," *Mathematical Philosophy,* Lecture 20 (New York, 1922), pp. 422–451; W. Johnson, *People in Quandaries: The Semantics of Personal Adjustment* (New York, 1946); I. J. Lee, *Language Habits in Human Affairs: An Introduction to General Semantics* (New York, 1941); G. A. Lundberg, *Can Science Save Us?* (New York, 1947); S. I. Hayakawa, "The Non-Aristotelian Revision of Morality," *ETC.: A Review of General Semantics,* III, 3 (Spring, 1946), 161–173, and *Language in Thought and Action* (New York, 1949).

Semi-Arianism. See *Antioch, Synods of; Arianism,* 3; *Basil of Ancyra; Macedonius.*

Semi-Pelagianism. Semi-Pelagians rejected Pelagianism (see *Pelagian Controversy,* 4–5) but did not deny freedom of the will and what they regarded as irresistible grace and predestination. They coordinated the human will and divine grace as factors in the work of salvation, holding that the reason why some are saved, others not, lies in an inner condition and receptivity in man, some making proper use of the will, others not; free will is only partially impaired but needs the help of divine grace; salvation is dependent on grace and the right use of natural powers. J. Cassianus* of Massilia (Marseilles) was an early leader of semi-Pelagians, who were first called Massilians.

Seminaries. See *Ministry, Education of,* IV–VI, IX–XIV.

Seminario Concordia. See *Ministry, Education of,* XI C; *Lutheran Church–Missouri Synod, Districts of The,* B 1, 2.

Seminole. See *Indians, American,* 7.

Semler, Johann Salomo (1725–91). Sometimes called "Father of Ger. rationalism"; b. Saalfeld, Thuringia, Ger.; raised under Pietistic influence; educ. Halle, where he came under rationalistic influence; prof. theol. Halle 1752–79. Tried to free science by distinguishing bet. "religion" and "theol." Prophecies and appeal to miracles are explained as accommodation to needs of the times. Rejected "natural" religion; regarded Christianity as originating in divine revelation. See also *Lutheran Theology After 1580,* 8.

Sendlinge. See *Lutheran Church – Missouri Synod, The,* I 2.

Sendomir, Consensus of (Consensus Sendomiriensis). See *Poland,* 2; *Reformed Confessions,* E 5.

Seneca, Lucius Annaeus (ca. 4 BC–65 AD). Roman rhetorician, eclectic Stoic philos., statesman, poet; b. Córdoba, Sp.; studied at Rome; entered legal profession; exiled to Corsica 41–49; returned to tutor young Nero*; later councillor of Nero, who turned against him; suicide by Nero's order. Held ethical goal to be life in harmony with nature; life is preparation for death. Seneca's apocryphal correspondence with Paul was known to Jerome.* Works include *De consolatione; De brevitate vitae; De constantia sapientis; De providentia;* dramatic writings.

Senegal, Republic of. See *Africa,* C 1.

Senestrey, Ignaz von (1818–1906). RC theol.; b. Bärnau, Upper Palatinate, NE Bav., Ger.; priest 1842; taught at sem. in Eichstätt; bp. Regensburg 1858; cardinal 1892. Advocate of doctrine of papal infallibility; worked for RC interests in Kulturkampf.*

Senfl, Ludwig (Senfel; Senffl; ca. 1486/92 [most probably 1486] – probably ca. 1542/43 [1555?]). RC composer; b. Basel [or Zurich?], Switz.; pupil of H. Isaak* and succeeded him at the court of Maximilian* I from ca. 1512/17; court conductor Munich ca. 1530–40. M. Luther thought highly of his music; some believe Senfl was a Luth. at heart. Compositions based on chorales used only pre-Reformation, not Luth., chorales. Works include masses, motets, Magnificats.

Sennert, Andreas (1606–89). B. Wittenberg, Ger.; prof. oriental languages Wittenberg. Works include *Hypotyposis harmonica linguarum orientalium; Grammatica orientalis eademque harmonica; De articulis fidei fundamentalibus exercitio theologica.*

Sensationalism (sensualism). Theory that all knowledge or ideas originate in sense perceptions. Philosophically it leads to empiricism,* ethically to hedonism.*

Sensualism. See *Sensationalism.*

Sensuality. Free indulgence in the lust* of the flesh.

Sensus literalis unus est. See *Hermeneutics,* 4.

Separate Baptists. See *Baptist Churches,* 24.

Separation of Church and State. See *Church and State,* 13–15; *Religious Liberty.*

Separatists. See *Communistic Societies,* 5; *United Church of Christ, The,* I A 1.

Sepp, Johann Nepomuk (Johannes; 1816–1909). RC hist.; b. Tölz, Upper Bav., Ger.; educ. Munich; traveled extensively; prof. Munich; deposed and expelled from the city 1847 for pol. reasons; reinstated 1850; retired 1867; opposed the doctrine of papal infallibility*; defended Old* Caths. Wrote *Das Leben Christi* in reply to D. F. Strauss,* *Das Leben Jesu,* adding a vol. on Acts; other works include writings on Christian archaeology and on the hist. of Bav.

Septuagesima Sunday. See *Church Year,* 3; *Quadragesima.*

Septuagint. See *Bible Versions,* A.

Sequence. In music, immediate repetition of a phrase at another pitch. In liturgics, additions that follow immediately after the Hallelujah.* Sequence texts are lengthy poems whose musical setting is usually syllabic. Sequences may have originated at least as early as the 8th c. The term "sequence" was apparently first used in the 9th c. Sequences include *Dies* irea; Veni, Sancte Spiritus; Victimae paschali laudes.* To be distinguished from trope.* See also *Canon; Notker* (ca. 840–912); *"Stabat mater"; Worship, Parts of,* 8.

Serampore Trio. Name applied to W. Carey,* J. Marshman,* and W. Ward* because of their assoc. with Serampore, Dan. India, where they est. a coll., library, schools, and a press, printed books and tracts, assembled translators from many parts of India, and pub. Bible versions. See also *India,* 10.

Seraphic Hymns. See *Worship, Parts of,* 11.

Seraphim. Heavenly beings described Is. 6:2-3 as having each 6 wings, and praising God with their voices. See also *Angels, Good,* 6–7.

Serapion (Sarapion; d. after 362). Bp. Thmuis, in the Nile delta, from before 339; friend of Athanasius* and supported him in his opposition against Arianism.*

Serbia. One of 6 republics in Yugoslavia; E of the Drina R.; Christianity was first introd. by the RC Ch. in the 7th c. under Heraclius,* who sent missionaries, who baptized some Serbs; but this led to no lasting results. In the 2d half of the 9th c. Basil I see *Schism,* 5) defeated the Serbian pirates and imposed Christianity by compulsion. The leading ch. is Serbian Orthodox, which 1879, as a result of Serbian revolt against the Turk, became free from the Ecumenical Patriarch under Turkish control.

Serbian Eastern Orthodox Church for the U. S. A. and Canada. See *Eastern Orthodox Churches,* 6.

Sergeant, John (Sargent; 1710–July 27, 1749). B. Newark, N. J.; educ. Yale coll. (called Yale U. since 1887), New Haven, Conn.; tutor Yale 1731–ca. 1734; ordained Cong. 1735; worked among Indians in the Housatonic Valley, Berkshire Co., Mass., till 1749 (see also *Indians, Lutheran Missions to North American*). Tr. prayers, portions of the Bible, and I. Watts's* shorter catechism into Indian.

Sergius (d. 638). Patriarch Constantinople 610–638; adviser of emp. Heraclius*; helped lead successful defense of Constantinople against Avars (a nation of Mongolian or Turkish origin) 626. Wrote Ecthesis.* See also *Acathistus.*

Sergius (Stragorodski; 1867–1944). Partriarch Moscow and all Russ.; b. Arsamas [Arzamas], near Nizhni Novgorod, Russ.; educ. Saint Petersburg; taught Moscow and Saint Petersburg; bp. Jamburg (Yamburg; called Kingisepp from 1922) 1901; abp. Fin. and Vyborg 1905; metropolitan Novgorod 1917; patriarch 1943. Tried to est. working relationship bet. ch. and state in Russ.

Sergius I (d. 701). B. Palermo, Sicily; pope 687–701; rejected the reforming decrees of the Quinisext* Syn.; interested in Eng. missions.

Serle, Ambrose (1742–1812). Commissioner in the Brit. Govt. Transport Office; hymnist. Works include *Horae solitariae;* hymns include "Thy Ways, O Lord, with Wise Design."

Sermon. See *Homiletics; Preaching, Christian, History of.*

Sernin, St. (ch. at Toulouse, Fr.). See *Church Architecture,* 7.

Serra, Junípero (Jose Miguel; Miguel Jose; 1713–84). B. Petra, Majorca, Sp.; Franciscan 1730; to Mexico City 1749; miss. to Indians NE of Querétaro 1750–58[59?]; then in coll. administration Mexico City; miss. in Dioceses of Mexico, Puebla, Oaxaca, Valladolid, and Guadalajara; to Lower Calif. 1767. Est. 9 missions, including San Diego 1769, San Francisco 1776, Santa Clara 1777.

Servetus, Michael (Miguel Serveto; probably 1511–53). Theol. and physician; b. probably Tudela, Navarre, N Sp. (or Villaneuva de Sigena, Huesca, NE Sp., in Aragon?); educ. Toulouse, Fr.; attended coronation of Charles* V at Bologna, It., 1530; anti-Trinitarian; arrested Vienne, Fr., 1553; escaped; arrested Geneva, It.; condemned; burned. Works include *De trinitatis erroribus; Christianismi restitutio.* See also *Calvin, John,* 6; *Socinianism,* 1; *Unitarianism.*

Service, Divine. See *Worship,* 4, 8.

Service Books. Books containing forms of worship. Before the Reformation there were many such books, including, e. g., breviaries (see *Breviary*), cantionales (see *Cantionale*), missals (see Missal), sacramentaries (see *Sacramentary*), troparia.* In Luth. chs., agenda* and lectionaries (see *Lectionary*) are common, in addition to books containing liturgies and hymnals with directives for conducting services. Antiphonaries (see *Antiphonary*) and other books containing musical settings are also used.

Service Centers. See *Armed Services Commission,* 5.

Service Pastors. See *Armed Services Commission,* 5.

Servites (Order of Friar Servants of St. Mary). Religious family of friars (priests and brothers), contemplative nuns, and conventual and secular tertiaries* founded 1233 when some cloth merchants of Florence, It., left their city and families to retire to an area near Florence for a life of poverty and penance. Miss. fields have included Arab., Philippines, Afr., Chile, and Brazil. See also *Annunciation, Orders of,* 5; *Mendicant Friars.*

Session. See *Elders,* 2; *Polity, Ecclesiastical,* 7; *Reformed Churches,* 1.

Sethians (Sethites). See *Gnosticism,* 7 i.

Settlements. In soc. work, institutions est. in congested city areas to supply educ., recreational, med., and other services.

Seuel, Johann Edmund (Apr. 21, 1865–May 9, 1951). B. Vincennes, Ind.; educ. Conc. Coll., Fort Wayne, Ind., and Conc. Sem., St. Louis, Mo.; ordained 1886; pastor Ogallala, Nebr., and miss. at large 1886–88; prof. Walther* Coll., St. Louis, 1888–1907; mgr. CPH, St. Louis, 1907–44; treas. to Mo. Syn. 1914–42; helped found Lutheran* Laymen's League.

Seven Cardinal Virtues. See *Cardinal Virtues.*

Seven Deadly Sins. See *Sins, Venial and Mortal.*

Seven Gifts of the Holy Spirit. Term often used in connection with Is. 11:2-3. Opinions vary as to the validity of "7." Some hold that the passage speaks of the Spirit as bestowing 6 gifts: wisdom, understanding, counsel, might, knowledge, fear of the Lord. Some arrive at the figure 7 in v. 2 by including the Spirit Himself as a gift bestowed. Some do not include the Spirit in the gifts, but find the 7th in v. 3a, where the LXX and Vulgate use a different term for "fear of the Lord" than in v. 2 at the end (though the Heb. is the same in both verses). The basic question persists: Must we find a list of 7 in this passage? See also *Gifts of the Spirit.* LP

Seven Hours (canonical). See *Hours, Canonical.*

Seven Joys of Mary. In RCm, the Annunciation, Visitation, Nativity of Christ, Adoration of the Magi, Finding the Child Jesus in the Temple, Appearance of the Risen Christ to Mary, Assumption and Coronation of Mary. Commemorated with a 7-decade rosary* called Franciscan Crown.

Seven Liberal Arts. See *Quadrivium;* Trivium.

Seven Penitential Psalms, The. Ps. 6, 32, 38, 51, 102, 130, 143. Used liturgically from ancient times, esp. in connection with penitential* days and seasons.

Seven Sages, or Wise Men of Greece. See *Thales.*

Seven Sleepers of Ephesus. Seven Christian youths who, acc. to a legend that originated perhaps in the 6th c., were walled up in a cave during the Decian persecution (see *Persecution of Christians,* 4), fell asleep, awoke and were released ca. 175/197 yrs. later. The legend varies considerably in details.

Seven Sorrows of Mary. In RCm, the Prophecy of Simeon, Flight into Egypt, Loss of the Child Jesus, Meeting Christ on the Way to Calvary, Standing at the Foot of the Cross, Taking Christ Down from the Cross, Burial of Christ. Commemorated on Fri. after Passion Sun. (Judica; 5th Sun. in Lent) and Sept. 15.

Seven Virtues. See *Cardinal Virtues.*

Seventh-day Adventists. See *Adventist Bodies,* 4; *Baptist Churches,* 16.

Seventh Day Baptist Youth Fellowship. See *Young People's Organizations, Christian,* III 20.

Seventh Day Baptists. See *Baptist Churches,* 16, 17; *Brethren,* 1.

Severians. See *Gnosticism,* 7 i.

Severinghaus, John Dietrich (July 22, 1834–Oct. 14, 1905). B. near Severinghausen, Hannover, Ger.; to Am. ca. 1850; educ. Wittenberg Sem. (theol. dept. of Wittenberg Coll. [see *Wittenberg University*]); ordained Miami Syn. 1862, later joined Wartburg Syn.; pastor Ohio, Ind., N. Y., Ill.; est. connection with C. Jensen* 1878 and arranged for students from Breklum, Ger., to enter the field of the Wartburg and Ger. Nebr. Synods. Pres. Wartburg Synod. Prof. German* Theol. Sem. of The General* Syn. of the Ev. Luth. Ch. in the USA, Chicago, Ill. Ed. *Lutherischer Hausfreund; Lutherischer Kirchenfreund; Chicago Banner.* See also *Breklum Missionary Society.*

Severinus (d. 482). Abbot and apostle Noricum; miss. on banks of Danube and Inn rivers in modern Bav. Founded monastery at Boiotro (near Passau) and another at Faviana.

Severus, Lucius Septimius (146–211). B. near Leptis, Afr.; Roman emp. 193–211. See also *Persecution of Christians,* 3.

Severus, Sulpicius. See *Sulpicius Severus.*

Sexagesima Sunday. See *Church Year,* 3; *Quadragesima.*

Sext (from Lat. for "6th"). One of the canonical hours,* at the 6th hour of the day acc. to old Roman reckoning.

Sexton (corruption of "sacristan*"). Originally an attendant on the clergy; now one in charge of ch. and parish bldgs. and their equipment and of related minor duties (often including bell ringing) as a custodian or janitor.

Sexual Life. See *Marriage.*

Seyffarth, Gustavus (July 13, 1796–Nov. 17, 1885). B. Übigau, Saxony, Ger.; educ. Leipzig; prof. archaeol. Leipzig; resigned; to Am. in the mid-1850s; prof. Mo. Syn. Gymnasium and Conc. Sem., Saint Louis, Mo., 1856–59; returned to archaeol. studies, this time in NYC.

The Literary Life of Gustavus Seyffarth . . . : An Autobiographical Sketch (New York, 1886).

Shabazz. See *Lost-Found Nation of Islam in the Wilderness of North America.*

Shabuoth (Shavuos; Shavuot; Shavuoth). See *Judaism,* 4.

Shaftesbury, Anthony Ashley Cooper, 3d Earl of (1671–1713). "Lord Ashley" 1683–99; Eng. moral philos.; freethinker.* B. London, Eng.; educ. by J. Locke* et al.; remained in Angl. ch.; opposed scholasticism* and enthusiasm*; tried to est. an ethic indep. of revelation. Collected treatises pub. as *Characteristicks of Men, Manners, Opinions, Times.* See also *Deism,* III 4.

Shahadah. See *Islam,* 1, 3.

Shakers. 1. Popular name of "The United Society of Believers in Christ's Second Appearing," or "The Millennial Church," a communistic sect also known as Alethians (from Gk. *aletheia,* "truth"). Originated in a Quaker revival in Eng. 1747; mems. called "Shaking Quakers" or "Shakers" because of their movements during religious excitement; joined 1758 by A. Lee* ca. 1757/58. Regarded celibacy as more perfect than marriage. To escape persecution, A. Lee led a small group to Am. 1774; settled at Niskeyuna, now Watervliet, near Troy, N. Y. First soc. organized 1787 Mount Lebanon, near New Lebanon, N. Y. Miss. work in the 1st half of the 19th c. extended the soc. to Ky., Ohio, and Ind.; membership is said to have reached ca. 5,000; decline began ca. 1860.

2. Teachings. God is dual, male and female. Christ is not God, but the highest spirit, and dual,

incarnate in Jesus (male) and A. Lee (female). Jesus and A. Lee are to be loved and honored (or respected), but not worshiped. Other tenets included communism, celibacy, non-resistance and non-participation in war, perfectionism, spiritism, insistence on pub. confession. Shakers rejected Trin., atonement, physical resurrection, final judgment, eternal damnation.

3. Community govt. was vested in 4 elders (2 men, 2 women). Services included addresses, hymns and anthems, and rhythmic marching. Sexes kept apart at table and worship.

Shakespeare, John Howard (1857–1928). Brit. Bap. preacher; pastor Norwich; secy. Baptist* Union of Gt. Brit. and Ireland 1898; leader in founding Bap. World Alliance (see *Union Movements,* 10) and Fed. Council of Ev. Free Chs. (see *Free Church Federal Council*). Works include *The Churches at the Cross-Roads; A United Free Church of England; Baptist and Congregational Pioneers.*

Shakespeare, William (Shakspere; many other variants; 1564–1616). Dramatist, poet; b. Stratford-upon-Avon, Warwickshire, Eng.; actor-playwright London 1592; bought New Place in Stratford 1597 but lived mainly in London till 1610; he and his children were bap. Angl.; he was buried in an Angl. ch., Stratford; but the question of his religious conviction and practice remains unanswered. Plays include *The Comedy of Errors; The Tragedy of Romeo and Juliet; The Merchant of Venice; The Tragedy of Julius Caesar; The Tragedy of Hamlet, Prince of Denmark; The Tragedy of King Lear; The Tragedy of Macbeth.*

R. M. Frye, *Shakespeare and Christian Doctrine* (Princeton, N. J., 1963).

Shaman. See *Indians, American,* 1; *Shamanism.*

Shamanism. Animistic cult of Ural-Altaic people of N. Asia and Eur. and of Eskimo and Am. Indian tribes. Named after Tungus term *shaman* for the priest-doctor, or medicine man, who heals the sick, divines the unknown, controls spirits, averts evil, accomplishes good, etc. by magic. Conjuring, trance, incantation, and use of drums are common in shamanism. In Korea shamanism is also called Sinkyo; the shaman is called pan-su. See also *Korea,* 4.

Shamash. See *Babylonians, Religion of the,* 1.

Shammai (fl. 1st c. BC). Rabbi; in tradition usually assoc. with Hillel* I; took a rigorous stand in religious and moral matters; mem. Sanhedrin.

Shang-ti. See *Chinese Term Question; Confucianism,* 3; *Taoism,* 4.

Shankaracharya (Shankara; Sankara; ca. 788–ca. 820/822). Hindu philos.; probably b. Malabar, India; advocated strict monism.* Works include commentaries on Vedanta philos. (see *Brahmanism,* 4).

Shapur II. See *Middle East,* L.

Shastras (sastras; shasters; Skt. "instruction"). Sacred books of the Hindus (see *Hinduism*). Often grouped in 4 classes: 4 Vedas, 4 Upa-vedas, 6 Ved-angas, 4 Up-angas. The 1st Up-anga includes the 18 Puranas, the Ramayana, and the Mahabharata; the 2d and 3d Up-angas consist of the main works on metaphysics and logic; the 4th Up-anga consists of the law. See also *Sacred Literature.*

Shavuos (Shavuot; Shavuoth; Shabuoth). See *Judaism,* 4.

Shaw, Barnabas (ca. 1793–1857). B. Elloughton, near Hull, Eng.; became Meth.; preacher; 1st Wesleyan miss. to S. Afr. 1816; worked esp. in Little Namaqualand.*

Shaw, George Bernard (1856–1950). Journalist; art, music, and dramatic critic; dramatist; b. Dublin, Eire; to London ca. 1876; exponent of socialism. Works include *The Quintessence of Ibsenism; Back to Methuselah; Saint Joan; The Intelligent Woman's Guide to Socialism, Capitalism, Sovietism, and Fascism.*

Shawnee. See *Indians, American,* 6.

Sheatsley, Clarence Valentine (Nov. 25, 1873–Jan. 19, 1943). Son of William Sheatsley; b. Paris, Ohio; educ. Capital U., coll. and sem. (Ev. Luth. Theol. Sem.), Columbus, Ohio, and Erlangen (Ger.) U.; ordained 1900. Pastor Pa. and Ohio. ALC miss. ex. Works include *Our Mission Field in India* (Ger. title *Unsere Mission in Indien*); *History of the Evangelical Lutheran Joint Synod of Ohio and Other States.*

Sheatsley, Jacob (June 20, 1859–Aug. 31, 1953). Son of John Frederick Sheatsley; b. Paris, Ohio; educ. Capital U., Columbus, Ohio, and German* Theol. Sem. of the Gen. Syn., Chicago, Ill.; ordained 1887; pastor Ohio. Ed. *Lutheran Standard* 1915–29. Other works include *Sermons on the Eisenach Gospels; The Bible in Religious Education;* S. S. literature.

Shedd, William Greenough Thayer (1820–94). Presb. educator; b. Acton, Mass.; educ. U. Vt. (at Burlington) and Andover (Mass.) Theol. Sem. Pastor Brandon, Vt., 1844–45; NYC 1862–63. Prof. U. Vt. 1845–52; Auburn (N. Y.) Theol. Sem. 1852–53; Andover 1855–62; Union Theol. Sem., NYC, 1863–74. Opposed higher* criticism. Works include *A History of Christian Doctrine; Dogmatic Theology.*

Sheeleigh, Matthias (Dec. 29, 1821–July 15, 1900). B. Charlestown [Charleston?], Chester Co., Pa. Educ. Pa. Coll., Gettysburg, Pa., and Lutheran Theol. Sem., Gettysburg, Pa. Pastor N. Y., Pa., and N. J. Dir. Lutheran Theol. Sem., Gettysburg. Ed. and coed. of several periodicals; author; poet.

Sheldon, Charles Monroe (1857–1946). B. Wellsville, N. Y.; educ. Brown U., Providence, R. I., and Andover (Mass.) Theol. Sem.; ordained Cong. 1886. Pastor Waterbury, Vt., 1886–89; Topeka, Kans., 1889–1912, 1915–19. Minister-at-large 1912–15. Exponent of social* gospel. Works include *In His Steps.*

Shem hammephorash (from Heb. *shem,* "name," and *parash,* "distinguished"). Term used by Jews in the Middle Ages to designate the tetragrammaton (Gk. "four-lettered"; specifically the Heb. divine name JHVH), commonly pronounced "Jehovah" by Christians, but not by Jews.

Shem hammephorash is a cabalistic term (*see Cabala*) which is not, but only represents, a real word of power, the use of which is said to have made possible the performance of many wonderful works. The exact meaning of the term is not known. M. Luther used the term in *Vom Schem Hamphoras und vom Geschlecht Christi* (WA 53, 573–648).

Shen. See *Chinese Term Question; Confucianism,* 3.

Sheol. See *Hereafter,* C 3.

Shepard, Thomas (ca. 1605–49). B. Towcester, S Northhamptonshire, Eng.; to Am. 1635; pastor Newtown (now Cambridge), Mass.; friend of J. Harvard*; helped est. Harvard coll., Cambridge; diary describes colonial life.

Shepherd of Hermas. See *Apostolic Fathers,* 5.

Sherlock, Thomas (1678–1761). B. London, Eng.; educ. Eton and Cambridge; master of Catherine Hall, Cambridge, and vice-chancellor of the U. 1714; dean Chichester 1715; canon Norwich 1719; bp. Bangor 1728; Salisbury 1734, London 1748. Advocated a measure of indep. for the ch.; opposed deism.* Works include *The Tryal of the Witnesses of the Resurrection of Jesus.*

Shi'ites (from Arab. *shi'ah,* "following; sect"). Mems. of Shi'a, one of the 2 major branches of Islam.* The main difference bet, them and the other major branch (Sunnites*) is the Shi'ite belief that the imamate (or caliphate; see also *Imam*) is hereditary, not elective, that it belonged to Ali, Muhammad's* son-in-law, and his descendants, and that all others who claim the office, including abu-Bakr,* are usurpers.

Shi'ites are found throughout the Muslim world.

They comprise 3 main groups: (1) *Zaidites* (named after Zaid, a grandson of Ali's son Husain) form the majority in Yemen (see *Middle East,* L 2). (2) Most *Ismailis* (named after Isma'il, son of Ja'far, the 6th imam; also called Seveners because they believe in 7 imams and the figure 7 is prominent also in other connections in their beliefs) are Khodjas (or neo-Ismailis) and are in India; other Ismaili groups include Assassins* (or Nizaris), Babists (see *Bahaism*), Carmathians (or Qarmatians; founded 9th c.; flourished in Middle Ages as a communistic secret soc.). (3) The creed of the *Twelvers* (so called because they believe in 12 imams) was est. as state religion in Iran 1502.

Shinto. 1. Ancient native religion of Japan. The word Shinto was coined from Chinese Mandarin for "way of the gods" (Jap. colloquial equivalent: *kami-no-michi*) to distinguish it from Buddhism.* Primitive Shinto was crude polytheistic nature worship of things called *kami* (Jap. "above; superior") that were dreaded and revered (e. g., various ancient deities of heaven [e. g., sun-goddess] and earth and their spirits; human being [mikados]; rain, thunder, wind; plants, trees, mountains, seas; echo; animals including dragon, fox, tiger, wolf, birds. The oldest surviving documents of Shinto are *Kojiki** (712 AD) and *Nihongi* (720 AD), but they are not sacred books in the common sense. Shinto has no supreme deity. The creator pair appears in the 7th generation of gods, when a male *kami,* Izanagi ("male who invites"), and a female *kami,* Izanami ("female who invites"), procreated the islands of Jap. and many gods and goddesses, including Amaterasu,* most eminent of Shinto deities and whose seat is at Ise.

2. Ancestor* worship was imported from China to Jap.

3. The gods are, as a rule, considered to be beneficent, thought they may cause illness and misfortune if their worship is neglected. On the other hand, the aid of the gods is sought as protection against plagues and disasters.

4. The emp. (or mikado; see also 1) came to be regarded as a descendant of Amaterasu and as the only "incarnate god." See also 9.

5. Shrines are simple, usually unpainted, wooden structures. Before them are torii (Jap. "bird residence"): gateways consisting of 2 uprights with a straight crosspiece near the top and a concave (ends curve upward) crosspiece at the top; both crosspieces (upper slightly longer than lower) extend beyond the uprights.

The spiritual emanation, or spiritual double of a deity is called *mitama.* The *mitama* has as its special place of residence the *shintai,* or god-body (e. g., a sword, stone, mirror, or other material object), which is usually in a shrine and usually in a box that is rarely or never opened.

6. Shinto has rituals and a hereditary priesthood; the emp. was chief priest (see 9); celibacy is not enjoined on priests, who wear distinctive dress only when engaged in worship. There is no cong. worship. Priests serve at local shrines only on special occasions, but worshipers may come at any time. Worship includes obeisance, handclaps. Formerly offerings of food, drink, and fabrics were made; in process of substitution these came to be replaced by *gohei* (wands with white paper strips attached as representations of the fabric formerly offered).

7. Shinto has no code of ethics; each one's heart tells him what he should do. Dirt is considered disrespectful of the deities; preliminaries to worship include bathing and putting on clean clothes. There is no sense of sin in the Christian sense, consequently no corresponding idea of forgiveness and redemption. Teachings regarding life beyond the grave are vague; there is no teaching regarding heaven and hell.

8. Shinto was absorbed by Buddhism ca. the 9th c. in a system called Ryobu (or Ryobu Shinto), more Buddhist than Shinto. Near the end of the 18th c. a reaction in favor of Shinto set in, leading to restoration 1868 of imperial power, which had been eclipsed since ca. 1300 by feudal lords called shoguns (or tycoons). But because it was so barren in ethical teachings, Shinto could not compete seriously with Buddhism. It was divided into State Shinto (patriotic ritual incumbent on all Japanese) and Sect or Religious Shinto and was kept alive mainly by festivals and pilgrimages, of which religion formed only a small part.

9. State Shinto was abolished 1947; the emp. disclaimed divinity. Sect Shinto expanded.

10. Buddhism awakened to new life early in the 20th c. and so encroached on Shinto that it is very hard to differentiate bet. Shintoists and Buddhists in Japan.

See bibliography under *Religion, Comparative.*

Shiva. See *Hinduism,* 4.

Shober. See *Schober.*

Shopar (Shofar; Heb. "trumpet"). Horn used in ancient Israel for battle call and on festivals (cf. Ju 3:27; Am 3:6). Used in synagogues on Day of Atonement.

Shore, James. See *England, Free Church of.*

Shoshoni. See *Indians, American,* 9.

Shriners. See *Freemasonry,* 9.

Shrovetide (Ger. *Festnacht; Fastenabend; Fastenienstag*). Three days immediately preceding Ash Wed., esp. Shrove Tue. (also called Mardi Gras [Fr. "fat Tue."]). The name is derived from Lat. *scribo,* "to write," in the sense of "prescribe," sc. penance; hence shrive: administer absolution; hear confession. Confession and absolution on these days were thought of as preparation for the proper observance of Lent.

Shrubsole, William (1759–1829). B. Sheerness, on the Isle of Sheppey, N Kent, Eng.; first a shipwright, then a clerk, then (in London) a bank clerk (or accountant) 1785, finally Secy. to the Committee of the Treasury. During the last 20 yrs. of his life he was a mem. of the Cong. Ch. and active in benevolent and reformatory institutions. Hymnist. Hymns include "When, Streaming from the Eastern Skies."

Shu. See *Confucianism,* 2.

Shulhan Aruk. See *Caro, Joseph ben Ephraim.*

Siam. See *Asia,* C 4.

Sibbs, Richard (Sibbes; 1575–1635). B. Tostock (or Sudbury?), Suffolk, Eng.; educ. Cambridge; noted preacher Cambridge and London; leading Puritan.

Sibel, Kaspar (1590–1658). Dutch Ref.; b. Unterbarmen, near Elberfeld, Ger.; educ. Herborn, Siegen, and Leiden. Pastor Randerath and Geilenkirchen, in principality of Jülich, 1609; Jülich 1611; Deventer 1617. Helped prepare for 1618–19 Syn. of Dordrecht.* Helped rev. Dutch Bible.

Sibylline Books and Oracles. A Sibyl (from a Gk. word of uncertain derivation) was an old prophetess. Acc. to tradition, the earliest was at Erythrae in Asia Minor (or at Marpessus, near Troy) and spoke of Helen and the Trojan war (ca. 1200 BC); next, say some, is the Sibyl of Cumae in Campania, It. (late 6th c. BC); the Cumaean Sibyl is often identified with the Erythraean. The next Sibyl was assoc. with Delphi, Greece. Sibyls were connected with many different places. All their old prophecies, in verse form, were apparently in Gk. Collections of them were lost or destroyed, some in Rome ca. 82, when the Capitol burned, and the rest ca. 400 AD. Jewish and Christian adaptations were mainly for propaganda. The 1st Jewish adaptation was probably made in Alexandria, Egypt, in the 1st half of the 2d c. BC. Some Christian writers, with Hermas apparently the 1st, speak of Sibyls and their oracles; some Christians were suspected of coining oracles for their own purposes. Fragments of oracles speak of a reign of peace and happiness; the coming of Christ, the Messiah; and eschatological details. See also *Roman Religion,* 2.

Sicarii. Party of Jewish terrorists that arose ca. 52 AD; mems. carried a hidden knife (Lat. *sica,* "dagger") as murder weapon used in attempts to drive the Romans out of the land. Some fled to Egypt, where they continued resistance against Roman authority (cf. Josephus, *Wars,* VII, x, 1).

Sichardus, Johannes (Ioannes; ca. 1499–1552). Humanist; jurist; b. Tauberbischofsheim, N Baden, Ger.; educ. Erfurt and Ingolstadt; taught at Munich and Basel; inspected monasteries and cathedral chaps. in the Rhineland; studied law in Freiburg; prof. Tübingen; held various positions, including that of counselor to Christoph* of Württemberg; irenic adherent of the Reformation. Ed. *Divi Clementis recognitionum libri X; Antidotum contra diversas omnium fere seculorum haereses.*

Sickingen, Franz von (1481–1523). B. Ebernburg, near Kreuznach, Lower Palatinate, W Ger.; champion of knights against princes (see *Knights' Revolt*); provided refuge in his castles for K. Aquila,* M. Bucer,* J. Oecolampadius.* Wrote in support of the Reformation.

Sickness. See *Healing.*

Siddhartha. See *Gautama Buddha.*

Sidgwick, Henry (1838–1900). Philos.; b. Skipton, Yorkshire, Eng.; educ. Rugby and Cambridge; prof. Cambridge 1883–1900; cofounder Soc. for Psychical* Research; advocated a form of utilitarianism.* Works include *The Methods of Ethics.* See also *Metaphysical Society, The.*

Sidney, Philip (1554–86). Prot. poet, statesman, soldier; b. Penhurst, Kent, Eng. Tr. a treatise by P. de Mornay* on the Christian religion from Fr. into Eng.; collaborated with his sister on a paraphrase of the Psalms.

Siebenbürgen. Ger. name of Transylvania.*

Sieck, Henry (Heinrich; July 1, 1850–Sept. 7, 1916). Father of L. J. Sieck; b. near Mannheim, Baden, Ger.; to US at age 4; educ. Conc. Coll., Fort Wayne, Ind., and Conc. Sem., St. Louis, Mo. Pastor Memphis, Tenn., 1873; South Bend, Ind., 1879; Erie, Pa., 1882; St. Louis, Mo., 1886; Stillwater, Minn., 1889–93; Milwaukee, Wis., 1895–1905. Dir. St. John's Coll., Winfield, Kans., 1893–95. Field Secy. (Ger. *Missionsdirektor*) Wis. Dist. of the Mo. Syn. 1905. Works include *Adventspredigten über ausgewählte Texte nebst Anhang: Reden zur Christfeier; Passionspredigten; Lenten Sermons; Sermons on the Gospels of the Ecclesiastical Year; Sermons on the Epistles of the Ecclesiastical Year.*

Sieck, Louis John (Mar. 11, 1884–Oct. 14, 1952). Son of H. Sieck*; b. Erie, Pa.; educ, Conc. Coll., Milwaukee, Wis., and Conc. Sem., St. Louis, Mo.; asst. to F. Pfotenhauer, Hamburg, Minn., 1904. Asst. Zion Luth. Ch., St. Louis, Mo.; pastor 1914–43. Teacher, pub. speaking, Walther Coll., St. Louis, 1909–10. Pres. Conc. Sem., St. Louis, 1943–52. Mem. Bd. of Dirs., Valparaiso (Ind.) U., 11 yrs. Pres. The Luth. Publicity Organization of St. Louis (organized Jan. 14, 1917); pres. St. Louis City Miss. Soc. (see also *Herzberger, Frederick William*); charter mem. Conc. Hist. Institute. Coauthor *The Glory of Golgotha.*

Sieffert, Friedrich Anton Emil (Fridericus Antonius Aemilius; 1843–1911). Prot. theol.; b. Königsberg, Prussia; educ. Königsberg, Halle, Berlin; privatdocent Königsberg 1867; inspector theol. sem. Bonn 1871; assoc. prof. U. Bonn 1873; prof. Erlangen 1878, Bonn 1889. Works include *Die Heidenbekehrung im Alten Testament und im Judentum; Nonnulla ad Apocryphi Libri Henochi originem et compositionem nec non ad opiniones de Regno Messiano eo prolatas pertinentia.*

Siegler, Richard (July 20, 1859–Nov. 6, 1941). B. Wolin (Wollin), Pomerania; to US 1863; educ. Northwestern Coll., Watertown, and the Luth. theol. sem. Milwaukee, Wis. Pastor first at Ellington, Wis., then at Barre Mills, Wis. Field representative of educ. institutions and missions of the Joint Ev. Luth. Syn. of Wis., Minn., Mich., and Other States (see *Wisconsin Evangelical Lutheran Synod*) 1910–35.

Siegmund-Schultze, Friedrich. See *World Alliance for Promoting International Friendship Through the Churches.*

Sieker, Johann Heinrich (Oct. 23, 1839–Dec. 30, 1904). B. Schweinfurth, Bav., Ger.; to US 1850; educ. Gettysburg, Pa.; ordained Ev. Luth. Syn. of Wis. and Other States 1861. Pastor Granville, Wis., 1861–67; St. Paul, Minn. (Minn. Syn.), 1867–76. Pres. Minnesota* Syn. 1869–76; induced it to withdraw from the General* Council of the Ev. Luth. Ch. in (N.) Am. 1871 and help form the Synodical* Conf. 1872. Pastor St. Matthew Luth. Ch., NYC, 1876; joined Mo. Syn. (Eastern Dist.) 1882, his cong. joined 1886. Helped found Conc. Collegiate Institute (see *Concordia College,* Bronxville, N. Y.) 1881 at St. Matthew Luth. Ch., which had an academy.

P. Rösener, *Ehrendenkmal des weiland ehrwürdigen Pastor Johann Heinrich Sieker* (West Roxbury, Mass., 1905).

Siemering, Rudolf. See *Luther Monuments.*

Sierra Leone. See *Africa,* C 6.

Sieveking, Amalie Wilhelmine (1794–1859). B. Hamburg, Ger.; orphaned at early age; influenced by Thomas* à Kempis and A. H. Francke*; served Hamburg hospitals during 1831 cholera epidemic; founded a women's soc. to care for poor and sick 1832.

Sievers, Georg Ernst Christian Ferdinand (May 18, 1816–Sept. 9, 1893). B. Lüneburg, Hannover, Ger.; educ. Göttingen; private tutor Amelungsborn, Brunswick; postgraduate work Berlin 1842, Halle 1842–43; private tutor Grünenplan, Brunswick, 1843–46; emergency asst. pastor Husum 1846–47; won through F. C. D. Wyneken's* "Notruf"; ordained 1847 for North Am. service but not with power to administer the sacraments; contacted J. K. W. Löhe*; to US 1847 with E. A. Brauer*; pastor Frankenlust, Mich., 1848; traveled as miss. in Mich., Minn., Ohio, and Wis., founding congs. in Bay City, Mich., Minneapolis, Minn., and elsewhere. Chm. Mo. Syn. Bd. for Missions 1850–93. Mo. Syn. chronologist 1864–66, 1872–90.

A. R. Suelflow, "The Life and Work of Georg Ernst Christian Ferdinand Sievers," *CHIQ,* XX (1947–48), 135–141, 180–187; XXI (1948–49), 36–41, 75–87, 100–114, 175–180; XXII (1949–50), 43–48, 77–84.

Siger de Brabant (Sigerus de Brabantia; Sigerius; Sighier; Sigieri; Sygerius; ca. 1235/40–ca. 1281/85). Fr. Averroist philos. (see *Arabic Philosophy*); opposed by Thomas* Aquinas and Albertus* Magnus; summoned to appear before Inquisition* 1276; said to have fled to Roman curia at Orvieto, It., where he was probably condemned to stay and was assassinated by a berserk attendant. Works include *Impossibilia; Quaestiones de necessitate et contingentia causarum; De aeternitate mundi; Tractatus de anima intellectiva.*

Sigismund (1368–1437). Margrave of Brandenburg 1378; king of Hung. 1387–1437, Boh. 1419–37; Holy Roman emp. 1411–37 (crowned 1433); moved the pope to convoke the Council of Constance* (see also *John XXIII,* 1). See also *Hussites.*

Sigismund III. See *Poland,* 3.

Sigismund, John. See *John Sigismund.*

Signatura, Supreme Tribunal of the Apostolic. See *Curia,* 2 e.

Signorelli, Luca (Luca d'Egidio di Ventura de' Signorelli; Luca da Cortona; ca. 1441/50–1523). Painter; b. Cortona, Umbria, It.; applied anatomical knowledge to painting. Works include *Life of Moses; Conversion of St. Paul; Last Judgment.*

Sigtuna Foundation *(Sigtunastiftelsen).* Center of Luth. faith and culture est. 1915 at Sigtuna, near Uppsala, Swed. A folk high school stressing religion and morals was est. 1917; a coll. was added 1926. Activities include conferences of pastors, doctors, artists, authors, workingmen. The Scand. Ecumenical Institute was est. there 1940. See also *Sweden, Lutheranism in,* 6.

Sihler, Wilhelm (Nov. 12, 1801–Oct. 27, 1885). 1. B. Bernstadt, near Breslau, Silesia; studied at Berlin 1826–29; influenced by F. D. E. Schleiermacher*; private tutor Breslau 1829–30; instructor at a private coll. Dresden 1830; hitherto a rationalist, he came under influence of J. G. Scheibel,* A. G. Rudelbach*; because of resultant confessional Lutheranism he found himself incompatible with the coll. at Dresden; private tutor in the Baltic area 1838–43. 2. Won through F. C. D. Wyneken's* "Notruf"; contacted J. K. W. Löhe*; to US 1843; preacher and teacher Pomeroy, Ohio, and vicinity 1844; ordained Ev. Luth. Joint Syn. of Ohio* and Other States June 1844.

3. Called to Fort Wayne, Ind., spring 1845; withdrew from Ohio Syn. 1845 (see *Document of Separation*); pastor Fort Wayne, Ind., and vicinity July 1845; fostered Christian educ. of the young.

4. Prominent in organization of the Mo. Syn. (see *Lutheran Church – Missouri Synod, The,* I, 1–III, 2); as its first vice-pres. he was overseer of Ohio, Ind., and Mich. 1847–54. First pres. Cen. Dist. 1854–60 (see also *Lutheran Church – Missouri Synod, Districts of The,* A 2). Helped est. a practical sem. *(Nothelferseminar)* at Fort Wayne, Ind., and served as pres. and prof. 1846–61. Pres. of the teachers sem. that moved from Milwaukee, Wis., to Fort Wayne 1857. Pres. and instructor Conc. Coll., Fort Wayne.

5. Works include *Gespräche zwischen zwei Lutheranern über den Methodismus* (Eng. tr. *A Conversation Between Two Lutherans on Methodism*); *Lebenslauf von W. Sihler; Predigten über die Sonn- und Festtags-Evangelien des Kirchenjahres; Zeit- und Gelegenheits-Predigten; Predigten über die Sonn- und Festtags-Episteln des Kirchenjahres.*

W. Sihler, *Lebenslauf von W. Sihler,* I (St. Louis, 1879), II (New York, 1880); E. G. Sihler, "Memories of Dr. William Sihler (1801–1885)," *CHIQ,* V (1932–33), 50–57; L. W. Spitz, *Life in Two Worlds: Biography of William Sihler* (St. Louis, 1968); J. H. Jox, "Zum Ehrengedächtniss des am 27. October 1885 selig heimgegangenen Dr. W. Sihler, treuverdienten Pastors zu St. Paul in Fort Wayne, Ind.," *Der Lutheraner,* XLII (1886), 17–18, 26–28, 34–35, 42–43, 50–51, 59–60, 67–69, 83–84, 91–92.

Sikhs (from Hindi for "disciple"). Mems. of a sect of dissenters from Brahmanical Hinduism; founded in the Punjab, India, by Nanak (Nanok; 1469–ca. 1533/39; b. near Lahore, India; in early yrs. a Hindu; 1st of 10 Sikh gurus [from Hindi for "teacher"]; comp. part of "Adi* Granth"; tried to unite Islam and Hinduism, rejecting the soc. and ceremonial restrictions of the latter). Chief tenet is monotheism in the Hindu-pantheistic sense. Defeated in the 1840s by Brit., who annexed the Punjab to Brit. India. They number perhaps ca. 6 million. See also *India,* 2; *Singh, Sadhu Sundar.*

Siloam Inscription. Heb. inscription found 1880 in a water tunnel near the pool of Siloam; describes work in the construction of the tunnel; cf. 2 K 20:20; 2 Ch 32:2-4; Ecclus 48:17.

Silvester. See *Sylvester.*

Silvesterabend (Ger. "evening of Silvester's day"). New Year's Eve; named after Sylvester I (see *Popes,* 1), commemorated Dec. 31, traditional day of his death.

Simeon, Charles (1759–1836). Angl.; b. Reading, Berkshire, S Eng.; educ. Eton and Cambridge; priest Cambridge 1783. Led evangelicals; helped found CMS. Works include *Helps to Composition; Horae homileticae* (reprint. 1956 as *Expository Outlines on the Whole Bible*); tracts.

Simeon ben Yohai (bar Yochai). See *Cabala.*

Simeon Metaphrastes. See *Symeon Metaphrastes.*

Simeon Stylites (Symeon; ca. 390–ca. 459/460). Syrian ascetic; began living on pillars (the first ca. 6 ft. high) at ca. 30; built and lived on pillars of increasing height; spent ca. last 30 yrs. of life on a pillar ca. 60 ft. high; exercised considerable influence through preaching and disciples. See also *Stylites.*

Simler, Johann Jakob (1716–88). Descendant of Josias Simler*; supt. Alumnat (boarding school; sem.) at Zurich, Switz.; gathered hist. documents (originals and copies) relating largely to events connected with the Reformation. Issued *Sammlung alter und neuer Urkunden zur Beleuchtung der Kirchengeschichte, vornemlich des Schweizerlandes.*

Simler, Josias (1530–76). Ancestor of Johann Jakob Simler*; son-in-law of J. H. Bullinger; b. Kappel, Switz.; educ. Basel, Strasbourg, Zurich; asst. pastor, teacher, and prof. Zurich. Works include *De republica Helveticorum.*

Simon, Martin Paul William (Feb. 16, 1903–Sept. 23, 1969). B. Zachow (or Angelica?), Wis.; educ. Conc. Coll., Milwaukee, Wis., and Conc. Sem., St. Louis, Mo.; miss. to China 1926–28. Pastor Eugene, Oreg.; Brussels and Okawville, Ill. Ed. *The Children's Hour; My Chum; The Christian Parent.* Other works include *The Unequal Yoke; How to Know and Use Your Bible; Meeting Current Family Problems.* Coauthor *Little Visits with God; More Little Visits with God.*

Simon, Richard (1638–1712). "Father of Biblical criticism"; RC theol.; b. Dieppe, Fr.; his critical study of the OT was opposed by RCs and Prots. Works include *Histoire critique du Vieux Testament; Histoire critique du Texte du Nouveau Testament; Histoire critique des versions du Nouveau Testament.*

Simon Magus (Lat *magus* [from a similar Gk. word], "sorcerer"). Samaritan magician; offered to buy the power to give the Holy Spirit (hence the term simony*), Acts 8:9-24. See also *Christs, False; Gnosticism,* 7 a.

Simons, Menno. See *Menno Simons.*

Simony (for derivation see *Simon Magus*). Buying or selling things spiritual or connected with the spiritual. Early ch. councils and syns. (e. g., Council of Chalcedon,* Canon II; 533 Council of Orléans,* Canons II and IV; 786–787 Council of Nicaea,* Canon V; Quinisext* Syn., Canons XXII and XXIII) condemned simony. Gregory I (see *Popes,* 4) vigorously and repeatedly denounced it. In the mid-11th c., until Gregory VII (see *Popes,* 7) opposed it, the papacy was bought. Simony also lent itself as an abuse that led to and was involved in the struggle about investiture.* During the Reformation many efforts to eliminate simony originated within and outside the ch.

Simpson, Albert Benjamin (1844–1919). Presb.; b. Cavendish, Prince Edward Is., Can., of Scot. background; educ. Knox Coll., Toronto, Can. Pastor Hamilton, Ont., 1865; Louisville, Ky., 1873; NYC 1880. See also *Evangelistic Associations,* 5.

Simpson, Matthew (1811–84). Meth. bp. and educ.; b. Cadiz, Ohio; deacon 1835, elder 1837. Pastor Pittsburgh, Pa., 1835; Williamsport, Pa., 1836. Vice-pres. and prof. Allegheny Coll., Meadville, Pa., 1837. Pres. Indiana Asbury (now De Pauw) U., Greencastle, Ind., 1839–48. Bp. 1852 with residence at Philadelphia, Pa. Pres. Garrett Biblical Institute, Evanston, Ill., 1859. Supported Union in Civil War; gave eulogy at Abraham Lincoln's funeral, Springfield, Ill., 1865.

Sin. Transgression of God's law (Ro 4:15; 1 Jn 3:4). Sin may be divided into original sin (see *Sin, Original*) and actual sin. Actual sin (every act, thought, emotion (e. g., lust*) conflicting with God's law) may be involuntary or may be done ignorantly (Acts 17:30) and includes sins of commission (cf., e. g., Mt 15:19; Ja 1:15) and sins of omission (Ja 4:17). Sin arouses God's righteous wrath and deserves His punishment. Willful sin sears conscience*; repeated, it hardens the heart; may lead to, but is not identical with, the unpardonable sin against the Holy Spirit (see *Sin, The Unpardonable*).

Sin, Mortal. See *Sins, Venial and Mortal.*

Sin, Original (inherited; hereditary; principal; capital; Adam's sin; nature-sin; person-sin). 1. In its ordinary meaning this term does not refer to the origin of sin but to the guilt of Adam's sin imputed to his offspring (hereditary guilt, Ro 5:12-19; Eph 2:3; cf. FC SD I 9) and the corruption of man's nature that occurred when sin entered and which inheres in the human will and inclinations. Cf. Gn 5:3; 6:5; 8:21; Jb 15:14; Ps 51:5; Jn 3:6; Ro 14:23. Original sin is not an activity but a quality, a state, an inherent condition. It exists, though there be no conscious, voluntary act of internal or external powers, of mind or body. It is "the chief sin, a root and fountainhead of all actual sins" (FC SD I 5).

2. FC Ep I 1: "There is a distinction between man's nature and original sin. . . . No one except God alone can separate the corruption of our nature from the nature itself. . . . We . . . reject the Manichaean error that original sin is an essential, self-existing something which Satan infused into and mingled with human nature." AC II: "Since the fall of Adam all men who are propagated according to nature are born in sin. That is to say, they are without fear of God, are without trust in God, and are concupiscent. And this disease or vice of origin is truly sin, which even now damns and brings eternal death on those who are not born again through Baptism and the Holy Spirit." "Concupiscent" (drawn from the Lat. text) is explained in the Ger. text as "unable by nature to have true fear of God and true faith in God."

3. The Luth. Confessions condemn Pelagianism,* which denies the reality of original sin. FC SD I 10: "Original sin is the complete lack or absence of the original concreated righteousness of paradise or of the image of God according to which man was originally created in truth, holiness, and righteousness, together with a disability and ineptitude as far as the things of God are concerned." FC SD I 11–12: "Original sin in human nature is not only a total lack of good in spiritual, divine things, but . . . at the same time it replaces the lost image of God in man with a deep, wicked, abominable, bottomless, inscrutable, and inexpressible corruption of his entire nature in all its powers, especially of the highest and foremost powers of the soul in mind, heart, and will. As a result, since the Fall man inherits an inborn wicked stamp, an interior uncleanness of the heart and evil desires and inclinations. By nature every one of us inherits from Adam a heart, sensation, and mind-set which, in its highest powers and the light of reason, is by nature diametrically opposed to God and his highest commands and is actually enmity against God, especially in divine and spiritual matters. True, in natural and external things which are subject to reason man still possesses a measure of reason, power, and ability, although greatly weakened since the inherited malady has so poisoned and tainted them that they amount to nothing in the sight of God." FC Ep I 8: "Original sin is not a slight corruption of human nature, but . . . it is so deep a corruption that nothing sound or uncorrupted has survived in man's body or soul, in his inward or outward powers. It is as the church sings, 'Through Adam's fall man's nature and essence are all corrupt.' "

4. Escape from the consequences of original sin is only by rebirth through Baptism and the Holy Spirit (see 2); cf. Mk 16:16.

Separation of the corruption of our nature from the nature itself (see 2) "will take place wholly by way of death in the resurrection. Then the nature which we now bear will arise and live forever, without original sin and completely separated and removed from it"; cf. Jb 19:26-27. (FC Ep I 10). FC SD L 46: "Precisely the substance of this our flesh, but without sin, shall arise, and . . . in eternal life we shall have and keep precisely this soul, although without sin." FC Ep I 6: "Christ . . . will not quicken [original sin] in the elect, will not glorify it or save it. On the contrary, in the resurrection it will be utterly destroyed."

See also *Traducianism.*

Sin, The Unpardonable. 1. Cf. Is 22:14; Mt 12:31; Mk 3:29; Lk 12:10; Heb 6:4-6; 1 Jn 5:16. The sin against the Holy Spirit, or the unpardonable sin, involves conscious, stubborn, malicious opposition to divine truth once recognized as such and blasphemous hostility against it. J. Gerhard (*Loci theologici,* Locus XI: "De peccatis actualibus," par. 109) defines it: "intentional denial of evangelical truth (which [truth] was acknowledged and approved by conscience) connected with a bold attack on [this truth] and voluntary blasphemy [of it]." J. A. Quenstedt* (*Theologia didactico-polemica,* ch. 2, section 1, thesis 104) has a similar definition.

The stubborn and malicious opposition, which is the essence of the unpardonable sin, may be further distinguished as follows: (1) Some have internally experienced the truth, given their assent to it, and outwardly confessed it, but have set themselves against it; all apostates belong to this class, to which Heb 6:4 applies. (2) Others have not outwardly confessed it but inwardly assented to it, yet obstinately and wickedly oppose it; to this class belong the scribes and Pharisees, who opposed Christ's teaching but were convinced by His works that He was true God and revealed divine truths.

Though Peter denied Christ and the truth and Paul was a reviler, blasphemer, and persecutor of divine truth before his conversion, they are not to be classed with those who commit the sin against the Holy Spirit; Peter transgressed hastily, through fear of men, and Paul did so through ignorance (1 Ti 1:13).

2. The unpardonable sin is called the sin against the Holy Spirit not with reference to the person of the Holy Spirit (who has no precedence over Father or Son) but to His office, in that He reveals and testifies to the heavenly truths. It is conscious resistance to the special work of the Holy Spirit, who calls, enlightens (Eph 1:17-18), converts, renews (Eph 1:19; Tts 3:5) and sanctifies man (1 Co 6:11; Eph 4:30; 2 Th 2:13).

3. This sin is unpardonable, not because of any unwillingness in God, or because His mercy and Christ's merits are not great enough, but because of the condition of him who commits it: he continues to the end (the action of his sin is linear, rather than punctiliar) in obdurate rejection of the Word of God, divine grace and mercy, and Christ's merits; cf. 1 Jn 5:16. Augustine of Hippo calls it final impenitence. One who does not repent does not receive forgiveness; cf. Rv 2:22.

Sinaiticus, Codex. See *Manuscripts of the Bible,* 3 a.

Singapore. See *Asia,* C 3; *Malaysia,* 1, 3.

Singh, Sadhu Sundar (1889–1929?). B. a Sikh (see *Sikhs*) at Rampur, near Ludhiana North Punjab, NW India; became Christian under Presb. influence;

began preaching; went to Sabathu; bap. 1905; donned saffron robe of a sadhu (Skt. "straight"), or "holy man," in an attempt to help make Christianity acceptable to others; miss. Punjab (including Rampur), Kashmir, Baluchistan, Afghanistan, Tibet; disappeared on 1929 trip to Tibet.

Singmaster, Elsie (Mrs. Harold Lewars; Aug. 29, 1879–Sept. 30, 1958). Daughter of J. A. Singmaster*; Luth. novelist and hist. writer; b. Schuylkill Haven, Pa.; educ. Radcliffe Coll., Harvard U., Cambridge, Mass. Works include *The Story of Lutheran Missions; Martin Luther; Stories of Pennsylvania.*

Singmaster, John Alden (Aug. 31, 1852–Feb. 27, 1926). Father of E. Singmaster*; b. Macungie, near Allentown, Pa.; educ. Pa. Coll. and Lutheran Theol. Sem., both at Gettysburg; ordained E. Pa. Syn. 1876 (see *United Lutheran Church, Synods of,* 23); pastor Pa. and N. Y. 1876–1900; prof. Biblical theol. 1900–03, systematic theol. from 1903, pres. from 1906 Luth. Theol. Sem., Gettysburg. Pres. The General* Syn. of the Ev. Luth. Ch. in the USA 1915–17. Ed. *The Lutheran Quarterly;* other works include *A Handbook of Christian Theology.*

Sins, Venial and Mortal. The Luth. Confessions speak of sin* that is mortal, or deadly, i. e., irreconcilable with faith (Ap IV 48, 64, 109, 115). When believers fall into open sin, faith has departed (SA-III III 43–44). One who obeys his lusts does not retain faith (Ap IV 144). Original sin (see *Sin, Original*) is mortal; it brings eternal death on those who are not born again (AC II 2 Lat.). One who is dead in sin is insensitive to sin (LC, V: The Sacrament of the Altar, 77–78). Sins remain in believers (SA-III III 40; FC SD II 34). Many regard the following as 7 deadly sins, fatal to spiritual progress: pride,* covetousness,* lust,* anger, gluttony, envy,* sloth. But man cannot weigh, distinguish, or differentiate sins; all sins manifest total corruption (SA-III III 36–38), merit God's wrath (Mt 5:18-19; Gl 3:10; Ja 2:10), and are deadly (Eze 18:4; Ro 6:23); every sin loses its deadly effect when Christ, apprehended by faith, intervenes (Ro 8:1; 1 Jn 1:7, 9; 2:1-2).

In RCm, mortal sin is held to be that which deprives the soul of sanctifying grace and supernatural life (and so causes death to the soul), makes one an enemy of God, takes away the merit of all good works, deprives one of everlasting happiness in heaven, and makes him deserving of hell. It is a seriously wrong thought, word, deed, or omission of which one is mindful and to which he fully consents. Venial sins are less seriously wrong (or seriously wrong sins which one believes to be only slightly, i. e., not seriously, wrong) and do not deprive of sanctifying grace. EL

See also *Confession,* 4; *Sacraments, Roman Catholic.*

Sioux. See *Indians, American,* 9; *Primitive Religion.*

Sirach, Wisdom of. See *Apocrypha,* A 3.

Siricius. See *Jovinian.*

Sisterhoods. RC sisterhoods (communities, institutes, or socs. for women) not treated in separate arts. (see, e.g., *Benedictines; Joseph, Sisters of St.*) include (1) Sisters of the Good Shepherd (popular name for Sisters [or the Religious] of Our Lady of Charity of the Good Shepherd). Founded 1641 Caen, Fr., by J. Eudes* to help delinquent girls and young women. (2) Cong. of the Little Sisters of the Poor. Founded 1839 St. Servan, on the N coast of Fr., to care for elderly, esp. those who are poor. (3) Soc. of the Holy Child Jesus. Founded 1846 Derby, Eng., for educ., esp. of girls. (4) Felician Sisters. A papal institute of the 3d Order Regular of St. Francis* of Assisi, known also Sisters of St. Felix of Cantalice (Capuchin lay brother; 1515–87; b. Cantalice, It.; patron of children and infirm). Founded 1855 Poland to care esp. for poor girls and aged women. (5) Sisters, Servants of the Immaculate Heart of Mary. Two orders by this name: (a) Founded 1845 Monroe, Mich. Stress the apostolate of teaching. (b) Founded 1850 Quebec, Can. Stress rehabilitation of wayward girls and Christian educ. of youth. See also *Brotherhood and Sisterhood; Servites.*

Sisters of Charity. Name of many RC congs. for women. See also *Grey Nuns; Vincent de Paul.*

Sisters of St. Joseph. See *Joseph, Sisters of St.*

Sisters of the Common Life. See *Brethren of the Common Life.*

Sisters of the Good Shepherd. See *Sisterhoods.*

Situation(al) Ethics (New Morality). Approach to human behavior that claims to make love the starting point and dominant control for every facet of human existence; cites such Bible passages as Lv 19:18; Mt 22:37-39; Ro 13:8-10; Gl 5:14; Ja 2:8; 1 Jn 2:10. Does not try to eliminate laws but seeks flexibility in their application; holds a midway position bet. antinomianism and legalism. Based on presuppositions: (1) Persons are more important than things; (2) Love is the ultimate criterion for making ethical decisions; (3) What love demands in any specific instance depends on the situation; (4) Situation(al) ethics is in harmony with Scripture and great teachers of the ch.

The name and some proponents of situation(al) ethics have caused the term to be assoc. with sexual freedom, anarchy, relativism, and lawlessness. EL

See also *Ethics,* 10.

J. A. T. Robinson, *Christian Morals Today* (Philadelphia, 1964); J. Fletcher, *Situation Ethics: The New Morality* (Philadelphia, 1966); J. Knox, *The Ethic of Jesus in the Teaching of the Church: Its Authority and Its Relevance* (New York, 1961); C. H. Dodd, *Gospel and Law: The Relation of Faith and Ethics in Early Christianity* (New York, 1951); O. S. Barr, *The Christian New Morality: A Biblical Study of Situation Ethics* (New York, 1969).

Sitwell, Frank. See *Catholic Apostolic Church,* 1.

Sitz im Leben (Ger. "place [or situation] in life; origin in life situation"). Term used for hist. context (e.g., activity of a community). Exegetes try to determine the Sitz im Leben of a book or passage to help determine its meaning. See also *Gunkel, Johann Friedrich Hermann; Hermeneutics,* 5; *Higher Criticism,* 16.

Siva. See *Hinduism,* 4.

Six Articles, The. See *Anglican Confessions,* 3.

Six Chapters. See *Eastern Orthodox Standards of Doctrine,* A 2.

Six-Principle Baptists, General (or Old). See *Baptist Churches,* 3, 21.

Sixtus IV. See *Popes,* 16.

Sixtus V. See *Popes,* 22.

Sixtus of Siena (1520–69). RC of Jewish descent; b. Siena, It.; Franciscan; condemned by Inquisition*; pardoned through intercession of M. Ghislieri (see *Popes,* 21); Dominican 1551. Noted for Biblical studies; distinguished proto- and deuterocanonical books. Works include *Bibliotheca sancta.*

Sixty-Seven Articles. See *Reformed Confessions,* A 1.

Skaar, Johannes Nilsson (1828–1904). B. Vikör, Norw.; educ. Oslo; pastor Aurdal 1857, Skien 1862, Gjerpen 1872; bp. Tromsö 1885, Trondheim 1892. Works include *Norsk salmehistorie.*

Skarga, Piotr (1536–1612). B. Grójec, Mazovia, Poland; educ. Kraków; Jesuit; court preacher to Sigismund III (see *Poland,* 3) 1588; helped reunite Ruthenians who had reverted to Eastern Orthodoxy at the beginning of the 16th c. with RCm.

Skepticism (from Gk. for "to look"). Antidogmatic philos. school which holds that truth may exist but cannot be known. Neither reason nor senses provide a trustworthy guide to existence. For every dogmatic statement there is an opposing statement of equal validity. Philosophically, one must suspend judgment. But the ancient skeptic does not despair; he continues to look for truth (hence the name skeptic). Practically, human action is possible by doing what is customary or gen. accepted. Thus one achieves quiet and freedom from fear, the goal of all philosophy.

Pyrrho (ca. 365–ca. 275 BC; followers called Pyrrhonists, doctrine Pyrrhonism) founded a skeptic school at Elis, Greece. Other ancient skeptics include Carneades,* Aenesidemus (Gk. philos.; probably 1st c. BC or AD; taught in Alexandria, Egypt), Cicero,* Sextus Empiricus (2d–3d c. AD; Gk. physician and philos.). Their doctrine was modified, e.g., by I. Kant* and B. Pascal.* EK

See also *Philosophy*.

V. C. L. Brochard, *Les sceptiques grecs* (Paris, 1887); A. Goedeckemeyer, *Die Geschichte des Griechischen Skeptizismus* (Leipzig, 1905); L. Robin, *Pyrrhon et le scepticisme grec* (Paris, 1944).

Skinner, John (1851–1925). Presb.; b. Inverurie, near Aberdeen, Scot.; educ. Aberdeen, Edinburgh, Leipzig, Göttingen; prof. Cambridge. Rejected Biblical account of creation as unscientific. Works include *A Critical and Exegetical Commentary on Genesis.*

Skjelderup, Jens Pedersson (1510–82). B. Den.; educ. Ger.; taught science and medicine at U. of Copenhagen; bp. Bergen 1557; iconoclast.

Skoptsy. See *Russian Sects.*

Skovgaard-Petersen, Carl Axel (1866–1955). Dan. theologian. Pastor Alslev-Hostrup, Jutland, 1893; Maarum, N. Sjaelland, 1901. Head of Bible school in Copenhagen 1912–29; cathedral provost Roskilde 1929–36; mem. of commission that produced new Dan. Bible tr.; pres. Dan. Bible Soc. (see *Bible Societies,* 4) 1936–49. Noted for devotional writing. Works include *Menneskheden uden Kristus; Evighedsordet i Slaegternes Gang; Korset i Kirke og Kunsten.*

Skoworoda, Gregory (1722–94). Ukrainian; educ. Kiev; prof. Charkow; journeyed through Ukraine with Bible and flute urging people to understand themselves; philos. combined Christian mysticism and enlightenment.

Skrefsrud, Lars Olsen (1840–1910). B. near Lillehammer, SE Norw.; imprisoned as youth; converted; studied at school of Gossner* Miss. Soc., Berlin, 1861–63; miss. to India 1863; worked among Santals with H. P. Börresen.* Works include a grammar of the Santal language. See also *Norwegian Foreign Missions,* 3.

Skydsgaard, Kristen Ejner. See *Dogmatics,* B 11.

Skytte, Martin (Martti). See *Finland, Lutheranism in,* 2.

Slander. A sin against the 8th Commandment ("Thou shalt not bear false witness against thy neighbor"); specifically, to speak evil of someone and so injure or destroy his good name. Cf. Ps 31:13; 50:20; 101:5; Pr 10:18; Jer 6:28; 9:4.

Slavery, Biblical Reference to. Slavery was practiced among Jews from the time of Abraham, but consciousness of caste is hardly noticeable in patriarchal days; master and slave lived together as mems. of a household (cf. Gn 15:2-3; 24; 1 Sm 9:5-10; Pr 29:19-21). During the period of the kings the condition of slaves became more intolerable (2 K 4:1; Am 2:6; 8:6). Nehemiah tried to rectify conditions that fostered slavery (Neh 5:4-11).

Servitude of Heb. slaves was regulated by laws that regarded them as hired servants (cf. Ex 21:1-11; Lv 25:39-55; Dt 15:12-18). The lot of for. slaves was less tolerable (cf. Dt 20:10-15; Ju 1:28), but they, too, lived as mems. of a religious community (Dt 12:12, 18; 16:11, 14; 21:10-14). The nations that sold Israelites into slavery were denounced (Jl 3:6; Am 1:6). The number of slaves in Israel was never as large as among the Gks. and Romans.

Christianity did not require masters to release their servants (cf. Eph 6:5-9) but invited all to be children of God, without soc. distinction (1 Co 7:21-22; Gl 3:28; Cl 3:11; Phmn 10, 16).

Slavery and Lutheranism in America. Luths. in Am. were in gen. opposed to slavery, but some owned slaves. The Franckean* Syn. was the 1st to adopt antislavery resolutions (1837). The Eng. Dist. Syn. of Ohio, Alleghany Syn., and Pittsburgh Syn. adopted similar resolutions in the 1840s, the Wittenberg Syn. and the Northern Ind. Syn. in the 1850s. See also *General Synod of the Evangelical Lutheran Church in the United States of America, The,* 4.

Disagreement over the slavery question in the Mo. Syn. was comparatively slight. The other syns., whose congs. were concentrated in N states, gen. opposed slavery and were not adversely affected by the issues. Northern and southern Luths. were reunited 1918 in The United* Luth. Ch. in Am. ARS

C. W. Heathcote, *The Lutheran Church and the Civil War* (New York, 1919).

Slavic Gospel Association, Inc. Founded 1934 Chicago, Ill.; long known as Russ. Gospel Assoc.; fields have included Can., Eur., Far East, S. Am., US; mem. IFMA; HQ Chicago.

Slavonic Bible Versions. See *Bible Versions,* H.

Slavs, Primitive Religion of. Slavs apparently developed as a people NE of the Carpathian Mountains several cents. BC. Ancient Slavs shared religious concepts of other peoples and developed them variously under influence of neighbors (Nordic, Indo-Iranian, Gk., Roman, Christian [the latter esp. among Slavs who remained pagan longest]). There was no Slavic mythology and cosmogony. Demonology was more important than theol. Chief aims of worship and magic rituals: to insure fertility and gain divine favor for military victory. Religion (basically animism influenced by fetishism and perhaps by totemism [see *Primitive Religion*]) lacked ethical content, came to include ancestor* worship. Death was gen. followed by cremation, but not as a denial of continuing life.

Early gods included Perun (god of stormy heavens), Svarog (god of sun, fire, and light), Veles (or Volos; god of flocks and herds, and perhaps agriculture). Stribog (wind god; sometimes war god) and Mokosh (or Mkosh; female god personifying mother earth; also god of trade) were worshiped esp. by E Slavs. Statues of gods were in stele form and many-faced, housed in temples (esp. among Baltic Slavs); priests offered sacrifices (sometimes human), served as oracles, and came to form a powerful caste; magicians, who claimed power over demons, exerted even more influence. Echoes of primitive beliefs continued far into the Christian era. RR tr. MSF)

L. Niederle, *Slovanské Starozitnosti.* Oddíl 2, kulturní, díl 1 (chaps. 1–5), *Zivot starych slovanu,* 2 vols. (Prague, 1911, 1913) and *Manuel de l'antiquité slave,* II (Paris, 1926); B. O. Unbegaun, "La Religion des anciens Slaves," in A. Grenier, *Les Religions étrusque et romaine* (Paris, 1948), pp. 389–445, and "Slawische Religion," *Die Religion in Geschichte und Gegenwart,* 3d ed. H. v. Campenhausen et al., VI (Tübingen, 1962), cols. 105–107; *The Mythology of All Races,* ed. L. H. Gray, III: J. Machal, *Slavic Mythology* (Boston, 1918).

Sleidanus, Johannes (Joannes; Philippi; Philippson; ca. 1506–56). Hist.; b. Schleiden, near Aachen, Ger.; educ. Liège, Cologne, Paris, and Orléans; diplomatic representative of Francis I (see *France,* 8) in 1537 negotiations with the Schmalkaldic* League; represented Strasbourg at Council of Trent* 1551. Annalist of the Reformation. Works include *De statu religionis et reipublicae, Carolo Quinto Caesare, commentarii.*

Slessor, Mary (1848–1915). B. near Aberdeen, Scot.; miss. to Calabar, SE Nigeria, Afr., 1876.

Sloth. See *Acedia; Sins, Venial and Mortal.*

Slovak Evangelical Lutheran Church. See *Synod of Evangelical Lutheran Churches.*

Slovak Evangelical Lutheran Zion Synod. See *United Lutheran Church, Synods of,* 26.

Slovakia. See *Czechoslovakia; Slovakia, Lutheran Theology in.*

Slovakia, Lutheran Theology in. 1. The Reformation spread to Slovakia in M. Luther's lifetime and there continued through the 16th and 17th c. largely to mirror the thought prevalent in Ger.

2. Jan Kollár (1793–1852; b. Mosovce, W Slovakia; educ. Pressburg [Bratislava] and Jena, Ger.; pastor Pest [now part of Budapest]; prof. Vienna 1849; poet), M. M. Hodza,* and Karol Kuzmány (Karel; Karl; Carl; 1806–66; b. Brezno, cen. Slovakia; educ. Jena, Ger.; pastor Banska Bystrica [Neusohl]; prof. Vienna; hymnist) were influenced by Hegelian idealism. The most significant 19th c. theol. figure was J. M. Hurban.* JP

See also *Czechoslovakia.*

J. Borbis, *Die evangelisch-lutherische Kirche Ungarns in ihrer geschichtlichen Entwicklung* (Nördlingen, 1861).

Slüter, Joachim (1490–1532). Reformer of Mecklenburg, Ger.; b. Dömitz, Mecklenburg; teacher 1521. chaplain 1523 Rostock. Issued prayerbook, catechism, and 2 hymnals in Low Ger.

Smalcald. See *Schmalkaldic.*

Smalcius, Valentinus (Valentin Schmalz; 1572–ca. 1622/24). B. Gotha, Thuringia, Ger.; became Unitarian while studying at Strasbourg; to Poland; rector of ch. school at Szmigel (Smigla); joined Socinian ch.; pastor Lublin 1598, Rakow 1605. Helped prepare Rakau* Catechism. See also *Socinianism,* 1.

"Smaller Questions, The." See *Reformed Confessions,* E 1.

Smend, Julius (1857–1930). B. Lengerich, Westphalia, Ger.; educ. Bonn, Halle, and Göttingen; served in the pastoral ministry at various places. Prof. at the sem. at Friedberg, Hesse, 1891; Strasbourg 1893; Münster 1914. Assoc. ed. with F. Spitta* *Monatschrift für Gottesdienst und kirchliche Kunst;* other works include *Der evangelische Gottesdienst.*

Smith, Adam (1723–90). B. Kirkcaldy, Fifeshire, Scot.; educ. Glasgow and Oxford; prof. logic and moral philos. Glasgow; lectured on theol., ethics, jurisprudence, pol. institutions. Stressed soc. sympathy and imitation in ethics. Laid foundation for science of pol. economy. Works include *The Theory of Moral Sentiments; An Inquiry into the Nature and Causes of the Wealth of Nations.*

Smith, Azariah (Feb. 16, 1817–June 3, 1851). B. Manlius, N. Y.; educ. Yale coll., New Haven, Conn.; studied medicine at Geneva, N. Y.; ordained Presb. 1842; ABCFM miss. in Armenia and Turkey 1842–51.

Smith, Eli (1801–57). B. Northford (now in North Branford), Conn.; educ. Yale coll., New Haven, Conn., and Andover (Mass.) Theol. Sem.; ABCFM Cong. miss. to Malta and the Near East. Tr. Bible into Arabic. See also *Dwight, Harrison Gray Otis.*

Smith, Gerald Birney (1868–1929). B. Middlefield, Hampshire Co., Mass. Educ. Brown U., Providence, R. I.; Columbia U., NYC; Union Theol. Sem., NYC. Prof. theol. U. of Chicago. Leader in modernizing and socializing theol. Influenced by A. B. Ritschl.*

Smith, Henry Preserved (1847–1927). Father of P. Smith*; b. Troy, Ohio. Educ. Lane Theol. Sem., Cincinnati; univs. Berlin Leipzig. Ordained Presb. 1875; taught at Lane 1877–93, Amherst (Mass.) Coll. 1898–1906, Meadville (Pa.) Theol. Sem. 1907–13; librarian Union Theol. Sem., NYC, 1913–25. Suspended 1893 for higher Biblical criticism; Cong. 1899. Works include *A Critical and Exegetical Commentary on the Books of Samuel; Essays in Biblical Interpretation.*

Smith, John (Smyth; perhaps ca. 1570–1612). Educ. Cambridge for the Angl. Ch.; lecturer or preacher Lincoln 1600; deposed 1602, apparently for nonconformist views; Cong. pastor Gainsborough several yrs. later; with T. Helwys led a group of separatists to Holland ca. 1607/08; became Anabap. under Mennonite influence ca. 1608/09; bap. himself by affusion (hence often called the Se-Baptist, and his followers Se-Baptists). See also *Baptist Churches,* 2.

R. G. Torbet, *A History of the Baptists,* rev. ed. (Valley Forge, Pa., 1963), pp. 33–37.

Smith, John (of Jamestown, Va.). See *Pocahontas.*

Smith, Joseph, Sr. (1805–44). Father of Joseph Smith* Jr.; uncle of J. F. Smith*; founded Latter* Day Saints; b. Sharon, Windsor Co., Vt.; claimed visions beginning 1820. Works include *A Book of Commandments; Doctrine and Covenants.*

Smith, Joseph, Jr. (1832–1914). Son of Joseph Smith* Sr.; cousin of J. F. Smith*; b. Kirtland, Ohio; pres. Reorganized Ch. of Jesus Christ of Latter Day Saints (see *Latter Day Saints,* g 2) 1860. Ed. *Saints' Herald.*

Smith, Joseph Fielding (1838–1918). Nephew of Joseph Smith* Sr.; cousin of Joseph Smith* Jr.; b. Far West, Mo.; to Utah 1848 with B. Young; held various positions; pres. The Ch. of Jesus Christ of Latter Day Saints 1901; announced to US Senate committee 1904 that Mormons no longer sponsored polygamy; fostered friendly relations with non-Mormons.

Smith, Preserved (1880–1941). Son of H. P. Smith*; b. Cincinnati, Ohio; educ. Amherst (Mass.) Coll. and Columbia U., NYC; prof. Cornell U., Ithaca. N. Y., 1922–41. Works include *The Age of the Reformation; The Life and Letters of Martin Luther; Luther's Table Talk: A Critical Study; Erasmus; A History of Modern Culture.*

Smith, Robert Pearsall (1827–98). B. Philadelphia, Pa.; Quaker; manufacturer in Philadelphia; claimed unique religious experience of confirmation in faith 1858; joined holiness* movement 1866/67; presented views on progressive sanctification at Oxford 1874; influenced T. Jellinghaus.*

Smith, Rodney (1860–1947). "Gipsy Smith"; b. Wanstead, Eng., of Gipsy parentage; converted in midteens; evangelist in Eng.; visited Am. several times.

Smith, Samuel Francis (1808–95). Bap. cleric and poet; b. Boston, Mass.; educ. Harvard coll., Cambridge, Mass., and Andover (Mass.) Theol. Sem. Pastor Waterville, Maine, 1834–42; Newton, Mass., 1842–54. Prof. modern languages Waterville Coll. 1834–42. Active in Christian journalism. Author of "My Country, 'Tis of Thee." Hymns include "The Morning Light is Breaking"; "Founded on Thee, Our Only Lord."

Smith, William Benjamin (1850–1934). B. Stanford, Ky.; educ. U. of Ky., at Lexington; held several teaching positions, finally as prof. math. (1893–1906) and philos. (1906–15) Tulane U. of La., New Orleans. Works include *Der vorchristliche Jesus; The Color Line; Ecce Deus: Die urchristliche Lehre des reingöttlichen Jesu; The Birth of the Gospel.*

Smith, William Robertson (1846–94). B. New Farm, near Keig, Aberdeenshire, Scot.; educ. Aberdeen. Prof. Oriental languages and OT exegesis Free Ch. Coll., Aberdeen, 1870–81; prof. Arabic, Cambridge, 1883–86, 1889–94. Exponent of higher* criticism and of comparative study of religions. Coed. 1880, ed.-in-chief 1887–88 9th ed. *The Encyclopaedia Britannica.*

Smyth, John. See *Smith, John.*

"Snick." See *Student Nonviolent Coordinating Committee.*

Snowden, James Henry (1852–1936). B. Hookstown, Pa. Educ. Washington and Jefferson Coll., Washington, Pa.; Western Theol. Sem., Allegheny (now part of Pittsburgh), Pa.; ordained Presb. 1879. Pastor Huron, Ohio, 1879–83; Sharon, Pa., 1883–86; Washington, Pa., 1886–1911; adjunct prof. pol. economy and ethics Washington and Jefferson Coll. 1893–98; prof. Western Theol. Sem. 1911–26. Ed. *The Presbyterian Banner; The Presbyterian Magazine; Snowden's Sunday School Book* (1922; called *Snowden's Sunday School Lessons* from 1923). Other works include *The Christian Belief in Immortality in the Light of Modern Thought; The Making and Meaning of the New Testament; The Basal Beliefs of Christianity; The Discovery of God; Jesus as Judged by His Enemies; Old Faith and New Knowledge; The Personality of God; The Coming of the Lord: Will It Be Premillennial?* See also *Isagogics,* 3.

Sobornost (from Russ. for "assembly; synod"). Term without exact Eng. equivalent; denotes a quality necessary for charitable cooperation in a free communion of all; disavows unity by authority alone on the one hand and fragmentation by an excess of individual liberty on the other; in application to the liturgy in corporate worship it stresses participation by the cong.; regards the ch. as consisting of those who are freely associated in Christ by faith and love (cf. the view of A. S. Khomyakov*). Related in concept to *koinonia** and *communio* sanctorum.* Its catholicity (see *Catholic*) is interior. Cf. Acts 2:42.

Social Action. Organized effort to change economic or soc. institutions; includes movements to reform politics, employer-employee relations, and race relations; operates, e. g., through propaganda and legislative lobbies. See also *Social Reform; Social Work.*

Social Contract. See *Government; Natural Law,* 5.

Social Creed of Methodism. See *Methodist Churches,* 2.

Social Ethics. Ethics* applied to soc. relations and problems. Christian soc. ethics have OT roots and involve man's inner and total life and his relation to Christ. M. Luther made the calling of the Christian man in family, community, and occupation the proving ground of spiritual vitality engendered by Christ. The ch. plays a proper part in soc. ethics not by invading functions of other agencies but by equipping individuals and groups to play their part in other agencies as citizens, mems. of professions, mems. of families, etc. RRC

See also *Situation(al) Ethics.*

P. F. Joachimsen, *Sozialethik des Luthertums* (Munich, 1927); H. E. Brunner, *Das Gebot und die Ordnungen,* tr. O. Wyon, *The Divine Imperative* (London, 1937); J. S. Schöffel and A. Köberle, *Luthertum und soziale Frage* (Leipzig, 1931); G. W. Forell, *Faith Active in Love: An Investigation of Principles Underlying Luther's Social Ethics* (New York, 1954); W. E. Bauer, *God and Caesar: A Christian Approach to Social Ethics* (Minneapolis, 1959); C. F. Sleeper, *Black Power and Christian Responsibility: Some Biblical Foundations for Social Ethics* (Nashville, Tenn., 1968); M. Luther, *On the Freedom of a Christian Man* (1520).

Social Gospel. Teaching of a soc. salvation whose objective is rebirth of soc. through change of the soc. order by mass or group action. Tries to persuade individuals to practice the social* ethics of Jesus. Makes little or no reference to reconciliation with God through Christ and to the regenerative work of the Holy Spirit. For many it is essentially a this-worldly gospel of works, not a Gospel of grace for this life and heaven. The term "Social Gospel" is inadequate, since it is hard to separate "soc." from "individual" gospel when applied to Christian life.

The Soc. Gospel movement, influenced by F. D. E. Schleiermacher,* A. B. Ritschl,* and K. G. A. v. Harnack,* came into prominence in the US in the 1870s, declined after WW I, perhaps affected adversely also by the Great Depression (began in the late 1920s, lasted far into the 1930s). Exponents include W. Gladden,* E. S. Jones,* S. Mathews,* W. Rauschenbusch,* C. M. Sheldon.* The Soc. Creed of the FCCCA was an adaptation and expansion of the Soc. Creed of Methodism (see *Methodism,* 2). The Soc. Gospel flourished esp. among Methodists, Baptists, Congregationalists, Unitarians, and Episcopalians.

Critics of the Soc. Gospel see in it an idealistic, purely humanitarian, falsely optimistic, utopian and pacifistic, soc. reformist movement not essentially Christian (since it bypasses essential elements of Christian doctrine and life). JD

See also *Modernism,* 3.

E. Troeltsch, *The Social Teaching of the Christian Churches,* 2 vols., tr. O. Wyon (London, 1931); C. H. Hopkins, *The Rise of the Social Gospel in American Protestantism 1865–1915* (New Haven, Conn., 1940); W. A. Visser 't Hooft, *The Background of the Social Gospel in America* (Haarlem, Neth., 1928); F. E. Johnson, *The Social Gospel Re-examined,* 3d ed. (New York, 1940); H. P. Douglass and E. de S. Brunner, *The Protestant Church as a Social Institution* (New York, 1935); H. R. Niebuhr, *The Social Sources of Denominationalism* (New York, 1929); J. N. Hughley, *Trends in Protestant Social Idealism* (New York, 1948); *The Hartwick Seminary Conference on the Social Mission of the Lutheran Church* (Princeton, N. J., 1944); C. C. Morrison, *The Social Gospel and the Christian Cultus* (New York, 1933); E. E. Fischer, *Social Problems: The Christian Solution* (Philadelphia, 1927); A. Cronbach, *The Bible and Our Social Outlook* (Cincinnati, Ohio, 1941); R. T. Handy, *The Social Gospel in America 1870–1920* (New York, 1966); P. A. Carter, *The Decline and Revival of the Social Gospel* [enl. ed.] (Hamden, Conn., 1971).

Social Reform. Soc. reform is not revolutionary; it does not aim at complete change of the soc. order, as social* action may. It accepts the existing fundamental soc. and economic structure of soc. but tries to eliminate the evils that result from improper or faulty functioning of the soc. system. Its motivation derives from individual and group distress that soc. work tries to alleviate; it proceeds beyond alleviation and tries to remedy the causes of distress insofar as they may seem to result from maladjustments in the soc. order. Temperance movements and antivice crusades are examples of soc. reform movements.

Social Security Act. See *Social Work,* D 1.

Social Service. See *Social Work.*

Social Work (soc. service; welfare work). A. *Definition.* Social (from Lat. *socialis,* from *socius,* "companion; ally; associate") work has been defined as any activity to promote soc. welfare and described as the processes involved in adjusting an individual's relationships with other persons and with his wider soc. and economic development. Since it deals with human personalities, created not only by heredity but also developed by many changing environmental factors, and with changing society, the best picture of soc. work is obtained through study of its hist., goals, and present stage of development.

B. *History.* 1. Soc. work arises out of the responsibility of one for the welfare of another (cf. Gn 4:9). The pre-Christian world did not lack humanitarian impulses; writings of all ancient nations tell of efforts in behalf of poor and sick. In the NT, Christian love of God and fellowman became the motive (Jn 13:34); resultant charitable service was regarded as a fruit of faith and love (Gl 5:6; 1 Jn 3:17).

2. In the early ch. this service was rendered personally or through others (Acts 6:1-6). A form of voluntary Christian communism was apparently practiced briefly (Acts 2:44-45). Later the ch. exercised almost complete control over work and institutions of charity. Institutional care was fostered by

religious orders; other work was supervised by priests. Encouragement of indiscriminate almsgiving led to widespread mendicancy requiring mass relief in large pop. centers. By the end of the Middle Ages, relief of poor was a major issue.

3. The Reformation and accompanying changes swept away old concepts of charity and the old system of relief. Recognition of poverty as a soc. rather than individual problem led to the Eng. poor-law system, beginning ca. 1573, and to later large-scale development of soc. work in Eng. and Am.

4. In the 1890s the concept of character deficiency as primary cause of poverty gave way to recognition of environmental causes. Soc. action movements developed to abolish soc. inequities and economic and pol. ills that seemed to produce poverty and attendant evils.

5. Modern soc. casework began after WW I. Mary Ellen Richmond (1861–1928; b. Belleville, Ill.; soc. worker) wrote *Social Diagnosis* (New York, 1917) and *What Is Social Case Work?* (New York, 1922). Thorough investigation, accurate diagnosis, and specific treatment came to be recognized as indispensable. Emphasis on self-help grew. The family was recognized as basic in society; relationships of the family to the soc. order received much attention. The psychol. approach was developed. Personality problems came to be recognized as a potent cause of soc. maladjustment, esp. since the start of WW II 1939. Growing knowledge of the dynamics of soc. behavior provides new tools for soc. workers.

C. *Types of Soc. Work.* 1. Soc. work may be classified as casework, group work, and community service. Casework: work with individuals or closely knit small groups. Group work: work with larger or more loosely knit groups. Community service: work with communities. Cf. "Social Casework," "Social Group Work," and "Community Organization" in *Encyclopedia of Social Work* (successor to *Social Work Year Book*), 15th issue, ed. H. L. Lurie (New York, 1965).

2. Casework tries to make specialized services available, e. g., in child welfare, family service, service to transients, med., soc. service, psychiatric soc. service.

D. *Organization of Social Work Agencies.* 1. Pub. agencies are gen. administered as a function of local, state, or nat. govt. They are created by legal enactment and are supported by taxes. Fed. govt. concern for soc. welfare is expressed, e. g., in the 1964 antipoverty legislation and the 1935 Soc. Security Act and its subsequent amendments. WW II and its aftermath led to expansion of govt. assistance, esp. to the internat. field through the UN Relief and Rehabilitation Administration. A Dept. of Health, Educ., and Welfare was est. 1953.

2. Services offered by pub. agencies exceed those of private agencies in terms of funds expended, number of clients served, and variety of services rendered.

3. Private agencies are agencies founded by private initiative, governed by privately chosen bds. or committees, and supported by voluntary contributions. Many private agencies have combined under United Funds (Community Chests) and similar movements in an endeavor to secure equitable distribution of funds. Some religious private agencies operate on basis of denominational support.

E. *Christian Soc. Service.* 1. Gen. follows methods, techniques, and service classifications of secular service. Sponsored by Christian groups. Governed by Christian principles that vary with the tenets of sponsoring groups.

2. Distinguished from secular service in motivation. Secular service is motivated by humanitarian principles, a sense of justice and fair play, or expediency. Christian service is motivated by Christian love, a fruit of faith (Gl 5:6).

3. Distinguished from secular service also in areas served. Secular service commonly deals with biological, psychological, and soc. needs. Christian service includes spiritual needs.

4. Looks beyond this world to the world to come.

F. *Lutheran Soc. Work.* 1. Exalts the love and mercy of God; goes beyond soc. action and soc. reform in that it both serves individuals in time and points the way to eternity with God.

2. Luth. soc. work in Am. was first called charity. Now it is gen. called soc. service or soc. work. HFW JCC

See also *Associated Lutheran Charities; Bünger, Johann Friedrich; Charities, Christian; Deaconesses; Child and Family Service Agencies; Duemling, Enno A.; Herzberger, Frederick William; Inner Mission; National Association of Social Workers; Passavant, William Alfred; Social Action; Social Reform; Sociology.*

Theology and Social Welfare: Redemption and Good Works. Papers delivered at the Soc. Work Conf. sponsored by the Luth. Academy for Scholarship, Mar. 29–30, 1968, Valparaiso (Ind.) U. (Saint Louis, 1968).

Social Work Research Group. See *National Association of Social Workers.*

Socialism. Form of soc. organization in which property is controlled for common good. It has appeared in several forms.

1. Socialization of resources in an originally capitalistic state, to prevent exploitation for private gain of natural or economic resources.

2. Soc. security for capitalistic purposes, as when the purpose of soc. security, med. and unemployment insurance, etc. is to thwart the rise of workers against capitalistic control.

3. Fascism (from It. for "bundle; pol. group"), assoc. with the dictatorship of Benito Mussolini (1883–1945) in It., and Nazism (Ger. fascism; see also *Germany,* C 4; *Kirchenkampf*) opposed socialism. In It., the organized socialist movement was destroyed when Fascism (see also *Pareto, Vilfredo*) came into power 1922. In Ger., socialism existed under Nazism only as an underground movement; many of its followers were imprisoned, some were executed, some fled the country. Fascism conflicts with socialism in that it operates with totalitarianism and concomitant exploitation and oppression; the socialist movement was outlawed in Fascist Sp. when Francisco Franco (b. 1892) came to power 1939.

4. Communism, a revolutionary movement, is also to be distinguished from socialism, which tries, in democratic and constitutional ways, gradually to nationalize only essential means of production and to distribute justly to all acc. to amount and quality of work; operates with the maxim "from each acc. to his capacity, to each acc. to his need." In Marxist theory, socialism is transitional bet. capitalism and communism; in areas under communist control socialist parties have been liquidated or become only nominally socialist.

To the extent that the individual is subordinated to social considerations, individual freedom is drawn into tension, including freedom of religion. Socialism and communism were promoted largely by agnostic and antiecclesiastical thinkers; as a result, chs. took an opposing stand (see, e. g., *Encyclicals*). But many aims of the Social* Gospel found parallels in socialism; hence, though motives differed, some criticism of socialism was blunted. The search continues for solution to problems involved without violence to Christian faith. RCC

See also *Christian Socialism; Engels, Friedrich; Marx, Karl Heinrich.*

K. H. Marx and F. Engels, *Manifest der Kom-*

munistischen Partei (London, 1848), tr., ed., and annotated F. Engels, *Manifesto of the Communist Party* (Chicago, 1945); V. I. Lenin, *The State and Revolution* (London, 1919); N. A. Berdyaev, *The Origin of Russian Communism,* tr. from the Russ. by R. M. French, new ed. (London, 1948); W. Temple, *Christianity and Social Order,* 3d ed. (London, 1950); E. Heimann, *Communism, Fascism, or Democracy?* (New York, 1938); Encyclicals of Leo XIII (cf., e. g., *Social Wellsprings,* selected, arranged, and annotated by J. Husslein, I [Milwaukee, 1940]); R. Niebuhr, *An Interpretation of Christian Ethics* (New York, 1935); H. E. Brunner, *Justice and the Social Order,* tr. M. Hottinger (New York, 1945); J. C. Bennett, *Christianity and Communism Today* (New York, 1960); M. Harrington, *Socialism* (New York, 1972).

Socialism, Christian. See *Christian Socialism.*

Società Cattolica Biblica Internazionale. See *Bible Societies,* 6.

Societas Divini Salvatoris (Salvatorians). Founded 1881 Rome, It., as *Societas Apostolica Instructiva;* received final papal approbation 1911; advances RCm through teaching.

Societas Mariae. See *Marianists.*

Société des missions évangéliques de Paris. See *Paris Evangelical Missionary Society.*

Société évangélique de Genève (Ev. Soc. of Geneva). Founded 1831 as a cen. of orthodoxy over against rationalism; est. a theol. school at Geneva, Switz., which stressed Bible-centered instruction; conducted S. S., Bible study, revival hrs., served Fr. prisoners of war in Germany; active also in France and It.; emphasized colportage. See also *Gaussen, François Samuel Robert Louis; Merle d'Aubigné, Jean Henri.*

Society Arch-Triumphant. See *Communistic Societies,* 5.

Society for Advancing the Christian Faith in the British West India Islands (Christian Faith Soc.). Began in the 1691 will of R. Boyle,* who directed part of his estate to be used to advance the Christian faith among infidels; the executors of the will bought an estate in Brafferton, Yorkshire, Eng., proceeds from which were used at William and Mary Coll., Willamsburg, Va., for instruction of Indian children; after the War of Am. Indep. (Revolutionary War) the Soc. for the Conversion and Religious Instruction and Educ. of the Negro Slaves in the Brit. West India Islands was est. by royal charter; slavery was abolished in the Brit. colonies 1834; a new charter (1836) changed the name; work later extended to Mauritius and other islands belonging to Gt. Brit.

Society for Missions in Africa and the East. See *Church Missionary Society.*

Society for Promoting Christian Knowledge. See *Bible Societies,* 3.

Society for the Conversion and Religious Instruction and Education of the Negro Slaves in the British West India Islands. See *Society for Advancing the Christian Faith in the British West India Islands.*

Society for the Diffusion of Christian and General Knowledge Among the Chinese. Organized 1887 under leadership of A. Williamson* in Shanghai, China. The Christian Literature Soc. for China was formed in Glasgow and Edinburgh, Scot., 1892 to help this soc. Pubs.: *The Review of the Times; Chinese Missionary Review.*

Society for the Promotion of Church Work Among the Blind. See *Blind,* 3.

Society for the Promotion of Mohammedan Missions, The. Formed 1944 under leadership of H. Nau* to disseminate information regarding Islam and promote missions to Muslim. Pub.: *The Minaret.*

Society for the Propagation of the Gospel Among the Danes in North America, The. Organized Oct. 1869 in Den.; missionaries included R. Andersen.* Known as Udvalget ("The Committee [or Commission]"). See also *Danish Lutherans in America,* 3.

Society for the Propagation of the Gospel in Foreign Parts. See *Bible Societies,* 3; *Society for the Propagation of the Gospel in New England; United Society for the Propagation of the Gospel.*

Society for the Propagation of the Gospel in New England. Organized 1649 in Eng., largely as a result of interest stimulated by J. Eliot's* work. Its work was later taken over by the Soc. for the Propagation of the Gospel in For. Parts (see *Bible Societies,* 3). See also *Mayhew, Experience.*

Society Islands (Iles de la Société). S Pacific islands named on basis of Eng. rediscovery in the late 1760s, in honor of the Brit. Royal Soc. Previous names of Tahiti: King George's Is. (1767) and La Nouvelle Cythère (1768); Tahiti and adjacent islands were first called Georgian Island (1769). *Area:* ca. 650 sq. mi.; 1962 *pop.:* ca. 68,000. Part of Fr. Polynesia,* which became an overseas territory of Fr. 1946; E of Cook* Islands, SW of Marquesas Islands; include 14 islands, 8 inhabited (including Tahiti and Mooréa [or Eimeo]). Discovered 1607 by P. F. de Quirós.*

LMS began work 1797. King Pomare II was bap. 1812. The whole Bible in Tahitian was pub. 1838. Fr. protectorate est. 1843. The Paris* Ev. Miss. Soc. took the place of the LMS. See also *Williams, John.*

Society of Friends. See *Friends, Society of.*

Society of Jesus. RC order of clerks* regular; mems. are called Jesuits, a term that was long derogatory.

Stated purpose: salvation and perfection of mankind. Emphasis on obedience (including special obedience to the pope) is reflected in use of military language. Main work is in educ. (esp. higher educ.) and missions.

The Soc. of Jesus was founded by I. (of) Loyola*; he and 6 companions made the first vows 1534; canonical establishment came 1540.

Jesuits were prominent in the Counter Reformation (see *Counter Reformation,* 8–9). Opposition, arising perhaps partly out of envy of success, partly out of Gallicanism* and Jansenism,* partly out of resentment and a variety of other causes, led to suppression of the order 1773 everywhere except Russ., where it was favored by Catherine II (Catherine the Great; Ekaterina Alekseevna; Sophia Augusta Frederica of Anhalt-Zerbst; 1729–96; empress of Russ. 1762–96) and perpetuated itself with papal approval until it was restored 1814 (see also *Bull; Popes,* 25).

Supreme authority is in a gen. cong., which elects superior generals (who serve for life) and deals with some grave problems; the cong. met 31 times 1558–1965 (25 times for election). A provincial heads each province (10 in the US: Md.; N. Y.; Mo.; New Orleans; Calif.; New Eng.; Chicago; Oreg.; Detroit; Wis.). Official directives are in writings collectively called the Institute.

Training (reduced in time and made more flexible in recent yrs.) leads to membership consisting of priests, scholastics (students), and temporal coadjutors. All spend 2 yrs. in a novitiate (see *Novice*), preceded in the case of brothers by 6-mo. postulancy (see *Postulant*).

Worldwide there were ca. 35,000 Jesuits in 1970 (ca. 7,900 in the US: 5,000 priests, 2,500 scholastics, 650 temporal coadjutors). Nearly 3,000 priests and scholastics left the order 1965–70, including ca. 500 Americans. In 1960 four hundred were admitted, in 1967 only 149. In 1970, efforts by Jesuits in Sp. to splinter off in order to preserve "the true spirit" of the order were suppressed. MAM

See also *Accommodation,* 5; *Jajus, Claudius; Paccanarists.*

Society of Mary. See *Marianists.*

Society of the Faith of Jesus. See *Paccanarists.*
Society of the Woman in the Wilderness. See *Communistic Societies,* 4.
Society People. See *Associated Reformed Church; Cameronians; Presbyterian Churches,* 3.
Socinianism. 1. Theol. system named after F. P. Sozzini (see *Socinus*) and his followers. Has roots in 16th-c. Eur. anti-Trinitarians and Anabaptists (e. g., G. Blandrata,* F. Davidis,* J. Denk,* G. V. Gentile,* M. Gribaldi,* L. Hetzer,* J. Kautz,* B. Ochino,* M. Servetus,* L. F. M. Sozini [see *Socinus*]). Some fled the Inquisition* to Switz., Transylvania, and Poland (where Unitarianism found favor among the ruling classes). F. P. Sozzini (see *Socinus*) unified and organized them. Rakow (Racow), Poland, became the cen. of the movement and seat of a flourishing school (see also *Rakau Catechism*). Leaders included V. Smalcius.*

RC reaction began under Sigismund III (see *Poland,* 3). The ch. at Lublin was destroyed 1627; the school at Rakow was suppressed 1638. All Socinians were banished from Poland 1658; some fled to Transylvania, others to Prussia and other parts of Ger. and to Holland and elsewhere, but without finding complete toleration. Socinians in Eng. found a kindred spirit in deism and included J. Biddle* and J. Priestley.* See also *Unitarianism.*

Socinianism as reflected, e. g., in the works of F. P. Sozzini and the Rakau Catechism, is supernaturalistic with the tendency toward increasing rationalism. The Bible is regarded as the revealed authority and source of religious truth, containing nothing contrary to reason; e. g., the deity of Christ, original sin, vicarious atonement of Christ, and resurrection of the body are denied; the ungodly, with the devil and his angels, shall be annihilated; Baptism and Communion are unnecessary; men save themselves, insofar as they need salvation.
Socinus. Latinized form of Sozini (Sozzini), name of 2 It. anti-Trinitarians connected with the beginnings of Socinianism.*

1. *Lelio Francesco Maria Sozini* (Laelius Socinus; 1525–62). Uncle of F. P. Sozzini (see 2); b. Siena; educ. as a jurist at Bologna; studied theol.; came to doubt the Trin. and other doctrines repugnant to reason; traveled widely in Reformation lands and became acquainted with P. Melanchthon and J. Calvin. Expressed his views in writings bequeathed to F. P. Sozzini. D. Zurich, Switz.

2. Fausto Paolo Sozzini (Faustus Socinus; 1539–1604). Nephew of L. F. M. Sozini (see 1); b. Siena; no regular educ.; studied theol.; lived at Lyons, Fr., 1559–62, at Zurich 1562; became firmly est. in anti-Trinitarianism; held court positions at Florence, It., 1562–74; lived at Basel, Switz., 1574–78; to Transylvania 1578 on invitation of G. Blandrata*; theol. turmoil and outbreak of the pest caused him to leave; to Poland 1579, where he freed scattered anti-Trinitarians from Anabap. and chiliastic accretions and unified and organized them; lived mainly in Kraków, under abuse and opposition, till driven out of the city 1598.
Sociological Positivism. See *Positivism, Sociological.*
Sociological Realism. See *Positivism, Sociological.*
Sociology. Science or study of society and of soc. institutions and relations with a view to understanding and improvement. Subdivisions include rural, urban, hist., and cultural sociology. See also *Social Work.*
Sockman, Ralph Washington (1889–1970). B. Mt. Vernon, Ohio. Educ. Ohio Wesleyan U., Delaware, Ohio; Columbia U. and Union Theol. Sem., NYC. Pastor NYC. Preacher NBC's Nat. Radio Pulpit 1928–62. Visiting prof. Yale U., New Haven, Conn.; Union Theol. Seminary. Pres. Church Peace Union (later Council* on Religion and Internat. Affairs) 1948. Works include *The Paradoxes of Jesus; The Meaning of Suffering; A Lift for Living; Suburbs of Christianity; Date with Destiny; The Higher Happiness; How to Believe.*
Socrates (ca. 470–399 BC). Philos.; b. Athens, Greece; rendered military service from time to time; twice defied govt. ruling which he regarded as unjust; criticized follies and vices of the govt. and inanities of the popular theol. of his day; convicted of charges of corrupting the youth and of being unfaithful to the religion and gods of the state; chose death by poison hemlock rather than suggest a lesser penalty.

Aristophanes (ca. 448–ca. 380 BC; Athenias playwright) caricatures him, probably playfully, in *The Clouds* as petty, bourgeoise, antidemocratic. Xenophon (ca. 434–ca. 355 BC; hist. and essayist; b. Athens, Greece; disciple of Socrates) describes him in *Memorabilia* as a practical man of action. Plato* (disciple of Socrates) idealizes him as a hero of dialectic. Aristotle* credits him with being the first to seek natural definitions or universal principles, but only in moral matters. The accuracy of the image thus secured is subject to debate.

Socrates developed a method of inquiry and instruction (known as the Socratic method) by questions and answers; it led to the notion that virtue is teachable, evil the result of ignorance, and the virtues one.

Other disciples of Socrates include Aristppus,* Antisthenes (see *Cynicism*), Euclid(es)* of Megara.

See also *Dialectic; Natural Law,* 2; *Philosophy.*
Socrates (surnamed Scholasticus; ca. 380 – after 440). Gk. ch. hist.; b. Constantinople. Wrote a ch. hist. covering the period 306–439, continuing the *Historia ecclesiastica* of Eusebius* of Caesarea. See also *Sozomen.*
Sodalities. See *Confraternity.*
Sodality of Our Lady. See *Young People's Organizations, Christian,* V 2.
Soden, Hans Karl Hermann von (1852–1914). Father of H. O. A. M. R. U. v. Soden*; b. Cincinnati, Ohio; educ. Tübingen, Ger., held various positions in the ministry at Wildbad (near Stuttgart), Dresden-Striesen, Chemnitz, and Berlin; prof. NT Berlin 1893; liberal of the Ritschlian school (see *Ritschl, Albrecht Benjamin*). Works include *Die Schriften des Neuen Testaments in ihrer ältesten erreichbaren Textgestalt.*
Soden, Hans Otto Arthur Marie Roderich Ulrich von (1881–1945). Son of H. K. H. v. Soden*; b. Dresden, Ger.; pupil of K. G. A. v. Harnack*; prof. Breslau 1918, Marburg 1924; became founder and leader of Confessing* Ch. in Hesse-Cassel. Works include *Geschichte der christlichen Kirche; Wahrheit in Christus.*
Söderblom, Nathan (Lars Olof Jonathan; 1866–1931). Luth. theol.; b. Trönö, Hälsingland province (included largely in Gävleborg Co.), E cen. Swed.; educ. Uppsala; ordained 1893; chaplain mental hosp. Uppsala; pastor Paris and sailors' pastor Calais and Dunkerque, Fr., 1894. Prof. Uppsala 1901–14, also Leipzig, Ger., 1912–14; abp. Uppsala 1914; received Nobel peace prize 1930. Sweden's most outstanding spiritual leader in modern times. Works include *Christian Fellowship;* The Nature of Revelation, tr. F. E. Pamp. See also *Ecumenical Movement, The,* 9; *Sweden, Lutheranism in,* 6. GH

T. J. E. Andrae, *Nathan Söderblom,* 5th ed. (Upsala, 1932); E. Berggrav, *Nathan Söderblom: Geni og karakter* (Oslo, 1931); E. J. Ehnmark, *Religionsproblemet hos Nathan Söderblom* (Lund, 1949); C. J. Curtis, *Söderblom: Ecumenical Pioneer* (Minneapolis, Minn., 1967); T. C. Graebner, "Nathan Soederblom," *CTM,* XV (1944), 314–328.
Södermann, August Johan (Johan August; 1832–76). Prot. composer; b. Stockholm, Swed.; received musical training in Ger. Works include a mass; *Benedictus; Agnus Dei.*

Soembawa. See Indonesia, 1, 11.

Soenda Isles. See *Indonesia,* 1, 3–6, 9–12.

Soetefleisch, Johann (1552–1620). Luth. theol.; b. Seesen, Brunswick, NW Ger.; educ. Gandersheim and Helmstedt; rector Burg, near Magdeburg; taught at Magdeburg 1581; gen. supt. Göttingen 1589, Calenberg 1608. Prepared Catechism questions based on M. Luther's text.

Sohm, Rudolph (Rudolf; 1841–1917). B. Rostock, Ger.; educ. Rostock, Berlin, Heidelberg, Munich; prof. Göttingen, Freiburg, Strasbourg, Leipzig. Works include *Das Verhältnis von Staat und Kirche; Trauung und Verlobung; Kirchenrecht; Institutionen des römischen Rechts; Kirchengeschichte im Grundriss.*

Sohn(ius), Georg (1551–89). Ref. theol.; b. Rossbach, Ger.; educ. Marburg and Wittenberg; prof. Marburg and Heidelberg; Philippist (see *Philippists*); opposed FC in Hesse. Works include *De verbo Dei et eius tractatione.*

Sohn, Otto Emanuel (Oct. 10, 1894–Apr. 15, 1969). B. Detroit, Mich.; educ. Conc. Coll., Fort Wayne, Ind., and Conc. Sem., St. Louis, Mo. Pastor Sturgis, Sherman Twp., St. Joseph Co., SW Mich., 1917–19; Berrien Springs, Niles, and Buchanan, Mich., Flint, Mich., 1930–47. Prof. Conc. Sem., St. Louis, 1947–66. Ed. *Der Lutheraner* 1954–69; other works include *What's the Answer?*

Soka Gakkai ("Value-creating Society"). Subsect of the Nichiren* branch of Buddhism.*

D. Neiswender, "Christianity and Nichiren in Japan," *CTM,* XXXVII (1966), 355–364.

Sola fide (Lat. "by faith alone"). Term referring to the Scriptural doctrine that "a man is justified by faith without the deeds of the Law" (Ro 3:28; cf. Ph 3:9). AC IV 1–2: "Men cannot be justified before God by their own strength, merits, or works but are freely justified for Christ's sake through faith when they believe that they are received into favor and that their sins are forgiven on account of Christ, who by His death made satisfaction for our sins." See also *Faith, Justifying; Material Principle.*

Sola gratia (Lat. "by grace alone"). Term referring to the Scriptural doctrine that man is saved by grace alone without the deeds of the Law (Eph 2:8-9). See also *Conversion,* II; *Faith, Justifying; Grace; Predestination.*

Sola Scriptura (Lat. "Scripture alone"). Term referring to the formal* principle of the Luth. Church. FC SD Rule and Norm 3: "We pledge ourselves to the prophetic and apostolic writings of the Old and New Testaments as the pure and clear fountain of Israel, which is the only true norm according to which all teachers and teachings are to be judged and evaluated." See also *Grace, Means of; Holy Scripture; Inspiration, Doctrine of; Norma normans.*

J. T. Mueller, "The Sola Scriptura and Its Modern Antithesis," *CTM, XVI* (1945), 5–24.

Solemn League and Covenant. See *Covenanters; League and Covenant, Solemn; Presbyterian Confessions,* 1, 3.

Solemn Mass. See *Missa solemnis.*

Solid Declaration. See *Lutheran Confessions,* C 2.

Solipsism. A subjective idealism* which holds that the self can know only its own states and modifications.

Sollicitudo Omnium. See *Bull.*

Solomon, Psalms of. See *Apocrypha,* A 4.

Solomon, Wisdom of. See *Apocrypha,* A 3.

Solomon Islands. See *Melanesia.*

Soma. See *Brahmanism,* 2.

Somalia. See *Africa,* E 5.

Somaliland. See *Africa,* E 4–5.

Somascha, Order of Clerks Regular of (Ordo Clericorum *Regularium a Somascha;* Somaschi; also called Regular Clerks of St. Majolus, or Majolites, after the Ch. of St. Majolus,* Pavia, It., which was given them by C. Borromeo*). RC order founded 1532 Somasca (or Somascho), bet. Milan and Bergamo; approved by pope 1540; united with Theatines* ca. 1546–55; made religious order under Augustinian rule and named after Majolus 1568. Work includes care of needy and teaching. See also *Counter Reformation,* 6.

Somerset Confession. See *Democratic Declarations of Faith,* 3.

Sommer, Martin Samuel (Mar. 31, 1869–Dec. 16, 1949). B. Blenheim, near Baltimore, Md.; educ. Baltimore City Coll. and Conc. Sem., St. Louis, Mo.; pastor Grace Luth. Ch., St. Louis 1892–1920 (he had begun preaching there 1891); pres. Eng. Dist. of the Mo. Syn. 1912–15; prof. Conc. Sem., Saint Louis, 1920–46. Coed. *The Lutheran Witness* 1914–49.

R. L. Sommer, "Martin Samuel Sommer," *CHIQ,* XXIII (1950–51), 123–131, 159–169.

Sommer, Peter Nicholas (Nicolaus; Jan. 9, 1709–Oct. 27, 1795). Luth. pastor; b. Hamburg, Ger.; educ. Germany; to US 1742/43; pastor Schoharie, N. Y., serving also Stone Arabia, Palatine Bridge, Cobleskill and other places from 1743.

Song of the Three Children. See *Apocrypha,* A 3.

Sonntag, Karl Gottlob (1765–1827). B. Radeberg, near Dresden, Ger.; educ. Leipzig; held various ministerial positions; gen. supt. Livonia (now in Latvia); originally rationalist, later stressed piety; tried to improve the lot of peasants. Poet. Helped draft const. for Luth. Ch. in Russia; issued catechisms. Works include *Wert und Notwendigkeit der christlichen Religion für den vernünftigen Menschen; Über Menschenleben, Christentum und Umgang.*

Sophianism. Theol. based on divine wisdom.

Sophists. See *Chinese Philosophy,* 4; *Philosophy; Philostratus.*

Sophocles. See *Religious Drama.*

Sophronius. See *Monothelitism.*

Sorbon, Robert de (1201–74). B. Sorbon, near Rethel, Fr.; chaplain and confessor of Louis* IX; founded a coll. for poor theol. students 1257, forerunner of Sorbonne Coll. of Paris U.

Sorley, William Ritchie (1855–1935). Brit. philos.; b. Selkirk, Scot.; prof. Cambridge 1900–33; exponent of moral argument for God (see *Apologetics, Christian,* 4, I, A; *God, Arguments for the Existence of*). Works include *The Moral Life and Moral Worth; A History of British Philosophy to 1900* (1st ed. pub. under title *A History of English Philosophy*).

Sorolainen, Eerikki Eerikinpoika (Fin. "Eric, son of Eric Sorolainen"; known also as Ericus Erici; 1545–1625). Luth. theol.; b. Laitila, Fin.; educ. Ger.; rector of Gymnasium at Gävle, Swed.; bp. Turku (Aabo), Fin., 1583. Helped tr. Bible into Fin. Other works include a ch. manual; catechism; postil.

Sororities, Student. See *Fraternities, Student.*

Soteriology. Branch of doctrinal theol. that deals with salvation by divine agency. In Luth. theol.: the Bible doctrine concerning the application of the merits of Christ to the individual sinner, whereby the sinner is led to the actual possession and enjoyment of the blessings which Christ has procured for all mankind. See also *Atonement.*

Soto, Francisco Domingo de (1494–1560). RC theol.; b. Segovia, Sp.; educ. Alcalá de Henares, Sp., and Paris, Fr.; prof. Alcalá 1520; Dominican 1525 (when he replaced his name Francisco with Domingo); taught at Segovia and Salamanca; imperial theol. of Charles* V at the Council of Trent*; confessor and spiritual adviser of Charles V 1547; prior at Salamanca. Works include commentary on Ro and on Aristotle's *De anima.*

Soto, Pedro de (1500–63). B. probably Alcalá de Henares (or Córdoba?), Sp.; Dominican ca. 1518/19; confessor and adviser of Charles* V 1542;

opposed Lutheranism; prof. Dillingen. Works include *Institutiones Christianae.*

Soul. Vital principle in man; without matter and form. Definitions of, and distinctions bet., soul, mind, and spirit vary. See also *Creationism; Democritus; Image of God,* 3–4; *Immortality; Materialism; Traducianism.*

Soul Care. See *Pastor as Counselor.*

Soul Sleep (psychopannychism). View that the soul of a dead person exists in a state of sleep. Scripture does not speak of soul sleep, but of souls after death in a state of awareness (Rv 6:10; cf. Lk 16: 22-31; "rest" in Rv 14:13 does not imply sleep; cf. Heb 4:9-11). When we speak of the dead as sleeping, this refers to the body.

Souls, Cure of. See *Pastor as Counselor.*

Source Hypothesis. See *Higher Criticism,* 6–13.

Souter, Alexander (1873–1949). NT Biblical and classical scholar; b. Perth, Scot.; educ. Aberdeen, Scot., and Cambridge, Eng.; taught at Aberdeen 1897–1903; prof. Oxford 1903–11, Aberdeen 1911–37. Works include *The Text and Canon of the New Testament; A Pocket Lexicon to the Greek New Testament.*

South, Liturgical. Right, as one faces the altar in a ch.; Epistle* side. See also *Orientation of Churches.*

South America. S continent, W hemisphere; 4th largest (after Asia, Afr., and N Am.). *Area:* figures vary from 6,795,000 to 6,970,706 sq. mi. *Pop.* (est.): more than 190,000,000. Political divisions: Argentina, Bolivia, Brazil, Chile, Colombia, Ecuador, Guyana, Paraguay, Peru, Uruguay, Venezuela. Surinam (Dutch Guiana) is part of the Kingdom of the Netherlands. Fr. Guiana is an overseas dept. of Fr. The Falkland Islands and dependencies are a colony of the United Kingdom of Gt. Brit. and N. Ireland. For the Neth. Antilles see *Caribbean Islands,* C, E 7. See also *Trinidad and Tobago.*

1. *Argentine Rep.* (Argentina). *Area:* figures vary from 1,072,067 to 1,079,520 sq. mi. *Pop.* (1972 est.): 25,000,000 (ca. 97% of Eur. origin [mainly Sp. and It.]; ca. 3% Indian, mestizo, et al.). Under Sp. influence and control from the 16th c.; indep. 1816. Official language: Spanish. RCm officially recognized in the const.; liberty provided for all religions; perhaps ca. 200,000 Prots. The Ger. Ev. La Plata Syn. (Luth-Ref.) was est. 1899. The *Iglesia Evangelica Luterana Unida* began 1908 as a N. Am. miss. venture. Other Luth. chs. include Swed., Dan., Norw., and Fin. See also 2; *Lutheran Church – Missouri Synod, Districts of The,* B 2; *United Lutheran Church The,* III.

2. *Tierra del Fuego,* largest is. in the Tierra del Fuego archipelago, S tip of S. Am. *Area:* figures vary from 18,530 to 18,800 sq. mi.; ca. W half belongs to Chile, ca. E half to Argentina. The Angl. Ch. continued work after unsuccessful efforts by A. F. Gardiner* and by The S. Am. Miss. Soc.

3. *Rep. of Bolivia.* Surrounded by Brazil, Paraguay, Argentina, Chile, Peru. *Area:* ca. 424,162 sq. mi. *Pop.* (1972 est.): 5,200,000 (perhaps ca. 63% Amerindian, 15% of Eur. origin, 22% mixed). Official language: Sp., spoken by perhaps ca. 40%. Under Sp. influence and control, as Upper Peru, from the 1530s; indep. 1825 and renamed after its liberator, Simón Bolívar (1783–1830). Official religion: RCm (perhaps ca. 95%); religious liberty extends to others. A Ger. Luth. cong. was est. 1923 in La Paz, the capital; related congs. were est. in the vicinity. The *Iglesia Evangelica Luterana* was est. 1938 by the World* Miss. Prayer League.

4. *Federative Rep. of Brazil* (22 states, 4 territories, 1 fed. dist.). *Area:* figures vary from 3,284,426 to 3,286,488 sq. mi. *Pop.* (1972 est.): 100,000,000 (perhaps ca. 62% of Eur. [mainly Port.] origin, 11% Negro, 26% mixed, 1% others). Under Port. influence and control from ca. 1500; indep. monarchy 1822; rep. 1889. Official language: portuguese. Religion: perhaps ca. 90–95% RC. Luths. have been in Brazil at least since 1552. Huguenot efforts at colonization 1555–68 and Ref. work 1636–44 came to nought. A Ger. Luth. cong. was est. 1823. The Rio Grande do Sul Syn. was organized 1886, other syns. 1905, 1911, 1912; these 4 formed a fed. 1950 which became the Ev. Ch. of the Luth. Confession 1954. Swed. and Norw. Luth. pastors serve seamen. The World* Miss. Prayer League began work 1953. See also *Lutheran Church – Missouri Synod, Districts of The,* B 1.

5. *Rep. of Chile* (narrow strip along S half of the W coast of S. Am.). *Area:* ca. 292,256 sq. mi. *Pop.* (1972 est.): 10,200,000 (ca. 68% of Sp.-Indian origin, 30% of Eur. [mainly Sp.] origin, 2% Indian). Under Sp. influence and control from the 16th c.; indep. 1818; under congressional dictatorship 1891–1925. Official and prevailing language: Spanish. RCm dominant. Hundreds of Ger. Luth. families came to Chile ca. 1849–59; the 1st parish was organized 1863, the Ger. Ev. Luth. Ch. in Chile 1905. After unsuccessful efforts 1920 and 1932, LCMS est. permanent work 1952; LCMS Argentine Dist. includes Chile. See also 2.

6. *Rep. of Colombia* (NW S. Am.). *Area:* ca. 439,735 sq. mi. *Pop.* (1972 est.): 22,900,000 (perhaps ca. 68% mestizo, 20% white, 7% Indian, 5% Negro). Under Sp. influence and control from ca. 1499; indep. 1819. Official and prevailing language: Spanish. State religion: RCm (perhaps ca. 96–99%); others tolerated. Indep. Luth. missionaries founded the Celmosa Miss. of Colombia 1936. The field was transferred to ELC/UELC 1946, to The ALC 1960. *Iglesia Evangelica Luterana – Sinodo de Colombia* was organized 1958. Luth. miss. work has also been done among Germans and Scandinavians.

7. *Rep. of Ecuador* (Pacific coast, NW S. Am.). *Area:* ca. 109,483 sq. mi. *Pop.* (1972 est.): 6,500,000 (ca. 40% Indian, 40% mestizo, 10% of Eur. [mainly Sp.] origin, 10% Negro). Under Sp. influence and control from ca. 1532; indep. of Sp. 1822; then part of confederacy of Greater Colombia till 1830, when it became an indep. rep. Official and prevailing language: Spanish. RCm predominates. The World* Miss. Prayer League began work among Indians 1951. Luth. ch. work among Gers. and Scands. began 1953 by extension from Colombia.

8. *Rep. of Paraguay* (cen. S. Am.; surrounded by Argentina, Brazil, Bolivia). *Area:* ca. 157,047 sq. mi. *Pop.* (1972 est.): 2,600,000 (ca. 95% of Sp.-Indian [Guarani] origin, 3% white, 2% Indian). Under Sp. influence and control from the 16th c.; indep. 1811. Official language: Sp.; nearly all speak also Guarani. State religion: RCm (ca. 90%); others tolerated. Ger. Ev. work began 1893. LCMS began Ger. work 1935; its Argentine Dist. includes Paraguay.

9. *Rep. of Peru* (Pacific coast, NW S. Am., bet. Ecuador and Chile). *Area:* ca. 496,222 sq. mi. *Pop.* (1972 est.): 14,500,000 (ca. 46% Indian, 43% mestizo, 11% white and others). Under Sp. influence and control from 1532; indep. 1824. Official language: Spanish. State religion: RCm; others tolerated. Ev. work among Gers. began ca. 1898, connected to the Prussian* Union 1905, est. legally as *Iglesia Evangelica Luterana del Peru* 1951.

10. *Eastern* (or *Oriental*) *Rep. of Uruguay* (echoing *Banda Oriental* ["East Bank," i.e., of the Uruguay and the Plata], the name under which it was inc. in the Sp. Viceroyalty of Río de la Plata 1776), smallest country of S. Am., on SE coast. *Area:* figures vary from 68,536 to 72,172 sq. mi. *Pop.* (1972 est.): 3,000,000 (ca. 90% of Eur. [mainly Sp. and It.] origin, 10% mestizo and mulatto). Settled by Sp. 1624; unsuccessfully challenged by Port.

from the 1680s to the 1770s; indep. from Sp. 1811–14; conquered by Port. from Brazil; province of Brazil 1820–25; revolted 1825; indep. rep. 1828; administered by a 9-mem. Nat. Council 1951–66. Official and universal language: Spanish. Ch. and state are separate; RCm predominant. Ger. evangelical work began 1843 and was carried on intermittently. LCMS (whose Argentine Dist. includes Uruguay) began work 1936. Work of the ULC began in the 1940s, was undergirded by the NLC in the early 1950s, transferred to the Augustana Bd. of World Mission 1956, to the LCA 1962.

11. *Rep. of Venezuela* (N coast of S. Am.); consists of 20 states, 2 territories, 1 fed. dist. *Area:* ca. 352, 143 sq. mi. *Pop.* (1972 est.): 11,500,000 (ca. 65% mestizo [mixed Indian and Eur. origin], 21% of Eur. [mainly Sp.] origin, 7% Negro, 2% Indian, 5% mulatto or of mixed Indian and Negro origin). Under Sp. influence and control from the 16th c.; indep. proclaimed 1811, assured 1821; part of confederacy of Greater Colombia 1819–29/30; indep. rep. 1830; unsettled times followed for many decades. Official and universal language: Sp. Official religion: RCm (perhaps ca. 96%); religious freedom guaranteed. Ger. Prot. miss. efforts began in the last half of the 19th c. The LWF supplied a pastor 1949 for Ger. and Latvian services. The NLC supplied additional pastors in the early 1950s. A Luth. Council of Venezuela was formed 1960. LCMS began work 1951. The Conf. of Luth. Chs. in Venezuela was formed in the early 1970s.

12. *Rep. of Guyana* (NE coast of S. Am.). *Area:* ca. 83,000 sq. mi. *Pop.* (1972 est.): 800,000 (ca. 48–50% East Indian, ca. 33–45% African, the rest Indian, Port., Chinese, and mixed). Settled by Dutch in 17th c.; alternated bet. Dutch and Brit. rule in 18th c., with Brit. rule est. by 1815; colony of Brit. Guiana est. 1831; indep. state in the Comm. 1966; rep. 1970. Official language: Eng.; various others spoken. Religion: perhaps ca. 57% Christian (mainly Angl.), 34% Hindu. 9% Muslim. The Luth. ch. est. by Dutch settlers in New Amsterdam lasted ca. 100 yrs., was then used by Meths., reopened for Luth. services 1875, affiliated with the E. Pa. Syn. 1890. The Ev. Luth. Ch. of (or in) Brit. Guiana, organized 1943 as ULC assoc. syn., became ULC-affiliated syn. 1950. See also *United Lutheran Church in America, The,* III.

13. *Surinam* (Dutch Guiana), autonomous part of the Kingdom of the Neth.; NE coast of S. Am. *Area:* figures vary from ca. 55,000 to 70,060 sq. mi. *Pop.* (1972 est.): 420,000 (perhaps ca. 40% Negro, 30% East Indian, 16% Indonesian, 10% native Indians, 2% Chinese, 2% European and others). Explored by Sp. in 16th c. Control changed hands several times when Brit., Fr., and Dutch competed for the area. Awarded to Dutch by Congress of Vienna 1815. Official language: Dutch; various others spoken. Religions include Christian, Hindu, Muslim, Jewish. Moravians began work in 1730s. See also *Weltz, Justinian(us) Ernst von.*

14. *French Guiana* (NE coast of S. Am.); consists of 2 arrondissements: coastal Cayenne and and hinterland Inini. *Area:* figures vary from 34,749 to 37,740 sq. mi. *Pop.* (1972 est.): 52,000 (ca. 75% Creole [b. in Fr. Guiana, but with some Eur. blood], 10% indigenous Indians and descendants of Negro slaves, 7% Eur., 5% Chinese, 3% others). First settled by Fr. early in the 17th c.; changed hands several times under Dutch and Brit. competition; Fr. sovereignity est. ca. 1676; captured by Anglo-Port. force ca. 1808/09; repossessed by Fr. 1817; penal colony est. ca. 1852; Fr. overseas dept. 1946; penal colony closed 1947. Official language: Fr. RCm predominates. Prots. include Salvation Army; Christian Missions in Many Lands; Angls.; Seventh-day Adventists. WED

South America Indian Mission. Founded 1914 by an Am. miss. as Paraguayan Mission. Joined a like-minded mission from Scot. 1919 and renamed Inland S. Am. Missionary Union. Present name adopted 1939. Avoided larger centers of civilization; sought Indians in jungles. Est. several Bible schools for natives. Fields include Bolivia, Brazil, Colombia, Peru. Mem. IFMA. US HQ Lake Worth, Fla.

South American Missionary Society, The. See *Gardiner, Allen Francis.*

South Andhra Lutheran Church. See *India,* 13.

South Australia, Evangelical Lutheran Synod of. See *Australia, Lutheranism in,* A 1.

South Carolina, Evangelical Lutheran Synod of. See *United Lutheran Church, Synods of,* 16, 27.

South China Boat Mission. See *International Missions, Inc.*

South-West Africa. See *Africa,* B 8.

Southcott, Joanna (1750–1814). B. Gittisham, near Exmouth, Devonshire, Eng.; domestic servant; originally Meth.; claimed to possess supernatural gifts and to be the woman of Rv 12; in spring 1814 she announced that she was pregnant with Shiloh, who, however, failed to appear; she died a few days after Christmas. Followers called Southcottians.* Works include *The Book of Wonders; The Strange Effects of Faith; The True Explanation of the Bible; Song of Moses and the Lamb.*

Southcottians. Followers of J. Southcott,* who obligated them to keep Mosaic laws regarding the Sabbath and clean and unclean meats. Once numbering perhaps 100,000, the sect dwindled, becoming extinct by the end of the 19th c. See also *Purnell, Benjamin.*

Southern Africa (Eastern Region), The Evangelical Lutheran Church in.
See *Africa,* B 5.

Southern Baptist Convention. See *Baptist Churches,* 9.

Southern Christian Leadership Conference. Organized 1957 by M. L. King* to help coordinate civil rights efforts in S US.

Southern Illinois, Evangelical Lutheran Synod of (Southern Ill. Syn.). See *Illinois, Evangelical Lutheran Synod of Southern.*

Southern Methodist Church. See *Methodist Churches,* 4 b.

Southern Presbyterians. See *Presbyterian Churches,* 4.

Southern Rhodesia. See *Africa,* B 2.

Southern Seminary, Lutheran Theological. See *Ministry, Education of,* X M.

Southwest, Synod of the (Syn. of the South West; Ev. Luth. Syn. of the Southwest [or South West]; Southwest Syn.). Organized 1846, when Ev. Luth. Syn. of the West* divided. Joined The General* Syn. of the Ev. Luth. Ch. in the USA 1848. Divided 1854, part helped form a Ky. Syn. (see *Kentucky Synod,* 3), part retained the name Southwest. Dissolved 1856 by mutual consent because it covered too much territory. Mems. in mid-Tenn. were directed to the Ky. Syn. Of the mems. in W Tenn., Mo., and Ill., some formed the Ev. Luth. Syn. of Southern Illinois,* others joined the Ev. Luth. Syn. of Illinois.*

South-West Africa. See *Africa,* B 8.

Southwestern Virginia Synod. See *Synods, Extinct; United Lutheran Church, Synods of,* 16, 29.

Sovereign Military Order of the Hospital of St. John of Jerusalem, of Rhodes, and of Malta. See *Military Religious Orders,* a.

Sovereignty of God. See *Calvin, John,* 10.

Sower, Christopher. See *Publicity, Church.*

Sozini (Sozzini). See *Socinus.*

Sozomen (full name includes various forms of Hermias Salamanes; ca. 375/400 – ca. 443/450). Gk.

ch. hist.; b. Bethelea (Bethelia), near Gaza, Palestine. Known for ch. hist. covering ca. 100 yrs. (1st part of the 4th c. to 1st part of the 5th c.), paralleling that of Socrates* (Scholasticus).

Space Age. See *Time.*

Spaeth, Philipp Friedrich Adolph Theodor (Oct. 29, 1839–June 25, 1910). B. Esslingen, Württemberg, Ger.; educ. Tübingen; ordained 1861; tutor; to US 1864; pastor Philadelphia, Pa., 1864–73; prof. Luth. Theol. Sem., Philadelphia, Pa., 1873–1910; pres. General* Council of the Ev. Luth. Ch. in (N.) Am. 1880–88, Pa. Ministerium 1892–95; liturgical and hymnological scholar; gifted pulpit orator. Works include *Charles Porterfield Krauth; D. Wilhelm Julius Mann, ein deutsch-amerikanischer Theologe: Erinnerungsblätter;* homiletical writings.

H. R. (Krauth) Spaeth, *Life of Adolph Spaeth, D. D., LL. D.* (Philadelphia, 1916).

Spain. W Eur. country occupying most of Iberian peninsula. *Area:* ca. 194,881 sq. mi.; *pop.* (1973 est.): 34,879,500.

1. A legend that arose in the 7th c. and acc. to which the apostle James the Elder preached in Sp. is now gen. abandoned as contrary to other tradition and to Ro 15:20, 24. Irenaeus (*Adversus haereses,* I, x, 2) and Tertullian (*Adversus Judaeos,* vii) note that there were Christians in Spain. Cyprian (ca. 200-258) mentions Christians at León, Astorga, Mérida, and Saragossa (Epistle lxvii). The Syn. of Elvira* addressed itself to the problem of laxity in morals and discipline. Suevians (Germanic) settled in Sp. early in the 5th c., veered unsteadily bet. RCm and Arianism, surrendered to Arian Visigoth king Leovigild (coregent with his brother Liuva [or Leova] 568; sole king 572, when his brother died; d. 586), disappeared as an indep. nation 585. The 589 Council of Toledo* marked the conversion of Reccared (or Recared), son and successor of Leovigild, to RCm. Saracens invaded Sp. from Afr. 711, brought Islam, and were not completely defeated till the fall of Granada 1492.

2. Reform movements in Sp. before the Luth. Reformation* were basically oriented on a RC axis esp. by Isabella (see *Inquisition,* 6), F. Jiménez* de Cisneros, and J. de Torquemada.* Many outward abuses, reflecting, e. g., a low moral level in convents and among the clergy, were corrected; papal authority was at times challenged, at least indirectly; yet the Span. pre-Reformation saw the est. of the Span. Inquisition,* not to oppose the "reform" but to undergird it.

3. The Luth. Reformation influenced, e. g., C. de Reina,* A. de Valdés,* J. de Valdés,* and F. de Enzinas.* M. Luther's writings and copies of Sp. Bibles found their way into Spain. See also *Lutheran Confessions,* A 5. But the Inquisition prevailed, esp. from 1557. See also *Auto-da-fé.* By 1570 Protestantism was practically dead in Spain.

4. 18th c. Fr. skepticism influenced Sp. and by the middle of the 19th c. helped bring a wave of liberalism and anticlericalism, with proclamation of religious freedom 1858 and 1868; but from 1876 religious dissidence was only tolerated, not recognized. Disestablishment was one of the main aims of the 2d Rep., installed 1931, but RCm gained the ascendancy after the 1936–39 civil war. The 1947 Const. assures official protection for RCm; no one shall be disturbed because of his religious beliefs or the private practices of his worship; but only RC outward ceremonies and demonstrations are permitted.

6. F. Fliedner* organized a Ger. Luth. cong. at Barcelona 1885; other Ger. Luth. congs. were est. elsewhere. Other Prots. in Sp. include Meths., Angls., Baps., and Plymouth Brethren.

Spalatin, Georg (family name: Burckhardt [Burkhardt]; changed to Spalatin from his birthplace; 1484–1545). B. Spalt, Middle Franconia, W cen. Bav., Ger.; priest 1508; tutored John* Frederick; served Frederick* III ("The Wise") in several capacities; friend of M. Luther. Moved to Altenburg 1525, where he had received a canonry 1511; took part in 1526 Diet of Speyer*; active in ch. visitations; attended the 1530 Diet of Augsburg and wrote an account of it; took sick Luther home from Schmalkalden 1537; helped reform Albertine Saxony under Henry* ("The Pious"); helped install N. v. Amsdorf as bp. Naumburg-Zeitz 1542. See also *Lutheran Confessions,* B 1.

Spalding, Henry Harmon (Spaulding; ca. 1803/04–Aug. 3, 1874). B. Bath, N. Y.; educ. Western Reserve Coll., Hudson, Ohio, and Lane Theol. Sem., Cincinnati, Ohio. ordained Presb. 1835; ABCFM miss. to Indians in the Northwest 1836; where he labored intermittently till his death. See also *Indians, American,* 13.

Spalding, Johann Joachim (1714–1804). B. Tribsees, Hither Pomerania; educ. Rostock and Greifswald; private tutor; pastor Pomerania 1749, Berlin 1764; provost and mem. of high consistory. Opposed Fr. materialism. Works include *Betrachtung über die Bestimmung des Menschen; Gedanken über den Werth der Gefühle in dem Christentum; Über die Nutzbarkeit des Predigtamtes und deren Beförderung.*

Spangenberg, Augustus Gottlieb (1704–92). B. Klettenberg, Ger.; educ. Jena; lectured at Jena; joined Moravians 1733; organizer and supervisor for his ch. in Eng., West Indies, Ga., N. C.; miss. to Am. Indians.* Hymnist. Works include *Idea fidei fratrum, oder kurzer Begrif der Christlichen Lehre in den evangelischen Brüdergemeinen; Von der Arbeit der evangelischen Brüder unter den Heiden.* See also *Moravian Church,* 5.

Spangenberg, Cyriacus (Cyriakus; 1528–1604). Son of J. Spangenberg*; b. Nordhausen, Ger.; study at Wittenberg interrupted by the Schmalkaldic* War; preacher Eislenben 1550, Mansfeld 1553; gen. dean of the county and assessor of the Eisleben consistory 1559; helped est. Lutheranism in Antwerp 1566–67; defended M. Flacius* Illyricus's view of original sin; excommunicated; fled to the dist. of Sangerhausen; expelled 1578; to Strasbourg; preacher Schlitzsee, on the Fulda, 1581; deprived of office 1591. Hymnist. Works include *Christliche und Gottselige Tagübung; Christlichs Gesangbüchlein; Christliche Erklärung dess streitigen Artickels Von der Erbsünde.*

Spangenberg, Johann (1484–1550). Father of C. Spangenberg*; b. Hardegsen, near Göttingen, Ger.; educ. Erfurt; rector Lat. School at Stolberg, also preacher Stolberg (ca. 1520); supported M. Luther; pastor Nordhausen 1524, where he est. Lutheranism and reest. a school; gen. county inspector, based at Eisleben, 1564. Hymnist. Works include *Postilla, Das ist: Auslegung der Episteln und Evangelien, Auf alle Sontage und vornehmsten Feste durch das ganze Jahr, Für die einfältigen Christen in Frag-Stücke verfasset; Cantiones ecclesiasticae Latinae.* See also *Medler, Nikolaus.*

Spanish Guinea. See *Africa,* C 18.

Spanish Inquisition. See *Inquisition,* 6.

Sparks, Jared (1789–1866). B. Willington, Conn.; educ. Harvard U., Cambridge, Mass.; ordained Unitarian 1819; pastor Baltimore, Md.; chaplain US Congress 1821; prof. Harvard 1829–39; pres. Harvard 1849–53. Historian.

Sparre, Aage (Jepsen). See *Denmark, Lutheranism in,* 1.

Spaulding, Levi (Aug. 22, 1791–June 18, 1873 [1874?]). B. Jaffrey, N. H.; educ. Dartmouth Coll., Hanover, N. H., and Andover (Mass.) Theol. Sem.; ordained Cong. 1818; ABCFM miss. to Ceylon (left 1819, arrived 1820). Educator. Hymnist. Helped tr. Bible into Tamil; revised Tamil OT. Other works include Tamil dictionary; rev. and enl. Eng.-Tamil dictionary; tracts; hymns; Bible History; tr. J. Bunyan's *Pilgrim's Progress.*

Speaking in Tongues. See *Pentecostalism; Tongues, Gift of.*

Speckhard, Georg Philipp (Jan. 22, 1821–Nov. 20, 1879). Father of H. Speckhard*; b. Wersau, Hesse, Ger.; educ. teachers' sem. at Friedberg; taught at a school for deaf, Friedberg; severed connection with state ch. for reasons of conscience 1859; to US soon thereafter; studied at the sem. in Fort Wayne, Ind. (see *Ministry, Education of,* X D). Pastor Hillsdale and Coldwater, Mich., 1861; Sandy Creek, near Monroe, Mich., 1863; Sebewaing, Mich., 1867; Royal Oak, Mich., 1873 (also 1st dir. of the Mo. Syn. school for deaf [see also *Deaf,* 10] and head of the Mo. Syn. orphanage there).

Speckhard, Hermann (Aug. 5, 1859–Dec. 28, 1916). Son of G. P. Speckhard*; b. Friedberg, Hesse, Ger.; bap. by F. A. Brunn*; to US soon thereafter; educ. Conc. Coll., Fort Wayne, Ind., and Conc. Sem., St. Louis, Mo. Pastor Hillsdale 1882, Ionia 1885, Saginaw 1894, all in Mich. Vice-pres. Mo. Syn. and Synodical* Conf. 1914.

Speculative Theology. See *Theology, Speculative.*

Speculum humanae salvationis. See *Biblia pauperum.*

Spee, Friedrich von (Spe; von Langenfeld; 1591–1635). B. Kaiserswerth, near Düsseldorf, Ger.; Jesuit 1610; educ. Fulda and Würzburg; ordained 1622; prof. philos. and cathedral preacher Paderborn 1623–26; then active 2 yrs. as teacher and miss. esp. at Cologne and Wesel; prof. moral theol. Cologne 1631–33, Trier 1633–35. Prominent leader in Counter* Reformation. Hymnist.

Speer, Robert Elliott (1867–1947). Presb. layman; b. Huntingdon, Pa.; educ. at the coll. and theol. sem. at Princeton, N. J.; secy. Student* Volunteer Movement 1889–90; instr. at coll. in Princeton 1890–91; secy. Presb. Bd. of For. Missions 1891–1937; made 4 extensive visitation tours to Asia, 2 to S. America. Works include *Presbyterian Foreign Missions; South American Problems; Studies of Missionary Leadership.*

Spegel, Haquin (Haqvin; 1645–1714). Abp. Uppsala, Swed., 1711; hymnist; collaborated with others in the hymnal prepared by J. Swedberg.* Hymns include "Waar Herres Jesu Kristi död" ("The Death of Jesus Christ, Our Lord").

Speier. See *Speyer.*

Spencer, Herbert (1820–1903). B. Derby, Derbyshire, N cen. Eng. His philos., a materialistic monism* influenced by A. Comte's* positivism,* distinguishes bet. the knowable and the unknowable. It is futile to try to investigate the unknowable (agnosticism*). To explain the knowable, he developed a system of philos. influenced by the theory of evolution, which he applied also to mental and soc. phenomena; coined the phrase "survival of the fittest." Held that all religion began in ancestor* worship. Works include a series projected as *A System of Philosophy,* of which the following appeared: *First Principles; The Principles of Biology; The Principles of Psychology; The Principles of Sociology; The Principles of Ethics.*

Spencer, John (1630–93). Angl. theol.; b. Bocton (Boghton), near Blean and Canterbury, Kent, Eng.; educ. Cambridge; served several parishes; prebendary at the cathedral of Ely 1671; archdeacon Sudbury 1677; dean Ely 1677. Pioneer in comparative religion. Works include *Dissertatio de Urim et Thummim; De legibus Hebraeorum ritualibus, et earum rationibus, libri tres.*

Spener, Philipp Jacob (Jakob; 1635–1705). "Father of Pietism*"; b. Rappoltsweiler, Upper Alsace; educ. Strasbourg (instructors included J. K. Dannhauer* and S. Schmidt*); asst. preacher at the Strasbourg cathedral 1663; minister and "senior" (supt.) Frankfurt am Main 1666, where he introd. (1670) *collegia pietatis,* private devotional gatherings, twice a week, in his house. Pub. *Pia desideria* 1657, in which he pictured the deplorable conditions in the ch. as he saw them and proposed measures for improvement (stressing Bible study and personal piety); result: controversy, in which some of his adherents left the ch., some emigrating to Pa. 1683. Spener became court preacher Dresden 1686. Influenced P. Anton* and A. H. Francke.* Provost St. Nicolai, Berlin, 1691. Helped est. Halle U. 1694. Spener's Lutheranism was marred by elements evidently from Ref. sources. Held a form of millennialism.* Hymnist. See also *Spizel, Theophil; Urlsperger, Samuel.*

Spengler, Lazarus (1479–1534). B. Nürnberg, Ger.; studies at Leipzig terminated by his father's death; town clerk 1507, mem. of council 1516 Nürnberg; met M. Luther 1518; leader of Reformation in and around Nürnberg; instrumental in opening a Gymnasium there; opposed P. Melanchthon's tendency to yield at Augsburg 1530. Hymnist. Hymns include "Durch Adams Fall ist ganz verderbt."

T. Pressel, *Lazarus Spengler,* in *Leben und Ausgewählte Schriften der Väter und Begründer der lutherischen Kirche,* ed. J. Hartmann et al., VIII (Elberfeld, 1862), separate paging 1–100.

Spengler, Oswald (1880–1936). Philos.; b. Blankenburg am Harz, Ger.; educ. Halle, Munich, Berlin; taught high school Hamburg 1908–11. Influenced by F. W. Nietzsche.* Works include *Der Untergang des Abendlandes* (Eng. tr. *The Decline of the West*).

Spenser, Edmund (ca. 1552–99). Poet; b. London, Eng.; educ. Cambridge. Works include *The Faerie Queene,* an allegory vindicating Protestantism and Puritanism over against enemies including RCm.

Speratus, Paul (Paulus; Spret; 1484–1551). B. Rötlen, near Ellwangen, Ger.; educ. various univs.; ordained ca. 1506; active in Salzburg, Dinkelsbühl, Würzburg; held ev. views; married; fled Würzburg; expelled from Salzburg; excommunicated at Ofen, Hung.; imprisoned at Iglau and condemned to death; escaped on condition he would leave Moravia; helped M. Luther prepare 1st Prot. hymnal; castle preacher Königsberg. Luth. bp. Pomerania 1530. Hymnist. Helped prepare Luth. Prussian ch. order. Hymns include "Es ist das Heil uns kommen her."

T. Pressel, *Paul Speratus,* in *Leben und Ausgewählte Schriften der Väter und Begründer der lutherischen Kirche,* ed. J. Hartmann et al., VIII (Elberfeld, 1862), separate paging 1–84.

Speyer, Cathedral at. See *Church Architecture,* 7.

Speyer, Diets of (Spire[s]; Speier). 1. *1526.* First ordered to meet Feb. 1 at Esslingen, later at Speyer May 1; began deliberations June 26 under Ferdinand (see *Reformed Confessions,* E 3) in the name of Charles* V; recess Aug. 27.

Background includes threatened invasion of Ger. by Turks and formation of the League of Torgau* (formed at Gotha Feb. 1526, ratified at Torgau in May, enlarged in the first part of June [and in Sept.]).

Charles V had claimed Lombardy, N It., for his empire. Francis I (see *France,* 8) challenged the claim with an army but was defeated and captured at Pavia 1525. To obtain release, he renounced claims in It. and over other disputed territories in the Jan. 1526 Peace (or Treaty) of Madrid. This would have left Charles V free to enforce the 1521 Edict of Worms.* But Francis I soon claimed that his concessions had been obtained by coercion and helped form the Holy League of Cognac (see *Holy Leagues and Alliances,* 5) in May. Problems besetting the emp. forced a tempering of imperial views in the interest of consolidating forces by winning evangelicals. Ferdinand agreed to a council within a yr.; meantime every state should be allowed so to arrange its religious affairs that it would be able to give account thereof to God and the emp. This opened the door for the spread of Lutheranism, allowing indep. from Rome; it divided Ger. religiously, gave Lutheranism a recognized existence, and offered hope for territorial constitutions on a formally legitimate basis. It was a great hist. landmark. See also *Augsburg, Religious Peace of.*

2. *1529.* Charles V neither signed nor opposed the 1526 edict of Speyer. The contemplated council did not materialize. The emp. dealt with the intractability of Francis I by engaging in a war (1527–29) against the Holy League of Cognac; Rome was sacked 1527 by rampant imperial forces, unpaid and mutinous; the pope was besieged in the Castle of St. Angelo. Naples was invaded by Fr.; but Genoa revolted (with indep. promised by the emp.) and a plague epidemic forced the Fr. to return home. See also *Cambrai, Peace of.*

Victorious over the Holy League of Cognac, Charles V appointed commissaries, headed by Ferdinand, and ordered another diet at Speyer, first set for Feb. 1, later for Feb. 21, finally Mar. 15. RCs were in the majority, strengthened and embittered by the O. v. Pack* episode. Decisions of the 1526 Diet of Speyer were declared ineffective. The 1521 Edict of Worms was declared in effect where it had been recognized; where RCm could not be reinstated without danger, evangelicals were to be tolerated but put under certain restrictions till the next gen. council. The evangelicals drew up and presented (Apr. 19/20) a protest ("We protest . . ."; hence the name Protestant), holding that in matters concerning God's honor and the salvation of souls each one must for himself stand before God and give account, so that herein no one can in any way (or to any extent) excuse himself by the action or resolution of others. Ferdinand rejected the protest. The recess of the diet was issued Apr. 22. Subsequent efforts by Prots to present their case to the emp. himself resulted in temporary imprisonment of their delegation late in 1529. Meanwhile the protest was pub. in Germany beginning in May.

3. *1542.* The 3d Diet of Speyer opened Feb. 9, 1542, under Ferdinand; purpose: to deal with needs for defense against Turks. Prots. refused support unless the 1532 Nürnberg* Religious Peace (extended by the 1541 Regensburg Interim [see *Regensburg Conference*] to the next gen. council) be observed. The Apr. 11 recess of the diet included a compromise recognizing Prot. claims in exchange for support against Turks.

4. *1544.* The 4th Diet of Speyer opened Feb. 20, 1544, under Charles V, who appealed for support against Turks and Francis I (who, he claimed, had made an alliance with Turks), with the first move to be made against Francis I. The Prots. demanded settlement of religious questions before giving war support. RCs were dissatisfied with some imperial proposals. Neither side was satisfied with the final compromise, which provided for maintenance of an army and a diet to be held at Worms within a yr.

In the upshot, Charles V defeated Francis I Sept. 1544 and so became free to move against Prots. (see *Schmalkaldic War*).

Spire(s). See *Speyer.*

Spirit (Spirit of Christ; Spirit of God). See *Holy Spirit.*

Spirit-baptized. See *Pentecostalism.*

Spiritans. See *Holy Ghost Under the Protection of the Immaculate Heart of Mary, Congregation of the.*

Spiritism (Spiritualism). Belief in intercommunication bet. mortals and departed spirits. Spiritists study psychic phenomena and explain them in terms of discarnate spirits. They believe development is continued in the hereafter, but deny the deity of Christ and the existence of devil, demons, and angels and try to unite evil and good, falsehood and truth, vice and virtue.

Marriage is not regarded as a divine institution but as based on laws of human nature and as the result of natural and spiritual affinities; the two parties united are not so much united into one flesh as virtually into one spirit and soul; divorces are to be freely given when desired by one or both.

The Nat. Spiritualists' Assoc. of the USA was organized 1893; name changed later to Nat. Spiritualist Assoc., Inc., and (in the 1950s) to Nat. Spiritualist Assoc. of Chs. The Morris Pratt Institute Assoc., founded 1901, supports and promotes the work of the NSAC.

Cf. Dt 18:9-14; see also *Fox, Margaret.*

Spirits. See *Angels.*

Spiritual Eating and Drinking. See *Grace, Means of,* IV 3.

"Spiritual Exercises" (Sp. *Ejercicios espirituales*). Book written by I. (of) Loyola* bet. 1521 and 1548; became a chief instrument of Jesuits. Consists of meditations in 4 divisions: 1. sin and its consequences; 2. kingdom of Christ; 3. Passion of Christ; 4. resurrection and ascension of Christ.

See also *Gerhard of Zutphen.*

Spiritual Life. See *Conversion,* II 2.

Spiritual Realism. Theory that only truly good will is free; causality based on spiritual activity; full realization of personality is achieved through self-forgetfulness.

Spiritual Sword. See *Two Swords.*

Spiritual Worship. See *Worship,* 8.

Spiritualism. See *Monism; Spiritism.*

Spirituals, Franciscan. Franciscans* who claim strictly to follow the rule and testament of Francis* of Assisi; accepted the teaching of Joachim* of Floris on the approaching "age of the Holy Spirit."

Spirituels. Pantheistic antinomian sect of the Reformation period; called Libertines* by opponents; originated perhaps at Lille, ca. 130 mi. NNE of Paris, Fr.; spread in Neth, and Fr. Held that since all visible existence is a manifestation of the one Spirit, nothing can be essentially bad; regenerate man attains the innocence that Adam had before he knew good and evil and recognizes that the distinction bet. good and bad is baseless.

Spiritus gladius. See *Symbolism, Christian,* 3.

Spitta, Friedrich Adolf Wilhelm (1852–1924). Son of K. J. P. Spitta*; brother of J. A. P. Spitta*; b. Wittingen, Ger.; educ. Erlangen and Göttingen; asst. preacher Bonn 1879; pastor Oberkassel, near Bonn, and privatdocent Bonn 1881; prof. Strasbourg 1887, Göttingen 1919. Assoc. ed. with J. Smend* *Monatschrift für Gottesdienst und kirchliche Kunst.* Other works include *Zur Reform des evangelischen Kultus; Zur Geschichte und Litteratur des Urchristentums; Über Chorgesang im evangelischen Gottesdienst; Heinrich Schütz, ein Meister der musica sacra.*

Spitta, Julius August Philipp (1841–94). Son of K. J. P. Spitta*; brother of F. A. W. Spitta*; b. Wechold, near Hoya, Hannover, Ger.; educ. Göttingen; taught at Reval, Sondershausen, Leipzig; prof. Berlin 1875; helped est. Leipzig Bach-Verein 1874. Ed. complete works of H. Schütz*; organ works of D. Buxtehude.* Other works include *Johann Sebastian Bach.*

Spitta, Karl Johann Philipp (1801–59). Father of F. A. W. Spitta* and J. A. P. Spitta*; b. Hanover, Hannover, Ger.; Hugenot ancestors, originally named de L'Hôpital (hence probably the name Spitta as abbreviated from Ger. *Hospital*), had fled Fr. to Brunswick after revocation of the Edict of Nantes* (see also *France,* 10); educ. Göttingen under rationalistic influence; private tutor Lüne, near Lüneburg, 1824–28; asst. pastor Sudwalde, near Hoya, 1828–30; military and prison chaplain Hameln 1830–37; pastor Wechold, near Hoya, 1837–47; supt. Wittingen 1847, Peine 1853, Burgdorf 1859. Hymnist. Works include *Psalter und Harfe;* hymns include "O selig Haus, wo man dich aufgenommen"; "Wir sind des Herrn, wir leben oder sterben."

Spittler, Christian Friedrich (1782–1867). B. Wimsheim, near Leonberg, Württemberg, Ger.; Luth. layman distinguished for services in behalf of missions; in civil revenue and administrative service 1796–1800; asst. in the Deutsche Christentumsgesellschaft* 1801; helped found Basel Bible Soc. 1804 (see *Bible Societies,* 2, 4); founded a pub. house at Basel 1812; helped found Basel* Miss. Soc. and (1834) a lending library; in 1841 he limited his est. to Bibles, tracts, and Christentumsgesellschaft literature. See also *Chrischona.*

Spittler, Ludwig Timotheus von (1752–1810). B. Stuttgart, Ger.; educ. Tübingen and Göttingen; prof. Göttingen 1779. Works include *Grundriss der Geschichte der christlichen Kirche,* which emphasizes ch. govt. and constitution.

Spizel, Theophil (Spitzel; Gottlieb; 1639–91). B. Augsburg, Ger.; educ. Leipzig, Wittenberg, Leiden, Strasbourg, Basel, Tübingen; pastor Augsburg; polymath; friend of P. J. Spener*; helped introd. Pietism in Augsburg.

Spleiss, David (1786–1854). B. Schaffhausen, Switz.; prof. physics and math Schaffhausen 1812, also pastor Buch, near Schaffhausen, 1813; revivalist; active in soc. and miss. work.

Spohr, Louis (bap. Ludewig; called himself Louis; 1784–1859). Luth. composer, violinist, conductor; b. Brunswick, Ger.; dir. music Theater an der Wien; conductor opera Frankfurt am Main; court kapellmeister Kassel. Works include 4 oratorios: *Das jüngste Gericht; Die letzten Dinge; Des Heilands letzte Studen; Der Fall Babylons.* See also *Passion, The.*

Sponsors (godparents; godfather; godmother). Persons making required professions and promises in the name of infants presented for Christian baptism (see *Grace, Means of,* III). Luths. follow ancient custom in having such persons present at baptism. Sponsors are 1. to testify that the children have been properly baptized; 2. to be concerned for the Christian educ. and training of their godchildren; 3. to pray for them.

Sprague, William Buell (1795–1876). B. Hebron (now in Andover), Conn.; educ. Yale Coll., New Haven, Conn., and Princeton (N. J.) Theol. Sem.; Cong. pastor West Springfield, Mass., 1819–29; Presb. pastor Albany, N. Y., 1829–69. Works include *Annals of the American Pulpit.*

Sprecher, Samuel (Dec. 28, 1810–Jan. 10, 1906). B. near Williamsport and Hagerstown, Washington Co., Md.; educ. Luth. Theol. Sem., Gettysburg, Pa. Pastor Harrisburg, Pa. Principal of Emmaus Institute, Middletown, Pa., 1840–42. Pastor Martinsburg, W. Va., 1842–43; Chambersburg, Pa., 1843–49. Influenced by S. S. Schmucker.* Pres. Wittenberg Coll., Springfield, Ohio, 1849–74; continued as prof. till 1884. At first supported the Definite* Syn. Platform; later regarded it as hopeless. See also *American Lutheranism.*

Spurgeon, Charles Haddon (1834–92). B. Kelvedon, Essex, Eng.; joined Baps. 1851; pastor Waterbeach 1852; pastor London 1854; trained young students for the ministry; est. a preachers' coll.; preacher Metropolitan Tabernacle (seated 6,000) from 1861; rejected the doctrine of baptismal regeneration; withdrew from Baptist* Union (organized 1813 Southwark, London, 1813) 1887, but remained Bap.; nonconformist. Works include *The Treasury of David; Lectures to My Students.*

Spurling, Richard G., Sr. (ca. 1812–86). Bap. minister near Cokercreek, Monroe Co., Tenn.; with son R. G. Spurling Jr. et al. organized Christian* Union in Barney Creek Meetinghouse, a crude log bldg. in Monroe Co., near confluence of Barney and Coker Creeks, ca. 2 mi. from Tenn.-N. C. boundary 1886. See also *Church of God,* 2; *Latter Rain Movement.*

Spy Wednesday. See *Church Year,* 8.

Sri Lanka, Republic of. See *Asia,* B 3.

"Stabat mater." One of the sequences (see *Sequence*) suppressed by the Council of Trent*; restored 1727. Probably of 13th-c. origin; authorship variously assigned, e. g., to Bonaventura,* Jacopone* da Todi, Innocent II (Gregorio Papareschi; d. 1143; b. Rome, It.; pope 1130–43). Named after its first 2 words in Lat., based on Jn 19:25. Includes reference to Lk 2:35. Used as a sequence in RCm on Sept. 15, as a hymn in Lent. Musical settings supplied by various composers including F. J. Haydn,* G. P. da Palestrina,* G. B. Pergolesi,* A. Scarlatti,* F. S. P. Schubert,* A. Steffani,* G. Verdi.* Used also in Prot. adaptations. See also *Seven Sorrows of Mary.*

Stach, Jacob (1865–1944). Luth. pastor; b. Grunau, South Russ.; studied at miss. school Basel, Switz. 1883–88 (see *Basel Missionary Society*); worked in Ger. settlements at Annenfeld (Transcaucasia), Hochheim (Crimea), Freudental, Eugenfeld; diaspora preacher for West Siberia 1916; to Moscow 1920; left Russ. 1922; pastor Brandenburg, Ger., 1925–36. Works include *Das Deutschtum in Sibirien, Mittelasien und dem Fernen Osten, von seinen Anfängen bis in die Gegenwart.*

Stade, Bernhard (1848–1906). B. Arnstadt, Ger.; educ. Leipzig and Berlin; worked and taught at Leipzig 1871–75; prof. Giessen 1875. Founded (1881) and ed. *Zeitschrift für die alttestamentliche Wissenschaft;* other works include *Lehrbuch der hebräischen Grammatik.* See also *Grammars,* A.

Staden, Johann Gottlieb (1581–1634). Luth. composer, organist; b. probably Nürnberg, Ger.; court organist Bayreuth and Kulmbach from ca. 1603/04; at Nürnberg from ca. 1616; influenced by baroque* style; contributed to transition from older style of pure vocal music to newer style of instrumental accompaniment. Works include *Harmoniae sacrae; Kirchen-Music; Hauss-Music.*

Stahl, Friedrich Julius (1802–61). B. Würzburg, Ger.; educ. Würzburg, Heidelberg, Erlangen; mem. Prussian chamber of deputies 1848; mem. cabinet 1854; mem. supreme council Ev. Ch. of Prussia 1852–59; pres. syn.; conservative; tried to develop a pol. science based on Christian world view. Works include *Die Philosophie des Rechts, nach geschichtlicher Ansicht.*

Stahl, Heinrich (ca. 1595–1657). B. Tallin(n) [Revel; Reval], Estonia; educ. Rostock, Greifswald, Wittenberg; pastor Estonia; provost 1627; mem. consistory 1637; supt. diocese Narva 1641. Works include an Estonian grammar; German-Estonian agenda.

Stählin, Adolf (von) (1823–97). Brother of L. Stählin*; Luth. cleric; b. Schmähingen, near Nördlingen, Ger.; educ. Erlangen; pastor Nördlingen 1864; preacher Ansbach 1866; mem. supreme consistory Munich 1879, pres. 1883. Works include *Justin der Märtyrer und sein neuester Beurtheiler.*

Stählin, Leonhard (1835–1907). Brother of A. (v.) Stählin*; Luth. theol.; b. Westheim, Bav., Ger.; educ. Erlangen; pastor Bayreuth and Ansbach. Works include *Katholicismus und Protestantismus: Darstellung und Erläuterung der kirchengeschichtlichen Ansicht Schelling's.*

Stainer, John (1840–1901). Composer; b. London, Eng.; organist at various places, notably St. Paul's Cathedral, London, 1872–88; prof. music Oxford 1889–99. Works include manuals *Harmony* and *The Organ.* Compositions include cantatas *(The Daughter of Jairus; St. Mary Magdalen);* anthems; oratorios *(Gideon; The Crucifixion).* See also *Passion, The.*

Stalker, James (1848–1927). B. Crieff, Perthshire, Scot.; educ. Edinburgh, Berlin, Halle. Pastor Kirkcaldy, Scot., 1874–87; Glasgow, Scot., 1887–1902. Prof. Aberdeen, Scot., 1902–26. Works include *The Life of Jesus Christ; The Trial and Death of Jesus Christ; The Life of St. Paul.* See also *Jesus, Lives of.*

Stall, Sylvanus (Oct. 18, 1847–Nov. 6, 1915). B. Elizaville, Columbia Co., N. Y.; educ. Union Theol. Sem., NYC, and Lutheran Theol. Sem., Gettysburg, Pa. Pastor Cobleskill, N. Y.; Martin's Creek, Pa.; Lancaster, Pa; Baltimore, Md. Assoc. ed. *The Lutheran Observer;* ed. *Stall's Lutheran Year-Book and Historical Quarterly.* Other works include *What a Young Boy Ought to Know; What a Young Man Ought to Know; What a Young Husband Ought to Know; What a Man of Forty-five Ought to Know.*

Stallmann, Heinrich (July 5, 1887–June 16, 1969). Son of H. Z. Stallmann*; b. Allendorf, on the Lumda, Hesse, Ger.; educ. Conc. Sem., St. Louis, Mo.; ordained by his father in Ger. 1911; miss. to Ambur, India; asst. in hosp. in Ger. during WW I; after WW I studied medicine at Giessen. Pastor Wittingen, then Berlin, then Bochum, then Wittingen again (1956). Pres. Ev. Luth. Free Ch. 1958.

Stallmann, Heinrich Zacharias (Aug. 15, 1847–Feb. 26, 1933). Father of H. Stallmann*; son-in-law of F. A. Brunn*; b. Bremen, Ger.; educ. Göttingen, Tübingen, Halle; influenced by C. F. W. Walther,* he left the Hannover state ch. and joined the Luth. free ch.; pastor Dresden 1876; later pastor Allendorf, on the Lumda, Hesse; secy. and (in WW I) pres. of the Luth. free ch.; head of theol. high school founded 1920 Leipzig, moved 1922 to Berlin-Zehlendorf. See also *Germany, Lutheran Free Churches in,* 5.

Stancarus, Franciscus (Francisco Stancaro; Stancari; ca. 1501–74). B. Mantua, It.; monk trained in scholastic theol.; opposed A. Osiander* the Elder at Königsberg; held that Christ is a mediator with God only in his human nature. Active in It., Switz., Ger., Poland, Hung., and Transylvania.

Standard Confession, The. See *Democratic Declarations of Faith,* 3.

Stanford, Charles Villiers (1852–1924). Composer, conductor, teacher; b. Dublin, Ireland; conductor London Bach Choir 1885–1902; mem. Royal Academy of Arts, Berlin, 1904. Works include Stabat mater; *Die Auferstehung;* motet: *The Lord of Might;* oratorios: *The Three Holy Children* and *Eden; Mass in G; Te Deum; Requiem.*

Stange, Carl (1870–1959). B. Hamburg, Ger.; educ. Halle, Göttingen, Leipzig, Jena; taught at Halle, Königsberg, Greifswald, Göttingen; active in Apologetic Seminar, Wernigerode, and Luther Academy, Sondershausen. Emphasized philos. and ethical aspects of Christianity. Founded and ed. *Zeitschrift für systematische Theologie.* Other works include *Die Religion als Erfahrung; Einleitung in die Ethik; Hauptprobleme der Ethik.*

Stanislas (Stanislaus; ca. 1030–79). Patron saint of Poland; b. Szczepanów, Poland, acc. to tradition; bp. Cracow 1071; denounced and excommunicated Boleslav II ("the Bold"; ca. 1039–83; king of Poland 1058–79); murdered by king's order.

Stanley, Arthur Penrhyn (1815–81). B. Alderly, Cheshire, Eng.; educ. Oxford; ordained 1839; canon Canterbury 1851; prof. Oxford 1856; dean Westminster 1864; favored union of ch. and state; liberal (see also *High Church*). Works include *The Life and Correspondence of Thomas Arnold, D. D.; Historical Memorials of Westminster Abbey.* See also *Metaphysical Society, The.*

Stanley, Henry Morton. See *Africa,* A 6; F 1; *Livingstone, David.*

Stanza. In poetry, a group of lines or verses (see *Verse*) arranged in a recurring pattern.

Stapfer, Johann Friedrich (1708–75). Ref. theol.; b. Brugg, Aargau canton, Switz.; studied at Bern and Marburg; chaplain 1738–40; tutor and pastor Dissbach. Influenced by C. v. Wolff*; exponent of mild rationalism. Works include *Institutiones theologiae polemicae universae ordine scientifico dispositae.*

Staphylus, Friedrich (Stapelage; 1512–64). B. Osnabrück, Ger.; educ. Kraków, Poland, and Padua, It.; at Danzig ca. 1533, Wittenberg from 1536 for ca. 10 yrs.; prof. 1545, rector 1547 U. of Königsberg; councillor of Abert* of Prussia 1548; involved in controversy with A. Osiander* the Elder and others; RC 1552; helped restore RCm in Austria and Bav.

Stapulensis. See *Lefèvre d'Étaples, Jacques.*

Starck, Johann Friedrich (1680–1756). B. Hildesheim, Ger.; educ. Giessen; preacher Sachsenhausen; pastor Frankfurt am Main 1723; exponent of mild, practical Pietism. Works include *Tägliches Handbuch.*

Starke, Christoph (Starcke; 1684–1744). B. Freienwalde, Ger.; studied at Halle; pastor and teacher Nennhausen, near Rathenow; chief pastor and military chaplain Driesen 1737. Works include *Synopsis bibliothecae exegeticae in Vetus et Novum Testamentum.*

State Church. The est. ch. of a realm; enjoys certain privileges, usually including state financial support. In medieval RCm and early Protestantism little tolerance was granted dissenting minorities. Intolerance was practiced esp. in Eng. and Scot. The Religious Peace of Augsburg* was a concession to territorialism rather than toleration, which began to emerge with the Peace of Westphalia.*

"Statement, A." Twelve propositions with comments signed 1945 by 44 Mo. Syn. clerics (sometimes called "The Forty-four"); deplored legalism; stressed ev. practice, also in inter-Luth. relations; emphasized privileges and responsibilities of local congs.

Statement of Baptist Faith and Message. Issued 1925 by Southern Bap. Convention. Consists of an introd. (which explains the role of creeds as voluntary statements among Baps.) and 25 sections. Draws largely on the New* Hampshire Confession. Additions include statements on the creation of man as a special act (section 3); on the virgin birth of Christ (section 4); on resurrection, return of Jesus, religious liberty, peace and war, education, soc. service, cooperation, evangelism and missions, stewardship, the Kingdom of God (sections 16–25).

J. H. Leith, *Creeds of the Churches* (Chicago, 1963), pp. 334–352.

Statement of Faith According to the Teachings of Congregational Christians, A. Issued by a theol. commission of the Cong. Christian chs. as a contribution to contemporary theol. thought and a statement of Cong. faith in light of contemporary issues and interpretations; 13 arts.; subject to further rev.

W. M. Horton, *Our Christian Faith* (Boston, 1945), pp. 127–137.

States Bible. See *Bible Versions,* K.

States of the Church. Also called Papal States. 1. Territory in cen. It. formerly ruled by the pope as a temporal king.

2. The "Donation of Pepin" (see *Pepin the Short*) 754 marks the beginning of the temporal rule of popes. In the papal decline of the 9th and 10th c. (see *Papacy,* 4) much territorial authority slipped away. By the middle of the 11th c. papal rule was not recognized beyond Rome and immediate vicinity. Gains achieved in tension with the Holy Roman Empire from the 12th to the 16th c. were largely only apparent. See also *Babylonian Captivity,* 2.

3. Julius II (see *Popes,* 19) regained Romagna. Ferrara was regained 1598. Annexation of Ravenna, Ancona, Bologna was also effected. Submerged by

the ground swell of the Fr. Revolution (see *France,* 5), the papal states were restored to the papacy 1815 by the Congress of Vienna (see *Popes,* 27). An 1831 insurrection was suppressed by Austrian and Fr. troops. Dissatisfaction continued. Attempts at conciliation by Pius IX (See *Popes,* 28) did not prevent another uprising in Rome 1848, which he survived only with the help of Eur. diplomacy and a Fr. expeditionary force.

4. In 1860 Romagna, Marches, and Umbria joined Piedmont (region in NW It.; nucleus around which the kingdom of It. grew in the early 1860s). Fr. troops left and Victor Emmanuel II (1820–78; b. Turin, It.; king Sardinia 1849–61; 1st "King of It." 1861–78) made Rome capital 1870. The pope was not a temporal ruler again till 1929 (see *Concordat,* 7).

Stations of the Cross. Series of 14 (or more, as in E Orthodox chs.) images or pictures portraying scenes (some legendary) in Christ's passion; usually placed at intervals around the nave in chs. or on the road to a shrine or ch. A popular devotion is to visit the stations in sequence, with prayers and meditations suited to each.

Statistics, Ecclesiastical. Branch of theol. science that uses techniques of science, in the framework of a theol. value system, to comprehend the whole kingdom of God in its earthly manifestations. Includes descriptive statistics (description of geog. distribution and expansion, numerical strength and growth, and the socio-economic nature and structure of Christendom); inferential statistics (comparison within and bet. various segments of Christendom, projection of growth and related trends in Christendom, and explanation of internal and external factors that influence the nature, structure, and development of Christendom).

Reference books in the field include editions of *World Christian Handbook* (Nashville, Tenn.); F. S. Mead, *Handbook of Denominations in the United States* (Nashville, Tenn.); *Yearbook of American Churches* (Nashville, Tenn.); *Catholic Almanac* (Huntington, Ind.); *Statistical Yearbook* of the Mo. Syn. (St. Louis, Mo). PRP

Statistics, Educational. See *Christian Education,* F; *Parish Education.*

Stauch, Johannes (John Stough; Jan. 25, 1762–July 1845). B. York Co., Pa.; wagonmaker; lay preacher in W Md., Va., and Pa. from 1787; licensed as catechist by Pa. Ministerium 1793, licensed candidate 1794, ordained pastor 1804; pioneer preacher in Ohio and Ky. ca. the turn of the c.; to Columbiana Co., Ohio, 1802 to organize congs. and conduct revivals; settled in Columbiana Co. 1806; to Crawford Co., Ohio, 1829; pres. of what later became The Ev. Luth. Joint Syn. of Ohio* and Other States 1818–20, 1822, 1824, 1828; said to have traveled 100,000 mi. preaching in 5 states.

Stäudlin, Karl Friedrich (Carl; 1761–1826). B. Stuttgart, Ger.; educ. Tübingen; prof. Göttingen 1790. Works include *Geschichte und Geist des Skepticismus; Universalgeschichte der christlichen Kirche; Geschichte der theologischen Wissenschaften.*

Stauff, Argula von. See *Grumbach, Argula von.*

Stauffer Mennonite Church. See *Mennonite Churches,* 3 a.

Staupitz, Johann von (ca. 1469/70–1524). B. Motterwitz, near Leisnig, Saxony, Ger.; educ. Cologne and Leipzig; Augustinian ca. 1490; prior Tübingen 1497, later Munich; charter mem. of the faculty of the U. of Wittenberg (see also *Frederick III*) and dean of theol. faculty; made Luther his successor as prof. of Bible (see also *Luther, Martin,* 6); influenced by Thomism* and mysticism*; emphasized Scripture; freed Luther from vow of obedience 1518 (see also *Luther, Martin,* 10).

Steady-state Theory. See *Cosmogony; Lucretius.*

Stearns, Shubael. See *Baptist Churches,* 24.

Steck, John Michael (Steg; Oct. 5, 1756–July 14, 1830). B. Germantown, Pa.; studied theol. under J. H. C. Helmuth*; without ordination or license he began his ministerial career at Chambersburg, Pa., 1784; served congs. in Bedford and Somerset counties, Pa., 1789–92, Westmoreland Co., Pa., 1792–1830 (licensed by Pa. Ministerium 1796; ordained 1806); active also in Ohio and in early convs. of The Ev. Luth. Joint Syn. of Ohio* and Other States.

Stedingers (Stedingo; Stetingi; Stadingi; Low Ger. for *Gestadebewohner,* "dwellers along the bank or shore"). Inhabitants (mostly Frisians) along the lower Weser, near the North Sea, in the 12th and 13th c.; revolted against ecclesiastical oppression; after many yrs. of war with the ch. they were nearly wiped out 1234 by a crusade under Gregory IX (see *Popes,* 11).

Steeden Proseminar. See *Brunn, Friedrich August; Germany, Lutheran Free Churches in,* 4.

Steele, Anne (1716–78). B. Broughton, Hampshire, Eng.; daughter of a timber merchant who served as an unsalaried Bap. minister; hymnist. Works include *Hymns, Psalms, and Poems.* Hymns include "Enslaved by Sin and Bound in Chains"; "The Savior Calls; Let Every Ear"; "To Our Redeemer's Glorious Name."

Steele, Richard (1672–1729). Essayist, dramatist; b. Dublin, Ireland; studied at Oxford. Ed. *The Tatler;* with J. Addison* coed. *The Spectator.* Other works include *The Christian Hero* (1701), a devotional book reflecting Puritan idealism in contrast to the licentiousness of the Restoration period (sometimes identified with the reign of Charles II, sometimes regarded as extending to the accession of Anne [1665–1714; queen of Gt. Brit. and Ireland 1702–14]).

Steenberg, Peder (Per; 1870–1947). Norw. Luth. composer and organist; studied in Oslo, Leipzig, Copenhagen; taught in various Oslo schools and 1935–47 at the conservatory of music there; specialized in G. P. da Palestrina.* Works include *Koralbok.*

Steffani, Agostino (ca. 1654–1728). RC composer, diplomat; b. Castelfranco, Near Venice, It.; studied organ with J. K. (v.) Kerll*; priest 1680; abbot Lepsing 1682; influenced G. F. Handel,* whom he recommended for kapellmeister Hanover. Works include *Stabat mater.*

Steffens, Henrik (1773–1845). Philos., naturalist; b. Stavanger, Norw.; educ. Copenhagen and Kiel; taught in Copenhagen 1802; prof. Halle 1804, Breslau 1811, Berlin 1831. Influenced N. F. S. Grundtvig.* Works include *Von der falschen Theologie und dem wahren Glauben; Wie ich wieder Lutheraner wurde und was mir das Luthertum ist; Christliche Religionsphilosophie; Was ich erlebte.* See also *Germany, Lutheran Free Churches in,* 1.

Stegmann, Josua (1588–1632). B. Sulzfeld, near Meiningen, Ger.; educ. Leipzig; adjunct philos, faculty Leipzig; supt. Schaumburg, also pastor Stadthagen and prof. Gymnasium there 1617; moved with the Gymnasium to Rinteln 1621; suffered in Thirty* Years' War, esp. under Edict of Restitution.* Hymnist. Hymns include "Ach bleib mit deiner Gnade."

Steimle, Friedrich Wilhelm Tobias (1827–Feb. 28, 1880). B. Württemberg, Ger.; educ. in the institute of the Basel* Miss. Soc.; to Am. 1851. Pastor Ellenville, N. Y.; asst. pastor St. Matthew's Luth. Ch., NYC, 1851–55; pastor Willamsburg (Brooklyn) and then in Brooklyn proper, N. Y. Helped found Ger. Ev. Luth. Syn. of New* York and Other States and was its only pres.; organized Ger. Pastoral Conf. of N. Y. and Brooklyn 1872, which disbanded at his death. See also *United Lutheran Church, Synods of,* 15.

Steimle Synod. See *United Lutheran Church, Synods of,* 15.

Steinbart, Gotthilf Samuel (1738–1809). Ev. theol.; b. Züllichau (Suelchow), Brandenburg; prof. Frankfurt am Main 1774; reduced the content of faith to a doctrine of happiness. Works include *System der reinen Philosophie oder Glückseligkeitslehre des Christenthums.*

Steinbüchel, Theodor (1888–1949). RC philos., theol.; b. Cologne, Ger.; taught at Bonn, Giessen, Munich, Tübingen. Works include *Der Sozialismus als sittliche Idee; Die philosophische Grundlegung der katholischen Sittenlehre.*

Steiner, Rudolf (1861–1925). B. Kraljevec (Kraljevic), Hung.; educ. Vienna; left RCm for theosophy,* but rejected the latter's Oriental associations. Founded anthroposophy: spiritual and mystical doctrine, acc. to which higher knowledge may be attained through concentration and meditation. Works include *Die Philosophie der Freiheit.*

Steinfelden, A. L. von. See *Lercheimer, Augustin.*

Steinhaeuser, Albert Theodore William (Sept. 30, 1876 –Nov. 1, 1924). B. Buffalo, N. Y.; educ. Luth. Theol. Sem., Mount Airy, Philadelphia, Pa.; ordained 1898; pastor in Pa. Tr. J. M. Reu's* *Homiletics* and excerpts from works of M. Luther; other works include *The Man of Sorrows.*

Steinhausen, Wilhelm (1846–1924). Painter; b. Sorau, Lower Lusatia; realist. Works include portrayals of events in the life of Christ.

Steinhofer, Friedrich Christoph (1706–61). B. Owen, Württemberg, Ger.; follower of N. L. v. Zinzendorf from the 1730s; leader among Moravians. Works include *Die Haushaltung des dreieinigen Gottes.*

Steinkopf, Karl Friedrich Adolf (1773–1859). B. Ludwigsburg, Ger.; pupil of J. A. Bengel*; secy. Deutsche Christentumsgesellschaft*; pastor London, Eng.; secy. BFBS; helped est. Bible socs. in Ger.

Steinle, Eduard Jakob von (1810–86). Painter; b. Vienna, Austria; worked in Rome, It., 1828–34; prof. hist. painting Frankfurt 1850–86. Works include religious and mythological subjects and portraits. See also *Nazarenes,* 3.

Steinmetz, Rudolf (1801–54). B. state of Waldeck, Ger.; pastor Rehburg; supt. Holtorf, near Nienburg; gen. supt. Klausthal; with A. F. O. Münchmeyer* and L. A. Petri* founded Gotteskasten.*

Steinmeyer, Franz Karl Ludwig (1811–1900). B. Beeskow, near Frankfurt an der Oder, Brandenburg; educ. Berlin; asst. Luth. pastor Wittenberg; chaplain navy officers' training school Kulm; taught at Berlin 1848; prof. Breslau 1852 Bonn 1854, Berlin 1858. Works include *Beiträge zur praktischen Theologie.*

Stellhorn, August Conrad (June 2, 1887–May 17, 1964). B. Red Bud, Ill.; educ. Ev. Luth. Teachers Sem., Addison, Ill. Elementary school teacher Red Bud, Ill., 1908–11; Indianapolis, Ind., 1911–18. Supt. of schools, Cen. Dist. of the Mo. Syn., 1918–21; 1st Secy. of Schools of the Mo. Syn. 1921–60. Ed. Conc. ed. *Bobbs-Merrill Readers; Comprehensive Bible History; Graded Memory Course for Lutheran Sunday Schools and Other Institutions.* Other works include *The Beginning Teacher; Schools of The Lutheran Church – Missouri Synod.* WAK

Stellhorn, Frederick William (Oct. 2, 1841–Mar. 17, 1919). B. Brüninghorstedt, Hannover, Ger.; to US 1854. Educ. at the practical sem., Fort Wayne, Ind. (see *Löhe, Johann Konrad Wilhelm*); Conc. Coll. and Conc. Sem., St. Louis, Mo. Asst. pastor St. Louis 1865–67; pastor De Kalb Co., Ind., 1867–69. Prof. Northwestern U. (also known as Northwestern Coll.), Watertown, Wis., 1869–74; Conc. Coll., Fort Wayne, Ind., 1874–81; Capital U., Columbus, Ohio, 1881–1919 (pres. Capital U. 1894–1900). Ed. *Lutherische Kirchenzeitung; Theologische Zeitblätter.* Other works include *The Epistle of St. Paul to the Romans;* commentaries on other NT books; a NT Gk. lexicon. See also *Ohio and Other States, The Evangelical Lutheran Joint Synod of,* 5.

Stender, Gotthard Friedrich 1714–96). Luth. pastor in Latvia; b. Kurland; promoted culture and soc. progress. Works include Latvian grammar; Latvian-Ger. dictionary; Latvian encyclopedia.

Stenersen, Stener Johannes (1789–1835). Luth. theol.; b. Jevnaker, Norw.; educ. Copenhagen (influenced by N. F. S. Grundtvig,* whom he followed till 1825); taught at Christiania (now Oslo) from 1814; his theol. was Biblical and represented moderate Luth. orthodoxy. Works include exegetical and hist. writings.

Stensen, Niels (Nicolaus Stenonis; 1638–86). Pioneer in anatomy, paleontology, geology, crystallography; b. Copenhagen, Den.; descendant of long line of Luth. pastors; MD Leiden 1664; impressed by Corpus Christi procession in Livorno, It.; RC 1667; vicar apostolic for Nordic missions 1677; titular bp. Titiopolis 1677; auxiliary bp. Münster 1680; left Münster 1683 in protest against simoniacal election; active in Hamburg and Schwerin.

Stephan, Martin, Sr. (Aug. 13, 1777–Feb. 21, 1846). Father of M. Stephan* Jr.; b. Stramberg, Moravia; studied theol. at Halle and Leipzig. Pastor Haber, Boh. 1809; Dresden, Ger., 1810–37; opposed rationalism; widely known as spiritual adviser; influenced C. F. W. Walther; resolved in the 1830s to emigrate to the US with his followers; placed under temporary suspension 1837; led Saxon emigration to Mo. 1838/39; deposed and taken to Ill. 1839; by 1841 he was living in or near Kaskaskia, Ill., and preaching there in the courthouse every 2 weeks; served a cong. at Horse Prairie, several miles SE of Red Bud, Ill., 1845–46. See also *Lutheran Church – Missouri Synod, The,* II 1–2.

Stephan, Martin, Jr. (July 23, 1823–Jan. 16, 1884). Son of M. Stephan* Sr.; b. Dresden, Ger.; to US 1838/39; studied architecture in Dresden; returned to US 1847; worked for a lithographer in NYC 1847 –49; private tutor Brattleboro, Vt., 1849; educ. Conc. Sem., St. Louis, Mo. Pastor Theresa, near Mayville, Dodge Co., Wis., 1853; Kalamazoo, Mich., 1856; served congs. in and near Oshkosh, Wis., 1857–58; asst. pastor Fort Wayne, Ind., 1858, also instructor in secular subjects at the sem. (see *Löhe, Johann Konrad Wilhelm*). Pastor Adams Twp., Allen Co., Ind., 1860–65; Wolcottsville, N. Y., 1865–66; Chester, Ill., 1866–75; Warren Twp., Bremer Co., Iowa, 1875–84. Drew bldg. plans for a number of chs., for the 1st bldg. of Conc. Sem., St. Louis 1849, and for the teachers' sem. at Addison, Ill., 1864.

Stephanus, Robert. See *Estienne, Robert, I.*

Stephen, Saint. See *Church Year,* 1, 16; *Symbolism, Christian,* 4–5.

Stephen I (of Hung.). See *Hungary.*

Stephen I (of Rome; fl. 3d c.). Pope 254–257. Opposed Cyprian* of Carthage in the question of heretical Baptism, holding that the validity of Baptism depends not on the officiating person but on the institution of Christ and on administration in conformity with that institution.

Stephen Báthory. See *Poland,* 3.

Stephensen, Magnús (1762–1833). Icelandic ch. leader; educ. Copenhagen, Den.; held offices in service of Dan. crown in Iceland; worked for cultural and soc. reform; rationalist; removed reference to divinity of Christ, atonement, and Holy Spirit in hymns in *Grallarinn* ("Gradual"; Order of Worship); removed significant parts of liturgy (Confiteor; Kyrie; Nicene Creed; Sanctus; Gloria in excelsis).

Stepinac, Alojzije (Aloys; Alois; 1898–1960). RC Yugoslav official; b. Krasic, Croatia; priest 1930; abp. Zagreb 1937; condemned to forced labor 1946 for cooperation with the enemy; released 1951; cardinal 1953.

Stern, Henry Aaron. See *Middle East,* H.

Sternhold, Thomas. See *Psalter, English.*

Steuber, Johannes (1590–1643). Luth. theol.; b. Schwickardshausen, Upper Hesse; prof. Giessen 1614, Marburg 1624. Helped restore Lutheranism in territory of Marburg and Schmalkalden.

Steudel, Friedrich (1866–1939). B. Tuttlingen, Württemberg; prof. Tübingen; pastor Maienfels and Bremen; radical theol.; rejected Biblical and dogmatic foundations of Christianity. Works include *Das Christusproblem und die Zukunft des Protestantismus; Im Kampf um die Christusmythe.*

Steuerlein, Johannes (1546–1613). B. Schmalkalden, Ger.; studied law; town clerk Wasungen (on the Werra, bet. Schmalkalden and Meiningen, Thuringia), cen. Ger., ca. 1580; secy. in chancery 1589, mayor ca. 1604 Meiningen. Crowned as poet by Rudolf* II for a metric Bible; also made a metrical version of Ecclus. Musician; works include melodies and 4-part settings.

Stewardship. Term used Lk 16:2–4 (in the parable of the unjust steward). A steward is a servant entrusted with administration of his master's property and interests (cf. Gn 39:4–6). The Bible uses the term in a secular sense but elevates it to a fruit of faith, permeating it with spiritual meaning and implications for pastors (1 Co 4:1; Tts 1:7) and Christians in gen. (1 Ptr 4:10).

Christian stewardship is recognition and fulfillment of the personal privilege and responsibility to administer all endowments of life acc. to God's will. Sometimes identified with sanctification, it is more properly sanctification in a narrower sense.

Christian stewardship acknowledges that God owns all (1 Ch 29:14; Ps 24:1; 100:3; 1 Co 4:7; 6:19), that we belong to Him by virtue of creation, preservation, redemption, and sanctification and are to glorify Him in all things (Ro 14:7–8; 1 Co 6:20; 10:31; 1 Ptr 4:11), that all our talents and endowments are temporarily in our charge (Lk 12:20; 16:2), and that we must render account to God (2 Co 5:10).

True motivation for Christian stewardship is supplied by the Gospel, not by the Law.

A proper ch. stewardship program is educational, aimed at lay participation in ch. work and at growth in the grace of giving. RGL, JEH

See also *Finances in the Church.*

P. Lindemann, *My God and I* (St. Louis, 1949); K. Kretzschmar, *The Stewardship Life* (St. Louis, 1929); W. C. Birkner, "Christian Stewardship," *The Abiding Word,* I, ed. T. Laetsch (St. Louis, 1946), 457–481; C. W. Berner, *Spiritual Power for Your Congregation* (St. Louis, 1956); T. A. Kantonen, *A Theology for Christian Stewardship* (Philadelphia, 1956); R. C. Rein, *First Fruits* (St. Louis, 1959); H. Rolston, *Stewardship in the New Testament Church* (Richmond, Va., 1946); J. E. Herrmann, *The Chief Steward.* (St. Louis, 1951).

Stewart, John. See *Indians, American,* 6.

Sthen, Hans Christensen (ca. 1544–1610). B. Roskilde, Den.; rector 1565, chaplain 1573 Helsingör (Elsinore); pastor and provost Malmö 1583; hymnist. Works include *En liden haandbog; En liden vandrebog.* Hymns include "Herre Jesu Krist!"

Sticharion. Ecclesiastical vestment similar to alb (see *Vestments, Clerical,* 2); worn by deacons and priests in Eastern Orthodox Ch.

Sticheron (pl. *stichera;* from Gk. for "verse"). In the Eastern Orthodox Ch., short hymn usually following a Ps verse.

Stiefel, Michael (Stifel; Stieffel; Styfel; 1487–1567). Augustinian monk at Esslingen, Ger.; follower of M. Luther 1522; pastor Mansfeld, Tollet (Austria), Lochau, Holzdorf (near Schweinitz), Memel, Haffstrom (near Königsberg); taught math at Jena 1559–67; predicted end of world for Oct. 19, 1533. Works include *Von der Christförmigen rechtgegründten leer Doctoris Martini Luthers; Ein Rechenbüchlein Vom End Christi.*

Stier, Rudolf Ewald (1800–62). B. Fraustadt, ca. 57 mi. NW of Breslau, Posen; studied at Berlin and Halle; pastor and supt. at various places, last at Eisleben; hymnist. Works include *Die Reden des Herrn Jesu* (tr. W. B. Pope, *The Words of the Lord Jesus*); commentaries. Hymns include "Wir sind vereint, Herr Jesu Christ."

Stigmatization (from Gk. *stigma,* "prick, or puncture of a pointed instrument"). Formation (some hold supernatural) of wounds resembling those received by Jesus from the crown of thorns, nails, and spear. Francis* of Assisi is alleged to have been so marked 1224. Since then the number of persons with stigmata increased considerably, but there is no reliable list of stigmatized persons. See also *Emmerich, Anna Katharine.*

Stilling, Heinrich. See *Jung-Stilling, Johann Heinrich.*

Stillingfleet, Edward (1635–99). Angl. prelate; b. Cranborne, NE Dorsetshire, Eng.; educ. Cambridge; held various positions; dean St. Paul's, London, 1678; bp. Worcester 1689. Works include *A Rational Account of the Grounds of Protestant Religion.*

Stip, Gerhard Chryno Hermann (1809–82). Luth. theol., hymnist; b. Norden, East Friesland; educ. Bonn and Göttingen; pastor Osteel, near Norden; resigned 1839; to Bern, Switz., and London, Eng. (where he lived with C. K. J. v. Bunsen*); settled at Alexandrowka, near Potsdam. Emphasized faith rather than traditional form of expression in hymnal reform. Ed. *Unverfälschter Liedersegen;* other works include *Hymnologische Reisebriefe.*

Stobäus, Johann(es) (Stobaeus; Stobeus; Stoboeus; 1580–1646). Composer; b. Graudenz, West Prussia; educ. Königsberg; studied music under J. Eccard 1599; bass singer ducal chapel 1601; cantor Domkirche 1602; kapellmeister to the Elector of Brandenburg, Königsberg, 1626. Works include *Cantiones sacrae; Geistliche Lieder.*

Stockbridge Indians. See *Indians, Lutheran Missions to North American.*

Stöckel, Leonhard (1510–60). B. Bartfeld, Hung.; studied at Wittenberg; won for Reformation esp. by P. Melanchthon*; school rector Bartfeld 1539. Perhaps drew up *Confessio Pentapolitana* (see *Lutheran Confessions,* A 5). See also *Hungary.*

Stöcker. See *Stoecker.*

Stockfleth, Nils Joachim Christian Vibe (1787–1866). "Apostle of the Laplanders"; b. Fredrikstad (Frederikstad; or Christiania?), Norw.; after serving in armed forces, studied theol. at Christiania; after ordination 1825, studied language of Laplanders. Tr. NT, Ps, and some of M. Luther's writings into Lapp; other works include a Lapp grammar and a Norw.-Lapp dictionary.

Stöckhardt, Karl Georg (Feb. 17, 1842–Jan. 9, 1913). B. Chemnitz, Saxony, Ger.; educ. Erlangen, Leipzig, Berlin; instructor at an academy for girls, Tharandt, 1866; asst. pastor of a Ger. Luth. ch. Paris June 1870. The Franco-Prussian war (began July 19, 1870) caused him to flee to Belg. in fall 1870; ministered to wounded and dying at Sedan 3 mo. Private tutor OT and NT exegesis Erlangen U. and teacher of religion Erlangen Gymnasium 1871. Pastor (diaconus) of a state ch. at Planitz 1873–76; influenced by F. C. T. Ruhland* and Mo. Syn. theol. literature; suspended; resigned; with part of his cong. he joined Ruhland's cong.; assoc. pastor there 1876–78; also conducted a Lat. school and prepared a number of boys for coll. To US 1878; pastor Holy Cross Luth. Ch., St. Louis, Mo., 1878; began teaching exegesis at Conc. Sem., St. Louis, 1878 (part-time prof. 1881, full-time 1887).

Stöckhardt was the only Ger. U. trained exegete in the early hist. of the Mo. Syn. His learning was coupled with firm belief in the verbal inspiration of the Bible, childlike acceptance of all Bible teachings, and great love of revealed truth. He concentrated on the written Word and unfolded its message in concise, clear, convincing language. He was a forceful preacher. In the Predestinarian* Controversy of the 1880s he sided with C. F. W. Walther.*

Works include *Adventspredigten; Ausgewählte Psalmen; Die biblische Geschichte; Commentar über den Brief Pauli an die Römer; Commentar über den Propheten Jesaia* (chaps. 1–12); *Gnade um Gnade: Ein Jahrgang Evangelienpredigten; Die Heilsame Lehre oder Erklärung des kleinen Katechismus Luthers; Die kirchlichen Zustände Deutschlands; Kommentar über den Brief Pauli an die Epheser; Kommentar über den Ersten Brief Petri; Passionspredigten.* WEG

O. Willkomm, *D. th. Georg Stöckhardt* (Zwickau, 1914); "Dr. George Stoeckhardt," *Theological Quarterly,* XVII (1913), 65–75, 136–153; XVIII (1914), 16–23; E. Biegener, "Karl Georg Stoeckhardt, D. Theol., 1842–1913," *CHIQ,* XXI (1948–49), 154–166; R. Baepler, "The Hermeneutics of Johannes Christian Konrad von Hofmann with Special Reference to His Influence on George Stoeckhardt," Conc. Sem., St. Louis, BD thesis 1954; W. R. Goerss, "Some of the Hermeneutical Presuppositions and Part of the Exegetical Methodology of Georg Stoeckhardt," Conc. Sem., St. Louis, ThD theses 1964.

Stockholm Blood Bath. To est. claim to the Swed. throne, Christian* II of Den. and Norw. repeatedly attacked Swed.; the 3d attack (1520) succeeded; he secured capitulation of Swed. in exchange for a promise of gen. amnesty; but a few days after coronation as king of Swed., he had more than 80 Swedes, mostly nobles, executed at Stockholm on charges of hostility to the pope. This blood bath was followed by successful revolution led by Gutavus* I, who est. Lutheranism in Swed.

Stockmann, Ernst (1634–1712). B. Lützen, near Merseburg, Ger.; educ. Jena; pastor Bayer-Naumburg, near Mansfeld, cen. Ger.; held various other positions; hymnist. Hymns include "Gott, der wird's wohl machen."

Stockmayer, Otto (1838–1917). Ev. theol.; b. Aalen, Württemberg, Ger.; tutor in Switz.; leader in holiness* movement; opposed Pentecostalism* and perfectionism.* Works include *Die Gabe des Heiligen Geistes; Die Gnade ist erschienen.*

Stoddard, Solomon (1643–1729). Grandfather of J. Edwards* the Elder; Cong. cleric; b. Boston, Mass.; educ. Harvard Coll., Cambridge, Mass.; chaplain to Dissenters* on Barbados; pastor Northhampton, Mass., 1672–1729; held that Lord's Supper is a means of regeneration; developed the practice, called Stoddardeanism, of admitting to full ch. privileges (e. g., Communion) also those who could not relate a specific experience of regeneration; pol. leader of W Mass. See also *Half-Way Covenant.*

Stoecker, Adolf (Stöcker; 1835–1909). B. Halberstadt, Ger.; educ. Halle and Berlin; private tutor 1857–62. Pastor Seggerde, near Halberstadt, 1863; Hamersleben, near Magdeburg, 1866. Military chaplain Metz 1871–74; court and cathedral preacher Berlin 1874; dismissed as court preacher 1890 because of his Socialist party activities. Organized Berlin City Miss. 1877 by merging 2 previously launched efforts; founded Christian Social Labor Party 1878. Helped found Ev. Social Congress 1890; left it 1896 because of its liberalism; founded the Ecclesiastical Social Conf. 1897, in Kassel, as a rival organization. Antisemite. See also *Christian Socialism; Inner Mission,* 3.

Stoeckhardt. See *Stöckhardt.*

Stoever, John Caspar, Sr. (Steffer; Casper; Jan. 13, 1685–1738). Father of J. C. Stoever* Jr.; b. Frankenberg, Hesse, Ger.; close relative of J. P. Fresenius*; schoolmaster; to US 1728; pastor Va.; to Ger. 1734 to gather funds; d. on return voyage.

Stoever, John Caspar, Jr. (Steffer; Casper; Dec. 21, 1707–May 13, 1779). Son of J. C. Stoever* Sr.; b. Luedorf, Ger.; privately educ.; to US 1728; ordained 1733; miss. in E Pa., Md., and Va.; joined Pa. Ministerium 1763; organized many congs.; opposed pietism of H. M. Mühlenberg.*

Records of Rev. John Caspar Stoever, Baptismal and Marriage, 1730–1779, tr. F. J. F. Schantz (Harrisburg, Pa., 1896); R. L. Winters, *John Caspar Stoever* (Norristown, Pa., 1948).

Stoever, Martin Luther (Feb. 17, 1820–July 22, 1870). Great-grandson of J. C. Stoever* Jr.; b. Germantown, Pa.; educ. Pa. Coll. and Lutheran Theol. Sem., both at Gettysburg; taught at Gettysburg from 1842. Coed. *The Evangelical Review;* ed. *The Evangelical Quarterly Review;* other works include *Memoir of The Life and Times of Henry Melchior Muhlenberg, D. D., Patriarch of the Evangelical Lutheran Church in America.*

Stoeylen, Bernt Andreas (Stöylen; 1858–1937). Norw. Luth. bp.; ordained 1887; pastor; dir. of teachers' coll. 1895; pres. of practical sem. Oslo 1902; bp. Kristiansand (Christiansand) 1914–30. Helped compile *Nyorsk salmebok;* issued *Hymns and Spiritual Songs;* other works include *Life with God* (sermon collection).

Stoicism (from Gk. *Stoa* [*Poikile*], "Painted Portico," where Zeno* of Citium taught in Athens). Craeco-Roman school of philos. founded ca. 300 BC by Zeno; divided philos. into logic (including definitions, syllogisms, paradoxes, etymology, grammar, dialectic, rhetoric), physics (including metaphysics, astronomy, religion, anthropology, psychology), and ethics.* Earlier Stoics (e. g., Chrysippus [3d c. BC; b. Soli, Cilicia; disciple of Cleanthes*]; Diogenes of Babylonia [or of Seleucia; 2d c. BC]) stressed logic, later Stoics (e. g., Epictetus*) stressed ethics.

Stoicism is a form of materialistic monism.* It is deterministic, regarding God as the all-pervading energy (spirit, *pneuma*), law, and reason *(logos)* that gives order and beauty to the world. Some regard Stoicism as pantheistic, others as panentheistic.

In ethics man must recognize that he cannot change the predetermined course of events; his function is to bring his will, which is free, into harmony with what happens, "to live according to scientific knowledge of the phenomena of nature" (Chrysippus). He can do this because he is kin to God. Absolutely self-sufficient, he can practice the Stoic virtues: practical wisdom, bravery, justice, self-control. He is not bound to things or life itself.

Despite similarities bet. Stoicism and Christianity, Stoic and Christian ethics are mutually exclusive. EK

E. V. Arnold, *Roman Stoicism* (New York, 1911); E. R. Bevan, *Stoics and Sceptics* (New York, 1913); M. Pohlenz, *Die Stoa,* 2 vols. (Göttingen, 1948–49); J. N. Sevenster, *Paul and Seneca* (Leiden, 1961).

Stoics. *Adherents of Stoicism.**

Stolberg, Friedrich Leopold von (or zu; 1750–1819). Poet; statesman; b. Bramstedt, Holstein, Ger.; friend of J. W. v. Goethe* and F. G. Klopstock*; at first Luth.; RC 1800; mem. Münster* Circle. Works include *Geschichte der Religion Jesu Christi; Betrachtungen und Beherzigungen der heiligen Schrift; Ein Büchlein von der Liebe.*

Stole. See *Vestments, Clerical,* 2.

Stoltz, Johann (Stolz; ca. 1514–56). B. Wittenberg, Ger.; educ. Wittenberg; diaconus Jessen; tutor August* (later elector Saxony); prof. Wittenberg 1544; court preacher Weimar 1547; opposed Interim.* Helped ed. the Jena ed. of M. Luther's works. See also *Synergistic Controversy.*

Stoltzer, Thomas (variants include Stolczer, Scholczer, Stollerus, Stollcerus; b. perhaps before 1450 or as late as 1485; d. perhaps 1526 or as late as 1544). Composer; b. Schweidnitz, Silesia; kapellmeister at Ofen or Buda to Louis II (1506–26; king of Hung. and Boh. 1516–26). Ch. music includes motet settings of Psalms.

Stone, Barton Warren (1772–1844). Evangelist; b. near Port Tobacco, Md.; licensed Presb. 1796; ordained 1798; withdrew from Syn. of Ky. 1803 and helped form Springfield Presbytery, which dissolved 1804, its mems. declaring that they would know no creed but the Bible and no designation but "Christian." Active in Ohio, Ky., and Tennessee. Ed. *The Christian Messenger;* other works include *An Address to the Christian Churches in Kentucky, Tennessee, and Ohio, on Several Important Doctrines of Religion.* See also *Churches of Christ; Disciples of Christ,* 2 c; *United Church of Christ, The,* I B.

Stone, Samuel (1602–63). Puritan; b. Hertford, Eng.; educ. Cambridge; to Am. with J. Cotton* and T. Hooker* 1633; pastor Cambridge, Mass., 1633–36; helped est. Puritan colony Hartford, Conn., 1636; pastor Hartford 1636–63.

Stone, Samuel John (1839–1900). B. Whitmore, Staffordshire, Eng.; educ. at the Charterhouse (Godalming, Surrey) and Oxford; held several positions as curate, vicar, and rector; mem. of the committee of *Hymns Ancient and Modern;* hymnist. Hymns include "The Church's One Foundation."

Stone Age. See *Time.*

Storch, Nikolaus. See *Zwickau Prophets.*

Stork, Charles August Gottlieb (Storch; Carl Augustus; June 16, 1764–Mar. 27, 1831). B. Helmstadt, Brunswick, Ger.; educ. Helmstadt; tutor and private teacher; ordained in Ger.; to US 1788; pastor N. C.; helped organize the Ev. Luth. Syn. and Ministerium of N. C. 1803 (see *United Lutheran Church, Synods of,* 16). See also *Velthusen, Johann Kaspar.*

Storr, Gottlob Christian (1746–1805). Son of J. C. Storr*; b. Stuttgart, Ger.; educ. Tübingen; prof. Tübingen 1775; chief court chaplain and consistorial councillor Stuttgart 1797. Founded Old Tübingen* School of theology. Biblico-apologetic supernaturalist; opposed J. S. Semler's* theory of accommodation. Works include *Opuscula academica ad interpretationem librorum sacrorum* [of the NT] *pertinentia; Die Geschichte der Auferstehung Jesu Christi.* See also *Flatt, Karl Christian.*

Storr, Johann Christian (1712–73. Father of G. C. Storr*; b. Heilbronn, Württemberg, Ger.; educ. Tübingen; held various positions, including that of court chaplain 1744 and city preacher 1757 Stuttgart; consistorial councillor and chaplain of collegiate ch. Stuttgart 1759; prelate Herrenalb 1765; consistorial councillor and prelate Alpirsbach. Pietist; pupil and follower of J. A. Bengel.* Works include *Christliches Hausbuch zur Uebung des Gebets.*

Stosch, Bartholomäus (1604–86). Ref. theol.; b. Silesia; educ. Frankfurt an der Oder; tutor; preacher Kurland 1640; court preacher 1643, consistorial councillor Berlin 1659; effective adviser of and spokesman for Frederick* William of Brandenburg in matters pertaining to ch. affairs; shaped a policy that favored the Ref., gave promise of tolerance, but oppressed Luths.

Stoss, Veit (Wit Stosz, or Stwosz; ca. 1438/47–1533). Sculptor, painter, engraver, and wood carver; b. Nürnberg, Germany. Works include the high altar for the Ch. of the Virgin Mary, Krakow.

Stössel, Johann (1524–78). B. Kitzingen, Lower Franconia, NW Bav., Ger.; educ. Wittenberg and Jena; diaconus Jena 1550; pastor and supt. Heldburg 1554; supt. 1561, prof. 1562 Jena. Sided with V. Strigel* against M. Flacius* Illyricus. Left Jena 1568. Supt. Pirna. Expelled from Thuringia 1573. Died in prison.

Stough, John. See *Stauch, Johannes.*

Strack, Hermann Lebrecht (1848–1922). B. Berlin, Ger.; educ. Berlin and Leipzig; taught in Berlin 1872–73; worked in the Imperial Library, St. Petersburg, 1873–76; prof. Berlin 1877. Coed. with O. Zöckler* *Kurzgefasster Kommentar zu den heiligen Schriften Alten und Neuen Testamentes sowie zu den Apokryphen;* other works include *Einleitung in das Alte Testament.*

Strang, James Jesse (1813–56). B. Scipio, N. Y.; Mormon 1843; claimed endorsement of Joseph Smith* Sr.; founded village of St. James, Beaver Is., Mich., 1849; crowned "king" 1850; mem. Mich. legislature 1852–54; sanctioned plural marriage 1850; assassinated. Followers called Strangites. Works include alleged discovery and tr. of Plates of Laban, mentioned in *The Book of Mormon* (1 Nephi 3–5); *The Book of the Law of the Lord.* See also *Latter Day Saints,* g 6.

Strasen, Carl Johann August (Karl; Strassen; May 30, 1827–Feb. 25 [26]?, 1909). B. Jürgenshagen, Mecklenburg-Schwerin, Ger.; to US 1846; educ. at the practical sem. Fort Wayne, Ind. (see *Löhe, Johann Konrad Wilhelm*). Pastor Horse Prairie, near Red Bud, Ill., 1847; Collinsville, Ill., 1850; Watertown, Wis., 1859. Pres. Northwestern Dist. 1875–82. Wis. Dist. 1882–85, both Districts of the Mo. Syn.

Stratigraphy. See *Geography, Christian,* 6.

Strauss, David Friedrich (1808–74). B. Ludwigsburg, Ger.; educ. Tübingen and Berlin; influenced by F. C. Baur,* F. D. E. Schleiermacher,* F. W. J. v. Schelling,* G. W. F. Hegel*; vicar at a village near Ludwigsburg 1830; taught in the sem. at Maulbronn 1831; taught at Tübingen 1832. Held mythical theory of the gospels: the Christian religion developed gradually, like heathen mythology, without intentional fabrication by the writers. Works include *Das Leben Jesu, kritisch bearbeitet; Der alte und der neue Glaube.* See also *Vatke, Johann Karl Wilhelm.*

Streeter, Burnett Hillman (1874–1937). Angl. theol. and religious philos.; b. Croydon, Eng.; educ. Oxford; prof. exegesis Oxford. Tried to correlate science and theol. Works include *The Four Gospels: A Study of Origins.*

Streissguth, Wilhelm (William; Apr. 10, 1827–May 20, 1915). B. Lahr, grand duchy of Baden, Ger.; educ. Basel, Switz.; ordained 1850; sent by ch. authorities of the canton of Glarus as miss. to the colonies at New Glarus and New Bilten, Green Co., Wis.; joined Wisconsin* Syn. 1856. Pastor Newton (Newtonburg and Liberty, Manitowoc Co., Wis., 1855–56; Milwaukee, Wis., 1856–68; Fond du Lac, Wis., 1868–72; St. Paul, Minn., 1872–81; Kenosha, Wis., 1881–86. Pres. Wis. Syn. 1865–67.

Streit, Christian (June 7, 1749–Mar. 10, 1812). B. near New Germantown, N. J., of Swiss extraction; studied theol. privately under H. M. Mühlenberg* and C. M. Wrangel*; educ. Coll. of Philadelphia (which later became U. of Pa.); ordained by Syn. of Pa. 1770; Pastor Easton, Pa., 1769–76. Chaplain 8th Va. Regt. 1776–77. Pastor Charleston, S. C., 1778–80. Chaplain 9th Va. Regt. Prisoner of Brit. 1780–82. Pastor New Hanover (Falckner's Swamp), Pa., 1782–85; Winchester, Va., 1785–1812. Helped prepare P. Henkel (see *Henkels, The,* 2) and W. Carpenter* for the ministry.

Streit, Robert (1875–1930). Pioneer in RC mission science; b. Fraustadt, Posen, Ger.; priest 1901. Works include *Bibliotheca missionum.*

Streufert, Frank Carl (Apr. 30, 1874–Sept. 17, 1953). B. Chicago, Ill.; educ. Conc. Coll., Fort Wayne, Ind., and Conc. Sem., St. Louis, Mo.; traveling miss. in N Calif. 1895; served various parishes in Calif. 1895–1902; pastor Chicago 1902–32; Mo. Syn. Secy. of Missions 1932–53; held various other positions.

Stribog. See *Slavs, Primitive Religion of.*

Strigel, Victorinus (Victorin; Strigelius; 1524–69). Melanchthonian Luth.; b. Kaufbeuren, Swabia; educ. Freiburg and Wittenberg; taught at Wittenberg, Erfurt, Jena; moved to Leipzig 1563, Heidelberg 1567. Failed to distinguish bet. philos. and theol. Works include *Loci theologici.* See also *Synergistic Controversy.*

Strodach, Paul Zeller (Mar. 27, 1876–May 30, 1947). B. Norristown, Pa.; educ. Muhlenberg Coll., Allentown, Pa., and Lutheran Theol. Sem., Mount Airy, Philadelphia, Pa.; ordained 1899; pastor Trenton, N. J., and in Pa. Edited *The Children's Hymnal and Service Book.* Other works include *The Church Year; A Manual on Worship; Oremus; In the Presence.*

Strohl, Henri-Adolphe (1874–1959). B. Brumath, near Strasbourg, Fr.; vicar Weissenburg (Wissembourg) and Ingweiler (Ingwiller), NE Fr., 1898; pastor Colmar 1906–19; taught in Strasbourg; noted for Luther studies. Works include *Luther: Esquisse de sa vie et de sa pensée; Le Protestantisme en Alsace.*

Strong, Augustus Hopkins (1836–1921). Bap. theo.; b. Rochester, N. Y. Educ. Yale coll., New Haven, Conn.; Rochester (N. Y.) Theol. Sem.; and in Ger. Pastor Haverhill, Mass., 1861–65; Cleveland, Ohio, 1865–72. Pres. and prof. Biblical theol. Rochester Theol. Sem. 1872–1912. Works include *Systematic Theology; The Great Poets and Their Theology.*

Strong, Nathan (1748–1816). B. Coventry, Conn.; educ. Yale coll., New Haven, Conn.; studied law; tutor Yale coll. 1772–73; studied theol.; Cong. pastor Hartford, Conn., 1774. Helped est. Conn. Home Mission Soc. 1801. Helped compile *The Hartford Selection of Hymns.* Hymnist. Hymns include "Swell the Anthem, Raise the Song."

Strossmayer, Joseph Georg (Josip Juraj; 1815–1905). RC prelate; b. Osijek (Eszék; Esseg), Croatia; priest 1838; bp. Bosnia, with see at Djakovo, 1849. Worked for reunion of Orthodox and Catholics; opposed doctrine of papal infallibility.

Ströter, Ernst Ferdinand (1846–1922). B. Barmen, Ger.; to US; became Meth.; preacher in Ger. congs. from 1869; worked for Jewish missions from 1894; returned to Eur. 1899; advocated evangelicalism in the spirit of neo-Darbyism (see *Brethren, Plymouth*); defended verbal inspiration (see *Inspiration, Doctrine of*). Works include *Das Evangelium Gottes von der Allversöhnung in Christus.*

Structuralism. See *Psychology,* J 2.

Stuart, Janet Erskine (1857–1914). B. Cottesmore, Rutland, Eng.; RC 1879; superior gen. Soc. of the Sacred Heart 1911. Known for teaching of asceticism and writings on educ. topics.

Stub, Hans Andreas (May 18, 1879–June 15, 1968). Son of H. G. Stub*; b. Koshkonong, Wis. Educ. U. of Minn.; Luther Coll., Decorah, Iowa; Luther Theol. Sem., St. Paul, Minn. Pastor Seattle, Wash., 1903–54. Works include *Music in the Church; Inspiration; Christ in the Old Testament; The Place of the Lutheran Church in America; The City Church; Home Mission Problems.*

Stub, Hans Gerhard (Feb. 23, 1849–Aug. 1, 1931). Father of H. A. Stub*; b. near Muskego, Wis. Educ. Bergen, Norway 1861–65; Luther Coll., Decorah, Iowa; Conc. Coll., Fort Wayne, Ind.; Conc. Sem., St. Louis, Mo. Pastor in Minn. 1872–78. Prof. Luther Theol. Sem. (see *Luther Theological Seminary,* 1) 1878–96. Pastor and prof. Decorah, Iowa, 1896–1900. Prof. and pres. Luth. Theol. Sem. 1900–17. Pres. Norw. Syn. (see *Evangelical Lutheran Church, The,* 8–13) 1910–17. Helped form The Norw. Luth. Ch. of Am. (see *Evangelical Lutheran Church, The,* 13–14) and was its pres. 1917–25. Pres. National* Luth. Council 1918–20. Works include *Om Naadevalget; Foredrag mod det humanistiske og saakaldte kristelige Frimureri.*

Stubnatzy, Wolfgang Simon (Stubnatzi; Feb. 15, 1829–Sept. 13, 1880). B. Fürth, Franconia, Bav., Ger.; sent to US by J. K. W. Löhe* 1847; educ. at the practical sem., Fort Wayne, Ind. (see *Ministry, Education of,* X C and D). Pastor Coopers Grove, Cook Co., Ill., 1849–62; asst. pastor to W. Sihler* in the Fort Wayne, Ind., area 1862–68; pastor Emmanuel Luth. Ch., Fort Wayne, 1868; pres. Cen. Dist. of the Mo. Syn. 1878–80.

Stuckenberg, John Henry Wilburn (Wilbrand; Willbrandt; Jan. 6, 1835–May 28, 1903). B. Bramsche, near Osnabrück, Hannover, Ger.; to US 1839. Educ. Wittenberg Coll., Springfield, Ohio. Studied at Halle 1859–61; Göttingen, Tübingen, and Berlin 1865–66. Pastor Davenport, Iowa, 1858–59; Erie, Pa., 1861–62, 1863–65; Indianapolis, Ind., 1867–68; Pittsburgh, Pa., 1868–73. Chaplain in Civil War 1862–63. Prof. Wittenberg Coll. 1873–80. Pastor Am. Ch. in Berlin 1880–94; lectured in Am. 1892. To US 1894; made his home at North Cambridge, Mass. Works include *The History of the Augsburg Confession, from Its Origin till the Adoption of the Formula of Concord; Christian Sociology; The Social Problem.*

Student Christian Movement. Nat. affiliate of World Student Christian Fed. (see *Students, Spiritual Care of,* A 5); sprang out of the Student* Volunteer Movement; formed 1893 in Eng. by combination of the Cambridge Inter-Collegiate Christian Union with several other university Christian organizations. See also *Ecumenical Movement, The,* 12.

Student Nonviolent Coordinating Committee (also known as "Snick" from its acronym SNCC). Formed 1960 to coordinate protests of students conducting sit-ins in behalf of Negro rights. Changed name 1969 to Student Nat. Coordinating Committee.

W. H. Burns, *The Voices of Negro Protest in America* (New York, 1963).

Student Service Commission. See *Students, Spiritual Care of,* B 3 and 4, C 2.

Student Volunteer Missionary Union. See *Student Volunteer Movement,* 3.

Student Volunteer Movement. 1. Began at the 1st internat. conf. of Christian coll. students at Mount Hermon (now part of Northfield), Mass., 1886; 100 participants in the conf. indicated desire to become for. missionaries; the Student Volunteer Movement for For. Missions was formed Dec. 1886 to expedite the movement.

2. Purposes: (a) to awaken and maintain among all Christian students of the US and Can. intelligent and active interest in for. missions; (b) to enroll a sufficient number of properly qualified student volunteers to meet the successive demands of the various missionary bds. of N. Am.; (c) to help all such intending missionaries to prepare for their lifework and to enlist their cooperation in developing the missionary life of home chs.; (d) to lay an equal burden of responsibility on all students who are to remain as ministers and lay workers at home, that they may actively promote the missionary enterprise by intelligent advocacy, gifts, and prayer.

3. The SVM led to formation of the Student Volunteer Missionary Union in Eng. 1892 and spread to the Continent and Asia.

4. The SVM joined the NCC 1953, and in 1959, with the United Student Christian Council (see *Young People's Organizations, Christian,* I 6) and the Interseminary Committee (see *National Council of the Churches of Christ in the United States of America*) formed the Nat. Student Christian Fed., of which the SVM became the Commission on World Mission (see also *Students, Spiritual Care of,* 5).

See also *Student Christian Movement.*

Students, Spiritual Care of. A. *General.* 1. Prominent in the beginning of Am. higher educ. was a determination to integrate religion with higher educ. Hundreds of denominational colleges were est. (for examples see *Ministry, Education of,* VI–VIII; *Protestant Education in the United States*). Rise of state univs., beginning with the U. of Va. (founded 1819 at Charlottesville), and progressive secularization of higher educ. led some local congs. and voluntary agencies to provide spiritual service for student mems. at secular colleges and univs. before 1900.

2. Gen. denominational support of student work did not come till early in the 20th c.

3. Main religious student organizations have included Canterbury Clubs (Episc.); United Student Fellowship (United Ch. of Christ); Roger Williams Clubs (Northern Baps.); Bap. Student Unions (Southern Baps.); Meth. Student Movement (Wesley Foundations in state institutions and Meth. fellowships in Meth. and indep. colleges); Westminster Foundation (Presb.); Gamma Delta (see C 9); Luth. Student Assoc. of Am. (organized Toledo, Ohio, 1922); Beta Sigma Psi Luth. Fraternity (founded 1928 as Conc. Club); Newman Club (RC); Pax Romana (RC internat. student movement founded 1921 Switz.); Hillel Foundations (founded 1923; supported by B'nai B'rith, a Jewish service organization founded 1843 NYC).

4. Christian student socs. in Am. began early in the 18th c. and antedate all other voluntary student organizations. The first student YMCAs were organized at the state univs. of Mich. and Va. 1858.

5. Major interdenom. student movements: World Student Christian Fed. (founded 1895 in Swed. by representatives of Am. and Eur. SCMs [see *Student Christian Movement*]; the US section is the Nat. Student Christian Fed. [see *Student Volunteer Movement,* 4]); Student For. Missions Fellowship (formerly Inter-Varsity Christian Fellowship; began in Eng. 1910 in the withdrawal of the Cambridge Inter-Collegiate Christian Union [see also *Student Christian Movement*] from the Brit. SCM; the name Student For. Missions Fellowship was first attached to the fellowship that arose 1936 among students in Christian colleges and Bible institutes in Am. and was absorbed 1945/46 as a dept. of the Inter-Varsity Christian Fellowship, which later became the Student For. Missions Fellowship); Campus* Crusade for Christ Internat.

B. *Lutheran in America.* 1. The General* Council of the Ev. Luth. Ch. in N. Am. placed a pastor in Madison, Wis., 1907 to serve Luth. students at the U. of Wis.

2. The ULC developed and expanded the work begun in its merging bodies.

3. The Am. Luth. Conf. created a Student Service Commission.

4. The NLC organized a Student Service Commission 1945 (gave it divisional status 1949), took over the student work of its constituent bodies 1946. See also *American Lutheran Conference, The,* 4.

The Nat. Luth. Campus Ministry of The ALC and the LCA is administered by the Lutheran* Council in the USA.

See also A 3, C.

C. *Mo. Syn.* 1. Before 1923 (see 3), spiritual care of students depended on individual initiative. A. T. E. Haentzschel* began campus work at the U. of Wis., Madison, 1920 under call issued by a joint bd. of the S. Wis. Dist. and the Wisconsin* Ev. Luth. Syn.; a bldg. containing chapel, parsonage, and soc. rooms for students, and located near the campus, was dedicated 1926.

2. Under impetus provided by the Student Welfare Committee (later names include Student Service Commission; Commission on Coll. and University Work; Campus Ministry) other Dists. began similar work.

3. 1923 and 1926 syn. resolutions expressed concern for spiritual care of students, but lack of financial means delayed action for yrs. Reuben W. Hahn, who had served as university pastor at the U. of Ala., Tuscaloosa, since 1929, served as Ex. Secy. for the work 1940–68. Secy. for Campus Ministry: W. J. Fields 1970–.

4. The program: soul conservation, reclamation, and winning; training for Christian service; Christian impact on the campus through evangelism and establishment of Luth. chairs of religion.

5. Since May 1, 1968, campus ministry has been part of the Bd. for Missions.

6. In most cases campus work is done by pastors of coll. community congs.; full-time campus pastors are called where conditions warrant it. Formation of student assemblies (or congs.) offers opportunity for students to prepare for service in congs. they will join later.

7. The Luth. Collegiate Assoc. (defunct ca. 1970), conceived as an extension of the student service program, was formally organized 1945 as an assoc. of persons with coll. training, to enlist talents of educ. laypersons for ch. work.

8. Nat. and regional study assemblies for Luths. on coll. and university faculties and staffs have been held, partly to consider and meet spiritual needs of students.

9. Gamma Delta, Internat. Assoc. of Luth. Students, was founded 1934 Chicago, Ill., by W. A. Maier* et al. The Gk. letters *gamma* and *delta* here stand for *gnosis* ("knowledge") and *diakonia* ("service") and reflect the origin of the assoc., which succeeded the Student Dist. of the Walther League (with its program of Christian knowledge and service; see also *Young People's Organizations, Christian,* II 3), which had been formed 1928. Aims: "to foster thorough study of the Bible; to disseminate the Scriptural philosophy of life; to train Lutheran students for Christian service to God and their fellowmen; to maintain and increase Lutheran consciousness on the campus; to maintain and increase local and inter-campus fellowship among students of our faith." Gamma Delta supports student-related for. miss. projects. RWH

Stump, Joseph (Oct. 6, 1866–May 24, 1935). B. Marietta, Pa.; educ. Capital U., Columbus, Ohio, and Luth. Theol. Sem., Philadelphia, Pa. Pastor Pa. and N. J. 1887–1915. Prof. Chicago Luth. Theol. Sem., Maywood, 1915–20; Chicago Luth. Divinity School 1920–21; pres. and prof. Northwestern* Luth. Theol. Sem. 1921–35. Works include *An Explanation of Luther's Small Catechism; The Christian Life: A Handbook of Christian Ethics; Life of Philip Melanchthon; The Christian Faith: A System of Christian Dogmatics.* See also *Ministry, Education of,* X I.

Stundists. See *Russian Sects.*

Sturm, Beata (Sturmin; 1682–1730). "Württembergische Tabea" ("Württemberg Tabitha"; cf. Acts 9: 36). B. Stuttgart, Ger.; became blind as a child; eyesight partly restored by an operation; said to have read the Bible from beginning to end 30 times; avid reader of M. Luther's works; known for helping poor, sick, and needy.

Sturm, Jakob (Jakob Sturm v. Sturmeck; 1489–1553). Reformer, statesman, educator; b. Strasbourg; educ. Heidelberg, Freiburg, Liège, Paris; aided Prots. at diets of Speyer 1526 and 1529, Augsburg 1530. Helped draw up Tetrapolitan Confession (see *Reformed Confessions,* D 1); helped found a Gymnasium at Strasbourg which became a pattern for many similar schools. See also *Higher Education,* 7; *Sturm, Johannes.*

Sturm, Johannes (1507–89). Educator; b. Schleiden, Ger.; educ. at school of the Brethren of the Common Life at Liege, Belg., and at Louvain; became Prot. under influence of M. Bucer*; helped found a Gymnasium at Strasbourg 1537/38 of which he was rector ca. 43 yrs. (see also *Higher Education,* 7; *Sturm,*

Jakob). Emphasized classical culture and training in rhetoric and eloquence, based on humanism and ev. piety. Deprived of rectorship in tension with Luths.

Sturm, Julius Karl Reinhold (Carl; 1816–96). Cleric, poet; b. Köstritz, Ger.; educ. Jena; tutor and pastor at various places. Works include *Fromme Lieder; Zwei Rosen, oder das Hohelied der Liebe; Israelitische Lieder.*

Sturm, Leonhard Christoph (1669–1719). Mathematician, architect; b. Altdorf, Ger.; influenced Prot. ch. architecture.

Stuttgart Declaration. Statement presented to representatives of the ch. at large at Stuttgart, Ger., 1945 by the council of EKD acknowledging guilt of ev. Christians in Ger.: 1. Confession of guilt for not confessing more courageously, praying more faithfully, believing more joyfully, and loving more fervently. 2. Resolution to make a new beginning. 3. Expression of gratitude for ecumenical fellowship. 4. Expression of hope that the spirit of power and revenge becoming evident everywhere will be curbed by the influence of the ch. 5. Plea for new beginning in all Christendom through the Holy Spirit.

Stutz, Georg Ulrich (1868–1938). B. Zurich, Switz.; educ. Zurich and Berlin; taught at Berlin, Basel, Freiburg, Bonn, and again Berlin (from 1917). Expert on ch. law. Works include *Geschichte des kirchlichen Benefizialwesens von seinen Anfängen bis auf die Zeit Alexanders III.*

Stylites (from Gk. *stylos,* "pillar"). Hermits who lived on pillar tops, esp. in Syria, but also Mesopotamia, Egypt, Greece, and elsewhere, 5th–10th cents., with isolated cases down to modern times. Also called pillar saints. See also *Simeon Stylites.*

Suárez, Francisco (1548–1617). Jesuit philos.; b. Granada, Sp.; held that the pope has power to depose temporal rulers. Works include Defensio fidei; commentary on Thomas* Aquinas' *Summa theologica* (or *Summa theologiae*).

Sub una specie; sub utraque specie. See *Grace, Means of,* IV 4.

Subdeacon. See *Clergy; Hierarchy.*

Sublapsarians. See *Infralapsarianism.*

Subordinationism. View that because Christ is begotten of the Father, He is subordinate to the Father in essence and majesty, being God is a secondary or lesser sense. Found in crass form in Arianism, Ritschlianism, and modernism, in subtler forms in other misinterpretations of Jn 14:28 (which is properly understood in reference to Christ's human nature in His state of humiliation, as the context shows).

Subscription to Confessions. See *Lutheran Confessions,* D.

Substance. See *Cause,* 4.

Succop, H. H. (Heinrich; July 13, 1845–Dec. 24, 1919). B. Pittsburgh, Pa.; educ. Conc. Coll., Fort Wayne, Ind., and Conc. Sem., St. Louis, Mo. Pastor Wallace and Harick, Ont., Can., 1869–72; Ellice, near Sebringville, Ont., 1872–75; Chicago, Ill., 1875–1919. Pres. Ill. Dist. of the Mo. Syn. 1891–1903; Mo. Syn. vice-pres. 1905–08.

Sudan, Republic of the. See *Africa,* E 1.

Sudan Bible School. See *Africa,* C 3.

Sudan Interior Mission. Interdenom. soc. organized as Africa Industrial Mission 1898 at Toronto, Ont., Can., to support work begun 1893 as Soudan Interior Mission on individual initiative; name changed 1905 to Africa Evangelistic Mission; merged with Sudan* United Miss. 1906; union dissolved and present name adopted 1907. The 1st station was est. 1902 at Patigi (or Patiji), several hundred miles up the Niger R., another at Bida 1903, another at Wushishi 1904. Fields have included Aden, Dahomey, Ethiopia, Ghana, Liberia, Niger, Nigeria, Somali Rep., Sudan, Upper Volta. Mem. IFMA. See also *Africa,* C 14.

Sudan United Mission. Also known as Sudan Pioneer Miss. Founded 1904 in Gt. Brit. First station opened 1904 at Wase, N Nigeria. Fields have included Cameroon, Chad, Nigeria, Sudan. Mem. IFMA. See also *Africa,* E 1.

Sudanese Republic. See *Africa,* C 3.

Sudra. See *Brahmanism,* 3.

Suffragan. 1. Bp. subordinate to abp. or metropolitan. 2. Asst. bp.

Suffrage. Intercessory prayer (as in a liturgy); usually used in pl.

Sufism (Sufiism; derivation uncertain). Ascetic Islamic mysticism; began 7th c. AD, largely under Christian influence; developed esp. in Persia; spread to other countries, including Eng. and Am. Includes elements of pantheism.

Suicer, Johann Caspar (Johannes Casparus Suicerus; Hans Kaspar Schweitzer; 1620–84). Ref. theol.; b. Frauenfeld, Thurgau canton, N Switz.; educ. Montauban, Saumur, and Paris; pastor; prof. Zurich 1646. Works include *Thesaurus ecclesiasticus e patribus Graecis ordine alphabetico concinnatus.*

Suicide (from Lat. for "take one's own life"). Self-murder. Christians regard it as a transgression of the 5th Commandment ("Thou shalt not kill"). Many non-Christians have either been indifferent to the problem of suicide or have advocated suicide.

Suidas (Suda; Gk. *Souidas* or *Souda;* before Eustathius* of Thessalonica; perhaps late 10th c.). Byzantine lexicographical compendium; includes comments on early Christian writings. Some have regarded "Suidas" (perhaps erroneously) as author's name.

Suidbert (d. 713). Northumbrian priest; assoc. with Egbert* and Willibrord* in Frisia; fled under Saxon attack; founded monastery Kaiserswerth on an is. in the Lower Rhine.

Sulawesi. See *Indonesia,* 1, 6.

Sullivan, Arthur Seymour (1842–1900). Composer, organist, choirmaster; b. Lambeth, London, Eng.; studied music at Leipzig, Ger. Wrote light operas to the librettos of William Schwenck Gilbert (1836–1911), including *H. M. S. Pinafore; The Pirates of Penzance; The Mikado; The Gondoliers.* Other works include oratorios *The Prodigal Son* and *The Light of the World;* songs, including "The Lost Chord"; hymn tunes, including St. Gertrude ("Onward, Christian Soldiers") and Heaven Is My Home ("I'm But a Stranger Here").

Sulpicians. Mems. of an order of secular priests named after the parish of St. Sulpice in Faubourg St. Germain, near Paris, Fr., with which the community became assoc. 1642 soon after it was founded; purpose: to prepare young men for the priesthood. Administer the Theol. Coll. at The Cath. U. of Am., Washington, D. C. See also *Olier, Jean Jacques; Roman Catholic Church,* E 4.

Sulpicius Severus (ca. 360–ca. 410/20). B. Aquitaine (hist. region SW Fr.); lawyer; influenced by Martin of Tours (see *Celtic Church,* 2); became monk. Works include *Historia sacra,* which reflects and summarizes world hist.

Sulze, Emil (1832–1914). Ev. theol.; b. Kamenz, Saxony, Ger.; pastor Dresden 1876–95; emphasized small congs., observance of parish lines, lay activity. Works include *Die Hauptpuncte der kirchlichen Glaubenslehre; Die Reform der evangelischen Landeskirchen nach den Grundsätzen des neueren Protestantismus.*

Sulzer, Simon (1508–85). Ref. theol.; b. Meiringen, Bern canton, S cen. Switz.; educ. Bern, Lucerne, Strasbourg, Basel; teacher and pastor Bern 1533; became follower of M. Luther 1536 after visiting Wittenberg; preacher and prof. Basel.

Sumatra. See *Indonesia,* 1, 3, 4.

Sumbawa. See *Indonesia,* 1, 11.

Summa (Lat. "compendium; whole"). Name often

used in Middle Ages for textbooks of philos. and theol. See also, e. g., *Thomas Aquinas.*

Summer Schools. See *Parish Education,* F 3.

Summus episcopus. See *Bishop,* 9.

Sumner, John Bird (1780–1862). B. Kenilworth, Warwickshire, cen. Eng.; educ. Eton and Cambridge; ordained 1803; bp. Chester 1828; opposed Oxford* Movement; abp. Canterbury 1848. Works include *Apostolical Preaching; A Treatise on the Records of the Creation; The Evidence of Christianity.* See also *Gorham, George Cornelius.*

Sunda Isles. See *Indonesia,* 1, 3–6, 9–12.

Sundar Singh, Sadhu. See *Singh, Sadhu Sundar.*

Sunday (from OE *sunne,* "sun," and *daeg,* "day," tr. of Lat. *dies solis,* tr. of Gk. *he tou heliou hemera,* "the day of the sun"). 1st day of the week; named after heathen consecration of it to the sun(god).

The "Sunday question" (whether to exclude from ch. fellowship those who held that the ch. had to set apart 1 day in 7 because God had rested 1 day in 7) was a point of controversy bet. the Ev. Luth. Syn. of Iowa* and Other States and the Mo. Syn. The latter summarized its position in the Brief* Statement: "We teach that in the New Testament God has abrogated the Sabbath and all the holy days prescribed for the Church of the Old Covenant, so that neither 'the keeping of the Sabbath nor of any other day' nor the observance of at least one specific day of the seven days of the week is ordained or commanded by God, Col. 2:16; Rom. 14:5 [AC XXVIII 51–60].

"The observance of Sunday and other church festivals is an ordinance of the Church, made by virtue of Christian liberty. [AC XXVIII 51–53, 60; LC I 83, 85, 89]. Hence Christians should not regard such ordinances as ordained by God and binding upon the conscience, Col. 2:16; Gal. 4:10. However, for the sake of Christian love and peace they should willingly observe them, Rom. 14:13; 1 Cor. 14:40. [AC XXVIII 53–56]"

See also *Lord's Day; Sabbath,* 6, 8.

Sunday, William Ashley ("Billy"; 1862[1863?]–1935). B. Ames, Iowa; professional baseball player 1883–90; YMCA worker 1891–95; evangelist and revivalist 1896; Presb. minister 1903; prohibitionist.

Sunday Letter (dominical letter). That letter, of the first 7 of the alphabet, which falls on Sun. when the letters are assigned in order to the days of the yr., beginning Jan. 1 (leap yr. requiring adjustments). Used with the Golden Number, or Prime, for the yr., and in connection with a calendar table found, e. g., in a prefix to the Book of Common Prayer, to determine the date of Easter in any given yr. The Golden Number is determined by mathematical calculation (e. g., for 1973: take 73, add 1, making 74; divide by 19; the remainder [17] is the Goldern Number for 1973; if, for another yr., there is no remainder, the Golden Number is 19). For dates of Easter see also *Easter Dates.*

"Sunday Question." See *Sunday.*

Sunday School. 1. Also called Sabbath school, or Sun. ch. school; primary agency of Christian educ. in most N. Am. Prot. chs. today.

2. It has been claimed that Sun. schools were begun in Scot. by J. Knox* ca. 1560. Sun. schools were est. in the 17th c. in Eng. and Am. The modern S. S. movement is usually traced to efforts of R. Raikes* 1780, when he opened his 1st S. S. (children worked on other days) in hope of preventing vice by educ. His movement originally was not ch.-related and was opposed by ch. leaders; yet it grew and spread.

3. The 1st S. S. of the Raikes type in N. Am. was organized in Va. in the mid-1780s. In course of time more emphasis was placed on religion, adults and small children were included, and volunteer teachers replaced professionals.

4. Local S. S. unions formed and crossed denominational lines. The Am. S. S. Union formed around some of these groups 1824; a nat. conv. was held Philadelphia 1832.

5. With the development of tax-supported "free schools" 1825–50, many Luth. parochial schools were replaced by Sun. schools. The General* Syn. of the Ev. Luth. Ch. in the USA est. a Luth. S. S. Union 1830. Sun. schools began to appear in the Mo. Syn. in the 1840s, but the syn. in gen., distrustful of doctrinal laxity often assoc. with Prot. Sun. schools, long continued rather to emphasize parochial schools and Christenlehre (see *Parish Education,* F 5); the S. S. was not officially accepted until ca. the time of WW I.

6. Curricular materials in the first Sun. schools were the Bible, catechisms, and hymnals. A wide assortment of other materials appeared in the early and middle 19th c. Internat. Uniform Lessons were adopted 1872. In the 20th c. a philos. of child-centered, rather than curriculum-centered, educ. found wide acceptance.

7. Sun. schools spread through the world. In the US, world leader, ca. 90% of the enrollment is Prot. PHP

See also *International Council of Religious Education; Parish Education,* B 2–4, E; *Protestant Education in the United States.*

J. D. Butler, Religious Education (New York, 1962); M. A. Haendschke, *The Sunday School Story: The History of the Sunday School in The Lutheran Church – Missouri Synod,* in *Lutheran Education Association 20th Yearbook* (River Forest, Ill., 1963).

Sunday School Council of Evangelical Denominations. See *International Council of Religious Education, The.*

Sunday School Literature. See *Parish Education,* E 5–6; *Sunday School,* 6.

Sunday School Union (Luth.). See *Sunday School,* 5.

Sundermann, Wilhelm Heinrich (Oct. 29, 1849–Apr. 24, 1919). B. Ladbergen (Tecklenburg), Westphalia, Ger.; Rhenish* Miss. Soc. miss. to Nias* 1815. Tr. Bible into Nias. Other works include *Kurzgefasste niassische Grammatik; Die Insel Nias und die Mission daselbst.*

Sung, John (Siong Chiat Sung; Sept. 27, 1901–Aug. 18, 1944). B. Hinghwa, China; outstanding Christian miss. in China, Thailand, SE Asia. Works include *My Testimony.*

Sung Mass. See *Missa cantata.*

Sunna. See *Islam,* 2.

Sunnites. Larger of the 2 main branches of Islam. See also *Islam,* 5.

Suomi. See *Finland.*

Suomi College. See *Lutheran Church in America,* V; *Ministry, Education of,* VIII C 1 g.

Suomi Synod. See *Canada,* A 16; *Finnish Lutherans in America,* 2.

Suomi Theological Seminary. See *Ministry, Education of,* X I.

Superego. See *Ego,* 3; *Psychology,* J 7.

Supererogation, Works of. In RCm, works done, esp. by mems. of holy orders, over and above those that are required for salvation; their merit may be credited to those who fall short of requirement.

Superintendents (S. S., weekday school, VBS). See *Parish Education,* K 6–7.

Superior. See *Abbot.*

Supernaturalism (supranaturalism). Term that came into prominence esp. in Eng. and Ger. ca. 1780–1830 in theol. discussions arising esp. out of tensions created by deism* and rationalism.* Supernaturalists held that the authenticity of divine revelation is attested, in part, by prophecies and miracles. After I. Kant* and G. W. F. Hegel* the term supernaturalist was applied to those who held the absolute transcendence of God; later the name supernaturalism was applied to many systems within Christianity that rejected reason as an absolute norm and held authoritarian, inner, emotional, or other criteria. Supernaturalists included L. F. O. Baumgarten-Crusius,* J. F. Flatt,* F. V. Reinhard,* J. M. Schröckh,* G. C. Storr,* F. G. v. Süskind,* J. A. H. Tittmann.*

Supervision, Educational (including supervision of teachers). See *Parish Education,* K. L. M; *Teachers,* 17.

Supplement Theory. See *Higher Criticism,* 14.

Supralapsarianism. View that predestination* in which God determined to save some and damn others preceded creation and that God allowed the fall as a means of carrying out his purpose. See also *Infralapsarianism.*

Supranaturalism. Supernaturalism.*

Supremacy, Act of. See *Church and State,* 9.

Supremacy, Papal. See *Luther, Chief Writings of,* 4, 7; *Papacy; Roman Catholic Confessions.*

Suras (surahs). See *Koran.*

Sure Salvation. See *Methodist Churches,* 2.

Surgant, Johann Ulrich (1450–1503). B. Altkirch, Alsace; educ. Basel and Paris; priest 1472; prof. Basel. Works include *Manuale curatorum predicandi prebens modum.*

Surinam. See *South America,* 13.

Surplice. See *Vestments, Clerical,* 2.

Survival of the Fittest. See *Spencer, Herbert.*

Susanna, History of. See *Apocrypha,* A 3.

Susi. Faithful servant of D. Livingstone*; with Chuma (native companion) and others carried Livingstone's body from the district of Ilala on the S shore of Lake Bangweulu to Zanzibar, a journey of ca. 8 mo.

Süskind, Friedrich Gottlieb von (Süsskind; 1767–1829). B. Neuenstadt am Kocher, N Württemberg, Ger.; prof. Tübingen; chief court chaplain; consistorial councillor; exponent of supernaturalism.* Works include *Über das Recht der Vernunft in Ansehung der negativen Bestimmung der Offenbarung.*

Suso, Heinrich (Henricus; Henry Suso; Sus; Suse; Seuse; also called Amandus; real surname v. Berg; ca. 1295/1300–1366). Mystic, poet; "Minnesinger of mysticism"; b. Konstanz (or Überlingen?), Ger.; itinerant preacher Swabia ca. 1335–48; settled at Ulm ca. 1348. Works include *Das Büchlein der Wahrheit* and *Das Büchlein der ewigen Weisheit* (titles occur in various forms). See also *Friends of God; Heresy,* 3.

Susquehanna Synod. See *United Lutheran Church, Synods of,* 23.

Susquehanna University. Began 1858 at Selinsgrove, Pa., as Missionary Institute, founded by B. Kurtz*; name changed 1895 to Susquehanna U.; theol. dept. disbanded 1933. See also *General Synod of the Evangelical Lutheran Church in the United States of America, The,* 8; *Lutheran Church in America,* V; *Ministry, Education of,* VIII A 3; *Universities in the United States, Lutheran,* 4.

Sutel, Johann (1504–75). B. Altmorschen, Hesse, Ger.; educ. Erfurt; teacher Melsungen; preacher and supt. Göttingen; went to Allendorf in Schmalkaldic* War; returned to Göttingen 1548; pastor Northeim 1555–75. Works include *Das Evangelion von der grausamen, erschrecklichen Zerstörung Jerusalem* (title occurs in various forms).

Suttee (sati; Skt. "good woman"). Hindu widow voluntarily cremated on her husband's funeral pyre; also: the act or custom of such cremation. The practice was made a statutory offense 1829/30 and became practically extinct soon thereafter.

Suttner, Bertha von (nee Countess Kinsky; 1843–1914). Austrian writer; b. Prague; founded Austrian Soc. of Friends of Peace 1891; was awarded Nobel peace prize 1905. Works include *Die Waffen nieder!*

Suzerainty Covenant. See *Covenant,* 2.

Svarog. See *Slavs, Primitive Religion of.*

Svebilius, Olavus (Olof Jöransson; 1624–1700). Luth. abp. Swed. 1681. Educ. Uppsala; headmaster Kalmar classical high school and court preacher Kalmar 1656; pastor Ljungby 1659; chief court chaplain Stockholm 1668; chief pastor and pres. of consistory Stockholm 1671. Helped rev. service book, hymnal, and catechism.

Svedberg. See *Swedberg.*

Sveinsson, Brynjulf (Bryniulf; Brynjúlfur; 1605–75). Bp. Skálholt diocese, Iceland; discovered the Poetic Edda (see *Eddas*), also called Elder Edda, ca. 1643 and called it *Edda Saemundi multiscii* (after Saemund Sigfusson [ca. 1055–1132], scion of the royal house of Norw., who was thus credited with collecting these poems).

Svenonius, Enevald. See *Finland, Lutheranism in,* 3.

Svensson, Olaf (16th c.). Swed. hymnist; school teacher Stockholm; secy. of city council; hymns opposed RCm.

Sverdrup, Georg (Dec. 16, 1848–May 3, 1907). B. Balestrand, near Bergen, Norw.; educ. Christiania (Oslo); to US 1874. Prof. Augsburg Theol. Sem., Minneapolis, Minn., 1874–1907; pres. 1876–1907. Pres. Friends of Augsburg 1894–97 (see also *Lutheran Free Church*). Ed. *Folkebladet* and other Norw. theol. periodicals.

Svetambara. See *Jainism.*

Swabian-Saxon Concordia. See *Lutheran Confessions,* C 2.

Swain, Joseph (1761–96). Hymnist; b. Birmingham, Eng.; became Bap. in London; Bap. minister Walworth, London, 1791. Works include *Walworth Hymns.*

Swami (swamy; from Skt. for "owner; lord"). 1. Form of address to a Hindu monk or religious teacher. 2. Initiated mem. of a Hindu religious order. See also *Vivekananda.*

Swaziland, Kingdom of. See *Africa,* B 7.

Swedberg, Jesper (Svedberg; 1653–1735). Father of E. Swedenborg*; b. near Falun, Swed.; educ. Uppsala; prof. Uppsala 1692; bp. Skara 1702; influenced by Pietism*; hymnist. Prepared a hymnal. See also *Spegel, Haquin.*

Sweden, Conversion of, to Christianity. Beginnings of Christianity in Swed. may be traced to Christian captives (presumably victims of Viking raids) found by Ansgar,* who began work ca. 830 at Birka, on an is. in Lake Mälaren, near Stockholm, and visited the land more than once; it is not known how long the Christian communities he est. continued.

Norway is also said to have contributed to early Swed. Christianity. Perhaps Christian influence entered Swed. also from Russ. But Eng. seems to have had the largest part in the latter stages of the conversion of Sweden. Christianity was probably introd. to Gotland, a trading center, through commercial contacts with England. Christianity was fully est. in Swed. under Olaf Skutkonung (Olof; Sköt[t]konung), 1st Christian ruler (ruled 993–1024). See also *Denmark.*

Eric IX (d. 1160; "the Saint"; king of Swed. 1150–60) led crusade to Finland* in the 1150s and imposed Christianity on the conquered. Bishoprics were est. at various places in Swed.; an archbishopric was est. at Uppsala 1164. The U. of Uppsala was founded 1477.

See also *Bridget; Eskil.*

Sweden, Lutheranism in. 1. For beginnings of the Luth. Reformation in Swed. see *Christian II; Gustavus I; Petri, Laurentius; Petri, Olaus; Stockholm Blood Bath.*

The pattern of religious thought that emerged out of the Swed. Reformation gen. followed Ger. models. Writings of O. Petri contributed esp. a lasting Luth. statement of faith; L. Petri set up an episc. structure consonant with Lutheranism. By 1552 RCm was practically dead in Swed. Attempts of John III (1537–92; son of Gustavus* I; king of Swed. 1568–92) to Romanize Swed. failed, as did Counter* Reformation measures under Sigismund III (see *Poland,* 2). The 1593 Council of Uppsala declared the Swed. ch. Luth. (see also *Lutheran Confessions,* A 5), but the program of Charles* IX (succeeded by Gustavus* II) savored somewhat of J. Calvin's* theocratic spirit.

2. A remarkable unity and balance of ch. and state prevailed in the 17th c. An excellent program of educ. and discipline resulted. Strong bps. (including J. Rudbeck,* O. Svebilius,* Erik Benzelius the Elder [1632–1709; abp. Other bps. and abps. in the family include his 3 sons; Erik Benzelius the Younger (1675–1743; librarian U. of Uppsala; bp. Gothenburg and Linköping; abp.; see also 3), Jacob Benzelius (1683–1745; succeeded E. Benzelius the Younger as abp.), and Henrik Benzelius (1689–1758; prof. U. of Lund; abp.); Karl Jesper Benzelius (1714–93, son of E. Benzelius the Younger; bp. Strängnäs)], J. Swedberg,* H. Spegel*) left their mark on nat. life. The age of strong bps. and great kings (Gustavus* II; Charles* X, XI, and XII) saw centralization of ch. govt. 1686, founding of schools for clergy and laity, a hymnal, manual of worship, new Bible tr., new catechism, and a system of ch. registers. The question of orthodoxy became critical in the last half of the 17th c.; the Book of Concord became part of ch. law 1686.

3. The next period (1718–72) began with the death of Charles XII and soon saw growing manifestations of Pietism,* which gained the support of E. Benzelius the Younger (see 2), A. Rydelius,* Erik Tolstadius (1693–1759; vicar and pastor Stockholm), et al. J. K. Dippel,* Ger. Pietist, lived for a time in Sweden. Herrnhut (see *Moravian Church,* 3) influenced esp. cen. and S Sweden. Anticonventicle measures were taken in the 1720s (see also 5). E. Swedenborg* was a child of this era.

The next period, which introd. modern Swed., began 1772, the yr. in which Swedenborg died. Gustavus III (1746–92; b. Stockholm; king 1771–92; has been called the prince of the Enlightenment) arrested council in a body and est. absolute govt. by means of a military coup d'état 1772. For. ideas and customs, esp. Fr., invaded the land; rationalism helped weaken orthodoxy; religious life reached low ebb reflected in a new catechism and other religious books.

4. Reaction against liberalism drew heavily on writings of A. Nohrborg.* Adherents of the protest movement esp. in N provinces were called "readers" because of their use of the Bible and other Christian literature. A nat. ecclesiastical council was authorized 1863, met first 1868. Lund became the cen. of ch. affairs. Outstanding figures in the 1st half of the 19th c. include Frans Mikael Franzén (Michael; 1772–1847; b. Oulu [Uleaaborg], Fin.; educ. Aabo; minister Kumla [Örebro Co., Swed.] and Stockholm, Swed.; bp. Hernösand [Härnösand] 1841; hymnist), E. G. Geijer,* H. Schartau,* E. Tegnér,* J. O. Wallin.* See also *Communistic Societies,* 5; *Scott, George.*

5. Anticonventicle measures taken in the 1720s were repealed 1858. Schism developed in the Evangeliska Fosterlands-Stiftelsen (see *Rosenius, Carl Olof*) 1878, when the Svenska Missionsförbundet was formed under leadership of P. P. Waldenström* (see also *Swedish Missionary Societies,* 4). Nearly one-fifth of the population emigrated in protest against religious and soc. conditions. The ch. began to take interest in current ills; Peter Jonasson Wieselgren (1800–77; b. Spaanhult, Swed.; scholar; cleric) advocated temperance reform; but with the growth of socialism and labor unions the ch. lost much of its influence on secular life.

6. In the 20th c. strong currents were set in motion in theol., missions, ch. art and music, the diaconate, and ecumenicity. Free Chs. developed. Leaders included E. M. Billing,* active in the "young ch. movement"; Manfred Björkquist, who helped raise the Sigtuna* Foundation into prominence; N. Söderblom,* scholar in the field of comparative religion and ecumenical leader; Y. T. Brilioth*; G. E. H. Aulen; A. T. S. Nygren. *Svensk Teologisk Kvartalskrift* began 1925. Other significant works include a new Bible tr., rev. handbook, new hymnal. Interest in litugical renewal, in some respects influenced by the Angl. Ch., led to new forms of ch. architecture and of vestments and produced a book* of hours. CB

For Swed. Luth. influence in the US see *Augustana Evangelical Lutheran Church;* entries beginning *Swedes . . .* and *Swedish. . . .*

See also *Laestadius, Lars Levi; Lund, Theology of.*

Swedenborg, Emanuel (1688–1772). Son of J. Swedberg*; scientist, philos.; b. Stockholm. Swed.; educ. Uppsala; assessor on Swed. bd. of mines 1716, resigned 1747; engaged in psychical and spiritual research; followers called Swedenborgians.* Works include *Opera philosophica et mineralia; Oeconomia regni animalis; Regnum animale; Arcana coelestia* [*caelestia*]; *Vera Christiana religio.*

Swedenborgians (Ch. of the New Jerusalem; New Ch.; New Jerusalem Ch.). 1. Followers of E. Swedenborg.* Held that the Trin. is not of persons, but of divine essentials, without division of the divine being. Redemption was accomplished by the incarnate Jehovah. Justification involves cooperation bet. man and God. Scripture has a literal and spiritual (inner, symbolic) sense; Swedenborg was chosen by God to reveal the latter. The New Ch. was identified with the new Jerusalem of Rv 21 and was dated from 1757, though not organized till the 1780s. Original sin, justification by faith alone, and resurrection of the body are denied. Man's spirit goes to heaven or hell through an intermediate realm after death.

2. Swedenborg was a prolific theosophical writer (see *Theosophy*).

3. Swedenborgians organized in London, Eng., in the 1780s.

4–5. The 1st New Ch. soc. in Am. was founded Baltimore 1792. The Gen. Convention of the New Jerusalem in the USA was organized 1817. The Academy of the New Ch. was founded 1876 as organic exponent of principles later adopted by the Pa. Assoc., connected with the Gen. Conv. The assoc. changed name 1883 to The Gen. Ch. of Pa., separated from the Gen. Conv. 1890, changed name 1892 to The Gen. Ch. of the Advent of the Lord, reorganized 1897 as The Gen. Ch. of the New Jerusalem.

Swedes on the Delaware. See *United States, Religious History of the,* 6.

Swedish Baptist General Conference of America. See *Baptist Churches,* 18.

Swedish Evangelical Free Church. See *Evangelical Free Church of America.*

Swedish Evangelical Lutheran Ansgarius Synod. See *Evangelical Covenant Church of America, The.*

Swedish Evangelical Lutheran Mission Synod. See *Evangelical Covenant Church of America, The; Evangelical Free Church of America.*

Swedish Evangelical Mission Covenant Church of America. See *Evangelical Covenant Church of America, The; Evangelical Free Church of America.*

Swedish Missionary Societies (Eur.). Include (1) Swedish Missionary Soc. (Svenska Missionssällskapet), founded 1835; absorbed the Lund Miss. Soc. founded 1845) 1855; united with the Swed. Ch. Miss. (see 3) 1876 but was not wholly absorbed by it. (2) Ev. Nat. Miss. Soc. (Evangeliska Fosterlands-Stiftelsen), founded 1856. This soc. (literally "foundation") consists of many socs.; est. a school for training missionaries 1863 at Johannelund, near Stockholm; fields have included Swed., Afr., India. (3) The Ch. of Swed. Miss. (Svenska Kyrkans Missionsstyrelse), founded 1874; state institution; headed by abp. Uppsala; united with Swed. Miss. Soc. 1876 (see 1) but did not wholly absorb it; fields have included China, India, Afr.; during the 2 World Wars the Ch. of Swed. Miss. administered the work of the Leipzig Ev. Luth. Miss. in India. See also *India,* 10. (4) Mission Covenant Ch. of Swed. (Swed. Miss. Covenant; Svenska Missionsförbundet), founded 1878; cong. free ch. denomination; fields have included Congo, China, Jap., East Turkestan, Fin., Russ., Armenia, Caucasus, Persia, North Afr., Alaska.

See also *Sweden, Lutheranism in,* 5.

Sweelinck, Jan Pieterszoon (or Pieters) (variants include Swelinck and Swelingh; 1562–1621). Calvinist composer; b. Deventer or Amsterdam, Neth.; organist Amsterdam; taught J. Praetorius,* S. Scheidt,* H. Scheidemann,* et al. Works include *Cantiones sacrae.* See also *Toccata.*

W. Apel, *Masters of the Keyboard* (Cambridge, Mass., 1947); H. Besseler, *Die Musik des Mittelalters und der Renaissance* (Potsdam, 1931); M. F. Bukofzer, *Music in the Baroque Era, from Monteverdi to Bach* (New York, 1947); G. Frotscher, *Geschichte des Orgelspiels und der Orgelkomposition,* 2 vols. (Berlin, 1935–36); R. M. Haas, *Die Musik des Barocks* (Potsdam, 1928); P. H. Láng, *Music in Western Civilization* (New York, 1941).

Swensson, Carl Aaron (June 25, 1857–Feb. 16, 1904). B. Sugar Grove (or Sugargrove), Warren Co., Pa.; educ. Augustana Theol. Sem., Rock Island, Ill.; pastor Lindsborg, Kans.; founded Bethany Academy (now Bethany Coll.), Lindsborg 1881; mem. Kans. legislature; pres. General* Council of the Ev. Luth. Ch. in N. Am. in the mid-1890s. Comp. hymnals. Ed. *Ungdoms Vaennen; Korsbanneret; Framaat.* Other works include *I Sverige; Aater I Sverige.*

Swete, Henry Barclay (1835–1917). Angl. textual critic; b. Bristol, Eng.; educ. Cambridge; priest 1859; curate and rector at various places; taught at King's Coll., London, and at Cambridge. Ed. *The Old Testament in Greek.* Other works include *The Apocalypse of St. John: The Greek Text, with Introduction, Notes, and Indices.*

Swift, Jonathan (1667–1745). Anglo-Irish satirist; cousin of J. Dryden*; b. Dublin, Ireland; priest 1695; dean St. Patrick's, Dublin, 1713. Works include *A Tale of a Tub:* story of 3 brothers (Peter = Romanists; Martin = Anglicans; Jack = Dissenters) altering 3 new coats (Christian truth) bequeathed to them by their father in his will (Bible), with instructions for wearing them.

Swiss Brethren. See *Mennonite Churches,* 1.

Switzerland. Mountainous cen. Eur. country. *Area:* 15,941 sq. mi.; *pop.* (1973 est.): 6,438,400. Languages: 75% German, 20% French, 4% Italian, 1% Romansh.

1. Christianity first reached Switzerland in the 3d or 4th c. By the end of the 15th c. Switz. was RC. See also *Gall; Meinrad; Nicholas of Flüe; Notker; Ratpert.*

2. The Swiss Reformation is often dated from 1516, when H. Zwingli* became priest at Einsiedeln (see *Meinrad*). He became priest Zurich 1518; the Reformation there was practically complete 1525. See also 3.

Another segment of the Swiss Reformation began with the work of B. Haller,* who became active in Bern at least as early as 1518. The Reformation in Bern progressed rapidly after the disputation at Baden 1526 (on the real presence, sacrifice of the mass, invocation of Mary and other saints, and on images, purgatory, and original sin; J. Eck* represented RCs; Haller and J. Oecolampadius* represented Prots.; RCs claimed victory, but reaction to RC measures gave impetus to Protestantism). This segment ends ca. 1531 with the death of Zwingli and defeat of Prots. at Kappel. See also 4.

The next period centers in Geneva, begins with the arrival there of G. Farel* 1532, and ends with the death of J. Calvin* 1564. See also 5.

Then follows a period of increased RC-Prot. tension and of Prot. consolidation under leadership of J. H. Bullinger* in Zurich and T. Beza* in Geneva. See also 5.

3. The Reformation reached Appenzell and Schaffhausen ca. 1521. Erasmus* est. 1522 that ca. 200,000 "abhorred the see of Rome" in Switz. The Council of Zurich required 1523 that "the pastors of Zurich should rest their discourses on the words of Scripture alone." Abolition of images in chs. soon followed; the clergy was no longer forbidden to marry; the mass was replaced 1525 by the simple ordinance of the Lord's Supper.

4. Five RC cantons (Lucerne, Uri, Schwyz, Unterwalden, Zug) banded together 1524 against Zurich and the Reformation; these 5 were joined 1528 by Fribourg and Solothurn. Zurich and Bern decided May 1531 to blockade the RC cantons; the blockade was supported by the bailiwicks of St. Gall, Toggenburg, Sargans, and the Rheinthal; Zwingli protested. The RC cantons took to arms. Zwingli rode to battle with the Zurichers but used no weapons. He was killed and the Zurichers defeated at Kappel Oct. 11, 1531.

5. Farel, who came to Geneva early in Oct. 1532, was banished almost immediately, but recalled early 1534. The city council proclaimed adherence to the Reformation 1535. Calvin came to Geneva 1536, was banished with Farel 1538, returned to Geneva early 1541, after favorable conditions had been restored. See also 2; *Calvin, John; Farel, Guillaume.*

RC reaction set in after 1564 and long seemed to predominate. RC-Prot. strife became more open toward the end of the 17th c. and intensified early in the 18th century. Prots. gained a decisive victory 1712 at Villmergen, Aargau canton, N Switz. See also 2.

6. Switz. is more than 50% Prot., more than 40% RC. There is complete freedom of worship. Non-RC Christian groups include Cantonal Ref. Chs., Meths., Seventh-day Adventists, Luths., Mennonites, Apostolic Ch., Baps., Old Caths., Moravians. Jews: perhaps ca. .6% of the pop. A Luth. cong. was organized at Geneva 1707, Zurich 1891; related groups were est. at Basel, Bern, Davos, Lausanne, St. Gall.

See also *Christian Catholic Church of Switzerland, The; Reformed Churches,* 1; *Reformed Confessions,* A.

Switzerland, Contemporary Theology in. 1. The theol. liberalism of F. D. E. Schleiermacher* and A. B. Ritschl* continued in the work of K. G. A. v. Harnack,* E. P. W. Troeltsch,* et al.

2. Ritschl, Harnack, and Troeltsch were intensely concerned with the relevance of Christian hist. for the modern ch. They believed that the hist. of Christianity must result in repudiation of classical Christian theol., but their interest in the hist. of Christian thought stimulated study and publication of many monuments of Christian hist., e. g., the NT and writings of M. Luther* and other Reformers. Under influence of Harnack's *Dogmengeschichte* (tr. N. Buchanan, *History of Dogma*), and Troeltsch's *Die Soziallehren der christlichen Kirchen und Gruppen* (tr. O. Wyon, *The Social Teaching of the Christian Churches*) the hist. of Christian thought found an important place in theol. scholarship and educ.

3. But this influence destroyed much of the liberalism it was intended to buttress. One of Har-

nack's pupils was K. Barth.* Hist. study of the NT (e. g., by the Formgeschichtliche Schule [see *Isagogics,* 3]; see also *Schweitzer, Albert*) had begun to stress the dynamic and prophetic character of NT religion as well as its essential unity in acknowledgment of Jesus as Messiah. Also, renewed interest in Luther's writings and thought, intensified since the 400th anniversary of his birth (see *Luther and the Reformation, Anniversaries of*) 1883 had helped make Barth and some of his contemporaries dissatisfied with the moralism and optimism of the Ritschlian school. Besides, Barth had been influenced by S. A. Kierkegaard* and F. M. Dostoevski.* WW I provided the occasion for his final break with Ritschlian idealism and for pub. of his epochal *Der Römerbrief* (1919).

4. Barth's new departure was that Paul, Luther, Calvin, Kierkegaard, etc. were to be interpreted not merely in terms of their own hist. environment but also in terms of how they speak to our situation. He denounced the ch., world, theol., and philos. in the name of the "wholly Other," who renders all things of earth fundamentally questionable.

5. Barth found kindred minds among both Luths. and Ref. His theol. has been called dialectical* theol. and crisis theol. (or theol. of crisis, in reference to the assoc. of the Gk. work *krisis* with concepts of separation, judgment, and catastrophe).

6. H. E. Brunner,* more systematic and scientific than Barth, helped relate many of the latter's insights to the problems of the modern mind and ch. Yet they parted company. Barth's increasing inclination to Calvinism and extreme Biblicism (the latter evident in his *Die Kirchliche Dogmatik,* tr. G. T. Thomson et al., *Church Dogmatics*) led him to deny validity to "natural" theol. and to ascribe not only preeminence but absolute uniqueness to all Biblical revelation. Brunner asserted also the revelation of God in creation but often made unfortunate concessions to modern thought.

7. Barth and Brunner shared both an insistence on Biblical realism and a certain arbitrariness in theol.

8. The theol. of Barth and Brunner is subject to valid criticism of all Ref. theol. on the means of grace, ch., distinction bet. Law and Gospel, etc. But it helped bring a large segment of Protestantism closer to true Christianity, JP

Swords, Two. See *Two Swords.*

Sydow, Karl Leopold Adolf (1800–82). B. Berlin, Ger.; pastor military school Berlin 1822; court preacher Potsdam 1836; pastor Berlin 1848–76. Tried to develop scientific and critical NT study. Cofounder *Unierte Kirchenzeitung* and Ger. Protestant* Union.

Syle, Henry Winter. See *Deaf,* 6.

Syllabus of Errors. Eighty RC theses condemning "the principal [Lat. *praecipuos*] errors of our time" condemned by Pius IX (see *Popes,* 28); issued 1864 with encyclical *Quanta cura* (see *Encyclicals*); not signed by Pius IX.

Propositions condemned include statements on pantheism, naturalism, rationalism, indifferentism, latitudinarianism, socialism, communism, secret socs., Bible socs., clerical-liberal socs., ch. rights, ch. and state, ethics.

Reactions varied. Some regarded the theses as absolute and untenable; others regarded them as relative and conditioned by hist. roots. The latter opinion seems to prevail in RCm today. JEG

See also *Roman Catholic Confessions,* D.

R. Aubert, "Monseigneur Dupanloup et le Syllabus," *Revue d'Histoire Ecclésiastique,* LXI (1956), 79–142, 471–512, 837–915; J. Schmidlin, *Papstgeschichte der neuesten Zeit,* II (Munich, 1934); E. E. Y. Hales, *Pio Nono* (New York, 1962).

Sylvester I. See *Popes,* 1.

Sylvester II. See *Popes,* 6.

Sylvester, Johannes (Johann; Janos; Erdösi; ca. 1504–ca. 1552). Hung. humanist, reformer; b. Szinyérváralja (Szinér-Váralja; Seine); educ. Kraków and Wittenberg; prof. Heb. 1544, hist. 1552 Vienna; banished by Jesuits. Tr. NT.

Sylvesterabend. See *Silvesterabend.*

Symbol. 1. Creed; summary of doctrine or faith; confession of faith used as a distinctive emblem. See also *Creeds and Confessions; Ecumenical Creeds; Symbolics; Symbolists.* 2. Visible sign of something. See also *Art, Ecclesiastical and Religious; Symbolism, Christian; Worship,* 8. 3. Anything (e. g., a word, abbreviation, name, nickname, sound, motion, color, action, pain or other sensation) that symbolizes, means, indicates, or designates something. See also *"D"; "E"; "J"; "P."*

Religious Symbolism, ed. F. E. Johnson (New York, 1955); C. W. Morris, *Signs, Language and Behavior* (NYC, 1946); N. O. Schedler, "Paul Tillich's Theory of Symbol," unpub. STM thesis (Conc. Sem., St. Louis, Mo., 1958); G. Ferguson, *Signs & Symbols in Christian Art* (NYC, 1959); T. A. Stafford, *Christian Symbolism in the Evangelical Churches* (NYC, 1942); F. R. Webber, *Church Symbolism* (Cleveland, Ohio, 1938).

Symbolic Books (symbolical books). Books containing creeds (see *Symbol,* 1) of a ch. See also *Book of Concord.*

Symbolics. Branch of theol. knowledge dealing with creeds of the ch. Comparative symbolics is the comparative study of creeds. See also *Symbol,* 1.

Symbolism, Christian. 1. A cross* or crucifix* has been used from early NT times as a symbol (see *Symbol,* 2) of Christ's crucifixion or of Christianity.

2. Figures of Christ and the evangelists came to be used, often with identifying objects (e. g., the instrument of death: Christ with cross in hand; the evangelists, each with a copy of his gospel, and Matthew with a battle-ax, Mark with a club, Luke with a short-handled ax). The evangelist John is sometimes pictured with his gospel and with a chalice out of which a serpent is rising (in reference to the tradition that a priest of Diana gave him poisoned wine to drink, but John made the sign of the cross over the cup and the poison left in the form of a serpent).

Matthew is sometimes shown as a winged man (because he stressed the incarnation of Christ), or with a lion* (symbol of royalty), or with 3 purses or a money chest (in reference to his original calling; cf. Mt 10:3; Lk 5:27); Mark is sometimes assoc. with the winged man, sometimes with a lion ("the voice of one crying in the wilderness," Mk 1:3), sometimes with an eagle (symbol of grace); Luke is sometimes assoc. with the lion or with a calf or ox (because he gives a full account of the sacrificial death of Christ); John is sometimes assoc. with a lion (because he speaks of the divine nature and kingly office of Christ) or eagle (because his gospel soars, as it were, on eagles' wings to the throne of heaven). Cf. Rv 4:7.

3. The 12 apostles are often similarly assoc. with identifying objects (e. g., Peter with 2 keys [for binding and loosing], Mt 16:19; Andrew with an X-shaped cross [on which he is said to have died], or with fish, or a boathook, or a fisherman's net [cf. Mk 1:16]; James with shells, or a pilgrim's staff, wallet, or hat [symbols of pilgrimage and missionary journeying], or a sword [cf. Acts 12:2]). Paul is sometimes assoc., e. g., with an open Bible bearing the Lat. words *Spiritus gladius* ("Sword of the Spirit") and a cross-hilted sword behind the Bible, or with a shield (cf. Eph 6:16), or with a serpent and fire (cf. Acts 28:3-6), or a scourge (cf. Acts 16:23, 37; 2 Co 11:24).

4–5. Stephen is pictured with several stones lying at his feet (cf. Acts 7:59-60). Columba (see *Celtic*

Church, 7) is pictured with a coracle (small boat with wicker frame covered by leather or hide; used by ancient Britons). Boniface* is pictured with a fallen oak at his feet (it is said that, when he was told at Geismar, Ger., that to touch the ancient oak sacred to Thor [god of thunder] meant instant death, he felled it with an ax) or with a Bible transfixed by a sword (it is said that at his martyrdom he held a Bible which was struck by the swords of those who killed him). Agnes* was called *agna sanctissima* ("most holy lamb") and is pictured with a lamb. Lawrence* is pictured with a gridiron, said to have been the instrument of his death.

6. IHC uses the 1st 3 letters of the Gk. word for "Jesus" as an abbreviation (I = J; H = Gk. for E [capital *eta*]; C = Gk. for S [capital *sigma*]). IHS is not a proper reproduction of the Gk. but a mixture of Gk. and Eng. Also not valid is the suggestion that the H is not an E and that the letters stand for the Ger. *Jesus, Heiland, Seligmacher* ("Jesus, Redeemer, Savior"), or for the Lat. *In Hoc Signo* (see *Constantine* I), or (as suggested by Bernardino* of Siena) for the Lat. *Iesus, Hominum Salvator* ("Jesus, Mankind's Savior"). In this symbol the "I" should, of course, not be changed to "J"; the Gk. had no "J."

The Chi-Rho symbol uses the 1st 2 letters of the Gk. word for "Christ" as an abbreviation (X is the capital Gk. letter for Eng. "Ch" and is called Chi; P is the capital Gk. letter for Eng. "R," is called Rho, and is sometimes pictured in the form of a shepherd's crook. The 2 letters are sometimes superimposed one on the other.

See also *Alpha and Omega; Constantine I; Fish.*

Symbolists (derived from "symbol*" in the sense of "confession of faith used as a distinctive emblem"). Name applied by adherents of "American* Lutheranism" to confessional Luths. (see *Old Lutherans*).

Symbolofideism. See *Fideism.*

Symeon Metaphrastes (Simeon; Logothetes [Gk., primarily "one who audits accounts"; administrative functionary under a Byzantine emp.]; fl. ca. 960; d. perhaps ca. 976/977). Byzantine hagiographer; reworked ("metaphrased") some biographies, hence his name. His compilation was later expanded. See also *Menologion,* 3.

Symeon Stylites. See *Simeon Stylites.*

Synagog (from Gk. *synagoge,* "assembly; meeting place"). Jewish place of worship, and, since the destruction of the temple, the only such place. Its furniture includes an "ark" (box, cabinet, or shrine for the sacred scrolls) and a platform from which Scripture is read. In some cases an area is set aside for women.

Synaxarion (synaxary; synaxarium; plurals: synaxaria or synaxaries; from the Greek *synaxis,* from *synagein,* "to gather together"). Term used in reference to E Orthodox cultus for 1. short life of a saint or exposition of a feast included in the Menaion* and appointed to be read at early morning service; 2. Greater Synaxarion: book containing synaxaria arranged acc. to calendar. At times used interchangeably with Menologion*; 3. Lesser Synaxarion: book listing feasts for each day, with pericopic notes (see *Pericope*).

Syncretism (from Gk. for "union; federation" and perhaps assoc. with Gk. for "mix, mingle"). Union, or effort to unite; in religious context practically a synonym for unionism.*

The term is used mainly in reference to 3 controversies: (1) That which began after the 1645 Colloquy of Thorn (see *Poland,* 4; *Reformed Confessions,* D 3 c), involved G. Calixtus,* and ended with the latter's death 1656; Calixtus tried to unite Prots. with each other and with RCs. (2) That which extended from the 1661 Colloquy of Cassel* to 1669, when an order (probably originating from Frederick* William of Brandenburg) to refrain from literary polemics was heeded. An interim of quiet followed till 1675. See also *Gerhardt, Paul(us).* (3) That which began 1675, when A. Calov(ius)* renewed the conflict, and ended with his death 1686.

Syncretistic notions of the 17th c. led to union movements in the 20th c. See *Union Movements,* 8–21; *Union and Unity Movements, Lutheran, in the United States.*

Syneidesis. See *Conscience.*

Synergism (from Gk. *synergeo,* "to work with"). In religious context the term refers to the concept of man cooperating with God in his own conversion.* The concept of synergism developed out of an attempt to solve an apparent contradiction. Scripture teaches the native corruption of man (Jn 3:6), that God provided all-inclusive redemption (Eze 33:11; Jn 3:16; 2 Co 5:19; 1 Ti 2:4), and that man is saved by faith (Mk 16:16; Gl 3:11).

Three views have been held regarding the "how" of conversion: (1) God alone brings man to faith; (2) man unilaterally decides to believe; (3) man cooperates with God (God begins, man completes conversion; or vice versa). Gen. speaking, the synergistic view holds that man is by nature not altogether spiritually dead and that some resist God's call to faith less violently than others.

The synergistic view rests on such arguments as these: (1) if one can do nothing in his conversion, he will become careless and fatalistic; (2) the call to repent (Mk 1:15; Acts 2:38) implies power to repent; (3) if man is entirely passive, conversion is mechanical; (4) God makes conversion possible, man makes it real; (5) since man can hinder conversion (Mt 23:37; Lk 7:30) he can also cooperate in it; (6) ability to resist implies ability to cease resisting.

Scripture teaches that man is by nature spiritually dead (Jn 5:24; Eph 2:1) and antagonistic to spiritual things (Ro 8:7-8; 1 Co 2:14) and that man is saved by God's grace, not by works (Eph 2:8-10). Whatever synergism there is, in the proper sense of the term, follows conversion and is a result of God's monergism in man's conversion (Jn 6:44, 63-65; Ro 9:16; 2 Co 4:6; 5:17; 6:1; Eph 4:24; Cl 1:13). EMP

See also *Synergistic Controversy.*

E. M. Plass, "Synergism," *The Abiding Word,* II, ed. T. F. C. Laetsch (St. Louis, 1947), 299–321.

Synergistic Controversy. In the 2d ed. of his *Loci* (1535), P. Melanchthon* taught 3 cooperating causes in conversion: (1) God's Word; (2) the Holy Spirit; (3) man's will not resisting God's Word. Like D. Erasmus,* he ascribed to man the ability to apply himself to grace. This synergistic view found expression in the Leipzig Interim* 1548. But controversy did not arise till J. Pfeffinger* formulated Melanchthonian theses on free* will 1555. J. Stoltz* countered with 110 theses 1556 and was supported by N. v. Amsdorf* and M. Flacius* Illyricus. V. Strigel* was imprisoned 1569 for opposing the 1568–69 Konfutationsbuch.* Synergism was debated at Weimar Aug. 2–8, 1560 (see also *Weimar, Colloquies and Conventions of*); Strigel held that the unconverted had latent power to cooperate in conversion; Flacius opposed Strigel and was supported by all true Luths. and by the Philippists* of Wittenberg.

The Konfutationsbuch was now enforced so rigorously, esp. by J. Wigand* and M. Judex,* that John* Frederick II countered July 8, 1561, by depriving ministers of the right to excommunicate and vesting this power in a consistory est. at Weimar. Flacius and his adherents protested against this measure in the name of freedom of conscience and of the ch., where only Christ and His Word are to decide. Flacius, Wigand, Judex, and J. Musäus* were suspended and expelled from Jena Dec. 10, 1561. Strigel was reinstated at Jena May 24, 1562, after signing an ambiguous declaration. J. Stössel* drew up a declaration intending to explain Strigel's declaration in an acceptable way, but only made matters worse; Strigel refused to sign it and 40 Thuringian pastors who refused to sign both Strigel's and Stössel's declarations were deposed and exiled.

Johann Wilhelm (d. 1573) succeeded John Frederick II 1567 and issued an edict Jan. 16, 1568, supporting Luth. orthodoxy; the Philippists left Jena; Flacians (except Flacius) returned. The 1568–69 Altenburg* Colloquy reached unsuccessfully for final solution, which came 1571 in the Final Report and Declaration of the Theologians of Both Universities Leipzig and Wittenberg; it includes this: "Consideration and reception of God's Word and voluntary beginning of obedience in the heart arises out of that which God has begun graciously to work in us." Difference of terminology in explanation persisted. FC I and II reject the extremes of Strigel and Flacius and teach that man is purely passive in his conversion but cooperates with God after conversion.

See also *Synergism.*

Synesius (ca. 370–ca. 414). B. Cyrene, Libya, Afr.; studied at Alexandria, Egypt, under Hypatia*; Neoplatonist; influenced by Origen*; married a Christian wife 403 with the blessing of Theophilus,* patriarch of Alexandria; bp. Ptolemais (chosen 410, consecrated 411 by Theophilus); opposed Anomoeans*; Credited with 10 hymns. Other works include *Oratio de regno; De providentia; De insomniis; Epistolae.*

MPG, 66, 1021–1616.

Synod. See *Councils and Synods; Polity, Ecclesiastical,* 3; *Reformed Churches,* 1.

Synod at the Oak. See *Quercum, Synodus ad.*

Synod of Bishops. See *Councils and Synods,* 1.

Synod of Dort (1574, 1578, and 1618–19). See *Dordrecht, Synods of.*

Synod of Evangelical Lutheran Churches. 1. A few Slovaks came to the US in the 1770s; others came as a result of the 1848 revolution in Hung., settling in Chicago, Ill., and elsewhere. Measures resulting from Hung. dominance led many more to leave their homeland (see *Czechoslovakia*) and settle in Pa., N. Y., Ill., Minn., Calif., and the Northwest, including Wash. and Alaska, in the last decades of the 19th and first decades of the 20th c.

2. In Eur. the founders of the Syn. of Ev. Luth. Chs. had been mems. of the Luth. Ch. (see *Czechoslovakia, 5–7; Slovakia, Lutheran Theology in*). Congs. were organized at Freeland, Pa., 1883; Streator, Ill., 1884; Mount Carmel and Nanticoke, Pa., and Minneapolis, Minn., 1888; Tabor, Minn., 1889. Others followed in the 1890s in Ill., Pa., Conn., N. J., Ohio, N. Y., Minn. For various reasons, including lack of regular and properly indoctrinated Slovak pastors and teachers, some congs. were not strictly confessional Luth.

3. A "Seniorate" was formed by a small group early June 1894 at Mahanoy City, Pa., but soon died, apparently for lack of real spiritual union. Official organ: *Cirkevné Listy* ("Church Letters").

4. Three pastoral conferences were held in Pa. (June 9, 1899, Wilkes-Barre; Jan. 16–17, 1900, and June 4, 1902, Braddock) with a view to organize a Slovak Luth. syn. Organization of the Slovak Ev. Luth. Ch. (*Slovensk-evanjelická augsburgského vyznania celocirkev v Spojenych státoch americkych,* "The Slovak Evangelical Church of the Augsburg Confession in the United States of America," abbreviated S. E. A. V. C.) took place at a meeting held Sept. 2–4, 1902, at St. Peter Luth. Ch., Connellsville, Pa. Official organ: *Lutherán* ("The Lutheran").

Original (1903) charter name: *Celocirkev cili Synoda ev. a. v. slovenská Pennsylvánská* ("The Slovak Evangelical Church or Synod of the Augsburg Confession in Pennsylvania"). Joined Synodical* Conf. 1908. New charter name (1913): Slovak Evangelical Lutheran Synod of the United States of America. See also 6.

5. Controversies threatening disruption and concerning confessional prayer (whether it is necessary to state Christ's deity in a prayer which mentions Him), announcement for Communion, and open Communion arose by 1905. The first was soon settled; the others continued to some extent for ca. 2 decades.

6. Charter amended Jan. 24, 1945, changed name to Slovak Ev. Luth. Ch. *(Slovenská Evanjelická Luteránska Cirkev).*

7. Name changed 1959 to Syn. of Ev. Luth. Chs.

8. SELC pastors and teachers were educ. in Mo. Syn. colleges and sems. For some time the SELC had a prof. of Slovak in Mo. Syn. schools (e. g., Conc. Coll., Fort Wayne, Ind., and Conc. Sem., Springfield, Ill.).

9. The SELC was governed by elected officers and a bd. of directors and held regular convs. every 2 yrs.

10. Funds for for., Negro, and Jewish missions were channeled through the Mo. Syn. and Syn. Conf. respectively; missions in Can. and Argentina were administered by the SELC.

11. Official SELC organs: *Svedok – The Witness* and *Lutheran Beacon* (the latter ceased pub. at end of 1970).

12. SELC youth organized the Slovak Luther League (later simply Luther League) at St. Paul Luth. Ch., Whiting, Ind., Sept. 5, 1927. Official organ: *The Courier.*

13. SELC created a Publication Department. Publications included *Symbolické knihy* (the Book of Concord) and *Písne Duchovní* (Slovak hymnal first issued 1636 by J. Tranovsky.*

14. Services were held in Eng. and Slovak; *The Lutheran Hymnal* was used.

15. SELC est. Lutheran Haven at Oviedo, Fla., with services for aging, families, and children.

16. The SELC Army and Navy Bd. operated in conjunction with the corresponding LCMS commission. JSB

17. SELC pres.: Daniel Jonaten Záboj Laucek 1902–05; John Pelikán 1905–13; Stephen Tuhy 1913–19; J. Pelikán 1919–21; John Somora 1921–22; John Samuel Bradác 1922–39; Andrew Daniel 1939–49; Paul Rafaj 1949–63; John Kovac 1963–69; Milan A. Ontko 1969–71.

18. SELC became an LCMS dist. Jan. 1, 1971. See *Lutheran Church – Missouri Synod, Districts of The,* A 49.

See also *Lutheran Council in the United States of America.*

Synod of Illinois and Other [Adjacent] States, Evangelical Lutheran. See *Illinois, Evangelical Lutheran Synod of,* b.

Synod of Ohio (ULC). See *United Lutheran Church, Synods of,* 19.

Synod of the Lutheran Church Emigrated from Prussia, The. See *Buffalo Synod.*

Synod of the Southwest (or South West). See *Southwest, Synod of the.*

Synod of the West. See *West, Evangelical Lutheran Synod of the.*

Synodical Conference. 1. Fed. of Am. Luth. synods organized 1872 as Evangelisch-lutherische Synodal-Conferenz (Ev. Luth. Synodical Conf.) Proceedings call it Ev. Luth. Syn. Conf. of N. Am.

In 1856 the hope was expressed in *Lehre und Wehre,* II, 3–5, that the Luth. Ch. in Am. would be one, united by sincere and unqualified acceptance of Scripture and the Luth. Confessions, and all Luths. who were confessionally minded were invited to meet with that in view. This led to conferences 1856–59 (see *Free Lutheran Conferences,* 1).

Renewed confessional crisis in the 1860s (see *United States, Lutheran Theology in the,* 8; *United*

States, Lutheranism in the, 8) and est. of the General* Council of the Ev. Luth. Ch. in (N.) Am. led to renewed interest in a confessional intersyn. body. See also *Four Points.* The more staunchly confessional syns. rallied around the Mo. Syn., which reached fellowship agreement with the Wisconsin* Syn. 1869, the Ohio Syn. 1868–72 (see Lutheran Church – Missouri Synod, The, V 15), the Ev. Luth. Syn. of Illinois* 1872; agreement bet. the Mo. Syn. and the Minnesota* Syn. was reached, at the June 1872 Minn. Syn. conv., after discussion bet. that syn. and Mo. Syn. representatives; fraternal relations had existed bet. the Mo. Syn. and the Norw. Syn. (see *Evangelical Lutheran Church, The,* 8–13) since 1857.

2. Preliminary meetings were held Jan. 11–13, 1871, Chicago, Ill., and Nov. 14–16, 1871, Fort Wayne, Ind. Formal organization took place at a meeting held July 10–16, 1872, Milwaukee, Wis. Charter mems.: Mo. Syn., Ohio Syn., Wis. Syn., Norw. Syn., Ill. Syn., Minn. Synod. Vice-pres. W. F. Lehmann*; secy. J. P. Beyer.* See also *United States, Lutheran Theology in the,* 12.

3. The recommendation adopted 1876 that the theol. schools of mem. syns. be combined into 1 school and that it and the teachers sem. come under Syn. Conf. supervision was frustrated by the predestinarian* controversy of the 1880s. State syns. were recommended 1876, to eliminate fragmentation and unite into 1 organization all congs. within a given State or territory, except for language divisions; accordingly, the Ev. Luth. Concordia* Syn. of Va., which joined the Syn. Conf. 1876, became the Conc. Dist. of the Ohio Syn. 1877 and the Ill. Syn. merged with the Ill. Dist. of the Mo. Syn. 1880. Disruption of the Syn. Conf. in the early 1880s prevented further moves in this direction.

4. As a result of the predestinarian* controversy the Ohio Syn. withdrew from the Syn. Conf. 1881, the Norw. Syn. 1883. Dissidents in the Ohio Syn. withdrew from this syn. and organized the Ev. Luth. Concordia* Syn. of Pa. and Other States, which joined the Syn. Conf. 1882, disbanded and merged with the Mo. Syn. 1886. The Gen. Eng. (Ev.) Luth. Conf. of Mo. and Other States (see *Missouri and Other States, The English Evangelical Lutheran Synod of*) joined the Syn. Conf. 1890, became a Mo. Syn. dist. 1911. The Michigan* Syn. joined the Syn. Conf. 1892. The Ev. Luth. Dist. Syn. of Nebr. and Other States joined the Syn. Conf. 1906 (final approval 1910), became a dist. of the Ev. Luth. Joint Syn. of Wis., Minn., Mich., and Other States 1917 (see also *Nebraska, German Evangelical Lutheran District Synod of*). The Slovak Ev. Luth. Ch. (see *Synod of Evangelical Lutheran Churches*) joined the Syn. Conf. 1906 (final approval 1910).

5. The Syn. Conf. acknowledged the canonical writings of the OT and NT as God's Word and the 1580 Book of Concord as her confessional standard.

6. Purposes: external expression of the spiritual unity of mem. syns.; mutual strengthening in faith and confession; promotion of unity in doctrine and practice and elimination of actual or threatening disturbance thereof; united action for common aims; geog. delimitation of mem. syns. except for necessary language divisions; consolidation of all Luth. syns. in Am. into 1 orthodox Am. Luth. Ch.

7. The Syn. Conf. was only an advisory body in all matters in which it had not been given decisive power by all mem. syns. Negro miss. work in the US and Afr. was the only major activity of the Syn. Conf. (see also *Africa,* C 14; *Missions,* 10).

8. Charges against the Mo. Syn. of improper relations with other Luth. bodies and of growing doctrinal laxity led to withdrawal 1963 of the Wisconsin* Ev. Luth. Syn. and the Evangelical* Luth. Syn. from the Syn. Conf., which became inactive 1966. It was dissolved 1967.

9. Pres.: C. F. W. Walther* (Mo. Syn.) 1872–73; W. F. Lehmann* (Ohio Syn.) 1873–76, 1877–80; H. A. Preus* (Norw. Syn.) 1876–77; P. L. Larsen* (Norw. Syn.) 1880–82; J. Bading* (Wis. Syn.) 1882–1912; C. F. W. Gausewitz* (Wis. Syn.) 1912–27; L. E. Fuerbringer* (Mo. Syn.) 1927–44; E. B. Schlüter* (Wis. Syn.) 1944–50; G. C. Barth (Mo. Syn.) 1950–52; W. A. Baepler* (Mo. Syn.) 1952–56; John Samuel Bradác (SELC) 1956–60; John Daniel of Bethlehem, Pa. (SELC) 1960–67. WDU

J. T. Mueller, *A Brief History of the Origin, Development, and Work of the Evangelical Lutheran Synodical Conference of North America, Prepared for Its Diamond Jubilee 1872–1947* (St. Louis, [1948]); W. D. Uhlig, "The Origin of the Synodical Conference," unpub. STM thesis (Con. Sem., St. Louis, Mo., 1965).

Synods. See entries beginning *Synod . . .* and *Synodical . . . .*

Synods, Extinct. Extinct (either no longer existing or no longer existing under the names given) syns. include Alleghany Syn.; Alpha Syn. of the Ev. Luth. Ch. of Freedmen in Am.; Augsburg Syn.; Buffalo Syn.; Cen. Can., Ev. Luth. Syn. of; Chicago Syn.; Conc. Syn. of Pa. and Other States, Ev. Luth.; Conc. Syn. of the West; Conc. Syn. of Va., Ev. Luth.; Franckean Syn.; Ga. Syn.; Hartwick Syn.; Hauge Syn.; Holston Syn.; Ill. Syn. (1846–67); Ill. Syn. (1867–80); Ill., Ev. Luth. Syn. of Cen.; Ill., Ev. Luth. Syn. of Cen. and Southern; Ill., Ev. Luth. Syn. of Northern; Ill., Ev. Luth. Syn. of Southern; Immanuel Syn. of the Ev. Luth. Ch. in N. Am.; Ind. Syn. (I); Ind. Syn. (II); Ind. Syn., Northern; Indianapolis, Ger. Ev. Luth. Syn. of; Iowa and Other States, Ev. Luth. Syn. of; Ky. Syn. (Ev. Luth. Syn. of Ky.); Man. and Other Provinces, The Ger. Ev. Luth. Syn. of; Man. and the NW Territories, Syn. of; Md., Ev. Luth. Syn. of (Md. Syn.); Md., Ger. Syn. of; Md. and Adjacent States, Ger. Ev. Luth. Syn. of (Ger. Syn. of Md. and the South; Ger. Syn. of Md.; Md. and the South Syn.); Md. and Va., The Ev. Luth. Syn. of; Melanchthon Syn.; Miami Syn.; Mich. Syn. (Missionary Syn. of the West); Mich. Syn. (Ev.-Luth. Synode von Michigan und andern Staaten); Mich. Syn. of the ULC; N. J., Ev. Luth. Syn. of (I); N. J., Ev. Luth. Syn. of (II); N. Y., Ev. Luth. Syn. of; N. Y., Ministerium of; N. Y., Syn. of, of the Ev. Luth. Ch.; N. Y., United Luth. Syn. of; N. Y. and New Eng., Ev. Luth. Syn. of; N. Y. and New Eng., United Luth. Syn. of; N. Y. and N. J., Ev. Luth. Syn. of; N. Y. and Other States, Ger. Ev. Luth. Syn. of (Steimle Syn.); N. C., Ev. Luth. Syn. and Ministerium of; N. C., United Ev. Luth. Syn. of; Norw. Syn. (The Norw. Ev. Luth. Ch. in Am.; The Syn. for the Norw. Ev. Luth. Ch. in Am.; see *Evangelical Lutheran Church, The,* 8–13); Syn. and Ministerium of the Eng. Ev. Luth. Chs. in Ohio and Adjacent States (The Eng. Ev. Luth. Syn. and Ministerium of Ohio and Adjacent States; see *Ohio and Other States, The Evangelical Lutheran Joint Synod of,* 4); East Ohio Syn. of the Ev. Luth. Ch. (see *General Synod of the Evangelical Lutheran Church in the United States of America, The,* 3); Ohio Syn. (known by various names 1818–1930); Eng. Ev. Luth. Dist. Syn. of Ohio and Adjacent States (see *Ohio and Other States, The Evangelical Lutheran Joint Synod of,* 4); Syn. of Ohio of the ULC (see *United Lutheran Church, Districts of,* 19); Pa., Ev. Luth. Syn. of Cen. (Cen. Pa. Syn.); Pa., Ev. Luth. Syn. of East (East Pa. Syn.); Pa., Ev. Luth. Syn. of West (West Pa. Syn.); Pa. and Adjacent States, Ministerium of; Pittsburgh Syn. (1845–1919); Pittsburgh Syn. (1867–1919); Southwest, Syn. of the; Steimle Syn. (see *New York and Other States, German Evangelical Lutheran*

Synod of); Susquehanna Syn. of the Ev. Luth. Ch. in the US (see *United Lutheran Church, Synods of,* 23); Susquehanna Syn. of Cen. Pa. of the Ev. Luth. Ch., shortened 1932 to Susquehanna Syn. (see *United Lutheran Church, Synods of,* 23); Tenn. Syn., Ev. Luth.; Tenn., Ev. Luth. Syn. of Middle; Union Syn. of the Evangelic Luth. Ch.; Va. Syn. (1829–1922); Va. Syn. (1922–62); Va. Syn., Cen.; Va. Syn., Southwestern; Va. Syn., Western; Wartburg Syn.; West, Ev. Luth. Syn. of the (Syn. of the West; 1835–46); West, Ev. Luth. Syn. of the (Syn. of the West; 1846; dissolved); West, Missionary Syn. of the (1840s; see *Michigan Synod,* 1; West,* Missionary Syn. of the (Franckean Syn. II; 1866–72); Wittenberg Syn.

See also entries for the synods.

Synthronon (Gk. "with-throne"). Structure combining clergy stalls and bishop's throne; placed against E wall behind altar; now mostly in E chs.

Syria. See *Middle East,* C; *Nonchalcedonian Churches,* 2.

Syriac Bible Versions. See *Bible Versions,* C.

Syrian Arab Republic. See *Middle East,* C.

Syrian Christians. See *India,* 4–8.

Syrian Jacobite Church. See *Monophysite Controversy.*

Syrian Mysteries. See *Mystery Religions.*

Syrian Orthodox Christians. See *India,* 7.

Syrian Orthodox Church of Antioch (Archdiocese of the U. S. A. and Canada). See *Eastern Orthodox Churches,* 6.

Syro-Malabar Rite. See *India,* 7.

Syro-Malankara Rite. See *India,* 7.

Systematic Theology. Branch of theology* that tries to express all religious truth in self-consistent statements forming an organized whole. See also *Revelation,* 10.

Syvstjernen. See *Norway, Lutheranism in,* 8.

T

Tabernacle (from Lat. *tabernaculum,* "tent"). Secure, safe-like receptacle (e. g., cupboard or closet), often richly ornamented, used in RCm for vessels containing host* reserved for Communion outside mass and for adoration; usually attached to an altar.

Tabernacles, Feast of. See *Judaism,* 4.

Table of Duties. See *Haustafel.*

Table of the Lord. See *Grace, Means of,* IV 1.

Table Talk. See *Luther, Table Talk of.*

Taboo (tabu; Tongan *tabu*). Set apart as venerable or as having dangerous supernatural power; forbidden to profane contact. Taboos have been used for various religious and soc. purposes. The term has also been used to designate warning signs used by primitive people.

Taborites. Radical group of Hussites*; named after Tabor, town S of Prague in the former kingdom of Boh. (later a province of W. Czechoslovakia) founded 1420 as a stronghold by J. Ziska (or Zizka) for his followers.

Tabula rasa (Lat. "blank tablet"). Term attached to a theory developed esp. by J. Locke,* who held that man's mind begins as a blank slate, which receives impressions by sense perception (see *Sensationalism*) and later reflection. See also *Psychology,* G 1.

Tacitus, Cornelius (ca. 55–after 117). Roman politician, orator, hist.; quaestor 79, praetor 88, consul 97. Works (titles occur in various forms) include *Historiae; Germaniae; Annales.*

Taffin, Jean (probably ca. 1528/30–1602). B. Tournai; (Tournay; Flemish *Doornik*), Hainaut province, SW Belg.; perhaps educ. Geneva, Switz., under T. Beza* and J. Calvin*; preacher Metz, Antwerp, and Heidelberg; court preacher of William* I (William the Silent; prince of Orange); pastor Haarlem and Amsterdam. Works include *Traicté de l'amendement de vie* (tr. *The Amendment of Life*).

Tahiti. See *Polynesia; Society Islands.*

Taiwan (Formosa). Is. ca. 90/110 mi. off the coast of Fukien province (SE mainland China). Taiwan (ca. 240 mi. long N to S, 85 mi. at its greatest width) is the seat of the Rep. of China (also known as Nationalist China), whose govt. uses the name Taiwan to include 13 or 14 other nearby islands and 64 more comprising the Penghu (Pescadores) group. Quemoy and Matsu, near the mainland, are also under control of the Rep. of China. Taiwan was ceded by China to Japan 1895, returned to China as a province 1945. "Taiwan" is a Chinese name meaning "Terraced Bay." "Formosa" is shortened from "Ilha Formosa" ("Beautiful Isle"), 16th-c. Port. name.

Religions include Confucianism, Buddhism, Taoism, Islam, Christianity. Christianity was brought to Taiwan by Dutch, who controlled the island from the 1620s to the 1660s. Eng. Presbs. began work 1865, Can. Presbs. 1872. RCs claim 2–3% of the pop. The Mustard Seed, Inc., HQ Glendale, Calif., was organized in the 1950s to support certain interdenom. work. LCMS work began 1951 (see *Gruen, Olive Dorothy*); a sem. was est. at Taipeh 1952, moved to Chia Yi 1954, combined with efforts of the Taiwan* Luth. Ch. (related to The ALC) in formation of a Federated Luth. Sem. at Taichung in the early 1970s. The 1st gen. conf. of The China Ev. Luth. Ch. (related to LCMS) was held Sept. 1966; a const. was adopted 1968. Conc. Middle School was est. by LCMS at Chia Yi in the late 1960s. HRR

See also *China,* 9.

Li-wu Hang (Han Lih-wu), *Taiwan Today,* rev. ed. (Taipei, Taiwan, 1952); *(The) Taiwan Christian Yearbook* (Taipei, 1960, 1964, 1968); H. K. Tong, *Christianity in Taiwan: A History* (Taipei, 1961); K. L. Wilson, *Angel at Her Shoulder: Lillian Dickson and Her Taiwan Mission* (New York, 1964).

Taiwan Lutheran Church. Autonomous Luth. body organized 1954; a sem. was est. at Taipei 1957, later moved to Taichung (see also *Taiwan*).

Taizé, Community of (Communauté de Taizé). Interdenom. and ecumenical Prot. monastic order founded 1940 at Taizé, near Cluny, Saône-et-Loire dept., E cen. Fr.

Talisman (from Gk. for "to complete; to initiate into mysteries"). Object engraved or cut with a character or sign and regarded as a good luck charm.

Talley-Rand-Périgord, Charles Maurice de (1754–1838). Statesman; b. Paris, Fr.; priest 1779; bp. Autun 1788; mem. States-Gen. 1789; proposed secularization of ch. property and termination of clergy privileges; excommunicated by pope 1791; minister of for. affairs 1797; helped frame 1801 Concordat (see *Concordat,* 5) and restore Bourbons at fall of Napoleon* I.

Talleyrand-Périgord, Alexandre Angélique de (1736–1821). B. Paris, Fr.; abp. Reims 1777; abp. Paris and cardinal 1817; exponent of ecclesiastical rights.

Tallis, Thomas (Tallys; Talys; probably ca. 1505/20–85). Eng. composer, organist; master of counterpoint. Hymn tunes include "Tallis' Canon," in which the tenor begins the melody when the soprano is on the 5th melody note, and sings the last 4 melody notes while the soprano sings the first 4 (a kind of perpetual fugue.* Other works include the motet *Spem in alium non habui* for eight 5-voice choirs.

Talmage, Thomas de Witt (1832–1902). Pulpit orator; b. near Bound Brook, N. J.; studied law NYC, theol. at Dutch Ref. sem., New Brunswick, N. J. Was pastor of Ref. chs. in N. J., N. Y., and Pa. 1856–69. Presb. pastor Brooklyn, N. Y., 1869–94; Washington, D. C., 1894–99. Works include *The Abominations of Modern Society; Around the Tea-table; The Bright and Morning Star; From Manger to Throne; Every-Day Religion.*

Talmud (Heb. "teaching"). Name of 2 compilations (Babylonian and Palestinian) comprising Mishna(h) and Gemara.

Jewish law rests on the Pentateuch.* But changing conditions, esp. after the exile (see *Babylonian Captivity,* 1) required new decisions and laws long transmitted orally as a rabbinical supplement to the Pentateuch. This material, called Mishna (from Heb. for "repeat"), complete ca. 200 AD, was reduced to writing 200–500, with some material added later.

The Mishna became the text of a still more extended commentary called Gemara (Aramaic "completion"), which is, in effect, an encyclopedia of the knowledge of its times.

The Talmud is a legal source book in the sense that it contains matter connected with Jewish law; that which deals exclusively with the Law is called halakah (halacha[h]; Heb. "way"), the rest (illus-

trative, ethical, hist., biographical, legendary) is called haggada(h) (from Heb. for "to tell").
See also *Judaism,* 2; *Midrash; Tradition.*

Tametsi. See *Ne temere.*

Tamil. 1. A Dravidian* language of Madras (in S India) and N and E Ceylon; closely related to Malayalam.* 2. Mem. of Tamil-speaking group. 3. Script used in writing Tamil.

Tamil Evangelical Lutheran Church. See *India,* 10.

Tamisier, Marie Marthe Emilia. See *Eucharistic Congresses.*

Tanchelm (Tanchelijn; Tanchelinus; Tanquelm[us]; Tanquelin; Tandemus; d. perhaps ca. 1115 [or 1124/25?]). Flemish layman; itinerant preacher Sjaelland (Zealand), Antwerp, and Brugge (Bruges); denounced sacraments of the ch.; opposed lazy and immoral priests; persuaded many that they would be conformed to Christ by asceticism; followers called Tanchelmians.

Tanganyika. See *Africa,* E 7.

Tangier, Voice of. See *Africa,* D 4.

Tanner, Jacob (Oct. 15, 1865–Jan. 25, 1964). B. Molde, Norw.; educ. Christiania (Oslo); ordained in Norw. 1893; to US 1893; pastor Iowa, N. Y., and other states. Taught at Conc. Coll., Moorhead, Minn., 1916–24; Luther Sem., St. Paul, Minn., 1924–38. After retirement taught at Waldorf* Coll.

Tanzania, United Republic of. See *Africa,* E 7.

Taoism. 1. One of the 3 main religions of China (the others: Buddhism* and Confucianism*); traditionally founded by Lao-tzu.*

2. Taoism was first only philos.; it became an organized religion in the 5th c. AD and was made a state cult 440. Embodies elements of quietism.* Named after *tao* (a key term in all ancient Chinese philos. schools; hard to translate; has been rendered, e. g., "way; truth; doctrine; path; road; course; reason; principle; logos [Gk. 'word'; cf. Jn 1:1]"); has been regarded as the eternal and ubiquitous, or universal, impersonal principle, or Spirit, by which the universe was produced and is supported and governed (see also *Chinese Philosophy,* 2), a kind of primary or first cause (see *Causa secunda*); other concepts include nature, providence, order of the universe, rotation of the seasons, time, absolute. Hence, acc. to Taoism, all true virtue and the highest goal of human development consists in being one with tao. He who in self-effacement, suppression of desire, and in meditation tries to understand tao will not perish in death but be saved. Lao-tzu emphasized welfare of the individual, advocating gentleness, moderation, modesty, and love for one's fellowmen.

3. Taoism began to degenerate after Chuang-tzu. It became intertwined with Buddhism, which was introd. into China during the Han dynasty (202 BC–220 AD).

4. Modern Taoism (regarded as founded by Chang Tao-ling [fl. 1st c. AD]) is characterized by superstitious magic, occultism, and a quest for the elixir of immortality. Its pantheon, which to some extent reflects docetic Buddhism, includes San-Ch'ing ("Three Pure Ones," of which Lao-tzu is the 3d). Yü Hwang Shang-ti (Yü-huang shang-ti) is the supreme Taoist god. There are gods for almost everything (e. g., stars, ancestors, parts of the body, ideals, famous hist. beings), temples, a priesthood, and a monastic system with a kind of "pope" (who, however, is not recognized as head by all the Taoist priesthood). Confucianism gained ascendancy over Taoism, but the latter's spirit of harmony, naturalism, peace, and simplicity continues to mark and mold Chinese life.

See also *Chinese Philosophy,* 5; *Chinese Term Question.*

See bibliography of *Religion, Comparative.*

Tappan, William Bingham (1794–1849). B. Beverly, Mass.; apprenticed to clockmaker Boston 1810; employed by American* S. S. Union 1822; licensed as Cong. minister 1840; poet. Hymns include "There Is an Hour of Peaceful Rest."

Tappert, Theodore Gerhardt (May 5, 1904–Dec. 25, 1973). B. Meriden, Conn.; educ. Wagner Coll., Staten Is., N. Y., and Lutheran Theol. Sem., Mount Airy, Philadelphia, Pa. Ordained ULC 1930. Prof. Lutheran Theol. Sem., Mount Airy. Tr. and ed. in collaboration with others, *The Book of Concord.* Coed. and cotr. *The Journals of Henry Melchior Muhlenberg.* Tr. and ed. M. Luther's *Letters of Spiritual Counsel.* Jt. tr. A. H. Böhmer's *Der junge Luther* (Eng. title *Road to Reformation*). Ed. *The Lutheran Quarterly; Lutheran World Review; Lutheran Confessional Theology in America 1840–1880; Selected Writings of Martin Luther.* Tr. *Here We Stand* (from the Ger. of H. Sasse). Other works include *The Church Through the Ages;* "Christology and Lord's Supper in the Perspective of History," *A Reexamination of Lutheran and Reformed Traditions,* II: *Christology, The Lord's Supper and Its Observance in the Church,* pp. 21–35; *The Church in the Changing World; The Lord's Supper: Past and Present Practices.*

Taranger, Absalon (1858–1930). Norw. Luth. jurist; studied theol. and jurisprudence; prof. hist. of law Christiania (Oslo) 1898–1928; also taught ch. law in practical sem. Christiania; advocated separation of ch. and state. Works include textbook on Norw. ch. law.

Targums. See *Bible Versions,* B.

Tarnow, Johann (Johannes Tarnov; Joannes Tarnovius; 1586–1629). Nephew of P. Tarnow*; Luth. theol.; b. Grevesmühlen, Mecklenburg, N Ger.; educ. Rostock, Strasbourg, Basel, Giessen; prof. Rostock 1614; used grammaticohistorical* method. Works include *Exercitationes biblicae.*

Tarnow, Paul (Tarnov; 1562–1633). Uncle of J. Tarnow*; b. Grevesmühlen, Mecklenburg, N Ger.; educ. Rostock; prof. Rostock 1607. Works include a commentary on John's Gospel; writings on ministry and Trin.

Tartaros. See *Hereafter,* C 7.

Tast, Hermann (1490–1551). B. Husum, Schleswig-Holstein, NW Ger.; vicar St. Mary, Husum, 1514; began preaching Luth. doctrine 1522; reformer of Husum and W coast of Schleswig.

Tate, Nahum. See *Psalter, English.*

Tatian (Tatianus; perhaps ca. 110/120 – perhaps ca. 172/180). Apologist; b. perhaps E Syria, perhaps of Gk. parents; studied philos.; to Rome perhaps ca. 150/152; pupil of Justin* Martyr; denounced Gk. mythology and philos.; after Justin Martyr's death Tatian engaged in Gnostic speculation (see *Gnosticism*); Encratite. Works include *Oratio ad Graecos; Diatessaron* (gen. dated shortly after the middle of the 2d c.).

See also *Apologists,* 8; *Encratism.*

Täufer. See *Brethren,* 1.

Tauler, Johann(es) (Taler; Taweler; Tauweler; ca. 1300–61). Ger. mystic; b. Strasbourg; Dominican ca. 1315/18; studied at Cologne; active in Strasbourg, from which he and other Dominicans were driven 1339 by interdict of John XXII (see *Popes,* 13) in conflict with Louis* IV; settled in Basel, Switz.; assoc. with Friends* of God; returned to Strasbourg. Noted preacher. Works include sermons; *Medulla animae.* See also *Mysticism.*

Taurellus, Nikolaus (1547–1606). B. Montbéliard, Fr.; educ. Tübingen, Ger.; prof. medicine and physics Altdorf, near Nürnberg; exponent of Luth. orthodoxy combined with Aristotelian humanism; held that the human spirit was not essentially changed by the fall; combined natural and revealed knowledge and made philos. basic to theol.

Tausen, Hans (1494–1561). Reformer; b. on Fyn,

Den.; entered a monastery; studied at Rostock 1516–19; taught Copenhagen; studied under M. Luther 1523; preached Reformation doctrines Viborg and Copenhagen, also taught Copenhagen; bp. Ribe 1542. Helped est. schools. Tr. Pentateuch into Dan.; helped provide a Dan. agenda. See also *Denmark, Lutheranism in,* 2.

Tavaszy, Sándor (1888–1951). Hung. ref. theol.; educ. Klausenburg (Cluj, in Transylvania*), Jena, Berlin; prof. Klausenburg. Works include *Weltmission des Calvinismus.*

Taverner, Richard (1505?–75). B. Brisley, Norfolk, Eng.; educ. Cambridge and Oxford; clerk of privy seal 1536; licensed to preach 1552; removed from office of accession of Mary* I; sheriff of Oxford under Elizabeth* I. Works include The confessyon of the fayth of the Germaynes; *The Epistles and Gospelles with a brief Postyl upon the same.* See also *Bible Versions,* L 6.

Taylor, James Hudson (1832–1905). B. Barnsley, Yorkshire, Eng.; studied medicine; left for China 1853 (arrived 1854) as 1st agent of short-lived Chinese Evangelization Soc., from which he resigned after ca. 3 yrs.; worked as indep. miss.; returned to Eng. 1860; founded China* Inland Mission 1865 and served it till he died. Works include *China: Its Spiritual Need and Claims.*

Taylor, Jeremy (1613–67). "The Chrysostom of Eng."; Angl. prelate; b. Cambridge, Eng.; educ. Cambridge; lectured at St. Paul's, London; renowned preacher; chaplain to W. Laud* and Charles* I (see *Presbyterian Confessions,* 1); after fall of Royalists, taught school in Wales; bp. Down and Connor 1661. Works include *A Discourse of the Liberty of Prophesying; The Rule and Exercises of Holy Living; The Rule and Exercises of Holy Dying; A Course of Sermons for All the Sundays of the Year; The Golden Grove* (devotions).

Taylor, John (1808–87). B. Milnthorpe, Westmoreland Co., Eng., of nominally Angl. parents; apprenticed to learn the trades of cooper and turner; Meth. preacher ca. 1825; to Toronto, Can., 1832; briefly assoc. with Irvingites (see *Irving, Edward*); bapt. Mormon 1836; with Mormons to Mo. 1838; Mormon apostle 1838. Ed. *Times and Seasons* (official Mormon periodical) and owned and pub. *Nauvoo Neighbor* (newspaper) at Nauvoo, Ill.; to Utah with B. Young*; mem. territorial legislature 1857–76; probate judge Utah Co. 1868–70; territorial supt. of schools 1877; acting pres. of the Utah branch of the Mormon Ch. 1877, pres. 1880. Miss. (from 1840) to Eng., Ireland, Scot., Isle of Man, Fr., Ger. Est. *The Mormon* (newspaper) N. Y. 1854. Practices plural marriage; went into voluntary exile to escape arrest 1884. Works include *An Examination into and an Elucidation of the Great Principle of the Mediation and Atonement of Our Lord and Savior Jesus Christ.* See also *Latter Day Saints,* b.

Taylor, Nathaniel William (1786–1858). Cong. theol.; b. New Milford, Conn.; educ. Yale Coll., New Haven, Conn.; prof. didactic theol. Yale Divinity School 1822–58; revival preacher; representative of New* Eng. theol. and New* Haven theol. Works include *Practical Sermons; Lectures on the Moral Government of God; Concio ad clerum* (sermon).

Taylor, Thomas Rawson (1807–35). Cong. minister; b. Ossett, near Wakefield, Yorkshire, Eng.; pastor Sheffield 1830; tutor Airedale Coll., Bradford; hymnist; died of consumption. Hymns include "I'm But a Stranger Here."

Taylor, William (1821–1902). Meth. Episc. miss.; b. Rockbridge Co., Va.; connected with Baltimore Conf. of the M. E. Ch. in the 1840s; miss. to Calif. 1849–56; evangelist in E US 1856–62, Eng. and Australia 1862–66, India 1870–75, Eng. 1875, S. Am. 1877–84; bp. for Afr. 1884–96. Works include *Ten Years of Self-supporting Missions in India.*

Tchaikovsky, Petr Ilich (Tschaikovsky; Chaikovski; Peter; 1840–93). Composer and conductor; b. Votkinsk, in W foothills of cen. Urals, Russ. Works include 6 symphonies; 3 piano concertos; a violin concerto; chamber music; music for Liturgy of St. John Chrysostom; a Russ. Vesper Service.

Teacher of Righteousness. See *Dead Sea Scrolls.*

Teachers. 1. The office of Christian teacher is a gift of Christ to the ch. and part of the church's ministry (Eph 4:11-12).

2. 1969 LCMS teachers: more than 6,500 in 1,236 elementary schools; more than 700 in 25 high schools; 600 in 14 colleges. Ratio bet. men and women teachers: similar to that in other schools except on the elementary level, where LCMS ratio of ca. 2,600 men to ca. 4,000 women is higher.

3. Most LCMS men teachers either are graduates of a syn. teachers coll. or became teachers by colloquy; they are certified by syn., classified as ministers of religion, eligible for call by an authorized calling group and for installation, advisory membership in syn., and for a variety of parish services.

4. Mo. Syn. founders included teacher training in the coll. est. 1843 Perry Co., Mo.; the school est. 1846 Fort Wayne, Ind. (see *Löhe, Johann Konrad Wilhelm*) included teacher training; both schools were acquired by the Mo. Syn. 1847. For Conc. Teachers Coll., River Forest, Ill., see *Lutheran Church – Missouri Synod, The,* V 6; includes a graduate program.

5. For the beginning of Conc. Teachers Coll., Seward, Nebr., see *Lutheran Church – Missouri Synod, The,* VI 6. This school became a full teachers sem. 1905; graduated its first teachers 1907; includes a graduate program.

6. Conc. Coll., St. Paul, Minn., prepared students for the teachers school at Addison, Ill. (see *Lutheran Church – Missouri Synod, The,* V 6) 1893–1908, then discontinued such training; included preparation of men and women for teacher training 1947; coll. women teacher trainees were enrolled beginning 1950; a 4-yr. coll. teacher educ. program for women was authorized 1959; male teacher training at the sr. coll. level was authorized 1965.

7. Colloquy requirements include 4 yrs. coll., attendance of at least 1 quarter at a syn. teachers coll., specified courses in educ. and religion, and 1 yr. successful teaching.

8. A call issued to a syn. certified teacher (see 3) conveys rights and obligations not conveyed by a call issued to other teachers.

9. LCMS resolved 1953 to "recognize those called by our congregations for the various activities included in the ministry of the Word as 'ministers of the Word,' whose specific area of responsibility is determined by the congregation which issues the call" (*Proceedings,* p. 327). He is not a pastor but may be called on for some pastoral work. The male teacher's ministerial status is recognized by the US govt.

10. Until recently (see 12) the status of certified women teachers was less clearly defined. Their call is often on a 9–12 mo. basis, renewable at the employer's discretion.

11. The role of women teachers in the ch. has been influenced by interpretations, e. g., of 1 Co 14:34-35; 1 Ti 2:11-15. Their rise to numerical importance has been relatively recent. Their role as wife and mother has often taken them out of school teaching during some of the most productive professional yrs.

12. LCMS resolved 1973 "that all teachers, male or female, who have met all requirements for inclusion in the official roster of the Synod be considered eligible for membership under the terms of Articles V and VI of the Constitution" (*Proceedings,* p. 190).

13. The professional lay teacher's status is a developing one, impossible to describe with finality.

14. Many teachers of elementary school classes are women serving temporarily and without intention of making a career of teaching in Luth. schools; their educ. attainment may range as high as a grad. degree.

15. Graduates of LCMS teachers colleges receive their 1st placement in syn. through the syn. Bd. of Assignments.

16. In LCMS, after 1st placement and assumption of teaching duties, a teacher comes under supervision of officers of the Dist. in which he teaches (see also 17). Synod's Personnel Dir. and the Secy. of Elementary and Secondary Schools keep personnel records and provide lists of candidates and biographical and professional information on teachers.

17. In LCMS, a teacher is under direct supervision of the cong. he serves.

18. Many Luth. professional teachers on the lower levels and most on the higher school levels continue their educ. in various formal ways.

19. Many continue their educ. in less formal ways (e. g., through conferences of the Assoc. of Luth. Secondary Schools, an LCMS organization).

20. Teachers on all levels are mems. of various professional organizations (e. g., LEA; Nat. Education Assoc.).

21. A journal for Luth. teachers has been pub. in the US since 1865; title: *Evangelisch-Lutherisches Schulblatt* (1865–1920), *Lutheran School Journal* (1921–47), *Lutheran Education* (1947–); it is the oldest educ. journal in continuous pub. in the US. Other publications have included *News Service* (from the early 1920s to 1947).

22. Authorized calling groups may secure a list of candidates drawn from names of teachers in service by application to the Dist. pres.; candidates for staff positions at colleges and sems. may be nominated by congs.

23. The decision to accept or not to accept a cali is ideally based on consideration of opportunities for most effective use of talents.

24. In 1972 LCMS had ca. 2,734 men teachers, 4,237 women teachers in 1,238 elementary schools with 151,482 pupils in the US.

25. In 1972 LCMS in the US and Can. had ca. 91,859 teachers and officers in 5,890 S. S. with 719,661 pupils; 43,025 teachers in 4,202 Vacation Bible Schools with 354,348 pupils; 13,600 staff mems. in 5,096 Weekday Religion Classes with 146,393 pupils.

26. LCMS congs. maintain the largest Prot. elementary and secondary school system in N. Am.

27. WELS maintains an extensive school system, many of whose teachers are graduates of Dr. Martin Luther Coll., New Ulm, Minn.; for Milwaukee Lutheran Teachers Coll. see *Ministry, Education of,* VIII C 1 f. WELS Bd. for Parish Educ. pub. *The Lutheran Educator.*

28. The ALC maintains an extensive school system. Wartburg Coll., Waverly, Iowa, reest. teacher training 1961. The Am. Luth. Education Assoc. was founded 1961. The ALC pub. *Lutheran Teacher.*

29. Other Luth. bodies maintaining school systems include LCA and Church* of the Luth. Confession.

30. Seventh-day Adventists maintain an extensive school system with many teachers graduates of such Seventh-day Adv. schools as Andrews U., Berrien Springs, Mich.; Atlantic Union Coll., South Lancaster, Mass.; Pacific Union Coll., Angwin, Calif.; Union Coll., Lincoln, Nebr.; Walla Walla Coll., College Place, Wash. Periodical: *Journal of Adventist Education.*

31. The Nat. Union of Christian Schools, founded 1920, composed of Calvinistic school socs., maintains an extensive school system with many teachers provided by Calvin Coll., Grand Rapids, Mich., an institution of the Christian Ref. Ch. Periodical: *Christian Home and School.*

32. The Prot. Episc. Ch. maintains many schools, many of which belong to the Nat. Assoc. of Episc. Schools, founded 1954.

33. The Nat. Assoc. of Christian Schools, founded 1947, affiliate of Nat. Assoc. of Evangelicals, serves many schools in N. Am. and several miss. fields. Periodical: *Christian Teacher.*

34. Mennonite and Amish bodies maintain many schools with many teachers provided by Eastern Mennonite Coll., Harrisonburg, Va., and Goshen Coll., Goshen, Ind.

35. Other ch. bodies that have maintained schools include Soc. of Friends, Los Angeles Bap. City Miss. Soc., Assemblies of God, Southern Bap. Conv. ACS, WAK, FN

See also *Roman Catholic Church,* E 4, 8, 14; *Schools, Church-Related.*

W. H. Beck, *Lutheran Elementary Schools in the United States,* 2d ed. (St. Louis, 1965); G. W. Brockopp, *The Parish Role of the Lutheran Teacher,* 18th LEA Yearbook (River Forest, Ill., 1961); A. J. Freitag, *College with a Cause: A History of Concordia Teachers College* (River Forest, Ill., 1964); M. A. Haendschke, *The Sunday School Story: The History of the Sunday school in The Lutheran Church – Missouri Synod,* 20th LEA Yearbook (River Forest, Ill., 1963); W. A. Kramer, *Lutheran Schools,* Information Bulletin on Christian Education No. 301 (St. Louis, 1961); V. C. Krause, *Lutheran Elementary Schools in Action* (St. Louis, 1963); A. L. Miller, *Educational Administration and Supervision of the Lutheran Schools of the Missouri Synod, 1914–50,* 8th LEA Yearbook (River Forest, Ill., 1951); R. S. Moore, "Protestant Full-Time Weekday Schools," *Religious Education: A Comprehensive Survey,* ed. M. J. Taylor (New York, 1960), pp. 236–246; A. C. Mueller, *The Ministry of the Lutheran Teacher* (St. Louis, 1964); A. C. Stellhorn, *Schools of The Lutheran Church – Missouri Synod* (St. Louis, 1963).

Te Deum. Opening Lat. words of a canticle (see *Canticles*) in matins; composed in Lat. ca. the beginning of the 5th c.; origin of text uncertain; various musical settings have been written, including one by M. Luther (WA 35, 521–524). *Te Deum laudamus* is Lat. for "We praise Thee, O God."

Te Punga, Hamuera. See *New Zealand,* 3.

Teague, Colin. See *Africa,* C 7; *Carey, Lot(t).*

Teed, Cyrus R. See *Communistic Societies,* 5.

Teellinck, Johannes (Jan.; d. 1674). Son of W. Teellinck*; brother of M. Teellinck*; b. Middelburg, Zeeland province, SW Neth. Pastor Maidstone, Eng.; Wemeldinge, Zeeland, 1641; Eng. ch. Middelburg 1646; Dutch ch. Vlissingen 1649, Utrecht 1654. Held that ch. wealth should remain in the hands of the ch. and not come into the hands of prominent families by inheritance. Forced to leave Utrecht, he was pastor Arnemuiden 1660, Kampen 1661, Leeuwarden 1674. Pietist. Works include *Den vruchtbaermakenden* [or *vrugtbaermakenden*] *wijnstok* [or *Wynstok*] Christus.

Teellinck, Maximiliaan (ca. 1606–53). Son of W. Teellinck*; brother of J. Teellinck*; b. Angers, Fr. Pastor Eng. ch. Vlissingen 1627; Ref. ch. Zierikzee 1628; Middelburg 1540. Pietist. Works include *Vredepredicaatsie.*

Teellinck, Willem (1579–1629). Father of J. Teellinck* and M. Teellinck*; b. Zierikzee, Zeeland prov. Neth.; studied law; lived in Eng. and was persuaded by Puritans to study theol.; studied in Leiden. Pastor Haamstede and Burcht 1606, Middelburg 1613. Works include *De volstandige Christen in dry tractaten; Huysboek over de kleine Catechismus.*

Tegetmeyer, Sylvester (d. 1552). B. Hamburg, Ger.;

influenced by Luth. Reformation* while chaplain Rostock; ev. preacher Riga 1522; called to Dorpat (Tartu) 1525 to restore order out of confusion wrought by M. Hofmann*; organized the ch. in Riga, Reval (Revel; Tallinn), Dorpat; chief pastor St. Peter, Dorpat. See also *Estonia,* 2; *Latvia.*

Tegnér, Esaias (1782–1846). Poet; b. Kyrkerud, near Saffle, Värmland Co., SW Swed.; prof. Gk. at Lund 1812; bp Växjö, Kronoberg Co., S Swed., 1824. Tried to combine Christianity with humanism. Works include *Svea; Tal vid jubelfesten 1817; Frithiofs* [or *Frithjofs*] *Saga.* See also *Sweden, Lutheranism in,* 4.

Teichmüller, Gustav (1832–88). B. Brunswick, Ger.; prof. Dorpat (Tartu); opposed positivism and developmental theories of religion; tried to form a new metaphysic based on the ego and consciousness of the divine; rejected the idea of a new life in Christ. Works include *Religionsphilosophie.*

Teilhard de Chardin, Pierre (1881–1955). Paleontologist and explorer; b. Sarcenat, near Clermont, Fr.; educ. Paris; Jesuit 1899; took part in geological expedition to Ordos, along Great Wall of China, 1923, and in later field studies of China and other parts of Asia; noted for work on Cenozoic geology; interested in the theory of evolution. Works include *Le phénomène humain; L'apparition de l'homme; La vision du passé; Le milieu divin; L'avenir de l'homme.*

Teilhard de Chardin, ed. N. Baybrooke (Greenwich, Conn., 1964).

Telemann, Georg Philipp (1681–1767). Luth. composer, organist, cantor; b. Magdeburg, Ger.; educ. Magdeburg, Zellerfeld, Hildesheim, and Leipzig; largely self-taught in music; active esp. in Hamburg. Works include oratorios *Der Tag des Gerichts; Der Tod Jesu; Die Auferstehung Christi.* Other works include cantatas, psalms, overtures, sonatas. See also *Passion, The.*

R. Hass, *Die Musik des Barocks* (Potsdam, 1927).

Teleological Argument. See *Apologetics, Christian,* I A, B; *God, Arguments for the Existence of; Immortality, Arguments for.*

Teleology (from Gk. for "doctrine, theory, or science of the end"). Branch of philos. that studies evidences of design or goal-directed activity, including purposive activity, systems of purposive activity, special concepts used to distinguish purposive from nonpurposive activity, identification of functions, systems of functional activity, and special concepts used to analyze activity. See also *Apologetics, Christian,* I A, B; *Finalism; God, Arguments for the Existence of; Immortality, Arguments for.*

Telepathy. See *Psychical Research.*

Television. See *Radio and Television Evangelism, Network.*

Teller, Romanus (1703–50). Father of W. A. Teller*; ev. theol.; b. Leipzig, Ger.; pastor and prof. Leipzig. Works include *Die Heilige Schrift des Alten und Neuen Testaments, nebst einer vollständigen Erklärung derselben, welche aus den auserlesensten Anmerkungen verschiedener Engländischen Schriftsteller zusammengetragen, und zuerst in der französischen Sprache an das Licht gestellet, nunmehr aber in dieser deutschen Uebersetzung auf das neue durchgesehen, und mit vielen Anmerkungen und einer Vorrede begleitet.*

Teller, Wilhelm Abraham (1734–1804). Son of R. Teller*; b. Leipzig, Ger.; educ Leipzig; prof. Helmstedt 1761; mem. of high consistory Berlin and provost Kölln (13th-c. Wendish village near Berlin; now part of Berlin) 1767; tried to surmount orthodoxy and pietism by use of rationalism. Works include *Lehrbuch des christlichen Glaubens; Wörterbuch des Neuen Testaments.*

Temperance. See *Intemperance.*

Temperance Movements and the Lutheran Church. Temperance movements, advocating abstinence from use of intoxicants, try to deal with an old problem (cf. Gn 9:21). Unsuccessful attempts to cope with the problem in the US by state and local laws in the 19th and 20th c. led to the 18th Amendment to the Const. of the US, which went into effect early 1920 and prohibited "the manufacture, sale, or transportation of intoxicating liquors within, the importation thereof into, or the exportation thereof from the United States and all territory subject to the jurisdiction thereof for beverage purposes." The Volstead Act (named after its author, congressman Andrew John Volstead; 1860–1947; b. Goodhue Co., Minn.; mem. US House of Representatives 1902–22), passed Oct. 1919, designed for enforcement of the 18th Amendment, defined intoxicants as beverages with "one-half of one per centum or more of alcohol by volume." The 21st Amendment, passed and ratified 1933, repealed the 18th or Prohibition Amendment.

Maine enacted a law 1846 prohibiting the sale of liquor by any except those designated by selectmen.

The General* Syn. of the Ev. Luth. Ch. in the USA resolved 1853 that "this General Synod views with pleasure the success thus far attending the efforts for the removal of Intemperance by the introduction of the Maine Liquor Law, and would be glad to see our ministers and people co-operating with others in extending its principles throughout our land" (Proceedings, p. 47); 1889: "The General Synod of the Evangelical Lutheran Church in the United States, in Allegheny assembled, in accord with previous deliverances of the Synod, bids the Prohibitory Constitutional Amendment in Pennsylvania Godspeed, and hopes her members, in the exercise of their Christian liberty as citizens, will all vote for it" (Proceedings, p. 8); but Pa. rejected the proposed amendment. In 1918 the Gen. Syn. adopted the report of its Committee on Temperance, which stated: "For this [widespread state ratification of the 18th Amendment] and all the great victories over the organized and nefarious liquor traffic we give devout thanks to the great Head of the Church, Who has beyond question providentially led and helped us in the great contest. Our Church of the General Synod has ever been found on the right side, and by her ministers and laymen has actively and practically assisted in achieving this most significant victory of moral reform of all time" (Proceedings, p. 111).

The Ev. Luth. Syn. of N. Illinois* resolved 1853 that "we, as a Synod, and as individuals, will give our influence to the introduction and establishment of a 'liquor law,' that shall be similar in its provisions to the 'Maine Law,' for the total suppression of this evil" (Minutes, p. 17).

In 1890 The United* Norw. Luth. Ch. in Am. resolved "that it is the duty of every church member and of every citizen to take active part by word and example in wiping out this impious and ruinous traffic" (Proceedings, p. 122).

The Scand. Ev. Luth. Augustana Syn. (see *Augustana Evangelical Lutheran Church*) resolved 1889 "I. That we regard it as the duty of the Christian Church earnestly to require of its members to lead a strictly temperate life.

"II. That it is the duty of every church-member to use all his or her influence and such lawful christian means as are at his or her disposal in the furtherance of true temperance in society and the state at large.

"III. That it is the special duty of parents and guardians to youth thoroughly to instruct them in the principle of true temperance, properly to present to them the evils of intemperance according to the teachings of God's Word, science and every-day experience" (Proceedings, p. 81).

1890 Augustana Syn. Proceedings, pp. 81–82: "Resolved by the Scand. Ev. Luth. Augustana Synod

. . . That it heartily endorses the action of the Nebraska Conference in making preparations for a vigorous campaign, and that it recommends to the voters of that state the adoption of the Prohibition Amendment to the State Constitution at the next November election;

"Furthermore that as material aid is in great need in this campaign, we as a Synod also recommend to our people to give liberal donations to the Nebraska Prohibitory Campaign fund."

In 1930 the Augustana Syn. resolved to "reaffirm our steadfast purpose to oppose any and all measures looking to the repeal of the Eighteenth Amendment" (Proceedings, p. 45).

Other syns. took similar stands and action.

LCMS passed no resolutions on manufacture and sale of intoxicating liquors (cf. Ro 14:3, 15-21) but holds that excessive drinking is sinful and that reform can be achieved only through the Gospel of Christ. ARS

See also *Alcoholism*.

Templars, Knights. See *Military Religious Orders,* b.

Temple, William (1881–1944). Angl. theol.; b. Exeter, Eng.; educ. Rugby and Oxford; headmaster Repton 1910–14; chaplain to king 1915–21; canon Westminster 1919–21; bp. Manchester 1921–29; abp. York 1929–42, Canterbury 1942–44. At first somewhat liberal, later more orthodox; active in educ. and soc. work and ecumenical* movement; mem. Labor Party. Works include *Christus Veritas* (Eng. title *Christ the Truth*); *Christian Faith and Life; Nature, Man and God; Christianity and Social Order; Fellowship with God.* See also *Dialectical Realism.*

Temporal Power. See *Church and State; Papacy; States of the Church.*

Temporal Sword. See *Two Swords.*

Temptation. The act of putting a quality of man to the test, specifically his life with and toward God. Purposes, acc. to the Bible: 1. God aims to make man's need of God clear and drive man to God as source of spiritual life (1 Co. 10:13); 2. Devil, world, and flesh aim to loosen man's grasp on God and plunge man into thoughts and acts contrary to his life in and for God (Ja 1:13-15; 4:1-5), but God can use also these tests for His purpose (Jb 1–42). The alert Christian will in soberness and patience recognize the struggle in his life bet. the forces of God and those of sin and will value every reminder to strengthen his spiritual life and grow in grace (Ph 2–3; 1 Th 5; 1 Ptr 5). RRC

R. R. Caemmerer, "Temptation," *The Abiding Word,* II, ed. T. Laetsch (St. Louis, 1947), 171–199.

Tempus clausum (Lat. "closed season"). Season in which festivities and merrymaking (e. g., weddings) were forbidden by the ch. The prohibition applied to Lent (or Quadragesima*) is in the 52d canon of the Syn. of Laodcea.* The 1091 Syn. of Benevento, It., extended the prohibition to Advent, the 1284 Syn. of Nimes (Nismes), Fr., to the period from the 1st of the Rogation* Days to the 1st Sun. after Pent. The Council of Trent,* Sess. XXIV, Chap 10 on the Reform of Matrimony, commands "that from the Advent of our Lord Jesus Christ till the day of the Epiphany, and from Ash Wednesday till the octave of Easter inclusive, the old prohibitions of solemn nuptials be carefully observed by all." CIC, Canon 1108, allows marriage to be contracted at any time of the yr.; only the solemn blessing of marriage is forbidden from the 1st Sun. of Advent to Christmas inclusively and from Ash Wed. to Easter inclusively. The Luth. Ch. gen. recommended observance of *tempus clausum,* esp. Lent.

Ten Articles. See *Anglican Confessions,* 1.

Ten Articles on the Church's Freedom and Service. Adopted 1963 by ch. leaders in East Ger. to guide Christians living under atheistic govt. The arts. treat 1. The Church's Mission; 2. Faith and Obedience; 3. Science and Faith; 4. Justification and Justice; 5. Reconciliation and Peace; 6. Work; 7. Government; 8. The Church's Life and Service; 9. The Church's Polity; 10. The Church's Hope.

Ten Commandments. See *Decalog.*

Ten Lost Tribes. Tribes of Israel carried into captivity (see *Babylonian Captivity,* 1) whose descendants did not return; various theories have tried to identify later descendants. See also *Anglo-Israelism.*

Ten Theses of Bern. See *Reformed Confessions,* A 2.

Tenebrae (Lat. "darkness"). In the W Ch., the service of matins* and lauds on the last 3 days of Holy Week. Acc. to ancient custom the lights in the ch. are extinguished one by one as the service proceeds. Lessons in the 1st nocturn are customarily from Lm.

Tengström, Jakob (Jaakko Tengstrom; 1755–1832). Luth. churchman, poet, and hist.; b. Kokkola, Fin.; educ. Turku (Aabo); prof. Turku 1790–1803; bp. Turku 1803; abp. Fin. 1817; interested in humanities. Works include *Handlingar till upplysning i Finlands kyrkohistoria.*

Tennent, Gilbert (1703–64). Son of W. Tennent*; b. Armagh Co., Ireland; to US with his father ca. 1717/18; educ. in his father's "log coll."; licensed to preach 1725; tutor in "log coll."; Presb. pastor New Brunswick, N. J., 1726; joined G. Whitefield* 1740; Presb. pastor Philadelphia, Pa., 1743–4. See also *Presbyterian Churches,* 4 a.

Tennent, William (1673–1746). Father of G. Tennent*; b. Ireland; educ. probably Dublin; Episc. priest 1706; to US ca. 1717/18; Presb. pastor N. Y. and Pa. See also *Presbyterian Churches,* 4 a.

Tennessee, Evangelical Lutheran Synod of Middle (Syn. of Middle Tenn.; Middle Tenn. Syn.). Formed 1878 by mems. of the Ev. Luth. Syn. of Southern Illinois*; joined The General* Syn. of the Ev. Luth. Ch. in the USA 1879; united with Olive Branch Syn. (see *Indiana Synod, Northern; United Lutheran Church, Synods of,* 8) 1894.

Tennessee Synod, Evangelical Lutheran. See *Henkels, The,* 2, 3; *United Lutheran Church, Synods of,* 16, 29.

Tennyson, Alfred (1809–92). Poet; b. Somersby, Lincolnshire, Eng.; educ. Cambridge. Works include *Timbuctoo; The Palace of Art; Oenone; The Lady of Shalott; Locksley Hall; The Princess; Ode on the Death of the Duke of Wellington; The Charge of the Light Brigade; Maud; The Idylls of the King; Enoch Arden; Crossing the Bar; In Memoriam* (tribute to Arthur Henry Hallam; offers a solution for conflicts bet. science and religion). See also *Metaphysical Society, The.*

Terce. See *Hours, Canonical.*

Terence. See *Religious Drama,* 2.

Teresa (Theresa; T[h]eresa de Jesus; 1515–82). B. Ávila, Sp.; mystic; visionary reformer; Carmelite. Works include autobiography and *El camino de la perfección* ("The Way of Perfection").

Teresa of Lisieux. See *Thérèse de Lisieux.*

Terminism. 1. View that has fixed a certain term of grace accorded man as an individual. The Terministic Controversy raged in Germany ca. 1699–1704. Attempts were made to defend terminism on basis, e. g., of Mt 3:10; 7:21; 20:1-16; Heb 6:4-12; 2 Ptr 2:20-22. Opposition to terminism was based, e. g., on Is 65:2; Lk 23:34-43; Ro 5:20 and held that God desires the salvation of everyone during his whole life and that an abbreviated day of grace is due to self-hardening of the heart against the means of grace.*

2. Nominalism.* See also *Ockham, William of.*

Territorial System (Territorialism). Theory that temporal rulers have, by virtue of their office, the right to govern the ch. and determine its doctrines; distinguished from collegialism.* See also *Augsburg, Religious Peace of; Polity, Ecclesiastical,* 4; *Thomasius, Christian.*

Terrores conscientiae. See *Contrition.*

Terry, Milton Spenser (1840–1914). M. E. cleric; b. Coeymans, Albany Co., N. Y.; educ. N. Y. Conf. sem. Charlotteville, N. Y., and Yale Divinity School, New Haven, Conn.; pastor near NYC; prof. Heb., OT exegesis, and theol. Garrett Biblical Institute, Evanston, Ill. Works include *Biblical Apocalyptics; Biblical Dogmatics; Biblical Hermeneutics.*

Tersanctus. See *Canticles.*

Tersteegen, Gerhard (Terstegen; TerSteegen; ter Steegen; Gerrit; 1697–1769). Prot. poet, devotional writer; b. Mörs (Moers), near Duisburg, Ger.; apprenticed 1713 to his brother-in-law, a merchant at Mülheim an der Ruhr; became an indep. merchant 1717, ribbon weaver 1719; turned to asceticism and seclusion; returned to society and began religious work ca. 1724, preaching, teaching, and helping the poor. Hymns, which include "Gott is gegenwärtig," pub. under title *Geistliches Blumengärtlein.*

Tertiaries (Third Orders Secular). Several RC orders, besides having rules for monks and nuns, have a so-called Third Rule (hence the term tertiaries), under which laymen (men and women) can join these orders; mems. are called Tertiaries, Lay Franciscans, etc. See also *Sisterhoods.*

Tertullian (Quintus Septimius Florens Tertullianus; ca. 155/160–ca. 220/230). B. probably Carthage, son of a pagan centurion; schooled in rhetoric and jurisprudence; Christian perhaps ca. 190/195; catechist (or presbyter) Carthage. Held that the end, preceded by troubles and apostasy, was near, and that only the empire held off impending doom. Espoused Montanism* in later life. Wrote Gk. and Lat., esp. the latter. Known for epigrams, e. g., "The blood of Christians is seed" (*Apol.*, chap. 50). Works include*Apologeticus* (defense of Christianity); *De baptismo; Adversus Marcionem.* See also *Apologists,* 10; *Gnosticism,* 9; *Philosophy; Schools, Early Christian; Tradition.* RPB

R. E. Roberts, *The Theology of Tertullian* (London, 1924); J. Morgan, *The Importance of Tertullian in the Development of Christian Dogma* (London, 1928); B. Nisters, *Tertullian: Seine Persönlichkeit und sein Schicksal* (Münster, 1950).

Test Act. Passed 1673 in Eng.; required one to renounce the doctrine of transubstantiation and to take the oaths of supremacy and allegiance to the king in order to be eligible for pub. office; practically nullified after 1689; repealed 1828. The Corporation* Act of 1661 was also a test act.

Testament of Abraham. See *Apocrypha,* A 4.

Testament of Job. See *Apocrypha,* A 4.

Testament of the Twelve Patriarchs. See *Apocrypha,* A 4.

Tetelbach, Johann(es) (1517–after 1580 [perhaps ca. 1598]). B. Dinkelsbühl, W Bav., Ger.; educ. Wittenberg; pastor Dinkelsbühl; expelled 1549 for refusing to submit to Augsburg Interim*; pastor and conrector Holy Cross Ch., Dresden; pastor Meissen; supt. Chemnitz; expelled 1568 on suspicion of being a follower of M. Flacius* Illyricus; pastor Schwandorf, in the Upper Palatinate; supt. Burglengenfeld, Upper Palatinate, 1580. Works include *Gülden Kleinrod Lutheri in Frag' und Antwort,* an explanation of M. Luther's catechism.

Tetragrammaton. See *Shem hammephorash.*

Tetrapolitan Confession. See *Reformed Confessions,* D 1.

Tetzel, Johann (Diez; Tietze; Tezel[ius]; ca. 1465–1519). B. Pirna, near Meissen, Ger.; educ. Leipzig; Dominican ca. 1487/90; indulgence salesman. See also *Indulgences; Luther, Martin,* 8; *Reformation, Lutheran,* 8.

Teutonic Knights. See *Military Religious Orders,* c.

Teutsch, Friedrich (1852–1933). Son of G. D. Teutsch*; b. Schässburg (Sighisoara; Segesvár), Sibiu province, cen. Romania, in Transylvania*; educ. Heidelberg, Leipzig, Berlin; held various positions; bp. of ev. Saxons in Transylvania 1906; bp. of ev. ch. in Romania 1927. Works include *Geschichte der ev. Kirche in Siebenbürgen.*

Teutsch, Georg Daniel (1817–93). Father of F. Teutsch*; b. Schässburg (Sighisoara; Segesvár), Sibiu province, cen. Romania, in Transylvania*; educ. Schässburg; teacher 1842, rector 1850 Gymnasium at Schässburg; pastor Agnetheln 1863; bp. of ev. Saxons in Transylvania 1867. Worked for ch. renewal and indep. of ch. from state.

Texas-Louisiana Synod. See *United Lutheran Church, Synods of,* 28.

Texas Lutheran College. See *Ministry, Education of,* VIII B 24.

Texas Synod. See *United Lutheran Church, Synods of,* 28.

Textual Criticism. 1. That branch of study which traces the hist. of the transmission of ancient texts with a view esp. to determine the most ancient form of a given text, thereby laying the basis for interpretation. Also called lower criticism because of its basic or primary character; cf. *Higher Criticism.*

2. There are perhaps ca. 200,000 variant readings in NT MSS (see *Manuscripts of the Bible,* 3 b); some arose inadvertently, others by design. Origen* tried to cope with some variants. A "Textus* receptus" gradually became standard; later studies hold some other readings in higher regard.

3. The importance of ancient versions and ch. fathers for NT textual criticism was recognized by J. Mills.* J. A. Bengel* noted "families" of MSS and formulated basic principles of textual criticism that emphasized preference for the more difficult readings. J. J. Wettstein* introd. a system of numbering MSS. See also *Griesbach, Johann Jakob; Hort, Fenton John Anthony; Lachmann, Karl Konrad Friedrich Wilhelm; Lake, Kirsopp; Soden, Hans Karl Hermann von; Tischendorf, Lobegott Friedrich Constantin von; Westcott, Brooke Foss.* FWD

See also *Theology.*

The New Testament in the Original Greek, ed. and rev. B. F. Westcott and F. J. A. Hort, 2 vols. (New York, 1882–89); A. Souter, *The Text and Canon of the New Testament,* rev. C. S. C. Williams, 2d ed. (London, 1954); W. Arndt, "The Chief Principles of New Testament Textual Criticism," *CTM,* V (1934), 577–584; F. G. Kenyon, *Our Bible and the Ancient Manuscripts,* rev. A. W. Adams (London, 1958); E. E. Flack, "The Sacred Text: The Lutheran Evaluation of Biblical Criticism," *What Lutherans Are Thinking,* ed. E. C. Fendt (Columbus, Ohio, 1947), pp. 48–71; I. M. Price, *The Ancestry of Our English Bible,* 3d rev. ed. W. A. Irwin and A. P. Wikgren (New York, 1956); B. M. Metzger, *Annotated Bibliography of the Textual Criticism of the New Testament 1914–39;* K. Aland, *Kurzgefasste Liste der Griechischen Handschriften des Neuen Testaments,* I (Berlin, 1963) and *Studien zur Überlieferung des Neuen Testaments und seines Textes* (Berlin, 1967); *Materialien zur neutestamentlichen Handschriftenkunde,* I, ed. K. Aland (Berlin, 1969); *Die alten Übersetzungen des Neuen Testaments, die Kirchenväterzitate und Lektionare,* ed. K. Aland (Berlin, 1972).

Textus receptus (Lat. "received text"). Gen. accepted text of a literary work. The Gk. NT textus receptus is said to be traceable to ca. 300 or earlier; its form spread widely and came to be known as the Byzantine text and is in substance the text of the Complutensian Polyglot (see *Lexicons,* B; *Polyglot Bibles*), of D. Erasmus,* R. Estienne* I, and T. Beza.* The Lat. name reflects a phrase in the preface of the 2d ed. pub. by the Dutch Elzevir (Elzevier; Elsevier) family of publishers 1633 and underlies the KJV (see *Bible Versions,* L 10). See also *Textual Criticism,* 2.

Thadden-Trieglaff, Adolf Ferdinand von (1796–1882). B. Berlin, Ger.; army officer; bought the Trieglaff estate in Pomerania; leader in revival movement; opposed Prussian* Union; joined Old Luth. Free Ch. (see *Old Lutherans*).

Thailand. See *Asia,* C 4.

Thales (ca. 640/624–ca. 548–543). One of the 7 Sages, or Wise Men, of Greece (the others, acc. to a gen. accepted list: Bias of Priene, Chilon of Sparta, Cleobulus of Lindus, Periander of Corinth, Pittacus of Mitylene, Solon of Athens). B. probably Miletus; regarded as founder of Gk. geometry, astronomy, and philos.; held a form of monism* acc. to which everything is a form of water. See also *Philosophy.*

Thalhofer, Valentin (1825–91). RC liturgist and exegete; b. Unterroth, near Ulm, Ger.; prof. Dillingen, Munich, Eichstätt. Works include *Handbuch der katholischen Liturgik.*

Thamer, Theobald (1502–69). B. Oberehnheim, Alsace; educ. Wittenberg; prof. Gk. at Frankfurt an der Oder 1540; prof. theol. Marburg 1543; championed Luth. doctrine of Lord's Supper over against A. G. Hyperius*; experiences in Schmalkaldic* War led him to write against faith without works; rejected Protestantism 1548; preacher Frankfurt am Main 1549, dismissed 1552; rejoined RC Ch. 1553/55; preacher Minden; canon Mainz; prof. Freiburg im Breisgau 1566.

Thangbrand (Dankbrand; Thangbrandur; Tangbrand; Thankbrandr; fl. toward end of 10th c. AD). Perhaps Anglo-Saxon or Flemish priest; miss. to Iceland 997–999 (see *Iceland,* 2), which he prepared for official acceptance of Christianity (1000). See also *Norway, Early Christianity in.*

Thanksgiving Day. Many special days of thanksgiving have been observed from time immemorial. In medieval Eng., Lammas (from "loaf" + "mass"; popularly apprehended as from "lamb" + "mass") Day (Aug. 1; feast of St. Peter's Chains in the RC calendar; cf. Acts 12:3, 6-7) was probably a thanksgiving at which bread from first ripe grain was used at mass. Special forms of thanksgiving for abundant harvests were occasionally authorized from the end of the 18th c. The custom of using bread from first ripe grain at mass was revived in the early 1840s; an annual thanksgiving soon replaced, or was combined with (cf. Ger. *Erntedankfest*), the traditional Harvest Home, which was a celebration in which thanksgiving was not necessarily prominent. The proposed Rev. Prayer Book of 1927–28 provided a collect, Epistle, and Gospel for such a day; the 1789 Am. Prayer Book has a form for thanksgiving.

In the US, the Pilgrim Fathers observed an occasion of thanksgiving perhaps on arrival 1620, surely no later than their 1st harvest 1621. In course of time other days of thanksgiving were observed. Thanksgiving Day as a nat. religious festival observed on the same day throughout the country dates from 1863. It was observed on the last Thu. in Nov. through 1938. In 1939 it was moved to the 2d-last Thu. in Nov. This met with widespread objection and led to confusion as to date of actual observance 1939–41. On basis on Dec. 1941 congressional action, Thanksgiving Day is the 4th Thu. in Nov. See also *Church Year,* 17.

Thayer, Joseph Henry (1828–1901). Congr. scholar; b. Boston, Mass.; educ. Harvard Coll., at Cambridge, Mass., and Andover (Mass.) Theol. Sem.; pastor Salem, Mass., 1859–64. Tr. J. G. B. Winer's* *Grammatik des neutestamentlichen Sprachidioms.* See also *Grammars,* B; *Lexicons,* B.

Theater. Ancient heathen authors (e. g., Xenophon, Plato, Plutarch, Ovid, Seneca, Tacitus) pointed out dangers of the theater. Early Christian leaders (e. g., Ambrose, Chrysostom, Clement of Rome, Cyril of Jerusalem, F. Lactantius, Salvianus, Tertullian) opposed the theater of their day as incompatible with Christianity. Classical drama was crushed for ca. 1,000 yrs.

On the theater in the Middle Ages see *Religious Drama,* 2.

M. Luther was interested in tragedies and comedies (St. L. ed. 22, 1826). He felt that comedies, despite their obscenity, should be read by youths in order that they might learn Lat. and because comedies urged youth to marry and taught the duties of various stations in life (Wa-T 3, 278 and 690). Though opposed to their immorality, idolatry, and other anti-Scriptural thought, Luther quoted ancient dramatists to illustrate or elucidate (e. g., WA 20, 122–123; 28, 523; 31 I, 440; 42, 511 and 534; 51, 228). He opposed theatrical (Ger. *schauspielerartig*) religious dramas as presented by RCs, but encouraged drama used for spreading the Word, pointing out that when preaching of the Word was forbidden in the Neth., many were converted through religious plays (St. L. ed. 21b, 2856). See also *Religious Drama,* 3.

Luth. theologians in Ger. (e. g., J. K. Dannhauer, J. F. Buddeus) included comedies among plays objectionable because they arouse evil desires. Luths. in Am. (e. g., C. F. W. Walther, A. L. and T. C. Graebner, C. C. Schmidt, L. Fuerbringer) continued to warn against the evils of the theater of their day.

1935 NLC resolutions include: "Motion-pictures might be at all times, and often are, legitimate entertainment as well as an important educational factor. . . . But at the present time many pictures stand charged with serious offenses against decency and morality. . . . We appeal to our Lutheran people to withhold their patronage from all motion-pictures which have a degrading influence and are a menace to home, church, and country. We call upon them to make their influence felt in creating a public opinion which will demand the suppression of that which corrupts and distorts life. We hold that as citizens they must bring pressure to bear to secure legislation which will deal with the evil at its source, that is, where the pictures are made."

The 1940s witnessed improvement in the type of pictures shown in response to aroused pub. opinion. There were indications that movies and theaters were at times being used for cultural and educ. purposes. EM

C. F. W. Walther, *Tanz und Theaterbesuch* (St. Louis, 1887), pp. 59–118, and "Etwas, den Theaterbesuch betreffend," *Der Lutheraner,* XXV 1868–69), 92–94; A. L. Graebner, "Das heutige Theater," *Der Lutheraner,* LVI (1900), 17–20; C. C. S[chmidt], "Das Theater im Gegensatz zum Christenthum," *Der Lutheraner,* XLVIII (1892), 72; L. Fuerbringer, "Das heutige Theater," *Der Lutheraner,* LX (1904), 18–19; T. C. Graebner, "Das heutige Theater," *Der Lutheraner,* LXX (1914), 154–157; "The National Lutheran Council Holds Its Election and Issues Pronouncements on War and Movies," *CTM,* VI (1935), 305–308.

Theatines (Theatine Fathers; Cong. of Clerics Regular). Founded 1524 Rome by Cajetan* of Thiene and others, including G. P. Caraffa (see *Paul IV*), first superior of the group, who had been bp. Chieti, It. (Lat. *Teate,* or *Theate;* hence the name Theatines); purpose: to elevate clerical and lay morality and combat Lutheranism; known for miss. work. See also *Christian Church, History of,* III 9; *Counter Reformation,* 6; *Somascha, Order of Clerks Regular of.*

Theban Legion. See *Maurice.*

Thebesius, Adam (Thebes; 1596–1652). B. Seifersdorf, near Liegnitz, Ger.; educ. Wittenberg. Pastor Mondschütz, near Wohlau, 1619; Wohlau 1627; Liegnitz 1639. Hymnist. Hymns include "O grosser Schmerzensmann."

Theiner, Augustin (1804–74). Brother of J. A. Theiner*; RC theol.; b. Breslau, Prussia; prefect of Vatican archives 1855; dismissed 1870 under charge of collaboration with the opposition. Works include *Geschichte der geistlichen Bildungsanstalten.*

Theiner, Johann Anton (1799–1860). Brother of A. Theiner*; RC theol.; b. Breslau, Prussia; prof. exegesis and canon law Breslau 1824; opposed celibacy. Works include *Die Einführung der erzwungenen Ehelosigkeit bei den christlichen Geistlichen und ihre Folgen* (2d ed. 1845 with A. Theiner).

Theism. In opposition to atheism,* gen. term for belief in God or gods; in restricted sense opposed to deism* and pantheism*: monotheistic belief in a personal God, who is Creator, Preserver, and Ruler of the world.

T. C. Graebner, *God and the Cosmos* (Grand Rapids, Mich., 1932); L. S. Keyser, *A System of Natural Theism* (Burlington, Iowa, 1917).

Theiss, John William (Johannes Wilhelm; Sept. 20, 1963–Mar. 3, 1932). B. Zelienople, Pa.; educ. Conc. Sem., St. Louis, Mo. Pastor Madisonville, Ohio, 1886–89; Portland, Oreg., 1889–93; Santa Rosa, Calif., 1894–1904; Los Angeles, Calif., 1904–28. Pres. Calif. and Nev. Dist. of the Mo. Syn. 1920–24. Watercolorist. Poet. Works include *Gepflückt am Wege; Sang und Klang fürs Christenhaus; Heimwärts; In der Feierstunde: Lieder und Gedichte.*

Theocracy. Form of govt., as that of ancient Israel, in which God is recognized as civil ruler.

Theodicy (from Gk. *theos,* "God," and *dike,* "right, judgment"). Vindication of God, esp. in His justice, wisdom, goodness, and love. The name is drawn from use of the term in the title of a work by G. W. v. Leibniz.*

Theodore of Mopsuestia (ca. 350–ca. 428). Brother of Polychronius*; exegete of the Antiochene school; presbyter Antioch ca. 383; bp. Mopsuestia, Cilicia, Asia Minor, on the Pyramus (Ceyhan) R., ca. 392. Works include commentaries on books of the Bible. See also *Exegesis,* 4; *Schools, Early Christian,* 4; *Three Chapters, Controversy of.*

Theodore of Studion (Theodore of Studios; Theodore of the Studion; Theodore the Studite; Theodorus Studita; Theodoros Studites; ca. 759–826. Brother of Joseph* of Thessalonica; b. Constantinople; priest ca. 787/788; abbot Saccudium, near Mt. Olympus, Bithynia, 794; banished to Thessalonica 796 for opposing adulterous 2d marriage of Constantine VI (771–ca. 797; Roman emp. 780–797 [under maternal guardianship 780–790]; killed by mother Irene, who usurped throne); recalled 797; moved with Saccudium community to dormant monastery of Studion (or Studios), Constantinople, 799; in conflict with Nicephorus*; in banishment 809–811; banished again ca. 814/815 for opposing iconoclasm; lived at various monasteries. Works include *Sermones catechetici;* commentaries; orations. See also *Hymnody, Christian,* 2; *Iconoclastic Controversy.*

MPG, 99.

Theodore of Tarsus (ca. 602–690). B. Tarsus, Cilicia; educ. Athens; monk in Tarsus and Rome; abp. Canterbury, Eng., 667/668; to Eng. 669; unified the ch. in Eng. and est. papal supremacy there.

Theodoret of Cyrrhus (or of Cyr; ca. 386/393–before 466). B. Antioch; lector Antioch; monk Apamea, W cen. Turkey; bp. Cyrrhus (Cyr), Syria, 423; influenced by Theodore* of Mopsuestia; deposed 449 by "Robber Syn." of Ephesus,* reinstated by Council of Chalcedon* 451. See also *Exegesis,* 4; *Three Chapters, Controversy of.*

Theodoric (Lat. Theodoricus; Ger. Dietrich; ca. 454–526). "The Great"; b. Pannonia; succeeded his father ca. 474 as king of Ostrogoths; invaded It. 488, completing conquest by 493. Called Dietrich von Bern (Theodoric of Verona) in Teutonic legends. Used as example of fable by M. Luther (e. g., LC, Longer Preface, 11).

Theodoros Studites (Theodorus Studita). See *Theodore of Studion.*

Theodosius I (Flavius Theodosius; ca. 346–395). "The Great"; grandfather of Theodosius* II; b. Sp.; co-Augustus (with Gratian*) for the E 379; made peace with Goths along the Danube 379–386; bap. 380; opposed Arianism* and other heresies and sects; ordered a massacre as countermeasure against a riot at Thessalonica ca. 390 and was barred from ch. and suspended from Communion by Ambrose till performing pub. penance; sole emp. Sept. 5, 394, till his death Jan. 17, 395. See also *Constantinople, Councils of,* 1.

Theodosius II (401–450). Grandson of Theodosius* I; E Roman emp. 408–450 (minority 408–421); fought against Persia, Vandal pirates, Huns; pub. Code of Theodosius (collection of imperial constitutions). See also *Ephesus, Third Ecumenical Council of; Justinian I; Natural Law.*

Theodotians. See *Monarchianism,* A 2.

Theodotus the Fuller (Theodotus of Byzantium [Constantinople; Istanbul]; the Cobbler; the Tanner; fl. end of 2d c. AD). Leading exponent of dynamic monarchianism at Rome; excommunicated by Victor* I. See also *Adoptionism; Gnosticism,* 7 g; *Monarchianism,* A 2.

Theodotus the Money Changer (fl. early 3d c. AD). Monarchian; follower of Theodotus* the Fuller; condemned by Zephyrinus.* See also *Monarchianism,* A 2.

Theodulf (ca. 750/760–821). B. apparently Sp.; abp. Orléans, Fr. 800; employed by Charlemagne* in affairs of state; cultural leader; banished 817/818 under charge of conspiracy. Hymnist. Hymns include "Gloria, laus et honor."

Theologia crucis (Lat. "theol. of the cross"). Term used by M. Luther* in reference to the fact that true theology derives from study of the humiliation and suffering of Christ, in contrast to the *theologia gloriae* (Lat. "theol. of glory") of mystic and scholastic speculation, which holds that true knowledge of God derives from the study of nature, which reflects God's glory. Cf., e. g., WA 1, 353–374, 613, 614.

"Theologia deutsch." See *"German Theology."*

Theological Argument for the Existence of God. See *God, Arguments for the Existence of.*

Theological Education. See *Ministry, Education of.*

Theological Education, Lutheran Graduate. Several Luth. sems in Am. offer graduate theol. educ. Two (former Augustana Theol. Sem., Rock Island, Ill., and former Chicago Luth. Theol. Sem., Maywood, Ill.) began to offer it in the 1890s; these schools are now consolidated in Luth. School of Theol. at Chicago, Ill. Others that have offered it beginning in the 1st part of the 20th c. include Conc. Sem., St. Louis, Mo.; Hamma School of Theol., Springfield, Ohio; Luth. Theol. Sem. at Philadelphia, Pa.; Luth. Theol. Sem., Gettysburg, Pa.

Theological Encyclopedia. See *Encyclopedia, Theological.*

Theological Individualism. See *Individualism.*

Theological Journals (partial list; background given when emphasized by the journal). I. *Scholarly;* quarterly unless otherwise indicated.

Academy: Lutherans in Profession (formerly *The Lutheran Scholar*); quarterly; CPH, 3558 S. Jefferson Ave., St. Louis, Mo.

Acta apostolicae sedis;* RC.

American Ecclesiastical Review, The; monthly except July, Aug.; RC; The Cath. U. of Am. Press, 620 Michigan Ave. NE, Washington, D. C.

Andover Newton Quarterly; Andover Newton Theol. School, 210 Herrick Rd., Newton Centre, Mass.

Andrews University Seminary Studies; Seventh-day Adv. Theol. Sem. of Andrews U., Berrien Springs, Mich.

Anglican Theological Review; Episc.; unofficial; 600 Haven St., Evanston, Ill.
Archive for Reformation History – Archiv für Reformationsgeschichte; annually; Am. Soc. for Reformation Research and Verein für Reformationsgeschichte; Gütersloher Verlagshaus Gerd Mohn, Gütersloh, NE North Rhine-Westphalia, West Ger.
Baptist Quarterly, The; Bap. Historical Soc.; 4 Southhampton Row, London, WC1B 4 AB, Eng.
Bible League Quarterly; Drayton House, Gordon St., London WC1H O AN, Eng.
Bible Today, The; 6 yearly; RC; The Liturgical Press, St. John's Abbey, Collegeville, Minn.
Bible Translator, The; United Bible Societies, 101 Queen Victoria St., London, EC4P, 4EP, Eng.
Biblica; RC; Pontificium Institutum Biblicum, Via della Pilotta, 25, Rome, It.; Biblical Institute Press, Piazza della Pilotta 35, Rome, It.
Biblical Archaeologist, The; The American Schools of Oriental Research, 126 Inman St., Cambridge, Mass.
Biblical Theology Bulletin; 3 yearly; RC; Piazza del Gesù, 45, Rome, It.
Bibliotheca Sacra; Bap.; Dallas Theol. Sem., 3909 Swiss Ave., Dallas, Tex.
Biblische Zeitschrift; 2 yearly; RC; Ferdinand Schöningh, D-4790 Paderborn, Jühenplatz 1, W. Ger.
Calvin Theological Journal, 2 yearly; Ref.; Calvin Theol. Sem., 3233 Burton St., S. E., Grand Rapids, Mich.
Catholic Biblical Quarterly, The; RC; The Cath. Biblical Assoc. of Am.; Cardinal Station, Washington, D. C.
Catholic Historical Review, The; RC; The Am. Cath. Historical Assoc.; The Cath. U. of Am. Press, Washington, D. C.
Christian Scholar's Review; 955 La Paz Rd., Santa Barbara, Calif.
Church History; The Am. Soc. of Ch. Hist.; Swift Hall, U. of Chicago, Chicago, Ill.
Churchman, The; Angl.; Ch. Soc.; Ch. Book Room Press, Ltd., Dean Wace House, 7 Wine Office Court, Fleet St., London, Eng.
Communion (continues *Verbum Caro*); La Communaute de Taize; Taizé-Communauté, Fr.
Concordia Historical Institute Quarterly; Luth.; 801 De Mun Ave., St. Louis, Mo.
Council on the Study of Religion Bulletin, The; 5 yearly; Wilfrid Laurier U., Waterloo, Ont., Can.
Criterion; The Divinity School of the U. of Chicago, Chicago, Ill.
Cross Currents; 103 Van Houten Fields, West Nyack, N. Y.
CTM (*Concordia Theological Monthly* through 1973); 5 yearly; Luth.; Faculty of Conc. Sem., St. Louis, Mo.; 3558 S. Jefferson Ave., St. Louis, Mo. Last issue Jan. 1974.
Dansk teologisk Tidsskrift; G. E. C. Gads Forlag, Copenhagen, Den.
Diakonia; 6 yearly; Matthias-Grünewald-Verlag, Mainz, and Herder Verlag, Vienna, Austria.
Diakonia; Orthodox-RC dialog; John XXIII Center, 2502 Belmont Ave., Bronx, N. Y.
Dialog; Luth.; 2375 Como Ave., St. Paul, Minn.
Duke Divinity School Review, The; 3 yearly; The Divinity School of Duke University; Durham, N. C.
Eastern Churches Review; 2 yearly; Oxford U. Press, Press Rd., Neasden, London, Eng.
Ecumenical Review, The; World Council of Chs.; 150 route de Ferney, 1211 Geneva 20, Switz.
église et théologie; 3 yearly; Faculty of Theol., St. Paul U.; 223 Main St., Ottawa, Ont., Can.
Encounter; Christian Ch.; Christian Theol. Sem., Box 88267, Indianapolis, Ind.
Études théologiques et religieuses; Theol. Faculties of Montpellier, Brussels, Paris, and Strasbourg; 26, boulevard Berthelot, Montpellier, Fr.
Evangelical Quarterly, The; Ref.; Paternoster House, 3 Mount Radford Crescent, Exeter, Devonshire, Eng.
Gereformeerd Theologisch Tijdschrift; Ref.; Kampen, Neth.
Gnomon: Kritische Zeitschrift für die gesamte Klassische Altertumswissenschaft; 8 yearly; C. H. Beck'sche Verlagsbuchhandlung, Wilhelmstrasse 9, Munich, W. Ger.
Greek Orthodox Theological Review, The; 2 yearly; 50 Goddard Ave., Brookline, Mass.
Harvard Theological Review; Harvard U. Press, 79 Garden St., Cambridge, Mass.
History of Religions; The U. of Chicago Press, Chicago, Ill.
Iliff Review, The; 3 yearly; Meth.; The Criterion Press, Inc., 2201 S. University Blvd., Denver, Colo.
Indian Church History Review; 2 yearly; The Ch. Hist. Assoc. of India; Wesley Press, Mysore City, India.
Indian Journal of Theology, The; 224 Acharya Jagadish Bose Rd., Calcutta, India.
International Journal for Philosophy of Religion; Martinus Nijhoff, 9–11 Lange Voorhout, P. O. B. 269, The Hague, Neth.
International Journal of Religious Education (see *Spectrum* under II below).
International Reformed Bulletin; 1677 Gentian Dr., S. E., Grand Rapids, Mich.
International Review of Mission; 150 route de Ferney, 1211 Geneva 20, Switz.
Internationale Kirchliche Zeitschrift; Old Cat.; Rabbentalstrasse 5, CH-3013 Bern, Switz.
Issues in Christian Education; 3 yearly; Luth.; Conc. Teachers Coll., Seward, Nebr.
Japan Christian Quarterly, The; Kyu Bun Kwan, 4-5-1 Ginza, Chuo-ku, Tokyo, 104, Jap.
Journal for the Scientific Study of Religion; U. of Conn., Storrs, Conn.
Journal of Bible and Religion (see *Journal of the Academy of Religion* below).
Journal of Biblical Literature; Soc. of Biblical Literature; Waterloo Luth. U., Waterloo, Ont., Can.
Journal of Ecclesiastical History, The; Cambridge U. Press, London and NYC.
Journal of Ecumenical Studies; Temple U., Philadelphia, Pa.
Journal of Religion, The; U. of Chicago Press, 5801 Ellis Ave., Chicago, Ill.
Journal of Religious Thought, The; 2 yearly; The Howard U. Press, Washington, D. C.
Journal of the Academy of Parish Clergy, The; 2 yearly; 3100 W. Lake, Minneapolis, Minn.
Journal of the American Academy of Religion (formerly *Journal of Bible and Religion*); U. of Mont., Missoula, Mont.
Journal of the American Society for Church Architecture; irregular; 15 Montevideo Rd., Avon, Conn.
Journal of the Evangelical Theological Society, The; Wheaton Coll., Wheaton, Ill.
Journal of Theological Studies, The; 2 yearly; Clarendon Press, Oxford, Eng.
Journal of Theology; 5 yearly; Ch. of the Luth. Confession, Eau Claire, Wis.
Kairos: Zeitschrift für Religionswissenschaft und Theologie; Otto Müller Verlag, Salzburg and Freilassing, W. Ger.
Kerygma und Dogma; Vandenhoeck and Ruprecht, Göttingen, W. Ger.
Listening: Journal of Religion and Culture; 3 yearly; 7200 W. Division St., River Forest, Ill.
Luther Theological Seminary Review; irregular; 2375 Como Ave., W., St. Paul, Minn.

Lutheran Education; 5 yearly; 3558 S. Jefferson Ave., St. Louis, Mo.
Lutheran Quarterly; Lutheran Theol. Sem., Gettysburg, Pa.
Lutheran Theological Journal; 3 yearly; 205 Halifax St., Adelaide, S. Australia.
Lutheran World; Luth. World Fed.; 150 route de Ferney, 1211 Geneva 20, Switz.
Mennonite Quarterly Review, The; Goshen Coll., Goshen, Ind.
Muslim World; The Hartford Sem. Foundation, Hartford, Conn.
Nederlands Theologisch Tijdschrift; Postbus 5176, The Hague, Neth.
Neue Zeitschrift für Systematische Theologie und Religionsphilosophie; 3 yearly; W. de Gruyter, Berlin and NYC.
New Pulpit Digest, The (continuing *Pulpit Preaching and Pulpit Digest*); P. O. Box 5195, 429 Miss. St., Jackson, Miss.
New Testament Studies; Studiorum Novi Testamenti Societas; Cambridge U. Press, London and NYC.
Norsk Teologisk Tidsschrift; Postboks 307, Blindern, Oslo 3, Norw.
Novum Testamentum: An International Quarterly for New Testament and Related Studies; E. J. Brill, Leiden, Neth.
Numen; 3 yearly; E. J. Brill, Leiden, Neth.
Perspective; 2 yearly; Pittsburgh Theol. Sem., 616 N. Highland Ave., Pittsburgh, Pa.
Princeton Seminary Bulletin, The; Princeton, N. J.
Pulpit Preaching and Pulpit Digest (see *New Pulpit Digest, The* above).
Quaker Religious Thought; Rio Grande Coll., Rio Grande, Ohio.
Recherches de Science Religieuse; 15, rue Monsieur, Paris, Fr.
Recherches de Théologie ancienne et médiévale; Abbaye du Mont Cesar, Louvain, Belg.
Reformation Review, The; Internat. Council of Christian Chs.; 24 Frederiksplein, Amsterdam-2, Neth.
Reformed Review; 3 yearly; New Brunswick Theol. Sem., New Brunswick, N. J., and Western Theol. Sem., Holland, Mich.
Religion in Life; Abingdon Press, 201 Eighth Ave., S., Nashville, Tenn.
Religious Education; The Religious Educ. Assoc. of the US and Can.; 545 W. 111 St., NYC.
Religious Studies; Cambridge U. Press, London and NYC.
Review and Expositor; Southern Bap. Theol. Sem., Louisville, Ky.
Review for Religious; RC; faculty mems. of the School of Divinity, St. Louis U., St. Louis, Mo.
Revue Biblique; L'Ecole Pratique D'Etudes Bibliques; J. Gabalda et Cie, 90, rue Bonaparte, Paris, Fr.
Revue de Theologie et de Philosophie; 6 yearly; 7 chemin des Cedres, Lausanne, Switz.
Revue d'Histoire et de Philosophie Religieuses; Prot. theol. faculties at Strasbourg, Montpellier, and Paris; Palais Universitaire, Strasbourg, Fr.
Rivista Biblica; RC; Paideia, Brescia, It.
Römische Quartalschrift für christliche Altertumskunde und Kirchengeschichte; Herder Verlag, Freiburg im Breisgau, W. Ger.
St. Luke's Journal of Theology, The; The School of Theology of the U. of the South; Sewanee, Tenn.
St. Vladimir's Theological Quarterly; faculty of St. Vladimir's Orthodox Theol. Sem.; 575 Scarsdale Rd., Crestwood, Tuckahoe, N. Y.
Scottish Journal of Theology; Cambridge U. Press, London and NYC.
South East Asia Journal of Theology, The; 2 yearly; Singapore.
Springfielder, The; faculty of Conc. Theol. Sem.; Springfield, Ill.
Studia Theologica: Scandinavia Journal of Theology; 2 yearly; Universitetsforlaget, P. O. Box 307, Blindern, Oslo 3, Norw.
Studies in Religion: Sciences Religieuses; U. of Toronto Press, Toronto, Ont., Can.
Svensk Teologisk Kvartalskrift; C. W. K. Gleerup, Lund, Swed.
Teologinen Aikakauskirja Teologisk Tidskrift; 6 yearly; Fabianinkatu 33, Helsinki, Fin.
Theological Studies (Theol. Faculties of the Soc. of Jesus in the US); Mt. Royal and Guilford Avenues, Baltimore, Md.
Theologische Quartalschrift; RC; Katholisch-Theologisches Seminar, Liebermeisterstrasse 12, Tübingen, W. Ger.
Theologische Rundschau; J. C. B. Mohr (Paul Siebeck), Tübingen, Ger.
Theologische Zeitschrift; 6 yearly; Basel, Switz.
Theology: A Monthly Review; SPCK; Holy Trin. Ch., Marylebone Rd., London, Eng.
Theology Digest; School of Divinity of St. Louis U., St. Louis, Mo.
Tidsskrift for teologi og Kirke; Universitetsforlaget, Postboks 307, Blindern, Oslo 3, Norw.
Tijdschrift voor Theologie; Utrecht, Neth., and Brugge, Belg.
Una Sancta: Zeitschrift für ökumenische Begegnung; Kyrios-Verlag, Freising, W. Ger.
Verbum Caro (see *Communion* above).
Vetus Testamentum; E. J. Brill, Leiden, Neth.
Westminster Theological Journal, The; 3 yearly; Presb.; Westminster Theol. Sem., Philadelphia, Pa.
Wisconsin Lutheran Quarterly; Northwestern Publishing House, Milwaukee, Wis.
Zeitschrift für die Alttestamentliche Wissenschaft; 3 yearly; W. de Gruyter, Berlin and NYC.
Zeitschrift für die Neutestamentliche Wissenschaft; W. de Gruyter, Berlin and NYC.
Zeitschrift für Kirchengeschichte; 3 yearly; W. Kohlhammer, Stuttgart, W. Ger.
Zeitschrift für Missionswissenschaft und Religionswissenschaft; Internationales Institut für missionswissenschaftliche Forschung; Aschendorffsche Verlagsbuchhandlung, Gallitzinstr. 13, Münster, Westphalia, W. Ger.
Zeitschrift für Religions- und Geistesgeschichte; E. J. Brill, Haus am Friesenplatz, Cologne, W. Ger.
Zeitschrift für Theologie und Kirche; J. C. B. Mohr (Paul Siebeck), Tübingen, W. Ger.
Zeitwende: Die neue Furche: Kultur, Theologie, Politik; 6 yearly; Gerd Mohn, Gütersloh, W. Ger.

II. *Popular;* weekly unless otherwise indicated.

A. D., Presbyterian Life Edition (formerly *Presbyterian Life*); monthly; Witherspoon Bldg., Philadelphia, Pa.
A. D., United Church Herald Edition (formerly United Church Herald); monthly; 297 Park Ave. So., NYC.
A. D. Correspondence; biweekly; RC; Ave Maria Press, Notre Dame, Ind.
Advance; monthly except July and Aug.; Luth.; CPH, 3558 S. Jefferson Ave., St. Louis, Mo.
Affirm; monthly; Balance, Inc.; Walther Memorial Luth. Ch., 4040 Fund du Lac Ave., Milwaukee, Wis.
Alliance Witness, The (formerly *The Alliance Weekly*); biweekly; Christian and Missionary Alliance; 260 W. 44th St., NYC.
America; RC; America Press, Inc., 106 W. 56th St., NYC.
American Bible Society Record (formerly *Bible Society Record*); monthly except June and Aug.; P. O. Box 3575, NYC.
American Review of Eastern Orthodoxy; 10 yearly; E. Orthodox Cath. Ch. in Am.; P. O. Box 390, Dobbs Ferry, N. Y.

Banner, The; Christian Ref. Ch.; 2850 Kalamazoo Ave., SE, Grand Rapids, Mich.
Bible Society Record (see *American Bible Society Record* above).
Biblical Missions; 10 yearly; Presb.; 246 W. Walnut Lane, Philadelphia, Pa.
Blue Banner Faith and Life; quarterly; Ref. Presb. (Covenanter) Ch.; Beaver Falls, Pa.
Catholic Mind; monthly except in July and Aug.; RC; America Press, 106 W. 56th St., NYC.
Catholic World, (The) (see *New Catholic World* below).
Chaplain, The; quarterly; The Gen. Commission on Chaplains and Armed Forces Personnel); 122 Maryland Ave., N. E., Washington, D. C.
Christ to the World; 6 yearly; RC; Via G. Nicotera, 31, Rome, It.
Christian Advocate; biweekly except the 2d issue in July and the 2d issue in Aug.; The United Meth. Ch.; Box 423 Park Ridge, Ill.
Christian Century, The; nondenom.; 407 S. Dearborn St., Chicago, Ill.
Christian Herald; monthly; nondenom.; Chappaqua, N. Y.
Christian Ministry, The (formerly *The Pulpit*); bimonthly; 407 S. Dearborn St., Chicago, Ill.
Christian News from Israel; quarterly; Ministry of Religious Affairs, Jerusalem, Israel.
Christianity and Crisis; 24 yearly; 537 W. 121st St., NYC.
Christianity Today; biweekly; nondenom.; 1014 Washington Bldg., Washington, D. C.
Church and Society (formerly *Social Progress*); bimonthly; The United Presb. Ch. USA and Presb. Ch. US; 475 Riverside Dr., Room 1244K, NYC.
Church Management; monthly; 115 N. Main St., Mt. Holly, N. C.
Churchman, The; monthly; 1074 23d Ave., N., St. Petersburg, Fla.
Commentary (formerly *Contemporary Jewish Record*); monthly; 165 E. 56th St., NYC.
Commonweal; RC; 232 Madison Ave., NYC.
Concordia Lutheran, The; monthly or double bimonthly; 10200 62d Ave. S., Seattle, Wash.
Contemporary Jewish Record (see *Commentary* above).
Context; 24 yearly; 180 N. Wabash Ave., Chicago, Ill.
Cresset, The; 10 yearly; Luth.; Valparaiso U. Press., Valparaiso, Ind.
East Asia Millions (formerly *The Millions*); bimonthly; 237 W. School House Lane, Philadelphia, Pa.
Ecumenist, The; bimonthly; RC; 1865 Broadway, NYC.
Episcopalian, The; monthly; 1930 Chestnut St., Philadelphia, Pa.
Eternity (formerly *Revelation*); monthly; Evangelical Foundation, Inc., 1716 Spruce St., Philadelphia, Pa.
Event, 11 yearly; Am. Luth. Ch. Men, 422 S. 5th St., Minneapolis, Minn.
Faith-Life; bimonthly; The Protes'tant Conference; Luth.; P. O. Box 130, Mosinee, Wis.
Faithful Word, The; quarterly; Luth. Chs. of the Reformation; Route 1, Shepherd, Mich.
Fellowship; monthly except for a combined July-Aug. issue; Fellowship of Reconciliation, Box 271, Nyack, N. Y.
Focus on Public Affairs; 20 yearly; LCUSA, 315 Park Ave., S., NYC.
Forum Letter; monthly; ALPB, 155 E. 22d St., NYC.
Friends Journal; twice a month, except monthly in June, July, and Aug.; Quaker; Friends Publishing Corp., 152-A N. 15th St., Philadelphia, Pa.
HIS: Magazine of Campus Christian Living; monthly except July–Sept; Inter-Varsity Christian Fellowship, 5206 Main St., Downers Grove, Ill.
Homiletic and Pastoral Review; monthly except bimonthly for Aug.–Sept.; RC; Cath. Polls, Inc., 86 Riverside Dr., NYC.
Interaction; monthly except July–Aug. bimonthly; Luth.; CPH, 3558 S. Jefferson Ave., St. Louis, Mo.
Interchange; monthly except combined May/June issue; LCUSA, 315 Park Ave., S., NYC.
Japan Harvest; quarterly; Japan Evangelical Mission Assoc.; 1, 2-chome, Surugadai, Kanda, Chiyoda-ku, Tokyo, Jap.
Journal of Church Music; monthly, except July–Aug. bimonthly; Fortress Press, 2900 Queen Lane, Philadelphia, Pa.
Journal of Pastoral Care, The; quarterly; Assoc. for Clinical Pastoral Education, Inc., 475 Riverside Dr., NYC.
Learning for Living; 5 annually; Christian Educ. Movement; pub. in assoc. with the SCM Press; Annandale, North End Rd., London NW 11 7 QX, Eng.
Link: A Magazine for Armed Forces Personnel; monthly; 122 Maryland Ave., NE, Washington, D. C.
Living Church, The; Episc.; 407 E. Michigan St., Milwaukee, Wis.
Lutheran, The; semimonthly except July and Aug.; 2900 Queen Lane, Philadelphia, Pa.
Lutheran Forum, quarterly; ALPB, 155 E. 22d St., NYC.
Lutheran Scholar, The; quarterly; CPH, 3558 S. Jefferson Ave., St. Louis, Mo. Now *Academy: Lutherans in Profession.*
Lutheran Sentinel; semimonthly; 204 N. 2d Ave. W., Lake Mills, Iowa.
Lutheran Spokesman; monthly; 22 N. State St., New Ulm, Minn.
Lutheran Standard, The; semimonthly; Augsburg Publishing House, 426 S. 5th St., Minneapolis, Minn.
Lutheran Synod Quarterly, The; Bethany Luth. Sem., 734 Marsh St., Mankato, Minn.
Lutheran Witness, The; monthly; CPH, 3558 S. Jefferson Ave., St. Louis, Mo.
Lutheran Women; monthly except Aug.; Lutheran Church Women; LCA; 2900 Queen Lane, Philadelphia, Pa.
Lutheraner, Der; 6 yearly; CPH, 3558 S. Jefferson Ave., St. Louis, Mo. Last issue Nov.-Dec. 1974.
Lutherans Alert – National; monthly; P. O. Box 7186, Tacoma, Wash.
Mennonite, The; Gen. Conference Mennonite Ch., 722 Main St., Box 347, Newton, Kans.
Midstream; monthly; Jewish; The Theodor Herzl Foundation, Inc., 515 Park Ave., NYC.
Moody Monthly; Moody Bible Institute of Chicago, 820 N. LaSalle St., Chicago, Ill.
National Christian Council Review; monthly; Christian Council Lodge, Nagpur, Maharashtra, India.
New Catholic World (formerly [*The*] *Catholic World*); bimonthly; Paulist Fathers, 1865 Broadway, NYC.
North India Churchman, The (formerly *The United Church Review*); monthly; Ch. of N. India; ISPCK, Kasmere Gate, Delhi, India.
Northwestern Lutheran, The; 24 yearly; Northwestern Publishing House, 3624 W. North Ave., Milwaukee, Wis.
positions luthériennes; quarterly; Église Evangélique Luthérienne de France, 16, rue Chaucat, Paris, Fr.
Presbyterian Life (see *A. D., Presbyterian Life Edition* above).
Pulpit, The (see *Christian Ministry, The* above).
Reformed Journal, The; 10 yearly; 255 Jefferson SE, Grand Rapids, Mich.
Revelation (see *Eternity* above).

Risk (formerly *Youth*); quarterly; pub. by an ed. group within the WCC; 150, route de Ferney, 1211 Geneva 20, Switz.
Seminar; pub. occasionally during the school year; Conc. Sem., St. Louis, Mo.
Shareletter; irregularly; Luth.; Conc. Literature Center, P. O. Box 507, Manila, Philippines.
Social Progress (see *Church and Society* above).
Sola Scriptura; bimonthly; Fed. for Authentic Lutheranism, 5244 Tujunga Ave., N., Hollywood, Calif.
South India Churchman, The; monthly; Ch. of S. India; Synod Office, Cathedral P. O., Madras 86, India.
Spectrum: International Journal of Religious Education (formerly *International Journal of Religious Education*); quarterly; NCC, 475 Riverside Dr., NYC.
Study Encounter; quarterly; WCC, 150, route de Ferney, 1211 Geneva 20, Switz.
Toward Wholeness: A Journal of Ministries to Blacks in Higher Education; quarterly; 890 Beckwith St., Atlanta, Ga.
United Church Review, The (see *North India Churchman, The* above).
United Evangelical Action; quarterly; Nat. Assoc. of Evangelicals, Box 28, Wheaton, Ill.
U. S. Catholic; monthly; 221 W. Madison St., Chicago, Ill.
Vanguard: Vision for the Seventies; 8 annually; nondenom.; Wedge Publishing Foundation, Toronto, Ont., Can.; 229 College St., Toronto 2B, Ont.
World Encounter; 5 yearly; Luth; 2900 Queen Lane, Philadelphia, Pa.
World Vision; monthly except combined July/Aug.; nondenom.; 919 W. Huntington Dr., Monrovia, Calif.
Worldmission; quarterly; RC; The Soc. for the Propagation of the Faith, 366 5th Ave., NYC.
Worldview (formerly *World Alliance News Letter*); monthly; Council on Religion and Internat. Affairs, 170 E. 64th St., NYC. *Youth* (see *Risk* above). EJS, EL, HLH, EFS

Theological Problems. See *Fundamental Doctrines,* 4; *Open Questions.*

Theological Propaedeutic. See *Propaedeutic, Theological.*

Theological Schools. See *Ministry, Education of.*

Theological Society, American. Organized 1912 NYC "to promote the interests of present-day constructive theology, by the holding of meetings for the discussion of theological problems and for the furthering of acquaintance and fellowship among those working in this field, and by arranging for cooperation in theological investigation." Membership limited to experts in the NYC area.

Theological Society, American – Midwest Division. Founded 1927. Not officially connected with Am. Theological* Society. HQ Luth. School of Theol. at Chicago, Ill.

Theological Training Program, Tokyo, Jap. See *Ministry, Education of,* XI B 18.

Theological Virtues. See *Cardinal Virtues.*

Theology. In the subjective concrete sense a practical, God-given ability, aptitude, habitude, quality, competence, or sufficiency (cf. 2 Co 3:5-6) by which one may understand, accept, expound, impart to others, and defend the truth of Scripture as containing the way of salvation. In the objective, abstract sense the whole body of knowledge pertaining to the understanding and exposition of Scripture. This knowledge is commonly divided into (1) exegetical theol., which includes Biblical isagogics* and the hist. of the Bible canon* and Bible* versions, hermeneutics* and textual* criticism, and OT and NT exegesis*; (2) systematic* theol., which includes dogmatics* or doctrinal* theol., study of Symbolic* Books, moral* philos. and Christian ethics (see *Ethics,* 2), and often Christian apologetics* and polemics*; (3) hist. theol., which includes Biblical archaeology* and hist. of the Christian* Ch., hist. of Christian doctrine* and confessions (see *Creeds and Confessions*), and patristics*; (4) practical* theol., which includes pastoral* theol. and ch. polity,* catechetics,* homiletics,* diaconics* and missions,* liturgics* and Christian hymnody,* and ecclesiastical and religious art* and church* architecture.

A. L. Graebner, *Outlines of Doctrinal Theology* St. Louis, 1898); pp. 1–3; F. Pieper, *Christliche Dogmatik,* I (St. Louis, 1924), 44–49; J. T. Mueller, *Christian Dogmatics* (St. Louis, 1934), pp. 30–33.

Theology, Dialectical. See *Dialectical Theology.*

Theology, Mediating. See *Mediating Theology.*

Theology, Natural. Man has a natural knowledge of God (Acts 14:16-17; 17:22-31; Ro 1:18-23; 2:14-15). This is not contradicted by passages which say that natural man does not "know" God (Gl 4:8; 1 Th 4:5), i. e., has no saving knowledge of Him. Saving faith through knowledge and acceptance of Christ is created by the Holy Spirit through the Word. Yet perception and reason are able to est. the existence of God and such of His attributes as power, wisdom, and justice. The mind of natural man, however, is vain, his understanding darkened, and his heart hardened; for the god of this world has blinded the minds of them which believe not (2 Co 4:4; Eph 4:17-18). God's handwriting in nature bears with it a natural conviction; the power of Scripture is supernatural, effecting in the heart of the reader or hearer spiritual discernment and divine assurance of the truths set forth therein (1 Co 2:6-16). See also *Apologetics, Christian,* I A; *Natural Knowledge of God.*

Theology, Speculative. Theol. founded on, or fundamentally influenced by, speculation or metaphysical philos.; includes all ordered and systematic reflection on matters of faith; founded by K. Daub.*

Theology, Systematic. See *Systematic Theology.*

Theology of Crisis. See *Switzerland, Contemporary Theology in,* 5.

Theopaschitism. View, defended esp. by adherents of Monophysitism,* that when Christ suffered and died the whole Godhead suffered and died; rejected by orthodox Christianity on basis of the fact that Scripture teaches that only the Son of God became incarnate, suffered, and died, not the Father and the Holy Spirit. See also *Monarchianism, B; Patripassianism.*

Theophany. Manifestation or visible appearance of a supreme being or deity; cf., e. g., Gn 12:7; 26:2; Ex 3:1–4:17; 33:11, 17-23; Is 6. See also *Revelation,* 3.

Theophilanthropism. Doctrines of deistic soc. founded 1796 in Fr. by theophilanthropists (from Gk. for "lovers of God and man"), who believed in God as the father of nature, in immortality of the soul, and in virtue, and who derived their thoughts from philosophies and religions of all times. See also *Kairis, Theophilos.*

Theophilus (d. ca. 181/186 AD). Bp. Antioch in Syria 169. Wrote against gnosticism.* See also *Apologists,* 8; *Christian Church, History of,* I 2.

Theophilus (345–ca. 412). Uncle of Cyril* of Alexandria; patriarch Alexandria 385–ca. 412; opposed remnants of paganism; first admired, then opposed Origenism (see *Origen*); opposed J. Chrysostom.*

Theophylact (ca. 1050–ca. 1108). Probably b. Euripus, on Euboea, in the Aegean Sea; abp. Ochrida (various spellings include Achrida) and metropolitan of Bulg. ca. 1078 (or 1090?). Works include commentaries on some OT books and on the NT except Rv.

Theopneustia (from Gk. *theopneustos,* "God-breathed"). Term drawn from 2 Ti 3:16 and used to describe divine inspiration. See also *Inspiration, Doctrine of.*

Theosebism. See *Kaïris, Theophilos.*

Theosophy. 1. Term used rather loosely for philos. systems that claim to enable man to know God and divine things by direct inspiration and direct contact with deity. Buddhism* and Jainism* theosophical religions. Neoplatonism* is theosophical.

2. E. P. Blavatsky* founded The Theosophical Soc. 1875 NYC. Objects: (1) To form a nucleus of the universal brotherhood of humanity, without distinction of race, creed, sex, caste, or color; (2) To encourage the study of comparative religion, philosophy, and science; (3) To investigate the unexplained laws of nature and the powers latent in man.

3. Theosophy is pantheistic; rejects a personal God; teaches reincarnation (confined to the human race) and fatalism; has no place for prayer, repentance, forgiveness, resurrection, and other Christian teachings.

4. Yoga* plays a large part in theosophy.

See also *Besant, Annie; Böhme, Jakob; Steiner, Rudolf; Swedenborg, Emanuel.*

Theotokos (Gk. "God-bearer"). Term used to describe Mary, mother of Jesus Christ, as mother of God (cf. Lk 1:35); upheld at 3d ecumenical council of Ephesus* and the council of Chalcedon.* FC Ep VIII 12: "Mary conceived and bore not only a plain, ordinary, mere man but the veritable Son of God"; cf. FC Ep VIII 15, SD VIII 24. See also *Mariology; Nestorianism,* 1.

Therapeutae. Ascetics in Egypt described by Philo* Judaeus in *De vita contemplativa.*

Therapeutic Technique. See *Psychology,* J 7.

Theresa. See *Teresa.*

Thérèse de Lisieux (Teresa of Lisieux; Thérèse Martin; 1873–97). "Little Flower of Jesus"; Fr. Carmelite nun; emphasized renunciation in the little things of life; held that the way to Jesus leads down, not up. Works include autobiography.

Thesaurus meritorum. See *Treasury of Merits.*

Theses, Altenburg. See *Altenburg Theses.*

Theses, Ninety-five, of Harms. C. Harms* pub. Luther's 95 Theses (see *Theses, Ninety-five of Luther*) with 95 of his own against rationalism* and the Prussian* Union; a great stir resulted.

C. Harms, *Das sind die 95* theses *oder Streitsätze Dr. Luthers, theuren Andenkens. Zum besondern Abdruck besorgt und mit andern 95 Sätzen als mit einer Uebersetzung aus* Ao. *1517 in 1817 begleitet* (Kiel, 1817) and *Briefe zu einer nähern Verständigung über verschiedene meine Thesen betreffende Puncte. Nebst Einem namhaften Briefe, an den Herrn* Dr. *Schleiermacher* (Kiel, 1818).

Theses, Ninety-five, of Luther. 1. When our Lord and Master Jesus Christ said, "Repent" [Mt 4:17], he willed the entire life of believers to be one of repentance.

2. This word cannot be understood as referring to the sacrament of penance, that is, confession and satisfaction, as administered by the clergy.

3. Yet it does not mean solely inner repentance; such inner repentance is worthless unless it produces various outward mortification of the flesh.

4. The penalty of sin remains as long as the hatred of self (that is, true inner repentance), namely till our entrance into the kingdom of heaven.

5. The pope neither desires nor is able to remit any penalties except those imposed by his own authority or that of the canons.

6. The pope cannot remit any guilt, except by declaring and showing that it has been remitted by God; or, to be sure, by remitting guilt in cases reserved to his judgment. If his right to grant remission in these cases were disregarded, the guilt would certainly remain unforgiven.

7. God remits guilt to no one unless at the same time he humbles him in all things and makes him submissive to his vicar, the priest.

8. The penitential canons are imposed only on the living, and, according to the canons themselves, nothing should be imposed on the dying.

9. Therefore the Holy Spirit through the pope is kind to us insofar as the pope in his decrees always makes exception of the article of death and of necessity.

10. Those priests act ignorantly and wickedly who, in the case of the dying, reserve canonical penalties for purgatory.

11. Those tares of changing the canonical penalty to the penalty of purgatory were evidently sown while the bishops slept [Mt 13:25].

12. In former times canonical penalties were imposed, not after, but before absolution, as tests of true contrition.

13. The dying are freed by death from all penalties, are already dead as far as the canon laws are concerned, and have a right to be released from them.

14. Imperfect piety or love on the part of the dying person necessarily brings with it great fear; and the smaller the love, the greater the fear.

15. This fear or horror is sufficient in itself, to say nothing of other things, to constitute the penalty of purgatory, since it is very near the horror of despair.

16. Hell, purgatory, and heaven seem to differ the same as despair, fear, and assurance of salvation.

17. It seems as though for the souls in purgatory fear should necessarily decrease and love increase.

18. Furthermore, it does not seem proved, either by reason of Scripture, that souls in purgatory are outside the state of merit, that is, unable to grow in love.

19. Nor does it seem proved that souls in purgatory, at least not all of them, are certain and assured of their own salvation, even if we ourselves may be entirely certain of it.

20. Therefore the pope, when he uses the words "plenary remission of all penalties," does not actually mean "all penalties," but only those imposed by himself.

21. Thus those indulgence preachers are in error who say that a man is absolved from every penalty and saved by papal indulgences.

22. As a matter of fact, the pope remits to souls in purgatory no penalty which, according to canon law, they should have paid in this life.

23. If remission of all penalties whatsoever could be granted to anyone at all, certainly it would be granted only to the most perfect, that is, to very few.

24. For this reason most people are necessarily deceived by that indiscriminate and high-sounding promise of release from penalty.

25. That power which the pope has in general over purgatory corresponds to the power which any bishop or curate has in a particular way in his own diocese or parish.

26. The pope does very well when he grants remission to souls in purgatory, not by the power of the keys, which he does not have, but by way of intercession for them.

27. They preach only human doctrines who say that as soon as the money clinks into the money chest, the soul flies out of purgatory.

28. It is certain that when money clinks in the money chest, greed and avarice can be increased; but when the church intercedes, the result is in the hands of God alone.

29. Who knows whether all souls in purgatory wish to be redeemed, since we have exceptions in St. Severinus and St. Paschal, as related in a legend.

30. No one is sure of the integrity of his own con-

trition, much less of having received plenary remission.

31. The man who actually buys indulgences is as rare as he who is really penitent; indeed, he is exceedingly rare.

32. Those who believe that they can be certain of their salvation because they have indulgence letters will be eternally damned, together with their teachers.

33. Men must especially be on their guard against those who say that the pope's pardons are that inestimable gift of God by which man is reconciled to him.

34. For the graces of indulgences are concerned only with the penalties of sacramental satisfaction established by man.

35. They who teach that contrition is not necessary on the part of those who intend to buy souls out of purgatory or to buy confessional privileges preach unchristian doctrine.

36. Any truly repentant Christian has a right to full remission of penalty and guilt, even without indulgence letters.

37. Any true Christian, whether living or dead, participates in all the blessings of Christ and the church; and this is granted him by God, even without indulgence letters.

38. Nevertheless, papal remission and blessing are by no means to be disregarded, for they are, as I have said [Thesis 6], the proclamation of the divine remission.

39. It is very difficult, even for the most learned theologians, at one and the same time to commend to the people the bounty of indulgences and the need of true contrition.

40. A Christian who is truly contrite seeks and loves to pay penalties for his sins; the bounty of indulgences, however, relaxes penalties and causes men to hate them – at least it furnishes occasion for hating them.

41. Papal indulgences must be preached with caution, lest people erroneously think that they are preferable to other good works of love.

42. Christians are to be taught that the pope does not intend that the buying of indulgences should in any way be compared with works of mercy.

43. Christians are to be taught that he who gives to the poor or lends to the needy does a better deed than he who buys indulgences.

44. Because love grows by works of love, man thereby becomes better. Man does not, however, become better by means of indulgences but is merely freed from penalties.

45. Christians are to be taught that he who sees a needy man and passes him by, yet gives his money for indulgences, does not buy papal indulgences but God's wrath.

46. Christians are to be taught that, unless they have more than they need, they must reserve enough for their family needs and by no means squander it on indulgences.

47. Christians are to be taught that the buying of indulgences is a matter of free choice, not commanded.

48. Christians are to be taught that the pope, in granting indulgences, needs and thus desires their devout prayer more than their money.

49. Christians are to be taught that papal indulgences are useful only if they do not put their trust in them, but very harmful if they lose their fear of God because of them.

50. Christians are to be taught that if the pope knew the exactions of the indulgence preachers, he would rather that the basilica of St. Peter were burned to ashes than built up with the skin, flesh, and bones of his sheep.

51. Christians are to be taught that the pope would and should wish to give of his own money, even though he had to sell the basilica of St. Peter, to many of those from whom certain hawkers of indulgences cajole money.

52. It is vain to trust in salvation by indulgence letters, even though the indulgence commissary, or even the pope, were to offer his soul as security.

53. They are enemies of Christ and the pope who forbid altogether the preaching of the Word of God in some churches in order that indulgences may be preached in others.

54. Injury is done the Word of God when, in the same sermon, an equal or larger amount of time is devoted to indulgences than to the Word.

55. It is certainly the pope's sentiment that if indulgences, which are a very insignificant thing, are celebrated with one bell, one procession, and one ceremony, then the gospel, which is the very greatest thing, should be preached with a hundred bells, a hundred processions, a hundred ceremonies.

56. The true treasures of the church, out of which the pope distributes indulgences, are not sufficiently discussed or known among the people of Christ.

57. That indulgences are not temporal treasures is certainly clear, for many indulgence sellers do not distribute them freely but only gather them.

58. Nor are they the merits of Christ and the saints, for, even without the pope, the latter always work grace for the inner man, and the cross, death, and hell for the outer man.

59. St. Lawrence said that the poor of the church were the treasures of the church, but he spoke according to the usage of the word in his own time.

60. Without want of consideration we say that the keys of the church, given by the merits of Christ, are that treasure.

61. For it is clear that the pope's power is of itself sufficient for the remission of penalties and cases reserved by himself.

62. The true treasure of the church is the most holy gospel of the glory and grace of God.

63. But this treasure is naturally most odious, for it makes the first to be last [Mt 20:16].

64. On the other hand, the treasure of indulgences is naturally most acceptable, for it makes the last to be first.

65. Therefore the treasures of the gospel are nets with which one formerly fished for men of wealth.

66. The treasures of indulgences are nets with which one now fishes for the wealth of men.

67. The indulgences which the demagogues acclaim as the greatest graces are actually understood to be such only insofar as they promote gain.

68. They are nevertheless in truth the most insignificant graces when compared with the grace of God and the piety of the cross.

69. Bishops and curates are bound to admit the commissaries of papal indulgences with all reverence.

70. But they are much more bound to strain their eyes and ears lest these men preach their own dreams instead of what the pope has commissioned.

71. Let him who speaks against the truth concerning papal indulgences be anathema and accursed.

72. But let him who guards against the lust and license of the indulgence preachers be blessed.

73. Just as the pope justly thunders against those who by any means whatever contrive harm to the sale of indulgences,

74. Much more does he intend to thunder against those who use indulgences as a pretext to contrive harm to holy love and truth.

75. To consider papal indulgences so great that they could absolve a man even if he had done the impossible and had violated the mother of God is madness.

76. We say on the contrary that papal indulgences

cannot remove the very least of venial sins as far as guilt is concerned.

77. To say that even St. Peter if he were now pope, could not grant greater graces is blasphemy against St. Peter and the pope.

78. We say on the contrary that even the present pope, or any pope whatsoever, has greater graces at his disposal, that is, the gospel, spiritual powers, gifts of healing, etc., as it is written 1 Co 12[:28].

79. To say that the cross emblazoned with the papal coat of arms, and set up by the indulgence preachers, is equal in worth to the cross of Christ is blasphemy.

80. The bishops, curates, and theologians who permit such talk to be spread among the people will have to answer for this.

81. This unbridled preaching of indulgences makes it difficult even for learned men to rescue the reverence which is due the pope from slander or from the shrewd questions of the laity,

82. Such as: "Why does not the pope empty purgatory for the sake of holy love and the dire need of the souls that are there if he redeems an infinite number of souls for the sake of miserable money with which to build a church? The former reason would be most just; the latter is most trivial."

83. Again, "Why are funeral and anniversary masses for the dead continued and why does he not return or permit the withdrawal of the endowments founded for them, since it is wrong to pray for the redeemed?"

84. Again, "What is this new piety of God and the pope that for a consideration of money they permit a man who is impious and their enemy to buy out of purgatory the pious soul of a friend of God and do not rather, because of the need of that pious and beloved soul, free it for pure love's sake?"

85. Again, "Why are the penitential canons, long since abrogated and dead in actual fact and through disuse, now satisfied by the granting of indulgences as though they were still alive and in force?"

86. Again, "Why does not the pope, whose wealth is today greater than the wealth of the richest Crassus, build this one basilica of St. Peter with his own money rather than with the money of poor believers?"

87. Again, "What does the pope remit or grant to those who by perfect contrition already have a right to full remission and blessings?"

88. Again, "What greater blessing could come to the church than if the pope were to bestow these remissions and blessings on every believer a hundred times a day, as he now does but once?"

89. "Since the pope seeks the salvation of souls rather than money by his indulgences, why does he suspend the indulgences and pardons previously granted when they have equal efficacy?"

90. To repress these very sharp arguments of the laity by force alone, and not to resolve them by giving reasons, is to expose the church and the pope to the ridicule of their enemies and to make Christians unhappy.

91. If, therefore, indulgences were preached according to the spirit and intention of the pope, all these doubts would be readily resolved. Indeed, they would not exist.

92. Away, then, with all those prophets who say to the people of Christ, "Peace, peace," and there is no peace! [Jer 6:14]

93. Blessed be all those prophets who say to the people of Christ, "Cross, cross," and there is no cross!

94. Christians should be exhorted to be diligent in following Christ, their Head, through penalties, death and hell,

95. And thus be confident of entering into heaven through many tribulations rather than through the false security of peace [Acts 14:22].

See also *Christian Church, History of,* III 1; *Luther, Martin,* 7; *Reformation, Lutheran,* 8.

Martin Luther's 95 Theses with the Pertinent Documents from the History of the Reformation, ed. K. Aland, various translators (St. Louis, 1967).

Theses of Agreement. Adopted by a joint pastoral conf. of The Ev. Luth. Ch. of Australia and The United Ev. Luth. Ch. of Australia at Walla Walla, New South Wales, Australia, Aug. 27, 1956. Contains I. Theses on Principles Governing Ch. Fellowship; II. Theses on Joint Prayer and Worship; III. Thesis on Conversion; IV. Theses on Election; V. Theses on the Ch.; VI. Theses on the Office of the Ministry; VII. Theses on Eschatological Matters; VIII. Theses on Scripture and Inspiration; IX. The Luth. Confessions. Appendix: I. Theses on Cooperation Between Chs. Not in Ch. Fellowship; II. Statements on Practical Matters. See also *Australia, Lutheranism in,* B 1.

Theses of Agreement adopted by the Intersynodical Committees of The Evangelical Lutheran Church of Australia and The United Evangelical Lutheran Church in Australia (Tanunda, South Australia, n. d.).

Theses on the Church. See *Church and Ministry, Walther's Theses on.*

Theses on the Ministry. See *Church and Ministry, Walther's Theses on.*

Theses on the Ministry of the Keys and the Public Ministry. See *Church of the Lutheran Confession.*

Theses on the Relation of Synod and Local Congregation to the Holy Christian Church. See *Church of the Lutheran Confession.*

Theudas. See *Christs, False.*

Thibaut IV. See *Crusades,* 7.

Thibaut, Anton Friedrich Justus (1772–1840). Jurist; b. Hameln, Ger.; musical amateur; regarded classical music as extending from G. P. d. Palestrina* to G. F. Handel.* Works include *Über Reinheit der Tonkunst.*

Thiel College. See *Lutheran Church in America,* V; *Ministry, Education of,* VIII B 25; *United Lutheran Church, Synods of,* 24.

Thielicke, Helmut. See *Dogmatics,* B 13.

Thieme, Karl (Carl; 1862–1932). B. Spremberg, Saxony, Ger.; educ. Leipzig; prof. Leipzig. Works include *Die sittliche Triebkraft des Glaubens: Eine Untersuching zu Luthers Theologie; Die christliche Demut; Jesus und seine Predigt; Von der Gottheit Christi; Die Augsburgische Konfession und Luthers Katechismen auf theologische Gegenwartswerte untersucht.*

Thierry of Chartres (Theodoricus, or Terricus, Carnotensis, or Brito; Thierry the Breton; ca. 1100–ca. 1156). Brother of Bernard* of Chartres; b. Fr.; taught at Chartres and later at Paris; archdeacon Dreux 1136; archdeacon and chancellor Chartres 1141. Works include *Heptateuchon.* See also *Chartres, School of.*

Thiersch, Heinrich Wilhelm Josias (1817–85). Ev. theol.; b. Munich, Ger.; taught at Basel, Switz.; prof. Marburg; joined Catholic* Apostolic Ch. 1847. Works include *De pentateuchi versione Alexandrina; Vorlesungen über Katholicismus und Protestantismus.*

Thing-in-Itself. See *Ding an sich.*

Third Orders Secular. See *Tertiaries.*

Third World. 1. See Jehovah's witnesses. 2. Group of nations esp. in Asia and Afr. outside the Communist and non-Communist blocs.

Thirteen Articles, The. See *Anglican Confessions,* 4.

Thirteen Theses. On election, or predestination; adopted 1881 by the Mo. Syn.: "1. We believe, teach and confess, that God loved the whole world from eternity, created all men unto salvation, none unto damnation, and that He earnestly wills the salvation of all men; and we therefore reject and condemn with all our heart the contrary Calvinistic doctrine.

"2. We believe, teach and confess, that the Son of God came into the world for all men, that He bore and expiated the sins of all men, and that He fully redeemed all men, none excepted; we therefore reject and condemn the contrary Calvinistic doctrine with all our heart.

"3. We believe, teach and confess, that God calls through the means of grace all men earnestly, that is, with the purpose that they should, through these means, be brought to repentance and faith, also be preserved therein unto their end, and thus be finally led to blessedness, conformable to which purpose God offers them through the means of grace the salvation wrought by Christ's atonement and the power to embrace this salvation by faith; and we therefore reject and condemn the contrary Calvinistic doctrine with all our heart.

"4. We believe teach and confess, that no one perishes because God was not willing that he be saved, passed him by with His grace, and because He had not also offered him the grace of perseverance and was not willing to bestow the same upon him. But all men that perish, perish because of their own fault, because of their unbelief and because they contumaciously resisted the Word and grace unto their end. The cause of this contempt of the Word is not God's foreknowledge *(vel praescientia vel praedestinatio)* but man's perverted will which rejects or perverts the means and the instrument of the Holy Spirit, which God offers unto it through the call, and it resists the Holy Spirit who would be efficacious and operate through the Word, as Christ says: Matth. 23:37, How often would I have gathered you together, and ye would not. (*Form. of Concord* p 718, par. 41.) Therefore we reject and condemn the contrary Calvinistic doctrine with all our heart.

"5. We believe, teach and confess, that the elect or predestinated persons are only the true believers, who truly believe unto their end or yet at the end of their life; we reject therefore and condemn the error of Huber, that election is not particular, but universal and pertains to all men.

"6. We believe, teach and confess, that the divine decree of election is unchangeable and that therefore no elect person can become a reprobate and perish, but that every one of the elect will surely be saved; and we therefore reject and condemn the contrary Huberian error with all our heart.

"7. We believe, teach and confess, that it is foolish and soul-endangering, leads either to carnal security or despair to endeavor to become or be sure of our own election or eternal happiness by means of searching out the eternal secret decree of God; and we reject and condemn the contrary doctrine as an injurious fanatic notion with all our heart.

"8. We believe, teach and confess, that a true believer ought to endeavor to become sure of his election from God's revealed will; and we therefore reject and condemn with all our heart the opposite Papistical error, that one may become or be sure of his election and salvation only by means of a new immediate revelation.

"9. We believe, teach and confess: 1. That election does not consist in the mere fact that God foresaw which men will secure salvation; 2. That election is also not the mere purpose of God to redeem and save men, which would make it universal and extend in general to all men; 3. That election does not embrace those 'which believe for awhile' (Luke 8:13.) 4. That election is not a mere decree of God to lead to bliss all those who would believe unto their end; we therefore reject and condemn the opposite errors of the Rationalists, Huberians and Arminians with all our heart.

"10. We believe, teach and confess, that the cause which moved God to elect, is alone His grace and the merit of Jesus Christ, and not anything good foreseen by God in the elect, not even faith foreseen in them by God; and we therefore reject and condemn the opposite doctrines of the Pelagians, Semi-Pelagians and Synergists as blasphemous, dreadful errors which subvert the Gospel and therewith the whole Christian religion.

"11. We believe, teach and confess, that election is not the mere divine foresight or prescience of the salvation of the elect, but also a cause of their salvation and of whatever pertains to it; and we therefore reject and condemn the opposite doctrines of the Arminians, Socinians, and of all Synergists with all our heart.

"12. We believe, teach and confess, that God has also concealed and kept secret many things concerning the mystery of election and reserved them for His wisdom and knowledge alone, into which no human being is able and ought to search; and we therefore reject every attempt to inquire curiously also into these things which have not been revealed, and to harmonize with our reason those things which seem contradictory to our reason, may such attempts be made by Calvinistic or Pelagianistic Synergistic doctrines of men.

"13. We believe, teach and confess, that it is not only not useless, much injurious, but necessary and salutary that the mysterious doctrine of election, in so far as it is clearly revealed in God's Word, be presented also publicly to Christian people, and we therefore do not agree with those who hold that entire silence should be kept thereon, or that its discussion should only be indulged in by learned theologians."

See also *Predestinarian Controversy*, 2.

Thirty-nine Articles. See *Anglican Confessions*, 6; *Democratic Confessions of Faith*, 6; *Protestant Episcopal Church, The*, 5.

Thirty Years' War. Religio-pol. Eur. war 1618–48; main campaigns in Ger. Some provisions of the Religious Peace of Augsburg* 1555 helped bring it on. Ferdinand* II introd. oppressive measures against Prots. in Boh. 1617. Prots. retaliated with force and uprising 1618 but were defeated 1620 by J. T. Tilly,* with more than 30,000 families driven out of the country. Prots. rallied under Dan. leadership but were defeated again by Tilly 1626. Den. was eliminated from the war 1629 by making separate peace with the emp. in the treaty of Lübeck. Gustavus* II (Adolphus) of Swed. took up the Prot. cause in Ger. but fell 1632 in the battle of Lützen, where the imperial army, now under A. E. W. v. Wallenstein,* was defeated. The Swed. Prot. army was defeated Sept. 1634 at Nördlingen, Bav., Ger. The elector of Saxony made peace with the emp. and turned against the Swedes 1635 in the treaty of Prague. Brandenburg and most of the other Prot. states accepted the peace. But conflict continued when Fr. joined Swed. in war against Austria and its allies. Gen. exhaustion led to the peace of Westphalia* 1648.

This Is the Life. See *Radio and Television Evangelism, Network*, 5, 8.

Thistedahl, Ole Christian (1813–76). Norw. Luth. theol.; taught high school; influenced G. C. Johnson* et al.; tr. OT into Norw.

Thoburn, James Mills (Mar. 7, 1836–Nov. 28, 1922). B. St. Clairsville, Ohio; educ. Allegheny Coll., Meadville, Pa.; M. E. miss. to India 1859–1908; miss. bp. India and Malaysia 1888–1908. Works include *My Missionary Apprenticeship; India and Malaysia; Light in the East; The Christian Conquest of India.*

Thököly, Imre (Tököly; Tökölyi; Tököli; Emerich;

1657–1705). Hung. Luth.; b. Kesmark (Kezmarok); educ. Eperjes (Presov); opposed RC Hapsburg rulers; sovereign prince Hung. 1682, Transylvania 1690–91.

Tholuck, Friedrich August (Gotttreu; Gottgetreu; 1799–1877). B. Breslau, Ger.; educ. Breslau and Berlin; influenced by H. E. v. Kottwitz,* J. A. W. Neander,* and F. D. E. Schleiermacher*; prof. Berlin and Halle; opposed rationalism and Luth. orthodoxy, favored Prussian* Union. Contributed to E. W. Hengstenberg's* *Evangelische Kirchen-Zeitung* and to J. J. Herzog's* *Real-Encyklopädie;* other works include commentaries on John's Gospel, Ro, and Heb. See also *Evangelical Alliance.*

Thoma, Hans (1839–1924). Realistic painter; b. Bernau, in the Black Forest, Ger. Works include *Paradise; Adam and Eve; Eve in Paradise; The Flight into Egypt; Christ and Nicodemus.*

Thomä, Nikolaus (1492–1546). B. Siegelsbach, Ger.; educ. Heidelberg; pastor Flinsbach; teacher Bergzabern 1524; rejected M. Luther's doctrine of the Lord's Supper in favor of K. v. Schwenkfeld's*; discussed infant baptism with J. Denk* 1527.

Thomander, Johan Henrik (1798–1865). Swed. theol.; prof. Lund 1833; cathedral provost Göteborg 1850; bp. Lund 1856. Introd. ch. reforms. Coed. *Theologisk Quartalskrift.*

Thomas, Gospel of. See *Apocrypha,* B 2.

Thomas, J. I. Wilhelm. See *New Guinea,* 5.

Thomas, John (1805–71). B. London, Eng.; studied medicine there; to US 1832; joined Disciples* of Christ but left them as a result of disagreement and founded Christadelphians.*

Thomas, William Henry Griffith (1861–1924). B. Oswestry, Shrophshire, Eng.; Angl. priest 1885; vicar St. Paul's, Portman Sq., St. Marylebone borough, London, 1896–1905; taught at Oxford 1905–10; prof. OT Wycliffe Coll., Toronto, Ont., Can., 1910–19; moved to Philadelphia, Pa.; engaged in continent-wide ministry. Works include *The Principles of Theology; Grace and Power; The Apostle John.*

Thomas à Becket. See *Becket, Thomas à.*

Thomas à Kempis (Thomas Hamerken [or Hemerken] von Kempen; other variants include Hamer, Hämerken, Hammerchen, Hämmerchen, Hämmerle, Hammerlein, Hämmerlein; Latinized: Malleolus ["Little Hammer"]; ca. 1379/80–1471). Ecclesiastic, mystic (see *Mysticism*); b. Kempen, former Prussian Rhine Province, near Cologne and Düsseldorf; educ. Deventer, Neth., by Brethren* of the Common Life; entered Mt. St. Agnes monastery, near Zwolle, Neth., 1399 and spent nearly all the rest of his life there; ordained 1413. See also *Imitation of Christ.*

Thomas Aquinas (ca. 1224/27–1274). "Doctor angelicus or communis; Princeps scholasticorum"; philos. and theol.; b. Roccasecca, near Aquino, It.; educ. by Benedictines at Monte Cassino and Naples; Dominican 1243/44; studied in Paris and Cologne 1245–52, influenced by Albertus* Magnus; taught in Paris 1252–59, 1269–72; in It. 1259–69, 1272–74.

His Aristotelianism (see *Aristotle*) was opposed by Franciscans* (e. g., J. Peckham*) et al.; but his teaching was made official in the Dominican order; he was canonized 1323, made a Doctor of the Ch. 1567. Study of Thomas Aquinas was made part of all theol. training; cf. CIC 589.1, 1366.2. Made patron of all RC univs. 1880; authority as teacher reaffirmed 1923 by Pius XI (see *Popes,* 32).

In his thought, the relation of reason to faith is one of subalternation, in which the lower (reason) accepts principles of the higher (faith). He rejects Anselm* of Canterbury's ontological argument and accepts the cosmological and teleological arguments for the existence of God.* There is a level of knowledge attainable by reason alone; another level is attainable by reason for skilled thinkers and by faith for unskilled thinkers; the highest level is attainable only by faith. Arguments for the existence of God are at the 2d level.

Aristotle's distinction bet. matter and form raised a question regarding immortality of the soul (since matter individuates, how could a nonmaterial soul be individual?) and regarding the doctrine that angels are beings in which individual and species are coterminous (since there is no individuating matter in them). The movement of reality is conceived as transition from potential to actual being, God being *actus purus.*

His cen. theol. problems were Christological (Incarnation) and sacramental; God is *esse ipsum,* man is in His image, Christ with the sacraments is the *via* ("way").

He had little direct influence on the Reformation, which knew him mainly through late medieval nominalism.* He had greater influence on 17th c. Protestantism, esp. as regards understanding of concepts, but his scholasticism* differs from 17th c. Prot. scholasticism in evaluation of formal thought and in relation of reason to theol. and faith.

Neo-Thomism* tries to preserve fundamental Thomistic philos. with adjustments to modern science and existentialism.*

His system is called Thomism, his followers Thomists.

Works ascribed to him include *Summa contra gentiles; Summa theologiae* (or *theologica*); *Quaestiones disputatae (De veritate; De potentia Dei; De malo;* etc.). RPS

See also *Analogia entis; Preaching, Christian, History of,* 8; *Psychology,* C 4–5; *Via antiqua.*

F. C. Copleston, *Aquinas* (Harmondsworth, Middlesex, Eng., 1955); M. Grabmann, *Thomas Aquinas,* tr. V. Michel (New York, 1963); R. P. Scharlemann, *Thomas Aquinas and John Gerhard* (New Haven, Conn., 1964).

Thomas Christians. See *India,* 4–8; *Malabar Christians.*

Thomas of Celano (fl. 1st half of 13th c. AD). B. Celano, near former lake Fucino, Aquila province, cen. It.; monk at Assisi; custos of some convents in Ger. Works include a life of Francis* of Assisi. See also *Dies irae.*

Thomas von Westen. See *Westen, Thomas von.*

Thomasius, Christian (Latinized from Thomas; 1655–1728). Luth. philos. and jurist; b. Leipzig, Ger.; educ. Frankfurt an der Oder; prof. Leipzig 1684; banished 1690 from the university for criticism of religion and of educ. methods; prof. Halle. Early champion of the Enlightenment* and territorial* system; opposed punishment for witchcraft and application of torture.

Thomasius, Gottfried (1802–75). Descendant of C. Thomasius*; Luth. theol.; b. Egenhausen, Middle Franconia, Ger.; educ. Erlangen, Halle, Berlin; pastor in various places 1825–42; prof. dogmatics Erlangen 1842 (and univ. preacher 1842–72); kenoticist. Works include *Beiträge zur kirchlichen Christologie; Christi Person und Werk.* See also *Kenosis; Pericope,* 2.

Thomism. Theol. and philos. system of Thomas* Aquinas.

Thomissön, Hans (1532–73). Dan. Luth. pastor and hymnist; educ. Wittenberg, Ger.; dean Ribe, Den.; pastor Copenhagen. Collected hymns for Dan. hymnal pub. 1569.

Thomists. Followers of Thomas* Aquinas.

Thompson, Elizabeth Maria. See *Middle East,* C.

Thompson, Francis (1859–1907). RC poet and critic; b. Preston, Lancashire, Eng.; Works include *The Hound of Heaven,* which describes God's pursuit of man's soul.

Thompson, Thomas. See *Africa,* C 11.

Thomsen, Niels (Aug. 5, 1842–Apr. 18, 1892). B. Den.; miss. to India 1865; ordained 1868; returned to Den. ca. 1869/70; to US 1870. Pastor Indianapolis, Ind., 1871; Neenah, Wis., 1874; Gowen and Greenville, Mich., 1881. Helped organize Kirkelig Missionsforening (see *Danish Lutherans in America,* 3); left Dan. Syn. ca. 1883/84. Ed. *Kirkelig Samler.*

Thor. See *Symbolism, Christian,* 4.

Thor Helle, Anton. See *Estonia,* 2.

Thorgrimson, Hans Baagöe (Thorgrims[s]en; Thergrimso; Aug. 21, 1853–Feb. 7, 1942). B. Eyrarbakki, Iceland; to US 1872; educ. Conc. Sem., St. Louis, Mo. Pastor N. Dak., S. Dak., and Wis. Helped found Icelandic Ev. Luth. Syn. in (N.) Am. See also *Canada,* A 13; *United Lutheran Church, Synods of,* 6.

Thorlaksson, Gudbrandur (ca. 1541/42–1627). Icelandic Luth.; educ. Copenhagen, Den.; called to be bp. Holar, N Iceland, 1570; ordained 1571. Pub. Icelandic Bible which includes his tr. of some OT books and O. Gottskalksson's* NT tr. See also *Iceland,* 4.

Thorlaksson, Paul. See *Canada,* A 13.

Thorn (Torun). City in N cen. Poland. Birthplace of N. Copernicus.* Meetings of Polish and Lith. Prots. (1595) and of Polish Prots. and RCs (1645) held here. Insolent and provocative conduct by Jesuit students in a Corpus Christi procession 1724 so enraged Prots. that they destroyed the RC school in the city, but without loss of life; Jesuits succeeded in having 10 leading Prot. citizens executed in retaliation (Massacre of Thorn). See also *Poland,* 4; *Reformed Confessions,* D 3 c; *Syncretism.*

Thorndike, Edward Lee (1874–1949). Psychologist; b. Williamsburg, Mass. Educ. Wesleyan U., Middletown, Conn.; Harvard U., Cambridge, Mass.; Columbia U., NYC. Prof. Columbia U. Engaged in research on animal intelligence; developed educ. and psychol. tests and applications of psychol. to math, reading, handwriting, and language. Works include *The Principles of Teaching; Educational Psychology; The Measurement of Intelligence.* See also *Educational Psychology,* D 3.

Thorndike, Herbert (1598–1672). Angl.; probably b. Suffolk, Eng.; educ. Cambridge; prebendary Westminster 1661. Works include *Of the Government of Churches; Of Religious Assemblies and the Publick Service of God; A Discourse of the Right of the Church in a Christian State; An Epilogue to the Tragedy of the Church of England; The Reformation of the Church of England Better Than That of the Council of Trent.*

Thornton, Henry (1760–1815). Eng. merchant and banker; placed his wealth in service of Meth. charities; with W. Wilberforce* worked for abolition of slavery.

Thornwell, James Henley (1812–62). B. Marlborough Dist., S. C. Educ. Andover (Mass.) Theol. Sem.; Harvard Divinity School, Cambridge, Mass.; held various pastorates; prof. 1841–51, later pres. S. C. Coll., Columbia; prof. Presb. Theol. Sem., Columbia, S. C. Logician, scholar, organizer. Works include *The Arguments of Romanists from the Infallibility of the Church and the Testimony of the Fathers in Behalf of the Apocrypha.*

Thorough Declaration. See *Lutheran Confessions,* C 2.

Thorvald Kodransson (Thorvaldur; Thorvaldr; Thorwald; 10th c. AD). Probably b. Iceland; said to have cruised the seas and met a bp. of Saxony, who bap. him; miss. in Iceland ca. 981; became unpopular; left Iceland ca. 985. See also *Iceland,* 2. SP

Thorvaldsen, Bertel (ca. 1768/70–1844). Sculptor; b. Copenhagen, Den.; studied and worked in Copenhagen and Rome. Works include *Christ and the Twelve Apostles; Christ's Entry into Jerusalem; The Risen Christ.*

Three Chapters, Controversy of. The "3 Chaps." in tension with monophysitism*: 1. Person and writings of Theodore* of Mopsuestia; 2. Writings of Theodoret* of Cyrrhus against Cyril* of Alexandria; 3. Letter of Ibas* to the Persian bp. Maris, in which he complains of outrages of Cyril's party in Edessa. Theodore was not mentioned, Theodoret and Ibas were upheld 451 at Chalcedon.* In hope of conciliating monophysites, Justinian* I condemned the 3 Chaps. 543/544 and 551. Controversy resulted. The 5th ecumenical council (see *Constantinople, Councils of,* 2) anathematized the 3 Chaps. A lasting schism resulted. See also *Christological Controversies; Popes,* 3.

Three Hours' Service. See *Tre ore.*

"Three Witnesses." See *Johannine Comma.*

Threlfall, Jeannette (1821–80). Hymnist; b. Blackburn, Lancashire, Eng.; orphaned early. Hymns include "Hosanna, Loud Hosanna."

Thring, Godfrey (1823–1903). Hymnist; b. Alford, Somersetshire, Eng.; educ. Oxford; held several curacies; rector Alford, Somersetshire, 1858–93. Hymns include "O God of Mercy, God of Might, In Love and Pity Infinite."

Thrupp, Adelaide (19th c.) Eng. hymnist; daughter or wife of Joseph Francis Thrupp (Eng. hymnist; 1827–67; educ. Cambridge; vicar Barrington, Cambridge, 1852). Wrote stanzas 1 and 3 of "Lord [or Thou], Who at Cana's Wedding-Feast."

Thulin, Oskar (1898–1971). B. Aschersleben, Ger.; dir. Lutherhalle, Wittenberg, 1930; prof. Halle. Ed. *Illustrated History of the Reformation,* various translators.

Thumm, Theodor (Thummius; 1586–1630). B. Hausen, Württemberg, Ger.; educ. Tübingen; served in various capacities at several places; prof. Tübingen 1618; controversialist, opposing RCs and Reformed. Works include *Synopsis praecipuorum articulorum fidei nostro saeculo maxime controversiorum.*

Thurificati. See *Lapsi.*

Thürlings, Adolf (Thuerlings; 1844–1915). B. Kaldenkirchen, Ger.; RC priest 1867; deposed 1870 for opposing Vatican Council I (see *Vatican Councils,* 1); Old Cath. (see *Old Catholics*) pastor Kempten, Allgäu, Ger., 1872; prof. Bern, Switz., 1877. Ed. *Liturgisches Gebetbuch nebst Liederbuch; Gesangbuch der christkatholischen Kirche für die Schweiz.*

Thurston, Asa (Oct. 12, 1787–Mar. 11, 1868). B. Fitchburg, Mass.; educ. Yale Coll., New Haven, Conn., and Andover (Mass.) Theol. Sem.; ABCFM miss. to Sandwich Islands (now Hawaii*) 1819; stationed at Kailua, ancient residence of Hawaiian kings; instructed Kamehameha II (Liholiho; 1797–1824; son of Kamehameha I; king 1819–24) and Kamehameha III (Kauikeaouli; 1813–54; brother of Kamehameha II; king 1825–54).

Thysius, Antonius (1565–1640). B. Antwerp; educ. Geneva, Heidelberg, Leiden, and France. Prof. Harderwijk 1601, Leiden 1619. Attended 1618–19 Syn. of Dordrecht.* Infralapsarian (see *Infralapsarianism*). Opposed Remonstrants.* Works include *Anglicana scripta de praedestinatione; Responsio in Remonstrantium remonstrantiam.*

Tiberius (Tiberius Claudius Nero Caesar; 42 BC–37 AD). Stepson of Caesar Augustus*; 2d Roman emp. 14–37. Cf. Mt 22:17; Mk 12:14; Lk 3:1; 20:21-22.

Tiberius Claudius Drusus Nero Germanicus. See *Claudius I.*

Tibet. See *Asia,* B 6.

Tichonius. See *Tychonius.*

Tieftrunk, Johann Heinrich (1759–1837). B. Stove, near Rostock, Ger.; follower of I. Kant*; prof. philos. and theol. Halle. Held that basic religious ideas could be derived from basic morality of practical reason indep. of revelation. Works include *Einzig möglicher Zweck Jesu aus dem Grundgesetze der Religion entwickelt; Censur des christlichen protestantischen Lehrbegriffs; Die Religion der Mündingen.*

Tiele, Cornelis Petrus (1830–1902). Neth. theol.;

pastor Arminian cong. Rotterdam 1856; prof. Amsterdam and Leiden. Works include *Manuel de l'histoire des religions,* tr. M. Varnes; *Elements of the Science of Religion.*

Tiele-Winckler, Eva von (1866–1930). Luth. deaconess; "Mutter Eva" ("Mother Eva"); b. Miechowitz, near Beuthen (Bytom), Upper Silesia; daughter of industrialist; death of mother and personal illness turned her to soc. work; founded Friedenshort (a deaconess house) at Miechowitz and homes for homeless elsewhere; miss. work was undertaken in China, Afr., and Guatemala.

T'ien. See *Chinese Term Question; Confucianism,* 3.

Tiepolo, Giovanni Battista (1696–1770). Painter; b. Venice, It.; last important figure in Venetian art; initiated the baroque period. Works include *The Sacrifice of Abraham; Crossing of the Red Sea; Repudiation of Hagar; Fall of the Rebel Angels; Rachel Hiding the Idols; Judgment of Solomon; John the Baptist Preaching; Baptism of Christ; Decapitation of John the Baptist.*

Tierce. See *Hours, Canonical.*

Tietze, Christoph (Titius; 1641–1703). Hymnist; b. Wilkau, near Breslau; educ. Altdorf (near Nürnberg) and Jena; pastor Laubenzeddel, Hanfenfeld, and Hersbruck. Hymns include "Ich armer Mensch, ich armer Sünder"; "Sollt es gleich bisweilen scheinen"; "Was ist unser Leben und nach dem wir streben? eitel Eitelkeit."

Tigurinus, Consensus. See *Reformed Confessions,* A 8.

Til, Salomo[n] van (1643–1713). Ref. theol.; b. Weesp, Neth.; educ Utrecht and Leiden; pastor at various places; prof. Leiden. Distinguished natural and revealed theol. but regarded them as connected since doctrinal truth is rational. Works include *Theologiae utriusque compendium cum naturalis tum revelatae.*

Tilak, Narayan Waman (1861–1919). Poet, patriot, Christian of India; b. a Brahman (see *Brahmanism*); bap. 1895; tried to est. indep. ch. in India. His *Christayan* (life of Christ in poetic form) completed by his wife, Lakshmibai.

Tillich, Paul Johannes Oskar (1886–1965). B. Starzeddel, near Guben, Prussia; son of a Luth. pastor; educ. Berlin, Tübingen, Halle, Breslau; ordained Luth. 1912; army chaplain WW I; privatdocent Berlin 1919. Prof. Marburg 1924, Dresden and Leipzig 1925, Frankfurt am Main 1929. Lost position under Nazis 1933. Prof. Union Theol. Sem., NYC; Harvard U., Cambridge, Mass.; U. of Chicago, Ill. Concerned with relation bet. revelation and human reality; tried to find a synthesis bet. neoorthodoxy and liberal humanism; theol. and philos. are interrelated in a process that also involves sociol., hist., art, literature, ethics, psychotherapy. Works include *Kirche und Kultur; Rechtfertigung und Zweifel; Systematic Theology; The Courage to Be; Biblical Religion and the Search for Ultimate Reality; Theology of Culture.*

Tillmanns, Walter Guenther (Nov. 16, 1913–June 10, 1966). B. Altenburg, Ger.; educ. Heidelberg and Tübingen; to US 1936; educ. Wartburg Theol. Sem., Dubuque, Iowa. Pastor Clifton, Tex., 1938–40; Giddings, Tex., 1942–45. Taught at Hebron (Nebr.) Jr. Coll. (ALC) 1941–42. Prof. Wartburg Coll., Waverly, Iowa, 1946. Works include *The World and Men Around Luther;* coauthor *The Synods of American Lutheranism.*

Tillotson, John Robert (1630–94). B. Sowerby, Yorkshire, Eng.; educ. Cambridge; held various positions including dean Canterbury and canon St. Paul's, London; abp. Canterbury 1691; ineffective against deism* and RCm because of his latitudinarianism (see *Latitudinarians*).

Tilly, Johan Tserclaes (of) (various spellings; 1559–1632). Flemish field marshal; commander in chief RC field forces at outbreak of Thirty* Years' War; repeatedly victorious, but was defeated by Gustavus* II at Breitenfeld 1631 and at Rain, on the Lech (near its confluence with the Danube), where he was mortally wounded.

Timan, Johann (various spellings; before 1500–57). Luth. theol.; b. Amsterdam; educ. Wittenberg; pastor and reformed Bremen; opposed Anabaps.; attended 1537 meeting of the Schmalkaldic League (see *Lutheran Confessions,* B 2) and the Colloquy of Worms* and Regensburg* Conf. 1540/41; opposed Interim.* Works include *Farrago sententiarum consentientium.*

Time. OT dating was based on the reign of kings and other important events (e. g., Exodus, 1 K 6:1; erection of Solomon's temple, 1 K 9:10; Babylonian Captivity, Eze 33:21; earthquake, Am 1:1). The Seleucid era (312–64 BC; named after founder Seleucus I [Nicator; ca. 358–280; king of Babylon 312–280] and 5 other of its kings called Seleucus; at height of power controlled Bactria, Persia, Babylonia, Syria, and part of Asia Minor) was widely used by Jews and continued at Alexandria till the 16th c. and later in S Arabia. Jews under for. rule often figured their eras acc. to the system of the conquerors. Shortly after the time of Christ, Jews began to figure from the time of creation, which they regarded as being ca. 4,000 yrs. before the destruction of the temple.

The Christian era is reckoned from the birth of Christ on basis of calculation by Dionysius* Exiguus.

J. Ussher* propounded a scheme of chronology said to be source of dates long printed in margin of KJV beginning 1701. Some of its OT dates:

4004 – Fall
2349 – Flood
1921 – Call of Abraham
1706 – Jacob's Family Enters Egypt
1491 – Exodus
1451 – Beginning of the Conquest of Canaan
1405 – Othniel Becomes Judge of Israel
1095 – Saul Becomes King of Israel
1004 – Dedication of Solomon's Temple
975 – Division of the Kingdom
721 – Captivity of Israel
587 – Captivity of Judah
536 – Return of Jews Under Zerubbabel
4 – Birth of Christ

By calculations of cause and effect a theory of a much longer time span has been developed: There was a vast period of astronomical time before the earth existed as such. Then a vast period of earth, or geological, time passed before living structures appeared. The period of living structures has been divided into eras: Archeozoic, Proterozoic, Paleozoic, Mesozoic, and Cenozoic (era of animals and man). The Cenozoic era is divided into 2 periods or systems: Tertiary (of mammals) and Quaternary (of man). The period or system of man is divided into ages (which are in turn divided into Eolithic etc.): Stone Age (prehistoric; characterized by use of stone tools), Bronze Age (beginning in Eur. ca. 3500 BC, in W Asia and Egypt somewhat earlier; characterized by use of bronze tools), Iron Age (beginning ca. 1000 BC in S Eur., somewhat earlier in W Asia and Egypt; characterized by the smelting of iron), and later ages to the present space age, which began soon after the middle of the 20th c., when man reached and began to explore outer space. See also *Evolution.*

Definition of time is elusive. "Time marches on" suggests that, whatever it is, it moves inexorably toward or into the future; as it does, future events become part of the past.

Philosophers disagree on the nature of time. Parmenides* regarded change and becoming as illusions. Heraclitus* held that change characterizes all.

I. Newton* regarded time as indep. of, and prior to, events. G. W. v. Leibniz* held time to be formed by relationship bet. events and dependent on events. A. Einstein* regarded time as relative to the point of observation. Augustine* of Hippo regarded time as essentially psychological (the future is the anticipated as such, the past is the remembered as such). H. Bergson,* A. N. Whitehead,* et al. regarded time as modal, or the way in which the determined ("past") is related to the potential ("future"). See also *Royce, Josiah.* EL

Timor. See *Indonesia,* 12.

Timpler, Clemens (ca. 1567/68–1624). B. Stolpen, Saxony, Ger.; prof. Steinfurt 1595; Crypto-Calvinist. Wrote textbooks for almost all areas of philos.; works include *Metaphysicae systema methodicum.*

Tindal, Matthew (probably ca. 1653/57–1733). Deist; b. Beer Ferrers (Ferris), Devonshire, Eng.; educ. Oxford; RC ca. 1685; returned to Angl. Ch. 1688. Works include *Christianity as Old as the Creation: Or, the Gospel a Republication of the Religion of Nature.* See also *Deism,* III 5.

Tindal(e), William. See *Tyndale, William.*

Tintoretto, Il (It. "The Little Dyer"; real name Jacopo Robusti; 1518–94). Painter; b. Venice, It.; active mainly in Venice. Works include *Adoration of the Golden Calf; Adoration of the Magi; The Agony in the Garden; Ascension; The Baptism of Christ; Belshazzar's Feast; Cain and Abel; Christ Among the Doctors; Christ and the Adulteress; Christ Before Pilate; The Creation of the Animals; Crucifixion; Samson and Delilah.*

Tipitaka. See *Buddhism,* 2, 5; *Sacred Literature.*

Tiro, Prosper. See *Prosper of Aquitaine.*

Tischendorf, Lobegott Friedrich Constantin von (Lobegott sometimes classicized: Aenotheus; Konstantin; 1815–74). Luth. scholar; b. Lengenfeld, near Plauen, in the Saxon Vogtland, Ger.; educ. Leipzig; prof. Leipzig; discovered Codex Sinaiticus; deciphered Codex Ephraemi. Ed. Gk NT and other MSS; other works include *Wann wurden unsere Evangelien verfasst?* See also *Harmony of the Gospels,* 2; *Manuscripts of the Bible,* 3 a.

Tischreden. See *Luther, Table Talk of.*

Tissot, James Joseph Jacques (1836–1902). Painter, engraver, enameler; b. Nantes, Fr.; active in London, Eng., ca. 1870–80; traveled in Palestine 1887. Works include hundreds of Biblical watercolor pictures, many pub. under the title *Vie de Notre-Seigneur Jésus-Christ.* Pictures include *The Childhood of St. John the Baptist; Nathanael Under the Fig Tree; Healing of the Lepers at Capernaum; Jesus Teaching on the Sea Shore.*

Titchener, Edward Bradford (1867–1927). Psychol.; b. Chichester, West Sussex, Eng.; educ. Oxford and Leipzig; taught at Oxford; to US 1893; prof. Cornell U., Ithaca, N.Y. Exponent of structuralism (see *Psychology,* J 2). Works include *Experimental Psychology; A Text-Book of Psychology; Systematic Psychology: Prolegomena.*

Tithing. See *Finances in the Church,* 6.

Titian (Tiziano Vecelli, or Vecellio; 1477–1576). Painter; b. Pieve di Cadore, Belluno province, Veneto, It.; chief master of Venetian school. Works include *Adam and Eve; Martyrdom of St. Peter; Christ and the Adulteress; Supper at Emmaus.*

Titius, Christoph. See *Tietze.*

Tittmann, Johann August Heinrich (1773–1831). Ev. theol.; b. Langensalza, near Erfurt, Ger.; prof. and preacher Leipzig. Exponent of confessional supernaturalism*; opposed Prussian* Union. Works include *Encyklopädie der theologischen Wissenschaften; Über Superanaturalismus, Rationalismus und Atheismus; De synonymis in Novo Testamento.*

Titular Bishop. RC bp. with title of bp. of a defunct see, hence without jurisdiction there. Conquests, e. g., by Muslim, destroyed many sees; many exiled bps. assisted other prelates and became known as *vicarii in pontificalibus* or bps. *in partibus infidelium.* After the 12th c. the papal see continued to nominate bps. to sees in which they could not reside or rule. Since the 16th c., bps. have also been assigned to sees long suppressed. An 1882 encyclical abolished the term *in partibus infidelium,* substituting "titular bp." and "titular see." Many higher prelates in the curia,* vicars apostolic, and prelates *nullius* are titular bps. and abps. See also *Roman Catholic Church,* C 4; *Vicar Apostolic.*

Titus Flavius Sabinus Vespasianus (ca. 40–81). Son of Vespasian*; b. Rome, It.; emp. Rome 79–81; as commander of legion in Judea, captured Jerusalem 70 (commemorated by the Arch of Titus, built by Domitian* in Rome 81). See also *Persecution of Christians,* 2.

Tlatscala. See *Mexico,* B.

Tobit. See *Apocrypha,* A 3.

Toccata (from It. for "to touch or strike"). Kind of brilliant freestyle keyboard composition, usually with many rapid equal-time notes; a small toccata is a toccatina. Composers of this kind of music include J. S. Bach,* D. Buxtehude,* G. Frescobaldi,* A. Gabrieli,* J. Pachelbel,* H. Scheidemann,* S. Scheidt,* J. P. Sweelinck.*

Toellner, Johann Gottlieb (1724–74). Ev. theol.; b. Charlottenburg (now part of West Berlin), Ger.; prof. Frankfurt an der Oder; accepted Bible and Confessions but regarded natural revelation as sufficient for salvation. Works include *Beweis, dass Gott die Menschen bereits durch seine Offenbarung in der Natur zur Seligkeit führt; Der thätige Gehorsam Jesu Christi untersucht.* See also *Lutheran Theology After 1580,* 8.

Togo, Republic of. See *Africa,* C 13.

Tokai Evangelical Lutheran Church. The Evangelical* Luth. Ch. began work 1949 in the Tokai area of Jap. bet. Tokyo and Nagoya. This work was continued by The American* Luth. Ch. and led to formation of the Tokai Ev. Luth. Ch. 1960. Merged 1963 with the Japan* Ev. Luth. Ch. to form the new Japan Ev. Luth. Ch. See also *Japan.*

Tokens, Communion. See *Communion Tokens.*

Toland, John (originally Junius Janus; 1670–1722). Deist; b. near Londonderry, Ireland, of RC parentage; changed name and became Prot. ca. 1686; educ. Glasgow, Edinburgh, and Leiden; controversialist. Works include *Christianity Not Mysterious; Amyntor; Tetradymus; Pantheisticon* (parodied the Angl. liturgy). See also *Deism,* III 4; *Pantheism,* 2.

Toledo, Councils of. Prominent among many councils held at Toledo, Sp., was that of 447 (which condemned Priscillianists*) and that of 589 (which condemned Arianism*). See also *Christian Church, History of,* II 1; *Spain,* 1.

Toledo Theses (1867). In 1856 the Ev. Luth. Syn. of Iowa* and Other States adopted 7 theses binding its pastors to the Book* of Concord but distinguishing bet. essentials (theses and antithesis) and nonessentials (proof, elucidation, etc., called "Accidens"), and holding that the Confessions must be interpreted only historically, not dogmatically without regard to their hist. origin. This view was attacked by the Buffalo Syn. et al. Controversy regarding millennialism involved also the Mo. Syn. The Iowa Syn. suffered from resultant doubt. C. S. Fritschel (see *Fritschel,* 1) went to Ger. 1866 for opinions of recognized Luth. faculties and theologians on basis of Iowa Syn. publications. Opinions rendered included those of the faculty at Dorpat (Tartu) and of C. E. Luthardt,* G. C. A. v. Harless,* K. K. Münkel,* and H. E. F. Guericke.* The Dorpat faculty and Münkel recognized the need for distinguishing bet. essentials and nonessentials in the Confessions but criticized the way in which an 1858 Iowa Syn. essay spelled out the distinction. In 1867, at Toledo, Ohio, the Iowa Syn. adopted 9 theses in answer to the question, "What Is Necessary for Church Unity?" Summary of theses: The unity of the visible ch. consists in concordant preaching of the Gospel and administration of the sacraments. By the preaching of the Gospel is meant not only preaching from the pulpit but the pub. confession of the ch. This confession must hold all arts. of faith without error. The doctrine of the Gospel is the doctrine of justification by faith. Accordingly, ch. unity is fundamental but never absolute. Essential, or fundamental, doctrines are all those which the ch. has fixed in its Confessions. Doctrinal agreement does not apply to all unessential and incidental teachings in the Confessions, but only to all arts. of faith est. by the ch.

Kirchenblatt der evangelisch-lutherischen Synode von Iowa, I, No. 1 (Jan. 1858), [pp. 1–2]; J. A. Deindörfer, *Geschichte der Evangel.-Luth. Synode von Iowa und anderen Staaten* (Chicago, 1897); *Quellen und Dokumente zur Geshichte und Lehrstellung der ev.-luth. Synode von Iowa u. a. Staaten,* comp. G. J. Fritschel (Chicago, n. d.)

Toledo Theses (1907). Revision of Michigan* City Theses; drawn up 1907 Toledo, Ohio, by representatives of the Ev. Luth. Syn. of Iowa* and Other States and the Ev. Luth. Joint Syn. of Ohio* and Other States; adopted by Iowa 1907, formally by Ohio 1914; basis of 1919 discussions bet. the 2 syns. that led to fellowship bet. them 1920.

"Thesis I. The Church. The Church, in the proper sense of the term, is the communion of true believers which is established and built up through the means of grace. . . . According to its real essence the church is and remains invisible on earth. Fellowship of the means of grace is the necessary form of the church's appearance and the infallible mark of its existence; and in so far the church is visible.

"Thesis II. The Office of the Ministry. . . . The office of the ministry rests on a special command of the Lord, valid throughout all time, and consists in the right and power conferred by special call to administer the means of grace publicly and by commission of the congregation. The call (to the pastorate) is a right of the congregation within whose bounds the minister is to discharge his office. . . .

"Thesis III. Attitude to the Confessions. A binding subscription to the Confessions pertains only to the doctrines of faith therein set forth, and to all these without exception. Since the doctrine of Sunday taught in the Confessions is a doctrine revealed in God's Word, it is not to be excluded from the body of obligatory dogmas.

"Thesis IV. Open Questions. All doctrines revealed clearly and plainly in God's Word are, by virtue of the absolute authority of the divine Word, dogmatically fixed and binding on conscience, whether they have been symbolically defined or not. In God's church there is no justification for departing from clearly revealed Scripture truths, be their content fundamental or nonfundamental, important or apparently unimportant. Full agreement in all articles of faith constitutes the indispensable condition of church-fellowship. Persistent error in an article of faith always causes division. Full agreement in all nonfundamental doctrines is not attainable on earth, but should nevertheless be sought as goal. Those who knowingly, obstinately, and stubbornly contradict God's Word, even if only in subordinate points, thereby overthrow the organic foundation (of the faith) and must be excluded from church-fellowship.

"Thesis V. Chiliasm. Any chiliasm that regards the kingdom of Christ as an external, earthly, and worldly kingdom of glory and teaches a resurrection of all believers before the last day is to be rejected as a doctrine in direct conflict with the analogy of faith. The belief . . . that the reign of Christ and His saints referred to in Rev. 20 is an event belonging to the future and that the resurrection spoken of there is to be understood as a bodily resurrection of some [Ger. *einzelner*] believers unto life everlasting does indeed not contradict the analogy of faith but can no more be strictly proved from Scripture than can the spiritual interpretation.

"Thesis VI. Predestination and Conversion. We find that the church-dividing error in the Missouri doctrine of predestination is the severance of the universal gracious will of God and the special decree of election into two contradictory wills *(contradictoriae voluntates)* formed one after the other and apart from and beside each other. . . . Concerning conversion . . . we confess that, viewed as the placing or planting of a new spiritual life, conversion does not consist of or depend to any extent whatsoever on any cooperation . . . but that it is wholely and solely the work of the Holy Spirit. . . . We deny that the Holy Spirit works conversion according to the mere pleasure of His elective will and accomplishes it in the elect despite the most willful resistance . . . but we hold that by such stubborn resistance both conversion in time and election in eternity are hindered." EL

Iowa Syn. *Synodal-bericht* 1907, p. 109; Ohio Syn. *Verhandlungen* 1908, pp. 8–10; Ohio Syn. *Proceedings* 1908, pp. 8–11; Ohio Syn. *Minutes* 1914, p. 125; *Quellen und Dokumente zur Geschichte und Lehrstellung der ev.-luth. Synode von Iowa u. a. Staaten,* comp. G. J. Fritschel (Chicago, n. d.); [G.] F. B[ente], "Die Toledoer Unionsthesen," *L. u. W.* LIII (1907), 278–284; F. W. Stellhorn, "Das Kolloquium zu Toledo, Ohio," *Theologische Zeitschrift,* XXVI (1907), 166–168; F. W. Meuser, *The Formation of the American Lutheran Church* (Columbus, Ohio, 1958); *Documents of Lutheran Unity in America,* ed. E. C. Wolf (Philadelphia, Pa., 1966); *Doctrinal Declarations* (St. Louis, 1957).

Toleration, Edict of. (1) 313. See *Constantine I; Milan, Edict of.* (2) 1781. See *Hungary; Joseph II and Josephinism; Roman Catholic Church,* D 14.

Tolstadius, Erik. See *Sweden, Lutheranism in,* 3.

Tolstoi, Lev Nikolaevich (Tolstoy; Lyev; Leo; Nikolayevich; other spellings; 1828–1910). B. Yasnaya Polyana, Tula Province, Russ.; army officer; fought in Crimean War (1854–56); then lived on family estate Yasnaya Polyana; renounced use of his wealth and lived as a peasant; excommunicated by Holy* Syn. 1901.

Began an intensive study of Christianity in the 1870s; rejected immortality, Christ's deity, and other Christian doctrines as well as organized religion; developed Tolstoyism, a kind of Christian naturalism, based on the Sermon on the Mount, emphasizing nonresistance to evil.

Works include *The Christian Teaching; Meine Beichte; My Religion; What I Believe; The Kingdom of God Is Within You; What Is Religion?*

Toltec. See *Mexico,* B.

Tomkins, Oliver. See *Chalmers, James.*

Tomlinson, Ambrose Jessup (1865–1943). Father of H. A. Tomlinson*; b. near Westfield, Ind., of Quaker parents; ABS colporter in N. C. in the 1890s; joined holiness movement (see *Holiness Churches,* 1) 1896. See also *Church of God,* 2; *Church of God of Prophecy, The.*

Tomlinson, Homer Aubrey (1892–1968). Son of A. J. Tomlinson*; b. Westfield, Ind.; organized The Church* of God (Queens Village, N. Y.).

Tomlinson Church of God. See *Church of God,* 2; *Church of God of Prophecy, The.*

Tommaso de Vio. See *Cajetan.*

Tonga (Tonga Islands; Friendly Islands). Ca. 150 small islands ESE of Fiji, SSW of Samoa. *Area:* ca. 269 sq. mi. (697 sq. km.); pop. perhaps ca. 90,000. Brit. protectorate 1900; indep. 1970. LMS attempted miss. work unsuccessfully 1797; Meths.

est. successful work in the 1820s. Taufaahau (also Siosi; King George I; ca. 1798–1893), ruler of Haabi Is., was bap. 1830. Meths. predominate; others include RCs, Angls., Seventh-day Advs., Latter Day Saints.

Tongues, Gift of (glossolalia, from Gk. *glossa,* "tongue," and *lalia,* "speaking"). Ecstatic religious speech usually unintelligible to hearers. The speaking in tongues of Acts 2:4-13 and 10:46 was understood; that in 1 Co 14 required interpretation (cf. verse 13). Scripture connects speaking in tongues with the Holy Spirit; but it does not say that all similar manifestations are evidences of His presence. See also *Gifts of the Spirit,* 8–10.

Tonstall. See *Tunstall.*

Tonsure (from Lat. *tondere,* "to shear"). Clipping or shaving part or all of the top of the head as a sacred rite. In RCm it is part of the ceremony admitting a layman to the clerical state. The shaven crown or patch is also called tonsure. Custom circumstances, and other factors determine size and other details.

Toplady, Augustus Montague (1740–78). Hymnist; b. Farnham, Surrey, Eng.; educ. Dublin, Ireland; ordained Angl. 1762; vicar Broadhembury (or Broad Hembury), Devonshire, Eng.; minister of the Chapel of the Fr. Calvinists in Leicester Fields ca. 1776. Hymns include "Rock of Ages."

Torah. Heb. term for divine law esp. as contained in the Pentateuch. See also *Judaism,* 2, 3.

Torgau, League of. Organized 1526 by Luth. princes in Ger. in reaction against the League of Dessau.* See also *Speyer, Diets of,* 1.

Torgau Articles. See *Lutheran Confessions,* A 2.

Torgau Book. See *Lutheran Confessions,* C 2.

Torgau Conference. See *Chemnitz, Martin; Lutheran Confessions,* C 2.

Torgau Confession. See *Crypto-Calvinistic Controversy.*

Torkillus, Reorus (1599–Sept. 7, 1643). First Luth. pastor of a parish in the US; b. Fässberg, Östergötland, Swed.; to New Swed. on the Del. with the 2d expedition from Swed. ca. 1639/40; served Fort Christina colonists, Wilmington, Del. See also *United States, Religious History of the,* 6.

Török, Pál (1808–83). B. Alsóvárad (Also-Varad, or Lower Varad, or Wardein), Hung.; educ. Debrecen and Vienna; est. the Prot. Budapest Theol. Academy 1855 and was its 1st rector; est. Ref. Gymnasium at Budapest 1857; bp. Danube Dist. 1860.

Torquemada, Juan de (Johannes de Turrecremata; 1388–1468). B. Valladolid, Sp.; studied at Paris, Fr.; prior of Valladolid and Toledo, Sp.; named *Defensor fidei* and made cardinal 1439; attended councils at Constance,* Basel,* Ferrara, and Florence*; regarded pope as supreme also over council; opposed doctrine of Immaculate* Conception. Works include treatise on Eucharist against Hussites; commentary on decrees of Gratian*; *Summe de ecclesia domini.*

Torquemada, Tomás de (Thomas; ca. 1420–98). B. Valladolid, Sp.; Dominican prior at Segovia; grand inquisitor (or inquisitor gen.) of the Span. Inquisition* 1483.

Torrey, Charles Cutler (1863–1956). B. East Hardwick, Vt.; educ. Andover (Mass.) Theol. Sem.; instructor in Semitic languages Andover 1892–1900; dir. (in Jerusalem) Am. School(s) of Oriental Research; prof. Semitics Yale U., New Haven, Conn., till 1932. Works include *The Composition and Date of Acts; Ezra Studies; Documents of the Primitive Church; The Jewish Foundation of Islam; Pseudo-Ezekiel and the Original Prophecy; The Second Isaiah.*

Torrey, Joseph (1797–1867). Cong. theol.; b. Rowley, Mass.; educ. Andover (Mass.) Theol. Sem.; miss.; pastor Royalton, Vt., 1819–27; prof. Gk. and Lat. 1827–42, intellectual and moral philos. 1842–67 U. of Vt., Burlington; pres. there 1862–66. Tr. J. A. W. Neander* *General History of the Christian Religion and Church;* other works include *A Theory of Fine Art.*

Torrey, Reuben Archer (1856–1928). Cong. evangelist; b. Hoboken, N. J.; educ. Yale Coll., New Haven, Conn., and at Leipzig and Erlangen, Ger.; pastor Garretsville, Ohio, 1878–82; active in Minneapolis, Minn., 1883–89; supt. Moody Bible Institute 1889–1908 (and pastor Chicago 1894–1905); dean Bible Institute, Los Angeles, Calif., 1912–24. Works include *The Fundamental Doctrines of the Christian Faith.* See also *Revivals,* 2.

Torrison, Isaac Bertinus (Nov. 17, 1859–Nov. 17, 1929). B. Manitowoc, Wis.; educ. Johns Hopkins U., Baltimore, Md., and Conc. Sem., St. Louis, Mo.; ordained 1885 Norw. Synod. Pastor Waco, Tex., 1885–89; Chicago, Ill., 1889–98; Decorah, Iowa, 1901–29. See also *Madison Settlement.*

Torun. See *Thorn.*

Totalitarianism. See *Government.*

Totemism (from an Ojibwa word indicating relationship). Belief in which an animal, plant, or other object serves as emblem (totem) of family or clan. Adherents hold that a mystic relationship exists bet. the totem and the family or clan and that characteristics (e. g., power) transfer from totem to people; a tribe is divided into totemic groups imposing restrictions (e. g., marriage forbidden within totemic group). See also *Durkheim, Émile; Primitive Religion.*

Totenfest. Ger. name of festival in commemoration of the dead. See also *Departed, Commemoration of.*

Toulouse, Synods of. Held 1056, 1119, 1161, 1229, and 1590 at Toulouse (ancient Tolosa), Haute-Garonne dept., S Fr. The syn of 1161 recognized Alexander III (see *Popes,* 9) to the exclusion of Victor IV. The syn. of 1229 adopted 45 canons for extinction of heresy and reest. of peace (see also *Inquisition,* 3).

Touptala, Danilo. See *Dimitrij of Rostov.*

Toussain, Daniel (Tossanus; 1541–1602). Son of Peter Toussain*; father of Paul Toussain*; b. Montbéliard, Fr. Educ. Basel, Switz.; Tübingen, Ger.; Paris, Fr. Pastor Orléans, Fr., 1562; forced to flee 1568, he found protection with Renata* of Ferrara in Montargis; returned to Montbéliard 1570; fled after Bartholomew's* Day Massacre to Basel; court preacher Heidelberg 1573; prof. Neustadt ca. 1576/77; pastor and prof. Heidelberg 1583.

Toussain, Paul (Tossanus; 1572–1634). Son of Daniel Toussain*; b. Montargis, Fr.; educ. Heidelberg, Altdorf, Geneva, and Leiden; rector Deventer and Amsterdam; pastor Frankenthal 1600, Heidelberg 1608; present 1618 at Syn. of Dordrecht.*

Toussain, Peter (Pierre; Tossanus; 1499–1573). Father of Daniel Toussain*; b. St. Laurent, near Marville (145 mi. ENE of Paris), Lorraine; educ. Metz, Basel, Cologne, Paris, Rome; canon Metz 1515, where he learned M. Luther's doctrine; fled to Basel; to Paris 1525; returned to Metz; imprisoned; escaped; deviously to Wittenberg; engaged to continue the reformation of Montbéliard; gave the ch. neither a strictly Ref. nor Luth. character; deposed after the 1559 Luth. ch. order for Württemberg was adopted.

Towianski, Andreas (1799–1878). Polish mystic; b. Antoszwince, Latvia; studied law in Wilna (Vilnius); lawyer; claimed to have visions; held that there is a secret connection bet. the visible world and the world of spirits.

Town and Country, Church in. See *Rural Church in America.*

Trach. See *Draconites, Johann(es).*

Tract (liturgical). Scripture verses recited or sung after the Gradual* or as part of it or instead of the Hallelujah* on penitential days from Septuagesima to Holy Saturday (see *Church Year,* 3, 4, 16; *Quadragesima*), on ember days (see *Quatember*), and certain other occasions. The term is derived from the Lat. for "drawn out," a tract being assigned to one voice without a break.

Tract [Tractatus] on the Power and Primacy of the Pope. See *Lutheran Confessions,* B 2.

Tractarianism. RC revival in the Ch. of Eng. that began 1833 at Oxford with pub. of *Tracts for the Times* (see *Newman, John Henry*); 90 tracts appeared 1833–41. Other tractarians include R. H. Froude,* J. Keble,* C. Marriott,* E. B. Pusey.* Newman resigned his incumbency in the Ch. of Eng. 1843, was received into the RC Ch. 1845; others, clerics and laymen, followed him. Effects of tractarianism include revival and strengthening of the high* ch. movement and increased emphasis on RC tradition in doctrine, sacraments, worship, and life. Reaction against it included formation of the Evangelical* Alliance. See also *Anglo-Catholics; England,* C 7.

Tracts, Religious. See *Religious Tracts; Tractarianism.*

Tracts for the Times. See *Tractarianism.*

Traditio-historical Research. See *Higher Criticism,* 16.

Tradition. In the ancient Christian Ch. the Lat. word *traditio* ("act of handing over"; equivalent of Gk. *paradosis*) was used of instruction, oral and written, given by one person to another. In course of time it came to refer to teaching not in Scripture.

Jews hold that God gave Moses an oral law which was handed down orally. Decisions of their doctors and priests became the source of their traditions (Mt 15:2-3; Mk 7:3-13; 2 Th 2:15; 3:6; see also *Talmud*).

Early ch. fathers (e. g., Clement* of Alexandria, Irenaeus,* Tertullian*) often appealed to oral tradition. But they warned against setting too high a value on it (e. g., Tertullian, *De virginibus velandis,* i; Cyprian, *Epist.* lxxiv [lxxv]). Augustine acknowledged the adequacy of Scripture (*De doctrina Christiana,* ii 9) but said that he would not believe the Gospel except as moved by the authority of the ch. (*Contra epistolam Manichaei quam vocant fundamenti,* v). See also *Vincent of Lérins.*

In the Dark* Ages extensive compilations of patristic writings (with more or less pagan learning included) were continued (e. g., by Alcuin,* F. M. A. Cassiodorus,* Isidore* of Seville, Rabanus* Maurus). Reliance on tradition was dealt a telling blow by P. Abelard.*

M. Luther* rejected extravagant RC claims for tradition and the spirit of radicals who tried to overthrow everything; tradition is reflected, e. g., in retention of the Creed; but he felt free to investigate traditional decisions even regarding the canon of Scripture. AC XXI: In our teaching nothing "departs from the Scriptures or the catholic church or the church of Rome, in so far as it is known from its writers." The Council of Trent* (Sess. IV, Decree Concerning the Canonical Scriptures) placed tradition on a level with Scripture *(omnes libros tam veteris quam novi testamenti . . . necnon traditiones ipsas . . . tamquam vel oretenus a Christo, vel a Spiritu Sancto dictatas et continua successione in ecclesia catholica conservatas, pari pietatis affectu ac reverentia suscipit et veneratur),* thus preparing the way for the doctrine of papal infallibility. EL

See also *Norma normans; Regensburg Conference.*

Traditions of Matthias. See *Apocrypha,* B 2.

Traditores. See *Donatist Schism, The; Lapsi.*

Traducianism. View that the soul* of a new infant is generated from the souls of its parents. Many prefer this view to creationism* because they feel that it helps to account for transmission of sin from parents to offspring (see also *Sin, Original*).

Traherne, Thomas (ca. 1636/37–74). Metaphysical poet and cleric; probably b. Hereford, Eng.; educ. Oxford. Works include *Roman Forgeries; Christian Ethicks* (also pub. under the title *The Way to Blessedness*); *Centuries of Meditations.*

Trajan (Marcus Ulpius Trajanus; 52 [53?] –117). Roman emp. 98–117; b. Italica, near Seville, Sp.; involved in persecutions of Christians (see *Persecutions of Christians,* 3).

Trandberg, Peter Christian (1832–96). B. on is. of Bornholm, Den.; educ. Copenhagen; influenced by S. A. Kierkegaard*; itinerant and revivalist on Bornholm 1860–63; left state ch. and organized a Luth. Free Ch. 1863; resigned as pastor 1877 because of ill health; to US 1882; prof. Chicago* Theol. Sem. 1885–90; dismissed because of his Luth. principles.

Tranoscius. See *Tranovsky.*

Tranovsky, Jirí (George Trzanowski; Georgius Tranoscius; Jerzy Tranowski; 1592–1637). Called "Polish Luther" by Slovaks because of his Polish descent; b. Cieszyn, Silesia; educ. Wittenberg, Ger.; teacher Prague; private tutor; headmaster of school at Holesov, Moravia; head of school 1615, pastor 1616 Valasské Mezirici, Moravia; returned to Cieszyn 1625 under anti-Prot. pressure; then to Bielsko, where he served first as court chaplain, then (till end of 1627) as municipal minister; under Counter* Reformation pressure to Budatyn, Slovakia, then to the castle of Orava; pastor Liptovsky Sväty Mikulás, Slovakia. Tr. AC into Czech 1620. See also *Czechoslovakia,* 7; *Synod of Evangelical Lutheran Churches,* 13.

A. Wantula, "The Slavonic Luther," *CTM,* XVII (1946), 728–737.

Tranquebar. See *India,* 10; *Ministry, Education of* XI B 9.

Transcendence of God. Quality or attribute acc. to which God is supermundane, absolutely free and superior to all earthly, material things; even the heaven and heaven of heavens cannot contain Him (1 K 8:27; cf. Jb 11:7-10). But He is not separate or apart (see *Deism*); cf. Jer 23:23; Acts 17:28. See also *Immanence of God; Panentheism.*

Transcendentalism. Idealistic philos. of I. Kant* acc. to which it is possible to know principles that transcend human experience. The term is also applied to a 19th c. New Eng. movement centering in R. W. Emerson.*

Transept. Extension of bema N and S. See also *Church Architecture,* 3; *Orientation of Churches.*

Transfiguration. See *Church Year,* 16.

Transjordan. See *Middle East,* G.

Translations, Bible. See *Bible Versions.*

Transmigration of Souls (Gk. *metempsychosis,* "animation after [death]").

1. View that at death the soul passes into another body (human, animal, or plant) or demonic or divine form. Based on animism (see *Primitive Religion*).

2. Prominent in religions of India. See *Brahmanism,* 3; *Hinduism,* 3.

3. Theoretically Buddhism* teaches neither the existence of the soul nor its transmigration; practically it does teach metempsychosis. See also *Karma.*

4. Plato,* Plutarch,* and other Gk. writers say that Egyptians taught metempsychosis.

5. In Greece, the view is assoc. with Pythagoreanism,* Empedocles,* Plato and Neoplatonism.*

6. The view is also assoc. with Gnosticism,* Manichaeism,* Judaism,* Druids,* Theosophy,* savage and barbarian peoples in many parts of the earth, and others. It is rejected by Christianity.

See also *Reincarnation.*

Transubstantiation. Change of one substance into another. Term for RC view that in the eucharistic rite the substance or basic reality of bread and wine are changed into the body and blood of Jesus Christ, while the outward appearances of bread and wine are not affected. RC theologians disagree as to whether bread and wine are annihilated in the process or if they pass into preexistent body and blood. See also *Eucharistic Controversies; Grace, Means of,* IV 3; *Lateran Councils.*

Transylvania (Hung. Erdély; Ger. Siebenbürgen). Region in NW and cen. Romania. Part of Dacia in Roman times; later overrun by Germanic and other tribes; conquered by Hungarians 1003; soon thereafter, Szeklers (probably akin to Magyars) settled in the east and southeast and "Saxons" (Germans from the Rhineland and Luxembourg) in northeastern and southern passes; origin and hist. of the Vlachs (after whom Walachia, or Wallachia, was named) is much debated (their authentic hist. begins ca. the end of the 13th c.). Invaded by Mongols 1241. Tributary to the sultan 1540 in reaction against royal Ger. Hapsburgs. Part of Hung. 1867. Made part of Romania 1918/20. N part assigned to Hung. 1940–45, returned to Romania 1947.

Christianity probably reached Transylvania in Roman times. Won decisively for RCm in the 11th c.; diocese of Transylvania erected 1103. Hussite* doctrines spread. When Transylvania became a vassal principality under Turkish rule in the 16th c. most of its Caths. became Prot.

M. Luther's writings reached Transylvania ca. 1519; a reform movement begun Hermannstadt 1519 was short-lived, but a more successful one began Kronstadt in the early 1540s under leadership of J. Honter(us).* The AC was adopted 1572 largely as result of leadership of M. Hebler.*

In the 17th and 18th c. the Luth. Ch. in Transylvania experienced various persecutions. The 1861 ch. const., adopted after negotiation with the Austrian govt. (which saw advantage in good relations), gave the ch. autonomy free from state rule and led to lay participation in ch. administration. Nazis took control of the ch. 1940, communists at the end of WW II; many ch. activities, esp. educ., are highly restricted. Hungs. and Gers. each organized their own Luth. ch.

Trappists (Order of Cistercians* of the Strict Observance). Arose out of a reform of Cistercians in the 1660s by A. J. Le B. de Rance.* Trappists rise at 2 (2:15 weekdays), retire at 7, devoting 4–6 hrs. to manual labor, the rest of the day, apart from meals, to worship services, prayer, meditative reading, and study. Meat, fish, and eggs are restricted to the sick. Silence is perpetual, except for necessary directions at work and consultation with superiors.

Trautmann, Philipp Jakob (Jacob; Feb. 21, 1815–Apr. 3, 1900). B. Lambsborn, Rhenish Palatinate, Bav., Ger.; trained by J. K. W. Löhe* at Neuendettelsau; to US 1845 with F. A. Crämer,* J. A. Detzer,* and F. J. C. Lochner.* Pastor Danbury, Ottawa Co., Ohio, in the Sandusky Bay area, 1845; mem. Mo. Syn. at its 1st conv. 1847. Pastor Liverpool, Medina Co., Ohio, 1849; Adrian, Mich., 1850; retired 1882; thereafter repeatedly supplied vacancies. See also *Michigan Synod,* 1.

Travers, Walter (ca. 1548–1635). Presb. cleric, educator; b. Nottingham, Eng.; educ. Cambridge and Geneva; refused to sign Thirty-nine Articles; ordained on the Continent to serve the Eng. cong. at Antwerp; lecturer London 1581; dismissed 1585; tried to make Eng. Calvinistic; provost Trin. Coll., Dublin, Ireland, in the mid-1590s. Works include *Ecclesiasticae disciplinae et Anglicanae ecclesiae ab illa aberrationis, plena e verbo Dei et dilucida . . . explicatio.*

Tre ore (from Lat. for "3 hours"). 3-hr. service (noon to 3) on Good Fri.; introd. in the 17th c.; commemorates Christ's hours on the cross.

Treasury of Merits (Lat. *thesaurus meritorum*). In RCm, alleged treasury of merits (filled by merits of Christ and superabundant works of saints) from which the ch. grants indulgences.*

Treatise on the Power and Primacy of the Pope. See *Lutheran Confessions,* B 2.

Treaty of Bergerac. See *France,* 9.

Treaty of Cambrai. See *Cambrai, Peace of.*

Treaty of Lübeck. See *Thirty Year's War.*

Treaty of Madrid (1526). See *Speyer, Diets of,* 1.

Treaty of Nemours. See *France,* 9.

Treaty of Prague. See *Thirty Years' War.*

Treaty of Utrecht. See *Utrecht, Treaty of.*

Tregelles, Samuel Prideaux (1813–75). B. Wodehouse Place, near Falmouth, Eng.; ironworker; largely self-educ. in original languages of the Bible. Issued a critical ed. of the Gk. NT. See also *Brethren, Plymouth; Lexicons,* A.

Treitschke, Heinrich von (1834–96). B. Dresden, Ger.; educ. Leipzig and Bonn; taught at Leipzig, Freiburg, Kiel, Heidelberg, Berlin. First opposed O. E. L. v. Bismarck, then supported him; opposed social democracy; first opposed Christianity later was more favorably inclined to it; emphasized power of state. Works include *Deutsche Geschichte in 19. Jahrhundert.*

Trelcatius. 1. *Lucas the Elder* (1542–1602). Father of 2; Ref. theol.; b. Erin, near Arras, N Fr.; educ. Paris and Orléans; refugee London, Eng.; preacher Walloon congs. in Neth.; prof. Leiden 1587. Works include *Synopsis theologiae.* 2. *Lucas the Younger* (1573–1607). Son of 1; Ref. theol.; b. London, Eng.; Walloon preacher Leiden 1595; prof. Leiden 1603. Works include *Scholastica et methodica locorum communium s. theologiae institutio.*

Tremellius, John Immanuel (Joannes; Tremellio; 1510–80). B. in ghetto at Ferrara, It.; bap. RC; prof. Heb. at Lucca, It.; fled to Switz. and became ev.; taught Strasbourg 1542–47, Cambridge 1548–53; helped write Book* of Common Prayer; tutor of princes at Zweibrücken 1554–58; rector Gymnasium at Hornbach 1559–61; taught at Heidelberg 1561–67, then at Metz, then at Sedan. Works include a Chaldean and Syriac grammar. See also *Junius, Franciscus.*

Trench, Richard Chenevix (1807–86). B. Dublin, Ireland; educ. Harrow and Cambridge, Eng.; held various positions; ordained Angl. priest 1835; lectured at Cambridge 1845–46; prof. King's Coll., London, 1846–58; dean Westminster 1856–64; abp. Dublin 1864–84. Works include *Notes on the Miracles of Our Lord; Notes on the Parables of Our Lord; Synonyms of the New Testament.*

Trent, Council of (Lat. *Tridentinum*). Regarded as 19th ecumenical council by RCs (see also *Councils and Synods,* 4). Met in 3 periods at Trent (It. Trento; Ger. Trient; ancient Tridentum), NE It.

Sess. 1–10; Dec. 13, 1545–Sept. 1547; under Paul* III; transferred to Bologna Mar. 1547 because of plague.

Sess. 11–16; May 1, 1551–Apr. 28, 1552; under Julius* III; at Trent; Prots. having been granted an improved safe-conduct, ambassadors and theologians of several estates (Brandenburg, Württemberg, Strasbourg) attended.

Sess. 17–25; Jan. 18, 1562–Dec. 4, 1563; under Pius* IV.

Issued a number of decrees, e. g., on the canonical Scriptures (see also *Tradition*), original sin, justification, sacraments, purgatory, indulgences.

Enacted various reforms, e. g., regarding educ. of clerics, conferring of benefices, administration of property.

See also *Counter Reformation,* 12; *Interim,* II; *Roman Catholic Church,* B 2–5; *Roman Catholic Confessions,* A; *"Stabat mater"; Tempus clausum.*

Trepka, Eustachy (1519–58). Polish Luth.; educ. Wittenberg; pastor Poznan, Poland; preacher and secy. at court of starost gen. of Poland 1548; privy councillor to Albert* of Prussia 1553; opposed J. Laski*; leader of congs. in Greater Poland which adopted AC. Tr. Luth. books into Polish.

Tressler, Victor George Augustine (Apr. 10, 1865–Sept. 1, 1923). B. Somerfield, former borough, Somerset Co., Pennsylvania. Educ. Gettysburg (Pa.) Coll. and McCormick Theol. Sem., Chicago, Ill.; also studied law in Chicago 1887–88. Pastor San Jose, Calif., 1891–98 (ordained 1892); lecturer San Jose Academy 1896–98; dean and prof. Ansgar Coll., Hutchinson, Minn., 1901–02. Prof. Wittenberg Coll., Springfield, Ohio, 1903–05; Hamma Divinity School, Springfield, Ohio, 1905–23. Pres. The General* Syn. of the Ev. Luth Ch. in the USA 1917–18.

Treutlen, John Adam (Johann; 1726–82). B. Berchtesgaden, in the Salzburg Alps, Austria; to US with Salzburgers*; helped form state of Ga. and was its 1st gov. 1777; defended Savannah against Brit. and Indians; repulsed by Brit. 1779; settled near Orangeburg S. C.; returned to Ga. 1781 upon election to pub. office; murdered by Tories.

Treves, Holy Coat of. See *Holy Coat of Treves.*

Tribunals of Curia. See *Curia,* 2 e.

Tridentine. Of, relating to, or based on Council of Trent.* See also *Roman Catholic Confessions,* A.

Trigland, Jacobus (1583–1654). Ref. theol.; b. Vianen, Neth.; pastor Stolwijk 1607, Amsterdam 1610; prof. Leiden 1634; opposed Remonstrants*; present at 1618–19 Syn. of Dordrecht.*

Triller, Valentin (ca. 1493–1573). Ev. pastor, hymnist; educ. Kraków, Poland; pastor Panthenau. Works include *Ein Schlesisch Singebüchlein.*

Trillhaas, Wolfgang. See *Dogmatics,* B 13.

Trimurti. See *Hinduism,* 4.

Trine, Ralph Waldo (1866–1959). B. Mount Morris, Ill.; mystic philos.; exponent of New* Thought; held that the message of Christianity is essentially the same as that of the other great religions. Works include *In Tune with the Infinite; In the Hollow of His Hand; My Philosophy and My Religion.*

Trinidad and Tobago. West Indies islands off the NE coast of Venezuela. *Area:* ca. 1,980 sq. mi.; *pop.* (1973 est.): ca. 1,167,330, mostly Negro and East Indian. Dscovered by Columbus 1498. Changed hands repeatedly. Trinidad Brit. crown colony 1802, Tobago 1877. Slaves, imported under Sp. rule in the 17th and 18th c., were emancipated in the early 1830s. Amalgamated into a single colony 1889. Mem. West Indies Fed. 1958–62. Indep. 1962. RC miss. began with coming of the Spaniards. Others have included Baps., Salv. Army, Seventh-day Adv., Presb., Pentecostal. Prot. community: perhaps ca. 90,000 in the late 1960s.

Trinitarians (Order of the Most Holy Trin. for the Redemption of Captives). RC order founded, acc. to tradition, by Jean* de Matha and approved 1198 by Innocent III (see *Popes,* 10). First object was to secure release of Christians held captive by Muslim; activities expanded later to larger soc. service. Also known as Mathurins, or Mathurines, from St. Mathurin, 3d c. AD priest to whom the Paris convent was dedicated.

Trinity. 1. The eternal, infinite Spirit (Jn 4:24), subsisting in 3 Persons, Father, Son, and Holy Spirit. God is one (Dt 6:4; Is 44:6; 48:12; 1 Ti 2:5). God is also three. Plurality is indicated in *Elohim* (Heb. "God"), pl. form expressing not a plurality of gods, but a plurality in one God (and hence construed with the singular verb form, e. g., Gn. 1:1)

Athanasian Creed (see *Ecumenical Creeds,* C): ". . . We worship one God in Trinity and Trinity in Unity, neither confounding the Persons nor dividing the Substance. For there is one Person of the Father, another of the Son, and another of the Holy Spirit. But the Godhead of the Father, of the Son, and of the Holy Spirit is all one: the glory equal, the majesty coeternal. Such as the Father is, such is the Son, and such is the Holy Ghost. The Father uncreate, the Son uncreate, and the Holy Spirit uncreate. The Father incomprehensible, the Son incomprehensible, and the Holy Spirit incomprehensible. The Father eternal, the Son eternal, and the Holy Spirit eternal. And yet they are not three Eternals, but one Eternal. As there are not three Uncreated nor three Incomprehensibles, but one Uncreated and one Incomprehensible. So likewise the Father is almighty, the Son almighty, and the Holy Spirit almighty. And yet they are not three Almighties, but one Almighty. So the Father is God, the Son is God, and the Holy Spirit is God. And yet they are not three Gods, but one God. So likewise the Father is Lord, the Son Lord, and the Holy Spirit Lord. And yet not three Lords, but one Lord. For like as we are compelled by the Christian verity to acknowledge every Person by Himself to be God and Lord, so are we forbidden by the catholic religion to say, There be three Gods or three Lords. The Father is made of none, neither created nor begotten. The Son is of the Father alone, not made nor created, but begotten. The Holy Ghost is of the Father and of the Son, neither made nor created nor begotten, but proceeding. So there is one Father, not three Fathers; one Son, not three Sons; one Holy Spirit, not three Holy Spirits. And in this Trinity none is before or after another; none is greater or less than another; but the whole three Persons are coeternal together and coequal, so that in all things, as is aforesaid, the Unity in Trinity and the Trinity in Unity is to be worshiped."

AC I 2–3: "There is one divine essence, which is called and which is truly God, and . . . there are three persons in this one divine essence, equal in power and alike eternal: God the Father, God the Son, God the Holy Spirit. All three are one divine essence, eternal, without division, without end, of infinite power, wisdom, and goodness, one creator and preserver of all things visible and invisible."

2. All similes, comparisons, images, or illustrations by which men have tried to represent the doctrine of three Persons in one Godhead fail to illustrate; much less do they explain. The Trin. has been compared to fire, which is said to possess the 3 "attributes" of flame, light, and heat; but this division is highly artificial, and the comparison is altogether faulty, because Father, Son, and Holy Spirit are not so many attributes of God, but are, each of them, God Himself. The Trin. has been compared to the division of a human being into body, soul, and mind; but each of these constituents is not separately a human being, whereas each of the divine Persons, separately considered, is truly God (cf. Cl 2:9).

3. The doctrine of the Trin. is beyond our powers of comprehension. The difficulty does not lie in the numeral terms but in the relation of the 3 Persons to each other and the way they are united in one Godhead without being only parts of it. AC I 4: "The word 'person' is to be understood as the Fathers employed the term in this connection, not as a part or a property of another but as that which exists of itself."

4. That the Father, Son, and Holy Spirit are 3 distinct Persons is evident from Mt 3:13-17. The Father speaks; the Son is baptized; the Holy Spirit descends like a dove. Cf. Gn 1:1-3 and Ps 33:6 with Jn 1:1; Gn 48:16 with Is 63:9-10; cf. also Is 48:16.

5. These 3 Persons are equal in works, rank, and attributes. Cf. Jb 33:4; Is 9:6; Jn 5:23; 8:58; 1 Co 2:10-14; Eph 1:10; 3:14-16.

See also *Christ Jesus; Church Year,* 6, 16; *Circumincession; Ecumenical Creeds; Father, God the; Fatherhood of God; Filioque Controversy; God; Holy Spirit; Perichoresis; Procession of the Holy Spirit.*

Trinity Seminary. See *Danish Lutherans in America,* 5; *Ministry, Education of,* X P.
Tripitaka. See *Buddhism,* 2, 5; *Sacred Literature.*
Trisagion (Trishagion; Gk. "thrice holy"). Doxology whose name is derived from its 3-fold "Holy": "Holy God, Holy and Mighty, Holy and Immortal, have mercy on us." Used in RCm since the 11th c. as part of the Improperia,* on other occasions, and for inscriptions on bells. Also used in E rites. To be distinguished from Sanctus (see *Worship, Parts of,* 11), sometimes also called Trisagion.
Tritheim, Johann(es) (Trithemius: 1462–1516). B. Trittenheim, near Trier, on Moselle river; educ. Heidelberg; abbot Sponheim and Würzburg. Works include *Sermones et exhortationes ad monachos;* histories.
Tritheism. Belief in 3 gods. Specifically, the heretical view that Father, Son, and Holy Spirit are not 3 distinct Persons in 1 God, but 3 distinct essences, or gods; hence a form of polytheism. Arose and developed within Monophysitism.* See also *Roscellinus.*
Trito-Isaiah Theory. See *Duhm, Bernhard.*
Tritone. See *Modes, Ecclesiastical.*
Triumph the Church and Kingdom of God in Christ. See *Holiness Churches,* 2.
Triumphal Arch. See *Church Architecture,* 3.
Trivium (from Lat. for "3 ways; place where 3 roads meet"). In Middle Ages, group of studies consisting of grammar, rhetoric, and logic; the lower group of the 7 liberal arts. See also *Quadrivium.*
Troeltsch, Ernst Peter Wilhelm (1865–1923). Prot. theol.; b. Haunstetten, near Augsburg, Ger.; educ. Erlangen, Berlin, Göttingen; taught at Göttingen 1890, Bonn 1892, Heidelberg 1894, Berlin ca. 1914/15; a leader of Religionsgeschichtliche* Schule. See also *Historicism,* 4; *Lutheran Theology After 1580,* 13; *Modernism,* 2; *Switzerland, Contemporary Theology in,* 1–2.
Tronchin, Theodore (1582–1657). B. Geneva, Switz.; prof. Heb. and theol. Geneva; present at 1618–19 Syn. of Dordrecht.* Works include *Harmonia confessionum.*
Troparia. Short hymns in rhythmic prose sung or chanted in E Orthodox chs. See also *Canon,* 1.
Trope. Addition of music, or words and music, by way of expansion or elaboration of the official text of RC mass or breviary office to be sung by the choir; incapable of artistic existence apart from the liturgical text and setting; in vogue ca. 9th–12th c. To be distinguished from sequence.*
Trotzendorf, Valentin (Valentinus Drossendorf; 1490–1556). Educator; original name Friedland; adopted name of birthplace on matriculation at Wittenberg; b. Trotzendorf (later called Troitschendorf), near Görlitz, Ger.; educ. Leipzig and Wittenberg; rector Lat. School Goldberg, near Liegnitz, Silesia, 1524; the school fell victim to pest and fire 1554.
Truber, Primus (Trubar; 1508–86). "Slovenian Luther"; b. Raschiza, near Auersperg (near Laibach [now Ljubljana], which is near Trieste); RC priest; preached justification by faith alone at Laibach ca. 1531; fled in the late 1540s; preacher Rothenburg; pastor Kempten 1552; to Laibach 1562; banished in the mid-1560s; pastor Laufen, on the Neckar, Württemberg, 1565–66, and then at Derendingen. Created the Slovenian literary language. Works include a catechism; *Abecedarium;* compendium of AC and the Württemberg and Saxon confessions; a ch. order; commentaries.
Trucial States (Trucial Oman; Trucial Coast). See *Middle East,* L 9.
True Dutch Reformed. See *Reformed Churches,* 4 c.
Trullan Synods (or Councils). See *Quinisext Synod.*
Trumball, Henry Clay (1830–1903). Cong. cleric; b. Stonington, Conn.; army chaplain in Civil War. Works include *War Memories of an Army Chaplain; The Blood Covenant; Kadesh-Barnea; The Threshold Covenant.*
Trumpets, Feast of. See *Judaism,* 4.
Trustees. See *Elders,* 3.
Truth. That which is eternal, ultimate, secure, steadfast. God is truth in contradistinction to all that is relative and derived (Ps 31:5; Is 65:16; Jn 17:3; 1 Jn 5:20); cannot lie (2 Ti 2:13; Heb. 6:18). All that comes from God is true (Ps 33:4). Truth is manifested in Christ (Jn 1:14, 17; 14:6). The Holy Spirit imparts the truth of Christ (1 Jn 2:20-21), through whom truth is known (Jn 8:31-32) and whose word is truth (Jn 17:17-19; 2 Co 4:2; Gl 5:7; Eph 1:13; Ja 1:18). Truth is known in sanctified life (Jn 17:17-19; 1 Jn 2:4-6).

In philos. various theories of truth are held, e. g., *correspondence theory* (truth consists in some form of correspondence bet. belief and fact); *coherence theory* (the truth of statements is determined by whether they cohere or fail to cohere with a system of other statements); *pragmatic theory* (truth is determined by experimental handling); *performative theory* (truth is a performative uterance).
Truth, Gospel of. See *Apocrypha,* B 2.
Trutvetter, Jodocus (Truttvetter; Trutfetter; ca. 1460–1519). B. Eisenach, Ger.; exponent of *via* moderna;* prof. philos. Erfurt under whom M. Luther studied; prof. Wittenberg 1507–10. Works include *Summulae totius logicae* (title occurs in various forms).
Tryggvesson, Olaf. See *Olaf I.*
Trygophorus, Johannes (Grecized from Hefenträger; Hefentreger; 1497–1542). B. Fritzlar, on the Eder, 15 mi. SW of Kassel, Ger.; educ. Erfurt; priest 1521; preached Reformation doctrine at Fritzlar, Waldeck, and Wildungen. Works include a catechism; order of worship.
Trypho. See *Apologists,* 4.
Trzanowski, George. See *Tranovsky, Jirí.*
Tschackert, Paul Moritz Robert (1848–1911). B. Freistadt (Freystadt), Lower Silesia; educ. Breslau, Halle, Göttingen; privatdocent Breslau 1875; prof. ch. hist. Halle 1877, Königsberg 1884, Göttingen 1890; followed J. Müller* and F. A. Tholuck* in theol. With G. N. Bonwetsch ed. 13th and 14th eds. of J. H. Kurtz's* *Lehrbuch der Kirchengeschichte.*
Tschernembl, Georg Erasmus von (1567–1626). Pol. leader of Prots. in Austria; finally fled to Geneva, Switz.
Tübingen School. Two theol. trends at U. of Tübingen, Ger. The theol. faculty was conservative till G. C. Storr* founded the so-called Old Tübingen School, which was continued by J. F. and K. C. Flatt* and F. G. Süskind* and advocated a Bible-based but rationalistic supernaturalism. The Later (or Younger, or New) Tübingen School, traced to F. C. Baur,* was more rationalistic and included, e. g., A. B. C. C. Hilgenfeld,* F. C. A. Schwegler,* K. H. v. Weizsäcker,* and E. Zeller.* See also *Isagogics,* 3; *Lutheran Theology After 1580,* 12.
Tübinger Bibelwerk. See *Pfaff, Christoph Matthäus.*
Tuch, Johann Christian Friedrich (1806–67). B. Quedlinburg, Ger.; educ. Halle; privatdocent and prof. Halle; prof. Leipzig; prof. and canon Zeitz. Works include *Kommentar über die Genesis.*
Tucher von Simmelsdorf, Christoph Karl Gottlieb von (1798–1877). B. Nürnberg, Ger.; educ. Erlangen, Heidelberg, and Berlin; held various positions, finally that of counsellor at supreme court in Munich 1856–68. Issued *Kirchengesänge der berühmtesten älteren italienischen Meister; Schatz des evangelischen Kirchengesangs in ersten Jahrhundert der Reformation.*
Tucker, Abraham (pseudonyms Cuthbert Comment and Edward Search; 1705–74). B. London, Eng.; educ. Oxford; exponent of utilitarianism.* Works include *Free Will, Foreknowledge, and Fate; Man in Quest of Himself; The Light of Nature Pursued.*
Tucker, Alfred R. See *Africa,* F 1.

Tucker, Charlotte Maria (pseudonym A. L. O. E. [for "A Lady of Eng."]; 1821–93). B. Barnet, S Hertfordshire, Eng.; after a successful literary career she went to India 1875 as an indep. miss.; d. Amritsar, India. Works include *Abbeokuta, or Sunrise Within the Tropics: An Outline of the Origin and Progress of the Yoruba Mission; Pearls of Wisdom from the Parables of Christ.*

Tucker, Josiah (1712–99). B. Laugharne, Carmarthenshire, Wales; educ. Oxford; pastor Bristol 1737; dean Gloucester 1758; opposed monopolies, Methodism, and "war for sake of trade"; favored separation of Am. colonies from Eng.

Tucker, William Jewett (1839–1926). Cong. cleric; b. Griswold, Conn.; educ. Andover (Mass.) Theol. Sem. Prof. Andover Theol. Sem. 1880–93; Dartmouth Coll., Hanover, N. H., 1893–1909. Works include *The Function of the Church in Modern Society.*

Tudor, John. See *Catholic Apostolic Church,* 1.

Tulloss, Rees Edgar (July 26, 1881–June 8, 1959). B. near Leipsic, Ohio; educ. Hamma Divinity School, Springfield, Ohio. Pastor Constantine, Mich., 1909–15; Mansfield, Ohio, 1918–20. Psychologist US Naval Radio School, Cambridge, Mass., 1917–18. Pres. Wittenberg Coll., Springfield, Ohio, 1920–49; active in NLC.

Tulsi Das (Tulsidas; Tulasidasa; 1532–1623). Hindu poet and reformer. Works include *Ramcarit-manas (Ramcharit-manas; Ramacaritamanesa;* tr. W. D. P. Hill, *The Holy Lake of the Acts of Rama),* sometimes called "Bible of N India."

Tunder, Franz (1614–67). Father-in-law of D. Buxtehude*; Luth. composer; b. Lübeck, Ger. (or at Burg [or Bannersdorf?], on Fehmarn is. in the Baltic Sea?); organist Lübeck 1641. Works include choral-variations *Komm, heiliger Geist, Herre Gott* and *Jesus Christus, unser Heiland.*

Tung Chung-shu. See *Chinese Philosophy,* 5.

Tunica talaris. See *Vestments, Clerical,* 1.

Tunicle. Short dalmatic* worn by subdeacon over alb during mass, or short close-fitting vestment worn by bp. under dalmatic at pontifical ceremonies.

Tunisia, Republic of. See *Africa,* D 2.

Tunker. See *Brethren,* 1.

Tunstall, Cuthbert (Tonstall; ca. 1474–1559). B. Hatchford, near Richmond, Yorkshire, Eng.; educ. Oxford, Cambridge, and Padua; bp. London 1522–30, Durham 1530; held RC dogma; tried to suppress W. Tyndale's* NT; imprisoned in the early 1550s; reinstated 1553; deprived of office 1559.

Tuptalo, Daniil Savic. See *Dimitrij of Rostov.*

Turkey. See *Middle East,* B.

Turks, Threatened Invasion by. See *Charles V; Speyer, Diets of.*

Turrettini, François (1623–87). B. Geneva, Switz.; educ. Geneva, Leiden, Utrecht, Paris, Saumur, Montauban, and Nimes; pastor It. cong. Geneva 1647; prof. theol. Geneva 1653. Helped write *Helvetic Consensus Formula* (see *Reformed Confessions,* A 10).

Tuttiett, Lawrence (Laurence; 1825–97). Angl. cleric and hymnist; b. Colyton, Devonshire, Eng.; educ. King's Coll., London; ordained 1848; vicar Lea Marston, Warwickshire, 1854–70; incumbent Episc. Ch. of St. Andrews, Fife, E Scot., 1870–93; canon St. Ninian's Cathedral, Perth, 1880. Works include *Hymns for Churchmen; Hymns for the Children of the Church.* Hymns include "Father, Let Me Dedicate."

Twelvers. See *Shi'ites.*

Twenty Articles. See *Canada,* B.

Twenty-eight Theses. See *Barmen Theses.*

Twenty-five Articles of Religion. See *Democratic Declarations of Faith,* 6.

Twenty-four Articles of the Faith, The. See *Presbyterian Confessions,* 4.

Twesten, August Detlev Christian (1789–1876). B. Glückstadt, near Hamburg, Ger.; educ. Kiel and Berlin; influenced by F. D. E. Schleiermacher*; prof. philos. and theol. Kiel 1814, dogmatics and NT exegesis Berlin 1835; held that Confessions of the Reformation period should be basis of ch. in Prussia; Luth.; worked for union of Luths. and Reformed. Works include *Die drey ökumenischen Symbola, die Augsburgische Confession, und die Repetitio confessionis Augustanae; Vorlesungen über die Dogmatik der evangelisch-lutherischen Kirche.*

Twisse, William (ca. 1578–1646). Puritan; educ. Oxford; pastor of rural parishes in Eng.; friend of W. Laud. Works include *A Briefe Catecheticall Exposition of Christian Doctrine; The Doctrine of the Synod of Dort and Arles Reduced to the Practise.*

Two-Seed-in-the-Spirit Predestinarian Baptists. See *Baptist Churches,* 13.

Two Swords. Term drawn from Lk 22:38 and used in reference to RC claim (expressed by Boniface VIII [see *Popes,* 12] in bull* *Unam Sanctam*) that there are 2 swords in the power of the ch., the spiritual to be used by, the temporal for, the ch. See also *Church and State,* 7.

Tychonius (Tichonius; Ticonius; Tyconius; fl. ca. 370/390). Donatist; opposed rebaptism of those who became Donatists; held that the ch. included good and bad. Works include a book on hermeneutics: *Liber de septem regulis.*

Tye, Christopher (ca. 1497/1500–1572). Eng. organist and composer; birthplace unknown, perhaps East Anglia; organist to Chapel Royal under Elizabeth* I. Tr. 1st half of Acts into Eng. verse set to music, some of which became hymn tunes, e. g., *Windsor.*

Tyler, Bennet (1783–1858). Cong. cleric; b. Middlebury, Conn.; educ. Yale Coll., New Haven, Conn. Pastor South Britain, Conn., 1808–22; Portland, Maine, 1828–33. Pres. Dartmouth Coll., Hanover, N. H., 1822–28; opposed New* Haven Theol., esp. as taught by N. W. Taylor*; prof. and pres. Theol. Institute of Conn., 1833/34–57 (founded at East Windsor, Conn., to offset the influence of New Haven Theol.; moved to Hartford 1865; reinc. 1913 as part of Hartford Sem. Foundation); his theol. became known as Tylerism.

Tylor, Edward Burnett. See *Primitive Religion.*

Tyndale William (Tindal[e]; ca. 1483/95 [most probably ca. 1494]–1536). B. "about the borders of Wales," probably Gloucestershire (or Monmouthshire?), perhaps in the hundred of Berkeley (at Stinchcombe? or North Nibley?); educ. Oxford and Cambridge; to the Continent 1524 on failing to receive support for Bible tr. from C. Tunstall*; was at Hamburg, Wittenberg, Cologne, and Marburg, but spent most of his remaining yrs. at Antwerp; influenced by M. Luther* but Zwinglian on the Lord's Supper; defended Reformation theol. against T. More*; strangled and burned near Brussels. Tr. NT and parts of the OT, including Pentateuch and Jon. See also *Bible Versions,* L 1–7; *England,* B 2. NST

R. Demaus, *William Tyndale,* rev. R. Lovett (London, 1886); J. F. Mozley, *William Tyndale* (London, 1937).

Tyndall, John (1820–93). Brit. physicist and natural philos.; b. Leighlin Bridge, County Carlow, Ireland; educ. Marburg, Ger.; prof. Royal Institution, London; visited Switz. often to study glaciers and meteorological conditions; defended determinism* and agnosticism; showed that the blue in the sky is due to fine particles in the air. See also *Metaphysical Society, The.*

Typological Exegesis. See *Exegesis,* 8.

Typology. See *Geography, Christian,* 6.

Tyro, Prosper. See *Prosper of Aquitaine.*

Tyrrell, George (1861–1909). B. Dublin, Ireland; raised Calvinist; RC 1879; Jesuit 1880; denied inerrancy of RC theol.; expelled from Jesuits 1906.

Works include *Christianity at the Cross-Roads.* See also *Modernism,* 1.

Tzschirner, Heinrich Gottlieb (1778–1828). B. Mittweida, near Chemnitz, Saxony, Ger.; educ. Leipzig; privatdocent Wittenberg 1800; soon adjunct of the philos. faculty there; then deacon Mittweida; prof. theol. Wittenberg 1805, Leipzig 1809. See also *Schröckh, Johann Matthias.*

U

Ubangi-Shari-Chad Colony. See *Africa,* F 3, 6.

Übergangstheologie. See *Neology.*

Übertragungslehre. See *Church and Ministry, Walther's Theses on.*

Ubiquity (from Lat. *ubique,* "everywhere"). Term that originated in medieval scholasticism and is sometimes used as a synonym of omnipresence. Originally used by Luths. in reference to Christ's omnipresence also acc. to His human nature (cf. Mt 28:20). Ref. theologians accused Luths. of teaching ubiquity in the FC in the sense of a *local* omnipresence or infinite extension of Christ's human nature. Luths. reject the charge and point out 1. The FC does not use the word "ubiquity." 2. The FC specifically rejects ubiquity in that sense. "We reject and condemn as contrary to the Word of God and our simple Christian Creed . . . that the human nature of Christ is locally extended to every place in heaven and earth" (Ep VIII, The Person of Christ, Antitheses, 10; cf. SD VIII 92). 3. FC SD VII, The Holy Supper, 98–101, quoting M. Luther*: "The one body of Christ has three different modes, or all three modes, of being at any given place. [First,] The comprehensible, corporeal mode of presence, as when he walked bodily on earth and vacated or occupied space according to his size. . . . Secondly, the incomprehensible, spiritual mode of presence according to which he neither occupies nor vacates space but penetrates every creature, wherever he wills. . . . He employed this mode of presence . . . in the bread and wine in the Lord's Supper. . . . Thirdly, since He is one person with God, the divine, heavenly mode, according to which all creatures are indeed much more penetrable and present to Him than they are according to the second mode." The 2d and 3d mode are *illocal.*

Uchimura, Kanzo (Kanso Utschimura; 1861–1930). Indep. Christian leader in Jap.; mem. warrior class (samurai); converted 1878; studied at Amherst (Mass.) Coll.; founded Non-Ch. Movement (popularly so called not because he opposed the ch. [he didn't] but because he rejected for. denominationalism and promoted a Jap. form of Christianity.

Udvalget. See *Society for the Propagation of the Gospel Among the Danes in North America, The.*

Uganda, Republic of. See *Africa,* F 1.

Uhde, Fritz Karl Hermann von (1848–1911). Painter; b. Wolkenburg, in the Erzgebirge, Saxony, Ger.; realist to the point of transferring Biblical episodes into modern settings. Works include *Lasst die Kindlein zu mir kommen; Die heilige Nacht; Komm, Herr Jesu, sei unser Gast; Christus und die Jünger von Emmaus.*

Uhland, Johann Ludwig (1787–1862). Poet, philol., literary hist.; b. Tübingen, Ger.; prof. Tübingen; Christian romantic; regarded Ger. myths as poetic developments of ancient revelation. Works include *Schäfers Sonntagslied; Des Sängers Fluch; Der Mythus von Thor; Alte hoch- und niederdeutsche Volkslieder.*

Uhlhorn, Johann Gerhard Wilhelm (1826–1901). Luth. cleric; b. Osnabrück, Ger.; educ. Göttingen; court chaplain Hanover; mem. consistory; abbot Loccum 1878. Works include *Die Christliche Liebesthätigkeit; Der Kampf des Christenthums mit dem Heidenthum.*

Uhlig, Hermann Daniel. See *Deaf,* 10.

Ukrainian Autocephalic Orthodox Church in Exile, Holy. See *Eastern Orthodox Churches,* 6.

Ukrainian Orthodox Church in the U. S. A. See *Eastern Orthodox Churches,* 6.

Ukrainian Orthodox Church of America (Ecumenical Patriarchate). See *Eastern Orthodox Churches,* 6.

Ulfilas (Ulfila; Wulfila; various other spellings; the name means "Little Wolf"; ca. 310/313–381/383). Birthplace unknown (some think N of the Danube; others Cappadocia); his mother is said to have been a Cappadocian Christian; said to have become bp. at 30; miss. to Goths; said to have been an adherent of the Nicene Creed and to have turned Arian only at a syn. in Constantinople 360. Tr. Bible into Gothic (for which he is said to have devised an alphabet based on Gk. uncials supplemented from Gothic runes). See also *Bible Versions,* I; *Goths, Conversion of.*

Ullmann, Karl (Carl; 1796–1865). B. Epfenbach, near Heidelberg, in the Palatinate, Ger.; educ. Heidelberg and Tübingen; prof. Heidelberg and Halle; prelate of the Ev. Ch. in Karlsruhe 1853; pres. supreme ecclesiastical council 1856–61; favored union of Luths. and Ref. in Baden; opposed rationalism. Ed. *Theologische Studien und Kritiken.* See also *Mediating Theology.*

Ullmann, Uddo Lechard (1837–1930). B. Göteborg, Swed.; taught at Uppsala and Göteborg; bp. Strängnäs 1889–1927; liturgical scholar. Works include *Om den kyrkliga psalmboken med särskild hänsyn till den svenska kyrkans psalmbok af aar 1819; Evangelisk-luthersk liturgik.*

Ulmann, Karl Christian (1793–1871). Leader of Luths. in Russ.; educ. Dorpat (Tartu), Jena, Göttingen; pastor Kremon, Livonia, 1817–35; prof. Dorpat 1835–42; deposed; gen. supt. and vice-pres. of gen. consistory, St. Petersburg (now Leningrad), 1856; bp. 1858; founded a treasury to aid Luth. congs. in Russ. 1859. Founded (1838) and ed. a periodical supplying information and news for the ev. ch. in Russ.

Ulmer, Friedrich (1877–1946). B. Munich, Ger.; educ. Munich, Erlangen, Leipzig; parish pastor; dean Dinkelsbühl 1920; prof. Erlangen 1924; retired under Nazis 1937; reinstated 1946; in 1928 he became leader of what came to be called Martin-Luther-Bund 1932 (see *Gotteskasten*); helped resettle Ger.-Russ. refugees from Manchuria in Brazil. Ed. *Lutherische Kirche.*

Ulrich (1487–1550). B. Alsace; duke Württemberg 1498 (assumed personal control 1503); introd. Reformation into Württemberg; mem. Schmalkaldic* League.

Ulrich von Augsburg. See *Saints, Veneration of,* 6.

Ulrich von Hutten. See *Hutten, Ulrich von.*

Ulrici, Hermann (1806–84). Theistic philos.; b. Pförten, Lower Lusatia, Ger.; privatdocent Berlin; prof. Halle; opposed G. W. F. Hegel.* Works include *Über Princip und Methode der Hegelschen Philosophie; Glauben und Wissen, Speculation und exacte Wissenschaft; Strauss as a Philosophical Thinker,* tr. C. P. Krauth.

Ulster, Synod of. See *Presbyterian Churches,* 3.

Ultramontanism (from Lat. *ultra montes,* "beyond the mountains," i. e., from the viewpoint of the N [e. g., Eng., Fr., Ger.]). 1. Policy of supporting papal authority and power over against Febronianism,* Gallicanism,* Jansenism,* Josephinism,* and later, secularism.* The term, originated in the 11th c., found its modern application to religious tensions beginning in the 17th c.

2. Basis for ultramontanism was laid in the Donation* of Constantine.

3. Est. of the Holy* Roman Empire led to complications and conflicts bet. emp. and pope. Gregory VII (see *Popes,* 7), Innocent III (see *Popes,* 10), Boniface VIII (see *Popes,* 12) and other popes were virtual world rulers. But their claims continued to be challenged. Rise of modern states and the spirit of nationalism curtailed the pope's temporal power. RC claims to spiritual power led to the dogma of papal infallibility,* also under challenge.

See also *Christian Church, History of,* III 12.

Umbreit, Friedrich Wilhelm Karl (1795–1860). B. Sonneborn, near Gotha, Ger.; educ. Göttingen; privatdocent Göttingen 1818; prof. Heidelberg 1820; mediating theol. with supernatural tendencies. Works include commentaries on Jb, OT prophets, and Ro. See also *Mediating Theology.*

Umfrid, Otto (1857–1920). Ev. pastor Stuttgart; pacifist; opposed rights of the strong as hist. rights; favored natural rights based on justice. Works include *Friede auf Erden.*

Unam sanctam. See *Bull.*

Unamuno y Jugo, Miguel de (1864–1936). Philos.; b. Bilbao, Sp.; educ. Madrid; prof. Salamanca 1891; influenced by H. Bergson,* W. James,* S. A. Kierkegaard,* and B. Pascal.*

Unchangeableness of God. See *Immutability of God.*

Uncials. See *Manuscripts of the Bible,* 2, 3.

Uncreated Grace. See *Gratia increata.*

Unction (Anointing of the Sick; Chrism; Chrismation; Extreme Unction; Holy Unction). 1. The NT speaks of elders anointing the sick (Ja 5:14).

2. The E Orthodox Ch. teaches that Holy Unction is a sacrament celebrated by more than 1 priest (except in emergency, when 1 suffices) in ch., if possible. The ceremony consists of 7 parts, each containing an Epistle reading, a Gospel reading, and a prayer. An oil lamp burns during the ceremony, at the end of which the priests take oil from the lamp and anoint forehead, breast, hands, and feet of the sick, praying for bodily and spiritual healing.

3. Present RC practice allows 2 kinds of anointing (one involving unction of the 5 senses, the other only of the forehead).

4. In RCm, a 1972 apostolic constitution, pub. 1973, effective Jan. 1, 1974, reduced anointings to those of forehead and hands. It is held that the rite confers comforting grace; remission of venial sins and unculpably unconfessed mortal sins, together with at least some temporal punishment due for sin; and, sometimes, improved physical health.

5. Some Prots. practice anointing of the sick but gen. reject it as a sacrament. EL

Undereyck, Theodor (Untereyck; Ondereick; 1635–93). Ref. theol.; b. Duisburg, Ger.; educ. Utrecht, Duisburg, Leiden; came in contact with Puritans; pastor Mülheim on the Ruhr 1660–68, Bremen 1670–93; founded Ref. pietistic conventicles in Ger. Works include *Wegweiser der Einfältigen zu den ersten Buchstaben des wahren Christentums.*

Underhill, Evelyn (Mrs. Stuart Moore; 1875–1941). Poet and writer on mysticism; b. Wolverhampton, Eng. Works include *A Bar-Lamb's Ballad Book; Mysticism; Immanence; Man and the Supernatural; Concerning the Inner Life; The Rhythm of Sacrifice; The Golden Sequence.*

Understanding Scripture. See *Hermeneutics.*

Unevangelized Fields Mission. Founded 1931 London, England. Miss fields have included Belg. Congo, Brazil, Dominican Rep., Egypt, Fr., Guyana (formerly Brit. Guiana), Haiti, Ivory Coast, Papua, West Irian.

Ungleich, Lucas. See *Lutheran Confessions,* A 5.

Ungnad von Weissenwolf, David. See *Crusius, Martin.*

Ungnad von Weissenwolf, Johann (Hans; Ungnade; von Son[n]egg [Soneg; Sonneck], Carinthia; ca. 1493/96–1564). B. province of Styria, Austria; Luth.; privy councillor to Ferdinand I (see *Reformed Confessions,* E 3); army gen.; sponsored tr. of the Bible, AC, and some of M. Luther's writings into Slovene, Serbo-Croatian, and Turkish and paid for their distribution. See also *Consul, Stipan.*

Uniate Churches (Uniat Chs.). E rite chs. in union with and submitting to the Roman papacy but not part of the Lat. patriarchate; retain resp. languages and canon law; usually observe Communion under both kinds, baptism by immersion, and marriage of clergy. See also *Union Movements,* 2.

Uniformity, Act of (1559). See *Roman Catholic Church,* D 9.

Uniformity, Act of (1662). See *Presbyterian Churches,* 2.

Unigenitus. Bull issued 1713 by Clement XI (Giovanni Francesco Albani; 1649–1721; b. Urbino, It.; pope 1700–21) against P. Quesnel,* condemning 101 propositions of his *Réflexions morales.* See also *Jansenism.*

Unio ecclesiastica der deutsch protestantischen Kirchen in Staate South Carolina. See *United Lutheran Church, Synods of,* 27.

Unio mystica. See *Mystical Union.*

Unio sacramentalis. See *Sacramental Union.*

Union, Prussian. See *Prussian Union.*

Union American Methodist Episcopal Church. See *Methodist Churches,* 4 c.

Union and Unity Movements in the United States, Lutheran. Until ca. the middle of the 18th c., attempts to organize Luths. in the US gen. did not go beyond the cong. level.

The Ministerium of Pa. was organized 1748 (see *United Lutheran Church, Synods of,* 22), Ministerium of N. Y. 1786 (see *United Lutheran Church, Synods of,* 15), Ev. Luth. Syn. and Ministerium of N. C. 1803 (see *United Lutheran Church, Synods of,* 10, 16), Ohio Syn. 1818 (see *Ohio and Other States, The Evangelical Lutheran Joint Synod of*), Md. and Va. Syn. 1820 (see *United Lutheran Church, Synods of,* 11, 29), Tenn. Syn. 1820 (see *Henkels, The,* 2, 3; *United Lutheran Church, Synods of,* 10, 16). Others followed.

Next step was organization of syns. into larger bodies. The General* Syn. of the Ev. Luth. Ch. in the USA organized 1820, suffered under tensions of war and liberal-conservative conflict in the 1860s. The General* Council of the Ev. Luth. Ch. in (N.) Am. organized 1867, The United* Syn. of the Ev. Luth. Ch. in the South 1886.

These 3 larger groups united 1918 in The United* Luth. Ch. in Am.

The Mo. Syn. organized 1847 (see *Lutheran Church – Missouri Synod, The*), the Synodical* Conf. 1872. For related efforts toward doctrinal unity with others see, e. g., *Brief Statement; Chicago Theses; Common Confession.*

The American* Luth. Ch. (ALC) organized 1930.

For union and unity movements among Norwegians see *Anti-Missouri Brotherhood; Eielsen Synod; Evangelical Lutheran Church, The; Hauge Synod; Madison Settlement; Norwegian-Danish Augustana Synod in America, The; United Norwegian Lutheran Church in America, The.*

For similar movements among Swedes see *Augustana Evangelical Lutheran Church; Baptist Churches,* 18; *Evangelical Covenant Church of America, The; Evangelical Free Church of America; Illinois, Evangelical Lutheran Synod of Northern.*

For similar movements among Danes see *Danish Lutherans in America.*

For similar movements among Finns see *Finnish*

Lutherans in America.

The American* Luth. Conf. formed 1930.

The American* Luth. Ch. (The ALC) organized 1960.

The Lutheran* Ch. in Am. formed 1962/63.

The Lutheran* Council in the USA organized 1966.

The Synod* of Ev. Luth. Chs. became an LCMS dist. 1971. EL

See also *United States, Lutheranism in the,* 8, 9.

Documents of Lutheran Unity in America, ed. R. C. Wolf (Philadelphia, 1966).

Union des Eglises evangeliques libres de France. See *France,* 13.

Union Movements. 1. Union movements in the ch. vary in character. (1) Some groups try to attain union based on strict doctrinal agreement. (2) Some favor union based on compromise expressed in the motto: "In essentials unity, in doubtful things liberty, in all things charity." (3) LCMS founders stressed the unity of the ch., based on unity of faith (Gl 3:28), and worked for unity in the ch. on confessional bases. (4) Purpose of some union movements is simply to draw Christians closer together with a view to cooperation in certain areas of activity and to present a united front against atheism and other foes.

2. Heresy has disrupted outward unity of Christendom since apostolic times. Unsuccessful attempts were made to unite the E and W chs. by the 1274 council of Lyons* and by the council of Florence.* Rome est. a uniate* relationship with some E rite chs.

3. During the Reformation era the ch. divided into several groups, including Luth., Ref., RC, Angl. Efforts toward reunion failed (see, e. g., *Lutheran Confessions,* A 2; P. Melanchthon* tried to unite Luths. and Ref. on basis of an altered AC [see *Lutheran Confessions,* B 3]). Luths. united on basis of the FC (see *Lutheran Confessions,* C 2).

4. Efforts toward union of Luths. and Anglicans in the 1530s failed (see *Lutheran Confessions,* A 5) as did efforts to unite Luths. and E Orthodox chs. in the last half of the 16th c. (see *Eastern Orthodox Churches,* 5) and efforts to unite Angls. and RCs in the 1st part of the 18th c. (see *Wake, William*). For some time after adoption of the FC Luths. gen. held that union with dissident groups can be achieved only on a confessional basis. But Pietism* and rationalism* encouraged unionism.* See also *Prussian Union.*

5. The Ev. Syn. of N. Am. grew out of the Prussian Union (see *United Church of Christ,* II B). Various Presb. groups (see *Presbyterian Churches,* 4). The Synodical* Conf. was organized 1872. Union of Meths. in Can. 1874 and 1883 resulted in the Meth. Ch. of Can. The United* Ev. Ch. was organized 1894. The Council of Ref. Chs. in the US holding the Presb. System was formed 1907.

6. In the 20th c., modernism* led to division and fundamentalism.*

7. 20th c. unions include that of N. Bap. Conv. and Free Baps. 1911 (see *Baptist Churches,* 8, 26); Presb. Ch. in the USA and Welsh Calvinistic Meth. Ch. 1920 (see *Presbyterian Churches,* 4 a); Ev. Assoc. and United* Ev. Ch. 1922 (see also *Evangelical Church,* 1); Ref. Ch. in the US and Hung. Ref. Ch. in the US 1921 (see *United Church of Christ,* II A 3); United Ch. of Can. 1925 (see *Canada,* B); Gen. Council of Cong. and Christian Chs. 1931 (see *United Church of Christ,* I); Ev. and Ref. Ch. 1934 (see *United Church of Christ,* II); The Methodist* Ch. 1939; The Evangelical* United Brethren Ch. 1946; United* Ch. of Christ 1957; Ref. Presb. Ch., Ev. Syn., 1965 (see *Presbyterian Churches,* 4 e); The United Meth. Ch. 1968 (see *Methodist Churches,* 1). See also *Union and Unity Movements in the United States, Lutheran.*

8. The Vereinigte Evangelisch-Lutherische Kirche Deutschlands (VELKD) was organized July 6–8, 1948, the Evangelische Kirche in Deutschland (EKD) July 9–15, 1948, both in Eisenach (see also *Germany,* C 5; *Germany, Lutheran Free Churches in,* 3).

9. VELKD is a ch. based on the Luth. Confessions. It is not a mem. of EKD, but its mem. chs. are also mems. of EKD. The latter is not a ch. but a fed. (Ger. *Bund*) of Luth., Ref., and Union (see *Prussian Union*) chs.

10. Other alliances, feds., assocs., and councils include Evangelical* Alliance 1846; Federal* Council of the Chs. of Christ in Am. (see also 13) 1908; Bap. World Alliance, organized 1905 London, Eng., as a free assoc.; The Lutheran* World Federation.

11. The Am. Council of Christian Chs. was organized 1941 in opposition to the FCC (see 10) by Carl McIntire (b. 1906; pastor Bible Presb. Ch., Collingswood, N. J.; founded Bible Presb. Ch., Collingswood Syn., 1956; pres. International* Council of Christian Chs. Founded [1936] and ed. *Christian Beacon;* other works include *The Death of a Church*). Demands "separation from apostasy."

12. The Nat. Assoc. of Evangelicals began 1942 St. Louis, Mo., as Evangelicals for United Action; advocates interch. cooperation.

13. The National* Council of the Chs. of Christ in the USA formed 1950 by merger of Federal* Councils of Chs. of Christ in Am.; The For. Missions Conference of N. Am. (began 1893 NYC; name adopted 1911); Home Mission Council of N. Am. (formed 1940 by merger of Council of Women of Home Missions [organized 1908] and Home Missions Council [organized 1908]); The International* Council of Religious Education; Missionary Education Movement of the US and Can. (began 1902 as Young People's Missionary Movement, a cooperative agency of 23 denominations); Nat. Prot. Council on Higher Educ. (founded 1911); United Council of Ch. Women (founded 1940); United Stewardship Council (founded 1920).

14. In a sense, the World* Council of Chs. began with the world missionary* conferences held 1900 NYC, 1910 Edinburgh (at which a permanent internat. organization was effected), for cooperation in life and work on miss. fields encouraged the meetings at Geneva 1920, Stockholm 1925, and Oxford 1937 (see *Ecumenical Movement, The,* 9–10) that led to the WCC.

15. Immediate antecedents of the WCC were the meeting of the Universal Christian Conference on Life and Work (Stockholm 1925; replaced by the Universal Christian Council for Life and Work [Oxford 1937]), the World Conf. on Faith and Order (Lausanne 1927, Edinburgh 1937), and world missionary conferences Jerusalem 1928 and Tambaram, Madras, India, 1938.

16. The WCC was organized 1948. ACM

Union of Arab Emirates. See *Middle East,* L 9.

Union of Brethren. See *Bohemian Brethren.*

Union of Evangelical Protestant Churches of Belgium. See *Belgium.*

Union of South Africa. See *Africa,* B 5.

Union protestante chrétienne. See *Evangelisch-christliche Einheit.*

Union Synod of the Evangelic Lutheran Church. Formed Nov. 5, 1859, Newtown Ch., Boone Co., Ind., by mems. of Indiana* Syn. (I), which disbanded Nov. 4, 1859. Purpose: to unite all unaffiliated Luths. in Ind. in 1 syn. Fraternal relations were at first maintained with the Ev. Luth. Joint Syn. of Ohio* and Other States, but in the early 1860s the Southern Dist. Syn. of the Ev. Luth. Joint Syn. of Ohio and Other States declared the Union

Syn. unlutheran in doctrine and practice; this made fraternization bet. them impossible. The Union Syn. changed name 1863 to Union Syn. of the Evangelical Luth. Ch. Dissolved 1871. Its mems helped form Indiana* Syn. (II). At one time or other 17 pastors and 27 congs. were mems. of the Union Syn. See also *Henkels, The,* 3.

M. L. Wagner, *The Chicago Synod and Its Antecedents* (Waverly, Iowa, n. d.).

Union Theological Seminary (NYC). See *Ministry, Education of,* XII.

Union Theological Seminary in Virginia. See *Ministry, Education of,* XII.

Unionism. Nonbiblical term applied to various dedegrees of coorganization, joint worship, and/or cooperation bet. religious groups of varying creeds and/or spiritual convictions.

Meyers Grosses Konversations-Lexikon, XIX, 921, speaks of unionists as adherents of the union est. 1817 bet. Luths. and Ref. (see *Prussian Union*); this sense of the term gained widespread acceptance also in Am. It also speaks of unionists in gen. as those who try to unite Christian denominations *(Religionsparteien)* in 1 ch.

E. Eckhardt, *Homiletisches Reallexikon nebst Index Rerum,* speaks of unionism as mingling of truth and error; ch. fellowship bet. true believers *(Rechtgläubigen)* and errorists *(Falschgläubigen)* or union of both into an external ch. organization. It includes all ecclesiastical cooperation in which error is tolerated and the Luth. Confession is not given proper consideration *(zu kurz kommt).*

The Concordia Cyclopedia (St. Louis, 1927), p. 774: "Religious unionism consists in joint worship and work of those not united in doctrine. Its essence is an agreement to disagree. In effect, it denies the doctrine of the clearness of Scripture."

See also *Altar Fellowship; Fellowship; Minneapolis Theses* (1925), III 1; *Syncretism.*

J. H. C. Fritz, *Religious Unionism* (St. Louis, 1930); W. A. Poovey, *Questions That Trouble Christians* (Columbus, Ohio, 1946); C. Bergendoff, "Lutheran Unity," *What Lutherans Are Thinking* (Columbus, Ohio, 1947), pp. 368–390; N. Söderblom, *Christian Fellowship or the United Life and Work of Christendom* (New York, 1923); J. S. Stowell, *The Utopia of Unity* (New York, 1930); M. Bach, *Report to Protestants* (New York, 1948); *CTM,* XV (1944), pp. 538–539, footnote 19; *The Abiding Word,* I, ed. T. Laetsch (St. Louis, 1953), 286–287, 301.

Unitarian Universalist Association. Formed May 1961 by consolidation of Am. Unitarian Assoc. (see *Unitarianism*) and Universalists Ch. of Am. (see *Universalists*).

Unitarianism. Belief that God is unipersonal; held by Monarchians (see *Monarchianism*); anti-Trinitarian (see *Trinity*). See also *Socinianism.*

Eng. Unitarians include J. Biddle,* S. Clarke,* W. H. Drummond,* T. Lindsey,* J. Martineau,* J. Priestley.*

In Am., Unitarianism gained foothold first in King's Chapel (Episc.), Boston, Mass., 1785, then in Cong. chs. in E Mass. (on Congregationalism see *United Church of Christ,* I A 1). See also *Ware, Henry, Sr.; Ware, Henry, Jr.; Ware, William.* Tension bet. Trinitarians and Unitarians among Congs. led to separation. W. E. Channing's* sermon on Unitarian Christianity at the ordination of J. Sparks* 1819 became the practical platform of Unitarianism. The Am. Unitarian Assoc., organized 1825 for ch. extension, was long ill supported for lack of enthusiasm to build a denomination. See also *Clarke, James Freeman; Emerson, Ralph Waldo; Parker, Theodore; Unitarian Universalist Association.*

Unitarianism has no creed in the common meaning of the term; holds that every individual is free to form his own religious beliefs; opposes all specifically Christian doctrines; emphasizes essential dignity and perfectibility of human nature; engages in philanthropy; promotes educ. FEM

See also *Universalism.*

Unitas fratrum. See *Bohemian Brethren; Czechoslovakia,* 5.

Unitatis redintegratio. See *Vatican Councils,* 2.

United Arab Republic. See *Middle East,* A 2.

United Baptists. See *Baptists Churches,* 28.

United Brethren. 1–2. The *Ch. of the United Brethren in Christ* formed in Frederick Co., Md., 1800 as United Brethren in Christ under leadership of Philipp Wilhelm Otterbein (1726–1813; b. Dillenburg, Ger.; educ. Herborn; pastor Herborn; to US 1752; Ger. Ref. pastor Lancaster and elsewhere in Pa. and in Md. 1752–1813; claimed a deep personal religious experience early in his ministry) and Martin Boehm (1725–1812; b. Lancaster Co., Pa.; Mennonite bp. 1759; met P. W. Otterbein 1768), who conducted evangelistic work together in Pa., Md., and Va. Because of opposition to revivals and to other features of their work, Otterbein became pastor 1774 of an indep. ch. Baltimore, Md., where revivalist preachers adopted a confession of faith and rules of discipline 1789. Otterbein and Boehm were elected bps. 1800. See also *Newcomer, Christian.* Otterbein came into close relations with F. Asbury,* but language differences kept the United Brethren and Meths. from uniting. The 1st gen. conf., held 1815 near Mount Pleasant, Pa., adopted a book discipline and allowed use of English. A const. was adopted 1841. The United Brethren and the Evangelical* Ch. merged 1946 to form The Evangelical* United Brethren Ch., which in turn merged 1968 with The Methodist* Ch. to form The United Meth. Ch. (see *Methodist Churches,* 1).

3. *Ch. of the United Brethren in Christ (Old Constitution).* Formed 1889 by a minority in protest against liberalizing the 1841 const. "(Old Constitution)" was dropped soon after the other Ch. of the United Brethren in Christ lost its identity.

4. *United Christian Ch.* Separated 1862–70 from Ch. of the United Brethren in Christ in conscientious objection against doctrines and practices which they regarded as liberal; organized 1878 Campbelltown, Pa. FEM

See also *United Church of Christ,* II A 2.

Cf. *Religious Bodies (US), Bibliography of.*

United Brethren in Christ, Church of the. See *United Brethren.*

United Christian Adult Movement. See *Adult Education.*

United Christan Church. See *United Brethren,* 4.

United Christian Youth Movement. See *Young People's Organizations, Christian,* I 6; IV.

United Church Board for World Ministries. Formed 1961 to carry on work done previously by American* Bd. of Commissioners for For. Missions; Bd. of Internat. Missions (1934) and Commission on World Service (1953) of the Ev. and Ref. Ch. (see *United Church of Christ,* II); Cong. Christian Service Committee (1943; see also *United Church of Christ,* I).

United Church of Canada. See *Canada,* B.

United Church of Christ. Formed June 25, 1957, by merger of the Gen. Council of Cong. Christian Chs. and the Ev. and Ref. Ch. See also III.

I. *Cong. and Christian Chs.* In 1931 the Nat. Council of the Cong. Chs. of the US and the Gen. Conv. of the Christian Ch. (HQ Dayton, Ohio) united to form the Gen. Council of the Cong. and Christian Chs. (later name: Gen. Council of Cong. Christian Chs.).

A. *Cong. Ch.* 1. One of the questions raised by the Reformation for many Eng. Prots. was whether a Christian could hold membership in the Angl.

Church. Puritans* believed they should remain in it and help purify it of papal elements. Separatists (also called Indeps. and Congregationalists) advocated congregationalism, holding that a cong. must be free of all ecclesiastical and pol. domination; see also *Nonconformist; Robinson, John.* After passage of the 1559 Act of Uniformity (see *Roman Catholic Church,* D 9), some intractables were executed, many dissident chs. were broken up. Robert Browne (ca. 1550–ca. 1633; b. Tolethorp, near Stamford, Rutlandshire, Eng.; educ. Cambridge; teacher; pastor based at Norwich ca. 1580; regarded by many as the founder of Congregationalism) emigrated to Holland with his cong. 1581; his views were called Brownism, his followers Brownists. Separatists in Holland developed a sense of being strangers and pilgrims in a for. land and became the Pilgrim Fathers who came to Am. 1620 on the *Mayflower,* est. the 1st permanent settlement in New Eng., and founded the 1st Cong. ch. in Am. at Plymouth, Mass. (see also *Bradford, William; Brewster, William*). Puritans est. Mass. Bay Colony 1629.

2. Pilgrims and Puritans agreed doctrinally, differing only on ch. govt. and membership, Pilgrims, as Separatists, denouncing the Angl. Ch., Puritans considering themselves mems. of it. The Cambridge Platform, adopted 1648, (see *Democratic Declarations* of Faith, 2) became standard of Congregationalism in Mass. and Conn.

The intolerance that developed in New Eng. seems to have originated among Puritans, who emphasized the purity of the ch. and its authority also in the pol. realm. Heresy and witchcraft were accordingly to be condemned by ch. and state and punished by death. But Pilgrim ideals gradually prevailed. Separatists claimed freedom for themselves and granted it to others and so gave Congregationalism its distinctive mark.

But doctrinal freedom made doctrinal discipline and uniformity impossible. The Confession of 1680 (see *Democratic Declarations of Faith,* 2) was not binding on congs.

3. The liberalism of Congregationalism went hand in hand with modernism,* rationalism,* and Unitarianism.* See also *Abbot, Lyman; Beecher, Henry Ward; Bushnell, Horace; Gladden, Washington; New England Theology.* The Plan of Union of Congregationalists and Presbs. (see *Presbyterian Churches,* 4 a) was abandoned 1837 by Old School Presbs., by Congregationalists 1852.

See also *Kansas City Platform; Statement of Faith According to the Teachings of Congregational Christians, A.*

B. *Christian Ch.* Resulted from a movement pioneered by J. O'Kelly,* who withdrew 1972 from the M. E. Ch. in protest against episcopacy, organized his followers as Republican Meths., who 1794 resolved to be known only as "Christians," taking the Bible as guide and discipline and accepting only Christian character as test of ch. fellowship. A little later a similar movement arose among New Eng. Baps. See also *Churches of Christ; Disciples of Christ,* 2. Gen. meetings were held beginning ca. 1809. Gen. conferences were held regularly 1819–32. Gen. convs. were held beginning 1833. In 1890 the denomination was called "Christians (Christian Connection)"; the name "Christian Ch. (Am. Christian Conv.)" was used 1916; the name "Christian Ch. (Gen. Conv. of the Christian Ch.)" was adopted 1922. Unitarianism found adherents in the group. The Social* Gospel was emphasized.

II. *Ev. and Ref. Ch.* Est. 1934 Cleveland, Ohio, by merger of Ev. Syn. of N. Am. and Ref. Ch. in the US.

A. *Ref. Ch. in the US.* 1. Beginning traced to controversies in Ger. after the Interim,* esp. the Crypto-Calvinistic* controversy. In the early 1560s elector Frederick* III (1515–76) and the Palatinate became Reformed. The Ref. chs. in Eur. had much in common.

2. Ref. emigrants to the US included Ger. settlers from the Palatinate at Germantown, near Philadelphia, Pa., 1683. Others came from Switz., and others, early in the 18th c., from Fr. The 1st Communion service of the Ref. Ch. in the US was celebrated 1725 at Falckner's Swamp, ca. 40 mi. N of Philadelphia. But for scarcity of ministers no organization was effected till 1747, when M. Schlatter* organized a *coetus* (Lat. practical equivalent of "synod") in Philadelphia, with ties to Holland. See also *United Brethren,* 1–2. The *coetus* became indep. 1793 as The Syn. of the Ger. Ref. Ch. Liberal-conservative tension developed. See also *Mercersburg Theology.*

3. Upon expansion of the Allegheny Mountains, The Syn. of the Ger. Ref. Ch. divided 1819 into 8 districts called Classes. The Ohio Classis organized itself into the Ohio Syn. 1824. The mother syn. and the Ohio Syn. united 1863 to form the Gen. Syn. Most of the Hung. Ref. Ch. in Am. joined the Ref. Ch. in the US 1921 (see *Reformed Churches,* 4 d–e). The Gen. Syn. ceased to function at the 1934 merger.

B. *Ev. Syn. of N. Am.* Grew out of the Prussian* Union. Six ministers formed the Ev. Union of the West (a kind of ministerial assoc.) at Gravois Settlement, near St. Louis, Mo., 1840, on basis of Luth.-Ref. compromise. Congregations began to join 1849. Similar assocs. sprang up in other states. They joined 1872 and 1877 adopted the name Ger. Ev. Syn. of N. America. Ref. theol. gained control; modernism* followed.

III. A proposal was made 1938 to merge the Cong. Christian Chs. and the Ev. and Ref. Ch. to form a body to be called United Ch. of Christ. A "Gen. Syn. of the United Ch. of Christ," composed of delegates from both groups, met 1957 Cleveland, Ohio, and elected a const. committee. Last meetings of the constituent bodies were held 1958. The 1st Gen. Syn. of the newly created United Ch. of Christ met 1959. The const. was adopted 1961 and says in its preamble: "The United Church of Christ acknowledges as its sole Head, Jesus Christ, the Son of God and the Saviour of men. It acknowledges as brethren in Christ all who share in this confession. It looks to the Word of God in the Scriptures, and to the presence and power of the Holy Spirit, to prosper its creative and redemptive work in the world. It claims as its own the faith of the historic Church expressed in the ancient creeds and reclaimed in the basic insights of the Protestant Reformers. It affirms the responsibility of the Church in each generation to make this faith its own in reality of worship, in honesty of thought and expression, and in purity of heart before God. In accordance with the teaching of our Lord and the practice prevailing among evangelical Christians, it recognizes two sacraments: Baptism and the Lord's Supper or Holy Communion." The const. describes the relationships of local chs., Assocs., Conferences, and ministers with the Gen. Syn. as "free and voluntary."

In 1959 a Statement of Faith was adopted expressing belief "in God, the Eternal Spirit, Father of our Lord Jesus Christ and our Father. . . . In Jesus Christ, the man of Nazareth, our crucified and risen Lord, ... He bestows upon us his Holy Spirit, creating and renewing the Church of Jesus Christ, binding in covenant faithful people of all ages, tongues, and races. . . . He calls us . . . to accept the cost and joy of discipleship . . . to share in Christ's baptism and eat at his table. . . . He promises to all who trust him forgiveness of sins and fullness of grace. . . ." Local chs. are neither bound by this Statement of Faith nor required to accept it.

1973 inclusive membership: more than 1,900,000. FEM, EL.

United Church Seminary. See *Luther Theological Seminary,* 4.

United Conference of Methodist Churches. See *Methodist Churches,* 1.

United Congregations. Name given the 3 congs. served by H. M. Mühlenberg (see *Mühlenberg, Henry Melchior and Family,* 1) 1742. As other congs. joined them, the name was applied to the larger group. See also *United Lutheran Church, Synods of,* 22.

United Council of Church Women. See *Union Movements,* 13.

United Danish Evangelical Lutheran Church in America. See *Danish Lutherans in America,* 5, 6.

United Domestic Missionary Society. See *American Home Missionary Society.*

United Evangelical Church. See *Evangelical Church; Evangelical Congregational Church.*

United Evangelical Lutheran Church. See *Danish Lutherans in America,* 5.

United Evangelical Lutheran Free Congregations of Denmark. See *Denmark, Evangelical Lutheran Free Church of.*

United Evangelical Lutheran Synod of North Carolina (ULC). See *United Lutheran Church, Synods of,* 16.

United Free Church of Scotland. Formed Oct. 1900 Edinburgh by merger of Free* Ch. of Scot. and United Presb. Ch. (see *Presbyterian Churches,* 1); united with Est. Ch. of Scot. 1929. See also *Scotland, Reformation in,* 2.

United Free Will Baptist Church, The. See *Baptist Churches,* 27.

United Holy Church of America, Inc. Traces its hist. to a meeting held 1886 Method, suburb of Raleigh, N. C. First called Holy Ch. of N. C., then Holy Ch. of N. C. and Va.; inc. under present name 1918.

United Kingdom of Great Britain and Northern Ireland. See *Great Britain.*

United Lutheran Church in America, The. Organized in a conv. Nov. 14–18, 1918, NYC, by merger of General* Council of the Ev. Luth. Ch. in N. Am., The General* Syn. of the Ev. Luth. Ch. in the USA, and The United* Syn. of the Ev. Luth. Ch. in the S.; ceased to exist 1962 with formation of the Lutheran* Ch. in Am.

I. Leaders of the 3 groups held meetings 1877, 1878, 1898, 1902, 1904 (see also *Diets, Lutheran, in America*). The 3 groups issued a Common Service 1888. By 1909 a Home Mission Arbitration Commission was formed. Doctrinal differences were removed 1911 by const. amendment in the Gen. Syn. Direct impetus for merger grew out of preparations for joint observance of the Reformation quadricentennial 1917, by work of the Nat. Luth. Commission for Soldiers' and Sailors' Welfare, and by formation of the National* Luth. Council.

All constituent syns. of the 3 groups, except the Augustana Syn. (see *Augustana Evangelical Lutheran Church,* 10), entered the merger. Preamble to the ULC const. said: "We . . . invite and until such end be attained continue to invite all Evangelical Lutheran congregations and synods in America, one with us in the faith, to unite with us."

Const., Art. II, Doctrinal Basis: "Section 1. The United Lutheran Church in America receives and holds the canonical Scriptures of the Old and New Testaments as the inspired Word of God, and as the only infallible rule and standard of faith and practice, according to which all doctrines and teachers are to be judged.

"Section 2. . . . accepts the three ecumenical creeds . . . as important testimonies drawn from the Holy Scriptures. . . .

"Section 3. . . . receives and holds the Unaltered Augsburg Confession as a correct exhibition of the faith and doctrine of the Evangelical Lutheran Church, founded upon the Word of God. . . .

"Section 4. . . . recognized the Apology of the Augsburg Confession, the Smalkald Articles, the Large and Small Catechisms of Luther, and the Formula of Concord, as in the harmony of one and the same pure Scriptural faith."

II. *Statistics.* As a result of realignment and other factors, the number of constituent syns. changed from 45 in 1918 to 32 in 1962. The Icelandic Ev. Luth. Syn. of (N.) Am. joined the ULC 1942; the Slovak Ev. Luth. Zion Syn. joined the ULC 1920. See also *United Lutheran Church, Synods of*).

The ULC grew from ca. 2,800 to more than 5,100 ministers, from ca. 3,700 to nearly 4,700 congs., from ca. 907,500 to nearly 2½ million bap. mems., from ca. 775,400 to nearly 1,7000,000 confirmed mems., from ca. 3,600 to ca. 4,700 Sun. Schools (from ca. 540,000 to more than 800,000 pupils, from ca. 53,900 to ca. 107,000 staff mems.). Ch. property value rose from ca. $54,900,000 to nearly $752 million and local expenditures from ca. $5½ million to more than $101,700,000 a yr.

III. Following chs. developed under auspices of the Bd. of For. Missions were received 1950 as affiliated chs.: (1) The Luth. Ch. in the Andhra Country of India; formed 1927 by amalgamation of the Guntur and Rajahmundry Syns.; reorganized 1944. (2) The Ev. Luth. Ch. in Jap.; traces its hist. to 1892; formally organized Tokyo 1931; reorganized after WW II; see also Japan. (3) The Ev. Luth. Ch. of (or in) Brit. Guiana (see *South America,* 12). (4) The United Ev. Luth. Ch. (Argentina); organized 1947/48. (5) The Ev. Luth. Ch. in Liberia; see *Africa,* C 7.

IV. The ULC held membership in National* Luth. Council, Federal* Council of the Chs. of Christ in Am., LWC, The Lutheran* World Fed., National* Council of the Chs. of Christ in the USA, World* Council of Chs.

V. ULC organizations included Luther League of Am. (see also *Young People's Organizations, Christian,* II 2), United Luth. Ch. Men., United Luth. Ch. Women.

VI. Pres.: F. H. Knubel* 1918–Dec. 31, 1944; F. C. Fry* Jan. 1, 1945–62. WT, TGT

See also *Lutheran Council in Canada,* 2; *Students, Spiritual Care of,* B 2.

T. E. Schmauk, "Historical Report of the Merger," *Minutes of the First Convention of The United Lutheran Church in America* (New York, [1918]), pp. 37–42; A. R. Wentz, *A Basic History of Lutheranism in America,* rev. ed. (Philadelphia, 1964), pp. 269–286; J. L. Neve, *History of the Lutheran Church in America,* 3d ed. W. D. Allbeck (Burlington, Iowa, 1934), pp. 342–356.

United Lutheran Church, Synods of. 1. *Can., Syn. of* (Canada Syn.). Pittsburgh Syn. (see 24) miss. efforts in Ont. led to formation 1853 of the Canada Conf. of the Pittsburgh Syn.; the Conf. resolved itself into the Ev. Luth. Syn. of Can. July 1861; helped form General* Council of the Ev. Luth. Ch. in (N.) Am. 1867, ULC 1918. The Ev. Luth. Syn. of Cen. Can., organized 1908 as a result of Gen. Council Eng. miss work in Ont., helped form ULC 1918, merged into the Ev. Luth. Syn. of Can. June 1925. See also 32.

The Ev. Luth. Sem. of Can. was founded 1911 at Waterloo, Ont., by the Ev. Luth. Syn. of Can. and the Ev. Luth. Syn. of Cen. Can.; Waterloo Coll. School was est. 1914 in connection with the sem. The coll. expanded 1924 into the Waterloo Coll. of Arts; the faculty of arts under the name Waterloo Coll. became affiliated with the U. of Western Ont. 1925; preparatory courses of the coll. school were abandoned 1929. The Ev. Luth. Sem. of Can. became Waterloo Luth. U. 1959/60, and at that time Waterloo Coll. terminated affiliation with the U. of Western Ont. and began granting degrees as Waterloo U. Coll. In 1973 Waterloo Luth. U. severed ties with the Eastern Canada Syn. (LCA) in order to become a provincially assisted school renamed Wilfrid Laurier U. The sem., federated with the new university, came under a separate bd. of governors.

1961 statistics: 141 pastors; 144 congs.; 68,312 bap. mems.

Jubiläums-Büchlein: Festschrift zur Feier des 50-jährigen Jubiläums der evang.-luther. Synode von Canada (n. p., 1911); V. J. Eylands, *Lutherans in Canada* (Winnipeg, Man., Can., 1945); C. R. Cronmiller, *A History of the Lutheran Church in Canada* (n. p., 1961).

See also *Canada,* A 4.

2. *Caribbean Ev. Luth. Syn. of the ULCA* (Caribbean Syn.). See *Caribbean Islands,* E 4, 8. 1961 statistics: 19 pastors; 21 congs.; 6,699 bap. mems.

J. P. M. Larsen, *Virgin Islands Story* (Philadelphia, 1950).

3. *Central States, Ev. Luth. Syn. in the* (Central States Syn.). The Ev. Luth. Syn. of Kans. (and Adjacent States) (also known as Kans. Syn.) organized early Nov. 1868 Topeka; joined The General* Syn. of the Ev. Luth. Ch. in the USA 1869. The Ev. Luth. Syn. of Nebr. (also known as Nebr. Syn.) organized early Sept. 1871 Omaha; joined Gen. Syn. 1875. Some Ger.-speaking mems. withdrew from the Nebr. Syn. and organized the Ger. Ev. Luth. Syn. of Nebr. (also known as Ger. Nebr. Syn.) 1890 Sterling, Nebr.; joined Gen. Syn. 1893; name changed 1937 to Ev. Luth. Syn. in the Midwest (also known as Midwest Syn.); est. Martin* Luther Sem. 1913 Lincoln, Nebr. The 3 syns. merged 1954 to form the Ev. Luth. Syn. in the Central States. 1961: 218 pastors; 197 congs.; 87,305 bap. mems.

H. A. Ott, *A History of the Evangelical Lutheran Synod of Kansas* (Topeka, Kans., 1907); *Story of the Midwest Synod U. L. C. A. 1890–1950* (n. p., n. d.).

4. *Fla. Syn. (of the ULCA)* (Syn. of Fla.). Organized 1928 Lakeland, Fla., by pastors and congs. formerly constituting the Fla. Conference of the Ev. Luth. Syn. and Ministerium of Ga. and Adjacent States (see 5); joined ULC 1928. 1961: 81 pastors; 55 congs.; 24,720 bap. mems.

5. *Ga.-Ala. Syn. (of the ULCA).* Organized July 1860 Spalding Co., Ga., as the Ev. Luth. Syn. in the State of Ga. (also known as Ga. Syn.). Helped organize The Gen. Syn. of the Ev. Luth. Ch. in the Confederate* States of Am. 1863. Became the Ev. Luth. Syn. and Ministerium of Ga. in the 1860s, the Ev. Luth. Syn. and Ministerium of Ga. and Adjacent States in the 1870s. Helped form The United* Syn. of the Ev. Luth. Ch. in the South 1886, ULC 1918. On the Fla. Syn. see 4. The Ga. Syn. changed name 1930 to Ga.-Ala. Syn. 1961: 52 pastors; 58 congs.; 17,986 bap. mems.

D. R. Poole, *History of the Georgia-Alabama Synod of The United Lutheran Church in America* 1860–1960 (n. p., n. d.).

6. *Icelandic Syn.* 19th-c. immigrants from Iceland to Am. settled mainly in Man., Can., and in Minn. and the Dakotas. An Icelandic Luth. service was conducted 1874 Milwaukee, Wis., by Jon Bjarnason. The Icelandic Syn. organized Winnipeg, Man., Can., June 1885 after a preliminary meeting Jan. 1885 Mountain, N. Dak.; Icelandic name: Hins evangeliska lúterska kirkjufélags Islendinga í Vesturheimi ("The Ev. Luth. Ch. Organization of Icelanders in the Western Hemisphere"); Eng. name since 1951: Icelandic Ev. Luth. Syn. in (or of) Am.; const. provided for female suffrage. In the 1st decade of the 20th c. the syn. was torn by strife over Biblical inspiration and the meaning of confessional subscription; some Icelanders and their pastors later became Unitarian. Joined ULC 1940. 1961: 18 pastors; 30 congs.; 7,476 bap. mems. See also *Canada,* A 13; *Thorgrimson, Hans Baagöe.*

K. K. Olafson, *The Icelandic Lutheran Synod* (Winnipeg, n. d.).

7. *Ill. Syn. (of the ULCA).* Organized June 1920 by merger of the Ev. Luth. Syn. of Cen. Illinois,* the Ev. Luth. Syn. of N. Illinois,* the Ev. Luth. Syn. of S. Illinois,* and part of the former Chicago* Syn. of the Ev. Luth. Church. 1961: 232 pastors; 167 congs.; 111,024 bap. mems.

M. L. Wagner, *The Chicago Synod and Its Antecedents* (Waverly, Iowa, n. d.); T. W. Brosche et al., *Progress of a Century: A History of The Illinois Synod of the United Lutheran Church in America 1851–1951* (n. p., n. d.).

8. *Ind. Syn. (of the ULCA).* The Ind. mems. of the Miami* Syn. helped form the Olive Branch Ev. Luth. Syn. of Ind. 1848, which joined The General* Syn. of the Ev. Luth. Ch. in the USA 1850, changed name 1898 to Olive Branch Syn. of the Ev. Luth. Ch., and merged 1920 with the Ind. mems. of the former Chicago* Syn. of the Ev. Luth. Ch. to form an Ind. Syn. with mems. in other states. By 1934 all mems. outside Ind. were dismissed to other syns. See also 10, 12. 1961: 136 pastors; 127 congs.; 46,569 bap. mems.

9. *Iowa, (Ev. Luth.) Syn. of* (Iowa Syn.). Organized in the 1850s; joined The General* Syn. of the Ev. Luth. Ch. in the USA 1857. 1961: 78 pastors; 45 congs.; 40,092 bap. mems.

M. Qualley, "United Lutheran Synod in Iowa," *The Palimpsest,* XXXV (1954), 245–260.

10. *Ky.-Tenn. Syn.* Formed 1934 by some mems. of the Ind. Syn. (see 8) and Ohio Syn. (see 19), but not congs. in eastern Tenn. which retained membership in the Va. Syn. (see 29). 1961: 43 pastors; 40 congs.; 12,272 bap. mems.

11. *Md., Ev. Luth. Syn. of* (Md. Syn.). Organized 1820 by the Va. Conf. of the Pa. Ministerium as "The Evangelical Lutheran Synod of Maryland, Virginia, and so forth"; name changed 1822 to "The Evangelical Lutheran Synod of Maryland and Virginia," 1833 to "The Evangelical Lutheran Synod of Maryland" (the Ev. Luth. Syn. of Va. [Va. Syn.] had been formed 1829). Helped form The General* Syn. of the Ev. Luth. Ch. in the USA. When the Md. Syn. refused to sanction the Definite* Syn. Platform, B. Kurtz* withdrew and led in organizing the Melanchthon Syn. 1857; the latter rejoined the Md. Syn. 1869. 1961: 191 pastors; 161 congs.; 113,105 bap. mems. See also 29.

A. R. Wentz, *History of the Evangelical Lutheran Synod of Maryland of The United Lutheran Church in America 1820–1920* (Harrisburg, Pa., 1920).

12. *Mich. Syn. (of the ULCA).* Formed 1920 by merger of N. Indiana* Syn. and part of the Chicago* Syn. of the Ev. Luth. Ch.; mems. in Ind. were transferred to the Ind. Syn. (see 8) 1934. 1961: 85 pastors; 68 congs.; 35,910 bap. mems.

13. *Miss., Ev. Luth. Syn. of* (Miss. Syn.). Organized 1855 by pastors of the S. C. Syn. (see 27) who had begun work in Miss. 1846; joined The Ev. Luth. **Gen. Syn. S.** (see *United Synod of the Evangelical Lutheran Church in the South, The,* 1) 1876; helped organize United Syn. of the S. 1886. 1961: 5 pastors; 10 congs.; 962 bap. mems.

14. *N. J., Ev. Luth. Syn. of* (N. J. Syn.). The Ev. Luth. Syn. of N. J. (II) organized 1950 by N. J. mems. of the United Syn. of N. Y. (see 15), Pa. Ministerium (see 22), and Cen. Pa. Syn. (see 23). 1961: 175 pastors; 154 congs.; 96,324 bap. mems.

A. Hiller, "History of the Lutheran Church in New Jersey," *The Lutheran Quarterly,* XXVIII (1898), 98–130, 165–196; T. G. Tappert, "Early Lutheranism in Southern New Jersey," *The Lutheran Church Quarterly,* XIX (1946), 305–314.

15. *N. Y. and New Eng., United (Luth.) Syn. of*

(N. Y. and New Eng. Syn.). Traced its hist. to organization of the N. Y. Ministerium at least as early as 1786 Albany, N. Y. under leadership of J. C. Kunze* (see also *Schwerdtfeger, Johann Samuel Wilhelm*); foundations had been laid in the 1770s by F. A. C. Muhlenberg (see *Mühlenberg, Henry Melchior, and Family,* 6). Its const. was based on that of the Pa. Ministerium (see 22) but differed from the latter in that (a) laymen were given voice and vote (see also *Ministerium*) and (b) the N. Y. Ministerium had no sessions limited to pastors.

The N. Y. Ministerium helped organize The General* Syn. of the Ev. Luth. Ch. in the USA 1820 but withdrew after the 1st meeting and did not return till 1837. Meantime it suffered internal strife. Some mems. withdrew 1830, formed the Hartwick* Syn. of the Ev. Luth. Ch. in the State of N. Y. on basis of a modified AC, and joined the Gen. Syn. 1831. Further liberalism in the Hartwick Syn. led to organization 1837 of the Franckean* Syn. of the Ev. Luth. Ch. in the State of N. Y. In 1859 some mems. of the N. Y. Ministerium withdrew and 1861 organized the Ev. Luth. Syn. of New* Jersey (I). In protest against reception of the Franckean Syn. into the Gen. Syn. 1864/66, the N. Y. Ministerium (which had rejoined the Gen. Syn. 1837) withdrew from the Gen. Syn. 1866/67 and helped form the General* Council of the Ev. Luth. Ch. in (N.) Am. But a minority of mems. withdrew 1866 from the N. Y. Ministerium in protest against this new alignment, formed the Ev. Luth. Syn. of New* York 1867, joined the Gen. Syn. 1868, and merged 1872 with the Ev. Luth. Syn. of N. J. (I) to form the Ev. Luth. Syn. of N. Y. and N. J. (mem. Gen. Syn.).

Meantime, F. W. T. Steimle* and others withdrew 1866 for confessional reasons from the N. Y. Ministerium and formed the Ger. Ev. Luth. Syn. of New* York and Other States (also known as Steimle Syn.); the syn., but not Steimle, rejoined the N. Y. Ministerium 1872.

Eng.-speaking mems. withdrew from the N. Y. Ministerium and formed the Ev. Luth. Syn. of N. Y. and New Eng. 1902, joined Gen. Council 1903.

The Hartwick Syn., Franckean Syn., and Ev. Luth. Syn. of N. Y. and N. J. merged 1908 to form the Syn. of N. Y. of the Ev. Luth. Ch. (also known as N. Y. Syn.), which joined the Gen. Syn. 1909.

The Syn. of N. Y. of the Ev. Luth. Ch., N. Y. Ministerium, and Ev. Luth. Syn. of N. Y. and New Eng. merged 1929 to form the United Luth. Syn., N. Y. In 1952 it became the United Luth. Syn. of N. Y. and New Eng.

1961: 515 pastors; 377 congs.; 220,274 bap. mems.

J. Nicum, *Geschichte des Evangelisch-Lutherischen Ministeriums vom Staate New York und angrenzenden Staaten und Ländern* (n. p., 1888); H. J. Kreider, *History of the United Lutheran Synod of New York and New England,* I, 1786–1860 (Philadelphia, 1954); N. van Alstine, *Historical Review of the Franckean Evangelical Lutheran Synod of New York* (Philadelphia, 1893); S. G. Trexler, *Crusaders of The Twentieth Century: A Lutheran Story in the Empire State* (New York, 1926).

16. *N. C., United (Ev. Luth.) Syn. of.* Ger. Luths. from Pa. began to settle in N. C. bet. 1745 and 1750. Congs. began to form. A special appeal to Eur. for a pastor 1772 brought A. Nussmann.* C. A. G. Stork* was sent 1788 from Ger. to help Nussmann. Paul Henkel (see *Henkels, The,* 2) was active in N. C. and helped organize the Ev. Luth. Syn. and Ministerium of N. C. (also known as N. C. Syn.) 1803, whose membership soon extended into S. C., Va., and Tenn.

When the N. C. Syn. planned to help form the Gen. Syn., Paul, Philip, and D. Henkel and others formed the Ev. Luth. Tenn. Syn. (see also 29) in protest 1820. The N. C. Syn. suffered other losses by organization of the Ev. Luth. Syn. of S. C. 1824 (see also 27), the Western Va. Syn. 1842 (see also 29), and the Ev. Luth. Syn. of Miss. 1855 (see also 13). In 1863 the N. C. Syn. withdrew from the Gen. Syn. and helped organize The Gen. Syn. of the Ev. Luth. Ch. in the Confederate* States of Am., which became The Ev. Luth. Gen. Syn. in N. Am. 1866. In 1870 the N. C. Syn. withdrew from the latter, which in 1876 became The Ev. Luth. Gen. Syn. South. The N. C. Syn. (re)joined the latter 1881. In 1886 the N. C. Syn. helped organize The United Syn. of the Ev. Luth. Ch. in the S. In 1921 the Tenn. Syn. reunited with the N. C. Syn. to form the United Ev. Luth. Syn. of N. C., which that yr. came into ownership and control of Lenoir Rhyne Coll.

1961: 226 pastors; 187 congs.; 70,316 bap. mems.

History of the Lutheran Church in North Carolina (1803–1953), ed. J. L. Morgan et al. (n. p., n. d.).

17. *Northwest, Syn. of the* (Northwest Syn.; Eng. Ev. Luth. Syn. of the Northwest; Eng. Northwest Syn.). Organized 1891 St. Paul, Minn.; joined General* Council of the Ev. Luth. Ch. in (N.) Am. 1893. Territory included Wis., Minn., N. and S. Dak., Mont., Idaho, Wash., Oreg. 1961: 236 pastors; 172 congs.; 160,308 bap. mems. See also *Northwestern Lutheran Theological Seminary.*

G. H. Trabert, *English Lutheranism in the Northwest* (Philadelphia, 1914); P. H. Roth, *Story of the English Evangelical Lutheran Synod of the Northwest* (1891–1941) (n. p., n. d.); D. A. Flesner, *70th Anniversary Review: The English Evangelical Lutheran Synod of the Northwest 1891–1961* (n. p., n. d.).

18. *Nova Scotia Syn.* See *Canada,* A 1–3. 1961: 13 pastors; 36 congs.; 7,812 bap. mems.

D. L. Roth, *Acadie and the Acadians* (Philadelphia, 1890); V. J. Eylands, *Lutherans in Canada* (Winnipeg, Man., Can., 1945); C. R. Cronmiller, *A History of the Lutheran Church in Canada* (n. p., 1961).

19. *Ohio Syn.* (Syn. of Ohio [of the ULCA]). Formed 1920 by merger of the East Ohio Syn. of the Ev. Luth. Ch. (see *General Synod of the Evangelical Lutheran Church in the United States of America, The,* 3), Miami* Syn., Wittenberg* Syn., Dist. Syn. of Ohio (organized 1857), and 1 parish of the Chicago* Syn. of the Ev. Luth. Ch. In 1934 some mems. were released to help form the Ky.-Tenn. Syn. (see 10). 1961: 368 pastors; 310 congs.; 177,657 bap. mems. See also *Ohio and Other States, Evangelical Lutheran Joint Synod of,* 1–4; *Wittenberg University.*

20. *Pacific Syn. (of the Ev. Luth. Ch.).* Organized 1901 by 10 pastors of the Northwest Syn. (see 17) living W of the Mo. R.; joined General* Council of the Ev. Luth. Ch. in (N.) Am. 1901; territory included Wash., Oreg., Idaho, British Columbia, Alaska. Pacific Sem., est. 1910 Portland, Oreg., moved 1914 to Seattle, Wash., suspended operation 1932, closed as a sem. 1934; its capital resources were used 1950 to help found Pacific Luth. Theol. Sem., Berkeley, Calif. (see also 21). 1961: 92 pastors; 66 congs.; 36,856 bap. mems.

E. Bracher, *The First Fifty Years of the Pacific Synod* (Seattle, Wash., 1951).

21. *Pacific Southwest Syn. of the ULCA* (Syn. of Pacific Southwest). The Ev. Luth. Syn. of Calif., result of Gen. Syn. missions beginning 1886, organized 1891; joined Gen. Syn. 1891; came to include chs. in Ariz., Nev., and Hawaii; name changed 1954 to Ev. Luth. Syn. of the Pacific Southwest. Helped est. Pacific Luth. Theol. Sem., Berkeley, Calif. (see also 20; *Lutheran Church in America,* V; *Ministry, Education of,* X O). 1961: 191 pastors; 131 congs.; 74,156 bap. mems.

22. *Pa. Ministerium* (Ministerium of Pa.; various other names and forms of the name). "Mother syn.

of the Luth. Ch. in Am." Organized 1748; outgrowth of United* Congregations. Meetings were not held 1755–59. 1781 const. name: An Ev. Luth. Ministerium in N. America. 1792 name: The Ger. Ev. Luth. Ministerium in Pa. and Adjacent States (adopted in view of organization of the N. Y. Ministerium; see 15). Called ministerium because originally only ministers were given voice and vote. After laymen were seated as regular delegates 1792, the meeting of ministers and laymen together was called a synodical meeting, but the body itself continued to be called a ministerium. Helped form The General* Syn. of the Ev. Luth. Ch. in the USA 1820; withdrew from the Gen. Syn. 1823 partly out of fear of unacceptable authority. But most congs. W of the Susquehanna R. withdrew from the Pa. Ministerium, formed the Ev. Luth. Syn. of West Pa. (West Pa. Syn.) 1825, and joined Gen. Syn. 1825. Pa. Ministerium mems. in E Pa. formed the Ev. Luth. Syn. of East Pa. (East Pa. Syn.) 1842, joined Gen. Syn. 1843. Resultant comparative isolation from new* measures left the Pa. Ministerium comparatively conservative. Rejoined Gen. Syn. 1853 but withdrew again 1866 in protest against the Definite* Synodical Platform (see also *Mann, Wilhelm Julius*) and admission of the Franckean* Syn. to the Gen. Syn. The Pa. Ministerium founded Lutheran Theol. Sem., Philadelphia, 1864. Helped form General* Council of the Ev. Luth. Ch. in (N.) Am. 1867. N. J. mems. were dismissed 1950 to the N. J. Syn. (see 14). 1961: 584 pastors; 542 congs.; 389,840 bap. mems. See also *Mühlenberg, Henry Melchior, and Family,* 2.

Documentary History of the Evangelical Lutheran Ministerium of Pennsylvania and Adjacent States: Proceedings of the Annual Conventions from 1748 to 1821 (Philadelphia, 1898); H. E. Pfatteicher, *The Ministerium of Pennsylvania* (Philadelphia, 1938); T. E. Schmauk, *A History of The Lutheran Church in Pennsylvania (1638–1820),* I (Philadelphia, 1903); T. G. Tappert, "Two Hundred Years of the Ministerium of Pennsylvania," 1948 *Minutes of the Proceedings of the Annual Convention of the Evangelical Lutheran Ministerium of Pennsylvania and the Adjacent States* (n. p., n. d.), pp. 297–303.

23. *Pa., Ev. Luth. Syn. of Central* (Central Pa. Syn. [of the ULCA]). Formed 1938 by merger of the West Pa. Syn. (see 22), Alleghany (Allegheny) Ev. Luth. Syn. of Pa. (Alleghany [Allegheny] Syn.; formed 1842 by mems. of the West Pa. Syn.), East Pa. Syn. (see 22), and Susquehanna Syn. (of the ULCA). The latter organized 1867 as the Susquehanna Syn. of the Ev. Luth. Ch. in the US; merged 1923/24 with the Ev. Luth. Syn. of Central Pa. [Central Pa. Syn.; formed 1855 by mems. who withdrew from the West Pa. Syn.] to form the Susquehanna Syn. of Central Pa. of the Ev. Luth. Ch. [name shortened 1932 to Susquehanna Syn.]). N. J. mems. were dismissed 1950 to the N. J. Syn. (see 14). 1961: 521 pastors; 618 congs.; 309,114 bap. mems.

W. H. B. Carney, *History of the Alleghany Evangelical Lutheran Synod of Pennsylvania,* 2 vols. (Philadelphia, 1918); *The Susquehanna Synod of the Evangelical Lutheran Church in the United States: A History 1867–1917,* ed. F. P. Manhart et al. (n. p., 1917); L. G. Shannon, *A Short History of the Central Pennsylvania Synod of the United Lutheran Church in America* (n. p., 1958).

24. *Pittsburgh Syn. (of the Ev. Luth. Ch.).* Organized 1845 (see also *Passavant, William Alfred*); became known for miss. work extending into other states and into Ont. and Nova Scotia. Joined The General* Syn. of the Ev. Luth. Ch. in the USA 1853. Majority joined the General* Council of the Ev. Luth. Ch. in (N.) Am. 1867; minority remained with the Gen. Syn.; both kept the same name and reunited 1919 under that name. Thiel Coll., Greenville, Pa., came under control of the Pittsburgh Syn. 1870. 1961: 318 pastors; 307 congs.; 161,859 bap. mems.

E. G. Heissenbuttel and R. H. Johnson, *Pittsburgh Synod History: Its Auxiliaries and Institutions, 1845–1962* (Pittsburgh, 1963).

25. *Rocky Mountain Syn.* (of the ULCA). Organized 1891 Manitou, Colo.; territory included Wyo., Colo., N. Mex., and part of Tex.; joined The General* Syn. of the Ev. Luth. Ch. in the USA 1891. 1961: 49 pastors; 31 congs.; 20,012 bap. mems.

26. *Slovak Ev. Luth. "Zion" Syn.* (Slovak Zion Syn.). Organized 1919 Braddock. Pa.; joined ULC 1920; represented mainly in Pa., N. J., and N. Y. 1961: 37 pastors; 48 congs.; 20,355 bap. mems.

27. *South Carolina, Ev. Luth. Syn of* (S. C. Syn.). Luth. chs. were est. in S. C. as early as the 1730s. The Unio Ecclesiastica der deutsch protestantischen Kirchen im Staate South Carolina, formed 1787, disappeared ca. the turn of the c. The S. C. Syn., organized 1824, joined The General* Syn. of the Ev. Luth. Ch. in the USA 1835, helped organize The Gen. Syn. of the Ev. Luth. Ch. in the Confederate* States of Am. 1863 and The United Syn. of the Ev. Luth. Ch. in the South 1886.

Lutheran Theol. Southern Sem. traces its hist. to a theol. institution est. 1830 by the S. C. Syn.; Lexington, S. C., chosen as its "permanent location" 1832; a classical dept. added; moved to Newberry, S. C.; classical dept. named Newberry Coll. 1856. Theol. instruction interrupted by the Civil War; work revived by the Gen. Syn. South first at Walhalla, S. C., 1868, then at Columbia, finally at Salem, Va.; closed 1884; theol. work resumed 1886 by the S. C. Syn. at Newberry Coll.; given new impetus by the United Syn. in the South ca. 1898; moved to Mount Pleasant, ca. 21 mi. SW of Columbia, S. C.; moved to Columbia, S. C., 1911. See also *Hazelius, Ernest Lewis; Lutheran Church in America,* V; *Ministry, Education of,* VIII B 20; *Repass Stephan Abion.*

1961: 144 pastors; 140 congs.; 45,922 bap. mems. See also 13.

History of the Evangelical Lutheran Synod of South Carolina 1824–1924, ed. S. T. Hallman (Columbia, S. C., n. d.).

28. *Tex. and La., (Ev. Luth.) Syn. of* (Tex. and La. Syn.). Preachers from St. Chrischona* and a missionary sent by W. A. Passavant* organized the First (Ger.) Ev. Luth. Syn. of Tex. (Tex. Syn.) 1851; joined The General* Syn. of the Ev. Luth. Ch. in the USA 1853; mem. the General* Council of the Ev. Luth. Ch. in (N.) Am. 1868–94. Most of the Tex. Syn. withdrew 1894 and joined the Ev. Luth. Syn. of Iowa* and Other States as a dist. 1896; The minority continued as Old Ger. Ev. Luth. Syn. of Tex. of the UAC (also known as Tex. Syn.); it experienced some losses to the Iowa Syn. 1913; joined the Gen. Council 1915; name changed 1954 to Ev. Luth. Syn. of Tex. and La. 1961: 60 pastors; 56 congs.; 19,258 bap. mems.

J. Mgebroff, *Geschichte der Ersten Deutschen Evangelisch-Lutherischen Synode in Texas* (n. p., 1902); *History of the First Evangelical Lutheran Synod of Texas,* comp. M. Heinrich (n. p., n. d); *History of the Evangelical Lutheran Texas Synod of the United Lutheran Church in America* (Philadelphia, 1926); H. C. Ziehe, *A Centennial Story of the Lutheran Church in Texas* (Seguin, Tex., 1951).

29. *Va., (Luth.) Syn. of* (Va. Syn.). For hist. up to 1829 see 11. Some mems. of the N. C. Syn. (see 16) and of the Va. Syn. formed the "Ev. Luth. Syn. and Ministerium of Western Va. and adjacent parts" (Western Va. Syn.) 1842. The Va. Syn. joined The General* Syn. of the Ev. Luth. Ch. in the USA 1839; the Western Va. Syn. joined the Gen. Syn.

1843. These 2 syns. helped organize The Gen. Syn. of the Ev. Luth. Ch. in the Confederate* States of Am. 1863. The Western Va. Syn. changed name 1867 to Ev. Luth. Syn. and Ministerium of Southwestern Va. (Southwestern Va. Syn.).

The Holston Syn., organized 1860 by mems. of the Tenn. Syn. (see 16) in western Va. and Tenn., was mem. of The Gen. Syn. of the Ev. Luth. Ch. in the Confederate States of Am. 1869–72 and of the General* Council of the Ev. Luth. Ch. in (N.) Am. 1874–86.

All 3 syns. (Va. Syn., Southwestern Va. Syn., Holston Syn.) helped organize The United Syn. of the Ev. Luth. Ch. in the South 1886. In 1922 they merged into the (Luth.) Syn. of Va. Est. Marion (Va.) Coll. 1873 (see also *Ministry, Education of,* VIII C 1 e). 1961: 142 pastors; 187 congs.; 45,901 bap. mems.

History of the Lutheran Church in Virginia and East Tennessee, ed. C. W. Cassell et al. (Strasburg, Va., 1930); W. E. Eisenberg, *The Lutheran Church in Virginia, 1717–1962, including an Account of the Lutheran Church in East Tennessee* (Roanoke, Va., 1967).

30. *Wartburg Syn.* (of the Ev. Luth. Ch.). Organization resolved on 1875, documentarily fixed 1876. Formed by Ger. mems. of the Ev. Luth. Syn. of Cen. Illinois,* who first met 1873 as the Ger. Conference of that syn. Joined The General* Syn. of the Ev. Luth. Ch. in the USA 1877. 1961: 64 pastors; 51 congs.; 34,181 bap. mems. See also *Severinghaus, John Dietrich.*

W. E. Kaitschuk, *History of the Wartburg Synod* (Burlington, Iowa, 1940).

31. *West Va., Ev. Luth. Syn. of* (West Va. Syn.). Organized 1912; joined The General* Syn. of the Ev. Luth. Ch. in the USA 1913. 1961: 31 pastors; 37 congs.; 10,611 bap. mems.

32. *Western Can., (Ev. Luth.) Syn. of* (Western Can. Syn.). Began in the 1890s as Northwest Conf. of the Ev. Luth. Syn. of Can. (see 1); organized 1897 as Ger. Ev. Luth. Syn. of Manitoba* and the Northwest Territories; name changed 1907 to The Ger. Ev. Luth. Syn. of Man. and other Provinces, 1947 to Ev. Luth. Syn. of Western Can. Territory came to include Man., Sask., Alta., and Brit. Columbia. Est. Luth. Coll. and Sem., Saskatoon, Sask., 1913 (see also *Ministry, Education of,* X L). 1961: 60 pastors; 104 congs.; 22,088 bap. mems. See also *Canada,* A 14.

See also *Lutheran Church in America; United Lutheran Church in America.*

V. J. Eylands, *Lutherans in Canada* (Winnipeg, Man., Can., 1945); C. R. Cronmiller, *A History of the Lutheran Church in Canada* (n. p., 1961).

United Lutheran Publication House, The. See *United Lutheran Publication Houses.*

United Lutheran Synod. See *England,* C 18.

United Lutheran Synod, New York. See *United Lutheran Church, Synods of,* 15.

United Lutheran Synod of New York and New England. See *United Lutheran Church, Synods of,* 15.

United Methodist Church, The. See *Methodist Churches,* 1.

United Methodist Free Churches. See *Methodist Churches,* 1.

United Methodist Youth Fellowship. See *Young People's Organizations, Christian,* III 12.

United Missionary Church. See *Mennonite Churches,* 1.

United Nations Relief and Rehabilitation Administration. See *Social Work,* D 1.

United Norwegian Lutheran Church in America, The. Organized June 1890 by The Norwegian-Danish* Augustana Syn. in Am., The Conf. for the Norw.-Dan. Ev. Luth. Ch. in Am., and the Anti-Missouri* Brotherhood. United 1917 with Hauge's Norw. Ev. Luth. Syn. and most of the Norw. Syn. to form The Norw. Luth. Ch. of Am. See also *Evangelical Lutheran Church, The,* 8–13.

E. C. Nelson and E. L. Fevold, *The Lutheran Church Among Norwegian-Americans,* 2 vols. (Minneapolis, Minn., 1960).

United Original Secession Church. See *Presbyterian Churches,* 1.

United Pentecostal Church. Formed by merger of Pentecostal Ch., Inc., and Pentecostal Assemblies of Jesus Christ 1945 St. Louis, Mo.; holds that there is only 1 person in the Godhead, namely Jesus Christ.

The Pent. Ch., Inc., formed 1924 by whites who withdrew from the interracial Pentecostal Assemblies of the World, Inc., organized 1914. The Pent. Assemblies of Jesus Christ organized Dec. 1931.

United Presbyterian Church in the United States of America, The. See *Presbyterian Churches,* 4 a.

United Presbyterian Church of North America, The. See *Associate Reformed Church; Presbyterian Churches,* 4 a.

United Presbyterian Church of Scotland. See *Gillespie, Thomas; Presbyterian Churches,* 1; *Scotland, Reformation in,* 1.

United Protestant Confession. See *Fraternal Appeal to the American Churches, with a Plan for Catholic Union, on Apostolic Principles.*

United Republic of Tanzania. See *Africa,* E 7.

United Secession Church. See *Gillespie, Thomas; Presbyterian Churches,* 1; *Scotland, Reformation in,* 1.

United Seventh Day Brethren. Adv. ch. formed 1947 by merger of 2 small indep. Sabbatarian premillennial chs.

United Society. Organized by J. Wesley* in connection with Moravians 1739/40.

United Society for the Propagation of the Gospel. Formed 1965 by merger of Society* for the Propagation of the Gospel in For. Parts and Universities'* Mission to Cen. Afr.

United Society of Believers in Christ's Second Appearing, The. See *Shakers.*

United States, Lutheran Theology in the. 1. The early Luths. in Am. came from Swed., Holland, and Ger. determined to adhere to the Luth. Confessions. The Swed. govt. instructed J. B. Printz (see *Campanius, Johan*) that services be performed acc. to the UAC, the Council of Uppsala (see *Sweden, Lutheranism in,* 1), and the ceremonies of the Swed. ch. Dutch and Ger. Luths. proceeded largely on basis of the Amsterdam Ch. Order, which required subscription to the UAC.

The Lutheranism of H. M. Mühlenberg (see *Mühlenberg, Henry Melchior, and Family,* 1–4) and of his fellow workers from Halle was tinged with Pietism.*

2. The Pa. Ministerium (see *United Lutheran Church, Synods of,* 22) had no const. or formal declaration on the Book* of Concord when it was organized. But J. N. Kurtz* promised at his ordination 1748 to teach only what harmonizes with the Word of God and the Confessions of the Ev. Luth. Ch. The dedication sermon of St. Michael's Ch., Philadelphia, 1748, reminded the cong. that Ev. Luth. doctrine should be taught in it acc. to the foundation of the prophets and apostles and acc. to the UAC and the other symbolical books. The 1781 Pa. Ministerium const., chap. 6, par. 2: "Every minister professes that he holds the Word of God and our Symbolical Books in doctrine and life; . . ."

3–4. H. M. Mühlenberg died 1787. Gen. deterioration of confessional Lutheranism followed. The 1792 Pa. Ministerium const. omitted all confessional tests. F. H. Quitman* of the N. Y. Ministerium (see *United Lutheran Church, Synods of,* 15) was a rationalist.

5. The General* Syn. of the Ev. Luth. Ch. in the USA was organized 1820 for closer relations bet. syns.; its const. made no ref. to Luth. confessions.

Gen. Syn. 1825 plan for a sem., resolution 1: "In this Seminary shall be taught . . . the fundamental doctrines of the Sacred Scriptures, as contained in the Augsburg Confession." Purpose of the sem. as expressed in its 1826 const., Art. I: "To provide . . . pastors who sincerely believe, and cordially approve of the doctrines of the Holy Scriptures, as they are fundamentally taught in the Augsburg Confession, . . ." The oath of prof. office required by the const. read in part: "I . . . believe the Scriptures of the Old and New Testament to be the inspired Word of God, and the only perfect rule of faith and practice. I believe the Augsburg Confession and the Catechisms of Luther to be a summary and just exhibition of the fundamental doctrines of the Word of God." The 1829 Gen. Syn. Const. of Syns. for dist. syns. candidates for licensing and ordination were required to say that they believed that the fundamental doctrines of the Word of God are taught in a manner substantially correct in the doctrinal articles of the Augsburg Confession. But these confessional obligations lacked necessary clearness and definiteness and opened the door to latitudinarianism. In a letter in the mid-1840s to the Ev. Ch. in Ger. the Gen. Syn. said: "In most of our church principles we stand on common ground with the Union Church of Germany. The distinctive views which separate the Old Lutherans and the Reformed Church we do not consider essential." Besides unionism,* doctrinal indifference, and rationalism, the influence of Puritanism was apparent. Works, external conduct, and "new* measures" were emphasized.

6. Paul Henkel (see *Henkels, The,* 2), C. F. W. Walther,* and others protested nonconfessional trends. See also *Lutheran Church–Missouri Synod, The.* Conservative Lutheranism was strengthened.

7. The Definite* Syn. Platform, an unsettling factor, led to Free* Luth. Conferences.

8. Admission of the Franckean* Syn. to the Gen. Syn. in the mid-1860s led to disruption of the Gen. Syn. and formation of the General* Council of the Ev. Luth. Ch. in (N.) Am. 1867. See also *Four Points; Galesburg Rule.*

9. After formation of the Gen. Council the doctrinal position of the Gen. Syn. became progressively more conservative. By 1913 all dist. syns. of the Gen. Syn. had approved revised arts. of the const. that recognized the OT and NT canonical scriptures as the Word of God and the only infallible rule of faith and practice; the UAC as a correct exhibition of faith and doctrine as founded on the Word; and the secondary symbols as expositions of Luth. doctrine of great hist. and interpretative value. The revised arts. especially commended the SC as a book of instruction.

10. The United* Syn. of the Ev. Luth. Ch. in the S. recognized "the Holy Scriptures, the Inspired Writings of the Old and New Testaments, the only standard of doctrine and church discipline"; the ecumenical symbols and the UAC "as a true and faithful exhibition of the doctrines of the Holy Scriptures in regard to matters of faith and practice"; and the other Confessions of the Book of Concord "as true and Scriptural developments of the doctrines taught in the Augsburg Confession, and in the perfect harmony of one and the same pure, Scriptural faith."

11. The doctrinal basis of The United* Luth. Ch. in Am. recognized the OT and NT canonical Scriptures as the inspired Word of God, and as the only infallible rule and standard of faith and practice, acc. to which all doctrines and teachers are to be judged; the 3 ecumenical* creeds as important testimonies drawn from the Holy Scriptures; the UAC as a correct exhibition of the faith and doctrine of the Ev. Luth. Ch., founded on the Word of God; the other Luth. Confessions as in the harmony of one and the same pure Scriptural faith. See also *Pittsburgh Agreement.*

12. On the confessional basis of the Mo. Syn. see *Lutheran Church – Missouri Synod, The,* III 4; see also other parts of that art., esp. V and VI.

The Synodical* Conference acknowledged "the canonical writings of the Old and New Testaments as God's Word, and the confession of the Evangelical Lutheran Church of 1580, called the 'Concordia,' as her own." See also *Predestinarian Controversy,* 2.

On the doctrine of the ALC (1930) see *American Lutheran Church,* II. On the doctrinal basis of The American* Lutheran Conference see *Chicago Theses; Minneapolis Theses* (1925). On the doctrinal basis of The ALC (1960) see *American Lutheran Church, The,* II. On the doctrinal basis of the LCA see *Lutheran Church in America,* III. Purposes of the Lutheran* Council in the USA include seeking to achieve theological consensus on basis of the Scriptures and the witness of the Luth. Confessions.

See also *American Lutheran Church,* V 1; *Brief Statement; Common Confession; Madison Settlement; Madison Theses.*

United States, Lutheranism in the. 1. Lutheranism was brought from Eur. to Am. beginning in the 17th c. See *Arensius Bernhardus Antonius; Campanius, Johan; Danish Lutherans in America; Fabritius, Jacob; Falckner, Daniel, Jr.; Falckner, Justus; Gutwasser, John Ernst; Kocherthal, Josua; Lock, Lars Carlson; Torkillus, Reorus.* Salzburgers* settled 1734 near Savannah, Ga. In pre-Revolutionary days Lutheranism spread esp. in N. Y., Pa., Del., and Md. See also *Berkenmeyer, Wilhelm Christoph; Henkels, The,* 1; *Stover, John Caspar, Sr.; Stoever, John Caspar, Jr.*

Through most of the 18th c. the hist. of Lutheranism in the US is the history of Luth. immigrants and of congs. in most Luth. settlements. It was a time of confusion. Congs. were widely scattered and poor. Pastors were few; some were adventurers and impostors.

2. The period of larger organizations or syns. began 1748 with the Pa. Ministerium (see *United Lutheran Church, Synods of,* 22). The N. Y. Ministerium was organized in the 1780s, the N. C. Syn. 1803 (see *United Lutheran Church, Synods of,* 15, 16).

3. After the death of H. M. Mühlenberg 1787, till 1817 (tercentenary of the Reformation), rationalism and indifference gripped the Luth. Ch. in the US. See also *Quitman, Frederick Henry; Schober, Gottlieb.*

4. Immigration from Luth. countries to the US reached its peak 1817–1860. New syns. were organized, some in reaction against unionism*: Ohio Syn. 1818 (see *Ohio and Other States, The Evangelical Lutheran Joint Synod of*), Md. Syn. 1820 (see *United Lutheran Church, Synods of,* 11), The General* Syn. of the Ev. Luth. Ch. in the USA 1820, Tenn. Syn. 1820 (see *United Lutheran Church, Synods of,* 16), Buffalo* Syn. 1845, Mo. Syn. 1847 (see *Lutheran Church – Missouri Synod, The*). The Gen. Syn. included ca. two-thirds of US Lutheranism 1860.

5. For lack of pastors some pastors trained students in their homes; some pastors were trained in sems. of other denominations. The Hartwick* Sem. lacked efficient direction. The Luth. Theol. Sem., Gettysburg, was est. 1826.

Adherence to the Ger. language drove many young Eng.-speaking people into Eng. denominations.

6. The Gen. Syn. carried on Home Mission work chiefly through dist. syns. See also *Central Mis-*

sionary Society of the Evangelical Lutheran Church in the United States; Keller, Ezra. J. C. F. Heyer* was sent as miss. to India by the Pa. Ministerium in the early 1840s. See also *Passavant, William Alfred.*

7. The Definite* Syn. Platform led to controversy. Other controverted matters: Antichrist,* Church* and Ministry, Open* Questions, Predestination* (see also *Predestinarian Controversy,* 2), Sunday.*

8. Reaction against indifference and confessional laxity and the impact of the Civil War (see *United Synod of the Evangelical Lutheran Church in the South, The,* 1) led to disruption of the Gen. Syn. and formation of the General* Council of the Ev. Luth. Ch. in (N.) Am. in the 1860s.

9. The Synodical* Conference was organized 1872. Intersynodical mergers saw formation of The Norw. Luth. Ch. of Am. 1917 (see *Evangelical Lutheran Church, The,* 13), The United* Luth. Ch. in Am. 1918, the American* Luth. Ch. 1930. For other similar developments see *Union and Unity Movements in the United States, Lutheran.* See also *Lutheran World Federation, The.* ARS

See also *United States, Lutheran Theology in the.*

I. Acrelius, *A History of New Sweden* (Philadelphia, 1874); E. L. Hazelius, *History of the American Lutheran Church from Its Commencement in the Year of Our Lord 1685, to the Year 1842* (Zanesville, Ohio, 1846); C. W. Schaeffer, *Early History of the Lutheran Church in America* (Philadelphia, 1857); A. L. Gräbner [Graebner], *Geschichte der Lutherischen Kirche in America* (St. Louis, 1892); *The American Church History Series,* ed. P. Schaff et al., IV: H. E. Jacobs, *A History of the Evangelical Lutheran Church in the United States,* 5th ed. (New York, 1907); O. Kraushaar, *Verfassungsformen der Lutherischen Kirche Amerikas* (Gütersloh, 1911); W. J. Finck, *Lutheran Landmarks and Pioneers in America* (Philadelphia, 1913); J. L. Neve, *History of the Lutheran Church in America,* 3d ed. W. D. Allbeck (Burlington, Iowa, 1934); F. Bente, *American Lutheranism,* 2 vols. (St. Louis, 1919); A. B. Faust, *The German Element in the United States,* 2 vols. (New York, 1909); A. R. Wentz, *A Basic History of Lutheranism in America,* rev. ed. (Philadelphia, 1964); V. Ferm, *The Crisis in American Lutheran Theology* (New York, 1927); C. Mauelshagen, *American Lutheranism Surrenders to Forces of Conservatism* (Athens, Ga., 1936); R. C. Wiederaenders and W. G. Tillmanns, *The Synods of American Lutheranism* ([St. Louis], 1968); E. C. Nelson and K. S. Knutson, *Lutheranism in North America 1914–70* (Minneapolis, Minn., 1972).

United States, Religious History of the. 1. The purpose of this art. is to indicate in a gen. way the basic trends and movements in the hist. of Am. Christianity.

2. Fr. Huguenots* est. Ft. Caroline in what is now Fla., on the St. Johns R., near its mouth, 1564. Sp. RCs destroyed this colony (see also *Martyr*) and founded St. Augustine 1565. By 1609 RCs founded Santa Fe in what is now N. M. For early RC missions in what is now Calif. see *Serra, Junípero.* Fr. RCs est. missions in the Miss. Valley, e. g., in what is now Ill. at Cahokia 1699, Kaskaskia 1700; Detroit, in what is now Mich., 1701; Vincennes, in what is now Ind., 1702 (fortified 1732).

3. The 1st permanent Prot. settlement in what is now the US was at Jamestown, in what is now Va., 1607. See also *Hunt, Robert; Pocahontas.* Anglicanism was completely est. in Va. soon after the colony became a royal province 1624. Est. of the Angl. Ch. in Md. was approved in Eng. 1702 (see also 5).

4. Separatists founded Plymouth in what is now Mass. 1620 (see also *United Church of Christ,* I A 1). Puritans* est. Mass. Bay Colony when they settled at Salem 1628. T. Hooker* and S. Stone* helped est. a Puritan colony at Hartford, Conn., 1636. R. Williams* laid the foundations of the State of Rhode Is. and Providence Plantations 1636; here dissenters (e. g., Baps. and Quakers) enjoyed freedom of conscience.

5. Cecilius Calvert* (Lord Baltimore), a RC, received a charter 1632 to est. Md. colony; first settlers arrived 1634; est. of the Angl. Ch. in Md. was approved in Eng. 1702. On resurgence of RCm in Md. toward the end of the 18th c. see *Carroll, John; Roman Catholic Church,* E 3–4. Under royal charter received 1681 W. Penn,* a Quaker (see *Friends, Society of*), est. Pa.; its assurances of civil and religious freedom attracted many persecuted from the Brit. Isles and the Continent.

6. On the Dutch Ref. Ch. in New Amsterdam (later NYC) and New Neth. (renamed N. Y. by the Eng. after they conquered the colony 1664) see *Reformed Churches,* 4 b. Dutch Luths. were in New Neth. at least as early as 1643. By the end of the 17th c. the Angl. Ch. was practically, if not officially, est. in N. Y.

New Swed. (in present Del.), est. 1638, included many Luths. from the outset; see also *Torkillus, Reorus.* There were 3 Luth. ministers, including L. C. Lock, in the colony when it fell to the Dutch 1655.

Ger. sectarians (e. g., Quakers, Mennonites) and Luths. settled at Germantown, near Philadelphia, Pa., beginning 1683 (see also *Communistic Societies,* 4; *Falckner, Daniel, Jr.; Falckner, Justus; Köster, Heinrich Bernhard*). Moravians settled in Pa. and Ga. in the 1730s (see also *Schwenkfelders,* 2; *Spangenberg, Augustus Gottlieb*).

7. H. M. Mühlenberg* had to counteract the influence of N. L. v. Zinzendorf* before he could est. his own position as Luth. pastor in and around Philadelphia 1742. Ger. Ref. also settled in Pa. For a time friendly relations existed bet. Luths., Ref., and Moravians.

8. Presbs. of Scotch-Irish origin came to the US beginning in the late 17th c., settled in all colonies by mid-18th c. See also *Presbyterian Churches,* 4 a.

9. Revivals under J. Edwards* the Elder and others ran ca. 1725–ca. 1750. Methodism (see *Methodist Churches*) came to the US.

10. The spirit of Am. indep. accompanied a movement for religious freedom. A bill for establishing religious freedom was adopted by Va. 1785. Separation of ch. and state in Va. was complete 1840. Other states followed similar patterns, e. g., Congregationalism was disestablished in N. H. 1817, Conn. 1818, Mass. 1833.

11. Denominationalism in the US arose as chs. began to develop an emerging Am. character. In the 19th c. many older chs. split over doctrinal and soc. issues. The 20th c. has seen movements toward union and reunion on the one hand, appearance of new groups on the other. Ecumenism came into ascendancy (see also *Ecumenical Movement, The*).

12. The influence of rationalism* and deism* led to decline in religious fervor in the last part of the 18th c., but by the 1790s revivals heralded the beginning of another awakening, e. g., at North Yarmouth, Maine, Lee, Mass., and East Haddam and Lyme, Conn. Yale Coll., New Haven, Conn., experienced a notable revival 1802.

13. The Aug. 1801 Cane Ridge, Bourbon Co., Ky., camp meeting drew attendance est. at 20–25 thousand. It had been set up under Presb. auspices but came to include large participation by Meth. and Bap. preachers. Despite a Plan of Union as basis for cooperation bet. Presbs. and Congregationalists, religious life on the frontier was soon dominated by Meths. (esp. in the Midwest) and Baps. (esp. in the South).

14. Slavery and the Civil War split some chs. bet. North and South; some split along confessional lines.

15. Miss. work was carried on, usually by miss. socs., at home (see *Immigrant and Emigrant Missions; Indians, American; Indians, Lutheran Missions to North American*) and abroad. Many colleges and sems. were est.

16. After the Civil War immigration and soc. concern dominated religious life. Cath. immigrants gravitated toward large urban centers, Luths. toward the northern Midwest. Soc. concerns (e. g., temperance) were reflected in a revival movement (see *Revivals*). The Social* Gospel came into prominence.

17. Liberal theol., with its optimistic view of man, went hand in hand with the Social Gospel but was opposed by Protestant Fundamentalism (see also *Five Points of Fundamentalism*), which survived far into the 20th c. and produced *The Fundamentals* (12 vols.). See also *Evangelicals,* 6.

Discouraging prospects for man after WW I and the Great Depression weakened liberal theol., which came to be replaced by neoorthodoxy.*

These and other theol. movements gen. crossed denominational lines and tended to divide denominations internally.

18. The Civil War helped est. separate Negro denominations, which came to be found in both North and South and survived far into the 20th c.

19. In the 20th c. many chs. organized highly and took over work of pub. educ., and for. missions previously carried on by societies.

20. The Federal* Council of the Chs. of Christ in Am., the National* Council of the Chs. of Christ in the USA, and the World* Council of Chs. were est. to help coordinate ch. work.

21. Many chs. are concerned about soc. responsibility and about the relationship bet. ch. and state; integration of mutual interests has taken place in institutional and military chaplaincies. Ch.-state relations in educ. continue to present difficulties. Many chs. look to ecumenism for the solution to many problems. JW

See also *Religious Bodies (US), Bibliography of;* bibliography of *Statistics Ecclesiastical; Union Movements,* 5–7, 10–13.

C. E. Olmstead, *History of Religion in the United States* (Englewood Cliffs, N. J., 1960); H. S. Smith, R. T. Handy, and L. A. Loetscher, *American Christianity,* 2 vols. (New York, 1960–63); *Religion in American Life,* ed. J. W. Smith and A. L. Jamison, vols. 1, 2, and 4 (in 2) (Princeton, N. J., 1961).

United States, Roman Catholicism in the. See *Roman Catholic Church.*

United Stewardship Council. See *Union Movements,* 13.

United Student Christian Council. See *Young People's Organizations, Christian,* I 6.

United Student Fellowship. See *Students, Spiritual Care of,* A 3.

United Synod of New York and New England. See *United Lutheran Church, Synods of,* 15.

United Synod of the Evangelical Lutheran Church in the South, The. 1. During the Civil War the N. C., S. C., Va., and SW Va. syns. took umbrage at certain resolutions passed by The General* Syn. of the Ev. Luth. Ch. in the USA in regard to the war. In 1863 they withdrew and, at Concord, N. C., together with the Ga. Syn., organized The Gen. Syn. of the Ev. Luth. Ch. in the Confederate* States of Am. The name changed 1866 to The Ev. Luth. Gen. Syn. in N. Am., 1876 to The Ev. Luth. Gen. Syn. South. The Miss. Syn. (see *United Lutheran Church, Synods of,* 13) joined 1876. When the confessionalism of The Ev. Luth. Gen. Syn. South had reached a point satisfactory to the Holston Syn. and Tenn. Syn. (see *United Lutheran Church, Synods of,* 16, 29), the latter 2 and the 6 syns. of The Ev. Luth. Gen. Syn. South joined to form The United Syn. of the Ev. Luth. Ch. in the South 1886 Roanoke, Va. See also *United States, Lutheran Theology in the,* 10.

2. Official organ: *Lutheran Church Visitor.*

3. Helped form The United* Luth. Ch. in Am. 1918.

4. Leaders included Socrates Henkel (see *Henkels, The,* 3), E. T. Horn.* M. G. G. Scherer,* A. G. Voigt.*

The theol. sem. of The United Syn. of the Ev. Luth. Ch. in the South is now Lutheran* Theol. Southern Sem.

Colleges included Newberry* Coll., Roanoke* Coll., Lenoir* Rhyne Coll.

Its miss. in Jap., est. in the early 1890s, was later supported also by the General* Council of the Ev. Luth. Ch. in (N.) Am.

Consisted of 8 syns., 262 pastors, 494 congs., 55,473 confirmed mems. when it helped form the ULC (*The Lutheran Church Year Book for 1919* [Philadelphia, n. d.], p. 85).

C. W. Heathcote, *The Lutheran Church and the Civil War* (New York, 1919); F. Bente, *American Lutheranism,* 2 vols. (St. Louis, 1919); *The American Church History Series,* ed. P. Schaff et al., IV: H. E. Jacobs, *A History of the Evangelical Lutheran Church in the United States,* 5th ed. (New York, 1907); J. L. Neve, *History of the Lutheran Church in America,* 3d ed. W. D. Allbeck (Burlington, Iowa, 1934); A. R. Wentz, *A Basic History of Lutheranism in America,* rev. ed. (Philadelphia, 1964).

United Testimony on Faith and Life. Statement approved 1952 by the ALC, ELC, and UELC; helped provide basis for merger that formed The ALC 1960. Part I, *Concerning Faith,* contains arts. I. God; II. Atonement; III. The Means of Grace; IV. Justification; V. Sanctification; VI. The Church. Part II. *Concerning Life and Practice,* contains arts. I. Liturgical Trends; II. Lay Activities in the Church; III. Elements in the Eucharist; IV. Christian Liberty; V. Concerning Evangelism; VI. Spiritual Fellowship. See also *American Lutheran Church, The,* 1.

United Wesleyan Methodist Church of America, The. See *Methodist Churches,* 4 c.

United Zion's Children. See *Brethren, River.*

Unity of Brethren. See *Bohemian Brethren; Moravian Church,* 2.

Unity School of Christianity. Est. ca. 1889 Kansas City, Mo., by C. Fillmore* and his wife; inc. 1903 as Unity School of Practical Christianity; present name adopted 1914. Also known as Unity. Somewhat similar to Christian Science (see *Church of Christ, Scientist*), New* Thought, and Theosophy.* Emphasizes spiritual healing, prosperity, and practical Christianity. Has no definite creed. Present location: Unity Village, near Lee's Summit (near Kansas City), Mo. Publications include *Unity; Daily Word; Wee Wisdom.*

Universal Christian Conference on Life and Work (1925). See *Ecumenical Movement, The,* 9.

Universal Christian Council for Life and Work. See *Ecumenical Movement, The,* 9.

Universal Education. See *Christian Education,* D.

Universal Negro Improvement Association. Organized 1914 by M. M. Garvey* Jr., who planned to build a state in Afr. which all Negroes could make their home.

E. D. Cronon, *Black Moses: The Story of Marcus Garvey and the Universal Negro Improvement Association* (Madison, Wis., 1955).

Universal Salvation. See *Methodist Churches,* 2.

Universalism. Belief that God will destroy all sin and save all mankind. See also *Universalists.*

Universalists. 1. Adherents of universalism.* Universalists find the doctrine of endless punishment incompatible with belief in a just and loving God.

Universalism can be traced at least to Zoroaster.* Universalists became a distinct denomination under leadership of J. Murray* 1785 Oxford, Mass., as Indep. Christian Society commonly called Universalists.

2. H. Ballou* became the recognized theol. leader of Am. universalists at the beginning of the 19th c.; directed them into Unitarianism.*

Profession of belief adopted 1803 Winchester, N. H.:

"Article I. We believe that the Holy Scriptures of the Old and New Testaments contain a revelation of the character of God and of the duty, interest, and final destination of mankind.

"Article II. We believe that there is one God, whose nature is Love, revealed in one Lord Jesus Christ, by one Holy Spirit of Grace, who will finally restore the whole family of mankind to holiness and happiness.

"Article III. We believe that holiness and true happiness are inseparably connected, and that believers ought to be careful to maintain order and practice good works; for these things are good and profitable unto men."

Essential principles of Universalist Faith adopted 1899: "1. The universal fatherhood of God; 2. The spiritual authority and leadership of his son, Jesus Christ; 3. The trustworthiness of the Bible as containing a revelation from God; 4. The certainty of just retribution for sin; 5. The final harmony of all souls with God."

3. Universalists hold that punishment for sin is inevitable, that its purpose is beneficent (namely, to deter from further sin), and that probation does not end with this life, but everyone after death will be able forever to develop upward and Godward. With regard to Christ, universalists are practically Unitarians. Sins are pardoned when the sinner ceases from sin and becomes obedient. Doctrines gen. denied by universalists include vicarious atonement, justification by imputation of Christ's righteousness, original sin, existence of the devil, resurrection of the body, Christ's final coming, the final judgment, efficacy of sacraments, real presence of Christ in the Lord's Supper.

4. In May 1961 the Universalist Ch. of Am., which traced its beginnings to the 1770s and its formal organization to the 1790s, joined the Am. Unitarian Assoc. to form the Unitarian* Universalist Assoc.

See *Religious Bodies (US), Bibliography of.*

Universities, Non-Lutheran. See *Higher Education,* 10; *Protestant Education in the United States.*

Universities in the United States, Lutheran. 1. Dedication to Christian educ. is reflected in est. and development of Luth. univs. in the US.

2. *Capital U.,* Columbus, Ohio; The ALC; est. 1830 Canton, Ohio, by the Ohio Syn. (see *Ohio and Other States, The Evangelical Lutheran Joint Synod of,* 3); moved to Columbus, Ohio, 1831; est. as a university 1850; moved 1853 to a site adjoining Goodale Park in northern Columbus, 1876 to a site E of Alum creek, now in the suburb of Bexley. Coeduc. introd. 1918. A music dept. organized 1918 was est. as a conservatory 1928.

Capital U. and the sem. became separate institutions 1959 in preparation for the merger that formed The ALC.

Pres.: W. M. Reynolds* 1850–54, C. Spielmann 1854–57, W. F. Lehmann* 1857–80, M. Loy* 1881–90, C. H. L. Schuette* 1890–94, F. W. Stellhorn* 1894–1900, L. H. Schuh* 1900–12, Otto Mees 1913–46 [called 1912, installed 1913], Harold L. Yochum 1946–69, Thomas H. Langevin 1970–.

See also *Ministry, Education of,* VI C; VIII A 1; X E.

3. *Pacific Luth. U.,* Tacoma, Wash.; The ALC; supported by LCA's Pacific Northwest Syn. Opened 1894 as an academy; closed 1918; reopened 1920 in merger with Columbia Coll., Everett, Wash., to form a jr. coll.; became a 3-yr. normal school 1932, 4-yr. normal coll. 1940, coll. of liberal arts 1941, university 1960.

Pres.: S. C. Eastvold 1960–62, Robert A. L. Mortvedt 1962–69, Eugene W. Wiegman 1969–74, Richard Jungkuntz (acting pres.) 1974–.

See also *Ministry, Education of,* VIII A 2.

4. *Susquehanna* U.,* Selinsgrove, Pa.; LCA. Began 1858 as Missionary Institute; coeduc. 1873; present name adopted 1895.

Pres.: B. Kurtz* 1858–65, Henry Ziegler 1865–81, Peter Born 1881–93, F. P. Manhart* 1893–95, Jonathan R. Dimm 1895–99, C. W. Heisler 1899–1901, John L. Woodruff (acting pres.) 1901–02, G. W. Enders 1902–04, J. B. Focht 1904–05, C. T. Aikens 1905–27, Jacob Diehl (acting pres.) 1927–28, G. Morris Smith 1928–59, Gustave W. Weber 1959–.

5. *Valparaiso U.,* Valparaiso, Ind. Owned and operated by Luth. U. Assoc. Opened 1859 as the Valparaiso Male and Female Coll. under supervision of a conference of the Meth. Ch. Operated for a number of yrs. Suspended operation several yrs. Reopened 1873 by Henry Baker Brown as Northern Ind. Normal School and Bus. Institute. School of Law added 1879. Brown was joined 1881 by Oliver Perry Kinsey. The Institution was renamed Valparaiso Coll. 1900, Valparaiso U. 1907. Difficulties after WW I made new support necessary. The newly organized Luth. U. Assoc. bought the school 1925.

Pres.: John C. Baur (acting pres.) 1926, W. H. T. Dau* 1926–29, (Ex. Committee 1929–30), O. C. Kreinheder* 1930–39, Walter George Friedrich (acting pres.) 1939–40, Otto Paul Kretzmann 1940–68, Albert G. Huegli 1968–.

See also *Ministry, Education of,* VIII A 4.

6. *Wittenberg U.,* Springfield, Ohio; LCA; in 1842 the Eng. Dist. Syn. of Ohio (see *Ohio and Other States, Evangelical Lutheran Joint Synod of,* 4) resolved to est. a literary and theol. institution; Wooster, Ohio, chosen as the place 1843; classes, taught by E. Keller,* began there 1844; the school received a charter, moved to Springfield, Ohio, and was called Wittenberg* Coll. 1845; coeduc. 1874; graduate program introd. 1883; reorganized as a university 1957; name changed to Wittenberg U. 1959.

Pres.: E. Keller 1845–48, S. Sprecher* 1849–74, John B. Helwig 1874–82, S. A. Ort* 1882–1900, J. Mosheim Ruthrauff 1900–02, Charles G. Heckert 1903–20, R. E. Tulloss* 1920–49, Clarence C. Stoughton 1949–63, John N. Stauffer 1963–68, G. Kenneth Andeen 1969–. AS

See also *Ministry, Education of,* VIII A 6.

H. H. Lentz, *A History of Wittenberg College (1845–1945)* (Columbus, Ohio, 1946); P. H. Buehring, D. B. Owens, and H. L. Yochum, *These Hundred Years: The Centennial History of Capital University* (Columbus, Ohio, 1950); J. H. Strietelmeier, *Valparaiso's First Century: A Centennial History of Valparaiso University* (Valparaiso, Ind., 1959); W. S. Clark and A. H. Wilson, *The Story of Susquehanna University* (Selinsgrove, Pa., 1958).

Universities' Mission to Central Africa. A miss. of the Ch. of Eng., formed by Cambridge, Oxford, London, Durham, and Dublin (for a time) univs. in answer to D. Livingstone's* 1857 plea to univs. to bring Christianity, commerce, and civilization to E and cen. Afr. Merged 1965 with Society* for the Propagation of the Gospel in For. Parts to form United* Soc. for the Propagation of the Gospel. See also *Africa,* B 2.

Unorganized Italian Christian Churches of North America. See *Christian Church of North America, General Council.*

Unpardonable Sin. See *Sin, The Unpardonable.*

Upanishads. Sanskrit treatises or dialogs containing

expression of philos. speculation of sages and teachers of India,* esp. 8th–6th c. BC. See also *Brahmanism,* 3, 4; *Hinduism,* 6.

Upper Volta, Republic of. See *Africa,* C 8.

Uppsala, Council of. See *Sweden, Lutheranism in,* 1.

Upsala College. See *Lutheran Church in America,* V; *Ministry, Education of,* VIII B 26.

Ur-Engur (Ur-Nammu). See *Law Codes,* 1.

Urban II (Odo [or Udo] of Châtillon-sur-Marne; ca. 1042–99). B. probably Châtillon-sur-Marne, N Fr.; archdeacon Reims 1064; monk, later prior, Cluny*; cardinal bp. Ostia ca. 1080; legate to Ger. in the 1080s; pope 1088–99. See also *Crusades,* 1; *Clermont, Council of.*

Urban V. See *Babylonian Captivity,* 2.

Urban VI. See *Jubilees.*

Urbanus Rhegius. See *Rhegius Urbanus.*

Urfa. See *Edessa.*

Urlsperger, Johann August (1728–1806). Son of S. Urlsperger*; b. Augsburg, Ger.; educ. Tübingen and Halle; pastor Augsburg; resigned 1776 because of ill health; founded Deutsche Christentumsgesellschaft* 1780. Engaged in intensive study of the doctrine of the Trinity. Controversialist.

Urlsperger, Samuel (1685–1772). Father of J. A. Urlsperger*; b. Kirchheim unter Teck; educ. Tübingen; influenced by A. H. Francke*; pastor Augsburg; friend of P. J. Spener*; helped introd. Pietism in Augsburg; agent for Salzburger colony in Ga. (see *Salzburgers, Banishment of*).

Ursinus, Zacharias (Beer; Bär; 1534–83). Ref. theol.; b. Breslau, Ger.: educ. Wittenberg and Paris; influenced by P. Melanchthon*; prof. Heidelberg. See also *Neostadiensium admonitio; Reformed Confessions,* D 2.

Ursula. Legendary RC saint; allegedly a Brit. princess martyred with maidens (numbered variously from 11 to 11,000) by Huns at Cologne sometime in the beginning of the 4th c.

Ursulines. RC order founded ca. 1535 by Angela Merici (ca. 1474–1540) to educ. girls. See also *Counter Reformation,* 6.

Uruguay. See *South America,* 10.

Ussher, James (Usher; 1581–1656). B. Dublin, Ireland; educ. Dublin; ordained Angl. 1601; prof. Dublin 1607–21; bp. Meath 1621; abp. Armagh 1625–40; to Eng. 1640; bp. Carlisle 1642; to Wales 1645; returned to Eng. 1646; preacher Lincoln's Inn, a London law academy, 1647–54; chronologist. See also *Time.*

Usteri, Leonhard (1799–1833). B. Zurich, Switz.; educ. Zurich and Berlin; influenced by F. D. E. Schleiermacher*; prof. Bern, Switz. Works include *Entwickelung des Paulinischen Lehrbegriffs.*

Usury. 1. More interest than legally allowed; or indiscriminate interest; or any interest.

The OT distinguishes bet. taking interest from a fellow believer and taking it from others. (Ex 22:25-27; Lv 25:35-37; Dt 23:20)

2. Gratuitous lending is commended Lk 6:34-35. Taking interest is allowed Mt 25:14-30; Lk 19:12-27.

3. In the ch., taking interest was condemned at least as early as the syn. of Elvira* 306. SC, Preface, 12: "Usury and avarice have burst in like a deluge and have taken on the color of legality."

4. Among Luths. in Am., C. F. W. Walther* especially opposed taking interest.

Utenhove, Jan (ca. 1520–65). B. Gent, Belg.; studied at Louvain; fled 1544 because of his Ref. faith; to Aachen, Cologne, Strasbourg; driven by Interim* to Eng.; with J. Laski* organized Neth. refugee chs.; went with cong. expelled from London by Mary* I through Den. to Emden, Wesel, and Frankfurt; promoted Ref. in Poland with Laski 1556–59. Works include *Rationes quaedam* (against Luth. doctrine of Lord's Supper); tr. of Laski's *Compendium doctrinae.*

Utilitarianism. Theory elaborated by J. Bentham,* J. S. Mill,* and others acc. to which the morality of conduct is determined by its ability to promote the greatest happiness of the greatest number of people. The term has come to be used in various meanings. See also *Ethics,* 4; *Gay, John; Paley, William; Sidgwick, Henry; Tucker, Abraham.*

Utopia. See *More, Thomas.*

Utraquists. See *Bohemia, Lutheran Theology in,* 4; *Bohemian Brethren; Hussites.*

Utrecht, Declaration of. Formalized declaration of doctrinal basis of Old* Caths. Reaffirmed the proposition of Vincent* of Lérins; subscribed to the ecumenical* creeds and the universally accepted dogmatic decisions of ecumenical councils of the first 1,000 yrs. Rejected the doctrine of papal infallibility and supremacy and of the immaculate* conception. Rejected Unigenitus,* the Syllabus* of Errors, and similar RC pronouncements. Rejected the Council of Trent* decisions regarding discipline and those of its doctrinal definitions that disagree with the early ch. Affirmed true reception of the body and blood of Christ in the Eucharist; rejected RC doctrine of the unbloody sacrifice of the mass.

Utrecht, Treaty of (Peace of Utrecht). Series of treaties signed at Utrecht, Neth., 1713–14, ending the War of the Sp. Succession; included recognition by Louis* XIV of Fr. of the Prot. succession in Eng.

Utrecht Missionary Society (Utrechtsche Zendings-Vereneging). Founded 1859 in the interest of miss. work in the Dutch (or Neth.) E. Indies; first missionaries sent 1863; combined 1951 with other agencies to form Netherlands* Ref. Ch., Bd. of For. Miss.

Utschimura, Kanso. See *Uchimura, Kanzo.*

Uytenbogaert, Johannes (Wtenbogaert; Jan Utenbogaert; 1557–1644). B. Utrecht, Neth.; educ. Utrecht and Geneva; pastor Utrecht 1584–90, The Hague 1591–1618; organized Remonstrants* in Antwerp; banished 1619; lived at Rouen, Fr., 1621–26; returned to Neth. Works include *Kerckelicke Historie;* helped write *Remonstrantie* (1610).

V

Vacation Bible School. See *Christian Education,* E 9, F 2; *Parish Education,* F 3.

Vacherot, Étienne (1809–97). Philos.; b. Torcenay, near Langres, Fr.; prof. Paris 1839–52. Held that the concept of God arises in human consciousness out of ideas of perfection that are incompatible with reality.

Vagabonds. See *Camisards.*

Vaihinger, Hans (1852–1933). Philos.; b. Nehren, near Tübingen, Württemberg, Ger.; educ. Tübingen; prof. Halle 1884–1906. Held that though religion is fictitious, Christianity has ethical value.

Vaisheshika. See *Brahmanism,* 4.

Vaisya. See *Brahmanism,* 3.

Valdés, Alfonso de (ca. 1500–32). Twin brother of J. de Valdés*; RC reformer; b. Cuenca, Castile, Sp.; met with P. Melanchthon* at Augsburg 1530. Works include *Lactantius.*

Valdés, Juan de (ca. 1500–41). Twin brother of A. de Valdés*; RC reformer; b. Cuenca, Castile, Sp.; to It. ca. 1530/31; adopted in part the ideas of the Luth. Reformation. Works include *Alfabeto cristiano; Diálogo de la lengua.* See also *Mantova, Benedetto da.*

Valdo, Peter. See *Waldenses.*

Valen, Olav Fartein (1887–1952). Luth. composer; b. Stavanger, Norw.; son of a miss.; lived in Madagascar in early childhood. Works include *Hvad est du dog Skiön; Vaagn op, min sjael; O store konge, David's sön; Kom regn fra det höie.*

Valentine, Milton (Jan. 1, 1825–Feb. 7, 1906). B. near Uniontown, Carroll Co., Md.; educ. Gettysburg, Pa.; licensed by W. Pa. Syn. 1852; ordained by Md. Syn. 1853; miss. and pastor Pa. 1853–55; principal Emmaus Institute, Middletown, Pa., 1855–59; pastor Reading, Pa., 1859–66; prof. Gettysburg 1866; pres. Pa. Coll., Gettysburg, 1868–84; pres. Luth. Theol. Sem., Gettysburg, 1884–1903. Coed. with J. A. Brown* *The Quarterly Review of the Evangelical Lutheran Church* and (with P. M. Biklé and E. J. Wolf*) *The Lutheran Quarterly;* other works include *Christian Theology.*

Valentinus. See *Gnosticism,* 7 g.

Valerian (Publius Licinius Valerianus; d. perhaps ca. 260/269 AD). Roman emp. 253–259 [260?]. See also *Persecutions of Christians,* 3, 4.

Valla, Lorenzo (Laurentius Vallensis; Lorenzo della Valle; ca. 1406/07–57). Humanist; b. Rome, It.; taught rhetoric at Pavia; secy. and hist. to king of Naples 1435–48; papal secy. 1448. Showed the Donation* of Constantine to be a forgery; ridiculed the Lat. of the Vulgate; denied apostolic origin of Apostles' Creed and genuineness of correspondence bet. Jesus and Abgar.*

Vallerius, Harald (1646–1716). Luth. composer; b. Vallerstad, Swed.; educ. Uppsala; dir. music 1676, prof. math 1690 Uppsala. Works include *Den svenska psalmboken.*

Vallombrosans (Congregatio Vallisumbrosae Ordinis S. Benedicti). Strict RC community founded by John* Gualbert at Vallombrosa forest near Florence, It. Tried to revive the Benedictine Rule in its integrity.

Valparaiso University. See *Universities in the United States, Lutheran,* 5.

Value Judgments. See *Ritschl, Albrecht Benjamin.*

Van Alstyne, Frances Jane (nee Crosby; also known as Fanny Crosby; 1820 [1823?]–1915). Hymnist; b. Southeast (or South East), Putnam Co., N. Y.; lost her sight when ca. 6 weeks old; educ. N. Y. (City) Institution for the Blind; taught there 1847–58; said to have written thousands of songs and hymns. Hymns include "Pass Me Not, O Gentle Savior"; "Sweet Hour of Prayer."

Van Woerden, Jan. See *De Bakker, Jan.*

Vanderkemp, Johannes Theodorus (1747–Dec. 15, 1811). B. Rotterdam, Holland; educ. Leiden; army officer; doctor; became interested in ch. work upon losing his first wife and only child in a drowning tragedy; ordained miss. to S. Afr. by LMS 1797; left for Afr. on a convict ship 1798; arrived Cape Town in Mar. 1799; labored among Hottentots, Kaffir, and others; removed his followers to a grant of land near Algoa Bay 1802; said to have redeemed many slaves with his own funds from cruel Boer masters; broke down much opposition of Europeans in Afr. to miss. work among natives. See also *Africa,* A 6; *Netherlands Missionary Society.*

Vane, Henry (Harry; 1613–62). B. Debden, Essex, Eng.; educ. Oxford and on Continent; opposed state ch.; to Puritans in Mass. 1635; gov. of colony 1636–37; returned to Eng.; sided with parliament and O. Cromwell* but did not support execution of Charles I (see also *England,* B 7; *Presbyterian Confessions,* 1); later championed rights of parliament against Cromwell; imprisoned 1656; executed for treason after Restoration (see *England,* C). Works include *The Retired Man's Meditations; An Epistle General to the Mystical Body of Christ on Earth; A Pilgrimage into the Land of Promise.*

Vardhamana Jnatiputra Mahavira. See *Jainism.*

Variata. See *Lutheran Confessions,* B 3; *Union Movements,* 3.

Varuna. See *Brahmanism,* 2.

Vasa. See *Gustavus I.*

Vassy, Massacre at. See *France,* 9.

Vatican City (State of Vatican City; Stato della Citta del Vaticano). Territorial seat of the papacy in Rome, It. Includes Vatican Palace, art galleries, astronomical observatory, bank, libraries, post office, gardens, museums, radio station, St. Peter's Basilica, and other bldgs.; extraterritorial rights include more than 10 other bldgs. in Rome. *Area:* 108.7 acres (.15 sq. mi.; .4 sq. km.). *Normal pop.:* ca. 1,000.

Basilica hist. is traced to the early 4th c., Vatican palace hist. to the 6th c. (palace now covers more than 13 acres); the palace became the chief papal residence after 1378 (see also *Babylonian Captivity,* 2; the older Lateran palace had been burned).

Various bldgs. (e. g., Sistine Chapel [see *Popes,* 16]) were designed and decorated by Michelangelo,* Raphael,* and other masters. The crypt of St. Peter's Basilica includes tombs of popes and other rulers (e. g., Christina*).

See also *Concordat,* 7; *Curia.*

Vatican Councils. 1. Vatican Council I (Dec. 8, 1869–Oct. 20, 1870). Regarded by RCs as the 20th ecumenical council (see Councils and Synods, 4). Convened by Pius IX (see *Popes,* 28). Prots. and Eastern Orthodox also invited.

a. The constitution on the catholic faith (*de fide catholica;* also known as *Dei filius*), adopted and promulgated Apr. 24, 1870, condemned pantheism, rationalism, materialism and contained 4 chaps. on

God the Creator, Revelation, Faith, and Faith and Reason.

b. The First Dogmatic Constitution of the Church of Christ (*Constitutio dogmatica prima de ecclesia Christi;* also known as *Pastor aeternus*), adopted July 18, 1870, treats in 4 chaps. the institution of the apostolic primacy in Peter, the perpetuity of Peter's primacy in Roman bps., the power and reason of the primacy of Roman bps., and the infallibility of Roman bps. See also *Infallibility, Papal; Old Catholics.*

2. Vatican Council II. Regarded by RCs as the 21st ecumenical council (see *Councils and Synods,* 4). Convened by John XXIII (see *Popes,* 34). Non-RCs invited as observers. Purpose: spiritual renewal of the ch. Discussions highlighted by insistence on return to liturgical, Biblical, and patristic sources of faith.

1st sess., Oct. 11–Dec. 8, 1962, got the council under way.

2d ses., Sept. 29–Dec. 4, 1963; Const. on the Sacred Liturgy *(Sacrosanctum concilium)* and Decree on the Instruments of Social Communication *(Inter mirifica)* promulgated Dec. 4.

3d sess., Sept. 14–Nov. 21, 1964; Dogmatic Const. on the Ch. *(Lumen gentium),* Decree on Ecumenism *(Unitatis redintegratio),* and Decree on Eastern Cath. Chs. *(Orientalium ecclesiarum)* promulgated Nov. 21.

4th sess., Sept. 14–Dec. 8, 1965; Decree on the Bishops' Pastoral Office in the Ch. *(Christus dominus),* Decree on Priestly Formation *(Optatam totius),* Decree on the Appropriate Renewal of the Religious Life *(Perfectae caritatis),* Declaration on the Relationship of the Ch. to Non-Christian Religions *(Nostra aetate),* and Declaration on Christian Educ. *(Gravissimum educationis)* promulgated Oct. 28; Dogmatic Const. on Divine Revelation *(Dei verbum)* and Decree on the Apostolate of the Laity *(Apostolicam actuositatem)* promulgated Nov. 18; Pastoral Const. on the Ch. in the Modern World *(Gaudium et spes),* Decree on the Ministry and Life of Priests *(Presbyterorum ordinis),* Decree on the Church's Missionary Activity *(Ad gentes),* and Declaration on Religious Freedom *(Dignitatis humanae)* promulgated Dec. 7. EL

H. Daniel-Rops, *The Second Vatican Council: The Story Behind the Ecumenical Council of Pope John XXIII,* tr. A. Guinan (New York, 1962); L. Jaeger, *The Ecumenical Council, the Church and Christendom,* tr. A. V. Littledale (New York, 1961); K. E. Skydsgaard, *The Papal Council and the Gospel: Protestant Theologians Evaluate the Coming Vatican Council* (Minneapolis, Minn., 1961); R. M. Brown, *Observer in Rome: A Protestant Report on the Vatican Council* (New York, 1964); X. Rynne (pseudonym), *Letters from Vatican City: Vatican Council II (First Session): Background and Debates* (New York, 1963), *The Second Session: The Debates and Decrees of Vatican Council II, September 29 to December 4, 1963* (New York, 1963/64), *The Third Session: The Debates and Decrees of Vatican Council II, September 14 to November 21, 1964* (New York, 1964/65), and *The Fourth Session: The Debates and Decrees of Vatican Council II, September 14 to Dec. 8, 1965* (New York, 1965/66); H. Küng, *The Council in Action: Theological Reflections on the Second Vatican Council,* tr. C. Hastings (New York, 1963); M. Novak, *The Open Church, Vatican II, Act II* (New York, 1964); G. C. Berkouwer, *The Second Vatican Council and the New Catholicism,* tr. L. B. Smedes (Grand Rapids, Mich., 1965); *Dialog on the Way: Protestants Report from Rome on the Vatican Council,* ed. G. A. Lindbeck (Minneapolis, 1965); *The Documents of Vatican II in a New and Definitive Translation with Commentaries and Notes by Catholic, Protestant and Orthodox Authorities,* ed. W. M. Abbott (New York, 1966).

Vaticanus, Codex. See *Manuscripts of the Bible,* 3 a.

Vatke, Johann Karl Wilhelm (1806–82). B. Behndorf, near Magdeburg, Ger.; prof. Berlin; friend of D. F. Strauss*; applied hist. criticism to OT; opposed by E. W. Hengstenberg.* Works include *Die Biblische Theologie, wissenschaftlich dargestellt, I: Die Religion des Alten Testamentes.*

Vautroullier, Thomas (Vautrollier; fl. 16th c.). Printer; Huguenot; to London ca. 1558; est. a press 1570; printed Eng. tr. of some of M. Luther's works; to Edinburgh, Scot., where he est. a press 1584.

Vázquez, Gabriel (1549–1604). RC theol.; b. Belmonte, Cuenca prov., E cen. Sp.; prof. Ocaña, Madrid, Alcalá (twice), Rome; follower of Thomas* Aquinas; exponent of Molinism (see *Molina, Luis [de]*).

Vedanta. See *Brahmanism* 4.

Vedanta Society. Extension in the US of the Ramakrishna Mission (see *Hinduism,* 7). Resulted from lectures on Vedanta philos. (see *Brahmanism,* 4) delivered 1894 in NYC by Vivekananda.* Organized and inc. 1898. Grew to 13 centers in the US 1973. Claims no attempt to form a new sect or creed; tries to set forth the end of wisdom and how it is attained and to give religion a philos. and scientific basis.

Vedas (from Skt. *veda,* "knowledge"). Sacred Hindu writings of ancient India. Rig-Veda ("praise of knowledge") is oldest of the 4 Vedas in the narrower sense; said to date from perhaps ca. 1000 BC. See also *Brahmanas; Brahmanism; Sacred Literature; Shastras.*

Vedic Religion. Early form of Hinduism* based on the Vedas.*

Vega, Andreas de (1498–1549). B. Segovia, Sp.; prof. Salamanca 1532–38; took part in Council of Trent,* esp. in formulating decrees on Biblical canon and justification.

Vega, Lope de (Lope Félix de Vega Carpio; pseudonyms El Licenciado Tome de Burguillos and Gabriel Padecopeo; 1562–1635). "El Fénix de España"; dramatic poet; b. Madrid, Sp.; educ. Alcalá de Henares; in military service; priest 1614; confidential officer of the Inquisition.* Works include *Los Pastores de Belén; Romances a la Pasión.*

Vegetius, Bartoldt (1654–1742). Luth. pastor in Russ.; educ. Bergedorf (part of Hamburg since 1938), Ger.; teacher Bergedorf; pastor for Luth. workers in foundry near Moscow, Russ., 1684; pastor Moscow 1689; supt. Luth. ch. in Russ. 1711.

Veghe, Johannes (ca. 1430–1504). B. Münster, Westphalia; exponent of *Devotio* moderna;* active in Münster and Rostock. Works include *Gheystlike jagd;* sermons.

Vehse, Carl Eduard (1802–June 18, 1870). Scholar, hist.; b. near Dresden, Ger.; studied law; curator Saxon state archives 1833; became adherent of M. Stephan* Sr.; to US 1839 with Saxon immigrants (see *Lutheran Church–Missouri Synod, The,* II); returned to Ger. disillusioned Dec. 1839. Works include *Die Stephan'sche Auswanderung nach Amerika.* See also *Altenburg Debate.*

Veil. See *Corporal.*

Veit, Friedrich (1861–1948). B. Augsburg, Ger.; educ. Erlangen and Leipzig; itinerant preacher in W Upper Bav. 1884. Pastor Schwarzenbach, Upper Franconia, NE Bav., 1887; Munich 1892, dean 1905, mem. high consistory 1915 and its pres. 1917. Worked for unification of Ger. chs. in gen. and Luth. union in particular.

Velázquez, Diego Rodríguez de Silva y (Velásquez; 1599–1660). Painter; b. Seville, Sp.; to Madrid 1622; court painter 1623. Works include *Adoration of the Magi; Christ in the House of Martha; Crucifixion; Christ and the Pilgrims of Emmaus.*

Veles. See *Slavs, Primitive Religion of.*
Velthusen, Johann Kaspar (Caspar; 1740–1814). B. Weimar, Ger.; educ. Göttingen; private tutor Bremervorde; deacon Hameln 1767; chaplain London 1770; prof. Kiel 1775, Helmstädt (Helmstedt) 1778, Rostock 1789; gen. supt. of the duchies of Bremen and Verden 1791; influenced by Enlightenment*; sent C. A. G. Stork* to N. C., with passage paid by pub. of religious and school books.
Veltwick, Gerhard (Gerard Veltwyckius; Veltwyk; Gerhard Veltwick v. Rabenstein; Dinius Gerard Volckruck; 16th c.). Orientalist, theol., statesman; counselor of Charles* V. Works include *Shevilé Thohu.* See also *Regensburg Book.*
Venantius Honorius Clementianus Fortunatus. See *Fortunatus, Venantius Honorius Clementianus.*
Venatorius, Thomas (Gechauf; Jähauf; ca. 1488–1551). Humanist; b. Nürnberg, Ger.; friend of W. Pir(c)kheimer*; helped reform Rothenburg. Works include *De virtute christiana.*
Venerabilis inceptor. See *Ockham, William of.*
Veneration of Relics. See *Relics.*
Veneration of Saints. See *Saints, Veneration of.*
Venetian School of Church Music. 16th-c. school of composers centered in Venice, It.; in some ways freer than the traditional. See also *Gabrieli, Andrea; Praetorius, Hieronymus; Willaert, Adrian.*
Venezuela. See *South America,* 11.
Veni, Creator Spiritus. Lat. hymn variously assigned (e. g., to Ambrose,* Charlemagne,* Charles* II, Gregory I [see *Popes,* 4], Rabanus* Maurus); tr. into Ger. by M. Luther* ("Komm, Gott Schöpfer, Heiliger Geist"); various Eng. translations.
Veni, Sancte Spiritus. See *Golden Sequence.*
Venial Sins. See *Sins, Venial and Mortal.*
Venite. Verses of Ps 95 (Vulgate 94) commonly assoc. with matins*; named after first word in Lat.
Venturini, Karl Heinrich Georg (1768–1849). Ev. theol.; b. Brunswick, Ger.; taught Helmstedt and Copenhagen; pastor Hordorf 1807. Makes Jesus instrument of Essenes. Works include *Natürliche Geschichte des grossen Propheten von Nazareth.*
Verbal Inspiration. See *Inspiration, Doctrine of,* A 3, B 7 c.
Verbeck, Guido Herman Fridolin (Verbeek; 1830–98). B. Zeist, Holland; brought up under Moravian influence; studied engineering at Utrecht; to US 1852; educ. Auburn* Theol. Sem.; (Dutch) Ref. Ch. miss. to Jap. 1859–98; instructor Nagasaki; head Imperial U., Tokyo; attached to Jap. senate 1863–78; taught in union theol. sem., Tokyo. Linguist, poet, musician.
Verbum audibile. See *Grace, Means of,* I 1.
Verbum visibile. See *Grace, Means of,* I 1.
Verdi, Guiseppe (1813–1901). Composer; b. (Le) Roncole, Parma province, It. Works include operas; *Messa da Requiem;* ch. music (e. g., *Stabat mater; Te Deum; Laudi alla virgine Maria*).
Vereinigte Evangelisch-Lutherische Kirche Deutschlands. See *Germany,* C 5; *Union Movements,* 8–9.
Verger (from Lat. *virga,* "twig, rod"). Official who carries a mace or verge before a dignitary. Also one who takes care of the interior of a ch. or an official who serves as sacristan* or usher or one who keeps order during services.
Vergerio Pietro Paolo (1370–ca. 1444/45). Called "the Elder" because a later mem. of the family had the same name (see next entry); humanist, educ., canonist, statesman; b. Capodistria, It.: educ. Padua, Florence, and Bologna; taught rhetoric and logic at Padua and Florence; tutor for princes of Carrara at Padua; papal secy. 1406–17; secy. to emp. Sigismund.* Works include *Pro redintegranda et unienda ecclesia.*
Vergerio, Pietro Paolo (Pier; Pierpaolo; Vergerius; Petrus Paulua; Peter Paul; ca. 1497/98–ca. 1564/65). Called "the Younger" because an earlier mem. of the family had the same name (see preceding entry); lawyer, poet, reformer; b. Capodistria, It.; educ. Padua; lawyer in Verona, Padua, Venice; sent with others to 1530 Augsburg Diet (see *Lutheran Confessions,* A 2) by Clement VII (see *Clement VII,* 2) to oppose Prots.; papal secy. and domestic chaplain 1532; sent to Ger. 1535 by Paul* III to negotiate with Ger. princes about a proposed council at Mantua, It. (the council, for which M. Luther* wrote the Schmalkaldic Arts. [see *Lutheran Confessions,* B 2], did not materialize); conferred with Luther (whom he, in a report to the papal secy., called a "beast" who was possibly possessed by a demon); bp. Modrus(z) May 1536, Capodistria Sept. 1536; attended the 1540 colloquy of Worms* (as commissioner for Francis* I) and 1541 Regensburg* Conference; studied writings of Luther; aroused RC suspicion for perhaps conceding too much to Prots.; broke with RCm 1545; applied unsuccessfully for admittance to the Council of Trent* to justify himself; excommunicated 1549; active in Switz. till 1553; spent rest of his life in service of Christoph,* duke of Württemberg. Works include many anti-RC polemical writings.
Verígin, Peter Vasilich (d. 1924). Russ. Doukhobor (from Russ. for "spirit wrestler") leader (see *Russian Sects*); banished 1887 by Russ. authorities from the Caucasus to Archangel; exiled to Siberia 1892; followers migrated to W Can. 1898/99; Verígin, released from exile 1911, became leader of Doukhobors in Can.
Veritas. See *Dogmatics,* B 3.
Veritates revelatae. See *Dogmatics,* B 3.
Vermigli, Pietro Martire. See *Peter Martyr.*
Veronica (variants include Berenice, Bernice, Venice, Venisse, Vernice, Veronce, Verone; Beronica, from Gk. *Bernike, Beronike*). Legendary woman of Jerusalem; said to have received an imprint of the face of Christ on a cloth, legends varying as to when, where, and how; possession of the cloth has been claimed by chs. in Rome, Milan, and Jaen (Sp.).
Verschoor, Jakob (1646–1700). Ref. separatist; educ. Leiden, Neth.; rejected by followers of G. Voetius*; active in conventicles around Middelburg; held that the redeemed had been made guiltless by Christ, with resultant possible innate righteousness; banished from Middelburg and Leiden; gained many followers. See also *Hebraeans.*
Verse. 1. In the Bible, the smallest division of a chapter. 2. In poetry one metrical line, or group of lines comprising a stanza.* See also *Chapters and Verses of the Bible.*
Versicle. Verse or sentence chanted or spoken in a service by a pastor to which the choir or cong. responds. See also *Response.*
Versions, Bible. See *Bible Versions.*
Verus, Lucius Aurelius. See *Marcus Aurelius.*
Verus, Marcus Annius. See *Marcus Aurelius.*
Vespasian (Titus Flavius Sabinus Vespasianus; 9–79). Father of Titus* Flavius Sabinus Vespasianus; b. Reate, Latium, It.; sent by Claudius* I to command legions in Ger. and Brit.; conquered Isle of Wight; consul 51; proconsul of Afr. 63 under Nero*; sent to Palestine to conduct war against Jews 66; joined 67 by son Titus, whom he left in charge of Roman forces 68; emperor 69–79; began bldg. Coliseum (or Colosseum) at Rome. See also *Josephus, Flavius; Persecution of Christians,* 2.
Vespers (from Gk. *hespera* and Lat. *vesper* and *vespera,* "evening"). Evening service of the Western Ch.; one of the canonical hours.* Its order has been used at various times during the day. See also *Canticles.*
Vespers of the Dead. See *Burial* 4; *Placebo.*
Vestiarian Controversy. Dispute about clerical dress begun under Edward VI (see *England,* B 4), became acute when J. Hooper* refused to wear pre-

scribed vestments at his consecration as bp. Gloucester 1550; burst forth again 1554, when an attempt was made to secure uniformity of vestments in Eng. See also *Puritans.*

Vestments Clerical. 1. Chief traditional vestments: The *tunica talaris* (from Lat. *talus,* "ankle, heel"), an ankle-length tunic, was fashioned after the common tunic. The *dalmatic** was practically an ungirdled over-tunic; worn at high mass (see *Missa solemnis*) by deacons, now also by some prelates (e. g., bps.); white linen. The *paenula* or *casula* (chasuble*) is the outermost vestment worn by the celebrant at mass. The *pallium* is a circular band of white wool, worn on the shoulders, with white wool pendant strips front and rear; marked with 6 dark purple crosses; originally apparently worn by abps. but without connection with Rome; now conferred by the pope as a symbol of office; its equivalent in the E Ch. is called *omophorion* (from Gk. for "bearing on the shoulders"). The *stole* is a white or colored neckcloth (see also 2; *Epitrachelion; Orarion*). The *maniple* was originally a napkin or handkerchief used by deacons in table ministration; now an ornamental band over the left forearm. The *amice* was probably originally a head covering; now an oblong cloth worn about the neck and shoulders. The *alb* is a white linen ankle-length garment with girdle and tight sleeves. The *cope,* or *pluvial* (from Lat. for "rain"), a long cloak, open in front except for closure at top, originally used for protection against inclement weather, is worn in nearly all functions in which the chasuble is not used. The girdle,* or cincture, serves as a belt.

2. Following are worn by a priest at mass: (1) amice; (2) alb; (3) girdle; (4) maniple; (5) stole (see also 1), a narrow strip of fabric worn about the neck and with the ends loose or crossed over the breast; (6) chasuble; (7) *surplice* (from Lat. for "over fur"), or *cotta,* a kind of alb but shorter, with loose sleeves and worn loose at the waist; designed for use over fur or fur-lined garments in unheated chs. in cold weather; used by clerics, acolytes, lay readers, choristers.

3. The hist. position of M. Luther* and the Luth. Ch. regarding use of vestments is conservative; vestments are to serve worship, not distract the eye or mind. Use of vestments in the Luth. Ch. has varied from time to time and place to place.

Biretta,* cassock (long close-fitting garment, now usually black and worn with clerical collar), Geneva bands (Ger. *Beffchen;* 2 narrow strips of white cloth pendant from front of collar of clerical dress of some Prots.; based on Ref. practice in Geneva, Switz.). Geneva gown (loose, large-sleeved, black academic gown; adopted by Ref. clergy at Geneva; also used by some other Prots.), and ruff (round, multilayered, lace or lace-edged collar) are not hist. service-oriented.

See also *Cuffs; Humeral Veil; Miter; Rochet; Sticharion; Tunicle.*

Vestry. 1. Room in, or attached to, a ch. (and usually near the altar) and used for some or all purposes of a sacristy.* 2. Esp. in the Angl. Ch. and Prot. Episc. Ch., a body of parish ch. officers or a parish or vestry meeting.

Veterans Administration Hospitals. See *Armed Services Commission.*

Veto Law (1834). See *Free Church of Scotland.*

Vetter, Daniel (ca. 1650–1721). Luth. musician; b. Breslau, Ger.; contemporary of J. Kuhnau* and G. Vopelius*; organist Nicolaikirche, Leipzig 1679–1721; composer. Works include *Musicalische Kirch- und Haus-Ergötzlichkeit,* which includes the hymn tune *Das walt' Gott Vater.*

Vetter Jakob (1872–1918). B. Worms, Ger.; worked with Pilgermission St. Chrischona*; est. Zeltmission ("tent mission") 1902 and served it till 1918.

Vetus Itala. See *Bible Versions,* J 1.

Via antiqua. Term for schools of Scotists (see *Duns Scotus, John*) and Thomists (see *Thomas Aquinas*). See also *Via moderna.*

Via moderna. Term for school formed by followers of W. of Ockham* in opposition to *via* antiqua.*

Viaticum. Originally a broad term for various ministrations of the ch. for a Christian at the time of his death. Now, in RCm, the Lord's Supper given to one in danger of death as food for his journey to the world beyond death. Not to be confused with unction.*

Vicar. One who substitutes for or represents another. Anciently, a secular cleric who officiated in a ch. owned by a religious order. In the Angl. Ch., the priest of a parish of which the tithes are owned by another. In the Prot. Episc. Ch., a deputy cleric in charge of a dependent chapel. In the Luth. Ch., an unordained student of theol. who serves as asst. in ch. or school.

Vicar Apostolic. Titular* bp. with ordinary jurisdiction over a miss. area; may also administer a vacant diocese or one whose bp. cannot function.

Vicar-General. Prelate appointed by a bp. to assist him in administration of the diocese by exercising ordinary jurisdiction in his name.

Vicar of Christ. Term current as exclusive title of pope since Innocent III (see *Popes,* 10); its claim that the pope is the vicar,* or representative, of Christ, is based on Jn 21:16-17. See also *Pope,* 2.

Vicarii in pontificalibus. See *Titular Bishop.*

Vicarious Satisfaction. See *Atonement; Atonement, Theories of.*

Vico, Giovanni Battista (Giambattista; 1668–1744). Philos., hist., jurisprudent; b. Naples, It.; prof. Naples 1699. Tried to put rationalism into its proper place and perspective; prepared the way for historicism*; held that the God-concept is the speculative means for regarding things not only acc. to their facticity and appearance but also acc. to their ground and meaning. Works include *Principi di una Scienza nouva d'intorno alla commune natura delle nazione.* See also *Philosophy.*

Victimae paschali laudes. See *Sequence.*

Victor, János (1888–1954). Hung. Ref. theol.; prof. and pastor Budapest. Works include *Die Sünden der Kirche;* sermons.

Victor I. Bp. Rome (pope) ca. 198/199; involved in Easter* controversy.

Victor IV. See *Popes,* 9; *Toulouse, Synods of.*

Victoria, Evangelical Lutheran Synod of. See *Australia, Lutheranism in,* B 1.

Victoria, Tomás Luis de (Tommaso Lodovico da Vittoria; ca. 1535/48–1611). Composer; b. Ávila Sp.; studied at Collegium Germanicum, Rome; organist Rome 1569; priest 1575. Works include many masses, motets, magnificats, hymns, psalm settings.

Victorines. Mems. of the Order of St.Victor, founded Paris, Fr., ca. 1108/10 by William* of Champeaux; extinct since the Fr. Revolution; identity of the saint to whom the abbey at Paris was dedicated seems uncertain. See also *Adam of St. Victor; Commentaries, Biblical; Free Spirit, Brothers and Sisters of the; Hugh of St. Victor; Richard of St. Victor; Walter of St. Victor.*

Victorious Life. Term assoc. with the concept of perfectionism.*

Vidalin, Jon Thorkelsson (1666–1720). Luth. cleric; b. Gardar, near Álftanes, near Reykjavík, Iceland; educ. Skalholt and Copenhagen; soldier 2 yrs.; teacher and pastor Skalholt 1691; pastor Gardar 1696; coadjutor of bp.; bp. 1697. Works include *Húss-Postilla* (sermons for the Christian home).

Vienna, Concordat of. See *Concordat,* 3.

Vienna, Congress of. See *Popes,* 27.

Vienne, Council of. Convoked by Clement* V; met 1311–12 at Vienne (ancient Vienna), Isère dept., SE

Fr.; regarded by RCs as 15th ecumenical council (see *Councils and Synods,* 4); suppressed Knights Templars (see *Military Religious Orders,* b); issued reform decrees.

Viénot, John Emmanuel (1859–1933). Ch. hist.; b. Asnières, near Bourges, Fr.; pastor Montbéliard 1883; prof. Paris 1900, also pastor 1907. Works include *Histoire de la Réforme dans le pays Montbéliard; Calvin et la conscience moderne; Luther et l'Allemagne.*

Vietnam. See *French Indochina.*

Vig, Peter Sorenson (Nov. 7, 1854–Mar. 21, 1929). B. Egtved, near Kolding, Den.; private tutor in Den.; to US 1879; worked and studied in Chicago, Ill.; returned to Den. 1882; educ. Missionary Institute, Copenhagen; returned to US 1884; instructor Dan. high school Elk Horn, Iowa, 1884–85; pastor Jacksonville, Iowa, 1885–88; prof. theol. sem., West Denmark, Wis., 1888–93; pastor Luck, Wis., 1888–93, 1905–09; prof. theol. sem. Elk Horn, Iowa, 1894–96; pres. Trin. Sem., Blair, Nebr., 1896–99, 1902–05, 1909–; pastor Elk Horn, Iowa, 1899–1902. Works include *Danske i Amerika; Elk Horn i Iowa; Nordboerne finder vei til Amerika; Trinitatis Seminarium; Den forenede danske Ev. Luth. Kirke i Amerika; Den Danske Udvandring til Amerika; Dens Aarsager og Veie; Danske i Kamp i og for Amerika.*

Vigilius. See *Popes,* 3.

Vigils (from Lat. *vigilia,* "wakefulness"). Nocturnal or evening prayers or devotions. See also *Hours, Canonical.*

Vigness, Lauritz Andreas (Jan. 14, 1864–Sept. 21, 1947). B. Fillmore Co., Minn.; educ. Augustana Sem., Beloit, Iowa (see *Beloit Seminary*). Prof. Augustana Coll., Canton, S. Dak., 1886–90; Highland Park Coll., Des Moines, Iowa, 1890–94. Ordained 1894. Pastor Des Moines, Iowa, 1894–95; Ottawa, Ill., 1901–14. Prof. Jewell (Iowa) Luth. Coll., 1894–95. Pres. Pleasant View Luth. Coll., Ottawa, Ill., 1895–1914; St. Olaf Coll., Northfield, Minn., 1914–18. Ed. *Lutheraneren.*

Vignola, Giacomo da (Giacomo Barocchio, or Barozzi, or Barozzio; 1507–73). Architect; b. Vignola, near Modena, It.; active in Fr. 1541–43, Bologna 1543–46, Rome from 1546; papal architect from 1551; succeeded Michelangelo* as chief architect of St. Peter's 1564. Works include writings on architectural theory.

Vikings. See *Iceland,* 1; *Norway, Early Christianity in.*

Villmergen, Switzerland. See *Switzerland,* 5.

Vilmar, August Friedrich Christian (1800–68). Brother of J. W. G. Vilmar*; theol., literary hist.; b. Solz, near Rotenburg, Electoral Hesse, Ger.; educ. Marburg; active as educator in Rotenburg 1823–27, Hersfeld from 1827; won for Lutheranism; dir. Gymnasium at Marburg 1833–50; consistorial counciller 1850; supt. Kassel 1851; prof. theol. Marburg 1855. Works include *Collegium biblicum.*

Vilmar, Jacob Wilhelm Georg (1804–84). Brother of A. F. C. Vilmar*; ev. theol.; b. Solz, near Rotenburg, Electoral Hesse, Ger.; pastor Rotenburg 1830–51; pastor and metropolitan Melsungen 1851–66. Leader in Luth. confessional movement to keep Hessian ch. free of Prussian domination. Works include *Der gegenwärtige Kampf der Hessischen Kirche um ihre Selbständigkeit; Protestantismus und Christenthum.*

Vincent, John Heyl (1832–1920). M. E. cleric; b. Tuscaloosa, Ala.; pastor N. J. and Ill.; leader in organization of S.S. Institute held at Chautauqua Lake, N. Y. 1874; chancellor Chautauqua Literary and Scientific Circle 1878; bp. 1888–94.

Vincent, Louis Hugues. See *Geography, Christian,* 8.

Vincent, Marvin Richardson (1834–1922). B. Poughkeepsie, N. Y.; educ. Columbia U., NYC; prof. Meth. U., Troy, N. Y., 1858–60; M. E. minister 1859; changed to Presb. Ch. 1863; pastor Troy 1863–73, NYC 1873–88; prof. Union Theol. Sem., NYC, 1888. Tr. J. A. Bengel,* *Gnomon Novi Testamenti;* other works include *Word Studies in the New Testament.*

Vincent de Paul (b. perhaps ca. 1580/81–1660). RC priest; b. Pouy (now Saint-Vincent de Paul), Landes, Fr.; ordained 1600; some say he was a slave of Muslim of Barbary ca. 1605–07; founded Lazarists*; with Louise de Marillac (Ludovica; Madame Le Gras; 1591–1660; b. probably Ferrières-en-Brie, near Meaux, Fr.) founded Sisters* of Charity (popular name for Daughters of Charity of St. Vincent de Paul; devoted to care of poor and other needy) 1633 in Fr.

Vincent Ferrer (Vicente; 1350–1419). B. Valencia, Sp.; Dominican 1367; prof. Lérida and Valencia; confessor of Benedict XIII (see *Benedict XIII,* 1) 1395–98; tried to heal papal schism (see *Schism,* 8); famous preacher; concerned esp. about conversion of Moors and Jews. Works include *Tractatus de vita spirituali,* which influenced I. (of) Loyola.*

Vincent of Beauvais (Vincentius; ca. 1190–ca. 1264). Dominican encyclopedist; b. Beauvais, Oise, Fr. Works include *Speculum maius.* See also *Encyclopedias and Dictionaries,* 1.

Vincent of Lérins (Vincentius Lerinensis [or Lirinensis]; d. 450 AD or sooner). B. probably Gaul; semi-Pelagian; monk in monastery on Saint-Honorat is., in Iles de Lérins, in Mediterranean, off SE Fr.; held that the Cath. faith is what has been believed everywhere, always, by all.

Vincent of Saragossa (d. ca. 304 AD). Sp. martyr; most details of his life are lost in the midst of legend and tradition.

Vincentians. See *Lazarists.*

Vinci, Leonardo da. See *Leonardo da Vinci.*

Vinet, Alexandre Rodolphe (Rudolf; 1797–1847). Ref.; b. Ouchy, near Lausanne, Switz.; taught Fr. language and literature at Basel from 1817; influenced by W. M. L. De Wette*; prof. practical theol. Lausanne 1837; led free ch. movement in Vaud canton 1845–47. Works include *Homiletics,* tr. and ed. T. H. Skinner; *Der Sozialismus in seinem Prinzip betrachtet,* tr. D. Hofmeister; *Über die Darlegung der religiösen Überzeugungen und über die Trennung der Kirche und des Staates als die nothwendige Folge sowie Garantie derselben,* tr. F. H. Spengler; *Über die Freiheit des religiösen Cultus,* tr. J. U. D. Volkmann; *Pastoral Theology,* tr. T. H. Skinner.

Viret, Pierre (1511–71). Reformer of W Switz.; b. Orbe, Vaud canton, Switz.; studied theol. in Paris, Fr.; co-worker of G. Farel* 1530; pastor and prof. Lausanne; active in Geneva, Switz., and S Fr. Works include *Disputations chrestiennes; Instruction chrestienne.*

Virgin Birth. See *Incarnation.*

Virgin Islands. See *Caribbean Islands,* E 5, 8.

Virginia Synod. See *United Lutheran Church, Synods of,* 29.

Virginia Synod, Central. Luth. syn. 1847–ca. 1851; fate unknown.

Virginia Synod, Southwestern. See *United Lutheran Church, Synods of,* 29.

Virginius, Adrian (1663–1706). Luth. pastor; b. Estonia; educ. Kiel. Tr. NT into South-Estonian; helped tr. OT into North-Estonian.

Virtues, Cardinal. See *Cardinal Virtues.*

Virtues, Stoic. See *Stoicism.*

Vischer, Christoph (Fischer; 1520–ca. 1597/1600). B. Joachimsthal, Bohemia (now Jáchymov, NW Czechoslovakia); educ. Wittenberg, Ger.; pastor Jüterbog 1544; cathedral preacher and supt. Schmalkalden 1552; pastor and gen. supt. Meiningen 1571; court preacher and asst. supt. Celle 1574; pastor Halberstadt 1577; gen. supt. Lüneburg (at Celle)

1583; hymnist. Hymns include "Wir danken dir, Herr Jesu Christ, dass du für uns gestorben bist."

Vischer, Peter (ca. 1460–1529). "The Elder"; sculptor; b. Nürnberg, Ger.; son of a worker in brass. He and his sons created the shrine of St. Sebald, Nürnberg (includes 12 Apostles, 12 Prophets, 72 lesser figures), whose conception is Gothic, but many of whose details are Renaissance.

Vishnu. See *Brahmanism,* 2; *Hinduism,* 4.

Visible Church. See *Church,* 3.

Visible Word. See *Grace, Means of,* I 1, 6.

Visigoths, Conversion of. See *Goths, Conversion of.*

Visions. Appearances, or revelations, of God or a representative of God. See also *Psychical Research; Revelation,* 3, 4; *Theophany.*

Visitatio liminum. See *Bishop,* 3.

Visitation, Feast of the. See *Church Year,* 13, 16.

Visitation Articles. See *Articles of Visitation; Crypto-Calvinistic Controversy; Melanchthon, Philipp.*

Visitation Nuns. Founded 1610 at Annecy, Fr., by J. F. F. de Chantal* under guidance of Francis* of Sales for visiting the sick poor in their homes; educ. work was added later.

Visitations, Church. Surveys made under authorization of Luth. princes in Ger. in the 1520s to organize the chs. and est. schools; inaugurated by John* the Constant in Ernestine Saxony because ch. life needed reform, clergy needed orientation, the Peasants* War and Zwickau* Prophets had caused confusion, and related matters needed attention; visitations began 1526 (WA 26, 178) and continued several yrs.; M. Luther,* P. Melanchthon,* and others prepared Articles* of Visitation by June 1527 (WA 26, 176 and 180). Needs were analyzed and recommendations for structures and procedures made. On later visits, progress was checked and further recommendations made. Result: organization of the Landeskirche (regional ch.) and est. of schools. The pattern was followed by other princes in other regions of Ger.

Visvakarman. See *Brahmanism,* 2.

Vital, Hayyim. See *Cabala.*

Vitoria, Francisco de (ca. 1480/86–1546). B. Vitoria, Old Castile, Sp.; Dominican; laid foundation for internat. law which he regarded as binding every state of the international community and the individuals who composed those states.

Vitringa, Campegius (1659–1722). Dutch Ref. OT scholar; b. Leeuwarden, Neth.; educ. Franeker and Leiden; prof. Oriental languages Franeker 1680/81; pioneered in using historicocritical* method. Works include a commentary on Is.

Vivekananda (Narendranath Datta [or Dutt]). Hindu philos.; 1862–1902; b. Calcutta, India; tried to combine W materialism and Indian spirituality; known as Swami* Vivekananda. See also *Hinduism,* 7; *Vedanta Society.*

Vladimir I (Vladimir the Great; ca. 956–1015). First Christian ruler of Russia* (980–1015); became Christian (E Orthodox) ca. 989. Father of Boris* and Gleb. Before conversion he opposed Christianity by force; among his victims were Theodore and Ivan, perhaps the first Russ. Christian martyrs. See also *Christian Church, History of,* II 1.

Voes, Hendrik (Vos; d. 1523). Augustinian monk at Antwerp, Belg.; imprisoned for ev. faith; tried by Inquisition*; burned at stake in Brussels with J. Esch.*

Voet, Gisbert (Gysbertus Voetius; 1588–1676). Dutch Calvinist theol.; b. Heusden, near Utrecht, Neth.; educ. Leiden; preacher Vlijmen (or Vlymen) 1611, Heusden 1617; delegate to 1618–19 Syn. of Dordrecht*; prof. Utrecht 1634; opposed Arminianism,* Cocceianism (see *Cocceius, Johannes*), and Cartesianism*; followers called Voetians.

Vogt, Karl Christoph (Carl; 1817–95). Naturalist; b. Giessen, Ger.; prof. Giessen 1847; dismissed; prof. geol. 1852, later also of zoology, at Geneva, Switz.; championed materialism* and Darwinism (see *Darwin, Charles Robert*) and their logical consequences. Works include *Köhlerglaube und Wissenschaft; Vorlesungen über den Menschen, seine Stellung in der Schöpfung und in der Geschichte der Erde.*

Voice of Prophecy. See *Radio and Television Evangelism, Network,* 5.

Voigt, Andrew George (Jan. 22, 1859–Jan. 2, 1933). B. Philadelphia, Pa. Educ. U. of Pa., Philadelphia; Lutheran Theol. Sem., Philadelphia; Erlangen, Ger. Pastor in N. J. 1883–85; Wilmington, N. C., 1898–1903. Prof. Newberry (S. C.) Coll. 1885–89, 1891–98. Prof. Thiel Coll., Greenville, Pa., 1889–91 (acting pres. 1890–91); Lutheran Theol. Southern Sem. (see *United Lutheran Church, Synods of,* 27) 1892–98. Dean Lutheran Theol. Southern Sem. 1903–33. Pres. The United* Syn. of the Ev. Luth. Ch. in the South 1906–10. Works include *Biblical Dogmatics* (2d ed. titled *Between God and Man*); commentary on Ephesians in *The Lutheran Commentary,* IX, ed. H. E. Jacobs, pp. 1–117.

Volborth, Frederick (1768–1840). Luth. ch. leader in Russia. Pastor Mogilev (or Mohilev) 1797, New-Saratovka (near St. Petersburg, which is called Leningrad since 1924); court preacher at Tver (called Kalinin since 1932) ca. 1810; pastor St. Petersburg 1813–39; gen. supt. 1832.

Volckmar, Tobias (1678–1756). Luth. composer; b. Reichenstein, Silesia; pupil of J. P. Krieger; studied at U. of Königsberg (now Kaliningrad); organist Geibsdorf, near Lauban; cantor and dir. of music Hirschberg ca. 1709/10–56. Works include much vocal and instrumental ch. music.

Volckmar, Wilhelm Valentin (1812–87). B. Hersfeld, Ger.; music teacher at Homberg Sem. 1835; organist; composer. Works include *Orgelschule.*

Voliva, Wilbur Glenn (1870–1942). B. near Newton, Ind.; studied at Hiram (Ohio) Coll. and Union Christian Coll., Merom, Sullivan Co., Ind.; pastor Christian Ch. (Disciples* of Christ); joined Christian* Cath. Ch. 1899; overseer of that ch. in Australia 1901–06; asst. to J. A. Dowie* 1906; gen. overseer of the ch. 1907.

Volkening, Johann Heinrich (1796–1877). B. Hille, near Minden, Westphalia, Ger.; educ. Jena; asst. pastor Minden; pastor Schnathorst (near Lübbecke) 1822, Gütersloh 1827, Jöllenbeck (near Bielefeld) 1838. Leader in awakening and influenced this movement also outside Westphalia; opposed conventicles; tried to keep the "awakened" in congs. Works include *Kleine Missionsharfe.*

Völker, Karl (Carl; 1886–1937). Ev. theol.; b. Lemberg; pupil of G. K. D. Loesche* and K. G. A. v. Harnack*; prof. Vienna. Works include *Die Entwicklung des Protestantismus in Österreich.*

Volos. See *Slavs, Primitive Religion of.*

Volstead Act. See *Temperance Movements and the Lutheran Church.*

Voltaire (real name François Marie Arouet; 1694–1778). Hist., philos.; b. Paris, Fr.; educ. by Jesuits; wrote provocative satire; imprisoned 1717–18, 1726; 1726–29 in Eng.; influenced by deism* and Enlightenment*; 1750–53 at court of Frederick II (1712–86; "the Great"; b. Berlin, Ger.; king of Prussia 1740–86); at Ferney, near Geneva, Switz., 1758–78; d. Paris.

Voltaire was a strong promotor of deism. Antagonized by RCm, he adopted the motto "Écrasez l'infame!" ("Crush the infamous one!") and bitterly opposed every form of Christianity. His opposition against all absolutism helped bring on the Fr. Revolution (see *Church and State,* 15; *France,* 5). Works include tragedies; novels; poems; *Dictionnaire philosophique; Essay sur l'Histoire générale et sur les moeurs et l'esprit des nations, depuis Charlemagne jusqu'à nos jours.*

See also *Encyclopedists.*

J. Morley, *Voltaire* (London, 1872); N. L. Torrey, *Voltaire and the English Deists* (New Haven, Conn., 1930) and *The Spirit of Voltaire* (New York, 1938).

Voluntarism. Theory based on voluntary action. In application it may lead, e.g., to voluntary support of a religious system as opposed to state support, or to a system of philos., ethics, theol., or metaphysics in which the will, rather than intellect or reason, is the dominant factor in experience or in the constitution of the universe.

Volunteers of America. Organization, an American secession from the Salvation* Army, formed 1896 by Ballington Booth (1859–1940; son of W. Booth, who founded Salv. Army; b. Brighouse, Eng.). Ev. in doctrine, democratic in govt.; concerned with soc. welfare; also offers spiritual aid.

Vondel, Joost van den (1587–1679). Poet, dramatist; b. Cologne, Ger., son of Mennonite immigrants from Antwerp, Belg., who settled in Amsterdam 1596/97; sided with Remonstrants.* Lack of Prot. unity and longing for pristine Christian unity led him into RCm 1639/41. Works include *Joseph in Dothan; Jeptha; Bespiegelingen van Godt en Godtsdienst.*

Voodooism (from Vodun, "god, spirit," in the Fon language of Dahomey). Religion brought from Afr. to Haiti; practiced also elsewhere in the West Indies and in parts of the US; based on mythology and superstition; includes, e. g., spells, snake dances, and alleged communication with the supernatural world.

Vopelius, Gottfried (1645–1715). B. Herwigsdorf, near Zittau, Ger.; cantor Nikolaikirche, Leipzig, 1677–1715. Ed. *Neu Leipziger Gesangbuch* 1682.

Vorst, Konrad (Conradus Vorstius; 1569–1622). Arminian theol.; b. Cologne, Ger., of RC Dutch parents, who later became Ref.; studied RC theol. at Cologne but differed with Council of Trent* and became a merchant; later continued studies at Herborn and elsewhere; prof. Leiden 1610. Works include *Tractatus theologicus de Deo, sive de natura & attributis Dei.*

Vos, Geerhardus (1862–1949). B. Heerenveen, Neth. Educ. at Amsterdam, Neth.; Christian Ref. sem., Grand Rapids, Mich.; Princeton (N. J.) Theol. Sem. Prof. Grand Rapids 1888, Princeton 1893. Ordained Presb. 1894. Works include *The Mosaic Origin of the Pentateuchal Codes; The Teaching of Jesus Concerning the Kingdom of God and the Church; The Pauline Eschatology; Old and New Testament Biblical Theology; The Self-Disclosure of Jesus.*

Vos, Gerrit Jan (1836–1912). Ref. theol.; b. Harderwijk, Neth.; pastor Amsterdam 1872; opposed modernism. Works include *Geschiedenis der Vaderlandsche Kerk van 1630–1842.*

Voskamp, Karl Johannes (Carl John; Sept. 18, 1859–Sept. 20, 1937). B. Antwerp, Belg. Educ. Duisburg, Berlin U. and sem. of Berlin Miss. Soc.; miss. to China 1884; active in Canton (S China), later in Shantung (N China); work was transferred to ULC 1925. Works include *Aus dem belagerten Tsingtau; Unter dem Banner des Drachen und im Zeichen des Kreuzes.*

Vossius, Gerardus Joannis (Voss; originally Gerrit Jansz. Vos; 1577–1649). Ref. theol.; b. near Heidelberg, Ger., of Dutch parents; held Remonstrant views; prof. Amsterdam, Neth. Works include *Historiae de controversiis, quas Pelagius eiusque reliquiae moverunt.*

Votive Mass. RC mass (1) in honor of the Trin., Christ, Mary, or saints; (2) for peace, the sick, in time of disaster, etc.; or (3) nuptial mass or mass for the dead. Not liturgically prescribed.

Votive Offering. Imprecise term denoting objects dedicated to deities, persons, institutions. Occur in ethnic cultures as well as OT (It 12:6, 11; Ps 22:25; 50:14; 56:12). In RCm objects (e. g., candles) used to express such personal feelings as gratitude, affection, dedication.

Vows. Vows of voluntary poverty, celibacy, and obedience made by those entering various RC orders. Vows may be solemn or simple. Solemn vows are for life; simple vows are either for a limited time or for life; further differentiation is difficult. Solemn vows are preceded by simple vows. The RC Ch. claims authority to release from vows, tries to compel observance if dispensation is withheld. M. Luther condemned RC practice of continued celibacy under vow if the gift of continence is found to be lacking (WA 10 II, 151).

Vuilleumier, Henri (1841–1925). B. Basel, Switz.; prof. OT at Academy (later U.) Lausanne. Coed. *Revue de Théologie et de Philosophie;* other works include *Histoire de l'Eglise réformée du Pays de Vaud.*

Vulgate. See *Bible Versions,* J 2.

Vulpius, Melchior (Vulpius is Latinization of Ger. Fuchs; ca. 1560/70–1615). Luth. composer; b. Wasungen, near Meiningen, Ger.; cantor Weimar ca. 1596/1602–15. Works include a Passion Oratorio (see *Passion, The*) based on Mt; chorale melodies (e.g., "Christus, der ist mein Leben"; "Die helle Sonn' leucht't jetzt herfür"; "Gelobt sei Gott" [also called *Vulpius*"]; "Jesu Kreuz, Leiden und Pein"; "Lobet den Herrn, ihr Heiden all'").

W

Wabag Lutheran Church. See *New Guinea,* 7.

Wach, Joachim (1898–1955). B. Chemnitz (called Karl-Marx-Stadt 1953), Ger.; taught at Leipzig; to US 1935; taught at Brown U., Providence, R. I., and at U. of Chicago (Ill.) Divinity School. Works include *Religionswissenschaft: Prolegomena zu ihrer wissenschaftstheoretischen Grundlegung; Einführung in die Religionssoziologie; Sociology of Religion; Das Verstehen; Types of Religious Experience Christian and Non-Christian; The Comparative Study of Religion; Church Denomination and Sect.*

"Wachende Kirche." See *Buffalo Synod,* 6.

Wacker, Peter Johannes Georg Emil (May 16, 1839–Apr. 2, 1913). B. Kotzenbüll near Tönning, Ger.; educ. Copenhagen, Kiel, and Berlin; pastor Rinkenis, near Flensburg, 1867–76; pastor and rector of the deaconess institution, Flensburg, 1876. Works include *Diakonissenspiegel; Die Laienpredigt und der Pietismus in der lutherischen Kirche; Der Diakonissenberuf nach seiner Vergangenheit und Gegenwart; Eins ist not; Die Heilsordnung.*

Wackernagel, Carl Heinrich Wilhelm (1806–69). Brother of K. E. P. Wackernagel*; b. Berlin, Ger.; prof. Basel, Switz., 1833. Works include *Poetik, Rhetorik und Stilistik; Altdeutsche Predigten und Gebete aus Handschriften.*

Wackernagel, Karl Eduard Philipp (Carl; 1800–77). Brother of C. H. W. Wackernagel*; b. Berlin, Ger.; educ. Berlin, Breslau, Halle; taught in Berlin, Stetten in Württemberg, Wiesbaden, Elberfeld; hymnologist. Works include *Das deutsche Kirchenlied von der ältesten Zeit bis zu Anfang des XVII. Jahrhunderts.*

Wafer. See *Altar Bread.*

Wagenseil, Johann Christoph (1633–1705). B. Nürnberg, Ger.; prof. hist. and law 1667, oriental languages 1674, canon law 1697 Altdorf. Tr. Mishna (see *Talmud*) and its commentary into Ger.; other works include *Belehrung der Jüdisch-Deutschen Rede- und Schreibart* (title is given in various forms).

Wagner, Anton (Jan. 20, 1830–Jan. 10, 1914). B. Allendorf, near Giessen, Hesse, Ger.; educ. Fort Wayne, Ind. Pastor Watertown, Wis., 1855; Freistadt, Wis., 1859; Pleasant Ridge, Ill., 1860; Chicago, Ill., 1867–1909.

Wagner, Charles (1852–1918). Prot. cleric and moral essayist; b. Vibersviller, Moselle, Fr.; educ. Strasbourg, Göttingen, Heidelberg; pastor Remiremont and Paris; liberal; tried to unify Fr. Protestantism.

Wagner, Georg Gottfried (1698–1756). Composer; b. Mühlberg, Saxony, Ger.; pupil of J. Kuhnau*; played violin in orchestra under J. S. Bach.* Studied theol. at Leipzig; cantor Plauen. Works include motet *Lob und Ehre* (pub. as J. S. Bach's); cantatas; oratorios.

Wagner, Richard. See *Wagner, Wilhelm Richard.*

Wagner, Tobias (1598–1680). Luth. theol.; great-grandfather of T. Wagner* (d. 1775); b. Heidenheim, N Württemberg, Ger.; pastor Esslingen; prof. theol. 1653, later provost, chancellor 1662 Tübingen; confessional opponent of skepticism, atheism, and Cartesianism.

Wagner, Tobias (d. 1775). Great-grandson of T. Wagner* (1598–1680); to US 1742; pastor in Maine and Pa.; befriended by H. M. Mühlenberg but turned against him; returned to Ger. 1759.

Wagner, Valentin (after 1510–57). Rector, printer, city pastor Kronstadt; visited Wittenberg ca. 1542; influenced Kronstadt reformation; friend of P. Melanchthon* and J. Camerarius.* Works include Gk. grammar; comedies; song book.

Wagner, Wilhelm Richard (dropped "Wilhelm" before he was 20; 1813–83). Dramatic composer, poet, essayist; b. Leipzig, Ger.; educ. Leipzig; choral dir. Würzburg 1833; active in various capacities in Magdeburg, Königsberg, Riga, Paris, Dresden, Zurich, London, and elsewhere. Works include *Tannhäuser; Lohengrin; Götterdämmerung; Parsifal; Die Meistersinger von Nürnberg.* See also *Sachs, Hans; Wartburg.*

Wagner College. See *Lutheran Church in America,* V; *Ministry, Education of,* VIII B 27.

Wahhabis (Wahabis). Also called Ikhwan ("brothers"); puritanical Muslim sect founded in Arabia by Muhammad ibn-Abdul Wahhab (ca. 1691/1703–ca. 1787/92); loyal to Koran* and traditions regarding Muhammad. See also *Islam,* 5.

Wahl, Christian Abraham (1773–1855). Prot. theol.; b. Dresden, Ger.; pastor Schneeberg 1808; supt. Oschatz 1823; mem. consistory Dresden 1835. Works include *Clavis novi testamenti philologica; Clavis librorum veteris testamenti apocryphorum philologica; Historisch-praktische Einleitung in die biblischen Schriften.* See also *Lexicons,* B.

Wakamba Mission. Miss. in E Afr. begun 1886 by a soc. organized for that purpose earlier in the yr. in Bav. Ger.; the field was taken over 1893 by the Leipzig* Ev. Luth. Miss.

Wakan (Wakanda). See *Primitive Religion.*

Wake, William (1657–1737). B. Blandford, Dorset, Eng.; educ. Oxford; to Paris, Fr., as chapalin of Eng. ambassador 1682; returned to Eng. 1685; held various appointments; bp. Lincoln 1705; abp. Canterbury 1716–37; negotiated with L. E. Du Pin* and others for reunion of Ch. of Eng. and Fr. Ch. Works include *Exposition of the Doctrine of the Church of England; The State of the Church and Clergy of England; The Genuine Epistles of the Apostolical Fathers; The Principles of the Christian Religion.* See also *Union Movements,* 4.

Wakon (Wakonda). See *Primitive Religion.*

Walaeus, Antonius (Antoine de Waele; 1573–1639). B. Gent, Belg.; educ. Leiden, Neth.; preached and lectured at Geneva, Switz.; city preacher Leiden; accepted a call to Koudekerke, near Middelburg, 1602; court chaplain 1604; preacher 1605, prof. dogmatics 1609 Middelburg; attended 1618–19 Syn. of Dordrecht* and helped write its canons; prof. theol. Leiden 1619. Opposed Arminianism.* Conducted a sem. for missionaries to the E. Indies 1622–32. Works include *Het ampt der Kerckendienaren; Compendium ethicae Aristotelicae ad normam veritatis Christianae revocatum.*

Walch, Christian Wilhelm Franz (1726–84). Son of J. G. Walch*; brother of J. E. I. Walch*; ev. theol.; b. Jena, Ger.; prof. Jena and Göttingen; exponent of supernaturalism; adopted and modified his father's moderate orthodoxy. Works include *Entwurf einer vollständigen Historie der Ketzereien, Spaltungen und Religionsstreitigkeiten, bis auf die Zeiten der Reformation; Entwurf einer vollständigen Historie der Kirchenversammlungen; Entwurf einer vollständigen Historie der römischen Päpste; Bibliotheca* *symbolica vetus; Compendium historiae ecclesiasticae recentissimae.*

Walch, Johann Ernst Immanuel (1725–78). Son of J. G. Walch*; brother of C. W. F. Walch*; prof. philos., logic, metaphysics, and other subjects Jena. Works include *Antiquitates Herculanenses litterariae oratione auspicali; Antiquitates symbolicae quibus symboli apostolici historia illustratur.*

Walch, Johann Georg (1693–1775). Father of the 2 foregoing; b. Meiningen, Ger.; educ. Leipzig; prof. philos., theol., and other subjects Jena; ecclesiastical councillor for Saxe-Weimar. Ed. works of M. Luther; other works include *Historische und theologische Einleitung in die Religions-Streitigkeiten Der Evangelisch-Lutherischen Kirchen, Von der Reformation bis auf ietzige Zeiten.*

Waldeland, Martin Enoch (Sept. 18, 1876–Dec. 30, 1933). B. Gunder, Clayton Co. (ca. 6 mi. E of Elgin, Fayette Co.), Iowa. Educ. St. Olaf Coll., Northfield, Minn.; United Ch. sem., Minneapolis, Minn. (see *Luther Theological Seminary,* 4). Pastor Fertile, Iowa, 1900–02; St. Ansgar, Iowa, 1902–27. Taught at St. Ansgar 1902–04, 1907–08. Literary ed. Augsburg Pub. House 1908–12.

Waldemar II (Den.). See *Estonia,* 1.

Waldenses (variants of the name include Waldensians; Wadoys; Valdesii; Vaudes; Vaudois). The Waldensian Ch. grew out of fusion of the work of P. Waldo* with movements of Arnold* of Brescia, P. de Bruys,* and others; banned by pope repeatedly; object of repeated crusades; under vicious persecution by the Inquisition*; driven from their homes. Granted civil and religious liberty 1848 by Charles Albert of Sardinia (Carlo Alberto; 1798–1849; b. Turin, It.; king of Sardinia 1831–49).

Waldenses rejected purgatory, masses for the dead, indulgences, prayers to saints, RC eucharist and hierarchy. Known for preaching, miss. zeal, Bible knowledge. Beginning at the time of the Reformation, they merged into Prot. groups. The 1655 Confession of the Waldenses, *A Brief Confession of Faith of the Reformed Churches of Piedmont,* is in part an abridgment of the 1559 *Gallican Confession* (see *Reformed Confessions,* B).

See also *Pacifism,* B; *Saints, Veneration of,* 7.

J. J. I. v. Döllinger, *Beiträge zur Sektengeschichte des Mittelalters,* 2 vols. (Munich, 1890); F. Bender, *Geschichte der Waldenser* (Ulm, 1850); H. C. Sartorio, *A Brief History of the Waldensians* (New York, 1921); K.-V. Selge, *Die ersten Waldenser,* 2 vols. (Berlin, 1967); G. B. Watts, *The Waldenses of Valdese* (Valdese, N. C., 1965).

Waldenström, Paul Peter (1838–1917). B. Luleaa, Swed.; educ. Uppsala; held various teaching positions and pub. offices. Held that the reconciliation through Christ is not of God to us, but of us to God. Helped found Svenska Missionsförbundet 1878 (see *Sweden, Lutheranism in,* 5; *Swedish Missionary Societies,* 4).

Waldis, Burkard (Burkhard; ca. 1490–1556). B. Allendorf, on the Werra R., Ger.; poet; Franciscan; Luth. 1524; imprisoned during persecution 1536–40. Works include *Die Parabel vom Verlorenen Sohn.* See also *Religious Drama,* 3.

Waldo, Peter (Valdo; Valdes; Valdez; Valdesius; Petrus Waldus; ca. 1140–ca. 1217/18). Fr. reformer; originally merchant of Lyons; renounced the world ca. 1173; devoted to religious study and preaching; he and his followers, known as Poor of Lyons, later as Waldenses,* used Scripture in the vernacular, preached without ch. authorization, and were excommunicated in the early 1180s. See also *Doctrine, Christian, History of,* 5.

Waldorf College, Forest City, Iowa. Founded 1903. ALC.

Wales. Peninsula on W of Gt. Brit.; principality of Eng. since 1284. Christianity did not come to Wales with Romans, but from the E, probably via Honoratus* and Martin of Tours (see *Celtic Church,* 2). Hostility of RC and Anglo-Saxon chs. drove early Christian Britons into mountainous districts of Wales, where they gradually diminished in numbers and finally became extinct. Then ignorance and superstition overspread the whole principality for cents. The Reformation reached Wales through England. Gospel truth spread rapidly among Welsh mountaineers, but under later Stuarts ignorance, vice, and immorality prevailed in Wales. A successful system of schools was est. in the 1st half of the 18th century. Meths. became most numerous among free chs.; Presbs. grew strong; other Prots. flourished; RCs, though few, became vigorous.

Walker, Jesse (d. 1835). M. E. miss.; b. N. C.; traveling preacher Tenn. and Ky. 1802, Ill. 1806; planted Methodism in St. Louis 1820; active among Indians along the upper Miss. R. 1823.

Walker, Martin F. (Apr. 2, 1877–July 12, 1967). B. York, Pa.; educ. Conc. Sem., St. Louis, Mo.; pastor NYC 1899; prof. Conc. Collegiate Institute, Hawthorne (school moved to Bronxville 1908–10; see also *Lutheran Church – Missouri Synod, The,* V 7), N. Y., 1902–10; pastor Buffalo, N. Y., 1910; pres. Mo. Syn. Eng. Dist. 1938–45. Coauthor *Greater Love Hath No Man.*

Walker, Williston (1860–1922). Cong.; b. Portland, Maine; educ. Hartford (Conn.) Theol. Sem.; taught at Bryn Mawr (Pa.) Coll. 1888–89. Prof. Hartford Theol. Sem. 1889–1901; Yale U., New Haven, Conn., 1901–22. Works include *A History of the Congregational Churches in the United States; The Reformation.*

Wall, Georg Wendelin (1811–67). B. Württemberg, Ger.; educ. Basel, Switz.; commissioned Basel 1836; to US 1836; arrived St. Louis, Mo., Nov. 1836; pastor Ger. Prot. Ev. Ch. of the Holy Ghost; built Ger. Prot. Ch. in St. Louis (dedicated Aug. 1840; first Ger. ch. in St. Louis); preached funeral sermon of O. H. Walther*; helped found The German* Ev. Ch. Soc. of the West.

Wallenstein, Albrecht Eusebius Wenzel von (Waldstein; Valdstejn; 1583–1634). Duke of Friedland and Mecklenburg; Prince of Sagan; Austrian gen.; b. Hermanic, Boh. (now Czechoslovakia), on the Elbe, near Arnau, of Luth. parents; became RC but without deep religious convictions; lost his estates when Boh. became Prot. in the Thirty* Years' War. Commander imperial armies 1625; removed 1630; recalled 1632; defeated by Gustavus* II at Lützen 1632; assassinated Feb. 25, 1634.

Wallin, Johan Olof (Olaf; 1779–1839). Hymnist; b. Stora Tuna, NW of Uppsala, in the Dalecarlia (Dalarne, "the Dales") region, Kopparberg district, Swed.; educ. Uppsala; ordained Luth. 1806; pastor Solna 1809, later at Stockholm, still later dean Västeraas; bp. 1824; abp. Uppsala 1837. Issued rev. Swed. hymnal 1819; other works include "The Angel of Death."

Walliser, Christoph Thomas (Wallisser; Waliser; Walleser; 1568–1648). Composer; b. Strasbourg; probably studied under M. Vulpius; taught in the Academy and dir. ch. music Strasbourg from 1599. Works include many Ger. Psalms set in the old contrapuntal style.

Walloons. Inhabitants of Walloni (Fr. *Wallonie*), Fr.-speaking part of Belg., including provinces Hainaut, Liège, Luxembourg, Namur, and S. Brabant. Became Cath after conversion of Clovis* I 496. Some became Prot. in the 16th c., and some of these fled under RC pressure, including the Inquisition,* to the neighborhood of Leiden, N Neth.; many Walloons from the Neth. settled in the mid-1620s at what came 1625 to be called New Amsterdam (now NYC).

Walter, Johann. See *Walther, Johann.*

Walter, Johannes Wilhelm von (1876–1940). Ger. Luth. theol.; b. St. Petersburg (now Leningrad,

Russ.); educ. Dorpat, Leipzig, Göttingen; taught at Göttingen, Breslau, Vienna, Rostock. Works include *Die Geschichte des Christentums; Die Theologie Luthers.*

Walter, Rudolf. See *Gualther, Rudolf.*

Walter of Mortagne (Gualterus de Mauretania; ca. 1090–1174). B. Mortagne, Flanders; studied at Reims; perhaps taught Paris; cathedral dean 1150, bp. 1155 Laon; indifferentist on the question of universals.

Walter of St. Victor (Saint-Victor; d. perhaps ca. 1180/90). Polemicist; opposed P. Abelard,* Gilbert* de la Porrée, Peter* the Lombard, et al.; attacked scholasticism; held that dialectics can reveal only formal, not material, truth.

Walther, Carl Ferdinand Wilhelm (Oct. 25, 1811–May 7, 1887). 1. Brother of O. H. Walther*; prominent Luth. theol.; b. Langenchursdorf near Waldenburg, Saxony, Ger.; his father, grandfather, and great-grandfather were Luth. pastors; educ. Leipzig, where rationalism ruled; influenced for Christianity by a group of earnest students, the F. W. Barthel* family, and M. Stephan* Sr.

2. Left the university ca. 6 mo. 1831–32 because of ill health; read M. Luther during illness; grad. Leipzig 1833; private tutor 1834; ordained Bräunsdorf, near Penig, Saxony, 1837.

3. Walther emigrated to the US 1839 with other Saxons (see *Lutheran Church – Missouri Synod, The,* II); pastor Dresden, Perry Co., Mo.; helped found log-cabin "coll." (see *Lutheran Church – Missouri Synod, The,* II 4).

4. For subsequent events, including organization of the Mo. Syn., see *Lutheran Church – Missouri Synod, The,* II 2 to III 2; *Ministry, Education of,* X C. Walther promoted Bible-centered educ. and growth on all levels.

5. Walther and F. C. D. Wyneken* went to Ger. 1851 to discuss doctrinal differences with J. K. W. Löhe*; returned 1852 without reaching unity. See also *Church and Ministry, Walther's Theses on.*

On Walther's connection with CPH see *Publication Houses, Lutheran.*

In 1854 the Mo. Syn. authorized pub. of a theol. journal ed. by Walther; he ed. *Lehre und Wehre* 1855–60, coed. 1861–64; see also *Lutheran Church – Missouri Synod, The,* V 2. Walther gave first impetus toward calling free* Luth. conferences beginning 1856, took part in the 1866 Buffalo* Colloquy and a colloquy with representatives of the Iowa Syn. Nov. 13–18, 1867, Milwaukee, on "open* questions," millennialism,* antichrist,* and the meaning of confessional subscription. He helped form the Synodical* Conference.

6. Walther gave direction to those who formed The Eng. Ev. Luth. Syn. of Missouri* and Other States. In 1878 Capital U., Columbus, Ohio (see *Universities in the United States, Lutheran,* 2), a school of the Ohio Syn., which was in doctrinal agreement with the Mo. Syn., conferred on him the title of DD (which he had refused for doctrinal reasons 1855 when offered by the U. of Göttingen). From the early 1870s much of his time was taken up by the predestinarian controversy (see *Predestinarian Controversy,* 2), which erupted in the open 1880.

7. Walther followed M. Luther in emphasizing justification by faith (see *Luther, Martin,* 6). In his doctrine of the ch., Walther distinguished ch. and structure.

8. Though criticized at times for his polemics, Walther is often described as the most prominent Luth. theol. of the US.

9. Pres. Mo. Syn. 1847–50, 1864–78.

10. In addition to works mentioned or referred to above: Walther issued an amplified ed. of J. W. Baier's* *Compendium theologiae positivae;* ed. *Der Lutheraner.* Other works include *Americanisch-Lutherische Pastoraltheologie; Casual-Predigten und -Reden; Communismus und Socialismus; Die Evangelisch-Lutherische Kirche die wahre sichtbare Kirche Gottes auf Erden; Festklänge; Gnadenjahr; Der Gnadenwahlslehrstreit; Licht des Lebens; Lutherische Brosamen; Die rechte Gestalt einer vom Staate unabhängigen Evangelisch-Lutherischen Ortsgemeinde; Die rechte Unterscheidung von Gesetz und Evangelium; Die Stimme unserer Kirche in der Frage von Kirche und Amt; Tanz und Theaterbesuch; Thesen über den Wucher.*

See also *Weimarische Bibelwerk, Das.*

M. Günther, *Dr. C. F. W. Walther: Lebensbild* (St. Louis, 1890); C. L. Janzow, *Life of Rev. Prof. C. F. W. Walther, D. D.* (Pittsburgh, 1899); D. H. Steffens, *Doctor Carl Ferdinand Wilhelm Walther* (Philadelphia, 1917); W. G. Polack, *The Story of C. F. W. Walther* (St. Louis, 1935); W. Dallmann, W. H. T. Dau, Th. Engelder (ed.), *Walther and the Church* (St. Louis, 1938); *Briefe von C. F. W. Walther . . . an seine Freunde, Synodalgenossen und Familienglieder,* ed. L. Fuerbringer, 2 vols. (St. Louis, 1915–16); J. L. Gruber, *Erinnerungen an Professor C. F. W. Walther und seine Zeit* (Burlington, Iowa, [1930]); L. W. Spitz, *The Life of Dr. C. F. W. Walther* (St. Louis, 1961); *Letters of C. F. W. Walther: A Selection,* tr. and ed. C. S. Meyer (Philadelphia, 1969); Walther Sesquicentennial No. of the *CTM* (Oct. 1961).

Walther, Johann (1496–1570). Composer; friend of M. Luther*; b. probably Kahla, on the Thuringian Saale, near Jena, cen. Ger.; active in Torgau from the mid-1520s to 1548, Dresden 1548–54; lived in Torgau 1554–70. Helped Luther prepare music for *Deudsche Messe* (see Luther, Liturgies of). Issued *Geystliche gesangk Buchleyn* 1524, for which Luther wrote the foreword; other works include 2 Passions (see *Passion, The*) and the text of the hymn "Der Bräut'gam wird bald rufen." Walther is regarded by some as the real founder of the musical liturgy of the Luth. ch. See also *Kantorei; Music, Church.*

Walther, Johann Gottfried (1684–1748). Composer; relative of J. S. Bach*; b. Erfurt, Ger.; organist Thomaskirche, Erfurt, 1702; town organist Weimar 1707. Issued *Musikalisches Lexikon Oder Musikalische Bibliothek;* other works include a prelude and fugue and 4 chorales with variations.

Walther, Michael (1593–1662). Luth. theol.; b. Nürnberg, Ger.; educ. Wittenberg, Giessen, Altdorf, Jena; court preacher Schöningen 1618, also prof. theol. Helmstedt 1622; gen. supt. Aurich 1626, Celle 1643. Works include *Officina biblica* (isagogics); *Harmonia totius s. scripturae;* catechism exposition. See also *Lutheran Theology After 1580,* 3.

Walther, Otto Hermann (Sept. 23, 1809–Jan. 21, 1841). Brother of C. F. W. Walther*; b. Langenchursdorf, near Waldenburg, Saxony; educ. Leipzig; private tutor; his father's asst. 1834; to US with other Saxons 1839 (see *Lutheran Church – Missouri Synod, The,* II); pastor St. Louis, Mo., 1839.

Walther, Rudolf. See *Gualther, Rudolf.*

Walther, Wilhelm Markus (1846–1924). Luth. theol.; b. Cuxhaven, Ger.; educ. Erlangen, Marburg, Göttingen; pastor Cuxhaven 1870; prof. Rostock 1895. Ed. WA XIX, XXIII. Other works include *Adolf Harnacks Wesen des Christentums für die christliche Gemeinde geprüft; Die Bibelübersetzungen des Mittelalters; Lehrbuch der Symbolik.*

Walther College. An assoc. was organized 1866 St. Louis, Mo., to est. a high school, which opened 1867 and was divided into *Höhere Bürgerschule* and *Höhere Töchterschule;* it was called Conc. Academy 1880, Lutheran High School 1881; a classic course was added to the academic course, coeduc. endorsed, and name changed to Walther-Coll. 1888; discontinued 1917. See also *Graebner, August(us) Law-*

rence; Graebner, Theodore Conrad; Lutheran Church – Missouri Synod, The, VI 7.

Walther League. See *Young People's Organizations, Christian,* II 3.

Walther von der Vogelweide (ca. 1170–ca. 1230). Middle High Ger. lyric poet and minnesinger; b. perhaps Austria; educ. at court in Vienna; wandering singer after 1198; championed authority of Ger. rulers; opposed efforts to extend papal power. Works include *Sprüche; Under der linden an der heide; Kreuzlied.*

Walton, Brian (Bryan; ca. 1600–61). Angl. scholar; b. Cleveland dist., North Riding, Yorkshire, Eng.; educ. Cambridge; rector St. Martin's Orgar, London, 1628; bp. Chester 1660. Ed. *London Polyglot* (see *Polyglot Bibles*).

Wambsganss, Philipp, Sr. See *Deaconesses,* 7.

Wambsganss, Philipp, Jr. See *Associated Lutheran Charities; Deaconesses,* 9, 11.

Wang Ch'ung. See *Chinese Philosophy,* 5.

Wangemann, Hermann Theodor (1818–94). B. Wilsnack, near Wittenberg, Ger.; rector and asst. preacher Wollin 1845; sem. dir. and archdeacon Kammin 1849; dir. Berlin* Miss. Soc. I 1865–94; visited Afr. twice. Works include *Kurze Geschichte des evangelischen Kirchenliedes; Das Opfer nach Lehre der heiligen Schrift alten und neuen Testaments; Sieben Bücher Preussischer Kirchengeschichte; Der Kirchenstreit unter den von der Landeskirche sich getrennt haltenden Lutheranern in Preussen.*

Wanradt and Koell's Catechism. See *Estonia,* 2.

War. 1. Hostile conflict bet. nations and states (internat. war) or bet. parties in the same nation or state (civil war); cold war falls short of engagement by arms.

2. The hist. of the Children of Israel from the conquest of Canaan to the Exile is mainly an account of wars.

3. Many of these wars were waged with God's consent or at His direction. Some of the wars were God's punishment (cf., e. g., Dt 28:47-68) for such sins as contempt of the Word of God (Lv 26:21-25; 1 Ki 8:33), shedding innocent blood (2 Sm 12:9-10).

4. AC XVI: "It is taught among us that all government in the world and all established rule and laws were instituted and ordained by God for the sake of good order, and that Christians may without sin occupy civil offices or serve as princes and judges, render decisions and pass sentences according to imperial and other existing laws, punish evildoers with the sword, engage in just wars, serve as soldiers, buy and sell, take required oaths, possess property, be married, etc."

War and Prophecy. Much prophetic literature usually appears in wartime; its writers seek materialistic contemporary evidence for their views regarding the meaning of prophetic Bible passages; they try to show that individual wars and nations were specifically foretold in detail; they emphasize, e. g., the battle of Armageddon (Rv 16:14, 16).

T. C. Graebner, *War in the Light of Prophecy* (St. Louis, 1942).

Ward, James (1843–1925). Philos., psychol.; b. Hull, Eng.; educ. Liverpool, Berlin, Göttingen, Cambridge; Cong. minister Cambridge 1 yr.; engaged in psychol. research; prof. Cambridge 1897–1925. Influenced by G. W. v. Leibniz* and R. H. Lotze.* Opposed pluralism.* Held a theistic view of the world. Works include *The Realm of Ends or Pluralism and Theism.* See also *Metaphysical Society, The.*

Ward, William (Oct. 20, 1769–Mar. 7, 1823). B. Derby, Eng.; learned printers' trade; studied for the ministry; missionary printer for Bap. Miss. Soc. 1798; sailed for India 1799; settled at Dan. settlement Serampore, near Calcutta; printed W. Carey's* Bengali NT and other translations. See also *India* 10; *Serampore Trio.*

Ward, William Hayes (1835–1916). Cong. cleric; orientalist; journalist; b. Abington, Mass.; educ. Union Theol. Sem., NYC, and Andover (Mass.) Theol. Sem.; pastor Oskaloosa, Kans.; teacher Utica (N. Y.) Free Academy 1863–65; prof. Ripon (Wis.) Coll. 1865–67; assoc. with *The Independent* (N. Y.) in various editorial capacities; led exploring expedition to Babylonia 1884–85; his surveys led to uncovering of Nippur; authority on Babylonian and Assyrian seals.

Ware, Henry, Sr. (1764–1845). Father of H. Ware* Jr. and W. Ware*; b. Sherborn, Mass.; educ. Harvard U., Cambridge, Mass.; Unitarian pastor Hingham, Mass., 1787–1805; prof. Harvard U. 1805–40, Harvard Divinity School 1816–45.

Ware, Henry, Jr. (1794–1843). Son of H. Ware* Sr.; brother of W. Ware*; b. Hingham, Mass.; educ. Harvard U., Cambridge, Mass.; Unitarian pastor Boston 1817–30; helped found Am. Unitarian Assoc. (see *Unitarianism*); prof. Harvard Divinity School 1828–42. Works include *The Life of the Saviour.*

Ware, William (1797–1852). Son of H. Ware* Sr.; brother of H. Ware* Jr.; b. Hingham, Mass.; educ. Harvard U., Cambridge, Mass. Unitarian pastor NYC 1821–36; Waltham, Mass., 1837–38; West Cambridge, Mass., 1844–45. Works include *Zenobia: or, The Fall of Palmyra: An Historical Romance.*

Waremund, Joannes. See *Flacius Illyricus, Matthias.*

Warfield, Benjamin Breckinridge (1851–1921). Presb. theol.; b. Lexington, Ky.; educ. Princeton (N. J.) Theol. Seminary. Prof. Western Theol. Sem., Allegheny (now part of Pittsburgh), Pa., 1878; Princeton Theol. Sem. 1887. Coed. *The Presbyterian and Reformed Review;* other works include *An Introduction to the Textual Criticism of the New Testament.*

Warneck, Gustav Adolf (1834–1910). Father of J. Warneck*; b. Naumburg, near Halle, Ger.; educ. Halle; served congs. in Roitzsch, Dommitzsch, and Rothenschirmbach; inspector of missions at Barmen 1870; founded Saxon provincial missionary conference 1879. With T. Christlieb* and P. R. Grundemann* founded *Allgemeine Missions-Zeitschrift* 1874. Other works include *Abriss einer Geschichte der protestantischen Missionen von der Reformation bis auf die Gegenwart; Evangelische Missionslehre.*

Warneck, Johannes (1867–1944). Son of G. A. Warneck*; Luth. miss. leader; b. Dommitzsch, near Torgau, Ger.; educ. Tübingen, Greifswald, Leipzig, Halle; miss. to Batak under dir. of L. I. Nommensen* 1892–1906; inspector Barmen 1908; taught at theol. school at Bethel 1912; ephor* Batak ch. 1920; dir. Rhenish* Miss. Soc. 1932–37. Works include *Tobabataksch-Deutsches Wörterbuch; Die Religion der Batak; D. Ludwig I. Nommensen; Sechzig Jahre Batakmission.*

Warner, Daniel Sidney (1842–1925). B. Bristol (now Marshallville), Ohio; mem. Churches* of God in N. Am.; preached in Ohio and Nebr. from 1872; expelled for advocating "entire sanctification" ca. 1877; founded Church* of God (Anderson, Ind.).

Warnshuis, Abbe Livingston (Nov. 22, 1877–Mar. 17, 1958). B. Clymer, N. Y.; educ. Hope Coll. Holland, Mich., and New Brunswick (N. J.) Theol. Sem.; Ref. Ch. in Am. (see *Reformed Churches,* 4 b) miss. Amoy, China, 1900–15; nat. evangelistic secy. China Continuation Com., Shanghai, 1915–20; Am. secy. IMC 1921. Coed. *The China Mission Year Book;* ed. *Directory of For. Missions* 1933.

Warren, Charles. See *Geography, Christian,* 5.

Warren Association. Formed 1767 at Warren, R. I., by 4 Bap. congs. (of Warren, R. I., and Haverhill, Bellingham, and Middleborough, Mass.) on the model of the Philadelphia Assoc. (see *Baptist Churches,* 4, 26), to secure denominational cooperation in educ., evangelization, and the struggle for religious liberty. Chief initial leader: J. Manning.* See also *Backus, Isaac.*

Wars of Religion. See *Reformation, Lutheran,* 12.

Wartburg. Castle, Thuringia, cen. Ger., on hill just SW of Eisenach; built ca. 1070; scene of Sängerkrieg (song contest) 1207; subject of W. R. Wagner's* *Tannhäeuser.* See also *Luther, Martin,* 13–14.

Wartburg College. See *Iowa and Other States, Evangelical Lutheran Synod of,* 3; *Ministry, Education of,* VIII B 28.

Wartburg Press, The. See *Publication Houses, Lutheran.*

Wartburg Synod. See *United Lutheran Church, Synods of,* 30.

Wartburg Theological Seminary. See *Iowa and Other States, Evangelical Lutheran Synod of,* 3; *Ministry, Education of,* X P.

Wasa, Gustav. See *Gustavus I.*

Washington, Booker Taliaferro (ca. 1856/58–1915). B. near Hale's Ford, Franklin Co., Va.; his mother was a slave; studied at Hampton (Va.) Institute; taught school 2 yrs. at Malden, W. Va.; studied at Wayland Sem., Washington, D. C.; taught at Hampton Institute 1879; organized and was principal of Tuskegee (Ala.) Normal and Industrial Institute; promoted educ. and elevation of the Negro race. Works include *Up from Slavery; The Story of the Negro.*

Washington Declaration (Declaration of Principles Concerning the Church and Its External Relationships). After the ULC was organized, its Ex. Bd. was often asked to define the attitude of the ULC toward cooperative movements looking toward ch. union and toward other organizations, tendencies, and movements. The ULC adopted the Washington Declaration 1920:

A. *Concerning the Cath. Spirit in the Ch.* This section declares and explains the belief in the one, holy, cath., apostolic ch., the existence of which cannot be demonstrated but rests on "our belief in the continued life of Christ in all His Christians." This ch. "performs its earthly functions and makes its presence known among men through groups of men who profess to be believers in Jesus Christ. In these groups the Word of God is preached and the Sacraments are administered." "Every group of professing Christians calling itself a Church will seek to express in its own life the attributes of the one, holy, catholic, and apostolic Church. . . . 1. By professing faith in Jesus Christ. . . . 2. By preaching the Word and administering the Sacraments. . . . 3. By works of serving love. . . . 4. By the attempt to secure universal acceptance of the truth which it holds and confesses." Every such group, even if partial and imperfect, is an expression of the one holy ch. But those groups in which the Word of God is most purely preached and confessed and the sacraments administered in the closest conformity to the institution of Christ "will be the most complete expression of the one, holy Church. For this reason it is necessary that, when occasion arises, any such group of Christians shall define its relationship to other groups which also claim the name of Church, as well as to other groups and organizations which do not bear that name." Hence each ch. should be ready "to declare unequivocally what it believes . . . approach others without hostility, jealousy, suspicion or pride . . . grant cordial recognition to all agreements which are discovered between its own interpretation of the Gospel and that which others hold . . . co-operate with other Christians in works of serving love . . . insofar as this can be done without surrender of its interpretation of the Gospel, without denial of conviction, and without suppression of its testimony as to what it holds to be the truth."

B. *Concerning the Relation of the Ev. Luth. Ch. Bodies to One Another.* The ULC "recognizes no doctrinal reasons against complete co-operation and organic union" with chs. calling themselves Ev. Luth. and subscribing the Luth. Confessions.

C. *Concerning the Organic Union of Prot. Chs.* ". . . we hold the union of Christians in a single organization to be of less importance than the agreement of Christians in the proclamation of the Gospel. . . . We believe that a permanent and valid union of churches must be based upon positive agreements concerning the truth for which the united Church Body is to stand."

D. *Concerning Cooperative Movements Among the Prot. Chs.* This section states the earnest desire to cooperate in "works of serving love . . . provided, that such co-operation does not involve the surrender of our interpretation of the Gospel, the denial of conviction, or the suppression of our testimony to what we hold to be the truth." The purpose, principles, and effect on "the independent position of our Church as a witness to the truth of the Gospel" must determine cooperation. Nine paragraphs list fundamental doctrines (including the Real Presence) which a movement or organization must hold before the ULC would enter cooperation with it. The ULC refused to enter cooperative organizations or movements "whose purposes lie outside the proper sphere of Church activity" and there are organizations (e.g., for soc. or pol. reform) which the ch. as such would not enter but commended to its pastors and mems. No syn., conference, or bd. had power of indep. affiliation with "general organizations and movements."

E. *Concerning Movements and Organizations Injurious to the Christian Faith.* This section warns against these.

In 1922 the ULC did not become a regular mem. of the FCC but resolved (in the so-called Buffalo Declaration) that the "relationship shall be of a consultative character by which The United Lutheran Church may have a voice but no vote; thus securing to it entire autonomy . . . in regard to the decisions and actions of the Federal Council of Churches, and, at the same time, the privilege of co-operating in such tasks and problems as it may elect." EL

Minutes of the Second Biennial Convention of The United Lutheran Church in America (Washington, D. C., 1920), pp. 92–100; *Minutes of the Third Biennial Convention of The United Lutheran Church in America* (Buffalo, N. Y., 1922), p. 86; *Documents of Lutheran Unity in America,* ed. R. C. Wolf (Philadelphia, 1966).

Wassmann, Dietrich (1897–1954). B. Grossenheidorn, Schaumburg-Lippe Ger.; educ. Hermannsburg; miss. to Ethiopia 1927. Works include *Durchbruch des Evangeliums im Gallaland.*

Watch Tower Bible and Tract Society. See *Jehovah's witnesses.*

Water, Holy. See *Holy Water.*

Waterland, Daniel (ca. 1682/83–1740). Angl. theol.; b. Walesby, Lincolnshire, Eng.; educ. Cambridge; king's chaplain 1717; chancellor York diocese 1722; canon Windsor 1727; archdeacon Middlesex 1730. Opposed deism.* Works include *The Importance of the Doctrine of the Holy Trinity Asserted; Scripture Vindicated.*

Waterland Confession. See *Democratic Declarations of Faith,* 1.

Waterloo (University) College. See *United Lutheran Church, Synods of,* 1.

Waterloo Lutheran Seminary. See *Canada,* A 9; *Lutheran Church in America,* V; *Ministry, Education of,* X Q; *United Lutheran Church, Synods of,* 1.

Waterloo Lutheran University. See *Canada,* A 9; *Lutheran Church in America,* V; *Ministry, Education of,* VIII A 5; *United Lutheran Church, Synods of,* 1.

Watson, John Broadus (1878–1958). Psychol.; b. Greenville, S. C. Educ. Furman U., Greenville; U.

of Chicago; prof. Johns Hopkins U., Greenville; U. 1908–20; entered business; exponent of behaviorism. See also *Educational Psychology,* D 4.

Watson, Richard (1737–1816). B. Heversham, Westmorland, Eng.; educ. Cambridge; prof. chemistry 1764, divinity 1771 Cambridge; prebendary 1774, archdeacon 1779 Ely. Rector Northwold, Norfolk, 1779; Knaptoft, Leicestershire, 1780. Bp. Llandaff 1782. Works include *An Apology for Christianity* (against E. Gibbon*); *An Apology for the Bible* (against T. Paine*).

Watson, Richard (1781–1833). B. Barton-upon-Humber, Lincolnshire, Eng.; Meth. lay preacher; mem. Meth. New Connection (see *Methodist Churches,* 1) for a time; supported for. missions. Works include *Theological Institutes.*

Watson, Thomas (d. 1686). Eng. Presb. preacher; educ. Cambridge; joined pastors opposed to O. Cromwell*; opposed execution of Charles I (see *England,* B 7); joined movement to est. Charles II (see *England,* C 1) as king; imprisoned 1651–52. Works include *The Godly Man's Picture; Heaven Taken by Storm; A Body of Practical Divinity.*

Watts, Isaac (1674–1748). B. Southampton, S Hampshire, Eng.; educ. at a nonconformist academy at Stoke Newington; tutor 1696–1702; pastor of an indep. ch. London 1702; failing health from 1703 led to severe illness 1712 and semiretirement. Works include *Logic.* Other works include more than 600 (perhaps ca. 750) hymns, many of which are in *Psalms of David, Imitated in the Language of the New-Testament.* See also *Sergeant, John.*

Watts Memorial College. Est. 1885 as Arthur G. Watts Memorial Coll., of Guntur, India. See also *General Synod of the Evangelical Lutheran Church in the United States of America, The,* 8.

Watzinger, Carl. See *Geography, Christian,* 6.

Wauwatosa Theology. Theol. tendency in the Ev. Luth. Joint Syn. of Wisconsin* and Other States which developed at the sem. in Wauwatosa, Wis., under leadership of J. P. Köhler* and emphasized hist. and exegesis over against dogmatics. See also *Protestant Conference, The.*

Webb, Thomas (ca. 1724–96). B. Eng.; to Am. 1755 as Brit. army officer under Gen. Braddock; one of the survivors of Braddock's defeat; saw action also elsewhere, e.g., at Quebec 1759; returned to Eng.; retired from military service; became Meth. 1765; returned to US as preacher in Albany, NYC, Philadelphia, and elsewhere; d. in Eng.

Weber, Ernst Heinrich. See *Psychology,* G 3.

Weber, Ferdinand Wilhelm (1836–79). B. Schwabach, near Nürnberg, N Bav., Ger.; educ. Erlangen; vicar under J. K. W. Löhe*; instructor at the miss. school in Neuendettelsau. Pastor Diebach, near Schillingsfürst, Middle Franconia, W Bav., Ger., 1864–72; Neuendettelsau 1872; Polsingen, Middle Franconia, 1876. Works include *System der altsynagogalen palästinischen Theologie aus Targum, Midrasch und Talmud.*

Weber, Hans Emil (1882–1950). B. München-Gladbach (now Mönchengladbach), near Düsseldorf, Ger.; student of K. M. A. Kähler*; taught at Halle, Bonn (twice), Münster. Works include *Reformation, Orthodoxie und Rationalismus;* writings on the NT.

Weber, Karl Maria Friedrich Ernst von (Carl; Ernest; 1786–1826). Composer, opera conductor, pianist; b. Eutin near Lübeck, Ger.; active esp. in Breslau, Stuttgart, Prague, Dresden, London. Works include piano music; orchestral compositions; operas and other dramatic works; cantatas (including *In seiner Ordnung schafft der Herr*); masses.

Weber, Max (1864–1920). Economist, sociologist, philos.; b. Erfurt, Ger.; studied law at Heidelberg, Berlin, Göttingen; prof. Freiburg, Heidelberg, Munich. Works include *Gesammelte Aufsätze zur Religionssoziologie.*

Weckmann, Matthias (ca. 1619/21–74). B. probably Niederdorla or Mühlhausen, Thuringia, Ger.; studied organ and composition under J. Praetorius; active in Dresden, Den., and Hamburg. Works include choral and organ music.

Wedding. See *Marriage.*

Wedding Ring. See *Ring, Engagement and Wedding.*

Wederdoper. See *Mennonite Churches.*

Wee, Mons Olson (May 13, 1871–Apr. 15, 1942). B. Etne, Bremnes canton, Hordaland Co. (which includes Sunnhordland, or Sönhordland), Norw.; to US 1891; educ. Red* Wing (Minn.) Sem.; miss. tour of inspection Persia 1898–99; pastor S. Dak., Minn., and Mont.; prof. Red Wing Sem. 1908–17, Luther Theol. Sem. (St. Paul, Minn.) 1917–41. Works include *Absolutionen; Men Who Knew God; Moses: Faith in Decision; Who Is Jesus?*

Weekday Schools. See *Parish Education,* F 2.

Weeks, Feast of. See *Judaism,* 4.

Wegelin, Josua (Wegelein; 1604–40). B. Augsburg, Ger.; educ. Tübingen; pastor Budweiler; 4th diaconus of the Franciscan Ch., Augsburg, 1627; forced to leave Augsburg by 1629 Edict of Restitution*; recalled as archidiaconus after Gustavus II gained control of the city 1632; forced to flee again as a result of the battle of Nördlingen (see *Thirty Years' War*); pastor Pressburg, Hung.; hymnist. Hymns include "Allein auf Christi Himmelfahrt" ("Auf Christi Himmelfahrt allein").

Wegelius, Johan, Sr. and Jr. See *Finland, Lutheranism in,* 4.

Wegner, Thomas Cortsen (1588–1654). B. Den.; pastor Copenhagen 1911–27; bp. Stavanger 1627–54; exponent of Luth. orthodoxy.

Wegs, Michael, See *Weisse, Michael.*

Wegscheider, Julius August Ludwig (1771–1849). B. Küblingen, near Schöppenstedt, Ger.; educ. Helmstedt; privatdocent Göttingen 1805; prof. Rinteln 1806, Halle 1810; regarded supernatural revelation as impossible. Works include *Institutiones theologiae christianae dogmaticae,* a representative dogmatic work of rationalism.

Weibezahn, Carl Friedrich August (1804–44). Luth. preacher; b. Springe, Hannover, Ger.; educ. Göttingen; morning preacher 1830, consistorial councillor 1842 Osnabrück; active in awakening, miss., and inner miss. movements.

Weidenheim, Johann (fl. ca. 1690). Ger. Luth. hymnist. Hymn "Herr, deine Treue ist so gross" ascribed to him.

Weidner, Revere Franklin (Nov. 22, 1851–Jan. 5, 1915). B. Center Valley, Lehigh Co., Pa.; educ. Lutheran Theol. Sem., Philadelphia. Pastor Phillipsburg, N. J., 1873–78; prof. Muhlenberg Coll., Allentown, Pa., 1875–77; pastor Philadelphia 1878–82; prof. Augustana Theol. Sem., Rock Island, Ill., 1882–91; pres. and prof. dogmatics and Heb. exegesis Chicago Luth. Theol. Sem. 1891–1915. Works include *Commentary on the Gospel of Mark; Biblical Theology of the Old Testament; An Introduction to Dogmatic Theology; Theological Encyclopaedia and Methodology.*

Weigel, Valentin (1533–88). Mystic; b. Naundorf, near Grossenhain, near Dresden, Ger.; educ. Leipzig and Wittenberg; pastor Zschopau 1567; subscribed FC. Writings published after his death reveal theosophic, pantheistic tendencies; influenced by Neoplatonism,* Erasmus,* Paracelsus*; influenced J. Böhme,* G. W. v. Leibniz,* et al.; followers called Weigelianer.

Weil, Simone (1909–43). B. Paris, Fr., of Jewish parents; taught philos. at girls' schools at Roanne, Bourges, and Saint-Quentin; fled Ger. troops to Marseille 1940, to Eng. via Am. 1942; known for radical views on soc. questions and alleged mystical experience of Christ. Works include *La pesanteur et la* *grâce; Attente de Dieu; La connaissance surnaturelle; Cahiers.*

Weimar, Colloquies and Conventions of. Weimar, Ger., was a stronghold of Gnesio-Lutherans* in the 16th c. Conventions and colloquys held there included: convention regarding the Interim* 1548; Flacian Syn. against Philippists* 1556; colloquy (or disputation) concerning the Konfutationsbuch* (rev. at Weimar) 1560; colloquy bet. theologians of Wittenberg and Jena 1568–69; syn. on original sin 1571.

Weimarische Bibelwerk, Das. Ger. Bible with annotations and other helps, first pub. 1640 Nürnberg, Ger.; put together in Weimar by order of Ernest* I by J. M. Dilherr,* J. Gerhard,* S. Glass(ius),* C. Löber,* J. Major,* et al. New ed. prefaced by C. F. W. Walther.* Also called Ernestinische Bible, Nürnberger Bibel, Weimarer Bibel, Gothaische Bibel, and (popularly) Kurfürstenbibel (or Churfürstenbibel).

Weinbrenner Johann. See *Winebrenner, John.*

Weinel, Heinrich (1874–1936). Ev. theol.; b. Vonhausen, near Büdingen, Hesse, Ger.; educ. Giessen and Berlin and at the theol. sem. at Friedberg, Hesse; taught at Berlin, Bonn, Jena. Tried to win unchurched intellectuals for ch. membership on their own terms. Works include *Die Nichtkirchlichen und die freie Theologie; Die Gleichnisse Jesu.*

Weingärtner, Sigismund (fl. early 17th c.). Ger. hymnist; details of life obscure. Hymn "Auf meinen lieben Gott" ascribed to him.

Weise, Christian (1642–1708). Hymnist; b. Zittau, Ger.; educ. Leipzig; prof. Weissenfels 1670; rector Gymnasium at Zittau 1678. Hymns include "Ach seht, was ich für Recht und Licht."

Weiser, John Conrad, Jr. (Nov. 2, 1696–July 13, 1760). Father-in-law of H. M. Mühlenberg*; son of J. C. Weiser Sr. (1660–1746; b. probably Gross Aspach, Württemberg, Ger.; to N. Y. 1710; soldier); b. Afstaedt, a small village in Herrenberg, a county contiguous to Backnang, Württemberg; to N. Y. 1710; learned Indian language and lore; served as interpreter and justice of the peace; in the struggle bet. Brit. and Fr. he kept the Indians on the Brit. side; arranged treaties with Indians; aided Moravian missions to Indians.

Weishaupt, Adam (1748–1830). Mystic, philos.; b. Ingolstadt, Ger.; studied at the Jesuit sem. and at the U. of Ingolstadt; prof. Ingolstadt; founded Illuminaten 1776 (see *Illuminati*).

Weismann, Christian Eberhard (1677–1747). Ev. theol.; b. Hirsau, S Württemberg, Ger.; educ. Tübingen; diaconus Calw 1701; court chaplain 1705; prof. Stuttgart 1707, Tübingen 1721. Works include *Introductio in memorabilia ecclesiastica historiae sacrae Novi Testamenti.*

Weiss, Carl Philipp Bernhard (1827–1918). Father of J. Weiss*; ev. theol.; b. Königsberg, Ger.; educ. Königsberg, Halle, Berlin; prof. Königsberg, Kiel, Berlin; consistorial councillor Berlin; theologian of the Prussian* Union. Works include commentaries in H. A. W. Meyer's* *Kritisch exegetischer Kommentar über das Neue Testament.*

Weiss, Johannes (1863–1914). Son of C. P. B. Weiss*; b. Kiel, Ger.; educ. Marburg, Berlin, Göttingen, Breslau; prof. Göttingen, Marburg, Heidelberg; mem. Religionsgeschichtliche* Schule. See also *Lutheran Theology After 1580,* 13.

Weisse, Christian Hermann (1801–66). B. Leipzig, Ger.; prof. philos. Leipzig; formulated a system of Christian theism.

Weisse, Michael (Weiss; Wiss; Wegs; Weys; Weyss; ca. 1480–1534). B. Neisse, Silesia; priest; monk at Breslau; joined Bohemian* Brethren in Boh. and became their preacher at Landskron in Boh. and Fulnek, Moravia; hymnist. Ed. 1st Ger. hymnal of the Boh. Brethren; hymns include "Christus ist erstanden"; "Nun lasst uns den Leib begraben."

Weissel, Georg (1590–1635). B. Domnau, near Königsberg (now Kaliningrad), Prussia; educ. Königsberg, Wittenberg, Leipzig, Jena, Strasbourg, Basel, Marburg; school rector Friedland, near Domnau, 1614–17; pastor Königsberg 1623–35; hymnist. Hymns include "Macht hoch die Tür, die Tor' macht weit"; "Such, wer da will, ein ander Ziel."

Weissenberg, Joseph. See *Evangelisch-Johannische Kirche.*

Weissenwolf, David Ungnad von. See *Crusius, Martin.*

Weissenwolf, Johann Ungnad von. See *Ungnad von Weissenwolf, Johann.*

Weisses Kreuz. Society organized 1882 to care for wounded or sick soldiers of the Austro-Hung. army and to place and care for officers and their widows and orphans in proper institutions. Not to be confused with White* Cross League.

Weitbrecht, Gottlieb Friedrich (1840–1911). Ev. theol.; b. Calw, in Black Forest, S Württemberg, Ger.; educ. Tübingen; pastor Stuttgart; prelate Ulm 1897; prelate and preacher Stuttgart 1900; exponent of conservative Biblical theol. Ed. *Der Christenbote* and *Jugendblätter;* other works include sermons and biographies.

Weizsäcker, Karl Heinrich von (1822–99). Ev. theol.; b. Öhringen, near Heilbronn, Württemberg, Ger.; educ. Tübingen; prof. ch. hist. Tübingen 1861; chancellor U. of Tübingen 1890; regarded himself as a disciple of F. C. Baur.* Works include writings on early Christianity. See also *Bible Versions,* M.

Welch, Adam Cleghorn (1864–1943). B. Jamaica; educ. Edinburgh, Scot.; pastor Scot. 1887–1913; prof. OT Edinburgh 1913; disciple of J. Wellhausen.* Works include *Deuteronomy: The Framework to the Code; Prophet and Priest in Old Israel.*

Welfare Agencies. See *Child and Family Service Agencies.*

Welfare Work. See *Social Work.*

Weller, Jakob (1602–64). B. Markneukirchen (im Vo[i]gtlande), near Plauen, Saxony, E cen Ger.; educ. Wittenberg; prof. Wittenberg 1635; supt. Brunswick 1640; court preacher Dresden from 1645/46. Works include writings against G. Calixtus.*

Weller von Molsdorf, Hieronymus (1499–1572). B. Freiberg (or Freyburg?), Ger.; educ. Wittenberg; converted by one of M. Luther's sermons; lived with Luther 1527–35; school rector Freiberg (Freyburg?) 1539; staunch Luth. in the adiaphoristic* and Majoristic* controversies. Works include commentaries; a postil; writings on propaedeutics, ethics, and homiletics.

Wellhausen, Julius (1844–1918). OT scholar, philol., textual critic; b. Hameln, Lower Saxony, Ger.; educ. Göttingen; prof. Greifswald, Halle, Marburg, Göttingen; held that the "Priestly writer" (see *Higher Criticism,* 7) is the latest of the Pentateuch sources. Works include *Das arabische Reich und sein Sturz; Geschichte Israels; Prolegomena zur Geschichte Israels; Israelitische und jüdische Geschichte; Die Pharisäer und die Sadducäer;* commentaries. See also *Duhm, Bernhard; Exegesis,* 9; *Higher Criticism,* 12; *Lods, Adolphe; Lutheran Theology After 1580,* 10.

Welsh Calvinistic Methodist Church. See *Presbyterian Churches,* 4 a.

Weltgeist. See *Historicism,* 3.

Wel(t)z, Justinian(us) Ernst von (Dec. 12, 1621–1668); Luth. miss.; b. probably Chemnitz (now Karl-Marx-Stadt), Ger., of Austrian extraction; issued several miss. treatises 1663–64; ordained by F. Breckling* at Zwolle, Holland, 1664; miss. to Dutch Guiana (see also *South America,* 13).

Wenceslas I. See *Czechoslovakia,* 2.

Wenceslaus (Wenzel; 1361–1419). King Wenceslaus IV of Boh. 1378–1419; king of Ger. and Holy Roman emp. 1378–1400; imprisoned by Boh. nobles 1393–94; deposed by Ger. electors 1400; imprisoned

1402; regained Boh. throne 1404. With J. Hus* he supported the claims of Alexander V (see *Schism,* 8).

Wendelin, Markus Friedrich (Marcus Frederik; Fridericus; 1584–1652). Ref. theol.; b. Sandhausen, near Heidelberg, Ger.; educ. Heidelberg; private tutor Geneva, Switz., 1609–10; rector Gymnasium Zerbst, Ger. Works include *Christianae theologiae systema maius; Collatio doctrinae Christianae Reformatorum et Lutheranorum.*

Wendt, Hans Hinrich (1853–1928). B. Hamburg, Ger.; educ. Tübingen and Göttingen; prof. Göttingen, Kiel, Heidelberg, Jena. Works include *Die Lehre Jesu; Das Johannesevangelium; System der christlichen Lehre.* See also *Lutheran Theology After 1580,* 12.

Wenger, Frederick Samuel (Feb. 8, 1878–July 11, 1963). B. Bern, Switz.; educ. Conc. Sem., St. Louis, Mo.; miss. at large for Minn. and Dak. dist. of the Mo. Syn.; pastor Fair Haven and Kimball, Minn., 1902; prof. Luther Coll., New Orleans, La., 1906; pastor Frohna, Mo., 1910; prof. Conc. Sem., Springfield, Ill., 1923. See also *Brief Statement.*

Wenner, George Unangst (May 17, 1844–Nov. 1, 1934). B. near Bethlehem, Pa.; educ. Union Theol. Sem., NYC; founded Ger. Luth. Christ Ch., NYC, 1869 and was its pastor till his death. Pres. Ev. Luth. Syn. of N. Y. and N. J. (see *United Lutheran Church, Synods of,* 15) 1904–08; N. Y. Syn. (see *United Lutheran Church, Synods of,* 15) 1908–10. Visited deaconess mother houses in Eur. 1888, and his report led to founding Deaconess Motherhouse, Baltimore, Md., 1895 (see also *Deaconesses,* 8). Helped found FCC. Wrote the "Germanicus" letters in *(The) Lutheran Observer;* issued *Der Sonntagsgast* 1872–1932; other works include an order of worship.

Wennerberg, Gunnar (1817–1901). Luth. composer; b. Lidköping, Swed.; educ. Uppsala; taught at Skara. Works include *Stycken ur Davids psalmer; Jesu födelse; Jesu dom; Jesu död.*

Wenth, Johan (ca. 1495–1541). Luth. theol.; b. Gandersheim, Brunswick, NW Ger.; educ. Wittenberg; reformer with E. Wildensee* of Haderslev and Törning, Schleswig-Holstein.

Werenfels, Peter (1627–1703). Father of S. Werenfels*; Ref. theol.; b. Liestal, Switz.; educ. Basel; archdiaconus Basel cathedral 1655; antistes Basel and prof. Basel U. 1675. Advocated receiving Huguenots and Waldensians as citizens. Works include *Disputationes theologicae.*

Werenfels, Samuel (1657–1704). Son of P. Werenfels*; Ref. theol.; b. Basel, Switz.; educ. Basel; prof. Basel; exponent of a humanistic, rational orthodoxy; dissociated himself from logomachy about verbal inspiration. Works include *Opuscula theologica, philosophica, et philogica;* sermons.

Werfel, Franz (1890–1945). Poet, dramatist, novelist; b. Prague of Jewish parents; to US 1940; tried to give life religious meaning; held that everything temporal is sacred because it comes out of the eternal; tried to depict man against the background of creation, fall, incarnation, and resurrection; his poems call for brotherhood and love.

Werner, Georg (1589–1643). B. Preussisch-Holland, near Elbing (or Elbląg), Prussia; school rector Preussisch-Holland 1616; diaconus Königsberg 1621; hymnist. Hymns include "Nun treten wir ins neue Jahr"; "Der Tod hat zwar verschlungen"; "Freut euch, ihr Christen alle, Gott schenkt uns seinen Sohn!"

Wertheim Bible. Ger. version of the Pentateuch* pub. anonymously at Wertheim, Ger., 1735; product of *rationalismus vulgaris* (a common or popular type of rationalism); printed secretly; a 1737 imperial mandate ordered its confiscation and the apprehension of its author.

Weseloh, Henry (Nov. 1, 1851–Aug. 30, 1925). B. Hanover, Ger.; to US 1868; educ. Conc. Sem., St. Louis, Mo.; pastor Cleveland, Ohio. Ed. *Amerikanischer Kalender für deutsche Lutheraner* 1909-22. Other works include *Das Buch des Herrn und seine Feinde; Gottes Wort eine Gotteskraft; Die Herrlichkeit Gottes in der Natur.*

Wesley Charles (1707[08?]–88). Brother of J. Wesley*; father of S. Wesley*; b. Epworth, Eng.; 18th child and youngest son in the family; educ. Oxford; coll. tutor; helped form Holy* Club; ordained 1735; to Ga. as secy. of James Edward Oglethorpe (1696–1785; b. London, Eng.; mem. parliament; founder of Ga.) 1735 (arrived Feb. 1736); returned to Eng. 1736; influenced by Moravians; nonconformist; itinerant preacher 1739–56. Wrote perhaps more than 6,000 hymns, including "Oh, for a Thousand Tongues to Sing"; "Jesus, Lover of My Soul." See also *Methodist Churches,* 1.

Wesley, John (1703–91). Brother of C. Wesley*; founder of Methodism; b. Epworth, Eng.; educ. Oxford; ordained 1728; joined Holy* Club and became its leader; with C. Wesley to Ga. as miss. 1735; influenced by Moravians; in London again by early 1738; felt his heart "strangely warmed" May 24, 1738, ca. 8:45 p. m., at a Moravian meeting in London while listening to a reading of M. Luther's Preface to Ro; to Herrnhut, Ger., to visit Moravian leaders; on return to Eng. was opposed by organized chs.; nonconformist; began preaching in fields 1739; sent out lay preachers; provided chapels; 1st soc. of followers formed 1740. Traveled extensively in Eng., Ireland, and Scot. For his theol. see *Methodist Churches,* 2. Hymns include tr. from Ger., e. g., "Jesus, Thy Blood and Righteousness"; "Jesus, Thy Boundless Love to Me." See also *Religious Tracts; Scotland, Reformation in,* 5; *United Society.*

M. L. Edwards, *John Wesley and the Eighteenth Century,* rev. ed. (London, 1955); C. W. Williams, *John Wesley's Theology Today* (New York, 1960); V. H. H. Green, *John Wesley* (London, 1964); R. C. Monk, *John Wesley: His Puritan Heritage* (Nashville, Tenn., 1966).

Wesley, Samuel (1766–1837). Son of C. Wesley*; father of S. S. Wesley*; b. Bristol, Eng.; leading Eng. organist of his day; revealed J. S. Bach's music to Eng. listeners. Works include music for RC services.

Wesley, Samuel Sebastian (1810–76). Son of S. Wesley*; b. London, Eng.; organist at various places; prof. of the organ at the Royal Academy of Music, London, 1850; leading Eng. organist of his day. Works include the hymn tune "Aurelia" and other ch. music.

Wesley Foundations. See *Students, Spiritual Care of,* A 3.

Wesleyan Church, The. Formed 1968 by merger of Pilgrim Holiness Ch. (emphasized new birth, sanctification, premillennialism, evangelism; see also *International Apostolic Holiness Union*) and The Wesleyan Methodist Church of America (see *Methodist Churches,* 4 b).

Wesleyan Methodist Association. See *Methodist Churches,* 1.

Wesleyan Methodist Church. See *Methodist Churches,* 1.

Wesleyan Methodist Church of America, The. See *Evangelistic Associations,* 13; *International Apostolic Holiness Union; Methodist Churches,* 4 b; *Wesleyan Church, The.*

Wesleyan Methodist Missionary Society. 1. Miss. soc. of the Meth. Ch. of Gt. Brit. and Ireland which traces its origin to miss. work among slaves on the is. of Antigua 1786 and was formally organized Leeds, Eng., 1813; usually called Meth. Missionary Soc. 2. The Missionary Soc. of the Wesleyan Meth. Ch. of Am. was founded Syracuse, N. Y., 1862;

dept. of world missions of The Wesleyan* Meth. Ch. of Am.; often called Wesleyan World Missions.

Wesleyan Reformers. See *Methodist Churches,* 1.

Wessel (Wessel [Harmeness; Harmenss] Gansfort; Goesevoyrdt; 1st name perhaps John, originally perhaps Johann[es]; ca. 1419/20–89). Mystic, philos.; b. Groningen, Neth.; studied at several univs.; active in various cities, esp. Paris, Fr.; spent last yrs. in the Neth.; regarded by many as a "reformer* before the Reformation" (see *Reformation, Lutheran,* 4). Works include *Farrago rerum theologicarum uberrima;* treatise on the Lord's Supper.

Wessel, Louis (July 14, 1864–Jan. 31, 1933). B. St. Louis, Mo.; educ. Conc. Sem., St. Louis; pastor near Nokomis, Ill., 1886–92; prof. Conc. Sem., Springfield, Ill., 1892–1933. Works include *Sermons and Addresses on Fundamentals; The Prooftexts of the Catechism with a Practical Commentary; Festival and Occasional Sermons.*

Wessenberg, Ignaz Heinrich von (1774–1860). RC theol.; b. Dresden, Ger.; educ. Dillingen, Würzburg, Vienna; priest 1812; administrator of the diocese of Constance 1817; fostered continued clerical educ. after ordination; promoted principles of J. H. Pestalozzi* in schools; introd. masses in the vernacular; relaxed laws of celibacy; advocated a Ger. Cath. ch. only loosely connected with Rome. Works include *Über die Folgen der Säcularisation; Die deutsche Kirche; Betrachtungen über die Verhältnisse der katholischen Kirche im Umfange des Deutschen Bundes; Die grossen Kirchenversammlungen des 15ten und 16ten Jahrhunderts.*

West, Evangelical Lutheran Synod of the. For beginnings see *Kentucky Synod,* 2; name Ev. Luth. Syn. of the West adopted 1835 (Syn. of the West I); included Tenn., Ky., Ind. Ill., and parts of Ohio, Mo., Iowa, and Wis. Joined The General* Syn. of the Ev. Luth. Ch. in the USA 1841. Split 1846 into Ev. Luth. Syn. of Illinois,* Syn. of the Southwest,* and Ev. Luth. Syn. of the West (Syn. of the West II). Shortly thereafter in 1846 a few mems. of the Syn. of the West (II), suspecting a move to attach that syn. to the Gen. Syn., withdrew and organized the Ger. Ev. Luth. Syn. of Indianapolis.* Some mems. of the Syn. of the West (II) were absorbed by the Miami* Syn. and by the Olive Branch Syn. (see *Indiana Synod, Northern; United Lutheran Church, Synods of,* 8). The ch. at Fort Wayne, Ind., of which W. Sihler* was pastor, helped form the Mo. Syn. 1847 and with ratification of its delegate action severed its connection with the Syn. of the West (II). There is no record of any further meeting of the Syn. of the West (II).

J. B. Gardner, "The Synod of the West," *CHIQ,* I, No. 4 (Jan. 1929), 84–91.

West, Gilbert (1703–56). Brit. author; educ. Oxford; served in army; employed by secy. of state; retired to Wickham ca. 1729. Works include *Observations on the Resurrection of Jesus Christ;* poetry, including "Education" and "Institution of the Order of the Garter." See also *Deism,* IV.

West, Liturgical. See *Orientation of Churches.*

West, Missionary Synod of the (1840s). See *Michigan Synod,* 1.

West, Missionary Synod of the (Franckean Syn. II). Organized 1866 by some pastors of the Franckean* Syn. and some pastors of the Iowa Syn. Disbanded 1872.

West, Synod of the. See *West, Evangelical Lutheran Synod of the.*

West, The German Evangelical Church Society of the. See *German Evangelical Church Society of the West, The.*

West Borneo. West Kalimantan (see *Indonesia,* 1, 5).

West Indies. See *Caribbean Islands.*

West Indies Federation, British. See *Caribbean Islands,* E 5.

West Indies Mission. The Cuba Bible Institute, *Los Pinos Nuevos,* from which the West Indies Mission developed, opened 1928 near Placetas, cen. Cuba. Fields have included Brazil, Cuba, Dominican Rep., Guadeloupe, Haiti, Jamaica, Surinam, Trinidad and Tobago, Windward Is.

West Irian. See *Indonesia,* 1, 7; *New Guinea,* 1, 2.

West New Guinea (West Irian). See *Indonesia,* 1, 7; *New Guinea,* 1, 2.

West Pennsylvania Synod. See *United Lutheran Church, Synods of,* 22, 23.

West Virginia Synod. See *United Lutheran Church, Synods of,* 31.

Westcott, Brooke Foss (1825–1901). B. near Birmingham, Eng.; educ. Cambridge; ordained 1851; canon Peterborough 1869–83; prof. divinity Cambridge 1870–90; mem. of committee for rev. Eng. tr. of NT 1870–81; bp. Durham 1890. Active in Christian Socialist movement (see also *Christian Social Union).* Textual critic. With F. J. A. Hort* pub. critical ed. of Gk. NT.

Westen, Thomas von (Sept. 13, 1682–Apr. 9, 1727). "Apostle to Norw. Finns"; b. Trondheim, Norw.; pastor on is. of Veoy (formerly Vedoy; Ger.. Weö, or Wedöen), in Romsdal Fjord, 1710; chief of miss. to Finns 1716; made miss. tours among Finns 1716, 1718, 1722. See also *Lapland; Norway, Lutheranism in,* 8.

Western Canada, Synod of. See *Canada,* A 14; *United Lutheran Church, Synods of,* 32.

Western Canada Synod (LCA–Can. Section). See *Canada,* A 27.

Western Christianity 500–1500. 1. The period of ca. 1,000 yrs. from the 6th to the 16th cents. is sometimes called Middle* Age(s) (a term that acquired some overtones of barbarism and superstition, but which is essentially time-oriented, referring to the middle bet. ancient times and the "last times"; as hist. unfolds it becomes increasingly meaningless).

2. Ca. 500 Christianity was largely limited to the Mediterranean basin. By 1000 it had spread throughout Eur., fostered by popes, princes, and monks. See *Augustine of Canterbury; Celtic Church; Clovis I; England,* A 2; *France,* 1; *Palladius* (5th c.); *Patrick; Popes,* 4.

3. In the 7th and 8th cents. missionaries from Eng. evangelized Belg., Holland, and the coasts of the North Sea. See *Boniface; Columban; Netherlands,* 1; *Suidbert; Symbolism, Christian,* 4–5; *Willibrord.*

4. On the conversion of Saxony see *Germany,* A. On Scandinavia see *Ansgar; Denmark; Iceland; Norway, Early Christianity in; Sweden, Conversion of, to Christianity.* On Christianization of E Eur. see *Charlemagne; Czechoslovakia,* 1–2; *Hungary; Poland.*

5. During much of the Middle Ages, Eur. Christianity was involved in feudalism, an economic and pol. system in which wealth was reckoned on basis of land, and the ch. and clergy, by holding lands (or estates, called feuds) under several forms of tenure, became an integral part of the soc. and economic fabric. Bps. and abbots often functioned as secular princes having obligations of service to other lords and in turn receiving homage from inferior vassals. Theoretically each ch. was under jurisdiction of a bp., but many were controlled by lay lords. This led to the struggle about investiture.* In some cases the church's victory led ecclesiastics to try to dominate secular princes. By the end of the Middle Ages both the prelates and the Holy Roman emperors (see *Holy Roman Empire*) had been discredited by this power struggle.

6. On the rise of the papacy see *Gregory III; Papacy, 1–4.* When Charlemagne was crowned by the pope 800, a new alliance bet. popes and W emps. began which largely ignored E emps. and patriarchs and marked the beginning of the Holy Roman em-

pire. In course of time popes came to be regarded as final arbiters in matters of dogma and discipline. They retained sole right to create cardinals, ratify election of bps., authenticate relics, canonize saints, and absolve grave sins.

7. The pope's advisors came to be called cardinals* (a term of uncertain derivation). In the 8th c. their number was increased from 25 (unchanged since the 6th c.) to 28. Since 1059 they are the papal electors.

8. Most potent of the church's means of enforcing ch. discipline* was the interdict*; excommunication* was another. Day-by-day ch. govt. on the local level was carried on by bps. (see *Bishop*), whose chs. were called cathedrals (see *Cathedral*). For assistants to bps. see *Archdeacon; Canon,* 2; *Chapter.* Theoretically bps. were to be elected by canons, asked for by the people, and consecrated by the abp; practically there often was external pressure from influential princes which dictated the choice.

9. Basic unit of ch. organization was the parish,* which was served by a priest.* Educ. of priests, derived from other priests, monasteries, or bps., often left much to be desired.

10. Canon* law was formulated gradually and enforced by ch. tribunals (see also *Curia,* 2 e). On councils see *Councils and Synods.*

11. Perhaps the most formative pre-Reformation influence on the W Ch. was monasticism.*

12. Medieval theol. primarily preserved tradition, most profoundly influenced by Augustine* of Hippo.

13. Medieval theol. was marked by adoptionist (see *Adoptionism*), eucharistic,* Filioque,* iconoclastic,* and predestinarian* controversies. The number of RC sacraments* was not defined till 1547. Superstition, ignorance, and abuses beclouded the light of the Gospel. Man sought serenity and stability in the practice of a groping faith.

14. Scholasticism* was the dominant philos. movement in the later Middle Ages. Mystics (see *Mysticism*) emphasized contemplation in reaching for the Infinite.

15. Struggle for power with secular rulers led to the Babylonian Captivity of the popes (see *Christian Church, History of,* II 3) and the conciliar* movement. These and other factors, including financial abuses, led to decline of the ecclesiastical hierarchy by the end of the 15th c. Primary object of M. Luther's* reform efforts was not removal of outward abuse (much, if not most, of which was corrected by the Council of Trent*) but restoration of the Gospel, difference in definition of which caused continuing cleavage bet. Luths. and RCs. CAV

See also *Latin Christianity.*

Western Schism. See *Schism,* 8.

Western Theological Seminary. 1. Sem. of The General* Syn. of the Ev. Luth. Ch. in the USA founded 1893 at Midland* Coll., Atchison, Kans.; moved to Fremont, Nebr., 1919; separate institution called Cen. Luth. Theol. Sem. 1949; merged with Luth. School of Theol. at Chicago 1966. See also *Ministry, Education of,* X B and X I. 2. Sem. of the Prot. Episc. Ch. est. Chicago, Ill., 1883, united 1933 with Seabury Divinity School (developed from a miss. and school est. 1858 at Faribault, Minn.) in Seabury-Western Theol. Sem., Evanston, Ill. 3. Sem. of the (Dutch) Ref. Ch. in Am. est. 1869 Holland, Ottawa Co., Mich.; suspended 1877–84. 4. See *Pittsburgh Theological Seminary.*

Westminster Assembly. Syn. appointed by the Long Parliament (see *Presbyterian Confessions,* 3) to reform the Eng. Ch.; 1st meeting July 1643; Scottish Commissioners absent after Nov. 1647; met irregularly till 1653. See also *Directory for the Public Worship of God; Henderson Alexander.*

Westminster Catechisms. The Larger Catechism is for ministers, to be explained from the pulpit; the Shorter Catechism is for instruction of the young. Both were approved by the Eng. parliament 1648; the Scot. Ch. adopted them 1648 and again 1690, after temporary repeal under Charles II (see *England,* C 1). The Shorter Catechism is noted for terse brevity and precision; it differs from most other catechisms in the following: (1) The question is embodied in the answer; (2) A new, logical order of topics is substituted for the old hist. order in the Apostles' Creed; (3) It deals in dogmas rather than facts, addressing the intellect rather than the heart; (4) The questions are put in an impersonal form, instead of addressing the learner directly; (5) The answers are theol. and metaphysical. See also *Scotland, Reformation in,* 1.

Westminster Confession. See *Presbyterian Confessions,* 3, 4.

Westminster Fellowship. See *Young People's Organizations, Christian,* III 6.

Westminster Foundation. See *Students, Spiritual Care of,* A 3.

Westminster Standards. Standards of Presbyterianism adopted at Westminster. See also *Presbyterian Confessions,* 3.

Westphal, Joachim (of Eisleben) (d. 1569). Ger. Luth. theol.; preacher Nausitz, near Artern, 1553; diaconus Sangerhausen; preacher Gerbstädt, Co. of Mansfeld; Gnesio-Lutheran. Works include *Der Faulteufel* and *Wider den Hoffartsteufel* (titles are cited in various forms).

Westphal, Joachim (of Hamburg) (1510–74). B. Hamburg, Ger.; educ. Wittenberg; pupil of M. Luther* and P. Melanchthon*; teacher at the Hamburg Johanneum*; lectured at Wittenberg; pastor 1541, supt. 1571 Hamburg. Held with J. Hoeck* that Christ's descent into hell was an expression of His complete humiliation and vicarious suffering; sided with M. Flacius* Illyricus in Adiaphoristic Controversy (see *Adiaphoristic Controversies,* 1); opposed Melanchthon and G. Major*; defended Luther's doctrine of the Lord's Supper against J. Calvin,* J. H. Bullinger,* et al. See also *Micron, Marten.*

Westphalia, Peace of. 1648 treaty that ended the Thirty* Years' War; drawn up in Münster and Osnabrück, Westphalia . Terms dealt with indemnification for various countries, secular affairs of the empire, and ecclesiastical affairs. The latter included: Approval and extension of the Convention of Passau* and the Religious Peace of Augsburg* to include Calvinists. Prots. and RCs to be equal in all affairs of empire. Jan. 1, 1624, to be the normative day (*annus normalis,* Lat. literally "normal year") for determining questions of ownership of ecclesiastical states and of exercise of religion; where this date was indecisive, territorial lords retained *ius reformandi* (Lat. "right of reformation," i.e. to determine religion by fiat); certain rights, including that of emigration, were given to subjects who differed from their ruler in religion. The imperial court was restored and divided equally bet. Prots. and RCs. See also *France,* 13.

Wette, De. See *De Wette.*

Wettstein, Johann Jakob (Wetstein; 1693–1754). NT textual critic; b. Basel, Switz.; educ. Basel; pastor Basel and taught at Basel U.; dismissed 1730; to Amsterdam. Ed. *Novum Testamentum graecum editionis receptae cum lectionibus variantibus.* See also *Arminianism; Textual Criticism,* 3.

Wetzel, Johann Caspar (1691–1755). Ger. ev. hymnist; lived in Meiningen and Römhild. Works include *Hymnopoeographia; Analecta hymnica.*

Wexels, Wilhelm Andreas (1797–1866). Norw. theol. and hymnist; b. Copenhagen, Den.; educ. Christiania (now Oslo); chaplain Oslo cathedral. Opposed rationalism; influenced by N. F. S. Grundtvig.* Works include *Andagtsbog for Menigmand; Christelige*

Psalmer; Psalmebog; Foredrag over Pastoraltheologien.

Weyer, Anthony (Anton; Weier; ca. 1760–Mar. 30, 1829). Early settler in Stark Co., Ohio; licensed by Pa. Ministerium 1812; ordained 1819 by Ohio Syn. (see *Ohio and Other States, The Evangelical Lutheran Joint Synod of*); pastor in Ohio.

Weyermüller, Friedrich (1810–77). Luth. poet; b. Niederbronn, at E foot of the lower Vosges, Alsace; acquired comprehensive acquaintance with Ger. poetry early on; mem. consistory Niederbronn 1852. Poems adapted as hymns include "O Jesu, Freund der Sünder."

Weygand, John Albert (Aug. 26, 1722–Mar. 1770). B. Hanau, Ger.; educ. Halle; to US 1748. Pastor on the Raritan, N. J., 1748; NYC and Hackensack, N. J., 1753. Tr. *The Whole System of the XXVIII Articles of the Evangelical unvaried Confession.*

Weygandt, G. Henry (May 2, 1779–Oct. 7, 1847). B. Northumberland Co., Pa.; licensed 1809 as catechist, 1810 as candidate, for Washington Co., Pa., by Pa. Ministerium; ordained deacon 1815. Pastor Washington Co., Pa., and Wayne Co., Ohio. Helped organize Special Conference 1812 which led 1818 to beginning of the Ohio Syn., in which he was also active (see *Ohio and Other States, The Evangelical Lutheran Joint Synod of,* 1–2).

Weys(s), Michael. See *Weisse, Michael.*

Whately, Richard (1787–1863). B. London, Eng.; educ. Oxford; prof. pol. economy Oxford 1829; abp. Dublin, Ireland, 1831. Works include *Apostolical Succession Considered; Essays on Some of the Difficulties in the Writings of the Apostle Paul; Essays on the Errors of Romanism; The Kingdom of Christ Delineated; Historic Doubts Relative to Napoleon Buonaparte; Elements of Logic.*

Wheat Ridge Foundation. Est. 1944 by the Walther League (see *Young People's Organizations, Christian,* II 3); continues work that traces its beginning to 1903, when a small group of Denver, Colo., Luths. organized The Ev. Luth. Sanitarium Assoc. of Denver, Colo.; this assoc. was inc. 1904; it bought land May 1905 near Denver; a tent colony, or "health farm," was dedicated Sept. 1905 and came to be known as Wheat Ridge; from the outset it received support from the Walther League, which assumed ownership and control 1927.

Whichcote, Benjamin (Whichcot; Whitchcote; 1609–83). B. Whichcote Hall, Stoke, Shropshire, Eng.; educ. Cambridge; priest; preacher Trin. Ch., Cambridge; provost King's Coll., Cambridge; vice-chancellor Cambridge U. 1650; deposed from provostship after the Restoration (see *England,* C); then served parishes in London; leading mem. Cambridge* Platonists. Works include *Select Sermons; Moral and Religious Aphorisms.*

Whipple, Fred Lawrence. See *Evolution, I.*

Whipple, Henry Benjamin (1822–1901). Prot. Episc. cleric; b. Adams, Jefferson Co., N. Y.; active in Rome, N. Y., 1850–57 and Chicago, Ill., 1857–59; bp. Minn. 1859; worked to remove injustice and cruelty to Indians. See also *Indians, American,* 9.

Whiston, William (1667–1752). Arian theol.; mathematician; b. Norton juxta Twycross, near Leicester, Leicestershire, Eng.; educ. Cambridge. Tr. works of F. Josephus.* Other works include *Primitive Christianity Revived; An Essay Towards Restoring the True Text of the Old Testament and for Vindicating the Citations Made Thence in the New Testament.*

Whitaker, William (1548–95). B. Holme, near Manchester, Eng.; educ. Cambridge; prof. Cambridge; anti-RC. Helped draft Lambeth Arts. (see *Anglican Confessions,* 7); other works include *A Disputation on Holy Scripture, Against the Papists, Especially Bellarmine and Stapleton.*

Whitby, Daniel (1638–1726). B. Rushden, Northamptonshire, Eng.; educ. Oxford; prebendary Salisbury; rector St. Edmund's, Salisbury; anti-RC; sought reconciliation with nonconformists. Works include *The Protestant Reconciler; A Paraphrase and Commentary on the New Testament; The Fallibility of the Roman Church Demonstrated; Last Thoughts.* See also *Arminianism.*

Whitby, Synod of. Assembly convened ca. 664 by the king of Northumbria to settle differences bet. Irish and RCs, e.g., date of Easter and shape of tonsure. See also *Easter Controversy; England,* 2; *Wilfrid.*

White, Ellen Gould (nee Harmon; 1827–1915). B. Gorham, Maine; originally Meth.; became Adv.; claimed visions of heavenly Jerusalem. Works include *Gospel Workers; Der Weg zu Christo.* See also *Adventist Bodies,* 3, 4.

White, Henry Julian (1859–1934). Biblical scholar; b. Islington, Greater London, Eng.; educ. Oxford; ordained priest 1886; domestic chaplain of bp. John Wordsworth (1843–1911) 1886; taught at Oxford from 1895, at King's Coll., London, from 1905. Worked on Wordsworth's ed. of Vulgate; coauthor *A Grammar of the Vulgate.*

White, Henry Kirke (1785–1806). Hymnist; b. Nottingham, Eng.; d. while a student at Cambridge; known for early development of his genius. Hymns include "Much in sorrow, oft in woe" (rev. as "Oft in sorrow, oft in woe").

White, Mrs. M. See *Evangelistic Associations,* 3.

White, Thomas. See *Baptist Churches,* 22.

White, William (1748–1836). Prot. Episc. cleric; b. Philadelphia, Pa.; educ. Coll. of Philadelphia; rector Christ Ch., Philadelphia; active at 1785 conv. (see *Protestant Episcopal Church, The,* 2); bp. Pa. 1787–1836; presiding bp. of the ch. 1796–1836. See also *Protestant Episcopal Church, The,* 3.

White Cross League (Ger.: Weisses Kreuz). Organized 1883 by J. B. Lightfoot* against immorality; spread to N. Am. 1885, Fr. 1889, Ger. 1890. Not to be confused with Weisses* Kreuz.

White Friars. See *Carmelites.*

White Horse Inn. See *England,* B 2.

White Monks. See *Cistercians.*

White Thursday. See *Gründonnerstag.*

Whitefield, George (1714–70). Founder of Calvinistic* Methodism; b. Gloucester, Eng.; educ. Oxford; mem. Holy* Club; deacon 1736; in Ga. 1738; returned to Eng. late in 1738 to raise funds for orphanage; ordained priest; began open-air preaching 1739; parted company with C. and J. Wesley* in the early 1740s; presided at 1st Calvinistic Meth. Conference, held at Waterford, Wales, Jan. 5, 1743; visited Scot. and Ireland; made 7 trips to US. See also *Presbyterian Churches,* 4 a.

Whitehead, Alfred North (1861–1947). Philos., mathematician; b. Ramsgate, on the Isle of Thanet, NE Kent, SE Eng.; educ. Cambridge. Taught at Cambridge 1885–1911; U. of London 1911–24; Harvard U., Cambridge, Mass., 1924–ca. 1938. His view, which he called philos. of organism, is based on the patterned process of events; only what appears, what is given in perception, is real; relations bet. things or events consist in a kind of feeling; every actual entity is a "prehensive occasion"; the actual world is a certain selection of eternal objects; God is the source of unactualized possibilities (his "primordial nature") and conserver of actualized values (his "consequent nature"). See also *Time.*

Whitehead, John (1630–96). Quaker; b. Owstwick in Holderness, Yorkshire, Eng.; itinerant preacher; often imprisoned. Works include *The Enmitie between the Two Seeds; For the Vineyard of the Lord of Hosts; Ministers among the People of God (Called Quakers) No Jesuites.*

Whitgift, John (ca. 1530–1604). B. Great Grimsby, Lincolnshire, Eng.; educ. Cambridge; prof. theol. Cambridge 1563; vice-chancellor Cambridge 1570;

bp. Worcester 1577; abp. Canterbury 1583. Helped draft Lambeth Arts. (see *Anglican Confessions, 7*).

Whitman, Marcus (Sept. 4, 1802–Nov. 29, 1847). B. Rushville, N. Y.; studied medicine at Berkshire Med. Coll., Pittsfield, Mass.; physician in Can. and Wheeler, N. Y.; ABCFM miss. to Oregon region; helped est. miss. stations at Waiilatpu (near present Walla Walla, Wash.), Lapwai (near present Lewiston, Idaho), and elsewhere. Massacred by Cayuse. See also *Indians, American,* 13.

Whitsunday (Pentecost). See *Church Year,* 5, 10, 16.

Wichern, Johann Hinrich (1808–81). Founder of Inner* Mission; b. Hamburg, Ger.; educ. Göttingen and Berlin; S. S. teacher Hamburg; founded Rauhes Haus in Horn, suburb of Hamburg, as rescue home for boys; girls were included later. Emphasized love, freedom, and joy; est. training school for helpers, later called Brüderanstalt. Ed. *Die fliegende Blätter aus dem Rauhen Hause.* Other works include *Nothstände der protestantischen Kirche und die innere Mission; Die innere Mission der deutschen evangelischen Kirche; Denkschrift.* See also *Charities, Christian,* 5; *Christian Socialism,* 4.

Wiclif, John. See *Wycliffe, John.*

Widensee, Eberhard (Weidensee; ca. 1486–1547). B. Hildesheim, Ger.; educ. Leipzig; Augustinian; began preaching Luth. sermons 1523; deposed 1524; preacher Magdeburg 1524, Hadersleben 1526; with J. Wenth* gave Luth. direction to Reformation in Haderslev and Törning, Schleswig-Holstein.

Widor, Charles Marie Jean Albert (1845–1937). B. Lyons, Fr.; organist Paris 1870–1933; prof. of organ and composition Paris 1890. Works include operas; orchestral music; chamber music; organ music; a mass, 2 Psalms, and other ch. music; with Albert Schweitzer* coed. organ works of J. S. Bach.* See also *Offertory.*

Wiebusch, C. A. See *Australia, Lutheranism in,* A 5.

Wiebusch Printery. See *Publication Houses, Lutheran.*

Wied, Hermann von. See *Hermann von Wied.*

Wiek, Amund Larson (Jan. 19, 1861–Sept. 30, 1922). B. Rio, Wis.; attended Northwestern Bible and Mission Training School, Minneapolis, Minn. Pastor Minneapolis, Cokato, and French Lake, Minn.; Sisseton, S. Dak.; mem. Eielsen* Synod. Ed. *Den Kristelige Laegmand.*

Wieland, Christoph Martin (1733–1813). Poet, prose writer; b. Oberholzheim, near Biberach, Ger.; educ. Magdeburg and Tübingen; lived mainly in Weimar from 1772. Held that poetry should serve religion. Saw in the sovereignty of the people advocated in the Fr. Revolution a new pol. religion.

Wiener, Paul (d. 1554). B. Laibach (ancient Emona; now Ljubljana, or Lyublyana, Slovenia, NW Yugoslavia); canon (or prebendary) and gen. vicar Laibach 1520; mem. diet Laibach 1530; joined P. Truber's* ev. movement ca. 1536; imprisoned 1547; released by the emp. 1548 on condition of emigration to Hermannstadt (now Sibiu), cen. Romania, Transylvania, where he became pastor 1549, city pastor 1552, bp. 1553.

Wieseler, Karl (1813–83). Luth. theol.; b. Altencelle, near Celle, Hannover, Ger.; educ. Göttingen; prof. Kiel and Greifswald; fields of activity: OT and NT exegesis, isagogics, NT criticism, Biblical and early Christian hist.; effectively opposed the concept and treatment of early Christendom developed by D. F. Strauss* and F. C. Baur.*

Wieselgren, Peter Jonasson. See *Sweden, Lutheranism in,* 5.

Wiesenmeyer, Burchard (Burkhard; 17th c.). Hymnist; b. Helmstädt (Helmstedt), Ger.; taught at Grey* Friars Gymnasium, Berlin, probably 1635–45; helped J. Crüger* prepare 1640 Luth. hymnal. Hymns include "Wie schön leucht't uns der Morgenstern"; "Das alte Jahr ist nun dahin."

Wigand, Johann(es) (1523–87). B. Mansfeld, Ger.; educ. Wittenberg; taught in Nürnberg 1541–44; preacher Mansfeld 1546; supt. and pastor Magdeburg 1553; prof. Jena 1560; deposed 1561; supt. Wismar 1562; returned to Jena 1568; deposed again 1573; prof. Königsberg; bp. Pomesania 1575, Samland 1577. Staunch Luth. in various controversies. Coauthor Magdeburg* Centuries. See also *Adiaphoristic Controversies,* 1; *Flacius Illyricus, Matthias; Gnesio-Lutherans; Synergistic Controversy.*

Wikner, Carl Pontus (1837–88). Swed. Luth. pastor, philos., author, poet; educ. Uppsala; taught at Uppsala; prof. philos. Christiania (now Oslo) 1884. Rejected the orthodox 2-nature doctrine and the liberal concept of Christ as ideal man; pictured Christ as "the friend."

Wilberforce, William (1759–1833). Philanthropist, pol.; b. Hull, Yorkshire, Eng.; educ. Cambridge; mem. House of Commons 1780; became ev. Christian ca. 1784/85; antislavery agitator; supported extension of miss. work in India. See also *Thornton, Henry.*

Wilbrord (Wilbrod). See *Willibrord.*

Wilbur, John. See *Friends, Society of,* 7.

Wilburites. See *Friends, Society of,* 7.

Wilbye, John (ca. 1574–1638). Madrigal* composer; b. Diss, S Norfolk, Eng.; resident musician Hengrave, near Bury Saint Edmunds ca. 1595; spent last 10 yrs. at Colchester. Works include 2 sacred compositions.

Wilcken, Hermann. See *Lercheimer, Augustin.*

Wilfrid (Wilfrith; 634–ca. 709). Eng. prelate; favored Rome at Syn. of Whitby* 664; bp. York ca. 668; exiled when he objected to division of see; evangelized south Saxons; bp. Hexham ca. 706. See also *Germany,* A 1.

Wilke, Christian Gottlob (1786–1854). NT exegete; b. Badrina, near Delitzsch, Saxony, Ger.; pastor Hermannsdorf 1821–36; RC 1846. Works include *Der Urevangelist; Die neutestamentliche Rhetorik; Die Hermeneutik des Neuen Testaments; Clavis Novi Testamenti philologica.* See also *Grimm, Karl Ludwig Willibald; Lexicons,* B.

Wilkens, Cornelius August (1829–1914). Ref. theol.; pastor Vienna 1861, The Hague 1879–81. Opposed rationalism, liberalism, and state ch. Works include biography of P. Abelard.*

Wilkinson, John Gardner (1797–1875). Traveler, Egyptologist; b. probably Hardendale, Westmorland, Eng.; educ. Oxford. Works include *The Mamners and Customs of the Ancient Egyptians.*

Wilkinson, William (d. 1613). Educ. Cambridge, Eng.; taught at Cambridge; opposed H. Niclaes.*

Will, Enslaved and Free. See *Conversion,* I; *Free Will; Luther, Chief Writings of,* 5.

Will, Robert (1869–1959). B. Assweiler, SE Saar; educ. Strasbourg, Berlin, Paris; pastor Masevaux 1894, Strasbourg 1901–22; prof. Strasbourg 1919–37, Clermont-Ferrand 1939–45; mem. consistory Ch. of the Augsburg Confession. Works include *Tauler; La Liberté chrétienne; Der Gottesdienst Augsburger Konfession in Elsass und Lothringen.*

Willaert, Adrian (Adriaan; Adriaen; Adrien; Villard; Villahert; Vuigliart; Hadrian; Adriano Fiammingo; ca. 1480/90–1562). B. perhaps Brugge (Bruges) or Roeselare (Roulers), West Flanders, NW Belg.; maestro di cappella St. Mark's, Venice, 1527; founded a singing-school. Works include masses, motets, madrigals, psalms, hymns. See also *Venetian School of Church Music.*

Willard, Frances Elizabeth Caroline (1839–98). B. Churchville, N. Y.; educ. Northwestern Female Coll., Evanston, Ill.; teacher; pres. 1871, dean of women 1873 Evanston Coll. for Ladies; corresponding secy. 1874, pres. 1879 Nat. Woman's Christian Temperance Union; pres. World's Woman's Christian Temperance Union. Favored woman's suffrage as early as 1877; mem. Ex. Committee of the Prohibition Party 1884.

William I (1533–84). "The Silent" because, though eloquent, he learned to hold his tongue; 1st stadholder of Holland 1579–84 (made hereditary 1581); b. Dillenburg, Hesse, Gerf., of Luth. parents; succeeded to principality of Orange 1544; Charles* V required 1544 that he be educ. RC in the Neth.; count of Nassau 1559; led revolt against Sp. 1568–76; Calvinist 1573. The 7 N provinces of the Neth. concluded the Union of Utrecht 1579, followed 1581 by proclamation of indep. from Spain. William I was assassinated.

William I (king of the Neth.). See *Netherlands,* 1.

William I (Ger. emp.). See *Kulturkampf.*

William III and Mary II. See *England,* C 2.

William of Auvergne (Guillaume de Paris; Guillaume d'Auvergne; ca. 1180/90–1248/49). Theol. and philos.; b. Aurillac, Fr.; taught theol. at Paris; bp. Paris 1228. Works, significant for the development of scholasticism, include *De universo.*

William of Auxerre (ca. 1150–1231). Scholastic theol.; b. Auxerre, Fr.; archdeacon Beauvais; taught at Paris; formulated the concept that the minimum required for the sacramental intention of a priest (see *Sacraments, Roman Catholic*) is that he will to do what the ch. does. Works include *Summa super quattuor libros sententiarum* (also known as *Summa aurea,* "Golden Compendium").

William of Champeaux (Guillaume de Champeaux; Guglielmus de Campellis; ca. 1070–1121). Scholastic philos.; b. Champeaux, Fr.; studied under Anselm* of Laon and Roscellinus*; taught in the cathedral school of Notre Dame, Paris; archdeacon of Paris ca. 1100 (retired 1108); founded Order of St. Victor (see *Victorines*); bp. Châlons-sur-Marne 1113; differed with P. Abelard,* one of his pupils, over universals (words that can be applied to more than 1 particular thing); realist.

William of Conches (Gulielmus de Conchis; ca. 1080–ca. 1154). B. Conches, Normandy; probably pupil of Bernard* of Chartres; taught at Chartres beginning in the early 1120s; pupils included John* of Salisbury. Works include *De philosophia mundi; Dragmaticon.*

William of Malmesbury (Gulielmus Malmesburiensis; ca. 1090/96–ca. 1143/45). Hist.; b. perhaps Somerset, Eng.; educ. Malmesbury Abbey; librarian Malmesbury Abbey. Works include *De gestis regum Anglorum* (to ca. 1125/28); *Historia novella* (to 1142); *De gestis pontificum Anglorum.*

William of Newburgh (1136–ca. 1198). Hist.; b. Bridlington, Yorkshire, Eng.; entered Augustinian priory of Newburgh as a boy; apparently remained there the rest of his life. Works include *Historia rerum Anglicarum.*

William of Ockham (Occam). See *Ockham, William of.*

William of Paris. See *William of Auvergne.*

William of Saint-Thierry (ca. 1085–1148). B. Liège, Belg.; studied under Anselm* of Laon; abbot of the monastery of Saint-Thierry, near Reims, 1119; joined Cistercians* at Signy, in the forest of the Ardennes, 1135; friend of Bernard* of Clairvaux; opposed P. Abelard* and William* of Conches.

William the Rich (of Nassau-Katzenelnbogen). See *Sarcerius, Erasmus.*

Williams, Eleazar (ca. 1789–Aug. 28, 1858). Probably b. Sault St. Louis (Caughnawaga), S Quebec, Can.; half-breed son of a St. Regis Indian; scout for Americans in War of 1812; appointed lay reader and catechist by an Episc. bp. for miss. work among Indians; led group of Oneida chiefs to Green Bay, Wis., to est. an Indian empire; lost favor of Indians for various reasons; claimed to be "lost dauphin" of France. Tr. selected prayers from the Book* of Common Prayer into Iroquois. See also *Indians, American,* 9.

Williams, George (1821–1905). Founder of YMCA; b. Dulverton, Somersetshire, Eng.; converted at a Cong. service; worked for soc. reform.

Williams, John (June 29, 1796–Nov. 20, 1839). "The apostle of Polynesia"; b. London, Eng.; LMS miss. to Society* Is. 1816; settled on Raiatea 1818; discovered Rarotonga (see *Cook Islands*) 1823, where he later tr. parts of the Bible into the native tongue; in Eng. 1833/34–38; returned to South Pacific with 16 other missionaries; killed and eaten by natives on Eromanga (Erromanga), New* Hebrides. See also *Samoa.*

Williams, Roger (ca. 1603–83). Founder of Rhode Is.; probably b. London, Eng.; to US 1630/31; active in Plymouth Colony and Salem; banished 1635 for criticizing civil authorities; founded Providence 1636, where obedience to the majority was promised by all, but "only in civil things"; Bap. a few months, then a "Seeker" or "Come-outer," holding that no ch. had all marks of the true ch. Works include *The Bloody Tenent* (title occurs in various forms). See also *Baptist Churches,* 3.

Williams, William (1717–91). Hymnist; b. Cefn-y-Coed, near Llandovery, Carmarthenshire, Wales, ordained deacon of the est. ch. 1740; served 2 curacies 3 yrs.; became Calvinistic Meth. preacher. Hymns include the one tr. as "Guide Me, O Thou Great Jehovah."

Williamson, Alexander (Dec. 5, 1829–Aug. 28, 1890). B. Falkirk, Scot.; educ. Glasgow; LMS miss. to China 1855–58; to China again 1863 as agent of the Nat. Bible Soc. of Scot. (see *Bible Societies,* 4) and in connection with the United Presb. Ch. of Scot. mission. Sold Christian books also to Koreans on the Manchurian border of Korea. Founded Book and Tract Soc. for China, which grew into the Society* for the Diffusion of Christian and Gen. Knowledge Among the Chinese.

Willibrord (Wilbrord; Wilbrod; ca. 657–ca. 738). "Apostle of the Frisians"; b. Northumbria; perhaps Anglo-Saxon; miss. to N Ger. and Denmark*; said to have been abp. of the Frisians ca. 695, residing at Utrecht. See also *Germany,* A 1; *Netherlands,* 1; *Suidbert.*

Willkomm, Karl Martin (1876–1946). Son of O. H. T. Willkomm*; b. Madura(i), S Tamil Nadu, S India; to Ger. 1876; educ. Conc. Sem., St. Louis, Mo.; asst. pastor Planitz, Ger., 1898. Pastor Mulhouse, Alsace, 1905–19; Planitz 1919–24; dir. theol. sem. at Klein Machnow, near Berlin-Zehlendorf, from 1923/24. Ed. *Die Evangelisch-Lutherische Freikirche* (alternate form: *Die Ev.-Luth. Freikirche*); *Schrift und Bekenntnis.*

Willkomm, Otto Heinrich Theodor (Nov. 30, 1847–Aug. 5, 1933). Father of K. M. Willkomm*; b. Ebersbach, Lusatia, Saxony, Ger.; educ. Leipzig; taught 1868–70 in a private school; active 1870–72 at Leipzig* Ev. Luth. Miss.; in Leipzig miss. in India 1873–76; with C. M. Zorn* and J. F. Zucker* severed connection with Leipzig Miss. and Saxon state ch. for confessional reasons. Pastor Free Ch. cong. Crimmitschau, Saxony, 1876–79; Planitz, near Zwickau, 1879–1917. Pres. Ev.-Luth. Free Ch. in Saxony and Other States 1879–1907. Ed. *Die Evangelisch-Lutherische Freikirche* (alternate form of title: *Die Ev.-Luth. Freikirche); Evangelisch-Lutherischer Hausfreund-Kalender.* See also *Germany, Lutheran Free Churches in,* 5.

Wilpert, Joseph (Josef; 1857–1944). Ger. authority on early Christian art, vestments; archaeologist; at Rome since 1884. Works include *Die römischen Mosaiken und Malereien der kirchlichen Bauten vom IV. bis XIII. Jahrhundert.*

Wilson, Robert Dick (1856–1930). Presb. orientalist; b. Indiana, Pa; prof. in OT dept. of Western Theol.

Sem.; prof. of Semitic philol. and OT introd. at Princeton 1900. Works include *Studies in the Book of Daniel; Elements of Syriac Grammar by an Inductive Method; Is the Higher Criticism Scholarly?*

Wilson, William. See *Associate Reformed Church.*

Wimmer, Richard (1836–1905). Ev. theol. and writer; b. Altenburg, Ger.; pastor Weisweil, Baden, Ger.; published theol., devotional, and poetic writings. Works include *Inneres Leben.*

Wimpfeling, Jakob (Jacob Wimpheling; 1450–1528). Ger. humanist; b. Sélestat, Alsace; educ. Freiburg, Erfurt, Heidelberg; held various positions including prof. of poetry and rhetoric at Heidelberg. Works include *Epitome Germanicarum rerum.*

Winchester Profession. See *Universalists,* 2.

Winckelmann, Johann Joachim (1717–68). Classical art critic and archaeologist; b. Stendal, Ger.; educ. Halle; librarian Nöthnitz; became RC 1754 and lived at Rome. Works include *Geschichte der Kunst des Altertums.*

Winckelmann, Johannes (1551–1626). B. Homburg, Hesse, Ger.; educ. Marburg; rector Homburg; court preacher Kassel 1582; prof. Marburg; deposed; to Giessen, helped found U.; supt. Giessen; champion of Luth. orthodoxy.

Winckler, Hugo (1863–1913). Orientalist; b. Graefenhainichen, near Wittenberg, Ger.; prof. Berlin 1904. Wrote numerous works on Assyriology and related subjects.

Winckler, Johann (1642–1705). Luth. pastor; b. Golzern, near Grimma, Ger.; educ. Grimma, Saint Thomas' in Leipzig, and Leipzig U.; pastor Homburg vor der Höhe 1671; supt. Braubach 1672; court preacher Darmstadt 1676; pastor Mannheim 1678; supt. Wertheim 1679; chief preacher Saint Michael's, Hamburg, 1684; senior minister there 1699. Friend of P. J. Spener,* whose conventicles he defended.

Wind, Henry Frederick (Jan. 2, 1891–Feb. 24, 1966). B. Millard, Nebr.; educ. Conc. Coll., Milwaukee, Wis., and Conc. Sem., St. Louis, Mo.; ordained 1916; pastor Brockport, N. Y.; camp pastor U. S. military 1917; institutional miss. Buffalo, N. Y., 1919–53; ex. secy., LCMS Dept. of Soc. Welfare 1953–66. Ed. *Good News; Associated Lutheran Charities Review; Lutheran Hospice and Institutional Missionary Bulletin; Welfare Review;* other works include *"Towering o'er the Wrecks of Time": Lenten Meditations;* devotional booklets.

Windelband, Wilhelm (1848–1915). B. Potsdam, Ger.; prof. Strasbourg and Heidelberg; held that science may ascertain facts but values must be supplied by philosophy; differentiated method in natural and historical science. Works include *Die Geschichte der neueren Philosophie.*

Windisch, Hans (1881–1935). B. Leipzig, Ger.; taught at Leipzig, Leiden, Kiel, Halle. Exponent of Religionsgeschichtliche* Schule. Works include *Johannes und die Synoptiker.*

Winward Islands. See *Caribbean Islands,* E 7.

Winebrenner, John (Johann Weinbrenner; 1797–1860). B. near Walkersville, Frederick Co., Md.; stud. theol. privately at Philadelphia, Pa.; ordained 1820 by Gen. Syn. of Ger. Ref. Ch.; pastor Harrisburg and neighboring rural parishes; excluded from ch. for Methodistic tendencies; itinerant preacher; leader in founding Gen. Eldership of the Ch. of God 1830 (name changed 1845 to Gen. Eldership of the Ch. of God in N Am., and in 1896 to Gen. Eldership of the Churches* of God in N Am.). Ed. *Gospel Publisher; Church Advocate.* Followers called Winebrennerians.

Winebrennerians. See *Churches of God in North America; Winebrenner, John.*

Winer, Johan Georg Benedikt (1789–1858). B. Leipzig, Ger.; rationalist, but later approached orthodox position; prof. Leipzig, Erlangen, Leipzig; noted for his *Grammatik des neutestamentlichen Sprachidioms,* a standard work for nearly 75 years and repeatedly tr. into Eng. See also *Grammars,* B; *Robinson, Edward.*

Winfrid. See *Boniface.*

Wingren, Gustav. See *Lund, Theology of.*

Winkler, Martin Theodore. See *New Zealand,* 3.

Winkworth, Catherine (1829–78). Sister of S. Winkworth*; b. London, Eng.; cultured, devoted mem. of Ch. of Eng.; active, ardent supporter of societies for educ. and uplift of women. Her lifework was the tr. into Eng. of the best Ger. hymns. This work is embodied in her published *Lyra Germanica* and her *Christian Singers of Germany.* Dr. John Julian says in *A Dictionary of Hymnology:* "Miss Winkworth, although not the earliest of modern translators from the German into English, is certainly the foremost in rank and popularity. Her translations are the most widely used of any from that language and have had more to do with the modern revival of the English use of the German hymns than the versions of any other writer."

Winkworth, Susanna (1820–84). Sister of C. Winkworth*; b. London, Eng.; tr. *Deutsche Theologie* (ed. and pub. by Luther 1516; see *German Theology, A*) into Eng. 1854; tr. J. Tauler's* sermons 1857; completed (1855) *The Life of Luther* begun by Julius Charles Hare.*

Winnebago. See *Indians, Lutheran Missions to North American.*

Winnington-Ingram, Arthur Foley (1858–1946). Anglican bp.; educ. Oxford; ordained 1884; leader of Oxford House in Bethnal Green, London; bp. Stepney 1897; bp. London 1901. Noted preacher. Works include *Fifty Years Work in London.*

Winnipeg Theses. Eight "Theses on the Sacrament of the Altar" adopted by theologians of Luth. chs. in Canada at a free conf. in Winnipeg, Man., Sept. 4–5, 1962.

Winstanley, Gerrard. See *Diggers.*

Winterfeld, Karl Georg August Vivigens von (1784–1852). B. Berlin, Ger.; jurist; among foremost musicologists of 19th c. His *Johannes Gabrieli und sein Zeitalter* (1834) and *Der evangelische Kirchengesang und sein Verhältniss zur Kunst des Tonsatzes* (3 vols.; 1843–47) are still regarded as monumental works. He underestimated the music of J. S. Bach* and of other composers of the Baroque era because he had come under the spell of A. F. J. Thibaut* and others who insisted that only a cappella music may be regarded as ideal choral music for the church.

Wirz, Johann Jakob. See *Nazarenes,* 2.

Wischan, F. (1845–1905). B. Ger.; Luth. pastor Philadelphia 1870; "the soul of the Board of German Missions" of the General Council; ed. *Lutherisches Kirchenblatt.*

Wisconsin Evangelical Lutheran Synod. 1. This body is a consolidation of several separate and indep. Luth. syns.: Wisconsin,* Minnesota,* and Michigan.* Organically it has passed through 2 distinct stages of development, an earlier one in which the constituent syns. retained their individuality and indep., being assoc. with one another only in certain phases of their work, and the present one in which they have reconstituted themselves as one syn. with a number of dists. The first assoc. was formed 1892, the amalgamation took place 1917.

2. The Joint Ev. Luth. Syn. of Wis., Minn., Mich., and Other States (name changed to Ev. Luth. Joint Syn. of Wis. and Other States 1919; Wis. Ev. Luth. Syn. [WELS] 1959) was organized Oct. 11, 1892, in Milwaukee. It united into one body the aforementioned neighboring syns. without destroying their identity, but provided for joint use of their several educ. institutions. Wis. was at that time replacing its old Milwaukee sem. with a new bldg. in Wauwa-

tosa, Wis. This new theol. sem. now became the property of the Joint Syn., with G. A. T. F. Hönecke* as director. Minnesota's Dr. Martin Luth. Coll. at New Ulm, Minn., was converted into a teachers sem. under the directorship of J. Schaller.* Michigan's theol. sem. was supposed to be discontinued and reorganized as a prep. school *(Progymnasium).* Northwestern Coll., Watertown, Wis. (A. F. Ernst,* pres.), was relieved of its normal dept. but provided the presem. course for the ministerial students of the entire body. Home missions were coordinated, but remained under the jurisdiction of the constituent syns. As a new venture the Joint Syn. undertook the evangelization of the Apache Indians of Ariz., first planned by Wis. alone. Wis. and Minn. had both taken part in the founding of the Synodical* Conf., 1872. Mich. had joined 1890. Their doctrinal position and confessional declarations were those of the Syn. Conf. In 1904 the Nebr. Conf. of the Wis. Syn. was given the status of a Dist. Syn. (see also *Nebraska, German Evangelical Lutheran District Synod of*). In the meantime the Joint Syn. had suffered a loss. A majority of the congs. and pastors of the Mich. Syn. had not taken kindly to the thought of closing their theol. sem. Other internal difficulties led to a split within this body, and in 1896 the majority left not only the Joint Syn. but also the Syn. Conf. A minority remained with the Joint Syn. as one of its dists. Ten years later the two groups reconciled their differences, with the result that since 1909 Mich. resumed its old place as a member of the Joint Syn. and also the Syn. Conf. In the following year Mich. Luth. Sem. at Saginaw, which had been closed for some time, was reorganized under the leadership of O. J. R. Hönecke as a prep. school in the growing educ. system of the Joint Syn.

3. By this time the need for redistricting was becoming obvious. As a result a new const. was presented in 1915, approved by the several constituent syns. and dists. 1916, rev. 1917, finally accepted 1919, when the name Ev. Luth. Joint Syn. of Wis. and Other States was adopted. The complete amalgamation which this new const. provided was a fruit of the ever closer cooperation that had been practiced by the member syns. and the mutual understanding which grew out of their joint work. In the new body the old Wis. Syn. accounted for 4 dists.: Northern, Southeastern, and Western Wis., and the Pacific Northwest Dist. (formerly a Wis. miss.). Minn. was made into 2: Minn. and Dak.-Mont.; Mich. and Nebr. (see also *Nebraska, German Evangelical Lutheran District Synod of*) each represented one dist. The Ariz.-Calif. Dist. was added 1954, and the South Atlantic Dist. 1973. The special needs of the Dak.-Mont. Dist. were recognized by the founding in 1928 of Northwestern Luth. Academy at Mobridge, S. Dak. In the following year the theol. sem. was transferred from Wauwatosa to a new set of bldgs. near Thiensville (Mequon), Wis., its present location. The educ. institutions of the WELS now represent a well-integrated system: academies and prep. depts. (on the high school level) at Saginaw, Mobridge, New Ulm, and Watertown; a 2-yr. coll. at Milwaukee, a teachers coll. at New Ulm, and a full 4-year coll. at Watertown; a theol. sem. at Mequon.

During the middle 20s a serious controversy occurred which grew out of some cases of discipline. As a result, a considerable number of pastors and congs. severed their connection with the syn. to form the Protes'tant* Conf. In 1961 the syn. terminated fellowship with the LCMS, and in 1963 it withdrew from the Syn. Conf. Since ca. 1965 the syn. has experienced vigorous growth, with expansion into all parts of the US and to other countries. The syn. is noted for its strict orthodoxy and its repudiation of unionism.*

4. Presidents during the first phase of the synod's existence were A. F. Ernst,* 1892–1901; C. F. W. Gausewitz,* 1901–07 and 1913–17; F. Soll, 1907–13. Since the reorganization of 1917: G. E. Bergemann,* 1917–33; John Brenner, 1933–53; Oscar Naumann, 1953–. Statistics (1972): congregations 990; pastors serving parishes 787; baptized members 385,077; communicant members 278,442; contributions for home purposes $26,587,709, for work at large $8,204,693 (for statistics on educ. see *Parish Education,* D 9, E 10, G 1). Official publications include *The Northwestern Lutheran* (established by Joint Synod 1913); *Wisconsin Theological Quarterly* (established in 1903 as *Theologische Quartalschrift*). The syn. also owns and operates Northwestern Pub. House, Milwaukee. Charitable institutions include homes for the aged in Belle Plaine, Minn.; Milwaukee and Fountain City, Wis.; and Holt, Saginaw, and South Lyon, Mich. ER

J. P. Köhler, *Geschichte der Allgemeinen Evangelisch-Lutherischen Synode von Wisconsin und andern Staaten* (Milwaukee, 1925), tr., rev., and updated by author, "The History of the Wisconsin Synod," *Faith–Life,* XI, 2–XVII, L (Feb. 1938–Jan. 1944), ed. L. D. Jordahl and pub. in book form 1970; A. P. Sitz and G. A. Westerhaus, "Brief History of the Wisconsin Synod," *Northwestern Lutheran,* May 5, 1940; Martin Lehninger, *Continuing in His Word,* 1951.

Wisconsin Synod. 1. Pastors J. Mühlhäuser,* John Weinmann (perished at sea 1858), and W. Wrede (later returned to Germany) founded The First Ev. Luth. Syn. of Wis. at Milwaukee, Dec. 8, 1849. It was formally organized May 1850 at Granville, a village near Milwaukee, as The Ger. Ev. Luth. Ministerium of Wis. The name was subsequently changed to The Ger. Ev. Luth. Syn. of Wis. and Other (Adjacent) States (Die Deutsche Evangelisch-Lutherische Synode von Wisconsin und Andern [Angrenzenden] Staaten; constitution 1853). There were 2 other pastors present, the 5 serving 18 congs. The founders were graduates of the Barmen Training School for Missionaries and were sent to Am. by the Langenberg Soc., for some years the chief source from which pastors were drawn. Mühlhäuser and his associates were Luths. and upheld the Luth. Confessions, as their first const. shows, but they did not espouse the strict confessionalism for which the syn. later became noted. Congregational delegates constituted the "synod" together with the pastors, but the "ministerium" reserved for itself certain privileges, for example, in the licensing and ordaining of ministers. The great problem was to secure suitable pastors. Mühlhäuser established connections with Pa. Ministerium (see *United Lutheran Church, Synods* of, 22) and with individual pastors in the E and also kept in close touch with the Langenberg Soc., which was soon reenforced in its Am. undertakings by the Berlin Society. The Barmen school furnished many of the early ministers. Others came from Basel. Among these pioneers were C. F. Goldammer, J. Bading,* P. Köhler,* W. Streissguth,* E. Mayerhoff, G. Reim, P. Sprengling, G. Fachtmann, E. F. Moldehnke,* T. Meumann.

2. As the tide of immigration spread and congs. were est. as far N as Green Bay and W as La Crosse, the need for trained men became increasingly acute. The syn., which had already shown a trend toward greater confessionalism, decided in 1863 to est. its own sem. and college. Bading was sent to Eur. to collect funds and a library. Though his mission was successful, the syn. did not reap the results; the money was retained by the Ger. authorities because the Wis. Syn. had clarified its confessional position to a positive and uncompromising Lutheranism which was distasteful to its former patrons, who belonged to the Prussian State Church. In the mean-

time the sem. had been opened in Sept. 1863 in a dwelling in Watertown, with 2 students and Moldehnke as prof. In the following yr. 11 were enrolled and ground was broken for the first bldg. of Northwestern University, as the combined sem. and coll. was now called. A. Martin* was its first president. G. A. T. F. Hönecke* was called as prof. of theol. in 1866. The Wis. Syn. broke with its unionistic friends in Ger. by its declaration of 1867 and at the same time took a stand against the General* Council because of the latter's lack of a definite position on altar and pulpit fellowship. It came to agreement in doctrine and practice with the Mo. Syn. 1869. At this time a plan was worked out to simplify and strengthen the educ. system. Mo. was to furnish a prof. and send some of its students to Watertown. Wisconsin was to discontinue its sem. and send its students and a prof. to St. Louis. Under this arrangement F. W. Stellhorn* represented Mo. at Watertown from 1869 to 1874. Hönecke was called to St. Louis, eventually declined, however, when the agreement to exchange profs. was suspended by common consent. In 1878 the arrangement was terminated, when Wis. reopened its own sem. under Hönecke, this time in Milwaukee.

3. Having now settled its doctrinal position and found its place in Am. Lutheranism, Wis. cooperated in the founding of the Synodical* Conf. 1872. While not entering upon C. F. W. Walther's* plan for the forming of state syns., Wis. did lend its wholehearted and active support to Mo. in the controversy on election which in 1881 led to the secession of Ohio and a division in the Norwegian Syn. of that time. This controversy did not materially weaken Wis.; it lost a few congs. and pastors, but gained internal strength and also added a few pastors who shared its position.

4. Since the early 60s relations with the Minnesota* Syn. had been friendly. Delegations at syn. meetings were exchanged. A working arrangement was est. whereby the Minn. students were sent to Northwestern Coll. At the same time the *Evangelisch-Lutherisches Gemeinde-Blatt* (founded in 1865 by Wis.) was made the official publication of Minn. as well. When Mich. severed its connection with the General Council in 1888, a closer approach became possible in that direction also and was sponsored particularly by Minn. As a result Mich. first became a member of the Syn. Conf. and then in 1892 joined the other 2 bodies in forming the Joint Syn. of Wis., Minn., Mich., and Other States, an assoc. in which the constituent syns. retained their individuality and indep. but pooled their resources in the field of higher educ. In 1904 Nebr., previously a conference of Wis., attained dist. status in the Joint Syn. (see also *Nebraska, German Evangelical Lutheran District Synod of*). This rather loose type of organization was eventually replaced by a complete amalgamation of these several bodies. A new const. was drafted 1915 and put into operation 1917. In this larger organization (Wisconsin* Ev. Luth. Syn.) the old Wis. Syn. lost its identity. Its presidents until 1917 were Mühlhäuser, 1850–60; Bading, 1860–64; Streissguth, 1864–67; Bading, 1867–89; P. A. von Rohr*, 1889–1908; G. E. Bergemann*, 1908–17. ER

J. P. Köhler, *Geschichte der Allgemeinen Evangelisch-Lutherischen Synode von Wisconsin und andern Staaten* (Milwaukee, 1925), tr., rev., and updated by author, "The History of the Wisconsin Synod," *Faith–Life,* XI, 2–XVII, 1 (Feb. 1938–Jan. 1944). ed. L. D. Jordahl and pub. in book form 1970; A. P. Sitz and G. A. Westerhaus, "Brief History of the Wisconsin Synod," *Northwestern Lutheran,* May 5, 1940.

Wisdom of God. Wisdom is the attribute of God by which He chooses, disposes, and directs the proper means to the proper ends (Jb 12:13; Is 55:8-9; 1 Co 2:7). The greatest exhibitions of the wisdom of God are the plan of creation and the plan of salvation. But though these counsels have been in a measure revealed to us, there are many things which God has reserved, in His wisdom, to Himself (Ro 11:33-36).

Wisdom of Sirach. See *Apocrypha,* A 3.

Wisdom of Solomon. See *Apocrypha,* A 3.

Wise, John (1625–1725). Cong. pastor at Ipswich, Mass.; upheld dem. ch. govt. in his *The Churches' Quarrel Espoused;* opposed a condemnation in a witchcraft trial.

Wiseman, Nicholas Patrick Stephen (1802–65). Eng. cardinal; b. Seville, Sp., of Irish stock; educ. Rome; sought to win Eng. for papacy; rector of Eng. Coll. at Rome 1828; bp. London 1840; influenced Oxford Movement; confirmed J. H. Newman*; vicar apostolic 1849; cardinal 1850; archb. of Westminster. Works include *Lectures on the Principal Doctrines and Practices of the Catholic Church; Three Lectures on the Catholic Hierarchy.*

Wishart, George (ca. 1513–46). Scottish martyr; little is known of early life; in Switz. and Ger. ca. 1539–40; tr. *Confessio Helvetica* into Eng.; taught at Cambridge 1543; worked with J. Knox*; burned as heretic at Edinburgh, Mar. 1, 1546. See *Presbyterian Churches,* 1.

Wiss, Michael. See *Weisse, Michael.*

Witchcraft. 1. The practice of occult arts by witches, or wizards, who perform their work with the aid of the devil. The Scriptures oppose witchcraft (LV 20:27; Dt 18:10-12; 1 Sm 28; Gl 5:20; Acts 8:9-11; 13:8; 19:19).

2. In the early Christian ch. witchcraft of every kind was forbidden, either on the ground of the emptiness of the practice or that of its positive godlessness and commerce with the devil. In the ch. of the early Middle Ages special rules of penance were made for women convicted of witchcraft. But at the beginning of the 13th c., when the Inquisition* was introduced, the use of magic and witchcraft was everywhere suspected and immediately branded as a desertion of God for the service of evil spirits. In 1231 a bull of Pope Gregory IX invoked the use of civil punishment against every form of heresy connected with sorcery. Toward the end of the 15th c. the provisions which brought witches under the power of the Inquisition were enlarged, so that trials for witchcraft became very common.

3. After the Reformation the crime of witchcraft was again the subject of legal enactments, also under the influence of the ch. Thus Elector August of Saxony supported a decree against sorcery, making it a capital offense. An epidemic of witch prosecution that had broken out in Ger. at the end of the 15th c. spread into Fr., It., Sp., the Neth., and Eng. and continued through the 16th, 17th, and 18th centuries. The number of its unfortunate victims, mems. of both the Cath. and Prot. chs., is estimated at many thousands. Some of the tortures and ordeals resorted to in the examination of persons suspected of witchcraft were almost of a diabolical nature.

4. In Am. the first witchcraft persecution broke out 1692 in Salem, Mass., the occasion being some meetings in the family of a minister by the name of Parrish. A company of girls had been in the habit of meeting a West Indian slave in order to study the "black art." Suddenly they allegedly began to act mysteriously, bark like dogs, and scream at things unseen. An old Indian servant was accused of bewitching them. A special court was formed to try the accused, as a result of which the jails filled rapidly, many persons being found guilty and condemned to death.

L. Kittredge, *Witchcraft in Old and New England,* (Cambridge, Mass., 1929); H. C. Lea, *Materials*

Toward a History of Witchcraft (Philadelphia, 1939), 3 vols.

Witekind, Hermann. See *Lercheimer, Augustin.*

Wither, George (Withers; 1588–1667). Eng., poet and hymnwriter; b. Bentworth, Hampshire; joined Puritans and wrote pamphlet for their cause; imprisoned for satire in *Abuses Stript and Whipt;* raised troops for parliamentary side in Eng. civil war; later imprisoned for *Vox Vulgi* against parliament. Works include *Hymnes and Songs of the Church; Halelviah.*

Witherspoon, John (1723–94). B. Yester, near Edinburgh, Scot.; educ. Edinburgh; ordained Presb. pastor 1745; pastor Beith (Ayrshire, Paisley); came to Am. to be pres. of the College of N. J. (later Princeton) 1768; represented N. J. in Continental Congress 1776–82; signed Declaration of Independence. Works include *Ecclesiastical Characteristics; A Serious Enquiry into the Nature and Effects of the Stage; The Trial of Religious Truth by Its Moral Influence; Essays on Important Subjects; Considerations on the Nature and Extent of the Legislative Authority of the British Parliament.*

Wits, Hermann (Witsius; 1636–1708). Dutch Calvinist; b. Enkhuizen; educ. Utrecht and Groningen; pastor Westwoud, Wormer, Goes, Leeuwarden; prof. Franeker, Utrecht, Leiden; regent of state coll. Leiden; exponent of modified federal* theology and mystical pietism; opposed Cartesianism* and antinomianism. Works include *De oeconomia foederum Dei cum hominibus.* See also *Dogmatics.* B 5.

Witt, Christian Friedrich (1665–1716). Author of *Psalmodia sacra* of Gotha (1715); wrote a number of hymn tunes still used today. Some attribute the tune "Es ist genug" (*Lutheran Hymnal* 196) to him.

Witt, Franz Xaver (1834–88). Ger. RC priest and music scholar; b. Walderbach, Palatinate; founded *Fliegende Blätter für die katholische Kirchenmusik* 1866 and *Cäcilienverein* 1868. Works include *Ausgewählte Aufsätze zur Kirchenmusik.*

Witte, Catechism of. See *Estonia,* 2.

Witte, Johannes (1877–1945). Ger. Ev. student of religion and missions; b. Silligsdorf, Pomerania; prof. Berlin. Works include *Ostasien und Europa; Japan zwischen zwei Kulturen; Das Jenseits im Glauben der Völker.*

Wittenberg Academy. Est. 1901 at Wittenberg, Wis.; operated jointly by Norw. Syn., Wis. Syn., and Mo. Syn.; closed 1913. See also *Homme, Even Johannes; Mueller, John Theodore.*

Wittenberg Articles. Outcome of Anglo-Luth. negotiations in spring 1536 when effort was made to reach doctrinal formula acceptable to govt. of Henry VIII and the Ger. Luth. theologians. The Eng. representatives at the conf. were Edward Fox, Nicholas Heath, and R. Barnes.* The Germans were represented by Luther,* Melanchthon,* Bugenhagen,* Cruciger,* and others. The *Wittenberg Articles,* agreed on by the conferees, were largely an explication of the AC, with considerable borrowing from Melanchthon's *Loci communes* and the Ap. Melanchthon appears to have been chiefly responsible for the writing of the formula. It was never formally adopted in Eng., but it did become the basis for the Eng. *Ten Articles* of 1536 and later became a chief source for the *Thirty-nine Articles,* the formal conf. statement of the Ch. of Eng. See also *Anglican Confessions; Lutheran Confessions,* A 5.

G. Mentz. *Die Wittenberger Artikel von 1536* (Leipzig, 1905); F. Pruser, *England und die Schmalkaldener* (Leipzig, 1929); E. G. Rupp, *Studies in the Making of the English Protestant Tradition* (Cambridge, 1949). NST

Wittenberg College. See *Hamma Divinity School; Universities in the United States, Lutheran,* 6.

Wittenberg Concord. When Philip* of Hesse could not bring about agreement between the Luth. theologians and the Swiss (at Marburg 1529) or the south Germans (at Augsburg 1530), M. Bucer* persisted till he got some of the highlanders to travel to Wittenberg and sign the *Wittenberg Concord* on May 26, 1536. It is quoted in FC SD 7. See also *Grynäus,* 1; *Lutheran Confessions,* B 1.

Wittenberg Seminary. Theol. dept. of Wittenberg Coll. (see *Wittenberg University*); later called Hamma* Divinity School.

Wittenberg Synod of The Evangelical Lutheran Church of Ohio. Organized June 8, 1847, by 8 pastors ("bishops") formerly belonging to the Eng. Syn. of Ohio (East Ohio). Territory: NW Ohio. Among prominent men of the syn. were E. Keller* and S. Sprecher.* Joined General* Syn. 1848; approved "Definite* Platform." In 1918 it entered the United Luth. Ch. and Nov. 3, 1920, merged with E Ohio, the Miami* Syn., and the Dist. Syn. of Ohio into the Ohio Syn. of the ULC. It then numbered 55 pastors, 74 congs., and 12,590 communicants. See *United Lutheran Church, Synods of,* 19.

C. S. Ernsberger, *A History of the Wittenberg Synod of the General Synod of the Evangelical Lutheran Church* (Columbus, Ohio, 1917).

Wittenberg University. See *Lutheran Church in America,* V; *Ministry, Education of,* VIII A 6; *Universities in the United States, Lutheran,* 6.

Wittenbergense, Corpus. See *Lutheran Confessions,* C 1.

Witter, Henning Bernhard (1683–1715). B. Hildesheim, Ger.; taught Helmstedt; pastor Hildesheim; pointed out differences between Gn 1 and 2. Regarded Gn 1 as older document used by Moses. Forerunner of literary criticism.

Wittgenstein, Ludwig (1889–1951). B. Vienna; fellow Trinity Coll., Oxford; prof. there; noted for his philos. of language. Works include *Tractatus logico-philosophicus; Philosophical Investigations.* See also *Logical Positivism.*

Wittich, Christoph (1625–87). Ref. theol. B. Brieg, Silesia; educ. Bremen Groningen, Leiden; prof. Herborn 1650; pastor Duisburg; prof. Nymwegen, Leiden. Influenced by Cartesianism* and federal* theology. Exponent of scientific world view. Works include *Consensus veritatis in scriptura divina et infallibili revelatae cum veritate philosophica a Renato DesCartes detecta; Theologia pacifica.*

Wittmann, George Michael. See *Bible Societies,* 6.

Witzel, Georg (1501–73). RC reformer; b. Vacha, Ger.; studied a semester at Wittenberg and came under influence of Luther and Melanchthon; pastor Wenigen-Lubnitz, Thuringia; preached against abuses in Roman Ch. and also oppression of lower classes; Peasants' Revolt brought him under suspicion; appealed to Luther for help and through him obtained position near Wittenberg. Felt there was a lack of piety and good works among the Evangelicals and concluded that their doctrine hindered works; favored Anabaptists and became friend of J. Campanus*; after latter became anti-Trinitarian, Witzel through patristic study and the influence of D. Erasmus* returned to RCm, which he sought to advance through reform; previous marriage brought him under suspicion of RCs; throughout remainder of his wandering life sought to gain adherence for his reform program which, however, was rejected at the Council of Trent.

Wizenmann, Thomas (1759–89). Swabian theol. and philos.; shared views of J. K. Lavater,* J. G. Hamann,* and M. Claudius*; joined Collenbusch circle; wrote *Geschichte Jesu nach Matthäus; Göttliche Entwicklung des Satans.*

Wladyslaw. See *Lithuania,* 1.

Wobbermin, Georg (1869–1943). Ger. Ev. theol.; b. Stettin; taught Berlin, Marburg, Breslau, Heidelberg, Göttingen, Berlin; influenced by J. W. M. Kaftan*;

sought transcendental basis for religion; advocated religious-psychological approach to theology. Works include *Systematische Theologie nach religionspsychologischer Methode.*

Woerden, Jan van. See *De Bakker, Jan.*

Wohlgemuth, Michel (1434–1519). Ger. painter, influenced by art of Neth., but with awkward style and flat modeling; his shop produced many altars, but few of intrinsic value.

Wold, Oscar Rudolph (Aug. 11, 1874–Oct. 11, 1929). B. Sibley Co., Minn.; educ. Red Wing Sem., Conc. Coll., Moorhead, Minn., Chicago Luth. Sem.; miss. China 1898–1905; prof. Red Wing Sem. (on furlough); miss. China 1910–29; pres. Central China Union Luth. Theol. Sem. 1913–29; pres. Chinese Luth. Ch. 1920–29.

Wolf, Edmund Jacob (Dec. 8, 1840–Jan. 10, 1903). Hist.; b. Rebersburg, Pa.; educ. Gettysburg Luth. Sem., Tübingen, Erlangen; Luth. pastor Baltimore; from 1873 prof. ch. hist. and NT exegesis Gettysburg Luth. Sem.; conservative. Coed. (with P. M. Biklé and M. Valentine*) *The Lutheran Quarterly;* other works include *The Lutherans in America.*

Wolfenbüttel Fragments. See *Reimarus, Hermann Samuel.*

Wolff, Christian von (Wolf; 1679–1754). Ger. philos.; b. Breslau; prof. math. and nat. philos. Halle 1707; deposed 1723 and banished from Prussia through influence of Halle Pietists; to Marburg; later recalled to Halle. Adopted theories of G. W. v. Leibniz*; coined term monism*. Though he accepted revelation, reason was his final authority. Logical consequence of his method was rationalism, which through his system gained increasingly strong foothold in Germany. See also *Lutheran Theology After 1580,* 8.

Wolff, Joseph. See *Middle East,* C. H.

Wolfgang von Anhalt (1492–1566).) Met Luther at Worms 1521 and favored Reformation; signed AC 1530; joined Schmalkaldic* League; exiled by emperor; present at Luther's death; opposed Interim.*

Wolfram von Eschenbach (ca. 1170–ca. 1220). Middle High Ger. poet and minnesinger; descended from Bavarian family of Eschenbach, near Ansbach; spent much time on Wildenburg in Odenwald and on Wartburg in Thuringia. Works include *Parzival.*

Wolfrum, Philipp (1854–1919). Ger. Luth. musicologist and composer; b. Schwarzenbach-am-Wald, Bavaria; educ. Altdorf, Munich, Leipzig; dir. of music at U. of Heidelberg. Works include *Johann Sebastian Bach; Evangelisches Kirchenlied; Luther und die Musik; Luther und Bach.*

Wolleb, Johannes (1586–1629). Swiss Ref. theol.; b. Basel; pastor and OT prof. Basel. Works include *Compendium theologiae christianae.*

Wolsey, Thomas (ca. 1475–1530). Eng. cardinal, statesman; b. Ipswich(?); educ. Oxford; fellow Magdalen Coll.; ordained priest ca. 1498; domestic chaplain of archbp. of Canterbury 1502; chaplain of Henry VII 1507; privy counsellor of Henry VIII; bp. of Lincoln 1514; archbp. of York 1514; cardinal 1515; Lord Chancellor of Eng. 1515. In his foreign policy he endeavored to hold the balance of power in struggle between Empire and France; endeavored to obtain papal dispensation for divorce of Henry VIII; blamed for his failure by Anne Boleyn and incurred King's displeasure; founded Christ Church, Oxford; arrested for high treason; died on way to London. See also *Praemunire, Statutes of.*

Wolter, C. L. August (Aug. 29, 1818–Aug. 31, 1849). Luth. scholar, educ.; b. Hamburg, Ger.; sent to Am. 1846 with C. J. H. Fick* and A. G. G. Francke* by J. K. W. Löhe* shortly after founding of practical sem. at Ft. Wayne; prof. there for 3 yrs.; d. of cholera. Noted for humility, clarity of thought, friendliness, and zeal for confessional Luth.

Wolter, Maurus and Placidus. See *Beuron, Abbey of.*

Woltersdorf, Ernst Gottlieb (1725–61). Ger. poet, educator, preacher, author; pietist; stud. Halle 1742; in 1744 was compelled by illness to discontinue and to travel; called as second pastor to Bunzlau 1748; became identified with an orphan asylum 1754.

Wolzogen, Ludovicus (1633–90). Dutch. theol.; b. Amersfoort; educ. Utrecht and Geneva; pastor Groningen, Middelburg, Utrecht; pastor and prof. Utrecht and Amsterdam; Cartesian. Works include *De scripturarum interpretate.*

Woman in Christian Society. I. *General.* A. The NT, in common with the OT, places woman on a high level and creates the basis for a noble concept of ethical equality with man. It does so by making woman equal to man as a shareholder in the gifts of the Holy Spirit, by removing sex as a factor in the reception and exercise of the life of God, and by presenting noble illustrations of Christian womanhood. This ideal is further implemented in the NT by the definition of woman's sphere of service as one unique to her and essential to the world. Paul emphasized the need of the Holy Spirit, both in man and in woman, and outlined the sphere of woman's service. Already in the apostolic age special spheres of labor in the ch. were devised for women without families. Under the influence of the ascetic ideal these spheres of service were broadened into the work of welfare, which is one of the most worthy aspects of RCm. Luther opposed the view, which had developed in the ch., that marriage* is an inferior state to celibacy.* He himself, the ex-monk, married an ex-nun as a symbol and testimony of this revolt. Thereby he sought not to afford himself or others a license for lust but to est. an object lesson in the concept of the Christian calling. This concept, basic to Luth. ethics, views man as living in the vocations of family, state, and occupation, and woman as likewise fulfilling her vocation as wife, mother, friend, and citizen; and the fulfilling of this vocation with the help and for the glory of God constitutes a lofty Christian service. See also *Asceticism; Monasticism.*

B. The NT ideal brought about vast changes in the attitude toward woman in the ancient world. Whereas woman had been regarded as a chattel or object of lust, she was enabled to assume the regard and worth due her in God's plan. Likewise the Prot. Reformation served to restore the family ideal, not only in its communions but also in RCm.

C. Women have been particularly active in the Luth. program of the Ch. and of welfare. The Deaconess (see *Deaconesses*) program originated in the attempt to utilize the NT method of providing definite areas of service for women not in families. Luth. women have found more and more opportunity for rendering service to objectives of the Ch. also when they were wives and mothers. Am. Luth. ch. life has imitated the custom of other chs. by organizing women of the parish in specific groupings (ladies' aid, women's guild, business-women's groups, young women's groups) and for specific services. The parish groups foster fellowship among the women of the ch., occupy themselves with study or mission enterprises, engage in fund-raising pursuits, and otherwise are at the disposal of specific parish programs. In more recent yrs. women's groups have organized on a nat. scale. RRC

II. *Denominational Organizations.* A. *General.* 1. The OT and NT speak favorably of women in God's service, including Miriam (Ex 2:4-10), Esther, Naomi and Ruth, Anna (Lk 2:36-38), Mary Magdalene (Mt 28:1), Mary and Martha (Lk 10:38-42), Lois and Eunice (2 Ti 1:5), Priscilla (Acts 18:2, 18, 26), Lydia (Acts 16:4-15, 40). These and other Bible women exerted a great influence before and after women's organizations.

2. In the early centuries of Christianity wives and

mothers helped to keep the faith alive through days of suffering, persecution, and martyrdom. Women like Monica,* mother of Augustine* of Hippo, with their prayers and training helped develop men who dedicated their lives to Christ.

3. Also in the post-Reformation era women made their influence felt in various ways. The Countess of Zinzendorf and Susanna Wesley (mother of John and Charles) are prominent names in the religious field of their day and active in the spiritual revolution in Eng.

4. In the 18th c. we find the name of Barbara Ruckle Heck,* "mother of Methodism in Am." Hannah Marshman carried the Word to North India and in 1800 made an attempt at female educ. there.

5. In the middle of the 19th c. and later, women were a great force in the proclamation of the Gospel to women in India and in est. the first women's hospital there 1869. Dr. Clara N. Swain, a Meth. from Am., is credited as being the first woman medical missionary. Dr. Ida Scudder founded the medical center at Vellore, India. Stirring and hazardous efforts by consecrated women (e. g., Mary Slessor*) were likewise put forth in Africa.

6. These briefly related efforts can be multiplied many times over in various parts of the world as a testimony to other heroic women in missions. During these earlier centuries women served the ch. as individuals, each in her own way. They became stimuli for women to organize for missions.

7. After the Revolutionary War a number of groups banded together to raise money for miss. purposes at home and abroad. Some of the earliest groups were Quakers. "The Female Cent Soc." of Bap. women was formed in Boston 1800. Organized miss. work of the Cong. women seems to have begun 1801, of the Presb. women 1803, of the Dutch Ref. 1851, of the Meth. 1819.

8. The significant thing is that in spite of the terrific handicap they faced, church women had the temerity to form societies in days when such a movement was not looked upon with favor by the brethren – not even by the male members of their own families, to say nothing of the pastors and elders.

9. These early women had no precedent to guide them. They developed their own idea and relied largely on prayer and the Holy Spirit to lead them. Their loyalty to Christ and missions, in prayer and Bible reading, is an example for Christian women also in this age.

10. Records of early organizations are scarce. They were known by such names as "Female Benevolent Soc.," the "Pious Female Praying Soc.," the "Female Mite Soc." and the "Female Soc. for the Support of a Female School in India."

B. *Catholic.* 1. For years, as in most chs., the women of the RC Ch. formed parochial or parish organizations concerned with assisting the priest in some phase of his mission in the parish. Also in the course of years various women rallied around specific causes within the ch. on the nat. scale.

2. Shortly after WW I steps were taken to provide a structure to affiliate every eligible Cath. organization of women within the diocesan and nat. councils so that each could work in harmony with the leadership of the ch.

3. In 1919, with approval of Pope Benedict XV, the bps. of the US met in Washington, D. C., to launch the Nat. Cath. Welfare Conf., which is recognized as the official agency of the bps. of the US intended to promote Christian life and to further the mission of Christ and His church. As in any agency the NCWC includes a number of depts. and bureaus to achieve its purposes. One of these is called the "Dept. of Lay Organizations" and includes the Nat. Council of Cath. Men and the Nat. Council of Cath. Women, organized in 1920. The NCCW is not a new or separate organization but is designed to federate existing organizations of women – nat., state, diocesan, and local. It was called into existence to unite the Cath. women of the US in organized effort in all useful fields of educ., soc., religious, and economic work, for the betterment and happiness of the people. It further provides for channeling information from NCWC depts. to all affiliated organizations, for assisting them through publications, correspondence, institutes, and biennial nat. convs., and it provides a nat. and internat. voice for the Cath. women of the US.

4. The NCCW includes ca. 30 affiliated organizations including Nat. Council of Cath. Nurses; Ladies Cath. Benevolent Association; Cath. War Veterans, Ladies Auxiliary; Cath. Daughters of Am.; organizations representing nationalities, alumnae, or college groups. The NCCW-affiliated organizations represent ca. 10 million women.

5. The NCCW makes no provision for individual membership. Rather, women belong to an organization. Organizations in turn affiliate with the federation, the NCCW.

6. The NCCW is affiliated with the internat. World Union of Cath. Women's Organizations, a worldwide fed. with mems. in 60 countries.

7. It is noted that a special service rendered by the Council of Men and Council of Women is to provide representation for the ch. at nat. and internat. meetings. Through their delegates the councils represent Cath. thinking and obtain information on developments in various fields that they relay to the bps. Important areas in which representatives recently participated are White House Conf. on Children and Youth, Nat. Conf. of Citizens for Decent Literature, Congressional Hearings on Indecent Literature, Special UN Briefings, Council of Nat. Organizations for Adult Educ., and many other meetings of nat. and internat. character.

C. *Lutheran.* 1. *Luth. Ch. Women (LCW).* Official auxiliary for women of the LCA. The LCW was initiated July/Aug. 1962, following the June/July 1962 merging of 4 Luth. bodies: the ULCA (Ger. background); the Augustana Luth. Ch. (Swed. background); the Suomi Syn. (Fin. background); and the AELC (Dan. background).

2. In order to give a clear picture of the LCW it is necessary to refer not only to the women's organizations of the 4 merging church bodies, but also to the antecedents of the ULCA.

3. In 1837, before any general organization was formed, women attending a conf. of the Gen. Syn. of the Luth. Ch in N. Y., with their husbands, gained the incentive to aid in educating missionaries, with the result that they formed the Female Association of Hartwick Syn. for the Educ. of Foreign Missionaries. Interest was extended beyond the Hartwick Syn. (N. Y.) into other parts of the ch. In 1875 several pastors were moved to action, and the women in the Iowa Syn. organized and adopted a constitution. Almost simultaneously the movement spread to Ohio. After much promotional work the Gen. Syn., through a committee, called a meeting in Canton, Ohio, in June 1879 to organize a gen. women's group. The formal action read as follows: "Resolved, that we hail the organization of this General Women's Home and Foreign Mission Society of the General Synod as the dawning of a new era in the history of women's work in the Lutheran Church, and will not rest until there is an auxiliary society in every congregation connected with the General Synod."

4. Several syn. societies in the United Syn. in the South formed the Women's Miss. Conf. 1906. Within the Gen. Council the women began organizing in 1885 but did not unite generally until Sept. 1911 into the *Women's Missionary Soc. of the Gen. Council.*

5. These 3 tributaries, after a history of 40 years, merged in Nov. 1918 immediately following the organization of the ULCA and became the *Women's Missionary Soc. of the ULCA.* The purpose of the organization has always been "missionary." The const., adopted 1919, states: "The objects of the Society shall be: to exert all possible effort, by the grace and power of God, to fulfill the great commission of our risen and triumphant Lord, set forth in Matthew 28:19-20, 'Go ye therefore, and teach all nations, baptizing them in the name of the Father, and of the Son, and of the Holy Ghost; Teaching them to observe all things whatsoever I have commanded you; and, lo, I am with you alway, even unto the end of the world'; to promote and stimulate the interest of the whole Church in the work of Missions; to disseminate missionary information, to promote missionary education, and financially to aid the missionary operations of the Church, through its regularly established boards; to co-ordinate and unite the work of synodical societies." The work has been carried on largely through the mission bds. of the ch. Numerous institutions have been built and maintained. Among them are hospitals, soc. institutions, and miss. residences.

6. Women missionaries have been educ. and supported in their respective fields. In a given year the number ranges from 50 to 75. More than $25,000,000 has been contributed to the ch. by this women's organization since 1919. At the conv. in 1955 the name was changed to United Luth. Ch. Women. This was the largest group in the 1962 merger; membership in 1959 was reported to be 171,815.

7. *The Augustana Luth. Ch. Women* voted to organize June 6, 1882, in Lindsborg, Kans., provided that the ch. in session at the same time would give its approval. In the afternoon of the same date a favorable resolution was passed by the ch. assembly. Their endeavor was "to awaken a greater interest for missions and a more general support of the same." The objective remained basically the same, but the scope of the miss. activity broadened to include all services in the parish, the community, the nation, and the world. In 1959 the membership had reached 82,423.

8. *Luth. Guild of Suomi Syn.* When the Suomi Syn. was organized 1890, it was an accepted fact among them that women had equal rights to speak and vote. This concept likely forestalled any formal women's organization for many years. On the local level, however, ladies' aids often preceded the forming of a cong. They brought not only monetary returns but had social and spiritual significance for the newly arrived imigrants. The Finnish language was generally used. In 1945 during the conv. of the synod women and interested pastors submitted a resolution advocating greater use of the Eng. language in all ch. activities and requesting that the women be permitted to organize. The requests were granted, and the Luth. Guild of Suomi Syn. was organized Hancock, Mich., June 12, 1946. The const. provided for the promotion of Christian knowledge, the advancement of the syn. through the development of the women of the ch., and cooperation with the Synod, and promised "to labor in behalf of missions" and to "cultivate interest in Synod institutions and work."

9. *Women's Mission Society of the AELC.* At the time of the annual syn. conv. in Chicago, Ill., in summer 1908 a number of young matrons gathered during the noon hour to discuss their growing world – beyond family, ladies' aid, and local church. They were concerned about the needs of home missions and how to arouse all the women of the ch. to action. While no formal organization was effected, the women's aid agreed to form a "Dan. Women's Mission Fund" to aid young pastors and small congs. and to cultivate a love for missions. This loosely formed organization was under the leadership of Mrs. Karoline Kjolhede for 30 yrs. Meetings were conducted in the Dan. language. After Mrs. Kjolhede resigned 1937, the younger women, born in this country, undertook a firmer organization. The Eng. language was used, a const. drafted, and a new name applied, "Women's Mission Soc."

10. *Am. Luth. Ch. Women* (ALCW). Founded 1960 by women of The ALC. Its purposes include: "To serve as an auxiliary to the American Lutheran Church in the achievement of its objectives of making the Gospel of Jesus Christ known among all men."

There were women's miss. groups in the 4 churches which 1960 organized The ALC. In the UELC it was called the Women's Missionary Society; in the ALC, ELC, and Luth. Free Ch., Women's Missionary Federation.

All confirmed women of The ALC are automatically considered members of the ALCW. The organization has no charter or membership lists. The ALC provides the operating funds. It has 2 depts.: educ. and stewardship. The educ. dept. fosters study of the Bible and of the nature and mission of the ch. The stewardship dept. encourages support of syn. and projects within syn.

The core of the ALCW is Bible study in small groups called "circles."

The const. gives the purpose of the organization as "to know and do the will of Jesus Christ by: inspiring in the individual member a deeper consecration to the Savior; developing stewardship of time, talents, and treasure; disseminating knowledge of the program of the church of Jesus Christ, particularly of The American Lutheran Church; spreading the Gospel of Jesus Christ throughout the world." AN (10)

11. *Luth. Women's Missionary League* (LWML). Women's soc. of the LCMS, organized Chicago, Ill., July 1942 as an expansion of women's groups that had been working successfully in various dists. of the Mo. Syn. In 1951 the use of the name "Internat. Luth. Women's Missionary League" for referring to the league at large was authorized.

Prior to 1928 a few pastors conceived the plan to secure the united efforts of women in support of missions. An educ. program was introduced. The women saw the need for special miss. projects not provided for in the syn. budget.

During 1928–42 the directors of missions and pastors, watching the development and the achievements of organized women's groups, recognized the need for united effort throughout the syn. At the 1938 syn. conv. in St. Louis 2 proposals regarding organized women's work were submitted. The syn. took the plans under advisement and appointed a com. to study the situation and prepare recommendations for the next conv. In 1941 the syn. conv. approved the creation of a synodwide organization of women.

The pres. of syn. appointed a com. for a synodwide women's organization. At the July 1942 meeting a const. was adopted and name chosen.

The organization meets in conv. biannually. During the biennium business is administered by the administrative com. and the ex. bd. The purpose of the organization is to promote miss. educ., miss. inspiration, and miss. service. Its freewill offerings support miss. projects for which no provision is made in dist. or syn. budgets. The "mite box" early became a noted collection device. The LWML has supported schools, sems., colls., hospitals, chapels, and other miss. projects around the world.

The major programs are directed toward Christian growth and miss. service.

The official pub. is the *Luth. Woman's Quarterly.* Headquarters: St. Louis, Mo. SFR

See also *Laymen's Activity in the Lutheran Church.*

III. *United Work of Prot. Women.* A. Prot. women were early influenced by the ideal of the oneness of the ch. Since the beginning of the 19th c. women met in local organized groups for the purpose of studying and supporting missions. In addition to appeals for help from foreign missions, immigrant families and the moving frontier opened up needs for women's work.

B. The *Union Missionary Society,* an interdenom. female soc., was formed in New York 1861 for sending out female missionaries.

C. In the next 2 decades women's boards were organized in nearly every Prot. denom., including *Women's Foreign Missionary Soc. of The Meth. Ch.* 1869, *Women's Foreign Missionary Soc. of the Presb. Ch. USA* 1870; *United Presb. Women* 1870.

D. 1. In 1890–91 an interdenom. committee of women was formed to help put on a program for the 1893 Chicago World's Fair. A "Day of Prayer" for home missions was est. 1887, and for foreign missions 1890; combined on first Friday in Lent 1919; became "World Day of Prayer for Missions" 1927. A Central Committee on the United Study of Foreign Missions was set up 1901. The Council of Women for Home Missions was organized 1908. In 1914 a Committee on Christian Literature for Women and Children was organized which produced magazines, leaflets, books, and illustrated material in various languages. Some local interdenom. groups were already organized in the late 19th and early 20th c., including The Woman's Missionary Union of Springfield, Mo. 1887, the Missionary Social Union of St. Louis 1898, the Missionary Federation of Kansas City 1909. The jubilee meetings arranged across the country 1911 contributed greatly to the formation of such groups and led to the founding of the *Federation of Women's Boards of Foreign Mission.* Membership in local groups was usually not linked with denom. representation. All ch. women were eligible.

2. Social reform and work early became a concern of women's organizations. Though the Social Gospel was successfully opposed by fundamentalists, women's organizations continued to work and pray for social betterment.

3. In May 1928 the *Nat. Commission of Prot. Ch. Women* was organized to plan for local interdenom. church women's groups, unify and enlarge their programs, advise new organizations, and cooperate with the Federal* Council of Churches. The *Nat. Council of Federated Ch. Women* (NCFCW) was formed 1929 for the purpose of "establishing a Christian social order in which all areas of life shall be brought into harmony with the teachings of Jesus Christ." It published a *News Bulletin* 1934 and *The Church Woman* 1936.

4. The Nat. Council of Federated Ch. Women, the Council of Women for Home Missions, and the Women's Committee of the Foreign Missions Conf. merged into *The United Council of Ch. Women* (UCCW), Dec. 11–13, 1941, with the purpose of uniting ch. women in their allegiance to their Lord and Savior, Jesus Christ, through a program looking to their integration in the total life and work of the ch. and to the building of "a world Christian community." At the constituting conv. the United Council of Ch. Women became the Gen. Dept. of United Ch. Women of the National* Council of Churches but kept its own charter, Dec. 1950. In 1965 it became one of five departments in the Division of Christian Unity of the NCC. It has continued to stress prayer, unity, missions, human and civil rights. EDH, EL, PGL

These Fifty Years: 1892–1942, ed. Mrs. P. Peterson (Chicago, 1942); *Revised Interim Report of a Study on the Life and Work of Women in the Church* (Geneva, 1948); I. M. Cavert, *Women in American Church Life* (New York, 1948); K. Bliss, *The Service and Status of Women in the Churches* (London, 1952); K. Lehmann, *And the Women Also* (Columbus, Ohio, 1952); *Men and Women in Church and Society* (Geneva, 1952); *Women of the Church* (Study Document of LWF, 1952); M. A. Wyker, *Church Women in the Scheme of Things* (St. Louis, 1953); C. P. Blackwood, *How to Be an Effective Church Woman* (Philadelphia, 1955); F. Zerbst, *The Office of Woman in the Church,* tr. A. Merkens (St. Louis, 1955); R. C. Prohl, *Woman in the Church* (Grand Rapids, Mich., 1957); M. Reishus, *Hearts and Hands Uplifted* (Minneapolis, 1958); R. J. Smith, *Their Sound Goes Forth* (Philadelphia, 1959); J. F. Danielou, *The Ministry of Women in the Early Church* (London, 1961); G. G. Calkins, *Follow Those Women* (New York, 1961); R. F. Meyer, *Women on a Mission* (St. Louis, 1967).

Woman's Christian Temperance Union. Organized Cleveland, Ohio, during great temperance crusade 1874; mems. required to sign pledge of total abstinence. It is largely due to WCTU that public school textbooks make special reference to effects of alcohol and narcotics; its Sunday school dept. secured the teaching of quarterly temperance lessons in the Internat. Sunday School Series.

Woman's Union Missionary Society. As result of efforts of Mrs. Thomas C. Doremus and Mrs. Francis Mason, a woman's miss. soc. was organized in Boston 1860 and in New York 1861. The two united 1861 to form the Woman's Union Miss. Soc. of Am. for Heathen Lands. The purpose of the interdenom. organization was to send single ladies to miss. fields. Fields (1966): India, Japan, West Pakistan. US headquarters: New York, N. Y. Member IFMA.

Woodd, Basil (1760–1831). B. Richmond, Surrey, Eng.; widowed mother exercised salutary influence; at 17 entered Trinity College, Oxford; holy orders 1783; lecturer St. Peter's, Cornhill, 1784; morning preacher Bentinck Chapel; purchased lease of chapel 1793 and held incumbency together with rectory of Drayton from 1808; took great interest in religious societies and antislavery movement. Wrote hymns including "Hail, Thou Source of Every Blessing."

Woodhouse, Francis V. See *Catholic Apostolic Church,* 1.

Woodruff, Wilfred. See *Latter Day Saints,* f.

Woolley, Charles Leonard. See *Geography, Christian,* 6.

Woolman, John (1720–72). Am. Quaker; his efforts to remove social ills are given in his *Journal;* known especially for his opposition to slavery.

Woolston, Thomas. See *Deism,* III 5.

Word of God. Word of God covers the whole field of God's revelation of Himself. His Word is the essential mode whereby God intervenes in the world: Through it He creates the heavens and the earth (Gn 1); through it He reveals Himself to men (Jn 1:1-14); and by its proclamation the history of the ch. develops and is fulfilled (Acts 4:29, 31). The term is used in a special way of Jesus Christ, who is the Heart and Center of God's revelation. In addition, the NT uses "Word of God" of (a) the OT law (Mk 7:13); (b) a particular passage from the OT (Jn 10:35); (c) in a more general sense, God's revealed will, or His whole plan of salvation (Lk 11:28; Ro 9:6); (d) the word preached by Jesus (Lk 5:1); (e) the Christian message (Acts 4:31); and (f) all that goes on in a cong. in terms of worship, proclamation, and life (Acts 6:7). The application of "the Word of God" to Scripture as the written Word is derived from use *b* above. While theologians distinguished bet. the incarnate, the proclaimed, and the written Word, all 3 testify to the purpose of God in creating, saving, and sanctifying His people. The uniqueness of the Bible consists of the fact that it is our source book of knowledge on what God has done within history for the redemption of mankind. From beginning to end the Scriptures are anchored in Jesus Christ (Jn 5:39), to whom all the prophets, apostles, and evangelists testify. The Lutheran* Confessions, therefore, speak of the Bible as the prophetic and apostolic Word.

See also *Bible; Inspiration; Grace, Means of; Logos; Revelation.*

R. Abba, *The Nature and Authority of the Bible* (Philadelphia, 1958); O. Cullmann, *The Christology of the New Testament* (Philadelphia, 1959); W. Keller, *The Bible as History* (New York, 1956); P. Schumm, "The Clearness and Sufficiency of Scripture" in *Abiding Word,* I, 58–66. MHS

Wordsworth, Christopher (1807–85). Nephew of W. Wordsworth*; educ. Cambridge; brilliant scholar; held positions as master and lecturer, then parish priest, finally bp. of Lincoln. Works include *The Holy Year,* containing "Songs of Thankfulness and Praise."

Wordsworth, William (1770–1850). Uncle of C. Wordsworth*; leading Eng. romantic poet; named poet laureate 1843; gave charm of novelty to things of everyday life; for many years strongly Platonic, but his *Ecclesiastical Sonnets,* written when in his 50s, reflect a return to Ch. of Eng.

Working Men's College. See *Ludlow, John Malcolm Forbes.*

Works. See *Good Works; Sanctification.*

Works, Merit of. See *Merit.*

Works of Spirit. See *Holy Spirit.*

World Alliance for Promoting International Friendship Through the Churches. Organized at Constance, Ger., Aug. 1, 1914, by ca. 80 people under the leadership of Friedrich Siegmund-Schultze (b. 1885) and the English Quaker Henry Theodore Hodgkin (1877–1933); officially dissolved June 30, 1948. See also *Ecumenical Movement, The,* 9.

World Alliance of Reformed Churches (Presbyterian and Congregational). Internat. agency of Ref. chs. formed by merger of the World Alliance of Ref. Chs. and the Internat. Cong. Council at Nairobi, Kenya, Aug. 20, 1970.

World Conference on Faith and Order. See *Ecumenical Movement, The,* 7; *Union Movements,* 15.

World Council of Christian Education and Sunday School Association. Fed. of nat. councils of Prot. chs. and nat. councils of Christian educ. In 1889 the first in a series of World's Sunday School Conventions assembled at London. At the 7th conv. the World's S. S. Assoc. was constituted (Rom 1907). The name was changed to World Council of Christian Educ. and S. S. Assoc. 1947. It promotes organized Christian educ. including Sun. schools, encourages study of Bible, and fosters world evangelization. It conducted world institutes on Christian educ. at Toronto 1950; Nishonomiya, Japan, 1958; Belfast 1962. Publication: *World Christian Education.* Headquarters: Geneva. See also *Ecumenical Movement, The,* 12.

World Council of Churches. "The World Council of Churches is a fellowship of churches which confess the Lord Jesus Christ as God and Saviour according to the Scriptures and therefore seek to fulfill together their common calling to the glory of the one God, Father, Son, and Holy Spirit" (constit., rev. 1961). The WCC had its origins in the Faith and Order and the Life and Work movements (see *Ecumenical Movement, The,* 7–10; *Union Movements,* 14, 15). These 2 movements converged 1937 when delegates from the majority of Prot. chs. met at Edinburgh and Oxford to discuss the possibilities of ch. union. The delegation at Edinburgh concerned itself primarily with Faith and Order, while the topic for discussion at Oxford was chiefly Life and Work. The two groups agreed to appoint continuation committees which were to lay the foundation for the proposed WCC and to prepare a draft for a const. Specific steps leading to the formation of the WCC were (1) The 1937 meeting of the Committee of 35 under W. Temple's* chairmanship at Westfield, Onson, Eng.; and the 1938 meeting of the Committee of 14 at Utrecht, Neth. The organizational meeting was scheduled for 1941 but had to be postponed until 1948 at Amsterdam. At New Delhi 1961 the International* Missionary Council merged with the WCC. The const. lists the following functions of the WCC:

1. To carry on the work of the world movements for Faith and Order and Life and Work and of the International Missionary Council;
2. To facilitate common action by the churches;
3. To promote cooperation in study;
4. To promote the growth of ecumenical and missionary consciousness in the members of all churches;
5. To support the churches in their worldwide missionary and evangelistic task;
6. To establish and maintain relations with national and regional councils, world confessional bodies, and other ecumenical organizations;
7. To call world conferences on specific subjects as occasion may require, such conferences being empowered to publish their own findings.

The work of the WCC is carried on by 3 commissions: The *Commission on Faith and Order,* continuing the work of the Faith and Order movement (see *Ecumenical Movement, The,* 7, 8, 10, 11); the *Commission of the Chs. on Internat. Affairs,* developed from the Life and Work movement (see *Ecumenical Movement, The,* 9–11); the *Commission on World Mission and Evangelism,* developed from the Internat. Missionary Council (see *Ecumenical Movement, The,* 6, 11).

As of 1972 the WCC comprised more than 260 chs. in more than 90 countries. The LCA and The ALC are members, but the LCMS and the WELS are not. Headquarters: Geneva.

G. K. A. Ball, *The Kingship of Christ: The Story of the World Council of Churches* (Baltimore, 1954); P. Gaines, *The World Council of Churches: A Study of Its Background and History* (Peterborough, N. H., 1966); G. A. Thiele, "The World Council of Churches," *CTM,* XXVII (May 1956), 532–369; R. Krieling, *Uppsala 1968* (Göttingen, 1968).

World Mission and Evangelism, Commission on. See *Ecumenical Movement, The,* 6, 11.

World Mission Prayer League. Indep. intersyn. Luth. mission soc. Began as prayer group among students 1932. Organized 1937. Sent out first missionaries 1938. Tries to go where other mission work is nonexistent or weak. See also *Mexico,* D 3.

World Missionary Conference. See *Ecumenical Movement, The,* 5.

World Presbyterian Alliance. See *Alliance of the Reformed Churches Througout the World Holding the Presbyterian System.*

World Student Christian Federation. See *Student Christian Movement; Students, Spiritual Care of,* A 5.

World View, Christian. See *History, Philosophy of.*

World's Christian Endeavor Union. See *Christian Endeavor.*

World's Evangelical Alliance. See *Evangelical Alliance.*

Worldwide Evangelization Crusade. Origin is traced to 1913 when Charles Thomas Studd (1860–1931) with a companion went from Eng. to Afr. to evangelize areas not worked by other missions. Studd called his work "Christ's Etceteras"; called Afr. mission "The Heart of Africa Mission"; name changed

1919 to "Worldwide Evangelization Crusade." Missionaries endeavor to live on level of nat. workers and make chs. endigenous and self-supporting; operates as worldwide fellowship rather than highly organized society; work coordinated through internat. secy. and coordinating council; theol. position fundamental but allows for varying interpretations; interdenom.; active in ca. 40 countries.

Worms, Colloquy of. Meeting held Nov. 1540 and Jan. 1541 to promote understanding between RC and Luth. theologians. There were 11 men on RC side, with Granvella as representative of Charles* V and the legate L. Campeggio* as chief spokesman, while Melanchthon* was leader of Luths. But a few days after the real opening, when a discussion between J. Eck* and Melanchthon was under way, the colloquy was adjourned to the Regensburg* Conf. without having accomplished anything. See also *Grynäus*, 1.

Worms, Concordat of. See *Concordat*, 2.

Worms, Consultation of. Meeting of Luth. and RC theols. held 1557. Those on Evangelical side were themselves at odds, because Flacian party had refused to acknowledge Wittenberg party unless the men in this group would cleanse themselves of synergism* (see also *Synergistic Controversy*) and Zwinglianism (see *Zwingli, Huldreich*). Preliminary efforts at effecting a united front having failed, the meeting was nevertheless called, Bp. J. v. Pflug* acting as chairman; greatest difficulty arose when RC refused to accept Bible as only final norm of doctrine; meeting adjourned in Dec. See also *Schnepf, Erhard*.

Worms, Diet of. First diet called by young Emperor Charles* V, where April 18, 1521, Luther made world-changing speech refusing to recant. He stood alone on Scripture against pope, prelates, and emperor. The diet also presented the *Centum gravamina*, "Hundred Grievances," which German nation had against abuses of papacy. Former diets had made similar protests. This time, as previously, no real reforms were effected. See also *Luther, Martin*, 13; *Reformation, Lutheran*, 9.

A. R. Wentz, *When Two Worlds Met, The Diet of Worms, 1521* (Philadelphia, 1921).

Worms, Edict of. Issued by Charles* V immediately after close of Diet of Worms*; put Luther* and followers under ban.

Worship. 1. In broadest definition worship is the response of the creature to the Creator. In this sense it includes all expressions of mind or voice or body which are motivated by or directed toward the Divine. Since all men live and move and have their being in God, the term worship may be as correctly applied to the conscious and unconscious responses of pagan peoples to God as they understand Him as to the devotion of Christians.

2. *Christian* worship can only be defined accurately, however, by adding to "Creator" the words "as He has revealed Himself in Jesus Christ and makes Himself known through the Holy Spirit." The recognition of the Holy Trinity as the one true God and the acceptance of the revelation of His nature and His purpose to save all men through Jesus Christ is basic to the Christian faith. Since no man can call Jesus "Lord" but by the Holy Spirit, the recognition of the Third Person of the Trinity is also basic to Christian worship. Since the Holy Spirit works among men through the means of grace – the Word of God in Scripture and sacraments – their impartation of the new life in Christ Jesus is the beginning of worship. Because the old nature of man must continually be killed by the Law, and the new man must constantly be revitalized by the Gospel and the sacraments, their use is a necessary part of any continuation in worship. So vital is this Word impetus to the existence and the practice of Christian worship that the Lutheran Confessions say: "We cannot offer anything to God unless we have first been reconciled and reborn. The greatest possible comfort comes from this doctrine that the highest worship in the Gospel is the desire to receive forgiveness of sins, grace, and righteousness" (Ap IV 310). Luther wrote in his Small Catechism: "We should fear and love God that we may not despise preaching and His Word, but hold it sacred and gladly hear and learn it."

3. In common usage the word "worship" is used to include this reception of the means of grace – hearing the Scriptures and participating in the sacraments. However, in its sharpest focus the word "worship" describes man's *response* to this power of God brought to his life by the Spirit. Man's *desiring* to receive forgiveness, grace, and righteousness is worship. "Gladly" is the adverb that carries the worship accent into the action of hearing the Word. It is not the mere participation in Holy Baptism or the Lord's Supper that is worship; but the reaching out to God by the believer during his participation or as he meditates on God's gift in the Sacrament, that is worship. Worship is more accurately man's "fearing and loving God," the heart of the First Commandment and the beating center of the Christian faith. Worship is "the all-pervading recognition of the absolute worth of God."

4. The word for "worship" commonly used in this specific sense in the OT is *hishtahawah*, from *shaha*, to bow, to prostrate oneself. In the NT the specific word is *proskuneo* – to prostrate oneself, to adore, to *worship*. The general concept of worship, however, included the broader aspects of "the service of God." The OT word for this idea is *abodah*, from *abad*, to labor, to serve. In the NT this idea is expressed in the word *latria*,* originally meaning servitude, the state of a hired laborer or slave. Later the word described a gratuitous act by a citizen for the state, as, for instance, if a ship were built at a citizen's expense and given to the navy. Christians use it in the terms "church service," "divine service," "religious service," or simply "service."

5. Since God is served not only by expressions of adoration but by acts of service to the least of our Lord's brethren, "worship" is often used to include all that a believing man does for God's sake. In this sense worship is everything that a child of God does in faith. The mutually edifying acts of Christians for one another, "teaching and admonishing one another in psalms and hymns and spiritual songs," are particularly described as aspects of worship. Every act of charity, done "as unto God" can well be called worship, especially since there is really nothing that a creature can do for the Creator except to show love and concerns for His other creatures. Such a definition of worship, however, equates it with the Christian life. To provide a workable definition of worship, the "recognition of the absolute worth of God" which pervades these actions could more helpfully be described as worship.

6. The interaction between Christians in worship ("Corporate worship") is the more readily included in some definitions because Christian worship is always corporate in nature. Frequently the corporateness is visibly expressed as congs. of Christians gather in one place to "worship." In such meetings the Scriptures and sacraments are used, and ritual and symbol are employed to make corporate expression possible. But even when Christians worship individually they are not alone, since all are "members one of another." That Christians "gather together" is the expressed will of God, and the mutual helpfulness of Christians as they worship together is God-pleasing. But narrowly considered, these actions, too, are focused in man's direction. What is

worship in them, in worship's narrow sense, is that they are offered to God by those who do them.

7. Forms which a group of Christians employ in order to express their worship of God are not worship, even though that word and the word "service" are sometimes used to label them (see also 4). The Luth. Confessions state that "the ceremonies or church usages which are neither commanded nor forbidden in the Word of God, but which have been introduced solely for the sake of good order and the general welfare, are in and for themselves no divine worship or even a part of it" (FC Ep X 3). It is here that the distinction between "spiritual" and "ceremonial" worship should be drawn. Our Lord's words to the woman at the well, "God is spirit, and they that worship Him must worship Him in spirit and in truth," do not deprecate the use of form in corporate or individual worship. They underline that the Lord must be loved with heart and soul and mind and strength, and not with heartless words or thoughtless ceremony. Our Lord Himself was the supreme example of such true worship of His Father; and He gave that example to us as a Jew participating in the ceremonial aspects of OT religion as well as in the times and ways that He went apart to pray to the Father in secret. The very creatureliness of humankind demands that worship be expressed in physical ways, even as God has revealed Himself in ways that are susceptible to the senses. God not only communicated His will and the revelation of His thoughts (which are not our thoughts) and His ways (which are not our ways) to the understanding of man, but He came into our world and time through the incarnation of His Son, Jesus Christ. His grace was made available to man through the very real dying of His Son, and our justification was secured through the coming to life again of the body of our Lord. His forgiving love is still mediated to us through print, through water and bread and wine. This alone would provide the adequate justification for the use of "things" in man's response to God. The detailed specification in the OT of the manner in which the action of worship was to be expressed is further evidence that it is correct for man to acknowledge his creatureliness by the use of ceremony and symbol in worship. Cultus, the embodiment of worship, is therefore divinely approved in principle but not specified in detail for NT Christians. The Luth. Ch., in Christian liberty, but with a very keen sense of the significance of the ch. as it has existed in the world through the centuries, has adopted the historic liturgy of the Western Cath. world. Even as this form is used in the recurring cycles of the church* yr., Christians must be mindful of the fact that worship is the adoring action of the participant, and not mere participation, in the liturgy.

8. The Christian worships when he gives to God the glory that is due His name; when he confesses his faults to Him whom he knows to be faithful and just to forgive his trespasses; when he gives thanks at all times and in all places for all things that a loving God directs in his life; and when he presents prayers and supplications for all sorts and conditions of men, and all this always as a member of the Kingdom and within the frame of the will of God, which is the basic premise of adoration. GWH

See also *Worship, Orders of; Worship, Park of; Worship, Private.*

Worship, Orders of. A few ancient ch. orders have either remained practically unchanged to the present time or have influenced present orders to a great extent.

1. The liturgy of the Roman Ch. was established in the basic features of its present form by Gregory the Great (590–604; see *Popes,* 4). Not only did the Roman rite, as fixed by him, tend to emphasize the difference bet. Rome and Constantinople, but it also brought out the sacerdotal idea as it gained ground in the West under the influence of Gregory. In spite of Gregory's conservative position, the Roman rite began to supersede other rites which had been in use in the West. In the Ger. Empire, which at that time included Gaul, Pepin* and Charlemagne* virtually succeeded in abolishing the Gallican Liturgy, the Roman Ordinary of the Mass being introduced by force.

2. In Eng. the Council of Clovesho prescribed the Roman rite for the entire country 747, although it never fully succeeded in replacing the ancient forms.

3. In Ireland the syns. of Tara 692, of Kells 1152, and of Cashel 1172 passed resolutions favoring the Roman rite alone.

4. In Sp. the Syn. of Burgos 1085 declared the Roman Liturgy valid for the entire country. Thus by the 12th c. the Roman forms had superseded or supplanted the rites previously in use in Sp., Fr., Ger., Eng., Scot., Ireland, and It., with the exception of the archbishopric of Milan and individual dioceses at Seville, Toledo, Salamanca, and Valladolid, in Sp.

5. There was a revision of the Roman Liturgy in the 16th c., the Breviary of Quignon appearing 1539 and the Breviary of Pius V (see *Popes*, 21) 1568. Since these efforts, however, did not meet with general satisfaction, Clement VIII issued a new Roman service book 1604 which was finally revised under Urban VIII and appeared 1634. It may be said to be a recast of the Gregorian Liturgy, the framework and much of the liturgical material having been retained.

6. The order of service in the celebration of Mass in the Roman Ch. at present contains the following parts: the solemn beginning of Mass, with the Introibo (Ps 43) and the Gloria Patri; the Confiteor, or confession of sins by the priest; the Introit of the day with the Gloria Patri; the Kyrie, followed by the Gloria in Excelsis; the Collect, introduced with the Salutation and Response; the reading of the Epistle; the Gradual, or Hallelujah; the Gospel, preceded by the Benediction and Salutation, with Response by the priest's assistants; the Nicene Creed; the Offertory, or the Oblation, with the Invocation and the Lavabo; the Preface, including everything from the Salutation to the Sanctus; the Canon of the Mass, including the offering of the unbloody sacrifice, the Consecration, the Elevation and Adoration, and the Commemoration for the living and the dead; the preparation for Communion; the prayers preceding the Distribution (Agnus Dei and several collects); the Distribution, the priest first taking bread and wine himself and then administering the bread, if there are communicants; the Communion Psalm, the Postcommunion; the end of the Mass; the Benediction.

7. The liturgy of the Ch. of Eng. and also of the Prot. Episc. Ch. in Am. was derived from Ephesine or Gallican sources, reaching Eng. in the last part of the 2d c. or in the 3d c. by way of Lyons. It was afterward modified by Augustine* of Canterbury and Theodore* of Tarsus. A revision by Osmund of Salisbury (1087) resulted in a compromise bet. the Roman and the Gallican rite. The ancient Use of Salisbury was amended and rev. 1516, a 2d rev. being undertaken 1541. For further hist. see *Book of Common Prayer.*

8. The order of the chief service in the Angl. Ch. is the following: Lord's Prayer; Collect for Purity; Ten Commandments, with the response Kyrie; Collect of the day; Epistle, the cong. seated; Gospel, the cong. standing; Nicene Creed; announcements; Psalm; Sermon; sentences relating to offering; General Prayer; Exhortation and Invitation; Confession

and Absolution; Comfortable Words; the Communion service.

9. In the liturgy of the Ref. chs. in Am. the sacrificial idea preponderates. In most denoms. a number of hymns, alternating with prayers and readings, precede the sermon, and the services close with prayer and benediction. Great emphasis is placed on the prayers in public worship, and the hymns and music are usually made an outstanding feature of the services. There is also a certain tendency to make the services more beautiful by introducing liturgical material, though the execution of liturgical parts is commonly left to a choir. See also *Worship, Parts of*.

10. The order of worship in the Luth. chs. of Am. is based largely on the work of Luther, whose *Formula missae* 1523 and *Deutsche Messe* 1526 exerted a wide influence. An abbreviated form of the Saxon and Prussian orders was used in many Ger. congs.

11. The chief parochial service of the Ch. of the Augsburg Conf. is the Holy Communion (AC XXIV 34; Ap XXIV 1). It is the historic rite of the Western Ch. in the language of the people. The invariable framework of the service (Ordinary) gives a cath. and evangelical direction to the devotion of the worshiper. The Propers, which change from Sun. to Sun., from week to week, from holiday to holiday, enable the worshiper to live in the regular rhythm of the ch. yr.

12. In the LCMS the Holy Communion may be divided into 2 parts: the liturgy of the Word and the liturgy of the Sacrament. The 1st part consists of (a) Introit, Kyrie, Gloria in Excelsis, Salutation, Collect; (b) Epistle and Holy Gospel; (c) Creed, Sermon, Hymn. The 2d part consists of (a) Salutation, Preface, Sanctus, Exhortation; (b) Lord's Prayer, Consecration, Distribution; (c) Post-Communion. A more detailed division of the service is the following: I. The Service of Preparation: Invocation, Confession, Absolution. II. The Liturgy of the Word: (a) Introit, Kyrie, Gloria in Excelsis, Salutation, Collect; (b) Epistle, Gradual and Hallelujah, Holy Gospel, Nicene Creed; (c) Hymn, Sermon. III. The Litury of the Sacrament: (a) Offertory, Prayer of the Ch.; (b) Salutation, Preface, Sursum Corda, Gratias Agimus, Dignum, Sanctus and Hosanna; (c) Lord's Prayer, Words of Institution, Pax Domini, Agnus Dei; (d) Distribution. IV. The Post-Communion: Nunc Dimittis, Versicle, Collects, Benedicamus, Benediction.

13. In addition to the above liturgy, which may be found in *The Lutheran Hymnal,* p. 15 (Conc. Pub. House, 1941), there are 3 alternate services suggested for cong. use and printed in the *Worship Supplement* (Conc. Pub. House, 1969). The 1st service is similar to the structure outlined above but provides a new musical setting for the liturgy. The Service of the Word is composed of Entrance Song, Lord Have Mercy, Glory and Praise, Salutation, Collect, Lesson, Gradual, Epistle, Holy Gospel, Sermon, Creed. The Service of the Sacrament is composed of Offering and Offertory, Intercessions, Preface, Holy Holy Holy, Prayer of Thanksgiving, Our Father, Greeting of Peace, Lamb of God, Distribution, Thanksgiving, Collect, and Benediction. This liturgy follows closely the sequence of the new RC Mass, especially in regard to the placement of the sermon immediately after the reading of the Holy Gospel.

14. The 2d service follows an order of worship used in St. Mark's in the Bowery Ch., NYC. The service is divided into 3 main parts: The Preparation, The Service of the Word, and The Meal. The Service of the Word includes Lessons, Sermon, and Intercessions. The Meal follows the 4-fold action of the Eucharist as outlined by Gregory Dix: Taking, Blessing, Breaking, and Sharing.

15. The 3d service is based on the so-called Dutch Canon. This order is divided into the Liturgy of the Word and the Liturgy of the Eucharist. The Liturgy of the Word includes Opening, Confession, Glory in the Highest, Prayer for the Day, Readings, Homily, Intercessory Prayers. The Liturgy of the Eucharist includes Prayer for Peace and Unity, Offertory, Invitation, Thanksgiving, Communion, and Dismissal.

16. There is also a Service of Holy Communion prepared by the Inter-Luth. Commission on Worship for provisional use. This order is printed in *Contemporary Worship Services, The Holy Communion* (Augsburg Pub. House, Bd. of Pub. – Luth. Ch. in Am., and Conc. Pub. House, 1970). The order of the liturgy is as follows: Entrance Hymn; The Liturgy of the Word: First Lesson, Second Lesson, Holy Gospel, Sermon, Hymn of the Day or Creed, Act of Reconciliation, the Intercessions; The Liturgy of the Eucharistic Meal, which includes all the traditional elements as found in the Order of Holy Communion, *The Luth. Hymnal* (p. 15); however, in order to emphasize the unity of the Eucharistic action, the various parts are not titled or distinguished.

17. The orders for the Holy Communion found in *The Luth. Hymnal* (p. 15), the *Worship Supplement,* and the Inter-Luth. Commission on Worship booklet are all based on the structure of the worship service employed by the early ch. They follow the historic 2-part division of the service: the Mass of the Catechumens and the Mass of the Faithful. JSD (11–17)

Worship, Parts of. In following the sequence of parts in the order of worship, their significance should be noted.

1. *Versicles* are short passages of Scripture intended to incite the worshipers to devotion and to suggest the central thought of the part following.

2. The *Confession of Sins* is properly made as a preparatory step, to obtain assurance of the forgiveness of God at the very beginning of worship. It has taken the place of the ancient Confiteor. In the Confiteor the priest knelt and made confession of his sins to "Almighty God, to the blessed Virgin Mary, the blessed archangel Michael, the blessed John the Baptist, the holy Apostles Peter and Paul," etc. The meaning of this confession was that the priest, having doffed his usual clothing and having donned his priestly vestments, was worthy of offering the sacrifice for the living and the dead. In Luth. worship the Confession is made for the entire cong.

3. The Office of the Word begins with the Introit and extends up to, but does not include, the Preface. The *Introit* (entrance) is the opening of the Ps. of the day, spoken or chanted after the preparation, to indicate the character of the day and the nature of the spiritual food offered to the cong. It is a remnant of the primitive psalmody, which was probably taken over into the early ch. from the services of the synagog. Originally the entire Ps. was chanted or sung antiphonally bet. the officiating clergy and the choir at the great entrance of the officiating priest and his assistants. Luther favored the use of the entire introductory Ps., but the abbreviated form remained, chiefly on account of lack of time.

4. The *Gloria Patri* or *Lesser Doxology* to the Holy Trinity distinguishes the use of the Psalter in NT times from its use in the synagog worship.

5. The *Kyrie* is a plea for the removal of misery and suffering, a confession of the wretchedness to be borne as a consequence of sins now forgiven. It is addressed to the Lord of mercy, in whom we not only have forgiveness of sins but also help and assistance in every need.

6. The *Gloria in excelsis* or *Greater Doxology* fittingly follows as a hymn of adoration, celebrating

God's glory as manifested in the merciful gift of His Son, who bore all our sins and infirmities.

7. The *Collects* are prayers in which the wants and perils, or the wishes and desires, of the people or the entire ch. are together presented to God.

8. The reading of the *Epistle* is followed by the *Hallelujah* on the part of the cong., which praises the Lord for the unspeakable gift of His Word. At this point may be sung the *Gradual* (sequence, prose, tract, trope), originally merely an extension of the last syllable of the Hallelujah, in order to permit the lector to proceed from the Epistle to the Gospel ambo, but later developed into a special hymn or a series of responses and versicles, from which the liturgical plays were developed. The announcement of the *Gospel* is hailed with the sentence "Glory be to Thee, O Lord," and the "Praise be to Thee, O Christ" at the close signifies the grateful acceptance or the Word by the cong. Then the *Creed* is said or chanted.

9. In the *Offertory* following the sermon the cong. confesses its grateful and humble acceptance of the Word which has just been proclaimed, all the faithful offering themselves, their substance, and the sacrifices of prayer, praise, and thanksgiving to the Lord.

10. The *Salutation,* with its *Response,* is sung at the opening of the Communion service to indicate the beginning of a new part of the service.

11. The Office of the Holy Communion begins with the Preface and extends to the end of the service. The *Preface* is preceded by the *prefatory sentences (Sursum* and *Gratias)* and is distinguished for impressiveness and beauty, setting forth the reason for the hymn of praise which follows the chanting of the Preface (whether common, for ordinary Sundays, or proper, for festival seasons). This hymn of praise is known as the *Sanctus,* or Tersanctus (also called Seraphic Hymn; cf. Is. 6:2-3), in which the combination of heaven's and earth's chorus results in an exalted strain of glorification and thanksgiving (to be distinguished from Trisagion*).

12. After the *Consecration* of the elements the pastor chants the *Pax,* to which the cong. responds with the *Agnus* Dei,* during which the communicants move to the altar.

13. The *Nunc dimittis* opens the Postcommunion. The believer, having received the fulness of God's grace and mercy, feels that he may now depart in peace to his home.

14. In the *Benedicamus* the cong. is called upon to give all honor to God alone, in order to receive from Him the final blessing.

15. The *Canticles,* among which the Benedictus (the song of Zacharias) and the Magnificat (the hymn of Mary) are best known, are as a rule used only in the minor services.

References for further reading are listed under *Liturgics;* see also *Propers; Response; Worship, Orders of.*

Worship, Private. 1. That the worship of God in the midst of the cong., in the assembly of those who confess the true God together, is required of all believers, appears from various parts of the Bible (Ps 26:12; 42:4; Heb 10:25).

2. Just as important, however, for the nurture of the Christian's spiritual life is the daily communication with the Lord by way of private worship, by prayer, by reading the Word of God and meditating on it, and by discussing its truths with others (Ps 1:2; 55:17; 109:4; Mt 6:6). Examples of consecrated men and women who remained in such communication with the Lord are Hannah (1 Sm 1:10); David (2 Sm 7:27; 1 Ch 17:25); Elisha (2 K 4:33; 6:17); Ezra (Ez 10:1); Daniel (Dn 6:10; 9:3-4); Mary, the mother of Jesus (Lk 2:19, 51); Anna, the prophetess (Lk 2:37); the Ethiopian eunuch (Acts 8:28 ff.); Cornelius (Acts 10:2, 30); Peter (Acts 10:9); the Bereans (Acts 17:11); Paul (Acts 20:36); the prophets (1 Ptr 1:10-11).

3. Home devotions may easily be arranged, either in the morning or in the evening, preferably right after meals, when all the members of the family are together. A few stanzas of a hymn may be sung, or the head of the house may at once read a chapter or a passage from the Bible or from some good book of exposition or a devotion based on a Bible passage. This will be followed by prayer suitable to the time or occasion and, possibly, by recital of part of the SC. The home service may close with the Lord's Prayer and the Benediction. The liturgical orders of Matins, Vespers, and Compline may well be used. See also *Hours, Canonical.*

Worship Hour, Family. A 15-minute radio program, sponsored by the Lutheran* Laymen's League, dedicated to the revival of the family altar. The idea of visiting in homes by radio with prayers, hymns, and meditations originated in the Pittsburgh, Pa., area 1943. Electrical transcriptions were prepared and offered to radio stations gratis on a sustaining basis. First broadcast was Sept. 27, 1948, over 11 stations; in less than a yr., over 100 stations; reached a peak of nearly 300 stations; discontinued 1971. TDM

Worthington, John (1618–71). Eng. theologian; ordained 1646; taught at Cambridge; Cambridge* Platonist. Ed. *Selected Discourses* of J. Smith.*

Wortman, Denis (1835–1922). B. Hopewell, N. Y.; grad. Amherst Coll. 1857 and New Brunswick Theol. Sem. 1860; ordained Ref. Ch. in Am.; pastor Brooklyn, Philadelphia, and Schenectady, N. Y.; served his denom. as sec. of ministerial relief and pres. of its Gen. Synod. Wrote "God of the Prophets, Bless the Prophets' Sons."

Wounds, Five Sacred. The wounds of Jesus, object of veneration by RCs during Middle Ages.

Wrangel, Carl Magnus (Aug. 23, 1727–June 12, 1786). Swed. Luth. pastor in Am.; b. Mölinta parish, Västmanland, Swed.; educ. Västeras, Uppsala, Strasbourg; ordained 1758; appointed pastor of Wicaco and provost of Swed. Luth. parishes in Am.; to Am. 1759; recalled to Sweden 1768; chief court chaplain.

Wrede, William (Wilhelm; 1859–1906). Ger. NT scholar; b. Bücken, Hannover; taught Göttingen; prof. Breslau; adherent of *Religionsgeschichtliche* Schule.* Held that Christ did not claim Messiahship but Gospels contain later beliefs and that Paul radically changed teachings of Jesus. Works include *Paulus; Das Messiasgeheimnis in den Evangelien.*

Wreford, John Reynell (1800–81). B. Barnstaple, Eng.; educ. Manchester Coll., York; nonconformist minister Birmingham; later withdrew from ministry and opened school. Among his hymns: "Lord, While for All Mankind We Pray."

Wright, Andreas (Sept. 13, 1835–Nov. 15, 1917). B. Norw.; pastor Coon Prairie, Rushford, and Highland, Wis.; one of founders of The Norwegian*-Dan. Augustana Syn. in Am. and The United* Norw. Luth. Ch. in Am.; served as secy. and later pres. of former; promoter of colls. and sems. (Augustana, Salem). Ed. *Luthersk Kirketidende* and *Bornebudet.*

Wright, George Ernest. See *Geography, Christian,* 8.

Wright, George Frederick (1838–1921). Congregationalist; b. Whitehall, N. Y.; grad. Oberlin; pastor; prof. Oberlin, first of NT language and literature, then of harmony of science and religion, 1881–1907; served on US Geological Survey. Ed. *Bibliotheca Sacra,* 1884–1921; works include *Scientific Confirmations of Old Testament History.*

Wright, Thomas, See *Evolution,* I.

Writings. See *Canon, Bible,* 2.

Wucherer, Johann Friedrich (1803–1881). Friend of J. K. W. Löhe* and cofounder with him of inner mission work in Bavaria; fought rationalism and championed cause of Luth. Confessions; prolific writer; throughout life active in inner missions.

Wulf, Maurice de (1867–1947). RC philos.; b. Belg.; educ. Löwen, Berlin, Paris; prof. Löwen. Works include *Histoire de la philosophie médiévale.*

Wulfila, See *Ulfilas.*

Wunder, Heinrich (Mar. 12, 1830–Dec. 22, 1913). B. Muggendorf, Bavaria; stud. at *Missionshaus* in Neuendettelsau; to Am.; stud. at Ft. Wayne and Altenburg; ordained Millstadt, Ill., 1849; to Chicago 1851, serving St. Paul's for 62 yrs. and contributing greatly to firm founding and rapid growth of Mo. Syn. in Chicago area; 1st pres. Ill. Dist. 1875–91.

Wunderle, Georg (1881–1950). Ger RC psychol. and theol.; b. Weissenburg; priest 1905; taught at Eichstätt; prof. and rector Würzburg; interested in piety of E. Orthodox Church. Ed. *Ostkirchliche Studien;* works include *Die gestaltende Kraft der Religion im Seelenleben des Menschen; Zur Psychologie der Stigmatisation; Das geistige Antlitz der Ostkirche.*

Wundt, Wilhelm Max (1832–1920). Ger. physiol., psychol.; b. Neckarau, Baden; educ. Tübingen, Heidelberg, Berlin; prof. Leipzig 1875. Works include writings on physiol., psychol., ethics. See also *Psychology,* G 4.

Wurm, Theophil (1868–1953). Ger. Luth.; b. Basel, Switz.; educ. Tübingen; vicar Stuttgart; pastor of social work Stuttgart 1899; pastor Ravensburg 1920; prelate Heilbronn 1927; pres. Luth. Ch. of Württemberg 1929; bp. 1933. In Kirchenkampf* preserved indep. of Württemberg ch.; became leader in confessing ch.; protested against euthanasia and extermination of Jews. Works include *Der lutherische Grundcharakter der württembergischen Landeskirche; Erinnerungen aus meinem Leben; Fünfzig Jahre im Dienste der Kirche.*

Wurster, Paul (1860–1923). Ger. Ev. theol.; b. Hohenstaufen; pastor Heilbronn; deacon Blaubeuren; prof. and dir. of sem. Friedberg; prof. practical theol. Tübingen; wrote devotional books and on inner missions. Works include *Was jedermann von der Inneren Mission wissen muss; Abendsegen.*

Württemberg Bible Society. See *Bible Societies,* 2.

Württemberg Confession. See *Brenz, Johann; Lutheran Confessions,* A 5.

Württemberg Pietists, See *Nazarenes,* 2.

Württemberger Summarien. Eberhard III, Duke of Württemberg, ordered these *Summarien* printed to take place of *Summarien* by V. Dietrich,* which through plundering of chs. in war had become scarce. They were written by Johann Jakob Heinlin (d. 1660), Jeremias Rebstock, and Johann Konrad Zeller (d. 1683) and were published 1669. To 2d ed. explanatory remarks were added by members of Tübingen faculty: Johann Wolfgang Jäger, Johann Christoph Pfaff, and A. A. Hochstetter.* An ed. was pub. as late as 1878. The books contain not a translation of the Bible but only *summaries* of the contents of the OT and NT books and at the end of each chapter useful applications.

Wuttke, Karl Friedrich Adolph (1819–70). Prof. Berlin and Halle; advocate of Luth. Confessions within Prussian* Union. Wrote on hist. of heathendom, contemporary superstitions of Ger. people, and an outstanding work on Christian ethics.

Wyandottes, See *Indians, American,* 6.

Wycliffe, John (Wiclif; Wyclif; 1320–84). 1. B. of noble parentage near Richmond, Yorkshire, Eng.; was connected with Oxford U. as student or teacher most of his life; was also parish priest, last at Lutterworth, a small market town in Leicestershire near Birmingham.

2. Wycliffe's repeated opposition to the pope's meddling in Eng. affairs of state and ch. and his other anti-Roman activities caused his citation before ecclesiastical tribunals, which, however, failed to silence him. Besides preaching himself, he trained and sent out itinerant preachers; also issued numerous Lat. treatises and many Eng. tracts against Roman errors. With aid of Nicholas* of Hereford, one of his pupils, he translated Bible from Lat. Vulgate and issued complete Eng. Bible. See also *Purvey, John.*

3. His attack on transubstantiation* aroused bitter controversy with mendicant* friars. At times he seems to teach the Luth. doctrine of the Lord's Supper, and then again speaks of the bread and wine as being "Christ's body and blood figuratively and spiritually." Considered the 2 sacraments real means of grace, but seemed to believe that an unbelieving priest could not administer them effectively. Confirmation and extreme unction were to him mere human institutions. Termed enforced auricular confession "a sacrament of the devil" and denounced purgatory as a blasphemous swindle. Although he taught that Christ is the only Mediator bet. God and man, and delighted to dwell on the love of Christ, he ascribed a certain degree of meritoriousness to the good works of a Christian. Upheld separation of ch. and state and taught that the ch. is the cong. of the elect. Considered enforced celibacy immoral and apparently also thought it unscriptural "that ecclesiastical men should have temporal possessions." Maintained that Christ is only Head of ch. and that pope is Antichrist, yet never left Roman Ch. After his death Council of Constance 1415 excommunicated him, and 1427 his bones were burned and their ashes thrown into the Swift.

J. Stacy, *John Wyclif and Reform* (Philadelphia, 1964).

Wycliffe Bible Translators, Inc. Organized 1934; goal: to make Bible available to all tribes.

Wycliffism. Term used to describe adherence to principles and doctrines of J. Wycliffe.* See also *Lollards,* 2.

Wyneken, Friedrich Conrad Dietrich (May 13, 1810–May 4, 1876). B. Verden, Hannover, Ger.; father was Luth. pastor; educ. Göttingen and Halle; as tutor of young nobleman traveled in Fr. and It.; rector of Lat. school at Bremerford. Influenced to Biblical faith by Pastor Hanfstengel at Leesum near Bremen, F. A. Tholuck,* and others. Arrived Baltimore 1838; assisted J. Haesbert; sent W by ex. bd. of Miss. Soc. of Pennsylvania* Ministerium; pastor Friedheim and Ft. Wayne, Ind.; also traveling miss. NW Ohio, S Mich., and N Ind. with undaunted courage in face of many hardships.

Failing health and the desire to obtain help, both men and money, for the cause of Lutheranism in Am. took him to Ger. 1841. His celebrated *Notruf* ("The Distress of the Ger. Luths. in N. Am.") and his lectures in Nürnberg, Erlangen, Dresden, Leipzig, and elsewhere gained the support of such influential men as J. K. W. Löhe,* L. A. Petri,* and K. G. v. Raumer* and stimulated not only W. Sihler,* F. J. C. Lochner,* F. A. Craemer,* G. E. C. F. Sievers,* and others to come to Am. but also caused colonies of people to emigrate with them. This plus the generous work of the Miss. Soc. of Stade, the Löhe *Nothelfer,* and the Soc. for N. Am. in Dresden resulted in such developments as the Franconian settlements in Mich. with their missions among the Indians and the coming of young men for work in the Midwest with the subsequent est. of a practical sem. at Ft. Wayne, all of which is accountable to the energetic and enthusiastic efforts of Wyneken.

In 1845 he was called to St. Paul's in Baltimore. Taking a firm stand against unionism, indifference, and the lodge, he emphasized confessionalism. He severed his connections with the General* Syn. for confessional reasons and, having in Ft. Wayne made the acquaintance of the Saxons in Mo. through the *Lutheraner,* took keen interest in the early deliberations which resulted in the organization of the Mo. Syn., being present at the Cleveland meeting where preliminary plans were drawn up. He joined Syn. at its 2d conv. and was elected its 2d pres. 1850, having previously been called to serve Old Trinity Cong. in St. Louis. The yr. after his election he and C. F. W. Walther* were sent to Ger. to adjust doctrinal differences which had arisen between Löhe and the Mo. Syn. During his early presidency the syn., because of rapid growth, was divided into 4 dists. and the heated Buffalo-Mo. controversy came to a head. With the burdens of office his health became impaired and he was granted a leave of absence by his cong. In 1859 he settled near Ft. Wayne, devoting full time to the presidency. He discharged his duties with vigor and enthusiasm, visiting as many as 60 congs. in 1 yr., stressing at convs. and visitations the necessity of doctrinal purity and a sound program of Christian educ., the importance of a sanctified Christian life, and the need for ceaseless warfare against sectarianism, lodges, worldliness, and indifference. The character of the Mo. Syn. is to a high degree the result of his influence.

In 1864, owing to increasing age and bodily infirmities, he was relieved of the presidency; took charge of Trinity Ch. in Cleveland, latterly as assistant to his son; retired 1875. EJS

W. A. Baepler, *A Century of Grace* (St. Louis, 1947); *Ebenezer,* ed. W. H. T. Dau (St. Louis, 1922); G. E. Hageman, "Friedrich Konrad Dietrich Wyneken," *Men and Missions,* ed. L. Fuerbringer, III (St. Louis, 1926); J. C. W. Lindemann, article on Wyneken in *Amerikanischer Kalender für Deutsche Lutheraner,* 1877; C. Mauelshagen, *American Lutheranism Surrenders to Forces of Conservatism* (Athens, Ga., 1936); *Moving Frontiers,* ed. C. S. Meyer (St. Louis, 1964).

Wyneken, Henry C. (Dec. 13, 1844–June 21, 1899). Son of F. C. D. Wyneken*; b. Ft. Wayne, Ind.; educ. Conc. Coll. and Sem.; instructor in institute of F. A. Brunn* at Steeden, Ger.; assistant to his father (later, first pastor) and principal Trinity Luth. School, Cleveland, Ohio; prof. exegesis, homiletics, catechetics, and other branches at Conc. Sem., Springfield, Ill., 1876; retired 1890 on account of ill health; served 2 small churches near Springfield; founder of Negro mission in Springfield. Rev. *Altenburger Bibelwerk.*

X

Xaverian Brothers. Religious teaching institute of laymen, founded in Belg. 1839, primarily for Am. work; entered US 1854.

Xavier, Francis (1506–52). Famous Jesuit miss.; man of extraordinary earnestness, energy, and devotion; one of the original number who, with I. Loyola*, formed the Society* of Jesus; ordained to priesthood 1537; began work in India 1542, Japan 1549; died while trying to enter China. See also *Malaysia,* 2.

Xenia Seminary. See *Pittsburgh Theological Seminary.*

Xenophanes (6th c. B. C.). Gk. philos.; regarded as founder of Eleatic* school; opposed anthropomorphic conceptions of God; regarded God as one. See also *Philosophy.*

Ximenes (Jimenes), Francisco. See *Jiménez do Cisneros, Francisco.*

XPI. First 3 Gk. capital letters of the word *Christos* (chi, rho, iota).

Y

Yahweh. See *Jahweh.*
Yahwist (Yahvist). Variants of Jahwist; Jahvist. See *Higher Criticism,* 7–12.
Yam. See *Canaanites, Religion of.*
Yang. See *Chinese Philosophy,* 4; *Confucianism,* 3.
Yang Chu. See *Chinese Philosophy,* 4.
Yaramanda. See *New Guinea,* 7.
Yaroslav (Jaroslav). See *Estonia,* 1.
Yearly Meeting. See *Friends, Society of.*
Yin. See *Chinese Philosophy,* 4; *Confucianism,* 3.
Ylvisaker, Ivar Daniel (May 26, 1868–Mar. 5, 1926). B. Trondhjem, Norw.; to Am. as child; educ. Luther Coll., Decorah, Iowa, Luther* Theol. Sem.; pastor Great Falls and Helena, Mont., Mayville, N. Dak.; pres. N. Dak. Dist. of The Norw. Luth. Ch. of Am. after 1917 merger; pres. of ministerium of same ch.; member of several committees and boards, including the one which brought about the merger. See also *Evangelical Lutheran Church, The,* 13–16.
Ylvisaker, Johannes Thorbjoernsen (Apr. 24, 1845–Oct. 10, 1917). Father of S. C. Ylvisaker; b. Sogndal, Norw.; to Am. 1871; educ. Luther Coll., Decorah, Iowa, Conc. Sem., St. Louis, Christiania, Leipzig; pastor Zumbrota Minn., 1877; prof. Luther* Theol. Sem. 1879. Coed. *Kirketidende;* works include *The Gospels.*
Ylvisaker, Sigurd Christian (June 15, 1884–Apr. 26, 1959). Son of J. T. Ylvisaker; b. Madison, Wis.; educ. Luther Coll., Decorah, Iowa, Minnesota U., Luther* Theol. Sem., St. Paul, Minn., Leipzig; pastor Minot, N. Dak., 1910; prof. Gk. and Heb. Luther Coll., Decorah, Iowa, 1911; prof. Conc. Coll., St. Paul, Minn., 1919; pastor Madison, Wis., 1923; pres. Bethany Lutheran Coll., Mankato, Minn., 1930; retired 1952. Ed. *Lutheran Sentinel;* chief ed. *Grace for Grace: Brief History of the Norwegian Synod;* works include *Zur Babylonischen und Assyrischen Grammatik.*
Yoga. One of the 6 systems of Indian philos. Teaches how, by ascetic discipline, concentration of thought, supression of breath, and sitting immovably, to unite the soul with the Supreme Spirit and thereby to obtain complete control over the body (culminating sometimes in ecstasy and catalepsy), miraculous powers, and finally release from rebirth, i. e., salvation. See *Brahmanism,* 4; *Theosophy.*
Yom Kippur. See *Judaism,* 4.
York Amendment. Amendment to Art. III, Sec. 3, of const. of Gen. Syn., drawn up by H. N. Pohlman* for conv. at York, Pa., 1864, after delegates of Pennsylvania* Ministerium had withdrawn. Favorably acted upon by Gen. Syn. and adopted by majority of 18 dist. syns. (but the 4 syns. which rejected it remained in Gen. Syn.). Amendment reads: "All regularly constituted Lutheran synods not now in connection with the General Synod, receiving and holding with the Evangelical Lutheran Church of our fathers, the Word of God as contained in the canonical Scriptures of the Old and New Testaments, as the only infallible rule of faith and practice, and the Augsburg Confession, as a correct exhibition of the fundamental doctrines of the Divine Word, and of the faith of our Church founded upon that Word, may, at any time, become associated with the General Synod by complying with the requisitions of this constitution and sending delegates according to the ratio specified in Art. II." *Proceedings of the 21st Conv. of the Gen. Syn. of the Ev. Luth. Ch. in the US, Assembled in York, Pa., May 1864* (Gettysburg, 1864), pp. 38–39. See also *General Synod of the Evangelical Lutheran Church in the United States of America, The,* 7.
York Resolution. Statement adopted by York conv. of The General* Syn. of the Ev. Luth. Ch. in the USA 1864. It reflected a resolution adopted by the Pittsburgh* Syn. at Zelienople Pa., 1856. Resolution reads: "The following preamble and resolutions in reference to alleged errors in the Augsburg Confession were presented and adopted: . . . *Resolved,* That while this Synod, resting on the Word of God as the sole authority in matters of faith, on its infallible warrant rejects the Romish doctrine of the real presence or transubstantiation and with it the doctrine of consubstantiation; rejects the mass, and all the ceremonies distinctive of the mass; denies any power in the sacrament as an *opus operatum,* or that the blessings of baptism, and the Lord's Supper, can be received without faith; rejects auricular confession and priestly absolution; holds that there is no priesthood on earth but that of all believers, and that God only can forgive sins; and maintains the divine obligations of the Sabbath, and while we would with our whole heart reject any part of any confession which taught doctrines in conflict with this our testimony, nevertheless, before God and his church, we declare that, in our judgment, the Augsburg Confession, properly interpreted, is in perfect consistence with this our testimony and with the Holy Scripture as regards the errors specified." *Proceedings of the 21st Conv. of the Gen. Syn. of the Ev. Luth. Ch. in the US, Assembled in York, Pa., May 1864* (Gettysburg, 1864), pp. 39–40.
Yorker Brethren. See *Brethren, River.*
Young, Brigham (1801–77). Mormon leader; b. Whitingham, Vt.; converted and baptized in Mormon faith 1832; itinerant miss.; mem. of the Twelve Apostles; directed Mormon settlement at Nauvoo, Ill.; miss. in Eng. 1839–41; successor of J. Smith* Sr. 1847; leader of migration to Salt Lake City, Utah, arriving 1847; governor of Territory of Utah 1850–57; removed by Pres. Buchanan; practiced polygamy. See also *Latter Day Saints.*
Young, Rosa Jinsey (May 14, 1890–June 30, 1971). B. Rosebud, Ala.; educ. Payne U., Selma, Ala.; teacher; instrumental in beginning permanent Luth. work among Negroes in Ala. 1916; prof. Ala. Luth. Acad. (see *Ministry, Education of*) 1946; received Litt. D. from Conc. Sem., Springfield, Ill., 1961. Works include *Light in the Dark Belt.*
Young Christian Workers. See *Jocists.*
Young Men's Christian Association. Founded in London, June 6, 1844, by G. Williams.* Original purpose was to win young men to faith and love of Jesus Christ. Soon the assoc. widened its scope of work by defining its object as being "improvement of the spiritual and mental condition of young men." Associations were est. in Montreal and Boston 1851 and in New York 1852. The New York assoc. in 1886 stated its objective to be "the improvement of the spiritual, mental, social, and physical condition of young men." This broad definition of the aim of the YMCA became characteristic of the N. Am. assoc. as a whole. While never claiming to be a ch., the YMCA stressed its purpose of serving the ch.,

seeking to cooperate with all denominations. In 1922 the various branches were permitted to elect or appoint up to 10 percent of their managing bd. from members of the assoc. not identified with chs. defined as evangelical. As far as the members are concerned, the YMCA long ago abandoned the evangelical test, except as to officers, its purpose being stated in terms so broad as to eliminate religious convictions as a condition of membership. The organization does not exact any religious pledge or confession from those who simply desire to have access to its colleges, business and vocational schools, gymnasia, reading rooms, etc. TG

Young People's Organizations, Christian. I. *Development of Youth Work in America.* 1. Young people's work in Prot. chs. did not begin in individual denoms. but with the interdenom. program known as the Young* Men's Christian Assoc. 1845, the first boys' dept. being est. in this organization 1866.

2. Another contribution to the youth movement in Prot. chs. was made by the Internat. Soc. of Christian* Endeavor, started by F. E. Clark* 1881, and the young people's societies which were brought into existence as a result of this program.

3. There were other movements which gave impetus to youth work in Prot. chs., such as the S. S. movement fostered esp. in Eng. by R. Raikes*; the Knights of King Arthur, started 1892 by William Byron Forbush; the Woodcraft Indians, founded 1902 by Ernest Thompson Seton, a program which may be called a forerunner of the Boy Scout* movement in Eng., coming to the US 1910; the Internat. S. S. Assoc., beginning to be recognized 1906.

4. Prot. denoms. at first used and adopted youth programs developed outside the ch. Gradually they began to pub. their own materials.

5. Boston U. set up a Dept. of Religious Educ. 1918. In 1920 this univ. set up a Dept. of Young People's Work. Since that time other colls. and univs. have est. courses dealing with youth work.

6. The trend in Prot. denoms. in later years has been toward cooperation in interdenom. activities. This trend is evident also in the Prot. youth programs, esp. in the United Christian Youth Movement (see V 1). Other cooperative efforts include the United Student Christian Council (est. 1944; joined NCC; see also *Student Volunteer Movement,* 4), a fed. on the nat. level of 12 ch. student movements, the Student YMCA and YWCA, the Student Volunteer Movement, and the interseminary movement; the World Student Christian Federation, seeking to unite internationally the efforts of Prot. students; the Youth for Christ movement; the Inter-Varsity Christian Fellowship (see *Students, Spiritual Care of,* A 5); the Campus* Crusade for Christ; and the Navigators. Teen Challenge, which grew out of the work of Rev. David Wilkerson (author of *The Cross and the Switchblade*) in NYC, concerns itself with prevention and treatment of drug addiction.

II. *Lutheran Youth Organizations.* 1. *The Luther League of The American Lutheran Church* (including the youth of the former ALC, ELC, LFC, and UELC) was organized at a constituting conv. in Milwaukee, Wis., Aug. 16–21, 1960.

The ALC has carried out a vigorous youth program, as can be seen in the strong representation of ALC youth at intersynodical youth gatherings. Nat. offices are at 422 S. Fifth St., Minneapolis, Minn. 55415.

2. *The Luther League of the Lutheran Church in America* (including the Luther Leagues of the former AELC, Augustana Ev. Luth. Ch., Suomi Syn., and ULCA) came into being at a constituting conv. in San Francisco, Calif., Aug. 20–26, 1962. At this conv. the Luther League adopted a const., elected officers, adopted a budget, and developed the Luther League program for the future. In 1968, however, the Luther League disbanded. See *Youth Work,* 7.

In addition, the LCA has a Commission on Youth Ministry, which is responsible for giving direction to the total youth ministry of the church. Nat. offices are at 2900 Queen Lane, Philadelphia, Pa. 19129.

3. *The Walther League* (youth organization of the former Synodical* Conference, with most societies in LCMS). Organized May 23, 1893, at Trinity Church, Buffalo, N.Y. The name *Walther Liga* (from C. F. W. Walther*) was adopted 1894. The const. of the Walther League stated: "The purpose of this association shall be to help young people grow as Christians through WORSHIP – building a stronger faith in the Triune God; EDUCATION – discovering the will of God for their daily life; SERVICE – responding to the needs of all men; RECREATION – keeping the joy of Christ in all activities; FELLOWSHIP – finding the power of belonging to others in Christ."

The League involved youth in worship, leadership training schools, camping, writing and publishing, various training projects of service (welfare), missions, vocational guidance, recruitment for ch. professions, opportunities for practical experience in roles of leadership, and opportunities for a wider circle of fellowship than the home parish. It had its own headquarters bldg., paid for by the young people, erected 1942 in Chicago.

The League sponsored the Arcadia Association, an adult educ. and conference program agency, whose directors were elected annually by the internat. ex. bd. of the Walther League. The Arcadia Assoc. owned, operated, and managed Camp Arcadia (Arcadia, Mich.) as a model summer camp and a site for experimentation and development of conference programs.

The League also sponsored the Wheat* Ridge Foundation, whose directors were elected annually by the internat. ex. bd. of the Walther League. The Wheat Ridge Foundation has established and/or supports sanitoria and hospitals in Wheat Ridge (Colo.), Japan, India, Hong Kong, New Guinea, and Nigeria, in addition to regular support of other Luth. welfare agencies in the US and Canada. It also contributes to the support of religious, educ., and scientific projects. Financial support is given through an annual Wheat Ridge seals campaign at Christmas.

Walther League publications included the *Walther League Messenger* (W. A. Maier,* ed.); the *Workers Quarterly* (Alfred P. Klausler, ed.), a quarterly topic discussion and program guide for societies; *Arena* (Alfred P. Klausler, ed.), a monthly magazine for young adults; *Spirit* (Walter Riess, ed.), a monthly magazine for teen-agers. For later developments see *Youth Work;* see also *Students, Spiritual Care of,* C 9.

The LCMS in 1920 elected a *Bd. for Young People's Work;* name changed 1969 to *Bd. of Youth Ministry;* composed (1973) of 1 pastor, 1 teacher, 1 representative of a synodical school, 2 laymen, and 5 young people. The syn. has charged this bd. to assist congs., pastors, and dists. to serve their youth, including those in organizations such as Boy Scouts, Girl Scouts, 4-H, Camp Fire Girls, etc. "The purpose of youth ministry is – a. To proclaim among youth the presence, love, and power of God through faith in our Lord Jesus Christ, whose life, death, and resurrection have redeemed all people; b. To equip youth for faithful service to God and His world by a ministry of the Holy Spirit through Word and Sacraments; c. To assist and train adults in building helpful Christian relationships with youth in contemporary culture; d. To enable youth and adults to share their unique gifts in ministry to one another within the Christian community and in ministry to the world as the witnessing people of God; e. To provide settings for Christian youth to demonstrate the mission of the church in word and life and for unclaimed youth to be exposed to the call of God in the Gospel" (*Handbook* of the LCMS).

4. *The Luther League of the Synod* of Evangelical Lutheran Churches* (formerly the Slovak. Ev. Luth. Ch.). Organized Sept. 5, 1927, in St. Paul's Luth. Ch., Whiting, Ind. Principal projects were the Luth. Haven seals campaign, *Lutheran Beacon* subscription campaign, scholarship fund campaign, mission projects such as supporting a vicar at a mission church, and pub. the Luther League periodical, the *Courier*. Since 1971 the SELC is a dist. of LCMS.

5. *Inter-Church Activities of Lutheran Youth Groups.* For a number of yrs. some of the Luth. youth organizations have planned and worked together in holding nationwide youth gatherings, discussing youth problems, sharing experiences and materials, and taking joint actions on some projects. *Lutheran Youth Research* was administered in most of the Luth. ch. bodies 1958–61. It established that the problems which are most troublesome to Luth. youth can be grouped into 5 areas to form the following scales: family, opposite sex, personal faith, self, school. The kinds of help youth want most from the ch. can be identified as guidance in the fields of vocations and boy-girl relationship. A summary of this research is found in *What Youth Are Thinking* and M. P. Strommen's *Profiles of Church Youth.*

III. *Protestant Youth Organizations.* 1. *Baptist Training Union* (Southern Bap. Convention). Organized 1934; successor to Bap. Young People's Union, 1896–1934; under guidance of S. S. bd.; began as an organization in Southern Bap. chs. primarily for young people ages 17–24; later expanded into a graded program to train mems., nursery through adult, in responsibilities of ch. membership and to help them mature and grow as Christians. Nat. office: 127 9th Ave., No., Nashville, Tenn. 37203.

2. *Baptist Youth Fellowship* (Am. Bap. Convention). Bap. Young People's Union of Am. organized 1891; name changed to Bap. Youth Fellowship 1941; program administered through Dept. of Youth Work; program: Sun. ch. school, evening fellowship, Boy Scouts, Fellowship Guild, Choir, and any other phase of the ch. youth ministry. Nat. office: Valley Forge, Pa. 19481.

3. *Baptist Young People's Union* (Bap. Convention of Ontario and Quebec). First conv. 1892; at first an integral part of the conv. of chs., indep. of any bd.; since 1934 the Young People's Dept. of the Dept. of Christian Education. Nat. office: 188–190 St. George St., Toronto 5, Ont., Canada.

4. *Christian Youth Fellowship* (Christian Ch. [Disciples of Christ]). Organized 1938; first nat. meeting 1943; activities offered through the United Christian Missionary Society; Youth mag.: *Vision.* Nat. office: 222 S. Downey Ave., Indianapolis, Ind. 46219.

5. *Presbyterian Youth Fellowship* (Presb. Ch. in the US). Period of beginnings 1861–94; period of Covenanters and Miriams 1895–1901; period of Westminster League 1902–09; period of Christian* Endeavor 1910–23; period of transitions 1923–29; period of development of the Kingdom Highways Program 1930–35; period of recent developments 1935–63; period of Covenant Life Curriculum, developed in cooperation with 4 other Presb. and Ref. denoms., 1964–. Nat. office: Presb. Bldg., 801 E. Main St., Richmond, Va. 23209.

6. *Westminster Fellowship* (The Presb. Ch. in the USA; 1958: The United Presb. Ch. in the USA). Work begun 1861; organization effected 1895; first nat. meeting 1903; 4 commissions: faith and life, stewardship, Christian fellowship, Christian outreach. Nat. office: 1105 Witherspoon Bldg., Philadelphia, Pa. 19107.

7. *Cumberland Youth Fellowship* (Cumberland Presb. Ch.). Nat. office: McKenzie, Tenn. 38118.

8. *Christian Union* (including all youth organizations of the Associate Ref. Presb. Ch. [Gen. Syn.]). Organized 1884; first nat. meeting 1895. Nat. office: 113 W. 11th St., Charlotte, N. C. 28202.

9. *Youth Fellowship* (The United Presb. Ch. of N. Am.; merged 1958 with 6 above). Organized 1874; first nat. meeting 1889.

10. *Youth Ministry* (United Ch. of Christ, the merged youth ministry of the former Pilgrim Fellowship of the Gen. Council of the Cong. Christian Chs. and the Youth Fellowship of the Ev. and Ref. Ch.). The Youth Ministry concept emphasizes the unity of the cong., denying an auxiliary or separate youth organization; 5 program areas: Christian faith, witness, outreach, citizenship, fellowship. Nat. office: 1505 Race St., Philadelphia, Pa. 19102.

11. *Reformed Youth Fellowship* (Ref. Ch. in Am.). Youth work was at first conducted without a nat. organization; plan for the nat. Reformed Youth Fellowship adopted 1960. Nat. office: 475 Riverside Dr., New York, N. Y. 10027.

12. *United Methodist Youth Fellowship* (The United Meth. Ch.). Organized 1939; first nat. meeting 1940; successor to Epworth League, which included youth of the former Meth. Episc. Ch. and Meth. Prot. Church. Nat. office: P. O. Box 871, Nashville, Tenn. 37202.

13. *Free Methodist Youth* (Free Meth. Ch. of N. Am.). First serious attempt to provide a distinctive program for youth 1903; Young People's Missionary Society launched 1919 as an auxiliary of the Women's Missionary Society; became official youth organization 1931; name changed to Free Methodist Youth 1955; 3-fold purpose: (1) bringing youth to Christ, (2) bringing youth up in Christ, (3) sending youth forth for Christ; strong mission and evangelism program; youth responsible for raising budget; motto: "Others"; slogan: "United to Make Christ Known." Nat. office: Winona Lake, Ind. 46590.

14. *Nazarene Young People's Society* (Ch. of the Nazarene). Organized 1923; first nat. meeting 1923. Nat. office: 6401 The Paseo, Kansas City, Mo. 64131.

15. *The American Moravian Youth Fellowship* (Moravian Ch. in Am. [*Unitas Fratrum*]). Nat. office: 69 W. Church St., Bethlehem, Pa. 18018.

16. *Church of the Brethren Youth Fellowship* (Ch. of the Brethren). Need of developing youth program recognized as early as 1904; youth fellowships organized in local chs. following a major study 1920. Nat. office: 1451 Dundee Ave., Elgin, Ill. 60120.

17. *The Anglican Young People's Association* (The Anglican Ch. of Canada). Organized 1902; first nat. meeting 1931. Nat. office: 604 Jarvis St., Toronto 5, Ont., Canada.

18. *The Youth Fellowship of the Evangelical United Brethren Church* (Ev. United Brethren Ch.; 1968: merged with 12 to form The United Meth. Ch.). Organized 1946; first nat. meeting 1946.

19. *Friends Youth Fellowship* (Friends United Meeting, formerly the Five Years Meeting of Friends). Organized 1935. Nat. office: 101 Quaker Hill Dr., Richmond, Ind. 47374.

20. *Seventh Day Baptist Youth Fellowship* (Seventh Day Bap. Gen. Conference). Organized 1940. Nat. office: Alfred Station, N. Y. 14803.

IV. *Nondenominational groups.* 1. *United Christian Youth Movement* began 1934 with denoms. working together in their youth movements or ministries; indep. movement; closely related to the Youth Dept. of the NCC (ex. staff same for both); close working relationship with the Youth Dept. of the WCC. Nat. office: 475 Riverside Dr., New York 27, N. Y.

2. For other interdenom. movements see I 6.

V. *Roman Catholic Youth Organizations.* 1. *The National Council of Catholic Youth* was est. 1951 and operates under the Youth Dept. of the National Catholic Welfare Conference. It has 3 divisions: for students in RC colls. (including the Nat. Fed. of Cath. Coll. Students); for students in other colls. (the Newman Clubs); and the diocesan section. The Nat. Council of Cath. Youth provides on a nat. scale a device by which all existing youth councils and organizations of the RC Ch. are unified. Nat. office: 1312 Massachusetts Ave., N. W., Washington, D. C. 20005.

2. *Sodalities.* The Sodality of Our Lady was founded 1563 in the Roman College of the Society of Jesus by a young Jesuit teacher, John Leunis, who wanted to band together in a lay religious order young men in colleges. The first sodality in the New World began 1574 at the Colegia Maxima in Mexico City. One was founded 1730 at the Ursuline school in New Orleans, La., and ca. 1789 one began functioning at Georgetown U. in Washington, D. C. The sodality magazine *Queen's Work* was launched 1913 in St. Louis, Mo. The World Fed. of Sodalities was est. 1953, and the Nat. Fed. of Sodalities 1956. Sodalities involve not only youth but the adult laity as well. Annual summer schools of Catholic* Action have been conducted since 1931. Nat. office: 4140 Lindell, St. Louis, Mo. 63108.

Bibliography of Historical Developments of Luth. Youth Programs: 1. Of all Luth. youth programs: G. Jenny, *The Youth Movement in the American Lutheran Church* (Minneapolis, 1928); C. H. Peters, "Developments of the Youth Programs of the Lutheran Churches in America," doctoral thesis at Conc. Sem., St. Louis, 1951 (duplicated); M. P. Strommen, *Profiles of Church Youth* (St. Louis, 1963).

2. Of youth work in LCMS: *ABC of Youth Work* (Chicago, 1949); T. C. Coates, "A Century of Youth Work," *Walther League Messenger,* LIII, 334-35, 363-65; C. H. Peters (see previous par.), pp. 83–144, and Appendix AA, pp. 505–23; H. E. Simon, "Background and Beginnings of Organized Youth Work in the Missouri Synod," unpub. thesis at Conc. Sem., St. Louis, 1944; O. H. Theiss, "The Way of the Years," *Walther League Messenger,* LI, 480–83, 508–10, 512; *Walther League Manual* (Chicago, 1935); W. F. Weiherman, ed., *Fifty Years* (Chicago, 1943). CP

Young People's Society of Christian Endeavor. See *Christian Endeavor.*

Young Women's Christian Association. A Young Women's Christian Association of Great Britain and Ireland was initiated 1855. In New York a Union Prayer Circle was formed by Mrs. Marshall O. Roberts 1858. The name was changed in the same year to Ladies' Christian Association. Its purpose was "to labor for the temporal, moral, and religious welfare of young self-supporting women." In 1866 the name was changed to Ladies' Christian Union, and the same year the Young Women's Christian Association of Boston was organized. In the course of years similar organizations were founded, which then developed into the present Young Women's Christian Association. Its purpose is to look after the mental, physical, social, and spiritual interests of young women. In character, work, and methods the organization closely resembles the Young* Men's Christian Association.

Youth Fellowship. See *Young People's Organizations, Christian,* III.

Youth Ministry. See *Young People's Organizations, Christian,* III 10.

Youth Work. 1. Youth work in the ch. could previously be called the "training of youth in Christian growth during the postconfirmation period." Most parishes could anticipate the presence of a relatively stable and satisfied nucleus of young people to form some type of Young Peoples' Group – in the LCMS usually a Walther League group, holding membership in the internat. Walther League, which was a youth auxiliary organization closely connected on the executive level with youth agencies directly responsible to the elected leadership of the Missouri Synod. Through resolutions presented and passed at the 1965 convention of the LCMS at Detroit, and through resolutions presented and passed at the internat. Walther League Gathering at Purdue in 1968, the Walther League underwent a drastic change; proposals for new conceptions of youth work were adopted by delegates who themselves could only guess at the shapes and forms youth and youth work might assume in the future.

2. The basic purpose underlying any ministry to youth is growth in the truths of the revealed Word of God, and a close relationship with Jesus Christ, through whom God offers justification by faith. When the young person confesses faith in Jesus Christ as personal Savior, the ch. through God's means attempts to open avenues for the Holy Spirit to assist people in the maturation of their faith and life and their understanding of God's will. Young people are thus helped to grow up to become "lights of the world" in their home and family, in the ch., and in society at large.

3. Throughout the 60s, however, adults and agencies working among youth found a fundamental lack of interest in the *hearts* of young people for the mission of the ch. and a lack of knowledge in the *minds* of young people about the nature of the Christian Gospel. Significantly, Strommen in his *Profiles of Church Youth* (St. Louis, 1963), discovered through a depth survey of a representative sampling of ALC and LCMS youth that the youth found themselves unable to offer meaningful explanations of the Gospel, of justification by faith, of the means of grace, and seemed to know little of the differences between the confessional stance of the Luth. Ch. and Prot. ch. bodies in America. The ch. symbolized in their minds an authority, an institution, serving as a repository for law and regulations that might lead to commendable moral behavior.

4. This image of the ch. and its representatives led to a great deal of stress and tension between youth and their parents, their teachers, and representatives of the church. Minorities of youth went through various experiences on the group level during the 60s in attempts to discover for themselves an identity different from the adult or so-called established world. A radical fringe attempted to foster revolution to reshape not only the institutions of this country, but to est. new ways of self-perception, of relationship, new models of reality. The radical or seriously revolutionary young person experimented with sexual practice in group and private life, with aggression and nonaggression, with sensitivity process, with drugs, with styles of dress and body care, with straight rock, acid rock, folk, soul, Gospel, blues, Oriental, and country and western forms of music, and demonstration and power process, hoping to arrive at ways of existence that would differ from an adult world thought to be hopelessly trapped by self-perpetuating forms of bureaucracy, economic competition, and a dehumanizing scientific perspective. Most youth seemed to have been profoundly affected in their abilities and willingness to acquire information and values by exposure from preschool yrs. to (1) TV and radio programming which presented knowledge in nonchronological, all-at-once, segments and settings (in contrast to a rectilinear,

formal, and graded method of information-gathering), and to (2) wars in Korea and Vietnam in which the necessity and morality of involvement by the US seemed ambiguous.

5. The great majority of young people through the 60s, however, remained only on the fringe of radical groups advocating a total change of life patterns and of understanding of man, God, and the world in our culture. Yet they were affected in obviously recognizable ways by radical pressures of youth upon youth and by feelings of differentness between themselves and adults. Many of the most conservative youth inside and outside the ch. adopted blue jeans and denim work shirts as a mode of dress, knew the trends in pop music and purchased expensive electronic hardware to make the sounds available at all times, tended to become disenchanted with school authorities, with formal curricula, with ch. rituals which brought little spiritual experience but rather a kind of mental and emotional blankness and fatigue. By the late 60s statistics revealed what leaders in ch. ministry had feared: Youth, conservative or liberal, were largely indifferent to the ch. and were disappearing from the ch. community. They failed to understand the rewards of Bible or even topic/Bible study. They said they did not experience the blessings their pastors promised would come through the means of grace, Word and sacraments. They said the social life of the typical parish was inferior to a variety of social settings available to them outside the ch. They found the pastor tedious in his preaching and teaching, and failed even to understand why he was needed in the parish. A 1970 survey conducted by a group of 4th-yr. Conc. Sem. students revealed that Luth. High School students were less sure than their public school counterparts in an adjacent school of the pastor's identity and function. They did not understand what he did other than preach and occasionally talk *to their parents.* A significant minority thought the role of the pastor to be effeminate, a role close to that of a homemaker or housekeeper.

6. Perhaps most startling, youth in the 60s became more and more insistent that their parents and other authority figures (especially teachers) were hypocritical, especially in failing to practice what they "advocated" as a Christian or moral way of life. Parents were said to "advocate" the way, not even to *preach* it in the home. The Christian way of life was absent in the week-to-week conversation in the home, was contradicted by vulgarity and profanity of language, by heavy drinking habits, by parties which seemed virtually an imitation of group experiences the youth themselves tried to create. The youth sensed that the nat. media were using their style of life and language as basic factors in the production of advertisements, and found their own parents eager to discover – despite their arguments to the contrary – new ways of living and of evaluating life in the ch. and the world.

7. All these extraordinary developments among youth, largely within a 10-yr. period, led to organized and disorganized change in the structure and shape of ch. youth work on the nat. and the local level. The Walther League, following the Purdue Gathering, dismantled its entire internat. organization. The intricate networks of districts, zones, and local societies were officially eliminated. The staff of the Walther League was reduced to 2 adult executives – with offices in Chicago, though the sale of the Youth Building at 875 N. Dearborn became necessary – and 6 post-high-school teen-agers who were strategically located in portions of the country to promulgate a new Walther League program among young people and counselors who had to join the League anew through a special membership form. The Walther League became issue-oriented and strongly promotive of youth movement causes. At Purdue the League began with the hunger issue. The League has since moved to the issues of draft counseling, race tensions, concern over the so-called "military-industrial" complex, pollution, all aspects of the ecology issue, the Am. Indian and Mexican problems, and the promotion of "power" groups to bring about changes in these problem areas afflicting the country. At a Gathering in Ghost Hawk Park, S. Dak., in Aug. 1970 a group of youth and adult advisors, limited to 350, spent 4 days in the discussion of these social issues. The large Walther League convention thereby was officially replaced by an entirely new concept in youth activity and ministry. The Walther League today publishes a newsletter called *Bridge,* publishes occasional information and data related to current issues under consideration, and alerts its constituency to materials and programs available through other agencies, chs., and pub. houses. The Walther League no longer publishes the *Worker's Quarterly* and publishes no magazine or curricular materials.

8. Replacing the international Walther League is a staffed agency known as the Board of Youth Ministry (replacing the old Board for Young Peoples' Work) with headquarters at 500 N. Broadway, St. Louis. The executive staff presently numbers 4 adults. Since 1969 they have attempted to discover a new basis for youth ministry in the LCMS through a study of ch. youth, of youth activities in congs. across the country, of pastoral involvement with youth, of parental/youth relationships, and the complex problem of shifting responsibilities for month-to-month programming from the now nonexistent Walther League district to the synodical district Youth Board or Committees and whatever remnants of the former Walther League zones yet exist. The new Board projects as an ideal a parish which involves all of its youth in Bible classes, confirmation classes, young peoples' groups (junior and senior high levels), young adult groups (virtually extinct in the LCMS), and even older elementary school groupings, in a common program with common goals of self-growth in the Gospel and mission to the local parish, the ch., and the world. At the same time both youth and adults everywhere are exhibiting a desire for interparish and district or geographical gatherings, with a strong emphasis on personal relationship to Christ as Savior, personal religious experience, commitments to Christ, which would serve as an alternate life-style to the various other styles offered in the 60s. Several nat. youth groups of this type have already developed esp. in Calif. and the Midwest. *Christ for Youth* is an example of a youth-inspired organization with its origins in the Midwest, gradually expanding across the country. Interest in courses in "religion" is mushrooming in colleges and is beginning to filter down to the senior high level.

9. What the youth seem to want from adults more than anything else is a self-sufficient and credible *older* Christian who by his faith and life makes Christianity believable, affirmative, and a source of responsible power. The psychiatrist Erik Erikson in his book *Young Man, Luther* suggested that every young person needs an adult guarantor in order to achieve maturity and adulthood. The young people of the ch. seem to desire in youth work an adult who will serve as a guarantee to them that Christianity is not outmoded or unbelievable but rather a perfectly creditable and powerful way of life superior in every way to all the other "styles" confronting them in their peer groups and through the media – a style which brings peace and security in these troubled times and promises joy throughout eternity. Pres. Jacob Preus of LCMS has suggested that youth need adults who will listen to them carefully in order to minister to them – not by becoming

overgrown youth themselves, which tended to be the trend of the 60s, but by becoming deeply responsive as adults to the tremendous needs of youth attempting to find a secure foothold in a kaleidoscopic culture. Or as Eugene Smith of the WCC stated at the end of 1970: "The nontraditional religious quest among young people is a major clue to our time. Not since the 1st or 16th centuries has there been such a combination of interest in Christian faith and disinterest in its institutional forms. The nontraditional search for God in our time may yet produce changes in institutional Christianity as far-reaching as in those fateful centuries."

10. For further study see Detroit LCMS convention *Proceedings,* 1965; "New Walther League Manifesto"; "Resources for Youth Ministry," pub. quarterly by the Bd. of Youth Ministry, 500 N. Broadway, St. Louis, Mo. (esp. *Don't Be Afraid,* Vol. 2, No. 2, and *Out into the Sunshine,* Vol. 3, No. 2); the "Nelson Youth Forum Series" (Camden, N. J.); D. M. Evans, *Shaping the Church's Ministry with Youth* (Valley Forge, Pa., 1965); C. F. H. Henry, *Answers for the Now Generation* (Chicago, 1969); R. Snyder, *Young People and Their Culture* (Nashville, 1969); M. P. Strommen, *Bridging the Gap* (Minneapolis, 1973) and *Five Cries of Youth* (New York, 1974). LW DPM

Yugoslavia (Jugoslavia). Republic in SE Europe. Area: 98,766 sq. mi. Population: ca. 21,232,000. The Kingdom of the Serbs, Croats, and Slovenes was founded 1918, after Allied victory in WW I. Name changed to Yugoslavia 1929. Proclaimed a communist republic 1945 and organized as a federated republic Jan. 1946. Composed of 6 republics: Serbia, Croatia, Slovenia, Montenegro, Bosnia-Herzegovina, and Macedonia. Const. adopted April 1963 gave the country the name Socialist Federal Republic of Yugoslavia. Political parties limited to communists and the communist-dominated Socialist Alliance of Working People.

Ca. 42% of the people are Serbian Orthodox, 32% RC, 12% Muslim, ca. 12% unchurched; less than 1% are Prot., including ca. 30,000 Reformed; ca. 1% other religions, including perhaps ca. 2,000 Jews.

At time of Reformation P. Truber* became the "Slovenian Luther," credited with creating the Slovenian literary language to bring the Gospel to his people. J. Ungnad* von Weissenwolf also espoused printing of Ev. literature. The Counter Reformation almost exterminated the Prot. movement.

After Emperor Joseph II of Austria granted religious tolerance 1781, many Ger. Luths. settled in lowland areas of what is now Yugoslavia. After WW I the Luth. people were largely neglected. In 1920 the Yugoslav government ordered all Luths. to unite. They formed the Ev. Ch. of the Augsburg Conf. in Yugoslavia. WW II and its aftermath brought expulsions and massacres. After WW II there were 4 Luth. chs. in Yugoslavia: 1. Ev. Christian Ch. of the Augsburg Conf. in the People's Republic of Slovenia-Yugoslavia (autonomous after WW II); 2. Ev. Ch. in the People's Republics of Croatia, Bosnia, and Herzegovina and the Autonomous Province of Voivodina (remnant of 300,000 Ger. Luths.); 3. Ev. Ch. in the People's Republic of Serbia (Hungarian Luths.); 4. Slovak Ev. Christian Ch. of the Augsburg Conf. in Yugoslavia (formerly part of the Luth. Ch. of Hungary; autonomous since 1918).

Yukon. See *Canada,* A 27.

Yung Chêng. See *China,* 6.

Yvo. See *Ivo.*

Yvon, Pierre (1646–1707). B. Montauban, Fr.; adherent of J. de Labadie.* Works include *Impietas convicta.*

Z

Zabarella, Francesco (1360–1417). RC canonist and diplomat; b. Padua, It.; educ. Bologna; prof. Florence, Padua; archpriest Padua 1398; bp. Florence 1410; cardinal deacon at Rome 1411; advocate of reform; supported antipope John XXIII. Works include *De schismate sui temporis; Commentaria in V libros Decretalium.*

Zabarella, Giacomo (Jacopo; 1533–89). Renaissance philos.; b. Padua, It.; prof. nat. philos. and logic Padua. Works include *Opera logica; De rebus naturalibus.*

Zaccaria, Antonio M. See *Barnabites.*

Zahn, Adolf (1834–1900). Cousin of F. M. Zahn and T. v. Zahn; b. Mützenow, Pomerania; pastor Halle, Elberfeld, Stuttgart; wrote on hist. and OT; defended orthodoxy; opposed Biblical criticism. Works include *Ernste Blicke in den Wahn der modernen Kritik des Alten Testaments; Israelitische und jüdische Geschichte; Abriss einer Geschichte der evangelischen Kirche auf dem europäischen Festlande im neunzehnten Jahrhundert.*

Zahn, Franz Michael (1833–1900). Brother of T. v. Zahn; cousin of A. Zahn; b. Moers, near Duisburg, Ger.; inspector of N. Ger. Missionary Soc. 1862; founder of Continental Missions Conference 1866. Works include *Das erste Evangelium; Ein Gang durch die heilige Geschichte.*

Zahn, Gottfried (1705–58). Founder of orphanage at Bunzlau, which, however, was closed by his enemies 1753, while he and the teacher were imprisoned; but he won E. G. Woltersdorf* for his cause, and the king granted him a permit to open another orphanage 1754.

Zahn, Johannes Christoph Andreas (1817–95). B. Eschenbach, Ger.; stud. theol. at Erlangen and Berlin; teacher at *Lehrerseminar* in Altdorf; lived in Neuendettelsau after retirement; prominent hymnologist and ch. musician. Ed. *Vierstimmiges Melodienbuch zum Gesangbuch der ev.-luth. Kirche in Bayern; Die Melodien der deutschen evangelischen Kirchenlieder.*

Zahn, Theodor von (1838–1933). Brother of F. M. Zahn; cousin of A. Zahn; NT scholar; b. Moers, near Duisburg, Ger.; educ. Basel, Erlangen, Berlin, Göttingen; prof. Göttingen, Kiel, Erlangen (as successor to J. C. K. v. Hofmann*), Leipzig, again Erlangen; leader of conservatives in NT criticism, in opposition to the radicalism of A. Harnack.* Works include the monumental *Einleitung in das Neue Testament; Die Geschichte des neutestamentlichen Kanons;* important parts of *Kommentar zum Neuen Testament.*

Zaidites. See *Shi'ites.*

Zaire. See *Africa,* F 2.

Zambia. See *Africa,* B 2.

Zanchi, Hieronymus (Girolamo; Jerome; 1516–90). Ref. theol.; b. It.; Augustinian; directed to ch. fathers and Reformers by Vermigli*; influenced by Bullinger* and Calvin*; forced to flee; prof. Geneva; canon Strasbourg; involved in controversies on Lord's Supper, predestination, and perseverance; preacher Chiavenna, It.; prof. Heidelberg 1568, Neustadt 1576. See also *Dogmatics,* B 5; *Grace, Means of,* IV 3.

Zänker, Otto Ewald Paul (1876–1960). Ger. Luth. bp.; b. Herzkamp, Westphalia; educ, Erlangen, Griefswald, Halle; dir. of sem. Soest; gen. supt. Breslau; bp. Silesia 1933; est. laymen's retreats; opposed Nazism; expelled from Silesia 1945. Works include *Katholische und evangelische Frömmigkeit; Seelsorge an Gebildeten; 20 Jahre kirchliches Leben in Schlesien.*

Zanzibar. See *Africa,* E 7.

Zarathustra. See *Zoroaster.*

Zauleck, Paul (1849–1917). B. Berlin; pastor Bremen; created *Kindergottesdienst* modeled after Brit. and Am. Sun. school. Est. periodical *Der Kindergottesdienst;* works include *Weide meine Lämmer; Deutsches Kindergesangbuch; Wie man den Kindern den Heiland zeigt.*

Zebul. See *Canaanites, Religion of.*

Zehner, Samuel (1594–1635). B. Suhl, Ger.; at time of his death superintendent at Schleusingen; wrote "Ach Gott, gib du uns deine Gnad" while a suburb was being sacked.

Zeisberger, David (Apr. 11, 1721–Nov. 17, 1808). Moravian miss. to Am. Indians; b. Zauchtenthal, Moravia; to Am. ca. 1739; present at founding of Moravian settlement, Bethlehem, Pa., 1741; worked among Indians, traveling to various places including Pa., Ohio, Canada; est. congs. which, however, did not survive.

Zell, Katharina (ca. 1497–1562). Wife of M. Zell*; maiden name Schütz; highly gifted; helped refugees and did other works of mercy; did literary work; carried on theol. correspondence with Luther,* Zwingli,* Bullinger,* and other famous theologians.

Zell, Matthäus (1477–1548). B. Kaisersberg, Ger.; educ. Mainz, Erfurt, Freiburg; pastor of cathedral in Strasbourg 1518; won for Ev. cause through influence of Bible, Luther, and Johann Geyler; began Reformation activity 1521 with series of sermons on Romans; citizens won for his cause; his *Christliche Verantwortung,* a reply to attacks of monks, became basis for Reformation in Strasbourg; refrained from participation in theol. quarrels; sheltered those persecuted because of religion (including K. v. Schwenkfeld*); excommunicated by Rome 1524 because of his marriage to K. Zell.*

Zeller, Christian Heinrich (1779–1860). B. in Castle Hohen-Entringen near Tübingen, Ger.; studied law Tübingen; instructor and school superintendent Zofingen, Switz.; helped est. a sem. and a home for poor children at Beuggen, near Basel, 1820, which he conducted according to ideas of J. H. Pestalozzi* and in a somewhat pietistic manner. Works include *Lehren der Erfahrung; Seelenlehre.*

Zeller, Eduard (1814–1908). Ger. theol., hist., philos.; b. Kleinbottwar, near Marbach; taught Tübingen, Bern, Marburg, Heidelberg, Berlin; adherent of school of F. C. Baur.* Ed. *Theologische Jahrbücher;* works include *Das theologische System Zwinglis; Die Philosophie der Griechen.*

Zenana Mission. See *India,* 12.

Zend-Avesta. I. e., Avesta with commentaries (Zend), sacred scriptures of Zoroastrianism* and the Parsis,* consisting of 3 parts: Yasna (liturgical texts), Vendidad (ritual laws), and Yashts (poems containing mythology and legends of ancient Iran). Most important and oldest part of Yasna are Gathas, hymns, most of which are attributed to Zoroaster.*

Zending Batak (Batak Missionary Society). Miss. movement which began ca. 1899 on Samosir Island in Lake Toba, Sumatra. It later was active on the Mentawai Islands. See also *Bataks.*

Zenkovsky, Basilius (1881–1962). B. Russia; taught philos. at Kiev, Belgrade, Prague, Paris. Works include *Geschichte der Russischen Philosophie.*

Zeno of Citium (ca. 336–264 B. C.). Greek philos.; founder of Stoicism.*

Zeno of Velia (Elea; b. ca. 490 B. C.). Gk. philos. of Eleatic* School; known for his paradoxes on motion. See also *Dialectic.*

Zeno(n) (426–491). B. Isauria, Asia Minor; E. Roman emp. 474–491; tried unsuccessfully to settle Monophysite* Controversy by issuing Henoticon.*

Zephyrinus. Pope (bp. Rome) ca. 198/200–217. See also *Monarchianism,* A 3; *Theodotus the Money Changer.*

Zepper, Wilhelm (1550–1607). Ref. theol.; b. Dillenburg, Ger.; educ. Marburg; pastor Herborn; court preacher Dillenburg; prof. Herborn; worked in area of catechetics, homiletics, pastoral theology, and canon law.

Zerbolt Gerhard (1367–98). B. Zutphen, Neth.; librarian of cong. of Brethren* of the Common Life at Deventer. Works include *Super modo vivendi devotorum hominum simul commorantium.*

Zeus. See *Greek Religion,* 2.

Zezschwitz, Carl Adolpf Gerhard von (1825–86). Conservative Luth. theol.; b. Bautzen, Ger.; prof. Leipzig, Giessen, Erlangen; prolific writer, chiefly on practical theol. and catechetics; exerted great personal influence as teacher and preacher. Works include *Über die Aufgaben welche die Selbständigkeitspflicht der Lutherischen auf Grund der Ereignisse der letzten Jahre stellt; Über die wesentliche Verfassungsziele der lutherischen Reformation.*

Ziegenbalg, Bartholomäus (June 24, 1683–Feb. 23, 1719). Ger. Luth. miss. to India; b. Pulsnitz, Saxony; educ. by A. H. Francke* at Halle. Ziegenbalg and H. Plütschau* were sent by Frederick IV of Denmark as missionaries to India, arriving at Tranquebar July 1706. Surmounting much opposition from both the Dan. governor and the Hindus, he learned the vernacular in a yr., did effective miss. work, founded a school for native helpers, built a ch., still in use today, engaged in much literary work, and translated the SC, NT, and OT as far as the Book of Ruth into Tamil.

In 1715 Ziegenbalg returned to Eur., calling forth much enthusiasm by his addresses and reports. In Halle he had his Tamil grammar printed. There he married Maria Dorothea Salzmann, a relative of P. J. Spener.* Ziegenbalg and his wife went to Eng., where he was presented to King George I, who later wrote him expressing satisfaction "not only because the work undertaken by you of converting the heathen to the Christian faith doth, by the grace of God, prosper, but also because that in this our kingdom such a laudable zeal for promotion of the Gospel prevails."

In 1716 Ziegenbalg, with his wife, returned to Tranquebar, where he continued his work. However, the dir. of the miss. in Den. criticized him severely for getting married, allegedly spending too much money, and staying too much in one place – a criticism that may well have contributed to his early death.

Ziegler, Jakob (ca. 1470–1549). B. Landau on the Isar, Ger.; educ. Ingolstadt, Vienna; traveled in Moravia and opposed Moravian Brethren; to Hungary, Rome; abuses in ch. and desire for inwardness caused him to seek contact with Reformers; to Strasbourg 1531; returned to RC Ch.; prof. Vienna.

Ziegler, Kaspar (1621–90). B. Leipzig; stud. law, also theol.; prof. of law Wittenberg; practiced law with great success; friend of A. Calov.* Wrote "Ich freue mich in dir und heisse dich willkommen."

Ziegler, Theobald (1846–1918). Ger. philos.; prof. Strasbourg; wrote on educ. and ethics; sought to separate ethics from the supranatural. Works include *Geschichte der Pädagogik mit besonderer Rücksicht auf das höhere Unterrichtswesen; Philipp Melanchthon, der humanistische Genosse Luthers.*

Ziethe, Wilhelm (1824–1901). Noted preacher; b. Senftenberg, Ger.; educ. Halle; mem. of Prussian* Union; Pastor Berlin 1861–95; very popular. Works include *Das Leben Jesu für das deutsche Volk; Matthias Claudius, der Wandsbecker Bote; Die Wahrheit und Herrlichkeit des Christentums.*

Zigabenus, Euthymius. See *Euthymius Zigabenus.*

Ziggurat. See *Babylonians, Religion of the,* 4.

Ziller, Tuiskon (1817–82). B. Wasungen, Ger.; educ. Meiningen, Leipzig; lectured at Leipzig; opened pedagogical sem. 1864; founded Association for Scientific Pedagogy 1869. Ziller developed and applied to public schools J. F. Herbart's* ideas, emphasized the moral end of educ., demanded that the different parts of study be graded, associated, and unified, history and religion forming the core around which all other subjects are grouped; theory of "concentration." All instruction to contribute to the training of a strong moral character. Works include *Grundlegung zur Lehre vom erziehenden Unterricht; Vorlesungen über allgemeine Pädagogik.*

Zillerthaler Emigration. Emigration of ca. 400 persons who, to escape persecution following their secession from RC Ch., left their native valley (Zillerthal) in Tyrol and found domicile in Silesia 1837; the exiles united with the Prot. Ch. of Prussia.

Zimmer, Friedrich (1855–1919). Ger. Ev. theol.; b. Gardelegen; taught at Bonn, Königsberg, Herborn; noted for inner miss. work and educ. of women for nursing and deaconess work.

Zimmerman, John L. (Mar. 18, 1856–Sept. 17, 1941). Prominent Luth. layman in General* Syn.; b. Mahoning Co., Ohio; grad. Wittenberg Coll. 1878; author of merger resolution that led to forming of The United* Luth. Ch. in Am. 1918; lived in Springfield, Ohio.

Zimmermann, Ernst Christoph Philipp (1786–1832). Ger. rationalistic theol.; b. Darmstadt; educ. Giessen; active exponent of ch. union in Baden (see *Germany,* C 2); published sermons; founded *Allgemeine Kirchenzeitung* (Darmstadt) and *Allgemeine Schulzeitung.*

Zimmermann, Johann Jakob (1695–1756). Ref. theol.; prof. Zürich; influenced by Arminians; exponent of a Biblical "simplicity" without dogmatic subtleties and disputes. Works include *Opuscula theologici, historici et philosophici argumenti.*

Zinzendorf, Christian Renatus von (1727–52). Son of N. L. v. Zinzendorf*; b. Dresden; wrote hymns.

Zinzendorf, Nikolaus Ludwig von (1700–60). Founder of reorganized Moravian Ch. or Unity of Brethren; b. Dresden, Ger.; grew up in Pietistic surroundings; to school in Halle; stud. law at Wittenberg; made friends with Cath. and Ref. notables on his travels; purchased Berthelsdorf, where he wished to build up a community of heart-and-soul Christians; settled body of Moravians on part of his estate (beginning 1722), colony being called Herrnhut (the Lord's Watch); expelled from Saxony; made Moravian bishop in Berlin 1737; traveled extensively in Eur. and Am., establishing Moravian colonies (e. g., Bethlehem, Pa., 1741); lived in London 1751–55, where he influenced Methodism; passed his latter days in somewhat depressing circumstances at Herrnhut. Wrote strongly subjective hymns, e. g., "Jesus, Thy Blood and Righteousness" (see *Wesley, John*), many not in keeping with the dignity of the ch. See also *David, Christian; Moravian Church,* 3. 4.

Zion City. See *Christian Catholic Church.*

Zion Union Apostolic Church. See *Methodist Churches,* 4 c.

Zionism. A modern Jewish movement whose objects

are to create an asylum for oppressed and persecuted Jews and to preserve Judaism from becoming submerged in the culture of other peoples. Throughout the centuries Jews have yearned for a Jewish homeland, and this yearning always became intense during persecutions. The anti-Semitism* in Eur. in the 2d half of the 19th c. resulted in attempts to settle Jews in Palestine; but no organization was effected until Theodor Herzl, a Viennese lawyer and journalist (1860–1904), wrote *Der Judenstaat* 1896, which resulted in the First Zionist Congress at Basel 1897, where the Zionist organization was formed and the program formulated "to establish for the Jewish people a publicly recognized, legally secured home in Palestine." Numerous congresses were held in the following yrs.

By WW I ca. 115,000 Jews had settled in Palestine. On Nov. 2, 1917, the Brit. govt. issued the Balfour Declaration (see *Balfour, Arthur J.; Middle East,* F), stating that "His Majesty's Government view with favor the establishment in Palestine of a national home for the Jewish people. . . ." Proposals intended to "ultimately render possible the creation of an autonomous commonwealth" for the Jews were adopted at the San Remo peace conference 1920, which later became part of the Palestine Mandate given the Brit. govt. by the League of Nations.

After WW I Jewish immigration increased, ca. 150,000 additional settlers coming by 1936, after which violent Arab opposition and Brit. restrictions held the number down until the end of WW II. Agricultural settlements were formed; the Heb. University was est. on Mt. Scopus; the all-Jewish city of Tel-Aviv grew rapidly; commerce and manufacture were promoted.

After WW II a flood of refugees from Hitler's concentration camps poured in despite all opposition. On Nov. 29, 1947, the UN decided to partition Palestine. On May 14, 1948, a momentous date in Jewish history, the indep. state of Israel was est.; the Zionist dream had come true. On Feb. 14, 1949, a const. setting up a republican form of govt. was adopted.

Since the est. of Israel, immigration has continued, with particular strength in the early yrs. In 1948 the Jewish pop. was ca. 750,000; in 1952 ca. 1,440,000; in 1966 ca. 2,300,000; in 1973 ca. 2,870,000. After 4 wars with the Arabs (1948-49, 1956, 1967, 1973) Zionism still faces the problem of reconciliation of the Arab world to the existence of this new Jewish state.

Zionites. See *Ellerians.*

Zoar Separatists. See *Communistic Societies,* 5.

Zöckler, Otto (1833–1906). Prominent Luth. theol.; b. Grünberg, Hesse; educ. Giessen; mem. of Prussian* Union; influenced by Erlangen school; prof. Giessen; prof. Greifswald to end of life. Zöckler was a prolific writer, chiefly on apologetic subjects regarding the inner harmony of revealed religion and true science. His best book on these is perhaps *Gottes Zeugen im Reich der Natur.* He wrote commentaries in J. P. Lange's* commentary; with H. L. Strack* ed. a commentary on the Bible; ed. *Handbuch der theologischen Wissenschaften* and *Evangelische Kirchen-Zeitung* (founded by E. W. Hengstenberg*).

Zöckler, Theodor (1867–1949). Ev. theol.; b. Greifswald, Ger.; miss. to Jews 1890; pastor at Stanislau (Stanislav), Galicia (after WW I Stanisławów, Poland; after WW II Ivano-Frankovsk, USSR) 1891; est. schools and active in inner missions; helped unite Polish chs. in "Council of Ev. Chs. in Poland; he and his institutions were forced to relocate in Ger. 1939; work continues in Stade, W. Ger.

Zoellner, Wilhelm (1860–1937). Ger. Luth. theol.; b. Minden, Westphalia; educ. Leipzig, Halle, Bonn; pastor Friedrichsdorf near Bielefeld and Barmen-Wupperfeld; dir. of deaconess institution at Kaiserswerth 1897; gen. supt. of Ch. of Westphalia 1905; chairman of the committee of the Ger. fed. of chs. in Kirchenkampf* 1935; exponent of confessional Lutheranism. Works include *Im Dienst der Kirche; Die Kirche der Geschichte und die Kirche des Glaubens.*

Zollikofer, Georg Joachim (1730–1788). Ref. preacher; rationalist; b. St. Gall, Switz.; pastor Morat, Switz., and Leipzig, Ger.; praised by J. W. v. Goethe* for sermons. Works include *Predigten; Predigten über die Würde des Menschen.*

Zonaras, Joannes (12 c.). Byzantine historian. Works include general history; commentaries on patristic canons.

Zorn, Carl Manthey (Mar. 18, 1846–July 12, 1928). B. Sterup, Schleswig, Ger.; grad. Leipzig 1870; miss. of Leipzig Mission Soc. in India 1871–76; pastor Sheboygan, Wis., 1876–81; Cleveland, Ohio (Zion), 1881–1911, when he retired. Among his books are many popular expositions of Bible books, the most comprehensive being that on Colossians; other works include *Bekehrung und Gnadenwahl; Eunike; Brosamlein; Auf den Weg; Handbook for Home Study; Christenfragen aus Gottes Wort beantwortet.*

C. M. Zorn, *Dies und das aus dem Leben eines ostindischen Missionars* (St. Louis, 1907); *Dies und das aus frühem Amtsleben* (St. Louis, 1912); *Abwärts, Aufwärts* (Milwaukee, 1910); F. D. Lueking, *Mission in the Making* (St. Louis, 1964).

Zoroaster. Grecized name of Zarathustra, founder of Zoroastrianism* and alleged author of Zend-Avesta.* Exact time and place of birth and place of activity unknown; but it seems assured that he lived a considerable time before the 6th c. BC in Iran. Details of his life also shrouded in obscurity, but tradition tells the following: B. 660 BC. At age 30 he received revelations from Ahura Mazdah regarding new monotheism which he was to preach in opposition to contemporary polytheism. For 11 yrs. he went from court to court in Iran without success, until he converted King Vishtaspa 618 BC, through whose influence the new religion spread widely. Was slain at age of 77 in a religious war.

Zoroastrianism. 1. The religion of Persia prior to the Mohammedan conquest. Its traditional founder is Zoroaster,* its sacred book the Avesta.* Other sources are texts written in Pahlavi, the medieval Persian, collected from the 3d to the 9th c., of which the most important is the *Bundahishn,* a work containing cosmogony, mythology, and legend.

2. Before Zoroaster the religion of the Persians was a polytheistic nature worship (see *Brahmanism*). Among their deities were Mithra, the sun god, Ahura Mazdah, or "Wise Lord," the sky god, a fire spirit, numerous evil spirits, called daevas. This nature worship was reformed by Zoroaster in the direction of a practical monotheism. Of the old gods he chose Ahura Mazdah (later Persian, Ormuzd) and ascribed to him absolute supremacy, rejecting all other gods. The name Mazdaism, therefore, is also applied to the Avestan religion. Zoroaster also taught an ethical dualism which, as Zoroastrianism, developed during the following centuries and became more and more pronounced until it was the most characteristic doctrine of the system.

3. Beside Ahura Mazdah, who is the creator of the universe, the guardian of mankind, the source of all that is good, and who demands righteousness of his people, there existed from eternity a powerful evil spirit, Angra Mainyu, or Ahriman, who is the source of all evil and the implacable opponent of Ahura Mazdah and who endeavors to lead men from the path of virtue. Between these two spirits is man, who has a free will to choose bet. good and evil and will be rewarded or punished accordingly.

Characteristic of the system also is a well-developed angelology and eschatology.

4. Associated with Ahura Mazdah are a large number of good spirits, presided over by 6 archangels, the Amesha Spentas, or "Immortal Holy Ones," who are personified attributes of the supreme deity and regarded as his main agencies. They are Good Thought, Best Righteousness, Wished-for Kingdom, Harmony on Earth, Salvation, Immortality.

5. Opposed to the good spirits and associated with Ahriman is a hierarchy of evil spirits. The conflict bet. these 2 forces will continue until the end of the world cycle, which consists of 12,000 years, when Ahura Mazdah will finally triumph and Ahriman be overthrown. The last period of 3,000 years of this cycle begins with Zoroaster's prophetic career.

6. Zoroaster's ethical code lays great stress on "good thoughts, good words, good deeds." To be good, however, means chiefly to abstain from demon worship and to worship Ahura Mazdah and follow his precepts. Body and soul must be kept pure. It is also man's religious duty to foster agriculture, cattle raising, and irrigation, to protect especially the cow and the dog, to abstain from lying and robbery. The elements of earth, fire, and water must be kept from defilement. Because of the last injunction Zoroastrians neither bury nor cremate their dead, as thereby earth and fire would be defiled, but expose them to vultures on "towers of silence." Forgiveness of sins has no place in the system; sins must be counterbalanced by good works. Three days after death the souls cross the Cinvat bridge to be judged, the righteous passing on to heaven, the wicked to the tortures of hell. If good and evil deeds balance exactly, the soul passes to an intermediate place, called Hamestakan (or Hamestagan; Hamistagan), where it experiences neither bliss nor torture.

7. At the Last Day all men will be raised from the dead and subjected to another ordeal. They must pass through molten metal, which causes joy to the good, but extreme pain to the wicked. After that all souls, even of the wicked, being purified, will be taken to heaven and a new world established, which shall endure to eternity.

8. Zoroaster's teachings did not involve a ritual. Later, however, a complete ceremonial worship and a priesthood developed (see *Magi*). Important rites were preparation of the *haoma,* a sacred drink, and in later centuries fire ceremonies (see *Fire Worshipers*). Marriage was a religious duty, and intermarriage of those closely related, even of brother and sister, was permitted. Zoroastrianism made considerable progress under the Achaemenian kings (558–331 B. C.); but whether it was universally accepted during that period is not known. It received a setback through the conquest of Persia by Alexander the Great and under Greek and Parthian rule had difficulty in maintaining itself. In the Neo-Persian empire (226–637), under the Sassanid dynasty, it again became the dominant religion; but after the Moslem conquest it began to decline rapidly, yielding to Shi'ite* Mohammedanism. Due to Moslem persecution many Zoroastrians emigrated to India, where they settled mainly at Bombay. See also *Parsi; Religion, Comparative, Bibliography.*

Zosimus (5th c.) Byzantine hist.; preferred paganism to Christianity. Works include *Nea historia* (Gk.)

Zscharnack, Leopold (1877–1955). B. Berlin; prof. Berlin; army chaplain 1916–18; prof. Breslau, Königsberg, Marburg. Works include *Lessings theologische Schriften; Die Trennung von Staat und Kirche.*

Zschiegner, Max Heinrich (Sept. 9, 1897–Jan. 23, 1940). B. New York State; grad. Conc. Sem., St. Louis, 1921; miss. to China from 1921 till his sudden death; pres. Conc. Theol. Sem., Hankow, from 1929; mem. *Chinese Lutheran Witness* ed. staff; translator; writer of books in Chinese language; artist.

Zuccheto. The skullcap worn by the RC hierarchy.

Zucker, Johann Friedrich (Sept. 2, 1842–Sept. 13, 1927). B. Breitenau, Bavaria; grad. Erlangen 1865; miss. of Leipzig Mission Soc. in India 1870–76; pastor Brooklyn, N. Y., 1876–79; prof. Conc. Coll., Ft. Wayne, Ind., 1881–1921; pres. there 1879–81.

Zündel, Friedrich (1827–1891). Ev. theol. and pastor; b. Schaffhausen, Switz.; adherent of J. C. Blumhardt.* Works include *Johann Christoph Blumhardt, Ein Lebensbild; Jesus; Aus der Apostelzeit.*

Zurich, Consensus of *(Consensus Tigurinus).* See *Calvin, John,* 12; *Reformed Confessions,* A 8.

Zütphen. See *Henry of Zutphen.*

Zwemer, Samuel Marinus (Apr. 12, 1867–Apr. 2, 1952). B. Vriesland, near Holland, Mich.; educ. New Brunswick Theol. Sem.; helped found Arabian Mission (see *Middle East,* L); miss. (of Ref. Ch. in Am.) to Arabia 1890–1912; then prof. of theol. sem. and Cairo Study Center, Cairo, Egypt, till 1929; founded periodical *The Moslem World* (later *Muslim World*); prof. of religion and missions, Princeton Theol. Sem. 1929–38. Works include *Cross Above the Crescent; Into All the World.*

Zwick, Johannes (ca. 1496–1542). Reformer of Constance; b. Constance; stud. law at various universities; taught law at Basel; stud. theol. and ordained priest; married; priest at Riedlingen, Ger., 1522–25, when he was driven out "for adhering to Luth. doctrine"; to Constance, where he est. the Reformation and worked effectively the rest of his life; befriended refugees; d. of pestilence in Bischofszelt, Switz., where he had gone to minister to a plague-stricken cong. Works include a hymnbook with an excellent preface and containing the hymn "Auf diesen Tag bedenken wir"; and his *Gebete und Lieder für die Jugend.*

Zwickau Prophets (Heavenly Prophets; *Bilderstürmer*). Name given to group of radical Anabaptists from Zwickaa, Ger., led by Nikolaus Storch (weaver; claimed prophetic power; d. 1525). Stressed rigid conformity to NT injunctions, separation of believer from unbelieving marriage partner; rejected infant baptism, use of oaths, use of civil power, military service; some were iconoclastic. Storch and others came to Wittenberg, Dec. 1521, influenced Karlstadt* and even Melanchthon* for a time, causing Luther to return to Wittenberg from the Wartburg, Mar. 1522. See also *Luther, M.,* 15; *Hausmann, Nicolaus; Luther, Controversies of,* d.

Zwilling, Gabriel (Didymus; ca. 1487–1558). B. near Annaberg, Ger.; educ. Wittenberg and Erfurt; left Augustinian order 1521; active in iconoclastic movement; yielded to Luther; preacher at Altenburg 1522; preacher 1523, pastor 1525, supt. 1529 at Torgau; deposed because of his opposition to Interim* 1549.

Zwingli, Confessions of. See *Reformed Confessions,* A 1–5.

Zwingli, Huldreich (Ulrich; 1484–1531). 1. Founder of Swiss Ref. Ch.; b. Wildhaus, Switz.; received humanistic educ.; parish priest at Glarus 1506–16 (took time out to be chaplain at battles of Novara 1513 and Marignano 1515, both in Italy; preached against hiring out of Swiss soldiers as mercenaries, arousing animosity against him); at Einsiedeln 1516–18 (opposed indulgences); and at Zurich, where he stayed from 1519 to end of life. Studied a great deal, esp. the NT and the ch. fathers; met Erasmus 1515. He gave up his papal pension 1520, but his reformatory work did not really begin until 1522, when he wrote against compulsory fasting. That yr. he contracted a secret marriage, which was publicly solemnized 1524. In a disputation Jan. 29, 1523, Zwingli successfully defended 67 theses he had drawn up, in which he maintained that the Gospel alone should be the rule of faith and practice, etc. In a few months he expanded these and published them under the title *Auslegung und Begründung der Schlussreden* – the 1st Ger. Ev. dogmatics. A 2d disputation (in which Zwingli attacked the RC Mass) took place Oct. 26–28, 1523, and a 3d on Jan. 19–20, 1524. Pictures and statues were removed from chs.; even ch. music was abolished; services were held in the vernacular; monasteries were closed. Ca. 1523 Zwingli adopted C. H. Hoen's* doctrine of the Eucharist. On Maundy Thurs., Apr. 13, 1525, the Lord's Supper was celebrated in Zurich with men and women sitting on opposite sides of a table extending down the middle aisle. Zwingli strongly opposed the Anabaptists. In 1529, in his only meeting with Luther, he attended the Marburg Colloquy (see *Luther, Controversies of,* g). When the Diet of Augsburg convened on June 30, 1530, Zwingli sent his own confession of faith to the emperor. He set on foot far-reaching politico-religious schemes, but the 5 Forest Cantons remained staunchly RC, and war broke out bet. them and Zurich. He went out with the army as chaplain and was killed.

2. It is hard to determine to what extent Zwingli was dependent on Luther. He always maintained that he arrived at his theol. conclusions independently, but he read Luther's writings and some influence is highly probably. Interesting comparisons can be drawn bet. the 2 men: Like Luther, Zwingli was a born musician and fond of company, also an excellent teacher; unlike Luther, he defended the death penalty for unbelievers and was always ready to engage in politics; both recognized Scripture as the only authority in religion, but Zwingli was inclined to be influenced by reason and humanism. See also *Reformed Confessions,* A 1; *Switzerland,* 2–4.

W. Köhler, *Zwingli and Luther* (1924 and 1953); J. Rilliet, tr. H. Knight, *Zwingli: Third Man of the Reformation* (Philadelphia, 1964); H. Sasse, *This Is My Body* (Minneapolis, 1959); J. P. Whitney, "The Helvetic Reformation," *Cambridge Modern History,* II, 305–41 (voluminous bibliography of material published to the time of the printing of this work on pp. 773–78).

Zygomalas, Thomasius (1498–1578). Secretary to the Eastern Orthodox patriarchs Joasaph II and Jeremias* II; favored cause of Protestants. See *Eastern Orthodox Churches,* 5; *Eastern Orthodox Standards of Doctrine,* 5.